DICCIONARIO

Cambridge
Klett
Pocket

D0039720

Español – Inglés
English – Spanish

PUBLISHED BY THE PRESS SYNDICATE OF THE UNIVERSITY OF CAMBRIDGE
The Pitt Building, Trumpington Street, Cambridge, United Kingdom

CAMBRIDGE UNIVERSITY PRESS

The Edinburgh Building, Cambridge CB2 2RU, UK
40 West 20th Street, New York NY10011-4211, USA
477 Williamstown Road, Port Melbourne, VIC 3207, Australia
Ruiz de Alarcón 13, 28014 Madrid, Spain
Dock House, The Waterfront, Cape Town 8001, South Africa

http://www.cambridge.org

First published 2002

Printed in Germany at Clausen & Bosse, Leck

Typeface: Weidemann, Stone Sans

A catalogue record for this book is available from the British Library

Library of Congress Cataloguing in Publication data applied for

ISBN 0521 753007 flexicover

ISBN 0521 802997 paperback

Defined words that we have reason to believe constitue trademarks have been labelled as such. However, neither the presence nor absence of such labels should be regarded as affecting the legal status of any trademarks.

The contents of this book are based on the **Diccionario Cambridge Klett Compact (Español-Inglés/English-Spanish)**

Editorial Management: María Teresa Gondar Oubiña

Contributors: Sonia Aliaga López, Alexander Burden, Majka Dischler, Tim Gutteridge, Yolanda Madarnás Aceña, Josep Ràfols i Ventosa, James Robert Gurney Salter, Stephen Alan Trott

Typesetting: Dörr und Schiller GmbH, Stuttgart
Data processing: Andreas Lang, conTEXT AG für Information und Kommunikation, Zürich
Illustrations: Terry McKenna, Anthony Morris
Maps: Klett-Perthes, Justus Perthes Verlag, Gotha

▶ ÍNDICE

▶ CONTENTS

El *Diccionario Cambridge Klett Pocket* es un diccionario bilingüe completamente nuevo destinado a estudiantes de inglés de habla española y a estudiantes de español de habla inglesa. Ha sido diseñado con el objetivo de satisfacer especialmente las necesidades de los estudiantes con un nivel intermedio y en su confección y edición ha participado un gran número de hablantes nativos de ambas lenguas, lo que lo convierte en una herramienta lingüística amplia y actualizada.

En el diccionario se halla reflejado tanto el inglés británico como el inglés americano y proporciona, de esta manera, una guía fiable del inglés como lengua internacional. Al mismo tiempo ofrece una amplia cobertura tanto del español peninsular como del español de América Latina y constituye, por tanto, una herramienta útil de aprendizaje para cualquier estudiante de español en cualquier país de lengua española.

El diccionario incluye, además, una ayuda complementaria para el aprendizaje de aquellos aspectos que acostumbran a resultar más dificultosos a los estudiantes; por ejemplo, modelos de conjugaciones de los dos idiomas y un gran número de páginas a todo color para facilitar el estudio de vocabularios específicos.

Le deseamos que la consulta de este diccionario y el aprendizaje del nuevo idioma le reporten unos momentos agradables.

Si desea obtener más información, visítenos en nuestra dirección:

dictionary.cambridge.org

▶ INTRODUCTION

The *Diccionario Cambridge Klett Pocket* is a completely new bilingual dictionary for Spanish-speaking learners of English and English-speaking learners of Spanish. It has been specially designed so that it meets the needs of intermediate-level learners and it has been written and edited by a large team of native speakers of both languages so that it provides an up-to-date and comprehensive language tool.

It covers British English and American English, so that it provides a reliable guide to English as an international language. It also has good coverage of the Spanish from Spain and Spanish from Latin America so that for learners of Spanish it can help them in all of the Spanish-speaking world.

The dictionary provides extra help with many areas that learners find difficult. For example, there is full information about the verb patterns of the the two languages and there are full-colour pages to help you learn the vocabulary from particular language areas.

We hope that you enjoy using this book and that you enjoy learning your new language.

You can also find out more information on our website at:

dictionary.cambridge.org

► LA PRONUNCIACIÓN DEL ESPAÑOL
SPANISH PRONUNCIATION

Remarkable differences can be observed in Spanish pronunciation, both within the various regions of the Iberian Peninsula and also in the individual countries where Spanish is spoken. Contrary to general opinion, these differences are stronger within Spain than between the various Spanish-speaking countries in America. In bilingual regions of the Iberian Peninsula like Catalonia, Valencia, the Balearic Islands, the Basque Provinces and Galicia, the pronunciation of Spanish is strongly influenced by the native languages of these areas. In other regions, on the other hand, the phonetic features of a range of dialects have been mixed into spoken Spanish. A particularly characteristic and autonomous note is evident in Andalusian pronunciation, for instance in the case of this dialect's own special **ceceo: s**, **z** and **c** are pronounced with an interdental fricative /th/ (**káza**, as opposed to *casa* **kása**).

Generally, Castilian pronunciation is considered the standard pronunciation as it represents the closest approximation to the written form. This is also the pronunciation on which the following descriptions are based.

► Vowels

Symbol	Graphic representation	Examples
[a]	a	san, acción
[e]	e	pez, saber
[i]	i	sí, mirar
[o]	o	con
[u]	u	tú, dibujo

► Semi-vowels resp. semi-consonants

Symbol	Graphic representation	Examples	Notes
[i̯]	i, y	baile, hoy, despreciéis	*occurs in the diphthongs **ai, ei, oi** resp. **ay, ey, oy** and as the final element in triphthongs*
[j]	i	bieldo, apreciáis	*when **i** is pronounced as the first element in diphthongs and triphthongs*

| [u̯] | u | auto, causa | *occurs in the diphthongs **au, eu, ou*** |
| [w] | u | bueno, cuerda | *when **u** is pronounced as the first element in diphthongs or triphthongs* |

▶ Consonants

Symbol	Graphic representation	Examples	Notes
[p]	p	pato	
[b]	b, v	vacío, hombre	*plosive: pronounced in the absolute initial sound after a pause and in the medial after a preceding nasal*
[β]	b, v	objeto, pueblo	*fricative: pronounced when it does not occur in the absolute initial sound or after **m, n.***
[m]	m, n	mamá, convivir	*every non-word-final **m** and **n** before [p] [b]*
[mg]	n	enfermo, infusión	*every **n** which comes before **f***
[n]	n	nadie, entre	
[n̪]	n	quince, conciencia	***n** together with a following [θ]*
[n̪]	n	condenar, cantar	*dentalised **n:** together with a following [t] or [d]*
[ŋ]	n	cinco, fingir	*syllable-final **n** together with a following velar consonant*
[ɲ]	ñ, n	viña, concha	***ñ** in the initial sound of the syllable and in syllable-final **n** before a palatal consonant*
[f]	f	café	
[k]	k, c, q	kilo, casa, que, actor	*occurs in the groupings **c + a,o,u** and **qu + e,i** and with syllable-final **c***
[g]	g, gu	garra, guerra,	*plosive: occurs in the absolute initial sound or in the medial sound with preceding nasal in the groupings **g + a,o,u** and **gu + e,i***

[x]	j, g	rojo, girar, gente	*equivalent to **j** and to the groupings **g** + **e,i***
[ɣ]	g, gu	agua, alegre, estigma	*fricative: occurs in the groupings **g** + **a,o,u** and **gu** + **e,i**, when it does not come in the absolute initial sound or follow **n***
[t]	t	letra, tío	*plosive: equivalent to **d** in the absolute initial sound or after **n** or **l***
[d]	d	dedo, conde, caldo	*plosive: equivalent to **d** when it occurs in the absolute initial sound or follows **n** or **l***
[ð]	d,t	cada, escudo, juventud	*fricative: equivalent to **d** when it does not occur in the absolute initial sound or follow **n** or **l***
[θ]	c, z	cero, zarza, cruz	*occurs in the groupings **c** + **e,i** and **z** + **a,o,u** and in the final sound*
[l]	l	libro, bloque, sal	
[l̪]	l	alce	*interdental **l**: occurs together with a following [θ]*
[l̪]	l	altura, caldo	*dental **l**: occurs together with a following [t] or [d]*
[ʎ]	ll, l	llueve, colcha	*equivalent to **ll** and syllable-final **l** before a palatal consonant*
[s]	s	así, coser	
[r]	r	caro, prisa	*equivalent to the letter **r** when it occurs at the beginning of a word or follows **n, l, s***
[rr]	r, rr	roca, honrado	*equivalent to -**rr**- and **r-**, -**r**- at the beginning of a word or at the beginning of a syllable after **n, l, s***
[tʃ]	ch	chino	
[ɟ]	y, hi	cónyuge, inyección, yunque	*palatal affricate: fricative when **y, hi** occurs in the initial sound of a syllable*
[ʃ]	sh	shock	*like English **shock, show***

Hispano-American pronunciation bears the closest similarity to that of the Andalusian region. Among the phonetic peculiarities to be encountered in the Hispano-American linguistic areas, the following phenomena are the most prominent:

yeísmo

The **ll** is pronounced like a **y** (**yovér**, as opposed to *llover* **llovér**). This phonetic phenomenon is usual not only in Spanish-speaking areas of America but also in various regions of Spain like Andalusia, the Canary Islands, Extremadura, Madrid and Castilian subregions. The assumption that the **yeísmo** is a phonetic feature of all Hispano-American countries is false. The standard pronunciation of **ll** is maintained in subregions of Chile, Peru, Columbia and Ecuador.

A further peculiarity is the pronunciation of **y** as a **dʒ** (**adʒér**, as opposed to *ayer* **aⱼér**) in Argentina, Uruguay and subregions of Ecuador and Mexico.

seseo

z and **c** (θ) are pronounced like **s** (**sínko**, as opposed to *cinco* **θínko**). This dialectal peculiarity is widespread not only in Hispano-America but also in subregions of Andalusia and on the Canary Islands.

In the vernacular pronunciation of some areas of Spain and Hispano-America, one also encounters aspiration of the **s** in the final sound (**lah kása**, as opposed to *las casas* – **las kásas**), which may even disappear altogether (**mímo**, as opposed to *mismo* **mísmo**). Both phenomena are considered vulgar and should therefore be avoided.

► SÍMBOLOS FONÉTICOS DEL INGLÉS
ENGLISH PHONETIC SYMBOLS

[ɑː]	plant, farm, father	[l]	lamp, oil, ill
[aɪ]	life	[m]	man, am
[aʊ]	house	[n]	no, manner
[æ]	man, sad	[ɒ]	not, long
[b]	been, blind	[ɔː]	law, all
[d]	do, had	[ɔɪ]	boy, oil
[ð]	this, father	[p]	paper, happy
[e]	get, bed	[r]	red, dry
[eɪ]	name, lame	[s]	stand, sand, yes
[ə]	ago, better	[ʃ]	ship, station
[ɛː]	bird, her	[t]	tell, fat
[eə]	there, care	[tʃ]	church, catch
[ʌ]	but, son	[ʊ]	push, look
[f]	father, wolf	[uː]	you, do
[g]	go, beg	[ʊə]	poor, sure
[ŋ]	long, sing	[v]	voice, live
[h]	house	[w]	water, we, which
[ɪ]	it, wish	[z]	zeal, these, gaze
[iː]	bee, me, beat, belief	[ʒ]	pleasure
[ɪə]	here	[dʒ]	jam, object
[j]	youth	[θ]	thank, death
[k]	keep, milk		

A a

A, a *f* A, a; ~ **de Antonio** A for Andrew *Brit*, A for Abel *Am*

a *prep* **1.**(*dirección*) to; **ir ~ Barcelona** to go to Barcelona; **llegar ~ Madrid** to arrive in Madrid **2.**(*posición*) at; ~ **la mesa** at the table; ~ **la derecha** on the right **3.**(*distancia*) ~ **10 kilómetros de aquí** 10 kilometres (away) from here **4.**(*tiempo*) at; (*hasta*) until; ~ **las tres** at three o'clock; ~ **mediodía** at noon **5.**(*modo*) ~ **pie** on foot; **ir ~ pie** to walk; ~ **mano** by hand; ~ **oscuras** in the dark **6.**(*precio*) ¿~ **cómo está?** how much is it?; ~ **2 euros el kilo** (at) 2 euros a kilo **7.**(*relación*) **dos ~ dos** two all **8.**(*complemento*) **oler ~ gas** to smell of gas; **he visto ~ tu hermano** I've seen your brother **9.**(*con infinitivo*) **empezó ~ correr** he/she began to run **10.**(+ *que*) **¡~ que llueve mañana!** I bet it'll rain tomorrow!

> [!] **a** in combination with the masculine definite article 'el' becomes 'al': "Mañana voy al teatro con algunos amigos; Segovia está al norte de Madrid."

abad(esa) *m(f)* abbot *m,* abbess *f*
abadía *f* abbey
abajo *adv* **1.**(*movimiento*) down; **calle ~** down the street; **de arriba ~** from top to bottom **2.**(*estado*) down (below); (*en casa*) downstairs; **hacia ~** down, downwards; **el ~ firmante** the undersigned; **de veinte para ~** twenty or under; **véase más ~** see below
abalanzarse <z→c> *vr* ~ **a la ventana** to dash (over) to the window; ~ **sobre algo** to pounce on sth
abandonado, -a *adj ser* (*descuidado*) neglected; (*desaseado*) slovenly
abandonar I. *vi* DEP to withdraw

II. *vt* **1.**(*dejar*) to leave; (*niño*) to abandon; (*fuerzas*) to desert **2.**(*renunciar*) to give up **3.**INFOR (*interrumpir*) to leave **III.** *vr:* ~**se** to give oneself over
abandono *m* **1.**(*abandonamiento*) abandonment **2.**(*renuncia*) renunciation; (*de una idea*) giving-up **3.**(*descuido*) neglect
abanicar <c→qu> *vt* to fan
abanico *m* fan; (*de posibilidades*) range
abaratar I. *vt* (*precios*) to lower; (*costes*) to cut **II.** *vr:* ~**se** to become cheaper
abarcar <c→qu> *vt* **1.**(*comprender*) to include; ~ **con la vista** to take in; **quien mucho abarca poco aprieta** don't bite off more than you can chew **2.**(*contener*) to contain
abarrotado *adj* completely full; (*de gente*) crowded
abastecer *irr como crecer vt* ~ **de** [*o* **con**] **algo** to provide with sth; COM to supply with sth
abastecimiento *m* supply
abasto *m* supply; **no dar ~ con algo** to be unable to cope with sth
abatido, -a *adj* dejected
abatimiento *m* dejection
abatir I. *vt* (*casa*) to demolish; (*árbol*) to fell, to chop down *Am;* (*avión*) to shoot down; (*respaldo*) to recline **II.** *vr:* ~**se 1.**(*desanimarse*) to become dejected **2.**(*precipitarse*) ~**se sobre algo** to pounce on sth
abdicación *f* abdication
abdicar <c→qu> *vt* **1.**(*monarca*) to abdicate **2.**(*ideales*) to renounce
abdomen *m* abdomen
abdominal I. *adj* abdominal **II.** *m* DEP press-up *Brit,* sit-up *Am*
abecedario *m* alphabet
abedul *m* birch
abeja *f* bee
abejorro *m* bumblebee
aberración *f* aberration
abertura *f* **1.**(*acción*) opening **2.**(*hueco*) hole **3.**(*franqueza*) openness
abeto *m* fir

abierto, -a I. *pp de* **abrir II.** *adj* **1.** (*cosa*) open; **en campo** ~ in the open country **2.** (*persona*) open--minded

abigarrado, -a *adj* many-coloured *Brit,* many-colored *Am*

abismal *adj* enormous

abismo *m* abyss

abjurar *vi, vt* ~ (**de**) **algo** to renounce sth

ablandar I. *vt* **1.** (*poner blando*) to soften **2.** (*calmar*) to soothe **II.** *vr:* ~**se 1.** (*ponerse blando*) to soften **2.** (*persona*) to relent

abnegación *f* self-denial

abnegado, -a *adj* selfless

abocado, -a *adj* (*vino*) smooth

abochornar I. *vt* **1.** (*calor*) to oppress; **estoy abochornado** I'm stifled **2.** (*avergonzar*) to embarrass **II.** *vr* ~**se de** [*o por*] **algo** to be embarrassed by sth

abofetear *vt* to slap

abogacía *f* legal profession

abogado, -a *m, f* **1.** JUR lawyer; (*en tribunal*) barrister, attorney *Am;* ~ **defensor** defense lawyer **2.** (*defensor*) advocate

abogar <g→gu> *vi* ~ **por algo** to advocate sth

abolengo *m* ancestry

abolición *f* abolition

abolir *irr vt* to abolish

abolladura *f* dent

abollar *vt* to dent

abominable *adj* abominable

abominación *f* abomination

abonado, -a *m, f* (*a revistas*) subscriber; (*a electricidad*) customer

abonar I. *vt* **1.** (*garantizar*) to guarantee **2.** (*pagar*) to pay; ~ **en cuenta** to credit to an account **3.** (*terreno*) to fertilize **II.** *vr:* ~**se** to subscribe

abono *m* **1.** (*metro*) t. TEAT season ticket **2.** PREN subscription **3.** (*pago*) payment; ~ **en cuenta** credit **4.** (*fertilizante*) fertilizer, manure

abordar *vt* **1.** (*barco*) to board **2.** (*persona*) to approach **3.** (*tema*) to discuss; (*problema*) to tackle

aborigen I. *adj* aboriginal **II.** *mf* aborigine

aborrecer *irr como crecer vt* to loathe

abortar I. *vi* **1.** (*provocado*) to have an abortion **2.** (*espontáneo*) to have a miscarriage **3.** (*fracasar*) to fail **II.** *vt* to abort

aborto *m* **1.** (*provocado*) abortion **2.** (*espontáneo*) miscarriage

abota(r)gado, -a *adj* bloated

abotonar *vt* to button up

abovedar *vt* to vault

abrasar I. *vi* (*sol*) to scorch; (*comida*) to be burning hot **II.** *vt* **1.** (*quemar*) to burn **2.** (*plantas*) to dry up

abrazadera *f* **1.** TIPO bracket **2.** TÉC clamp

abrazar <z→c> **I.** *vt* **1.** (*persona*) to embrace **2.** (*abarcar*) to take in; (*religión*) to adopt **II.** *vr:* ~**se** to embrace (each other)

abrazo *m* embrace; **dar un** ~ **a alguien** to give sb a hug

abrebotellas *m inv* bottle opener

abrecartas *m inv* letter opener

abrelatas *m inv* tin opener, can opener *Am*

abreviar *vt* (*palabras*) to abbreviate; (*texto*) to abridge

abreviatura *f* abbreviation

abridor *m* opener

abrigar <g→gu> **I.** *vt* **1.** (*del viento*) to protect **2.** (*cubrir*) to cover **3.** (*tener*) to hold; (*esperanzas*) to cherish; (*proyectos*) to harbour *Brit,* to harbor *Am* **II.** *vr:* ~**se** to wrap up (warm)

abrigo *m* coat; **al** ~ **de** protected by

abril *m* April; *v.t.* **marzo**

abrillantar *vt* to polish

abrir *irr* **I.** *vt* **1.** (*algo cerrado*) to open; (*paraguas*) to put up; (*grifo*) to turn on; (*con la llave*) to unlock; (*luz*) to turn on; **a medio** ~ (*puerta*) half-open **2.** (*canal, túnel*) to dig; (*agujero*) to bore **3.** (*perspectivas, mercado*) to open up **II.** *vr:* ~**se 1.** (*puerta, herida*) to open **2.** (*confiar*) to confide **3.** *inf* (*irse*) to beat it

abrochar *vt* (*con broches*) to fasten; (*con botones*) to button (up)

abrumar *vt* **1.** (*agobiar*) to over-

whelm **2.** (*con elogios*) to wear out
abrupto, -a *adj* **1.** (*camino*) steep
2. (*carácter*) abrupt
absceso *m* abscess
absentismo *m* absenteeism
absolución *f* **1.** JUR acquittal **2.** REL
absolution
absoluto, -a *adj* absolute; **en ~** not at
all
absolver *irr como volver* vt **1.** JUR to
acquit **2.** REL to absolve
absorbente *adj* **1.** (*esponja*) absorbent **2.** (*trabajo*) demanding
absorber vt **1.** t. FÍS to absorb **2.** (*empresa*) to take over
absorción *f* **1.** (*de líquidos*) t. FÍS absorption **2.** ECON takeover
absorto, -a *adj* **1.** (*pasmado*) amazed
2. (*entregado*) absorbed
abstención *f* t. POL abstention
abstenerse *irr como tener* vr t. POL to
abstain; (*del tabaco*) to refrain
abstinencia *f* abstinence
abstracción *f* abstraction
abstracto, -a *adj* abstract
abstraer *irr como traer* **I.** vt to abstract **II.** vr ~se en algo to be absorbed in sth
abstraído, -a *adj* lost in thought
absurdo, -a *adj* absurd
abuchear vt to boo; (*silbando*) to
hiss
abuelo, -a *m, f* grandfather *m*,
grandmother *f;* **los ~s** the grandparents
abulense *adj* of/from Avila
abulia *f* apathy
abúlico, -a *adj* weak-willed
abultado, -a *adj* bulky; (*labios*) thick
abultar vt **1.** (*aumentar*) to increase
2. (*exagerar*) to exaggerate
abundancia *f* abundance; **vivir en
la ~** to be affluent
abundante *adj* abundant; (*lluvia*)
heavy; (*cosecha*) plentiful
abundar vi to abound; ~ **en algo** to
be rich in sth
aburrido, -a *adj* **1.** *estar* (*harto*)
bored **2.** *ser* (*pesado*) boring
aburrimiento *m* **1.** (*tedio*) boredom
2. (*fastidio*) bore
aburrir **I.** vt **1.** (*hastiar*) to bore

2. (*fastidiar*) to weary **II.** vr: ~se to
be bored
abusar vi **1.** (*usar indebidamente*) ~
de algo to misuse sth **2.** (*aprovecharse*) ~ **de alguien** to take advantage of sb
abusivo, -a *adj* improper; (*precios*)
outrageous
abuso *m* misuse
abyecto, -a *adj* wretched
a.C. *abr de* **antes de Cristo** AD
acá *adv* here
acabado, -a *adj* **1.** (*completo*) finished **2.** (*salud*) ruined
acabar **I.** vi **1.** (*terminar*) to end; ~
bien/mal to turn out well/badly; ~
de hacer algo to have just done sth;
ella acaba de llegar she's just arrived **2.** (*destruir*) ~ **con algo** to finish sth off; ~ **con alguien** to put paid
to sb **II.** vt **1.** (*terminar*) to finish
2. (*consumir*) to finish off **III.** vr: ~se
to come to an end; **se ha acabado**
there's no left; **todo se acabó** it's all
over
acabóse *m inf* **¡esto es el ~!** that
really is the limit!
acacia *f* acacia
academia *f* **1.** (*corporación*) academy **2.** (*colegio*) (private) school
académico, -a *adj* academic
acaecer *irr como crecer* vi to happen
acallar vt **1.** (*hacer callar*) to silence
2. (*apaciguar*) to pacify
acalorado, -a *adj* heated
acalorarse vr **1.** (*sofocarse*) to get
hot **2.** (*enfadarse*) to get angry
acampar vi to camp
acanalar vt to furrow
acantilado *m* cliff
acantilado, -a *adj* steep
acaparar vt **1.** (*objetos*) to hoard
2. (*miradas*) to captivate
acariciar vt **1.** (*persona*) to caress
2. (*plan*) to toy with
acarrear vt **1.** (*transportar*) to transport **2.** (*ocasionar*) to cause
acaso **I.** *m* chance **II.** *adv* maybe; **por
si ~** (*en caso de*) in case; (*en todo
caso*) just in case
acatamiento *m* **1.** (*respeto*) respect
2. (*de las leyes*) compliance

acatar *vt* **1.** (*respetar*) to respect **2.** (*obedecer*) to obey

acatarrarse *vr* to catch a cold

acaudalado, -a *adj* well-off

acaudillar *vt* to lead

acceder *vi* **1.** (*consentir*) to agree **2.** (*tener acceso*) to gain access **3.** (*ascender*) to accede

accesible *adj* **1.** (*persona*) approachable **2.** (*lugar*) accessible **3.** (*precios*) affordable

acceso *m t.* INFOR access

accesorio *m* accessory

accidentado, -a I. *adj* **1.** (*terreno*) rugged **2.** (*difícil*) difficult **II.** *m, f* injured person

accidental *adj* **1.** (*no esencial*) incidental **2.** (*casual*) casual

accidentarse *vr* to have an accident

accidente *m* **1.** (*de tráfico*) accident **2.** (*desnivel*) unevenness

acción *f* **1.** (*acto*) act **2.** *t.* MIL, JUR (*influencia*) action **3.** FIN share

accionar *vt* TÉC to operate

accionista *mf* shareholder, stockholder

acebo *m* holly

acecho *m* **estar al** ~ to lie in wait

aceite *m* oil

aceitera *f* **1.** (*recipiente*) oil-can **2.** *pl* (*vinagreras*) cruet

aceitoso, -a *adj* oily

aceituna *f* olive

aceitunado, -a *adj* olive(-green)

acelerador *m* AUTO accelerator *Brit,* gas pedal *Am*

acelerar *vt* to accelerate; ~ **el paso** to walk faster

acelga *f* chard

acento *m* **1.** (*prosódico*) stress **2.** (*pronunciación*) accent **3.** (*énfasis*) emphasis

acentuar <*I. pres:* acentúo> *vt* **1.** (*al pronunciar*) to stress; (*al escribir*) to write with an accent **2.** (*resaltar*) to highlight

acepción *f* sense, meaning

aceptación *f* **1.** (*aprobación*) approval **2.** COM, JUR acceptance

aceptar *vt* **1.** (*recibir*) to accept **2.** (*conformarse*) to agree

acequia *f* irrigation ditch

acera *f* pavement *Brit,* sidewalk *Am*

acerado, -a *adj* **1.** (*de acero*) steel **2.** (*mordaz*) biting

acerbo, -a *adj* **1.** (*gusto*) sharp **2.** (*despiadado*) cruel; (*crítica, tono*) harsh

acerca *prep* ~ **de** (*sobre*) about; (*en relación a*) concerning

acercar <c→qu> **I.** *vt* **1.** (*poner más cerca*) to bring nearer **2.** (*traer*) to bring over **II.** *vr:* ~**se 1.** (*aproximarse*) ~**se a alguien/algo** to approach sb/sth **2.** (*ir*) to come round

acerico *m* pincushion

acero *m* steel

acérrimo, -a I. *superl de* **acre**[1] **II.** *adj* (*defensor*) staunch; (*enemigo*) bitter

acertado, -a *adj* **1.** (*correcto*) correct **2.** (*atinado*) accurate **3.** (*conveniente*) apt

acertar <e→ie> *vt* **1.** (*dar en el blanco*) to hit **2.** (*encontrar*) to find; ~ **con algo** to come across sth **3.** (*conseguir*) ~ **a** to manage to **4.** (*adivinar*) to get right

acertijo *m* riddle

acervo *m* store; ~ **cultural** cultural heritage

achacar <c→qu> *vt* to attribute

achacoso, -a *adj* sickly

achaque *m* ailment

achicar <c→qu> **I.** *vt* **1.** (*empequeñecer*) to make smaller **2.** (*intimidar*) to intimidate **3.** (*agua*) to bale out **II.** *vr:* ~**se 1.** (*ropa*) to shrink **2.** (*acoquinarse*) to take fright

achicharrar I. *vt* **1.** (*calor*) to scorch **2.** (*comida*) to burn **II.** *vr:* ~**se** to be sweltering

achicoria *f* chicory

aciago, -a *adj* ill-fated

acicalarse *vr* to get dressed up

acicate *m* **1.** (*espuela*) spur **2.** (*estímulo*) stimulus

acidez *f* acidity

ácido *m* acid

ácido, -a *adj* sour

acierto *m* **1.** (*en el tiro*) accuracy **2.** (*éxito*) success; (*en la lotería*) right number **3.** (*habilidad*) skill

aclamación *f* applause; **por** ~ by acclamation

aclamar *vt* **1.**(*vitorear*) to cheer **2.**POL to acclaim

aclaración *f* **1.**(*clarificación*) clarification **2.**(*explicación*) explanation

aclarar I. *vt* **1.**(*hacer más claro*) to lighten; (*voz*) to clear **2.**(*un líquido*) to thin (down) **3.**(*explicar*) to explain **4.**(*crimen*) to solve II. *vr:* ~**se** **1.**(*problema*) to be clarified **2.***inf* (*entender*) to catch on

aclaratorio, -a *adj* explanatory

aclimatación *f* acclimatization *Brit,* acclimation *Am*

aclimatar I. *vt* to acclimatize *Brit,* to acclimate *Am* II. *vr:* ~**se** to get acclimatized

acné *m o f sin pl* acne

acobardar I. *vt* to frighten; (*con palabras*) to intimidate II. *vr:* ~**se** **1.**(*desanimarse*) to flinch from **2.**(*intimidarse*) to be frightened

acogedor(a) *adj* welcoming, inviting

acoger <g→j> I. *vt* to welcome; (*recibir*) to receive II. *vr:* ~**se 1.**(*refugiarse*) to take refuge **2.**(*ampararse*) to shelter **3.**(*basarse*) to resort

acogida *f* welcome; (*recibimiento*) reception; **tener una buena** ~ (*persona*) to be well received; (*proyecto*) to meet with approval

acolchar *vt* to quilt

acometer *vt* **1.**(*embestir*) to attack **2.**(*emprender*) to undertake

acometida *f* **1.**(*embestida*) attack **2.**TÉC connection

acomodado, -a *adj* **1.**(*cómodo*) comfortable **2.**(*rico*) well-off, reasonable

acomodador(a) *m(f)* TEAT, CINE usher

acomodar I. *vt* **1.**(*adaptar*) to adapt **2.**(*colocar*) to place **3.**(*albergar*) to accommodate II. *vr:* ~**se** to adapt oneself, to put up with everything

acomodaticio, -a *adj* **1.**(*adaptable*) adaptable **2.***pey* (*oportunista*) opportunistic

acompañante *mf* **1.**(*de una dama*) escort **2.**(*en el coche*) passenger

acompañar *vt* **1.**(*ir con*) *t.* MÚS to accompany **2.**(*hacer compañía*) ~ **a**

alguien to keep sb company **3.**(*adjuntar*) to enclose

acomplejar I. *vt* to give a complex II. *vr:* ~**se** to get a complex

acondicionar *vt* **1.**(*preparar*) to prepare **2.**(*climatizar*) to air-condition

acongojar *vt* to distress

aconsejar *vt* to advise

acontecer *irr como crecer vi* to happen

acontecimiento *m* event

acopio *m* store; **hacer** ~ **de algo** to stock up with sth

acoplamiento *m* coupling

acoplar *vt* **1.**(*ajustar*) to adjust **2.**FERRO to fit together **3.**ELEC to connect

acorazar <z→c> I. *vt* to armourplate *Brit,* to armorplate *Am* II. *vr:* ~**se** to arm oneself

acordar <o→ue> I. *vt* **1.**(*convenir*) to agree **2.**(*decidir*) to decide II. *vr* ~**se de** to remember

acorde I. *adj* **1.**(*conforme*) agreed; **estar** ~ **con** to be in agreement with **2.**MÚS harmonious II. *m* MÚS chord

acordeón *m* accordion

acordonar *vt* **1.**(*botas*) to lace up **2.**(*un sitio*) to cordon off

acorralar *vt* **1.**(*ganado*) to round up **2.**(*intimidar*) to intimidate

acortar I. *vt* to shorten; (*duración*) to cut down II. *vr:* ~**se** to become shorter

acosar *vt* **1.**(*perseguir*) to hound **2.**(*asediar*) to harass; (*con preguntas*) to pester

acoso *m* relentless pursuit; ~ **sexual** sexual harassment

acostar <o→ue> I. *vt* to put to bed II. *vr:* ~**se 1.**(*descansar*) to lie down **2.**(*ir a la cama*) to go to bed

acostumbrado, -a *adj* accustomed; **mal** ~ spoilt

acostumbrar I. *vi* ~ **a hacer algo** to be used to doing sth II. *vr:* ~**se a algo** to get accustomed to sth

acotación *f* **1.**(*nota*) margin note **2.**TEAT stage direction **3.**(*cota*) elevation mark

acre[1] *adj* <acérrimo> **1.**(*áspero*) bitter **2.**(*ácido*) sour **3.**(*mordaz*) scathing

acre² *m* acre

acrecentar <e→ie> *vt,* **acrecer** *irr como crecer vt* to increase

acreditar I. *vt* 1. (*atestiguar*) to vouch for 2. (*autorizar*) to authorize 3. (*diplomático*) to accredit 4. FIN to credit II. *vr:* ~se to get a reputation

acreedor(a) I. *adj* ~ **a** [*o* de] **algo** worthy of sth II. *m(f)* FIN creditor

acribillar *vt* 1. (*abrir agujeros*) to riddle 2. (*a preguntas*) to pester

acróbata *mf* acrobat

acta *f* 1. (*de una reunión*) minutes *pl;* **levantar** ~ **de algo** to draw up a document of sth 2. (*certificado*) certificate 3. JUR act

actitud *f* 1. (*corporal*) posture 2. (*disposición*) attitude 3. (*comportamiento*) behaviour *Brit,* behavior *Am*

activar *vt* 1. (*avivar*) to stimulate 2. QUÍM, FÍS, INFOR to activate; (*bomba*) to detonate

actividad *f* (*general*) activity; **volcán en** ~ active volcano

activo *m* FIN assets *pl*

activo, -a *adj* active

acto *m* 1. (*acción*) action; ~ **seguido...** immediately after ...; **en el** ~ immediately, on the spot 2. (*ceremonia*) ceremony 3. TEAT act

actor, actriz *m, f* TEAT, CINE actor *m,* actress *f*

actuación *f* 1. (*conducta*) conduct 2. (*actividad*) activity 3. TEAT, MÚS performance; ~ **en directo** live performance 4. *pl* JUR legal proceedings *pl*

actual *adj* 1. (*de ahora*) present 2. (*corriente*) current

actualidad *f* present; **en la** ~ at present; **ser de gran** ~ to be topical

actualizar <z→c> *vt* to bring up to date

actualmente *adv* at the moment, currently

actuar <*1. pres:* actúo> *vi* 1. (*hacer*) to work; ~ **sobre algo** to have an effect on sth 2. TEAT to act; ~ **en directo** to perform live

acuarela *f* watercolour *Brit,* watercolor *Am*

acuario *m* aquarium

Acuario *m* Aquarius

acuático, -a *adj* aquatic; **parque** ~ waterpark

acuchillar *vt* 1. (*herir*) to knife 2. (*parqué*) to sand down; (*muebles*) to scrape

acuciar *vt* to hurry up

acudir *vi* 1. (*ir*) to go 2. (*recurrir*) to turn to

acuerdo *m* 1. (*convenio*) *t.* POL agreement; **¡de** ~**!** I agree!, OK!; **de** ~ **con** in accordance with 2. (*decisión*) decision

acumular *vt* 1. (*reunir*) to collect 2. (*amontonar*) *t.* ELEC to accumulate

acuñar *vt* 1. (*monedas*) to mint 2. (*palabras*) to coin

acuoso, -a *adj* watery

acupuntura *f* acupuncture

acurrucarse <c→qu> *vr* to curl up; (*agacharse*) to crouch

acusación *f* accusation; JUR charge

acusar *vt* 1. (*culpar*) to accuse 2. (*en juicio*) to charge 3. (*en la escuela*) to tell on 4. ECON to confirm

acuse *m* ~ **de recibo** acknowledgement of receipt

acústico, -a *adj* acoustic

adagio *m* 1. (*proverbio*) adage 2. MÚS adagio

adaptable *adj* adaptable

adaptación *f* adaptation

adaptador *m* TÉC adapter

adaptar I. *vt* 1. *t.* CINE (*acomodar*) to adapt 2. (*edificio*) to convert 3. (*ajustar*) to adjust II. *vr:* ~se to adapt

adecuado, -a *adj* 1. (*apto*) appropriate 2. (*palabras*) fitting

adecuar *vt, vr:* ~se to adapt

a. de (J)C. *abr de* **antes de (Jesu)cristo** BC

adelantado, -a *adj* advanced; **por** ~ in advance

adelantamiento *m* 1. (*avance*) advance 2. (*del coche*) overtaking *Brit,* passing *Am*

adelantar I. *vi* 1. (*reloj*) to be fast 2. (*progresar*) to progress 3. (*coche*) to overtake *Brit,* to pass *Am* II. *vt*

1. (*reloj*) to put forward 2. (*avanzar*) to move forward 3. (*coche*) to overtake *Brit,* to pass *Am* 4. (*viaje*) to bring forward 5. (*paga*) to advance 6. (*ganar*) to gain III. *vr:* ~se 1. (*reloj*) to be fast 2. (*avanzarse*) to go forward 3. (*llegar antes*) to get ahead 4. (*anticiparse*) to anticipate

adelante *adv* forward, ahead *Am;* ¡~! come in!; **seguir** ~ to go (straight) on

adelanto *m* 1. (*progreso*) progress 2. (*anticipo*) advance

adelgazar <z→c> I. *vi, vr:* ~se to lose weight II. *vt* (*peso*) to reduce

ademán *m* 1. (*gesto*) gesture 2. (*actitud*) attitude

además *adv* besides, moreover

adentrarse *vr* 1. (*entrar*) to go into 2. (*estudiar*) to study thoroughly

adentro *adv* inside; **mar** ~ out to sea; **tierra** ~ inland

adentros *mpl* **para sus** ~ inwardly

aderezar <z→c> *vt* (*condimentar*) to season; (*ensalada*) to dress

aderezo *m* (*condimentación*) seasoning; (*de, para una ensalada*) dressing

adeudar I. *vt* (*deber*) to owe; (*en cuenta*) to debit II. *vr:* ~se to run into debt

adherir *irr como sentir* I. *vt* (*sello*) to stick II. *vr:* ~se 1. (*pegarse*) to adhere 2. (*a una opinión*) to support 3. (*a un partido*) to join

adhesión *f* 1. (*adherencia*) adhesion 2. (*a una opinión*) support

adicción *f* addiction

adición *f* t. MAT addition

adicionar *vt* to add

adicto, -a I. *adj* addicted II. *m, f* addict

adiestrar *vt* to train

adinerado, -a *adj* wealthy

adiós *interj* 1. (*despedida*) goodbye, bye 2. (*al pasar*) hello, hi

aditivo *m* additive

aditivo, -a *adj* additional

adivinanza *f* riddle

adivinar *vt* 1. (*el futuro*) to foretell 2. (*conjeturar*) to guess

adjetivo *m* adjective

adjudicación *f* 1. (*de un premio*)

award(ing) 2. (*en una subasta*) sale

adjudicar <c→qu> I. *vt* 1. (*premio*) to award 2. (*en una subasta*) to knock down *Brit,* to sell at auction *Am* II. *vr:* ~se (*apropiarse*) to appropriate

adjuntar *vt* to enclose

adjunto, -a *adj* 1. (*junto*) enclosed 2. (*auxiliar*) assistant

administración *f* 1. (*dirección*) administration; **la** ~ **española** the Spanish authorities; ~ **municipal** town/city council 2. (*de sacramentos*) administering

administrador(a) *m(f)* administrator; (*gerente*) manager

administrar *vt* administer

administrativo, -a I. *adj* administrative II. *m, f* clerk

admirable *adj* admirable

admiración *f* 1. (*respeto*) admiration 2. (*signo*) exclamation mark

admirar *vt* 1. (*adorar, apreciar*) to admire 2. (*asombrar*) to amaze

admisible *adj* admissible

admisión *f* admission, acceptance

admitir *vt* 1. (*en universidad*) to admit, to accept 2. (*aceptar*) to accept 3. (*reconocer*) to recognize 4. (*permitir*) to permit

admonición *f* warning

ADN *m abr de* **ácido desoxirribonucleico** DNA

adobar *vt* 1. (*con salsa*) to marinade 2. (*piel*) to tan

adobe *m* adobe

adoctrinar *vt* to indoctrinate

adolecer *irr como crecer vi* to suffer

adolescencia *f* adolescence

adolescente I. *adj* adolescent II. *mf* teenager, teen *Am, inf*

adonde *adv* (*relativo*) where

adónde *adv* (*interrogativo*) where

adopción *f* adoption

adoptar *vt* to adopt

adoptivo, -a *adj* 1. (*personas*) adoptive, foster *Am* 2. (*cosas*) adopted, foster *Am*

adoquín *m* cobblestone

adorar *vt* to adore; (*idolatrar*) to worship

adormecer *irr como crecer* I. *vt* to

make sleepy **II.** *vr:* ~**se** to fall asleep

adornar *vt* to adorn

adorno *m* adornment; (*decoración*) decoration

adosado, -a *adj* **casa adosada** semi-detached house

adquirir *irr vt* **1.** (*conseguir*) to acquire **2.** (*comprar*) to purchase

adquisición *f* acquisition; (*de una empresa*) takeover

adrede *adv* on purpose

Adriático *m* Adriatic

adscribir *irr como escribir vt* **1.** (*atribuir*) to assign **2.** (*destinar*) to appoint

aduana *f* **1.** (*tasa*) customs duty; **sin ~** duty-free **2.** (*oficina*) customs office

aduanero, -a **I.** *adj* customs **II.** *m, f* customs officer

aducir *irr como traducir vt* (*razón, motivo*) to put forward; (*prueba*) to provide

adueñarse *vr* to take possession

adulación *f* flattery

adular *vt* to flatter

adulterar *vt* to adulterate

adulterio *m* adultery

adúltero, -a **I.** *adj* adulterous **II.** *m, f* adulterer

adulto, -a **I.** *adj* adult **II.** *m, f* adult

adusto, -a *adj* **1.** (*persona*) stern **2.** (*región*) austere

advenedizo, -a **I.** *adj* upstart **II.** *m, f pey* upstart

advenimiento *m* advent

adverbio *m* adverb

adversario, -a *m, f* opponent

adversidad *f* **1.** (*contrariedad*) adversity **2.** (*desgracia*) setback

adverso, -a *adj* adverse

advertencia *f* **1.** (*amonestación*) warning **2.** (*indicación*) advice

advertir *irr como sentir vt* **1.** (*reparar*) to notice **2.** (*indicar*) to point out **3.** (*avisar*) to warn

adviento *m* Advent

adyacente *adj* adjacent

aéreo, -a *adj* aerial; (*tráfico*) air; **compañía aérea** airline (company); **por vía aérea** (by) airmail

aeróbic *m* aerobics

aerodeslizador *m* hovercraft

aerodinámico, -a *adj* aerodynamic

aeromodelismo *m* construction of model airplanes

aeronáutica *f* aeronautics

aeronave *f* airship

aeroplano *m* aeroplane *Brit,* airplane *Am*

aeropuerto *m* airport

aerosol *m* **1.** (*suspensión*) aerosol **2.** (*espray*) spray

aerotrén *m* aerotrain

afabilidad *f* affability

afable *adj* affable

afamado, -a *adj* famous

afán *m* **1.** (*ahínco*) eagerness; **con ~** eagerly **2.** (*anhelo*) longing

afanar **I.** *vi* to work hard **II.** *vr:* ~**se** to toil (away)

afanoso, -a *adj* **1.** (*trabajoso*) laborious **2.** (*persona*) industrious

afear *vt* to disfigure

afección *f* **1.** MED condition **2.** (*inclinación*) inclination

afectación *f* affectation

afectado, -a *adj* affected

afectar **I.** *vt* **1.** (*influir*) to concern **2.** (*dañar*) to harm; MED to attack **3.** (*impresionar*) to affect **II.** *vr:* ~**se** *AmL* to fall ill

afectísimo, -a *adj* **suyo ~** yours truly

afectivo, -a *adj* affective

afecto *m* ~ **a algo/alguien** affection for sth/sb

afecto, -a *adj* ~ **a algo/alguien** inclined towards sth/sb

afectuoso, -a *adj* affectionate

afeitadora *f* ~ **eléctrica** electric razor

afeitar **I.** *vt* (*persona*) to shave; **máquina de ~** (safety) razor **II.** *vr:* ~**se** to shave

afeminado, -a *adj* effeminate

aferrar **I.** *vt* to grasp **II.** *vr* ~**se a algo** to cling on sth

Afganistán *m* Afghanistan

afgano, -a *adj, m, f* Afghan

afianzamiento *m* **1.** (*sujeción*) fastening **2.** (*aseguramiento*) securing

afianzar <z→c> **I.** *vt* **1.** (*sujetar*) to fasten **2.** (*dar firmeza*) to strengthen; (*asegurar*) to secure **II.** *vr:* ~**se** to become established

afiche *m AmL* poster

afición *f* **1.** (*inclinación*) liking; **tener una ~ hacia algo** to be fond of sth **2.** (*pasatiempo*) hobby **3.** (*hinchada*) fans *pl*

aficionado, -a *adj* amateur **II.** *m, f* **1.** (*entusiasta*) lover; DEP fan **2.** (*no profesional*) amateur

aficionar I. *vt* ~ **a alguien a algo** to get sb interested in sth **II.** *vr* **~se a algo** to take a liking to sth

afilado, -a *adj* (*cuchillo*) sharp; (*nariz*) pointed; (*cara*) thin

afilar I. *vt* to sharpen **II.** *vr:* ~**se** (*cara*) to grow thin

afín *adj* related

afinar I. *vi* to play in tune **II.** *vt* **1.** (*hacer más fino*) to refine **2.** MÚS to tune

afincarse <c→qu> *vr* to become established

afinidad *f* **1.** (*semejanza*) similarity **2.** (*por parentesco*) relationship

afirmación *f* affirmation

afirmar I. *vt* **1.** (*decir sí*) to affirm **2.** (*aseverar*) to state **II.** *vr:* ~**se** to reaffirm

afirmativo, -a *adj* affirmative; **en caso ~** if so

aflicción *f* grief

afligir <g→j> **I.** *vt* **1.** (*apenar*) to upset **2.** (*atormentar*) to afflict **II.** *vr:* ~**se** to get upset

aflojar I. *vt* **1.** (*nudo*) to loosen **2.** (*cuerda*) to slacken (off) **3.** (*velocidad*) to reduce **II.** *vr:* ~**se** to slacken

aflorar *vi* to come to the surface; (*agua subterránea*) to emerge

afluente *m* tributary

afluir *irr como huir* *vi* **1.** (*río*) to flow into **2.** (*gente*) to flock

afónico, -a *adj* hoarse

aforo *m* **1.** (*en un estadio*) capacity **2.** TÉC gauging

afortunado, -a *adj* fortunate

afrenta *f* insult

África *f* Africa

africano, -a *adj, m, f* African

afrontar *vt* to face up to; (*problema*) to tackle

afuera *adv* outside; **¡~!** *inf* get out of here!

afueras *fpl* outskirts *pl*

agachar I. *vt* (*cabeza*) to lower **II.** *vr:* ~**se** **1.** (*encogerse*) to crouch **2.** *AmL* (*ceder*) to give in

agalla *f* (*de un pez*) gill; **tener ~s** *fig* to have guts

agarrado, -a *adj* stingy

agarrar I. *vi* **1.** (*echar raíces*) to take root **2.** (*coche*) to grip the road **II.** *vt* **1.** (*tomar*) to take **2.** (*asir*) to grasp **3.** (*delincuente*) to seize **4.** (*enfermedad*) to catch **III.** *vr:* ~**se** **1.** (*asirse*) to hold on **2.** (*reñir*) to have a fight **3.** (*comida*) to stick **4.** *AmL* (*coger*) to catch

agarrotar I. *vt* **1.** (*entumecer*) to stiffen up **2.** (*atar*) to tie tight **II.** *vr:* ~**se** (*entumecerse*) to go numb

agasajar *vt* **1.** (*recibir*) to receive in great style **2.** (*con comida*) to wine and dine

agencia *f* **1.** (*empresa*) agency; ~ **inmobiliaria** estate agency; ~ **de viajes** travel agency **2.** (*sucursal*) branch

agenciar I. *vt* *inf* to get **II.** *vr:* ~**se** to get hold of

agenda *f* **1.** (*calendario*) diary, engagement book *Am* **2.** (*cuaderno*) notebook

agente *mf* **1.** (*representante*) representative; (*de un artista*) agent; ~ **de bolsa** stockbroker **2.** (*funcionario*) ~ **de aduanas** customs officer; ~ **de policía** policeman

ágil *adj* **1.** (*de movimiento*) agile **2.** (*mental*) alert, quick-witted

agilidad *f* **1.** (*física*) agility **2.** (*mental*) acumen

agilizar <z→c> *vt* to speed up

agitación *f* **1.** (*movimiento*) movement; (*de un líquido*) stirring **2.** *t.* POL (*intranquilidad*) agitation

agitar I. *vt* **1.** (*mover*) to move; (*bandera*) to wave; (*botella*) to shake **2.** (*intranquilizar*) to worry **II.** *vr:* ~**se** **1.** (*moverse*) to move about **2.** (*excitarse*) to get excited; (*preocuparse*) to get upset

aglomeración *f* agglomeration

aglomerarse *vr* to crowd (together)

agnóstico, -a *adj, m, f* agnostic

agobiar I. *vt* **1.** (*abrumar*) to overwhelm **2.** (*calor*) to suffocate **II.** *vr:* ~**se 1.** (*sentirse abatido*) to feel overwhelmed **2.** (*angustiarse*) to be weighed down

agolparse *vr* to crowd (together)

agonía *f* **1.** (*del moribundo*) death throes *pl* **2.** (*angustia*) anguish

agonizar <z→c> *vi* to be dying

agosto *m* August; **hacer su** ~ to make a killing; *v.t.* **marzo**

agotado, -a *adj* **1.** (*producto*) out of stock **2.** (*persona*) exhausted

agotamiento *m* exhaustion

agotar I. *vt* **1.** (*existencias*) to use up **2.** (*mercancía*) to deplete **3.** (*paciencia*) to exhaust **4.** (*cansar*) to tire (out) **II.** *vr:* ~**se 1.** (*mercancía*) to run out **2.** (*pilas*) to run down [*o* out *Am*]

agraciado, -a *adj* **1.** (*bien parecido*) attractive **2.** (*afortunado*) lucky

agraciar *vt* **1.** (*conceder*) to award **2.** (*vestido*) to enhance

agradable *adj* pleasant

agradar *vi* to please; **me agrada oír música** I like listening to music

agradecer *irr como crecer vt* to thank; **les agradezco que...** I'm grateful to you for ...; **le ~ía mucho si** +*subj* I'd be very grateful if

agradecido, -a *adj* grateful

agradecimiento *m* gratitude

agrado *m* **1.** (*afabilidad*) affability **2.** (*complacencia*) willingness; **esto no es de mi** ~ this isn't to my liking

agrandar *vt* **1.** (*hacer más grande*) to make bigger **2.** (*exagerar*) to exaggerate

agrario, -a *adj* agrarian; **población agraria** rural population

agravante I. *adj* aggravating **II.** *m o f* aggravating factor

agravar I. *vt* (*enfermedad*) to make worse, to aggravate **II.** *vr:* ~**se** (*situación*) to worsen

agraviar *vt* to offend

agravio *m* (*ofensa*) offence *Brit,* offense *Am*

agredir *vt* to attack

agregado *m* aggregate

agregado, -a *adj, m, f* **1.** (*diplomático*) attaché **2.** UNIV assistant professor *Brit,* associate professor *Am*

agregar <g→gu> **I.** *vt* **1.** (*añadir*) to add **2.** (*persona*) to appoint **II.** *vr:* ~**se** to join

agresión *f* aggression

agresivo, -a *adj* aggressive

agriar I. *vt* to sour **II.** *vr:* ~**se** to turn sour

agrícola *adj* agricultural

agricultor(a) *m(f)* farmer

agricultura *f* agriculture

agridulce *adj* bittersweet; GASTR sweet-and-sour

agrietarse *vr* to crack; (*piel*) to become chapped

agrimensor(a) *m(f)* surveyor

agrio, -a *adj* bitter

agronomía *f* agronomy

agropecuario, -a *adj* agricultural, farming

agroturismo *m* agrotourism

agrupación *f* **1.** (*agrupamiento*) grouping **2.** (*conjunto*) group

agrupar I. *vt* to group (together) **II.** *vr:* ~**se** to form a group

agua *f* **1.** (*líquido*) water; ~ **de colonia** eau de cologne; ~ **con gas** sparkling water; ~ **del grifo** tap water; ~ **potable** drinking water; ~**s residuales** sewage; **caer mucha** ~ to rain a lot; **como** ~ **de mayo** *fig* very welcome; **estoy con el** ~ **hasta el cuello** *fig* I'm up to my neck in it; **¡hombre al** ~**!** man overboard! **2.** *pl* (*mar*) waters *pl;* ~**s abajo/arriba** downstream/upstream; ~**s menores** urine; **estar entre dos** ~**s** *fig* to be sitting on the fence

---

! With words like **agua** which begin with a stressed a- or ha- the masculine singular article is used even though these words are feminine: "el agua sucia; las aguas del mar Mediterráneo". Other examples include: "el águila, el ala, el alma, el ama, el área, el arte, el aula, el hacha, el hada, el hambre".

aguacate *m* avocado, alligator pear *Am*

aguacero *m* downpour

aguado, -a *adj* watered-down; (*fruta*) tasteless

aguafiestas *mf inv, inf* spoilsport, party pooper *Am*

aguafuerte *m* etching

aguanieve *f* sleet

aguantar I. *vt* **1.**(*sostener*) to hold; (*sujetar*) to hold tight; (*risa*) to hold back **2.**(*soportar*) to bear, to stand **II.** *vr:* ~**se 1.**(*contenerse*) to restrain oneself **2.**(*soportar*) to put up with it; (*tener paciencia*) to be patient **3.**(*sostenerse*) to support oneself

aguante *m* **1.**(*paciencia*) patience **2.**(*resistencia*) endurance

aguar <gu→gü> *vt* to water (down)

aguardar *vt* to wait for

aguardiente *m* brandy

aguarrás *m* turpentine

agudeza *f* **1.**(*del cuchillo*) sharpness **2.**(*ingenio*) wittiness

agudizar <z→c> **I.** *vt* **1.**(*hacer agudo*) to sharpen **2.**(*agravar*) to make worse **II.** *vr:* ~**se** to worsen

agudo, -a *adj* **1.**(*afilado*) sharp **2.**(*ingenioso*) witty; (*mordaz*) scathing **3.**(*dolor*) acute **4.**(*sonido*) piercing

agüero *m* **de mal** ~ ill-omened; **ser de buen** ~ to augur well

aguijón *m* **1.**ZOOL, BOT sting, stinger *Am* **2.**(*estímulo*) stimulus

águila *f* **1.**(*animal*) eagle **2.**(*persona*) very clever

aguileño, -a *adj* aquiline; **rostro** ~ angular face

aguinaldo *m* tip (*given at Christmas*)

aguja *f* **1.**(*general*) needle **2.**(*del reloj*) hand; (*de otros instrumentos*) pointer **3.**FERRO point

agujerear *vt* to make holes in; (*orejas*) to pierce

agujero *m* hole; ~ (**en la capa**) **de**

ozono hole in the ozone layer

agujetas *fpl* stiffness

aguzar <z→c> *vt* **1.**(*afilar*) to sharpen **2.**(*atención*) to heighten; (*sentidos*) to sharpen

ahí I. *adv* (*lugar*) there; ~ **está** there he/she/it is; **me voy por** ~ I'm going that way **II.** *conj* **de** ~ **que...** that is why ...

ahijado, -a *m, f* **1.**(*del padrino*) godchild **2.***fig* protégé *m,* protégée *f*

ahínco *m* **1.**(*afán*) zeal **2.**(*empeño*) effort

ahogar <g→gu> **I.** *vt* **1.**(*en el agua*) to drown **2.**(*estrangular*) to strangle **3.**(*asfixiar*) to suffocate **II.** *vr:* ~**se 1.**(*en el agua*) to drown **2.**(*asfixiarse*) to suffocate

ahogo *m* **1.**(*sofocación*) breathlessness **2.**(*asfixia*) asphyxiation

ahondar I. *vi* ~ **en algo** to go deeply into sth **II.** *vt* to deepen

ahora *adv* now; (*dentro de poco*) very soon; ~ **bien** now then; **de** ~ **en adelante** from now on; **hasta** ~ up to now; **por** ~ for the present; ~ **mismo vengo** I'm just coming; **acaba de salir** ~ **mismo** he/she has just gone out; **¿y** ~ **qué?** what now?

ahorcar <c→qu> **I.** *vt* to hang **II.** *vr:* ~**se** to hang oneself

ahorita *adv AmL* (*ahora*) right away

ahorrar I. *vt* **1.**(*dinero, fuerzas*) to save; (*explicaciones*) to spare **2.**(*economizar*) to economize **II.** *vr:* ~**se** to save oneself

ahorro *m* saving

ahuecar <c→qu> **I.** *vt* to hollow out **II.** *vr:* ~**se 1.**(*ave*) to ruffle (up) its feathers **2.**(*envanecerse*) to give oneself airs

ahumado, -a *adj* **1.**(*color*) smoky; (*cristal*) tinted **2.**(*salmón*) smoked

ahumar I. *vi* to smoke **II.** *vt* **1.**GASTR to smoke **2.**(*llenar de humo*) to fill with smoke **III.** *vr:* ~**se** to become blackened

ahuyentar *vt* **1.**(*espantar*) to frighten off **2.**(*dudas*) to dispel

airar *irr* **I.** *vt* to anger **II.** *vr:* ~**se** to get angry

airbag *m* airbag

aire *m* **1.**(*atmósfera*) air; **al ~ libre** in the open air; **tomar el ~** to go for a stroll **2.**(*viento*) wind; **corriente de ~** draught *Brit*, draft *Am* **3.**(*aspecto*) appearance **4.**(*garbo*) elegance

airear I. *vt* to air **II.** *vr:* **~se 1.**(*ventilarse*) to air **2.**(*coger aire*) to get some fresh air

airoso, -a *adj* graceful

aislado, -a *adj* isolated

aislar I. *vt* **1.**(*general*) to isolate **2.** TÉC to insulate **II.** *vr:* **~se** to isolate oneself

ajar *vt* to wear out

ajardinado, -a *adj* landscaped

ajedrez *m sin pl* DEP chess

ajeno, -a *adj* **1.**(*de otro*) somebody else's; **la felicidad ajena** other people's happiness **2.** *ser* (*impropio*) inappropriate **3.** *estar* (*ignorante*) ignorant **4.**(*carente*) **~ a** [*o* **de**] lacking

ajetreo *m* bustle

ají *m AmS, Ant* **1.**(*arbusto*) pepper (plant) **2.**(*pimentón*) chilli *Brit*, chili *Am*

ajo *m* garlic; **estar en el ~** *inf* to be mixed up in it; **tieso como un ~** *inf* stuck-up

ajuar *m* **1.**(*de la novia*) trousseau **2.**(*de una casa*) furnishings *pl*

ajustado, -a *adj* **1.**(*ropa*) tight **2.**(*adecuado*) fitting

ajustar I. *vi* to fit **II.** *vt* **1.**(*adaptar*) *t.* TÉC to adjust; (*vestido*) to take in **2.**(*una pieza en otra*) to fit **III.** *vr:* **~se 1.**(*acordar*) to come to an agreement **2.**(*adaptarse*) to adapt; **~se a la verdad** to stick to the truth

ajuste *m* **1.**(*adaptación*) adjustment **2.**(*graduación*) graduation **3.**(*encaje*) fitting **4.**(*acuerdo*) compromise

al = a + el *v.* **a**

ala *f* wing; (*de hélice*) propeller blade; (*de sombrero*) brim; (*del tejado*) eaves *pl;* **dar ~s a alguien** to encourage sb; **estar tocado del ~** *inf* to be crazy

Alá *m* Allah

alabanza *f* praise

alabar *vt* to praise

alacena *f* larder

alacrán *m* scorpion

alado, -a *adj* winged

alambicado, -a *adj* subtle

alambique *m* still

alambrada *f* (*valla*) wire fence

alambre *m* wire

alameda *f* **1.**(*lugar*) poplar grove **2.**(*paseo*) avenue

álamo *m t.* BOT poplar; **~ temblón** aspen

alarde *m* show

alargar <g→gu> **I.** *vt* **1.**(*la extensión*) to lengthen; (*pierna*) to stretch; (*cuello*) to crane; (*mano*) to hold out **2.**(*la duración*) to prolong **3.**(*retardar*) to delay **II.** *vr:* **~se 1.**(*en la extensión*) to lengthen **2.**(*retardarse*) to be delayed

alarido *m* shriek

alarma *f* alarm; **dar la ~** to raise the alarm

alarmar I. *vt* to alarm **II.** *vr:* **~se** to get worried

alavés, -esa *adj* of/from Álava

alba *f* dawn

albacea *mf* executor

albaceteño, -a *adj* of/from Albacete

albahaca *f* basil

albanés, -esa *adj, m, f* Albanian

Albania *f* Albania

albañil *mf* **1.**(*constructor*) builder **2.**(*artesano*) bricklayer

albarán *m* delivery note, invoice

albaricoque *m* apricot

albedrío *m* whim; **libre ~** free will

alberca *f* reservoir

albergar <g→gu> **I.** *vt* to house **II.** *vr:* **~se** to lodge

albergue *m* (*refugio*) refuge; (*alojamiento*) lodging; **~ juvenil** youth hostel

albóndiga *f* meatball

albornoz *m* bathrobe

alborotar I. *vi* to make a racket; (*niños*) to romp about **II.** *vt* **1.**(*desordenar*) to agitate **2.**(*sublevar*) to stir up **III.** *vr:* **~se** to get excited

alboroto *m* **1.**(*vocerío*) racket **2.**(*bulla*) uproar

alborozar <z→c> **I.** *vt* to delight **II.** *vr:* ~**se** to be overjoyed

alborozo *m* joy

albricias *fpl inf* ¡~! good news!

álbum *m* <álbum(e)s> album

albumen *m* albumen

alcachofa *f* **1.** BOT artichoke **2.** (*de ducha*) shower head

alcalde(sa) *m(f)* mayor

alcaldía *f* **1.** (*oficio*) post of mayor **2.** (*oficina*) mayor's office

alcance *m* **1.** (*distancia*) range; **al ~ de la mano** within reach; **dar ~ a alguien** to catch up with sb; **estar al ~** to have within one's grasp **2.** (*importancia*) importance **3.** (*déficit*) deficit

alcancía *f* money box *Brit,* piggy bank *Am*

alcantarilla *f* **1.** (*cloaca*) sewer **2.** (*sumidero*) drain

alcanzar <z→c> **I.** *vi* to reach **II.** *vt* **1.** (*dar alcance*) to catch up (with) **2.** (*llegar*) to reach; ~ **fama** to become famous **3.** (*entender*) to grasp

alcaparra *f* caper

alcatraz *m* ZOOL gannet

alcaucil *m* artichoke

alcázar *m* MIL fortress

alcoba *f* bedroom

alcohol *m* alcohol; **bebida sin ~** non-alcoholic drink

alcohólico, -a *adj, m, f* alcoholic

alcoholismo *m sin pl* alcoholism

alcornoque *m* **1.** BOT cork oak **2.** (*persona*) idiot

alcurnia *f* ancestry

aldaba *f* doorknocker

aldea *f* small village

aldeano, -a I. *adj* village **II.** *m, f* villager

aleación *f* alloy

aleatorio, -a *adj* random, fortuitous

aleccionar *vt* to instruct

alegación *f* **1.** JUR (*declaración*) declaration; (*escrito*) statement **2.** *pl* (*objeciones*) objections *pl*

alegar <g→gu> **I.** *vt* to cite; (*pruebas*) to produce **II.** *vi* AmL (*discutir*) to argue

alegato *m* **1.** (*escrito*) bill of indictment; (*oral*) plea **2.** AmL (*disputa*) argument

alegoría *f* allegory

alegrar I. *vt* to make happy **II.** *vr:* ~**se 1.** (*sentir alegría*) ~**se de** [*o* **con**] **algo** to be glad about sth; **me alegro de...** I'm pleased ... **2.** (*beber*) to get tipsy

alegre *adj* **1.** (*contento*) happy; (*color*) bright; (*habitación*) pleasant **2.** (*frívolo*) frivolous **3.** *inf* (*achispado*) merry; **estar ~** to be tipsy

alegría *f* **1.** (*gozo*) happiness **2.** (*buen humor*) cheerfulness

alegrón *m inf* thrill; **llevarse un ~** to have been thrilled

alejamiento *m* removal; *fig* aloofness

alejar I. *vt* **1.** (*distanciar*) to remove **2.** (*ahuyentar*) to drive away **II.** *vr:* ~**se** to move away; (*retirarse*) to withdraw

aleluya I. *interj* hallelujah **II.** *m o f* REL hallelujah

alemán *m* (*lengua*) German

alemán, -ana *adj, m, f* German

Alemania *f* Germany

alentar <e→ie> *vt* to encourage

alergia *f* allergy; ~ **a la primavera** hay fever

alero *m* **1.** ARQUIT eaves *pl* **2.** AUTO wing, fender *Am* **3.** DEP winger

alerta I. *adj* alert **II.** *f* alert; **dar la ~** to give the alarm

aleta *f* **1.** (*general*) wing **2.** (*de un buzo*) flipper; (*de un pez*) fin

aletargar <g→gu> **I.** *vt* to become drowsy **II.** *vr:* ~**se** to get drowsy

aletear *vi* **1.** (*ave*) to flutter **2.** (*pez*) to wriggle **3.** *inf* (*cobrar fuerza*) to regain one's strength

alevín *m* fry, young fish

alevosía *f* treachery

alfabeto *m* alphabet

alfalfa *f* alfalfa, lucerne

alfarería *f* pottery

alfarero, -a *m, f* potter

alféizar *m* windowsill

alférez *m* MIL second lieutenant

alfil *m* (*en ajedrez*) bishop

alfiler *m* **1.** (*aguja*) pin; **no caber un ~** *fig* to be bursting at the seams **2.** (*broche*) brooch

alfiletero *m* needle case
alfombra *f* carpet
alfombrar *vt* to carpet
alfombrilla *f* 1.(*estera*) mat; ~ **de baño** bath mat 2.INFOR mousemat *Brit*, mousepad *Am*
alforja *f* saddlebag
alga *f* alga
algarabía *f* uproar
algarroba *f* 1.BOT carob 2.(*fruto*) carob bean
algarrobo *m* carob tree
algazara *f* clamour *Brit*, clamor *Am*; (*de alegría*) jubilation
álgebra *f* MAT algebra
álgido, -a *adj* 1.(*culminante*) **el período** ~ the high point 2.(*muy frío*) freezing
algo I. *pron indef* (*en frases afirmativas*) something; (*en negativas, interrogativas*) anything; ~ **es** ~ it's better than nothing; **¿quieres** ~? do you want anything?; **me suena de** ~ it seems familiar to me; **se cree** ~ he/she thinks he/she is something II. *adv* a little; ~ **así como** something like
algodón *m* 1.(*planta, tejido*) cotton 2.(*cosmético*) cotton wool *Brit*, cotton *Am*
algodonero, -a I. *adj* cotton II. *m*, *f* cotton grower
alguacil *m* bailiff
alguien *pron indef* (*en frases afirmativas*) somebody, someone; (*en interrogativas*) anybody, anyone; **¿hay** ~ **aquí?** is anybody there?; ~ **me lo ha contado** somebody told me
algún *adj v.* **alguno¹**
alguno, -a¹ *adj* <algún> 1.(*antepuesto*) some; (*en frases negativas e interrogativas*) any; **¿alguna pregunta?** any questions?; **de alguna manera** somehow; **en algún sitio** somewhere; **alguna vez** sometimes; **algún día** some day 2.(*postpuesto: ninguno*) no, not any; **en sitio** ~ nowhere
alguno, -a² *pron indef* somebody, someone; ~**s ya se han ido** some have already gone; **¿tienes caramelos? – sí, me quedan** ~**s** do you

have any sweets? – yes, I still have some left
alhaja *f* piece of jewellery [*o* jewelry *Am*]; (*de bisutería*) costume jewellery [*o* jewelry *Am*]
alhelí *m* <alhelíes> wallflower
alheña *f* 1.BOT privet 2.(*polvo*) henna
aliado, -a I. *adj* allied II. *m*, *f* ally
alianza *f* 1.(*pacto*) alliance 2.(*anillo*) wedding ring
aliar <1. *pres:* alío> I. *vt* to ally II. *vr:* ~**se** to ally oneself
alias *adv* alias
alicantino, -a *adj* of/from Alicante
alicates *mpl* pliers *pl*
aliciente *m* incentive
alienación *f* alienation
aliento *m* 1.(*respiración*) breath; **sin** ~ out of breath 2.(*ánimo*) courage; **dar** ~ **a alguien** to encourage sb
aligerar *vt* 1.(*cargas*) to lighten 2.(*aliviar*) to alleviate 3.(*acelerar*) to quicken
alimaña *f* pest
alimentación *f* 1.(*nutrición*) food; (*acción*) feeding 2.(*de un horno*) stoking; (*de una máquina*) feeding; ~ **de papel** INFOR sheetfeed
alimentador *m* TÉC feeder; ~ **de hojas sueltas** INFOR cut-sheet feed
alimentar I. *vt* 1.(*nutrir*) to feed 2.TEC to stoke; (*máquina*) to feed 3.INFOR to feed II. *vr* ~**se de algo** to live on sth
alimenticio, -a *adj* nourishing; **productos** ~**s** foodstuffs *pl*
alimento *m* 1.(*sustancia*) food; **los** ~**s** foodstuffs *pl* 2.(*alimentación*) nourishment
alineación *f*, **alineamiento** *m* 1.(*general*) alignment 2.DEP line-up
alinear I. *vt* 1.(*poner en línea*) to line up; **país no alineado** POL non-aligned country 2.DEP to select; (*para un partido*) to field II. *vr:* ~**se** to line up
aliñar *vt* to season; (*ensalada*) to dress
aliño *m* seasoning; (*para ensalada*) dressing

alisar *vt* (*superficie*) to smooth down; (*terreno*) to level (off); (*pelo*) to smooth

aliso *m* alder

alistar I. *vt* **1.** (*inscribir*) to enrol **2.** (*enumerar*) to list **3.** MIL to recruit **II.** *vr:* ~**se** MIL to enlist

aliviar *vt* **1.** (*carga*) to lighten **2.** (*de una preocupación*) to relieve **3.** (*dolor*) to alleviate

alivio *m* **1.** (*aligeramiento*) relief; **ser de** ~ *inf* to be horrible. **2.** (*de una enfermedad*) recovery; (*mejoría*) improvement

aljibe *m* cistern

allá *adv* **1.** (*dirección*) there; **el más** ~ REL the hereafter; **ponte más** ~ move further over; **¡~ tú!** *inf* that's your problem! **2.** (*tiempo*) back; ~ **por el año 1964** round about 1964

allanamiento *m* levelling *Brit*, leveling *Am*; ~ **de morada** JUR breaking and entering

allanar I. *vt* **1.** (*terreno*) to level (out); ~ **una casa** JUR to break into a house **2.** (*dificultades*) to remove **II.** *vr:* ~**se** to agree

allegado, -a I. *adj* close **II.** *m, f* relative

allí *adv* **por** ~ over there; **¡~ viene!** he's/she's just coming!; **hasta** ~ as far as that

alma *f* **1.** (*espíritu*) soul; **lo siento en el** ~ I'm terribly sorry; ~ **de cántaro** simpleton; ~ **en pena** lost soul; **estar con el** ~ **en un hilo** *inf* to have one's heart in one's mouth **2.** (*ánimo*) spirit **3.** TÉC core

almacén *m* **1.** (*depósito*) warehouse; **tener en** ~ to have in stock **2.** (*tienda*) **grandes almacenes** department store

almacenaje *m,* **almacenamiento** *m t.* INFOR storage

almacenar *vt t.* INFOR to store

almanaque *m* almanac

almeja *f* clam

almendra *f* almond

almendro *m* almond tree

almeriense *adj* of/from Almería

almíbar *m* syrup

almidón *m* starch; (*cola*) paste

almidonar *vt* to starch

almirantazgo *m* admiralty

almirante *m* admiral

almirez *m* mortar

almizcle *m* musk

almohada *f* (*cojín*) cushion; (*de la cama*) pillow

almohadilla *f* small cushion; ~ **de tinta** inkpad

almohadón *m* cushion

almorranas *fpl* piles *pl*

almorzar *irr como forzar* **I.** *vi* to have lunch **II.** *vt* to have for lunch

almuerzo *m* lunch

alocado, -a *adj* **1.** (*loco*) crazy **2.** (*imprudente*) reckless

alojamiento *m* **1.** (*lugar*) accommodation **2.** (*acción*) housing

alojar I. *vt* **1.** (*albergar*) to accommodate **2.** (*procurar alojamiento*) to house **3.** (*cosa*) to lodge **II.** *vr:* ~**se 1.** (*hospedarse*) to stay **2.** (*meterse*) ~**se en algo** to put up at sth

alondra *f* lark

alpaca *f* (*tela*) *t.* ZOOL alpaca

alpargata *f* espadrille

Alpes *mpl* **los** ~ the Alps

alpinismo *m sin pl* mountaineering, mountain climbing

alpinista *mf* mountaineer, mountain climber

alpino, -a *adj* Alpine

alpiste *m* **1.** BOT canary grass **2.** (*para pájaros*) birdseed; **le gusta mucho el** ~ *inf* he's/she's a boozer

alquilar *vt* **1.** (*dejar*) to rent (out), to let **2.** (*tomar en alquiler*) to rent; **se alquila** to let *Brit*, for rent *Am*

alquimia *f* alchemy

alquitrán *m* tar

alrededor *adv* around; ~ **de** (*aproximadamente*) around

alrededores *mpl* surroundings *pl*

Alsacia *f* Alsace

alta *f* **1.** (*documento*) (certificate of) discharge; **dar de** ~ **del hospital** to discharge from hospital **2.** (*inscripción*) registration; (*ingreso*) membership; **darse de** ~ (*en una ciudad*) to register as being resident; (*en asociación*) to become a member

altanería *f* arrogance, haughtiness

A a

altanero, -a *adj* arrogant, haughty
altar *m* altar
altavoz *m* (loud)speaker
alteración *f* **1.** (*de planes*) alteration **2.** (*perturbación*) disturbance
alterar I. *vt* **1.** (*cambiar*) to alter **2.** (*perturbar*) to disturb **II.** *vr:* ~**se** (*aturdirse*) to get upset; (*irritarse*) to be irritated
altercado *m* argument
alternar I. *vi* **1.** (*turnarse*) to alternate **2.** (*tratar*) ~ **con alguien** to associate with sb **3.** (*en un club nocturno*) to go clubbing **II.** *vr* ~**se en algo** to take turns at sth
alternativa *f* alternative
alternativo, -a *adj* **1.** (*opcional*) alternative **2.** (*con alternación*) alternating
alterno, -a *adj* alternate
alteza *f* highness
altibajos *mpl* ups *pl* and downs
altiplanicie *f*, **altiplano** *m* high plateau
altisonante *adj* high-flown
altitud *f* height, altitude
altivo, -a *adj* arrogant, haughty
alto I. *interj* halt **II.** *m* **1.** (*descanso*) stop **2.** (*altura*) height; **medir 8 metros de** ~ to be 8 metres high **3.** (*collado*) hill **III.** *adv* high (up); **pasar por** ~ to ignore; **por todo lo** ~ splendidly
alto, -a *adj* **1.** (*en general*) high; **un** ~ **cargo** a high-ranking position; **alta calidad** high-quality; **a altas horas de la noche** late at night **2.** (*persona*) tall; (*edificio*) high, tall **3.** (*arriba*) upper; **clase alta** upper class **4.** (*río*) in spate *Brit*, swollen *Am* **5.** (*sonido*) loud; **en voz alta** loudly
altoparlante *m AmL* loudspeaker
altramuz *m* lupin
altruismo *m sin pl* altruism
altura *f* **1.** (*estatura*) height; **de gran** ~ high; **de poca** ~ low; **a estas** ~**s at** this point **2.** (*de un sonido*) pitch **3.** *pl* (*cielo*) heaven
alubia *f* bean
alucinación *f* hallucination
alucinante *adj inf* **1.** (*estupendo*) fantastic **2.** (*increíble*) incredible

alucinar I. *vi inf* **1.** (*hablando*) to hallucinate **2.** (*quedar fascinado*) to be fascinated **II.** *vt inf* **1.** (*pasmar*) to amaze **2.** (*fascinar*) to fascinate
alud *m* avalanche
aludir *vi* (*referirse*) to allude; **darse por aludido** to take it personally
alumbrado *m* lighting
alumbramiento *m* **1.** (*iluminación*) lighting **2.** (*parto*) childbirth
alumbrar I. *vi* **1.** (*iluminar*) to give off light **2.** (*parir*) to give birth **II.** *vt* **1.** (*iluminar*) to light (up) **2.** (*parir*) to give birth to
aluminio *m* aluminium *Brit,* aluminum *Am*
alumno, -a *m, f* (*de escuela*) pupil; (*de universidad*) student
alusión *f* **1.** (*mención*) ~ **a algo** mention of sth **2.** (*insinuación*) allusion
alusivo, -a *adj* ~ **a algo** regarding sth, about sth
aluvión *m* **1.** (*inundación*) *t. fig* flood **2.** (*sedimento*) alluvium
alza *f* **1.** (*elevación*) rise **2.** (*de un zapato*) raised insole
alzamiento *m* uprising
alzar <z→c> **I.** *vt* **1.** (*levantar*) to lift (up); (*precio, voz*) to raise **2.** (*mesa*) to put away; (*campamento*) to break **3.** (*construir*) to erect **4.** AGR (*cosecha*) to gather in **II.** *vr:* ~**se 1.** (*levantarse*) to rise (up) **2.** JUR to appeal **3.** *AmL* (*animales*) to become wild **4.** *AmL* (*sublevarse*) to revolt
ama *f* (*dueña*) mistress; (*propietaria*) owner; ~ **de casa** housewife; ~ **de cría** wet nurse
amabilidad *f* kindness
amable *adj* kind
amaestrar *vt* (*animales*) to train; (*caballos*) to break in
amagar <g→gu> *vt* to threaten
amago *m* **1.** (*amenaza*) threat **2.** DEP feint
amainar I. *vi* to abate **II.** *vt* NÁUT to shorten
amalgama *f* amalgam
amalgamar *vt* TÉC to amalgamate
amamantar *vt* (*bebé*) to breastfeed; (*cachorro*) to suckle

amanecer I. *vimpers* to dawn; **está amaneciendo** it's getting light **II.** *irr como crecer vi* to wake up **III.** *m* dawn

amanecida *f AmL* dawn

amanerado, -a *adj* affected

amansar I. *vt* **1.** (*animal*) to tame **2.** (*persona*) to subdue **II.** *vr:* ~**se** to become tame

amante I. *adj* **ser** ~ **de algo** to like doing sth **II.** *mf* lover

amapola *f* poppy

amar *vt* to love

amargar <g→gu> **I.** *vt* to make bitter **II.** *vr:* ~**se** to become bitter

amargo, -a *adj* bitter

amarillento, -a *adj* yellowish; (*fotografía, papel*) yellowed

amarillo, -a *adj* **1.** (*color*) yellow **2.** (*pálido*) pale

amarra *f* **1.** NÁUT hawser **2.** *pl* (*apoyo*) connections *pl*

amarrar I. *vt* **1.** (*atar*) to tie up **2.** NÁUT to moor **II.** *vr:* ~**se** *AmL* to get married

amartillar *vt* to cock

amasar *vt* **1.** (*masa*) to knead **2.** (*fortuna*) to amass

amasijo *m* **1.** (*acción*) kneading **2.** *inf* (*mezcla*) mixture

amateur *adj, mf* <amateurs> amateur

amatista *f* amethyst

amazona *f* amazon; DEP rider

ámbar *adj inv, m* amber

Amberes *m* Antwerp

ambición *f* ambition; ~ **de poder** hunger for power

ambicionar *vt* to aspire to

ambicioso, -a *adj* ambitious

ambientación *f* **1.** CINE, LIT setting **2.** (*ambiente*) atmosphere

ambientador *m* air freshener

ambientar I. *vt* **1.** (*novela*) to set **2.** (*fiesta*) to enliven **II.** *vr:* ~**se 1.** (*aclimatarse*) to adjust **2.** (*en una fiesta*) to get into the mood

ambiente *m* **1.** (*aire*) air **2.** (*medio*) surroundings *pl;* **medio** ~ environment **3.** (*atmósfera*) atmosphere

ambigüedad *f* ambiguity

ambiguo, -a *adj* ambiguous

ámbito *m* area; ~ **nacional** national level

ambos, -as *adj* both

ambulancia *f* ambulance

ambulante *adj* walking; **circo** ~ travelling circus; **venta** ~ peddling

ambulatorio *m* outpatient department

ameba *f* amoeba *Brit,* ameba *Am*

amedrentar *vt* **1.** (*asustar*) to scare **2.** (*intimidar*) to intimidate

amén I. *m* amen; **decir** ~ **a todo** to agree to everything **II.** *prep* ~ **de** except for

amenaza *f* **1.** (*intimidación*) threat **2.** (*peligro*) menace

amenazar <z→c> *vt, vi* to threaten

amenidad *f* **1.** (*lo agradable*) pleasantness **2.** (*entretenimiento*) entertainment

amenizar <z→c> *vt* **1.** (*hacer agradable*) to make pleasant **2.** (*entretener*) to entertain

ameno, -a *adj* **1.** (*agradable*) pleasant **2.** (*entretenido*) entertaining

América *f* America; ~ **Central** Central America; ~ **Latina** Latin America; ~ **del Norte/del Sur** North/ South America

---

[?] Many Spaniards emigrated to Latin America in the 19th and 20th centuries. The expression "hacer **las Américas**" refers directly to this fact and more or less means to make one's fortune in the Americas.

---

americana *f* jacket

americano, -a *adj, m, f* (*de América del Sur*) South American; (*estadounidense*) American

amerindio, -a *adj, m, f* Amerindian

amerizar <z→c> *vi* to land on water

ametralladora *f* machine gun

amianto *m* asbestos

amigable *adj* friendly

amígdala *f* tonsil

amigo, -a I. *adj* **es muy amiga mía**

she's a good friend of mine; **somos (muy)** ~**s** we've been close friends; **ser** ~ **de algo** to be fond of sth; **¡y tan** ~**s!** and that's that! **II.** *m, f* friend; ~ **por correspondencia** penfriend *Brit,* penpal *Am;* **hacerse** ~ **de alguien** to make friends with sb

amilanar *vt* **1.** (*intimidar*) to intimidate **2.** (*desanimar*) to discourage

aminorar I. *vi* to diminish **II.** *vt* to reduce

amistad *f* **1.** (*entre amigos*) friendship **2.** *pl* (*amigos*) friends *pl*

amistoso, -a *adj* friendly, amicable; **partido** ~ friendly match

amnesia *f sin pl* amnesia

amnistía *f* amnesty

amo *m* **1.** (*propietario*) owner **2.** (*patrón*) boss

amodorrarse *vr* to become drowsy

amoldar I. *vt* **1.** (*moldear*) to mould *Brit,* to mold *Am* **2.** (*acomodar*) to adapt **II.** *vr:* ~**se** to adapt oneself

amonestación *f* **1.** (*advertencia*) warning; **tarjeta de** ~ DEP yellow card **2.** (*de los novios*) marriage banns *pl*

amonestar *vt* **1.** (*advertir*) to warn **2.** (*los novios*) to publish the banns

amoníaco *m* ammonia

amontonar I. *vt* **1.** (*tierra*) to pile up **2.** (*dinero*) to accumulate **II.** *vr:* ~**se 1.** (*cosas*) to pile up **2.** (*personas*) to crowd together **3.** (*noticias*) to accumulate

amor *m* love; **hacer el** ~ to make love; **hacer algo con** ~ to do sth lovingly; **¡por** ~ **de Dios!** for God's sake!

amoratado, -a *adj* purple; (*ojo*) black; (*labios*) blue

amordazar <z→c> *vt* to gag

amorfo, -a *adj* shapeless, amorphous

amorío(s) *m(pl) pey* love affair

amoroso, -a *adj* **1.** (*de amor*) loving **2.** (*cariñoso*) affectionate

amortiguador *m* AUTO shock absorber

amortiguar <gu→gü> *vt* (*sonido*) to muffle; (*golpe*) to cushion

amortización *f* repayment

amortizar <z→c> *vt* **1.** (*deuda*) to pay off **2.** (*inversión*) to recover

amotinar I. *vt* to stir up **II.** *vr:* ~**se** to rebel

amparar I. *vt* to protect **II.** *vr:* ~**se** to seek protection

amparo *m* protection

amperio *m* amp

ampliación *f* **1.** (*engrandecimiento*) enlargement; (*de un territorio*) expansion; (*de un edificio*) extension **2.** (*de un sonido*) amplification; ~ **de RAM** INFOR RAM expansion

ampliar <1. pres: amplío> *vt* **1.** (*hacer más grande*) to enlarge; (*territorio*) to expand; (*edificio*) to extend **2.** (*conocimientos*) to broaden **3.** (*sonido*) to amplify

amplificador *m* amplifier

amplificar <c→qu> *vt* to amplify

amplio, -a *adj* **1.** (*casa*) spacious; (*parque*) extensive **2.** (*vestido*) loose-fitting **3.** (*informe*) detailed; (*experiencia*) wide-ranging

amplitud *f* **1.** (*extensión*) extent; (*de conocimientos*) range; (*de un informe, parque*) extensiveness **2.** (*de una casa*) roominess **3.** FÍS amplitude

ampolla *f* **1.** (*en la piel*) blister; **levantar** ~**s** *fig* to get people's backs up **2.** (*para inyecciones*) ampoule *Brit,* ampule *Am*

ampuloso, -a *adj* pompous

amputar *vt* to amputate

amueblar *vt* to furnish

amuleto *m* amulet

amurallar *vt* to wall

anabolizante *m* anabolic steroid

ánade *mf* duck

anagrama *m* anagram

anales *mpl* HIST annals *pl*

analfabetismo *m sin pl* illiteracy

analfabeto, -a *m, f* illiterate (person)

analgésico *m* painkiller

análisis *m inv* **1.** (*general*) *t.* MAT analysis; ~ **de sistemas** INFOR systems analysis **2.** MED test; ~ **de sangre** blood test

analista *mf* **1.** (*de anales*) chronicler **2.** (*que analiza*) analyst; ~ **de siste-**

mas INFOR systems analyst

analizar <z→c> *vt t.* MED to analyse *Brit,* to analyze *Am*

analogía *f* analogy

análogo, -a *adj* analogous

ananá(s) *m CSur* pineapple

anaquel *m* shelf

anarquía *f* anarchy

anarquismo *m sin pl* anarchism

anarquista *adj, mf* anarchist

anatomía *f* anatomy

anca *f* **1.** (*de animal*) haunch; **~s de rana** frogs' legs **2.** *pl, inf* (*nalgas*) backside

ancestral *adj* ancestral

ancho *m* width; **~ de vía** AUTO, FERRO gauge *Brit,* gage *Am*

ancho, -a *adj* (*vasto*) wide; (*vestidos*) loose-fitting; **~ de espaldas** broad-shouldered; **estar a sus anchas** to feel at ease

anchoa *f* anchovy

anchura *f* width; (*de un vestido*) looseness

ancianidad *f* old age

anciano, -a I. *adj* old **II.** *m, f* old man

ancla *f* anchor

ancladero *m* anchorage

anclar *vi, vt* to anchor

Andalucía *f* Andalusia

andaluz(a) *adj, m(f)* Andalusian

andamiaje *m,* **andamio** *m* scaffolding

andar *irr* **I.** *vi* **1.** (*caminar*) to walk; (*a caballo*) to ride; **~ a gatas** to go on all fours; (*bebés*) to crawl **2.** (*reloj, coche*) to go *Brit,* to run *Am;* (*máquina*) to work **3.** (*tiempo*) to pass **4.** (*estar*) **~ atareado** to be busy; **~ mal de dinero** to be short of money; **~ por los 30** to be about 30; **~ a la que salta** to seize the opportunity **II.** *m* walk, gait

andariego, -a I. *adj* fond of travelling **II.** *m, f* wanderer

andén *m* **1.** FERRO platform **2.** (*de muelle*) quayside

Andes *mpl* **los ~** the Andes + *pl vb*

Andorra *f* Andorra

? **Andorra** is a small democratic state (only 467 square kilometres in area) that has a parlamentary principality as its form of government. It borders France to the north and east and Spain to the west and south.

andorrano, -a *adj, m, f* Andorran

andrajo *m* rag

andrajoso, -a *adj* ragged

andurrial(es) *m(pl)* godforsaken place

anécdota *f* anecdote

anegar <g→gu> **I.** *vt* **1.** (*inundar*) to flood **2.** (*ahogar*) to drown **II.** *vr:* **~se** **1.** (*campo*) to flood **2.** (*ahogarse*) to drown

anejo *m* **1.** (*edificio*) annexe *Brit,* annex *Am* **2.** (*carta, libro, revista*) supplement; (*en un libro*) appendix

anejo, -a *adj* (*a edificios*) joined; (*a cartas*) enclosed

anemia *f sin pl* anaemia *Brit,* anemia *Am*

anestesia *f* anaesthesia *Brit,* anesthesia *Am*

anestesiar *vt* to anaesthetize *Brit,* to anesthetize *Am*

anexión *f* annexation

anexionar *vt* to annex

anexo *m v.* **anejo**

anexo, -a *adj v.* **anejo, -a**

anfibio *m* ZOOL (*t. vehículo*) amphibian

anfibio, -a *adj* amphibious

anfiteatro *m* amphitheatre *Brit,* amphitheater *Am*

anfitrión, -ona *m, f* host *m,* hostess *f*

ánfora *f* amphora

ángel *m* angel; **tener mucho ~** *fig* to be very charming

angelical *adj* angelic(al); **rostro ~** angelic face

angina *f* **~ de pecho** angina (pectoris); **~s** sore throat

anglicismo *m* anglicism

angoleño, -a *adj, m, f* Angolan

angosto, -a *adj* narrow

anguila *f* **1.** ZOOL eel **2.** NÁUT slipway

angula *f* elver

ángulo *m* 1.MAT angle; **en ~** angled 2.(*rincón*) corner 3.(*arista*) edge

angustiar I. *vt* 1.(*acongojar*) to distress 2.(*afligir*) to worry II. *vr:* ~**se** to get worried

anhelante *adj* longing

anhelar I. *vi* to pant II. *vt* to long for

anhelo *m* ~ **de algo** longing for sth

anidar I. *vi* 1.(*hacer nido*) to nest 2.(*morar*) to live II. *vt* to take in

anilla *f* ring; (*de puro*) band; ~**s** DEP rings *pl*

anillo *m* ring; **venir como ~ al dedo** *fig* to be just right

ánima *f* soul

animación *f* 1.(*acción*) *t.* CINE, INFOR animation 2.(*viveza*) liveliness

animado, -a *adj* 1.(*persona*) in high spirits 2.(*lugar*) busy 3.(*actividad*) lively; ~ **por ordenador** INFOR computer-animated

animador(a) *m(f)* 1.(*artista*) entertainer 2.(*presentador*) presenter

animadversión *f* hostility

animal I. *adj* 1.(*de los animales*) animal 2.(*grosero*) rude II. *m* 1.ZOOL animal; ~**es de caza** game; ~ **de compañía** pet 2. *pey* (*ignorante*) fool; (*bruto*) brute

animar I. *vt* 1.(*infundir vida*) to liven up 2.(*alentar*) to encourage 3.(*persona triste*) to cheer up 4.(*economía*) to stimulate II. *vr:* ~**se** 1.(*cobrar vida*) to liven up 2.(*atreverse*) to dare 3.(*decidirse*) to decide; **¿te animas?** will you have a go? 4.(*alegrarse*) to cheer up

ánimo *m* 1.(*espíritu*) spirit; **no estoy con ~s de...** I don't feel like ... 2.(*energía*) energy; **cobrar ~** to take heart; **dar ~** to encourage; **¡~!** cheer up! 3.(*intención*) intention; **sin ~ de lucro** non-profit-making

animoso, -a *adj* (*valeroso*) brave

aniquilar *vt* to annihilate; (*esperanzas*) to destroy

anís <anises> *m* 1.(*planta*) anise 2.(*licor*) anisette

aniversario *m* anniversary

anoche *adv* last night

anochecer I. *irr como crecer vimpers* **anochece** it's getting dark II. *m* nightfall

anodino, -a *adj* 1.(*cosa*) insipid 2.(*persona*) bland

anomalía *f* anomaly

anonadar *vt* to astound

anonimato *m* anonymity

anónimo *m* 1.(*autor*) anonymous author; (*escrito*) anonymous work 2.(*anonimato*) anonymity

anónimo, -a *adj* anonymous

anorak <anoraks> *m* anorak

anorexia *f* anorexia

anormal *adj* (*no normal*) abnormal

anotación *f* 1.(*acción de anotar*) annotation; (*en un registro*) record 2.(*nota*) note

anotar *vt* (*apuntar*) to note (down); (*en un registro*) to record

anquilosamiento *m* paralysis

anquilosar I. *vt* to paralyze II. *vr:* ~**se** 1.(*las articulaciones*) to get stiff 2.(*paralizarse*) to become paralyzed

ansia *f* 1.(*angustia*) anguish 2.(*intranquilidad*) anxiety

ansiar <1. *pres:* ansío> *vt* to long for; **el momento ansiado** the long--awaited moment

ansiedad *f* anxiety

ansioso, -a *adj* 1.(*intranquilo*) anxious 2.(*anheloso*) eager

antagónico, -a *adj* 1.(*opuesto*) opposed 2.(*rival*) antagonistic

antagonista *mf* antagonist

antaño *adv* long ago

antártico, -a *adj* Antarctic; **el polo ~** the South Pole

Antártida *f* Antarctica

ante I. *m* 1.ZOOL elk 2.(*piel*) suede II. *prep* 1.(*posición*) before 2.(*en vista de*) in view of 3.(*adversario*) faced with

anteanoche *adv* the night before last

anteayer *adv* the day before yesterday

antebrazo *m* ANAT forearm

antecedente I. *adj* foregoing II. *m pl* history; (*de una persona*) background; ~**s penales** JUR criminal record; **estar en ~s** to be well informed

anteceder *vt* to precede

antecesor(a) *m(f)* predecessor

antedicho, -a *adj* aforementioned

antelación *f* con ~ in advance
antemano *adv* de ~ in advance
antena *f* 1. (*de telecomunicaciones*) *t.* ZOOL antenna; ~ **colectiva** communal aerial; **estar en** ~ TV to be on the air 2. NÁUT lateen yard
anteojo *m* 1. (*catalejo*) telescope 2. *pl* (*gemelos*) opera glasses *pl;* (*prismáticos*) binoculars *pl*
antepasado, -a *m, f* ancestor
antepecho *m* (*de ventana*) window--sill
anteponer *irr como poner vt* 1. (*poner delante*) ~ **algo a algo** to place sth in front of sth 2. (*dar preferencia*) to give priority to
anteproyecto *m* draft
anterior I. *adj* previous; **la noche** ~ the night before II. *prep* ~ **a** prior to
anterioridad *prep* con ~ **a** prior to, before
antes I. *adv* 1. (*de tiempo*) before; (*hace un rato*) just now; (*antiguamente*) formerly; (*primero*) first; **poco** ~ shortly before; **cuanto** ~ as soon as possible; ~ **de nada** first of all; ~ **que nada** above all 2. (*comparativo*) rather II. *prep* ~ **de** before III. *conj* (*temporal*) before
antesala *f* anteroom
antiaéreo, -a *adj* MIL anti-aircraft
antibiótico *m* antibiotic
anticiclón *m* anticyclone
anticipación *f* anticipation; **con** ~ (*pago*) in advance
anticipado, -a *adj* (*elecciones*) early; **pagar por** ~ to pay in advance
anticipar I. *vt* 1. (*fecha*) to bring forward *Brit,* to move up *Am* 2. (*suceso*) to anticipate 3. (*dinero*) to advance II. *vr* ~**se a alguien** to beat sb to it
anticipo *m* 1. (*del sueldo*) advance 2. (*de un pago*) advance payment
anticonceptivo *m* contraceptive
anticongelante *m* antifreeze
anticuado, -a *adj* old-fashioned
anticuario, -a *m, f* (*vendedor*) antique dealer
anticuerpo *m* antibody
antídoto *m* antidote
antiestético, -a *adj* unattractive

antifaz *m* mask
antigualla *f* pey 1. (*objeto*) piece of junk 2. (*costumbre, estilo*) relic
antiguamente *adv* once, long ago
antigüedad *f* 1. (*edad antigua*) antiquity 2. (*objeto*) antique 3. (*en una empresa*) seniority
antiguo, -a *adj* <antiquísimo> 1. (*objeto*) old; (*relación*) long--standing 2. (*anticuado*) antiquated 3. (*de la antigüedad*) ancient 4. (*anterior*) former
antílope *m* antelope
antinatural *adj* unnatural
antipatía *f* antipathy; ~ **a** [*o* contra] **alguien** antipathy for sb
antipático, -a *adj* unpleasant
antiquísimo, -a *adj superl de* **antiguo**
antirrobo *m* anti-theft device
antiséptico, -a *adj* antiseptic
antiterrorista *adj* antiterrrorist; **lucha** ~ fight against terrorism
antítesis *f inv* antithesis
antojadizo, -a *adj* capricious
antojarse *vimpers* 1. (*encapricharse*) **se le antojó hacer algo** he/she took it into his/her head to do sth; **hace lo que se le antoja** he/she does as he/she pleases 2. (*tener la sensación*) **se me antoja que...** I've a feeling that ...
antojo *m* 1. (*capricho*) whim; **a mi** ~ as I please 2. (*de una embarazada*) craving
antología *f* anthology; **de** ~ (*memorable*) excellent
antonomasia *f* **por** ~ par excellence
antorcha *f* torch
antro *m* pey (*local*) dive
antropófago, -a *m, f* cannibal
antropología *f* anthropology
antropólogo, -a *m, f* anthropologist
anual *adj* annual
anualidad *f* annuity; ~ **vitalicia** life annuity
anualmente *adv* annually, yearly
anuario *m* yearbook
anudar I. *vt* 1. (*hacer un nudo*) to knot 2. (*juntar*) to join II. *vr:* ~**se** to become knotted
anulación *f* 1. (*de una ley*) repeal

2.(*de una sentencia*) overturning **3.**(*de un matrimonio*) annulment **4.**(*de un contrato*) cancellation
anular I. *vt* **1.**(*ley*) to repeal **2.**(*sentencia*) to overturn **3.**(*matrimonio*) to annul **4.**(*contrato*) to cancel **5.**(*tren, autobús*) to cancel **6.** DEP (*gol*) to disallow **II.** *adj* **1.**(*relativo al anillo*) annular **2.**(*de forma de anillo*) ring-shaped
anunciación *f* announcement
anunciar *vt* **1.**(*dar noticia*) to announce **2.**(*dar publicidad*) to advertise **3.**(*presagiar*) to herald
anuncio *m* **1.**(*de una noticia*) announcement **2.**(*publicidad: en la TV*) advertisement, commercial *Am;* (*en un periódico*) advertisement, ad *inf*
anzuelo *m* **1.**(*para pescar*) (fish-) hook **2.** *inf* (*aliciente*) bait; **morder el ~** to take the bait
añadidura *f* addition; **por ~** in addition
añadir *vt* **1.**(*agregar*) to add **2.**(*alargar*) to lengthen
añejo, -a *adj* old; (*vino*) mature
añicos *mpl* fragments *pl;* **hacer algo ~** to smash sth up
añil *m* **1.** BOT indigo **2.**(*color*) indigo blue
año *m* year; **~ natural** calendar year; **~ nuevo** New Year; **cumplir ~s** to have a birthday; **cumplir 60 ~s** to turn sixty; **¿cuántos ~s tienes?** how old are you?; **a mis ~s** at my age; **los ~s 60** the sixties; **en el ~ 1960** in 1960
añoranza *f* yearning; (*morriña*) homesickness
añorar *vt* to yearn for; (*tener morriña*) to be homesick for
aorta *f* aorta
apabullar *vt* *elev* to crush; **me quedé apabullado al oírlo** I was devastated when I heard it
apacentar <e→ie> *vt, vr:* **~se** to graze
apacible *adj* **1.**(*persona*) placid **2.**(*tiempo*) mild **3.**(*viento*) gentle
apaciguar <gu→gü> **I.** *vt* (*persona*) to calm down; (*dolor*) to ease

II. *vr:* **~se** to calm down
apadrinar *vt* **1.**(*ser padrino*) **~ a alguien** to be sb's godfather **2.**(*patrocinar*) to sponsor
apagado, -a *adj* **1.**(*volcán*) extinct **2.**(*sonido*) muffled **3.**(*persona*) lifeless **4.**(*color*) dull
apagar <g→gu> **I.** *vt* **1.**(*luz, fuego*) to put out; **estar apagado** *fig* (*person*) to not be in form **2.**(*sed*) to quench **3.**(*hambre*) to satisfy **4.**(*radio*) to switch off **5.**(*vela*) to snuff **II.** *vr:* **~se 1.**(*fuego, luz*) to go out **2.**(*sonido*) to die away **3.**(*color*) to fade
apagón *m* blackout; ELEC power cut
apaisado, -a *adj* landscape; **formato ~** landscape format
apalabrar *vt* to arrange
apalear *vt* to thrash, to beat
apañado, -a *adj* skilful *Brit,* skillful *Am;* **estar ~ si...** to be quite mistaken if ...
apañar I. *vt* (*remendar*) to mend; **¡ya te ~é yo!** I'll give you what for! **II.** *vr:* **~se 1.**(*darse maña*) to contrive to **2.**(*arreglárselas*) to manage
aparador *m* **1.**(*mueble*) sideboard **2.**(*escaparate*) shop window
aparato *m* **1.**(*utensilio*) *t.* DEP apparatus; **~ de televisión** television set **2.** TEL receiver; **estar al ~** to be on the phone **3.** ANAT system; **~ digestivo** digestive system **4.**(*ostentación*) pomp
aparatoso, -a *adj* **1.**(*ostentoso*) spectacular **2.**(*desmedido*) excessive
aparcamiento *m* **1.**(*acción*) parking **2.**(*lugar*) car park *Brit,* parking lot *Am*
aparcar <c→qu> *vt* to park
aparear I. *vt* **1.**(*animales*) to mate **2.**(*formar un par*) to pair **II.** *vr:* **~se 1.**(*animales*) to mate **2.**(*formar un par*) to form a pair
aparecer *irr como crecer* **I.** *vi* to appear; (*algo inesperado*) to turn up **II.** *vr:* **~se** to appear
aparejado, -a *adj* (*adecuado*) suitable; **llevar** [*o* **traer**] **~** to entail
aparejador(a) *m(f)* foreman builder *m,* forewoman builder *f*

aparejo *m* 1. (*arnés*) harness 2. (*poleas*) block and tackle 3. (*jarcia*) tackle 4. *pl* (*utensilios*) equipment

aparentar *vt* to feign; **trata de ~ que es...** he/she tries to make out that ...; ~ **estar enfermo** to pretend to be ill

aparente *adj* 1. (*que parece y no es*) apparent 2. (*de buen aspecto*) attractive

aparición *f* 1. (*acción*) appearance 2. (*visión*) apparition

apariencia *f* appearance; **las ~s engañan** appearances can be deceptive

apartado *m* paragraph; ~ **de Correos** ADMIN post office box

apartado, -a *adj* 1. (*lugar*) isolated 2. (*persona*) unsociable

apartamento *m* apartment, flat *Brit*

apartamiento *m* (*separación*) separation

apartar I. *vt* 1. (*separar*) to separate 2. (*poner a un lado*) to put aside 3. (*de un cargo*) to remove 4. (*disuadir*) to dissuade 5. (*la vista*) to avert 6. (*la atención*) to divert II. *vr:* ~**se** 1. (*separarse*) to separate 2. (*de un camino*) to turn off; **¡apártate!** get out of the way! 3. (*del tema*) to deviate

aparte I. *adv* (*en otro sitio*) apart II. *prep* 1. (*separado*) **él estaba ~ del grupo** he was separated from the group 2. (*además de*) ~ **de** apart from; ~ **de mala está fría** besides tasting bad, it is cold as well III. *m* (*de un escrito*) paragraph; **punto y ~** new paragraph IV. *adj inv* separate

apasionado, -a I. *adj* 1. (*con pasión*) passionate 2. (*entusiasta*) enthusiastic II. *m, f* enthusiast

apasionante *adj* exciting

apasionar I. *vt* to fill with enthusiasm II. *vr:* ~**se** 1. (*por algo*) to become enthusiastic 2. (*por alguien*) to fall passionately in love with

apatía *f* apathy

apático, -a *adj* apathetic

apátrida *adj* stateless

Apdo. *abr de* **Apartado de Correos** PO Box

apeadero *m* FERRO halt

apearse *vr* (*de un vehículo*) to get out; (*de un caballo*) to dismount

apechugar <g→gu> *vi* ~ **con** to put up with

apedrear *vt* to throw stones at; (*lapidar*) to stone (to death)

apegarse <g→gu> *vr* to become attached

apego *m* **tener ~ a algo** to be attached to sth

apelación *f* 1. JUR (*recurso*) appeal 2. *fig* remedy

apelar *vi* 1. *t.* JUR (*invocar*) to appeal; (*referirse*) to refer 2. (*recurrir: a alguien*) to turn; (*a algo*) to resort

apellidar I. *vt* to name II. *vr* **se apellida Martínez** his/her surname is Martínez

apellido *m* surname; ~ **de soltera** maiden name

? Every Spaniard has two surnames (**apellidos**): the first one is the father's name and the second is the mother's. If, for example, Señora Iglesias Vieira and Señor González Blanco were to become parents, the child's surname would be González Iglesias.

---

apenas I. *adv* 1. (*casi no*) hardly; ~ **había nadie** there was hardly anybody there 2. (*tan solo*) just; (*escasamente*) barely; ~ **hace un mes** just a month; ~ **hace una hora** barely an hour ago II. *conj* (*tan pronto como*) as soon as

apéndice *m t.* ANAT appendix

apendicitis *f inv* appendicitis

apercibir I. *vt* 1. (*preparar*) to prepare 2. (*avisar*) to warn II. *vr* ~**se de algo** to notice sth

aperitivo *m* 1. (*bebida*) aperitif 2. (*comida*) appetizer

apertura *f* 1. (*reunión*) opening 2. (*testamento*) reading

apesadumbrar I. *vt* to sadden II. *vr* ~**se por algo** to grieve over sth

apestar I. *vi* ~ **a algo** to stink of sth II. *vt* ~ **algo** to stink sth out

apetecer *irr como crecer vi* to feel like; **¿qué te apetece?** what would you like?; **me apetece un helado** I feel like an ice cream; **una copa de vino siempre apetece** a glass of wine is always welcome; **este libro me apetece más** this book appeals to me more

apetecible *adj* attractive

apetito *m* **1.** (*de comida*) appetite; **abrir el ~** to whet one's appetite **2.** (*deseo*) desire

apetitoso, -a *adj* **1.** (*que abre el apetito*) appetizing **2.** (*sabroso*) tasty

apiadarse *vr* ~ **de** to take pity on; **¡Dios, apiádate de nosotros!** may God have mercy on us!

ápice *m* **1.** (*punta*) apex **2.** (*nada*) iota; **no ceder un ~** not to yield an inch; **no entender un ~** not to understand the slightest thing

apilar **I.** *vt* to pile up **II.** *vr:* ~**se** to pile up

apiñar **I.** *vt* **1.** (*cosas*) to cram **2.** (*personas*) to crowd together **II.** *vr:* ~**se** to crowd together

apio *m* celery

apisonadora *f* steamroller

aplacar <c→qu> **I.** *vt* **1.** (*persona*) to calm down **2.** (*dolor*) to soothe **3.** (*hambre*) to satisfy; (*sed*) to quench **II.** *vr:* ~**se** to calm down

aplanar **I.** *vt* **1.** (*allanar*) to level **2.** (*aplastar*) to flatten **II.** *vr:* ~**se** to get discouraged

aplastar *vt* **1.** (*chafar*) to flatten **2.** (*con la mano*) to squash; (*cigarrillo*) to stub out **3.** (*con el pie*) to crush

aplaudir *vi, vt* to applaud

aplauso *m* applause; **salva de ~s** storm of applause

aplazamiento *m* postponement

aplazar <z→c> *vt* **1.** (*posponer*) to postpone; (*decisión*) to defer **2.** *AmL* (*suspender*) to fail

aplicación *f* application

aplicado, -a *adj* (*trabajador*) hard-working

aplicar <c→qu> **I.** *vt* **1.** (*pintura*) to apply; (*lazo*) to sew **2.** (*utilizar*) to use; (*tipo de interés*) to apply; ~ **una**

sanción JUR to impose **II.** *vr:* ~**se** **1.** (*esforzarse*) to apply oneself **2.** (*emplearse*) to be used

aplique *m* wall lamp, sconce

aplomo *m* self-confidence, composure

apocamiento *m* timidity

apocarse <c→qu> *vr* to lose heart

apodar *vt* to nickname

apoderado, -a *m, f* **1.** JUR proxy **2.** COM agent

apoderar **I.** *vt* **1.** (*en general*) to authorize **2.** JUR to grant power of attorney to **II.** *vr:* ~**se** to take possession

apodo *m* nickname

apogeo *m* **1.** ASTR apogee **2.** (*cumbre*) summit

apolillarse *vr* to get moth-eaten

apología *f* defence *Brit,* defense *Am*

apoltronarse *vr* to get lazy

apoplejía *f* stroke

apoquinar *vt inf* to fork out

aporrear *vt* **1.** (*dar golpes*) to beat; (*piano, puerta*) to bang on **2.** (*molestar*) to bother

aportación *f* **1.** (*contribución*) contribution **2.** (*donación*) donation **3.** ECON (*capital*) investment

aportar **I.** *vt* **1.** (*contribuir*) to contribute **2.** (*información, pruebas*) to provide **3.** (*traer*) to bring **II.** *vi* to reach port

aposentar *vt* to lodge, to put up

aposento *m* **1.** (*hospedaje*) lodging; **nos dieron ~** they put us up **2.** (*cuarto*) room

apósito *m* (*vendaje*) dressing

aposta *adv* on purpose

apostar <o→ue> **I.** *vi* ~ **por algo/ alguien** to back sth/sb **II.** *vt, vr:* ~**se** to bet; **¿qué apostamos?** what much shall we bet?; **¿qué te apuestas a que no lo hace?** I bet you he/ she won't do it

a posteriori *adv* with hindsight

apostilla *f* marginal note

apóstol *m* apostle

apóstrofo *m* LING apostrophe

apoyacabezas *m inv* headrest

apoyar **I.** *vt* **1.** (*colocar sobre*) to rest; (*contra*) to lean **2.** (*fundar*) to base;

(con pruebas) to support **3.** *(patrocinar)* to back; *(ayudar)* to stand by **II.** *vi* ARQUIT to rest **III.** *vr:* ~**se 1.** *(descansar sobre)* to rest; ~**se en** [*o* **contra**] **algo** to lean on sth **2.** *(fundarse)* to be based

apoyo *m* **1.** *(sostén)* support **2.** *(respaldo)* backing; *(ayuda)* help; **cuenta con mi ~** you can rely on me; **en ~ de** in support of

apreciable *adj* **1.** *(observable)* noticeable **2.** *(considerable)* considerable

apreciación *f* **1.** *(juicio)* assessment **2.** ECON appreciation **3.** *(de una casa)* valuation **4.** *(del tamaño)* estimation

apreciado, -a *adj (en cartas)* ~**s Sres** Dear Sirs

apreciar *vt* **1.** *(estimar)* to appreciate; **aprecio los perros** I like dogs; **aprecio la libertad** I value my liberty **2.** ECON to appreciate **3.** *(una casa)* to value **4.** *(tamaño, distancia)* to estimate **5.** *(captar)* to detect **6.** *(valorar)* to assess

aprecio *m* **1.** *(afecto)* affection; **te tengo un gran ~** I'm very fond of you **2.** *(estima)* esteem; **gran ~** high opinion **3.** ECON valuation

aprehender *vt* **1.** *(coger)* to apprehend; *(botín)* to seize **2.** *(percibir)* to perceive

aprehensión *f* **1.** *(acción de coger)* apprehension; *(del botín)* seizure **2.** *(percepción)* perception **3.** *(comprensión)* understanding

apremiante *adj* pressing

apremiar **I.** *vt* to urge (on) **II.** *vi (urgir)* to be urgent

apremio *m* urgent situation

aprender *vt* to learn; **~ a leer** to learn to read; **~ de memoria** to learn by heart; **siempre se aprende algo nuevo** you live and learn

aprendiz(a) *m(f)* apprentice

aprendizaje *m* **1.** *(acción de aprender)* learning; **~ en línea** online training **2.** *(formación profesional)* apprenticeship

aprensión *f* **1.** *(recelo)* apprehension; **me da ~ decírtelo** I daren't tell you **2.** *(asco)* disgust; **he cogido**

~ a la leche I've taken a strong dislike to milk **3.** *(temor)* fear; **tener la ~ de que...** +*subj (temer)* to be afraid that ...; *(creer)* to have the impression that ...; **son aprensiones suyas** *(figuración)* those are just his/her strange ideas

aprensivo, -a *adj* overanxious

apresar *vt* **1.** *(hacer presa)* to seize **2.** *(delincuente)* to capture

aprestar **I.** *vt* **1.** *(preparar)* to prepare **2.** *(telas)* to size **II.** *vr:* ~**se** to prepare

apresurado, -a *adj* hurried, hasty

apresuramiento *m* hurry, haste

apresurar **I.** *vt* **1.** *(dar prisa)* to hurry **2.** *(acelerar)* to speed up; **~ el paso** to quicken one's step **II.** *vr:* ~**se** to hurry; **¡no te apresures!** take your time!

apretado, -a *adj (vestido, tornillo)* tight; *(cinta, cuerda)* taut; **estar ~ de dinero/de tiempo** to be short of money/of time

apretar <e→ie> **I.** *vi* **1.** *(calor)* to become oppressive; *(dolor)* to become intense **2.** *(vestido)* to be too tight **3.** *(problemas)* ~ **a alguien** to weigh heavily on sb **4.** *(esforzarse)* to make more of an effort **5.** *(exigir)* to demand **II.** *vt* **1.** *(presionar: botón)* to press; *(el tubo de la pasta)* to squeeze; *(acelerador)* to step on **2.** *(estrechar: nudo, tornillo)* to tighten; *(dientes)* to grit; *(manos)* to clasp; *(puño)* to clench **III.** *vr:* ~**se 1.** *(estrecharse)* to become narrower; ~**se el cinturón** to tighten one's belt **2.** *(agolparse)* to crowd together

apretón *m* **1.** *(presión)* squeeze **2.** *(sprint)* sprint

aprieto *m* jam, fix; **~ económico** financial difficulties; **estar en un ~** to be in a jam

a priori *adv* a priori

aprisa *adv* quickly

aprobación *f* approval; *(de una ley)* passing

aprobado *m* ENS pass

aprobar <o→ue> **I.** *vt* **1.** *(decisión)* to approve; *(ley)* to pass **2.** *(examen)*

to pass **II.** *vi* ENS to pass
apropiación *f* appropriation; ~ **in-
debida** misappropriation
apropiado, -a *adj* **1.** (*adecuado*) ~
para suitable for **2.** (*oportuno*) appropriate
apropiar *vr* ~**se de algo** to appropriate sth
aprovechado, -a *adj* **1.** (*alumno, trabajador*) hardworking **2.** (*calcula-
dor*) opportunistic
aprovechamiento *m* exploitation; ~
del tiempo libre use of one's leisure
time
aprovechar I. *vi* to be of use; **¡que
aproveche!** enjoy your meal! **II.** *vt*
to make good use of; (*abusar*) to exploit; ~ **una idea** to exploit an idea
III. *vr:* ~**se 1.** (*sacar provecho*) ~**se
de algo** to profit by sth **2.** (*abusar*) to
take advantage **3.** (*explotar*) to exploit
aproximación *f* **1.** (*acercamiento*)
approach **2.** (*en una lotería*) consolation prize
aproximado, -a *adj* approximate
aproximar I. *vt* to bring nearer;
(*opiniones*) to bring closer **II.** *vr:*
~**se** to approach; ~**se a los 50** to be
getting on for 50
aptitud *f* **1.** (*talento*) aptitude
2. (*conveniencia*) suitability; ~ **para
algo** fitness for sth
apto, -a *adj* suitable; ~ **para menores** suitable for minors
apuntador(a) *m(f)* TEAT prompter
apuntalar *vt* to prop up
apuntar I. *vi* to appear; (*día*) to break
II. *vt* **1.** (*con un arma*) ~ **a algo** to
aim at sth **2.** (*con el dedo*) ~ **a algo**
to point at sth **3.** (*anotar*) to note
(down) **4.** (*inscribir*) to enroll; (*en
una lista*) to enter **5.** (*dictar*) to dictate; TEAT to prompt **6.** (*insinuar*) to
hint at **7.** (*indicar*) to point out; **todo
apunta en esta dirección** every-
thing points in this direction **III.** *vr:*
~**se 1.** (*inscribirse*) ~**se a algo** to
enrol in sth; (*en una lista*) to enter
one's name in sth; (*a un club*) to join
2. (*victoria*) to achieve
apunte *m* **1.** (*escrito*) note **2.** (*bos-*

quejo) sketch **3.** FIN entry
apuñalar *vt* to stab
apurado, -a *adj* **1.** (*falto*) ~ **de dinero** hard up; ~ **de tiempo** short of
time **2.** (*dificultoso*) difficult; **verse**
~ to be in a fix **3.** *AmL* (*apresurado*)
hurried
apurar I. *vt* **1.** (*vaso*) to drain; (*plato*)
to finish off **2.** (*paciencia*) to exhaust; **¡no me apures, mi paciencia tiene un límite!** don't hassle
me, my patience is limited! **3.** (*investigación*) to examine thoroughly
4. (*avergonzar*) to embarrass **5.** *AmL*
(*dar prisa*) to hurry **II.** *vr:* ~**se
1.** (*preocuparse*) to worry **2.** *AmL*
(*darse prisa*) to hurry up
apuro *m* **1.** (*aprieto*) fix; (*dificultad*)
difficulty; **estar en un** ~ to be in a
fix; **poner en** ~ to put in an awkward position **2.** (*estrechez*) financial need **3.** (*vergüenza*) embarrassment; **me da** ~**...** it's embarrassing
for me ... **4.** *AmL* (*prisa*) hurry
aquejado, -a *adj* ~ **de** afflicted by
aquejar *vt* to grieve; (*enfermedad*)
to afflict
aquel, -ella I. *adj dem* <aquellos,
-as> that, those *pl* **II.** *pron dem v.*
aquél, aquélla, aquello
aquél, aquélla, aquello <aqué-
llos, -as> *pron dem* that (one), those
(ones); **¿qué es aquello?** what's
that?; **como decía** ~ as the former
said; **esta teoría se diferencia de
aquélla** this theory differs from that
one; **oye, ¿qué hay de aquello?** *inf*
hey, how about it?
aquí *adv* **1.** (*lugar*) here; (**por**) ~
cerca around here; ~ **dentro** in
here; **éste de** ~ this fellow here;
¡ah, ~ estás! oh, there you are!;
mira ~ **dentro** look in here; **mejor
ir por** ~ it's better to go this way
2. (*de tiempo*) **de** ~ **en adelante**
from now on; **de** ~ **a una semana** a
week from now
aquietar I. *vt* to calm (down) **II.** *vr:*
~**se** to calm down
ara¹ *f* altar; **en** ~**s de la paz** *fig* in the
interests of peace
ara² *m AmL* parrot

árabe I. *adj* **1.** (*país*) Arab **2.** (*palabra*) Arabic **3.** (*península*) Arabian **4.** (*de los moros*) Moorish **II.** *mf* **1.** (*de un país árabe*) Arab **2.** (*lengua*) Arabic

Arabia *f* Arabia; ~ **Saudita** Saudi Arabia

arado *m* plough *Brit,* plow *Am*

Aragón *m* Aragon

aragonés, -esa *adj, m, f* Aragonese

arancel *m* (*tarifa*) tariff; (*impuesto*) duty

arandela *f* TÉC washer

araña *f* **1.** ZOOL spider **2.** (*candelabro*) chandelier

arañar *vt* **1.** (*rasguñar*) to scratch **2.** *inf* (*reunir*) to scrape together **3.** (*tocar*) to play

arañazo *m* scratch; **dar un** ~ to scratch

arar *vt* to plough *Brit,* to plow *Am*

arbitraje *m* **1.** (*juicio*) arbitration **2.** DEP refereeing

arbitrar I. *vt* **1.** (*disputa*) ~ **algo** to arbitrate in sth **2.** (*medios*) to provide **3.** DEP to referee **II.** *vi* JUR to adjudge

arbitrariedad *f* **1.** (*cualidad*) arbitrariness **2.** (*acción*) arbitrary act

arbitrario, -a *adj* arbitrary

arbitrio *m* **1.** (*de un juez*) adjudication **2.** (*voluntad*) free will; **dejar algo al** ~ **de alguien** to leave sth to sb's discretion **3.** *pl* (*impuesto*) ~**s municipales** municipal taxes

árbitro, -a *m, f* **1.** (*mediador*) arbitrator **2.** (*fútbol*) referee; (*tenis*) umpire

árbol *m* **1.** BOT tree **2.** TÉC (*eje*) shaft **3.** NÁUT mast

arbolado *m,* **arboleda** *f* woodland

arbusto *m* shrub, bush

arca *f* chest; (*para dinero*) safe; **las** ~**s del estado** the treasury; ~ **de Noé** Noah's Ark

arcada *f* **1.** ARQUIT arcade **2.** *pl* (*náusea*) retching

arcaico, -a *adj* archaic

arce *m* maple

arcén *m* edge; (*de carretera*) hard shoulder *Brit,* shoulder *Am*

archipiélago *m* archipelago

archivador *m* **1.** (*mueble*) filing cabinet **2.** (*carpeta*) file

archivar *vt* (*documentos*) to file; INFOR to store; (*asunto*) to put on file

archivo *m* **1.** (*lugar*) archive(s); ~ **fotográfico** picture library **2.** *pl* (*documentos*) archives *pl* **3.** INFOR file

arcilla *f* clay

arco *m* **1.** ARQUIT, MAT arc; ~ **iris** rainbow **2.** (*arma*) *t.* MÚS bow **3.** *AmL* DEP goal

arder *vi* to burn; ~ **con fuerza** to blaze; ~ **sin llama** to smoulder; ~ **de rabia** to be mad with rage; **estoy que ardo** (*enfadado*) I'm furious

ardid *m* ruse

ardiente *adj* **1.** (*pasión*) burning **2.** (*persona*) passionate **3.** (*color*) bright

ardilla *f* squirrel

ardor *m* **1.** (*calor*) heat; ~ **de estómago** heartburn **2.** (*fervor*) ardour *Brit,* ardor *Am*

ardoroso, -a *adj* ardent

arduo, -a *adj* arduous

área *f* *t.* MAT area; ~ **de descanso** AUTO lay-by *Brit,* rest stop *Am;* ~ **de castigo** DEP penalty area

arena *f* **1.** (*materia*) sand **2.** (*escenario*) arena

arenal *m* sandy area

arengar <g→gu> *vt* to harangue

arenoso, -a *adj* sandy

arenque *m* herring; ~**s ahumados** kippers *pl*

argamasa *f* mortar

Argel *m* Algiers

Argelia *f* Algeria

argelino, -a *adj, m, f* Algerian

Argentina *f* Argentina

⯈ **Argentina** (official title: **República Argentina**) lies in the southern part of South America. It is the second largest country in South America after Brazil. The capital of Argentina is **Buenos Aires**. The official language of the country is Spanish and the monetary unit is the **peso argentino**.

argentino, -a *adj, m, f* Argentinian
argolla *f* ring
argot <argots> *m* slang
argucia *f* **1.** (*falacia*) fallacy **2.** (*truco*) trick
argüir *irr como huir* **I.** *vt* **1.** (*alegar*) to argue **2.** (*deducir*) to deduce **3.** (*probar*) to prove **II.** *vi* to argue
argumentación *f* line of argument
argumentar *vi, vt* to argue
argumento *m* **1.** (*razón*) argument; (*razonamiento*) reasoning **2.** LIT, CINE, TEAT plot **3.** *AmL* (*discusión*) discussion
aria *f* aria
aridez *f t. fig* aridity
árido, -a *adj* (*terreno*) arid, dry; (*tema*) dry
Aries *m inv* Aries
ariete *m* **1.** MIL battering ram **2.** DEP striker
ario, -a *adj, m, f* Aryan
arisco, -a *adj* (*persona*) surly, unfriendly; (*animal*) skittish
aristocracia *f* aristocracy
aristócrata *mf* aristocrat
aritmética *f* arithmetic
arma *f* **1.** (*instrumento*) weapon, arm; ~ **blanca** knife; ~ **de fuego** firearm; ¡apunten ~**s**! take aim!; ¡descansen ~**s**! order arms!; **ser un** ~ **de doble filo** to be a double-edged sword; **ser de** ~**s tomar** to be bold **2.** (*del ejército*) arm **3.** *pl* (*blasón*) arms *pl*
armadillo *m* armadillo
armado, -a *adj* armed
armador(a) *m(f)* shipowner
armadura *f* **1.** (*de caballero*) armour *Brit*, armor *Am* **2.** (*de gafas*) frame; (*de edificio*) framework
armamento *m* (*de una persona*) arms *pl*; (*de un país*) armaments *pl*
armar I. *vt* **1.** (*ejército*) to arm **2.** (*embarcación*) to fit out **3.** TÉC to assemble; ~**la** *inf* to start a row; ~ **un Cristo** *inf* to kick up a stink **II.** *vr* ~**se de paciencia** to muster one's patience; ~**se de valor** to pluck up courage
armario *m* cupboard
armatoste *m* monstrosity

armazón *m o f* (*armadura*) frame; (*de edificio*) skeleton
Armenia *f* Armenia
armenio, -a *adj, m, f* Armenian
armiño *m* **1.** (*animal*) stoat **2.** (*piel*) ermine
armisticio *m* armistice
armonía *f* harmony
armónica *f* harmonica, mouth organ
armonioso, -a *adj* harmonious
armonizar <z→c> *vi, vt* to harmonize
arnés *m* **1.** (*armadura*) armour, armor *Am* **2.** *pl* (*caballería*) harness
aro *m* **1.** (*argolla*) ring; (*para jugar*) hoop; **pasar por el** ~ *inf* to knuckle under **2.** *AmL* (*anillo de boda*) wedding ring
aroma *m* aroma
aromático, -a *adj* aromatic
aromatizar <z→c> *vt* **1.** (*perfumar*) to scent **2.** GASTR to flavour *Brit*, to flavor *Am*
arpa *f* harp
arpía *f t. fig* harpy
arpón *m* harpoon
arquear I. *vt* **1.** (*doblar*) to bend; (*espalda*) to arch **2.** (*cejas*) to raise **II.** *vr*: ~**se** to bend
arqueo *m* **1.** (*de espalda*) *t.* ARQUIT arching **2.** NÁUT capacity
arqueología *f* archaeology, archeology *Am*
arqueólogo, -a *m, f* archaeologist, archeologist *Am*
arquero, -a *m, f* archer
arquetipo *m* archetype
arquitecto, -a *m, f* architect; ~ **interiorista** interior designer
arquitectura *f* architecture
arrabal *m* (*periferia*) suburb; (*barrio bajo*) slum area
arraigado, -a *adj* deep-rooted
arraigar <g→gu> *vi, vr*: ~**se** *t. fig* to take root
arraigo *m t. fig* rooting; **de mucho** ~ deep-rooted
arrancar <c→qu> **I.** *vt* **1.** (*planta*) to pull up **2.** (*pegatina*) to tear off; (*página*) to tear out **3.** (*muela*) to extract; (*clavo*) to pull (out) **4.** (*quitar*) to snatch (away); **le** ~**on el**

arma they wrenched the weapon from him/her; **el ladrón le arrancó el bolso** the thief snatched her handbag **5.** (*motor*) to start **6.** (*conseguir: aplausos*) to draw; (*promesa*) to force; (*victoria*) to snatch **II.** *vi* **1.** (*motor*) to start **2.** (*persona*) to start; ~ **a cantar** to burst out singing **3.** (*provenir*) to stem; (*comenzar*) to begin

arranque *m* **1.** (*comienzo*) start **2.** AUTO starting; ~ **automático** self-starter **3.** (*arrebato*) outburst **4.** (*prontitud*) promptness **5.** ARQUIT base **6.** INFOR start-up

arrasar I. *vt* (*edificios*) to demolish; (*región*) to devastate **II.** *vi* to triumph; POL to sweep the board **III.** *vr:* ~**se** (*ojos*) to fill with tears

arrastrado, -a *adj* poor, wretched

arrastrar I. *vt* **1.** (*tirar de*) to pull; (*algo pesado*) to drag **2.** (*impulsar*) ~ **a alguien a hacer algo** to lead sb to do sth **3.** (*producir*) to cause **II.** *vi* (*vestido*) to trail on the ground **III.** *vr:* ~**se 1.** (*reptar*) to crawl **2.** (*humillarse*) to grovel

arrastre *m* (*de objetos*) dragging; (*en pesca*) trawling; **estar para el ~** *inf* (*cosa*) to be ruined; (*persona*) to be a wreck

arre *interj* gee up *Brit,* giddap *Am*

arrear *vt* **1.** (*ganado*) to drive **2.** *inf* (*golpe*) to give

arrebatado, -a *adj* **1.** (*alocado*) hasty **2.** (*impetuoso*) rash

arrebatar I. *vt* **1.** (*arrancar*) to snatch (away) **2.** (*extasiar*) to captivate **3.** (*conmover*) to move **II.** *vr:* ~**se** (*exaltarse*) to get carried away

arrebato *m* **1.** (*arranque*) outburst **2.** (*éxtasis*) ecstasy

arrecife *m* reef

arredrar I. *vt* to drive back **II.** *vr:* ~**se 1.** (*ante algo*) to draw back; (*ante alguien*) to shrink (away) **2.** (*asustarse*) to get scared

arreglado, -a *adj* **1.** (*ordenado*) tidy; (*cuidado*) neat; **¡estamos ~s!** *inf* now we're in trouble! **2.** (*elegante*) smart **3.** (*moderado: precio*) reasonable

arreglar I. *vt* **1.** (*reparar*) to repair; (*ropa*) to mend; **¡ya te ~é yo!** *inf* I'll sort you out! **2.** (*ordenar*) to tidy up **3.** (*preparar*) to get ready **4.** (*pelo*) to do **5.** (*resolver: asunto*) to sort out **6.** (*acordar*) to arrange **7.** MÚS to arrange **II.** *vr:* ~**se 1.** (*vestirse, peinarse*) to get ready **2.** (*componérselas*) to manage **3.** (*ponerse de acuerdo*) to come to an agreement; (*solucionarse*) to work out; **al final todo se arregló** everything worked out all right in the end **4.** (*mejorar*) to get better

arreglo *m* **1.** (*reparación*) repair **2.** (*solución*) solution **3.** (*acuerdo*) agreement; **con ~ a lo convenido** as agreed **4.** MÚS arrangement

arrellanarse *vr* to settle comfortably; ~ **en algo** to settle oneself in sth

arremangar <g→gu> *vt, vr:* ~**se** to roll up

arremeter *vi* **1.** (*criticar*) to attack **2.** (*embestir*) to charge

arrendador(a) *m(f)* landlord *m,* landlady *f*

arrendamiento *m* **1.** (*alquiler*) rent; (*de negocio*) lease **2.** (*contrato*) contract

arrendar <e→ie> *vt* (*propietario*) to rent, to let; (*inquilino*) to rent

arrendatario, -a *m, f* tenant

arreos *mpl* harness

arrepentido, -a *adj* **1.** REL repentant; **estar ~ de algo** to regret sth **2.** (*delincuente*) reformed

arrepentimiento *m* (*lamento*) regret; REL repentance

arrepentirse *irr como sentir vr* (*lamentar*) to regret

arrestar *vt* to arrest

arresto *m* **1.** (*detención*) arrest **2.** (*reclusión*) imprisonment **3.** *pl* (*arrojo*) daring; **tener ~s** to be bold

arriar < *1. pres:* arrío> *vt* **1.** (*bandera*) to lower **2.** (*cabo, cadena*) to loosen

arriba *adv* **1.** (*posición*) above; (*en una casa*) upstairs; **más** ~ higher up; **el piso de** ~ (*el último*) the top floor; **de** ~ **abajo** from top to bottom; (*persona*) from head to foot;

¡manos ~! hands up! **2.** (*dirección*) up, upwards; **río** ~ upstream **3.** (*cantidad*) **tener de 60 años para** ~ to be over 60

arribar *vi* **1.** NÁUT to reach port **2.** *AmL* (*llegar*) to arrive

arribista *mf* arriviste; (*en sociedad*) social climber

arriendo *m v.* **arrendamiento**

arriesgado, -a *adj* **1.** (*peligroso*) risky **2.** (*atrevido*) daring

arriesgar <g→gu> **I.** *vt* **1.** (*vida*) to risk **2.** (*en el juego*) to stake **II.** *vr:* ~**se** to take a risk

arrimar I. *vt* to bring closer **II.** *vr:* ~**se 1.** (*acercarse*) to come close(r) **2.** (*apoyarse*) to lean against

arrinconar I. *vt* **1.** (*objeto*) to put in a corner **2.** (*enemigo*) to corner **II.** *vr:* ~**se** to withdraw from the world

arroba *f* INFOR at

arrobarse *vr* to become entranced

arrodillarse *vr* to kneel (down)

arrogancia *f* arrogance

arrogante *adj* arrogant

arrojar I. *vt* **1.** (*lanzar*) to throw **2.** (*emitir*) to emit, to give off **3.** (*expulsar*) to throw out **4.** *AmL, inf* (*vomitar*) to throw up **5.** (*un resultado*) to produce; (*beneficios*) to yield **II.** *vr:* ~**se** to throw oneself; ~**se al agua** to jump into the water

arrojo *m* daring

arrollador(a) *adj* **1.** (*mayoría*) overwhelming **2.** (*carácter*) irresistible

arrollar *vt* **1.** (*enrollar*) to roll up **2.** (*atropellar*) to run over **3.** DEP (*derrotar*) to crush **4.** (*riada*) to sweep away

arropar I. *vt* to wrap up **II.** *vr:* ~**se** to wrap oneself up

arrostrar *vt* to face up to

arroyo *m* **1.** (*riachuelo*) stream **2.** (*cuneta*) gutter

arroz *m* rice

arrozal *m* ricefield

arruga *f* **1.** (*en la piel*) wrinkle **2.** (*tela*) crease

arrugar <g→gu> **I.** *vt* **1.** (*piel*) to wrinkle **2.** (*tela*) to crease **II.** *vr:* ~**se 1.** (*piel*) to get wrinkled **2.** (*tela*) to get creased

arruinar I. *vt* to ruin; (*plan*) to wreck **II.** *vr:* ~**se** to be ruined

arrullar I. *vt* to lull to sleep **II.** *vi* (*paloma*) to coo

arsenal *m* **1.** MIL arsenal **2.** NÁUT dockyard

arsénico *m* arsenic

arte *m o f* (*m en sing, f en pl*) **1.** (*disciplina*) art; ~**s y oficios** arts and crafts; **bellas ~s** fine arts; **el séptimo** ~ the cinema *Brit,* the movies *Am;* **como por** ~ **de magia** as if by magic; **no tener** ~ **ni parte en algo** to have nothing whatsoever to do with sth **2.** (*habilidad*) skill

artefacto *m* (*aparato*) appliance; (*mecanismo*) device

arteria *f* ANAT artery

arterio(e)sclerosis *f inv* arteriosclerosis

artesanía *f* **1.** (*arte*) craftsmanship **2.** (*obras*) handicrafts *pl*

artesano, -a *m, f* artisan, craftsman *m,* craftswoman *f*

ártico *m* **1.** (*océano*) Arctic Ocean **2.** (*región*) Arctic

ártico, -a *adj* Arctic

articulación *f* **1.** ANAT joint **2.** LING articulation

articulado, -a *adj* articulated

articular *vt* **1.** TÉC to join together **2.** LING to articulate

articulista *mf* feature writer

artículo *m* **1.** (*objeto*) article; COM commodity; ~**s de consumo** consumer goods **2.** PREN, LING article **3.** (*en un diccionario*) entry

artífice *mf* **1.** (*artista*) artist **2.** *fig* architect

artificial *adj* artificial

artificio *m* (*habilidad*) skill; (*truco*) trick

artillería *f* artillery

artillero *m* gunner

artilugio *m* gadget

artimaña *f* (sly) trick

artista *mf* **1.** (*de bellas artes*) artist **2.** (*de circo, teatro*) artist(e) *m(f)*

artístico, -a *adj* artistic

artritis *f inv* arthritis

arzobispo *m* archbishop

get creased

as *m t. fig* ace

asa *f* handle

asado *m* GASTR roast

asador *m* **1.** (*pincho*) spit **2.** (*aparato*) spit roaster

asadura *f* offal

asalariado, -a **I.** *adj* wage-earning **II.** *m, f* wage earner

asaltante *mf* attacker; (*de banco*) raider

asaltar *vt* **1.** (*fortaleza*) to storm; (*banco*) to break into, to raid **2.** (*persona*) to attack, to assault

asalto *m* **1.** (*a una fortaleza*) storming **2.** (*a un banco*) raid

asamblea *f* assembly; (*reunión*) meeting

asar **I.** *vt* **1.** GASTR to roast; ~ **a la parrilla** to grill **2.** (*a preguntas*) to pester **II.** *vr:* ~**se** to roast

asbesto *m* asbestos

ascendencia *f* **1.** (*linaje*) ancestry; **de** ~ **escocesa** of Scottish descent **2.** (*antepasados*) ancestors *pl*

ascender <e→ie> **I.** *vi* **1.** (*subir*) to rise; DEP to go up **2.** (*escalar*) to climb **3.** (*de empleo*) to be promoted **II.** *vt* to promote

ascendiente¹ *mf* ancestor

ascendiente² *m* influence

ascensión *f* **1.** (*subida*) ascent **2.** (*de Cristo*) Ascension

ascenso *m* **1.** (*de precio*) rise **2.** (*a una montaña*) ascent **3.** (*de equipo*) promotion

ascensor *m* lift *Brit,* elevator *Am*

ascético, -a *adj* ascetic

asco *m* **1.** (*sensación*) disgust, loathing; **dar** ~ (*olor*) to make feel sick; (*comida*) to loathe; (*persona*) to detest **2.** (*situación*) **estar hecho un** ~ (*lugar*) to be a mess; (*persona*) to feel low

ascua *f* ember; **arrimar el** ~ **a su sardina** *fig* to feather one's nest; **en** ~**s** on tenterhooks

aseado, -a *adj* (*limpio*) clean; (*arreglado*) smart

asear **I.** *vt* to clean up **II.** *vr:* ~**se** to tidy oneself up

asediar *vt* **1.** MIL to besiege **2.** (*importunar*) to bother

asedio *m* **1.** MIL siege **2.** (*fastidio*) nuisance

asegurado, -a *adj, m, f* insured

asegurador(a) *m(f)* insurance agent

aseguradora *f* (*empresa*) insurance company

asegurar **I.** *vt* **1.** (*fijar*) to secure **2.** (*afirmar*) to affirm **3.** (*prometer*) to assure; (*garantizar*) to ensure **4.** (*con un seguro*) to insure **II.** *vr:* ~**se** **1.** (*comprobar*) to make sure **2.** (*con un seguro*) to insure oneself

asemejarse *vr* to be alike

asentado, -a *adj* **1.** (*juicioso*) sensible **2.** (*estable*) settled

asentar <e→ie> **I.** *vt* **1.** (*poner*) to place **2.** (*sentar*) to seat **3.** (*población*) to found **II.** *vr:* ~**se** to settle

asentir *irr como sentir vi* to agree

aseo *m* **1.** (*estado*) cleanliness; ~ **personal** personal hygiene **2.** *pl* (*servicios*) toilets *pl Brit,* restrooms *pl Am*

aséptico, -a *adj* aseptic

asequible *adj* **1.** (*precio*) reasonable; (*plan*) feasible **2.** (*persona*) approachable

aserradero *m* sawmill

aserrar <e→ie> *vt* to saw

asesinar *vt* to murder; POL (*personaje público*) to assassinate

asesinato *m* murder; POL assassination

asesino, -a **I.** *adj t. fig* murderous **II.** *m, f* murderer; POL assassin

asesor(a) **I.** *adj* advisory **II.** *m(f)* **1.** (*consejero*) adviser, consultant **2.** JUR assessor

asesoramiento *f* advice

asesorar **I.** *vt* to advise **II.** *vr* ~**se en algo** to take advice about sth

asesoría *f* **1.** (*oficio*) consultancy **2.** (*oficina*) consultant's office

asestar *vt* (*propinar*) to deal; (*puñalada*) to stab; (*tiro*) to fire

asfaltar *vt* to asphalt

asfalto *m* asphalt

asfixia *f* suffocation, asphyxia

asfixiar *vt* (*persona*) to suffocate; (*humo*) to asphyxiate

así **I.** *adv* **1.** (*de este modo*) in this way; ¡~ **es!** that's right!; **¿no es** ~**?**

isn't it? **2.** (*ojalá*) ¡~ **revientes!** I hope you die! **3.** (*de esta medida*) ~ **de grande** this big **II.** *adj inv* like this, like that

Asia *f* Asia

asiático, -a *adj, m, f* Asian, Asiatic

asidero *m* handle

asiduidad *f* frequency

asiduo, -a *adj* frequent

asiento *m* **1.** (*silla*) seat **2.** (*sitio*) site **3.** (*en una cuenta*) entry

asignación *f* **1.** *t.* INFOR assignment; (*de recursos*) allocation **2.** FIN allowance

asignar *vt t.* INFOR to assign; (*recursos*) to allocate

asignatura *f* subject

asilado, -a *m, f* POL political refugee

asilo *m* **1.** POL asylum **2.** (*refugio*) refuge **3.** (*de ancianos*) (old people's) home

asimilación *f* assimilation

asimilar *vt t.* BIO to assimilate

asimismo *adv* likewise, also

asir *irr* **I.** *vt* (*sujetar*) to seize **II.** *vr* ~**se a algo** to seize sth

asistencia *f* **1.** (*presencia*) attendance **2.** (*ayuda*) assistance, help; ~ **médica** medical care

asistenta *f* cleaning woman

asistente *mf* assistant; ~ **social** social worker

asistido, -a *adj* assisted; ~ **por ordenador** computer-assisted

asistir I. *vi* **1.** (*ir*) ~ **a algo** to attend sth **2.** (*estar presente*) to be present; ~ **a algo** to witness sth **II.** *vt* **1.** (*estar presente en*) to attend **2.** (*ayudar*) to help, assist

asma *m sin pl* asthma

asno *m* **1.** ZOOL donkey, ass **2.** *inf* (*persona*) ass

asociación *f* association

asociado, -a I. *adj* associate **II.** *m, f* **1.** (*socio*) associate **2.** COM partner

asociar I. *vt* **1.** *t.* POL to associate **2.** (*juntar*) to join **3.** COM to take into partnership **II.** *vr:* ~**se** to associate; COM to become partners

asolar <o→ue> *vt* (*destruir*) to devastate

asomar I. *vt* **1.** (*mostrar*) to show **2.** (*cabeza*) to put out **II.** *vi* (*verse*) to show; (*aparecer*) to appear **III.** *vr:* ~**se 1.** (*mostrarse*) to show up **2.** (*cabeza*) to put out

asombrar I. *vt* (*pasmar*) to amaze **II.** *vr:* ~**se** to be amazed

asombro *m* amazement

asombroso, -a *adj* amazing

asomo *m* hint

aspa *f* **1.** (*figura*) cross **2.** (*de molino*) sail

aspaviento *m* fuss

aspecto *m* **1.** (*apariencia*) appearance **2.** (*punto de vista*) aspect

áspero, -a *adj* **1.** (*superficie*) rough **2.** (*persona*) harsh **3.** (*clima*) tough

aspersión *f* sprinkling

aspersor *m* sprinkler

aspiración *f* **1.** (*inspiración*) breathing in **2.** (*pretensión*) aspiration

aspiradora *f* vacuum cleaner, hoover *Brit;* **pasar la** ~ to vacuum

aspirante *mf* aspirant

aspirar I. *vt* **1.** (*inspirar*) to breathe in **2.** (*aspirador*) to suck in **II.** *vi* **1.** (*inspirar*) to breathe in **2.** (*pretender*) to aspire

aspirina® *f* aspirin®

asquear I. *vt* to disgust **II.** *vr:* ~**se** to feel disgusted

asqueroso, -a *adj* disgusting; (*sucio*) filthy

asta *f* **1.** (*mango*) handle; **a media** ~ at half mast **2.** (*cuerno*) horn

asterisco *m* asterisk

asteroide *m* asteroid

astilla *f* **1.** (*esquirla*) splinter; **clavarse una** ~ to get a splinter **2.** *pl* (*para fuego*) firewood

astillero *m* shipyard

astro *m t. fig* star

astrología *f* astrology

astrólogo, -a *m, f* astrologer

astronauta *mf* astronaut

astronave *f* spaceship

astronomía *f* astronomy

astronómico, -a *adj t. fig* astronomical

astrónomo, -a *m, f* astronomer

astucia *f* **1.** (*sagacidad*) astuteness **2.** (*ardid*) trick

Asturias *f* Asturias

astuto, -a *adj* astute

asueto *m* time off; (**día de**) ~ day off

asumir *vt* **1.** (*responsabilidad*) to assume; (*cargo*) to take over **2.** (*suponer*) to assume

asunción *f* assumption

asunto *m* **1.** (*cuestión*) matter; **ir al** ~ to get to the point **2.** (*negocio*) business **3.** (*amorío*) affair

asustar I. *vt* to frighten II. *vr:* ~**se** to be frightened

atacar <c→qu> I. *vt* **1.** (*agredir*) to attack **2.** (*problema*) to tackle II. *vi t.* DEP to attack

atadura *f* tie, bond

atajar I. *vi* to take a short cut II. *vt* **1.** (*detener*) to stop **2.** (*discurso*) to interrupt

atajo *m* short cut

atañer <*3. pret:* atañó> *vimpers* **eso no te atañe** that doesn't concern you

ataque *m* attack; ~ **al** [*o* **de**] **corazón** heart attack; ~ **de nervios** nervous breakdwon

atar I. *vt* to tie (up) II. *vr:* ~**se** to do up; (*zapatos*) to lace up

atardecer I. *irr como crecer vimpers* **atardece** it's getting dark II. *m* dusk

atareado, -a *adj* busy

atascar <c→qu> I. *vt* to block II. *vr:* ~**se** **1.** (*cañería*) to get blocked (up) **2.** (*coche*) to get stuck **3.** (*mecanismo*) to jam

atasco *m* **1.** (*de una cañería*) blockage **2.** (*de un mecanismo*) blocking **3.** (*de tráfico*) traffic jam

ataúd *m* coffin

ataviar <*1. pres:* me atavío> *vt, vr:* ~**se** to dress up

atavío *m* attire

atemorizar <z→c> I. *vt* to scare, to frighten II. *vr:* ~**se** to get scared

Atenas *f* Athens

atención *f* **1.** (*interés*) attention; ¡~, **por favor!** your attention please!; **llamar la** ~ **a alguien** to rebuke sb; **prestar** ~ **a algo** to pay attention to sth; (*escuchar*) to listen to sth **2.** (*cuidado*) attention, care; ~ **médica** medical care **3.** (*en cartas*) **a la** ~ **de...** for the attention of ...

4. (*cortesía*) kindness

atender <e→ie> I. *vt* **1.** (*prestar atención a*) to pay attention to; (*escuchar*) to listen to **2.** (*consejo*) to heed; (*deseo*) to comply with **3.** (*cuidar*) ~ **a alguien** to care for sb **4.** (*tratar*) to treat **5.** (*despachar*) to serve; **¿lo atienden?** are you being served? **6.** (*llamada*) to answer II. *vi* **1.** (*prestar atención*) to pay attention; (*escuchar*) to listen **2.** (*tener en cuenta*) ~ **a algo** to take sth into account

atenerse *irr como tener vr* ~ **a** (*reglas*) to abide by; (*lo dicho*) to stand by, to keep to

atentado *m* (*ataque*) attack; (*crimen*) crime

atentamente *adv* (*final de carta*) (**muy**) ~ yours sincerely *Brit,* sincerely yours *Am*

atentar *vi* ~ **contra alguien** to make an attempt on sb's life

atento, -a *adj* **1.** (*observador*) attentive **2.** (*cortés*) kind

atenuantes *f pl* JUR extenuating circumstances *pl*

atenuar <*1. pres:* atenúo> *vt* **1.** to attenuate; (*dolor*) to ease **2.** JUR to extenuate

ateo, -a I. *adj* atheistic II. *m, f* atheist

aterciopelado, -a *adj* velvety

aterirse *irr como abolir vr* to become numb; **quedarse aterido** to be stiff with cold

aterrador(a) *adj* terrifying

aterrar I. *vt* (*atemorizar*) to terrify; (*sobresaltar*) to startle II. *vr:* ~**se** (*sobresaltarse*) to be startled; (*tener miedo*) to be afraid

aterrizaje *f* landing

aterrizar <z→c> *vi* to land

aterrorizar <z→c> *vt* **1.** POL, MIL to terrorize **2.** (*causar terror*) to terrify

atesorar *vt* **1.** (*tesoros*) to store up **2.** ECON to hoard

atestado *m* ~ (**policial**) statement

atestar *vt* **1.** JUR to attest **2.** (*llenar*) to pack

atestiguar <gu→gü> *vt* to testify to

atiborrar I. *vt* to stuff II. *vr:* ~**se** to

stuff oneself

ático *m* attic; (*de lujo*) penthouse

atildado, -a *adj* elegant

atildar I. *vt* to tidy (up) II. *vr:* ~**se** to dress up

atinado, -a *adj* accurate

atinar *vi* **1.** (*acertar*) to hit on sth **2.** (*al disparar*) to hit the target

atípico, -a *adj* atypical

atisbar *vt* to spy on

atizar <z→c> *vt* **1.** (*fuego*) to poke **2.** (*pasión*) to rouse **3.** (*bofetada*) to give

atlántico, -a *adj* Atlantic

Atlántico *m* **el** ~ the Atlantic

atlas *m inv* atlas

atleta *mf* athlete

atlético, -a *adj* athletic

atletismo *m sin pl* athletics

atmósfera *f* atmosphere

atolladero *m* **estar en un** ~ to be in a fix

atolondrado, -a *adj* bewildered

atolondramiento *m* **1.** (*de los sentidos*) bewilderment **2.** (*irreflexión*) thoughtlessness

atómico, -a *adj* atomic

atomizador *m* spray

átomo *m* atom

atónito, -a *adj* amazed

atontado, -a *adj* **1.** (*tonto*) stupid **2.** (*distraído*) inattentive

atontar I. *vt* to stun II. *vr:* ~**se** to be stunned

atormentar *vt* **1.** (*torturar*) to torture **2.** (*molestar*) to harass

atornillador *m* screwdriver

atornillar *vt* to screw down, to screw on

atosigar <g→gu> *vt* to harass

atracador(a) *m(f)* bank robber

atracar <c→qu> I. *vi* NÁUT to berth II. *vt* **1.** NÁUT to moor **2.** (*asaltar*) to hold up III. *vr inf* ~**se** to stuff oneself

atracción *f t.* FÍS attraction; **parque de atracciones** amusement park

atraco *m* hold-up; ~ **a un banco** bank robbery

atracón *m inf* **darse un** ~ to stuff oneself

atractivo *m* attraction

atractivo, -a *adj* attractive

atraer *irr como traer* I. *vt* to attract II. *vr:* ~**se** (*ganarse*) to win

atragantarse *vr* ~ **con algo** to choke on sth

atrancar <c→qu> *vt* to bolt

atrapar *vt* to trap; (*ladrón*) to catch

atrás *adv* **1.** (*hacia detrás*) back, backwards; **ir marcha** ~ to reverse *Brit,* to back up *Am;* **volver** ~ to go back; **¡**~**!** get back! **2.** (*detrás*) back, behind; **rueda de** ~ rear wheel; **sentarse** ~ to sit at the back **3.** (*de tiempo*) **años** ~ years ago

atrasado, -a *adj* **1.** (*en el estudio*) behind; (*país*) backward **2.** (*pago*) overdue

atrasar I. *vt* **1.** (*aplazar*) to postpone **2.** (*reloj*) to put back II. *vr:* ~**se** **1.** (*quedarse atrás*) to remain behind **2.** (*retrasarse*) to be late

atraso *m* **1.** (*de un tren*) delay **2.** (*de un país*) backwardness **3.** *pl* FIN arrears *pl*

atravesar <e→ie> I. *vt* **1.** (*calle*) to cross; (*río*) to swim across **2.** (*con aguja*) to pierce; (*taladrando*) to bore through **3.** (*poner de través*) to lay across II. *vr:* ~**se** **1.** (*ponerse entremedio*) to get in one's way **2.** (*en una conversación*) ~**se en algo** to butt into sth

atrayente *adj* attractive

atreverse *vr* to dare

atrevido, -a *adj* **1.** (*valiente*) daring **2.** (*insolente*) insolent

atrevimiento *m* **1.** (*audacia*) boldness **2.** (*descaro*) cheek *Brit,* nerve *Am*

atribución *f* **1.** (*de un hecho*) attribution **2.** (*competencia*) authority

atribuir *irr como huir* *vt* **1.** (*hechos*) to attribute; (*culpa*) to blame **2.** (*funciones*) to confer

atributo *m* attribute

atril *m* **1.** MÚS music stand **2.** (*de mesa*) lectern

atrincherar *vt, vr:* ~**se** to entrench (oneself)

atrocidad *f* atrocity

atropellar I. *vt* **1.** (*vehículo*) to run over **2.** (*derribar*) to knock down **3.** (*agraviar*) to insult II. *vr:* ~**se** to rush

atropello *m* **1.**(*accidente*) accident **2.**(*empujón*) push; (*derribo*) knocking down **3.**(*insulto*) insult

atroz *adj* atrocious

atuendo *m* outfit

atún *m* tuna (fish)

aturdir **I.** *vt* **1.**(*los sentidos*) to stupefy **2.**(*pasmar*) to stun **II.** *vr:* ~**se** *t. fig* to be stunned

atusar *vt* **1.**(*el peinado*) to smooth **2.**(*la barba*) to trim

audacia *f* boldness, audacity

audaz *adj* bold, audacious

audible *adj* audible

audición *f* **1.**(*acción*) hearing **2.**(*concierto*) concert **3.** TEAT audition

audiencia *f* **1.** TEL audience **2.** JUR court

audífono *m* hearing aid

auditivo, -a *adj* ANAT hearing

auditor(a) *m(f)* ECON, FIN auditor

auditorio *m* **1.**(*público*) audience **2.**(*sala*) auditorium

auge *m* **1.**(*cumbre*) peak; (*de una época*) heyday **2.**(*mejora*) improvement

augurar *vt* to predict

augurio *m* prediction

aula *f* classroom

aullar *irr vi* to howl

aullido *m* howl

aumentar **I.** *vi, vt* **1.**(*en general*) to increase; (*precios*) to rise **2.**(*en extensión*) to extend **II.** *vr:* ~**se** **1.**(*en cantidad*) to increase **2.**(*en extensión*) to extend

aumentativo *m* LING augmentative

aumento *m* increase

aun *adv* even; ~ **así** even so

aún *adv* still; ~ **más** even more

aunar *irr* como aullar *vt, vr:* ~**se** to unite

aunque *conj* even though; ~ **es viejo, aún puede trabajar** although he's old, he can still work; **la casa,** ~ **pequeña, está bien** the house is nice, even if it's small

aúpa *interj* up, up you get

aura *f* (*atmósfera*) aura; **tiene una** ~ **misteriosa** he/she has a mysterious aura

aureola *f* halo

auricular *m* **1.** TEL receiver **2.** *pl* (*de música*) headphones *pl*

aurora *f t. fig* dawn

auscultar *vt* to sound

ausencia *f* absence

ausentarse *vr*(*irse*) to go away; ~ **de la ciudad** to leave town

ausente *adj* **1.**(*no presente*) absent **2.**(*distraído*) distracted

auspicios *mpl* **1.**(*protección*) protection **2.**(*patrocinio*) auspices *pl*

austeridad *f* austerity

austero, -a *adj* austere

austral *adj* southern

Australia *f* Australia

australiano, -a *adj, m, f* Australian

Austria *f* Austria

austriaco, -a, austríaco, -a *adj, m, f* Austrian

auténtico, -a *adj* authentic

auto *m* **1.**(*resolución*) decision **2.** *pl* JUR (*actas*) proceedings *pl* **3.** AUTO car

autoadhesivo, -a *adj* self-adhesive

autobús *m* bus

autocar <autocares> *m* coach *Brit,* bus *Am*

autóctono, -a *adj* indigenous

autodefensa *f* self-defence *Brit,* self--defense *Am*

autoescuela *f* driving school

autoestop *m* **hacer** ~ to hitch-hike

autogestión *f* self-management

autógrafo *m* autograph

autómata *m* automaton

automático *m* press stud *Brit,* snap fastener *Am*

automático, -a *adj* automatic

automatización *f* automation

automotivarse *vr* to motivate oneself

automóvil *m* car

automovilismo *m* DEP motoring

automovilista *mf* motorist, driver

automovilístico, -a *adj* car

autonomía *f* **1.**(*de una persona*) autonomy **2.**(*territorio*) autonomous region

autonómico, -a *adj* autonomous; **política autonómica** regional policy

autónomo, -a *adj* **1.** POL autonomous

2. (*trabajador*) self-employed
autopista *f* motorway *Brit,* freeway *Am;* ~ **de datos** INFOR data highway; ~ **de la información** INFOR information highway
autopsia *f* MED autopsy
autor(a) *m(f)* **1.** (*de una obra*) author **2.** (*de un atentado*) assassin
autoridad *f* **1.** (*en general*) authority **2.** (*pl*) (*policía*) authorities *pl*
autoritario, -a *adj* authoritarian
autorización *f* authorization
autorizado, -a *adj* **1.** (*facultado*) authorized **2.** (*oficial*) official
autorizar <z→c> *vt* **1.** (*consentir*) to approve **2.** (*facultar*) to authorize **3.** (*dar derecho*) to entitle
autorretrato *m* self-portrait
autoservicio *m* self-service
autostop *m* **hacer** ~ to hitch-hike
autostopista *mf* hitch-hiker
autosuficiencia *f* self-sufficiency; *pey* smugness
autosuficiente *adj* self-sufficient; *pey* smug
autosugestión *f* autosuggestion
autovía *f* dual carriageway *Brit,* divided highway *Am*
auxiliar[1] **I.** *mf* assistant **II.** *vt* to help
auxiliar[2] *m* LING auxiliary verb
auxilio *m* help
avalancha *f* avalanche
avance *m* **1.** *t.* MIL advance **2.** (*presupuesto*) estimate **3.** CINE trailer
avanzado, -a *adj* advanced
avanzar <z→c> *vi t.* MIL to advance
avaricia *f* **1.** (*codicia*) greed **2.** (*tacañería*) avarice
avaricioso, -a *adj,* **avariento, -a** *adj* **1.** (*codicioso*) greedy **2.** (*tacaño*) avaricious
avaro, -a **I.** *adj* miserly **II.** *m, f* miser
avasallar *vt* to subjugate
Avda. *abr de* **Avenida** Av(e).
ave *f* bird
AVE *m abr de* **Alta Velocidad Española** high-speed train
avecinarse *vr* to approach
avellana *f* hazelnut
avellano *m* hazel (tree)
avemaría *f* Hail Mary
avena *f* oats *pl*

avenida *f* avenue
avenir *irr como venir* **I.** *vt* to reconcile **II.** *vr:* ~**se** **1.** (*entenderse*) to get on **2.** (*ponerse de acuerdo*) to agree on
aventajado, -a *adj* outstanding
aventajar *vt* to surpass
aventura *f* **1.** (*extraordinaria*) adventure **2.** (*amorosa*) affair
aventurado, -a *adj* risky
aventurero, -a *adj* adventurous
avergonzar *irr* **I.** *vt* to shame **II.** *vr:* ~**se** to be ashamed of
avería *f* **1.** AUTO breakdown **2.** NÁUT average
averiar <*l. pres:* averío> **I.** *vt* to damage **II.** *vr:* ~**se** **1.** AUTO to break down **2.** TÉC to fail
averiguación *f* **1.** (*haciendo pesquisas*) inquiry **2.** (*al dar con*) discovery
averiguar <gu→gü> *vt* **1.** (*inquiriendo*) to inquire into **2.** (*dar con*) to discover
aversión *f* aversion
avestruz *m* ostrich
aviación *f* **1.** AERO aviation **2.** MIL air force
aviador(a) *m(f)* aviator
aviar <*l. pres:* avío> **I.** *vt* (*maleta*) to pack; (*comida*) to prepare; (*mesa*) to set **II.** *vr:* ~**se** to get ready
avícola *adj* poultry
avicultura *f* poultry farming
avidez *f* eagerness
ávido, -a *adj* eager
avilés, -esa *adj* of/from Ávila
avinagrarse *vr* to turn sour
avío *m* preparation; ~**s de coser** sewing things
avión *m* AERO aeroplane *Brit,* airplane *Am*
avioneta *f* light aircraft
avisar *vt* **1.** (*dar noticia*) to notify **2.** (*advertir*) to warn **3.** (*llamar*) to call
aviso *m* **1.** (*notificación*) notification; (*en una cartelera*) notice; (*por el altavoz*) announcement; **sin previo** ~ without notice **2.** (*advertencia*) warning; ~ **de bomba** bomb warning **3.** (*consejo*) advice **4.** (*pruden-*

cia) prudence
avispa *f* wasp
avispado, -a *adj* sharp
avispero *m* wasps' nest
avispón *m* hornet
avistar *vt* to sight
avituallar *vt* to supply with food
avivar *vt* to enliven; (*fuego*) to stoke; (*color*) to brighten
axila *f* armpit
axioma *m* axiom
ay *interj* **1.** (*de dolor*) ouch **2.** (*de pena*) oh **3.** (*de miedo*) oh, my God
ayer *adv* yesterday; ~ (**por la**) **noche** last night
ayo, -a *m, f* tutor
ayuda *f* help; **perro de** ~ watchdog
ayudante *mf* **1.** (*que ayuda*) helper **2.** (*cargo*) assistant
ayudar *vt* to help
ayunar *vi* to fast
ayunas *adv* **estar en** ~ to not have eaten anything
ayuno *m* fast
ayuntamiento *m* **1.** (*de una ciudad*) town/city council **2.** (*edificio*) town/city hall
azada *f* hoe
azafata *f* AERO air hostess; ~ **de congresos** conference hostess
azafrán *m* saffron
azahar *m* orange blossom
azalea *f* azalea
azar *m* **1.** (*casualidad*) chance; **al** ~ at random; **por** ~ by chance **2.** (*imprevisto*) misfortune
Azerbaiyán *m* Azerbaijan
azogue *m* mercury
azoramiento *m* **1.** (*nerviosismo*) excitement **2.** (*turbación*) confusion
azorar I. *vt* **1.** (*poner nervioso*) to excite **2.** (*turbar*) to confuse **II.** *vr:* ~**se** to get upset
Azores *fpl* **las** ~ the Azores
azotar *vt* (*con un látigo*) to whip; (*con la mano*) to thrash, to spank
azote *m* **1.** (*látigo*) whip **2.** (*golpe*) lash
azotea *f* terrace roof
azteca *adj, mf* Aztec
azúcar *m* sugar

[?] The Indian tribe of the **aztecas** built up a vast and powerful empire between the 14th and 16th centuries in the southern and central part of Mexico, which was conquered by the Spanish in 1521. The language of the **aztecas** was **náhuatl**.

azucarar I. *vt* to sugar **II.** *vr:* ~**se** to crystallize
azucarero *m* sugar basin, sugar bowl *Am*
azucena *f* Madonna lily
azufre *m* sulphur, sulfur *Am*
azul *adj* blue; ~ **celeste** sky blue; ~ **marino** navy blue
azulejo *m* (glazed) tile
azuzar <z→c> *vt* to incite

B b

B, b *f* B, b; ~ **de Barcelona** B for Benjamin *Brit,* B for Baker *Am*
baba *f* **1.** (*de la boca*) spittle **2.** (*del caracol*) slime
babear *vi* to dribble, to drool
babel *m o f* bedlam
babero *m* bib
babor *m* NÁUT port; **a** ~ on the port side
baboso, -a *adj* **1.** (*con baba*) slimy **2.** *AmL* (*tonto*) silly
babucha *f* slipper
baca *f* roof rack
bacalao *m* **1.** (*pescado*) cod; **cortar el** ~ *fig* to run the show **2.** MÚS techno music
bachata *f* RDom, PRico party
bache *m* **1.** (*en la calle*) pothole **2.** (*psíquico*) bad patch
bachillerato *m* *high school education for 14–17-year-olds*

backup *m* <backups> INFOR backup
bacteria *f* bacteria
bacteriológico, -a *adj* bacteriological
bacteriólogo, -a *m, f* bacteriologist
báculo *m* crosier
badajocense *adj* of/from Badajoz
bádminton *m* DEP badminton
bafle *m* (loud)speaker
bagaje *m* 1. MIL baggage 2. (*saber*) knowledge
bagatela *f* trifle
Bahamas *fpl* **las** (**islas**) ~ the Bahamas
bahía *f* bay
bailador(a) *m(f)* dancer (of flamenco)
bailar *vi, vt* 1. (*danzar*) to dance 2. (*objetos*) to move; (*peonza*) to spin
bailarín, -ina *m, f* dancer; (*de ballet*) ballet dancer
baile *m* 1. (*danza*) dance 2. (*fiesta*) dance party; (*de etiqueta*) ball
baja *f* 1. (*disminución*) decrease; (*de precio*) drop 2. (*laboral*) vacancy; ~ **por maternidad** maternity leave; **dar de ~ a alguien** to expel sb 3. (*documento*) discharge certificate; (*del médico*) sick note 4. MIL casualty 5. FIN slump
bajada *f* 1. (*descenso*) descent; (*de intereses*) fall 2. (*camino*) way down 3. (*pendiente*) slope
bajamar *f* low tide
bajar I. *vi* 1. (*ir hacia abajo*) to go down, to come down 2. (*de un caballo*) to get down; (*de un coche*) to get out of 3. (*las aguas*) to fall 4. (*disminuir*) to decrease; (*temperatura*) to drop; (*hinchazón*) to go down II. *vt* 1. (*transportar*) to bring down, to take down 2. (*persiana, voz*) to lower; (*radio*) to turn down 3. (*ojos*) to drop
bajeza *f* 1. (*acción*) vile act 2. (*carácter*) baseness
bajo I. *m* 1. (*instrumento*) bass 2. (*persona*) bass player 3. *pl* (*piso*) ground floor *Brit*, first floor *Am* II. *adv* 1. (*posición*) below 2. (*voz*) quietly III. *prep* 1. (*colocar debajo*)

below 2. (*por debajo de*) underneath
bajo, -a <más bajo *o* inferior, bajísimo> *adj* 1. **estar** (*en lugar inferior*) low 2. **ser** (*de temperatura*) low; (*de estatura*) short 3. (*voz*) low; (*sonido*) soft 4. (*color*) pale 5. (*metal*) base 6. (*comportamiento*) mean 7. (*clase social*) humble 8. (*calidad*) poor
bajón *m* 1. (*descenso*) decline; (*de precios*) drop 2. (*de la salud*) worsening
bakalao *m* MÚS techno music
bala *f* bullet; ~ **de fogueo** blank cartridge; **como una** ~ *fig* like a flash
balacear *vt AmL* (*herir o matar*) to shoot; (*disparar contra*) to shoot at
baladí *adj* <baladíes> trivial, worthless
balance *m* 1. COM (*resultado*) balance; **hacer un** ~ to draw up a balance 2. (*comparación*) comparison
balancear I. *vt* 1. (*mecer*) to sway 2. (*equilibrar*) to balance II. *vr:* ~**se** to swing
balanceo *m* swaying
balanza *f* 1. (*pesa*) scales *pl* 2. COM balance
Balanza *f* ASTR Libra
balar *vi* to bleat
balaustrada *f* balustrade
balazo *m* shot
balbucear *vi, vt v.* **balbucir**
balbuceo *m* stammering
balbucir *vi, vt* to stammer
Balcanes *mpl* **los** ~ the Balkans
balcón *m* balcony
baldar *vt* to disable
balde *m* bucket; **de** ~ for nothing; **en** ~ in vain
baldío *m* AGR wasteland
baldío, -a *adj* 1. (*terreno*) uncultivated 2. (*en balde*) vain
baldosa *f* floor tile
baldosín *m* tile
balear *AmL* I. *vt* ~ **a alguien** to shoot at sb II. *vr:* ~**se** to exchange shots
Baleares *fpl* **las** (**islas**) ~ the Balearics
balido *m* bleat

balística *f sin pl* ballistics
baliza *f* buoy
balizar <z→c> *vt* **1.** (*con boyas*) to mark with buoys **2.** (*iluminar*) to light
ball *f AmL* **1.** (*balón*) ball **2.** (*proyectil*) shell
ballena *f* whale
ballesta *f* HIST crossbow
ballet <ballets> *m* ballet
balneario *m* spa, health resort
balón *m* ball; **echar balones fuera** *fig* to evade the question
baloncesto *m* basketball
balonmano *m* handball
balonvolea *m* volleyball
balsa *f* **1.** (*charca*) pool; (*estanque*) pond **2.** (*plataforma*) raft
bálsamo *m* balm
baluarte *m* bastion
bambolearse *vr* to swing, to sway
bambú *m* bamboo
banalidad *f* banality
banalizar <z→c> *vt* to trivialize
banana *f AmL* banana
banano *m AmL* banana tree
banca *f* **1.** *AmL* (*asiento*) bench **2.** FIN banking; ~ **electrónica** electronic banking **3.** (*en juegos*) bank
bancario, -a *adj* bank(ing); **cuenta bancaria** bank account
bancarrota *f* bankruptcy
banco *m* **1.** (*asiento*) bench **2.** FIN bank; ~ **en casa** home banking; **Banco Mundial** World Bank; ~ **de datos** INFOR databank; ~ **de sangre** bloodbank **3.** TÉC bench, work table **4.** (*de peces*) shoal
banda *f* **1.** (*cinta*) band; ~ **sonora** CINE soundtrack **2.** (*pandilla*) gang; ~ **terrorista** terrorist group **3.** (*de música*) band **4.** (*insignia*) sash
bandada *f* (*de pájaros*) flock; (*de peces*) shoal
bandazo *m* **dar** ~**s** to roll from side to side
bandeja *f* tray; ~ **de entrada** in-tray; **servir en** ~ to hand on a plate
bandera *f* flag; **estar hasta la** ~ *fig* to be packed full
banderilla *f* **1.** TAUR banderilla (*short decorated lance*) **2.** (*tapa*) cocktail

snack on a stick
banderín *m* small flag
banderola *f* MIL pennant
bandido, -a *m, f* bandit
bando *m* edict
bandolera *f* bandoleer
bandolero, -a *m, f* bandit
banquero, -a *m, f* banker
banqueta *f* **1.** (*taburete*) stool; (*para los pies*) footstool **2.** *AmC* (*acera*) pavement *Brit*, sidewalk *Am*
banquete *m* banquet
banquillo *m* **1.** (*banco*) bench; (*para pies*) footstool **2.** JUR dock
bañador *m* (*de mujer*) swimming costume *Brit*, swimsuit *Am*; (*de hombre*) swimming trunks
bañar **I.** *vt* **1.** (*lavar*) to bath *Brit*, to bathe *Am* **2.** (*en el mar*) to bathe **3.** (*recubrir*) to coat **II.** *vr*: ~**se** **1.** (*lavarse*) to have a bath *Brit*, to bathe *Am* **2.** (*en el mar*) to bathe, to have a swim
bañera *f* bath, bathtub *Am*
bañero, -a *m, f* (swimming) pool attendant
bañista *mf* bather
baño *m* **1.** (*acto*) bathing; ~ **de sangre** bloodbath; ~**s termales** hot springs **2.** (*cuarto*) bathroom; **ir al** ~ to go to the toilet **3.** (*de pintura*) coat
baptista *mf* REL Baptist
baqueta *m* drumstick
bar *m* (*café*) café; (*tasca*) bar
barahúnda *f* uproar
baraja *f* pack [*o* deck *Am*] of cards
barajar *vt* **1.** (*naipes*) to shuffle **2.** (*posibilidades*) to consider **3.** *CSur* (*detener*) to catch
baranda *f,* **barandilla** *f* handrail
baratijas *fpl* cheap goods *pl; pey* junk
baratillo *m* **1.** (*tienda*) junk shop **2.** (*artículos*) junk
barato *adv* cheap(ly)
barato, -a *adj* cheap
barba *f* **1.** (*mentón*) chin **2.** (*pelos*) beard; **por** ~ per head
barbacoa *f* barbecue
barbaridad *f* **1.** (*crueldad*) barbarity; **¡qué** ~! how terrible! **2.** (*disparate*) nonsense

barbarie f savagery
bárbaro, -a I. adj 1. (cruel) savage 2. inf (estupendo) tremendous II. m, f 1. (grosero) brute 2. HIST barbarian
barbecho m fallow (land)
barbería f barber's (shop)
barbero m barber
barbilla f chin
barbitúrico m barbiturate
barbo m barbel
barbudo, -a adj bearded
barca f 1. (embarcación) (small) boat 2. pl (columpio) swing boat
barcaza f barge
Barcelona f Barcelona
barcelonés, -esa adj of/from Barcelona
barco m ship; ~ **de pasajeros** passenger ship; ~ **de vapor** steamer
baremo m table; (de tarifas) price list
barítono m MÚS baritone
barman m <bármanes> barman
barniz m polish; (para madera) varnish
barnizar <z→c> vt to put a gloss on; (madera) to varnish
barómetro m barometer
barón, -onesa m, f baron m, baroness f
barquero, -a m, f boatman m, boatwoman f
barquillo m wafer
barra f 1. (pieza larga) bar; (de cortina) rail; ~ **de labios** lipstick 2. INFOR ~ **de comandos** taskbar; ~ **espaciadora** space bar; ~ **de desplazamiento** scroll bar 3. (de pan) loaf; (de chocolate) bar 4. (en un bar) bar 5. AmL (pandilla) gang
barraca f 1. (choza) hut 2. AmL MIL barracks 3. AmL (almacén) storage shed
barranco m cliff
barrena f drill
barrenar vt to drill
barrendero, -a m, f sweeper
barrer vt to sweep; (un obstáculo) to sweep aside; ~ **para** [o **hacia**] **dentro** fig to look after number one
barrera f 1. (barra) barrier 2. (valla) fence 3. DEP wall 4. TAUR barrier

barriada f 1. (barrio) district 2. AmL (barrio pobre) shanty town
barricada f barricade
barriga f 1. (vientre) belly 2. (de una pared) bulge
barrigón, -ona adj pottbellied
barril m barrel; **cerveza de** ~ draught beer
barrio m district, neighbourhood Brit, neighborhood Am; ~ **chino** red-light district; ~ **comercial** business quarter
barro m 1. (lodo) mud 2. (arcilla) clay; **de** ~ earthenware
barroco m sin pl baroque
barrote m (heavy) bar; **entre** ~**s** fig behind bars
barruntar(se) vt, vr to conjecture
bartola f inf **tumbarse a la** ~ to be idle
bártulos mpl belongings pl
barullo m inf 1. (ruido) din 2. (desorden) confusion
basalto m basalt
basar I. vt 1. (asentar) to base 2. (fundar) to ground II. vr ~**se en algo** to be based on sth
basca f 1. (espasmo) nausea; **tener** ~**s** to feel sick 2. inf (gentío) gang
báscula f scales pl
base f 1. (lo fundamental) basis; ~ **de datos** INFOR database; **a** ~ **de algo** on the basis of sth; **a** ~ **de bien** inf really well 2. ARQUIT, MIL, DEP base 3. POL rank and file
básico, -a adj (t. quím) basic
Basilea f Basle, Basel
basílica f basilica
basket m sin pl basketball
bastante I. adj enough; **tengo** ~ **frío** I'm quite cold II. adv (suficientemente) sufficiently; (considerablemente) rather; **con esto tengo** ~ this is enough for me
bastar I. vi to be enough; **¡basta!** that's enough! II. vr ~**se (uno) solo** to be self-sufficient
bastardilla f TIPO italics pl
bastardo, -a adj, m, f bastard
bastidor m TÉC frame(work); (de coche) chassis inv; (de ventana) frame

basto, -a *adj* **1.** (*grosero*) rude; (*vulgar*) coarse **2.** (*superficie*) rough

bastón *m* stick; (*de esquí*) ski pole

bastoncillo *m dim de* **bastón** ~ **de algodón** cotton bud *Brit,* Q-tip® *Am*

basura *f* rubbish *Brit,* garbage *Am*

basurero *m* **1.** (*vertedero*) rubbish dump *Brit,* garbage dump *Am* **2.** (*recipiente*) dustbin *Brit,* trashcan *Am*

bata *f* **1.** (*albornoz*) dressing gown **2.** (*guardapolvos*) overalls *pl Brit,* coverall *Am* **3.** (*de laboratorio*) lab coat

batalla *f* **1.** MIL battle **2.** (*lucha*) struggle

batallar *vi* to fight

batallón *m* MIL battalion

batata *f* sweet potato; ~ **de la pierna** *AmL* calf

bate *m* DEP bat

bateador(a) *m(f)* DEP batter

batería¹ *f* **1.** *t.* TÉC battery; ~ **de cocina** pots and pans **2.** MÚS (*en conjunto*) drums *pl*

batería² *mf,* **baterista** *mf* drummer

batida *f* **1.** (*de cazadores*) beat **2.** (*de policía*) raid **3.** *AmL* (*paliza*) thrashing

batido *m* milk shake

batidora *f* (*de mano*) whisk; (*eléctrica*) mixer, blender

batir **I.** *vt* **1.** (*golpear, récord*) to beat; ~ **palmas** to clap **2.** (*enemigo*) to defeat **3.** (*un terreno*) to comb **II.** *vr:* ~**se** **1.** (*combatir*) to fight **2.** (*en duelo*) to fight a duel

baturro, -a *m, f* Aragonese peasant

batuta *f* MÚS baton; **llevar la** ~ to be in charge

baúl *m* **1.** (*mueble*) trunk **2.** *AmL* (*portamaletas*) boot *Brit,* trunk *Am*

bautismo *m* baptism; ~ **de sangre** first combat

bautizar <z→c> *vt* REL to baptize; (*nombrar*) to christen

bautizo *m* baptism; (*ceremonia*) christening

bayeta *f* washing-up cloth, dish cloth

bayoneta *f* bayonet

baza *f* (*naipes*) trick; **meter** ~ **en algo** *inf* to butt in on sth; **sacar** ~ **de algo** to profit from sth

bazar *m* bazaar

bazo *m* ANAT spleen

bazofia *f* **1.** (*comida*) pigswill **2.** (*cosa*) filthy thing

be *f* letter B

beatificar <c→qu> *vt* to beatify

beato, -a *adj* **1.** (*piadoso*) devout **2.** (*feliz*) blessed

bebé *m* baby

bebedero *m* drinking trough

bebedor(a) *m(f)* drinker

bebé-probeta *m* <bebés-probeta> test-tube baby

beber **I.** *vi, vt* to drink; (*a sorbos*) to sip; (*de un trago*) to gulp **II.** *vr:* ~**se** to drink up

bebida *f* drink, beverage *form*

bebido, -a *adj* (*borracho*) drunk

beca *f* (*de estudios*) grant; (*por méritos*) scholarship

becar <c→qu> *vt* to award a grant to

bedel(a) *m(f)* beadle, proctor

beduino, -a *adj* Bedouin

befarse *vr* to jeer

beicon *m sin pl* bacon

beige *adj* beige

béisbol *m sin pl* DEP baseball

beldad *f elev* beauty

Belén *m* Bethlehem

belga *adj, mf* Belgian

Bélgica *f* Belgium

Belgrado *m* Belgrade

Belice *m* Belize

bélico, -a *adj* warlike

belicoso, -a *adj* aggressive

beligerante *adj* belligerent

bellaco, -a **I.** *adj* cunning **II.** *m, f* rascal

bellaquería *f* dirty trick

belleza *f* beauty

bello, -a *adj* beautiful

bellota *f* acorn

bemol *m* MÚS flat; **tener** ~**es** *fig* to be difficult

bencina *f* benzine

bendecir *irr como* **decir** *vt* to bless; ~ **la mesa** to say grace

bendición *f* blessing

bendito, -a *adj* **1.** REL blessed; (*agua*) holy; ¡~ **sea!** *inf* thank God! **2.** (*dichoso*) lucky

benedictino, -a *m, f* REL Benedictine
beneficencia *f* charity
beneficiar I. *vt* 1. (*favorecer*) to benefit 2. *AmL* (*animal*) to slaughter II. *vr:* ~**se** 1. (*sacar provecho*) ~**se de algo** to benefit from sth 2. *pey* (*enriquecerse*) ~**se de algo** to take advantage of sth
beneficiario, -a *m, f* beneficiary; (*de un crédito*) assignee
beneficio *m* 1. (*bien*) good 2. (*provecho*) *t.* FIN profit; **a ~ de** for the benefit of 3. *AmL* (*matanza*) slaughter
beneficioso, -a *adj* 1. (*favorable*) beneficial 2. (*útil*) profitable
benéfico, -a *adj* charitable
benévolo, -a *adj* (*clemente*) indulgent
benigno, -a *adj* 1. (*persona*) kind 2. (*clima*) mild 3. MED benign
beodo, -a *adj* drunk
berberecho *m* cockle
berenjena *f* aubergine *Brit,* eggplant *Am*
Berlín *m* Berlin
berlinés, -esa I. *adj* Berlin II. *m, f* Berliner
bermejo, -a *adj* red
bermudas *mpl* Bermuda shorts *pl*
Berna *f* Berne
berrear *vi* 1. (*animal*) to bellow 2. (*llorar*) to howl 3. (*chillar*) to screech
berrido *m* 1. (*de animales*) bellow 2. (*lloro*) howl 3. (*chillido*) screech
berrinche *m inf* rage
berro *m* watercress
berza *f* cabbage
besar *vt* to kiss
beso *m* kiss
bestia[1] *mf* 1. (*bruto*) brute 2. (*ignorante*) ignoramus
bestia[2] *f* (wild) beast
bestial *adj* 1. (*salvaje*) bestial 2. *inf* (*muy intensivo*) tremendous; (*muy grande*) huge
bestialidad *f* 1. (*cualidad*) bestiality 2. *inf* (*gran cantidad*) huge amount
best seller *m inv,* **bestséller** *m inv* bestseller
besugo *m* bream; **ojos de ~** *inf* bulging eyes
besuquear *vt* to cover with kisses
betún *m* 1. QUÍM bitumen 2. (*para el calzado*) shoe polish
biberón *m* feeding bottle
Biblia *f* Bible
bibliografía *f* bibliography
biblioteca *f* 1. (*local*) library; **~ de consulta** reference library 2. (*mueble*) bookcase
bibliotecario, -a *m, f* librarian
bicarbonato *m* bicarbonate
bíceps *m inv* ANAT biceps *inv*
bicho *m* 1. (*animal*) (small) animal; (*insecto*) bug 2. TAUR bull 3. *inf* (*persona*) ~ **raro** weirdo; **mal** ~ rogue
bici *f inf abr de* **bicicleta** bike
bicicleta *f* bicycle; **~ de carreras** racing bike; **~ de montaña** mountain bike
bidé *m* <bidés>, **bidet** *m* <bidets> bidet
bidón *m* steel drum
Bielorrusia *f* Belorussia
bielorruso, -a *adj, m, f* Belorussian
bien I. *m* 1. (*bienestar*) well-being 2. (*bondad moral*) good 3. (*provecho*) benefit 4. *pl* ECON goods *pl;* **~es inmuebles** real estate II. *adv* 1. (*de modo conveniente*) properly; (*correctamente*) well; **¡~!** well done!; ~ **mirado** well thought of; **estar** (**a**) ~ **con alguien** to get on well with sb; **hacer algo** ~ to do sth well; **¡pórtate** ~! behave yourself!; **te está** ~ *inf* that serves you right; **ahora** ~ however 2. (*con gusto*) willingly 3. (*seguramente*) surely 4. (*muy*) very; (*bastante*) quite 5. (*asentimiento*) all right; **¡está** ~! OK! III. *conj* 1. (*aunque*) ~ **que** although; **si** ~ even though 2. (*o ... o*) ~ **...** ~ **...** either ... or ...

| ! | **bien** is an adverb and qualifies the verb: "Mi tío cocina muy bien." **bueno** is an adjective and qualifies a noun: "Él tiene siempre buenas ideas." |

bienal *adj* biennial

bienaventurado *adj* **1.** REL blessed **2.** (*feliz*) fortunate

bienestar *m* **1.** (*estado*) well-being **2.** (*riqueza*) prosperity; **estado del ~** welfare state

bienhechor(a) **I.** *adj* beneficent **II.** *m(f)* benefactor

bienvenida *f* welcome; **dar la ~ a alguien** to welcome sb

bienvenido, -a *interj* welcome; **¡~ a casa!** welcome home!; **¡~ a España!** welcome to Spain!

bies **cortar al ~** to cut on the bias

bife *m* *CSur* steak

bifocal *adj* bifocal

bifurcación *f* **1.** (*de un camino*) fork **2.** INFOR branch

bifurcarse <c→qu> *vr* to fork

bigamia *f* bigamy

bígamo, -a **I.** *adj* bigamous **II.** *m, f* bigamist

bigote *m* **1.** (*de hombre*) moustache, mustache *Am* **2.** *pl* (*de animal*) whiskers *pl*

bigotudo, -a *adj* with a big moustache

bikini *m* bikini

bilateral *adj* bilateral

bilingüe *adj* bilingual

billar *m* **1.** (*juego*) billiards; **~ americano** pool **2.** (*mesa*) billiard table

billete *m* **1.** (*pasaje*) ticket; **~ de ida y vuelta** return ticket *Brit*, roundtrip ticket *Am* **2.** FIN note *Brit*, bill *Am* **3.** (*de lotería*) ticket

billetera *f*, **billetero** *m* wallet *Brit*, billfold *Am*

billón *m* billion *Brit*, trillion *Am*

bimensual *adj* twice-monthly

bimotor *m* twin-engined plane

bingo *m* (*juego*) bingo; (*sala*) bingo hall

binóculo *m* pince-nez

bioactivo, -a *adj* bioactive

biobasura *f* biorefuse

biodegradable *adj* biodegradable

biodiversidad *f* biodiversity

bioenergía *f* bioenergy

biogenética *f* biogenetics

biografía *f* biography

biógrafo *m* *CSur* (*cine*) cinema

biógrafo, -a *m, f* (*persona*) bi-ographer

biología *f* biology

biólogo, -a *m, f* biologist

biombo *m* (folding) screen

biopsia *f* biopsy

biosfera *f* biosphere

biquini *m* bikini

birlar *vt inf* to pinch *Brit*, to swipe *Am*

Birmania *f* Burma

birome *m o f* *CSur* ballpoint pen, biro® *Brit*

birra *f inf* beer

birria *f* **1.** (*persona*) drip **2.** (*objeto*) rubbish, trash

bis **I.** *m* MÚS encore **II.** *adv* **1.** MÚS bis **2.** (*piso*) **7 ~** 7A

bisabuelo, -a *m, f* great-grandfather *m*, great-grandmother *f*

bisagra *f* hinge

bisbis(e)ar *vt inf* to mutter

bisexual *adj* bisexual

bisiesto *adj* **año ~** leap year

bisnieto, -a *m, f* great-grandson *m*, great-granddaughter *f*

bisonte *m* bison

bisté *m* <bistés>, **bistec** *m* <bis-tecs> steak

bisturí *m* scalpel

bisutería *f* costume jewellery [*o* jewelry *Am*]

bit *m* <bits> INFOR bit

bizco, -a *adj* cross-eyed

bizcocho *m* GASTR sponge cake

biznieto, -a *m, f v.* **bisnieto**

bizquear *vi* to squint

blanca *f* MÚS minim *Brit*, half note *Am*; **estar sin ~** to be broke

blanco *m* **1.** (*color*) white; **noche en ~** sleepless night **2.** (*diana*) target; **dar en el ~** *fig* to hit the mark

blanco, -a **I.** *adj* **1.** (*de tal color*) white **2.** (*tez*) pale **II.** *m, f* white man *m*, white woman *f*

blancura *f* whiteness

blandir **I.** *vt* to brandish **II.** *vi, vr:* **~se** to wave about

blando, -a *adj* **1.** (*objeto*) soft **2.** (*ca-rácter*) mild; **~ de corazón** soft-hearted **3.** (*constitución*) weak

blandura *f* **1.** (*de una cosa*) softness **2.** (*del carácter*) mildness

blanquear vt 1.(*pintar*) to whiten; (*pared*) to whitewash 2.(*dinero*) to launder 3.(*tejido*) to bleach

blanquecino, -a *adj* whitish

blanqueo *m* 1.(*de una pared*) whitewashing 2.(*de dinero*) laundering

blasfemar *vi* 1.REL to blaspheme 2.(*maldecir*) ~ **de algo** to swear about sth

blasfemia *f* 1.REL blasphemy 2.(*injuria*) insult 3.(*taco*) swearword

blasfemo, -a *m, f* blasphemer

blasón *m* 1.(*escudo*) coat of arms 2.(*honor*) honour *Brit,* honor *Am*

blasonar I.*vt* to emblazen II.*vi* ~ **de algo** to boast about sth

bledo *m* (**no**) **me importa un** ~ I couldn't care less

blindado *m* MIL armour-plated *Brit,* armor-plated *Am;* **puerta blindada** reinforced door

blindaje *m* armour (plating) *Brit,* armor (plating) *Am*

bloc *m* <blocs> 1.(*cuaderno*) notepad 2.(*calendario*) calendar pad

bloque *m* 1.INFOR block 2.POL bloc

bloquear I.*vt* 1.(*cortar el paso*) to block 2.(*aislar*) to cut off 3.TÉC to jam 4.MIL (*asediar*) to blockade 5.FIN to freeze II.*vr:* ~**se** 1.(*cosa*) to jam 2.(*persona*) to have a mental block

bloqueo *m* 1.(*de un paso*) blocking; ~ **comercial** COM trade embargo 2.(*aislamiento*) cutting off 3.TÉC (*de un mecanismo*) jamming 4.MIL blockade

blusa *f* blouse

boa *f* boa

bobada *f* silly thing; **decir** ~**s** to talk nonsense

bobina *f* 1.ELEC coil 2.(*de papel*) reel

bobo, -a I.*adj* 1.(*tonto*) silly 2.(*simple*) simple II. *m, f* fool

boca *f* 1.ANAT mouth; ~ **abajo** face down(ward); ~ **arriba** face up(ward); **con la** ~ **abierta** dumbfounded; **a pedir de** ~ perfectly 2.MÚS mouthpiece 3.INFOR slot

bocacalle *f* street entrance

bocadillo *m* sandwich

bocado *m* 1.(*mordisco*) mouthful 2.(*freno*) bit

bocajarro *adv* a ~ (*tirar*) point-blank

bocanada *f* 1.(*de humo*) puff 2.(*de comida, bebida*) mouthful

boceto *m* sketch

bocha *f* (*bola*) bowl; **las** ~**s** bowls, bowling *Am*

bochinche *m* uproar

bochorno *m* 1.METEO sultry weather 2.(*vergüenza*) shame; **me da** ~ **que...** +*subj* it embarrasses me that ...

bochornoso, -a *adj* 1.METEO sultry 2.(*vergonzoso*) shameful

bocina *f* 1.(*de auto*) horn; **tocar la** ~ to blow the horn 2.MÚS trumpet

boda *f* 1.(*ceremonia*) wedding 2.(*fiesta*) wedding reception

bodega *f* 1.(*de vino*) wine cellar 2.(*tienda*) wine shop; (*taberna*) bar 3.(*en un buque*) hold

bodegón *m* ARTE still life

BOE *m abr de* **Boletín Oficial del Estado** ≈ Hansard *Brit,* ≈ The Congressional Record *Am*

bofe *m* lung; **echar los** ~**s** *inf* to slog one's guts out

bofetada *f* cuff, smack *Am;* **dar una** ~ **a alguien** to slap sb

boga *f* **estar en** ~ to be in vogue

bogar <g→gu> *vi* 1.(*remar*) to row 2.(*navegar*) to sail

bogavante *m* lobster

Bohemia *f* Bohemia

bohemio, -a *adj, m, f* bohemian

boicot <boicots> *m* boycott

boicotear *vt* to boycott

boicoteo *m* boycott

boina *f* beret

bola *f* 1.(*pelota*) ball; ~ **de nieve** snowball; **en** ~**s** *inf* naked 2.(*canica*) marble 3.*inf* (*mentira*) fib

bolchevique *adj, mf* POL Bolshevik

boleadoras *fpl AmS* bolas *pl*

bolera *f* bowling alley

bolero *m* MÚS bolero

boleta *f* 1.(*entrada*) ticket 2.*AmL* (*documento*) permit 3.*AmL* (*para votar*) ballot (paper)

boletería *f AmL* TEAT box office

boletín *m* **1.**(*publicación*) bulletin **2.**(*informe*) report
boleto *m AmL* (*entrada, billete*) ticket
boli *m inf abr de* **bolígrafo** (ballpoint) pen, biro®
boliche *m* **1.**(*bola*) jack **2.**(*juego*) bowls; (*de bolos*) skittles **3.***AmL* (*establecimiento*) grocery shop
bólido *m* **1.**ASTR meteorite **2.**AUTO racing car
bolígrafo *m* (ballpoint) pen, biro®
bolívar *m* bolivar
Bolivia *f* Bolivia

> **?** **Bolivia** is the fifth largest country in South America. Although **Sucre** is the capital, the seat of government is in **La Paz**, the largest city in the country. In addition to Spanish, the official languages of Bolivia are **quechua** and **aimara** (also known as **aimará**). The monetary unit is the **boliviano**.

boliviano *m* (*moneda*) boliviano
boliviano, -a *adj, m, f* Bolivian
bollo *m* **1.**(*panecillo*) bun; (*pastelillo*) cake **2.**(*abolladura*) dent
bolo *m* **1.**DEP skittle **2.**(*píldora*) large pill
bolsa *f* **1.***t.* (*saco*) bag **2.**(*bolso*) handbag, purse *Am* **3.**(*pliegue*) crease **4.**FIN stock exchange **5.***AmL* (*bolsillo*) pocket
bolsillo *m* pocket; **de ~** pocket; **rascarse el ~** *inf* to fork out
bolsista *mf* FIN stockbroker
bolso *m* bag; (*de mujer*) handbag, purse *Am*
bomba I.*f* **1.***t.* MIL bomb; **a prueba de ~s** bomb-proof **2.**TÉC pump **3.***AmL* (*bola*) ball **4.***AmL, inf* (*borrachera*) **pegarse una ~** to get drunk II. *adj inf* astounding; **pasarlo ~** to have a great time
bombardear *vt* **1.**MIL to bomb **2.**FÍS to bombard
bombardeo *m* **1.**MIL bombing **2.**FÍS bombardment
bombardero *m* (*avión*) bomber
bombero *m* **1.**(*oficio*) fireman **2.***pl* (*cuerpo*) fire brigade; **coche de ~s** fire engine
bombilla *f* ELEC (light)bulb
bombín *m* bowler hat
bombo *m* **1.**MÚS bass drum **2.**(*en un sorteo*) drum
bombón *m* chocolate; **ser un ~** *inf* to be gorgeous
bombona *f* cylinder
bonachón, -ona *adj* **1.**(*buenazo*) kindly **2.**(*crédulo*) naive
bonaerense *adj* of/from Buenos Aires
bonanza *f* **1.**NÁUT calm conditions *pl* **2.**(*prosperidad*) prosperity
bondad *f* **1.**(*de bueno*) goodness **2.**(*amabilidad*) kindness
bondadoso, -a *adj* good-natured
bonito I. *m* ZOOL bonito II. *adv AmL* nicely
bonito, -a *adj* pretty
bono *m* **1.**(*vale*) voucher **2.**COM bond
bonoloto *f* state-run lottery
boquear I. *vi* to gape II. *vt* to utter
boquerón *m* (fresh) anchovy
boquiabierto, -a *adj* astonished
boquilla *f* **1.**MÚS mouthpiece **2.**(*de cigarrillos*) cigarette holder **3.**TÉC nozzle
borbotón *m* **salir a borbotones** to gush out
borda *f* NÁUT gunwale; **echar algo por la ~** *t. fig* to throw sth overboard
bordado *m* embroidery
bordar *vt* to embroider
borde I. *adj inf* (*persona*) difficult, stroppy II. *m* **1.**(*de camino*) verge; (*de mesa*) edge **2.**(*de río*) bank
bordear I. *vt* **1.**(*ir por el borde*) to skirt **2.**(*estar en el borde*) to border on II. *vi* NÁUT to tack
bordillo *m* kerb *Brit,* curb *Am*
bordo *m* NÁUT board; **ir a ~** to go on board
borla *f* tassel
borrachera *f* drunkenness; **agarrar una ~** to get drunk
borracho, -a *adj, m, f* drunk

borrador *m* **1.**(*escrito*) rough draft **2.**(*cuaderno*) scribbling pad **3.**(*trapo*) duster

borrar I. *vt* **1.**(*con goma*) to rub out, to erase; (*con esponja*) to wipe off **2.**INFOR to delete **3.**(*huellas*) to remove **II.** *vr:* ~**se 1.**(*difuminarse*) to blur **2.**(*retirarse*) ~**se de algo** to resign from sth

borrasca *f* (*temporal*) squall; (*tempestad*) storm

borrico, -a *m, f* donkey

borrón *m* (*mancha*) stain; **hacer ~ y cuenta nueva** to wipe the slate clean

borroso, -a *adj* **1.**(*escritura*) unclear **2.**(*foto*) blurred

Bósforo *m* Bosphorus

Bosnia Herzegovina *f* Bosnia and Herzegovina

bosnio, -a *adj, m, f* Bosnian

bosque *m* wood

bosquejar *vt* to sketch

bostezar <z→c> *vi* to yawn

bostezo *m* yawn

bota *f* **1.**(*calzado*) boot **2.**(*cuba*) large barrel

botánica *f sin pl* botany

botánico, -a I. *adj* botanical **II.** *m, f* botanist

botar I. *vi* **1.**(*pelota*) to bounce **2.**(*persona*) to jump **II.** *vt* **1.**(*lanzar*) to throw; (*la pelota*) to bounce **2.**NÁUT (*barco*) to launch **3.**AmL (*expulsar*) to fire; (*del colegio*) to expell

bote *m* **1.**(*golpe*) blow; **a ~ pronto** (*adj*) sudden; (*adv*) suddenly **2.**(*salto*) jump; **pegar un ~** to jump **3.**(*de pelota*) bounce **4.**(*vasija*) jar **5.**(*en la lotería*) jackpot **6.**NÁUT boat

botella *f* bottle; **~ de cerveza** bottle of beer; **cerveza de ~** bottled beer

botica *f* pharmacy, chemist's *Brit,* drugstore *Am*

boticario, -a *m, f* chemist *Brit,* druggist *Am*

botijo *m* **1.**(*vasija*) earthenware drinking jug **2.**(*tren*) excursion train

botín *m* high shoe

botiquín *m* **1.**(*en casa*) medicine chest **2.**(*de emergencia*) first-aid kit

botón *m* **1.**(*en vestidos*) button **2.**ELEC knob; **~ de opciones** INFOR option button **3.**(*en instrumento*) key

botones *m inv* bellboy

boxeador(a) *m(f)* boxer

boxear *vi* to box

boxeo *m* boxing

boya *f* buoy

boyante *adj* **1.**(*flotante*) buoyant; (*barco*) high in the water **2.**(*próspero*) prosperous

bozal *m* muzzle

bracear *vi* **1.**(*mover los brazos*) to swing one's arms **2.**(*nadar*) to swim

bracero *m* labourer *Brit,* laborer *Am*

braga *f* **1.**(*de bebé*) nappy *Brit,* diaper *Am* **2.***pl* (*de mujer*) panties *pl*

bragapañal *m* disposable nappy *Brit,* disposable diaper *Am*

bragueta *f* flies *pl Brit,* fly *Am*

braille *m* Braille

bramar *vi* to roar; (*ciervo*) to bellow

bramido *m* (*animales*) roar; (*ciervos*) bellow

brasa *f* ember; **a la ~** grilled

brasero *m* brazier

Brasil *m* (**el**) **~** Brazil

brasileño, -a *adj, m, f* Brazilian

bravata *f* threat

bravío, -a *adj* **1.**(*animal*) wild **2.**(*persona*) impetuous

bravo, -a *adj* **1.**(*valiente*) brave **2.**(*bueno*) excellent **3.**(*salvaje: animal*) wild; (*mar*) stormy

bravura *f* **1.**(*de los animales*) ferocity **2.**(*de las personas*) bravery

braza *f* **1.**NÁUT fathom **2.**DEP breast stroke

brazada *f* stroke

brazalete *m* **1.**(*pulsera*) bracelet **2.**(*banda*) armband

brazo *m* **1.**ANAT arm; **ir cogidos del ~** to walk arm-in-arm **2.**ZOOL foreleg **3.**BIO limb

brea *f* tar

brecha *f* **1.**MIL breach **2.**(*agujero*) gap

brega *f* struggle

Bretaña *f* Brittany; **Gran ~** Great Britain

bretón, **-ona** *adj, m, f* Breton
breva *f* **1.** (*higo*) early fig **2.** (*cigarro*) flat cigar; **¡no caerá esa ~!** no such luck!
breve **I.** *adj* **1.** (*de duración*) brief **2.** (*de extensión*) short **II.** *m* PREN short news item
brevedad *f* shortness
brezo *m* heather
bribón, **-ona** **I.** *adj* idle **II.** *m*, *f* rogue, rascal
bricolaje *m* do-it-yourself
brida *f* **1.** (*de caballo*) bridle **2.** TÉC clamp
bridge *m* bridge
brigada¹ *f* **1.** (*de obreros*) gang **2.** (*de policía*) squad
brigada² *m* MIL sergeant-major
brillante **I.** *m* diamond **II.** *adj* (*luz*) bright; (*joya*) sparkling, brilliant
brillar *vi* to shine
brillo *m* **1.** (*cualidad*) shine; (*reflejo*) glow; **dar ~ a algo** to polish sth **2.** (*gloria*) splendour *Brit,* splendor *Am*
brincar <c→qu> *vi* to hop; (*hacia arriba*) to jump
brinco *m* hop
brindar **I.** *vi* to drink a toast **II.** *vt* (*ofrecer*) to offer
brindis *m inv* toast
brioso, **-a** *adj* spirited
brisa *f* breeze
británico, **-a** **I.** *adj* British **II.** *m*, *f* Briton *Brit,* Britisher *Am*
brizna *f* **1.** (*hebra*) strand **2.** BOT blade **3.** (*porción diminuta*) scrap
broca *f* TÉC bit
brocal *m* rim
brocha *f* brush; **~ de afeitar** shaving brush
broche *m* clasp; (*de adorno*) brooch
broma *f* joke; **decir algo en ~** to be kidding; **no estoy para ~s** I'm in no mood for jokes
bromear *vi* to joke, to kid *Am*
bromista **I.** *adj* fond of jokes **II.** *mf* joker
bronca *f* **1.** (*riña*) row **2.** (*reprimenda*) ticking-off *Brit*
bronce *m* bronze
bronceado, **-a** *adj* **1.** (*objeto*) bronze

2. (*piel*) tanned
bronceador *m* suntan lotion
broncear **I.** *vt* to tan **II.** *vr:* **~se** to get a (sun)tan
bronco, **-a** *adj* **1.** (*voz*) gruff **2.** (*genio*) surly
bronquedad *f* **1.** (*de la voz*) gruffness **2.** (*del genio*) surliness
bronquio *m* ANAT bronchial tube
bronquitis *f inv* MED bronchitis
brotar *vi* **1.** BOT to sprout **2.** (*agua*) to flow **3.** (*enfermedad*) to break out
brote *m* **1.** BOT shoot; **~s de soja** bean sprouts **2.** (*erupción*) outbreak
bruces *adv* **caer de ~** to fall headlong
bruja *f* witch
Brujas *f* Bruges
brujería *f* witchcraft
brujo *m* **1.** (*hechicero*) wizard **2.** *AmL* (*curandero*) medicine man
brújula *f* compass
bruma *f* mist
brumoso, **-a** *adj* misty
bruñir <3. pret: bruñó> *vt* to polish
brusco, **-a** *adj* **1.** (*repentino*) sudden **2.** (*person*) abrupt
Bruselas *f* Brussels
brutal *adj* brutal
brutalidad *f* brutality
bruto *adj* **1.** (*diamante*) rough **2.** (*peso*) gross
bruto, **-a** **I.** *adj* brutal **II.** *m*, *f* brute
bucal *adj* (of the) mouth
bucear *vi* **1.** (*nadar*) to dive **2.** (*investigar*) **~ en algo** to delve into sth
buceo *m* diving
bucle *m* **1.** (*cabello*) curl **2.** INFOR loop
budismo *m sin pl* Buddhism
budista *adj, mf* Buddhist
buen *adj v.* **bueno**
buenamente *adv* **1.** (*fácilmente*) easily **2.** (*voluntariamente*) voluntarily
buenaventura *f* **echar la ~ a alguien** to tell sb's fortune
bueno, **-a** *adj* <mejor *o* más bueno, el mejor *o* bonísimo *o* buenísimo> *delante de un substantivo masculino:* **buen** **1.** (*calidad*) good; (*tiempo*) fine; (*constitución*) sound; **~s días** good morning; **hace ~** it's nice weather; **estar de buenas** to

be in a good mood **2.** (*apropiado*) suitable **3.** (*fácil*) easy **4.** (*honesto*) honest **5.** *inf* (*atractivo*) attractive

> ⚠ **bueno** is not used before a masculine noun; **buen** is used instead: "Hoy hace buen tiempo."

Buenos Aires *m* Buenos Aires
buey *m* ox
búfalo *m* buffalo
bufanda *f* scarf
bufar *vi* to snort
bufete *m* lawyer's office
bufido *m* **1.** (*resoplido*) snort **2.** (*exabrupto*) sharp remark **3.** (*gato*) hiss
bufón, -ona *m, f* TEAT buffoon
buhardilla *f* **1.** (*desván*) loft **2.** (*vivienda*) garret
búho *m* owl
buhonero *m* pedlar *Brit*, peddler *Am*
buitre *m* vulture
buje *m* hub
bujía *f* **1.** (*vela*) candle **2.** AUTO sparking plug *Brit*, spark plug *Am* **3.** ELEC candlepower
bula *f* (papal) bull
bulbo *m* bulb
bulevar *m* boulevard
Bulgaria *f* Bulgaria
búlgaro, -a *adj, m, f* Bulgarian
bulimia *f sin pl* MED bulimia
bulla *f* **1.** (*ruido*) racket **2.** (*aglomeración*) mob
bullicio *m* **1.** (*ruido*) uproar **2.** (*tumulto*) commotion
bullicioso, -a *adj* noisy
bullir <3. pret: bulló> *vi* **1.** (*hervir*) to boil; (*borbotar*) to bubble **2.** (*agitarse*) to move
bulto *m* **1.** (*fardo*) bundle; **escurrir el ~** *inf* to pass the buck **2.** (*paquete*) piece of luggage
buñuelo *m* doughnut *Brit*, donut *Am*
BUP *m abr de* **Bachillerato Unificado Polivalente** (*secondary studies for pupils aged 14–17, now supplanted by the ESO*)
buque *m* ship; **~ de carga** freighter;

~ de vapor steamer
burbuja *f* bubble
burbujear *vi* to bubble
burdel *m* brothel
Burdeos *m* Bordeaux
burdo, -a *adj* (*tosco*) coarse; (*excusa*) clumsy
burgalés, -esa *adj* of/from Burgos
burgués, -esa **I.** *adj t. pey* middle-class **II.** *m, f t. pey* bourgeois *m*, bourgeoise *f*
burguesía *f* bourgeoisie
Burkina Faso *f* Burkina-Faso
burla *f* joke; **hacer ~ de alguien** to make fun of sb
burlador(a) *m(f)* **1.** (*mofador*) mocker **2.** (*bromista*) joker
burlar **I.** *vt* **1.** (*mofarse*) to mock **2.** (*engañar*) to cheat **3.** (*eludir*) to evade **II.** *vr:* **~se** to joke
burlesco, -a *adj* burlesque
burlón, -ona *adj* mocking
burocracia *f* bureaucracy
burócrata *mf* bureaucrat
burocrático, -a *adj* bureaucratic
burrada *f* silly thing; **decir ~s** to talk nonsense
burro, -a **I.** *adj* stupid **II.** *m, f* **1.** ZOOL donkey **2.** (*persona*) idiot
bursátil *adj* stock exchange
bus *m t.* INFOR bus
busca¹ *f* search
busca² *m* bleeper *Brit*, beeper *Am*
buscador *m* INFOR searcher
buscar <c→qu> *vi, vt* to look for; **me viene a buscar a las 7** he/she is picking me up at 7; **él se lo ha buscado** he brought it on himself
buscona *f* whore
búsqueda *f t.* INFOR search
busto *m* bust
butaca *f* **1.** (*silla*) armchair **2.** (*de cine*) stall *Brit*, seat *Am*
butano *m* butane (gas)
buzo *m* **1.** (*buceador*) diver **2.** (*mono*) overalls *pl Brit*, coverall *Am*
buzón *m* (*de correos*) letterbox *Brit*, mailbox *Am*; **~ (electrónico)** INFOR mailbox
byte *m* INFOR byte

Cc

C, c *f* C, c; ~ **de Carmen** C for Charlie

C/ *abr de* **calle** St

cabal I. *adj* honest II. *m* **no estar en sus ~es** not to be in one's right mind

cábala *f* 1. REL cabbala 2. *pl* (*suposición*) supposition

cabalgadura *f* mount

cabalgar <g→gu> *vi, vt* to ride

cabalgata *f* procession

caballa *f* mackerel

caballeresco, -a *adj* chivalrous

caballería *f* 1. (*montura*) mount 2. MIL cavalry

caballeriza *f* stable

caballerizo *m* groom

caballero *m* 1. (*señor, galán*) gentleman 2. HIST knight

caballerosidad *f* gentlemanliness

caballete *m* 1. (*de mesa*) trestle 2. (*de cuadro*) easel

caballito *m* 1. ZOOL ~ **de mar** sea horse 2. *pl* (*en una feria*) merry-go-round, carousel *Am*

caballo *m* 1. (*animal*) horse 2. (*ajedrez*) knight 3. DEP ~ jumper 4. AUTO horsepower 5. (*naipes*) queen

cabaña *f* cabin

cabaré *m*, **cabaret** *m* <cabarets> cabaret

cabecear I. *vi* to nod off II. *vt* DEP to head

cabecera *f* 1. (*de cama*) head; **médico de** ~ general practioner 2. (*del periódico*) masthead

cabecilla *mf* ringleader

cabellera *f* 1. (*de la cabeza*) hair 2. (*de cometa*) tail

cabello *m* hair

cabelludo, -a *adj* hairy

caber *irr vi* 1. (*tener espacio*) to fit 2. (*ser posible*) to be possible

cabestrillo *m* MED sling

cabeza¹ *f* 1. *t.* ANAT, TÉC head; ~ **de lectura** INFOR read head; ~ **abajo** upside down; **levantar** ~ to pull through; **tener** ~ *fig* to be clever;

traer de ~ to drive crazy; **de** ~ headfirst; **por** ~ a head 2. (*extremo*) top; **ir en** ~ DEP to be in the lead 3. AGR (*res*) head

cabeza² *m* head; ~ **rapada** skinhead

cabezada *f* blow

cabezazo *m* 1. (*golpe*) blow 2. DEP header

cabezón, -ona *adj* 1. (*de cabeza grande*) with a big head 2. *inf* (*obstinado*) pigheaded

cabezota *mf inf* pigheaded person

cabida *f* space

cabina *f* cabin; (*en la playa*) cubicle; ~ **de teléfonos** telephone box *Brit*, phone booth *Am*

cabizbajo, -a *adj* with head bowed; (*triste*) dejected

cable *m t.* ELEC cable; **echar un** ~ *inf* to help out

cabo *m* 1. (*extremo*) end; **al fin y al** ~ in the end; **llevar a** ~ to carry out; **al** ~ **de** after 2. GEO cape; **Ciudad del Cabo** Cape Town 3. MIL corporal 4. NÁUT rope

cabra *f* goat; **estar como una** ~ *inf* to be off one's head

cabrear I. *vt inf* to infuriate II. *vr:* ~**se** *inf* to get angry

cabrío, -a *adj* goatish

cabriola *f* caper

cabritillo, -a *m, f* kid

cabrón, -ona *m, f vulg* bastard

cabronada *f vulg* dirty trick

caca *f inf* 1. (*excremento*) pooh *Brit*, poop *Am* 2. (*chapuza*) rubbish

cacahuete *m* peanut

cacao *m* cacao

cacarear *vi* 1. (*gallinas*) to cackle 2. *inf* (*presumir*) to brag

cacería *f* (*partida*) hunting

cacerola *f* saucepan

cachalote *m* sperm whale

cacharro *m* 1. (*recipiente*) pot 2. *pey, inf* (*aparato*) gadget 3. *pey, inf* (*trasto*) piece of junk

cachear *vt* to frisk

cachemir *m* cashmere

cacheo *m* searching, frisking

cachete *m* 1. (*golpe*) slap 2. (*carrillo*) cheek

cachimba *f AmL* pipe

cachiporra *f* truncheon

cachivache *m* junk; **tienes la coci-na llena de ~s** your kitchen is full of junk

cachondeo *m* 1. *inf* (*broma*) joke; (*juerga*) good time 2. *vulg* (*burla*) farce

cachondo, -a *adj* 1. *vulg* (*sexual*) sexy, horny 2. *inf* (*gracioso*) funny

cachorro, -a *m, f* (*de tigre*) cub; (*de perro*) pup(py)

cacique *m* 1. (*jefe indio*) chief 2. (*ti-rano*) tyrant

caco *m inf* burglar

cacto *m* cactus

cada *adj* each; ~ **uno/una** each one; ~ **hora** hourly; ~ **día** daily; ¿~ **cuán-to?** how often?

cadalso *m* scaffold

cadáver *m* corpse

cadena *f* 1. *t. fig* (*objeto*) chain; ~ **perpetua** JUR life imprisonment; **tra-bajo en** ~ assembly-line work 2. GEO mountain chain 3. TV network

cadencia *f* cadence

cadera *f* hip

cadete *m* MIL cadet

caducar <c→qu> *vi* to expire

caducidad *f* 1. (*de un documento*) expiry 2. (*de productos*) sell-by date

caduco, -a *adj* 1. perishable 2. (*ár-bol*) deciduous

caer *irr* I. *vi* 1. (*objeto, persona*) to fall (down); (*precio*) to fall; ~ **bien/mal** *fig* to like/not to like 2. (*presi-dente*) to fall from power 3. (*vesti-dos*) to suit 4. *inf* (*encontrarse*) to be (located) II. *vr:* ~**se** (*desplomar-se*) to collapse; (*un avión*) to crash; (*pelo, dientes*) to fall out

café *m* 1. (*bebida*) coffee; ~ **con leche** white coffee; ~ **solo** black cof-fee 2. (*local*) café 3. (*planta*) coffee tree

cafeína *f* caffeine

cafetal *m* coffee plantation

cafetera *f* coffee pot

cafetería *f* café

cagalera *f inf* **tener** ~ to have the runs

cagar <g→gu> I. *vi vulg* to have a shit II. *vt vulg* to mess up III. *vr:* ~**se**

vulg to shit oneself

caída *f* 1. (*bajada brusca*) fall; (*de aviones*) crash; (*del cabello*) loss; ~ **del sistema** INFOR system crash 2. (*de agua*) waterfall 3. FIN fall in prices

caído, -a I. *adj* drooping II. *m, f* **los ~s** the fallen

caigo *1. pres de* **caer**

caimán *m* caiman

Cairo *m* **El** ~ Cairo

caja *f* 1. (*recipiente*) box; ~ **fuerte** safe; ~ **de herramientas** *t.* INFOR tool box 2. (*carcasa*) case 3. FIN fund

cajero, -a *m, f* cashier; ~ **automáti-co** cash dispenser

cajetilla *f* packet of cigarettes *Brit,* pack of cigarettes *Am*

cajón *m* 1. (*caja*) big box; (*de em-balaje*) crate 2. (*de mueble*) drawer

cal *f* lime; **a** ~ **y canto** firmly

cala *f* 1. (*bahía*) cove 2. NÁUT hold

calabacín *m* courgette *Brit,* zucchini *Am*

calabaza *f* 1. BOT pumpkin 2. *pey* (*persona*) dummy

calabozo *m* 1. (*mazmorra*) dungeon 2. (*celda*) (prison) cell

calado *m* 1. (*bordado*) open work 2. NÁUT draught

calamar *m* squid

calambre *m* 1. (*eléctrico*) electric shock 2. (*muscular*) cramp

calamidad *f* (*catástrofe*) calamity; (*desastre*) disaster

calaña *f* **ser de mala** ~ to be bad

calar I. *vi* 1. (*líquido*) to soak in 2. (*material*) to be permeable II. *vt* 1. (*líquido*) to soak 2. (*con un obje-to*) to pierce III. *vr:* ~**se** 1. (*mojarse*) to get soaked 2. (*motor*) to stall 3. (*gorra*) to pull down

calavera *f* skull

calcañar *m* ANAT heel

calcar <c→qu> *vt* 1. (*dibujar*) to trace 2. (*imitar*) to copy

calceta *f* knitting

calcetín *m* sock

calcinar *vt* to burn

calcio *m* calcium

calco *m* tracing

calcomanía *f* transfer

calculadora *f* calculator
calcular *vt* to calculate
cálculo *m* **1.** *t.* ECON calculation **2.** MED stone
caldear *vt* **1.** (*calentar*) to heat (up) **2.** (*acalorar*) to inflame
caldera *f* TÉC boiler
calderilla *f* small change
caldero *m* cauldron *Brit,* caldron *Am*
caldo *m* **1.** GASTR broth **2.** (*vino*) wine
caldoso, -a *adj* soggy
calefacción *f* heating
caleidoscopio *m* kaleidoscope
calendario *m* calendar
calentador *m* heater; (*para la cama*) bed-warmer
calentamiento *m* DEP warm-up
calentar <e→ie> **I.** *vi* (*dar calor*) to be warm **II.** *vt* **1.** (*caldear*) to heat (up); (*con calefacción*) to warm (up) **2.** (*enfadar*) to anger **3.** *vulg* (*sexualmente*) to turn on **III.** *vr:* ~**se 1.** (*caldearse*) to heat up **2.** (*enfadarse*) to get angry **3.** DEP to warm up
calentura *f* **1.** (*fiebre*) fever **2.** (*en los labios*) cold sore
calenturiento, -a *adj* feverish
calibre *m* **1.** (*diámetro*) calibre *Brit,* caliber *Am* **2.** (*instrumento*) gauge, gage *Am*
calidad *f* **1.** (*clase*) quality; **en** ~ **de** as **2.** (*prestigio*) importance
cálido, -a *adj* (*país*) hot; *fig* warm
caliente *adj* **1.** (*cálido*) warm **2.** (*acalorado*) heated **3.** (*sexualmente*) randy
califa *m* caliph
calificación *f* **1.** (*cualificación*) qualification **2.** (*nota*) mark, grade
calificar <c→qu> *vt* **1.** (*definir*) ~ **de algo** to describe as sth **2.** (*evaluar*) to assess **3.** ENS to mark
caligrafía *f* calligraphy
calina *f* mist
cáliz *m* **1.** REL chalice **2.** BOT calyx
caliza *f* limestone
callado, -a *adj* (*sin hablar*) silent; (*silencioso*) quiet
callar I. *vi, vr:* ~**se** to keep quiet; **¡cállate!** shut up! **II.** *vt* to keep (quiet)
calle *f* street; DEP lane; ~ **peatonal** pedestrian street; **hacer la** ~ *inf* to

streetwalk; **quedarse en la** ~ *inf* to be out of a job
callejear *vi* to stroll around
callejero *m* street directory
callejón *m* alley; ~ **sin salida** cul-de--sac
callista *mf* chiropodist
callo *m* **1.** (*callosidad*) callus; (*en el pie*) corn **2.** *pl* GASTR tripe
calma *f* **1.** (*tranquilidad*) calm; ~ **chicha** NÁUT dead calm **2.** (*serenidad*) calmness
calmante I. *adj* sedative **II.** *m* tranquillizer *Brit,* tranquilizer *Am*
calmar I. *vi* (*viento*) to abate **II.** *vt* **1.** (*tranquilizar*) to calm (down) **2.** (*dolor*) to relieve **III.** *vr:* ~**se 1.** (*tranquilizarse*) to calm down **2.** (*dolor*) to ease off
calmoso, -a *adj* calm
calor *m* **1.** (*de un cuerpo*) warmth **2.** (*clima*) heat
caloría *f* calorie
calorífero, -a *adj* heat-producing, heat-emitting
calumnia *f* slander
caluroso, -a *adj* **1.** (*clima*) hot **2.** *fig* warm
calva *f* bald patch
calvario *m* REL Stations *pl* of the Cross
calvicie *f* baldness
calvo, -a I. *adj* **1.** (*sin pelo*) bald **2.** (*sin vegetación*) bare **II.** *m, f* bald person
calzada *f* (paved) road
calzado *m* footwear
calzador *m* shoehorn
calzar <z→c> **I.** *vt* **1.** (*poner*) to put on **2.** (*llevar puesto*) to wear **3.** (*una cuña*) to wedge **II.** *vr:* ~**se** to put one's shoes on
calzón *m* AmL trousers *pl*
calzoncillo(s) *m(pl)* men's underpants *pl*
cama *f* **1.** (*mueble*) bed; **caer en** ~ to fall ill **2.** (*de animales*) lair
camada *f* **1.** (*de animales*) litter **2.** *pey* (*cuadrilla*) gang
camafeo *m* cameo
camaleón *m t. fig* chameleon
cámara¹ *f* **1.** FOTO camera; ~ **web**

web camera **2.** POL (*consejo*) house
3. (*receptáculo*) chamber
cámara² *mf* CINE cameraman *m*,
camerawoman *f*
camarada *mf* **1.** POL comrade
2. (*amigo*) companion
camarero, -a *m*, *f* **1.** (*en restaurantes*) waiter *m*, waitress *f*; ¡~!
waiter! **2.** (*en la barra*) barman *m*,
barmaid *f*
camarilla *f t. pey* clique
camarín *m* dressing room
camarón *m* prawn, shrimp
camarote *m* NÁUT cabin, berth
cambiable *adj* **1.** COM exchangeable
2. (*variable*) changeable
cambiante *adj* changeable
cambiar **I.** *vi* (*transformarse*) to
change; ~ **de casa** to move (house)
II. *vt* to (ex)change; (*dinero*) to
change; ~ **algo de lugar** to move sth
III. *vr* **1.** (*transformarse*) to change
2. (*de casa*) to move
cambiazo *m* big change; **dar el ~ a
alguien** *inf* to pull a fast one on sb
cambio *m* **1.** (*transformación*)
change; **en ~** however **2.** (*intercambio*) exchange; **a ~ de algo** in exchange for sth **3.** FIN exchange rate; ~
de divisa foreign exchange **4.** (*suelto*) change **5.** TÉC gear change *Brit*,
gearshift *Am*
cambista *mf* foreign exchange clerk
Camboya *f* Cambodia
camelar *vt inf* **1.** (*engañar*) to cajole
2. (*seducir*) to seduce
camelia *f* camellia
camello, -a *m*, *f* **1.** ZOOL camel **2.** *inf*
(*persona*) drug dealer
camelo *m inf* con
camerino *m* TEAT dressing room
Camerún *m* Cameroon
camilla *f* stretcher
caminar **I.** *vi* **1.** (*ir*) to go; (*a pie*) to
walk **2.** *AmL* (*funcionar*) to work
II. *vt* (*distancia*) to cover
caminata *f* long walk
camino *m* **1.** (*senda*) path; (*más
estrecho*) track; (*calle*) road; **ponerse en ~** to set out; **ir por buen
~** *fig* to be on the right track **2.** (*distancia*) way **3.** INFOR path

camión *m* AUTO lorry *Brit*, truck *Am*
camionero, -a *m*, *f* lorry driver *Brit*,
truck driver *Am*
camioneta *f* **1.** (*furgoneta*) van
2. *AmL* (*autobús*) bus
camisa *f* **1.** (*prenda*) shirt **2.** (*funda*)
case
camiseta *f* **1.** (*exterior*) T-shirt **2.** (*interior*) vest *Brit*, undershirt *Am*
3. DEP shirt
camisón *m* nightdress, nightgown
Am
camorra *f* **1.** *pey*, *inf* (*escándalo*)
row **2.** (*mafia*) Camorra
camorrista *mf* troublemaker
camote *m AmL* sweet potato
campamento *m* camp; ~ **de veraneo** summer camp
campana *f* bell
campanada *f* chime
campanario *m* bell tower
campanilla *f* **1.** (*campana*) bell
2. ANAT uvula
campaña *f* **1.** (*campo*) countryside;
tienda de ~ tent **2.** MIL campaign
campechano, -a *adj* straightforward
campeón, -ona *m*, *f* champion
campeonato *m* championship
campesino, -a **I.** *adj* rural **II.** *m*, *f*
1. (*que vive*) countryman *m*,
countrywoman *f* **2.** *t. pey* (*labrador*)
peasant
camping *m* **1.** (*campamento*) camping site **2.** (*actividad*) camping
campiña *f* countryside
campo *m* **1.** (*no ciudad*) countryside
2. *t.* DEP, INFOR (*de cultivo*) field; ~
para entradas INFOR input field; ~
de opción INFOR option field **3.** (*cam-*

pamento) camp; ~ **de trabajo** work camp

camposanto *m* cemetery

campus *m inv* campus

camuflaje *m* camouflage

camuflar *vt t. fig* to camouflage

cana *f* white hair

Canadá *m* (**el**) ~ Canada

canal *m o f* **1.** *t. ANAT* (*cauce artificial*) canal **2.** GEO, TV channel

canalizar <z→c> *vt* **1.** (*un río*) to canalize **2.** (*encauzar*) to channel

canalla *mf pey* swine

canalón *m* gutter

Canarias *fpl* **las Islas** ~ the Canary Islands

canario *m* canary

canario, -a *adj* of/from the Canary Islands

canasta *f* basket

canastilla *f* **1.** (*cestita*) small basket **2.** (*del bebé*) layette

cancel *m* inner door

cancelación *f* cancellation

cancelar *vt* **1.** (*anular*) to cancel **2.** FIN (*una cuenta*) to close; (*una deuda*) to pay (off)

cáncer *m* MED cancer

Cáncer *m* Cancer

cancerígeno, -a *adj* carcinogenic

cancha *f* (*de deporte*) sports field; (*de tenis*) court

canciller *mf* POL chancellor

canción *f* song

cancionero *m* songbook

candado *m* padlock

candela *f* candle

candelero *m* candlestick

candente *adj* **1.** (*al rojo*) red-hot **2.** (*palpitante*) burning

candidato, -a *m, f* **1.** (*aspirante*) applicant **2.** POL candidate

candidez *f v.* **candor**

cándido, -a *adj v.* **candoroso**

candil *m* oil lamp

candilejas *fpl* TEAT footlights *pl*

candor *m* **1.** (*inocencia*) innocence **2.** (*ingenuidad*) naivety *Brit,* naiveté *Am*

candoroso, -a *adj* **1.** (*inocente*) innocent **2.** (*ingenuo*) naive

canela *f* cinnamon

canelones *m pl* GASTR cannelloni

cangrejo *m* (*crustáceo*) crab

canguro¹ *m* ZOOL kangaroo

canguro² *mf inf* (*persona*) baby-sitter

caníbal *adj, mf* cannibal

canica *f* marble

canijo, -a *adj pey* (*endeble*) feeble; (*pequeñajo*) puny

canilla *f* **1.** ANAT shinbone **2.** TÉC (*carrete*) bobbin

canino *m* canine (tooth)

canjear *vt* **1.** (*intercambiar*) to exchange **2.** (*cambiar*) to cash (in)

canoa *f* canoe

canon *m* rule

canónigo *m* REL canon

canonizar <z→c> *vt* REL to canonize

canoso, -a *adj* grizzled

cansado, -a *adj* **1.** *estar* (*fatigado*) tired **2.** *estar* (*harto*) tired **3.** *ser* (*fatigoso*) tiring **4.** *ser* (*aburrido*) boring

cansancio *m* tiredness

cansar I. *vt* **1.** (*fatigar*) to tire (out) **2.** (*hastiar*) to bore **II.** *vr:* ~**se 1.** (*fatigarse*) to tire oneself out **2.** (*hartarse*) to get bored

Cantabria *f* Cantabria

cantábrico, -a *adj* Cantabrian; **el Mar Cantábrico** the Bay of Biscay

cantante I. *adj* singing **II.** *mf* singer

cantar I. *vi, vt* **1.** (*personas*) to sing; (*gallo*) to crow **2.** (*alabar*) to sing the praises of **3.** *inf* (*confesar*) to talk **II.** *m* song

cántaro *m* pitcher

cantautor(a) *m(f)* singer-songwriter

cante *m* singing; ~ **jondo** Flamenco singing

cantera *f* quarry

cantidad *f* **1.** (*porción*) quantity; (*número*) number **2.** (*suma*) sum

cantilena *f* song; **la misma** ~ *inf* the same old story

cantina *f* (*en estaciones*) buffet; (*en cuarteles*) canteen

cantinela *f v.* **cantilena**

canto *m* **1.** (*acción*) singing; (*canción*) song **2.** (*esquina*) corner; (*arista*) edge **3.** (*en un cuchillo*) back; (*en un libro*) fore-edge

cantor(a) I. *adj* singing **II.** *m(f) elev*

singer

canuto m 1.(*tubo*) tube 2. *inf* (*porro*) joint

caña f 1.BOT reed; (*tallo*) stalk; (*junco*) cane 2. ANAT shinbone 3.(*de pescar*) (fishing) rod

cañada f 1.(*barranco*) gully 2.(*camino*) cattle track

cáñamo m hemp

cañería f pipe

caño m 1.(*tubo*) tube; (*de la fuente*) jet 2.(*desagüe*) drainpipe

cañón m 1.(*tubo*) tube; (*de escopeta*) barrel 2.MIL cannon 3.GEO canyon

caoba f mahogany

caos m *inv* chaos

caótico, -a *adj* chaotic

cap. *abr de* **capítulo** ch.

capa f 1. t. TAUR (*prenda*) cape 2.(*cobertura*) covering; (*baño*) coating 3.(*de ozono*) layer 4.GEO stratum

capacho m (large) basket, hamper

capacidad f 1. t. FÍS (*cabida*) capacity 2.(*aptitud*) aptitude

capacitación f (*capacidad*) capacity; (*formación*) training

capacitar I.*vt* to train; (*preparar*) II.*vr:* ~**se** to qualify

capar *vt* to castrate

caparazón m t. *fig* shell

capataz m foreman

capaz *adj* 1.(*con cabida*) capacious 2.(*en condiciones*) capable

capcioso, -a *adj* deceitful

capea f bullfight with young bulls

capellán m 1.(*con capellanía*) chaplain 2.(*clérigo*) clergyman

caperuza f (*pointed*) hood

capicúa m symmetrical number

capilla f REL chapel

capital[1] I. *adj* essential II. m ECON, FIN capital

capital[2] f capital (city)

capitalismo m capitalism

capitalista I. *adj* capitalist(ic) II.*mf* capitalist

capitalizar <z→c> *vt* to capitalize

capitán m 1.MIL, DEP captain 2.*fig* leader

capitanear *vt* to captain

capitolio m capitol; **el Capitolio** the Capitol

capitulación f 1.MIL surrender 2.(*acuerdo*) agreement

capitular *vi* 1.(*acordar*) to agree to 2.(*rendirse*) to surrender

capítulo m t. REL chapter

capo m mob boss

capó m bonnet *Brit,* hood *Am*

capón m capon

caporal m 1.MIL squadron leader, corporal *Am* 2.(*jefe*) leader

capota f AUTO convertible roof *Brit,* convertible top *Am*

capote m 1.(*abrigo*) cloak 2.TAUR cape

capricho m whim

caprichoso, -a *adj* capricious

Capricornio m Capricorn

cápsula f capsule

captar *vt* 1.(*percibir*) to make out 2.TEL to pick up 3.CINE, FOTO to take 4.INFOR to capture

captura f 1.(*apresamiento*) capture 2.(*detención*) arrest

capturar *vt* 1.(*apresar*) to capture 2.(*detener*) to arrest

capucha f, **capuchón** m hood

capullo m 1.BOT bud 2.ZOOL cocoon

caqui m khaki

cara I. f 1.(*rostro*) face; **echar en** ~ to reproach; **plantar** ~ **a** to face up to; **tener mucha** ~ to have some nerve 2.(*aspecto*) look 3.(*lado*) side; (*de una moneda*) face; ~ **o cruz** heads or tails II. *prep* (**de**) ~ **a** facing

carabina f carbine

caracol m 1.ZOOL snail 2.(*concha*) conch (shell)

carácter <caracteres> m 1.t. TIPO, INFOR (*general*) character 2.(*índole*) nature

característica f characteristic

caracterizar <z→c> I.*vt* 1.(*marcar*) to characterize 2.TEAT to play II. *vr:* ~**se** to be characterized

caradura *mf inf* shameless person

carajillo m *inf: coffee with a dash of brandy*

carajo m *vulg* prick; **irse al** ~ to go to hell; (*estropearse*) to go to the dogs; ¡~! hell!

caramba *interj inf* damn
carámbano *m* icicle
caramelo *m* **1.**(*azúcar*) caramel **2.**(*golosina*) sweet *Brit,* candy *Am*
carantoña *f* **hacer ~s** to butter up
caraqueño, -a *adj* of/from Caracas
carátula *f* **1.**(*careta*) mask **2.**(*de un disco*) cover
caravana *f* **1.**(*remolque*) caravan *Brit,* trailer *Am* **2.**(*de coches*) tailback
carbón *m* coal
carbonilla *f* coal dust
carbonizar <z→c> *vt* **1.**(*abrasar*) to char **2.** QUÍM to carbonize
carbono *m* carbon
carburador *m* TÉC carburettor *Brit,* carburetor *Am*
carburante *m* fuel
carcajada *f* guffaw
carcajearse *vr* to roar with laughter
cárcel *f* prison
carcelero, -a *m, f* prison officer
carcoma *f* woodworm
carcomer **I.** *vt* **1.**(*corroer*) to eat away **2.**(*minar*) to undermine **II.** *vr:* **~se** *fig* to decay
carcomido, -a *adj* (*madera*) eaten away; *fig* decayed
cardar *vt* to card
cardenal *m* **1.** REL cardinal **2.**(*hematoma*) bruise
cárdeno, -a *adj* (*color*) purple; (*res*) black and white; (*agua*) opaline blue
cardiaco, -a *adj,* **cardíaco, -a** *adj* heart; MED cardiac; **ataque ~** heart attack
cardinal *adj* cardinal
cardo *m* BOT thistle
carear **I.** *vt* **1.** JUR (*confrontar*) to bring face to face **2.**(*cotejar*) to compare **II.** *vr:* **~se** to come face to face
carecer *irr como crecer vi* **~ de algo** to lack sth
carencia *f* **1.**(*falta*) lack **2.**(*escasez*) shortage
carente *adj* lacking
carestía *f sin pl* **1.**(*escasez*) scarcity **2.** ECON high cost
careta *f* mask
carga *f* **1.**(*acto*) loading **2.**(*cargamento*) load; (*flete*) freight; **buque**

de ~ freighter **3.**(*obligación*) obligation **4.** MIL, FIN charge; **~ fiscal** tax burden
cargado, -a *adj* **1.**(*con cargamento*) loaded; (*lleno*) full **2.** FÍS, TÉC charged **3.**(*pesado*) heavy **4.**(*fuerte*) strong
cargamento *m* (*acto*) loading; (*carga*) load, cargo
cargar <g→gu> **I.** *vt* **1.** *t.* MIL to load; **~ con algo** to carry sth **2.**(*achacar*) to attribute **3.** FIN (*en una cuenta*) to charge **4.** *inf* (*irritar*) to annoy **5.** INFOR to load **6.** *AmL* (*llevar*) to have **II.** *vr:* **~se 1.**(*llenarse*) to fill up **2.** *inf* (*romper*) to smash up
cargo *m* **1.** FIN (*cantidad debida*) charge **2.**(*puesto*) post **3.**(*responsabilidad*) responsibility; (*deber*) duty
carguero *m* NÁUT freighter
Caribe *m* **el** (**Mar**) **~** the Caribbean (Sea)
caribeño, -a *adj* Caribbean
caricatura *f* caricature
caricia *f* caress
caridad *f* charity
caries *f inv* MED tooth decay
cariño *m* (*afecto*) affection; (*amor*) love; **¡~** (**mío**)**!** (my) dear!
cariñoso, -a *adj* **~ con alguien** affectionate towards sb
carisma *m* charisma
caritativo, -a *adj* charitable
cariz *m* (*aspecto*) look
carmesí *adj, m* carmine
carnal *adj* carnal
carnaval *m* carnival; REL shrovetide
carne *f* **1.**(*del cuerpo*) flesh; **~ de gallina** gooseflesh; **de ~ y hueso** real; **uña y ~** inseparable **2.**(*alimento*) meat
carné *m* <carnés> identity card; **~ de conducir** *AmL* driving licence *Brit,* driver's license *Am*
carnero *m* ram
carnet *m* <carnets> *v.* **carné**
carnicería *f* **1.**(*tienda*) butcher's (shop) **2.**(*masacre*) massacre
carnicero, -a **I.** *adj* carnivorous **II.** *m, f* butcher
carnívoro, -a *adj* carnivorous
carnoso, -a *adj* fleshy
caro *adv* dear(ly) *Brit*

caro, -a *adj* expensive, dear *Brit*

carpa *f* **1.** ZOOL carp **2.** (*de circo*) marquee **3.** *AmL* (*de campaña*) tent

Cárpatos *mpl* **los** (**Montes**) ~ the Carpathians

carpeta *f* **1.** (*portafolios*) folder **2.** (*de un disco*) cover

carpintería *f* carpentry

carpintero, -a *m, f* carpenter

carpir *vt AmL* to hoe

carraspear *vi* to clear one's throat

carraspera *f* hoarseness

carrera *f* **1.** (*movimiento*) run **2.** (*recorrido*) journey; (*de un astro*) course **3.** DEP (*competición*) race **4.** (*estudios*) ~ **profesional** career; **hacer una** ~ to study

carreta *f* wagon

carrete *m t.* FOTO spool, reel

carretera *f* (main) road

carretilla *f* wheelbarrow

carril *m* **1.** (*en la carretera*) lane **2.** *t.* TÉC (*raíl*) rail

carrillo *m inf* cheek

carro *m* **1.** (*vehículo*) cart; **el Carro Mayor** ASTR the Big Dipper **2.** *AmL* (*coche*) car **3.** (*de máquina de escribir*) carriage

carrocería *f* bodywork

carroña *f* carrion

carroza *f* carriage

carruaje *m* carriage

carrusel *m* merry-go-round, carousel *Am*

carta *f* **1.** (*escrito*) letter; **echar una** ~ to post a letter **2.** (*documento*) document; **Carta Magna** Magna Carta; **tomar ~s en algo** to intervene in sth **3.** (*naipes*) card; **echar las ~s** **n** to tell fortune **4.** GEO (*mapa*) map **5.** (*menú*) menu

cartabón *m* set square

cartearse *vr* to correspond

cartel *m* poster; (*rótulo*) sign; TEAT bill

cártel *m* ECON cartel

cartelera *f* **1.** (*en periódico*) entertainment guide **2.** (*tablón*) notice board; TEAT, CINE publicity board

cartera *f* (*de bolsillo*) wallet; (*de mano*) handbag, purse *Am*; (*portafolios*) portfolio; (*escolar*) (school)

satchel; ~ **de valores** FIN securities portfolio

carterista *mf* pickpocket

cartero, -a *m, f* postman *m Brit,* postwoman *f Brit*

cartilla *f* first reader; ~ **de ahorros** FIN savings book

cartografía *f* cartography

cartón *m* **1.** (*material*) cardboard **2.** (*envase*) carton

cartucho *m* **1.** *t.* MIL cartridge **2.** (*envoltura*) cone

cartulina *f* thin cardboard

casa *f* **1.** (*edificio*) house; **tirar la** ~ **por la ventana** *inf* to spare no expense **2.** (*vivienda*) flat **3.** (*hogar*) home; **ir a** ~ to go home **4.** ECON (*empresa*) firm; ~ **editorial** publishing house

casadero, -a *adj* marriageable

casamiento *m* marriage, wedding

casar **I.** *vt* **1.** (*dos personas*) **estar casado** to be married; **los recién casados** the newlyweds **2.** (*combinar*) to combine **II.** *vr:* ~se to get married

cascabel *m* (little) bell; **serpiente de** ~ rattlesnake

cascada *f* waterfall

cascanueces *m inv* nutcracker

cascar <c→qu> **I.** *vi inf* (*charlar*) to chatter **II.** *vt* **1.** (*romper*) to crack **2.** *inf* (*pegar*) to clout **III.** *vr:* ~se **1.** (*romperse*) to crack **2.** *inf* (*envejecer*) to get old

cáscara *f* (*de huevo*) shell; (*de limón*) peel

casco *m* **1.** (*para la cabeza*) helmet **2.** *inf* (*cabeza*) head **3.** (*pezuña*) hoof **4.** (*de un barco*) hull **5.** (*botella*) (empty) bottle **6.** (*centro ciudad*) city centre *Brit,* downtown *Am* **7.** *pl* (*auriculares*) headphones *pl*

cascote *m* piece of rubble

caserío *m* farmhouse

casero, -a **I.** *adj* **1.** (*hecho en casa*) homemade **2.** (*hogareño*) home-loving **II.** *m, f* landlord *m*, landlady *f*

caseta *f* hut; (*de feria*) booth; (*de muestras*) stand

casete¹ *m o f* (*cinta*) cassette

casete² *m* **1.** (*aparato*) cassette re-

corder **2.** (*pletina*) cassette deck
casi *adv* almost
casilla *f* **1.** (*caseta*) hut **2.** (*en la cua-drícula*) box **3.** (*en un tablero*) square **4.** (*en un casillero*) pigeon-hole
casillero *m* set of pigeonholes
casino *m* **1.** (*casa de juego*) casino **2.** (*club*) club
caso *m* **1.** (*hecho*) case; **yo, en tu ~…** If I were you …; **en ~ de** +*infin* in the event of; **dado el ~ de que** +*subj* supposing (that); **en ~ contrario** otherwise; **en todo ~** in any case **2.** (*atención*) notice; **hacer ~** to pay attention
caspa *f* dandruff
Caspio *m* (**el**) **Mar ~** (the) Caspian Sea
casquillo *m* **1.** (*de bala*) cartridge case **2.** (*de bombilla*) light fitting
cassette¹ *m o f v.* **casete¹**
cassette² *m v.* **casete²**
casta *f* **1.** (*raza*) race **2.** (*linaje*) lin-eage
castaña *f* **1.** (*fruto*) chestnut **2.** *inf* (*golpe*) blow **3.** *inf* (*puñetazo*) thump **4.** *inf* (*borrachera*) drunken-ness
castañetear *vi* **1.** (*dedos*) to snap **2.** (*castañuelas*) to play
castaño *m* chestnut tree
castaño, -a *adj* brown
castañuela *f* castanet
castellano *m* LING (*español*) Spanish; (*variedad*) Castilian
castellano, -a *adj, m, f* Castilian; **la lengua castellana** the Spanish lan-guage
castidad *f* chastity
castigar <g→gu> *vt* **1.** (*punir*) to punish **2.** (*físicamente*) to beat
castigo *m* punishment
Castilla *f* Castile
Castilla-La Mancha *f* Castile and La Mancha
Castilla-León *f* Castile and León
castillo *m* castle
castizo, -a *adj* typical
casto, -a *adj* chaste
castor *m* beaver
castrar *vt* **1.** AGR to geld **2.** *t.* MED to

castrate
casual *adj* chance
casualidad *f* chance; **por ~** by chance; **¡qué ~!** what a coincidence!
cataclismo *m* cataclysm
catacumbas *fpl* catacombs *pl*
catador(a) *m(f)* taster
catalán *m* (*lengua*) Catalan
catalán, -ana *adj, m, f* Catalan, Catalonian
catalejo *m* telescope
catalizador *m* **1.** *t.* QUÍM, TÉC catalyst **2.** AUTO catalytic converter
catalogar <g→gu> *vt* **1.** (*registrar*) to catalogue *Brit,* to catalog *Am* **2.** (*clasificar*) to class
catálogo *m* catalogue *Brit,* catalog *Am*
Cataluña *f* Catalonia
cataplasma *f* **1.** MED poultice **2.** *inf* (*pesado*) bore
catapulta *f* catapult
catar *vt* to taste
catarata *f* **1.** (*salto*) waterfall **2.** MED cataract
catarro *m* cold; MED catarrh
catarsis *f inv* catharsis
catastro *m* cadastre *Brit,* cadaster *Am*
catástrofe *f* catastrophe
catear *vt inf* to fail, to flunk *Am*
catecismo *m* REL catechism
cátedra *f* **1.** ENS (*púlpito*) lectern **2.** ENS (*docencia*) chair
catedral *f* cathedral
catedrático, -a *m, f* ENS professor
categoría *f* **1.** *t.* FILOS (*clase*) cat-egory **2.** (*calidad*) quality; **de pri-mera ~** first-class **3.** (*rango*) rank
catequesis *f inv* REL catechesis
cateto, -a *m, f* yokel
catolicismo *m* REL (Roman) Catholi-cism
católico, -a *adj, m, f* (Roman) Cath-olic
catorce *adj inv, m* fourteen; *v.t.* **ocho**
catre *m* plank bed
Cáucaso *m* **el ~** the Caucasus
cauce *m* **1.** GEO (*lecho*) river bed **2.** (*camino*) channel, course
caucho *m* **1.** (*sustancia*) rubber **2.** *AmL* (*neumático*) tyre *Brit,* tire

Am

caución *f* 1.(*cautela*) caution 2.JUR security

caudal I. *adj* tail II. *m* 1.(*de agua*) volume 2.(*dinero*) fortune 3.(*abundancia*) abundance

caudaloso, -a *adj* 1.(*río*) large 2.(*rico*) rich 3.(*cantidad*) abundant

caudillo *m* MIL, POL leader; **el Caudillo** Franco

causa *f* 1. *t.* POL (*origen*) cause; (*motivo*) reason; **a ~ de** on account of 2.JUR lawsuit

causar *vt* to cause; **~ alegría** to make happy; **~ efecto** to have an effect

cautela *f* (*precaución*) caution

cauteloso, -a *adj* (*prudente*) cautious

cautivar *vt* 1.(*apresar*) to capture 2.(*fascinar*) to captivate

cautiverio *m,* **cautividad** *f* captivity

cautivo, -a *adj, m, f* captive

cauto, -a *adj* cautious

cava *m* cava

[?] **Cava** is referred to as the Spanish Champagne. This quality sparkling white wine is produced in champagne cellars in the north--east of Spain.

---

cavar *vi, vt* to dig

caverna *f* (*cueva*) cave; (*gruta*) cavern

caviar *m sin pl* caviar

cavidad *f t.* MED cavity

cavilar *vt* to ponder (on)

caviloso, -a *adj* suspicious

cayado *m* 1.(*del pastor*) crook 2.(*del prelado*) crozier

caza¹ *f* 1.(*montería*) hunting 2.(*animales*) game

caza² *m* MIL fighter plane

cazador(a) I. *adj* hunting II. *m(f)* (*persona*) hunter *m,* huntress *f*

cazadora *f* jacket

cazar <z→c> *vt* 1.(*atrapar*) to hunt; (*perseguir*) to pursue 2.(*coger*) to catch

cazavirus *adj inv* INFOR anti-virus; **programa** ~ anti-virus programme

cazo *m* saucepan; (*cucharón*) ladle

cazuela *f* casserole

cazurro, -a I. *adj* sullen II. *m, f* sullen person

CC.OO. *fpl abr de* **Comisiones O-breras** *Spanish communist federation of trade unions*

CE *f* HIST *abr de* **Comunidad Europea** EC

cebada *f* BOT barley

cebar I. *vt* 1.(*engordar*) to fatten (up) 2.(*un arma*) to prime 3.(*el anzuelo*) to bait II. *vr:* ~**se** to vent one's anger

cebo *m* 1.(*alimento*) feed 2.(*de anzuelo*) bait 3.(*en un arma*) primer

cebolla *f* onion

cebolleta *f* spring onion *Brit,* scallion *Am*

cebra *f* ZOOL zebra; **paso de ~** AUTO zebra crossing *Brit,* crosswalk *Am*

cecear *vi* to lisp

ceceo *m* lisp

[?] In certain regions, for example in certain areas of Andalusia, the Spanish 's' is pronounced as a 'z'. This linguistic phenomenon is referred to as **ceceo**, e.g. 'cocer' instead of 'coser'.

---

cedazo *m* sieve

ceder I. *vi* 1.(*renunciar*) to give up 2.(*disminuir*) to diminish 3.(*capitular*) to give in 4.(*cuerda*) to give way II. *vt* 1.(*dar*) to hand over 2.(*transferir*) to transfer 3.DEP (*balón*) to pass

cedro *m* BOT cedar

cédula *f* certificate; ~ **personal** identity card

CEE *f* HIST *abr de* **Comunidad Económica Europea** EEC

cegar *irr como fregar* I. *vi* to go blind II. *vt* 1.(*la vista*) to blind 2.(*ventana*) to wall up III. *vr:* ~**se** to be blinded

ceguera *f t. fig* blindness

Ceilán *m* Ceylon

ceja *f* eyebrow

cejar *vi* to give up

celada *f* **1.** ambush **2.** (*trampa*) trap
celador(a) *m(f)* watchman; (*de aparcamientos*) attendant
celda *f* cell
celebración *f* celebration
celebrar I. *vt* **1.** (*acontecimiento*) to celebrate **2.** (*reuniones*) to hold **3.** (*alegrarse*) to be delighted II. *vi* REL to celebrate Mass III. *vr:* ~**se** **1.** (*fiesta*) to be celebrated **2.** (*reunión*) to be held
célebre <celebérrimo> *adj* famous
celebridad *f* **1.** (*alguien ilustre*) celebrity **2.** (*renombre*) fame
celeste *adj* **1.** (*célico*) celestial **2.** (*color*) sky blue
celestial *adj* celestial, heavenly
celibato *m* celibacy
célibe I. *adj* celibate II. *mf* unmarried person
celo *m* **1.** (*afán*) zeal **2.** *pl* (*por amor*) jealousy; **tener** ~**s** to be jealous; **estar en** ~ (*macho*) to be in rut; (*hembra*) to be on heat **3.** (*autoadhesivo*) adhesive tape *Brit,* Scotch® tape
celoso, -a *adj* **1.** (*con fervor*) zealous **2.** jealous
celta I. *adj* Celtic II. *mf* Celt
célula *f* cell
celulitis *f inv* MED cellulitis
cementerio *m* cemetery; ~ **de coches** used-car scrapyard
cemento *m* cement
cena *f* supper
cenagal *m* bog
cenar I. *vi* to have supper II. *vt* to have for supper
cenicero *m* ashtray
cenit *m* zenith
ceniza *f* ash
censar *vt* to take a census of
censo *m* census
censura *f* censorship; **moción de** ~ POL motion of censure
censurar *vt* **1.** (*juzgar*) to censure **2.** (*vituperar*) to condemn
centella *f* spark
centell(e)ar *vi* **1.** (*fuego*) to spark **2.** (*estrella*) to twinkle
centelleo *m* **1.** (*de las llamas*) sparking **2.** (*de las estrellas*) twinkling

centena *f* hundred
centenar *m* hundred
centenario *m* centenary *Brit,* centennial *Am*
centenario, -a *adj, m, f* centenarian
centeno *m* BOT rye
centésimo, -a *adj, m, f* hundredth
centígrado *m* centigrade
centímetro *m* centimetre *Brit,* centimeter *Am*
céntimo I. *adj* hundredth II. *m* **1.** (*centésima parte*) hundredth part **2.** (*moneda*) hundredth part of a peseta
centinela *mf* **1.** (*de museo*) guard **2.** MIL sentry
centollo *m* spider crab
central I. *adj* central; **Europa Central** Central Europe; **estación** ~ main station II. *f* **1.** (*oficina*) head office **2.** TÉC plant; ~ **eléctrica** electric power station
centralita *f* TEL switchboard
centralización *f* centralization
centralizar <z→c> *vt* to centralize
centrar *vt* **1.** TÉC, DEP to centre *Brit,* to center *Am* **2.** (*atención*) to focus
céntrico, -a *adj t.* TÉC central
centrifugadora *f* spin-dryer; TÉC centrifuge
centrifugar <g→gu> *vt* to spin-dry; TÉC to centrifuge
centrífugo, -a *adj* centrifugal
centrista *adj, mf* POL centrist
centro *m* **1.** *t.* POL, DEP centre *Brit,* center *Am;* (*de la ciudad*) town centre *Brit,* downtown; ~ **nervioso** ANAT nerve centre **2.** (*institución*) centre *Brit,* center *Am;* ~ **de computación** computer centre
Centroamérica *f* Central America
centroamericano, -a *adj, m, f* Central American
Centroeuropa *f* Central Europe
ceñido, -a *adj* tight-fitting
ceñir *irr* I. *vt* **1.** (*rodear*) to surround **2.** (*ponerse*) to put on; (*cinturón*) to buckle on **3.** (*acortar*) to shorten II. *vr:* ~**se** **1.** (*ajustarse*) to limit oneself **2.** (*vestido*) to be close-fitting
ceño *m* frown

cepa *f* stock

cepillar I. *vt* 1. (*traje*) to brush 2. TÉC (*madera*) to plane II. *vr:* ~**se** 1. *inf* (*robar*) to rip off 2. *inf* (*matar*) to bump off 3. *vulg* (*seducir*) to make it with

cepillo *m* 1. (*para el cabello*) brush; ~ **de dientes** toothbrush 2. (*para madera*) plane

cepo *m* 1. (*caza*) trap 2. *pl* AUTO wheel clamp

cera *f* wax

cerámica *f* ceramics *pl*

cerca I. *adv* 1. (*en el espacio*) near; **aquí** ~ near here; ~ **de** near 2. (*en el tiempo*) close II. *f* fence

cercanía *f* 1. (*proximidad*) closeness; (*vecindad*) 2. *pl* (*alrededores*) outskirts *pl*

cercano, -a *adj* near

cercar <c→qu> *vt* 1. (*vallar*) to fence in 2. (*rodear*) to surround

cerciorar I. *vt* to convince II. *vr:* ~**se** to make sure

cerco *m* 1. (*círculo*) circle 2. (*valla*) fence 3. MIL siege

cerda *f* 1. ZOOL sow 2. (*pelo*) bristle

cerdada *f pey* dirty trick

Cerdeña *f* Sardinia

cerdo, -a I. *adj* (*sucio*) dirty II. *m, f* 1. ZOOL pig; (*carne*) pork 2. (*insulto*) swine

cereales *mpl* cereals *pl*, grain

ceremonia *f* ceremony

ceremonial *adj, m* ceremonial

ceremonioso, -a *adj* 1. (*solemne*) ceremonious 2. (*formal*) formal

cereza *f* cherry

cerilla *f* match

cerner <e→ie> *vt* to sieve, to sift

cero *m* zero; **partir de** ~ to start from scratch

cerrado, -a *adj* 1. *estar* (*no abierto*) closed; (*con llave*) locked 2. *estar* (*cielo*) overcast 3. *ser* (*actitud*) reserved 4. *ser* (*curva*) sharp

cerradura *f* 1. (*dispositivo*) lock 2. (*acción*) closing; (*con llave*) locking

cerrajero, -a *m, f* locksmith

cerrar <e→ie> I. *vt* 1. (*paraguas, carretera*) to close; (*carta*) to seal; ~

archivo INFOR to close a file 2. (*con llave*) to lock 3. (*agujero*) to block (up); (*agua*) to turn off 4. (*terreno*) to close off II. *vi* 1. (*puerta*) to close 2. (*acabar*) to end III. *vr:* ~**se** 1. (*puerta*) to close 2. (*herida*) to heal (up)

cerro *m* hill

cerrojo *m* bolt

certamen *m* competition

certero, -a *adj* accurate

certeza *f* certainty

certificado *m* certificate

certificado, -a *adj* 1. JUR certified 2. (*correos*) registered

certificar <c→qu> *vt* 1. *t.* JUR (*afirmar*) to certify 2. (*correos*) to register

cervato *m* fawn

cervecería *f* 1. (*bar*) pub *Brit,* bar 2. (*fábrica*) brewery

cerveza *f* beer

cervical *adj* 1. ANAT neck 2. MED cervical

Cervino *m* **el Monte** ~ the Matterhorn

cesación *f,* **cesamiento** *m* cessation

cesante I. *adj* 1. (*suspendido*) suspended 2. *AmL* (*parado*) unemployed II. *mf* laid-off civil servant

cesar I. *vi* 1. (*parar*) to stop 2. (*en una profesión*) to leave II. *vt* 1. (*pagos*) to stop 2. (*despedir*) to dismiss

cesárea *f* caesarean

cese *m* 1. (*que termina*) cessation; (*interrupción*) suspension 2. (*de obrero*) sacking 3. JUR (*proceso*) abandonment

césped *m* grass

cesta *f* basket

cesto *m t.* DEP basket

cetro *m* sceptre *Brit,* scepter *Am*

cf. *abr de* **compárese** cf.

chabacano, -a *adj* vulgar

chabola *f* 1. (*casucha*) shack 2. *pl* (*barrio*) shanty town

chacal *m* jackal

chacha *f inf* maid

cháchara *f inf* chatter

chacra *f AmL* (*granja*) small farm

Chad *m* Chad

chafar I. *vt* **1.** (*aplastar*) to flatten, to squelch; (*arrugar*) to crease **2.** (*estropear*) to spoil **II.** *vr:* ~**se** to be flattened

chal *m* shawl

chalado, -a *adj inf* crazy

chalé *m* chalet

chaleco *m* waistcoat *Brit,* vest *Am;* ~ **salvavidas** life jacket

chalupa *f* NÁUT launch

chamaco, -a *m, f* (*muchacho*) boy; (*muchacha*) girl

champán *m,* **champaña** *m* champagne

champiñón *m* mushroom

champú *m* shampoo

chamuscar <c→qu> **I.** *vt* to scorch; (*aves*) to singe **II.** *vr:* ~**se** to get scorched

chancho *m AmL* pig

chanchullo *m inf* swindle, fiddle

chándal *m* <chándals> tracksuit

chapa *f* **1.** (*metal*) sheet **2.** (*lámina*) plate **3.** (*contrachapado*) plywood **4.** (*tapón*) (bottle)cap **5.** *AmL* (*cerradura*) lock

chaparrón *m* downpour; (*chubasco*) cloudburst

chapista *mf* **1.** (*planchista*) tinsmith **2.** (*de carrocería*) panel beater

chapotear I. *vi* to splash (around) **II.** *vt* to moisten

chapucero, -a I. *adj* shoddy **II.** *m, f* bungler

chapurr(e)ar *vt* to speak badly

chapuza *f* shoddy job

chapuzón *m* dip

chaqué *m* morning coat

chaqueta *f* jacket

chaquetón *m* long jacket

charca *f* pond

charco *m* puddle, pool

charcutería *f* **1.** (*productos*) pork products *pl* **2.** (*tienda*) ≈ delicatessen

charla *f* **1.** (*conversación*) chat **2.** (*conferencia*) talk

charlar *vi* to chat

charlatán, -ana *m, f* **1.** (*hablador*) chatterbox **2.** (*chismoso*) gossip

charol *m* **1.** (*barniz*) varnish **2.** (*cuero*) patent leather

chárter *adj inv* charter

chascarrillo *m* funny story

chasco *m* **1.** (*burla*) joke **2.** (*decepción*) disappointment

chasis *m inv* **1.** AUTO chassis **2.** FOTO plateholder

chasquear *vi* **1.** (*con la lengua*) to click; (*con los dedos*) to snap **2.** (*madera*) to creak

chasquido *m* **1.** (*de lengua*) click; (*de látigo*) crack **2.** (*de la madera*) creak

chatarra *f* scrap (metal)

chato, -a *adj* **1.** (*nariz*) snub **2.** (*persona*) snub-nosed

chaval(a) *m(f)* *inf* (*chico*) kid; (*joven*) young man *m,* young woman *f*

checo, -a *adj, m, f* Czech

checo(e)slovaco, -a *adj, m, f* Czechoslovakian

cheque *m* cheque, check *Am;* ~ **en blanco/cruzado** blank/crossed cheque; ~ **de viaje** traveller's cheque; **cobrar un** ~ to cash a cheque

chequear I. *vt AmL* (*comprobar*) to check **II.** *vr:* ~**se** to have a checkup

chequeo *m* (*de la salud*) checkup; (*de un mecanismo*) service

Chequia *f* Czech Republic

chica I. *adj* **1.** (*pequeña*) small **2.** (*joven*) young **II.** *f* **1.** (*niña*) girl **2.** (*joven*) young woman

chicharrón *m* GASTR crackling (of pork)

chichón *m* bump

chicle *m* chewing gum

chico I. *adj* **1.** (*pequeño*) small **2.** (*joven*) young **II.** *m* **1.** (*niño*) boy **2.** (*joven*) young man

chiflado, -a I. *adj inf* crazy **II.** *m, f inf* nutcase

chiflar I. *vt inf* (*gustar*) to be crazy about **II.** *vr:* ~**se** *inf* **1.** (*pirrarse*) to be crazy about sb **2.** (*volverse loco*) to go crazy

chiíta *adj, mf* Shiite

chile *m t.* BOT (*especia*) chilli, chili *Am*

Chile *m* Chile

? The capital of **Chile** (official title: **República de Chile**) is **Santiago** (de Chile). Running from north to south, the country is over four thousand kilometres in length with an average width of just one hundred and eighty kilometres. The official language of the country is Spanish and the monetary unit is the **peso chileno**.

chileno, -a *adj, m, f* Chilean
chillar *vi* 1. (*persona*) to yell 2. (*animal salvaje*) to howl 3. *AmL* (*sollozar*) to sob
chillido *m* 1. (*de persona*) yell 2. (*de animal*) howl; *AmL* (*sollozo*) sob
chillón, -ona I. *adj* 1. (*persona*) loud 2. (*voz*) shrill II. *m, f* loudmouth
chimenea *f* 1. *t.* GEO chimney 2. (*hogar*) fireplace
chimpancé *mf* chimpanzee
china *f* pebble
China *f* (**la**) ~ China
chinche¹ *m* o *f* ZOOL bedbug
chinche² *mf inf* (*pelmazo*) pain
chincheta *f* drawing pin *Brit*, thumbtack *Am*
chingar <g→gu> I. *vt* 1. *vulg* (*joder*) to fuck 2. *inf* (*molestar*) to annoy II. *vr*: ~**se** *inf* 1. (*emborracharse*) to get plastered 2. *AmL, inf* (*frustrarse*) to be a washout
chino, -a I. *adj* Chinese II. *m, f* Chinese man *f*; **engañar a alguien como a un** ~ *inf* to take sb for a ride
chip *m* INFOR chip
Chipre *f* Cyprus
chipriota *adj, mf* Cypriot
chiquillo, -a I. *adj* young II. *m, f* (*niño*) (small) child; (*chico*) (little) boy; (*chica*) (little) girl
chiquito, -a *adj inf* very small
chiringuito *m* kiosk
chiripa *f inf* fluke
chirriar <1. *pres:* chirrío> *vi* 1. (*metal*) to squeak 2. (*pájaros*) to chirp

chirrido *m* 1. (*del metal*) squeaking 2. (*de los pájaros*) chirping
chis *interj* (*silencio*) sh; (*oye*) hey
chisme *m* 1. (*habladuría*) piece of gossip 2. (*objeto*) thingummyjig
chismoso, -a I. *adj* gossiping II. *m, f* gossip
chispa *f* 1. *t.* ELEC spark 2. (*ingenio*) wit 3. *inf* (*borrachera*) drunkenness
chispear *vimpers* (*lloviznar*) to drizzle
chisporrotear *vi* (*echar chispas*) to throw off sparks; (*el fuego*) to crackle
chiste *m* (*cuento*) funny story; (*broma*) joke; ~ **verde** dirty joke
chistera *f* top hat
chistoso, -a I. *adj* funny II. *m, f* joker
chivatazo *m inf* tip-off
chivo, -a *m, f* ~ **expiatorio** scapegoat
chocante *adj* 1. (*raro*) strange 2. (*escandaloso*) shocking
chocar <c→qu> I. *vi* 1. (*vehículos*) to collide, to crash 2. (*discutir*) to have words II. *vt* 1. (*copas*) to clink 2. (*sorprender*) to surprise
chochear *vi* to dodder (around)
chocho, -a *adj* (*senil*) doddering
choclo *m* 1. (*zueco*) clog 2. *AmS* (*maíz*) maize *Brit*, corn *Am*
chocolate *m* 1. (*para comer*) chocolate 2. *inf* (*hachís*) dope, hash *inf*
chofer *m,* **chófer** *m* driver; (*personal*) chauffeur
chollo *m inf* 1. (*suerte*) luck 2. (*ganga*) bargain 3. (*trabajo*) cushy job
chopera *f* poplar grove
chopo *m* BOT black poplar
choque *m* 1. (*impacto*) impact 2. (*colisión*) crash 3. (*encuentro*) clash
chorizo *m* chorizo
chorizo, -a *m, f inf* petty thief
chorrada *f* 1. *inf* (*tontería*) stupid remark 2. *inf* (*cosa superflua*) trivial thing
chorrear *vi* 1. (*fluir*) to gush (out) 2. (*gotear*) to drip
chorro *m* 1. (*hilo*) trickle 2. (*torrente*) stream; *t.* TÉC jet; **llover a ~s**

to pour

choza *f,* **chozo** *m* hut

chubasco *m* (heavy) shower

chubasquero *m* raincoat, wind-breaker *Am*

chuchería *f* (*dulce*) sweet

chulería *f* **1.** (*jactancia*) bragging **2.** (*frescura*) boldness

chuleta *f* **1.** (*costilla*) chop **2.** *inf* (*apunte*) crib (sheet)

chulo, -a I. *adj* **1.** (*jactancioso*) boast-ful; (*presumido*) conceited **2.** (*fres-co*) cheeky **II.** *m, f* **1.** (*fanfarrón*) flashy type **2.** (*exagerador*) brag-gart

chungo, -a *adj inf* **1.** (*malo*) bad; (*co-mida*) **2.** (*persona: rara*) odd; (*enfer-miza*) poorly

chupa *f inf* (*chaqueta*) leather jacket

chupado, -a *adj* **1.** (*flaco*) skinny; (*consumido*) emaciated **2.** *inf* (*fácil*) dead easy *Brit,* a cinch *Am* **3.** *AmL* (*borracho*) drunk

chupar I. *vt* **1.** (*caramelo*) to suck; (*helado*) to lick **2.** (*cigarrillo*) to smoke, to puff on **II.** *vi* **1.** *inf* (*mamar*) to suckle **2.** (*aprovecharse*) to sponge

chupete *m* dummy, pacifier *Am*

chupetón *m* suck

churrasco *m* **1.** (*carne*) steak **2.** (*bar-bacoa*) barbecue

---

| ? | **Churro** is the term for fritters. The most typical of Spanish break-fasts comprises **chocolate** (hot chocolate) **con churros. Churros** can be obtained either in a **chu-rrería,** in a **cafetería,** or they can be bought **en un puesto de chu-rros** (at a kiosk in the street). |

---

chusco *m* crust (of bread)

chusma *f* rabble, riffraff

chutar I. *vt* to shoot **II.** *vr:* ~**se** *inf* to shoot up

Cía *abr de* **compañía** Co.

cianuro *m* cyanide

ciberbar *m,* **cibercafé** *m* cybercafé

ciberespacio *m* cyberspace

cibernauta *mf* cybernaut

cicatriz *f* scar

cicatrizar <z→c> **I.** *vi, vr:* ~**se** to heal (up) **II.** *vt* to heal

ciclamen *m* BOT cyclamen

ciclismo *m* DEP cycling

ciclista I. *adj* cycle **II.** *mf* cyclist

ciclo *m* cycle

ciclomotor *m* moped, motorbike

ciclón *m* cyclone

cicloturismo *m* cycle touring

ciego, -a I. *adj* blind; **a ciegas** blindly **II.** *m, f* blind man *m,* blind woman *f*

cielo *m* **1.** (*atmósfera*) sky; **a ~ raso** in the open air; **como caído del ~** out of the blue; **¡~s!** good heavens! **2.** (*cariño*) darling

ciempiés *m inv* centipede

cien *adj inv* a hundred; **al ~ por ~** one hundred per cent; *v.t.* **ocho-cientos**

ciénaga *f* swamp

ciencia *f* **1.** (*saber*) knowledge; **a ~ cierta** for sure **2.** (*disciplina*) science

ciencia-ficción *f sin pl* science fic-tion

científico, -a I. *adj* scientific **II.** *m, f* scientist

ciento *adj* <cien> *inv* a hundred; *v.t.* **ochenta**

cierre *m* **1.** (*conclusión*) closing; (*clausura*) closure; **hora de ~** clos-ing time **2.** (*dispositivo*) closing de-vice; ~ **centralizado** AUTO central locking

cierto *adv* certainly; **por ~** by the way

cierto, -a *adj* <certísimo> **1.** (*ver-dadero*) true; (*seguro*) sure; **estar en lo ~** to be right **2.** (*alguno*) a cer-tain; ~ **día** one day

ciervo, -a *m, f* deer

cierzo *m* north wind

cifra *f* **1.** (*guarismo*) figure; ~ **de ne-gocios** ECON turnover **2.** (*clave*) code

cifrar *vt* **1.** (*codificar*) to code **2.** (*cal-cular*) to reckon

cigala *f* crayfish

cigarra *f* cicada

cigarrillo *m* cigarette

cigarro *m* cigar

cigüeña *f* **1.** (*ave*) stork **2.** (*manive-*

la) crank
cilindro *m* cylinder
cima *f t. fig* summit
cimbrar, cimbrear I. *vt* to shake **II.** *vr:* ~**se** to sway
cimentar <e→ie> *vt* **1.** (*fundamentar*) to lay the foundations of **2.** (*consolidar*) to strengthen
cimiento *m* foundation
cinc *m* zinc
cincel *m* chisel
cincelar *vt* to chisel
cinco *adj inv, m* five; *v.t.* **ocho**
cincuenta *adj inv, m* fifty; *v.t.* **ochenta**
cine *m* **1.** (*arte*) cinema, movies *pl Am;* ~ **mudo** silent films; ~ **negro** film noir **2.** (*sala*) cinema, movie theater *Am*
cineasta *mf* film-maker
cinematógrafo *m* **1.** (*proyector*) projector **2.** (*cine*) cinema
cínico, -a I. *adj* **1.** (*descarado*) shameless **2.** (*escéptico*) cynical **II.** *m, f t.* FILOS cynic
cinismo *m* **1.** (*descaro*) shamelessness **2.** (*escepticismo*) cynicism
cinta *f* band; (*transportadora*) belt; ~ **adhesiva** adhesive tape; ~ **de vídeo** videotape
cinto *m* belt
cintura *f* waist
cinturón *m* **1.** (*correa*) belt **2.** (*de una ciudad*) belt
ciprés *m* cypress
circo *m* circus
circuito *m* **1.** *t.* ELEC circuit; **corto** ~ short circuit **2.** DEP circuit, track
circulación *f* **1.** *t.* ECON (*ciclo*) circulation **2.** (*tránsito*) traffic
circular I. *adj* circular **II.** *vi* **1.** (*recorrer*) to circulate **2.** (*personas*) to walk (around) **3.** (*vehículos*) to drive (around) **III.** *f* circular
círculo *m* circle
circuncidar *vt* to circumcise
circundar *vt* to surround
circunferencia *f t.* MAT circumference
circunscribir *irr como* **escribir I.** *vt t.* MAT to circumscribe **II.** *vr:* ~**se** to limit oneself

circunscripción *f* **1.** (*distrito*) electoral district **2.** *t.* MAT (*concreción*) circumscription
circunspecto, -a *adj* circumspect
circunstancia *f* circumstance
circunvalación *f* **carretera de** ~ bypass
cirio *m* candle
cirrosis *f inv* MED cirrhosis
ciruela *f* plum; ~ **pasa** prune
cirugía *f* MED surgery; ~ **estética** cosmetic surgery
cirujano, -a *m, f* MED surgeon
cisne *m* swan
cisterna *f* cistern, tank *Am*
cita *f* **1.** (*convocatoria*) appointment **2.** (*encuentro*) meeting; (*romántico*) date; ~ **a ciegas** blind date **3.** (*mención*) quotation
citación *f* JUR summons
citar I. *vt* **1.** (*convocar*) to arrange to meet **2.** (*mencionar*) to quote **3.** JUR to summon **II.** *vr:* ~**se** to arrange to meet
cítrico, -a *adj* citric
cítricos *mpl* citrus fruits *pl*
ciudad *f* town; (*más grande*) city; ~ **universitaria** university campus
ciudadanía *f* citizenship
ciudadano, -a I. *adj* civic **II.** *m, f* **1.** (*residente*) resident **2.** (*súbdito*) citizen
cívico, -a *adj* **1.** (*de la ciudad*) civic **2.** (*del civismo*) public-spirited
civil I. *adj* civil **II.** *m* **1.** *inf* (*persona*) civil guard **2.** (*paisano*) civilian
civilización *f* civilization
civilizar <z→c> *vt* to civilize
civismo *m* community spirit, civic-mindedness
cizaña *f* (*enemistad*) discord
cl *abr de* **centilitro** centilitre *Brit,* centiliter *Am*
clamar I. *vi* to cry out **II.** *vt* to demand
clamor *m* lament
clan *m* clan
clandestino, -a *adj* **1.** (*secreto*) secret **2.** (*movimiento*) underground
clara *f* (*del huevo*) white
claraboya *f* skylight
clarear I. *vi* **1.** (*amanecer*) to grow

light **2.** (*despejarse*) to clear up **II.** *vr:* ~**se** (*transparentarse*) to be transparent

clarete *m* rosé (wine)

claridad *f* **1.** (*luminosidad*) brightness **2.** (*lucidez*) clarity

clarificar <c→qu> *vt* to clarify

clarín *m* bugle

clarinete *m* clarinet

clarividencia *f* **1.** (*instinto*) intuition **2.** (*percepción*) clairvoyance

claro I. *interj* of course **II.** *m* **1.** (*hueco*) gap **2.** (*calvero*) clearing **3.** (*calva*) bald patch **III.** *adv* clearly

claro, -a *adj* **1.** (*iluminado*) bright; **azul** ~ light blue **2.** (*ilustre*) famous **3.** (*evidente*) clear; **sacar en** ~ to clarify

clase *f* **1.** (*tipo*) kind **2.** *t.* BIO (*categoría*) class **3.** ENS class; (*aula*) classroom

clásico, -a I. *adj* classical; *fig* classic **II.** *m, f* classic

clasificación *f* **1.** (*ordenación*) sorting **2.** *t.* BIO classification

clasificar <c→qu> **I.** *vt* **1.** (*ordenar*) to sort **2.** BIO to classify **II.** *vr:* ~**se** to qualify

claudicar <c→qu> *vi* **1.** (*principios*) to abandon **2.** (*ceder*) to give way

claustro *m* **1.** (*convento*) cloister **2.** (*de profesores*) senate

claustrofobia *f* PSICO claustrophobia

cláusula *f* JUR, LING clause; (*ley*) article

clausura *f* **1.** (*cierre*) closure **2.** (*en un convento*) cloister

clausurar *vt* to close

clavar *vt* **1.** (*hincar*) to knock in **2.** (*enclavar*) to nail **3.** (*vista*) to fix **4.** *inf* (*cobrar*) to rip off

clave I. *adj inv* key **II.** *f* **1.** (*secreto*) **de algo** key to sth **2.** (*código*) code; ~ **de acceso** password

clavel *m* carnation

clavícula *f* collar bone

clavija *f* **1.** TÉC pin **2.** (*de guitarra*) peg **3.** (*enchufe*) plug

clavo *m* **1.** (*punta*) nail **2.** (*especia*) clove

claxon *m* horn

clemencia *f* mercy

cleptómano, -a *m, f* kleptomaniac

clerical *adj* clerical

clérigo *m* clergyman

clero *m* clergy

clic *m* click

cliché *m* **1.** (*tópico*) cliché **2.** FOTO negative

cliente, -a *m, f* customer

clientela *f* customers *pl;* (*de un abogado*) clients *pl*

clima *m* **1.** (*atmósfera*) atmosphere **2.** GEO climate

climatización *f* air conditioning

climatizar <z→c> *vt* to air-condition

clímax *m inv* climax

clínica *f* clinic

clínico *m* clinical

clip *m* paper clip

clítoris *m inv* clitoris

cloaca *f* sewer; ZOOL cloaca

clonar *vt* to clone

cloro *m* chlorine

clorofila *f* chlorophyl(l)

club <clubs *o* clubes> *m* club; ~ **de alterne** hostess bar

cm *abr de* **centímetro** cm.

coacción *f* coercion

coaccionar *vt* to coerce

coagular I. *vt* to coagulate **II.** *vr:* ~**se** to coagulate, to clot

coágulo *m* clot

coalición *f* coalition

coartada *f* alibi

coartar *vt* **1.** (*libertad*) to restrict **2.** (*persona*) to inhibit

coba *f* **dar** ~ **a alguien** to suck up to sb

cobarde I. *adj* cowardly **II.** *m* coward

cobaya *m o f* guinea pig

cobertizo *m* shed

cobertor *m* bedspread, counterpane *Brit*

cobertura *f* **1.** (*cobertor*) cover **2.** COM (*acción*) coverage

cobija *f AmL* (*manta*) blanket

cobijar I. *vt* **1.** (*cubrir*) to cover **2.** (*proteger*) to shelter **II.** *vr:* ~**se** to take shelter

cobijo *m* shelter

cobra *f* cobra

cobrador(a) *m(f)* **1.** COM (*que cobra*) collector **2.** (*de tranvía*) conductor

cobrar I. *vt* **1.** (*recibir*) to receive; (*suma*) to collect; (*cheque*) to cash; (*sueldo*) to earn; **¿me cobra, por favor?** can I pay, please? **2.** (*exigir*) to levy; (*intereses*) to charge; (*deudas*) to recover II. *vi* (*sueldo*) to get one's wages

cobre *m* **1.** QUÍM copper **2.** *AmL* (*moneda*) copper coin

cobro *m* **1.** FIN (*impuestos*) collection; (*pago*) payment; **llamar a ~ revertido** to reverse the charges **2.** *pl* COM arrears *pl*

cocaína *f* cocaine

cocción *f* **1.** (*acto*) cooking **2.** (*duración*) cooking time

cocear *vi* to kick

cocer *irr* I. *vt* **1.** (*cocinar*) to cook; (*hervir*) to boil; (*al horno*) to bake **2.** (*cerámica*) to fire II. *vi* **1.** (*cocinar*) to cook **2.** (*hervir*) to boil III. *vr:* ~**se 1.** (*cocinarse*) to be cooked **2.** (*tramarse*) to be going on

coche *m* **1.** (*automóvil*) car; ~ **de bomberos** fire engine; **ir en** ~ to go by car **2.** (*de caballos*) coach, carriage

coche-bomba <coches-bomba> *m* car bomb

coche-cama <coches-cama> *m* FERRO sleeping car

cochera *f* garage; (*de tranvías*) depot

coche-restaurante <coches-restaurante> *m* FERRO dining car

coche-vivienda <coches-vivienda> *m* (large) caravan

cochinillo *m* piglet

cochino, -a I. *adj inf* filthy II. *m, f* **1.** ZOOL pig **2.** *inf* (*guarro*) swine

cocido *m* stew

cociente *m* quotient

cocina *f* **1.** (*habitación*) kitchen **2.** (*aparato*) cooker, stove *Am* **3.** (*arte*) cookery, cooking

cocinar *vt, vi* to cook

cocinero, -a *m, f* cook

coco *m* **1.** (*fruto*) coconut **2.** (*árbol*) coconut palm **3.** *inf* (*cabeza*) head; **comerse el** ~ to worry

cocodrilo *m* crocodile

cocotero *m* coconut palm

coctel <coctels> *m,* **cóctel** <cócteles> *m* cocktail

codazo *m* nudge (with one's elbow)

codear I. *vi* to nudge II. *vr:* ~**se** to rub shoulders

codicia *f* greed

codiciar *vt* to covet

codicioso, -a *adj* covetous

codificar <c→qu> *vt* **1.** JUR to codify **2.** (*con señales*) to code; *t.* INFOR to encode

código *m* code; ~ **de circulación** highway code; ~ **bancario** bank sorting code; ~ **postal** postcode *Brit,* zip code *Am*

codillo *m* **1.** ZOOL elbow **2.** TÉC (*doblez*) elbow joint

codo *m* **1.** ANAT elbow; **empinar el** ~ *inf* to go on the booze **2.** TÉC elbow joint

codorniz *f* quail

coerción *f* constraint; *t.* JUR coercion

coetáneo, -a *adj, m, f* contemporary

coexistir *vi* to coexist

cofradía *f* brotherhood

cofre *m* **1.** (*caja*) chest; (*baúl*) trunk **2.** (*de joyas*) jewel case

coger <g→j> I. *vt* **1.** (*agarrar*) to take hold; (*flor*) to pick; (*objeto caído*) to pick up; (*cosecha*) to harvest; (*trabajo*) to take (up); (*hábito*) to acquire; (*enfermedad*) to catch; ~ **del brazo** to take by the arm **2.** (*tocar*) to touch **3.** (*quitar*) to take away **4.** (*atrapar*) to catch; (*apresar*) to capture **5.** RADIO to pick up **6.** (*tren*) to take **7.** *AmL, vulg* (*copular*) to screw II. *vi* **1.** (*planta*) to take **2.** (*tener sitio*) to fit **3.** *AmL, vulg* (*copular*) to screw III. *vr:* ~**se 1.** (*pillarse*) catch **2.** *inf* (*robar*) to steal

cogollo *m* **1.** (*de lechuga*) heart **2.** (*núcleo*) core

cogorza *f* **pillar una buena** ~ to get plastered

cohabitar *vi* to live together

cohecho *m* bribery

coherencia *f* coherence

coherente *adj* coherent

cohesión *f* cohesion

cohete *m* rocket

cohibido, **-a** *adj* **1.** (*tímido*) shy **2.** (*inhibido*) inhibited

cohibir *irr como prohibir* **I.** *vt* **1.** (*intimidar*) to intimidate **2.** (*incomodar*) to inhibit **II.** *vr:* **~se** to feel inhibited

coima *f And, CSur* (*soborno*) bribe; (*dinero*) rake-off

coincidencia *f* coincidence

coincidir *vi* **1.** (*sucesos*) to coincide **2.** (*con alguien*) to meet **3.** (*estar de acuerdo*) to agree

coito *m* coitus, (sexual) intercourse

cojear *vi* (*persona*) to limp; (*mueble*) to wobble

cojera *f* limp

cojín *m* cushion

cojinete *m* TÉC bearing

cojo, **-a** **I.** *adj* **1.** (*persona*) lame; **a la pata coja** on one leg **2.** (*mueble*) wobbly **II.** *m, f* lame person

cojón *m vulg pl* (*testículos*) balls *pl;* **¡cojones!** God damn it!, bloody hell! *Brit*

cojudo, **-a** *adj AmL* (*tonto*) stupid

col *f* BOT cabbage; **~es de Bruselas** Brussels sprouts

cola *f* **1.** (*rabo*) tail **2.** (*de vestido*) train **3.** (*al esperar*) queue, line; **hacer ~** to queue (up), to line up **4.** (*de un cometa*) tail **5.** (*pegamento*) glue

colaboración *f* collaboration; (*periódico*) contribution

colaborador(a) **I.** *adj* collaborating **II.** *m(f)* collaborator; LIT contributor

colaborar *vi* **1.** (*cooperar*) to collaborate **2.** LIT to contribute

colado, **-a** *adj inf* crazy

colador *m* sieve

colapsar *vt* (*tráfico*) to bring to a standstill

colapso *m* **1.** MED collapse **2.** (*paralización*) standstill

colar <o→ue> **I.** *vt* **1.** (*filtrar*) to filter **2.** (*metal*) to cast **II.** *vi* **1.** (*penetrar: líquido*) to seep (through); (*aire*) to get in **2.** *inf* (*información*) to be credible **III.** *vr:* **~se 1.** *inf* (*entrar*) to slip in **2.** (*en una cola*) to jump the queue

colcha *f* bedspread, counterpane *Brit*

colchón *m* mattress

colchoneta *f* DEP mat

colear *vi* to wag

colección *f* collection

coleccionar *vt* to collect

coleccionista *mf* collector

colecta *f* collection

colectivo, **-a** *adj* **1.** (*todos juntos*) collective **2.** (*global*) comprehensive

colector *m* **1.** ELEC collector **2.** (*canalización*) (main) sewer

colega *mf* colleague

colegiado, **-a** **I.** *adj* collegiate **II.** *m, f* DEP (*árbitro*) referee

colegial(a) **I.** *adj* school **II.** *m(f)* (*alumno*) schoolboy *m,* schoolgirl *f*

colegio *m* **1.** ENS school; **ir al ~** to go to school **2.** AmL (*universidad*) college **3.** (*corporación*) **~ de abogados** bar association

colegir *irr como elegir vt* **1.** (*juntar*) to collect **2.** (*deducir*) to gather

cólera[1] *m* MED cholera

cólera[2] *f* (*ira*) anger

colérico, **-a** *adj* furious

colesterol *m* cholesterol

colgante **I.** *adj* hanging; **puente ~** suspension bridge **II.** *m* **1.** ARQUIT festoon **2.** (*joya*) pendant

colgar *irr* **I.** *vt* **1.** (*pender*) to hang; (*teléfono*) to put down **2.** (*suspender*) to fail **II.** *vi* **1.** (*pender*) to hang **2.** TEL (*auricular*) to hang up **III.** *vr:* **~se** to hang oneself

cólico *m* MED colic

coliflor *f* cauliflower

colilla *f* cigarette end, fag end, butt

colina *f* hill

colindar *vi* to adjoin

colisión *f* collision

collar *m* (*adorno*) necklace; (*de perro*) collar

colmado *m* grocer's shop, grocery

colmado, **-a** *adj* full

colmar **I.** *vt* **1.** (*vaso*) to fill to the brim **2.** (*esperanzas*) to fulfil *Brit,* to fulfill *Am* **II.** *vr:* **~se** to be fulfilled

colmena *f* beehive

colmillo *m* eyetooth; (*de elefante*) tusk; (*de perro*) fang

colmo *m* **¡esto es el ~!** this is the last straw!

colocación *f* **1.** (*empleo*) job **2.** (*disposición*) placing **3.** DEP (*posición*) position

colocar <c→qu> **I.** *vt* **1.** (*emplazar*) to place; (*según un orden*) to arrange; (*poner*) to put **2.** COM (*invertir*) to invest; (*mercancías*) to sell **3.** (*empleo*) to find a job for **II.** *vr:* ~**se 1.** (*empleo*) to get a job **2.** (*gafas*) to put on **3.** (*posicionarse*) to place oneself **4.** *inf* (*alcohol*) to get plastered; (*drogas*) to get high

Colombia *f* Colombia

> **?** **Colombia** (official title: **República de Colombia**) lies in the northwestern part of South America, between the Caribbean and the Pacific Ocean. The capital (**Santa Fe de**) **Bogotá** is also the largest city in the country. The official language of **Colombia** is Spanish and the monetary unit is the **peso**.

colombiano, -a *adj, m, f* Colombian
colombicultura *f* pigeon breeding
colonia *f* **1.** BIO, POL colony **2.** (*barrio*) suburb **3.** (*perfume*) cologne
colonización *f* colonization
colonizar <z→c> *vt* to colonize
colono *m* **1.** (*de una colonia*) settler **2.** (*labrador*) tenant farmer
coloquial *adj* LING colloquial
coloquio *m* **1.** (*conversación*) conversation **2.** (*congreso*) conference
color *m* **1.** (*en general*) colour *Brit,* color *Am;* **un hombre de** ~ a coloured man; **mudar de** ~ (*palidecer*) to turn pale; (*ruborizarse*) to blush **2.** (*sustancia*) dye **3.** POL (*ideología*) hue
colorado, -a *adj* **1.** (*rojo*) red; **ponerse** ~ to blush **2.** (*coloreado*) coloured *Brit,* colored *Am*
colorante *m* colouring *Brit,* coloring *Am*
colorar *vt* to colour *Brit,* to color *Am*
colorear *vt* (*dar color*) to colour *Brit,* to color *Am;* (*pintar*) to paint; (*teñir*)

to dye, to tint
colorido *m* colour(ing) *Brit,* color(ing) *Am*
coloso *m* colossus
columna *f* column; ~ **vertebral** ANAT spinal column
columpiar **I.** *vt* (*balancear*) to swing (to and fro) **II.** *vr:* ~**se** to swing
columpio *m* (*para niños*) swing
colza *f* rape
coma¹ *m* MED coma
coma² *f* LING comma
comadre *f* **1.** *inf* (*comadrona*) midwife **2.** (*madrina*) godmother **3.** *inf* (*vecina*) neighbour *Brit,* neighbor *Am* **4.** *inf* (*chismosa*) gossip
comadrear *vi inf* to gossip
comadreja *f* weasel
comadrona *f* midwife
comandancia *f* command
comandante *m* commander
comandar *vi, vt* to command
comando *m* MIL command; ~ **de arranque** INFOR start command
comarca *f* (*zona*) area; (*región*) region
comba *f* **1.** (*curvatura*) bend **2.** (*cuerda*) skipping rope; **saltar a la** ~ to skip
combar **I.** *vt* to bend **II.** *vr:* ~**se** to bend; (*madera*) to warp
combate *m* **1.** (*lucha*) combat; (*batalla*) battle **2.** (*de boxeo*) match
combatiente *adj, mf* combatant
combatir *vt, vi* to fight
combi *m* fridge-freezer, refrigerator-freezer *Am*
combinación *f* **1.** (*composición*) combination **2.** QUÍM compound **3.** (*de transportes*) connection **4.** (*lencería*) slip
combinar **I.** *vi* to go **II.** *vt* **1.** (*componer*) to combine **2.** (*unir*) to unite **3.** (*coordinar*) to coordinate **4.** MAT to permutate **III.** *vr:* ~**se** to combine
combustible **I.** *adj* combustible **II.** *m* fuel
combustión *f* combustion
comedia *f* **1.** TEAT (*obra*) play; (*divertida*) comedy **2.** CINE comedy **3.** *inf* (*farsa*) farce
comediante, -a *m, f* CINE, TEAT actor

comedido, -a *adj* moderate

comedor *m* (*sala*) dining room; (*en una empresa*) canteen

comensal *mf* fellow diner

comentar *vt* **1.** (*hablar sobre algo*) to talk about; (*hacer comentarios*) to comment on **2.** (*criticar*) to discuss

comentario *m* **1.** (*general*) comment; (*análisis*) commentary **2.** *pl* (*murmuraciones*) gossip

comentarista *mf* commentator

comenzar *irr como empezar vt, vi* to begin, to commence

comer **I.** *vi* **1.** (*alimentarse*) to eat **2.** (*almorzar*) to have lunch; **antes/después de ~** before/after lunch **II.** *vt* **1.** (*ingerir*) to eat **2.** *fig* (*consumir*) to consume **III.** *vr:* **~se 1.** (*ingerir*) to eat up **2.** (*corroer*) to eat away

comercial¹ **I.** *adj* commercial **II.** *mf* (*profesión*) sales representative

comercial² *m AmL* (*anuncio*) commercial

comerciante, -a *m, f* shopkeeper; (*negociante*) dealer

comerciar *vi* **1.** COM to trade **2.** (*traficar*) to deal

comercio *m* **1.** (*actividad*) trade **2.** (*tienda*) shop

comestibles *mpl* foods; **tienda de ~** grocer's (shop), grocery

cometa¹ *m* ASTR comet

cometa² *f* (*de papel*) kite

cometer *vt t. t.* JUR to commit **2.** COM to give commission

cometido *m* **1.** (*encargo*) assignment **2.** (*obligación*) commitment

comezón *f* itch

cómic *m* <cómics> comic

comicios *mpl* POL elections *pl*

cómico, -a **I.** *adj* (*de la comedia*) comedy; (*divertido*) comical **II.** *m, f* comedian

comida *f* **1.** (*alimento*) food; (*plato*) meal; (*cocina*) cooking; **~ principal** main meal **2.** (*almuerzo*) lunch

comidilla *f inf* **ser la ~** to be the talk

comienzo *m* (*principio*) beginning; **al ~** at first

comillas *fpl* inverted commas; **entre ~** in inverted commas

comilona *f inf* feast, blowout *inf*

comino *m* cumin; **no valer un ~** *inf* not to be worth anything

comisaría *f* **1.** (*depolicía*) police station, precinct *Am* **2.** (*cargo*) commissionership

comisario, -a *m, f* **1.** (*delegado*) commissioner **2.** (*de policía*) chief police inspector

comisión *f* **1.** (*cometido*) assignment **2.** (*delegación*) commission; (*comité*) committee; **Comisión Europea** POL European Commission **3.** COM commission

comité *m* committee

comitiva *f* procession

como **I.** *adv* **1.** (*del modo que*) as, like; **hazlo ~ quieras** do it any way you like **2.** (*comparativo*) as; **tan alto ~...** as tall as … **3.** (*aproximadamente*) about **4.** (*y también*) as well as **5.** (*en calidad de*) as; **trabajar ~ ...** to work as… **II.** *conj* **1.** (*causal*) as, since **2.** (*condicional*) if

cómo *adv* **1.** (*exclamativo*) how; **¿~ estás?** how are you?; **¿~?** sorry? **2.** (*por qué*) why

cómoda *f* chest (of drawers), dresser *Am*

comodidad *f* **1.** (*confort*) comfort **2.** (*conveniencia*) convenience

comodín *m* **1.** (*en juegos*) joker **2.** INFOR wild card **3.** (*pretexto*) pretext

cómodo, -a *adj* **1.** *ser* (*conveniente*) convenient **2.** *ser* (*perezoso*) lazy **3.** *estar* (*a gusto*) comfortable

compact (**disc**) *m* compact disc

compacto, -a *adj* compact

compadecer *irr como crecer* **I.** *vt* to feel sorry for **II.** *vr:* **~se** to (take) pity

compadre *m* **1.** (*padrino*) godfather **2.** (*amigo*) friend, mate *Brit,* buddy

compaginar **I.** *vt* **1.** (*combinar*) to combine **2.** (*paginar*) to page up **II.** *vr:* **~se** to combine

compañerismo *m* comradeship; DEP team spirit

compañero, -a *m, f* companion; (*amigo*) friend

compañía *f* company; **animal de ~** pet

comparación *f* comparison
comparar I. *vt* to compare II. *vr:* ~**se** to be compared
comparativo *m* comparative
comparecer *irr como crecer vi t.* JUR to appear (in court)
comparsa *mf* extra
compartim(i)ento *m* compartment
compartir *vt* 1. (*tener en común*) to share 2. (*repartirse*) to share (out)
compás *m* 1. (*en dibujo*) compass 2. (*ritmo*) beat; MÚS time 3. AERO, NÁUT (*brújula*) compass
compasión *f* pity, compassion
compasivo, -a *adj* compassionate
compatibilidad *f* compatibility
compatible *adj* compatible
compatriota *mf* compatriot, fellow citizen
compendiar *vt* to summarize
compendio *m* 1. (*resumen*) summary 2. (*manual*) textbook
compenetrarse *vr* to reach an understanding
compensación *f* compensation
compensar *vt* to compensate
competencia *f* 1. *t.* COM, DEP competition 2. *t.* LING competence 3. (*responsabilidad*) responsibility
competente *adj* competent
competición *f* competition
competir *irr como pedir vi* to compete
competitivo, -a *adj* competitive
compilador *m* INFOR compiler
compilar *vt t.* INFOR to compile
compinche *mf pey, inf* mate *Brit,* buddy
complacencia *f* 1. (*agrado*) willingness; (*placer*) pleasure 2. (*indulgencia*) indulgence
complacer *irr como crecer* I. *vt* (*gustar*) to please II. *vr:* ~**se** to be pleased
complaciente *adj* obliging
complejo, -a *adj* complex
complemento *m* 1. *t.* LING complement 2. (*paga*) supplementary payment 3. *pl* (*accesorio*) accessory
completar I. *vt* to complete II. *vr:* ~**se** to complete each other
completo, -a *adj* 1. (*íntegro*) complete 2. (*lleno*) full; (*espectáculo*) sold out
complexión *f* constitution
complicar <c→qu> *vt* to complicate
cómplice *mf t.* JUR accomplice
complo *m* <complós>, **complot** *m* <complots> conspiracy
componente *m t.* TÉC component; MAT, QUÍM constituent
componer *irr como poner* I. *vt* 1. (*formar*) to put together; (*organizar*) to organize 2. (*constituir*) to make up 3. *t.* MÚS to compose 4. TIPO to set (up) 5. (*recomponer*) to repair II. *vr:* ~**se** to consist
comportamiento *m* conduct, behaviour *Brit,* behavior *Am; t.* TÉC performance
comportar I. *vt* to involve II. *vr:* ~**se** to behave
composición *f* composition
compositor(a) *m(f)* composer
compost *m sin pl* compost
compostura *f* 1. (*corrección*) repair 2. (*aspecto*) tidiness 3. (*comedimiento*) composure
compra *f* purchase; **ir de** ~**s** to go shopping
comprador(a) *m(f)* buyer
comprar *vt* to buy
comprender *vt* 1. (*entender*) to understand; ~ **mal** to misunderstand 2. (*contener*) to comprise; (*incluir*) to include
comprensible *adj* understandable
comprensión *f* 1. (*capacidad*) understanding 2. (*entendimiento*) comprehension
comprensivo, -a *adj* 1. (*benévolo*) understanding 2. (*tolerante*) tolerant
compresa *f* 1. *t.* MED (*apósito*) compress 2. (*higiénica*) sanitary towel *Brit,* sanitary napkin *Am*
comprimido *m* pill
comprimir I. *vt* 1. *t.* FÍS, TÉC to compress 2. (*reprimir*) to restrain II. *vr:* ~**se** to control oneself
comprobante *m* voucher, proof
comprobar <o→ue> *vt* 1. (*controlar*) to check 2. (*verificar*) to verify; (*probar*) to prove
comprometer I. *vt* 1. (*implicar*) to

involve **2.**(*exponer*) to endanger **3.**(*arriesgar*) to put at risk **II.** *vr:* **~se 1.**(*implicarse*) to compromise oneself **2.**(*obligarse*) to commit oneself
compromiso *m* **1.**(*vinculación*) commitment; (*obligación*) obligation **2.**(*promesa*) promise **3.**(*acuerdo*) agreement **4.**(*aprieto*) awkward situation **5.**(*cita*) engagement
compuesto *m t.* QUÍM compound
compungido, -a *adj* **1.**(*contrito*) remorseful **2.**(*triste*) sad
computador *m AmL* computer
computadora *f AmL* computer
cómputo *m* calculation; (*de votos*) count
comulgar <g→gu> *vi* REL to take communion
común *adj* common; **sentido ~** common sense; **poco ~** unusual
comunicación *f* **1.**(*en general*) communication **2.**(*conexión*) connection; **~ telefónica** telephone call
comunicado *m* communiqué
comunicar <c→qu> **I.** *vi* **1.**(*conectar*) to connect **2.**(*teléfono*) to be engaged [*o* busy *Am*] **II.** *vt* **1.**(*informar*) to inform **2.**(*transmitir*) to communicate **3.**(*unir*) to connect **III.** *vr:* **~se 1.**(*entenderse*) to communicate **2.**(*relacionarse*) to be connected
comunicativo, -a *adj* communicative
comunidad *f* community; **~ autónoma** autonomous region
comunión *f* communion
comunismo *m* POL communism
comunista *adj, mf* communist
comunitario, -a *adj* **1.**(*colectivo*) communal **2.**(*municipal*) community **3.** POL (*Comunidad Europea*) Community
con *prep* **1.**(*compañía, modo*) with; **~ el tiempo...** with time ... **2.** MAT **3 ~ 5** 3 point 5 **3.**(*actitud*) (**para**) **~** to, towards **4.**(*circunstancia*) **~ este tiempo...** in this weather ...; **~ sólo que** +*subj* if only
conato *m* attempt
concebir *irr como pedir vt, vi* to conceive

conceder *vt* **1.**(*otorgar*) to grant; (*palabra*) **2.**(*admitir*) to concede
concejal(a) *m(f)* town councillor *Brit,* councilman *m Am,* councilwoman *f Am*
concejo *m* council
concentración *f* concentration
concentrar *vt* to concentrate
concepción *f* conception
concepto *m* concept; **bajo ningún ~** on no account
concertación *f* coordination; **~ social** social harmony
concertar <e→ie> **I.** *vi* to agree **II.** *vt* **1.**(*arreglar*) to arrange **2.** MÚS (*afinar*) to tune **3.**(*armonizar*) to harmonize
concesión *f* **1.** *t.* COM concession **2.**(*de un premio*) awarding
concesionario, -a *m, f* dealer
concha *f* shell
conciencia *f* **1.**(*conocimiento*) awareness **2.**(*moral*) conscience; (**sin**) **cargo de ~** (without) remorse
concienciar **I.** *vt* to make aware **II.** *vr:* **~se** to become aware
concienzudo, -a *adj* conscientious
concierto *m* MÚS (*función*) concert; (*obra*) concerto
conciliar *vt* to reconcile; **~ el sueño** to get to sleep
concilio *m t.* REL council
conciso, -a *adj* concise
conciudadano, -a *m, f* fellow citizen
concluir *irr como huir* **I.** *vt* **1.**(*terminar*) to complete **2.**(*deducir*) to conclude **II.** *vr:* **~se** to end
conclusión *f* conclusion; **en ~** (*en suma*) in short; (*por último*) in conclusion
concluyente *adj* conclusive
concordar <o→ue> **I.** *vi* **1.**(*coincidir*) to coincide **2.** LING to agree **II.** *vt* to reconcile
concordia *f* harmony
concretar **I.** *vt* **1.**(*precisar*) to put in concrete form **2.**(*limitar*) to limit **II.** *vr:* **~se** to limit oneself
concreto, -a *adj* concrete; **en ~** specifically
concurrido, -a *adj* crowded

concurrir *vi* 1.(*en un lugar*) to come together; (*en el tiempo*) to coincide 2.(*participar*) to take part

concursante *mf* competitor, contestant

concursar *vi* to compete

concurso *m* 1.*t.* DEP competition 2.(*ayuda*) help

conde(sa) *m(f)* count *m*, countess *f*

condecoración *f* MIL decoration

condecorar *vt* MIL to decorate

condena *f* sentence, conviction

condenar I.*vt* 1.(*sentenciar*) to condemn 2.REL to damn II.*vr:* ~**se** 1.REL to be damned 2.(*acusarse*) to confess

condensar *vt* to condense

condesa *f v.* **conde**

condescender <e→ie> *vi* 1.(*avenirse*) to agree 2.(*rebajarse*) to condescend

condición *f* 1.(*índole de una cosa*) nature 2.(*estado*) condition; **a** ~ **de que** +*subj* providing that 3.(*clase*) social class

condicional *adj t.* LING conditional

condicionar *vt* 1.(*supeditar*) ~ **a algo** to make conditional on sth 2.(*acondicionar*) to condition

condimento *m* seasoning

condolerse <o→ue> *vr* to sympathize

condón *m* condom

conducir *irr como traducir* I.*vt* 1.(*llevar*) to take 2.(*guiar*) to guide 3.(*arrastrar*) to lead 4.(*pilotar*) to drive II.*vi* 1.(*dirigir*) to lead 2.(*pilotar*) to drive III.*vr:* ~**se** to behave

conducta *f* conduct, behaviour *Brit*, behavior *Am*

conducto *m* 1.(*tubo*) pipe 2.MED canal 3.(*mediación*) channels *pl*

conductor *m* FÍS conductor

conductor(a) I.*adj* conductive II.*m(f)* 1.(*chófer*) driver 2.(*jefe*) leader

conectar I.*vt* 1.(*enlazar*) to connect 2.(*enchufar*) to plug in II.*vi* to communicate

conejillo *m* ~ **de Indias** *t. fig* guinea pig

conejo, -a *m, f* rabbit

conexión *f t.* TEL connection

confección *f* making; (*de vestidos*) dressmaking

confeccionar *vt* to make; (*plan*) to draw up

confederación *f* confederation

conferencia *f* 1.(*charla*) lecture 2.(*encuentro*) conference 3.(*telefónica*) call

conferir *irr como sentir vt* to confer

confesar <e→ie> *vt, vr:* ~**se** to confess

confesión *f* confession

confes(i)onario *m* confessional (box)

confeti *m* confetti

confiado, -a *adj* 1.*ser* (*crédulo*) trusting 2.*estar* (*de sí mismo*) self--confident

confianza *f* 1.(*crédito*) trust 2.(*esperanza*) confidence 3.(*en uno mismo*) self-confidence 4.(*familiaridad*) familiarity

confiar <1.*pres:* confío> I.*vi* to trust II.*vt* to entrust III.*vr:* ~**se** to confide

confidencia *f* secret

confidencial *adj* confidential

confidente *mf* 1.(*cómplice*) confidant *m* 2.(*espía*) informer

configurar I.*vt* 1.(*formar*) to shape 2.INFOR to configure II.*vr:* ~**se** to take shape

confinar I.*vi* to border II.*vt* to confine

confirmación *f t.* REL confirmation

confirmar I.*vt t.* REL to confirm II.*vr:* ~**se** to be confirmed

confiscar <c→qu> *vt* to confiscate

confitura *f* jam

conflicto *m* conflict

confluir *irr como huir vi* (*ríos, calles*) to meet

conformar I.*vt* 1.(*contentar*) to satisfy 2.(*formar*) to shape II.*vr:* ~**se** 1.(*contentarse*) to be satisfied 2.(*ajustarse*) to adjust

conforme I.*adj* satisfied II.*prep* according to III.*conj* (*como*) as

conformidad *f* 1.(*afinidad*) similarity 2.(*aprobación*) approval

confort *m sin pl* comfort

confortable *adj* comfortable
confortar I. *vt* 1. (*vivificar*) to encourage 2. (*consolar*) to comfort II. *vr*: ~se 1. (*reanimarse*) to regain one's strength 2. (*consolarse*) to take comfort
confraternizar <z→c> *vi* to fraternize
confrontar I. *vt* 1. (*comparar*) to compare 2. (*enfrentar*) to confront II. *vr*: ~se to face up
confundir I. *vt* 1. (*trastocar*) to mistake 2. (*mezclar*) to mix up II. *vr*: ~se 1. (*mezclarse*) to mix 2. (*embrollarse*) to get confused
confusión *f* confusion
confuso, -a *adj* confused
congelador *m* freezer
congelar(se) *vt*, (*vr*) *t. fig* to freeze
congénere *mf* **el ladrón y sus ~s** the likes of the thief
congeniar *vi* to get on
congestión *f t.* MED congestion
congestionar I. *vt t.* MED to congest II. *vr*: ~se *t.* MED to become congested
congoja *f* 1. (*pena*) sorrow 2. (*desconsuelo*) anguish
congraciar I. *vt* to win over II. *vr*: ~se to ingratiate oneself
congratular(se) *vt*, (*vr*) to congratulate
congregación *f* 1. (*reunión*) meeting 2. REL congregation
congregar <g→gu> I. *vt* to bring together II. *vr*: ~se to gather
congresista *mf* POL delegate, congressman *m*, congresswoman *f*
congreso *m* congress
cónico, -a *adj* conical
conífera *f* conifer
conjetura *f* conjecture
conjeturar *vt* to speculate
conjugación *f* conjugation
conjugar <g→gu> *vt* 1. (*combinar*) to combine 2. LING to conjugate
conjunción *f* conjunction
conjuntivitis *f inv* conjunctivitis
conjunto *m* 1. (*unido*) unit 2. (*totalidad*) whole; **en** ~ as a whole 3. (*ropa*) outfit 4. MAT set
conjurar I. *vt* 1. (*invocar*) to beseech

2. (*alejar*) to ward off II. *vr*: ~se to conspire
conmemoración *f* commemoration
conmemorar *vt* to commemorate
conmigo *pron pers* with me
conminar *vt* to threaten
conmoción *f* 1. MED concussion 2. *fig* shock
conmovedor(a) *adj* 1. (*conmocionando*) stirring 2. (*sentimental*) moving
conmover <o→ue> I. *vt* 1. (*emocionar*) to move 2. (*sacudir*) to shake II. *vr*: ~se to be moved
conmutador *m* ELEC switch
cono *m* cone

[?] The economic union between the four countries in the most southerly part of Latin America, **Argentina, Chile, Paraguay** and **Uruguay**, is referred to as **Cono Sur.**

conocedor(a) I. *adj* knowledgeable II. *m(f)* expert
conocer *irr como crecer* I. *vt* 1. (*saber, tener trato*) to know 2. (*reconocer*) to recognize 3. (*por primera vez*) to meet II. *vi* ~ **de algo** to know about sth III. *vr*: ~se to know each other
conocido, -a I. *adj* (well-)known II. *m, f* acquaintance
conocimiento *m* 1. (*saber*) knowledge 2. (*consciencia*) consciousness 3. *pl* (*nociones*) knowledge
conque *conj inf* so
conquense *adj* of/from Cuenca
conquista *f* conquest
conquistar *vt* to conquer
consagrar I. *vt* 1. REL to consecrate 2. (*dedicar*) to dedicate II. *vr*: ~se to devote oneself
consciencia *f* consciousness
consciente *adj* conscious; **ser** ~ to be aware
consecución *f* attainment
consecuencia *f* 1. (*efecto*) consequence 2. (*coherencia*) consistency
consecuente *adj* consistent

consecutivo, -a *adj* consecutive
conseguir *irr como seguir* vt **1.**(*obtener*) to get **2.**(*beca*) to obtain
consejero, -a *m, f* **1.**(*guía*) adviser **2.**(*miembro de un consejo*) member **3.**(*de una autonomía*) minister
consejo *m* **1.**(*recomendación*) piece of advice **2.**(*organismo*) council; **Consejo Europeo** Council of Europe **3.**(*reunión*) meeting
consenso *m* consensus
consentimiento *m* ~ **para algo** consent to sth
consentir *irr como sentir* I. *vi* (*admitir*) to agree II. *vt* **1.**(*autorizar*) to allow; (*tolerar*) to tolerate **2.**(*mimar*) to spoil
conserje *mf* **1.**(*hotel*) concierge, receptionist **2.**(*portero*) (hall) porter
conserva *f* **1.**(*enlatado*) tinned food *Brit,* canned food *Am* **2.**(*conservación*) preserving
conservación *f* **1.**(*mantenimiento*) maintenance **2.**(*guarda*) conservation
conservador(a) *adj, m(f)* conservative
conservante *m* preservative
conservar I. *vt* **1.**(*mantener*) to maintain **2.**(*guardar*) to conserve **3.**(*hacer conservas*) to can **4.**(*tradición*) to preserve II. *vr:* ~**se** to survive; (*mantenerse*) to keep
conservatorio *m* conservatory
considerable *adj* considerable
consideración *f* **1.**(*reflexión*) consideration **2.**(*respeto*) respect
considerado, -a *adj* **1.**(*tener en cuenta*) considered **2.**(*apreciado*) respected
considerar *vt* to consider
consigna *f* **1.** MIL motto **2.** POL instruction **3.**(*de equipajes*) left-luggage (office) *Brit,* checkroom *Am*
consigo *pron pers* (*con él*) with him; (*con ella*) with her

⚠ **consigo** (= with him, with himself): "Jaime lleva siempre un bolígrafo consigo; Él habla a menudo consigo mismo." **consigo** is also the first person of the verb conseguir (= to achieve, to manage to): "Siempre consigo lo que me propongo."

consiguiente *adj* resulting; **por** ~ consequently
consistente *adj* consistent; (*argumento*) sound; GASTR thick; ~ **en** consisting of
consistir *vi* **1.**(*componerse*) to consist **2.**(*radicar*) to lie
consola *f* **1.**(*mesa*) console table **2.** ELEC console; (*de videojuegos*) video console
consolación *f* consolation
consolar <o→ue> *vt* to console
consolidar I. *vt* to consolidate II. *vr:* ~**se** to be consolidated
consomé *m* consommé
consonante I. *adj* **1.**(*que rima*) rhyming **2.**(*armonioso*) harmonious II. *f* LING consonant
consorcio *m* consortium
conspiración *f* conspiracy
conspirar *vi* to conspire
constancia *f* **1.**(*firmeza*) constancy **2.**(*certeza*) certainty; **dejar** ~ to show evidence
constante *adj* constant
constar *vi* **1.**(*ser cierto*) to be clear **2.**(*figurar*) to put on record **3.**(*componerse*) to consist
constatar *vt* to confirm
constelación *f* constellation
consternación *f* consternation
consternar I. *vt* to dismay II. *vr:* ~**se** to be dismayed
constipado *m* cold
constipado, -a *adj* **estar** ~ to have a cold
constiparse *vr* to catch a cold
constitución *f t.* POL constitution
constitucional *adj* constitutional
constituir *irr como huir* I. *vt* **1.**(*formar*) to constitute **2.**(*ser*) to be **3.**(*establecer*) to establish II. *vr:* ~**se** to become
constitutivo, -a *adj* constituent

constreñir *irr como ceñir vt* **1.** *(obligar)* to constrain **2.** *(cohibir)* to restrict

construcción *f* **1.** *(acción)* construction **2.** *(edificio)* building

constructivo, -a *adj* constructive

constructor(a) *m(f)* builder

construir *irr como huir vt* to build

consuelo *m* consolation

cónsul *mf* consul

consulado *m* consulate

consulta *f* **1.** *(acción)* consultation **2.** *(de un médico)* surgery

consultar *vt* to consult

consultorio *m* *(establecimiento)* consultancy; *(de un médico)* surgery

consumar *vt* to carry out; *(matrimonio)* to consummate

consumición *f* **1.** *(bar)* drink **2.** *(agotamiento)* consumption

consumidor(a) *m(f)* consumer

consumir I. *vt* **1.** *(gastar)* to consume **2.** *(acabar)* to use **3.** *(comer)* to eat II. *vr:* ~**se** **1.** *(persona)* to waste away **2.** *(gastarse)* to be consumed

consumismo *m* consumerism

consumo *m* consumption; **sociedad de** ~ consumer society

contabilidad *f* **1.** *(sistema)* accounting **2.** *(profesión)* accountancy

contabilizar <z→c> *vt* to enter

contable I. *adj* countable II. *mf* accountant

contactar *vi, vt* to contact

contacto *m* contact

contado *m* **pagar al** ~ to pay (in) cash

contador *m* meter

contagiar I. *vt* to transmit, to infect II. *vr:* ~**se** to become infected

contagio *m* contagion

contagioso, -a *adj* contagious; **tener una risa contagiosa** to have a contagious laugh

contaminación *f* pollution

contaminar I. *vt* **1.** *(infestar)* to pollute **2.** *(contagiar)* to infect II. *vr:* ~**se** **1.** *(infectarse)* to become contaminated **2.** *(contagiarse)* to become infected

contante *adj* ~ **y sonante** in hard

cash

contar <o→ue> I. *vi* to count; ~ **con** *(confiar)* to rely on; *(tener en cuenta)* to expect II. *vt* **1.** *(numerar, incluir)* to count **2.** *(narrar)* to tell

contemplación *f* contemplation

contemplar *vt* **1.** *(mirar)* to look at **2.** *(considerar)* to consider

contemplativo, -a *adj* contemplative

contemporáneo, -a *adj, m, f* contemporary

contendiente *mf* contender

contenedor *m* **1.** *(general)* container **2.** *(escombros)* skip *Brit,* dumpster *Am*

contener *irr como tener* I. *vt* **1.** *(encerrar)* to contain **2.** *(refrenar)* to hold back II. *vr:* ~**se** to contain oneself

contenido *m* **1.** *(incluido)* contents *pl* **2.** *(concentración)* content

contentar I. *vt* to satisfy II. *vr:* ~**se** to be contented

contento, -a *adj* **1.** *(alegre)* happy **2.** *(satisfecho)* content

contestación *f* **1.** *(respuesta)* answer **2.** *(protesta)* protest

contestador *m* answering machine

contestar *vt* to answer back

contestatario, -a *m, f* rebel

contexto *m* context

contienda *f* dispute

contigo *pron pers* with you

contiguo, -a *adj* adjoining

continental *adj* continental

continente *m* continent

contingencia *f* **1.** *(eventualidad)* eventuality **2.** *t.* FILOS contingency **3.** *(riesgo)* risk

contingente I. *adj* possible II. *m* **1.** ECON quota **2.** MIL contingent

continuación *f* continuation; **a** ~ next

continuar <1. pres: continúo> *vi, vt* to continue

continuidad *f* continuity

continuo, -a *adj* continuous

contorno *m* **1.** *(de una figura)* outline **2.** *(pl)* *(territorio)* surrounding area

contra[1] I. *prep* against; **tener en** ~

to object **II.** *m* **los pros y los** ~**s** the pros and the cons

contra² *f* **1.** (*oposición*) **llevar la** ~ to contradict **2.** (*guerilla*) contra

contraataque *m* MIL counterattack

contrabajo *m* double bass

contrabandista *mf* smuggler

contrabando *m sin pl* **1.** (*comercio*) smuggling **2.** (*mercancía*) contraband

contracción *f* contraction

contrachapado *m* plywood

contracorriente *f sin pl* crosscurrent

contradecir *irr como decir vt* to contradict

contradicción *f* contradiction

contradictorio, -a *adj* contradictory

contraer *irr como traer* **I.** *vt* **1.** (*encoger*) to contract **2.** (*enfermedad*) to catch **3.** (*limitar*) to limit **II.** *vr:* ~**se 1.** (*encogerse*) to contract **2.** (*limitarse*) to limit oneself

contraespionaje *m* counterespionage

contrafuerte *m* ARQUIT buttress

contraluz *m o f* back light(ing)

contramanifestación *f* counterdemonstration

contraofensiva *f* counteroffensive

contrapartida *f* **1.** (*compensación*) compensation **2.** (*contabilidad*) balancing entry

contrapelo *adv* **a** ~ *t. fig* the wrong way

contrapesar *vt* to counterbalance, to offset

contrapeso *m* counterweight

contraportada *f* back cover

contraproducente *adj* counterproductive

contrariar <*1. pres:* contrarío> *vt* **1.** (*oponerse*) to oppose **2.** (*disgustar*) to upset

contrariedad *f* **1.** (*inconveniente*) obstacle **2.** (*disgusto*) annoyance

contrario, -a **I.** *adj* (*opuesto*) contrary; (*perjudicial*) harmful; **en caso** ~ otherwise; **de lo** ~ or else **II.** *m, f* opponent

contrarrestar *vt* to counteract

contrasentido *m* contradiction

contraseña *f* password

contrastar **I.** *vi* to contrast **II.** *vt* **1.** (*oro*) to hallmark **2.** (*peso*) to verify

contraste *m* contrast

contratar *vt* **1.** (*trabajador*) to hire **2.** (*encargar*) to contract

contratiempo *m* setback

contratista *mf* contractor

contrato *m* contract

contravenir *irr como venir vt* to contravene

contraventana *f* shutter

contribución *f* **1.** (*aportación*) contribution **2.** (*impuesto*) tax

contribuir *irr como huir* **I.** *vi* **1.** (*ayudar*) to contribute **2.** (*tributar*) to pay taxes **II.** *vt* to contribute

contribuyente *mf* taxpayer

contrincante *mf* opponent

control *m* control; (*inspección*) inspection; ~ **a distancia** TÉC remote control

controlador *m* INFOR driver

controlador(a) *m(f)* controller

controlar **I.** *vt* (*confirmar*) to check; (*regir*) to control **II.** *vr:* ~**se** to control oneself

controversia *f* controversy

contundente *adj* **1.** (*objeto*) contusive **2.** *fig* convincing **3.** (*prueba*) conclusive

contusión *f* MED bruise

convalecencia *f* convalescence

convalecer *irr como crecer vi* to convalesce

convaleciente *mf* convalescent

convalidar *vt* **1.** (*título*) to (re)validate **2.** (*confirmar*) to confirm, to recognize

convencer <c→z> **I.** *vt* to persuade **II.** *vr:* ~**se** to be convinced

convencimiento *m sin pl* conviction

convención *f* convention

convencional *adj* conventional

conveniencia *f* **1.** (*provecho*) usefulness **2.** (*acuerdo*) agreement

conveniente *adj* **1.** (*adecuado*) suitable **2.** (*provechoso*) advisable

convenio *m* agreement

convenir *irr como venir* **I.** *vi* **1.** (*acordar*) to agree **2.** (*ser oportuno*) to be advisable **II.** *vr:* **~se** to agree

convento *m* **1.** (*de monjes*) monastery **2.** (*de monjas*) convent

convergencia *f* convergence

converger <g→j> *vi,* **convergir** <g→j> *vi* **1.** (*líneas*) to converge **2.** (*coincidir*) to coincide

conversación *f* conversation

conversar *vi* to talk

conversión *f* conversion

convertir *irr como sentir* **I.** *vt* **1.** (*transformar*) to turn into **2.** REL, TÉC to convert **II.** *vr:* **~se 1.** (*transformarse*) to turn into **2.** REL to convert

convexo, -a *adj* convex

convicción *f* conviction

convicto, -a *adj* convicted

convidado, -a *m, f* guest

convidar *vt* to invite

convincente *adj* convincing

convite *m* **1.** (*invitación*) invitation **2.** (*banquete*) banquet

convivencia *f* living together; *fig* co-existence

convivir *vi* to live together; *fig* to co-exist

convocar <c→qu> *vt* **1.** (*citar*) to summon; (*reunir*) to call (together); MIL to call up **2.** (*concurso*) to announce

convocatoria *f* **1.** (*citación*) summons **2.** (*de un concurso*) official announcement **3.** (*de una conferencia*) notification

convulsión *f* **1.** MED convulsion **2.** POL upheaval **3.** GEO tremor

conyugal *adj* marital

cónyuge *mf form* spouse

coñá *m,* **coñac** *m* <coñacs> cognac

coñazo *m vulg* pain in the arse [*o ass Am*] *vulg*

coño **I.** *interj vulg* damn, bloody hell *Brit* **II.** *m vulg* cunt, fanny *Brit,* pussy *Am* **III.** *adj Chile, pey* Spaniard

cooperación *f* cooperation

cooperar *vi* **1.** (*juntamente*) to cooperate **2.** (*participar*) to collaborate

cooperativa *f* cooperative, co-op

coordinador(a) **I.** *adj* coordinating **II.** *m(f)* coordinator

coordinar *vt* to coordinate

copa *f* **1.** (*vaso*) glass; **ir de ~s** to go out for a drink **2.** (*de árbol*) top **3.** (*de sujetador*) cup **4.** DEP cup

copar *vt* **1.** MIL (*rodear*) to surround **2.** (*acorralar*) to corner **3.** (*premios*) to win

Copenhague *m* Copenhagen

copia *f* **1.** (*de un escrito*) copy; **~ de seguridad** INFOR back-up copy **2.** ARTE (*réplica*) replica **3.** FOTO print

copiar *vt* to copy

copiloto, -a *m, f* AERO copilot; AUTO co-driver

copioso, -a *adj* (*exuberante*) copious; (*abundante*) abundant

copla *f* **1.** LIT verse **2.** MÚS popular song

copo *m* flake; **~ de nieve** snowflake; **~s de maíz** cornflakes

coprocesador *m* INFOR co-processor

copropietario, -a *m, f* co-owner

copular *vi* to copulate

coqueta *f* **1.** (*chica*) flirt **2.** (*mueble*) dressing table

coquetear *vi* to flirt

coraje *m* **1.** (*valor*) courage **2.** (*ira*) anger

coral **I.** *adj* choral **II.** *m t.* ZOOL coral **III.** *f* (*coro*) choir

coraza *f* **1.** MIL cuirass **2.** NÁUT armour-plating *Brit,* armor-plating *Am* **3.** ZOOL shell

corazón *m* **1.** *t. fig* ANAT heart; **~ (mío)** darling; **de todo ~** with all one's heart; **no tener ~** to be heartless; **hacer de tripas ~** to pluck up courage **2.** BOT core

corazonada *f* **1.** (*presentimiento*) hunch **2.** (*impulso*) sudden impulse

corbata *f* tie

Córcega *f* Corsica

corchea *f* quaver

corchete *m* **1.** (*broche*) hook and eye **2.** TIPO square bracket

corcho *m* **1.** (*material, tapón*) cork **2.** (*en la pesca*) float

cordel *m* cord

cordero *m* **1.** (*carne*) lamb **2.** (*piel*) lambskin

cordero, -a *m, f* lamb

cordial *adj, m* cordial

cordialidad *f* cordiality

cordillera *f* mountain range

cordón *m* **1.** (*cordel*) cord; (*del uniforme*) braid; (*de zapatos*) shoelace **2.** ELEC flex *Brit,* cord *Am* **3.** MIL cordon

cordura *f* **1.** (*razón*) good sense **2.** (*prudencia*) prudence

Corea *f* Korea

coreografía *f* choreography

córner *m* DEP corner

corneta *f* cornet; (*en el ejército*) bugle

cornisa *f* cornice; **la ~ cantábrica** the Cantabrian Coast

coro *m* ARQUIT, MÚS choir

corona *f* **1.** (*adorno*) crown **2.** (*de flores*) garland, wreath **3.** ASTR corona

coronación *f* **1.** (*de un rey*) coronation **2.** (*de una acción*) culmination

coronar *vt* to crown

coronel(a) *m(f)* colonel

coronilla *f* crown (of the head); **estar hasta la ~** *inf* to be fed up to the back teeth

corporación *f* corporation

corporal *adj* physical

corporativo, -a *adj* corporate

corpulento, -a *adj* **1.** (*persona*) hefty **2.** (*cosa*) massive

corral *m* **1.** (*cercado*) yard; (*redil*) stockyard **2.** (*para niños*) playpen

correa *f* **1.** (*tira*) strap **2.** (*cinturón*) belt; **~ de transmisión** TÉC driving belt

corrección *f* **1.** (*de errores*) correction **2.** (*represión*) rebuke **3.** (*comportamiento*) (good) manners *pl*

correccional *m* reformatory

correcto, -a *adj* correct

corrector(a) *m(f)* TIPO proofreader

corredizo, -a *adj* (*puerta*) sliding; **nudo ~** slipknot

corredor *m* corridor

corredor(a) *m(f)* **1.** DEP (*a pie*) runner **2.** COM agent; **~ de fincas** estate agent *Brit,* real estate broker *Am*

corregir *irr como elegir* **I.** *vt* **1.** TIPO to correct **2.** (*reprender*) to rebuke **II.** *vr:* **~se 1.** (*en la conducta*) to change one's ways **2.** (*al expresarse*) to correct oneself

correo *m* **1.** (*persona*) courier **2.** (*correspondencia*) post *Brit,* mail *Am;* **~ aéreo** airmail; **~ certificado** registered mail; **~ electrónico** e-mail; **echar al ~** to post *Brit,* to mail *Am*

Correos *mpl* post office

correr **I.** *vi* **1.** (*caminar*) to run; **eso corre de mi cuenta** I'm paying for that **2.** (*apresurarse*) to rush; **a todo ~** at top speed **3.** (*conducir*) to go fast **4.** (*tiempo*) to pass (quickly) **5.** (*líquido*) to flow **6.** (*viento*) to blow **7.** (*rumor*) to circulate **II.** *vt* (*un mueble*) to move; (*una cortina*) to draw; **corre prisa** it's urgent; **dejar ~ algo** not to worry about sth **III.** *vr:* **~se 1.** (*moverse*) to move **2.** *vulg* (*eyacular*) to come

correspondencia *f* **1.** (*correo*) post *Brit,* mail *Am;* (*de cartas*) correspondence **2.** (*equivalente*) correspondence

corresponder **I.** *vi* **1.** (*equivaler*) to correspond **2.** (*armonizar*) to match **3.** (*convenir*) to tally **4.** (*incumbir*) to concern **5.** (*trenes*) to connect **II.** *vr:* **~se 1.** (*ser equivalente*) to correspond; (*armonizar*) to match; (*convenir*) to agree **2.** (*comunicarse*) to communicate with each other

correspondiente *adj* **1.** (*oportuno*) corresponding **2.** (*respectivo*) respective

corresponsal *mf* correspondent

corrida *f* TAUR bullfight

corrido, -a *adj* **1.** *t.* ARQUIT (*sin interrupción*) continuous **2.** (*cantidad: larga*) large **3.** *estar* (*avergonzado*) embarrassed

corriente **I.** *adj* **1.** (*fluente*) running **2.** (*actual*) current; **estar al ~** to be aware **3.** (*ordinario*) ordinary **II.** *f* **1.** (*electricidad*) current; (*de aire*) draught *Brit,* draft *Am* **2.** (*tendencia*) tendency

corro *m* **1.** (*círculo*) circle **2.** (*juego*) ring-a-ring-a-roses

corroborar *vt* to corroborate

corroer *irr como roer* **I.** *vt* **1.** (*un material*) to corrode **2.** (*una persona*) consume **II.** *vr:* ~**se** to corrode

corromper I. *vt* **1.** (*descomponer*) to rot; (*un texto*) to corrupt **2.** (*sobornar*) to bribe **3.** (*enviciar*) to corrupt **II.** *vr:* ~**se 1.** (*descomponerse*) to rot; (*alimentos*) to go bad **2.** (*degenerar*) to become corrupted

corrosión *f* corrosion

corrosivo, -a *adj* corrosive

corrupción *f* **1.** (*descomposición*) decay **2.** (*moral*) corruption

corrupto, -a *adj* corrupt

corsé *m* corset

cortacésped *m* lawnmower

cortado *m* GASTR *coffee with only a little milk*

cortado, -a *adj* **1.** (*leche*) sour **2.** (*tímido*) shy; (*avergonzado*) self-conscious

cortar I. *vt* **1.** (*en pedazos*) to cut up; (*un árbol*) to cut down; (*leña*) to chop; (*el césped*) to mow; (*pelo*) to trim **2.** (*el agua*) to cut off; (*la corriente*) to switch off **II.** *vi* **1.** (*tajar*) cut **2.** (*con alguien*) to split **III.** *vr:* ~**se 1.** (*persona*) to cut oneself **2.** (*turbarse*) to become embarrassed **3.** (*leche*) to turn **4.** TEL to get cut off

cortaúñas *m inv* nailclippers *pl*

corte¹ *m* **1.** (*tajo*) cut; ~ **de corriente** ELEC power cut **2.** (*de pelo*) haircut

corte² *f* court

cortedad *f* **1.** (*escasez*) shortness **2.** (*de poco entendimiento*) stupidity

cortejar *vt* to court

cortejo *m* **1.** (*séquito*) retinue **2.** (*desfile*) procession

cortés *adj* polite

cortesía *f* courtesy

corteza *f* (*de un tronco*) bark; (*del queso*) rind; (*de una fruta*) peel; (*del pan, terrestre*) crust

cortina *f* curtain; ~ **de la ducha** shower curtain

corto, -a *adj* **1.** (*pequeño*) short; **a la corta o a la larga...** sooner or later ... **2.** (*breve*) brief **3.** (*de poco entendimiento*) slow

cortocircuito *m* ELEC short circuit

cortometraje *m* CINE short

coruñés, -esa *adj* of/from Corunna

corva *f* back of the knee

cosa *f* **1.** (*en general*) thing; **¿sabes una** ~**?** do you know what?; **ser una** ~ **nunca vista** to be unique; **como si tal** ~ as if nothing had happened **2.** *pl* (*pertenencias*) things *pl*

coscorrón *m* bump on the head

cosecha *f* **1.** AGR harvest **2.** (*conjunto de frutos*) crop

cosechar *vi, vt* to harvest

coser *vt* **1.** (*un vestido*) to sew **2.** MED to stitch (up), to sew; **esto es** ~ **y cantar** this is child's play

cosmética *f* cosmetics *pl*

cosmético, -a *adj* cosmetic

cosmos *m sin pl* cosmos

cosquillas *fpl* **tener** ~ to be ticklish

costa *f* **1.** GEO coast; **Costa de Marfil** Ivory Coast **2.** FIN cost; **a toda** ~ at any price **3.** *pl* JUR costs *pl*

? **Costa del Sol** is the name of a coast in southern Spain, running from **Tarifa** (in the west) to **Almería** (in the east). It incorporates the following four **provincias: Cádiz, Málaga, Granada** and **Almería.** The coast of **Málaga** is probably the most well known (especially **Marbella** and **Fuengirola**) and is where Spanish celebrities particularly like taking their holidays.

---

costado *m* **1.** (*lado*) side **2.** MIL flank

costal *m* sack

costar <o→ue> *vi, vt* **1.** (*de precio*) to cost **2.** (*un esfuerzo*) to be difficult

Costa Rica *f* Costa Rica

? **Costa Rica** lies in Central America and borders the countries Nicaragua and Panama as well as the Pacific and the Caribbean. The capital of **Costa Rica** is **San José.** Spanish is the official language of the country and the monetary unit is the **colón.**

costarriqueño, -a *adj, m, f* Costa Rican

coste *m* **1.** (*costo*) cost **2.** (*precio*) price

costear I. *vt* **1.** (*pagar*) to pay for **2.** NÁUT to sail along the coast of **II.** *vr:* ~**se** to cover the expenses

costero, -a *adj* coastal

costilla *f* **1.** *t.* ANAT rib **2.** GASTR chop

costo *m* cost

costoso, -a *adj* **1.** (*en dinero*) expensive **2.** (*en esfuerzo*) difficult

costra *f* **1.** MED scab **2.** (*corteza*) crust

costumbre *f* **1.** (*hábito*) habit; **como de** ~ as usual **2.** (*tradición*) custom

costura *f* **1.** (*coser*) sewing, needlework **2.** (*confección*) dressmaking

costurera *f* dressmaker

costurero *m* sewing box

cota *f* **1.** (*armadura*) doublet **2.** GEO height above sea level

cotejar *vt* to compare

cotidiano, -a *adj* daily

cotilla *mf inf* gossip

cotillear *vi inf* to gossip

cotilleo *m inf* gossip

cotización *f* **1.** (*de acciones*) price **2.** (*de cuota*) contribution

cotizar <z→c> **I.** *vt* **1.** FIN to stand at **2.** (*estimar*) to value **II.** *vr:* ~**se 1.** FIN to sell at **2.** (*ser popular*) to be valued

coto *m* ~ **de caza** game preserve

cotorra *f* **1.** (*papagayo*) parrot **2.** *inf* (*persona*) chatterbox

COU *m abr de* **Curso de Orientación Universitaria** *one-year pre-university course*

coyote *m* coyote

coyuntura *f* **1.** ANAT joint **2.** (*oportunidad*) opportunity **3.** ECON current economic situation

coz *f* kick

cráneo *m* ANAT skull

cráter *m* crater

creación *f* creation

creador(a) I. *adj* creative **II.** *m(f)* creator

crear I. *vt* **1.** (*hacer*) to create **2.** (*fundar*) to establish **3.** INFOR ~ **archivo** to make a new file **II.** *vr:* ~**se** to be created

creativo, -a *adj* creative

crecer *irr* **I.** *vi* **1.** (*aumentar*) to grow, to increase **2.** (*relativo a la luna*) to wax **3.** (*relativo al agua*) to rise **II.** *vr:* ~**se** (*persona*) to grow more confident

creces *fpl* **con** ~ fully

crecida *f* **1.** (*riada*) flood **2.** (*crecimiento*) (sudden) growth

creciente *adj* growing, increasing

crecimiento *m* **1.** *t.* ECON growth **2.** (*moneda*) appreciation

credencial *fpl* credentials

crédito *m* **1.** FIN (*préstamo*) credit; **dar a** ~ to loan **2.** (*fama*) reputation **3.** (*confianza*) **dar** ~ **a algo/alguien** to believe in sth/sb

credo *m* creed

crédulo, -a *adj* credulous

creencia *f* belief; REL faith

creer *irr como leer* **I.** *vi,* *vr:* ~**se** to believe **II.** *vt* to believe; **¡ya lo creo!** I should think so!

creíble *adj* credible, believable

creído, -a *adj* conceited

crema I. *adj* cream **II.** *f* **1.** creme *Brit,* cream *Am* **2.** (*natillas, pasta*) custard

cremallera *f* zip (fastener) *Brit,* zipper *Am*

crematorio *m* crematorium

crepitar *vi* to crackle

crepúsculo *m* twilight, dusk; ~ **matutino** dawn

crespo, -a *adj* curly

crespón *m* (*tela*) crepe

cresta *f* **1.** (*del gallo*) (cocks)comb **2.** (*de una ola*) crest

Creta *f* Crete

cretino, -a *m,* *f t. fig* cretin

creyente *mf* believer

cría *f* **1.** (*cachorro*) young **2.** (*camada*) litter **3.** (*pájaro*) brood

criadero, -a *adj* fertile

criado, -a *m,* *f* servant

criador(a) *m(f)* breeder

crianza *f* **1.** (*lactancia*) lactation **2.** (*educación*) upbringing

criar < *l. pres:* **crío**> **I.** *vt* **1.** (*alimentar*) to feed **2.** (*cuidar*) to breed **3.** (*ser propicio*) to produce **4.** (*educar*) to bring up **II.** *vi* (*animal*) to have young **III.** *vr:* ~**se** to grow up

criatura *f* creature; (*niño*) child
criba *f* sieve
cribar *vt* to sieve
crimen *m* crime
criminal *adj, mf* criminal
crin *f* mane
crío, -a *m, f inf* kid
cripta *f* crypt
crisis *f inv* crisis; ~ **nerviosa** nervous breakdown
crisma *f inf* (*cabeza*) head
crispación *f* **1.** (*contracción*) contraction **2.** (*irritación*) tension
crispar I. *vt* **1.** (*contraer*) to contract **2.** (*exasperar*) to exasperate II. *vr:* ~**se** **1.** (*contraerse*) to contract **2.** (*exasperarse*) to become exasperated
cristal *m* **1.** (*cuerpo*) crystal **2.** (*de ventana*) glass
cristalino *m* MED crystalline lens
cristalino, -a *adj* **1.** (*de cristal*) crystalline **2.** (*transparente*) crystal--clear
cristalizar <z→c> *vi, vt, vr:* ~**se** to crystallize
cristiandad *f* Christendom
cristiano, -a *adj, m, f* Christian
Cristo *m* Christ
criterio *m* **1.** (*norma*) criterion **2.** (*discernimiento*) judgement **3.** (*opinión*) opinion
crítica *f* criticism
criticar <c→qu> *vt* to criticize
crítico, -a I. *adj* critical II. *m, f* critic
Croacia *f* Croatia
croar *vi* (*rana*) to croak
croata *adj, mf* Croat(ian)
crol *m* crawl
cromar *vt* to chromium-plate
cromo *m* **1.** QUÍM chromium **2.** (*estampa*) (picture) card
cromosoma *m* chromosome
crónica *f* **1.** HIST chronicle **2.** (*prensa*) (feature) article
crónico, -a *adj t.* MED chronic
cronología *f* chronology
cronológico, -a *adj* chronological
cronometrar *vt* to time
cronómetro *m* chronometer; DEP stopwatch
croqueta *f* ≈ croquette

cruce *m* **1.** (*acción*) crossing; ~ **de peatones** pedestrian crossing **2.** (*interferencia*) interference **3.** BIO cross
cruceiro *m* FIN cruzeiro
crucero *m* **1.** ARQUIT transept **2.** NÁUT (*buque*) cruiser **3.** (*viaje*) cruise
crucial *adj* crucial
crucificar <c→qu> *vt* to crucify
crucifijo *m* crucifix
crucigrama *m* crossword (puzzle)
crudo *m* crude oil
crudo, -a *adj* **1.** (*sin cocer*) raw **2.** (*tiempo*) harsh **3.** (*color*) yellowish-white **4.** (*cruel*) cruel
cruel *adj* <crudelísimo> cruel
crueldad *f* cruelty
crujido *m* **1.** (*de papel*) rustling **2.** (*de madera*) creaking
crujiente *adj* **1.** (*dientes*) grinding **2.** (*pan tostado*) crunchy
crujir *vi* **1.** (*papel, hojas*) to rustle **2.** (*madera*) creak **3.** (*huesos*) crack
cruz *f* **1.** (*aspa*) cross; ~ **gamada** swastika; **Cruz Roja** Red Cross **2.** (*de una moneda*) reverse; **¿cara o ~?** heads or tails?
cruzada *f* crusade
cruzado *m* crusader
cruzado, -a *adj* **1.** (*animal*) crossbred **2.** (*chaqueta*) double-breasted
cruzar <z→c> I. *vt* to cross II. *vr:* ~**se** **1.** (*caminos*) to cross **2.** (*encontrarse*) to meet **3.** *t.* MAT to intersect
cuaderno *m* notebook
cuadra *f* **1.** (*de caballos*) stable **2.** (*lugar sucio*) pigsty **3.** AmL (*manzana de casas*) block (of houses)
cuadrado *m* MAT square
cuadrado, -a *adj* square
cuadragésimo, -a *adj* fortieth; *v.t.* **octavo**
cuadrar I. *vi* **1.** (*ajustarse*) to fit in **2.** (*coincidir*) to tally II. *vt t.* MAT to square III. *vr:* ~**se** MIL to stand to attention
cuadrícula *f* grid squares *pl*
cuadricular *adj* squared
cuadrilátero *m* **1.** (*polígono*) quadrilateral **2.** DEP ring
cuadrilla *f* **1.** (*de amigos*) group **2.** (*de trabajo*) work team **3.** *pey* (*de*

maleantes) gang

cuadro *m* **1.** (*cuadrado*) square; **a ~s** plaid, chequered *Brit,* check(er)ed *Am;* ~ **sinóptico** synoptic chart **2.** (*pintura*) painting **3.** (*escena*) scene

cuádruple I. *adj* quadruple, four-fold **II.** *m* quadruple

cuádruplo, -a *adj* quadruple

cuajar I. *vi* **1.** (*espesarse*) to thicken; (*la nieve*) to lie **2.** *inf* (*realizarse*) to come off **II.** *vt* **1.** (*leche*) to curdle **2.** (*cubrir*) to cover **III.** *vr:* ~**se** **1.** (*coagularse*) to coagulate **2.** (*llenarse*) to fill (up)

cuajo *m* **de** ~ completely

cual *pron rel* **el/la** ~ (*persona*) who, whom; (*cosa*) which; **lo** ~ which; **los/las** ~**es** (*personas*) who, whom; (*cosas*) which; **cada** ~ everyone; **hazlo tal** ~ **te lo digo** do it just as I tell you (to)

cuál I. *pron interrog* which (one); **¿~ es el tuyo?** which is yours? **II.** *pron indef* ~ **más** ~ **menos** some more, some less

cualesquier(a) *pron indef pl de* **cualquiera**

cualidad *f* quality

cualquiera I. *pron indef* any; **en un lugar** ~ anywhere; **a cualquier hora** at any time; **cualquier cosa** anything **II.** *mf* **ser una** ~ *pey* to be a whore

cuando *conj* **1.** (*presente*) when; **de** ~ **en** ~ from time to time; **~ quieras** when(ever) you want; **el lunes es** ~ **no trabajo** I don't work on Mondays **2.** (*condicional*) if; ~ **menos** at least **3.** (*aunque*) **aun** ~ even if

cuándo *adv* when

cuantía *f* **1.** (*suma*) amount **2.** (*importancia*) importance

cuantioso, -a *adj* substantial

cuanto I. *adv* ~ **antes** as soon as possible **II.** *prep* **en** ~ **a** as regards **III.** *conj* **1.** (*temporal*) **en** ~ (**que**) as soon as **2.** (*puesto que*) **por** ~ **que** inasmuch as

cuanto, -a I. *pron rel* (*neutro*) all that (which); **dije** (**todo**) ~ **sé** I said all that I know **II.** *pron indef* **unos**

~**s/unas cuantas** some, several

cuánto *adv* **1.** (*interrogativo*) how much **2.** (*exclamativo*) how

cuánto, -a I. *adj* **¿~ vino?** how much wine?; **¿~s libros?** how many books?; **¿~ tiempo?** how long?; **¿cuántas veces?** how often? **II.** *pron interrog* how much

cuarenta *adj inv, m* forty; *v.t.* **ochenta**

cuarentena *f* **1.** (*aislamiento*) quarantine **2.** (*cuarenta unidades*) **una** ~ **de veces** about forty times

cuaresma *f* REL Lent

cuarta *f* **1.** (*cuarta parte*) quarter **2.** (*medida*) span

cuartear I. *vt* (*dividir*) to quarter **II.** *vr:* ~**se** to crack

cuartel *m* **1.** MIL (*acuartelamiento*) encampment; ~ **general** headquarters *pl* **2.** MIL (*edificio*) barracks *pl*

cuarteto *m* MÚS quartet

cuartilla *f* (*hoja*) sheet of paper

cuarto *m* **1.** (*habitación*) room; ~ **de aseo** lavatory; ~ **de baño** bathroom; ~ **de estar** living room **2.** (*pl*), *inf* (*dinero*) money, dough *inf*

cuarto, -a I. *adj* fourth **II.** *m, f* quarter; ~ **de final** DEP quarterfinal; **un** ~ **de hora** a quarter of an hour; *v.t.* **octavo**

cuarzo *m* quartz

cuatrimestre *m* four-month period

cuatro *adj inv, m* four; *v.t.* **ocho**

cuatrocientos, -as *adj* four hundred; *v.t.* **ochocientos**

cuba *f* (*tonel*) barrel; **estar como una** ~ *inf* (*borracho*) to be plastered

Cuba *f* Cuba

❓ **Cuba** (official title: **República de Cuba**) is the largest of the West Indian Islands. The capital and also the largest city in Cuba is **La Habana**. The official language of the country is Spanish and the monetary unit is the **peso cubano**.

cubano, -a *adj, m, f* Cuban
cúbico, -a *adj t.* MAT cubic
cubierta *f* 1.(*cobertura*) cover; (*de un libro*) jacket; (*de una rueda*) tyre *Brit*, tire *Am* 2.NÁUT deck 3.ARQUIT roof
cubierto *m* 1.(*de mesa*) place setting 2.(*cubertería*) set of cutlery; **los ~s** the cutlery, the silverware *Am*
cubierto, -a I.*pp de* **cubrir** II.*adj* 1.(*cielo*) overcast; **ponerse a ~** to take cover 2.FIN **cheque no ~** bounced cheque
cubil *m* lair
cubilete *m* cup
cubito *m* ~ **de hielo** ice cube
cúbito *m* ANAT ulna
cubo *m* 1.(*recipiente*) bucket; ~ **de basura** dustbin *Brit*, trash can *Am* 2.*t.* MAT cube 3.(*de una rueda*) hub
cubrecama *m* bedspread
cubrir *irr como* **abrir** I.*vt* 1.*t. fig* (*tapar*) to cover 2.(*vacante*) to fill II.*vr:* ~**se** 1.(*taparse*) to cover oneself 2.(*el cielo*) to become overcast 3.MIL to take cover
cucaracha *f* cockroach
cuchara *f* spoon
cucharada *f* (*porción*) spoonful
cucharadita *f* 1.(*cuchara*) teaspoon 2.(*medida*) teaspoonful
cucharilla *f* teaspoon
cucharón *m* ladle
cuchichear *vi* to whisper
cuchilla *f* 1.(*de afeitar*) razor blade 2.(*de cocina*) kitchen knife 3.(*hoja*) blade
cuchillada *f* 1.(*navajazo*) slash 2.(*herida*) stab wound
cuchillo *m* knife
cuchitril *m* 1.(*pocilga*) pigsty 2.*fig* (*habitación*) hole
cuclillas *fpl* **en ~** squatting
cuco *m* cuckoo
cuco, -a *adj* 1.(*astuto*) crafty 2.(*bonito*) pretty
cucurucho *m* 1.(*de papel*) cone 2.(*de helado*) ice-cream cone
cuello *m* 1.ANAT neck; ~ **de botella** *t. fig* bottleneck 2.(*de una prenda*) collar
cuenca *f* 1.GEO basin 2.(*región*) val-

ley 3.(*de los ojos*) socket
cuenco *m* 1.(*vasija*) bowl 2.(*concavidad*) hollow
cuenta *f* 1.(*cálculo*) counting; (*calculación final*) calculation; ~ **atrás** countdown; **a ~ de alguien** on sb's account; **caer en la ~** to catch on; **a fin de ~s** after all; **en resumidas ~s** in short 2.(*en el banco*) account; ~ **corriente** [*o de giros*] current account; **pagar la ~** to pay the bill; **abonar en ~** to credit 3.(*consideración*) **tener en ~** to bear in mind; **tomar en ~** to take into consideration 4.(*de un collar*) bead
cuentakilómetros *m inv* speedometer, odometer *Am*
cuento *m* story; ~ **chino** *inf* tall story; ~ **de hadas** fairy tale; **venir a ~** to matter
cuerda *f* 1.(*gruesa*) rope; (*delgada*) string; ~ **floja** tightrope 2.(*del reloj*) spring; **dar** ~ **al reloj** to wind up one's watch 3.ANAT ~**s vocales** vocal chords 4.(*de instrumentos*) string
cuerdo, -a *adj* 1.(*sano*) sane 2.(*razonable*) sensible
cuerno *m* 1.MÚS, ZOOL horn 2.*inf*(*exclamativo*) **¡y un ~!** my foot!; **irse al ~** to be ruined; (*plan*) to fall through
cuero *m* leather
cuerpo *m* 1.(*de un ser*) body; (*tronco*) trunk; (*de una mujer*) figure; **tomar ~** to take shape 2.*t.* FÍS (*objeto, grupo*) body; ~ **de bomberos** fire brigade *Brit*, fire department *Am*
cuervo *m* raven, crow
cuesta *f* slope; ~ **abajo** downhill; **un camino en ~** an uphill road
cuestión *f* question, matter; ~ **de gustos** question of taste; ~ **secundaria** minor matter; **la ~ es...** the main thing is ...
cuestionario *m* questionnaire
cueva *f* cave; (*sótano*) cellar
cuidado *m* care; **¡~!** careful!; **¡~ con el escalón!** mind the step!
cuidadoso, -a *adj* careful
cuidar I.*vi* to take care II.*vt* to look after III.*vr:* ~**se** to look after oneself
cuita *f* worry
culata *f* (*del fusil*) butt

culebra *f* snake
culebrón *m* 1. *aum de* **culebra** big snake 2. TV soap opera
culinario, -a *adj* culinary
culminación *f* culmination
culminar *vi* to culminate
culo *m* 1. (*trasero*) bottom, backside 2. (*de botella*) bottom
culpa *f* fault; JUR guilt; **echar la ~** to blame
culpabilidad *f* guilt
culpable I. *adj* guilty II. *mf* culprit
culpar(se) *vt*, (*vr*) to blame (oneself)
cultivar *vt* 1. *t. fig* AGR to cultivate 2. (*bacterias*) to culture
cultivo *m* 1. AGR (*acto*) cultivation; (*resultado*) crop 2. (*de bacterias*) culture
culto *m* worship
culto, -a *adj* educated, cultured
cultura *f* culture
cultural *adj* cultural
culturismo *m* body-building
cumbre *f* 1. (*cima*) summit 2. (*reunión*) summit meeting
cumpleaños *m inv* birthday
cumplido *m* compliment
cumplido, -a *adj* 1. (*acabado*) completed 2. (*abundante*) plentiful 3. (*cortés*) courteous
cumplidor(a) I. *adj* reliable II. *m(f)* reliable person
cumplimentar *vt* 1. (*felicitar*) to congratulate 2. (*una orden*) to carry out 3. (*un impreso*) to complete
cumplimiento *m* 1. (*observación*) fulfilment; (*de un deber*) performance 2. (*cumplido*) compliment
cumplir I. *vi* 1. (*deber*) to do; (*promesa*) to keep 2. (*plazo*) to end II. *vt* 1. (*una orden*) to carry out 2. (*una promesa*) to keep 3. (*un plazo*) to keep to 4. (*el servicio militar*) to do 5. (*una pena*) to serve 6. (*las leyes*) to observe III. *vr*: **~se** to be fulfilled
cúmulo *m* 1. (*amontonamiento*) heap 2. METEO cumulus
cuna *f* cradle; **canción de ~** lullaby
cundir *vi* 1. (*dar mucho de sí*) to be productive 2. (*un trabajo*) to go well 3. (*rumor*) to spread
cuneta *f* ditch

cuña *f* 1. (*traba*) wedge 2. *fig* (*enchufe*) influence 3. MED bedpan
cuñado, -a *m*, *f* brother-in-law *m*, sister-in-law *f*
cuota *f* 1. (*porción*) quota; **~ de mercado** market share 2. (*contribución*) fee
cupo I. 3. *pret de* **caber** II. *m* ECON quota
cupón *m* coupon; (*de lotería*) lottery ticket
cúpula *f* ARQUIT dome
cura[1] *m* priest
cura[2] *f* 1. (*curación*) cure 2. (*tratamiento*) treatment; **~ de desintoxicación** detoxification
curación *f* treatment
curandero, -a *m*, *f* quack (doctor)
curar I. *vi* to recover II. *vt* 1. (*tratar*) to treat; (*sanar*) to cure 2. (*ahumar*) to cure 3. (*pieles*) to tan III. *vr*: **~se** to recover
curdo, -a I. *adj* Kurdish II. *m*, *f* Kurd
curiosear *vi* to look round; (*fisgar*) to snoop
curiosidad *f* curiosity
curioso, -a I. *adj* 1. (*indiscreto*) curious 2. (*aseado*) neat II. *m*, *f* 1. (*indiscreto*) busybody 2. (*mirón*) onlooker 3. *AmL* (*curandero*) quack doctor
currante *mf inf* worker
currar *vi inf*, **currelar** *vi inf* to work
currículo *m* curriculum
curriculum (**vitae**) *m*, **currículum** (**vitae**) *m* curriculum vitae
curro *m inf* (*trabajo*) job
cursar *vt* 1. (*cursos*) to study 2. (*tramitar*) to issue
cursi *adj inf* affected
cursillo *m* short course
cursiva *f* italics *pl*
cursivo, -a *adj* cursive
curso *m* 1. (*transcurso*) course 2. (*de enseñanza*) course; **~ acelerado** crash course; **estar en ~** FIN to be in circulation
cursor *m* 1. INFOR cursor 2. TÉC slide
curtido, -a *adj* 1. *fig* hardened 2. (*cuero*) tanned
curtir *vt* 1. (*pieles*) to tan 2. (*persona*) to harden

curva *f* curve
curvo, -a *adj* curved
cúspide *f* **1.** MAT apex **2.** *fig* pinnacle
custodia *f* (*guarda*) custody; **bajo ~** in custody
custodiar *vt* to guard
custodio, -a *m, f* guardian
cutáneo, -a *adj* skin
cutícula *f* cuticle
cutis *m inv* skin, complexion
cutre **I.** *adj* **1.** (*tacaño*) stingy, mean *Brit* **2.** (*sórdido*) seedy, grotty, crummy *inf* **II.** *mf* miser
cuyo, -a *pron rel* whose; **por cuya causa** for which reason
C.V. **1.** *abr de* **curriculum vitae** CV **2.** *abr de* **caballos de vapor** HP, h.p.

D d

D, d *f* D, d; **~ de Dolores** D for David *Brit,* D for dog *Am*
dádiva *f* gift
dadivoso, -a *adj* generous
dado¹ *m* **1.** (*cubo*) die; **~s** dice *pl* **2.** *pl* (*juego*) dice
dado² *conj* **~ que...** (*ya que*) given that ...; (*supuesto que*) supposing ...
dado, -a *adj* given; **en el caso ~** in this particular case
daltónico, -a *adj* colour-blind *Brit,* color-blind *Am*
dama *f* **1.** (*señora*) lady; **~ de honor** (*de la reina*) lady-in-waiting; (*de la novia*) bridesmaid **2.** *pl* (*juego*) draughts *Brit,* checkers *pl Am*
damasco *m* damask
damnificar <c→qu> *vt* (*persona*) to injure; (*cosa*) to damage
danés, -esa **I.** *adj* Danish **II.** *m, f* Dane
Danubio *m* Danube
danza *f* dance
danzar <z→c> *vt, vi* to dance
danzarín, -ina *m, f* dancer

dañar **I.** *vt* (*cosa*) to damage; (*persona*) to injure **II.** *vr:* **~se** to get damaged
dañino, -a *adj* harmful
daño *m* **1.** (*perjuicio*) damage; **~s y perjuicios** JUR damages **2.** (*dolor*) hurt
dar *irr* **I.** *vt* **1.** (*entregar*) to give; (*patada*) to kick; (*abrazo*) to hug; **~ forma** to shape sth; **¡qué más da!** *inf* what does it matter? **2.** (*producir*) to yield **3.** (*fiesta*) to give; **~ clases** to teach **4.** (*causar*) **~ gusto** to please; **~ miedo** to be frightening **5.** (*película*) to show; (*buenas noches*) to say; (*recuerdos*) to send; **~ un paseo** to go for a walk **6.** (*luz*) to turn on; **el reloj ha dado las dos** the clock has chimed two o'clock **7.** (+ *'de'*) **~ de alta** MED to discharge; **~ de baja** MED to put on sick leave **II.** *vi* **1.** (+ *'a'*) **el balcón da a la calle** the balcony faces the street; **~ a conocer** to let be known **2.** (+ *'con'*) **~ con** (*persona*) to run into; (*solución*) to find **3.** (*acertar*) **~ en el blanco** *fig* to hit the target **4.** (+ *'para'*) **da para vivir** it's enough to live on **5.** (+ *'por'*) **~ por muerto** to take for dead; **~ por concluido** to treat as concluded; **le ha dado por...** he/she has decided to ... **6.** (+ *'que'*) **~ que...** to give cause for ...; **~ de sí** (*jersey*) to stretch **III.** *vr:* **~se** **1.** (*suceder*) to happen; **~se un baño** to have a bath; **~se cuenta** to realize **2.** (+ *'a'*: *consagrarse*) to devote oneself; (*entregarse*) to surrender; **~se a conocer** (*persona*) to make oneself known; (*noticia*) to become known **3.** (+ *'contra'*) to hit **4.** (+ *'de'*) **~se de baja** to sign off; **dárselas de...** *inf* to pretend to be ... **5.** (+ *'por':*) **~se por vencido** to give up
dardo *m* dart
dársena *f* dock
datar *vi, vt* to date
dátil *m* date
dativo *m* dative
dato *m* **1.** (*circunstancia*) fact **2.** (*cantidad*) figure **3.** (*fecha*) date

4. *pl* INFOR data *pl;* ~**s de entrada** input data

dcha. *abr de* **derecha** rt.

d. de J.C. *abr de* **después de Jesu-cristo** AD

de *prep* **1.**(*posesión*) **el reloj ~ mi padre** my father's watch **2.**(*origen*) from; **ser ~ Italia** to come from Italy; **un libro ~ Goytisolo** a book by Goytisolo **3.**(*material*) of; ~ **oro** of gold, gold; ~ **madera** of wood, wooden **4.**(*temporal*) from; ~ **niño** as a child **5.**(*condición*) ~ **haberlo sabido...** if we had known ...

> ! **de** in combination with the masculine definite article 'el' becomes 'del': "Matilde vuelve normalmente pronto del trabajo; Él es el hijo del alcalde."

deambular *vi* to wander around

debajo I. *adv* underneath **II.** *prep* ~ **de** (*local*) below; (*con movimiento*) under

debate *m* **1.** POL debate **2.**(*charla*) discussion

debatir I. *vt* **1.** POL to debate **2.**(*considerar*) to discuss **II.** *vr:* ~**se** to struggle

deber I. *vi* (*suposición*) **debe de estar al llegar** he/she should arrive soon; **deben de ser las nueve** it must be nine o'clock **II.** *vt* **1.**(*estar obligado*) to have to **2.**(*tener que dar*) to owe **III.** *vr:* ~**se 1.**(*tener por causa*) ~**se a algo** to be due to sth **2.**(*estar obligado*) to have a duty **IV.** *m* **1.**(*obligación*) duty **2.** *pl* (*tareas*) homework *sin pl*

debido *prep* ~ **a** due to

debido, -a *adj* **como es** ~ as is proper

débil *adj* weak; (*sonido*) faint; (*luz*) dim

debilidad *f* ~ **por algo** weakness for sth

debilitar *vt* to weaken

debutar *vi* to make one's debut

década *f* decade

decadencia *f* **1.**(*decaimiento*) de-cay **2.**(*de un imperio*) decline

decaer *irr como caer vi* to decline; ~ **el ánimo** to get discouraged

decaído, -a *adj* **1.**(*abatido*) down-hearted **2.**(*débil*) weak

decano, -a *m, f* UNIV dean

decapitar *vt* to decapitate

decena *f* ten; ~**s** MAT tens

decencia *f* decency

decente *adj* **1.**(*decoroso*) decent **2.**(*respetable*) respectable

decepción *f* disappointment

decepcionar *vt* to disappoint

decidir I. *vi* to decide **II.** *vt* **1.**(*determinar*) to decide **2.**(*mover a*) to per-suade

decimal *adj* decimal; **número** ~ decimal number

décimo *m* (*de lotería*) tenth share of *a lottery ticket*

décimo, -a *adj* tenth; *v.t.* **octavo**

decimoctavo, -a *adj* eighteenth; *v.t.* **octavo**

decimocuarto, -a *adj* fourteenth; *v.t.* **octavo**

decimonoveno, -a *adj* nineteenth; *v.t.* **octavo**

decimoquinto, -a *adj* fifteenth; *v.t.* **octavo**

decimoséptimo, -a *adj* seventeenth; *v.t.* **octavo**

decimosexto, -a *adj* sixteenth; *v.t.* **octavo**

decimotercero, -a *adj* thirteenth; *v.t.* **octavo**

decir *irr* **I.** *vi* **1.**(*expresar*) to say; **diga** TEL hello; **es ~** in other words; **¡no me digas!** *inf* really!; **y no diga-mos** not to mention; **ser un ~** to be a manner of speaking **2.**(*contener*) to say **II.** *vt* (*expresar*) to say; (*comunicar*) to tell; **dicho y hecho** no sooner said than done; **como se ha dicho** as has been said **III.** *vr* ¿**cómo se dice en inglés?** how do you say it in English?

decisión *f* **1.**(*resolución*) decision; **tomar una** ~ to take a decision **2.**(*firmeza*) determination

decisivo, -a *adj* decisive

declamar *vt* to declaim; (*versos*) to recite

declaración f **1.** (*a la prensa*) declaration **2.** JUR statement; ~ **de la renta** FIN income-tax return

declarar I. vi **1.** (*testigo*) to testify **2.** (*a la prensa*) to make a statement II. vt (*ingresos*) to declare III. vr: ~**se 1.** (*aparecer*) to break out **2.** (*manifestarse*) to declare oneself; ~**se inocente** to plead innocent

declinar I. vi **1.** (*disminuir*) to decline **2.** (*extinguirse*) to come to an end II. vt to decline

declive m **1.** (*del terreno*) slope **2.** (*decadencia*) decline

decolorar vt **1.** QUÍM to discolour *Brit,* to discolor *Am* **2.** (*el sol*) to bleach

decomisar vt to confiscate

decoración f decoration

decorado m TEAT set

decorar vt to decorate

decorativo, -a adj decorative

decoro m **1.** (*dignidad*) dignity **2.** (*respeto*) respect **3.** (*pudor*) decency

decoroso, -a adj **1.** (*decente*) decent **2.** (*digno*) dignified

decrecer irr como crecer vi to decrease; (*nivel*) to fall

decrépito, -a adj decrepit

decretar vt to decree

decreto m decree

dedal m thimble

dedicación f dedication; ~ **plena** (*en el trabajo*) full-time

dedicar <c→qu> I. vt **1.** (*destinar*) to dedicate **2.** (*consagrar*) to consecrate II. vr: ~**se** to devote oneself; (*profesionalmente*) to work as

dedicatoria f dedication

dedo m (*de mano*) finger; (*de pie*) toe; ~ **anular** ring finger; ~ **gordo** big toe; ~ **índice** index finger, forefinger; ~ **pulgar** thumb; **chuparse el** ~ *inf* to suck one's thumb; **hacer** ~ to hitch-hike; **no mover un** ~ to not lift a finger

deducción f deduction

deducir irr como traducir vt **1.** (*derivar*) to deduce **2.** (*descontar*) to deduct

defecto m **1.** (*carencia*) lack **2.** (*falta*) defect

defectuoso, -a adj faulty, defective

defender <e→ie> I. vt **1.** (*ideas*) t. JUR to defend **2.** (*proteger*) to protect II. vr: ~**se 1.** (*contra ataques*) to defend oneself **2.** (*arreglárselo*) to get by

defendible adj defensible

defensa[1] f defence *Brit,* defense *Am;* **tener** ~**s** MED to have resistance

defensa[2] mf DEP defender

defensiva f defensive

defensivo, -a adj defensive

defensor(a) I. adj defending II. m(f) defender

deferente adj deferential

deficiencia f **1.** (*insuficiencia*) lack **2.** (*defecto*) deficiency

deficiente adj **1.** (*insuficiente*) lacking **2.** (*defectuoso*) deficient

déficit m inv **1.** FIN deficit **2.** (*escasez*) shortage

deficitario, -a adj (*empresa*) loss-making; (*cuenta*) in deficit

definición f t. TV definition

definir I. vt to define II. vr: ~**se** to take a stand

definitivo, -a adj **1.** (*irrevocable*) final **2.** (*decisivo*) decisive; **en definitiva** in short

deforestación f deforestation

deformación f **1.** (*alteración*) distortion **2.** (*desfiguración*) deformation

deformar I. vt **1.** (*alterar*) to distort **2.** (*desfigurar*) to deform II. vr: ~**se** to become deformed; (*jersey*) to lose its shape

deforme adj **1.** (*imagen*) distorted **2.** (*cuerpo*) deformed

defraudar vt **1.** (*estafar*) to cheat; (*impuestos*) to evade **2.** (*decepcionar*) to disappoint

defunción f death

degeneración f (*proceso*) degeneration; (*estado*) degeneracy

degenerar vi to degenerate

degollar <o→ue> vt ~ **a alguien** to slit sb's throat

degradar I. vt **1.** (*en el cargo*) to demote **2.** (*calidad*) to worsen **3.** (*color*) to tone down II. vr: ~**se** to degrade oneself

D d

degustación *f* tasting
deificar <c→qu> *vt* to deify
dejadez *f* **1.** (*pereza*) laziness **2.** (*negligencia*) neglect
dejado, -a *adj* **1.** *ser* (*descuidado*) slovenly **2.** *estar* (*abatido*) dejected
dejar **I.** *vi* ~ **de hacer algo** to stop doing sth; **no dejes de escribirles** don't fail to write them; **¡no deje de venir!** make sure you come! **II.** *vt* **1.** (*abandonar*) to leave; ~ **acabado** to finish; ~ **caer** to drop; ~ **en libertad** to set free; ~ **a alguien en paz** to leave sb in peace **2.** (*permitir*) to allow, to let **3.** (*entregar*) to give; (*prestar*) to lend **III.** *vr:* ~**se 1.** (*descuidarse*) to neglect oneself **2.** (*olvidar*) to forget
dejo *m* accent
del = **de** + **el** *v.* **de**
delantal *m* apron, pinafore *Brit*
delante **I.** *adv* **1.** (*ante*) in front; **de** ~ from the front **2.** (*enfrente*) opposite **II.** *prep* ~ **de** in front of
delantera *f* **1.** (*parte anterior*) front (part) **2.** (*distancia*) lead **3.** DEP forward line
delantero *m* DEP forward
delantero, -a *adj* front
delatar *vt* **1.** (*denunciar*) to inform on **2.** (*manifestar*) to reveal
delegación *f* **1.** (*comisión*) delegation **2.** (*oficina*) local office; (*filial*) branch
delegado, -a *m, f* delegate
delegar <g→gu> *vt* to delegate
deletrear *vt* to spell
deleznable *adj* **1.** (*frágil*) fragile **2.** (*despreciable*) contemptible
delfín *m* dolphin
delgado, -a *adj* thin; (*esbelto*) slender
deliberar *vi, vt* to deliberate
delicadeza *f* **1.** (*finura*) delicacy **2.** (*debilidad*) weakness
delicado, -a *adj* **1.** (*fino*) delicate **2.** (*atento*) thoughtful **3.** (*enfermizo*) frail **4.** (*asunto*) delicate
delicia *f* delight
delicioso, -a *adj* (*cosa*) delightful; (*comida*) delicious
delimitar *vt* to mark out

delincuencia *f* crime, delinquency
delincuente *adj, mf* criminal
delineante *mf* draughtsman *m*, draughtswoman *f*
delinear *vt* to draw
delinquir <qu→c> *vi* to commit an offence
delirante *adj* **1.** *t* MED delirious **2.** (*idea*) crazy
delirar *vi* to be delirious
delirio *m* **1.** (*enfermedad*) delirium **2.** (*ilusión*) delusion
delito *m* crime
delta *m* GEO delta
demagogia *f* demagogy
demanda *f* **1.** (*petición*) request; ~ **de empleo** job application **2.** COM demand **3.** JUR action, lawsuit
demandante *mf* claimant; JUR plaintiff
demandar *vt* to ask for; ~ **por algo** JUR to sue for sth
demarcación *f* demarcation
demás **I.** *adj* other; **...y ~... (***y otros***)** ... and other ...; **y ~ (***etcétera***)** and so on; **por lo** ~ otherwise **II.** *adv* **por** ~ more
demasía *f* **1.** (*exceso*) excess **2.** (*insolencia*) insolence
demasiado *adv* (+ *adj*) too; (+ *verbo*) too much; **comió** ~ he/she ate too much
demasiado, -a *adj* (*singular*) too much; (*plural*) too many
demencia *f* madness
demencial *adj,* **demente** *adj* mad
democracia *f* democracy
demócrata **I.** *adj* democratic **II.** *mf* democrat
democrático, -a *adj* democratic
demoler <o→ue> *vt* to demolish
demonio *m* **1.** (*espíritu*) demon **2.** (*diablo*) devil; **cómo/dónde/qué** ~**s...** *inf* how/where/what the hell ...
demora *f* delay
demorar **I.** *vt* to delay **II.** *vr:* ~**se 1.** (*retrasarse*) ~**se en hacer algo** to delay in doing sth **2.** (*detenerse*) to be held up
demostración *f* **1.** (*prueba*) test **2.** (*argumentación*) proof

demostrar <o→ue> vt 1.(*probar*) to demonstrate 2.(*exhibir*) to show

demostrativo, -a adj demonstrative

demudado, -a adj (*pálido*) pale

denegar irr como fregar vt 1.(*negar*) to deny 2.(*rechazar*) to refuse

denigrar vt 1.(*humillar*) to denigrate 2.(*injuriar*) to insult

denominación f naming

denominador m MAT denominator

denotar vt to denote

densidad f density

denso, -a adj 1.(*compacto*) dense 2.(*espeso*) thick 3.(*pesado*) heavy

dentadura f teeth pl

dental adj dental

dentera f **dar ~ a alguien** (*dar grima*) to set sb's teeth on edge; inf (*dar envidia*) to make sb jealous

dentífrico m toothpaste

dentista I. adj dental II. mf dentist

dentro I. adv inside; **desde ~** from within; **por ~** inside II. prep **de** (*local*) inside; (*con movimiento*) into, within; **~ de poco** soon; **~ de lo posible** as far as possible

denuncia f 1.(*acusación*) accusation 2.(*de una injusticia*) denunciation

denunciar vt 1.(*acusar*) **~ a alguien por algo** to accuse sb of sth 2.(*delatar*) to betray 3.(*hacer público*) to expose

departamento m 1.(*de un edificio*) t. UNIV department 2.(*de un objeto*) compartment 3.FERRO compartment 4.*AmL* (*apartamento*) flat *Brit,* apartment *Am*

departir vi to converse

dependencia f 1.(*sujeción*) dependency 2.(*sucursal*) branch 3. pl (*habitaciones*) rooms pl

depender vi to depend; **depende de ti** it's up to you

dependiente adj dependent

dependiente, -a m, f shop assistant

depilarse vr (*cejas*) to pluck; (*a la cera*) to wax

depilatorio, -a adj depilatory

deplorable adj deplorable

deponer irr como poner I. vt 1.(*de un cargo*) to remove; (*monarca*) to depose 2.(*armas*) to set aside II. vi JUR to give evidence, to testify

deportar vt to deport

deporte m sport; **hacer ~** to practise sports

deportista I. adj sporty II. mf sportsman m, sportswoman f

deportivo m sports car

deportivo, -a adj sporting; **noticias deportivas** sports news

depositar I. vt to put; FIN to deposit II. vr: **~se** to settle

depósito m 1.(*almacén*) warehouse; (*de coches*) pound; (*de cadáveres*) morgue, mortuary; **~ de equipajes** FERRO left-luggage office *Brit,* checkroom *Am* 2.AUTO petrol tank *Brit,* gas tank *Am* 3. t. FIN deposit

depravar I. vt to corrupt II. vr: **~se** to become depraved

depreciar vt, vr: **~se** to depreciate

depredador(a) I. adj predatory II. m(f) predator

depresión f 1.(*tristeza*) depression 2.GEO hollow 3.METEO depression

deprimir I. vt (*abatir*) to depress II. vr: **~se** (*abatirse*) to become depressed

deprisa adv fast, quickly

depuración f purification; POL purge

depuradora f (*de agua*) water-treatment plant; **~ de aguas residuales** sewage plant

depurar vt 1.(*purificar*) to purify; **~ el estilo** to polish one's style 2.POL to purge

derecha f 1.(*diestra*) right 2.(*lado*) right-hand side; **a la ~** (*estar*) on the right; (*ir*) to the right 3.POL right (wing)

derecho I. adv straight II. m 1.(*legitimidad*) right; **con ~ a** with the right to; **¡no hay ~!** inf it's not fair! 2.(*jurisprudencia*) law; **estudiar ~** to study law 3.(*de hoja*) right side 4. pl (*impuestos*) duties pl

derecho, -a adj 1.(*diestro*) right 2.(*recto*) straight 3.(*erguido*) upright

derivado m derivative

derivar I. vi 1.(*proceder*) to derive

2. to drift **II.** *vt* **1.** *t.* MAT, LING (*deducir*) to derive **2.** (*desviar*) to divert **III.** *vr:* ~**se** to come from

dermoprotector(a) *adj* kind to the skin, skin-friendly

derramamiento *m* spilling; (*de sangre*) shedding

derramar I. *vt* to pour; (*sin querer*) to spill; (*lágrimas*) to shed **II.** *vr:* ~**se** (*líquidos*) to spill; (*otros*) to scatter

derrame *m* MED haemorrhage *Brit,* hemorrhage *Am*

derrapar *vi* to skid

derredor *m* en ~ around

derretir *irr como pedir vt, vr:* ~**se** to melt

derribar *vt* **1.** (*edificio*) to demolish; (*árbol*) to fell; (*avión*) to shoot down **2.** (*boxeador*) to knock down **3.** (*gobierno*) to overthrow

derrocar <c→qu> *vt* **1.** (*edificio*) to knock down **2.** (*destituir*) to remove

derrochar *vt* **1.** (*despilfarrar*) to squander **2.** *inf* (*tener mucho*) to be brimming with

derroche *m* **1.** (*despilfarro*) waste **2.** (*exceso*) profusion

derrota *f* **1.** (*fracaso*) defeat **2.** NÁUT course

derrotar *vt* to defeat

derrotero *m* course

derruir *irr como huir vt* to knock down

derrumbar I. *vt* to knock down **II.** *vr:* ~**se** to fall down

desabotonar(se) *vt,* (*vr*) to unbutton

desabrido, -a *adj* **1.** (*comida*) insipid **2.** (*persona*) disagreeable

desabrochar(se) *vt,* (*vr*) (*botón*) to undo; (*cordón*) to untie

desacato *m* disrespect

desacertado, -a *adj* **1.** (*equivocado*) mistaken **2.** (*inapropiado*) unfortunate

desacierto *m* mistake

desaconsejado, -a *adj* not advised

desaconsejar *vt* to advise against

desacorde *adj* **1.** MÚS discordant **2.** (*opinión*) conflicting

desacreditar *vt* to discredit

desacuerdo *m* disagreement

desafiar <*1. pres:* desafío> *vt* **1.** (*retar*) to challenge **2.** (*hacer frente a*) to defy

desafilado, -a *adj* blunt

desafinar *vi* MÚS to be out of tune

desafío *m* **1.** (*reto*) challenge **2.** (*duelo*) duel

desaforado, -a *adj* **1.** (*fuera de la ley*) lawless **2.** (*desmedido*) excessive

desafortunado, -a *adj* unlucky

desagradable *adj* unpleasant

desagradar *vi* to displease

desagradecido, -a *adj* ungrateful

desagrado *m* displeasure

desagraviar *vt* to make amends for

desagravio *m* amends *pl;* **en ~ de** as amends for

desagüe *m* plughole, drain

desaguisado *m* offence *Brit,* offense *Am*

desaguisado, -a *adj* outrageous

desahogado, -a *adj* spacious

desahogar <g→gu> **I.** *vt* to relieve **II.** *vr:* ~**se 1.** (*desfogarse*) to let off steam **2.** (*confiarse*) to tell one's troubles

desahogo *m* **1.** (*alivio*) relief **2.** (*económico*) comfort

desahuciar *vt* **1.** (*enfermo*) to declare past saving **2.** (*inquilino*) to evict

desahucio *m* JUR eviction

desairar *irr como airar vt* **1.** (*humillar*) to insult **2.** (*desestimar*) to slight

desaire *m* **1.** (*humillación*) insult **2.** (*desprecio*) disdain

desajustar *vt* to put out of balance; (*aparato*) to put out of order

desajuste *m* **1.** (*desorden*) imbalance **2.** (*de aparatos*) breakdown

desalentador(a) *adj* discouraging

desalentar <e→ie> *vt* to discourage

desaliento *m* dismay

desaliñado, -a *adj* shabby

desaliño *m* shabbiness

desalmado, -a *adj* heartless

desalojar *vt* (*casa*) to vacate; (*puesto*) to leave

desamor *m* **1.** (*falta de amor*) indifference **2.** (*aborrecimiento*) dislike

desamparado, -a *adj* **1.** (*persona*) defenceless *Brit,* defenseless *Am* **2.** (*lugar*) exposed

desamparar *vt* to abandon

desandar *irr como andar vt* ~ **lo andado** to retrace one's steps

desangrar I. *vt* to bleed **II.** *vr:* ~**se** to bleed to death

desanimado, -a *adj* downhearted

desanimar I. *vt* to discourage **II.** *vr:* ~**se** to lose heart

desapacible *adj* unpleasant

desaparecer *irr como crecer vi* to disappear; (*en guerra*) to go missing

desaparecido, -a I. *adj* missing **II.** *m, f* missing person

desaparición *f* disappearance

desapego *m* indifference

desaprensivo, -a *adj* unscrupulous

desaprobar <o→ue> *vt* to disapprove

desaprovechado, -a *adj* wasted

desaprovechar *vt* to waste

desarmar *vt, vi* POL to disarm

desarme *m* POL disarmament

desarraigar <g→gu> *vt* **1.** (*árbol*) to uproot **2.** (*costumbre*) to eradicate

desarraigo *m* **1.** (*de árbol*) uprooting **2.** (*de costumbre*) eradication

desarreglado, -a *adj* (*cuarto*) untidy; (*vida*) disorganized

desarreglar *vt* **1.** (*desordenar*) to mess up **2.** (*perturbar*) to disturb

desarreglo *m* **1.** (*de un cuarto*) untidiness; (*de la vida*) confusion **2.** (*desperfecto*) problem; (*en el coche*) trouble

desarrollar I. *vt* **1.** (*aumentar*) to develop **2.** (*detallar*) to expound **II.** *vr:* ~**se 1.** (*progresar*) to develop **2.** (*tener lugar*) to take place

desarrollo *m* **1.** *t.* FOTO development **2.** (*crecimiento*) growth

desarticular *vt* **1.** (*mecanismo*) to dismantle **2.** (*articulación*) to dislocate **3.** (*grupo*) to break up

desaseado, -a *adj* dirty

desasir *irr como asir* **I.** *vt* to let go of **II.** *vr:* ~**se** to come off

desasosegar *irr como fregar* **I.** *vt* to

worry **II.** *vr:* ~**se** to become uneasy

desasosiego *m* unease

desastrado, -a *adj* (*desaliñado*) untidy; (*harapiento*) shabby

desastre *m* disaster

desastroso, -a *adj* disastrous

desatado, -a *adj* **1.** (*desligado*) untied **2.** (*desenfrenado*) wild

desatar I. *vt* **1.** (*soltar*) to untie; (*nudo*) to undo **2.** (*causar*) to unleash **II.** *vr:* ~**se 1.** (*soltarse*) to untie oneself; (*nudo*) to come undone **2.** (*tormenta*) to break; (*crisis*) to erupt

desatascar <c→qu> *vt* to unblock; (*coche*) to pull out

desatender <e→ie> *vt* **1.** (*desoír*) to ignore **2.** (*abandonar*) to neglect

desatento, -a *adj* (*distraído*) inattentive; (*negligente*) careless

desatinado, -a *adj* **1.** (*desacertado*) foolish **2.** (*irreflexivo*) rash

desatino *m* **1.** (*error*) mistake **2.** (*tontería*) rubbish

desatornillar *vt* to unscrew

desatrancar <c→qu> *vt* **1.** (*puerta*) to unbolt **2.** (*desatascar*) to unblock

desautorizado, -a *adj* unauthorized

desautorizar <z→c> *vt* (*inhabilitar*) to deprive of authority; (*desmentir*) to deny

desavenencia *f* **1.** (*desacuerdo*) disagreement **2.** (*discordia*) friction

desaventajado, -a *adj* **1.** (*poco ventajoso*) unfavourable *Brit,* unfavorable *Am* **2.** (*inferior*) inferior

desayunar I. *vi* to have breakfast **II.** *vt* to have for breakfast

desayuno *m* breakfast

desazón *f* **1.** (*desasosiego*) unease **2.** (*malestar*) discomfort

desazonar I. *vt* to annoy **II.** *vr:* ~**se** to get annoyed

desbarajuste *m* chaos

desbaratar I. *vt* **1.** (*dispersar*) to break up **2.** (*desmontar*) to take apart **II.** *vr:* ~**se 1.** (*separarse*) to break up **2.** (*estropearse*) to break down

desbloquear *vt t.* POL to unblock

desbocado, -a *adj* **1.** (*persona: enlo-*

quecida) mad **2.** (*caballo*) runaway
desbocarse <c→qu> *vr* **1.** (*enloquecer*) to go mad **2.** (*caballo*) to bolt
desbordar I. *vr:* ~**se** (*río*) to overflow **II.** *vi* to overflow; ~ **de emoción** to be full of emotion **III.** *vt* (*exceder*) to exceed
descabalgar <g→gu> *vi* to dismount
descabellado, -a *adj* preposterous
descabellar *vt* TAUR to give the coup de grâce to the bull
descafeinado, -a *adj* decaffeinated
descalabro *m* setback
descalificación *f* disqualification
descalificar <c→qu> *vt* to disqualify
descalzar <z→c> *vt* (*calzado*) to take off
descalzo, -a *adj* **1.** (*sin zapatos*) barefoot **2.** *fig* (*indigente*) destitute
descambiar *vt inf* to exchange
descampado *m* open ground
descansado, -a *adj* rested
descansar *vi* **1.** (*reposar*) to rest **2.** (*recuperarse*) to recover **3.** (*dormir*) to sleep **4.** (*apoyar*) to rest
descansillo *m* landing
descanso *m* **1.** (*reposo*) rest; **día de** ~ day off **2.** (*tranquilidad*) peace **3.** (*pausa*) *t.* DEP break; (*alto*) pause **4.** (*alivio*) relief **5.** (*apoyo*) support
descapotable *m* convertible
descarado, -a *adj* **1.** (*desvergonzado*) shameless **2.** (*evidente*) blatant
descarga *f* **1.** (*de mercancías*) unloading **2.** *t.* ELEC (*disparo*) discharge
descargar <g→gu> **I.** *vi* **1.** (*desembocar*) to flow **2.** (*tormenta*) to break **II.** *vt* **1.** (*carga*) to unload **2.** ELEC, FÍS to discharge **3.** (*disparar*) to fire **4.** (*desahogar*) to vent **5.** (*aliviar*) to relieve; FIN to discharge **6.** JUR (*absolver*) to acquit **7.** INFOR to download **III.** *vr:* ~**se** to empty; ELEC, FÍS to discharge; (*pila*) to go flat, to run out
descargo *m* **1.** (*descarga*) unloading **2.** FIN discharge **3.** (*liberación*) release
descarnado, -a *adj* **1.** (*sin carne*) scrawny **2.** (*acre*) brutal **3.** *fig* bare

descaro *m* cheek
descarriarse <*l. pres:* descarrío> *vr* **1.** (*perderse*) to get lost **2.** (*descaminarse*) to go astray
descarrilamiento *m* derailment
descarrilar *vi* to be derailed
descartar *vt* (*propuesta*) to reject; (*posibilidad*) to rule out
descascarillarse *vr* (*loza*) to chip; (*pintura*) to peel
descendencia *f* descendents *pl*
descender <e→ie> *vi* **1.** (*ir abajo*) to descend; (*a un valle*) to go down **2.** (*disminuir*) to diminish **3.** (*proceder*) to be descended
descendiente *mf* descendant
descenso *m* **1.** (*bajada*) descent **2.** (*cuesta*) slope **3.** (*disminución*) decline
descifrar *vt* (*código*) to decipher; (*problema*) to figure out
descodificador *m* decoder
descodificar <c→qu> *vt* to decode
descolgar *irr como* colgar **I.** *vt* **1.** (*quitar*) to take off **2.** (*teléfono*) to pick up **3.** (*bajar*) to take down **II.** *vr:* ~**se 1.** (*bajar*) to come down **2.** (*aparecer*) to turn up
descollar <o→ue> *vi* to stand out
descompaginar *vi* to upset
descompasado, -a *adj* **1.** (*sin proporción*) out of all proportion **2.** MÚS out of time
descompensar *vt* to unbalance
descomponer *irr como* poner **I.** *vt* **1.** (*desordenar*) to mess up **2.** (*separar*) to take apart **3.** (*corromper*) *t.* QUÍM to decompose **II.** *vr:* ~**se 1.** (*desmembrarse*) to come apart **2.** (*corromperse*) to decay
descomposición *f* **1.** QUÍM decomposition; ~ (**de vientre**) diarrhoea *Brit,* diarrhea *Am* **2.** (*corrupción*) decay
descompostura *f* disorder
descompuesto, -a I. *pp de* **descomponer II.** *adj* **1.** (*desordenado*) untidy **2.** (*podrido*) rotten
descomunal *adj* enormous
desconcertar <e→ie> *vt* **1.** to ruin; (*planes*) to upset **2.** (*pasmar*) to confuse; **estar desconcertado** to be

disconcerted

desconchado *m* (*de loza*) chip; (*en la pared*) *place where paint has come off*

desconcierto *m* **1.** (*desarreglo*) disorder **2.** (*desorientación*) confusion

desconectar *vi, vt* to disconnect; (*radio*) to switch off; (*desenchufar*) to unplug

desconfianza *f* distrust

desconfiar <*1. pres:* desconfío> *vi* ~ **de alguien/algo** to mistrust sb/ sth

descongelar *vt* **1.** (*comida*) to thaw out; (*el frigorífico*) to defrost **2.** FIN to unfreeze

descongestionar *vt* to unblock; MED to clear

desconocer *irr como* crecer *vt* **1.** (*ignorar*) to be unaware of **2.** (*subestimar*) to underestimate

desconocido, -a **I.** *adj* unknown; **estar** ~ to be unrecognizable **II.** *m, f* stranger

desconocimiento *m* **1.** (*ignorancia*) ignorance **2.** (*ingratitud*) ingratitude

desconsiderado, -a *adj* inconsiderate

desconsolar <o→ue> **I.** *vt* to distress **II.** *vr:* ~**se** to lose hope

desconsuelo *m* distress

descontado, -a *adj* (*descartado*) discounted; **dar por** ~ **que...** to take it for granted that ...; **por** ~ of course

descontar <o→ue> *vt* **1.** (*restar*) to take away **2.** (*letras*) to discount

descontento *m* dissatisfaction

descontento, -a *adj* dissatisfied

descontrol *m* loss of control

descontrolarse *vr* to go wild

descorazonar **I.** *vt* to discourage **II.** *vr:* ~**se** to lose heart

descorchar *vt* (*botella*) to uncork

descorrer *vt* to draw; (*cerrojo*) to unbolt

descortés *adj* impolite

descoser **I.** *vt* to unpick *Brit,* to unstitch **II.** *vr:* ~**se** **1.** (*costura*) to come apart at the seam **2.** *inf* to fart

descosido, -a *adj* **como un** ~ (*loco*) like mad

descrédito *m* discredit

descreído, -a *adj* sceptical *Brit,* skeptical *Am*

descremar *vt* (*milk*) to skim

describir *irr como* escribir *vt* **1.** (*explicar*) to describe **2.** (*trazar*) to trace

descripción *f* description

descuartizar <z→c> *vt* to cut up

descubierto *m* **1.** (*lugar*) **al** ~ in the open **2.** (*bancario*) overdraft; **quedar al** ~ to be revealed

descubierto, -a **I.** *pp de* descubrir **II.** *adj* open; (*cielo*) clear; (*cabeza*) uncovered

descubrimiento *m* **1.** (*invento*) discovery **2.** (*revelación*) disclosure

descubrir *irr como* abrir **I.** *vt* **1.** (*destapar*) to uncover **2.** (*encontrar*) to discover **3.** (*averiguar*) to find out **4.** (*inventar*) to invent **II.** *vr:* ~**se** to come out

descuento *m* **1.** (*deducción*) discount **2.** (*rebaja*) reduction

descuidado, -a *adj* **1.** *ser* (*falto de atención*) inattentive; (*de cuidado*) careless; (*desaseado*) slovenly **2.** *estar* (*abandonado*) neglected; (*desprevenido*) unprepared

descuidar **I.** *vt* **1.** (*desatender*) to neglect; **¡descuida!** don't worry! **2.** (*ignorar*) to overlook **II.** *vr:* ~**se** to neglect oneself, to let oneself go

descuido *m* **1.** (*falta de atención*) inattentiveness; (*de cuidado*) carelessness **2.** (*error*) oversight

desde **I.** *prep* **1.** (*pasado*) since; (*a partir de*) from; **¿~ cuándo vives aquí?** how long have you lived here (for)?; ~ **entonces** since then; ~ **hace un mes** for a month **2.** (*local*) from; **te llamo ~ el aeropuerto** I'm calling from the airport **II.** *adv* ~ **luego** of course **III.** *conj* ~ **que** since

desdecir *irr como* decir **I.** *vi* to be unworthy **II.** *vr:* ~**se** to take back

desdén *m* disdain

desdeñar *vt* to scorn

desdicha *f* **1.** (*desgracia*) misfortune **2.** (*miseria*) misery

desdichado, -a *adj* unfortunate

desdoblar *vt* (*desplegar*) to unfold; (*extender*) to open out

desear *vt* to want; (*sexualmente*) to

desire; **¿desea algo más?** would you like anything else?

desecarse <c→qu> *vr* to dry up

desechable *adj* **1.** (*de un solo uso*) disposable **2.** (*despreciable*) despicable

desechar *vt* **1.** (*tirar*) to throw away **2.** (*descartar*) to rule out

desecho(s) *m(pl)* (*restos*) remains *pl;* (*residuos*) residue

desembalar *vt* to unpack

desembarazado, -a *adj* **1.** (*expedito*) free **2.** (*desenvuelto*) free and easy

desembarazar <z→c> **I.** *vt* (*despejar*) to clear; (*librar*) to free **II.** *vr:* ~**se** to free oneself

desembarcar <c→qu> **I.** *vi* to disembark **II.** *vt* to unload

desembocadura *f* mouth

desembocar <c→qu> *vi* to flow into

desembolso *m* payment

desembragar <g→gu> *vi* AUTO to release the clutch

desembrollar *vt inf* **1.** (*madeja*) to disentangle **2.** (*asunto*) to sort out

desempatar *vi* to break the tie

desempate *m* breakthrough

desempeñar *vt* (*cargo*) to hold; (*trabajo*) to carry out; ~ **un papel** to play a role

desempeño *m* (*ejercicio*) fulfilment *Brit,* fulfillment *Am;* (*realización*) performance

desempleado, -a *m, f* unemployed person

desempleo *m* unemployment

desempolvar *vt* (*limpiar*) to dust

desencadenar **I.** *vt* **1.** (*soltar*) to unleash **2.** (*provocar*) to trigger **II.** *vr:* ~**se** to break loose

desencajar *vt* (*sacar*) to dismantle; MED to dislocate

desencanto *m* disillusion

desenchufar *vt* to unplug

desenfadado, -a *adj* **1.** (*carácter*) easy-going **2.** (*ropa*) casual

desenfado *m* openness

desenfocado, -a *adj* FOTO out of focus

desenfrenado, -a *adj* frantic

desenfreno *m* lack of restraint

desenganchar *vt* **1.** (*gancho*) to unhook **2.** (*soltar*) to take off **3.** FERRO to uncouple

desengañar **I.** *vt* to disillusion **II.** *vr:* ~**se** to be disappointed

desengaño *m* disillusion

desenlace *m* outcome

desenmarañar *vt* to untangle

desenmascarar *vt* to unmask; *fig* to expose

desenredar *vt t. fig* to unravel; (*pelo*) to untangle

desentenderse <e→ie> *vr* **1.** (*despreocuparse*) ~ **de algo** to want nothing to do with sth **2.** (*fingir ignorancia*) to pretend to not know about

desenterrar <e→ie> *vt* to dig up; (*cadáver*) to exhume

desentonar *vi* **1.** (*cantar*) to sing out of tune **2.** (*no combinar*) to not go

desentrañar *vt* to unravel

desentumecer *irr como crecer* *vt* to loosen up; DEP to warm up

desenvoltura *f* self-confidence

desenvolver *irr como volver* **I.** *vt* **1.** (*desempaquetar*) to unwrap **2.** (*desarrollar*) to develop **II.** *vr:* ~**se** **1.** (*llevarse*) to get on with **2.** (*manejarse*) to handle oneself

deseo *m* **1.** (*anhelo*) wish **2.** (*necesidad*) need **3.** (*sexual*) desire

deseoso, -a *adj* eager

desequilibrado, -a *adj* unbalanced; (*persona*) (mentally) disturbed

desertar *vi* MIL to desert

desértico, -a *adj* desert

desertor(a) *m(f)* deserter

desesperación *f* **1.** (*desmoralización*) desperation, despair **2.** (*enojo*) exasperation

desesperado, -a *adj* **1.** (*desmoralizado*) desperate; (*situación*) hopeless **2.** (*enojado*) exasperated

desesperar **I.** *vt* **1.** (*quitar la esperanza*) ~ **a alguien** to cause sb to lose hope **2.** (*exasperar*) to exasperate **II.** *vi* to despair **III.** *vr:* ~**se** **1.** (*perder la esperanza*) to give up hope **2.** (*lamentarse*) to despair

desestimar *vt* **1.** (*despreciar*) to have a low opinion of **2.** (*rechazar*) to reject

desfachatez *f* cheek

desfalco *m* embezzlement

desfallecer *irr como crecer vi* **1.**(*debilitarse*) to weaken **2.**(*perder el ánimo*) to lose heart

desfasado, -a *adj* **1.**(*persona*) old--fashioned; (*cosa*) antiquated **2.** TÉC out of phase

desfase *m* (*diferencia*) gap

desfavorable *adj* unfavourable *Brit,* unfavorable *Am*

desfigurar *vt* **1.**(*las facciones*) to disfigure; (*el cuerpo*) to deform **2.**(*deformar*) to deface; (*una imagen*) to distort

desfiladero *m* GEO gorge

desfilar *vi* to parade

desfile *m* **1.**(*de tropas*) march-past; (*parada*) parade; **~ de modelos** fashion show **2.**(*personas*) procession

desfogar <g→gu> **I.** *vt* (*sentimiento*) to vent **II.** *vi* (*tormenta*) to break **III.** *vr:* ~**se** to let off steam

desgajar I. *vt* **1.**(*arrancar*) to tear off **2.**(*despedazar*) to tear to pieces **II.** *vr:* ~**se** to come off

desgana *f* **1.**(*inapetencia*) lack of appetite **2.**(*falta de interés*) lack of enthusiasm

desganado, -a *adj* **estar ~** (*sin apetito*) to have no appetite; (*sin entusiasmo*) to have lost one's enthusiasm

desgarrador(a) *adj* heartrending

desgarrar I. *vt* to tear; **esto me desgarra el corazón** *fig* this breaks my heart **II.** *vr:* ~**se 1.**(*romperse*) to tear **2.**(*anímicamente*) to break one's heart

desgarro *m* **1.**(*rotura*) tear **2.**(*descaro*) cheek

desgastar I. *vt* **1.**(*estropear*) to wear out **2.**(*consumir*) to use up **II.** *vr:* ~**se** to wear out

desgaste *m* **1.**(*fricción*) wear **2.**(*consumo*) consumption

desglosar *vt* to treat separately

desgracia *f* **1.**(*suerte adversa*) bad luck; **por ~** unfortunately **2.**(*acontecimiento*) misfortune; **es una ~**

que... +*subj* it's a terrible shame that … **3.**(*pérdida de gracia*) disgrace; **caer en ~** to fall into disgrace

desgraciado, -a I. *adj* **1.**(*sin suerte*) unlucky **2.**(*infeliz*) miserable **3.**(*que implica desgracia*) unfortunate **II.** *m, f* **1.**(*sin suerte*) unlucky person **2.** *pey* (*miserable*) scoundrel, rotter

desgravación *f* **1.**(*de un impuesto*) tax allowance, tax deduction **2.**(*de un gasto*) tax relief

desgravar *vt* to reduce the tax on

desgreñado, -a *adj* dishevelled

desguace *m* scrapyard *Brit,* breaker's yard

desguazar <z→c> *vt* to scrap *Brit,* to break up, to wreck

deshabitado, -a *adj* (*edificio*) empty

deshacer *irr como hacer* **I.** *vt* **1.**(*paquete*) to unwrap; (*costura*) to unpick; (*un nudo*) to undo; (*cama*) to mess up; (*maleta*) to unpack **2.**(*romper*) to break **3.**(*arruinar*) to ruin; (*plan*) to spoil **4.**(*hielo*) to melt; (*contrato*) to dissolve **II.** *vr:* ~**se 1.**(*descomponerse*) to come apart; (*hielo*) to melt; ~**se en llanto** to cry one's heart out; ~**se de nervios** to be a nervous wreck **2.**(*romperse*) to break **3.**(*desprenderse*) to come away; (*librarse*) to get rid of

deshecho, -a I. *pp de* **deshacer** **II.** *adj* **1.**(*deprimido*) devastated **2.**(*cansado*) tired

deshelar <e→ie> *vt* (*hielo*) to melt; (*nieve*) to thaw; (*una nevera*) to defrost

desheredar *vt* to disinherit

deshidratar *vt* to dry; (*cuerpo*) to dehydrate

deshielo *m* thaw

deshinchar I. *vt* **1.**(*sacar el aire*) to deflate **2.**(*una inflamación*) to reduce **II.** *vr:* ~**se 1.**(*perder aire*) to deflate **2.**(*una inflamación*) to go down

deshonesto, -a *adj* **1.**(*inmoral*) indecent **2.**(*tramposo*) dishonest

deshonra *f* disgrace

deshonrar *vt* to disgrace; (*ofender*) to offend; (*humillar*) to humiliate

deshora *f* inconvenient time; **hablar a** ~(**s**) to interrupt; **venir a** ~(**s**) to arrive too late

desierto *m* GEO desert

desierto, -a *adj* **1.** (*sin gente*) deserted **2.** (*como un desierto*) desert

designar *vt* **1.** (*dar un nombre*) to designate **2.** (*destinar*) to assign; (*fecha*) to set; (*nombrar*) to appoint; (*candidato*) to select

designio *m* **1.** (*plan*) plan **2.** (*propósito*) intention

desigual *adj* **1.** (*distinto*) unequal **2.** (*injusto*) unfair **3.** (*inconstante*) inconsistent

desigualdad *f* **1.** (*diferencia*) inequality **2.** (*irregularidad*) unevenness **3.** (*del carácter*) inconsistency

desilusión *f* **1.** (*desengaño*) disappointment **2.** (*desencanto*) disillusion

desilusionar **I.** *vt* **1.** (*quitar la ilusión*) to disillusion **2.** (*decepcionar*) to disappoint **II.** *vr:* ~**se** to become disillusioned

desinfectar *vt* to disinfect

desinflar **I.** *vt* to deflate **II.** *vr:* ~**se** to go down

desintegración *f* disintegration; (*debido al clima*) erosion; Fís fission

desinterés *m* **1.** (*indiferencia*) indifference **2.** (*altruismo*) altruism

desistir *vi* **1.** (*de un proyecto*) to give up **2.** (*de un derecho*) to waive; (*de un cargo*) to resign from

desleal *adj* (*infiel*) disloyal; (*competencia*) unfair; (*publicidad*) misleading

deslealtad *f* disloyalty

desleír *irr como* reír *vt, vr:* ~**se** to dissolve

deslenguado, -a *adj* foul-mouthed

desligar <g→gu> **I.** *vt* **1.** (*un nudo*) to undo **2.** (*un asunto*) to clear up **3.** (*separar*) to separate **II.** *vr:* ~**se** (*de un compromiso*) to be released

desliz *m* **1.** (*error*) slip **2.** (*adulterio*) affair

deslizar <z→c> **I.** *vt, vi* to slip; ~ **la mano sobre algo** to run one's hand over sth **II.** *vr:* ~**se 1.** (*sobre algo*) to slide over; (*por un tobogán*) to go

down **2.** (*escaparse*) to slip away **3.** (*un errror*) to slip up

deslucido, -a *adj* **1.** (*actuación*) lacklustre *Brit,* lackluster *Am* **2.** (*sin gracia*) dull

deslucir *irr como* lucir *vt* **1.** (*estropear*) to ruin **2.** (*metal*) to tarnish; (*colores*) to fade **3.** (*desacreditar*) to discredit

deslumbrar *vt* to dazzle

desmadrarse *vr inf* to go wild

desmadre *m* outrageous behaviour

desmán *m* **1.** (*salvajada*) outrage **2.** (*exceso*) excess

desmandarse *vr* **1.** (*rebelarse*) to rebel; (*descontrolarse*) to get out of control **2.** (*insolentarse*) to be insolent

desmano *m* **a** ~ out of the way

desmantelar *vt* **1.** (*un edificio*) to demolish **2.** (*desmontar*) to take apart; (*bomba*) to dismantle; (*escenario*) to take down **3.** NÁUT (*desarbolar*) to unmast

desmaquillador *m* make-up remover

desmaquillarse *vr* to take one's make-up off

desmayado, -a *adj* **1.** (*sin conocimiento*) unconscious **2.** (*sin fuerza*) exhausted

desmayar **I.** *vi* (*desanimarse*) to lose heart **II.** *vr:* ~**se** to faint

desmayo *m* **1.** (*desvanecimiento*) faint **2.** (*desánimo*) dismay **3.** (*debilidad*) weakness

desmedido, -a *adj* excessive; (*apetito*) enormous

desmejorar **I.** *vt* (*estropear*) to ruin; (*gastar*) to wear out **II.** *vi* to deteriorate

desmembrar <e→ie> *vt* **1.** (*desunir*) to break up **2.** (*escindir*) to separate; (*un cuerpo*) to dismember

desmentir *irr como* sentir **I.** *vt* **1.** (*negar*) to deny; (*contradecir*) to contradict **2.** (*sospecha*) to refute **II.** *vr:* ~**se** to contradict oneself

desmenuzar <z→c> *vt* **1.** (*deshacer*) to break into pieces; (*con un cuchillo*) to chop up; (*con los dedos*) to crumble **2.** (*analizar*) to scrutinize

desmerecer *irr como crecer* **I.** *vt* (*no merecer*) to not deserve **II.** *vi* **1.** (*decaer*) to decline; (*belleza*) to lose one's looks **2.** (*ser inferior*) ~ **de alguien/algo** to be worse than sb/sth

desmesurado, -a *adj* **1.** (*enorme*) enormous **2.** (*excesivo*) excessive; (*ambición*) boundless **3.** (*desvergonzado*) shameless

desmontable *adj* (*que se puede quitar*) detachable; (*sacar*) removable; (*doblar*) foldable

desmontar **I.** *vt* **1.** (*un mecanismo*) to disassemble **2.** (*una pieza*) to detach, to remove **3.** (*una estructura*) to take down **4.** (*una pistola*) to uncock **5.** (*de un caballo*) to throw **II.** *vi* (*de un caballo*) to dismount; (*de una moto*) to help get down from

desmoralizar <z→c> **I.** *vt* to demoralize **II.** *vr:* ~**se** to lose heart

desmoronar **I.** *vt* (*deshacer*) to wear away; GEO to erode **II.** *vr:* ~**se** **1.** (*un edificio*) to fall down **2.** (*disminuir*) to decline

desnatar *vt* (*la leche*) to skim

desnivel *m* **1.** (*de altura*) drop **2.** (*disparidad*) inequality; ~ **cultural** cultural difference **3.** (*altibajo*) unevenness

desnucarse <c→qu> *vr* to break one's neck

desnudar **I.** *vt* **1.** (*desvestir*) to undress **2.** (*descubrir*) to strip **II.** *vr:* ~**se** to undress

desnudez *f* **1.** (*persona*) nudity **2.** *fig* bareness

desnudo *m* ARTE nude

desnudo, -a *adj* **1.** (*desvestido*) naked, nude **2.** (*despojado*) bare **3.** (*claro*) clear; **al** ~ clearly; **la verdad desnuda** the plain truth

desnutrición *f* malnutrition

desnutrido, -a *adj* undernourished

desobedecer *irr como crecer* *vi, vt* to disobey

desobediencia *f* disobedience

desocupación *f* **1.** (*paro*) unemployment **2.** (*ociosidad*) leisure

desocupado, -a **I.** *adj* **1.** (*parado*) unemployed **2.** (*vacío*) empty; (*vivienda*) vacant **II.** *m, f* unemployed person

desocupar **I.** *vt* **1.** (*evacuar*) to evacuate; (*vivienda*) to vacate **2.** (*vaciar*) to empty **II.** *vr:* ~**se 1.** (*de una ocupación*) to get away **2.** (*quedarse vacante*) to be vacant

desodorante *m* deodorant; ~ **en espray** deodorant spray

desolación *f* **1.** (*devastación*) desolation **2.** (*desconsuelo*) distress

desolar <o→ue> **I.** *vt* to devastate **II.** *vr:* ~**se** to be devastated

desollar <o→ue> *vt* (*quitar la piel*) to flay, to skin

desorbitado, -a *adj* **1.** (*ojos*) bulging **2.** (*exagerado*) exaggerated; (*desmedido*) exhorbitant

desorbitar **I.** *vt* (*exagerar*) to exaggerate **II.** *vr:* ~**se** to get out of control

desorden *m* **1.** (*desarreglo*) mess; (*confusión*) chaos; ~ **público** public disturbance **2.** (*exceso*) excess **3.** *pl* (*alboroto*) disorders *pl* **4.** MED disorder

desordenado, -a *adj* (*desorganizado*) jumbled; (*cosa*) messy; (*vida*) chaotic

desordenar *vt* (*turbar*) to mess up; (*mezclar*) to mix up; (*pelo*) to ruffle

desorganizar <z→c> *vt* to disrupt; (*planes*) to disturb

desorientación *f* **1.** (*extravío*) disorientation **2.** (*confusión*) confusion

desorientar **I.** *vt* **1.** (*extraviar*) to lose one's bearings **2.** (*confundir*) to confuse **II.** *vr:* ~**se** to become disorientated *Brit,* to become disoriented *Am*

desovar *vi* (*pez, anfibio*) to spawn; (*insecto*) to lay eggs

despabilado, -a *adj* **1.** (*listo*) smart **2.** (*despierto*) alert

despabilar **I.** *vt* **1.** (*despertar*) to wake up **2.** (*avivar*) to sharpen up **3.** (*acabar deprisa*) to finish off **II.** *vi* (*darse prisa*) to hurry up **III.** *vr:* ~**se 1.** (*despertar*) to waken up **2.** (*darse prisa*) to hurry up

despachar **I.** *vt* **1.** (*mercancías*) to dispatch **2.** (*concluir*) to finish off

3.(*resolver*) to decide **4.**(*atender*) to serve, to wait on **5.**(*vender*) to sell **6.**(*matar*) to kill **7.**inf (*despedir*) to dismiss, to sack *Brit,* to fire *Am* **II.** *vi* **1.**(*acabar*) to finish **2.**(*atender*) to do business **3.**(*con alguien*) to consult with **III.** *vr:* ~**se 1.**(*darse prisa*) to hurry up **2.**(*desahogarse*) to let off steam; ~**se a (su) gusto** to speak frankly

despacho *m* **1.**(*oficina*) office; (*en casa*) study; ~ **de aduana** customs office; ~ **de billetes** [*o* **boletos**] *AmL* FERRO ticket office; ~ **de localidades** TEAT, CINE box office; **mesa de** ~ desk **2.**(*envío*) sending **3.**(*de un asunto*) resolution; (*entrevista*) consultation **4.**(*de clientes*) service **5.**(*venta*) sale **6.**(*despido*) dismissal **7.**(*de un pedido*) dispatch, shipping; (*de la correspondencia, el equipaje*) sending **8.**(*muebles*) office furniture **9.**(*comunicado*) dispatch

despacio **I.** *adv* **1.**(*lentamente*) slowly **2.**(*calladamente*) quietly **II.** *interj* take it easy

despampanante *adj* (*mujer*) stunning

desparpajo *m* **1.**(*desenvoltura*) self--confidence; (*en el hablar*) ease; **con** ~ confidently **2.**(*frescura*) cheek; **con** ~ cheekily

desparramar *vt* **1.**(*dispersar*) to scatter **2.**(*un líquido*) to spill **3.**(*malgastar*) to waste

despavorido, -a *adj* terrified

despecho *m* spite, rancour *Brit,* rancor *Am;* **a** ~ **de algo** in spite of sth

despectivo, -a *adj* **1.**(*despreciativo*) contemptuous; (*desdeñoso*) disdainful **2.**LING pejorative

despedazar <z→c> *vt* (*romper*) to smash; (*en mil pedazos*) to tear to pieces; (*con una tijera*) to cut up

despedida *f* **1.**(*separación*) goodbye, farewell **2.**(*acto oficial*) send--off; (*fiesta*) leaving party; ~ **de soltero** stag night; ~ **de soltera** hen night **3.**(*en una carta*) close

despedir *irr como pedir* **I.** *vt* **1.**(*decir adiós*) to say goodbye; **vinieron a** ~**me al aeropuerto** they came to the airport to see me off **2.**(*echar*) to throw out; (*de un empleo*) to dismiss, to sack *Brit,* to fire *Am* **3.**(*emitir*) to emit; **el volcán despide fuego** the volcano gives off flames **4.**(*lanzar*) to launch **II.** *vr:* ~**se 1.**(*decir adiós*) to say goodbye; **despídete de ese dinero** say goodbye to that money **2.**(*dejar un empleo*) to leave

despegar <g→gu> **I.** *vt* to unstick **II.** *vi* (*avión*) to take off **III.** *vr:* ~**se 1.**(*desprenderse*) to come off **2.**(*perder el afecto*) to lose one's feelings for

despego *m* **1.**(*falta de cariño*) coldness **2.**(*falta de afecto*) lack of feeling

despegue *m* AERO, ECON take-off; (*cohete*) blast-off

despeinado, -a *adj* unkempt

despeinar *vt* to ruffle

despejado, -a *adj* **1.**(*sin nubes, cabeza*) clear **2.**(*ancho*) wide; (*habitación*) spacious **3.**(*listo*) smart

despejar **I.** *vt* **1.** *t.* DEP (*lugar*) to clear; (*sala*) to tidy up **2.**(*situación*) to clarify; (*misterio*) to clear up **II.** *vr:* ~**se 1.**(*cielo, misterio*) to clear up **2.**(*despabilarse*) to wake up

despellejar *vt* **1.**(*desollar*) to flay, to skin **2.** inf (*criticar*) to cut to bits

despeluznante *adj* terrifying

despensa *f* **1.**(*fresquera*) larder, pantry **2.**(*provisiones*) provisions *pl*

despeñadero *m* GEO precipice

despeñar *vt* to throw down

desperdiciar *vt* to waste; (*ocasión*) to miss

desperdicio *m* **1.**(*residuo*) rubbish *Brit,* garbage *Am* **2.**(*malbaratamiento*) waste

desperdigar <g→gu> *vt, vr:* ~**se** to scatter

desperezarse <z→c> *vr* to stretch

desperfecto *m* **1.**(*deterioro*) damage **2.**(*defecto*) fault, defect

despertador *m* alarm clock

despertar <e→ie> *vt, vr:* ~**se** to wake up

despiadado, -a *adj* (*inhumano*) ruthless; (*cruel*) cruel

despido *m* (*descontratación*) dismissal, sack

despierto, **-a** *adj* **1.** (*insomne*) awake **2.** (*listo*) smart

despilfarrar *vt* to waste; (*dinero*) to squander

despilfarro *m* (*derroche*) waste; (*de dinero*) squandering

despiojar *vt* to delouse

despistado, -a *adj* absent-minded

despistar **I.** *vt* (*confundir*) to confuse; (*desorientar*) to mislead **II.** *vr:* ~se **1.** (*perderse*) to get lost **2.** (*desconcertarse*) to become confused

despiste *m* **1.** (*distracción*) confusion **2.** (*error*) slip

desplazamiento *m* **1.** (*traslado*) displacement **2.** (*remoción*) removal

desplazar <z→c> *vt* **1.** (*mover*) to move **2.** (*suplantar*) to displace

desplegar *irr como* **fregar** *vt* **1.** (*abrir*) to open out; (*desdoblar*) to unfold; (*bandera*) to unfurl **2.** MIL to deploy

despliegue *m* **1.** (*desdoblamiento*) unfolding **2.** MIL deployment

desplomarse *vr* to collapse

desplumar *vt* **1.** (*plumas*) to pluck **2.** (*robar*) to fleece

despoblado *m* deserted place

despoblado, -a *adj* depopulated

despojar **I.** *vt* to strip; (*de un derecho*) to deprive **II.** *vr:* ~se **1.** (*desistir*) to give up **2.** (*quitar*) to remove; (*ropa*) to take off

despojo *m* **1.** (*presa*) spoils *pl* **2.** *pl* (*restos*) leftovers *pl;* (*del matadero*) offal

desposado, -a *adj* newly wed

desposar **I.** *vt* to marry **II.** *vr:* ~se to get married to

desposeer *irr como* **leer** **I.** *vt* **1.** (*expropiar*) to dispossess **2.** (*no reconocer*) to not recognize; (*de derechos*) to deprive **II.** *vr:* ~se **1.** (*renunciar*) to give up **2.** (*desapropiarse*) to relinquish

déspota *mf* despot

despotismo *m* despotism

despotricar <c→qu> *vi inf* to rant and rave about

despreciar **I.** *vt* **1.** (*menospreciar*) to

despise **2.** (*rechazar*) to spurn; (*oferta*) to turn down **II.** *vr:* ~se to run oneself down

desprecio *m* contempt

desprender **I.** *vt* **1.** (*soltar*) to release **2.** (*gas*) to give off **3.** (*deducir*) to deduce **II.** *vr:* ~se **1.** (*soltarse*) to untie oneself **2.** (*deshacerse*) to come undone; (*desembarazarse*) to get rid of

desprendimiento *m* **1.** (*separación*) separation; ~ **de tierras** landslide **2.** (*generosidad*) generosity

despreocupado, -a *adj* **1.** (*negligente*) careless **2.** (*tranquilo*) unconcerned

despreocuparse *vr* **1.** (*tranquilizarse*) to stop worrying **2.** (*desatender*) to neglect

desprestigiar *vt* to discredit

desprevenido, -a *adj* unprepared

desproporcionado, -a *adj* disproportionate

despropósito *m* stupid remark

desprovisto, -a *adj* ~ **de** lacking

después **I.** *adv* **1.** (*tiempo*) after; **una hora** ~ an hour later; ~ **de todo** after all **2.** (*espacio*) ~ **de la torre** behind the tower **II.** *conj* ~ (**de**) **que** after

desquiciado, -a *adj inf* disturbed

desquite *m* **1.** (*satisfacción*) satisfaction **2.** (*venganza*) revenge

destacado, -a *adj* outstanding

destacar <c→qu> **I.** *vi* to stand out **II.** *vt* (*realzar*) to emphasize **III.** *vr:* ~se to stand out

destajo *m* piecework; **trabajar a** ~ to do piecework; *fig* to work hard

destapar **I.** *vt* **1.** (*abrir*) to open; (*olla*) to take the lid off **2.** (*desabrigar*) to uncover **3.** (*secretos*) to reveal **II.** *vr:* ~se **1.** (*perder la tapa*) to lose its lid **2.** (*desabrigarse*) to be uncovered **3.** (*descubrirse*) to be revealed

destaponar *vt* **1.** (*una botella*) to uncork **2.** (*obstrucción*) to unplug

destartalado, -a *adj* ramshackle

destello *m* **1.** (*reflejo*) glint **2.** (*resplandor*) sparkle

destemplado, -a *adj* **1.** (*voz*) harsh **2.** (*tiempo*) unpleasant **3.** (*persona*) bad-tempered

desteñir *irr como ceñir vi, vt* to fade

desternillarse *vr* ~ **de risa** to laugh one's head off

desterrar <e→ie> *vt* **1.** (*exiliar*) to exile **2.** (*alejar*) to banish

destetar *vt* to wean

destiempo *m* **a** ~ at the wrong moment

destierro *m* exile

destilar **I.** *vi* to distil *Brit*, to distill *Am* **II.** *vt* **1.** (*alambicar*) to distil *Brit*, to distill *Am* **2.** (*sentimiento*) to exude

destilería *f* distillery; ~ **de petróleo** oil refinery

destinar *vt* **1.** (*dedicar*) to dedicate **2.** (*enviar*) to send **3.** (*designar*) to appoint

destinatario, -a *m, f* (*correo*) addressee; (*mercancía*) consignee

destino *m* **1.** (*hado*) fate **2.** (*empleo*) job, post *Brit* **3.** (*destinación*) destination; **estación de** ~ destination station; **el barco sale con** ~ **a México** the boat is bound for Mexico **4.** (*finalidad*) purpose

destituir *irr como huir vt* to dismiss

destornillador *m* screwdriver, turnscrew *Brit*

destornillar *vt* to unscrew

destreza *f* skill; ~ **manual** dexterity

destrozar <z→c> *vt* **1.** (*despedazar*) to smash; (*libro*) to rip up; (*ropa*) to tear up **2.** (*moralmente*) to shatter **3.** *inf* (*físicamente*) to shatter; **el viaje me ha destrozado** I'm absolutely exhausted from the journey **4.** (*planes*) to ruin **5.** (*enemigo*) to destroy

destrozo *m* **1.** (*daño*) damage **2.** (*acción*) destruction

destrucción *f* destruction

destruir *irr como huir vt* **1.** (*destrozar*) to destroy **2.** (*físicamente*) to shatter **3.** (*aniquilar*) to annihilate

desunión *f* **1.** (*separación*) separation **2.** (*discordia*) disunity

desunir **I.** *vt* **1.** (*separar*) to separate **2.** (*enemistar*) to cause discord **II.** *vr:* ~**se 1.** (*separar*) to separate **2.** (*enemistar*) to fall out

desuso *m* **caer en** ~ to fall into disuse; (*máquina*) to become obsolete

desvalido, -a *adj* needy

desvalijar *vt* to clean out *inf*

desvalorización *f* FIN depreciation

desvalorizar <z→c> *vt* to devalue

desván *m* loft, attic

desvanecer *irr como crecer* **I.** *vt* **1.** (*color*) to tone down **2.** (*dudas*) to dispel; (*sospechas*) to allay **II.** *vr:* ~**se 1.** (*desaparecer*) to disappear; (*esperanzas*) to fade **2.** (*desmayarse*) to faint

desvanecimiento *m* **1.** (*desaparición*) disappearance **2.** (*mareo*) faint

desvariar <1. pres: desvarío> *vi* (*delirar*) to be delirious; (*decir incoherencias*) to talk nonsense

desvarío *m* **1.** (*locura*) madness **2.** (*delirio*) delirium

desvelar **I.** *vt* **1.** (*sueño*) ~ **a alguien** to keep sb awake **2.** (*revelar*) to reveal **II.** *vr:* ~**se 1.** (*no dormir*) to stay awake **2.** (*por alguien*) to devote oneself to

desvencijado, -a *adj* dilapidated

desventaja *f* disadvantage, drawback

desventura *f* misfortune

desventurado, -a *adj* unfortunate

desvergonzado, -a *adj* **1.** (*sinvergüenza*) shameless **2.** (*descarado*) brazen

desvergüenza *f* shamelessness

desvestir *irr como pedir vt, vr:* ~**se** to undress

desviación *f* **1.** (*torcedura*) deviation **2.** (*del tráfico*) diversion, detour

desviar <1. pres: desvío> **I.** *vt* (*del camino, dinero*) to divert; (*de un propósito*) to distract **II.** *vr:* ~**se 1.** (*del camino*) to be diverted; (*del tema*) to be distracted; (*de una intención*) to be put off **2.** (*extraviarse*) to get lost

desvío *m* **1.** (*desviación*) deviation **2.** (*carretera*) detour

desvirgar <g→gu> *vt* to deflower

desvirtuar <1. pres: desvirtúo> *vt* (*argumento*) to undermine; (*rumor*) to scotch

desvivirse *vr* **1.** (*por alguien*) to be

crazy about **2.** (*afanarse*) to be devoted to

detallar *vt* to detail, to itemize

detalle *m* **1.** (*pormenor*) detail; **venta al** ~ retail sales **2.** (*finura*) nice gesture

detallista **I.** *adj* precise **II.** *mf* COM retailer

detectar *vt* to detect

detective *mf* detective

detector *m* detector

detención *f* **1.** (*parada*) stopping **2.** JUR arrest **3.** (*dilación*) delay

detener *irr como tener* **I.** *vt* **1.** (*parar*) to stop; (*progresos*) to halt **2.** JUR to arrest **II.** *vr:* ~**se** to stop; ~**se en algo** to pass one's time doing sth

detenidamente *adv* thoroughly, carefully

detenido, -a **I.** *adj* **1.** (*minucioso*) thorough **2.** (*arrestado*) arrested **II.** *m, f* person under arrest

detenimiento *m* care; **con** ~ thoroughly

detergente *m* detergent; (*para la ropa*) washing powder *Brit,* laundry detergent *Am*

deteriorar **I.** *vt* **1.** (*empeorar*) to worsen **2.** (*romper*) to break **II.** *vr:* ~**se** **1.** (*empeorarse*) to worsen **2.** (*estropearse*) to spoil

deterioro *m* **1.** (*desmejora*) deterioration **2.** (*daño*) damage

determinación *f* **1.** (*fijación*) establishment; (*de objetivos*) setting **2.** (*decisión*) decision; **tomar una** ~ to take a decision **3.** (*audacia*) determination

determinado, -a *adj* **1.** (*cierto*) *t.* LING definite **2.** (*atrevido*) determined **3.** (*preciso*) specific

determinar **I.** *vt* **1.** (*fijar*) to establish; (*plazo*) to fix **2.** (*decidir*) to decide **3.** (*causar*) to determine **II.** *vr* ~**se a hacer algo** to decide to do sth

detestable *adj* loathsome

detestar *vt* to detest, to loathe

detonación *f* **1.** (*acción*) detonation **2.** (*ruido*) explosion

detonante *m* (*causa*) cause

detonar *vt, vi* to detonate, to set off

detractor(a) **I.** *adj* denigrating **II.** *m(f)* detractor

detrás **I.** *adv* **1.** (*local*) behind; **allí** ~ over there, behind that **2.** (*en el orden*) **el que está** ~ the next one **II.** *prep* ~ **de** (*de una puerta*) behind; (*de una hoja*) on the back of; **ir** ~ **de alguien** to be looking for sb; **uno** ~ **de otro** one after another

detrimento *m* **1.** (*daño*) harm **2.** (*perjuicio*) detriment; **en** ~ **de su salud** at cost to his/her health

deuda *f* debt; **contraer** ~**s** to get into debt; **estar en** ~ **con** to be indebted to

deudor(a) *m(f)* debtor

devaluación *f* devaluation

devaluar <*1. pres:* devalúo> *vt* to devalue

devastar *vt* to devastate

devengar <g→gu> *vt* **1.** (*salario*) to earn **2.** (*intereses*) to yield

devenir *irr como venir vi* **1.** (*acaecer*) to occur **2.** (*convertirse*) to become

devoción *f* **1.** (*religión*) religious belief; (*a un santo*) to venerate **2.** (*respeto*) devotion; **amar con** ~ to love devotedly

devolución *f* return; ~ **de impuestos** tax refund, tax return

devolver *irr como volver* **I.** *vt* **1.** to return; *fig* to restore; ~ **cambio** to give change; ~ **la pelota** to pass the ball back **2.** (*vomitar*) to throw up **II.** *vr:* ~**se** *AmL* (*volver*) to return

devorar *vt* to devour; (*comida*) to wolf down; **me devora la impaciencia** I am consumed with impatience

devoto, -a **I.** *adj* **1.** (*religioso*) devout **2.** (*adicto*) devoted **II.** *m, f* **1.** (*creyente*) devotee **2.** (*admirador*) enthusiast

día *m* day; ~ **de año nuevo** New Year's day; ~ **hábil** [*o* **laborable**] working day; **el** ~ **del juicio final** Judgement Day; ~ **libre** day off; ~ **de Reyes** Epiphany; **el** ~ **de hoy** nowadays; **un** ~ **sí y otro no,** ~ **por medio** *AmL* every other day; **un** ~ **y otro** ~ again and again; **cualquier** ~ any day; **hoy** (**en**) ~ nowadays; **de hoy en ocho** ~**s** eight days from now; **de un ~ a otro** from one day to the next; **todo el santo ~** the whole day long; **estar al ~** to be up to date; **hace buen ~** it's nice weather; **tiene los ~s contados** his/her days are numbered; **vivir al ~** to live from day to day; **¡buenos ~s!** hello; (*por la mañana*) good morning; **de ~** by day

diabetes *f inv* diabetes

diabético, -a *adj, m, f* diabetic

diablo *m* devil; **¡~s!** damn!; **de mil ~s** hellish; **¡vete al ~!** go to hell!; **¿cómo ~s…?** how on earth …?; **¿qué ~s pasa aquí?** what the hell is going on here?

diablura *f* prank

diadema *f* (*corona*) diadem; (*joya*) tiara; (*del pelo*) hairband

diáfano, -a *adj* transparent

diafragma *m* **1.** FOTO, ANAT diaphragm **2.** (*anticonceptivo*) (Dutch) cap *Brit,* diaphragm *Am*

diagnosis *f inv* diagnosis

diagnosticar <c→qu> *vt* to diagnose

diagonal *adj, f* diagonal

diagrama *m* diagram

dial *m* dial

dialecto *m* dialect

dialogar <g→gu> *vi* (*hablar*) to talk; **~ con alguien** to have a conversation with sb

diálogo *m* dialogue *Brit,* dialog *Am*

diamante *m* diamond

diámetro *m* diameter

diana *f* **1.** MIL reveille **2.** (*objeto*) target **3.** (*del blanco*) bull's-eye

diapositiva *f* slide

diario *m* **1.** (*periódico*) (daily) newspaper **2.** (*dietario*) journal **3.** (*memorias*) diary

diario, -a *adj* daily

diarrea *f* diarrhoea *Brit,* diarrhea *Am*

dibujante *mf* (*lineal*) draughtsman *m,* draughtswoman *f;* (*de caricaturas*) cartoonist

dibujar **I.** *vt* **1.** (*trazar*) to draw **2.** (*describir*) to describe **II.** *vr:* **~se** to be outlined

dibujo *m* **1.** (*acción*) drawing **2.** (*resultado*) drawing; **~s animados** cartoons **3.** (*muestra*) illustration

diccionario *m* dictionary

dicha *f* (*suerte*) luck

dicho *m* **1.** (*ocurrencia*) observation **2.** (*refrán*) saying

dicho, -a I. *pp de* **decir** II. *adj* **dicha gente** the said people; **~ y hecho** no sooner said than done

dichoso, -a *adj* **1.** (*feliz*) happy **2.** *irón* (*maldito*) blessed

diciembre *m* December; *v.t.* **marzo**

dictado *m* **1.** (*escuela*) dictation **2.** *fig* (*dela conciencia*) dictate

dictador(a) *m(f)* dictator

dictadura *f* dictatorship

dictamen *m* **1.** (*peritaje*) opinion **2.** (*informe*) report **3.** (*opinión*) opinion

dictar *vt* **1.** (*un dictado*) to dictate **2.** (*una sentencia*) to pass **3.** (*un discurso*) to give **4.** *AmS* (*clases*) to teach

didáctico, -a *adj* didactic

diecinueve *adj inv, m* nineteen; *v.t.* **ocho**

dieciocho *adj inv, m* eighteen; *v.t.* **ocho**

dieciséis *adj inv, m* sixteen; *v.t.* **ocho**

diecisiete *adj inv, m* seventeen; *v.t.* **ocho**

diente *m* **1.** (*de la boca*) tooth; **~s postizos** false teeth **2.** TÉC tooth; (*de horquilla*) prong; **~ de ajo** BOT clove of garlic; **decir algo entre ~s** to mumble sth; **tener buen ~** to have a healthy appetite

diesel *m* diesel

diestro *m* (*torero*) matador

diestro, -a <destrísimo *o* diestrísimo> *adj* **1.** (*a la derecha*) right **2.** (*hábil*) skilful *Brit,* skillful *Am* **3.** (*no zurdo*) right-handed

dieta *f* **1.** (*para adelgazar*) diet; **estar a ~** to be on a diet **2.** *pl* (*retribución*) allowance

dietético, -a *adj* dietary

diez *adj inv, m* ten; *v.t.* **ocho**

diezmar *vt* (*aniquilar*) to decimate

difamación *f* defamation; (*escrita*) libel; (*oral*) slander

difamar *vt* to defame; (*por escrito*) to libel; (*hablando*) to slander

diferencia *f* **1.** *t.* MAT (*desigualdad*) difference; **a ~ de...** unlike ... **2.** (*desacuerdo*) disagreement

diferenciar **I.** *vt* **1.** (*distinguir*) to distinguish **2.** MAT to differentiate **II.** *vr:* **~se** to differ

diferente **I.** *adj* different; **~s veces** several times **II.** *adv* differently

diferir *irr como* **sentir** **I.** *vi* to differ **II.** *vt* to postpone; (*pago*) to delay payment

difícil *adj* difficult

dificultad *f* difficulty

dificultar *vt* to hinder; (*circulación*) to obstruct

difuminar *vt* (*dibujo*) to blur; (*luz*) to diffuse

difundir **I.** *vt* to spread; (*gas*) to give off; TV, RADIO to broadcast **II.** *vr:* **~se** to spread

difunto, -a **I.** *adj* deceased **II.** *m, f* deceased person; **día de ~s** All Souls' Day

difusión *f* (*divulgación*) dissemination; TV, RADIO broadcast

difuso, -a *adj* **1.** (*extendido*) widespread **2.** (*vago*) diffuse

digerir *irr como* **sentir** *vt* **1.** (*la comida*) to digest **2.** (*a una persona*) to stomach

digestión *f* (*de alimentos*) digestion; **corte de ~** stomach cramp

digestivo, -a *adj* digestive

digital *adj* **1.** (*dactilar*) finger; **huellas ~es** fingerprints *pl* **2.** INFOR, TÉC digital; **ordenador ~** digital computer

digitalizar <z→c> *vt* to digitize *Brit,* to digitalize *Am*

dígito *m* MAT, INFOR digit; **~ de control** check bit

dignarse *vr* to condescend to

dignidad *f* **1.** (*respeto*) dignity **2.** (*decencia*) decency

digno, -a *adj* **1.** (*merecedor*) worthy; **~ de ver** worth seeing **2.** (*noble*) noble

dilapidar *vt* to squander; **~ una fortuna** to squander a fortune

dilatar **I.** *vt* **1.** (*extender*) to expand; MED to dilate **2.** (*aplazar*) to postpone **3.** (*retrasar*) to delay **4.** (*prolongar*) to prolong **II.** *vr:* **~se** **1.** (*extenderse*) to expand **2.** AmL (*demorar*) to delay

dilema *m* dilemma

diligencia *f* **1.** (*esmero*) diligence **2.** (*agilidad*) skill **3.** (*trámite*) paperwork **4.** (*administrativa*) procedure **5.** (*carreta*) stagecoach

diligente *adj* diligent

diluir *irr como* **huir** **I.** *vt* **1.** (*líquidos*) to dilute **2.** (*sólidos*) to dissolve **II.** *vr:* **~se** to dissolve

diluvio *m* **1.** (*lluvia*) downpour **2.** *inf* (*abundancia*) shower; **~ de balas** hail of bullets

dimensión *f* dimension; *fig* magnitude; **la ~ cultural** the cultural aspect

diminutivo *m* LING diminutive

diminuto, -a *adj* tiny

dimisión *f* resignation

dimitir *vt, vi* to resign

Dinamarca *f* Denmark

dinamarqués, -esa **I.** *adj* Danish **II.** *m, f* Dane

dinámica *f* dynamics *pl*

dinámico, -a *adj* dynamic

dinamita *f* dynamite

dinamo *f,* **dínamo** *f* dynamo

dinastía *f* dynasty

dineral *m* fortune

dinero *m* money; **~ electrónico** e-money; **~ metálico** hard cash; **~ negro** undeclared money; **~ suelto** loose change; **estar mal de ~** to be short of money

dinosaurio *m* dinosaur

dio *3. pret de* **dar**

diócesis *f inv* diocese

dios(a) *m(f)* god *m,* goddess *f*

Dios *m* God; **~ te bendiga** God bless you; **~ dirá** time will tell; **¡~ mío!** my God!; **todo ~** everyone; **¡por ~!** for God's sake!; **¡válgame ~!** good God!; **¡vaya por ~!** for Heaven's sake!; **a la buena de ~** at random; **armar la de ~ es Cristo** *inf* to raise a hell of a row; **hacer algo como ~ manda** to do sth properly; **vivir como ~** to live like a lord; **~ los cría y ellos se juntan** *prov* birds of a feather flock together

diploma *m* diploma
diplomacia *f* diplomacy
diplomado, -a *adj* qualified
diplomático, -a I. *adj* diplomatic II. *m, f* diplomat
diptongo *m* diphthong
diputación *f* 1.(*delegación*) deputation; ~ **provincial** provincial delegation of government 2.(*personas*) delegation
diputado, -a *m, f* member of parliament
dique *m* 1.(*rompeolas*) dike 2. NÁUT dry dock
dirección *f* 1.(*rumbo*) direction; ~ **única** one-way; ~ **prohibida** no entry; **salir con** ~ **a España** to leave for Spain 2.(*mando*) direction; ~ **general** head office; ~ **comercial** business management 3.(*guía*) direction; **bajo la** ~ **de** directed by 4.(*señas*) address 5. AUTO steering
directiva *f* 1.(*dirección*) board (of directors) 2.(*instrucción*) directive
directivo, -a I. *adj* managing II. *m, f* 1.(*manager*) manager 2.(*de la junta directiva*) member of the board of directors
directo *m* 1. FERRO through train 2. DEP straight (punch)
directo, -a *adj* 1.(*recto*) straight 2.(*franco*) direct; (*transmisión*) live; **un tren** ~ a through train
director(a) *m(f)* director; (*gerente*) manager; (*de escuela*) headmaster *m Brit,* headmistress *f Brit,* principal *mf Am;* ~ **de orquesta** conductor; ~ **invitado** guest conductor; ~ **de la tesis** doctoral advisor
directorio *m* INFOR directory; ~ **raíz** root directory
dirigente *mf* leader; **los** ~**s** the leadership
dirigir <g→j> I. *vt* 1.(*un coche, un buque*) to steer 2.(*el tráfico*) to direct 3.(*palabras*) to address 4.(*la vista*) to turn 5.(*empresa*) to manage; (*orquesta, debate*) to conduct; ~ **una casa** to run a household 6.(*por un camino*) to lead 7. CINE, TEAT to direct II. *vr:* ~**se** 1.(*a un lugar*) to head for 2.(*a una persona*)

to address
discernir *irr como cernir vt* to differentiate, to distinguish
disciplina *f* discipline
disciplinario, -a *adj* disciplinary
discípulo, -a *m, f* 1.(*alumno*) pupil 2.(*seguidor*) disciple
disco *m* 1.(*lámina*) disc *Brit,* disk *Am;* (*en el teléfono*) dial 2. MÚS record; ~ **de larga duración** LP 3. DEP discus 4.(*semáforo*) traffic light 5. INFOR disk; ~ **de arranque** boot disk; ~ **duro** hard disk; ~ **flexible** floppy (disk)
discográfico, -a *adj* record
disconforme *adj* 1.(*persona*) in disagreement 2.(*cosa*) incompatible
discontinuo, -a *adj* 1.(*inconstante*) discontinuous 2.(*interrumpido*) interrupted
discordancia *f* 1.(*disconformidad*) disagreement 2. MÚS discordance, dissonance
discorde *adj* 1.(*persona*) in disagreement 2. MÚS discordant
discordia *f* discord
discoteca *f* disco(thèque)
discreción *f* discretion; ~ **absoluta** strict privacy; **a** ~ at one's discretion; **con** ~ tactfully
discrecional *adj* discretional; **parada** ~ request stop
discrepancia *f* 1.(*entre cosas*) discrepancy 2.(*entre personas*) disagreement
discrepar *vi* 1.(*diferenciarse*) to differ 2.(*disentir*) to dissent
discreto, -a *adj* (*reservado*) discreet; (*cantidad*) modest
discriminación *f* 1.(*perjuicio*) discrimination 2.(*diferenciación*) differentiation
discriminar *vt* 1.(*diferenciar*) to differentiate (between) 2.(*perjudicar*) to discriminate against
disculpa *f* 1.(*perdón*) apology; **pedir** ~**s** to apologize 2.(*pretexto*) excuse
disculpar I. *vt* 1.(*perdonar*) to forgive 2.(*justificar*) to justify II. *vr:* ~**se** to apologize
discurrir I. *vi* 1.(*pensar*) to ponder

on **2.**(*andar*) to roam **3.**(*río*) to flow **4.**(*transcurrir*) to pass **II.** *vt* to come up with

discurso *m* **1.**(*arenga*) speech; **pronunciar un ~** to make a speech **2.**(*plática*) talk **3.**(*raciocinio*) reasoning **4.**(*transcurso*) passing

discusión *f* **1.**(*debate*) discussion; **~ pública** public debate **2.**(*riña*) argument; **sin ~** without argument

discutible *adj* **1.**(*disputable*) debatable **2.**(*dudoso*) doubtful

discutir **I.** *vi, vt* **1.**(*asunto*) to discuss, to debate **2.**(*opinar diferentemente*) to argue about **II.** *vt* (*contradecir*) to contradict

disecar <c→qu> *vt* **1.** ANAT to dissect **2.**(*animal*) to stuff **3.**(*flor*) to press

diseminar *vt* **1.**(*semillas*) to disperse **2.**(*noticias*) to spread

disentir *irr como sentir vi* to dissent, to disagree

diseñador(a) *m(f)* designer

diseñar *vt* **1.**(*crear*) to design **2.**(*delinear*) to draught *Brit,* to draft *Am*

diseño *m* **1.**(*dibujo*) drawing; (*boceto*) sketch **2.**(*forma*) design; **~ de página** *t.* INFOR page design **3.**(*en tejidos*) pattern

disertación *f* (*escrita*) dissertation; (*oral*) presentation

disfraz *m* **1.**(*para engañar*) disguise; (*para la cara*) mask; (*traje*) fancy dress **2.**(*disimulación*) pretence *Brit,* pretense *Am*

disfrazar <z→c> **I.** *vt* **1.**(*enmascarar*) to disguise **2.**(*escándalo*) to cover up; (*voz*) to disguise; (*sentimiento*) to hide **II.** *vr:* **~se** to disguise oneself as

disfrutar *vi, vt* **1.**(*gozar*) to enjoy **2.**(*poseer*) to have **3.**(*utilizar*) to have the use; (*sacar provecho*) to have the benefit

disgregar(se) <g→gu> *vt,* (*vr*) **1.**(*gente*) to disperse **2.**(*materia*) to disintegrate; FÍS to split

disgustar **I.** *vt* **1.**(*desagradar*) to displease; **me disgusta** I don't like it **2.**(*enfadar*) to anger **II.** *vr:* **~se** **1.**(*enfadarse*) **~se por** [*o* de] **algo**

to get angry about sth **2.**(*ofenderse*) **~se por algo** to be offended about sth **3.**(*reñir*) **~se con alguien** to quarrel with sb

disgusto *m* **1.**(*desagrado*) displeasure; **estar a ~** to be ill at ease **2.**(*aflicción*) suffering; (*molestia*) annoyance

disidente *adj, mf* dissident

disimulado, -a *adj* **1.**(*fingido*) feigned **2.**(*encubierto*) concealed

disimular **I.** *vi* to pretend **II.** *vt* **1.**(*ocultar*) to conceal; **~ el miedo** to hide one's fear **2.**(*paliar*) to make better

disimulo *m* pretence *Brit,* pretense *Am;* (*engaño*) deceit; **con ~** furtively

disipar **I.** *vt* **1.**(*niebla*) to disperse; (*dudas*) to dispel **2.**(*derrochar*) to squander **II.** *vr:* **~se** to disperse; (*dudas*) to vanish

dislexia *f* dyslexia

dislocar <c→qu> **I.** *vt* **1.** MED to dislocate **2.**(*desplazar*) to displace **II.** *vr:* **~se** **1.**(*deshacerse*) to come apart **2.**(*desarticularse*) to be dislocated

disminución *f* decrease; (*de natalidad*) decline; (*de la pena*) JUR remission; (*de peso*) weight loss; (*de precios*) fall

disminuir *irr como huir* **I.** *vi* (*en intensidad*) to diminish; (*número*) to decrease **II.** *vt* to diminish; (*precio*) to lower; (*velocidad*) to reduce

disolución *f* **1.**(*dilución*) dissolution; (*de la familia*) break-up **2.**(*de las costumbres*) dissoluteness **3.** QUÍM solution

disolvente *m* QUÍM solvent; (*para pintura*) thinner

disolver *irr como volver vt, vr:* **~se** (*manifestación*) to dissolve; (*reunión*) to break up

dispar *adj* dissimilar

disparador *m* **1.**(*de un arma*) trigger **2.** FOTO shutter release

disparar **I.** *vt* (*el arma*) to fire; (*piedra*) to throw **II.** *vi* **1.**(*tirar*) to fire **2.** *AmL* (*caballo*) to bolt **III.** *vr:* **~se** **1.**(*arma*) to go off **2.**(*precios*) to shoot up **3.** (*salir corriendo*) to rush off

disparatado, -a *adj* **1.** (*absurdo*) nonsensical **2.** *inf* (*desmesurado*) outrageous

disparate *m* (*insensatez*) foolish act; (*comentario*) foolish remark; (*idea*) foolish idea

disparo *m* shot

dispensar *vt* **1.** (*otorgar*) to give out; (*favores*) to lavish; (*ovación*) to shower **2.** (*de molestias, de un cargo*) to relieve; (*de la mili*) to exempt **3.** (*excusar*) to forgive

dispersar *vt* to spread; (*personas*) to disperse; (*una manifestación*) to break up

dispersión *f* dispersion; FÍS diffusion

disperso, -a *adj* scattered

displicencia *f* displeasure; **tratar con ~** to treat with contempt

disponer *irr como poner* **I.** *vi* to have the use; **~ de tiempo** to have time **II.** *vt* **1.** (*colocar*) to place, to set out **2.** (*preparar*) to prepare; (*la mesa*) to lay **3.** (*determinar*) to stipulate **III.** *vr:* **~se 1.** (*colocarse*) to position oneself **2.** (*prepararse*) to get ready

disponible *adj* available

disposición *f* **1.** (*colocación*) arrangement **2.** (*de ánimo, salud*) disposition **3.** (*para algún fin*) preparation; **estar en ~ de** to be ready to **4.** (*disponibilidad*) availability; **poner a ~** to make available **5.** (*talento*) aptitude **6.** (*resolución*) agreement; **~ legal** legal provision; **última ~** last will and testament

dispositivo *m* device; **~ de visualización** INFOR monitor; **~ intrauterino** MED intrauterine device

dispuesto, -a I. *pp de* **disponer II.** *adj* **1.** (*preparado*) ready; **estar ~ para salir** to be ready to go out; **estar ~ a trabajar** to be prepared to work **2.** (*persona*) **estar bien ~** (*ánimo*) to be in a good frame of mind; (*de salud*) to be well

disputa *f* (*pelea*) fight; (*conversación*) argument

disputar I. *vi* to argue **II.** *vt* **1.** (*controvertir*) to dispute **2.** (*competir*) to compete for

disquete *m* INFOR floppy disk; **~ de arranque** start-up disk; **~ para instalación** setup disk

disquetera *f* disk drive

distancia *f t. fig* distance; **a ~** (*lejos*) far away; (*desde lejos*) from a distance; **acortar ~s** to close the gap; **guardar las ~s** *fig* to keep one's distance; **¿a qué ~?** how far?

distanciar I. *vt* to distance **II.** *vr:* **~se 1.** (*de alguien*) to drift apart **2.** (*de un lugar*) to move away

distante *adj t. fig* distant

distar *vi* to be distant

distensión *f* **1.** (*relajación*) easing of tension; POL détente **2.** MED strain

distinción *f* **1.** (*diferenciación*) distinction; **sin ~ de** irrespective of **2.** (*claridad*) clarity **3.** (*honor*) distinction

distinguible *adj* **1.** (*diferenciable*) distinguishable **2.** (*visible*) visible

distinguido, -a *adj* **1.** (*ilustre*) distinguished **2.** (*elegante*) refined **3.** (*en cartas*) Dear

distinguir <gu→g> **I.** *vt* **1.** (*diferenciar*) to distinguish **2.** (*señalar*) to single out **3.** (*divisar*) to make out **4.** (*condecorar*) to honour *Brit,* to honor *Am* **II.** *vr:* **~se 1.** (*poder ser visto*) to be noticeable **2.** (*ser diferente*) to be different

distintivo *m* emblem

distintivo, -a *adj* distinguishing

distinto, -a *adj* **1.** (*diferente*) different **2.** (*nítido*) distinct **3.** *pl* (*varios*) various

distorsión *f* **1.** MED sprain **2.** FÍS distortion **3.** (*falseamiento*) distortion

distorsionar I. *vt* to distort **II.** *vr:* **~se** MED to sprain

distracción *f* **1.** (*entretenimiento*) pastime **2.** (*falta de atención*) distraction

distraer I. *vt* **1.** (*entretener*) to entertain **2.** (*dinero*) to embezzle **3.** (*desviar*) to divert **II.** *vr:* **~se 1.** (*entretenerse*) to amuse oneself **2.** (*no atender*) to be distracted

distraído, -a *adj* **1.** (*desatento*) distracted; **hacerse el ~** to pretend to not notice **2.** (*entretenido*) entertaining

distribución *f* **1.** *t.* COM (*repartición*) distribution; (*de correo*) delivery; **armario de** ~ ELEC connection cabinet **2.** FIN sharing out; ~ **de beneficios** profit breakdown

distribuidor *m* **1.** TÉC distributor; ~ **automático** automatic dispenser **2.** COM dealer

distribuir *irr como huir* **I.** *vt* **1.** (*repartir*) to distribute; (*disponer*) to arrange; (*el correo*) to deliver **2.** COM to distribute **3.** FIN to share out **II.** *vr:* ~**se** to divide up

distrito *m* district; ~ **electoral** constituency

disturbio *m* disturbance, riot

disuadir *vt* to dissuade

disuelto, -a *pp de* **disolver**

disyuntiva *f* choice

DIU *m* MED *abr de* **dispositivo intrauterino** IUD

diurno, -a *adj* daily; **trabajo** ~ day work

diva *f* diva

divagar <g→gu> *vi* **1.** (*desviarse*) to digress **2.** (*hablar sin concierto*) to ramble

diván *m* divan

divergencia *f* divergence

divergente *adj* divergent; (*opiniones*) differing opinions

diversidad *f* diversity

diversificar <c→qu> **I.** *vt* to diversify; ~ **los horizontes** to broaden one's horizons **II.** *vr:* ~**se** to diversify

diversión *f* **1.** (*entretenimiento*) entertainment **2.** (*pasatiempo*) pastime

diverso, -a *adj* **1.** (*distinto*) distinct **2.** (*variado*) diverse **3.** ~**s** (*varios*) various; (*muchos*) many

divertido, -a *adj* **1.** (*alegre*) amusing **2.** (*que hace reír*) funny

divertir *irr como sentir* **I.** *vt* to amuse **II.** *vr:* ~**se 1.** (*alegrarse*) to amuse oneself **2.** (*distraerse*) to be distracted

dividendo *m* dividend

dividir **I.** *vt* **1.** (*partir*) to divide; ~ **algo entre** [*o por*] **dos** MAT to divide sth by two **2.** (*distribuir*) to dis-

tribute **3.** (*separar*) to separate **4.** (*agrupar*) to divide up **II.** *vr:* ~**se 1.** (*partirse*) to divide **2.** (*agruparse*) to divide up into

divinizar <z→c> *vt* to deify

divino, -a *adj* divine, heavenly

divisa *f* **1.** (*insignia*) emblem **2.** *pl* (*moneda*) (foreign) currency

divisar *vt* to make out

divisible *adj* divisible

división *f* **1.** (*partición*) *t.* MAT division **2.** (*separación*) separation

divisor *m* MAT divisor

divorciado, -a **I.** *adj* divorced **II.** *m, f* divorcee

divorciar **I.** *vt* to divorce **II.** *vr:* ~**se** to get divorced

divorcio *m* **1.** (*separación*) divorce **2.** (*discrepancia*) disagreement

divulgar <g→gu> **I.** *vt* (*propagar*) to spread; (*popularizar*) to popularize **II.** *vr:* ~**se** (*propagarse*) to spread; (*conocerse*) to become known

DNI *m abr de* **Documento Nacional de Identidad** ID

Dña. *abr de* **doña** ≈ Mrs *Brit,* ≈ Mrs. *Am*

do <does> *m* MÚS (*de la escala*) C; (*de la solfa*) doh

dobladillo *m* (*pliegue*) hem; (*del pantalón*) turn-up, cuff

doblaje *m* CINE dubbing

doblar **I.** *vt* **1.** (*arquear*) to bend **2.** (*plegar*) to fold; **no** ~ do not bend **3.** (*duplicar*) to be twice as much as **4.** (*una película*) to dub **5.** (*la esquina*) to turn **6.** (*convencer*) to convince **II.** *vi* (*torcer*) to turn **2.** (*campanas*) to toll **III.** *vr:* ~**se 1.** (*inclinarse*) to bend down **2.** (*ceder*) to give in

doble¹ **I.** *adj inv* double; ~ **nacionalidad** dual nationality; ~ **personalidad** split personality **II.** *mf t.* CINE double

doble² *m* double; (**partido de**) ~**s** DEP doubles (match)

doble³ *f* doubles *pl*

doblegar <g→gu> **I.** *vt* **1.** (*torcer*) to **2.** (*persuadir*) to persuade **II.** *vr:* ~**se** to give in

doblez[1] *m* (*pliegue*) fold
doblez[2] *m o f* (*hipocresía*) duplicity
doce *adj inv, m* twelve; *v.t.* **ocho**
docena *f* dozen
docente I. *adj* teaching II. *mf* UNIV lecturer *Brit*, professor *Am*
dócil *adj* **1.** (*sumiso*) obedient **2.** (*manso*) docile
doctor(a) *m(f)* doctor
doctorado *m* doctorate
doctrina *f* doctrine
documentación *f* (*documentos*) documentation; (*del coche*) vehicle documents *pl*, car papers *pl*
documental *adj, m* documentary
documentar I. *vt* to document II. *vr:* ~**se** to inform oneself
documento *m* document
dogma *m* dogma
dogmático, -a *adj* dogmatic
dogo *m* bulldog
dólar *m* dollar
doler <o→ue> I. *vi* to hurt; **me duele la cabeza** I have a headache II. *vr:* ~**se 1.** (*quejarse*) to complain about **2.** (*arrepentirse*) to regret
dolor *m* pain; ~ **de cabeza** headache; ~ **de barriga** stomach ache
dolorido, -a *adj* **1.** (*dañado*) painful **2.** (*apenado*) sad
doloroso, -a *adj* **1.** (*lastimador*) painful **2.** (*lamentable*) regrettable
domador(a) *m(f)* tamer
domar *vt,* **domeñar** *vt* to tame
domesticar <c→qu> *vt* to domesticate
doméstico, -a I. *adj* domestic; **animal** ~ pet; **gastos** ~**s** household expenses II. *m, f* (domestic) servant
domiciliación *f* (*de recibos*) direct debit
domiciliar I. *vt* **1.** (*un recibo*) to pay by standing order **2.** (*dar domicilio*) to house II. *vr:* ~**se** to reside
domicilio *m* (*una empresa*) address; **reparto a** ~ home delivery
dominante *adj* dominant
dominar I. *vi* **1.** (*imperar*) to rule **2.** (*sobresalir*) to stand out II. *vt* **1.** (*conocer*) to have a good knowledge of **2.** (*reprimir*) to control **3.** (*sobresalir*) to dominate III. *vr:* ~**se** to control oneself

domingo *m* Sunday; ~ **de Resurrección** Easter Sunday; *v.t.* **lunes**
dominguero, -a *m, f pey* Sunday driver
dominical I. *adj* Sunday II. *m* PREN Sunday supplement
dominicano, -a *adj, m, f* Dominican
dominio *m* **1.** (*dominación*) control **2.** (*poder*) authority **3.** (*territorio*) domain
don *m* gift
don, doña *m, f* Mr *m*, Mrs *f*
donación *f* donation; JUR gift
donaire *m* grace
donante *mf* donor
donar *vt* to donate
doncella *f* maid
donde *adv* where; **de** ~... where ... from; **estuve** ~ **Luisa** I was at Luisa's
dónde *pron interrog, rel* where; **¿a** [*o* **hacia**] ~? where to?
dondequiera *adv* anywhere
donostiarra *adj* of/from San Sebastian
doña *f v.* **don**
dopar *vt, vr:* ~**se** DEP to take drugs
doping *m sin pl* drug-taking
dorado, -a *adj* golden
dorar I. *vt* **1.** (*sobredorar*) to gild **2.** (*tostar*) to brown II. *vr:* ~**se** to go brown
dormir *irr* I. *vi* **1.** (*descansar*) to sleep; **quedarse dormido** to fall asleep **2.** (*pernoctar*) to spend the night **3.** (*reposar*) to rest II. *vt* (*a un niño*) to get to sleep; (*borrachera*) to sleep off III. *vr:* ~**se 1.** (*parte del cuerpo*) to fall asleep **2.** (*descuidarse*) to not pay attention
dormitar *vi* to doze
dormitorio *m* bedroom
dorsal I. *adj* ANAT dorsal; **espina** ~ backbone II. *m* DEP number
dorso *m* (*reverso*) *t.* ANAT back
dos I. *adj inv* two II. *m* two; **los/las** ~ both; **cada** ~ **por tres** all the time; *v.t.* **ocho**
doscientos, -as *adj* two hundred; *v.t.* **ochocientos**
dosis *f inv* dose

dotado, -a *adj* **1.** (*con talento*) gifted **2.** (*hombre:genitales*) endowed

dotar *vt* **1.** (*constituir dote*) to give as a dowry **2.** (*equipar*) to equip with **3.** (*financiar*) to provide funds for **4.** (*con sueldo*) to provide

dote¹ *m o f* (*ajuar*) dowry

dote² *f* (*aptitud*) gift

doy *1. pres de* **dar**

dragón *m* dragon

drama *m* drama; TEAT play

dramático, -a *adj* dramatic

dramatizar <z→c> *vt* dramatize

dramaturgo, -a *m, f* playwright

drástico, -a *adj* drastic

drenar *vt* to drain

droga *f* drug, dope *inf;* ~ **sintética** synthetic drug

drogadicto, -a I. *adj* addicted to drugs **II.** *m, f* drug addict

drogar <g→gu> **I.** *vt* to drug **II.** *vr:* ~**se** to take drugs

drogodependencia *f* drug addiction

droguería *f* shop selling soap, shampoo, cleaning materials etc.

dromedario *m* dromedary

ducha *f* shower; **recibir una** ~ **de agua fría** *fig* to receive a shock

duchar I. *vt* to shower **II.** *vr:* ~**se** to have a shower

duda *f* doubt; **sin** ~ (**alguna**) without a doubt; **poner algo en** ~ to question sth

dudar I. *vi* **1.** (*desconfiar*) to doubt **2.** (*vacilar*) to hesitate **II.** *vt* to doubt

dudoso, -a *adj* **1.** (*inseguro*) doubtful **2.** (*indeciso*) undecided

duelo *m* **1.** (*desafío*) duel **2.** (*pesar*) grief **3.** (*funerales*) mourning

duende *m* elf; **tener** ~ *fig* to have charm

dueño, -a *m, f* **1.** (*propietario*) owner; (*amo*) boss; **hacerse** ~ **de algo** (*apropiarse*) to take possession of sth; (*dominar*) to take command of sth **2.** (*de familia*) head

dulce I. *adj* **1.** (*referente al sabor*) sweet **2.** (*agradable*) pleasant **II.** *m* **1.** (*postre*) dessert **2.** (*almíbar*) syrup

dulcificar <c→qu> *vt* **1.** (*azucarar*) to sweeten **2.** (*suavizar*) to soften

dulzor *m,* **dulzura** *f* **1.** (*sabor*) sweetness **2.** (*suavidad*) softness

duna *f* dune

dúo *m* duet

duodécimo, -a *adj* twelfth; *v.t.* **octavo**

duodeno *m* ANAT duodenum

dúplex *m* ARQUIT duplex

duplicar <c→qu> *vt, vr:* ~**se** to duplicate

duplo *m* double

duque(sa) *m(f)* duke, duchess *m, f*

duración *f* duration; **de larga** ~ long-term

duradero, -a *adj* long-lasting

durante *prep* during; **hablar** ~ **una hora** to talk for an hour

durar *vi* **1.** (*extenderse*) to last **2.** (*permanecer*) to stay **3.** (*resistir*) to last

durazno *m AmL* (*fruta*) peach; (*árbol*) peach tree

dureza *f* **1.** (*rigidez*) hardness **2.** (*callosidad*) hard skin

durmiente I. *adj* sleeping **II.** *mf* sleeper

duro I. *m* five-peseta coin **II.** *adv* hard

duro, -a *adj* hard; ~ **de corazón** hard-hearted; **a duras penas** barely

DVD *abr de* **videodisco digital** DVD

Eₑ

E, e *f* E, e; ~ **de España** E for Edward *Brit,* E for easy *Am*

e *conj* (*before 'hi' or 'i'*) and; **madres** ~ **hijas** mothers and daughters

E *abr de* **Este** E

ea *interj* come on

ebanista *mf* cabinetmaker, woodworker

ébano *m* ebony

ebrio, -a *adj elev* inebriated

ebullición *f* boiling

eccema *m* eczema

echar I. *vt* **1.** (*tirar*) to throw; (*carta*)

to post *Brit,* to mail *Am;* (*a la basura, al suelo*) to throw out **2.** (*verter*) to pour **3.** (*expulsar*) to throw out; (*despedir*) to sack *Brit,* to fire *Am* **4.** (*hojas, flores*) to sprout **5.** (*emitir*) to give off; ~ **humo** to let out smoke **6.** (*tumbar*) to lie down **7.** (*proyectar*) to show; TEAT to stage; **en el cine echan 'Titanic'** 'Titanic' is on at the cinema **8.** (*calcular*) **te echo 30 años** I reckon you're 30 **II.** *vi* to begin; ~ **a correr** to break into a run **III.** *vr:* ~**se 1.** (*postrarse*) to lie down **2.** (*lanzarse*) to jump; ~**se atrás** *fig* to have second thoughts **3.** (*empezar*) to begin; ~**se a llorar** to burst into tears **4.** *inf* (*iniciar una relación*) ~**se un novio** to get a boyfriend
eclesiástico *m* clergyman
eclesiástico, -a *adj* ecclesiastical
eclipsar *vt t. fig* to eclipse
eclipse *m* eclipse
eco *m* echo
ecografía *f* ultrasound scan
ecología *f* ecology
ecológico, -a *adj* ecological; **daños** ~**s** environmental damage
ecologista I. *adj* ecological **II.** *mf* ecologist, environmentalist
economato *m* cooperative store
economía *f* **1.** (*situación, sistema*) economy **2.** (*ciencia*) economics
económico, -a *adj* **1.** ECON economic; **año** ~ financial year; **Ciencias Económicas** economics **2.** (*barato*) cheap; (*ahorrador*) economical
economista *mf* economist
ecosistema *m* ecosystem
ecotest *m* ecotest
ecu, ECU *m* *abr de* **European Currency Unit** ecu, ECU
ecuación *f* equation
ecuador *m* equator
Ecuador *m* Ecuador

? Ecuador lies in the northwestern part of South America. It borders Colombia to the north, Peru to the east and south and the Pacific Ocean to the west. The capital is **Quito**. The official language of the country is Spanish and the monetary unit of **Ecuador** is the **sucre**.

ecuánime *adj* level-headed
ecuatoriano, -a *adj* of/from Ecuador
ecuestre *m* equestrian
eczema *m* eczema
edad *f* **1.** (*años*) age; ~ **del pavo** adolescence; **mayor de** ~ adult; **menor de** ~ minor; **ser mayor/menor de** ~ to be of/under age; **la tercera** ~ old age; **a la** ~ **de...** at the age of ...; **¿qué** ~ **tiene?** how old is he/she? **2.** (*época*) age, era; **la** ~ **media** the Middle Ages
edición *f* **1.** (*impresión*) edition; ~ **de bolsillo** paperback edition **2.** (*de un acontecimiento*) **la presente** ~ **del Festival de Cine** this year's Film Festival
edicto *m* edict
edificar <c→qu> *vt* to build
edificio *m* building
Edimburgo *m* Edinburgh
editar *vt* **1.** (*publicar*) to publish **2.** (*preparar*) to edit
editor(a) *m(f)* **1.** (*que publica*) publisher **2.** (*que prepara textos*) editor
editorial¹ I. *adj* publishing; **casa** ~ publishing house; **éxito** ~ best-seller **II.** *f* publisher
editorial² *m* editorial
edredón *m* eiderdown; ~ **nórdico** duvet
educación *f* **1.** (*instrucción*) education; ~ **de adultos** adult education; ~ **ambiental** environmental education; ~ **física** physical education **2.** (*comportamiento*) manners *pl;* **no tener** ~ to have no manners **3.** (*crianza*) upbringing
educar <c→qu> *vt* **1.** (*dar instrucción*) to educate **2.** (*criar*) to bring up
educativo, -a *adj* educational
edutenimiento *m sin pl* edutainment
EE.UU. *mpl abr de* **Estados Unidos** USA
efectista *adj* for effect

efectivamente *adv* in fact
efectivo *m* cash; **en** ~ (in) cash
efectivo, -a *adj* **1.** (*que hace efecto*) effective **2.** (*auténtico*) real; **hacer** ~ to put into action; (*cheque*) to cash
efecto *m* effect; ~ **retardado, ~s secundarios** side effects; **hacer** ~ to have an effect; **hacer buen/mal** ~ (*impresión*) to make a good/bad impression; **tener** ~ to take effect; **en** ~ indeed; **para los ~s** effectively
efectuar <*1. pres*: efectúo> *vt* to carry out; (*viaje*) to go on; ~ **una compra** to make a purchase
eficacia *f* efficiency; (*de medida*) effectiveness; **con** ~ effectively; **sin** ~ useless
eficaz *adj* efficient; (*medida*) effective
eficiente *adj* efficient; (*medida*) effective
efusivo, -a *adj* effusive
EGB *f* HIST *abr de* **Educación General Básica** *education for children aged 6 to 14*
Egeo *m* Aegean; **el mar** ~ the Aegean Sea
egipcio, -a *adj, m, f* Egyptian
Egipto *m* Egypt
egoísmo *m sin pl* selfishness, egoism
egoísta **I.** *adj* selfish, egoistical; **ser un** ~ to be very selfish **II.** *mf* selfish person, egoist
egregio, -a *adj* eminent, illustrious
ej. *abr de* **ejemplo** example
eje *m* axle
ejecución *f* execution
ejecutar *vt* to execute
ejecutiva *f* executive (body)
ejecutivo, -a *adj, m, f* executive
ejemplar **I.** *adj* exemplary; **un alumno** ~ a model student **II.** *m* (*ejemplo*) example; (*de libro*) copy; (*de revista*) issue; ~ **de muestra** sample
ejemplo *m* example; **dar buen** ~ to set a good example; **poner por** ~ to give as an example; **por** ~ for example; **sin** ~ unprecedented
ejercer <c→z> *vt* (*profesión*) to practise *Brit*, to practice *Am*; (*derechos*) to exercise
ejercicio *m* **1.** (*de una profesión*) practice **2.** DEP exercise; (*entrenamiento*) training; **tener falta de** ~ to be out of practice **3.** ENS (*para practicar*) exercise; (*prueba*) test **4.** ECON ~ (**económico**) financial year
ejercitar *vt* **1.** (*profesión*) to practise *Brit*, to practice *Am*; (*actividad*) to carry out **2.** (*adiestrar*) to train
ejército *m* MIL army; ~ **del aire** air force
ejote *m* *AmC, Méx* string bean
el, la, lo <los, las> *art def* **1.** the; **el perro** the dog; **la mesa** the table; **los amigos/las amigas** the friends; **prefiero** ~ **azul al amarillo** I prefer the blue one to the yellow one **2.** *lo* + *adj* **lo bueno/malo** the good/bad thing; **lo antes** [*o* **más pronto**] **posible** as soon as possible; **hazlo lo mejor que puedas** do it the best you can **3.** + *nombres geográficos* **el Canadá** Canada; **la China/India** China/India **4.** + *días de semana* **llegaré el domingo** I'll arrive on Sunday; **los sábados no trabajo** I don't work on Saturdays **5.** + *que* **lo que digo es...** what I'm saying is ...; **lo que pasa es que...** the thing is that ...
él *pron pers, 3. sing m* **1.** (*sujeto*) he **2.** (*tras preposición*) him; **el libro es de** ~ (*suyo*) the book is his
elaboración *f* manufacture; **de** ~ **casera** home-made
elaborar *vt* **1.** (*fabricar*) to manufacture; (*preparar*) to prepare **2.** (*idea*) to develop
elasticidad *f* elasticity
elástico *m* elastic
elástico, -a *adj* elastic; *fig* flexible
Elba *m* **1.** (*río*) **el** ~ the (river) Elbe **2.** (*isla*) Elba
elección *f* choice; *t.* POL election; **elecciones legislativas** general elections; **lo dejo a su** ~ the choice is yours
electorado *m* electorate
electoral *adj* electoral
electricidad *f* electricity
electricista *mf* electrician
eléctrico, -a *adj* electric, electrical

electrificar <c→qu> *vt* electrify
electrizar <z→c> *vt t. fig* to electrify
electrocardiograma *m* electrocardiogram
electrocución *f* electrocution
electrocutar *vt* to electrocute
electrodo *m* electrode
electrodoméstico *m* household appliance
electroimán *m* electromagnet
electromagnético, -a *adj* electromagnetic
electrón *m* electron
electrónica *f* electronics
electrónico, -a *adj* electronic; **correo** ~ e-mail
electrotecnia *f* electrical engineering
elefante, -a *m, f* elephant *m*
elegancia *f* elegance; (*buen gusto*) tastefulness
elegante *adj* elegant
elegir *irr* **I.** *vi, vt* (*escoger*) choose; **a ~ entre** to be chosen from **II.** *vt* POL to elect
elemental *adj* basic
elemento *m* **1.** (*componente, persona*) element **2.** *pl* (*fuerzas naturales*) elements *pl*
elepé *m* LP, album
elevación *f* **1.** (*subida*) rise **2.** GEO elevation
elevador *m* AmC lift *Brit,* elevator *Am*
elevar *vt* **1.** (*subir*) to raise **2.** MAT ~ **a** to raise to the power of; **tres elevado a cuatro** three to the power of four
eliminar *vt* to eliminate
eliminatoria *f* (*competición*) knockout competition *Brit,* playoff; (*vuelta*) qualifying round; (*atletismo*) heat
elite *f,* **élite** *f* elite; **de** ~ top-class
elitista *adj* elitist
elixir *m* elixir
ella *pron pers, 3. sing f* **1.** (*sujeto*) she **2.** (*tras preposición*) her; **el abrigo es de** ~ (*suyo*) the coat is hers
ellas *pron pers, 3. pl f* **1.** (*sujeto*) they **2.** (*tras preposición*) them; **el coche es de** ~ (*suyo*) the car is theirs

ello *pron pers, 3. sing neutro* **1.** (*sujeto*) it **2.** (*tras preposición*) it; **para** ~ for it; **por** ~ that is why; **estar en** ~ to be doing it; **¡a** ~! let's do it!
ellos *pron pers, 3. pl m* **1.** (*sujeto*) they **2.** (*tras preposición*) them; **estos niños son de** ~ (*suyos*) these children are theirs
elocuencia *f* eloquence; **con** ~ eloquently
elocuente *adj* eloquent; **las pruebas son** ~**s** *fig* the evidence speaks for itself
elogiar *vt* to eulogize *form,* to praise
elogio *m* eulogy, praise; **digno de** ~ praiseworthy
elote *m* AmC maize [*o* corn *Am*] cob
eludir *vt* to elude; (*preguntas*) to evade; ~ **su responsabilidad** to shirk one's responsibility
emanar **I.** *vi* ~ **de** to emanate from *form;* (*líquido*) to ooze from **II.** *vt* to give off
emancipar **I.** *vt* to free; (*feminismo*) to emancipate **II.** *vr:* ~**se** to become emancipated
embadurnar **I.** *vt* **1.** (*manchar*) ~ **algo de** [*o* con] **algo** to smear sth with sth **2.** (*pintar*) to daub **II.** *vr* ~**se de** [*o* con] **algo** to be smeared with sth
embajada *f* embassy
embajador(a) *m(f)* ambassador
embalar *vt* to pack
embalsamar *vt* to embalm
embalse *m* reservoir
embarazada **I.** *adj* (*encinta*) pregnant; **estar** ~ **de seis meses** to be six months pregnant; **quedarse** ~ to become pregnant **II.** *f* pregnant woman
embarazar <z→c> *vt* **1.** (*estorbar*) to get in the way **2.** (*cohibir*) ~ **a alguien** to make sb feel awkward **3.** (*dejar encinta*) ~ **a alguien** to get sb pregnant
embarazo *m* **1.** (*gravidez*) pregnancy **2.** (*cohibición*) awkwardness; **causar** ~ **a alguien** to make sb feel awkward **3.** (*impedimento*) obstacle
embarazoso, -a *adj* awkward
embarcación *f* (*barco*) vessel

embarcadero *m* pier, wharf

embarcar <c→qu> I. *vi* to go on board; (*avión*) to board II. *vt* (*en barco*) to stow; (*en avión*) to put on board III. *vr:* ~se (*en barco*) to embark; (*avión*) to board

embargar <g→gu> *vt* 1. (*retener*) to confiscate 2. (*absorber*) to overcome

embargo I. *m* 1. COM embargo 2. (*retención*) confiscation II. *conj* sin ~ however

embarque *m* (*de material*) loading; (*de personas*) boarding

embaucar <c→qu> *vt* to cheat

embeber I. *vt* 1. (*absorber*) to absorb 2. (*empapar*) to soak up II. *vr:* ~se to become absorbed

embellecer *irr como crecer vt* to beautify

embestida *f* onslaught

embestir *irr como pedir* I. *vi* to charge II. *vt* to attack

emblema *m* emblem; (*de marca*) logo

émbolo *m* piston

embolsar *vt* to pocket

emborrachar I. *vt* to make drunk II. *vr:* ~se to get drunk

emboscada *f* ambush

embotellamiento *m* jam

embotellar *vt* to bottle

embragar <g→gu> *vi* to engage the clutch

embrague *m* clutch

embriagar <g→gu> I. *vt* to inebriate II. *vr:* ~se to get drunk

embriaguez *f* inebriation

embrión *m* embryo

embrollar *vt* to mess up; lo embrollas más de lo necesario you're overcomplicating things

embrollo *m* 1. (*lío*) mess; (*de hilos*) tangle 2. (*embuste*) swindle; no me vengas con ~s don't try and fool me

embromar *vt* to play a joke on

embrujado, -a *adj* bewitched; casa embrujada haunted house

embudo *m* funnel

embuste *m* lie

embustero, -a I. *adj* lying II. *m, f* liar

embutido *m* sausage

embutir *vt* to pack

emergencia *f* 1. (*acción*) appearance 2. (*suceso*) emergency

emerger <g→j> *vi* to emerge

emeritense *adj* of/from Mérida

emigración *f* emigration

emigrar *vi* to emigrate

eminencia *f* 1. (*talento*) expert 2. (*título*) Eminence

eminente *adj* outstanding

emisión *f* 1. TV, RADIO (*difusión*) broadcast; (*programa*) programme *Brit*, program *Am* 2. (*de radiación, calor, luz*) emission

emisora *f* ~ (de radio) radio station

emitir *vt* 1. TV, RADIO to broadcast 2. (*despedir*) to emit, to give off

emoción *f* emotion; (*conmoción*) excitement; llorar de ~ to cry with emotion

emocionante *adj* 1. (*excitante*) exciting, thrilling 2. (*conmovedor*) moving

emocionar I. *vt* 1. (*apasionar*) to excite 2. (*conmover*) to move; tus palabras me ~on I found your words very moving II. *vr:* ~se 1. (*conmoverse*) to be moved 2. (*alegrarse*) to get excited

emotivo, -a *adj* 1. (*persona*) emotional 2. (*palabras*) moving

empacar <c→qu> *vt* to pack

empacho *m* indigestion

empadronarse *vr* to register (for a census)

empalagoso, -a *adj* 1. (*alimento*) oversweet 2. (*persona*) cloying

empalmar I. *vi* 1. (*trenes*) to link up 2. (*caminos, ríos*) ~ con algo to meet sth II. *vt* to connect; (*maderos, tubos*) to fit together

empalme *m* connection; (*de maderos, tubos*) join; FERRO transfer station

empanada *f* pie (*usually containing meat or tuna*)

empantanarse *vr* to flood

empañarse *vr* to mist up

empapar I. *vt* to soak; la lluvia ha empapado el suelo the rain has soaked the floor; estar empapado de sangre to be soaked with blood

E e

II. *vr:* ~**se** to get soaked

empapelar *vi, vt* to (wall)paper

empaquetar *vt* to pack

emparedado *m* sandwich

empastar *vt* to fill

empaste *m* filling

empatar *vi* **1.** DEP to draw; ~ **a uno** to draw one-all; **estar empatados a puntos** to have the same points **2.** POL to tie

empate *m* **1.** DEP draw; **gol del** ~ the equalizer **2.** POL tie

empedernido, -a *adj* incorrigible; **bebedor** ~ hardened drinker; **fumador** ~ chain smoker; **solterón** ~ confirmed bachelor

empeine *m* instep

empeñado, -a *adj* **estar** ~ (**en hacer algo**) to be determined (to do sth)

empeñar I. *vt* (*objetos*) to pawn **II.** *vr:* ~**se 1.** (*insistir*) to insist; **se empeña en hablar contigo** he/she insists on speaking to you; **no te empeñes** don't go on about it **2.** (*endeudarse*) to get into debt

empeño *m* **1.** (*afán*) determination; **con** ~ determinedly; **tener** ~ **por** [*o* **en**] **hacer algo** to be determined to do sth; **pondré** ~ **en...** I will try my best to ... **2.** (*de objetos*) pawning; **casa de** ~**s** pawnbroker's

empeorar I. *vt* to make worse **II.** *vi, vr:* ~**se** to worsen

empequeñecer *irr como crecer vt* **1.** (*disminuir*) to make smaller **2.** (*quitar importancia*) to trivialize

emperador *m* emperor

emperatriz *f* empress

empezar *irr vi, vt* to begin, to start; ~ **de la nada** to start with nothing; ~ **con buen pie** to get off to a good start; **¡no empieces!** don't start!; **para** ~ **me leeré el periódico** to begin with, I'll read the newspaper; **para** ~ **no tengo dinero y, además, no tengo ganas** first of all, I have no money, and what's more, I don't feel like it

empinar I. *vt* to raise; ~ **el codo** *inf* to have a drink, to booze *inf* **II.** *vr:* ~**se** to stand on tiptoes

empírico, -a *adj* empirical

emplaste *m* plaster

emplasto *m* poultice

emplazamiento *m* **1.** (*lugar, situación*) location **2.** JUR summons *pl*

emplazar <z→c> *vt* **1.** (*citar*) to call; JUR to summon **2.** (*situar*) to locate

empleado, -a *m, f* employee; ~ **de oficina** office worker; ~ **de ventanilla** clerk

emplear *vt* **1.** (*usar*) to use; (*tiempo*) to spend; (*dinero*) to invest; **¡podrías** ~ **mejor el tiempo!** you could use your time better! **2.** (*colocar*) to employ; (*ocupar*) to engage

empleo *m* **1.** (*trabajo*) job, post *Brit;* (*ocupación*) employment; **pleno** ~ full employment; **no tener** ~ to be out of work **2.** (*uso*) use; (*de tiempo*) spending; **modo de** ~ instructions for use

empobrecer *irr como crecer* **I.** *vt* to impoverish **II.** *vi, vr:* ~**se** to become poorer

empollar I. *vi inf* to swot **II.** *vt* **1.** (*ave*) to brood **2.** *inf* (*lección*) to swot up

empollón, -ona *m, f inf* swot

emporio *m* centre, center *Am*

empotrado, -a *adj* fitted, built-in

emprendedor(a) *adj* resourceful, enterprising

emprender *vt* **1.** (*trabajo*) to begin; (*negocio*) to set up; ~ **la marcha** to set out; ~ **el vuelo** to take off; ~ **la vuelta** to go back **2.** *inf* (*principiar una acción*) ~**la con alguien** to take it out on sb; ~**la a insultos con alguien** to begin insulting sb

empresa *f* enterprise; (*compañía*) company

empresario, -a *m, f* **1.** ECON businessman *m*, businesswoman *f* **2.** TEAT impresario

empréstito *m* loan

empujar *vi, vt* to push; (*con violencia*) to shove

empuje *m* **1.** FÍS force **2.** (*energía*) energy; (*resolución*) drive

empujón *m* push; (*violento*) shove; **entrar en un local a empujones** to push one's way into a place

empuñar *vt* to take; (*asir*) to grip

emular *vt* to emulate

emulsión *f* emulsion

en *prep* **1.** (*lugar: dentro*) in; (*encima de*) on; (*con movimiento*) in, into; **el libro está ~ el cajón** the book is in the drawer; **coloca el florero ~ la mesa** put the vase on the table; **~ la pared hay un cuadro** there is a painting on the wall; **estar ~ el campo/~ la ciudad/~ una isla** to be in the countryside/in the city/on an island; **~ Escocia** in Scotland; **vacaciones ~ el mar** holidays at the seaside; **jugar ~ la calle** to play in the street; **vivo ~ la calle George** I live in George Street; **estoy ~ casa** I'm at home; **estoy ~ casa de mis padres** I'm at my parents' house; **trabajo ~ una empresa japonesa** I work in a Japanese company **2.** (*tiempo*) in; **~ el año 2005** in 2005; **~ mayo/invierno/el siglo XIX** in may/winter/the 19th century; **~ otra ocasión** on another occasion; **~ aquellos tiempos** in those times; **~ un mes/dos años** in a month/two years; **lo terminaré ~ un momento** I'll finish it in a moment; **~ todo el día** all day **3.** (*modo, estado*) **~ absoluto** not at all; **~ construcción** under construction; **~ flor** in flower; **~ venta** for sale; **~ vida** while living; **~ voz alta** aloud; **de dos ~ dos** two at a time; **~ español** in Spanish; **pagar ~ libras** to pay in pounds **4.** (*medio*) **papá viene ~ tren/~ coche** dad is coming by train/by car; **he venido ~ avión** I came by air; **lo reconocí ~ la voz** I recognised him by his voice **5.** (*ocupación*) **doctor ~ filosofía** PhD in Philosophy; **estar ~ la mili** to be doing military service; **trabajar ~ Correos** to work in the postal service **6.** (*con verbo*) **pienso ~ ti** I am thinking of you; **no confío ~ él** I don't trust him; **ingresar ~ un partido** to join a party; **ganar ~ importancia** to gain in importance **7.** (*cantidades*) **aumentar la pro-**

ducción ~ un 5% to increase production by 5%; **me he equivocado sólo ~ 3 euros** I was only wrong by 3 euros **8.** ECON **~ fábrica** ex-works; **franco ~ almacén** ex-store

enajenación *f* **1.** (*de una propiedad*) transfer **2.** (*de la mente*) derangement; **~ mental** insanity

enajenar *vt* **1.** (*una posesión*) to transfer **2.** (*enloquecer*) to drive mad

enamorado, -a I. *adj* **estar ~ (de alguien/algo)** to be in love (with sb/sth) **II.** *m, f* lover; **día de los ~s** St Valentine's Day

enamorar I. *vt* (*conquistar*) to win the heart of; **mi profesora me ha enamorado** I've fallen in love with my teacher **II.** *vr* **~se (de alguien/algo)** to fall in love (with sb/sth)

enano, -a I. *adj* tiny **II.** *m, f* dwarf

enardecer *irr como crecer vt* to fire with enthusiasm

encabezamiento *m* heading

encabezar <z→c> *vt* to head

encadenar *vt* to chain (up)

encajar I. *vi* to fit; **la puerta encaja mal** the door doesn't fit properly; **las dos declaraciones encajan** the two statements fit together **II.** *vt* **1.** *t.* TÉC to fit; **~ dos piezas** to fit two pieces together **2.** *inf* (*dar*) **~ un golpe a alguien** to hit sb **3.** (*gol*) to let in

encaje *m* lace

encalar *vt* to whitewash

encallar *vi* to run aground

encaminar I. *vt* to direct; **~ sus pasos hacia el pueblo** to head towards the village; **~ los esfuerzos hacia algo** to focus one's efforts on sth **II.** *vr* **~se a/hacia algo** to head for/towards sth

encandilar *vt* to dazzle; **escuchar encandilado** to listen in raptures

encantado, -a *adj* (*satisfecho*) **estar ~ (de [*o* con] algo/alguien)** to be delighted (with sth/sb); **¡~ (de conocerle)!** pleased to meet you!; **estoy ~ con mi nuevo trabajo** I love my new job; **estoy ~ de la vida** I am thrilled

encantador(a) *adj* charming; (*bebé*) lovely, adorable

encantar *vt* **1.**(*hechizar*) to bewitch **2.**(*gustar*) **me encanta viajar** I love to travel; **me encantan los dulces** I love sweet things; **me encanta que te preocupes por mí** I love the fact that you care about me **3.**(*cautivar*) to captivate; (*fascinar*) to fascinate

encanto *m* **1.**(*hechizo*) spell **2.**(*atractivo*) charm; **¡es un ~ de niño!** what an adorable child!

encarcelar *vt* to imprison

encarecer *irr como crecer vt* to raise the price of

encarecimiento *m* price increase

encargado, -a I. *adj* in charge **II.** *m, f* person in charge; **~ de obras** site manager; **~ de prensa** press officer

encargar <g→gu> **I.** *vt* **1.**(*comprar*) to order **2.**(*mandar*) to ask **II.** *vr* ~**se de algo** to take responsibility for sth; **tengo que ~me aún de un par de cosas** I still have to get a couple of things done

encargo *m* **1.**(*pedido*) order **2.**(*trabajo*) job; **de ~** to order; **hacer ~s** to run errands

encariñarse *vr* ~ **con algo** to get attached to sth; ~ **con alguien** to grow fond of sb

encarnación *f* incarnation; **la ~ del horror** the embodiment of horror

encarnizado, -a *adj* **1.**(*lucha*) bloody **2.**(*herida*) sore; (*ojo*) bloodshot **3.**(*persona*) cruel

encarrilar *vt* FERRO to put on rails; **ir encarrilado** *fig* to be on the right track

encasillar *vt* to pigeonhole

encasquetar I. *vt* **1.**(*dar*) ~ **un golpe a alguien** to hit sb **2.**(*una idea*) to get into one's head **3.**(*endilgar*) to lumber with; **nos ~on la parte peor** we were lumbered with the worst part; **me encasquetó un rollo tremendo** I had to listen to him going on and on **II.** *vr:* ~**se 1.**(*sombrero*) to put on one's head **2.**(*idea*) **se te ha encasquetado esa idea** you've got this idea into your head

encauzar <z→c> *vt* to channel

encendedor *m* lighter

encender <e→ie> **I.** *vt* **1.**(*cigarrillo*) to light **2.**(*conectar*) to switch on **II.** *vr:* ~**se 1.**(*inflamarse*) to ignite **2.**(*luz*) go come on; (*ruborizarse*) to blush

encendido *m* ignition

encendido, -a *adj* **1.**(*conectado*) **estar ~** to be on **2.**(*ardiente*) burning; (*cigarrillo*) lighted; **estar ~** to be lit

encerado *m* blackboard

encerar *vt* to wax

encerrar <e→ie> *vt* **1.**(*depositar, recluir*) to lock in; ~ **entre paréntesis** to put in brackets **2.**(*contener*) to contain

encestar *vi* to score a basket

enchilada *f AmC* enchilada

enchufar *vt* **1.** ELEC to plug in **2.** *inf* (*persona*) ~ **a alguien** to get a job for sb (by pulling strings)

enchufe *m* **1.**(*clavija*) plug **2.**(*toma*) socket **3.** *inf* (*contactos*) **tener ~** *inf* to have connections **4.**(*trabajo*) good job (*which has been obtained by pulling strings*)

encía *f* gum

enciclopedia *f* encyclopaedia *Brit,* encyclopedia *Am*

encierro *m* **1.**(*reclusión*) confinement **2.** TAUR *running of bulls in the San Fermín festival in Pamplona*

? Strictly speaking, **encierro**, a term from the **tauromaquia** (art of bullfighting), refers to the following two processes: the bulls are first driven into the arena pens and then locked up in the **toril** (bull cage). For many people this represents the actual **fiesta** (public festival).

---

encima I. *adv* **1.**(*arriba: con contacto*) on top; (*sin tocar*) above **2.** *fig* **echarse ~ de alguien** to attack sb; **quitarse algo de ~** to get sth off one's back; **llevaba mucho dinero**

En la cocina

In the kitchen

1	fregadero *m*	sink
2	escurreplatos *m inv*, escurridero *m*	washing-up bowl [*o* basin], dishpan *Am*
3	(líquido *m*) lavavajillas *m inv*	washing-up liquid, dishsoap *Am*
4	grifo *m*	tap *Brit*, faucet *Am*
5	cubiertos *mpl*	cutlery, silverware *Am*
6	colador *m*	sieve
7	cucharón *m*, cazo *m*	ladle
8	cuchara *f*	spoon
9	cafetera *f* eléctrica	coffee machine [*o* maker]
10	panera *f*	bread bin, breadbox *Am*
11	enchufe *m*	socket
12	hervidor *m* de agua	electric kettle
13	armario *m* colgado [*o* de pared]	wall-cupboard, cupboard *Am*
14	encimera *f*	work surface [*o* worktop], counter *Am*
15	trapo *m* de cocina, paño *m* de cocina	tea towel *Brit*, dish towel *Am*
16	lavadora *f*	washing machine
17	nevera *f*, frigorífico *m*	fridge, refrigerator
18	armario *m*	cupboard
19	cubo *m* de (la) basura	(rubbish) bin, trashcan *Am*
20	cocina *f*	cooker, stove *Am*
21	horno *m*	oven
22	olla *f*, cazuela *f*	(sauce)pan
23	sartén *f*	frying pan
24	cajón *m*	drawer
25	silla *f* de cocina	kitchen chair
26	jarra *f*	jug, pitcher *Am*
27	botella *f* de leche	milk bottle
28	tetera *f*	teapot
29	salvamanteles *m inv*	table mat, place mat *Am*
30	vaso *m*	glass
31	tostada *f*, rebanada *f* de pan tostado	piece of toast
32	plato *m*	plate
33	taza *f*	mug
34	cuchillo *m*	knife
35	tenedor *m*	fork
36	huevo *m* frito	fried egg
37	tiras *fpl* de beicon	rashers of bacon
38	tarro *m* de mermelada de naranja	jar of marmalade
39	fuente *f*	bowl
40	azucarero *m*	sugar basin, sugar bowl *Am*
41	tapa *f*	lid
42	mantel *m*	tablecloth

~ he/she had a lot of money on him/her; **se me ha quitado un peso de** ~ that's a weight off my mind; **se nos echa el tiempo** ~ time is running out **3.** (*además*) besides; **te di el dinero y** ~ **una botella de vino** I gave you the money and a bottle of wine as well **4. por** ~ (*superficialmente*) superficial(ly) **II. prep 1.** (*local: con contacto*) ~ **de** on top of; **con queso** ~ with cheese on top; **el libro está** ~ **de la mesa** the book is on the table; **estar** ~ **de alguien** *fig* to be on sb's case **2.** (*local: sin contacto*) (**por**) ~ **de** above; **viven** ~ **de nosotros** they live above us; **por** ~ **de todo** above all; **por** ~ **de la media** above average **3.** (*con movimiento*) (**por**) ~ **de** over; **pon esto** ~ **de la cama** put this over the bed; **cuelga la lámpara** ~ **de la mesa** hang the light above the table; **¡por** ~ **de mí!** *fig* over my dead body!; **ése pasa por** ~ **de todo** *fig* he only cares about himself **4.** (*más alto*) **el rascacielos está por** ~ **de la catedral** the skyscraper is higher than the cathedral **5.** (*en contra de*) **por** ~ **de alguien** against one's will

encimera *f* work surface, counter *Am*

encina *f* holm oak

encinta *adj* pregnant

enclave *m* enclave

enclenque *adj* (*enfermizo*) sickly; (*débil*) weak

encoger <g→j> **I.** *vi, vt* to shrink **II.** *vr:* ~**se 1.** (*reducirse*) to shrink **2.** *fig, inf* ~**se de hombros** to shrug one's shoulders

encolar *vt* to glue

encolerizar <z→c> **I.** *vt* to incense **II.** *vr:* ~**se** to be incensed

encomendar <e→ie> **I.** *vt* **1.** (*recomendar*) to recommend **2.** (*confiar*) ~ **algo a alguien** to entrust sth to sb **II.** *vr* ~**se a Dios** to commend one's soul to God

encomiar *vt* to praise

encomienda *f* **1.** (*encargo*) assignment **2.** *AmL* (*postal*) parcel

encono *m* spite

encontrado, -a *adj* opposite; **opiniones encontradas** conflicting opinions

encontrar <o→ue> **I.** *vt* **1.** (*hallar, considerar*) to find **2.** (*coincidir con*) to come across **II.** *vr:* ~**se 1.** (*estar*) to be **2.** (*sentirse*) to feel **3.** (*citarse*) ~**se con alguien** to meet sb **4.** (*coincidir*) ~**se con alguien** to run into sb **5.** (*hallar*) to find; **me encontré con que el coche se había estropeado** I found that the car had broken down

encorvar *vt* to bend

encrespar I. *vt* **1.** (*rizar*) to frizz **2.** (*irritar*) to annoy **II.** *vr:* ~**se 1.** (*rizarse*) to curl **2.** (*irritarse*) to get annoyed

encrucijada *f t. fig* crossroads *inv*

encuadernación *f* cover; ~ **en pasta** hardback; ~ **en rústica** paperback

encuadernador(a) *m(f)* bookbinder

encuadrar *vt* to frame

encubrir *irr como* abrir *vt* **1.** (*cubrir*) to cover **2.** (*ocultar*) to hide; (*escándalo, crimen*) to cover up; (*delincuente*) to harbour *Brit,* to harbor *Am*

encuentro *m* **1.** (*acción*) *t.* MIL encounter **2.** (*cita, reunión*) meeting **3.** DEP match, game

encuesta *f* **1.** (*sondeo*) opinion poll; ~ **estadística** statistical survey **2.** (*investigación*) inquiry

encumbrar *vt* elevate; ~ **a alguien a la fama** to make sb famous

endeble *adj* weak

endémico, -a *adj* endemic

endemoniado, -a *adj* **1.** (*poseso*) possessed **2.** (*malo*) bado

enderezar <z→c> *vt* **1.** (*poner derecho*) to straighten **2.** (*corregir*) to straighten out

endeudarse *vr* to get into debt

endiablado, -a *adj* bad

endibia *f* chicory *Brit,* endive *Am*

endilgar <g→gu> *vt inf* ~ **algo a alguien** to offload sth onto sb; **me** ~**on el trabajo sucio** I got stuck with the dirty work

endomingarse <g→gu> *vr* to put on one's Sunday best

endosar *vt* to endorse

endulzar <z→c> *vt* **1.** (*poner dulce*) to sweeten **2.** (*suavizar*) to soften

endurecer *irr como crecer vt, vr:* ~**se** to harden

enemigo, -a <enemicísimo> *adj, m, f* enemy; **ser** ~ **de algo** to be opposed to sth

enemistad *f* enmity

enemistar **I.** *vt* to make enemies of **II.** *vr:* ~**se** to become enemies

energía *f* energy; **con/sin** ~ *fig* forcefully/feebly; **con toda su** ~ with all one's force

enérgico, -a *adj* **1.** (*fuerte*) energetic **2.** (*decidido*) firm **3.** (*estricto*) tough

energúmeno, -a *m, f inf* lout, boor

enero *m* January; **la cuesta de** ~ the post-Christmas slump; *v.t.* **marzo**

enésimo, -a *adj* MAT nth; **por enésima vez** *inf* for the thousandth time

enfadar **I.** *vt* to anger; **estar enfadado con alguien** to be angry with sb **II.** *vr:* ~**se** to get angry

enfado *m* (*enojo*) anger; (*molestia*) annoyance

énfasis *m o f inv* emphasis

enfático, -a *adj* emphatic

enfermar *vi, vr* ~(**se**) **de algo** to get ill with sth

enfermedad *f* illness; (*específica*) disease

enfermera *f* nurse

enfermería *f* infirmary

enfermero *m* male nurse

enfermizo, -a *adj* sickly

enfermo, -a **I.** *adj* ill, sick; ~ **del corazón** suffering heart disease; **caer** ~ **de algo** to come down with sth **II.** *m, f* ill person; (*paciente*) patient

enflaquecer *irr como crecer* **I.** *vi, vr:* ~**se** to become thin **II.** *vt* to make thin

enfocar <c→qu> *vt* **1.** (*ajustar*) to focus; **mal enfocado** out of focus **2.** (*una cuestión*) to approach

enfoque *m* **1.** (*punto de vista*) opinion, stance **2.** (*planteamiento*) approach

enfrascarse <c→qu> *vr* to get wrapped up in

enfrentamiento *m* confrontation

enfrentar **I.** *vt* **1.** (*encarar*) to bring face to face **2.** (*hacer frente*) to face up to; ~ **los hechos** to face the facts **II.** *vr:* ~**se** **1.** (*encararse*) to come face to face **2.** (*afrontarse*) ~**se con alguien** to face up to sb

enfrente **I.** *adv* opposite; **allí** ~ over there; **la casa de** ~ the house opposite **II.** *prep* (*local: frente a*) ~ **de** opposite; ~ **mío** [*o* **de mí**] opposite me; ~ **del teatro** opposite the theatre; **vivo** ~ **del parque** I live opposite the park

enfriamiento *m* **1.** (*pérdida de temperatura*) cooling **2.** (*resfriado*) cold

enfriar <*1. pres:* enfrío> **I.** *vi* to cool (down) **II.** *vt* to cool; *fig* to cool down; ~ **el vino** to chill the wine **III.** *vr:* ~**se** **1.** (*perder calor*) to cool (down) **2.** (*refrescar, apaciguarse*) to cool off **3.** (*acatarrarse*) to catch a cold

enfurecer *irr como crecer* **I.** *vt* to enrage **II.** *vr:* ~**se** to be furious

engalanar *vt* to decorate

enganchar **I.** *vt* to hook; (*remolque*) to hitch up; (*caballerías*) to harness; FERRO, TÉC to couple **II.** *vr* ~**se de** [*o* **en**] **algo** to get caught on sth

enganche *m* **1.** (*gancho*) hook **2.** (*acto*) hooking

engañar **I.** *vi* to deceive; **las apariencias engañan** *prov* looks are deceiving *prov* **II.** *vt* (*mentir*) to deceive; (*estafar*) to cheat; ~ **a alguien** (*ser infiel*) to cheat on sb; ~ **el hambre** to stave off one's hunger; **dejarse** ~ to fall for it *inf*

engaño *m* **1.** (*mentira*) deceit **2.** (*truco*) trick

engañoso, -a *adj* **1.** (*persona*) deceitful **2.** (*falaz*) false

engarzar <z→c> *vt* (*trabar*) to join together; (*montar*) to set

engatusar *vt* to sweet-talk; ~ **a alguien para que haga algo** to coax sb into doing sth

engendrar *vt* **1.** (*concebir*) to beget *liter* **2.** (*causar*) to give rise to

engendro *m* **1.** (*persona fea*) freak **2.** (*idea*) piece of claptrap

englobar *vt* **1.** (*incluir*) to include, to comprise **2.** (*reunir*) to bring together

engomar *vt* to put glue on

engordar *vi* **1.** (*ponerse gordo*) to get fat; (*aumentar de peso*) to gain weight; **he engordado tres kilos** I've gained three kilos **2.** (*poner gordo*) to be fattening

engorroso, -a *adj* awkward; (*molesto*) bothersome

engranaje *m* **1.** TÉC gear; (*mecanismo*) cogs *pl* **2.** (*sistema*) gearing

engrandecer *irr como crecer vt* to enlarge

engrasar *vt* to grease; (*enaceitar*) to oil

engreído, -a *adj* conceited, spoilt

engrosar <o→ue> **I.** *vi* **1.** (*engordar*) to become fatter **2.** (*aumentar*) to increase **II.** *vt* to increase

enhebrar *vt* to thread

enhorabuena *f* congratulations *pl*; **dar la ~ a alguien** to congratulate sb

enigma *m* enigma

enjabonar *vt* to soap

enjambre *m* swarm

enjaular *vt* to lock up; (*en una jaula*) to cage

enjuagar <g→gu> *vt* to rinse

enjuague *m* rinse

enjugar <g→gu> *vt* to dry

enjuiciar *vt* **1.** (*juzgar*) to judge **2.** (*procesar*) to prosecute

enjuto, -a *adj* ~ (**de carnes**) thin

enlace *m* **1.** (*conexión*) connection; ELEC, FERRO, INFOR link **2.** (*boda*) wedding

enlazar <z→c> **I.** *vi* (*transporte*) to link up **II.** *vt* (*atar*) to tie; (*conectar*) to connect

enloquecer *irr como crecer* **I.** *vi, vr:* ~**se** to go mad **II.** *vt* to madden, to drive crazy

enlutado, -a *adj* dressed in mourning

enmarañar I. *vt* **1.** (*enredar*) to mix up **2.** (*confundir*) to confuse **II.** *vr:* ~**se 1.** (*enredarse*) to get mixed up

2. (*confundirse*) to get confused

enmarcar <c→qu> *vt* to frame

enmascarar *vt* **1.** (*poner máscara*) to mask **2.** (*ocultar*) to hide

enmendar <e→ie> **I.** *vt* to correct **II.** *vr:* ~**se** to mend one's ways

enmienda *f* correction

enmohecer *irr como crecer vi, vr:* ~**se** to go mouldy *Brit,* to go moldy *Am*

enmudecer *irr como crecer* **I.** *vi* **1.** (*perder el habla*) to be struck dumb; ~ **de miedo** to be struck speechless with fear **2.** (*callar*) to go silent **II.** *vt* to silence

ennegrecer *irr como crecer vt, vr:* ~**se** to blacken

ennoblecer *irr como crecer vt* to ennoble

enojar I. *vt* to annoy; (*enfadar*) to anger **II.** *vr:* ~**se** to get cross; (*enfadarse*) to get angry

enojo *m* annoyance; (*enfado*) anger

enojoso, -a *adj* annoying

enorgullecer *irr como crecer* **I.** *vt* to fill with pride **II.** *vr:* ~**se** to be proud

enorme *adj* enormous

enormidad *f* enormity; **una ~ (de algo)** *fig* a lot (of sth)

enraizar *irr vi* to set down roots

enredadera *f* climbing plant

enredar I. *vt* (*liar*) to mix up; (*confundir*) to confuse **II.** *vr:* ~**se** to get mixed up

enredo *m* **1.** (*de alambres*) tangle **2.** (*asunto*) muddle

enrevesado, -a *adj* complicated

enriquecer *irr como crecer vt* to enrich

enrojecer *irr como crecer vi, vr:* ~**se** to blush; ~ **de ira** to go red with anger

enrolar *vt* **1.** NÁUT to enrol *Brit,* to enroll *Am* **2.** MIL to enlist

enrollar I. *vt* (*cartel*) to roll up; (*cuerda*) to coil **II.** *vr:* ~**se** *inf* **1.** (*demasiado*) ~**se** (**como una persiana**) to go on and on **2.** (*ligar*) ~**se con alguien** to take up with sb

enroscar <c→qu> **I.** *vt* (*tornillo*) to screw in; (*tapa*) to twist on **II.** *vr:* ~**se** to curl up

? Anyone who visits **Mallorca** brings **ensaimadas** with them, at least every Spanish tourist does. An **ensaimada** is a light spiral--shaped pastry that can be filled with sweet **cabello de ángel**, a type of mashed pumpkin filling.

ensalada *f* salad

? **Ensaladilla rusa**: Take jacket potatoes, cooked vegetables (carrots, green beans, peas), olives, and hard-boiled eggs. Finely chop all these ingredients (similar to potato salad), then add tuna and dress the dish with mayonnaise and a little vinegar.

ensalzar <z→c> *vt* to praise
ensamblar *vt* to assemble
ensanchar *vt, vr:* ~**se** to widen
ensanche *m* widening; **zona de** ~ area for urban development
ensangrentar <e→ie> *vt* to cover in blood
ensartar *vt* to string
ensayar *vt* 1. TEAT to rehearse 2. (*probar*) to test
ensayo *m* 1. TEAT rehearsal; ~ **general** dress rehearsal 2. LIT essay 3. (*prueba*) test
enseguida *adv* at once, straight away
ensenada *f* inlet
enseñanza *f* 1. (*sistema*) education; ~ **superior** higher education 2. (*docencia*) teaching; ~ **a distancia** distance learning
enseñar *vt* 1. (*instruir, dar clases*) to teach 2. (*mostrar*) to show; **te enseñé a hacer las camas** I showed you how to make beds
enseres *mpl* belongings *pl*
ensillar *vt* to saddle
ensimismarse *vr* to become absorbed
ensordecer *irr como crecer vi* to go deaf

ensortijado, -a *adj* curly
ensuciar I. *vt* to dirty II. *vr:* ~**se** to get dirty; ~**se de algo** to be stained with sth
ensueño *m* dream; **de** ~ fantastic
entablar *vt* (*conversación*) to strike up; (*negociaciones*) to begin; (*juicio*) to file
entablillar *vt* to splint
entallado, -a *adj* taken in at the waist
entallar *vt* to take in at the waist
ente *m* 1. FILOS being 2. (*autoridad*) body
entender <e→ie> I. *vi* 1. (*comprender*) to understand 2. (*saber*) ~ **mucho de algo** to know a lot about sth; **no** ~ **nada de algo** to know nothing about sth II. *vt* 1. (*comprender*) to understand; **dar a** ~ **que...** to imply that ...; **lo entendieron mal** they misunderstood it; **si entiendo bien Ud. quiere decir que...** am I right in saying that what you mean is that ...; **no entiende una broma** he/she can't take a joke 2. (*creer*) to think; **yo no lo entiendo así** that's not the way I see it; **tengo entendido que...** (*según creo*) I believe that ...; (*según he oído*) I've heard that ... III. *vr:* ~**se** 1. (*llevarse*) to get on; (*liarse*) to have an affair 2. (*ponerse de acuerdo*) to reach an agreement 3. *inf* (*desenvolverse*) **no me entiendo con este lío de cables** I can't manage with this tangle of leads; **¡que se las entienda!** let him/her get on with it! IV. *m* opinion; **a mi** ~ the way I see it
entendido, -a *adj* ~ **en algo** expert on sth
entendimiento *m sin pl* (*razón*) reason; (*comprensión*) understanding; **obrar con** ~ to act reasonably
enterado, -a *adj* ~ **de algo** (*iniciado*) aware of sth; (*conocedor*) knowledgeable about sth; **yo ya estaba** ~ **del incidente** I already knew about the incident; **no se dio por** ~ he pretended not to have understood

enteramente *adv* wholly

enterarse *vr* ~ (**de algo**) (*descubrir*) to find out (about sth); (*saber*) to hear (about sth); **no me enteré** (**de nada**) I didn't notice anything; **pasa las hojas sin ~ de lo que lee** he/she spends hours reading without taking anything in; **¡para que te enteres!** *inf* that'll teach you!; **para que te enteres...** for your information ...

entereza *f sin pl* **1.** (*determinación*) strength of mind **2.** (*integridad*) integrity; (*aguante*) fortitude

enternecer *irr como crecer* **I.** *vt* to move **II.** *vr:* ~**se** to be touched

entero, -a *adj* **1.** (*completo*) *t.* MAT whole, entire; (*intacto*) intact; **por ~** completely; **se pasa días ~s sin decir ni una palabra** he/she goes for days at a time without speaking; **el juego de café no está ~** some of the coffee service is missing **2.** (*persona*) honest

enterrador(a) *m(f)* gravedigger

enterrar <e→ie> *vt* to bury

entibiar *vt, vr:* ~**se** to cool

entidad *f* (*asociación*) organization; (*compañía*) company; ~ **bancaria** bank

entierro *m* **1.** (*inhumación*) burial **2.** (*funeral*) funeral

entonación *f* intonation

entonar I. *vi* to go well **II.** *vt* to sing

entonces *adv* then; **desde ~** from then on; **hasta ~** until then; **en** [*o* **por**] **aquel ~** at that time, then; **¿pues ~ por qué te extraña si no vienen?** then why are you surprised that they don't come?

entornar *vt* to leave slightly open

entorno *m* surroundings *pl;* (*medio ambiente*) environment

entorpecer *irr como crecer vt* **1.** (*dificultar*) to hamper; (*retrasar*) to slow down **2.** (*sentidos*) to dull

entrada *f* **1.** (*acción, comienzo*) *t.* TEAT, LING entry; ~ **en vigor** coming into force; **de ~** (*desde un principio*) right from the start; (*al principio*) at first; **se prohíbe la ~** no entry **2.** (*puerta*) entrance; ~ **a la autopis-**ta motorway slip road *Brit,* (entry) ramp *Am* **3.** (*billete*) ticket **4.** GASTR first course, entrée **5.** *pl* (*pelo*) **tiene ~s** his/her hair is receding **6.** (*depósito*) deposit; **dar una ~ to pay a** deposit **7.** INFOR input

entrado, -a *adj* **un señor ~ en años** an elderly gentleman; **hasta muy ~ el siglo XVII** until well into the seventeeth century; **llegamos entrada la noche** we arrived when it was already dark

entrante¹ *adj* next

entrante² *m* first course, starter

entrañable *adj* (*amistad*) intimate; (*película, persona*) endearing; (*recuerdo*) fond

entrañar *vt* to entail

entrañas *fpl* (*órganos*) entrails *pl;* **echar las ~** *inf* to throw up

entrar I. *vi* **1.** (*pasar*) to enter; ~ **por la fuerza** to break in; **me entró por un oído y me salió por otro** it went in one ear and out the other; **¡entre!** come in! **2.** (*caber*) to fit; **no me entra el anillo** I can't get the ring on **3.** (*penetrar*) to go in; **el clavo entró en la pared** the nail went into the wall; **¡no me entra en la cabeza cómo pudiste hacer eso!** I can't understand how you could do this! **4.** (*empezar*) to begin; ~ **en calor** to warm up; **no ~ en detalles** not to go into details; **me entró el hambre/el sueño/un mareo** I became hungry/sleepy/dizzy; **me entró la tentación** I was tempted **5.** (*formar parte*) **en un kilo entran tres panochas** you can get three corncobs to the kilo; **eso no entraba en mis cálculos** I hadn't reckoned on this **6.** INFOR to access **7.** *inf* (*entender*) **las matemáticas no me entran** I can't get the hang of mathematics **8.** (*opinar*) **yo en eso no entro** [*o* **ni entro ni salgo**] *inf* I've got nothing to do with this **II.** *vt* to put

entre *prep* **1.** (*dos cosas*) between; (*más de dos cosas*) among(st); **salir de ~ las ramas** to emerge from among(st) the branches; **pasar por**

~ **las mesas** to go between the tables; ~ **semana** during the week; **ven** ~ **las cinco y las seis** come between five and six; ~ **tanto** meanwhile; **un ejemplo** ~ **muchos** one of many examples; **lo hablaremos** ~ **nosotros** we'll speak about it among(st) ourselves; ~ **el taxi y la entrada me quedé sin dinero** what with the taxi and the ticket I had no money left; **me senté** ~ **los dos** I sat down between the two of them **2.** MAT **ocho** ~ **dos son cuatro** eight divided by two is four

entreabrir *irr como abrir* vt to open slightly

entrecejo *m* brow; **fruncir el** ~ to frown

entrecortado, -a *adj* (*respiración*) uneven, laboured *Brit,* labored *Am;* (*voz*) halting

entredicho *m* **poner algo en** ~ to put sth in question

entrega *f* **1.** (*dedicación*) dedication **2.** (*fascículo*) instalment *Brit,* installment *Am;* **novela por** ~**s** serialized novel **3.** (*de documentos*) delivery; ~ **de premios** prizegiving; ~ **de títulos** UNIV graduation ceremony; **hacer** ~ **de algo** to hand sth over **4.** COM delivery; ~ **a domicilio** home delivery; ~ **contra reembolso** collect on delivery

entregar <g→gu> **I.** vt to give, to hand over; (*carta*) to deliver; ~**la** *inf* to kick the bucket **II.** vr: ~**se 1.** (*desvivirse*) ~**se a la bebida** to take to drink **2.** (*delincuente*) to give oneself up; MIL to surrender

entrelazar <z→c> vt, vr: ~**se** to join, to (inter)weave

entremeses *mpl* hors d'oeuvres *pl,* appetizers *pl Am*

entremeterse *vr* to interfere

entremezclar vt to intermingle

entrenador(a) *m(f)* coach

entrenamiento *m* training

entrenar vt, vr: ~**se** to train

entrepierna *f* crotch

entresacar <c→qu> vt to pick out

entresuelo *m* first floor

entretanto *adv* meanwhile

entretejer vt **1.** (*meter*) to weave in **2.** (*entrelazar*) to interweave

entretener *irr como tener* **I.** vt **1.** (*divertir*) to entertain **2.** (*detener*) to hold up **II.** vr: ~**se 1.** (*pasar el rato*) to amuse oneself; ~**se con revistas** to amuse oneself by reading magazines **2.** (*tardar*) to delay; **¡no te entretengas!** don't dilly dally!

entretenido, -a *adj* entertaining

entretenimiento *m* entertainment; (*pasatiempo*) activity

entretiempo *m sin pl* **chaqueta de** ~ jacket for spring and autumn

entrever *irr como ver* vt **1.** (*objeto*) to glimpse **2.** (*sospechar*) to surmise; (*intenciones*) to guess

entrevista *f* **1.** (*inteviú*) interview **2.** (*reunión*) meeting

entrevistar **I.** vt to interview **II.** vr: ~**se** to have a meeting

entristecer *irr como crecer* **I.** vt to sadden **II.** vr: ~**se** to be saddened

entrometerse *vr* to interfere

entroncar <c→qu> vi ~ **con alguien** to be related to sb

entumecerse *irr como crecer* vr (*frío*) to go numb; (*músculo*) to stiffen

entumecido, -a *adj* (*frío*) numb; (*rígido*) stiff

enturbiar vt to darken

entusiasmar **I.** vt to enthuse **II.** vr: ~**se** to get enthusiastic

entusiasmo *m sin pl* enthusiasm

entusiasta **I.** *adj* enthusiastic **II.** *mf* enthusiast

enumerar vt to enumerate; (*escrito*) to set down

enunciado *m* **1.** (*de un problema*) setting out **2.** LING statement

envalentonar **I.** vt to spur **II.** vr: ~**se** to become brave

envanecer *irr como crecer* **I.** vt to make vain **II.** vr: ~**se** to become vain

envasar vt to package; (*en latas*) to tin *Brit,* to can *Am;* (*en botellas*) to bottle

envase *m* **1.** (*paquete*) package; (*recipiente*) container; (*botella*) bottle **2.** (*acción*) packing

envejecer *irr como crecer* vt, vr: ~**se**

to age
envenenar *vt* to poison
envergadura *f* (*importancia*) magnitude; (*alcance*) scope
envés *m* back
enviar <*1. pres:* envío> *vt* to send
envidia *f* envy; **dar ~ a alguien** to make sb envious; **tener ~ a alguien** to envy sb; **tener ~ de algo** to be jealous of sth
envidiar *vt* to envy
envío *m* sending; **~ a domicilio** home delivery; **gastos de ~** postage and packing *Brit,* shipping and handling *Am;* **~ contra reembolso** cash on delivery
enviudar *vi* to be widowed
envoltura *f* (*capa*) covering; (*embalaje*) wrapping
envolver *irr como* volver *vt* **1.**(*en papel, ropa*) to wrap; (*empaquetar*) to pack **2.**(*implicar*) to involve
enyesar *vt* to plaster
enzarzarse *vr* to get involved
epicentro *m* epicentre *Brit,* epicenter *Am*
épico, -a *adj* epic
epidemia *f* epidemic
epidermis *f inv* epidermis
epilepsia *f* epilepsy
epiléptico, -a *adj, m, f* epileptic
epílogo *m* epilogue *Brit,* epilog *Am*
episodio *m* episode
época *f* **1.** HIST epoch, age; **un invento que hizo ~** an epoch-making invention; **muebles de ~** antique furniture **2.**(*tiempo*) time; **~ de las lluvias** rainy season; **en aquella ~** at that time
equidad *f sin pl* fairness
equilibrar *vt, vr:* **~se** to balance
equilibrio *m* balance; **mantener/perder el ~** to keep/loose one's balance
equilibrista *mf* tightrope artist
equipaje *m* baggage, luggage *Am;* **hacer el ~** to pack
equipar *vt* to equip; (*de ropa*) to fit out
equiparar *vt* **1.**(*igualar*) to put on the same level **2.**(*comparar*) to compare

equipo *m* **1.**(*grupo*) *t.* DEP team; (*turno*) shift; **el ~ de casa/de fuera** the home/visiting team **2.**(*utensilios*) equipment; **~ de alta fidelidad** hi-fi system
equis I. *adj inv* X; **~ euros** X number of euros II. *f inv* X, x
equitación *f sin pl* horseriding
equitativo, -a *adj* equitable
equivalente *adj, m* equivalent; **el ~ a diez días de trabajo** the equivalent of ten days' work
equivaler *irr como* valer *vi* to be equivalent; **la negativa equivaldría a la ruptura de las negociaciones** saying no would mean the breakdown of negotiations; **lo que equivale a decir que...** which is the same as saying that ...
equivocación *f* mistake; (*error*) error; (*malentendido*) misunderstanding; **por ~** by mistake
equivocado, -a *adj* wrong
equivocarse <c→qu> *vr* **~ (en** [*o* de] **algo**) to be wrong (about sth); **~ de camino** to take the wrong way; **~ al escribir/al hablar** to make a mistake (when) writing/speaking; **~ de número (de teléfono)** to dial the wrong number
equívoco *m* (*doble sentido*) ambiguity; (*malentendido*) misunderstanding
equívoco, -a *adj* (*con dos sentidos*) ambiguous; (*dudoso*) doubtful
era¹ *f* **1.**(*período*) era **2.**(*para trigo*) threshing floor
era² **3.** *imper de* ser
erario *m* revenue; **el ~ público** the public treasury
erección *f* erection
eres **2.** *pres de* ser
erguir *irr vt* (*levantar*) to raise; (*poner derecho*) to straighten; **con la cabeza erguida** with one's head held high
erigir <g→j> I. *vt* **1.**(*construir*) to build; **~ un andamio** to put up scaffolding **2.**(*fundar*) to establish II. *vr* **~se en algo** (*declararse*) to declare oneself to be sth; (*hacer de*) to act as sth

E
e

erizado, -a *adj* **1.** BOT prickly **2.** (*pelo*) on end

erizarse <z→c> *vr* to stand on end; **se me erizó el vello de tanto frío** it was so cold I had goose pimples

erizo *m* hedgehog

ermita *f* hermitage

ermitaño, -a *m, f* hermit

erosión *f t. fig* erosion

erosionar *vt t. fig* to erode

erótico, -a *adj* erotic

erotismo *m* eroticism, erotism

erradicar <c→qu> *vt* to eradicate

errar *irr* **I.** *vi* **1.** (*equivocarse*) to err; ~ **en algo** to make a mistake in sth; ~ **en el camino** to take the wrong road; ~ **en la respuesta** to give the wrong answer **2.** (*andar vagando*) to wander; **ir errando por las calles** to wander the streets **II.** *vt* to miss

errata *f* errata

erróneo, -a *adj* erroneous; **decisión errónea** wrong decision

error *m* **1.** (*falta, equivocación*) fault; ~ **de cálculo** miscalculation; ~ **de imprenta** misprint; ~ **de operación** INFOR operative error; ~ **ortográfico** spelling mistake; **estar en el** [*o* **un**] ~ to be wrong; **por** ~ by mistake **2.** FÍS, MAT (*diferencia*) error

eructar *vi* to belch, to burp

eructo *m* belch, burp

erudito, -a **I.** *adj* **1.** (*persona*) erudite **2.** (*obra*) scholarly; **conocimientos** ~s extensive knowledge **II.** *m, f* scholar; (*experto*) expert

erupción *f* **1.** GEO eruption **2.** MED rash

es *3. pres de* **ser**

esa(s) *adj, pron dem v.* **ese, -a**

ésa(s) *pron dem v.* **ése**

esbelto, -a *adj* slender

esbozo *m* **1.** (*dibujo*) sketch **2.** (*de un proyecto*) outline

escabeche *m* marinade; **atún en** ~ pickled tuna

escabroso, -a *adj* **1.** (*áspero*) rough; (*terreno*) uneven **2.** (*asunto*) thorny

escabullirse <3. pret: se escabulló> *vr* **1.** (*desaparecer*) to slip away; ~ (**por**) **entre la multitud** to slip away through the crowd **2.** (*escurrirse*) to slip through; **la trucha se me escabulló** (**de entre las manos**) the trout slipped through my fingers

escacharrar *vt* **1.** (*objeto*) to break **2.** (*proyecto*) to spoil; (*plan*) to wreck

escafandra *f* diving suit

escala *f* **1.** (*serie, proporción, de mapa, medida*) *t.* MÚS scale; **a** ~ to scale; **un mapa a** ~ **1:100.000** a map with a 1:100,000 scale; **en gran** ~ on a large scale; **a** ~ **mundial** on a world scale **2.** (*parada, puerto*) stop; AERO stopover; **hacer** ~ NÁUT to stop; AERO to land

escalafón *m* (*de cargos*) ranking; (*de sueldos*) salary scale

escalar *vi, vt* to climb; ~**on la habitación por la ventana** they got into the room through the window

escalera *f* **1.** (*escalones*) staircase, stairs; AERO stairway; ~ **abajo/arriba** downstairs/upstairs; ~ **mecánica** [*o* **automática**] escalator **2.** (*escala*) ladder; ~ **de cuerda** rope ladder; ~ **de incendios** fire escape; ~ **de mano** ladder; ~ **doble** [*o* **de tijera**] stepladder

escalfar *vt* to poach

escalinata *f* main staircase; (*fuera*) outside steps *pl*

escalofriante *adj* chilling; **película** ~ scary film *Brit*, scary movie *Am*

escalofrío *m* shiver; **al abrir la ventana sentí** ~**s** I felt a chill when I opened the window; **cierra la puerta, tengo** ~**s** close the door, I feel chilly; **el libro me produjo** ~**s** the book sent shivers down my spine

escalón *m* **1.** (*peldaño*) step; (*de una escala*) rung **2.** (*nivel*) step; **subir un** ~ to move up the ladder

escalope *m* escalope

escama *f t.* ZOOL, BOT scale; ~**s de jabón** soap flakes

escamar *vt* **1.** (*el pescado*) to scale **2.** *inf* (*inquietar*) to make suspicious

escamotear *vt* **1.** (*ilusionista*) to whisk out of sight **2.** (*robar*) to palm **3.** (*ocultar*) to cover up

escampar *vimpers* **espera hasta que escampe** wait until it clears

escanciar *vt* to pour

escandalizar <z→c> **I.** *vt* **1.** (*indignar, impactar*) to scandalize **2.** (*alborotar*) **escandalizaste la casa con tus gritos** you woke up the whole house with your shouting **II.** *vr* **~se de** [*o por*] **algo** to be scandalized by sth

escándalo *m* **1.** (*ruido*) uproar; **armar un** [*o dar el*] **~** to make a scene; **se armó un ~** there was a terrible uproar **2.** (*hecho*) scandal; **de ~** scandalous; **causar ~** to cause a scandal; **estos precios son un ~** these prices are outrageous; **tu comportamiento es un ~** your behaviour is a disgrace

escandaloso, -a *adj* **1.** (*ruidoso*) noisy **2.** (*inmoral, irritante*) scandalous; **precios ~s** outrageous prices

Escandinavia *f* Scandinavia

escandinavo, -a *adj, m, f* Scandinavian

escáner *m* scanner

escaño *m* **1.** (*banco*) bench **2.** POL seat

escapar I. *vi, vr:* **~se 1.** (*de la cárcel, de un peligro*) to escape **2.** (*deprisa, ocultamente*) to get away; **~ de casa** to run away from home **II.** *vr:* **~se 1.** (*agua, gas*) to leak **2.** (*involuntariamente*) **se me ha escapado que te vas a casar** I let it slip that you were getting married; **se me ha escapado su nombre** I've forgotten your name; **se me ha escapado el autobús** I've missed the bus; **se me ha escapado la mano** my hand slipped; **se me escapó un suspiro** I let out a sigh **3.** (*pasar inadvertido*) **no se te escapa ni una** you don't miss a thing

escaparate *m* shop window

escape *m* **1.** (*de un gas, líquido*) leak **2.** (*solución*) way out; **no había ningún ~ a la situación** there was no way out of the situation

escaquearse *vr inf* to skive off

escarabajo *m* beetle

escaramuza *f* skirmish

escarbar *vi, vt* **1.** (*en la tierra*) **~ (en) algo** to dig sth **2.** (*escudriñar*) **~ (en)**

algo to investigate sth; (*entremeterse*) to pry into sth

escarceo *m* **~ amoroso** fling; **~s políticos** political comings and goings; **sin ~s** without hesitation

escarcha *f* frost

escarlata *adj* scarlet

escarlatina *f* scarlet fever

escarmentar <e→ie> **I.** *vi* to learn one's lesson **II.** *vt* to teach a lesson; **quedar** [*o estar*] **escarmentado de algo** to learn one's lesson from sth

escarmiento *m* lesson; **me sirvió de ~** it taught me a lesson

escarnio *m* scorn; **con ~** scornfully

escarola *f* curly endive

escarpado, -a *adj* (*terreno*) rugged; (*montaña*) steep and craggy

escasear *vi* to be scarce

escasez *f* shortage

escaso, -a *adj* (*insuficiente*) insufficient, scant(y); (*tiempo*) little; **andar ~ de dinero** to be short of money; **estar ~ de tiempo** to be short of time; **tener escasas posibilidades de ganar** to have little chance of winning; **en dos horas escasas** in only two hours

escatimar *vt* to skimp; **no ~ gastos** not to skimp on costs; **me escatimó parte del dinero** he/she didn't give me some of the money

escayola *f* plaster

escayolar *vt* to put a plaster-cast on; **llevar el brazo escayolado** to have an arm in plaster

escena *f* **1.** (*parte del teatro*) stage; **aparecer en ~** to appear on stage; **poner en ~** to stage; **puesta en ~** staging; **salir a/de la ~** to go on/off stage **2.** (*de una obra, lugar, suceso, reproche*) scene

escenario *m* **1.** (*parte del teatro*) stage **2.** (*lugar, situación*) scene

escenografía *f* **1.** (*decoración*) set design **2.** (*decorados*) set

escepticismo *m sin pl* scepticism *Brit*, skepticism *Am*

escéptico, -a *adj, m, f* sceptic *Brit*, skeptic *Am*

escisión *f* split

esclarecer *irr como crecer vt* to clear

up; (*crimen, misterio*) to shed light upon

esclavitud *f* slavery

esclavizar <z→c> *vt* to enslave

esclavo, -a *adj, m, f* slave; **eres esclava de tu familia** you do everything your family wants; **eres (un) ~ del alcohol** you can't live without alcohol

esclusa *f* lock

escoba *f* broom, brush *Brit;* **no vender ni una ~** *inf* to be completely useless

escobilla *f* brush; (*de baño*) toilet brush

escocer *irr como cocer vi* to sting

escocés *m* (Scottish) Gaelic

escocés, -esa I. *adj* Scottish; **cuadros escoceses** tartan; **falda escocesa** kilt; (*para mujeres*) tartan skirt **II.** *m, f* Scot, Scotsman *m,* Scotswoman *f*

Escocia *f* Scotland

escoger <g→j> *vi, vt* to choose; **no has sabido ~** you've made the wrong choice

escogido, -a *adj* 1. *ser* (*selecto*) finest 2. *estar* (*elegido*) **estos plátanos están ya muy ~s** all the good bananas have gone

escolar I. *adj* academic; **curso ~** academic year **II.** *mf* schoolboy *m,* schoolgirl *f*

escollo *m* 1. (*peñasco*) rock 2. (*riesgo*) pitfall; (*obstáculo*) obstacle

escolta *f* escort

escoltar *vt* to escort

escombro(s) *m(pl)* rubble

esconder *vt, vr:* ~**se** to hide

escondidas *adv* **a** ~ secretly; **a** ~ **de alguien** behind sb's back

escondite *m* 1. (*juego*) hide and seek 2. (*lugar*) hiding place

escondrijo *m* hideout

escopeta *f* shotgun

escoria *f* 1. (*residuo*) slag 2. (*despreciable*) scum

Escorpio *m* Scorpio

escorpión *m* scorpion

Escorpión *m* Scorpio

escotado *m* neckline

escotado, -a *adj* with a low neckline

escote *m* 1. (*en el cuello*) neckline; ~

en pico V-neck 2. (*busto*) bust 3. (*dinero*) share; **pagar a ~** to split the price; **pagaron la cena a ~** they went Dutch on the dinner bill

escotilla *f* hatchway

escozor *m* burning

escribano *m* court clerk

escribiente *mf* scribe

escribir *irr* **I.** *vi, vt* write; **escrito a mano** handwritten; **escrito a máquina** typewritten; **¿cómo se escribe tu nombre?** how do you spell your name? **II.** *vr:* ~**se** to write (to each other)

escrito *m* (*carta*) letter; (*literario, científico*) text; **por ~** in writing

escrito, -a I. *pp de* **escribir II.** *adj* written

escritor(a) *m(f)* writer

escritorio *m* desk(top)

escritura *f* 1. (*acto*) writing 2. (*signos*) script 3. (*documento*) deed; ~ **de propiedad** title deeds; ~ **de seguro** insurance certificate; **las Sagradas Escrituras** the Holy Scriptures

escrúpulo *m* 1. (*duda*) scruple; ~**s de conciencia** pangs of conscience; **ser una persona sin ~s** to be completely unscrupulous; **no tener ~s en hacer algo** to have no qualms about doing sth 2. (*asco*) disgust; **me da ~ beber de latas** I think it's disgusting to drink out of cans

escrupuloso, -a *adj* 1. (*meticuloso*) scrupulous 2. (*quisquilloso*) fussy

escrutar *vt* 1. (*mirar*) to scrutinize 2. (*recontar*) to count

escrutinio *m* 1. (*examen*) scrutiny 2. (*recuento*) count

escuadra *f* 1. (*para dibujar*) set square; **a** ~ at right angles 2. MIL squad; NÁUT, AERO squadron

escuadrilla *f* squadron

escuadrón *m* squadron

escuálido, -a *adj* scrawny

escualo *m* shark

escucha¹ *m* scout

escucha² *f* listening; ~ **telefónica** telephone tapping

escuchar I. *vi* to listen **II.** *vt* to listen to; ~ **una conversación telefónica**

to tap into a telephone conversation

escudarse *vr* ~ **en algo** to use sth as an excuse

escudilla *f* bowl

escudo *m* **1.** (*arma*) shield **2.** (*emblema*) ~ (**de armas**) coat of arms

escudriñar *vt* **1.** (*examinar*) to scrutinize **2.** (*mirar*) to scour

escuela *f* school; ~ **de párvulos** nursery school; ~ **superior técnica** polytechnic

escueto, -a *adj* **1.** (*sin adornos*) bare **2.** (*lenguaje*) concise

escuincle *m Méx, inf* baby, kid

esculpir *vt* **1.** (*modelar*) to sculpt; ~ **en madera** to carve in wood **2.** (*grabar*) to engrave

escultor(a) *m(f)* sculptor *m,* sculptress *f*

escultura *f* sculpture

escupidera *f* spittoon

escupir I. *vi* to spit **II.** *vt* to spit out; ~ **sangre** to spit blood

escupitajo *m* gob of spit

escurreplatos *m inv,* **escurridero** *m* plate rack

escurridizo, -a *adj* slippery

escurrir I. *vt* **1.** (*ropa*) to wring out; (*platos, verdura*) to drain **2.** (*una vasija*) to empty; ~ **la** (**botella de**) **cerveza** to empty the bottle of beer **II.** *vr:* ~**se 1.** (*resbalar*) to slip **2.** (*escaparse*) to slip out; **el pez se me escurrió de** (**entre**) **las manos** the fish slipped out of my hands **3.** (*desaparecer*) to slip away; ~**se** (**por**) **entre la gente** to slip away in the crowd **4.** (*gotear*) to drip

ese *f* S, s

ese, -a I. *adj* <esos, -as> that; **esas sillas están en el medio** those chairs are in the way **II.** *pron dem v.* **ése, ésa, eso**

ése, ésa, eso <ésos, -as> *pron dem* that, that one; **me lo ha dicho ésa** that girl told me; **¿por qué no vamos a otro bar?** – ~ **no me gusta** why don't we go to another bar? – I don't like that one; **llegaré a eso de las doce** I'll arrive at about twelve o'clock; **estaba trabajando, en eso** (**que**) **tocaron al timbre** I

was working when I heard the bell; **¡no me vengas con ésas!** come off it!; **eso mismo te acabo de decir** that's what I've just said; **aun con eso prefiero quedarme en casa** even so, I'd rather stay at home; **no es eso** it's not that; **por eso** (**mismo**) that's why; **¿y eso?** what do you mean?; **¿y eso qué?** so what?; **¡eso sí que no!** defintely not!; *v.t.* **ese, -a**

esencia *f* essence

esencial *adj* essential; (*fundamental*) fundamental; **lo** ~ the main thing

esfera *f* **1.** *t.* MAT sphere **2.** (*del reloj*) face, dial

esférico, -a *adj* spherical

esforzado, -a *adj* courageous

esforzarse *irr como forzar vr* (*moralmente*) to strive; (*físicamente*) to make an effort

esfuerzo *m* effort; **sin** ~ effortlessly; **me ha costado muchos** ~**s conseguirlo** it took me a lot of effort to manage it

esfumarse *vr* **1.** (*desaparecer*) to fade away; (*contornos*) to blur **2.** *inf* (*marcharse*) to beat it; **¡esfúmate!** beat it!

esgrima *f* fencing

esgrimir *vt* **1.** (*blandir*) to wield **2.** (*argumento*) to use

esguince *m* sprain; **hacerse un** ~ **en el tobillo** to sprain one's ankle

eslabón *m* link

eslalon *m* slalom

eslavo, -a *adj, m, f* Slav

eslogan *m* slogan

eslovaco, -a I. *adj* Slovakian **II.** *m, f* Slovak

Eslovaquia *f* Slovakia

Eslovenia *f* Slovenia

esloveno, -a *adj, m, f* Slovenian

esmaltar *vt* to enamel

esmalte *m* enamel; ~ (**de uñas**) nail polish

esmerado, -a *adj* **1.** (*persona*) painstaking **2.** (*obra*) professional

esmeralda *adj, f* emerald

esmerarse *vr* **1.** (*obrar con esmero*) to take pains; ~ **en la limpieza** to clean conscientiously **2.** (*esforzarse*)

E e

~ **en algo** to make an effort with sth **3.** (*lucirse*) to make a good impression; **hoy te has esmerado en la comida** today's lunch was wonderful

esmero *m* care; **con** ~ with great care

esnob I. *adj* snobbish **II.** *mf* snob

esnobismo *m* snobbery

eso *pron dem v.* **ése**

esófago *m* oesophagus *Brit,* esophagus *Am*

esos *adj v.* **ese**

ésos *pron dem v.* **ése**

esotérico, -a *adj* esoteric

espabilado, -a *adj* smart

espachurrar I. *vt inf* to squash **II.** *vr:* ~**se** to get squashed

espacial *adj* space

espaciar *vt* to space out

espacio *m* **1.** (*área*) *t.* ASTR space; (*superficie*) area; (*trayecto*) distance; **a doble** ~ double-spaced **2.** (*que ocupa un cuerpo*) room, space **3.** (*de tiempo*) period; **en el ~ de dos meses** in a period of two months; **por** ~ **de tres horas** for a three hour period **4.** TV programme *Brit,* program *Am;* ~ **informativo** news bulletin; ~ **publicitario** advertising spot

espacioso, -a *adj* spacious, roomy

espada¹ *m* bullfighter

espada² *f* **1.** (*arma*) sword; **estar entre la** ~ **y la pared** to be between the devil and the deep blue sea; **el despido era mi** ~ **de Damocles** the possibility of losing my job hung over me like a sword of Damocles **2.** (*naipes*) spade

espagueti(s) *m(pl)* spaghetti; ~**s a la boloñesa** spaghetti bolognese

espalda *f* **1.** (*parte posterior*) back; **ancho de** ~**s** broad-shouldered; **atacar por la** ~ to attack from the rear; **estar a** ~**s de alguien** to be behind sb; **estar de** ~**s a la pared** to have one's back to the wall; **hablar a** ~**s de alguien** to talk behind sb's back; **volver la** ~ **a alguien** *t. fig* to turn one's back on sb; **la responsabilidad recae sobre mis** ~**s** the re-

sponsibility is on my shoulders **2.** DEP backstroke

espaldilla *f* **1.** (*de una res*) shoulder **2.** ANAT shoulder blade

espanglis *m* Spanglish

espantadizo, -a *adj* jittery

espantajo *m,* **espantapájaros** *m inv* scarecrow

espantar *vt* **1.** (*dar miedo*) to frighten **2.** (*ahuyentar*) to frighten off

espanto *m* **1.** (*miedo*) fright; **¡qué ~!** how awful!; **hace un calor de** ~ it's terribly hot; **los precios son de** ~ prices are outrageous **2.** (*terror*) horror

espantoso, -a *adj* **1.** (*horroroso*) horrible **2.** (*feo*) hideous

España *f* Spain

> **?** **España** (official title: **Reino de España**) is a constitutional monarchy with a two-chamber system. The king, **Juan Carlos I,** was appointed Head of State on 22.11.1975. The successor to the throne is Crown Prince **Felipe de Asturias.** The official language of the country is Spanish. Since 1978, **el gallego** (Galician), **el catalán** (Catalan) and **el euskera/el vasco** (Basque) have also been recognised as national languages.

español *m* Spanish; **clases de** ~ Spanish classes; **aprender** ~ to learn Spanish; **traducir al** ~ to translate into Spanish

español(a) I. *adj* Spanish; **a la** ~**a** Spanish-style **II.** *m(f)* Spaniard

esparadrapo *m* adhesive tape

esparcimiento *m* fun

esparcir <c→z> **I.** *vt* **1.** (*cosas*) to spread (out) **2.** (*noticia*) to spread **II.** *vr:* ~**se 1.** (*cosas*) to spread (out) **2.** (*noticias*) to spread **3.** (*distraerse*) to relax; **¿qué haces para** ~**te?** what do you do for fun?

espárrago *m* asparagus; **estar**

hecho un ~ *fig* to be as thin as a rake; **¡vete a freír ~s!** *inf* get lost!

esparto *m* esparto

espasmo *m* spasm

espátula *f* **1.** TÉC trowel; (*manualidades*) palette knife **2.** MED spatula

especia *f* spice

especial *adj* **1.** (*no habitual*) special; **en** ~ in particular; **¿qué has hecho hoy? – nada en** ~ what did you do today? – nothing special; **no pensaba en nada en** ~ I wasn't thinking of anything in particular; **él es para mí alguien muy** ~ he means a lot to me **2.** (*raro*) peculiar

especialidad *f* **1.** (*de un restaurante, una empresa*) speciality *Brit,* specialty *Am* **2.** (*rama*) field; DEP speciality *Brit,* specialty *Am*

especialista *mf* specialist

especializarse <z→c> *vr* to specialize; **personal especializado** skilled staff

especialmente *adv* (*específicamente*) specially; (*particularmente, sobre todo*) especially

especie *f* **1.** BOT, ZOOL species *inv;* **la** ~ **animal** animals *pl* **2.** (*clase*) kind; **ese es una** ~ **de cantante** he's a kind of singer; **gente de todas las** ~**s** all kinds of people **3.** COM **pagar en** ~**s** to pay in kind

especificar <c→qu> *vt* to specify

específico, -a *adj* specific

espécimen *m* <especímenes> specimen

espectáculo *m* **1.** TEAT show; ~ **de circo** circus; ~ **deportivo** sporting event **2.** *inf* (*escándalo*) **dar el** [*o* **un**] ~ to make a spectacle

espectador(a) *m(f)* spectator

espectro *m* **1.** (*fantasma*) phantom, spectre *Brit,* specter *Am* **2.** FÍS spectrum

especulación *f* speculation

especular *vi* to speculate; ~ **en la Bolsa** to speculate on the stock market

espejismo *m* mirage

espejo *m* mirror; ~ **retrovisor** car mirror, rear-view mirror; **mirarse al** ~ to look at oneself in the mirror

espeluznante *adj* horrific

espera *f* wait; **lista de** ~ waiting list; **no tener** ~ to be urgent; **sin** ~ immediate; **en** ~ **de su respuesta** looking forward to hearing from you; **en** ~ **de tu carta, te mando el paquete** I'm sending you the parcel and look forward to hearing from you; **tuvimos dos horas de** ~ we had a two-hour wait; **estoy a la** ~ **de recibir la beca** I'm waiting to hear about the grant; **esta** ~ **me saca de quicio** this waiting around is really getting to me

esperanza *f* hope; ~ **de vida** life expectancy; **estar en estado de buena** ~ to be pregnant; **poner las** ~**s en algo** to put one's hopes into sth; **no tener** ~**s** to have no hope; **veo el futuro con** ~ I'm hopeful about the future

esperanzar <z→c> **I.** *vt* to give hope to **II.** *vr* ~**se en algo** to become hopeful about sth

esperar I. *vi* (*aguardar*) to wait; **hacerse** ~ to keep people waiting; **es de** ~ **que** +*subj* it is to be expected that; **¿a qué esperas?** what are you waiting for?; **espera, que no lo encuentro** hold on, I can't find it; **ganaron la copa tan esperada** they won the long-awaited cup **II.** *vt* **1.** (*aguardar*) to wait for; **hacer** ~ **a alguien** to keep sb waiting; **la respuesta no se hizo** ~ the answer was not long in coming; **te espero mañana a las nueve** I'll be waiting for you tomorrow at nine o'clock; **me van a** ~ **al aeropuerto** they're meeting me at the airport; **nos esperan malos tiempos** there are bad times in store for us; **espero su decisión con impaciencia** (*final de carta*) I'm looking forward to hearing from you; **te espera una prueba dura** a hard test awaits you **2.** (*un bebé, recibir, pensar*) to expect; **ya me lo esperaba** I expected it **3.** (*confiar*) to hope; **esperando recibir noticias tuyas...** looking forward to hearing from you ...; **espero que sí** I hope so; **espero que**

nos veamos pronto I hope to see you soon

esperma *m* sperm

espermatozoide *m* spermatozoid

espesar *vt* to thicken

espeso, -a *adj* thick

espesor *m* thickness; (*nieve*) depth

espía *mf* spy

espiga *f* ear; **dibujo de ~** herringbone

espina *f* 1.(*de pescado*) bone 2. BOT thorn 3. ANAT ~ (**dorsal**) spine 4. *fig, inf* **esto me da mala ~** I don't like the look of this

espinaca *f* spinach

espinazo *m* spinal column

espinilla *f* 1. ANAT shin 2.(*grano*) blackhead

espino *m* 1. BOT ~ (**albar**) hawthorn 2. TÉC **alambre de ~** barbed wire

espinoso, -a *adj* 1.(*planta*) thorny; (*pescado*) bony 2.(*problema*) tricky

espionaje *m* espionage

espiral *adj, f* spiral

espirar *vi* to exhale

espiritista *adj* spiritualist

espíritu *m* spirit; (*alma*) soul; (*inteligencia*) mind; (*idea principal*) essence, nature; ~ **de contradicción** contrariness; ~ **deportivo** sportsmanship; ~ **emprendedor** hard-working nature; **el Espíritu Santo** the Holy Spirit; **levantar el ~ a alguien** to lift sb's spirits

espiritual *adj* spiritual

espita *f* tap *Brit,* faucet *Am*

espléndido, -a *adj* 1.(*generoso*) generous 2.(*magnífico*) splendid; (*ocasión*) excellent

esplendor *m* splendour *Brit,* splendor *Am*

espolear *vt* 1.(*al caballo*) to spur 2.(*a alguien*) to spur on

espoleta *f* fuse

espolvorear *vt* to sprinkle

esponja *f* sponge; **beber como una ~** *inf* to drink like a fish; **¡pasemos la ~!** *inf* let's forget about it!

esponjoso, -a *adj* (*masa*) fluffy; (*pan*) light

espontaneidad *f* spontaneity

espontáneo, -a *adj* spontaneous

esporádico, -a *adj* sporadic

esposar *vt* to handcuff

esposas *fpl* handcuffs *pl;* **colocar las ~ a alguien** to handcuff sb

esposo, -a *m, f* spouse; (*marido*) husband; (*mujer*) wife; **los ~s** the bride and groom

espray *m* spray; ~ **desodorante** deodorant spray

espuela *f* 1.(*de caballo*) spur; **poner las ~s a alguien** to spur sb on 2. *inf* (*la última copa*) **tomar la ~** to have one for the road

espuma *f* (*burbujas*) foam; (*de jabón*) lather; (*de cerveza*) head; ~ **de afeitar** shaving foam

espumadera *f* skimmer

espumoso, -a *adj* foamy; **vino ~** sparkling wine

esqueje *m* cutting

esquela *f* 1.(*nota*) notice of death 2.(*necrológica*) ~ (**mortuoria**) obituary notice

esquelético, -a *adj* scrawny

esqueleto *m* 1. ANAT skeleton; **mover el ~** *inf* to dance 2.(*de un avión, barco*) shell; (*de un edificio*) framework

esquema *m* 1.(*gráfico*) sketch; **en ~** in rough 2.(*resumen*) outline

esquemático, -a *adj* schematic

esquí *m* 1.(*patín*) ski; ~ **de fondo** cross-county ski 2.(*deporte*) skiing; ~ **acuático** water-skiing

esquiar *vt* <1. pres: esquío> *vi* to ski

esquilar *vt* to shear

esquimal *adj, mf* Eskimo; **perro ~** husky

esquina *f* corner; **casa que hace ~** house on the corner; **a la vuelta de la ~** around the corner; **doblar la ~** to turn the corner; **hacer un saque de ~** to take a corner

esquinazo *m* *inf* corner; **dar ~ a alguien** (*dejar plantado*) to stand sb up; (*rehuir*) to avoid sb

esquirol *mf* scab, blackleg

esquivar *vt* 1.(*golpe*) to dodge 2.(*problema*) to shirk; (*a alguien*) to avoid

esquivo, -a *adj* (*huidizo*) evasive; (*arisco*) aloof

esta *adj v.* **este, -a**

ésta *pron dem v.* **éste**

estabilidad *f* stability

estabilizar <z→c> *vt, vr:* ~**se** to stabilize

estable *adj* stable; (*trabajo*) steady

establecer *irr como crecer* **I.** *vi* to **II.** *vt* **1.** (*fundar*) to establish; (*grupo de trabajo*) to set up; (*sucursal, tienda*) to open; (*principio, récord*) to set; (*orden, escuela*) to found **2.** (*colocar*) to place; (*campamento*) to set up; (*conexión*) to establish **III.** *vr* ~**se de algo** to set oneself up as sth

establecimiento *m* establishment; (*de un grupo de trabajo*) setting-up; (*de una sucursal*) opening; (*de un principio, récord*) setting; (*del orden, de una escuela*) founding

establo *m* stable, barn

estaca *f* (*palo*) post; (*para una tienda*) peg; (*garrote*) stick

estacada *f* fence; **dejar a alguien en la** ~ to leave sb in the lurch; **quedarse en la** ~ to be left in the lurch

estación *f* **1.** (*año, temporada*) season; ~ **de las lluvias** rainy season **2.** (*centro*) *t.* RADIO, TV, FERRO station; (*parada*) stop; ~ **de autobuses** bus station; ~ **de destino** destination; ~ **meteorológica** weather station; ~ **de servicio** service station

estacionamiento *m* **1.** AUTO parking **2.** MIL positioning

estacionar *vt* **1.** AUTO to park **2.** MIL to position

estacionario, -a *adj* stable

estadio *m* **1.** DEP stadium **2.** MED stage

estadística *f* statistics *pl*

estado *m* **1.** (*condición*) condition; (*situación*) state; ~ **civil** marital status; ~ **de las cosas** (*general*) state of affairs; ~ **financiero** financial situation; **estar en** ~ (*de buena esperanza*) to be pregnant **2.** POL state; ~ **totalitario** police state **3.** FIN ~ **de cuentas** balance statement

Estados Unidos *mpl* United States *pl* of America

estadounidense *adj, mf* of/from the United States, American

estafa *f* swindle

estafar *vt* to swindle; **la cajera me ha estafado el cambio** the checkout assistant has shortchanged me

estafeta *f* sub-post office *Brit,* branch post office *Am*

estallar *vi* **1.** (*globo, neumático*) to burst; (*bomba*) to explode, to go off; (*cristales*) to shatter; (*látigo*) to crack; **estalló una ovación** applause broke out; **me estalla la cabeza** I have a splitting headache **2.** (*revolución, guerra, incendio*) to break out; (*tormenta*) to break **3.** (*persona*) ~ **en carcajadas** to burst out laughing; ~ **en llanto** to burst into tears; **estaba enfadado y al final estalló** he was angry and he finally snapped

estallido *m* **1.** (*ruido*) explosion; (*de un globo*) bursting **2.** (*de una revolución, guerra*) outbreak

Estambul *m* Istanbul

estampa *f* **1.** (*dibujo*) illustration; ~ **de la Virgen** image of the Virgin Mary **2.** (*aspecto*) appearance; **un caballo de magnífica** ~ a splendid--looking horse; **tienes mala** ~ you look terrible **3.** (*image*) **ser la viva** ~ **de la pobreza** to be the incarnation of poverty; **ser la viva** ~ **de su padre** *inf* to be the spitting image of one's father

estampado *m* **1.** (*tejido*) print; **no me gusta este** ~ I don't like this design **2.** (*metal*) engraving

estampado, -a *adj* printed

estampar *vt* to print; (*con relieve*) to stamp; **se me quedó estampado en la cabeza** *fig* it imprinted itself on my memory

estampida *f* stampede

estampido *m* bang; **dar un** ~ to bang

estampilla *f* rubber stamp; *AmL* (*de correos*) stamp

estancar <c→qu> **I.** *vt* **1.** (*un río*) to stagnate; **aguas estancadas** stagnant water **2.** (*mercancía*) to monopolize **3.** (*proceso*) to hold up **II.** *vr:* ~**se** to stagnate

estancia *f* **1.** (*permanencia*) stay

2. (*habitación*) room **3.** *AmL* (*hacienda*) estate

estanciero, -a *m, f CSur, Col, Ven* farmer

estanco *m* tobacconist's (*also selling stamps*)

estanco, -a *adj* watertight

estándar *adj, m* standard

estandarizar <z→c> *vt* to standardize

estandarte *m* banner

estanque *m* pool, pond; (*para el riego*) tank

estanquero, -a *m, f* tobacconist

estante *m* shelf

estantería *f* shelves *pl;* (*para libros*) bookcase

estaño *m* tin; ~ (**para soldar**) solder

estar *irr* **I.** *vi* **1.** (*hallarse*) to be; (*un objeto: derecho*) to stand; (*tumbado*) to lie; (*colgando*) to hang; **Valencia está en la costa** Valencia is on the coast; **¿está Pepe?** is Pepe there?; **ya lo hago yo, para eso estoy** I'll do it, that's why I'm here; **¿está la comida?** is lunch ready? **2.** (*sentirse*) to be; **¿cómo estás?** how are you?; **ya estoy mejor** I'm better **3.** (+ *adjetivo, participio*) to be; ~ **cansado/sentado** to be tired/sitting; **está visto que...** it is obvious that ... **4.** (+ *bien, mal*) ~ **mal de azúcar** to be running out of sugar; ~ **mal de la cabeza** to be off one's head; ~ **mal de dinero** to be short of money; **eso te está bien empleado** *inf* it serves you right; **esa blusa te está bien** that blouse suits you **5.** (+ *a*) ~ **al caer** (*persona*) to be about to arrive; (*suceso*) to be about to happen; **están al caer las diez** it's almost ten o'clock; ~ **al día** to be up to date; **¿a qué estamos?** what day is it?; **estamos a uno de enero** it's the first of January; **las peras están a 2 euros el kilo** pears cost 2 euros a kilo; **las acciones están a 12 euros** the shares are at 12 euros; **Sevilla está a 40 grados** it is 40 degrees in Seville; **el termómetro está a diez grados** the thermometer shows ten degrees;

están uno a uno they're drawing one-all; **estoy a lo que decida la asamblea** I will follow whatever the assembly decides **6.** (+ *con*) to be; **en la casa estoy con dos más** I share the house with two others; **estoy contigo en este punto** I agree with you on that point **7.** (+ *de*) to be; ~ **de broma** to be joking; ~ **de mal humor** to be in a bad mood; ~ **de pie** to be standing; ~ **de secretario** to be working as a secretary; ~ **de viaje** to be travelling; **en esta reunión estoy de más** I'm not needed in this meeting; **esto que has dicho estaba de más** there's no call for what you've just said **8.** (+ *en*) **el problema está en el dinero** the problem is the money; **yo estoy en que él no dice la verdad** I believe he's not telling the truth; **no estaba en sí cuando lo hizo** he/she wasn't in control of himself/herself when he/she did it; **siempre estás en todo** you don't miss a thing **9.** (+ *para*) ~ **para morir** to feel like dying; **hoy no estoy para bromas** today I'm in no mood for jokes; **el tren está para salir** the train is about to leave **10.** (+ *por*) **estoy por llamarle** I think we should call him/her; **eso está por ver** we don't know that yet; **la historia de esta ciudad está por escribir** the history of this city has not been written yet; **este partido está por la democracia** this party believes in democracy **11.** (+ *gerundio*) to be; **¿qué estás haciendo?** what are you doing; **¡lo estaba viendo venir!** I saw it coming! **12.** (+ *que*) **estoy que no me tengo** I can hardly stand up I'm so tired; **está que trina** he/she's furious **13.** (+ *sobre*) **estáte sobre este asunto** look after this matter; **siempre tengo que ~ sobre mi hijo para que coma** I always have to force my son to eat **14.** (*entendido*) **a las 10 en casa, ¿estamos?** 10 o'clock at home, OK? **II.** *vr:* ~**se** to be; (*permanecer*) to stay; ~**se de charla** to be chatting;

te puedes ~ **con nosotros** you can stay with us; **me estuve con ellos toda la tarde** I spent the whole afternoon with them; **¡estáte quieto!** keep still; **¡estáte callado!** shut up!

estárter *m* choke

estatal *adj* state

estático, -a *adj* static

estatua *f* statue

estatura *f* stature; (*altura*) height; **¿qué ~ tienes?** how tall are you?; **hombre de ~ pequeña** short man

estatus *m inv* status

estatuto *m* statute

este *m* east; **el ~ de España** eastern Spain; **en el ~ de Inglaterra** in the east of England; **al ~ de** east of

este, -a I. *adj* <estos, -as> this; ~ **perro es mío** this dog is mine; **esta casa es nuestra** this house is ours; **estos guantes son míos** these gloves are mine **II.** *pron dem v.* **éste, ésta, esto**

éste, ésta, esto <éstos, -as> *pron dem* him, her, this; (a) **éstos no los he visto nunca** I've never seen them; ~ **se cree muy importante** this guy thinks he's very important; **antes yo también tenía una camisa como ésta** I used to have a shirt like this before, too; (**estando**) **en esto** [*o* **en éstas**], **llamaron a la puerta** and then, someone called at the door; **¡ésta sí que es buena!** *irón* that's a good one!; *v.t.* **este, -a**

estela *f* NÁUT wake; AERO slipstream, vapour [*o* vapor *Am*] trail

estelar *adj* stellar

estenografía *f* shorthand

estepa *f* steppe

estera *f* matting

estéreo *adj, m* stereo

estereotipo *m* stereotype

estéril *adj* sterile; (*mujer*) infertile; (*tierra*) barren

esterilizar <z→c> *vt* to sterilize

esterlina *adj* **libra ~** pound sterling

estética *f* aesthetics *Brit,* esthetics *Am*

estético, -a *adj* aesthetic *Brit,* esthetic *Am;* **cirugía estética** plastic

surgery; **no ~** unaesthetic *Brit,* unesthetic *Am*

estiércol *m* manure

estigma *m* stigma; (*en el cuerpo*) mark

estilarse *vr* to be in fashion

estilo *m* style; ~ (**de**) **pecho** breaststroke; ~ **de vida** lifestyle; ~ **directo/indirecto** direct/indirect speech; ~ **libre** freestyle; **al ~ de** in the style of; **algo por el ~** something similar; **¿estás mal?, pues yo estoy por el ~** are you not feeling well? neither am I; **ya me habían dicho algo por el ~** I'd already been told something like that

estima *f* esteem; **tener a alguien en mucha ~** to hold sb in high esteem

estimación *f* **1.** (*aprecio*) esteem **2.** (*evaluación*) estimate

estimado, -a *adj* respected; ~ **Señor** Dear Sir

estimar *vt* **1.** (*apreciar*) to appppreciate; ~ **a alguien poco** not to think much of sb; ~ **en demasía** to overrate **2.** (*tasar*) to estimate; ~ **algo en algo** to value sth at sth **3.** (*considerar*) to judge

estimulante *m* stimulant

estimular *vt* **1.** (*excitar*) to stimulate; (*en la sexualidad*) to excite, to turn on *inf* **2.** (*animar*) to encourage; ECON to stimulate

estímulo *m* stimulus

estío *m elev* summer

estipulación *f* agreement; JUR stipulation

estipular *vt* to stipulate; (*fijar*) to fix

estirado, -a *adj* (*adusto*) severe; (*engreído*) haughty, snooty *inf*

estirar I. *vi* to stretch; **no estires más que se rompe la cuerda** if you stretch it any more the rope will break **II.** *vt* **1.** (*extender, alargar*) to stretch; (*suma*) to spin out; (*discurso*) to draw out; ~ **el bolsillo** to spin out one's resources **2.** (*alisar*) to smoothe; ~ **la cama** to make the bed; ~ **la masa** to roll out the dough **3.** (*tensar*) to tighten **4.** (*piernas, brazos*) to stretch out; ~ **el cuello** to crane (one's neck); ~ **demasiado un**

músculo to overstretch a muscle; **voy a salir a ~ un poco las piernas** I'm going to stretch my legs a little; **~ la pata** *inf* to kick the bucket *inf* **III.** *vr:* **~se** to stretch; (*crecer*) to shoot up

estirón *m* **1.**(*tirón*) pull **2.**(*crecimiento*) **dar un ~** *inf* to shoot up

estirpe *f* stock

estival *adj* summer

esto *pron dem v.* **éste**

Estocolmo *m* Stockholm

estofa *f pey* class

estofado *m* (meat) stew

estofar *vt* to stew

estómago *m* stomach; **tener buen ~** *fig* to be tough

Estonia *f* Estonia

estonio, -a *adj, m, f* Estonian

estorbar I. *vi* **1.**(*obstaculizar*) to get in the way **2.**(*molestar*) to be annoying **II.** *vt* **1.**(*impedir*) to stop; (*obstaculizar*) to hinder **2.**(*molestar*) to bother

estorbo *m* **1.**(*molestia*) nuisance **2.**(*obstáculo*) obstacle

estornudar *vi* to sneeze

estornudo *m* sneeze

estos *adj v.* **este, -a**

estrado *m* dais

estrafalario, -a *adj inf* (*extravagante*) outlandish; (*ridículo*) preposterous

estrago *m* damage; **hacer grandes ~s en la población civil** to wreak havoc upon the civil population

estragón *m* tarragon

estrambótico, -a *adj* eccentric

estrangulador *m ~* (**de aire**) choke

estrangulador(a) *m(f)* strangler

estrangulamiento *m* **1.**(*de una persona*) strangulation **2.**(*estorbo*) blockage

estrangular *vt* **1.**(*asesinar*) to strangle **2.** MED to strangulate

estraperlo *m* black market; **adquirir algo de ~** to buy sth on the black market

Estrasburgo *m* Strasbourg

estratagema *m* **1.**(*artimaña*) ploy **2.** MIL strategy

estrategia *f* strategy

estratégico, -a *adj* strategic

estrato *m* stratum

estrechar I. *vt* **1.**(*angostar*) to narrow; (*ropa*) to take in **2.**(*abrazar*) to hug; (*la mano*) to shake **II.** *vr:* **~se 1.**(*camino*) to become narrower **2.** *inf* (*en un asiento*) to squeeze in

estrechez *f* narrrowness

estrecho *m* GEO strait

estrecho, -a *adj* **1.**(*angosto*) narrow **2.**(*amistad*) close **3.**(*ropa, lugar*) tight

estrella *f* **1.** ASTR, CINE star; **~ fugaz** shooting star; **haber nacido con buena ~** to have been born under a lucky star; **poner a alguien por las ~s** to praise sb to the skies; **tener buena/mala ~** to be lucky/unlucky; **ver las ~s (de dolor)** to see stars **2.** TIPO asterisk **3.** ZOOL **~ de mar** starfish

estrellado, -a *adj* **1.**(*esteliforme*) star-shaped **2.**(*noche, cielo*) starry

estrellar I. *adj* star **II.** *vt* (*romper*) to smash; (*arrojar*) to hurl **III.** *vr* **~se contra** [*o* **en**] **algo** to crash into sth

estremecer *irr como crecer* **I.** *vt* **1.**(*conmover*) to move **2.**(*hacer tiritar*) to make tremble **II.** *vr:* **~se 1.**(*suceso, susto*) to be shocked **2.**(*temblar*) to shiver

estremecimiento *m* **1.**(*emoción*) shock **2.**(*de frío, miedo*) shivering

estrenar I. *vt* **1.**(*usar*) to use for the first time; (*ropa*) to wear for the first time; (*edificio*) to inaugurate; **~ un piso** to move into a new flat; **sin ~** brand new **2.** CINE, TEAT to première **II.** *vr:* **~se 1.**(*carrera artística*) to make one's debut; (*trabajo*) to start work **2.** CINE, TEAT to be premièred

estreno *m* **1.**(*uso*) first use; (*de un edificio*) opening; **ser de ~** to be brand new **2.**(*de un actor, músico*) debut; (*de una obra*) première

estreñido, -a *adj* constipated

estreñimiento *m* constipation

estreñir *irr como ceñir vt* to constipate; **~ a alguien** to give sb constipation

estrépito *m* **1.**(*ruido*) din **2.**(*ostentación*) fanfare; **con gran ~** ostentatiously

estrepitoso, -a *adj* (*sonido*) loud; (*fracaso*) spectacular

estrés *m* stress; **producir** ~ to be stressful

estría *f* groove; (*en la piel*) stretch--mark

estribación *f* foothills *pl*

estribar *vi* to lie

estribillo *m* MÚS chorus; LIT refrain

estribo *m* **1.** (*de jinete*) stirrup; **perder los** ~**s** *fig* to fly off the handle **2.** (*del coche*) running board; (*de moto*) footrest

estribor *m* starboard

estricnina *f* strychnine

estricto, -a *adj* strict

estridente *adj* shrill; (*vestir*) loud

estrofa *f* (*de poema*) stanza; (*de canción*) verse

estropajo *m* scourer; **poner a alguien como un** ~ *inf* to lay into sb

estropear I. *vt* to spoil; (*romper*) to break; (*arruinar*) to ruin; **desde la muerte de su mujer está muy estropeado** since his wife died he looks terrible; **está muy estropeado por la enfermedad** the disease has had a very bad effect on him **II.** *vr:* ~**se** (*averiarse*) to break down; (*romperse*) to break; (*comida*) to go off; (*planes*) to be spoilt

estructura *f* structure

estruendo *m* **1.** (*ruido*) din **2.** (*alboroto*) uproar

estrujar I. *vt* to squeeze; (*machacar*) to crush; (*papel*) to crumple up **II.** *vr* ~**se los sesos** *inf* to rack one's brains

estuche *m* case; ~ **de joyas** jewel box

estudiante *mf* **1.** (*de universidad*) student; ~ **de ciencias** science student **2.** (*de escuela*) pupil

estudiantil *adj* student

estudiar *vi, vt* to study; ~ **para médico** to study to be a doctor; **dejar de** ~ to drop out

estudio *m* **1.** (*trabajo intelectual*) studying; **dedicarse tres horas todos los días al** ~ to devote three hours every day to studying **2.** (*obra,* *investigación*) study; **estar en** ~ to be under study **3.** ARTE, TV studio; ~ **cinematográfico/radiofónico** cinema/radio studio **4.** (*piso*) bedsit **5.** *pl* (*carrera*) studies *pl;* **cursar** ~**s** to study; **tener** ~**s** to have studied; **no se me dan bien los** ~**s** I'm not good at studying

estudioso, -a *adj* studious

estufa *f* heater

estupefaciente *m* MED narcotic; (*droga*) drug

estupefacto, -a *adj* amazed

estupendo, -a *adj* fantastic

estupidez *f* stupidity

estúpido, -a I. *adj* stupid **II.** *m, f* idiot

estupor *m* amazement

estupro *m* rape (*of a minor*)

esvástica *f* swastika

ETA *abr de* **Euzkadi Ta Askatasuna** ETA (*radical Basque separatist movement*)

etapa *f* (*fase*) stage; (*época*) phase; **por** ~**s** in stages

etarra I. *adj* **un comando** ~ an ETA cell **II.** *mf* ETA member

etc. *abr de* **etcétera** etc.

etcétera etcetera

eternidad *f* eternity

eternizarse <z→c> *vr* to take ages

eterno, -a *adj* eternal; (*discurso*) long-winded

ética *f* ethics; ~ **profesional** professional code of conduct

ético, -a *adj* ethical

etíope *adj, mf* Ethiopian

Etiopía *f* Ethiopia

etiqueta *f* **1.** (*rótulo*) label; ~ **del precio** price tag **2.** (*convenciones*) etiquette; ~ **de la red** netiquette; **de** ~ formal; **ir de** ~ *inf* to be dressed up

etnia *f* (*pueblo*) ethnic group

étnico, -a *adj* ethnic

eucaristía *f* Eucharist

eufemismo *m* euphemism

euforia *f* euphoria

eunuco *m* eunuch

Eurasia *f* Eurasia

euro *m* euro

eurodiputado, -a *m, f* member of the European Parliament, MEP

euroescéptico, -a *m, f* eurosceptic
Europa *f* Europe
europarlamentario, -a *m, f* member of the European Parliament, MEP
europeidad *f* Europeanness
europeísmo *m sin pl* Europeanism
europeísta *adj, mf* pro-European
europeizar *irr como enraizar vt* to Europeanize
europeo, -a *adj, m, f* European
eurotúnel *m* Channel tunnel
Euskadi *m* Basque Country
euskera *adj,* **eusquera** *adj* Basque
eutanasia *f* euthanasia
evacuación *f* evacuation
evacuar *vt* to evacuate
evadir I. *vt* to avoid II. *vr:* **~se** to get away
evaluación *f* assessment
evaluar <*l. pres:* evalúo> *vt* to assess
evangélico, -a I. *adj* evangelical II. *m, f* evangelist
evangelio *m* Gospel
evaporar *vt, vr:* **~se** to evaporate
evasión *f* evasion; (*fuga*) escape; **lectura de ~** escapist literature
evasiva *f* 1. (*rodeo*) evasions *pl;* **dar ~s** to hedge 2. (*pretexto*) excuse
evasivo, -a *adj* evasive; (*ambiguo*) ambiguous, non-committal
evento *m* event; **a todo ~** in any event
eventual *adj* (*posible*) possible; (*provisional*) temporary; **trabajo ~** casual job
evidencia *f* (*certidumbre*) evidence; **poner algo en ~** (*probar*) to prove sth; (*hacer claro*) to make sth clear; **poner a alguien en ~** to make sb look bad
evidenciar *vt* to show
evidente *adj* evident
evitar *vt* to avoid; (*prevenir*) to prevent
evocar <c→qu> *vt* (*traer a la memoria*) to evoke; (*tener en la memoria*) to remember; **tu presencia evocó en mí el recuerdo de tu madre** your being there made me remember your mother

evolución *f* 1. (*desarrollo*) development; (*progreso*) progress; (*cambio*) transformation 2. BIO evolution
evolucionar *vi* 1. (*desarrollarse*) to develop; (*avanzar*) to progress; (*cambiar*) to transform 2. BIO to evolve
ex I. *adj* ~ **novia** ex-girlfriend II. *mf inf* ex
exacerbar *vt* to aggravate
exactitud *f* 1. (*precisión*) accuracy 2. (*veracidad*) exactitude 3. (*puntualidad*) punctuality
exacto, -a *adj* 1. (*con precisión*) accurate; (*al copiar*) faithful 2. (*correcto*) correct; **eso no es del todo ~** that's not exactly true 3. (*puntual*) punctual
exageración *f* exaggeration
exagerar *vi, vt* to exaggerate; **pienso que ese paso sería ~** I think such a step would be going too far
exaltado, -a *adj* (*sobreexcitado*) over-excited; (*apasionado*) passionate
exaltar I. *vt* to exalt II. *vr* **~se (con algo)** to become excited (about sth)
examen *m* examination; ENS exam; ~ **de conductor** driving test; ~ **de ingreso** entrance exam; ~ **de selectividad** *Spanish university entrance exam;* **presentarse a un ~** to sit for an exam; **someterse a un ~** (*médico*) to have a check-up
examinar I. *vt* to examine; TÉC, AUTO to inspect II. *vr:* **~se** to sit an exam; **mañana me examino de francés** tomorrow I've got my French exam; **volver a ~se** to resit an exam
excavadora *f* excavator
excavar *vt* to excavate
excedencia *f* (*laboral*) leave
excedente *adj, m* surplus
exceder I. *vi* to be greater; ~ **de algo** to exceed sth II. *vt* (*aventajar: persona*) to outdo; (*cosa*) to be better than III. *vr:* **~se** 1. (*sobrepasar*) **~se (a sí mismo)** to excel oneself 2. (*pasarse*) to go too far
excelencia *f* 1. (*exquisitez*) excellence; **por ~** par excellence 2. (*cargo*) Excellency
excelente *adj* excellent

excelso, -a *adj elev* illustrious

excentricidad *f* eccentricity

excéntrico, -a *adj, m, f* eccentric

excepción *f* exception; ~ **de la regla** exception to the rule; **a** [*o* **con**] ~ **de** with the exception of, except (for); **de** ~ exceptional; (*privilegiado*) special; **la** ~ **confirma la regla** (*prov*) it is the exception which proves the rule

excepcional *adj* exceptional

excepto *adv* except

exceptuar <*1. pres:* exceptúo> *vt* to except

excesivo, -a *adj* excessive

exceso *m* excess; FIN surplus; ~ **de alcohol** excessive drinking; ~ **de capacidad** overcapacity; ~ **de demanda/equipaje** excess demand/baggage; ~ **de velocidad** speeding; **con** [*o* **en**] ~ too much

excitación *f* **1.** (*exaltación*) excitement; (*sexual*) arousal **2.** (*irritación*) nervousness **3.** (*incitación*) stimulation

excitar I. *vt* **1.** (*incitar*) to incite; (*apetito*) to stimulate **2.** (*poner nervioso*) to put on edge **3.** (*sexualmente*) to arouse II. *vr:* ~**se 1.** (*enojarse*) to get all worked up **2.** (*sexualmente*) to become aroused

exclamación *f* exclamation; (*grito*) cry; **signo de** ~ exclamation mark

exclamar *vi, vt* to exclaim; (*gritar*) to cry

excluir *irr como huir vt* to exclude; (*descartar*) to rule out

exclusión *f* exclusion; **a/con** ~ **de** excluding

exclusiva *f* **1.** (*privilegio*) sole rights *pl* **2.** PREN exclusive; (*primicia*) scoop

exclusivo, -a *adj* exclusive

excomulgar <g→gu> *vt* REL to excommunicate

excomunión *f* excommunication

excremento *m* excretion

excursión *f* **1.** (*paseo*) excursion, trip; ~ **a pie** hike; **ir de** ~ to go on an excursion **2.** (*de estudios*) field trip

excursionista *mf* daytripper, excursionist; (*a pie*) hiker

excusa *f* excuse; (*disculpa*) apology; **presentar sus** ~**s** to apologize

excusado *m* toilet

excusar I. *vt* **1.** (*disculpar*) to excuse **2.** (*evitar*) to avoid **3.** (+ *inf*) **excusas venir** you don't have to come II. *vr* ~**se de algo** to apologize for sth

exento, -a *adj* exempt, free; ~ **de aranceles** duty-free; ~ **de impuestos** tax free

exequias *fpl* funeral rites *pl*

exfoliar *vt* to exfoliate

exhalar *vt* **1.** (*emanar*) to give off **2.** (*suspiros, quejas*) to let out

exhaustivo, -a *adj* exhaustive; **de forma exhaustiva** thoroughly

exhausto, -a *adj* exhausted

exhibición *f* **1.** (*ostentación*) display **2.** (*exposición*) exhibition **3.** (*presentación*) show

exhibir I. *vt* **1.** (*mostrar*) to exhibit **2.** (*ostentar*) to show off II. *vr:* ~**se** to put on a show; ~**se en público** to expose oneself

exhortación *f* exhortation

exhortar *vt* to exhort

exigencia *f* **1.** (*demanda*) demand **2.** (*requisito*) requirement

exigente *adj* demanding

exigir <g→j> *vt* to demand

exil(i)ado, -a I. *adj* exiled II. *m, f* exile

exilio *m* exile

eximio, -a *adj elev* illustrious

eximir *vt* to exempt; ~ **de obligaciones** to free from obligations; ~ **de responsabilidades** to release from responsibilities

existencia *f* **1.** (*vida*) existence **2.** (*pl*) COM stock; **renovar las** ~**s** to renew stocks

existir *vi* to exist; (*haber*) to be

éxito *m* success; ~ **de taquilla** box office hit; **con** ~ successfully; **tener** ~ to be successful

éxodo *m* exodus; ~ **rural** rural depopulation; (*de tecnicos, científicos*) brain drain

exonerar *vt* **1.** (*eximir*) to exempt **2.** (*culpa*) to exonerate **3.** (*relevar*) to relieve; ~ **a alguien de su cargo** to remove sb from his/her position

Ee

exótico, -a *adj* exotic

expandir *vt, vr:* ~**se 1.**(*dilatar*) to expand **2.**(*divulgar*) to spread

expansión *f* **1.**(*dilatación, desarrollo*) expansion; (*crecimiento*) growth **2.**(*difusión*) spread **3.**(*diversión*) recreation

expansionarse *vr* **1.**(*dilatarse*) to expand **2.** *inf*(*sincerarse*) ~ **con alguien** to talk openly to sb **3.** *inf*(*divertirse*) to relax

expansivo, -a *adj* **1.**(*dilatable*) expansive **2.**(*comunicativo*) open

expatriar <*1.pres:* expatrío> **I.** *vt* to exile **II.** *vr:* ~**se** to go into exile

expectativa *f* **1.**(*expectación*) expectation; **estar a la** ~ **de algo** to be on the lookout for sth **2.**(*perspectiva*) prospect; ~ **de vida** life expectancy

expedición *f* **1.**(*viaje, grupo*) expedition **2.**(*remesa*) shipment; (*acción*) shipping; (**empresa de**) ~ shipping agent **3.**(*de documentos*) issue

expediente *m* **1.**(*asunto*) proceedings *pl* **2.**(*legajo*) file; (*sumario*) record; ~ **académico** student record

expedir *irr como pedir vt* **1.**(*carta*) to send; (*pedido*) to ship; ~ **por avión** to send by air mail **2.**(*documento*) to issue

expedito, -a *adj* free

expendedor *m* ~ **automático** vending machine; ~ **de bebidas** soft drink vending machine

expendedor(a) I. *adj* **máquina** ~**a de billetes/tabaco** ticket/cigarette vending machine **II.** *m(f)* vendor

expensas *fpl* costs *pl;* **a** ~ **de** at the expense of; **vivir a** ~ **de alguien** to live off sb

experiencia *f* experience; **saber algo por** ~ **propia** to know sth from experience

experimentado, -a *adj* experienced

experimentar I. *vi* to experiment **II.** *vt* **1.**(*sentir*) to experience **2.**(*hacer experimentos*) to experiment with; (*probar*) to test **3.**(*tener*) to register

experimento *m* experiment

experto, -a *adj, m, f* expert

expiar <*1. pres:* expío> *vt* to expiate

expirar *vi* to expire

explayarse *vr* **1.**(*extenderse*) to spread **2.**(*expresarse*) to speak at length; ~ **con alguien** (*confiarse*) to talk openly to sb **3.**(*divertirse*) to enjoy oneself

explicación *f* explanation; (*motivo*) reason

explicar <c→qu> **I.** *vt* **1.**(*manifestar*) to tell **2.**(*aclarar, exponer*) to explain **II.** *vr:* ~**se 1.**(*comprender*) to understand; **no me lo explico** I don't understand it **2.**(*articularse*) to express oneself; **¿me explico?** do I make myself clear?

explícito, -a *adj* explicit

explorador(a) *m(f)* **1.**MIL scout **2.**(*investigador*) explorer

explorar *vt* **1.**MIL to reconnoitre *Brit,* to reconnoiter *Am* **2.**MED to analyze **3.**(*investigar*) to explore

explosión *f* explosion; (*arrebato*) outburst; **hacer** ~ to explode

explosivo, -a *adj* explosive

explotación *f* **1.**(*aprovechamiento, abuso*) exploitation; AGR plantation; MIN working; ~ **minera** mine **2.**(*empresa*) management

explotar I. *vi* to explode **II.** *vt* **1.**(*usar, abusar*) to exploit; AGR to cultivate **2.**(*empresa*) to manage

exponer *irr como poner* **I.** *vt* **1.**(*mostrar*) to show, to display **2.**(*exhibir*) to exhibit **3.**(*hablar, escribir*) to set out; (*proponer*) to put forward; (*explicar*) to explain **4.**(*arriesgar*) to endanger **II.** *vr* ~**se a que** +*subj* to risk that; ~**se a hacer algo** to run the risk of doing sth

exportación *f* export

exportar *vt* to export

exposición *f* **1.**(*explicación*) explanation **2.**(*informe*) report **3.**(*exhibición*) exhibition; ~ **universal** world('s) fair

exprés I. *adj inv* express; **café** ~ espresso; **olla** ~ pressure cooker **II.** *m* (*tren*) express

expresar I. *vt* to express **II.** *vr:* ~**se** to

express oneself

expresión f expression

expreso m, adv express

expreso, -a adj express; **enviar una carta por (correo)** ~ to send a letter by special delivery

exprimidor m squeezer

exprimir vt to squeeze

expropiar vt to expropriate

expuesto, -a I. pp de **exponer** II. adj 1. (peligroso) risky 2. (sin protección) exposed

expulsar vt to expel; ~ **a alguien (del campo de juego)** to send sb off (the pitch); ~ **a alguien de la sala** to eject sb from the room

expulsión f expulsion

exquisito, -a adj exquisite; (comida) delicious

éxtasis m inv ecstacy

extender <e→ie> I. vt 1. (papeles, mantequilla, pintura) to spread 2. (desplegar) to unfold; ~ **la mano** to reach out one's hand 3. (ensanchar) to widen; (agrandar) to enlarge 4. (escribir) to write out; (documento) to draw up II. vr: ~**se** 1. (terreno) to extend; (en la cama) to stretch out 2. (prolongarse) to last

extendido, -a adj 1. (amplio, conocido) widespread 2. (mano, brazos) outstretched

extensión f 1. (dimensión) extent; (longitud, duración) length 2. TEL extension

extenso, -a adj extensive

extenuar <1. pres: extenúo> vt (agotar) to exhaust; (debilitar) to weaken

exterior I. adj 1. (de fuera) external, exterior; **espacio** ~ outer space 2. (extranjero) foreign; **relaciones** ~**es** external relations pl II. m exterior

exteriorizar <z→c> vt to show

exterminar vt to exterminate

exterminio m extermination

externo, -a adj external

extinguir <gu→g> I. vt 1. (apagar) to extinguish 2. (finalizar) to terminate II. vr: ~**se** 1. (apagarse) to be extinguished 2. (finalizar) to be termin-

ated; ECOL to become extinct

extinto, -a adj 1. (especie, volcán) extinct 2. (fuego) extinguished

extintor m ~ (de incendios) fire extinguisher

extra¹ I. adj 1. (adicional) extra; **horas** ~**s** overtime; **paga** ~ bonus 2. (excelente) extra special; **de calidad** ~ top quality II. prep ~ **de** in addition to III. m 1. (complemento) extra; (en periódico, revista) special supplement 2. (paga) bonus

extra² mf extra

extracción f extraction; (lotería) draw

extracto m extract

extractor m ~ (de humo) extractor fan

extraer irr como traer vt to extract

extrajudicial adj extrajudicial

extralimitarse vr to go too far; ~ (en sus funciones) to overstep one's bounds

extranjero m abroad

extranjero, -a I. adj foreign II. m, f foreigner

extrañamente adv strangely

extrañar I. vt 1. (sorprender) to surprise; ¡**no me extraña!** I'm not surprised! 2. (echar de menos) to miss II. vr ~**se de que** +subj to be surprised that

extrañeza f 1. (rareza) strangeness 2. (perplejidad) surprise

extraño, -a I. adj strange; (extranjero) foreign II. m, f (forastero) stranger

extraordinario m special supplement

extraordinario, -a adj extraordinary; (por añadidura) special

extrarradio m outskirts pl

extraterrestre adj, mf extraterrestrial, alien

extravagancia f eccentricity

extravagante adj, mf eccentric

extraviado, -a adj lost; (animal) stray

extraviar <1. pres: extravío> I. vt 1. (despistar) to confuse 2. (perder) to lose; (dejar) to leave II. vr: ~**se** to get lost; fig to go astray

Extremadura *f* Extremadura
extremar I. *vt* ~ **la prudencia** to be extremely cautious; ~ **las medidas de seguridad** to tighten security measures II. *vr* ~**se en algo** to put a lot of work into sth
extremaunción *f* extreme unction
extremeño, -a *adj* of/from Extremadura
extremidad *f* 1. (*cabo*) end; (*punta*) tip 2. *pl* ANAT limb
extremista *adj, mf* extremist
extremo *m* 1. (*cabo*) end; **a tal** ~ to such an extreme; **con** [*o* **en**] ~ a lot; **en último** ~ in the last resort 2. (*asunto*) matter; **en este** ~ on this point 3. (*punto límite*) extreme; **esto llega hasta el** ~ **de...** this goes so far as ...
extremo, -a I. *adj* 1. (*intenso, limit*) extreme 2. (*distante*) outermost II. *m, f* ~ (*derecha*) (right) winger
extrovertido, -a *adj* outgoing
exuberancia *f* exuberance
exuberante *adj* exuberant; (*vegetación*) lush
eyaculación *f* ejaculation
eyacular *vi* to ejaculate

Ff

F, f *f* F, f; ~ **de Francia** F for Frederick *Brit,* F for Fox *Am*
fa *m inv* F
fabada *f* bean stew (*typical dish of Asturias*)
fábrica *f* factory; ~ **de cerveza** brewery
fabricación *f* manufacturing; ~ **en masa** mass production
fabricante *mf* 1. (*que fabrica*) manufacturer 2. (*dueño*) factory owner
fabricar <c→qu> *vt* 1. (*producir*) to manufacture 2. (*construir*) to build 3. (*inventar*) to fabricate
fábula *f* LIT fable; *inf* (*invención*)

tale; ¡**de** ~! terrific!, smashing!
fabuloso, -a *adj* fabulous; **personaje** ~ ficticious character
facción *f* 1. (*de un partido*) faction 2. *pl* (*rasgos*) (facial) features *pl*
faceta *f* facet; (*aspecto*) aspect, side
facha¹ *mf pey, inf* fascist
facha² *f inf* appearance, look; **estar hecho una** ~ *inf* to look a sight; **tener una** ~ **sospechosa** to look suspicious
fachada *f* 1. (*de un edificio*) façade 2. (*apariencia*) façade, front; **su buen humor es pura** ~ his/her good humour is pure pretence
facial *adj* facial
fácil *adj* 1. (*sin dificultades*) easy, simple; **es más** ~ **de decir que de hacer** *prov* easier said than done *prov* 2. (*cómodo*) undemanding 3. (*probable*) probable; **es** ~ **que** +*subj* it is likely that; **es** ~ **que nieve** it may well snow 4. (*carácter*) easy-going
facilidad *f* 1. (*sin dificultad*) ease 2. (*dotes*) facility; **tener** ~ **para algo** to have an ability for sth; **tener** ~ **para los idiomas** to have a flair for languages 3. *pl* facilities *pl*
facilitar *vt* 1. (*favorecer*) to facilitate; (*posibilitar*) to make possible 2. (*suministrar*) to furnish, to supply
fácilmente *adv* 1. (*sin dificultad*) easily 2. (*con probabilidad*) probably
facsímil(e) *m* fax
factible *adj* feasible, viable
factor *m* (*causa*) factor
factura *f* bill; (*recibo*) receipt
facturar *vt* 1. (*cobrar*) to bill; ~ **los gastos de transporte** to bill for transport costs 2. AERO ~ (**el equipaje**) to check in
facultad *f* 1. (*atribuciones*) authority; **conceder** ~**es a alguien** (**para hacer algo**) to authorize sb (to do sth); **tener** ~ **para hacer algo** to have the authority to do sth 2. (*aptitud*) *t.* UNIV faculty
facultativo, -a *adj* 1. (*potestativo*) optional 2. (*del médico*) medical
faena *f* 1. (*tarea*) task; ~**s domésticas** chores *pl* 2. *inf* (*mala pasada*)

dirty trick; **hacer una ~ a alguien** to play a dirty trick on sb

fagot *m* bassoon

faisán *m* pheasant

faja *f* corset, girdle; (*para abrigar*) sash

fajo *m* bundle

falange *f* phalanx; **la Falange** (**Española**) the (Spanish) Falange

falda *f* **1.**(*vestido*) skirt; **~ tubo** straight skirt **2.**(*regazo*) lap **3.**(*de una montaña*) lower slope

falla *f* (*defecto*) defect; (*en un sistema*) fault

fallar **I.** *vi* **1.** JUR to pronounce sentence **2.**(*malograrse: proyecto*) to fail; (*plan, intento*) to miscarry **3.**(*no funcionar*) to go wrong; **le ~on los nervios** his/her nerves let him/her down; **no falla nunca** (*cosa*) it never fails; (*persona*) you can always count on her/him **4.**(*romperse*) to break **5.**(*no cumplir con su palabra*) **~ a alguien** to let sb down; (*en una cita*) to stand sb up **II.** *vt* **1.** JUR **~ la absolución** to acquit **2.** DEP to miss

[?] The **Fallas** is the name of the largest public festival in Valencia on March 19th, which is **día del padre** (Father's Day) in Spain. **Fallas** are figures made from papier-mâché that are humorous caricatures, mainly of well-known public figures. They are burned during the "**noche del fuego**" on March 19th.

fallecer *irr como crecer vi* to pass away, to die

fallecimiento *m* death

fallido, -a *adj* (*proyecto*) unsuccessful; (*intento*) abortive

fallo *m* **1.** JUR sentence **2.**(*error*) error; (*omisión*) omission; **este asunto solo tiene un pequeño ~** this matter only has one small shortcoming **3.** TÉC breakdown **4.**(*fracaso*) failure **5.** MED **~ cardíaco/renal**

heart/kidney failure

falo *m elev* phallus

falsear *vt* **1.**(*al referir*) to misrepresent; (*verdad*) to distort **2.**(*materialmente*) to counterfeit

falsedad *f* falseness; (*hipocresía*) hypocrisy

falsificar <c→qu> *vt* to forge, to falsify; **~ la verdad** to distort the truth

falso, -a *adj* false; (*no natural*) artificial; **¡~!** not true!

falta *f* **1.**(*carencia*) lack; (*ausencia*) absence; **echar en ~ algo/alguien** to miss sth/sb; **me hace ~ dinero** I need money; **¡ni ~ que hace!** there is absolutely no need! **2.**(*equivocación*) error; **sin ~s** with no mistakes; **sin ~** without fail **3.** DEP foul

faltar *vi* **1.**(*no estar*) to be missing; (*persona*) to be absent; **~ a clase** to miss class **2.**(*necesitarse*) **~ (por) hacer** to be still to be done; **me falta tiempo para hacerlo** I need time to do it; **falta (por) saber si...** we need to know if ...; **¡no ~ía** [*o* **faltaba**] **más!** it is the limit!; (*respuesta a agradecimiento*) you are welcome!; (*asentir amablemente*) of course!; **¡lo que faltaba!** that is the last straw! **3.**(*temporal*) to be left; **faltan cuatro días para tu cumpleaños** your birthday is in four days; **falta mucho para que vengan** they won't be here for a long time yet; **falta poco para las doce** it is nearly twelve o'clock; **me faltó poco para llorar** I was on the verge of tears **4.**(*no cumplir*) **~ a una promesa** to break a promise; **nunca falta a su palabra** he/she never goes back on his/her word **5.**(*ofender*) to be rude; **~ a alguien** to be disrespectful to sb

falto, -a *adj* (*escaso*) **~ de algo** short of sth; (*desprovisto*) lacking in sth

fama *f* **1.**(*gloria*) glory; (*celebridad*) fame; **dar ~ a algo/alguien** to make sth/sb famous; **tener ~** to be famous **2.**(*reputación*) reputation; **tener ~ de fanfarrón** to have a reputation of being boastful

famélico, -a *adj* starving

familia *f* family; (*hogar*) household; (*parentela*) relatives *pl;* ~ **numerosa** large family; ~ **política** in-laws *pl;* **en** ~ with the family; **ser de la** ~ to be one of the family; **eso viene de** ~ that runs in the family

familiar I. *adj* **1.** (*íntimo*) intimate; **asunto** ~ personal matter **2.** (*conocido*) familiar **3.** LING colloquial **II.** *mf* relative

familiaridad *f* (*confianza*) intimacy; (*trato familiar*) familiarity

familiarizar <z→c> *vr:* ~**se** to familiarize oneself, to get to know

famoso, -a *adj* famous

fan *mf* <fans> fan

fanático, -a I. *adj* fanatical **II.** *m, f* **1.** *inf* (*hincha*) fan **2.** *pey* (*extremista*) fanatic

fanatismo *m sin pl* fanaticism

fanfarrón, -ona I. *adj inf* swanky **II.** *m, f inf* braggart, swank

fanfarronear *vi inf* to brag

fango *m* mud

fangoso, -a *adj* muddy

fantasía *f* (*imaginación*) imagination; (*cosa imaginada*) fantasy; **¡déjate de** ~**s!** come down to earth! *inf*

fantasma *m* ghost

fantástico, -a *adj* **1.** (*irreal*) fantastic, imaginary **2.** *inf* (*fabuloso*) fantastic, fabulous

faquir *m* fakir

faraón *m* Pharaoh

faraónico, -a *adj* pharaonic

faringe *f* pharynx, throat

faringitis *f inv* pharyngitis

farmacéutico, -a I. *adj* pharmaceutical **II.** *m, f* chemist *Brit,* druggist *Am*

farmacia *f* **1.** (*tienda*) chemist's *Brit,* drugstore *Am;* ~ **de guardia** all-night chemist's **2.** (*ciencia*) pharmacy

fármaco *m* medicine, drug

faro *m* **1.** AUTO headlight; ~ **antiniebla** fog light **2.** NÁUT lighthouse

farol *m* **1.** (*lámpara*) lamp; ~ (**de calle**) streetlight **2.** *inf* (*fanfarronada*) **tirarse un** ~ to show off

farola *f* street light; (*poste*) lamppost

farsa *f* sham

farsante *mf inf* charlatan

fascículo *m* instalment *Brit,* installment *Am*

fascinar *vt* to fascinate; (*libro*) to enthral *Brit,* to enthrall *Am*

fascismo *m sin pl* fascism

fascista I. *adj* fascist(ic) **II.** *mf* fascist

fase *f* phase

fastidiar I. *vt* **1.** (*molestar*) to annoy; **¡no te fastidia!** *inf* you must be joking! **2.** *inf* (*estropear*) ruin **II.** *vr:* ~**se** *inf* **1.** (*enojarse*) to get cross; **¡fastídiate!** stuff it! *inf;* **¡hay que** ~**se!** it's unbelievable! **2.** (*aguantarse*) to put up with it

fastidio *m* nuisance

fastidioso, -a *adj* annoying

fastuoso, -a *adj* sumptuous; (*persona*) flashy

fatal I. *adj* **1.** (*inevitable*) unavoidable **2.** (*funesto*) fatal; (*mortal*) mortal; **mujer** ~ femme fatale **3.** *inf* (*muy mal*) awful **II.** *adv inf* awfully; **el examen me fue** ~ my exam was a disaster

fatalidad *f* **1.** (*desgracia*) misfortune **2.** (*destino*) fate

fatiga *f* weariness, fatigue *form*

fatigar <g→gu> *vt* to tire, to fatigue *form*

fatigoso, -a *adj* (*trabajo*) tiring; (*persona*) tiresome

fatuo, -a *adj* **1.** (*presumido*) conceited; (*jactancioso*) boastful **2.** (*necio*) fatuous

fauces *fpl* fauces *pl*

fauna *f* fauna

favor *m* favour *Brit,* favor *Am;* **a** [*o* **en**] ~ **de alguien** in sb's favour; **por** ~ please; **estar a** ~ **de algo** to be in favour of sth; **hacer un** ~ **a alguien** to do sb a favour; **votar a** ~ **de alguien** to vote for sb; **¡hágame el** ~ **de dejarme en paz!** would you please leave me alone!; **te lo pido por** ~ I am begging you

favorable *adj* favourable *Brit,* favorable *Am*

favorecer *irr como crecer vt* **1.** (*beneficiar*) to benefit **2.** (*ayudar*) to help **3.** (*prendas de vestir*) to become

favorito, -a *adj, m, f* favourite *Brit,* favorite *Am*

fax *m inv* fax

faz *f elev* (*rostro*) face; (*anverso*) obverse

fe *f* **1.** faith; **de buena/mala** ~ in good/bad faith; **digno de** ~ worthy of trust; **dar** ~ **de algo** to certify sth; **tener** ~ **en alguien** to believe in sb **2.** (*certificado*) certificate; ~ **de erratas** errata; ~ **de matrimonio** marriage certificate

fealdad *f* ugliness

febrero *m* February; *v.t.* **marzo**

febril *adj* (*fiebre*) feverish; **acceso** ~ sudden temperature; (*actividad*) hectic

fecha *f* **1.** (*data*) date; (*señalada*) day; ~ **de caducidad** expiry date; (*de comida*) sell-by date; ~ **de cierre** closing date; ~ **clave** decisive day; ~ **límite/tope** deadline; **sin** ~ undated; **en la** ~ **fijada** on the agreed day; **hasta la** ~ until now, so far **2.** *pl* (*época*) days *pl;* **en estas** ~**s** around this time

fechar *vt* to date

fechoría *f* **1.** (*delito*) misdemeanour *Brit,* misdemeanor *Am* **2.** (*travesura*) prank

fecundar *vt* to fertilize

fecundo, -a *adj* **1.** (*prolífico*) prolific **2.** (*tierra*) fertile; (*campo*) productive

federación *f* federation

federal *adj* federal

felicidad *f* happiness; **¡**~**es!** congratulations!; (*Navidad*) Merry Christmas!; (*cumpleaños*) happy birthday!; **te deseamos muchas** ~**es** we wish you all the best

felicitación *f* **1.** (*enhorabuena*) congratulation **2.** (*tarjeta*) greetings card

felicitar I. *vt* ~ **a alguien por algo** to congratulate sb on sth II. *vr* ~**se por algo** to be glad about sth; ~**se de que** +*subj* to be glad that

feligrés, -esa *m, f* parishioner, church member

felino, -a *adj* feline

feliz *adj* **1.** (*dichoso*) happy; **¡**~ **Navi-**

dad! merry Christmas!; **¡**~ **viaje!** have a good journey! **2.** (*exitoso*) fortunate, successful

felpudo *m* doormat

femenino, -a *adj* **1.** (*sexo*) female; **equipo** ~ women's team **2.** (*afeminado*) effeminate **3.** LING feminine

feminista *adj, m f* feminist

fenomenal I. *adj* phenomenal; *inf* (*tremendo*) tremendous II. *adv inf* terrifically

fenómeno *m* phenomenon; (*genio*) genius

feo, -a *adj* **1.** (*espantoso*) ugly; **dejar** ~ **a alguien** *fig* to show sb up; **la cosa se está poniendo fea** things aren't looking too good **2.** (*reprobable*) bad

féretro *m* coffin

feria *f* **1.** (*exposición*) fair, show; ~ **de muestras** trade fair **2.** (*verbena*) fair; **puesto de** ~ stand

feriado, -a *adj AmL* holiday; **día** ~ bank holiday

fermentar *vi, vt* to ferment

ferocidad *f* **1.** (*salvajismo*) ferocity **2.** (*crueldad*) savagery

feroz *adj* **1.** (*salvaje*) fierce **2.** (*cruel*) savage

férreo, -a *adj* **1.** *t. fig* iron **2.** (*del ferrocarril*) railway *Brit,* railroad *Am*

ferretería *f* ironmonger's, hardware store

ferrocarril *m* **1.** (*vía*) railway line *Brit,* railroad *Am* **2.** (*tren*) railway; **por** ~ by rail

ferroviario, -a *adj* railway *Brit,* railroad *Am*

fértil *adj* fertile; (*rico*) rich

fertilidad *f* fertility; (*productividad*) productiveness

fertilizante *m* fertilizer

fertilizar <z→c> *vt* to fertilize

ferviente *adj* fervent

fervor *m* fervour *Brit,* fervor *Am;* (*entusiasmo*) enthusiasm; **con** ~ ardently

fervoroso, -a *adj* fervent

festejar *vt* **1.** (*celebrar*) to celebrate **2.** (*galantear*) to court, to woo

festejo *m* **1.** (*conmemoración*) celebration **2.** (*galanteo*) courtship

F f

3. pl (actos públicos) festival, public festivities pl

festín m feast

festival m festival

festividad f **1.** (conmemoración) festivity **2.** (día) feast

festivo, -a adj festive, celebratory; **día** ~ bank holiday

fétido, -a adj fetid form

feto m foetus Brit, fetus Am

fiable adj reliable; (persona) trustworthy

fiaca f CSur (pereza) laziness

fiador(a) m(f) backer, bondsman; **salir** ~ **por alguien** to stand surety for sb

fiambre m **1.** GASTR cold meat **2.** inf (cadáver) stiff; **ese está** ~ that one is stone-dead

fianza f (garantía) security; (depósito) deposit; (fiador) surety, bail; **en libertad bajo** ~ free on bail

fiar <1. pres: fío> **I.** vi **1.** (al vender) to give credit; **en esa tienda no fían** that shop does not give credit **2.** (confiar) to trust; **es de** ~ he/she is trustworthy **II.** vt (dar crédito) to sell on credit **III.** vr ~**se de algo/alguien** to trust sth/sb

fibra f fibre Brit, fiber Am; ~ **de vidrio** fibreglass Brit, fiberglass Am

ficción f fiction; (simulación) simulation

ficha f **1.** (de ruleta) chip; (de dominó) domino; (de ajedrez) piece, man **2.** (para una máquina, de guardarropa) token **3.** (tarjeta informativa) (index) card; (en el trabajo) card; ~ **policial** police record

fichar **I.** vi **1.** DEP to sign **2.** (en el trabajo) to clock in **II.** vt **1.** (policía) to open a file on; **estar fichado** to have a police record **2.** inf (desconfiar) to mistrust **3.** DEP to sign up

fichero m **1.** (archivador) filing-cabinet; (caja) box file **2.** INFOR file

ficticio, -a adj ficticious

fidelidad f **1.** (lealtad) fidelity, faithfulness **2.** (precisión) precision; **alta** ~ high fidelity

fideo m (fine) noodle

fiebre f fever; ~ **del heno** hay fever; ~ **del juego** compulsive gambling; ~ **del oro** gold rush; ~ **palúdica** malaria; **tener poca** ~ to have a slight temperature

fiel **I.** adj faithful; (memoria) accurate; **ser** ~ **a una promesa** to keep a promise **II.** m **1.** (de una balanza) needle, pointer **2.** pl REL the faithful

fieltro m felt

fiera f wild animal; **llegó hecho una** ~ inf he arrived in a furious state

fiero, -a adj **1.** (feroz) fierce **2.** (cruel) cruel **3.** (feo) ugly **4.** (fuerte) terrible

fiesta f **1.** (día) holiday; **¡Felices Fiestas!** Merry Christmas and a Happy New Year!; **hoy hago** ~ I have taken the day off today **2.** (celebración) celebration; ~ (**mayor**) festival **3.** inf (humor) **estar de** ~ to be in a very cheerful mood

figura f **1.** figure; (imagen) image; **se distinguía la** ~ **de un barco** you could make out the shape of a boat **2.** TEAT character; (personaje) figure

figurado, -a adj figurative

figurante mf extra

figurar **I.** vi to figure; **figura en el puesto número tres** he appears in third place **II.** vr: ~**se** to imagine; **¡figúrate!** just think!; **no vayas a** ~**te que...** don't go thinking that ...

fijador m **1.** (para el pelo) hair gel **2.** FOTO fixer

fijar **I.** vt **1.** (sujetar) to fix; (con cuerdas) to tie up; (con cola) to glue on; (con clavos) to nail; (con cadenas) to chain; (con tornillos) to screw on; ~ **con chinchetas** to stick up with drawing pins; **prohibido** ~ **carteles** bill posters prohibited **2.** (la mirada) to fix; ~ **la atención en algo** to concentrate on sth **3.** (residencia, precio) to establish **II.** vr: ~**se 1.** (en un lugar) to establish oneself **2.** (atender) to pay attention; **no se ha fijado en mi nuevo peinado** he/she has not noticed my new hairdo; **ese se fija en todo** nothing escapes him; **fíjate bien en lo que te digo** listen carefully to what I have to say **3.** (mirar) to notice; **no se fijó en**

mí he/she did not notice me

fijo, -a adj **1.** (estable) stable; (trabajador) permanent; **cliente** ~ regular client; **precio** ~ fixed price **2.** (idea) fixed **3.** (mirada) steady

fila f **1.** (hilera) row; ~ **de coches** line of cars; **en** ~ in line; **en** ~ **india** in single file; **aparcar en doble** ~ to double-park; **salir de la** ~ to step out of line **2.** MIL rank; **¡en** ~**s!** fall in!; **¡rompan** ~**s!** fall out! **3.** pl (de un partido) ranks pl

filántropo mf philanthropist

filatelia f philately, stamp collecting

filete m fillet Brit, filet Am; (solomillo) steak

filial f subsidiary

Filipinas fpl **las** ~ the Philippines

filipino, -a adj, m, f Philippine

film m film Brit, movie Am

filmar vt to film, to shoot

filme m film Brit, movie Am

filo m blade

filología f philology

filón m seam; fig (negocio) gold mine

filosofía f philosophy

filósofo, -a m, f philosopher

filtrar I. vt to filter; (llamadas) to screen II. vr: ~**se 1.** (líquido) to seep; (luz) to filter **2.** (noticia) to percolate **3.** (dinero) to dwindle

filtro m filter; **cigarrillo con** ~ filter tip cigarette; ~ **solar** sunscreen

fin m **1.** (término) end; ~ **de semana** weekend; **a** ~**(es) de mes** at the end of the month; **al** ~ **y al cabo, a** ~ **de cuentas** after all; **sin** ~ never-ending; **poner** ~ **a algo** to put an end to sth **2.** (propósito) aim; **a** ~ **de que** +subj so that

final¹ I. adj (producto, resultado) end; (fase, examen) final; (solución) ultimate; **palabras** ~**es** last words II. m end; (de un libro) ending; MÚS finale; **al** ~ **no nos lo dijo** in the end he did not tell us

final² f DEP (partido) final; (ronda) finals pl

finalidad f purpose

finalista mf finalist

finalizar <z→c> I. vi to finish;

(plazo) to end II. vt to end; (discurso) to conclude

financiar vt to finance

financiero, -a I. adj financial II. m, f financier

finanzas fpl finances pl

finca f property, real estate Am

finés, -esa I. adj Finnish II. m, f Finn

fingir <g→j> I. vi to pretend II. vt to pretend; (sentimiento) to feign

finlandés, -esa I. adj Finnish II. m, f Finn

Finlandia f Finland

fino m dry sherry

fino, -a adj **1.** (delgado, de calidad) fine **2.** (liso) smooth, even **3.** (sentido) acute **4.** (cortés) polite; **modales** ~**s** refined manners **5.** (astuto) shrewd

firma f **1.** (en documentos) signature **2.** (empresa) firm

firmamento m firmament

firmante mf signatory, signer; **el/la abajo** ~ the undersigned

firmar vi, vt to sign

firme I. adj firm; (estable) steady; (seguro) secure; (carácter) resolute; (postura corporal) straight; **con mano** ~ with a firm hand; **¡~s!** MIL attention! II. m **1.** (cubierta) road surface **2.** (de guijo) roadbed

firmeza f firmness; (solidez) solidity; (perseverancia) perseverance; ~ **de carácter** resolution

fiscal I. adj (del fisco) fiscal; (de los impuestos) tax II. mf public prosecutor Brit, district attorney Am

fisco m exchequer, treasury

fisgar <g→gu> vi ~ **en algo** to snoop into sth

fisgón, -ona m, f pey nosy Parker

física f physics pl

físico m physique; **tener un buen** ~ (cuerpo) to have a good physique; (aspecto) to be good-looking

físico, -a I. adj physical II. m, f physicist

fisioterapia f physiotherapy

flaco, -a adj **1.** (delgado) thin **2.** (débil) weak

flagrante I. adj (evidente) flagrant II. adv **en** ~ red-handed

flamante *adj inf* 1. (*vistoso*) flamboyant 2. (*nuevo*) brand-new

flamenco *m* 1. ZOOL flamingo 2. (*cante*) flamenco 3. (*lengua*) Flemish

> [?] The **flamenco**, a very traditional form of song and dance from **Andalucía**, is known the world over. The origins of the **flamenco** can be found in the rich traditions of three national groups: the Andalusians, the Moors and the Gypsies. The song and dance movements (solo or duet) are always accompanied by a rhythmic clapping of hands and clicking of fingers together with various cries.

flamenco, -a I. *adj* 1. (*andaluz*) flamenco; **cante** ~ flamenco 2. (*de Flandes*) Flemish 3. (*chulo*) cocky II. *m, f* Fleming

flan *m* crème caramel; **estar hecho un** ~ to be shaking like a leaf

Flandes *m* Flanders

flaquear *vi* 1. (*fuerzas*) to flag; (*salud*) to decline 2. (*en un examen*) to be poor

flaqueza *f* 1. (*de flaco*) thinness 2. (*debilidad*) weakness

flash *m inv* flash

flauta¹ *f* ~ (**dulce**) recorder; ~ (**travesera**) flute

flauta² *mf* flautist *Brit,* flutist *Am*

flecha *f* arrow; **ser rápido como una** ~ to be as quick as lightning

flechazo *m inf* **lo nuestro fue un** ~ ours was love at first sight

fleco *m* fringe

flema *f* 1. (*calma*) imperturbability 2. (*mucosidad*) phlegm

flemón *m* gumboil

flequillo *m* fringe

flete *m* 1. (*carga*) cargo, freight 2. (*tasa*) freight

flexible *adj* flexible; (*músculo*) supple

flexión *f* 1. (*del cuerpo*) flexion, bending; (*plancha*) press-up 2. LING inflection

flexo *m* desk lamp

flipper *m* pinball machine

flirt *m* <flirts> flirt

flirtear *vi* to flirt

flojear *vi* 1. (*disminuir*) to diminish; (*calor*) to ease up 2. (*en una materia*) ~ **en algo** to be poor at sth

flojera *f inf* weakness

flojo, -a *adj* 1. (*cuerda*) slack; (*nudo*) loose 2. (*vino, café, argumento*) weak; (*viento*) light; (*luz*) feeble; ~ **de carácter** spineless; **estoy** ~ **en inglés** I am weak in English

flor *f* (*planta*) flowering plant; (*parte de la planta*) flower, bloom; **estar en** ~ to be in flower; **camisa de ~es** flowery shirt; **la** ~ **de la canela** *fig* the best; **la** ~ **y la nata de la sociedad** the cream of society; **la** ~ **de la vida** the prime of life; **tengo los nervios a** ~ **de piel** my nerves are frayed

flora *f* flora

florecer *irr* *como crecer* I. *vi* to flower, to bloom; *fig* to flourish II. *vr:* ~**se** to grow mould *Brit,* to grow mold *Am*

floreciente *adj* flowering; *fig* flourishing

Florencia *f* Florence

florentino, -a *adj, m, f* Florentine

florero *m* vase; **estar de** ~ *fig* to be just for decoration

florista *mf* florist

floristería *f* florist's, flower shop

flota *f* fleet

flotador *m* float; (*para niños*) rubber ring; (*de cisterna*) ballcock; *inf* (*michelines*) roll of fat

flotar *vi* float; (*activamente*) to stay afloat

flote *m* **estar a** ~ to be afloat; **mantenerse a** ~ *t. fig* to manage to keep one's head above water; **sacar a** ~ **una empresa** to get a business going

fluctuar <1. *pres:* fluctúo> *vi* to fluctuate

fluidez *f* **hablar con** ~ **un idioma extranjero** to speak a foreign language fluently

fluido *m* fluid

fluido, -a *adj* **1.** (*líquido*) fluid **2.** (*expresión*) fluent; **es ~ de palabra** he speaks with ease **3.** (*tráfico*) free--flowing

fluir *irr como huir vi* to flow

flujo *m* flow; (*de la marea*) rising tide; **~ de palabras** stream of words

flúor *m* fluorine

fluorescente *adj* fluorescent

fluvial *adj* fluvial

FMI *m abr de* **Fondo Monetario Internacional** IMF

foca *f* seal

foco *m* **1.** FÍS, MAT focus; (*centro*) focal point; **~ de infección** source of infection **2.** (*lámpara*) light; (*estadio*) floodlight; (*teatro*) spotlight **3.** *AmL* (*bombilla*) light bulb

fofo, -a *adj* flabby

fogón *m* **1.** (*de la cocina*) stove **2.** (*de máquinas de vapor*) furnace; FERRO firebox **3.** (*de un cañón*) vent **4.** *AmL* (*fogata*) fire

fogoso, -a *adj* (*pasión*) passionate; (*persona*) ardent

folclor(e) *m* folklore

folclórico, -a *adj* traditional

fólder *f AmL* (*carpeta*) folder

follaje *m* foliage

follar *vi, vt vulg* to fuck, to shag *Brit, vulg*

folleto *m* pamphlet; **~ publicitario** advertising leaflet, flier

follón *m inf* **1.** (*alboroto*) row; **armar un ~** to cause a commotion **2.** (*asunto enojoso*) trouble

fomentar *vt* (*empleo*) to promote; (*economía*) to boost

fomento *m* (*del empleo*) promotion; (*de la economía*) boosting

fonda *f* inn

fondo *m* **1.** (*de un cajón*) back; (*del río*) bed; NÁUT sea bed; (*de un valle*) bottom; **los bajos ~s** the underworld; **en el ~ de su corazón** in his/her heart of hearts; **irse a ~** to sink; **tocar ~** to touch bottom; ECON to hit bottom **2.** (*de un edificio*) depth; **al ~ del pasillo** at the end of the corridor; **mi habitación está al** **~ de la casa** my bedroom is at the back of the house **3.** (*lo esencial*) essence; **artículo de ~** editorial; **en el ~** at bottom; **ir al ~ de un asunto** to go to the heart of the matter; **tratar un tema a ~** to seriously discuss a subject **4.** (*índole*) nature, disposition; **persona de buen ~** a good person at heart **5.** (*de un cuadro*) background; (*de una tela*) background colour; **ruido/música de ~** background noise/music **6.** DEP long--distance; **corredor de ~** long-distance runner **7.** FIN, POL fund; **~ común** kitty; **Fondo Monetario Internacional** International Monetary Fund **8.** *pl* (*medios*) funds *pl;* **cheque sin ~s** bad cheque *Brit,* bad check *Am*

fonética *f* phonetics *pl*

fontanería *f* **1.** (*acción, conducto*) plumbing **2.** (*establecimiento*) plumber's

fontanero, -a *m, f* plumber

footing *m sin pl* jogging; **hacer ~** to jog

forastero, -a *m, f* stranger; (*extranjero*) foreigner

forcejear *vi* to struggle

fórceps *m inv* forceps *pl*

forense **I.** *adj* forensic **II.** *mf* pathologist

forestal *adj* forest, woodland; **guarda ~** forester *Brit,* forest ranger *Am*

forjar *vt* **1.** (*metal*) to forge **2.** (*inventar*) to invent; (*crear*) to forge; (*imperio*) to build

forma *f* **1.** (*figura*) form, shape; **las ~s de una mujer** a woman's curves; **en ~ de gota** in the shape of a drop; **dar ~ a algo** (*formar*) to shape sth; (*precisar*) to spell out **2.** (*manera*) way; LIT, JUR form; **defecto de ~** JUR defect of form; **~ de pago** method of payment; **de ~ libre** freely; **en ~ escrita** written; **en (buena y) debida ~** duly; **de ~ que** so that; **de todas ~s, ...** anyway, ...; **lo haré de una ~ u otra** I will do it one way or another; **no hay ~ de abrir la puerta** this door is impossible to open **3.** (*comportamiento*) manners *pl*

4. (*molde*) mould *Brit,* mold *Am* **5.** (*condición*) **estar en** ~ to be fit **6.** DEP form

formación *f* **1.** (*creación, grupo*) *t.* GEO formation; ~ **política** political group **2.** (*educación*) education; ~ **escolar/de adultos** school/adult education; ~ **profesional** vocational training

formal *adj* **1.** (*relativo a la forma*) formal; **requisito** ~ formal requirement **2.** (*serio*) serious; (*polite*) educated; (*cumplidor*) reliable **3.** (*oficial*) official; **una invitación** ~ a formal invitation; **tiene novio** ~ she has a steady boyfriend

formalidad *f* **1.** (*seriedad*) seriousness; (*exactitud*) correctness **2.** *pl* ADMIN, JUR formalities *pl* **3.** (*norma de comportamiento*) formality

formalizar <z→c> **I.** *vt* to formalize; ~ **un noviazgo** (*comprometerse*) to become engaged; (*casarse*) to marry **II.** *vr:* ~**se** to grow up

formar I. *vt* **1.** (*dar forma*) to form, to shape **2.** (*constituir*) to form; MIL to form up **3.** (*educar*) to train; (*enseñar*) to teach **II.** *vr:* ~**se** **1.** (*crearse*) to form; MIL to fall in **2.** (*ser educado*) to be educated; **se ha formado a sí mismo** he is self-taught **3.** (*desarrollarse*) to develop **4.** (*hacerse*) to form; ~**se una idea de algo** to form an impression of sth

formatear *vt* to format

formato *m* format

formica® *f sin pl* Formica®

formidable *adj* **1.** *inf* (*estupendo*) fantastic **2.** (*enorme*) enormous **3.** (*temible*) awesome

fórmula *f* formula

formular *vt* to formulate; ~ **demanda** to file a claim; ~ **denuncia** to lodge a complaint

formulario *m* form

fornido, -a *adj* well-built, husky

foro *m* forum

forrar I. *vt* (*el exterior, una pared*) to face; (*el interior, una prenda*) to line; (*una butaca*) to upholster; (*un libro*) to cover **II.** *vr:* ~**se** *inf* to make a packet

forro *m* (*exterior, de una pared*) facing; (*interior, de una prenda*) lining; (*de una butaca*) upholstery; (*de un libro*) cover

fortalecer *irr* **I.** *vt* **1.** (*vigorizar*) to invigorate **2.** (*reforzar*) to fortify **II.** *vr:* ~**se** **1.** (*vigorizarse*) to fortify oneself **2.** (*volverse más fuerte*) to become stronger

fortaleza *f* **1.** (*fuerza*) strength; **de poca** ~ not very tough **2.** (*virtud*) fortitude **3.** (*robustez*) robustness **4.** MIL fortress, stronghold

fortuito, -a *adj* fortuitous, chance

fortuna *f* **1.** (*suerte, capital*) fortune **2.** (*destino*) fate

forzar *irr* *vt* **1.** (*obligar*) to force; (*voz*) to strain; (*obligar a entrar*) to push in; (*a abrirse*) to force open **2.** (*un acontecimiento*) to bring about **3.** (*violar*) to rape

forzoso, -a *adj* forced, necessary; **aterrizaje** ~ forced landing; **venta forzosa** compulsary sale

fosa *f* **1.** (*hoyo*) pit; (*alargado*) trench; ~ **séptica** septic tank **2.** (*sepultura*) grave **3.** ANAT ~ **nasal** nostril

fosforescente *adj* phosphorescent

fósforo *m* **1.** QUÍM phosphorus **2.** (*cerilla*) match

fósil *m* fossil

foso *m* **1.** (*hoyo*) hole; (*alargado*) ditch; MIL trench; (*fortaleza*) moat **2.** MÚS, TEAT orchestra pit **3.** (*en un garaje*) inspection pit

foto *f* photo; ~ (**tamaño**) **carnet** passport photo

fotocopia *f* photocopy

fotocopiadora *f* photocopier

fotocopiar *vt* to photocopy

fotogénico, -a *adj* photogenic

fotografía *f* **1.** (*imagen*) photograph; ~ **en color** colour photograph; ~ (**tamaño**) **carnet** passport photograph **2.** (*arte*) photography

fotografiar < 1. pres: fotografío> *vi, vt* to photograph

fotógrafo, -a *m, f* photographer

fotomatón *m* photo booth

fotonovela *f* photostory

frac *m* <fracs *o* fraques> tails *pl*

fracasar *vi* to fail; **la película fracasó** the film was a flop
fracaso *m* failure
fracción *f* fraction; ~ **parlamentaria** parliamentary faction
fractura *f* break; MED fracture
fragancia *f* fragrance
fragata *f* frigate
frágil *adj* 1.(*objeto*) fragile 2.(*constitución, salud*) delicate; (*anciano*) frail
fragmento *m* fragment
fragua *f* forge
fraguar <gu→gü> I. *vi* to set II. *vt* to forge; **¿qué estás fraguando?** *fig* what are you scheming?
fraile *m* friar
frambuesa *f* raspberry
francés, -esa I. *adj* French; **tortilla francesa** plain omelette II. *m, f* Frenchman *m,* Frenchwoman *f*
Francfort *m* Frankfurt
Francia *f* France
franco *m* 1.(*moneda*) franc 2.(*lengua*) Frankish
franco, -a *adj* 1.(*sincero*) frank 2.(*libre*) free; ~ **a bordo** free on board; ~ **de derechos** duty-free
francotirador *m* sniper
franela *f* flannel
franja *f* strip; (*guarnición*) border
franquear *vt* 1.(*carta*) to pay postage on; **a** ~ **en destino** postage paid at destination 2.(*desobstruir*) to clear 3. *inf* (*río*) to cross; (*obstáculo*) to get round
franqueo *m* postage; **sin** ~ without stamps
franqueza *f* frankness; **admitir algo con** ~ to openly admit sth
franquismo *m sin pl* 1.(*régimen*) Franco's regime 2.(*movimiento*) Francoism
franquista *adj, mf* Francoist
fraques *pl de* **frac**
frasco *m* flask
frase *f* 1.(*oración*) sentence 2.(*locución*) expression; ~ **hecha** idiom
fraternal *adj* fraternal, brotherly
fraude *m* fraud
fraudulento, -a *adj* fraudulent
frazada *f AmL* blanket

frecuencia *f* frequency; **con** ~ frequently
frecuentar *vt* 1.(*lugar*) to frequent 2.(*a alguien*) to be in touch with
frecuente *adj* 1.(*repetido*) frequent 2.(*usual*) common
fregadero *m* (kitchen) sink
fregar *irr vt* 1.(*frotar*) to rub 2.(*limpiar: el suelo*) to scrub; (*con fregona*) to mop; (*los platos*) to wash up 3. *AmL, inf* (*molestar*) to annoy
fregona *f* 1.(*utensilio*) mop 2. *pey* (*sirvienta*) drudge, skivvy *Brit*
freidora *f* fryer
freír *irr* I. *vt* to fry; **mandar a alguien a** ~ **espárragos** *inf* to tell sb to get lost II. *vr:* ~**se** to fry
frenar I. *vt* 1.(*hacer parar*) to stop 2.(*un impulso, persona*) to restrain; (*un desarollo*) to check, to curb II. *vi* to brake; ~ **en seco** to slam on the brakes
frenazo *m* sudden braking; **pegar un** ~ to step on the brakes
frenesí *m* frenzy
frenético, -a *adj* 1.(*exaltado*) frenzied 2.(*furioso*) furious
freno *m* 1. TÉC brake; ~ **de mano** handbrake *Brit,* emergency brake *Am* 2.(*para un caballo*) bit
frente¹ *f* forehead; ~ **a** ~ face to face; **fruncir la** ~ to frown; **hacer** ~ **a alguien** to stand up to sb; **hacer** ~ **a algo** to face up to sth
frente² I. *m* front; (*de un edificio*) façade, face; **al** ~ (*dirección*) ahead; (*lugar*) in front; **de** ~ head-on; **estar al** ~ **de algo** to be in charge of sth; **ponerse al** ~ to take charge II. *prep* 1. ~ **a** (*enfrente de*) opposite; (*delante de*) in front of; (*contra*) as opposed to; (*ante*) in the face of 2. **en** ~ **de** opposite
fresa *f* strawberry
fresco *m* 1.(*frescor*) cool air; **salir a tomar el** ~ to go out to get some fresh air; **hoy hace** ~ it is cool today 2. ARTE fresco 3. *AmL* (*refresco*) soft drink
fresco, -a *adj* 1.(*frío*) cool; (*prenda*) lightweight, cool 2.(*sano, descansado, reciente*) fresh; **queso** ~ cottage

cheese **3.** *inf* (*desvergonzado*) fresh, cheeky **4.** (*impasible*) cool

frescura *f* **1.** (*frescor*) freshness **2.** (*desvergüenza*) cheek **3.** (*desembarazo*) naturalness; **con** ~ freely

frialdad *f* **1.** (*frío*) coldness **2.** (*despego, impasibilidad*) coolness; **me trató con** ~ he/she was cool towards me

fricción *f* **1.** (*resistencia, desavenencia*) friction **2.** (*del cuerpo*) rub; (*con linimento*) massage

frigidez *f* frigidity

frígido, -a *adj* frigid

frigorífico *m* fridge, refrigerator

frigorífico, -a *adj* refrigeratory

frijol *m*, **fríjol** *m AmL* bean

frío *m* cold; **hace** ~ it is cold; **hace un** ~ **que pela** *inf* it is bitterly cold; **coger** ~ to catch cold; **tener** ~ to be cold; **no dar a alguien ni** ~ **ni calor** to leave sb indifferent

frío, -a *adj* cold; *fig* cool

frito *m* fry

frito, -a I. *pp* de **freír** II. *adj* **1.** (*comida*) fried **2.** *inf* (*dormido*) **quedarse** ~ to fall fast asleep **3.** *inf* (*harto*) **estar** ~ **con algo** to be fed up with sth; **me tienen** [*o* **traen**] ~ **con sus preguntas** I am fed up with their questions

frívolo, -a *adj* frivolous

frontal *adj* head-on

frontera *f* border; **atravesar la** ~ to cross the frontier

fronterizo, -a *adj* frontier; (*país*) border(ing); **paso** ~ border post

frontón *m* pelota

frotamiento *m* rubbing

frotar *vt* to rub

fructífero, -a *adj* fruitful

frugal *adj* frugal

fruncir <c→z> *vt* **1.** (*tela*) to gather, to shirr **2.** (*frente*) to wrinkle; ~ **el entrecejo** to frown

frustración *f* frustration

frustrar *vt* **1.** (*estropear*) to thwart; ~ **las esperanzas de alguien** to frustrate sb's hopes **2.** (*decepcionar*) to discourage

fruta *f* fruit; ~ **del tiempo** seasonal fruit

frutería *f* greengrocer's

frutero *m* fruit bowl

frutilla *f AmL* strawberry

fruto *m t. fig* fruit; (*ganancia*) profit; (*provecho*) benefit

fue I. *3. pret de* **ir** **2.** *3. pret de* **ser**

fuego *m* **1.** fire; **¿me das** ~? can you give me a light?; ~**s artificiales** fireworks *pl*; **a** ~ **lento** over a low heat; **prender** [*o* **pegar**] ~ **a algo** to set sth alight **2.** MIL firing **3.** (*ardor*) ardour *Brit*, ardor *Am;* **en el** ~ **de la discusión** in the heat of the discussion

fuente *f* **1.** (*manantial*) spring **2.** (*construcción*) fountain **3.** (*plato llano*) platter; (*plato hondo*) (serving) dish **4.** (*origen*) source; ~**s bien informadas** reliable sources

fuera I. *adv* **1.** (*lugar*) outside; **por** ~ on the outside; **el nuevo maestro es de** ~ the new teacher is not from here **2.** (*dirección*) out; **hacia** ~ outwards; **salir** ~ to go out; **¡**~ **con esto!** no way! **3.** (*tiempo*) out; ~ **de plazo** past the deadline **4.** *inf* (*de viaje*) away; **me voy** ~ **una semana** I am going away for a week II. *prep* **1.** *t. fig* (*local*) out of; **estar** ~ **de casa** to be away from home; ~ **de juego** DEP offside; ~ **de serie** exceptional **2.** (*excepto*) ~ **de** outside of III. *conj* ~ **de que** +*subj* apart from the fact that

fuero *m* privilege

fuerte I. *adj* <fortísimo> **1.** (*resistente, poderoso, valiente*) strong; **caja** ~ safe; **ser** ~ **de carácter** to be strong-willed **2.** (*musculoso*) strong; (*gordo*) fat **3.** (*intenso*) intense; (*duro*) hard; (*sonido*) loud; (*comida, golpe*) heavy; (*abrazo, beso*) big; **un vino** ~ a full-bodied wine **4.** (*genio*) **tener un carácter** [*o* **genio**] **muy** ~ to be quick-tempered **5.** (*versado*) **estar** ~ **en matemáticas** to be good at mathematics **6.** (*violento*) disturbing; (*expresión*) nasty; **palabra** ~ rude word II. *m* **1.** (*de una persona*) strong point **2.** MIL fort III. *adv* **1.** (*con fuerza*) strongly; (*con intensidad*) intensely; (*en voz alta*) aloud

2.(*en abundancia*) copiously; **desayunar** ~ to have a large breakfast
fuerza *f* **1.**(*capacidad física*) strength; *t.* FÍS (*potencia*) force; ~ **de ánimo** strength of mind; ~ **de voluntad** willpower; **sin** ~**s** weak, drained; **tiene más** ~ **que yo** he/she is stronger than I am; **se le va la** ~ **por la boca** he/she is all talk **2.**(*capacidad de soportar*) toughness; (*eficacia*) effectiveness **3.**(*poder*) power; ~ **mayor** act of God, force majeure **4.**(*violencia*) force; **a** [*o* **por**] **la** ~ willy-nilly; **por** ~ (*por necesidad*) out of necessity; (*con violencia*) by force; **recurrir a la** ~ to resort to violence **5.**(*intensidad*) intensity **6.**(*expresividad*) expressiveness **7.** *pl* POL political groups *pl;* MIL forces *pl* **8.** ELEC power **9.**(*usando*) **a** ~ **de** by means of; **lo ha conseguido todo a** ~ **de trabajo** he/she has achieved everything through hard work
fuga *f* **1.**(*huida*) flight; (*de la cárcel*) escape; **darse a la** ~ to escape; ~ **de cerebros** brain drain **2.**(*en tubos*) leak
fugarse <g→gu> *vr* to flee; (*de casa*) to run away; (*para casarse*) to elope; ~ **de la cárcel** to escape from prison
fugaz *adj* fleeting; (*caduco*) short-lived; **estrella** ~ shooting star
fugitivo, -a I. *adj* fugitive; (*belleza*) transitory II. *m, f* fugitive; (*de la cárcel*) escapee
fulano, -a *m, f* **1.**(*evitando el nombre*) so-and-so **2.**(*persona indeterminada*) guy, Joe Bloggs *Brit,* John Doe *Am;* **no me importa lo que digan** ~ **y mengano** I do not care what Tom, Dick or Harry say
fulgor *m* (*centelleo*) sparkle; (*de una superficie*) gleam
fulminante *adj* **1.** *t.* MED (*inesperado*) sudden **2.**(*mirada*) withering
fulminar *vt* to strike down; **un rayo/el cáncer lo fulminó** he was struck down by lightning/cancer
fumador(a *m(f)* smoker; **no** ~ non-smoker; **zona de no** ~**es** no-smoking area

fumar I. *vi, vt* to smoke II. *vr:* ~**se** **1.**(*fumar*) to smoke **2.** *inf*(*gastar*) to squander
fumigar <g→gu> *vt* to fumigate
funámbulo, -a *m, f* tightrope walker
función *f* **1.** *t.* BIO, MAT (*papel*) function; **el precio está en** ~ **de la calidad** the price depends on the quality **2.**(*cargo*) office; (*tarea*) duty; **entrar en** ~ to take up one's duties; (*cargo*) to enter into office **3.**(*acto formal*) function; CINE showing; TEAT performance; ~ **doble** double feature; ~ **de noche** late show
funcional *adj* functional
funcionamiento *m* **1.**(*marcha*) running; ~ **administrativo** running of the administration; ~ **del mercado** market organization; **poner en** ~ to bring into operation **2.**(*rendimiento*) performance; (*manera de funcionar*) operation; **en estado de** ~ in working order; (*máquina*) working
funcionar *vi* to function; (*estar trabajando*) to be working; **el coche no funciona bien** the car is not going properly; **la televisión no funciona** the television does not work; **No Funciona** (*cartel*) out of order
funcionario, -a *m, f* (*de una organización*) employee; (*del Estado*) civil servant
funda *f* cover; (*para gafas*) glasses case; (*de almohada*) pillowcase
fundación *f* foundation
fundamental *adj* fundamental
fundamentalismo *m sin pl* fundamentalism
fundamentalista *adj, mf* fundamentalist
fundamentar *vt* to base
fundamento *m* **1.** ARQUIT foundations *pl* **2.**(*base*) basis **3.**(*motivo*) grounds; **sin** ~ groundless **4.**(*formalidad*) sensibleness; (*seriedad*) seriousness; **hablar sin** ~ to not talk seriously **5.** *pl* (*conocimientos*) fundamentals *pl*
fundar I. *vt* **1.**(*crear*) to found

F f

2. (*basar*) to base; (*justificar*) to found **II.** *vr:* ~**se** (*basarse*) to base oneself; (*tener su justificación*) to be founded

fundición *f* **1.** (*de un metal*) smelting **2.** (*en una forma*) casting **3.** (*taller*) foundry

fundir I. *vt* **1.** (*deshacer*) to melt **2.** (*dar forma*) to found, to cast **3.** (*bombilla*) to fuse; (*plomo*) to blow **4.** (*unir*) to unite; (*empresas*) to merge **5.** *inf* (*gastar*) to squander **II.** *vr:* ~**se 1.** (*deshacerse*) to melt **2.** (*bombilla*) to fuse; (*plomo*) to blow **3.** (*unirse*) to unite; (*empresas*) to merge

fúnebre *adj* **1.** (*triste*) mournful; (*sombrío*) gloomy **2.** (*de los difuntos*) funerary; **coche** ~ hearse; **pompas** ~**s** (*ceremonia*) funeral; (*empresa*) undertaker's

funeral *m* **1.** (*entierro*) burial **2.** *pl* (*misa*) funeral, obsequies *pl*

funeraria *f* funeral parlour

funerario, -a *adj* funeral

funesto, -a *adj* **1.** (*aciago*) ill-fated **2.** (*desgraciado*) terrible

furgón *m* (*carro*) wagon; (*camioneta*) van

furgoneta *f* van

furia *f* **1.** (*ira, ímpetu*) fury **2.** (*persona*) **estaba hecha una** ~ she was furious

furibundo, -a *adj* furious

furioso, -a *adj* furious

furor *m* **1.** (*ira*) fury **2.** (*auge*) **hacer** ~ to be the (latest) thing

furtivo, -a *adj* furtive

furúnculo *m* boil

fusible I. *adj* fusible **II.** *m* fuse

fusil *m* rifle

fusilar *vt* to execute

fusión *f* **1.** (*fundición*) fusion **2.** (*unión*) union; ECON merger

fusta *f* riding whip

fútbol *m* football *Brit,* soccer *Am;* ~ **americano** American football, football *Am*

futbolín *m* table football

futbolista *mf* football player *Brit,* soccer player *Am*

futileza *f Chile* trifle

futilidad *f* triviality

futuro *m* future

futuro, -a *adj* future

G, g *f* G, g; ~ **de Granada** G for George

gabacho, -a *m, f pey* Froggy

gabán *m* overcoat

gabardina *f* raincoat

gabinete *m* **1.** (*estudio*) study; (*de médico, abogado*) office; ~ **de prensa** press office **2.** POL cabinet

Gabón *m* Gabon

gabonés, -esa *adj, m, f* Gabonese

gaceta *f* newspaper, gazette

gaditano, -a *adj* of/from Cadiz

gafar *vt inf* to jinx

gafas *fpl* glasses *pl;* ~**s de bucear** diving mask

gafe *m* jinx

gaita *f* bagpipes *pl*

gajes *mpl* ~ **de oficio** occupational hazards

gajo *m* (*de naranja, limón*) segment; (*racimo*) bunch

gala *f* **1.** (*fiesta*) gala; **hacer** ~ **de algo** to take pride in sth **2.** *pl* (*vestido*) finery

galaico, -a *adj* Galician

galán *m* handsome man

galante *adj* gallant

galantear *vt* to woo

galápago *m* turtle

galardón *m* prize

galardonar *vt* to award a prize to; ~ **a alguien con un título** to confer a title on sb

galaxia *f* galaxy

galera *f* galley

galería *f* gallery

galés, -esa I. *adj* Welsh **II.** *m, f* Welshman, Welshwoman *m, f*

Gales *m* (**el País de**) ~ Wales

galgo, -a *m, f* greyhound

Galicia *f* Galicia
galimatías *m inv* **1.**(*lenguaje*) gibberish **2.**(*enredo*) jumble
gallardía *f* poise
gallego, -a *adj, m, f* Galician
galleta *f* biscuit *Brit,* cookie *Am*
gallina *f* hen; ~ **clueca** brooding hen; **acostarse/levantarse con las ~s** to go to bed/to get up very early; **jugar a la ~ ciega** to play blind man's buff
gallinero *m* chicken coop
gallo *m* **1.**(*ave*) cock, rooster *Am;* **en menos que canta un ~** in an instant **2.**(*pez*) (John) dory
galón *m* **1.**(*cinta*) braid; MIL. stripe, decoration **2.**(*medida*) gallon
galopante *adj* galloping
galopar *vi* to gallop
gama *f* **1.**(*escala*) range; **una ~ amplia/reducida de productos** a wide/narrow range of products **2.** MÚS scale
gamba *f* prawn, shrimp
gamberrada *f* act of hooliganism; **hacer ~s** to horse around *inf*
gamberro, -a *m, f* hooligan, yobbo *inf*
gamuza *f* **1.**(*animal*) chamois **2.**(*piel*) chamois leather **3.**(*paño*) duster
gana *f* desire; **de buena/mala ~** willingly/unwillingly; **tener ~s de hacer algo** to feel like doing sth; **me quedé con las ~s de verlo** I wish I'd been able to see him; **no me da la (real) ~** *inf* I can't be bothered; **este es feo con ~s** *inf* he's bloody ugly
ganadería *f* **1.**(*ganado*) livestock *pl* **2.**(*crianza*) livestock farming
ganadero, -a **I.** *adj* livestock **II.** *m, f* farmer
ganado *m* livestock *pl;* **~ bovino** [*o* **vacuno**] cattle *pl;* **~ cabrío** goats *pl;* **~ ovino** sheep *pl;* **~ porcino** pigs *pl*
ganador(a) **I.** *adj* winning **II.** *m(f)* winner
ganancia *f* profit
ganar **I.** *vi* **1.**(*vencer*) to win **2.**(*mejorar*) ~ **en algo** to improve at sth;

con esto sólo puedes salir ganando you can't lose with this; **no gana para sustos** with him/her it is one thing after another **II.** *vt* **1.**(*vencer: persona*) to beat **2.**(*trabajando*) to earn; **con ese negocio consiguió ~ mucho dinero** he/she made a lot of money out of that business **3.**(*jugando*) win; **le he ganado 30 euros** I won 30 euros from him/her **4.**(*adquirir*) to gain; (*libertad*) to win; ~ **peso** to put on weight; **¿qué esperas ~ con esto?** what do you hope to gain by that? **5.**(*aventajar*) ~ **a alguien en algo** to be better than sb at sth **III.** *vr:* ~**se 1.**(*dinero*) to earn; **¡te la vas a ~!** *inf* you're for it **2.**(*a alguien*) to win over
ganchillo *m* **1.**(*gancho*) hook **2.**(*labor*) crochet; **hacer ~** to crochet
gancho *m* **1.**(*instrumento*) hook **2.**(*atractivo*) **tener ~** to be attractive
gandul(a) **I.** *adj* lazy **II.** *m(f)* layabout
ganga *f* bargain
gangrena *f* gangrene
gansada *f inf* silly thing; **decir ~s** to talk nonsense; **hacer ~s** to clown about
ganso, -a *m, f* **1.**(*ave: hembra*) goose; (*macho*) gander **2.** *inf* (*estúpido*) **hacer el ~** to clown about
Gante *m* Ghent
ganzúa[1] *f* (*llave*) picklock
ganzúa[2] *mf* (*ladrón*) burglar
garabatear *vt, vi* to scribble
garabato *m* scribble
garaje *m* garage
garante *mf* guarantor
garantía *f* guarantee
garantizar <z→c> *vt* to guarantee

? **garapiña** (or **garrapiña**) is a refreshing Latin American drink, which is prepared from pineapple rinds, water and milk.

garbanzo *m* chickpea; **ganarse los ~s** *inf* to earn one's living
garbo *m* elegance; (*de movimiento*) grace(fulness)

G g

garete *m* **ir(se) al ~** *inf* to go down the tubes
garfio *m* hook
garganta *f* **1.** (*gaznate*) throat; (*cuello*) neck; **tener buena ~** to have a good voice **2.** GEO gorge, ravine
gargantilla *f* necklace
gárgaras *fpl* gargles *pl;* **hacer ~** to gargle; **¡vete a hacer ~!** *inf* get lost!
garita *f* **1.** (*de centinelas*) sentry box **2.** (*de portero*) lodge
garito *m* gambling den
garra *f* **1.** (*de animal*) claw; **caer en las ~s de alguien** to fall into sb's clutches **2.** *pey* (*mano*) paw **3.** *inf* (*brío*) **tener ~** to be compelling; **este equipo tiene ~** this team has real class
garrafa *f* carafe
garrapata *f* tick
garrote *m* **1.** (*palo*) stick **2.** (*ligadura*) tourniquet **3.** (*de ejecución*) ~ (**vil**) garotte
garza *f* heron
gas *m* **1.** (*fluido*) gas; **agua con/sin ~** carbonated/still water; **bombona de ~** gas cylinder; **cocina de ~** gas cooker *Brit* [*o* stove *Am*] **2.** *inf* AUTO **dar ~** to accelerate; **ir a todo ~** to go at full speed **3.** *pl* (*en el estómago*) wind
gasa *f* gauze
gascón, -ona I. *adj* from Gascony **II.** *m, f* Gascon
gaseosa *f* lemonade, soda
gaseoso, -a *adj* fizzy
gasoil *m*, **gasóleo** *m* diesel
gasolina *f* petrol *Brit,* gas(oline) *Am;* ~ **sin plomo** unleaded petrol *Brit* [*o* gasoline *Am*]; ~ **súper** three-star petrol *Brit* [*o* gasoline *Am*]; **echar ~** to fill up with petrol *Brit* [*o* gasoline *Am*]
gasolinera *f* petrol station *Brit,* gas station *Am*
gastado, -a *adj* (*vestido, zapato*) worn out; (*talón*) worn down; (*suelo*) worn; (*neumático*) bare; (*expresión*) hackneyed
gastar I. *vt* **1.** (*dinero, tiempo*) to spend **2.** (*desgastar*) to wear out

3. (*usar*) use; **¿qué talla/número gastas?** what size are you? **II.** *vr:* ~**se 1.** (*dinero*) to spend **2.** (*desgastarse*) to wear out **3.** (*consumirse*) to run out
Gasteiz *m* Vitoria
gasto *m* *pl* (*de dinero*) spending; (*costes*) costs *pl;* ECON, COM (*desembolso*) expenditure; (*costos adicionales*) expenses *pl;* ~**s adicionales** extra charges; ~**s corrientes** running costs; ~**s generales** overhead (expenses); ~**s pagados** all expenses paid
gastronomía *f sin pl* gastronomy
gata *f* (she-)cat
gatas andar a ~ to crawl
gatear *vi* to crawl
gatillo *m* trigger; **apretar el ~** to pull the trigger
gato *m* **1.** (*félido*) cat; (*macho*) tomcat; **dar ~ por liebre a alguien** *inf* to rip sb off; **llevarse el ~ al agua** *inf* to bring it off; **cuando el ~ no está los ratones bailan** when the cat's away, the mice will play; **éramos cuatro ~s** *inf* there was hardly anyone else there; **aquí hay ~ encerrado** *inf* there's something fishy going on here; ~ **escaldado del agua fría huye** *prov* once bitten twice shy; **de noche todos los ~s son pardos** all cats are grey in the night **2.** (*de coche*) jack
gaucho *m AmL* gaucho

[?] **Gauchos** were the cattle drovers or "cowboys" of the South American **Pampa**.

gaveta *f* drawer
gaviota *f* (sea)gull
gay *adj, m* gay
gazapo *m* young rabbit
gazpacho *m* gazpacho

[?] **Gazpacho**, a cold vegetable soup made from **tomates** (tomatoes), **pepinos** (cucumbers), **pimientos** (peppers), **aceite de oliva** (olive oil) and a little **pan** (bread), is prepared in summer, especially in the south of Spain, in **Andalucía** and **Extremadura**.

GB *m* **1.** *abr de* **gigabyte** GB **2.** *abr de* **Gran Bretaña** GB
gel *m* gel
gelatina *f* gelatine, gelatin *Am*
gema *f* gem, jewel
gemelo, -a *adj, m, f* twin; **hermanos ~s** twin brothers
gemelos *mpl* **1.** (*prismáticos*) binoculars *pl;* **~ de teatro** opera glasses **2.** (*de la camisa*) cufflinks *pl*
gemido *m* (*de dolor*) groan; (*de pena*) moan
Géminis *m inv* Gemini
gemir *irr como pedir vi* (*de dolor*) to groan; (*de pena*) to moan
gen *m* gene
generación *f* generation
general **I.** *adj* (*universal*) general; **cultura ~** general knowledge; **por regla ~** as a (general) rule; **de uso ~** (*para todo uso*) multi-purpose, all--purpose; (*para todo el mundo*) for general use; **en ~, por lo ~** in general, generally; **en ~ me siento satisfecho** overall, I'm satisfied; **en ~ hace mejor tiempo aquí** generally speaking, the weather is better here **II.** *m* general; **~ en jefe** supreme commander
generalizar <z→c> *vi* to generalize
generalmente *adv* generally
generar *vt* to generate
género *m* **1.** BIO genus; **~ humano** mankind, human race **2.** (*clase*) type, sort; **sin ningún ~ de dudas** without a shadow of a doubt; **tomar todo ~ de precauciones** to take every possible precaution **3.** LING gender **4.** LIT, ARTE genre; **el ~ narrativo** fiction **5.** (*mercancía*) merchandise; (*tela*) cloth; **~s de punto** knitwear
generosidad *f* generosity
generoso, -a *adj* generous; **ser ~ con alguien** to be generous to sb
genética *f sin pl* BIO genetics
genético, -a *adj* genetic

genial *adj* brilliant
genio *m* **1.** (*carácter*) character; **tener mal ~** to be bad-tempered; **tener mucho ~** to be very temperamental **2.** (*talento*) genius
genital *adj* genital
genitales *mpl* genitals *pl*
Génova *f* Genoa
gente *f* **1.** (*personas*) people *pl;* **la ~ joven/mayor** young/old people; **~ menuda** (*niños*) children; **tener don de ~s** to have a way with people; **¿qué dirá la ~?** what will people say? **2.** *inf* (*parentela*) family; **¿qué tal tu ~?** how are your folks?

! **gente** is used with a singular verb: "La gente está inquieta."

---

gentil *adj* kind
gentileza *f* kindness; **¿tendría Ud. la ~ de ayudarme?** would you be so kind as to help me?
gentío *m sin pl* crowd
genuino, -a *adj* genuine
geografía *f sin pl* geography
geográfico, -a *adj* geographical
geología *f sin pl* geology
geometría *f sin pl* geometry
Georgia *f* Georgia
georgiano, -a *adj, m, f* Georgian
geranio *m* geranium
gerencia *f* management
gerente *mf* manager
geriatría *f sin pl* geriatrics *pl*
geriátrico, -a *adj* geriatric
germen *m* germ; **~ de trigo** wheatgerm
germinar *vi* **1.** BOT to germinate **2.** (*sospechas*) **~ en** to give rise to
gerundense *adj* of/from Gerona
gerundio *m* gerund
gestación *f* gestation
gesticulación *f* gesticulation
gesticular *vi* to gesticulate
gestión *f* **1.** (*diligencia*) measure; **hacer gestiones** to take measures **2.** (*de una empresa*) *t.* INFOR management; **~ de ficheros** file management
gestionar *vt* **1.** (*asunto*) to conduct

2. (*negocio*) to manage
gesto *m* **1.** (*con la mano*) gesture; (*con el rostro*) expression; (*con el cuerpo*) movement; **torcer el ~** to scowl **2.** (*acto*) gesture
gestoría *f* agency handling official matters
ghanés, -esa *adj, m, f* Ghanese
Gibraltar *m* Gibraltar
gibraltareño, -a *adj, m, f* Gibraltarian
gigante *adj, m* giant
gilipollas *mf inv, vulg* jerk, wanker
gilipollez *f vulg* bullshit; **decir gilipolleces** to talk rubbish
gimnasia *f* **1.** DEP gymnastics *pl;* **~ rítmica** rhythm gymnastics; **hacer ~** to do gymnastics **2.** (*ejercicio*) **hacer ~** to do exercises **3.** ENS gym
gimnasio *m* gymnasium
gimnasta *mf* gymnast
gimotear *vi* **1.** (*gemir*) to groan **2.** (*lloriquear*) to whimper, to whine
ginebra *f* gin
Ginebra *f* Geneva
ginebrino, -a *adj* of/from Geneva
ginecología *f sin pl* gynaecology *Brit,* gynecology *Am*
ginecólogo, -a *m, f* gynaecologist *Brit,* gynecologist *Am*
gira *f* **1.** (*de un artista*) tour; **estar de ~** to be on tour **2.** (*de un día*) (day)trip, excursion; (*más larga*) tour
girar I. *vi* **1.** (*dar vueltas*) to revolve; (*con rapidez*) to spin **2.** (*conversación*) **~ en torno a algo** to revolve around sth **3.** (*torcer*) to turn II. *vt* **1.** (*dar la vuelta*) to turn; **~ la vista** to look round **2.** (*dinero*) to send
giratorio, -a *adj* revolving
giro *m* **1.** (*vuelta, cariz*) turn; **un ~ de volante** a turn of the steering wheel; **tomar un ~ favorable/ negativo** to take a turn for the better/worse; **me preocupa el ~ que toma este asunto** I don't like the way this issue is developing **2.** LING expression **3.** FIN draft; **~ postal** money order
gitano, -a *adj, m, f* gipsy *Brit,* gypsy *Am;* **brazo de ~** GASTR Swiss roll *Brit,* jelly roll *Am*

glacial *adj* icy cold; **zona ~** polar region
glaciar *m* glacier
glándula *f* gland
global *adj* **1.** (*total*) overall **2.** (*cantidad*) total **3.** (*informe*) comprehensive **4.** (*mundial*) global
globo *m* **1.** (*esfera*) sphere; **~ de una lámpara** (round) lampshade; **~ ocular** eyeball **2.** (*tierra, mapa*) globe **3.** (*para niños*) balloon; **~** (*aerostático*) hot-air balloon
glóbulo *m* ANAT corpuscle
gloria *f* **1.** (*fama, esplendor*) glory **2.** (*paraíso*) heaven; **conseguir la ~** to go to heaven; **estar en la ~** *inf* to be in seventh heaven; **oler/saber a ~** to smell/taste delicious
glorieta *f* **1.** (*plazoleta*) (small) square **2.** (*rotonda*) roundabout **3.** (*cenador*) arbour *Brit,* arbor *Am*
glorificar <c→qu> *vt* to glorify
glorioso, -a *adj* glorious
glosa *f* **1.** **~ a algo** (*aclaración*) explanation on sth; (*anotación*) note on sth; (*comentario*) comment on sth **2.** LIT gloss
glosar *vt* **1.** (*anotar*) to annotate **2.** LIT to gloss; (*comentar*) to comment on
glosario *m* glossary
glotón, -ona I. *adj* gluttonous, greedy II. *m, f* glutton, gannet *inf*
gobernación *f* government
gobernador(a) I. *adj* governing II. *m(f)* governor
gobernante *mf* ruler
gobernar <e→ie> *vt* **1.** POL to govern **2.** (*dirigir*) to manage; (*nave*) to steer; **~ una casa** to run a household
gobierno *m* government; (*ministros*) cabinet; **~ autonómico** regional government; **~ en la sombra** shadow cabinet
goce *m* pleasure, enjoyment
gol *m* goal; **~ del empate** equalizer; **meter un ~** to score (a goal)
golf *m sin pl* golf
golfa *f inf* slut
golfo *m* **1.** GEO gulf **2.** (*persona*) rogue
golondrina *f* swallow

golosina *f* sweet *Brit,* candy *Am*
goloso, -a I. *adj* sweet-toothed II. *m, f* **ser un** ~ to have a sweet tooth
golpe *m* *t. fig* (*impacto*) blow; (*choque*) bump; (*puñetazo*) punch; (*ruido*) bang; ~ **de Estado** coup (d'état); **un** ~ **de tos** a fit of coughing; **al primer** ~ **de vista** at a glance; **de** ~ (**y porrazo**) (*al mismo tiempo*) at the same time; (*de repente*) suddenly; **abrirse de** ~ to fly open; **andar a** ~**s** to be always fighting; **cerrar la puerta de** ~ to slam the door shut; **me he dado un** ~ **en la cabeza** I've banged my head; **me lo tragué de un** ~ I downed it in one go; **no pegó ni** ~ *inf* he didn't lift a finger
golpear *vt* to hit; (*puerta*) to knock on
golpista *mf* participant in a coup (d'état)
goma *f* 1. (*sustancia*) rubber; ~ **de borrar** rubber *Brit,* eraser *Am;* ~ **elástica** (*sustancia*) rubber; (*objeto*) elastic band; ~ **de pegar** glue 2. *inf* (*preservativo*) condom, johnny *Brit,* rubber *Am*
gomina® *f* hair gel
gordo *m* 1. (*grasa*) fat 2. (*lotería*) **el** ~ the jackpot
gordo, -a I. *adj* 1. (*persona*) fat; (*tejido*) thick 2. *fig* **una mentira gorda** a big lie; **ha pasado algo muy** ~ something serious has happened; **se armó la gorda** *inf* all hell broke loose; **me cae** ~ I don't like him II. *m, f inf* fat man, fat woman *m, f*
gordura *f* 1. (*obesidad*) fatness; (*corpulencia*) corpulence 2. (*tejido adiposo*) fat
gorila *m* 1. (*animal*) gorilla 2. *inf* (*portero*) bouncer 3. *inf* (*guardaespaldas*) bodyguard
gorjear *vi* to twitter
gorra *f* cap; (*para niños*) bonnet; ~ **de visera** peaked cap *Brit,* baseball cap *Am;* **de** ~ *inf* (*gratis*) free; **andar** [*o* **vivir**] **de** ~ *inf* to sponge
gorrión *m* sparrow
gorro *m* hat; (*de uniforme*) cap; ~ (**para bebés**) (baby's) bonnet; ~ **de** natación bathing cap; **estar hasta el** ~ **de algo/alguien** to be fed up with sth/sb
gorrón, -ona *m, f inf* scrounger
gorronear *vi inf* to scrounge
gota *f* drop; **café con unas** ~**s de ron** coffee with a dash of rum; **el agua salía** ~ **a** ~ **del grifo** the water dripped out of the tap; **parecerse como dos** ~**s de agua** to be like two peas in a pod; **no tiene ni** (**una**) ~ **de paciencia** he/she doesn't have an ounce of patience; **la** ~ **que colma el vaso** the last straw
gotear I. *vi* 1. (*líquido*) to drip; (*escurrir*) trickle 2. (*salirse*) to leak II. *vimpers* **está goteando** it's drizzling, it's spitting (with rain) *Brit*
gotera *f* 1. (*filtración, grieta*) leak 2. (*mancha*) stain
gótico, -a *adj* Gothic
gozar <z→c> *vi* to enjoy oneself; ~ **de algo** to enjoy sth; ~ **de una increíble fortuna** to be incredibly wealthy
gozne *m* hinge
gozo *m* (*delicia*) delight; (*placer*) pleasure; (*alegría*) joy
grabación *f* 1. (*de disco*) recording 2. INFOR saving
grabado *m* 1. (*acción*) engraving 2. (*copia*) print; ~ **al agua fuerte** etching; ~ **en madera** woodcut
grabador(a) *m(f)* engraver
grabadora *f* TÉC tape recorder
grabar I. *vt* 1. ARTE to engrave; (*en madera*) to cut 2. (*disco*) to record 3. INFOR to save II. *vr:* ~**se** to become engraved
gracia *f* 1. *pl* (*agradecimiento*) **¡**(**muchas**) ~**s!** thanks (a lot)!; **¡**~**s a Dios!** thank God!; **te debo las** ~**s** I owe you my thanks; **no me ha dado ni las** ~**s** he/she didn't even say "thank you"; ~**s a** thanks to 2. REL grace 3. (*perdón*) mercy 4. (*garbo*) elegance; **está escrito con** ~ it's elegantly written 5. (*chiste*) joke; **no tiene** (**ni**) **pizca de** ~ it's not in the least bit funny; **no me hace nada de** ~ I don't find it funny in the least; **si lo haces se va la** ~ if you do it it

loses its charm; **este cómico tiene poca** ~ this comedian isn't very funny; **la ~ es que...** the funny thing is that ...

gracioso, -a *adj* **1.** (*atractivo*) attractive **2.** (*chistoso*) funny

grada *f* **1.** (*de un estadio*) tier; **las ~s** the terraces **2.** (*peldaño*) step **3.** *pl* (*escalinata*) steps *pl*

gradación *f* gradation

grado *m* **1.** *t.* FÍS, MAT degree; **quemaduras de primer ~** MED first-degree burns; **en ~ sumo** greatly, highly **2.** ENS year; **~ elemental** basic level

graduación *f* **1.** (*regulación*) adjustment **2.** (*en grados*) graduation; (*en niveles, de personas*) grading; (*de precios*) regulation **3.** (*de un vino*) strength; **~ alcohólica** alcohol content **4.** UNIV graduation

gradual *adj* gradual

graduar < *I. pres:* gradúo > **I.** *vt* **1.** (*regular*) to regulate **2.** TÉC to graduate; **~ la vista a alguien** to test sb's eyesight **3.** (*en niveles*) to classify; (*precios*) to regulate **4.** UNIV to confer a degree on **II.** *vr:* **~se** to graduate

gráfica *f* graph

gráfico *m* graph; **~ de tarta** pie chart; **tarjeta de ~s** INFOR graphics card

gráfico, -a *adj* graphic; (*de la escritura*) written; **diccionario ~** visual dictionary

grajo *m* rook

gral. *abr de* **general** gen.

gramática *f* grammar

gramático, -a *m, f* grammarian

gramo *m* gramme *Brit*, gram *Am*

gran *adj v.* **grande**

grana *adj* scarlet

granada *f* **1.** (*fruto*) pomegranate **2.** (*proyectil: de mano*) grenade; (*de artillería*) shell

granadino, -a *adj* of/from Granada

granate *adj* burgundy

Gran Bretaña *f* Great Britain

grancanario, -a *adj* of/from Grand Canary

grande *adj* <más grande *o* mayor, grandísimo> (*precediendo un sustantivo singular:* gran) big; (*en número, cantidad*) large; (*moralmente*) great; **una habitación ~** a large room; **un gran hombre/una gran idea** a great man/idea; **una gran suma de dinero** a large sum of money; **gran velocidad** high speed; **ir ~ a alguien** *fig* to be too much for sb; **pasarlo en ~** to have a great time; **vivir a lo ~** to live in style; **vino gran cantidad de gente** a lot of people came; **tengo un gran interés por...** I'm very interested in ...; **no me preocupa gran cosa** I'm not very worried about it

> ⚠ **grande** is used after a noun and emphasizes the size of something/someone: "un restaurante grande; una fiesta grande"; **gran** (= of standing, important) is used before a noun and stresses the quality of someone/something: "un gran restaurante; una gran fiesta".

grandeza *f* greatness

grandioso, -a *adj* impressive

granel *m* **carga a ~** bulk order; **a ~** (*sin envase*) loose; (*líquido*) by volume; (*en abundancia*) in abundance

granero *m* granary; (*de granja*) barn

granito *m* granite

granizado *m* iced drink; **~ de café** ≈ iced coffee

granizar <z→c> *vimpers* to hail

granizo *m* hail

granja *f* farm

granjearse *vr* (*respeto*) to earn

granjero, -a *m, f* farmer

grano *m* **1.** (*de cereales, sal, arena*) *t.* TÉC grain; **~s** grain; **~ de café** coffe bean; **de ~ duro** coarse-grained; **de ~ fino** fine-grained; **apartar el ~ de la paja** *t. fig* to separate the wheat from the chaff; **aportó su ~ de arena** he/she did his/her bit; **ir al ~** to get to the point **2.** (*en piel*) spot

granuja *m* **1.** (*pilluelo*) rascal **2.** (*bribón*) scoundrel

grapa *f* staple

grapadora *f* stapler
grasa *f* **1.** (*animal, vegetal*) fat; **tener mucha ~ en los muslos** to have fat thighs **2.** (*lubricante*) oil, grease
grasiento, -a *adj* fatty; (*de aceite*) greasy
graso, -a *adj* fatty; **piel grasa** oily skin; **pelo graso** greasy hair
gratificación *f* **1.** (*recompensa*) reward **2.** (*del sueldo*) bonus **3.** (*propina*) tip
gratificar <c→qu> *vt* **1.** (*recompensar*) ~ **a alguien por algo** to reward sb for sth; **se ~á a quien lo encuentre** there is a reward for the finder **2.** (*en el trabajo*) ~ **a alguien** to give sb a bonus
gratinar *vt* to cook au gratin, to brown on top
gratis *adv* free
gratitud *f* gratitude
grato, -a *adj* pleasant; ~ **al paladar** tasty; **tu novio me ha causado una grata impresión** your boyfriend seems very nice; **tu visita me es muy grata** I'm very glad you could come; **me es ~ comunicarle que...** I am pleased to inform you that ...
gratuito, -a *adj* **1.** (*gratis*) free **2.** (*infundado*) groundless; **este rumor es** ~ this rumour is without foundation; **lo que has hecho ha sido bastante** ~ what you did was quite unnecessary
grava *f* gravel
gravamen *m* **1.** (*carga*) burden **2.** (*impuesto*) tax
gravar *vt* **1.** (*cargar*) to burden **2.** FIN to tax; ~ **algo con un impuesto** to impose a tax on sth
grave *adj* (*enfermedad, situación*) serious; **está** ~ he/she is very ill; **este es un momento ~ para la industria** this is a difficult time for the industry
gravedad *f* **1.** FÍS gravity **2.** (*de una situación*) seriousness
gravilla *f* gravel
gravitar *vi* FÍS to gravitate; ~ **sobre algo** (*cuerpo*) to rest on sth
gravoso, -a *adj* **1.** (*pesado*) burden-

some **2.** (*costoso*) expensive
graznar *vi* (*cuervo*) to caw; (*ganso*) to honk; (*pato*) to quack
Grecia *f* Greece
gremio *m* association, guild
greña *f* mop of hair, rats' tails *pl;* **andar a la ~ con alguien** to squabble with sb
gresca *f* **1.** (*bulla*) uproar, racket **2.** (*riña*) quarrel
griego, -a *adj, m, f* Greek
grieta *f* **1.** (*en la pared, una taza*) crack; (*en la piel*) chap **2.** (*desacuerdo*) rift
grifo *m* **1.** TÉC tap *Brit,* faucet *Am;* **agua del ~** tap water; **abrir/cerrar el ~** to turn the tap on/off; **he dejado el ~ abierto** I've left the tap running **2.** *Perú, Ecua, Bol* (*gasolinera*) petrol station *Brit,* gas station *Am*
grillete *m* shackle, fetter
grillo *m* **1.** ZOOL cricket **2.** *pl* (*grilletes*) shackles *pl*
grima *f* **me da** ~ it's disgusting
gripe *f* flu, influenza
gris *adj* grey *Brit,* gray *Am*
gritar **I.** *vt* to shout at **II.** *vi* to shout, to yell
grito *m* shout; ~ **de protesta** cry of protest; **a** ~ **limpio** [*o* pelado] at the top of one's voice; **pedir algo a ~s** to be crying out for sth; **pegar un ~** to shout, to yell; **poner el ~ en el cielo por algo** to raise hell about sth; **ser el último** ~ to be the (latest) rage; **me lo dijo a ~s** he/she told me in a very loud voice
groenlandés, -esa **I.** *adj* Greenland **II.** *m, f* Greenlander
Groenlandia *f* Greenland
grosella *f* (red)currant
grosería *f* **1.** (*descortesía, ordinariez*) rudeness **2.** (*tosquedad*) crudeness **3.** (*observación*) rude comment; (*palabrota*) swearword
grosero, -a *adj* **1.** (*descortés, ordinario*) rude **2.** (*tosco*) crude
grosor *m* thickness
grotesco, -a *adj* grotesque
grúa *f* **1.** (*máquina*) crane **2.** (*vehículo*) tow truck, breakdown van *Brit,* wrecker *Am*

G
g

grueso *m* **1.** (*espesor*) thickness **2.** (*parte principal*) main part

grueso, -a *adj* **1.** (*objeto*) thick **2.** (*persona*) stout

grulla *f* crane

grumo *m* lump; ~ **de sangre** blood clot

gruñido *m* grunt; (*del perro*) growl; *fig* (*queja*) grumble

gruñir <*3. pret:* gruñó> *vi* to grunt; (*perro*) to growl; *fig* (*quejarse*) to grumble

grupa *f* hindquarters *pl*

grupo *m* **1.** (*conjunto*) group; ~ (**industrial**) corporation; ~ **principal** INFOR main group; **trabajo en** ~ groupwork **2.** TÉC unit

gruta *f* (*natural*) cave; (*artificial*) grotto

guadalajareño, -a *adj* of/from Guadalajara

guadaña *f* scythe

guagua *f* AmC (*autobús*) bus

guante *m* glove; **colgar los** ~**s** (*boxeador*) to hang up one's gloves; (*futbolista*) to hang up one's boots; **echar el** ~ **a alguien** to catch sb; **ir** [*o* **sentar**] **como un** ~ to fit like a glove; **recoger el** ~ to take up the challenge

guapo *m* **1.** (*galán*) handsome man **2.** AmL, pey (*pendenciero*) bully

guapo, -a *adj* good-looking; (*mujer*) pretty; (*hombre*) handsome; **estar** [*o* **ir**] ~ to look smart

guarda¹ *mf* guard; (*cuidador*) custodian, keeper; ~ **forestal** forester *Brit,* forest ranger *Am;* ~ **jurado** security guard

guarda² *f* **1.** (*acto*) guarding, safekeeping; (*protección*) protection **2.** (*de un libro*) flyleaf

guardabarros *m inv* wing *Brit,* fender *Am*

guardabosque(s) *mf* (*inv*) **1.** (*de caza*) gamekeeper **2.** (*guarda forestal*) forester *Brit,* forest ranger *Am*

guardacostas *m inv* coastguard

guardaespaldas *mf inv* bodyguard

guardameta *mf* goalkeeper

guardapolvo *m* overalls *pl*

guardar *vt* **1.** (*vigilar*) to guard; (*proteger*) to protect **2.** (*ley*) to observe **3.** (*conservar, poner*) to keep; ~ **algo en el bolsillo** to put sth in one's pocket; **guárdame un trozo de pastel** save a piece of cake for me; **guárdame esto** keep this for me; **¿dónde has guardado las servilletas?** where did you put the serviettes? **4.** INFOR to save

guardarropa *m* **1.** (*cuarto*) cloakroom *Brit,* checkroom *Am* **2.** (*armario*) wardrobe

guardería *f* nursery

guardia¹ *f* **1.** (*vigilancia*) duty; **estar de** ~ to be on duty; MIL to be on guard duty; **¿cuál es la farmacia de** ~**?** which chemist is on the emergency rota? *Brit,* which pharmacy is open 24 hours? *Am* **2.** (*cuerpo armado*) **la Guardia Civil** the Civil Guard; ~ **municipal** [*o* **urbana**] local police

guardia² *mf* ~ **civil** civil guard; ~ **municipal** [*o* **urbano**] local policeman; ~ **de tráfico** traffic policeman *m,* traffic policewoman *f*

guardián, -ana *m, f* guardian; (*en el zoo*) (zoo)keeper; **perro** ~ watchdog

guarecer *irr como crecer* **I.** *vt* **1.** (*proteger*) to protect **2.** (*albergar*) to shelter; **lo guarecí en mi casa** I took him in **II.** *vr:* ~**se** (*cobijarse*) to take refuge; ~ **de la lluvia** to take shelter from the rain

guarida *f* **1.** (*de animales*) den, lair **2.** (*de ladrones*) hideout

guarnecer *irr como crecer vt* ~ **algo con** [*o* **de**] **algo** to adorn sth with sth; GASTR to garnish sth with sth; (*vestido*) to trim sth with sth

guarnición *f* **1.** GASTR garnish; **chuletas de cordero con** ~ **de patatas y ensalada** lamb chops served with salad and potatoes **2.** (*adorno*) adornment; (*en un vestido*) trimming

guarrada *f,* **guarrería** *f inf* **1.** (*mala pasada*) dirty trick **2.** (*palabras*) swear word(s) **3.** (*asquerosidad*) **ser una** ~ (*sucio*) to be filthy; (*asqueroso*) to be disgusting

guarro, -a I. *adj* 1. (*cosa*) disgusting; **chiste** ~ dirty joke 2. (*persona*) dirty; (*moralmente*) smutty II. *m, f* pig

guasa *f* joke; **estar de** ~ to be joking; **tiene** ~ **que...** +*subj* it's ironic that ...

guasón, -ona *m, f* joker

Guatemala *f* Guatemala

> [?] **Guatemala** (official title: **República de Guatemala**) lies in Central America. The capital is also called **Guatemala**. The official language of the country is Spanish and the monetary unit of **Guatemala** is the **quezal**.

guatemalteco, -a *adj, m, f* Guatemalan

guay *adj inf* great, cool

Guayana *f* Guyana

guayanés, -esa *adj, m, f* Guyanese

gubernamental *adj* governmental

gubernativo, -a *adj* governmental; **policía gubernativa** national police

güero, -a *adj, m, f AmL* blond(e)

guerra *f* war; **la** ~ **civil española** the Spanish Civil War; **guerra química/psicológica** chemical/psychological warfare; **la Segunda Guerra Mundial** the Second World War; **en** ~ at war; **dar mucha** ~ *inf* to be a real handful; **ir a la** ~ to go to war; **tener la** ~ **declarada a alguien** *fig* to have it in for sb

guerrear *vi* to wage war

guerrero, -a I. *adj* warlike II. *m, f* warrior

guerrilla *f* 1. (*guerra*) guerrilla warfare 2. (*partida*) guerrilla band

guerrillero, -a *m, f* guerrilla (fighter)

gueto *m* ghetto

guía¹ *mf* (*persona*) guide; ~ **turístico** tourist guide

guía² *f* 1. (*pauta*) guidance, guideline 2. (*manual*) handbook; ~ **comercial** trade directory; ~ **de ferrocarriles** railway timetable; ~ **telefónica** telephone directory, phone book *Am*; ~

turística travel guide(book)

guiar <*1. pres:* guío> I. *vt* 1. (*a alguien*) to guide 2. (*conversación*) to direct II. *vr* ~**se por algo** to be guided by sth; **me guío por mis instinto** I follow my instincts

guijarro *m* pebble

guillotina *f* guillotine; **ventana de** ~ sash window

guinda *f* morello cherry

guindilla *f* chilli pepper *Brit,* chili pepper *Am*

guiñapo *m* 1. (*trapo*) rag 2. (*andrajoso*) **estar hecho un** ~ to be a wreck

guiñar *vt, vi* to wink; ~ **el ojo a alguien** to wink at sb

guiño *m* wink; **hacer un** ~ **a alguien** to wink at sb

guión *m* 1. CINE, TV script 2. (*de una conferencia*) outline 3. LING hyphen; (*en diálogo*) dash

guionista *mf* CINE screenwriter; TV scriptwriter

guipuzcoano, -a *adj* of/from Guipuzcoa

guiri *mf pey, inf* foreigner

guirnalda *f* garland

guisa *f* a ~ **de** like; **de tal** ~ in such a way; **no puedes hacerlo de esta** ~ you can't do it like that

guisado *m* stew

guisante *m* pea

guisar *vt* 1. (*cocinar*) to cook 2. (*tramar*) to prepare

guiso *m* dish; (*en salsa*) stew

guitarra *f* guitar

guitarrista *mf* guitarist

gula *f* gluttony

gusano *m* 1. (*lombriz*) worm; ~ **de luz** glow-worm 2. (*oruga*) caterpillar 3. (*larva de mosca*) maggot

gustar I. *vi* 1. (*agradar*) **me gusta nadar/el helado** I like swimming/ice cream; **¿te gusta estar aquí?** do you like it here?; **¡así me gusta!** well done! 2. (*ser aficionado*) ~ **de hacer algo** to enjoy doing sth 3. (*atraer*) **me gusta tu hermano** I fancy your brother 4. (*querer*) **me gustas** I like you 5. (*condicional*) **me** ~**ía saber...** I would like to know ... **II.** *vt* to taste

⚠️ The verb **gustar** is used only in two persons, the third person singular and the third person plural, according to its grammatical subject. It is always used with the definite article when the subject is a noun: "Me gusta mucho el chocolate; A Mario no le gustan los niños." It can also be used with a verb in the infinitive: "A Beatriz le gusta bailar el tango."

gusto *m* **1.** (*sentido*) taste; **una broma de mal** ~ a joke in bad taste; **no hago nada a tu** ~ nothing I do pleases you; **lo ha hecho a mi** ~ he/she did it to my satisfaction; **sobre ~s no hay nada escrito** there's no accounting for tastes **2.** (*sabor*) taste, flavour *Brit,* flavor *Am;* **tener** ~ **a algo** to taste of sth; **huevos al** ~ eggs cooked to order **3.** (*placer*) pleasure; **con** ~ with pleasure; **coger** ~ **a algo** to take a liking to sth; **estar a** ~ to feel comfortable; **tanto** ~ **en conocerla – el** ~ **es mío** pleased to meet you – the pleasure is all mine; **cantan que da** ~ they sing wonderfully
gutural *adj* guttural, throaty

Hh

H, h *f* H, h; ~ **de Huelva** H for Harry *Brit,* H for How *Am*
haba *f* broad bean; **son ~s contadas** there's no doubt about it; **en todas partes cuecen ~s** *prov* it's the same the world over
Habana *f* **la** ~ Havana
habanero, -a *adj, m, f* Havanan

habano *m* Havana cigar
haber *irr* **I.** *aux* **1.** (*en tiempos compuestos*) to have; **he comprado el periódico** I've bought the newspaper **2.** (*de obligación*) ~ **de hacer algo** to have to do sth; **has 'de hacerlo** (*sin falta*) you must do it **3.** (*futuro*) **han de llegar pronto** they will be here soon **4.** (*imperativo*) **¡~ venido antes!** you should have come earlier! **II.** *vimpers* **1.** (*ocurrir*) **ha habido un terremoto en Japón** there has been an earthquake in Japan; **¿qué hay?** what's the news?; **¿qué hay, Pepe?** how's it going, Pepe? **2.** (*efectuarse*) **hoy no hay cine** the cinema is closed today; **ayer hubo reunión** there was a meeting yesterday **3.** (*existir*) **aquí no hay agua** there is no water here; **eso es todo... ¡y ya no hay más!** that's all ... and nothing more!; **¿hay algo entre tú y ella?** is there something going on between you two?; **hay poca gente que...** there are few people who ...; **hay quien cree que...** some people think that ...; **¡muchas gracias! – no hay de qué** thanks a lot! – not at all; **no hay quien me gane al ping-pong** nobody can beat me at table tennis **4.** (*hallarse, estar*) **hay un cuadro en la pared** there is a painting on the wall; **no hay platos en la mesa** there are no plates on the table; **¿había mucha gente?** where there many people? **5.** (*tiempo*) **había una vez...** once there was ... **6.** (*obligatoriedad*) **¡hay que ver cómo están los precios!** my God! look at those prices!; **hay que trabajar más** we have to work harder; **no hay que olvidar que...** we must not forget that ... **III.** *vr* **habérselas con alguien** to be up against sb **IV.** *m* **1.** (*capital*) assets *pl* **2.** (*en cuenta corriente*) balance, account; **pasaré la cantidad a tu** ~ I'll pay the amount into your account

⚠️ **hay** is used for both singular and plural. It can also be used with the indefinite article, with numbers, without the article or with indefinite articles such as 'mucho' and 'poco': "Hay un libro/diez libros de español en la mesa; Hay gente/mucha gente en la calle."

habichuela *f* (kidney) bean; (*judía blanca*) haricot bean

hábil *adj* **1.** (*diestro*) skilled; **ser ~ para algo** to be skilled at sth **2.** (*en el oficio*) **ser ~ en algo** to be good at sth

habilidad *f* **1.** (*destreza*) skill; **no tengo gran ~ con las manos** I'm not very skilful with my hands **2.** (*facultad*) ability

habilitar *vt* JUR to entitle, to empower; (*documentos*) to authorize

habitación *f* room; (*dormitorio*) bedroom

habitante *mf* inhabitant; **¿cuántos habitantes tiene Madrid?** what is the population of Madrid?

habitar I. *vi* to live II. *vt* to live in

hábitat *m* <hábitats> habitat

hábito *m t.* REL habit; **he dejado el ~ de fumar** I gave up smoking; **el ~ no hace al monje** *prov* clothes don't make the man

habitual *adj* regular; **bebedor ~** habitual drinker; **lo dijo con su ironía ~** he said it with his customary irony

habituar <*1. pres:* habitúo> *vt, vr* **~(se) a algo** to get used to sth

habla *f* **1.** (*facultad*) speech, diction; **quedarse sin ~** to be left speechless **2.** (*acto*) speech; (*manera*) way of speaking; **un país de ~ inglesa** an English-speaking country; **¡Juan al ~!** TEL Juan speaking!

hablador(a) I. *adj* talkative II. *m(f)* **1.** (*cotorra*) chatterbox **2.** (*chismoso*) gossip

habladuría *f* rumour *Brit,* rumor *Am;* **~s** gossip

hablante *mf* speaker

hablar I. *vi* **1.** (*decir*) to speak, to talk; **~ alto/bajo** to speak loudly/softly; **~ entre dientes** to mutter; **~**

claro to speak frankly; **por no ~ de...** not to mention ...; **déjeme terminar de ~** let me finish; **el autor no habla de este tema** the author does not address this topic; **la policía le ha hecho ~** the police have made him talk; **los números hablan por sí solos** the figures speak for themselves; **¡no ~ás en serio!** you must be joking!; **¡ni ~!** no way! **2.** (*conversar*) **~ con alguien** to talk to sb; **~ por teléfono** to talk on the telephone; **~ por los codos** *inf* to talk nineteen to the dozen II. *vt* **1.** (*idioma*) to speak **2.** (*decir*) **~ a alguien (de algo/alguien)** to talk to sb (about sth/sb); **no me habló en toda la noche** he/she didn't say a word all night **3.** (*asunto*) **lo ~é con tu padre** I'll talk about it with your father III. *vr* **no se hablan** they are not on speaking terms; **no se habla con su madre** he/she doesn't talk to his/her mother

hacedor(a) *m(f)* maker

hacendado, -a I. *adj* landowning II. *m, f* landowner

hacendoso, -a *adj* hard-working

hacer *irr* I. *vt* **1.** (*producir, crear*) *t.* GASTR to make; (*patatas*) to do; (*textos*) to write; (*construir*) to build; **la casa está hecha de madera** the house is made of wood; **Dios hizo al hombre** God created man; **quiero la carne bien hecha** I want the meat well done **2.** (*realizar*) to do; **~ una llamada** to make a phone call; **a medio ~** half-finished; **¿qué hacemos hoy?** what shall we do today?; **hazlo por mí** do it for me; **lo hecho, hecho está** there's no use crying over spilt milk; **¿qué haces por aquí?** what are you doing round here?; **¡me la has hecho!** you've let me in for it; **la has hecho buena** you've really messed things up; **hicimos la trayectoria en tres horas** we did the journey in three hours **3.** (*pregunta*) to ask; (*observación, discurso*) to make **4.** (*ocasionar: ruido*) to make; (*daño*) to cause; **~**

destrozos to wreak havoc; ~ **sombra** to cast a shadow; **no puedes ~me esto** you can't do this to me **5.** (*procurar*) to make; **¿puedes ~me sitio?** can you fit me in? **6.** (*transformar*) ~ **pedazos algo** to smash sth up; **estás hecho un hombre** you're a man now **7.** (*conseguir: dinero, amigos*) to make **8.** (*limpiar*) ~ **las escaleras** *inf* to do the steps **9.** TEAT ~ **una obra** to do a play; ~ **el papel de Antígona** to play the role of Antigone **10.** ENS to study, to do; **¿haces francés o inglés?** are you doing French or English? **11.** (*más sustantivo*) ~ **el amor** to make love; ~ **caso a alguien** to pay heed to sb; ~ **cumplidos** to pay compliments; ~ **deporte** to do sport; ~ **frente a algo/alguien** to face up to sth/sb; ~ **noche en...** to spend the night in ...; ~ **uso de algo** to make use of sth **12.** (*más verbo*) ~ **creer algo a alguien** to make sb believe sth; ~ **venir a alguien** to make sb come; **hazle pasar** let him in; **no me hagas contarlo** don't make me say it **II.** *vi* **1.** (*convenir*) **eso no hace al caso** that's not relevant **2.** (*oficio*) ~ **de algo** to work as sth **3.** (*con preposición*) **por lo que hace a Juan...** as regards Juan ...; **hizo como que no me vio** he pretended he hadn't seen me **III.** *vr:* **~se 1.** (*volverse*) to become; **~se del Madrid** to become a Madrid supporter **2.** (*simular*) **~se el sueco** to pretend not to hear; **~se la víctima** to act like a victim **3.** (*habituarse*) **~se a algo** to get used to sth **4.** (*dejarse hacer*) **~se una foto** to have one's picture taken **5.** (*conseguir*) **~se respetar** to instill respect; **~se con el poder** to seize power **6.** (*resultar*) to be; **se me hace muy difícil creer eso** it's very difficult for me to believe that **IV.** *vimpers* **1.** (*tiempo*) **hace frío/calor** it is cold/hot; **hoy hace un buen día** it's a nice day today **2.** (*temporal*) **hace tres días** three days ago; **no hace mucho** not long ago; **desde hace un día** since yesterday

hacha *f* axe, hatchet

hachazo *m* stroke of the axe

hachís *m* hashish

hacia *prep* **1.** (*dirección*) towards, to; **el pueblo está más ~ el sur** the village lies further to the south; **fuimos ~ allí** we went that way; **vino ~ mí** he/she came towards me **2.** (*cerca de*) near **3.** (*respecto a*) regarding

hacienda *f* **1.** (*finca*) country estate **2.** FIN, POL ~ **pública** public finance

Hacienda *f* (*ministerio*) the Treasury, the Exchequer *Brit;* (*administración*) the Inland Revenue; **el Ministro de Economía y ~** the Chancellor of the Exchequer; **¿pagas mucho a ~?** do you pay a lot of tax?

hada *f* fairy; **cuento de ~s** fairy tale; ~ **madrina** fairy godmother

Haití *m* Haiti

haitiano, -a *adj, m, f* Haitian

halagar <g→gu> *vt* to flatter

halago *m* **1.** (*acción*) flattery **2.** (*palabras*) flattering words *pl,* compliment

halagüeño, -a *adj* flattering

halcón *m* falcon

hálito *m* breath

hall *m* hall

hallar **I.** *vt* to find; (*sin buscar*) to come across **II.** *vr:* **~se** to be

hallazgo *m* **1.** discovery **2.** *pl* findings *pl*

halógeno *m* halogen

halterofilia *f* weightlifting

hamaca *f* hammock; (*tumbona*) deckchair

hambre *f t. fig* hunger; ~ **de poder** hunger for power; **matar el ~** to kill one's hunger; **morirse de ~** to die of hunger; **tener ~** to be hungry; **a buen ~ no hay pan duro** *prov* hunger is the best sauce; **ser más listo que el ~** to be no fool

hambriento, -a *adj t. fig* hungry; **estar ~ de poder** to be hungry for power

hambruna *f AmL* famine

hamburguesa *f* GASTR hamburger; ~ **con queso** cheeseburger

hampón *m* **1.** (*maleante*) crook

2. (*valentón*) thug
haragán, -ana *m, f* loafer
harapiento, -a *adj* ragged, in tatters
harapo *m* rag
harina *f* flour; ~ **integral** wholemeal flour; **esto es ~ de otro costal** this is a horse of a different colour
hartar *irr* I. *vt* **1.** (*saciar*) ~ **a alguien** to give sb their fill **2.** (*fastidiar*) **me harta con sus chistes** I'm getting sick of his/her jokes II. *vr:* ~**se 1.** (*saciarse*) to eat one's fill; (*en exceso*) to eat too much **2.** (*cansarse*) to get fed up; ~**se de reír** to laugh oneself silly; **me he hartado de este tiempo** I'm sick of this weather
hartazgo *m* glut; **darse un ~** (**de dulces**) to have a binge (on the sweets)
harto, -a I. *adj* **1.** (*repleto*) full; (*en exceso*) too full **2.** (*cansado*) **estar ~ de alguien/algo** to be sick of sb/sth II. *adv* (*sobrado*) (more than) enough; (*muy*) a lot of
hartura *f* (over)abundance
hasta I. *prep* **1.** (*de lugar*) to; **te llevo ~ la estación** I'll give you a lift to the station; **volamos ~ Madrid** we're flying to Madrid; ~ **cierto punto** to a certain degree **2.** (*de tiempo*) until, up to; ~ **ahora** up to now; ~ **el próximo año** up until next year **3.** (*en despedidas*) ¡~ **luego!** see you later!; ¡~ **la vista!** see you again!; ¡~ **la próxima!** until next time! II. *adv* even III. *conj* ~ **cuando come lee el periódico** he/she even reads the newspaper while he's/she's eating; **no consiguió un trabajo fijo ~ que cumplió 40 años** he/she didn't get a steady job until he/she was forty
hastiar <*1. pres:* hastío> I. *vt* to bore II. *vr* ~**se de alguien/algo** to get fed up with sb/sth
hastío *m* boredom; ¡**qué ~!** what a bore!
hatillo *m* belongings *pl;* (*de ropa*) bundle
Hawai *m* Hawaii
hawaiano, -a *adj, m, f* Hawaian
Haya *f* **La ~** the Hague

haz *m* bunch
hazaña *f* feat, exploit
hazmerreír *m inv* laughing stock; **es el ~ de la gente** he's the butt of everyone's jokes
he *1. pres de* **haber**
hebilla *f* buckle
hebra *f* thread
hebreo *m* Hebrew
hebreo, -a *adj, m, f* Hebrew
hechicero, -a *m, f* sorcerer
hechizar <z→c> *vt* to cast a spell on; *fig* to captivate
hechizo *m* spell
hecho *m* **1.** (*circunstancia*) fact; **de ~** in fact **2.** (*acto*) action, deed; ~ **delictivo** criminal act **3.** (*suceso*) event; JUR deed; **lugar de los ~s** scene of the crime
hecho, -a *adj* **1.** (*cocido*) cooked; **me gusta la carne hecha** I like meat well done; **el pollo está demasiado ~** the chicken is overcooked **2.** (*acabado*) finished; **frase hecha** set phrase; **traje ~** ready-made suit **3.** (*adulto*) **un hombre ~ y derecho** a real man
hechura *f* making; (*de un vestido*) tailoring; **de buena ~** well-made
hectárea *f* hectare
heder <e→ie> *vi* ~ **a algo** to stink of sth
hediondo, -a *adj* fetid
hedor *m* stench; ~ **a huevos podridos** stench of rotten eggs
hegemonía *f* hegemony
helada *f* frost; **anoche cayó una ~** there was a frost last night
heladera *f Arg* refrigerator, fridge; **este sitio es una ~** it's absolutely freezing here
heladería *f* ice cream parlour *Brit* [*o* parlor *Am*]
helado *m* ice cream
helado, -a *adj* (*congelado*) frozen; (*frío*) freezing; **me quedé ~** I was freezing; *fig: pasmado* I was left speechless; (*de miedo*) I was petrified
helar <e→ie> I. *vt, vimpers* to freeze II. *vr:* ~**se 1.** (*congelarse*) to freeze; (*lago, ventana*) to freeze over

H
h

2. (*morir*) to freeze to death
3. (*pasar frío*) ~**se** (**de frío**) to be freezing
helecho *m* fern, bracken
hélice *f* propeller
helicóptero *m* helicopter
helio *m* helium
helvético, -a *adj, m, f* Swiss
hematoma *m* bruise; MED haematoma *Brit*, hematoma *Am*
hembra *f* female
hemiciclo *m* semicircle; (*Congreso de Diputados*) Parliament chamber
hemisferio *m* hemisphere
hemorragia *f* haemorrhage *Brit*, hemorrhage *Am*
hemorroides *fpl* haemorrhoids *pl Brit*, hemorrhoids *pl Am*
hendidura *f* crack
heno *m* hay; **fiebre del ~** hay fever
hepatitis *f inv* MED hepatitis
herbicida *m* herbicide
herbívoro *m* herbivore
herboristería *f* health food shop
heredad *f* piece of land; (*finca*) estate
heredar *vt* to inherit
heredero, -a *m, f* heir; **el príncipe ~** the crown prince; **el ~ del trono** the heir to the throne
hereditario, -a *adj* hereditary
hereje *mf* heretic
herencia *f* **1.** JUR inheritance **2.** (*legado*) legacy
herida *f* wound; **tocar a alguien en la ~** *fig* to find somebody's weak spot
herido, -a I. *adj* **1.** (*lesionado*) injured; MIL wounded; **~ de gravedad** seriously injured **2.** (*ofendido*) hurt, offended **II.** *m, f* **los ~s** the wounded; **en el atentado no hubo ~s** nobody was wounded in the attack
herir *irr como sentir vt* **1.** (*lesionar*) to injure; MIL to wound **2.** (*ofender*) to hurt, to offend; **no quisiera ~ susceptibilidades** I wouldn't want to hurt anybody's feelings
hermana *f* sister; *v.t.* **hermano**
hermanastro, -a *m, f* stepbrother *m*, stepsister *f*
hermandad *f* (*de hombres*) brother-

hood; (*de mujeres*) sisterhood; REL religious association
hermano, -a *m, f* brother *m*, sister *f*; **~ político** brother-in-law; **hermano de leche** foster brother; **tengo tres ~s** (*sólo chicos*) I have three brothers; (*chicos y chicas*) I have three brothers and sisters
hermético, -a *adj* hermetic(al); (*al aire*) airtight; (*al agua*) watertight
hermoso, -a *adj* beautiful; (*hombre*) handsome; (*sanote*) robust; (*día*) lovely
hermosura *f* beauty
hernia *f* hernia
herniarse *vr* to rupture oneself; *irón* to work very hard; **¡no te herniarás, no!** *irón* don't burst a blood vessel!
héroe *m* hero; (*protagonista*) main character
heroína *f* **1.** (*de héroe*) heroine; (*protagonista*) main character **2.** (*droga*) heroin
heroinómano, -a *m, f* heroin addict
heroísmo *m sin pl* heroism
herradura *f* horseshoe
herramienta *f* tool
herrería *f* blacksmith's, smithy
herrero *m* blacksmith
herrumbre *f* rust
hervidero *m* **1. un ~ de intrigas** a hotbed of intrigue **2.** (*multitud*) throng
hervidor *m* **~ (de agua)** electric kettle
hervir *irr como sentir* **I.** *vi* to boil; (*burbujear*) to bubble; **~ (a fuego lento)** to simmer **II.** *vt* to boil
hervor *m* **dar un ~ a algo** to bring sth to the boil; **levantar el ~** to come to the boil
heterosexual *adj, mf* heterosexual
híbrido, -a *adj* hybrid
hidratante *adj* moisturizing; **crema ~** moisturizer
hidratar *vt* to moisturize
hidrato *m* hydrate
hidráulica *f* hydraulics *pl*
hidráulico, -a *adj* hidraulic
hidroeléctrico, -a *adj* hydroelectric; **central hidroeléctrica** hydroelec-

tric power station
hidrofobia *f* hydrophobia
hiedra *f* ivy
hiel *f* bile
hielo *m* ice; **romper el ~** *t. fig* to break the ice; **quedarse de ~** to be stunned
hiena *f* hyena
hierba *f* grass; (*comestible*) *t.* MED herb; **infusión de ~s** herbal tea; **tenis sobre ~** lawn tennis; **mala ~** weed; **como la mala ~** like wildfire; **mala ~ nunca muere** *prov* the Devil looks after his own
hierbabuena *f* mint
hierro *m* iron; **salud/voluntad de ~** iron constitution/will
hígado *m* **1.** ANAT liver **2.** *pl* (*valor*) guts *pl*
higiene *f* hygiene
higiénico, -a *adj* hygienic; **compresa higiénica** sanitary towel *Brit,* sanitary napkin *Am;* **papel ~** toilet paper
higo *m* fig; **estar hecho un ~** to be crumpled
higuera *f* fig tree
hijastro, -a *m, f* stepson *m,* stepdaughter *f*
hijo, -a *m, f* **1.** (*parentesco*) son *m,* daughter *f;* **un ~ de papá** Daddy's boy; **pareja sin ~s** childless couple; **~ político** son-in-law; **~ de puta** *vulg* bastard; **~ único** only child **2.** *pl* (*descendencia*) children *pl,* offspring
hilar *vt* **1.** (*hilo, araña*) to spin **2.** (*inferir*) to work out
hilera *f* row, line; MIL file; **colocarse en la ~** to get into line
hilo *m* **1.** (*para coser*) thread; (*más resistente*) yarn; TÉC wire; **~ conductor** thread; **~ dental** dental floss; **~ de perlas** string of pearls; **mover los ~s** *fig* to pull the strings; **pender de un ~** *fig* to hang by a thread **2.** (*tela*) linen **3.** (*curso*) gist; **perder el ~** (**de la conversación**) to lose the thread (of the conversation) **4.** (*de un líquido*) trickle
hilvanar *vt* to tack, to baste *Am*
himno *m* hymn; **~ nacional** national anthem
hincapié *m* **hacer ~ en algo** to emphasize sth
hincar <c→qu> **I.** *vt* to stick; **~ el diente en algo** *fig, inf* to get one's teeth into sth **II.** *vr* **~se de rodillas** to kneel down
hincha *mf* (*seguidor*) fan
hinchada *f* supporters *pl*
hinchado, -a *adj* **1.** (*pie, madera*) swollen **2.** (*estilo*) wordy, verbose
hinchar **I.** *vt* **1.** (*globo*) to blow up; (*neumático*) to inflate **2.** (*exagerar*) to exaggerate; **¡no lo hinches!** come off it! **II.** *vr:* **~se 1.** (*pierna*) to swell; **se me ha hinchado el pie** my foot's swollen **2.** (*engreírse*) to become conceited **3.** *inf* (*de comer*) **~se** (**de algo**) to stuff oneself (with sth) **4.** (*hacer mucho*) **~se a escuchar algo** to listen to sth non-stop; **~se a insultar a alguien** to go overboard insulting sb
hinchazón *f* swelling
hindú *mf* **1.** (*indio*) Indian **2.** (*del hinduismo*) Hindu
hinojo *m* fennel
hiperenlace *m* hyperlink
hipermercado *m* superstore, hypermarket *Brit*
hipertensión *f* high blood pressure
hipertexto *m* hypertext
hípico, -a *adj* equestrian, horse
hipnosis *f inv* hypnosis
hipnotismo *m* hypnotism
hipnotizar <z→c> *vt* to hypnotize
hipo *m* hiccup; **tener ~** to have (the) hiccups; **...que quita el ~** *fig* ... that takes your breath away
hipocresía *f* hypocrisy
hipócrita **I.** *adj* hypocritical **II.** *mf* hypocrite
hipódromo *m* racecourse, racetrack *Am*
hipopótamo *m* hippopotamus
hipoteca *f* mortgage
hipotecar <c→qu> *vt* to mortgage
hipótesis *f inv* hypothesis
hiriente *adj* hurtful
hispalense *adj* of/from Seville
hispánico, -a *adj* **1.** (*de España*) Spanish **2.** (*de Hispania*) Hispanic;

Hh

Filología Hispánica Spanish Language and Literature
hispano, -a I. *adj* **1.**(*español*) Spanish **2.**(*en EE.UU.*) Hispanic II. *m, f* **1.**(*español*) Spaniard **2.**(*en EE.UU.*) Hispanic
Hispanoamérica *f* Spanish America

? Hispanoamérica is a generic term that includes all countries of Central and South America, where Spanish is (officially) spoken. There are nineteen states in total: **Argentina, Bolivia, Chile, Colombia, Costa Rica, Cuba, Ecuador, El Salvador, Guatemala, Honduras, México, Nicaragua, Panamá, Paraguay, Perú, Puerto Rico, República Dominicana, Uruguay** and **Venezuela**. In contrast, the collective term **Latinoamérica** (or **América Latina**) applies to all those countries of Central and South America that were colonised by the Spaniards, Portugese and French.

hispanoamericano, -a *adj, m, f* Spanish American
histeria *f* hysteria
histérico, -a I. *adj* hysterical II. *m, f* hysterical person
historia *f* **1.**(*antigüedad*) history; **pasar a la ~** to go down in history **2.** *t. inf* story; **¡déjate de ~s!** stop fooling around; **ésa es la misma ~ de siempre** it's the same old story; **¡no me vengas con ~s!** come off it; **ya sabes la ~** you know what I'm talking about
historiador(a) *m(f)* historian
historial *m* record; (*currículo*) curriculum vitae; **~ delictivo** police record; **~ profesional** professional background
histórico, -a *adj* historical; (*acontecimiento*) historic
historieta *f* **1.**(*anécdota*) anecdote

2.(*cómic*) comic strip
hito *m* milestone
hocico *m* muzzle; (*de cerdo*) snout
hockey *m sin pl* hockey; **~ sobre hielo/hierba** ice/field hockey
hogar *m* **1.**(*casa*) home; **artículos para el ~** household items; **persona sin ~** homeless person **2.**(*familia*) family; **la vida del ~** family life; **crear un ~** to start a family **3.**(*de cocina, de tren*) boiler; (*de chimenea*) hearth
hogareño, -a *adj* **1.**(*ambiente*) family **2.**(*persona*) homeloving
hoguera *f* bonfire
hoja *f* **1.** BOT leaf; **árbol sin ~s** leafless tree **2.**(*de papel*) sheet; **~ de lata** tinplate; **~ volante** leaflet, flyer *Am* **3.**(*formulario*) form; **~ de estudios** educational record; **~ de servicios** service record **4.**(*de arma*) blade; **~ de afeitar** razor blade **5.**(*de ventana*) pane
hojalata *f* tinplate
hojaldre *m* puff pastry; **pastel de ~** puff
hojear *vt* to browse through
hola *interj* hello
Holanda *f* the Netherlands
holandés, -esa I. *adj* Dutch II. *m, f* Dutchman *m*, Dutchwoman *f*
holgado, -a *adj* loose
holgar *irr como colgar vi* **1.**(*sobrar*) to be unnecessary; **huelga decir que...** needless to say that ... **2.**(*descansar*) to relax
holgazán, -ana *m, f* layabout
holgura *f* **1.**(*de vestido*) looseness **2.** TÉC play **3.**(*bienestar*) **vivir con ~** to live comfortably
hollín *m* soot
hombre I. *m* **1.**(*varón*) man; **el ~ de la calle** *fig* the man in the street; **~ de estado** statesman; **~ de negocios** businessman; **¡está hecho un ~!** he's become a man! **2.**(*especie humana*) **el ~** mankind II. *interj* (*sorpresa*) well, well; (*duda*) well; **¡~!, ¿qué tal?** hey! how's it going?; **¡cállate, ~!** give it a rest, eh!; **¡pero, ~!** but, come on!; **¡sí, ~!** yes, of course!

hombrera *f* shoulder pad

hombro *m* shoulder; **ancho de ~s** broad-shouldered; **cargado de ~s** round-shouldered; **encogerse de ~s** to shrug one's shoulders

hombruno, -a *adj* mannish

homenaje *m* tribute; **rendir ~ a alguien** to pay homage to sb

homeopatía *f sin pl* homeopathic medicine

homeopático, -a *adj* homeopathic

homicida **I.** *adj* homicidal; **el arma ~** the murder weapon **II.** *mf* murderer *m*, murderess *f*

homicidio *m* homicide; (*planeado*) murder; (*no planeado*) manslaughter; **~ frustrado** attempted murder

homologar <g→gu> *vt* **1.** (*escuela*) to validate **2.** TÉC to authorize

homólogo, -a *m*, *f* counterpart

homosexual *adj*, *mf* homosexual

hondo, -a *adj* deep; **respirar ~** to breathe deeply

hondonada *f* depression, hollow

hondura *f* depth

Honduras *f* Honduras

> [?] Honduras lies in Central America and borders **Nicaragua, El Salvador** and **Guatemala** as well as the Caribbean and the Pacific Ocean. The capital is **Tegucigalpa.** Spanish is the official language of the country and the monetary unit of **Honduras** is the **lempira.**

hondureño, -a *adj*, *m*, *f* Honduran

honestidad *f sin pl* honesty

honesto, -a *adj* honest

hongo *m* **1.** BOT fungus; (*comestible*) mushroom **2.** (*sombrero*) bowler (hat)

honor *m* honour *Brit,* honor *Am;* **¡palabra de ~!** word of honour!

honorable *adj* honourable *Brit,* honorable *Am*

honorario, -a *adj* honorary

honorarios *mpl* fees *pl*

honra *f* **1.** (*honor*) honour *Brit,* honor *Am* **2.** REL **~s fúnebres** funeral proceedings

honradez *f* (*honestidad*) honesty; (*integridad*) integrity

honrado, -a *adj* honourable *Brit,* honorable *Am*

honrar *vt* to honour *Brit,* to honor *Am*

honroso, -a *adj* honourable *Brit,* honorable *Am*

hora *f* **1.** (*de un día*) hour; **~s de consulta** surgery hours; **~s extraordinarias** overtime; **~(s) punta** rush hour; **una ~ y media** an hour and a half; **un cuarto de ~** a quarter of an hour; **a última ~** at the last minute; **a primera/última ~ de la tarde** in the early/late afternoon; **noticias de última ~** last-minute news; **esperar ~s y ~s** to wait for hours and hours; **estar a dos ~s de camino** to be two hours' walk away; **a la ~** on time **2.** (*del reloj*) time; **adelantar/retrasar la ~** to put the clock forward/back; **¿qué ~ es?** what's the time?; **¿a qué ~ vendrás?** what time are you coming?; **me ha dado ~ para el martes** I've got an appointment for Tuesday **3.** (*tiempo*) time; **a la ~ de la verdad…** when it comes down to it …; **no lo dejes para última ~** don't leave it till the last minute; **ven a cualquier ~** come at any time; **ya va siendo ~ que** +*subj* it is about time that

horadar *vt* to perforate

horario *m* timetable, schedule *Am;* **~ de oficina** office hours; **~ flexible** flexitime; **tenemos ~ de tarde** we work evenings

horario, -a *adj* hourly

horca *f* **1.** (*para colgar*) gallows *pl* **2.** (*horquilla*) pitchfork

horcajadas a ~ astride

> [?] Horchata is a refreshing drink from Valencia made from **chufas** (a specific type of almond), **azúcar** (sugar) and **agua** (water).

Hh

horda *f* horde
horizontal *adj* horizontal
horizonte *m* horizon
horma *f* mould *Brit,* mold *Am*
hormiga *f* ant
hormigón *m* concrete
hormigueo *m* pins and needles; **tengo un ~ en la espalda** my back is itching
hormiguero *m* anthill; **la plaza era un ~ de gente** the square was seething with people
hormona *f* hormone
hornada *f* batch, ovenload
hornillo *m* stove
horno *m* 1.(*cocina*) oven; **asar al ~** to oven roast 2.TÉC furnace
horóscopo *m* horoscope
horquilla *f* 1.(*del pelo*) hairclip *Brit,* bobby pin *Am;* (*de moño*) hairpin 2.(*de bicicleta, árbol*) fork
horrendo, -a *adj v.* **horroroso**
horrible *adj* horrible; **un crimen ~** a ghastly crime
horripilante *adj* horrifying
horror *m* 1.(*miedo, aversión*) horror; **tener ~ a algo** to have a horror of sth; **siento ~ a la oscuridad** I'm terrified of the dark; **¡qué ~!** *inf* how horrible! 2. *pl* (*actos*) **los ~es de la guerra** the atrocities of war 3.*inf* (*mucho*) **ganar un ~ de dinero** to earn a lot of money
horrorizar <z→c> *vt* to horrify; **me horrorizó ver el accidente** I was horrified by the accident
horroroso, -a *adj* horrifying; (*malo*) awful
hortaliza *f* vegetable
hortelano, -a *m, f* market gardener *Brit,* truck gardener *Am*
hortera I. *adj* vulgar, tasteless II. *m* *inf* vulgar person
horterada *f* *inf* tasteless thing; **este vestido es una ~** this dress is completely tasteless
hortofrutícula *adj* fruit and vegetable gardening
hosco, -a *adj* 1.(*persona*) gruff 2.(*ambiente*) unpleasant, hostile
hospedar I. *vt* to accommodate II. *vr:* ~**se** to stay

hospital *m* hospital
hospitalario, -a *adj* welcoming, hospitable
hospitalidad *f sin pl* hospitality
hospitalizar <z→c> *vt* to hospitalize; **ayer ~on a mi madre** yesterday my mother went into hospital; **estoy hospitalizado desde el domingo** I've been in hospital since Sunday
hostal *m* cheap hotel
hostelería *f* 1.ECON hotel business 2.ENS hotel management
hostia I. *f* 1.REL host 2. *vulg* (*bofetada*) clout, smack; (*golpe*) bash 3. *fig, vulg* **¡me cago en la ~!** for fuck's sake; **¡este examen es la ~!** fucking hell! what an exam!; **hace un tiempo de la ~** (*malo*) the weather's really shitty; (*bueno*) the weather's fantastic; **iba a toda ~** he was going full speed II. *interj vulg* Jesus
hostigar <g→gu> *vt* 1.(*fustigar*) to whip 2.(*molestar*) to bother; (*con observaciones*) to harrass
hostil *adj* hostile
hostilidad *f* hostility
hotel *m* hotel
hotelero, -a I. *adj* hotel; **industria hotelera** hotel business II. *m, f* hotelier, hotelkeeper
hoy *adv* today; ~ (**en**) **día** nowadays; **llegará de ~ a mañana** it will arrive any time now; **los niños de ~** (**en día**) children nowadays; **de ~ en adelante** from now on
hoyo *m* hole
hoyuelo *m* dimple
hoz *f* 1.AGR sickle 2.GEO gorge
huacal *m And, Méx: wooden box*
hubo 3. *pret de* **haber**
hucha *f* moneybox, piggy bank
hueco *m* 1.(*agujero*) hole; ~ **de la mano** hollow of the hand; ~ **de la ventana** window space 2.(*lugar*) space; **hazme un ~** move over 3.(*tiempo*) time; **hazme un ~ para mañana** make time for me tomorrow
hueco, -a *adj* 1.(*ahuecado*) hollow; (*vacío*) empty 2.(*sonido*) resonant 3.(*tierra*) soft

huelga *f* strike; **declararse en** [*o* **hacer**] ~ to go on strike; **estar en** ~ to be on strike

huelguista *mf* striker

huella *f* **1.** (*señal*) mark; ~ (**de un animal**) (animal) track; ~ (**dactilar**) fingerprint **2.** (*vestigio*) trace

huelveño, -a *adj* of/from Huelva

huérfano, -a I. *adj* orphan; **quedarse** ~ to become an orphan; **ser** ~ **de padre** to have no father **II.** *m, f* orphan

huerta *f* (*frutales*) orchard; (*hortalizas*) market garden *Brit,* truck garden *Am*

huerto *m* (*hortalizas*) vegetable patch; (*frutales*) orchard

hueso *m* **1.** ANAT bone; **carne sin** ~ boneless meat; **te voy a romper los** ~**s** *inf* I'm going to kick your face in; **estar en los** ~**s** to be a rack of bones **2.** (*de fruto*) stone, pit *Am*

huésped(a) *m(f)* guest

huesudo, -a *adj* **1.** (*persona*) big--boned **2.** (*carne*) bony

hueva *f* roe

huevera *f* egg cup; (*cartón*) egg crate

huevo *m* **1.** BIO egg; ~ **duro/pasado por agua** hard-boiled/soft-boiled egg; ~**s revueltos** scrambled eggs **2.** *vulg* (*testículo*) ball; **¡estoy hasta los** ~**s!** I've had it up to here!; **me importa un** ~ I don't give a shit; **me costó un** ~ (*dinero*) it cost loads; (*dificultades*) it was damn difficult

huida *f* flight

huidizo, -a *adj* elusive

huir *irr* **I.** *vi* (*escapar*) to flee; ~ **de casa** to run away from home; **el tiempo huye** time flies **II.** *vt, vi* (*evitar*) ~ (**de**) **algo** to keep away from sth; ~ (**de**) **alguien** to avoid sb

hule *m* **1.** (*para la mesa*) tablecloth **2.** (*tela*) oilcloth

humanidad *f* **1.** (*género humano*) **la** ~ mankind; **un crimen contra la** ~ a crime against humanity **2.** (*naturaleza, caridad*) humanity

humanitario, -a *adj* humanitarian

humano, -a *adj* **1.** (*del hombre*) human **2.** (*manera de ser*) humane

humareda *f* cloud of smoke

humedad *f* humidity; (*agradable*) moisture; (*desagradable*) dampness

humedecer *irr como crecer* *vt* to moisten

húmedo, -a *adj* (*mojado*) wet; (*agradable*) moist; (*desagradable*) damp; (*con vapor*) humid

humildad *f* humility

humilde *adj* humble; **ser de orígenes** ~**s** to be of humble origin

humillación *f* humiliation

humillante *adj* humiliating

humillar *vt* to humiliate

humo *m* **1.** (*de combustión*) smoke **2.** (*vapor*) steam **3.** *pl* (*vanidad*) conceit; **bajar los** ~**s a alguien** to take sb down a peg; **tener muchos** ~**s** to be very conceited

humor *m* **1.** (*cualidad, humorismo*) humour *Brit,* humor *Am*; ~ **negro** gallows humour **2.** (*ánimo*) mood; **estar de buen/mal** ~ to be in a good/bad mood; **no estoy de** ~ **para bailar** I'm not in the mood for dancing

humorismo *m sin pl* comedy

humorista *mf* comic, humorist; (*dibujante*) cartoonist

humorístico, -a *adj* comic

hundimiento *m* **1.** (*de un barco*) sinking **2.** (*de un edificio*) *t.* ECON collapse

hundir I. *vt* **1.** (*barco*) to sink **2.** (*destrozar*) to destroy; (*arruinar*) to ruin **II.** *vr:* ~**se 1.** (*barco*) to sink **2.** (*edificio*) *t.* ECON to collapse; (*suelo*) to cave in

húngaro, -a *adj, m, f* Hungarian

Hungría *f* Hungary

huracán *m* hurricane

huraño, -a *adj* (*insociable*) unsociable; (*hosco*) surly

hurgar <g→gu> *vt, vi* **1.** (*remover*) ~ **en algo** to poke about in sth; ~ **el fuego** to poke the fire; ~ **la nariz** to pick one's nose **2.** (*fisgonear*) ~ (**en**) **algo** to look through sth

hurón, -ona *m, f* ferret

hurtadillas a ~ secretly; **lo hizo a** ~ **de su novia** he did it behind his girlfriend's back

hurtar I. *vt* to steal; (*en tiendas*) to

shoplift **II.** *vr* ~**se a algo** to keep away from sth

hurto *m* **1.** (*acción*) stealing; (*en tiendas*) shoplifting **2.** (*cosa*) stolen property

husmear I. *vt* (*perro*) to sniff **II.** *vi* (*perro*) to sniff around; (*fisgonear*) to nose around

huso *m* spindle

huy *interj* (*de dolor*) ow; (*de asombro*) wow

I, i *f* I, i; ~ **de Italia** I for Isaac *Brit*, I for Item *Am*

ibérico, -a *adj* Iberian; **Península Ibérica** Iberian Peninsula

Iberoamérica *f* Latin America

iberoamericano, -a *adj, m, f* Latin American

ibicenco, -a *adj* of/from Ibiza

Ibiza *f* Ibiza

iceberg *m* <icebergs> iceberg

icono *m*, **ícono** *m* REL, INFOR icon

iconoclasta I. *adj* iconoclastic **II.** *mf* iconoclast

ictericia *f sin pl* MED jaundice

ictiología *f sin pl* ichthyology

I+D *abr de* **Investigación y Desarrollo** R & D

ida *f* departure; **de** ~ **y vuelta** return

idea *f* **1.** *t.* FILOS idea; **ni** ~ no idea **2.** (*propósito*) intention **3.** *pl* (*convicciones*) ideas *pl*

ideal *adj, m* ideal

idealista I. *adj* idealistic **II.** *mf* idealist

idealizar <z→c> *vt* to idealize

idear *vt* **1.** (*concebir*) to conceive **2.** (*inventar*) to think up

ídem *pron* ditto

idéntico, -a *adj* **1.** (*igual*) identical **2.** (*semejante*) same

identidad *f* **1.** (*personalidad*) identity; **carné de** ~ identity card **2.** (*coincidencia*) sameness

identificación *f* **1.** (*de alguien*) identification **2.** INFOR password

identificar <c→qu> **I.** *vt* to identify **II.** *vr:* ~**se 1.** (*con el DNI*) to identify **2.** (*con alguien*) ~**se con alguien/algo** to identify oneself with sb/sth

ideología *f* ideology

idilio *m* love affair

idioma *m* language

idiota I. *adj* idiotic, stupid **II.** *mf* idiot

idiotez *f* **1.** *t.* MED imbecility **2.** (*estupidez*) idiocy

idolatrar *vt* **1.** (*rendir culto*) to worship **2.** (*adorar*) to idolize

ídolo *m* idol

idóneo, -a *adj* apt

iglesia *f* church

iglú *m* igloo

ignominia *f* ignominy, disgrace

ignorancia *f* **1.** (*desconocimiento*) ignorance **2.** (*incultura*) lack of culture

ignorante I. *adj* **1.** (*desconocedor*) ignorant **2.** (*inculto*) uncultured **II.** *mf pey* dunce, ignoramus

ignorar *vt* **1.** (*no saber*) to be ignorant of **2.** (*no hacer caso*) to ignore

igual¹ I. *adj* **1.** (*idéntico*) identical; (*semejante*) same; **¡es ~!** it doesn't matter; **al ~ que...** as well as ... **2.** (*llano*) flat **3.** (*constante*) stable; (*ritmo*) steady **4.** MAT equal **II.** *mf* equal **III.** *adv inf* (*quizá*) ~ **no viene** he/she might not come

igual² *m* MAT equal(s) sign

igualada *f* equalizer

igualado, -a *adj* **1.** (*parecido*) similar **2.** (*empatado*) level

igualar I. *vt* **1.** (*hacer igual*) to equalize; (*equiparar*) to match **2.** (*nivelar*) to level **3.** (*ajustar*) to even out **II.** *vi* **1.** (*equivaler*) to be equal **2.** (*combinar*) to match **III.** *vr:* ~**se 1.** (*parecerse*) to be similar to **2.** (*compararse*) to equate **3.** (*ponerse igual*) to make equal

igualdad *f* **1.** equality; (*uniformidad*) sameness, uniformity; ~ **de derechos** equal rights **2.** (*semejanza*) similarity **3.** (*regularidad*) steadiness

igualmente I. *interj* and the same to

you **II.** *adv* equally

ikurriña *f flag of the Basque Country*

ilegal *adj* illegal, unlawful

ilegítimo, -a *adj* **1.** (*asunto*) illegal **2.** (*hijo*) illegitimate

ileso, -a *adj* unharmed, unhurt

ilícito, -a *adj* illegal, illicit

ilimitado, -a *adj* unlimited

ilógico, -a *adj* illogical

iluminación *f* **1.** (*el alumbrar*) *t.* ARTE illumination **2.** (*alumbrado*) lighting **3.** REL enlightenment

iluminar *vt* **1.** (*alumbrar*) *t.* ARTE to illuminate **2.** *fig* to enlighten

ilusión *f* **1.** (*alegría*) excitement **2.** (*esperanza*) hope **3.** (*sueño*) illusion **4.** (*espejismo*) (optical) illusion

ilusionar I. *vt* **1.** (*entusiasmar*) to excite; **estar ilusionado con algo** to be excited about sth; **me ilusiona mucho hacer ese viaje** I'm very excited about that journey **2.** (*hacer ilusiones*) to raise false hopes **II.** *vr:* ~**se 1.** (*alegrarse*) to be excited **2.** (*esperanzarse*) **el proyecto le ilusiona mucho** the project has got his hopes up

ilusionista *mf* illusionist

iluso, -a I. *adj* gullible **II.** *m, f* dreamer

ilusorio, -a *adj* **1.** (*engañoso*) illusory **2.** (*de ningún efecto*) ineffective

ilustración *f* **1.** (*imagen*) illustration **2.** HIST **la Ilustración** the Enlightenment

ilustrado, -a *adj* **1.** (*con imágenes*) illustrated **2.** (*instruido*) enlightened

ilustrar I. *vt* **1.** (*con imágenes, aclarar*) to illustrate **2.** (*instruir*) to enlighten **II.** *vr:* ~**se** to enlighten oneself

ilustre *adj* illustrious

imagen *f* **1.** (*general*) image **2.** TV picture **3.** REL graven image

imaginación *f* imagination

imaginar I. *vt* to imagine **II.** *vr:* ~**se 1.** (*representarse*) to imagine oneself **2.** (*figurarse*) to imagine, to suppose

imaginario, -a *adj t.* MAT imaginary, unreal

imaginativo, -a *adj* imaginative

imán *m* magnet

imbatible *adj* unbeatable

imbécil *adj t.* MED imbecile

imborrable *adj* **1.** (*tinta*) indelible **2.** (*acontecimiento*) unforgettable

imbuir *irr como huir vt* to imbue

IME *m abr de* **Instituto Monetario Europeo** EMI

imitación *f* imitation

imitar *vt* to imitate; (*parodiar*) to impersonate; (*firma*) to forge

impaciencia *f* impatience

impaciente *adj* impatient

impacto *m* **1.** (*de un proyectil*) impact; *fig* repercussions *pl* **2.** *AmL* (*en el boxeo*) punch **3.** (*emocional*) shock, impact

impar *m* odd number

imparcial *adj* **1.** (*justo*) impartial **2.** (*sin prejuicios*) unbiased

imparcialidad *f* impartiality, fairness

impartir *vt* to give

impasibilidad *f* impassiveness

impávido, -a *adj* self-possessed, intrepid

impecable *adj* impeccable

impedimento *m* impediment, hindrance

impedir *irr como pedir vt* **1.** (*imposibilitar*) to prevent **2.** (*obstaculizar*) to impede

impeler *vt* **1.** (*impulsar*) to impel, to drive **2.** (*incitar*) to urge

impenetrable *adj* impenetrable

impensable *adj* unthinkable

imperar *vi* to reign; *fig* to prevail

imperativo, -a *adj* **1.** (*autoritario*) imperative **2.** (*imperioso*) imperious

imperceptible *adj* **1.** (*inapreciable*) imperceptible **2.** (*minúsculo*) minute

imperdible *m* safety pin

imperdonable *adj* unpardonable, inexcusable

imperfección *f* imperfection, flaw

imperfecto *m* LING imperfect

imperfecto, -a *adj* imperfect, flawed

imperial *adj* imperial

imperialismo *m* POL imperialism

imperio *m* empire; *t. fig* realm

imperioso, -a *adj* **1.** (*autoritario*) imperious **2.** (*urgente, forzoso*) imperative

impermeable I. *adj* impermeable II. *m* raincoat
impersonal *adj t.* LING impersonal
impertérrito, -a *adj* imperturbable
impertinencia *f* impertinence
impertinente *adj* impertinent
imperturbable *adj* imperturbable
ímpetu *m* 1.(*vehemencia*) vehemence 2.(*brío*) impetus
impetuosidad *f* impetuousity
impetuoso, -a *adj* 1.(*temperamento*) impetuous 2.(*movimiento*) hasty
impío, -a *adj* 1.(*irrespetuoso*) impious 2.(*inclemente*) pitiless
implacable *adj* implacable
implantar I. *vt* 1. *t.* MED to implant 2.(*instituir*) to found, to institute 3.(*introducir*) to introduce II. *vr:* ~se to become established
implicar <c→qu> I. *vt* 1.(*incluir*) to involve 2.(*significar*) to imply; **eso implica que...** this means that ... II. *vr:* ~se to be involved
implícito, -a *adj* 1.(*incluido*) implicit 2.(*tácito*) tacit
implorar *vt* (*a alguien*) to implore; (*algo*) to beg
imponente *adj* 1.(*impresionante*) imposing 2.(*que infunde respeto*) awesome 3.(*inmenso*) enormous
imponer *irr como poner* I. *vt* 1.(*sanciones*) to impose 2.(*nombre*) to give 3.(*respeto*) to command 4. FIN to levy, to tax II. *vr:* ~se 1.(*hacerse necesario*) to become necessary 2.(*prevalecer*) to prevail over 3.(*como obligación*) to impose oneself
imponible *adj* 1. FIN taxable 2.(*importación*) dutiable
impopular *adj* unpopular
importación *f* 1.(*acción*) importation 2.(*producto*) import
importancia *f* 1.(*interés*) importance; **restar** ~ to play down 2.(*extensión*) scope, magnitude 3.(*trascendencia*) significance
importante *adj* 1.(*de gran interés*) important 2.(*dimensión*) considerable 3.(*cantidad*) significant
importar I. *vt* 1.(*mercancía*) to import 2.(*precio*) to cost, to amount to; (*valer*) to be worth II. *vi* to matter, to mind; **¿a ti qué te importa?** what has it got to do with you?
importe *m* (*cuantía*) value; (*total*) amount
importunar *vt* to pester
imposibilidad *f* impossibility
imposibilitar *vt* 1.(*impedir*) to make impossible 2.(*evitar*) to prevent
imposible *adj* 1.(*irrealizable*) impossible 2. *inf*(*insoportable*) impossible, unbearable
imposición *f* 1.(*obligación*) imposition 2.(*de impuestos*) taxation
impostor(a) *m(f)* impostor, imposter
impotencia *f* 1.(*falta de poder*) *t.* MED impotence 2.(*incapacidad*) incapacity
impotente *adj* 1. *t.* MED (*sin poder*) impotent, powerless 2.(*incapaz*) incapable
impracticable *adj* 1.(*irrealizable*) unfeasible 2.(*intransitable*) impassable
imprecar <c→qu> *vt* to curse, to imprecate *form*
impreciso, -a *adj* imprecise
impregnar I. *vt* 1.(*empapar, un tejido*) to impregnate 2.(*penetrar*) to penetrate II. *vr:* ~se to become impregnated
imprenta *f* 1.(*técnica*) printing 2.(*taller*) printer's 3. BIO ~ **genética** genetic imprint 4.(*máquina*) press
imprescindible *adj* (*ineludible*) essential; (*insustituible*) indispensable
impresión *f* 1.(*huella*) imprint 2. TIPO printing 3. INFOR print-out 4. FOTO print 5.(*sensación*) impression
impresionable *adj* impressionable
impresionante *adj* 1.(*emocionante*) impressive 2.(*magnífico*) magnificent
impresionar I. *vt* 1.(*emocionar*) to impress; (*conmover*) to move 2. FOTO to print II. *vr:* ~se (*emocionarse*) to be impressed; (*conmoverse*) to be moved

impreso *m* **1.** (*hoja*) sheet **2.** (*formulario*) form
impresora *f* printer; ~ **láser** laser printer
imprevisto, -a *adj* (*no previsto*) unforeseen; (*inesperado*) unexpected
imprevistos *mpl* unexpected expenses
imprimir *irr vt* **1.** TIPO, INFOR to print **2.** (*editar*) to publish
improbable *adj* improbable, unlikely
improcedente *adj* **1.** (*inoportuno*) inopportune **2.** (*inadecuado*) inappropriate
improductivo, -a *adj* unproductive
impropiedad *f* impropriety
impropio, -a *adj* **1.** (*inoportuno*) improper **2.** (*inadecuado*) inappropriate
improvisación *f* improvisation
improvisado, -a *adj* impromptu, improvised
improvisar *vt* to improvise; *inf* TEAT to ad-lib
improviso, -a *adj* unexpected; **de ~** unexpectedly
imprudencia *f* **1.** (*irreflexión*) imprudence **2.** JUR negligence
imprudente *adj* **1.** (*irreflexivo*) imprudent **2.** (*indiscreto*) indiscreet **3.** JUR negligent
impúdico, -a *adj* indecent; (*obsceno*) lewd
impudor *m* shamelessness
impuesto *m* FIN tax; ~ **sobre el valor añadido** Value Added Tax; **libre de ~s** duty-free
impugnar *vt* **1.** *t.* JUR to contest **2.** (*combatir*) to dispute
impulsar *vt* **1.** (*incitar*) to incite **2.** (*estimular*) to motivate, to instigate
impulsivo, -a *adj* impulsive
impulso *m* **1.** impulse **2.** (*empuje*) drive
impune *adj* unpunished
impureza *f* **1.** *t.* REL impurity **2.** (*obscenidad*) foulness
impuro, -a *adj* **1.** *t.* REL impure **2.** (*obsceno*) lewd
imputar *vt* to impute
inacabable *adj* never-ending

inaccesible *adj* inaccessible
inacción *f* inaction
inaceptable *adj* unacceptable
inactividad *f* inactivity
inactivo, -a *adj* inactive
inadaptación *f* inability to adapt
inadecuado, -a *adj* inadequate
inadmisible *adj* inadmissible
inadvertido, -a *adj* **1.** (*descuidado*) inadvertent **2.** (*desapercibido*) unnoticed
inagotable *adj* inexhaustible
inaguantable *adj* unbearable, intolerable
inalámbrico, -a *adj* TEL cordless, wireless
inalterable *adj* **1.** (*invariable*) unalterable **2.** (*imperturbable*) impassive
inanición *f* starvation
inanimado, -a *adj,* **inánime** *adj* inanimate
inapreciable *adj* inappreciable
inaudito, -a *adj* unprecedented
inauguración *f* **1.** (*puente, exposición*) opening **2.** (*comienzo*) inauguration
inaugurar *vt* **1.** (*puente*) to open **2.** (*comenzar*) to inaugurate
inca *adj, m* Inca

? The **incas** were a small Indian tribe, who lived in **Perú**. In the 15th century, however, they expanded their empire, which ultimately covered present-day Colombia, Ecuador, Peru and Bolivia, and extended south into the northern part of Argentina and Chile.

---

incaico, -a *adj* Inca
incalculable *adj* incalculable
incandescente *adj* incandescent
incansable *adj* tireless
incapacidad *f* **1.** (*ineptitud*) incompetence **2.** (*psíquica*) incapacity; (*física*) disability
incapacitado, -a *adj* **1.** (*incapaz*) incapacitated **2.** (*incompetente*) incompetent

incapacitar *vt* 1. (*para negocios*) to incapacitate 2. (*impedir*) to impede
incapaz *adj* 1. (*inepto*) incapable 2. JUR incapacitated
incautación *f* seizure, confiscation
incautarse *vr* 1. (*confiscar*) to confiscate 2. (*adueñarse*) to appropriate
incauto, -a *adj* 1. (*sin cautela*) incautious 2. (*ingenuo*) naive
incendiar I. *vt* to set fire to II. *vr:* ~**se** to catch fire
incendiario, -a *adj, m, f* incendiary
incendio *m* fire; (*intencionado*) arson
incentivo *m* incentive
incertidumbre *f* 1. (*inseguridad*) incertitude 2. (*duda*) uncertainty
incesante *adj* incessant
incesto *m* incest
incidencia *f* 1. *t.* MAT incidence 2. (*efecto*) impact
incidente I. *adj* incidental II. *m* incident
incidir *vi* 1. (*tener consecuencias*) to impinge on 2. (*en un error*) to fall into 3. FÍS to incise in
incienso *m* incense
incierto, -a *adj* uncertain
incineradora *f* incinerator
incinerar *vt* 1. TÉC to incinerate 2. (*cadáveres*) to cremate
incisión *f t.* MED incision
incitar *vt* to incite
incívico, -a *adj* antisocial
incivil *adj,* **incivilizado, -a** *adj* 1. (*inculto*) uncivilised 2. (*rudo*) uncivil
inclemencia *f* 1. (*personal*) unmercifulness 2. (*del clima*) inclemency
inclinación *f* 1. (*declive*) slope 2. (*reverencia*) bow 3. (*afecto*) inclination
inclinado, -a *adj* inclined
inclinar I. *vt* to incline II. *vr:* ~**se** 1. (*reverencia*) to bow 2. (*propender*) to incline
incluir *irr como huir vt* to include
inclusive *adv* inclusively
incluso I. *adv* inclusively II. *prep* including
incluso, -a *adj* included
incógnita *f* 1. MAT (*magnitud*) vari-

able 2. (*enigma*) enigma; (*secreto*) secret
incógnito, -a *adj* incognito
incoherente *adj* incoherent
incoloro, -a *adj* colourless *Brit,* colorless *Am*
incólume *adj* intact, unscathed
incomodar I. *vt* to inconvenience II. *vr:* ~**se** to trouble oneself
incomodidad *f,* **incomodo** *m* 1. (*inconfortable*) uncomfortableness 2. (*molestia*) inconvenience
incómodo, -a *adj* 1. (*inconfortable*) uncomfortable 2. (*molesto*) tiresome
incomparable *adj* incomparable
incompatible *adj* incompatible
incompetencia *f* incompetence
incompetente *adj* incompetent
incompleto, -a *adj* incomplete
incomprensible *adj* incomprehensible
incomunicado, -a *adj* incommunicado
incomunicar <c→qu> *vt* 1. (*aislar*) to isolate 2. (*bloquear*) to cut off
inconcebible *adj* inconceivable
inconcluso, -a *adj* unfinished
inconcreto, -a *adj* imprecise
incondicional I. *adj* unconditional II. *mf* faithful friend
inconexo, -a *adj* unconnected
inconformista *mf* nonconformist
inconfundible *adj* unmistakable
incongruente *adj* incongruous
inconmensurable *adj* incommensurate
inconsciencia *f* 1. (*desmayo*) unconsciousness 2. (*irresponsabilidad*) thoughtlessness
inconsciente *adj* 1. *estar* (*desmayado*) unconscious 2. *ser* (*irresponsable*) thoughtless
inconsistente *adj* 1. (*irregular*) uneven 2. (*argumento*) weak
inconstancia *f* inconstancy
inconstante *adj* 1. (*irregular*) inconstant 2. (*caprichoso*) changeable
incontable *adj* 1. (*innumerable*) countless 2. LING uncountable
incontestable *adj* 1. (*innegable*) incontestable 2. (*pregunta*) unanswerable

incontinencia *f t.* MED incontinence
inconveniencia *f* 1.(*descortesía*) discourtesy 2.(*disparate*) absurd remark
inconveniente I. *adj* 1.(*descortés*) discourteous 2.(*disparate*) absurd II. *m* 1.(*desventaja*) disadvantage 2.(*obstáculo*) inconvenience
incordiar *vt* to bother
incorporación *f* incorporation; ~ **a filas** MIL induction
incorporar I. *vt* 1.(*a un grupo*) to incorporate in 2.(*a una persona*) to include II. *vr:* ~**se** 1.(*enderezarse*) to sit up 2.(*agregarse*) to join; (*a filas*) to join up
incorrección *f* 1.(*no correcto*) inaccuracy 2.(*falta*) mistake
incorrecto, -a *adj* 1.(*erróneo*) erroneous 2.(*descortés*) impolite
incorregible *adj* incorrigible
incredulidad *f* 1.(*desconfianza*) incredulity 2. REL lack of faith
incrédulo, -a *adj* 1.(*desconfiado*) incredulous 2. REL (*sin fe*) unbelieving
increíble *adj* incredible
incrementar *vt* to increase
incremento *m* 1.(*aumento*) increment 2.(*crecimiento*) increase
increpar *vt* to rebuke
incruento, -a *adj* bloodless
incrustar I. *vt* (*con madera*) to inlay II. *vr:* ~**se** to embed itself
incubar I. *vt* to incubate II. *vr:* ~**se** to incubate
inculcar <c→qu> I. *vt* 1.(*enseñar*) to instil, to instill *Am* 2.(*infundir*) to inculcate II. *vr:* ~**se** to be obstinate
inculpar *vt* to accuse of; JUR to charge with
inculto, -a *adj* uneducated
incumbencia *f* **no es de tu** ~ it's none of your business
incumplimiento *m* non-compliance
incurable *adj* incurable
incurrir *vi* (*en una falta*) to commit; (*en un viejo hábito*) to go back to
indagación *f* investigation
indagar <g→gu> *vt* to investigate
indecencia *f* indecency; (*obscenidad*) obscenity

indeciso, -a *adj* 1.(*irresoluto*) irresolute 2.(*que vacila*) indecisive
indefenso, -a *adj* defenceless *Brit,* defenseless *Am*
indefinido, -a *adj t.* LING indefinite
indemne *adj* 1.(*persona*) unharmed 2.(*cosa*) undamaged
indemnizar <z→c> *vt* to indemnify
independiente *adj* independent
indeseable *adj* undesirable
indeterminado, -a *adj* 1.(*inconcreto*) indeterminate 2.(*indeciso*) indecisive
indexación *f* INFOR indexing
indexar *vt* INFOR to index
India *f* **la** ~ India
indicación *f* 1.(*señal*) indication 2. MED (*síntoma*) symptom 3.(*consejo*) advice; **por** ~ **de...** on the advice of ...
indicado, -a *adj* indicated; **lo más** ~ the most suitable
indicador *m* indicator; TÉC gauge, gage *Am;* ECON index; (*de carretera*) roadsign
indicar <c→qu> *vt* 1. TÉC (*aparato*) to register 2.(*señalar*) to indicate; (*mostrar*) to show 3. MED to prescribe
indicativo, -a *adj t.* LING indicative
índice *m* 1.(*catálogo*) index; (*libro*) table of contents 2.(*dedo*) index finger, forefinger 3.(*estadísticas*) rate
indicio *m* 1.(*señal*) sign 2.(*vestigio*) trace
indiferencia *f* indifference
indiferente *adj* indifferent
indígena I. *adj* indigenous, native II. *mf* native
indigencia *f* poverty
indigestión *f* MED indigestion
indigesto, -a *adj ser* indigestible
indignación *f* indignation
indignar I. *vt* to infuriate, to outrage II. *vr:* ~**se** to become indignant
indigno, -a *adj* unworthy
indio, -a *adj, m, f* 1.(*de la India*) Indian 2.(*de América*) American Indian; **hacer el** ~ *fig* to fool around
indirecto, -a *adj* indirect
indiscreción *f* indiscretion

indiscreto, -a *adj* indiscreet
indiscriminado, -a *adj* indiscriminate
indiscutible *adj* indisputable
indispensable *adj* indispensable; **lo (más)** ~ the most essential
indisponer *irr como poner* **I.** *vt* **1.** (*enemistar*) to set someone against another **2.** (*de salud*) to indispose **II.** *vr:* ~**se 1.** (*enemistarse*) to quarrel **2.** (*ponerse mal*) to become indisposed
indisposición *f* indisposition
indistinto, -a *adj* **1.** (*igual*) indistinguishable **2.** (*difuso*) vague
individual *adj* **1.** (*personal*) personal **2.** (*simple*) single
individuo *m* individual
índole *f* nature, kind
indolencia *f* **1.** (*apatía*) apathy **2.** (*desgana*) indolence
indomable *adj* **1.** (*que no se somete*) indomitable **2.** (*indomesticable*) untameable
indómito, -a *adj* **1.** (*indomable*) indomitable **2.** (*rebelde*) rebellious
inducir *irr como traducir* *vt* ELEC to induce; ~ **a error** to mislead
indudable *adj* undeniable
indulgencia *f* indulgence
indultar *vt* **1.** JUR (*perdonar*) to pardon; (*tras un proceso*) to reprieve **2.** (*eximir*) to exempt
indulto *m* **1.** (*perdón total*) pardon **2.** (*exención*) exemption
industria *f* **1.** COM industry **2.** (*empresa*) business; (*fábrica*) factory **3.** (*dedicación*) industry
industrial **I.** *adj* industrial **II.** *mf* industrialist
industrializar <z→c> *vt, vr:* ~**se** to industrialize
inédito, -a *adj* **1.** (*no publicado*) unpublished **2.** (*desconocido*) unknown
inefable *adj* ineffable, inexpressible
ineficaz *adj* **1.** (*cosa*) ineffective **2.** (*persona*) ineffectual
ineficiente *adj* inefficient
INEM *m abr de* **Instituto Nacional de Empleo** *national employment agency*

ineptitud *f* **1.** (*incapacidad*) ineptitude **2.** (*incompetencia*) incompetence
inepto, -a *adj* **1.** (*incapaz*) inept **2.** (*incompetente*) incompetent
inequívoco, -a *adj* unequivocal
inercia *f t.* FÍS inertia
inerme *adj* **1.** (*desarmado*) unarmed **2.** BIO (*indefenso*) defenceless
inerte *adj* **1.** (*sin vida*) inanimate **2.** (*inmóvil*) inert
inescrutable *adj elev* inscrutable
inesperado, -a *adj* unexpected
inestable *adj* unstable
inestimable *adj* inestimable
inevitable *adj* inevitable, unavoidable
inexactitud *f* **1.** (*no exacto*) inaccuracy **2.** (*error*) incorrection
inexacto, -a *adj* inaccurate
inexistente *adj* non-existent
inexorable *adj elev* inexorable
inexperto, -a *adj* inexperienced
infalible *adj* infallible
infame *adj* **1.** (*vil*) wicked **2.** (*muy malo*) vile
infamia *f* **1.** (*canallada*) infamy **2.** (*deshonra*) dishonour *Brit,* dishonor *Am*
infancia *f* **1.** (*niñez*) childhood **2.** (*etapa*) infancy
infante, -a *m, f* **1.** *elev* (*niño, niña*) infant **2.** (*príncipe*) infante *m*, infanta *f*
infantería *f* MIL infantry
infantil *adj* **1.** (*de la infancia*) infant; **trabajo** ~ child labour *Brit,* child labor *Am* **2.** *pey* (*ingenuo*) infantile
infarto *m* heart attack
infatigable *adj* tireless
infección *f* MED **1.** (*contaminación*) contagion **2.** (*afección*) infection
infeccioso, -a *adj* MED infectious
infectar **I.** *vt* **1.** MED (*contagiar*) to transmit **2.** *inf* (*contaminar*) to infect **II.** *vr:* ~**se** to become infected
infeliz **I.** *adj* **1.** (*no feliz*) unhappy **2.** *inf* (*ingenuo*) ingenuous **II.** *mf inf* **1.** (*desgraciado*) wretch **2.** (*buenazo*) kind-hearted person
inferior **I.** *adj* **1.** (*debajo*) lower; (*a algo*) lesser; **labio** ~ lower lip **2.** (*de*

menos calidad) inferior **3.** (*subordinado*) subordinate **II.** *mf* inferior
inferioridad *f* inferiority
inferir *irr como sentir* **I.** *vt* to infer **II.** *vr:* ~**se** to be deducible
infernal *adj* infernal
infestar *vt* **1.** (*inundar*) to overrun **2.** (*infectar*) to infect
infidelidad *f* infidelity
infiel *adj* <infidelísimo> unfaithful
infierno *m* **1.** *t.* REL hell; **vete al** ~ go to hell **2.** (*en la mitología*) underworld
infiltración *f t.* POL infiltration
infiltrar **I.** *vt* to infiltrate; (*inculcar*) to imbue **II.** *vr:* ~**se** **1.** (*penetrar*) to penetrate **2.** (*introducirse*) to infiltrate
ínfimo, -a *adj* **1.** (*muy bajo*) very low **2.** (*mínimo*) minimal **3.** (*vil*) vile
infinidad *f* infinity
infinitivo *m* infinitive
infinito *m t.* MAT infinity
infinito, -a *adj* **1.** (*ilimitado*) limitless **2.** (*incontable*) infinite
inflación *f* inflation
inflacionista *adj* inflationist
inflamar **I.** *vt* **1.** (*encender*) to ignite **2.** (*excitar*) *t.* MED to inflame **II.** *vr:* ~**se** *t.* MED to become inflamed
inflar **I.** *vt* to inflate **II.** *vr:* ~**se** **1.** (*hincharse*) ~**se de algo** to swell with sth **2.** *inf* (*de comida*) to stuff oneself
inflexible *adj* **1.** (*rígido*) inflexible **2.** (*firme*) firm
infligir <g→j> *vt* (*dolor*) to inflict
influencia *f* influence
influenciar **I.** *vt* to influence **II.** *vr:* ~**se** to be influenced
influir *irr como huir* **I.** *vi* to have an influence on **II.** *vt* to influence
influjo *m* influence
influyente *adj* influential
información *f* **1.** information **2.** (*noticias*) news + *sing vb*
informal *adj* **1.** (*desenfadado*) informal **2.** (*no cumplidor*) unreliable
informante *mf* informant
informar **I.** *vt* to inform; (*periodista*) to report **II.** *vi* JUR to plead **III.** *vr:* ~**se** to find out

informática *f* computer science
informático, -a **I.** *adj* computer **II.** *m, f* computer expert
informativo *m* news programme *Brit,* news program *Am*
informativo, -a *adj* informative
informatizar <z→c> *vt* to computerize
informe *m* report
infortunio *m* misfortune
infotainment *m* infotainment
infracción *f* infraction; (*administrativa*) breach; (*de tráfico*) offence, offense *Am*
infrahumano, -a *adj* subhuman
infranqueable *adj* impassable
infrautilizar <z→c> *vt* to underuse
infravalorar *vt* to undervalue, to underestimate
infringir <g→j> *vt* to infringe; (*la ley*) to break
infructuoso, -a *adj* fruitless
infundado, -a *adj* unfounded
infundir *vt* (*deseo*) to infuse; (*temor*) to intimidate
infusión *f* infusion; (*de hierbas*) herb(al) tea
ingeniar **I.** *vt* to devise **II.** *vr:* ~**se** to manage
ingeniería *f* engineering
ingeniero, -a *m, f* engineer
ingenio *m* **1.** (*inventiva*) ingenuity, ingeniousness **2.** (*talento*) wit **3.** (*maña*) aptitude **4.** (*máquina*) device
ingenioso, -a *adj* **1.** (*hábil*) skilful *Brit,* skillful *Am* **2.** (*listo*) ingenious
ingenuidad *f* **1.** (*inocencia*) ingenuousness **2.** (*torpeza*) naivety
ingenuo, -a *adj* ingenuous
ingerir *irr como sentir* *vt* **1.** (*medicamentos*) to take **2.** (*comida*) to ingest
Inglaterra *f* England
ingle *f* ANAT groin
inglés, -esa **I.** *adj* English **II.** *m, f* Englishman *m,* Englishwoman *f*
ingratitud *f* ingratitude
ingrato, -a *adj* ungrateful
ingrediente *m* **1.** (*sustancia*) ingredient **2.** (*elemento*) element
ingresar **I.** *vi* **1.** (*en organiyación*) to

become a member of **2.** (*en hospital*) to be admitted to **II.** *vt* **1.** FIN (*cheque*) to pay in, to deposit **2.** (*hospitalizar*) to hospitalize **3.** (*percibir*) to earn

ingreso *m* **1.** (*inscripción*) entry **2.** (*alta*) incorporation **3.** (*en una cuenta*) deposit **4.** *pl* (*retribuciones*) income

inhábil *adj* **1.** (*persona: torpe*) clumsy; (*incompetente*) inept **2.** (*día*) non-working

inhabilitar *vt* **1.** (*incapacitar*) to incapacitate **2.** (*prohibir*) to disqualify

inhabitable *adj* uninhabitable

inhalar *vt t.* MED to inhale, to breathe in

inherente *adj* inherent

inhibir I. *vt* **1.** (*reprimir*) to repress **2.** BIO, JUR to inhibit **II.** *vr* to abstain from; (*de hacer algo*) to refrain from

inhumano, -a *adj* (*no humano*) inhuman; (*sin compasión*) inhumane

INI *m abr de* **Instituto Nacional de Industria** *national industry institute*

inicial *adj, f* initial

iniciar I. *vt* **1.** (*comenzar*) to begin **2.** (*introducir*) to initiate **3.** INFOR to log in **II.** *vr:* ~**se 1.** (*comenzar*) to begin **2.** (*introducirse en*) to tech to

iniciativa *f* initiative; ~ **privada** ECON private enterprise

inicio *m* beginning

inigualable *adj* unrivalled *Brit,* unrivaled *Am*

ininterrumpido, -a *adj* uninterrupted

injerencia *f* interference

injertar *vt* (*plantas*) *t.* MED to graft

injerto *m t.* MED graft

injuria *f* (*palabras*) affront; (*acciones*) harm

injuriar *vt* (*con palabras*) to insult; (*con acciones*) to injure

injurioso, -a *adj* injurious

injusticia *f* injustice, unfairness

injusto, -a *adj* unjust, unfair

inmadurez *f sin pl* immaturity

inmaduro, -a *adj* immature

inmediatamente *adv* **1.** (*sin demora*) immediately **2.** (*directamente*) directly

inmediato, -a *adj* **1.** (*sin demora*) immediate; **de** ~ immediately **2.** (*directo*) direct **3.** (*próximo*) adjacent

inmejorable *adj* unbeatable

inmenso, -a *adj* immense

inmerecido, -a *adj* undeserved

inmigración *f* immigration

inmigrante *mf* immigrant

inmigrar *vi* to immigrate

inminente *adj* imminent

inmiscuirse *irr como huir vr* to interfere, to meddle

inmobiliaria *f* **1.** (*construcción*) construction company **2.** (*alquiler*) estate agency *Brit,* real estate office *Am*

inmodesto, -a *adj* immodest

inmolar(se) *vt,* (*vr*) to sacrifice oneself

inmoral *adj* immoral

inmortal *adj* immortal

inmortalizar <z→c> **I.** *vt* to immortalize **II.** *vr:* ~**se** to be immortalized

inmóvil *adj* immobile; (*inamovible*) unmovable

inmovilizar <z→c> **I.** *vt* **1.** (*paralizar*) to paralyse **2.** MED to immobilize **II.** *vr:* ~**se** to become immobilized

inmueble *adj, m* property

inmundicia *f* filth

inmundo, -a *adj* filthy

inmune *adj* MED immune

inmunidad *f* immunity

inmunizar <z→c> *vt* to immunize

inmutable *adj* **1.** (*inmodificable*) immutable **2.** (*imperturbable*) imperturbable

inmutarse *vr* to be affected; **sin** ~ impassively

innato, -a *adj* innate; (*talento*) natural

innavegable *adj* **1.** (*aguas*) unnavigable **2.** (*embarcación*) unseaworthy

innegable *adj* undeniable

innoble *adj* ignoble

innovación *f* innovation

inocencia *f* innocence

inocentada *f* (*comentario*) naive remark; (*acción*) naive action; **gastar una** ~ to play a practical joke

inocente *adj* **1.** (*sin culpa*) innocent

Mi habitación

1	libros *mpl*	books
2	espejo *m*	mirror
3	lámpara *f* (de mesa)	table lamp
4	taza *f*	mug
5	radiocasete *m*	radio cassette recorder, boom box *Am*
6	mesilla *f* de noche	bedside table, nightstand *Am*
7	cómoda *f*	chest of drawers, dresser *Am*
8	moqueta *f*	fitted carpet, carpet *Am*
9	zapatilla *f* de deporte	trainer, sneaker *Am*
10	raqueta *f* (de tenis)	tennis racket
11	cartera *f*, mochila *f*	school bag, backpack *Am*

My bedroom

12	edredón *m*	duvet, quilt *Brit*, comforter *Am*
13	almohada *f*	pillow
14	despertador *m*	alarm clock
15	antepecho *m*	windowsill
16	persiana *f*	blind
17	lector *m* de CD portátil	portable CD-player
18	lámpara *f* de escritorio, flexo *m*	desk lamp
19	(teléfono *m*) móvil *m*	mobile (phone), cellphone *Am*
20	escritorio *m*	desk
21	teclado *m*	keyboard
22	pantalla *f*, monitor *m*	screen

2. (*sin malicia*) harmless
inodoro *m* toilet (bowl)
inodoro, -a *adj* odourless *Brit,* odorless *Am*
inofensivo, -a *adj* inoffensive
inolvidable *adj* unforgettable
inoperante *adj* ineffective
inopinado, -a *adj* unexpected
inoportuno, -a *adj* **1.** (*fuera de lugar*) inappropriate **2.** (*fuera de tiempo*) inopportune
inoxidable *adj* rustproof; (*acero*) stainless
input *m* <inputs> INFOR input
inquebrantable *adj* (*decisión*) unwavering; (*cosa*) unbreakable
inquietar I. *vt* to worry II. *vr:* ~**se** to worry about
inquieto, -a *adj* **1.** estar (*intranquilo*) anxious **2.** ser (*desasosegado*) restless
inquietud *f* **1.** (*intranquilidad*) anxiety **2.** (*preocupación*) worry
inquilino, -a *m, f* tenant; COM lessee
inquirir *irr como adquirir* *vt* to enquire *Brit,* to inquire *Am*
insaciable *adj* insatiable
insalubre *adj* unhealthy
insano, -a *adj* (*loco*) insane
insatisfecho, -a *adj* dissatisfied
inscribir *irr como escribir* I. *vt* **1.** (*registrar*) to register **2.** *t.* MAT (*grabar*) to inscribe II. *vr:* ~**se 1.** (*registrarse*) to register **2.** *t.* UNIV (*alistarse*) to enrol *Brit,* to enroll *Am*
inscripción *f* **1.** (*registro*) registration **2.** *t.* UNIV (*alistamiento*) enrolment *Brit,* enrollment *Am* **3.** (*grabado*) inscription
insecticida *m* insecticide
insecto *m* insect
inseguridad *f* insecurity
inseguro, -a *adj* insecure
inseminación *f* insemination
insensato, -a *adj* foolish
insensibilidad *f* **1.** (*sin sensibilidad*) insensitivity **2.** (*resistencia*) immunity
insensible *adj* **1.** (*no sensible*) insensitive **2.** (*resistente*) immune
inseparable *adj* inseparable
insertar *vt* **1.** (*llave, moneda*) to in-

sert **2.** (*anuncio*) to place
inservible *adj* useless
insidioso, -a *adj* **1.** (*intrigante*) scheming **2.** (*enfermedad*) insidious
insignia *f* **1.** (*de asociación*) badge; (*militar*) insignia **2.** (*bandera*) flag, ensign
insignificante *adj* insignificant
insinuar < *1. pres:* insinúo> I. *vt* to insinuate; **¿quién te ha insinuado eso?** who has put that into your head? II. *vr:* ~**se** (*a alguien*) to get in with; (*amorosamente*) to flirt with
insípido, -a *adj* **1.** (*comida*) insipid **2.** (*persona*) dull
insistencia *f* **1.** (*perseverancia*) persistence **2.** (*énfasis*) insistence
insistir *vi* **1.** (*perseverar*) to persist **2.** (*recalcar*) to insist
insociable *adj,* **insocial** *adj* unsociable
insolación *f* MED sunstroke
insolencia *f* impertinence, disrepect
insolente *adj* **1.** (*impertinente*) impertinent **2.** (*arrogante*) insolent
insólito, -a *adj* unusual, uncommon
insoluble *adj* insoluble
insolvencia *f* bankruptcy; ECON insolvency
insomnio *m* MED insomnia, sleeplessness
insondable *adj* bottomless
insonorizar <z→c> *vt* to soundproof
insoportable *adj* unbearable
insospechado, -a *adj* **1.** (*no esperado*) unexpected **2.** (*no sospechado*) unsuspected
inspección *f t.* TÉC (*reconocimiento*) inspection; **Inspección Técnica de Vehículos** ≈ MOT test
inspeccionar *vt t.* TÉC to inspect
inspector(a) *m(f)* inspector
inspiración *f* **1.** (*de aire*) inhalation **2.** (*ideas*) inspiration
inspirar I. *vt* **1.** (*aire*) to inhale **2.** (*ideas*) to inspire II. *vr:* ~**se** to be inspired
instalación *f* **1.** (*acción*) installation; **instalaciones deportivas** sports facilities *pl* **2.** TÉC fitting; (*objeto fijo*) fixture

instalador(a) *m(f)* installer, fitter
instalar I. *vt* 1. (*calefacción*) to install, to instal *Am;* (*baño*) to plumb 2. (*alojar*) to accommodate 3. (*negocio*) to set up II. *vr:* ~**se** to settle
instancia *f* 1. (*solicitud*) application 2. JUR instance; **en última ~** *fig* as a last resort
instantánea *f* FOTO snapshot
instantáneo, -a *adj* instantaneous; (*café*) instant
instante *m* instant; **en un ~** in an instant; **¡un ~!** one moment!
instar *vi, vt* (*pedir*) to urge; ~ **a algo** to press for sth
instaurar *vt* 1. (*democracia*) to establish 2. (*plan*) to implement
instigar <g→gu> *vt* to instigate; (*a algo malo*) to incite
instinto *m* instinct
institución *f* institution; ~ **penitenciaria** prison
instituir *irr como huir* *vt* 1. (*fundar*) to found 2. (*comisión*) to set up; (*norma*) to introduce
instituto *m* 1. ENS (*de bachillerato*) secondary school, high school *Am* 2. (*científico*) institute; **Instituto Monetario Europeo** European Monetary Institute; **Instituto Nacional de Empleo** Employment Service
institutriz *f* governess
instrucción *f* 1. (*enseñanza*) teaching 2. (*formación*) training 3. *pl* (*órdenes*) instructions *pl,* directions *pl* 4. JUR (*proceso*) proceedings *pl*
instructivo, -a *adj* instructive
instruir *irr como huir* *vt* 1. (*enseñar*) to teach; (*en una máquina*) to instruct; (*en tarea específica*) to train 2. JUR (*proceso*) to prepare
instrumento *m* instrument
insubordinarse *vr* to rebel
insuficiencia *f* 1. (*cualidad*) insufficiency 2. (*escasez*) deficiency; (*falta*) lack 3. MED failure
insuficiente I. *adj* insufficient; (*conocimientos*) inadequate II. *m* ENS fail
insufrible *adj* insufferable
insular *adj* insular

insulina *f* MED insulin
insultar *vt* to insult
insulto *m* insult
insumisión *f* MIL *refusal to do military service*
insumiso *m* one who refuses to do military service *or* its alternative
insuperable *adj* (*dificultad*) insuperable, insurmountable; (*persona*) unrivalled *Brit,* unrivaled *Am*
insurgente *adj, mf* insurgent
insurrección *f* insurrection
intacto, -a *adj* 1. (*no tocado*) untouched 2. (*no dañado*) intact
integral I. *adj* 1. (*completo*) integral, full 2. (*pan*) wholemeal, wholegrain; (*arroz*) brown II. *f* MAT integral
integrar I. *vt* 1. (*constituir*) to constitute, to comprise 2. *t.* MAT (*en conjunto*) to integrate II. *vr:* ~**se** to integrate
integridad *f* 1. (*totalidad*) entirety 2. (*honradez*) integrity
integrismo *m* fundamentalism
integrista *mf* fundamentalist
íntegro, -a *adj* 1. (*completo*) whole 2. (*persona*) honest
intelectual I. *adj* intellectual; (*facultad*) intelligent, scholarly II. *mf* intellectual
inteligencia *f* 1. (*capacidad*) intelligence; **servicio de ~** POL MI5 *Brit,* CIA *Am* 2. (*comprensión*) comprehension
inteligente *adj* intelligent
inteligible *adj* 1. (*comprensible*) comprehensible 2. (*sonido*) *t.* FILOS intelligible
intemperie *f* **a la ~** out in the open; **dormir a la ~** to sleep outdoors
intempestivo, -a *adj* 1. (*observación*) inopportune 2. (*visita*) ill-timed
intención *f* 1. (*propósito*) intention; **con ~** deliberately 2. (*idea*) idea
intencionado, -a *adj* intentional; JUR premeditated; **mal ~** unkind; (*persona*) malicious
intensidad *f* 1. (*fuerza*) *t.* FÍS intensity 2. (*de viento*) force
intensivo, -a *adj* intensive
intenso, -a *adj* 1. (*fuerza*) strong

2.(*tormenta*) severe **3.**(*frío, calor*) intense

intentar *vt* **1.**(*probar*) to attempt, to try **2.**(*proponerse*) to intend, to mean

intento *m* **1.**(*tentativa*) attempt **2.**(*propósito*) aim

interactivo, -a *adj* interactive

intercalar *vt* (*en un periódico*) to insert

intercambio *m* exchange

interceder *vi* to intercede

interceptar *vt* (*comunicaciones*) to cut off; (*mensaje*) to intercept; (*tráfico*) to hold up

intercesión *f* intercession

interés *m* **1.**(*importancia*) concern **2.**(*atención*) interest **3.** FIN interest; (*rendimiento*) yield

interesado, -a I. *adj* **1.**(*con interés*) interested **2.**(*parcial*) biased, prejudiced **II.** *m, f* (*egoísta*) selfish person

interesante *adj* interesting

interesar I. *vi* to be of interest **II.** *vt* **1.**(*inspirar interés*) to interest **2.**(*atraer*) to attract, to appeal **III.** *vr*: ~**se 1.**(*mostrar interés*) ~**se por algo** to become interested in sth **2.**(*preguntar por*) ~**se por algo** to ask about sth

interface *m* INFOR interface

interferir *irr como sentir vi t.* FÍS to interfere

interfono *m* intercom

interino, -a I. *adj* **1.**(*funcionario*) temporary **2.** POL interim **II.** *m, f* **1.**(*suplente*) stand-in **2.**(*maestro*) supply teacher

interior I. *adj* interior; (*vida*) inner; **mercado** ~ COM home market; **ropa** ~ underwear **II.** *m* **1.**(*lo de dentro*) interior; **Ministerio del Interior** POL Home Office *Brit,* Department of the Interior *Am;* **en el** ~ **de...** inside ... **2.** DEP inside-forward

interjección *f* LING interjection

interlocutor(a) *m(f)* speaker

intermediario, -a I. *adj* intermediary **II.** *m, f* **1.**(*mediador*) mediator, intermediary; (*enlace*) go-between **2.**(*comerciante*) middleman

intermedio *m* interval

intermedio, -a *adj* **1.**(*capa*) intermediate; **mandos** ~**s** middle management **2.**(*tamaño*) medium

interminable *adj* interminable, endless

intermitente *m* intermittence; AUTO indicator *Brit,* turn signal *Am*

internacional *adj* international

internado *m* boarding school

internado, -a I. *adj* boarding **II.** *m, f* **1.**(*alumno*) boarder **2.**(*demente*) inmate

internar I. *vt* **1.**(*penetrar*) to lead inland; MIL to intern **2.**(*en hospital*) to admit; (*en asilo*) to commit **II.** *vr*: ~**se 1.**(*penetrar*) *t.* DEP to enter **2.**(*en tema*) to delve into

internauta *mf* INFOR Internet user

internet *f sin pl* INFOR Internet

interno, -a I. *adj* internal **II.** *m, f* (*en colegio*) boarder; (*en cárcel*) inmate

interponer *irr como poner* **I.** *vt* **1.**(*poner*) to interpose **2.** JUR to bring, to lodge **II.** *vr*: ~**se** to intervene

interpretación *f* **1.**(*de texto*) interpretation **2.**(*traducción oral*) interpreting **3.** TEAT performance; MÚS rendering

interpretar *vt* **1.**(*texto, oralmente*) to interpret **2.** TEAT to perform; MÚS to render

intérprete¹ *mf* **1.**(*de texto*) scholar **2.**(*actor*) performer **3.**(*traductor*) interpreter

intérprete² *m* INFOR interpreter

interrogación *f* **1.**(*de policía*) interrogation **2.**(*signo*) question mark

interrogante I. *adj* questioning **II.** *m* question

interrogar <g→gu> *vt* **1.**(*hacer preguntas*) to question **2.**(*policía*) to interrogate

interrumpir *vt* **1.**(*cortar*) to interrupt; (*tráfico*) to hold up **2.**(*estudios*) to terminate

interrupción *f* **1.**(*corte*) break; (*del tráfico*) hold-up **2.**(*de los estudios*) termination

interruptor *m* ELEC switch, socket *Am*

intersección *f* intersection; (*de ca-*

rreteras) crossing

intersticio *m* (*espacio*) *t.* BIO interstice; (*en pared*) crack; (*entre placas*) fissure

interurbano, -a *adj* intercity

intervalo *m*, **intérvalo** *m* *t.* MÚS interval

intervención *f* 1. (*participación*) participation 2. (*en conflicto*) intervention 3. POL intervention 4. MED operation 5. (*del teléfono*) tapping

intervenir *irr como venir* I. *vi* 1. (*tomar parte*) to participate 2. (*en conflicto*) to intervene 3. (*mediar*) to mediate II. *vt* 1. MED to operate on 2. (*incautar*) to seize 3. (*teléfono*) to tap 4. COM to audit

interventor(a) *m(f)* 1. COM auditor 2. POL supervisor

interviú *m* o *f* interview

intestino *m* 1. ANAT intestine 2. *pl* (*tripas*) intestines *pl*, bowels *pl*

íntimamente *adv* 1. (*estrechamente*) closely 2. (*en lo íntimo*) intimately

intimar I. *vi* to become intimate II. *vt* to require

intimidad *f* 1. (*privacidad*) privacy 2. (*vida privada*) private life 3. *pl* (*sexuales*) private parts *pl*; (*asuntos*) personal matters *pl*

intimidar *vt* to intimidate

íntimo, -a *adj* 1. (*interior*) inner, innermost 2. (*amigo*) intimate, close 3. (*conversación*) private

intolerable *adj* intolerable

intolerancia *f* intolerance

intoxicación *f* (*de alimentos*) food poisoning; (*de alcohol*) intoxication

intranet *f sin pl* INFOR Intranet

intranquilizar <z→c> *vt, vr:* ~**se** to worry

intranquilo, -a *adj* 1. (*nervioso*) edgy 2. (*preocupado*) worried

intransigente *adj* intransigent

intransitable *adj* impassable

intransitivo, -a *adj* LING intransitive

intrepidez *f* intrepidity, fearlessness

intrépido, -a *adj* intrepid

intriga *f* 1. (*maquinación*) intrigue 2. CINE suspense

intrigar <g→gu> I. *vi* to scheme

II. *vt* to intrigue

intrincado, -a *adj* 1. (*nudo*) intricate; (*camino*) twisting 2. (*situación*) complicated

intrínseco, -a *adj* 1. (*interior*) intrinsic 2. (*propio*) inherent

introducción *f* 1. (*de una llave, medida*) insertion, introduction; INFOR (*de datos*) input 2. (*de mercancías*) launching 3. (*de libro*) preface

introducir *irr como traducir* I. *vt* 1. (*llave, disquete*) to insert, to put in; (*medidas*) to introduce; INFOR (*datos*) to enter, to input 2. (*discordia*) to sow II. *vr:* ~**se** 1. (*meterse*) to get in(to) 2. (*en un ambiente*) to enter into 3. (*moda*) to be introduced

intromisión *f* interference

introvertido, -a *adj* introverted

intruso, -a I. *adj* intrusive II. *m, f* intruder

intuición *f* intuition

intuir *irr como huir* *vt* 1. (*reconocer*) to intuit *form* 2. (*presentir*) to sense; **intuyo que...** I have a hunch that ...

inundación *f* flood(ing)

inundar *vt* to flood

inusitado, -a *adj* unusual, uncommon

inusual *adj* unusual

inútil *adj* 1. (*que no sirve*) useless; MIL unfit 2. (*esfuerzo*) vain

inutilidad *f* uselessness; (*laboral*) incapacity; MIL unfitness

inutilizar <z→c> *vt* 1. (*objeto*) to render useless 2. (*al enemigo*) to defeat

invadir *vt* 1. (*país*) to invade 2. (*plaga*) to infest 3. (*tristeza, dudas*) to assail

invalidar *vt* 1. (*anular*) to invalidate 2. JUR (*matrimonio*) to annul

inválido, -a I. *adj* 1. MED disabled 2. (*acuerdo*) invalid II. *m, f* disabled person, invalid

invariable *adj t.* MAT invariable

invasión *f* 1. *t.* MIL, MED invasion 2. (*de plaga*) plague

invasor(a) I. *adj* invasive II. *m(f)* invader

invencible *adj* **1.** (*inderrotable*) invincible **2.** (*obstáculo*) unsurmountable

invención *f* invention; (*mentira*) lie

inventar *vt* to invent

inventario *m* **1.** COM stocktaking **2.** (*lista*) inventory

inventiva *f* inventiveness

invento *m* invention

inventor(a) *m(f)* inventor

invernadero *m* BOT greenhouse

invernar <e→ie> *vi* ZOOL to hibernate

inverosímil *adj* **1.** (*increíble*) implausible **2.** (*improbable*) improbable

inversión *f* COM, FIN investment

inverso, -a *adj* inverse, opposite; **en orden** ~ in reverse order

inversor(a) *m(f)* investor

invertebrado, -a *adj* invertebrate

invertir *irr como sentir vt* **1.** (*orden*) to invert **2.** (*dar la vuelta*) to turn upside down **3.** (*dinero*) to invest

investigación *f* **1.** (*indagación*) investigation; (*averiguación*) enquiry *Brit,* inquiry *Am* **2.** (*ciencia*) research

investigar <g→gu> *vt* **1.** (*indagar*) to investigate; (*averiguar*) to enquire *Brit,* to inquire *Am* **2.** (*en la ciencia*) to research

investir *irr como pedir vt* to confer; **la investieron doctor honoris causa** she was given an honorary PhD; ~ **doctor honoris causa** to be given an honorary PhD

inviable *adj* non-viable, unfeasible

invicto, -a *adj* unbeaten

invidencia *f* blindness

invidente **I.** *adj* blind **II.** *mf* blind person

invierno *m* winter

invisible *adj* invisible

invitación *f* **1.** (*a una fiesta*) invitation **2.** (*tarjeta*) invitation card

invitado, -a **I.** *adj* invited **II.** *m, f* guest

invitar *vt* **1.** (*convidar*) to invite; **esta vez invito yo** this time it's on me **2.** (*instar*) to press; (*rogar*) to beg

invocar <c→qu> *vt* (*dirigirse*) to invoke; (*suplicar*) to implore, to appeal

involucrar **I.** *vt* to involve **II.** *vr:* ~**se** **1.** (*inmiscuirse*) to interfere **2.** (*intervenir*) to become involved

involuntario, -a *adj* **1.** (*sin querer*) unintentional **2.** (*por obligación*) involuntary

invulnerable *adj* **1.** (*no vulnerable*) invulnerable **2.** (*insensible*) insensitive

inyección *f* **1.** MED injection **2.** TÉC fuel injection

inyectar *vt* to inject

ion *m* ion

IPC *m* ECON *abr de* **Índice de Precios al Consumo** RPI

ir *irr* **I.** *vi* **1.** (*general*) to go; **¡voy!** I'm coming!; ~ **a pie** to go on foot; ~ **en bicicleta** to go by bicycle; **¿cómo va la tesina?** how is the dissertation going?; **¿cómo te va?** how are things? **2.** (*ir a buscar*) **iré por el pan** I'll go and get the bread **3.** (*diferencia*) **de dos a cinco van tres** two from five leaves three **4.** (*referirse*) **eso no va por ti** I'm not referring to you; **¿tú sabes de qué va?** do you know what it is about? **5.** (*sorpresa*) **¡vaya coche!** what a car!; **¡qué va!** of course not! **6.** (*con verbo*) **iban charlando** they were chatting; **voy a hacerlo** I'm going to do it **II.** *vr:* ~**se** **1.** (*marcharse*) to leave **2.** (*dirección*) to go **3.** (*resbalar*) to slip **4.** (*perder*) to leak

ira *f* anger, wrath *form*

iracundo, -a *adj* irate

Irán *m* Iran

iraní *adj, mf* Iranian

Iraq *m* Iraq

iraquí *adj, mf* Iraqi

irascible *adj* irascible

iris *m* ANAT iris; **arco** ~ rainbow

Irlanda *f* Ireland

irlandés, -esa **I.** *adj* Irish **II.** *m, f* Irishman *m,* Irishwoman *f*

ironía *f* irony

irónico, -a *adj* ironic

IRPF *m abr de* **Impuesto sobre la Renta de las Personas Físicas** personal income tax

irracional *adj* (*contra la razón*) ir-

rational; (*contra la lógica*) illogical
irreal *adj* unreal
irrecuperable *adj* irretrievable
irreflexión *f* recklessness, thought-lessness
irregular *adj* 1. (*desigual*) irregular, uneven 2. (*contra las reglas*) irregular
irregularidad *f* 1. (*desigualdad*) irregularity, unevenness 2. (*contra las reglas*) irregularity
irremediable *adj* 1. (*inevitable*) inevitable 2. (*daño físico*) irreversible
irrenunciable *adj* 1. (*imprescindible*) indispensable 2. (*destino*) inescapable
irreparable *adj* 1. (*máquina*) irreparable 2. (*daño físico*) irreversible
irreprochable *adj* irreproachable
irresistible *adj* 1. (*atractivo*) irresistible 2. (*inaguantable*) unbearable
irresoluble *adj* unsolvable
irresolución *f* 1. (*indecisión*) indecisiveness 2. (*vacilación*) irresolution
irresoluto, -a *adj* 1. (*indeciso*) indecisive 2. (*vacilante*) irresolute
irrespetuoso, -a *adj* disrespectful
irresponsable *adj* irresponsible
irreversible *adj* irreversible
irrevocable *adj* 1. (*no revocable*) irrevocable 2. (*inamovible*) unalterable
irrigar <g→gu> *vt* 1. AGR (*regar*) to irrigate 2. (*la sangre*) to oxygenate
irrisorio, -a *adj* derisory; (*precios*) ridiculously
irritación *f* 1. MED inflammation 2. (*enfado*) irritation
irritar I. *vt* 1. (*molestar*) to irritate 2. MED to inflame II. *vr:* ~**se** 1. (*enojarse*) to become irritated 2. MED to become inflamed
irrupción *f* 1. (*entrada*) irruption 2. MIL (*invasión*) invasion; (*ataque*) raid
IRTP *m abr de* **impuesto sobre el rendimiento del trabajo personal** PAYE
isla *f* island
Islam *m* REL Islam
islámico, -a *adj* Islamic
islandés, -esa I. *adj* Icelandic II. *m, f*

Icelander
Islandia *f* Iceland
isleño, -a I. *adj* island II. *m, f* islander
isotónico, -a *adj* isotonic
Israel *m* Israel
israelí *adj, mf* Israeli
israelita *adj, mf* Israelite
istmo *m* GEO isthmus
Italia *f* Italy
italiano, -a *adj, m, f* Italian
itinerario *m* itinerary; AERO route
ITV *f abr de* **Inspección Técnica de Vehículos** MOT test
IVA *m abr de* **impuesto sobre el valor añadido** VAT
izar <z→c> *vt* NÁUT to hoist
izda. *adj,* **izdo.** *adj abr de* **izquierda, izquierdo** left
izquierda *f* 1. (*mano*) left hand 2. POL left 3. (*lado*) left side
izquierdista *adj, mf* POL leftist
izquierdo, -a *adj* left; (*zurdo*) left-handed

J, j *f* J, j; ~ **de Juan** J for Jack *Brit,* J for Jig *Am*
jabalí *m* <jabalíes> wild boar
jabato, -a *adj* brave
jabón *m* soap; **pastilla de** ~ bar of soap; **dar** ~ **a alguien** to soft-soap sb
jabonar *vt* to soap
jaca *f* 1. (*yegua*) mare 2. *pey* (*caballo*) nag
jacinto *m* hyacinth
jactancioso, -a I. *adj* boastful II. *m, f* boaster
jactarse *vr* to boast of
jadear *vi* to pant
Jaén *m* Jaen
jaenero, -a, jaenés, -esa *adj* of/from Jaen
jaguar *m* jaguar
jalar I. *vt* AmL 1. (*cuerda*) to pull

2. (*persona*) to attract **3.** *inf* (*comer*) to guzzle **II.** *vr:* ~**se** *AmL* (*emborracharse*) to get drunk
jalea *f* jelly
jalear *vt* (*animar*) to encourage
jaleo *m* **1.** (*barullo*) commotion; **armar** ~ to kick up a row **2.** (*desorden*) confusion
jalón *m* **1.** (*vara*) pole **2.** (*hito*) landmark
jalonar *vt* **1.** (*un terreno*) to stake out **2.** (*marcar*) to mark
jamás *adv* never; **¿habías leído ~ algo parecido?** had you ever read anything like it?; **nunca** ~ never again
jamón *m* ham; ~ **dulce/serrano** boiled/cured ham; **¡y un ~!** *inf* get away!
Japón *m* Japan
japonés, -esa *adj, m, f* Japanese
jaque *m* DEP check; ~ **mate** checkmate; **dar** ~ to check
jaqueca *f* (severe) headache, migraine
jarabe *m* syrup; (*para la tos*) cough mixture
jarcia *f* NÁUT rigging
jardín *m* garden; (*de una ciudad*) parks *pl;* ~ **de infancia** creche *Brit,* nursery school
jardinería *f* gardening
jardinero, -a *m, f* gardener
jarra *f* jar; (*de agua*) jug, pitcher *Am;* (*de café*) mug; **ponerse en ~s** to stand with arms akimbo
jarro *m* jug, pitcher; (*de agua*) pitcher
jarrón *m* vase
jaula *f* cage
jauría *f* pack of hounds
jazmín *m* jasmine
jazz *m sin pl* MÚS jazz
J.C. *abr de* **Jesucristo** J.C.
jeep *m* <jeeps> jeep
jefatura *f* **1.** (*cargo*) leadership **2.** (*sede*) ~ **del gobierno** seat of government; ~ **de policía** police headquarters
jefazo *m inf* big boss
jefe, -a *m, f* (*de empresa*) head, boss; (*de una banda*) leader; ~ **de(l) Esta-**

do head of state; ~ **de gobierno** head of the government; **redactor** ~ editor-in-chief
jengibre *m* ginger
jeque *m* sheik(h)
jerarquía *f* hierarchy
jerárquico, -a *adj* hierarchical
jerez *m* sherry
jerga *f* (*lenguaje*) jargon
jerigonza *f* **1.** (*galimatías*) gibberish **2.** (*jerga*) jargon
jeringa *f* syringe
jeringar <g→gu> *vt* **1.** (*con la jeringa*) to syringe **2.** *inf* (*molestar*) to pester
jeringuilla *f* syringe
jeroglífico *m* (*signo*) hieroglyph(ic)
jeroglífico, -a *adj* hieroglyphic
jersey *m* pullover, jumper *Brit*
Jerusalén *m* Jerusalem
Jesucristo *m* Jesus Christ
jesuita *adj, m* Jesuit
Jesús *m* Jesus; **¡~!** (*al estornudar*) bless you!; (*interjección*) good heavens!
jet¹ *m* <jets> (*avión*) jet
jet² *f sin pl* (*alta sociedad*) jet set
jeta *f inf* (*cara*) mug; **ése tiene una ~ increíble** *fig* what incredible cheek that guy has
jíbaro, -a *adj* **1.** *AmL* (*campesino*) country; (*costumbres*) rural **2.** *AmL* (*animal*) wild
jienense, -a *adj* of/from Jaen
jilguero *m* goldfinch
jinete *m* (*persona*) horseman; (*profesional*) rider
jirafa *f* giraffe
jirón *m* shred
jitomate *m Méx* (*tomate*) tomato
JJ.OO. *abr de* **Juegos Olímpicos** Olympic Games
jockey *m* jockey
jocoso, -a *adj* humourous, jocular
joder I. *vt vulg* **1.** (*copular*) to fuck, to screw **2.** (*fastidiar*) to piss off; **¡no me jodas!** piss off! **3.** (*echar a perder*) to fuck up **4.** (*robar*) to pinch **II.** *vr:* ~**se** *vulg* to get pissed off; **¡¡jódete!** piss off!
Jordania *f* Jordan
jordano, -a *adj, m, f* Jordanian

jornada *f* **1.** (*de trabajo*) working day; **~ partida** split shift; **trabajo media ~** I work part-time **2.** (*viaje*) day's journey **3.** *pl* (*congreso*) conference

jornal *m* (*paga*) day's wage

jornalero, -a *m*, *f* day labourer *Brit*, day laborer *Am*

joroba *f* **1.** (*de persona*) hunched back **2.** (*de camello*) hump

jorobado, -a **I.** *adj* hunchbacked **II.** *m*, *f* hunchback

jota *f* **1.** (*letra*) j; **no saber ni ~** *inf* not to have a clue **2.** (*baile*) Aragonese dance

joven **I.** *adj* young **II.** *mf* young man *m*, young woman *f*

jovial *adj* cheerful, jovial

joya *f* **1.** (*alhaja*) jewel; (*piedra*) gem; **las ~s** jewellery, jewelry *Am* **2.** *fig* (*persona*) gem

joyería *f* jeweller's shop *Brit*, jeweler's shop *Am*

joyero *m* jewel case

joyero, -a *m*, *f* jeweller *Brit*, jeweler *Am*

joystick *m* joystick

juanete *m* (*del pie*) bunion

jubilación *f* **1.** (*acción*) retirement **2.** (*pensión*) pension

jubilado, -a *m*, *f* pensioner, retiree

jubilar **I.** *vt* **1.** (*a alguien*) to pension off **2.** *inf* (*un objeto*) to take out of circulation **II.** *vr:* **~se** to retire

júbilo *m* joy, jubilation

jubiloso, -a *adj* jubilant

judía *f* bean

judicial *adj* judicial

judío, -a **I.** *adj* Jewish **II.** *m*, *f* Jew

judo *m* DEP judo

juego *m* **1.** (*diversión*) game; **~ de mesa** board game; **hacer ~s malabares** to juggle; **perder dinero en el ~** to gamble money away; **vérsele a alguien el ~** *fig* to know what sb is up to **2.** DEP play; **~ limpio** fair play; **fuera de ~** (*persona*) offside; (*balón*) out of play **3.** (*conjunto*) set; **~ de café** coffee set; **~ de mesa** dinner service; **hacer ~** to match **4.** TÉC play

juerga *f* spree; **correrse unas cuan-** tas **~s** *inf* to go out at night quite a bit

jueves *m inv* Thursday; **Jueves Santo** Maundy Thursday; *v.t.* **lunes**

juez *mf t.* JUR judge; **~ de línea** DEP linesman; **ser ~ y parte** to be biased

jugada *f* **1.** DEP play; **~ de ajedrez** chess move **2.** (*jugarreta*) bad turn; **gastar una ~ a alguien** to play a dirty trick on sb

jugador(a) *m(f) t.* DEP player

jugar *irr* **I.** *vi* **1.** (*a un juego, deporte*) to play; **¿puedo ~?** can I join in?; **¿a qué juegas?** *fig* what are you playing at? **2.** (*bromear*) to play about; **hacer algo por ~** to do sth for fun **3.** (*hacer juego*) to match **II.** *vt* **1.** (*un juego*) to play; (*ajedrez*) to move; **¿quién juega?** whose turn is it? **2.** (*apostar*) to gamble **III.** *vr:* **~se** **1.** (*la lotería*) to be drawn; **jugársela a alguien** *fig* to take sb for a ride **2.** (*apostar*) to gamble on **3.** (*arriesgar*) to risk

juglar *m* HIST, LIT, MÚS minstrel

jugo *m* **1.** (*de fruta*) juice **2.** (*esencia*) essence

jugoso, -a *adj* juicy

juguete *m* toy

juguetear *vi* to play

juguetería *f* toyshop

juguetón, -ona *adj* playful

juicio *m* **1.** (*facultad para juzgar*) reason **2.** (*razón*) sense; **tú no estás en tu sano ~** you're not in your right mind **3.** (*opinión*) opinion; **a mi ~** to my mind **4.** JUR trial; **el** (*día del*) **Juicio final** REL the Last Judgement

juicioso, -a *adj* (*sensato*) sensible; (*acertado*) fitting

julio *m* **1.** (*mes*) July; *v.t.* **marzo** **2.** FÍS joule

jumo, -a *adj* AmL (*borracho*) drunk

junco *m* **1.** BOT reed **2.** (*embarcación*) junk

jungla *f* jungle

junio *m* June; *v.t.* **marzo**

junta *f* **1.** (*comité*) committee; (*consejo*) council; **~ directiva** COM board of directors; **~ militar** MIL military junta **2.** (*reunión*) meeting; **~ de accionistas** shareholders' meeting

3. TÉC joint; (*de dos tubos*) junction
juntar I. *vt* **1.** (*aproximar*) to put together **2.** (*unir*) to join **3.** (*reunir: personas*) to assemble; (*dinero*) to collect **II.** *vr:* ~**se 1.** (*reunirse*) to meet **2.** (*unirse*) to come together **3.** (*aproximarse*) to come closer **4.** (*vivir juntos*) to move in (together)
junto *prep* **1.** (*local*) ~ **a** near to; **¿quién es el que está ~ a ella?** who's the man at her side?; ~ **a la entrada** at the entrance; **pasaron ~ a nosotros** they walked past us **2.** (*con movimiento*) ~ **a** beside; **pon la silla ~ a la mesa** put the chair next to the table **3.** (*con*) ~ **con** together with
junto, -a *adj* joined; **todos ~s** all together
jurado *m* **1.** JUR (*miembro*) juror; (*tribunal*) jury **2.** (*de un examen*) qualified examiner **3.** (*de un concurso*) panel member
jurado, -a *adj* qualified; **intérprete** ~ sworn interpreter
juramento *m* **1.** *t.* JUR (*jura*) oath; **falso** ~ perjury **2.** (*blasfemia*) swearword
jurar *vt, vi* to swear; ~ **en falso** to commit perjury; **jurársela(s) a alguien** *inf* to swear vengeance on sb
jurídico, -a *adj* legal, lawful
jurisdicción *f* **1.** JUR (*potestad*) jurisdiction; ~ **militar** military law **2.** (*territorio*) administrative district
jurisprudencia *f* jurisprudence
jurista *mf* jurist
justamente *adv* **1.** (*con justicia*) justly **2.** (*precisamente*) precisely
justicia *f* **1.** (*cualidad*) justice **2.** (*derecho*) law
justiciero, -a *adj* (*justo*) just; (*severo*) strict
justificación *f* **1.** (*disculpa*) justification **2.** (*prueba*) proof, evidence
justificante *m* supporting evidence; (*de ausencia*) note of absence
justificar <c→qu> **I.** *vt* **1.** (*disculpar*) to justify **2.** (*probar*) to prove; (*con documentos*) to substantiate **II.** *vr:* ~**se** to justify oneself
justo *adv* **1.** (*exactamente*) right; ~ **a**

tiempo just in time **2.** (*escasamente*) scarcely; ~ **para vivir** just enough to live on
justo, -a *adj* **1.** (*persona, decisión*) just **2.** (*exacto*) exact **3.** (*vestido*) close-fitting
juvenil *adj* youthful
juventud *f* **1.** (*edad*) youth **2.** (*estado*) early life **3.** (*jóvenes*) young people
juzgado *m* court; ~ **de guardia** police court
juzgar <g→gu> **I.** *vt* **1.** *t.* JUR (*opinar*) to judge; (*condenar*) to sentence; ~ **mal** to misjudge **2.** (*considerar*) to consider **II.** *vi* to judge; **a** ~ **por...** judging by ...

K, k *f* K, k; ~ **de Kenia** K for King
karaoke *m* karaoke
karate *m*, **kárate** *m* DEP karate
kart *m* <karts> go-cart
Kazajstán *m* Kazakhstan
KB *m* INFOR *abr de* **kilobyte** KB
keniano, -a *adj, m, f* Kenyan
keniata *adj, mf* Kenyan
ketchup *m* <ketchups> ketchup
kg *abr de* **kilogramo** kg
kibutz *m* <kibutzs> kibbutz
kikirikí *m* cock-a-doodle-doo
kilo *m* kilo

> [!] **kilo** is always used with the preposition 'de': "Déme dos kilos de naranjas, por favor."

kilogramo *m* kilogramme *Brit,* kilogram *Am*
kilometraje *m* AUTO mileage *Brit,* milage *Am* (*distance in kilometres*)
kilómetro *m* kilometre *Brit,* kilometer *Am*
kilovatio *m* kilowatt

kínder *m inv,* **kindergarten** *m inv,* *AmL* kindergarten, nursery school
kit *m* <kits> kit
kleenex® *m inv,* **klínex®** *m inv* Kleenex®, tissue
km *abr de* **kilómetro** km
Kremlin *m* Kremlin
Kurdistán *m* Kurdistan
kurdo, -a I. *adj* Kurdish **II.** *m, f* Kurd
kuwaití *adj, mf* Kuwaiti
kv *abr de* **kilovatio** kw

L

L, l *f* L, l; ~ **de Lisboa** L for Lucy *Brit,* L for Love *Am*
la I. *art def v.* **el, la, lo II.** *pron pers, f sing* **1.** *objeto directo* her; *cosa* it; **mi bicicleta y** ~ **tuya** my bicycle and yours **2.** *(con relativo)* ~ **que...** the one that ...; ~ **cual** which **III.** *m* MÚS A
laberinto *m* labyrinth, maze
labia *f inf* glibness; **tener mucha** ~ to be a smooth talker
labial *adj* labial
labio *m* **1.** *(boca)* lip **2.** *(borde)* rim
labor *f* work; *(de coser)* needlework; *(labranza)* ploughing *Brit,* plowing *Am;* **no estoy por la** ~ I don't feel like it
laborable *adj* **día** ~ working day
laboral *adj* labour *Brit,* labor *Am*
laborar *vi* **1.** *(gestionar)* to strive for **2.** *(intrigar)* to scheme
laboratorio *m* laboratory, lab
laborioso, -a *adj* **1.** *(trabajador)* hard-working **2.** *(difícil)* arduous
laborista *adj* **partido** ~ Labour Party
labrado *m* *(campo)* cultivated land
labrado, -a *adj* **1.** *(madera)* carved; *(cristal)* etched **2.** AGR tilled; **campo** ~ ploughed field
labrador(a) *m(f)* farmhand
labranza *f* tillage
labrar *vt* **1.** *(cultivar)* to work; *(arar)*

to plough *Brit,* to plow *Am* **2.** *(causar)* to bring about
labriego, -a *m, f* farmworker
laca *f* **1.** *(pintura)* lacquer **2.** *(para el pelo)* hairspray; *(para las uñas)* nail varnish
lacayo *m* lackey
lacerar *vt* **1.** *(herir)* to injure **2.** *(magullar)* to bruise
lacio, -a *adj* *(cabello)* straight, lank
lacónico, -a *adj* laconic
lacra *f* **1.** *(de una enfermedad)* mark **2.** *(vicio)* blight
lacrar *vt* to seal
lacre *m* sealing wax
lacrimógeno, -a *adj* *(gas)* tear; *(sentimental)* soupy
lactancia *f* breastfeeding
lactar *vt, vi* to nurse
lácteo, -a *adj* milk, dairy
ladear I. *vt* **1.** *(inclinar)* to slant; *(un sombrero)* to tip **2.** *(desviar)* to skirt **II.** *vi* *(caminar)* to walk lopsided **III.** *vr:* **~se** to lean
ladera *f* slope, hillside
ladino, -a *adj* *(taimado)* cunning
lado *m* **1.** *t.* MAT *(parte)* side; **ir de un** ~ **a otro** to go back and forth; **por todos** ~**s** everywhere; **al** ~ nearby; **la casa de al** ~ the house next-door; **al** ~ **de** *(junto a)* beside, next to; **su** ~ **débil** his weak spot; **dejar de** ~ to ignore; **me puse de tu** ~ I sided with you; **por un** ~**..., y por el otro** ~**...** on the one hand..., and on the other hand... **2.** *(borde)* edge; *(extremo)* end
ladrar *vi* *(perro)* to bark
ladrido *m* bark
ladrillo *m* brick
ladrón, -ona *m, f* *(bandido)* thief, robber
lagar *m* *(aceite)* oil press; *(vino)* winepress
lagartija *f* small lizard
lagarto *m* **1.** *(reptil)* lizard **2.** *AmL* *(caimán)* alligator
lago *m* lake
lágrima *f* tear
lagrimal **I.** *adj* lachrymal **II.** *m* corner of the eye
laguna *f* **1.** *(agua)* lagoon **2.** *(omi-*

sión) gap
laico, -a I. *adj* lay **II.** *m, f* layman *m,* laywoman *f*

> [?] The term **laísmo** refers to the incorrect or perhaps non-standard usage of **la(s)** as the indirect object instead of **le(s)**, e.g. "**La regalé una novela de Borges**" instead of "**Le regalé una novela de Borges.**" Such use is commonly accepted in certain regions but not accepted by most Spanish speakers.

lamentable *adj* regrettable
lamentar I. *vt* to regret; **lo lamento** I'm sorry **II.** *vr* ~**se de algo** to complain about
lamento *m* lament
lamer *vt* to lick
lámina *f* **1.** (*hojalata*) tin plate **2.** (*ilustración*) print
laminar *vt* **1.** (*cortar*) to split **2.** (*guarnecer*) to laminate
lámpara *f* **1.** (*luz*) lamp, light; ~ **de escritorio** desk lamp **2.** TV, RADIO valve *Brit,* tube *Am* **3.** (*mancha*) grease stain
lamparón *m* **1.** (*mancha*) grease stain **2.** MED scrofula
lampiño, -a *adj* (*sin barba*) beardless; (*sin pelo*) hairless
lana *f* **1.** (*material*) wool **2.** *inf* (*dinero*) dough
lance *m* **1.** (*trance*) critical moment **2.** (*pelea*) quarrel **3.** (*de juego*) move **4.** (*golpe*) stroke
lancha *f* (*bote*) motorboat; ~ **de salvamento** lifeboat
lanero, -a *adj* wool
langosta *f* **1.** (*insecto*) locust **2.** (*crustáceo*) lobster
langostino *m* prawn
languidecer *irr como crecer vi* to languish
languidez *f* **1.** (*debilidad*) weakness **2.** (*espíritu*) listlessness
lánguido, -a *adj* **1.** (*débil*) weak **2.** (*espíritu*) languid
lanilla *f* (*pelillo*) nap

lanudo, -a *adj* woolly, wooly *Am;* (*oveja*) wool-bearing
lanza *f* lance
lanzadera *f* shuttle; (*plataforma*) platform, launch(ing) pad
lanzado, -a *adj* **1.** (*decidido*) determined **2.** (*impetuoso*) impetuous
lanzamiento *m* throw; (*de bombas*) dropping; (*espacial*) launch; (*comercial*) promotion; ~ **de peso** DEP shot put
lanzamisiles *m inv* missile-launcher
lanzar <z→c> **I.** *vt* **1.** (*arrojar*) to throw; ~ **peso** to put the shot **2.** (*al mercado*) to launch **II.** *vr:* ~**se** to throw oneself; ~**se al agua** to dive into the water
lapa *f* limpet
La Paz *f* La Paz
lapicero *m* pencil
lápida *f* stone tablet
lapidar *vt* to stone
lapidario, -a *adj* lapidary
lápiz *m* pencil; ~ **de labios** lipstick; ~ **de color** crayon, wax crayon *Brit*
lapón, -ona *adj, m, f* Lapp
Laponia *f* Lapland
lapso *m* **1.** (*de tiempo*) lapse **2.** *v.* **lapsus**
lapsus *m inv* blunder; ~ **linguae** slip of the tongue
largar <g→gu> **I.** *vt* **1.** (*soltar*) to release **2.** *inf* (*golpe*) to land **3.** *inf* (*discurso*) to give **4.** (*revelar*) to tell **II.** *vr:* ~**se 1.** (*irse*) to leave; (*de casa*) to leave home **2.** *AmL* (*comenzar*) to begin **III.** *vi inf* to yack
largo I. *adv* (*en abundancia*) plenty; ¡~ (**de aquí**)! clear off! **II.** *m* (*longitud*) length
largo, -a *adj* **1.** (*tamaño, duración*) long; **a** ~ **plazo** in the long term; **a lo** ~ **de los años** throughout the years; **ir de** ~ to be in a long dress; **pasar de** ~ to pass by; *fig* to ignore; **tener las manos largas** *fig* to be light-fingered **2.** (*extensivo*) lengthy; (*mucho*) abundant **3.** *inf* (*astuto*) shrewd
largometraje *m* full-length film
largura *f* length
laringe *f* larynx

laringitis *f inv* laryngitis

larva *f* larva

las I. *art def v.* el, la, lo II. *pron pers f pl* 1. (*objeto directo*) them 2. (*con relativo*) ~ **que**... the ones that ...; ~ **cuales** those which

lascivo, -a *adj* lewd

láser *m* laser

lástima *f* 1. (*compasión*) pity; **me da** ~ I feel sorry for him/her; **por** ~ out of pity; **¡qué** ~**!** what a pity! 2. (*lamentación*) complaint

lastimar I. *vt* 1. (*herir*) to hurt 2. (*agraviar*) to offend II. *vr:* ~**se** 1. (*herirse*) to hurt oneself 2. (*quejarse*) to complain about

lastimero, -a *adj*, **lastimoso, -a** *adj* 1. (*daño*) harmful 2. (*lástima*) pitiful

lastre *m* 1. NÁUT ballast 2. (*estorbo*) dead weight

lata *f* 1. (*metal*) tin 2. (*envase*) tin *Brit,* can *Am* 3. *inf* (*pesadez*) bore; **dar la** ~ to be a nuisance; **¡vaya** ~**!** what a pain!

latente *adj* latent

lateral *adj* lateral

latido *m* heartbeat

latifundio *m* large landed estate

latifundista *mf* owner of a large estate

latigazo *m* 1. (*golpe*) whiplash 2. (*chasquido*) crack 3. (*reprimenda*) tongue lashing

látigo *m* whip

latín *m* Latin

latino, -a I. *adj* Latin; **América Latina** Latin America II. *m, f AmL* Latin American

Latinoamérica *f* Latin America

latinoamericano, -a *adj, m, f* Latin American

latir *vi* to beat

latitud *f* 1. GEO latitude 2. (*extensión*) breadth

latón *m* brass

latoso, -a *adj* bothersome

latrocinio *m* larceny

laúd *m* MÚS lute

laurel *m* 1. (*árbol*) laurel 2. (*condimento*) bay leaf

lava *f* lava

lavabo *m* 1. (*pila*) washbasin, sink *Am* 2. (*cuarto*) toilet *Brit,* bathroom *Am*

lavadero *m* laundry

lavado *m* wash; ~ **de cerebro** *fig* brainwashing

lavadora *f* washing machine

lavanda *f* lavender

lavandería *f* laundry, launderette *Brit,* laundromat *Am*

lavaplatos *m inv* dishwasher

lavar I. *vt* (*limpiar*) to wash; ~ **los platos** to wash up II. *vr:* ~**se** to wash; ~**se los dientes** to brush one's teeth

lavavajillas *m inv* dishwasher, dishsoap *Am*

lavotearse *vr inf* to wash quickly

laxante *m* laxative

lazada *f* bow

lazo *m* 1. (*nudo*) bow 2. (*para caballos*) lasso 3. (*cinta*) ribbon 4. (*vínculo*) tie

le *pron pers* 1. *objeto indirecto: m sing* him; *f sing* her; *forma cortés* you; **¡da~ un beso!** give him/her a kiss!; ~ **puedo llamar el lunes** if you like, I can phone you on Monday 2. *m sing reg: objeto directo* him

leal *adj* loyal

lealtad *f* loyalty

lebrel *m* greyhound

lección *f t. fig* lesson; UNIV lecture; **dar una** ~ **a alguien** *fig* to teach sb a lesson

leche *f* 1. (*líquido*) milk 2. *vulg* (*esperma*) spunk 3. *inf* (*golpe*) blow 4. *inf* (*hostia*) **¡~s!** damn it!; **ser la** ~ to be too much; **estar de mala** ~ to be in a foul mood

lechera *f v.* **lechero**

lechería *f* dairy

lechero, -a *m, f* milkman *m,* milkwoman *f*

lecho *m* bed; (*río*) riverbed

lechón, -ona *m, f* suckling pig

lechoso, -a *adj* milky

lechuga *f* lettuce

lechuza *f* barn owl

lectivo, -a *adj* ENS school; UNIV academic

lector *m* 1. (*aparato*) player; ~ **de CD** CD player 2. INFOR reader

lector(a) *m(f)* **1.** *(que lee)* reader **2.** *(profesor)* conversation assistant

lectura *f t.* INFOR reading

leer *irr vt* to read

legado *m* **1.** POL legacy; REL legate **2.** *(herencia)* legacy

legajo *m* dossier

legal *adj* **1.** *(determinado por la ley)* legal **2.** *(conforme a la ley)* lawful

legalidad *f* legality

legalizar <z→c> *vt* **1.** *(autorizar)* to legalize **2.** *(atestar)* to authenticate

legaña *f* sleep, rheum

legar <g→gu> *vt* **1.** *(legado)* to bequeath **2.** *(enviar)* to delegate

legendario, -a *adj* legendary

legión *f* **1.** MIL legion **2.** *(multitud)* crowd

legionario, -a I. *adj* legionary **II.** *m, f* legionnaire

legislación *f* **1.** *(acción)* lawmaking **2.** *(leyes)* legislation

legislar *vi* to legislate

legislativo, -a *adj* legislative

legislatura *f* **1.** *(período)* term of office **2.** *AmL (parlamento)* legislative body

legitimar *vt* **1.** *(dar legitimidad)* to authenticate **2.** *(hijo)* to make legitimate

legítimo, -a *adj* **1.** *(legal)* legitimate **2.** *(verdadero)* genuine

lego, -a I. *adj* **1.** *(no eclesiástico)* lay **2.** *(ignorante)* uninformed **II.** *m, f* layman

legua *f* league; **se ve a la ~ que...** it's obvious that ...

legumbre *f* *(seca)* pulse; *(fresca)* vegetable; **frutas y ~s** fruit and vegetables

leído, -a *adj* **1.** *(persona)* well-read **2.** *(revista)* widely-read

---

? The term **leísmo** refers to the incorrect or perhaps non-standard usage of **le(s)** as the indirect object instead of **lo(s)** or **la(s)**, e.g. "**Les visité ayer, a mis hermanas**" instead of "**Las visité ayer, a mis hermanas.**" Such use is commonly accepted in certain regions but not accepted by most Spanish speakers.

---

lejanía *f* distance

lejano, -a *adj* faraway; *(parentesco)* distant

lejía *f* bleach

lejos I. *adv* far; **~ de algo** far from sth; **a lo ~** in the distance; **de ~** from afar; **sin ir más ~** *fig* to take an obvious example **II.** *prep* **~ de** far from

lelo, -a I. *adj inf* **1.** *ser (tonto)* silly **2.** *estar (pasmado)* stunned **II.** *m, f* *(persona)* dolt

lema *m* **1.** *(mote)* motto **2.** *(contraseña)* watchword

lencería *f* **1.** *(telas)* linen **2.** *(ropa interior)* underwear

lengua *f* ANAT, LING tongue; **~ materna** mother tongue; **~ oficial** official language; **dar a la ~** to gab; **en la punta de la ~** on the tip of my tongue; **se me trabó la ~** I got tongue-tied; **tener la ~ demasiado larga** *fig* to talk too much; **irse de la ~** to spill the beans; **tirar a alguien de la ~** *fig* to pump sb for information

lenguado *m* sole

lenguaje *m* language

lenguaraz *adj* talkative

lengüeta *f* **1.** *(zapato)* tongue; *(balanza)* pointer **2.** MÚS reed

lenitivo, -a *adj* alleviating

lente *m o f* **1.** *(gafas)* eyeglasses *pl;* **llevar ~s** to wear glasses **2.** *t.* FOTO *(cristal)* lens

lenteja *f* lentil; **ganarse las ~s** *fig* to earn one's daily bread

lentejuela *f* sequin, spangle

lentilla *f* contact lens

lentitud *f* slowness; *fig* slow-wittedness

lento, -a *adj* slow; *fig* slow-witted; **a paso ~** slowly; **a fuego ~** low heat

leña *f* *sin pl* **1.** *(madera)* firewood; **echar ~ al fuego** *fig* to add fuel to the flames **2.** *(castigo)* beating; **repartir ~** to dish out blows

leñador(a) *m(f)* woodcutter, lumber-

jack
leño *m* log
Leo *m* Leo
león *m* lion; *AmL* (*puma*) puma, cougar *Am*
leonino, -a *adj* **1.** (*animal*) leonine **2.** (*contrato*) unfair
leopardo *m* leopard
leotardo(s) *m(pl)* leotards *pl*, tights *pl*
lepra *f* MED *sin pl* leprosy
leproso, -a I. *adj* leprous **II.** *m, f* leper
lerdo, -a *adj* slow, sluggish
les *pron pers* **1.** *mf pl* (*objeto indirecto*) them; (*forma cortés*) you **2.** *m pl, reg* (*objeto directo*) them
lesbiana *f* lesbian
lesión *f* injury
lesionar I. *vt* **1.** (*herir*) to injure **2.** (*dañar*) to damage **II.** *vr:* ~**se** to get hurt
letal *adj elev* lethal
letanía *f* litany
letárgico, -a *adj* lethargic
letargo *m* lethargy
letón, -ona *adj, m, f* Latvian
Letonia *f* Latvia
letra *f* **1.** (*signo*) letter; ~ **mayúscula/minúscula** capital/small letter; **al pie de la** ~ to the letter; ~ **por** ~ word for word; **poner cuatro** ~**s a alguien** to drop sb a line **2.** (*escritura*) handwriting **3.** *pl* (*saber*) learning, letters; UNIV arts *pl*; **hombre de** ~**s** man of letters **4.** MÚS lyrics *pl* **5.** COM ~ (**de cambio**) bill of exchange; ~ **al portador** draft payable to the bearer
letrado, -a I. *adj* learned **II.** *m, f* lawyer
letrero *m* notice, sign
leucemia *f sin pl* MED leukaemia *Brit,* leukemia *Am*
leucocito *m* leucocyte *Brit,* leukocyte *Am*
levadizo, -a *adj* **puente** ~ drawbridge
levadura *f* leavening yeast; ~ **en polvo** baking powder
levantamiento *m* **1.** (*amotinamiento*) uprising **2.** (*alzar*) lifting

levantar I. *vt* **1.** (*alzar*) to lift; (*voz*) to raise; (*del suelo*) to pick up; (*algo inclinado*) to straighten; (*un campamento*) to strike; (*las anclas*) to weigh; ~ **el vuelo** to take off **2.** (*despertar*) to awaken; (*sospechas*) to arise **3.** (*construir*) to build; (*monumento*) to erect **4.** (*embargo*) to lift **5.** (*acta*) to draw up **II.** *vr:* ~**se 1.** (*de la cama*) to get up **2.** (*sobresalir*) to stand out **3.** (*sublevarse*) to rebel **4.** (*viento, telón*) to rise **5.** (*sesión*) to adjourn
levante *m sin pl* **1.** (*Este*) east **2.** (*viento*) east wind
levar *vt* (*anclas*) to weigh
leve *adj* (*enfermedad*) mild; (*peso, sanción*) light
levedad *f sin pl* lightness
léxico *m* **1.** (*diccionario*) lexicon **2.** (*vocabulario*) vocabulary
ley *f* **1.** JUR, REL, FÍS law; ~ **orgánica** constitutional law; **la** ~ **seca** the Prohibition; **proyecto de** ~ POL bill; **ser de** ~ *inf* to be reliable **2.** *pl* (*estudio*) Law
leyenda *f* **1.** LIT, REL legend **2.** (*moneda*) inscription
liar <*1. pres:* lío> **I.** *vt* **1.** (*fardo*) to tie up **2.** (*cigarrillo*) to roll **3.** *inf* (*engañar*) to take in; (*enredar*) to mix up **II.** *vr:* ~**se 1.** *inf* (*juntarse*) to become lovers **2.** (*embarullarse*) to get complicated
libanés, -esa *adj, m, f* Lebanese
Líbano *m* **El** ~ Lebanon
libar *vi* (*abeja*) to suck
libelo *m* libel
libélula *f* dragonfly
liberación *f* liberation, release
liberal *adj, mf* liberal
liberalidad *f* (*generosidad*) generosity
liberalizar <z→c> *vt* to liberalize
liberar *vt* to liberate, to set free
libertad *f* liberty; ~ **de expresión** freedom of speech; **en** ~ **bajo fianza** on bail; **en** ~ **condicional** on parole; **poner en** ~ to set free
libertar *vt* to liberate
libertinaje *m* libertinage
libertino, -a I. *adj* dissolute **II.** *m, f*

libertine
Libia *f* Libya
libidinoso, -a *adj* lustful
libido *f sin pl* libido
libio, -a *adj, m, f* Libyan
libra *f* pound; ~ **esterlina** pound sterling
Libra *f* Libra
libramiento *m,* **libranza** *f* order of payment; (*de un cheque*) payment
librar I. *vt* 1. (*dejar libre*) to free from; (*salvar*) to save from 2. COM (*letra*) to draw II. *vi inf* (*tener libre*) **hoy libro** I have today off III. *vr* 1. (*deshacerse*) to get rid of 2. (*salvarse*) to escape from
libre <libérrimo> *adj* 1. (*en general*) free; (*independiente*) independent; **zona de ~ cambio** free trade area 2. (*soltero*) single
librería *f* 1. (*tienda*) bookshop 2. (*biblioteca*) library 3. (*estantería*) bookcase
librero, -a *m, f* bookseller
libreta *f* 1. (*cuaderno*) notebook; (*para notas*) notepad 2. (*de ahorros*) bank book
libro *m* (*escrito*) book; ~ **de bolsillo** paperback; ~ **de consulta** reference book; ~ **de escolaridad** school record; **los Libros Sagrados** the Holy Scriptures; ~ **de texto** textbook; **colgar los ~s** *fig* to abandon one's studies
licencia *f* 1. (*permiso*) licence *Brit,* license *Am;* ~ **de armas** gun licence; **estar de ~** MIL to be on leave 2. (*libertad*) liberty
licenciado, -a *m, f* 1. (*estudiante*) graduate 2. (*soldado*) discharged soldier
licenciar I. *vt* (*despedir*) to dismiss; (*soldado*) to discharge II. *vr:* ~**se** to graduate
licencioso, -a *adj* licentious
liceo *m* 1. (*sociedad*) literary society 2. *AmL* (*colegio*) secondary school
licitar *vt* to bid
lícito, -a *adj* 1. (*permitido*) allowed 2. (*justo*) fair 3. (*legal*) lawful
licor *m* liquor; (*de frutas*) liqueur
licuadora *f* (*batidora*) blender; (*para*

fruta) liquidizer
licuar <*l. pres:* licúo> *vt* to liquefy
líder *mf* leader
liderato *m,* **liderazgo** *m sin pl* leadership
lidia *f* fight; TAUR bullfight
lidiar *vt, vi* to fight
liebre *f* hare
lienzo *m* 1. (*para cuadros*) canvas 2. (*óleo*) painting
liga *f* 1. *t.* DEP (*alianza*) league 2. (*prenda*) suspender, garter
ligadura *f* 1. (*lazo*) bond 2. *fig* (*traba*) tie
ligamento *m* ANAT ligament
ligar <g→gu> I. *vi inf* (*tontear*) to flirt II. *vt* 1. (*atar*) to tie 2. (*metal*) to alloy 3. (*unir*) to join 4. MÚS (*notas*) to slur III. *vr:* ~**se** 1. (*unirse*) to join 2. *inf* (*tontear*) to flirt
ligereza *f* 1. (*rapidez*) swiftness 2. (*levedad*) lightness 3. (*error*) thoughtless act
ligero, -a *adj* 1. (*leve*) light; (*ruido*) soft; ~ **de ropa** lightly clad; **a la ligera** without thinking; **tomarse algo a la ligera** to not take sth seriously 2. (*ágil*) nimble
ligue *m inf* chat-up, pick-up
liguero *m* suspender belt, garter belt *Am*
lija *f* sandpaper
lijar *vt* to sand
lila[1] I. *adj* lilac coloured *Brit,* lilac colored *Am* II. *f* BOT lilac
lila[2] *m* (*color*) lilac
lima *f* 1. (*instrumento*) file; **comer como una ~** *inf* to eat like a horse 2. BOT (*fruta*) lime
limar *vt* 1. (*pulir*) to file; *fig* to perfect 2. (*consumir*) to wear (down)
limbo *m* REL limbo; **estar en el ~** (*distraído*) to be distracted
limitación *f* limitation; (*de una norma*) restriction; **sin limitaciones** unlimited
limitar I. *vi* (*con algo*) to border on II. *vt* to limit; (*libertad*) to restrict; (*definir*) to fix the boundaries of III. *vr:* ~**se** to confine oneself
límite *m* limit; **situación ~** extreme situation

limítrofe *adj* bordering; (*país*) neighbouring *Brit,* neighboring *Am*

limón *m* lemon

limonada *f* lemonade

limonero *m* lemon tree

limosna *f* alms *pl;* **pedir** ~ to beg

limpiabotas *mf inv* bootblack

limpiacristales *mf inv* window cleaner

limpiaparabrisas *m inv* windsreen wiper, windshield wiper *Am*

limpiar I. *vt* 1. (*suciedad*) to clean; (*dientes*) to brush; (*chimenea*) to sweep; ~ **el polvo** to dust 2. (*librar*) to clear; (*de culpas*) to exonerate 3. *inf* (*robar*) to nick II. *vi* (*quitar la suciedad*) to clean III. *vr:* ~**se** to clean; (*nariz*) to wipe; (*dientes*) to brush

limpieza *f* 1. (*lavar*) washing; (*zapatos*) cleaning; **señora de la** ~ cleaning lady 2. (*estado*) cleanness, cleanliness 3. (*eliminación*) cleansing; POL purge

limpio *adv* (*sin trampas*) fairly; **escribir en** ~ to make a clean copy; **jugar** ~ to play fair

limpio, -a *adj* 1. (*no sucio*) clean; (*aire*) pure; **dejar a alguien** ~ *inf* to clean sb out 2. *fig* honorable

linaje *m* lineage

linaza *f* flax seed; **aceite de** ~ linseed oil

lince *m* lynx; **ser un** ~ *fig* to be very sharp

linchar *vt* to lynch

lindar *vi* ~ **con algo** to border on sth

linde *m o f,* **lindero** *m* boundary; (*camino*) edge

lindo, -a *adj* pretty; (*niño*) lovely, cute; **divertirse de lo** ~ to have a great time

línea *f* 1. *t.* MAT (*raya*) line; ~ **aérea** airline; ~ **en blanco** blank line; **coche de** ~ coach *Brit,* long-distance bus *Am;* **en toda la** ~ completely; **leer entre** ~**s** to read between the lines; **por** ~ **materna** on his mother's side 2. TEL telephone line; ~ **roja** hotline; **no hay** ~ the line is dead 3. (*tipo*) figure 4. (*directriz*) policy

lingote *m* ingot

lingüista *mf* linguist

lingüística *f* linguistics

linimento *m* liniment

lino *m* 1. BOT flax 2. (*tela*) linen

linóleo *m* linoleum

linterna *f* 1. (*de mano*) torch, flashlight 2. (*farol*) lantern

lío *m* 1. (*embrollo*) mess 2. (*de ropa*) bundle 3. *inf* (*relación*) affair

lipotimia *f* blackout

liquen *m* lichen

liquidación *f* 1. (*de una mercancía*) sale 2. (*de una empresa*) liquidation 3. (*de una factura*) payment; (*cuenta*) settlement

liquidar *vt* 1. (*mercancía*) to sell; ~ **las existencias** to sell off all merchandise 2. (*cerrar*) to close 3. (*factura*) to settle 4. *inf* (*acabar*) to liquidate; (*matar*) to kill

liquidez *f* 1. (*agua*) fluidity 2. COM liquidity

líquido *m* 1. (*agua*) liquid 2. (*saldo*) cash

líquido, -a *adj* 1. (*material, consonante*) liquid 2. (*dinero*) cash; **renta líquida** disposable income

lira *f* 1. (*moneda*) lira 2. (*instrumento*) lyre

lírica *f* poetry

lírico, -a *adj* lyric(al)

lirio *m* lily

lirón *m* dormouse

Lisboa *f* Lisbon

lisiado, -a I. *adj* crippled II. *m, f* cripple

lisiar I. *vt* (*mutilar*) to maim II. *vr:* ~**se** to become disabled

liso, -a *adj* 1. (*superficie*) smooth; (*pelo*) straight 2. (*tela*) plain

lisonja *f* flattery

lisonjear *vt* to flatter

lisonjero, -a I. *adj* flattering II. *m, f* flatterer

lista *f* 1. (*enumeración*) list; ~ **de espera** waiting list; **pasar** ~ (*leer*) to take roll call; (*controlar siempre*) to check on 2. (*de madera*) strip; (*estampado*) stripe

listado *m* list

listado, -a *adj* striped

listar *vt* to list

listo, -a *adj* **1.** *ser* (*inteligente*) clever; (*sagaz*) shrewd; **pasarse de ~** to be too clever by half **2.** *estar* (*preparado*) ready; **~ para enviar** *t.* INFOR ready to send

listón *m* lath

litera *f* (*cama*) bunk; FERRO couchette; NÁUT berth

literal *adj* literal

literario, -a *adj* literary

literato, -a *m, f* man *m* of letters, woman *f* of letters

literatura *f* literature; **~ barata** pulp fiction

litigar <g→gu> *vt* **1.** *t.* JUR (*disputar*) to dispute **2.** (*llevar a juicio*) to be in dispute

litigio *m* **1.** (*disputa*) dispute **2.** (*juicio*) lawsuit

litografía *f* **1.** ARTE (*proceso*) lithography **2.** (*grabado*) lithograph

litoral **I.** *adj* coastal **II.** *m* (*costa*) coast; (*playa*) shore

litro *m* litre *Brit,* liter *Am*

> ⚠ **litro** is always used with the preposition 'de': "He comprado un litro y medio de leche."

Lituania *f* Lithuania

liturgia *f* liturgy

liviano, -a *adj* **1.** (*trivial*) light **2.** (*ligero*) light

lívido, -a *adj* **1.** (*amoratado*) livid **2.** (*pálido*) ashen

llaga *f* wound

llama *f* **1.** (*fuego*) flame **2.** ZOOL llama

llamada *f* **1.** (*voz*) call; **~ del programa** INFOR program call **2.** (*de teléfono*) phonecall; **~ a cobro revertido** reverse charge call **3.** (*a la puerta golpeando*) knock; (*con el timbre*) ring **4.** MIL call-up, conscription *Brit,* draft *Am*

llamamiento *m* (*exhortación*) appeal; (*soldado*) call-up; **~ a filas** MIL call to arms

llamar **I.** *vt* **1.** (*voz*) to call; (*por teléfono*) to telephone, to ring up *Brit;* **~ a filas** MIL to call up *Brit,* to draft *Am* **2.** (*despertar*) to wake up; **~ la atención** (*reprender*) to reprimand; (*ser llamativo*) to attract attention **II.** *vi* (*a la puerta golpeando*) to knock; (*con el timbre*) to ring; **¿quién llama?** who is it? **III.** *vr:* **~se** to be called; **¿cómo te llamas?** what's your name?

llamarada *f* **1.** (*llama*) blaze **2.** (*rubor*) sudden flush

llamativo, -a *adj* (*traje*) flashy; (*color*) loud

llamear *vi* to blaze

llano *m* plain

llano, -a *adj* **1.** (*liso*) flat; (*terreno*) level **2.** (*campechano*) straightforward

llanta *f* **1.** AmL (*rueda*) tyre *Brit,* tire *Am* **2.** (*cerco*) (metal) rim

llanto *m* crying

llanura *f* plain

llave *f* **1.** *t. fig* (*instrumento*) key; **~ de contacto** AUTO ignition key; **ama de ~s** housekeeper; **echar la ~** to lock **2.** MÚS (*trompeta*) valve **3.** (*grifo*) tap *Brit,* faucet *Am* **4.** (*tuerca*) spanner **5.** (*interruptor*) switch **6.** TIPO bracket **7.** DEP hold, armlock

llavero *m* (*utensilio*) key ring

llegada *f* **1.** (*al destino*) arrival **2.** (*meta*) finishing line

llegar <g→gu> *vi* **1.** (*al destino*) to arrive; (*avión*) to land; (*barco*) to dock; **~ a Madrid/al hotel** to arrive in Madrid/at the hotel; **~ tarde** to be late; **¡todo llegará!** all in good time! **2.** (*recibir*) to receive **3.** (*durar*) to live; **~ a los ochenta** to reach the age of eighty **4.** (*ascender*) to amount to; **no llega a 20 euros** it's less than 20 euros; **~ lejos** to go far; **~ a ser muy rico** to become very rich **5.** (*alcanzar*) **~ a** [*o* **hasta**] **algo** to reach sth

llenar **I.** *vt* **1.** (*atestar*) to fill; **nos llenó de regalos** we were showered with gifts **2.** (*comida*) to be filling **3.** (*cumplimentar*) to fill in **4.** (*satisfacer*) to satisfy **II.** *vr:* **~se** *inf* (*decomida*) to stuff oneself with

lleno, -a *adj* full; **luna llena** full moon; **estoy ~** *inf* I'm full

L

llevadero, -a *adj* bearable
llevar I. *vt* 1. (*a un destino*) to take; (*transportar*) to transport; (*en brazos*) to carry, to induce sth; ~ **a alguien en el coche** to give sb a lift; **dos pizzas para** ~ two pizzas to take away; ~ **a algo** to lead to sth 2. (*cobrar*) to charge; (*costar*) to cost 3. (*tener*) ~ **consigo** to be carrying, to have 4. (*conducir*) to lead 5. (*ropa*) to wear 6. (*coche*) to drive 7. (*estar*) to have been; **llevo dos días aquí** I've been here for two days 8. (*gestionar*) to manage II. *vr:* ~**se** 1. (*coger*) to take; ~**se dos años** to be two years older 2. (*estar de moda*) to be in fashion 3. (*soportarse*) to get along
llorar I. *vi* to cry, to weep; (*ojos*) to water II. *vt* 1. (*lágrimas*) to cry over 2. (*lamentar*) to bemoan
lloriquear *vi* to whimper, to snivel
lloro(s) *m(pl)* crying
llorón, -ona I. *adj* always crying II. *m, f* crybaby, whiner
lloroso, -a *adj* tearful
llover <o→ue> *vi, vt, vimpers* to rain; **está lloviendo** it's raining; **llueve a mares** [*o* **a cántaros**] it's pouring; **como llovido del cielo** heaven sent
llovizna *f* drizzle
lloviznar *vimpers* **está lloviznando** it's drizzling
lluvia *f* 1. (*chubasco*) rain; ~ **ácida** acid rain; ~ **radiactiva** fallout 2. (*cantidad*) shower 3. *AmL* (*ducha*) shower
lluvioso, -a *adj* rainy
lo I. *art def v.* **el, la, lo** II. *pron pers m y neutro sing* 1. (*objeto: masculino*) him; (*neutro*) it; **¡lláma~!** call him!; **¡haz~!** do it! 2. (*con relativo*) ~ **que...** what; ~ **cual** which

⚠️ **lo** is used to turn adjectives or relative clauses into nouns: "Lo importante es participar; Lo más me importa es la salud."

loa *f* praise

loable *adj* commendable
loar *vt* to praise
lobato *m* 1. (*lobo*) wolf cub 2. (*cachorro*) cub
lobo, -a *m, f* wolf; ~ **de mar** old salt; **en la boca del** ~ in the lion's den; **tener un hambre de** ~**s** to be as hungry as a wolf
lóbrego, -a *adj* gloomy
lóbulo *m* ANAT lobe
local I. *adj* local II. *m* locale; COM premises *pl*
localidad *f* 1. (*municipio*) town 2. (*entrada*) ticket; (*asiento*) seat
localizar <z→c> *vt* 1. (*encontrar*) to find 2. (*limitar*) to localize; AERO to track
loción *f* lotion; ~ **tónica** after-shave
loco, -a I. *adj* 1. (*chalado*) mad, crazy; ~ **por la música** crazy about music; **estar** ~ **de contento** to be elated 2. (*maravilloso*) tremendous II. *m, f* madman; **casa de** ~**s** *t. fig* madhouse
locomoción *f* locomotion
locomotora *f* locomotive
locuaz *adj* loquacious; (*charlatán*) talkative
locución *f* (*expresión*) phrase
locura *f* 1. (*mental*) madness; ~ **bovina** mad cow disease 2. (*disparate*) crazy thing
locutor(a) *m(f)* speaker
locutorio *m* TEL telephone box *Brit,* telephone booth *Am*
lodo *m* mud
lógica *f* logic
lógico, -a *adj* logical; (*normal*) natural
logística *f* logistics *pl*
logístico, -a *adj* logistic
logotipo *m* logo
logrado, -a *adj* successful, well done
lograr I. *vt* to achieve; (*premio*) to win II. *vr:* ~**se** to be successful
logro *m* achievement
loma *f* hill
lombriz *f* worm
lomo *m* 1. (*espalda*) back 2. (*solomillo*) loin 3. (*de libro*) spine 4. (*de cuchillo*) back
lona *f* canvas

loncha *f* slice; (*beicon*) rasher
londinense I. *adj* London II. *mf* Londoner
Londres *m* London
longaniza *f* spicy pork sausage
longevidad *f sin pl* longevity
longitud *f* length; GEO longitude; **salto de** ~ DEP long jump; **cuatro metros de** ~ four metres long
longitudinal *adj* **corte** ~ longitudinal section
lonja *f* **1.** COM public exchange **2.** (*loncha*) slice
Lorena *f* Lorraine
loro *m* parrot
los I. *art def v.* **el, la, lo** II. *pron pers m y neutro pl* **1.** (*objeto directo*) them; **¡lláma~!** call them! **2.** (*con relativo*) ~ **que...** the ones that ...; ~ **cuales** which
losa *f* **1.** (*piedra*) slab **2.** (*lápida*) gravestone
lote *m* (*parte*) share; COM lot
lotería *f* lottery
loza *f* earthenware; (*vajilla*) crockery; ~ **fina** china
lozanía *f sin pl* (*robustez*) vigour *Brit,* vigor *Am;* (*salud*) healthiness
lozano, -a *adj* (*robusta*) vigorous; (*saludable*) healthy
lubri(fi)cante *m* lubricant
lubri(fi)car <c→qu> *vt* to lubricate
lucense *adj* of/from Lugo
lucero *m* bright star
lucha *f* fight; DEP wrestling
luchar *vi* to fight for
lucidez *f sin pl* lucidity
lúcido, -a *adj* **1.** (*clarividente*) clear-sighted **2.** (*sobrio*) clear-headed
luciérnaga *f* firefly
lucir *irr* I. *vi* **1.** (*brillar*) to shine **2.** (*verse*) to look good II. *vt* (*exhibir*) to display, to show III. *vr:* ~**se 1.** (*exhibirse*) to display **2.** (*destacarse*) to stand out
lucro *m* profit; **con ánimo de** ~ for profit
lúdico, -a *adj* ludic
luego I. *adv* **1.** (*después*) later; **¡hasta** ~**!** see you later!; **desde** ~ of course **2.** (*entonces*) then II. *conj* **1.** (*así que*) and so **2.** (*después de*) ~

que as soon as
lugar *m* **1.** (*sitio, situación*) place; **en primer/segundo** ~ first/second; **tener** ~ to take place; **en algún** ~ somewhere; **en** ~ **de** instead of; **yo en** ~ **de usted...** if I were you ... **2.** (*motivo*) **dar** ~ **a...** to give rise to ...
lugarteniente *m* deputy
lúgubre *adj* (*sombrío*) gloomy
lujo *m* luxury
lujoso, -a *adj* luxurious
lujuria *f* lechery, lust
lumbago *m* MED lumbago
lumbre *f sin pl* (*llamas*) fire; (*brasa*) glow; **¿me das** ~**?** can you give me a light?
lumbrera *f* **1.** (*claraboya*) skylight **2.** (*talento*) leading light
luminoso, -a *adj* **1.** (*brillante*) bright, luminous; (*día*) light **2.** (*excelente*) brilliant
luna *f* **1.** ASTR moon; (*luz*) moonlight; ~ **creciente/menguante/llena** waxing/waning/full moon; ~ **de miel** honeymoon; **estar en la** ~ to be daydreaming **2.** (*cristal*) plate glass; (*espejo*) mirror
lunar I. *adj* lunar II. *m* **1.** (*en la piel*) mole **2.** (*en una tela*) polka-dot
lunes *m inv* Monday; ~ **de carnaval** the last Monday before Lent; ~ **de Pascua** Easter Monday; **el** ~ on Monday; **el** ~ **pasado** last Monday; **el** ~ **que viene** next Monday; **el** ~ **por la noche/al mediodía/por la mañana/por la tarde** Monday night/at midday/morning/afternoon; (**todos) los** ~ every Monday, on Mondays; **en la noche del** ~ **al martes** in the small hours of Monday; **el** ~ **entero** all day Monday; **cada dos** ~ (**del mes**) every other Monday; **hoy es** ~**, once de marzo** today is Monday, March 11th
lupa *f* magnifying glass
lustrabotas *mf inv, AmL* shoeshine
lustrar *vt* to polish; (*zapatos*) to shine
lustre *m* **1.** (*brillo*) lustre *Brit,* luster *Am;* **sacar** ~ to polish **2.** *AmL* (*betún*) shoe polish

lustroso, -a *adj* shiny
luto *m* mourning
Luxemburgo *m* Luxembourg
luz *f* **1.** (*resplandor*) light; ~ **larga**
full beam; **traje de luces** bull-
fighter's suit; **a la ~ del día** in daylight; **dar a ~** to give birth; **salir a la
~** *fig* to come to light; **a todas luces**
evidently **2.** (*energía*) electricity;
(*lámpara*) light; **apagar/encender
la ~** to turn off/on the light

M m

M, m *f* M, m; ~ **de María** M for Mary
Brit, M for Mike *Am*
macabro, -a *adj* macabre
macarrones *mpl* macaroni
macedonia *f* ~ (**de frutas**) fruit
salad
macerar *vt* **1.** (*con golpes*) to macer-
ate **2.** GASTR to marinate
maceta *f* flowerpot
machacar <c→qu> *vt* **1.** (*triturar*)
to pound **2.** (*insistir*) to insist on, to
harp on **3.** *inf* (*estudiar*) to swot up
4. *inf* (*destruir*) to crush
machete *m* machete
machismo *m* male chauvinism; (*virilidad*) manliness
machista *adj* (male) chauvinistic
macho **I.** *m* **1.** ZOOL (*masculino*) male
2. *inf* (*machote*) tough guy **3.** (*pieza*) male part **II.** *adj* **1.** (*masculino*)
male **2.** (*fuerte*) macho
macizo *m* **1.** (*masa*) solid mass **2.** GEO
massif **3.** (*plantas*) flowerbed
macizo, -a *adj* **1.** (*oro*) solid **2.** (*sólido*) solid **3.** *inf* (*mujer*) stacked;
(*hombre*) well-built
macramé *m* macramé
mácula *f* (*mancha*) spot; *fig* stain;
sin ~ *fig* pure
madeja *f* skein, hank
madera *f* **1.** (*de los árboles*) wood;

(*cortada*) timber, lumber *Am;* **de ~**
wooden; **tocar ~** to touch wood;
tener ~ de to have the makings of
2. *inf* (*policía*) **la ~** the law
madero *m* **1.** (*viga*) beam; (*tablón*)
board **2.** (*persona*) oaf
madrastra *f* **1.** (*pariente*) stepmother **2.** *pey* (*mala madre*) bad
mother
madre *f* **1.** (*de familia*) mother; ~ **de
alquiler** surrogate mother; ~ **patria**
mother country; ~ **política** mother-
-in-law; ¡~ (**mía**)! goodness me!; ¡**tu
~**! *inf* up yours! *vulg;* **de puta ~** *vulg*
(fucking) great! *vulg* **2.** GEO river bed
3. GASTR dregs *pl*
madreperla *f* mother of pearl
madreselva *f* honeysuckle
Madrid *m* Madrid
madriguera *f* burrow
madrileño, -a *adj* of/from Madrid
madrina *f* **1.** (*de bautismo*) godmother **2.** (*de boda*) ~ (**de boda**)
maid of honour
madrugada *f* (*alba*) dawn; **en la** [*o*
de] ~ in the early morning; **a las
cinco de la ~** at five in the morning
madrugador(a) *adj* **ser ~** to be an
early riser
madrugar <g→gu> *vi* to get up
early
madurar *vt, vi* **1.** (*fruta*) to ripen
2. (*persona*) to mature **3.** (*reflexionar*) to think over
madurez *f* **1.** (*de fruta*) ripeness
2. (*de persona*) maturity; **estar en
la ~** to be middle-aged **3.** (*de un
plan*) readiness
maduro, -a *adj* **1.** (*fruta*) ripe **2.** (*persona: prudente*) mature; (*mayor*)
adult; (*plan*) ready
maestría *f* **1.** (*habilidad*) mastery;
con ~ skilfully *Brit,* skillfully *Am*
2. (*título*) Master's degree
maestro, -a **I.** *adj* master; **obra
maestra** masterpiece **II.** *m, f*
1. (*profesor*) teacher **2.** (*experto*)
master **3.** (*capataz*) overseer
mafia *f* **la Mafia** the Mafia
mafioso, -a **I.** *adj* of the Mafia **II.** *m,
f* mafioso
magia *f* magic

mágico, -a I. *adj* 1. (*misterioso*) magic 2. (*maravilloso*) marvellous *Brit,* marvelous *Am* II. *m, f* magic
magisterio *m* teaching; **estudiar ~** to study to become a teacher
magistrado, -a *m, f* JUR magistrate
magistral *adj* 1. ENS teaching 2. (*con maestría*) masterly
magnanimidad *f* magnanimity
magnánimo, -a *adj* magnanimous
magnate *m* tycoon; **~ de las finanzas** finance magnate
magnesio *m* magnesium
magnético, -a *adj* magnetic
magnetismo *m* magnetism
magnetizar <z→c> *vt* to magnetize
magnetofón *m* tape recorder
magnetofónico, -a *adj* recording; **cinta magnetofónica** (recording) tape
magnífico, -a *adj* 1. (*valioso*) valuable 2. (*excelente*) magnificent 3. (*liberal*) lavish
magnitud *f* magnitude
magno, -a *adj* great
magnolia *f* magnolia
magnolio *m* magnolia
mago, -a *m, f* magician; **los Reyes Magos** the Magi, the Three Kings
magro, -a *adj* lean
magullar *vt* to bruise
mahometano, -a *adj, m, f* Muslim, Mohammedan
mahonesa *f* mayonnaise
maíz *m* sweetcorn *Brit,* corn *Am*
maizal *m* maize field *Brit,* cornfield *Am*
majadería *f* 1. (*tontería*) idiocy 2. (*imprudencia*) foolishness
majadero, -a *adj* 1. (*insensato*) silly 2. (*porfiado*) pestering
majestad *f* 1. (*título*) Majesty; **Su Majestad** Your Majesty 2. (*majestuosidad*) majesty
majestuosidad *f* majesty
majestuoso, -a *adj* majestic
majo, -a *adj* 1. (*bonito*) lovely; (*guapo*) attractive 2. (*agradable*) pleasant
mal I. *adj v.* **malo** II. *m* 1. (*daño*) harm; (*injusticia*) wrong; **el ~ de ojo** the evil eye; **no hay ~ que por**

bien no venga every cloud has a silver lining 2. (*lo malo*) bad thing; **el ~ menor** the lesser evil; **menos ~** thank goodness 3. (*inconveniente*) problem 4. (*enfermedad*) illness; **~ de vientre** stomach complaint 5. (*desgracia*) misfortune III. *adv* 1. (*de mala manera*) badly; **estar ~ de dinero** to be badly off; **tomarse algo a ~** to take sth badly; **me cae ~** I don't like him/her; **vas a acabar ~** you are going to come to a bad end; **~ que bien, sigue funcionando** better or worse, it is still working; **~ que bien, tendré que ir** whether I like it or not, I will have to go 2. (*equivocadamente*) wrongly

! **mal** is an adverb and qualifies the verb: "Mi primo canta muy **mal**." **malo** is an adjective and qualifies a noun: "David es un niño muy **malo**."

malabarismo *m* juggling
malabarista *mf* (*artista*) juggler
malaconsejar *vt* to badly advise; **actuar malaconsejado** to act on bad advice
malacostumbrado, -a *adj* (*mimado*) spoilt; (*sin modales*) badly brought-up
malacostumbrar I. *vt* 1. (*mimar*) to spoil 2. (*educar mal*) to bring up badly II. *vr:* **~se** to get into a bad habit
malaria *f* malaria
Malasia *f* Malaysia
malcriado, -a *adj* 1. (*mal educado*) spoilt 2. (*descortés*) rude
malcriar <1. *pres:* malcrío> *vt* to bring up badly; (*mimar*) to spoil
maldad *f* evil, wickedness
maldecir *irr* I. *vt* to curse, to damn II. *vi* 1. (*jurar*) to swear 2. (*hablar mal*) to speak ill
maldición *f* 1. (*imprecación*) curse 2. (*juramento*) swear word
maldito, -a I. *pp de* **maldecir** II. *adj* 1. (*endemoniado*) damned; **¡maldita sea!** *inf* damn (it)!; **¡maldita la**

M

gracia (que me hace)! I don't find it in the least bit funny!; **¡malditas las ganas!** I haven't the slightest wish to! **2.** (*maligno*) wicked

maleante I. *adj* **1.** (*delincuente*) delinquent **2.** (*maligno*) miscreant **II.** *mf* delinquent

malecón *m* **1.** (*dique*) dyke **2.** (*rompeolas*) breakwater **3.** (*embarcadero*) jetty

maledicencia *f* (evil) talk

maleducado, -a *adj* **1.** (*sin modales*) ill-mannered; (*niño*) ill-bred **2.** (*descortés*) rude

maléfico, -a I. *adj* **1.** (*perjudicial*) harmful **2.** (*que hechiza*) who casts spells; **poder ~** evil power **II.** *m, f* sorcerer

malentendido *m* misunderstanding

malestar *m* **1.** (*físico*) malaise **2.** (*espiritual*) uneasiness

maleta *f* suitcase; **hacer la ~** to pack one's suitcase

maletera *f* Col, Méx, **maletero** *m* AUTO boot Brit, trunk Am

maletín *m* (*de documentos*) briefcase; (*de aseo*) toilet bag; (*para herramientas*) tool box; (*en una bici*) pannier

malévolo, -a *adj* malevolent

maleza *f* **1.** (*hierbas malas*) weeds *pl* **2.** (*matorral*) thicket

malgastar *vt* to waste; (*dinero*) to squander

malhechor(a) *adj, m(f)* delinquent

malherir *irr como sentir* *vt* to seriously injure

malhumorado, -a *adj* **1.** *ser* bad--tempered **2.** *estar* **estar ~** to be in a bad mood

malicia *f* **1.** (*mala intención*) malice **2.** (*maldad*) wickedness **3.** (*picardía*) mischievousness

malicioso, -a *adj* **1.** (*con mala intención*) malicious **2.** (*maligno*) malign

maligno, -a *adj* (*pernicioso*) malign; (*persona*) spiteful; (*sonrisa*) malicious; MED malignant

malintencionado, -a *adj* unkind

malinterpretar *vt* to misinterpret

malla *f* **1.** (*de un tejido*) mesh, weave **2.** (*vestido*) leotard **3.** *pl*

(*pantalones*) leggings *pl* **4.** AmL (*de baño*) swimming costume Brit, swimsuit Am

Mallorca *f* Majorca

mallorquín, -ina *adj* of/from Majorca

malnutrido, -a *adj* malnourished

malo, -a I. *adj* <peor, pésimo> (*delante de sustantivo masculino: mal*) **1.** (*en general*) bad; **de mala gana** unwillingly; **tener mala suerte** to be unlucky; **hace un tiempo malísimo** the weather is really bad **2.** *ser* (*falso*) false **3.** *ser* (*malévolo*) nasty **4.** *estar* (*enfermo*) ill **5.** *ser* (*travieso*) naughty **6.** *estar* (*leche*) off Brit, gone bad; (*ropa*) worn-out **II.** *adv* **andar a malas** to be on bad terms; **estar a malas con alguien** to be at daggers drawn with sb; **se pusieron a malas por una tontería** they fell out with each other over an insignificance **III.** *m, f* (*persona*) bad man *m,* bad woman *f*; CINE baddie

malograr I. *vt* **1.** (*desaprovechar*) to waste **2.** (*frustrar*) to frustate **3.** (*estropear*) to ruin **II.** *vr:* **~se 1.** (*fallar*) to fail **2.** (*estropearse*) to be ruined **3.** (*desarrollarse mal*) to turn out badly **4.** (*morir*) to die an untimely death

maloliente *adj* foul-smelling

malparar *vt* (*persona*) to come off badly; **salir malparado de algo** to come off worse in sth

malpensado, -a *adj* evil-minded

malsano, -a *adj* unhealthy

malta *f* **1.** *t.* AGR malt **2.** Arg (*cerveza*) beer

maltés, -esa *adj, m, f* Maltese

maltratar *vt* to maltreat

maltrato *m* maltreatment, abuse

maltrecho, -a *adj* **1.** (*golpeado*) battered **2.** (*deprimido*) low

malva I. *adj* mauve **II.** *f* mallow

malvado, -a *adj* wicked

malvavisco *m* marsh mallow

malversar *vt* to misappropriate, to embezzle

Malvinas *fpl* Falkland Islands *pl*

mama *f* (*pecho*) breast; (*ubre*) udder

mamá *f inf* mummy *Brit,* mommy *Am*

mamar *vt, vi* **1.** (*en el pecho*) to breastfeed **2.** (*adquirir*) to acquire

mamarracho *m* **1.** (*persona que viste mal*) sight; (*ridícula*) ridiculous person **2.** (*cosa mal hecha*) botch; (*fea*) hideous thing; (*sin valor*) piece of junk **3.** (*persona despreciable*) despicable person

mamífero **I.** *adj* mammalian **II.** *m* mammal

mamón, -ona *m, f* **1.** *vulg* jerk; (*hombre*) prick; (*mujer*) bitch **2.** *AmL, inf* (*borracho*) drunk

mampara *f* screen (door), (room) divider

mamporro *m inf* clout; **darse un ~ contra algo** to bash oneself against sth

mampostería *f* **1.** (*obra*) rubblework **2.** (*oficio*) drystone walling

mamut <mamuts> *m* mammoth

manada *f* (*de vacas, ciervos*) herd; (*de ovejas, aves*) flock; (*de lobos*) pack; **~ de gente** crowd of people

Managua *m* Managua

manantial *m* **1.** (*natural*) spring **2.** (*artificial*) fountain **3.** (*origen*) source

manar **I.** *vt* to flow with **II.** *vi* **1.** (*surgir*) to well **2.** (*fluir fácilmente*) to flow

mancha *f* **1.** (*en la ropa*) dirty mark; (*de tinta*) stain; (*salpicadura*) spot **2.** (*toque de color*) fleck **3.** (*deshonra*) stain

Mancha *f* **canal de la ~** the (English) Channel

manchado, -a *adj* **1.** (*ropa, mantel*) stained **2.** (*cara, fruta*) dirty **3.** (*caballos*) dappled

manchar **I.** *vt* **1.** (*ensuciar*) to dirty **2.** (*desprestigiar*) to sully **II.** *vr:* **~se** (*ensuciarse*) to get dirty

manchego, -a *adj* of/from la Mancha

mancilla *f* stain

manco, -a *adj* **1.** (*de un brazo*) one-armed; (*de una mano*) one-handed; **no ser (cojo ni) ~** (*ser hábil*) to be dexterous; (*ser largo de manos*) to

be light-fingered **2.** (*defectuoso*) faulty; (*incompleto*) incomplete

mancomunar **I.** *vt* to join together **II.** *vr:* **~se** to unite

mancomunidad *f* **1.** (*comunidad*) community **2.** JUR joint ownership

mandado *m* (*encargo*) errand; (*orden*) order

mandamiento *m* **1.** (*orden*) order **2.** (*precepto*) precept **3.** REL commandment

mandar *vt* **1.** (*ordenar*) to order **2.** (*prescribir*) to prescribe **3.** (*dirigir*) to lead; (*gobernar*) to govern **4.** (*encargar*) to ask to do **5.** (*enviar*) to send **6.** TÉC to control

mandarín *m* **1.** (*idioma*) Mandarin **2.** *pey, inf* (*funcionario*) mandarin

mandarina *f* mandarin, tangerine

mandatario, -a *m, f* **primer ~** POL head of state; JUR attorney

mandato *m* **1.** (*orden*) order; (*prescripción*) prescription; (*delegación*) delegation **2.** POL mandate

mandíbula *f* **1.** ANAT jaw **2.** TÉC clamp

mandil *m* apron

mando *m* **1.** (*poder*) control; MIL command **2.** (*persona*) **~s intermedios** middle management; **alto ~** MIL high command **3.** TÉC control; **~ a distancia** remote control

mandolina *f* MÚS mandolin

mandón, -ona *adj* bossy

manecilla *f* **1.** (*del reloj*) hand **2.** TÉC pointer

manejable *adj* **1.** (*objeto*) user-friendly **2.** (*persona*) tractable

manejar **I.** *vt* **1.** (*usar*) to use; (*máquina*) to operate; *fig* to handle **2.** INFOR to use **3.** (*dirigir*) to handle **4.** *AmL* (*un coche*) to drive **II.** *vr:* **~se** to manage

manejo *m* **1.** (*uso*) use; (*de una máquina*) operation; *fig* handling; **~ a distancia** remote control **2.** INFOR management; **~ de errores** error management **3.** (*de un negocio*) running **4.** *AmL* (*de un coche*) driving

manera *f* **1.** (*modo*) manner, way; **~ de pensar** way of thinking; **~ de**

ver las cosas way of seeing things; **a mi** ~ my way; **de la** ~ **que sea** somehow or other; **de cualquier** ~, **de todas** ~s anyway; **de** ~ **que** so that; **de ninguna** ~ no way; **en cierta** ~ in a way; **no hay** ~ **de...** there is no way that ...; **¡qué** ~ **de llover!** just look at the rain!; **sobre** ~ a lot; **de mala** ~ (*responder*) rudely; (*hacer*) badly **2.** pl (*modales*) manners pl

manga f **1.** (*del vestido*) sleeve; **en ~s de camisa** in shirt-sleeves; **tener ~ ancha** *fig* to be lenient **2.** (*tubo*) hose **3.** GASTR (*filtro*) muslin strainer; (*pastelera*) pastry bag, icing bag *Brit*

mangar <g→gu> vt inf to swipe, to nick; (*en tiendas*) to shoplift

mango m **1.** (*puño*) knob, (*alargado*) handle **2.** (*fruta*) mango

mangonear I. vi inf to meddle II. vt inf to wangle

manguera f hose

maní m peanut

manía f **1.** (*locura*) mania **2.** (*extravagancia*) eccentricity, quirk **3.** (*obsesión*) obsession **4.** inf (*aversión*) aversion; **coger ~ a alguien** to take a dislike to sb

maniaco, -a, maníaco, -a I. adj maniacal II. m, f maniac

maniatar vt to tie sb's hands up

maniático, -a I. adj **1.** (*extravagante*) fussy **2.** (*loco*) manic II. m, f **1.** (*extravagante*) fusspot **2.** (*loco*) maniac

manicomio m psychiatric hospital; *fig* (*casa de locos*) madhouse

manicura f manicure

manicuro, -a m, f manicurist

manifestación f **1.** (*expresión*) expression **2.** (*reunión*) demonstration

manifestante mf demonstrator

manifestar <e→ie> I. vt **1.** (*declarar*) to declare **2.** (*mostrar*) to show II. vr: ~se **1.** (*declararse*) to declare oneself **2.** (*políticamente*) to demonstrate

manifiesto m manifesto

manifiesto, -a adj (*evidente*) manifest; **poner de** ~ (*revelar*) to show; (*expresar*) to declare

manija f handle

manillar m handlebars pl

maniobra f **1.** (*operación manual*) handling **2.** (*ardid*) ploy **3.** MIL manoeuvre *Brit,* maneuver *Am*

maniobrar I. vi **1.** MIL to carry out manoeuvres **2.** (*intrigar*) to scheme II. vt **1.** (*manejar*) to handle **2.** (*manipular*) to manipulate

manipulación f **1.** (*empleo*) handling **2.** (*alteración*) manipulation

manipular vt **1.** (*maniobrar*) to manoeuvre *Brit,* to maneuver *Am;* (*máquina*) to operate **2.** (*elaborar*) to make **3.** (*alterar*) to manipulate **4.** (*interferir*) to interfere with **5.** (*manosear*) to fiddle with

maniquí <maniquíes> m **1.** (*modelo*) model **2.** (*muñeco*) puppet, dummy

manirroto, -a adj spendthrift

manita f **hacer ~s** inf to canoodle, to snog *Brit;* **ser un ~s** to be dexterous

manivela f handle

manjar m **1.** (*comestible*) food **2.** (*exquisitez*) delicacy

mano f **1.** t. ANAT (*trabajador, naipes*) hand; ~ **de obra** labour *Brit,* labor *Am;* **a** ~ **alzada** (*votación*) by a show of hands; **a** ~ **armada** armed; **apretón de ~s** handshake; **bajo** ~ underhand; **echar una** ~ to give a hand; **echar** ~ **de algo** to draw on sth; **irse a las ~s** to come to blows; **meter** ~ to take action; **tener** ~ **con** to have a way with; **tener** ~ **izquierda** to be tactful; **traer entre ~s** to be up to sth; **hecho a** ~ handmade; ~ **a** ~ *fig* hand in hand; **¡~s a la obra!** to work!; **con las ~s en la masa** red-handed; **poner las ~s en el fuego por alguien** to risk ones neck for somebody **2.** (*lado*) ~ derecha/izquierda right-/left-hand side **3.** (*de pintura*) coat

manojo m bunch; (*de nervios*) bundle

manopla f flannel *Brit,* washcloth *Am*

manoseado, -a adj **1.** (*sobado*) worn **2.** (*trillado*) hackneyed

manosear *vt* to handle; *pey* to paw
manotazo *m* smack
mansalva *adv* **a** ~ in abundance
mansedumbre *f* **1.** (*suavidad*) gentleness **2.** (*sumisión*) meekness
mansión *f* **1.** (*casa*) mansion **2.** (*morada*) dwelling
manso, -a *adj* **1.** (*dócil*) docile **2.** (*animales*) tame
manta *f* **1.** (*de cama*) blanket; **a** ~ in abundance **2.** (*zurra*) beating **3.** ZOOL manta
manteca *f* **1.** (*grasa*) fat **2.** (*mantequilla*) butter
mantecado *m* **1.** (*bollo*) pastry cake **2.** (*helado*) icecream
mantel *m* tablecloth
mantener *irr como* **tener** **I.** *vt* **1.** (*conservar*) to maintain; (*orden*) to keep; (*correspondencia*) to keep up **2.** (*sostener*) to support **3.** (*proseguir*) to continue; (*conversación*) to hold **II.** *vr:* ~**se** **1.** (*sostenerse*) to support oneself **2.** (*continuar*) to continue **3.** (*perseverar*) to keep **4.** (*sustentarse*) to support oneself
mantenimiento *m* **1.** (*alimentos*) sustenance **2.** TÉC maintenance; ~ **de datos** INFOR database update
mantequilla *f* butter
mantilla *f* **1.** (*de mujer*) mantilla **2.** (*de niño*) swaddling clothes *pl*
manto *m* **1.** (*prenda*) cloak **2.** (*capa*) layer; ~ **terrestre** GEO earth's crust
mantón *m* shawl
manual **I.** *adj* **1.** (*con las manos*) manual, hand; **trabajos** ~**es** handicrafts *pl* **2.** (*manejable*) user-friendly **II.** *m* manual, handbook
manubrio *m* **1.** (*puño*) stock **2.** (*manivela*) handle
manufactura *f* **1.** (*acción, producto*) manufacture **2.** (*taller*) factory
manufacturar *vt* to manufacture
manuscrito *m* manuscript
manuscrito, -a *adj* handwritten
manutención *f* **1.** (*alimentos*) keep **2.** TÉC maintenance
manzana *f* **1.** (*fruta*) apple **2.** (*de casas*) block **3.** *AmL* ANAT (*nuez*) Adam's apple
manzanilla *f* **1.** (*planta*) camomile **2.** (*infusión*) camomile tea **3.** (*vino*) manzanilla
manzano *m* apple tree
maña *f* **1.** (*habilidad*) skill **2.** (*astucia*) craftiness
mañana¹ **I.** *f* morning; **a las 5 de la** ~ at 5 a.m.; **de la noche a la** ~ overnight; **de** ~ in the early morning; ~ **por la** ~ tomorrow morning **II.** *adv* tomorrow; **¡hasta** ~**!** see you tomorrow!
mañana² *m* tomorrow; **pasado** ~ the day after tomorrow; **el día de** ~ in the future
mañanero, -a *adj* early-rising
maño, -a *adj* of/from Aragón
mañoso, -a *adj* **1.** (*hábil*) dexterous, handy **2.** (*sagaz*) guileful
mapa *m* map
maqueta *f* **1.** ARQUIT (scale) model **2.** (*formato*) format; (*de libro*) dummy
maquetación *f* layout
maquetar *vt* to lay out
maquillaje *m* make-up
maquillar **I.** *vt* **1.** (*con maquillaje*) to apply make-up to **2.** (*disimular*) to disguise **II.** *vr:* ~**se** to put on make-up
máquina *f* **1.** (*artefacto*) machine; ~ **de afeitar** electric shaver; ~ **fotográfica** camera; **a toda** ~ (at) full speed; **escrito a** ~ typed **2.** (*de monedas*) vending machine; (*de tabaco*) dispenser **3.** (*tren*) engine
maquinación *f* plot
maquinal *adj* mechanical, automatic
maquinar *vt* to scheme
maquinaria *f* **1.** (*máquinas*) machinery **2.** (*mecanismo*) mechanism
maquinilla *f* (safety) razor
maquinista *mf* **1.** (*conductor*) machinist; ~ **de trenes** train driver *Brit,* engineer *Am* **2.** (*constructor*) engineer
mar *m o f* GEO sea; **Mar de las Antillas** Caribbean Sea; **Mar Ártico** Artic Ocean; **Mar Báltico** Baltic Sea; **Mar de Irlanda** Irish Sea; **Mar Mediterráneo** Mediterranean Sea; **Mar del Norte** North Sea; **en alta** ~ offshore; **por** ~ by sea; **al otro lado**

Mm

del ~ overseas; **llueve a ~es** it is pouring with rain; **ser la ~ de aburrido** to be excruciatingly boring; **ser la ~ de bonita** to be incredibly pretty

maraca *f* maraca

maraña *f* 1.(*maleza*) thicket 2.(*lío*) mess; (*de cabello*) tangle

maratón *m o f* marathon

maravilla *f* 1.(*portento*) marvel 2.(*admiración*) wonder

maravillar I. *vt* to amaze II. *vr:* ~se to marvel at

maravilloso, -a *adj* marvellous *Brit,* marvelous *Am*

marca *f* 1.(*distintivo*) mark 2.(*de productos, ganado*) brand; ~ **registrada** registered trademark; **ropa de** ~ designer label 3.(*huella*) impression 4.DEP record 5.INFOR bookmark

marcado, -a *adj* 1.(*señalado*) marked 2.(*evidente*) clear

marcador *m* scoreboard; **abrir el** ~ to open the scoring

marcapaso(s) *m* (*inv*) pacemaker

marcar <c→qu> *vt* 1.(*señalar*) to mark; (*ganado*) to brand; (*mercancías*) to label; (*época*) to denote; (*compás*) to beat 2.(*resaltar*) to emphasize 3.(*teléfono*) to dial 4.(*cabello*) to style 5.DEP (*gol*) to score 6.DEP (*a un jugador*) to mark, to cover

marcha *f* 1.(*movimiento*) progress; **poner en** ~ to start; **la** ~ **de los acontecimientos** the course of events; **sobre la** ~ along the way 2.(*caminata*) hike 3.(*velocidad*) gear; ~ **atrás** reverse; **a toda** ~ at full speed 4. *t.* MIL, MÚS march 5.(*salida*) departure 6. *inf*(*acción*) action

marchar I. *vi* 1.(*ir*) to go; **¡marchando!** let's go! 2.(*funcionar*) to work II. *vr:* ~se 1.(*irse*) to leave 2.(*huir*) to flee

marchitar I. *vi* 1.(*plantas*) to wither 2.(*personas*) to be on the wane II. *vr:* ~se to wither

marchito, -a *adj* withered

marchoso, -a *adj* fun-loving

marcial *adj* martial

marciano, -a *adj, m, f* Martian

marco *m* 1.(*recuadro*) frame; (*armazón*) framework 2.(*ambiente*) background 3.(*moneda*) mark

marea *f* 1.(*mar*) tide; ~ **negra** oil slick 2.(*multitud*) flood

mareado, -a *adj* (*en el mar*) seasick; (*al viajar*) travel-sick; **estoy** ~ I feel sick

marear I. *vt* 1.*inf* (*molestar*) to pester 2.MED to nauseate II. *vr:* ~se 1.(*enfermarse*) to feel sick; (*en el mar*) to get seasick 2.(*quedar aturdido*) to become dizzy 3.(*emborracharse*) to get tipsy

maremoto *m* tidal wave; (*seísmo*) seaquake

mareo *m* 1.(*malestar*) nausea; (*en el mar*) seasickness; (*al viajar*) travel-sickness, motion sickness 2.(*vértigo*) dizziness

marfil *m* ivory

margarina *f* margarine

margarita *f* daisy

margen *m o f* 1.(*borde*) edge; **el** ~ **del río** the riverside; **al** ~ apart; **dejar al** ~ to leave out; **mantenerse al** ~ *fig* to keep out of 2.(*página*) margin 3.(*ganancia*) profit margin

marginal *adj* 1.(*al margen*) apart 2.(*secundario*) secondary

marginar *vt* (*algo*) to disregard; (*a alguien*) to marginalize

mariachi *m* mariachi musician

marica *m,* **maricón** *m vulg* 1.(*homosexual*) queer, poof *Brit,* fag *Am* 2.(*cobarde*) sissy

marido *m* husband; **mi** ~ my husband

marihuana *f sin pl* marijuana, marihuana

marimacho *m inf* butch (woman); (*niña*) tomboy; *pey* (*lesbiana*) dyke

marina *f* 1.(*flota*) navy; **la** ~ **mercante** the merchant marine 2.ARTE seascape

marinero *m* sailor

marinero, -a *adj* 1.(*del mar*) marine; (*pueblo*) coastal 2.(*de la marina*) marine

marino *m* sailor, seaman

marino, -a *adj* marine
marioneta *f* puppet, marionette
mariposa *f* **1.** ZOOL butterfly **2.** DEP butterfly stroke
mariquita[1] *f* ZOOL ladybird
mariquita[2] *m inf* poof *Brit,* fag *Am*
marisco *m* seafood
marisma *f* marsh
marítimo, -a *adj* maritime, marine
marmita *f* pot
mármol *m* marble
marqués, -esa *m, f* marquis *m,* marquise *f*
marranada *f inf* filthiness; (*acción*) a dirty trick
marrano *m* **1.** (*cerdo*) pig **2.** *pey* (*hombre*) dirty man; (*grosero*) rude man
marrano, -a *adj* filthy
marrón *adj* brown
marroquí *adj, mf* Moroccan
Marruecos *m* Morocco
Marsella *f* Marseilles
Marte *m* Mars
martes *m inv* Tuesday; ¡~ **y trece!** Friday the thirteenth!; *v.t.* **lunes**
martill(e)ar *vt* to hammer
martillo *m* **1.** (*herramienta*) hammer; ANAT malleus; **pez** ~ ZOOL hammerhead **2.** (*subasta*) gavel
mártir *mf* martyr
martirio *m* REL martyrdom; *fig* torture
marxismo *m* Marxism
marxista *adj, mf* Marxist
marzo *m* March; **en** ~ in March; **a principios/a mediados/a fin(al)es de** ~ at the beginning/in the middle/at the end of March; **el 21 de** ~ the 21st of March; **el mes de** ~ **tiene 31 días** the month of March has 31 days; **el pasado** ~ **fue muy frío** last March was very cold
mas *conj* LIT but, yet
más I. *adv* **1.** (*cantidad, comparativo*) more; ~ **inteligente** more intelligent; ~ **grande/pequeño** bigger/smaller; **correr** ~ to run more; **esto me gusta** ~ I like this better; ~ **adelante** (*local*) further forward; (*temporal*) later; ~ **guapo que tú** more

handsome than you; **son** ~ **de las diez** it is after ten **2.** (*superlativo*) **el/la** ~ the most; **la** ~ **bella** the most beautiful; **el** ~ **listo de la clase** the cleverest in the class; **lo** ~ **pronto posible** as early as possible; ~ **que nunca** more than ever; **a** ~ **no poder** to the utmost **3.** (*con interrogativo, indefinido*) **¿algo** ~**?** anything else? **4.** MAT plus **5.** (*locuciones*) ~ **bien** rather; ~ **o menos** (*ni bien ni mal*) so-so; (*aproximadamente*) more or less; **estar de** ~ not to be needed; **hay comida de** ~ there is food to spare; **por** ~ **que...** however hard I ...; **el** ~ **allá** the beyond; **quien** ~ **y quien menos** everyone; ~ **aún** what is more II. *m* MAT plus sign
masa *f* **1.** (*pasta*) mixture; (*para hornear*) dough **2.** (*volumen*) mass; ~ **monetaria** money supply; **en** ~ en masse **3.** ELEC earth *Brit,* ground *Am*
masacre *f* massacre
masaje *m* massage; **dar** ~**s** to massage
mascar <c→qu> *vt* **1.** (*masticar*) to chew **2.** (*mascullar*) to mumble
máscara *f* **1.** *t.* INFOR mask; **traje de** ~ fancy dress **2.** (*enmascarado*) masquerade
mascarada *f* **1.** (*baile*) masquerade **2.** (*farsa*) farce
mascarilla *f* **1.** (*máscara*) mask; ~ **facial** face pack **2.** (*molde*) cast
mascota *f* mascot
masculino *m* LING masculine
masculino, -a *adj* masculine; **moda masculina** men's fashion
mascullar *vt* to mumble
masificación *f* overcrowding
masilla *f* putty
masivo, -a *adj* mass
masón, -ona *m, f* Mason, Freemason
masoquista I. *adj* masochistic II. *mf* masochist
mastectomía *f* mastectomy
máster <másters> *m* master's degree
masticar <c→qu> *vt* **1.** (*mascar*) to chew **2.** (*meditar*) to ponder

M m

mástil *m* 1. NÁUT mast, spar 2. (*de guitarra*) neck

mastín *m* mastiff

masturbación *f* masturbation

masturbarse *vr* to masturbate

mata *f* 1. (*matorral*) clump; ~ **de pelo** mop of hair 2. (*planta*) plant; (*arbusto*) bush

matadero *m* slaughterhouse

matador(a) *m(f)* 1. TAUR matador 2. (*asesino*) killer

matamoscas *m inv* 1. (*insecticida*) fly-spray 2. (*objeto*) fly-swat

matanza *f* slaughter; **hacer una** ~ to massacre

matar I. *vt* 1. (*asesinar*) to kill; (*el aburrimiento*) to alleviate; ~ **a tiros** to shoot dead 2. (*hambre*) to satisfy; (*sed*) to quench 3. (*sellos*) to postmark 4. (*molestar*) to annoy II. *vr:* ~**se** 1. (*suicidarse*) to kill oneself 2. (*trabajando*) ~**se trabajar** to work oneself to death

matasellos *m inv* postmark

mate I. *adj* dull II. *m* 1. (*ajedrez*) mate; **jaque** ~ checkmate 2. (*acabado*) matte 3. *pl inf* (*matemáticas*) maths *Brit,* math *Am*

? In South America **mate** means: 1. The maté plant, 2. The leaves of the maté plant, from which tea is made, 3. The tea itself, and 4. A container in which the tea is kept.

---

matemáticas *fpl* mathematics

matemático, -a I. *adj* mathematical II. *m, f* mathematician

materia *f* 1. *t.* (*substancia*) matter; ~ **gris** ANAT grey matter; ~ **prima** raw material 2. *t.* ENS (*tema*) subject

material I. *adj* (*real*) tangible; (*daño*) physical II. *m* material; ~ **de oficina** office equipment

materialismo *m* materialism

materialista I. *adj* materialistic II. *mf* materialist

materializar <z→c> I. *vt* 1. (*hacer material*) to bring into being 2. (*realizar*) to carry out II. *vr:* ~**se** to materialize

materialmente *adv* materially

maternal *adj* maternal, motherly

maternidad *f* 1. (*el ser madre*) maternity 2. (*hospital*) maternity hospital

materno, -a *adj* maternal; **lengua materna** mother tongue

matinal *adj* morning

matiz *m* 1. (*gradación*) shade 2. (*toque*) touch 3. (*sentido*) nuance

matizar <z→c> *vt* 1. (*con colores*) to blend 2. (*graduar*) to tint 3. (*de un sentido*) to tinge

matón, -ona *m, f* 1. (*chulo*) bully 2. (*guardaespaldas*) bodyguard

matorral *m* thicket

matraca *f* (*carraca*) rattle, noise-maker

matrícula *f* 1. (*documento*) registration document 2. (*inscripción*) enrolment *Brit,* enrollment *Am;* UNIV matriculation 3. AUTO number plate *Brit,* license plate *Am;* **número de la** ~ registration number *Brit,* license number *Am*

matricular *vt* to register; UNIV to enrol *Brit,* to enroll *Am*

matrimonial *adj* matrimonial; (*vida*) married; **agencia** ~ dating agency

matrimonio *m* 1. marriage; ~ **civil** civil wedding; **contraer** ~ to marry 2. (*marido y mujer*) married couple; **cama de** ~ double bed

matriz I. *f* 1. (*útero*) womb 2. (*molde*) cast 3. TIPO, MAT matrix II. *adj* **casa** ~ parent company

matrona *f* 1. (*comadrona*) midwife 2. (*de familia*) matron

matutino, -a *adj* morning

maullar *irr como aullar vi* to miaow *Brit,* to meow *Am*

mausoleo *m* mausoleum

maxilar I. *adj* ANAT maxillary II. *m* jaw

máxima *f* maxim

máxime *adv* particularly

máximo, -a I. *adj* maximum; (*volumen*) as high as possible II. *m, f* maximum; **como** ~ at most; (*temporal*) at the latest

maya *adj, m* Mayan

? The **mayas** were an Indian race of people native to Central America (present-day Mexico, Guatemala and Honduras) with a civilisation that was highly advanced in many fields. The great number of ruins bear witness to this fact, such as the pyramids constructed from blocks of stone, numerous inscriptions and drawings, and not least the very accurate calendar that these people possessed.

mayo m May; v.t. **marzo**
mayonesa f mayonnaise
mayor I. adj 1. (tamaño) bigger; **comercio al por** ~ wholesale trade; **la** ~ **parte** the majority, most; ~ **que** bigger than 2. (edad) older; ~ **que** older than; **mi hermano** ~ my older brother; **ser** ~ to be grown-up; ~ **de edad** adult; **persona** ~ elderly person 3. MÚS major II. m 1. MIL major 2. (superior) superior 3. pl (ascendientes) ancestors pl

! **mayor** (= elder, taller): "Margarita es la mayor de todos los nietos." In contrast **más grande** is used with objects to indicate size: "La cocina es más grande que el cuarto de baño."

mayoral m (capataz) foreman
mayordomo, -a m, f butler
mayoría f majority; ~ **de edad** (age of) majority; **la** ~ **tiene un coche** most have a car
mayorista I. adj wholesale II. mf wholesaler
mayoritario, -a adj majority
mayúscula f capital (letter)
mayúsculo, -a adj (grande) big
mazapán m marzipan
mazazo m blow
mazo m 1. (martillo) mallet 2. (del mortero) pestle; (grande) sledgehammer 3. (manojo) bundle

mazorca f corn cob, corn Am
me I. pron pers 1. (objeto directo) me; ¡míra~! look at me! 2. (objeto indirecto) me; **da~ el libro** give me the book II. pron refl ~ **lavo** I wash myself; ~ **voy** I am going; ~ **he comprado un piso** I have bought myself a flat
meandro m (curva) meander
mear vi, vr: ~**se** inf to piss; ~**se de risa** to die laughing
mecánica f mechanics
mecánico, -a I. adj mechanical II. m, f mechanic
mecanismo m mechanism; (dispositivo) device
mecanografía f typewriting
mecanógrafo, -a m, f typist
mecate m AmC, Col, Méx, Ven (cuerda) rope
mecedora f rocking chair
mecer <c→z> I. vt (balancear) to rock II. vr: ~**se** (balancearse) to rock; (columpiarse) to swing
mecha f 1. (pabilo) wick; (de explosivos) fuse; **a toda** ~ inf very fast 2. pl (de pelo) highlights pl
mechero m lighter
mechón m tuft
medalla f medal
media f 1. (promedio) average 2. (calceta) stocking; AmL (calcetín) sock
mediación f mediation
mediado, -a adj (medio lleno) half full; (work) half-completed
mediana f 1. AUTO central reservation Brit, median strip Am 2. MAT median
mediano, -a adj 1. (calidad) average 2. (tamaño) medium 3. ECON medium-sized
medianoche f midnight
mediante prep by means of; (a través de) through
mediar vi 1. (intermediar) to mediate 2. (por alguien) to intercede 3. (existir) to exist
medicación f medication
medicamento m medicine
medicina f medicine
medicinal adj medicinal

Mm

medición *f* measurement

médico, -a I. *adj* medical II. *m, f* doctor; ~ **de cabecera** family doctor; ~ **forense** forensic surgeon; ~ **naturista** homeopath

medida *f* 1. (*dimensión*) measurement; **a la** ~ (*ropa*) made-to-measure; **hasta cierta** ~ up to a point; **en la** ~ **de lo posible** as far as possible; **a** ~ **que** as 2. LIT metre *Brit,* meter *Am* 3. (*moderación*) moderation 4. (*acción*) measure; **tomar** ~**s** to take measures

medieval *adj* medieval

medio *m* 1. (*mitad*) middle; **en** ~ **de** in the middle of; **meterse por** ~ to intervene; **quitar de en** ~ to get rid of 2. (*instrumento*) means; **por** ~ **de** by means of 3. TV medium; ~**s de comunicación** the media 4. (*entorno*) surroundings *pl;* ~ **ambiente** environment 5. DEP halfback

medio, -a I. *adj* 1. (*mitad*) half; **a las cuatro y media** at half past four; **litro y** ~ one and a half litres 2. (*promedio*) **ciudadano** ~ average person II. *adv* half; ~ **vestido** half dressed; **tomar a medias** to share; **ir a medias** to go halves

> ⚠ **medio** is used without an indefinite article: "medio kilo de tomates; media botella de agua."

medioambiental *adj* environmental

mediocre *adj* mediocre

mediodía *m* 1. (*hora*) midday; **al** ~ at noon 2. (*sur*) south

medir *irr como pedir* I. *vt* 1. (*calcular*) to measure; **¿cuánto mides?** how tall are you? 2. (*sopesar*) to weigh II. *vi* to measure III. *vr:* ~**se** (*con alguien*) to measure oneself against

meditabundo, -a *adj* meditative

meditar *vt, vi* to meditate

mediterráneo, -a *adj* Mediterranean

Mediterráneo *m* Mediterranean

médula *f* 1. ANAT marrow; ~ **espinal** spinal cord 2. BOT pith 3. (*meollo*) core; **hasta la** ~ to the core

medusa *f* jellyfish

megaciclo *m* megacycle

megáfono *m* megaphone

megalómano, -a *adj* megalomaniac

mejicano, -a *adj, m, f* Mexican

Méjico *m* Mexico

mejilla *f* cheek

mejillón *m* mussel

mejor I. *adj* 1. (*compar*) better; ~ **que** better than; **es** ~ **que** +*subj* it is better that; **pasar a** ~ **vida** to pass away 2. (*superl*) **el/la/lo** ~ the best; ~ **postor** highest bidder; **el** ~ **día** the best day II. *adv* better; **a lo** ~ maybe; ~ **que** ~ better still; **en el** ~ **de los casos** at best

mejora *f* improvement; ~ **salarial** (pay) rise *Brit,* (pay) raise *Am*

mejorar I. *vt* 1. (*perfeccionar*) to improve 2. (*superar*) to surpass II. *vi, vr:* ~**se** 1. (*enfermo*) to get better 2. (*tiempo*) to improve

mejunje *m pey* concoction

melancolía *f* melancholy

melancólico, -a *adj* melancholic

melena *f* 1. (*crin*) mane 2. (*pelo*) long hair

mellizo, -a *adj, m, f* twin

melocotón *m* peach

melocotonero *m* peach tree

melodía *f* melody

melodrama *m* melodrama

melodramático, -a *adj* melodramatic

melón *m* melon

meloso, -a *adj* sweet

membrana *f* membrane

membrillo *m* quince; **carne** [*o* **dulce**] ~ quince jelly

memorable *adj* memorable

memorándum *m* <memorandos> memorandum

memoria *f* 1. *t.* INFOR (*facultad*) memory; **de** ~ by heart; **hacer** ~ to try and remember; **venir a la** ~ to come to mind 2. (*informe*) report 3. *pl* (*autobiografía*) autobiography

memorizar <z→c> *vt* 1. (*aprender*) to memorize 2. INFOR to store

menaje *m* household furnishings *pl*

mención *f* mention; **hacer** ~ **de** to

mention
mencionar *vt* to mention
mendigar <g→gu> *vi, vt* to beg
mendigo, -a *m, f* beggar
mendrugo *m* crust
menear I. *vt* to move; (*cabeza*) to shake; (*cola*) to wag II. *vr*: ~**se** 1. (*moverse*) to move 2. *inf* (*apresurarse*) to get a move on
menester *m* 1. (*necesidad*) need; **ser** ~ to be necessary 2. *pl* (*tareas*) jobs *pl*
menestra *f* vegetable stew
menguante *f* 1. (*marea*) ebb 2. (*mengua*) decrease
menguar <gu→gü> I. *vi* to diminish II. *vt* to decrease; (*punto*) to reduce
menopausia *f* MED menopause
menor I. *adj* 1. (*tamaño*) smaller; **al por ~** COM retail; **no dar la ~ importancia** not to give the least importance 2. (*edad*) younger; ~ **de edad** underage; **el ~ de mis hermanos** the youngest of my brothers 3. MÚS minor II. *mf* (*persona*) minor; **apta para ~es** (*película*) suitable for under-eighteens

> ⚠️ **menor** (= younger, shorter): "Antonio es el menor de sus hermanos." In contrast **más pequeño** is used with objects to indicate size: "Tu coche es más pequeño que el mío."

Menorca *f* Minorca
menorquín, -ina *adj, m, f* Minorcan
menos I. *adv* 1. (*contrario de más*) less; **a ~ que** unless; **el coche (el) ~ caro** the least expensive car; **al** [*o* **por lo**] ~ at least; **echar de ~** to miss; **ir a ~** to decrease; ~ **de 20 personas** fewer than 20 people; ~ **mal** thank goodness; **¡ni mucho ~!** not at all!; **son las ocho ~ diez** it's ten minutes to eight 2. MAT minus 3. (*excepto*) except; **todo ~ eso** anything but that II. *m* MAT minus
menoscabar *vt* 1. (*dañar*) to impair; *fig* to damage 2. (*desacreditar*) to

discredit
menospreciar *vt* 1. (*despreciar*) to underrate 2. (*desdeñar*) to despise
mensaje *m* message; ~ **de error** INFOR error message
mensajero, -a *adj, m, f* messenger
menstruación *f* menstruation
menstruar <*l. pres:* menstrúo> *vi* to menstruate
mensual *adj* monthly
mensualidad *f* 1. (*sueldo*) monthly salary 2. (*compra aplazada*) monthly instalment
menta *f* mint
mental *adj* mental
mentalidad *f* mentality
mentalizar <z→c> I. *vt* (*preparar*) to prepare (mentally); (*concienciar*) to make aware; ~ **a alguien de algo** to make sb aware of sth II. *vr*: ~**se** (*prepararse*) to prepare oneself (mentally); (*concienciarse*) to make oneself aware
mente *f* 1. (*pensamiento*) mind; **tener en (la)** ~ to have in mind; **traer a la** ~ to bring to mind; **tengo la** ~ **en blanco** my mind is a complete blank 2. (*intelecto*) intellect
mentecato, -a I. *adj* silly II. *m, f* fool
mentir *irr como sentir* *vi* to lie; **¡miento!** I tell a lie!, I am wrong!
mentira *f* (*embuste*) lie; **¡parece ~!** I can hardly believe it!
mentiroso, -a I. *adj* (*persona*) lying II. *m, f* liar
menú *m* <menús> *t.* INFOR menu
menudo, -a *adj* 1. (*minúsculo*) minuscule 2. (*pequeño y delgado*) slight 3. (*fútil*) futile 4. (*exclamación*) **¡menuda película!** what a film! 5. *fig* **a** ~ often
meñique *m* little finger, pinkie, pinky *Am*
meollo *m* essence, crux
mercader *m* merchant
mercado *m* market; ~ **exterior/interior** overseas/domestic market; ~ **de trabajo** labour market; ~ **único europeo** European Single Market
mercancía *f* goods *pl*
mercantil *adj* mercantile
mercenario, -a *adj, m, f* mercenary

M
m

mercería f **1.** (*tienda*) haberdasher's shop *Brit*, notions store *Am* **2.** (*artículos*) haberdashery *Brit*, notions pl *Am*

mercurio m mercury

Mercurio m Mercury

merecer *irr como crecer* **I.** *vt* **1.** (*ser digno de*) to deserve **2.** (*valer*) to be worthy of **II.** *vr:* ~**se** to deserve

merecido m deserts pl; **se llevó su** ~ he got his just deserts

merendar <e→ie> **I.** *vt* to have for tea **II.** *vi* to have tea; (*en el campo*) to picnic

merengue m meringue

meridiano m meridian

merienda f **1.** (*comida*) tea **2.** (*picnic*) picnic; ~ **de negros** *fig* free-for-all

mérito m **1.** (*merecimiento*) merit **2.** (*valor*) worth; **hacer ~s** to prove oneself worthy

merluza f **1.** ZOOL hake **2.** *vulg* (*borrachera*) **coger una buena** ~ to get sloshed

merluzo, -a *adj inf* silly

merma f decrease; (*de peso*) loss

mermar **I.** *vt* to lessen; (*peso*) to reduce **II.** *vi* to decrease

mermelada f jam; ~ **de naranja** marmalade

mero **I.** *adv AmC* (*pronto*) soon **II.** m grouper

mero, -a *adj* **1.** (*sencillo*) simple **2.** (*sin nada más*) mere

merodear *vi* to prowl; ~ **por un sitio** to hang about a place

mes m **1.** (*período*) month; **todos los ~es** every month; **hace un** ~ a month ago **2.** (*sueldo*) monthly salary **3.** *inf* (*menstruación*) period

mesa f **1.** (*mueble*) table; ~ **de despacho** office desk; ~ **digitalizadora** INFOR digitizer; ~ **electoral** POL *officials in charge of a polling station;* **vino de** ~ table wine; **bendecir la** ~ to say grace; **poner/quitar la** ~ to lay/to clear the table, at the table; **¡a la** ~**!** food's ready! **2.** GEO plateau

mesero, -a m, f *AmL* (*camarero*) waiter m, waitress f

meseta f GEO plateau

mesilla f small table; ~ **de noche** bedside table, nightstand *Am*

mesón m inn, tavern

mesonero, -a m, f innkeeper

mestizo, -a *adj* **1.** (*entre blancos e indios*) mestizo **2.** (*entre dos razas*) mixed-race

[?] A **mestizo** in Latin America means a person of mixed race whose parents were of white (i.e. European) and Indian origin. (In Brazil, **mestizos** are known as **mamelucos**.)

mesura f **1.** (*moderación*) moderation **2.** (*calma*) calm

meta¹ f **1.** *t. fig* winning post; (*portería*) goal **2.** (*objetivo*) aim, goal

meta² mf (*portero*) goalkeeper *Brit*, goaltender *Am*

metabolismo m metabolism

metáfora f metaphor

metal m **1.** (*material*) metal **2.** (*de voz*) timbre **3.** (*instrumento*) brass instrument **4.** (*dinero*) **el vil** ~ filthy lucre

metálico m (*monedas*) coins pl; **en** ~ in cash

metálico, -a *adj* metallic

metalurgia f metallurgy

metalúrgico, -a **I.** *adj* metallurgical **II.** m, f metallurgist

metedura f **¡vaya** ~ **de pata!** *inf* what a clanger *Brit* [o blooper *Am*]!

meteorito m meteorite

meteoro m meteor

meteorología f sin pl meteorology

meter **I.** *vt* **1.** (*introducir*) to insert; (*poner*) to put; **¡mete el enchufe!** put the plug in! **2.** (*invertir*) to invest **3.** (*en costura*) to take in **4.** DEP (*gol*) to score **5.** *inf* (*encasquetar*) to palm off; (*vender*) to sell **6.** *inf* (*dar*) ~ **prisa** to hurry (up); ~ **un puñetazo** to punch **7.** (*provocar*) ~ **miedo** to frighten; ~ **ruido** to be noisy **8.** (*hacer participar*) to involve **II.** *vr:* ~**se** **1.** (*introducirse*) to put; ~**se en la cabeza que...** to get into ones head that ... **2.** (*entrar en un lugar*) to enter; **¿dónde se habrá metido?** where has he/she got to? **3.** (*inmiscuirse*) to meddle; **¡no te metas donde no te llaman!** mind your own business! **4.** (*con alguien*) to provoke **5.** (*convertirse en*) ~**se a actor** to become an actor

meticuloso, -a *adj* meticulous

metódico, -a *adj* methodical

metodismo *m* Methodism

metodista *adj, mf* Methodist

método *m* **1.** (*sistema*) method **2.** (*libro*) manual

metodología *f* methodology

metralla *f* **1.** (*munición*) shell **2.** (*trozos*) shrapnel

metralleta *f* sub-machine gun, tommy gun

métrico, -a *adj* metric

metro *m* **1.** (*unidad*) metre *Brit,* meter *Am;* ~ **cuadrado/cúbico** square/cubic metre **2.** (*para medir*) ruler **3.** FERRO underground *Brit,* subway *Am* **4.** *t.* MÚS (*poesía*) metre *Brit,* meter *Am*

metrópoli *f* (*urbe*) metropolis; (*capital*) capital

México *m* Mexico

[?] **México** or **Méjico** (official title: **Estados Unidos Mexicanos**) lies in Central America and borders the USA in the north. The capital, **Ciudad de México** (Mexico City), has almost twenty million inhabitants. Spanish is the official language of the country and the monetary unit is the **peso**. The original inhabitants of Mexico, the **aztecas** (Aztecs), referred to themselves as **mexica**.

---

mezcla *f* **1.** (*sustancia*) mixture **2.** (*acto*) mixing

mezclar I. *vt* **1.** (*unir*) to blend; GASTR (*añadir*) to mix **2.** (*revolver*) to muddle; (*confundir*) to mix up II. *vr:* ~**se 1.** (*inmiscuirse*) to meddle; ~**se entre los espectadores** to mingle

with the spectators **2.** (*revolverse*) to mix

mezquino, -a I. *adj* **1.** (*tacaño*) stingy, mean *Brit* **2.** (*miserable*) small-minded II. *m, f* miser

mezquita *f* mosque

mg. *abr de* **miligramo** mg.

mi I. *adj* (*antepuesto*) my II. *m inv* MÚS E

mí *pron pers* me; **a** ~ (*objeto directo*) me; (*objeto indirecto*) to me; **para** ~ for me; **¿y a** ~ **qué?** so what?; **por** ~ as far as I'm concerned

miaja *f* crumb

miau miaow *Brit,* meow *Am*

michelín *m inf* roll of fat, spare tyre

micro *m* (*micrófono*) mike

microbio *m* microbe

microbús *m* minibus

microchip *m* microchip

microfilm *m* <microfilm(e)s> microfilm

micrófono *m* microphone

microonda *f t.* FÍS (*cocina*) microwave; **horno** (**de**) ~**s** microwave (oven)

microscópico, -a *adj* microscopic

microscopio *m* microscope

miedo *m* **1.** (*angustia*) fear; **por** ~ **de que** +*subj* for fear that; **dar** ~ to be frightening; **morirse de** ~ to be petrified **2.** *inf* **de** ~ (*maravilloso*) terrific; **de** ~ (*terrible*) dreadful

miedoso, -a *adj ser* fearful

miel *f* (*de abeja*) honey; **luna de** ~ honeymoon

miembro *m* **1.** *pl* (*extremidades*) limbs *pl* **2.** *t.* LING, MAT (*socio*) member **3.** (*pene*) ~ (**viril**) male member

mientes *fpl* **parar** ~ **en algo** to give sth great thought; **traer a las** ~ to recall

mientras I. *adv* meanwhile; ~ (**tanto**) in the meantime II. *conj* ~ (**que**) while; ~ (**que**) +*subj* as long as

miércoles *m inv* Wednesday; ~ **de ceniza** Ash Wednesday; *v.t.* **lunes**

mierda *f vulg* **1.** (*heces*) shit **2.** (*porquería*) muck **3.** (*expresiones*) **¡a la ~!** to hell with it!; **¡(vete) a la ~!** get lost!; ¡~! shit!

miga f 1.(*trocito*) crumb; **hacer buenas ~s con alguien** to get on well with sb; **estar hecho ~** (*cansado*) to be shattered 2.(*esencia*) essence; **esto tiene su ~** there is something behind this

migaja f 1.(*trocito*) crumb; **una ~ de** a scrap of 2. pl (*sobras*) leftovers pl

migración f migration

mil adj inv, m thousand

milagro m miracle; **hacer ~s** to work wonders

milagroso, -a adj miraculous

mili f inf military service

milicia f 1.(*tropa*) military 2.(*actividades*) military operation

miligramo m milligram

milímetro m millimetre Brit, millimeter Am

militante adj, mf militant

militar I. vi 1.(*en el ejército*) to serve 2.(*en un partido*) to be an active member of II. adj military III. m soldier

milla f mile

millar m thousand

millón m million; **mil millones** a billion

> **!** **millón** is always used with the preposition 'de': "En esta ciudad viven dos millones de habitantes."

millonario, -a m, f millionaire, millionairess f

mimar vt to indulge; (*excesivamente*) to spoil

mimbre m wicker; **de ~** wicker

mímica f 1.(*facial*) mime 2.(*señas*) sign language

mimo m 1.(*actor*) mimic 2.(*caricia*) caress; **necesitar ~** to need affection 3.(*condescencia*) spoiling

mina f 1. MIN mine; **~ de carbón** coal mine 2.(*explosivo*) mine; **~ de tierra** landmine 3.(*de lápiz*) lead

minar vt 1.(*con minas*) to mine 2.(*debilitar*) to undermine

mineral I. adj mineral II. m 1. GEO mineral 2. MIN ore

minero, -a I. adj mining II. m, f miner

miniatura f miniature

minifalda f miniskirt

minifundio m smallholding

minimizar <z→c> vt to minimize

mínimo m minimum; **como ~** (*cantidad*) as a minimum; (*al menos*) at least

mínimo, -a adj superl de **pequeño** minimum; **sin el más ~ ruido** without the least noise; **no ayudar en lo más ~** to be no help at all

minino, -a m, f inf pussy (cat)

ministerio m 1.(*edificio*) ministry 2.(*cargo*) ministerial office

ministro, -a m, f minister; **Ministro de Economía y Hacienda** Chancellor of the Exchequer Brit, Treasury Secretary Am; **Ministro del Interior** Home Secretary Brit, Secretary of the Interior Am; **Primera Ministra** prime minister

minoría f minority

minorista I. adj retail II. mf retailer

minucioso, -a adj meticulous

minúscula f LING lower case; **en ~s** in lower case letters

minúsculo, -a adj minuscule, minute; **letra minúscula** lower-case letter

minusválido, -a adj handicapped

minuta f 1.(*cuenta*) lawyer's bill 2.(*menú*) menu

minutero m minute hand

minuto m minute; **sin perder un ~** at once

mío, -a pron pos 1.(*de mi propiedad*) mine; **el libro es ~** the book is mine; **la botella es mía** the bottle is mine; **¡ya es ~!** I have it! 2.(*tras artículo*) **el ~/la mía** mine; **los ~s** (*cosas*) mine; (*parientes*) my family; **ésta es la mía** inf this is just what I want; **he vuelto a hacer una de las mías** inf I have been up to it again; **eso es lo ~** that is my strong point 3.(*tras substantivo*) of mine; **una amiga mía** a friend of mine; **(no) es culpa mía** it is (not) my fault; **¡amor ~!** my darling!

miope *adj* myopic, short-sighted

miopía *f* myopia, short-sightedness

mira *f* 1. (*para apuntar*) sight; **estar en la ~ de alguien** to be in sb's sights 2. MIL watchtower 3. (*pl*) (*intención*) intention; **con amplias ~s** broad-minded; **de ~s estrechas** narrow-minded; **con ~s a** with a view to

mirada *f* look; **echar una ~ a algo** to glance at sth; **apartar la ~** to look away

mirado, -a *adj* 1. (*respetuoso*) respectful 2. *inf* (*delicado*) considerate 3. (*cuidadoso*) discreet; **bien ~, ...** all things considering, ...

mirador *m* (*atalaya*) viewpoint

mirar I. *vt* 1. (*observar*) to observe; (*ver*) to look at; **~ fijamente** to stare 2. (*buscar*) to look for 3. (*prestar atención*) to watch; **¡mira el bolso!** keep an eye on the bag! 4. (*meditar*) to think about 5. (*tener en cuenta*) to take into account; **~ el dinero** to be careful of the money II. *vi* 1. (*dirigir la vista*) to look; (*por agujero*) to look through; **~ atrás** to look back; **~ alrededor** to look around; **la casa mira al este** the house faces east 2. (*buscar*) to look for 3. (*expresiones*) **mira (a ver) si...** go and see if ...; **¡mira por donde...!** surprise, surprise ...!; **mira que si se cae este jarrón** just imagine if the vase fell; **mira que es tonta, ¿eh?** she really is silly, isn't she? III. *vr:* **~se** to look at oneself; **se mire como se mire** no matter how you look at it

mirilla *f* peephole *Brit,* eyehole *Am*

mirlo *m* blackbird

misa *f* REL (*ceremonia*) mass; **~ del gallo** midnight mass; **decir ~** to say mass; **no saber de la ~ la mitad** *inf* not to know the half of it; **eso va a ~** *inf* and that's a fact

miserable I. *adj* 1. (*pobre*) poor 2. (*lamentable*) pitiful 3. (*tacaño*) stingy 4. (*cantidad*) miserable II. *mf* (*desdichado*) wretch; (*que da pena*) poor thing

miseria *f* 1. (*pobreza*) poverty 2. (*poco dinero*) pittance 3. (*taca-ñería*) stinginess 4. *pl* (*infortunios*) misfortunes *pl*

misericordia *f* 1. (*compasión*) compassion 2. (*perdón*) forgiveness

misil *m* missile

misión *f* mission; POL assignment

misionero, -a *m, f* missionary

mismo *adv* 1. (*manera*) **así ~** in that way 2. (*justamente*) **ahí ~** just there; **aquí ~** right here; **ayer ~** only yesterday

mismo, -a *adj* 1. (*idéntico*) same; **al ~ tiempo** at the same time; **da lo ~** it does not matter; **por lo ~** for that reason; **lo ~ no vienen** they might not come; **¡eso ~!** exactly! 2. (*reflexivo*) myself; **te perjudicas a ti ~** you harm yourself; **yo misma lo vi** I myself saw him/it

misterio *m* mystery

misterioso, -a *adj* mysterious

mitad *f* 1. (*parte igual*) half; **a ~ de precio** at half price; **reducir a la ~** to halve 2. (*medio*) middle

mitigar <g→gu> *vt* 1. (*dolores*) to alleviate; (*sed*) to quench; (*hambre*) to take the edge off 2. (*colores*) to subdue; (*calor*) to mitigate

mitin *m* political meeting

mito *m* myth

mitología *f* mythology

mixto *m* (*fósforo*) match

mixto, -a *adj* mixed

ml. *abr de* **mililitro** ml

mm. *abr de* **milímetro** mm

mobiliario *m* furniture

mocasín *m* moccasin

mochila *f* rucksack *Brit,* backpack *Am*

mochuelo *m* small owl; **cargar a alguien con el ~** *inf* to stick sb with the dirty work

moción *f t.* POL motion

moco *m* mucus; (*de la nariz*) snot; **limpiarse los ~s** to wipe one's nose; **no ser~ de pavo** *fig* to be nothing to sneeze at; **llorar a ~ tendido** *inf* to cry one's eyes out

moda *f* fashion; **vestido de ~** fashionable dress; **ponerse de ~** to come into fashion

modal I. *adj* modal II. *mpl* manners

M m

pl

modalidad *f* form; **~es de un contrato** types of contract

modelar *vt* to model; *fig* to fashion

modelo *mf* model

modelo *m* 1.(*ejemplo*) model 2.(*esquema*) design

módem *m* INFOR modem

moderado, -a I. *adj* moderate; (*precio, petición*) reasonable II. *m, f* POL moderate

moderar I. *vt* 1.(*disminuir*) to moderate 2. TV, RADIO to present II. *vr:* **~se** to calm down

modernización *f* modernization

modernizar <z→c> *vt* to modernize

moderno, -a *adj* modern

modestia *f* modesty

modesto, -a *adj* modest

módico, -a *adj* modest

modificar <c→qu> I. *vt* to modify II. *vr:* ~se to adapt

modismo *m* idiom

modisto, -a *m, f* dressmaker

modo *m* 1.(*manera*) way; **de este ~** in this way; **de ningún ~** no way; **hacer algo de cualquier ~** to do sth any old how; **de cualquier ~ no hubieran ido** anyway they would not have gone; **de ~ que** so; **en cierto ~** in a way; **de todos ~s no hubo heridos** at any rate no one was injured; **de todos ~s, lo volvería a intentar** anyway, I would try again 2. LING mood 3. INFOR mode; **~ de operación** operational mode 4. *pl* (*comportamiento*) manners *pl*

modorra *f* drowsiness

módulo *m* 1. *t.* ARQUIT, ELEC (*de un mueble*) unit 2.(*de una prisión*) wing 3. ENS, INFOR module

mogollón *m* 1. *inf* (*cantidad*) load(s); **~ de gente** loads of people 2. *inf* (*lío*) mess

moho *m* 1. BOT mould *Brit,* mold *Am* 2.(*óxido*) rust

mohoso, -a *adj* 1.(*de moho*) mouldy *Brit,* moldy *Am* 2.(*oxidado*) rusty

mojar I. *vt* 1.(*con un líquido*) to wet; (*ligeramente*) to moisten; (*para planchar*) to dampen 2.(*el pan*) to dunk 3. *inf* (*celebrar*) to celebrate II. *vi inf* (*en un asunto*) to get involved III. *vr:* **~se** 1.(*con un líquido*) to get wet 2. *inf* (*comprometerse*) to get involved

mojón *m* 1.(*hito*) boundary stone; **~ kilométrico** milestone 2.(*poste*) post

moldavo, -a *adj, m, f* Moldavian

molde *m* 1. TÉC, GASTR mould *Brit,* mold *Am*; TIPO form; **letras de ~** block letters 2.(*modelo*) model

moldeador *m* **~ eléctrico** curling tongs *pl,* curling iron *Am*

moldear *vt* 1.(*formar*) to mould *Brit,* to mold *Am* 2.(*vaciar*) to cast

mole¹ *f* (*masa*) mass

mole² *m* *Méx* GASTR 1.(*salsa*) sauce 2.(*guiso*) stew

> **?** **Mole** is the name given to a Mexican chilli sauce. Cayenne pepper from the chilli plant gives this sauce its characteristic sharp taste.

molécula *f* molecule

moler <o→ue> *vt* 1.(*café*) to grind; (*aceitunas*) to press 2.(*fatigar*) to exhaust

molestar I. *vt* (*estorbar*) to inconvenience; (*fastidiar*) to bother II. *vr:* ~se 1.(*tomarse la molestia*) to bother; **ni siquiera te has molestado en...** you haven't even taken the trouble to ...; **no te molestes por mí** don't put yourself out for me 2.(*ofenderse*) to take offence *Brit,* to take offense *Am*

molestia *f* 1.(*fastidio*) bother; (*por dolores*) discomfort 2.(*inconveniente*) trouble; **tomarse la ~** to take the trouble; **perdonen las ~s** we apologize for the inconvenience caused 3.(*dolor*) discomfort

molesto, -a *adj* 1. *ser* (*desagradable*) unpleasant; (*fastidioso*) troublesome 2. *estar* (*enfadado*) annoyed; (*ofendido*) hurt by sth 3. *estar* (*incómodo*) uncomfortable

molido, -a *adj inf* (*cansado*) worn

out

molinillo m **1.**(*aparato*) ~ **de café** coffee grinder **2.**(*juguete*) windmill *Brit,* pinwheel *Am*

molino m mill; ~ **de papel** paper mill

molusco m mollusc

momentáneo, -a *adj* **1.**(*instantáneo*) momentary **2.**(*provisional*) provisional

momento m **1.**(*instante*) instant, moment; **de un ~ a otro** at any time now; **al ~** immediately; **en cualquier** [o **en todo**] ~ at any time; **en este ~** at the moment; **en este ~ estaba...** I was just ...; **de ~** for the moment; **en todo ~** at all times; **hace un ~** a moment ago **2.**(*período*) period; **atravieso un mal ~** I am going through a bad patch **3.**(*actualidad*) present; **la música del ~** present-day music **4.**FÍS momentum

momia f mummy

mona f **coger una ~** *inf* to get drunk; ~ **de Pascua** GASTR Easter cake

monaguillo, -a m, f altar boy

monarca mf monarch

monarquía f monarchy

monárquico, -a I. *adj* **1.**(*de la monarquía*) monarchic **2.**(*partidario*) monarchist **II.** m, f monarchist

monasterio m monastery

mondadientes m inv toothpick

mondar I. *vt* (*plátano*) to peel; (*guisantes*) to shell **II.** *vr:* ~**se** (*dientes*) to clean with a toothpick; ~**se (de risa)** *inf* to die laughing

moneda f **1.**(*pieza*) coin; ~ **suelta** change; **teléfono de ~s** pay phone **2.**(*de un país*) currency; ~ **de curso legal** legal tender; ~ **extranjera/nacional** foreign/local currency

monedero m purse

monetario, -a *adj* monetary

mongólico, -a I. *adj* of Down's syndrome **II.** m, f person with Down's syndrome

mongolismo m sin pl Down's syndrome

monigote m **1.**(*dibujo mal hecho*) childlike drawing; (*figura*) stick figure **2.**(*muñeco*) rag doll **3.**(*persona*) wimp

monitor m TÉC, TV, INFOR monitor; (*pantalla*) screen

monja f nun

monje m monk

mono m **1.**ZOOL monkey **2.**(*traje*) overalls pl **3.** inf (*de drogas*) withdrawal symptoms pl

mono, -a *adj* (*niño*) cute; (*chica*) pretty; (*vestido*) lovely

monóculo m monocle

monógamo, -a *adj* monogamous

monografía f monograph

monólogo m monologue

monopatín m skateboard

monopolio m monopoly

monopolizar <z→c> *vt* COM to monopolize, to corner (a market)

monotonía f monotony

monótono, -a *adj* monotonous

monstruo I. m monster **II.** *adj inv* magnificent

monstruoso, -a *adj* **1.**(*desfigurado*) disfigured **2.**(*terrible*) monstrous **3.**(*enorme*) huge

monta f total; **de poca ~** *fig* unimportant

montacargas m inv (service) lift *Brit,* (freight) elevator *Am*

montaje m **1.**TÉC assembly **2.**CINE editing; FOTO montage **3.**TEAT decor **4.**(*engaño*) set-up

montaña f **1.**GEO (*monte*) mountain; ~ **rusa** big dipper **2.**(*de cosas*) difficulty

montañero, -a m, f mountaineer

montañés, -esa *adj* **1.**(*de la montaña*) highlander **2.**(*de Santander*) of/from Santander

montañismo m mountaineering

montañoso, -a *adj* mountainous

montar I. *vi* **1.**(*a un caballo*) to get on; (*en un coche*) to get in **2.**(*ir a caballo, bici*) to ride **3.**(*una cuenta*) ~ **a** to come to **II.** *vt* **1.**(*en un caballo*) to mount **2.**(*ir a caballo*) to ride **3.**(*máquina*) to assemble **4.**(*tienda*) to open **5.**(*huevo*) to beat **6.**(*negocio*) to set up **7.**CINE to edit **8.** inf (*organizar*) to organize; ~ **un número** to make a scene **III.** *vr:* ~**se 1.**(*subir*) to climb **2.** inf (*arreglárselas*) to manage

montaraz *adj* **1.** (*salvaje*) wild **2.** (*tosco*) coarse **3.** (*arisco*) unsociable

monte *m* **1.** (*montaña*) mountain **2.** (*bosque*) ~ **alto** woodland; ~ **bajo** scrub **3.** *pl* (*cordillera*) mountain range

monto *m* total

montón *m* (*de ropa*) heap; (*de gente*) a lot of; **problemas a montones** *inf* loads of problems; **ser del** ~ to be ordinary

monumental *adj* monumental; **el Madrid** ~ the sights of Madrid

monumento *m* memorial; (*grande*) monument; **los** ~**s de una ciudad** the sights of a city

monzón *m o f* monsoon

moño *m* bun; **estar hasta el** ~ **de algo** *inf* to be fed up to the back teeth with sth

moqueta *f* carpet

mora *f* **1.** BOT (*del moral*) mulberry; (*de la zarzamora*) blackberry **2.** JUR delay

morada *f* **1.** (*casa*) abode **2.** (*residencia*) residence

morado, -a *adj* purple; (*ojo*) black; **pasarlas moradas** to have a bad time

moral I. *adj* moral; **código** ~ code of ethics **II.** *f* morals *pl*; **levantar la** ~ **a alguien** to boost sb's morale

moraleja *f* moral

moralidad *f* (*cualidad*) morality

moralizar <z→c> **I.** *vi* to moralize **II.** *vt* to improve the morals of

moratón *m* bruise

moratoria *f t.* FIN moratorium

morbo *m* **1.** (*enfermedad*) illness **2.** (*interés malsano*) morbid fascination

morboso, -a *adj* **1.** (*clima*) unhealthy **2.** (*placer*) morbid

morcilla *f* black pudding, blood sausage

mordaz *adj* (*comentario*) caustic; (*crítica*) scathing

mordaza *f* **1.** (*en la boca*) gag **2.** TÉC clamp

morder <o→ue> **I.** *vt* **1.** (*con los*

dientes) to bite; **está que muerde** *inf* he/she is furious **2.** (*corroer*) to corrode **3.** AmL (*estafar*) to cheat **II.** *vr:* ~**se** to bite; **no** ~**se la lengua** to say what one thinks

mordisco *m* bite, nibble

morena *f* moray eel

moreno, -a I. *adj* brown; (*de piel*) swarthy; (*de cabello*) dark-haired **II.** *m, f* **1.** (*negro*) coloured person *Brit,* colored person *Am* **2.** *Cuba* (*mulato*) mulatto

morfina *f* morphine

moribundo, -a *adj* dying

morir *irr* **I.** *vi* **1.** (*perecer*) to die; (*en guerra*) to be killed; (*ahogado*) to drown; (*en humo*) **2.** (*tradición*) to die out; (*camino*) to peter out; (*sonido*) to die away **II.** *vr:* ~**se 1.** (*perecer*) to die; (*planta*) to wither; **¡así te mueras!** *inf* good riddance to you! **2.** (*con 'de'*) ~**se de hambre** to die of starvation; ~**se de frío** to freeze to death; ~**se de risa** to die laughing **3.** (*con 'por'*) **me muero por...** I am dying to …

mormón, -ona *adj, m, f* Mormon

moro, -a *adj, m, f* Muslim

moroso, -a I. *adj* **1.** (*deudor*) slow to pay up **2.** *elev* (*lento*) slow **II.** *m, f* debtor in arrears, defaulter

morral *m* nosebag

morriña *f sin pl, inf* homesickness

morro *m* **1.** ZOOL (*hocico*) snout **2.** *inf* (*de persona*) lip; (*boca*) mouth; **beber a** ~ to drink straight from the bottle; **caerse de** ~**s** to fall flat on ones face; **partirle los** ~**s a alguien** to smash sb his/her face in; **tener** ~ to have a real nerve; **estar de** ~(**s**) *fig* to be angry

morsa *f* walrus

morse *m* Morse code

mortadela *f* mortadella, ≈ bologna

mortaja *f* **1.** (*sábana*) shroud **2.** AmL (*de cigarrillo*) cigarette paper

mortal *mf* mortal

mortalidad *f* mortality

mortero *m* mortar

mortífero, -a *adj* deadly

mortificar <c→qu> **I.** *vt* **1.** (*atormentar*) to torment **2.** *t.* REL (*humi-*

llar) to mortify **II.** *vr:* ~**se 1.** (*atormentarse*) to be tormented **2.** REL to mortify oneself

mosaico *m* mosaic

mosca *f* **1.** ZOOL fly; **por si las** ~**s** *inf* just in case; **tener la** ~ **detrás de la oreja** *inf* to be suspicious; **estar** ~ *inf* (*receloso*) to be suspicious; (*enfadado*) to be cross **2.** (*barba*) goatee

moscovita *adj, mf* Muscovite

Moscú *m* Moscow

mosquearse *vr inf* **1.** (*ofenderse*) to take offence *Brit,* to take offense *Am* **2.** (*enfadarse*) to get angry

mosquita *f* **hacerse la** ~ **muerta** to look as if butter wouldn't melt in one's mouth

mosquitero *m* mosquito net(ting)

mosquito *m* mosquito; (*pequeño*) gnat

mostaza *f* mustard

mosto *m* grape juice

mostrador *m* **1.** (*tienda*) counter **2.** (*bar*) bar

mostrar <o→ue> **I.** *vt* (*enseñar*) to show; (*presentar*) to display **II.** *vr:* ~**se** to appear

mota *f* **1.** (*partícula*) speck; (*de polvo*) speak **2.** (*mancha*) spot

mote *m* nickname

motín *m* uprising; (*militar*) mutiny; (*en la cárcel*) riot

motivación *f* motivation

motivar *vt* **1.** (*incitar*) to motivate **2.** (*explicar*) to explain **3.** (*provocar*) to cause

motivo *m* **1.** (*causa*) reason behind; (*de un crimen*) motive; **con** ~ **de...** on the occasion of ...; **por este** ~ for this reason **2.** (*tela*) motif

moto *f inf* motorbike; ~ **acuática** jet ski; ~ **para la nieve** snowmobile

motocicleta *f* motorcycle

motociclismo *m sin pl* motorcycling

motor *m* **1.** *t. fig* motor; ~ **de búsqueda** INFOR search engine; ~ **de reacción** jet engine **2.** (*causa*) cause

motor(a) *adj* motor; **nervio** ~ motor nerve

motora *f* motorboat

motorista *mf* DEP motorcyclist

motorizar <z→c> *vt* to motorize

motosierra *f* chain saw

motriz *adj* driving

movedizo, -a *adj* **1.** (*móvil*) moving **2.** (*inconstante*) changeable

mover <o→ue> **I.** *vt* **1.** *t.* INFOR (*desplazar*) to move; (*cola*) to wag; ~ **archivo** move file; ~ **la cabeza** (*asentir*) to nod (one's head); (*negar*) to shake one's head **2.** (*incitar*) to rouse **II.** *vr:* ~**se** to move; **¡venga, muévete!** come on! get a move on!

movido, -a *adj* **1.** (*foto*) blurred **2.** (*activo*) active; (*vivo*) lively **3.** MÚS rhythmic

móvil I. *adj* mobile **II.** *m* **1.** (*para colgar*) mobile **2.** (*crimen*) motive **3.** TEL mobile (phone), cellphone *Am*

movilidad *f sin pl* mobility

movilización *f* mobilization

movilizar <z→c> *vt* to mobilize

movimiento *m* **1.** *t.* FÍS, COM movement; **poner en** ~ to put in motion; ~ **de cuenta** debit/credit in an account; ~**s bursátiles** stock-market movements **2.** (*ajedrez*) move **3.** MÚS (*velocidad*) tempo; (*tiempo*) movement

mozo *m* **1.** (*de café*) waiter; (*de estación*) porter; (*de hotel*) bellboy **2.** (*soldado*) recruit

mozo, -a I. *adj* **1.** (*joven*) young **2.** (*soltero*) single **II.** *m, f* (*chico*) lad; (*chica*) girl; (*joven*) youth, young man

muchacho, -a *m, f* (*chico*) boy; (*chica*) girl

muchedumbre *f* **1.** (*de cosas*) collection **2.** (*de personas*) crowd

mucho, -a I. *adj* a lot of; ~ **vino** a lot of wine, much wine; ~**s libros** a lot of books, many books; **hace ya** ~ **tiempo que...** it has been a long time since ... **II.** *adv* (*intensidad*) very; (*cantidad*) a lot; (*mucho tiempo*) for a long time; (*a menudo*) often; **trabajar** ~ to work hard; **lo sentimos** ~ we are very sorry; **no hace** ~ not long ago; **ni** ~ **menos** far from it; **como** ~ at (the) most

muda *f* **1.** (*ropa interior*) change of underwear **2.** (*serpiente*) slough

mudanza *f* (*de casa*) move

mudar I. *vi, vt* to change **II.** *vr:* ~**se**
1. (*de casa*) to move (house) **2.** (*de ropa*) to change clothes

mudo, -a I. *adj* dumb; **cine** ~ silent
films *Brit,* silent movies *Am;* **quedarse** ~ to be speechless **II.** *m, f*
mute person

mueble I. *m* **1.** (*pieza*) piece of furniture; ~ **bar** drinks cabinet; ~ **de
cocina** kitchen unit **2.** *pl* furniture
II. *adj* JUR **bienes** ~**s** movable goods,
personal property

mueca *f* face; **hacer** ~**s** to pull faces

muela *f* **1.** (*diente*) molar; ~**s del
juicio** wisdom teeth; **dolor de** ~**s**
toothache **2.** (*molino*) millstone
3. (*para afilar*) grindstone

muelle I. *m* **1.** (*resorte*) spring;
(*reloj*) mainspring **2.** (*puerto*) wharf
3. (*andén*) loading dock **II.** *adj* (*blando*) soft; (*cómodo*) comfortable

muerte *f* **1.** (*acción*) death; ~ **forestal** forest destruction; **pena de** ~
death penalty; **lecho de** ~ deathbed;
morir de ~ **natural** to die of natural
causes; **a** ~ to death **2.** (*asesinato*)
murder; **de mala** ~ *fig* lousy, crummy; **un susto de** ~ a dreadful fright

muerto, -a I. *pp de* **morir II.** *adj*
dead; **punto** ~ AUTO neutral; **horas
muertas** period of inactivity; **naturaleza muerta** still life **III.** *m, f* dead
person; (*difunto*) deceased; (*cadáver*) corpse; **cargar el** ~ **a alguien** *inf* to lay the blame on sb; **hacerse el** ~ (*quieto, t. fig*) to play
dead; (*nadando*) to float; **ser un** ~
de hambre to be a nobody

muesca *f* nick

muestra *f* **1.** (*mercancía*) sample;
feria de ~**s** trade fair **2.** (*prueba*)
proof; ~ **de sangre** MED blood
sample; ~ **de amistad** token of
friendship **3.** (*demostración*) demonstration; **dar** ~(**s**) **de...** to give a
demonstration of ...

muestreo *m* sampling

mugir <g→j> *vi* (*vaca*) to moo

mugre *f sin pl* grime

mugriento, -a *adj* grubby

mujer *f* woman; ~ **fatal** femme
fatale; ~ **de la limpieza** cleaning
lady; ~ **de la calle** prostitute

mujeriego *m* womanizer

mulato, -a I. *adj* (*mestizo*) mulatto;
(*color*) brown-skinned **II.** *m, f* mulatto

muleta *f* **1.** (*apoyo*) crutch **2.** TAUR
*red cloth attatched to a stick used by
a matador*

mullido, -a *adj* soft

mulo, -a *m, f* mule

multa *f* fine

multar *vt* to fine

multicines *mpl* multiplex

multicolor *adj* multicoloured *Brit,*
multicolored *Am;* TIPO polychromatic

multicopista *f* duplicator

multimedia *adj inv* multimedia

multimillonario, -a *m, f* multimillionaire

multinacional *adj, f* multinational

múltiple *adj* multiple; ~**s veces** numerous times

multiplicar <c→qu> **I.** *vi, vt* MAT to
multiply; **tabla de** ~ multiplication
table **II.** *vr:* ~**se 1.** (*reproducirse*) to
multiply **2.** (*desvivirse*) to be everywhere at the same time

multiplicidad *f* multiplicity

múltiplo, -a *adj, m, f* multiple

multitud *f* **1.** (*cantidad*) multitude
2. (*gente*) multitude, crowd

mundanal *adj,* **mundano, -a** *adj*
(*del mundo*) of the world; (*terrenal*)
worldly

mundial *adj* world; **guerra** ~ world
war; **a nivel** ~ worldwide

mundo *m* (*globo*) world; (*tierra*)
earth; **el** ~ **antiguo** the ancient
world; **el otro** ~ the next world;
todo el ~ everyone, everybody;
venir al ~ to be born; **irse de este**
~ to die; **ver** ~ to travel a lot; **con
toda la tranquilidad del** ~ with the
utmost calm; **este** ~ **es un pañuelo**
it is a small world; **nada del otro** ~
nothing out of this world; **tener
mucho** ~ to be worldly-wise

munición *f* (*de armas*) ammunition

municipal *adj* municipal

municipio *m* **1.** (*población*) municipality, borough **2.** (*ayuntamiento*)

town hall **3.** (*concejo*) town council
muñeca *f* **1.** (*brazo*) wrist **2.** (*juguete*) doll
muñeco *m* **1.** (*juguete*) doll; ~ **de nieve** snowman **2.** *pey* (*monigote*) puppet
muñequera *f* wristband
mural I. *adj* wall **II.** *m* mural
muralla *f* wall
murciélago *m* bat
murmullo *m* **1.** (*voz*) whisper; (*cuchicheo*) murmur **2.** (*hojas*) rustling; (*agua*) murmur
murmuración *f* **1.** (*calumnia*) slander **2.** (*cotilleo*) gossip
murmurar I. *vi, vt* (*entre dientes*) to mutter; (*susurrar*) to murmur **II.** *vi* **1.** (*gruñir*) to grumble **2.** (*criticar*) to criticize **3.** (*agua*) to murmur; (*hojas*) to rustle
muro *m* wall; **Muro de las Lamentaciones** the Wailing Wall
mus *m* card game
musa *f* muse
musaraña *f* shrew; **pensar en las ~s** *fig* to have one's head in the clouds
muscular *adj* muscular
músculo *m* muscle
musculoso, -a *adj* muscular
museo *m* museum
musgo *m* moss
música *f* music; (*partituras*) score; ~ **ambiental** muzak, canned music; **banda de** ~ band; **caja de** ~ music box; **¡vete con la ~ a otra parte!** *inf* get out of here!
musical *adj, m* musical
músico, -a I. *adj* musical **II.** *m, f* musician; (*compositor*) composer
musitar *vi* (*balbucear*) to mumble; (*susurrear*) to whisper
muslo *m* (*persona*) thigh; (*animal*) leg
mustio, -a *adj* **1.** (*flores*) wilting **2.** (*triste*) low
musulmán, -ana *adj, m, f* Muslim
mutación *f* **1.** (*transformación, genes*) mutation **2.** TEAT scene change
mutilar *vt* **1.** (*cuerpo*) to mutilate **2.** (*recortar*) to cut

mutismo *m* silence
mutuo, -a *adj* mutual
muy *adv* very; ~ **a pesar mío** much to my dismay; ~ **atentamente,** (*en cartas*) yours faithfully; **¡eso es ~ de María!** that is typical of María!

> ⚠ **muy** is an adverb and is used with adjectives and other adverbs: "El edificio es muy antiguo; Ella hace siempre su trabajo muy bien." **mucho** is used with verbs: "Hoy hemos trabajado mucho" and also with nouns: "Actualmente no tengo mucho tiempo libre."

N n

N, n *f* N, n; ~ **de Navarra** N for Nelly *Brit,* N for Nan *Am*
nabo *m* turnip
nácar *m* mother-of-pearl, nacre
nacer *irr como crecer vi* **1.** (*venir al mundo*) to be born; (*de un huevo*) to hatch; **volver a** ~ to have a very narrow escape **2.** (*germinar*) to germinate **3.** (*originarse*) to stem; (*arroyo*) to begin; (*surgir*) to arise
nacido, -a I. *pp de* nacer **II.** *m, f* **recién** ~ newborn
naciente *adj fig* incipient, budding
nacimiento *m* birth; **ciego de** ~ born blind; **lugar de** ~ birthplace; **de** ~ by birth
nación *f* nation
nacional *adj* national; **vuelos ~es** domestic flights
nacionalidad *f* nationality, citizenship
nacionalismo *m sin pl* nationalism
nacionalista *adj, mf* nationalist
nacionalizar <z→c> **I.** *vt* to natu-

ralize, to nationalize **II.** *vr* ~**se español** to obtain Spanish nationality
nada I. *pron indef* nothing; **¡gracias! – ¡de ~!** thank you! – not at all!; **¡pues ~!** well all right then; **por ~ se queja** he/she complains about the slightest thing; **como si ~** as if nothing had happened; **le costó ~ más y ~ menos que...** it cost him/her the fine sum of ...; **no servir para ~** to be useless **II.** *adv* not at all; **antes de ~** (*sobre todo*) above all; (*primero*) first of all; **~ más** (*solamente*) only; (*no más*) no more; **de ~** absolutely nothing; **para ~** not in the slightest; **no ser ~ difícil** to not be difficult at all; **¡y ~ de llegar tarde!** no arriving late!; **¡casi ~!** hardly anything! **III.** *f* nothing; **salir de la ~** to appear out of nowhere
nadador(a) *m(f)* swimmer
nadar *vi* to swim
nadie *pron indef* nobody, anybody, no one; **no ví a ~** I didn't see anybody, I saw nobody; **no vino ~** nobody came; **tú no eres ~ para decir...** who are you to say ...?; **un don ~** a nobody; **tierra de ~** no man's land
nado *adv* **a ~** afloat, swimming; **cruzar algo a ~** to swim across sth
nafta *f CSur* petrol *Brit*, gasoline *Am*
naipe *m* card
nalga *f* buttock
namibio, -a *adj, m, f* Namibian
nana *f* lullaby
napia(s) *f(pl) inf* conk
Nápoles *m* Naples
napolitano, -a *adj, m, f* Neapolitan
naranja *f* orange; **tu media ~** *fig* your better half
naranjo *m* orange tree
narcisista *adj* narcissistic
narciso *m* **1.** BOT daffodil, narcissus *inv* **2.** (*persona*) narcissist
narcótico *m* narcotic
narcótico, -a *adj* narcotic
narcotizar <z→c> *vt* to narcotize
narcotráfico *m* drug dealing
narigón, -ona *adj*, **narigudo, -a** *adj* big-nosed
nariz *f* **1.** ANAT nose **2.** *inf* **dar a al-**

guien con la puerta en las narices to slam the door in sb's face; **estar hasta las narices** to have had it up to here; **hasta que se me hinchen las narices** until I lose my rag; **lo hizo por narices** he/she did it because he/she felt like it; **¡(qué) narices!** no way; **romper las narices a alguien** to smash sb's face in; **¡tócate las narices!** would you believe it?
narración *f* narration
narrador(a) *m(f)* narrator
narrar *vt* to narrate
narrativa *adj, f* narrative
nata *f* **1.** (*producto*) cream; ~ **montada** whipped cream **2.** (*sobre la leche*) skin
natación *f* swimming
natal *adj* native; **ciudad ~** home town
natalidad *f* birth; (**índice de**) ~ birth rate
natillas *fpl* custard
natividad *f* nativity
nativo, -a *adj, m, f* native
nato, -a *adj* born
natural *adj* **1.** (*no artificial, sencillo*) natural; **de tamaño ~** life-sized **2.** (*nacido*) **ser ~ del Reino Unido** to be a British natural
naturaleza *f* nature
naturalidad *f sin pl* naturalness; **con ~** naturally
naturalizar <z→c> **I.** *vt* to naturalize **II.** *vr:* ~**se** to become naturalized
naufragar <g→gu> *vi* (*barco*) to be wrecked; (*personas*) to be shipwrecked
naufragio *m* shipwreck
náufrago, -a *m, f* castaway
nauseabundo, -a *adj* nauseating
náuseas *fpl* sick feeling; **dar ~ a alguien** to make sb feel sick; **tener ~** to feel sick
náutica *f sin pl* navigation
náutico, -a *adj* nautical; **club ~** yacht club
navaja *f* (pocket) knife; ~ **de afeitar** razor
navajazo *m* stab wound
naval *adj* naval

navarro, -a *adj* of/from Navarra
nave *f* 1. NÁUT ship, vessel 2. AVIAT ~
(**espacial**) spaceship, spacecraft
3. (*en una iglesia*) nave 4. (*almacén*)
warehouse; (*fábrica*) factory unit
navegación *f* navigation
navegador *m* INFOR browser
navegante *mf* navigator; ~ **de internet** Net surfer
navegar <g→gu> *vi, vt* to navigate;
~ **por la web** to surf the net
Navidad *f* Christmas; **¡feliz ~!** merry
Christmas!
navideño, -a *adj* Christmas
navío *m* ship
nazi *adj, mf* Nazi
nazismo *m sin pl* Nazism
NE *abr de* **Nordeste** NE
neblina *f* mist
nebuloso, -a *adj* 1. (*brumoso*) misty;
(*nuboso*) cloudy 2. (*vago*) hazy; (*oscuro*) obscure
necedad *f* stupidity; **no decir más
que ~es** to talk a lot of nonsense
necesario, -a *adj* necessary; **es ~
que haya más acuerdo** there is a
need for more agreement
neceser *m* (*de aseo*) toilet bag; (*de
costura*) sewing box
necesidad *f* 1. (*ser preciso*) need,
necessity; **no tiene ~ de trabajar**
there is no need for him/her to work
2. (*requerimiento*) need; **tener ~ de
algo** to be in need of sth
necesitado, -a I. *adj* in need II. *m, f*
los ~s the poor
necesitar I. *vt* 1. (*precisar*) to need;
se necesita piso flat wanted
2. (*tener que*) to need to II. *vi* ~ **de
algo** to need sth
necio, -a I. *adj* idiotic II. *m, f* idiot
necrología *f* obituary
néctar *m* nectar
nectarina *f* nectarine
neerlandés, -esa I. *adj* Dutch II. *m,
f* Dutchman *m,* Dutchwoman *f*
nefasto, -a *adj* awful
negación *f* 1. (*desmentir*) denial
2. (*denegar*) refusal 3. LING negative
negado, -a *adj, m, f* (**ser un**) ~ **para
algo** (to be) useless at sth
negar *irr como fregar* I. *vt* 1. (*des-*

mentir) to deny 2. (*rehusar*) to refuse II. *vr:* ~**se** to refuse
negativa *f* 1. (*desmentir*) denial
2. (*denegar*) refusal
negativo *m* negative
negativo, -a *adj* negative
negligencia *f* negligence
negligente *adj* negligent
negociable *adj* negotiable
negociación *f* negotiation
negociado *m* section
negociante *mf* dealer; *pey* money-
-grubber
negociar I. *vi* (*comerciar*) to deal
II. *vi, vt* (*dialogar, concertar*) to negotiate
negocio *m* business; ~ **al detalle** retail business; **hombre/mujer de ~s**
businessman/businesswoman; **eso
no es ~ mio** it's none of my business
negra *f* crotchet *Brit,* quarter note
Am
negro, -a *adj, m, f* black; ~ **como la
boca del lobo** pitch-black; **estar/
ponerse** ~ *inf* to be/get furious;
pasarlas negras *inf* to have a terrible time; **verse** ~ [*o* **pasarlas negras**] **para hacer algo** *inf* to have a
hard time doing sth; **verlo todo** ~ to
be very pessimistic
negrura *f* blackness
nene, -a *m, f inf* baby
nenúfar *m* water lily
neologismo *m* neologism
neón *m* neon
neoyorquino, -a I. *adj* of/from New
York II. *m, f* New Yorker
neozelandés, -esa I. *adj* of/from
New Zealand II. *m, f* New Zealander
nepalés, -esa *adj, m, f* Nepalese
nepotismo *m sin pl* nepotism
nervio *m* nerve; **ataque de ~s** nervous breakdown; **crispar los ~s a alguien, poner a alguien los ~s de
punta** *inf* to get on sb's nerves
nerviosismo *m* nervousness
nervioso, -a *adj* nervous
neto, -a *adj* net
neumático *m* tyre *Brit,* tire *Am*
neura *f inf* obsession
neurólogo, -a *m, f* neurologist
neurona *f* neuron, neurone *Brit*

N
n

neutral *adj* neutral
neutralizar <z→c> *vt* to neutralize
neutro, -a *adj* neuter
neutrón *m* neutron
nevada *f* snowfall; (*tormenta*) snow-storm
nevado, -a *adj* snow-covered
nevar <e→ie> *v impers* to snow
nevera *f* fridge; (*portátil*) cool box
nevisca *f* light snowfall
nexo *m* link
ni *conj* ~... ~... neither ... nor ...; **no fumo ~ bebo** I don't smoke or drink, I neither smoke nor drink; ~ (**siquiera**) not even; **¡~ lo pienses!** don't even let it cross your mind!; **sin más ~ más** without any further ado; **¡~ que fueras tonto!** anyone would think you were stupid!; ~ **bien...** *Arg* as soon as ...
Nicaragua *f* Nicaragua

[?] **Nicaragua** lies in Central America, bordering Honduras to the north, Costa Rica to the south, the Caribbean to the east and the Pacific Ocean to the west. The capital of Nicaragua is **Managua**. The official language of the country is Spanish and the monetary unit is the **córdoba**.

nicaragüense *adj, mf* Nicaraguan
nicho *m* niche
nicotina *f* nicotine
nido *m* nest
niebla *f* fog; **hay** ~ it is foggy
nieto, -a *m, f* grandson *m*, grand-daughter *f*; **los nietos** the grand-children
nieve *f* snow; **a punto de** ~ GASTR stiff
NIF *m abr de* **Número de Identificación Fiscal** Fiscal Identity Number
nigeriano, -a *adj, m, f* Nigerian
Nilo *m* Nile
nimiedad *f* trifle
nimio, -a *adj* insignificant
ninfa *f* nymph
ninfómana *f* nymphomaniac

ningún *adj indef v.* **ninguno**
ninguno, -a I. *adj indef* (*precediendo un sustantivo masculino singular: ningún*) any; **por ningún lado** anywhere; **de ninguna manera** in no way; **ninguna vez** never; **no hay ningún peligro** there is no danger II. *pron indef* anything, nothing; (*personas*) anybody, nobody; **no quiso venir** ~ nobody wanted to come
niña *f* **1.** (*chica*) girl **2.** ANAT pupil; **eres** (**como**) **la** ~ **de mis ojos** you are the apple of my eye
niñera *f* nanny
niñería *f* childish act
niñez *f* childhood
niño *m* child; (*chico*) boy; (*bebé*) baby; ~ **de pecho** babe-in-arms
nipón, -ona *adj, m, f* Japanese *inv*
níquel *m* nickel
nitidez *f* brightness; FOTO clarity
nítido, -a *adj* bright; FOTO clear
nitrato *m* nitrate
nitrógeno *m* nitrogen
nitroglicerina *f* nitroglycerine
nivel *m* level, standard; **paso a** ~ level crossing *Brit,* grade crossing *Am;* **sobre el** ~ **del mar** above sea level; ~ **de vida** standard of living
nivelar I. *vt* to level II. *vr:* ~**se** to level out; ~**se con alguien** to catch up with sb
no *adv* **1.** (*respuesta*) no **2.** + *adjetivo* non- **3.** + *verbo* not; ~**...** **nada** not ... anything; ~**...** **nunca** not ... ever, never; **ya** ~ not any more, no longer; **o, si** ~ otherwise; ~ **tiene más que un abrigo** he/she only has one coat; **¡a que** ~**!** do you want to bet?; **¿cómo** ~**?** of course **4.** (*retórica*) **¿**~**?** isn't he/she?, don't we/they?

[!] The negation **no** is followed by other negative particles when the speaker wants to give special emphasis or express a nuance: "No entiendo nada; No he estado nunca en Japón." When these negative particles go before the verb, 'no' is omitted: "Nunca he estado en Jamaica."

NO *abr de* **Noroeste** NW
noble *adj* <nobilísimo> noble
nobleza *f* nobility
noche *f* **1.** (*contrario de día*) night; **de la ~ a la mañana** overnight; **buenas ~s** (*saludo*) good evening; (*despedida*) good night; **a media ~** at midnight; **Noche Vieja** New Year's Eve; **ayer** (**por la**) **~** last night; **hacerse de ~** to get dark; **hacer ~ en...** to spend the night in ...; **ser como la ~ y el día** to be as different as night and day **2.** (*tarde*) evening **3.** (*oscuridad*) darkness; **es de ~** it's dark
Nochebuena *f* Christmas Eve
Nochevieja *f* New Year's Eve
noctámbulo, -a *m, f* night owl
nocturno *m* nocturne
nocturno, -a *adj* night; ZOOL nocturnal
nodriza *f* wet-nurse
nogal *m* walnut tree
nómada I. *adj* nomadic **II.** *mf* nomad
nombramiento *m* appointment
nombrar *vt* **1.** (*mencionar*) to mention **2.** (*designar*) to appoint
nombre *m* **1.** (*designación*) name; **~ de familia** surname *Brit,* last name *Am;* **~ de pila, primer ~** first name; **~ de soltera** maiden name; **~ artístico** stage name; **a ~ de alguien** in sb's name; **en ~ de** on behalf of; **llamar a las cosas por su ~** *fig* to call a spade a spade **2.** LING noun
nomenclatura *f* nomenclature
nomeolvides *f inv* forget-me-not
nómina *f* payroll
nominal *adj* nominal; LING noun
nominar *vt* to nominate
nominativo, -a *adj* nominative
non I. *adj* odd **II.** *m* odd number
nonagésimo, -a *adj* ninetieth; *v.t.* **octavo**
nono, -a *adj* ninth; *v.t.* **octavo**
nordeste *m* north-east
nórdico, -a *adj* northern, northerly; (*escandinavo*) Scandinavian
noreste *m* north-east

noria *f* **1.** (*para agua*) water wheel **2.** (*de feria*) big wheel *Brit,* Ferris wheel *Am*
norirlandés, -esa I. *adj* Northern Irish **II.** *m, f* native/inhabitant of Northern Ireland
norma *f* norm, standard; (*regla*) rule
normal *adj* normal; **gasolina ~** two--star petrol *Brit,* regular gas *Am*
normalizar <z→c> *vt* to normalize
normalmente *adv* normally; (*habitualmente*) usually
normando, -a *adj, m, f* Norman
normativa *f* rules *pl*
normativo, -a *adj* normative
noroeste *m* north-west
norte *m* north; **el ~ de España** northern Spain; **en el ~ de Inglaterra** in the north of England; **al ~ de** north of
norteamericano, -a *adj, m, f* North American; (*de los EE.UU.*) American
Noruega *f* Norway
noruego, -a *adj, m, f* Norwegian
nos I. *pron pers* us; **tu primo nos pegó** your cousin hit us; **nos escribieron una carta** they wrote a letter to us **II.** *pron refl* ourselves, each other
nosotros, -as *pron pers, 1.pl* **1.** (*sujeto*) we **2.** (*tras preposición*) us
nostalgia *f* (*de lugar*) homesickness; (*del pasado*) nostalgia
nostálgico, -a *adj* (*de un lugar*) homesick; (*del pasado*) nostalgic
nota *f* **1.** (*anotación, apunte*) *t.* MÚS note; **~ circular** circular; **~ al pie de la página** footnote; **~ preliminar** preliminary notes; **tomar ~** to take notes; **tomar** (**buena**) **~ de algo** to take (good) note of sth **2.** (*calificación*) mark *Brit,* grade *Am;* **sacar malas ~s** to get bad marks **3.** (*detalle*) touch
notable I. *adj* remarkable; (*suma*) considerable **II.** *m* qualification *equivalent to 7 or 8 on a scale of ten*
notar *vt* to notice; **no se te nota nada** you wouldn't notice
notarial *adj* legal

N
n

notario, -a *m, f* notary
noticia *f* (piece of) news; **las ~s** the news; **ser ~** to be in the news; **no tener ~ de alguien** to not have heard from sb; **tener ~ de algo** to have heard about sth
noticiario *m* news report, newscast *Am;* **~ deportivo** sports news
notificar <c→qu> *vt* to notify; **hacer ~** to let it be known
notoriedad *f* fame
notorio, -a *adj* well-known
novato, -a *m, f* beginner
novecientos, -as *adj* nine hundred; *v.t.* **ochocientos**
novedad *f* **1.** (*acontecimiento*) new development; **¿hay alguna ~?** anything new? **2.** (*cosa*) novelty; (*libro*) new publication
novedoso, -a *adj AmL* novel
novel I. *adj* inexperienced **II.** *mf* beginner
novela *f* novel; **~ policíaca** detective story
novelesco, -a *adj* novel; *fig* amazing
novelista *mf* novelist
noveno, -a *adj* ninth; *v.t.* **octavo**
noventa *adj inv, m* ninety; *v.t.* **ochenta**
noviazgo *m* (*para casarse*) engagement; *inf* (*relación*) relationship
novicio, -a *m, f* novice
noviembre *m* November; *v.t.* **marzo**
novillada *f TAUR* bullfight with young bulls and less experienced bullfighters
novillero, -a *m, f* apprentice bullfighter
novillo, -a *m, f* young bull
novio, -a *m, f* **1.** (*para casarse*) bridegroom *m,* bride *f;* **los ~s** (*en la boda*) the bride and groom; (*después de la boda*) the newly-weds; **viaje de ~s** honeymoon **2.** (*en relación amorosa*) boyfriend *m,* girlfriend *f*
nubarrón *m* storm cloud
nube *f* cloud; **estar por las ~s** (*precios*) to be sky-high; **poner a alguien por las ~s** to praise sb to the skies
nublado *adj* cloudy

nublar I. *vt* to cloud **II.** *vr:* **~se** to cloud over
nuca *f* nape, back of the neck
nuclear *adj* nuclear
núcleo *m* nucleus
nudillo *m* knuckle
nudo *m* **1.** (*atadura, madera*) *t.* NÁUT knot; **se me hizo un ~ en la garganta** I got a lump in my throat **2.** (*centro*) centre *Brit,* center *Am;* **~ ferroviario** junction
nudoso, -a *adj* knotty; (*madera*) gnarled
nuera *f* daughter-in-law
nuestro, -a I. *adj* our **II.** *pron pos* **1.** (*propiedad*) **la casa es nuestra** the house is ours; **¡ya es ~!** *fig* we've got it! **2.** *tras artículo* **el ~/la nuestra/lo ~** ours; **los ~s** our people; (*parientes*) our family; **¡eso es lo ~!** that's what we're good at!; **ésta es la nuestra** *fig, inf* this is our chance **3.** *tras substantivo* of ours, our; **una amiga nuestra** a friend of ours; **es culpa nuestra** it is our fault
nueva *f* piece of news; **esto me coge de ~s** this is news to me; **no te hagas de ~s** don't pretend you didn't know
nuevamente *adv* again
Nueva York *f* New York
Nueva Zelandia *f* New Zealand
nueve *adj inv, m* nine; *v.t.* **ocho**
nuevo, -a *adj* new; **de ~** again; **sentirse como ~** to feel like a new man; **¿qué hay de ~?** what's new?
nuez *f* **1.** BOT walnut; **~ moscada** nutmeg **2.** ANAT Adam's apple
nulidad *f* **1.** (*no válido*) nullity; **declarar la ~ de algo** to declare sth invalid **2.** *inf* (*persona*) **ser una ~** to be useless
nulo, -a *adj* **1.** (*inválido*) invalid **2.** (*incapaz*) useless
núm. *abr de* **número** No.
numeración *f* numbering system; **~ arábiga** Arabic numerals
numerador *m* numerator
numeral *m* number
numerar *vt* to number; **sin ~** unnumbered
numérico, -a *adj* numerical

número *m* number; ~ **quebrado**
fraction; ~ **de zapatos** shoe size;
hacer ~**s para ver si…** to calculate
if …; **montar un** ~ to make a scene

numeroso, -a *adj* numerous; **familia**
numerosa large family

nunca *adv* never; ~ **jamás** never
ever; **más que** ~ more than ever

nuncio *m* nuncio

nupcial *adj* nuptial

nupcias *fpl* nuptials *pl;* **segundas** ~
remarriage

nutria *f* otter

nutrición *f* nutrition

nutrido, -a *adj* **bien** ~ well-fed; **mal**
~ undernourished

nutrir *vt* to feed; (*piel*) to nourish

nutritivo, -a *adj* nutritious; **valor** ~
nutritional value

Ñ, ñ *f* Ñ, ñ

> **?** The **eñe** is the trade mark of the
> Spanish **alfabeto**. Up until a few
> years ago, the 'ch' – **la che** – (di-
> rectly after the 'c') and the 'll' – **la**
> **elle** – (after the 'l') were also part
> of the alphabet, as they are both
> independent sounds in their own
> right. This had to be changed,
> however, in order to internation-
> alise the Spanish alphabet, i.e. bring
> it into line with other languages.

ñato, -a *adj CSur* snub-nosed

ñoñería *f* **1.** (*simpleza*) inanity
2. (*dengues*) silliness

ñoño, -a I. *adj inf* **1.** (*soso*) insipid;
(*aburrido*) boring **2.** (*tonto*) inane
3. (*remilgado*) prudish **II.** *m, f inf*
1. (*tonto*) idiot **2.** (*aburrido*) bore

O, o *f* O, o; ~ **de Oviedo** O for Oliver
Brit, O for Oboe *Am*

o, ó *conj* or; ~…, ~… either …, or
…; ~ **sea** in other words; ~ **bien** or
else; ~ **mejor dicho** or rather

> **!** **o** always becomes **u** before a
> word beginning with o- or ho-:
> "siete u ocho, Marta u Olga, orien-
> tal u occidental, ayer u hoy." Be-
> tween numbers the 'o' has a
> written accent to distinguish it
> from the number zero: "20 ó 30."

O *abr de* **oeste** W

oasis *m inv* oasis

obcecar <c→qu> **I.** *vt* to blind **II.** *vr:*
~**se** to be blinded

obedecer *irr como crecer vt* to obey;
(*instrucciones*) to follow

obediencia *f* obedience

obediente *adj* obedient

obertura *f* overture

obesidad *f* obesity

obeso, -a *adj* obese

obispo *m* bishop

objeción *f* objection

objetar *vt* to object; **tengo algo que**
~ I have an objection

objetivo *m* **1.** (*finalidad*) goal **2.** FOTO
lens **3.** (*blanco*) target

objetivo, -a *adj* objective

objeto *m* **1.** (*cosa*) object; ~ **de**
valor valuables *pl;* ~**s perdidos** lost
property **2.** (*motivo*) purpose; **con**
(**el**) [*o* **al**] ~ **de…** in order to …
3. LING object

objetor(a) *m(f)* ~ **de conciencia**
conscientious objector

oblicuo, -a *adj* oblique, slanted

obligación *f* **1.** (*deber*) obligation;
faltar a sus obligaciones to neglect
one's duties; **tener la** ~ **de hacer**
algo to be obliged to do sth
2. (*deuda*) liability; (*documento*)
bond

obligar <g→gu> *vt* (*forzar*) to force; (*comprometer*) to oblige

obligatorio, -a *adj* obligatory; **asignatura obligatoria** compulsory subject; **es ~ llevar puesto el casco** helmets must be worn

oboe *m* oboe

obra *f* **1.** (*creación, labor*) work; ~ **benéfica** charitable act; ~ **maestra** masterpiece; ~ **de teatro** play **2.** (*construcción*) building work; (*lugar en construcción*) construction site; (*edificio*) building; **mano de** ~ labour *Brit*, labor *Am;* ~**s públicas** public works; ~ **de reforma** renovation

obrar *vi* to act

obrero, -a *m, f* worker

obscenidad *f* obscenity

obsceno, -a *adj* obscene

obsequiar *vt* (*con regalos*) to bestow; ~ **a alguien con un banquete** to hold a banquet in sb's honour

obsequio *m* (*regalo*) gift; (*agasajo*) treat

obsequioso, -a *adj* attentive

observación *f* **1.** (*contemplación, vigilancia*) observation **2.** (*comentario*) remark **3.** (*observancia*) observance

observador(a) **I.** *adj* observant **II.** *m(f)* observer

observancia *f* observance

observar *vt* **1.** (*contemplar, cumplir*) to observe **2.** (*notar*) to notice

observatorio *m* observatory; ~ **meteorológico** weather station

obsesión *f* obsession

obsesionar *vt* to obsess; **el fútbol lo obsesiona** he is obsessed with football

obseso, -a *adj* obsessed

obsoleto, -a *adj* obsolete

obstaculizar <z→c> *vt* to hinder; ~ **la carretera** to obstruct the road

obstáculo *m* obstacle; COM barrier; **poner ~s a alguien** to hinder sb

obstante *adv* **no ~** nevertheless

obstetra *mf* obstetrician

obstetricia *f* obstetrics *pl*

obstinado, -a *adj* obstinate

obstinarse *vr* to persist

obstrucción *f* obstruction

obstruir *irr como* huir *vt* to obstruct; (*una tubería*) to block

obtener *irr como* tener *vt* to obtain; (*resultado, ventaja*) to gain

obturador *m* shutter

obtuso, -a *adj* blunt

obviar *vt* (*evitar*) to avoid; (*eliminar*) to remove

obvio, -a *adj* obvious

oca *f* **1.** ZOOL goose **2.** (*juego*) snakes *pl* and ladders

ocasión *f* occasion; **coche de** ~ second hand car; **libros de** ~ bargain books; **con ~ de** on the occasion of; **en esta** ~ on this occasion; **en ocasiones** sometimes; **en la primera** ~ at the first opportunity; **dar a alguien** ~ **para quejarse** to give sb cause to complain

ocasionar *vt* to cause

ocaso *m* **1.** (*del sol*) sunset **2.** (*decadencia*) decline

occidental *adj* western

occidente *m* GEO west; **el** ~ the West

OCDE *f abr de* **Organización para la Cooperación y el Desarrollo Económicos** OECD

océano *m* ocean

ochenta *adj inv, m* eighty; **los años** ~ the eighties; **un hombre de alrededor de** ~ **años** a man of about eighty years of age; **una mujer en sus** ~ a woman in her eighties

ocho *adj inv, m* eight; **jornada de** ~ **horas** eight-hour day; ~ **veces mayor/menor que...** eight times bigger/smaller than ...; **a las** ~ at eight (o'clock); **son las** ~ **y media de la mañana/tarde** it is half past eight in the morning/evening; **las** ~ **y cuarto/menos cuarto** a quarter past/to eight; **a las** ~ **en punto** at eight o'clock precisely; **el** ~ **de agosto** the eighth of August; **dentro de** ~ **días** in a week's time; **de aquí a** ~ **días** a week from now

ochocientos, -as *adj* eight hundred; **esta basílica fue construida hace** ~ **años** this basilica was built eight hundred years ago; **vinieron más**

de **ochocientas personas** more than eight hundred people came

ocio *m* leisure

ociosidad *f* idleness

ocioso, -a *adj* idle

octava *f* octave

octavilla *f* leaflet

octavo, -a *adj* eighth; **en ~ lugar** in eighth place; **estoy en ~ curso** I am in eighth year; **la octava parte** an eighth

octogésimo, -a *adj* eightieth; *v.t.* **octavo**

octubre *m* October; *v.t.* **marzo**

ocular *adj* ocular; **examen ~** eye test

oculista *mf* ophthalmologist

ocultar *vt* 1. *(información, delito)* to conceal

oculto, -a *adj* hidden; *(secreto)* secret

ocupación *f* occupation; **zona de ~** occupied zone; **~ temporal** temporary job; **sin ~** unemployed

ocupado, -a *adj* 1. *(sitio)* occupied 2. *(persona)* busy 3. *(teléfono)* engaged *Brit*, busy *Am*

ocupar I. *vt* 1. *(lugar, teléfono)* *t.* MIL to occupy; *(tiempo, espacio, asiento)* to take up 2. *(vacante)* to fill 3. *(un cargo)* to hold 4. *(a una persona)* to keep busy **II.** *vr* **~se de alguien/algo** *(cuidar)* to look after sb/sth; **~se de algo** *(tratar)* to deal with sth; *(encargarse)* to take care of sth

ocurrencia *f* 1. *(idea)* idea; **tener la ~ de...** to have the bright idea of ...; **¡qué ~ pensar que es mi culpa!** imagine saying that it was my fault!; **dijo que podía comerse 20 panecillos, ¡qué ~!** he/she said that he/she could eat 20 rolls, what nonsense!; **se bañó en el mar en pleno invierno, ¡qué ~!** he/she swam in the sea in the middle of winter, what a thing to do! 2. *(suceso)* occurrence

ocurrir I. *vi* to happen; **¿qué ocurre?** what's wrong?; **¿qué te ocurre?** what's the matter?; **lo que ocurre es que...** the thing is that ...

II. *vr:* **~se** to occur; **no se me ocurre nada** I can't think of anything; **no se le ocurre más que decir tonterías** he/she does nothing but talk nonsense; **¿cómo se te ocurrió esa tontería?** what on earth made you think of a stupid thing like that?; **nunca se me hubiese ocurrido pensar que...** I never would have imagined that ...

odiar *vt* to hate

odio *m* hate, hatred; **tener ~ a alguien** to hate sb

odioso, -a *adj* 1. *(hostil)* nasty 2. *(repugnante)* horrible

odisea *f* odyssey

odontólogo, -a *m, f* dentist

OEA *f abr de* **Organización de los Estados Americanos** OAS

oeste *m* west; **el ~ de España** western Spain; **en el ~ de Inglaterra** in the west of England; **al ~ de** west of; **el lejano ~** the wild west; **película del ~** western

ofender I. *vt* to offend **II.** *vr:* **~se** to take offence; **¡no te ofendas conmigo!** don't get angry with me!

ofensa *f* offence, offense *Am*

ofensiva *f* offensive; **tomar la ~** to go on the offensive

ofensivo, -a *adj* offensive

oferta *f* 1. *(propuesta)* offer; *(para contratar)* tender, bid; **estar de ~** to be on special offer 2. ECON **~ (y demanda)** supply (and demand)

offset *m* offset

oficial *adj* official; **boletín ~** official gazette

oficial(a) *m(f)* *(oficio manual)* worker; *(administrativo)* clerk; MIL officer; *(funcionario)* civil servant; **~a (de secretaría)** secretary

oficina *f* office; **~ de empleo** job centre *Brit*, job office *Am*

oficinista *mf* office worker

oficio *m* 1. *(trabajo manual)* trade; **~ de ebanista** cabinet-making 2. *(profesión)* profession; **de ~** by trade; **gajes del ~** occupational hazards 3. *(función)* function; **de ~** ex officio 4. *(escrito)* official document 5. REL service; **Santo Oficio** Holy Office

oficioso, -a *adj* unofficial

ofimática *f* office automation

ofrecer *irr como crecer* **I.** *vt* to offer; ~ **un banquete** to give a meal; ~ **grandes dificultades** to present a lot of difficulties **II.** *vr:* ~**se** to offer oneself; **¿se le ofrece algo?** do you need anything?; **¿qué se le ofrece?** may I help you?

ofrecimiento *m* offer

ofrendar *vt* to offer

oftalmólogo, -a *m, f* ophthalmologist

ofuscación *f,* **ofuscamiento** *m* confusion

ofuscar <c→qu> *vt* **1.** (*cegar*) to blind **2.** (*la mente*) ~ (**la mente**) **a alguien** to confuse sb

oída *f* **conocer a alguien/saber algo de** ~**s** to have heard about sb/sth

oído *m* **1.** (*sentido*) hearing; **duro de** ~ hard of hearing; **aguzar el** ~ to prick up one's ears; **tener buen** ~ to have a good ear **2.** ANAT ear; **ser todo** ~**s** to be all ears

oír *irr vt* (*sentir*) to hear; (*escuchar*) to listen; ~ **decir que...** to hear that ...; **¡oye!** hey!; **¿oyes?** do you understand?; **¡oiga!** excuse me!; ~**, ver y callar** *prov* hear no evil, see no evil, speak no evil

ojal *m* buttonhole

ojalá *interj* I hope so, I wish; **¡~ tuvieras razón!** if only you were right!

ojeada *f* glance; **echar una** ~ **a algo** to glance at sth; (*vigilar*) to keep an eye on sth

ojeras *fpl* **tener** ~ to have dark circles under one's eyes

ojeriza *f* **tener** ~ **a alguien** to bear a grudge against sb

ojeroso, -a *adj* haggard, tired

ojo **I.** *m* **1.** ANAT eye; **en un abrir y cerrar de** ~**s** in a flash; ~ **de buey** NÁUT porthole; **a** ~**s cerrados** without thinking; **con los** ~**s cerrados** with complete confidence; **a** ~ by eye; **andar con cien** ~**s** to be on one's guard; **costar un** ~ **de la cara** to cost an arm and a leg; **echar el** ~ **a algo/alguien** to have one's eye on

sth/sb; **echar un** ~ **a algo/alguien** to take a look at sth/sb; (*vigilar*) to keep an eye on sth/sb; **mirar con buenos/malos** ~**s** to approve/disapprove of; **no parecerse ni en el blanco de los** ~**s** to be as different as chalk and cheese *Brit;* **no pegar** ~ to not sleep a wink; **ser el** ~ **derecho de alguien** to be the apple of sb's eye; ~**s que no ven, corazón que no siente** *prov* out of sight, out of mind *prov;* **cuatro** ~**s ven más que dos** *prov* two heads are better than one *prov;* ~ **por** ~ (**y diente por diente**) *prov* an eye for an eye (a tooth for a tooth) **2.** (*agujero*) hole; ~ **de aguja** eye of a needle; ~ **de cerradura** keyhole **II.** *interj* (be) careful

ojota *f AmL* sandal

okupa *mf inf* squatter

ola *f* wave; ~ **de calor** heatwave

olé *interj* ≈ bravo

? **Olé** (or **ole**) is not only a cry of encouragement during a bullfight or a Flamenco dance, but also a general cry of enthusiasm and joy. **¡Olé!** is associated worldwide with Spain and its folklore.

---

oleada *f* wave

oleaje *m* swell, surf

óleo *m* (**cuadro al**) ~ oil painting; **pintar al** ~ to paint in oil

oleoducto *m* pipeline

oleoso, -a *adj* oily

oler *irr vi, vi* ~ (**a algo**) to smell of sth

olfatear **I.** *vt* **1.** (*oliscar*) to sniff **2.** (*husmear*) to smell out **II.** *vi* **1.** (*oliscar*) to sniff **2.** (*curiosear*) to nose about

olfato *m* sense of smell; **tener** (**buen**) ~ *fig* to have a good nose

oligarquía *f* oligarchy

olimpiada *f* **la**(**s**) ~(**s**) the Olympics

olímpico, -a *adj* Olympic

oliva *f* olive

olivo *m* olive tree

olla *f* **1.** (*para cocinar*) saucepan; ~

exprés pressure cooker **2.** GASTR stew

olmo *m* elm

olor *m* smell; (*fragancia*) scent; **tener ~ a** to smell of

oloroso, -a *adj* fragrant

olote *m Méx* corncob

olvidadizo, -a *adj* forgetful

olvidar(se) *vt, vr* to forget; **se me ha olvidado** [*o* **me he olvidado de**] **tu nombre** I've forgotten your name

olvido *m* forgetting; (*omisión*) oversight; **caer en (el) ~** to sink into oblivion

ombligo *m* navel

ominoso, -a *adj* despicable

omisión *f* omission

omiso, -a *adj* **hacer caso ~ de algo** to take no notice of sth

omitir *vt* **1.** (*no hacer*) to fail to do **2.** (*pasar por alto*) to omit

omnipotente *adj* almighty, omnipotent

omnívoro, -a I. *adj* omnivorous **II.** *m, f* omnivore

omoplato *m,* **omóplato** *m* scapula, shoulder blade

OMS *f abr de* **Organización Mundial de la Salud** WHO

once *adj inv, m* eleven; *v.t.* **ocho**

onceno, -a *adj* eleventh; *v.t.* **octavo**

onda *f* wave

ondear *vi* to ripple; (*bandera*) to flutter

ondulación *f* wave; (*agua*) ripple

ondulado, -a *adj* wavy; **cartón ~** corrugated cardboard

ondular *vt* to wave

oneroso, -a *adj* onerous

ONG *f abr de* **Organización No Gubernamental** NGO

ONU *f abr de* **Organización de las Naciones Unidas** UNO

onubense *adj* of/from Huelva

opaco, -a *adj* **1.** (*no transparente*) opaque **2.** (*sin brillo, persona*) dull

ópalo *m* opal

opción *f* option; (*elección*) choice; (*derecho*) right

opcional *adj* optional

ópera *f* opera; **teatro de la ~** opera house

operación *f* operation; (*negocio*) transaction

operador(a) *m(f)* **1.** CINE projectionist; **~ (de cámara)** cameraman **2.** INFOR, TEL operator

operar I. *vi* to operate; COM to do business **II.** *vt* to operate on **III.** *vr:* **~se** to have an operation

opereta *f* operetta

opinar I. *vi, vt* to think; **~ bien/mal de algo/alguien** to have a good/ bad opinion of sth/sb; **¿tú qué opinas de** [*o* **sobre**] **esto?** what do you think about this?; **¿qué opinas del nuevo jefe?** what's your opinion of the new boss? **II.** *vi* to give an opinion; **¿puedo ~?** can I say what I think?

opinión *f* opinion; **tener buena/ mala ~ de algo/alguien** to have a good/bad opinion of sth/sb

opio *m* opium

oponente *mf* opponent

oponer *irr como* **poner I.** *vt* **1.** (*enfrentar*) to oppose; (*confrontar*) to confront **2.** (*objetar*) to object; **~ reparos** to raise objections; **~ resistencia** to offer resistance **II.** *vr:* **~se 1.** (*rechazar*) to object; **~se a algo** to oppose sth **2.** (*enfrentarse*) to oppose each other **3.** (*obstaculizar*) to hinder

oporto *m* port (wine)

oportunidad *f* (*posibilidad*) chance; (*ocasión*) opportunity; **(no) tener ~ de...** (not) to have the opportunity of ...

oportunismo *m* opportunism

oportunista *mf* opportunist

oportuno, -a *adj* **1.** (*adecuado, apropiado*) appropriate; **en el momento ~** at the right moment **2.** (*propicio*) opportune

oposición *f* **1.** *t.* POL opposition; **presentar ~** to oppose **2.** *(pl)* UNIV (competetive) examination (*for a public-sector job*); **por ~** by examination; **presentarse a unas oposiciones** to sit an examination

opositar *vi* **~ a algo** to sit an examination for sth

opositor(a) *m(f)* candidate (*in exam-*

ination for a public-sector job)
opresión *f* oppression
opresivo, -a *adj* oppressive
opresor(a) **I.** *adj* oppressive **II.** *m(f)* oppressor
oprimir *vt* **1.** (*presionar*) to press; (*comprimir*) to compress **2.** (*reprimir*) to oppress
oprobio *m* disgrace
optar *vi* **1.** (*escoger*) ~ **por algo/alguien** to opt for sth/sb **2.** (*aspirar*) to aspire
optativo, -a *adj* optional; (*asignatura*) optional subject
óptica *f* **1.** FÍS optics *pl* **2.** (*establecimiento*) optician's
óptico, -a **I.** *adj* **1.** ANAT optic **2.** FÍS optical **II.** *m, f* optician
optimismo *m* optimism
optimista **I.** *adj* optimistic **II.** *mf* optimist
óptimo, -a **I.** *superl de* **bueno** **II.** *adj* (very) best; (*excelente*) excellent
opuesto, -a **I.** *pp de* **oponer** **II.** *adj* opposite; (*diverso*) different; (*enfrentado*) opposing; **al lado** ~ on the other side
opulencia *f* opulence
opulento, -a *adj* opulent
oración *f* **1.** REL prayer **2.** (*frase*) sentence; LING clause
oráculo *m* oracle
orador(a) *m(f)* orator
oral *adj* oral; **por vía** ~ orally
órale *interj Méx* (*animar*) come on; (*oiga*) hey; (*acuerdo*) OK, right
orangután *m* orang-utan
orar *vi elev* to pray
oratoria *f* oratory
órbita *f* **1.** ASTR, FÍS orbit **2.** ANAT eye socket
orden¹ <órdenes> *m* order; ~ **constitucional** constitution; **del** ~ **de** in the order of; **en** [*o* **por**] **su** (**debido**) ~ in the right order; **por** ~ **de antigüedad** in order of seniority
orden² <órdenes> *f* order; ~ **de arresto** arrest warrant; **estar a las órdenes de alguien** to be at sb's command; **estar a la** ~ **del día** *fig* to be the order of the day; **hasta nueva** ~ until further notice; **por** ~ by

order; **por** ~ **de** to the order of; **¡a la** ~! yes, sir!
ordenado, -a *adj* **1.** *estar* (*en orden*) tidy, neat **2.** *ser* (*persona*) organized
ordenador *m* computer; ~ **portátil** laptop (computer)
ordenamiento *m* legislation; ~ **constitucional** constitution
ordenanza¹ *f* **1.** (*medida*) order **2.** *pl* ADMIN, MIL regulations *pl*
ordenanza² *m* MIL orderly; (*botones*) office assistant
ordenar *vt* **1.** (*arreglar*) to organize; (*habitación, armario*) to tidy; (*colocar*) to arrange; (*clasificar*) to order **2.** (*mandar*) to order
ordeñar *vt* to milk
ordinario, -a *adj* **1.** (*habitual*) usual; **de** ~ usually **2.** (*grosero*) rude **3.** *t.* JUR (*regular*) ordinary
orégano *m* oregano
oreja *f* **1.** ANAT ear; **calentar las ~s a alguien** to box sb's ears; *fig* to give sb a dressing-down; **ver las ~s al lobo** to have a close shave **2.** (*lateral*) flap; **sillón de ~s** wing chair
orensano, -a *adj* of/from Orense
orfanato *m* orphanage
orfanatorio *m Méx* orphanage
orfandad *f* orphanhood
orfebrería *f* gold and silver work
orgánico, -a *adj* organic; **Ley Orgánica del Estado** basic law
organigrama *m* organization chart; ~ (**del programa**) INFOR flowchart
organillo *m* barrel organ
organismo *m* **1.** ANAT, BIO organism **2.** (*institución*) body
organista *mf* organist
organización *f* organization
organizar <z→c> **I.** *vt* to organize **II.** *vr:* ~**se** **1.** (*asociarse, ordenarse*) to organize oneself **2.** (*surgir*) to break out; **¡menuda se organizó!** all hell broke loose!
órgano *m* organ
orgasmo *m* orgasm
orgía *f* orgy
orgullo *m* pride; ~ **por** [*o* **de**] **algo** pride in sth
orgulloso, -a *adj* proud
orientación *f* **1.** (*situación*) situ-

ation; (*posición*) position; (*dirección*) direction **2.**(*ajuste*) adjustment **3.**(*asesoramiento*) advice; ~ **profesional** career guidance **4.**(*tendencia*) tendency

oriental I. *adj* **1.**(*del Este*) eastern; **Alemania Oriental** East Germany **2.**(*del Extremo Oriente*) oriental II. *mf* Oriental

orientar I. *vt* **1.**(*dirigir*) to direct; **orientado a la práctica** with a practical focus **2.**(*ajustar*) to adjust **3.**(*asesorar*) to advise II. *vr:* ~**se** **1.**(*dirigirse*) to orientate oneself; *fig* to find one's bearings **2.**(*tender*) to tend

oriente *m* east; **el Oriente Próximo, el Cercano Oriente** the Near East; **el Extremo** [*o* **Lejano**] **Oriente** the Far East

origen *m* origin; **dar** ~ **a algo, ser** ~ **de algo** to give rise to sth

original *adj, m* original

originalidad *f* originality

originar I. *vt* **1.**(*causar*) to cause **2.**(*provocar*) to provoke II. *vr:* ~**se** **1.**(*tener el origen*) to originate **2.**(*surgir*) to arise

originario, -a *adj* **1.**(*oriundo*) native; **es** ~ **de Chile** he comes from Chile **2.**(*original*) original

orilla *f* **1.**(*borde*) edge **2.**(*ribera*) bank; **a ~s del Ebro** on the banks of the Ebro

orín *m* **1.**(*óxido*) rust; **cubierto de** ~ rusty **2.** *(pl)* (*orina*) urine

orina *f* <orines> urine

orinal *m* chamber pot; (*de niño*) potty

orinar I. *vi, vt* to urinate; **ir a** ~ to go to the lavatory II. *vr:* ~**se** to wet oneself; ~**se en la cama** to wet the bed

oriundo, -a *adj* ~ **de** native to; **es** ~ **de Méjico** he comes from Mexico

ornar *vt* to adorn

oro *m* gold; **color** ~ golden; ~ **de ley** fine gold; **bañado en** ~ gold-plated; **de** ~ *fig* golden; **tener un corazón de** ~ to have a heart of gold; **prometer a alguien el** ~ **y el moro** to promise sb the earth; **no es** ~ **todo lo que reluce** *prov* all that

glitters is not gold *prov*

oropel *m* tinsel

orquesta *f* orchestra

orquestar *vt* to orchestrate

orquídea *f* orchid

ortiga *f* nettle

ortodoncia *f* orthodontics *pl*

ortodoxo, -a *adj* orthodox

ortografía *f* spelling; **falta de** ~ spelling mistake

ortopedia *f* orthopaedics *Brit,* orthopedics *Am*

ortopédico, -a *adj* orthopaedic *Brit,* orthopedic *Am*

oruga *f* caterpillar

orzuelo *m* stye

os I. *pron pers* (*objeto directo e indirecto*) you II. *pron refl* yourselves; **¿~ marcháis?** are you leaving?

osa *f* **1.** ZOOL she-bear **2.** ASTR **la Osa Mayor/Menor** the Great/Little Bear

osadía *f* daring; (*desfachatez*) boldness

osar *vi* to dare

oscense *adj* of/from Huesca

oscilación *f* **1.**(*vaivén*) oscillation **2.**(*variación*) fluctuation

oscilar *vi* **1.**(*en vaivén*) to oscillate; (*péndulo*) to swing **2.**(*variar*) to fluctuate

oscurecer *irr como crecer* I. *vimpers* to get dark II. *vt, vr:* ~**se** to darken

oscuridad *f* darkness; *fig* obscurity; **en la** ~ in the dark; *fig* in obscurity

oscuro, -a *adj* dark; *fig* obscure; **a oscuras** in the dark

óseo, -a *adj* bony

oso *m* bear; ~ **blanco** polar bear; ~ **de peluche** teddy bear

ostensible *adj* obvious; **hacer** ~ to make evident

ostentación *f* display; (*jactancia*) ostentation; **hacer** ~ **de algo** to show sth; (*jactarse*) to flaunt sth

ostentar *vt* **1.**(*mostrar*) to show; (*jactarse*) to flaunt **2.**(*poseer*) to have; (*puesto, poder*) to hold

ostentoso, -a *adj* **1.**(*jactancioso*) ostentatious **2.**(*llamativo*) showy

ostra *f* oyster; **aburrirse como una** ~ *inf* to be bored to death; **¡~s!** *inf*

O_o

Jesus!

OTAN *f abr de* **Organización del Tratado del Atlántico Norte** NATO

otear *vt* (*escudriñar*) to scan; (*observar*) to watch

otitis *f sin pl* inflammation of the ear

otoñal *adj* autumnal

otoño *m* autumn, fall *Am*

otorgamiento *m* **1.** (*conferir*) conferring **2.** (*concesión*) concession **3.** (*de un documento*) drawing up

otorgar <g→gu> *vt* **1.** (*conferir*) to confer **2.** (*conceder*) to concede; (*ayudas*) to offer **3.** (*expedir*) to issue; ~ **licencia** to grant a license

otorrinolaringólogo, -a *m, f* ear, nose and throat specialist

otro, -a I. *adj* another, other; **al ~ día** the next day; **el ~ día** the other day; **en otra ocasión** another time; **la otra semana** the other week; **en ~ sitio** in another place, somewhere else; **otra cosa** another thing; **~ tanto** as much again; **otra vez** again; **¡otra vez será!** maybe another time!; **es ~ Mozart** he is another Mozart; **eso ya es otra cosa** that is much better; **¡hasta otra (vez)!** until the next time! II. *pron indef* **1.** (*distinto: cosa*) another (one); (*persona*) someone else; **~s** others; **el ~/la otra/lo ~** the other (one); **ninguna otra persona** nobody else; **de un sitio a ~** from one place to another; **no ~ que...** none other than ...; **ésa es otra** (*cosa distinta*) that is different; *irón* (*aún peor*) that is even worse **2.** (*uno más*) another; **otras tres personas** three more people; **¡otra, otra!** more!

> ⚠ **otro** is used with the definite article or without an article, never with the indefinite article: "¿Me trae otro café con leche, por favor?; El otro día conocí a tu madre."

ovación *f* ovation

oval *adj*, **ovalado, -a** *adj* oval

óvalo *m* oval

ovario *m* ovary

oveja *f* sheep

overol *m AmL* overall

ovetense *adj* of/from Oviedo

ovillo *m* ball; *fig* tangle; **hacerse un ~** (*enredarse*) to get tangled up; (*encogerse*) to curl up into a ball; (*al hablar*) to get all tangled up

ovni *m* UFO

ovulación *f* ovulation

óvulo *m* ovule

oxidación *f* rusting

oxidar *vt, vr:* ~**se** to rust; **hierro oxidado** rusty iron

óxido *m* rust

oxigenar *adj* **1.** (*cabello*) to bleach; (**rubio**) **oxigenado** platinum blond(e) **2.** QUÍM **agua oxigenada** (hydrogen) peroxide

oxígeno *m* oxygen

oyente *mf* listener; (**libre**) ~ UNIV unmatriculated student

P p

P, p *f* P, p; ~ **de París** P for Peter

pabellón *m* **1.** (*tienda*) bell tent **2.** (*bandera*) flag **3.** ARQUIT pavillion

pabilo *m* wick

pacer *irr como crecer* *vi, vt* to graze

paciencia *f* patience

paciente *adj, mf* patient

pacificación *f* pacification

pacificar <c→qu> *vt* to pacify

pacífico, -a *adj* peaceful

Pacífico *m* Pacific (Ocean)

pacifismo *m* pacifism

pacifista *adj, mf* pacifist

pacotilla *f* **de ~** (*mercancía*) shoddy; (*restaurante*) second-rate

pactar I. *vi* to come to an agreement II. *vt* to agree on

pacto *m* agreement

padecer *irr como crecer* I. *vi* to suffer II. *vt* **1.** (*sufrir*) ~ **algo** to suffer from

sth **2.** (*soportar*) to endure
padecimiento *m* **1.** (*sufrimiento*) suffering **2.** (*enfermedad*) ailment
padrastro *m* stepfather
padre *m* father; **mis ~s** my parents; **¡tu ~!** *inf* up yours!
padrino *m* (*de bautizo*) godfather; (*de boda*) best man
padrón *m* (census) register
paella *f* paella

> **?** **Paella** is a Spanish rice dish containing various types of meat and fish, **marisco** (seafood) and **azafrán** (saffron), which gives the rice its characteristic dark-yellow colour. Originally from **Valencia**, Paella is known today throughout the world.

paga *f* **1.** (*sueldo*) pay **2.** (*acto*) payment
pagadero, -a *adj* payable
pagano, -a *adj, m, f* pagan
pagar <g→gu> *vt* to pay; (*deuda*) to repay, to pay off; **~ un anticipo** to make an advance payment; **una cuenta sin ~** an unpaid bill; **¡me las ~ás!** you'll pay for this!
pagaré *m* IOU
página *f* page; **~s amarillas** yellow pages; **~s blancas** telephone directory
pago *m* **1.** (*reintegro*) payment; (*salario*) pay; **~ adicional** supplement; **~ anticipado** advance payment; **~ contra entrega** payment on delivery, C.O.D. *Am;* **~ extraordinario** one-off payment, bonus; **~ inicial** down payment **2.** (*recompensa*) reward
país *m* country; **~ comunitario** member state (of the EU)
paisaje *m* landscape
paisano, -a *m, f* **1.** (*no militar*) civilian; **ir de ~** to be in plain clothes **2.** (*compatriota*) compatriot
Países Bajos *mpl* Netherlands
paja *f* straw; **hacerse una ~** *vulg* to wank *Brit,* to jerk off *Am*

pajar *m* hayloft; **buscar una aguja en un ~** *fig* to search for a needle in a haystack
pajarita *f* bow tie
pájaro *m* bird; **~ carpintero** woodpecker; **tener la cabeza llena de ~s** to be scatterbrained; **más vale ~ en mano que ciento volando** *prov* a bird in the hand is worth two in the bush
pajita *f* (drinking) straw
Pakistán *m* Pakistan
pakistaní *adj, mf* Pakistani
pala *f* **1.** (*para cavar*) spade; (*cuadrada*) shovel **2.** (*del timón*) rudder **3.** (*raqueta*) racket; (*bate*) bat
palabra *f* word; **~ clave** keyword; **de ~** (*oral*) by word of mouth; (*que cumple sus promesas*) honourable *Brit,* honorable *Am;* **juego de ~s** pun, play on words; **libertad de ~** freedom of speech; **de pocas ~s** quiet; **coger a alguien la ~** to take sb at his word; **dejar a alguien con la ~ en la boca** to interrupt sb; **dirigir la ~ a alguien** to speak to sb; **poner dos ~s a alguien** to write sb a short note; **quitar a alguien la ~ de la boca** to take the words right out of sb's mouth
palabrota *f* swearword
palacio *m* palace; **Palacio de Justicia** law courts; **~ municipal** town hall
paladar *m* palate
paladear *vt* **1.** (*degustar*) to taste **2.** (*saborear*) to savour *Brit,* to savor *Am*
palanca *f* **1.** (*pértiga*) lever; **~ de cambio** gear lever *Brit,* gearshift *Am;* **~ de mando** AERO, INFOR joystick **2.** (*influencia*) influence
palangana *f* washbasin
palco *m* box
Palestina *m* Palestine
palestino, -a *adj, m, f* Palestinian
paleta *f* **1.** (*del albañil*) trowel **2.** (*del pintor*) palette
paleto, -a **I.** *adj* uncouth **II.** *m, f* yokel, hick *Am*
paliar <*I. pres:* palío, palio> *vt* **1.** (*delito*) to mitigate **2.** (*enferme-*

P
p

dad) to alleviate

paliativo *m* palliative

palidecer *irr como crecer vi* to turn pale

palidez *f* paleness

pálido, -a *adj* pale

palillo *m* (small) stick; (*para los dientes*) toothpick

palio *m* canopy

paliza *f* **1.** (*zurra*) beating; **dar una buena ~ a alguien** (*pegar*) to beat sb up; (*derrotar*) to thrash sb; **¡no me des la ~!** *fig* give me a break! **2.** *inf* (*esfuerzo*) slog; **¡qué ~ me he pegado subiendo la montaña!** climbing that mountain has exhausted me!

palma *f* **1.** (*palmera*) palm (tree); (*hoja*) palm leaf **2.** (*triunfo*) **llevarse la ~** to be the best **3.** ANAT palm; **conozco el barrio como la ~ de mi mano** *inf* I know the area like the back of my hand **4.** *pl* (*ruido*) clapping; (*aplauso*) applause; **tocar las ~s** to clap

palmada *f* **1.** (*golpe*) pat **2.** *pl* (*ruido*) clapping; **dar ~s** to clap

palmar *vi inf* **~la** to kick the bucket

palmear *vi* to clap

palmense *adj* of/from Las Palmas

palmera *f* palm (tree)

palmero, -a *adj* of/from the island of Palma

palmo *m* (hand)span

palmotear *vi* to clap

palmoteo *m* clapping

palo *m* **1.** (*bastón*) stick; (*vara*) pole; (*garrote*) club; (*estaca*) post; **de tal ~, tal astilla** *prov* like father, like son **2.** NÁUT mast **3.** (*madera*) wood **4.** (*paliza*) **echar a alguien a ~s** to throw sb out

paloma *f* pigeon; (*blanca, símbolo*) dove

palomilla *f* **1.** ZOOL moth **2.** (*tornillo*) wing nut

palomitas *fpl* popcorn

palpar *vt* to touch

palpitación *f* beating

palpitante *adj* throbbing

palpitar *vi* to throb

palta *f AmS* avocado (pear)

palúdico, -a *adj* **fiebre palúdica** malaria

paludismo *m* malaria

pamela *f* (road-brimmed ladies') hat

pampa *f* pampas + *sing/pl vb*

> **?** The **pampa** is a flat, treeless, grassy steppe in Argentina. It is a very fertile agricultural area, because the moist soil, which consists mainly of fine sand, clay and earth, is ideally suited to the cultivation of cereals.

pamplonés, -esa *adj* of/from Pamplona

pamplonica *adj, mf inf v.* **pamplonés**

pan *m* bread; **~ con mantequilla** bread and butter; **~ de molde** sliced bread; **~ rallado** breadcrumbs *pl*; (*llamar*) **al ~, ~ y al vino, vino** *inf* to call a spade a spade; **ser un pedazo de ~, ser más bueno que el ~** to be very good-natured

pana *f* corduroy

panadería *f* bakery

panadero, -a *m, f* baker

Panamá *m* Panama

> **?** **Panamá** is divided in two by the Panama Canal and links Central America to North America. The capital, which is also called **Panamá**, is the largest city in the country. Spanish is the official language of the country, although English is widely used. The monetary unit of Panama is the **balboa**.

panameño, -a *adj, m, f* Panamanian

pancarta *f* placard

páncreas *m inv* pancreas

panda¹ *m* ZOOL panda

panda² *f v.* **pandilla**

pandereta *f* tambourine

pandilla *f* group; **~ de ladrones**

gang of thieves
panecillo *m* roll
panel *m* panel
panera *f* bread bin, breadbox *Am*
panfleto *m* pamphlet
pánico *m* panic; **entrar en** ~ to panic; **tener** ~ **a algo** to be terrified of sth
panocha *f* corn cob, corn *Am*
panorama *m* panorama; *fig* outlook
pantalla *f* screen; (*de la lámpara*) shade
pantalón *m* (pair of) trousers *pl,* pants *pl;* ~ **tejano** [*o* **vaquero**] jeans *pl*
pantano *m* **1.** (*ciénaga*) marsh; (*laguna*) swamp **2.** (*embalse*) reservoir
pantera *f* panther
pantis *mpl inf* tights *pl Brit,* pantyhose
pantomima *f* pantomime
pantorrilla *f* calf
pantufla *f* slipper
panza *f* belly
panzudo, -a *adj* potbellied
pañal *m* nappy *Brit,* diaper *Am*
pañería *f* **1.** (*comercio*) drapery *Brit,* dry goods *pl Am* **2.** (*tienda*) draper's (shop) *Brit,* dry goods store *Am*
paño *m* cloth; ~ **de cocina** (*para fregar*) dishcloth; (*para secar*) tea towel *Brit,* dish towel *Am*
pañuelo *m* **1.** (*moquero*) handkerchief; **el mundo es un** ~ it's a small world **2.** (*pañoleta*) fichu; (*de cabeza*) scarf
papa[1] *m* pope
papa[2] *f reg, AmL* potato; **no entender ni** ~ not to understand a thing
papá *m inf* dad; **Papá Noel** Father Christmas; **los** ~**s** mum and dad
papada *f* (*persona*) double chin, jowl; (*animal*) dewlap
papagayo *m* parrot; **hablar como un** ~ to be a real chatterbox
papalote *m Ant, Méx* paper kite
papanatas *m inv, inf* halfwit
paparrucha *f inf,* **paparruchada** *f inf* piece of nonsense
papaya *f* pawpaw, papaya
papel *m* **1.** (*para escribir, material*) paper; (*hoja*) piece of paper; (*escritura*) piece of writing; ~ **de aluminio** aluminium foil; ~ **de envolver** wrapping paper; ~ **de estraza** brown paper; ~ **de fumar** cigarette paper; ~ **higiénico** toilet paper; ~ **de lija** sandpaper; ~ **moneda** banknotes *pl;* ~ **pintado** wallpaper; ~ **de regalo** giftwrap **2.** (*rol*) role; ~ **protagonista/secundario** leading/supporting role; **hacer buen/mal** ~ to make a good/bad impression; **hacer su** ~ to play one's part **3.** *pl* (*documentos*) documentation; (*de identidad*) identity papers *pl*
papeleo *m* paperwork
papelera *f* wastepaper basket; (*en la calle*) litter bin
papelería *f* stationer's
papeleta *f* slip of paper; (*en el examen*) result slip; **menuda** ~ **le ha tocado** *inf* that's a nasty problem he's got
paperas *fpl* mumps *pl*
papilla *f* baby food
paquete *m* packet; ~ (**postal**) parcel
paquistaní *adj, mf* Pakistani
par I. *adj* **1.** (*número*) even **2.** (*igual*) equal; **a la** ~ at the same time; **de** ~ **en** ~ wide open; **sin** ~ without equal; **abrir una ventana de** ~ **en** ~ to open a window wide; **esta película entretiene a la** ~ **que instruye** this film is both entertaining and educational II. *m* **1.** (*dos cosas*) pair; **un** ~ **de zapatos** a pair of shoes **2.** (*algunos*) **un** ~ **de minutos** a couple of minutes
para I. *prep* **1.** (*destino*) for; **un regalo** ~ **el niño** a present for the child; **asilo** ~ **ancianos** old people's home **2.** (*finalidad*) for; **gafas** ~ **bucear** diving goggles; **servir** ~ **algo** to be useful for sth; *¿*~ **qué es esto?** what is this for? **3.** (*dirección*) to; **voy** ~ **Madrid** I'm going to Madrid; **mira** ~ **acá** look over here **4.** (*duración*) for; ~ **siempre** forever; **con esto tenemos** ~ **rato** with this we've got enough for quite a while; **vendrá** ~ **Navidad/finales de marzo** he/she will come for Christ-

P
p

mas/towards the end of March; **estará listo ~ el viernes** it will be ready for Friday; **diez minutos ~ las once** *AmL* ten to eleven **5.**(*contra-posición*) for; **es muy activo ~ la edad que tiene** he is very active for his age **6.**(*trato*) ~ (**con**) with; **es muy amable ~ con nosotros** he/she is very kind to us **7.**(+ *estar*) **estar ~...** (*a punto de*) to be about to ...; **no estoy ~ bromas** I'm in no mood for jokes; **está ~ llover** it's about to rain; **está ~ llegar** he/she is about to arrive **8.**(*a juicio de*) ~ **mí, esto no es lo mismo** in my opinion, this is not the same; **~ mí que va a llover** I think it's going to rain **II.** *conj* **1.** + *inf* to; **he venido ~ darte las gracias** I've come to thank you **2.** + *subj* so; **te mando al colegio ~ que aprendas algo** I send you to school so that you learn sth

> [!] **para** expresses aim or purpose: "El regalo es para mi madre; Estudio español para ir a Ecuador." In contrast **por** expresses cause: "Lo ha hecho por sus hijos."

parabién *m* congratulations *pl;* **dar el ~ a alguien** to congratulate sb
parábola *f* **1.**(*alegoría*) parable **2.** MAT curve, parabola
parabólica *f* satellite dish
parabrisas *m inv* windscreen *Brit,* windshield *Am*
paracaídas *m inv* parachute
paracaidista *mf* DEP parachutist; MIL paratrooper
parachoques *m inv* bumper; ~ **trasero** rear bumper
parada *f* **1.**(*lugar*) stop; ~ **de taxis** taxi rank **2.**(*acción*) stopping; ~ **de una fábrica** factory stoppage; **hacer una ~** to stop
paradero *m* (*de alguien*) whereabouts + *sing/pl vb;* (*de algo*) destination; **está en ~ desconocido** his whereabouts are unknown; **no logramos descubrir el ~ del paquete** we didn't manage to find out

where the packet ended up
parado, -a *adj* **1.**(*que no se mueve*) stationary; **estar ~** to be motionless; (*fábrica*) to be at a standstill; **quedarse ~** to remain motionless; *fig* to be surprised; **me has dejado ~** you have really surprised me **2.**(*sin empleo*) unemployed **3.**(*tímido*) shy **4.**(*resultado*) **salir bien/mal ~ de algo** to come out of sth well/badly
paradoja *f* paradox; **esto es una ~** this is absurd
parador *m* (state-run) luxury hotel
paráfrasis *f inv* paraphrase
paraguas *m inv* umbrella
Paraguay *m* Paraguay

> [?] **Paraguay** lies in South America and borders Bolivia, Brazil and Argentina. It is a landlocked country. The capital of Paraguay is **Asunción**. The official languages of the country are Spanish and **guaraní**. The monetary unit of the country is also called the **guaraní**.

paraguayo, -a *adj, m, f* Paraguayan
paraíso *m* paradise
paraje *m* (*lugar*) place; (*punto*) spot
paralelo *m* parallel
paralelo, -a *adj* parallel
parálisis *f inv* paralysis; **sufre ~ de las piernas** his/her legs are paralysed
paralítico, -a I. *adj* (*persona*) paralysed *Brit,* paralyzed *Am* **II.** *m, f* paralytic
paralizar <z→c> *vt* to paralyse *Brit,* to paralyze *Am;* **el miedo la paralizó** she was paralysed by fear
paramilitar *adj* paramilitary
páramo *m* (*terreno infértil*) wasteland; (*altiplano*) barren plateau
parangón *m* **sin ~** incomparable
paranoia *f* paranoia
paranoico, -a *adj* paranoid
paranormal, -a *adj* paranormal
parapléjico, -a *adj, m, f* paraplegic
parar I. *vi* **1.**(*detenerse, cesar*) to stop; **la máquina funciona sin ~**

the machine works non-stop; **mis hijos no me dejan** ~ my kids never give me a break; **mis remordimientos de conciencia no me dejan** ~ my guilty conscience doesn't give me any peace; **no para (de trabajar)** he/she never stops (working) **2.** (*acabar*) **si sigues así irás a** ~ **a la cárcel** if you carry on like this you'll end up in jail; **la maleta fue a** ~ **a Bilbao** the suitcase ended up in Bilbao; **por fin, el paquete fue a** ~ **a tus manos** the packet finally reached you; **¿en qué irá a** ~ **esto?** where will it all end?; **siempre venimos a** ~ **al mismo tema** we always end up talking about the same thing **3.** (*alojarse*) to stay; (*vivir*) to live; **no para en casa** he/she is never at home **II.** *vt* (*detener*) to stop; (*golpe*) to block; (*gol*) to save; (*motor*) to turn off **III.** *vr:* ~**se** to stop

pararrayos *m inv* lightning conductor

parásito, -a I. *adj* parasitic **II.** *m, f* parasite

parcela *f* plot

parche *m* patch

parchís *m* ludo *Brit,* parcheesi *Am*

parcial *adj* **1.** (*incompleto*) partial **2.** (*arbitrario*) biased

parcialidad *f* bias, favoritism

parco, -a *adj* (*moderado*) moderate; (*escaso*) meagre *Brit,* meager *Am;* ~ **en palabras** of few words

pardillo *m* linnet

pardillo, -a I. *adj inf* uncouth **II.** *m, f* yokel

pardo, -a *adj* **1.** (*color*) greyish-brown; **oso** ~ brown bear; **de ojos** ~**s** brown-eyed **2.** (*oscuro*) dark

parear *vt* (*formar parejas*) to pair; (*ropa*) to match up

parecer I. *irr como crecer vi* to seem; (*aparentar*) to appear; **a lo que parece** [*o al* ~] apparently; **tu idea me parece bien** I think your idea is a good one; **parece mentira que** +*subj* it seems incredible that; **me parece que no tienes ganas** I don't think you want to; **parece que**

va a llover it looks like rain; **¿qué te parece (el piso)?** what do you think (of the flat)?; **si te parece bien, ...** if you agree, ...; **me ha parecido oír un grito** I thought I heard a scream; **parecen hermanos** they look like brothers **II.** *irr como crecer vr:* ~**se** to look alike; ~**se a alguien** to look like sb; **¡esto se te parece!** this looks like you! **III.** *m* opinion; **a mi** ~ in my opinion

parecido *m* similarity, likeness; **tienes un gran** ~ **con tu hermana** you and your sister look very alike

parecido, -a *adj* **1.** (*semejante*) similar **2.** (*de aspecto*) **ser bien/mal** ~ to be good/bad-looking

pared *f* wall; **subirse por las** ~**es** *fig* to go up the wall

pareja *f* **1.** (*par*) pair; (*amantes*) couple; **¿dónde está la** ~ **de este guante?** where is the other glove? **2.** (*compañero*) partner

parejo, -a *adj* (*igual*) equal; (*semejante*) similar

parentela *f* relations *pl*

parentesco *m* relationship, kinship

paréntesis *m inv* bracket; **entre** ~ in brackets; *fig* by the way

paridad *f* parity; ~ (**de cambio**) exchange parity

pariente, -a *m, f* relative

parir *vi, vt* to give birth (to)

París *m* Paris

parisiense *adj, mf* Parisian

paritario, -a *adj* equal; **comité** ~ joint committee

parking *m* <parkings> car park, parking lot *Am*

parlamentar *vi* to negotiate

parlamentario, -a I. *adj* parliamentary **II.** *m, f* member of parliament

parlamento *m* parliament

parlanchín, -ina I. *adj inf* talkative **II.** *m, f inf* chatterbox; (*indiscreta*) gossip

parlar *vi,* **parlotear** *vi* to chatter

paro *m* **1.** (*huelga*) ~ (**laboral**) strike **2.** (*desempleo*) ~ (**forzoso**) unemployment; **cobrar el** ~ to be on the dole; **estar en** ~ to be unemployed

parodia *f* parody

parodiar *vt* to parody

parpadear *vi* **1.**(*ojos*) to blink **2.**(*luz*) to flicker

párpado *m* eyelid

parque *m* **1.**(*jardín*) park; ~ **de a-tracciones** funfair *Brit*, amusement park *Am*; ~ **zoológico** zoo **2.**(*depósito*) depot; ~ **de bomberos** fire station **3.**(*para niños*) playpen

parqué *m*, **parquet** *m* parquet

parquímetro *m* parking meter

parra *f* (grape)vine; **subirse a la** ~ (*enfadarse*) to hit the roof; (*darse importancia*) to get above oneself

párrafo *m* paragraph

parranda *f* spree; **ir de** ~ to go out on the town

parrilla *f* **1.**(*para la brasa*) grill; (*de un horno*) oven rack **2.***AmL* AUTO roof-rack

parrillada *f* grill; ~ **de carne** mixed grill; ~ **de pescado** grilled fish

párroco *m* parish priest

parroquia *f* parish

parroquiano, -a *m, f* parishioner

parte¹ *f* **1.**(*porción, elemento*) part; **una cuarta** ~ a quarter; **en** ~ in part; **en gran** ~ largely; **tomar** ~ **en algo** to be involved in sth **2.**(*repartición*) share; ~ **hereditaria** share of the inheritance; **tener** ~ **en algo** to have a share in sth; **llevarse la peor/mejor** ~ to come off (the) worst/best **3.**(*lugar*) part; **en cualquier** ~ anywhere; **a/en ninguna** ~ nowhere; **en otra** ~ somewhere else; **por todas (las)** ~s everywhere; **no llevar a ninguna** ~ to lead nowhere; **¿a qué** ~ **vas?** where are you going? **4.***t.* JUR party; (*en una discusión*) participant **5.**(*lado*) side; ~ **de delante/de atrás** front/back; **por otra** ~ on the other hand; (*además*) what's more; **estar de** ~ **de alguien** to be on sb's side; **ponerse de** ~ **de alguien** to take sb's side; **dale recuerdos de mi** ~ give him/her my regards; **somos primos por** ~ **de mi padre/de mi madre** we are cousins on my father's/mother's side; **por mi** ~ **puedes hacer lo que quieras** as far as I'm concerned

you can do what you like **6.** *pl* (*genitales*) (private) parts *pl*

parte² *m* report; **dar** ~ **(de algo)** to report (sth)

partera *f* midwife *f*

partición *f* partition; MAT division

participación *f* **1.**(*intervención*) participation; ~ **en los beneficios** profit-sharing **2.**(*parte*) share

participante *mf* participant

participar I. *vi* **1.**(*tomar parte*) to participate; ~ **en un juego** to take part in a game **2.**(*tener parte*) to have a part; ~ **de/en algo** to share in sth **II.** *vt* to inform

partícipe *mf* participant; **hacer a alguien** ~ **de algo** (*compartir*) to share sth with sb; (*informar*) to inform sb of sth

particular¹ *adj* **1.**(*propio*) peculiar; (*especial*) special; (*individual*) individual; (*típico*) typical; (*personal*) personal; **en** ~ in particular **2.**(*raro*) peculiar **3.**(*privado*) private; **envíamelo a mi domicilio** ~ send it to my home address **4.**(*determinado*) particular

particular² *m* matter

particularizar <z→c> *vt* **1.**(*explicar*) to go into details about **2.**(*distinguir*) to distinguish

partida *f* **1.**(*salida*) departure **2.**(*envío*) consignment **3.** FIN item; ~ **doble** double entry **4.**(*certificado*) certificate **5.**(*juego*) game **6.**(*grupo*) party

partidario, -a I. *adj* **ser** ~ **de algo** to be in favour of sth **II.** *m, f* supporter

partido *m* **1.** POL party **2.** DEP (*juego*) match; ~ **amistoso** friendly **3.**(*determinación*) **tomar** ~ **a favor de alguien** to take sb's side **4.**(*provecho*) advantage; **de esto aún se puede sacar** ~ something can still be made of this; **no sacarás** ~ **de él** you'll get nothing out of him; **saqué** ~ **del asunto** I profited from the affair

partir I. *vt* (*dividir*) to divide; (*cortar*) to cut; (*romper*) to break; (*madera*) to chop; (*nuez*) to crack; ~ **la cabeza a alguien** to crack sb's head open **II.** *vi* to start; (*salir de viaje*) to leave; **a ~ de ahora** from now on; **a ~ de entonces** since then; **a ~ de mañana** from tomorrow; **a ~ de las seis** from six o'clock onwards; **partimos de Cádiz a las cinco** we left Cadiz at five o'clock **III.** *vr:* ~**se** to split; (*cristal*) to crack; ~**se** (**de risa**) *inf* to split one's sides laughing

partitura *f* MÚS score; (*hojas*) sheet music

parto *m* birth; **dolores de ~** labour pains; **estar de ~** to be in labour

pasa *f* raisin

pasable *adj* passable

pasada *f* **1.** (*paso*) **de ~** in passing **2.** (*mano*) **dar una ~ a algo** to give sth another going-over; (*con la plancha*) to give sth a quick iron **3.** *inf* (*comportamiento*) **¡vaya** (**mala**) **~!** what a thing to do!; **hacer una mala ~ a alguien** to play a dirty trick on sb **4.** *inf* (*exageración*) **¡es una ~!** it's way over the top!

pasadizo *m* corridor; (*entre dos calles*) alley

pasado *m* past; **son cosas del ~** it's all in the past

pasado, -a *adj* **1.** (*de atrás*) past; **el año ~** last year; **la conferencia del año ~** last year's conference; **~ mañana** the day after tomorrow; **~s dos meses** after two months; **~ de moda** unfashionable **2.** (*estropeado: alimentos*) bad; (*fruta*) overripe; (*leche*) off, sour; (*mantequilla*) rancid; (*flores*) wilted; **el yogur está ~ de fecha** the yogurt is past its sell-by date **3.** GASTR **un huevo ~ por agua** a soft-boiled egg; **estar (muy) ~** to be overcooked; **¿quieres el filete muy ~?** do you want the steak very well done?

pasador *m* **1.** (*para el cabello*) hairclip **2.** (*cerrojo*) bolt

pasaje *m* **1.** (*acción*) crossing **2.** (*derecho*) toll **3.** (*billete*) ticket; (*precio*) fare **4.** (*pasillo*) passage

pasajero, -a **I.** *adj* passing **II.** *m, f* passenger; **tren de ~s** passenger train

pasamano(s) *m(pl)* handrail

pasamontañas *m inv* balaclava, ski mask *Am*

pasaporte *m* passport

pasar **I.** *vi* **1.** (*en general*) to pass; **~ por un control** to pass a checkpoint; **~ corriendo** to run past; **dejar ~** to allow to go past; **~ desapercibido** to go unnoticed; **~ de largo** to go past; **no dejes ~ la oportunidad** don't miss the opportunity; **cuando pasen las vacaciones...** when the holidays are over ...; **han pasado dos semanas sin llover** we have had two weeks without rain; **lo pasado, pasado** what's done is done; **arreglándolo aún puede ~** if we fix it it should still be okay **2.** (*por un hueco*) to go through; **el sofá no pasa por la puerta** the sofa won't go through the door; **el Ebro pasa por Zaragoza** the Ebro flows through Zaragoza; **~ por una crisis** to go through a crisis **3.** (*trasladarse*) to move; **pasemos al comedor** let's go to the dining room **4.** (*acaecer*) to happen; **¿qué pasa?** what's up?; **¿qué te pasa?** what's wrong?; **pase lo que pase** whatever happens; **lo que pasa es que...** the thing is that ... **5.** (*poder existir*) to get by; **vamos pasando** we manage **6.** (*aparentar*) **~ por** to pass for; **hacerse ~ por médico** to pass oneself off as a doctor; **pasa por nuevo** it looks new; **podrías ~ por inglesa** you could be taken for an Englishwoman **7.** (*cambiar*) to go; **paso a explicar porqué** and now I will (go on to) explain why; **~ a mayores** to go from bad to worse **8.** *inf* (*no necesitar*) **yo paso de salir** I don't want to go out; **paso de esta película** I can't be bothered with this film; **pasa de todo** he/she couldn't care less about anything **II.** *vt* **1.** (*atravesar*) to cross; **~ el semáforo en rojo** to go through a red light **2.** (*por un hueco*) **~ algo por debajo de la puerta** to slide sth under the door; **~ la tarjeta por la ranura** to swipe the card through the slot **3.** (*trasladar*) to transfer; **~ a**

limpio to make a fair copy **4.**(*dar*) to pass; ~ **la pelota** to pass the ball **5.**(*una temporada*) to spend; **~lo en grande** to have a whale of a time; **~lo mal** to have a bad time; **¡que lo paséis bien!** enjoy yourselves! **6.**(*sufrir*) to experience; ~ **hambre** to go hungry; **has pasado mucho** you have been through a lot; **pasé un mal rato** I went through a difficult time **7.**(*transmitir*) to send; (*una película*) to show; ~ **un recado** to pass on a message; **me has pasado el resfriado** you've given me your cold; **le paso a la Sra. Ortega** I'll put you through to Señora Ortega **8.**(*sobrepasar*) to exceed; **he pasado los treinta** I am over thirty; **te paso en altura** I am taller than you **9.**(*hacer deslizar*) ~ **la aspiradora** to vacuum; ~ **la mano por la mesa** to run one's hand over the table **10.**(*colar*) to strain **11.**(*las hojas de un libro*) to turn **12.**(*géneros prohibidos*) to smuggle **III.** *vr:* **~se 1.**(*acabarse*) to pass; **~se de fecha** to miss a deadline; **~se de moda** to go out of fashion; **se me han pasado las ganas** I don't feel like it any more; **ya se le ~á el enfado** his anger will soon subside **2.**(*exagerar*) to go too far; **~se de listo** to be too clever by half; **~se de la raya** to go over the line; **te has pasado un poco con la sal** you've overdone the salt a bit **3.**(*por un sitio*) **~se la mano por el pelo** to run one's hand through one's hair; **pásate un momento por mi casa** drop round to my house; **me pasé un rato por casa de mi tía** I popped round to my aunt's house for a while; **se me pasó por la cabeza que...** it occurred to me that ...; **no se te pasará ni por la imaginación** you'll never be able to guess **4.**(*cambiar*) to go over; **se ha pasado de trabajadora a perezosa** she has gone from being hard-working to being lazy **5.**(*olvidarse*) **se me pasó tu cumpleaños** I forgot your birthday **6.**(*estropearse*) to spoil, to go off; (*fruta*) to overripen;

(*mantequilla*) to go rancid; (*flores*) to wilt; **se ha pasado el arroz** the rice is overcooked **7.**(*escaparse*) **se me pasó la oportunidad** I missed my chance; **se me pasó el turno** I missed my turn

pasarela *f* **1.**(*para desfiles*) catwalk **2.**(*de un barco*) gangway **3.**(*para peatones*) walkway

pasatiempo *m* **1.**(*diversión*) pastime; **los ~s del periódico** the games and puzzles section of the newspaper **2.**(*hobby*) hobby

Pascua *f* **1.**(*de resurrección*) Easter; **de Pascuas a Ramos** once in a blue moon **2.** *pl* (*navidad*) Christmas time; **felices ~s** Merry Christmas

pase *m* **1.** DEP pass **2.** CINE showing **3.**(*permiso*) pass; (*para entrar gratis*) free pass; FERRO rail pass

pasear I. *vt* to take for a walk; ~ **al perro** to walk the dog **II.** *vi, vr:* **~se** to go for a walk

paseo *m* **1.**(*acción*) walk; **dar un ~** to go for a walk; **mandar a alguien a ~** *inf* to tell sb to get lost; **¡vete a ~!** *inf* get lost **2.**(*lugar*) avenue; ~ **marítimo** promenade **3.**(*distancia*) short walk; **de aquí al colegio sólo hay un ~** it's only a short walk from here to the school

pasillo *m* passage; (*entre habitaciones, pisos*) corridor

pasión *f* passion; **sentir ~ por el fútbol** to be passionate about football

pasional *adj* passionate; **crimen ~** crime of passion

pasivo *m* **1.**(*deuda*) liabilities *pl* **2.** LING passive

pasivo, -a *adj* passive

pasmar I. *vt* to astonish; **me has dejado pasmado** you have left me completely stunned; **no te quedes pasmado** don't just stand there **II.** *vr:* **~se** to be astonished

pasmo *m* astonishment

pasmoso, -a *adj* amazing

paso *m* **1.**(*acción de pasar*) passing; **al ~** on the way; **de ~** (*indirectamente*) by the way; **ceder el ~** to make way; (*en el tráfico*) to give way, to yield *Am;* **estar de ~** to be passing through; **de ~ que vas al centro,...** on your way to the centre, ... **2.**(*movimiento, medida*) step; **~ a ~** step by step; **bailar a ~ de vals** to dance a waltz; **dar un ~ adelante/atrás** to take a step forwards/backwards; **dar un ~ en falso** to trip; *fig* to make a false move; **dar todos los ~s necesarios** to take all the necessary steps; **no dar ~** not to do anything; **marcar el ~** to mark the rhythm; **he dado un enorme ~ en mis investigaciones** I have made enormous progress in my research **3.**(*velocidad*) pace; **a ~s agigantados** with giant steps; *fig* by leaps and bounds; **a buen ~** quickly; **a ~ de tortuga** at snail's pace; **a este ~ no llegarás** at this speed you'll never get there; **a este ~ no conseguirás nada** *fig* at this rate you won't achieve anything **4.**(*sonido*) footstep **5.**(*pisada*) footprint; (*de un animal*) track; **seguir los ~s de alguien** to follow sb; *fig* to follow in sb's footsteps **6.**(*distancia*) **vive a dos ~s de mi casa** he lives very near to my house **7.**(*pasillo*) passage; (*en el mar*) strait; (*entre montañas*) pass; **abrirse ~** to open up a path for oneself; *fig* to make one's way; **esta puerta da ~ al jardín** this door leads to the garden; **¡prohibido el ~!** (*pasar*) no throughfare! *Am;* (*entrar*) no entry!; **con este dinero puedo salir del ~** with this money I can solve my problems; **sólo lo has dicho para salir del ~** you only did it to get out of a jam **8.**(*para atravesar algo*) crossing; **~ de cebra** zebra crossing; **~ a nivel** level crossing; **¡~!** make way! **9.**(*de un contador*) unit **10.**(*de un escrito*) passage

pasota *mf inf* drop-out; **es un ~ total** he/she doesn't give a damn about anything

pasta *f* **1.**(*masa*) paste; (*para un pastel*) pastry; **~ de dientes** toothpaste **2.**(*comida italiana*) pasta **3.** *pl* (*pastelería*) pastries *pl* **4.**(*encuadernación*) cover; **de ~ dura/blanda** hardback/softback **5.** *inf* (*dinero*)

dough

pastar *vt, vi* to graze

pastel *m* (*tarta*) cake; (*bollo*) pastry; (*de carne, pescado*) pie

pastelería *f* (*comercio*) pastry shop; (*arte*) pastrymaking

pasteurizar <z→c> *vt* to pasteurize

pastilla *f* **1.** MED tablet **2.**(*trozo*) **~ de chocolate** bar of chocolate; **~ de jabón** bar of soap; **ir a toda ~** *inf* to go at full pelt

pasto *m* **1.**(*pastizal*) pasture **2.**(*hierba*) grass; (*alimento*) feed; **~ seco** fodder; **ser ~ de las llamas** to go up in flames; **ser ~ de la murmuración** to be the subject of gossip

pastor *m* **1.** REL minister **2.** ZOOL **~ alemán** Alsatian *Brit,* German shepherd *Am*

pastor(a) *m(f)* shepherd

pata *f* **1.** *inf.* ANAT leg; (*de un perro, un gato*) paw; **a cuatro ~s** on all fours; **~s de gallo** (*del rostro*) crow's feet; **mala ~** *inf* bad luck; **estirar la ~** *inf* to kick the bucket; **meter la ~** *fig, inf* to put one's foot in it; **la habitación está ~s arriba** the room has been turned upside down **2.** ZOOL (female) duck

patada *f* **1.**(*contra algo*) kick; (*en el suelo*) stamp; **a ~s** *fig* by the bucketload; **dar una ~ contra la pared** to kick the wall; **dar ~s en el suelo** to stamp one's feet **2.** *fig, inf* **dar la ~ a alguien** to give sb the boot; **echar a alguien a ~s** to kick sb out; **romper una puerta a ~s** to kick a door down; **tratar a alguien a ~s** to treat sb like dirt; **me da cien ~s** he/she really gets on my nerves

Patagonia *f* Patagonia; **ir a la ~** to go to Patagonia

? **Patagonia** lies in the southernmost part of Chile and Argentina, to the south of the Pampa. Unlike the Pampa, this vast, scantily cultivated, barren steppe is unsuited to the growth of cereals and is used mainly for rearing sheep.

patalear *vi* to kick; (*en el suelo*) to stamp one's feet

patata *f* potato; **~s fritas** chips *pl Brit,* French fries *pl Am;* **una bolsa de ~s fritas** a bag of crisps *Brit,* a bag of potato chips *Am*

paté *m* pâté

patear I. *vt* 1. (*dar golpes*) to kick; **~ el estómago a alguien** to kick sb in the stomach 2. (*pisotear*) to trample II. *vi* to stamp

patentar *vt* to patent

patente I. *adj* (*visible*) clear; (*evidente*) patent II. *f* patent

patera *f* boat

paternal *adj* paternal

paterno, -a *adj* paternal; **casa paterna** parental home

patético, -a *adj* 1. (*conmovedor*) moving; (*tierno*) tender; (*manifestando dolor*) painful 2. *pey* (*exagerado*) pathetic

patilla *f* 1. (*gafas*) sidepiece 2. *pl* (*pelo*) sideburns *pl*

patín *m* 1. (*de hielo*) ice skate; (*de ruedas*) roller skate; (*de ruedas en línea*) roller blade 2. (*de pedales*) pedal boat

patinaje *m* skating; **~ artístico** figure skating

patinar *vi* 1. (*sobre patines*) to skate 2. (*un vehículo*) to skid

patio *m* courtyard

pato, -a *m, f* duck

patológico, -a *adj* pathological

patoso, -a *adj* clumsy

patraña *f* lie

patria *f* native land

patrimonio *m* 1. (*herencia*) inheritance 2. (*riqueza*) wealth

patriota *mf* patriot

patriótico, -a *adj* patriotic

patriotismo *m* patriotism

patrocinador(a) *m(f)* sponsor

patrocinar *vt* to sponsor

patrocinio *m* 1. (*protección*) patronage 2. DEP sponsorship

patrón *m* pattern

patrón, -ona *m, f* 1. (*jefe*) boss 2. (*de una casa*) landlord *m,* landlady *f* 3. REL patron saint

patronal *adj* ECON employers'; **cierre ~** lockout

patronato *m* foundation

patrulla *f* patrol; **estar de ~** to be on patrol

pausa *f* pause; **con ~** unhurriedly

pausado, -a *adj* deliberate

pauta *f* standard

pavimento *m* surface; (*en una casa*) floor

pavo, -a *m, f* 1. ZOOL turkey; **~ real** peacock 2. (*persona*) idiot; **estar en la edad del ~** *inf* to be at an awkward stage (*of one's adolescence*)

pavor *m* terror

payaso, -a *m, f* clown

paz *f* peace; **hacer las paces** to make up; **¡déjame en ~!** leave me alone!

P.D. *abr de* **posdata** P.S.

peaje *m* toll

peatón, -ona *m, f* pedestrian

peca *f* freckle

pecado *m* sin; **~ capital** deadly sin; **sería un ~ rechazarlos** it would be a crying shame to reject them

pecador(a) *m(f)* sinner

pecar <c→qu> *vi* to sin; **~ por exceso** to go too far; **éste no peca de hablador** he's not exactly talkative

pecera *f* fish tank; (*globo*) fishbowl

pecho *m* chest; (*mama*) breast; **dar el ~ al bebé** to breastfeed the baby; **tomarse algo muy a ~** to take sth to heart; **el bebé toma el ~** the baby breastfeeds

pechuga *f* breast; **~ de pollo** chicken breast

pecoso, -a *adj* freckly

peculiar *adj* 1. (*especial*) distinctive 2. (*raro*) peculiar

peculiaridad *f* 1. (*singularidad*) peculiarity 2. (*distintivo*) distinguishing feature

pedagogía *f sin pl* pedagogy

pedal *m* pedal

pedalear *vi* to pedal

pedante I. *adj* pedantic II. *mf* pedant

pedantería *f* pedantry

pedazo *m* piece; **caerse ~s** to fall apart; **estoy que me caigo a ~s** *inf* I'm absolutely exhausted; **hacerse ~s** to fall to pieces; **hacer ~s** to break; (*madera*) to smash up; (*pas-*

El cuerpo		The body	
1 espejo *m*	mirror	24 zapatilla *f*, pantufla *f*	slipper
2 frente *f*	forehead	25 lavabo *m*	washbasin, sink *Am*
3 ceja *f*	eyebrow	26 grifo *m*	tap *Brit*, faucet *Am*
4 ojo *m*	eye	27 manopla *f* (para baño)	flannel *Brit*, washcloth *Am*
5 nariz *f*	nose	28 cepillo *m* del pelo	hairbrush
6 mejilla *f*	cheek	29 cepillo *m* de dientes	toothbrush
7 oreja *f*	ear	30 pasta *f* dentífrica	toothpaste
8 boca *f*	mouth	[*o* de dientes],dentífrico *m*	
9 cabeza *f*	head	31 bastoncillos *mpl* de algodón	cotton buds, Q-tips® *Am*
10 codo *m*	elbow	32 máquina *f* de afeitar,	electric razor
11 brazo *m*	arm	afeitadora *f* eléctrica	
12 espalda *f*	back	33 brocha *f* de afeitar	shaving brush
13 pecho *m*	breast, chest *Am*	34 espuma *f* de afeitar	shaving foam
14 mano *f*	hand	35 maquinilla *f* de afeitar	razor
15 barriga *f*	stomach	36 moldeador *m* eléctrico,	(electric) curling tongs,
16 ombligo *m*	navel	rizador *m* eléctrico	curling iron *Am*
17 culo *m*, trasero *m*	bottom, backside	37 interruptor *m*	switch, socket *Am*
18 muslo *m*	thigh	38 secador *m* (de pelo)	hair dryer
19 corva *f*	back [*o* hollow] of the knee	39 estante *m*, anaquel *m*	shelf
20 pantorrilla *f*	calf	40 toalla *f*	towel
21 tobillo *m*	ankle	41 toallero *m*	towel rail, towel rack *Am*
22 talón *m*	heel	42 suelo *m*, piso *m*	floor
23 pie *m*	foot		

tel) to cut up; (*papel*) to tear up;
(*con tijeras*) to cut to pieces; **ser un
~ de pan** *fig* to be very good-natured
pedernal *m* flint
pedestal *m* pedestal
pediatra *mf* paediatrician *Brit,* pediatrician *Am*
pedicuro, -a *m, f* chiropodist
pedido *m* order
pedigrí *m* pedigree
pedir *irr vt* **1.** (*rogar*) to ask for; ~
algo a alguien to ask sb for sth; ~
(*limosna*) to beg; ~ **la mano de alguien** to ask for sb's hand in marriage; **os pido que hagáis menos
ruido** I'm asking you to make less
noise; **están pidiendo para la Cruz
Roja** they are collecting for the Red
Cross **2.** (*exigir, cobrar*) to demand;
(*necesitar*) to need; (*solicitar, demandar*) to request **3.** (*encargar*) to
order
pedo *m vulg* **1.** (*ventosidad*) fart; **tirarse un** ~ to fart **2.** *inf* (*borrachera*)
drunkenness; **estar en** ~ to be blind
drunk
pedrada *f* **matar a alguien a** ~**s** to
stone sb to death; **pegar una** ~ **a alguien** to throw a stone at sb
pega *f inf* (*dificultades*) difficulty;
(*desventaja*) drawback, snag; **poner
~s a** to find fault with
pegadizo, -a *adj* sticky; **melodía pe-
gadiza** catchy tune
pegajoso, -a *adj* **1.** (*adhesivo*) sticky,
adhesive **2.** (*persona*) tiresome; (*niño*) clinging
pegamento *m* glue
pegar <g→gu> **I.** *vt* **1.** (*poner*) to
stick; ~ **la mesilla a la cama** to put
the side table right next to the bed;
no ~ **ojo** not to sleep a wink; ~ **un
sello** to attach a stamp **2.** (*contagiar*) to give **3.** (*fuego*) ~ **fuego a
algo** to set fire to sth **4.** (*golpear*) to
hit; ~ **una paliza a alguien** to beat
sb up **5.** (*grito*) to let out; (*tiro*) to
fire; ~ **una bofetada** to slap; ~ **una
patada** to kick; ~ **un salto** to jump;
~ **un susto a alguien** to frighten sb
II. *vi* **1.** (*hacer juego*) to go together;
te pegan bien los zapatos con el

bolso those shoes go really well with
the bag; **esto no pega ni con cola**
this really doesn't go **2.** *inf* (*dar*)
¡cómo pega el sol hoy! the sun is
really hot today!; **no** ~ **golpe** [*o* **palo
al agua**| not to do a thing **III.** *vr:* ~**se
1.** (*impactar*) ~**se con algo** to bump
into sth; ~**se con alguien** to fight
with sb; ~**se un tortazo en el
coche** *inf* to crash one's car
2. (*quemarse*) to stick to the pot
3. (*contagiarse*) **finalmente se me
pegó el sarampión** I finally caught
the measles **4.** *inf* (*darse*) ~**se la
gran vida** to live it up; ~**se un tiro**
to shoot oneself
pegatina *f* sticker
pegote *m* **1.** (*emplasto*) patch **2.** *pey,
inf* (*guisote*) stodgy mess **3.** *inf* (*persona*) hanger-on **4.** *inf* (*chapuza*)
botch
peinado *m* hairstyle
peinar **I.** *vt* to comb; (*acicalar*) to
style **II.** *vr:* ~**se** to comb one's hair;
(*arreglar el pelo*) to style one's hair
peine *m* comb; **¡te vas a enterar de
lo que vale un** ~! *fig* you'll soon
find out what's what!
peineta *f* ornamental comb
p.ej. *abr de* **por ejemplo** e.g.
Pekín *m* Peking
pelado, -a *adj* **1.** (*rapado*) shorn
2. (*escueto, despojado*) bare **3.** *inf*
(*sin dinero*) broke
pelaje *m* **1.** (*piel*) coat, fur **2.** *pey*
(*pinta*) appearance, looks *pl*
pelambre *m o f* mop (of hair)
pelar **I.** *vt* **1.** (*animales*) to skin; (*plumas*) to pluck; ~ **a alguien** to cut
sb's hair **2.** (*frutas, verduras*) to peel
3. (*robar*) to fleece **II.** *vi inf* **hace un
frío que pela** it's freezing cold
III. *vr:* ~**se 1.** (*pelo*) to have one's
hair cut **2.** (*piel*) to peel
peldaño *m* step; (*escalera portátil*)
rung
pelea *f* fight; (*verbal*) quarrel, argument
pelear **I.** *vi* to fight; (*discutir*) to
argue **II.** *vr:* ~**se 1.** (*luchar*) ~**se** (*por
algo*) to fight (over sth); (*verbal*) to
argue (about sth) **2.** (*enemistarse*) to

P
p

fall out

peletería f (costura) furrier's; (venta) fur shop

peliagudo, -a adj tricky

pelícano m pelican

película f film, movie Am; de ~ fig, inf sensational; ~ del oeste western; ~ de suspense thriller; ¡allí ~s! it's nothing to do with me!

peligrar vi to be in danger

peligro m danger; ~ de incendio fire risk; correr (un gran) ~ to be at (great) risk; correr ~ de hacer algo to run the risk of doing sth; poner en ~ to endanger; poniendo en ~ su propia vida risking one's own life

peligroso, -a adj dangerous

pelirrojo, -a adj red-haired

pellejo m (de animal) hide; (de persona) skin; salvar el ~ inf to save one's skin; arriesgar el ~ inf to risk one's neck

pellizcar <c→qu> vt 1.(repizcar) to pinch 2. inf (comida) to nibble

pellizco m 1.(pizco) pinch; dar un ~ a alguien to pinch sb 2.(de sal) pinch; (de bocadillo) nibble

pelma m inf, **pelmazo** m inf bore, drag

pelo m 1.(cabello) hair; (de animal) fur; (de ave) plumage; no tocar un ~ (de la ropa) a alguien inf not to lay a finger on sb; tomar el ~ a alguien inf to pull sb's leg; se me pusieron los ~s de punta my hair stood on end; no se te ve el ~, ¿por dónde andas? inf I haven't seen you for ages, where have you been hiding? 2.(vello) down; (pelusa) fluff; (de alfombra) pile 3.(+ al) al ~ perfectly; venir al ~ to be just right, to happen at just the right time; todo irá al ~ everything will be fine; el traje ha quedado al ~ the suit looks great 4. inf (poco) escaparse por un ~ to escape by the skin of one's teeth; no tener (un) ~ de tonto inf to be nobody's fool; por un ~ te caes you very nearly fell; no se mueve ni un ~ de aire the air is completely still

pelón, -ona adj bald

pelota f 1.(balón, juego) ball; hacer la ~ a alguien inf to suck up to sb 2.(juego) pelota 3. pl, vulg (testículos) balls pl, ballocks pl; en ~s starkers; tocarse las ~s fig to do absolutely nothing; y esto lo hago así porque me sale de las ~s I do it like this because I bloody well feel like it!

pelotón m crowd; (en carreras) pack

peluca f wig

peluche m plush; oso ~ teddy bear

peludo, -a adj hairy

peluquería f hairdresser's; ir a la ~ to go to the hairdresser's

peluquero, -a m, f hairdresser

pelusa f 1.(vello) down; (tejido, de polvo) fluff 2. inf (celos) sentir ~ to be jealous

pelvis f inv pelvis

pena f 1.(tristeza) sorrow 2.(lástima) ser una ~ to be a pity; me da mucha ~ el gato I feel really sorry for the cat; me da mucha ~ el tener que verlo así it really upsets me to see him like this; ¡qué ~! what a shame! 3.(sanción) punishment; ~ pecuniaria fine 4.(dificultad) trouble; valer la ~ to be worth the effort; ¡allá ~s! it's not my problem! 5. AmL (vergüenza) shame; tener ~ to be ashamed

penal I. adj penal; antecedentes ~es criminal record II. m 1.(prisión) prison 2. AmL penalty

penalidad f 1.(molestia) hardship 2.(sanción) punishment

penalizar <z→c> vt to penalize

penalti m penalty

penar I. vt to punish II. vi 1.(padecer) to suffer 2.(ansiar) ~ por algo to long for sth

pendiente[1] I. adj 1.(colgado) hanging 2.(problema, asunto) unresolved; (cuenta, trabajo, pedido) outstanding; quedar ~ una asignatura to have one subject left to pass 3. inf (ocuparse) estate ~ del arroz keep an eye on the rice; ¡tú estate ~ de lo tuyo! mind your own business!; estoy ~ de si me conceden la beca o no I'm waiting to see whether or not they'll give me the grant **II.** *m* earring

pendiente[2] *f* slope

péndulo *m* pendulum

pene *m* penis

penetración *f* **1.** (*acción*) penetration **2.** (*comprensión*) insight

penetrante *adj* (*profundo*) deep; (*dolor*) fierce; (*frío*) biting; (*hedor*) strong; (*olor*) pervasive; (*sonido*) penetrating; (*grito*) piercing

penetrar *vi, vt* to penetrate

penicilina *f* penicillin

península *f* peninsula

? The **Península Ibérica** (Iberian Peninsula) includes Spain and Portugal. The Spanish language makes use of this term (and the corresponding adjective **peninsular**), in order to differentiate between the Spanish mainland and the two Spanish island groups (**Baleares y Canarias**) as well as the country's territories in Africa (**Ceuta y Melilla**).

---

peninsular *adj* peninsular

penique *m* penny

penitencia *f* penance

penitenciaría *f* prison, penitentiary *Am*

penitenciario, -a *adj* prison, penitentiary *Am*

penoso, -a *adj* **1.** (*arduo*) laborious **2.** (*dificultoso*) difficult

pensador(a) *m(f)* thinker

pensamiento *m* **1.** (*acción, idea, objeto*) thought **2.** (*mente*) mind; ¿cuándo te vino esa idea al ~? when did that idea occur to you? **3.** BOT pansy

pensar <e→ie> *vi, vt* to think; **pensándolo bien** on reflection; ¿en qué piensas? what are you thinking about?; **todo pasa cuando menos se piensa** (**en ello**) everything happens when you least expect it;

¡ni ~lo! don't even think about it!; ¡no quiero ni ~lo! I don't even want to think about it!; **nos dio mucho que ~ que no hubiera regresado aún** the fact that he/she hadn't returned yet gave us a lot to think about; **lo hicimos sin ~lo** we did it without thinking; **sin ~lo me dio una bofetada** he suddenly slapped me; **pienso que deberíamos irnos** I think we should go; **pensábamos venir este fin de semana** we were thinking of coming this weekend; **lo pensó mejor y no lo hizo** he/she thought better of it and didn't do it

pensativo, -a *adj* thoughtful, pensive

pensión *f* **1.** (*paga*) pension; ~ **alimenticia** maintenance **2.** (*para huéspedes*) guesthouse **3.** (*precio*) (charge for) board and lodging; ~ **completa** full board

pensionista *mf* pensioner

penúltimo, -a *adj* penultimate

penumbra *f* semi-darkness

penuria *f* poverty

peña *f* **1.** (*roca*) crag **2.** (*grupo*) group; (*de aficionados*) club

peñasco *m* boulder

peñón *m* crag; **el Peñón** the Rock (of Gibraltar)

peón *m* **1.** (*obrero*) unskilled labourer **2.** (*en ajedrez*) pawn

peonza *f* spinning top

peor *adv, adj* **1.** *comp de* **mal(o)** worse; **vas de mal en ~** you're going from bad to worse; ~ **es nada** it's better than nothing **2.** *superl de* **mal(o) en el ~ de los casos** at worst; **si pasa lo ~** if worst comes to worst; **pero lo ~ de todo fue...** but the worst thing of all was ...

pepinillo *m* gherkin

pepino *m* cucumber; **eso me importa un ~** *inf* I don't give two hoots about that

pepita *f* seed

pequeñez *f* **1.** (*tamaño*) smallness **2.** (*minucia*) trifle

pequeño, -a I. *adj* small, little; **ya desde ~ solía venir a este sitio** I've been coming here since I was

P
p

little; **esta camisa me queda** ~ this shirt is too small for me **II.** *m, f* little one

pera I. *adj* **niño** ~ posh brat *Brit,* little rich kid **II.** *f* pear

peral *m* pear tree

percance *m* (*contratiempo*) setback; (*por culpa propia*) blunder; (*de plan, proyecto*) hitch

per cápita *adv* per capita

percatarse *vr* ~ **de algo** (*darse cuenta*) to notice sth; (*comprender*) to realize sth

percepción *f* **1.** (*acción*) perception; FIN receipt **2.** (*idea*) notion

perceptible *adj* **1.** (*que puede comprenderse*) perceptible **2.** FIN payable

percha *f* **1.** (*en el armario*) hanger **2.** (*perchero*) coat stand; (*en la tienda*) clothes rail **3.** *inf* (*tipo*) **tener buena** ~ to have a good figure

percibir *vt* **1.** (*notar*) to perceive; (*darse cuenta*) to notice; (*comprender*) to realize **2.** (*cobrar*) to receive

percusión *f* percussion

perdedor(a) I. *adj* losing **II.** *m(f)* loser

perder <e→ie> **I.** *vt* **1.** (*en general*) to lose **2.** (*no aprovechar*) **si llego tarde al espectáculo pierdo la entrada** if I arrive late for the show my ticket will be wasted **3.** (*oportunidad, tren*) to miss **II.** *vi* **1.** (*en general*) to lose; **llevar todas las de** ~ to be fighting a losing battle; **Portugal perdió por 1 a 2 frente a Italia** Portugal lost 2–1 to Italy; **vas a salir perdiendo** you're going to come off worst; **lo echó todo a** ~ he/she lost everything; **la comida se quemó y todo se echó a** ~ the food was burnt and everything was completely ruined **2.** (*decaer*) to decline **III.** *vr:* ~**se 1.** (*extraviarse*) to get lost; **¡qué se le habrá perdido por allí?** *fig* what is he/she doing there? **2.** (*bailando, leyendo*) to lose oneself **3.** (*desaparecer*) to disappear **4.** (*arruinarse*) ~**se por algo/alguien** to be ruined by sth/sb **5.** (*ocasión*) to miss out; **si no te vienes, tú te lo**

pierdes if you don't come, you'll be the one who misses out

perdición *f* ruin

pérdida *f* loss; ~**s humanas** victims *pl;* **esto es una** ~ **de tiempo** this is a waste of time; **es fácil de encontrar, no tiene** ~ it's easy to find, you can't miss it; **el coche tiene una leve** ~ **de aceite** the car has a slight oil leak

perdido, -a *adj* **1.** (*en general*) lost; **dar algo por** ~ to give sth up for lost; *fig* to give up on sth; **estar loco** ~ *inf* to be completely insane **2.** (*sucio*) **poner algo** ~ *inf* to make sth completely dirty; **ponerse** ~ **de pintura** *inf* to get covered in paint

perdigón *m* pellet

perdiz *f* partridge; **... y fueron felices y comieron perdices** ... and they lived happily ever after

perdón *m* **1.** (*absolución, indulto*) pardon **2.** (*disculpa*) **pedir** ~ **a alguien** to ask for sb's forgiveness; (*disculparse*) to apologize to sb; **¡**~**!** sorry!; **¿**~**?** pardon?; **¡con** ~**!** if you'll excuse me!; **no cabe** ~ it's inexcusable

perdonar *vt* **1.** (*ofensa, pecado*) to forgive; **perdona que te interrumpa** forgive me for interrupting; **perdona, ¿puedo pasar?** excuse me, can I come through? **2.** (*obligación*) to let off; **te perdono los 20 euros** I'll forget about the 20 euros you owe me

perdurable *adj* **1.** (*duradero*) long-lasting **2.** (*eterno*) everlasting

perdurar *vi* **1.** (*todavía*) to persist **2.** (*indefinidamente*) to last for ever; **su recuerdo** ~**á para siempre entre nosotros** his memory will always be with us

perecedero, -a *adj* **1.** (*pasajero*) transitory **2.** (*alimento*) perishable

perecer *irr como crecer vi* die

peregrinación *f* pilgrimage; **ir en** ~ to make a pilgrimage

peregrino, -a I. *adj* strange **II.** *m, f* pilgrim

perejil *m* parsley

perenne *adj* everlasting; BOT perennial

perentorio, -a *adj* **1.** (*urgente*) pressing **2.** plazo ~ fixed time limit

pereza *f* laziness; **me dio ~ ir y me quedé en casa** I couldn't be bothered going so I stayed at home

perezoso, -a *adj* lazy; **y ni corto ni ~ me soltó un sopapo** *inf* without stopping to think he slapped me

perfección *f* perfection; **hacer algo a la ~** to do sth to perfection

perfeccionar *vt* to perfect; (*mejorar*) to improve

perfecto *m* perfect tense

perfecto, -a *adj* perfect

perfidia *f* **1.** (*deslealtad*) disloyalty **2.** (*traición*) betrayal

perfil *m* **1.** (*de cara, descripción*) *t.* TÉC profile; **de ~** in profile **2.** (*contorno*) outline

perfilar I. *vt* **1.** (*retocar*) to touch up **2.** (*sacar perfil*) to outline **II.** *vr:* ~se **1.** (*distinguirse*) to stand out **2.** (*tomar forma*) to take shape

perforación *f* perforation

perforadora *f* drill; (*de papel*) card--punch

perforar *vt* (*con máquina*) to drill; (*oreja*) to pierce; (*papel*) to punch; (*para decorar*) to perforate

perfume *m* **1.** (*sustancia*) perfume **2.** (*olor*) fragrance

pericia *f* (*habilidad*) expertise; (*práctica*) skill

periferia *f* periphery; (*de ciudad*) outskirts *pl*

periférico, -a *adj* peripheral

perilla *f* goatee

perímetro *m* perimeter

periódico *m* newspaper

periódico, -a *adj* periodic; **sistema ~** periodic table

periodismo *m* journalism

periodista *mf* journalist

periodo *m*, **período** *m* period

peripecia *f* vicissitude; **ha pasado por muchas ~s en esta vida** he/she has had many ups and downs in his/her life

perito, -a *adj, m, f* expert; **~ mercantil** accountant

perjudicar <c→qu> *vt* **1.** (*causar*

daño) to damage; (*naturaleza, intereses*) to harm; (*proceso, desarrollo*) to hinder; **fumar perjudica la salud** smoking is bad for your health **2.** (*causar desventaja*) to disadvantage

perjudicial *adj* **1.** (*que causa daño*) harmful; **~ para la salud** harmful to health **2.** (*desventajoso*) disadvantageous

perjuicio *m* **1.** (*daño: de imagen, naturaleza*) harm; (*de objeto*) damage; (*de libertad*) infringement; **causar ~s** to cause harm **2.** (*detrimento*) detriment; **ir en ~ de alguien** to be to sb's detriment

perjurar *vi* to commit perjury

perla *f* pearl

permanecer *irr como crecer vi* to remain; **~ quieto** to keep still; **~ dormido** to carry on sleeping

permanencia *f* **1.** (*estancia*) stay **2.** (*continuación*) continuation

permanente I. *adj* permanent **II.** *f* perm

permisible *adj* permissible

permiso *m* **1.** (*aprobación, autorización*) permission **2.** (*licencia*) permit; **~ de conducir** driving licence *Brit,* driver's license *Am* **3.** (*vacaciones*) leave; **estar de ~** to be on leave

permitir I. *vt* **1.** (*consentir*) to permit; **¿me permite entrar/salir/pasar?** may I enter/leave/get past?; **no está permitido fumar** smoking is not allowed; **si me permite la expresión** if you will excuse the phrase **2.** (*tolerar*) to allow; **no permito que me levantes la voz** I won't allow you to raise your voice to me **II.** *vr:* ~**se** to allow oneself

pernicioso, -a *adj* (*tumor*) malignant; **~ (para algo/alguien)** damaging (to sth/sb)

perno *m* bolt

pero I. *conj* but; (*sin embargo*) however; **¡~ si todavía es una niña!** but she is still only a child!; **¡~ si ya la conoces!** but you already know her!; **¿~ qué es lo que quieres?** what do you want? **II.** *m* objection;

sin un ~ no buts; **poner ~s a algo** to object to sth; **el proyecto tiene sus ~s** there are lots of problems with the project

perol *m,* **perola** *f* (metal) cooking pot

perpendicular *adj, f* perpendicular

perpetrar *vt* to perpetrate

perpetuar <*I. pres:* perpetúo> **I.** *vt* (*recuerdo*) to preserve; (*situación, error*) to perpetuate **II.** *vr:* ~**se** to be perpetuated

perpetuo, -a *adj* perpetual; **cadena perpetua** life sentence; **nieves perpetuas** permanent snow

perplejo, -a *adj* perplexed

perra *f* **1.** ZOOL bitch **2.** (*obstinación*) obsession **3.** *inf* (*rabieta*) tantrum; **coger una** ~ to throw a tantrum **4.** *inf* (*dinero*) penny; **no tener una** ~ to be broke

perrera *f* (*casita*) kennel; (*de perros callejeros*) dog pound

perro, -a *m, f* dog; (*hembra*) bitch; ~ **callejero** stray dog; **se llevan como el** ~ **y el gato** *inf* they fight like cat and dog; ~ **ladrador, poco mordedor** *prov* his bark is worse than his bite

persa *adj, mf* Persian

persecución *f* **1.** (*seguimento*) pursuit; ~ **en coche** car chase **2.** (*acoso*) persecution

perseguir *irr como seguir* *vt* to chase; (*contrato, chica*) to pursue; **me persigue la mala suerte** I am dogged by bad luck; **me persiguen los remordimientos** I am tormented by remorse; **el jefe me persigue todo el día** the boss is always on my back; **¡qué persigues con esto?** what do you hope to achieve by this?

perseverante *adj* persevering

perseverar *vi* to persevere

Persia *f* Persia

persiana *f* blind

pérsico, -a *adj* Persian

persignarse *vr* to cross oneself

persistente *adj* persistent

persistir *vi* to persist

persona *f* person; ~ **jurídica** legal entity; ~ **mayor** adult, grown-up; **ser buena/mala** ~ to be good/bad; **había muchas ~s** there were a lot of people; **no había ninguna** ~ **allí** there was nobody there

personaje *m* **1.** (*personalidad*) personality **2.** TEAT, LIT character

personal I. *adj* personal; **datos ~es** personal details **II.** *m* **1.** (*plantilla*) personnel; (*en empresa*) staff **2.** *inf* (*gente*) people + *pl vb*

personalidad *f* personality

personalizar <z→c> **I.** *vt* to personalize **II.** *vi* to get personal

personarse *vr* to appear; ~ **en juicio** to appear before the court; **el lunes tengo que personarme en el INEM** on Monday I have to go to the job centre; **persónese ante el director** report to the director

personificar <c→qu> *vt* to personify

perspectiva *f* **1.** (*general*) perspective **2.** (*vista*) view **3.** *pl* (*posibilidad*) prospects *pl*

perspicacia *f* insight

perspicaz *adj* perceptive

persuadir I. *vt* to persuade **II.** *vr:* ~**se** to be persuaded

persuasión *f* **1.** (*acto*) persuasion **2.** (*convencimiento*) belief

persuasivo, -a *adj* persuasive

pertenecer *irr como crecer* *vi* **1.** (*ser de*) ~ (**a algo/alguien**) to belong (to sth/sb); **esta cita pertenece a Hamlet** this is a quotation from Hamlet **2.** (*tener obligación*) **te pertenece a ti hacerlo** it is your duty to do it; **esto pertenece al Ministerio de Asuntos Exteriores** that's the Foreign Office's *Brit* [*o* State Department's *Am*] responsibility

perteneciente *adj* ~ **a** belonging to; **los países ~s a la ONU** the countries which are members of the UN; **todo lo** ~ **al caso** everything which is relevant to the case

pertenencia *f* **1.** (*acción*) belonging; (*afiliación*) membership **2.** *pl* (*bienes*) belongings *pl*

pértiga *f* pole; **salto de** ~ pole vault

pertinaz *adj* persistent

pertinente *adj* 1.(*oportuno*) appropriate 2.(*relevante*) pertinent 3.(*relativo*) **en lo ~ a ...** with regard to ...

perturbación *f* disturbance
perturbador(a) *adj* disturbing
perturbar *vt* to disturb
Perú *m* Peru

? Perú lies in the western part of South America. It is the third largest country after Brazil and Argentina. The capital and also the largest city in Peru is **Lima**. Both Spanish and **quechua** are the official languages of the country and the monetary unit is the **sol**. The original inhabitants of Peru were the **incas**.

peruano, -a *adj, m, f* Peruvian
perversión *f* perversion
perverso, -a *adj* 1.(*malo*) wicked 2.(*sexual*) perverse
pervertido, -a I. *adj* perverted II. *m, f* pervert
pervertir *irr como sentir vt* to corrupt
pesa *f* weight; **hacer (entrenamiento de) ~s** to do weight training
pesadez *f* 1.(*de objeto*) heaviness 2.(*aburrido*) dullness
pesadilla *f* nightmare
pesado, -a *adj* 1.(*que pesa*) heavy 2.(*molesto*) tiresome 3.(*duro*) hard 4.(*aburrido*) boring 5.(*sueño*) deep; (*viaje*) tedious
pesadumbre *f* affliction
pésame *m* condolences *pl;* **dar el ~** to offer one's condolences; **reciba mi más sincero ~ por la muerte de su hermana** please accept my condolences for the loss of your sister
pesar I. *vi* 1.(*tener peso*) to weigh; **esta caja pesa mucho** this box is very heavy; **pon encima lo que no pese** put the lightest things on top 2.(*cargo, responsabilidad*) **~ sobre alguien** to weigh heavily on sb; (*problemas*) to weigh sb down II. *vt*

1.(*objeto, persona*) to weigh; (*cantidad concreta*) to weigh out 2.(*ventajas*) to weigh up 3.(*disgustar*) **pese a...** in spite of ...; **pese a que...** although ...; **me pesa haberte mentido** I regret having lied to you; **mal que te pese...** much as you may dislike it ... III. *m* 1.(*pena*) sorrow; **muy a ~ mío** to my great sadness 2.(*remordimiento*) regret 3.(*prep, conj*) **a ~ de** in spite of; **a ~ de que...** although
pesca *f* 1.(*acción, oficio, industria*) fishing; **ir de ~** to go fishing 2.(*lo pescado*) catch
pescadería *f* fishmonger's *Brit*, fishmarket
pescadilla *f* whiting
pescado *m* fish
pescador(a) *m(f)* (*de caña*) angler; (*de mar*) fisherman
pescar <c→qu> I. *vt* 1.(*con caña, en barco*) to fish for 2. *t. fig* (*coger*) to catch; *inf* (*novio*) to land; *inf* (*entender*) to understand II. *vi* to fish
pescuezo *m* (scruff of the) neck
pesebre *m* manger
peseta *f* peseta
pesimismo *m sin pl* pessimism
pesimista I. *adj* pessimistic II. *mf* pessimist
pésimo, -a *adj* dreadful
peso *m* 1.(*de objeto, importancia*) weight; **coger ~** to gain weight; **tener una razón de ~** to have a good reason; **vender a ~** to sell by weight; **¿qué ~ tiene?** how much does it weigh? 2.(*carga*) burden; **llevar el ~ de algo** to bear the burden of sth; **me saco un ~ de encima** that's taken a load off my mind 3.(*moneda*) peso
pesquero, -a *adj* fishing
pesquisa *f* inquiry
pestaña *f* eyelash
pestañ(e)ar *vi* to blink; **sin ~** without batting an eyelid
peste *f* 1.(*plaga*) plague 2.(*olor*) stench; **aquí hay una ~ increíble** it really stinks here 3.(*crítica*) **echar ~s de alguien** to heap abuse on sb
pesticida *m* pesticide

P
p

pestilencia *f* stench

pestillo *m* bolt

petaca *f* (*para cigarros*) cigarette case; (*para tabaco*) tobacco pouch

pétalo *m* petal

petanca *f* bowls, petanque

petardo *m* 1. (*de fiesta*) firecracker; **tirar ~s** to let off firecrackers 2. *inf* (*persona o cosa mala*) **ser un ~** to be a pain

petición *f* 1. (*ruego, solicitud*) request; **a ~ de...** at the request of ... 2. (*escrito*) petition

petrificar <c→qu> *vt* to petrify

petróleo *m* petroleum, (crude) oil

petrolero *m* oil tanker

petrolero, -a *adj* petrol, oil

peyorativo, -a *adj* pejorative; **un comentario ~** a derrogatory remark

pez *m* fish; **un ~ gordo** a bigshot; **estar como (el) ~ en el agua** to be in one's element

pezón *m* nipple

pezuña *f* hoof

pianista *mf* pianist

piano *m* piano

piar <*1. pres:* pío> *vi* 1. (*pájaro*) to chirp 2. (*clamar*) **~ por algo** to cry out for sth

PIB *m abr de* **Producto Interior Bruto** GDP

pibe, -a *m, f Arg* (*chico*) boy; (*chica*) girl

picadero *m* riding school

picadillo *m* mince *Brit,* ground meat *Am*

picado, -a *adj* 1. (*fruta*) rotten; (*muela*) decayed 2. *inf* (*enfadado*) annoyed

picador *m* picador (*mounted bullfighter who goads the bull with a lance*)

picadura *f* 1. (*de insecto*) sting; (*de serpiente*) bite 2. (*caries*) cavity

picante *adj* spicy, hot; *fig* risqué

picaporte *m* 1. (*aldaba*) doorknocker 2. (*tirador*) door handle

picar <c→qu> I. *vi* 1. (*sol, ojos*) to sting 2. (*chile, pimienta*) to be hot 3. (*pez, clientes*) to take the bait 4. (*de la comida*) to snack 5. (*tener picazón*) to itch; **me pica la espal-**da my back is itchy II. *vt* 1. (*con punzón*) to prick, to pierce 2. (*sacar*) **~ una aceituna de la lata** to fish an olive from the tin 3. (*insecto*) to sting; (*serpiente*) to bite; **¿qué mosca te ha picado?** *fig* what's eating you? 4. (*ave*) to peck 5. (*desmenuzar*) to chop up; (*carne*) to mince 6. (*ofender*) to irritate; **estar picado con alguien** ~ I said it out of a sense of annoyed by sb 7. (*incitar*) to goad 8. INFOR to click on III. *vr:* **~se** 1. (*metal*) to rust; (*muela*) to decay 2. (*ofenderse*) to become irritated; (*mosquearse*) to become angry; **~se por nada** to get irritated about the slightest thing

picardía *f* 1. (*malicia*) roguishness; **lo dije con ~** I said it out of a sense of mischief 2. (*travesura*) naughty trick; (*broma*) joke

pícaro, -a I. *adj* 1. (*granuja*) roguish 2. (*astuto*) cunning 3. (*comentario*) naughty II. *m, f* rogue

pichón *m* young pigeon

pico *m* 1. (*del pájaro*) beak 2. *inf* (*boca*) mouth, gob *Brit* 3. (*herramienta*) pickaxe *Brit,* pickax *Am* 4. (*montaña*) peak 5. (*punta*) corner; (*de jarra*) lip 6. *inf* (*cantidad*) **llegar a las cuatro y ~** to arrive just after four o'clock; **tiene cuarenta y ~ de años** he/she is forty-something; **salir por un ~** to cost a lot

picor *m* stinging, burning; (*en la piel*) itching

picotear *vt* to peck

picudo, -a *adj* pointed

pie *m* foot; **al ~ de la carta** at the bottom of the letter; **~ de página** foot of the page; **estar de ~** to be standing; **no hacer ~** to be out of one's depth; **ponerse de ~** to stand up; **seguir algo al ~ de la letra** to follow sth to the letter; **¿qué ~ calza Ud.?** what shoe size do you take?; **hoy no doy ~ con bola** I can't seem to do anything right today; **andarse con ~s de plomo** to tread very carefully

piedad *f sin pl* 1. REL piety 2. (*compasión*) pity; **¡ten ~ de nosotros!**

have pity on us!

piedra *f* stone; **no dejar ~ sobre ~** to raze to the ground; **poner la primera ~** to lay the foundation stone; **cuando lo supimos nos quedamos de ~** we were absolutely stunned when we found out about it

piel *f* **1.** (*de persona, fruta*) skin; **~ de gallina** goose-pimples *pl*; **se me puso la ~ de gallina oyendo su historia** hearing his story made my flesh crawl **2.** (*de animal*) skin, hide; (*con pelo*) fur; (*cuero*) leather; **un abrigo de ~es** a fur coat

pienso *m* fodder

pierna *f* leg

pieza *f* **1.** (*en general*) piece; (*parte*) part; **un traje de dos ~s** a two-piece suit; **vender a ~s** to sell by the piece; **me quedé de una ~** *inf* I was absolutely dumbfounded **2.** *AmL* (*habitación*) room

pigmento *m* pigment

pigmeo, -a *adj, m, f* pigmy

pijama *m* pyjamas *pl*, pajamas *pl Am*

pijo, -a I. *adj inf* posh II. *m, f inf* posh youth; **niño ~** *pey* upper-class twit

pila *f* **1.** (*lavadero*) sink; **~ (bautismal)** (baptismal) font; **nombre de ~** first name **2.** FÍS battery **3.** (*montón*) pile

pilar *m* pillar

píldora *f* pill

pileta *f RíoPl* **1.** (*de cocina*) kitchen sink **2.** (*piscina*) swimming pool

pillaje *m* pillage

pillar *vt* **1.** (*atropellar*) to knock down, to run over **2.** (*encontrar*) to catch; **la noche nos pilló en el monte** when night came we were still on the mountain; **eso no me pilla de sorpresa** that doesn't surprise me **3.** (*hallarse*) **tu casa nos pilla de camino** your house is on our way; **Correos no nos pilla cerca** the Post Office isn't very near

pillo, -a I. *adj inf* crafty II. *m, f inf* rascal

pilotar *vt* (*barco*) to steer; (*coche*) to drive; (*avión*) to fly

piloto¹ *mf* AERO, NÁUT pilot; AUTO driver; **~ de carreras** racing driver

piloto² *m* TÉC pilot light

pimentón *m* paprika

pimienta *f* pepper

pimiento *m* pepper

pinacoteca *f* art gallery

pinar *m* pine grove

pincel *m* brush

pinchadiscos *mf inv* disc jockey

pinchar I. *vt* **1.** (*alfiler*) to prick **2.** (*estimular*) to prod; (*fastidiar*) to needle **3.** (*inyección*) to give an injection II. *vr:* **~se 1.** (*alfiler*) to prick oneself **2.** (*rueda*) **se nos ha pinchado una rueda** one of our wheels has a puncture **3.** MED to give oneself an injection; *inf* (*drogarse*) to shoot up

pinchazo *m* **1.** (*espina*) prick; **me dieron unos ~s insoportables en el estómago** I had some really horrible shooting pains in the stomach **2.** (*neumático*) puncture

pincho *m* **1.** (*avispa*) sting; (*rosa*) thorn **2.** GASTR snack

pinciano, -a *adj* of/from Valladolid

ping-pong *m sin pl* ping-pong

pingüino *m* penguin

pino *m* **1.** (*árbol, madera*) pine; **en el quinto ~** *fig* in the back of beyond **2.** DEP handstand

pinta¹ *f* **1.** (*mancha*) spot; **a ~s** spotted **2.** *inf* (*aspecto*) appearance; **tener buena ~** to look good; **tener ~ de caro** to look expensive

pinta² *f* (*medida*) pint

pintada *f* graffiti

pintado, -a *adj* **eso viene como ~** *inf* that is just what was needed; **el traje te sienta que ni ~** *inf* the suit really suits you; **no lo puedo ver ni ~** *inf* I can't stand even the sight of him

pintar I. *vi* **1.** ARTE to paint **2.** (*bolígrafo*) to write II. *vt* **1.** (*pared*) to paint; (*con dibujos*) to decorate; **~ de azul** to paint blue; **¡recién pintado!** wet paint! **2.** (*cuadro*) to paint; (*dibujo*) to draw; (*colorear*) to colour in **3.** *fig* **no ~ nada** (*persona*) to have no influence; (*asunto*) to be completely irrelevant; **¿qué pinta eso aquí?** what's that doing here?, to describe

P p

III. *vr:* ~**se** to do one's make-up

pintor(a) *m/f)* painter

pintoresco, -a *adj* picturesque

pintura *f* **1.** (*arte, cuadro*) painting; ~ **al óleo** oil painting; **no lo puedo ver ni en** ~ *inf* I can't stand him **2.** (*color*) paint; **caja de** ~**s** paintbox

pinza(s) *f(pl)* **1.** (*tenacilla*) tongs *pl;* TÉC pincers *pl* **2.** (*para la ropa*) (clothes) peg, (clothes) pin *Am* **3.** (*para depilar*) tweezers *pl* **4.** (*costura*) pleat **5.** (*de cangrejo*) claw

piña *f* **1.** (*pino*) pine cone **2.** (*fruta*) pineapple

piñón *m* **1.** (*pino*) pine nut **2.** TÉC pinion

pío *m* cheep; **no decir ni** ~ not to say a word

pío, -a *adj* pious

piojo *m* louse

pionero, -a *m, f* pioneer

pipa *f* **1.** (*fumador*) pipe; **fumar en** ~ to smoke a pipe **2.** (*de fruta*) pip, seed **3.** *pl* (*de girasol*) sunflower seed **4.** *inf* (*muy bien*) **lo pasamos** ~ we had a great time

pipí *m inf* pee, wee wee *childspeak*

pique *m* **1.** (*rivalidad*) rivalry **2.** (*hundirse*) **irse a** ~ (*barco*) to sink; (*plan*) to fail

piqueta *f* pickaxe *Brit,* pickax *Am*

piquete *m* **1.** (*huelga*) (strike) picket **2.** MIL squad

piragua *f* canoe

piragüismo *m* canoeing

pirámide *f* pyramid

piraña *f* piranha

pirarse *vr inf* to clear off

pirata *mf* pirate; INFOR hacker; ~ **aéreo** hijacker

Pirineos *mpl* Pyrenees *pl*

pirómano, -a *m, f* pyromaniac

piropo *m inf* flirtatious comment; **echar** ~**s** to make flirtatious comments

pirueta *f* pirouette

pis *m inf* piss

pisada *f* **1.** (*acción*) footstep **2.** (*huella*) footprint

pisar *vt* **1.** (*poner el pie*) ~ **algo** to tread on sth; ~ **los talones a alguien** *fig* to follow on sb's heels **2.** (*entrar*) to enter **3.** (*tierra*) to tread down **4.** (*humillar*) to walk all over

piscina *f* swimming pool; ~ **cubierta** indoor swimming pool

Piscis *m inv* Pisces

piso *m* **1.** (*pavimento*) floor; (*calle*) surface **2.** (*planta*) floor, storey *Brit,* story *Am;* **de dos** ~**s** with two floors **3.** (*vivienda*) flat *Brit,* apartment *Am*

pisotear *vt* to trample; *fig* to walk all over

pisotón *m* stamp; **dar un** ~ **a alguien** to tread on sb's foot

pista *f* **1.** (*huella*) trail; (*indicio*) clue; **seguir la** ~ **a alguien** to follow sb's trail **2.** (*para atletismo, coches*) track; (*de tenis*) court; (*de baile*) floor; ~ **de aterrizaje** runway; ~ **de esquí** ski slope **3.** INFOR track

pisto *m* vegetable stew

pistola *f* pistol

pistolera *f* holster

pistolero *m* gunman

pistón *m* piston

pitar I. *vt, vi* **1.** (*claxon*) to blow; **me pitan los oídos** my ears are buzzing **2.** *AmS* (*fumar*) to smoke **II.** *vi inf* **salir pitando** to rush off; **¡con la mitad vas que pitas!** half of it should be more than enough!

pitido *m* whistle

pitillera *f* cigarette case

pitillo *m* cigarette

pito *m* **1.** (*silbato*) whistle; (*claxon*) horn; **entre** ~**s y flautas** *inf* what with one thing and another; **no me importa un** ~ *inf* I don't give a damn about it; *inf* to be completely worthless **2.** (*cigarro*) cigarette

pitón *m* python

pitonisa *f* fortune teller

pitorreo *m inf* joking; **¡esto es un** ~**!** this is a joke!

pizarra *f* **1.** (*roca*) slate **2.** (*encerado*) blackboard

pizca *f inf* (*poco*) pinch, little bit; **no tienes ni** ~ **de vergüenza** you have no shame whatsoever

placa *f* **1.** (*tabla, plancha*) plate; (*lámina*) sheet; INFOR board; ~ **base** INFOR motherboard **2.** (*cartel*) plaque; AUTO number plate *Brit,* license plate *Am*

placenta *f* placenta

placentero, -a *adj* pleasant

placer I. *m* pleasure II. *irr como crecer vi* to please; **¡haré lo que me plazca!** I will do as I please!

plácido, -a *adj* calm

plaga *f* plague; *fig* (*abundancia*) glut

plagar <g→gu> *vt* to infest; ~ **de algo** *fig* to fill with sth; **el texto estaba plagado de faltas** the text was full of mistakes; **la casa está plagada de cucarachas** the house is infested with cockroaches

plagiar *vt* 1. (*copiar*) to plagiarize 2. *AmL* (*secuestrar*) to kidnap

plagio *m* 1. (*copia*) plagiarism 2. *AmL* (*secuestro*) kidnapping

plan *m* 1. (*proyecto*) plan; **si no tienes** ~ **para esta noche paso a buscarte** if you don't have anything planned for tonight I'll come round and fetch you 2. *inf* (*ligue*) date 3. *inf* (*actitud*) **esto no es** ~ it's just not on; **en ~ de... as ...; está en un** ~ **que no lo soporto** I can't stand him when he behaves like this

plana *f* page; **un artículo en primera** ~ a front-page article

plancha *f* 1. (*tabla*) plate; (*lámina*) sheet 2. (*para ropa*) iron 3. GASTR grill; **a la** ~ grilled

planchado *m* ironing

planchar *vt* to iron

planeador *m* glider

planear I. *vi* to glide II. *vt* to plan

planeta *m* planet

planicie *f* plain

planificación *f* planning

plano *m* 1. MAT plane 2. (*mapa*) map 3. CINE **primer** ~ close-up; **en primer** ~ (*delante*) in the foreground 4. (*totalmente*) **de** ~ directly; (*negar*) flatly; **aceptó de** ~ **nuestra propuesta** she accepted our suggestion straight away

plano, -a *adj* flat

planta *f* 1. BOT plant 2. (*pie*) sole 3. (*piso*) floor; ~ **alta** top floor; ~ **baja** ground floor *Brit,* first floor *Am* 4. (*aspecto*) **tener buena** ~ to be

good-looking

plantación *f* plantation

plantar I. *vt* 1. (*bulbo*) to plant 2. (*terreno*) **han plantado el monte** they have planted trees on the hillside 3. (*clavar*) to stick in; ~ **una tienda de campaña** to pitch a tent 4. *inf* (*golpe*) to land; ~ **un tortazo a alguien** to slap sb 5. *inf* (*cita*) to stand up; **desapareció y me dejó plantado** he/she disappeared and left me standing; **lo** ~**on en la calle** they chucked him out II. *vr:* ~**se** 1. (*resistirse*) ~**se ante algo** to stand firm in the face of sth 2. (*aparecer*) to get to; **se** ~**on en mi casa en un periquete** they arrived at my house in no time

plantear I. *vt* 1. (*asunto, problema*) to approach; **este problema está mal planteado** this problem has been incorrectly formulated 2. (*causar*) to cause 3. (*proponer*) to put forward, to pose II. *vr:* ~**se** to think about; **ahora me planteo la pregunta si...** now I ask myself whether ...

plantilla *f* 1. (*empleados*) staff 2. (*de zapato*) insole

plantón *m* *inf* (*espera*) **dar un** ~ **a alguien** to stand sb up; **y ahora estoy de** ~ I've been left waiting around

plañir <3. *pret:* plañó> *vi* to wail

plasma *m* plasma

plástico *m* plastic

plástico, -a *adj* 1. (*materia*) *t.* ARTE plastic 2. (*expresivo*) expressive

plastilina® *f* plasticene *Brit,* modelling clay *Brit,* modeling clay *Am*

plata *f* 1. (*metal*) silver; ~ **de ley** sterling silver; **bodas de** ~ silver wedding anniversary 2. *AmL* (*dinero*) money

plataforma *f* platform; ~ **petrolífera** oil rig

plátano *m* banana

platea *f* stalls *pl Brit,* orchestra *Am*

plateado, -a *adj* (*con plata*) silver-plated; (*color*) silver

platense *adj* 1. (*de La Plata*) of/from La Plata 2. (*de Río de La Plata*) of/

P
p

from the River Plate region

plática *f* chat; **estar de ~** to be chatting

platicar <c→qu> *vi inf* to chat

platillo *m* 1.(*de una taza*) saucer 2.(*de una balanza*) pan 3. MÚS cymbal

platina *f* 1.(*de microscopio*) slide 2. TYP platen 3.(*de tocadiscos, casete*) deck

platino *m* 1. QUÍM platinum 2. *pl* AUTO contact points *pl*

plato *m* 1.(*vajilla*) plate; **tener cara de no haber roto un ~ en la vida** *inf* to look as if butter wouldn't melt in one's mouth; **ahora tengo que pagar los ~s rotos** *fig* now I've got to pay the consequences 2.(*comida*) dish; **hoy hay ~ único** today there is only one dish; **nos sirvieron tres ~s y postre** we were served three courses and dessert 3.(*de la bicicleta*) sprocket

plató *m* (film) set

platónico, -a *adj* platonic

playa *f* 1.(*mar*) beach 2. *AmL* **~ de estacionamiento** car park, parking lot *Am*

playera *f Guat, Méx* (*camiseta*) T-shirt

playeras *fpl* (*zapatillas*) gym shoes *pl*

plaza *f* 1.(*espacio*) square; (*mercado*) market(place); **~ (de toros)** bullring 2.(*asiento*) seat; (*de garage, parking*) space 3.(*empleo*) post 4.(*en instituciones, viajes*) place

plazo *m* 1.(*vencimiento*) period; **a corto/largo ~** in the short/long term; **~ de entrega** delivery date; **fuera del ~** after the closing date; **en el ~ de un mes** within a month; **tengo dos millones a ~ fijo** I have two million in a fixed-term deposit; **¿cuándo vence el ~?** when is the deadline? 2.(*cantidad*) instalment *Brit,* installment *Am;* **a ~s** by instalments

plazoleta *f dim de* **plaza**

pleamar *f* high tide

plebe *f sin pl* masses *pl*

plebeyo, -a *adj* 1. *t.* HIST plebeian 2.(*grosero*) uncouth

plebiscito *m* plebiscite

plegable *adj* folding

plegar *irr como fregar vt* to fold; (*muebles*) to fold away

pleito *m* 1. JUR lawsuit 2.(*disputa*) dispute

plenitud *f* 1.(*totalidad*) fullness 2.(*apogeo*) height; **en la ~ de sus facultades físicas** at the height of his/her physical powers

pleno *m* plenary session

pleno, -a *adj* full; **en ~ verano** at the height of summer; **le robaron a plena luz del día** they robbed him in broad daylight

pliego *m* sheet

pliegue *m* fold

plomero *m AmL* (*técnico fontanero*) plumber

plomo *m* 1.(*metal*) lead; **gasolina sin ~** unleaded petrol *Brit,* unleaded gas *Am* 2. *pl* ELEC fuse

pluma *f* 1.(*ave*) feather 2.(*escribir*) pen

plumero *m* feather duster; **vérsele el ~ a alguien** *fig* to be obvious what sb is up to

plumón *m* down

plural *adj, m* plural

pluralidad *f* plurality

pluriempleo *m* one person filling various positions

plus *m* bonus

plusvalía *f sin pl* appreciation

plutocracia *f sin pl* plutocracy

PNB *m abr de* **producto nacional bruto** GNP

población *f* 1. *t.* BIO (*habitantes*) population; **~ activa** working population 2.(*ciudad*) city; (*ciudad pequeña*) town; (*pueblo*) village

poblado *m* (*pueblo*) village; (*colonia*) settlement

poblado, -a *adj* 1.(*habitado*) inhabited; (*con árboles*) wooded 2.(*cejas*) bushy; (*barba*) thick

poblador(a) *m(f)* settler

poblar <o→ue> I. *vi, vt* 1.(*colonizar*) to colonize 2.(*de plantas*) to plant; (*de peces*) to stock; **han poblado el monte de pinos** they have planted the hillside with pines

3. (*habitar*) to inhabit **II.** *vr:* ~**se** to fill; **la costa se pobló rápidamente** the coast quickly filled with people
pobre I. *adj* poor; ~ **de algo** poor in sth; **es una lengua ~ de expresiones** it is a language with few expressions; **¡~ de ti si dices mentiras!** you'll be sorry if you lie! **II.** *mf* poor person; (*mendigo*) beggar; **los pobres** the poor *pl*
pobreza *f* poverty
pocilga *f* pigsty
pocillo *m AmL* (*taza*) cup
pócima *f,* **poción** *f* potion
poco I. *m* **1.** (*cantidad*) **un ~ de azúcar** a little sugar; **acepta el ~ de dinero que te puedo dar** accept what little money I can give you; **espera un ~** wait a little **2.** *pl* few; **es un envidioso como hay ~s** there are few people who are as jealous as him **II.** *adv* little; ~ **a ~** bit by bit; **dentro de ~** soon; **desde hace ~** since recently; ~ **después** shortly afterwards; **hace ~** recently, not long ago; ~ **a ~ dejamos de creerle** we gradually stopped believing him; **es ~ simpático** he is not very friendly; **nos da ~ más o menos lo mismo** it really doesn't make much difference to us; **a ~ de llegar...** shortly after arriving ...; **por ~ me estrello** I very nearly crashed; **y por si fuera ~...** and as if that wasn't enough ...
poco, -a <poquísimo> *adj* little; ~**s** few; **aquí hay poca comida para dos personas** there's not much food here for two people; **tiene pocas probabilidades de aprobar** he has little chance of passing
podar *vt* to prune
poder I. *irr vi* (*ser capaz*) to be able to; **puedo/puedes** (*en general*) I/you can; **a ~ ser** if possible; **no puede ser** it is impossible; **no puedes cogerlo sin permiso** you can't take it witout permission; **yo a ti te puedo** *inf* I'm stronger than you; **¡bien pod(r)ías habérmelo dicho!** you could have told me!; **bien puede haber aquí un millón de abejas** there could easily be a million bees here; **no puedo verlo todo el día sin hacer nada** I can't stand seeing him do nothing all day long; **no puedo con mi madre** I can't cope with my mother; **no ~ con el alma** to be completely exhausted; **de ~ ser, no dudes que lo hará** if it is at all possible, have no doubt that he/she will do it **II.** *irr vimpers* **puede** (**ser**) **que después vuelva** he/she may come back afterwards; **¡puede!** maybe!; **¿se puede?** may I (come in)? **III.** *m* power; ~ **adquisitivo** buying power; **el partido en el ~** the party in power; **subir al ~** to achieve power; **haré todo lo que está en mi ~** I will do everything in my power
poderoso, -a *adj* powerful
podio *m* podium
podólogo, -a *m, f* podiatrist, chiropodist
podrido, -a *adj* rotten
podrir *irr vt, vr v.* **pudrir**
poema *m* poem
poesía *f* **1.** (*género*) poetry **2.** (*poema*) poem; **libro de ~s** poetry book
poeta, -isa *m, f* poet *mf,* poetess *f*
poético, -a *adj* poetic
poetisa *f v.* **poeta**
póker *m sin pl* poker
polaco, -a I. *adj* Polish **II.** *m, f* (*persona*) Pole; (*idioma*) Polish
polar *adj* polar; **la estrella ~** Polaris, Pole Star
polaridad *f* polarity
polea *f* pulley; (*roldana*)
polémica *f* controversy, polemic
polémico, -a *adj* polemical
polen *m* pollen; **tengo alergia al ~** I have hay fever
policía¹ *f* police; **agente de ~** police officer; **comisaría de ~** police station
policía² *mf* policeman *m,* policewoman *f;* **perro ~** police dog
policiaco, -a *adj,* **policíaco, -a** *adj* police; **película/novela policíaca** detective film/novel
polideportivo *m* sports centre
poliéster *m* polyester

P
p

polietileno *m* polythene *Brit,* polyethylene *Am*

poligamia *f sin pl* polygamy

polígono *m* **1.** MAT polygon **2.** (*terreno*) ~ **industrial** industrial estate

polilla *f* moth

polio *f inv* polio, poliomyelitis

politécnico, -a *adj, m, f* (**centro**) ~ polytechnic

política *f* politics; ~ **interior/exterior** domestic/foreign policy

político, -a I. *adj* **1.** POL political **2.** (*parentesco*) in-law; **hermana política** sister-in-law II. *m, f* politician

póliza *f* **1.** JUR policy; **hacerse una ~ de seguros** to have taken out an insurance policy **2.** (*sello*) stamp

polizón *mf* stowaway

pollera *f AmL* (*falda*) skirt

pollería *f* poultry shop

pollo *m* **1.** GASTR chicken **2.** (*cría*) young; (*de gallina*) chick **3.** (*joven*) kid *inf*

polo *m* **1.** GEO, FÍS, ASTR pole; ~ **norte** North Pole **2.** DEP polo **3.** (*camiseta*) polo neck **4.** (*helado*) ice lolly

Polonia *f* Poland

poltrona *f* easy chair, recliner

polución *f* pollution

polvera *f* powder compact

polvo *m* **1.** (*suciedad*) dust; **quitar el ~** to dust; **hacer algo ~** to smash sth; **hacer ~ a alguien** to annihilate sb; **estoy hecho ~** *inf* I'm exhausted **2.** (*sustancia*) powder; **levadura en ~** powdered yeast **3.** *vulg* (*coito*) screw; **echar un ~** to screw **4.** *pl* (*cosmética*) powder

pólvora *f* gunpowder

polvoriento, -a *adj* dusty

pomada *f* ointment

pomelo *m* grapefruit

pómez *f* pumice

pomo *m* handle

pompa *f* **1.** (*burbuja*) bubble **2.** (*esplendor*) pomp

pomposo, -a *adj* magnificent; (*estilo*) pompous

pómulo *m* cheekbone

ponche *m* punch

poncho *m* poncho

ponderar *vt* **1.** (*sopesar*) to weigh up **2.** (*encomiar*) to praise

poner *irr* I. *vt* **1.** (*colocar, exponer*) to put, pegar, to stick on; (*inyección*) to give; (*huevos*) to lay; **lo pongo en tus manos** *fig* I leave it in your hands; ~ **la mesa** to lay the table; ~ **algo a disposición de alguien** to make sth available to sb; ~ **la ropa a secar al sol** to put the clothes out to dry in the sun; ~ **la leche al fuego** to put the milk on the stove; ~ **en peligro** to endanger **2.** (*encender*) to switch on; ~ **en marcha** to start; **pon el despertador para las cuatro** set the alarm for four o'clock **3.** (*convertir*) to make; ~ **de buen/mal humor a alguien** to put sb in a good/bad mood **4.** (*suponer*) to assume; **pon que no viene** let's assume he doesn't come; **pongamos el caso que no llegue a tiempo** let's consider what happens if she doesn't arrive on time **5.** (*contribuir*) to put in; (*juego*) to bet; **¿cuánto has puesto tú en el fondo común?** how much have you put into the kitty?; **pusimos todo de nuestra parte** we did all that we could **6.** (*una expresión*) to take on; ~ **mala cara** to look angry **7.** (*denominar*) to give; **le pusieron por** [*o* **de**] **nombre Manolo** they called him Manolo; **¿qué nombre le van a ~?** what are they going to call him/her? **8.** (*espectáculo*) to put on; ~ **en escena** to stage; **¿qué ponen hoy en el cine?** what's on at the cinema today? **9.** (*imponer*) to impose; **nos han puesto muchos deberes** they have given us a lot of homework **10.** (*instalar*) to install *Brit,* to instal *Am* **11.** (*añadir*) to add **12.** (*escribir*) to write; ~ **un anuncio** to place an advertisement; ~ **entre comillas** to put in inverted commas; ~ **la firma** to sign; ~ **por escrito** to put in writing **13.** (*estar escrito*) to say **14.** (*vestido, zapato*) to put on **15.** (*teléfono*) to put through II. *vr:* ~**se 1.** (*vestido, zapato*) to put on; **ponte guapo** make yourself look nice **2.** ASTR to set; **el sol se pone por el oeste** the sun sets in the west **3.** (*mancharse*) **se pusieron perdidos de barro** they got mud all over themselves **4.** (*comenzar*) to begin; **por la tarde se puso a llover** in the evening it started to rain **5.** (+ *adj o adv*) to become; **~se chulo** to become rude; **ponte cómodo** make yourself comfortable

poniente *m* west

pontevedrés, -esa *adj* of/from Pontevedra

pontífice *m* pontiff

ponzoña *f* poison

pop *adj, m inv* pop

popa *f* stern

popular *adj* **1.** (*del pueblo*) folk; **aire ~** folk song **2.** (*conocido*) well--known; (*admirado*) popular

popularidad *f* popularity

por *prep* **1.** (*lugar: a través de*) through; (*vía*) via; (*en*) in; **~ aquí** near here; **~ dentro/fuera** inside/ outside; **pasé ~ Madrid hace poco** I passed through Madrid recently; **adelantar ~ la izquierda** to overtake on the left; **volar ~ encima de los Alpes** to fly over the Alps; **ese pueblo está ~ Castilla** that town is in Castile; **la cogió ~ la cintura** he grasped her waist **2.** (*tiempo*) in; **~ la(s) mañana(s)** in the morning; **mañana ~ la mañana** tomorrow morning; **~ la tarde** in the evening; **ayer ~ la noche** last night; **~ fin** finally **3.** (*a cambio de*) for; (*en lugar de*) instead of; (*sustituyendo a alguien*) in place of; **cambié el libro ~ el álbum** I exchanged the book for the album **4.** (*agente*) by; **una novela ~ Dickens** a novel by Dickens **5.** MAT (*multiplicación*) by **6.** (*reparto*) per; **toca a cuatro ~ cabeza** it comes out at four each; **el ocho ~ ciento** eight per cent **7.** (*finalidad*) for **8.** (*causa*) because of; (*en cuanto a*) regarding; **lo merece ~ los esfuerzos que ha hecho** he/she deserves it for all his/her effort; **lo hago ~ ti** I'm doing it for you; **~**

consiguiente consequently; **~ eso, ~** (**lo**) **tanto** therefore, because of that; **~ lo que a eso se refiere** as far as that is concerned; **~ mí que se vayan** as far as I'm concerned, they can go **9.** (*preferencia*) in favour *Brit,* in favor *Am;* **estoy ~ comprarlo** I think we should buy it; **estar loco ~ alguien** to be crazy about sb **10.** (*dirección*) **voy** (**a**) **~ tabaco** I'm going to get some cigarettes **11.** (*pendiente*) **este pantalón está ~ lavar** these trousers need to be washed **12.** (*aunque*) however; **~ muy cansado que esté no lo dejará a medias** however tired he is, he won't leave it unfinished **13.** (*medio*) by means of; (*alguien*) through; **poner ~ escrito** to put in writing; **al ~ mayor** wholesale **14.** (*interrogativo*) **¿~** (**qué**)? why? **15.** **~ si acaso** just in case **16.** (*casi*) **~ poco** almost; **~ poco me ahogo** I nearly drowned

porcelana *f* porcelain

porcentaje *m* percentage

porción *f* portion

pordiosero, -a *m, f* beggar

porfía *f* persistence

porfiar < *1. pres:* porfío> *vi* **1.** (*insistir*) **~ en algo** to insist on sth **2.** (*disputar*) to quarrel

pormenor *m* detail

porno *adj, m inf* porn

pornografía *f* pornography

poro *m* pore

poroso, -a *adj* porous

porque *conj* **1.** (*causal*) because; **lo hizo ~ sí** he/she did it because he/ she wanted to **2.** + *subj* (*final*) so that; **recemos ~ llueva** let us pray that it rains

porqué *m* reason

porquería *f inf* **1.** (*suciedad*) filth **2.** (*comida*) pigswill **3.** (*cacharro*) piece of junk **4.** (*pequeñez*) trifle

porra *f* **1.** (*bastón*) truncheon **2.** *inf* (*expresión*) **¡vete a la ~!** *inf* go to hell!; **¡~(s)!** *inf* damn!

porrazo *m* blow

porro *m* **1.** *inf* (*canuto*) joint, spliff *Brit* **2.** (*puerro*) leek

porrón *m* bottle with a long spout

portaaviones *m inv* aircraft carrier

portada *f* **1.** (*fachada*) front **2.** TIPO title page; PREN cover

portador(a) *m(f)* **1.** (*de gérmenes*) carrier **2.** COM bearer

portaequipaje(s) *m* (*inv*) **1.** (*maletero*) boot *Brit*, trunk *Am* **2.** (*baca, en tren*) luggage rack

portafolios *m inv* briefcase

portal *m* hall; (*soportal*) arcade

portamaletas *m inv* boot *Brit*, trunk *Am*

portarse *vr* to behave; ~ **bien con alguien** to treat sb well; ~ **como un hombre** to act like a man

portátil *adj* portable; **ordenador** ~ laptop

portavoz *mf* spokesperson, spokesman *m*, spokeswoman *f*

portazo *m* slam; **dar un** ~ to slam the door; **dar a alguien un** ~ **en las narices** *inf* to slam the door in sb's face

porte *m* **1.** (*transporte*) transport; (*gastos*) transport costs *pl*, shipping; ~ **aéreo** air freight; **gastos de** ~ transport costs **2.** (*correo*) postage

portento *m* marvel

portentoso, -a *adj* marvellous *Brit*, marvelous *Am*

porteño, -a *adj* of/from Buenos Aires

portería *f* **1.** caretaker's office *Brit*, superintendent's office *Am* **2.** DEP goal

portero, -a *m, f* **1.** (*conserje*) caretaker *Brit*, superintendent *Am;* (*de la entrada*) doorman; ~ **automático** entryphone **2.** DEP (*fútbol*) goalkeeper, goaltender

pórtico *m* (*porche*) porch; (*galería*) arcade

portilla *f* porthole

portillo *m* gap; (*postigo*) gate

portorriqueño, -a *adj, m, f* Puerto Rican

Portugal *m* Portugal

portugués, -esa *adj, m, f* Portuguese

porvenir *m* future

pos *adv* **ir en** ~ **de algo/alguien** to pursue sth/sb; **van en** ~ **del éxito** they are striving for success

posada *f* **1.** (*parador, fonda*) inn; (*pensión*) guest house **2.** (*hospedaje*) **dar** ~ **a alguien** to give sb lodging

posaderas *fpl inf* bottom, backside

posar **I.** *vi* to pose **II.** *vt* to place **III.** *vr:* ~**se** to settle; **el gorrión se posó en la rama** the sparrow alighted on the branch

posdata *f* postscript

pose *f* pose

poseedor(a) *m(f)* owner; (*póliza, acciones*) holder

poseer *irr como leer vt* to possess, to have; ~ **una importante posición social** to occupy an important position in society

poseído, -a *adj* possessed; ~ **de odio** full of hatred

posesión *f* possession

posesivo, -a *adj* possessive

posibilidad *f* possibility; **tener grandes** ~**es de éxito** to have a good chance of success

posibilitar *vt* to make possible

posible *adj* possible; **lo antes** ~ as soon as possible; **en lo** ~ as far as possible; **hacer lo** ~ **para que** +*subj* to do everything possible so that; **hacer todo lo** ~ to do everything one can; **es muy** ~ **que** +*subj* it is very likely that; **es** ~ **que** +*subj* it is possible that; **es muy** ~ **que lleguen tarde** they may very well arrive late; **¡no es** ~! I can't believe it!; **¿será** ~? surely not!; **si es** ~ if possible; **no lo veo** ~ I don't think it's possible

posición *f* position; **en buena** ~ in a good position

positivo, -a *adj* positive

poso *m* sediment

posponer *irr como poner vt* to postpone

postal **I.** *adj* postal, mail *Am* **II.** *f* postcard

poste *m* post; ELEC pylon

póster *m* poster

postergar <g→gu> *vt* to postpone; (*demorar*) to delay; ~ **la fecha** to put back the date

posteridad *f* posterity; **pasar a la** ~ to be remembered by posterity

posterior *adj* **1.** (*de tiempo*) later; ~ **a** after **2.** (*de lugar*) back; ~ **a alguien** behind sb; **la parte** ~ **la** the back

posterioridad *f* posteriority; **con** ~ subsequently

postizo *m* hairpiece

postizo, -a *adj* artificial; **dentadura postiza** false teeth

postor(a) *m(f)* bidder; **mejor** ~ highest bidder

postrado, -a *adj* prostrate; ~ **de dolor** (*físico*) in great pain; (*pena*) beside oneself with grief

postre *m* dessert

postrero, -a *adj* last

postulado *m* proposition

póstumo, -a *adj* posthumous

postura *f* **1.** (*colocación*) position; (*del cuerpo*) posture **2.** (*actitud*) attitude

potable *adj* drinkable; **agua** ~ drinking water

potaje *m* (*sopa*) soup; (*guiso*) stew

pote *m* pot

potencia *f* power

potencial *adj*, *m* potential

potente *adj* powerful; (*sexualidad*) potent

potro *m* **1.** ZOOL colt **2.** DEP vaulting horse

pozo *m* **1.** (*manantial*) well **2.** (*hoyo*) shaft; ~ **petrolífero** oil well

práctica *f* practice; (*experiencia*) experience; **en la** ~ in practice; **adquirir** ~ to gain experience; **llevar a la** ~ to carry out; **perder la** ~ to get out of practice; **poner en** ~ to put into practice

practicable *adj* **1.** (*realizable*) feasible **2.** (*camino, calle*) passable

practicar <c→qu> *vi, vt* to practise *Brit,* to practice *Am*; ~ **deporte** to do sports; ~ **una operación** to perform an operation; **estudió medicina, pero no practica** he/she studied medicine, but he/she doesn't work as a doctor

práctico, -a *adj* practical

pradera *f* grassland; (*Norteamérica*) prairie; (*prado*) meadow

prado *m* meadow

Praga *f* Prague

pragmático, -a *adj* pragmatic

preámbulo *m* introduction, preamble; **sin** ~s *fig* without further ado; **no andarse con** ~s not to beat about the bush; **¡déjese de** ~s! get to the point!

precalentar <e→ie> I. *vt* to preheat II. *vr:* ~se DEP to warm up

precario, -a *adj* precarious

precaución *f* precaution

precaver I. *vt* (*prevenir*) to prevent; (*evitar*) to avoid II. *vr* ~se **de algo/ alguien** to take precautions against sth/sb

precavido, -a *adj* cautious

precedencia *f* precedence

precedente I. *adj* preceding II. *m* precedent; **sentar un** ~ to establish a precedent; **sin** ~s unprecedented

preceder *vt* to precede

precepto *m* precept

preciado, -a *adj* prized

preciarse *vr* ~ **de algo** to boast about sth

precintar *vt* to seal

precinto *m* seal

precio *m* price; **a buen** ~ for a good price; ~ **al consumidor** [o **al detalle**] retail price, retail price; **a mitad de** ~ at half price; **a** ~ **de oro** for a very high price; **no tener** ~ *fig* to be priceless; **de todos los** ~s at all prices; **¿qué** ~ **tiene el libro?** how much does this book cost?

preciosidad *f* **ser una** ~ to be lovely

precioso, -a *adj* **1.** (*valioso*) valuable **2.** (*hermoso*) lovely

precipicio *m* precipice

precipitación *f* **1.** (*prisa*) haste; **con** ~ hastily **2.** METEO rainfall

precipitado, -a *adj* hasty

precipitar I. *vt* **1.** (*arrojar*) to throw down; **lo** ~**on por la ventana** they threw him out of the window **2.** (*apresurar*) to hasten; (*acelerar*) to hurry II. *vr:* ~se **1.** (*arrojarse*) to throw oneself down **2.** (*atacar*) ~se **sobre algo/alguien** to hurl oneself

P
p

at sth/sb **3.**(*acontecimientos*) to happen very quickly; (*personas*) to act hastily; **¡no se precipite!** don't be hasty!

precisamente *adv* exactly; **¿tiene que ser ~ hoy?** does it have to be today, of all days?; **~ por eso** for that very reason

precisar *vt* **1.**(*determinar*) to specify **2.**(*necesitar*) to need

precisión *f* precision

preciso, -a *adj* **1.**(*necesario*) necessary; **es ~ que** +*subj* it is necessary to; **es ~ que nos veamos** we need to see each other; **si es ~...** if necessary ... **2.**(*exacto*) precise; **a la hora precisa** punctually

preconcebido, -a *adj* preconceived

precoz *adj* (*persona*) precocious; (*diagnóstico, cosecha*) early

precursor(a) *m(f)* precursor

predecesor(a) *m(f)* predecessor

predecir *irr como decir vt* to predict; (*tiempo*) to forecast

predestinado, -a *adj* predestined; **estar ~ al crimen** to be destined for a life of crime

predeterminar *vt* to predetermine

predicado *m* predicate

predicador(a) *m(f)* preacher

predicar <c→qu> *vt* to preach

predicción *f* prediction; **~ económica** economic forecast

predilecto, -a *adj* favourite *Brit,* favorite *Am*

predisponer *irr como poner vt* to predispose; **~ a alguien a favor/en contra de alguien** to bias sb in favour of/against sb

predisposición *f* predisposition; (*tendencia*) tendency; **tener ~ a engordar** to have a tendency to put on weight

predominar *vi, vt* to predominate; (*sobresalir*) to stand out; **~ en algo/sobre alguien** to stand out at sth/over sb

predominio *m* predominance; **~ sobre alguien** superiority over sb

preescolar *adj* pre-school; **edad ~** pre-school age

prefabricado, -a *adj* prefabricated

prefacio *m* preface

preferencia *f* **1.**(*elección, trato*) preference; **mostrar ~ por alguien** to show a preference for sb **2.**(*predilección*) predilection; **sentir ~ por alguien** to be biased in favour of sb **3.**(*prioridad*) priority; **de ~** preferably; **~ de paso** right of way; **dar ~** to give preference; **tener ~ ante alguien** to have priority over sb

preferible *adj* preferable; **sería ~ que lo hicieras** it would be better if you did it

preferir *irr como sentir vt* to prefer; **prefiero ir a pie** I prefer to walk; **prefiero que no venga** I would rather he/she didn't come

prefijo *m* **1.**LING prefix **2.**TEL (dialling) code *Brit,* area code *Am*

pregonar *vt* to proclaim; (*lo que estaba oculto*) to make public

pregunta *f* question; **a tal ~ tal respuesta** ask a silly question, get a silly answer

preguntar **I.** *vi, vt* to ask; **~ por alguien** to ask after sb **II.** *vr* **~se si/cuándo/qué...** to wonder if/when/what ...

preguntón, -ona *adj* inquisitive, nosy *pej*

prehistórico, -a *adj* prehistoric

prejuicio *m* prejudice

preliminar *adj* preliminary

preludio *m* prelude

premamá *adj inv* **vestido ~** maternity dress

prematuro, -a *adj* premature

premeditación *f* premeditation; **con ~** premeditated

premeditar *vt* **1.**(*pensar*) to think about **2.**(*planear*) to plan; JUR to premeditate

premiar *vt* **1.**(*recompensar*) to reward **2.**(*dar un premio*) to give a prize to

premio *m* **1.**(*galardón, lotería*) prize; **el ~ gordo** the jackpot **2.**(*recompensa*) reward **3.**(*remuneración*) bonus

premisa *f* premise

premonición *f* premonition

premura *f* (*urgencia*) urgency;

(*prisa*) haste

prenatal *adj* prenatal

prenda *f* 1. (*fianza*) guarantee; **en ~** as security; **no soltar ~** *fig, inf* not to say a word 2. (*pieza de ropa*) garment; **~s interiores** underwear

prendar *vt* to captivate

prendedor *m* brooch, pin

prender I. *vi* to take root II. *vt* 1. (*sujetar*) to hold down; (*con alfileres*) to pin 2. (*detener*) to catch 3. (*fuego*) **el coche prendió fuego** the car caught fire 4. *AmL* (*luz*) to turn on

prensa *f* 1. (*máquina*) press; **~ de uvas** wine press 2. (*imprenta*) printer's, press; **estar en ~** to be at the printer's 3. PREN press; **~ amarilla** tabloids *pl;* **libertad de ~** freedom of the press; **tener buena/mala ~** to get a good/bad press

prensar *vt* to press

preñado, -a *adj* 1. BIO pregnant 2. (*lleno*) full; **~ de emoción** full of emotion

preocupación *f* worry; (*obsesión*) concern; **~ por algo/alguien** worry about sth/sb; **tu única ~ es el dinero** the only thing you care about is money

preocupado, -a *adj* worried; **~ por algo/alguien** worried about sth/sb

preocupar I. *vt* to worry II. *vr:* **~se** 1. (*inquietarse*) **~se por algo/alguien** to worry about sth/sb 2. (*encargarse*) to take care; **no se preocupa de arreglar el asunto** he/she doesn't do anything to solve the problem

preparación *f* preparation; (*formación*) training; **~ académica** education; **~ de datos** INFOR data processing

preparado *m* preparation

preparado, -a *adj* (*listo*) ready; **~ (para funcionar)** ready for use; **¡~s, listos, ya!** ready, steady, go!

preparar I. *vt* to prepare; ENS to train; **~ un buque para zarpar** to get a boat ready for a journey; **~ datos** INFOR to process data; **~ las maletas** to pack one's bags II. *vr:* **~se** to get

ready; **~se para un examen** to prepare for an exam; **se prepara una tormenta** there's a storm brewing; **me preparaba a salir, cuando empezó a llover** I was getting ready to leave when it started raining

preparativo *m* preparation

preparativo, -a *adj* preparatory

preposición *f* preposition

prepotente *adj* arrogant

prerrogativa *f* prerogative

presa *f* 1. (*acción*) capture; **ave de ~** bird of prey 2. (*objeto, de caza*) prey; **animal de ~** prey 3. (*dique*) dam

presagiar *vt* tp predict; **estas nubes presagian tormenta** these clouds mean there will be a storm

presagio *m* 1. (*señal*) warning sign 2. (*presentimiento*) premonition

prescindir *vi* **~ de algo/alguien** (*renunciar a*) to do without sth/sb; (*pasar por alto*) to overlook sth/sb; (*no contar*) to disregard sth/sb; **tenemos que ~ del coche** we will have to get rid of the car; **han prescindido de mi opinión** they have ignored my opinion

prescribir *irr como escribir vt* to prescribe

prescripción *f* prescription

presencia *f* 1. (*asistencia, existencia*) presence; **sin la ~ del ministro** without the minister being present 2. (*aspecto*) appearance; **buena ~** stylish appearance

presencial *adj* **testigo ~** eyewitness

presenciar *vt* 1. (*ver*) to witness 2. (*asistir*) to attend

presentación *f* presentation; (*de personas*) introduction; **el plazo de ~ de solicitudes finaliza hoy** the period for presenting requests ends today

presentador(a) *m(f)* presenter; (*de telediario*) newsreader

presentar I. *vt* 1. (*en general*) to present; (*mostrar*) to show 2. (*instancia, dimisión, trabajo*) to submit 3. (*argumentos*) to put forward 4. (*persona*) to introduce; **te presento a mi marido** may I introduce

you to my husband? **II.** *vr:* **~se**
1. (*comparecer*) to present oneself;
(*aparecer*) to turn up **2.** (*participar*)
~se a una elección to stand in an
election; **~se a un concurso** to
enter a competition

presente¹ I. *adj* present; **la ~ edi-**
ción this edition; **hay que tener ~**
las circunstancias one must consider the circumstances; **ten ~ lo**
que te he dicho bear in mind what
I have told you; **por la ~ deseo co-**
municarle que... I write in order to
tell you that ... **II.** *mf* **los/las ~s**
those present

presente² *m* **1.** (*actualidad*) present;
hasta el ~ until now; **por el ~** for
the moment **2.** LING present (tense)
3. (*regalo*) present, gift

presentimiento *m* premonition;
tengo el ~ de que... I have a feeling that ...

presentir *irr como sentir vt* to have a
premonition of; **presiento que**
mañana lloverá I have a feeling it's
going to rain tomorrow

preservación *f* preservation

preservar *vt* to protect

preservativo *m* condom

presidencia *f* presidency

presidente *mf* **1.** POL president; **el ~**
del gobierno español the Spanish
Prime Minister **2.** (*de asociación*)
chairperson

presidiario, -a *m, f* convict

presidio *m* prison; **condenar a 20**
años de ~ to sentence to 20 years in
prison

presidir *vt* **1.** (*ocupar presidencia*)
to be president of **2.** (*reunión*) to
chair

presión *f* pressure; **~ arterial** blood
pressure

presionar *vt* **1.** (*apretar*) to press
2. (*coaccionar*) to put pressure on

preso, -a *m, f* prisoner, (prison) inmate

prestación *f* **1.** (*de ayuda, servicio*)
provision **2.** (*subsidio*) **~ por des-**
empleo unemployment benefit

prestado, -a *adj* borrowed; **vivir de**
~ en casa de alguien to live off sb

else; **voy de ~, el traje me lo han**
dejado I'm wearing borrowed
finery, sb lent me the suit

prestamista *mf* moneylender

préstamo *m* **1.** (*acción*) lending
2. (*lo prestado*) loan; **~ hipotecario**
mortgage

prestar I. *vt* **1.** (*dejar*) to lend; **¿me**
prestas la bici, por favor? can I
borrow your bike?; **el banco me ha**
prestado el dinero I have borrowed money from the bank
2. (*dedicar*) **~ apoyo** to support; **~**
ayuda to help; **~ servicios** to provide services **3.** (*tener*) **~ atención**
to pay attention; **~ silencio** to remain silent **II.** *vr:* **~se 1.** (*ofrecerse*)
to offer oneself; **se prestó a ayu-**
darme he/she offered to help me
2. (*avenirse*) **~se a algo** to accept
sth

presteza *f* speed

prestigio *m* prestige

prestigioso, -a *adj* prestigious

presto *adv* (*rápidamente*) quickly; (*al*
instante) at once

presto, -a *adj* **1.** (*listo*) ready **2.** (*rápi-*
do) quick

presumido, -a *adj* (*arrogante*) arrogant; (*vanidoso*) vain

presumir I. *vi* **~ de algo** to boast
about sth **II.** *vt* to presume

presunción *f* **1.** (*sospecha*) assumption **2.** (*petulancia*) arrogance;
(*vanidad*) vanity

presunto, -a *adj* **1.** (*supuesto*) pre-
sumed; **el ~ asesino** the alleged
murderer **2.** (*equivocadamente*) so-
-called

presuntuoso, -a *adj* conceited

presuponer *irr como poner vt* to presuppose

presupuesto *m* **1.** POL, ECON budget
2. (*cálculo*) estimate **3.** (*suposición*)
assumption

presuroso, -a *adj* hurried; **iba ~ por**
la calle he hurried down the street

pretender *vt* **1.** (*aspirar a*) to aspire
to **2.** (*pedir*) to expect; **¿qué pre-**
tendes que haga? what do you
want me to do? **3. ~ hacer algo**
(*tener intención*) to mean to do sth;

(*intentar*) to try to do sth

pretendiente *m* (*de trabajo*) applicant; (*de mujer*) suitor

pretensión *f* 1. (*derecho*) claim 2. (*ambición*) ambition 3. *pl* (*desmedidas, vanidad*) pretensions *pl;* **tiene pretensiones de actor** he fancies himself as an actor

pretérito I. *adj* past II. *m* past (tense); ~ **indefinido** preterite (tense)

pretexto *m* pretext; **a ~ de...** on the pretext of ...

prevalecer *irr como crecer vi* to prevail; **en esta ciudad prevalecen los de derechas sobre los de izquierdas** in this city there are more right-wingers than left-wingers

prevención *f* 1. (*precaución*) precaution 2. (*acción*) prevention; ~ **del cáncer** cancer prevention

prevenido, -a *adj* 1. *estar* (*alerta*) **estar** ~ to be prepared 2. *ser* (*previsor*) prudent

prevenir *irr como venir* I. *vt* 1. (*protegerse de, evitar*) to prevent; **más vale ~ que curar** *prov* prevention is better than cure, a stitch in time saves nine *prov* 2. (*advertir*) to warn 3. (*preparar*) to prepare II. *vr:* ~**se** 1. (*tomar precauciones*) to take precautions 2. (*contra alguien*) to protect oneself 3. (*prepararse*) to get ready

preventivo, -a *adj* preventive

prever *irr como ver vt* to foresee; (*esperar*) to expect

previo, -a *adj* previous; (*sin*) ~ **aviso** (without) prior warning; **previa presentación del D.N.I.** on presentation of identity documents

previsión *f* 1. (*de prever*) prediction 2. (*precaución*) precaution; **en ~ de...** as a precaution against ... 3. (*cálculo*) forecast

previsor(a) *adj* 1. (*con visión*) far-sighted 2. (*precavido*) prudent

previsto, -a *adj* predicted; **el éxito estaba** ~ the success had been expected; **todo lo necesario está** ~ everything necessary has been prepared

prima *f* 1. (*pariente*) cousin; ~ **hermana** first cousin 2. FIN bonus; (*seguro*) insurance premium

primacía *f* 1. (*supremacía*) supremacy 2. (*prioridad*) priority

primario, -a *adj* primary; **enseñanza primaria** primary education; **necesidades primarias** basic necessities

primavera *f* spring

primer *adj v.* **primero, -a**

primera *f* 1. AUTO first (gear); **ir en** ~ to be in first (gear) 2. FERRO, AERO first class; **viajar en** ~ to travel first class

primero *adv* 1. (*en primer lugar*) first 2. (*antes*) rather

primero, -a I. *adj ante sustantivo masculino: primer* first; **de primera calidad** top quality; **de primera** first-rate; **a primera hora** (*de la mañana*) first thing (in the morning); **en primer lugar** in the first place; **a ~s de mes** at the beginning of the month; **el Primer Ministro** the Prime Minister; **desde un primer momento** from the outset; **ocupar una de las primeras posiciones** to occupy one of the top positions; **lo hice a la** ~ I did it at the first attempt; **lo ~ es lo** ~ first things first; **para mí tú eres lo** ~ for me you are more important than anything else; **lo ~ es ahora la familia** the most important thing now is the family II. *m, f* first; **el ~ de la carrera** the winner of the race; **el ~ de la clase** the top of the class; **eres el ~ en llegar** you are the first to arrive

> ⚠ **primero** is always used after a masculine noun or on its own as a pronoun: "Voy al piso primero; Su teléfono móvil es el primero de la estantería." In contrast **primer** is always used before a masculine singular noun: "Hoy es el primer día de mis vacaciones."

primicia *f* 1. PREN, TV, RADIO scoop 2. *pl* (*frutos*) **las ~s** the first fruits

primitivo, -a *adj* primitive

primo *m* **1.** (*pariente*) cousin; **~ hermano** first cousin **2.** *inf* (*ingenuo*) mug; **he hecho el ~:** he pagado 100 euros por esto I've been taken for a ride: I paid 100 euros for this; **¡no seas ~!** don't be such a fool!

primo, -a *adj* **1.** (*primero*) **materia prima** raw material **2.** MAT **número ~** prime number

primogénito, -a *adj, m, f* first-born

primor *m* **1.** (*habilidad*) skill **2.** (*esmero*) care; **hacer algo con ~** to take great care in doing sth

primordial *adj* essential, fundamental

primoroso, -a *adj* **1.** (*hábil*) skilful *Brit*, skillful *Am* **2.** (*con esmero*) exquisite

princesa *f v.* **príncipe**

principal **I.** *adj* main, principal; **su carrera profesional era lo ~ para él** his career was his main priority **II.** *mf* (*propietario*) owner; (*jefe*) boss

príncipe, princesa *m, f* prince *m,* princess *f;* **~ azul** Prince Charming; **~ heredero** crown prince

principiante *mf* beginner, novice

principio *m* **1.** (*comienzo*) beginning; **al ~** at the beginning; **ya desde el ~** right from the beginning; **desde un ~** from the first; **a ~s de diciembre** at the beginning of December; **dar ~ a algo** to start sth **2.** (*causa*) cause; (*origen*) origin **3.** (*de ética*) *t.* FÍS principle; **en ~** in principle; **por ~** on principle

pringar <g→gu> **I.** *vt* **1.** (*manchar*) **~ algo de** [*o* con] **algo** to smear sth with sth **2.** (*mojar*) to dip **II.** *vr* **~se de** [*o* con] **algo** to cover oneself with sth

pringoso, -a *adj* **1.** (*grasiento*) greasy **2.** (*pegajoso*) sticky

pringue *m* **1.** (*grasa*) grease **2.** (*suciedad*) grime

prioridad *f* priority; AUTO right of way

prisa *f* hurry; **de ~** quickly; **de ~ y corriendo** quickly; (*con demasiada prisa*) in a rush; **meter ~ a alguien**

to hurry sb; **no corre ~** there's no hurry; **¡date ~!** hurry up!; **tengo ~** I'm in a hurry; **no tengas ~** take your time

prisión *f* **1.** (*reclusión*) imprisonment **2.** (*edificio*) prison

prisionero, -a *m, f* prisoner

prismáticos *mpl* binoculars *pl*

privación *f* **1.** (*desposesión*) deprivation; **~ de libertad** loss of liberty **2.** (*carencia*) privation

privado, -a *adj* private; (*sesión*) closed; **en ~** in private, privately

privar **I.** *vt* **1.** (*desposeer*) to deprive; **~ a alguien de libertad** to deprive sb of his freedom; **~ a alguien del permiso de conducir** to take away sb's driving licence **2.** (*prohibir*) **~ a alguien de hacer algo** to forbid sb to do sth; **no me prives de visitarte** don't stop me from visiting you **II.** *vr* **~se de algo** to deny oneself sth; **no se privan de nada** they don't want for anything

privativo, -a *adj* **~** (*de alguien*) exclusive to sb; **esta facultad es privativa del presidente** that power belongs exclusively to the president

privatizar <z→c> *vt* to privatize

privilegiado, -a **I.** *adj* privileged; (*memoria*) exceptional **II.** *m, f* privileged person

privilegiar *vt* to grant a privilege to

privilegio *m* privilege

pro **I.** *m o f* **1.** (*provecho*) advantage; **valorar los ~s y los contras** to weigh up the pros and cons **2.** (*favor*) **en ~ de** for **II.** *prep* for

proa *f* NÁUT bow; AERO nose

probabilidad *f* **1.** (*verosimilitud*) probability; **con toda ~** in all likelihood **2.** (*posibilidad*) prospect; **hay ~es de rescatar los rehenes** there is a good chance of rescuing the hostages

probable *adj* likely, probable; **lo más ~ es que...** +*subj* chances are that ...

probador *m* fitting room

probar <o→ue> **I.** *vt* **1.** (*demostrar*) to prove; **todavía no está probado que sea culpable** it still hasn't been proved that he is guilty **2.** (*experimentar*) to try; (*aparato*) to test **3.** (*vestido*) to try on **4.** GASTR to taste; **no he probado nunca una paella** I have never tried paella **II.** *vi* (*intentar*) to try

probeta *f* test tube

problema *m* problem

procedencia *f* origin; **anunciar la ~ del tren** to announce where the train has come from

procedente *adj* **1.** (*oportuno*) appropriate **2.** (*que viene de*) **~ de** from

proceder I. *m* behaviour *Brit,* behavior *Am* **II.** *vi* **1.** (*de un lugar*) to come; (*familia*) to descend **2.** (*actuar*) to act **3.** (*ser oportuno*) to be appropriate; **ahora procede guardar silencio** now we should remain silent **4.** (*pasar a*) to proceed

procedimiento *m* **1.** (*actuación*) procedure; JUR proceedings *pl* **2.** (*método*) method

procesado, -a *m, f* **el ~** the accused

procesador *m* processor *Brit,* computer *Am; ~* **de textos** word processor

procesar *vt* **1.** JUR to prosecute; **le procesan por violación** he is being prosecuted for rape **2.** TÉC to process

procesión *f* procession

proceso *m* **1.** (*método*) process **2.** (*procedimiento*) procedure **3.** JUR trial

proclamar *vt* to announce; **~ la República** to proclaim a Republic

procrear *vt* to procreate

procurador(a) *m(f)* attorney

procurar *vt* **1.** (*intentar*) to try; **procura hacerlo lo mejor que puedas** do it to the best of your abilities; **procura que no te vean más por aquí** make sure you're not seen around here any more; **procura que no te oigan** make sure they don't hear you **2.** (*proporcionar*) to obtain

prodigar <g→gu> I. *vt* **1.** (*malgastar*) to waste **2.** (*dar*) to lavish **II.** *vr* **~se en elogios hacia alguien** to shower sb with praise; **se prodigó en toda clase de atenciones con nosotros** he attended to our every

need

prodigio *m* prodigy; **niño ~** child prodigy

prodigioso, -a *adj* marvellous *Brit,* marvelous *Am*

pródigo, -a *adj* **1.** (*malgastador*) wasteful; **el hijo ~** the prodigal son **2.** (*generoso*) generous; **la pródiga naturaleza** bountiful nature

producción *f* **1.** *t.* TÉC, CINE production **2.** (*productos*) output

producir *irr como* traducir I. *vt* to produce; (*intereses*) to yield; (*causar*) to cause **II.** *vr:* **~se** **1.** (*fabricarse*) to be produced **2.** (*tener lugar*) to take place; (*ocurrir*) to occur; **se ha producido una mejora** there has been an improvement; **cuando se produzca el caso...** as the case arises ...

productividad *f* productivity; (*de negocio*) profitability

productivo, -a *adj* productive; (*negocio*) profitable

producto *m* **1.** (*objeto, resultado*) *t.* QUÍM, MAT product; **~ alimenticio** food item; **~s alimenticios** foodstuffs *pl; ~***s químicos** chemicals *pl* **2.** (*de un negocio*) profit; (*de una venta*) proceeds *pl;* **Producto Interior/Nacional Bruto** Gross Domestic/National Product

productor(a) I. *adj* producing II. *m(f)* producer

proeza *f* exploit

profanar *vt* (*templo, cementerio*) to desecrate; (*memoria, nombre*) to profane

profano, -a *adj* **1.** (*secular, irreverente*) profane **2.** (*ignorante*) ignorant; **soy ~ en esta materia** I am not an expert in this subject

profecía *f* prophecy

proferir *irr como* sentir *vt* (*palabra, grito*) to utter; (*insulto*) to hurl; (*queja*) to express

profesar *vt* **1.** (*oficio*) to practise *Brit,* to practice *Am* **2.** (*declarar*) to profess

profesión *f* profession

profesional *adj* professional

profesor(a) *m(f)* teacher; UNIV lecturer; (*catedrático*) professor

profesorado *m* **1.**(*cargo*) teaching post; UNIV lectureship *Brit;* (*catedrático*) professorship *Am* **2.**(*conjunto*) teaching staff *Brit,* faculty *Am*

profeta, -isa *m,* *f* prophet *mf,* prophetess *f*

profetizar <z→c> *vt* to prophesy

prófugo *m* MIL deserter

prófugo, -a *m,* *f* JUR fugitive

profundidad *f* depth; **tener poca ~** to be not very deep; **una cueva de cinco metros de ~** a cave five metres deep

profundizar <z→c> *vi,* *vt* (*hoyo, zanja*) *~* (**en**) **algo** to study sth in depth

profundo, -a *adj* deep; (*pena*) heartfelt; (*pensamiento, misterio*) profound; (*conocimiento*) thorough; **en lo más ~ de mi corazón** from the very bottom of my heart

profusión *f* profusion; **con ~ de detalles** with a wealth of details

progenitor(a) *m(f)* father *m,* mother *f;* **los ~es** the parents

programa *m* programme *Brit,* program *Am;* **~ de las clases** timetable

programación *f* **1.**(*acción*) programming **2.**TV, RADIO programme *Brit,* program *Am*

programador(a) *m(f)* programmer

programar *vt* **1.**(*planear*) to plan; **la conferencia está programada para el domingo** the talk is scheduled for Sunday **2.**TÉC, INFOR to programme *Brit,* to program *Am*

progre *adj inf* trendy; POL left-wing

progresar *vi* to make progress; (*enfermedad, ciencia*) to develop

progresión *f* **1.**(*avance*) progress **2.**MAT, MÚS progression

progresista *adj* progressive

progresivo, -a *adj* progressive

progreso *m* progress

prohibición *f* prohibition

prohibir *irr vt* to prohibit, to ban; **prohibida la entrada** no entry; **prohibido fumar** no smoking; **en los hospitales prohiben fumar** in hospitals smoking is not allowed

prójimo *m* fellow man; **amor al ~** love of one's neighbour

proletariado *m* proletariat

proletario, -a *adj, m,* *f* proletarian

proliferación *f* proliferation; *t.* MED (*incontrolada*) spread

proliferar *vi* to proliferate; (*epidemia, rumor*) to spread

prolífico, -a *adj* prolific

prolijo, -a *adj* (*extenso*) protracted; (*cargante*) long-winded

prólogo *m* prologue

prolongación *f* extension

prolongado, -a *adj* long

prolongar <g→gu> I. *vt* to extend; (*decisión*) to postpone; (*estado*) to prolong II. *vr:* **~se** to continue; (*estado*) to be prolonged; (*reunión*) to overrun; **la fiesta se prolongó hasta bien entrada la noche** the party carried on well into the night; **las negociaciones se están prolongando demasiado** the negotiations are dragging on for too long

promedio *m* average

promesa *f* promise; **el jefe me ha dado su ~ de que...** the boss has promised me that ...

prometer I. *vt* to promise; **te prometo que lo haré** I promise you I'll do it II. *vr:* **~se** to get engaged

prometido, -a *m,* *f* fiancé *m,* fiancée *f*

prominente *adj* prominent

promiscuo, -a *adj* promiscuous

promoción *f* **1.**(*de empresa, categoría, producto*) promotion **2.**(*de licenciados*) year, graduating class

promocionar *vt* to promote

promontorio *m* promontory

promotor(a) *m(f)* **1.**(*de altercado*) instigator **2.**(*patrocinador*) sponsor; (*deportivo, de espectáculo*) promoter

promover <o→ue> *vt* **1.**(*querella, escándalo*) to cause **2.**(*en el cargo*) to promote **3.**(*altercado*) to instigate

promulgar <g→gu> *vt* to enact; (*divulgar*) to announce

pronombre *m* pronoun

pronosticar <c→qu> *vt* to forecast

pronóstico *m* forecast; MED prognosis; DEP prediction

pronto I. *adv* **1.** (*rápido*) quickly; (*enseguida*) at once; **de** ~ suddenly; **¡hasta** ~**!** see you! **2.** (*temprano*) early II. *conj* **tan** ~ **como** as soon as; **tan** ~ **como llegaron/lleguen** as soon as they arrived/arrive

pronto, -a *adj* quick

pronunciación *f* pronunciation

pronunciar *vt* to pronounce; ~ **un discurso** to make a speech; ~ **unas palabras** to say a few words; ~ **sentencia** to pass sentence

propagación *f* **1.** (*multiplicación, reproducción*) propagation **2.** (*extensión, transmisión*) spreading

propaganda *f* **1.** (*publicidad, promoción*) publicity; **hacer** ~ to advertise **2.** MIL, POL propaganda

propagar <g→gu> *vt, vr:* ~(**se**) **1.** (*multiplicar, reproducir*) to propagate **2.** (*extender, divulgar*) to spread

propano *m* propane

propasarse *vr* to go too far

propensión *f* ~ **a algo** tendency towards sth; MED predisposition to sth

propenso, -a *adj* ~ **a algo** inclined to sth; MED susceptible to sth

propiamente *adv* (*realmente*) really; (*exactamente*) exactly; ~ **dicho** strictly speaking

propicio, -a *adj* favourable *Brit,* favorable *Am;* **en el momento** ~ at the right moment

propiedad *f* **1.** (*en general*) property; ~ **industrial** patent rights; ~ **inmobiliaria** real assets *Brit,* real estate *Am;* **tener algo en** ~ to own sth **2.** (*corrección*) **con** ~ correctly

propietario, -a *m, f* owner; (*casero*) landlord

propina *f* tip; **dejar** ~ to leave a tip; **me dió dos libras de** ~ he/she gave me a two pound tip

propio, -a *adj* **1.** (*de uno mismo*) own; **en defensa propia** in self-defence *Brit,* in self-defense *Am;* **con la propia mano** with one's own hand; **tengo piso** ~ I own my flat **2.** (*mismo*) same; **lo** ~ the same; **el** ~ **jefe** the boss himself; **nombre** ~ proper noun; **al** ~ **tiempo** at the same time **3.** (*característico*) charac-

teristic; (*típico*) typical; **eso** (**no**) **es** ~ **de ti** that is (not) like you **4.** (*apropiado*) proper

proponer *irr como* **poner** I. *vt* to propose II. *vr:* ~**se** to intend, to propose *form;* **¿qué te propones?** what are you trying to do?

proporción *f* proportion; **no guardar** ~ **con algo** to be out of proportion with sth; **en una** ~ **de 8 a 1** in a ratio of 8 to 1; **un accidente de enormes proporciones** a major accident

proporcional *adj* proportional

proporcionar *vt* **1.** (*facilitar*) to provide; (*conseguir, procurar*) to obtain; ~ **víveres a alguien** to provide sb with supplies **2.** (*ocasionar*) to cause; ~ **disgustos a alguien** to upset sb

proposición *f* **1.** (*propuesta*) proposal; ~ **de ley** bill; ~ **de matrimonio** marriage proposal **2.** (*oración*) sentence; (*parte*) clause

propósito I. *m* **1.** (*intención*) intention; **tener el** ~ **de...** to intend to ... **2.** (*objetivo*) purpose; **a** ~ (*adrede*) on purpose; (*adecuado*) suitable; (*por cierto*) by the way II. *prep* **a** ~ **de** with regard to

propuesta *f* proposal; (*recomendación*) suggestion; **a** ~ **de alguien** on sb's suggestion

propugnar *vt* (*defender*) to defend; (*apoyar, promover*) to advocate

propulsar *vt* **1.** TÉC to propel **2.** (*fomentar*) to promote

propulsión *f* propulsion; ~ **trasera** AUTO rear-wheel drive

prórroga *f* **1.** (*prolongación*) prolongation; ECON extension **2.** (*dilatoria, retraso*) delay; (*aplazamiento*) deferral; (*cambio de fecha*) postponement **3.** DEP extra time, overtime

prorrogar <g→gu> *vt* **1.** (*prolongar*) to prolong; ECON to extend **2.** (*dilatar, retrasar*) to delay; *t.* JUR (*aplazar*) to defer; (*cambiar de fecha*) to postpone

prorrumpir *vi* **1.** (*salir*) to burst forth **2.** (*estallar*) ~ **en algo** to break out into sth

P
p

prosa *f* prose; **texto en** ~ piece of prose

prosaico, -a *adj* prosaic

proscrito, -a *m, f* exile

prosecución *f* continuation

proseguir *irr como seguir* I. *vi* (*alguien*) to continue; (*mal tiempo*) to persist II. *vt* to continue

prospección *f* prospecting

prospecto *m* (*folleto*) prospectus; (*de instrucciones*) instructions *pl;* (*informativo*) (information) leaflet; (*de un medicamento*) directions *pl* for use

prosperar *vi* to prosper

prosperidad *f* prosperity

próspero, -a *adj* prosperous; **¡Próspero Año Nuevo!** Happy New Year!

prostíbulo *m* brothel

prostitución *f* prostitution

prostituirse *irr como huir vr* to prostitute oneself

prostitutoa *f* prostitute *f*

protagonista *mf* key participant; CINE, TEAT leading actor *m*, leading actress *f;* LIT main character

protagonizar <z→c> *vt* to play; **un gran actor protagoniza esta película** a famous actor stars in this film

protección *f* protection; *t.* POL (*mecenazgo*) patronage

protector(a) I. *adj* protective II. *m(f)* protector; *t.* POL (*mecenas*) patron

proteger <g→j> I. *vt* to protect; *t.* POL (*como mecenas*) to act as a patron to II. *vr:* ~**se** to protect oneself; ~**se los ojos** to protect one's eyes

protegido, -a I. *adj* protected; ~ **contra escritura** INFOR write-protected II. *m, f* protégé *m*, protégée *f*

proteína *f* protein

prótesis *f inv* prosthesis

protesta *f* protest; JUR objection

protestante *adj, mf* Protestant

protestar I. *vi* to protest II. *vt* to avow

protocolo *m* protocol; **de** ~ formal

protón *m* proton

prototipo *m* prototype

protuberancia *f* protuberance;

(*bulto*) bulge

provecho *m* 1. (*aprovechamiento*) use; (*ventaja*) advantage; (*producto*) yield; (*beneficio*) benefit; **de** ~ useful; **en** ~ **de alguien** to sb's advantage; **nada de** ~ nothing of use; **sacar** ~ **de algo/alguien** to benefit from sth/sb 2. (*en comidas*) **¡buen** ~! enjoy your meal!, bon appétit!

proveer *irr* I. *vi* to provide; ~ **a algo** to provide for sth II. *vt* 1. (*abastecer, suministrar*) to supply; ~ **a alguien de algo** to furnish sb with sth; (*dotar*) to provide sb with sth 2. (*un puesto*) to fill III. *vr:* ~**se** to supply oneself; ~**se de algo** to provide oneself with sth

provenir *irr como venir vi* ~ **de** to come from

proverbio *m* proverb

providencia *f* 1. (*prevención*) precaution; (*medida, disposición*) measure 2. REL Providence

provincia *f* province

The 17 **Comunidades Autónomas** in Spain are subdivided into 52 **provincias**. Consequently, the **Comunidad de Castilla-León**, for example, consists of the following nine **provincias: Ávila, Burgos, León, Palencia, Salamanca, Segovia, Soria, Valladolid** and **Zamora**.

provinciano, -a *adj* provincial

provisión *f* 1. (*reserva*) supply; **provisiones** provisions *pl* 2. (*suministro*) supply 3. (*medida*) provision 4. (*de un cargo*) filling

provisional *adj* provisional

provocación *f* 1. (*ataque*) provocation; (*instigación*) instigation 2. (*causa*) cause

provocar <c→qu> *vt* 1. (*incitar, irritar*) to provoke; (*excitar*) to arouse; (*instigar*) to instigate; POL to agitate 2. (*causar*) to cause; ~ **un cambio** to bring about a change; ~ **una guerra** to start a war; ~ **risa a al-**

guien to make sb laugh
provocativo, -a *adj* provocative
próximamente *adv* soon
proximidad *f* proximity
próximo, -a *adj* **1.**(*cercano*) near; (*temporal*) close; **estar ~ a...** to be close to ... **2.**(*siguiente*) next; **el ~ año** next year; **el ~ 3 de octubre** on the 3rd of October this year; **la próxima vez** the next time; **¡hasta la próxima!** see you soon!
proyectar *vt* **1.** FÍS, FOTO, CINE to project **2.**(*lanzar*) to throw **3.**(*luz*) to shine; (*sombra*) to cast **4.**(*planear, proponerse*) to plan **5.** *t.* TÉC (*diseñar*) to design
proyectil *m* projectile; MIL missile
proyecto *m* project, plan; (*proyección*) draft; **en ~** planned; **~ de ley** bill; **tener algo en ~** to be planning sth
proyector *m* projector; **~ de cine** film projector
prudencia *f* **1.**(*precaución, previsión*) prudence; (*cautela*) caution **2.**(*cordura*) good sense **3.**(*moderación*) moderation
prudente *adj* **1.**(*precavido, previsor*) prudent; (*cauteloso*) cautious **2.**(*razonable*) reasonable **3.**(*adecuado*) sufficient
prueba *f* **1.** *t.* TÉC (*test*) test; **a ~ de agua** waterproof; **~ al azar** random trial; **~ de fuego** *fig* acid test; **período de ~** trial period; **poner a ~** to try out; **someter a ~** to test; **sufrir una dura ~** to be put through a stern test **2.**(*de ropa*) trying on; **~ (de degustación)** tasting **3.**(*examen*) exam **4.** DEP (*competición*) event; **~ clasificatoria/eliminatoria** qualifier/eliminator **5.**(*comprobación*) proof; (*testimonio*) piece of evidence; **~ (de imprenta)** proof; **dar ~s de afecto** to show one's affection; **en ~ de nuestro reconocimiento** as a token of our gratitude; **ser ~ de algo** to be proof of sth; **tener ~s de que...** to have evidence that ...
prurito *m* **1.**(*picor*) itch **2.**(*afán*) urge

(p)sicoanálisis *m sin pl* psychoanalysis
(p)sicología *f sin pl* psychology
(p)sicológico, -a *adj* psychological
(p)sicólogo, -a *m, f* psychologist
(p)sicópata *mf* psychopath
(p)sicosis *f inv* psychosis
(p)sicosomático, -a *adj* psychosomatic
(p)siquiatra *mf* psychiatrist
(p)siquiátrico *m* mental hospital
(p)siquiátrico, -a *adj* psychiatric
(p)síquico, -a *adj* mental, psychic
PSOE *m abr de* **Partido Socialista Obrero Español** *Spanish Socialist Party*
púa *f* **1.**(*espina*) spike; (*de planta*) thorn; (*de animal, pez*) spine, quill **2.**(*del peine*) tooth **3.** MÚS plectrum
pub <pubs> *m* bar
pubertad *f* puberty
publicación *f* publication
publicar <c→qu> I. *vt* to publish; (*proclamar*) to make known II. *vr:* **~se** to be published
publicidad *f* **1.**(*carácter público*) publicity; **dar ~ a algo** to publicize sth; **este programa le ha dado mucha ~** this programme has given him/her a lot of publicity **2.**(*propaganda*) advertising; **~ en TV** TV advertisement; **hacer ~ de algo** to advertise sth
publicitario, -a *adj* advertising
público *m* **1.**(*colectividad*) public; **el gran ~** the general public **2.**(*asistente*) audience; **hoy hay poco ~** there aren't many people today
público, -a *adj* public; **deuda pública** national debt; **de utilidad pública** of general use; **hacer ~** to make public; **hacerse ~** to become known
puchero *m* **1.**(*olla*) pot **2.** GASTR stew
púdico, -a *adj* **1.**(*recatado*) shy; (*vergonzoso*) bashful; (*decente*) decent **2.**(*modesto*) modest
pudiente *adj* (*poderoso*) powerful; (*rico*) well-off
pudor *m* **1.**(*recato*) shyness; (*decencia*) decency; (*vergüenza*) shame **2.**(*modestia*) modesty
pudrir *irr vt, vr:* **~se** to rot; **¡ahí te**

pudras! *vulg* go to hell!

pueblo *m* **1.** (*nación*) people; **el ~ bajo** the common people; **un hombre del ~** a man of the people **2.** (*aldea*) village; (*población*) (small) town; **~ de mala muerte** *inf* dead-end town

puente *m* **1.** (*en general*) bridge; **~ colgante** suspension bridge; **~ dental** bridge; **~ de mando** (compass) bridge; **hacer un ~ a un coche** to hot-wire a car **2.** (*fiesta*) long weekend (*public holiday plus an additional day off*); **hacer ~** to take a long weekend

puenting *m sin pl* bungee jumping

puerco, -a I. *adj* **1.** *estar inf* (*sucio*) filthy **2.** *ser* (*indecente*) gross **II.** *m, f* pig

pueril *adj* childish

puerro *m* leek

puerta *f* door; (*portal*) doorway; (*acceso*) entry; AERO, INFOR gate; **~ de la calle** front door; **~ de socorro** emergency exit; **a ~ abierta** in public; **de ~s adentro** *fig,* **a ~ cerrada** in private; **estar a las ~s** *fig* to be on the brink; **poner a alguien en la ~ (de la calle)** to throw sb out

puerto *m* **1.** NÁUT harbour *Brit,* harbor *Am;* (*ciudad*) port; **~ deportivo** marina; **~ franco** free port; **~ interior** river port; **~ marítimo** seaport **2.** (*de montaña*) pass **3.** INFOR port

Puerto Rico *m* Puerto Rico

? **Puerto Rico**, a state associated with the USA since 1952, consists of a main island and several small islands situated in the Greater Antilles. The capital of Puerto Rico is **San Juan**. The official languages of the country are both Spanish and English.

---

puertorriqueño, -a *adj, m, f* Puerto Rican

pues I. *adv* **1.** (*bueno*) well; (*entonces*) then; (*así que*) so; **~ bien**

okay; **la consecuencia es, ~, ...** so the result is ...; **Ana quiere conocerte – ~ que venga** Ana wants to meet you – well, she should come then; **~ entonces, nada** well that's it, then **2.** (*expletivo*) **estudio inglés – ¡ah, ~ yo también!** I study English – ah, me too!; **¿estuviste por fin en Toledo? – ~ no/sí** did you go to Toledo in the end? – no, I didn't/yes, I did; **¡~ esto no es nada!** this is nothing compared with what's to come!; **estoy muy cansado – ~ aún queda mucho camino** I'm very tired – well, there's still a long way to go; **¡qué caro! – ¿sí? ~ a mí me parece barato** how expensive! – do you think so? it seems cheap to me **3.** (*exclamativo*) **¡~ vaya lata!** what a pain!; **¡~ no faltaría más!** (*naturalmente*) but of course!; (*el colmo*) that's all we need! **4.** (*interrogativo*) **no voy a salir – ¿~ cómo es eso?** I'm not going out – why not?; **¿~ qué quieres?** what do you want, then?; **¿y ~?** and? **5.** (*atenuación*) well; **¿por qué no viniste a la fiesta? – ~ es que tenía mucho que hacer** why didn't you come to the party? – well, I was really busy **6.** (*insistencia*) **~ así es** well that's how it is; **~ claro** but of course **II.** *conj* **– no me queda otro remedio, venderé el coche** so I don't have any choice, I'll sell the car; **no voy de viaje, ~ no tengo dinero** I'm not going on holiday because I don't have any money

puesta *f* **1.** (*en general*) putting; **~ a cero** resetting; **~ en escena** staging; **~ en funcionamiento** activation (*of time*); **~ en libertad** release; **~ en marcha** start button; AUTO starter; **~ en práctica** putting into effect; **~ a punto** final check; AUTO service; **~ de sol** sunset **2.** (*en el juego*) bet

puesto *m* **1.** (*lugar*) place; (*posición*) position; **~ de información** information point **2.** (*empleo*) job; (*cargo*) post; (*posición*) position **3.** (*tenderete*) stall; (*feria de muestras*) stand; **~ de periódicos** newspaper stand **4.** *t.* MIL post; ~ **de poli-cía** police post; ~ **de socorro** first--aid station

puesto, -a I. *pp de* **poner** II. *adj inf* **ir muy bien** ~ to be very smartly dressed; **tienen la casa muy bien puesta** they've done the house up very nicely III. *conj* ~ **que** given that

pugna *f* (*lucha*) struggle; (*conflicto*) conflict

pugnar *vi* to fight; ~ **por algo/por hacer algo** (*esforzarse*) to struggle for sth/to do sth; (*intentar*) to strive for sth/to do sth

pujar *vi* **1.** (*esforzarse*) to struggle **2.** (*en una subasta*) to bid

pulcro, -a <pulquérrimo> *adj* neat

pulga *f* flea; INFOR bug

pulgada *f* inch

pulgar *m* thumb

pulir I. *vt* to polish; *fig* to polish up II. *vr*: ~**se** *inf* to squander

pulla *f* jibe *Brit,* gibe *Am*

pulmón *m* lung

pulmonía *f* pneumonia

pulpa *f* pulp, flesh

pulpería *f AmL* general store

> [?] In Latin America a **pulpería** is a general store selling alcoholic drinks, where all kinds of items can be bought. **Pulperías** are very similar to the small **tiendas de pueblo** that are still frequently encountered in small villages in Spain.

pulpo *m* octopus

pulquería *f AmC, Méx* general store

pulsación *f* **1.** ANAT beat, throbbing **2.** (*de una tecla*) striking; (*mecanografía*) keystroke; ~ **doble** INFOR strikeover

pulsador *m* button; (*conmutador*) switch

pulsar *vt* to press; (*teclado*) to strike; ~ **el timbre** to ring the bell

pulsera *f* bracelet; **reloj de** ~ wrist-watch

pulso *m* pulse; *fig* steadiness of hand;

a ~ (*sin apoyarse*) freehand; (*por su propio esfuerzo*) on one's own; **con** ~ carefully; **tener buen** ~ to have a steady hand; **tomar el** ~ **a alguien** to take sb's pulse

pulverizador *m* spray

pulverizar <z→c> *vt* **1.** (*reducir a polvo*) to pulverize **2.** (*atomizar*) to atomize

puna *f AmS* altitude sickness

punición *f* punishment

punitivo, -a *adj* punitive

punki *adj, mf* punk

punta *f* **1.** (*extremo*) end; (*de lengua, iceberg*) tip; **hora(s)** ~ rush hour; **lo tenía en la** ~ **de la lengua** it was on the tip of my tongue **2.** (*pico*) point; **de** ~ **en blanco** all dressed up; **acabar en** ~ to come to a point; **sacar** ~ (*afilar*) to sharpen

puntada *f* stitch

puntal *m* prop; *fig* mainstay

puntapié *m* kick; **pegar un** ~ **a alguien** to kick sb; **tratar a alguien a** ~**s** *fig* to walk all over sb

puntear *vt* **1.** (*marcar*) to dot **2.** MÚS to pluck

puntería *f* **1.** (*apuntar*) aim **2.** (*destreza*) marksmanship; **tener buena/mala** ~ to be a good/bad shot

puntero *m* pointer

puntero, -a I. *adj* leading; **el equipo** ~ the top team II. *m, f* leader

puntiagudo, -a *adj* (sharp-)pointed

puntilla *f* **1.** (*encaje*) lace (edging) **2.** (*del pie*) **de** ~**s** on tiptoe; **ponerse de** ~**s** to stand on tiptoe

punto *m* **1.** (*general*) point; ~ **de destino** destination; ~ **de encuentro** meeting place; ~ **de intersección** intersection; ~ **muerto** AUTO neutral; ~ **a tratar** item (on the agenda); ~ **de venta** point of sale; ~ **de vista** point of view; **en** ~ **a** with reference to; **en su** ~ *fig* just right; **hasta cierto** ~ up to a point; **hasta tal** ~ **que...** to such a degree that ...; **la una en** ~ exactly one o'clock; **dar el** ~ **a algo** to get sth just right; **ganar por** ~**s** to win on points; **no hay** ~ **de comparación** there's no comparison; **¿hasta qué ~?** how far?; **está a ~ de llover** it's about to rain; **¡y ~!** *inf* and that's that! **2.** TIPO full stop; INFOR dot; **~ y aparte** full stop, new paragraph; **~ y coma** semicolon; **dos ~s** LING colon; **~ final** full stop; **~ y seguido** full stop, new sentence; **~s suspensivos** suspension points; **con ~s y comas** *fig* very precise; **poner ~ final a algo** *fig* to bring sth to an end **3.** (*labor*) knitting; **chaqueta de ~** knitted jacket; **hacer ~** to knit **4.** (*puntada*) stitch; **~** (**de sutura**) stitch **5.** GASTR **en su ~** done; **batir a ~ de nieve** to beat until stiff **6.** (*preparado*) **a ~** ready; **poner a ~** TÉC to fine-tune; (*ajustar*) to adjust

puntuación *f* **1.** LING punctuation; **signo de ~** punctuation mark **2.** (*calificación*) mark *Brit*, grade *Am*; DEP score

puntual *adj* **1.** (*concreto*) specific **2.** (*exacto*) precise **3.** (*sin retraso*) punctual

puntualidad *f* punctuality

puntualizar <z→c> *vt* to specify

puntuar <*l. pres:* puntúo> *vt* **1.** (*un escrito*) to punctuate **2.** (*calificar*) to mark *Brit*, to grade *Am*

punzada *f* sharp pain

punzante *adj* **1.** (*puntiagudo*) sharp **2.** (*mordaz*) scathing

punzar <z→c> *vt* to prick

puñado *m* handful; **a ~s** by the handful

puñal *m* dagger

puñalada *f* stab; (*herida*) stab wound

puñetazo *m* punch

puño *m* **1.** (*mano*) fist; **~ cerrado** clenched fist; **como un ~** (*huevo, mentira*) enormous; (*casa, habitación*) tiny; **apretar los ~s** *fig* to struggle hard; **comerse los ~s** to be starving; **tener a alguien en un ~** to have sb under one's thumb **2.** (*puñado*) handful **3.** (*mango*) handle **4.** (*de la ropa*) cuff

pupila *f* pupil

pupitre *m* desk; **~ de control** control panel

puré *m* purée; **~ de patatas** mashed potatoes; **hacer ~** to purée

pureza *f* purity

purga *f* **1.** (*medicamento*) purgative **2.** (*eliminación*) purge

purgante *m* purgative

purgar <g→gu> *vt* to purge

purgatorio *m* purgatory

purificar <c→qu> *vt* to purify

puritano, -a *adj* puritanical

puro *m* cigar

puro, -a *adj* (*sin imperfecciones*) pure; (*auténtico*) authentic; **pura casualidad** sheer chance; **por pura cortesía** as a matter of courtesy; **de ~ miedo** from sheer terror; **la pura verdad** the honest truth

púrpura *f* purple

purpúreo, -a *adj* purple

pus *m sin pl* pus

pústula *f* pustule

puta *f vulg* whore; **hijo de ~** son of a bitch; **pasarlas ~s** to go through hell

putada *f vulg* **¡qué ~!** what a bloody nuisance!; **hacer una ~ a alguien** to play a dirty trick on sb

putrefacción *f* decay

pútrido, -a *adj* putrid

puzzle *m* jigsaw (puzzle)

PVP *m abr de* **Precio de Venta al Público** RRP

PYME *f abr de* **Pequeña y Mediana Empresa** SME

Q q

Q, q *f* Q, q; **~ de Quebec** Q for Queenie *Brit*, Q for Queen *Am*

que I. *pron rel* **1.** (*con antecedente: personas, cosas*) that, which (*often omitted when referring to object*); **la pelota ~ está pinchada** the ball that is punctured; **la pelota ~ compraste** the ball you bought; **la historia de ~ te hablé** the story I told you about; **reacciones a las ~ es-**

tamos **acostumbrados** reactions which we are accustomed to; **el proyecto en el ~ trabajo** the project that I am working on; **la empresa para la ~ trabajo** the company that I work for **2.**(*con antecedente: personas*) who, whom (*often omitted when referring to the object*); **la mujer que trabaja conmigo** the woman who works with me; **el rey al ~ sirvo** the king (whom) I serve **3.**(*sin antecedente*) **el/la/lo ~...** the one (that/who/which) ...; **los ~ hayan terminado** those who have finished; **el ~ quiera, ~ se marche** whoever wants to, can leave; **es de los ~...** he/she/it is the type that ...; **el ~ más y el ~ menos** every single one; **es todo lo ~ sé** that's all I know; **lo ~ haces** what you do; **no sabes lo difícil ~ es** you don't know how difficult it is **4.**(*con preposición*) **de lo ~ habláis** what you are talking about **II.** *conj* **1.**(*completivo*) that; **me pidió ~ le ayudara** he/she asked me to help him/her **2.**(*estilo indirecto*) that; **ha dicho ~...** he/she said that ... **3.**(*comparativo*) **más alto ~** taller than; **lo mismo ~** the same as; **yo ~ tú...** if I were you ... **4.**(*porque*) because; **le ayudaré, seguro, ~ se lo he prometido** I'll help him/her, of course, because I promised **5.**(*para que*) **dio órdenes a los trabajadores ~ trabajaran más rápido** he/she ordered the workers to work faster **6.**(*de manera que*) **corre ~ vuela** he/she runs like the wind **7.**(*o, ya*) **~ paguen, ~ no paguen, eso ya se verá** we'll see whether they pay or not **8.**(*frecuentativo*) **y él dale ~ dale con la guitarra** and he kept on playing and playing the guitar **9.**(*explicativo*) **hoy no vendré, es ~ estoy cansado** I'm not coming in today because I'm tired; **no es ~ no pueda, es ~ no quiero** it's not that I can't, it's that I don't want to **10.**(*enfático*) **¡~ sí/no!** yes/no!, I said "yes"/"no"!; **sí ~ lo hice** I did

do it! **11.**(*de duda*) **¿~ no está en casa?** are you saying he/she isn't at home? **12.**(*exclamativo*) **¡~ me canso!** I'm getting tired! **13.**(*con verbo*) **hay ~ trabajar más** you/we/they have to work harder; **tener ~ hacer algo** to have to do something; **dar ~ hablar** to set tongues wagging

qué *adj, pron interrog* **1.**(*general*) what; (*cuál*) which; (*qué clase de*) what kind of; **¿por ~?** why?; **¿en ~ piensas?** what are you thinking about?; **¿para ~?** what for?; **¿de ~ hablas?** what are you talking about?; **¿a ~ esperas?** what are you waiting for?; **¿~ día llega?** what day is he/she arriving?; **¿~ cerveza tomas?** what kind of beer do you drink?; **¿a ~ vienes?** what are you here for?; **¿~ edad tienes?** how old are you?; **según ~ gente no la soporto** some people I just can't stand **2.**(*exclamativo*) **¡~ alegría!** how nice!; **¡~ gracia!** how funny!; **¡~ suerte!** what luck! **3.**(*cuán*) **¡~ magnífica vista!** what a magnificent view!; **¡mira ~ contento está!** look how happy he is! **4.**(*cuánto*) **¡~ de gente!** what a lot of people! **5.¿~ tal?** how are you?; **¿~ tal si salimos a cenar?** how about going out to dinner?; **¿y ~?** so what?; **¿y a mí ~?** and what about me?; **¿~?** well?; **~, ¿vienes o no?** well, are you coming, or not?

quebrada *f* ravine
quebradizo, -a *adj* fragile
quebrado *m* fraction
quebrado, -a *adj* **1.**(*empresa*) bankrupt **2.**(*terreno*) rough
quebrantar *vt* to break
quebranto *m* **1.**(*romper*) breaking **2.**(*pérdida*) loss
quebrar <e→ie> **I.** *vt* to break **II.** *vi* to go bankrupt **III.** *vr:* **~se** to break; (*herniarse*) to rupture oneself
quechua **I.** *adj* Quechua **II.** *mf* Quechuan

? Quechua is the name given both to the original inhabitants of

Perú as well as their language. **Quechua** is the second official language of **Perú**.

quedar I. *vi* 1. (*permanecer*) to remain; **los problemas quedan atrás** the problems are a thing of the past; **¿cuánta gente queda?** how many people are left? 2. (*sobrar*) to be left; **no nos queda dinero/otro remedio** we have no money/alternative (left); **no queda pan** there's no bread left 3. (*resultar, estar, faltar*) to be; ~ **cojo** to go lame; ~ **en ridículo** to make a fool of oneself; **todo quedó en una simple discusión** it ended up in a mere argument; **aún queda mucho por hacer** there's still a lot to do; **por mí que no quede** I'll do all that I can 4. (*acordar*) ~ **en algo** to agree to sth; **¡en qué habéis quedado?** what have you decided?; **quedamos a las 10** we agreed to meet at 10; **¿quedamos a las 10?** shall we meet at 10? 5. (*terminar*) to end 6. (+ *por*) **algo queda por ver** sth remains to be seen 7. (+ *bien/mal*) ~ **bien/mal** to come off well/badly 8. (+ *como*) ~ **como un señor** to behave like a real gentleman; ~ **como un idiota** to look a fool II. *vr:* ~**se** 1. (*permanecer*) to stay; ~**se atrás** to stay behind; **durante la tormenta nos quedamos a oscuras** during the storm the lights went out 2. (*resultar*) ~**se ciego** to go blind; ~**se viuda** to become a widow 3. ~**se con algo** (*adquirir*) to take sth; (*conservar*) to keep sth; ~**se sin nada** to be left with nothing 4. (*burlarse*) ~**se con alguien** to make fun of sb

quehacer *m* work; **los ~es de la casa** the housework

queja *f* complaint

quejarse *vr* 1. (*formular queja*) ~ (**de algo**) to complain (about sth) 2. (*gemir*) to moan

quejido *m* moan

quejoso, -a *adj* complaining; **estar ~**

de alguien to be annoyed at sb

quemado, -a *adj* burnt; *fig* (*agotado*) finished; **estar ~ con alguien** *inf* (*enfadado*) to have had it with sb

quemadura *f* burn

quemar I. *vi* to burn; (*estar caliente*) to be boiling hot II. *vt* to burn; (*completamente*) to burn down; *fig* (*fortuna*) to squander III. *vr:* ~**se** to burn; (*sunburn*) to get burnt

quemarropa **disparar a ~** to shoot at very close range; **hacer preguntas a ~** to ask pointblank

quemazón *f* **sentir una ~ en el estómago** to have a burning sensation in one's stomach

quepo 1. *pres de* **caber**

querella *f* dispute

querellarse *vr* 1. (*quejarse*) ~ (**por algo**) to complain (about sth) 2. JUR to bring an action

querer *irr* *vt* 1. (*desear*) to desire; (*más suave*) to want; **como tú quieras** as you like; **has ganado, ¿qué más quieres?** you win, what more do you want?; **lo hice sin ~** I didn't mean to do it; **quisiera tener 20 años menos** I wish I were 20 years younger; **quiero que sepáis que…** I want you to know that …; **y yo, ¡qué quieres que le haga!** what do you expect me to do? 2. (*amar*) to like; (*más fuerte*) to love 3. (*pedir*) to require; (*necesitar*) to need

querido, -a I. *adj* dear II. *m, f* (*amante*) lover; (*vocativo*) darling

queso *m* cheese

quicio *m* hinge post; **sacar a alguien de ~** to drive sb up the wall *inf*

quiebra *f* 1. (*rotura*) break 2. (*pérdida*) loss, breakdown; COM bankruptcy

quiebro *m* dodge

quien *pron rel* 1. (*con antecedente*) who, that, whom (*often omitted when referring to object*); **el chico de ~ te hablé** that boy I told you about; **las chicas con ~es…** the girls with whom … 2. (*sin antecedente*) that; **hay ~ dice que…** some people say that …; **no hay ~ lo aguante** nobody can stand him; ~

opine eso... whoever thinks so ...; ~ **más,** ~ **menos, todos tenemos problemas** everybody has problems
quién *pron interrog* who; ¿~ **es?** (*llama*) who is it?; ¿~**es son tus padres?** who are your parents?; ¿a ~ **has visto?** who did you see?; ¿a ~ **se lo has dado?** who did you give it to?; ¿~ **eres tú para decirme esto?** who do you think you are telling me this?; ¿**por** ~ **me tomas?** what do you take me for?; **¡~ tuviera 20 años!** If only I were 20!
quienquiera <quienesquiera> *pron indef* whoever; ~ **que sea que pase** whoever it is, come in
quieto, -a *adj* still; **estar/quedarse** ~ to keep/stand still
quietud *f* stillness
quijada *f* jaw(bone)
quilate *m* carat *Brit,* karat *Am*
quilla *f* keel
quimera *f* chimera *form*
química *f* chemistry
químico, -a I. *adj* chemical **II.** *m, f* chemist
quimioterapia *f* chemotherapy
quince I. *adj inv* fifteen; **dentro de** ~ **días** in a fortnight *Brit,* in fifteen days **II.** *m* fifteen; *v.t.* **ocho**
quincena *f* fortnight *Brit,* fifteen days
quincenal *adj* fortnightly *Brit,* twice-monthly
quincuagésimo, -a *adj* fiftieth; *v.t.* **octavo**
quiniela *f* sports pools *pl;* **jugar a las** ~**s** to do the pools
quinientos, -as *adj* five hundred; *v.t.* **ochocientos**
quinina *f* quinine
quinqui *mf inf* delinquent
quinteto *m* quintet
quinto *m* conscript, draftee *Am*
quinto, -a *adj* fifth; *v.t.* **octavo**
quiosco *m* ~ (**de periódicos**) news-stand
quirófano *m* operating theatre *Brit* [*o* room *Am*]
quirúrgico, -a *adj* surgical
quiso *3. pret de* **querer**
quisquilloso, -a *adj* **1.** (*susceptible*) touchy **2.** (*meticuloso*) fussy

quiste *m* cyst
quitaesmalte *m* nail varnish remover
quitamanchas *m inv* stain remover
quitanieves *f inv* snowplough *Brit,* snowplow *Am*
quitar I. *vt* **1.** (*separar, apartar*) to remove; (*tapa, ropa*) to take off; ~ **la mesa** to clear the table; **de quita y pon** detachable **2.** (*desposeer*) to take; (*robar*) to steal; **me lo has quitado de la boca** *fig* you took the words right out of my mouth **3.** (*mancha*) to get out; (*obstáculo*) to remove; (*dolor*) to relieve **4.** MAT to take away **II.** *vr:* ~**se** to take off; (*barba*) to shave off; ~**se de la bebida** to give up drinking; ~**se la vida** to commit suicide; ~**se de encima algo/a alguien** to get rid of sth/sb; **quítate de mi vista** get out of my sight
Quito *m* Quito
quizá(s) *adv* perhaps, maybe; ~ **y sin** ~ without a doubt

R, r *f* R, r; ~ **de Ramón** R for Roger
rabadilla *f* coccyx
rábano *m* radish; ~ **picante** [*o* blanco] horseradish
rabia *f* **1.** MED rabies *pl* **2.** (*furia*) rage; **¡qué** ~**!** how infuriating! **3.** (*enfado, manía*) **tener** ~ **a alguien** (*enfado*) to be furious with sb; (*manía*) not to be able to stand sb; **me da** ~ **sólo pensarlo** just thinking about it makes me mad
rabiar *vi* **1.** (*enfadarse*) to be furious; **hacer** ~ **a alguien** to infuriate sb **2.** (*desear*) ~ **por hacer algo** to be dying to do sth
rabieta *f* tantrum; **coger una** ~ to throw a tantrum
rabino *m* rabbi

rabioso, -a *adj* **1.** (*hidrofóbico*) rabid **2.** (*furioso*) furious

rabo *m* tail

racha *f* **1.** (*de aire*) gust of wind **2.** (*fase*) series; **a** [*o* **por**] **~s** in fits and starts; **tener buena/mala ~ to** have a good/bad run

racial *adj* racial; **disturbios ~es** race riots

racimo *m* bunch; **~ de uvas** grapes *pl*

raciocinio *m* **1.** (*razón*) reason **2.** (*proceso mental*) reasoning

ración *f* portion; MIL ration; **una ~ de queso** a plate of cheese

racional *adj* rational

racionalizar <z→c> *vt* to rationalize

racionar *vt* to ration

racismo *m sin pl* racism

racista *adj, mf* racist

radar *m* radar

radiactividad *f* radioactivity

radiactivo, -a *adj* radioactive

radiador *m* radiator

radiante *adj* radiant; **~ de alegría** radiant with joy

radical *adj* radical

radicar <c→qu> I. *vi* **~ en algo** to lie in sth II. *vr:* **~se** to settle

radio¹ *f* RADIO, TEL radio; **por la ~** on the radio

radio² *m* **1.** MAT, ANAT radius **2.** (*en la rueda*) spoke **3.** (*ámbito*) range; (*esfera*) field; **~ de acción** operational range; *fig* sphere of influence; **~ de alcance** reach

radioaficionado, -a *m, f* radio ham

radiocasete *m o f* radio cassette recorder, boom box *Am*

radiodifusión *f* broadcasting

radioemisora *f* radio station

radiografía *f* X-ray

radiotaxi *m* radiocab

radioterapia *f* radiotherapy

radioyente *mf* listener

RAE *f abr de* **Real Academia Española** Spanish Royal Academy

[?] Since its inception in 1714, the **Real Academia Española (RAE)** has made the standardisation and purity of the Spanish language one of its objectives.

ráfaga *f* (*de aire*) gust; (*de lluvia*) squall; (*de luz*) flas; (*de disparos*) burst

raído, -a *adj* worn-out

raigambre *f* roots *pl*

raíz *f* root; **~ cuadrada/cúbica** square/cube root; **a ~ de** because of; **de ~** completely; **arrancar de ~** to destroy; **extraer la ~** to calculate the root; **tener su ~ en algo** to be due to sth

raja *f* **1.** (*grieta*) crack; (*hendedura*) split **2.** (*rodaja*) slice

rajar I. *vt* **1.** (*cortar*) to cut; (*hender*) to split **2.** *inf* (*apuñalar*) to knife II. *vr:* **~se 1.** (*abrirse*) to split open; (*agrietarse*) to crack **2.** *inf* (*echarse atrás*) to back out

rajatabla a ~ (*estrictamente*) strictly; (*exactamente*) to the letter

rallador *m* grater

rallar *vt* (*fino*) to grate; (*menos fino*) to shred

ralo, -a *adj* (*árboles*) sparse; (*cabello*) thin

rama *f* branch; (*sector*) sector; **andarse** [*o* **irse**] **por las ~s** to beat about the bush

ramaje *m* branches

ramal *m* **1.** (*cabo*) strand **2.** (*ramificación*) branch; FERRO branch line

rambla *f* boulevard

ramera *f pey* whore

ramificación *f* ramification

ramificarse <c→qu> *vr* to branch out

ramillete *m* bouquet

ramo *m* **1.** (*de flores*) bunch **2.** (*de un árbol*) (small) branch; **Domingo de Ramos** Palm Sunday **3.** (*sector*) sector

rampa *f* ramp; **en ~** sloping

ramplón, -ona *adj* coarse

rana *f* frog; **hombre ~** frogman; **salir ~ a alguien** *inf* to be a disappointment to sb

ranchero, -a *m, f* rancher

rancho *m* **1.** (*comida*) food **2.** (*granja*) ranch

rancio, -a *adj* **1.** (*grasas*) rancid **2.** (*antiguo*) ancient

rango *m* rank; **de** (**alto**) ~ high-ranking; **de primer** ~ first-level

ranura *f* groove; (*fisura*) slot

raparse *vr* ~ **el pelo** (*afeitar*) to shave one's head; (*cortar*) to have one's hair cut very short

rapaz *adj, f* (*ave*) ~ bird of prey

rapaz(a) *m(f)* kid; (*niño*) boy, lad *Brit;* (*niña*) girl, lass *Brit*

rape *m* **1.** ZOOL monkfish **2.** *inf* **al** ~ (*pelo*) closely cropped

rapé *m* snuff; **polvos de** ~ snuff powder

rapidez *f* speed; **con** (**gran**) ~ (very) quickly

rápido *m* **1.** (*tren*) express **2.** *pl* (*de un río*) rapids *pl*

rápido, -a *adj* **1.** (*veloz*) fast **2.** (*breve*) quick

rapiña *f* robbery; (*saqueo*) pillage

raptar *vt* to kidnap

rapto *m* **1.** (*secuestro*) kidnapping **2.** (*arrebato*) fit

raqueta *f* racket

raquítico, -a *adj* **1.** (*débil*) weak **2.** (*insuficiente*) measly

raquitismo *m sin pl* rickets *pl*

rareza *f* rarity; (*curiosidad*) strangeness; (*peculiaridad*) peculiarity; (*manía*) eccentricity

raro, -a *adj* **1.** (*extraño, inesperado*) strange **2.** (*inusual*) unusual; (*poco común*) rare; **raras personas** few people; **rara vez** rarely; **no es** ~ **que...** +*subj* it's not surprising that ...

ras *m* level; **al** ~ level; **a(l)** ~ **de** on a level with; **a** ~ **de agua** at water level; **volar a** ~ **de suelo** to hedge-hop

rasar *vt* **1.** (*igualar*) to level **2.** (*rozar*) to skim

rascacielos *m inv* skyscraper

rascar <c→qu> **I.** *vt* to scrape; (*con las uñas*) to scratch **II.** *vr:* ~**se** to scratch

rasgar <g→gu> *vt, vr:* ~**se** to tear

rasgo *m* **1.** (*del rostro*) feature; (*del carácter*) trait **2.** (*trazo*) stroke; **a grandes** ~**s** in outline

raspado *m* MED scrape

raspadura *f* scraping; (*arañar*) scratching

raspar **I.** *vi* to be rough **II.** *vt* to scrape; (*arañar*) to scratch

rastra *f* rake; **ir a** ~**s** *inf* to drag along behind; **llevar a alguien a** ~**s** to drag sb along

rastrear *vt* **1.** (*seguir*) to track **2.** (*investigar*) ~ **algo** to make inquiries about sth

rastrero, -a *adj* **1.** (*por el suelo*) creeping; **planta rastrera** creeper **2.** *pey* (*despreciable*) despicable

rastrillar *vt* to rake

rastrillo *m* **1.** (*herramienta*) rake **2.** (*mercadillo*) flea market

rastro *m* **1.** (*indicio, pista*) trace; **sin dejar** (**ni**) ~ without trace; **seguir el** ~ **a** [*o* **de**] **alguien** to follow sb's trail **2.** (*mercadillo*) flea market **3.** (*herramienta*) rake

rastrojo *m* stubble

rasurar *vt, vr:* ~**se** to shave

rata *f* rat

ratear *vt inf* to nick

ratero, -a *m, f* petty thief

ratificar <c→qu> *vt* **1.** JUR, POL to ratify **2.** (*confirmar*) to confirm

rato *m* while; **un buen** ~ for quite a time; **a cada** ~ all the time; **un** ~ (**largo**) *inf* a lot; **en un** ~ **perdido** in a quiet moment; **al** (**poco**) ~ shortly after; **todo el** ~ the whole time; **a** ~**s** from time to time; **de** ~ **en** ~ from time to time; **hacer pasar un mal** ~ **a alguien** to give sb a rough time; **pasar un buen/mal** ~ to have a good/bad time; **pasar el** ~ to pass the time; **tener para** ~ to have lots to do; **¡hasta otro** ~! see you later!; **aún hay para** ~ there's still plenty left to do

ratón *m t.* INFOR mouse

ratonera *f* **1.** (*trampa*) mousetrap **2.** (*agujero*) mousehole

raudal *m* torrent; **por la ventana entra la luz a** ~**es** the light came flooding through the window

raya *f* line; (*guión*) dash; (*del pelo*)

R

parting *Brit,* part *Am;* **a** ~**s** (*paper*) lined; (*shirt*) striped; **pasarse de la** ~ *inf* to go too far; **tener a alguien a** ~ *inf* to keep sb in place

rayar I. *vi* ~ **con algo** to border on sth **II.** *vt* to scratch **III.** *vr:* ~**se** to get scratched

rayo *m* **1.** (*de luz, radiación*) ray; ~ **láser** laser beam; ~**s** **X** X-rays *pl* **2.** (*relámpago*) (bolt of)lightning; **como un** ~ in a flash

raza *f* race; **de** ~ (*perro*) pedigree; (*caballo*) thoroughbred

razón I. *f* **1.** (*discernimiento, motivo*) reason; ~ **de ser** raison d'être; **la** ~ **por la que ...** the reason why ...; **por** ~ **de algo** due to sth; **por razones de seguridad** for security reasons; **entrar en** ~ to come to one's senses **2.** (*acierto*) **dar la** ~ **a alguien** to agree with sb; **llevar la** ~ to be right; **tener** (**mucha**) ~ to be (absolutely) right; **en eso** (**no**) **tienes** ~ you are (not) right about that; **¡con** (**mucha**) ~! quite rightly! **II.** *prep* **en** ~ **de** (*en cuanto a*) as far as; (*a causa de*) because of

razonable *adj* reasonable

razonamiento *m* reasoning

razonar *vi* to reason

RDSI *f abr de* **Red Digital de Servicios Integrados** ISDN

re *m* D

reacción *f* reaction; ~ **en cadena** chain reaction; ~ **excesiva** overreaction

reaccionar *vi* **1.** (*ante un estímulo*) ~ **a** [*o* ante] **algo** to react to sth **2.** (*responder*) ~ **a algo** to respond to sth

reaccionario, -a *adj* reactionary

reacio, -a *adj* reluctant; **ser** ~ **a hacer algo** to be reluctant to do sth

reactivar *vt* to reactivate; ECON to revive

reactor *m* **1.** FÍS reactor **2.** (*avión*) jet

readaptación *f* ~ **profesional** professional retraining

readmitir *vt* to readmit

reajuste *m* readjustment; (*reorganización*) reorganization

real *adj* **1.** (*verdadero*) real; **basado en hechos** ~**es** based on a true story **2.** (*del rey*) royal

realce *m* **dar** ~ **a algo** to highlight sth

realidad *f* reality; (*verdad*) truth; **en** ~ in fact; **hacer algo** ~ to make sth come true; **hacerse** ~ to happen; (*cumplirse*) to come true

realismo *m sin pl* realism

realista *adj* realistic

realización *f* **1.** (*ejecución*) execution **2.** (*materialización*) realization; (*cumplimiento*) fulfilment *Brit,* fulfillment *Am* **3.** CINE production

realizador(a) *m(f)* producer

realizar <z→c> **I.** *vt* **1.** (*efectuar*) to carry out; (*hacer*) to make **2.** (*hacer realidad*) to make real; (*sueños*) to fulfil *Brit,* to fulfill *Am* **3.** CINE, TV to produce **II.** *vr:* ~**se** to come true

realmente *adv* really; (*de hecho*) in fact

realquilar *vt* to sublet

realzar <z→c> *vt* (*acentuar*) to bring out; (*subrayar*) to highlight

reanimar I. *vt* **1.** (*reavivar*) to revive **2.** (*animar*) to liven up **3.** MED to resuscitate **II.** *vr:* ~**se** **1.** MED to regain consciousness **2.** (*animarse*) to liven up

reanudar *vt* to resume

reaparición *f* reappearance; TEAT, CINE comeback

rearme *m* rearmament

reavivar *vt, vr:* ~**se** to revive

rebaja *f* **1.** (*oferta*) sale; **estar de** ~**s** to have a sale on **2.** (*descuento*) discount; (*reducción*) reduction

rebajar *vt* **1.** (*reducir, abaratar*) to reduce **2.** (*humillar*) to put down **3.** (*mitigar*) to soften **4.** (*una bebida*) to dilute

rebanada *f* slice

rebañar *vt* ~ **el plato** to wipe the plate clean

rebaño *m* herd

rebasar *vt* to exceed; ~ **el límite** *fig* to overstep the mark

rebatir *vt* **1.** (*refutar*) to refute; (*rechazar*) to reject **2.** (*repeler*) to repel

rebeca *f* cardigan

rebelarse *vr* to rebel

rebelde I. *adj* 1. (*indócil*) unruly; (*difícil*) troublesome 2. (*insurrecto*) rebellious II. *mf* rebel

rebeldía *f* rebelliousness

rebelión *f* rebellion

reblandecer *irr como crecer vt, vr:* ~**se** to soften

rebobinar *vt* to rewind

rebosante *adj* overflowing; ~ **de alegría** brimming with hapiness; ~ **de salud** glowing with health

rebosar *vi* 1. (*desbordar*) to overflow 2. (*tener mucho*) ~ **de algo** to be brimming with sth

rebotar *vi* to bounce

rebote *m* rebound; **de** ~ on the rebound

rebozar <z→c> *vt* (*con pan rallado*) to coat with breadcrumbs; (*con masa*) to coat with batter

rebuscado, -a *adj* pedantic; (*estilo*) contrived

rebuscar <c→qu> *vi* to search thoroughly

rebuznar *vi* to bray

recabar *vt* to manage to obtain

recado *m* 1. (*mensaje*) message 2. (*encargo*) errand

recaer *irr como caer vi* 1. (*enfermedad*) to relapse 2. (*delito*) to reoffend; ~ **en el mismo error una y otra vez** to repeat the same mistake again and again; ~ **en la bebida** to start drinking again 3. ~ **en alguien** (*culpa*) to fall on sb; (*herencia*) to fall to sb

recaída *f* relapse

recalcar <c→qu> *vt* to stress

recalcitrante *adj* recalcitrant

recalentamiento *m* ~ **global** global warming

recalentar <e→ie> I. *vt* 1. (*comida*) to reheat 2. (*aparato*) to overheat II. *vr:* ~**se** (*motor*) to overheat

recámara *f* 1. (*para ropa*) dressing room 2. (*arma*) chamber

recambio *m* spare (part); (*envase*) refill

recapacitar I. *vt* to consider II. *vi* to think things over

recapitular *vt* to summarize, to sum up

recargable *adj* (*pila*) rechargeable

recargado, -a *adj* overelaborate

recargar <g→gu> *vt* 1. (*pila*) to recharge 2. (*decorar*) to overdecorate 3. (*impuesto*) to increase 4. (*carga*) to overload; ~ **a alguien de trabajo** to overload sb with work

recargo *m* (*aumento*) increase; (*sobreprecio*) surcharge; **llamada sin** ~ freephone call *Brit,* toll-free call *Am*

recatado, -a *adj* 1. (*decoroso*) decent; (*modesto*) modest 2. (*cauto*) cautious

recato *m* 1. (*decoro*) decency; (*pudor*) modesty 2. (*cautela*) caution

recauchutado *adj* **neumático** ~ retread

recaudación *f* (*cobro*) collection; (*cantidad*) takings *pl*

recaudar *vt* to collect

recelar I. *vt* to fear II. *vi* to be suspicious; **recelo de mi secretaria** I don't trust my secretary

recelo *m* mistrust; **mirar algo con** ~ to be suspicious of sth

receloso, -a *adj* distrustful; **estar** ~ **de alguien** to be suspicious of sb; **ponerse** ~ to become suspicious

recepción *f* reception

recepcionista *mf* receptionist

receptáculo *m* receptacle

receptivo, -a *adj* receptive

receptor *m* receiver; ~ **de televisión** TV set

receptor(a) *m(f)* recipient, receiver

recesión *f* recession

receta *f* 1. GASTR *t. fig* recipe 2. MED prescription; **con** ~ **médica** on prescription; **venta con** ~ available on prescription

recetar *vt* to prescribe

rechazar <z→c> *vt* 1. (*no aceptar*) to reject; (*denegar, no tolerar*) to refuse; ~ **las acusaciones** to deny the accusations 2. (*ataque*) to repel, to push back

rechazo *m* rejection; (*denegación*) refusal

rechinar *vi* to squeak; (*puerta*) to creak; (*dientes*) to grind

R
r

rechistar *vi* to grumble; **sin** ~ without complaining

rechoncho, -a *adj inf* tubby

rechupete de ~ delicious

recibidor *m* entry (hall)

recibimiento *m* welcome

recibir *vt* to receive; (*personas*) to welcome

recibo *m* receipt; (*de la luz, del agua*) bill; **acusar** ~ to acknowledge receipt

reciclaje *m* **1.** TÉC recycling **2.** ENS **curso de** ~ refresher course; ~ **profesional** professional retraining

reciclar *vt* **1.** TÉC to recycle **2.** ENS to retrain

recién *adv* recently; **los** ~ **casados** the newly weds; ~ **cocido/pintado** freshly cooked/painted; **el** ~ **nacido** the newborn baby

reciente *adj* **1.** (*nuevo*) new; (*fresco*) fresh **2.** (*que acaba de suceder*) recent; **un libro de** ~ **publicación** a book which has recently been published

recientemente *adv* recently

recinto *m* enclosure; ~ **universitario** university campus

recio, -a **I.** *adj* strong **II.** *adv* (*hablar*) loudly; (*llover*) heavily

recipiente *m* container; (*de vidrio, barro*) vessel

reciprocidad *f* reciprocity

recíproco, -a *adj* reciprocal; ... **y a la recíproca** ...and vice versa

recital *m* MÚS concert, recital; LIT reading

recitar *vt* to recite

reclamación *f* **1.** (*recurso*) protest; (*queja*) complaint **2.** (*exigencia*) claim; (*de deuda*) demand

reclamar **I.** *vi* (*protestar*) to protest; ~ (**por algo**) (*quejarse*) to complain (about sth) **II.** *vt* to claim; (*una deuda*) to demand; **nos reclaman el dinero que nos prestaron** they want us to repay the money which they lent us; **el terrorista es reclamado por la justicia sueca a Italia** the Swedish courts have asked Italy to hand over the terrorist

reclamo *m* **1.** (*caza, utensilio*) decoy; (*grito*) decoy call **2.** COM advert(isement)

reclinar **I.** *vt* to lean **II.** *vr:* ~**se** to lean back

recluir *irr como huir* **I.** *vt* (*cárcel*) to imprison; (*hospital*) to confine **II.** *vr:* ~**se** to shut oneself away

reclusión *f* **1.** JUR imprisonment **2.** (*aislamiento*) seclusion

recluta *mf* (*voluntario*) recruit; (*obligado*) conscript, draftee *Am*

reclutamiento *m* recruiting

recobrar *vt, vr:* ~**se** to recover; ~ **las fuerzas** to regain one's strength; ~ **las pérdidas** to make good one's losses; ~ **el sentido** to regain consciousness; ~ **la vista** to regain one's sight

recodo *m* bend

recoger <g→j> **I.** *vt* **1.** (*buscar*) to collect; **te voy a** ~ **a la estación** I'll meet you at the station **2.** (*coger*) to collect; (*ordenar*) to tidy; (*guardar*) to put away; ~ (**del suelo**) to pick up (from the floor) **3.** (*juntar*) to gather together **4.** (*cosecha*) to gather; ~ **el fruto de su trabajo** to reap the fruits of one's labour **5.** (*acoger*) to take in **6.** (*cabello*) to gather up **II.** *vr:* ~**se** (*a casa*) to go home; (*a la cama*) to go to bed

recogida *f* collection; ~ **de equipajes** baggage reclaim *Brit*, baggage claim *Am*

recogido, -a *adj* **1.** (*acogedor*) welcoming **2.** (*retirado*) secluded

recolección *f* harvest; (*período*) harvest time

recomendación *f* recommendation; **por** ~ **de mi médico** on my doctor's advice

recomendar <e→ie> *vt* recommend; (*aconsejar*) to advise

recompensa *f* reward; **en** ~ as a reward

recompensar *vt* **1.** (*por un servicio*) ~ (**a alguien por algo**) to reward sb (for sth) **2.** (*de daño*) to compensate; **fue recompensado por sus gastos** his/her expenses were paid

recomponer *irr como poner vt* to repair

reconciliación *f* reconciliation
reconciliar **I.** *vt* to reconcile **II.** *vr:* ~**se** to be reconciled
recóndito, -a *adj* hidden; **en lo más** ~ **del bosque** in the depths of the forest; **en lo más** ~ **de mi corazón** in my heart of hearts
reconfortar *vt* to comfort
reconocer *irr como crecer* *vt* **1.** (*identificar*) *t.* POL to recognize **2.** (*admitir*) to accept; (*un error*) to acknowledge; ~ **a alguien como hijo** to recognize sb as one's son
reconocido, -a *adj* **1.** (*agradecido*) grateful **2.** (*aceptado*) recognized
reconocimiento *m* **1.** POL, JUR recognition **2.** MED examination **3.** (*gratitud*) gratefulness; **en** ~ **de mi labor** in recognition of my work
reconquista *f* reconquest

[?] The **Reconquista** was ended after eight centuries of Moorish occupation by the reconquest of the Kingdom of **Granada**. For eight centuries, the sole objective of the Christian rulers had been to drive the arabs out of the **Península Ibérica**. Those Moors and Jews who wished to remain in Spain had to convert to the Christian faith.

---

reconstituyente *m* reconstituent
reconstruir *irr como huir* *vt* **1.** (*reedificar*) to rebuild **2.** (*componer*) to reconstruct
recopilación *f* compilation
recopilar *vt* to compile
récord <récords> *m* record
recordar <o→ue> **I.** *vi, vt* **1.** (*acordarse*) to remember **2.** (*traer a la memoria, semejar*) to remind; **recuérdale que me traiga el libro** remind him/her to bring me the book; **este paisaje me recuerda (a) la Toscana** this landscape reminds me of Tuscany; **si mal no recuerdo** if I remember correctly **II.** *vr:* ~**se** to re-

member
recordatorio *m* **1.** (*comunión*) communion card; (*fallecimiento*) *card which commemorates sb's death* **2.** (*advertencia*) reminder
recorrer *vt* **1.** (*atravesar*) to cross; (*viajar por*) to travel around **2.** (*trayecto*) to travel; **recorrimos tres kilómetros a pie** we walked three kilometres
recortado, -a *adj* (*hoja*) uneven; (*costa*) rugged
recortar *vt* (*figuras*) to cut out; (*barba, uñas*) to trim; (*quitar*) to cut off
recorte *m* **1.** (*periódico*) cutting **2.** *pl* (*cortaduras*) cuttings *pl;* ~**s de tela** scraps of cloth
recostar <o→ue> **I.** *vt* **1.** (*apoyar*) to rest **2.** (*inclinar*) ~ **algo contra/ en algo** to lean sth on sth **II.** *vr:* ~**se** **1.** (*inclinarse*) ~**se contra/en algo** to lean on sth **2.** (*tumbarse*) to lie down
recoveco *m* bend
recreación *f* recreation
recrear **I.** *vt* **1.** (*reproducir*) to reproduce **2.** (*divertir*) to entertain **II.** *vr:* ~**se** to entertain oneself; **se recrea contemplando cuadros** he/she enjoys looking at pictures
recreativo, -a *adj* recreational; (**salón de juegos**) ~**s** amusement arcade
recreo *m* **1.** (*recreación*) recreation; **de** ~ recreational; **casa de** ~ holiday home **2.** (*en el colegio*) break, recess *Am*
recriminar *vt* to reproach
recrudecer *irr como crecer* *vi, vr:* ~**se** to worsen; (*conflicto*) to intensify
recta *f* straight; **entrar en la** ~ **final** *t.* DEP to enter the final straight
rectangular *adj* rectangular
rectángulo *m* rectangle
rectángulo, -a *adj* rectangular
rectificar <c→qu> *vt* **1.** (*corregir*) to correct **2.** (*carretera*) to straighten
rectitud *f* uprightness
recto *m* rectum
recto, -a *adj* **1.** (*forma*) straight;

ángulo ~ right angle **2.** (*honrado*) upright

rector(a) **I.** *adj* principal; (*responsable*) governing **II.** *m(f)* ENS, REL rector; UNIV vice-chancellor *Brit,* president *Am*

recuadro *m* box

recubrir *irr como abrir vt* to cover

recuento *m* count; **hacer el ~ de votos** to count the votes

recuerdo *m* **1.** (*evocación*) memory; **en** [*o* **como**] ~ **de nuestro encuentro** in memory of our meeting; **tener un buen ~ de algo** to have good memories of sth **2.** (*de un viaje*) souvenir **3.** *pl* (*saludos*) regards *pl;* **dales muchos ~s de mi parte** send them my regards; **María te manda muchos ~s** María sends you her regards

recular *vi inf* to back down

recuperación *f* recovery; ~ **de datos** INFOR data retrieval; **exámen de** ~ ENS re-sit (exam)

recuperar **I.** *vt* **1.** (*recobrar*) to recover **2.** (*tiempo*) to make up **3.** ENS to pass (*a re-sit*); **no recuperé la física en el examen de septiembre** I failed my physics re-sit **II.** *vr:* ~**se** to recover

recurrir *vi* **1.** JUR to appeal **2.** (*acudir*) ~ **a alguien** to turn to sb; ~ **a algo** to resort to sth; ~ **a la justicia** to turn to the law; **si no me pagas ~é a un abogado** if you don't pay me I'm going to see a lawyer

recurso *m* **1.** JUR appeal; ~ **de apelación** appeal **2.** (*remedio*) solution; **no me queda otro ~ que...** I have no alternative but ...; **como último** ~ as a last resort **3.** *pl* (*bienes*) means *pl* **4.** *pl* (*reservas*) resources *pl*

recusar *vt* to reject; JUR to challenge

red *f* **1.** (*malla*) net; **caer en la ~** *fig* to fall into the trap **2.** (*sistema*) network; ~ **vial** road network **3.** ELEC mains *pl Brit,* power lines *pl*

redacción *f* **1.** ENS writing; **hacer una ~ sobre el mar** to write a composition on the sea **2.** PREN editing

redactar *vt* to write; (*documento*) to edit; (*testamento*) to draw up

redactor(a) *m(f)* writer; PREN editor

redada *f* raid

redención *f* redemption

redentor(a) *m(f)* redeemer

redicho, -a *adj inf* pretentious

redil *m* fold

redimir *vt* to redeem

rédito *m* yield, revenue

redoblar *vt* to intensify

redomado, -a *adj* **1.** (*astuto*) sly **2.** (*total*) utter

redonda *f* **en tres kilómetros a la** ~ for three kilometres in all directions

redondear *vt* to round off; ~ **por defecto/por exceso** to round up/down

redondel *m* circle

redondo, -a *adj* (*circular*) round; (*redondeado*) rounded; **caer** ~ (*derrumbarse*) to fall flat; (*quedarse mudo*) to be struck dumb; **negarse en** ~ to flatly refuse

reducción *f* reduction

reducido, -a *adj* (*pequeño*) small

reducir *irr como traducir* **I.** *vt* to reduce; (*someter*) to subdue **II.** *vr* ~**se a algo** to come down to sth

redundancia *f* redundancy

reedición *f* reissue

reeditar *vt* to republish

reelección *f* re-election

reelegir *irr como elegir vt* to re-elect

reembolsar *vt* to repay, to reimburse

reembolso *m* repayment; **enviar algo contra** ~ to send sth cash on delivery

reemplazar <z→c> *vt* to replace

reemplazo *m* replacement

reenganchar *vt, vr:* ~**se** to re-enlist

reestreno *m* rerun

reestructurar *vt* to restructure

referencia *f* reference; **hacer una pequeña ~ a alguien** to make a slight reference to sb; **hacer una ~ a algo** to refer to sth

referéndum <referéndums> *m* referendum

referente *adj* ~ **a algo** regarding sth; **(en lo)** ~ **a su queja** with regard to your complaint

referir *irr como sentir* I. *vt* 1.(*relatar*) to recount 2.(*remitir*) to refer II. *vr* ~se a algo/alguien to refer to sth/sb; en [*o* por] lo que se refiere a nuestras relaciones with regard to our relationship

refilón mirar de ~ a alguien to look sideways at sb

refinado, -a *adj* refined

refinamiento *m* refinement

refinar *vt* to refine

refinería *f* refinery

reflejar *vi, vt* to reflect

reflejo *m* 1.(*luz, imagen*) reflection 2. MED, PSICO reflex; para ello hay que ser rápido de ~s you need fast reflexes for that

reflejo, -a *adj* movimiento ~ reflex

reflexión *f* reflection

reflexionar *vi, vt* to reflect; reflexiona bien antes de dar ese paso think carefully before doing that

reflexivo, -a *adj* 1.(*sensato*) thoughtful 2. LING reflexive

reflujo *m* ebb

reforma *f* 1.(*mejora, modificación*) reform 2.(*renovación*) renovation; hacer una ~ en el cuarto de baño to have one's bathroom refurbished

reformar I. *vt* 1.(*mejorar, modificar*) to reform; ~ su conducta to change one's ways 2.(*renovar*) to renovate II. *vr:* ~se to mend one's ways

reformatorio *m* reformatory; ~ para delincuentes juveniles borstal *Brit*

reformista *adj, mf* reformist

reforzar *irr como forzar vt* 1.(*fortalecer*) to reinforce; (*con vigas*) to strengthen 2.(*animar*) to encourage

refractario, -a *adj* 1. QUÍM, FÍS heat--resistant 2.(*opuesto*) ser ~ a algo to be opposed to sth

refrán *m* saying, proverb

refregar *irr como fregar vt* to rub; (*con un cepillo, estropajo*) to scrub

refrenar I. *vt* to check II. *vr:* ~se to restrain oneself

refrendar *vt* to approve

refrescante *adj* refreshing

refrescar I. *vt* to refresh; (*cosas olvidadas*) to brush up; (*sentimiento*) to revive; ~ la memoria to refresh one's memory; el baño me ha refrescado the bath has revived me II. *vi* to cool down III. *vr:* ~se to cool down; (*beber*) to have a refreshing drink; (*reponerse*) to freshen up; el día se ha refrescado the weather has become cooler IV. *vimpers* to get cooler

refresco *m* soft drink

refriega *f* MIL skirmish; *inf* (*pelea*) scuffle; (*violenta*) brawl

refrigeración *f* refrigeration; (*de una habitación*) air conditioning; ~ por aire/agua air/water-cooling

refrigerador *m*, **refrigeradora** *f Perú* refrigerator

refrigerar *vt* to refrigerate; (*una habitación*) to air-condition

refuerzo *m* reinforcement

refugiado, -a *m, f* refugee

refugiarse *vr* (*en un lugar*) to take refuge; ~ en la bebida to turn to drink; ~ en una mentira to hide behind a lie

refugio *m* refuge; *t.* MIL (*construcción*) shelter; ~ (montañero) mountain shelter

refulgir <g→j> *vi* to shine

refunfuñar *vi* to grumble

refutar *vt* to refute

regadera *f* watering can; estar como una ~ *inf* to be as mad as a hatter

regadío *m* irrigation; de ~ irrigated

regalado, -a *adj* very cheap; a este precio el vestido es ~ at this price they are practically giving the dress away

regalar *vt* to give; en esta tienda regalan la fruta *fig* in this shop the fruit is dirt-cheap

regalía *f* privilege; (*del Estado, la Corona*) prerogative

regaliz *m* liquorice *Brit*, licorice *Am*

regalo *m* 1.(*obsequio*) present, gift; a este precio el coche es un ~ at this price the car is a steal 2.(*gusto*) pleasure; un ~ para la vista a sight for sore eyes

R

regañadientes a ~ reluctantly, grudgingly

regañar I. *vt inf* to scold **II.** *vi* to argue; (*dejar de tener trato*) to fall out; **ha regañado con su novio** (*reñir*) she has had a fight with her boyfriend; (*separarse*) she has split up with her boyfriend

regañón, -ona *adj* grumpy

regar *irr como fregar vt* **1.** (*una planta, el jardín*) to water; (*las calles*) to hose down; AGR to irrigate **2.** (*con un líquido*) to wet; (*con algo menudo*) to sprinkle; ~ **el suelo con arena** to sprinkle sand on the ground

regatear I. *vi* **1.** (*mercadear*) to haggle **2.** (*con el balón*) to dribble **II.** *vt* to haggle over

regateo *m sin pl* **1.** (*negociar*) haggling **2.** DEP dribbling

regazo *m* lap

regencia *f* regency

regeneración *f* regeneration

regenerar *vt, vr:* ~**se** to regenerate

regentar *vt* **1.** (*dirigir*) to manage **2.** (*ejercer*) to hold

regente *mf* **1.** (*que gobierna*) regent **2.** (*que dirige*) director; (*un negocio*) manager

régimen *m* <regímenes> **1.** (*sistema*) system; (*reglamentos*) regulations *pl* **2.** POL government **3.** (*dieta*) diet; **estar a** ~ to be on a diet; **poner a alguien a** ~ to put sb on a diet

regimiento *m* regiment

regio, -a *adj* royal

región *f* **1.** (*territorio*) region **2.** (*espacio*) area; (*del cuerpo*) region

regional *adj* regional

regir *irr como elegir* **I.** *vt* **1.** (*gobernar*) to govern; (*dirigir*) to direct **2.** (*ley*) to govern **3.** LING to take **II.** *vi* **1.** (*tener validez*) to apply **2.** *inf* (*estar cuerdo*) **¡tú no riges!** you're out of your mind!

registrador(a) *m(f)* registrar

registrar I. *vt* **1.** (*examinar*) to search **2.** (*inscribir*) to register (*anotar*) to record **3.** (*señalar, grabar*) to record **II.** *vr:* ~**se** **1.** (*inscribirse*) to register **2.** (*observarse*) to be re-

ported

registro *m* **1.** (*inspección*) search; ~ **de la casa** house search **2.** (*con un instrumento*) measurement; (*grabación*) recording **3.** (*inscripción*) registration (*anotación*) recording **4.** (*nota*) note; (*protocolo*) record; (*libro*) register; (*lista*) list; ~ **de inventario** inventory **5.** (*oficina, archivo*) registry; ~ **civil** registry office; ~ **de la propiedad** land registry

regla *f* **1.** (*instrumento*) ruler; ~ **de cálculo** slide rule **2.** (*norma*) rule; ~**s de exportación** export regulations; **por** ~ **general** as a rule; **estar en** ~ to be in order; **salir de la** ~ to go too far; **por qué** ~ **de tres...** *inf* why on earth ...; **la excepción confirma la** ~ *prov* the exception confirms the rule *prov* **3.** MAT **las cuatro** ~**s** addition, subtraction, multiplication and division **4.** (*menstruación*) period; **está con la** ~ she has her period

reglamentación *f* **1.** (*acción*) regulation **2.** (*reglas*) rules *pl*

reglamentar *vt* to regulate

reglamentario, -a *adj* **1.** (*relativo al reglamento*) regulatory **2.** (*conforme al reglamento*) regulatory

reglamento *m* rules *pl*; (*de una organización*) regulations *pl*; ~ **de tráfico** traffic regulations

reglar *vt* to regulate

regocijar I. *vr:* ~**se** **1.** (*alegrarse*) ~**se con algo** to delight in sth **2.** (*divertirse*) to amuse oneself **II.** *vt* to delight

regocijo *m* (*alegría*) delight; (*diversión*) pleasure

regodearse *vr* ~ **con** [*o* **en**] **algo** (*gozar*) to enjoy sth; (*alegrarse*) to delight in sth

regodeo *m* pleasure

regresar *vi, vr:* ~**se** to return, to go back

regresivo, -a *adj* regressive

regreso *m* (*vuelta*) return; (*viaje de*) ~ return journey; **estar de** ~ to have returned

reguero *m* trail

regulación *f* regulation; (*ajustación*)

adjustment; **de ~ automática** self-regulating

regulador *m* regulator; (*mecanismo*) control knob

regular I. *vt* to regulate; (*ajustar*) to adjust **II.** *adj* regular; (*mediano*) average; **de tamaño ~** normal size; **por lo ~** as a rule **III.** *adv* so-so

regularidad *f* regularity; **con ~** regularly

regularizar <z→c> *vt* to regularize

regusto *m* aftertaste

rehabilitación *f* rehabilitation

rehabilitar I. *vt* to rehabilitate **II.** *vr:* **~se** to be rehabilitated

rehacer *irr como hacer* **I.** *vt* **1.** (*volver a hacer*) to redo; **~ una carta** to rewrite a letter **2.** (*reconstruir*) to rebuild; (*reparar*) to repair; **~ su vida con alguien** to rebuild one's life with sb **II.** *vr:* **~se** to recover one's strength

rehén *m* hostage

rehogar <g→gu> *vt* to sauté

rehuir *irr como huir* *vt* to avoid; **~ una obligación** to shirk an obligation

rehusar *vt* to refuse; (*una reclamación*) to reject; **~ una invitación** to decline an invitation

reina *f* queen; *inf* (*cariño*) darling

reinado *m* reign

reinar *vi* **1.** (*gobernar*) to reign **2.** (*dominar*) to prevail

reincidir *vi* **~ en algo** to relapse into sth; **~ en un delito** to reoffend; **~ siempre en el mismo error** to keep making the same mistake

reincorporarse *vr* to return; **~ a una organización** to rejoin an organization; **~ al trabajo** to return to work

reino *m* realm; (*de un monarca*) kingdom; **Reino Unido** United Kingdom

reintegrar I. *vt* **1.** (*reincorporar*) to reintegrate; (*en un cargo*) to reinstate; **~ a alguien a su puesto de trabajo** to reinstate sb in his/her job **2.** (*dinero*) to repay **II.** *vr:* **~se** to return; **~se a una organización** to rejoin an organization; **~se al trabajo** to return to work

reír *irr vi, vr:* **~se** to laugh; **~se tontamente** to giggle; **echarse a ~** to burst out laughing; **~se de algo** to laugh at sth; **~se hasta de su sombra** to laugh at the slightest provocation; **me río de tu dinero** *fig* I don't give a damn about your money

reiterar *vt* to repeat

reivindicación *f* **~ (de algo)** claim (to sth)

reivindicar <c→qu> *vt* to claim; (*exigir*) to demand

reja *f* grill; **estar entre ~s** *fig, inf* to be behind bars

rejilla *f* **1.** (*enrejado*) grating **2.** (*parrilla*) grill **3.** (*tejido*) wickerwork

rejuvenecer *irr como crecer* *vt* to rejuvenate; **este peinado te rejuvenece** this haircut makes you look much younger

relación *f* **1.** (*entre cosas, hechos*) relationship, relation; **~ entre la causa y el efecto** relationship between cause and effect; **hacer ~ a algo** to refer to sth; **con** [*o* **en**] **~ a tu petición...** as regards your request ... **2.** (*entre dos magnitudes*) relationship, ratio; **~ calidad-precio** value for money; **los gastos no guardan ~ con el presupuesto** the expenses bear no relation to the budget **3.** *pl* (*noviazgo, amorío*) relationship; **relaciones públicas** public relations; **tienen buenas/malas relaciones** they have a good/bad relationship; **mantener relaciones sexuales con alguien** to have a sexual relationship with sb; **mantienen relaciones** they are going out with each other; **han roto sus relaciones** they have broken up

relacionar *vt* **~ algo (con algo)** to relate (sth to sth)

relajación *f* relaxation

relajado, -a *adj* relaxed

relajar *vt, vr:* **~se** to relax

relamer I. *vt* to lick **II.** *vr:* **~se** to lick one's lips

relamido, -a *adj* **1.** (*arreglado*) prim and proper **2.** (*afectado*) affected

relámpago *m* flash of lightning; **ser (veloz como) un ~** to be as fast as lightning

relampaguear I. *vi* to sparkle II. *vimpers* **relampagueaba** there was lightning

relatar *vt* (*información*) to report; (*una historia*) to tell

relatividad *f sin pl* relativity

relativo, -a *adj* relative; **un artículo ~ a...** an article about ...; **ser ~ a algo** to be relative to sth

relato *m* report; LIT story

relegar <g→gu> *vt* to relegate; **ser relegado al olvido** to be consigned to oblivion

relevante *adj* (*importante*) important; (*sobresaliente*) outstanding

relevar I. *vt* 1. (*liberar*) **~ a alguien de un juramento/de sus deudas** to release sb from an oath/from his/her debts; **~ a alguien de sus culpas** to exonerate sb from blame for his/her actions 2. (*destituir*) **~ a alguien de un cargo** to relieve sb of his/her post 3. (*reemplazar*) to relieve II. *vr*: **~se** to take turns

relevo *m* 1. DEP relay; **carrera de ~s** relay race 2. MIL changing of the guard

relieve *m* 1. ARTE, GEO relief; **en bajo ~** in bas-relief 2. (*renombre*) prominence; **de ~** important; **poner de ~** to emphasize

religión *f* religion

religioso, -a *adj* religious

relinchar *vi* to neigh, to whinny

relincho *m* neigh, whinny

reliquia *f* relic

rellano *m* landing

rellenar *vt* 1. (*llenar*) **~ algo de [o con] algo** to fill sth with sth; GASTR to stuff sth with sth 2. (*volver a llenar*) to refill 3. (*completar*) to fill out

relleno *m* filling; GASTR stuffing

relleno, -a *adj* 1. GASTR stuffed 2. *inf* (*gordo*) chubby

reloj *m* clock; (*de pulsera*) watch; **~ de arena** hourglass; **~ despertador** alarm clock; **~ para fichar** time clock; **~ de sol** sundial

relojero, -a *m, f* clockmaker; (*de relojes de pulsera*) watchmaker

reluciente *adj* shining; **~ de limpio**

shiny clean

relucir *irr como* lucir *vi* to shine; **sacar algo a ~** to bring sth up; **salir a ~** to come up

relumbrar *vi* to shine

remachar *vt* 1. (*golpear*) to hammer 2. (*subrayar*) to stress

remanente *m* surplus

remangarse <g→gu> *vr* **~** (**las mangas**) to roll up one's sleeves

remanso *m* pool; **~ de paz** haven of peace

remar *vi* to row

rematado, -a *adj* absolute

rematar I. *vt* to finish (off); (*animal*) to put out of its misery; DEP to shoot II. *vi* to end; DEP to shoot

remate *m* end; DEP shot; **para ~** to cap it all *Brit*, to top it all off *Am;* **por ~** finally; **estar loco de ~** to be completely mad

remediar *vt* 1. (*evitar*) to prevent; **no me cae bien, no puedo ~lo** I don't like him/her, I can't help it 2. (*reparar*) to repair; (*compensar*) to make up for; (*corregir*) to correct; **llorando no remedias nada** crying won't solve anything

remedio *m* remedy; (*compensación*) compensation; (*corrección*) correction; **sin ~** (*inútil*) hopeless; (*sin falta*) inevitable; **buscar ~ en sus amigos** to turn to one's friends for help; **buscar ~ en la bebida** to turn to drink; **no tener ~** to be a hopeless case; **tu problema no tiene ~** there is no solution to your problem; **no llores, ya no tiene ~** don't cry, there's nothing that can be done now; **no hay ~** there's nothing we can do; **no tenemos [o no hay] más ~ que...** there is no choice but to ...

remedo *m* 1. (*imitación*) imitation; (*mal hecha*) travesty 2. (*parodia*) parody

remendar <e→ie> *vt* to mend; (*con parches*) to patch; (*zurcir*) to darn

remesa *f* COM consignment; FIN remittance

remiendo *m* patch

remilgado, -a *adj* prim; (*quisquilloso*) fussy

remilgo *m* primness; (*quisquilloso*) fussiness; **sin ~s** without making a fuss; **hacer ~s** to make a fuss

reminiscencia *f* reminiscence; **la ópera tiene ~s wagnerianas** the opera shows Wagnerian influences

remiso, -a *adj* reluctant; **mostrarse ~ a hacer algo** to be reluctant to do sth

remite *m* sender's name and address

remitente *mf* sender

remitir *vt* 1.(*enviar*) to send; FIN to remit 2.(*referirse*) to refer

remo *m* 1.(*pala: con soporte*) oar; (*sin soporte*) paddle; **a ~** by rowing boat *Brit*, by rowboat *Am* 2. DEP rowing

remojar *vt* to soak; (*galleta*) to dip

remojo *m* soaking; **poner en ~** to leave to soak

remolacha *f* beet; (*roja*) beetroot; (*de azúcar*) (sugar) beet

remolcador *m* 1.(*camión*) breakdown truck *Brit,* tow truck *Am* 2.(*barco*) tug

remolcar <c→qu> *vt* to tow

remolino *m* 1.(*movimiento*) whirl; (*de agua*) whirlpool; **~ de viento** whirlwind 2.(*pelo*) cowlick 3.(*gente*) throng

remolque *m* 1.(*arrastre*) tow; **hacer algo a ~** *fig* to do sth reluctantly; **llevar algo a ~** to tow sth 2.(*vehículo*) trailer

remontar I. *vt* 1.(*superar*) to overcome 2.(*subir*) to go up II. *vr:* 1.(*ave*) to soar 2.(*gastos*) **~se a** to amount to 3.(*pertenecer, retroceder*) **~se a** to go back to

remorder <o→ue> *vt* to torment

remordimiento *m* remorse; **tener ~s (de conciencia) por algo** to feel remorseful about sth; **el ~ no lo deja dormir** he can't sleep for remorse

remoto, -a *adj* remote; **en tiempos ~s** long ago; **no existe ni la más remota posibilidad** there is not the slightest possibility; **no tener ni la más remota idea** to not have the slightest idea

remover <o→ue> *vt* 1.(*mover*) to remove 2.(*agitar*) to shake; (*dar vueltas*) to stir; (*la ensalada*) to toss 3.(*activar*) to stir up

remozar <z→c> *vt* to renovate

remuneración *f* remuneration

remunerar *vt* to pay

renacer *irr como crecer vi* 1.(*volver a nacer*) to be reborn 2.(*regenerarse*) to revive; **sentirse renacido** to feel completely revived

renacimiento *m* 1. ARTE, LIT **el ~** the renaissance 2.(*regeneración*) revival

renacuajo *m* tadpole

renal *adj* renal

rencilla *f* quarrel

rencor *m* ill feeling; **guardar ~ a alguien** to bear a grudge against sb

rencoroso, -a *adj* 1.(*vengativo*) spiteful 2.(*resentido*) resentful

rendición *f* surrender

rendido, -a *adj* 1.(*cansado*) exhausted 2.(*sumiso*) submissive; **cayó ~ ante su belleza** he was enchanted by her beauty

rendija *f* crack

rendimiento *m* 1.(*productividad*) yield; ECON (*máximo*) capacity 2.(*beneficio*) profit

rendir *irr como pedir* I. *vt* 1.(*rentar*) to yield; **la inversión ha rendido mucho** the investment has been very profitable 2.(*trabajar*) to produce; **estas máquinas rinden mucho** these machines are very productive 3.(*tributar*) to attribute; **las gracias a alguien** to thank sb 4.(*vencer*) to defeat 5.(*cansar*) to exhaust II. *vr:* **~se** 1.(*entregarse*) to surrender; **~se a las razones de alguien** to yield to sb's arguments 2.(*cansarse*) **~se de cansancio** to give in to one's exhaustion

renegado, -a *adj, m, f* apostate

renegar *irr como fregar* I. *vi* to renounce; **~ de la fe** to renounce one's faith II. *vt* to deny

RENFE *f abr de* **Red Nacional de Ferrocarriles Españoles** *Spanish state railway company*

renglón *m* line; **a ~ seguido** straight away

renombrado, -a *adj* renowned

renombre *m* renown; **de ~** well--known

renovación *f* renewal; (*de un edificio*) renovation

renovar <o→ue> *vt* to renew; (*casa*) to renovate

renta *f* 1.(*beneficio*) profit; (*ingresos*) income 2.(*pensión*) pension 3.(*alquiler*) rent; **en ~** for rent

rentable *adj* profitable

rentar *vt* 1.(*beneficio*) to yield 2.*AmL* (*alquilar*) to rent

renuencia *f* reluctance

renunciar *vi* 1.(*desistir*) **~ a** [*o de*] **algo** to renounce sth; **~ al trono** to abdicate the throne; **~ a un cargo** to resign from a post; **~ a un proyecto** to give up a project 2.(*rechazar*) **~ a algo** to reject sth

reñido, -a *adj* 1.(*enojado*) **estoy ~ con él** I have fallen out with him 2.(*encarnizado*) bitter

reñir *irr como ceñir* I. *vi* (*discutir*) to quarrel; (*enemistarse*) to fall out II. *vt* to scold

reo, -a *m, f* (*culpado*) defendant; (*autor*) culprit

reojo *m* **mirar de ~** (*con hostilidad*) to look askance at; (*con disimulo*) to look out of the corner of one's eye at

reparación *f* 1.(*arreglo*) repair 2.(*indemnización, enmienda*) compensation; **~ de perjuicios** damages *pl*

reparar I. *vt* 1.(*arreglar*) to repair 2.(*indemnizar, enmendar*) to compensate II. *vi* **~ en** (*advertir*) to notice; (*considerar*) to consider; **sin ~ en gastos** regardless of the cost; **no ~ en sacrificios/gastos** to spare no effort/expense III. *vr:* **~se** to restrain oneself

reparo *m* 1.(*inconveniente*) problem; **sin ~ alguno** without any difficulty; **me da ~ decírselo** I don't like to say it 2.(*objeción*) objection; **sin ~** without reservation; **no andar con ~s** to have no reservations; **poner ~s a algo** to raise objections to sth

repartición *f* (*distribución*) distribution; (*división*) division

repartir *vt* to distribute; (*correos*) to deliver

reparto *m* 1.(*distribución*) distribution; (*división*) division; **~ domiciliario** home delivery 2.CINE, TEAT cast

repasar *vt* 1.(*ropa*) to mend 2.(*texto, lección*) to revise 3.(*cuenta, lista*) to check

repaso *m* 1.(*revisión*) review 2.(*inspección*) check

repatriar *vt* to repatriate

repelente *adj* 1.(*rechazador*) repellent; **~ al agua** water-repellent 2.(*repugnante*) repulsive

repeler *vt* 1.(*rechazar*) to repel 2.(*repugnar*) to disgust

repente *m* **de ~** suddenly, all of a sudden

repentino, -a *adj* sudden

repercusión *f* repercussion; **tener gran ~** to have a great impact

repercutir *vi* 1.(*efecto*) **~ en algo** to have an effect on sth 2.(*del choque*) to rebound 3.(*eco*) to reverberate

repertorio *m* 1.(*lista*) list 2.*t.* TEAT repertoire, repertory

repesca *f* resit

repetición *f* repetition

repetir *irr como pedir* I. *vi* to repeat; **los ajos repiten mucho** garlic comes back on you II. *vt* (*reiterar, recitar*) to repeat; **~ curso** to stay down III. *vr:* **~se** to repeat oneself

repicar <c→qu> *vi, vt* to ring

repipi *adj inf* (*redicho*) la-di-da; **niño ~** (*sabelotodo*) little know-all

repique *m*, **repiqueteo** *m* peal

repisa *f* shelf; **~ de chimenea** mantelpiece; **~ de ventana** window ledge

replantear *vt* to raise again; (*reconsiderar*) to rethink

replegarse *irr como fregar* *vr* to fall back

repleto, -a *adj* **~ de algo** full of sth; (*demasiado*) crammed with sth; **el tren está ~** the train is packed

réplica *f* 1. (*respuesta*) reply; (*objeción*) rebuttal 2. ARTE replica

replicar <c→qu> I. *vt* to answer II. *vi* 1. (*replicar*) to reply 2. (*contradecir*) to answer back

repliegue *m* withdrawal

repoblación *f* (*personas*) repopulation; (*plantas*) replanting; ~ **forestal** reafforestation *Brit,* reforestation *Am*

repoblar <o→ue> *vt* (*personas*) to repopulate; (*plantas*) to replant; (*árboles*) to reafforest *Brit,* to reforest *Am*

repollo *m* cabbage

reponer *irr como* **poner** I. *vt* 1. (*reemplazar*) to replace 2. (*completar*) to replenish II. *vr:* ~**se** to recover

reportaje *m* report; PREN article; ~ **gráfico** illustrated report

reportero, -a *m, f* reporter; ~ **gráfico** press photographer

reposacabezas *m inv* headrest

reposado, -a *adj* peaceful; (*agua*) calm

reposar *vi* 1. (*descansar*) to rest; **aquí reposan los restos mortales de...** here lie the mortal remains of ... 2. (*líquidos*) to settle

reposición *f* replacement

reposo *m* (*tranquilidad*) peace; (*descanso*) rest; **en** ~ at rest

repostar *vt* 1. (*provisiones*) to stock up (with) 2. (*vehículo*) to refuel; (*combustible*) to fill up with

repostería *f* 1. (*pastelería*) cake shop 2. (*oficio*) pastrymaking 3. (*productos*) pastries *pl*

repostero, -a *m, f* pastrycook

reprender *vt* to reprimand; ~**le algo a alguien** to scold sb for sth

represa *f* 1. (*estancamiento*) pool 2. (*construcción*) dam

represalia *f* reprisal

representación *f* representation; TEAT performance; **en** [*o* **por**] ~ **de** representing

representante *mf* representative; TEAT, CINE agent, manager; (*actor*) actor, actress *m, f*

representar *vt* to represent; (*actuar*)

to play; (*una obra*) to perform; (*significar*) to mean; (*aparentar*) to seem; **representa ser más joven** he/she seems younger

representativo, -a *adj* representative

represión *f* repression

reprimenda *f* reprimand

reprimir I. *vt* to suppress II. *vr:* ~**se** to control oneself; ~**se de hablar** to refrain from speaking

reprobar <o→ue> *vt* to condemn

réprobo, -a *adj, m, f* reprobate

reprochar *vt* to reproach

reproche *m* reproach; **hacer** ~**s a alguien** (**por algo**) to reproach sb (for sth)

reproducción *f* reproduction

reproducir *irr como* **traducir** I. *vt* to reproduce; (*repetir*) to repeat II. *vr:* ~**se** to reproduce

reproductor(a) *adj* reproductive

reptar *vi* to crawl

reptil *m* reptile

república *f* republic

republicano, -a *adj, m, f* republican

repudiar *vt* to repudiate

repudio *m* repudiation

repuesto *m* 1. (*pieza*) spare part; **rueda de** ~ spare tyre *Brit,* spare tire *Am* 2. (*de alimentos*) supply

repuesto, -a *pp de* **reponer**

repugnancia *f* ~ **a algo** (*repulsión*) repugnance for sth; (*asco*) disgust for sth

repugnante *adj* disgusting

repugnar *vi* to be disgusting; **me repugna la carne grasosa** fatty meat makes me sick

repujar *vt* to emboss

repulsa *f* rejection

repulsión *f* (*aversión*) aversion; (*asco*) disgust

repulsivo, -a *adj* repulsive

reputación *f* reputation; **tener buena/mala** ~ to have a good/bad reputation

reputar *vt* ~ **a alguien de** [*o* **por**] **algo** to consider sb to be sth

requemado, -a *adj* brown; (*piel*) tanned

requerimiento *m* ~ (**de algo**) re-

R

quest (for sth); (*demanda*) demand (for sth); **a ~ de...** on the request of ...

requerir *irr como sentir vt* **1.** (*necesitar*) to require **2.** (*intimar*) to urge; **~ a alguien que... +*subj*** to urge sb to ...

requesón *m* cottage cheese

réquiem *m* requiem

requisa *f* **1.** (*inspección*) inspection **2.** (*confiscación*) confiscation; MIL requisition

requisar *vt* to confiscate; MIL to requisition

requisito *m* requirement; **ser ~ indispensable** to be absolutely essential; **~ previo** prerequisite

res *f* beast

resabio *m* **1.** (*sabor*) unpleasant aftertaste **2.** (*costumbre*) bad habit

resaca *f* **1.** (*olas*) undertow, undercurrent **2.** *inf* (*malestar*) hangover

resaltar *vi* to stand out; **hacer ~** to highlight

resarcir <c→z> I. *vt* **1.** (*compensar*) **~ a alguien de algo** to compensate sb for sth **2.** (*reparar*) to repay II. *vr* **~se de algo** to make up for sth

resbaladizo, -a *adj* slippery

resbalar *vi* to slide; (*sin querer*) to slip; (*coche*) to skid

resbalón *m* slip; **dar un ~** to slip

rescatar *vt* **1.** (*prisionero*) to rescue; (*con dinero*) to pay the ransom for **2.** (*náufrago*) to pick up **3.** (*cadáver*) to recover **4.** (*algo perdido*) to recover

rescate *m* **1.** (*de un prisionero*) rescue; (*con dinero*) ransoming **2.** (*recuperación*) recovery **3.** (*dinero*) ransom

rescindir *vt* to annul

rescisión *f* annulment

rescoldo *m* embers *pl*

resecar <c→qu> *vt* to dry out

reseco, -a *adj* **1.** (*muy seco*) very dry **2.** (*flaco*) skinny

resentido, -a *adj* **1.** *estar* (*ofendido*) resentful **2.** *ser* (*rencoroso*) bitter

resentimiento *m* resentment

resentirse *irr como sentir vr* **1.** (*ofenderse*) **~ por** [*o de*] **algo** to feel resentful about sth **2.** (*sentir dolor*) **~ de** [*o con*] **algo** to suffer from sth; **~ del costado** to have a sore side

reseña *f* **1.** (*de un libro*) review **2.** (*de una persona*) description **3.** (*narración*) report

reseñar *vt* **1.** (*libro*) to review **2.** (*persona*) to describe **3.** (*resumir*) to summarize

reserva *f* **1.** (*previsión, de plazas*) reservation; **a ~ de que +*subj*** unless; **tener algo en ~** to hold sth in reserve **2.** (*depósito*) *t.* FIN reserve; (*fondos*) reserves *pl* **3.** MIL reserves *pl* **4.** (*discreción*) secrecy; **guardar la ~** to be discrete **5.** (*circunspección*) reserve; **sin la menor ~** unreservedly **6.** (*vino*) vintage **7.** (*lugar*) reserve; (*para personas*) reservation; (*para animales*) wildlife reserve

reservado *m* **1.** FERRO reserved compartment **2.** (*habitación*) reserved room

reservado, -a *adj* **1.** (*derecho, callado*) reserved; **quedan ~s todos los derechos** all rights reserved **2.** (*confidencial*) confidential

reservar *vt* **1.** (*plaza*) to reserve; **~ un asiento** (*ocupar*) to save a seat; (*para un viaje*) to reserve a seat **2.** (*guardar*) to put by

resfriado *m* cold

resfriarse <3. *pres:* resfría> *vr* to catch a cold

resguardar I. *vt* to protect II. *vr* **~se de algo** to protect oneself from sth

resguardo *m* **1.** (*protección*) protection **2.** (*recibo*) receipt; (*vale*) voucher

residencia *f* residence; **~ de ancianos** old people's home; **~ de huérfanos** children's home; **~ habitual** usual place of residence; **cambiar de ~** to change one's address

residencial I. *adj* residential II. *m* housing development

residente *adj* resident

residir *vi* **1.** (*habitar*) to reside **2.** (*radicar*) **~ en** to lie in

residuo *m* **1.** (*resto*) residue **2.** *pl* (*basura*) waste

resignación *f* resignation

resina *f* resin
resistencia *f* resistance; ~ (**física**) stamina; ~ **al choque** shock resistance; **oponer** ~ to offer resistance
resistente *adj* resistant; ~ **al calor** heat-resistant
resistir I. *vi, vt* **1.** (*oponer resistencia*) to resist; ~ **a una tentación** to resist a temptation; **resistió la enfermedad** he/she overcame the illness **2.** (*aguantar*) **no resisto la comida pesada** I can't cope handle heavy food; **no puedo ~ a esta persona** I can't stand this person; **¡no resisto más!** I can't take any more! **II.** *vr:* ~**se** to resist
resollar *vi* to breathe heavily
resolución *f* **1.** (*firmeza*) resolve **2.** (*decisión*) decision; POL resolution; **tomar una** ~ to take a decision **3.** (*solución*) solution
resoluto, -a *adj* resolute
resolver *irr como* volver **I.** *vt* **1.** (*acordar*) to agree **2.** (*solucionar*) to solve; (*dudas*) to resolve **3.** (*decidir*) to decide **4.** (*disolver*) to dissolve **II.** *vr:* ~**se 1.** (*solucionarse*) to be solved **2.** (*decidirse*) to decide **3.** (*disolverse*) to dissolve
resonancia *f* resonance; **tener** ~ (*suceso*) to have an impact
resonante *adj* **con éxito** ~ with tremendous success; **una victoria** ~ a resounding victory
resonar <o→ue> *vi* to resound; ~ **fuera de las fronteras** *fig* to be heard beyond the borders
resoplar *vi* to huff and puff; ~ **de rabia** to snort angrily
resorte *m* **1.** (*muelle*) spring **2.** *fig* (*medio*) means *pl;* **tocar todos los** ~**s** to pull out all the stops
respaldar I. *vt* to support **II.** *vr:* ~**se** (*apoyarse*) to lean; (*hacia atrás*) to lean back
respaldo *m* **1.** (*de un asiento*) back **2.** (*apoyo*) support
respectivo, -a *adj* respective
respecto *m* **al** ~, **con** ~ **a eso** in that regard; **a este** ~ in this regard; **al** ~ **de** with regard to; (**con**) ~ **a** with regard to

respetable *adj* respectable
respetar *vt* **1.** (*honrar*) to respect; **hacerse** ~ to command respect **2.** (*cumplir*) to observe
respeto *m* respect; **de** ~ respectable; **faltar al** ~ **a alguien** to be disrespectful to(wards) sb; **ofrecer los** ~**s a alguien** to pay one's respects to sb
respetuoso, -a *adj* respectful; **ser** ~ **con las leyes** to respect the law
respingo *m* **dar un** ~ to start, to jump
respiración *f* (*inhalación*) breathing; (*aliento*) breath; ~ **artificial** artificial respiration; ~ **boca a boca** mouth to mouth resuscitation
respirar *vi* to breathe; **sin** ~ *fig* without stopping; **escuchar sin** ~ to listen with bated breath; **no me atrevo a** ~ **delante de él** I don't dare to open my mouth when he's around; **¡déjame que respire!** leave me in peace! *Brit,* give me a break! *Am*
respiratorio, -a *adj* respiratory; **vías respiratorias** air passages
respiro *m* **1.** (*pausa*) rest **2.** (*de alivio*) sign
resplandecer *irr como* crecer *vi* to shine
resplandeciente *adj* shining
resplandor *m* brightness
responder *vi* **1.** (*contestar*) to reply; **el perro responde al nombre de...** the dog answers to the name of ... **2.** (*contradecir*) to contradict **3.** (*corresponder*) to correspond **4.** (*ser responsable*) ~ **por algo** to answer for sth
respondón, -ona *adj* cheeky *Brit,* sassy *Am*
responsabilidad *f* responsibility; (*por un daño*) liability; ~ **de** [*o* **por**] **alguien** responsibility for sb
responsabilizar <z→c> **I.** *vt* ~ **a alguien de algo** to make sb responsible for sth **II.** *vr* ~**se de algo** to accept the responsibility for sth
responsable *adj* ~ (**de algo**) responsible (for sth); **ser** (**civilmente**) ~ to be liable
respuesta *f* answer; ~ **negativa**

negative reply; **en ~ a su carta del...** in reply to your letter of ...
resquebrajar *vt, vr:* ~**se** to crack
resquemor *m* resentment, ill-feeling
resquicio *m* crack
resta *f* subtraction
restablecer *irr como crecer* I. *vt* to re-establish; (*democracia, paz*) to restore II. *vr:* ~**se** to recover
restallar *vi* to crack; **hacer ~ el látigo** to crack the whip
restante *adj* remaining; **cantidad ~** remainder
restar I. *vi* to be left II. *vt* to take away; MAT to subtract
restauración *f* restoration
restaurante *m* restaurant
restaurar *vt* to restore
restitución *f* return
restituir *irr como huir* 1. (*devolver*) to return 2. (*restablecer*) to restore
resto *m* rest; MAT remainder; **los ~s** GASTR te leftovers; **los ~s** (**mortales**) the (mortal) remains
restregar *irr como fregar* I. *vt* to rub II. *vr* ~**se los ojos** to rub one's eyes
restricción *f* restriction; **sin restricciones** freely
restrictivo, -a *adj* restrictive
restringir <g→j> *vt* to restrict
resucitar I. *vi* to resuscitate II. *vt* 1. (*de la muerte*) to resuscitate 2. (*estilo, moda*) to revive
resuello *m* breathing; **sin ~** out of breath
resuelto, -a I. *pp de* resolver II. *adj* determined
resultado *m* result, outcome; **~ del reconocimiento** (**médico**) results of the medical examination; **dar buen ~** (*funcionar*) to work; (*no desgastarse*) to last; **dar mal ~** (*no funcionar*) to fail; (*desgastarse*) to wear out fast
resultar *vi* 1. (*deducirse*) ~ **de algo** to result from sth 2. (*surtir*) to be; ~ **muerto en un accidente** to be killed in an accident; ~ **en beneficio de alguien** to be to sb's benefit 3. (*comprobarse*) to turn out to be
resumen *m* summary; **en ~** in short

resumir *vt* to summarize
resurgir <g→j> *vi* 1. (*reaparecer*) to reappear 2. (*revivir*) to revive
resurrección *f* resurrection; **Domingo de Resurrección** Easter Sunday
retablo *m* reredos, altarpiece
retaguardia *f* rearguard; **a ~ de** behind
retahíla *f* string
retal *m* remnant
retar *vt* to challenge
retardar *vt* to delay
retardo *m* delay
retazo *m* 1. (*retal*) remnant 2. (*fragmento*) fragment; (*de conversación*) snippet
retener *irr como tener* *vt* to retain; (*detener*) to detain
reticente *adj* 1. (*discurso*) insinuating 2. (*reacio*) reluctant
retina *f* retina
retintín *m* 1. (*tonillo*) sarcastic tone 2. (*son*) ringing
retirada *f* 1. MIL retreat 2. (*eliminación*) withdrawal 3. (*jubilación*) retirement
retirado, -a *adj* 1. (*lejos*) remote 2. (*jubilado*) retired
retirar I. *vt* 1. (*apartar, echar*) to remove; (*tropas, dinero*) to withdraw 2. (*recoger, quitar*) to take away 3. (*negar*) to deny 4. (*jubilar*) to retire II. *vr:* ~**se** 1. (*abandonar*) ~**se de algo** to withdraw from sth 2. *t.* MIL (*retroceder*) to retreat 3. (*jubilarse*) to retire
retiro *m* 1. (*pensión*) pension 2. (*refugio*) retreat 3. (*retraimiento*) withdrawal
reto *m* challenge
retocar <c→qu> *vt* 1. (*corregir*) FOTO to retouch, to touch up 2. (*perfeccionar*) to perfect
retoño *m* 1. (*vástago*) shoot 2. (*niño*) kid
retoque *m* alteration; FOTO retouch
retorcer *irr como cocer* I. *vt* to twist II. *vr:* ~**se** 1. (*enroscarse*) to twist 2. (*de dolor*) to writhe
retorcido, -a *adj* 1. (*complicado*) **pensar de manera retorcida** to

think in a very confused way; ¡qué
~! how complicated! **2.** (*maligno*)
twisted; **una mente retorcida** a
warped mind

retorcimiento *m* twist

retórica *f* rhetoric

retórico, -a *adj* rhetorical

retornable *adj* **botella** (**no**) ~
(non-)returnable bottle

retornar I. *vi* to return **II.** *vt* to give
back

retorno *m* return

retortijón *m* **1.** (*ensortijamiento*)
twist **2.** (*dolor*) **tener un ~ de estómago** to have stomach cramp(s)

retozar <z→c> *vi* to frolic

retozón, -ona *adj* playful

retracción *f* retraction

retractarse *vr* ~ **de algo** to withdraw from sth

retraer *irr como traer vt, vr:* ~**se** to
withdraw

retraído, -a *adj* (*reservado*) reserved; (*poco sociable*) withdrawn

retraimiento *m* reserve

retransmisión *f* broadcast; ~ **de-
portiva** sports programme *Brit,*
sport(s) program *Am*

retransmitir *vt* to broadcast

retrasado, -a *adj* **1.** (*región*) backward **2.** MED ~ **mental** mentally re-
tarded

retrasar I. *vt* **1.** (*demorar*) to delay
2. (*reloj*) to put back **II.** *vi* to be slow
III. *vr:* ~**se** to be late

retraso *m* **1.** (*demora*) delay **2.** FIN arrears *pl;* **tener ~ en los pagos** to be
in arrears

retratar *vt* **1.** (*describir*) to depict, to
portray **2.** (*fotografiar*) to photograph **3.** (*pintar*) to paint a portrait of

retrato *m* **1.** (*representación*) portrait; **ser el vivo ~ de alguien** to be
the spitting image of sb **2.** (*descripción*) description

retrato-robot <retratos-robot> *m*
photofit® picture

retreta *f* retreat

retrete *m* lavatory, toilet

retribución *f* reward; (*sueldo*) payment

retribuir *irr como huir vt* to pay

retroactivo, -a *adj* retroactive

retroceder *vi* **1.** (*regresar*) to go
back **2.** (*desistir*) to give up;
(*echarse atrás*) to back down

retroceso *m* **1.** (*regresión*) ~ **en las
negociaciones** setback in the negotiations **2.** MED relapse

retrógrado, -a *adj pey* reactionary

retropropulsión *f* jet propulsion

retrospectivo, -a *adj* retrospective

retrovisor *m* rearview mirror; ~ **exterior** wing mirror *Brit,* side mirror
Am

retumbar *vi* to boom; (*resonar*) to
resound

reuma *m o f,* **reumatismo** *m sin pl*
rheumatism

reunificar <c→qu> *vt* to reunify

reunión *f* **1.** (*encuentro, asamblea,
conferencia*) meeting; ~ **de anti-
guos alumnos** class reunion **2.** (*el
juntar*) collection **3.** (*grupo, invitados*) gathering

reunir *irr* **I.** *vt* **1.** (*congregar*) to assemble **2.** (*unir*) to gather **3.** (*juntar*)
to reunite **4.** (*poseer*) to have **II.** *vr:*
~**se** **1.** (*congregarse*) to meet; (*informal*) to get together **2.** (*juntarse*) to
reunite

revalidar *vt* to confirm

revalorización *f* appreciation

revancha *f* **1.** revenge; **tomarse la ~**
to take one's revenge **2.** DEP return
match

revelación *f* revelation

revelado *m* developing

revelar *vt* **1.** (*dar a conocer*) to reveal, to disclose **2.** FOTO to develop

reventa *f* resale; (*entradas*) touting
Brit, scalping *Am*

reventar <e→ie> **I.** *vi* to burst
II. *vt* to break; (*globo, neumático*)
to burst, to annoy **III.** *vr:* ~**se** to
burst

reventón *m* **tener un ~** to have a flat
tyre

reverberación *f* (*de la luz*) reflection; (*del sonido*) reverberation

reverberar *vi* (*luz*) to reflect; (*sonido*) to reverberate

reverencia *f* **1.** (*veneración*) reverence **2.** (*inclinación*) bow

R
r

reverenciar *vt* to revere
reverendo, -a *adj* revered
reverente *adj* respectful
reversible *adj* reversible
reverso *m* other side
revertir *irr como sentir vi* to revert; **revirtió en mi beneficio** it worked to my advantage
revés *m* **1.**(*reverso*) other side; **al** [*o* **del**] ~ back to front; (*con lo de arriba abajo*) upside down; (*dentro para fuera*) inside out **2.**(*golpe*) blow with the back of the hand **3.** DEP backhand **4.**(*infortunio*) setback; ~ **de fortuna** stroke of bad luck
revestir *irr como pedir* I. *vt* **1.**(*recubrir*) ~ **algo con** [*o* **de**] **algo** to cover sth with sth **2.**(*tener*) ~ **importancia** to assume importance II. *vr:* ~**se** (*aparentar*) ~**se con** [*o* **de**] **algo** to arm oneself with sth
revisar *vt* to check; TÉC to inspect; (*textos, edición*) to revise
revisión *f* check; TÉC inspection; JUR, TIPO revision; MED checkup
revisor(a) *m(f)* **1.**(*controlador*) inspector; ~ **de cuentas** auditor **2.** FERRO ticket inspector
revista *f* **1.** PREN magazine; **las ~s del corazón** the gossip magazines **2.**(*inspección*) inspection; **pasar ~ a las tropas** to inspect the troops **3.**(*espectáculo*) revue, variety show
revivir *vi, vt* to revive
revocación *f* annulment
revocar <c→qu> *vt* **1.**(*anular*) to annul **2.**(*enlucir*) to plaster
revolcarse *irr como volcar vr* **1.**(*restregarse*) ~ (**por algo**) to roll around (in sth) **2.**(*obstinarse*) ~ **en algo** to insist on sth
revolotear *vi* to flutter about
revoltijo *m* jumble
revoltoso, -a *adj* mischievous
revolución *f* revolution
revolucionar *vt* **1.**(*amotinar*) to stir up **2.**(*transformar*) to revolutionize
revolucionario, -a *adj, m, f* revolutionary
revolver *irr como volver* I. *vt* **1.**(*mezclar*) to mix **2.**(*desordenar*) to mess up **3.**(*soliviantar*) to stir up II. *vr:*

~**se 1.**(*moverse*) to toss and turn; **se me revuelve el estómago** it makes my stomach turn **2.**(*el tiempo*) to break
revólver *m* revolver
revuelo *m* stir
revuelta *f* **1.**(*rebelión*) revolt **2.**(*encorvadura*) bend
revuelto, -a I. *pp de* **revolver** II. *adj* **1.**(*desordenado*) chaotic **2.**(*tiempo*) unsettled **3.**(*huevos*) scrambled
rey *m* king; **los Reyes** The King and Queen; **los Reyes Magos** the Magi, the Three Wise Men; **el día de Reyes** Epiphany, Twelfth Night
reyerta *f* quarrel, fight
rezagado, -a *m, f* straggler
rezagar <g→gu> I. *vt* **1.**(*dejar atrás*) to leave behind **2.**(*suspender*) to postpone II. *vr:* ~**se** to fall behind
rezar <z→c> I. *vt* ~ **una oración** to say a prayer II. *vi* **1.**(*decir*) to pray **2.**(*corresponder*) ~ **con algo** to apply to sth
rezo *m* prayer
rezongar <g→gu> *vi* to grumble
rezumar *vi* **1.**(*filtrarse*) ~ **por algo** to ooze from sth **2.**(*rebosar*) ~ **algo** to ooze with sth
RFA *abr de* **República Federal de Alemania** FRG
ría *f* estuary
riachuelo *m* stream
riada *f* flood
ribera *f* **1.**(*orilla*) bank **2.**(*tierra*) riverside
ribete *m* **1.**(*galón*) trimming **2.**(*adorno*) adornment; (*de una narración*) embellishment
ribetear *vt* to trim
ricino *m* castor oil plant
rico, -a I. *adj* **1.**(*acaudalado, abundante*) rich; (*fructífero*) fertile **2.**(*sabroso*) delicious **3.**(*simpático*) lovely, cute II. *m, f* **1.**(*rico*) rich person; **los ~s** the rich; **nuevo ~** nouveau riche **2.** *inf* (*apelativo*) mate *Brit*
ridiculez *f* **1.**(*lo ridículo, nimiedad*) ridiculousness **2.**(*tontería*) stupidity
ridiculizar <z→c> *vt* to ridicule

ridículo, -a *adj* ridiculous; **ponerse en ~** to make a fool of (oneself)

riego *m* irrigation

riel *m* **1.** FERRO rail **2.** (*barra*) bar; **los ~es de la cortina** the curtain rod

rienda *f* **1.** (*correa*) rein; **a ~ suelta** wildly; **dar ~ suelta a** to give free rein to; **llevar las ~s** to be in control **2.** *pl* (*gobierno*) reins *pl*

riesgo *m* risk; **~ profesional** occupational hazard; **a ~ de que** +*subj* at the risk of +*inf*

rifa *f* raffle

rifar *vt* to raffle

rifle *m* rifle

rigidez *f* **1.** (*inflexibilidad*) rigidity **2.** (*severidad*) strictness

rígido, -a *adj* **1.** (*inflexible*) rigid **2.** (*severo*) strict

rigor *m* **1.** (*severidad*) strictness **2.** (*exactitud*) rigorousness; **en ~** strictly speaking

riguroso, -a *adj* **1.** (*severo*) strict **2.** (*exacto*) rigorous

rimar *vi* to rhyme

rimbombante *adj* grandiloquent

rímel® *m* mascara

Rin *m* Rhine

rincón *m* **1.** (*esquina*) corner **2.** (*lugar*) nook

rinoceronte *m* rhinoceros

riña *f* quarrel

riñón *m* **1.** ANAT kidney; **costar un ~** to cost an arm and a leg **2.** *pl* (*parte de la espalda*) lower back

río *m* river; **~ abajo** downstream; **~ arriba** upstream; **cuando el ~ suena, algo lleva** *prov* where there's smoke, there's fire

riojano, -a *adj* of/from La Rioja

rioplatense *adj* of/from the River Plate region

riqueza *f* riches *pl*

risa *f* laughter; **mondarse de ~** to split one's sides laughing; **tomar algo a ~** to treat sth as a joke; **no estoy para ~s** I'm in no mood for jokes; **¡qué ~!** what a joke!

risco *m* crag

risotada *f* guffaw

ristra *f* string

risueño, -a *adj* smiling

ritmo *m* rhythm

rito *m* ritual; REL rite

ritual *adj*, *m* ritual

rival *adj*, *mf* rival

rivalidad *f* rivalry

rivalizar <z→c> *vi* to compete

rizado, -a *adj* curly

rizador *m* **~ eléctrico** curling tongs *pl*, curling iron *Am*

rizar <z→c> *vt*, *vr*: **~se** to curl

rizo *m* curl

RNE *f abr de* **Radio Nacional de España** *Spanish national radio network*

robar *vt* **1.** (*hurtar: algo*) to steal; (*a alguien*) to rob; (*a alguien con violencia*) to mug; **me ~on en París** I was robbed in Paris; **esto roba mucho tiempo** this takes up a lot of time **2.** (*en juegos*) to draw

roble *m* oak; **estar como un ~** to be as fit as a fiddle

robo *m* robbery; **ser un ~** *fig* to be a rip-off; **¿20 libras? ¡qué ~!** twenty pounds? that's highway robbery!

robot <robots> *m* robot

robustecer *irr como crecer* *vt* to strengthen

robusto, -a *adj* robust

roca *f* rock

roce *m* **1.** (*fricción*) brush **2.** (*huella*) scrape **3.** (*contacto*) contact

rociar <3. *pres:* rocía> *vt* to sprinkle

rocín *m* nag

rocío *m* dew

rock *m* rock

rockero, -a **I.** *adj* rock **II.** *m, f* (*fan*) rock fan; (*músico*) rock musician

rocoso, -a *adj* rocky

rodado, -a *adj* **tráfico ~** vehicular traffic

rodaja *f* slice

rodaje *m* shooting

Ródano *m* Rhone

rodar <o→ue> **I.** *vi* to roll; (*sobre el eje*) to turn; **~ por el suelo** to roll across the floor; **echarlo todo a ~** to spoil everything **II.** *vt* to shoot

rodear **I.** *vi* **~ por algo** to go round sth **II.** *vt* **~ (de algo)** to surround (with sth) **III.** *vr*: **~se de algo/alguien** to surround oneself with sth/

sb
rodeo *m* detour; **dar un ~** to take a detour; **hablar sin ~s** to speak plainly; **¡no (te) andes con** [*o* **déjate de**] **~s!** don't beat about the bush!
rodilla *f* knee; **de ~s** on one's knees; **ponerse de ~s** to kneel
rodillo *m* **1.** TÉC roller **2.** (*de cocina*) rolling pin
roedor *m* rodent
roer *irr vt* **1.** (*ratonar*) ~ **algo** to gnaw at sth; **los ratones royeron mi libro** the mice gnawed my book **2.** (*concomer*) **las preocupaciones me roen el alma** I'm worrying my life away
rogar <o→ue> *vt* to ask; (*con humildad*) to beg; **rogamos nos contesten inmediatamente nuestra carta** we would be grateful if you could give us an immediate reply
rojizo, -a *adj* reddish
rojo, -a *adj* red; **al ~ (vivo)** red-hot; *fig* at fever pitch; **poner ~ a alguien** to make sb blush; **ponerse ~** to go red
rol *m* **1.** (*papel*) role **2.** (*lista*) list; **~ de pago** payroll
rollizo, -a *adj* plump
rollo *m* **1.** (*de papel, alambre*) *t.* FOTO, GASTR roll; **hacer un ~ de algo** to roll sth up **2.** *inf* **ir a su ~** to do as one likes; **soltar siempre el mismo ~** to always come out with the same old stuff; **tener mucho ~** to be full of crap *inf*; **¡qué ~ de película!** what a boring film!; **acaba con el ~, muchacho** get on with it, son; **corta el ~** cut the crap *inf*; **¿de qué va el ~?** what's it all about?
Roma *f* Rome
romance I. *adj* Romance II. *m* **1.** LIT ballad **2.** HIST (*castellano*) Castilian; **hablar en ~** *fig* to speak plainly
románico, -a *adj* Romanesque
romano, -a *adj, m, f* Roman
romanticismo *m sin pl* romanticism
romántico, -a *adj, m, f* romantic
rombo *m* rhombus; **en forma de ~** diamond-shaped
romería *f* **1.** (*peregrinaje*) pilgrimage

2. (*fiesta*) festival
romero *m* rosemary
romero, -a *m, f* pilgrim
romo, -a *adj* blunt
rompecabezas *m inv* (*juego*) brain-teaser; (*acertijo*) riddle
rompehielos *m inv* icebreaker
rompeolas *m inv* breakwater
romper I. *vi* **1.** (*olas*) to break **2.** (*empezar*) to burst; **~ a llorar** to burst into tears **3.** (*día*) to break; **al ~ el día** at the break of day **4.** (*separarse*) to break up II. *vt* **1.** (*destrozar, quebrar*) to break; (*cristal*) to shatter; (*plato*) to smash; (*papel, tela*) to tear; (*zapatos*) to wear out; **~ algo a golpes** to bash sth to pieces **2.** (*negociaciones, relaciones*) to break off; (*contrato, promesa*) to break; **~ el silencio/el encanto** to break the silence/the spell III. *vr:* **~se** to break; **~se la cabeza** *fig* to rack one's brains; **~se la pierna** to break one's leg
rompimiento *m* breaking; (*de negociaciones, relaciones*) breakdown
ron *m* rum
roncar <c→qu> *vi* to snore
roncha *f* (*hinchazón*) swilling; (*cardenal*) bruise; (*picadura*) sting
ronco, -a *adj* (*afónico*) voiceless; (*áspero*) hoarse
ronda *f* round; **hacer una ~ de inspección por la fábrica** to do an inspection tour of the factory; **pagar una ~** to buy a round
rondar I. *vi* to be on patrol II. *vt* to patrol
ronquido *m* snore
ronronear *vi* to purr
roña *f* **1.** (*mugre*) filth **2.** (*mezquindad*) meanness **3.** (*sarna*) scab
roñoso, -a *adj* **1.** (*tacaño*) mean, tight **2.** (*sucio*) filthy **3.** (*sarnoso*) scabby
ropa *f* **1.** (*géneros de tela*) **~ blanca** white wash + *pl vb* whites *pl Brit;* **~ de cama** bedclothes *pl;* **~ de color** colored wash + *pl vb* coloureds *pl Brit;* **~ delicada** delicates *pl;* **~ (interior)** underwear **2.** (*vestidos, traje*) clothes *pl*

ropa (= clothing, clothes) is used in the singular: "Normalmente lavo la ropa delicada a mano."

ropaje *m* clothing; (*ropa elegante*) finery
ropero *m* wardrobe
rosa I. *adj* pink; ~ **fucsia** fuchsia II. *f* rose; **color de** ~ pink; **no hay** ~ **sin espinas** *prov* every rose has its thorn *prov*
rosado, -a *adj* pink; **vino** ~ rosé (wine)
rosal *m* rosebush
rosario *m* rosary; **rezar el** ~ to say the rosary
rosca *f* 1. TÉC thread; **el tornillo se pasó de** ~ the screw broke the thread 2. (*bollo*) (ring-shaped) bread roll; (*torta*) sponge ring; **no comerse una** ~ *fig* not to get off with anyone; **hacer la** ~ **a alguien** to suck up to sb; **pasarse de** ~ *fig* to go too far
rosetón *m* rose window
rosquilla *f* doughnut
rostro *m* face
rotación *f* rotation; ~ **de mercancías** stock turnover
rotativo *m* newspaper
rotativo, -a *adj* rotary
roto *m* (*desgarrón*) tear; (*agujero*) hole
roto, -a I. *pp de* **romper** II. *adj* 1. (*despedazado*) broken; **un vestido** ~ a torn dress 2. (*destrozado*) destroyed
rótula *f* knee joint
rotulador *m* felt-tip pen
rotular *vt* (*letreros*) to make; (*mercancías*) to label
rótulo *m* sign; (*encabezamiento*) heading; (*etiqueta*) ticket
rotundo, -a *adj* emphatic; **un éxito** ~ a resounding success; **una negativa rotunda** a flat refusal, sonorous
rotura *f* (*acción*) breaking; (*parte quebrada*) break; ~ (**de hueso**) fracture

roturar *vt* to plough *Brit*, to plow *Am*
rozadura *f* scratch; (*de la piel*) graze
rozar <z→c> I. *vi* to rub II. *vt* (*tocar ligeramente*) to brush; (*frotar*) to rub; ~ **la ridiculez** to border on the ridiculous, to graze III. *vr:* ~**se** 1. (*restregarse*) to rub 2. (*relacionarse*) to rub shoulders
rte. *abr de* **remitente** sender
RTVE *f abr de* **Radio Televisión Española** Spanish state broadcasting corporation
rubí *m* ruby
rubio, -a I. *adj* fair; **tabaco** ~ Virginia tobacco II. *m*, *f* blond; (*mujer*) blonde
rubor *m* 1. (*color*) blush 2. (*vergüenza*) shame
ruboroso, -a *adj* 1. (*vergonzoso*) ashamed 2. (*ruborizado*) blushing
rúbrica *f* 1. (*después del nombre*) flourish 2. (*epígrafe*) heading
rubricar <c→qu> *vt* 1. (*firmar*) to sign 2. (*sellar*) to seal
rudeza *f* 1. (*brusquedad*) rudeness 2. (*tosquedad*) coarseness
rudimentario, -a *adj* rudimentary
rudo, -a *adj* 1. (*material*) rough; (*sin trabajar*) raw 2. (*persona tosca*) coarse; (*brusca*) rude
rueda *f* 1. (*que gira*) wheel; ~ **de repuesto** spare tyre; **todo marcha sobre** ~**s** everything is going smoothly 2. (*de bicicleta*) tyre *Brit*, tire *Am* 3. (*de personas*) ring; ~ **de prensa** press conference
ruedo *m* bullring
ruego *m* request; ~**s y preguntas** POL any other business
rufián *m* 1. (*chulo*) pimp 2. (*granuja*) scoundrel
rugby *m* rugby
rugido *m* roar
rugir <g→j> *vi* to roar
rugoso, -a *adj* wrinkled
ruido *m* noise; **hacer** ~ *fig* to cause a stir
ruidoso, -a *adj* noisy
ruin *adj* 1. (*malvado*) wicked; (*vil*) despicable 2. (*tacaño*) mean
ruina *f* 1. (*destrucción*) destruction 2. ARQUIT ruin; **convertir una ciu-**

R
r

dad en ~**s** to raze a city to the ground; **este hombre está hecho una** ~ this man is a wreck **3.**(*perdición*) downfall; **estar en la** ~ ECON to be bankrupt

ruindad *f* **1.**(*maldad*) wickedness **2.**(*tacañería*) meanness

ruinoso, -a *adj* **1.**(*edificios*) dilapidated **2.**(*perjudicial*) disastrous; ECON ruinous

ruiseñor *m* nightingale

ruleta *f* roulette

rulo *m* roller

rulot *f* caravan *Brit,* trailer *Am*

Rumanía *f* Romania

rumano, -a *adj, m, f* Romanian

rumba *f* rumba

rumbo *m* direction; AERO, NÁUT course; **con** ~ **a** bound for; **tomar** ~ **a un puerto** to head for a port; **tomar otro** ~ POL to change course; **no tengo** ~ **fijo** I'm not going anywhere in particular

rumboso, -a *adj* generous

rumiante *m* ruminant

rumiar *vt* **1.**(*vacas*) to ruminate **2.** *inf*(*cavilar*) to think over

rumor *m* **1.**(*chisme*) rumour *Brit,* rumor *Am;* **corren ~es de que...** it is rumoured that ... **2.**(*ruido*) murmur; ~ **de voces** buzz of conversation

runrún *m inf* **1.**(*ruido*) buzz; (*murmullo*) murmur **2.**(*chisme*) rumour *Brit,* rumor *Am*

rupestre *adj* **pintura** ~ cave painting

ruptura *f* breaking; (*de relaciones*) breaking-off

rural *adj* rural; **vida** ~ country life

Rusia *f* Russia

ruso, -a *adj, m, f* Russian

rústico, -a **I.** *adj* **1.**(*campestre*) rural **2.**(*tosco*) rough; **en rústica** TIPO paperback **II.** *m, f* peasant; *pey* yokel

ruta *f* route

rutina *f* routine

rutinario, -a *adj* routine

S, s *f* S, s; ~ **de Soria** S for Sugar

S. *abr de* **San** St

S.A. *f* **1.** *abr de* **Sociedad Anónima** plc **2.** *abr de* **Su Alteza** Your Highness

sábado *m* Saturday; *v.t.* **lunes**

sábana *f* sheet; **se me han pegado las ~s** *inf* I've overslept

sabandija *f* **1.**(*insecto*) bug **2.** *pey* (*persona*) wretch

sabañón *m* chilblain

sabelotodo *mf inv, inf* know-all *Brit,* know-it-all *Am*

saber *irr* **I.** *vt* **1.**(*estar informado*) to know; **¿se puede** ~ **si... ?** could you tell me if ...?; **sin ~lo yo** without my knowing; **¡cualquiera sabe!** who knows?; **vete tú a** ~ it's anyone's guess; (**al menos**) **que yo sepa** as far as I know; **para que lo sepas** for your information; **¡y qué sé yo!** how should I know! **2.**(*tener habilidad*) **él sabe ruso** he can speak Russian **3.**(*descubrir*) to find out; **lo supe por mi hermano** I heard about it from my brother **II.** *vi* **1.**(*tener sabor*) to taste **2.**(*agradar*) **me supo mal aquella respuesta** that reply upset me **3.**(*tener noticia*) to have news **III.** *m sin pl* knowledge

sabiduría *f* **1.**(*conocimientos*) knowledge **2.**(*sensatez*) wisdom **3.**(*erudición*) learning

sabiendas a ~ knowingly

sabio, -a **I.** *adj* wise **II.** *m, f* scholar

sable *m* sabre *Brit,* saber *Am*

sabor *m* taste; **tiene** (**un**) ~ **a...** it tastes of ...

saborear *vt* to savour *Brit,* to savor *Am;* (*triunfo*) to relish

sabotaje *m* sabotage

sabotear *vt* to sabotage

sabroso, -a *adj* **1.**(*sazonado*) tasty **2.**(*gracioso*) racy **3.**(*salado*) slightly salty

sacacorchos *m inv* corkscrew

sacapuntas *m inv* pencil sharpener

sacar <c→qu> **I.** *vt* **1.** (*de un sitio*) to take out, to remove; (*agua*) to draw; (*diente*) to pull (out); ~ **a bailar** to invite to dance; **¿de dónde lo has sacado?** where did you get it from? **2.** (*de una situación*) to get; ~ **adelante** (*persona*) to look after; (*negocio*) to run; (*niño*) to bring up **3.** (*solucionar*) to solve **4.** (*reconocer*) to recognize **5.** (*obtener*) to obtain; (*premio, entrada*) to get; ~ **en claro** (**de**) to gather (from) **6.** MIN to extract **7.** *inf* (*foto*) to take **8.** (*producto*) to bring out; ~ **a la venta** to put on sale **II.** *vi* (*tenis*) to serve; (*fútbol*) to take a goal kick **III.** *vr* to take out

sacarina *f sin pl* saccharin

sacerdote *m* priest

saciar I. *vt* to satisfy, to satiate; (*sed*) to quench **II.** *vr:* ~**se** *t. fig* to satiate oneself

saco *m* **1.** (*bolsa*) bag; (*costal*) sack; ~ **de dormir** sleeping bag **2.** (*prenda*) jacket

sacramento *m* sacrament

sacrificar <c→qu> **I.** *vt* **1.** (*ofrecer*) to sacrifice; *t. fig* to give up **2.** (*animal*) to slaughter **II.** *vr* ~**se** to sacrifice oneself

sacrificio *m* sacrifice

sacrilegio *m* sacrilege

sacrílego, -a *adj* sacrilegious

sacristán *m* sacristan

sacristía *f* vestry, sacristy

sacro, -a *adj* **1.** (*sagrado*) sacred **2.** ANAT **hueso** ~ sacrum

sacudida *f* shake; ~ **eléctrica** electric shock; ~ **sísmica** earthquake

sacudir I. *vt* **1.** (*agitar*) to shake; (*cola*) to swish **2.** (*pegar*) to belt **II.** *vr:* ~**se** (*a alguien*) to get rid of

sádico, -a I. *adj* sadistic **II.** *m, f* sadist

sadismo *m sin pl* sadism

sadomasoquismo *m sin pl* sadomasochism

sadomasoquista I. *adj* sadomasochistic **II.** *mf* sadomasochist

saeta *f* **1.** (*flecha*) arrow **2.** MÚS *pious song typically sung in the religious processions in Spain during Easter week*

safari *m* safari

sagacidad *f sin pl* astuteness

sagaz *adj* astute

Sagitario *m* Sagittarius

sagrado, -a <sacratísimo> *adj* sacred

Sáhara *m* **el** ~ the Sahara

Sajonia *f* Saxony

sal *f* **1.** (*condimento*) salt; ~ **común** table salt **2.** (*gracia*) wit; (*encanto*) charm **3.** AmL (*mala suerte*) bad luck

sala *f* **1.** (*habitación*) room; (*grande*) hall; ~ **de espera/estar** waiting/living room **2.** JUR courtroom

salado, -a *adj* **1.** (*comida*) salty **2.** (*gracioso*) witty **3.** AmL (*infortunado*) unfortunate

salami *m* salami

salar *vt* **1.** (*condimentar*) to add salt to **2.** (*para conservar*) to salt

salarial *adj* wage

salario *m* wages *pl*

salchicha *f* sausage; **perro** ~ *inf* (*dachshund*) sausage dog *Brit,* hotdog *Am*

salchichón *m* salami-type cured sausage

saldar *vt* **1.** (*cuenta*) to pay; (*deuda*) to pay off; (*diferencias*) to settle **2.** (*mercancía*) to sell off

saldo *m* **1.** (*de cuenta*) balance; (*pago*) payment **2.** *pl* (*rebajas*) sales *pl*

salero *m* **1.** (*objeto*) salt cellar *Brit,* salt shaker *Am* **2.** (*gracia*) wit

salida *f* **1.** (*puerta*) way out; (*para coches, de emergencia*) exit; **callejón sin** ~ dead end **2.** (*de un tren*) departure; (*de un barco*) sailing **3.** (*astr*) rising; ~ **del sol** sunrise **4.** DEP start **5.** COM sale; (*partida*) consignment; ~ **de capital** capital outflow **6.** *inf* (*ocurrencia*) witty remark **7.** (*solución*) way out

salido, -a *adj inf* randy, horny

saliente *adj* **1.** (*excelente*) outstanding **2.** (*ojos*) protruding

salir *irr* **I.** *vi* **1.** *t.* INFOR (*ir al exterior*) to go out; (*ir fuera*) to go away; ~ **con alguien** *inf* to go out with sb; ~ **adelante** to make progress **2.** (*de* *viaje*) to leave; (*avión*) to depart; ~ **ileso/ganando** to come out unscathed/the better **3.**(*sol*) to rise; ~ **a la luz** to come to light **4.**(*convertirse*) to turn into **5.**(*parecerse*) to look like **6.** DEP to start **7.**(*costar*) to cost **II.** *vr:* ~**se 1.**(*líquido*) to overflow; (*leche*) to boil over **2.**(*de una organización*) to leave

saliva *f* saliva

salmantino, -a *adj* of/from Salamanca

salmo *m* psalm

salmón I. *adj* salmon-pink **II.** *m* salmon

salmuera *f* brine

salón *m* **1.**(*de casa*) living-room **2.**(*local*) hall; ~ **de actos** assembly hall

salpicadero *m* AUTO dashboard

salpicar <c→qu> *vt* **1.**(*rociar*) to sprinkle; (*con pintura*) to splash **2.**(*manchar*) to spatter

salpicón *m* **1.** GASTR ≈ salmagundi (*chopped seafood or meat with oil, vinegar and seasoning*) **2.** Col, Ecua (*bebida*) cold drink of fruit juice **3.**(*mancha*) spatter

---

? In **Colombia** and **Ecuador** the **salpicón** is a cold fruit drink. In Spain, however, **salpicón** is a cold meat, fish or seafood dish.

---

salsa *f* **1.** GASTR sauce **2.**(*gracia*) humour *Brit,* humor *Am* **3.** MÚS salsa

saltador(a) *m(f)* DEP jumper; ~ **de altura** high-jumper; ~ **de longitud** long-jumper

saltamontes *m inv* grasshopper

saltar I. *vi* **1.**(*botar, lanzarse*) to jump; (*chispas*) to fly up; ~ **por los aires** to blow up; *fig* to get furious; ~ **de alegría** to jump for joy; ~ **a la cuerda** to skip; ~ **al agua** to jump into the water **2.**(*explotar*) to explode; (*los plomos*) to blow **3.**(*picarse*) to explode **4.**(*irrumpir*) to come out **5.**(*desprenderse*) to come off **II.** *vt* **1.**(*movimiento*) to jump (over) **2.**(*animal*) to cover **III.** *vr:*

~**se 1.**(*botón*) to come off **2.**(*ley*) to break

salteador(a) *m(f)* holdup man *m,* holdup woman *f*

saltear *vt* GASTR to sauté

saltimbanqui *m* acrobat

salto *m* **1.**(*bote*) jump; **dar un** ~ to jump **2.** DEP jump; ~ **de altura** high jump; ~ **de longitud** long jump **3.** INFOR ~ **de página** page break **4.**(*trabajo*) rapid promotion **5.**(*bata*) ~ **de cama** negligée

saltón, -ona *adj* **1.**(*saltarín*) restless **2.**(*sobresaliente*) protruding

salubre *adj* <salubérrimo> (*saludable*) healthy; (*curativo*) curative

salud *f sin pl* (*estado físico*) health; **¡~!** (*al estornudar*) bless you!; (*al brindar*) good health!; **beber a la ~ de...** to drink to the health of ...

saludable *adj* **1.**(*sano*) healthy **2.**(*provechoso*) beneficial

saludar *vt* **1.**(*al encontrar*) to greet; (*con la mano*) to wave; MIL to salute; **le saluda atentamente su...** *form* yours faithfully ... **2.**(*recibir*) to welcome **3.**(*mandar saludos*) to send regards to

saludo *m* **1.**(*palabras*) greeting; **con un cordial** ~ *form* yours sincerely; **¡déle ~s de mi parte!** give him/her my regards **2.**(*recibimiento*) welcome

salva *f* salvo; (*de aplausos*) round

salvación *f* rescue; REL salvation

salvado *m* bran

salvador(a) I. *adj* saving; REL salvational **II.** *m(f)* rescuer; REL saviour *Brit,* savior *Am*

Salvador *m* **El** ~ El Salvador

? The Republic of **El Salvador** lies in the northeastern part of Central America. The capital is **San Salvador.** The official language of the country is Spanish and the monetary unit of **El Salvador** is the **colón.** The country is the smallest and most densely populated in Central America.

salvadoreño, -a *adj, m, f* Salvadoran
salvaguardar *vt* to safeguard; (*derechos*) to protect
salvajada *f* savage deed, atrocity
salvaje I. *adj* (*animal*) wild; (*persona*) uncivilized; (*acto*) savage **II.** *mf* savage
salvajismo *m sin pl* savagery
salvamanteles *m inv* table mat, place mat *Am*
salvamento *m* salvation; (*accidente*) rescue
salvar I. *vt* **1.** *t.* REL (*del peligro*) to save **2.** (*obstáculo*) to get round; (*problema*) to overcome; (*apariencias*) to keep up **II.** *vr:* ~**se** to save oneself
salvavidas *m inv* lifebelt; **bote** ~ lifeboat; **chaleco** ~ lifejacket
salvia *f* sage
salvo *prep* except; ~ **que** [*o* **si**] +*subj* unless
salvo, -a *adj* safe
salvoconducto *m* safe-conduct
samba *f* samba
san *adj* Saint

> [!] **san** is used before masculine proper nouns not beginning with do- o to-: "San Antonio, San Francisco"; **santo** is used with names beginning with do- o to-: "Santo Domingo, Santo Tomás."

sanar I. *vi* to recover **II.** *vt* to cure
sanatorio *m* sanatorium
sanción *f* **1.** (*multa*) penalty **2.** ECON sanction
sancionar *vt* **1.** (*castigar*) to punish **2.** ECON to impose sanctions on
sandalia *f* sandal
sandez *f* stupid action
sandía *f* watermelon
sandinista *adj, mf Nic* Sandinista
sándwich *m* GASTR toasted sandwich
saneamiento *m* **1.** (*de un edificio*) repair; (*de un terreno*) drainage **2.** (*de economía*) reform
sanear *vt* **1.** (*edificio*) to clean up; (*tierra*) to drain **2.** (*economía*) to reform **3.** JUR to compensate

Sanfermines *mpl Pamplona bull-running festival*
sangrar *vi, vt* to bleed
sangre *f* blood; **a** ~ **fría** in cold blood; **de** ~ **azul** blue-blooded; **pura** ~ thoroughbred
sangría *f* **1.** MED bleeding **2.** TIPO indentation **3.** (*bebida*) sangria

> [?] **Sangría** is a punch made from red wine, water, sugar, lemon and orange. It is normally served in a **jarra de barro** (earthenware jug).

sangriento, -a *adj* bloody; (*injusticia*) cruel; **hecho** ~ bloody event
sanguijuela *f* leech
sanguinario, -a *adj* bloodthirsty
sanguíneo, -a *adj* **1.** MED blood **2.** (*temperamento*) sanguine
sanidad *f sin pl* health
sanitario *m* (*wáter*) toilet
sanitario, -a *adj* health; (*medidas*) sanitary
sano, -a *adj* **1.** (*robusto*) healthy; ~ **de juicio** of sound mind; ~ **y salvo** safe and sound **2.** (*no roto*) intact
Santiago *m* ~ (**de Chile**) Santiago
santiaguino, -a *adj* of/from Santiago (in Chile)
santiamén *m* **en un** ~ in a jiffy
santidad *f* holiness
santificar <c→qu> *vt* to sanctify
santiguarse <gu→gü> *vr* to cross oneself
santo, -a I. *adj* sacred, holy; (*piadoso*) saintly; **la Santa Sede** the Holy See **II.** *m, f* **1.** (*personaje*) saint; **día de Todos los Santos** All Saint's Day; **se le fue el** ~ **al cielo** he/she forgot what he/she was going to say **2.** (*fiesta*) saint's day, name day **3.** (*imagen*) (religious) illustration **4.** *fig* ~ **y seña** password
santuario *m* **1.** (*templo*) shrine **2.** (*refugio*) sanctuary, refuge
sapo *m* toad
saque *m* DEP (*fútbol*) goal kick, throw-in; **tener buen** ~ *fig* to have a hearty appetite
saquear *vt* to loot

S
s

saqueo *m* looting
sarampión *m sin pl* MED measles
sarcasmo *m sin pl* sarcasm
sarcástico, -a *adj* sarcastic
sarcófago *m* sarcophagus
sardina *f* sardine
sardónico, -a *adj* sardonic
sargento *m* sergeant
sargo *m* sea bream, sheepshead
sarmiento *m* (*tallo*) vine shoot
sarna *f sin pl* MED scabies
sarpullido *m* MED (*irritación*) rash
sarro *m* **1.** MED (*de los dientes*) tartar **2.** (*poso*) deposit
sartén *f* frying pan
sastre, -a *m, f* tailor
sastrería *f* **1.** (*tienda*) tailor's shop **2.** (*oficio*) tailoring
satélite *m* satellite
sátira *f* LIT satire
satisfacción *f* satisfaction
satisfacer *irr como* **hacer** **I.** *vt* **1.** (*pagar*) to honour *Brit*, to honor *Am* **2.** (*deseo*) to satisfy; (*sed*) to quench; (*demanda*) to settle **3.** (*requisitos*) to meet **4.** (*agravio*) to make amends for **II.** *vr:* ~**se 1.** (*contentarse*) to satisfy oneself **2.** (*agravio*) to obtain redress
satisfecho, -a **I.** *pp de* **satisfacer** **II.** *adj* (*contento*) contented; (*exigencias*) satisfied
saturación *f* saturation
saturar *vt* to saturate
sauce *m* willow; ~ **llorón** weeping willow
saudí <saudíes>, **saudita** *adj, mf* Saudi; **Arabia Saudí** Saudi Arabia
sauna *f* sauna
savia *f* sap
saxofón *m*, **saxófono** *m* saxophone
sazonado, -a *adj* **1.** (*comida*) seasoned **2.** (*fruta*) ripe **3.** (*frase*) witty
sazonar *vt* **1.** (*comida*) to season **2.** (*madurar*) to ripen
scanner *m* scanner
se *pron pers* **1.** *forma reflexiva: m sing* himself; *f sing* herself; *de cosa* itself; *pl* themselves; *de Ud.* yourself; *de Uds.* yourselves **2.** *objeto indirecto: m sing* to him; *f sing* to her; *a una cosa* to it; *pl* to them; *a Ud., Uds.* to

you; **mi hermana** ~ **lo prestó a su amiga** my sister lent it to her friend **3.** (*oración impers*) you; ~ **aprende mucho en esta clase** you learn a lot in this class **4.** (*oración pasiva*) ~ **confirmó la sentencia** the sentence was confirmed
sé 1. *pres de* **saber**
sebo *m* grease; (*vela*) tallow; **hacer** ~ *Arg, inf* to idle
seca *f* (*sequía*) drought
secador *m* (*para la ropa*) clothes horse; (*para el pelo*) hair dryer
secadora *f* tumble dryer
secano *m* dry land
secar <c→qu> **I.** *vt* **1.** (*deshumedecer*) to dry **2.** (*enjugar*) to wipe **II.** *vr:* ~**se 1.** (*deshumedecer*) to dry up **2.** (*enjugar*) to wipe up
sección *f* **1.** (*perfil*) cross-section **2.** (*parte*) section **3.** (*departamento*) branch
seco, -a *adj* **1.** (*sin agua*) dry; **golpe** ~ dull blow; **frutos** ~**s** dried fruit and nuts **2.** (*flaco*) skinny **3.** (*tajante*) curt; **en** ~ suddenly
secretaría *f* **1.** (*oficina*) secretary's office **2.** (*cargo*) secretaryship **3.** *AmL* (*ministerio*) ministry
secretario, -a *m, f* **1.** (*de oficina*) secretary **2.** *AmL* (*ministro*) minister
secreto *m* **1.** (*misterio*) secret **2.** (*reserva*) secrecy
secreto, -a *adj* secret
secta *f* sect
sectario, -a *adj* sectarian
sector *m* **1.** *t.* MAT, INFOR sector **2.** (*grupo*) group
secuela *f* consequence; (*de enfermedad*) after-effect
secuencia *f t.* CINE sequence; ~ **de caracteres** *t.* INFOR series of characters
secuestrar *vt* **1.** (*raptar*) to kidnap **2.** (*embargar*) to confiscate
secuestro *m* **1.** (*rapto*) kidnapping **2.** (*bienes*) confiscation
secular *adj* secular
secundar *vt* to second
secundario, -a *adj* (*segundo*) secondary; **papel** ~ CINE, TEAT supporting role

sed *f* thirst; **tener** ~ to be thirsty

seda *f* silk

sedal *m* (fishing) line

sedante I. *adj* (de efecto) ~ soothing **II.** *m* sedative

sedativo, -a *adj* sedative

sede *f* seat; **la Santa Sede** the Holy See

sedentario, -a *adj* sedentary

sediento, -a *adj* thirsty

sedimentar I. *vt* to deposit **II.** *vr:* ~**se** to settle

sedimento *m* deposit

sedoso, -a *adj* silky, silken

seducir *irr como traducir vt* **1.** (persuadir) to seduce **2.** (fascinar) to charm

seductor(a) I. *adj* seductive **II.** *m(f)* seducer

sefardí, sefardita I. *adj* Sephardic **II.** *mf* Sephardi

> **?** A **sefardí** is the descendant of a Jewish person who originated from Spain or Portugal. The language is also called **sefardí** (or **ladino**). The **sefardíes** were driven out of the Iberian Peninsula at the end of the 15th century. They subsequently settled in North Africa and some European countries.

segadora *f* mower

segar *irr como fregar vt* **1.** (cortar) to reap; (hierba) to mow **2.** (frustrar) to dash

seglar *adj* lay, secular

segmento *m* segment

segregación *f* segregation

segregar <g→gu> *vt* to segregate

seguido, -a *adj* **1.** (continuo) consecutive **2.** (en línea recta) straight; **todo** ~ straight on

seguidor(a) *m(f)* follower, supporter; DEP fan

seguimiento *m* (persecución) chase; (sucesión) continuation

seguir *irr* **I.** *vt* **1.** (suceder) to follow; ~ **adelante** to carry on **2.** (perse-

guir) to chase **II.** *vi* (por una calle) to follow **III.** *vr:* ~**se** to ensue

según I. *prep* according to; ~ **eso** according to that; ~ **la ley** in accordance with the law; ~ **tus propias palabras** judging by your own words **II.** *adv* **1.** (como) as; ~ **lo convenido** as we agreed **2.** (mientras) while **3.** (eventualidad) ~ (**y como**) it depends

segunda *f* AUTO second gear; FERRO second class; **con ~s** *fig* with veiled meaning

segundero *m* second hand

segundo *m* (tiempo) second

segundo, -a *adj* second; *v.t.* **octavo**

seguramente *adv* **1.** (de modo seguro) certainly **2.** (probablemente) probably

seguridad *f* **1.** (protección) security; **Seguridad Social** ADMIN Social Security **2.** (certeza) certainty **3.** (firmeza) confidence **4.** (garantía) surety

seguro I. *m* **1.** (contrato) insurance **2.** (mecanismo) safety device **II.** *adv* for sure; **sobre** ~ on safe ground

seguro, -a *adj* **1.** (exento de peligro) safe **2.** (firme) secure **3.** (convencido) certain; ~ **de sí mismo** confident; ¿**estás** ~? are you sure?

seis *adj inv, m inv* six; *v.t.* **ocho**

seiscientos, -as *adj* six hundred; *v.t.* **ochocientos**

seísmo *m* (temblor) tremor; (terremoto) earthquake

selección *f* selection; ~ **nacional** national team; ~ **natural** natural selection

seleccionar *vt* to select

selectividad *f* UNIV university entrance exam

> **?** The **selectividad** is a state school leaving exam, which all pupils must successfully sit after having completed the **bachillerato**, if they wish to enrol at a Spanish university.

selecto, -a *adj* select; (ambiente) exclusive

S

sellar *vt* **1.** (*timbrar*) to stamp **2.** (*precintar*) to seal; (*cerrar*) to close
sello *m* **1.** (*tampón, de correos*) stamp **2.** (*precinto*) seal
selva *f* (*bosque*) forest; (*tropical*) jungle
semáforo *m* traffic lights *pl*
semana *f* week; **fin de ~** weekend
semanal *adj* weekly
semblante *m* **1.** (*cara*) face **2.** (*expresión*) appearance
sembrar <e→ie> *vt* **1.** (*plantar*) to sow **2.** (*esparcir*) to scatter; (*terror*) to spread
semejante **I.** *adj* **1.** (*similar*) similar **2.** (*tal*) such; **~ persona** such a person **II.** *m* fellow man
semejanza *f* (*similitud*) similarity; (*físico*) resemblance
semejar **I.** *vi* to resemble **II.** *vr:* **~se** to look alike
semen *m* semen
semental *m* stud
semestral *adj* half-yearly
semiautomático, -a *adj* semi-automatic
semicírculo *m* semicircle
semiconsciente *adj* half-conscious
semidesnatado, -a *adj* semi--skimmed
semidiós, -osa *m, f* demigod
semidormido, -a *adj* half-asleep
semifinal *f* semi-final
semilla *f* seed
seminario *m* seminary
sémola *f* semolina
sempiterno, -a *adj* everlasting
Sena *m* Seine
senado *m* senate
senador(a) *m(f)* senator
sencillez *f* **1.** (*simplicidad*) simplicity **2.** (*naturalidad*) naturalness
sencillo, -a *adj* **1.** (*simple*) simple; (*fácil*) easy **2.** (*natural*) natural
senda *f*, **sendero** *m* path
senderismo *m* hillwalking, hiking
sendos, -as *adj* each of two
senil *adj* senile
seno *m* **1.** ANAT, MAT sinus **2.** (*pecho*) breast **3.** (*de organización*) heart
sensación *f* **1.** (*sentimiento*) feeling **2.** (*novedad*) sensation

sensacional *adj* sensational
sensatez *f* good sense
sensato, -a *adj* sensible
sensibilidad *f* sensitivity
sensibilizar <z→c> *vt* to sensitize
sensible *adj* **1.** (*sensitivo*) sensitive; (*impresionable*) impressionable **2.** (*perceptible*) noticeable
sensiblero, -a *adj* (over)sentimental
sensitivo, -a *adj* **1.** (*sensorial*) sensory **2.** (*sensible*) sensitive
sensor *m* sensor
sensorial *adj,* **sensorio, -a** *adj* sensory
sensual *adj* sensual
sentada *f* sit-in, sit-down protest
sentado, -a **I.** *pp de* sentar **II.** *adj* (*sensato*) sensible; **dar por ~** to take for granted
sentar <e→ie> **I.** *vi* (*ropa*) to suit; **~ bien/mal** (*comida*) to agree/disagree **II.** *vt* to sit; **estar sentado** to be sitting down **III.** *vr:* **~se 1.** (*asentarse*) to sit down; **¡siéntese!** have a seat! **2.** (*establecerse*) to settle down
sentencia *f* **1.** (*proverbio*) maxim **2.** JUR sentence
sentenciar *vt* to sentence
sentido *m* **1.** (*facultad*) sense; **doble ~** (*significado*) double meaning; (*dirección*) two-way; **sin ~** unconscious **2.** (*dirección*) direction; **en el ~ de las agujas del reloj** clockwise; **~ único** one-way **3.** (*significado*) meaning
sentido, -a *adj* **1.** (*conmovido*) deeply felt **2.** (*sensible*) sensitive
sentimental *adj* sentimental
sentimiento *m* **1.** (*emoción*) feeling **2.** (*pena*) sorrow; **le acompaño en el ~** please accept my condolences
sentir *irr* **I.** *vt* **1.** (*percibir*) to feel **2.** (*lamentar*) to be sorry for; **lo siento mucho** I am very sorry **II.** *vr:* **~se** to feel; **~se bien/mal** to feel good/bad **III.** *m* opinion
seña *f* **1.** (*gesto*) sign; **hablar por ~s** to use sign language **2.** (*particularidad*) distinguishing mark; **por más ~s** to be more specific **3.** *pl* (*dirección*) address
señal *f* **1.** (*signo*) sign; **~ de tráfico**

road sign; **en ~ de** as a sign of; **dar ~es de vida** *fig* to show oneself **2.**(*teléfono*) tone; **~ de comunicar** engaged tone *Brit,* busy signal *Am* **3.**(*huella*) mark; **ni ~** no trace **4.**(*cicatriz*) scar **5.**(*adelanto*) deposit; **paga y ~** first payment

señalado, -a *adj* **1.**(*famoso*) distinguished **2.**(*importante*) special

señalar *vt* **1.**(*anunciar*) to announce **2.**(*marcar*) to mark **3.**(*mostrar*) to show **4.**(*indicar*) to point out

señalizar <z→c> *vt* to signpost

señor(a) **I.** *adj inf* lordly **II.** *m(f)* **1.**(*dueño*) owner **2.**(*hombre*) (gentle)man; (*mujer*) wife; (*dama*) lady; **¡~as y ~es!** ladies and gentlemen! **3.**(*título*) Mister *m,* Mrs *f;* **muy ~ mío:** Dear Sir; **¡no, ~!** not a bit of it!; **¡sí, ~!** it certainly is! **4.** REL **el Señor** Our Lord

señorita *f* **1.**(*tratamiento*) Miss **2.**(*chica*) young lady

señorito *m* young gentleman

señuelo *m* decoy; *fig* lure

separación *f* **1.**(*desunión*) separation **2.**(*espacio*) distance

separado *adv* **por ~** separately; **contar por ~** to count one by one

separar **I.** *vt* **1.**(*desunir*) to separate **2.**(*apartar*) to remove **II.** *vr:* **~se** to separate

sepia *f* cuttlefish

septentrional *adj elev* northern

septiembre *m* September; *v.t.* **marzo**

séptimo, -a *adj* seventh; *v.t.* **octavo**

septuagésimo, -a *adj* seventieth; *v.t.* **octavo**

sepulcral *adj* sepulchral; (*silencio*) deathly

sepulcro *m* tomb

sepultar *vt* **1.** *t. fig* (*inhumar*) to bury **2.**(*cubrir*) to conceal **II.** *vr:* **~se** (*sumergir*) to hide away

sepultura *f* **1.**(*sepelio*) burial **2.**(*tumba*) grave

sepulturero, -a *m, f* gravedigger

sequedad *f* **1.**(*aridez*) dryness **2.**(*descortesía*) bluntness; **con ~** curtly

sequía *f* drought

séquito *m* retinue

ser *irr* **I.** *aux* **1.**(*construcción de la pasiva*) **las casas fueron vendidas** the houses were sold **2.**(*en frases pasivas*) **era de esperar** it was to be expected **II.** *vi* **1.**(*existir, constituir*) to be; **4 y 4 son ocho** 4 and 4 make eight; **éramos cuatro** there were four of us; **¿quién es?** who is it?; (*teléfono*) who's calling?; **soy Pepe** (*a la puerta*) it's me, Pepe; (*al teléfono*) this is Pepe; **son las cuatro** it's four o'clock **2.**(*costar*) **¿a cuánto es el pollo?** how much is the chicken? **3.**(*convertirse en*) to become; **¿qué es de él?** what's he doing now?; **¿qué ha sido de ella?** whatever happened to her? **4.**(*con 'de'*) **el paquete es de él** the parcel belongs to him; **el anillo es de plata** the ring is made of silver; **~ de Escocia** to be from Scotland **5.**(*con 'para'*) **¿para quién es el vino?** who is the wine for?; **no es para ponerse así** there's no need to get so angry **6.**(*con 'que'*) **esto es que no lo has visto bien** you can't have seen it properly; **es que ahora no puedo** the thing is I can't at the moment **7.**(*enfático, interrogativo*) **¡esto es!** that's the way!; (*correcto*) that's right!; **¿pero qué es esto?** what's this then?; **¡no puede ~!** that can't be! **8.**(*en infinitivo*) **manera de ~** manner; **a no ~ que +**subj unless **9.**(*en indicativo, subjuntivo*) **es más** what is more; **siendo así** that being so; **y eso es todo** and that's that **III.** *m* being; **~ vivo** living creature; **~ humano** human being

> [!] **ser** expresses inherent characteristics of people or objects: "Mis primos son altos y delgados."
> **estar** is used to express temporary characteristics which may change: "Enrique está muy enamorado de su novia; Está enfermo desde hace una semana."

S
s

Serbia *f* Serbia

serbio, -a *adj, m, f* Serb

serenarse *vr* (*calmarse*) to calm down; (*tiempo*) to clear up

serenidad *f sin pl* calmness

sereno *m* (*vigilante*) night watchman

sereno, -a *adj* 1. (*sosegado*) calm 2. (*sin nubes*) clear

serial *m* RADIO, TV serial

serie *f* 1. (*sucesión*) series *inv;* **fuera de ~** out of order; *fig* outstanding, special 2. *t.* MAT (*gran cantidad*) set; **fabricar en ~** to mass produce 3. DEP competition

seriedad *f sin pl* seriousness

serigrafía *f* TIPO serigraphy

serio, -a *adj* 1. (*grave*) serious; **¿en ~?** are you serious? 2. (*severo*) solemn 3. (*responsable*) trustworthy

sermón *m* sermon

seropositivo, -a *adj* HIV-positive

serpentear *vi* to creep; *fig* to wind

serpentina *f* (*de papel*) streamer

serpiente *f* snake; **~ de cascabel** rattlesnake

serranía *f* mountainous area

serrano, -a *adj* highland

serrar <e→ie> *vt* to saw

serrín *m* sawdust

serrucho *m* (*sierra*) handsaw

servicio *m* 1. (*acción de servir*) service; **~ militar** military service; **estar de ~** to be on duty; **hacer el ~** to do military service; **hacer un flaco ~ a alguien** to do sb more harm than good 2. (*servidumbre*) (domestic) service; **entrada de ~** tradesman's entrance *Brit,* service entrance *Am* 3. (*cubierto*) set 4. (*retrete*) lavatory 5. DEP serve

servidor *m* INFOR server

servidor(a) *m(f)* (*criado*) servant; **¿quién es el último?** – **~** who is the last in the queue? – I am

servidumbre *f* 1. (*personal*) servants *pl* 2. (*esclavitud*) servitude

servil *adj* servile

servilleta *f* napkin

servir *irr como pedir* I. *vi* 1. (*ser útil*) to be of use; **no sirve de nada** it's no use 2. (*ser soldado*) to serve 3. (*ayudar*) to assist; **¿en qué puedo**

~le? can I help you? 4. DEP to serve 5. (*suministrar*) to supply 6. (*comida*) to serve; (*bebida*) to pour out II. *vr:* **~se** to make use

sesenta *adj inv, m* sixty; *v.t.* **ochenta**

sesgo *m* 1. (*oblicuidad*) slant; **al ~** aslant 2. (*orientación*) direction

sesión *f* 1. (*reunión*) session 2. (*representación*) show(ing)

seso *m* 1. ANAT brain 2. (*inteligencia*) brains *pl;* **calentarse los ~s** *inf* to rack one's brains

sesudo, -a *adj* 1. (*inteligente*) brainy 2. (*sensato*) sensible

set *m* <sets> 1. DEP set 2. (*conjunto*) service

seta *f* mushroom

setecientos, -as *adj* seven hundred; *v.t.* **ochocientos**

setenta *adj inv, m* seventy; *v.t.* **ochenta**

seudónimo *m* pseudonym

Seúl *m* Seoul

severidad *f sin pl* severity

severo, -a *adj* severe, harsh; (*brusco*) rough; (*riguroso*) strict

Sevilla *f* Seville

sevillano, -a *adj, m, f* Sevillian

sexagésimo, -a *adj* sixtieth; *v.t.* **octavo**

sexo *m* 1. (*práctica*) sex 2. (*órganos*) sex organs *pl*

sexto, -a *adj* sixth; *v.t.* **octavo**

sexual *adj* sexual

sexualidad *f sin pl* sexuality

si I. *conj* 1. (*condicional*) if; **~ acaso** maybe; **~ no** otherwise; **por ~ acaso** just in case 2. (*en preguntas indirectas*) whether, if; **¿y ~...?** what if ...? 3. (*en oraciones concesivas*) **~ bien** although 4. (*comparación*) **como ~...** +*subj* as if ... 5. (*en frases desiderativas*) **¡~ hiciera más calor!** if only it were warmer! 6. (*protesta, sorpresa*) but; **¡pero ~ se está riendo!** but he/she's laughing! II. *m* MÚS B

sí I. *adv* yes; **¡(claro) que ~!** of course!; **creo que ~** I think so; **porque ~** (*es así*) because that's the way it is; (*lo digo yo*) because I say so; **volver en ~** to regain conscious-

El (cuarto de) baño

The bathroom

1	alcachofa f de la ducha	shower head
2	barra f	rail
3	tubo m	hose
4	azulejo m	tile
5	grifo m	tap Brit, faucet Am
6	esponja f	sponge
7	bañera f	bath, bathtub Am
8	desagüe m	plughole, drain Am
9	pastilla f de jabón	bar of soap
10	cortina f de la ducha	shower curtain
11	cesta f para la ropa sucia	dirty clothes basket
12	toalla f de baño	bath towel
13	alfombrilla f de baño	bath mat

14	zapatillas fpl	slippers
15	taburete m	stool
16	escobilla f del wáter [o retrete]	toilet brush
17	inodoro m, taza f (del wáter)	toilet bowl
18	asiento m del wáter	toilet seat
19	tapa f, tapadera f (del wáter)	lid
20	cisterna f, depósito m (del wáter)	cistern, tank Am
21	papel m higiénico	toilet paper
22	albornoz m	bathrobe
23	polvos mpl de talco	talcum powder
24	desodorante m en espray, espray m desodorante	deodorant spray
25	persiana f	blind

ness **II.** *pron pers: m sing* himself; *f sing* herself; *cosa, objeto* itself; **a ~ mismo** to himself; **de ~** in itself; **dar de ~** to be extensive; (*tela*) to give; **en** [*o* **de por**] **~** separately; **estar fuera de ~** to be beside oneself; **hablar entre ~** to talk among themselves; **por ~** in itself; **mirar por ~** to be selfish **III.** *m* consent; **dar el ~** to agree

siamés, -esa *adj* Siamese

sibarita I. *adj* sybaritic **II.** *mf* sybarite, pleasure seeker

sicalíptico, -a *adj* saucy

sicario *m* hired assassin

Sicilia *f* Sicily

sida, SIDA *m abr de* **síndrome de inmunodeficiencia adquirida** Aids, AIDS

siderúrgico, -a *adj* iron and steel

sidra *f* cider

siembra *f* sowing

siempre *adv* always; **a la hora de ~** at the usual time; **¡hasta ~!** see you!; **por ~ jamás** for ever and ever; **~ que** [*o* **y cuando**] +*subj* provided that, as long as

sien *f* ANAT temple

sierra *f* **1.** (*herramienta*) saw **2.** (*lugar*) sawmill **3.** GEO mountain range

siervo, -a *m, f* **1.** (*esclavo*) slave **2.** (*servidor*) servant

siesta *f* siesta; **echar** [*o* **dormir**] **la ~** to have a nap

siete *adj inv, m* seven; *v.t.* **ocho**

sífilis *f* syphilis

sifón *m* **1.** TÉC trap **2.** (*botella*) siphon **3.** (*soda*) soda

sigilo *m* **1.** (*discreción*) discretion **2.** (*secreto*) stealth

sigla *f* **1.** (*letra inicial*) initial **2.** (*rótulo de siglas*) acronym

siglo *m* century; **el ~ XXI** the 21st century; **el Siglo de Oro** the Golden Age; **por los ~s de los ~s** for ever and ever

significación *f* significance

significado *m* meaning

significar <c→qu> *vt, vi* to mean

significativo, -a *adj* significant

signo *m* **1.** *t.* MAT (*señal*) sign **2.** (*de puntuación*) mark

siguiente I. *adj* following **II.** *mf* next

silbar *vi, vt* **1.** (*persona*) to whistle; (*bala*) to whizz **2.** (*abuchear*) to boo

silbato *m* whistle

silbido *m* whistle; (*de los oídos*) ringing

silenciador *m* silencer

silenciar *vt* **1.** (*suceso*) to hush up **2.** (*persona*) to silence

silencio *m* **1.** silence; **guardar ~** to remain silent; **¡~!** quiet! **2.** MÚS rest

silencioso, -a *adj* **1.** (*poco hablador*) quiet **2.** (*callado*) silent

silicio *m* silicon

silla *f* **1.** *t.* REL (*asiento*) chair; **~ giratoria** swivel chair; **~ plegable** folding chair; **~ de ruedas** wheelchair **2.** (*montura*) saddle

sillín *m* saddle *Brit*, seat *Am*

sillón *m* (*butaca*) armchair

silueta *f* silhouette; **cuidar la ~** to look after one's figure

silvestre *adj* wild

simbólico, -a *adj* symbolic

simbolizar <z→c> *vt* to symbolize

símbolo *m* symbol

simétrico, -a *adj* symmetrical

simiente *f* seed

similar *adj* similar

simio *m* ape

simpatía *f* **1.** (*agrado*) liking; **tener ~ por** to have a liking for **2.** (*carácter*) friendliness

simpático, -a *adj* friendly

simpatizante *mf* sympathizer

simpatizar <z→c> *vi* **1.** (*congeniar*) to get on *Brit*, to get along *Am* **2.** (*identificarse con*) to sympathize

simple <simplísimo *o* simplicísimo> **I.** *adj* **1.** (*sencillo, persona*) simple **2.** (*fácil*) easy **3.** (*mero*) pure; **a ~ vista** with the naked eye **II.** *m* **1.** (*persona*) simpleton **2.** (*tenis*) singles *inv*

simpleza *f* **1.** (*bobería*) simpleness **2.** (*tontería*) silly thing

simplicidad *f sin pl* simplicity

simplificar <c→qu> *vt* to simplify

simposio *m* symposium

simulacro *m* **1.** (*apariencia*) simulacrum **2.** (*acción simulada*) sham

simular *vt* to simulate

simultáneo, -a *adj* simultaneous

sin I. *prep* without; ~ **dormir** without sleep; ~ **querer** unintentionally; ~ **más** nothing more; ~ **más ni más** without thinking about it, without further ado; **estar ~ algo** to be out of sth **II.** *adv* ~ **embargo** however

sinagoga *f* REL synagogue

sinceridad *f* sincerity

sincero, -a *adj* sincere

sincronizar <z→c> *vt* to synchronize

sindical *adj* union

sindicalista I. *adj* (*sindical*) union **II.** *mf* trade unionist

sindicato *m* trade union *Brit,* labor union *Am*

síndrome *m* syndrome

sinfín *m* huge number

sinfonía *f* symphony

sinfónico, -a *adj* symphonic

Singapur *m* Singapore

singular I. *adj* **1.** (*único*) singular **2.** (*excepcional*) outstanding **II.** *m* LING singular

singularidad *f* **1.** (*unicidad*) singularity **2.** (*excepcionalidad*) exceptional nature

singularizar <z→c> **I.** *vt* (*particularizar*) to single out **II.** *vr:* ~**se** to stand out

siniestro *m* (*accidente*) accident; (*catástrofe*) natural disaster; (*incendio*) fire

siniestro, -a *adj elev* **1.** (*maligno*) evil **2.** (*funesto*) disastrous **3.** (*izquierdo*) left

sinnúmero *m* huge number

sino I. *m* fate **II.** *conj* **1.** (*al contrario*) but **2.** (*solamente*) **no espero ~ que me creas** I only hope that you believe me **3.** (*excepto*) except

sinónimo *m* synonym

sinónimo, -a *adj* synonymous

sinrazón *f* unreasonableness

sinsentido *m* absurdity

sintáctico, -a *adj* syntactic

sintaxis *f inv* syntax

síntesis *f inv* synthesis

sintético, -a *adj* synthetic

sintetizar <z→c> *vt* **1.** QUÍM to synthesize **2.** (*resumir*) to summarize

síntoma *m* symptom

sintomático, -a *adj* symptomatic

sintonía *f* **1.** (*adecuación*) tuning **2.** (*melodía*) signature tune

sintonizar <z→c> *vt* to tune in; (*emisora*) to pick up

sinvergüenza I. *adj* shameless **II.** *mf pey* rotter

sionismo *m* Zionism

siquiera I. *adv* at least; **ni ~** not even **II.** *conj* + *subj* even if

sirena *f* **1.** (*bocina*) siren **2.** (*mujer pez*) mermaid

Siria *f* Syria

sirio, -a *adj, m, f* Syrian

siroco *m* METEO sirocco

sirviente *mf* servant

sisear *vt* to hiss

sísmico, -a *adj* seismic; **movimiento ~** earth tremor

sistema *m* system; ~ **montañoso** mountain range; ~ **operativo** INFOR operating system; ~ **periódico** QUÍM periodic table; **por ~** on principle

sistemático, -a *adj* systematic

sitiar *vt* to besiege

sitio *m* **1.** (*lugar*) place; (*espacio*) room; ~ **de veraneo** holiday resort; **en cualquier/ningún ~** anywhere/nowhere; **en todos los ~s** everywhere **2.** MIL siege

situación *f* **1.** (*ubicación*) location **2.** (*estado*) situation

situado, -a *adj* situated

situar <*1. pres:* sitúo> **I.** *vt* (*colocar*) to place; (*emplazar*) to locate **II.** *vr:* ~**se 1.** (*ponerse en un lugar*) to situate oneself **2.** (*abrirse paso*) to make one's way

S.M. *mf abr de* **Su Majestad** H.M.

SME *m abr de* **Sistema Monetario Europeo** EMS

smog *m sin pl* smog; ~ **electrónico** e-smog

so I. *interj* whoa **II.** *prep* under; ~ **pena de...** on pain of ...; ~ **pretexto de que...** under the pretext of ... **III.** *m inf* ¡~ **imbécil!** you idiot!

SO *abr de* **sudoeste** SW

sobaco *m* armpit

sobar *vt* **1.** *inf* (*a persona*) to paw, to

touch up *Brit,* to feel up *Am* **2.** (*un objeto*) to finger **3.** (*molestar*) to pester **4.** *inf* (*dormir*) to sleep, to kip *Brit*

soberanía *f* sovereignty

soberano, -a I. *adj* **1.** POL sovereign **2.** (*excelente*) supreme **II.** *m, f* (*monarca*) sovereign

soberbia *f* **1.** (*orgullo*) pride **2.** (*suntuosidad*) magnificence

soberbio, -a *adj* **1.** (*orgulloso*) proud **2.** (*suntuoso*) magnificent

sobornar *vt* to bribe

soborno *m* **1.** (*acción*) bribery **2.** (*dinero*) bribe

sobra *f* **1.** (*exceso*) surplus; **saber de ~** to know only too well **2.** *pl* (*desperdicios*) leftovers *pl*

sobrante I. *adj* **1.** (*que sobra*) spare **2.** (*de más*) excess **II.** *m* (*que sobra*) remainder; (*superávit*) surplus

sobrar *vi* **1.** (*quedar*) to remain **2.** (*abundar*) to be more than enough **3.** (*estar de más*) to be superfluous

sobrasada *f* sausage spread, *typical of the Balearic Islands*

sobre I. *m* **1.** (*para carta*) envelope **2.** *inf* (*cama*) bed **II.** *prep* **1.** (*por encima de*) on; **estar ~ alguien** to keep constant watch on sb **2.** (*aproximadamente*) about; **~ las tres** about three o'clock **3.** (*tema*) about **4.** (*reiteración*) on top of **5.** (*además de*) as well as **6.** (*superioridad*) over; **triunfar ~ alguien** to triumph over sb **7.** (*porcentajes*) out of; **tres ~ cien** three out of a hundred **8.** FIN **un préstamo ~ una casa** a loan on a house

sobrecama *f* bedspread

sobrecarga *f* ELEC overload; COM surcharge

sobrecoger I. *vt* **1.** (*sorprender*) to take by surprise **2.** (*espantar*) to frighten **II.** *vr:* **~se 1.** (*asustarse*) to be startled **2.** (*sorprenderse*) to be surprised

sobredosis *f inv* overdose

sobreentender <e→ie> **I.** *vt* **1.** (*adivinar*) to infer **2.** (*presuponer*) to presuppose **II.** *vr:* **~se** to be obvious

sobre(e)stimar *vt* to overestimate

sobrehumano, -a *adj* superhuman

sobrellevar *vt* to bear

sobremesa *f* **de ~** (*tras la comida*) after-dinner; INFOR desktop; **programa de ~** TV afternoon programme

sobrenatural *adj* supernatural

sobrenombre *m* nickname

sobrentender <e→ie> *vt, vr v.* **sobreentender**

sobrepasar *vt* **1.** (*en cantidad*) to surpass; (*límite*) to exceed **2.** (*aventajar*) to pass

sobreponer *irr como poner* **I.** *vt* **1.** (*encima de algo*) to put on top; (*funda*) cover **2.** (*añadir*) to add **II.** *vr:* **~se** (*a una enfermedad*) to overcome; (*a un susto*) to recover from

sobresaliente I. *adj* **1.** (*excelente*) outstanding **2.** UNIV first class; ENS excellent **II.** *m* ENS (*nota*) distinction

sobresalir *irr como salir vi* to stand out

sobresaltar I. *vt* to startle **II.** *vr:* **~se** to be startled

sobresalto *m* **1.** (*susto*) scare **2.** (*turbación*) sudden shock

sobretodo *m* overcoat

sobrevenir *irr como venir vi* (*epidemia*) to ensue; (*tormenta*) to break

sobreviviente *mf* survivor

sobrevivir *vi* (*acontecimientos*) to survive; (*a alguien*) to outlive

sobrevolar <o→ue> *vt* to fly over

sobriedad *f sin pl* **1.** (*sin beber*) soberness **2.** (*moderación*) moderation

sobrino, -a *m, f* nephew *m,* niece *f*

sobrio, -a *adj* **1.** (*no borracho*) sober **2.** (*moderado*) moderate **3.** (*estilo*) plain

socarrón, -ona *adj* ironic

socavar *vt* to dig under; *fig* to undermine

socavón *m* **1.** MIN subsidence **2.** (*en el suelo*) hole

sociable *adj* **1.** (*tratable*) sociable **2.** (*afable*) friendly

social *adj* **1.** (*de la sociedad*) society; **razón ~** JUR, ECON company name **2.** (*de la convivencia*) social; **asis-**

tente ~ social worker

socialdemócrata I. *adj* social-democratic II. *mf* social democrat

socialista *adj, mf* socialist

socializar <z→c> *vt* to socialize

sociedad *f* 1. (*población*) society; ~ **del bienestar** welfare society 2. (*empresa*) company; ~ **anónima** corporation

socio, -a *m, f* 1. (*de una asociación*) member 2. COM partner 3. *inf* (*compañero*) mate

sociología *f sin pl* sociology

sociólogo, -a *m, f* sociologist

socorrer *vt* to help, to come to the aid of

socorrismo *m* live-saving

socorrista *mf* (*de playas*) lifeguard; (*en piscinas*) pool attendant

socorro *m* (*ayuda*) help; (*salvamento*) rescue; **pedir** ~ to ask for help

soda *f* (*bebida*) soda water

sódico, -a *adj* sodium

sodio *m* sodium

sofá <sofás> *m* sofa

sofá-cama <sofás-cama> *m* sofa-bed

sofisticación *f* sophistication

sofisticado, -a *adj* 1. (*afectado*) affected 2. TÉC sophisticated

sofocar <c→qu> I. *vt* 1. (*asfixiar*) to suffocate 2. *t. fig* (*apagar*) to stifle; (*fuego*) to put out II. *vr:* ~**se** 1. (*sonrojar*) to blush 2. (*excitarse*) to get worked up 3. (*ahogarse*) to suffocate

sofoco *m* 1. (*ahogo*) suffocation 2. (*excitación*) shock

sofreír *irr como reír vt* to fry lightly

soga *f* rope

sois 2. *pres pl de* **ser**

soja *f* soya *Brit,* soy *Am*

sojuzgar <g→gu> *vt* to subdue

sol *m* 1. (*astro*) sun; (*luz*) sunlight; **de** ~ **a** ~ from dawn to dusk; **día de** ~ sunny day; **tomar el** ~ to sunbathe 2. (*moneda*) sol 3. MÚS G

solamente *adv* only

solapa *f* 1. (*chaqueta*) lapel 2. (*libro*) flap

solapado, -a *adj* underhand *Brit,* underhanded *Am*

solar I. *adj* solar II. *m* 1. (*terreno*) plot 2. (*casa*) family seat

solaz *m* (*recreo*) recreation; (*esparcimiento*) relaxation

solazar <z→c> I. *vt* to amuse II. *vr:* ~**se** to enjoy oneself

soldado, -a *m, f* MIL soldier; ~ **de infantería** infantryman, foot soldier; ~ **raso** private

soldador *m* TÉC soldering iron

soldador *mf* welder

soldar <o→ue> *vt* 1. TEC to weld 2. (*unir*) to join

soleado, -a *adj* sunny

soledad *f* (*estado*) solitude; (*sentimiento*) loneliness

solemne *adj* 1. (*ceremonioso*) solemn 2. (*mentira*) monstruous

solemnidad *f* solemnity

soler <o→ue> *vi* to be in the habit of; **solemos...** we usually ...; **suele ocurrir que...** it often occurs that ...

solfeo *m* MÚS singing of scales

solicitar *vt* 1. (*pedir*) to ask for; (*un trabajo*) to apply for 2. (*atención*) to seek

solícito, -a *adj* (*diligente*) diligent; (*cuidadoso*) solicitous

solicitud *f* 1. (*diligencia*) diligence; (*cuidado*) solicitude 2. (*petición*) request; ~ **de empleo** job application

solidaridad *f sin pl* solidarity

solidarizarse <z→c> *vr* to feel solidarity with; (*con una opinión*) to share

solidez *f* solidity

sólido *m* solid

sólido, -a *adj t.* FÍS solid; (*ingreso*) steady

soliloquio *m* soliloquy

solista *mf* MÚS soloist

solitaria *f* ZOOL tapeworm

solitario *m* solitaire

solitario, -a I. *adj* (*sin compañía*) alone; (*abandonado*) lonely II. *m, f* loner

sollozar <z→c> *vi* to sob

sollozo *m* sob

solo *m t.* MÚS (*baile*) solo

solo, -a *adj* 1. (*sin compañía*) alone; (*solitario*) lonely; **a solas** alone; **por sí** ~ on one's own 2. (*único*) only

3. (*café*) black; (*alcohol*) straight, neat

sólo *adv* **1.** (*únicamente*) only; ~ **que...** except that ...; **tan** ~ just; **aunque** ~ **sean 10 minutos** even if it's only 10 minutes **2.** (*expresamente*) expressly

solomillo *m* sirloin

solsticio *m* solstice

soltar *irr* **I.** *vt* **1.** (*dejar de sujetar*) to let go of; **¡suéltame!** let me go! **2.** (*liberar*) to free **3.** (*dejar caer*) to drop **4.** (*expresión*) to let out **5.** (*frenos*) to release; (*cinturón*) to undo **6.** *inf* (*dinero*) to cough up **II.** *vr:* ~**se 1.** (*liberarse*) to escape **2.** (*un nudo*) to come undone

soltero, -a I. *adj* single **II.** *m, f* bachelor *m*, unmarried woman *f*; **apellido de soltera** maiden name

solterón *m* confirmed bachelor

soltura *f* **1.** (*del pelo*) looseness **2.** (*carácter*) ease

soluble *adj* **1.** (*líquido*) soluble; (*café*) instant **2.** (*problema*) solvable

solución *f* solution

solucionar *vt* to solve

solventar *vt* **1.** (*problema*) to resolve; (*asunto*) to settle **2.** (*deuda*) to pay

solvente *adj, m* solvent

sombra *f* **1.** (*proyección*) shadow; ~ **de ojos** (*producto cosmético*) eyeshadow; **tener buena** ~ *fig* to have charm **2.** (*contrario de sol*) shade; **hacer** ~ to give shade **3.** (*clandestinidad*) **trabajar en la** ~ to work illegally **4.** ARTE shading **5.** *inf* (*cárcel*) **a la** ~ in the nick *Brit,* in the slammer *Am*

sombrero *m* (*prenda*) hat; ~ **de copa** top hat; ~ **hongo** bowler (hat) *Brit,* derby *Am*

sombrilla *f* parasol

sombrío, -a *adj* **1.** (*en la sombra*) shady **2.** (*triste*) sad; (*pesimista*) gloomy

somero, -a *adj* superficial

someter I. *vt* **1.** (*dominar*) to force to submit **2.** (*subyugar*) to conquer **II.** *vr:* ~**se 1.** (*en una lucha*) to give in **2.** (*a un tratamiento*) to undergo

somier <somieres> *m* bed base

somnífero *m* sleeping pill

somnífero, -a *adj* sleep-inducing

somnolencia *f* (*sueño*) drowsiness

somnoliento, -a *adj* (*con sueño*) drowsy; (*al despertarse*) half asleep

somos *1. pres pl de* **ser**

son I. *m* (*sonido*) sound; **en** ~ **de paz** in peace **II.** *3. pres pl de* **ser**

sonajero *m* (baby's) rattle

sonambulismo *m sin pl* sleepwalking

sonámbulo, -a *m, f* sleepwalker

sonar <o→ue> **I.** *vi* **1.** (*timbre*) to ring; (*instrumento*) to be heard **2.** *t.* LING, MÚS (*parecerse*) to sound; **esto me suena** this sounds familiar **II.** *vt* **1.** (*instrumento*) to play **2.** (*la nariz*) to blow **III.** *vr:* ~**se** to blow one's nose

sonda *f* **1.** (*acción*) sounding **2.** MED probe, catheter

sondear *vt* to sound out

sondeo *m* **1.** MED probing **2.** MIN boring **3.** NÁUT sounding **4.** (*averiguación*) investigation

sonido *m* **1.** (*ruido*) sound **2.** *t.* MÚS (*manera de sonar*) tone **3.** FÍS resonance

sonoro, -a *adj* **1.** (*que puede sonar*) resonant **2.** (*fuerte*) loud **3.** FÍS resonant; **banda sonora** CINE soundtrack

sonreír *irr como* reír *vi, vr:* ~**se** to smile

sonrisa *f* smile

sonrojar I. *vt* to make blush **II.** *vr:* ~**se** to blush

sonrojo *m* **1.** (*acción*) blushing **2.** (*rubor*) blush

sonsacar <c→qu> *vt* **1.** (*indagar*) to find out; (*secreto*) to worm out **2.** (*empleado*) to pump for information

soñador(a) I. *adj* dreamy **II.** *m(f)* dreamer

soñar <o→ue> *vi, vt* to dream; ~ **con algo** to dream of sth; ~ **despierto** to daydream; **¡ni** ~**lo!** no way!

soñoliento, -a *adj* drowsy

sopa *f* soup; ~**s de leche** bread and

S_s

milk

sopera *f* soup tureen

sopero, -a I. *adj* soup II. *m, f* soup plate

sopesar *vt* to try the weight of; *fig* to weigh up

soplar I. *vi* to blow II. *vt* 1. (*con la boca*) to blow on; (*velas*) to blow out; (*hinchar*) to blow up 2. (*en un examen*) TEAT to prompt 3. *inf* (*delatar*) to inform on; (*entre alumnos*) to tell on

soplo *m* 1. (*acción*) puff 2. (*viento leve*) breeze; **~ de viento** breath of wind 3. (*denuncia*) tip-off

soplón, -ona *m, f* 1. (*de la policía*) informer 2. (*entre alumnos*) talebearer *Brit,* tattletale *Am*

sopor *m* lethargy

soporífero *m* sleeping pill

soporífero, -a *adj* 1. (*que da sueño*) sleep-inducing 2. (*aburrido*) soporific, dull

soportable *adj* bearable

soportar *vt* 1. (*sostener*) to support 2. (*aguantar*) to stand

soporte *m* 1. *t. fig* (*apoyo*) support 2. (*pilar*) support pillar 3. INFOR **~ físico** hardware; **~ lógico** software

soprano *f* MÚS soprano

sor *f* REL sister

sorber *vt* 1. (*con los labios*) to sip; (*por una pajita*) to suck 2. (*emparparse de*) to soak up

sorbete *m* GASTR sorbet *Brit,* sherbet *Am*

sorbo *m* sip; **beber a ~s** to sip

sordera *f* deafness

sórdido, -a *adj* sordid

sordo, -a I. *adj* 1. (*que no oye*) deaf; **hacer oídos ~s** to turn a deaf ear 2. (*que oye mal*) hard of hearing 3. (*sonido*) dull II. *m, f* deaf person; **hacerse el ~** to pretend not to hear

sordomudo, -a I. *adj* deaf and dumb II. *m, f* deaf mute

sorna *f* 1. (*al obrar*) slyness 2. (*al hablar*) sarcasm

sorprendente *adj* 1. (*inesperado*) unexpected; (*evolución*) surprising 2. (*que salta a la vista*) striking 3. (*extraordinario*) incredible

sorprender I. *vt* 1. (*coger desprevenido*) to take by surprise; (*asombrar*) to startle, to amaze; (*extrañar*) to surprise 2. (*pillar*) to catch (in the act) II. *vr:* **~se** 1. (*asombrarse*) to be amazed 2. (*extrañarse*) to be surprised

sorpresa *f* surprise

sortear *vt* 1. (*decidir*) to draw lots for; (*rifar*) to raffle 2. (*esquivar*) to avoid

sorteo *m* 1. (*rifa*) raffle; (*lotería*) draw 2. (*esquivación*) avoidance

sortija *f* 1. (*joya*) ring 2. (*rizo*) curl

sosegado, -a *adj* 1. (*apacible*) peaceful 2. (*tranquilo*) calm

sosegar *irr como fregar* I. *vt* (*calmar*) to calm II. *vi, vr:* **~(se)** to rest III. *vr:* **~se** (*calmarse*) to calm down

sosiego *m* calm

soslayar *vt* 1. (*objeto*) to put sideways 2. (*evitar*) to avoid

soslayo, -a *adj* sideways; **de ~** out of the corner of one's eye

soso, -a *adj* 1. (*sin sabor*) tasteless, insipid 2. (*persona*) dull

sospecha *f* suspicion; **bajo ~ de...** suspected of ...

sospechar I. *vt* 1. (*creer posible*) to suppose 2. (*recelar*) to suspect II. *vi* to be suspicious

sospechoso, -a I. *adj* suspicious II. *m, f* suspect

sostén *m* 1. *t. fig* (*apoyo*) support 2. (*prenda*) bra 3. (*alimentos*) sustenance

sostener *irr como tener* I. *vt* 1. (*sujetar*) to support 2. (*aguantar*) to bear 3. (*afirmar*) to maintain; (*idea, teoría*) to stick to 4. (*mantener*) to keep up; (*conversación*) to have II. *vr:* **~se** 1. (*sujetarse*) to hold oneself up 2. (*aguantarse*) to keep going 3. (*en pie*) to stand up 4. (*en una opinión*) to insist on

sostenido, -a *adj* 1. (*esfuerzo*) sustained 2. MÚS sharp

sota *f* (*naipe*) jack

sotana *f* cassock

sótano *m* 1. (*piso*) basement 2. (*habitación*) cellar

soy *I. pres de* **ser**

spot *m* <spots> TV commercial
spray *m* <sprays> spray
squash *m sin pl* DEP squash
Sr. *abr de* **señor** Mr; (*en direcciones*) Esquire
Sra. *abr de* **señora** Mrs
S.R.C. *abr de* **se ruega contestación** R.S.V.P.
Srta. *f abr de* **señorita** Miss
Sta. *f abr de* **santa** St
stand *m* <stands> stand
status *m inv* status
Sto. *abr de* **santo** St.
stop *m* **1.** (*acción*) stop **2.** (*señal*) stop sign
su *adj* (*de él*) his; (*de ella*) her; (*de cosa, animal*) its; (*de ellos*) their; (*de Ud., Uds.*) your; (*de uno*) one's
suave *adj* **1.** (*piel*) smooth; (*jersey, droga*) soft; (*viento*) gentle **2.** (*aterrizaje*) smooth **3.** (*temperatura*) mild **4.** (*carácter*) docile; (*palabras*) kind
suavidad *f sin pl* **1.** (*de piel*) smoothness; (*de jersey*) softness; (*de viento, temperatura*) gentleness **2.** (*de aterrizaje*) smoothness **3.** (*de carácter*) docility; (*de palabras*) kindness
suavizante *m* **1.** (*para la ropa*) fabric softener **2.** (*para el cabello*) conditioner
suavizar <z→c> *vt* **1.** (*hacer suave*) to smooth; (*pelo*) to soften **2.** (*expresión*) to soften; (*situación*) to relax **3.** (*persona*) to mollify **4.** (*recorrido*) to make easy
subalimentación *f* undernourishment
subalimentado, -a *adj* undernourished
subasta *f* auction
subastar *vt* **1.** (*vender*) to auction **2.** (*contrato público*) to put out to tender
subcampeón, -ona *m, f* runner-up
subconsciencia *f* subconscious
subconsciente *adj* subconscious
subdesarrollado, -a *adj* underdeveloped
subdirector(a) *m(f)* assistant director
súbdito, -a *m, f* subject
subdividir *vt* to subdivide

subempleo *m* underemployment
subestimar *vt* to underestimate; (*propiedad*) to undervalue
subida *f* **1.** (*de una calle*) rise **2.** (*cuesta*) slope **3.** (*de precios, temperaturas*) increase **4.** (*acción de subir*) ascent; (*en coche*) climb; ~ **al poder** POL rise to power
subido, -a *adj* **1.** (*color*) bright **2.** *inf* (*persona*) vain **3.** (*precio*) high
subir **I.** *vi* **1.** (*ascender: calle*) to go up; (*sol, río*) to rise; (*cima*) to climb; (*marea*) to come in **2.** (*aumentar*) to increase **3.** (*montar: al coche*) to get in; (*al tren*) to get on **II.** *vt* **1.** (*precio, voz*) to raise **2.** (*música*) to turn up **3.** (*en coche*) to go up; (*montaña*) to climb **4.** (*levantar: brazos*) to lift up; (*persiana*) to raise **5.** (*llevar*) to take up **6.** (*pared*) to build **III.** *vr:* ~**se** (*al coche*) to get in; (*al tren*) to get on; (*a un árbol*) to climb
súbito, -a *adj* **1.** (*repentino*) sudden **2.** (*inesperado*) unexpected
subjetivo, -a *adj* subjective
subjuntivo *m* subjunctive
sublevación *f* uprising
sublevar **I.** *vt* to rouse to revolt **II.** *vr:* ~**se** to revolt
sublime *adj* sublime
subliminal *adj* subliminal
submarinismo *m sin pl* scuba-diving, skin-diving
submarinista *mf* scuba diver
submarino *m* submarine
submarino, -a *adj* submarine; (*vida*) underwater
subnormal **I.** *adj* subnormal **II.** *mf* (*persona*) subnormal person
subordinado, -a *adj, m, f* subordinate
subrayar *vt* **1.** (*con raya*) to underline **2.** (*recalcar*) to emphasize
subrepticio, -a *adj* surreptitious
subsanar *vt* **1.** (*falta*) to make up (for) **2.** (*error*) to rectify
subscripción *f v.* **suscripción**
subsidiariedad *f* subsidiarity
subsidiario, -a *adj* **1.** (*de subsidio*) subsidiary **2.** (*secundario*) complementary
subsidio *m* subsidy; ~ **de desem-**

S

pleo unemployment benefit *Brit*, unemployment compensation *Am*
subsistencia *f* subsistence
subsistir *vi* **1.** (*vivir*) to subsist **2.** (*perdurar*) to endure; (*empresa*) to survive
subterráneo, -a *adj* underground, subterranean
subtítulo *m t.* CINE subtitle
suburbano, -a *adj* suburban
suburbio *m* **1.** (*alrededores*) (poor) suburb **2.** (*barrio*) slum area
subvención *f* grant; POL subsidy
subvencionar *vt* to subsidize
subversión *f* subversion
subversivo, -a *adj* subversive
subyugar <g→gu> *vt* **1.** (*oprimir*) to subjugate **2.** (*sugestionar*) to dominate
succión *f* suction
sucedáneo *m* substitute; (*imitación*) imitation
sucedáneo, -a *adj* substitute
suceder **I.** *vi* **1.** (*seguir*) to succeed **2.** (*occurir*) to happen; **¿qué sucede?** what's happening?; **por lo que pueda** ~ just in case; **suceda lo que suceda** whatever happens; **sucede que...** the thing is that ... **3.** (*en cargo*) to follow on **II.** *vt* (*heredar*) to inherit; (*seguir*) to succeed
sucesión *f* **1.** (*acción*) succession **2.** (*cargo*) succession **3.** (*descendencia*) issue
sucesivo, -a *adj* following; **en lo** ~ henceforth; **dos días** ~**s** two consecutive days
suceso *m* (*hecho*) event; (*repentino*) incident; **página de** ~**s** PREN accident and crime reports
suciedad *f* **1.** (*cualidad*) dirtiness **2.** (*porquería*) dirt
sucinto, -a *adj* succinct
sucio, -a *adj* dirty; (*jugada*) foul
Sucre *m* Sucre
suculento, -a *adj* **1.** (*sabroso*) tasty **2.** (*jugoso*) juicy, succulent
sucumbir *vi* **1.** (*rendirse*) to succumb **2.** (*morir*) to die
sucursal *f* (*de empresa*) subsidiary; (*de banco*) branch

Sudáfrica *f* South Africa
sudafricano, -a *adj, m, f* South African
Sudamérica *f* South America
sudamericano, -a *adj, m, f* South American
sudar **I.** *vi, vt* to sweat **II.** *vi inf* (*trabajar*) to sweat it out
sudeste *m* south-east
sudoeste *m* south-west
sudor *m* sweat
Suecia *f* Sweden
sueco, -a **I.** *adj* Swedish **II.** *m, f* Swede; **hacerse el** ~ *inf* to pretend not to hear
suegro, -a *m, f* father-in-law *m*, mother-in-law *f*
suela *f* sole
sueldo *m* pay; (*mensual*) salary; (*semanal*) wage
suelo *m* **1.** (*de la tierra*) ground **2.** (*de casa*) floor; **ejercicios de** ~ DEP floor exercises **3.** (*terreno*) land; ~ **edificable** building land
suelto *m* **1.** (*dinero*) loose change **2.** (*artículo*) short item
suelto, -a *adj* **1.** (*tornillo, pelo*) loose; (*broche*) unfastened; **dinero** ~ ready money; **no dejar ni un cabo** ~ to leave no loose ends; **un prisionero anda** ~ a prisoner is on the loose **2.** (*separado*) separate; **pieza suelta** individual piece **3.** (*vestido*) loose-fitting **4.** (*estilo*) free; (*lenguaje*) fluent
sueño *m* **1.** (*acto de dormir*) sleep; **descabezar** [*o* echarse] **un** ~ to have a nap **2.** (*ganas de dormir*) sleepiness; **tener** ~ to be sleepy; **caerse de** ~ to be falling asleep
suero *m* **1.** (*de leche*) whey **2.** MED serum
suerte *f* **1.** (*fortuna*) luck; **¡(buena)** ~**!** good luck!; **estar de** ~ to be in of luck; **por** ~ fortunately; **probar** ~ to try one's luck **2.** (*destino*) fate; **echar algo a** ~(**s**) to draw lots for sth **3.** (*casualidad*) chance **4.** (*manera*) way; **de tal** ~ **que** so that **5.** (*tipo*) kind
suéter *m* sweater
suficiente **I.** *adj* **1.** (*bastante*)

enough; **ser** ~ to be sufficient **2.** (*presumido*) self-important, smug **II.** *m* ENS (*nota*) pass

sufragar <g→gu> **I.** *vt* **1.** (*ayudar*) to aid **2.** (*gastos*) to meet; (*tasa*) to pay **II.** *vi AmL* (*votar*) ~ **por alguien** to vote for sb

sufragio *m* **1.** (*voto*) vote **2.** (*derecho*) suffrage

sufrido, -a *adj* **1.** (*persona*) patient, uncomplaining **2.** (*color*) fast; (*tela*) hard-wearing

sufrimiento *m* suffering

sufrir *vt* **1.** (*aguantar*) to bear; (*a alguien*) to put up with **2.** (*padecer*) to suffer; ~ **una operación** to have an operation

sugerencia *f* **1.** (*propuesta*) suggestion **2.** (*recomendación*) recommendation

sugerir *irr como* **sentir** *vt* **1.** (*proponer*) to suggest **2.** (*insinuar*) to hint **3.** (*evocar*) to prompt

sugestión *f* **1.** (*de sugestionar*) hypnotic power **2.** (*propuesta*) suggestion

sugestionar I. *vt* to influence **II.** *vr:* ~**se** to indulge in autosuggestion

sugestivo, -a *adj* **1.** (*que sugiere*) evocative **2.** (*que influencia*) thought-provoking **3.** (*plan*) attractive

suicida I. *adj* suicidal **II.** *mf* **1.** (*muerto*) person who has committed suicide **2.** (*loco*) suicidal person

suicidarse *vr* to commit suicide

suicidio *m* suicide

Suiza *f* Switzerland

suizo *m* GASTR sweet bun

suizo, -a *adj, m, f* Swiss

sujeción *f* **1.** (*agarre*) hold **2.** (*aseguramiento*) support **3.** (*a una promesa*) binding

sujetador *m* **1.** (*sostén*) bra **2.** (*del bikini*) fastener

sujetar I. *vt* **1.** (*agarrar*) to seize **2.** (*someter*) to subject **3.** (*asegurar*) to support; (*pelo*) to hold in place; (*con clavos*) to nail down **II.** *vr:* ~**se** **1.** (*agarrarse*) to subject oneself **2.** (*a reglas*) to abide

sujeto *m* **1.** (*tema*) subject **2.** *pey* (*individuo*) individual

sujeto, -a *adj* (*expuesto a*) subject; **estar** ~ **a fluctuaciones** to be subject to fluctuation

sulfuro *m* sulphide *Brit,* sulfide *Am*

suma *f* **1.** MAT (*acción*) adding (up); (*resultado*) total; **en** ~ in short **2.** (*cantidad*) sum

sumar I. *vt* **1.** MAT to add (up) **2.** (*hechos*) to summarize **II.** *vr:* ~**se** to join; (*a una discusión*) to participate in

sumario *m* **1.** JUR committal proceedings *pl* **2.** (*resumen*) summary

sumergir(se) <g→j> *vt,* (*vr*) to submerge

sumidero *m* (*rejilla*) drain; (*de la calle*) sewer

suministrar *vt* **1.** *t.* COM (*información*) to supply **2.** (*abastecer*) to stock **3.** (*facilitar*) to supply

suministro *m* **1.** *t.* COM (*de información*) supply **2.** (*abastecimiento*) stock

sumir I. *vt* (*hundir*) to sink **II.** *vr:* ~**se** to sink; (*en el trabajo*) to become absorbed

sumisión *f* **1.** (*acción*) submission **2.** (*carácter*) submissiveness

sumiso, -a *adj* submissive

sumo, -a *adj* **1.** (*más alto*) high(est); **a lo** ~ at most **2.** (*mayor*) great

suntuoso, -a *adj* **1.** (*lujoso*) sumptuous **2.** (*opulento*) lavish

supeditar I. *vt* **1.** (*subordinar*) to subordinate **2.** (*someter*) to subdue **II.** *vr:* ~**se** to submit

súper[1] I. *adj inf* super **II.** *m* supermarket

súper[2] *f* four-star petrol *Brit,* Premium (gas) *Am*

superación *f* improvement

superar I. *vt* **1.** (*sobrepasar a alguien*) to surpass; (*límite*) to exceed; (*récord*) to beat **2.** (*prueba*) to pass **3.** (*situación*) to overcome **II.** *vr:* ~**se** to excel oneself

superávit *m* <superávit(s)> surplus

superficial *adj* superficial

superficialidad *f* superficiality

superficie *f* **1.** *t.* MAT (*parte externa*) surface **2.** (*área*) area

superfluo, -a *adj* superfluous
superintendente *mf* supervisor; (*de policía*) superintendent
superior *adj* **1.** (*más alto*) higher **2.** (*en calidad*) better; (*en inteligencia*) superior **3.** (*excelente*) excellent
superior(a) *m(f)* superior
superioridad *f* superiority
superlativo *m* LING superlative
superlativo, -a *adj t.* LING superlative
supermercado *m* supermarket
superponer *irr como* poner *vt* **1.** (*dos cosas*) to superimpose **2.** (*dar prioridad*) to give more importance to
superproducción *f* **1.** COM overproduction **2.** CINE big-budget movie
supersónico, -a *adj* supersonic
superstición *f* superstition
supersticioso, -a *adj* superstitious
supervisar *vt* to supervise; (*en un examen*) to invigilate
supervisor(a) *m(f)* supervisor
supervivencia *f* survival
superviviente **I.** *adj* surviving **II.** *mf* survivor
suplantar *vt* to supplant
suplementario, -a *adj* supplementary
suplemento *m* **1.** (*complemento*) supplement **2.** (*precio*) extra charge; (*del tren*) excess fare
suplente *adj, mf* substitute
supletorio *m* TEL extension
supletorio, -a *adj* supplementary; **cama supletoria** extra bed
súplica *f* request; JUR petition
suplicar <c→qu> *vt* **1.** (*rogar*) to implore **2.** JUR to appeal against
suplicio *m* **1.** (*tortura*) torture **2.** (*tormento*) torment
suplir *vt* **1.** (*completar*) to make up for **2.** (*sustituir*) to substitute
supo *3. pret de* **saber**
suponer *irr como* poner *vt* **1.** (*dar por sentado*) to suppose; **supongamos que...** let us assume that ...; **dar por supuesto** to take for granted **2.** (*figurar*) to imagine; **puedes** ~ **que...** you can imagine that ... **3.** (*atribuir*) **no le suponía**

tan fuerte I didn't realize he/she was so strong **4.** (*significar*) to mean; ~ **un duro golpe** to be a real blow
suposición *f* supposition
supositorio *m* MED suppository
supremacía *f* supremacy
supremo, -a *adj* supreme
supresión *f* **1.** (*eliminación*) suppression; (*de obstáculos*) removal; (*de una regla*) abolition **2.** (*omisión*) omission
suprimir *vt* **1.** (*poner fin*) to suppress; (*fronteras*) to eliminate; (*obstáculos*) to remove; (*regla*) to abolish **2.** (*omitir*) to omit
supuesto *m* **1.** (*suposición*) assumption **2.** (*hipótesis*) hypothesis
supuesto, -a *adj* (*asesino*) alleged; (*testigo*) assumed; (*causa*) supposed; **por** ~ of course
sur *m* south; **el** ~ **de España** southern Spain; **en el** ~ **de Inglaterra** in the south of England; **al** ~ **de** south of
surafricano, -a *adj, m, f* South African
surcar <c→qu> *vt* to plough *Brit*, to plow *Am*
surco *m* **1.** (*en tierra*) furrow **2.** (*en disco*) groove
sureste *m* south-east
surf *m* DEP *sin pl* surfing
surfear *vi* to windsurf; INFOR to surf
surgir <g→j> *vi* **1.** (*agua*) to gush **2.** (*dificultad*) to arise; (*pregunta*) to come up
suroeste *m* south-west
surtido *m* selection, assortment
surtido, -a *adj* **1.** (*mezclado*) mixed **2.** (*variado*) varied
surtidor *m* **1.** (*aparato*) petrol pump *Brit,* gas pump *Am* **2.** (*chorro*) jet; (*fuente*) fountain
surtir **I.** *vt* (*proveer*) to supply **II.** *vi* to spout
susceptible *adj* **1.** (*cosa*) ~ **de** capable of **2.** (*persona: sensible*) sensitive; (*irritable*) touchy
suscitar *vt* (*sospecha*) to cause; (*discusión*) to start; (*conflicto*) to stir up
suscribir *irr como* escribir **I.** *vt* **1.** (*escrito*) to sign **2.** (*opinión*) to endorse

II. *vr:* ~**se** to subscribe
suscripción *f* subscription
susodicho, -a *adj* above-mentioned
suspender *vt* **1.** (*tener en el aire*) to hang from **2.** (*trabajador*) to suspend **3.** (*en un examen*) to fail **4.** (*sesión*) to adjourn; (*embargo*) to lift; (*función*) to call off
suspense *m* suspense
suspensión *f* **1.** (*acción de colgar*) suspension **2.** (*de sesión*) adjournment; (*de embargo*) lifting; (*de pagos*) suspension
suspenso *m* **1.** ENS fail; **sacar un ~** to fail, to flunk *Am* **2.** *AmL v.* **suspense**
suspenso, -a *adj* (*perplejo*) perplexed
suspicacia *f* suspicion
suspicaz *adj* suspicious
suspirar *vi* to sigh
suspiro *m* sigh
sustancia *f* substance; ~ **gris** ANAT grey matter *Brit,* gray matter *Am*
sustancial *adj* substantial
sustancioso, -a *adj* (*comida*) substantial
sustantivo *m* noun
sustantivo, -a *adj* **1.** (*esencial*) vital **2.** LING nominal
sustentar I. *vt* **1.** (*una cosa*) to hold up **2.** (*esperanza*) to sustain **3.** (*familia*) to feed **II.** *vr:* ~**se 1.** (*alimentarse*) to sustain oneself **2.** (*aguantarse*) to rely on
sustento *m* **1.** (*mantenimiento*) maintenance **2.** (*apoyo*) support
sustituir *irr como huir vt t.* DEP to substitute, to replace
sustituto, -a *m, f* substitute, replacement
susto *m* scare; **dar un ~** to give a fright; **llevarse un ~** to get scared
sustraer *irr como traer vt* **1.** (*restar*) to subtract **2.** (*robar*) to steal
susurrar *vi* to whisper
susurro *m* whisper
sutil *adj* **1.** (*sabor*) subtle; (*aroma*) delicate **2.** (*diferencia*) fine **3.** (*persona*) sharp
sutileza *f,* **sutilidad** *f* **1.** (*de sabor*) subtlety; (*de aroma*) delicacy **2.** (*de diferencia*) fineness **3.** (*de persona*)

sharpness
suturar *vt* to stitch
suyo, -a *adj, pron* (*de él*) his; (*de ella*) hers; (*de cosa, animal*) its; (*de ellos*) theirs; (*de Ud., Uds.*) yours; (*de uno*) one's; **este encendedor es ~** this lighter is his/hers; **siempre habla de los ~s** he/she is always talking about his/her family; ~ **afectísimo** yours truly; **ya ha hecho otra de las suyas** *inf* he/she has been up to his/her tricks again; **eso es muy ~** that's typical of him/her; **ir a lo ~** to go one's own way
Swazilandia *f* Swaziland

T t

T, t *f* T, t; ~ **de Tarragona** T for Tommy *Brit,* T for Tare *Am*
tabaco *m* **1.** (*producto*) tobacco **2.** (*cigarrillo*) cigarettes *pl*
taberna *f* tavern, bar
tabernero, -a *m, f* (*dueño*) landlord *m,* landlady *f;* (*camarero*) barman *m,* barmaid *f*
tabique *m* partition; ~ **nasal** nasal septum
tabla *f* **1.** (*plancha*) board; ~ **de surf** surfboard; ~ **de windsurf** sailboard; **a raja ~** *fig* to the letter **2.** (*lista*) list; (*cuadro*) table; **las Tablas de la Ley** the Tables of the Law **3.** (*de vestido*) pleat **4.** (*pintura*) panel **5.** *pl* DEP draw, tie **6.** *pl* TEAT stage **7.** *pl* (*experiencia*) **tener ~s** to be experienced
tablado *m* **1.** (*suelo*) plank floor **2.** (*entarimado*) wooden platform **3.** (*del escenario*) stage
tablao *m* bar or place where a Flamenco show is performed
tablero *m* **1.** (*de madera*) board; ~ **de anuncios** notice board *Brit,* bulletin board *Am* **2.** (*pizarra*) blackboard; ~ **de ajedrez/damas** chess/

draught board **3.** AUTO dashboard

tableta *f* **1.** (*de chocolate*) bar **2.** MED tablet

tablón *m* **1.** (*de andamio*) plank **2.** (*de anuncios*) notice board *Brit,* bulletin board *Am*

tabú *m* <tabúes> taboo

tabulador *m* tab

tabular *vt* to tabulate

taburete *m* stool

tacaño, -a *adj* stingy, mean *Brit*

tacha *f* **1.** (*defecto*) blemish; **sin ~** flawless **2.** (*tachuela*) large tack

tachar *vt* **1.** (*rayar*) to cross out **2.** (*atribuir*) to brand as sth **3.** (*acusar*) to accuse; **le ~on de incompetente** they accused him of being incompetent

tacho *m* AmL **1.** (*vasija*) metal basin **2.** (*cubo*) dustbin *Brit,* garbage can *Am*

tácito, -a *adj* tacit

taciturno, -a *adj* **1.** (*callado*) taciturn **2.** (*melancólico*) melancholy

taco *m* **1.** (*pedazo*) piece **2.** (*de billar*) cue **3.** (*de papel*) pad; (*de billetes*) wad **4.** (*de jamón*) cube **5.** TÉC plug; (*para tornillo*) Rawlplug® **6.** *inf* (*palabrota*) swearword, four--letter word; **decir ~s** to swear **7.** *inf* (*lío*) mess **8.** AmL (*tacón*) heel

tacón *m* heel

taconear *vi* to tap one's heel

taconeo *m* heel clicking

táctico, -a I. *adj* tactical **II.** *m, f* tactician

tacto *m* **1.** (*sentido*) sense of touch **2.** (*contacto*) touch **3.** (*habilidad*) tact

tafetán *m* (*tela*) taffeta

tahona *f* bakery

tahúr *m* cardsharp

tailandés, -esa *adj, m, f* Thai

Tailandia *f* Thailand

taimado, -a *adj* sly, crafty

Taiwán *m* Taiwan

tajada *f* **1.** (*porción*) slice; **sacar ~ de algo** to get something out of sth **2.** *inf* (*borrachera*) **pillar una ~** to get smashed

tajante *adj* **1.** (*respuesta*) categorical **2.** (*absoluto*) in no uncertain terms

tajar *vt* **1.** (*cortar*) to cut **2.** AmL (*afilar*) to sharpen

tajo *m* **1.** (*corte*) cut; **ir al ~** *inf* to go to work **2.** GEO gorge **3.** (*filo*) cutting edge

tal I. *adj* **1.** (*igual*) such; **en ~ caso** in that case; **no digas ~ cosa** don't say any such thing **2.** (*tanto*) so; **la distancia es ~ que...** it's so far away that ... **II.** *pron* **1.** (*alguien*) **el ~** that fellow; **~ o cual** someone or other **2.** (*cosa*) **hablar de ~ y cual** to talk about one thing and another; **y ~ y cual** and so on and so forth **III.** *adv* **1.** (*así*) so **2.** (*de la misma manera*) just; **son ~ para cual** they're two of a kind; **estar ~ cual** to be just as it was; **~ y como** just as **3.** (*cómo*) **¿qué ~ (te va)?** how are things?; **¿qué ~ te lo has pasado?** did you have a good time?; **~ y como están las cosas** the way things are now **IV.** *conj* **con ~ de** +*inf,* **con ~ que** +*subj* (*mientras*) as long as; (*condición*) provided; **~ vez** (*quizás*) perhaps

taladradora *f* pneumatic drill

taladrar *vt* **1.** (*con taladro*) to drill **2.** (*oídos*) to pierce

taladro *m* drill; (*agujero*) (drill) hole

talante *m* **1.** (*modo*) disposition; **de buen ~** willingly **2.** (*humor*) mood

talar *vt* **1.** (*árboles*) to fell **2.** (*destruir*) to lay waste

talco *m* **1.** (*mineral*) talc **2.** (*polvos*) talcum powder

talega *f* bag

talego *m* **1.** (*talega*) sack **2.** *inf* (*cárcel*) nick *Brit,* slammer *Am*

talento *m* (*capacidad*) talent; **de gran ~** very talented; **tener ~ para los idiomas** to have a gift for languages

talentoso, -a *adj* talented

talero *m* *Arg, Chile, Urug* whip

Talgo *m* *abr de* **Tren Articulado Ligero Goicoechea Oriol** *high speed light articulated train of Spanish invention for intercity passenger transportation*

talismán *m* talisman, lucky charm

talla *f* **1.** (*de diamante*) cutting **2.** (*en madera*) carving; (*en piedra*) sculpting **3.** (*estatura*) height; **ser de poca ~** to be short **4.** (*de vestido*) size **5.** (*moral*) stature

tallar *vt* **1.** (*diamante*) to cut **2.** (*madera*) to carve **3.** (*estatura*) to measure **4.** (*en juego*) to deal

tallarín *m* noodle

talle *m* **1.** (*cintura*) waist **2.** (*figura*) figure

taller *m* **1.** TÉC workshop **2.** (*estudio*) studio **3.** (*auto*) garage

tallo *m* **1.** BOT stem **2.** (*renuevo*) shoot

talón *m* **1.** (*del pie*) heel; **~ de Aquiles** Achilles' heel; *fig* weak point **2.** (*cheque*) cheque *Brit,* check *Am*

talonario *m* **1.** (*de cheques*) cheque-book *Brit,* checkbook *Am* **2.** (*de recibos*) receipt book

tamaño *m* size; **en ~ bolsillo** pocket size

tamaño, -a *adj* **1.** (*grande*) such a big **2.** (*pequeño*) such a small, so small a **3.** (*semejante*) such a

tamarindo *m* tamarind

tambalear *vi, vr:* **~se** to stagger; *fig* to totter

también *adv* also, as well, too; **yo lo ví ~** I also saw him, I saw him too

tambor *m* **1.** (*instrumento*) drum **2.** (*músico*) drummer **3.** ANAT eardrum

Támesis *m* **el ~** the Thames

tamiz *m* sieve

tamizar <z→c> *vt* to sieve

tampoco *adv* not either, nor, neither; **~ me gusta éste** I don't like this one either

tampón *m* **1.** (*de tinta*) ink pad **2.** (*para la mujer*) tampon

tan *adv* so; **~... como...** as ... as ...; **~ siquiera una vez** just once; **ni ~ siquiera** not even

tanatorio *m* funeral parlour *Brit,* funeral parlor *Am*

tanda *f* **1.** (*turno*) shift, turn; **¿me puedes guardar la ~?** will you keep my place for me? **2.** (*serie*) series *inv;* **por ~s** in batches

tanga *m* tanga, G-string

tangente *f* tangent; **salirse por la ~** *fig* to go off on a tangent

Tánger *m* Tangier(s)

tangible *adj* tangible

tango *m* MÚS tango

tanque *m* **1.** MIL tank **2.** (*cisterna*) tanker

tanteador *m* scoreboard

tantear *vt* **1.** (*calcular: cantidad*) to calculate; (*tamaño*) to weigh up; (*a ojo*) to size up; (*precio*) to estimate **2.** (*probar*) to try out; (*persona: sondear*) to sound out **3.** (*ir a tientas*) to grope

tanteo *m* **1.** (*cálculo: cantidad*) calculation; (*de tamaño*) weghing up; (*a ojo*) sizing up; (*de precio*) estimate **2.** (*sondeo*) sounding out **3.** DEP (*de puntos*) score

tanto **I.** *m* **1.** (*cantidad*) certain amount; COM rate; **~ alzado** lump sum basis; **~ por ciento** percentage; **un ~** a bit; **estoy un ~ sorprendido** I'm somewhat surprised **2.** (*punto*) point; (*gol*) goal **3.** *fig* **estar al ~ de algo** to be up to date on sth **II.** *adv* **1.** (*de tal modo*) so much; **no es para ~** there's no need to make such a fuss **2.** (*de duración*) so long; **tu respuesta tardó ~ que...** your answer took so long that ... **3.** (*comparativo*) **~ mejor/peor** so much the better/worse; **~ como** as much as; **~ si llueve como si no...** whether it rains or not ...; **~... como...** both ... and ... **4.** (*locuciones*) **en ~ (que +subj)** as long as, provided; **entre ~** meanwhile, in the meantime; **por (lo) ~** therefore, so

tanto, -a **I.** *adj* **1.** (*comparativo*) as much, as many; **no ~ dinero como...** not as much money as ...; **~s días como...** as many days as ... **2.** (*tal cantidad*) so much; **¡hace ~ tiempo!** such a long time ago!; **~ gusto en conocerle** a pleasure to meet you **3.** *pl* (*número indefinido*) **uno de ~s** one of many; **a ~s de enero** on such and such a day of January; **tener 40 y ~s años** to be 40-odd years old; **quedarse des-**

pierto hasta las tantas to stay up until all hours **II.** *pron dem* ~**s** as many; **coge** ~**s como quieras** take as many as you like; **no llego a** ~ I won't go that far

Tanzania *f* Tanzania

taoísmo *m* Taoism

tapa *f* **1.**(*cubierta*) lid; ~ **de rosca** screw-top; **libro de** ~**s duras** hardback **2.**(*de zapato*) heelpiece **3.** GASTR tapa

---

? **Tapa** is the synonym for **pincho**, i.e. a snack or a bite to eat between meals. In **Andalucía**, however, a **tapa** consists exclusively of **embutido y/o jamón** (cured sausage and/or ham), which is served with wine or beer.

---

tapacubos *m inv* AUTO hubcap

tapadera *f* **1.**(*de vasija*) lid **2.**(*negocio*) cover

tapar **I.** *vt* **1.**(*cuerpo*) to cover; (*cazuela*) to put a lid on; (*en cama*) to cover up **2.**(*desagüe*) to obstruct; (*agujero*) to fill in; **¿te tapo?** am I blocking your view? **3.**(*ocultar*) to hide **II.** *vr:* ~**se 1.**(*con ropa*) to wrap up; (*en cama*) to cover up; (*completamente*) to hide **2.**(*oídos*) to get blocked; (*la cara*) to cover

tapete *m* table runner; **estar sobre el** ~ *fig* to be under consideration

tapia *f* wall; (*de jardín*) garden wall

tapiar *vt* to wall in

tapicería *f* **1.**(*tapices*) tapestries *pl,* wall-hangings *pl* **2.**(*tienda*) upholstery; (*taller*) upholsterer's **3.**(*tela*) upholstery

tapiz *m* tapestry; (*en el suelo*) rug

tapizar <z→c> *vt* **1.**(*muebles*) to upholster **2.**(*acolchar*) to quilt

tapón *m* **1.**(*obturador*) stopper; (*de fregadero*) drain plug **2.** MED tampon **3.**(*cerumen*) wax (in the ear)

taquicardia *f* MED tachycardia

taquigrafía *f* shorthand

taquigrafiar <*I. pres:* taquigrafío> *vt* to take down in shorthand

taquígrafo, -a *m, f* shorthand writer

taquilla *f* **1.** TEAT, CINE box office; DEP gate money; FERRO ticket window **2.**(*recaudación*) receipts *pl,* takings *pl* **3.**(*armario*) locker; (*archivador*) filing cabinet

taquillero, -a **I.** *adj* película taquillera box-office draw **II.** *m, f* ticket clerk

taquimecanógrafo, -a *m, f* shorthand typist

tara *f* **1.**(*defecto*) defect **2.** COM (*peso*) tare

tarántula *f* tarantula

tararear *vt* to hum

tardanza *f* delay

tardar *vi* to take time; ~ **en llegar** to take a long time to arrive; FERRO to be late arriving; **no tardo nada** I won't be long; **no** ~**é en volver** I'll be right back; **¡no tardes!** don't be gone long!; **a más** ~ at the latest; **sin** ~ without taking long

tarde **I.** *f* **1.**(*primeras horas*) afternoon; **por la** ~ in the afternoon; **¡buenas** ~**s!** good afternoon! **2.**(*últimas horas*) evening; **¡buenas** ~**s!** good evening! **II.** *adv* late; ~ **o temprano** sooner or later; **de** ~ **en** ~ now and then, occasionally; **se me hace** ~ it's getting late

tardío, -a *adj* **1.**(*atrasado*) late **2.**(*lento*) slow

tardo, -a *adj* slow

tarea *f* **1.**(*faena*) task **2.**(*trabajo*) job **3.** *pl* ENS homework

tarifa *f* rate; (*transporte*) fare

tarima *f* platform

tarjeta *f t.* INFOR card; ~ **de crédito** credit card; ~ **de memoria** memory chip; ~ **postal** postcard; ~ **de sonido** sound card; ~ **de visita** visiting-card *Brit,* calling-card *Am*

tarro *m* (*envase*) pot; (*de cristal*) jar

tarta *f* cake; (*pastel*) pie

tartamudear *vi* to stammer, to stutter

tartamudo, -a **I.** *adj* stammering, stuttering **II.** *m, f* stammerer, stutterer

tasa *f* **1.**(*valoración*) valuation **2.**(*precio*) fee; (*de impuesto*) tax

3. (*porcentaje*) rate; ~ **de desempleo** unemployment rate; ~ **de interés** interest rate

tasación *f* **1.** (*de producto*) fixing of a price **2.** (*de joya*) appraisement

tasar *vt* **1.** (*precio*) to fix the price of; (*impuesto*) to tax **2.** (*valorar*) to value

tasca *f* bar

tata¹ *f inf* (*niñera*) nanny

tata² *m AmL* (*papá*) daddy

tatarabuelo, -a *m, f* great-great-grandfather

tatuaje *m* tattoo

tatuar <*l. pres:* tatúo> *vt* to tattoo

taurino, -a *adj* bullfighting

Tauro *m* Taurus

tauromaquia *f sin pl* art of bullfighting

taxi *m* taxi, taxicab

taxista *mf* taxi driver *Brit,* cabdriver *Am*

taza *f* **1.** (*de café*) cup, mug **2.** (*del wáter*) toilet bowl

tazón *m* (*taza grande*) large cup; (*cuenco*) bowl

te **I.** *f* **la letra** ~ the letter t **II.** *pron pers* (*objeto directo, indirecto*) you; ¡**míra**~! look at yourself! **III.** *pron refl* ~ **vistes** you get dressed; ~ **levantas** you get up; **no** ~ **hagas daño** don't hurt yourself; ¿~ **has lavado los dientes?** have you brushed your teeth?

té *m* tea

tea *f* torch

teatral *adj* theatre

teatro *m* **1.** (*t. fig*) TEAT theatre *Brit,* theater *Am;* **obra de** ~ play; **hacer** ~ *fig* to playact **2.** (*escenario*) stage

tebeo *m* comic

techo *m* **1.** (*de habitación*) ceiling **2.** (*de casa*) roof

tecla *f* key; ~ **de mayúsculas** shift key; ~ **de retroceso** backspace key; ~ **de intro** enter key; **tocar demasiadas** ~**s** *fig* to do too many things at once

teclado *m* keyboard

teclear *vi* **1.** (*piano*) to play; (*ordenador*) to type **2.** (*dedos*) to drum

técnica *f* **1.** (*método*) technique

2. (*tecnología*) technology

técnicamente *adv* technically

técnico, -a **I.** *adj* technical **II.** *m, f* **1.** TÉC technician **2.** (*especialista*) expert

tecnicolor *m* Technicolor®

tecnócrata **I.** *adj* technocratic **II.** *mf* technocrat

tecnología *f* **1.** TÉC, ECON technology **2.** (*técnica*) technique

tecnológico, -a *adj* **1.** TÉC technological **2.** (*técnico*) technical

tedio *m* boredom

tedioso, -a *adj* tedious

teja *f* **1.** (*del tejado*) roof tile **2.** (*sombrero*) shovel hat

tejado *m* roof

tejano, -a *adj, m, f* Texan

tejanos *mpl* jeans

tejemaneje *m inf* **1.** (*actividad*) to-do **2.** (*intriga*) scheming

tejer *vt* **1.** (*tela*) to weave; (*tricotar*) to knit **2.** (*cestos*) to plait **3.** (*araña*) to spin **4.** (*intrigas*) to plot

tejido *m* **1.** *t.* ANAT (*textura*) tissue **2.** (*tela*) fabric; **los** ~**s** textiles *pl*

tejón *m* badger

tela *f* **1.** (*tejido*) material, fabric; ~ **de araña** spider's web *Brit,* spiderweb *Am* **2.** (*en leche*) film **3.** *inf* (*asunto*) matter; **este asunto tiene** ~ it's a complicated matter **4.** (*lienzo*) painting; **poner algo en** ~ **de juicio** (*dudar*) to question sth; (*tener reparos*) to raise objections about sth

telar *m* (*máquina*) loom

telaraña *f* cobweb *Brit,* spiderweb *Am*

tele *f inf abr de* **televisión** TV, telly *Brit*

telebanca *f* e-bank

telebanking *m sin pl* e-banking

telebasura *f* junk TV

telecompra *f sin pl* teleshopping

telecomunicación *f* telecommunication

teleconferencia *f* COM teleconference, video-phone conference

telecontrol *m* remote control

telediario *m* TV news; **el** ~ **de las 3** the 3 o'clock news

teledifusión *f* telecast

teledirigido, -a *adj* remote-controlled

teléf. *abr de* **teléfono** tel.

teleférico *m* cable car

telefonear *vi* to telephone

Telefónica *f national telephone company in Spain*

telefónico, -a *adj* telephone; **cabina telefónica** phone box; **guía telefónica** telephone directory, phone book

telefonista *mf* telephone operator

teléfono *m* 1. (*aparato*) telephone; ~ **móvil** mobile phone, cellphone *Am;* ~ **rojo** *fig* hotline; **hablar por** ~ to talk on the phone; **llamar por** ~ to telephone 2. (*número*) phone number 3. *pl* (*compañía*) telephone company

telegrafía *f* telegraphy

telegrafiar <3. *pret:* telegrafió> *vt, vi* to telegraph

telégrafo *m* 1. (*aparato*) telegraph 2. *pl* (*administración*) post office

telegrama *m* telegram

teleimpresor *m* teleprinter

telele *m* *inf* fit

telemando *m* remote control

telenovela *f* TV soap opera

teleobjetivo *m* FOTO telephoto lens

telepatía *f sin pl* telepathy

telepático, -a *adj* telepathic

telescópico, -a *adj* telescopic

telescopio *m* telescope

telesilla *f* chair-lift

telespectador(a) *m(f)* TV viewer

telesquí *m* ski-lift

teletexto *m* teletext

teletipo *m* teletype®

teletrabajo *m* teleworking (from home)

televidente *mf v.* **telespectador**

televisar *vt* to televise

televisión *f* television; ~ **de pago** pay-television; ~ **en color** colour TV *Brit,* color TV *Am*

televisor *m* television set

télex *m* telex

telón *m* curtain; **el** ~ **de acero** the iron curtain; ~ **de fondo** backdrop

tema *m* t. MÚS, LIT theme; ~s **de actualidad** current issues

---

⚠ Words such as **tema** ending in -ma are always masculine: "el tema." Other examples include: "el clima, el drama, el idioma, el problema, el programa, el sistema."

---

temario *m* 1. (*lista de temas*) programme *Brit,* program *Am* 2. (*para un examen*) list of topics

temática *f* subjects *pl*

temático, -a *adj* thematic

temblar <e→ie> *vi* to tremble; ~ **por alguien** to fear for sb; ~ **de frío** to shiver (with cold)

tembleque *m* *inf* 1. (*temblor*) shaking 2. (*persona*) weakling

temblón, -ona *adj* *inf* trembling

temblor *m* (*tembleque*) tremor; (*escalofrío*) shiver

tembloroso, -a *adj* shaky

temer I. *vt* 1. (*sentir temor*) to fear 2. (*sospechar*) to be afraid II. *vi, vr:* ~**se** to be afraid

temerario, -a *adj* 1. (*imprudente*) reckless 2. (*sin fundamento*) rash

temeridad *f sin pl* 1. (*imprudencia*) recklessness 2. (*insensatez*) rashness

temeroso, -a *adj* 1. (*medroso*) fearful 2. (*temible*) dreadful

temible *adj* fearsome

temor *m* 1. (*miedo*) fear 2. (*sospecha*) suspicion

témpano *m* 1. (*pedazo*) chunk; (*de hielo*) ice floe 2. (*tambor*) kettledrum

temperamento *m* temperament; **tener mucho** ~ to have a strong character

temperatura *f* temperature

tempestad *f* storm

tempestuoso, -a *adj* stormy

templado, -a *adj* 1. (*tibio*) lukewarm 2. (*temperado*) tempered 3. (*moderado*) moderate 4. (*sereno*) composed 5. MÚS tuned

templanza *f* 1. (*moderación*) temperateness 2. (*clima*) mildness 3. (*virtud*) temperance

templar I. *vt* 1. (*moderar*) to moderate; (*calmar*) to calm down **2.**(*calentar*) to warm up **3.**(*entibiar*) to cool down **4.**MÚS (*afinar*) to tune **5.**(*acero*) to temper **II.** *vr:* ~**se 1.**(*moderarse*) to control oneself **2.**(*calentarse*) to get warm **3.**AmL (*enamorarse*) to fall in love

temple *m* **1.**(*valentía*) courage **2.**(*carácter*) disposition; (*humor*) mood **3.**(*del acero*) tempering **4.**ARTE tempera

templo *m* temple; (*iglesia*) church

temporada *f* (*tiempo*) season; (*época*) period; **fruta de ~** seasonal fruit

temporal I. *adj* **1.**(*relativo al tiempo*) stormy **2.**(*no permanente*) temporary; (*no eterno*) temporal; **contrato ~** temporary contract **II.** *m* (*tormenta*) storm; (*marejada*) stormy seas *pl*

tempranero, -a I. *adj* (*fruta*) early **II.** *m, f* early riser, earlybird

temprano *adv* early

temprano, -a *adj* early

tenacidad *f sin pl* **1.**(*persona*) tenacity **2.**(*dolor*) persistence; (*mancha*) stubbornness

tenacillas *fpl* tongs *pl*; (*para rizar*) curling iron

tenaz *adj* **1.**(*perserverante*) persevering **2.**(*cabezota*) stubborn **3.**(*persistente*) persistent

tenaza(s) *f(pl)* pliers *pl*

tendedero *m* **1.**(*lugar*) drying place **2.**(*armazón*) clothes horse; (*cuerdas*) clothes line

tendencia *f* **1.**(*inclinación*) tendency **2.**(*dirección*) trend; ~**alcista** upward trend; ~**s de la moda** fashion trends

tendencioso, -a *adj pey* tendentious

tender <e→ie> **I.** *vt* **1.**(*esparcir*) to spread over; ~ **la cama** *AmL* to make the bed; ~ **la mesa** *AmL* to lay the table **2.**(*tumbar*) to lay **3.**(*la ropa*) to hang out; (*puente*) to build; (*línea, vía*) to lay **4.**(*aproximar*) to hold out; ~ **la mano a alguien** *fig* to give sb a hand **II.** *vi* to tend

tenderete *m* COM stall, stand

tendero, -a *m, f* shopkeeper *Brit,* storekeeper *Am*

tendido *m* **1.**(*de un cable*) laying **2.**(*cables*) cables *pl,* wiring **3.**(*ropa*) washing *Brit,* wash *Am* **4.**TAUR *front rows of seats* **5.**AmL (*de la cama*) bed linen

tendido, -a *adj* (*galope*) full; **largo y ~** long and hard

tendón *m* ANAT tendon

tenebroso, -a *adj* *t. fig* (*oscuro*) dark; (*tétrico*) gloomy

tenedor *m* fork

tenedor(a) *m(f)* holder; ~ **de tierras** landowner

teneduría *f* bookkeeping

tenencia *f* JUR possession

tener *irr* **I.** *vt* **1.**(*poseer, sentir*) to have; ~ **los ojos azules** to have blue eyes; ~ **29 años** to be 29 years old; ~ **hambre/calor/sueño** to be hungry/hot/sleepy; ¿(**con que**) **ésas tenemos?** so that's the way it is?; **no** ~**las todas consigo** not to be sure of something; ¿**tienes frío?** are you cold? **2.**(*considerar*) to consider; ~ **a alguien en menos/mucho** to think all the less/more of sb; **me tienes preocupada** I'm worried about you **3.**(*guardar*) to keep **4.**(*coger*) to take; (*sujetar*) to hold **II.** *vr:* ~**se 1.**(*por algo*) to consider oneself **2.**(*sostenerse*) to stand; ~**se firme** to stand upright; *fig* to stand firm **III.** *aux* **1.**(*con participio*) ~ **pensado hacer algo** to plan to do sth; **ya me lo tenía pensado** I had already thought of that **2.**(*obligación*) ~ **que** to have to; ~ **mucho que hacer** to have a lot to do

tenia *f* tapeworm

teniente *m* MIL lieutenant

tenis *m sin pl* tennis

tenista *mf* tennis player

tenor *m t.* MÚS tenor

tensar *vt* (*músculo*) to tense; (*cuerda*) to tighten

tensión *f* **1.**FÍS tension **2.**(*mental*) stress; (*de una cuerda*) tautness; (*de músculos*) tension; ~ **arterial** blood pressure **3.**(*impaciencia*) anxiety; **estar en** ~ (*nervioso*) to be nervous; (*impaciente*) to be anxious **4.**ELEC voltage

tenso, -a adj (situación) tense; (cuerda) taut; (impaciente) anxious

tentación f temptation; **caer en la ~** to succumb to the temptation

tentáculo m tentacle

tentador(a) I. adj tempting II. m(f) tempter m, temptress f

tentar <e→ie> vt 1. (palpar) to feel 2. (atraer) to tempt; (seducir) to entice

tentativa f attempt

tentempié m inf bite to eat

tenue adj 1. (delgado) fine 2. (débil) weak; (luz) faint 3. (sencillo) simple

teñir irr como ceñir vt, vr: ~se to dye

teología f theology

teorema m theorem

teoría f theory; **en ~** in theory

teórico, -a I. adj theoretical II. m, f theorist, theoretician

teorizar <z→c> vi, vt to theorize

tequila m tequila

terapéutica f therapeutics pl

terapéutico, -a adj therapeutic(al)

terapia f therapy

tercer adj v. **tercero**

tercermundista adj third-world, underdeveloped

tercero I. m t. JUR third party II. adv third

tercero, -a adj (delante de un sustantivo masculino: tercer) third; **tercera edad** retirement years; v.t. **octavo**

> ! **tercero** is always used after a masculine singular noun or on its own as a pronoun: "Vive en el piso tercero; Es el tercero de su clase." In contrast **tercer** is always used before a masculine singular noun: "Lo consiguió al tercer intento."

terceto m MÚS trio

terciar I. vt 1. (dividir) to divide into three parts 2. (atravesar) to place diagonally across 3. (la carga) to balance 4. AmL (aguar) to water down II. vi 1. (intervenir) to intervene 2. (mediar) to have a word III. vr, v impers: ~se to arise; **si se tercia** should the occasion arise

terciario m GEO Tertiary period

terciario, -a adj tertiary

tercio m third; v.t. **octavo**

terciopelo m velvet

terco, -a I. adj stubborn, obstinate II. m, f stubborn person

tergal® m type of synthetic fabric

tergiversar vt (hechos) to misrepresent; (la verdad) to distort

termal adj thermal; **aguas ~es** hot springs

termas fpl hot baths pl

térmico, -a adj thermal, thermic; **central térmica** power station

terminación f 1. (acción) termination; (de un proyecto) completion; (producción) finish; (de un plazo) end 2. (final) end

terminal¹ I. adj terminal; **parte ~** final part; **un enfermo ~** a terminally ill patient II. m INFOR terminal

terminal² f 1. (estación) terminal, terminus; FERRO station 2. (de aeropuerto) terminal

terminante adj 1. (claro) clear 2. (definitivo) categorical

terminar I. vt 1. (finalizar) to finish; (proyecto) to complete 2. (consumir) to finish up; (comer) to eat up II. vi 1. (tener fin) to finish; (plazo) to end; ~ **bien** to have a happy ending; ~ **de construir** to finish building; **la escuela termina a las dos** school is out at 2 pm; **ya termina la película** the film is almost over 2. (destruir) to do away 3. (separarse) to break up III. vr: ~se 1. (aproximarse al final) to be almost over 2. (no haber más) (for) there to be no more

término m 1. (fin) end; **llevar a ~** to carry out; **sin ~** endless 2. (plazo) period 3. (linde) boundary; ~ **municipal** township 4. (vocablo) term; **en otros ~s** in other words; **en malos ~s** rudely 5. pl (de un contrato) terms pl, conditions pl 6. (expresiones) **en ~s generales** generally speaking; **en primer ~**

first of all; **en último** ~ as a last resort; **por** ~ **medio** on the average
terminología *f* terminology
termita *f* termite
termo *m* thermos
termodinámica *f* thermodynamics *pl*
termómetro *m* thermometer
termonuclear *adj* thermonuclear
termostato *m*, **termóstato** *m* thermostat, thermal switch
ternera *f* (*carne*) beef, veal
ternero, -a *m*, *f* calf
terno *m* 1. (*conjunto*) set of three 2. (*traje*) three-piece suit
ternura *f* 1. (*cariño*) tenderness 2. (*dulzura*) sweetness 3. (*delicadeza*) gentleness
terquedad *f* stubbornness, obstinacy
terrado *m* flat roof; (*terraza*) terrace
Terranova *f* Newfoundland
terraplén *m* 1. (*protección*) rampart 2. (*desnivel*) slope 3. FERRO embankment
terráqueo, -a *adj* terrestrial, terraqueous; **globo** ~ globe
terrateniente *mf* landowner, landholder
terraza *f* 1. (*jardín*) terrace; (*balcón*) balcony; (*azotea*) flat roof 2. (*of a café*) terrace
terremoto *m* earthquake
terrenal *adj* worldly; **paraíso** ~ earthly paradise
terreno *m* 1. (*suelo*) land; GEO terrain 2. (*espacio*) lot; (*campo*) field; DEP playing field; **vehículo todo** ~ all-terrain vehicle; ~ **desconocido** unfamiliar territory; **estar en su propio** ~ to be on one's own ground; **explorar el** ~ to see how the land lies; **ganar/perder** ~ to gain/lose ground; **sobre el** ~ on the spot
terreno, -a *adj* earthly
terrestre *adj* 1. (*de la Tierra*) terrestrial 2. (*en la tierra*) earthly; **transporte** ~ ground transport
terrible *adj* terrible
territorial *adj* territorial
territorio *m* territory
terrón *m* lump; ~ (**de tierra**) clod

terror *m* terror
terrorífico, -a *adj* terrifying
terrorismo *m sin pl* terrorism
terrorista *adj, mf* terrorist
terroso, -a *adj* earthy
terruño *m* 1. (*trozo*) clod 2. (*patria*) native land 3. (*terreno*) piece of land
terso, -a *adj* 1. (*liso*) smooth 2. (*limpio*) clean 3. (*fluido*) flowing
tertulia *f* 1. (*reunión*) gathering; **estar de** ~ to talk; ~ **literaria** literary circle 2. (*para jugar*) games room
tesina *f* project; UNIV (*trabajo*) minor thesis
tesis *f inv* 1. (*proposición*) theory 2. UNIV (*trabajo*) thesis
tesón *m* tenacity
tesorero, -a *m*, *f* treasurer
tesoro *m* 1. (*de gran valor*) treasure 2. (*fortuna*) fortune; ~ (**público**) Exchequer, Treasury 3. (*cariño*) dear
test *m* test
testaferro *m* man of straw
testamentario, -a I. *adj* testamentary II. *m*, *f* executor *m*, executrix *f*
testamento *m* will
testar *vi* to make a will
testarudo, -a *adj* pigheaded
testículo *m* ANAT testicle
testificar <c→qu> I. *vt* 1. (*declarar*) to testify; (*testigo*) to witness 2. (*testigo*) to attest II. *vi* to testify
testigo *mf t.* JUR witness; ~ **de cargo** witness for the prosecution; ~ **ocular** eyewitness; **ser** ~ **de algo** to witness sth
testimonial *adj* 1. (*que afirma*) attesting 2. (*que prueba*) testificatory
testimoniar *vt* 1. (*declarar*) to testify 2. (*dar muestra*) to show 3. (*probar*) to be proof of
testimonio *m* 1. (*declaración*) testimony; **dar** ~ to testify; **falso** ~ false witness 2. (*muestra*) evidence 3. (*prueba*) proof
teta *f* 1. *inf* (*pecho*) breast 2. (*ubre*) udder 3. (*pezón*) nipple
tétano(s) *m* (*inv*) MED tetanus
tetera *f* (*para té*) teapot; (*para hervir*) kettle
tetilla *f* 1. (*biberón*) nipple 2. (*animal*) teat

tétrico, -a *adj* dismal

textil *adj, m* textile

texto *m* text

textual *adj* textual; **con palabras** ~**es** with those exact words

textura *f* **1.** (*tejido*) weave **2.** (*estructura*) structure; QUÍM texture

tez *f* complexion; **de** ~ **morena** dark

ti *pron pers* **a** ~ (*objeto directo, indirecto*) you; **de** ~ from you; **para/ por** ~ for you

tía *f* **1.** (*pariente*) aunt; ¡(**cuéntaselo a**) **tu** ~**!** *inf* tell that to the marines! **2.** *inf* (*mujer*) woman; ¡**qué** ~ **más buena!** what a babe!

tibieza *f* lukewarmness; (*en el trato*) coolness

tibio, -a *adj* **1.** (*temperatura*) lukewarm **2.** (*carácter*) unenthusiastic **3.** *AmL, inf* (*enfadado*) angry

tiburón *m* **1.** ZOOL shark **2.** FIN raider

tic I. *interj* tick II. *m* <tics> tic; (*manía*) habit

tiempo *m* **1.** (*periodo*) time; ~ **libre** spare time; **al poco** ~ shortly after; **a** ~ in time; **a su** ~ in due course; **cada cosa a su** ~ there is a time for everything; **al** ~ **que...** while ...; **antes de** ~ early; **llegar antes de** ~ to arrive ahead of time; **desde hace mucho** ~ for a long time; **en estos** ~**s** nowadays; **en otros** ~**s** in the past; **dar** ~ **al** ~ to give it time; **hace** ~ **que...** it's a long time since ...; ¡**cuánto** ~ **sin verte!** long time no see!; **hay** ~ there's time; **matar el** ~ to kill time; **mucho/demasiado** ~ long/too long; **perder el** ~ to waste time; **ya es** ~ **que** +*subj* it's about time; **tomarse** ~ to take one's time **2.** (*época*) time; (*estación*) season **3.** METEO weather; **si el** ~ **no lo impide** weather permitting **4.** LING tense **5.** (*edad*) age **6.** DEP (**medio**) ~ half-time; ~ **muerto** time out

tienda *f* **1.** (*establecimiento*) shop, store; ~ **de comestibles** grocer's *Brit,* grocery store *Am;* **ir de** ~**s** to go shopping **2.** (*de campaña*) tent

tienta *f* **1.** MED probe **2.** (*astucia*) cleverness; **andar a** ~**s** *fig* to feel one's way

tiento *m* **1.** (*acción*) touch **2.** (*tacto*) tact **3.** (*cautela*) caution; **con** ~ carefully; (*cuidado*) care **4.** (*pulso*) sureness of hand

tierno, -a *adj* **1.** (*blando*) soft; (*pan*) fresh **2.** (*suave*) tender **3.** (*cariñoso*) affectionate

tierra *f* **1.** (*materia, superficie*) earth; **toma de** ~ ELEC earth *Brit,* ground *Am;* **bajo** ~ MIN underground; **echar por** ~ to knock down; *fig* to ruin **2.** (*firme*) mainland; **tomar** ~ AERO to land, to touch down; NÁUT to land **3.** (*región*) land; **Tierra Santa** Holy Land; **poseer** ~**s** to own land

tieso *adv* firmly

tieso, -a *adj* **1.** (*rígido*) stiff **2.** (*erguido*) erect; (*orejas*) pricked up **3.** (*serio*) stiff **4.** (*engreído*) conceited **5.** (*tirante*) taut

tiesto *m* flowerpot

tifoideo, -a *adj* typhoid

tifón *m* **1.** (*huracán*) typhoon **2.** (*tromba*) waterspout

tifus *m inv* MED typhus

tigre, -a *m, f AmL* ZOOL jaguar

tigre(sa) *m(f)* tiger *m,* tigress *f;* **oler a** ~ *inf* to stink

tijera(s) *f (pl)* scissors *pl;* (*grandes*) shears *pl;* **silla de** ~ folding chair

tijeretear I. *vt* to snip II. *vi inf* (*entrometerse*) to meddle

tila *f* linden-blossom tea

tildar *vt* ~ **de algo** to brand as sth

tilde *f* **1.** (*acento*) accent **2.** (*de la ñ*) tilde

tilín *m sin pl* (*sonido*) tinkle

tilo *m* linden

timar I. *vt* to con II. *vr:* ~**se** (*hacerse guiños*) to make eyes at each other; (*tontear*) to flirt

timbal *m* MÚS small drum

timbrar *vt* (*pegar*) to put a stamp on; (*estampar*) to postmark

timbre *m* **1.** (*aparato*) bell; (*de la puerta*) doorbell **2.** *t.* MÚS (*sonido*) timbre **3.** (*sello que se pega*) stamp; (*que se estampa*) seal

timidez *f* shyness

tímido, -a *adj* shy

timo *m* (*fraude*) con; **dar un** ~ to

swindle

timón *m* rudder; **llevar el ~** *inf* to be at the helm

timonel *mf* helmsman

tímpano *m* 1. ANAT (*membrana*) eardrum 2. (*instrumento*) kettledrum

tina *f* vat; *AmL* (*bañera*) bathtub

tinaja *f* large earthenware jar

tinglado *m* 1. (*cobertizo*) shed 2. *inf* (*lío*) tangle 3. (*artimaña*) intrigue

tiniebla *f* darkness

tino *m* 1. (*puntería*) aim 2. (*destreza*) skill 3. (*moderación*) moderation; **sin ~** recklessly

tinta *f* 1. (*para escribir*) ink; **cargar las ~s** to exaggerate; **saber algo de buena ~** to know sth from a reliable source; **sudar ~** to sweat blood 2. (*color*) hue

tinte *m* 1. (*teñidura*) dye 2. (*colorante*) colouring *Brit,* coloring *Am* 3. (*tintorería*) dry cleaner's 4. (*matiz*) tinge; (*apariencia*) touch

tintero *m* inkwell; **dejar(se) en el ~** *fig* to leave unsaid

tintin(e)ar *vi* to clink

tinto, -a *adj* red; **vino ~** red wine

tintorería *f* dry cleaner's

tintura *f* 1. (*tinte*) tint 2. (*colorante*) dye 3. MED tincture

tío *m* 1. (*pariente*) uncle 2. *inf* (*hombre*) bloke *Brit,* guy

tiovivo *m* merry-go-round, carrousel *Am*

típico, -a *adj* typical

tiple[1] *mf* MÚS (*persona*) soprano

tiple[2] *m* MÚS (*voz*) soprano

tipo *m* 1. (*modelo*) model 2. (*muestra*) sample; (*espécimen*) type 3. (*cuerpo*) build; **aguantar el ~** to hold out; **arriesgar el ~** *inf* to risk one's neck; **tener buen ~** to have a good figure 4. (*clase*) type, kind 5. FIN rate; **~ de cambio** exchange rate

tipo, -a *m, f inf* guy *m,* woman *f*

tipografía *f* (*impresión*) printing; (*taller*) printing press

tipográfico, -a *adj* printing

tipógrafo, -a *m, f* printer

tiquet *m* <tiquets> (*de espectáculos*) ticket; (*de compra*) sales slip, re-

ceipt

tiquismiquis[1] *mf inv* (*remilgado*) fusspot

tiquismiquis[2] *mpl* 1. (*remilgo*) silly scruples *pl* 2. (*ñoñería*) finickiness

tira *f* 1. (*banda*) strip, band; **~ cómica** comic strip 2. *inf* (*mucho*) **esto me ha gustado la ~** I really liked this a lot

tirabuzón *m* 1. (*rizo*) ringlet, curl 2. (*sacacorchos*) corkscrew

tirada *f* 1. (*edición*) print run; **de una ~** *fig* without stopping 2. (*distancia*) stretch

tirado, -a I. *adj* 1. *estar inf* (*barato*) dirt cheap 2. *ser pey* (*descuidado*) slovenly 3. *estar inf* (*fácil*) very easy; **estar ~** to be dead easy II. *m, f inf* nohoper

tirador *m* 1. (*agarradero*) handle, knob 2. (*cordón*) pull chain

tirador(a) *m(f)* (*disparador*) shot, marksman

tiralíneas *m inv* ruling pen

tiranía *f* tyranny

tiránico, -a *adj* tyrannical

tiranizar <z→c> *vt* to tyrannize

tirano, -a I. *adj* tyrannic II. *m, f* tyrant

tirante I. *adj* 1. (*tieso*) taut; (*pantalón*) tight 2. (*conflictivo*) tense II. *m* 1. (*travesaño*) strut 2. *pl* (*elásticos*) braces *pl Brit,* suspenders *pl Am* 3. (*de un vestido*) strap 4. (*de caballería*) trace

tirantez *f* tension

tirar I. *vi* 1. (*arrastrar*) to pull on; **a todo ~** at the most; **¿qué tal? – vamos tirando** *inf* how are you? – we're managing 2. (*atraer*) to attract 3. (*chimenea*) to draw 4. (*vestido: ser estrecho*) to be tight 5. (*disparar*) to shoot II. *vt* 1. (*lanzar*) to throw 2. (*malgastar*) to waste 3. (*disparar*) to shoot; (*bombas*) to drop 4. (*derribar*) to knock down; (*edificio*) to pull down 5. (*imprimir*) to print 6. FOTO to take III. *vr:* **~se** 1. (*lanzarse*) to throw oneself 2. (*echarse*) to lie down 3. *inf* (*pasar tiempo*) to spend

tirita *f* plaster *Brit,* Band Aid®

Tt

tiritar *vi* to shiver

tiro *m* **1.** (*lanzamiento*) shot; ~ **al aire** warning shot; **a** ~ in range; *fig* accessible; **dar un** ~ to fire a shot; **pegarse un** ~ to shoot oneself; **me salió el** ~ **por la culata** *inf* it backfired on me **2.** (*caballerías*) team; **sentar como un** ~ (*comida*) to disagree; (*noticia*) to upset

tiroides *m inv* MED thyroid

tirón *m* (*acción*) snatch; **de un** ~ (*bruscamente*) suddenly; (*de una vez*) without stopping, in one go *Brit*

tiroteo *m* shooting

tísico, -a *m, f* consumptive person

tisis *f inv* MED tuberculosis

titánico, -a *adj* titanic

títere *m* **1.** *t. fig* (*muñeco*) puppet **2.** (*tipejo*) weakling **3.** *pl* (*espectáculo*) puppet show

titilar *vi* **1.** (*temblar*) to quiver **2.** (*centellear*) to twinkle

titiritero, -a *m, f* **1.** (*que maneja los títeres*) puppeteer **2.** (*acróbata*) acrobat

titubear *vi* **1.** (*vacilar*) to waver; *fig* to hesitate **2.** (*balbucear*) to stutter

titubeo *m* tottering; *fig* hesitation

titulado, -a **I.** *adj* titled **II.** *m, f* degree holder; ~ (**universitario**) university graduate

titular¹ **I.** *adj* **profesor** ~ full professor **II.** *mf* holder; ~ **de acciones** shareholder

titular² **I.** *m* headline **II.** *vt* (*poner título*) to title **III.** *vr:* ~**se** to be entitled

título *m* **1.** (*rótulo*) title **2.** (*diploma*) diploma; ~ **universitario** university degree **3.** (*motivo*) reason; **a** ~ **de** by way of; **a** ~ **gratuito** for free

tiza *f* chalk

tiznar **I.** *vt* to blacken **II.** *vr:* ~**se** (*entiznarse*) to get dirty

tizón *m* **1.** (*palo*) partly-burned stick **2.** (*deshonra*) stain

toalla *f* towel; ~ **de baño** bath towel

toallero *m* towel rail, towel rack *Am*

tobillo *m* ankle

tobogán *m* **1.** (*deslizadero*) slide **2.** (*pista*) chute

toca *f* headdress

tocadiscos *m inv* record player

tocado *m* headdress

tocado, -a *adj* **1.** (*perturbado*) slightly touched; **estar** ~ to be not all there **2.** (*lesionado*) injured **3.** (*medio podrido*) going bad

tocador *m* **1.** (*mueble*) dressing table **2.** (*habitación*) ladies' dressing room; (*servicios*) ladies' room

tocante *adj* ~ **a** concerning

tocar <c→qu> **I.** *vt* **1.** (*contacto*) to touch, to feel; ~ **fondo** to hit bottom; **¡no lo toques!** don't touch it! **2.** MÚS to play; (*timbre*) to ring; (*tambor*) to beat; (*bocina*) to blow; (*alarma*) to sound; ~ **a la puerta** to knock at the door; **el reloj tocó las tres** the clock struck three **3.** (*modificar*) to change **4.** (*chocar*) to run into **II.** *vi* **1.** (*obligación*) to have to **2.** (*corresponder*) **te toca jugar** it's your turn **3.** (*premio*) to win; **le tocó hacerlo** it fell to him/her to do it **III.** *vr:* ~**se 1.** (*estar en contacto*) to touch **2.** (*peinarse*) to do one's hair

tocateja **a** ~ cash

tocayo, -a *m, f* namesake

tocino *m* (*lardo*) pork fat; (*carne*) bacon

tocólogo, -a *m, f* MED obstetrician

todavía *adv* **1.** (*aún*) still; ~ **no** not yet; **es** ~ **más caro que…** it is even more expensive than … **2.** (*sin embargo*) **pero** ~ however

todo **I.** *pron indef* all; ~ **lo que** [*o* **cuanto**]… all …; (**o**) ~ **o nada** all or nothing; ~ **lo más** at the most; **es** ~ **uno** it's all one and the same; **ante** [*o* **sobre**] ~ above all; ~ **lo contrario** quite the contrary; **antes que** ~ first of all; **después de** ~ *inf* after all; **con** ~ nevertheless; **estar en** ~ *inf* to be on the ball **II.** *adv inf* all, completely **III.** *m sin pl* (*la totalidad*) the whole; **del** ~ completely; **no del** ~ not entirely; **jugarse el** ~ **por el** ~ to risk all

todo, -a *art indef* **1.** (*entero*) all; **toda la familia** the whole family; **toda España** all Spain; **en toda Europa** all over Europe; **a toda prisa** as fast as possible **2.** (*cada*) every; **a toda**

costa at all cost; ~ **Dios** [*o* **quisqui**] *inf* absolutely everyone **3.** *pl* all; **~s y cada uno** each and every one; **a todas horas** at all hours; **en todas partes** everywhere; **de ~s modos** anyway

todopoderoso, -a *adj* almighty

todoterreno **I.** *adj inv* all-purpose, versatile **II.** *m* AUTO all-terrain vehicle

toga *f* robe

toldo *m* **1.** (*marquesina*) marquee; (*en una tienda*) awning *Brit,* sunshade *Am* **2.** (*de carro*) tarpaulin

tole *m* **1.** (*bulla*) hubbub **2.** (*rumor*) rumour *Brit,* rumor *Am*

tolerancia *f* tolerance

tolerante *adj* tolerant

tolerar *vt* **1.** (*soportar*) to tolerate **2.** (*permitir*) to allow sth

toma *f* **1.** (*adquisición*) taking; ~ **de datos** INFOR data acquisition **2.** (*conquista*) capture **3.** (*dosis*) dose **4.** TÉC inlet; ~ **de tierra** ground **5.** (*grabación*) take **6.** FOTO shot

tomar **I.** *vi* to turn **II.** *vt* **1.** (*coger, llevar*) to take; (*préstamo*) to borrow; (*decisión*) to take; (*fuerzas*) to gather **2.** (*beber, comer*) to have **3.** (*interpretar*) ~ **algo a mal** to take offence at sth *Brit,* to take offense at sth *Am;* ~ **en serio** to take seriously; ~ **conciencia de** to become aware of **4.** (*contratar*) to hire; (*piso*) to rent **5.** (*filmar*) to shoot **6.** *AmL* (*beber alcohol*) to drink **III.** *vr:* ~**se** **1.** (*coger*) to take **2.** (*beber, comer*) to have **3.** *AmL* (*emborracharse*) ~ **de puerta**) to get drunk

tomate *m* tomato

tomatera *f* tomato plant

tomavistas *m inv* FOTO film camera *Brit,* movie camera *Am*

tomillo *m* thyme

tomo *m* volume

ton *inf* **sin ~ ni son** for no particular reason

tonada *f* **1.** (*canción*) song **2.** (*melodía*) tune

tonalidad *f* **1.** LING intonation **2.** MÚS tonality, tone

tonel *m* **1.** (*barril*) barrel **2.** *inf* (*persona gorda*) fatso

tonelada *f* (*peso*) ton

tonelaje *m* tonnage

tonelero *m* cooper

tongo *m* DEP fixing

tónica *f* **1.** MÚS tonic **2.** (*bebida*) tonic water

tónico *m* MED tonic

tónico, -a *adj* **1.** LING stressed **2.** MÚS tonic

tonificar <c→qu> *vt* to tone up

tono *m* **1.** *t.* MED (*altura, estilo*) tone, pitch; **bajar el ~** to lower one's voice; **dar el ~** to set the tone; **en ~ de reproche** reproachfully; **fuera de ~** out of place **2.** MÚS key **3.** (*del teléfono*) tone

tontería *f* **1.** (*memez*) foolishness **2.** (*nadería*) trifle

tonto, -a **I.** *adj* silly **II.** *m, f* fool; **hacer el ~** to clown around; **hacerse el ~** to play dumb

topacio *m* MIN topaz

topar *vi, vr* ~(**se**) **con algo** to run into sth; ~(**se**) **con alguien** to bump into sb

tope **I.** *adj* top, maximum; **fecha ~** latest date **II.** *m* **1.** (*extremo*) end; **estoy a ~ de trabajo** I'm swamped with work **2.** (*parachoques*) buffer; AUTO bumper **3.** (*de puerta*) doorstop

tópico *m* **1.** (*lugar común*) commonplace **2.** (*estereotipo*) cliché

tópico, -a *adj* trite; **de uso ~** MED for external use only

topo *m* **1.** (*roedor*) mole **2.** (*torpe*) clumsy clot

topógrafo, -a *m, f* surveyor, topographer

topónimo *m* place name

toque *m* **1.** (*roce*) touch **2.** (*golpe*) tap **3.** (*de campanas*) ringing; (*de teléfono*) ring; ~ **de queda** curfew **4.** (*advertencia*) warning **5.** (*lo principal*) crux

toquetear *vt inf* to fiddle with, to finger

tórax *m inv* thorax

torbellino *m* whirlwind

torcedura *f* MED sprain

torcer *irr como cocer* **I.** *vi* to turn **II.** *vt* **1.** (*encorvar*) to bend **2.** (*dar vueltas, desviar*) to wind; ~ **la vista**

T_t

to squint III. *vr:* ~**se 1.** (*encorvarse*) to bend; (*madera*) to warp **2.** (*dislocarse*) to sprain; (*pie*) to twist **3.** (*corromperse*) to go astray; (*fracasar*) to go wrong

torcido, -a *adj* **1.** (*ladeado*) lopsided **2.** (*encorvado*) crooked

tordo *m* thrush

tordo, -a *adj* **1.** (*color*) dapple-grey **2.** (*torpe*) dim

torear I. *vi* (*lidiar*) to fight; (*toros*) to bullfight **II.** *vt* **1.** (*lidiar*) to fight; (*toros*) to bullfight **2.** (*evitar*) to dodge

toreo *m* bullfighting

torero, -a I. *adj inf* bullfighting **II.** *m, f* bullfighter, matador

tormenta *f* **1.** *t. fig* (*temporal*) storm **2.** (*agitación*) turmoil

tormento *m* **1.** (*castigo*) torment **2.** (*congoja*) anguish

tormentoso, -a *adj* stormy; (*situación*) turbulent

tornar I. *vi* to return **II.** *vt* **1.** (*devolver*) to return **2.** (*cambiar*) to make **III.** *vr:* ~**se** to turn

tornasol *m* **1.** (*girasol*) sunflower **2.** (*reflejo*) iridescence

torneo *m* tournament

tornillo *m* **1.** (*clavo con rosca*) screw; **apretar los** ~**s a alguien** *fig* to put pressure on sb; **te falta un** ~ *inf* you have a screw loose **2.** *inf* (*deserción*) desertion

torniquete *m* **1.** (*puerta*) turnstile **2.** MED tourniquet

torno *m* **1.** (*máquina, para madera*) lathe; (*de alfarero*) potter's wheel; (*de banco*) vice *Brit,* vise *Am* **2.** (*cabrestante*) winch **3.** (*giro*) turn

toro *m* **1.** (*animal*) bull **2.** *pl* (*toreo*) bullfighting

toronja *f* **1.** (*naranja*) bitter orange **2.** (*pomelo*) grapefruit

torpe *adj* **1.** (*inhábil*) clumsy **2.** (*pesado*) sluggish

torpedo *m* torpedo

torpeza *f* **1.** (*pesadez*) heaviness **2.** (*inhabilidad*) clumsiness **3.** (*tontería*) stupidity **4.** (*error*) blunder

torre *f* **1.** *t.* ARQUIT tower; ~ **de alta tensión** electricity plyon; ~ **de per-**

foración derrick; ~ **de mando** control tower **2.** NÁUT turret **3.** DEP rook, castle

torrefacto, -a *adj* dark roasted

torrente *m* torrent

tórrido, -a *adj elev* torrid

torrija *f* ≈ French toast

torso *m* torso

torta *f* **1.** (*tarta*) cake; *AmL* (*pastel*) pie **2.** *inf* (*bofetada*) slap **3.** *inf* (*borrachera*) drunkenness; **no saber ni** ~ *inf* not to know a thing

tortazo *m inf* **1.** (*bofetada*) slap **2.** (*choque*) crash

tortilla *f* (*de huevos*) ≈ omelette *Brit,* ≈ omelet *Am; AmL* (*de harina*) tortilla

> **?** **Tortilla** is a type of Spanish omelette. A **tortilla de patatas** is an omelette with potatoes and onions, but there are also **tortillas** made from other ingredients, such as spinach, tuna, asparagus, etc. In Latin America, particularly in Mexico, a **tortilla** is a flat pancake prepared with maize and is one of the staple foods of this region.

tórtola *f* turtledove

tortuga *f* turtle

tortuoso, -a *adj* winding

tortura *f* (*suplicio*) torture

torturar *vt* to torture

tos *f* cough; ~ **ferina** whooping cough

tosco, -a *adj* rough, coarse

toser *vi* to cough

tostada *f* toast

tostador *m* toaster

tostar <o→ue> **I.** *vt* **1.** (*pan*) to toast **2.** (*curtir*) to brown **II.** *vr:* ~**se** to tan

total I. *adj* total; **en** ~ in all **II.** *m* MAT sum **III.** *adv* so, in the end

totalidad *f sin pl* totality, whole

totalitario, -a *adj* totalitarian

totalmente *adv* entirely, totally

tóxico *m* toxic substance

tóxico, -a *adj* toxic

toxicómano, -a I. *adj* addicted to drugs II. *m, f* drug addict

toxina *f* toxin

tozudo, -a I. *adj* obstinate II. *m, f* stubborn person

traba *f* 1. (*trabamiento*) tie 2. (*obstáculo*) hindrance; **poner ~s a...** to put obstacles in the way of ...

trabajador(a) I. *adj* hard-working II. *m(f)* worker

trabajar I. *vi* to work; **~ de vendedora** to work as a saleswoman; **~ por cuenta propia** to be self-employed; **~ a tiempo completo/parcial** to work full-time/part-time II. *vt* 1. (*tratar*) to work; (*caballo*) to train 2. (*perfeccionar*) to work on 3. (*inquietar*) to disturb 4. (*amasar*) to knead III. *vr:* **~se** to work

trabajo *m* 1. (*acción*) work 2. (*puesto*) job; **~s manuales** handicrafts *pl;* **~s forzados** hard labour *Brit,* hard labor *Am;* **~ en equipo** teamwork; **puesto de ~** job; **¡buen ~!** well done!; **costar ~** to be difficult; **tomarse el ~ de hacer algo** to take the trouble to do sth

trabajoso, -a *adj* hard

trabalenguas *m inv* tongue twister

trabar I. *vt* 1. (*juntar*) to join 2. (*coger*) to seize 3. (*comenzar*) to start; (*contactos*) to strike up II. *vi* to take hold III. *vr:* **~se** to get stuck; **~se la lengua** to get tongue-tied

tracción *f* 1. (*tirar*) pulling 2. (*accionar*) drive, traction; **~ a cuatro ruedas** four-wheel drive

tractor *m* tractor

tradición *f* tradition

tradicional *adj* traditional

traducción *f* translation; **~ al/del inglés** translation into/from English

traducir *irr vt* to translate

traductor(a) I. *adj* translating II. *m(f)* translator; **~ jurado** sworn translator

traer *irr* I. *vt* 1. (*llevar: a alguien*) to bring along; (*consigo*) to bring; (*vestido*) to wear; **¿qué te trae por aquí?** what brings you here?; **me trae sin cuidado** I couldn't care less 2. (*ir a por*) to fetch 3. (*atraer*) to attract 4. (*dar*) to give 5. (*más sustantivo*) **~ retraso** to be late; **~ prisa** to be in a hurry II. *vr:* **~se** 1. (*llevar a cabo*) **~se algo entre manos** to be up to something 2. (*ser difícil*) **este examen se las trae** the exam is really tough; **hace un frío que se las trae** it's really cold

traficar <c→qu> *vi* to deal; (*con drogas*) to traffic; (*con personas*) to smuggle

tráfico *m* 1. (*de vehículos*) traffic 2. COM trade; (*de drogas*) traffic; (*de personas*) smuggling

tragaluz *m* skylight

tragaperras *f inv* slot machine

tragar <g→gu> I. *vt, vr:* **~se** 1. (*engullir*) to swallow 2. (*mentira*) to fall for II. *vt* 1. (*soportar*) **no ~ a alguien** to not be able to stand sb 2. (*consumir*) to down; (*absorber*) to soak up

tragedia *f* tragedy

trágico, -a I. *adj* tragic II. *m, f* TEAT, LIT tragedian *m,* tragedienne *f*

trago *m* 1. (*de bebida*) swig; **a ~s cortos** in sips; **de un ~** in one gulp 2. (*bebida*) drink 3. (*experiencia*) experience; **pasar un mal ~** to have a bad time of it

traición *f* 1. (*acto desleal*) treachery, betrayal 2. JUR treason

traicionar *vt* to betray; (*la memoria*) to fail

traicionero, -a I. *adj* (*persona*) perfidious; (*acción*) traitorous II. *m, f* traitor

traidor(a) I. *adj* traitorous; (*falso*) deceitful II. *m(f)* traitor

traigo I. *pres de* **traer**

traje *m* 1. (*vestidura*) dress; **~ de baño** bathing suit; **~ de luces** bullfighter's costume 2. (*de hombre*) suit 3. (*de mujer*) outfit 4. (*popular*) regional costume 5. (*de época*) period costume

trajín *m* 1. (*de mercancías*) haulage 2. (*ajetreo*) rush

trajinar I. *vt* to transport II. *vi* to rush about

trama *f* 1. (*de hilos*) weft 2. LIT plot

3. (*intriga*) scheme

tramar *vt* **1.** (*traición*) to plot; (*plan*) to scheme **2.** (*tejidos*) to weave

tramitar *vt* **1.** (*asunto*) to attend to; (*negocio*) to transact **2.** (*expediente*) to process

trámite *m* **1.** (*diligencias*) proceedings *pl* **2.** (*formalidad*) formality; **estar en ~s de hacer algo** to be in the process of doing sth

tramo *m* **1.** (*de camino*) stretch; FERRO section **2.** (*de escalera*) flight

tramoya *f* **1.** TEAT stage machinery **2.** (*engaño*) scheme

trampa *f* **1.** (*para animales*) trap; **caer en la ~** to fall into the trap **2.** (*engaño*) trick; **hacer ~** (*engañar*) to cheat

trampilla *f* **1.** (*en habitación*) trapdoor **2.** (*portezuela*) oven door **3.** AUTO hatch

trampolín *m* (*de piscina*) diving board; (*de gimnasia*) trampoline

tramposo, -a I. *adj* cheating **II.** *m, f* **1.** (*estafador*) swindler **2.** (*en los juegos*) cheat

tranca *f* **1.** (*palo*) cudgel **2.** *inf* (*borrachera*) binge; **a ~s y barrancas** through fire and water

trance *m* **1.** (*momento*) **pasar un ~ difícil** to go through a difficult time **2.** (*hipnótico*) trance **3.** (*situación*) **en ~ de muerte** at death's door

tranco *m* stride; **a ~s** in a hurry

tranquilamente *adv* calmly

tranquilidad *f* **1.** (*calma*) tranquility; **~ de conciencia** ease of mind **2.** (*autocontrol*) calmness

tranquilizante *m* tranquillizer *Brit,* tranquilizer *Am*

tranquilizar <z→c> **I.** *vt* to calm down; (*con palabras*) to reassure **II.** *vr:* **~se** to calm down

tranquilo, -a *adj* **1.** (*no agitado, mar*) calm; **¡déjame ~!** leave me alone! **2.** (*persona: serena*) serene; (*con autocontrol*) calm

transacción *f* **1.** JUR settlement **2.** POL agreement **3.** COM deal **4.** FIN transaction

transatlántico *m* ocean liner

transatlántico, -a *adj* transatlantic

transbordador *m* **1.** NÁUT ferry **2.** AERO shuttle

transbordar I. *vt* **1.** (*por río*) to ferry across **2.** (*mercancías*) to transfer **II.** *vi* to change, to transfer

transbordo *m* **1.** (*cambio*) change **2.** (*mercancías*) transfer

transcribir *irr como escribir vt* to transcribe

transcurrir *vi* **1.** (*el tiempo*) to elapse, to pass **2.** (*acontecer*) to take place

transcurso *m* course

transeúnte I. *adj* transient **II.** *mf* passer-by, pedestrian

transferencia *f* **1.** (*traslado*) transfer **2.** FIN transfer **3.** (*de propiedad*) transfer

transferir *irr como sentir vt* **1.** (*trasladar*) to transfer **2.** (*posponer*) to postpone **3.** FIN to make over

transformación *f* transformation; (*de costumbres*) change

transformador *m* ELEC transformer

transformar *vt* to transform; (*costumbres*) to change

tránsfuga *mf* **1.** MIL deserter **2.** POL turncoat

transfusión *f t.* MED transfusion

transgénico, -a *adj* genetically engineered

transgredir *irr como abolir vt* (*ley*) to break

transición *f* transition

transido, -a *adj elev* (*de dolor*) racked; (*de emoción*) overcome

transigir <g→j> *vi* **1.** (*ceder*) to yield **2.** (*tolerar*) to tolerate **3.** JUR to compromise

transistor *m* ELEC transistor

transitar *vi* (*en coche*) to go along; (*a pie*) to walk along; **una calle transitada** a busy street

transitivo, -a *adj* LING transitive

tránsito *m* **1.** (*circulación*) traffic; **de mucho ~** very busy **2.** COM transit

transitorio, -a *adj* temporary; (*ley*) transitional

transmisión *f* **1.** (*de noticia*) broadcast **2.** TV, INFOR transmission **3.** TÉC drive; (*mecanismo*) transmission **4.** JUR transfer

transmisor *m* TÉC transmitter

transmitir *vt* **1.** (*noticia*) to broadcast **2.** TV, RADIO, TÉC to transmit **3.** (*enfermedad*) to give **4.** (*por herencia*) to pass on

transparencia *f* **1.** (*calidad*) transparency **2.** (*de intención*) openness **3.** FOTO slide

transparentar **I.** *vt* to reveal **II.** *vr:* ~**se** **1.** (*ser transparente*) to be transparent **2.** (*adivinar*) to show through

transparente **I.** *adj* **1.** (*material*) transparent **2.** (*intenciones*) clear **II.** *m* curtain

transpirar *vi* (*persona*) to perspire

transponer *irr como poner* **I.** *vt* (*persona*) to move; (*trasplantar*) to transplant **II.** *vr:* ~**se** **1.** (*persona*) to move **2.** (*sol*) to go out of sight

transportar **I.** *vt* to transport; (*en brazos*) to carry **II.** *vr:* ~**se** to be transported

transporte *m* **1.** COM transport **2.** *t.* TÉC (*de personas*) carriage

transversal *adj* transverse; **calle** ~ cross street

tranvía *m* tram *Brit*, streetcar *Am*

trapecio *m* trapeze

trapecista *mf* trapeze artist

trapero, -a *m, f* ragman

trapicheo *m inf* **1.** (*enredo*) jiggery--pokery; (*negocio*) dealing **2.** (*intriga*) scheming

trapo *m* **1.** (*tela*) rag **2.** (*para limpiar*) cleaning cloth; ~ **de cocina** tea towel, dish towel *Am* **3.** *pl*, *inf* (*vestidos*) clothes *pl* **4.** NÁUT sails *pl*

tráquea *f* ANAT trachea, windpipe *inf*

traqueteo *m* banging; (*de vajilla*) clattering; (*de motor*) rattling

tras *prep* **1.** (*temporal*) after; **día** ~ **día** day after day **2.** (*espacial: detrás de*) behind; (*orden*) after; **ir** ~ **alguien** (*perseguir*) to go after sb **3.** (*con movimiento*) after; **ponerse uno** ~ **otro** to put one after the other **4.** (*además de*) besides

trascendencia *f* consequence

trascendental *adj* **1.** (*importante*) important **2.** FILOS transcendental

trascender <e→ie> *vi* **1.** (*hecho*) to become known **2.** (*tener efecto*) to have a wide effect on **3.** (*ir más allá*) to go beyond **4.** (*olor*) to smell

trasegar *irr como fregar* *vt* **1.** (*objetos*) to switch around **2.** (*líquidos*) to decant

trasera *f* back

trasero *m* **1.** (*animal*) hindquarters *pl* **2.** *inf* (*persona*) bottom, backside

trasero, -a *adj* back; **asiento** ~ back seat; **luz trasera** rear light

trasfondo *m* background

trasladar **I.** *vt* **1.** (*cosas*) to move; (*tienda*) to relocate **2.** (*funcionario*) to transfer **3.** (*fecha*) to postpone **4.** (*orden*) to notify **II.** *vr:* ~**se** **1.** (*mudarse*) to move **2.** (*ir a*) to go to

traslado *m* **1.** (*de cosas*) movement; (*de tienda*) relocation **2.** (*de funcionario*) transfer **3.** (*de fecha*) postponement **4.** (*mudanza*) removal **5.** (*de orden*) notification

traslucir *irr como lucir* **I.** *vt* (*cara*) to reveal **II.** *vr:* ~**se** **1.** (*ser translúcido*) to be translucent **2.** (*verse, notarse*) to show through

trasluz *m* **mirar algo al** ~ to hold sth up to the light

trasnochado, -a *adj* **1.** (*comida*) stale **2.** (*idea*) outdated

trasnochador(a) *m(f) fig* night owl

trasnochar *vi* **1.** (*no dormir*) to spend a sleepless night **2.** (*acostarse tarde*) to stay up late **3.** (*pernoctar*) to spend the night

traspasar *vt* **1.** (*atravesar*) to go through, to pierce; (*calle*) to cross **2.** (*pasar a*) to transfer; FIN to make over **3.** (*límite*) to go beyond; (*ley*) to break

traspaso *m* **1.** (*de dinero*) transfer **2.** (*de límite*) exceeding; (*ley*) infringement

traspié(s) *m* (*inv*) stumble; *fig* slip-up

trasplantar *vt* to transplant

trasplante *m* transplant

trastada *f* **1.** *inf* (*travesura*) prank **2.** (*mala pasada*) dirty trick

trastazo *m inf* bump

traste *m* **1.** (*de guitarra*) fret; **irse al** ~ *fig* to fall through **2.** *AmL* (*trasto*) piece of junk

trastero, -a *adj* **cuarto** ~ lumber room

trastienda *f* back room

trasto *m* **1.** (*mueble*) piece of furniture; **tirarse los ~s a la cabeza** to have a knock down drag out fight **2.** *pl* (*para tirar*) junk

trastornado, -a *adj* (*confundido*) confused; (*loco*) mad, crazy

trastornar **I.** *vt* **1.** (*cosa*) to disarrange **2.** (*plan*) disrupt; (*orden público*) to disturb **3.** (*psicológicamente*) to traumatize **II.** *vr:* ~**se** **1.** (*enloquecer*) to go mad **2.** (*estropearse*) to fall through

trastorno *m* **1.** (*desorden*) disorder **2.** (*del orden público*) disturbance

trastrocar <c→qu> *vt* **1.** (*el orden*) to invert **2.** (*de sitio*) to switch around

trasvase *m* transfer; (*de río*) diversion

tratable *adj* sociable

tratado *m* **1.** *t.* POL treaty **2.** (*científico*) treatise

tratamiento *m* **1.** *t.* MED, QUÍM (*de asunto*) treatment **2.** *t.* INFOR (*elaboración*) processing; ~ **de texto** word processing

tratar **I.** *vt* **1.** (*a alguien*) to deal with **2.** MED, QUÍM to treat **3.** *t.* INFOR (*procesar*) to process **4.** (*dar tratamiento*) to address **5.** (*tema*) to discuss **II.** *vi* **1.** (*libro*) ~ **de** [*o* **sobre**] **algo** to be about sth, to deal with sth **2.** (*intentar*) to try **3.** (*con alguien*) to have contact with **4.** COM to deal **III.** *vr:* ~**se 1.** (*tener trato*) to have to do **2.** (*ser cuestión de*) to be a question; **¿de qué se trata?** what's it about?; **tratándose de ti...** in your case ...

trato *m* **1.** (*personal*) treatment; **malos ~s** ill-treatment **2.** (*contacto*) contact **3.** (*pacto*) agreement; (*negocio*) deal; **¡~ hecho!** it's a deal!

trauma *m* trauma

través **I.** *m* **mirar a alguien de** ~ to look at sb out of the corner of one's eye; **de** ~ crossways, crosswise **II.** *prep* **a** ~ **de** (*de un lugar*) across; (*de alguien*) from, through

travesaño *m* **1.** ARQUIT crosspiece **2.** DEP crossbar

travesía *f* **1.** (*por aire*) flight; (*por mar*) crossing **2.** (*calle*) cross street

travesti *mf,* **travestido, -a** *m, f* transvestite

travesura *f* prank

traviesa *f* **1.** FERRO sleeper **2.** (*de poste*) crossbar

travieso, -a *adj* **1.** (*niño*) mischievous, naughty **2.** (*de través*) across; **a campo traviesa** cross-country

trayecto *m* (*trecho*) distance; (*ruta*) route

trayectoria *f* **1.** (*de cuerpo*) path **2.** (*profesional*) career

traza *f* **1.** *t.* ARQUIT (*plan*) plan **2.** (*habilidad*) ability **3.** (*aspecto*) appearance **4.** (*rastro*) trace

trazado *m* **1.** *t.* ARQUIT (*de plan*) design **2.** (*recorrido*) route; FERRO line **3.** (*disposición*) layout

trazado, -a *adj* **bien** ~ nice-looking

trazar <z→c> *vt* **1.** (*líneas*) to trace; (*dibujos*) to sketch **2.** *t.* ARQUIT (*plan*) to draw up **3.** (*describir*) to describe

trazo *m* **1.** (*de escritura*) stroke **2.** (*dibujo*) sketch **3.** (*de la cara*) feature

trébol *m* **1.** (*planta*) clover **2.** (*cartas*) clubs

trece *adj inv, m* thirteen; *v.t.* **ocho**

trecho *m* **1.** (*distancia*) distance, way **2.** (*tiempo*) period, spell

tregua *f* **1.** MIL truce **2.** (*descanso*) respite; **sin** ~ relentlessly

treinta *adj inv, m* thirty; *v.t.* **ochenta**

tremendo, -a *adj* **1.** (*temible*) frightful **2.** (*enorme*) tremendous **3.** (*niño*) full of mischief

trémulo, -a *adj elev* tremulous; (*luz*) flickering

tren *m* **1.** FERRO train; ~ **de cercanías** suburban train; ~ **de alta velocidad** high-speed train; ~ **directo** through train; **coger el** ~ to catch the train; **ir en** ~ to go by train; ~ **de lavado** TÉC carwash; **estar como un** ~ *inf* to be very good-looking **2.** (*lujo*) ~ **de vida** lifestyle **3.** (*ritmo*) pace

trenca *f* duffle coat

trenza *f* plait *Brit,* braid *Am*

trenzar <z→c> *vt* (*pelo*) to plait *Brit,* to braid *Am*

trepar I. *vi, vt* **1.** (*al árbol*) to climb **2.** (*planta*) to creep **II.** *vt* to climb

trepidar *vi* to vibrate

tres *adj inv, m inv* three; *v.t.* **ocho**

trescientos, -as *adj* three hundred; *v.t.* **ochocientos**

tresillo *m* **1.** (*mueble*) three-piece living room suite **2.** MÚS triplet

treta *f* trick

triangular *adj* triangular

triángulo *m* **1.** (*figura*) triangle **2.** MÚS triangle

tribu *f* tribe

tribuna *f* **1.** (*en parlamento*) rostrum **2.** (*en estadio*) stand; ~ **de la prensa** press box

tribunal *m* **1.** JUR court; **Tribunal de Cuentas** National Audit Office; **Tribunal Europeo de Cuentas** European Court of Auditors; **Tribunal de Justicia Europeo** European Court of Justice **2.** (*comisión*) ~ **examinador** board of examiners

tributar *vt* **1.** (*impuestos*) to pay **2.** (*honor*) to render

tributo *m* tax

triciclo *m* tricycle

tricotar *vt* to knit

trifulca *f inf* rumpus

trigal *m* wheat field

trigésimo, -a *adj* thirtieth; *v.t.* **octavo**

trigo *m* **1.** (*planta*) wheat **2.** (*grano*) wheat

trigueño, -a I. *adj* (*pelo*) dark blond; (*piel*) olive-skinned **II.** *m, f AmL* coloured person

trillado, -a *adj inf* (*asunto*) overworked

trilladora *f* threshing machine

trillar *vt* **1.** (*grano*) to thresh **2.** (*usar*) to overuse

trillón *m* trillion

trimestral *adj* **1.** (*duración*) three-month **2.** (*cada tres meses*) quarterly

trimestre *m* **1.** (*período*) three-month period **2.** (*educación*) term *Brit,* semester *Am* **3.** (*paga*) quarterly payment

trinar *vi* **1.** (*pájaro*) to sing, to warble **2.** *inf* (*rabiar*) to fume

trincar <c→qu> *vt* **1.** (*con cuerdas*) to tie up **2.** (*detener*) to nab **3.** *inf* (*robar*) to steal

trinchar *vt* to carve

trinchera *f* **1.** MIL trench **2.** (*gabardina*) trench coat

trineo *m* sledge *Brit,* sled *Am*

trinidad *f* trinity

trino *m* MÚS trill

trío *m* trio

tripa *f* **1.** (*intestino*) intestine; (*comestibles*) tripe; **hacer de ~s corazón** *fig* to pluck up courage, to grin and bear it **2.** (*vientre*) tummy; **echar ~** *inf* to get a paunch

triple *adj* triple

triplicado, -a *adj* triplicate

triplicar <c→qu> *vt* to triple, to treble

trípode *m* FOTO tripod

tripulación *f* crew

tripulante *m* crew member

tripular *vt* **1.** (*proveer de tripulación*) to man **2.** (*coche*) to drive; (*avión*) to pilot

triquiñuela *f* trick

tris *m inv* crack; **estar en un ~ de hacer algo** to be within an inch of doing sth

triste *adj* sad; (*mustio*) gloomy; (*descolorido*) dreary

tristeza *f* sadness, sorrow

triturar *vt* **1.** (*desmenuzar*) to chop; (*moler*) to grind **2.** (*destruir*) to pulverize **3.** (*criticar*) to tear to pieces

triunfal *adj* triumphal, triumphant

triunfar *vi* **1.** (*salir triunfador*) to triumph **2.** (*ganar*) to succeed **3.** (*naipes*) to trump

triunfo *m* **1.** (*victoria*) triumph; **arco de ~** victory arch **2.** (*naipe*) trump

trivial *adj* trivial

trivializar <z→c> *vt* **1.** (*restar importancia*) to trivialize **2.** (*simplificar*) to play down

triza *f* shred; **hacer ~s** *fig* to tear to pieces

trocar *irr como volcar* **I.** *vt* **1.** (*cambiar*) to exchange for **2.** (*confundir*)

T
t

to confuse **II.** *vr:* **~se** (*cambiar*) to change; (*transformarse*) to turn

trocear *vt* to cut up

trocha *f* **1.** (*senda*) trail; (*atajo*) shortcut **2.** *AmL* FERRO gauge

trochemoche a ~ helter-skelter

trofeo *m* trophy

trola *f inf* lie, whopper

tromba *f* (*de agua*) water spout; **en** ~ *fig* en masse

trombón *m* MÚS trombone

trombosis *f inv* MED thrombosis

trompa[1] *f* **1.** (*de elefante*) trunk **2.** MÚS (*instrumento*) horn **3.** *inf* (*nariz*) conk **4.** *AmL, inf* (*labios*) lips *pl* **5.** *inf* (*borrachera*) drunkenness

trompa[2] *mf* MÚS horn player

trompada *f*, **trompazo** *m* (*porrazo*) bash; (*choque*) crash; (*puñetazo*) punch

trompeta[1] *mf* (*músico*) trumpet player

trompeta[2] *f* (*instrumento*) trumpet

trompicón *m* stumble; **a trompicones** in fits and starts

trompo *m* spinning top

tronar <o→ue> *vi, vimpers t.* METEO to thunder

tronchar I. *vt* **1.** (*tronco*) to cut down **2.** (*vida*) to cut short; (*esperanzas*) to shatter **II.** *vr:* **~se** to split; **~se de risa** *inf* to split one's sides laughing

tronco *m* (*de árbol*) trunk; (*de flor*) stem; **dormir como un** ~ *inf* to sleep like a log

trono *m* throne

tropa *f* **1.** MIL troop **2.** (*multitud*) crowd; *pey* (*grupo*) horde

tropel *m* **1.** (*mucha gente*) throng; **en** ~ in a mad rush **2.** (*prisa*) rush **3.** (*desorden*) jumble

tropelía *f* abuse of authority; (*acto violento*) violent act

tropezar *irr como empezar* **I.** *vi* **1.** (*con los pies*) to trip **2.** (*topar*) to come across **3.** (*cometer un error*) to make a mistake **II.** *vr:* **~se** to run into

tropezón *m* **1.** (*acción*) stumble; **dar un** ~ to trip **2.** (*error*) mistake; (*desliz*) lapse

tropical *adj* tropical

trópico *m* tropic

tropiezo *m* **1.** (*en el camino*) stumbling block; **dar un** ~ to trip **2.** (*error*) blunder **3.** (*revés*) setback **4.** (*discusión*) quarrel

trotamundos *mf inv* globetrotter

trotar *vi* **1.** (*caballos*) to trot **2.** (*con prisas*) to hustle

trote *m* **1.** (*caballos*) trot **2.** (*con prisa*) bustle; **a(l)** ~ quickly

trozo *m* **1.** (*pedazo*) piece, bit; **a ~s** in pieces **2.** LIT, MÚS excerpt, passage

trucar *vt* **1.** (*amañar*) to fix; FOTO to alter **2.** *inf* AUTO to soup up

trucha *f* **1.** (*pez*) trout **2.** *AmC* COM (*caseta*) stand

truco *m* trick; **coger el** ~ **a alguien** to catch on to sb

trueno *m* **1.** (*ruido*) clap of thunder **2.** *inf* (*juerguista*) madcap

trueque *m* exchange; COM (*sin dinero*) barter

trufa *f* **1.** *t.* BOT truffle **2.** (*mentira*) lie **3.** (*bombón*) (chocolate) truffle

truhán *m* rogue

truncar <c→qu> *vt* **1.** (*cortar*) to truncate **2.** (*texto*) to abridge **3.** (*desarrollo*) to stunt; (*esperanzas*) to shatter

tu *art pos* your; ~ **padre** your father; **~s hermanos** your brothers

tú *pron pers* you; **tratar de** ~ *to address in the familiar manner using 'tú'*; **de** ~ **a** ~ on equal footing

tubérculo *m* tuber

tuberculosis *f inv* tuberculosis

tubería *f* pipe

tubo *m* tube; ~ **digestivo** alimentary canal; ~ **de escape** exhaust pipe *Brit,* tailpipe *Am*

tuerca *f* nut

tuerto, -a *adj* **1.** (*de sólo un ojo*) one-eyed **2.** (*torcido*) crooked, twisted

tuétano *m* **1.** (*médula*) marrow **2.** (*corazón, esencia*) core, heart; **hasta los ~s** through and through

tufo *m* **1.** (*olor malo*) foul smell **2.** (*vapor*) fume

tugurio *m* **1.** (*chabola*) hovel **2.** *pl* (*barrio*) slums *pl* **3.** *pey* (*bar*) joint

tul *m* tulle

tulipán *m* tulip

tullido, -a I. *adj* (*persona*) disabled; *pey* crippled **II.** *m, f* cripple

tumba *f* grave, tomb; **ser** (**como**) **una** ~ (*callado*) to keep quiet

tumbar I. *vt* **1.** (*tirar*) to knock down; **estar tumbado** to be lying down **2.** *inf* ENS (*suspender*) to fail, to flunk *Am* **II.** *vr:* ~**se** to lie down

tumbo *m* **1.** (*caída*) fall, tumble **2.** (*vaivén*) roll; **dar un** ~ to jolt

tumbona *f* deck chair

tumor *m* MED tumour *Brit,* tumor *Am*

tumulto *m* tumult; (*de gente*) crowd

tuna *f* tuna

> **[?]** The **tuna** is a group of students who get together to sing and play music. Up until recently, only male students were admitted to **tunas**, but in the last few years new **tunas** have been formed for female students. In order to become a member of a **tuna**, certain initiation rites involving trials of courage have to be successfully completed.

tunante *mf v.* **tuno**

tunda *f* beating

túnel *m* tunnel; ~ **de lavado** car wash

Túnez *m* **1.** (*país*) Tunisia **2.** (*capital*) Tunis

tuno, -a I. *adj* **1.** (*astuto*) cunning **2.** (*pícaro*) roguish **II.** *m, f* member of a student 'tuna'

tuntún *m* *inf* **al** (**buen**) ~ any old way

tupé *m* quiff *Brit,* pompadour *Am*

tupido, -a *adj* **1.** (*denso*) thick **2.** *AmL* (*obstruido*) blocked

turba *f* peat

turbación *f* **1.** (*disturbio*) disturbance **2.** (*vergüenza*) embarrassment

turbante *m* turban

turbar I. *vt* **1.** (*perturbar*) to disturb **2.** (*avergonzar*) to embarrass **3.** (*desconcertar*) to unsettle **II.** *vr:* ~**se** **1.** (*ser disturbado*) to be disturbed **2.** (*alarmarse*) to get worried **3.** (*avergonzarse*) to get embarrassed

turbina *f* turbine

turbio, -a *adj* (*líquido*) cloudy; (*asunto*) turbid; (*negocio*) shady

turbo *m t.* AUTO turbo

turbulencia *f* **1.** (*agua*) turbulence **2.** (*alboroto*) commotion

turbulento, -a *adj* **1.** (*agua, aire*) turbulent **2.** (*alborotado*) stormy; (*confuso*) confused **3.** (*rebelde*) disorderly

turco, -a I. *adj* Turkish **II.** *m, f* Turk; **cabeza de** ~ *fig* scapegoat

turismo *m* **1.** (*viajar*) tourism; ~ **verde** ecotourism; **oficina de** ~ visitors' bureau **2.** AUTO private car

turista *mf* tourist

turístico, -a *adj* tourist

turnar *vi, vr:* ~**se** to take turns

turno *m* **1.** (*en la fábrica*) shift; **estar de** ~ to be on duty; ~ **de día** day shift **2.** (*orden*) turn; **es tu** ~ it's your turn; **pedir** ~ to ask who is last in line

turquesa *f* MIN turquoise

Turquía *f* Turkey

turrón *m* ≈ nougat

> **[?]** Like the British Christmas cake **turrón** is a must in Spain at Christmas. The traditional **turrón** is either a soft or hard bar, rather like nougat, containing nuts or honey--coated almonds. The **turrón** is made particularly in **Levante**, and especially in **Jijona** and **Alicante**.

tute *m* Spanish card game

tutear I. *vt* to address in the familiar manner using 'tú' **II.** *vr:* ~**se** to be on familiar terms

tutela *f* **1.** (*cargo*) guardianship **2.** (*amparo*) protection

tutelar *adj* JUR tutelary

tutor(a) *m(f)* **1.** JUR guardian **2.** (*profesor*) teacher **3.** ENS, UNIV tutor

tutoría *f* **1.** JUR guardianship, tutelage **2.** UNIV tutorship; (*class*) tutorial

T_t

tuyo, -a *pron pos* **1.** (*propiedad*) **el perro es** ~ the dog is yours; **¡ya es** ~**!** all yours! **2.** (*tras artículo*) **el** ~**/la tuya/lo** ~ yours; **los** ~**s** yours; (*parientes*) your family; **no cojas mi lápiz, tienes el** ~ don't take my pencil, you have your own **3.** (*tras substantivo*) of yours; **una amiga tuya** a friend of yours; **una hermana tuya** one of your sisters; **es culpa tuya** it's your fault **4.** (*tras impersonal 'lo'*) **lo** ~ what is yours; **tú a lo** ~ you mind your own business; **esto no es lo** ~ this isn't your strong point

TVE *f abr de* **Televisión Española** *the Spanish state-owned television broadcasting company*

U u

U, u *f* <úes> U, u; ~ **de Uruguay** U for Uncle

u *conj* (*before 'o' or 'ho'*) or

ubicar <c→qu> **I.** *vi* to be (situated) **II.** *vt AmL* to situate, to place **III.** *vr:* ~**se** to be (situated)

ubre *f* udder

Ucrania *f* Ukraine

Ud(s). *abr de* **usted(es)** you

UE *f abr de* **Unión Europea** EU

UEFA *f abr de* **Unión de Asociaciones Europeas de Fútbol** UEFA

UEME *abr de* **Unión Económica y Monetaria Europea** EEMU

UEO *f abr de* **Unión Europea Occidental** WEU

ufanarse *vr* to boast

ufano, -a *adj* **1.** (*orgulloso*) proud **2.** (*engreído*) conceited

UGT *f abr de* **Unión General de Trabajadores** socialist trade union

ujier *m* **1.** (*de un tribunal*) usher **2.** (*de un palacio*) gatekeeper

úlcera *f* MED ulcer

ulcerar *vt, vr:* ~**se** to ulcerate

ulterior *adj* (*posterior*) later, subsequent; (*más*) further

últimamente *adv* **1.** (*recientemente*) recently, lately **2.** (*por último*) lastly, finally

ultimar *vt* **1.** (*proyecto*) to finish; (*acuerdo*) to conclude **2.** *AmL* (*matar*) to murder

ultimátum *m sin pl* ultimatum

último, -a *adj* **1.** (*en orden*) last; **el** ~ **de cada mes** the last day of each month; **a** ~**s de mes** at the end of the month; **el** ~ **de la clase** the worst student in the class; **por última vez** for the last time; **la última moda** the lastest fashion; **por** ~ lastly, finally; **estar en las últimas** to be on one's last legs **2.** (*espacio*) **en el** ~ **piso** on the top floor; **el** ~ **rincón del mundo** *inf* the back of beyond *Brit,* the boondocks *pl Am*

ultra I. *adj* extreme **II.** *mf* extreme right-winger, neo-fascist

ultracongelado, -a *adj* deep-frozen

ultracongelar *vt* to deep-freeze

ultrajar *vt* **1.** (*insultar*) to insult **2.** (*humillar*) to humiliate

ultraje *m* abuse

ultramar *m sin pl* foreign parts *pl,* overseas *pl*

ultramarinos *mpl* **1.** (*tienda*) grocer's *Brit,* grocery store *Am* **2.** (*víveres*) groceries *pl*

ultranza 1. (*a muerte*) **defender algo a** ~ to defend sth with ones life; **luchar a** ~ to fight to the death **2.** (*resueltamente*) **ecologista a** ~ radical ecologist

ultrasónico, -a *adj* ultrasonic

ultratumba *f* **la vida de** ~ the next life

ultravioleta *adj inv* ultraviolet

ulular *vi* (*animal*) to howl; (*búho*) to hoot

umbilical *adj* umbilical

umbral *m* threshold; ~ **de rentabilidad** ECON break even point

UME *f abr de* **Unión Monetaria Europea** EMU

un, una <unos, -as> **I.** *art indef* **1.** (*no determinado*) a; (*before a vowel or initial silent 'h'*) an; **un**

perro a dog; **un elefante** an elephant **2.** pl (algunos) some, a few **3.** pl (aproximadamente) approximately, about **II.** adj v. **uno, -a**

unánime adj unanimous

unanimidad f unanimity

unción f anointing

uncir <c→z> vt to yoke

undécimo, -a adj eleventh; v.t. **octavo**

UNED f abr de **Universidad Nacional de Educación a Distancia** ≈ OU

ungir <g→j> vt t. REL to anoint

ungüento m **1.** MED ointment **2.** (remedio) salve

únicamente adv only, solely

único, -a adj **1.** (solo) only; **plato ~** main course **2.** (extraordinario) unique

unidad f **1.** t. MIL, TÉC (entidad) unit; **Unidad de Cuidados Intensivos** intensive care unit; **~ externa de disco duro** INFOR external hard disc unit; **~ monetaria** currency unit **2.** LIT unity

unido, -a adj united; **estamos muy ~s** we are very close

unifamiliar adj (casa) detatched

unificar <c→qu> vt to unite; (posiciones) to unify

uniformar vt to standardize

uniforme adj, m uniform

uniformidad f **1.** (movimiento) steadiness **2.** (similaridad) uniformity

unilateral adj (visión) one-sided; POL unilateral

unión f **1.** t. TÉC joint **2.** t. ECON, POL (territorial) union; **Unión Europea** European Union; **~ monetaria** monetary union; **en ~ con** (together) with **3.** COM merger **4.** (armonía) unity, closeness

unir I. vt **1.** t. TÉC (dos elementos) to join **2.** (territorios) to unite **3.** (ingredientes) to mix **4.** (esfuerzos) to combine **II.** vr: **~se** to join together; ECON to merge

unisex adj unisex

unísono, -a adj **1.** (de un solo tono) unisonal **2.** (de una sola voz) in unison; **al ~** unanimously

universal adj **1.** (del universo) universal **2.** (del mundo) worldwide; **historia ~** world history; **regla ~** general rule

universidad f university

universitario, -a I. adj university **II.** m, f **1.** (estudiante) university student **2.** (no licenciado) undergraduate; (licenciado) graduate

universo m universe

uno m one

uno, -a I. adj one; **la una** (hora) one o'clock **II.** pron indef **1.** (alguno) one, somebody; **cada ~** each (one), every one; **~s cuantos** some, a few; **~..., el otro...** one ..., the other ...; **~ de tantos** one of many; **de ~ en ~** one by one; **no acierto una** inf I can't do anything right **2.** pl (algunos) some **3.** (indeterminado) one, you

untar I. vt **1.** (con mantequilla) to spread **2.** (mojar) to dip **3.** (con grasa) to grease **4.** (sobornar) to bribe **II.** vr: **~se** (mancharse) to smear; **~se de algo** to become smeared with sth

uña f **1.** (de persona) nail; (de gato) claw; **~s de los pies** toenails pl; **enseñar las ~s** fig to show on's teeth; **ser ~ y carne** fig to be inseparable **2.** (pezuña) hoof

uperizado, -a adj **leche uperizada** UHT milk

Urales mpl Urals pl

uralita® f asbestos (cement)

uranio m uranium

urbanidad f urbanity, courtesy

urbanismo m town planning

urbanización f **1.** (acción) urbanization **2.** (de casas) housing estate

urbanizar <z→c> **I.** vt to urbanize **II.** vt, vr: **~se** to become civilized

urbano m traffic policeman

urbano, -a adj **1.** (de la ciudad) urban **2.** (cortés) urbane, courteous

urbe f large city, metropolis

urdir vt (conspiración) to scheme

urgencia f **1.** (cualidad) urgency **2.** (caso) emergency; **llamada de ~** urgent call **3.** pl (en hospital) casual-

U u

ty room *Brit,* emergency room *Am*
urgente *adj* urgent, pressing; (*carta*) express; **un pedido ~** a rush order
urgir <g→j> *vi* to be urgent, to be pressing
urinario *m* urinal, public lavatory
urinario, -a *adj* urinary
urna *f* 1. (*para cenizas*) urn 2. POL ballot box; **acudir a las ~s** to go and vote, to go to the polls
urología *f* urology
urraca *f* magpie
URSS *f abr de* **Unión de Repúblicas Socialistas Soviéticas** USSR
Uruguay *m* Uruguay

? **Uruguay** (official title: **República Oriental del Uruguay**) lies in the southeastern part of South America. The capital and the most important city in Uruguay is **Montevideo**. The official language of the country is Spanish and the monetary unit is the **peso uruguayo**.

---

uruguayo, -a *adj, m, f* Uruguayan
usado, -a *adj* 1. (*no nuevo*) second-hand; (*sello*) used 2. (*gastado*) worn
usanza *f* usage, custom
usar I. *vt* to use; (*ropa, gafas*) to wear; **sin ~** brand new II. *vr* 1. (*utilizar*) to use 2. (*ropa*) to be in fashion
uso *m* 1. (*utilización*) use; **de ~ externo** MED for external application; **en buen ~** *inf* in good condition; **desde que tengo ~ de razón...** since I have been old enough to reason ...; **en pleno ~ de sus facultades** sound of mind 2. (*moda*) fashion 3. (*costumbre*) custom, usage
usted *pron* 1. *sing, pl, form* you; **tratar de ~ a alguien** to address sb courteously 2. *pl, AmL* (*vosotros*) you
usual *adj* usual
usuario, -a *m, f t.* INFOR user
usurero, -a *m, f* usurer

usurpar *vt* to usurp
utensilio *m* utensil; (*herramienta*) tool
útero *m* uterus, womb
útil I. *adj* 1. (*objeto*) useful, handy 2. (*persona*) useful 3. (*ayuda*) helpful II. *mpl* tools *pl,* implements *pl*
utilidad *f* 1. *t.* INFOR (*de objeto*) utility 2. (*de persona*) usefulness 3. (*de inversión*) profit
utilizar <z→c> I. *vt* to use; (*derecho*) to avail oneself of; (*tiempo*) to make use of II. *vr:* ~**se** to be used
utopía *f* utopia
utópico, -a *adj* utopian
uva *f* grape; ~ **pasa** raisin; **estar de mala ~** *inf* to be in a bad mood

---

? It is customary in Spain on New Year's Eve at exactly twelve seconds to midnight to eat one (white) **uva** (grape) for every **campanada** (chime of the bell), which can be heard on television at intervals of one second. This is supposed to bring good fortune for the coming year.

---

uve *f* v; ~ **doble** w
UVI *f abr de* **Unidad de Vigilancia Intensiva** ICU
Uzbekistán *m* Uzbekistan

V, v *f* V, v; ~ **de Valencia** V for Victor
vaca *f* 1. ZOOL cow; **síndrome de las ~s locas** mad cow disease; ~**s gordas/flacas** *fig* prosperous/lean period 2. (*carne*) beef 3. (*cuero*) cow-hide
vacaciones *fpl* holidays *pl Brit,* vacation *Am;* **irse de ~** to go on holiday *Brit,* to go on vacation *Am*

vacante I. *adj* vacant II. *f* vacancy
vaciar <*1. pres:* vacío> *vt* 1. (*dejar vacío*) to empty; (*con bomba*) to pump out 2. (*ahuecar*) to hollow out 3. (*información*) to extract
vaciedad *f sin pl* 1. (*vacío*) emptiness 2. *fig* silliness
vacilación *f* hesitation
vacilante *adj* 1. (*persona*) hesitant 2. (*estructura*) unsteady 3. (*voz*) faltering
vacilar *vi* 1. (*objeto*) to sway; (*borracho*) to stagger; (*llama*) to flicker 2. (*dudar*) to hesitate
vacío *m sin pl* (*espacio*) emptiness; Fís vacuum; (*hueco*) gap; **envasado al ~** vacuum-packed; **hacer el ~ a alguien** to give sb the cold shoulder
vacío, -a *adj* 1. (*sin nada*) empty; (*hueco*) hollow; **con las manos vacías** emptyhanded 2. (*insustancial*) insubstantial
vacuna *f* vaccine
vacunar I. *vt* to vaccinate II. *vr:* ~se to get vaccinated
vacuno, -a *adj* bovine; (**carne de**) ~ beef
vacuo, -a *adj* vacuous
vadear *vt* 1. (*río*) to ford 2. (*dificultad*) to overcome
vado *m* 1. (*río*) ford 2. AUTO ~ **permanente** keep clear
vagabundo, -a I. *adj* wandering; (*perro*) stray II. *m, f* wanderer; *fig* tramp, bum
vagancia *f sin pl* laziness
vagar I.<g→gu> *vi* 1. (*vagabundear*) to wander 2. (*descansar*) to be idle II. *m* leisure
vagina *f* ANAT vagina
vago, -a I. *adj* 1. (*perezoso*) lazy 2. (*impreciso*) vague II. *m, f* 1. (*vagabundo*) tramp 2. (*holgazán*) layabout
vagón *m* (*de pasajeros*) coach *Brit,* car *Am;* (*de mercancías*) goods wagon *Brit,* freight car *Am*
vaguear *vi* to laze about
vaguedad *f* vagueness
vaho *m* 1. (*vapor*) vapour *Brit,* vapor *Am* 2. (*aliento*) breath
vaina¹ *f* sheath

vaina² *m pey* twit *Brit,* dork *Am*
vainilla *f* vanilla
vaivén *m* swaying; **los vaivenes de la vida** life's ups and downs
vajilla *f* crockery, dishes *pl*
vale *m* voucher; FIN promissory note; (*pagaré*) IOU
valedero, -a *adj* (*válido*) valid; (*vigente*) in force
valenciano, -a *adj, m, f* Valencian
valentía *f* 1. (*valor*) bravery 2. (*hazaña*) brave deed
valentón, -ona *adj pey* boastful
valer *irr* I. *vt* 1. (*costar*) to cost 2. (*equivaler*) to equal 3. (*expresiones*) **hacer ~ sus derechos** to assert one's rights; **vale más que ...** +*subj* you'd best...; **¡vale ya!** that's enough!; **¡vale!** OK! II. *vi* 1. (*ropa*) to be of use 2. (*tener validez*) to be valid 3. (*funcionar*) to be of use; **no sé para qué vale este trasto** I don't know what this piece of junk is for 4. (*tener mérito*) to be worthy; **no ~ nada** to be worthless; **~ poco** to be worth little 5. (*estar permitido*) to be allowed III. *vr:* ~se 1. (*servirse*) to make use 2. (*desenvolverse*) to manage
valía *f sin pl* worth
validar *vt* to validate
validez *f sin pl* validity; **tener ~** to be valid; (*ley*) to be in force
válido, -a *adj* valid
valiente *adj* brave
valija *f* case; (*del cartero*) mailbag; ~ **diplomática** diplomatic bag
valioso, -a *adj* valuable
valla *f* 1. (*tapia*) wall; (*alambrada*) fence 2. (*publicitaria*) hoarding *Brit,* billboard *Am* 3. DEP hurdle
vallar *vt* to fence in
valle *m* valley
valor *m* 1. (*valentía*) bravery; **armarse de ~** to pluck up courage 2. (*desvergüenza*) cheek 3. (*valía*) *t.* COM, MÚS value; (*cuantía*) amount; ~ **adquisitivo** purchasing power; ~ **nominal** face value 4. (*significado*) meaning 5. *pl* FIN securities *pl;* **~es bursátiles** stock exchange securities 6. *pl* (*ética*) **~es morales** moral

V
v

principles
valoración *f* valuation
valorar *vt* to value; (*apreciar*) to appreciate
vals *m* MÚS waltz
válvula *f* ANAT, TÉC valve
vampiresa *f* vamp, femme fatale
vampiro *m* vampire; *fig* bloodsucker
vanagloriarse *vr* to boast
vandalismo *m sin pl* vandalism
vándalo, -a *m, f* HIST Vandal; *fig* vandal, hooligan
vanguardia *f* 1. MIL van 2. (*movimiento*) forefront; LIT avant-garde; **de** ~ ultra-modern
vanguardista I. *adj* ultra-modern II. *mf* ultra-modern individual; *fig* pioneer
vanidad *f* vanity
vanidoso, -a *adj* vain
vano *m* ARQUIT space
vano, -a *adj* 1. (*ineficaz*) vain; **en** ~ in vain 2. (*infundado*) groundless
vapor *m* (*vaho*) vapour *Brit,* vapor *Am;* (*de agua*) steam; (**barco de**) ~ steamer
vaporizador *m* vaporizer; (*perfume*) atomizer
vaporizar <z→c> I. *vt* 1. (*evaporar*) to vaporize 2. (*perfume*) to spray II. *vr:* ~se to vaporize
vaporoso, -a *adj* 1. (*tela*) light 2. (*humeante*) steamy
vapulear *vt* 1. (*zurrar*) to beat 2. (*criticar*) to slate *Brit,* to slam *Am*
vaquero, -a I. *adj* cattle II. *m, f* cowboy *m,* cowgirl *f*
vaquero(s) *m(pl)* jeans *pl*
vaquilla *f* heifer
vara *f* 1. (*palo*) stick; ~ **mágica** magic wand 2. TÉC (*bastón de mando*) rod
variable *adj, f* variable
variación *f* 1. MAT, MÚS variation 2. (*cambio*) change
variado, -a *adj* (*distinto*) mixed, assorted
variante *f* 1. (*variedad*) variety 2. (*carretera*) bypass
variar <*1. pres:* varío> I. *vi* 1. (*modificarse*) to vary 2. (*cambiar*) to change II. *vt* 1. (*cambiar*) to change

2. (*dar variedad*) to vary; **y para** ~... and for a change ...
varicela *f sin pl* MED chickenpox
variedad *f* 1. (*clase*) variety 2. (*pluralidad*) variation 3. *pl* (*espectáculo*) variety show; **teatro de** ~**es** music hall
vario, -a *adj pl* 1. (*diferente*) several 2. (*algunos*) some
variopinto, -a *adj* 1. (*diverso*) diverse 2. (*color*) colourful *Brit,* colorful *Am*
variz *f* MED varicose vein
varón *m* (*hombre*) male; (*niño*) boy
varonil *adj* manly
Varsovia *f* Warsaw
vasco, -a I. *adj* Basque; **País Vasco** Basque Country II. *m, f* Basque
Vascongadas *fpl* Basque Provinces *pl*
vascuence *m* 1. (*lengua*) Basque 2. *inf* (*incomprensible*) Greek
vasectomía *f* MED vasectomy
vaselina® *f* Vaseline®
vasija *f* (*recipiente*) container
vaso *m* 1. (*recipiente*) glass; ~ **de papel** paper cup 2. ANAT vessel
vástago *m* 1. BOT shoot 2. *fig* (*hijo*) scion *liter;* ~**s** offspring 3. TÉC rod
vasto, -a *adj* vast; (*saber*) wide
Vaticano *m* Vatican; **la Ciudad del** ~ the Vatican City
vaticinio *m* prediction, prophecy
vatio *m* watt
Vd. *pron pers abr de* **usted** you
vecindad *f,* **vecindario** *m* 1. (*comunidad*) neighbourhood *Brit,* neighborhood *Am* 2. (*ciudadanos*) neighbours *pl Brit,* neighbors *pl Am*
vecino, -a I. *adj* near; **pueblo** ~ next village II. *m, f* 1. (*que vive cerca*) neighbour *Brit,* neighbor *Am* 2. (*habitante*) inhabitant
vector *m* vector
veda *f* 1. (*prohibición*) prohibition 2. (*temporada*) close season
vedado *m* reserve *Brit,* preserve *Am*
vedar *vt* to prohibit, to ban
vega *f* fertile plain
vegetación *f* vegetation
vegetal *adj, m* vegetable
vegetar *vi* to vegetate

vegetariano, -a *adj, m, f* vegetarian
vehemencia *f sin pl* **1.** (*ímpetu*) impetuosity **2.** (*fervor*) vehemence
vehemente *adj* **1.** (*impetuoso*) impetuous **2.** (*ardiente*) passionate
vehículo *m* **1.** (*transporte*) vehicle **2.** MED carrier
veinte *adj inv, m* twenty; *v.t.* **ochenta**
vejación *f,* **vejamen** *m* **1.** (*molestia*) annoyance **2.** (*humillación*) humiliation
vejar *vt* **1.** (*molestar*) to annoy **2.** (*humillar*) to humiliate
vejatorio, -a *adj* **1.** (*molesto*) annoying **2.** (*humillante*) humiliating
vejez *f sin pl* **1.** (*ancianidad*) old age **2.** (*envejecimiento*) ageing *Brit,* aging *Am*
vejiga *f* **1.** ANAT bladder **2.** (*ampolla*) blister
vela *f* **1.** NÁUT sail; **a toda ~** at full sail; *fig* energetically **2.** (*luz*) candle; **pasar la noche en ~** *fig* to have a sleepless night; **estar a dos ~s** *fig* to be broke
velada *f* evening gathering; LIT, MÚS, TEAT soirée
velar **I.** *vi* **1.** (*no dormir*) to stay awake **2.** (*cuidar*) to watch over, to look after **II.** *vt* **1.** (*vigilar*) to keep watch over **2.** (*ocultar*) to hide **III.** *vr:* **~se** FOTO to blur
velatorio *m* wake, vigil
veleidad *f* **1.** (*inconstancia*) fickleness **2.** (*capricho*) whim
velero *m* NÁUT sailing ship
veleta¹ *f* weather vane, weathercock *Brit*
veleta² *mf* (*persona*) changeable person
vello *m sin pl* **1.** (*corporal*) (body) hair **2.** BOT, ZOOL down, fuzz
velo *m* **1.** (*tela*) veil **2.** ANAT **~ del paladar** soft palate
velocidad *f* **1.** *t.* FÍS, INFOR speed; **exceso de ~** speeding **2.** (*marcha*) gear
velocímetro *m* speedometer
veloz *adj* swift
vena *f* **1.** ANAT vein **2.** (*filón*) lode; **~ de agua** underground stream **3.** *inf*

(*disposición*) mood
venado *m* **1.** (*ciervo*) deer **2.** (*carne*) venison **3.** (*caza mayor*) big game
vencedor(a) **I.** *adj* winning **II.** *m(f)* winner
vencer <c→z> **I.** *vi* **1.** (*ganar*) to win **2.** (*plazo*) to expire **II.** *vt* **1.** (*ganar*) to win; (*enemigos*) to defeat **2.** (*obstáculo*) to overcome; (*dificultad*) to get round
vencimiento *m* COM expiry
venda *f* MED bandage
vendaje *m* bandaging
vendar *vt* to bandage
vendaval *m* (*viento*) strong wind; (*huracán*) hurricane
vendedor(a) *m(f)* seller; **~ ambulante** hawker; **~ a domicilio** door--to-door salesman
vender **I.** *vt* to sell **II.** *vr:* **~se 1.** COM to sell, to be for sale; **se vende** for sale **2.** (*persona*) to give oneself away
vendimia *f* grape harvest
vendimiar *vi* to harvest grapes
Venecia *f* Venice
veneno *m* poison
venenoso, -a *adj* poisonous
venerable *adj* venerable
venerar *vt* **1.** (*adorar*) to worship **2.** (*respetar*) to venerate
venéreo, -a *adj* MED venereal
venezolano, -a *adj, m, f* Venezuelan
Venezuela *f* Venezuela

> ❓ **Venezuela** (official title: **República de Venezuela**) borders both the Caribbean Sea and the Atlantic Ocean to the north, Guyana to the east, Brazil to the south and Colombia to the west. The capital is **Caracas**. Spanish is the official language of the country and the monetary unit is the **bolívar**.

---

venganza *f* vengeance
vengar <g→gu> **I.** *vt* to avenge **II.** *vr:* **~se** to take revenge
vengativo, -a *adj* vengeful

venia *f sin pl, elev* permission
venial *adj* venial
venida *f* **1.** (*llegada*) arrival; (*vuelta*) return **2.** (*de un río*) floodwater
venidero, -a *adj* future
venir *irr* I. *vi* **1.** (*trasladarse*) to come; (*llegar*) to arrive; **el mes que viene** next month **2.** (*ocurrir*) to happen; **vino la guerra** the war came **3.** (*proceder*) to come; ~ **de una familia rica** to come from a rich family **4.** (*entrar*) **me vinieron ganas de reír** I felt like laughing **5.** (*figurar*) to appear **6.** (*prenda*) to suit **7.** (*expresiones*) **es una familia venida a menos** that family has come down in the world; **a mí eso ni me va ni me viene** to me that's neither here nor there II. *vr:* ~**se** to come back
venta *f* **1.** COM sale; ~ **al contado** cash sale; ~ **a plazos** hire purchase; **precio de** ~ **al público** retail price; **en** ~ for sale **2.** (*posada*) inn
ventaja *f t.* DEP advantage
ventajoso, -a *adj* advantageous
ventana *f* window; ~ **corrediza** sliding window; ~ **de guillotina** sash window; ~ **de la nariz** nostril
ventanilla *f* **1.** (*de coche*) side window **2.** (*taquilla*) ticket office
ventilación *f* ventilation
ventilador *m* **1.** (*aparato*) fan **2.** (*conducto*) ventilator (shaft)
ventilar I. *vt* **1.** (*airear*) to ventilate **2.** (*resolver*) to clear up II. *vr:* ~**se** (*persona*) to get some air
ventisca *f* blizzard
ventisquero *m* snowdrift
ventosidad *f* fart
ventoso, -a *adj* windy
ventrílocuo, -a *m, f* ventriloquist
ventura *f* (good) fortune; **mala** ~ ill luck; **por** ~ fortunately; **probar** ~ to try one's luck
venturoso, -a *adj* fortunate
ver *irr* I. *vi, vt* **1.** (*con los ojos*) to see; **lo nunca visto** something unheard of; **¡habráse visto!** did you ever!; **¡~ás!** just you wait!; **a** ~ let's see; **a** ~, **venga** come on, hurry up; **a** ~ **cómo lo hacemos** let's see how we

can do this; **no veas la que se armó** there was a tremendous row; **hay que** ~ **lo tranquilo que es Pedro** Pedro is such a quiet fellow; **¡vamos a** ~! let's see!; **luego ya** ~**emos** we'll see about that later; **si te he visto, no me acuerdo** out of sight, out of mind **2.** (*con la inteligencia*) to see, to understand; **a mi modo de** ~ as I see it; **¿no ves que...?** don't you see that ...? **3.** (*observar*) to watch; (*documentos*) to examine; **te veo venir** *fig* I know what you're up to **4.** JUR (*causa*) to hear **5.** (*relación*) **tener que** ~ **con alguien/algo** to have to do with sb/sth II. *vr:* ~**se 1.** (*encontrarse*) to meet **2.** (*estado*) to be; ~**se apurado** to be in a jam **3.** (*parecer*) **se ve que no tienen tiempo** it seems they have no time
vera *f* **1.** (*orilla*) bank **2.** (*lado*) **a la** ~ **de** beside
veracidad *f* truthfulness
veranear *vi* to spend the summer
veraneo *m* summer holiday *Brit,* summer vacation *Am;* **lugar de** ~ holiday resort *Brit,* vacation spot *Am*
veraniego, -a *adj* summer
verano *m* summer
veras *fpl* **de** ~ (*de verdad*) really; (*en serio*) in earnest; **esto va de** ~ this is serious
veraz *adj* truthful
verbal *adj* **1.** (*del verbo*) verbal **2.** (*oral*) oral
verbena *f* street party
verbo *m* verb
verboso, -a *adj* verbose
verdad *f* truth; ~ **de Perogrullo** truism; **a decir** ~, ... to tell you the truth, ...; **¡de** ~! really!; **faltar a la** ~ to be untruthful; **pues la** ~, **no lo sé** I don't know, to tell you the truth; **un héroe de** ~ a real hero; **¿~?** isn't it?, aren't you?; **¿~ que no fuiste tú?** it wasn't you, was it?
verdadero, -a *adj* **1.** (*cierto*) true **2.** (*real*) real **3.** (*persona*) truthful
verde I. *adj* **1.** (*color*) *t.* POL green **2.** (*fruta*) unripe, green **3.** (*chistes*) dirty **4.** (*personas*) randy II. *m* green

verdear *vi,* **verdecer** *irr como crecer vi* to turn green

verdor *m* **1.** (*verde*) greenness **2.** BOT lushness **3.** (*juventud*) youth

verdugo *m* **1.** (*de ejecuciones*) executioner **2.** (*hematoma*) weal **3.** BOT shoot

verdulero, -a *m, f* greengrocer

verdura *f* **1.** (*hortalizas*) vegetable, greens *pl* **2.** (*verdor*) greenness

vereda *f* **1.** (*sendero*) path **2.** *AmL* (*acera*) pavement *Brit,* sidewalk *Am;* **hacer entrar en ~ a alguien** *fig* to make sb toe the line

veredicto *m* JUR verdict

vergel *m elev* orchard

vergonzoso, -a *adj* **1.** (*persona*) bashful; (*tímido*) shy **2.** (*acción*) disgraceful

vergüenza *f* **1.** (*rubor*) shame; **me da ~...** I'm ashamed to ...; **pasar ~** to feel embarrassed; **¡qué ~!** shame on you! **2.** (*pundonor*) shyness **3.** (*timidez*) timidity **4.** (*escándalo*) disgrace

verídico, -a *adj* **1.** (*verdadero*) true **2.** (*muy probable*) credible

verificar <c→qu> **I.** *vt* **1.** (*comprobar*) to check **2.** (*controlar*) to verify **3.** (*realizar*) to carry out **II.** *vr:* **~se 1.** (*acto*) to be held **2.** (*una profecía*) to come true; (*deseos*) to be fulfilled

verja *f* (*cerca*) grille; (*puerta*) iron gate

vermú *m,* **vermut** *m* <vermús> (*licor*) vermouth

verosímil *adj* **1.** (*probable*) likely **2.** (*creíble*) credible

verruga *f* wart

versado, -a *adj* expert

versátil *adj* versatile

versión *f* **1.** (*interpretación*) version **2.** (*traducción*) translation

verso *m* line

vértebra *f* ANAT vertebra

vertebrado *m* vertebrate

vertebral *adj* vertebral; **columna ~** spinal column

verter <e→ie> **I.** *vt* **1.** (*vaciar*) to empty; (*líquido*) to pour **2.** (*traducir*) to translate **II.** *vi* to flow

vertical *adj, f* vertical

vértice *m* vertex

vertiente *f* slope

vertiginoso, -a *adj* giddy

vértigo *m* **1.** (*mareo*) dizziness; (*por la altura*) vertigo; **de ~** *inf* (*velocidad*) giddy **2.** (*desmayo*) fainting fit

vesícula *f* ANAT vesicle; **~ biliar** gall bladder

vespa® *f* motor scooter

vespertino, -a *adj* evening

vespino® *m* moped

vestíbulo *m* (*de un piso*) hall; (*de un hotel*) lobby; TEAT foyer

vestido *m* **1.** (*de mujer*) dress **2.** (*ropa*) clothing

vestigio *m* **1.** (*huella*) vestige **2.** (*señal*) trace

vestimenta *f* clothing

vestir *irr como pedir* **I.** *vt* **1.** (*persona*) to dress **2.** (*llevar*) to wear; (*ponerse*) to put on **II.** *vi* to dress; **~ de uniforme** to wear a uniform **III.** *vr:* **~se** to get dressed

vestuario *m* **1.** (*conjunto*) clothes *pl;* (*de una misma person*) wardrobe **2.** (*lugar*) TEAT dressing room; DEP changing room

veta *f* **1.** MIN seam **2.** (*en madera*) grain; (*en mármol*) vein

vetar *vt* to veto

veterano *m* MIL veteran

veterano, -a *adj, m, f* veteran

veterinaria *f sin pl* veterinary science

veterinario, -a *m, f* vet *inf,* veterinary surgeon *Brit,* veterinarian *Am*

veto *m* veto

vetusto, -a *adj elev* very old; *pey* ancient

vez *f* **1.** (*acto repetido*) time; **a la ~** at the same time; **a veces** sometimes; **cada ~ que...** each time that ...; **de una ~** in one go; **de ~ en cuando** from time to time; **aquella ~** on that occasion; **alguna ~** sometimes; **muchas veces** many times; **¿cuántas veces ...?** how often ...?; **tal ~** perhaps; **una y otra ~** time and time again; **érase una ~...** once upon a time ... **2.** (*con número*) time; **una ~** once; **dos veces** twice; **una y mil veces** a thousand times; **por enési-**

V
v

ma ~ for the umpteenth time **3.**(*turno*) turn; **cuando llegue mi ~...** when it's my turn ...; **en ~ de** instead of

vía *f* **1.**(*camino*) road; (*calle*) street; ~ **láctea** Milky Way; ~ **pública** public thoroughfare; **por ~ aérea** (*correos*) by air mail **2.**(*ruta*) via **3.**(*carril*) line; FERRO track; ~ **férrea** railway *Brit,* railroad *Am* **4.**ANAT tract; **por ~ oral** by mouth **5.**(*procedimiento*) proceedings *pl* **6.**INFOR track

viable *adj* viable

viada *f And* speed

viaducto *m* viaduct

viajante *mf* travelling salesman *Brit,* traveling salesman *Am*

viajar *vi* to travel

viaje *m* **1.**(*general*) travel; **estar de ~** to be away (on a trip); ~ **de negocios** business trip; ~ **de ida y vuelta** return trip *Brit,* round trip *Am;* **¡buen ~!** bon voyage!, have a good trip! **2.**(*carga*) load; (*recorrido*) trip **3.** *inf*(*drogas*) trip

viajero, -a **I.** *adj* travelling *Brit,* traveling *Am;* ZOOL migratory **II.** *m, f* traveller *Brit,* traveler *Am;* (*pasajero*) passenger

vial **I.** *adj* (*caminos*) road; FERRO rail **II.** *m* avenue

víbora *f* viper

vibración *f* vibration

vibrador *m* vibrator

vibrante *adj* **1.**(*sonoro*) resonant **2.**(*entusiasta*) vibrant

vibrar **I.** *vi* **1.**(*oscilar*) to vibrate **2.**(*voz*) to quiver **II.** *vt* to shake

vicario *m* vicar

vicedirector(a) *m(f)* **1.**COM deputy manager **2.**ENS deputy head teacher *Brit,* vice principal *Am*

vicepresidente, -a *m, f* POL vice president; (*en juntas*) vice-chairperson

viceversa *adv* vice versa

viciado, -a *adj*(*aire*) stuffy

viciar **I.** *vt* **1.**(*falsear*) to falsify; (*deformar*) to distort **2.**(*anular*) to invalidate **II.** *vr:* **~se 1.**(*persona*) to get a bad habit **2.**(*ser adicto*) ~**se**

con algo to become addicted to sth

vicio *m* **1.**(*mala costumbre*) bad habit **2.**(*adicción*) vice **3.**(*objeto*) defect

vicioso, -a *adj* **1.**(*carácter*) dissolute **2.**(*que produce vicio*) habit-forming **3.**(*consentido*) spoilt

vicisitud *f* **1.**(*acontecimiento*) important event **2.** *pl* (*alternancia*) ups *pl* and downs

víctima *f* victim; (*de accidente*) casualty

victoria *f* victory

victorioso, -a *adj* victorious

vid *f* (grape)vine

vida *f* **1.**(*existencia*) life; ~ **íntima** private life; **costo de la** ~ cost of living; **pasar a mejor** ~ to pass away; **salir con** ~ to survive; **¿qué es de tu ~?** what have you been up to lately? **2.**(*sustento*) livelihood **3.**(*biografía*) life; **de toda la** ~ all my life; **la otra** ~ afterlife **4.**(*cariño*) **¡mi ~!** my darling!

vidente *mf* **1.**(*que ve*) sighted person **2.**(*que adivina*) clairvoyant

vídeo *m* **1.**(*aparato*) video (cassette) recorder, VCR *Am;* **cámara de ~** video camera **2.**(*película*) video

videocámara *f* video camera

videocasete *m* videocassette

videoclip *m* music video

videoconferencia *f* INFOR video conference

videojuego *m* video game

videoteléfono *m* videophone

videotexto *m* teletext

vidriera *f* **1.**(*ventana*) stained-glass window **2.**AmL (*escaparate*) shop window

vidriero, -a *m, f* glazier

vidrio *m* glass; (*de una ventana*) window pane

vidrioso, -a *adj* **1.**(*como vidrio*) glassy; (*mirada*) glazed **2.**(*transparente*) like glass

viejo, -a **I.** *adj* old; **Noche Vieja** New year's Eve **II.** *m, f* old man *m,* old woman *f*

Viena *f* Vienna

vienés, -esa *adj, m, f* Viennese

viento *m* wind; **a los cuatro ~s** in all

directions; **¡vete a tomar ~!** *inf* get lost!; **contra ~ y marea** against all odds, come hell or high water; **el negocio va ~ en popa** business is going well

vientre *m* **1.** (*abdomen*) abdomen **2.** (*barriga*) belly **3.** (*matriz*) womb

viernes *m inv* Friday; **Viernes Santo** Good Friday; *v.t.* **lunes**

vietnamita *adj, mf* Vietnamese

viga *f* (*de madera*) beam; (*de metal*) girder

vigencia *f* validity; **entrar en ~** to come into effect

vigente *adj* valid

vigésimo, -a *adj* twentieth; *v.t.* **octavo**

vigía[1] *f* watchtower

vigía[2] *mf* lookout

vigilancia *f* vigilance

vigilante **I.** *adj* (*despierto*) awake; (*en alerta*) alert **II.** *mf* (*guardián*) guard; (*de cárcel*) warder *Brit*, warden; (*en tienda*) night watchman

vigilar **I.** *vt* to guard; (*niños*) to watch **II.** *vi* to keep watch over

vigilia *f* **1.** (*no dormir*) wakefulness **2.** (*víspera*) vigil **3.** (*sin comer*) abstinence

vigor *m* **1.** (*fuerza*) vigour *Brit*, vigor *Am*; (*energía*) energy **2.** (*vigencia*) validity; **entrar en ~** to come into effect

vigoroso, -a *adj* **1.** (*fuerte*) vigorous; (*resistente*) tough **2.** (*protesta*) strong

VIH *m sin pl abr de* **virus de inmunodeficiencia humana** HIV

vil *adj* (*malo*) vile; (*bajo*) base

vileza *f* **1.** (*cualidad*) vileness **2.** (*acción*) vile act

vilipendiar *vt* **1.** (*despreciar*) to revile **2.** (*insultar*) to vilify

villa *f* **1.** HIST (*población*) town **2.** (*casa*) villa

villancico *m* ~ (**de Navidad**) (Christmas) carol

villorrio *m pey, inf* one-horse town

vilo *adv* **en ~** suspended; *fig* in suspense

vinagre *m* vinegar

vinagrera *f* **1.** (*recipiente*) vinegar bottle **2.** *pl* (*para la mesa*) cruet set

vinagreta *f* vinaigrette

vincha *f AmS* (*cinta*) hairband

vinculación *f* link

vincular *vt* **1.** (*ligar*) to link; (*unir*) to join **2.** (*obligar*) to bind

vínculo *m* **1.** (*unión*) tie; **el ~ conyugal** the bond of matrimony **2.** (*obligación*) bond

vino *m* wine; ~ **rosado/tinto** rosé/red wine; ~ **de la casa** house wine; ~ **peleón** cheap wine, plonk *Brit*

viña *f*, **viñedo** *m* vineyard

viola *f* MÚS viola

violación *f* **1.** (*infracción*) violation; (*de una ley*) breaking **2.** (*de una mujer*) rape

violar *vt* **1.** (*mujer*) to rape **2.** (*ley*) to violate; (*contrato*) to break

violencia *f* **1.** (*condición*) violence; (*fuerza*) force; **con ~** by force **2.** (*acción*) violent action

violentar **I.** *vt* **1.** (*obligar*) to force; (*sexualmente*) to assault **2.** (*una casa*) to break into **3.** (*principio*) to break **II.** *vr:* **~se** (*obligarse*) to force oneself

violento, -a *adj* **1.** (*impetuoso*) impetuous; (*esfuerzo*) violent **2.** (*brutal*) aggressive; (*persona*) violent **3.** (*postura*) unnatural

violeta *adj, f* violet

violín *m* MÚS violin, fiddle *inf*

violón *m* MÚS double bass

viraje *m* **1.** (*giro*) turn; (*curva*) bend **2.** (*cambio*) switch; (*de opinión*) shift **3.** NÁUT tack

virar **I.** *vi* **1.** (*girar*) to turn; (*curva*) to bend **2.** (*cambiar*) to switch; (*de opinión*) to shift **3.** NÁUT to tack **II.** *vt* (*girar*) to turn

virgen **I.** *adj* virgin; *fig* pure; (*cinta*) blank; (*tierras*) virgin **II.** *f* REL **la Virgen** the Virgin; **la Santísima Virgen** the Blessed Virgin

virginidad *f sin pl* virginity

Virgo *m* Virgo

viril *adj* virile

virilidad *f sin pl* virility

virtual *adj* virtual

virtud *f* virtue; **en ~ de** by virtue of

virtuoso, -a *adj* **1.** (*con gran habilidad*) virtuoso **2.** (*lleno de virtudes*) virtuous

viruela *f* MED smallpox; **picado de ~s** pockmarked

virulento, -a *adj* MED virulent

virus *m* *inv* MED, INFOR virus

visa *m* *o* *f AmL,* **visado** *m* visa

vísceras *fpl* entrails *pl*

viscoso, -a *adj* viscous

visera *f* **1.** MIL visor **2.** (*de una gorra*) peak

visibilidad *f* visibility

visible *adj* **1.** (*perceptible*) visible **2.** (*obvio*) clear

visillo *m* net curtain

visión *f* **1.** (*vista*) sight, vision **2.** (*aparición*) vision; **ver visiones** *fig* to be seeing things **3.** (*punto de vista*) view; **~ de conjunto** overview

visionario, -a **I.** *adj* **1.** (*con imaginación*) visionary **2.** (*soñador*) idealistic, dreamy *pej* **II.** *m, f* **1.** (*con imaginación*) vision **2.** (*soñador*) idealist; *pey* dreamer

visita *f* **1.** (*visitante*) visitor **2.** (*acción*) visit; **~ del médico** doctor's call; **~ guiada** guided tour

visitar *vt* **1.** (*ir a ver*) to visit **2.** MED to call (on)

vislumbrar *vt* (*ver*) to make out, to distinguish

vislumbre *f* **1.** (*resplandor*) glimmer **2.** (*idea*) sign

viso *m* **1.** (*resplandor*) glow **2.** (*aspecto*) sign; **tener ~s de...** to look like ...

visón *m* mink

visor *m* **1.** MIL sights *pl* **2.** FOTO viewfinder

víspera *f* (*noche anterior*) night before, eve; (*día anterior*) day before; **en ~s de** just before

vista *f* **1.** (*visión*) sight, vision; (*mirada*) look; **~ cansada** MED eye strain; **apartar la ~** to look away; **hacer la ~ gorda** to turn a blind eye; **saltar a la ~** to be patently obvious; **tener ~** to be shrewd; **volver la ~** (**atrás**) to look back; **a primera ~** at first sight; **a simple ~** just by looking; *fig* super-

ficially; **al alcance de la ~** within view; **fuera del alcance de la ~** out of sight; **a la ~ de todos** in full view of everyone; **con ~s a...** with a view to ...; **en ~ de que...** in view of the fact that ...; **pagadero a la ~** COM due on demand; **¡hasta la ~!** see you!; **¡fuera de mi ~!** get out of my sight! **2.** (*panorama*) view; (*mirador*) viewpoint; **con ~s al mar** with sea views, overlooking the sea **3.** (*imagen*) image; FOTO picture; **~ general** overall view **4.** JUR hearing; **~ oral** hearing

vistazo *m* look; **de un ~** at a glance

visto, -a **I.** *pp de* ver **II.** *adj* **~ para sentencia** JUR conclusion of the trial; **estar muy ~** to have been seen before; **está ~ que...** it's clear that ...; **por lo ~** apparently **III.** *conj* **~ que...** since ...

vistoso, -a *adj* (*atractivo*) colourful *Brit,* colorful *Am;* (*llamativo*) striking

visual *adj* visual; **campo ~** field of vision

vital *adj* **1.** *t.* MED vital **2.** (*necesario*) essential **3.** (*vivaz*) lively

vitalicio, -a *adj* ADMIN, FIN life

vitalidad *f sin pl* **1.** (*alegría de vivir*) vitality **2.** (*importancia*) vital importance

vitamina *f* vitamin

viticultor(a) *m(f)* vine grower

viticultura *f* viticulture

vítor *m* cheer, hurrah

vitorear *vt* to cheer

vítreo, -a *adj* vitreous

vitrina *f* glass cabinet; *AmL* (*escaparate*) shop window

vituperio *m* **1.** (*censura*) criticism **2.** (*injuria*) vituperation *liter*

viudedad *f* **1.** (*estado*) widowhood **2.** (*pensión: de viuda*) widow's pension; (*de viudo*) widower's pension

viudo, -a **I.** *adj* widowed **II.** *m, f* widower *m,* widow *f*

viva **I.** *interj* hurray; **¡~ el rey!** long live the King! **II.** *m* cheer

vivacidad *f sin pl* **1.** (*viveza*) vivacity **2.** (*energía*) vigour *Brit,* vigor *Am*

vivaracho, -a *adj* **1.** (*vivo*) vivacious **2.** (*despierto*) bright

vivaz *adj* **1.**(*vivaracho*) vivacious **2.**(*enérgico*) lively **3.**(*despierto*) bright

vivencia *f* experience

víveres *mpl* provisions *pl*

vivero *m* **1.**(*de plantas*) nursery **2.**(*de peces*) hatchery

vivienda *f* **1.**(*habitaje*) housing **2.**(*casa*) house; **sin** ~ homeless

viviente *adj* living

vivir I. *vi* **1.**(*estar vivo*) to be alive **2.**(*habitar*) to live **3.**(*perdurar*) to live on II. *vt* to live

vivo *m* **1.**(*borde*) edge, trim **2.**(*tira*) strip

vivo, -a *adj* **1.**(*viviente*) alive; **ser** ~ living being; **al rojo** ~ red-hot; **en** ~ MÚS live; **estar** ~ to be alive **2.**(*vivaz*) lively **3.**(*enérgico*) vigorous **4.**(*color*) bright **5.**(*vívido*) vivid **6.**(*avispado*) sharp; *pey* crafty

V.O. *abr de* **versión original** original version

vocablo *m* word, term

vocabulario *m* **1.**(*léxico*) vocabulary **2.**(*lista*) vocabulary (list)

vocación *f* vocation; **tener** ~ to have a calling

vocal[1] I. *adj* MÚS vocal II. *f* LING vowel

vocal[2] *mf* **1.**(*de consejo*) member **2.**(*portavoz*) spokesperson, spokesman *m*, spokeswoman *f*

vocalizar <z→c> *vt* to vocalize

vocear I. *vi* to shout II. *vt* **1.**(*pregonar*) to cry **2.**(*aclamar*) to acclaim

vocerío *m* clamour *Brit*, clamor *Am*

vocero, -a *m, f AmL* spokesman *m*, spokeswoman *f*

vociferar I. *vi* to yell II. *vt* **1.**(*gritar*) to shout **2.** *pey* (*proclamar*) to shout from the rooftops

vodka *m o f* vodka

vol. *abr de* **volumen** vol.

volador(a) *adj* flying

volandas *fpl* **en** ~ (*en el aire*) up in the air; (*deprisa*) in a rush

volante I. *adj* (*móvil*) flying; **platillo** ~ flying saucer II. *m* **1.** AUTO steering wheel **2.** TÉC flywheel **3.**(*del reloj*) balance wheel **4.**(*escrito*) leaflet

volar <o→ue> I. *vi* **1.**(*en el aire*) to fly; **¡voy volando!** I'm on my way!

2.(*desaparecer*) to disappear **3.**(*apresurarse*) to dash II. *vt* **1.**(*hacer explotar*) to blow up **2.**(*hacer volar*) to fly

volátil *adj* **1.** QUÍM volatile **2.**(*inconstante*) unpredictable

volcán *m* volcano

volcánico, -a *adj* volcanic

volcar *irr* I. *vi* (*tumbarse*) to overturn; (*barco*) to capsize II. *vt* **1.**(*hacer caer*) to knock over **2.**(*dar la vuelta*) to turn over III. *vr:* ~**se** **1.**(*darse la vuelta*) to overturn; (*caer*) to get knocked over **2.**(*esforzarse*) to make an effort; (*en algo*) to throw oneself into

voleibol *m* DEP volleyball

volquete *m* dumper truck *Brit,* dump truck *Am*

voltaje *m* voltage

voltear I. *vi* **1.**(*dar vueltas: persona*) to roll over; (*cosa*) to spin; (*campana*) to peal **2.**(*volcar*) to overturn **3.** *AmL* (*torcer*) to turn **4.** *AmL* (*pasear*) to go for a walk II. *vt* **1.**(*invertir*) to turn over **2.**(*hacer girar*) to spin **3.** *AmL* (*volcar*) to knock over; (*volver*) to turn III. *vr:* ~**se** **1.**(*dar vueltas*) to turn over **2.** *AmL* (*volcar*) to overturn; (*darse la vuelta*) to turn around

voltereta *f* (*cabriola*) handspring; (*en el aire*) to turn a somersault

voltio *m* volt

voluble *adj* **1.** QUÍM unstable **2.**(*inconstante*) fickle

volumen *m* **1.**(*tamaño*) size; *t.* FÍS, MAT volume **2.**(*cantidad*) amount; ~ **de ventas** turnover **3.**(*de sonido*) volume

voluminoso, -a *adj* sizeable; (*corpulento*) heavy

voluntad *f* **1.**(*intención*) will; **última** ~ JUR last will; **buena/mala** ~ goodwill/evil intent; **a** ~ at one's discretion; **con buena** ~ with good intentions **2.**(*fuerza de voluntad*) willpower **3.**(*cariño*) affection

voluntario, -a *adj* voluntary

voluntarioso, -a *adj* willing

voluptuoso, -a *adj* voluptuous

volver *irr* I. *vi* **1.**(*dar la vuelta*) to go

back **2.** (*regresar*) to return; ~ **a casa** to go home; ~ **en sí** to come round **3.** (*repetir*) ~ **a hacer algo** to do sth again **II.** *vt* **1.** (*dar la vuelta*) to turn over **2.** (*poner del revés*) to turn inside out **3.** (*transformar*) to make; ~ **loco a alguien** to drive sb crazy **4.** (*devolver*) to return **III.** *vr:* ~**se 1.** (*darse la vuelta*) to turn around towards; ~**se** (**para**) **atrás** to retrace one's steps; *fig* to back out **2.** (*regresar*) to return **3.** (*convertirse*) to become; ~**se viejo** to grow old

vomitar *vi* to vomit

vómito *m* (*acción*) vomiting; (*lo vomitado*) vomit

voracidad *f* voraciousness

voraz *adj t. fig* voracious; (*hambriento*) ravenous

vórtice *m* (*de agua*) whirlpool; (*de viento*) whirlwind

vos *pron pers* **1.** *AmL* (*tú*) you; **esto es para** ~ this is for you; **voy con** ~ I'll go with you **2.** HIST (*usted*) thou

> **?** The term **vosear** means so address someone in a familiar way using '**vos**' instead of '**tu**'. This is very common practice in **Argentina** and other Spanish-speaking countries of Latin America.

vosotros, -as *pron pers, pl* you; **esto es para** ~ this is for you

votación *f* vote; ~ **a mano alzada** vote by show of hands

votar I. *vi* (*elegir*) to vote; ~ **por alguien** to vote for sb **II.** *vt* POL to vote for; (*presupuesto*) to approve

voto *m* **1.** POL (*opinión*) vote; (*acción*) voting; ~ **en blanco** unmarked ballot (paper); ~ **de censura** vote of no confidence **2.** REL (*promesa*) vow

voy *1. pres de* **ir**

voz *f* **1.** (*facultad*) voice; **levantar/bajar la** ~ to raise/lower one's voice; **hablar en** ~ **alta/baja** to speak loudly/softly; **leer en** ~ **alta**

to read aloud **2.** (*grito*) shouting; **dar voces** to shout; **dar la** ~ **de alarma** to raise the alarm **3.** (*sonido*) tone **4.** (*rumor*) rumour *Brit,* rumor *Am* **5.** (*vocablo*) word

vuelco *m* **1.** (*tumbo*) turning over **2.** (*cambio*) drastic change; **dar un** ~ to overturn; *fig* to change completely

vuelo *m* **1.** (*en el aire*) flight; ~ **sin motor** gliding; **levantar el** ~ (*pájaro*) to fly off; (*avión*) to take off; **de altos** ~**s** *fig* high-powered **2.** (*de la ropa*) looseness

vuelta *f* **1.** (*giro*) turn; **dar la** ~ (*rodear*) to go around; (*volver*) to turn back; (*llave*) to turn; **darse la** ~ to turn over; **dar media** ~ to turn around; **dar una** ~ to have a walk around; **dar** ~**s a algo** to think over sth; **dar una** ~ **de campana** to turn over; **a la** ~ **de la esquina** around the corner; **poner a alguien de** ~ **y media** to tear sb off a strip *Brit,* to tell sb off *Am* **2.** (*regreso*) return; (*viaje*) trip; **de** ~ **a casa** back home; **estar de** ~ to be back **3.** (*dinero*) change; **dar la** ~ to give change **4.** DEP lap; ~ **ciclista** cycle race

vuelto *m AmL* (*cambio*) change; **dar el** ~ to give change

vuelto, -a *pp de* **volver**

vuestro, -a I. *adj* your; ~ **coche** your car; **vuestra hija** your daughter; ~**s libros** your books **II.** *pron pos* **1.** (*de vuestra propiedad*) yours; **¿es** ~**?** is this yours? **2.** (*tras artículo*) **el** ~ yours **3.** (*tras substantivo*) (of) yours; **un amigo** ~ a friend of yours

vulgar *adj* **1.** (*común*) common **2.** (*ordinario*) vulgar

vulgaridad *f* **1.** (*normalidad*) ordinariness **2.** *pey* (*grosería*) vulgarity

vulgarizar <z→c> *vt* **1.** (*simplificar*) to vulgarize **2.** (*popularizar*) to popularize

vulgo *m* ordinary people

vulnerable *adj* vulnerable

vulnerar *vt* (*persona*) to hurt; (*derecho*) to violate

vulva *f* ANAT vulva

W w

W, w *f* W, w; **~ de Washington** W for William
walkie-talkie *m* walkie-talkie
walkman® *m* Walkman®
wáter *m* toilet
waterpolo *m* DEP water polo
web *m o f* web
webcam *f* web camera
whisky *m* whisky
windsurf *m* **1.** DEP windsurfing **2.** (*tabla*) windsurfer
WWW *abr de* World Wide Web WWW

X x

X, x *f* X, x; **~ de xilófono** X for Xmas *Brit,* X for X *Am;* **rayos ~** X-rays *pl*
xenofobia *f* xenophobia
xenófobo, -a *adj* xenophobic
xerografía *f* xerography
xilófono *m* MÚS xylophone

Y y

Y, y *f* Y, y; **~ de yema** Y for Yellow *Brit,* Y for Yoke *Am*
y *conj* and; **días ~ días** days and days; **¿~ qué?** so what?; **me voy de vacaciones – ¿~ tu trabajo?** I'm going on holiday – what about your job?

⚠ **y** becomes **e** before a word beginning with i- or hi-: "par e impar, Javier e Isabel." Before y- however,

'y' is used: "ella y yo, Rubén y Yolanda."

ya I. *adv* **1.** (*en el pasado*) already; **~ en 1800** as early as 1800 **2.** (*pronto*) soon; **!~ voy!** coming!; **~ verás** you'll see **3.** (*ahora*) now; **~ falta poco para Navidades** Christmas is near now **4.** (*negación*) **~ no fumo** I don't smoke any more; **~ no... sino...** not only ..., but ... **5.** (*afirmación*) yes; **¡ah ~!** I get it now! **II.** *conj* **1.** (*porque*) **~ que** since, as **2.** (*aprovechando que*) **~ que lo mencionas...** now that you mention it ... **III.** *interj* that's it
yacer *irr vi elev* to lie
yacimiento *m* GEO deposit; (*capa*) layer
yagual *m AmC* padded ring
yanqui I. *adj* Yankee **II.** *mf* Yank
yate *m* yacht
yedra *f* ivy
yegua *f* **1.** ZOOL mare **2.** *AmC* (*colilla*) cigar stub
yema *f* **1.** (*de un huevo*) yolk **2.** (*de un dedo*) fingertip **3.** BOT young shoot
yendo *gerundio de* **ir**
yergo *1. pres de* **erguir**
yermo *m* waste land
yermo, -a *adj* **1.** (*inhabitado*) uninhabited **2.** AGR uncultivated
yerno *m* son-in-law
yerto, -a *adj* stiff
yesca *f* tinder
yeso *m* **1.** (*material*) plaster **2.** GEO gypsum
yo *pron pers* I; **entre tú y ~** between you and me; **¿quién lo hizo? – ~ no** who did it? – not me; **soy ~, Susan** it's me, Susan; **~ mismo** myself
yodo *m* iodine
yoga *m* yoga
yogur *m* yogurt
yuca *f* yucca
yudo *m* judo
yugo *m* yoke
Yugoslavia *f* Yugoslavia
yugular *f* jugular vein
yunque *m t.* ANAT anvil

yunta *f* yoke
yute *m* jute
yuxtaponer *irr como poner* **I.** *vt* (*a otra cosa*) to join; (*dos cosas*) to juxtapose **II.** *vr:* ~**se** to join together
yuxtaposición *f* juxtaposition

Z z

Z, z *f* Z, z; ~ **de Zaragoza** Z for Zebra
zafar I. *vt* NÁUT to free **II.** *vr:* ~**se 1.** (*de una persona*) to get away **2.** (*de un compromiso*) to get out
zafio, -a *adj* **1.** (*grosero*) rude **2.** (*tosco*) rough
zafiro *m* MIN sapphire
zafo *adv AmL* (*salvo*) except
zaga *f* **1.** (*parte posterior*) rear; **ir a la** ~ **de alguien** to be behind sb **2.** DEP defence
zagal(a) *m(f)* (*muchacho*) boy, lad *Brit;* (*muchacha*) girl, lass *Brit*
zaguán *m* hall
zaherir *irr como sentir* *vt* **1.** (*reprender*) to reprimand **2.** (*mortificar*) to humiliate
zaino, -a *adj* **1.** (*persona*) treacherous **2.** (*caballo*) chestnut
zalamería *f* flattery
zalamero, -a *adj* flattering
zamarra *f* **1.** (*de pastor*) shepherd's waistcoat **2.** (*piel*) sheepskin
Zambia *f* Zambia
zambullirse <*3. pret:* se zambulló> *vr* **1.** (*en el agua*) to dive **2.** (*en un asunto*) to plunge into
zampar I. *vt* **1.** (*comer*) to scoff *Brit,* to scarf down *Am* **2.** (*ocultar*) to whip out of sight **II.** *vr:* ~**se 1.** (*comer*) to scoff **2.** (*en un lugar*) to crash
zanahoria *f* carrot
zancada *f* stride
zancadilla *f* **poner la** ~ to trip up
zanco *m* stilt
zancudo *m AmL* mosquito

zancudo, -a *adj* long-legged
zángano *m* **1.** (*vago*) idler **2.** *t.* ZOOL drone
zanja *f* **1.** (*excavación*) ditch **2.** *AmL* (*arroyada*) watercourse
zanjar *vt* **1.** (*abrir zanjas*) to dig ditches **2.** (*asunto*) to settle
zapallo *m AmL* (*calabaza*) pumpkin
zapata *f* TÉC shoe; (*arandela*) washer; ~ **de freno** brake shoe
zapatear I. *vt* (*golpear*) to kick **II.** *vi* to tap dance
zapatería *f* **1.** (*tienda*) shoeshop **2.** (*fábrica*) shoe factory **3.** (*oficio*) shoemaking
zapatero, -a *m, f* shoemaker
zapatilla *f* **1.** (*para casa*) slipper **2.** (*de deporte*) trainer, sneaker *Am*
zapato *m* shoe
zapear *vt inf* TV to channel-hop, to zap (channels)
zapping *m* channel-hopping
zar, zarina *m, f* tsar *m,* tsarina *f*
zarandear *vt* **1.** (*sacudir*) to shake hard **2.** (*cribar*) to sieve
zarina *f v.* **zar**
zarpa *f* (*del león*) paw; **echar la** ~ (*animal*) to claw; *inf* (*persona*) to grab
zarpar *vi* NÁUT to set sail
zarza *f* bramble
zarzal *m* bramble patch
zarzuela *f* MÚS zarzuela (*Spanish musical comedy or operetta*)
zigzag *m* <zigzagues *o* zigzags> zigzag
zigzaguear *vi* to zigzag
Zimbabue *m* Zimbabwe
zinc *m* <cines *o* zincs> zinc
zócalo *m* **1.** (*de pared*) skirting board **2.** *Méx* (*plaza*) (town) square
zodíaco *m* zodiac
zona *f* zone; (*área*) region; ~ **franca** (duty-)free zone; ~ **peatonal** pedestrian precinct; ~ **verde** green belt
zoo *m* zoo
zoología *f sin pl* zoology
zoológico, -a *adj* zoological
zoólogo, -a *m, f* zoologist
zopenco, -a I. *adj* oafish **II.** *m, f* dolt
zoquete *m* **1.** (*madera*) block **2.** (*tonto*) blockhead

zorra *f* **1.** ZOOL vixen **2.** *inf* (*prostituta*) whore; (*insulto*) bitch **3.** *inf* (*borrachera*) drunkenness

zorro *m* fox

zozobra *f* anxiety

zozobrar *vi* **1.** (*barco*) to capsize **2.** (*plan*) to fail

zueco *m* clog

zumbar **I.** *vi* **1.** (*abeja*) to buzz **2.** (*oídos*) to hum **II.** *vt* **1.** (*golpe*) to deal **2.** *AmL* (*arrojar*) to throw **III.** *vr:* ~**se** to make fun

zumbido *m* **1.** (*ruido*) hum **2.** *inf* (*golpe*) clout

zumo *m* juice

zurcir <c→z> *vt* to mend

zurdo, -a *adj* left-handed

zurrar *vt* **1.** (*pieles*) to tan **2.** *inf* (*apalizar*) to beat

zutano, -a *m, f* **fulano y** ~ Tom, Dick and Harry

Z
z

Apéndice I

Supplement I

► CORRESPONDENCIA
CORRESPONDENCE

► What do I write, when I want to apply for work experience?

Paul Westney
6 Wordsworth Road
Middletown MD8 1NP

IBERIA
Apartado de Correos 675
E-28080 Madrid

Middletown, a 13 de febrero de 2002

Solicitud de un puesto en prácticas

Estimados señores:

Con la presente quisiera solicitar un puesto en prácticas en su delegación en Madrid.

Estoy en el penúltimo curso de bachillerato, en el instituto de Middletown. Mis asignaturas principales son el francés y las matemáticas, y desde hace tres años estudio también español. Después del instituto y de realizar el examen de Selectividad correspondiente me gustaría estudiar Ingeniería mecánica.

Antes de empezar con mi último curso de bachillerato me gustaría aprovechar mis vacaciones de verano, del 20 de julio al 30 de agosto, para perfeccionar mis conocimientos de español y para poder conocer al mismo tiempo el mundo laboral.

En el caso de que ustedes acepten mi solicitud, les estaría muy agradecido si pudieran ayudarme a buscar alojamiento.

Les agradezco de antemano todo su interés.

Les saluda muy atentamente,

Paul Westney

Anexos: Currículum vitae
         Expedientes escolares compulsados

Note: Spanish writers put both their name and address at the top left of the page, with the name and address of the other person below and to the left.

▶ ¿Qué escribo cuando quiero solicitar un puesto en prácticas?

Pza. Padre Silvino, 35
09001 Burgos

18th March 2002

British Airways
PO Box 12345
London W12 3PT

Application for work experience

Dear Sir or Madam,

This is an application to undertake a period of work experience at your offices in London.

I am at present in Year 12 of the local Grammar School, specializing in English and Mathematics. After my A-levels I intend to study mechanical engineering.

I would like to use the period from July 20th to August 30th of the summer holidays before Year 13 and my A-level exams to improve my English and experience a little of the world of work.

Should you offer me a place, I would be very grateful if you could help me to find accommodation.

Thank you in advance for taking the trouble to read my application.

Yours sincerely,

Juan Pérez

Juan Pérez Montoya

<u>Enclosures:</u>   CV
certified copies of reports

¡Atención! En una carta inglesa el nombre no suele aparecer en el membrete. La dirección del remitente se pone arriba a la derecha, la dirección del destinatario a la izquierda.

► Curriculum vitae

Currículum vitae

Datos personales:

Nombre y apellido:	Paul Westney
Dirección particular:	6 Wordsworth Road Middletown MD8 1NP
Fecha de nacimiento:	2.3.1984
Lugar de nacimiento:	Middletown
Nacionalidad:	Inglés

Formación escolar:

1990–1994	Escuela primaria en Middletown
1994–2002	Instituto en Middletown (previsiblemente terminaré mis estudios de bachillerato, la Selectividad incluida, en julio del año 2003)

Idiomas: excelente dominio del francés y del español (tanto a nivel escrito como oral)

Otros conocimientos: conocimientos de Informática a nivel de usuario (Windows '98; lenguajes de programación C, C++)

Aficiones: idiomas, automovilismo

▶ **Currículum vitae**

Juan Pérez Montoya
Pza. Padre Silverino, 35
09001 Burgos

Date of Birth: 28/03/1983
Spanish
Single

SCHOOLS
1989–1993   Primary School in Burgos
1993–2002   Grammar School in Burgos
(A-levels expected July 2003)

LANGUAGES
Fluent spoken and written French and English

HOBBIES
Foreign languages, Motor racing

▶ What do I write, when I want to apply for an au pair job?

Ann Roberts
5 Rogers Road,
Rickland GN8 4BY

Rickland, a 8 de noviembre 2002

Familia González
Avda. de Mirat, 13–4ºA
E- 37002 Salamanca

Puesto de aupair

Estimada Familia González:

Con fecha del 4 de noviembre de 2002 he leído su anuncio en el periódico Daily Post, en el que solicitan una chica aupair.

Actualmente curso la 10ª clase de la Grammar School en Rickland. Estudio español desde hace cuatro años. Concluiré mis estudios en julio. Para perfeccionar mis conocimientos de español me gustaría trabajar en España como aupair. Podría ocuparme de sus hijos a partir del día 1 de agosto, por un periodo de un mes.

Tengo dos hermanos más pequeños, un hermano de 10 años y una hermana de 6. Como mis padres trabajan los dos, estoy acostumbrada a cuidar de ellos. Mi padre trabaja en un banco y mi madre en una boutique.

Al mismo tiempo que cuidaría de sus hijos, me gustaría aprovechar la ocasión de conocer su país, que, por cierto, me encanta.

Espero su respuesta.
Atentamente,

Ann Roberts

▶ ¿Qué escribo cuando quiero solicitar un puesto de aupair?

Carmen Rodríguez Santos
c/Serafín, 53, 2^0, 3^a
08014 Barcelona

Mr and Mrs Arnold
23 Fernleigh Crescent
Cheltenham
GL32 5IQ

1st September 2002

Application for the post of au pair

Dear Mr and Mrs Arnold,

I read your advertisement in the 28/3/02 edition of
The Times and would like to apply for the post of au pair
with you.

At present I am in Year 10 of the local Grammar School and
have been learning English for five years. I expect to leave
school in July with my school leaving certificate (equivalent of
GCSEs). I would therefore be delighted to be allowed to look
after your two children for one month from August 1st.

I have one younger brother (10) and one sister (6) whom I
regularly have to look after because our parents both work.
My father works in a bank and my mother works part-time in
a boutique.

I would very much like to be allowed to look after your
children and at the same time learn more about the British
way of life, which I find very attractive.

Please let me know soon.

Yours sincerely

Carmen Rodríguez

Carmen Rodríguez Santos

► What do I say, when I want to find out about a holiday language course?

Laura Benson
38, Swinburne Avenue
Howdray
MY7 9PL

Howdray, a 5 de noviembre 2002

Curso de Verano de Español en Santander

Estimados señores:

Mi profesor de español me informó acerca de su Facultad. Me gustaría matricularme, para agosto del próximo año, en un curso de español en Santander.

Voy al instituto, al noveno curso. Estudio español desde hace tres años, sin embargo, mis calificaciones en esta asignatura no son demasiado buenas.

¿Podrían enviarme folletos informativos acerca de sus cursos? Quisiera saber si tengo que realizar un examen para poder asistir a los cursos, aparte, me interesaría saber de antemano los horarios exactos de clase. Me ha comentado mi profesor que ustedes se encargarían de mi alojamiento. ¿Sería posible vivir en casa de una familia que tuviera una hija de mi edad?

Me gustaría recibir pronto noticias suyas.

Saludos cordiales,

Laura Benson

▶ ¿Qué escribo cuando deseo solicitar información más detallada acerca de un curso de verano de idiomas?

Manuel Gómez Marcos
C/Estrecha, 10
18020 Granada

19th November 2002

Your holiday language course in Brighton

Dear Sir or Madam,

I have received some information about your institute from my English teacher and would like to attend a language course in Brighton in August of next year.

I am in Year 9 of the local Grammar School and have been learning English for three years. My marks in English are not particularly good however.

Please send me detailed information on your courses. I would particularly like to know if I will have to take an assessment test. I would also like to know how much tuition there is each day and at what time. My teacher has told me that you will arrange accommodation. Would it be possible to live with a family with a son of my own age?

I hope to hear from you soon.

Yours sincerely

Manuel Gómez

Manuel Gómez Marcos

▶ **What do I say, when I write to a pen friend for the first time?**

Querida María:

Me llamo Jessica Blackhill y tengo 16 años. Ayer nuestro profesor de español nos entregó una lista en clase con nombres de chicos y chicas hispanohablantes que desean mantener correspondencia con chicos y chicas en Alemania. Yo te he escogido a ti, porque prácticamente somos de la misma edad y porque compartimos las mismas aficiones.

Vivo con mis padres y mi hermano pequeño Mark en Mingley. Mi padre es ingeniero. Mi madre es ama de casa. Mi hermano Mark sólo tiene ocho años. Yo estoy ahora en el décimo curso, en el instituto, y desde séptimo estudio español. Mis asignaturas preferidas son, naturalmente, el español, la educación física y las matemáticas. ¿En qué curso estás tú, y cuáles son tus asignaturas preferidas? ¿También tienes hermanos, y en qué trabajan tus padres? Mis hobbys, igual que los tuyos, son leer, escuchar música y montar en bici, además toco el piano desde hace ya seis años. ¿Tú también tocas algún instrumento?

Espero recibir pronto noticias tuyas, pues me gustaría saber muchas más cosas acerca de ti y de Méjico, por ejemplo, qué música te gusta y qué sueles hacer con tus amigas los fines de semana.

Muchos saludos,

Jessica

▶ ¿Qué escribo cuando me dirijo por primera vez a una amiga por correspondencia?

Dear Elisabeth,

My name is Carmen and I am 16 years old. Yesterday in class my English teacher gave us a list of boys and girls from Britain who are looking for pen friends in Spain. I picked you out because we are almost exactly the same age and have the same hobbies.

I live with my parents and my younger brother Marco in Madrid. My father works as an engineer and my brother Marco is only eight and still goes to primary school. I am in Year 10 and have been learning English since Year 5. My favourite subjects are English (of course), Sport and Maths. What Year are you in and what are your favourite subjects? Do you have any brothers or sisters and what do your parents do? Like you, my hobbies are listening to music, surfing the net and in-line skating.

I hope you write back soon, as I want to know so much about you and Britain, e.g. what sort of music you like and what you and your friends do at weekends.

With love from,

Carmen Bermúdez Díaz

▶ **What do I write, when I want to write a thank-you letter to my hosts?**

Estimado José, estimada Carmen, querido Luis:

Quisiera agradeceros de nuevo la agradable estancia en vuestra casa. ¡Qué pena que el tiempo con vosotros se me haya hecho tan corto!

Sabréis que he disfrutado muchísimo de la estancia en vuestro refugio el último fin de semana. Os envío algunas de las fotos que hice allí.

Mi profesora me ha comentado que mi español ha mejorado mucho después de haber pasado estas dos semanas con vosotros. Le ha recomendado a todos mis compañeros participar en el mismo programa de intercambio.

Tengo muchas ganas de que llegue abril y Luis venga a Cambridge. Mis padres y yo ya hemos pensado en todo aquello que queremos enseñarle. Espero que se lo pase al menos tan bien como me lo he pasado yo con vosotros.

Saludos también para Ana e Isabel de mi parte. Espero poder volver a veros muy pronto.

Un fuerte abrazo,

Charles Harris

► ¿Qué escribo cuando quiero enviar una carta de agradecimiento a mi familia anfitriona?

Dear Mr and Mrs Seaton, dear Elisabeth,

I'd like to thank you once again for the really lovely time I spent with you. I am a little sad that it all went so quickly.

I especially liked the weekend we spent together at your holiday home. I enclose a few of the photos I took there.

My English teacher said that I had really made great progress in those two weeks. She suggested the rest of the class should go on an exchange too.

I'm already looking forward to April, when Elisabeth comes over to Sevilla. My parents and I have already planned where we want to go with her. I hope she will like it here as much as I did with you.

Please give my regards to Jenny and Kate too. I hope to see you again soon.

With love from

Sonia Gómez

FÓRMULAS ÚTILES PARA LA CORRESPONDENCIA
USEFUL EXPRESSIONS IN LETTERS

▶ THE BEGINNING OF A LETTER
EL ENCABEZAMIENTO EN UNA CARTA

When you're writing ...	Cuando escribes...
... to someone you know or to a friend	**...a un conocido o a un amigo**
• Querido Felipe: • Querida Inés: • ¡Hola Silvia! Gracias por tu carta. Me alegra saber que te encuentras bien. Perdóname por/Siento por no haberte escrito antes.	• Dear Mark, • Dear Janet, Many thanks for your letter. I was really glad/delighted to hear from you. I apologize/I'm sorry for not having written for so long.
... to someone you know or to business contacts	**...a alguien a quien conoces a nivel personal o profesional**
• Estimada Srta. Hernández: • Estimada Sra. Gómez: • Estimado Sr. González:	• Dear Mrs Arnold, • Dear Mr Arnold,
... to companies or organizations	**...a una empresa o a una persona cuyo nombre desconoces**
• Muy señores míos: • Estimados Sres./Estimados señores: Me gustaría saber si... Quisiera saber si... Por favor, ¿podría(n) enviarme...?	• Dear Sir or Madam, • Dear Sirs, I wonder if you could let me know whether ... I would like to enquire whether ... Could you kindly/please send me ...?
... to someone whose title you know	**...a una persona cuyo título o grado académico conoces**
• Distinguido/Estimado Dr. Pedro Santos: • Distinguida/Estimada Catedrática D.ª Cristina Suárez:	• Dear Sir, • Dear Madam, • Dear Doctor, *(dirigiéndose a un médico)*

▶ THE ENDING OF A LETTER
  LA DESPEDIDA EN UNA CARTA

Informally:	Menos formal o familiar:
• Un abrazo muy fuerte,	• Love,
• Un fuerte abrazo,	• (With) warmest regards,
• Besos,	
• ¡Chao!	• Cheerio!
• Un abrazo,	• (With) kind regards,
• Un cordial saludo,	• With best wishes,
• Un afectuoso saludo,	
• Saludos cordiales,	
• Muchos saludos,	• Regards,
• Saludos,	• Yours,
• ¡Hasta pronto!	• Yours ever,
	• Yours with best wishes
	• See you soon!

Formal:	Formal:
• Atentamente,	• Yours sincerely,
• Le saluda atentamente,	*(Si la carta comienza con "Dear*
• Muy atentamente,	*Mr/Mrs ...")*
	• Yours faithfully,
	(Si la carta comienza con "Dear
	Sir/Madam")

Very formal:	Muy respetuoso:
• Sin otro particular, aprovechamos la oportunnidad para saludarles muy atentamente/muy cordialmente.	• Yours sincerely, *(Si la carta comienza con "Dear Mr/Mrs ...")*
• Sin otro particular, le saludo muy atentamente.	• Yours faithfully, *(Si la carta comienza con "Dear Sir/Madam")*
• Quedando en todo momento a su disposición, aprovecho la oportunidad para saludarles muy atentamente.	

► EXPRESIONES ÚTILES
USEFUL PHRASES

What do I say, when I want to greet someone? / **¿Qué digo cuando quiero saludar a alguien?**

¡Buenos días! (*until 2 pm*)	Good morning!
¡Buenas tardes! (*from 2 pm onwards until 9 pm*)	Good afternoon!
¡Buenas noches! (*from 9 pm onwards*)	Good evening!
¡Hola!	Hello!
Hola, ¿qué tal?	Hi (there)!
¿Cómo está(n) usted(es)/estás tú?/ Como le(s)/te va?	How are you?
¿Qué tal?/¿Qué hay?	How are things?

What do I say, when I want to say goodbye to someone? / **¿Qué digo cuando quiero despedirme de alguien?**

Adiós!	Goodbye!
¡Hasta luego!	Bye!/Cherrio!/See you later!
¡Hasta mañana!	See you tomorrow!/Until tomorrow!/Goodnight!
¡Que te lo pases/os lo paséis bien!/ ¡Que te diviertas/os divertáis!	Have fun!
¡Buenas noches!	Good night!
Salude(n) a/Saluda a María de mi parte.	Give María my regards./Say hello to María for me.

What do I say, when I want to ask for something or express my thanks? / **¿Qué digo cuando quiero pedir o agradecer algo?**

Sí, por favor.	Yes, please.
No, gracias.	No, thank you.
Gracias, con mucho gusto.	Yes please!
Gracias, ¡igualmente!	Thank you, (and) the same to you!

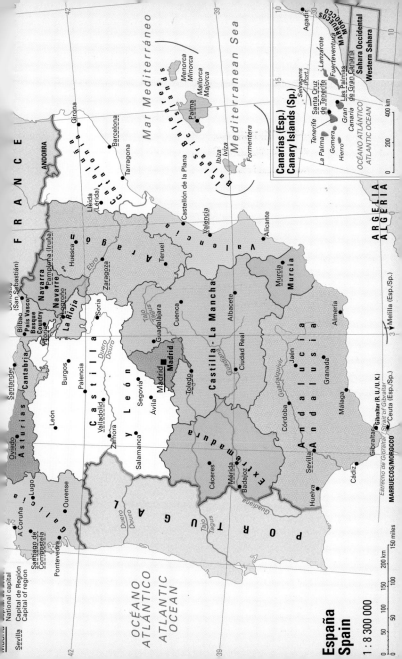

España
Spain

1 : 8 300 000

Canarias (Esp.)
Canary Islands (Sp.)

Sahara Occidental
Western Sahara

MARRUECOS/MOROCCO

MARRUECOS
MOROCCO

ARGELIA
ALGERIA

Gibraltar (R.U./U.K.)
Ceuta (Esp./Sp.)
Melilla (Esp./Sp.)

Estrecho de Gibraltar / Strait of Gibraltar

ANDORRA
FRANCE
PORTUGAL

OCÉANO ATLÁNTICO
ATLANTIC OCEAN

Mar Mediterráneo
Mediterranean Sea

Islas Baleares
Balearic Islands

Menorca
Minorca
Mallorca
Majorca
Palma
Ibiza
Iviza
Formentera

Canary Islands inset:
Selvagens (Port.)
Lanzarote
Fuerteventura
Las Palmas de Gran Canaria
Gran Canaria
Santa Cruz de Tenerife
Tenerife
La Palma
Gomera
Hierro
Agadir
OCÉANO ATLÁNTICO
ATLANTIC OCEAN
MARRUECOS
MOROCCO

Regions and cities

Galicia — A Coruña, Lugo, Santiago de Compostela, Pontevedra, Ourense

Asturias — Oviedo

Cantabria — Santander

País Vasco / Basque Country — Bilbao (San Sebastián), Vitoria, Donostia (San Sebastián)

Navarra / Navarre — Pamplona (Iruña)

La Rioja — Logroño

Castilla y León — León, Burgos, Palencia, Valladolid, Zamora, Salamanca, Soria, Segovia, Ávila

Aragón — Huesca, Zaragoza, Teruel

Cataluña — Girona, Lleida (Lérida), Barcelona, Tarragona

Madrid — Madrid

Extremadura — Cáceres, Mérida, Badajoz

Castilla - La Mancha — Guadalajara, Cuenca, Toledo, Albacete, Ciudad Real

Valencia — Castellón de la Plana, Valencia, Alicante

Murcia — Murcia

Andalucía — Huelva, Sevilla, Córdoba, Jaén, Cádiz, Málaga, Granada, Almería

Rivers — Ebro, Duero / Douro, Tajo / Tagus, Guadiana, Guadalquivir

OCÉANO ATLÁNTICO
ATLANTIC OCEAN

Madrid — National capital
Sevilla — Capital de Región / Capital of region

0 50 100 150 200 km
0 50 100 150 miles

0 200 400 km

El mundo hispanohablante
The spanish-speaking world

1 : 124 000 000

Países donde el español es lengua oficial y materna
Countries where Spanish is official la
and mother tongue

Países donde el español es lengua ofic
Countries where Spanish is official lan

Países donde el español es practicado por una minoría
Countries where Spanish is spoken by a minority

B.   Islas Baleares (Esp.)
      Balearic Islands (Sp.)
D.   REPÚBLICA DOMINICANA
      DOMINICAN REPUBLIC
G.   Islas de los Galápagos (Esp.)
      Galapagos Islands (Sp.)
G.-E. GUINEA ECUATORIAL
      EQUATORIAL GUINEA
P.   PANAMÁ
      PANAMA
P. R. Puerto Rico (EE. UU./U. S.)

Hispanoamérica
Spanish América

ESTADOS UNIDOS/UNITED STATES

Golfo de México
Gulf of México

Trópico de Cán
Tropic of Canc

La Habana
Havana

CUBA

JAMAICA

Mar Caribe
Caribbean Sea

Santo Domingo
San Juan

OCÉANO
ATLÁNTIC

Cd. de México
Mexico City

Cd. de Guatemala
Guatemala City

San Salvador

HONDURAS
Tegucigalpa

NICARAGUA

Managua

San José

COSTA RICA

Panamá
Panamá City

Caracas

Orinoco

VENEZUELA

GUYANA

SURI-
NAME

G. F.

Santa Fe de Bogotá
Bogotá

COLOMBIA

Quito

ECUADOR

Amazonas

B R A S I L
B R A Z I L

OCÉANO PACÍFICO
PACIFIC OCEAN

Ecuador
Equator

PERÚ

Lima

La Paz

BOLIVIA

Paraguay

PARAGUAY

Asunción

Paraná

Paraná

Trópico de Capricornio
Tropic of Capricorn

Santiago

Buenos
Aires

URUGUAY

Montevideo

Río de la Plata

ATLANTIC
OCEAN

ARGENTINA

CHILE

Est.   de Drake
Drake   Passage

Círculo Polar Antártico   Antarctic Circle

1 : 78 100 000

| 0 | 500 | 1000 | 1500 | 2000 km |
| 0 | 500 | | 1000 miles | |

D.	REPÚBLICA DOMINICANA DOMINICAN REPUBLIC	H.	HAITÍ HAITI
E.	EL SALVADOR	P.	PANAMÁ PANAMA
G.	GUATEMALA	P. R.	Puerto Rico (EE. UU./U. S.)
G. F.	Guayana Francesa French Guiana		

tish Isles
as Británicas

50   100   150   200 km

50   100   150 miles

500 000

Shetland Islands
Islas Shetland

60

Orkney Islands
Islas Orcadas

Western Isles
Islas Hébridas

Spey

57

ATLANTIC
OCEAN

S c o t l a n d

OCÉANO
ATLÁNTICO

Tay

E s c o c i a

Edinburgh
Edinburgo

North Sea
Mar del Norte

North Channel/Canal del Norte

Tweed

UNITED KINGDOM

Northern
Ireland
Irlanda
del Norte

E

Belfast

n

g

Isle of Man
Isla de Man

l

54

IRELAND

Irish Sea
Mar de Irlanda

REINO UNIDO

a

IRLANDA

n

Shannon

Dublin
Dublín

d

Trent

Barrow

Wales
País de Gales

Ouse

t

Suir

e

Severn

r

St. George's Channel
Canal de San Jorge

Cardiff

Thames
Támesis

r

a

London
Londres

51

Isle of Wight
Isla de Wight

Scilly Isles
Islas Scilly

English Channel
Canal de la Mancha

Channel Is. (U. K.)
Islas Anglo-
normandas (R. U.)   Alderney

Guernsey   Sark

Seine

Jersey

FRANCE
FRANCIA

9   6   3   0   3

80 **140** **160** **180** **160** **140** **120** **100** **80** **60** **40** **20** **0**

Arctic Circle
Círculo Polar Ártico

C A N A D A
C A N A D Á

UNITED KINGDOM
REINO UNIDO

Québec

IRELAND
IRLANDA

UNITED STATES
OF AMERICA
ESTADOS UNIDOS
DE AMÉRICA

Gi.

Bermuda (U. K.)
Bermudas (R. U.)

Tropic of Cancer
Trópico de Cáncer

BAHAMAS

BELIZE
BELICE **P. R.**

JAMAICA

G.

NIGERIA

S. L.
LIBERIA **GHANA**

C.

GUYANA

Equator
Ecuador

P A C I F I C
O C E A N
O C É A N O
P A C Í F I C O

A T L A N T I C
O C E A N
O C É A N O
A T L Á N T I C O

Tropic of Capricorn
Trópico de Capricornio

Falkland Islands (U. K.)
Islas Malvinas (R. U.)

Antarctic Circle
Círculo Polar Antártico

180 **160** **140** **120** **100** **80** **60** **40** **20** **0** **20**

The english-speaking world
El mundo angloparlante

1 : 124 000 000

| 0 | 1000 | 2000 | 3000 km |
| 0 | 1000 | | 2000 miles |

Countries where English is official language
and mother tongue
Países donde el inglés es lengua oficial y mate

Countries where English is one of the
official languages
Países donde el inglés es una de las
lenguas oficiales

PACIFIC
OCEAN

OCÉANO
PACÍFICO

N.

Gu.

Equator
Ecuador

P.

S. I.

VANUATU

AUSTRALIA

NEW ZEALAND
NUEVA ZELANDA

PAKISTAN
PAKISTÁN

INDIA

HONG
KONG

SRI
LANKA

S.

PALAU

KENYA
KENIA

TANZANIA

SEYCHELLES

MALAWI

Z.

MAURITIUS
MAURICIO

SW.

ANDA

MBIA

L.

INDIAN
OCEAN

OCÉANO
ÍNDICO

BOTSWANA
BOTSUANA
CAMEROON
CAMERÚN
THE GAMBIA
GAMBIA
Gibraltar (U. K./R. U.)
Guam (U.S./EE.UU.)
LESOTHO
LESOTO

N. Northern Mariana Is. (U. S.)
    Is. Marianas del Norte
    (EE. UU.)
P. PAPUA NEW GUINEA
    PAPÚA NUEVA GUINEA
P. R. Puerto Rico (U. S./EE. UU.)
S. SINGAPORE
    SINGAPUR
SW. SWAZILAND
    SWAZILANDIA

S. A. SOUTH AFRICA
      SUDÁFRICA
S. I. SOLOMON ISLANDS
      ISLAS SALOMÓN
S. L. SIERRA LEONE
      SIERRA LEONA
Z.   ZIMBABWE

Countries in the Pacific Ocean:
Países en el Océano Pacífico:

1 Midway (U. S./EE. UU.)
2 MARSHALL ISLANDS
   ISLAS MARSHALL
3 NAURU
4 KIRIBATI
5 TUVALU

6 Western Samoa
   Samoa Occidental
7 American Samoa
   Samoa Americana
8 FIJI
9 TONGA

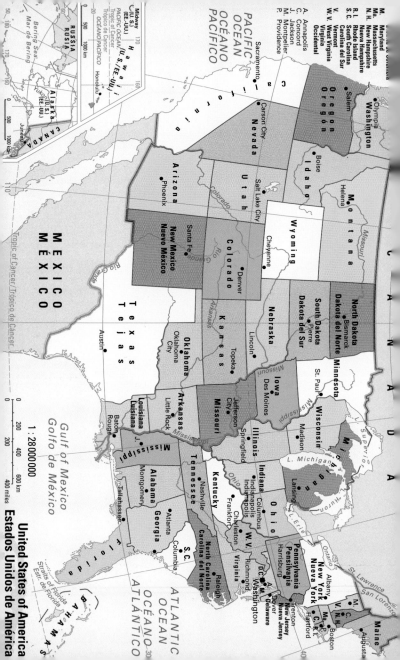

United States of America
Estados Unidos de América

1 : 28 000 000

PACIFIC OCEAN
OCÉANO PACÍFICO

MEXICO
MÉXICO

Gulf of Mexico
Golfo de México

CANADA

ATLANTIC OCEAN
OCÉANO ATLÁNTICO

M. Maryland
Ma. Massachusetts
N. H. Nueva Hampshire
R. I. Rhode Island
S. C. Carolina del Sur
V. Vermont
W. V. Virginia Occidental

A. Annapolis
C. Concord
J. Jackson
M. Montpelier
P. Providence

RUSSIA
RUSIA

Alaska (U.S.) (EE-UU.)

Hawai (U.S.) (EE-UU.)

Midway (U.S.)

States and capitals

Washington — Olympia
Oregon / Oregón — Salem
California — Sacramento
Nevada — Carson City
Idaho — Boise
Montana — Helena
Wyoming — Cheyenne
Utah — Salt Lake City
Arizona — Phoenix
New Mexico / Nuevo México — Santa Fe
Colorado — Denver
North Dakota / Dakota del Norte — Bismarck
South Dakota / Dakota del Sur — Pierre
Nebraska — Lincoln
Kansas — Topeka
Oklahoma — Oklahoma City
Texas / Tejas — Austin
Minnesota — St. Paul
Iowa — Des Moines
Missouri — Jefferson City
Arkansas — Little Rock
Louisiana / Luisiana — Baton Rouge
Wisconsin — Madison
Illinois — Springfield
Michigan — Lansing
Indiana — Indianapolis
Ohio — Columbus
Kentucky — Frankfort
Tennessee — Nashville
Mississippi — Jackson
Alabama — Montgomery
Georgia — Atlanta
Florida — Tallahassee
South Carolina / Carolina del Sur — Columbia
North Carolina / Carolina del Norte — Raleigh
Virginia — Richmond
W. V. — Charleston
Pennsylvania / Pensilvania — Harrisburg
New York / Nueva York — Albany
New Jersey / Nueva Jersey — Trenton
Delaware — Dover
Maine — Augusta

Washington D.C.

Tropic of Cancer / Trópico de Cáncer

Rio Grande
Colorado
Columbia
Missouri
Mississippi
Arkansas
Ohio
St. Lawrence / San Lorenzo

L. Superior
L. Michigan
L. Huron
L. Erie
L. Ontario

Bering Sea / Mar de Bering
Strait of Florida / Estr. de Florida

Por favor, ¿podría ayudarme?/¿podría echarme una mano?	Can you help me, please?
De nada./No hay de qué.	Not at all./You're welcome.
¡Muchas gracias!	Thanks a lot.
No tiene importanica.	Don't mention it.

What do I say, when I want to apologise or express my regrets? **¿Qué digo cuando quiero disculparme?**

¡Perdón!	Sorry!/Excuse me!
Debo disculparme.	I must/I'd like to apologize.
Lo siento.	I'm sorry (about it).
No era esa mi intención.	It wasn't meant like that.
¡Qué pena!/¡Qué lástima!	Pity!/Shame!

What do I say, when I want to congratulate someone or wish someone good luck? **¿Qué digo cuando quiero felicitar a alguien?**

¡Felicidades!/¡Enhorabuena!	Congratulations!
¡Suerte!/¡Le/te deseo mucha suerte!	Good luck!
¡Que se mejore/te mejores!	(Hope you) get well soon!
¡Que lo pases/paséis bien en las vacaciones!/¡Que disfrutes/disfrutéis de las vacaciones!	Have a nice holiday!
¡Felices Pascuas!	Happy Easter!
¡Feliz Navidad y un próspero año nuevo!	Merry Christmas and a Happy New Year!
¡Feliz cumpleaños!	Happy Birthday!
¡Que cumpla(s) muchos más!	Many happy returns of the day!
¡Suerte!	I'll keep my fingers crossed for you.

What do I say, when I want to say something about myself? **¿Qué digo cuando quiero hablar de mí mismo?**

| Me llamo... | My name is ... |
| Soy español/española./Soy de España. | I'm Spanish./I'm from Spain. |

Vivo en Málaga.	I live in Málaga.
Está cerca de…	That's near …
Está al norte/sur/oeste/este de…	That's north/south/west/east of …
Estoy aquí de vacaciones.	I'm on holiday here.
Estoy matriculado en un curso de idiomas.	I'm doing a language course here.
Estoy aquí como estudiante de intercambio.	I'm on a school exchange.
Estoy aquí con mi equipo de fútbol.	I'm with my football club here.
Me quedaré un día/cinco días/una semana/dos semanas.	I'm staying for a day/for five days/for a week/for two weeks.
Durante mi estancia vivo en/en casa de…	During my time here I'm staying in/at/with …
Mi padre es…/trabaja (como…) en la empresa…	My father is a(n) …/works (as a(n) …) at …
Mi madre es…	My mother is …
Tengo una hermana/dos hermanas y un hermano/dos hermanos.	I've got a sister/two sisters and a brother/two brothers.
Voy a la escuela en…	I go to school in …
Estoy en… curso.	I'm in Year …
Tengo… años.	I'm … (years old).
Me gusta jugar al fútbol./Me gusta jugar al ajedrez.	I like playing football./I like chess.

What do I say, when I want to find out something about other people?

Qué digo cuando quiero averiguar algo acerca de otras personas?

¿Cómo te llamas?	What's your name?
¿De dónde eres?	Where do you come from?
¿Dónde vives?	Where do you live?
¿Dónde queda eso?	Where is that?
¿Qué estás haciendo aquí?/¿Qué haces aquí?	What are you doing/do you do here?
¿Cuánto tiempo te vas a quedar (aquí)?	How long are you staying (here)?
¿Y aquí dónde vives?	Where are you staying?

¿En qué trabaja tu padre/madre? ¿Dónde trabaja?	What does your father/mother do? Where does he/she work?
¿Tienes hermanos?	Have you got any brothers or sisters?/ Do you have any brothers or sisters?
¿A qué escuela vas?	What school do you go to?
¿En qué curso estás?	What year are you in?
¿Cuántos años tienes?	How old are you?
¿Qué (es lo que) te gusta hacer?	What do you like doing?
¿Cuáles son tus hobbys/aficiones?	What are your hobbies?

What do I say, when I agree?	¿Qué digo cuando soy de la misma opinión?
¡Cierto!/¡Eso es!/¡Exactamente!	(That's) right!/Exactly!
¡Yo también!	Me too!/I do too!/So do I!
¡Yo tampoco!	Nor me!/Neither do I!
Sí, a mí también me parece bien/ fantástico/estupendo/genial.	Yes, I think it's good/brilliant/great/ ace too.

What do I say, when I disagree?	¿Qué digo cuando no comparto la misma opinión?
¡Eso no es así (en absoluto)!	That's not right (at all)!/That's (all) wrong!/That's not true!
¡(Qué) no!	No!
¡(Qué) sí!	Yes I am/was/will/can/could/do/ did!
¡No!, a mí me parece estúpido/ horrible.	No, I think it's stupid/revolting!

What do I say, when I want to say what I think?	¿Qué digo cuando quiero manifestar mi opinión?
Yo creo/pienso/opino que…	I believe/think that …
Yo no creo/pienso/opino que…	I don't believe/think that …
En mi opinión…	In my opinion …

What do I say, when I want to show that I'm listening?	**¿Qué digo cuando quiero demostrar que estoy prestando atención?**
¿De verdad?	Really?/Honestly?
¡Ah!/¡No me digas!	I see!

What do I say, when I want to ask the way?	**¿Qué digo cuando quiero preguntar por una dirección?**
¿Dónde está el... más próximo?	Where is the (nearest) ...?
¿Por dónde se va al... más cercano?	How do I get to the (nearest) ...?
¿Me podría decir/explicar dónde se encuentra/dónde está el... más cercano?	Could you tell me where the (nearest) ... is?

What do I say, when I want to say that I'm feeling good?	**¿Qué digo cuando quiero expresar que me encuentro bien?**
¡Hoy me encuentro realmente bien!	I feel really good!
¡Hoy me encuentro fenomenal!	I'm in a really good mood!
¡Hoy me siento estupendo/fenomenal!	I feel great/fantastic!

What do I say, when I want to say that I'm not feeling well?	**¿Qué digo cuando quiero expresar que me encuentro mal?**
¡Hoy no me encuentro bien!	I don't feel/I'm not feeling well!
¡Hoy me encuentro fatal!	I feel really terrible!
¡Hoy estoy en un humor de perros!	I'm in a foul/really bad mood!
¡Hoy (es que) me siento fatal/mal!	I feel really lousy!

What do I say, when I want to say that I like something?	**¿Qué digo cuando algo me gusta?**
¡Es realmente genial/guay/fantástico/intrigante/flipante!	It's really brilliant/ace/great/exciting!

What do I say, when I want to say that I don't like something?	¿Qué digo cuando algo no me gusta?
¡Es realmente estúpido/aburrido/insoportable!	It's really stupid/boring/revolting!

What do I say, when I ring/phone a friend?	Qué digo cuando llamo a un amigo/una amiga por teléfono?
Hola, soy…	Hello, it's … here/speaking.
Hola, soy yo,…	Hello, it's me, …
¡Bueno, entonces hasta la(s)…/mañana/más tarde!	OK then, see you at … (o'clock)/tomorrow/later!
¡Hasta luego!/¡Chao!	Bye!/Cheerio!

What do I say, when I speak to adults on the phone?	¿Qué digo cuando hablo con personas adultas por teléfono?
Buenas tardes, señor/señora…, soy…	Good morning/afternoon, Mr/Mrs …, it's … here/speaking.
Por favor, ¿podría hablar con… ?	Could I speak to … ?
¿Está… ?/¿Podría ponerse… ?	Is … there/at home?
(¿Quiere(s) dejar un mensaje?)	(Would you like to leave a message?)
No gracias. No es necesario.	No, thank you. That's OK.
Volveré a llamar más tarde.	I'll ring/try again later.
Sí, ¿podría decirle/comentarle que… ?	Yes, could you please tell him/her that/to …
¡Muchas gracias! ¡Adiós!	Many thanks! Goodbye!

What do I say, when I have to speak to an answering machine?	¿Qué digo cuando tengo que dejar un mensaje en el contestador (automático)?
¡Buenas tardes!/¡Hola! Soy…	Good morning/afternoon./Hello! This is … (speaking).
(Sólo) llamaba para preguntar si…/para comentarte/comentaros/comentarle/comentarles que…	I (just) wanted to ask if …/say that …
Me puede(s) localizar (hasta la(s)…) en el número…	You can reach me (until … o'clock) on … (number).
¡Gracias y hasta pronto/hasta luego!	Thanks, bye!

What do I say, when I want to give somebody my e-mail/Internet address?

¿Qué digo cuando quiero dar a alguien mi dirección de correo electrónico/de internet?

Mi dirección de correo electrónico es (la siguiente): <u>tom.robert@aol.com</u> (es decir, tom punto robert arroba a o l punto com)	My e-mail address is: <u>tom.robert@aol.com</u> (say: tom dot robert at a o l dot com)
Mi página de web es: <u>http://www.aol.com/~robert</u> (es decir, h t t p dos puntos dos barras w w w punto a o l punto com barra tilde robert)	My homepage address is: <u>http://www.aol.com/~robert</u> (say: h t t p colon forward slash forward slash w w w dot a o l dot com forward slash tilde robert)

Aa

A, a [eɪ] *n* **1.** (*letter*) A, a *f*; ~ *for An-drew*; *Brit* ~ *for Abel*; *Am* A de Anto-nio; **to get from ~ to B** ir de un lugar a otro **2.** MUS la *m*

a [ə, *stressed:* eɪ] *indef art before consonant,* **an** [ən, *stressed:* æn] *before vowel* **1.** (*in general*) un, una; ~ **car** un coche; ~ **house** una casa; **in ~ day or two** en unos días; **she is** ~ **teacher** es maestra; **he is an Eng-lishman** es inglés **2.** (*to express rates*) **£6** ~ **week** 6 libras por sema-na

A *n abbr of* **answer** R

AA [ˌeɪ'eɪ] *abbr of* **Alcoholics Anonymous** AA *mpl*

AB *Am abbr of* **Artium Baccalaureus** licenciatura *f* en Letras

aback [ə'bæk] *adv* **to be taken ~** (**by sth**) quedarse desconcertado (por algo)

abandon [ə'bændən] *vt* abandonar; **to ~ ship** evacuar el barco; **to ~ oneself to sth** entregarse a algo

abandoned [ə'bændənd] *adj* aban-donado

abashed [ə'bæʃt] *adj* avergonzado

abate [ə'beɪt] *vi* disminuir

abattoir ['æbətwɑːʳ, *Am:* -twɑːr] *n* matadero *m*

abbey ['æbɪ] *n* abadía *f*

abbot ['æbət] *n* REL abad *m*

abbreviation [əˌbriːvɪ'eɪʃn] *n* abre-viatura *f*

abdicate ['æbdɪkeɪt] *vi* abdicar

abdication [ˌæbdɪ'keɪʃn] *n no pl* abdicación *f*

abdomen ['æbdəmən] *n* abdomen *m*

abdominal [æb'dɒmɪnl, *Am:* -'dɑːmə-] *adj* abdominal

abduct [æb'dʌkt] *vt* secuestrar, pla-giar *AmL*

abduction [æb'dʌkʃn] *n* secuestro *m*, plagio *m AmL*

aberration [ˌæbə'reɪʃn] *n* aberra-ción *f*

abhor [əb'hɔːʳ, *Am:* æb'hɔːr] <-rr-> *vt* aborrecer

abhorrent *adj* aborrecible

abide [ə'baɪd] <-d *o* abode, -d *o* abode> *vt* soportar

ability [ə'bɪlətɪ, *Am:* -ət̬ɪ] <-ies> *n no pl* capacidad *f*; (*talent*) aptitud *f*

abject ['æbdʒekt] *adj* **1.** (*wretched*) abyecto **2.** (*absolute*) absoluto

ablaze [ə'bleɪz] *adj* en llamas

able ['eɪbl] *adj* capaz; **to be ~ to do sth** poder hacer algo

able-bodied [ˌeɪbl'bɒdɪd, *Am:* -'bɑːdɪd] *adj* sano y fuerte

abnormal [æb'nɔːml, *Am:* -'nɔːr-] *adj* anormal

abnormality [ˌæbnə'mælɪtɪ, *Am:* -nɔːr'mælət̬ɪ] <-ies> *n* anormali-dad *f*

aboard [ə'bɔːd, *Am:* ə'bɔːrd] **I.** *adv* a bordo **II.** *prep* a bordo de

abode [ə'bəʊd, *Am:* ə'boʊd] *n of* **no fixed** ~ sin domicilio fijo

abolish [ə'bɒlɪʃ, *Am:* -ɑːl-] *vt* abolir

abolition [əbəl'ɪʃn] *n no pl* aboli-ción *f*

abominable [ə'bɒmɪnəbl, *Am:* ə'bɑːm-] *adj* abominable

abomination [əˌbɒmɪ'neɪʃn, *Am:* ə'bɑːm-] *n* abominación *f*

aboriginal [ˌæbə'rɪdʒənl] *adj* abo-rigen

Aborigine [ˌæbə'rɪdʒɪnɪ] *n* abori-gen *mf* (de Australia)

abort [ə'bɔːt, *Am:* ə'bɔrt] *vt, vi* abortar

abortion [ə'bɔːʃn, *Am:* ə'bɔːr-] *n* aborto *m* (provocado)

abortive [ə'bɔːtɪv, *Am:* ə'bɔːrt̬ɪv] *adj* malogrado

abound [ə'baʊnd] *vi* abundar

about [ə'baʊt] **I.** *prep* **1.** (*on subject of*) sobre, acerca de; **a book ~ foot-ball** un libro sobre fútbol; **what is the film ~?** ¿de qué trata la pelícu-la?; **how ~ that!** ¡vaya!; **what ~ it?** ¿quieres? **2.** (*surrounding*) alrededor de **3.** (*in and through*) por **II.** *adv* **1.** (*around*) **all ~** por todas partes; **to be the other way ~** ser exacta-mente al revés; **is Paul ~?** ¿está Paul por ahí? **2.** (*approximately*) aproximadamente; ~ **5 years ago** hace unos cinco años; ~ **twenty** unos veinte **3.** (*almost*) casi; **to be** (**just**) ~ **ready** estar casi listo; **to be ~ to do sth** estar a punto de hacer algo

above [ə'bʌv] **I.** *prep* **1.** (*on the top of*) encima de **2.** (*over*) sobre; ~ **suspicion** por encima de toda sospecha **3.** (*greater than*) por encima de; ~ **3** más de 3; ~ **all** sobre todo **II.** *adv* encima, arriba; **the floor** ~ la planta de arriba

abrasion [ə'breɪʒn] *n* MED abrasión *f*

abrasive [ə'breɪsɪv] *adj* abrasivo

abreast [ə'brest] *adv* **three** ~ en fila de a tres; **to keep** ~ **of sth** mantenerse al corriente de algo

abroad [ə'brɔːd, *Am:* ə'brɑːd] *adv* **to be** ~ estar en el extranjero; **to go** ~ ir al extranjero

abrupt [ə'brʌpt] *adj* (*sudden*) repentino; (*brusque*) brusco

abscess ['æbses] *n* absceso *m*

abscond [əb'skɒnd, *Am:* -'skɑːnd] *vi* fugarse

absence ['æbsəns] *n no pl* ausencia *f*; **on leave of** ~ MIL de permiso

absent ['æbsənt] *adj* ausente

absentee [ˌæbsən'tiː] *n* ausente *mf*

absent-minded [ˌæbsənt'maɪn-dɪd] *adj* despistado, volado *AmL*

absolute ['æbsəluːt] *adj* absoluto

absolutely *adv* totalmente; ~! *inf* ¡claro que sí!; ~ **not!** ¡de ninguna manera!

absolutism ['æbsəluːtɪzəm, *Am:* -səluːt̬-] *n no pl* absolutismo *m*

absolve [əb'zɒlv, *Am:* -'zɑːlv] *vt* absolver

absorb [əb'sɔːb, *Am:* -'sɔːrb] *vt* absorber; **to get ~ed in sth** *fig* estar completamente absorbido por algo

absorbent [əb'sɔːbənt, *Am:* -'sɔːrb-] *adj* absorbente

absorbing *adj* absorbente, apasionante

absorption [əb'sɔːpʃn] *n no pl* absorción *f*

abstain [əb'steɪn] *vi* **to** ~ (**from doing sth**) abstenerse (de hacer algo)

abstinence ['æbstɪnəns] *n no pl* abstinencia *f*

abstract ['æbstrækt] *adj* abstracto

abstraction [əb'strækʃn] *n* abstracción *f*

absurd [əb'sɜːd, *Am:* -'sɜːrd] *adj* absurdo

absurdity [əb'sɜːdətɪ, *Am:* -'sɜːr-dət̬ɪ] <-ies> *n no pl* absurdo *m*

abundance [ə'bʌndəns] *n no pl* abundancia *f*

abundant [ə'bʌndənt] *adj* abundante

abuse[1] [ə'bjuːs] *n* **1.** *no pl* (*insults*) insultos *mpl*, insultadas *fpl AmL* **2.** *no pl* (*mistreatment*) maltrato *m*; **sexual** ~ abuso sexual

abuse[2] [ə'bjuːz] *vt* **1.** (*insult*) insultar **2.** (*mistreat*) maltratar; (*sexually*) abusar de

abusive [ə'bjuːsɪv] *adj* insultante

abysmal [ə'bɪzməl] *adj* pésimo

abyss [ə'bɪs] *n a. fig* abismo *m*

AC [ˌeɪ'siː] *n abbr of* **alternating current** CA *f*

academic [ˌækə'demɪk] *adj* académico; (*theoretical*) teórico

academy [ə'kædəmɪ] <-ies> *n* academia *f*

accede [æk'siːd] *vi* **to** ~ **to sth** acceder a algo

accelerate [ək'seləreɪt] *vt, vi* acelerar

acceleration [əkˌselə'reɪʃn] *n no pl* aceleración *f*

accelerator [ək'seləreɪtəʳ, *Am:* -eɪt̬ɚ] *n* acelerador *m*, chancleta *f* *Ven, Col*

accent ['æksənt, *Am:* -sent] *n* acento *m*

accentuate [ək'sentʃʊeɪt] *vt* acentuar

accept [ək'sept] *vt, vi* aceptar

acceptable *adj* aceptable

acceptance [ək'septəns] *n no pl* aceptación *f*

access ['ækses] *n no pl* entrada *f*, aproches *mpl AmL*; *a.* INFOR acceso *m*; **to gain** ~ **to sth** acceder a algo

accessibility [ækˌsesə'bɪlətɪ, *Am:* -ət̬ɪ] *n no pl* accesibilidad *f*

accessible [ək'sesəbl] *adj* accesible

accession [æk'seʃn] *n no pl* ascenso

m

accessory [ək'sesərɪ] <-ies> *n* accesorio *m*

accident ['æksɪdənt] *n* accidente *m*; **by** ~ (*accidentally*) sin querer; (*by chance*) por casualidad

accidental [ˌæksɪ'dentl, *Am:* -ţl] *adj* accidental, fortuito

acclaim [ə'kleɪm] *vt* aclamar

accommodate [ə'kɒmədeɪt, *Am:* -'kɑː-] *vt* alojar; (*satisfy*) complacer

accommodating [ə'kɒmədeɪtɪŋ, *Am:* ə'kɑːmədeɪţɪŋ] *adj* servicial

accommodation [əˌkɒmə'deɪʃn, *Am:* -kɑː-] *n* Aus, Brit, **accommodations** *npl* Am alojamiento *m*

accompaniment [ə'kʌmpənɪmənt] *n* acompañamiento *m*

accompany [ə'kʌmpənɪ] <-ie-> *vt* acompañar

accomplice [ə'kʌmplɪs, *Am:* -'kɑːm-] *n* cómplice *mf*

accomplish [ə'kʌmplɪʃ, *Am:* -'kɑːm-] *vt* efectuar

accomplished [ə'kʌmplɪʃt, *Am:* -'kɑːm-] *adj* consumado

accomplishment *n* 1. (*achievement*) logro *m* 2. (*skill*) talento *m*

accord [ə'kɔːd, *Am:* -'kɔːrd] I. *n* acuerdo *m* II. *vt form* conceder

accordance [ə'kɔːdəns, *Am:* -'kɔːrd-] *prep* **in** ~ **with** conforme a

accordingly *adv* (*therefore*) por consiguiente

according to [ə'kɔːdɪŋ tʊ, *Am:* ə'kɔːrdɪŋ tə] *prep* según; ~ **the law** con arreglo a la ley

accordion [ə'kɔːdɪən, *Am:*-'kɔːrd-] *n* acordeón *m*, filarmónica *f Méx*

accost [ə'kɒst, *Am:* -'kɑːst] *vt form* abordar

account [ə'kaʊnt] *n* 1. (*with bank*) cuenta *f* 2. *pl* (*financial records*) cuentas *fpl* 3. (*description*) relato *m*; **by all ~s** a decir de todos; **to take sth into** ~ tomar [o tener] algo en cuenta

◆ **account for** *vt* (*explain*) explicar

accountability [əˌkaʊntə'bɪlɪtɪ, *Am:* -kaʊntə'bɪləţɪ] *n no pl* responsabilidad *f*

accountable [ə'kaʊntəbl, *Am:* -ţə-] *adj* responsable

accountancy [ə'kaʊntənsɪ, *Am:* -'kaʊntnsɪ] *n no pl* contabilidad *f*

accountant [ə'kaʊntənt] *n* contable *mf*, contador(a) *m(f) And*

accrue [ə'kruː] *vi* **to** ~ **to sb** corresponder a alguien; **to** ~ **from** proceder de

accumulate [ə'kjuːmjʊleɪt] I. *vt* acumular II. *vi* acumularse

accumulation [əˌkjuːmjʊ'leɪʃn] *n* acumulación *f*

accuracy ['ækjərəsɪ, *Am:* -jəˈəsɪ] *n no pl* exactitud *f*

accurate ['ækjərət, *Am:* -jəˈət] *adj* 1. (*on target*) certero 2. (*correct*) preciso, exacto

accusation [ˌækjuː'zeɪʃn] *n* acusación *f*

accusative [ə'kjuːzətɪv, *Am:* -ţɪv] *adj* acusativo

accuse [ə'kjuːz] *vt* acusar

accused [ə'kjuːzd] *n* **the** ~ el acusado, la acusada

accustom [ə'kʌstəm] *vt* acostumbrar

accustomed [ə'kʌstəmd] *adj* **to be** ~ **to doing sth** estar acostumbrado a hacer algo

ace [eɪs] *n* as *m*; **to come within an** ~ **of doing sth** estar a punto de hacer algo

ache [eɪk] I. *n* dolor *m* II. *vi* doler

achieve [ə'tʃiːv] *vt* alcanzar; (*objective, victory*) lograr, conseguir

achievement *n* logro *m*

acid ['æsɪd] *n* ácido *m*

acidic [ə'sɪdɪk] *adj* ácido

acknowledge [ək'nɒlɪdʒ, *Am:* -'nɑːlɪdʒ] *vt* 1. (*admit*) admitir 2. (*recognize*) reconocer

acknowledg(e)ment *n no pl* 1. (*admission*) admisión *f* 2. (*recognition*) reconocimiento *m*

acne ['æknɪ] *n no pl* acné *m*

acorn ['eɪkɔːn, *Am:* -kɔrn] *n* bellota *f*

acoustic [ə'kuːstɪk] *adj* acústico

acoustic guitar *n* guitarra *f* acústica

acquaint [ə'kweɪnt] *vt* **to be/become** ~ed **with sb** conocer a alguien

acquaintance [əˈkweɪntəns] n conocido, -a m, f; **to make sb's ~** conocer a alguien

acquiesce [ˌækwɪˈes] vi form **to ~ in sth** estar conforme con algo

acquiescence [ˌækwɪˈesns] n no pl, form conformidad f

acquire [əˈkwaɪəʳ, Am: -ˈkwaɪəʳ] vt adquirir

acquisition [ˌækwɪˈzɪʃn] n adquisición f

acquit [əˈkwɪt] <-tt-> vt **1.** LAW absolver **2. to ~ oneself well** salir bien parado

acquittal [əˈkwɪtl, Am: -ˈkwɪt̬-] n no pl absolución f

acre [ˈeɪkəʳ, Am: ˈeɪkəʳ] n acre m

acreage [ˈeɪkrədʒ] n no pl superficie f (en acres)

acrimonious [ˌækrɪˈməʊnɪəs, Am: -ˈmoʊnɪ-] adj reñido

acrobat [ˈækrəbæt] n acróbata mf

across [əˈkrɒs, Am: əˈkrɑːs] I. prep **1.** (on other side of) al otro lado de; **just ~ the street** justo al otro lado de la calle; **~ from** enfrente de **2.** (from one side to other) a través de; **to walk ~ the bridge** cruzar el puente andando; **to go ~ the sea to France** ir a Francia cruzando el mar II. adv de un lado a otro; **to run/swim ~** cruzar corriendo/a nado; **to be 2m ~** tener 2 m de ancho

act [ækt] I. n **1.** (action) acto m; **to catch sb in the ~** coger a alguien con las manos en la masa **2.** (performance) número m; **to get one's ~ together** fig arreglárselas **3.** (pretence) fingimiento m **4.** THEAT acto m **5.** LAW ley f II. vi **1.** (take action) actuar; **to ~ for sb** representar a alguien **2.** (take effect) dar resultados **3.** THEAT actuar

♦**act on** vt obrar de acuerdo con

♦**act out** vt representar

♦**act up** vi inf hacer de las suyas

acting [ˈæktɪŋ] I. adj en funciones II. n no pl THEAT arte m dramático

action [ˈækʃn] n **1.** no pl (activeness) acción f; **to be out of ~** (person) estar inactivo; (machine) no

funcionar; **to take ~** tomar medidas; **~s speak louder than words** prov hechos son amores y no buenas razones **2.** LAW demanda f

activate [ˈæktɪveɪt] vt activar

active [ˈæktɪv] adj activo, enérgico; **to be ~ in sth** participar en algo

activist [ˈæktɪvɪst] n POL activista mf

activity [ækˈtɪvəti, Am: -ət̬i] <-ies> n actividad f

actor [ˈæktəʳ, Am: -təʳ] n actor m

actress [ˈæktrɪs] n actriz f

actual [ˈæktʃʊəl] adj verdadero

actually [ˈæktʃʊlɪ] adv en realidad; **~, I saw her yesterday** pues la vi ayer

acupuncture [ˈækjʊpʌŋktʃəʳ, Am: -tʃəʳ] n no pl acupuntura f

acute [əˈkjuːt] adj agudo

ad [æd] n inf abbr of **advertisement** anuncio m

AD [ˌeɪˈdiː] abbr of **anno Domini** d. (de) C.

Adam [ˈædəm] n Adán m

adamant [ˈædəmənt] adj firme

adapt [əˈdæpt] I. vt adaptar II. vi adaptarse

adaptable adj adaptable

adaptation [ˌædæpˈteɪʃn] n no pl adaptación f

adaptor [əˈdæptəʳ, Am: əˈdæptəʳ] n ELEC adaptador m

add [æd] vt añadir, agregar AmL; MAT sumar

♦**add up** I. vi **to ~ to ...** ascender a... II. vt sumar

adder [ˈædəʳ, Am: ˈædəʳ] n víbora f

addict [ˈædɪkt] n adicto, -a m, f

addicted [əˈdɪktɪd] adj adicto

addiction [əˈdɪkʃən] n no pl adicción f

addictive [əˈdɪktɪv] adj adictivo

addition [əˈdɪʃn] n **1.** no pl (act of adding) adición f; **in ~** además **2.** (added thing) añadido m, añadidura f

additional [əˈdɪʃənl] adj adicional

additionally [əˈdɪʃənəlɪ] adv por añadidura

additive [ˈædɪtɪv, Am: -ət̬ɪv] n aditivo m

address [əˈdres, Am: ˈædres] I. n

1. *a.* INFOR dirección *f* **2.** (*speech*) discurso *m* **II.** *vt* (*person*) dirigirse a

addressee [ˌædreˈsiː] *n* destinatario, -a *m, f*

adept [ˈædept, *Am:* əˈdept] *adj* experto

adequacy [ˈædɪkwəsɪ] *n no pl* suficiencia *f*

adequate [ˈædɪkwət] *adj* (*sufficient*) suficiente; (*good enough*) adecuado

adhere [ədˈhɪəʳ, *Am:* -ˈhɪr] *vi* **to ~ to** (*rule*) observar; (*belief*) aferrarse a

adherence [ədˈhɪərəns, *Am:* -ˈhɪrns] *n no pl* observancia *f*; (*to belief*) adhesión *f*

adherent [ədˈhɪərənt] *n form* partidario, -a *m, f*

adhesive [ədˈhiːsɪv] *n no pl* adhesivo *m*

adjacent [əˈdʒeɪsnt] *adj* contiguo

adjective [ˈædʒɪktɪv] *n* adjetivo *m*

adjoin [əˈdʒɔɪn] *vt* lindar con

adjoining *adj* colindante

adjourn [əˈdʒɜːn, *Am:* -ˈdʒɜːrn] **I.** *vt* aplazar **II.** *vi* aplazarse; **to ~ to another room** trasladarse a otra habitación

adjust [əˈdʒʌst] **I.** *vt* ajustar **II.** *vi* **to ~ to sth** adaptarse a algo

adjustment *n* ajuste *m*

adjutant [ˈædʒʊtənt] *n* ayudante *mf*

admin [ˈædmɪn] *n abbr of* **administration** admón.

administer [ədˈmɪnɪstəʳ, *Am:* -stəʳ] *vt* administrar

administration [ədˌmɪnɪˈstreɪʃn] *n* **1.** *no pl* (*organization*) administración *f* **2.** POL gobierno *m*

administrative [ədˈmɪnɪstrətɪv] *adj* administrativo

administrator [ədˈmɪnɪstreɪtəʳ, *Am:* -təʳ] *n* administrador(a) *m(f)*

admirable [ˈædmərəbl] *adj* admirable

admiral [ˈædmərəl] *n* almirante *m*

Admiralty [ˈædmərəltɪ, *Am:* -t̬ɪ] *n no pl, Brit* Almirantazgo *m*

admiration [ˌædməˈreɪʃn] *n no pl* admiración *f*

admire [ədˈmaɪəʳ, *Am:* ədˈmaɪəʳ]

vt admirar

admirer [ədˈmaɪərəʳ, *Am:* -əʳ] *n* admirador(a) *m(f)*

admission [ədˈmɪʃn] *n* **1.** *no pl* (*entry: to building*) admisión *f*; (*to organization*) ingreso *m* **2.** (*fee*) entrada *f* **3.** (*acknowledgement*) confesión *f*; **by his own ~, ...** por confesión propia...

admit [ədˈmɪt] <-tt-> **I.** *vt* dejar entrar; (*permit*) admitir; (*acknowledge*) reconocer **II.** *vi* **to ~ to sth** confesarse culpable de algo

admittedly [ədˈmɪtɪdlɪ, *Am:* -ˈmɪt̬ɪdlɪ] *adv* **~, ...** es cierto que...

admonish [ədˈmɒnɪʃ, *Am:* -ˈmɑː-nɪʃ] *vt* amonestar

admonition [ˌædməˈnɪʃn] *n* amonestación *f*

ado [əˈduː] *n no pl* **without further ~** sin más preámbulos

adolescence [ˌædəˈlesns] *n no pl* adolescencia *f*

adolescent [ˌædəˈlesnt] *n* adolescente *mf*

adopt [əˈdɒpt, *Am:* -ˈdɑːpt] *vt* adoptar

adoption [əˈdɒpʃn, *Am:* -ˈdɑːp-] *n* adopción *f*

adoration [ˌædəˈreɪʃn] *n no pl* adoración *f*

adore [əˈdɔːʳ, *Am:* -ˈdɔːr] *vt* adorar

adorn [əˈdɔːn, *Am:* -ˈdɔːrn] *vt form* adornar

adrenalin(e) [əˈdrenəlɪn] *n no pl* adrenalina *f*

Adriatic [ˌeɪdriˈætɪk] *n* **the ~ (Sea)** el (mar) Adriático

adrift [əˈdrɪft] *adv* a la deriva; **to come** *fig* **~** fallar

adult [ˈædʌlt, *Am:* əˈdʌlt] *n* adulto, -a *m, f*

adult education *n no pl* educación *f* para adultos

adulterate [əˈdʌltəreɪt, *Am:* -t̬ə-reɪt] *vt* adulterar

adultery [əˈdʌltərɪ, *Am:* -t̬əʳɪ] <-ies> *n no pl* adulterio *m*; **to commit ~** cometer adulterio

advance [ədˈvɑːns, *Am:* -ˈvæːns] **I.** *vi* avanzar **II.** *vt* **1.** (*move forward*) avanzar **2.** (*pay in advance*) anticipar

III. *n* **1.** (*movement*) avance *m;* **in ~** de antemano; **unwelcome ~s** *fig* molestias *fpl* **2.** FIN anticipo *m*

advanced [əd'vɑ:nst, *Am:* -'væ:nst] *adj* avanzado

advantage [əd'vɑ:ntɪdʒ, *Am:* -'væ:n̪t̪ɪdʒ] *n* ventaja *f;* **to take ~ of sth** aprovecharse de algo

advantageous [ˌædvən'teɪdʒəs, *Am:* -væn'-] *adj* ventajoso

advent ['ædvənt] *n no pl* **1.** (*coming*) llegada *f* **2.** REL **Advent** Adviento *m*

adventure [əd'ventʃər, *Am:* -tʃɚ] *n* aventura *f*

adventurer *n* aventurero, -a *m, f*

adventurous [əd'ventʃərəs] *adj* aventurero

adverb ['ædvɜ:b, *Am:* -vɜ:rb] *n* adverbio *m*

adversary ['ædvəsərɪ, *Am:* -vɚseri] <-ies> *n* adversario, -a *m, f*

adverse ['ædvɜ:s, *Am:* -vɜ:rs] *adj* adverso

adversity [əd'vɜ:sətɪ, *Am:* -'vɜ:rsət̪ɪ] <-ies> *n* adversidad *f*

advert ['ædvɜ:t, *Am:* -vɜ:rt] *n s.* **advertisement**

advertise ['ædvətaɪz, *Am:* -vɚ-] *vt* anunciar

advertisement [əd'vɜ:tɪsmənt, *Am:* ˌædvər'taɪzmənt] *n* anuncio *m,* aviso *m AmL;* **job ~** oferta *f* de empleo

advertiser ['ædvətaɪzər, *Am:* -vɚtaɪzɚ] *n* anunciante *mf*

advertising ['ædvəˌtaɪzɪŋ, *Am:* -vɚˌtaɪzɪŋ] *n* publicidad *f*

advertising agency <-ies> *n* agencia *f* de publicidad **advertising campaign** *n* campaña *f* publicitaria

advice [əd'vaɪs] *n no pl* consejo *m;* **a piece of ~** un consejo

---

! **advice** con c es un sustantivo y no se usa nunca en plural: "a piece of advice, some advice". **advise** con s es un verbo: "Jane advised him to go to Oxford."

---

advisable [əd'vaɪzəbl] *adj* aconse-

jable

advise [əd'vaɪz] **I.** *vt* aconsejar; **to ~ sb against sth** desaconsejar algo a alguien; **to ~ sb of sth** informar a alguien sobre algo **II.** *vi* **to ~ against sth** desaconsejar algo

adviser [əd'vaɪzər, *Am:* -zɚ] *n,* **advisor** *n* asesor(a) *m(f)*

advisory [əd'vaɪzərɪ] *adj* consultivo

advocate¹ ['ædvəkeɪt] *vt* recomendar

advocate² ['ædvəkət] *n* abogado, -a *m, f* defensor(a)

aegis ['i:dʒɪs] *n no pl* **under the ~ of ...** bajo los auspicios de...

aerial ['eərɪəl, *Am:* 'erɪ-] **I.** *adj* aéreo **II.** *n Brit* antena *f*

aerobics [eə'rəubɪks, *Am:* er'ou-] *n + sing/pl vb* aeróbic *m*

aeronautics [ˌeərə'nɔ:tɪks, *Am:* ˌerə'nɑ:t̪ɪks] *n + sing vb* aeronáutica *f*

aeroplane ['eərəpleɪn, *Am:* 'erə-] *n Aus, Brit* avión *m*

aerosol ['eərəsɒl, *Am:* 'erəsɑ:l] *n* aerosol *m*

aesthetic [i:s'θetɪk(l), *Am:* es'θet̪-] *adj* estético

aesthetics [i:s'θetɪks, *Am:* es'θet̪-] *n + sing vb* estética *f*

afar [ə'fɑ:r, *Am:* -'fɑ:r] *adv form* lejos

affable ['æfəbl] *adj* afable

affair [ə'feər, *Am:* -'fer] *n* **1.** (*matter*) asunto *m* **2.** (*sexual*) aventura *f* amorosa

affect [ə'fekt] *vt* afectar

affected [ə'fektɪd] *adj* afectado

affection [ə'fekʃn] *n* cariño *m*

affectionate [ə'fekʃənət] *adj* afectuoso

affidavit [ˌæfɪ'deɪvɪt] *n* declaración *f* jurada

affiliate [ə'fɪlɪeɪt] *vt* afiliar

affiliation [əˌfɪlɪ'eɪʃn] *n* afiliación *f*

affinity [ə'fɪnətɪ, *Am:* -ət̪ɪ] <-ies> *n* afinidad *f*

affirm [ə'fɜ:m, *Am:* -'fɜ:rm] *vt* afirmar

affirmation [ˌæfə'meɪʃn, *Am:* -ɚ-] *n* afirmación *f*

affirmative [ə'fɜ:mətɪv, *Am:* -'fɜ:rmət̪ɪv] *adj* afirmativo

affix [əˈfɪks] *vt* poner
afflict [əˈflɪkt] *vt* afligir
affliction [əˈflɪkʃn] *n* aflicción *f*
affluence [ˈæfluəns] *n no pl* riqueza *f*
affluent [ˈæfluənt] *adj* rico
afford [əˈfɔːd, *Am:* -ˈfɔːrd] *vt* **1.** (*be able to pay for*) permitirse **2.** (*offer*) **to ~ protection** ofrecer protección
affordable [əˈfɔːdəbl, *Am:* -ˈfɔːr-] *adj* asequible
affront [əˈfrʌnt] **I.** *n* afrenta *f* **II.** *vt* afrentar; **to be ~ed by sth** ofenderse por algo
Afghan [ˈæfgæn] *adj* afgano
Afghanistan [æfˈgænɪstæn, *Am:* -ə-] *n* Afganistán *m*
afield [əˈfiːld] *adv* **far ~** muy lejos
afloat [əˈfləʊt, *Am:* -ˈfloʊt] *adj* a flote
afoot [əˈfʊt] *adj* **there's sth ~** se está tramando algo
aforementioned [əˌfɔːˈmenʃnd, *Am:* -ˌfɔːr-], **aforesaid** [əˌfɔːˈsed, *Am:* -ˈfɔːr-] *adj form* anteriormente mencionado
afraid [əˈfreɪd] *adj* **to be ~** tener miedo; **to be ~ of doing sth** tener miedo de hacer algo; **to be ~ of sb** tener miedo a alguien; **I'm ~ so** lo siento, pero así es
afresh [əˈfreʃ] *adv* de nuevo
Africa [ˈæfrɪkə] *n no pl* África *f*
African [ˈæfrɪkən] *adj* africano
Afro-American [ˌæfrəʊəˈmerɪkən, *Am:* -roʊ-] *adj* afroamericano
after [ˈɑːftər, *Am:* ˈæftər] **I.** *prep* **1.** (*at later time*) después de; **~ two days** al cabo de dos días **2.** (*behind*) detrás de; **to run ~ sb** correr detrás de alguien **3.** (*following*) después de **4.** (*about*) por; **to ask ~ sb** preguntar por alguien **5.** (*despite*) **~ all** después de todo **II.** *adv* después; **soon ~** poco después; **the day ~** el día después **III.** *conj* después de que +*subj*
after-effects *npl* efectos *mpl* secundarios
afterlife [ˈɑːftəlaɪf, *Am:* ˈæftər-] *n no pl* **the ~** el más allá
aftermath [ˈɑːftəmɑːθ, *Am:* ˈæftərmæθ] *n no pl* secuelas *fpl*

afternoon [ˌɑːftəˈnuːn, *Am:* ˌæftər-] *n* tarde *f*; **this ~** esta tarde; **in the ~** por la tarde; **tomorrow ~** mañana por la tarde; **good ~!** ¡buenas tardes!
afterthought [ˈɑːftəθɔːt, *Am:* ˈæftərθɑːt] *n* idea *f* a posteriori
afterward *adv Am*, **afterwards** [ˈɑːftəwədz, *Am:* ˈæftərwərdz] *adv* más tarde
again [əˈgen] *adv* otra vez, de nuevo; **never ~** nunca más; **once ~** otra vez; **yet ~** una vez más; **~ and ~** una y otra vez
against [əˈgenst] *prep* **1.** (*in opposition to*) (en) contra (de) **2.** (*in contact with*) contra
age [eɪdʒ] **I.** *n* **1.** (*of person, object*) edad *f*; **old ~** vejez *f*; **what is your age?** ¿qué edad tienes?; **when I was her ~** cuando tenía su edad; **to be seven years of ~** tener siete años **2.** (*era*) época *f*; **in this day and ~** en estos tiempos; **I haven't seen you in ~s!** ¡hace siglos que no te veo! **II.** *vi, vt* envejecer
aged [eɪdʒd] *adj* **children ~ 8 to 12** niños de entre 8 y 12 años de edad
age group *n* grupo *m* de edad
agency [ˈeɪdʒənsɪ] <-ies> *n* agencia *f*
agenda [əˈdʒendə] *n* orden *m* del día
agent [ˈeɪdʒənt] *n* agente *mf*
aggravate [ˈægrəveɪt] *vt* agravar
aggravation [ˌægrəˈveɪʃn] *n no pl, inf* fastidio *m*
aggregate [ˈægrɪgɪt] *n* suma *f* total
aggression [əˈgreʃn] *n no pl* agresión *f*
aggressive [əˈgresɪv] *adj* agresivo
aggressor [əˈgresər, *Am:* -ər] *n* agresor(a) *m(f)*
aggrieved [əˈgriːvd] *adj* ofendido
aghast [əˈgɑːst, *Am:* -ˈgæst] *adj* horrorizado
agile [ˈædʒaɪl, *Am:* ˈædʒl] *adj* ágil
agility [əˈdʒɪlətɪ, *Am:* -ţɪ] *n no pl* agilidad *f*
agitate [ˈædʒɪteɪt] **I.** *vt* **1.** (*make nervous*) inquietar; **to become ~d** inquietarse, ponerse inquieto

2. (*shake*) agitar **II.** *vi* **to ~ for sth** hacer campaña en favor de algo

agitation [,ædʒɪ'teɪʃn] *n no pl* agitación *f*

AGM [,eɪdʒiː'em] *n abbr of* **annual general meeting** junta *f* general anual

ago [ə'gəʊ, *Am:* -'goʊ] *adv* **a year ~** hace un año; **long ~** hace mucho tiempo

agonize ['ægənaɪz] *vi* atormentarse

agonizing ['ægənaɪzɪŋ] *adj* (*pain*) atroz; (*delay*) angustiante

agony ['ægənɪ] <-ies> *n* agonía *f;* **to be in ~** sufrir fuertes dolores

agree [ə'griː] **I.** *vi* **1.** (*hold same opinion*) estar de acuerdo; **to ~ on sth** estar de acuerdo en algo; **to ~ to do sth** consentir en hacer algo **2.** (*be good for*) **to ~ with sb** sentar bien a alguien **3.** (*match up*) concordar **II.** *vt* **1.** (*concur*) acordar **2.** *Brit* (*accept*) acceder a

agreeable *adj* **1.** *form* (*acceptable*) aceptable; **to be ~** (**to sth**) estar conforme (con algo) **2.** (*pleasant*) agradable

agreement *n* acuerdo *m;* **to be in ~ with sb** estar de acuerdo con alguien; **to reach ~** llegar a un acuerdo

agricultural [,ægrɪ'kʌltʃərəl] *adj* agrícola

agriculture ['ægrɪkʌltʃəʳ, *Am:* -tʃəʳ] *n no pl* agricultura *f*

agrotourism [ægrəʊ'tʊərɪzəm, *Am:* ægroʊ'tʊrɪ-] *n no pl* agroturismo

ah [ɑː] *interj* ah

aha [ɑː'hɑː] *interj* ajá

ahead [ə'hed] *adv* delante; **to go ~** adelantarse; **to look ~** anticiparse

ahead of *prep* **1.** (*in front of*) delante de; **to walk ~ sb** caminar delante de alguien; **to be ~ one's time** anticiparse a su época **2.** (*before*) antes de

AI [,eɪ'aɪ] *n abbr of* **artificial intelligence** IA

aid [eɪd] *n no pl* ayuda *f;* **in ~ of sth** en beneficio de algo; **to come to the ~ of sb** ir en ayuda de alguien; **what's all this in ~ of?** *Brit, inf* ¿a

qué viene todo eso?

aide [eɪd] *n* asistente *mf*

AIDS [eɪdz] *n no pl abbr of* **Acquired Immune Deficiency Syndrome** sida *m*

ailing ['eɪlɪŋ] *adj* enfermo

ailment ['eɪlmənt] *n* dolencia *f*

aim [eɪm] **I.** *vi* **to ~ at sth** apuntar a algo; **to ~ to do sth** tener como objetivo hacer algo **II.** *vt* apuntar; **to ~ sth at sb** apuntar algo hacia alguien **III.** *n* **1.** *no pl* (*ability*) puntería *f;* **to take ~** apuntar **2.** (*goal*) objetivo *m*, meta *f*

ain't [eɪnt] *inf s.* **am not, are not, is not**

air [eəʳ, *Am:* er] **I.** *n* **1.** *a.* MUS aire *m;* **by ~** AVIAT por avión; **to be on (the) ~** estar en antena [*o* en el aire]; **to be up in the ~** *fig* estar en el aire **2.** *no pl* (*aura, quality*) aire *m* **II.** *vt* **1.** TV, RADIO emitir **2.** (*expose to air*) airear

air bag *n* airbag *m* **air conditioning** *n no pl* aire *m* acondicionado

aircraft ['eəkrɑːft, *Am:* 'erkræft] *n* avión *m* **aircraft carrier** *n* porta(a)viones *m inv*

airfield *n* aeródromo *m* **air force** *n* fuerza *f* aérea **air gun** *n* pistola *f* de aire comprimido

airline *n* línea *f* aérea, aerolínea *f AmL* **airliner** *n* avión *m* de pasajeros **airmail** *n no pl* correo *m* aéreo **airplane** *n Am* avión *m* **airport** *n* aeropuerto *m* **air raid** *n* ataque *m* aéreo **airstrip** *n* pista *f* de aterrizaje

airtight ['eətaɪt, *Am:* 'er-] *adj* hermético

air traffic *n no pl* tráfico *m* aéreo

airway ['eəweɪ, *Am:* 'er-] *n* ANAT vía *f* respiratoria

airy ['eərɪ, *Am:* 'er-] *adj* ARCHIT espacioso

aisle [aɪl] *n* pasillo *m;* (*in church*) nave *f* lateral

ajar [ə'dʒɑːʳ, *Am:* -'dʒɑːr] *adj* entreabierto

akin [ə'kɪn] *adj* ~ **to** parecido a

alarm [ə'lɑːm, *Am:* -'lɑːrm] **I.** *n* alarma *f;* **to cause sb ~** alarmar a alguien; **to give the ~** dar la (voz de) alarma *m* **II.** *vt* alarmar

alarm clock *n* reloj *m* despertador
alarming *adj* alarmante
Albania [æl'beɪnɪə] *n* Albania *f*
Albanian *adj* albanés
albatross ['ælbətrɒs, *Am:* -tra:s] *n* albatros *m*
albeit [ɔːl'biːɪt] *conj* aunque
albino [æl'biːnəʊ, *Am:* -'baɪnoʊ] *adj* albino
album ['ælbəm] *n* álbum *m*

[?] **Alcatraz** es una antigua cárcel situada en la Isla de Alcatraz, que a su vez se encuentra en la bahía de San Francisco. Dado que la isla se erige sobre una base de cinco hectáreas de rocosos acantilados, la cárcel recibe el sobrenombre de '**La Roca**'. Allí eran confinados presos considerados especialmente peligrosos.

alcohol ['ælkəhɒl, *Am:* -ha:l] *n no pl* alcohol *m*
alcoholic [ˌælkə'hɒlɪk, *Am:* -'ha:lɪk] *n* alcohólico, -a *m, f*
alcoholism *n no pl* alcoholismo *m*
ale [eɪl] *n* cerveza *f*
alert [ə'lɜːt, *Am:* -'lɜːrt] I. *adj* despierto II. *n* **to be on the** ~ estar alerta III. *vt* alertar
A-level ['eɪlevəl] *n Brit abbr of* **Advanced-level** ≈ bachillerato *m*

[?] El **A-Level** es un tipo de examen final que realizan los alumnos al finalizar la enseñanza secundaria. La mayoría de los alumnos elige tres asignaturas de examen, pero también es posible examinarse de una sola asignatura. Aprobar los **A-Levels** le da al alumno la posibilidad de acceder a los estudios universitarios.

algebra ['ældʒɪbrə] *n no pl* álgebra *f*
Algeria [æl'dʒɪərɪə, *Am:* -'dʒɪ-] *n* Argelia *f*

Algerian *adj* argelino
Algiers [æl'dʒɪəz, *Am:* -'dʒɪrz] *n* Argel *m*
alias ['eɪlɪəs] I. *n* alias *m inv* II. *conj* alias
alibi ['ælɪbaɪ] *n* coartada *f*
alien ['eɪlɪən] I. *adj* extranjero II. *n form* (*foreigner*) extranjero, -a *m, f*
alienate ['eɪlɪəneɪt] *vt* enajenar
alienation [ˌeɪlɪə'neɪʃn] *n no pl* enajenación *f*
alight¹ [ə'laɪt] *adj* (*on fire*) **to be** ~ estar ardiendo; **to set sth** ~ prender fuego a algo; **to set sb's imagination** ~ despertar la imaginación a alguien
alight² [ə'laɪt] *vi form* apearse
align [ə'laɪn] *vt* alinear; **to** ~ **oneself with sb** *fig* alinearse con alguien
alignment *n no pl* alineación *f*
alike [ə'laɪk] *adj* **to look** ~ parecerse
alive [ə'laɪv] *adj* **1.** (*not dead*) vivo **2.** (*active*) activo
all [ɔːl] I. *adj* todo, toda; ~ **the butter** toda la mantequilla; ~ **the wine** todo el vino; ~ **my sisters** todas mis hermanas; ~ **my brother** todos mis hermanos II. *pron* **1.** (*everybody*) todos, todas **2.** (*everything*) todo; ~ **but...** todo menos...; **most of** ~ sobre todo; **for** ~ **I know** que yo sepa; ~ **I want is ...** lo único que quiero es... **3.** SPORTS **two** ~ dos a dos III. *adv* totalmente
Allah ['ælə] *n* Alá *m*
all-around *adj Am s.* **all-round**
allay ['əleɪ] *vt* calmar
allegation [ˌælɪ'geɪʃn] *n* acusación *f*
allege [ə'ledʒ] *vt* afirmar
alleged [ə'ledʒd] *adj* supuesto
allegedly [ə'ledʒɪdlɪ] *adv* (*según*) se dice
allegiance [ə'liːdʒəns] *n no pl* lealtad *f*
allegoric(al) [ˌælɪ'gɒrɪk(l), *Am:* -'gɔːr-] *adj* alegórico
allegory ['ælɪgərɪ, *Am:* -gɔːrɪ] <-ies> *n* alegoría *f*
allergic [ə'lɜːdʒɪk, *Am:* -'lɜːr-] *adj* alérgico
allergy ['ælədʒɪ, *Am:* -ɚ-] <-ies> *n*

alergia *f*

alleviate [ə'li:vɪeɪt] *vt* aliviar

alley ['ælɪ] *n* callejón *m*

alliance [ə'laɪəns] *n* alianza *f;* **to be in ~ with sb** estar aliado con alguien

allied ['ælaɪd] *adj* aliado; **~ with** unido a

alligator ['ælɪgeɪtə', *Am:* -t̬ə-] *n* caimán *m*

allocate ['æləkeɪt] *vt* asignar

allocation [ˌælə'keɪʃn] *n no pl*
1. (*assignment*) asignación *f*
2. (*share*) ración *f*

allotment *n Brit* ≈ huerto *m* particular

all-out *adj* total

allow [ə'laʊ] *vt* **1.** (*permit*) permitir; **to ~ sb to do sth** dejar a alguien hacer algo; **smoking is not ~ed** se prohíbe fumar **2.** (*allocate*) asignar **3.** (*admit*) **to ~ that ...** reconocer que...

◆ **allow for** *vt* tener en cuenta

allowance [ə'laʊəns] *n* **1.** (*permitted amount*) cantidad *f* permitida **2.** (*excuse*) **to make ~s for sb** ser indulgente con alguien

alloy ['ælɔɪ] *n* aleación *f*

all-purpose *adj* universal

all right *adv* bien; **that's ~** (*after thanks*) de nada; (*after excuse*) no pasa nada; **to be ~** estar bien (de salud)

all-round *adj* completo

all-time *adj* histórico

allude [ə'lu:d] *vi* **to ~ to sth** aludir a algo

allure [ə'lʊə', *Am:* -'lʊr] *n no pl* encanto *m*

allusion [ə'lu:ʒn] *n* alusión *f*

ally ['ælaɪ] **I.** <-ies> *n* aliado, -a *m, f* **II.** <-ie-> *vt* **to ~ oneself with sb** aliarse con alguien

almanac ['ɔ:lmənæk] *n* almanaque *m*

almighty [ɔ:l'maɪtɪ, *Am:* -t̬ɪ] **I.** *adj inf* todopoderoso **II.** *n* **the Almighty** el Todopoderoso

almond ['ɑ:mənd] *n* (*nut*) almendra *f;* (*tree*) almendro *m*

almost ['ɔ:lməʊst, *Am:* -moʊst] *adv* casi; **we're ~ there** casi hemos llegado

alone [ə'ləʊn, *Am:* -'loʊn] **I.** *adj* solo, -a; **to do sth ~** hacer algo solo; **to leave sb ~** dejar a alguien en paz; **to leave sth ~** dejar algo como está; **let ~ ...** mucho menos... **II.** *adv* solamente, sólo

along [ə'lɒŋ, *Am:* -'lɑ:ŋ] **I.** *prep* por; **~ the road** por la carretera; **~ the river** a lo largo del río **II.** *adv* **all ~** todo el tiempo; **to bring sb ~** traer a alguien

alongside [ˌə.lɒŋ'saɪd, *Am:* ə'lɑ:ŋ-saɪd] **I.** *prep* junto a **II.** *adv* al lado

aloof [ə'lu:f] *adj* **to keep ~ from sth** mantenerse alejado de algo

aloud [ə'laʊd] *adv* en voz alta

alpha ['ælfə] *n* alfa *f*

alphabet ['ælfəbet] *n* alfabeto *m*

alphabetical [ˌælfə'betɪkl, *Am:* -'bet̬-] *adj* alfabético

alpine ['ælpaɪn] *adj* alpino

Alps [ælps] *npl* **the ~** los Alpes

already [ɔ:l'redɪ] *adv* ya

alright [ɔl'raɪt] *adv s.* **all right**

also ['ɔ:lsəʊ, *Am:* 'ɔ:lsoʊ] *adv* también

altar ['ɔ:ltə', *Am:* -t̬ə-] *n* altar *m*

alter ['ɔ:ltə', *Am:* -t̬ə-] *vt* cambiar

alteration [ˌɔ:ltə'reɪʃn, *Am:* -t̬ə-] *n* modificación *f;* (*in house*) reforma *f*

alternate¹ ['ɔ:ltəneɪt, *Am:* 'ɔ:ltə-] *vi, vt* alternar

alternate² [ɔ:l't3:nət, *Am:* -'t̬3:r-] *adj* alterno

alternating ['ɔ:ltəneɪtɪŋ, *Am:* -t̬ɪŋ] *adj* alterno

alternative [ɔ:l't3:nətɪv, *Am:* -'t3:r-nət̬ɪv] **I.** *n* alternativa *f* **II.** *adj* alternativo

alternatively *adv* si no

although [ɔ:l'ðəʊ, *Am:* -'ðoʊ] *conj* aunque

altitude ['æltɪtju:d, *Am:* -tətu:d] *n* altitud *f*

alto ['æltəʊ, *Am:* -toʊ] *n* (*woman*) contralto *f;* (*man*) contralto *m*

altogether [ˌɔ:ltə'geðə', *Am:* -ə-] *adv* **1.** (*completely*) totalmente **2.** (*in total*) en total

altruism ['æltru:ɪzəm] *n no pl* altruismo *m*

aluminium [ˌæljʊ'mɪnɪəm] *n no pl* aluminio *m*

aluminium foil *n* papel *m* de plata

aluminum [ə'lu:mɪnəm] *n Am s.* **aluminium**

always ['ɔ:lweɪz] *adv* siempre

am [əm, *stressed:* æm] *vi 1st pers sing of* **be**

a.m. [ˌeɪ'em] *abbr of* **ante meridiem** a.m.

amalgamate [ə'mælgəmeɪt] *vi* fusionarse

amass [ə'mæs] *vt* amasar

amateur ['æmətər, *Am:* -tʃər] *n* aficionado, -a *m, f*

amaze [ə'meɪz] *vt* asombrar

amazement *n no pl* asombro *m*

amazing *adj* asombroso, sorpresivo *AmL*

Amazon ['æməzən, *Am:* -zɑ:n] *n* **the** ~ el Amazonas

ambassador [æm'bæsədər, *Am:* -dər] *n* embajador(a) *m(f)*

amber ['æmbər, *Am:* -bər] I. *n* ámbar *m* II. *adj* ambarino

ambiguity [ˌæmbɪ'gju:ətɪ, *Am:* -bə'gju:əʈɪ] <-ies> *n* ambigüedad *f*

ambiguous [æm'bɪgjʊəs] *adj* ambiguo

ambition [æm'bɪʃn] *n* ambición *f*

ambitious [æm'bɪʃəs] *adj* ambicioso

amble ['æmbl] *vi* andar tranquilamente

ambulance ['æmbjʊləns] *n* ambulancia *f*

ambush ['æmbʊʃ] I. *vt* **to** ~ **sb** tender una emboscada a alguien II. *n* <-es> emboscada *f*

ameba [ə'mi:bə] <-s *o* -bae> *n Am s.* **amoeba**

amen [ɑ:'men, *Am:* eɪ'men] *interj* amén

amenable [ə'mi:nəbl] *adj* receptivo; **to be ~ to sth** mostrarse receptivo a (aceptar) algo

amend [ə'mend] *vt* (*text*) enmendar

amendment *n* enmienda *f*

amends *npl* **to make ~ for sth** reparar algo

amenities [ə'mi:nətɪz, *Am:* -'menəʈɪz] *npl* comodidades *fpl;* (**public**) ~ instalaciones públicas

America [ə'merɪkə] *n* América *f* (del Norte)

American [ə'merɪkən] *adj* (*from USA*) estadounidense; (*from American continent*) americano

amiable ['eɪmɪəbl] *adj* amable

amicable ['æmɪkəbl] *adj* amistoso

amid(st) [ə'mɪd(st)] *prep* en medio de

amiss [ə'mɪs] *adv* **there's something** ~ algo va mal; **to take sth** ~ tomar algo a mal

ammonia [ə'məʊnɪə, *Am:* -'moʊnjə] *n no pl* amoniaco *m*

ammunition [ˌæmjʊ'nɪʃn, *Am:* -jə-] *n no pl* municiones *fpl*

amnesia [æm'ni:zɪə, *Am:* -ʒə] *n no pl* amnesia *f*

amnesty ['æmnəstɪ] <-ies> *n* amnistía *f*

amoeba [ə'mi:bə] <-bas *o* -bae> *n* ameba *f*

among(st) [ə'mʌŋ(st)] *prep* entre

amorous ['æmərəs] *adj* amoroso

amount [ə'maʊnt] I. *n* cantidad *f;* (*of money*) suma *f* II. *vi* **to** ~ **to sth** ascender a algo

amphibian [æm'fɪbɪən] *n* anfibio *m*

ample ['æmpl] *adj* **1.** (*plentiful*) abundante **2.** (*large*) amplio

amplifier ['æmplɪfaɪər, *Am:* -ər] *n* amplificador *m*

amplify ['æmplɪfaɪ] <-ie-> *vt* amplificar

amputate ['æmpjʊteɪt] *vt* amputar

amuse [ə'mju:z] *vt* **1.** (*entertain*) entretener; **to** ~ **oneself** entretenerse **2.** (*cause laughter*) divertir

amusement [ə'mju:zmənt] *n* **1.** *no pl* (*entertainment*) entretenimiento *m*, entretención *f AmL* **2.** (*mirth*) diversión *f*

amusement arcade *n Brit* sala *f* de juegos recreativos

amusing *adj* divertido

an [ən, *stressed:* æn] *indef art before vowel s.* **a**

⚠ **an** se utiliza delante de palabras que empiezan con las vocales a, e, i, o, u: "an apple, an egg, an ice-cream, an oyster, an umbrella" y también delante de h cuando la h no suena: "an hour, an honest man." Pero si se pronuncia una u como [ju], entonces se utiliza **a**: "a unit, a university."

anachronistic [əˌnækrəˈnɪstɪk] *adj* anacrónico
anaesthetic [ˌænɪsˈθetɪk] *n* anestésico *m*
analogous [əˈnæləgəs] *adj* análogo
analogue [ˈænəlɒg] *n Brit* equivalente *m*
analogy [əˈnælədʒɪ] <-ies> *n* analogía *f*
analyse [ˈænəlaɪz] *vt Aus, Brit* analizar
analysis [əˈnæləsɪs] <-ses> *n* análisis *m inv*
analyst [ˈænəlɪst] *n* **1.** (*analyzer*) analista *mf* **2.** PSYCH psicoanalista *mf*
analytic(al) [ˌænəˈlɪtɪk(l), *Am:* -ˈlɪt̬-] *adj* analítico
analyze [ˈænəlaɪz] *vt Am s.* **analyse**
anarchism [ˈænəkɪzəm, *Am:* -ɚ-] *n no pl* anarquismo *m*
anarchist [ˈænəkɪst, *Am:* -ɚ-] *n* anarquista *mf*
anarchy [ˈænəkɪ, *Am:* -ɚ-] *n no pl* anarquía *f*
anatomy [əˈnætəmɪ, *Am:* -ˈnæt̬-] <-ies> *n no pl* anatomía *f*
ancestor [ˈænsestəʳ, *Am:* -sestɚ] *n* antepasado, -a *m, f*
ancestral [ænˈsestrəl] *adj* ancestral
ancestry [ˈænsestrɪ] <-ies> *n* ascendencia *f*
anchor [ˈæŋkəʳ, *Am:* -kɚ] **I.** *n* NAUT ancla *f*, sacho *m Chile*; **to drop/weigh ~** echar/levar anclas **II.** *vt* (*secure*) sujetar
anchorage [ˈæŋkərɪdʒ] *n* fondeadero *m*
anchovy [ˈæntʃəvɪ, *Am:* -tʃoʊ-] <-ies> *n* anchoa *f*

ancient [ˈeɪnʃənt] *adj* antiguo
and [ən, ənd, *stressed:* ænd] *conj* y; (*before 'i' or 'hi'*) e; **black ~ white** blanco y negro; **parents ~ children** padres e hijos; **2 ~ 3 is 5** 2 más 3 son 5; **more ~ more** cada vez más; **I tried ~ tried** lo intenté una y otra vez; **he cried ~ cried** lloraba sin parar
Andalusia [ˌændəˈluːsɪə, *Am:* -ˈluːʒə] *n* Andalucía *f*
Andalusian *adj* andaluz
Andean [ˈændɪən] *adj* andino
Andes [ˈændiːz] *npl* Andes *mpl*
Andorra [ænˈdɔːrə] *n* Andorra *f*
anecdotal [ˌænɪkˈdəʊtl, *Am:* -ˈdoʊt̬l] *adj* anecdótico
anecdote [ˈænɪkdəʊt, *Am:* -doʊt] *n* anécdota *f*
anesthetic [ˌænɪsˈθetɪk, *Am:* -ˈθet̬ɪk] *n Am s.* **anaesthetic**
anew [əˈnjuː, *Am:* -ˈnuː] *adv* de nuevo
angel [ˈeɪndʒl] *n* ángel *m*
anger [ˈæŋgəʳ, *Am:* -gɚ] **I.** *n no pl* enfado *m*, enojo *m AmL* **II.** *vt* enfadar, enojar *AmL*
angle¹ [ˈæŋgl] *n* **1.** *a.* MAT ángulo *m*; **to be at an ~** (**to sth**) formar un ángulo (con algo) **2.** *fig* perspectiva *f*
angle² [ˈæŋgl] *vi* pescar (con caña)
angler [ˈæŋgləʳ, *Am:* -glɚ] *n* pescador(a) *m(f)* de caña
Anglican [ˈæŋglɪkən] *adj* anglicano
Anglo-Saxon [ˌæŋgləʊˈsæksən, *Am:* -gloʊ-] *adj* anglosajón, -ona
Angola [æŋˈgəʊlə, *Am:* -ˈgoʊ-] *n* Angola *f*
Angolan *adj* angoleño
angry [ˈæŋgrɪ] *adj* enfadado, enojado *AmL*; **to make sb ~** enfadar [*o* enojar *AmL*] a alguien; **to get ~ about sth** enfadarse [*o* enojarse *AmL*] por algo
anguish [ˈæŋgwɪʃ] *n no pl* angustia *f*
angular [ˈæŋgjʊləʳ, *Am:* -lɚ] *adj* angular
animal [ˈænɪml] *n* animal *m*; *fig* bestia *mf*
animate [ˈænɪmeɪt] *vt* animar
animated *adj* animado
animation [ˌænɪˈmeɪʃn] *n no pl* ani-

mación *f*

animosity [ˌænɪ'mɒsəti, *Am:* -'mɑː-
səti] *n no pl* animosidad *f*

ankle ['æŋkl] *n* tobillo *m*

annals ['ænlz] *npl* anales *mpl*

annex ['æneks] *vt* (*territory*) anexionar

annexation [ˌænek'seɪʃn] *n no pl*
anexión *f*

annexe ['æneks] *n* anexo *m*

annihilate [ə'naɪəleɪt] *vt* aniquilar

annihilation [əˌnaɪə'leɪʃn] *n* ani-
quilación *f*

anniversary [ˌænɪ'vɜːsərɪ, *Am:*
-'vɜːr-] <-ies> *n* aniversario *m*

annotation [ˌænə'teɪʃn] *n* anotación *f*

announce [ə'naʊns] *vt* anunciar;
(*result*) comunicar

announcement *n* anuncio *m*; **to
make an ~ about sth** anunciar algo

announcer [ə'naʊnsər, *Am:* -səʳ] *n*
locutor(a) *m(f)*

annoy [ə'nɔɪ] *vt* molestar, fastidiar,
embromar *AmL;* **to get ~ed with sb**
enfadarse [*o* enojarse *AmL*] con alguien

annoyance [ə'nɔɪəns] *n* fastidio *m*,
enojo *m AmL;* (*thing*) molestia *f*

annoying *adj* molesto, chocante
AmL; (*person*) pesado

annual ['ænjʊəl] **I.** *adj* anual **II.** *n*
anuario *m*

annually ['ænjʊəlɪ] *adv* anualmente

annuity [ə'njuːəti, *Am:* -'nuːəti]
<-ies> *n* renta *f* anual

annul [ə'nʌl] <-ll-> *vt* anular

annulment [ə'nʌlmənt] *n* anulación *f*

anoint [ə'nɔɪnt] *vt* untar

anomalous [ə'nɒmələs, *Am:*
-'nɑː-] *adj* anómalo

anomaly [ə'nɒməlɪ, *Am:* -'nɑː-]
<-ies> *n* anomalía *f*

anonymity [ˌænə'nɪmətɪ, *Am:* -ti]
n no pl anonimato *m*

anonymous [ə'nɒnɪməs, *Am:*-'nɑː-
nə-] *adj* anónimo

anorexic [ˌænər'eksɪk] *adj* anoréxi-
co

another [ə'nʌðəʳ, *Am:* -əʳ] **I.** *pron*
1. (*one more*) otro, otra **2.** (*mutual*)

one ~ uno a otro; **they love one ~**
se quieren **II.** *adj* otro, otra; ~ **£30**
otras 30 libras

answer ['ɑːnsəʳ, *Am:* 'ænsəʳ] **I.** *n*
1. (*reply*) respuesta *f* **2.** (*solution*)
solución *f* **II.** *vt* **1.** (*respond to*) contestar a; **to ~ the door** abrir la puer-
ta **2.** (*fit, suit*) responder a **III.** *vi* contestar

◆ **answer back** *vi* contestar

◆ **answer for** *vt* (*action*) responder
de; (*person*) responder por

◆ **answer to** *vt* corresponder a

answerable ['ɑːnsərəbl, *Am:* 'æn-]
adj **to be ~ for sth** ser responsable
de algo; **to be ~ to sb** tener que rendir cuentas a alguien

answering machine *n* contestador
m automático

ant [ænt] *n* hormiga *f*

antagonism [æn'tægənɪzəm] *n*
antagonismo *m*

antagonistic [ænˌtægə'nɪstɪk] *adj*
antagónico

antagonize [æn'tægənaɪz] *vt* enfadar, enojar *AmL*

Antarctic [æn'tɑːktɪk, *Am:* -'tɑːrk-]
I. *adj* antártico **II.** *n* **the ~** el Antártico

Antarctica [æn'tɑːktɪkə] *n* la Antártida

Antarctic Ocean *n* Océano *m* Antártico

anteater ['æntˌiːtəʳ, *Am:* -təʳ] *n* oso
m hormiguero

antecedent [ˌæntɪ'siːdnt] *n* antecedente *m*

antelope ['æntɪləʊp, *Am:* -ţloʊp]
<-(s)> *n* antílope *m*

antenatal [ˌæntɪ'neɪtl, *Am:* -ţɪ-] *adj*
prenatal

antenna [æn'tenə] <-nae *o* -s> *n*
Am antena *f*

anthem ['ænθəm] *n* himno *m*

anthology [æn'θɒlədʒɪ, *Am:* -θɑː-
lə-] <-ies> *n* antología *f*

anthropological [ˌænθrəpə'lɒ-
dʒɪkl] *adj* antropológico

anthropologist [ˌænθrəpə'lɒ-
dʒɪst] *n* antropólogo, -a *m, f*

anthropology [ˌænθrə'pɒlədʒɪ,
Am: -'pɑːlə-] *n no pl* antropología *f*

anti ['ænti, *Am:* 'ænt̬i] *prep* en contra de

anti-abortion [ˌæntiə'bɔːʃən, *Am:* -t̬iə'bɔːr-] *adj* antiabortista

anti-aircraft [ˌænti'eəkrɑːft, *Am:* -t̬i'erkræft] *adj* antiaéreo

antibiotic [ˌæntɪbaɪ'ɒtɪk, *Am:* -t̬ɪbaɪ'ɑːt̬ɪk] *n* antibiótico

antibody ['æntɪbɒdɪ, *Am:* -t̬ɪbaːdɪ] <-ies> *n* anticuerpo *m*

anticipate [æn'tɪsɪpeɪt, *Am:* -ə-] *vt* **1.** (*expect*) prever; **to ~ doing sth** tener previsto hacer algo **2.** (*look forward to*) esperar (con ilusión) **3.** (*act in advance of*) anticiparse a

anticipation [ænˌtɪsɪ'peɪʃn, *Am:* ænˌtɪsə-] *n no pl* previsión *f;* **in ~** de antemano

anticlerical [ˌæntɪ'klerɪkl, *Am:* -t̬ɪ-] *adj* anticlerical

anti-clockwise [ˌæntɪ'klɒkwaɪz, *Am:* -t̬ɪ'klaːk-] *adv Aus, Brit* en sentido contrario al de las agujas del reloj

antics ['æntɪks, *Am:* -t̬ɪks] *npl* payasadas *fpl*

anticyclone [ˌæntɪ'saɪkləʊn, *Am:* -t̬ɪ'saɪkloʊn] *n* anticiclón *m*

antidote ['æntɪdəʊt, *Am:* -t̬ɪdoʊt] *n* antídoto *m*

antifreeze ['æntɪfriːz, *Am:* -t̬ɪ-] *n no pl* anticongelante *m*

Antilles [æn'tɪliːz] *npl* **the ~** las Antillas

antipathy [æn'tɪpəθɪ] <-ies> *n* antipatía *f*

antiperspirant [ˌæntɪ'pɜːspərənt, *Am:* -t̬ɪ'pɜːrspɚ-] *n* antitranspirante *m*

antiquarian [ˌæntɪ'kweərɪən, *Am:* -t̬ə'kwerɪ-] *n* anticuario, -a *m, f*

antiquated ['æntɪkweɪtɪd, *Am:* -t̬əkweɪt̬ɪd] *adj* anticuado

antique [æn'tiːk] *n* antigüedad *f*

antique shop *n* tienda *f* de antigüedades

antiquity [æn'tɪkwətɪ, *Am:* -t̬ɪ] <-ies> *n no pl* antigüedad *f*

anti-Semitic [ˌæntɪsɪ'mɪtɪk, *Am:* -t̬ɪsə'mɪt̬-] *adj* antisemita

anti-Semitism [æntɪ'semɪtɪsm, *Am:* -t̬ɪ'semə-] *n no pl* antisemi-

tismo *m*

antiseptic [ˌæntɪ'septɪk, *Am:* -t̬ə-] *n* antiséptico *m*

antisocial [ˌæntɪ'səʊʃl, *Am:* -t̬ɪ'soʊ-] *adj* antisocial

antithesis [æn'tɪθəsɪs] <-ses> *n* antítesis *f inv*

antithetic(al) [ˌæntɪ'θetɪk(l), *Am:* -t̬ə'θet̬-] *adj* antitético

antler ['æntləʳ, *Am:* -lɚ] *n* cuerno *m*

Antwerp ['æntwɜːp] *n* Amberes *m*

anus ['eɪnəs] *n* ano *m*

anvil ['ænvɪl, *Am:* -vl] *n* yunque *m*

anxiety [æŋ'zaɪətɪ, *Am:* -t̬ɪ] *n* inquietud *f;* **~ to do sth** ansias de hacer algo

anxious ['æŋkʃəs] *adj* **1.** (*concerned*) preocupado; **an ~ moment** un momento de preocupación **2.** (*eager*) ansioso, chingo *Ven;* **to be ~ to do sth** estar ansioso por hacer algo

any ['enɪ] **I.** *adj* **1.** (*some*) algún, alguna; **~ books** algunos libros; **do they have ~ money?** ¿tienen dinero?; **do you want ~ more soup?** ¿quieres más sopa? **2.** (*not important which*) cualquier **3.** (*negative sense*) ningún, ninguna; **I haven't ~ money** no tengo dinero; **there aren't ~ cars** no hay ningún coche **II.** *adv* **1.** (*not*) **~ more** no más; **she does not come ~ more** ya no viene más **2.** (*at all*) **does she feel ~ better?** ¿se siente algo mejor? **III.** *pron* **1.** (*some*) alguno, alguna; **~ of you** alguno de vosotros **2.** (*negative sense*) ninguno, ninguna; **not ~** ninguno

anybody ['enɪbɒdɪ, *Am:* -baːdɪ] *pron indef* **1.** (*someone*) alguien, alguno; **did you hear ~?** ¿has oído a alguien? **2.** (*not important which*) cualquiera; **~ but him** cualquiera menos él; **she's not just ~** no es cualquiera **3.** (*no one*) nadie, ninguno

anyhow ['enɪhaʊ] *adv* **1.** (*in any case*) de todas maneras **2.** (*well*) bueno; **~, as I was saying ...** bueno, como iba diciendo... **3.** (*in a disorderly way*) de cualquier manera

anyone ['enɪwʌn] *pron indef s.* **anybody**

anyplace ['enɪpleɪs] *adv Am s.* **anywhere**

anything ['enɪθɪŋ] *pron indef* **1.** (*something*) algo; ~ **else?** ¿algo más? **2.** (*each thing*) cualquier cosa; **it is** ~ **but funny** es todo menos gracioso; ~ **and everything** cualquier cosa; **to be as fast as** ~ *inf* ser rapidísimo **3.** (*nothing*) nada; **I was afraid, if** ~ estaba asustado, si acaso; **not for** ~ (**in the world**) por nada del mundo

anyway ['enɪweɪ] *adv*, **anyways** ['enɪweɪz] *adv Am, inf* **1.** (*in any case*) de todas maneras **2.** (*well*) bueno; ~**, as I was saying ...** bueno, como iba diciendo...

anywhere ['enɪweəʳ, *Am:* -wer] *adv* **1.** (*interrogative*) en alguna parte; **have you seen my glasses** ~? ¿has visto mis gafas en alguna parte?; **are we** ~ **near finishing yet?** *inf* ¿nos queda mucho para terminar? **2.** (*positive sense*) en cualquier parte; **I can sleep** ~ puedo dormir en cualquier sitio; ~ **else** en cualquier otro sitio; **to live miles from** ~ *inf* vivir en el quinto pino **3.** (*negative sense*) en ninguna parte; **you won't see this** ~ no verás esto en ningún sitio

? El **Anzac Day** (**A**ustralian and **N**ew **Z**ealand **A**rmed **C**orps) se celebra el 25 de abril y es un día de luto en Australia y Nueva Zelanda. Con misas y marchas fúnebres se conmemora el desembarco de las **Anzacs** en la península griega de Gallipoli que tuvo lugar el día 25 de abril de 1915, durante el transcurso de la I Guerra Mundial. Las **Anzacs** fueron derrotadas posteriormente. El significado simbólico de este acontecimiento radica en que los australianos luchaban por primera vez como ejército australiano fuera de sus fronteras.

apart [ə'pɑːt, *Am:* -'pɑːrt] *adv* **1.** (*separated*) aparte; **to be 20 km** ~ estar a 20 km de distancia; **far** ~ lejos; **to come** ~ desprenderse; **to live** ~ vivir separados; **to move** ~ apartarse; **to set** ~ apartar; **to take sth** ~ desmontar algo **2.** (*except for*) **you and me** ~ excepto tú y yo; **joking** ~ bromas aparte

apart from *prep* **1.** (*except for*) ~ **that** excepto eso **2.** (*in addition to*) aparte de

apartheid [ə'pɑːtheɪt, *Am:* -'pɑːrteɪt] *n no pl* apartheid *m*

apartment [ə'pɑːtmənt, *Am:* -'pɑːrt-] *n Am* apartamento *m*, departamento *m AmL*

apartment building *n Am* edificio *m* de apartamentos, edificio *m* de departamentos *AmL*

apathetic [ˌæpə'θetɪk, *Am:* -'θet̬-] *adj* apático

apathy ['æpəθɪ] *n no pl* apatía *f*

ape [eɪp] **I.** *n* mono *m* **II.** *vt* imitar

aperitif [əˌperə'tiːf] *n* aperitivo *m*

aperture ['æpətʃəʳ, *Am:* -ətʃʊr] *n* (*hole, gap*) abertura *f*; PHOT apertura *f*

apex ['eɪpeks] <-es *o* apices> *pl n* ápice *m*; *fig* cima *f*

aphorism ['æfərɪzəm, *Am:* -ə-] *n* aforismo *m*

apiece [ə'piːs] *adv* cada uno

apocalypse [ə'pɒkəlɪps, *Am:* -'pɑːkə-] *n no pl* apocalipsis *m inv*

apocalyptic [əˌpɒkə'lɪptɪk, *Am:* -ˌpɑːkə-] *adj* apocalíptico

apologetic [əˌpɒlə'dʒetɪk, *Am:* -ˌpɑːlə'dʒet̬-] *adj* de disculpa; **to be** ~ **about sth** disculparse por algo

apologize [ə'pɒlədʒaɪz, *Am:* -'pɑːlə-] *vi* disculparse; **to** ~ **to sb for sth** pedir perdón a alguien por algo

apology [ə'pɒlədʒɪ, *Am:* -'pɑːlə-] <-ies> *n* disculpa *f*; **to make an** ~ disculparse; **an** ~ **for a breakfast** *fig* una birria de desayuno

apostle [ə'pɒsl, *Am:* -'pɑːsl] *n* apóstol *m*

apostrophe [ə'pɒstrəfɪ, *Am:* -'pɑːs-trə-] *n* apóstrofo *m*

appal [ə'pɔːl] <-ll-> *vt,* **appall** *vt Am* horrorizar

appalling *adj* horroroso

apparatus [ˌæpə'reɪtəs, *Am:* -ə-'ræt-] *n (equipment)* equipo *m;* (*organization*) aparato *m;* **a piece of** ~ un aparato

apparel [ə'pærəl, *Am:* -'per-] *n no pl, form* indumentaria *f*

apparent [ə'pærənt, *Am:* -'pernt] *adj* **1.** (*clear*) evidente; **to become** ~ hacerse evidente **2.** (*seeming*) aparente

apparition [ˌæpə'rɪʃn] *n* aparición *f,* azoro *m AmC*

appeal [ə'piːl] **I.** *vi* **1.** (*attract*) atraer **2.** LAW apelar **3.** (*plead*) **to** ~ **to sb for sth** pedir algo a alguien; **to** ~ **for help** solicitar ayuda **II.** *n* **1.** (*attraction*) atractivo *m;* **to have** ~ tener gancho *inf;* **to lose one's** ~ perder su atractivo **2.** LAW apelación *f;* **to lodge an** ~ interponer una apelación

appealing [ə'piːlɪŋ] *adj* atractivo

appear [ə'pɪəʳ, *Am:* -'pɪr] *vi* **1.** (*be seen*) aparecer; (*newspaper*) salir; (*book*) publicarse; **to** ~ **in court** LAW comparecer ante un tribunal **2.** (*seem*) parecer; **so it** ~**s** eso parece

appearance [ə'pɪərəns, *Am:* -'pɪrəns] *n* **1.** (*instance of appearing*) aparición *f;* LAW comparecencia *f;* **to make an** ~ aparecer **2.** *no pl* (*looks*) aspecto *m;* **to all** ~**s** según parece; **to keep up** ~**s** guardar las apariencias

appease [ə'piːz] *vt form* apaciguar; (*hunger*) aplacar; POL contemporizar

appeasement *n no pl* apaciguamiento *m;* (*of hunger*) aplacamiento *m;* POL contemporización *f*

appendicitis [əˌpendɪ'saɪtɪs] *n no pl* apendicitis *f inv*

appendix [ə'pendɪks] *n* <-es> apéndice *m*

appetite ['æpɪtaɪt, *Am:* -ə-] *n* apetito *m,* antojo *m Méx*

appetizer ['æpɪtaɪzəʳ, *Am:* -ətaɪ-zɚ] *n* aperitivo *m,* botana *f Méx,* pasabocas *m inv Col*

appetizing ['æpɪtaɪzɪŋ, *Am:* -ə-] *adj* apetitoso

applaud [ə'plɔːd, *Am:* -'plɑːd] *vi, vi* aplaudir

applause [ə'plɔːz, *Am:* -'plɑːz] *n no pl* aplauso *m;* **a round of** ~ un aplauso

apple ['æpl] *n* manzana *f*

apple juice *n* zumo *m* de manzana

apple pie *n* pastel *m* de manzana

apple tree *n* manzano *m,* manzanero *m Ecua*

appliance [ə'plaɪəns] *n* aparato *m;* **electrical** ~ electrodoméstico *m*

applicable ['æplɪkəbl] *adj* aplicable; **delete where not** ~ táchese lo que no proceda

applicant ['æplɪkənt] *n* solicitante *mf,* candidato, -a *m, f*

application [ˌæplɪ'keɪʃn] *n* **1.** (*request*) solicitud *f;* **on** ~ mediante solicitud **2.** (*use*) aplicación *f* **3.** INFOR aplicación *f*

applied [ə'plaɪd] *adj* aplicado

apply [ə'plaɪ] **I.** *vi* **1.** (*request*) presentarse; **to** ~ **to sb** dirigirse a alguien; **to** ~ **for a job** solicitar un puesto de trabajo; **to** ~ **in writing** dirigirse por escrito **2.** (*be relevant*) **to** ~ **to sb** concernir a alguien **II.** *vt* **1.** (*coat*) aplicar **2.** (*use*) aplicar; **to** ~ **force** hacer uso de la fuerza; **to** ~ **pressure** ejercer presión; **to** ~ **oneself to sth** dedicarse a algo

appoint [ə'pɔɪnt] *vt* **1.** (*select*) nombrar **2.** *form* **at the** ~**ed time** a la hora señalada

appointed *adj form* equipado

appointment *n* **1.** (*selection*) nombramiento *m* **2.** (*meeting*) cita *f;* **to keep an** ~ acudir a una cita; **by** ~ **only** sólo con cita previa

apportion [ə'pɔːʃn] *vt* repartir

appraisal [ə'preɪzl] *n* evaluación *f*

appraise [ə'preɪz] *vt* evaluar

appreciate [ə'priːʃreɪt] **I.** *vt* **1.** (*value*) apreciar **2.** (*understand*) comprender **3.**(*be grateful*) agradecer **II.** *vi* FIN revalorizarse

appreciation [əˌpriːʃɪˈeɪʃn] *n no pl* **1.**(*gratitude*) agradecimiento *m* **2.**(*understanding*) aprecio *m* **3.** FIN revalorización *f*

appreciative [əˈpriːʃɪətɪv] *adj* agradecido

apprehend [ˌæprɪˈhend] *vt form* entender; (*arrest*) detener

apprehension [ˌæprɪˈhenʃn] *n form* comprensión; (*arrest*) detención *f*; (*fear*) aprensión *f*

apprehensive [ˌæprɪˈhensɪv] *adj* aprensivo, flatoso *AmL;* **to be ~ that** temer que +*subj*

apprentice [əˈprentɪs, *Am:* -t̬ɪs] *n* aprendiz(a) *m(f)*

apprenticeship [əˈprentɪʃɪp, *Am:* -t̬əsʃɪp] *n* aprendizaje *m*

approach [əˈprəʊtʃ, *Am:* -ˈproʊtʃ] **I.** *vt* **1.**(*get close to*) acercarse a **2.**(*ask*) dirigirse a **3.**(*deal with*) abordar **II.** *vi* acercarse **III.** *n* **1.**(*coming*) aproximación *f*; **at the ~ of winter** al acercarse el invierno **2.**(*access*) acceso *m;* **to make ~es to sb** dirigirse a alguien **3.**(*methodology*) enfoque *m*

approachable [əˈprəʊtʃəbl, *Am:* -ˈproʊ-] *adj* accesible

approbation [ˌæprəˈbeɪʃn] *n no pl, form* aprobación *f*

appropriate [əˈprəʊprɪət, *Am:* -ˈproʊ-] *adj* apropiado

appropriation [əˌprəʊprɪˈeɪʃn, *Am:* -ˌproʊ-] *n* apropiación *f*

approval [əˈpruːvl] *n no pl* aprobación *f*

approve [əˈpruːv] *vi* **to ~ of sth** aprobar algo

approved *adj* aprobado

approving [əˈpruːvɪŋ] *adj* de aprobación

approximate [əˈprɒksɪmət, *Am:* -ˈprɑːk-] *adj* aproximado

approximately [əˈprɒksɪmətlɪ] *adv* aproximadamente

approximation [əˌprɒksɪˈmeɪʃn, *Am:* -ˌprɑːk-] *n form* aproximación *f*

APR [ˌeɪpiˈɑːʳ, *Am:* -ˈɑːr] *n abbr of* **annual percentage rate** TAE *f*

apricot [ˈeɪprɪkɒt, *Am:* -kɑːt] *n* albaricoque *m*, chabacano *m Méx,* damasco *m AmS*

April [ˈeɪprəl] *n* abril *m;* **in ~** en abril; **every ~** todos los meses de abril; **the month of ~** el mes de abril; **at the beginning/end of ~** a principios/finales de abril; **at the beginning/end of ~** a principios/finales de abril; **on ~ the fourth** el cuatro de abril

April Fools' Day *n no pl* ≈ Día *m* de los Santos Inocentes (*en Gran Bretaña, el 1 de abril*)

apron [ˈeɪprən] *n* delantal *m*

apt [æpt] *adj* apropiado; **to be ~ to do sth** tener tendencia a hacer algo

APT *n abbr of* **advanced passenger train** tren de alta velocidad

aptitude [ˈæptɪtjuːd, *Am:* -tuːd] *n* aptitud *f*

aquarium [əˈkweərɪəm, *Am:* -ˈkwer-] <-s *o* -ria> *n* acuario *m*

Aquarius [əˈkweərɪəs, *Am:* -ˈkwer-] *n* Acuario *m*

aquatic [əˈkwætɪk, *Am:* -ˈkwæt̬-] *adj* acuático

Arab [ˈærəb, *Am:* ˈer-] *adj* árabe

Arabia [əˈreɪbɪə] *n* Arabia *f*

Arabian *adj* árabe, arábigo

Arabic [ˈærəbɪk, *Am:* ˈer-] *n* LING árabe *m*

arable [ˈærəbl, *Am:* ˈer-] *adj* cultivable

arbiter [ˈɑːbɪtəʳ, *Am:* ˈɑːrbɪt̬əʳ] *n* árbitro, -a *m, f*

arbitrary [ˈɑːbɪtrərɪ, *Am:* ˈɑːrbətrerɪ] *adj* arbitrario

arbitrate [ˈɑːbɪtreɪt, *Am:* ˈɑːrbə-] *vi, vt* arbitrar

arbitration [ˌɑːbɪˈtreɪʃn, *Am:* ˌɑːrbə-] *n no pl* arbitraje *m*

arbitrator [ˈɑːbɪtreɪtəʳ, *Am:* ˈɑːrbə-] *n* árbitro, -a *m, f*

? Con motivo del **Arbor Day** se plantan árboles en los EE.UU. En algunos estados es, incluso, un día festivo. La fecha exacta del **Arbor Day** varía en cada uno de los distintos estados, ya que la época

apropiada para plantar árboles no
es la misma en todos los sitios.

arc [ɑːk, *Am:* ɑːrk] *n* arco *m*

arcade [ɑːˈkeɪd, *Am:* ɑːr-] *n* ARCHIT
arcada *f;* (*of shops*) galería *f* comercial

arch [ɑːtʃ, *Am:* ɑːrtʃ] **I.** *n* arco *m*
II. *vi* arquearse

archaeological [ˌɑːkɪəˈlɒdʒɪkl, *Am:*
ˌɑːrkɪəˈlɑːdʒɪ-] *adj* arqueológico

archaeologist [ˌɑːkɪˈɒlədʒɪst, *Am:*
ˌɑːrkɪˈɑːlə-] *n* arqueólogo, -a *m, f*

archaeology [ˌɑːkɪˈɒlədʒɪ, *Am:*
ˌɑːrkɪˈɑːlə-] *n no pl* arqueología *f*

archaic [ɑːˈkeɪɪk, *Am:* ɑːr-] *adj* arcaico

archbishop [ˌɑːtʃˈbɪʃəp, *Am:* ˌɑːrtʃ-]
n arzobispo *m*

archdeacon [ˌɑːtʃˈdiːkən, *Am:*
ˌɑːrtʃ-] *n* arcediano *m*

archdiocese [ˌɑːtʃˈdaɪəsɪs, *Am:*
ˌɑːrtʃ-] *n* archidiócesis *f inv*

archeological [ˌɑːrkɪəˈlɑːdʒɪkəl] *adj*
Am s. **archaeological**

archeologist [ˌɑːrkiˈɑːlədʒɪst] *n Am*
s. **archaeologist**

archeology [ˌɑːrkiˈɑːlədʒi] *n Am s.*
archaeology

archer [ˈɑːtʃəʳ, *Am:* ˈɑːrtʃɚ] *n* arquero, -a *m, f*

archetype [ˈɑːkɪtaɪp, *Am:* ˈɑːr-] *n*
arquetipo *m*

archipelago [ˌɑːkɪˈpeləgəʊ, *Am:*
ˌɑːrkəˈpeləgoʊ] <-(e)s> *n* archipiélago *m*

architect [ˈɑːkɪtekt, *Am:* ˈɑːrkə-] *n*
arquitecto, -a *m, f*

architecture [ˈɑːkɪtektʃəʳ, *Am:*
ˈɑːrkətektʃɚ] *n no pl* arquitectura *f*

archive [ˈɑːkaɪv, *Am:* ˈɑːr-] *n* archivo *m*

archway [ˈɑːtʃweɪ, *Am:* ˈɑːrtʃ-] *n*
arco *m*

Arctic [ˈɑːktɪk, *Am:* ˈɑːrk-] *no pl* **I.** *n*
the ~ el Ártico **II.** *adj* ártico

Arctic Circle *n* círculo *m* Polar Ártico

Arctic Ocean *n* Océano *m* Glacial
Ártico

ardent [ˈɑːdnt, *Am:* ˈɑːr-] *adj* ferviente

arduous [ˈɑːdjʊəs, *Am:* ˈɑːrdʒu-]
adj arduo

are [əʳ, *stressed:* ɑːʳ, *Am:* ɚ,
stressed: ɑːr] *vi s.* **be**

area [ˈeəɹɪə, *Am:* ˈerɪ-] *n a.* MAT,
SPORTS área *f; fig* campo *m;* **in the ~
of** alrededor de

arena [əˈriːnə] *n a. fig* arena *f*

Argentina [ˌɑːdʒənˈtiːnə, *Am:* ˌɑːr-]
n Argentina *f*

Argentine [ˈɑːdʒəntaɪn, *Am:* ˈɑːr-
dʒn-], **Argentinian** [ˌɑːdʒənˈtɪn-
ɪən, *Am:* ˌɑːr-] *adj* argentino

arguably *adv* posiblemente

argue [ˈɑːgjuː, *Am:* ˈɑːrg-] **I.** *vi*
1. (*disagree*) discutir, alegar *AmL*
2. (*reason*) razonar; **to ~ against/
for sth** abogar contra/a favor de algo
II. *vt* sostener; **to ~ sb into doing
sth** persuadir a alguien de hacer algo

argument [ˈɑːgjʊmənt, *Am:* ˈɑːr-
gjə-] *n* **1.** (*disagreement*) discusión
f **2.** (*reasoning*) argumento *m*

aria [ˈɑːrɪə] *n* MUS aria *f*

arid [ˈærɪd, *Am:* ˈer-] *adj* árido

Aries [ˈeəriːz, *Am:* ˈeriːz] *n* Aries *m*

arise [əˈraɪz] <arose, -n> *vi* surgir

aristocracy [ˌærɪˈstɒkrəsɪ, *Am:*
ˌerəˈstɑːkrə-] <-ies> *n + sing/pl vb*
aristocracia *f*

aristocrat [ˈærɪstəkræt, *Am:* əˈrɪs-]
n aristócrata *mf*

aristocratic [ˌærɪstəˈkrætɪk, *Am:*
eˌrɪstəˈkrætɪk] *adj* aristocrático

arithmetic [əˈrɪθmətɪk, *Am:* ˌerɪθ-
ˈmetɪk] *n no pl* aritmética *f*

ark [ɑːk, *Am:* ɑːrk] *n no pl* arca *f;*
Noah's ark el Arca de Noé

arm¹ [ɑːrm] *n* ANAT brazo *m;* **to put
one's ~s round sb** abrazar a
alguien; **~ in ~** (agarrados) del
brazo

arm² [ɑːm, *Am:* ɑːrm] MIL **I.** *vt*
armar **II.** *n* arma *f*

armchair [ˌɑːmˈtʃeəʳ, *Am:* ˈɑːrm-
tʃer] *n* sillón *m*

armed [ɑːmd, *Am:* ɑːrmd] *adj* armado

armed forces *npl* **the ~** las fuerzas
armadas

Armenia [ɑːˈmiːnɪə, *Am:* ɑːr-] *n* Armenia *f*

Armenian *adj* armenio

armistice [ˈɑːmɪstɪs, *Am:* ˈɑːrmə-] *n* armisticio *m*

armor [ˈɑːrməʳ] *n Am*, **armour** [ˈɑːməʳ] *n no pl, Brit* armadura *f*

armoured [ˈɑːməd, *Am:* ˈɑːrməd] *adj Brit* blindado

armpit [ˈɑːmpɪt, *Am:* ˈɑːrm-] *n* axila *f*

arms control *n* MIL control *m* de armamentos **arms race** *n* **the ~** la carrera armamentista

army [ˈɑːmɪ, *Am:* ˈɑːr-] <-ies> *n* MIL ejército *m; fig* multitud *f;* **to join the ~** alistarse

aroma [əˈrəʊmə, *Am:* -ˈroʊ-] *n* aroma *m*

aromatic [ˌærəˈmætɪk, *Am:* ˌerə-ˈmæt̬-] *adj* aromático

around [əˈraʊnd] **I.** *prep* **1.** (*surrounding*) alrededor de **2.** (*here and there*) por; **to go all ~ the world** viajar por el mundo **3.** (*approximately*) alrededor de; **somewhere ~ here** en algún lugar por aquí **II.** *adv* **1.** (*round about*) alrededor; **all ~** en todas partes; **to walk ~** dar una vuelta; **to hang ~** andar por ahí **2.** (*near by*) por ahí

arouse [əˈraʊz] *vt* suscitar

arrange [əˈreɪndʒ] **I.** *vt* arreglar; (*organize*) organizar **II.** *vi* **to ~ to do sth** quedar en hacer algo

arrangement *n* **1.** *pl* (*preparations*) preparativos *mpl;* **to make ~s** (**for sth**) hacer los preparativos (de algo) **2.** (*agreement*) acuerdo *m;* **to come to an ~** llegar a un acuerdo

array [əˈreɪ] *n* colección *f*

arrears [əˈrɪəz, *Am:* -ˈrɪrz] *npl* FIN atraso *m;* **to be in ~** estar atrasado en el pago

arrest [əˈrest] **I.** *vt* detener **II.** *n* detención *f;* **to put sb under ~** detener a alguien

arrival [əˈraɪvl] *n* llegada *f*

arrive [əˈraɪv] *vi* llegar

arrogance [ˈærəgəns, *Am:* ˈer-] *n no pl* arrogancia *f*

arrogant [ˈærəgənt, *Am:* ˈer-] *adj* arrogante

arrow [ˈærəʊ, *Am:* ˈeroʊ] *n* flecha *f,* jara *f Guat, Méx*

arse [ɑːs, *Am:* ɑːrs] *n Aus, Brit, vulg* culo *m,* siete *m AmS, Méx;* **to make an ~ out of oneself** *inf* quedar como un gilipollas

arsenal [ˈɑːsənl, *Am:* ˈɑːr-] *n* arsenal *m*

arsenic [ˈɑːsnɪk, *Am:* ˈɑːr-] *n no pl* arsénico *m*

arson [ˈɑːsn, *Am:* ˈɑːr-] *n* incendio *m* provocado

art [ɑːt, *Am:* ɑːrt] *n* arte *m*

artefact [ˈɑːtɪfækt, *Am:* ˈɑːrt̬ə-] *n Brit* artefacto *m*

artery [ˈɑːtərɪ, *Am:* ˈɑːrt̬əʳ] <-ies> *n* arteria *f*

artful [ˈɑːtfl, *Am:* ˈɑːrt-] *adj* ingenioso

art gallery *n* galería *f* de arte

arthritis [ɑːˈθraɪtɪs, *Am:* ɑːr-ˈθraɪt̬əs] *n no pl* artritis *f inv*

artichoke [ˈɑːtɪtʃəʊk, *Am:* ˈɑːrt̬ə-tʃoʊk] *n* alcachofa *f*

article [ˈɑːtɪkl, *Am:* ˈɑːrt̬ɪ-] *n* **1.** (*object*) objeto *m; ~* **of clothing** prenda *f* de vestir **2.** LAW, LING artículo *m*

articulate [ɑːˈtɪkjʊlət, *Am:* ɑːrˈtɪk-jə-] *adj* que se expresa con claridad; (*speech*) claro

articulation [ɑːˌtɪkjʊˈleɪʃn, *Am:* ɑːrˌtɪkjə-] *n no pl* expresión *f*

artifact [ˈɑːtɪfækt, *Am:* ˈɑːrt̬ə-] *n Am* artefacto *m*

artifice [ˈɑːtɪfɪs, *Am:* ˈɑːrt̬ə-] *n form* artificio *m*

artificial [ˌɑːtɪˈfɪʃl, *Am:* ˌɑːrt̬ə-] *adj* artificial

artillery [ɑːˈtɪlərɪ, *Am:* ɑːr-] *n no pl* artillería *f*

artisan [ˌɑːtɪˈzæn, *Am:* ˈɑːrt̬əzn] *n* artesano, -a *m, f*

artist [ˈɑːtɪst, *Am:* ˈɑːrt̬əst-] *n* artista *mf*

artistic [ɑːˈtɪstɪk, *Am:* ɑːr-] *adj* artístico

artistry [ˈɑːtɪstrɪ, *Am:* ˈɑːrt̬ə-] *n no pl* arte *m* o *f*

artwork [ˈɑːtwɜːk, *Am:* ˈɑːrtwɜːrk] *n no pl* material *m* gráfico

as [əz, *stressed:* æz] **I.** *prep* como; **dressed ~ a clown** vestido de payaso; **~ a baby, I ...** de bebé, (yo)...

II. *conj* **1.** (*in comparison*) como; **the same name ~ ...** el mismo nombre que...; **~ fast ~ ...** tan rápido como...; **as soon ~ possible** lo antes posible **2.** (*like*) (tal) como; **~ it is** tal como es; **I came ~ promised** vine, como (lo) prometí; **~ if it were true** como si fuese verdad **3.** (*because*) como; **~ he is here I'm going** como él está aquí, yo me voy **4.** (*while*) mientras **5.** (*although*) (~) **fine ~ the day is, ...** aunque el día está bien,...; **try ~ I would, I couldn't** por más que me esforzara, no podía **III.** *adv* **~ far ~** en la medida en que; **~ long as** mientras que +*subj;* **~ much as** tanto como; **~ soon as** en cuanto; **~ well** también

asbestos [æz'bestɒs, *Am:* -təs] *n no pl* asbesto *m*

ascend [ə'send] *vt form* subir, ascender

ascendancy [ə'sendəntsɪ] *n no pl* ascendencia *f*

ascendant [ə'sendənt] *n no pl, form* **to be in the ~** estar en alza

ascension [ə'senʃn] *n* ascensión *f;* **the Ascension** REL la Ascensión

ascent [ə'sent] *n form* ascensión *f*

ascertain [ˌæsə'teɪn, *Am:* -ɚ-] *vt form* averiguar

ascetic [ə'setɪk, *Am:* -'seṭ-] *adj* ascético

ASCII ['æski:] *abbr of* **American Standard Code for Information Interchange** ASCII

> [?] **Ascot** es el nombre de una pequeña localidad en Berkshire en la que se encuentra un hipódromo construido en 1711 por expreso deseo de la Reina Anne. Con el nombre de **Royal Ascot** se conocen unas jornadas hípicas, de cuatro días de duración, que se celebran con carácter anual durante el mes de Junio y a las que la reina suele acudir casi siempre.

ascribe [ə'skraɪb] *vt* atribuir

ash¹ [æʃ] *n no pl* (*powder*) ceniza *f*

ash² *n* (*tree*) fresno *m*

ashamed [ə'ʃeɪmd] *adj* avergonzado; **to be ~ of** avergonzarse de

ashcan ['æʃkæn] *n Am* cubo *m* de basura, bote *m* de basura *Méx*

ashore [ə'ʃɔ:ʳ] *adv* **to go ~** desembarcar

ashtray ['æʃˌtreɪ] *n* cenicero *m*

Asia ['eɪʃə, *Am:* -ʒə] *n no pl* Asia *f*

Asian ['eɪʃən, *Am:* -ʒən] *adj* asiático

aside [ə'saɪd] **I.** *n* comentario *m* aparte **II.** *adv* **to stand ~** hacerse a un lado

aside from *prep* aparte de

ask [ɑ:sk, *Am:* æsk] **I.** *vt* **1.** (*request information*) preguntar; **to ~ sb sth** preguntar algo a alguien; **to ~ (sb) a question about sth** hacer (a alguien) una pregunta acerca de algo; **if you ~ me ...** en mi opinión... **2.** (*request*) pedir; **to ~ advice** pedir consejo **3.** (*invite*) invitar; **to ~ sb to do sth** invitar a alguien a hacer algo **4.** (*demand a price*) pedir; **to ~ 100 euros for sth** pedir 100 euros por algo; **to ~ too much of sb** pedir demasiado de alguien **II.** *vi* **1.** (*request information*) preguntar **2.** (*make request*) pedir

◆ **ask for** *vt* pedir; **to ~ trouble** buscar complicaciones

asleep [ə'sli:p] *adj* dormido; **to fall ~** quedarse dormido

asparagus [ə'spærəgəs, *Am:* -'sper-] *n* espárrago *m*

aspect ['æspekt] *n* **1.** (*point of view*) punto *m* de vista **2.** (*appearance*) aspecto *m*

asphalt ['æsfælt, *Am:* -fɑ:lt] *n* asfalto *m*, asfaltado *m AmL*

asphyxiate [əs'fɪksɪeɪt] *vi form* asfixiarse

aspiration [ˌæspə'reɪʃn] *n* aspiración *f*

aspire [ə'spaɪəʳ, *Am:* -'spaɪɚ] *vi* **to ~ to sth** aspirar a algo

aspirin® ['æsprɪn] *n no pl* aspirina® *f*

aspiring [ə'spaɪərɪŋ, *Am:* -'spaɪɚ-] *adj* en ciernes

ass [æs] <-es> *n* **1.** (*donkey*) asno *m*

2. *inf* (*person*) burro, -a *m, f* **3.** *Am, vulg* (*bottom*) culo *m*, siete *m AmS, Méx*

assail [əˈseɪl] *vt* atacar

assailant *n* asaltante *mf*

assassin [əˈsæsɪn, *Am:* -ən] *n* asesino, -a *m, f*

assassinate [əˈsæsɪneɪt] *vt* asesinar

assassination [əˌsæsɪˈneɪʃn] *n no pl* asesinato *m*

assault [əˈsɔːlt] **I.** *n* asalto *m* **II.** *vt* atacar

assault course *n* pista *f* americana

assemble [əˈsembl] **I.** *vi* congregarse **II.** *vt* reunir

assembly [əˈsemblɪ] <-ies> *n* reunión *f*

assent [əˈsent] **I.** *n no pl, form* consentimiento *m* **II.** *vi* **to ~ to sth** asentir a algo

assert [əˈsɜːt, *Am:* -ˈsɜːrt] *vt* afirmar; **to ~ oneself** imponerse

assertion [əˈsɜːʃn, *Am:* -ˈsɜːr-] *n* afirmación *f*

assertive [əˈsɜːtɪv, *Am:* -ˈsɜːrt̬ɪv] *adj* confiado

assess [əˈses] *vt* evaluar

assessment *n* evaluación *f*

assessor [əˈsesəʳ, *Am:* -ˈsesəʳ] *n* evaluador(a) *m(f)*

asset [ˈæset] *n* **1.** (*benefit*) ventaja *f* **2.** *pl* FIN activo *m*

assign [əˈsaɪn] *vt* asignar, apropiar *AmL;* **to ~ sb to a position** destinar a alguien a un puesto

assignment *n* tarea *f;* **to send sb on an ~** mandar a alguien a una misión

assimilate [əˈsɪməleɪt] *vt* asimilar

assimilation [əˌsɪməˈleɪʃn] *n no pl* asimilación *f*

assist [əˈsɪst] *vt, vi* ayudar

assistance [əˈsɪstəns] *n no pl* asistencia *f;* **to be of ~** ser de ayuda

assistant [əˈsɪstənt] *n* ayudante *mf,* suche *m Chile*

associate¹ [əˈsəʊʃiət, *Am:* -ˈsoʊʃɪt] *n* asociado, -a *m, f;* **business ~** socio, -a *m, f*

associate² [əˈsəʊʃiət, *Am:* -ˈsoʊ-] **I.** *vt* asociar; **to ~ oneself with sth** relacionarse con algo **II.** *vi* relacionarse

association [əˌsəʊsɪˈeɪʃn, *Am:* -ˌsoʊ-] *n* asociación *f*

assorted [əˈsɔːtɪd, *Am:* -ˈsɔːrt̬ɪd] *adj* surtido, variado

assortment [əˈsɔːtmənt, *Am:* -ˈsɔːrt-] *n* surtido *m*

assume [əˈsjuːm, *Am:* -ˈsuːm] *vt* **1.** (*regard as true*) suponer, asumir *AmL* **2.** (*power*) tomar

assumed [əˈsjuːmd, *Am:* -ˈsuːmd] *adj* supuesto

assumption [əˈsʌmpʃn] *n* supuesto *m;* **to act on the ~ that ...** actuar suponiendo que...

assurance [əˈʃʊərəns, *Am:* ˈʃʊrns] *n* **1.** (*self-confidence*) seguridad *f* **2.** (*promise*) garantía *f* **3.** *Brit* FIN seguro *m*

assure [əˈʃʊəʳ, *Am:* -ˈʃʊr] *vt* **1.** (*guarantee*) asegurar **2.** (*promise*) **to ~ sb of sth** asegurar algo a alguien

assured *adj* seguro

asterisk [ˈæstərɪsk] *n* asterisco *m*

asteroid [ˈæstərɔɪd] *n* asteroide *m*

asthma [ˈæsmə, *Am:* ˈæz-] *n no pl* asma *m*

astonish [əˈstɒnɪʃ, *Am:* -ˈstɑːnɪʃ] *vt* asombrar; **to be ~ed** asombrarse

astonishing *adj* asombroso

astonishment *n no pl* asombro *m;* **to her ~** para gran sorpresa suya

astound [əˈstaʊnd] *vt* asombrar; **to be ~ed** quedarse atónito

astounding *adj* asombroso

astray [əˈstreɪ] *adv* **to go ~** extraviarse; **to lead sb ~** llevar a alguien por mal camino

astrologer [əˈstrɒlədʒəʳ, *Am:* -ˈstrɑːlədʒəʳ] *n* astrólogo, -a *m, f*

astrology [əˈstrɒlədʒɪ, *Am:* -ˈstrɑːlə-] *n no pl* astrología *f*

astronaut [ˈæstrənɔːt, *Am:* -nɑːt] *n* astronauta *mf*

astronomer [əˈstrɒnəməʳ, *Am:* -ˈstrɑːnəməʳ] *n* astrónomo, -a *m, f*

astronomical [ˌæstrəˈnɒmɪkl, *Am:* -ˈnɑːmɪkl] *adj a. fig* astronómico

astronomy [əˈstrɒnəmɪ, *Am:* -ˈstrɑːnə-] *n no pl* astronomía *f*

Asturian [æsˈtʊəriən, *Am:* əˈstʊri-] *adj* asturiano

astute [əˈstjuːt, *Am:* -ˈstuːt] *adj* astuto

astuteness *n no pl* astucia *f*

asylum [ə'saɪləm] *n* asilo *m;* **mental** ~ manicomio *m*

at¹ [ət] *prep* 1. (*place*) en; ~ **home/ school** en casa/la escuela; ~ **the table** en la mesa; ~ **the window** a la ventana 2. (*time*) ~ **Easter** en Pascua; ~ **night** por la noche; ~ **once** en seguida; **all** ~ **once** de repente; ~ **present** en este momento; ~ **three o'clock** a las tres; ~ **the same time** al mismo tiempo 3. (*towards*) **to laugh** ~ **sb** reírse de alguien; **to look** ~ **sth** mirar algo; **to point** ~ **sb** señalar a alguien 4. (*in reaction to*) ~ **sb's request** a petición de alguien; **to be astonished** ~ **sth** estar asombrado por algo; **to be mad** ~ **sb** estar enfadado con alguien 5. (*in amount of*) ~ **120 km/h** a 120 km/h 6. (*in state of*) ~ **20** a los 20 (años); ~ **best** en el mejor de los casos; ~ **first** al principio; ~ **least** al menos; **to be** ~ **a loss** estar sin saber qué hacer; **I feel** ~ **ease** me siento tranquilo 7. (*in ability to*) **to be good** ~ **English** ser bueno en inglés 8. **not** ~ **all!** ¡de nada!; **to hardly do sth** ~ **all** apenas hacer algo

at² [ɑːt, æt] INFOR arroba *f*

ate [et, *Am:* eɪt] *pt of* **eat**

atheism ['eɪθɪɪzəm] *n no pl* ateísmo *m*

atheist ['eɪθɪɪst] *n* ateo, -a *m, f*

Athens ['æθənz] *n* Atenas *f*

athlete ['æθliːt] *n* atleta *mf*

athletic [æθ'letɪk, *Am:* -'let̬-] *adj* atlético

athletics [æθ'letɪks, *Am:* -'let̬-] *npl* atletismo *m*

Atlantic [ət'læntɪk, *Am:* -t̬ɪk] I. *n no pl* **the** ~ (**Ocean**) el (Océano) Atlántico II. *adj* atlántico

atlas ['ætləs] <-es> *n* atlas *m inv*

ATM [,eɪtiː'em] *n abbr of* **automated teller machine** cajero *m* automático

atmosphere ['ætməsfɪəʳ, *Am:* -fɪr] *n* atmósfera *f*

atmospheric [,ætməs'ferɪk] *adj* atmosférico

atoll ['ætɒl, *Am:* -ɑːl] *n* atolón *m*

atom ['ætəm, *Am:* 'æt̬-] *n* átomo *m*

atomic [ə'tɒmɪk, *Am:* -'tɑːmɪk] *adj* atómico

atomic bomb *n* bomba *f* atómica
  atomic energy *n* energía *f* atómica

atone for [ə'təʊn, *Am:* -'toʊn] *vi* expiar

atonement *n no pl, form* expiación *f*

atrocious [ə'trəʊʃəs, *Am:* -'troʊ-] *adj* atroz

atrocity [ə'trɒsəti] <-ies> *n* atrocidad *f*

at-sign *n* INFOR arroba *f*

attach [ə'tætʃ] *vt* 1. (*fix*) fijar; (*label*) pegar; **to be ~ed to sb** tenerle cariño a alguien; **to** ~ **oneself to sb** unirse a alguien; **to** ~ **importance to sth** dar importancia a algo 2. INFOR adjuntar

attaché [ə'tæʃeɪ, *Am:* ,æt̬ə'ʃeɪ] *n* agregado, -a *m, f*

attachment [ə'tætʃmənt] *n* 1. (*device*) accesorio *m* 2. INFOR archivo *m* adjunto

attack [ə'tæk] I. *n* ataque *m;* **to be on the** ~ emprender una ofensiva; **to come under** ~ ser atacado II. *vt* atacar, cachorrear *Col;* (*problem*) afrontar

attain [ə'teɪn] *vt form* alcanzar; (*independence*) lograr

attainment *n form* logro *m*

attempt [ə'tempt] I. *n* intento *m;* **to make an** ~ **at doing sth** intentar hacer algo II. *vt* intentar

attend [ə'tend] *vt* asistir a; (*take care of*) atender

attendance [ə'tendəns] *n* 1. *no pl* (*presence*) asistencia *f;* **in** ~ presente 2. (*people present*) concurrencia *f*

attendant [ə'tendənt] *n* asistente, -a *m, f*

attention [ə'tenʃn] *n no pl* atención *f;* **for the** ~ **of** *form* a la atención de; **to pay** ~ prestar atención; ~**!** MIL ¡firmes!

attentive [ə'tentɪv, *Am:* -t̬ɪv] *adj* atento

attenuate [ə'tenjʊeɪt] *vt form* atenuar

attest [əˈtest] *vt* testimoniar
attic [ˈætɪk, *Am:* ˈæt̬-] *n* desván *m*, tabanco *m AmC*, entretecho *m CSur*
attitude [ˈætɪtjuːd, *Am:* ˈæt̬ətuːd] *n* actitud *f*
attorney [əˈtɜːnɪ, *Am:* -ˈtɜːr-] *n Am* abogado, -a *m*, *f*
attract [əˈtrækt] *vt* atraer, jalar *AmL*; **to be ~ed by sth** sentirse atraído por algo
attraction [əˈtrækʃn] *n* **1.** (*force, place of enjoyment*) atracción *f* **2.** *no pl* (*appeal*) atractivo *m*
attractive [əˈtræktɪv] *adj* atractivo
attribute¹ [əˈtrɪbjuːt] *vt* atribuir; **to ~ the blame to sb** achacar la culpa a alguien; **to ~ importance to sth** dar importancia a algo
attribute² [ˈætrɪbjuːt] *n* atributo *m*
attrition [əˈtrɪʃn] *n no pl* desgaste *m*
aubergine [ˈəʊbəʒiːn, *Am:* ˈoʊbə-] *n Brit* berenjena *f*
auburn [ˈɔːbən, *Am:* ˈɑːbən] *adj* castaño
auction [ˈɔːkʃn, *Am:* ˈɑːkʃn] **I.** *n* subasta *f*; **to put sth up for ~** subastar algo **II.** *vt* **to ~ sth** (**off**) subastar algo
audacious [ɔːˈdeɪʃəs, *Am:* ɑː-] *adj* audaz
audacity [ɔːˈdæsəti, *Am:* ɑːˈdæsət̬ɪ] *n no pl* audacia *f*
audible [ˈɔːdəbl, *Am:* ˈɑː-] *adj* perceptible
audience [ˈɔːdɪəns, *Am:* ˈɑː-] *n* **1.** (*spectators*) público *m* **2.** (*interview*) audiencia *f*
audio [ˌɔːdɪəʊ, *Am:* ˌɑːdɪoʊ] *adj inv* de sonido
audit [ˈɔːdɪt, *Am:* ˈɑː-] *vt* FIN auditar
audition [ɔːˈdɪʃn, *Am:* ɑː-] *n* audición *f*
auditor [ˈɔːdɪtə, *Am:* ˈɑːdət̬ə] *n* COM auditor(a) *m(f)*
auditorium [ˌɔːdɪˈtɔːrɪəm, *Am:* ˌɑːdə-] <-s *o* auditoria> *n* auditorio *m*
augment [ɔːgˈment, *Am:* ɑːg-] *vt form* aumentar
augur [ˈɔːgə, *Am:* ˈɑːgə] *vi* **to ~ badly/well** ser de mal/buen agüero
August [ˈɔːgəst, *Am:* ˈɑː-] *n* agosto *m*; *s. a.* **April**

aunt [ɑːnt, *Am:* ænt] *n* tía *f*
au pair [ˌəʊˈpeə, *Am:* oʊˈper] *n* au pair *f*
aura [ˈɔːrə] *n* aura *f*
aurora [ɔːˈrɔːrə] *n* aurora *f*
auspices [ˈɔːspɪsɪz, *Am:* ˈɑː-] *n pl* auspicios *mpl*
austere [ɔːˈstɪə, *Am:* ɑːˈstɪr] *adj* austero
austerity [ɔːˈsterəti, *Am:* ɑːˈsterət̬ɪ] <-ies> *n* austeridad *f*
Australia [ɒˈstreɪlɪə, *Am:* ɑːˈstreɪlʒə] *n* Australia *f*

> [?] El **Australia Day**, 26 de enero, conmemora la fundación del primer asentamiento británico en 1788 en Sydney Cove. Para los **Aborigines**, los primeros habitantes de Australia, es el día de la invasión de su país. Durante ese día tienen lugar distintos acontecimientos de tipo multicultural que suelen reunir a australianos de todas las procedencias.

Australian [ɒˈstreɪlɪən, *Am:* ɑːˈstreɪlʒən] *adj* australiano
Austria [ˈɒstrɪə, *Am:* ˈɑː-] *n* Austria *f*
Austrian [ˈɒstrɪən, *Am:* ˈɑː-] *adj* austriaco
authentic [ɔːˈθentɪk, *Am:* ɑːˈθen-t̬ɪk] *adj* auténtico
authenticity [ˌɔːθənˈtɪsəti, *Am:* ˌɑːθənˈtɪsət̬ɪ] *n no pl* autenticidad *f*
author [ˈɔːθə, *Am:* ˈɑːθə] *n* autor *m*; *fig* creador(a) *m(f)*
authoritarian [ɔːˌθɒrɪˈteərɪən, *Am:* əːˌθɔːrəˈteri-] *adj* autoritario
authoritative [ɔːˈθɒrɪtətɪv, *Am:* əːˈθɔːrəteɪt̬ɪv] *adj* autorizado; (*assertive*) autoritario
authority [ɔːˈθɒrəti, *Am:* əːˈθɔː-rət̬ɪ] <-ies> *n* **1.** *no pl* (*power*) autoridad *f*; **to be in ~** tener autoridad **2.** *no pl* (*permission*) autorización *f* **3.** (*knowledge*) **to be an ~ on sth** ser una autoridad en algo
authorization [ˌɔːθəraɪˈzeɪʃn, *Am:*

ˌɑːθəˈraɪ] *n no pl* autorización *f*

authorize [ˈɔːθəraɪz, *Am:* ˈɑː-] *vt* autorizar

authorship [ˈɔːθəʃɪp, *Am:* ˈɑːθɚ-] *n no pl* autoría *f*

autistic [ɔːˈtɪstɪk] *adj* autista

auto [ˈɔːtəʊ, *Am:* ˈɑːt̬oʊ] *n Am* coche *m*, carro *m AmL*

autobiographical [ˌɔːtəbaɪəˈɡræfɪkl, *Am:* ˌɑːt̬ə-] *adj* autobiográfico

autobiography [ˌɔːtəbaɪˈɒɡrəfi, *Am:* ˌɑːt̬əbaɪˈɑːɡrə-] *n* autobiografía *f*

autocratic [ˌɔːtəˈkrætik, *Am:* ˌɑːt̬əˈkræt̬-] *adj* autocrático

autograph [ˈɔːtəɡrɑːf, *Am:* ˈɑːt̬əɡræf] *n* autógrafo *m*

automate [ˈɔːtəmeɪt, *Am:* ˈɑːt̬ə-] *vt* automatizar

automated [ˈɔːtəmeɪtɪd, *Am:* ˈɑːt̬əmeɪt̬ɪd] *adj* automatizado

automatic [ˌɔːtəˈmætɪk, *Am:* ˌɑːt̬əˈmæt̬-] **I.** *n* coche *m* automático; (*pistol*) pistola *f* automática **II.** *adj* automático

automation [ˌɔːtəˈmeɪʃn, *Am:* ˌɑːt̬ə-] *n no pl* automatización *f*

automobile [ˈɔːtəməbiːl, *Am:* ˈɑːt̬əmoʊ-] *n Am* automóvil *m*

automotive [ˌɔːtəˈməʊtɪv, *Am:* ˌɑːt̬əˈmoʊt̬ɪv] *adj inv* automovilístico

autonomous [ɔːˈtɒnəməs, *Am:* ɑːˈtɑːnə-] *adj* autónomo; **to be ~ of sth** ser independiente de algo

autonomy [ɔːˈtɒnəmi, *Am:* ɑːˈtɑːnə-] *n no pl* autonomía *f*

autopsy [ˈɔːtɒpsi, *Am:* ˈɑːtɑːp-] <-ies> *n* autopsia *f*

autumn [ˈɔːtəm, *Am:* ˈɑːt̬əm] *n* otoño *m*

auxiliary [ɔːɡˈzɪlɪəri, *Am:* ɑːɡˈzɪljri] <-ies> *adj* auxiliar

avail [əˈveɪl] **I.** *n* **to no ~** en vano **II.** *vt* **to ~ oneself of sth** aprovecharse de algo

available [əˈveɪləbl] *adj* disponible; **to make sth ~ to sb** poner algo a la disposición de alguien; **to be ~ to do sth** tener tiempo para hacer algo

avalanche [ˈævəlɑːnʃ, *Am:* -æntʃ] *n*

alud *m; fig* torrente *m*

avant-garde [ˌævɒŋˈɡɑːd, *Am:* ˌɑːvɑːntˈɡɑːrd] *adj* de vanguardia

avarice [ˈævərɪs] *n no pl, form* avaricia *f*

avenge [əˈvendʒ] *vt* vengar

avenue [ˈævənjuː, *Am:* -nuː] *n* avenida *f*, carrera *f AmL*

average [ˈævərɪdʒ] **I.** *n* promedio *m;* **on ~** por término medio **II.** *adj* **1.** MAT medio **2.** (*mediocre*) mediocre **III.** *vt* **1.** (*have value*) promediar **2.** (*calculate value of*) sacar la media de

averse [əˈvɜːs, *Am:* -ˈvɜːrs] *adj* **to be ~ to sth** ser contrario a algo

aversion [əˈvɜːʃn, *Am:* -ˈvɜːrʒn] *n* aversión *f*

avert [əˈvɜːt, *Am:* -ˈvɜːrt] *vt* prevenir; (*turn away*) desviar

aviation [ˌeɪviˈeɪʃn] *n no pl* aviación *f*

avid [ˈævɪd] *adj* ávido

avocado [ˌævəˈkɑːdəʊ, *Am:* -doʊ] <-s *o* -es> *n* aguacate *m*, abocado *m AmL*, ahuacatl *m Méx*

avoid [əˈvɔɪd] *vt* evitar

avoidance *n no pl* evasión *f*

await [əˈweɪt] *vt* aguardar

awake [əˈweɪk] <awoke, awoken *o Am:* -d, awoken> **I.** *vi* despertarse **II.** *adj* despierto; **to be ~ to sth** *fig* estar alerta ante algo

awakening [əˈweɪknɪŋ] *n no pl* despertar *m*

award [əˈwɔːd, *Am:* -ˈwɔːrd] **I.** *n* **1.** (*prize*) premio *m* **2.** (*reward*) recompensa *f* **II.** *vt* otorgar; **to ~ sb a grant** conceder a alguien una beca

aware [əˈweər, *Am:* -ˈwer] *adj* **to be ~ of sth** ser consciente de algo; **as far as I'm ~ ...** por lo que yo sé...; **not that I'm ~ of** no, que yo sepa

awareness [əˈweənɪs, *Am:* -ˈwer-] *n no pl* conciencia *f*

away [əˈweɪ] *adv* **1.** (*distant*) **10 km ~** a 10 km; **as far ~ as possible** lo más lejos posible; **to stay ~ from sb** mantenerse alejado de alguien **2.** (*absent*) fuera; **to be ~ on holiday** estar de vacaciones **3.** (*in future time*) **to be only a week ~** no faltar más que una semana; **right ~!** ¡enseguida!

awe [ɔ:, *Am:* ɑ:] *n no pl* respeto *m*
awesome ['ɔːsəm, *Am:* 'ɑː-] *adj* imponente
awful ['ɔːfl, *Am:* 'ɑː-] *adj* terrible; **an ~ lot** mucho
awfully ['ɔːflɪ, *Am:* 'ɑː-] *adv* terriblemente; **~ clever** muy inteligente
awkward ['ɔːkwəd, *Am:* 'ɑːkwəd] *adj* **1.** (*difficult*) difícil **2.** (*embarrassing*) incómodo **3.** (*clumsy*) torpe
awoke [ə'wəʊk, *Am:* -'woʊ-] *pp of* **awake**
awoken [ə'wəʊkən, *Am:* -'woʊ-] *pp of* **awake**
awry [ə'raɪ] *adj* **to go ~** salir mal
ax *n Am*, **axe** [æks] *n* hacha *f*; **to get the ~** *fig* ser despedido; **to have an ~ to grind** *fig* tener un interés personal
axiom ['æksɪəm] *n form* axioma *m*
axis ['æksɪs] *n* eje *m*
axle ['æksl] *n* eje *m*, cardán *m AmC, Ven, Col*
ayatollah [ˌaɪjə'tɔlə, *Am:* ˌaɪə'toʊlə] *n* ayatolá *m*
aye [aɪ] *n POL* **the ~s** los votos a favor
Azerbaijan [ˌæzəbaɪ'dʒɑːn, *Am:* ˌɑːzɚ-] *n* Azerbaiyán *m*
Azerbaijani *adj* azerbaiyano
Aztec ['æztɛk] *adj* azteca

B b

B, b [biː] *n* **1.** (*letter*) B, b *f*; **~ for Benjamin** *Brit,* **~ for Baker** *Am* B de Barcelona **2.** MUS si *m*
B & B [ˌbiːənd'biː] *n s.* **bed and breakfast** pensión *f* familiar
BA [ˌbiː'eɪ] *n abbr of* **Bachelor of Arts** Ldo., -a *m, f* (en Filosofía y Letras)
baa [bɑː, *Am:* bæ] <-ed> *vi* balar
babble ['bæbl] I. *n no pl* balbuceo *m* II. *vi* balbucear
baboon [bə'buːn, *Am:* bæb'uːn] *n* babuino *m*
baby ['beɪbi] *n* bebé *m*

baby food *n no pl* comida *f* para bebés
babysitter ['beɪbɪˌsɪtər, *Am:* -ˌsɪt̬ɚ] *n* canguro *mf*, nana *f Méx*
bachelor ['bætʃələr, *Am:* -lɚ] *n* **1.** (*man*) soltero *m* **2.** UNIV **Bachelor of Arts/Science** Licenciado, -a *m, f* en Filosofía y Letras/Ciencias

▌**B** b

? El **Bachelor's degree** es el título que obtienen los estudiantes después de haber cursado carreras universitarias de tres años (en algunos casos, de cuatro o cinco años). Este título recibe varios nombres según las disciplinas. Los títulos más importantes son: **BA (Bachelor of Arts)** en las disciplinas de humanidades, **BSc (Bachelor of Science)** en las disciplinas científicas, **BEd (Bachelor of Education)** en las disciplinas de tipo pedagógico, **LLB (Bachelor of Laws)** para los estudiantes de Derecho y **BMus (Bachelor of Music)** para los estudiantes de Musicología.

back [bæk] I. *n* **1.** (*opposite of front*) parte *f* trasera; (*of hand, piece of paper*) dorso *m*; (*of chair*) respaldo *m*; **~ to front** al revés; **to know sth like the ~ of one's hand** conocer algo como la palma de la mano *inf* **2.** (*end: of book*) final *m* **3.** ANAT espalda *f*; (*of animal*) lomo *m*; **to be on one's ~** estar boca arriba; **to do sth behind sb's ~** *a. fig* hacer algo a espaldas de alguien; **to turn one's ~ on sb** *a. fig* dar la espalda a alguien; **to have one's ~ against the wall** *fig* estar entre la espada y la pared **4.** SPORTS defensa *mf* II. *adj* trasero III. *adv* **to be ~** estar de vuelta; **to come ~** volver; **to want sb ~** querer que alguien vuelva; **~ and forth** adelante y atrás; **to look ~** mirar hacia atrás; **to sit ~** recostarse IV. *vt* apoyar
◆ **back down** *vi* retirarse

◆**back up** *vt* respaldar; **to ~ data** INFOR hacer copias de seguridad de datos

backbone ['bækbəʊn, *Am:* -boʊn] *n* columna *f* vertebral

backer ['bækəʳ, *Am:* -ɚ] *n* partidario, -a *m, f*

backfire [ˌbæk'faɪəʳ, *Am:* -'faɪɚ] *vi* (*go wrong*) fallar

backgammon [bæk'gæmən] *n no pl* backgamon *m*

background ['bækgraʊnd] *n* **1.** (*rear view*) fondo *m*; **in the ~** *fig* en segundo plano **2.** (*circumstances*) antecedentes *mpl*

backhand ['bækhænd] *n no pl* revés *m*

backing ['bækɪŋ] *n no pl* (*support*) apoyo *m*

backlash ['bæklæʃ] *n* reacción *f*

backlog ['bæklɒg, *Am:* -lɑ:g] *n* atraso *m*

backpack ['bækpæk] *n* mochila *f*

backstage [bæk'steɪdʒ] *adv* THEAT entre bastidores

backup ['bækʌp] *n* **1.** (*support*) apoyo *m* **2.** INFOR copia *f* de seguridad

backward ['bækwəd, *Am:* -wɚd] **I.** *adj* (*slow*) retrasado **II.** *adv Am s.* **backwards**

backwards ['bækwədz, *Am:* -wɚdz] *adv* **1.** (*towards back*) hacia atrás **2.** (*in reverse order*) al revés

back yard *n Brit* (*yard*) patio *m* trasero; *Am* (*garden*) jardín *m* trasero

bacon ['beɪkən] *n* beicon *m*, tocino *m AmL*

bacteria [bæk'tɪərɪə] *n pl of* **bacterium**

bacterium [bæk'tɪərɪəm] *n* <-ria> bacteria *f*

bad [bæd] <worse, worst> **I.** *adj* **1.** (*not good*) malo; **to feel ~** sentirse mal; **to look ~** tener mal aspecto; **to have a ~ heart** estar mal del corazón; **to use ~ language** decir palabrotas; **in ~ taste** de mal gusto; **to have a ~ temper** tener mal carácter; **~ times** tiempos *mpl* difíciles; **to go from ~ to worse** ir de mal en peor **2.** (*harmful*) dañino; **to be ~ for sb**

ser perjudicial para alguien **3.** (*spoiled*) malo; **to go ~** echarse a perder **4.** (*serious: accident*) grave; (*pain*) fuerte **II.** *adv inf* mal

badge [bædʒ] *n* insignia *f*, placa *f Méx*

badger ['bædʒəʳ, *Am:* -ɚ] *n* tejón *m*

badly ['bædli] <worse, worst> *adv* **1.** (*poorly, negatively*) mal; **to think ~ of sb** pensar mal de alguien **2.** (*very much*) desesperadamente

badminton ['bædmɪntən] *n no pl* bádminton *m*

baffle ['bæfl] *vt* desconcertar

baffling *adj* desconcertante

bag [bæg] *n* **1.** (*container*) bolsa *f*, busaca *f Col, Ven*; (*handbag*) bolso *m*; (*sack*) saco *m*; **to pack one's ~s** *a. fig* hacer las maletas; **to have ~s under one's eyes** tener ojeras **2.** *pej, inf* (*grumpy woman*) bruja *f*; **to have ~s of money/time** *inf* tener un montón de dinero/tiempo

baggage ['bægɪdʒ] *n no pl* equipaje *m*

baggy ['bægi] *adj* holgado

Bahamas [bə'hɑ:məz] *npl* **the ~** las (Islas) Bahamas

bail [beɪl] *n* fianza *f*; **on ~** bajo fianza

bailiff ['beɪlɪf] *n* **1.** *Brit* (*landlord's agent*) administrador(a) *m(f)* **2.** *Am* (*court official*) alguacil *mf*

bait [beɪt] **I.** *n* (*for fish*) cebo *m*; **to swallow the ~** *fig* morder el anzuelo **II.** *vt* (*harass*) acosar

bake [beɪk] **I.** *vi* **1.** (*cook*) cocerse **2.** *inf* (*be hot*) achicharrarse **II.** *vt* cocer al horno

baker ['beɪkəʳ, *Am:* -kɚ] *n* panadero, -a *m, f*

bakery ['beɪkəri] *n* panadería *f*

baking *adj* **it's ~ hot** hace un calor achicharrante

balance ['bælənts] **I.** *n* **1.** (*device*) balanza *f* **2.** *no pl* (*equilibrium*) equilibrio *m*; **to lose one's ~** perder el equilibrio **3.** FIN saldo *m*; (*difference*) balance *m* **II.** *vi* equilibrarse **III.** *vt* equilibrar; **to ~ sth against sth** comparar algo con algo; **to ~ the books** hacer cuadrar los libros de cuentas

balance sheet *n* balance *m*

balcony ['bælkəni] *n* balcón *m*
bald [bɔːld] *adj* calvo, pelón *Méx*
bale [beɪl] *n* fardo *m*
Balearic Islands [ˌbæli'ærɪk-, *Am:* ˌbɑːli'-] *n* the ~ las Islas Baleares
balk [bɔːk] *vi* to ~ **at sth** resistirse a algo
Balkans ['bɔlkəns] *n* the ~ los Balcanes
ball [bɔːl] *n* **1.** (*for golf, tennis*) pelota *f*; (*for football, basketball*) balón *m*; **to play** ~ jugar a la pelota; *fig* cooperar **2.** (*shape*) bola *f* **3.** (*dance*) baile *m*; **to have a** ~ *fig* divertirse
ballad ['bæləd] *n* balada *f*
ballast ['bæləst] *n no pl* NAUT lastre *m*
ballet dancer ['bæleɪˌdɑːntsər, *Am:* 'bæleɪˌdæːntsər] *n* bailarín, -ina *m, f*
balloon [bə'luːn] *n* globo *m*
ballot ['bælət] *n* votación *f*
ballpoint (pen) [ˌbɔːlpɔɪnt (pen)] *n* bolígrafo *m*, birome *m RíoPl*
ballroom ['bɔːlrʊm] *n* salón *m* de baile
Baltic ['bɔːltɪk] *n* the ~ (**Sea**) el (Mar) Báltico
bamboo [bæm'buː] *n no pl* bambú *m*
ban [bæn] **I.** *n* prohibición *f* **II.** *vt* <-nn-> prohibir
banal [bə'nɑːl] *adj* banal
banana [bə'nɑːnə, *Am:* -'nænə] *n* plátano *m*, banana *f AmL*; **to go ~s** *inf* (*mad*) volverse majara
band¹ [bænd] *n* **1.** (*strip: of cloth, metal*) banda *f*; (*ribbon*) cinta *f* **2.** (*stripe*) franja *f*
band² [bænd] *n* MUS grupo *m*; (*of friends*) pandilla *f*; (*of robbers*) banda *f*
bandage ['bændɪdʒ] *n* vendaje *m*
band-aid ['bændeɪd] *n* tirita® *f*, curita *f AmL*
bandit ['bændɪt] *n* bandido, -a *m, f*, carrilano, -a *m, f Chile*
bandwagon ['bændwægən] *n* **to jump on the** ~ *fig* subirse al carro
bang [bæŋ] **I.** *n* (*noise, blow*) golpe *m*; (*explosion*) detonación *f*; **to go with a** ~ *fig* ser todo un éxito **II.** *adv*

1. *inf* (*exactly*) ~ **in the middle** justo en medio **2.** (*making noise*) **to go** ~ estallar **III.** *vi* cerrarse de golpe **IV.** *vt* golpear
Bangladesh [bæŋglə'deʃ] *n* Bangladesh *m*
banish ['bænɪʃ] *vt a. fig* desterrar
banister ['bænɪstər, *Am:* -əstər] *n* pasamano(s) *m* (*inv*)
bank¹ [bæŋk] *n* **1.** FIN banco *m* **2.** (*storage place*) depósito *m*
bank² [bæŋk] *n* (*of river*) orilla *m*
bank³ [bæŋk] *n* (*of earth*) terraplén *m*; (*of fog*) banco *m*
bank account *n* cuenta *f* bancaria
banker ['bæŋkər, *Am:* -kər] *n* banquero, -a *m, f*
bank holiday *n Am, Brit* día *m* festivo, día *m* feriado *AmL*
banking *n no pl* banca *f*
bank manager *n* gerente *mf* de banco
bankrupt ['bæŋkrʌpt] *adj* **to be** ~ estar en quiebra; **to go** ~ quebrar
bankruptcy ['bæŋkrəptsi] *n* <-ies> bancarrota *f*
banner ['bænər, *Am:* -ər] *n* bandera *f*
banquet ['bæŋkwɪt, *Am:* -kwət] *n* banquete *m*
banter ['bæntər, *Am:* -ţər] *n* bromas *fpl*
baptise [bæp'taɪz] *vt Aus, Brit s.* **baptize**
baptism ['bæptɪzəm] *n* bautismo *m*
Baptist ['bæptɪst] *n* bautista *mf*
baptize [bæp'taɪz, *Am:* 'bæp-] *vt* bautizar
bar¹ [bɑːr, *Am:* bɑːr] **I.** *n* **1.** (*of metal, wood*) barra *f*; (*of cage, prison*) barrote *m*; (*of chocolate*) tableta *f*; (*of gold*) lingote *m*; (*of soap*) pastilla *f*; **to be behind ~s** *inf* estar entre rejas **2.** (*place to drink*) bar *m*; (*counter*) mostrador *m* **II.** *vt* <-rr-> **1.** (*fasten: door, window*) a-trancar **2.** (*obstruct*) obstruir **3.** (*prohibit*) prohibir
bar² [bɑːr, *Am:* bɑːr] *prep Brit* excepto; ~ **none** sin excepción
barb [bɑːb, *Am:* bɑːrb] *n* púa *f*
Barbados [bɑː'beɪdɒs, *Am:* bɑːr-

'bɑɪdoʊs] n Barbados m

barbarian [bɑːˈbeərɪən, *Am:* bɑːrˈberɪ-] n bárbaro, -a m, f

barbaric [bɑːˈbærɪk, *Am:* bɑːrˈber-] adj, **barbarous** [ˈbɑːbərəs, *Am:* ˈbɑːr-] adj bárbaro

barbecue [ˈbɑːbɪkjuː, *Am:* ˈbɑːr-] n barbacoa f, parrillada f *Col, Ven,* asado m *Chile*

barbed wire [bɑːbd-, *Am:* bɑːrbd-] n alambre m de púas

barber [ˈbɑːbəʳ, *Am:* ˈbɑːrbɚ] n barbero m

bare [beəʳ, *Am:* beʳ] I. adj 1. (naked) desnudo; (uncovered) descubierto; **with one's ~ hands** con las propias manos; **to fight with one's ~ hands** luchar sin armas; **to tell sb the ~ facts** decir a alguien la pura verdad; **the ~ minimum** lo mínimo 2. (empty) vacío II. vt **to ~ one's heart to sb** abrir el corazón a alguien

barely [ˈbeəli, *Am:* ˈber-] adv apenas, agatas *Arg, Urug, Par*

bargain [ˈbɑːgɪn, *Am:* ˈbɑːr-] n 1. (agreement) trato m; **to drive a hard ~** saber regatear; **to strike a ~** cerrar un trato; **into the ~** por añadidura 2. (item) ganga f, pichincha f *Arg, Bol, Par, Urug,* mamada f *AmC, Bol, Chile, Perú*

♦ **bargain for** vi **to get more than one bargained for** recibir más de lo que uno se esperaba

barge [bɑːdʒ, *Am:* bɑːrdʒ] n barcaza f

♦ **barge in** vi entrar sin avisar

baritone [ˈbærɪtəʊn, *Am:* ˈberətoʊn] n barítono m

bark¹ [bɑːk, *Am:* bɑːrk] I. n (of dog) ladrido m; **his ~ is worse than his bite** perro ladrador, poco mordedor *prov* II. vi ladrar

bark² n no pl (of tree) corteza f

barley [ˈbɑːli, *Am:* ˈbɑːr-] n no pl cebada f

barmaid [ˈbɑːmeɪd, *Am:* ˈbɑːr-] n camarera f

barman [ˈbɑːmən, *Am:* ˈbɑːr-] n <-men> camarero m

barn [bɑːn, *Am:* bɑːrn] n granero

barnacle [ˈbɑːnəkl, *Am:* ˈbɑːr-] n bálano m

barometer [bəˈrɒmɪtəʳ, *Am:* -ˈrɑːmətɚ] n barómetro m

baron [ˈbærən, *Am:* ˈber-] n barón m

baroness [ˈbærənɪs, *Am:* ˈbernəs] n baronesa f

baroque [bəˈrɒk, *Am:* -ˈroʊk] adj barroco

barracks [ˈbærəks, *Am:* ˈber-] npl cuartel m

barrage [ˈbærɑːʒ, *Am:* bəˈrɑːʒ] n (of questions) aluvión m

barrel [ˈbærəl, *Am:* ˈber-] n 1. (container) barril m 2. (of gun) cañón m

barren [ˈbærən, *Am:* ˈber-] adj estéril

barricade [ˌbærɪˈkeɪd, *Am:* ˌberə-] n barricada f

barrier [ˈbærɪəʳ, *Am:* ˈberɪɚ] n barrera f

barring [ˈbɑːrɪŋ] prep excepto; **~ complications** a menos que se presenten complicaciones

barrister [ˈbærɪstəʳ, *Am:* ˈberɪstɚ] n *Aus, Brit* abogado, -a m, f

barrow [ˈbærəʊ, *Am:* ˈberoʊ] n (wheelbarrow) carretilla f; (cart) carreta f

bartender [ˈbɑːtendəʳ, *Am:* ˈbɑːrtendɚ] n camarero, -a m, f

barter [ˈbɑːtəʳ, *Am:* ˈbɑːrt̬ɚ] vt **to ~ sth for sth** trocar algo por algo

basalt [ˈbæsɔːlt, *Am:* bəˈsɔːlt] n no pl basalto m

base [beɪs] I. n 1. (lower part) base f 2. (bottom) fondo m 3. MIL base f II. vt basar; **to be ~d on** basarse en

baseball [ˈbeɪsbɔːl] n béisbol m

bash [bæʃ] vt golpear

bashful [ˈbæʃfl] adj tímido

basic [ˈbeɪsɪk] adj básico

basically adv básicamente

basil [ˈbæzəl, *Am:* ˈbeɪzəl] n albahaca f

basin [ˈbeɪsn] n 1. (for cooking) cuenco m; (for washing) lavabo m 2. GEO cuenca f

basis [ˈbeɪsɪs] n <bases> base f; **on a weekly ~** semanalmente; **to be**

the ~ **for sth** ser el fundamento de
algo
bask [bɑːsk, *Am:* bæsk] *vi* **to ~ in
the sun** tomar el sol
basket ['bɑːskɪt, *Am:* 'bæskət] *n*
cesto *m;* SPORTS canasta *f*
basketball ['bɑːskɪtbɔːl, *Am:* 'bæs-
kətbɔːl] *n* baloncesto *m*
Basque [bæsk] *adj* vasco; ~
Country País *m* Vasco
bass [beɪs] *n* (*voice, electrical*) bajo
m; (*instrument*) contrabajo *m*
bastard ['bɑːstəd, *Am:* 'bæstəd] *n*
vulg cabrón, -ona *m, f*
bastion ['bæstɪən, *Am:* -tʃən] *n a.*
fig baluarte *m*
bat[1] [bæt] *n* ZOOL murciélago *m;* **to
be as blind as a ~** no ver tres en un
burro
bat[2] *vt* **to ~ one's eyelids** pestañear;
she didn't ~ an eyelid ni siquiera
pestañeó
bat[3] SPORTS **I.** *n* bate *m* **II.** *vt, vi* <-tt-*>
batear
batch [bætʃ] *n* <-es> tanda *f;* COM,
INFOR lote *m*
bath [bɑːθ, *Am:* bæθ] **I.** *n* **1.** (*container*) bañera *f*, tina *f AmL*, bañadera *f Arg* **2.** (*action*) baño *m*, bañada *f*
Méx; **to have a ~** bañarse **II.** *vt*
bañar
bathe [beɪð] **I.** *vi* bañarse **II.** *vt*
(*wound, eyes*) lavar; (*person, ani-
mal*) bañar; **to be ~d in sweat** estar
bañado en sudor
bathing *n no pl* baño *m*
bathing cap *n* gorro *m* de baño
bathing costume *n Aus, Brit,*
bathing suit *n Am* traje *m* de baño,
bañador *m*
bathroom ['bɑːθruːm] *n* (cuarto *m*
de) baño *m*
bathtub ['bɑːθtʌb, *Am:* 'bæθ-] *n*
bañera *f*, tina *f AmL*, bañadera *f Arg*
baton ['bætən, *Am:* bə'tɑːn] *n* MUS
batuta *f;* (*of policeman*) porra *f;*
SPORTS testigo *m*
batsman ['bætsmən] <-men> *n* ba-
teador *m*
battalion [bə'tælɪən, *Am:* -jən] *n*
batallón *m*
batter ['bætər, *Am:* 'bæʈər] **I.** *n*

1. GASTR (*for fried food*) rebozado *m;*
(*for pancake*) masa *f* **2.** *Am* SPORTS
bateador(a) *m(f)* **II.** *vt* **1.** (*assault*)
maltratar, pegar **2.** (*hit*) golpear
3. GASTR rebozar
battered ['bætəd, *Am:* -əd] *adj*
1. (*injured*) maltratado **2.** (*damaged*) estropeado
battering ['bætərɪŋ, *Am:* 'bæʈ-] *n*
paliza *f*
battery ['bætəri, *Am:* 'bæʈ-] <-ies>
n **1.** (*for radio, torch*) pila *f;* (*for car*)
batería *f* **2.** (*large number*) serie *f;* **a
~ of questions** una sarta de pregun-
tas
battle ['bætl, *Am:* 'bæʈ-] **I.** *n* MIL batalla *f;* (*struggle*) lucha *f;* **to fight a
losing ~** *fig* luchar por una causa
perdida **II.** *vi* luchar
battle cry *n* grito *m* de guerra
battlefield *n* campo *m* de batalla
battleground *n* campo *m* de batalla
battleship *n* acorazado *m*
bawl [bɔːl, *Am:* bɑːl] *vi* (*bellow*) vociferar; **to ~ at sb** gritar a alguien
bay[1] [beɪ] *n* GEO bahía *f*
bay[2] *n* BOT laurel *m*
bay[3] [beɪ] **I.** *vi* aullar **II.** *n* **to bring
sb to ~** acorralar a alguien; **to hold
sth at ~** mantener algo a raya
bayonet ['beɪənɪt, *Am:* ˌbeɪə'net] *n*
bayoneta *f*
bazaar [bə'zɑːʳ, *Am:* -'zɑːr] *n* bazar
m
BBC ['biːbiːˈsiː] *n abbr of* **British
Broadcasting Corporation** BBC *f*
BC [ˌbiːˈsiː] *adv abbr of* **before
Christ** a.C.
be [biː] <was, been> **I.** *vi* **1.** + *adj/n*
(*permanent state, quality, identity*)
ser; **she's a cook** es cocinera; **she's
Spanish** es española; **to ~ good** ser
bueno; **to ~ able to do sth** ser capaz
de hacer algo; **to ~ married** estar [*o*
ser *CSur*] casado **2.** + *adj* (*mental
and physical states*) estar; **to ~ fat**
estar gordo; **to ~ hungry** tener
hambre; **to ~ happy** estar contento
3. (*age*) tener; **I'm 21** tengo 21 años
4. (*measurement*) medir; (*weight*)
pesar; **to ~ 2 metres long** medir 2

metros de largo 5. (*exist, live*) **there is/are …** hay… 6. (*location, situation*) estar; **to ~ in Rome** estar en Roma 7. *pp* (*go*) **I've never ~en to Mexico** nunca he estado en Méjico 8. (*expresses possibility*) **can it ~ that …?** *form* ¿puede ser que… +*subj*? II. *impers vb* (*expressing physical conditions, circumstances*) **it's cloudy** está nublado; **it's sunny** hace sol; **it's two o'clock** son las dos III. *aux vb* 1. (*expresses continuation*) estar; **to ~ doing sth** estar haciendo algo; **don't sing while I'm reading** no cantes mientras estoy leyendo [*o* mientras leo]; **she's leaving tomorrow** se va mañana 2. (*expresses passive*) ser; **to ~ discovered by sb** ser descubierto por alguien; **he was left speechless** se quedó sin habla 3. (*expresses future*) **we are to visit Peru in the winter** vamos a ir a Perú en invierno; **what are we to do?** ¿qué podemos hacer? 4. (*expresses future in past*) **she was never to see her brother again** nunca más volvería a ver a su hermano 5. (*expresses subjunctive possibility in conditionals*) **if he was to work harder, he'd get better grades** si trabajara más, tendría mejores notas 6. (*expresses obligation*) **you are to come here right now** tienes que venir aquí ahora mismo 7. (*in question tags*) **she is tall, isn't she?** es alta, ¿no?

beach [bi:tʃ] *n* playa *f*

beacon ['bi:kən] *n* baliza *f*

bead [bi:d] *n* (*of glass*) abalorio *m*; **~s of sweat** gotas *fpl* de sudor

beak [bi:k] *n* pico *m*

beaker ['bi:kər, *Am:* -kɚ] *n* vaso *m*

beam [bi:m] I. *n* 1. (*ray*) rayo *m* 2. ARCHIT viga *f* II. *vt* transmitir III. *vi* brillar; (*smile*) sonreír (abiertamente)

bean [bi:n] *n* (*vegetable: fresh*) judía *f* verde, ejote *m Méx*, chaucha *f RíoPl*; (*dried*) alubia *f*; **coffee ~** grano *m* de café; **to be full of ~s** *fig* estar lleno de vida; **to spill the ~s** *fig* descubrir el pastel

bear[1] [beər, *Am:* ber] *n* ZOOL oso, -a *m, f*

bear[2] [beər, *Am:* ber] <bore, borne> I. *vt* 1. (*carry*) llevar; **to ~ arms** *form* portar armas 2. (*display*) **to ~ a resemblance to …** parecerse a… 3. (*have, possess*) tener 4. (*support: weight*) aguantar 5. (*accept: cost*) correr con; (*responsibility*) cargar con 6. (*endure: hardship, pain*) soportar; **what might have happened doesn't ~ thinking about** da miedo sólo de pensar lo que podía haber pasado 7. (*tolerate*) soportar 8. **to ~ sb a grudge** tener rencor a alguien; **to ~ sth in mind** tener algo presente; **to ~ witness to sth** atestiguar algo 9. (*give birth to*) dar a luz 10. (*fruit*) dar II. *vi* (*tend*) **to ~ east** dirigirse al este; **to ~ left** torcer a la izquierda

◆ **bear down on** *vt* avanzar hacia

◆ **bear on** *vt* tener que ver con

◆ **bear up** *vi* aguantar

beard [bɪəd, *Am:* bɪrd] *n* barba *f*

bearer ['beərər, *Am:* 'berɚ] *n* portador/a *m(f)*

bearing ['beərɪŋ, *Am:* 'berɪŋ] *n* NAUT rumbo *m*; **to get one's ~s** a. *fig* orientarse; **to lose one's ~s** a. *fig* desorientarse; **to have some ~ on sth** tener que ver con algo

beast [bi:st] *n* 1. (*animal*) bestia *f* 2. *inf* (*person*) animal *m*

beat [bi:t] I. *n* 1. (*pulsation: of heart*) latido *m*; (*of pulse*) pulsación *f*; (*of hammer*) martilleo *m* 2. MUS (*stress*) tiempo *m*; (*rhythm*) ritmo *m* 3. *no pl* (*of police officer*) ronda *f* II. <beat, beaten> *vt* 1. (*strike*) golpear; (*metal, eggs*) batir; (*carpet*) sacudir, festejar *Méx*; **to ~ sb black and blue** dar una paliza soberana a alguien; **to ~ a confession out of sb** hacer confesar a alguien a base de palos 2. (*wings*) batir 3. (*defeat*) ganar; **if you can't ~ them, join them** *prov* si no puedes con ellos, únete a ellos; **it ~s me why …** no llego a comprender por qué… 4. MUS (*drum*) tocar III. <beat, beaten> *vi* (*pulsate*) latir; (*wings*) batir; (*drum*) redoblar

◆ **beat back** *vt* rechazar

◆ **beat up** *vt* dar una paliza a

beaten ['biːtn, *Am:* 'biːt̬n] *pp of* **beat**

beating ['biːtɪŋ, *Am:* 'biːt̬ɪŋ] *n* **1.** (*assault*) paliza *f,* cueriza *f AmL;* **to give sb a** ~ dar una paliza a alguien **2.** (*defeat*) derrota *f* **3.** (*of heart*) latido *m*

beautiful ['bjuːtɪfl, *Am:* -t̬ə-] *adj* precioso; (*weather, meal*) estupendo

beauty ['bjuːti, *Am:* -t̬i] <-ies> *n* **1.** *no pl* (*property*) belleza *f;* ~ **is in the eye of the beholder** *prov* todo depende del color del cristal con que se mira **2.** (*woman*) belleza *f*

beaver ['biːvəʳ, *Am:* -vɚ] *n* castor *m*

became [bɪ'keɪm] *pt of* **become**

because [bɪ'kɒz, *Am:* -'kɑːz] **I.** *conj* porque **II.** *prep* ~ **of** a causa de; ~ **of illness** por enfermedad

beck [bek] *n* **to be at sb's** ~ **and call** estar siempre a la entera disposición de alguien

beckon ['bekən] *vt* llamar por señas; **to** ~ **sb over** hacer señas a alguien para que se acerque

become [bɪ'kʌm] <became, become> *vi* (+ *adj*) volverse; (+ *n*) llegar a ser; **to** ~ **a lawyer/teacher** hacerse abogado/profesor; **to** ~ **angry** enfadarse; **to** ~ **famous** hacerse famoso; **to** ~ **sad/happy** ponerse triste/contento; **to** ~ **interested in sth** interesarse por algo

bed [bed] *n* **1.** (*furniture*) cama *f;* **to get out of** ~ levantarse de la cama; **to go to** ~ acostarse; **to go to** ~ **with sb** acostarse con alguien; **to make the** ~ hacer la cama; **to put sb to** ~ acostar a alguien **2.** (*flower patch*) arriate *m,* cantero *m RíoPl* **3.** (*base*) base *f* **4.** (*bottom: of sea*) fondo *m;* (*of river*) lecho *m;* **a** ~ **of roses** un lecho de rosas *f*

BEd [biːˈed] *abbr of* **Bachelor of Education** Ldo., -a *m, f* en Magisterio

bed and breakfast *n* pensión *f* familiar

bedding ['bedɪŋ] *n no pl* ropa *f* de

cama; (*for animal*) cama *f*

bedrock ['bedrɒk, *Am:* -rɑːk] *n no pl* **1.** GEO roca *f* firme **2.** *fig* cimientos *mpl*

bedroom ['bedrʊm, *Am:* -ruːm] *n* dormitorio *m,* recámara *f Méx*

bedside ['bedsaɪd] *n no pl* cabecera *f* (de la cama)

bedside table *n* mesita *f* de noche, nochero *m Col, Chile, Urug,* búro *m Méx*

bedtime ['bedtaɪm] *n no pl* hora *f* de acostarse

bee [biː] *n* abeja *f;* **to have a** ~ **in one's bonnet about sth** tener algo metido entre ceja y ceja

beech [biːtʃ] *n* haya *f*

beef [biːf] *n no pl* carne *f* de ternera [*o* de res *AmC, Méx*]

beefburger ['biːfˌbɜːgəʳ, *Am:* -ˌbɜːr-gɚ] *n* hamburguesa *f*

beehive ['biːhaɪv] *n* colmena *f*

been [biːn, *Am:* bɪn] *pp of* **be**

beep [biːp] **I.** *n* pitido *m* **II.** *vi* pitar

beer [bɪəʳ, *Am:* bɪr] *n* cerveza *f*

beet [biːt] *n* **1.** (*sugar beet*) remolacha *f* (azucarera) **2.** *Am* (*beetroot*) remolacha *f,* betabel *f Méx*

beetle ['biːtl, *Am:* -t̬l] *n* escarabajo *m*

beetroot ['biːtruːt] *n* remolacha *f,* betabel *f Méx;* **to go as red as a** ~ ponerse rojo como un tomate

before [bɪ'fɔːʳ, *Am:* -'fɔːr] **I.** *prep* **1.** (*earlier*) antes de; **to leave** ~ **sb** salir antes que alguien; ~ **doing sth** antes de hacer algo **2.** (*in front of*) delante de; ~ **our eyes** ante nuestros ojos **3.** (*having priority*) antes que; ~ **everything** antes que nada; **to put sth** ~ **sth else** anteponer algo a algo **II.** *adv* antes; **the day** ~ el día anterior; **two days** ~ dos días antes; **as** ~ como antes **III.** *conj* antes de que +*subj;* **he spoke** ~ **she went out** habló antes de que ella se saliera; **he had a glass** ~ **he went** se tomó una copa antes de irse

beforehand [bɪ'fɔːhænd, *Am:* -'fɔːr-] *adv* de antemano

befriend [bɪ'frend] *vt* hacerse amigo de

beg [beg] <-gg-> **I.** *vt* (*request*)

rogar; **to ~ sb to do sth** suplicar a alguien que haga algo; **to ~ sb's pardon** pedir disculpas a alguien; **I ~ your pardon!** ¡disculpe! **II.** *vi* pedir (limosna); **to ~ for sth** pedir algo; **there are jobs going ~ging** *inf* hay trabajos a patadas

began [bɪˈgæn] *pt of* **begin**

beget [bɪˈget] <begot, begotten> *vt* engendrar

beggar [ˈbegəʳ, *Am:* -ɚ] **I.** *vt* **to ~ belief** parecer absolutamente inverosímil; **to ~ description** resultar indescriptible **II.** *n* mendigo, -a *m*, *f*, limosnero, -a *m*, *f AmL;* **~s can't be choosers** *prov* a buen hambre no hay pan duro *prov*

begin [bɪˈgɪn] <began, begun> **I.** *vt* empezar; **to ~ a conversation** entablar una conversación; **to ~ doing sth** empezar a hacer algo; **to ~ work** empezar a trabajar **II.** *vi* empezar; **the film ~s at eight** la película comienza a las ocho; **to ~ with ...** al principio...; (*enumeration*) primero...

beginner [bɪˈgɪnəʳ, *Am:* -ɚ] *n* principiante *mf*

beginning *n* **1.** (*start*) principio *m*, empiezo *m Arg, Col, Ecua, Guat;* **at the ~** al principio; **from ~ to end** de principio a fin **2.** (*origin*) origen *m*

begot [bɪgɒt, *Am:* -ˈgɑt] *pt of* **beget**

begotten [bɪˈgɒtn, *Am:* -ˈgːɑtn] *pp of* **beget**

begun [bɪˈgʌn] *pp of* **begin**

behalf [bɪˈhɑːf, *Am:* -ˈhæf] *n no pl* **on ~ of sb** (*for*) en beneficio de alguien; (*from*) de parte de alguien

behave [bɪˈheɪv] *vi* comportarse; **to ~ badly** portarse mal

behavior *n no pl, Am, Aus,* **behaviour** [bɪˈheɪvjəʳ, *Am:* -vjɚ] *n no pl, Aus, Brit* comportamiento *m*

behind [bɪˈhaɪnd] **I.** *prep* **1.** (*to the rear of*) detrás de; **right ~ sb** justo detrás de alguien; **~ the wheel** al volante; **there is somebody ~ this** *fig* hay alguien detrás de todo esto **2.** (*in support of*) **to be ~ sb** (**all the way**) estar con alguien (hasta el final) **3.** (*late for*) **~ time** retrasado;

to be ~ schedule ir con retraso; **to be ~ the times** estar atrasado con respecto a la época **II.** *adv* **1.** (*at the back*) por detrás; **to fall ~** (*be slower*) quedarse atrás; (*in work, studies*) atrasarse; **to come from ~** venir desde atrás; **to leave sb ~** dejar a alguien atrás; **to stay ~** quedarse atrás **2.** (*overdue*) **to be ~** retrasarse; **he is a long way ~** está muy retrasado; **to be ~** (**in sth**) estar atrasado (en algo) **III.** *n inf* trasero *m*

behold [bɪˈhəʊld, *Am:* -ˈhoʊld] *vt* contemplar

beige [beɪʒ] *adj* beige *inv*

being [ˈbiːɪŋ] **I.** *n* **1.** (*creature*) ser *m;* **to come into ~** nacer **2.** (*soul*) alma *f* **II.** *pres p of* be

Belarus [beləˈrʌs] *n* Bielorrusia *f*

belated [bɪˈleɪtɪd, *Am:* -ţɪd] *adj* tardío

belch [beltʃ] *vi* eructar

beleaguered [bɪˈliːgəʳd, *Am:* -gɚd] *adj* (*city*) asediado; (*person*) acosado

Belgian [ˈbeldʒən] *adj* belga

Belgium [ˈbeldʒəm] *n* Bélgica *f*

belie [bɪˈlaɪ] *irr vt* desmentir

belief [bɪˈliːf] *n a.* REL creencia *f;* **to the best of my ~** *Brit* que yo sepa; **to be beyond ~** ser increíble; **in the ~ that ...** con la convicción de que...

believable [bɪˈliːvəbl] *adj* creíble

believe [bɪˈliːv] **I.** *vt* creer; **she couldn't ~ her eyes** no podía dar crédito a sus ojos; **I can't ~ how ...** me cuesta creer cómo...; **~ it or not, ...** aunque parezca mentira,... **II.** *vi* creer; **to ~ in sth** (*support*) ser partidario de algo

believer [bɪˈliːvəʳ, *Am:* -vɚ] *n* **1.** REL creyente *mf* **2.** (*supporter*) partidario, -a *m*, *f;* **to be a ~ in sth** ser partidario de algo

belittle [bɪˈlɪtl, *Am:* -ˈlɪt̬-] *vt* menospreciar

bell [bel] *n* (*of church*) campana *f;* (*handbell*) campanilla *f;* (*on hat, cat*) cascabel *m;* (*of bicycle, door*) timbre *m;* **his name/face rings a ~** me suena su nombre/cara

belligerent [bɪ'lɪdʒərənt] *adj* beligerante

bellow ['beləʊ, *Am:* -oʊ] *vi* (*animal*) bramar; (*person*) gritar

bellows ['beləʊz, *Am:* -oʊz] *npl* fuelle *m*

belly ['beli] <-ies> *n inf* barriga *f*, guata *f Chile*

belly button *n inf* ombligo *m*

belong [bɪ'lɒŋ, *Am:* -'lɑːŋ] *vi* 1. (*be property of*) **to ~ to** sb/sth pertenecer a alguien/algo 2. (*be member of*) **to ~ to** (*club*) ser socio de; (*party*) estar afiliado a 3. (*have a place*) **this doesn't ~ here** esto no va aquí; I **feel I don't ~ here** no me encuentro a gusto aquí; **they ~ together** están hechos el uno para el otro

belongings *npl* pertenencias *fpl*

beloved [bɪ'lʌvɪd] *n no pl* amado, -a *m, f*

below [bɪ'ləʊ, *Am:* -'loʊ] I. *prep* 1. (*lower than, underneath*) debajo de; **~ the table** debajo de [*o* bajo] la mesa; **~ us** debajo de nosotros; **~ sea level** por debajo del nivel del mar 2. (*less than*) **~ average** por debajo de la media; **~ freezing** bajo cero; **it's 4 degrees ~ zero** estamos a 4 grados bajo cero; **children ~ the age of twelve** niños menores de doce años; **to be ~** sb (*unworthy of*) no ser digno de alguien II. *adv* abajo; **from ~** desde abajo; **see ~** (*in a text*) ver más adelante

belt [belt] I. *n* 1. FASHION cinturón *m*; **to fasten one's ~** abrocharse el cinturón; **to tighten one's ~** *fig* apretarse el cinturón 2. TECH correa *f* 3. (*area*) zona *f* 4. *inf* (*punch*) golpe *m* II. *vt inf* (*hit*) zurrar

bemoan [bɪ'məʊn, *Am:* -'moʊn] *vt form* lamentar

bemused [bɪ'mjuːzd] *adj* desconcertado

bench [bentʃ] *n* banco *m*; **the ~** SPORTS el banquillo; LAW la judicatura

benchmark ['bentʃmɑːk, *Am:* -mɑːrk] *n* punto *m* de referencia

bend [bend] <bent, bent> I. *n* (*of river, road*) curva *f*; (*of pipe*) codo *m*; **to take a ~** tomar una curva; **to go round the ~** *fig* volverse loco II. *vi* (*person*) inclinarse; (*thing*) doblarse III. *vt* (*arms, legs*) doblar; (*head*) inclinar; **to ~ the rules** interpretar las reglas a su manera; **to ~ sb to one's will** doblar a alguien a su voluntad

◆ **bend over** *vi* inclinarse

beneath [bɪ'niːθ] I. *prep* (*lower than, underneath*) debajo de; **~ the table** debajo de la mesa; **to be ~ sb in rank** tener un rango por debajo de alguien; **to be ~ sb** (*unworthy of*) no ser digno de alguien II. *adv* abajo

benefactor ['benɪfæktəʳ] *n* benefactor *m*

beneficiary [ˌbenɪ'fɪʃəri] *n* <-ies> beneficiario, -a *m, f*

benefit ['benɪfɪt] I. *n* 1. (*profit*) beneficio *m;* **for the ~ of sb** a beneficio de alguien 2. (*welfare payment*) subsidio *m* II.<-t- *o* -tt-> *vi* **to ~ from sth** beneficiarse de algo III.<-t- *o* -tt-> *vt* beneficiar

Benin [ben'iːn] *n* Benín *m*

bent [bent] I. *pt, pp of* **bend** II. *n* **to have a ~ for sth** tener una inclinación por algo; **to follow one's ~** obrar de acuerdo a sus inclinaciones III. *adj* 1. (*not straight*) torcido 2. (*determined*) **to be ~ on** (*doing*) sth estar empeñado en (hacer) algo 3. *inf* (*corrupt*) corrupto

bequeath [bɪ'kwiːð] *vt* legar

bequest [bɪ'kwest] *n* legado *m*

berate [bɪ'reɪt] *vt form* reprender

bereaved *n* **the ~** la familia del difunto

bereavement [bɪ'riːvmənt] *n* muerte *f* (de un familiar)

bereft [bɪ'reft] *adj form* **to be ~ of sth** estar privado de algo; **to feel ~** sentirse desolado

beret ['bereɪ, *Am:* bə'reɪ] *n* boina *f*

Bermuda [bɜː'mjuːdə, *Am:* bə-] *n* las Bermudas

berry ['beri] <-ies> *n* baya *f*

berth [bɜːθ, *Am:* bɜːrθ] *n* (*on ship*) camarote *m;* (*on train*) litera *f;* (*in harbour*) amarradero *m;* **to give sb a wide ~** *fig* evitar a alguien

beseech [bɪ'siːtʃ] <beseeched, be-

sought> *vt form* **to ~ sb to do sth** suplicar a alguien que haga algo

beset [bɪˈset] <beset, beset> *vt* **to be ~ by sth** estar acosado por algo

beside [bɪˈsaɪd] *prep* **1.** (*next to*) al lado de; **right ~ sb** justo al lado de alguien **2.** (*in comparison to*) frente a **3.** (*overwhelmed*) **to be ~ oneself** estar fuera de sí **4.** (*irrelevant*) **to be ~ the point** no venir al caso

besides [bɪˈsaɪdz] **I.** *prep* **1.** (*in addition to*) además de **2.** (*except for*) excepto **II.** *adv* además

besiege [bɪˈsiːdʒ] *vt* sitiar; (*with questions*) acosar

best [best] **I.** *adj superl of* **good** mejor; **the ~** el/la mejor; **the ~ days of my life** los mejores días de mi vida; **the ~ part** (*the majority*) la mayor parte; **may the ~ man win** que gane el mejor; **with the ~ will** con la mejor voluntad **II.** *adv superl of* **well** mejor; **the ~** lo mejor; **we'd ~ stay here** lo mejor es quedarse aquí **III.** *n no pl* **1.** (*the finest*) **all the ~!** *inf* (*congratulation*) ¡felicidades!; (*end of letter*) un abrazo; **to be the ~ of friends** ser muy buenos amigos; **to bring out the ~ in sb** sacar lo mejor de alguien; **to turn out for the ~** ir para bien; **to wear one's Sunday ~** llevar el traje de los domingos; **to the ~ of my knowledge** que yo sepa; **at ~** como mucho, a lo mucho *Méx* **2.** SPORTS récord *m*

bestow [bɪˈstəʊ, *Am:* -ˈstoʊ] *vt form* **to ~ sth on sb** otorgar algo a alguien

bestseller [ˈbestselər, *Am:* -ɚ] *n* éxito *m* de ventas

bet [bet] <bet *o* -ted, bet *o* -ted> **I.** *n* apuesta *f*; **it is a safe ~ that ...** es casi seguro que... +*subj*; **to be the best ~** ser la mejor opción; **to place a ~ on sth** apostar por algo **II.** *vt* apostar; **I ~ you don't!** ¡a que no lo haces! **III.** *vi* apostar; **to ~ on sth** apostar por algo; **I wouldn't ~ on it** yo no estaría tan seguro; **you ~!** *inf* ¡ya lo creo!

beta [ˈbiːtə, *Am:* ˈbeɪtə] *n* beta *f*

betray [bɪˈtreɪ] *vt* **1.** (*be disloyal to*) traicionar; **to ~ a promise** romper una promesa; **to ~ sb's trust** defraudar la confianza de alguien **2.** (*reveal*) delatar; **to ~ one's ignorance** demostrar ignorancia

betrayal [bɪˈtreɪəl] *n* traición *f*; **an act of ~** una traición

better [ˈbetər, *Am:* ˈbeṭɚ] **I.** *adj comp of* **good** mejor; **to be ~** MED estar mejor; **~ than nothing** mejor que nada **II.** *adv comp of* **well** mejor; **I like this ~** me gusta más esto; **there is nothing I like ~ than ...** nada me gusta más que...; **It'll be ~ to tell her** más vale decírselo; **you had ~ go** (será) mejor que te vayas; **to think ~ of sth** cambiar de opinión respecto a algo; **or ~ still ...** o mejor... **III.** *n no pl* el/la mejor; **to change for the ~** cambiar para bien; **the sooner, the ~** cuanto antes, mejor; **so much the ~** tanto mejor; **for ~ or (for) worse** para lo bueno y lo malo; **to get the ~ of sb** vencer a alguien

betting [ˈbetɪŋ] *n no pl* apuestas *fpl*; **the ~ is that ...** lo más probable es que... +*subj*

between [bɪˈtwiːn] **I.** *prep* entre; **to eat ~ meals** comer entre horas; **nothing will come ~ them** nada se interpondrá entre ellos; **the 3 children have £10 ~ them** entre los 3 niños tienen 10 libras **II.** *adv* (**in**) ~ en medio; (*time*) a mitad

beverage [ˈbevərɪdʒ] *n form* bebida *f*

beware [bɪˈweər, *Am:* ˈwer] *vi* tener cuidado; **~ of pickpockets!** ¡cuidado con los carteristas!

bewilder [bɪˈwɪldər, *Am:* -dɚ] *vt* desconcertar

bewildered *adj* desconcertado

bewildering *adj* desconcertante

bewilderment *n no pl* desconcierto *m*

beyond [bɪˈjɒnd, *Am:* -ˈɑːnd] **I.** *prep* **1.** (*on other side of*) más allá de; **~ the mountain** al otro lado de la montaña; **~ the wall** más allá del muro **2.** (*after*) después de; (*more than*) más allá de; **8:00 ~** después de las 8:00 **3.** (*further than*) más allá de; **to**

see/go (way) ~ **sth** ver/ir (mucho) más allá de algo; **it goes** ~ **a joke** va más allá de una broma; ~ **belief** increíble **4.** (*too difficult for*) **to be** ~ **sb** ser demasiado difícil de entender para alguien **5.** (*above*) por encima de; **to live** ~ **one's means** vivir por encima de sus posibilidades **6.** *with neg or interrog* (*except for*) excepto **II.** *adv* **the house** ~ la casa de más allá; **the next ten years and** ~ los próximos diez años y más

bias ['baɪəs] *n* **1.** (*prejudice*) prejuicio *m;* **to have** ~**es against sb** tener prejuicios contra alguien **2.** *no pl* (*one-sidedness*) parcialidad *f;* **without** ~ imparcial **3.** (*tendency*) tendencia *f;* **to have a** ~ **towards sth** sentir inclinación por algo

biased *adj Am*, **biassed** *adj Brit* parcial; ~ **in sb's favour** predispuesto a favor de alguien; ~ **opinions** opiniones parciales

bib [bɪb] *n* babero *m*

Bible ['baɪbl] *n* **the** ~ la Biblia

biblical ['bɪblɪkl] *adj* bíblico

bibliography [ˌbɪblɪ'ɒgrəfi, *Am:* -'ɑːgrə-] <-ies> *n* bibliografía *f*

biceps ['baɪseps] *n inv* bíceps *m inv*

bicycle ['baɪsɪkl] *n* bicicleta *f;* **to ride a** ~ montar en bicicleta; **by** ~ en bicicleta

bid [bɪd] **I.** *n* **1.** (*offer*) oferta *f;* **to make a** ~ **for sth** hacer una oferta por algo **2.** (*attempt*) intento *m* **II.** <bid, bid> *vi* pujar; **to** ~ **for a contract** COM concursar por un contrato

bidder ['bɪdəʳ, *Am:* -ɚ] *n* postor(a) *m(f)*

bidding ['bɪdɪŋ] *n no pl* **1.** FIN puja *f* **2.** (*command*) **to do sb's** ~ cumplir las órdenes de alguien

bidet ['biːdeɪ, *Am:* brɪ'deɪ] *n* bidé *m*

biennial [baɪ'enɪəl] *adj a.* BOT bienal

bier [bɪəʳ, *Am:* bɪr] *n* andas *fpl*

big [bɪg] <-gg-> *adj* **1.** (*in size, amount*) grande; (*before singular nouns*) gran; **a** ~ **book** un libro grande; **a** ~ **house** una casa grande; ~ **letters** mayúsculas *fpl;* ~ **words** *inf* palabras *fpl* altisonantes; **the** ~**ger the better** cuanto más grande mejor **2.** (*grown-up*) mayor; ~ **boy/girl** chico/chica mayor; ~ **sister/brother** hermana/hermano mayor **3.** (*significant*) gran(de); **a** ~ **day** un día importante; **to make it** ~ *inf* triunfar a lo grande; **this group is** ~ **in Spain** este grupo es muy popular en España

bigamy ['bɪgəmi] *n no pl* bigamia *f*

Big Apple *n* **the** ~ la gran manzana (*nombre que se aplica a la ciudad de Nueva York*)

> **?** **Big Ben** era, originariamente, el sobrenombre de una gran campana, fundida en 1856, que se encontraba en la torre de las **Houses of Parliament.** Sir Benjamin Hall, entonces **Chief Commissioner of Works,** es el que la bautizó con este nombre. Hoy en día, por **Big Ben,** se conocen tanto la campana como la torre. Las campanadas con las que el **Big Ben** da la hora se pueden oír en los telediarios de algunas cadenas de radio y televisión.

big business *n* el gran capital

bigoted *adj* intolerante; REL fanático

bigotry ['bɪgətri] *n no pl* intolerancia *f;* REL fanatismo *m*

big toe *n* dedo *m* gordo del pie **big wheel** *n* noria *f*

bike [baɪk] *n inf* (*bicycle*) bici *f;* (*motorcycle*) moto *f*

bikini [bɪ'kiːni] *n* bikini *m*

bilateral [ˌbaɪ'lætərəl, *Am:* -'læt̬ɚl] *adj* bilateral

bile [baɪl] *n* **1.** *no pl* ANAT bilis *f* **2.** *fig* mal genio *m*

bilingual [baɪ'lɪŋgwəl] *adj* bilingüe

bill¹ [bɪl] **I.** *n* **1.** (*invoice*) factura *f;* **phone** ~ factura del teléfono; **the** ~, **please** la cuenta, por favor **2.** *Am* (*banknote*) billete *m* **3.** POL proyecto *m* de ley; **to give sth a clean** ~ **of health** dar a algo el visto bueno **II.** *vt*

to ~ sb for sth facturar algo a alguien

bill² [bɪl] *n* (*of bird*) pico *m*

billboard ['bɪlbɔːd, *Am:* -bɔːrd] *n* valla *f* publicitaria

billfold ['bɪlfəʊld, *Am:* -foʊld] *n Am* cartera *f*

billiards ['bɪliədz, *Am:* '-jədz] *n no pl* billar *m*

billion ['bɪliən, *Am:* -jən] *n* mil millones *mpl*

billy goat *n* macho *m* cabrío

bimbo ['bɪmbəʊ, *Am:* -boʊ] <-(e)s> *n pej, inf:* mujer *joven y guapa, pero tonta*

bin [bɪn] *n Aus, Brit* cubo *m* de basura, basurero *m Méx*

binary ['baɪnəri] *adj* binario

bind [baɪnd] **I.** *n no pl, Brit, inf* apuro *m;* **to be in a ~** estar en un apuro **II.** <bound, bound> *vt* **1.** (*tie*) atar; **to be bound hand and foot** estar atado de pies y manos; **to ~ together** *fig* unir; **to be bound to sb** *fig* estar ligado a alguien; **to ~ sb to do sth** obligar a alguien a hacer algo **2.** (*book*) encuadernar

binder ['baɪndəʳ, *Am:* -dɚ] *n* carpeta *f*

binding ['baɪndɪŋ] **I.** *n no pl* TYPO encuadernación *f* **II.** *adj* vinculante

binge [bɪndʒ] *n inf* (*of drinking*) borrachera *f,* vacilada *f Méx;* (*of eating*) comilona *f;* **to go on a ~** ir de farra

bingo ['bɪŋgəʊ, *Am:* -goʊ] *n no pl* bingo *m*

binoculars [bɪ'nɒkjʊləz, *Am:* -'nɑːkjəlɚz] *npl* prismáticos *mpl,* binoculares *mpl AmL*

biochemical *adj* bioquímico **biochemist** *n* bioquímico, -a *m, f* **biochemistry** *n no pl* bioquímica *f* **biodegradable** *adj* biodegradable **biodegrade** *vi* biodegradarse **biodiversity** *n no pl* biodiversidad *f* **bioengineering** *n no pl* bioingeniería *f* **biofuel** *n* combustible *m* biológico

biographical [ˌbaɪəʊ'græfɪkəl] *adj* biográfico

biography [baɪ'ɒgrəfi, *Am:* -'ɑː-grə-] <-ies> *n* biografía *f*

biological [ˌbaɪə'lɒdʒɪkəl, *Am:* -'lɑːdʒɪ-] *adj* biológico

biologist [baɪ'ɒlədʒɪst, *Am:* -'ɑːlə-] *n* biólogo, -a *m, f*

biology [baɪ'ɒlədʒi, *Am:* -'ɑːlə-] *n no pl* biología *f*

biopsy ['baɪɒpsi, *Am:* -ɑːp-] *n* MED biopsia *f*

biorhythm *n* biorritmo *m* **biotechnology** *n no pl* biotecnología *f*

biotope ['baɪətəʊp, *Am:* -toʊp] *n* biótopo *m*

bipartisan [ˌbaɪpɑːtɪ'zæn, *Am:* -'pɑːrtəzən] *adj* bipartidista

birch [bɜːtʃ, *Am:* bɜːrtʃ] *n* (*tree*) abedul *m*

bird [bɜːd, *Am:* bɜːrd] *n* **1.** ZOOL pájaro *m;* (*larger*) ave *f* **2.** *Aus, Brit, inf* (*girl, woman*) chica *f,* chava *f Méx,* piba *f RíoPl*

birdcage *n* pajarera *f* **birdseed** ['bɜːdsiːd, *Am:* 'bɜːrd-] *n no pl* alpiste *m* **bird's-eye view** [ˌbɜːdzaɪ'vjuː, *Am:* ˌbɜːrdz-] *n no pl* vista *f* panorámica **birdwatching** *n no pl* observación *f* de aves

biro® ['baɪərəʊ, *Am:* -roʊ] *n* bolígrafo *m,* birome *m RíoPl*

birth [bɜːθ, *Am:* bɜːrθ] *n* **1.** nacimiento *m,* paritorio *m Cuba, Ven;* MED parto *m;* **at/by ~** al/de nacer; **date/place of ~** fecha/lugar de nacimiento; **to give ~ to a child** dar a luz a un niño **2.** *no pl* (*origin*) origen *m*

birth certificate *n* partida *f* de nacimiento **birth control** *n* control *m* de natalidad

birthday ['bɜːθdeɪ, *Am:* 'bɜːrθ-] *n* cumpleaños *m inv;* **happy ~!** ¡feliz cumpleaños!

birthday present *n* regalo *m* de cumpleaños

birthplace *n* lugar *m* de nacimiento

biscuit ['bɪskɪt] *n Aus, Brit* galleta *f;* **that (really) takes the ~!** *inf* ¡eso es el colmo!

🔲 Con la expresión **biscuits and gravy** se designa un desayuno típico de los EE.UU. procedente de los estados del sur. Los **biscuits** son una clase de panecillos planos servidos con **gravy** (un tipo de salsa de asado). En algunas zonas, este tipo de desayuno sólo se sirve en **truck stops** (locales frecuentados por camioneros).

bishop ['bɪʃəp] n 1. REL obispo m 2. (chess piece) alfil m

bishopric ['bɪsəprɪk] n obispado m

bison ['baɪsən] n bisonte m

bit¹ [bɪt] n 1. inf (small piece) trozo m; (of glass) fragmento m; **a ~ of paper** un trozo de papel; **little ~s** pedacitos mpl; **to smash sth to ~s** romper algo en pedazos 2. (some) **a ~ of** un poco de; **a ~ of news** una noticia 3. (part) parte f; **the difficult ~ of sth** la parte difícil de algo; **~ by ~** poco a poco; **to do one's ~** inf hacer su parte 4. pl, inf (things) ~**s and pieces** cosas fpl 5. inf (short time) momento m; **for a ~** (por) un momento 6. (somewhat) **a ~** algo; **a ~ stupid** un poco tonto; **quite a ~** bastante; **not a ~** en absoluto

bit² [bɪt] n 1. (for horses) bocado m 2. (for drill) broca f

bit³ [bɪt] n INFOR bit m

bit⁴ [bɪt] pt of **bite**

bitch [bɪtʃ] I. n 1. ZOOL perra f 2. inf (woman) zorra f, tusa f AmL, Cuba II. vi inf quejarse; **to ~ about sb** poner verde a alguien

bite [baɪt] I. <bit, bitten> vt morder; (insect) picar; **to ~ one's nails** morderse las uñas II. <bit, bitten> vi (dog, person) morder; (insect, fish) picar; **once bitten twice shy** prov (el) gato escaldado del agua fría huye prov III. n 1. (of dog, person) mordisco m; (of insect) picadura f 2. (mouthful) bocado m

biting ['baɪtɪŋ, Am: -tɪŋ] adj (wind) cortante; (criticism) mordaz

bitten ['bɪtn] pp of **bite**

bitter ['bɪtəʳ, Am: 'bɪtɚ] I. adj <-er, -est> agrio; (fruit) amargo; (dispute)

encarnizado; (disappointment) amargo; **to be ~ about sth** estar amargado por algo; **to carry on to the ~ end** seguir hasta el final II. n Aus, Brit (beer) cerveza f (amarga)

bitterness n no pl 1. (animosity) amargura f; (resentment) resentimiento m 2. (taste) amargor m

bizarre [bɪ'zɑːʳ, Am: -'zɑːr] adj (behaviour) extraño; (clothes) estrafalario

black [blæk] I. adj negro; **~ man** negro m; **~ woman** negra f; **to beat sb ~ and blue** inf moler a alguien a palos II. n negro m; **in ~** de negro; **in ~ and white** en blanco y negro; **in the ~** FIN con saldo positivo
◆**black out** vi perder el conocimiento

blackberry ['blækbəri, Am: -ˌber-] <-ies> n (fruit) zarzamora f; (plant) zarza f

blackbird n mirlo m

blackboard n pizarra f

blackcurrant [ˌblæk'kʌrənt, Am: 'blækˌkɜːr-] n grosella f negra

blacken ['blækən] vt ennegrecer; **to ~ sb's name** manchar la reputación de alguien

black eye n ojo m morado

blacklist n lista f negra

blackmail ['blækmeɪl] I. n chantaje m II. vt chantajear

black market n mercado m negro

blackness ['blæknɪs] n no pl (colour) negrura f; (darkness) oscuridad f

blackout ['blækaʊt] n 1. (faint) desmayo m 2. (censorship) bloqueo m 3. ELEC apagón m

black pudding n Brit morcilla f, moronga f Méx **Black Sea** n Mar m Negro

blacksmith ['blæksmɪθ] n herrero m

bladder ['blædəʳ, Am: -ɚ] n ANAT vejiga f

blade [bleɪd] n (of tool, weapon) hoja f; (of oar) pala f; **~ of grass** brizna f de hierba

blame [bleɪm] I. vt culpar; **to ~ sb for sth** echar la culpa a alguien de

algo; **I don't ~ you** te comprendo
II. *n no pl* culpa *f;* **to take the ~** declararse culpable
blameless ['bleɪmlɪs] *adj* inocente
blanch [blɑːntʃ, *Am:* blænʃ] *vi* palidecer
bland [blænd] *adj* (*insipid*) soso
blank [blæŋk] **I.** *adj* **1.** (*empty*) en blanco; **~ cheque** cheque *m* en blanco; **~ tape** cinta *f* virgen; **to go ~** quedarse en blanco; **the screen went ~** la pantalla se quedó negra **2.** (*unemotional: look*) inexpresivo **3.** (*complete*) absoluto; (*despair*) completo; **to be met by a ~ refusal** encontrarse con un rechazo absoluto **II.** *n* espacio *m* en blanco; **to draw a ~** no encontrar nada
blanket ['blæŋkɪt] **I.** *n* (*cover*) manta *f,* cobija *f Méx;* (*of snow*) capa *f* **II.** *vt* cubrir **III.** *adj* general
blare [bleə^r, *Am:* bler] *vi* resonar
blasphemy ['blæsfəmi] *n no pl* blasfemia *f*
blast [blɑːst, *Am:* blæst] **I.** *vt* **1.** (*with explosive*) volar **2.** (*criticize*) criticar duramente **II.** *n* **1.** (*detonation*) explosión *f* **2.** (*noise*) toque *m;* (**at**) **full ~** *a. fig* a toda marcha **III.** *interj inf* **~ it!** ¡maldita sea!
blasted *adj inf* (*damned*) maldito
blatant ['bleɪtnt] *adj* descarado
blaze [bleɪz] **I.** *vi* resplandecer; (*fire*) arder; **to ~ with anger** echar chispas **II.** *vt* **to ~ a trail** abrir camino **III.** *n* **1.** (*fire*) fuego *m;* (*flames*) llamarada *f* **2.** (*colour*) resplandor *m;* **a ~ of glory** un rayo de gloria; **a ~ of publicity** una campaña de publicidad a bombo y platillo
◆ **blaze up** *vi* encenderse vivamente
blazer ['bleɪzə^r, *Am:* -zɚ] *n* chaqueta *f*
blazing ['bleɪzɪŋ] *adj* **1.** (*heat*) abrasador; (*light*) brillante; (*fire*) vivo **2.** (*argument*) violento
bleach [bliːtʃ] **I.** *vt* blanquear **II.** *n* lejía *f*
bleak [bliːk] *adj* (*future*) sombrío; (*weather*) gris; (*landscape*) desolador

bleat [bliːt] *vi* balar
bled [bled] *pt, pp of* **bleed**
bleed [bliːd] <bled, bled> *vi* sangrar; **to ~ to death** morir desangrado
bleep [bliːp] **I.** *n* pitido *m* **II.** *vi* pitar
blemish ['blemɪʃ] *n a. fig* mancha *f*
blend [blend] **I.** *n* mezcla *f* **II.** *vt* mezclar **III.** *vi* **to ~ in** no desentonar
blender [blendə^r, *Am:* -dɚ] *n* licuadora *f*
bless [bles] *vt* bendecir; **~ you!** (*on sneezing*) ¡Jesús!
blessed ['blesɪd] *adj* **1.** (*holy*) bendito; (*ground*) santo **2.** *inf* dichoso
blessing ['blesɪŋ] *n* **1.** (*benediction*) bendición *f;* **to give one's ~ to sth** dar su aprobación a algo **2.** (*advantage*) ventaja *f;* **it's a ~ in disguise** no hay mal que por bien no venga *prov*
blew [bluː] *pt of* **blow**
blight [blaɪt] **I.** *vt a. fig* arruinar **II.** *n* AGR añublo *m;* **to cast a ~ on sth** arruinar algo
blimey ['blaɪmi] *interj Brit, inf* caray
blind [blaɪnd] **I.** *n* **1.** *pl* (*person*) **the ~** los ciegos **2.** (*window shade*) persiana *f* **II.** *vt* cegar; (*dazzle*) deslumbrar **III.** *adj* **1.** (*unable to see*) ciego; **to be ~ in one eye** ser tuerto; **to be ~ to sth** no ver algo **2.** (*without reason*) sin razón; (*devotion*) ciego, apasionado **3.** *Brit, inf* (*as intensifier*) **not to take a ~ bit of notice of sth** no conceder la más mínima importancia a algo **IV.** *adv* **to be ~ drunk** estar más borracho que una cuba; **to swear ~ that ...** jurar y perjurar que...
blind alley <-s> *n a. fig* callejón *m* sin salida
blindfold ['blaɪndfəʊld, *Am:* -foʊld] **I.** *n* venda *f* **II.** *vt* vendar los ojos a
blindness *n* ceguera *f*
blink [blɪŋk] **I.** *vt* **to ~ one's eyes** pestañear **II.** *vi* pestañear; **she didn't even ~** ni se inmutó **III.** *n* pestañeo *m;* **in the ~ of an eye** en un abrir y cerrar de ojos; **to be on the ~** *inf* estar averiado

blinkered *adj* estrecho de miras

bliss [blɪs] *n no pl* dicha *f*; **marital ~** felicidad *f* conyugal

blissful ['blɪsfl] *adj* (*happy*) bienaventurado

blister ['blɪstər, *Am:* -təʳ] *n* **1.** ANAT ampolla *f* **2.** (*bubble*) burbuja *f*

Blitz [blɪts] *n* **the ~** el bombardeo alemán de Londres en 1940–41

blizzard ['blɪzəd] *n* ventisca *f*

bloated ['bləʊtɪd, *Am:* 'bloʊt̬ɪd] *adj* hinchado

blob [blɒb, *Am:* blɑːb] *n* goterón *m*

bloc [blɒk] *n* POL bloque *m*

block [blɒk, *Am:* blɑːk] **I.** *n* **1.** (*solid lump*) bloque *m*; (*of wood*) zoquete *m*; (*toy*) cubo *m* **2.** (*tall building*) edificio *m*; (*group of buildings*) manzana *f*, cuadra *f* AmL; **~ of flats** *Brit* bloque *m* de viviendas **3.** (*barrier*) barrera *f* **II.** *vt* (*road, pipe*) bloquear; (*sb's progress*) obstaculizar
 ◆ **block off** *vt* cortar

blockade [blɒ'keɪd, *Am:* blɑː'keɪd] **I.** *n* bloqueo *m* **II.** *vt* bloquear

bloke [bləʊk] *n Brit, inf* tío *m*

blond(e) [blɒnd, *Am:* blɑːnd] **I.** *adj* (*hair*) rubio, güero *Méx, Guat, Ven* **II.** *n* rubio, -a *m, f*, güero *Méx, Guat, Ven*

blood [blʌd] *n no pl* sangre *f*; **in cold ~** a sangre fría

blood bank *n* banco *m* de sangre

bloodbath *n* baño *m* de sangre

blood pressure *n no pl* tensión *f* arterial

bloodshed ['blʌdʃed] *n no pl* derramamiento *m* de sangre

bloodstained ['blʌdsteɪnd] *adj* manchado de sangre

bloodstream *n* corriente *f* sanguínea

blood test *n* análisis *m inv* de sangre

bloodthirsty ['blʌd͵θɜːsti, *Am:* -͵θɜːr-] *adj* sanguinario

bloody ['blʌdi] <-ier, -iest> **I.** *adj* **1.** (*with blood*) ensangrentado **2.** *Aus, Brit, inf* (*for emphasis*) puñetero; **~ hell!** ¡coño! **II.** *adv Aus, Brit, inf* (*very*) muy; **to be ~ useless** no servir para nada; **I don't ~ know** no tengo ni puñetera idea

bloom [bluːm] **I.** *n no pl, a. fig* flor *f*; **to come into ~** florecer **II.** *vi* florecer

blossom ['blɒsəm, *Am:* 'blɑːsəm] **I.** *n* flor *f*; **in ~** en flor; **orange ~** azahar *m* **II.** *vi* florecer; (*mature*) madurar

blot [blɒt, *Am:* blɑːt] **I.** *n* mancha *f* **II.** *vt* **1.** (*mark*) emborronar **2.** (*dry*) secar

blotch [blɒtʃ, *Am:* blɑːtʃ] *n* borrón *m*; (*on skin*) mancha *f*

blouse [blaʊz] *n* blusa *f*

blow[1] [bləʊ, *Am:* bloʊ] *n a. fig* golpe *m*; **to come to ~s** llegar a las manos

blow[2] [bləʊ, *Am:* bloʊ] **I.** <blew, blown> *vi* **1.** (*expel air*) soplar **2.** (*fuse*) fundirse; (*tyre*) reventar **II.** *vt* **1.** (*instrument*) tocar; **to ~ one's nose** sonarse la nariz **2.** (*fuse*) fundir
 ◆ **blow away** *vt* llevar
 ◆ **blow out** *vt* apagar
 ◆ **blow over** *vi* (*scandal*) pasar al olvido; (*argument, dispute*) calmarse
 ◆ **blow up I.** *vi* (*storm, gale*) levantarse **II.** *vt* **1.** (*fill with air*) inflar **2.** PHOT ampliar **3.** (*explode*) volar

blown [bləʊn, *Am:* bloʊn] *vt, vi pp of* **blow**

blowtorch ['bləʊtɔːtʃ, *Am:* 'bloʊtɔːrtʃ] *n* soplete *m*

blubber[1] ['blʌbər, *Am:* -əʳ] *vi* lloriquear

blubber[2] ['blʌbər, *Am:* -əʳ] *n* grasa *f* (de ballena)

blue [bluː] **I.** *adj* **1.** (*colour*) azul *m* **2.** (*sad*) triste; **to feel ~** sentirse triste **II.** *n* azul *m*; **sky ~** azul cielo; **out of the ~** cuando menos se espera

bluebell ['bluːbel] *n* campánula *f* azul

blueberry ['bluːbəri, *Am:* -͵ber-] <-ies> *n* arándano *m*

bluebottle ['bluː͵bɒtl, *Am:* -͵bɑːt̬l] *n* mosca *f* azul

blueprint ['bluːprɪnt] *n* plano *m*

blue whale *n* ballena *f* azul

bluff [blʌf] **I.** *vi* tirarse un farol **II.** *n* farol *m*, bluff *m* AmL; **to call sb's ~**

descubrir a alguien la farolada

blunder ['blʌndər, *Am:* -dɚ] I. *n* error *m* garrafal, embarrada *f AmL* II. *vi* to ~ into sth tropezar con algo

blunt [blʌnt] *adj* 1. (*not sharp*) desafilado, pompo *Ecua, Col* 2. (*direct*) directo

bluntly *adv* sin rodeos

blur [blɜːʳ, *Am:* blɜːr] I. *vt* <-rr-> desdibujar II. *n no pl* (*shape*) contorno *m* borroso; (*memory*) vago recuerdo *m*

blurred [blɜːd, *Am:* blɜːrd] *adj* indistinto; (*picture*) borroso

blush [blʌʃ] *vi* ruborizarse

bluster ['blʌstəʳ, *Am:* -tɚ] I. *vi* 1. (*speak*) bravuconear 2. (*blow*) rugir II. *n no pl* bravuconería *f*

BO [ˌbiː'əʊ, *Am:* -'oʊ] *n abbr of* **body odour** olor *m* corporal

boa ['bəʊə, *Am:* 'boʊə] *n* boa *f*

boar [bɔːʳ, *Am:* bɔːr] *n* (**wild**) ~ jabalí *m*

board [bɔːd, *Am:* bɔːrd] I. *n* 1. (*wood*) tabla *f*; (*blackboard*) pizarra *f*; (*notice board*) tablero *m*; **across the ~** *fig* en general 2. ADMIN consejo *m* de administración; ~ **of directors** junta directiva; **Board of Trade** *Am* Cámara *f* de Comercio 3. (*in hotel*) **full ~** pensión *f* completa; **half ~** media pensión *f* 4. NAUT **on ~** a bordo II. *vt* (*ship*) subir a bordo de; (*bus, train*) subir a III. *vi* (*stay*) alojarse; (*in school*) estar interno

boarding school *n* internado *m*

boardroom *n* sala *f* de juntas

boardwalk *n Am:* paseo marítimo entablado

boast [bəʊst, *Am:* boʊst] *vi* alardear; **to ~ about/of sth** vanagloriarse sobre/de algo

boat [bəʊt, *Am:* boʊt] *n* barco *m*; (*small*) barca *f*; (*large*) buque *m*; **to go by ~** ir en barco

boating ['bəʊtɪŋ, *Am:* 'boʊt̬ɪŋ] *n no pl* **to go ~** dar un paseo en barca

---

[?] La anual **Boat Race** (competición de remo) se celebra un sába-

---

do de marzo en el río **Thames** (Támesis). Ocho remeros de las universidades de Oxford y Cambridge compiten en dicha carrera. Es un acontecimiento nacional muy importante seguido por 460 millones de espectadores de todo el mundo.

---

bob [bɒb, *Am:* bɑːb] <-bb-> *vi* **to ~** (**up and down**) agitarse

bobby ['bɒbi, *Am:* 'bɑːbi] <-ies> *n Brit, inf* poli *mf*

bode [bəʊd, *Am:* boʊd] *vi* **to ~ well/ill** ser una buena/mala señal

bodily ['bɒdəli] *adj* corpóreo; (*harm*) corporal; (*function*) fisiológico

body ['bɒdi, *Am:* 'bɑːdi] <-ies> *n* 1. *a.* ANAT, ASTR cuerpo *m*; (*corpse*) cadáver *m*; (*of water*) masa *f*; **over my dead ~** ¡por encima de mi cadáver! 2. ADMIN, POL organismo *m*; **in a ~** en bloque

bodyguard *n* guardaespaldas *mf inv*, espaldero *m Ven* **body language** *n no pl* lenguaje *m* corporal

bog [bɒg, *Am:* bɑːg] *n* ciénaga *f*, estero *m Bol, Col, Ven*

bogey ['bəʊgi, *Am:* 'boʊ-] *n* 1. *inf* (*snot*) moco *m* seco 2. (*golf score*) bogey *m*

boggle ['bɒgl, *Am:* 'bɑːgl] *vi* quedarse atónito

boggy ['bɒgi, *Am:* 'bɑːgi] <-ier, -iest> *adj* pantanoso

bogus ['bəʊgəs, *Am:* 'boʊ-] *adj* (*document*) falso; (*argument*) falaz

bohemian [bəʊ'hiːmiən, *Am:* boʊ-] *adj* bohemio

boil [bɔɪl] I. *vi, vt* hervir II. *n* 1. *no pl* **to bring sth to the ~** calentar algo hasta que hierva 2. MED furúnculo *m*
◆ **boil down to** *vt fig* reducirse a
◆ **boil over** *vi* 1. GASTR rebosar 2. (*situation*) estallar

boiler ['bɔɪləʳ, *Am:* -lɚ] *n* caldera *f* **boiler suit** *n Aus, Brit* mono *m*

boiling *adj* hirviendo; (*day, weather*) abrasador; **I am ~** me estoy asando

boisterous [ˈbɔɪstərəs] *adj* bullicioso

bold [bəʊld, *Am:* boʊld] <-er, -est> *adj* 1. (*brave*) audaz 2. (*colour*) llamativo 3. INFOR, TYP ~ (**type**) negrita *f*; **in** ~ en negrita

boldness *n* audacia *f*

Bolivia [bəˈlɪvɪə] *n* Bolivia *f*

Bolivian [bəˈlɪvɪən] *adj* boliviano

bolster [ˈbəʊlstə, *Am:* ˈboʊlstə] *vt* 1. (*support*) reafirmar 2. (*encourage*) alentar

bolt [bəʊlt, *Am:* boʊlt] I. *vi* fugarse II. *vt* 1. (*food*) engullir 2. (*lock*) echar el pestillo a 3. (*fix*) atornillar III. *n* 1. (*on door*) pestillo *m* 2. (*screw*) tornillo *m* 3. (*of lightning*) rayo *m*; **a ~ from the blue** un acontecimiento inesperado IV. *adv* ~ **upright** rígido

bomb [bɒm, *Am:* bɑːm] I. *n* bomba *f*; **to cost a ~** costar un dineral; **to go like a ~** *Brit, inf* ser un exitazo II. *vt* bombardear

bombard [bɒmˈbɑːd, *Am:* bɑːmˈbɑːrd] *vt* bombardear

bombardment [bɒmˈbɑːdmənt, *Am:* bɑːmˈbɑːrd-] *n* bombardeo *m*

bomber [ˈbɒmə, *Am:* ˈbɑːmə] *n* 1. AVIAT bombardero *m* 2. (*terrorist*) terrorista *mf* (que coloca bombas)

bombing *n* 1. MIL bombardeo *m* 2. (*by terrorists*) atentado *m*

bombshell [ˈbɒmʃel, *Am:* ˈbɑːm-] *n* 1. MIL obús *m* 2. (*surprise*) bombazo *m inf*

bona fide [ˌbəʊnəˈfaɪdɪ, *Am:* ˌboʊ-] *adj* genuino

bonanza [bəˈnænzə] *n* bonanza *f*

bond [bɒnd, *Am:* bɑːnd] I. *n* 1. (*connection*) vínculo *m*; (*of friendship*) lazo *m* 2. FIN bono *m* 3. LAW garantía *f*; *Am* (*bail*) fianza *f* II. *vt* pegar; **to ~** (**together**) vincular

bondage [ˈbɒndɪdʒ, *Am:* ˈbɑːn-] *n no pl, liter* esclavitud *f*

bone [bəʊn, *Am:* boʊn] I. *n* ANAT hueso *m*; (*of fish*) espina *f*; ~ **of contention** manzana *f* de la discordia; **to make no ~s about sth** no ocultar algo; **to have a ~ to pick with sb** *inf* tener que ajustar cuentas con

alguien II. *vt* deshuesar

bone idle *adj inf* vago **bone marrow** *n no pl* médula *f* ósea

bonfire [ˈbɒnfaɪə, *Am:* ˈbɑːnfaɪə] *n* hoguera *f*

bonkers [ˈbɒŋkəz, *Am:* ˈbɑːŋkəz] *adj inf* **to go** ~ volverse loco

bonnet [ˈbɒnɪt, *Am:* ˈbɑːnɪt] *n* 1. (*hat*) sombrero *m*; (*baby's*) gorrito *m* 2. *Aus, Brit* AUTO capote *m*

bonus [ˈbəʊnəs, *Am:* ˈboʊ-] *n* 1. (*money*) prima *f*, abono *m AmL*; **productivity** ~ plus *m* 2. (*advantage*) ventaja *f*

bony [ˈbəʊni, *Am:* ˈboʊ-] *adj* <-ier, -iest> huesudo; (*fish*) con muchas espinas

boo [buː] *vi* abuchear, pifiar *Chile, Méx*

booby prize [ˈbuːbi-] *n* premio *m* al peor **booby trap** *n* trampa *f*

book [bʊk] I. *n* libro *m*; (*of stamps*) taco *m*; (*of tickets*) talonario *m*; **the ~s** COM las cuentas; **to be in sb's bad ~s** estar en la lista negra de alguien; **to bring sb to** ~ pedir cuentas a alguien; **to cook the ~s** *inf* amañar las cuentas; **to throw the ~ at sb** castigar duramente a alguien; **in my** ~ en mi opinión II. *vt* 1. (*reserve*) reservar 2. (*register*) fichar

◆ **book in** *vi* inscribirse

bookcase [ˈbʊkkeɪs] *n* estantería *f*

bookie [ˈbʊki] *n inf* corredor(a) *m(f)* de apuestas

booking [ˈbʊkɪŋ] *n* reserva *f*

bookkeeping [ˈbʊkˌkiːpɪŋ] *n no pl* contabilidad *f*

booklet [ˈbʊklɪt] *n* folleto *m*

bookmaker [ˈbʊkˌmeɪkə, *Am:* -kə] *n* corredor(a) *m(f)* de apuestas

bookmark [ˈbʊkmɑːk, *Am:* -mɑːrk] *n a.* INFOR marcador *m*

book review *n* crítica *f* de libros **book reviewer** *n* crítico, -a *m, f* de libros

bookseller [ˈbʊkˌselə, *Am:* -ə] *n* (*person*) librero, -a *m, f*; (*shop*) librería *f*

bookshelf [ˈbʊkʃelf] <-shelves> *n* estante *m*

bookshop [ˈbʊkʃɒp, *Am:* -ʃɑːp] *n*

librería *f*

bookstall ['bʊkstɔːl, *Am:* -stɔːl] *n* quiosco *m*

bookstore ['bʊkstɔːʳ, *Am:* -stɔːr] *n Am* librería *f*

bookworm ['bʊkwɜːm, *Am:* -wɜːrm] *n* ratón *m* de biblioteca

boom¹ [buːm] ECON **I.** *vi* estar en auge **II.** *n* boom *m*

boom² [buːm] *n* (*sound*) estruendo *m*

boon [buːn] *n no pl* **to be a ~ (to sb)** ser de gran ayuda (para alguien)

boost [buːst] **I.** *n no pl* incentivo *m* **II.** *vt* estimular; (*morale*) reforzar

booster [buːstəʳ, *Am:* -stɚ] *n* MED vacuna *f* de refuerzo

boot [buːt] **I.** *n* **1.** (*footwear*) bota *f;* **to give sb the ~** *inf* echar a alguien; **to put the ~ in** *inf* emplear la violencia; **to ~** además **2.** *Brit, Aus* AUTO maletero *m*, baúl *m AmL* **II.** *vt inf* **1.** (*kick*) dar un puntapié a **2.** INFOR arrancar

◆ **boot out** *vt inf* poner de patitas en la calle

booth [buːð] *n* (*cubicle*) cubículo *m;* (*telephone*) cabina *f;* (*polling*) casilla *f;* (*at fair, market*) caseta *f*

bootlace ['buːtleɪs] *n* cordón *m*

bootleg ['buːtleg] <-gg-> *adj* (*alcohol*) de contrabando; (*software*) pirata

booty ['buːti, *Am:* -ţi] *n* botín *m*

booze [buːz] *n inf* bebida *f*

border ['bɔːdəʳ, *Am:* 'bɔːrdɚ] **I.** *n* (*frontier*) frontera *f;* (*edge, boundary*) borde *m;* FASHION cenefa *f;* (*in garden*) arriate *m* **II.** *vt* limitar con

◆ **border on** *vi* limitar con; *fig* rayar en

borderline ['bɔːdəlaɪn, *Am:* 'bɔːrdɚ-] *adj* dudoso

bore¹ [bɔːʳ, *Am:* bɔːr] **I.** *n* (*thing*) aburrimiento *m;* (*person*) pesado, -a *m, f;* **what a ~!** ¡qué lata! **II.** <bored> *vt* aburrir

bore² [bɔːʳ, *Am:* bɔːr] **I.** *n* (*of pipe*) alma *f;* (*of gun*) calibre *m* **II.** *vt* perforar; **to ~ a hole** abrir un agujero

bore³ [bɔːʳ, *Am:* bɔːr] *pt of* **bear**

bored *adj* aburrido

boredom ['bɔːdəm, *Am:* 'bɔːr-] *n no pl* aburrimiento *m*

boring ['bɔːrɪŋ] *adj* aburrido, cansador *Arg, Chile, Urug,* fome *Chile;* **to find sth ~** encontrar algo pesado

born [bɔːn, *Am:* bɔːrn] *adj* **1.** (*person*) **to be ~** nacer; **where were you ~?** ¿dónde naciste?; **I wasn't ~ yesterday** *inf* no nací ayer **2.** (*ability*) nato

borne [bɔːn, *Am:* bɔːrn] *pp of* **bear**

borough ['bʌrə, *Am:* 'bɜːroʊ] *n* municipio *m*

borrow ['bɒrəʊ, *Am:* 'bɑːroʊ] *vt* tomar prestado; (*ask for*) pedir prestado; **may I ~ your bag?** ¿me prestas tu bolso?

borrower *n* prestatario, -a *m, f*

borrowing *n no pl* préstamo *m*

Bosnia ['bɒzniə, *Am:* 'bɑːz-] *n* Bosnia *f*

Bosnia-Herzegovina [-ˌhɜːzəˈgʊvɪnə, *Am:* -ˌhertsəgoʊviːnə] *n* Bosnia *f* Herzegovina

Bosnian ['bɒznɪən, *Am:* 'bɑːz-] *adj* bosnio

bosom ['bʊzəm] *n no pl* pecho *m*

boss [bɒs, *Am:* bɑːs] **I.** *n* (*person in charge*) jefe, -a *m, f;* (*owner*) patrón, -ona *m, f* **II.** *vt inf* **to ~ sb about** mandonear a alguien

bossy ['bɒsi, *Am:* 'bɑːsi] <-ier, -iest> *adj* mandón

botanical [bəˈtænɪkəl] *adj* botánico

botanist ['bɒtənɪst, *Am:* 'bɑːtnɪst] *n* botánico, -a *m, f*

botany ['bɒtəni, *Am:* 'bɑːtni] *n no pl* botánica *f*

botch [bɒtʃ, *Am:* bɑːtʃ] **I.** *n* chapuza *f* **II.** *vt* **to ~ sth (up)** hacer una chapuza de algo

both [bəʊθ, *Am:* boʊθ] **I.** *adj, pron* los dos, las dos, ambos, ambas; **~ of them** ellos dos; **~ of us** nosotros dos; **~ (the) brothers** los dos hermanos; **on ~ sides** en ambos lados **II.** *adv* **~ Mathilde and Sara** tanto Mathilde como Sara; **to be ~ sad and pleased** estar a la vez triste y satisfecho

bother ['bɒðəʳ, *Am:* 'bɑːðɚ] **I.** *n* molestia *f*, friega *f AmL;* **it is no ~** no es ninguna molestia; **it is not worth the ~** no vale la pena; **to get into a spot of ~** *Brit, inf* meterse en un lío **II.** *vt* **1.** (*annoy*) molestar **2.** (*worry*) preocupar; (**not**) **to ~ to do sth** (no) molestarse en hacer algo; **what ~s me is …** lo que me preocupa es…

Botswana [ˌbɒtˈswɑːnə, *Am:* bɑːt-] *n* Botsuana *f*

bottle [ˈbɒtl, *Am:* ˈbɑːt̬l] **I.** *n* **1.** (*container*) botella *f*; (*of ink, perfume*) frasco *m*; (*baby's*) biberón *m*; **to hit the ~** *inf* empinar el codo **2.** *no pl, Brit, inf* (*courage*) agallas *fpl* **II.** *vt Brit* embotellar

bottled [ˈbɒtld, *Am:* ˈbɑːt̬ld] *adj* embotellado

bottle opener *n* abrebotellas *m inv*

bottom [ˈbɒtəm, *Am:* ˈbɑːt̬əm] **I.** *n* *no pl* **1.** (*of stairs, page*) pie *m*; (*of sea, street, glass*) fondo *m*; (*of chair*) asiento *m*; **from the ~ of one's heart** de todo corazón; **to get to the ~ of sth** llegar al fondo de algo; **at ~** en el fondo **2.** (*lower part*) parte *f* inferior; **from top to ~** de arriba a abajo **3.** (*buttocks*) trasero *m* **II.** *adj* (*lower*) más bajo; **in ~ gear** en primera

bought [bɔːt, *Am:* bɑːt] *vt pt, pp of* **buy**

boulder [ˈbəʊldəʳ, *Am:* ˈboʊldəʳ] *n* roca *f*

bounce [baʊnts] **I.** *vi* (re)botar; **to ~ an idea off sb** pedir la opinión a alguien; **to ~ sb into doing sth** presionar a alguien para hacer algo **II.** *vt* hacer (re)botar **III.** *n* **1.** (*rebound*) (re)bote *m* **2.** *no pl* (*vitality*) vitalidad *f*
♦ **bounce back** *vi* recuperarse

bouncer [ˈbaʊntsəʳ, *Am:* -səʳ] *n inf* gorila *m*

bound¹ [baʊnd] **I.** *vi* (*leap*) saltar **II.** *n* salto *m*

bound² [baʊnd] *adj* **to be ~ for …** ir rumbo a…

bound³ [baʊnd] **I.** *pt, pp of* **bind II.** *adj* **1.** (*sure*) **she's ~ to come** seguro que viene; **it was ~ to happen sooner or later** tarde o temprano tenía que suceder **2.** (*obliged*) **to be**

~ to do sth estar obligado a hacer algo

boundary [ˈbaʊndri] <-ies> *n* **1.** *a. fig* (*line*) límite *m* **2.** (*border*) frontera *f*

boundless [ˈbaʊndlɪs] *adj* (*love, patience*) sin límites; (*energy*) ilimitado

bounds [baʊndz] *n pl* límites *mpl*; **to know no ~** no conocer límites; **to be beyond the ~ of possibility** no ser posible; **this area is out of ~ to civilians** los civiles tienen prohibido la entrada en esta zona; **within ~** dentro de ciertos límites

bounty [ˈbaʊnti, *Am:* -t̬i] <-ies> *n* recompensa *f*

bouquet [bʊˈkeɪ, *Am:* boʊ-] *n* (*of flowers*) ramo *m*

bout [baʊt] *n* **1.** (*of illness*) ataque *m*; **~ of insanity** período *m* de locura; **drinking ~** borrachera *f* **2.** SPORTS combate *m*

bow¹ [bəʊ, *Am:* boʊ] *n* **1.** (*weapon*) *a.* MUS arco *m* **2.** (*knot*) lazo *m*, moño *m AmL*, moña *f Urug*, rosa *f Chile*

bow² [baʊ] *n* NAUT proa *f*

bow³ [baʊ] **I.** *vi* **1.** (*greet*) hacer una reverencia **2.** (*yield*) **to ~ to sth** someterse a algo **II.** *vt* (*one's head*) inclinar; (*body*) doblegar **III.** *n* reverencia *f*, venia *f CSur, Col*, caravana *f Méx*; **to take a ~** recibir un aplauso
♦ **bow out** *vi* retirarse

bowel [ˈbaʊəl] *n* intestino *m* grueso

bowl¹ [bəʊl, *Am:* boʊl] *n* cuenco *m*; (*larger*) bol *m*

bowl² [bəʊl, *Am:* boʊl] SPORTS **I.** *vi* (*in cricket*) lanzar **II.** *n pl juego semejante a la petanca o las bochas que se juega sobre el césped*

bowler [ˈbəʊləʳ, *Am:* ˈboʊləʳ] *n* **1.** (*in cricket*) lanzador(a) *m(f)* **2.** (*at bowling, bowls*) jugador(a) *m(f)* **3.** (*hat*) bombín *m*

bowling *n no pl* (*game*) bolos *mpl*

bowling alley *n* bolera *f*

bow tie *n* pajarita *f*, corbatín *m Col*, moñita *f Urug*

box¹ [bɒks, *Am:* bɑːks] *vi* SPORTS boxear

box² [bɒks, *Am:* bɑːks] I. *n* **1.** (*container*) caja *f;* **the ~ inf** (*television*) la caja tonta **2.** (*rectangular space*) casilla *f;* (*in soccer*) área *f* **3.** THEAT palco *m;* (*booth*) cabina *f* II. *vt* poner en una caja
◆**box in** *vt* acorralar

boxer ['bɒksər, *Am:* 'bɑːksər] *n* **1.** (*dog*) bóxer *m* **2.** (*person*) boxeador(a) *m(f)*

boxer shorts *npl* calzoncillos *mpl*

boxing ['bɒksɪŋ, *Am:* 'bɑːksɪŋ] *n no pl* boxeo *m,* box *m AmL*

⚠ El **Boxing Day** se celebra el 26 de diciembre. El nombre de este día proviene de cuando los aprendices de un oficio, el día después de Navidad, recogían en **boxes** (cajas) las propinas que los clientes del taller de su maestro les daban. Antiguamente se denominaba **Christmas box** a la paga navideña que recibían los empleados.

box office *n* taquilla *f,* boletería *f AmL*

boy [bɔɪ] *n* (*child*) niño *m;* (*young man*) chico *m,* chamaco, -a *m, f Méx,* pibe *m Arg*

boycott ['bɔɪkɒt, *Am:* -kɑːt] I. *vt* boicotear II. *n* boicot *m*

boyfriend ['bɔɪfrend] *n* novio *m*

boyhood ['bɔɪhʊd] *n no pl* niñez *f*

boyish ['bɔɪɪʃ] *adj* (*woman*) de chico; (*enthusiasm*) de niño

bra [brɑː] *n* sujetador *m,* brasier *m Col, Méx,* corpiño *m RíoPl*

brace [breɪs] I. *vt* reforzar; **to ~ oneself for sth** prepararse para algo II. *n* **1.** (*for teeth*) aparato(s) *m(pl)* **2.** (*for back*) aparato *m* ortopédico **3.** *pl, Aus, Brit* (*suspenders*) tirantes *mpl,* tiradores *mpl RíoPl* **4.** *pl, Am* (*callipers*) corrector *m*

bracelet ['breɪslɪt] *n* pulsera *f*

bracken ['brækn] *n no pl* helechos *mpl*

bracket ['brækɪt] I. *n* **1.** *pl* TYPO paréntesis *m inv;* **in ~s** entre paréntesis **2.** (*category*) categoría *f;* **age ~** grupo *m* etario; **tax ~** banda *f* impositiva **3.** (*for shelf*) soporte *m* II. *vt* **1.** TYPO poner entre paréntesis **2.** (*include*) agrupar

brag [bræg] <-gg-> *vi inf* **to ~ about sth** alardear de algo

braid [breɪd] *n* **1.** *no pl* FASHION galón *m* **2.** *Am* (*plait*) trenza *f*

brain [breɪn] *n* **1.** (*organ*) cerebro *m* **2.** *pl* (*substance*) sesos *mpl* **3.** (*intelligence*) cerebro *m;* **to have ~s** ser inteligente **4.** *inf* (*intelligent person*) cerebro *m*

brainchild ['breɪntʃaɪld] *n no pl* creación *f*

brain damage *n* lesión *f* cerebral

brainless ['breɪnləs] *adj* estúpido

brainwash ['breɪnwɒʃ, *Am:* -wɑːʃ] *vt* lavar el cerebro a

brainwave ['breɪnweɪv] *n inf* idea *f* brillante, lamparazo *m Col*

brake [breɪk] I. *n* freno *m* II. *vi* frenar

bramble ['bræmbl] *n* **1.** (*bush*) zarza *f* **2.** (*fruit*) zarzamora *f*

bran [bræn] *n no pl* salvado *m*

branch [brɑːntʃ, *Am:* bræntʃ] I. *n* **1.** (*of tree*) rama *f;* (*of river, road*) ramal *m* **2.** (*of company*) sucursal *f;* (*of union*) delegación *f* II. *vi* bifurcarse
◆**branch off** *vi* bifurcarse
◆**branch out** *vi* diversificarse

brand [brænd] I. *n* COM marca II. *vt* **to ~ sb** (**as**) **sth** tachar a alguien de algo

brandish ['brændɪʃ] *vt* blandir

brand name ['brændneɪm] *n* marca *f*

brand-new *adj inv* completamente nuevo

brandy ['brændi] <-ies> *n* brandy *m*

brash [bræʃ] *adj* **1.** (*attitude*) chulo **2.** (*colours*) chillón

brass [brɑːs, *Am:* bræs] *n no pl* latón *m*

brat [bræt] *n inf* mocoso, -a *m, f*

bravado [brəˈvɑːdəʊ, *Am:* -doʊ] *n no pl* bravuconada *f*

brave [breɪv] *adj* valiente

bravery ['breɪvəri] *n no pl* valentía *f*
brawl [brɔːl, *Am:* brɑːl] I. *n* pelea *f*
II. *vi* pelearse
bray [breɪ] *vi* rebuznar
brazen ['breɪzn] *adj* descarado
brazier ['breɪziəʳ, *Am:* -ʒɚ] *n* brasero *m*
Brazil [brə'zɪl] *n* Brasil *m*
Brazilian [brə'zɪliən, *Am:* -jən] *adj* brasileño
breach [briːtʃ] I. *n* 1. (*infraction: of regulation*) infracción *f*; (*of agreement*) ruptura *f*; (*of confidence*) abuso *m*; (*of contract*) incumplimiento *m*; **to be in ~ of the law** infringir la ley 2. (*opening*) brecha *f* II. *vt* (*law*) infringir; (*agreement*) romper; (*contract*) incumplir; (*security*) poner en peligro
bread [bred] *n* 1. pan *m*; **a loaf of ~** un pan 2. *inf* (*money*) pasta *f*
breadbin *n* panera *f*
breadth ['bretθ] *n no pl* anchura *f*
break [breɪk] I. *n* 1. (*crack*) grieta *f*; **the ~ of day** el amanecer; **to make a clean ~** *fig* cortar por lo sano 2. (*interruption*) interrupción *f*; (*rest period*) descanso *m*; *Brit* SCHOOL recreo *m* 3. (*divergence*) ruptura *f* 4. (*opportunity*) oportunidad *f*; **give me a ~!** ¡déjame en paz! II. <broke, broken> *vt* 1. (*damage*) romper 2. (*interrupt: circuit*) cortar 3. (*put an end to: deadlock*) salir de; (*peace, silence*) romper; (*strike*) poner fin a; (*habit*) dejar 4. (*violate: agreement*) incumplir; (*treaty*) violar III. <broke, broken> *vi* 1. (*shatter*) romperse; **to ~ even** salir sin ganar ni perder; **to ~ free** liberarse; **to ~ loose** soltarse; **to ~ into pieces** hacerse añicos; **the boy's voice is ~ing** la voz del niño está cambiando 2. (*interrupt*) **shall we ~ (off) for lunch?** ¿paramos para comer? 3. METEO (*weather*) cambiar
♦**break away** *vi* desprenderse; (*region*) escindirse
♦**break down** I. *vi* dejar de funcionar; (*car, machine*) averiarse; (*marriage*) romperse; (*negotiation*) fracasar; (*psychologically*) derrum-

barse II. *vt* 1. (*door*) echar abajo 2. (*resistance*) acabar con
♦**break in** I. *vi* 1. (*burgle*) entrar (para robar) 2. (*interrupt*) interrumpir II. *vt* domar
♦**break into** *vi* 1. (*enter: car, house*) entrar (para robar) 2. (*start doing*) **to ~ laughter/tears** echarse a reir/llorar
♦**break off** I. *vt* 1. (*detach*) partir 2. (*relationship*) romper II. *vi* desprenderse
♦**break out** *vi* 1. (*escape*) escaparse 2. (*begin*) estallar; **to ~ out in a sweat** empezar a sudar
♦**break through** *vi* penetrar; (*sun*) salir
♦**break up** I. *vt* (*meeting*) terminar; (*coalition, union*) disolver II. *vi* 1. (*end relationship*) separarse 2. (*come to an end: marriage*) fracasar; (*meeting*) terminar
breakaway ['breɪkəweɪ] *adj* disidente
breakdown ['breɪkdaʊn] *n* (*of negotiations, relationship*) ruptura *f*; TECH avería *f*; (**nervous**) ~ PSYCH crisis *f inv* nerviosa
breaker ['breɪkəʳ, *Am:* -kɚ] *n* (*wave*) gran ola *f*
breakfast ['brekfəst] *n* desayuno *m*; **to have ~** desayunar
breakthrough ['breɪkθruː] *n* (*in science*) adelanto *m*; MIL avance *m*
breakup ['breɪkʌp] *n* (*of marriage*) separación *f*; (*of group, empire*) disolución *f*; (*of talks*) fracaso *m*; (*of family, physical structure*) desintegración *f*
breast [brest] *n* 1. ANAT pecho *m* 2. GASTR pechuga *f*
breast cancer *n no pl* cáncer *m* de mama
breastfeed ['brestfiːd] *vt* amamantar
breath [breθ] *n* aliento *m*; **to be out of ~** estar sin aliento; **to be short of ~** ahogarse; **to draw ~** respirar; **to hold one's ~** *a. fig* contener la respiración; **to mutter sth under one's ~** decir algo entre dientes; **in the same ~** a continua-

ción; **to take sb's ~ away** dejar a alguien sin habla

breathe [briːð] *vi, vt* respirar; **to ~ again** respirar tranquilo

breather ['briːðəʳ, *Am:* -ðɚ] *n* **to take a ~** descansar

breathing *n no pl* respiración *f*

breathless ['breθlɪs] *adj* sin aliento

breathtaking ['breθteɪkɪŋ] *adj* imponente

bred [bred] *pt, pp of* **breed**

breed [briːd] **I.** *vt* <bred, bred> criar; (*disease, violence*) engendrar **II.** *vi* <bred, bred> reproducirse **III.** *n* ZOOL raza *f;* BOT variedad *f*

breeder ['briːdəʳ, *Am:* -dɚ] *n* criador(a) *m(f)*

breeding *n no pl* **1.** (*of animals*) cría *f* **2.** *fig* educación *f*

breeze [briːz] *n* brisa *f;* **to be a ~** *inf* ser pan comido, ser un bollo *RíoPl*

brew [bruː] **I.** *vi* **1.** (*beer*) fermentar; (*tea*) hacerse; **to let the tea ~** dejar reposar el té **2.** (*storm, trouble*) avecinarse; **there's something ~ing** se está cociendo algo **II.** *vt* (*beer*) elaborar; (*tea*) hacer

brewer ['bruːəʳ, *Am:* -ɚ] *n* cervecero, -a *m, f*

brewery ['bruəri, *Am:* 'bruːɚi] <-ies> *n* fábrica *f* de cerveza

bribe [braɪb] **I.** *vt* sobornar **II.** *n* soborno *m*

bribery ['braɪbəri] *n no pl* soborno *m*, coima *f Perú, CSur,* mordida *f Méx*

brick [brɪk] *n* ladrillo *m*
 ◆ **brick up** *vt* tapiar

bricklayer ['brɪkˌleɪəʳ, *Am:* -ɚ] *n* albañil *mf*

bridal ['braɪdəl] *adj* (*suite*) nupcial; (*gown*) de novia

bride [braɪd] *n* novia *f*

bridegroom ['braɪdgrʊm, *Am:* -gruːm] *n* novio *m*

bridesmaid ['braɪdzmeɪd] *n* dama *f* de honor

bridge [brɪdʒ] *n* **1.** ARCHIT puente *m* **2.** NAUT puente *m* (de mando) **3.** *no pl* GAMES bridge *m*

bridle ['braɪdl] **I.** *n* brida *f* **II.** *vi* **to ~ at sth** molestarse por algo

brief [briːf] **I.** *adj* (*short*) corto; (*concise*) conciso, sucinto; **in ~** en resumen **II.** *n Aus, Brit* (*instructions*) instrucciones *fpl* **III.** *vt* informar

briefcase ['briːfkeɪs] *n* maletín *m*

briefing *n* **1.** (*instructions*) instrucciones *fpl* **2.** (*information session*) reunión *f* informativa

briefly *adv* (*for short time*) por poco tiempo; (*concisely*) brevemente; **~, ...** en resumen,...

brigade [brɪ'geɪd] *n* MIL brigada *f*

brigadier [ˌbrɪgə'dɪəʳ] *n Brit* MIL general *m* de brigada

bright [braɪt] *adj* **1.** (*light*) brillante; (*room*) con mucha luz **2.** (*colour*) vivo **3.** (*intelligent: person*) inteligente; (*idea*) brillante **4.** (*promising*) prometedor; **to look on the ~ side of sth** mirar el lado bueno de algo

brightness *n no pl* brillo *m;* (*of sound*) claridad *f*

brilliance ['brɪlɪəns] *n no pl* **1.** (*cleverness*) brillantez *f* **2.** (*brightness*) resplandor *m*

brilliant ['brɪlɪənt, *Am:* -jənt] *adj* **1.** (*colour*) brillante; (*sunlight, smile*) radiante **2.** (*clever*) brillante; (*idea*) genial **3.** *Brit, inf* (*excellent*) fantástico

brim [brɪm] *n* (*of hat*) ala *f;* (*of vessel*) borde *m;* **to fill sth to the ~** llenar algo hasta el borde

brine [braɪn] *n no pl* GASTR salmuera *f*

bring [brɪŋ] <brought, brought> *vt* **1.** (*carry*) traer; **to ~ sth in** entrar algo; **to ~ news** traer noticias **2.** (*take*) llevar; **to ~ sth with oneself** llevar algo consigo; **to ~ sb luck** traer suerte a alguien **3.** LAW **to ~ an action** (**against sb**) interponer una demanda (contra alguien) **4.** (*force*) **to ~ oneself to do sth** resignarse a hacer algo
 ◆ **bring about** *vt* provocar
 ◆ **bring back** *vt* **1.** (*reintroduce*) volver a introducir **2.** (*call to mind*) recordar **3.** (*return*) devolver
 ◆ **bring down** *vt* **1.** (*benefits, level*) reducir; (*temperature*) hacer bajar **2.** (*person*) derribar; (*govern-*

ment) derrocar
◆ **bring in** *vt* **1.**(*introduce*) introducir **2.**(*call in*) llamar
◆ **bring on** *vt* **1.**(*cause to occur*) provocar **2.**(*improve*) mejorar
◆ **bring out** *vt* sacar; (*book*) publicar
◆ **bring to** *vt always sep* reanimar
◆ **bring up** *vt* **1.**(*child*) criar; **to bring sb up to do sth** educar a alguien para que haga algo **2.**(*mention*) sacar
brink [brɪŋk] *n no pl* borde *m;* **to drive sb to the ~ of sth** llevar a alguien al borde de algo
brisk [brɪsk] *adj* **1.**(*fast*) rápido **2.**(*breeze*) fresco **3.**(*manner*) enérgico
bristle ['brɪsl] **I.** *n* (*of animal*) cerda *f;* (*on face*) barba *f* **II.** *vi* erizarse; **to ~ with anger** *fig* enfurecerse
Britain ['brɪtən] *n* Gran Bretaña *f*
British ['brɪtɪʃ, *Am:* 'brɪt̬-] **I.** *adj* británico **II.** *n pl* **the ~** los británicos
British Columbia *n* Columbia *f* Británica **British Isles** *n* **the ~** las Islas Británicas
Briton ['brɪtn] *n* británico, -a *m, f*
Brittany ['brɪtænɪ] *n* Bretaña *f*
brittle ['brɪtl, *Am:* 'brɪt̬-] *adj* quebradizo
broach [brəʊtʃ, *Am:* broʊtʃ] *vt* mencionar
broad [brɔːd, *Am:* brɑːd] *adj* ancho; ~ **interests** intereses diversos; **a ~ mind** una mente abierta
broad bean *n* haba *f*
broadcast ['brɔːdkɑːst, *Am:* 'brɑːdkæst] **I.** *n* TV, RADIO programa *m;* (*of concert*) emisión *f* **II.** *vi, vt* <broadcast *Am:* broadcasted, broadcast *Am:* broadcasted> TV transmitir; RADIO emitir; (*rumour*) difundir
broadcaster *n* (*person*) locutor(a) *m(f);* (*station*) emisora *f*
broadcasting *n no pl* TV transmisión *f;* RADIO radiodifusión *f*
broaden ['brɔːdn, *Am:* 'brɑː-] *vt* **to ~ the mind** abrir la mente
broadly ['brɔːdlɪ] *adv* (*generally*) en líneas generales

broadsheet ['brɔːdʃiːt, *Am:* ˌbrɑːd-] *n Aus, Brit: periódico de formato grande*
broadside ['brɔːdsaɪd, *Am:* ˌbrɑːd-] *n* **1.** NAUT andanada *f* **2.**(*verbal attack*) ataque *m*

? **Broadway** es el nombre que recibe una larga calle de New York City. En esta calle se localiza el conocido barrio de **Broadway** famoso por su intensa actividad teatral. Prácticamente todas las piezas dramáticas americanas de importancia se representan allí. Aquellas que, bien por tratarse de producciones baratas, bien por ser de carácter experimental no se representan, reciben el nombre de **off-Broadway plays.**

broccoli ['brɒkəli, *Am:* 'brɑːkl-] *n no pl* brócoli *m*
brochure ['brəʊʃəʳ, *Am:* broʊ'ʃʊr] *n* folleto *m*
broke [brəʊk, *Am:* broʊk] **I.** *pt of* **break II.** *adj inf* pelado, planchado *Chile;* **to go for ~** *inf* jugarse el todo por el todo
broken ['brəʊkən, *Am:* 'broʊ-] **I.** *pp of* **break II.** *adj* roto; ~ **heart** corazón destrozado
broker ['brəʊkəʳ, *Am:* 'broʊkə-] *n* FIN corredor(a) *m(f)* de bolsa; (*of agreement*) agente *mf*
bronchitis [brɒŋ'kaɪtɪs, *Am:* brɑːŋ'kaɪt̬ɪs] *n no pl* bronquitis *f*
bronze [brɒnz, *Am:* brɑːnz] *n* bronce *m*
brooch [brəʊtʃ, *Am:* broʊtʃ] *n* broche *m*
brood [bruːd] **I.** *n* (*of mammals*) camada *f;* (*of birds*) nidada *f* **II.** *vi* **to ~ over sth** dar vueltas a algo
brook [brʊk] *n* arroyo *m*
broom [bruːm] *n* (*brush*) escoba *f*
broth [brɒθ, *Am:* brɑːθ] *n no pl* caldo *m*
brothel ['brɒθl, *Am:* 'brɑːθl] *n* bur-

del *m*

brother ['brʌðəʳ, *Am:* -ɚ] *n* hermano *m*

brotherhood ['brʌðəhʊd, *Am:* '-ɚ-] *n* + *sing/pl vb* fraternidad *f*

brother-in-law ['brʌðərɪnlɔː, *Am:* -ɚɪnlɑː] <brothers-in-law *Brit:* brother-in-laws> *n* cuñado *m*, concuño *m AmL*

brought [brɔːt, *Am:* brɑːt] *pt, pp of* **bring**

brow [braʊ] *n no pl, liter* (*forehead*) frente

brown [braʊn] I. *n* marrón *m Col* II. *adj* marrón; (*eyes, hair*) castaño; (*bread, rice*) integral

brownie ['braʊni] *n Am* bizcocho *m* de chocolate y nueces

browse [braʊz] *vi* echar un vistazo; INFOR navegar

browser [braʊzə, *Am:* -ɚ] *n* INFOR navegador *m*

bruise [bruːz] I. *n* morado *m*; (*on fruit*) magulladura *f* II. *vt* (*person*) contusionar; (*fruit*) magullar; **to ~ one's arm** hacerse morados en el brazo

brunch [brʌntʃ] *n* desayuno-almuerzo *m*

brunt [brʌnt] *n no pl* **to bear the ~ of sth** aguantar lo más duro de algo

brush [brʌʃ] I. *n* 1. (*for hair*) cepillo *m* 2. (*broom*) escoba *f* 3. (*for painting*) pincel *m*; (*bigger*) brocha *f* II. *vt* 1. (*teeth, hair*) cepillar; (*floor*) barrer 2. (*touch lightly*) rozar

◆**brush aside** *vt* 1. (*push to one side*) apartar 2. (*disregard*) hacer caso omiso de; (*criticism*) pasar por alto

◆**brush off** *vt* (*person*) no hacer caso a; (*criticism*) pasar por alto

Brussels ['brʌsəlz] *n* Bruselas *f*

Brussels sprouts *npl* coles *fpl* de Bruselas

brutal ['bruːtəl, *Am:* -ṭəl] *adj* (*attack*) brutal; (*words*) cruel; (*honesty*) crudo

brutality [bruːˈtæləti, *Am:* -əṭi] *n* (*of attack*) brutalidad *f*; (*of words*) crueldad *f*; (*of truth*) crudeza *f*

brute [bruːt] *n* bestia *f*; **~ force** fuerza *f* bruta

BSc [ˌbiːesˈsiː] *abbr of* **Bachelor of Science** Ldo., -a *m, f* (en Ciencias)

BSE [ˌbiːesˈiː] *n abbr of* **bovine spongiform encephalopathy** BSE *f*

bubble ['bʌbl] I. *n* burbuja *f*; (*in cartoons*) bocadillo *m* II. *vi* borbotear

bubble gum *n* chicle *m*

buccaneer [ˌbʌkəˈnɪəʳ, *Am:* -ˈnɪr] *n* bucanero *m*

buck¹ [bʌk] <-(s)> *vi* corcovear

buck² [bʌk] *n Am, Aus, inf* (*dollar*) dólar *m*; **to make a fast ~** hacer dinero fácil

buck³ [bʌk] *n no pl, inf* **to pass the ~** escurrir el bulto

bucket ['bʌkɪt] *n* cubo *m*; **to kick the ~** *fig,* inf estirar la pata

bucketful ['bʌkɪtfʊl] <-s *o* bucketsful> *n* cubo *m* (lleno)

? El **Buckingham Palace** es la residencia londinense de la familia real británica. El palacio dispone de unas 600 habitaciones y fue construido por John Nash por expreso deseo del rey George IV entre los años 1821–1830. El edificio fue inaugurado en 1837 con motivo de la subida al trono de la reina Victoria.

buckle ['bʌkl] I. *n* hebilla *f* II. *vt* 1. (*fasten*) abrochar 2. (*bend*) torcer III. *vi* (*bend*) torcerse

bud [bʌd] *n* (*of leaf*) brote *m*; (*of flower*) capullo *m*

Buddhism ['bʊdɪzəm, *Am:* 'buː-dɪ-] *n no pl* budismo *m*

Buddhist *adj* budista

budding ['bʌdɪŋ] *adj* en ciernes

buddy ['bʌdi] *n Am, inf* colega *m*, cuate *m Méx*

budge [bʌdʒ] I. *vi* moverse; (*change opinion*) cambiar de opinión II. *vt* (*move*) mover; (*cause to change opinion*) hacer cambiar de opinión a

budget ['bʌdʒɪt] I. *n* presupuesto *m* II. *vt* presupuestar; (*wages, time*) administrar III. *vi* **to ~ for sth** presupuestar algo

budgetary [ˈbʌdʒɪtəri] *adj* presupuestario

buff [bʌf] **I.** *adj* color de ante **II.** *n inf* entusiasta *mf;* **film** ~ cinéfilo, -a *m, f* **III.** *vt* pulir

buffalo [ˈbʌfələʊ, *Am:* -əloʊ] <-(es)> *n* búfalo *m*

buffer [ˈbʌfəʳ, *Am:* -ɚ] *n* **1.** (*of car*) parachoques *m inv;* (*of train*) tope *m* **2.** INFOR memoria *f* intermedia

buffet¹ [ˈbʊfeɪ, *Am:* bəˈfeɪ] *n* **1.** (*meal*) buffet *m* **2.** (*bar*) cafetería *f*

buffet² [ˈbʌfɪt] *vt* zarandear

bug [bʌg] **I.** *n* **1.** ZOOL chinche *f;* (*any insect*) bicho *m* **2.** MED virus *m inv;* **she's caught the travel** ~ *fig* le ha picado el gusanillo de viajar **3.** INFOR error *m* **II.** *vt* <-gg-> **1.** (*telephone*) pinchar; (*conversation*) escuchar clandestinamente **2.** *inf* (*annoy*) fastidiar

buggy [ˈbʌgi] *n* **1.** *Brit* (*pushchair*) sillita *f* de paseo **2.** *Am* (*pram*) cochecito *m* (de niño)

build [bɪld] **I.** *vt* <built, built> (*house*) construir; (*car*) fabricar; (*trust*) cimentar; (*relationship*) establecer **II.** *vi* <built, built> **1.** (*construct*) edificar **2.** (*increase*) aumentar **III.** *n* complexión *f*
♦ **build on** *vt* **to build sth on sth** agregar algo a algo
♦ **build up** **I.** *vt* **1.** (*increase*) acrecentar **2.** (*accumulate*) acumular **3.** (*strengthen*) fortalecer **II.** *vi* **1.** (*increase*) ir en aumento **2.** (*accumulate*) acumularse

builder [ˈbɪldəʳ, *Am:* -dɚ] *n* (*company*) constructor(a) *m(f);* (*worker*) albañil *mf*

building *n* edificio *m*

building society *n Aus, Brit* sociedad *f* de crédito hipotecario

build-up [ˈbɪldʌp] *n* acumulación *f*

built [bɪlt] *pt, pp of* **build**

built-in *adj* **1.** (*cupboard*) empotrado **2.** (*feature*) incorporado **3.** (*advantage*) intrínseco

bulb [bʌlb] *n* **1.** BOT bulbo *m* **2.** ELEC bombilla *f,* bombillo *m AmL*

Bulgaria [bʌlˈgeərɪə, *Am:* -ˈgerɪ-] *n*

Bulgaria *f*

Bulgarian [bʌlˈgeərɪən, *Am:* -ˈgerɪ-] *adj* búlgaro

bulge [bʌldʒ] **I.** *vi* sobresalir **II.** *n* bulto *m*

bulk [bʌlk] *n* **1.** *no pl* (*magnitude*) volumen *m* **2.** *no pl* (*mass*) mole *f;* **in** ~ a granel; **the** ~ **of** la mayor parte de

bulky [ˈbʌlki] <-ier, iest> *adj* (*large*) voluminoso; (*heavy*) pesado

bull [bʊl] *n* toro *m*

bulldog [ˈbʊldɒg, *Am:* -dɑ:g] *n* bulldog *m*

bulldozer [ˈbʊldəʊzəʳ, *Am:* -doʊzɚ] *n* buldozer *m,* topadora *f Arg, Méx, Urug*

bullet [ˈbʊlɪt] *n* bala *f*

bulletin [ˈbʊlətɪn, *Am:* -ət̬ɪn] *n* boletín *m*

bulletin board *n Am a.* INFOR tablón *m* de anuncios

bulletproof [ˈbʊlɪtpruːf] *adj* a prueba de balas

bullfight [ˈbʊlfaɪt] *n* corrida *f* de toros

bullfighter [ˈbʊlfaɪtəʳ, *Am:* -t̬ɚ] *n* torero, -a *m, f*

bullock [ˈbʊlək] *n* buey *m*

bullring [ˈbʊlrɪŋ] *n* plaza *f* de toros

bullshit [ˈbʊlʃɪt] *n no pl, inf* gilipolleces *fpl*

bully [ˈbʊli] **I.** <-ies> *n* (*person*) matón, -ona *m, f* **II.** <-ie-> *vt* intimidar

bulwark [ˈbʊlwək, *Am:* -wɚk] *n* baluarte *m*

bum [bʌm] *n* **1.** *Am* (*lazy person*) vago, -a *m, f* **2.** *Am* (*tramp*) vagabundo, -a *m, f* **3.** *Aus, Brit, inf* (*bottom*) culo *m*

bumble [ˈbʌmbl] *vi* andar a tropezones

bumblebee [ˈbʌmblbiː] *n* abejorro *m*

bump [bʌmp] **I.** *n* **1.** (*lump*) bulto *m;* (*on head*) chichón *m;* (*on road*) bache *m* **2.** (*thud*) golpe *m* **II.** *vt* chocar contra; **to** ~ **one's head against sth** darse un golpe en la cabeza contra algo
♦ **bump into** *vt insep* **1.** (*collide*

with) chocar contra **2.** (*meet*) topar con

◆**bump off** *vt inf* **to bump sb off** cargarse a alguien

bumper ['bʌmpəʳ, *Am:* -pɚ] **I.** *n Brit, Aus* AUTO parachoques *m inv,* paragolpes *m inv AmL* **II.** *adj* (*crop*) abundante

bumpy ['bʌmpi] <-ier, iest> *adj* (*surface*) desigual; (*journey*) zarandeado

bun [bʌn] *n* **1.** (*pastry*) bollo *m* **2.** *Am* (*roll*) panecillo *m* **3.** (*hair*) moño *m*

bunch [bʌntʃ] <-es> **I.** *n* (*of bananas, grapes*) racimo *m;* (*of carrots, keys*) manojo *m;* (*of flowers*) ramo *m;* (*of people*) grupo *m;* **to be the best of the ~** ser lo mejor **II.** *vi* **to ~** (**together**) amontonarse

bundle ['bʌndl] *n* (*of clothes*) fardo *m Col;* (*of money*) fajo *m;* (*of sticks*) haz *f;* **to be a ~ of laughs** ser muy divertido; **to be a ~ of nerves** ser un manojo de nervios

bungalow ['bʌŋgələʊ, *Am:* -oʊ] *n* bungaló *m,* bóngalo *m AmL*

bunk [bʌŋk] *n* NAUT litera *f,* cucheta *f RíoPl*

bunk bed *n* litera *f*

bunker ['bʌŋkəʳ, *Am:* -kɚ] *n* búnker *m*

bunting ['bʌntɪŋ, *Am:* -t̬ɪŋ] *n no pl* banderitas *fpl*

buoyant ['bɔɪənt, *Am:* -jənt] *adj* flotante

burden ['bɜːdən, *Am:* 'bɜːr-] **I.** *n* carga *f* **II.** *vt* cargar

bureau ['bjʊərəʊ, *Am:* 'bjʊroʊ] <-x *Am, Aus:* -s> *n* **1.** *Brit* (*desk*) escritorio *m* **2.** *Am* (*chest of drawers*) cómoda *f*

bureaucracy [bjʊə'rɒkrəsi, *Am:* bjʊ'rɑːkrə-] *n* burocracia *f*

bureaucrat ['bjʊərəkræt, *Am:* 'bjʊrə-] *n* burócrata *mf*

bureaucratic [ˌbjʊərə'krætɪk, *Am:* ˌbjʊrə'kræt̬-] *adj* burocrático

burger ['bɜːgəʳ, *Am:* 'bɜːrgɚ] *n inf* hamburguesa *f*

burglar ['bɜːgləʳ, *Am:* 'bɜːrglɚ] *n* ladrón, -ona *m, f*

burglary ['bɜːgləri, *Am:* 'bɜːr-] <-ies> *n* robo *m*

burgle ['bɜːgl, *Am:* 'bɜːr-] *vt* robar

burial ['berɪəl] *n* entierro *m*

Burkina Faso [bɜːˌkiːnə'fæsəʊ] *n* Burkina *f* Faso

burly ['bɜːli, *Am:* 'bɜːr-] <-ier, -iest> *adj* fornido

Burma ['bɜːmə, *Am:* 'bɜːr-] *n* Birmania *f*

burn [bɜːn, *Am:* bɜːrn] **I.** <burnt *o* -ed, burnt *o* -ed> *vi* arder; **to be ~ing to do sth** estar deseando hacer algo; **to ~ with desire** desear ardientemente **II.** <burnt *o* -ed, burnt *o* -ed> *vt* quemar; (*building*) incendiar **III.** *n* quemadura *f,* quemada *f Méx*

◆**burn down** *vi* (*house*) incendiarse; (*fire, candle*) apagarse

◆**burn out** **I.** *vi* (*engine*) quemarse; (*fire, candle*) apagarse **II.** *vt* **to burn oneself out** agotarse

burner ['bɜːnəʳ, *Am:* 'bɜːrnɚ] *n* fogón *m;* TECH quemador *m*

burning ['bɜːnɪŋ, *Am:* 'bɜːrnɪŋ] *adj* **1.** (*hot*) ardiente **2.** (*issue*) candente

---

⚠ La **Burns Night** tiene lugar el 25 de enero. En este día se conmemora el nacimiento del poeta escocés Robert Burns (1759–1796). A la celebración acuden entusiastas de la obra de Burns, no sólo de Escocia sino de todas las partes del mundo. En ese día se sirve una comida especial llamada **Burns Supper** que se compone de **haggis** (una especie de asado de carne picada hecha de vísceras especiadas de oveja mezclado con avena y cebolla. Todo ello es cocido dentro de la tripa de la oveja y después dorado al horno), **neeps** (nabos) y **mashed tatties** (puré de patatas).

---

burnt [bɜːnt, *Am:* 'bɜːrnt] **I.** *pt, pp*

of **burn** II. *adj* quemado

burp [bɜ:p, *Am:* bɜ:rp] I. *n* eructo *m* II. *vi* eructar

burr [bɜ:^r, *Am:* bɜ:r] *n* **1.** BOT abrojo *m* **2.** (*noise*) zumbido *m* **3.** LING sonido *m* gutural

burrow ['bʌrəʊ, *Am:* 'bɜ:roʊ] I. *n* madriguera *f* II. *vi* excavar un agujero

burst [bɜ:st, *Am:* bɜ:rst] I. *n* (*explosion*) explosión *f;* MIL (*of fire*) ráfaga *f;* **a ~ of applause** una salva de aplausos II.<burst *Am:* bursted, burst *Am:* bursted> *vi* reventar; **to ~ into tears** romper a llorar; **to be ~ing to do sth** morirse de ganas de hacer algo III.<burst *Am:* bursted, burst *Am:* bursted> *vt* reventar; **to ~ its banks** (*river*) desbordarse
♦ **burst in** *vi* entrar de sopetón
♦ **burst out** *vi* **1.** (*exclaim*) saltar **2.** (*break out*) **to ~ laughing/crying** echarse a reír/llorar

Burundi [bʊ'rʊndi] *n* Burundi *m*

bury ['beri] <-ie-> *vt* enterrar; **to ~ oneself in sth** enfrascarse en algo

bus [bʌs] <-es> *n* autobús *m*, colectivo *m Arg, Ven*, guagua *f Cuba;* **to miss the ~** *fig* perder el (último) tren

bus driver *n* conductor(a) *m(f)* de autobús

bush [bʊʃ] <-es> *n* **1.** BOT arbusto *m* **2.** *no pl* (*land*) **the ~** el monte; **to beat about the ~** *fig* andarse con rodeos

bushel ['bʊʃl] *n* **to hide one's light under a ~** ocultar sus talentos

bushy ['bʊʃi] <-ier, -iest> *adj* (*hair*) tupido; (*beard*) espeso; (*eyebrows*) poblado

busily *adv* afanosamente

business ['bɪznɪs] <-es> *n* **1.** *no pl* (*trade, commerce*) negocios *mpl;* **to do ~ with sb** hacer negocios con alguien; **to get down to ~** empezar a trabajar; **to go out of ~** cerrar; **to mean ~** *fig* hablar en serio; **like nobody's ~** *inf* como loco **2.** (*sector*) industria *f* **3.** (*firm*) empresa *f;* **to start up a ~** poner un negocio **4.** *no pl* (*matter*) asunto *m;* **an unfin-**ished **~** un asunto pendiente; **it's none of your ~!** *inf* ¡no es asunto tuyo!

businesslike ['bɪznɪslaɪk] *adj* eficiente

businessman ['bɪznɪsmæn] <-men> *n* hombre *m* de negocios

businesswoman ['bɪznɪs‚wʊmən] <-women> *n* mujer *f* de negocios

bus stop *n* parada *f* de autobús

bust¹ [bʌst] *n* busto *m*

bust² [bʌst] I. *adj* *inf* **1.** (*broken*) destrozado **2.** (*bankrupt*) **to go ~** quebrar II.<bust *Am:* busted, bust *Am:* busted> *vt inf* (*break*) destrozar

bustle ['bʌsl] *vi* **to ~ about** ir y venir

busy ['bɪzi] <-ier, -iest> *adj* **1.** (*occupied*) atareado; **to be ~ with sth** estar ocupado con algo **2.** (*full of activity*) activo; (*exhausting*) agotador **3.** *Am* TEL **to be ~** estar comunicando

busybody ['bɪzi‚bɒdi, *Am:* -‚ba:di] <-ies> *n inf* entrometido, -a *m, f*

but [bʌt] I. *prep* excepto; **all ~ one** todos excepto uno; **anything ~ ...** lo que sea menos...; **nothing ~ ...** nada más que...; **there is nothing for it ~ to go in** no hay nada que hacer excepto entrar II. *conj* pero; **I'm not an Englishman ~ a Scot** no soy inglés sino escocés; **he has paper ~ no pen** tiene papel pero no una pluma III. *adv* sólo; **he is ~ a baby** no es más que un bebé; **I can't help ~ cry** no puedo evitar llorar IV. *n* pero *m;* **there are no ~s about it!** ¡no hay peros que valgan!

butch [bʊtʃ] *adj* (*man*) macho; (*woman*) marimacho

butcher ['bʊtʃə^r, *Am:* -ɚ] I. *n* carnicero, -a *m, f* II. *vt* **1.** (*animal*) matar **2.** (*murder*) masacrar

butler ['bʌtlə^r, *Am:* -lɚ] *n* mayordomo *m*

butt [bʌt] I. *n* **1.** (*of rifle*) culata *f* **2.** (*of cigarette*) colilla *f* **3.** (*blow: with head*) cabezada *f* **4.** (*target*) blanco *m* **5.** *Am, inf* (*buttocks*) culo *m* II. *vt* (*with horns*) topetar; (*with head*) dar una cabezada contra

butter ['bʌtər, *Am:* 'bʌt̬ər] I. *n no pl* mantequilla *f* II. *vt* untar con mantequilla

butterfly ['bʌtəflaɪ, *Am:* 'bʌt̬ə-] <-ies> *n* mariposa *f*

buttock ['bʌtək, *Am:* 'bʌt̬-] *n* nalga *f*

button ['bʌtən] I. *n* botón *m* II. *vt*, *vi* abrochar(se)

buttress ['bʌtrɪs] <-es> *n* contrafuerte *m*

buy [baɪ] I. *n* compra *f*; **a good** ~ una ganga II.<bought, bought> *vt* 1.(*purchase*) comprar; **to** ~ **sth from sb** comprar algo a alguien 2. *inf*(*believe*) creer
  ◆ **buy in** *vt always sep, Brit* aprovisionarse de
  ◆ **buy up** *vt insep* acaparar

buyer ['baɪər, *Am:* -ə-] *n* comprador(a) *m(f)*

buzz [bʌz] I. *vi* zumbar; (*bell*) sonar II. *n* zumbido *m*; **to give sb a** ~ llamar a alguien

buzzard ['bʌzəd, *Am:* -əd] *n* 1. *Brit* (*hawk*) ratonero *m* común 2. *Am* (*turkey vulture*) gallinazo *m* común

buzzer ['bʌzər, *Am:* -ə-] *n* timbre *m*

by [baɪ] I. *prep* 1.(*near*) cerca de; **close** ~ **...** cerca de...; ~ **the sea** junto al mar 2.(*during*) ~ **day/ night** durante el día/la noche; ~ **moonlight** a la luz de la luna 3.(*at the latest time*) para; ~ **tomorrow/ midnight** para mañana/la medianoche; ~ **then/now** para entonces/ este momento 4.(*cause*) por; **a novel** ~ **Joyce** una novela de Joyce; **to be killed** ~ **sth/sb** ser matado por algo/alguien 5.(*through means of*) ~ **rail/plane** en tren/avión; **made** ~ **hand** hecho a mano; **to hold sb** ~ **the arm** tomar a alguien por el brazo; ~ **chance/mistake** por suerte/error 6.(*under*) **to call sb** ~ **his name** llamar a alguien por su nombre 7.(*alone*) **to be** ~ **oneself** estar solo; **to do sth** ~ **oneself** hacer algo solo 8.(*as promise to*) **to swear** ~ **God** jurar por Dios 9.(*in measurement, arithmetic*) **to buy** ~ **the kilo** comprar por kilo; **to divide**

~ **6** dividir entre 6; **to increase** ~ **10%** aumentar en un 10%; **to multiply** ~ **4** multiplicar por 4; **paid** ~ **the hour** pagado por hora II. *adv* **to put sth** ~ poner algo a mano; ~ **and** ~ dentro de poco; **to go** ~ pasar; ~ **and large** en general

bye(-bye) [,baɪ('baɪ)] *interj inf* adiós

bye-law ['baɪlɔː] *n Brit* s. **by-law**

by-election *n Brit* elección *f* parcial

bygone ['baɪɡɒn, *Am:* -ɡɑːn] I. *adj inv* pasado II. *n* **let** ~**s be** ~**s** lo pasado pasado está

by-law ['baɪlɔː, *Am:* -lɑː] *n* (*regional law*) reglamento *m* local; (*of organization*) estatuto *m*

> **?** El **BYO-restaurant** (**B**ring **Y**our **O**wn) se encuentra en Australia. Es un tipo de restaurante que no tiene licencia para servir bebidas alcohólicas. Por ello, si los clientes desean consumir esta clase de bebidas, deben de traerlas ellos mismos.

by-pass ['baɪpɑːs, *Am:* -pæs] *n* 1. AUTO carretera *f* de circunvalación 2. MED by-pass *m*

by-product ['baɪprɒdʌkt, *Am:* -prɑːdəkt] *n* subproducto *m*; *fig* derivado *m*

bystander ['baɪstændər, *Am:* -də-] *n* espectador(a) *m(f)*

byte [baɪt] *n* byte *m*

C, c [siː] *n* 1.(*letter*) C, c *f*; ~ **for Charlie** C de Carmen 2. MUS do *m*

C *after n abbr of* **Celsius** C

c. *abbr of* **century** s.

cab [kæb] *n Am, Aus* (*taxi*) taxi *m*; **by** ~ en taxi

CAB [ˌsiːerˈbiː] *n Am abbr of* **Civil Aeronautics Board** Oficina *f* de Aviación Civil

cabaret [ˈkæbəreɪ, *Am:* ˌkæbəˈreɪ] *n* cabaret *m*

cabbage [ˈkæbɪdʒ] *n* col *f*

cabin [ˈkæbɪn] *n* 1. (*in a vehicle*) cabina *f* 2. (*house*) cabaña *f*

cabinet [ˈkæbɪnɪt] *n* 1. (*storage place*) armario *m;* **filing** ~ archivador *m* 2. + *sing/pl vb* (*group of ministers*) gabinete *m*

cable [ˈkeɪbl] I. *n* cable *m* II. *vt* HIST cablegrafiar

cable car *n* teleférico *m* **cable television** *n no pl,* **cable TV** *n no pl* televisión *f* por cable

cache [kæʃ] *n* 1. (*secret stockpile*) alijo *m* 2. INFOR caché *m;* ~ **memory** memoria *f* caché

cackle [ˈkækl] I. *vi* cacarear II. *n* cacareo *m*

cactus [ˈkæktəs] <-es *o* cacti> *n* cactus *m inv,* ulala *f Bol*

caddie [ˈkædi], **caddy** [ˈkædɪ] <-ies> I. *n* caddie *mf,* caddy *mf* II. <caddied, caddied, caddying> *vi* **to** ~ **for sb** hacer de caddy de alguien

cadet [kəˈdet] *n a.* MIL cadete *mf*

cadre [ˈkɑːdər, *Am:* ˈkædriː] *n* cuadro *m*

Caesar [ˈsiːzər, *Am:* -zɚ] *n* César *m;* **Julius** ~ HIST Julio César

cafe [ˈkæfeɪ, *Am:* kæfˈeɪ] *n,* **café** *n* café *m*

cafeteria [ˌkæfɪˈtɪərɪə, *Am:* -ˈtɪrɪ-] *n* restaurante *m* autoservicio

cage [keɪdʒ] I. *n* jaula *f* II. *vt* enjaular

cairn [keən, *Am:* kern] *n* mojón *m* (de piedras)

Cairo [ˈkeərəʊ, *Am:* ˈkeroʊ] *n* El Cairo

cake [keɪk] *n* 1. GASTR pastel *m;* **to want to have one's** ~ **and eat it** *fig* quererlo todo 2. (*of soap*) pastilla *f*

cal. *n abbr of* **calorie** cal *f*

calamity [kəˈlæmətɪ, *Am:* -ət̪ɪ] <-ies> *n* calamidad *f*

calcium [ˈkælsɪəm] *n no pl* calcio *m*

calculate [ˈkælkjʊleɪt, *Am:* -kjə-]

I. *vt* calcular; **to** ~ **sth at …** calcular algo en… II. *vi* calcular

calculated *adj* calculado; **to be** ~ **to do sth** estar pensado para hacer algo

calculation [ˌkælkjʊˈleɪʃn, *Am:* -kjə-] *n* cálculo *m*

calculator [ˈkælkjʊleɪtər, *Am:* -kjəleɪtɚ] *n* calculadora *f*

calculus [ˈkælkjʊləs, *Am:* -kjə-] *n no pl* cálculo *m*

calendar [ˈkælɪndər, *Am:* -dɚ] I. *n* calendario *m,* exfoliador *m Chile, Méx* II. *adj* ~ **year** año *m* civil

calf¹ [kɑːf, *Am:* kæf] <calves> *n* (*young cow or bull*) ternero, -a *m, f*

calf² [kɑːf, *Am:* kæf] <calves> *n* (*lower leg*) pantorrilla *f*

California [ˌkælɪˈfɔːnɪə, *Am:* -əˈfɔrnjə] *n* California *f*

call [kɔːl] I. *n* 1. (*telephone*) llamada *f* 2. (*visit*) visita *f;* **to be on a** ~ estar haciendo una visita; **to be on** ~ estar de guardia; **to pay a** ~ **on sb** hacer una visita a alguien 3. (*shout*) grito *m* 4. (*bird*) canto *m* 5. (*request*) *a.* POL llamamiento *m;* **a** ~ **for help** una llamada de socorro II. *vt* 1. (*name*) llamar; **what's that actor** ~**ed?** ¿cómo se llama ese actor?; **to** ~ **sb's attention** llamar la atención de alguien 2. (*telephone*) llamar, telefonear *AmL* 3. (*decide to have: meeting*) convocar; (*strike*) declarar III. *vi* 1. (*telephone*) llamar 2. (*drop by*) pasar

◆ **call for** *vi insep* 1. (*come to get*) pasar a recoger 2. (*demand, require*) exigir; **this calls for a celebration** esto hay que celebrarlo

◆ **call in** *vt* llamar

caller [ˈkɔːlər, *Am:* -lɚ] *n* 1. (*on the telephone*) persona *f* que llama por teléfono; **hold the line please,** ~ espere, por favor 2. (*visitor*) visita *f;* (*in a shop*) cliente *mf*

calling [ˈkɔːlɪŋ] *n form* vocación *f*

callous [ˈkæləs] *adj* cruel

calm [kɑːm] I. *adj* 1. (*not nervous*) tranquilo; **to keep** ~ mantenerse tranquilo 2. (*peaceful*) pacífico II. *n* tranquilidad *f;* **the** ~ **before the storm** *a. fig* la calma que precede a la tormenta **III.** *vt* tranquilizar; **to ~ oneself** calmarse

calmness *n* *no pl* (*lack of agitation*) tranquilidad *f*

calorie ['kælərɪ] *n* caloría *f*

Calvinist ['kælvɪnɪst] *n* calvinista *mf*

CAM [kæm] *n* *abbr of* **computer assisted manufacture** FAO *f*

Cambodia [kæm'bəʊdɪə, *Am:* -'boʊ-] *n* Camboya *f*

Cambodian [kæm'bəʊdɪən, *Am:* -'boʊ-] *adj* camboyano

camcorder ['kæmkɔdər] *n* videocámara *f*

came [keɪm] *vi* *pt of* **come**

camel ['kæml] *n* camello *m*

cameo ['kæmɪəʊ, *Am:* -oʊ] *n* CINE, TV aparición *f* breve, papel *m* corto

camera ['kæmərə] *n* PHOT máquina *f* fotográfica; CINE cámara *f*; **to be on ~** estar en imagen

cameraman <-men> *n* cámara *m*

Cameroon [ˌkæmə'ruːn] *n* Camerún *m*

Cameroonian [ˌkæmə'ruːnɪən, *Am:* -'roʊ-] *adj* camerunés

camomile ['kæməmaɪl, *Am:* -miːl] *n* **~ tea** manzanilla *f*

camouflage ['kæməˌflɑːʒ] **I.** *n* *no pl* camuflaje *m* **II.** *vt* camuflar; **to ~ oneself** camuflarse

camp¹ [kæmp] **I.** *n* **1.** (*encampment*) campamento *m*; **to pitch ~** acampar; **summer ~** *Am* campamento de verano **2.** MIL **army ~** campamento militar **II.** *vi* acampar; **to go ~ing** ir de acampada, campear *AmL*

camp² [kæmp] *adj* (*effeminate*) amanerado

campaign [kæm'peɪn] **I.** *n* (*organized action*) *a.* MIL campaña *f*; **~ trail** campaña *f* electoral **II.** *vi* hacer campaña; **to ~ for sth/sb** hacer campaña a favor de algo/alguien

campaigner [kæm'peɪnər, *Am:* -ɚ] *n* defensor(a) *m(f)*; **a ~ for sth** un luchador a favor de algo

camper ['kæmpər, *Am:* -pɚ] *n* campista *mf*

camping ['kæmpɪŋ] *n* *no pl* cámping *m*; **to go ~** ir de acampada

campsite ['kæmpsaɪt] *n* cámping

m; *Am* (*for one tent*) parcela *f* de cámping

campus ['kæmpəs] <-ses> *n* campus *m inv*

can¹ [kæn] **I.** *n* (*container*) lata *f*; (*of oil*) bidón *m* **II.** *vt* **1.** (*put in cans*) enlatar **2.** *Am, inf* (*stop*) ~ **it!** ¡basta ya!

can² [kən] <could, could> *aux* **1.** (*be able to*) poder; **if I could** si pudiera; **I think she ~ help you** creo que ella te puede ayudar; **I could have kissed her** hubiera podido besarla **2.** (*be permitted to*) poder; **you can't go** no puedes ir; **could I look at it?** ¿podría verlo? **3.** (*know how to*) saber; ~ **you swim?** ¿sabes nadar?

Canada ['kænədə] *n* Canadá *m*

Canadian [kə'neɪdɪən] *adj* canadiense

canal [kə'næl] *n* canal *m*

canary [kə'neəri, *Am:* -'neri] <-ies> *n* canario *m*

Canary Islands *n* Islas *fpl* Canarias

cancel ['kænsl] <*Brit:* -ll-, *Am:* -l-> **I.** *vt* (*reservation, meeting*) cancelar; (*party, concert*) suspender **II.** *vi* anular

cancellation [ˌkænsə'leɪʃn] *n* (*of reservation, meeting*) cancelación *f*; (*of party, concert*) suspensión *f*

cancer ['kænsər, *Am:* -sɚ] *n* MED *no pl* cáncer *m*, cangro *m* *Col, Guat*; ~ **specialist** oncólogo, -a *m, f*; ~ **cell** célula *f* cancerígena

Cancer ['kænsər, *Am:* -sɚ] *n* Cáncer *m*

candid ['kændɪd] *adj* franco

candidacy ['kændɪdəsɪ] *n* *no pl* candidatura *f*

candidate ['kændɪdət] *n* **1.** POL candidato, -a *m, f* **2.** (*possible choice*) aspirante *mf*

candle ['kændl] *n* vela *f*; **to burn one's ~ at both ends** *fig* hacer de la noche día

candlelight ['kændllaɪt] *n* *no pl* luz *f* de una vela; **to do sth by ~** hacer algo a la luz de una vela

candlestick ['kændlstɪk] *n* candelero *m*

candor *n Am*, **candour** ['kændə', *Am:* -də'] *n no pl*, *Brit*, *Aus*, *form* franqueza *f*

candy ['kændɪ] <-ies> *n Am* (*sweets*) golosinas *fpl*

cane [keɪn] *n* 1. *no pl* (*dried plant stem*) caña *f* 2. *no pl* (*furniture*) mimbre *m*

canine ['keɪnaɪn] *adj* canino

canister ['kænɪstə', *Am:* -əstə'] *n* (*metal*) lata *f*; (*plastic*) bote *m*

cannabis ['kænəbɪs] *n no pl* cannabis *f*

canned [kænd] *adj* 1. enlatado 2. MUS, TV ~ **laughter** risas *fpl* grabadas

cannibal ['kænɪbl] *n* caníbal *mf*

cannibalism ['kænɪbəlɪzəm] *n no pl* canibalismo *m*

canning ['kænɪŋ] *n no pl* enlatado *m*; ~ **factory** fábrica *f* de conservas

cannon ['kænən] *n* cañón *m*

cannot ['kænɒt, *Am:* -ɑ:t] *aux =* can not *s.* **can²**

canny ['kænɪ] <-ier, -iest> *adj* astuto

canoe [kə'nuː] *n* canoa *f*; *Brit* (*kayak*) piragua *f*; **to paddle one's own** ~ *fig* arreglárselas solo

canoeing *n no pl* piragüismo *m*

can opener ['kæn,əʊpənə', *Am:* -oʊpnə'] *n* abrelatas *m inv*

canopy ['kænəpɪ] <-ies> *n* toldo *m*

can't [kɑːnt, *Am:* kænt] *=* cannot *s.* **can²**

canteen¹ [kæn'tiːn] *n* (*cafetería*) cantina *f*

canteen² *n* (*drink container*) cantimplora *f*

Cantonese [,kæntə'niːz] *adj* cantonés, -esa

canvas ['kænvəs] <-es> *n* 1. *no pl* (*cloth*) lona *f* 2. ART lienzo *m*, holán *m AmC*

canvass ['kænvəs] I. *vt* 1. (*gather opinion*) sondear; **to** ~ **sth** hacer una encuesta de algo 2. POL (*votes*) solicitar II. *vi* POL hacer campaña

canyon ['kænjən] *n* cañón *m*

CAP [,siː'eɪ'piː] *n abbr of* **Common Agricultural Policy** PAC *f*

cap¹ [kæp] I. *n* 1. (*without peak*) gorro *m* 2. (*with peak*) gorra *f*; **to**

put on one's thinking ~ *fig, inf* hacer uso de la materia gris; ~ **and gown** UNIV toga *f* y birrete *m* 3. (*cover*) tapón *m*; **screw-on** ~ casquete *m* 4. (*limit*) tope *m*; **salary** ~ *Am* salario *m* máximo II. <-pp-> *vt* 1. (*limit*) limitar 2. SPORTS **he has been** ~**ped two times for Spain** ha integrado dos veces la selección española

cap² *n abbr of* **capital** (**letter**) mayúscula *f*

capability [,keɪpə'bɪlətɪ, *Am:* -t̬ɪ] <-ies> *n* 1. *no pl* (*ability*) capacidad *f* 2. (*skill*) aptitud *f*

capable ['keɪpəbl] *adj* 1. (*competent*) competente 2. (*able*) capaz; **to be** ~ **of doing sth** ser capaz de hacer algo

capacity [kə'pæsətɪ, *Am:* -t̬ɪ] <-ies> *n* 1. *no pl* (*volume,*) cabida *f*; capacidad *f*; **to be full to** ~ estar completamente lleno 2. *no pl* (*ability, amount*) capacidad *f*; **seating** ~ aforo *m* 3. (*output*) rendimiento *m*

cape¹ [keɪp] *n* GEO cabo *m*

cape² [keɪp] *n* (*cloak*) capa *f*

caper¹ ['keɪpə', *Am:* -ə'] *n* (*joyful leaping movement*) cabriola *f*; **to cut** ~**s** hacer cabriolas

caper² ['keɪpə', *Am:* -pə'] *n* BOT alcaparra *f*

Cape Town ['keɪptaʊn] *n* Ciudad *f* del Cabo

Cape Verde ['keɪpvɜːd, *Am:* -vɜːrd] *n* Cabo *m* Verde

capital ['kæpɪtl, *Am:* -ət̬l] I. *n* 1. (*principal city*) capital *f* 2. TYPO mayúscula *f* 3. FIN capital *m*; **to make** ~ (**out**) **of sth** *fig* sacar partido de algo II. *adj* 1. (*principal*) primordial; ~ **city** capital *f* 2. TYPO (*letter*) mayúscula 3. LAW capital; ~ **punishment** pena *f* capital [*o* de muerte]

capital investment *n* FIN inversión *f* de capital

capitalism ['kæpɪtəlɪzəm, *Am:* 'kæpət-] *n no pl* capitalismo *m*

capitalist ['kæpɪtəlɪst, *Am:* 'kæpət̬əl-] *adj* capitalista

capitalize ['kæpɪtəlaɪz, *Am:* 'kæpətəlaɪz] *vt* capitalizar

capital letter [ˈkæpɪtl ˈletəʳ, *Am:* -ətl ˈletɚ] *n* mayúscula *f;* **in ~s** con mayúsculas **capital punishment** *n* *no pl* pena *f* de muerte

cappuccino [ˌkæpʊˈtʃiːnəʊ, *Am:* ˌkæpəˈtʃiːnoʊ] *n* capuchino *m*

Capricorn [ˈkæprɪkɔːn, *Am:* -rəkɔːrn] *n* Capricornio *m*

Caps. *n abbr of* **capitals** mayúsculas *fpl*

capsize [kæpˈsaɪz, *Am:* ˈkæpsaɪz] *vt, vi* NAUT hacer zozobrar; *fig* volcar

capsule [ˈkæpsjuːl, *Am:* -sl] *n* cápsula *f*

captain [ˈkæptɪn] I. *n* capitán, -ana *m, f* II. *vt* capitanear

caption [ˈkæpʃn] *n* (*heading*) título *m;* (*for cartoon*) leyenda *f*

captivate [ˈkæptɪveɪt, *Am:* -tə-] *vt* cautivar

captive [ˈkæptɪv] *adj* cautivo; **to hold sb ~** tener prisionero a alguien

captivity [kæpˈtɪvətɪ, *Am:* -t̬ɪ] *n no pl* cautiverio *m;* **to be in ~** estar en cautividad

capture [ˈkæptʃəʳ, *Am:* -tʃɚ] I. *vt* 1. (*take prisoner*) prender 2. (*take possession of*) capturar II. *n* captura *f*

car [kɑːʳ, *Am:* kɑːr] *n* 1. AUTO coche *m,* carro *m AmL,* auto *m Arg, Chile, Urug* 2. RAIL vagón *m*

caramel [ˈkærəmel, *Am:* ˈkɑːrml] *n* 1. *no pl* (*burnt sugar*) azúcar *m* quemado 2. (*sweet*) caramelo *m*

carat [ˈkærət, *Am:* ˈker-] *<-(s)>* *n* quilate *m*

caravan [ˈkærəvæn, *Am:* ˈker-] *n Brit* (*vehicle*) caravana *f;* **gypsy ~** carromato *m* de gitanos

carbohydrate [ˌkɑːbəʊˈhaɪdreɪt, *Am:* ˌkɑːrboʊ-] *n* CHEM hidrato *m* de carbono; **~ content** contenido *m* de carbohidratos

carbon [ˈkɑːbən, *Am:* ˈkɑːr-] *n no pl* CHEM carbono *m*

carbon dioxide *n no pl* dióxido *m* de carbono **carbon monoxide** *n no pl* monóxido *m* de carbono

carcass [ˈkɑːkəs, *Am:* ˈkɑːr-] *<-es>* *n* cadáver *m* de animal

card [kɑːd, *Am:* kɑːrd] *n* 1. *no pl a.* FIN, INFOR tarjeta *f* 2. GAMES carta *f,* naipe *m;* **pack of ~s** baraja *f;* **to play ~s** jugar a las cartas; **to play one's ~s right** *fig* hacer una buena jugada 3. **membership ~** carnet de socio

cardboard [ˈkɑːdbɔːd, *Am:* ˈkɑːrdbɔːrd] *n no pl* cartón *m*

cardiac [ˈkɑːdiæk, *Am:* ˈkɑːr-] *adj* MED cardíaco; (*disease*) cardiovascular

cardigan [ˈkɑːdɪgən, *Am:* ˈkɑːr-] *n* chaqueta *f* de punto

cardinal [ˈkɑːdɪnl, *Am:* ˈkɑːr-] I. *n* 1. REL, ZOOL cardenal *m* 2. (*number*) cardinal *m* II. *adj* (*importance: rule*) fundamental

care [keəʳ, *Am:* ker] I. *n* 1. (*attention*) cuidado *m;* **to take ~ of** cuidar de; **take ~ (of yourself)!** ¡cuídate!; **handle with ~** frágil 2. (*worry*) preocupación *f;* **to not have a ~ in the world** no tener ninguna preocupación II. *vi* 1. (*be concerned*) preocuparse; **to ~ about sb/sth** preocuparse por alguien/algo; **who ~s?** ¿qué más da? 2. (*feel affection*) importar

career [kəˈrɪəʳ, *Am:* -ˈrɪr] I. *n* 1. (*profession*) profesión *f* 2. (*working life*) carrera *f* profesional II. *vi* ir a toda velocidad; **to ~ out of control** (*car*) perder el control

carefree [ˈkeəfriː, *Am:* ˈker-] *adj* despreocupado

careful [ˈkeəfl, *Am:* ˈker-] *adj* cuidadoso; **to be ~ of sth** tener cuidado con algo

carefulness *n no pl* (*caution*) cuidado *m*

careless [ˈkeəlɪs, *Am:* ˈker-] *adj* descuidado

carelessness *n no pl* (*lack of attention*) falta *f* de atención

caress [kəˈres] I. *<-es>* *n* caricia *f* II. *vi, vt* acariciar, barbear *AmC*

caretaker [ˈkeəˌteɪkəʳ, *Am:* ˈkerˌteɪkɚ] *n* 1. *Brit* (*janitor*) conserje *mf* 2. *Am* (*job*) portero, -a *m, f*

cargo [ˈkɑːgəʊ, *Am:* ˈkɑːrgoʊ] *<-(e)s>* *n* 1. *no pl* (*goods*) carga *f* 2. (*load*) cargamento *m*

Caribbean [ˌkærɪˈbiːən, *Am:* ˌkerɪ-ˈbiː-] I. *adj* caribeño, caribe *AmL* II. *n* the ~ el Caribe

caricature [ˈkærɪkətjʊəʳ, *Am:* ˈkerə-kətjʊr] I. *n a.* ART caricatura *f* II. *vt* LIT caricaturizar

caring *adj* compasivo

carnation [kɑːˈneɪʃn, *Am:* kɑːr-] *n* clavel *m*

carnival [ˈkɑːnɪvl, *Am:* ˈkɑːrnə-] *n* carnaval *m*, chaya *f Arg, Chile*

carol [ˈkærəl, *Am:* ˈker-] *n* villancico *m*

carol singer *n* persona *f* que canta villancicos

car park [ˈkɑːpɑːk, *Am:* ˈkɑːrpɑːrk] *n Brit, Aus* aparcamiento *m*, párking *m*

carpenter [ˈkɑːpəntəʳ, *Am:* ˈkɑːr-pn̩təʳ] *n* carpintero, -a *m, f*

carpet [ˈkɑːpɪt, *Am:* ˈkɑːrpət] *n* moqueta *f*, alfombra *f AmL;* (*not fitted*) alfombra *f;* **to sweep sth under the ~** *fig* correr un velo sobre algo

carriage [ˈkærɪdʒ, *Am:* ˈker-] *n* 1. (*horse-drawn vehicle*) carruaje *m* 2. *Brit* (*train wagon*) vagón *m* 3. (*posture*) andares *mpl*

carrier [ˈkærɪəʳ] *n* 1. (*person who carries*) transportista *mf* 2. (*vehicle*) vehículo *m* transportador; **aircraft ~** portaviones *m inv* 3. MED portador(a) *m(f)*

carrot [ˈkærət, *Am:* ˈker-] *n* zanahoria *f*

carry [ˈkærɪ, *Am:* ˈker-] <-ies, -ied> *vt* 1. (*transport in hands or arms*) llevar 2. (*transport*) transportar, acarrear 3. (*have on one's person*) llevar encima 4. MED transmitir

◆ **carry away** *vt* 1. (*remove*) arrastrar 2. **to be carried away (by sth)** dejarse llevar (por algo)

◆ **carry on** I. *vt insep* continuar con; ~ **the good work!** ¡sigue con el buen trabajo! II. *vi* 1. (*continue*) seguir; **to ~ doing sth** continuar haciendo algo 2. *inf* (*make a fuss*) montar un número

◆ **carry out** *vt* llevar a cabo

cart [kɑːt, *Am:* kɑːrt] *n* 1. (*vehicle*) carreta *f*, carro *m;* **to put the ~ before the horse** *fig* empezar la casa por el tejado 2. *Am* (*supermarket trolley*) carrito *m*

cartel [kɑːˈtel, *Am:* kɑːr-] *n* cartel *m*

carton [ˈkɑːtn, *Am:* ˈkɑːr-] *n* envase *m* de cartón

cartoon [kɑːˈtuːn, *Am:* kɑːr-] *n* 1. ART viñeta *f* 2. CINE dibujos *mpl* animados

cartoonist *n* dibujante *mf*

cartridge [ˈkɑːtrɪdʒ, *Am:* ˈkɑːr-] *n* cartucho *m*, cachimba *f AmL*

cartwheel [ˈkɑːθwiːl, *Am:* ˈkɑːrt-] *n* 1. (*wheel*) rueda *f* de carro 2. (*playing*) rueda *f;* **to do a ~** hacer la rueda

carve [kɑːv, *Am:* kɑːrv] *vt* 1. (*cut*) cortar; **to ~ (out) a name for oneself** *fig* hacerse un nombre 2. (*stone, wood*) tallar 3. (*cut meat*) trinchar

carving *n* ART escultura *f;* (*of wood*) talla *f*

cascade [kæˈskeɪd] *n* cascada *f*

case[1] [keɪs] *n* 1. *a.* MED caso *m;* **in any ~** en cualquier caso; **just in ~** por si acaso; **in ~ it rains** en caso de que llueva 2. LING caso *m*

case[2] [keɪs] *n* 1. *Brit* (*suitcase*) maleta *f* 2. (*container*) caja *f;* (*for jewels, spectacles*) estuche *m;* (*for camera, musical instrument*) funda *f;* **glass ~** vitrina *f*

cash [kæʃ] I. *n no pl* dinero *m* en efectivo; ~ **in advance** adelanto *m* II. *vt* cobrar; **to ~ sth in** canjear algo

cash flow [ˈkæʃˌfləʊ, *Am:* -ˌfloʊ] *n* FIN flujo *m* de caja

cashier [kæˈʃɪəʳ, *Am:* kæˈʃɪr] *n* cajero, -a *m, f*

casino [kəˈsiːnəʊ, *Am:* -noʊ] *n* casino *m*

cask [kɑːsk, *Am:* kæsk] *n* tonel *m;* (*of wine*) barril *m*

casket [ˈkɑːskɪt, *Am:* ˈkæskɪt] *n* cofre *m*

Caspian Sea [ˈkæspiən] *n* Mar *m* Caspio

casserole [ˈkæsərəʊl, *Am:* -əroʊl] *n* 1. (*cooking vessel*) cazuela *f* 2. GASTR guiso *m*

cassette [kəˈset] *n* casete *m o f;*

video ~ videocasete *m*

cassette player *n*, **cassette recorder** *n* casete *m*

cast [kɑst, *Am:* kæst] I. *n* 1. THEAT, CINE reparto *m*; **supporting** ~ reparto secundario 2. (*mould*) molde *m* 3. MED escayola *f* II. <cast, cast> *vt* 1. (*throw*) lanzar 2. (*direct*) **to** ~ **doubt on sth** poner algo en duda; **to** ~ **one's mind back** hacer un esfuerzo de memoria 3. (*allocate roles*) asignar; **to** ~ **sb as sb/sth** dar a alguien el papel de alguien/algo 4. (*give*) dar; (*vote*) emitir
◆**cast off** I. *vt* 1. (*stitch*) cerrar 2. (*throw off*) desechar II. *vi* 1. NAUT soltar amarras 2. (*in knitting*) terminar

castaway ['kɑːstəweɪ, *Am:* 'kæstə-] *n* náufrago, -a *m, f*

caste [kɑst, *Am:* kæst] *n* (*social class*) casta *f*; ~ **system** sistema *m* de castas

casting ['kɑːstɪŋ, *Am:* 'kæstɪŋ] *n* 1. (*forming in a mould*) vaciado *m* 2. THEAT reparto *m* de papeles

cast iron [ˌkɑːst'aɪən] I. *n no pl* hierro *m* fundido II. *adj* 1. (*made of cast iron*) de hierro fundido 2. *fig* irrefutable

castle ['kɑːsl, *Am:* 'kæsl] I. *n* 1. (*building*) castillo *m;* **to build ~s in the air** *fig* construir castillos en el aire 2. (*chess piece*) torre *f* II. *vi* (*in chess*) enrocar

casual ['kæʒʊəl, *Am:* 'kæʒuː-] *adj* 1. (*relaxed*) relajado 2. (*not permanent*) casual 3. (*informal*) informal

casualty ['kæʒʊəltɪ, *Am:* 'kæʒuː-] <-ies> *n* 1. (*injured person*) herido, -a *m, f*; MIL baja *f* 2. *no pl* (*hospital department*) urgencias *fpl*

cat [kæt] *n* gato, -a *m, f*; **to let the ~ out of the bag** *fig* descubrir el pastel; **to rain ~s and dogs** *fig* llover a cántaros

CAT [kæt] *n* 1. INFOR *abbr of* **computer-assisted translation** TAO *f* 2. MED *abbr of* **computerized axial tomography** TAC *m o f;* ~ **scan** (escáner *m*) TAC *m*

Catalan [ˌkætə'læn, *Am:* 'kætəlæn] *adj* catalán

catalog ['kætəlɒg] *Am*, **catalogue** ['kætəlɑːg] *Brit* I. *n* catálogo *m;* **a** ~ **of mistakes** *fig* un error detrás de otro II. *vt* catalogar

Catalonia [ˌkætələʊniə, *Am:* -'loʊ-] *n* Cataluña *f*

Catalonian [ˌkætələʊniən, *Am:* -'loʊ-] *adj s.* **Catalan**

catalyst ['kætəlɪst, *Am:* 'kæt̬-] *n a. fig* catalizador *m*

catapult ['kætəpʌlt, *Am:* 'kæt̬-] *n* tirachinas *m inv;* HIST catapulta *f*

catastrophe [kə'tæstrəfɪ] *n* catástrofe *f*

catastrophic [ˌkætə'strɒfɪk, *Am:* ˌkæt̬ə'strɑːfɪk] *adj* catastrófico

catch [kætʃ] <-es> I. *n* 1. *no pl* (*fish caught*) pesca *f* 2. (*fastening device*) pestillo *m* 3. *inf* (*suitable partner*) **he's a good** ~ es un buen partido II. <caught, caught> *vt* 1. (*hold moving object*) agarrar; **to** ~ **sb at a bad moment** pillar a alguien en un mal momento 2. (*get*) coger, tomar *AmL;* **to** ~ **the bus** coger el bus 3. (*discover by surprise*) **to** ~ **sb** (**doing sth**) sorprender [*o* pillar] a alguien (haciendo algo); **to** ~ **sb red handed** *fig* coger [*o* pillar] a alguien con las manos en la masa 4. MED contagiarse de
◆**catch on** *vi* 1. (*be popular*) ponerse de moda 2. *inf* (*understand*) entender
◆**catch up** I. *vi* **to** ~ **with sb** alcanzar el nivel de alguien; **to** ~ **with sth** (*make up lost time*) ponerse al corriente de algo II. *vt* **to catch sb up** *Brit, Aus* alcanzar a alguien

catchy ['kætʃɪ] <-ier, -iest> *adj* pegadizo

categorise *vt Brit, Aus*, **categorize** ['kætəgəraɪz, *Am:* 'kæt̬əgəraɪz] *vt Am* clasificar

category ['kætɪgərɪ, *Am:* 'kæt̬əgɔːr-] <-ies> *n* categoría *f*

cater ['keɪtər, *Am:* -t̬ə] *vi* encargarse del servicio de comidas

catering ['keɪtərɪŋ] *n no pl* restauración *f;* (*service*) servicio *m* de comidas

caterpillar ['kætəpɪlə', *Am:* 'kæṭə-pɪlə'] *n* **1.** ZOOL oruga *f* **2.** (*vehicle*) tractor *m* oruga

cathedral [kə'θi:drəl] *n* catedral *f*; **~ city** ciudad *f* episcopal

Catholic ['kæθəlɪk] *adj* católico

Catholicism [kə'θɒləsɪzəm, *Am:* -'θɑ:lə-] *n* *no pl* catolicismo *m*

cattle ['kætl, *Am:* 'kæṭ-] *npl* ganado *m*; **beef ~** ganado vacuno; **dairy ~** vacas *fpl* lecheras

> ⚠ **cattle** (= el ganado) es plural en inglés: "The cattle are in the field."

catty ['kætɪ, *Am:* 'kæṭ-] <-ier, -iest> *adj* malicioso

cat-walk ['kæt,wɔ:k, *Am:* -wɑ:k] *n* pasarela *f*

caucus ['kɔ:kəs, *Am:* 'kɑ:-] *n* <-es> comité *m*

caught [kɔ:t, *Am:* kɑ:t] *pt, pp of* **catch**

cauliflower ['kɒlɪflaʊə', *Am:* 'kɑ:lɪ,flaʊə'] *n* coliflor *f*

cause [kɔ:z] I. *n* **1.** (*a reason for*) causa *f*; **this is no ~ for ...** esto no justifica... **2.** *no pl* (*objective*) causa *f* II. *vt* causar; (*an accident*) provocar; **to ~ sb/sth to do sth** hacer que alguien/algo haga algo

causeway ['kɔ:z,weɪ, *Am:* 'kɑ:z-] *n* carretera *f* elevada

caution ['kɔ:ʃn, *Am:* 'kɑ:-] *n* *no pl* **1.** (*carefulness*) cautela *f*; **to treat sth with ~** tratar algo con cuidado; **~ is advised** se recomienda prudencia **2.** (*warning*) advertencia *f*; **a note of ~** un aviso; **~!** ¡cuidado!

cautious ['kɔ:ʃəs, *Am:* 'kɑ:-] *adj* cauto; **to be ~ in sth** ser prudente en algo

cavalry ['kævlrɪ] *n pl vb* MIL caballería *f*

cave *n* (*natural*) cueva *f*; (*manmade*) caverna *f*

cavern ['kævən, *Am:* -ə'n] *n* caverna *f*

caviar(e) ['kævɪɑ:', *Am:* -ɑ:r] *n no pl* caviar *m*

cavity ['kævɪtɪ, *Am:* -ṭɪ] <-ies> *n* cavidad *f*; **nasal ~** fosa *f* nasal

Cayman Islands ['keɪmən] *n* Islas *fpl* Cayman

CBI [,si:bi:'aɪ] *n Brit abbr of* **Confederation of British Industry** ≈ CEOE *f*

cc [,si:'si:] *abbr of* **cubic centimetres** cc

CCTV [,si:si:ti:'vi:] *n abbr of* **closed--circuit television** circuito *m* cerrado de televisión

CD [,si:'di:] *n abbr of* **compact disc** CD *m*

CD-player *n abbr of* **compact disc player** reproductor *m* de CD **CD--ROM** [,si:di:'rɒm, *Am:* -'rɑ:m] *n abbr of* **compact disc read-only memory** CD-ROM *m*; **on ~** en CD--ROM **CD-ROM drive** *n* unidad *f* de CD-ROM

cease [si:s] *form* I. *vi* cesar; **to ~ from sth** cesar de (hacer) algo II. *vt* suspender; **it never ~s to amaze me** nunca deja de sorprenderme; **~ firing!** MIL ¡alto el fuego!

cease-fire [si:s'faɪə', *Am:* -'faɪə'] *n* MIL alto *m* el fuego, cese *m* del fuego *AmL*

ceiling ['si:lɪŋ] *n* **1.** ARCHIT, AVIAT techo *m* **2.** (*upper limit*) tope *m*; **to impose a ~ on sth** poner un tope a algo

celebrate ['selɪbreɪt] I. *vi* celebrar; **let's ~!** ¡vamos a celebrarlo! II. *vt* celebrar; **they ~d him as a hero** lo agasajaron como a un héroe

celebration [,selɪ'breɪʃn] *n* **1.** (*party*) fiesta *f* **2.** (*of an occasion*) celebración *f*; **this calls for a ~!** ¡esto hay que celebrarlo!

celebrity [sɪ'lebrətɪ, *Am:* sə'le-brəṭɪ] *n* <-ies> famoso, -a *m, f*

celery ['selərɪ] *n no pl* apio *m*, panul *m CSur*

celibacy ['selɪbəsɪ] *n no pl* **1.** *a.* REL celibato *m* **2.** (*being single*) soltería *f*

celibate ['selɪbət] *adj* **1.** *a.* REL célibe **2.** (*unmarried*) soltero

cell [sel] *n* **1.** (*in prison*) celda *f*, separo *m Méx* **2.** BIO, POL célula *f*; **a single ~ animal** un animal unicelular

cellar ['selər, *Am:* -ə'] *n* (*basement*) sótano *m*; (*for wine*) bodega *f*

cellist ['tʃelɪst] *n* MUS violoncelista *mf*

cello ['tʃeləʊ, *Am:* -oʊ] <-s *o* -li> *n* MUS violoncelo *m*

celluloid ['seljʊlɔɪd] **I.** *n no pl* celuloide *m* **II.** *adj* de celuloide

Celsius ['selsiəs] *adj* PHYS Celsius

Celt [kelt, selt] *n* HIST celta *mf*

Celtic ['keltik, 'seltik] *adj* céltico; (*language*) celta

cement [sɪ'ment] *n no pl* cemento *m*

cement mixer *n* hormigonera *f*

cemetery ['semətrɪ, *Am:* -terɪ] <-ies> *n* cementerio *m*, panteón *m* AmL

censor ['sensər, *Am:* -sə'] **I.** *n* censor(a) *m(f)* **II.** *vt* censurar

censorship ['sensəʃɪp, *Am:* -sə'-] *n no pl* censura *f*

census ['sensəs] <-ses> *n* censo *m*

cent [sent] *n Am* centavo *m*

centenary [sen'tiːnərɪ, *Am:* 'sentner-] **I.** <-ies> *n* centenario *m* **II.** *adj* (*once every century*) secular; ~ **year** año *m* del centenario

center ['sentə'] *n Am s.* **centre**

centimeter *n Am*, **centimetre** ['sentɪˌmiːtər, *Am:* -t̬əˌmiːtə'] *n Brit, Aus* centímetro *m*

central ['sentrəl] *adj* **1.** (*at the middle*) central; (*street*) céntrico; **in** ~ **Madrid** en el centro de Madrid **2.** (*important*) fundamental; **to be** ~ **to sth** ser vital para algo; **the** ~ **character** el protagonista

Central African *adj* centroafricano

Central African Republic *n* República *f* Centroafricana

Central Bank *n* Banco *m* Central

centralization [ˌsentrəlaɪ'zeɪʃn, *Am:* -lɪ'-] *n no pl* centralización *f*

centralize ['sentrəlaɪz] *vt* centralizar

centre ['sentə'] *n Brit* **1.** *a.* PHYS, POL, SPORTS centro *m*; ~ **party** partido *m* de centro **2.** (*of population*) núcleo *m*

◆**centre on** *vi* concentrarse en

centrifugal [sen'trɪfjʊgl, *Am:* -jə-gl] *adj* PHYS centrífugo

century ['sentʃərɪ] <-ies> *n* siglo *m*; **the twentieth** ~ el siglo veinte

CEO [ˌsiːiː'əʊ, *Am:* -'oʊ] *n abbr of* **chief executive officer** director(a) *m(f)* general

ceramic [sɪ'ræmɪk, *Am:* sə-] *adj* de cerámica

ceramics *n pl* cerámica *f*

cereal ['sɪərɪəl, *Am:* 'sɪrɪ-] *n* **1.** *no pl* (*cultivated grass*) cereal *m* **2.** (*breakfast food*) cereales *mpl*

cerebral ['serɪbrəl, *Am:* ˌserə-] *adj* cerebral; ~ **palsy** parálisis *f inv* cerebral

ceremonious [ˌserɪ'məʊnɪəs, *Am:* -ə'moʊ-] *adj* ceremonioso

ceremony ['serɪmənɪ, *Am:* -ə-moʊ-] <-ies> *n a.* REL ceremonia *f*; **to go through the** ~ **of sth** *fig* cumplir con todas las formalidades de algo

certain ['sɜːtn, *Am:* 'sɜːr-] **I.** *adj* **1.** (*sure*) seguro; **to be** ~ **about sth** estar convencido de algo; **for** ~ con certeza **2.** (*specified*) cierto; **a** ~ **Steve Rukus** un tal Steve Rukus; **to a** ~ **extent** hasta cierto punto **II.** *pron* ~ **of** algunos/algunas de

certainly *adv* **1.** (*surely*) por supuesto; **she** ~ **is a looker, isn't she?** es guapa, ¿verdad? **2.** (*gladly*) desde luego; ~ **not!** ¡desde luego que no!

certainty ['sɜːtəntɪ, *Am:* 'sɜːr-] <-ies> *n* certeza *f*

certificate [sə'tɪfɪkət, *Am:* sə'-] *n* (*document*) certificado *m*; (*of baptism, birth, death*) partida *f*

certification [ˌsɜːtɪfɪ'keɪʃn, *Am:* ˌsɜːrt̬ə-] *n no pl* **1.** (*process*) certificación *f* **2.** (*document*) certificado *m*

certify ['sɜːtɪfaɪ, *Am:* 'sɜːrt̬ə-] <-ie-> *vt* certificar; **certified copy** copia *f* legalizada; **he is certified to practise medicine** está habilitado para ejercer la medicina

cervical ['sɜːvɪkl, sɜː'vaɪkl, *Am:* 'sɜːrvɪ-] *adj* **1.** (*neck*) cervical *m*; ~ **vertebra** vértebra *f* cervical **2.** (*cervix*) del cuello del útero

Ceylon [sɪˈlɒn, *Am:* -ˈlɑːn] *n no pl* HIST Ceilán *m*

Ceylonese [sɪlɒˈniːz, *Am:* ˌsiːləˈniːz] *adj* HIST ceilanés, -esa

cf. *abbr of* **confer** cf.

CFC [ˌsiːefˈsiː] *n abbr of* **chlorofluorocarbon** clorofluorocarbono *m*

Chad [tʃæd] *n no pl* Chad *m*

Chadian *adj* chadiano

chain [tʃeɪn] I. *n* cadena *f;* ~ **gang** cuerda *f* de presos; **to be in** ~**s** estar encadenado II. *vt* encadenar; **to** ~ **sth/sb (up) to sth** encadenar algo/a alguien a algo

chain store *n* tienda *f* de una cadena

chair [tʃeəʳ, *Am:* tʃer] I. *n* 1. (*seat*) silla *f* 2. (*head*) presidente, -a *m, f;* **to be** ~ **of a department** ser jefe de un departamento II. *vt* (*a meeting*) presidir

chairman [ˈtʃeəmən, *Am:* ˈtʃer-] <-men> *n* presidente *m*

chairmanship [ˈtʃeəmənʃɪp, *Am:* ˈtʃer-] *n* presidencia *f*

chalet [ˈʃæleɪ, *Am:* ʃælˈeɪ] *n* chalet *m*

chalk [tʃɔːk] *n no pl* 1. (*stone*) caliza *f* 2. (*stick*) tiza *f*, gis *m Méx;* **to be as different as** ~ **and cheese** *fig* ser (como) la noche y el día

challenge [ˈtʃælɪndʒ] I. *n* (*a call to competition*) desafío *m;* **to be faced with a** ~ enfrentarse a un reto II. *vt* 1. (*ask to compete*) desafiar; **to** ~ **sb to a duel** retar a alguien a un duelo 2. (*question*) cuestionar, poner en tela de juicio

challenger [ˈtʃælɪndʒəʳ, *Am:* -ɚ] *n* desafiador(a) *m(f);* (*for a title*) aspirante *mf*

chamber [ˈtʃeɪmbəʳ, *Am:* -bɚ] *n* 1. (*a. anat, pol*) cámara *f;* ~ **of Deputies** cámara de los diputados; **Upper/Lower** ~ cámara alta/baja 2. TECH (*of a gun*) recámara *f;* **combustion** ~ cámara de combustión

chamberlain [ˈtʃeɪmbəlɪn, *Am:* -bɚ-] *n* HIST chambelán *m*

chambermaid [ˈtʃeɪmbəmeɪd, *Am:* -bɚ-] *n* camarera *f*

champ [tʃæmp] *n inf* campeón, -ona *m, f*

champagne [ʃæmˈpeɪn] *n no pl* champán *m*

champion [ˈtʃæmpiən] *n* 1. SPORTS campeón, -ona *m, f* 2. (*supporter*) defensor(a) *m(f)*

championship [ˈtʃæmpiənʃɪp] *n* campeonato *m*

chance [tʃɑːns, *Am:* tʃæns] *n* 1. *no pl* (*random force*) casualidad *f;* **by** ~ por casualidad 2. *no pl* (*likelihood*) probabilidad *f;* **there's not much of a** ~ **of my coming to the party** no es muy probable que vaya a la fiesta 3. (*opportunity*) oportunidad *f;* **to give sb a** ~ **(to do sth)** dar a alguien una oportunidad (de hacer algo)

chancellor [ˈtʃɑːnsələʳ, *Am:* ˈtʃæn-] *n* 1. POL canciller *mf;* ~ **of the Exchequer** ministro, -a *m, f* de Hacienda 2. UNIV rector(a) *m(f)*

chandelier [ˌʃændəˈlɪəʳ, *Am:* -ˈlɪr] *n* araña *f*

change [tʃeɪndʒ] I. *n* 1. (*alteration*) cambio *m;* **for a** ~ para variar; **that would make a (nice)** ~ no estaría mal hacer eso para variar 2. *no pl* (*coins*) cambio *m*, sencillo *m AmL*, feria *f Méx;* **small** ~ calderilla *f inf* 3. *no pl* (*money returned*) cambio *m*, vuelto *m AmL;* **no** ~ **given** se ruega importe exacto II. *vi* 1. (*alter*) cambiar; **to** ~ **into sth** convertirse en algo 2. (*put on different clothes*) cambiarse III. *vt* (*exchange*) cambiar; **to** ~ **sth/sb into sth** convertir algo/a alguien en algo

channel [ˈtʃænl] I. *n* canal *m;* **The (English) C**~ el Canal de la Mancha; **irrigation** ~ acequia *f* II. <*Brit:* -ll-, *Am:* -l-> *vt* canalizar; *fig* encauzar

Channel Tunnel *n no pl* túnel *m* del Canal de la Mancha

chant [tʃɑːnt, *Am:* tʃænt] I. *n* REL canto *m;* (*singing*) salmodia *f;* **gregorian** ~ canto gregoriano II. *vi* 1. (*intone*) salmodiar 2. (*repeat*) gritar al unísono III. *vt* 1. (*sing*) cantar; (*speak in a monotone*) salmodiar 2. (*repeat*) repetir al unísono

chaos [ˈkeɪɒs, *Am:* -ɑːs] *n no pl* caos *m inv*

chaotic [keɪˈɒtɪk, *Am:* -ˈɑːt̬ɪk] *adj*

caótico

chap [tʃæp] *n* (*fellow, friend*) tío *m*

chap. *n abbr of* **chapter** cap. *m*

chapel ['tʃæpl] *n* **1.** (*room*) capilla *f;* **funeral** ~ capilla ardiente **2.** *Brit* (*church*) templo *m*

chaplain ['tʃæplɪn] *n* REL capellán *m*

chapter ['tʃæptəʳ, *Am:* -t̬əʳ] *n a. fig* capítulo *m;* **to quote** ~ **and verse** citar textualmente

character ['kærəktəʳ, *Am:* 'kerək-t̬əʳ] *n* **1.** *no pl* (*qualities*) carácter *m;* **to be in/out of** ~ **with sb/sth** ser/ no ser típico de alguien/algo **2.** (*unique person, acted part*) personaje *m*, carácter *m* Col, Méx; **in the** ~ **of ...** en el papel de...

characteristic [ˌkærəktə'rɪstɪk, *Am:* ˌker-] **I.** *n* característica *f* **II.** *adj* característico; **with her** ~ **dignity** con la dignidad que le caracteriza

characterization [ˌkærəktəraɪ'zeɪ-ʃən, *Am:* ˌkerəktɚɪ-] *n* caracterización *f*

characterize ['kærəktəraɪz, *Am:* 'kerək-] *vt a.* CINE, THEAT caracterizar

charcoal ['tʃɑ:kəʊl, *Am:* 'tʃɑ:rkoʊl] *n no pl* **1.** (*fuel*) carbón *m* vegetal **2.** ART carboncillo *m*, carbonilla *f* RíoPl; **to draw in** ~ dibujar al carboncillo

charge [tʃɑ:dʒ, *Am:* tʃɑ:rdʒ] **I.** *n* **1.** (*load*) carga *f* **2.** (*cost*) precio *m;* **overhead** ~**s** gastos *mpl* generales; **free of** ~ gratis **3.** (*accusation*) cargo *m;* **to bring** ~**s against sb** presentar cargos contra alguien **4.** *no pl* (*authority*) responsabilidad *f;* **to be in** ~ **of sb/sth** tener algo/a alguien a su cargo; **who is in** ~ **here?** ¿quién es el responsable aquí? **5.** *no pl* ELEC carga *f* **II.** *vi* **1.** FIN cobrar **2.** (*attack*) **to** ~ **at sb/sth** arremeter contra alguien/algo; MIL cargar contra alguien/algo; ~**!** ¡al ataque! **3.** ELEC cargarse **III.** *vt* **1.** FIN cobrar; **to** ~ **sth to sb's account** cargar algo en la cuenta de alguien **2.** LAW acusar; **she's been** ~**d with murder** se le acusa de asesinato **3.** MIL cargar contra **4.** ELEC cargar

charitable ['tʃærɪtəbl, *Am:* 'tʃer-]

adj (*with money*) generoso; (*gifts, donation*) benéfico

charity ['tʃærəti, *Am:* 'tʃerət̬ɪ] <-ies> *n* **1.** *no pl* (*generosity of spirit*) caridad *f;* **to depend on** ~ depender de limosnas **2.** (*organization*) institución *f* benéfica

Charles [tʃɑ:lz, *Am:* tʃɑ:rlz] *n* Carlos *m;* ~ **the Fifth** (**of Spain**) Carlos V (de España)

Charlie [tʃɑ:li, *Am:* tʃɑ:rli] *n inf* Carlitos

charm [tʃɑ:m, *Am:* tʃɑ:rm] **I.** *n* **1.** (*quality*) encanto *m;* **she used all her** ~**s** usó todos sus encantos **2.** (*talisman*) amuleto *m*, payé *m* CSur **II.** *vt* cautivar; **to** ~ **sb into doing sth** embelesar a alguien para que haga algo

charming ['tʃɑ:mɪŋ, *Am:* 'tʃɑ:r-] *adj* encantador; **oh, that's just** ~**!** ¡es de lo más encantador!

chart [tʃɑ:t, *Am:* tʃɑ:rt] **I.** *n* **1.** (*display of information*) tabla *f;* **weather** ~ mapa *m* meteorológico **2.** *pl* MUS **the** ~**s** la lista de éxitos **II.** *vt a. fig* trazar; **the map** ~**s the course of the river** el mapa reproduce gráficamente el curso del río

charter ['tʃɑ:təʳ, *Am:* 'tʃɑ:rt̬əʳ] **I.** *n* **1.** (*government statement*) estatutos *mpl* **2.** (*document stating aims*) carta *f* **3.** *no pl* COM fletamiento *m* **II.** *vt* **1.** (*sign founding papers*) estatuir **2.** COM fletar

chartered ['tʃɑ:təd, *Am:* 'tʃɑ:rt̬ɚd] *adj* **1.** COM fletado **2.** Brit, Aus (*qualified*) jurado

chase [tʃeɪs] **I.** *n* **1.** (*pursual*) persecución *f;* **to give** ~ **to sb** salir en busca de alguien **2.** (*hunt*) caza *f* **II.** *vt* perseguir

chasm ['kæzəm] *n* abismo *m*

chaste [tʃeɪst] *adj form* casto

chastity ['tʃæstəti, *Am:* -t̬ɪ] *n no pl* castidad *f;* **vow of** ~ voto *m* de castidad

chat [tʃæt] **I.** *n* **1.** (*pursual*) charla *f* **II.** *vi* <-tt-> charlar, versar *AmC*

chat room *n* foro *m* de chat

chatter ['tʃætəʳ, *Am:* 'tʃæt̬əʳ] **I.** *n no pl* cháchara *f* **II.** *vi* (*converse superfi-*

cially) **to ~ about sth** charlar sobre algo

chauffeur [ˈʃəʊfə^r, *Am:* ˈʃɑːfɚ] *n* chófer *mf*

cheap [tʃiːp] *adj* **1.** (*inexpensive*) barato; **dirt ~** tirado **2.** (*inexpensive but bad quality*) ordinario; **~ and cheerful** *Brit, Aus, inf* bueno, bonito y barato

cheat [tʃiːt] **I.** *n* estafador(a) *m(f)* **II.** *vi* **to ~ at sth** hacer trampa en algo **III.** *vt* engañar; **to ~ the taxman** timar a Hacienda

check [tʃek] **I.** *n* **1.** (*inspection*) control *m;* **security ~** control de seguridad; **to keep sth in ~** mantener algo bajo control **2.** (*a look*) vistazo *m* **3.** GAMES jaque *m;* **to be in ~** estar en jaque **4.** *Am* cheque *m;* **open ~** cheque al portador **II.** *adj* a cuadros **III.** *vt* **1.** (*inspect for problems*) comprobar, chequear *AmL* **2.** (*prevent*) frenar **IV.** *vi* (*examine*) revisar
  ◆ **check in** *vi* **1.** (*at airport*) facturar **2.** (*at hotel*) registrarse

checkbook [ˈtʃekˌbʊk] *n Am* talonario *m* de cheques **checkpoint** [ˈtʃekpɔɪnt] *n* punto *m* de control

cheek [tʃiːk] *n* **1.** (*soft skin connecting jaws*) mejilla *f* **2.** *no pl* (*impertinence*) descaro *m,* empaque *m AmL;* **to have a ~** ser un caradura

cheeky [ˈtʃiːkɪ] <-ier, -iest> *adj* descarado, fregado *AmL;* **to be ~ to sb** ser descarado con alguien

cheer [tʃɪə^r, *Am:* tʃɪr] **I.** *n* ovación *f;* **three ~s for the champion!** ¡tres hurras por el campeón!; **to give a ~** vitorear **II.** *interj* *pl* **1.** (*said when drinking*) salud **2.** *Brit* (*thanks*) gracias **III.** *vi* **to ~ for sb** animar a alguien

cheerful [ˈtʃɪəfʊl, *Am:* ˈtʃɪr-] *adj* alegre

cheerleader [ˈtʃɪəˌliːdə^r, *Am:* ˈtʃɪrˌliːdɚ] *n Am* animadora *f*

[?] Con el nombre de **cheerleaders** se designa en los EE.UU. a aquellas chicas jóvenes que animan a un equipo deportivo. Su labor consiste fundamentalmente en guiar las canciones y gritos de ánimo de los fans y entretener al público asistente con pequeñas coreografías en las que utilizan los característicos **pompoms**. Su vestuario suele consistir en un vestido corto o falda y blusa además de calcetines y zapatos de cuero, todo ello en los colores de su equipo o colegio.

---

cheery [ˈtʃɪərɪ, *Am:* ˈtʃɪr-] <-ier, -iest> *adj* alegre

cheese [tʃiːz] *n no pl* queso *m;* **hard ~** queso curado

chef [ʃef] *n* jefe, -a *m,* f de cocina, chef *mf*

chemical [ˈkemɪkl] **I.** *n* sustancia *f* química **II.** *adj* químico

chemist [ˈkemɪst] *n* **1.** (*of chemistry*) químico, -a *m,* f **2.** *Brit, Aus* (*store*) farmacia *f;* (*person*) farmacéutico, -a *m,* f

chemistry [ˈkemɪstrɪ] *n no pl* química *f*

chemotherapy [ˌkiːməˈθerəpi, *Am:* ˌkiːmoʊ-] *n no pl* quimioterapia *f;* **to undergo ~** seguir un tratamiento de quimioterapia

cheque [tʃek] *n Brit, Aus s.* **check** **cheque book** *n Brit, Aus* talonario *m* de cheques

cherish [ˈtʃerɪʃ] *vt* apreciar

cherry [ˈtʃerɪ] <-ies> *n* cereza *f*

cherub [ˈtʃerəb] <-s *o* -im> *n* querubín *m*

chess [tʃes] *n no pl* ajedrez *m*

chest [tʃest] *n* **1.** (*human torso*) pecho *m;* **~ pains** dolores *mpl* pectorales; **to get sth off one's ~** *fig* desahogarse confesando algo **2.** (*breasts*) senos *mpl* **3.** (*trunk*) baúl *m,* petaca *f AmL;* **medicine ~** botiquín *m*

chestnut [ˈtʃesnʌt] **I.** *n* castaña *f* **II.** *adj* castaño

chew [tʃuː] **I.** *n* (*bite*) bocado *m* **II.** *vt* masticar

chic [ʃiːk] *adj* chic, a la moda

chick [tʃɪk] *n* **1.** (*baby chicken*) pollito, -a *m, f* **2.** (*young bird*) polluelo, -a *m, f* **3.** *inf* (*young woman*) tía *f*

chicken ['tʃɪkɪn] *n* **1.** (*farm bird*) pollo, -a *m, f* **2.** *no pl* (*meat*) carne *f* de pollo; **fried/roasted** ~ pollo frito/asado

chief [tʃiːf] **I.** *n* **1.** (*boss*) jefe, -a *m, f* **2.** (*of a tribe*) jerarca *m* **II.** *adj* principal

chiefly *adv* principalmente

child [tʃaɪld] <children> *n* **1.** (*person who's not fully grown*) niño, -a *m, f*; **unborn** ~ feto *m* **2.** (*offspring*) hijo, -a *m, f*; **illegitimate** ~ hijo bastardo

child abuse ['tʃaɪldəbjuːs] *n no pl* abuso *m* (sexual) de los niños **child-birth** *n no pl* parto *m*, parición *f* *AmL* **childhood** *n no pl* infancia *f*

childish ['tʃaɪldɪʃ] *adj pej* infantil, achiquillado *Méx;* **don't be** ~**!** ¡no seas niño!

childless ['tʃaɪldlɪs] *adj* sin hijos

childlike ['tʃaɪldlaɪk] *adj* infantil

children ['tʃɪldrən] *n pl of* **child**

Chile ['tʃɪlɪ] *n* Chile *m*

Chilean ['tʃɪlɪən, *Am:* tʃɪ'lɪː-] *adj* chileno

chili ['tʃɪlɪ] <-es> *n Am s.* **chilli**

chill [tʃɪl] **I.** *n* **1.** (*coldness*) frío *m;* **to catch a** ~ resfriarse **2.** (*shiver*) escalofrío *m* **II.** *vt* enfriar

chilli ['tʃɪlɪ] <-es> *n* chile *m*, ají *m* (picante) *AmS, Ant*

chilly ['tʃɪlɪ] <-ier, -iest> *adj a. fig* frío; **to feel** ~ tener frío

chime [tʃaɪm] **I.** *n* repique *m;* **wind** ~**s** carillón *m* **II.** *vi* repicar

chimney ['tʃɪmnɪ] *n* (*in a building*) chimenea *f*, tronera *f Méx*

chin ['tʃɪn] *n* barbilla *f;* **to keep one's** ~ **up** *fig* no desanimarse

china ['tʃaɪnə] *n no pl* porcelana *f*

China ['tʃaɪnə] *n* China *f*

Chinese [tʃaɪ'niːz] *adj* chino

chink [tʃɪŋk] *n* hendidura *f*

chip [tʃɪp] **I.** *n* **1.** (*flake*) pedazo *m;* **he's a** ~ **off the old block** *fig, inf* de tal palo tal astilla **2.** *pl, Brit* (*French fries*) patatas *fpl* fritas, papas *fpl* fri-

tas *AmL; Am* (*crisp potato snack*) patatas *fpl* fritas (de churrería), papas *fpl* fritas (de churrería) *AmL* **3.** INFOR chip *m* **II.** *vt* <-pp-> desportillar **III.** *vi* <-pp-> desportillarse

chisel ['tʃɪzl] **I.** *n* cincel *m* **II.** <*Brit:* -ll-, *Am:* -l-> *vt* (*cut*) esculpir

chivalry ['ʃɪvlrɪ] *n no pl* **1.** (*gallant behavior*) caballerosidad *f* **2.** HIST caballería *f*

chlorine ['klɔːriːn] *n no pl* cloro *m*

chocolate ['tʃɒklət, *Am:* 'tʃɑː-k-] *n* **1.** *no pl* (*sweet*) chocolate *m;* **a bar of** ~ una tableta de chocolate **2.** (*piece of chocolate*) bombón *m*

choice ['tʃɔɪs] *n* **1.** *no pl* (*possibility of selection*) elección *f;* **to make a** ~ elegir **2.** *no pl* (*selection*) selección *f;* **a wide** ~ **of sth** un amplio surtido de algo

choir ['kwaɪəʳ, *Am:* 'kwaɪəʳ] *n* coro *m*

choke [tʃəʊk, *Am:* tʃoʊk] **I.** *vi* sofocarse; **to** ~ **to death** morir asfixiado **II.** *n* AUTO estárter *m* **III.** *vt* asfixiar

cholera ['kɒlərə, *Am:* 'kɑːlə-] *n no pl* cólera *m*

cholesterol [kə'lestərɒl, *Am:* kə-'lestərɑːl] *n no pl* colesterol *m*

choose [tʃuːz] <chose, chosen> *vi, vt* elegir

choos(e)y ['tʃuːzɪ] <-ier, -iest> *adj inf* quisquilloso

chop [tʃɒp, *Am:* tʃɑːp] **I.** *vt* <-pp-> cortar **II.** *n* chuleta *f*

chopper ['tʃɒpəʳ, *Am:* 'tʃɑːpəʳ] *n inf* helicóptero *m*

choral ['kɔːrəl] *adj* coral; ~ **society** coral *f*

chord ['kɔːd, *Am:* 'kɔːrd] *n* MUS acorde *m*

chore [tʃɔːʳ, *Am:* tʃɔːr] *n* (*routine job*) tarea *f;* **household** ~**s** quehaceres *mpl* domésticos

choreography [ˌkɒrɪ'ɒɡrəfɪ, *Am:* ˌkɔːrɪ'ɑːɡrə-] *n no pl* coreografía *f*

chorus ['kɔːrəs, *Am:* 'kɔːrəs] <-es> *n* **1.** (*refrain*) estribillo *m;* **to join in the** ~ cantar el estribillo **2.** + *sing/pl vb* (*group of singers*) coral *f* **3.** + *sing/pl vb* (*supporting singers*) coro *m;* ~ **girl** corista *f;* **in** ~ a coro

chose [tʃəʊz, *Am:* tʃoʊz] *pt of*
choose
chosen ['tʃəʊzn, *Am:* 'tʃoʊ] *pp of*
choose
Christ [kraɪst] I. *n* Cristo *m* II. *interj*
inf ¡Dios!, ¡Jesús!; **for** ~**'s sake** ¡por
amor de Dios!
christen ['krɪsn] *vt* 1. (*baptise*) bautizar 2. (*give name to*) **they** ~**ed
their second child Sara** a su segundo bebé le pusieron Sara
Christendom ['krɪsndəm] *n no pl*
HIST cristiandad *f*
Christian ['krɪstʃən] *n* cristiano, -a
m, f
Christianity [ˌkrɪstɪ'ænətɪ, *Am:* -tʃɪ-
'ænətɪ] *n no pl* cristianismo *m*
Christmas ['krɪstməs, *Am:* 'krɪs-]
<-es *o* -ses> *n no pl* Navidad *f;* **at** ~
en Navidad; **Merry** [*o* **Happy**] ~!
¡Feliz Navidad!; **Father** ~ Papá *m*
Noel, viejo *m* Pascuero *Chile*

[?] En Gran Bretaña el envío de
Christmas cards (postales de
Navidad) comienza a principios
del mes de diciembre. Esta costumbre surgió a mediados del siglo
XIX. Otra de las tradiciones na-
videñas británicas consiste en colgar los **Christmas stockings**
(unos grandes calcetines) o fundas
de almohadas para que aparezcan
llenas de regalos a la mañana siguiente. Este ritual navideño es
llevado a cabo por los niños durante el **Christmas Eve** (día de
Nochebuena) que es día laborable
en Gran Bretaña. La comida tradicional del **Christmas Day** consiste
en pavo acompañado de patatas
salteadas y de postre **Christmas
pudding** o **plum pudding** que es
un pastel hecho al vapor con diversos tipos de pasas, entre otras,
pasas sultanas y de Corinto. Los
Christmas crackers (otro invento

británico de mediados del siglo
XIX) son unos pequeños cilindros
de cartón muy decorados que con-
tienen en su interior un pequeño
regalo, un proverbio y una corona
de papel. Este cilindro de cartón se
abre durante la comida de Navidad tirando dos personas de él simultáneamente, una por cada
lado.

Christmas Day *n* día *m* de Navidad,
día *m* de Pascua *Perú, Chile* **Christmas Eve** *n* Nochebuena *f*
Christopher ['krɪstəfəʳ, *Am:* -fɚ] *n*
Cristóbal *m;* ~ **Columbus** HIST Cristóbal Colón
chrome [krəʊm, *Am:* kroʊm] *n no
pl* cromo *m*
chromosome ['krəʊməsəʊm, *Am:*
'kroʊməsoʊm] *n* cromosoma *m*
chronic ['krɒnɪk, *Am:* 'krɑːnɪk] *adj*
crónico
chronicle ['krɒnɪkl, *Am:* 'krɑːnɪ-]
I. *vt* registrar II. *n* crónica *f*
chronicler ['krɒnɪklər, *Am:* 'krɑːnɪ-
klɚ] *n* cronista *mf*
chronological [ˌkrɒnə'lɒdʒɪkl, *Am:*
ˌkrɑːnə'lɑːdʒɪ-] *adj* cronológico; **in**
~ **order** en orden cronológico
chronology [krə'nɒlədʒɪ, *Am:* krə-
'nɑːlə-] *n no pl* cronología *f*
chuck [tʃʌk] *vt* 1. *inf* (*throw*) tirar
2. *inf* (*give up*) dejar; **to** ~ **sb** cortar
con alguien
chuckle ['tʃʌkl] I. *n* risita *f* II. *vi* reírse
chum [tʃʌm] *n inf* amigo, -a *m, f,* colega *mf,* cuate *m Méx*
chunk [tʃʌŋk] *n* pedazo *m,* trozo *m,*
troncho *m CSur*
church [tʃɜːtʃ, *Am:* tʃɜːrtʃ] *n* iglesia *f;*
to go to ~ ir a misa
churchyard [ˌtʃɜːtʃ'jɑːd, *Am:*
ˌtʃɜːrtʃjɑːrd] *n* cementerio *m*
churn [tʃɜːn, *Am:* tʃɜːrn] I. *n* lechera
f II. *vt* batir; *fig* agitar III. *vi* arremo-
linarse; **my stomach was** ~**ing**
tenía un nudo en el estómago

chute [ʃuːt] *n* (*sloping tube*) rampa *f*; **rubbish** ~ *Brit*, **garbage** ~ *Am* vertedero *m* de basuras

CIA [ˌsiːaɪˈeɪ] *n Am abbr of* **Central Intelligence Agency** CIA *f*

cider [ˈsaɪdəʳ, *Am:* -dəˈ] *n* sidra *f*

cigar [sɪˈgɑːʳ, *Am:* -gɑːr] *n* puro *m*
cigar-cutter *n* cortapuros *m inv*

cigarette [ˌsɪgəˈret] *n* cigarrillo *m*

Cinderella [ˌsɪndəˈrelə] *n* Cenicienta *f*

cinema [ˈsɪnəmə] *n* cine *m*, biógrafo *m Arg, Chile, Urug*

cinnamon [ˈsɪnəmən] *n no pl* canela *f*; **a ~ stick** un trozo de canela en rama

circa [ˈsɜːkə, *Am:* ˈsɜːr-] *prep* hacia; **~ 1850** hacia (el año) 1850

circle [ˈsɜːkl, *Am:* ˈsɜːr-] **I.** *n* círculo *m*; **to go round in ~s** dar vueltas **II.** *vt* rodear **III.** *vi* dar vueltas

circuit [ˈsɜːkɪt, *Am:* ˈsɜːr-] *n* circuito *m*

circular [ˈsɜːkjʊləʳ, *Am:* ˈsɜːrkjələˈ] *adj* circular

circulate [ˈsɜːkjʊleɪt, *Am:* ˈsɜːrkjə-] **I.** *vt* divulgar **II.** *vi* circular

circulation [ˌsɜːkjʊˈleɪʃn, *Am:* ˌsɜːr-] *n no pl* circulación *f*; **to be out of ~** estar fuera de circulación

circumference [səˈkʌmfərəns, *Am:* səˈ-] *n* circunferencia *f*

circumstance [ˈsɜːkəmstəns, *Am:* ˈsɜːrkəmstæns] *n* circunstancia *f*; **in no ~s** bajo ningún concepto

circumstantial [ˌsɜːkəmˈstænʃl, *Am:* ˌsɜːr-] *adj* circunstancial

circus [ˈsɜːkəs, *Am:* ˈsɜːr-] <-es> *n* circo *m*

CIS [ˌsiːaɪˈes] *n abbr of* **Commonwealth of Independent States** CEI *f*

citadel [ˈsɪtədəl, *Am:* ˈsɪt̬-] *n* ciudadela *f*

citizen [ˈsɪtɪzn, *Am:* ˈsɪt̬-] *n* **1.** (*subject*) ciudadano, -a *m, f* **2.** (*resident of town*) habitante *mf*

citizenship [ˈsɪtɪzənʃɪp, *Am:* ˈsɪt̬] *n no pl* ciudadanía *f*

citrus [ˈsɪtrəs] <citrus *o* citruses> *n* cítrico *m*

city [ˈsɪtɪ, *Am:* ˈsɪt̬-] <-ies> *n* ciudad *f*

? Muchas **cities** (grandes ciudades) americanas son conocidas entre sus ciudadanos por sus sobrenombres. Así **New York** es conocida como **Gotham** o **The Big Apple**. **Los Angeles** como **The Big Orange** o como **The City of the Angels**. De la misma manera **Chicago** es conocida como **The Windy City**. La expresión **The City of Brotherly Love** se usa para referirse a **Philadelphia**. **Denver**, debido a su situación, es conocida como **The Mile-High City** y **Detroit**, a causa de su industria automovilística, como **Motor City**.

city hall *n Am* ayuntamiento *m*

civic [ˈsɪvɪk] *adj* civil

civil [ˈsɪvl] *adj* civil

civilian [sɪˈvɪliən, *Am:* -jən] *n* civil *mf*

civility [sɪˈvɪləti, *Am:* -t̬i] <-ies> *n no pl* urbanidad *f*

civilization [ˌsɪvəlaɪˈzeɪʃn, *Am:* ˌsɪvəlɪ-] *n* civilización *f*

civil rights *npl* derechos *mpl* civiles
civil servant *n* funcionario, -a *m, f*
Civil Service *n* Administración *f* Pública

? En Gran Bretaña el **Civil Service** forma parte de la administración central del país. Dentro de él se encuentran el cuerpo diplomático, **Inland Revenue** (Hacienda), la Seguridad Social y los centros de enseñanza estatales. Los **civil servants** (funcionarios) son fijos y, dado que su puesto no es político, no se ven afectados por los cambios de gobierno.

civil war *n* guerra *f* civil

claim [kleɪm] **I.** *n* **1.** (*assertion*) afirmación *f* **2.** (*written demand*) demanda *f* **II.** *vt* **1.** (*assert*) asegurar, afirmar **2.** (*declare ownership*) reclamar; (*reward, title*) reivindicar; **to ~ damages** reclamar daños y perjuicios

claimant ['kleɪmənt] *n* solicitante *mf*

clam [klæm] *n* almeja *f*; **to shut up like a ~** *fig* quedarse como una tumba

clamor ['klæməʳ] *n Am*, **clamour** ['klæməʳ] *n Brit* clamor *m*

clamp [klæmp] **I.** *n* ARCHIT abrazadera *f* **II.** *vt* **1.** (*fasten together*) sujetar con abrazaderas **2.** *Brit* (*immobilise a vehicle*) **to ~ a car** poner el cepo a un coche

clan [klæn] *n* + *sing/pl vb, Scot* clan *m*

clandestine [klæn'destɪn] *adj form* clandestino

clap [klæp] <-pp-> *vi, vt* aplaudir

claret ['klærət, *Am:* 'kler-] *n* (*wine*) burdeos *m inv*

clarification [ˌklærɪfɪ'keɪʃn, *Am:* ˌkler-] *n no pl* aclaración *f*

clarify ['klærɪfaɪ, *Am:* 'kler-] <-ie-> *vt* aclarar

clarinet [ˌklærɪ'net, *Am:* ˌkler-] *n* clarinete *m*

clarity ['klærətɪ, *Am:* 'klerət̬ɪ] *n no pl* claridad *f*

clash [klæʃ] **I.** *vi* **1.** (*fight*) tener un enfrentamiento **2.** (*contradict*) contradecirse **3.** (*not match: colours*) desentonar **II.** <-es> *n* **1.** (*hostile encounter*) enfrentamiento *m* **2.** (*incompatibility*) choque *m*

clasp [klɑːsp, *Am:* klæsp] **I.** *n* broche *m*, cierre *m* **II.** *vt* (*grip*) agarrar, sujetar; **to ~ sb in one's arms** estrechar a alguien entre sus brazos

class [klɑːs, *Am:* klæs] **I.** <-es> *n* clase *f* **II.** *vt* catalogar; **to ~ sb as sth** catalogar a alguien de algo; **to ~ sb among sth** considerar a alguien como algo

classic ['klæsɪk] *adj*, **classical**
['klæsɪkl] *adj* clásico

classification [ˌklæsɪfɪ'keɪʃn, *Am:* ˌklæsə-] *n* clasificación *f*

classified ['klæsɪfaɪd] *adj* confidencial, secreto

classify ['klæsɪfaɪ] <-ie-> *vt* clasificar

classmate *n* compañero, -a *m, f* de clase **classroom** *n* clase *f*, aula *f*

clause [klɔːz, *Am:* klɑːz] *n* cláusula *f*; LING oración *f*

claw [klɔː, *Am:* klɑː] *n* garra *f*; (*of sea creatures*) pinza *f*

clay [kleɪ] *n no pl* arcilla *f*

clean [kliːn] **I.** *adj* **1.** (*free of dirt*) limpio **2.** (*morally acceptable*) decente; **~ police record** registro *m* de antecedentes penales limpio **II.** *n* limpieza *f* **III.** *vt* limpiar **IV.** *vi* hacer la limpieza; **the coffee stain ~ed off easily** la mancha de café salió fácilmente

◆**clean up I.** *vt* limpiar; (*tidy up*) ordenar; **to ~ the city** limpiar la ciudad **II.** *vi* limpiar

cleaner ['kliːnəʳ, *Am:* -nɚ] *n* asistente, -a *m, f*

cleaning [kliːnɪŋ] *n no pl* limpieza *f*

cleanly ['klenlɪ] *adv* limpiamente

clear [klɪəʳ, *Am:* klɪr] **I.** *adv* claramente **II.** *adj* **1.** claro; **to make oneself ~** explicarse con claridad; **as ~ as day** más claro que el agua **2.** (*certain*) evidente **III.** *vt* **1.** (*remove obstacles*) limpiar **2.** (*remove blockage*) desatascar; **to ~ the way** abrir el camino **3.** (*remove doubts*) aclarar; **to ~ one's head** despejar la cabeza **IV.** *vi* (*water*) aclararse; (*weather*) despejarse

◆**clear up I.** *vt* aclarar; (*tidy*) ordenar **II.** *vi* despejarse

clearance ['klɪərəns, *Am:* 'klɪr-] *n no pl* **1.** (*act of clearing*) despeje *m* **2.** (*permission*) autorización *f*

clear-cut ['klɪə'kʌt, *Am:* ˌklɪr'kʌt] *adj* bien definido

clearing ['klɪərɪŋ, *Am:* 'klɪrɪŋ] *n* claro *m*

clearly ['klɪəlɪ, *Am:* 'klɪr-] *adv* claramente

cleavage ['kliːvɪdʒ] *n* **1.** *no pl* (*in a*

dress) escote *m* **2.** *form* (*division*) división *f*

cleft [kleft] **I.** *adj* dividido **II.** *n* grieta *f*

clench [klentʃ] *vt* apretar

clergy ['klɜːdʒɪ, *Am:* 'klɜːr-] *n* + *sing/pl vb* clero *m*

clergyman ['klɜːdʒɪmən, *Am:* 'klɜːr-] <-men> *n* sacerdote *m;* (*protestant*) pastor *m*

clerical ['klerɪkl] *adj* **1.** (*of the clergy*) clerical **2.** (*of offices*) de oficina; ~ **worker** oficinista *mf*

clerk [klɑːk, *Am:* klɜːrk] *n* oficinista *mf*

clever ['klevəʳ, *Am:* -ɚ] *adj* inteligente

click [klɪk] **I.** *vi* **1.** (*make short, sharp sound*) chasquear **2.** INFOR hacer clic; **to** ~ **on a symbol** hacer clic en un símbolo **3.** (*become friendly*) congeniar **4.** (*become clear*) caer en la cuenta **II.** *vt* **1.** (*make short, sharp sound*) chasquear **2.** (*press button on mouse*) pulsar

client ['klaɪənt] *n* cliente *mf*

clientele [ˌkliːɒn'tel, *Am:* ˌklaɪən-] *n* clientela *f*

cliff [klɪf] *n* precipicio *m;* (*on coast*) acantilado *m*

climactic [ˌklaɪ'mæktɪk] *adj* culminante

climate ['klaɪmɪt] *n* **1.** (*weather*) clima *m* **2.** (*general conditions*) ambiente *m;* **the** ~ **of opinion** la opinión general

climatic [klaɪ'mætɪk] *adj* climático

climax ['klaɪmæks] <-es> *n* clímax *m inv*

climb [klaɪm] **I.** *n* subida *f* **II.** *vt* (*stairs*) subir; (*mountain*) escalar **III.** *vi* subir

climber ['klaɪməʳ, *Am:* -mɚ] *n* (*of mountains*) alpinista *mf*, andinista *mf AmL;* (*of rock faces*) escalador(a) *m(f)*

climbing ['klaɪmɪŋ] *n no pl* **1.** (*ascending mountains*) alpinismo *m*, andinismo *m AmL* (*ascending rock faces*) escalada *f*

clinch [klɪntʃ] *vt* (*settle decisively*) resolver; (*a deal*) cerrar

cling [klɪŋ] <clung, clung> *vi* agarrarse

clinic ['klɪnɪk] *n* clínica *f*

clinical ['klɪnɪkl] *adj* **1.** clínico **2.** (*emotionless*) frío

clink [klɪŋk] *vi* tintinear

clip¹ [klɪp] **I.** *n* **1.** (*fastener*) clip *m;* (*for paper*) sujetapapeles *m inv* **2.** (*gun part*) cargador *m* **II.** <-pp-> *vt* sujetar

clip² [klɪp] <-pp-> **I.** *vt* **1.** (*cut*) recortar; (*hair, nails*) cortar **2.** (*attach*) sujetar **II.** *n* fragmento *m*

clipper ['klɪpəʳ, *Am:* -ɚ] *n* NAUT clíper *m*

clipping ['klɪpɪŋ] *n* recorte *m*

clique [kliːk] *n* pandilla *f*

cloak [kləʊk, *Am:* kloʊk] *n a. fig* capa *f*

cloakroom ['kləʊkrʊm, *Am:* 'kloʊkruːm] *n* guardarropa *m*

clock [klɒk, *Am:* klɑːk] *n* (*for time*) reloj *m;* **alarm** ~ despertador *m;* **round the** ~ las 24 horas; **to run against the** ~ correr contra reloj

clockwise *adj, adv* en el sentido de las agujas del reloj

clockwork *n no pl* mecanismo *m* de relojería; **to go like** ~ salir todo bien

cloister ['klɔɪstəʳ, *Am:* -stɚ] *n* pl claustro *m*

clone [kləʊn, *Am:* kloʊn] **I.** *n* **1.** BIO clon *m* **2.** INFOR clónico *m* **II.** *vt* clonar

cloning ['kləʊnɪŋ, *Am:* 'kloʊn-] *n no pl* clonación *f*

close¹ [kləʊs, *Am:* kloʊs] *adj* **1.** (*near in location*) cercano; ~ **combat** combate *m* cuerpo a cuerpo **2.** (*intimate*) íntimo; ~ **relatives** parientes *mpl* cercanos **3.** (*stuffy*) cargado

close² [kləʊz, *Am:* kloʊz] **I.** *n no pl* (*end*) fin *m;* (*finish*) final *m;* **to bring sth to a** ~ terminar algo **II.** *vt* **1.** (*shut*) cerrar **2.** (*end*) terminar; **to** ~ **a deal** cerrar un trato **III.** *vi* **1.** (*shut*) cerrarse **2.** (*end*) terminarse

◆ **close down I.** *vi* cerrarse (definitivamente) **II.** *vt* cerrar (definitivamente)

◆**close in** vi 1.(*surround*) rodear
2.(*get shorter*) acortarse
◆**close up** I.vi (*wound*) cicatrizar
II.vt cerrar del todo
closed adj cerrado; **behind ~ doors**
a puerta cerrada
closely ['kləʊslɪ, Am: 'kloʊs-] adv
1.(*near*) de cerca 2.(*carefully*) atentamente
closeness ['kləʊsnɪs, Am: 'kloʊs-] n
1.no pl (*nearness*) proximidad f
2.no pl (*intimacy*) intimidad f
closet ['klɒzɪt, Am: 'klɑ:zɪt] n ropero m; **to come out of the ~** fig
declararse homosexual
close to prep 1.(*near*) cerca de; **to
live ~ the airport** vivir cerca del
aeropuerto 2.(*almost*) **~ tears/
death** a punto de llorar/morir 3.(*in
friendship with*) **to be ~ sb** estar
unido a alguien
close-up ['kləʊsʌp, Am: 'kloʊs-] n
CINE primer plano m
closing I.adj último; (*speech*) de
clausura II.n no pl (*ending*) conclusión f; (*act*) clausura f
closing date n fecha f límite **closing down** n no pl cierre m **closing
price** n cotización f de cierre **closing time** n Brit hora f de cierre
closure ['kləʊʒəʳ, Am: 'kloʊʒɚ] n
(*closing*) cierre m; (*in Parliament*)
clausura f
clot [klɒt, Am: klɑ:t] I.n MED coágulo m II.<-tt-> vi cuajar; (*blood*) coagular
cloth [klɒθ, Am: klɑ:θ] n (*material*)
tela f; (*for cleaning*) trapo m
clothe [kləʊð, Am: kloʊð] vt vestir;
fig revestir de
clothes [kləʊðz, Am: kloʊðz] npl
ropa f

> ⚠ Para **clothes** (= la ropa) no hay
> singular: "Susan's clothes are al-
> ways smart."

clothing ['kləʊðɪŋ, Am: 'kloʊ-] n
no pl ropa f; **article of ~** prenda f de
vestir

> ⚠ **clothing** (= la ropa) nunca se
> utiliza en plural: "In winter we
> wear warm clothing."

cloud [klaʊd] I.n nube f; **every ~
has a silver lining** prov no hay mal
que por bien no venga prov; **to be
on ~ nine** fig estar en el séptimo
cielo II.vt. fig anublar
cloudy ['klaʊdɪ] <-ier, -iest> adj
1.(*overcast*) nublado 2.(*liquid*) turbio
clove [kləʊv, Am: kloʊv] n clavo m;
(*of garlic*) diente m
clover ['kləʊvəʳ, Am: 'kloʊvɚ] n no
pl trébol m
clown [klaʊn] n payaso, -a m, f
club [klʌb] I.n 1.(*group*) asociación
f 2.(*team*) club m 3.SPORTS palo m
de golf 4.(*weapon*) cachiporra f
5.(*playing card*) trébol m; (*in Spanish cards*) basto m 6.(*disco*) sala f
de fiestas, club m II.<-bb-> vt aporrear
clue [klu:] n 1.(*hint*) pista f 2.(*idea*)
idea f; **I haven't a ~** inf no tengo ni
idea
clumsy ['klʌmzɪ] <-ier, -iest> adj
torpe
clung [klʌŋ] pt, pp of **cling**
cluster ['klʌstəʳ, Am: -tɚ] I.n grupo
m II.vi agruparse
clutch [klʌtʃ] I.vi **to ~ at sth** agarrarse a algo II.vt agarrar III.n
1.AUTO embrague m 2.(*control*) **to
be in the ~s of sb/sth** estar en las
garras de alguien/algo
clutter ['klʌtəʳ, Am: 'klʌtɚ] n no pl
desorden m
cm inv abbr of **centimetre** cm
Co [kəʊ, Am: koʊ] abbr of **company**
Cía.
coach [kəʊtʃ, Am: koʊtʃ] I.<-es> n
1.(*private bus*) autocar m 2.(*railway carriage*) vagón m 3.SPORTS
entrenador(a) m(f) II.vt **to ~ sb**
entrenar a alguien
coagulate [kəʊˈægjʊleɪt, Am: koʊ-
ˈægjə-] I.vi coagularse II.vt coagular
coagulation [kəʊˌægjʊˈleɪʃn, Am:

kou͵ægjə-] *n no pl* coagulación *f*

coal [kəʊl, *Am:* koʊl] *n no pl* carbón *m*

coalition [͵kəʊə'lɪʃn, *Am:* ͵koʊə-] *n* coalición *f*

coal mine *n* mina *f* de carbón

coarse [kɔːs, *Am:* kɔːrs] <-r, -st> *adj* **1.** (*rough*) basto **2.** (*vulgar*) grosero

coast [kəʊst, *Am:* koʊst] *n* costa *f;* **the ~ is clear** *fig, inf* no hay moros en la costa

coastal ['kəʊstl, *Am:* 'koʊ-] *adj* costero *AmL;* **~ traffic** cabotaje *m*

coat [kəʊt, *Am:* koʊt] *n* (*overcoat*) abrigo *m*, tapado *m AmS;* (*jacket*) chaqueta *f*

coat-hanger *n* percha *f*

cobra ['kəʊbrə, *Am:* 'koʊbrə] *n* cobra *f*

cobweb ['kɒbweb, *Am:* 'ka:b-] *n* telaraña *f*

cocaine [kəʊ'keɪn, *Am:* koʊ-] *n no pl* cocaína *f*

cock [kɒk, *Am:* ka:k] *n* **1.** (*male chicken*) gallo *m* **2.** *vulg* (*penis*) polla *f*, pichula *f Chile*

cockerel ['kɒkərəl, *Am:* 'ka:kɚ-] *n* gallo *m* joven

cockney ['kɒknɪ, *Am:* 'ka:k-] *n* cockney *m* (*dialecto de un barrio del East End londinense*)

cockpit ['kɒkpɪt, *Am:* 'ka:k-] *n* cabina *f*

cockroach ['kɒkrəʊtʃ, *Am:* 'ka:k-roʊtʃ] <-es> *n* cucaracha *f*, surupa *f Ven*

cocktail ['kɒkteɪl, *Am:* 'ka:k-] *n* cóctel *m*, copetín *m Arg*

cocky ['kɒkɪ, *Am:* 'ka:kɪ] <-ier, -iest> *adj inf* engreído

cocoa ['kəʊkəʊ, *Am:* 'koʊkoʊ] *n no pl* cacao *m*

coconut ['kəʊkənʌt, *Am:* 'koʊ-] *n* coco *m*

cocoon [kə'kuːn] *n* capullo *m*

cod [kɒd, *Am:* ka:d] *n inv* bacalao *m*

COD [͵siːəʊ'diː, *Am:* -oʊ'-] *abbr of* **cash on delivery** pago *m* contra reembolso

code [kəʊd, *Am:* koʊd] *n* **1.** (*ciphered language*) clave *f* **2.** LAW código *m*

coded *adj* codificado

code name *n* nombre *m* en clave **code of conduct** *n* código *m* de conducta

codify ['kəʊdɪfaɪ, *Am:* 'ka:-] <-ie-> *vt* codificar

co-ed ['kəʊed, *Am:* 'koʊed] *adj inf* mixto

co-education [͵kəʊedʒʊ'keɪʃən, *Am:* ͵koʊ-] *n no pl* educación *f* mixta

co-educational [͵kəʊedʒʊ'keɪʃə-nəl, *Am:* ͵koʊedʒə'-] *adj* mixto

coefficient [͵kəʊɪ'fɪʃnt, *Am:* ͵koʊ-] *n* coeficiente *m*

coffee ['kɒfɪ, *Am:* 'ka:fɪ] *n* café *m*

coffee break *n* pausa *f* para tomar café

coffee table *n* mesa *f* baja

coffin ['kɒfɪn, *Am:* 'kɔ:fɪn] *n Aus, Brit* ataúd *m*

cog [kɒg, *Am:* ka:g] *n* TECH diente *m;* (*wheel*) rueda *f* dentada; **to be a ~ in a machine** ser una pieza más de una organización

cognac ['kɒnjæk, *Am:* 'koʊnjæk] *n* coñac *m*

cognition [kɒg'nɪʃn, *Am:* ka:g-] *n* cognición *f*

cognitive ['kɒgnɪtɪv, *Am:* 'ka:g-nət̬ɪv] *adj* cognitivo

cohere [kəʊ'hɪər, *Am:* koʊ'hɪr] *vi* ser coherente

coherence [kəʊ'hɪərəns, *Am:* koʊ-'hɪr-] *n no pl* coherencia *f*

coherent ['kəʊ'hɪərənt, *Am:* 'koʊ-'hɪr-] *adj* coherente

coherently *adv* coherentemente

cohesion [kəʊ'hiːʒn, *Am:* koʊ-] *n no pl* cohesión *f*

cohesive [kəʊ'hiːsɪv, *Am:* koʊ-] *adj* cohesivo

coil [kɔɪl] **I.** *n* **1.** rollo *m* **2.** ELEC bobina *f* **II.** *vi* enrollarse **III.** *vt* enrollar

coiled *adj* enrollado

coin [kɔɪn] **I.** *n* moneda *f;* **to toss a ~** echar una moneda al aire **II.** *vt* acuñar; **to ~ a phrase ...** como se suele decir...

coincide [͵kəʊɪn'saɪd, *Am:* ͵koʊ-] *vi* coincidir

coincidence [kəʊ'ɪnsɪdəns, *Am:*

koʊ-] *n* casualidad *f*
coincidental [kəʊˌɪnsɪ'dentəl, *Am:* koʊˌɪnsɪ'dent̬əl] *adj* coincidente
coincidentally *adv* por casualidad
coke [kəʊk, *Am:* koʊk] *n no pl* 1. (*fuel*) coque *m* 2. *inf* coca *f*, pichicata *f Arg*

cold [kəʊld, *Am:* koʊld] I. *adj* frío; **to be ~** tener frío; **to go ~** (*soup, coffee*) enfriarse II. *n* 1. METEO frío *m* 2. MED resfriado *m;* **to catch a ~** acatarrarse; **to have a ~** estar acatarrado
coldish ['kəʊldɪʃ, *Am:* 'koʊl-] *adj* fresquito
coldness ['kəʊldnɪs, *Am:* 'koʊld-] *n no pl* frialdad *f*
cold war *n* guerra *f* fría
coleslaw ['kəʊlslɔː, *Am:* 'koʊlslɑː] *n no pl* ensalada *f* de col con salsa
collaborate [kə'læbəreɪt] *vi* colaborar
collaboration [kəˌlæbə'reɪʃn] *n* colaboración *f*
collaborator [kə'læbəreɪtəʳ, *Am:* -t̬ɚ] *n* 1. colaborador(a) *m(f)* 2. *pej* colaboracionista *mf*
collage ['kɒlɑːʒ, *Am:* kəlɑːʒ] *n* collage *m*
collapse [kə'læps] I. *vi* derrumbarse II. *n* derrumbamiento *m*
collar ['kɒləʳ, *Am:* 'kɑːlɚ] *n* 1. FASHION cuello *m* 2. (*of a dog, cat*) collar *m*
collateral [kə'lætərəl, *Am:* -'læt̬-] I. *n* FIN garantía *f* subsidiaria II. *adj* colateral
colleague ['kɒliːg, *Am:* 'kɑːliːg] *n* colega *mf*
collect [kə'lekt, *Am:* 'kɑːl-] I. *vi* 1. (*gather*) reunirse 2. (*money: contributions*) hacer una colecta; (*money: payments due*) cobrar II. *vt* 1. (*gather*) reunir; (*money*) recaudar; (*objects*) coleccionar 2. (*pick up*) recoger
collection [kə'lekʃn] *n* 1. (*money gathered*) recaudación *f*; REL colecta *f* 2. (*object collected*) colección *f* 3. (*act of getting*) recogida *f*
collective [kə'lektɪv] *adj* colectivo
collectively *adv* colectivamente
collector [kə'lektəʳ, *Am:* -ɚ] *n*

1. (*one who gathers objects*) coleccionista *mf* 2. (*one who collects payments*) cobrador(a) *m(f)*
college ['kɒlɪdʒ, *Am:* 'kɑːlɪdʒ] *n* 1. (*school*) colegio *m* 2. (*university*) universidad *f*

? El término **college** designa el tiempo necesario en la universidad para alcanzar el **bachelor's degree**, aproximadamente 4–5 años. Las universidades en las que los estudiantes sólo pueden obtener el **bachelor's degree** se llaman **colleges**, el mismo nombre reciben algunas escuelas profesionales. Las universidades, en sentido estricto, son aquellas que ofrecen también **higher degrees** (títulos superiores) como por ejemplo, **master's degrees** y **doctorates**. En los **junior colleges** se pueden cursar los dos primeros años de estudios universitarios o capacitarse para aprender una profesión técnica.

collide [kə'laɪd] *vi* chocar
collision [kə'lɪʒn] *n* choque *m*
colloquial [kə'ləʊkwɪəl, *Am:* -'loʊ-] *adj* coloquial
cologne [kə'ləʊn, *Am:* -loʊn] *n no pl, Am* (*perfume*) colonia *f*
Colombia [kə'lʌmbɪə] *n* Colombia *f*
Colombian [kə'lʌmbɪən] *adj* colombiano
colon ['kəʊlən, *Am:* 'koʊ-] *n* 1. ANAT colon *m* 2. LING dos puntos *mpl*
colonel ['kɜːnl, *Am:* 'kɜːr-] *n* coronel *mf*
colonial [kə'ləʊnɪəl, *Am:* -'loʊ-] I. *adj* colonial II. *n* colono, -a *m, f*
colonialism [kə'ləʊnɪəlɪzəm, *Am:* -'loʊ-] *n no pl* colonialismo *m*
colonialist *n* colonialista *mf*
colonisation ['kɒlənaɪzeɪʃn, *Am:* 'kɑːl-] *n Aus, Brit* colonización *f*
colonise ['kɒlənaɪz, *Am:* 'kɑːlənaɪz] *vt Aus, Brit* colonizar

colonization [ˌkɒlənaɪ'zeɪʃn, *Am:* ˌkɑːlənɪ-] *n no pl, Am* colonización *f*

colonize ['kɒlənaɪz, *Am:* 'kɑːlə-] *vt* colonizar

colony ['kɒlənɪ, *Am:* 'kɑːlə-] <-ies> *n a.* zool colonia *f*

color ['kʌləʳ, *Am:* -ɚ] *n Am s.* **colour**

colored *adj Am s.* **coloured**

colorful *adj Am s.* **colourful**

coloring *n no pl, Am s.* **colouring**

colorless *adj Am s.* **colourless**

colossal [kə'lɒsl, *Am:* -'lɑːsl] *adj* colosal

colour ['kʌləʳ, *Am:* -ɚ] *n* color *m;* **primary ~** color primario

coloured *adj* coloreado; *(pencil, people)* de color

colourful ['kʌləfl, *Am:* -ɚ-] *adj* lleno de colorido

colouring ['kʌlərɪŋ] *n no pl* **1.** *(complexion)* color *m* **2.** *(chemical)* colorante *m*

colourless ['kʌlələs, *Am:* -ɚ-] *adj* **1.** *(having no colour)* incoloro **2.** *(bland)* soso; **a grey, ~ city** una ciudad gris, apagada

colour scheme *n* combinación *f* de colores

colt [kəʊlt, *Am:* koʊlt] *n* potro *m,* potranco *m AmL*

Columbia [kə'lʌmbiə] *n* **the District of ~** el distrito de Columbia

Columbus Day [kə'lʌmbəsˌdeɪ] *n no pl, Am* día *m* de la Hispanidad, día *m* de la Raza *AmL*

? **Columbus Day** es el día en el que se conmemora que Colón descubrió el Nuevo Mundo el 12 de octubre de 1492. Desde 1971 este día se celebra siempre el segundo lunes del mes de octubre.

column ['kɒləm, *Am:* 'kɑːləm] *n a.* ARCHIT, ANAT, TYPO columna *f;* **spinal ~** columna vertebral

columnist ['kɒləmnɪst, *Am:* 'kɑːləm-] *n* columnista *mf*

coma ['kəʊmə, *Am:* 'koʊ-] *n* coma *m;* **to go into a ~** entrar en coma

comb [kəʊm, *Am:* koʊm] *n* **1.** *(hair device)* peine *m* **2.** zool cresta *f* de gallo

combat ['kɒmbæt, *Am:* 'kɑːm-] **I.** *n no pl (wartime fighting)* combate *m;* **hand-to-hand ~** combate cuerpo a cuerpo **II.** *vt* luchar contra

combination [ˌkɒmbɪ'neɪʃn, *Am:* ˌkɑːmbə-] *n* combinación *f*

combine [kəm'baɪn, *Am:* 'kɑːm-baɪn] *vt* combinar

combined [kəm'baɪnd, *Am:* 'kɑːm-] *adj* combinado

combustion [kəm'bʌstʃən] *n no pl* combustión *f*

come [kʌm] <came, come, coming> *vi* **1.** *(move towards)* venir; **to ~ towards sb** venir hacia alguien **2.** *(go)* venirse; **are you coming to the pub with us?** ¿te vienes al pub con nosotros? **3.** *(arrive)* llegar; **January ~s before February** enero precede a febrero; **the year to ~** el próximo año; **to ~ to an agreement** llegar a un acuerdo; **to ~ to a decision** llegar a una decisión; **to ~ home** volver a casa; **to ~ to sb's rescue** socorrer a alguien; **to ~ first/second/third** *Aus, Brit* ser primero/segundo/tercero **4.** *(become)* hacerse, llegar a; **my dream has ~ true** mi sueño se ha hecho realidad; **I like it as it ~s** me gusta tal cual; **to ~ open** abrirse **5.** *vulg (have an orgasm)* correrse, acabar *AmL*

◆ **come about** *vi* suceder

◆ **come across I.** *vt insep* encontrarse con, dar con; **to ~ a problem** topar con un problema **II.** *vi* **1.** *(be evident)* ser entendido **2.** *(create an impression)* dar una imagen

◆ **come from** *vt* ser de; *(a family)* descender de; **where do you ~?** ¿de dónde eres?; **to ~ a good family** ser de buena familia

◆ **come in** *vi* entrar

◆ **come on I.** *vi* **1.** *(improve)* progresar **2.** *(begin: film, programme)* empezar; **what time does the news ~?** ¿a qué hora dan las noticias? **II.** *vt insep* encontrar **III.** *interj* (*hurry*) ¡date prisa!, ¡ándale! *Méx;* (*encouragement*) ¡ánimo!, ¡órale! *Méx*

comeback ['kʌmbæk] *n* vuelta *f;* SPORTS recuperación *f*

comedian [kə'miːdɪən] *n* cómico, -a *m, f*

comedy ['kɒmədɪ, *Am:* 'kɑːmə-] <-ies> *n* comedia *f*

comet ['kɒmɪt, *Am:* 'kɑːmɪt] *n* cometa *m*

comfort ['kʌmfət, *Am:* -fət] *n* comodidad *f*

comfortable ['kʌmftəbl, *Am:* 'kʌmfətə-] *adj* **1.** (*offering comfort*) cómodo; **to make oneself ~** ponerse cómodo **2.** (*financially stable*) acomodado; **~ life** vida *f* holgada

comfortably ['kʌmftəblɪ, *Am:* 'kʌmfətə-] *adv* **1.** (*in a comfortable manner*) cómodamente **2.** (*in financially stable manner*) **to live ~** vivir de forma acomodada

comforting ['kʌmfətɪŋ, *Am:* -fə-tɪŋ] *adj* (*thought, words*) reconfortante

comfy ['kʌmfɪ] <-ier, -iest> *adj inf* (*furniture, clothes*) cómodo

comic ['kɒmɪk, *Am:* 'kɑːmɪk] I. *n* **1.** (*cartoon magazine*) cómic *m* **2.** (*person*) cómico, -a *m, f* II. *adj* cómico; **~ play** comedia *f*

comical ['kɒmɪkl, *Am:* 'kɑːmɪ-] *adj* cómico

coming ['kʌmɪŋ] *adj* próximo; **the ~ year** el año que viene

comma ['kɒmə, *Am:* 'kɑːmə] *n* coma *f*

command [kə'mɑːnd, *Am:* -'mænd] I. *vt* **1.** (*order*) **to ~ sb to do sth** ordenar a alguien que haga algo **2.** (*have command over*) estar al mando de II. *n* **1.** (*order*) mandato *m;* **to obey a ~** acatar una orden **2.** (*control*) mando *m;* **to be in ~ of sth** estar al mando de algo

commandant [ˌkɒmən'dænt, *Am:* 'kɑːməndænt] *n* MIL comandante *mf*

commander [kə'mɑːndə, *Am:* -'mændə] *n* comandante *mf*

commanding [kə'mɑːndɪŋ, *Am:* -'mæn-] *adj* dominante

Commandment [kə'mɑːndmənt, *Am:* -'mænd-] *n* **the Ten ~s** REL los diez mandamientos

commando [kə'mɑːndəʊ, *Am:* -'mændoʊ] <-s *o* -es> *n* MIL comando *m*

commemorate [kə'meməreɪt] *vt* conmemorar

commemoration [kəˌmemə'reɪʃn] *n no pl* conmemoración *f;* **in ~ of ...** en conmemoración de...

commence [kə'ments] *vi form* empezar; **to ~ speaking** comenzar un discurso

commend [kə'mend] *vt* **1.** (*praise*) elogiar; **to ~ sth/sb (on sth)** alabar algo/a alguien (por algo) **2.** (*entrust*) encomendar; **to ~ sth to sb** encomendar algo a alguien

comment ['kɒment, *Am:* 'kɑːment] I. *n* comentario *m;* **no ~** sin comentarios II. *vi* comentar; **to ~ that ...** observar que...

commentary ['kɒməntrɪ, *Am:* 'kɑːmənter-] <-ies> *n* comentario *m*

commentator ['kɒmənteɪtə, *Am:* 'kɑːmənteɪtə-] *n* TV, RADIO comentarista *mf*

commerce ['kɒmɜːs, *Am:* 'kɑːmɜːrs] *n no pl* comercio *m*

commercial [kə'mɜːʃl, *Am:* -'mɜːr-] I. *adj* comercial II. *n* RADIO, TV anuncio *m*, comercial *m AmL*

commission [kə'mɪʃn] I. *vt* encargar II. *n* **1.** (*order*) encargo *m* **2.** (*system of payment, investigative body*) comisión *f*

commissioner [kə'mɪʃənə, *Am:* -ə-] *n* comisario, -a *m, f*

commit [kə'mɪt] <-tt-> *vt* **1.** (*carry out*) cometer; **to ~ suicide** suicidarse **2.** (*institutionalize*) **to ~ sb to prison** encarcelar a alguien; **to ~ sb to hospital** internar a alguien en un hospital **3.** (*bind oneself*) **to ~ oneself to sth** comprometerse a algo

commitment [kə'mɪtmənt] *n* obligación *f*

committee [kə'mɪtɪ, *Am:* -'mɪt-] *n*

comité *m*

commodity [kə'mɒdətɪ, *Am:* -'mɑːdət̬ɪ] <-ies> *n* mercancía *f*

common ['kɒmən, *Am:* 'kɑːmən] *adj* **1.** corriente; **a ~ disease** una enfermedad común; **to be ~ knowledge** ser de dominio público **2.** (*shared*) común; **~ property** propiedad *f* comunal; **by ~ assent** por unanimidad; **for the ~ good** en beneficio de todos **3.** (*vulgar*) vulgar

common law *n no pl* ≈ derecho *m* consuetudinario

commonly *adv* (*often*) frecuentemente; (*usually*) normalmente

commonplace ['kɒmənpleɪs, *Am:* 'kɑːmən-] *adj* corriente; **it is ~ to see that ...** es frecuente ver que...

common sense *n no pl* sentido *m* común; **a ~ solution** una solución lógica

Commonwealth ['kɒmənwelθ, *Am:* 'kɑːmən-] *n* **the ~** la Commonwealth

[?] La **Commonwealth of Nations** (antiguamente la **British Commonwealth**) es una organización libre de estados independientes, que se ha ido desarrollando a partir del antiguo **British Empire**. Fue fundada oficialmente en 1931 a partir de los **Statute of Westminster**. En aquel momento, Canadá, Australia, Sudáfrica y Nueva Zelanda ya habían alcanzado la independencia y junto con el Reino Unido fueron los primeros miembros. La mayoría de los países que formaban el antiguo Imperio Británico al alcanzar la independencia han ido engrosando la lista de los países pertenecientes a dicha organización. Hoy en día esta organización trabaja en la línea de la colaboración económica y cultural. Los jefes de estado de los países integrantes de la **Commonwealth** se reúnen dos veces al año.

commotion [kə'məʊʃn, *Am:* -'moʊ-] *n* alboroto *m*

communal ['kɒmjʊnl, *Am:* kə-'mjuː] *adj* comunal

commune [kə'mjuːn] *n* comuna *f*

communicate [kə'mjuːnɪkeɪt] *vi, vt* comunicar(se)

communication [kə,mjuːnɪ'keɪʃn] *n* comunicación

communicative [kə'mjuːnɪkətɪv, *Am:* -nəkeɪt̬ɪv] *adj* comunicativo

communion [kə'mjuːnɪən, *Am:* -njən] *n no pl* comunión *f*; **to take ~** comulgar

communism ['kɒmjʊnɪzəm, *Am:* 'kɑːmjə-] *n no pl* comunismo *m*

communist ['kɒmjʊnɪst, *Am:* 'kɑːmjə-] *n* comunista *mf*

community [kə'mjuːnətɪ, *Am:* -nət̬ɪ] <-ies> *n* **1.** (*of people*) comunidad *f*; **the local ~** el vecindario **2.** (*of animals, plants*) colonia *f*

commute [kə'mjuːt] *vi* viajar (diariamente) al lugar de trabajo

commuter [kɒ'mjuːtər, *Am:* -t̬ər] *n* persona que debe viajar diariamente para ir al trabajo

Comoran ['kɒmərən, *Am:* 'kɑːm-] *adj* comorano

Comoros ['kɒmərəʊz, *Am:* 'kɑːmə-roʊz] *npl* **the ~** las Islas Comoras

compact ['kɒmpækt, *Am:* 'kɑːm-] **I.** *adj* compacto **II.** *vt* condensar

compact disc *n* compact *m*, disco *m* compacto

compact disc player *n* reproductor *m* de discos compactos

companion [kəm'pænjən] *n* compañero, -a *m, f*; **travelling ~** compañero de viaje

companionship *n no pl* compañerismo *m*

company ['kʌmpənɪ] <-ies> *n* **1.** (*firm, enterprise*) empresa *f*; **Duggan and C~** Duggan y Compañía **2.** *no pl* (*companionship*) compañía *f*; **you are in good ~** estás en buena compañía; **to keep sb** ~ hacer compañía a alguien

comparable ['kɒmpərəbl, *Am:* 'kɑːm-] *adj* comparable; ~ **to** equiparable a

comparative [kəm'pærətɪv, *Am:* -'perəṭɪv] *adj* comparativo

comparatively *adv* (*by comparison*) comparativamente; (*relatively*) relativamente

compare [kəm'peəʳ, *Am:* -'per] **I.** *vt* comparar; **to** ~ **sth/sb to** [*o* **with**] **sth/sb** comparar algo/a alguien con algo/alguien **II.** *vi* compararse; **to** ~ **favourably with sth** ser mejor que algo

comparison [kəm'pærɪsn, *Am:* -'per-] *n* comparación *f*; **by** ~ **with sb/sth** en comparación con alguien/algo

compartment [kəm'pɑːtmənt, *Am:* -'pɑːrt-] *n* compartimiento *m*

compass ['kʌmpəs] <-es> *n* a. NAUT brújula *f*

compassion [kəm'pæʃn] *n no pl* compasión *f*

compassionate [kəm'pæʃənət] *adj* compasivo

compatibility [kəmˌpætə'bɪləti, *Am:* -ˌpætə'bɪləṭɪ] *n no pl* a. MED, INFOR compatibilidad *f*

compatible [kəm'pætəbl, *Am:* -'pæṭ-] *adj* a. MED, INFOR compatible

compatriot [kəm'pætrɪət, *Am:* -'peɪtrɪ-] *n* compatriota *mf*

compel [kəm'pel] <-ll-> *vt* obligar

compensate ['kɒmpənseɪt, *Am:* 'kɑːm-] *vt* (*make up for*) compensar; (*for loss, damage*) indemnizar

compensation [ˌkɒmpen'seɪʃn, *Am:* ˌkɑːm-] *n no pl* (*award*) compensación *f*; (*for loss, damage*) indemnización *f*

compete [kəm'piːt] *vi* competir; **to** ~ **for sth** competir por algo

competence ['kɒmpɪtəns, *Am:* 'kɑːm-] *n no pl* a. LAW competencia *f*

competent ['kɒmpɪtənt, *Am:* 'kɑːmpɪṭənt] *adj* competente; **to be** ~ **at sth** ser competente en algo

competition [ˌkɒmpə'tɪʃn, *Am:* ˌkɑːm-] *n* **1.** (*state of competing*)

competencia *f* **2.** (*contest*) concurso *m*

competitive [kəm'petətɪv, *Am:* -'peṭətɪv] *adj* competitivo *m*; ~ **sports** deportes *mpl* de competición

competitiveness [kəm'petətɪvnəs] *n no pl* competitividad *f*

competitor [kəm'petɪtəʳ, *Am:* -'peṭəṭəˈ] *n* **1.** *a.* ECON competidor(a) *m(f)* **2.** SPORTS rival *mf*

compilation [ˌkɒmpɪ'leɪʃn, *Am:* ˌkɑːmpə-] *n* **1.** (*act of compiling*) compilación *f* **2.** (*collection*) recopilación *f*

compile [kəm'paɪl] *vt* **1.** *a.* INFOR compilar **2.** (*collect*) recopilar

complacence [kəm'pleɪsns(ɪ)] *n*, **complacency** *n no pl* complacencia *f* (excesiva)

complacent [kəm'pleɪsnt] *adj* satisfecho de sí mismo

complain [kəm'pleɪn] *vi* quejarse

complaint [kəm'pleɪnt] *n* queja *f*; **to lodge a** ~ formular una queja

complement ['kɒmplɪmənt, *Am:* 'kɑːm-] *vt* complementar

complementary [ˌkɒmplɪ'mentrɪ, *Am:* ˌkɑːmplə'menṭəˈɪ] *adj* complementario

complete [kəm'pliːt] **I.** *vt* completar **II.** *adj* completo, entero

completely *adv* totalmente

completeness *n no pl* totalidad *f*

completion [kəm'pliːʃn] *n no pl* finalización *f*; **to be nearing** ~ estar a punto de terminarse

complex ['kɒmpleks, *Am:* 'kɑːm-] **I.** *adj* complejo **II.** <-es> *n* PSYCH, ARCHIT complejo *m*; **guilt/inferiority** ~ complejo de culpabilidad/inferioridad

complexion [kəm'plekʃn] *n* (*skin*) cutis *m inv*; (*colour*) tez *f*

complexity [kəm'pleksəti, *Am:* -səṭɪ] *n no pl* complejidad *f*

compliance [kəm'plaɪəns] *n no pl* obediencia *f*; **to act in** ~ **with sth** actuar de acuerdo con algo

complicate ['kɒmplɪkeɪt, *Am:* 'kɑːmplə-] *vt* complicar

complicated *adj* complicado

complication [ˌkɒmplɪ'keɪʃn, *Am:*

‚kɑːmplə-] *n a.* MED complicación *f*
complicity [kəmˈplɪsətɪ, *Am:* -ət̬ɪ] *n no pl* complicidad *f*
compliment [ˈkɒmplɪmənt, *Am:* ˈkɑːmplə-] **I.** *n* **1.** (*expression of approval*) cumplido *m;* (*flirt*) piropo *m;* **to pay sb a** ~ hacer un cumplido a alguien **2.** *pl* saludos *mpl;* **with ~s** con un atento saludo **II.** *vt* **to** ~ **sb on sth** felicitar a alguien por algo
complimentary [ˌkɒmplɪˈmentrɪ, *Am:* ˌkɑːmpləmenˈter-] *adj* **1.** (*praising*) positivo; **to be** ~ **about sth** hablar en términos muy favorables de algo **2.** (*free*) gratuito
comply [kəmˈplaɪ] <-ie-> *vi* cumplir; **to** ~ **with the law/the rules** acatar la ley/las normas
component [kəmˈpəʊnənt, *Am:* -ˈpoʊ-] *n* componente *m;* **key** ~ pieza *f* clave
compose [kəmˈpəʊz, *Am:* -ˈpoʊz] *vi, vt* componer
composer [kəmˈpəʊzər, *Am:* -ˈpoʊzɚ] *n* compositor(a) *m(f)*
composition [ˌkɒmpəˈzɪʃn, *Am:* ˌkɑːm-] *n* **1.** composición *f* **2.** *no pl* (*make-up*) formación *f*
compost [ˈkɒmpɒst, *Am:* ˈkɑːmpoʊst] *n no pl* abono *m* orgánico
composure [kəmˈpəʊʒər, *Am:* -ˈpoʊʒɚ] *n no pl* compostura *f;* **to lose/regain one's** ~ perder/recobrar la compostura
compound [ˈkɒmpaʊnd, *Am:* ˈkɑːm-] **I.** *vt* agravar **II.** *n* **1.** (*combination*) mezcla *f* **2.** CHEM compuesto *m*
comprehend [ˌkɒmprɪˈhend, *Am:* ˌkɑːm-] *vi, vt* comprender
comprehensible [ˌkɒmprɪˈhensəbl, *Am:* ˌkɑːm-] *adj* comprensible
comprehension [ˌkɒmprɪˈhenʃn, *Am:* ˌkɑːm-] *n no pl* comprensión *f*
comprehensive [ˌkɒmprɪˈhensɪv, *Am:* ˌkɑːmprə-] **I.** *adj* (*exhaustive*) exhaustivo; ~ **coverage** cobertura *f* global **II.** *n Brit* SCHOOL *escuela para niños mayores de once años en la que no hay separación de alumnos*

según su nivel de aptitud

> **?** La **comprehensive school** es una escuela integrada para chicos de edades comprendidas entre los 11–18 años. La **comprehensive school** es el resultado de la unificación de la **secondary modern school** y la **grammar school** (para alumnos que habían aprobado el **eleven-plus examination**), producida en los años 60 y 70.

compress [kəmˈpres] *vt* comprimir
compressed [kəmˈprest] *adj* comprimido
compression [kəmˈpreʃn] *n a.* INFOR compresión *f*
compressor [kəmˈpresər, *Am:* -ɚ] *n* compresor *m*
comprise [kəmˈpraɪz] *vt* componerse de
compromise [ˈkɒmprəmaɪz, *Am:* ˈkɑːm-] **I.** *n* transigencia *f;* **to make a** ~ hacer una concesión **II.** *vi* transigir **III.** *vt* (*betray*) comprometer; **to** ~ **one's beliefs/principles** dejar de lado sus creencias/principios
compromising *adj* comprometido
comptroller [kənˈtrəʊlər, *Am:* -ˈtroʊlə-] *n* interventor(a) *m(f),* contralor(a) *m(f) AmL*
compulsion [kəmˈpʌlʃn] *n no pl* obligación *f*
compulsive [kəmˈpʌlsɪv] *adj* compulsivo
compulsory [kəmˈpʌlsərɪ] *adj* obligatorio
compute [kəmˈpjuːt] *vt* computar
computer [kəmˈpjuːtər, *Am:* -ɚ] *n* ordenador *m,* computador(a) *m(f) AmL*
computer game *n* videojuego *m*
computer graphics *n* + *sing/pl vb* gráficos *mpl* por ordenador [*o* computadora *AmL*]
computer network *n* red *f* de ordenadores [*o* computadoras *AmL*]
computer science *n no pl* informática *f;* ~ **course** curso *m* de in-

formática
comrade ['kɒmreɪd, Am: 'kɑːm-ræd] n **1.** (friend) compañero, -a m, f **2.** POL camarada mf
con [kɒn, Am: kɑːn] <-nn-> vt inf engañar; **to ~ sb** (into doing sth) engañar a alguien (para que haga algo)
conceal [kən'siːl] vt esconder
concealment [kən'siːlmənt] n no pl encubrimiento m
concede [kən'siːd] vt **1.** (acknowledge) conceder **2.** (surrender) ceder
conceit [kən'siːt] n no pl (vanity) vanidad f; **to be full of ~** tener muchas presunciones
conceive [kən'siːv] I. vt **1.** (imagine, become pregnant with) concebir **2.** (devise) idear II. vi concebir
concentrate ['kɒnsəntreɪt, Am: 'kɑːn-] I. vi concentrarse; **to ~ on sth** concentrarse en algo II. vt concentrar
concentrated adj concentrado
concentration [ˌkɒnsn'treɪʃn, Am: ˌkɑːn-] n no pl concentración f; ~ **on sth** concentración en algo
concept ['kɒnsept, Am: 'kɑːn-] n concepto m; **to grasp a ~** coger una idea
conception [kən'sepʃn] n **1.** (idea) idea f **2.** no pl BIO concepción f
conceptual [kən'septjʊəl, Am: -tʃu-] adj conceptual
concern [kən'sɜːn, Am: -'sɜːrn] I. vt **1.** (apply to) referirse a; **to ~ oneself about sth** interesarse por algo **2.** (worry) preocuparse; **to be ~ed about sth** estar preocupado por algo II. n **1.** (matter of interest) asunto m; **to be of ~ to sb** interesar a alguien **2.** (worry) preocupación f
concerning prep acerca de
concert ['kɒnsət, Am: 'kɑːnsɚt] n (musical performance) concierto m; **~ hall** sala f de conciertos
concerto [kən'tʃeətəʊ, Am: -'tʃer-toʊ] <-s o -ti> n concierto m
concession [kən'seʃn] n concesión f
conciliate [kən'sɪlɪeɪt] I. vi conciliarse II. vt conciliar
conciliation [kənˌsɪlɪ'eɪʃn] n no pl,

form conciliación f
concise [kən'saɪs] adj conciso
conclude [kən'kluːd] I. vi concluir II. vt **1.** (finish) finalizar; **to ~ by doing sth** terminar haciendo algo **2.** (infer) **to ~** (from sth) **that ...** deducir (de algo) que...
concluding adj final
conclusion [kən'kluːʒn] n conclusión f
conclusive [kən'kluːsɪv] adj concluyente
concrete ['kɒnkriːt, Am: 'kɑːn-] n no pl hormigón m
condemn [kən'dem] vt condenar; **to ~ sb for sth** censurar a alguien por algo
condemnation [ˌkɒndem'neɪʃn, Am: ˌkɑːn-] n condena f
condensation [ˌkɒnden'seɪʃn, Am: ˌkɑːn-] n no pl condensación f
condense [kɒn'dens] I. vt (concentrate) **to ~ a liquid** condensar un líquido II. vi condensarse
condition [kən'dɪʃn] I. n condición f; **in perfect ~** en perfecto estado II. vt **1.** (influence) condicionar **2.** (treat hair) acondicionar
conditional [kən'dɪʃənl] I. adj (provisory) condicional; **~ on sth** condicionado a algo II. n LING **the ~** el condicional
conditioner [kən'dɪʃənəʳ, Am: -ɚ] n **1.** (for hair) acondicionador m **2.** (for clothes) suavizante m
condom ['kɒndəm, Am: 'kɑːn-] n condón m
condone [kən'dəʊn, Am: -'doʊn] vt condonar
conduct [kən'dʌkt, Am: 'kɑːn-] I. vt **1.** (carry out) llevar a cabo **2.** (behave) **to ~ oneself** comportarse **3.** ELEC, PHYS conducir II. vi MUS llevar la batuta III. n no pl conducta f
conductor [kən'dʌktəʳ, Am: -tɚ] n **1.** (director) director(a) m(f) **2.** PHYS, ELEC conductor m **3.** (of train) revisor m
cone [kəʊn, Am: koʊn] n **1.** a. MAT cono m **2.** (cornet for ice cream) cucurucho m
confectionery [kən'fekʃənərɪ, Am:

-erɪ] *n no pl* confitería *f*

confederacy [kən'fedərəsɪ] <-ies>
n + sing/pl vb (*union*) confederación *f*; **the Confederancy** *Am* HIST
la Confederación

confederate [kən'fedərət] *adj* HIST,
POL confederado

confederation [kənˌfedə'reɪʃn] *n +
sing/pl vb* POL confederación *f*

> **?** El **Confederation Day** o **Cana-
> da Day** es la fiesta nacional de Ca-
> nadá que se celebra el día 1 de
> julio.

confer [kən'fɜːʳ, *Am:* -'fɜːr] <-rr->
I. *vi* consultar II. *vt* otorgar

conference ['kɒnfərəns, *Am:* 'kɑːn-
fə˞-] *n* conferencia *f*

confess [kən'fes] I. *vi* confesarse; **to
~ to a crime** confesarse de un
crimen II. *vt* confesar

confession [kən'feʃn] *n* confesión *f*

confidant [ˌkɒnfɪ'dænt, *Am:* ˌkɑːn-
fə-] *n* confidente *m*

confide [kən'faɪd] *vt* confiar; **to ~
(to sb) that ...** decir (a alguien) en
confidencia que...

confidence ['kɒnfɪdəns, *Am:*
'kɑːnfə-] *n* **1.** (*trust*) confianza *f*; **to
place one's ~ in sb/sth** poner la
confianza en alguien/algo; **he certainly doesn't lack ~** desde luego
no le falta confianza en sí mismo
2. *no pl* (*secrecy*) confidencia *f*

confident ['kɒnfɪdənt, *Am:* 'kɑːnfə-] *adj* **1.** (*sure*) seguro; **to be ~
about sth** estar seguro de algo
2. (*self-assured*) confiado

confidential [ˌkɒnfɪ'denʃl, *Am:*
ˌkɑːnfə-] *adj* confidencial

confine ['kɒnfaɪn, *Am:* 'kɑːn-] *vt*
1. (*limit*) **to ~ sth to sth** restringir
algo a algo; **to be ~d to doing sth** limitarse a hacer algo **2.** (*imprison*)
confinar

confinement [kən'faɪnmənt] *n no
pl* confinamiento *m*

confirm [kən'fɜːm, *Am:* -'fɜːrm]
I. *vt* **1.** (*verify*) verificar **2.** REL **to ~
sb's faith** confirmar la fe de alguien

II. *vi* confirmarse

confirmation [ˌkɒnfə'meɪʃn, *Am:*
ˌkɑːnfə˞-] *n a.* REL confirmación *f*

confiscate ['kɒnfɪskeɪt, *Am:* 'kɑːn-
fə-] *vt* confiscar

conflict ['kɒnflɪkt, *Am:* 'kɑːn-] *n*
conflicto *m*

conflicting [kən'flɪktɪŋ] *adj* opuesto

confluence ['kɒnfluːəns, *Am:*
'kɑːn-] *n* confluencia *f*

conform [kən'fɔːm, *Am:* -'fɔːrm] *vi*
conformarse; **to ~ to the law** ser
conforme a la ley

conformity [kən'fɔːmɪtɪ, *Am:*
-'fɔːrmətɪ] *n no pl* conformidad *f*;
in ~ with sth conforme con algo

confront [kən'frʌnt] *vt* enfrentarse a

confrontation [ˌkɒnfrʌn'teɪʃn, *Am:*
ˌkɑːnfrən-] *n* confrontación *f*

confuse [kən'fjuːz] *vt* confundir

confused [kən'fjuːzd] *adj* confundido

confusing [kən'fjuːzɪŋ] *adj* confuso

confusion [kən'fjuːʒn] *n no pl* confusión *f*

congested [kən'dʒestɪd] *adj* con-
gestionado

congestion [kən'dʒestʃən] *n no pl*
congestión *f*

conglomerate [kən'glɒmərət, *Am:*
-'glɑːmə˞-] *n* conglomerado *m*

Congo ['kɒŋgəʊ, *Am:* 'kɑːŋgoʊ]
I. *n* **the ~** el Congo II. *adj* del Congo

Congolese [ˌkɒŋgəʊ'liːz, *Am:*
ˌkɑːŋgə'-] *adj* congoleño

congratulate [kən'grætʃʊleɪt, *Am:*
-'grætʃə-] *vt* felicitar; **to ~ sb** (**on
sth**) felicitar a alguien (por algo)

congratulations [kənˌgrætʃʊ'leɪ-
ʃnz, *Am:* -ˌgrætʃə-] *npl ~!* ¡felicidades!

> **!** **congratulations** (= felicidades,
> enhorabuena) se utiliza en plural:
> "Congratulations on passing the
> exam!"

congregate ['kɒŋgrɪgeɪt, *Am:*
'kɑːŋ-] *vi* congregarse

congregation [ˌkɒŋgrɪ'geɪʃn, *Am:*
ˌkɑːŋ-] *n* congregación *f*

congress ['kɒŋgres, *Am:* 'kɑ:ŋ-] *n* congreso *m*

congressional [kən'greʃənəl, *Am:* kəŋ-] *adj Am* congresista

congressman ['kɒŋgresmən, *Am:* 'kɑ:ŋ-] *n* <-men> *Am* congresista *m*

conjecture [kən'dʒektʃəʳ, *Am:* -tʃɚ] *n* conjetura *f*

connect [kə'nekt] **I.** *vi* conectar(se); **to ~ to the Internet** conectarse a internet **II.** *vt* conectar

connected *adj* conectado

connecting *adj* comunicado; **~ link** enlace *m* de conexión

connection *n*, **connexion** [kə'nek-ʃən] *n* conexión *f*

connoisseur [ˌkɒnə'sɜːʳ, *Am:* ˌkɑ:-nə'sɜːr] *n* entendido, -a *m, f*; **art/wine ~** experto, -a *m, f* en arte/vino

connotation [ˌkɒnə'teɪʃn, *Am:* ˌkɑ:nə-] *n* connotación *f*

conquer ['kɒŋkəʳ, *Am:* 'kɑ:ŋkɚ] *vt* conquistar

conqueror ['kɒŋkərəʳ, *Am:* 'kɑ:ŋ-kɚɚ] *n a.* HIST conquistador(a) *m(f)*

conquest ['kɒŋkwəst, *Am:* 'kɑ:n-] *n no pl, a. iron* conquista *f*

conscience ['kɒnʃəns, *Am:* 'kɑ:n-] *n* conciencia *f*; **a clear ~** una conciencia limpia

conscious ['kɒnʃəs, *Am:* 'kɑ:n-] *adj* consciente; **fashion ~** preocupado por la moda

consciousness ['kɒnʃəsnɪs, *Am:* 'kɑ:n-] *n no pl* **1.** (*state of being conscious*) conocimiento *m* **2.** (*awareness*) conciencia *f*; **political/social ~** conciencia política/social

consecutive [kən'sekjʊtɪv, *Am:* -jət̬ɪv] *adj* consecutivo

consensus [kən'sensəs] *n no pl* consenso *m*

consent [kən'sent] **I.** *n form* consentimiento *m*; **by common ~** de común acuerdo **II.** *vi* (*agree*) **to ~ to do sth** consentir en hacer algo

consequence ['kɒnsɪkwəns, *Am:* 'kɑ:n-] *n* consecuencia *f*; **as a ~** como consecuencia; **in ~** por consiguiente

consequent ['kɒnsɪkwənt, *Am:* 'kɑ:n-] *adj*, **consequential** [ˌkɒn-sɪ'kwenʃl, *Am:* ˌkɑ:n-] *adj* consiguiente

consequently ['kɒnsɪkwəntlɪ, *Am:* ˌkɑ:n-] *adv* por consiguiente

conservation [ˌkɒnsə'veɪʃn, *Am:* ˌkɑ:nsɚ-] *n no pl* conservación *f*

conservationist [ˌkɒnsə'veɪʃənɪst, *Am:* ˌkɑ:nsɚ-] *n* conservacionista *mf*

conservatism [kən'sɜːvətɪzəm, *Am:* -'sɜːr-] *n no pl* conservadurismo *m*

conservative [kən'sɜːvətɪv, *Am:* -'sɜːrvət̬ɪv] *adj* conservador

conservatory [kən'sɜːvətrɪ, *Am:* -'sɜːrvətɔ:rɪ] *n* conservatorio *m*

conserve [kən'sɜːv, *Am:* -sɜːrv] *vt* conservar; **to ~ energy** ahorrar energía

consider [kən'sɪdəʳ, *Am:* -ɚ] *vt* considerar

considerable [kən'sɪdərəbl] *adj* considerable

considerate [kən'sɪdərət] *adj* considerado

consideration [kənˌsɪdə'reɪʃn] *n no pl* consideración *f*; **the project is under ~** el proyecto se está estudiando

considering [kən'sɪdərɪŋ] **I.** *prep* teniendo en cuenta; **~ the weather** en vista del tiempo **II.** *conj* **~ (that) ...** ya que...

consignment [kən'saɪnmənt] *n* remesa *f*

consist [kən'sɪst] *vi* **to ~ of sth** consistir en algo

consistency [kən'sɪstənsɪ] *n no pl* **1.** (*degree of firmness*) consistencia *f* **2.** (*being coherent*) coherencia *f*

consistent [kən'sɪstənt] *adj* consecuente

consolation [ˌkɒnsə'leɪʃn, *Am:* ˌkɑ:n-] *n no pl* consuelo *m*; **it was ~ to him to know that ...** le reconfortó saber que...

console[1] ['kɒnsəʊl, *Am:* 'kɑ:nsɔʊl] *vt* (*comfort*) consolar

console[2] [kən'səʊl, *Am:* -'sɔʊl] *n*

(*switch panel*) consola *f*

consolidate [kən'sɒlɪdeɪt, *Am:* -'sɑːlə-] I. *vi* consolidarse II. *vt* consolidar

consolidated *adj* consolidado

consolidation [kən,sɒlɪ'deɪʃn, *Am:* -,sɑːlə-] *n no pl* 1. (*becoming stronger*) fortalecimiento *m* 2. ECON consolidación *f*

consonant ['kɒnsənənt, *Am:* 'kɑːn-] *n no pl* consonante *f*

consortium [kən'sɔːtɪəm, *Am:* -'sɔːrt̬-] *n* <consortiums *o* consortia> consorcio *m*; ~ **of companies** grupo *m* de empresas

conspicuous [kən'spɪkjʊəs] *adj* llamativo; **to be ~ by one's absence** *iron* brillar por su ausencia

conspiracy [kən'spɪrəsɪ] <-ies> *n* conspiración *f*; **a ~ against sb** un complot contra alguien

conspirator [kən'spɪrətə^r, *Am:* -t̬ə^r] *n* conspirador(a) *m(f)*

conspire [kən'spaɪə^r, *Am:* -'spaɪə^r] *vi* conspirar; **to ~ to do sth** conspirar para hacer algo

constable ['kʌnstəbl, *Am:* 'kɑːn-] *n Brit* policía *mf*

constant ['kɒnstənt, *Am:* 'kɑːn-] *adj* constante; ~ **use** uso *m* frecuente

constantly *adv* constantemente

constipate ['kɒnstɪpeɪt, *Am:* 'kɑːnstə-] *vt* MED estreñir

constipated *adj* estreñido

constipation [,kɒnstɪ'peɪʃn, *Am:* 'kɑːnstə-] *n* MED estreñimiento *m*, prendimiento *m CSur*

constituency [kən'stɪtjʊənsɪ, *Am:* -'stɪtʃu-] *n* (*electoral district*) distrito *m* electoral

constituent [kən'stɪtjʊənt, *Am:* -'stɪtʃu-] *n* constituente *m*

constitute ['kɒnstɪtjuːt, *Am:* 'kɑːnstətuːt] *vt* constituir

constitution [,kɒnstɪ'tjuːʃn, *Am:* ,kɑːnstə'tuː-] *n* constitución *f*

constitutional [,kɒnstɪ'tjuːʃənl, *Am:* ,kɑːnstə'tuː-] *adj* constitucional; ~ **law** derecho político

constrain [kən'streɪn] *vt* constreñir

constraint [kən'streɪnt] *n* 1. *no pl* (*compulsion*) coacción *f*; **under** ~ bajo coacción 2. (*limit*) restricción *f*; **to impose ~s on sb/sth** imponer limitaciones a alguien/algo

construct [kən'strʌkt] I. *n* construcción *f* II. *vt* construir

construction [kən'strʌkʃn] *n* construcción *f*

constructive [kən'strʌktɪv] *adj* constructivo

constructor [kən'strʌktə^r, *Am:* -t̬ə^r] *n* constructor(a) *m(f)*

consul ['kɒnsl, *Am:* 'kɑːn-] *n* cónsul *mf*

consulate ['kɒnsjʊlət, *Am:* 'kɑːn-] *n* consulado *m*

consult [kən'sʌlt] *vi, vt* consultar

consultancy [kən'sʌltənsɪ] <-ies> *n* asesoría *f*

consultant [kən'sʌltənt] *n* 1. ECON asesor(a) *m(f)*; **management** ~ asesor de gestión; **tax** ~ asesor fiscal 2. *Brit* MED especialista *mf*

consultation [,kɒnsʌl'teɪʃn, *Am:* ,kɑːn-] *n* consulta *f*

consume [kən'sjuːm, *Am:* -'suːm] *vt* consumir

consumer [kən'sjuːmə^r, *Am:* -'suːmə^r] *n* consumidor(a) *m(f)*; ~ **credit** crédito *m* al consumidor

consumerism [kən'sjuːmərɪzəm, *Am:* -'suːmɚ-] *n no pl* consumismo *m*

consumption [kən'sʌmpʃn] *n no pl* 1. consumo *m* 2. HIST, MED tisis *f inv*

contact ['kɒntækt, *Am:* 'kɑːn-] *n* (*state of communication*) contacto *m*; (*connection*) relación *f*; **to have ~s** tener contactos

contact lens *n* lentilla *f*

contagious [kən'teɪdʒəs] *adj a. fig* contagioso

contain [kən'teɪn] *vt* contener

container [kən'teɪnə^r, *Am:* -nɚ] *n* contenedor *m*

contaminate [kən'tæmɪneɪt] *vt* contaminar

contamination [kən,tæmɪ'neɪʃn] *n no pl* contaminación *f*

contemplate ['kɒntempleɪt, *Am:* 'kɑːnt̬em-] *vt* contemplar

contemplation [,kɒntem'pleɪʃn,

Am: ˌkɑːnt̬em-] *n no pl* contemplación *f*

contemporary [kən'temprərɪ, *Am:* -pərer-] *adj* contemporáneo

contempt [kən'tempt] *n no pl* desprecio *m*

contemptuous [kən'temptʃʊəs] *adj* desdeñoso; **to be ~ of sb** menospreciar a alguien

contend [kən'tend] *vi* competir; **to ~ for sth** competir por algo; **to have sb/sth to ~ with** tener que enfrentarse a alguien/algo

contender *n* aspirante *mf*

content¹ ['kɒntent, *Am:* 'kɑːn-] *n* contenido *m*

content² [kən'tent] I. *vi* contentarse II. *adj* contento

contented *adj* satisfecho

contention [kən'tenʃn] *n no pl* 1. (*disagreement*) controversia *f* 2. (*competition*) **to be out of ~ for sth** no tener posibilidades de algo

contentment [kən'tentmənt] *n no pl* satisfacción *f*

contents ['kɒntents, *Am:* 'kɑːntents] *n pl* contenido *m*; (*index*) índice *m*

contest [kən'test, *Am:* 'kɑːn-] I. *n* concurso *m*; **beauty ~** certamen *m* de belleza II. *vt* impugnar

contestant [kən'testənt] *n* concursante *mf*

context ['kɒntekst, *Am:* 'kɑːn-] *n* contexto *m*

continent ['kɒntɪnənt, *Am:* 'kɑːntnənt] *n* continente *m*

continental [ˌkɒntɪ'nentl, *Am:* ˌkɑːntn'entl] *adj* continental; **~ drift** movimiento *m* de los continentes

contingency [kən'tɪndʒənsɪ] <-ies> *n form* contingencia *f*

contingent [kən'tɪndʒənt] I. *n* 1. (*part of a larger group*) representación *f* 2. MIL contingente *m* II. *adj* eventual

continual [kən'tɪnjʊəl] *adj* continuo

continually *adv* continuamente

continuation [kənˌtɪnjʊ'eɪʃn] *n no pl* continuación *f*

continue [kən'tɪnjuː] I. *vi* 1. (*persist*) continuar; **he ~d by saying that …** prosiguió diciendo que… 2. (*remain unchanged*) seguir; **to be ~d** continuará II. *vt* seguir con

continuity [ˌkɒntɪ'njuːətɪ, *Am:* ˌkɑːntn'uːət̬ɪ] *n no pl* continuidad *f*

continuous [kən'tɪnjʊəs] *adj* continuo

contour ['kɒntʊəʳ, *Am:* 'kɑːntʊr] *n* contorno *m*

contraception [ˌkɒntrə'sepʃn, *Am:* ˌkɑːn-] *n no pl* anticoncepción *f*

contraceptive [ˌkɒntrə'septɪv, *Am:* ˌkɑːn-] *n* anticonceptivo *m*

contract¹ [kən'trækt] I. *vi* contraerse II. *vt* 1. (*make shorter*) contraer 2. (*catch*) **to ~ smallpox/AIDS/a cold** contraer la viruela/el SIDA/un resfriado

contract² ['kɒntrækt, *Am:* 'kɑːn-] I. *n* contrato *m*; **~ of employment** contrato laboral II. *vt* contratar

contraction [kən'trækʃn] *n a.* MED, LING contracción *f*

contractor [kən'træktəʳ, *Am:* 'kɑːntræktɚ] *n* contratista *mf*

contradict [ˌkɒntrə'dɪkt, *Am:* ˌkɑːn-] I. *vi* contradecirse II. *vt* contradecir

contradiction [ˌkɒntrə'dɪkʃn, *Am:* ˌkɑːn-] *n* contradicción *f*

contradictory [ˌkɒntrə'dɪktərɪ, *Am:* ˌkɑːn-] *adj* contradictorio

contrary ['kɒntrərɪ, *Am:* 'kɑːntrɚ-] *n no pl* **on the ~** al contrario

contrary to *prep* al contrario de

contrast [kən'trɑːst, *Am:* -'træst] I. *n* contraste *m*; **by** [*o* **in**] **~** por contraste II. *vt* contrastar

contribute [kən'trɪbjuːt] *vi, vt* contribuir

contribution [ˌkɒntrɪ'bjuːʃn, *Am:* ˌkɑːn-] *n* contribución *f*

contributor [kən'trɪbjuːtəʳ, *Am:* -'trɪbjət̬ɚ] *n* contribuyente *mf*

contrive [kən'traɪv] *vt* 1. (*plan*) ingeniar 2. (*manage*) **to ~ to do sth** ingeniárselas para hacer algo

contrived *adj* artificial

control [kən'trəʊl, *Am:* -'troʊl] I. *n* control *m*; **to be in ~** mandar II. *vt*

<-ll-> controlar
controlled [kən'trəʊld, *Am:* -'troʊld] *adj* controlado
controversial [ˌkɒntrə'vɜːʃl, *Am:* ˌkɑːntrə'vɜːr-] *adj* polémico
controversy ['kɒntrəvɜːsɪ, kən-'trɒvəsɪ, *Am:* 'kɑːntrəvɜːr-] *n* <-ies> polémica *f*; **to be beyond ~** ser incuestionable
convene [kən'viːn] *vt* convocar
convenience [kən'viːnɪəns, *Am:* -'viːnjəns] *n no pl* conveniencia *f*
convenient [kən'viːnɪənt, *Am:* -'viːnjənt] *adj* conveniente
convent ['kɒnvənt, *Am:* 'kɑːn-] *n* convento *m*
convention [kən'venʃn] *n* (*custom*) convención *f*; **~ dictates that** es costumbre que +*subj*
conventional [kən'ventʃənəl] *adj* convencional
converge [kən'vɜːdʒ, *Am:* -'vɜːrdʒ] *vi a. fig* converger
convergence [kən'vɜːdʒəns, *Am:* -'vɜːr-] *n* convergencia *f*
conversation [ˌkɒnvə'seɪʃn, *Am:* ˌkɑːnvɚ-] *n* (*word exchange*) conversación *f*, plática *f AmL*; **to strike up a ~ with sb** entablar conversación con alguien
converse¹ [kən'vɜːs, *Am:* -'vɜːrs] *vi form* **to ~ with sb** conversar con alguien, platicar con alguien *AmL*
converse² ['kɒnvɜːs, *Am:* 'kɑːnvɜːrs] *n* **the ~** lo opuesto
conversion [kən'vɜːʃn, *Am:* -'vɜːr-ʒn] *n a.* REL, POL conversión *f*
convert [kən'vɜːt, *Am:* -'vɜːrt] I. *n* converso, -a *m, f* II. *vi* REL, POL convertirse III. *vt a.* REL, INFOR convertir
convey [kən'veɪ] *vt* transmitir
convict ['kɒnvɪkt, *Am:* 'kɑːn-] I. *n* presidiario, -a *m, f* II. *vt* condenar
conviction [kən'vɪkʃn] *n* 1. LAW condena *f* 2. (*firm belief*) convicción *f*
convince [kən'vɪnts] *vt* convencer; **I'm not ~d** no estoy convencido
convincing [kən'vɪntsɪŋ] *adj* convincente
convoy ['kɒnvɔɪ, *Am:* 'kɑːn-] *n* convoy *m*; **in** [*o* **under**] **~** en caravana
coo [kuː] I. *vi* arrullar II. *vt* susurrar

cook [kʊk] GASTR I. *n* cocinero, -a *m, f*; **too many ~s spoil the broth** *prov* muchas manos en un plato hacen mucho garabato *prov* II. *vi* hacerse III. *vt* cocinar
cookbook ['kʊkbʊk] *n* libro *m* de cocina
cooker ['kʊkəʳ, *Am:* -ɚ] *n Brit* (*stove*) cocina *f*, estufa *f Col, Méx*
cookery ['kʊkərɪ] *n no pl* cocina *f*
cookie ['kʊkɪ] *n Am* (*biscuit*) galleta *f*
cooking ['kʊkɪŋ] *n no pl* **to do the ~** hacer la comida
cool [kuːl] I. *adj* 1. (*slightly cold*) fresco 2. (*calm*) tranquilo; **keep ~** tómatelo con calma 3. *inf* (*fashionable*) **to be ~** estar en la onda; **that disco is very ~** esa discoteca está muy de moda II. *interj inf* ¡genial! III. *vt* enfriar; **just ~ it** *inf* ¡calma! IV. *vi* (*become cooler*) enfriarse
coop [kuːp] *n* gallinero *m*
cooperate [kəʊ'ɒpəreɪt, *Am:* koʊ-'ɑːpəreɪt] *vi* cooperar
cooperation [kəʊˌɒpə'reɪʃn, *Am:* koʊˌɑːpə-] *n* cooperación *f*
cooperative [kəʊ'ɒpərətɪv, *Am:* koʊ'ɑːpəɹ̩ətɪv] I. *n* cooperativa *f* II. *adj* cooperativo
coordinate [ˌkəʊ'ɔːdɪneɪt, *Am:* ˌkoʊ'ɔːr-] I. *n* coordenada *f* II. *vi* 1. (*work together effectively*) coordinar(se) 2. (*match*) combinar III. *vt* coordinar
coordination [ˌkəʊˌɔːdɪ'neɪʃn, *Am:* ˌkoʊˌɔːrdə'neɪ-] *n no pl* coordinación *f*
coordinator *n* coordinador(a) *m(f)*
cop [kɒp, *Am:* kɑːp] *n inf* (*police officer*) poli *mf*
cope [kəʊp, *Am:* koʊp] *vi* 1. (*master a situation*) aguantar 2. (*problem*) hacer frente
Copenhagen [ˌkəʊpən'heɪgən, *Am:* 'koʊpən̩heɪ-] *n* Copenhague *m*
copper ['kɒpəʳ, *Am:* 'kɑːpɚ] *n no pl* (*metal*) cobre *m*
copy ['kɒpɪ, *Am:* 'kɑːpɪ] I. <-ies> *n* (*facsimile*) copia *f*; (*of a book*) ejemplar *m* II. <-ie-> *vt* 1. *a.* INFOR, MUS

copiar **2.** (*imitate*) imitar

copyright *n* derechos *mpl* de autor; **to hold the ~ of sth** tener los derechos de autor de algo

coral ['kɒrəl, *Am:* 'kɔ:r-] *n no pl* coral *m*

cord [kɔ:d, *Am:* kɔ:rd] *n* **1.** (*rope*) cuerda *f*, piola *f AmS* **2.** ELEC cable *m* **3.** ANAT **umbilical ~** cordón *m* umbilical

cordial ['kɔ:dɪəl, *Am:* 'kɔ:rdʒəl] *adj* cordial

core [kɔ:ʳ, *Am:* kɔ:r] *n* **1.** (*centre*) centro *m;* **to be rotten to the ~** *fig* estar podrido hasta la médula **2.** (*centre with seeds*) corazón *m*

cork [kɔ:k, *Am:* kɔ:rk] *n* corcho *m*

corn [kɔ:n, *Am:* kɔ:rn] *n no pl* (*maize*) maíz *m*, choclo *m AmS*, abatí *m Arg;* **~ on the cob** mazorca *f* de maíz

corner ['kɔ:nəʳ, *Am:* 'kɔ:rnəʳ] **I.** *n* **1.** (*junction of two roads*) esquina *f;* **to be round the ~** estar a la vuelta de la esquina **2.** (*of a room*) rincón *m* **3.** (*place*) **a distant ~ of the globe** un rincón remoto de la tierra **4.** (*manoevre in sport*) córner *m* **II.** *vt* **1.** (*hinder escape*) acorralar **2.** ECON **to ~ the market** acaparar el mercado

cornerstone ['kɔ:nəstəʊn, *Am:* 'kɔ:rnəstoʊn] *n a. fig* piedra *f* angular

Cornwall ['kɔ:rnwɔ:l] *n* Cornualles *m*

corny ['kɔ:nɪ, *Am:* 'kɔ:r-] <-ier, -iest> *adj* **1.** *inf* viejo; (*joke*) gastado **2.** (*emotive*) sensiblero

coronary ['kɒrənrɪ, *Am:* 'kɔ:rənər-] *adj* coronario

coronation [ˌkɒrə'neɪʃn, *Am:* ˌkɔ:r-] *n* coronación *f*

coroner ['kɒrənəʳ, *Am:* 'kɔ:rənəʳ] *n* funcionario encargado de investigar muertes no naturales

corporal ['kɔ:pərəl, *Am:* 'kɔ:r-] **I.** *n* MIL cabo *mf* **II.** *adj form* corporal

corporate ['kɔ:pərət, *Am:* 'kɔ:r-] *adj* corporativo; **~ capital** capital *m* social

corporation [ˌkɔ:pə'reɪʃn, *Am:*

ˌkɔ:rpə-] *n + sing/pl vb* **1.** (*business*) sociedad *f* anónima; **a public ~** *Brit* una empresa pública **2.** (*local council*) ayuntamiento *m*

corpse [kɔ:ps, *Am:* kɔ:rps] *n* cadáver *m*

correct [kə'rekt] **I.** *vt* (*put right*) corregir **II.** *adj* correcto

correction [kə'rekʃən] *n* corrección *f*

correlate ['kɒrəleɪt, *Am:* 'kɔ:rə-] **I.** *vt* correlacionar **II.** *vi* (*relate*) poner en correlación

correlation [ˌkɒrə'leɪʃn, *Am:* ˌkɔ:rə-] *n* correlación *f*

correspond [ˌkɒrɪ'spɒnd, *Am:* ˌkɔ:rə-] *vi* **1.** (*be equal to*) corresponder a **2.** (*write*) cartearse

correspondence [ˌkɒrɪ'spɒndəns, *Am:* ˌkɔ:rə'spɑ:n-] *n no pl* correspondencia *f*

correspondent [ˌkɒrɪ'spɒndənt, *Am:* ˌkɔ:rə'spɑ:n-] *n* corresponsal *mf;* **special ~** enviado, -a *m, f* especial

corresponding [ˌkɒrɪ'spɒndɪŋ, *Am:* ˌkɔ:rə-] *adj* correspondiente

corridor ['kɒrɪdɔ:ʳ, *Am:* 'kɔ:rədəʳ] *n* (*passage*) pasillo *m*

corroborate [kə'rɒbəreɪt, *Am:* -'rɑ:bə-] *vt* corroborar

corrupt [kə'rʌpt] **I.** *vt* corromper **II.** *adj* corrupto; **~ practices** prácticas *fpl* corruptas

corruption [kə'rʌpʃn] *n no pl* corrupción *f*

corset ['kɔ:sɪt, *Am:* 'kɔ:r-] *n* corsé *m*

Corsica ['kɔ:sɪkə, *Am:* 'kɔ:r-] *n* Córcega *f*

Corsican ['kɔ:sɪkən, *Am:* 'kɔ:r-] *adj* corso

cosmetic [kɒz'metɪk, *Am:* kɑ:z'meṭ-] **I.** *n* cosmético *m;* **~s** cosméticos *mpl* **II.** *adj* cosmético; **~ cream** crema *f* cosmética

cosmic ['kɒzmɪk, *Am:* 'kɑ:z-] *adj fig* cósmico; **of ~ proportions** de proporciones astronómicas

cosmology [kɒz'mɒlədʒɪ, *Am:* kɑ:z'mɑ:lə-] *n* cosmología *f*

cosmonaut ['kɒzmənɔ:t, *Am:* 'kɑ:zmənɑ:t] *n* cosmonauta *mf*

cosmopolitan [ˌkɒzmə'pɒlɪtən, *Am:* ˌkɑ:zmə'pɑ:lɪ-] *adj* cosmopolita

cosmos ['kɒzmɒs, *Am:* 'kɑ:zmoʊs] *n no pl* cosmos *m inv*

cost [kɒst, *Am:* kɑ:st] I. *vt* 1.<cost, cost> (*amount to*) costar 2.<costed, costed> (*calculate price*) calcular el precio de II. *n* 1. (*price*) precio *m;* **at no extra ~** sin costes adicionales 2. *pl* (*expence*) costes *mpl*

Costa Rica [ˌkɒstə'ri:kə, *Am:* ˌkoʊstə-] *n* Costa Rica *f*

Costa Rican [ˌkɒstə'ri:kən, *Am:* ˌkoʊstə-] *adj* costarricense

costly ['kɒstlɪ, *Am:* 'kɑ:st-] <-ier, -iest> *adj* costoso; (*mistake*) caro; **to prove ~** *a. fig* resultar muy caro

costume ['kɒstju:m, *Am:* 'kɑ:s-tu:m] *n* 1. (*national dress*) traje *m;* **to dress in ~** ir trajeado 2. (*decorative dress*) disfraz *m*

cosy ['kəʊzɪ, *Am:* 'koʊ-] <-ier, -iest> *adj* (*comfortable*) cómodo; (*place*) acogedor

cot [kɒt, *Am:* kɑ:t] *n* cuna *f*

cottage ['kɒtɪdʒ, *Am:* 'kɑ:t̬ɪdʒ] *n* **country ~** casa *f* de campo

cottage cheese *n no pl* requesón *m*

cotton ['kɒtn, *Am:* 'kɑ:tn] *n* algodón *m*

couch [kaʊtʃ] <-es> *n* canapé *m;* **psychiatrist's ~** diván *m*

cough [kɒf, *Am:* kɑ:f] I. *n* tos *f;* **chesty ~** tos seca II. *vi* toser

could [kʊd] *pt, pp of* **can²**

council ['kaʊnsl] *n* + *sing/pl vb* ADMIN **city ~** ayuntamiento *m;* MIL consejo *m;* **local ~** consejo local; **the United Nations Security Council** el Consejo de Seguridad de las Naciones Unidas

councillor ['kaʊnsələ'], *Am:* -ə˞] *n*, **councilor** *n Am* concejal(a) *m(f)*

counseling *n Am*, **counselling** *n no pl* asesoramiento *m*

counsellor ['kaʊnsələ'] *n*, **counselor** *n Am* asesor(a) *m(f);* **marriage guidance ~** consejero, -a *m, f* matrimonial

count¹ [kaʊnt] *n* conde *m*

count² [kaʊnt] I. *vt* contar; **to ~ sth a success/failure** considerar algo un éxito/fracaso II. *vi* contar

countenance ['kaʊntɪnəns, *Am:* -tənəns] *n no pl, form* rostro *m*

counter ['kaʊntə', *Am:* -tə˞] I. *n* (*service point*) mostrador *m;* **over the ~** sin receta médica; **under the ~** *fig* subrepticiamente II. *vt* contrarrestar

counteract [ˌkaʊntər'ækt, *Am:* -t̬ə˞-] *vt* contrarrestar

counterattack ['kɑ:ʊntərətæk, *Am:* 'kaʊnt̬ə˞-] I. *n* contraataque *m* II. *vt* contraatacar III. *vi* (*attack in return*) contraatacar

counterfeit ['kaʊntəfɪt, *Am:* -t̬ə˞-] I. *adj* (*money*) falso II. *vt* falsificar

counterpart ['kaʊntəpɑ:t, *Am:* -t̬ə˞pɑ:rt] *n* contrapartida *f;* POL homólogo, -a *m, f*

counterproductive [ˌkaʊntəprə'dʌktɪv, *Am:* -t̬ə˞-] *adj* contraproducente

countess ['kaʊntɪs, *Am:* -t̬ɪs] *n* condesa *f*

country ['kʌntrɪ] *n* 1. *no pl* (*rural area*) campo *m* 2.<-ies> (*political unit*) país *m*

country house *n* casa *f* solariega

countryside ['kʌntrɪsaɪd] *n no pl* campo *m*, verde *m AmC, Méx*

county ['kaʊntɪ, *Am:* -t̬ɪ] <-ies> *n* condado *m*

coup [ku:] <coups> *n* golpe *m*

couple ['kʌpl] *n* 1. *no pl* par *m;* **the first ~ of weeks** las primeras dos semanas 2. + *sing/pl vb* (*two people*) pareja *f;* (*married*) matrimonio *m*

coupon ['ku:pɒn, *Am:* -pɑ:n] *n* 1. (*voucher*) vale *m* 2. (*return-slip of advert*) cupón *m*

courage ['kʌrɪdʒ] *n* coraje *m;* **to show great ~** mostrar gran valor

courageous [kə'reɪdʒəs] *adj* valiente

courier ['kʊrɪə', *Am:* 'kʊrɪə˞] *n* 1. (*tour guide*) guía *mf* 2. (*delivers post*) mensajero, -a *m, f*

course [kɔ:s, *Am:* kɔ:rs] *n* curso *m;* **to be off ~** *a. fig* desviarse; SPORTS pista *f*; (*golf*) campo *m*

court [kɔːt, *Am:* kɔːrt] I. *n* 1. (*room for trials*) juzgado *m* 2. (*judicial body*) tribunal *m* 3. (*marked out area for playing*) cancha *f*; (*tennis*) pista *f* 4. (*sovereign*) corte *f* II. *vt* (*woman*) cortejar

courteous ['kɜːtɪəs, *Am:* 'kɜːrt̬ɪ-] *adj* cortés

courtesy ['kɜːtəsɪ, *Am:* 'kɜːrt̬ə-] <-ies> *n* gentileza *f*, cortesía *f*

courtroom ['kɔːtrʊm, *Am:* 'kɔːrtru:m] *n* sala *f* de tribunal **courtship** *n* noviazgo *m*, cortejo *m* **courtyard** *n* patio *m*

cousin ['kʌzn] *n* primo, -a *m*, *f*

cove [kəʊv, *Am:* koʊv] *n* cala *f*

covenant ['kʌvənənt, *Am:* -ænt] *n* contrato *m*

cover ['kʌvəʳ, *Am:* -ɚ] I. *n* 1. (*top*) tapa *f* 2. (*outer sheet: of a book*) cubierta *f*; (*of a magazine*) portada *f* II. *vt* 1. (*hide: eyes, ears*) tapar; (*head*) cubrir 2. (*put over*) tapar 3. (*keep warm*) abrigar 4. (*deal with*) contemplar

♦**cover up** I. *vt* (*protect*) cubrir II. *vi* to ~ **for sb** encubrir a alguien

coverage ['kʌvərɪdʒ] *n no pl* cobertura *f*

covered *adj* cubierto

covering *n* capa *f*

cow [kaʊ] *n* vaca *f*

coward ['kaʊəd, *Am:* 'kaʊɚd] *n* cobarde *mf*

cowardice ['kaʊədɪs, *Am:* 'kaʊɚ-] *n no pl* cobardía *f*

cowardly ['kaʊədlɪ, *Am:* 'kaʊɚd-] *adj* cobarde

cowboy ['kaʊbɔɪ] *n* vaquero *m*, cowboy *m*, tropero *m Arg*

cox ['kɒksn, *Am:* 'kɑːk-] <-es> *n*, **coxswain** *n form* timonel *mf*

coy [kɔɪ, *Am:* -ɚ] <-er, -est> *adj* coqueto

coyote [kɔɪ'əʊt, *Am:* kaɪ'oʊt̬ɪ] *n* coyote *m*

cozy ['kəʊzɪ, *Am:* 'koʊ-] *adj Am* cómodo

CP *n abbr of* **Communist Party** PC *m*

crab [kræb] *n* cangrejo *m*, jaiba *f AmL*

crack [kræk] I. *n* 1. (*fissure*) grieta *f* 2. (*sharp sound*) estallido *m* 3. *inf* (*drug*) crack *m* II. *adj* de primera III. *vt* 1. (*break*) romper 2. (*resolve*) resolver IV. *vi* romperse; (*paintwork*) agrietarse

♦**crack down** *vi* to ~ **on sb/sth** tomar medidas enérgicas contra alguien/algo

crackdown ['krækdaʊn] *n* ofensiva *f*

cracked [krækt] *adj* agrietado; (*crazy*) chiflado

cracker ['krækəʳ, *Am:* -ɚ] *n* 1. (*dry biscuit*) galleta *f* 2. *Brit* (*device*) sorpresa *f*

crackle ['krækl] I. *vi* (*of paper*) crujir; (*telephone line*) hacer ruido II. *vt* hacer crujir III. *n* (*of paper*) crujido *m*; (*of a telephone line*) ruido *m*

cradle ['kreɪdl] *n* (*baby's bed*) cuna *f*; **from the ~ to the grave** durante toda la vida

craft [krɑːft, *Am:* kræft] *n* 1. (*means of transport*) nave *f* 2. *no pl* (*special skill*) arte *m*

craftiness *n no pl* astucia *f*

craftsman ['krɑːftsmən, *Am:* 'kræfts-] <-men> *n* artesano *m*

crafty ['krɑːftɪ, *Am:* 'kræf-] <-ier, -iest> *adj* astuto

crag [kræg] *n* peñasco *m*

cram [kræm] <-mm-> I. *vt* meter; to ~ **sth with** llenar algo de II. *vi* memorizar

cramp [kræmp] *n Brit, Aus* calambre *m*

cranberry ['krænbərɪ, *Am:* -ˌber-] <-ies> *n* arándano *m*

crane [kreɪn] *n* 1. (*vehicle for lifting*) grúa *f* 2. ZOOL grulla *f*

crap [kræp] *n vulg* 1. (*excrement*) mierda *f* 2. (*nonsense*) estupidez *f*

crash [kræʃ] I. *n* <-es> 1. (*accident*) accidente *m*; (*of a car*) choque *m* 2. (*noise*) estrépito *m* II. *vi* 1. (*have an accident*) chocar; (*plane*) estrellarse 2. (*make loud noise*) retumbar III. *vt* chocar

crass [kræs] *adj* grosero

crate [kreɪt] *n* cajón *m*

crater ['kreɪtər, *Am:* -t̬ər] *n* cráter *m*

crave [kreɪv] *vt* ansiar

craving ['kreɪvɪŋ] *n* ansia *f*

crawl [krɔːl, *Am:* krɑːl] *vi* gatear

crayon ['kreɪən, *Am:* -ɑːn] *n* lápiz *m* de color

craze [kreɪz] *n* manía *f*

craziness ['kreɪzɪnɪs] *n no pl* locura *f*

crazy ['kreɪzi] <-ier, -iest> *adj* loco, tarado *AmL;* **to go** ~ volverse loco

creak [kriːk] I. *vi* chirriar II. *n* chirrido *m*

cream [kriːm] *n* 1. *no pl* (*milk fat*) nata *f;* **single** ~ *Brit* crema *f* de leche; **double** ~ *Brit* nata *f* para montar 2. (*cosmetic product*) crema *f*

cream cheese *n no pl* queso *m* para untar

creamy ['kriːmi] <-ier, -iest> *adj* 1. (*smooth*) cremoso 2. (*off-white*) de color hueso

crease [kriːs] I. *n* (*fold*) arruga *f;* (*hat*) pliegue *m* II. *vt* arrugar

create [kriːˈeɪt] *vt* crear

creation [kriːˈeɪʃn] *n* creación *f*

creative [kriːˈeɪtɪv, *Am:* -t̬ɪv] *adj* creativo

creator [kriːˈeɪtər, *Am:* -t̬ər] *n* creador(a) *m(f)*

creature ['kriːtʃər, *Am:* -tʃər] *n* criatura *f*

creche [kreɪʃ] *n Brit, Aus* guardería *f*

credentials [krɪˈdenʃlz] *npl* credenciales *fpl*

credibility [ˌkredɪˈbɪləti, *Am:* -əˈbɪləti] *n no pl* credibilidad *f*

credible ['kredəbl] *adj* verosímil

credit ['kredɪt] *n* 1. (*honour*) honor *m;* (*recognition*) mérito *m;* **to be a** ~ **to sb** ser un orgullo [*o* honor] para alguien 2. FIN crédito *m;* **to buy sth on** ~ comprar algo a plazos 3. *pl* CINE títulos *mpl* de crédito

credit card *n* tarjeta *f* de crédito

creditor ['kredɪtər, *Am:* -t̬ər] *n* acreedor(a) *m(f)*

creed [kriːd] *n* credo *m;* **the Creed** el Credo

creek [kriːk] *n* 1. *Brit* (*narrow bay*) cala *f* 2. *Am, Aus* (*stream*) riachuelo *m*

creep [kriːp] I. <crept, crept> *vi* 1. (*crawl*) arrastrarse 2. (*move imperceptibly*) deslizarse II. *n* 1. *inf* (*sycophant*) pelotillero, -a *m, f,* lambiscón, -ona *m, f Méx,* lambón, -ona *m, f Col* 2. (*pervert*) pervertido, -a *m, f*

crepe [kreɪp] *n* GASTR crepé *f,* crêpe *f*

crept [krept] *pt, pp of* **creep**

crescent ['kresnt] *n* media luna *f*

crest [krest] *n* cresta *f*

Crete [kriːt] *n* Creta *f*

crew [kruː] *n + sing/pl vb* NAUT, AVIAT tripulación *f;* **ground/flight** ~ personal de tierra/de vuelo

crib [krɪb] I. *n* 1. *Am, Brit* (*baby's bed*) cuna *f* 2. (*nativity scene*) belén *m* 3. *inf* SCHOOL chuleta *f,* acordeón *m Méx,* machete *m RíoPl* II. <-bb-> *vi inf* SCHOOL copiar; **to** ~ **from sb** copiar de alguien

cricket¹ ['krɪkɪt] *n no pl* SPORTS cricket *m*

cricket² ['krɪkɪt] *n* grillo *m,* siripita *f Bol*

crime [kraɪm] *n* 1. (*illegal act*) delito *m;* (*more serious*) crimen *m;* **a** ~ **against humanity** un crimen contra la humanidad 2. (*criminal activity*) delincuencia *f;* ~ **rate** índice *m* de criminalidad

criminal ['krɪmɪnl] I. *n* (*offender*) delincuente *mf;* (*more serious*) criminal *mf* II. *adj* (*illegal*) delictivo; (*more serious*) criminal

crimson ['krɪmzn] *adj* (*colour*) carmesí; **to blush** ~ ponerse como un tomate

cripple ['krɪpl] I. *n* lisiado, -a *m, f* II. *vt* lisiar

crippling *adj fig* terrible

crisis ['kraɪsɪs] <crises> *n* crisis *f inv;* **to go through a** ~ atravesar una crisis

crisp [krɪsp] I. <-er, -est> *adj* 1. (*snow, bacon*) crujiente 2. (*apple, lettuce*) fresco 3. (*sharp*) nítido II. *n Brit pl* (*thin fried potatoes*) patatas *fpl* de churrero, papas *fpl* fritas *AmL*

criterion [kraɪˈtɪəriən, *Am:* -ˈtɪri-] <-ria> *n* criterio *m*

critic ['krɪtɪk, *Am:* 'krɪt̬-] *n* crítico, -a *m, f*

critical ['krɪtɪkl, *Am:* 'krɪt̬-] *adj* crítico

criticism ['krɪtɪsɪzəm, *Am:* 'krɪt̬-] *n* crítica *f;* **to take** ~ admitir la crítica

criticize ['krɪtɪsaɪz, *Am:* 'krɪt̬-] *vt, vi* criticar

croak [krəʊk, *Am:* kroʊk] **I.** *vi* (*crow*) graznar; (*frog*) croar **II.** *vt* decir con voz ronca **III.** *n* (*crow*) graznido *m;* (*frog*) croar *m*

Croat ['krəʊæt, *Am:* 'kroʊ-] *n* croata *mf*

Croatia [krəʊ'eɪʃɪə, *Am:* kroʊ-] *n* Croacia *f*

Croatian [krəʊ'eɪʃɪən, *Am:* kroʊ-] *adj* croata

crockery ['krɒkərɪ, *Am:* 'krɑːkə-] *n no pl* vajilla *f*

crocodile ['krɒkədaɪl, *Am:* 'krɑː-kə-] <-(s)> *n* cocodrilo *m*

crook [krʊk] *n* **1.** (*criminal*) delincuente *mf* **2.** (*staff: of shepherd*) cayado *m*

crooked ['krʊkɪd] *adj* **1.** (*not straight*) torcido **2.** *inf* (*dishonest*) deshonesto

crop [krɒp, *Am:* krɑːp] *n* cultivo *m*
◆ **crop up** *vi* surgir

cross [krɒs, *Am:* krɑːs] **I.** *vt* **1.** (*go across: road, threshold*) cruzar; (*desert, river, sea*) atravesar **2.** (*place crosswise*) **to** ~ **one's legs** cruzar las piernas **3.** BIO cruzar **4.** (*mark with a cross*) marcar con una cruz **II.** *vi* **1.** (*intersect*) cruzarse **2.** (*go across*) cruzar **III.** *n* **1.** *a.* REL cruz *f;* **the sign of the** ~ la señal de la cruz **2.** (*crossing: of streets, roads*) cruce *m* **3.** BIO cruce *m,* cruza *f AmL* **4.** (*mixture*) mezcla *f* **IV.** *adj* enfadado; **to be** ~ **about sth** estar enfadado por algo

crossbar *n* barra *f* transversal

cross-country *adj* a campo traviesa

crossing ['krɒsɪŋ, *Am:* 'krɑːsɪŋ] *n* paso *m;* **level** ~ RAIL paso *m* a nivel; **border** ~ paso fronterizo; **pedestrian** ~ paso de peatones

crossroads *n inv* cruce *m* **cross-section** *n* sección *f* transversal **cross-**

word (**puzzle**) *n* crucigrama *m*

crotch [krɒtʃ, *Am:* krɑːtʃ] <-es> *n* entrepierna *f*

crouch [kraʊtʃ] *vi* **to** ~ (**down**) agacharse; **to be** ~**ing** estar en cuclillas

crow [krəʊ, *Am:* kroʊ] *n* cuervo *m;* **as the** ~ **flies** *fig* en línea recta

crowd [kraʊd] **I.** *n* + *sing/pl vb* **1.** (*throng*) multitud *f;* **there was quite a** ~ había mucha gente **2.** (*masses*) masas *fpl;* **to stand out from the** ~ *fig* destacar(se) **II.** *vt* llenar; **to** ~ **the streets/a stadium** abarrotar las calles/un estadio

crowded *adj* lleno; ~ **together** amontonados; **the bar was** ~ había mucha gente en el bar

crown [kraʊn] **I.** *n* corona *f;* **the Crown** (*monarchy*) la Corona **II.** *vt* coronar; **to** ~ **sb queen** coronar reina a alguien

crucial ['kruːʃl] *adj* (*decisive*) decisivo; (*moment*) crucial; **it is** ~ **that ...** es de vital importancia que... +*subj*

crucible ['kruːsɪbl] *n a. fig* crisol *m*

crucifix [ˌkruːsɪ'fɪks] <-es> *n* crucifijo *m*

crucifixion [ˌkruːsɪ'fɪkʃn] *n* crucifixión *f*

crucify ['kruːsɪfaɪ] <-ie-> *vt* crucificar

crude [kruːd] *adj* **1.** (*unrefined*) bruto; (*oil*) crudo **2.** (*vulgar*) basto

cruel [krʊəl] <-(l)ler, -(l)lest> *adj* cruel; **to be** ~ **to sb** ser cruel con alguien

cruelty ['krʊəltɪ, *Am:* -t̬ɪ] <-ies> *n* crueldad *f*

cruise [kruːz] **I.** *n* crucero *m;* ~ **ship** transatlántico *m;* **to go on a** ~ hacer un crucero **II.** *vi* hacer un crucero

cruiser ['kruːzər, *Am:* -ɚ] *n* **1.** (*warship*) crucero *m* **2.** (*pleasure boat*) embarcación *f* de recreo

crumb [krʌm] *n* **1.** (*of bread*) miga *f* **2.** (*small amount*) pizca *f;* **a small** ~ **of ...** un poco de...

crumble ['krʌmbl] **I.** *vt* **1.** (*bread, biscuit*) desmigajar **2.** (*stone, cheese*) desmenuzar **II.** *vi* (*empire*) desmoronarse; (*plaster, stone*) desmenuzarse

crumple ['krʌmpl] *vt* arrugar

crunch [krʌntʃ] I. *vt* 1. (*in the mouth*) masticar (haciendo ruido) 2. (*grind*) hacer crujir II. *vi* crujir

crunchy [krʌntʃi] *adj* crujiente

crusade [kru:'seɪd] *n* 1. REL, HIST cruzada *f* 2. *fig* campaña *f;* **a ~ for/against sth** una campaña a favor/en contra de algo

crush [krʌʃ] I. *vt* 1. (*compress*) aplastar; **to be ~ed to death** morir aplastado 2. (*grind*) machacar 3. (*shock severely*) abatir II. *vi* 1. (*clothes, paper*) arrugarse 2. (*people*) apretujarse III. <-es> *n* 1. *no pl* (*throng*) muchedumbre *f;* **there was a great ~** había una gran aglomeración 2. *inf* (*temporary infatuation*) enamoramiento *m;* **to have a ~ on sb** encapricharse de alguien

crushing I. *n* aplastamiento *m* II. *adj* aplastante

crust [krʌst] *n* 1. GASTR, BOT corteza *f;* (*dry bread*) mendrugo *m;* **~ of the Earth** GEO corteza terrestre 2. (*hard external layer*) capa *f;* **a ~ of ice/dirt** una capa de hielo/suciedad

crutch [krʌtʃ] <-es> *n* MED muleta *f*

cry [kraɪ] I. <-ie-> *vi* 1. (*weep*) llorar; **to ~ for joy** llorar de alegría 2. (*shout*) gritar; (*animal*) aullar; **to ~ for help** pedir ayuda a gritos II. <-ie-> *vt* gritar III. *n* 1. *no pl* (*weeping*) llanto *m;* **to have a ~** llorar 2. (*shout*) grito *m* 3. ZOOL aullido *m*

crypt [krɪpt] *n* cripta *f*

cryptic ['krɪptɪk] *adj* críptico

crystal ['krɪstl] I. *n* cristal *m* II. *adj* de cristal

cub [kʌb] *n* cachorro *m*

Cuba ['kju:bə] *n* Cuba *f*

Cuban ['kju:bən] *adj* cubano

cube [kju:b] *n* cubo *m;* **ice ~** cubito *m* de hielo

cubic ['kju:bɪk] *adj* cúbico

cubicle ['kju:bɪkl] *n* cubículo *m*

cuckoo ['kʊku:, *Am:* 'ku:ku:] *n* cuco *m*

cucumber ['kju:kʌmbəʳ, *Am:* -bɚ] *n* pepino *m;* (**as**) **cool as a ~** *inf* más fresco que una lechuga

cuddle ['kʌdl] I. *vi* abrazarse II. *n* abrazo *m;* **to give sb a ~** abrazar a alguien

cuddly <-ier, -iest> *adj* mimoso; **~ toy** juguete *m* de peluche

cue [kju:] *n* 1. THEAT pie *m* 2. (*billiards*) taco *m;* **~ ball** bola *f* blanca

cuff [kʌf] I. *n* 1. (*end of sleeve*) puño *m* 2. (*slap*) cachete *m* II. *vt* (*slap playfully*) dar un cachete a

cuisine [kwɪ'zi:n] *n no pl* cocina *f*

cul-de-sac ['kʌldəsæk] <-s *o* culs--de-sac> *n a. fig* callejón *m* sin salida

culinary ['kʌlɪnerɪ, *Am:* -əner-] *adj* culinario

culprit ['kʌlprɪt] *n* culpable *mf*

cult [kʌlt] *n* 1. (*worship*) culto *m;* **fitness ~** culto al cuerpo 2. (*sect*) secta *f*

cultivate ['kʌltɪveɪt, *Am:* -t̬ə-] *vt a. fig* cultivar

cultivated *adj* 1. AGR cultivado 2. (*person*) culto

cultivation [ˌkʌltɪ'veɪʃn, *Am:* -t̬ə-] *n no pl* 1. AGR cultivo *m;* **to be under ~** estar en cultivo 2. (*of a person*) cultura *f*

cultural ['kʌltʃərəl] *adj* cultural

culture ['kʌltʃəʳ, *Am:* -tʃɚ] I. *n* 1. (*way of life*) cultura *f;* **enterprise ~** cultura de empresa 2. *no pl* (*arts*) cultura *f* 3. AGR cultivo *m* II. *vt* cultivar

cultured ['kʌltʃəd, *Am:* -tʃɚd] *adj* 1. AGR cultivado 2. (*intellectual*) culto

cumbersome ['kʌmbəsəm] *adj* engorroso

cunning ['kʌnɪŋ] I. *adj* astuto II. *n no pl* astucia *f*

cunt [kʌnt] *n* 1. *vulg* coño *m* 2. *vulg* (*despicable person*) cabrón, -a *m, f*

cup [kʌp] *n* 1. (*container*) taza *f;* **egg ~** huevera *f* 2. (*trophy*) copa *f;* **the World Cup** la copa del mundo

cupboard ['kʌbəd, *Am:* -ɚd] *n* armario *m;* **built-in ~** armario empotrado

curator [kjʊə'reɪtəʳ, *Am:* 'kjʊreɪt̬ɚ] *n* director(a) *m(f)* (*de museo o galería*)

curb [kɜ:b, *Am:* kɜ:rb] *vt* frenar

cure ['kjʊə^r, *Am:* 'kjʊr] I. *vt* **1.** MED, GASTR curar **2.** (*leather*) curtir II. *vi* curar; (*meat, fish*) curarse III. *n* cura *f*

curfew ['kɜːfjuː, *Am:* 'kɜːr-] *n* (toque *m* de) queda *f*

curiosity [ˌkjʊərɪ'ɒsətɪ, *Am:* ˌkjʊrɪ'ɑːsətɪ] <-ies> *n* curiosidad *f*

curious ['kjʊərɪəs] *adj* curioso; **it is ~ that** es curioso que +*subj*

curl [kɜːl, *Am:* kɜːrl] I. *n* rizo *m* II. *vt* rizar; **to ~ oneself up** acurrucarse

curly ['kɜːlɪ, *Am:* 'kɜːr-] <-ier, -iest> *adj* (*hair*) rizado

currant ['kʌrənt, *Am:* 'kɜːr-] *n* pasa *f* de Corinto

currency ['kʌrənsɪ, *Am:* 'kɜːr-] <-ies> *n* **1.** FIN moneda *f*; **foreign ~** divisas *fpl* **2.** *no pl* (*acceptance*) difusión *f*

current ['kʌrənt, *Am:* 'kɜːr-] I. *adj* actual II. *n a.* ELEC corriente *f*

currently *adv* **1.** (*at present*) actualmente **2.** (*commonly*) comúnmente

curry¹ ['kʌrɪ, *Am:* 'kɜːr-] <-ies> *n* curry *m*

curry² *vt* **to ~ favour with sb** buscar el favor de alguien

curse [kɜːs, *Am:* kɜːrs] I. *vi* **1.** (*swear*) soltar palabrotas **2.** (*blaspheme*) blasfemar II. *vt* **1.** (*swear at*) insultar **2.** (*damn*) maldecir; **~ it!** ¡maldito sea! III. *n* **1.** (*oath*) palabrota *f*; **to let out a ~** soltar un taco **2.** (*evil spell*) maldición *f*; **to put a ~ on sb** echar una maldición a alguien

curtain ['kɜːtn, *Am:* 'kɜːrtn] *n* **1.** *a. fig* cortina *f*; **to draw the ~s** correr las cortinas **2.** THEAT telón *m*; **to raise/lower the ~** subir/bajar el telón

curve [kɜːv, *Am:* kɜːrv] I. *n a.* MAT curva *f* II. *vi* estar curvado; (*path, road*) hacer una curva; **to ~ round to the left** (*path*) torcer a mano izquierda

cushion ['kʊʃn] *n* cojín *m*

cushy ['kʊʃɪ] <-ier, -iest> *adj inf* fácil; **a ~ job** un chollo

custard ['kʌstəd, *Am:* -təd] *n no pl* GASTR ≈ natillas *fpl*

custody ['kʌstədɪ] *n no pl* **1.** (*care*) cuidado *m;* **in the ~ of sb** al cuidado de alguien **2.** (*guardianship*) custodia *f*

custom ['kʌstəm] *n* **1.** (*tradition*) costumbre *f* **2.** *no pl* (*clientele*) clientela *f* **3.** *pl* (*place*) aduana *f*

customary ['kʌstəmərɪ, *Am:* -mer-] *adj* **1.** (*traditional*) tradicional; **it is ~ to** +*infin* es costumbre +*infin* **2.** (*usual*) habitual

customer ['kʌstəmə^r, *Am:* -mɚ] *n* cliente, -a *m, f*; **regular ~** cliente habitual

cut [kʌt] I. *n* **1.** (*incision*) *a.* FASHION corte *m* **2.** (*gash, wound*) herida *f*, cortada *f* AmL **3.** (*decrease*) reducción *f*; **a ~ in staff** una reducción de plantilla II. *adj* cortado; (*glass, diamond*) tallado III. <cut, cut, -tt-> *vt* **1.** (*make an incision*) cortar; **to have one's hair ~** cortarse el pelo **2.** (*saw down: trees*) talar **3.** (*decrease size, amount, length*) reducir **4.** (*cease*) dejar de; **~ all this noise!** ¡basta ya de hacer ruido!

◆ **cut back** *vt* reducir; **to ~ (on) sth** hacer recortes en algo

◆ **cut down** I. *vt* **1.** (*tree*) talar **2.** (*reduce: production*) reducir; **to ~ expenses** recortar gastos II. *vi* **to ~ on sth** reducir el consumo de algo; **to ~ on smoking** fumar menos

◆ **cut in** *vi* (*interrupt*) **to ~ (on sb)** interrumpir (a alguien)

◆ **cut off** *vt* **1.** (*sever*) *a.* ELEC, TEL cortar **2.** (*amputate*) amputar **3.** (*stop talking*) interrumpir **4.** (*separate, isolate*) aislar; **to be ~ by the snow** estar incomunicado por la nieve

cute [kjuːt] *adj* mono *inf*

cutlery ['kʌtlərɪ] *n no pl* cubiertos *fpl*

cutting ['kʌtɪŋ, *Am:* 'kʌt̬-] *n* **1.** (*act*) corte *m* **2.** (*piece*) recorte *m*

CV [ˌsiː'viː] *n abbr of* **curriculum vitae** CV *m*

cybercafé ['saɪbəˌkæfeɪ] *n* cibercafé *m*

cybercash ['saɪbəˌkæʃ] *n no pl* dinero *m* electrónico

cybernaut [ˌsaɪbə'nɔːt] *n* ciber-

nauta *mf*
cyberspace *n no pl* ciberespacio *m*
cycle[1] ['saɪkl] **I.** *n* bicicleta *f* **II.** *vi* ir en bicicleta
cycle[2] ['saɪkl] *n* ciclo *m*
cyclic ['saɪklɪk] *adj,* **cyclical** ['saɪklɪkl] *adj* cíclico
cycling ['saɪklɪŋ] *n no pl* SPORTS ciclismo *m*
cyclist ['saɪklɪst] *n* SPORTS ciclista *mf*
cyclone ['saɪkləʊn, *Am:* -kloʊn] *n* METEO ciclón *m*
cylinder ['sɪlɪndəʳ, *Am:* -dəʳ] *n* cilindro *m*
cynic ['sɪnɪk] *n* cínico, -a *m, f,* valemadrista *mf Méx*
cynical ['sɪnɪkl] *adj* cínico
cynicism ['sɪnɪsɪzəm] *n no pl* cinismo *m*
Cypriot ['sɪprɪət] *adj* chipriota
Cyprus ['saɪprəs] *n* GEO Chipre *m*
czar [zɑːʳ, *Am:* zɑːr] *n Am* zar *m*
Czech [tʃek] *adj* checo
Czech Republic *n* República *f* Checa

D d

D, d [diː] *n* **1.** (*letter*) D, d *f;* ~ **for David** *Brit,* ~ **for dog** *Am* D de Dolores **2.** MUS re *m*
DA [ˌdiːˈeɪ] *n Am abbr of* **District Attorney** fiscal *mf* del distrito
dab [dæb] <-bb-> *vt* tocar ligeramente
dabble ['dæbl] <-ling> *vi* **to** ~ **in sth** interesarse superficialmente por algo
dad ['dæd] *n inf* papá *m*
daddy ['dædi] *n childspeak, inf* papaíto *m,* tata *m AmL*
daffodil ['dæfədɪl] *n* narciso *m*
daft [dɑːft, *Am:* dæft] *adj Brit, inf* tonto; **to be** ~ **about sth** estar loco por algo
dagger ['dægəʳ, *Am:* -ɚ] *n* puñal *m;* **to look** ~**s at sb** fulminar a alguien

con la mirada
dahlia ['deɪliə, *Am:* 'dæljə] *n* dalia *f*

> **[?]** El **Dáil** es la cámara baja del Oireachtas, parlamento de la **Irish Republic.** Tiene 166 diputados, elegidos democráticamente para un mandato de cinco años. La cámara alta, el **Seanad** (senado), consta de 60 senadores, de los cuales 11 son nombrados por el **taoiseach** (primer ministro), 6 por las universidades irlandesas y otros 43 son nombrados de forma que todos los intereses profesionales, culturales y económicos estén representados.

daily ['deɪli] **I.** *adj* diario; **on a ~ basis** por días; **to earn one's ~ bread** *inf* ganarse el pan de cada día **II.** *adv* a diario; **twice ~** dos veces al día **III.** <-ies> *n* PUBL diario *m*
dainty ['deɪnti, *Am:* -ti] <-ier, -iest> *adj* delicado
dairy ['deəri, *Am:* 'deri] *n* **1.** (*shop*) lechería *f* **2.** *Am* (*farm*) vaquería *f,* tambo *m Arg*
dairy produce *n* productos *mpl* lácteos
dais ['deɪɪs] *n* ARCHIT tarima *f*
daisy ['deɪzi] <-ies> *n* margarita *f;* **to fell as fresh as a ~** sentirse tan fresco como una rosa
dally ['dæli] <-ie-> *vi* perder el tiempo; **to ~ over sth** perder el tiempo haciendo algo; **to ~ with sb** coquetear con alguien
dam [dæm] **I.** *n* presa *f* **II.** <-mm-> *vt* represar
damage ['dæmɪdʒ] **I.** *vt* (*building, object*) dañar; (*health, reputation*) perjudicar **II.** *n no pl* **1.** (*harm: to objects*) daño *m;* (*to pride, reputation*) perjuicio *m* **2.** *pl* LAW daños *mpl* y perjuicios
dame [deɪm] *n* **1.** *Brit* (*title*) dama *f* **2.** *Am, inf* (*woman*) tía *f,* tipa *f AmL*
damn [dæm] *inf* **I.** *interj* mierda

II. *adj* maldito; **to be a ~ fool** ser tonto de remate **III.** *vt* **1.**(*curse*) maldecir **2.** REL condenar **IV.** *adv* **to be ~ lucky** tener una suerte increíble; **~ all** *Brit* absolutamente nada **V.** *n no pl* **I don't give a ~!** ¡me importa un comino!

damnation [dæm'neɪʃən] *n no pl* a. REL condenación *f*

damned *adj inf* maldito

damp [dæmp] **I.** *adj* húmedo **II.** *n no pl, Brit, Aus* humedad *f* **III.** *vt* humedecer

dampen ['dæmpən] *vt* humedecer; **to ~ sb's enthusiasm** apagar el entusiasmo de alguien

dampness *n no pl* humedad *f*

dance [dɑːnts, *Am:* dænts] **I.** <-cing> *vi, vt* bailar; **to go dancing** ir a bailar; **to ~ with joy** dar saltos de alegría **II.** *n* baile *m*

dance music *n no pl* música *f* de baile

dancer ['dɑːntsə^r, *Am:* 'dæntsə-] *n* bailarín, -ina *m, f*

dancing *n no pl* baile *m*

dandelion ['dændɪlaɪən, *Am:* -də-] *n* diente *m* de león

dandruff ['dændrʌf, *Am:* -drəf] *n no pl* caspa *f*

dandy ['dændi] **I.** <-ies> *n* dandi *m* **II.** <-ier, -iest> *adj Am* estupendo

Dane [deɪn] *n* danés, -esa *m, f*

danger ['deɪndʒə^r, *Am:* -dʒə-] *n* peligro *m;* **to be in ~** correr peligro

dangerous ['deɪndʒərəs] *adj* peligroso, riesgoso *AmL*

dangle ['dæŋgl] **I.** <-ling> *vi* colgar **II.** <-ling> *vt fig* **to ~ sth before sb** tentar a alguien con algo

Danish ['deɪnɪʃ] *adj* danés, -esa

dank [dæŋk] *adj* húmedo

Danube ['dænjuːb] *n* Danubio *m*

dapper ['dæpə^r, *Am:* -ə-] *adj* atildado

dare [deə^r, *Am:* der] <-ring> *vt* **1.**(*risk doing*) **(not) to ~ to do sth** (no) atreverse a hacer algo; **don't you ~!** ¡ni se te ocurra! **2.**(*challenge*) **to ~ sb (to do sth)** retar a alguien (a hacer algo) **3.** I **~ say** me lo imagino

daring ['deərɪŋ, *Am:* 'derɪŋ] **I.** *adj* **1.**(*courageous*) temerario **2.**(*provocative: dress*) atrevido **II.** *n no pl* osadía *f*

dark [dɑːk, *Am:* dɑːrk] **I.** *adj* (*without light, black*) oscuro; (*complexion, hair*) moreno; *fig* sombrío; **~ chocolate** *Am, Aus* chocolate *m* sin leche; **to look on the ~ side of things** ver el lado malo de las cosas **II.** *n no pl* oscuridad *f;* **to be afraid of the ~** tener miedo de la oscuridad; **to do sth after ~** hacer algo después de que anochezca; **to keep sb in the ~ about sth** ocultar algo a alguien

Dark Ages *npl* HIST **the ~** la Alta Edad Media; *fig* la prehistoria

darken ['dɑːkən, *Am:* 'dɑːr-] *vi* oscurecerse; (*sky*) nublarse; *fig* ensombrecerse

darkness *n no pl* oscuridad *f*

darkroom *n* cámara *f* oscura

darling ['dɑːlɪŋ, *Am:* 'dɑːr-] *n* cariño *mf*

darn [dɑːn, *Am:* dɑːrn] *vt* zurcir

dart [dɑːt, *Am:* dɑːrt] **I.** *n* **1.**(*arrow*) dardo *m;* **to play ~s** jugar a los dardos **2.**(*movement*) **to make a ~ for sth** precipitarse hacia algo **II.** *vi* **to ~ for sth** precipitarse hacia algo

dash [dæʃ] **I.** <-es> *n* **1.**(*rush*) **to make a ~ for it** huir precipitadamente **2.**(*pinch*) poquito *m;* **a ~ of colour** una nota de color **3.** TYPO guión *m* **II.** *vi* precipitarse **III.** *vt* romper; (*hopes*) defraudar

dashboard *n* salpicadero *m*

dashing *adj* gallardo

DAT [dæt] *n abbr of* **digital audio tape** DAT *m*

data ['deɪtə, *Am:* 'deɪtə] *n* + *sing/pl vb* a. INFOR datos *mpl*

database *n* base *f* de datos **data processing** *n no pl* procesamiento *m* de datos

date¹ [deɪt] **I.** *n* **1.**(*calendar day*) fecha *f; what ~ is it today?* ¿a qué fecha estamos?; **to be out of ~** estar pasado de moda **2.**(*appointment*) cita *f;* **to make a ~ with sb** quedar con alguien **3.** *Am, inf* (*person*) novio, -a *m, f* **II.** *vt* **1.** (*recognize age of*) fechar **2.** *Am, inf* (*have relationship with*) **to ~ sb** salir con alguien **III.** *vi* **to ~ back to** remontarse a

date² *n* (*fruit*) dátil *m;* (*tree*) palmera *f* datilera

dated ['deɪtɪd, *Am:* -ṭɪd] *adj* anticuado

daub [dɔːb, *Am:* dɑːb] *vt* **to ~ sth with sth** manchar algo de algo

daughter ['dɔːtəʳ, *Am:* 'dɑːt̬ə] *n* hija *f*

daughter-in-law <daughters-in--law> *n* nuera *f*

daunting [dɔːntɪŋ, *Am:* dɑːnt-] *adj* amedrentador

dawdle ['dɔːdl, *Am:* 'dɑː-] *vi* holgazanear

dawn [dɔːn, *Am:* dɑːn] **I.** *n* alba *f,* amanezca *f Méx; fig* nacimiento *m;* **at ~** al alba **II.** *vi* amanecer; *fig* nacer; **it ~ed on him that ...** cayó en la cuenta de que...

day [deɪ] *n* día *m;* (*working period*) jornada *f;* **~ after ~** día tras día; **~ by ~** día a día; **all ~** (**long**) todo el día; **any ~ now** cualquier día de estos; **by ~** de día; **from that ~ on(wards)** desde ese día, de aquí en adelante; **from one ~ to the next** de un día para otro; **two ~s ago** hace dos días; **the ~ before yesterday** anteayer; **the ~ after tomorrow** pasado mañana; **in the** (**good**) **old ~s** en los buenos tiempos; **in this ~ and age** en estos tiempos nuestros; **to have seen better ~s** haber conocido tiempos mejores; **to call it a ~** dejarlo para otro día; **~ in ~ out** un día sí y otro también

daybreak *n no pl* alba *m*

daydream I. *vi* soñar despierto **II.** *n* ensueño *m*

daylight *n no pl* luz *f* del día; **in broad ~** a plena luz del día; **to scare the living ~s out of sb** *inf* dar un susto de muerte a alguien

daytime *n* día *m;* **in the ~** de día

day-to-day *adj* cotidiano

daze [deɪz] **I.** *n* **to be in a ~** estar aturdido **II.** *vt* aturdir

dazzle ['dæzl] *vt* deslumbrar

dB *n abbr of* **decibel** dB

deacon ['diːkən] *n* diácono *m*

dead [ded] **I.** *adj a. fig* muerto; (*fire*) apagado; (*town*) desierto; (*numb*) dormido; **to be a ~** ser un desastre total; **as ~ as a doornail** muerto y bien muerto; **she wouldn't be seen ~ wearing that** *inf* por nada del mundo se pondría eso **II.** *n* **the ~** los muertos; **in the ~ of night** en plena noche **III.** *adv inf* **to be ~ set on sth** estar completamente decidido a algo

deaden ['dedən] *vt* (*pain*) aliviar; (*noise*) amortiguar

dead-end *n* callejón *m* sin salida; **~ job** trabajo *m* sin porvenir

deadline *n* plazo *m* límite

deadlock *n* **to reach ~** llegar a un punto muerto

deadly ['dedli] <-ier, -iest> *adj* **1.** mortal **2.** *inf* (*very boring*) aburridísimo

Dead Sea *n* Mar *m* Muerto

deaf [def] **I.** *adj* sordo; **to go ~** volverse sordo; **to be ~ to sth** *fig* hacer oídos sordos a algo **II.** *npl* **the ~** los sordos

deafen ['defən] *vt* ensordecer

deafening *adj* ensordecedor

deaf-mute *n* sordomudo, -a *m, f*

deafness *n no pl* sordera *f*

deal¹ [diːl] *n no pl* (*large amount*) cantidad *f;* **a great ~** una gran cantidad; **a great ~ of effort** mucho esfuerzo

deal² **I.** *n* (*agreement*) pacto *m;* COM negocio *m;* (*of cards*) reparto *m;* **to do a ~** (**with sb**) hacer un trato (con alguien); **it's no big ~!** *fig, inf* ¡no es para tanto! **II.** <dealt, dealt> *vi* **to ~ in sth** comerciar con algo **III.** <dealt, dealt> *vt* (*cards*) repartir; **to ~ sb a blow** propinar un golpe a alguien

◆ **deal with** *vt* (*problem*) ocuparse de; (*person*) tratar con

dealer ['diːləʳ, *Am:* -lə] *n* **1.** COM negociante *mf;* **drug ~** traficante *mf* de drogas **2.** GAMES (*in cards*) mano *mf*

dealing ['diːlɪŋ] *n* COM comercio *m;*

to have ~s with sb *fig* tratar con alguien

dealt [delt] *pt, pp of* **deal**

dean [di:n] *n* 1. UNIV decano, -a *m, f* 2. REL deán

dear [dɪərˈ, *Am:* dɪr] I. *adj* 1. (*much loved*) querido; (*in letters*) estimado 2. (*expensive*) caro II. *interj inf* oh ~! ¡Dios mío!

dearly *adv* 1. (*very*) mucho 2. *fig* he paid ~ for his success su éxito le costó caro

dearth [dɜ:θ, *Am:* dɜ:rθ] *n no pl* escasez *f*

death [deθ] *n* muerte *f*; to put sb to ~ matar a alguien; to be at ~'s door estar a las puertas de la muerte; to be bored to ~ with sth morirse de aburrimiento con algo

deathbed *n* lecho *m* de muerte **death certificate** *n* certificado *m* de defunción **death penalty** *n* pena *f* de muerte **death row** *n Am* corredor *m* de la muerte **death sentence** *n* pena *f* de muerte **death squad** *n* escuadrón *m* de la muerte

debacle [deɪˈbɑ:kl, *Am:* dɪ-] *n* debacle *f*

debar [dɪˈbɑ:ˈ, *Am:* -ˈbɑ:r] <-rr-> *vt* excluir

debase [dɪˈbeɪs] *vt* degradar

debatable [dɪˈbeɪtəbl, *Am:* dɪˈbeɪtə-] *adj* discutible

debate [dɪˈbeɪt] I. *n no pl* debate *m* II. *vt, vi* debatir

debauchery [dɪˈbɔ:tʃəri, *Am:* ˈbɑ:-] *n no pl* vicio *m*

debenture [dɪˈbentʃəˈ, *Am:* -ˈbentʃɚ] *n Brit* FIN obligación *f*

debilitate [dɪˈbɪlɪteɪt] *vt* debilitar

debilitating [dɪˈbɪlɪteɪtɪŋ] *adj* debilitante

debility [dɪˈbɪləti, *Am:* dɪˈbɪləʈi] *n no pl* debilidad *f*

debit [ˈdebɪt] *n* débito *m*

debris [ˈdeɪbri:, *Am:* dəˈbri:] *n no pl* escombros *mpl*

debt [det] *n* deuda *f*; to be in ~ tener deudas

debtor [ˈdetəˈ, *Am:* ˈdeʈɚ] *n* deudor(a) *m(f)*

debug [ˌdi:ˈbʌg] <-gg-> *vt* INFOR depurar

debunk [di:ˈbʌŋk] *vt* desacreditar

debut [ˈdeɪbju:, *Am:* -ˈ-] *n* debut *m*; to make one's ~ debutar

decade [ˈdekeɪd] *n* década *f*

decadence [ˈdekədəns] *n no pl* decadencia *f*

decadent [ˈdekədənt] *adj* decadente

decaffeinated [ˌdi:ˈkæfɪneɪtɪd] *adj* descafeinado

decanter [dɪˈkæntəˈ, *Am:* -ʈɚ] *n* licorera *f*

decapitate [dɪˈkæpɪteɪt] *vt* decapitar

decathlon [dɪˈkæθlən, *Am:* -lɑ:n] *n* decatlón *m*

decay [dɪˈkeɪ] I. *n no pl* (*of food*) descomposición *f*; (*dental*) caries *f inv* II. *vi* (*food*) pudrirse; (*building, intellect*) deteriorarse; (*teeth*) cariarse

deceased [dɪˈsi:st] *n* difunto, -a *m, f*

deceit [dɪˈsi:t] *n* engaño *m*, transa *f Méx*

deceitful [dɪˈsi:tfəl] *adj* engañoso

deceive [dɪˈsi:v] *vt* engañar; to ~ oneself engañarse a sí mismo

December [dɪˈsembəˈ, *Am:* -bɚ] *n* diciembre *m*; *s. a.* **April**

decency [ˈdi:səntsi] *n* 1. *no pl* (*respectability*) decencia *f* 2. *pl* (*approved behaviour*) buenas costumbres *fpl*

decent [ˈdi:sənt] *adj* 1. (*socially acceptable*) decente 2. *inf* (*kind*) amable

decentralize [di:ˈsentrəlaɪz] *vt* descentralizar

deception [dɪˈsepʃən] *n* engaño *m*

deceptive [dɪˈseptɪv] *adj* engañoso

decibel [ˈdesɪbel] *n* decibel(io) *m*

decide [dɪˈsaɪd] I. *vi* decidirse; to ~ on sth decidirse [*o* optar] por algo II. *vt* decidir

decided [dɪˈsaɪdɪd] *adj* (*person, manner*) decidido; (*improvement*) indudable

deciduous [dɪˈsɪdjʊəs, *Am:* -ˈsɪdʒʊ-] *adj* caducifolio

decimal [ˈdesɪml] *adj* decimal

decimate [ˈdesɪmeɪt] *vt* diezmar

decipher [dɪ'saɪfəʳ, *Am:* -fəʳ] *vt* descifrar

decision [dɪ'sɪʒən] *n* **1.** (*choice*) decisión *f;* **to make a ~** tomar una decisión **2.** LAW fallo *m* **3.** *no pl* (*resoluteness*) resolución *f*

decision-making process *n* proceso *m* decisorio

decisive [dɪ'saɪsɪv] *adj* decisivo

deck [dek] I. *n* **1.** (*of ship*) cubierta *f;* **to go below ~s** ir bajo cubierta; **to clear the ~s** *fig* prepararse para algo **2.** (*of bus*) piso *m* **3.** (*cards*) baraja *f* II. *vt* **~ out** adornar

deckchair *n* tumbona *f,* reposera *f Arg*

declamatory [dɪ'klæmətəri, *Am:* dɪ'klæmətɔːri] *adj form* declamatorio

declaration [ˌdeklə'reɪʃən] *n* declaración *f*

declare [dɪ'kleəʳ, *Am:* dɪ'kler] I. *vt* declarar; **to ~ war on sb** declarar la guerra a alguien II. *vi* declararse

decline [dɪ'klaɪn] I. *vi* **1.** (*price*) bajar; (*power, influence*) disminuir; (*civilization*) decaer **2.** (*refuse*) rehusar II. *n no pl* **1.** (*of price, power*) disminución *f;* (*of civilization*) decadencia *f;* **to be in ~** estar en declive **2.** MED debilitación *f* III. *vt* rehusar

decode [ˌdiː'kəʊd, *Am:* -'koʊd] *vi, vt* descodificar

decompose [ˌdiː.kəm'pəʊz, *Am:* -'poʊz] *vi* descomponerse

decontaminate [ˌdiːkən'tæmɪneɪt] *vt* descontaminar

decor ['deɪkɔːʳ, *Am:* 'deɪkɔːr] *n* decorado *m*

decorate ['dekəreɪt] *vt* **1.** (*adorn*) decorar; (*paint*) pintar **2.** (*honour*) condecorar

decoration [ˌdekə'reɪʃən] *n* **1.** (*ornament*) adorno *m* **2.** (*medal*) condecoración *f*

decorative ['dekərətɪv, *Am:* -ṭɪv] *adj* decorativo

decorator ['dekəreɪtəʳ, *Am:* -ṭəʳ] *n Brit* (*painter*) pintor(a) *m(f)*

decorum [dɪ'kɔːrəm] *n no pl* decoro *m*

decoy ['diːkɔɪ] *n a. fig* señuelo *m*

decrease [dɪ'kriːs, *Am:* 'diːkriːs] *vi* disminuir; (*prices*) bajar

decree [dɪ'kriː] I. *n* decreto *m* II. *vt* decretar

decrepit [dɪ'krepɪt] *adj* deteriorado

decriminalize [ˌdiː'krɪmɪnəlaɪz] *vt* despenalizar

decry [dɪ'kraɪ] *vt form* censurar

dedicate ['dedɪkeɪt] *vt* **to ~ oneself to sth** dedicarse a algo; **to ~ sth to sb** dedicar algo a alguien

dedicated *adj* dedicado

dedication [ˌdedɪ'keɪʃən] *n* **1.** (*devotion*) dedicación *f* **2.** (*inscription*) dedicatoria *f*

deduce [dɪ'djuːs, *Am:* dɪ'duːs] *vt,* **deduct** [dɪ'dʌkt] *vt* deducir

deductible *adj* deducible

deduction [dɪ'dʌkʃən] *n* deducción *f*

deed [diːd] *n* **1.** (*act*) acto *m;* (*feat*) hazaña *f* **2.** LAW escritura *f*

deem [diːm] *vt form* considerar

deep [diːp] *adj* **1.** (*not shallow*) profundo; **to take a ~ breath** respirar hondo; **to be in ~ thought** estar absorto en sus pensamientos; **~ red** rojo intenso **2.** (*regret, disappointment*) gran(de) **3.** (*sound*) grave

deepen ['diːpən] *vi, vt* **1.** (*make deeper*) hacer(se) más profundo **2.** (*increase*) aumentar

deep-fry *vt* freir (en aceite abundante)

deeply *adv* profundamente; (*breathe*) hondo

deep-rooted [ˌdiːp'ruːtɪd, *Am:* -ṭɪd] *adj* profundamente arraigado

deep-seated *adj* profundamente arraigado

deer [dɪəʳ, *Am:* dɪr] *n inv* ciervo *m*

deface [dɪ'feɪs] *vt* pintarrajear

defamatory [dɪ'fæmətəri, *Am:* -tɔːri] *adj* difamatorio

default [dɪ'fɔːlt, *Am:* dɪ'fɑːlt] I. *vi* FIN no pagar II. *n* **by ~** por defecto

defeat [dɪ'fiːt] I. *vt* derrotar II. *n* derrota *f;* **to admit ~** darse por vencido

defeatism *n* derrotismo *m*

defecate ['defəkeɪt] *vi form* defecar

defect¹ ['diːfekt] *n* defecto *m*

defect² [dɪ'fekt] *vi* huir

defection [dɪˈfekʃən] *n* defección *f*

defective [dɪˈfektɪv] *adj* defectuoso

defence [dɪˈfens] *n Aus, Brit a.* LAW, SPORTS defensa *f;* **to rush to sb's ~** acudir en defensa de alguien

defence minister *n* ministro, -a *m, f* de defensa

defend [dɪˈfend] *vt a.* LAW, SPORTS defender; **to ~ oneself (from sth)** defenderse (de algo)

defendant [dɪˈfendənt] *n* (*in civil case*) demandado, -a *m, f;* (*in criminal case*) acusado, -a *m, f*

defense [dɪˈfens] *n Am s.* **defence**

defensive [dɪˈfensɪv] **I.** *adj* defensivo **II.** *n* **to be on the ~** estar a la defensiva

defer [dɪˈfɜːʳ, *Am:* dɪˈfɜːr] <-rr-> *vt* aplazar

deference [ˈdefərənts] *n no pl* deferencia *f*

deferential [ˌdefəˈrentʃəl] *adj* respetuoso

defiance [dɪˈfaɪənts] *n no pl* desafío *m*

defiant [dɪˈfaɪənt] *adj* rebelde; **to be in a ~ mood** mostrar una actitud desafiante

deficiency [dɪˈfɪʃəntsi] *n* escasez *f*

deficient [dɪˈfɪʃənt] *adj* deficiente

deficit [ˈdefɪsɪt] *n* déficit *m*

defile [dɪˈfaɪl] *vt form* profanar

define [dɪˈfaɪn] *vt* definir; (*rights*) formular; (*characterize*) caracterizar

definite [ˈdefɪnət] *adj* **1.** (*final*) definitivo **2.** (*certain*) seguro; (*opinion*) claro

definite article *n* artículo *m* determinado

definitely *adv* definitivamente

definition [ˌdefɪˈnɪʃən] *n* definición *f*

definitive [dɪˈfɪnətɪv, *Am:* -t̬ɪv] *adj* **1.** (*final*) definitivo; rajante *Arg* **2.** (*best*) de mayor autoridad

deflate [dɪˈfleɪt] *vt* desinflar; *fig* (*hopes*) frustrar

deflation [dɪˈfleɪʃən] *n no pl* ECON deflación *f*

deflect [dɪˈflekt] *vt* desviar

deforestation [diːˌfɒrɪˈsteɪʃən, *Am:* diːˌfɔːr-] *n no pl* deforestación *f*

deform [dɪˈfɔːm, *Am:* dɪˈfɔːrm] *vt* deformar; (*person*) desfigurar

deformation [ˌdiːfɔːˈmeɪʃən, *Am:* ˌdiːfɔːr-] *n no pl* deformación *f;* (*of person*) desfiguración *f*

deformed *adj* deformado

deformity [dɪˈfɔːməti, *Am:* dɪˈfɔːr-mət̬i] *n* deformidad *f*

defraud [dɪˈfrɔːd, *Am:* dɪˈfrɑːd] *vt* estafar

defrost [ˌdiːˈfrɒst, *Am:* -ˈfrɑːst] *vt* deshelar; (*fridge*) descongelar

deft [deft] *adj* hábil

defunct [dɪˈfʌŋkt] *adj* difunto; (*institution*) extinto

defy [dɪˈfaɪ] *vt* **1.** (*challenge*) desafiar **2.** (*resist*) resistirse a; **it defies description** es indescriptible

degenerate[1] [dɪˈdʒenəreɪt] *vi* degenerar; (*health*) deteriorarse

degenerate[2] [dɪˈdʒenərət] *adj* degenerado

degeneration [dɪˌdʒenəˈreɪʃən] *n no pl* degeneración *f*

degrade [dɪˈgreɪd] *vt* degradar; **to ~ oneself** rebajarse

degree [dɪˈgriː] *n* **1.** MAT, METEO grado *m;* **5 ~s below zero** 5 grados bajo cero **2.** (*amount*) nivel *m;* **by ~s** gradualmente **3.** UNIV título *m;* **to have a ~ in sth** ser licenciado en algo; **to do a ~ in chemistry** estudiar la carrera de química

dehydrated [ˌdiːhaɪˈdreɪtɪd] *adj* deshidratado; **to become ~** deshidratarse

dehydration [ˌdiːhaɪˈdreɪʃən] *n no pl* deshidratación *f*

deign [deɪn] *vi* **to ~ to do sth** dignarse a hacer algo

deity [ˈdeɪɪti, *Am:* ˈdiːət̬i] *n* deidad *f*

dejected [dɪˈdʒektɪd] *adj* desanimado

dejection [dɪˈdʒekʃən] *n no pl* desánimo *m*

delay [dɪˈleɪ] **I.** *vt* aplazar; **to be ~ed** retrasarse; **to ~ doing sth** posponer el momento de hacer algo **II.** *vi* **to ~ in doing sth** dejar algo para más tarde **III.** *n* retraso *m;* **without ~** sin dilación

delegate[1] [ˈdelɪgət] *n* delegado, -a

D d

m, f

delegate² ['delɪgeɪt] *vt* delegar

delegation [ˌdelɪ'geɪʃən] *n* delegación *f*

delete [dɪ'liːt] *vt* borrar; INFOR suprimir; (*file*) eliminar; ~ **as appropriate** táchese lo que no corresponda

deliberate¹ [dɪ'lɪbərət] *adj* deliberado; (*movement*) pausado

deliberate² [dɪ'lɪbəreɪt] *vi* to ~ **on sth** reflexionar sobre algo

deliberately *adv* adrede

deliberation [dɪˌlɪbə'reɪʃən] *n* deliberación *f;* **after due** ~ después de pensarlo bien

delicacy ['delɪkəsi] *n* 1. *no pl* (*tact*) delicadeza *f* 2. (*food*) manjar *m*

delicate ['delɪkət] *adj* delicado; (*fragile*) frágil; **to be in** ~ **health** estar delicado (de salud)

delicatessen [ˌdelɪkə'tesən] *n* delicatessen *m*

delicious [dɪ'lɪʃəs] *adj* delicioso

delight [dɪ'laɪt] I. *n* placer *m;* **to take** ~ **in sth** disfrutar con algo II. *vt* deleitar

◆**delight in** *vi* to ~ **doing sth** deleitarse haciendo algo

delightful [dɪ'laɪtfəl] *adj* delicioso; (*person*) encantador

delineate [dɪ'lɪnieɪt] *vt* delinear

delinquency [dɪ'lɪŋkwəntsi] *n* delincuencia *f*

delinquent [dɪ'lɪŋkwənt] *n* LAW delincuente *mf*

delirious [dɪ'lɪriəs] *adj* MED **to be** ~ delirar; **to be** ~ **with joy** estar delirante de alegría

deliver [dɪ'lɪvəʳ, *Am:* dɪ'lɪvɚ] *vt* entregar; (*to addressee*) repartir a domicilio; (*lecture*) dar; (*speech, verdict*) pronunciar; **to** ~ **a baby** asistir al parto de un niño; **to** ~ **the goods** *fig* cumplir lo prometido

delivery [dɪ'lɪvəri] *n* (*distribution*) reparto *m;* **to take** ~ **of sth** recibir algo

delta ['deltə, *Am:* -tə] *n* delta *m*

delude [dɪ'luːd] *vt* engañar

deluge ['deljuːdʒ] I. *n* diluvio *m;* (*of complaints*) aluvión *m* II. *vt* inundar

delusion [dɪ'luːʒən] *n* error *m;* ~**s**

of grandeur megalomanía *f*

delve [delv] *vi* **to** ~ **into sth** ahondar en algo

demand [dɪ'mɑːnd, *Am:* dɪ'mænd] I. *vt* exigir; (*right*) reclamar; **to** ~ **that...** exigir que... +*subj* II. *n* 1. (*request*) exigencia *f;* **by popular** ~ a petición del público 2. ECON demanda *f*

demanding [dɪ'mɑːndɪŋ, *Am:* dɪ'mæn-] *adj* exigente

demarcation [ˌdiːmɑː'keɪʃən, *Am:* -mɑːr'-] *n* demarcación *f*

demean [dɪ'miːn] *vt* **to** ~ **oneself** rebajarse

demeaning *adj* degradante

demeanor *n Am, Aus,* **demeanour** [dɪ'miːnəʳ, *Am:* dɪ'miːnɚ] *n Brit, Aus no pl* (*behaviour*) conducta *f;* (*bearing*) porte *m*

demented [dɪ'mentɪd, *Am:* -'mentɪd] *adj inf* demente

demilitarize [ˌdiː'mɪlɪtəraɪz, *Am:* -təraɪz] *vt* desmilitarizar

demise [dɪ'maɪz] *n no pl* deceso *m; fig* desaparición *f*

democracy [dɪ'mɒkrəsi, *Am:* dɪ'mɑː-] *n* democracia *f*

democrat ['deməkræt] *n* demócrata *mf*

democratic [ˌdemə'krætɪk, *Am:* -'kræt-] *adj* democrático

demolish [dɪ'mɒlɪʃ, *Am:* dɪ'mɑːlɪʃ] *vt* demoler

demolition [ˌdemə'lɪʃən] *n* demolición *f*

demon ['diːmən] *n* demonio *m*

demonic [dɪ'mɒnɪk, *Am:* dɪ'mɑːnɪk] *adj* diabólico

demonstrable [dɪ'mɒntstrəbl, *Am:* dɪ'mɑːnt-] *adj* demostable

demonstrate ['demənstreɪt] I. *vt* (*show clearly*) mostrar; (*prove*) demostrar II. *vi* POL manifestarse

demonstration [ˌdemən'streɪʃən] *n* demostración *f;* POL manifestación *f*

demonstrator ['demənstreɪtəʳ, *Am:* -tɚ] *n* 1. COM demostrador(a) *m(f)* 2. POL manifestante *mf*

demoralize [dɪ'mɒrəlaɪz, *Am:* -'mɔːr-] *vt* desmoralizar

demote [dɪ'məʊt, *Am:* -'moʊt] *vt*

bajar de categoría; MIL degradar

den [den] *n* **1.** (*lair*) guarida *f* **2.** *Am* (*small room*) estudio *m*

denial [dɪ'naɪəl] *n* negación *f;* **to issue a ~ of sth** desmentir algo

denigrate ['denɪgreɪt] *vt* denigrar

denim ['denɪm] *n no pl* tela *f* vaquera

Denmark ['denmɑːk, *Am:* 'denmɑːrk] *n* Dinamarca *f*

denomination [dɪˌnɒmɪ'neɪʃən, *Am:* -ˌnɑːmə-] *n* **1.** REL confesión *f* **2.** FIN denominación *f*

denominator [dɪ'nɒmɪneɪtəʳ, *Am:* -'nɑːməneɪtɚ] *n* denominador *m*

denote [dɪ'nəʊt, *Am:* -'noʊt] *vt* denotar

denounce [dɪ'naʊnts] *vt* denunciar

dense [dents] *adj* **1.** (*thick*) espeso; (*closely packed*) denso; (*compact*) compacto **2.** *inf* (*stupid*) duro de mollera

densely *adv* densamente

density ['dentsɪti, *Am:* -səti] *n* densidad *f*

dent [dent] **I.** *n* abolladura *f* **II.** *vt* abollar

dental ['dentəl] *adj* dental

dentist ['dentɪst, *Am:* -tɪst] *n* dentista *mf*

denunciation [dɪˌnʌntsi'eɪʃən] *n* denuncia *f*

deny [dɪ'naɪ] *vt* **1.** (*declare untrue*) negar **2.** (*refuse*) denegar; **to ~ oneself sth** privarse de algo

deodorant [di'əʊdərənt, *Am:* -'oʊ-] *n* desodorante *m*

depart [dɪ'pɑːt, *Am:* dɪ'pɑːrt] *vi* (*person*) partir; (*plane*) despegar; (*train*) salir

◆ **depart from** *vi* desviarse de

department [dɪ'pɑːtmənt, *Am:* dɪ'pɑːrt-] *n* (*of organization*) departamento *m;* (*of shop*) sección *f;* ADMIN, POL ministerio *m*

departmental [ˌdiːpɑːt'mentəl, *Am:* -pɑːrt'mentəl] *adj* departamental

department store *n* grandes almacenes *mpl,* tienda *f* por departamentos *AmS*

departure [dɪ'pɑːtʃəʳ, *Am:* dɪ'pɑːr-

tʃɚ] *n* **1.** (*act of leaving*) partida *f* form; (*of vehicle*) salida *f;* (*of plane*) despegue *m* **2.** (*deviation*) desviación *f*

depend [dɪ'pend] *vi* **to ~ on sb** (*trust*) confiar en alguien; **to ~ on sth** (*be determined by*) depender de algo; **~ing on the weather...** según el tiempo que haga...

dependable [dɪ'pendəbl] *adj* (*thing*) seguro; (*person*) serio

dependant [dɪ'pendənt] *n* familiar *m* dependiente

dependence [dɪ'pendənts] *n no pl* dependencia *f*

dependency *n* **1.** *no pl* (*overreliance*) dependencia *f* **2.** POL posesión *f*

dependent [dɪ'pendənt] **I.** *adj* **to be ~ on sth** depender de algo **II.** *n Am s.* **dependant**

depict [dɪ'pɪkt] *vt* representar

depiction [dɪ'pɪkʃən] *n* representación *f*

deplete [dɪ'pliːt] *vt* reducir

depleted *adj* agotado

depletion [dɪ'pliːʃən] *n* agotamiento *m*

deplorable [dɪ'plɔːrəbl] *adj* deplorable

deplore [dɪ'plɔːʳ, *Am:* -'plɔːr] *vt* deplorar

deploy [dɪ'plɔɪ] *vt* desplegar

deployment [dɪ'plɔɪmənt] *n no pl* despliegue *m*

deport [dɪ'pɔːt, *Am:* dɪ'pɔːrt] *vt* deportar

deportation [ˌdiːpɔː'teɪʃən, *Am:* -pɔːr'-] *n* deportación *f*

depose [dɪ'pəʊz, *Am:* dɪ'poʊz] *vt* destituir

deposit [dɪ'pɒzɪt, *Am:* dɪ'pɑːzɪt] **I.** *vt* depositar; FIN ingresar **II.** *n* **1.** (*sediment*) sedimento *m* **2.** (*payment*) depósito *m;* **to leave sth as a ~** dejar algo en garantía

depot ['depəʊ, *Am:* 'diːpoʊ] *n* (*storehouse*) almacén *m;* Brit (*for vehicles*) cochera *f*

depraved *adj* depravado

depravity [dɪ'prævəti, *Am:* dɪ'prævəti] *n no pl* depravación *f*

depreciate [dɪ'priːʃɪeɪt] *vi* depreciarse

depreciation [dɪ,priːʃi'eɪʃən] *n no pl* depreciación *f*

depress [dɪ'pres] *vt* **1.** (*sadden*) deprimir; **it ~es me that ...** me deprime que... +*subj* **2.** (*reduce activity*) disminuir

depressed *adj* deprimido, apolismado *Méx, Ven;* **to feel ~** sentirse abatido

depressing [dɪ'presɪŋ] *adj* deprimente

depression [dɪ'preʃən] *n a.* METEO, FIN depresión *f*

deprivation [,deprɪ'veɪʃən] *n* privación *f*

deprive [dɪ'praɪv] *vt* **to ~ sb of sth** privar a alguien de algo

deprived *adj* desvalido

depth [depθ] *n* profundidad *f;* (*intensity*) intensidad *f;* **to get out of one's ~** *fig* perder pie; **in ~** *fig* en detalle

deputize ['depjətaɪz] *vi* **to ~ for sb** suplir a alguien

deputy ['depjəti, *Am:* -ţi] *n* delegado, -a *m, f; ~* **manager** subdirector(a) *m(f)*

derail [dɪ'reɪl] *vt* hacer descarrilar

deranged [dɪ'reɪndʒd] *adj* trastornado

deregulation [,dɪregjə'leɪʃən] *n no pl* deregulación *f*

derelict ['derəlɪkt] *adj* abandonado

deride [dɪ'raɪd] *vt* burlarse de

derision [dɪ'rɪʒən] *n no pl* burla *f*

derisory [dɪ'raɪsəri] *adj* irrisorio

derivation [,derɪ'veɪʃən] *n* origen *m*

derivative [dɪ'rɪvətɪv, *Am:* dɪ'rɪvəţɪv] *n* derivado *m*

derive [dɪ'raɪv] I. *vt* **to ~ sth from sth** obtener algo de algo II. *vi* **to ~ from sth** derivar de algo

dermatitis [,dɜːmə'taɪtɪs, *Am:* ,dɜːrmə'taɪţəs] *n no pl* dermatitis *f inv*

dermatology [,dɜːmə'tɒlədʒi, *Am:* ,dɜːrmə'tɑːlə-] *n no pl* dermatología *f*

derogatory [dɪ'rɒgətəri, *Am:* dɪ-'rɑːgətɔːri] *adj* desdeñoso

desalination [diː,sælɪ'neɪʃən] *n no pl* desalinización *f*

descend [dɪ'send] I. *vi* descender; **to ~ from sb** provenir de alguien II. *vt* descender

descendant [dɪ'sendənt] *n* descendiente *mf*

descent [dɪ'sent] *n* **1.** (*landing*) descenso *m* **2.** *no pl* (*ancestry*) origen *m*

describe [dɪ'skraɪb] *vt* describir

description [dɪ'skrɪpʃən] *n* descripción *f;* **to answer a ~** corresponder a una descripción; **of every ~** de todo tipo

descriptive [dɪ'skrɪptɪv] *adj* descriptivo

desecrate ['desɪkreɪt] *vt* profanar

desegregation [,diː'segrɪgeɪʃən, *Am:* diː,segrɪ'geɪʃən] *n no pl* desegregación *f*

desert[1] [dɪ'zɜːt, *Am:* -'zɜːrt] I. *vi* MIL desertar II. *vt* abandonar; MIL desertar de

desert[2] ['dezət, *Am:* -ɚt] *n* desierto *m*

deserted *adj* desierto

deserter *n* MIL desertor(a) *m(f)*

desertion [dɪ'zɜːʃən, *Am:* dɪ'zɜːr-] *n* MIL deserción *f*

deserts [dɪ'zɜːts, *Am:* dɪ'zɜːrts] *npl* **to get one's ~** tener su merecido

deserve [dɪ'zɜːv, *Am:* dɪ'zɜːrv] *vt* merecer

deserving *adj* meritorio

design [dɪ'zaɪn] I. *vt* diseñar II. *n* diseño *m;* (*pattern*) dibujo *m;* **to do sth by ~** hacer algo adrede

designate ['dezɪgneɪt] *vt* nombrar; **to ~ sb to do sth** designar a alguien para hacer algo

designation [,dezɪg'neɪʃən] *n* nombramiento *m*

designer [dɪ'zaɪnəʳ, *Am:* dɪ'zaɪnɚ] I. *n* diseñador(a) *m(f)* II. *adj* de marca

desirable [dɪ'zaɪərəbl, *Am:* dɪ'zaɪ-] *adj* **1.** (*necessary*) conveniente **2.** (*popular*) codiciado; (*sexually attractive*) deseable

desire [dɪ'zaɪəʳ, *Am:* dɪ'zaɪɚ] I. *vt*

desear II. n deseo m
desired adj deseado
desist [dɪˈsɪst] vi form desistir
desk [desk] n escritorio m; (counter) mostrador m
desktop computer n INFOR microordenador m de mesa **desktop publishing** n autoedición f
desolate [ˈdesələt] adj desierto; **to feel** ~ sentirse desconsolado
desolation [ˌdesəˈleɪʃən] n no pl 1. (barrenness) desolación f 2. (sadness) aflicción f
despair [dɪˈspeəʳ, Am: dɪˈsper] I. n no pl desesperación f; **to drive sb to** ~ desesperar a alguien II. vi **to** ~ **of sb** perder las esperanzas con alguien
despairing adj desesperado
desperate [ˈdespərət] adj (person, solution) desesperado; (poverty) extremo; (situation) difícil; **to be in** ~ **need of help** tener necesidad extrema de ayuda; **to be** ~ **for sth** necesitar algo con suma urgencia
desperation [ˌdespəˈreɪʃən] n no pl desesperación f; **in** ~ a la desesperada; **to drive sb to** ~ desesperar a alguien
despicable [dɪˈspɪkəbl] adj despreciable
despise [dɪˈspaɪz] vt despreciar
despite [dɪˈspaɪt] prep a pesar de
despondent [dɪˈspɒndənt, Am: -ˈspɑːn-] adj desalentado
despotism [ˈdespətɪzəm] n no pl despotismo m
dessert [dɪˈzɜːt, Am: -ˈzɜːrt] n postre m
destabilize [ˌdiːˈsteɪbəlaɪz] vt desestabilizar
destination [ˌdestɪˈneɪʃən] n destino m
destiny [ˈdestɪni] n destino m
destitute [ˈdestɪtjuːt, Am: -tuːt] adj necesitado
destitution [ˌdestɪˈtjuːʃən, Am: -ˈtuː-] n no pl (poverty) miseria f
destroy [dɪˈstrɔɪ] vt destruir; (animal) sacrificar
destroyer [dɪˈstrɔɪəʳ, Am: dɪˈstrɔɪə·] n NAUT destructora f
destruction [dɪˈstrʌkʃən] n no pl

destrucción f
destructive [dɪˈstrʌktɪv] adj destructivo
detach [dɪˈtætʃ] vt separar
detached adj (aloof) indiferente
detachment [dɪˈtætʃmənt] n 1. no pl (disinterest) desinterés m 2. (group of soldiers) destacamento m
detail [ˈdiːteɪl, Am: dɪˈteɪl] I. n detalle m; (unimportant) minucia f; **in** ~ en detalle; **to go into** ~ entrar en detalles II. vt detallar; **to** ~ **sb to do sth** destacar a alguien para que haga algo
detailed adj detallado; (report) pormenorizado
detain [dɪˈteɪn] vt 1. LAW detener 2. (delay) retener
detainee [ˌdiːteɪˈniː] n detenido, -a m, f
detect [dɪˈtekt] vt descubrir
detection [dɪˈtekʃən] n no pl descubrimiento m
detective [dɪˈtektɪv] n detective mf
detector [dɪˈtektəʳ, Am: -tə·] n detector m
detention [dɪˈtenʃən] n 1. LAW arresto m 2. SCHOOL castigo f
deter [dɪˈtɜːʳ, Am: -ˈtɜːr] <-rr-> vt disuadir
detergent [dɪˈtɜːdʒənt, Am: -ˈtɜːr] n detergente m
deteriorate [dɪˈtɪərɪəreɪt, Am: -ˈtɪrɪ-] vi deteriorarse
deterioration [dɪˌtɪərɪəˈreɪʃən, Am: -ˈtɪrɪ-] n no pl deterioro m
determinant [dɪˈtɜːmɪnənt, Am: -ˈtɜːr-] n determinante m
determinate [dɪˈtɜːmɪnət, Am: -ˈtɜːr-] adj determinado
determination [dɪˌtɜːmɪˈneɪʃən, Am: -ˌtɜːr-] n no pl resolución f
determine [dɪˈtɜːmɪn, Am: -ˈtɜːr-] vt determinar
determined [dɪˈtɜːmɪnd, Am: -ˈtɜːr-] adj decidido; **to be** ~ **to do sth** estar resuelto a hacer algo
deterrence [dɪˈterəns] n no pl disuasión f
deterrent [dɪˈterənt] n **to act as a** ~ **to sb** disuadir a alguien
detest [dɪˈtest] vt detestar

Dd

detestable [dɪ'testəbl] *adj* detestable

detonate ['detəneɪt] **I.** *vi* detonar **II.** *vt* hacer detonar

detour ['diːtʊəʳ, *Am:* 'diːtʊr] *n* desvío *m*; **to make a ~** desviarse

detract [dɪ'trækt] *vi* **1.** (*devalue*) **to ~ from sth** quitar mérito a algo **2.** (*take away*) apartar

detractor [dɪ'træktəʳ, *Am:* -təʳ] *n* detractor(a) *m(f)*

detriment ['detrɪmənt] *n no pl* **to the ~ of sth** en detrimento de algo; **without ~ to sth** sin perjuicio de algo

detrimental [ˌdetrɪ'mentəl, *Am:* -t̬l] *adj* nocivo

devaluation [ˌdiːvæljuˈeɪʃən] *n* devaluación *f*

devalue [ˌdiːˈvæljuː] *vt* devaluar

devastate ['devəsteɪt] *vt* devastar

devastating *adj* devastador; (*beauty*) arrollador; (*charm*) irresistible

devastation [ˌdevəˈsteɪʃən] *n no pl* devastación *f*

develop [dɪ'veləp] **I.** *vi* desarrollarse; **to ~ into sth** transformarse en algo **II.** *vt* **1.** (*expand*) desarrollar **2.** (*create*) crear **3.** PHOT revelar

developed *adj* desarrollado

developer [dɪ'veləpəʳ, *Am:* -pəʳ] *n* inmobiliaria *f*

developing *adj* de desarrollo

development [dɪ'veləpmənt] *n* **1.** (*process*) desarrollo *m* **2.** (*event*) acontecimiento *m* **3.** (*building*) construcción *f*

deviant ['diːviənt] *adj* desviado

deviate ['diːviːeɪt] *vi* **to ~ from sth** desviarse de algo

deviation [ˌdiːviˈeɪʃən] *n* desviación *f*

device [dɪ'vaɪs] *n* dispositivo *m*; **to leave sb to their own ~s** abandonar a alguien a su suerte

devil ['devəl] *n* diablo *m*; **lucky ~!** ¡qué suerte!; **the poor ~!** ¡pobre diablo!; **between the ~ and the deep blue sea** entre la espada y la pared; **better the ~ you know** más vale malo conocido que bueno por conocer *prov*; **speak of the ~** hablando del rey de Roma, por la puerta asoma; **what the ~ ...?** ¿qué diablos...?

devious ['diːviəs] *adj* insincero

devise [dɪ'vaɪz] *vt* idear

devoid [dɪ'vɔɪd] *adj* **to be ~ of sth** estar desprovisto de algo

devolution [ˌdiːvəˈluːʃən, *Am:* ˌdevəˈluː-] *n no pl* POL delegación *f*

devolve [dɪ'vɒlv, *Am:* dɪ'vɑːlv] *vt* delegar

devote [dɪ'vəʊt, *Am:* -'voʊt] *vt* dedicar; **to ~ oneself to sth** dedicarse a algo

devoted [dɪ'vəʊtɪd, *Am:* -'voʊt̬ɪd] *adj* dedicado; (*husband, mother*) devoto

devotee [ˌdevəˈtiː, *Am:* -əˈtiː] *n* (*supporter*) partidario, -a *m, f*; (*admirer*) fanático, -a *m, f*

devotion [dɪ'vəʊʃən, *Am:* dɪ'voʊ-] *n no pl* (*loyalty*) lealtad *f*; (*affection*) afecto *m*

devour [dɪ'vaʊəʳ, *Am:* dɪ'vaʊəʳ] *vt* devorar; **to be ~ed by jealousy** estar consumido por los celos

devout [dɪ'vaʊt] *adj* devoto

dew [djuː, *Am:* duː] *n no pl* rocío *m*

diabetes [ˌdaɪəˈbiːtiːz, *Am:* -t̬əs] *n no pl* diabetes *f*

diabetic [ˌdaɪəˈbetɪk, *Am:* -'bet̬-] *n* diabético, -a *m, f*

diabolical [ˌdaɪəˈbɒlɪk(əl), *Am:* -'bɑːlɪk-] *adj* diabólico

diagnose ['daɪəgnəʊz, *Am:* ˌdaɪəgˈnoʊs] *vt* diagnosticar

diagnosis [ˌdaɪəgˈnəʊsɪs, *Am:* -'noʊ-] <-ses> *n* diagnóstico *m*

diagnostic [ˌdaɪəgˈnɒstɪk, *Am:* -'nɑːstɪk] *adj* diagnóstico

diagonal [daɪˈægənl] *adj* diagonal

diagram ['daɪəgræm] *n* diagrama *m*; (*plan*) esquema *m*

dial ['daɪəl] **I.** *n* esfera *f* **II.** <*Brit:* -ll-, *Am:* -l-> *vt* marcar

dialect ['daɪəlekt] *n* dialecto *m*

dialectical [ˌdaɪəˈlektɪkəl] *adj* dialéctico

dialog *n Am*, **dialogue** ['daɪəlɒg, *Am:* -lɑːg] *n* diálogo *m*

diameter [daɪˈæmɪtəʳ, *Am:* -ət̬əʳ] *n* diámetro *m*

diamond ['daɪəmənd] *n* **1.**(*precious stone*) diamante *m*; **a rough ~** *fig* un diamante en bruto **2.**(*rhombus*) rombo *m*

diaper ['daɪəpəʳ, *Am:* -pɚ] *n Am* pañal *m*

diaphragm ['daɪəfræm] *n* diafragma *m*

diarrhea *n*, **diarrhoea** [ˌdaɪə'rɪə, *Am:* -'riːə] *n no pl* diarrea *f*

diary ['daɪəri] *n* (*journal*) diario *m*; (*planner*) agenda *f*

diatribe ['daɪətraɪb] *n* diatriba *f*

dice [daɪs] I. *npl* (*cubes*) dados *mpl*; **to roll the ~** echar los dados II. *vt* cortar en tacos

dichotomy [daɪ'kɒtəmi, *Am:* -'kɑː-tə-] *n* dicotomía *f*

dick [dɪk] *n vulg* (*penis*) polla *f*, pija *f AmL*, pajarito *m RíoPl*

dictate [dɪk'teɪt, *Am:* 'dɪkteɪt] I. *vi* **to ~ to sb** dictar a alguien II. *vt* imponer

dictator [dɪk'teɪtəʳ, *Am:* 'dɪkteɪtɚ] *n* dictador(a) *m(f)*

dictatorial [ˌdɪktə'tɔːriəl] *adj* dictatorial

dictatorship [dɪk'teɪtəʃɪp, *Am:* -tɚ-] *n* dictadura *f*

diction ['dɪkʃən] *n no pl* dicción *f*

dictionary ['dɪkʃənəri, *Am:* -eri] *n* diccionario *m*

did [dɪd] *pt of* **do**

didactic [dɪ'dæktɪk, *Am:* daɪ-] *adj* didáctico

die¹ [daɪ] *n* **1.** dado *m*; **the ~ is cast** *fig* la suerte está echada **2.** TECH molde *m*

die² <dying, died> *vi* (*cease to live*) morir; **the secret will ~ with her** se llevará el secreto a la tumba; **to ~ hard** persistir; **to be dying to do sth** tener muchas ganas de hacer algo
◆ **die away** *vi* desaparecer; (*sound*) apagarse
◆ **die off** *vi*, **die out** *vi* (*species*) extinguirse; (*customs*) desaparecer

diehard ['daɪhɑːd, *Am:* -hɑːrd] *n* intransigente *mf*

diesel ['diːzəl, *Am:* -səl] *n no pl* diesel *m*

diet ['daɪət] I. *n* dieta *f*; **to be on a ~** estar a dieta II. *vi* estar a dieta

dietary ['daɪətəri, *Am:* 'daɪətɚ-] *adj* (*food*) dietético; (*habit*) de alimentación

dietary fibre *n* fibra *f* dietética

differ ['dɪfəʳ, *Am:* -ɚ] *vi* **1.**(*be unlike*) **to ~ from sth** ser distinto de algo **2.**(*disagree*) no estar de acuerdo

difference ['dɪfərənts] *n* diferencia *f*; **to make a ~** importar; **to not make any ~** ser igual; **to pay the ~** pagar la diferencia

different ['dɪfərənt] *adj* diferente; **to be as ~ as chalk and cheese** *Brit, Aus,* **to be as ~ as night and day** *Am* ser la noche y el día

differentiate [ˌdɪfə'rentʃieɪt] *vt* distinguir

differentiation [ˌdɪfərentʃi'eɪʃən] *n* diferenciación *f*

difficult ['dɪfɪkəlt] *adj* difícil

difficulty ['dɪfɪkəlti, *Am:* -ʈi] <-ies> *n* dificultad *f*; **with ~** difícilmente; **to have ~ doing sth** tener problemas para hacer algo

diffident ['dɪfɪdənt] *adj* tímido

diffuse¹ [dɪ'fjuːz] *vi*, *vt* difundir(se)

diffuse² [dɪ'fjuːs] *adj* difuso

diffusion [dɪ'fjuːʒən] *n no pl* difusión *f*

dig [dɪg] I. *n* (*excavation*) excavación *f*; **to have a ~ at sb** *fig* meterse con alguien II.<-gg-, dug, dug> *vt* cavar; (*well, canal*) abrir
◆ **dig in** *vi inf* atacar
◆ **dig up** *vt* desenterrar; *fig* (*information*) descubrir

digest [daɪ'dʒest] *vt* digerir; *fig* (*information*) asimilar

digestion [daɪ'dʒestʃən] *n* digestión *f*

digestive [daɪ'dʒestɪv] *adj* digestivo

digger ['dɪgəʳ, *Am:* -ɚ] *n* excavadora *f*

digit ['dɪdʒɪt] *n* **1.**(*number*) dígito *m* **2.**(*finger, toe*) dedo *m*

digital ['dɪdʒɪtl, *Am:* -ʈl] *adj* digital

dignified ['dɪgnɪfaɪd] *adj* (*person*) digno; (*occasion*) solemne

dignify ['dɪgnɪfaɪ] <-ie-> *vt* dignifi-

D d

car

dignitary ['dɪgnɪtəri, *Am:* -nəter-]
<-ies> *n* dignatario, -a *m, f*

dignity ['dɪgnəti, *Am:* -ţi] *n no pl*
dignidad *f;* **to be beneath sb's ~** no
ser digno de alguien

dike [daɪk] *n* dique *m*

dilapidated [dɪ'læpɪdeɪtɪd, *Am:*
-ţɪd] *adj* derruido

dilate [daɪ'leɪt, *Am:* 'daɪleɪt] *vi* dilatarse

dilemma [dɪ'lemə, daɪ'lemə] *n*
dilema *m;* **to be in a ~** estar en un
dilema

dilettante [ˌdɪlɪ'tænti, *Am:* -ə-
'tɑ:nt] *n* <-s *o* -ti> diletante *mf*

diligence ['dɪlɪdʒəns] *n no pl* diligencia *f*

diligent ['dɪlɪdʒənt] *adj* diligente

dill [dɪl] *n no pl* eneldo *m*

dilute [daɪ'lju:t, *Am:* -'lu:t] *vt* diluir

dim [dɪm] I.<-mm-> *vt* apagar
II.<-mm-> *adj* **1.**(*light*) tenue
2.(*stupid*) lerdo

dime [daɪm] *n* moneda *f* de diez
centavos; **a ~ a dozen** *inf* del montón

dimension [ˌdaɪ'mentʃən, *Am:* dɪ-
'mentʃən] *n* dimensión *f*

diminish [dɪ'mɪnɪʃ] *vi, vt* disminuir

diminutive [dɪ'mɪnjʊtɪv, *Am:* -jə-
ţɪv] *n* diminutivo *m*

din [dɪn] *n no pl* estrépito *m*

dine [daɪn] *vi* cenar

diner ['daɪnər, *Am:* -nɚ] *n* **1.**(*person*) comensal *mf* **2.***Am* (*restaurant*) restaurante *m* de carretera

dinghy ['dɪŋgi, *Am:* 'dɪŋi] *n* <-ies>
bote *m*

dingy ['dɪndʒi] <-ier, -iest> *adj* deslustrado

dinner ['dɪnər, *Am:* -ɚ] *n* (*evening
meal*) cena *f;* (*lunch*) almuerzo *m*

dinner jacket *n* esmoquin *m*
dinner party *n* cena *f*

dinosaur ['daɪnəsɔ:r, *Am:* -sɔ:r] *n*
dinosaurio *m*

diocese ['daɪəsɪs] *n* diócesis *f*

dioxide [daɪ'ɒksaɪd, *Am:* -'ɑ:k-] *n
no pl* dióxido *m*

dip [dɪp] I. *n* **1.**(*sudden drop*) caída
f **2.**GASTR salsa *f* **3.**(*brief swim*)

chapuzón *m* II. *vi* **1.**(*drop down*)
descender **2.**(*slope down*) inclinarse III. *vt* sumergir

diploma [dɪ'pləʊmə, *Am:* -'ploʊ-]
n diploma *m*

diplomacy [dɪ'pləʊməsi, *Am:*
-'ploʊ-] *n no pl* diplomacia *f*

diplomat ['dɪpləmæt] *n* diplomático, -a *m, f*

diplomatic [ˌdɪplə'mætɪk, *Am:*
-'mæţ-] *adj* diplomático

dire ['daɪər, *Am:* 'daɪɚ] *adj* horrendo

direct [dɪ'rekt] I. *vt* dirigir; (*command*) ordenar; **to ~ sth at sb** dirigir algo a alguien; **to ~ sb to a place**
indicar a alguien el camino hacia un
sitio II. *adj* directo; **the ~ opposite
of sth** exactamente lo contrario de
algo III. *adv* directamente

direction [dɪ'rekʃən] *n no pl* dirección *f;* **in the ~ of sth** en dirección a
[*o* hacia] algo; **sense of ~** sentido *m*
de la orientación; **can you give me
directions?** ¿me puedes indicar el
camino?

directive [dɪ'rektɪv] *n* directriz *f,* directiva *f AmL*

directly [dɪ'rektli] *adv* **1.**(*frankly*)
directamente **2.**(*immediately*) inmediatamente

director [dɪ'rektər, *Am:* dɪ'rektɚ] *n*
(*manager*) director(a) *m(f);* (*board
member*) miembro *m* del consejo

directory [dɪ'rektəri] *n* **1.**(*book*)
guía *f,* directorio *m Méx* **2.**INFOR directorio *m*

dirt [dɜ:t, *Am:* dɜ:rt] *n no pl* **1.**(*unclean substance*) suciedad *f;* **to treat
sb like ~** tratar a alguien como basura **2.**(*soil*) tierra *f*

dirty ['dɜ:ti, *Am:* 'dɜ:rţi] I. *n Brit,
Aus* **to do the ~ on sb** hacer una
mala pasada a alguien II. *vt* ensuciar
III.<-ier, -iest> *adj* **1.**(*unclean*)
sucio, chancho *AmL;* **to do the ~
work** *fig* hacer el trabajo sucio
2.(*nasty*) bajo **3.**(*lewd*) obsceno;
(*joke*) verde

disability [ˌdɪsə'bɪləti, *Am:* -əţi] *n*
discapacidad *f,* invalidez *f AmL*

disable [dɪ'seɪbl] *vt* incapacitar

disabled I. *npl* **the** ~ los discapacitados II. *adj* incapacitado

disabuse [ˌdɪsəˈbjuːz] *vt form* **to** ~ **sb of sth** desengañar a alguien de algo

disadvantage [ˌdɪsədˈvɑːntɪdʒ, *Am:* -ˈvæntɪdʒ] I. *n* desventaja *f;* **to be at a** ~ estar en desventaja II. *vt* perjudicar

disadvantaged *adj* desfavorecido

disaffected [ˌdɪsəˈfektɪd] *adj* desafecto

disagree [ˌdɪsəˈgriː] *vi* **to** ~ **on sth** no estar de acuerdo en algo; **the answers** ~ las respuestas no concuerdan; **spicy food** ~**s with me** la comida picante me sienta mal

disagreeable [ˌdɪsəˈgriːəbl] *adj* desagradable

disagreement [ˌdɪsəˈgriːmənt] *n no pl* desacuerdo *m*

disappear [ˌdɪsəˈpɪəʳ, *Am:* -ˈpɪr] *vi* desaparecer; **to** ~ **from sight** desaparecer de la vista

disappearance [ˌdɪsəˈpɪərənts, *Am:* -ˈpɪr-] *n no pl* desaparición *f*

disappoint [ˌdɪsəˈpɔɪnt] *vt* decepcionar, enchilar *AmC*

disappointed *adj* decepcionado

disappointing *adj* decepcionante

disappointment [ˌdɪsəˈpɔɪntmənt] *n* decepción *f*

disapproval [ˌdɪsəˈpruːvəl] *n no pl* desaprobación *f*

disapprove [ˌdɪsəˈpruːv] *vi* desaprobar; **to** ~ **of sth** desaprobar algo

disarm [dɪsˈɑːm, *Am:* -ˈɑːrm] *vt* desarmar

disarmament [dɪsˈɑːməmənt, *Am:* -ɑːr-] *n no pl* desarme *m*

disarray [ˌdɪsəˈreɪ] *n no pl* desorden *m*

disaster [dɪˈzɑːstəʳ, *Am:* dɪˈzæstəʳ] *n* desastre *m*

disastrous [dɪˈzɑːstrəs, *Am:* dɪˈzæstrəs] *adj* catastrófico

disbelief [ˌdɪsbɪˈliːf] *n no pl* incredulidad *f*

disbelieve [ˌdɪsbɪˈliːv] *vt* no creer

disc [dɪsk] *n* disco *m*

discard [dɪˈskɑːd, *Am:* -skɑːrd] *vt* desechar

discern [dɪˈsɜːn, *Am:* dɪˈsɜːrn] *vt* percibir

discernible [dɪˈsɜːnəbl, *Am:* dɪˈsɜːr-] *adj* perceptible

discerning [dɪˈsɜːnɪŋ, *Am:* dɪˈsɜːr-] *adj* perspicaz

discharge¹ [ˈdɪstʃɑːdʒ, *Am:* ˈdɪstʃɑːrdʒ] *n no pl* 1. (*release*) liberación *f* 2. (*emission*) emisión *f;* (*of liquid*) secreción *f*

discharge² [dɪsˈtʃɑːdʒ, *Am:* -ˈtʃɑːrdʒ] *vt* 1. MIL, COM despedir 2. (*let out*) emitir

disciple [dɪˈsaɪpl] *n* discípulo, -a *m, f*

disciplinary [ˌdɪsəˈplɪnəri, *Am:* ˈdisəplɪnər-] *adj* disciplinario

discipline [ˈdɪsəplɪn] I. *n* disciplina *f* II. *vt* 1. (*punish*) castigar 2. (*train*) disciplinar

disciplined *adj* disciplinado

disclaimer [dɪsˈkleɪməʳ, *Am:* -məʳ] *n form* repudio *m*

disclose [dɪsˈkləʊz, *Am:* -ˈkloʊz] *vt* divulgar

disclosure [dɪsˈkləʊʒəʳ, *Am:* -ˈkloʊʒəʳ] *n* divulgación *f*

disco [ˈdɪskəʊ, *Am:* -koʊ] *n* discoteca *f*

discomfort [dɪˈskʌmfət, *Am:* -fəʳt] *n* 1. *no pl* (*uneasiness*) malestar *m* 2. (*inconvenience*) molestia *f*

disconcert [ˌdɪskənˈsɜːt, *Am:* -ˈsɜːrt] *vt* desconcertar

disconnect [ˌdɪskəˈnekt] *vt* separar; (*phone*) desconectar; (*customer*) cortar el suministro a

discontent [ˌdɪskənˈtent] *n no pl* descontento *m*

discontented *adj* descontento

discontinue [ˌdɪskənˈtɪnjuː] *vt* suspender

discontinuity [ˌdɪsˌkɒntɪˈnjuːəti, *Am:* ˌdɪskəntənˈuːəti] <-ies> *n* discontinuidad *f*

discord [ˈdɪskɔːd, *Am:* -kɔːrd] *n* 1. *no pl* (*disagreement*) discordia *f* 2. (*noise*) discordancia *f*

discount¹ [ˈdɪskaʊnt] *n* descuento *m;* **at a** ~ con descuento

discount² [dɪˈskaʊnt] *vt* 1. COM descontar 2. (*disregard*) no hacer caso

de
discourage [dɪˈskʌrɪdʒ, Am: -ˈskɜːr-] vt desanimar; **to ~ sb from doing sth** disuadir a alguien de hacer algo
discouraging adj desalentador
discourse [ˈdɪskɔːs, Am: -kɔːrs] n discurso m
discover [dɪˈskʌvəʳ, Am: -ɚ] vt descubrir
discoverer n descubridor(a) m(f)
discovery [dɪˈskʌvəri] <-ies> n descubrimiento m
discredit [dɪˈskredɪt] vt desacreditar
discreet [dɪˈskriːt] adj discreto
discrepancy [dɪˈskrepəntsi] <-ies> n discrepancia f
discrete [dɪˈskriːt] adj separado
discretion [dɪˈskreʃən] n no pl discreción f
discriminate [dɪˈskrɪmɪneɪt] vi discernir; **to ~ against sb** discriminar a alguien
discrimination [dɪˌskrɪmɪˈneɪʃən] n no pl discriminación f
discriminatory [dɪˈskrɪmɪnətəri, Am: -tɔːri] adj discriminatorio
discursive [dɪˈskɜːsɪv, Am: -ˈskɜːr-] adj digresivo
discuss [dɪˈskʌs] vt discutir
discussion [dɪˈskʌʃən] n discusión f, argumento m AmL
disdain [dɪsˈdeɪn] n no pl desdén m
disease [dɪˈziːz] n a. fig enfermedad f; **to catch a ~** contraer una enfermedad
diseased adj a. fig enfermo
disembark [ˌdɪsɪmˈbaːk, Am: -ˈbaːrk] vi desembarcar
disenchanted adj desencantado
disengage [ˌdɪsɪnˈgeɪdʒ] vi, vt separar(se)
disfigure [dɪsˈfɪgəʳ, Am: -jɚ] vt desfigurar
disgrace [dɪsˈgreɪs] I. n no pl 1.(loss of honour) deshonra f 2.(thing, person) vergüenza f II. vt deshonrar
disgraceful [dɪsˈgreɪsfəl] adj vergonzoso
disgruntled [dɪsˈgrʌntld, Am:

-tld] adj contrariado
disguise [dɪsˈgaɪz] I. n disfraz m; **to be in ~** estar disfrazado II. vt disfrazar; **to ~ oneself as sth** disfrazarse de algo
disgust [dɪsˈgʌst] I. n no pl 1.(repugnance) asco m 2.(indignation) indignación f II. vt 1.(sicken) dar asco a, chocar AmL 2.(revolt) indignar
disgusting [dɪsˈgʌstɪŋ] adj 1.(repulsive) repugnante, chocante AmL 2.(unacceptable) indignante
dish [dɪʃ] <-es> n 1.(for food) plato m; **to do the ~es** fregar los platos 2. TV (antena f) parabólica f
♦ **dish out** vt, **dish up** vt servir
disharmony [dɪsˈhaːməni, Am: -ˈhaːr-] n no pl falta f de armonía
dishcloth n trapo m de cocina, repasador m Arg, Urug
dishearten [dɪsˈhaːtən, Am: -ˈhaːr-] vt descorazonar
disheveled adj Am, **dishevelled** [dɪˈʃevəld] adj desaliñado
dishonest [dɪsˈɒnɪst, Am: -ˈsaːnɪst] adj deshonesto
dishonesty [dɪsˈɒnɪsti, Am: -ˈsaːnə-] n no pl falta f de honestidad
dishonor n Am, **dishonour** [dɪsˈɒnəʳ] n Aus, Brit no pl deshonor m
dishpan n Am escurreplatos m inv
dishsoap n Am lavavajillas m inv
dishwasher n (machine) lavavajillas m inv
disillusioned [ˌdɪsɪˈluːʒənd] adj **to be ~ with sth** estar desilusionado con algo; **to be ~ with sb** estar desilusionado de alguien
disinclined [ˌdɪsɪnˈklaɪnd] adj **to be ~ to do sth** tener pocas ganas de hacer algo
disinfectant [ˌdɪsɪnˈfektənt] n desinfectante m
disingenuous [ˌdɪsɪnˈdʒenjuəs] adj insincero
disintegrate [dɪsˈɪntɪgreɪt, Am: -tə-] vi desintegrarse
disintegration [dɪˌsɪntɪˈgreɪʃən, Am: -tə-] n no pl desintegración f

disinterested [dɪ'sɪntrəstɪd, *Am:* -'sɪntrɪstɪd] *adj* **1.** (*impartial*) imparcial **2.** (*uninterested*) desinteresado

disk [dɪsk] *n* INFOR disco *m*

disk drive *n* disquetera *f*

diskette [dɪs'kæt] *n* disquete *m*

dislike [dɪs'laɪk] **I.** *vt* tener aversión a **II.** *n* *no pl* aversión *f;* **to take a ~ to sb** tomar aversión a alguien

dislocate ['dɪsləkeɪt, *Am:* dɪ'sloʊ-] *vt* dislocar

dislodge [dɪ'slɒdʒ, *Am:* -'slɑːdʒ] *vt* desalojar

dismal ['dɪzməl] *adj* **1.** (*depressing*) deprimente **2.** *inf* (*awful*) terrible

dismantle [dɪ'smæntl, *Am:* dɪ'smæn̪t̬l] *vt* desmontar

dismay [dɪ'smeɪ] **I.** *n* *no pl* consternación *f;* **to sb's** (**great**) **~** para (gran) consternación de alguien **II.** *vt* consternar

dismayed *adj* consternado

dismiss [dɪ'smɪs] *vt* **1.** (*not consider*) descartar **2.** (*let go*) dejar ir; (*from job*) despedir

dismissal [dɪ'smɪsəl] *n* *no pl* (*from job*) despido *m*

disobedience [ˌdɪsəʊ'biːdiənts, *Am:* -ə'-] *n* *no pl* desobediencia *f*

disobedient [ˌdɪsəʊ'biːdiənt, *Am:* -ə'-] *adj* desobediente

disobey [ˌdɪsəʊ'beɪ, *Am:* -ə'-] *vi, vt* desobedecer

disorder [dɪ'sɔːdər, *Am:* -'sɔːrdɚ] *n* **1.** *no pl* (*lack of order*) desorden *m* **2.** MED trastorno *m*

disorderly [dɪ'sɔːdəli, *Am:* -'sɔːrdɚ-] *adj* **1.** (*untidy*) desordenado **2.** (*unruly*) escandaloso

disorient [dɪ'sɔːriənt, *Am:* -ent] *vt Am,* **disorientate** [dɪ'sɔːriənteɪt] *vt* desorientar; **to get ~ed** desorientarse

disown [dɪ'səʊn, *Am:* dɪ'soʊn] *vt* repudiar

disparage [dɪ'spærɪdʒ, *Am:* -'sper-] *vt* menospreciar

disparaging *adj* despreciativo

disparate ['dɪspərət] *adj* dispar

disparity [dɪ'spærəti, *Am:* -'perət̬i] *n* disparidad *f*

dispassionate [dɪ'spæʃənət] *adj* desapasionado

dispatch [dɪ'spætʃ] *vt* despachar

dispel [dɪ'spel] <-ll-> *vt* disipar

dispensary [dɪ'spensəri] *n Brit* dispensario *m*

dispensation [ˌdɪspen'seɪʃən] *n* **1.** (*permission*) dispensa *f* **2.** (*distribution*) administración *f*

dispense [dɪ'spens] *vt* repartir; (*medicine*) administrar

♦ **dispense with** *vt* prescindir de

disperse [dɪ'spɜːs, *Am:* -'spɜːrs] *vi, vt* dispersar(se)

dispirited [dɪ'spɪrɪtɪd, *Am:* -t̬ɪd] *adj* desanimado

displace [dɪs'pleɪs] *vt* **1.** (*eject*) desplazar **2.** (*take the place of*) reemplazar

display [dɪ'spleɪ] **I.** *vt* **1.** (*arrange*) exhibir **2.** (*show*) demostrar **II.** *n* **1.** (*arrangement*) exposición *f* **2.** *no pl* (*demonstration*) demostración *f*

displease [dɪ'spliːz] *vt* disgustar

displeasure [dɪ'spleʒər, *Am:* -ɚ] *n* *no pl* disgusto *m*

disposable [dɪ'spəʊzəbl, *Am:* -'spoʊ-] *adj* desechable

disposal [dɪ'spəʊzl, *Am:* dɪ'spoʊ-] *n* **to be at sb's ~** estar a disposición de alguien

dispose [dɪ'spəʊz, *Am:* -'spoʊz] *vi* **to ~ of sth** (*throw away*) desechar algo; (*get rid of*) deshacerse de algo

disposed *adj* **to be well ~ towards sb** estar bien dispuesto hacia alguien

disposition [ˌdɪspə'zɪʃən] *n* disposición *f*

dispossess [ˌdɪspə'zes] *vt* desposeer

disproportionate [ˌdɪsprə'pɔːʃənət, *Am:* -'pɔːr-] *adj* desproporcionado

disprove [dɪ'spruːv] *vt* refutar

dispute [dɪ'spjuːt] **I.** *vt* (*argue*) discutir; (*doubt*) poner en duda **II.** *n* discusión *f*

disqualify [dɪ'skwɒlɪfaɪ, *Am:* dɪ'skwɑːlə-] <-ie-> *vt* descalificar

disquiet [dɪ'skwaɪət] *n* *no pl* inquietud *f*

disregard [ˌdɪsrɪ'gɑːd, *Am:* -rɪ'gɑːrd] **I.** *vt* desatender **II.** *n* *no pl* despreocupación f

disreputable [dɪs'repjətəbl, Am: -jəṭə-] adj de mala fama

disrespect [ˌdɪsrɪ'spekt] n no pl falta f de respeto

disrespectful [ˌdɪsrɪ'spektfəl] adj descortés

disrupt [dɪs'rʌpt] vt (interrupt) interrumpir; (disturb) trastornar

disruption [dɪs'rʌpʃən] n (interruption) interrupción f; (disturbance) perturbación f; fig (disorder) desorganización f

disruptive [dɪs'rʌptɪv] adj que trastorna

dissatisfaction [dɪsˌsætɪs'fækʃən, Am: ˌdɪssæṭəs'-] n no pl insatisfacción f

dissatisfied [dɪs'sætɪsfaɪd, Am: -'sæṭəs-] adj insatisfecho

dissect [dɪ'sekt] vt diseccionar; fig examinar

dissent [dɪ'sent] I. n no pl disidencia f II. vi disentir

dissertation [ˌdɪsə'teɪʃən, Am: -əʳ'-] n UNIV tesis f inv

disservice [ˌdɪs's3:vɪs, Am: -'s3:r-] n no pl perjuicio m; **to do sb a ~** perjudicar a alguien

dissident ['dɪsɪdənt] n disidente

dissimilar [ˌdɪs'sɪmɪləʳ, Am: -ləʳ] adj diferente, disímbolo Méx

dissipate ['dɪsɪpeɪt] vi disiparse

dissociate [dɪ'səʊʃieɪt, Am: -'soʊ-] vt **to ~ oneself from sb** disociarse de alguien

dissolution [ˌdɪsə'lu:ʃən] n no pl disolución f

dissolve [dɪ'zɒlv, Am: -'zɑ:lv] I. vi 1. CHEM disolverse 2. fig deshacerse II. vt CHEM disolver

dissuade [dɪ'sweɪd] vt disuadir

distance ['dɪstəns] I. n distancia f; **to keep one's ~** guardar las distancias II. vt **to ~ oneself from sb** distanciarse de alguien

distant ['dɪstənt] adj (far away) distante; (not closely related) lejano

distaste [dɪ'steɪst] n no pl aversión f

distasteful [dɪ'steɪstfəl] adj desagradable

distil [dɪ'stɪl] <-ll-> vt, **distill** vt Am,

Aus destilar

distillery [dɪ'stɪləri] n destilería f

distinct [dɪ'stɪŋkt] adj 1. (separate) distinto 2. (marked) definido

distinction [dɪ'stɪŋkʃən] n distinción f

distinctive [dɪ'stɪŋktɪv] adj característico

distinguish [dɪ'stɪŋgwɪʃ] vt distinguir; **to ~ oneself in sth** destacar en algo

distinguished adj distinguido

distort [dɪ'stɔ:t, Am: -'stɔ:rt] vt torcer; (facts, the truth) tergiversar

distortion [dɪ'stɔ:ʃən, Am: -'stɔ:r-] n (of facts, the truth) distorsión f

distract [dɪ'strækt] vt distraer

distraction [dɪ'strækʃən] n 1. (disturbing factor) distracción f 2. (pastime) entretenimiento m

distraught [dɪ'strɔ:t, Am: -'strɑ:t] adj turbado

distress [dɪ'stres] I. n no pl (anguish) congoja f II. vt afligir

distressed adj 1. (unhappy) afligido 2. (in difficulties) apurado

distressing adj angustioso

distribute [dɪ'strɪbju:t] vt repartir

distribution [ˌdɪstrɪ'bju:ʃən] n no pl 1. (giving out) reparto m 2. (spread) distribución f

distributor [dɪ'strɪbjətəʳ, Am: -ṭəʳ] n COM distribuidora f

district ['dɪstrɪkt] n (defined area) distrito m, intendencia f CSur; (region) región f

district attorney n Am fiscal m de distrito **district court** n Am tribunal m federal

distrust [dɪ'strʌst] I. vt desconfiar de II. n no pl desconfianza f

disturb [dɪ'st3:b, Am: -'st3:rb] vt (bother) molestar; (worry) preocupar

disturbance [dɪ'st3:bəns, Am: -'st3:r-] n 1. (bother) molestia f 2. (public incident) disturbio m

disturbing adj (annoying) molesto; (worrying) preocupante

disused [dɪ'sju:zd] adj en desuso

ditch [dɪtʃ] I. <-es> n zanja f; (road) cuneta f; (for defense) foso m II. vt

1. (*discard*) abandonar **2.** *inf* (*end relationship*) cortar con

dive [daɪv] **I.** *n* (*jump into water*) salto *m* de cabeza; *fig* descenso *m* en picado; **to take a ~** *fig* caer en picado *m* **II.** *vi* <dived *Am:* dove, dived *Am:* dove> (*plunge into water*) zambullirse; (*jump head first into water*) tirarse de cabeza; *fig* bajar en picado

diver ['daɪvəʳ, *Am:* -vɚ] *n* **1.** SPORTS buceador(a) *m(f)* **2.** (*worker*) buzo *m*

diverge [daɪ'vɜːdʒ, *Am:* -'vɜːrdʒ] *vi* divergir

divergence [daɪ'vɜːdʒəns, *Am:* dɪ'vɜːr-] *n no pl* divergencia *f*

divergent [daɪ'vɜːdʒənt, *Am:* dɪ-'vɜːr-] *adj* divergente

diverse [daɪ'vɜːs, *Am:* dɪ'vɜːrs] *adj* **1.** (*varied*) variado **2.** (*not alike*) diverso

diversification [daɪˌvɜːsɪfɪ'keɪʃən, *Am:* dɪˌvɜːr-] *n no pl* diversificación *f*

diversify [daɪ'vɜːsɪfaɪ, *Am:* dɪˌvɜːr-] <-ie-> *vi* diversificarse

diversion [daɪ'vɜːʃən, *Am:* dɪ'vɜːr-] *n no pl* desviación *f*; (*of railway, river*) desvío *m*

diversity [daɪ'vɜːsəti, *Am:* dɪ'vɜːr-sət̬i] *n no pl* diversidad *f*

divert [daɪ'vɜːt, *Am:* dɪ'vɜːrt] *vt* **1.** (*change direction*) desviar **2.** (*distract*) distraer

divest [daɪ'vest, *Am:* dɪ-] *vt* despojar de

divide [dɪ'vaɪd] **I.** *n* separación *f* **II.** *vt* **1.** *a.* MAT dividir **2.** (*allot*) repartir **III.** *vi* dividirse; **~ and rule** divide y vencerás

dividend ['dɪvɪdend] *n* dividendo *m*

divine [dɪ'vaɪn] **I.** *adj a. fig* divino **II.** *vt* adivinar

diving *n no pl* buceo *m*

divinity [dɪ'vɪnəti, *Am:* -ət̬i] <-ies> *n* **1.** *no pl* (*state*) divinidad *f* **2.** *pl* (*god*) deidad *f*

division [dɪ'vɪʒən] *n* **1.** *a.* MIL, MAT división *f* **2.** *no pl* (*splitting up*) reparto *m*

divorce [dɪ'vɔːs, *Am:* -'vɔːrs] **I.** *n* divorcio *m* **II.** *vt* **to get ~d from sb** divorciarse de alguien **III.** *vi* divorciarse

divulge [daɪ'vʌldʒ, *Am:* dɪ-] *vt* divulgar

DIY [ˌdiːaɪ'waɪ] *abbr of* **do-it-yourself** bricolaje *m*

dizzy ['dɪzi] <-ier, -iest> *adj* mareado

DJ [ˌdiː'dʒeɪ, *Am:* 'diːdʒeɪ] *n abbr of* **disc jockey** DJ *m*

DNA [ˌdiːen'eɪ] *n no pl abbr of* **deoxyribonucleic acid** ADN *m*

do [duː] **I.** *n Brit, Aus, inf* (*party*) fiesta *f* **II.** <does, did, done> *aux* **1.** (*to form questions*) **~ you own a dog?** ¿tienes un perro? **2.** (*to form negatives*) **Frida ~esn't like olives** a Frida no le gustan las aceitunas **3.** (*to form imperatives*) **~ come in!** ¡pero pasa, por favor! **4.** (*used for emphasis*) **he did ~ it** sí que lo hizo **5.** (*replaces a repeated verb*) **so ~ I** yo también; **neither ~ I** yo tampoco; **she speaks more fluently than he ~es** ella habla con mayor fluidez que él **6.** (*requesting affirmation*) ¿verdad?; **you ~n't want to answer, ~ you?** no quieres contestar, ¿verdad? **III.** <does, did, done> *vt* **1.** (*carry out*) hacer; **what on earth are you ~ing** (**there**)? ¿que diablos haces (ahí)?; **to ~ something for sb** hacer algo por alguien; **to ~ one's shoes** limpiar los zapatos; **to ~ one's teeth** lavarse los dientes **2.** (*act*) actuar; **to ~ as others ~** hacer como hacen los demás **3.** (*learn*) estudiar **4.** (*be satisfactory*) **I only have beer – will that ~ you?** sólo tengo cerveza – ¿te va bien **5.** (*cook*) cocer; **to ~ sth for sb** cocinar algo para alguien **IV.** <does, did, done> *vi* **this behaviour just won't ~!** ¡no se puede tolerar este comportamiento!; **how are you ~ing?** ¿qué tal estás?; **that will never ~** eso no sirve; **that will ~!** ¡ya basta!

◆ **do away with** *vt inf* liquidar

◆ **do in** *vt always sep* **to do sb in** acabar con alguien

◆ **do up** *vt* **1.** (*fasten: button*) abro-

char; (*shoes*) atar **2.**(*restore*) renovar

◆**do without** *vi* apañarse sin

docile ['dəʊsaɪl, *Am:* 'dɑ:səl] *adj*
dócil

dock¹ [dɒk, *Am:* dɑ:k] NAUT **I.** *n*
muelle *m* **II.** *vi* atracar

dock² [dɒk, *Am:* dɑ:k] *n no pl, Brit*
LAW **to be in the** ~ estar en el banquillo

docker ['dɒkər, *Am:* 'dɑ:kɚ] *n* esti-
bador *m*

dockyard ['dɒkjɑ:d, *Am:* 'dɑ:k-
jɑ:rd] *n* astillero *m*

doctor ['dɒktər, *Am:* 'dɑ:ktɚ] **I.** *n*
1. MED médico, -a *m, f;* **to go to the**
~**'s** ir al médico **2.** UNIV doctor(a)
m(f) **II.** *vt* (*alter*) falsear

doctorate ['dɒktərət, *Am:*'dɑ:k-] *n*
doctorado *m*

[?] El **doctorate** o **doctor's degree**
en una disciplina es el título académico más alto que se puede obtener en una universidad. En las
universidades anglosajonas los
doctorados reciben diversas de-
nominaciones según las materias.
El doctorado más común es el
PhD, también llamado **Dphil**
(**Doctor of Philosophy**). Este título se concede tras la realización de
una tesis doctoral en cualquier materia exceptuando Derecho y
Medicina. Otros títulos de doctorado son: **Dmus** (**Doctor of
Music**), **MD** (**Doctor of Medicine**), **LLD** (**Doctor of Laws**) y
DD (**Doctor of Divinity**, Doctor
en Teología). Las universidades
también pueden conceder el título
de doctor a aquellas personali-
dades de alto rango que han destacado por su contribución a la investigación científica, su trabajo o
sus importantes publicaciones.

Este tipo de doctorado se denomi-
na doctorado Honoris Causa. A
esta modalidad pertenecen el **Dlitt**
(**Doctor of Letters**) o el **DSc**
(**Doctor of Science**).

doctrine ['dɒktrɪn, *Am:* 'dɑ:k-] *n*
doctrina *f*

document ['dɒkjʊmənt, *Am:*
'dɑ:kjə-] **I.** *n* documento *m* **II.** *vt*
documentar

documentary [ˌdɒkjʊ'mentəri,
Am: ˌdɑ:kjə'mentɚ-] <-ies> *n*
documental *m*

documentation [ˌdɒkjʊmen'teɪʃən, *Am:* ˌdɑ:kjə-] *n no pl* documentación *f*

dodge [dɒdʒ, *Am:* dɑ:dʒ] *vt* esquivar; (*question*) eludir; **to** ~ **doing
sth** escaquearse de hacer algo

dodgy ['dɒdʒi, *Am:* 'dɑ:dʒi] <-ier,
-iest> *adj Brit, Aus, inf* (*person*)
tramposo; (*situation*) delicado

doe [dəʊ, *Am:* doʊ] *n* (*deer*) cierva
f, venada *f AmL*

DoE *n Brit abbr of* **Department of
the Environment** Departamento *m*
de Medioambiente

does [dʌz] *vt, vi, aux 3rd pers sing of*
do

dog [dɒg, *Am:* dɑ:g] **I.** *n* perro, -a
m, f; **the** (**dirty**) ~**!** *inf*¡el muy canalla!; **a** ~**'s breakfast** *inf* un revoltijo;
to lead a ~**'s life** llevar una vida de
perros; **to go to the** ~**s** *inf* ir de capa
caída **II.** <-gg-> *vt* acosar

dogged ['dɒgɪd, *Am:* 'dɑ:gɪd] *adj*
obstinado

dogma ['dɒgmə, *Am:* 'dɑ:g-] *n*
dogma *m*

dogmatic [dɒg'mætɪk, *Am:* dɑ:g-
'mæt̬-] *adj* dogmático

doing ['du:ɪŋ] *n no pl* **to be sb's** ~
ser asunto de alguien; **to take some**
~ requerir esfuerzo

doldrums ['dɒldrəmz, *Am:* 'doʊl-]
npl **to be in the** ~ (*person*) estar deprimido; (*business*) estar estancado

dole [dəʊl, *Am:* doʊl] *n* **to be on
the** ~ estar cobrando el paro

◆**dole out** *vt* repartir

doleful ['dəʊlfəl, *Am:* 'doʊl-] *adj* (*person*) triste; (*expression*) compungido

doll [dɒl, *Am:* dɑːl] *n* **1.** (*toy*) muñeco, -a *m, f;* ~**'s house** casa *f* de muñecas **2.** *Am, inf* (*term of address*) muñeca *f*

dollar ['dɒlə^r, *Am:* 'dɑːlɚ] *n* dólar *m;* **to feel like a million** ~**s** sentirse a las mil maravillas

dolly ['dɒli, *Am:* 'dɑːli] <-ies> *n* **1.** (*doll*) muñequita *f* **2.** CINE travelín *m*

dolphin ['dɒlfɪn, *Am:* 'dɑːl-] *n* delfín *m,* bufeo *m Perú*

domain [dəʊ'meɪn, *Am:* doʊ-] *n* **1.** POL, INFOR dominio *m;* (*lands*) propiedad *f* **2.** (*sphere of activity*) ámbito *m;* **to be in the public** ~ ser de dominio público

dome [dəʊm, *Am:* doʊm] *n* (*roof*) cúpula *f;* (*ceiling*) bóveda *f*

domestic [də'mestɪk] *adj* **1.** (*of the house*) doméstico **2.** (*home-loving*) casero **3.** (*produce, flight*) nacional; (*market, policy*) interior

domestic appliance *n* electrodoméstico *m*

domesticate [də'mestɪkeɪt] *vt* domesticar

dominance ['dɒmɪnənts, *Am:* 'dɑːmə-] *no pl n* **1.** (*rule*) dominación *f* **2.** MIL supremacía *f*

dominant ['dɒmɪnənt, *Am:* 'dɑːmə-] *adj* dominante

dominate ['dɒmɪneɪt, *Am:* 'dɑː-mə-] *vi, vt* dominar

domination [ˌdɒmɪ'neɪʃən, *Am:* ˌdɑːmə-] *no pl n* dominación *f*

Dominican [də'mɪnɪkən, *Am:* doʊ'mɪn-] *adj* dominicano

Dominican Republic *n* República *f* Dominicana

dominion [də'mɪnjən] *n* dominio *m*

domino ['dɒmɪnəʊ, *Am:* 'dɑː-mənoʊ] <-es> *n* **1.** *pl* (*games*) dominó *m* **2.** (*piece*) ficha *f* de dominó

don [dɒn, *Am:* dɑːn] I. *n* UNIV profesor(a) *m(f)* II. *vt* (*of clothing*) poner

donate [dəʊ'neɪt, *Am:* 'doʊneɪt] *vt* donar

donation [dəʊ'neɪʃən, *Am:* doʊ-'neɪ-] *n* **1.** (*contribution*) donativo *m* **2.** *no pl* (*act*) donación *f*

done [dʌn] *pp of* **do**

donkey ['dɒŋki, *Am:* 'dɑːŋ-] *n a. fig* burro *m*

donor ['dəʊnə^r, *Am:* 'doʊnɚ] *n* donante *mf*

donut ['dəʊnʌt, *Am:* 'doʊ] *n Am, Aus* donut *m*

doom [duːm] I. *n* (*destiny*) suerte *f* II. *vt* condenar

door [dɔː^r, *Am:* dɔːr] *n* puerta *f;* **there's someone at the** ~ llaman a la puerta; **to answer the** ~ abrir la puerta; **to live next** ~ vivir al lado de alguien; **to show sb the** ~ echar a alguien; **out of** ~**s** al aire libre

doorbell *n* timbre *m* **doorknob** *n* pomo *m* de la puerta **doorman** <-men> *n* portero *m* **doormat** *n* felpudo *m* **doorstep** *n* peldaño *m* (*de la puerta de entrada*)*;* **to be right on the** ~ *fig* estar a la vuelta de la esquina

door-to-door *adj, adv* de puerta a puerta

doorway *n* entrada *f*

dope [dəʊp, *Am:* doʊp] I. *n* **1.** *no pl, inf* (*drugs*) drogas *fpl;* (*marijuana*) marihuana *f;* ~ **test** SPORTS control *m* antidoping; **to give sb the** ~ **on sth** *fig* pasar informes a alguien sobre algo **2.** *inf* (*stupid person*) idiota *mf* II. *vt* SPORTS dopar

dopey *adj,* **dopy** ['dəʊpi, *Am:* 'doʊ-] *adj* <-ier, -iest> **1.** (*drowsy*) atontado **2.** (*stupid*) tonto

dormant ['dɔːmənt, *Am:* 'dɔːr-] *adj* inactivo

dormitory ['dɔːmɪtəri, *Am:* 'dɔːr-mətɔːri] <-ies> *n* **1.** dormitorio *m* **2.** *Am* UNIV residencia *f* de estudiantes

dose [dəʊs, *Am:* doʊs] *n a. fig* dosis *f inv;* **a nasty** ~ **of flu** una gripe muy fuerte

dossier ['dɒsieɪ, *Am:* 'dɑːsieɪ] *n* expediente *m*

dot [dɒt, *Am:* dɑːt] **I.** *n* **1.** punto *m;* **on the** ~ en punto **2.** *pl* TYPO puntos *mpl* suspensivos **II.** <-tt-> *vt* **to** ~ **one's i's and cross one's t's** poner los puntos sobre las íes

dote (up)on [dəʊt-, *Am:* doʊt̬-] *vt* adorar

dotty ['dɒti, *Am:* 'dɑːt̬i] *adj* <-ier, -iest> (*person*) chiflado; (*idea*) descabellado

double ['dʌbl] **I.** *adj* **1.** (*twice as much/many*) doble; **to have a** ~ **meaning** tener un doble sentido; **to lead a** ~ **life** llevar una doble vida **2.** (*composed of two*) **in** ~ **figures** más de diez; ~ **'s'** dos eses; **his number is** ~ **two five three five six** su número es el dos dos cinco tres cinco seis **3.** (*for two*) ~ **room** habitación *f* doble **II.** *adv* **to see** ~ ver doble; **to fold sth** ~ doblar algo por la mitad; **to be bent** ~ estar encorvado **III.** *vt* (*increase*) doblar; (*efforts*) redoblar **IV.** *vi* duplicarse **V.** *n* **1.** (*double quantity*) doble *m;* **at** [*o* **on**] **the** ~ *inf* inmediatamente **2.** (*person*) doble *mf* **3.** *pl* SPORTS **to play** ~**s** jugar una partida de dobles
◆**double back** *vi* volver sobre sus pasos

double bed *n* cama *f* de matrimonio **double chin** *n* papada *f* **double--glazing** *no pl n* doble acristalamiento *m* **double standard** *n* **to have** ~**s** no medir con el mismo rasero **double take** *n* **to do a** ~ tardar en reaccionar

doubly ['dʌbli] *adv* **to make** ~ **sure that ...** asegurarse bien de que... +*subj*

doubt [daʊt] *no pl* **I.** *n* duda *f;* **to be in** ~ **whether to ...** dudar si...; **no** ~ sin duda; **without a** ~ sin duda alguna; **beyond all reasonable** ~ más allá de toda duda fundada; **to raise** ~**s about sth** hacer dudar de algo; **to cast** ~ **on sth** poner algo en tela de juicio **II.** *vt* dudar de; (*capability, sincerity*) poner en duda; **to** ~ **that** dudar que +*subj*; **to** ~ **if** [*o* **whether**] ... dudar si...

doubtful ['daʊtfəl] *adj* **1.** (*uncer-tain, undecided*) indeciso; **to be** ~ **whether to ...** dudar si...; **to be** ~ **about going** estar indeciso respecto a si ir o no **2.** (*unlikely*) incierto **3.** (*questionable*) dudoso

doubtless ['daʊtlɪs] *adv* sin duda

dough [dəʊ, *Am:* doʊ] *n* **1.** GASTR masa *f* **2.** *Am, inf* (*money*) pasta *f,* plata *f AmS*

doughnut ['dəʊnʌt, *Am:* 'doʊ-] *n Brit* donut *m*

dour [dʊəʳ, *Am:* dʊr] *adj* (*manner*) adusto; (*appearance*) austero

douse [daʊs] *vt* **1.** (*throw liquid on*) mojar; **to** ~ **sth in petrol** mojar algo con gasolina **2.** (*extinguish*) apagar

dove[1] [dʌv] *n* ZOOL paloma *f*

dove[2] [dəʊv, *Am:* doʊv] *Am pt, pp of* **dive**

down[1] [daʊn] *n* (*feathers*) plumón *m;* (*hairs*) pelusa *f*

down[2] [daʊn] **I.** *adv* abajo; **to fall** ~ caerse; **to lie** ~ acostarse; **to go** ~ **to the sea** bajar al mar; **the price is** ~ el precio ha bajado; **to be** ~ **on sb** *fig* tener manía a alguien; ~ **with the dictator!** ¡abajo el dictador! **II.** *prep* **to go** ~ **the stairs** bajar las escaleras; **to run** ~ **the slope** correr cuesta abajo; **to go** ~ **the street** ir por la calle

down-and-out *n* vagabundo, -a *m, f*

downcast ['daʊnkɑːst, *Am:* 'daʊnkæst] *adj* alicaído

downfall ['daʊnfɔːl] *n* (*of government*) caída *f;* (*of person*) perdición *f*

downgrade [ˌdaʊn'greɪd] *vt* **1.** (*lower category of*) bajar de categoría **2.** (*disparage*) minimizar; **to** ~ **the importance of sth** minimizar la importancia de algo

downhill [ˌdaʊn'hɪl] *adv* **to go** ~ ir cuesta abajo; *fig* ir de mal en peor

download [ˌdaʊn'ləʊd, *Am:* 'daʊnloʊd] *vt* INFOR bajar

down payment *n* entrada *f,* cuota *f* inicial *AmL*

downpour ['daʊnpɔːʳ, *Am:* -pɔːr] *n* chaparrón *m*

downright ['daʊnraɪt] *adj* (*refusal, disobedience*) completo; (*lie*) abierto; **it is a ~ disgrace** es una auténtica vergüenza

downside ['daʊnsaɪd] *n no pl* inconveniente *m*

downstairs [ˌdaʊn'steəz, *Am:* -'sterz] **I.** *adv* abajo; **to go ~** bajar **II.** *adj* (del piso) de abajo

downstream [ˌdaʊn'stri:m] *adv* río abajo

down-to-earth *adj* práctico

downtown ['daʊntaʊn, *Am:* ˌdaʊn'-] **I.** *n no pl, Am* centro *m* (de la ciudad) **II.** *adv Am* **to go ~** ir al centro; **to live ~** vivir en el centro

downturn ['daʊntɜ:n, *Am:* -tɜ:rn] *n* empeoramiento *m*

downward ['daʊnwəd, *Am:* -wəd] **I.** *adj* (*direction*) hacia abajo; (*tendency*) a la baja **II.** *adv Am* hacia abajo

downwards ['daʊnwədz, *Am:* -wədz] *adv* hacia abajo

dowry ['daʊəri] <-ies> *n* dote *f*

doze [dəʊz, *Am:* doʊz] *vi* dormitar

dozen ['dʌzn] *n* docena *f;* **half a ~** media docena; **two ~ eggs** dos docenas de huevos; **~s of times** montones de veces; **it's six of one and half a ~ of the other** *inf* da lo mismo; **to talk nineteen to the ~** *inf* hablar por los codos

dozy ['dəʊzi, *Am:* 'doʊ-] *adj* <-ier, -iest> **1.** (*sleepy*) soñoliento **2.** *Brit, inf* (*stupid*) tonto, abombado *AmL*

Dr *abbr of* **Doctor** Dr. *m*, Dra. *f*

drab [dræb] *adj* <drabber, drabbest> (*colour*) apagado; (*existence*) monótono

draconian [drə'kəʊniən, *Am:* -'koʊ-] *adj* draconiano

draft [dra:ft, *Am:* dræft] **I.** *n* **1.** (*preliminary version*) borrador *m;* (*drawing*) boceto *m* **2.** *no pl, Am* MIL reclutamiento *m* **II.** *vt* **1.** (*prepare preliminary version*) hacer un borrador de **2.** *Am* MIL llamar a filas

drag [dræg] <-gg-> **I.** *vt* arrastrar; **to ~ one's heels** *fig* dar largas a un asunto **II.** *vi* **1.** (*trail along*) arrastrarse por el suelo **2.** (*time*) pasar lentamente; (*meeting, conversation*) hacerse interminable **3.** (*lag be-*

hind) rezagarse **III.** *n* **1.** *no pl* PHYS resistencia *f* **2.** *fig, inf* **to be a ~ on sb** ser una carga para alguien; **what a ~!** ¡qué rollo!; **to be in ~** ir vestido de mujer

◆**drag on** *vi* hacerse interminable
◆**drag up** *vt* sacar a relucir

dragon ['drægən] *n* dragón *m*

dragonfly ['drægənflaɪ] <-ies> *n* libélula *f,* alguacil *m RíoPl*

drain [dreɪn] **I.** *vt* **1.** AGR, MED drenar; (*pond*) vaciar; (*river*) desaguar; (*food*) escurrir **2.** (*empty by drinking: glass, cup*) apurar; (*bottle*) acabar **3.** (*exhaust: person*) dejar agotado; (*resources*) agotar **II.** *n* (*conduit*) canal *m* de desagüe; (*sewer*) alcantarilla *f,* resumidero *m AmL;* (*plughole*) desagüe *m;* **to be a ~ on sb's resources** consumir los recursos de alguien

drainage ['dreɪnɪdʒ] *n no pl* **1.** AGR, MED drenaje *m* **2.** TECH desagüe *m*

drainpipe *n* tubo *m* de desagüe

drake [dreɪk] *n* pato *m* (macho)

drama ['drɑ:mə] *n* **1.** LIT drama *m* **2.** THEAT arte *m* dramático

drama school *n* escuela *f* de arte dramático

dramatic [drə'mætɪk, *Am:* -'mæt̬-] *adj* **1.** THEAT dramático **2.** (*rise*) espectacular

dramatist ['dræmətɪst, *Am:* 'drɑ:-mət̬ɪst] *n* dramaturgo, -a *m, f*

dramatize ['dræmətaɪz, *Am:* 'drɑ:-mə-] *vt* **1.** THEAT adaptar al teatro **2.** (*exaggerate*) dramatizar

drank [dræŋk] *pt of* **drink**

drape [dreɪp] **I.** *vt* **1.** (*cover*) cubrir **2.** (*place*) colocar **II.** *npl Am, Aus* cortinas *fpl*

drastic ['dræstɪk] *adj* (*measure*) drástico; (*change*) radical

draught [drɑ:ft, *Am:* dræft] *n* **1.** (*air current*) corriente *f* de aire **2.** (*drink*) trago *m* **3.** *pl* GAMES damas *fpl*

draughtsman ['drɑ:ftsmən, *Am:* 'dræfts-] <-men> *n* delineante *m*

draw [drɔ:, *Am:* drɑ:] **I.** <drew, drawn> *vt* **1.** ART dibujar; (*line*) trazar; (*character*) perfilar **2.** (*pull*) a-

rrastrar; **to ~ the curtains** correr las cortinas; **to ~ sb aside** llevarse a alguien aparte; **to ~ sth from sb** conseguir algo de alguien; **to ~ a conclusion** sacar una conclusión; **to ~ an inference** inferir **3.** (*attract*) atraer; **to ~ applause** arrancar aplausos; **to be ~n toward(s) sb** sentirse atraído por alguien **4.** (*take out*) sacar; (*money*) retirar; **to ~ blood** *fig* hacer sangrar **5.** (*salary*) ganar; (*pension*) cobrar **II.** <drew, drawn> *vi* **1.** ART dibujar **2.** (*move*) **to ~ ahead** adelantarse; **to ~ away** apartarse; **to ~ level with sb** *Brit* alcanzar a alguien; **to ~ to a close** finalizar **3.** SPORTS empatar **III.** *n* **1.** (*attraction*) atracción *f* **2.** SPORTS empate *m* **3.** (*drawing of lots*) sorteo *m*
◆**draw in** *vi* **1.** (*arrive*) llegar **2.** (*days*) acortarse
◆**draw on** *vi* **1.** (*continue*) seguir su curso **2.** (*approach*) acercarse
◆**draw out** *vt* **1.** (*prolong*) alargar **2.** (*elicit*) sacar; **to draw sb out (of** *himself*) hacer que alguien se desinhiba
◆**draw up I.** *vt* (*draft*) redactar **II.** *vi* (*vehicle*) pararse
drawback *n* desventaja *f*
drawer ['drɔːʳ, *Am:* 'drɔːr] *n* cajón *m*
drawing *n* ART dibujo *m*
drawing board *n* tablero *m* de delineación; **back to the ~!** ¡vuelta a empezar! **drawing pin** *n Brit, Aus* chincheta *f* **drawing room** *n* salón *m*
drawl [drɔːl, *Am:* drɑːl] *vi* hablar arrastrando las vocales
drawn [drɔːn, *Am:* drɑːn] *pp of* **draw**
dread [dred] **I.** *vt* temer **II.** *n no pl* terror *m*
dreadful ['dredfəl] *adj* atroz; (*mistake*) terrible; (*atrocity*) espantoso; **I feel ~ about it** me da mucha pena
dreadfully ['dredfəli] *adv* terriblemente
dream [driːm] **I.** *n* **1.** sueño *m*; **a bad ~** una pesadilla **2.** (*daydream*) ensueño *m*; (*fantasy*) ilusión *f*; **to be**

in a ~ estar en las nubes; **he cooks like a ~** cocina de maravilla; **a ~ come true** un sueño hecho realidad **II.** <dreamt *o* dreamed, dreamt *o* dreamed> *vi* soñar; **to ~ about** (**doing**) **sth** soñar con (hacer) algo; **I would not ~ of** (**doing**) **that** no se me pasaría por la cabeza (hacer) eso **III.** <dreamt *o* dreamed, dreamt *o* dreamed> *vt* soñar; **I never ~t that...** nunca se me había ocurrido que...
◆**dream up** *vt* idear
dreamer ['driːməʳ, *Am:* -məᵊ] *n* soñador(a) *m(f)*; *pej* iluso, -a *m, f*
dreamt [dremt] *pt, pp of* **dream**
dreary ['drɪəri, *Am:* 'drɪr-] *adj* <-ier, -iest> deprimente; (*weather*) gris
dredge [dredʒ] *vt* TECH dragar
drench [drentʃ] *vt* empapar
dress [dres] **I.** *n* <-es> vestido *m* **II.** *vi* vestirse; **to ~ in blue** vestir de azul; **to ~ smartly for sth** ponerse elegante para algo **III.** *vt* **1.** (*put clothes on*) vestir **2.** GASTR (*salad*) aliñar **3.** MED (*wound*) vendar
◆**dress up** *vi* ponerse elegante; **to ~ as sth** disfrazarse de algo
dresser ['dresəʳ, *Am:* -əᵊ] *n* **1.** THEAT encargado, -a *m, f* de vestuario **2.** (*sideboard*) aparador *m; Am, Can* (*dressing table*) tocador *m*
dressing ['dresɪŋ] *n* **1.** GASTR aliño *m* **2.** MED vendaje *m*
dressing gown *n* bata *f;* (*towel*) albornoz *m* **dressing room** *n* vestidor *m;* THEAT camerino *m*
dressmaker *n* modisto, -a *m, f*
dress rehearsal *n* ensayo *m* general
drew [druː] *pt of* **draw**
dribble ['drɪbl] **I.** *vi* **1.** (*person*) babear; (*water*) gotear **2.** SPORTS regatear **II.** *vt* (*water*) dejar caer gota a gota **III.** *n no pl* (*saliva*) baba *f;* (*water*) chorrito *m*
dried [draɪd] *pt, pp of* **dry**
dried-up *adj* seco
drift [drɪft] **I.** *vi* **1.** (*on water*) dejarse llevar por la corriente; **to ~ out to sea** ir a la deriva **2.** (*move aimlessly*) dejarse llevar **3.** (*sand, snow*) amontonarse **II.** *n* **to catch sb's ~**

caer en la cuenta de lo que alguien quiere decir
♦**drift apart** *vi* distanciarse (progresivamente)
♦**drift off** *vi* dormirse lentamente
drill¹ [drɪl] **I.** *n* taladro *m;* (*dentist's*) fresa *f* **II.** *vt* TECH perforar
drill² **I.** *n* MIL, SCHOOL ejercicios *fpl* **II.** *vt* **1.** SCHOOL instruir; **to ~ sth into sb** inculcar algo a alguien **2.** MIL enseñar la instrucción a
drink [drɪŋk] **I.**<drank, drunk> *vi* beber; **to ~ to sb** brindar por alguien; **to ~ like a fish** beber como una esponja **II.**<drank, drunk> *vt* beber; **to ~ a toast** (**to sb**) brindar (por alguien); **to ~ sb under the table** tener mucho más aguante que alguien **III.** *n* bebida *f;* (*alcoholic beverage*) copa *f;* **to have a ~** tomar algo; **to drive sb to ~** llevar a alguien a la bebida
♦**drink in** *vt* beber; (*words*) estar pendiente de
drinkable [drɪŋkəbl] *adj* potable
drinker *n* bebedor(a) *m(f)*
drinking water *no pl n* agua *f* potable
drip [drɪp] **I.**<-pp-> *vi* gotear **II.** *n* **1.** (*of water*) goteo *m* **2.** MED gota *f* a gota **3.** *inf* (*person*) pánfilo, -a *m, f*
dripping ['drɪpɪŋ] *adj* que gotea; **to be ~ wet** estar empapado
drive [draɪv] **I.**<drove, driven> *vt* **1.** AUTO conducir, manejar *AmL;* **to ~ sb home** llevar a alguien a casa (en coche) **2.** (*urge*) empujar; **to ~ sb to** (**do**) **sth** forzar a alguien a (hacer) algo; **to ~ sb mad** sacar a alguien de quicio **II.**<drove, driven> *vi* conducir, manejar *AmL* **III.** *n* **1. to go for a ~** ir a dar una vuelta en coche **2.** (*driveway*) entrada *f* **3.** *no pl* PSYCH impulso *m* **4.** (*campaign*) campaña *f*
♦**drive at** *vt inf* insinuar
♦**drive off** *vt always sep* ahuyentar
♦**drive out** *vt* expulsar
drive-in *n Am, Aus* (*restaurant*) restaurante donde se sirve a los clientes en su propio coche; (*cinema*) autocine *m*
drivel ['drɪvəl] *n no pl* tonterías *fpl*

driven ['drɪvən] *pp of* **drive**
driver ['draɪvəʳ, *Am:* -vɚ] *n* conductor(a) *m(f)*

? Las **Drive through bottle shops** son un tipo de tiendas que se pueden encontrar por toda Australia. Generalmente pertenecen a hoteles y por su aspecto se parecen a un garaje abierto o a un granero en el que se puede entrar con el coche. A este tipo de tiendas también se las conoce como **liquor barns**. En ellas, sin tener que apearse del vehículo, se puede comprar vino, cerveza y cualquier bebida alcohólica. El cliente es servido directamente en la ventanilla de su coche.

driveway ['draɪvweɪ] *n* camino *m* de entrada
driving I. *n* conducción *f,* manejo *m AmL* **II.** *adj* **1.** (*rain*) torrencial **2.** (*ambition, force*) impulsor
driving force *n no pl* fuerza *f* motriz
driving licence *n Brit* carné *m* de conducir **driving school** *n* autoescuela *f* **driving test** *n* examen *m* de conducir
drizzle ['drɪzl] **I.** *n no pl* METEO llovizna *f,* garúa *f AmL* **II.** *vi* METEO lloviznar, garuar *AmL*
drone [drəʊn, *Am:* droʊn] **I.** *n no pl* **1.** ZOOL zángano *m* **2.** (*tone*) zumbido *m* **II.** *vi* zumbar
drool [druːl] *vi* babear; **to ~ over sth** *fig* caérsele a uno la baba con algo
droop [druːp] *vi* colgar; (*flowers*) marchitarse; *fig* (*mood, spirits*) decaer
drop [drɒp, *Am:* drɑːp] **I.** *n* **1.** (*of liquid*) gota *f;* **by ~** gota a gota; **just a ~** sólo un poco; **it's a ~ in the ocean** es una gota de agua en el mar **2.** (*vertical distance*) declive *f;* **a sheer ~** un profundo precipicio **3.** (*decrease*) disminución *f;* (*of temperature*) descenso *m* **4.** (*fall*) caída

f; **at the ~ of a hat** en seguida
II. <-pp-> *vt* 1. (*allow to fall*) dejar
caer; **to ~ a hint** soltar una indirecta
2. (*lower*) bajar; **to ~ one's voice**
bajar la voz 3. (*give up*) renunciar a
4. (*leave out*) omitir III. <-pp-> *vi*
bajar; **to ~ with exhaustion** caer
rendido; **he is ready to ~** está que
no se tiene; **~ dead!** *inf* ¡muérete!

◆**drop behind** *vi* quedarse atrás
◆**drop in** *vi inf* **to ~ on sb** ir a ver a
alguien
◆**drop out** *vi* darse de baja

dropout *n* automarginado, -a *m, f*;
UNIV, SCHOOL *persona que ha abandonado los estudios*

drought [draʊt] *n* sequía *f*

drove [drəʊv, *Am:* droʊv] *pt of*
drive

drown [draʊn] I. *vt* 1. (*cause to die*)
ahogar; **to ~ one's sorrows** ahogar
las penas 2. (*engulf in water*) anegar
3. (*make inaudible*) apagar II. *vi*
ahogarse; **to be ~ing in work** *inf*
estar hasta arriba de trabajo

drowse [draʊz] *vi* dormitar

drowsy ['draʊzi] <-ier, -iest> *adj* soñoliento

drug [drʌg] I. *n* 1. MED fármaco *m*
2. (*narcotic*) droga *f* II. <-gg-> *vt*
drogar

drug addict *n* toxicómano, -a *m, f*
drug dealer *n* traficante *mf* de drogas

drugstore *n Am* farmacia *f* (*donde
suelen venderse otros artículos, además de productos farmacéuticos*)

druid ['druːɪd] *n* druida *m*

drum [drʌm] I. *n* 1. MUS, TECH tambor *m* 2. *pl* (*in band*) batería *f* 3. (*for
oil*) bidón *m* II. <-mm-> *vi* MUS
tocar el tambor III. *vt inf* **to ~ sth
into sb** meter a alguien algo en la
cabeza

drummer ['drʌmər, *Am:* -ɚ] *n* (*in
band*) tambor *m*; (*in group*) batería *f*

drumstick ['drʌmstɪk] *n* 1. MUS palillo *m* 2. GASTR pierna *f* de pollo

drunk [drʌŋk] I. *vt, vi pp of* **drink**
II. *adj* borracho, jumo *AmL*, ido
AmC; **to get ~** emborracharse; **to be
~ with joy** estar ebrio de alegría

drunken ['drʌŋkən] *adj* borracho
drunkenness ['drʌŋkənɪs] *n no pl*
embriaguez *f*, bomba *f AmL*

dry [draɪ] I. <-ier *o* -er, -iest *o* -est>
adj seco; (*climate, soil*) árido; **to go
~** secarse; **to run ~** *fig* agotarse
II. <-ie-> *vt* secar; (*tears*) enjugarse
III. <-ie-> *vi* secarse

◆**dry up** *vi* 1. (*become dry*) secarse
2. (*dry the dishes*) secar los platos

dry-clean *vt* limpiar en seco

dry cleaner's *n no pl* tintorería *f*

dryer ['draɪər, *Am:* -ɚ] *n* (*for hair*)
secador *m*; (*for clothes*) secadora *f*

dual ['djuːəl, *Am:* 'duː-] *adj inv*
doble

dual carriageway *n Brit* autovía *f*,
autocarril *m Bol, Chile, Nic*

dub [dʌb] <-bb-> *vt* CINE doblar

dubious ['djuːbɪəs, *Am:* 'duː-] *adj*
dudoso

duchess ['dʌtʃɪs] *n* duquesa *f*

duchy ['dʌtʃi] *n* ducado *m*

duck [dʌk] I. *n* pato *m*; **to take to
sth like a ~ to water** *inf* sentirse
como pez en el agua II. *vi* agachar la
cabeza; **to ~ out of sth** escabullirse
de algo III. *vt* **to ~ one's head** agachar la cabeza; **to ~ an issue** eludir
un tema

duckling ['dʌklɪŋ] *n* patito *m*

duct [dʌkt] *n* conducto *m*; ANAT
canal *m*

dud [dʌd] *adj* falso

dude [djuː] *n Am, inf* (*guy*) individuo *m*

due [djuː, *Am:* duː] I. *adj* 1. (*payable*) pagadero; (*owing*) debido; **to
fall ~** vencer 2. (*appropriate*) **with
(all) due respect** con el debido respeto; **to treat sb with the respect
~ to him** *Brit, Aus* tratar a alguien
con el respeto que se merece; **in ~
course** a su debido tiempo 3. (*expected*) **I'm ~ in Berlin this evening** esta noche me esperan en Berlín
4. (*owing to*) **~ to** debido a II. *n* to
give sb his ~ dar a alguien lo que se
merece; **to pay one's ~s** *fig* cumplir
con sus obligaciones III. *adv* **~ north**
derecho hacia el norte

duel ['djuːəl, *Am:* 'duː-] *n* duelo *m*

duet [dju'et, *Am:* du-] *n* dúo *m*

dug [dʌg] *pt, pp of* **dig**

dugout ['dʌgaʊt] *n* **1.** MIL refugio *m* subterráneo; SPORTS banquillo *m* **2.** (*canoe*) piragua *f* (*hecha de un tronco*)

duke [djuːk, *Am:* duːk] *n* duque *m*

dull [dʌl] *adj* **1.** (*boring*) aburrido; **as ~ as ditchwater** más aburrido que un entierro de tercera **2.** (*not bright: surface*) deslustrado; (*colour*) apagado **3.** (*ache, thud*) sordo

duly ['djuːli, *Am:* 'duː-] *adv* debidamente

dumb [dʌm] *adj* **1.** (*mute*) mudo; **deaf and ~** sordomudo; **to be struck ~** quedarse mudo de asombro **2.** *inf* (*stupid*) estúpido

dumbfounded *adj* mudo de asombro

dummy ['dʌmi] <-ies> *n* **1.** (*mannequin*) maniquí *m* **2.** *Brit, Aus* (*for baby*) chupete *m* **3.** (*fool*) tonto

dump [dʌmp] **I.** *n* **1.** (*for waste*) vertedero *m*, botadero *m Ven;* MIL depósito *m* **2.** *inf* (*nasty place*) tugurio *m* **II.** *vt* **1.** (*waste*) verter **2.** *inf* (*end relationship*) dejar

dumpy ['dʌmpi] <-ier, -iest> *adj* regordete

dune [djuːn, *Am:* duːn] *n* duna *f*

dung [dʌŋ] *n no pl* estiércol *m*

dungarees [ˌdʌŋgə'riːz] *npl Brit* (*overall*) peto *m; Am* (*denim clothes*) mono *m*

dungeon ['dʌndʒən] *n* mazmorra *f*

dunk [dʌŋk] *vt* mojar

duo ['djuːəʊ, *Am:* 'duːoʊ] *n* dúo *m*

dupe [djuːp, *Am:* duːp] *n* inocentón, -ona *m, f*

duplex ['djuːpleks, *Am:* 'duː-] *n Am* dúplex

duplicate ['djuːplɪkət, *Am:* 'duː-] **I.** *vt* **1.** (*replicate*) duplicar **2.** (*copy*) copiar **II.** *adj* duplicado

duplicity [dju'plɪsəti, *Am:* duː-'plɪsəti] *n no pl* duplicidad *f*

durability [ˌdjʊərə'bɪləti, *Am:* ˌdʊrə'bɪləti] *n no pl* durabilidad *f*

durable ['djʊərəbl, *Am:* 'dʊrə-] *adj* duradero

duration [djʊ'reɪʃən, *Am:* dʊ-] *n*

no pl duración *f;* **for the ~** hasta que se acabe

during ['djʊərɪŋ, *Am:* 'dʊrɪŋ] *prep* durante

dusk [dʌsk] *n no pl* **at ~** al atardecer

dust [dʌst] **I.** *n no pl* polvo *m;* **to bite the ~** morder el polvo **II.** *vt* **1.** (*clean*) quitar el polvo a **2.** (*spread over*) salpicar

dustbin *n Brit* cubo *m* de (la) basura

duster ['dʌstər, *Am:* -təʳ] *n* trapo *m*

dustman <-men> *n Brit* basurero *m*

dusty ['dʌsti] <-ier, -iest> *adj* polvoriento

Dutch [dʌtʃ] **I.** *adj* holandés; **to go ~** *inf* pagar a escote **II.** *npl* **the ~** los holandeses

Dutchman ['dʌtʃmən] <-men> *n* holandés *m*

Dutchwoman ['dʌtʃˌwʊmən] <-women> *n* holandesa *f*

dutiful ['djuːtɪfəl, *Am:* 'duːt̬ɪ-] *adj* obediente

duty ['djuːti, *Am:* 'duːt̬i] <-ies> *n* **1.** (*moral*) deber *m;* (*obligation*) obligación *f;* **to do sth out of ~** hacer algo por compromiso; **to do one's ~** cumplir con su obligación **2.** *no pl* ⊣(*work*) **to be suspended from ~** ser suspendido del servicio; **to be on/off ~** estar/no estar de servicio **3.** (*tax*) impuesto *m;* (*revenue on imports*) derechos *mpl* de aduana

duty-free *adj* libre de impuestos

duvet ['djuːveɪ, *Am:* duː'veɪ] *n Brit* edredón *m* nórdico

DVD *n inv* INFOR *abbr of* **Digital Versatile Disk** DVD *m*

dwarf [dwɔːf, *Am:* dwɔːrf] <-s *o* -ves> *n* enano, -a *m, f*

dwell [dwel] <dwelt *o* -ed, dwelt *o* -ed> *vi* morar; **to ~ on sth** *fig* insistir en algo

dwelling ['dwelɪŋ] *n* morada *f*

dwelt ['dwelt] *pt, pp of* **dwell**

dwindle ['dwɪndl] *vi* menguar

dye [daɪ] **I.** *vt* teñir **II.** *n* tinte *m*

dying ['daɪɪŋ] *adj* (*person, animal*) moribundo; (*words*) último

dyke [daɪk] *n* dique *m*

dynamic [daɪ'næmɪk] *adj* dinámico

dynamics [daɪ'næmɪks] *n* dinámica *f*

dynamite ['daɪnəmaɪt] *n no pl* dinamita *f*

dynamo ['daɪnəməʊ, *Am:* -moʊ] <-s> *n* dinamo *f*

dynasty ['dɪnəsti, *Am:* 'daɪnə-] <-ies> *n* dinastía *f*

dysentery ['dɪsəntəri, *Am:* -teri] *n no pl* disentería *f*

dyslexia [dɪ'sleksiə] *n no pl* dislexia *f*

Ee

E, e [iː] *n* 1.(*letter*) E, e *f; ~* **for Edward** E de España 2. MUS mi *m*

E *n abbr of* **east** E *m*

each [iːtʃ] I. *adj* cada; *~* **one of you** cada uno de vosotros II. *pron* cada uno, cada una; *~* **of them** cada uno de ellos; **£70** *~* £70 cada uno; **he gave us £10** *~* nos dió a cada uno £10; **I'll take one kilo of** *~* tomaré un kilo de cada (uno)

each other *pron* uno a otro, una a la otra; **to help** *~* ayudarse mutuamente

eager ['iːgər, *Am:* -gɚ] *adj* ansioso; **to be** *~* **for sth** ansiar algo

eagle ['iːgl] *n* águila *f*

ear[1] [ɪər, *Am:* ɪr] *n* ANAT oído *m;* (*outer part*) oreja *f;* **to have a good** *~* tener buen oído; **to smile from** *~* **to** *~* sonreír de oreja a oreja; **to be up to one's** *~***s in debt** *inf* estar endeudado hasta la camisa

ear[2] [ɪər, *Am:* ɪr] *n* BOT espiga *f*

earache ['ɪəreɪk, *Am:* 'ɪr-] *n* dolor *m* de oído **eardrum** *n* tímpano *m*

earl [ɜːl, *Am:* ɜːrl] *n* conde *m*

earlobe ['ɪələʊb] *n* lóbulo *m* de la oreja

early ['ɜːlɪ, *Am:* 'ɜːr-] I. <-ier, -iest> *adj* 1.(*ahead of time, near the beginning*) temprano; **to be** *~* llegar temprano; **the** *~* **hours** la madrugada; **in the** *~* **morning** de madruga-

da; **in the** *~* **afternoon** a primera hora de la tarde; **at an** *~* **age** a una edad temprana; **in the** *~* **15th century** a principios del siglo XV; **to have an** *~* **night** acostarse temprano; **the** *~* **days/years of sth** los primeros tiempos de algo 2. *form* (*prompt: reply*) rápido 3.(*first*) primero II. *adv* 1.(*ahead of time*) temprano; **to get up** *~* madrugar; *~* **in the morning** por la mañana temprano; **to be half an hour** *~* llegar media hora antes 2.(*soon*) pronto; **as** *~* **as possible** tan pronto como sea posible

earmark ['ɪəmɑːk, *Am:* 'ɪrmɑːrk] *vt* (*put aside*) reservar; (*funds*) destinar

earn [ɜːn, *Am:* ɜːrn] *vt* 1.(*be paid*) ganar; **to** *~* **a living** ganarse la vida 2.(*bring in*) dar; (*interest*) devengar 3.(*obtain*) **to** *~* **money from sth** obtener dinero de algo

earnest ['ɜːnɪst, *Am:* 'ɜːr-] I. *adj* (*serious*) serio; (*sincere*) sincero II. *n no pl* seriedad *f;* **in** *~* en serio

earnings ['ɜːnɪŋz, *Am:* 'ɜːr-] *npl* 1.(*of a person*) ingresos *mpl* 2.(*of a company*) beneficios *mpl*, utilidades *fpl AmL*

earphones ['ɪəfəʊnz, *Am:* 'ɪrfoʊnz] *npl* auriculares *mpl*

earplug ['ɪəplʌg, *Am:* 'ɪr-] *n pl* tapón *m* para el oído

earring ['ɪərɪŋ, *Am:* 'ɪrɪŋ] *n* pendiente *m*, caravana *f CSur,* candonga *f Col;* **a pair of** *~***s** unos pendientes

earshot ['ɪəʃɒt, *Am:* 'ɪrʃɑːt] *n no pl* **in/out of** *~* al alcance/fuera del alcance del oído

earth [ɜːθ, *Am:* ɜːrθ] I. *n no pl* 1.(*planeta*) tierra *f;* **on** *~* en el mundo; **to cost the** *~* costar un ojo de la cara; **what/who** *~* **...?** *inf* ¿qué/quién diablos...? 2. ELEC toma *f* de tierra II. *vt* conectar a tierra

earthenware ['ɜːθənweər, *Am:* 'ɜːrθənwer] *n* objetos *mpl* de barro

earthquake ['ɜːθkweɪk, *Am:* 'ɜːrθ-] *n* terremoto *m*, temblor *m AmL*

earthy ['ɜːθɪ, *Am:* 'ɜːr-] <-ier, -iest> *adj* 1.(*with earth*) terroso 2.(*direct*)

llano **3.** (*vulgar*) grosero
ease [i:z] I. *n* **1.** (*without much effort*) facilidad *f;* **to do sth with ~** hacer algo con facilidad **2.** (*comfort, uninhibitedness*) comodidad *f;* **to be at** (**one's**) **~** estar a sus anchas; **to put sb at** (**his/her**) **~** hacer que alguien se relaje; (**stand**) **at ~!** MIL ¡descansen! II. *vt* **1.** (*relieve: pain*) aliviar; (*tension*) hacer disminuir; **to ~ one's conscience** descargarse la conciencia **2.** (*burden*) aligerar; (*screw*) aflojar III. *vi* (*tension, prices*) disminuir; (*wind*) amainar
 ◆ **ease off** *vi,* **ease up** *vi* (*pain*) aliviarse; (*fever, sales*) bajar; (*tension*) disminuir; (*person*) relajarse
easel ['i:zl] *n* caballete *m*
easily ['i:zəlɪ] *adv* fácilmente
east ['i:st] I. *n* este *m;* **in the ~ of Spain** en el este de España; **the East** el Oriente; POL el Este II. *adj* del este, oriental III. *adv* al este
Easter ['i:stəʳ, *Am:* -stɚ] *n* Pascua *f*

> [?] **At Easter** (En Semana Santa) es costumbre en Gran Bretaña consumir dos tipos de dulce: los **hot cross buns,** por un lado, panecillos especiados que tienen una cruz en la parte de arriba hecha con la misma masa, y el **simnel cake,** por otro lado, un denso pastel de pasas, que se decora con mazapán. Durante estos días es costumbre que los niños jueguen a arrojar huevos cocidos cuesta abajo para ver cuál es el huevo que llega más lejos. Hoy en día con el término de **Easter egg** (huevo de Pascua) se denomina al huevo de chocolate relleno de dulces y golosinas que se suele regalar durante estos días.

Easter Day *n* Domingo *m* de Pascua
Easter egg *n* huevo *m* de Pascua
easterly ['i:stəlɪ, *Am:* -stɚ-] I. *adj*

del este; **in an ~ direction** en dirección este II. *adv* (*towards*) hacia el este; (*from*)
Easter Monday *n* lunes *m* de Pascua
eastern ['i:stən, *Am:* -stɚn] *adj* del este, oriental
Easter Sunday *n s.* **Easter Day**
East Germany [ˌi:st'dʒɜ:mənɪ] *n* HIST Alemania *f* oriental
eastward(**s**) ['i:stwəd(z), *Am:* -wɚd(z)] *adv* hacia el este
easy ['i:zɪ] <-ier, -iest> I. *adj* **1.** (*simple*) fácil; **~ money** *inf* dinero *m* fácil; **~ to get on with** de trato fácil; **to be as ~ as anything** *inf* estar tirado; **that's easier said than done** *inf* es más fácil decirlo que hacerlo **2.** (*comfortable, carefree*) cómodo; **to feel ~ about sth** estar tranquilo por algo **3.** (*relaxed: manners*) natural; **to be on ~ terms with sb** estar en confianza con alguien **4.** FIN (*price, interest rate*) bajo; **on ~ terms** con facilidades de pago; (*loan*) con condiciones favorables II. *adv* con cuidado; **to go ~ on sb** *inf* no ser demasiado severo con alguien; **take it ~!** *inf* ¡cálmate!
easy chair *n* poltrona *f* **easy-going** [-'gou-] *adj* (*person*) de trato fácil; (*attitude*) tolerante
eat [i:t] <ate, eaten> *vi, vt* comer; **to ~ lunch/supper** comer/cenar
 ◆ **eat away** *vt* (*acid*) corroer; (*termites*) carcomer
 ◆ **eat away at** *vt,* **eat into** *vt* corroer
 ◆ **eat out** *vi* comer fuera
 ◆ **eat up** *vt* comerse
eau de Cologne [ˌəʊ də kə'ləʊn, *Am:* ˌoʊ də kə'loʊn] *n* (agua *f* de) colonia *f*
eaves [i:vz] *npl* ARCHIT alero *m,* tejaván *m* AmL
eavesdrop ['i:vzdrɒp, *Am:* -drɑ:p] <-pp-> *vi* **to ~ on sth/sb** escuchar algo/a alguien a escondidas
ebb [eb] I. *vi* **1.** (*tide*) bajar **2.** *fig* decaer II. *n no pl* **1.** (*tide*) reflujo *m* **2.** *fig* **the ~ and flow of sth** los altibajos de algo; **to be at a low ~** (*person*) estar deprimido III. *adj* = **tide**

marea *f* menguante

ebony ['ebənɪ] *n* ébano *m*

EC [ˌiːˈsiː] *n abbr of* **European Community** CE *f*

e-car ['iːkɑːʳ, *Am:* -kɑːr] *n* automóvil *m* eléctrico

e-cash ['iːkæʃ] *n* dinero *m* electrónico

ECB [ˌiːsiːˈbiː] *n abbr of* **European Central Bank** BCE *m*

eccentric [ɪkˈsentrɪk] *adj* excéntrico

ECG [ˌiːsiːˈdʒiː] *n abbr of* **electrocardiogram** electrocardiograma *m*

echo ['ekəʊ, *Am:* -oʊ] I. <-es> *n* eco *m* II. <-es, -ing, -ed> *vi* resonar III. <-es, -ing, -ed> *vt* repetir

eclipse [ɪˈklɪps] I. *n* eclipse *m* II. *vt* eclipsar

ecological [ˌiːkəˈlɒdʒɪkl, *Am:* -ˈlɑːdʒɪ-] *adj* ecológico

ecologist [iːˈkɒlədʒɪst, *Am:* -ˈkɑːlə-] *n* 1. (*expert*) ecólogo, -a *m, f* 2. POL ecologista *mf*

ecology [iːˈkɒlədʒi, *Am:* -ˈkɑːlə-] *n no pl* ecología *f*

e-commerce ['iːkɒmɜːs, *Am:* -kɑːmɜːrs] *n* comercio *m* electrónico

economic [ˌiːkəˈnɒmɪk, *Am:* -ˈnɑːmɪk] *adj* 1. POL, ECON económico 2. (*profitable*) rentable

economical [ˌiːkəˈnɒmɪkl, *Am:* -ˈnɑːmɪ-] *adj* económico

economics [ˌiːkəˈnɒmɪks, *Am:* -ˈnɑːmɪks] *n* 1. + *sing vb* (*discipline*) economía *f* 2. + *pl vb* (*matter*) aspecto *m* económico

economist [ɪˈkɒnəmɪst, *Am:* -ˈkɑːnə-] *n* economista *mf*

economize [ɪˈkɒnəmaɪz, *Am:* -ˈkɑːnə-] *vi* ahorrar

economy [ɪˈkɒnəmi, *Am:* -ˈkɑːnə-] <-ies> *n* economía *f*

economy class *n* AVIAT clase *f* turista

ecosystem *n* ecosistema *m* **ecotourism** *n* ecoturismo *m* **eco-tourist** *n* ecoturista *mf*

ecstasy ['ekstəsɪ] <-ies> *n* éxtasis *m inv*

ecstatic [ɪkˈstætɪk, *Am:* ekˈstæt̬-] *adj* extático; (*rapturous*) eufórico

ECT [ˌiːsiːˈtiː] *n abbr of* **electrocon-**

vulsive therapy terapia *f* de electroshock

ecu, ECU ['eɪkjuː, 'iːkjuː, *Am:* 'eɪkuː] *n abbr of* **European Currency Unit** ecu *m*, ECU *m*

Ecuador ['ekwədɔːʳ, *Am:* -dɔːr] *n* Ecuador *m*

Ecuadorian [ˌekwəˈdɔːrɪən] *adj* ecuatoriano

ecumenical [ˌiːkjuːˈmenɪkl, *Am:* ˌekjʊˈ-] *adj* ecuménico

eczema ['eksɪmə, *Am:* -sə-] *n no pl* eczema *m*

edge [edʒ] I. *n sing* 1. (*limit*) borde *m;* (*of a lake, pond*) orilla *f;* (*of a page*) margen *m;* (*of a table, coin*) canto *m;* **to be on ~** tener los nervios a flor de piel 2. (*cutting part*) filo *m* II. *vt* 1. (*border*) bordear 2. (*in sewing*) ribetear; **to ~ one's way through sth** ir abriéndose paso por algo III. *vi* **to ~ closer to sth** ir acercándose a algo; **to ~ forward** ir avanzando

edgeways ['edʒweɪz] *adv,* **edgewise** *adv Am* de lado

edgy ['edʒɪ] <-ier, -iest> *adj inf* nervioso

edible ['edɪbl] *adj* comestible

edict ['iːdɪkt] *n* edicto *m*

Edinburgh ['edɪnbrə, *Am:* -bʌrə] *n* Edimburgo *m*

⁇ Desde 1947 tiene lugar cada año en **Edingburgh**, la capital de Escocia, el **Edinburgh International Festival**. Se celebra en torno a mediados de agosto y dura tres semanas. En el marco de este festival tienen lugar numerosos espectáculos de tipo cultural: teatro, música, ópera y baile. Al mismo tiempo se celebran un **Film Festival**, un **Jazz Festival** y un **Book Festival**. Paralelamente al **Festival** oficial se ha ido desarrollando un **Festival Fringe** con alrededor de 1.000 espectáculos diferentes que se caracteriza por su vivacidad y su capacidad de innovación.

edit ['edɪt] *vt* **1.** (*correct*) corregir; (*articles*) editar **2.** (*newspaper*) dirigir **3.** CINE montar **4.** INFOR editar
♦ **edit out** *vt* suprimir

edition [ɪ'dɪʃn] *n* TYPO edición *f*; (*set of books*) tirada *f*; **limited** ~ edición limitada

editor ['edɪtər, *Am:* -tər] *n* **1.** (*of book*) editor(a) *m(f)*; (*of article*) redactor(a) *m(f)*; (*of a newspaper*) director(a) *m(f)*; **chief** ~ redactor(a) *m(f)* jefe **2.** CINE montador(a) *m(f)*

editorial [ˌedɪ'tɔːrɪəl, *Am:* -ə'-] **I.** *n* editorial *m* **II.** *adj* editorial; ~ **staff** redacción *f*

EDP [ˌiːdiː'piː] *n abbr of* **electronic data processing** PED *m*

educate ['edʒʊkeɪt] *vt* **1.** (*bring up*) educar **2.** (*teach*) instruir

education [ˌedʒʊ'keɪʃn] *n no pl* **1.** SCHOOL educación *f*; **primary/secondary** ~ enseñanza *f* primaria/secundaria **2.** (*training*) enseñanza *f* **3.** (*teaching*) enseñanza *f*; (*study of teaching*) pedagogía *f*

educational [ˌedʒʊ'keɪʃənl] *adj* **1.** SCHOOL (*system*) educativo; (*establishment*) docente **2.** (*instructive*) instructivo

EEC [ˌiːiː'siː] *n no pl* HIST *abbr of* **European Economic Community** CEE *f*

eel [iːl] *n* anguila *f*

eerie ['ɪəri, *Am:* 'ɪri] <-r, -st> *adj*, **eery** <-ier, -iest> *adj* espeluznante

effect [ɪ'fekt] **I.** *n* **1.** (*consequence*) efecto *m*; **to have an** ~ **on sth** afectar a algo **2.** (*result*) resultado *m*; **to be of little/no** ~ dar poco/no dar resultado; **to take** ~ LAW entrar en vigor; (*medicine*) surtir efecto **3.** (*impression*) impresión *f*; **the overall** ~ la impresión general **4.** *pl* (*belongings*) efectos *mpl* **II.** *vt* realizar; (*payment*) efectuar; (*cure*) lograr

effective [ɪ'fektɪv] *adj* **1.** (*giving result*) eficaz **2.** (*real*) efectivo **3.** (*op-*

erative) vigente **4.** (*striking*) impresionante

effectively *adv* **1.** (*giving result*) eficazmente **2.** (*really*) en efecto **3.** (*strikingly*) de manera impresionante

effeminate [ɪ'femɪnət] *adj* afeminado

efficiency [ɪ'fɪʃnsɪ] *n no pl* **1.** (*of a person*) eficiencia *f* **2.** (*of a machine*) rendimiento *m*

efficient [ɪ'fɪʃnt] *adj* (*person*) eficiente; (*machine*) de buen rendimiento

effort ['efət, *Am:* -ət] *n* esfuerzo *m*; **to be worth the** ~ valer la pena

effortless ['efətləs, *Am:* -ət-] *adj* fácil

effusive [ɪ'fjuːsɪv] *adj form* efusivo

EFL [ˌiːef'el] *n*, **Efl** *n abbr of* **English as a foreign language** inglés *m* como idioma extranjero

e.g. [ˌiː'dʒiː] *abbr of* **exempli gratia** (= **for example**) p.ej.

egg [eg] *n* huevo *m*; **hard-boiled** ~ huevo duro; **scrambled** ~s huevos revueltos
♦ **egg on** *vt* incitar

eggcup *n* huevera *f*

eggplant *n Am, Aus* berenjena *f*

eggshell *n* cáscara *f* de huevo

egg yolk *n* yema *f* de huevo

ego ['egəʊ, *Am:* 'iːgoʊ] *n* <-s> ego *m*

egotism ['egəʊtɪzəm, *Am:* 'iːgoʊ-] *n no pl* egotismo *m*

egotist ['egəʊtɪst, *Am:* 'iːgoʊ-] *n* egotista *mf*

Egypt ['iːdʒɪpt] *n* Egipto *m*

Egyptian [ɪ'dʒɪpʃn] *adj* egipcio

eiderdown ['aɪdədaʊn, *Am:* -də-] *n* edredón *m*

Eiffel tower [ˌaɪfl'taʊər, *Am:* -'taʊə-] *n* **the** ~ la torre Eiffel

eight [eɪt] *adj* ocho *inv*; **there are** ~ **of us** somos ocho; ~ **and a quarter/half** ocho y cuarto/medio; ~ **o'clock** las ocho; **it's** ~ **o'clock** son las ocho; **it's half past** ~ son las ocho y media; **at** ~ **twenty/thirty** a las ocho y veinte/media

eighteen [ˌeɪ'tiːn] *adj* dieciocho *inv*;

s. a. **eight**

eighteenth [ˌeɪˈtiːnθ] *adj* decimoctavo, -a

eighth [eɪtθ] *adj* octavo

eightieth [ˈeɪtɪəθ, *Am:* -t̬ɪəθ] *adj* octogésimo, -a

eighty [ˈeɪtɪ, *Am:* -t̬ɪ] *adj* ochenta *inv;* **he is ~ (years old)** tiene ochenta años; **a man of about ~ years of age** un hombre de alrededor de ochenta años

Eire [ˈæərə, *Am:* ˈerə] *n* Eire *m*

either [ˈaɪðə, *Am:* ˈiːðə] **I.** *adj* **1.** (*one of two*) **I'll do it ~ way** lo hará de una manera u otra **2.** (*each*) cada **II.** *pron* cualquiera (de los dos); **which one? – ~** ¿cuál? – cualquiera **III.** *adv* tampoco **IV.** *conj* **... or ... o... o...**

eject [ɪˈdʒekt] **I.** *vt* echar, expulsar; (*liquid, gas*) expeler **II.** *vi* eyectarse

eke out [iːk aʊt] *vt* (*money, food*) hacer durar; **to ~ a living** ganarse la vida a duras penas

elaborate [ɪˈlæbərət] **I.** *adj* (*complicated*) complicado; (*plan*) minucioso **II.** *vt* elaborar; (*plan*) idear **III.** *vi* entrar en detalles

elapse [ɪˈlæps] *vi form* transcurrir

elastic [ɪˈlæstɪk] *adj* elástico

elastic band *n Brit* gomita *f*

elated *adj* eufórico

elation [ɪˈleɪʃn] *n no pl* regocijo *m*

Elba [ˈelbə] *n* Elba *f*

elbow [ˈelbəʊ, *Am:* -boʊ] **I.** *n* codo *m* **II.** *vt* dar un codazo a; **to ~ one's way through the crowd** abrirse paso a codazos entre la multitud

elder¹ [ˈeldə, *Am:* -də] **I.** *n* **1.** (*older person*) mayor *mf;* **she is my ~ by three years** es tres años mayor que yo **2.** (*senior person*) anciano, -a *m, f* **II.** *adj* mayor

> [!] **elder, eldest** se pueden utilizar en lugar de **older, oldest** delante de los miembros de la familia: "Bob has two elder brothers and his eldest brother is six years older than him."

elder² [ˈeldə, *Am:* -də] *n* BOT saúco *m*

elderly [ˈeldəlɪ, *Am:* -də-] *adj* anciano; **the ~** los ancianos

eldest [ˈeldɪst] *adj* mayor; **the ~** el/la mayor

elect [ɪˈlekt] **I.** *vt* elegir; **to ~ to resign** optar por dimitir **II.** *n no pl* REL **the ~** los elegidos **III.** *adj* **the president ~** el presidente electo, la presidente electa

election [ɪˈlekʃn] *n* elección *f;* **to call/hold an ~** convocar/celebrar elecciones

election campaign *n* campaña *f* electoral

electioneering [ɪˌlekʃəˈnɪərɪŋ, *Am:* -ˈnɪr-] *n no pl* campaña *f* electoral

elector [ɪˈlektə, *Am:* -t̬ə] *n* elector(a) *m(f)*

electoral [ɪˈlektərəl] *adj* electoral; **~ college** colegio *m* electoral; **~ roll** censo *m* electoral

electorate [ɪˈlektərət] *n* electorado *m*

electric [ɪˈlektrɪk] *adj* eléctrico; **~ blanket** manta eléctrica; **~ chair** silla eléctrica; **~ cooker** cocina eléctrica; **~ light** luz eléctrica

electrical [ɪˈlektrɪkl] *adj* eléctrico

electrician [ɪˌlekˈtrɪʃn] *n* electricista *mf*

electricity [ɪˌlekˈtrɪsəti] *n no pl* electricidad *f;* **to run on ~** funcionar con electricidad

electricity board *n Brit* compañía *f* eléctrica

electrify [ɪˈlektrɪfaɪ] *vt* electrificar

electrocardiogram [ɪˌlektrəʊˈkɑːdɪəʊɡræm, *Am:* -troʊˈkɑːrdɪə-] *n* electrocardiograma *m*

electrocute [ɪˈlektrəkjuːt] *vt* electrocutar

electrocution [ɪˌlektrəˈkjuːʃn] *n* electrocución *f*

electrode [ɪˈlektrəʊd, *Am:* -troʊd] *n* electrodo *m*

electron [ɪˈlektrɒn, *Am:* -trɑːn] *n* electrón *m*

electronic [ˌɪlekˈtrɒnɪk, *Am:* ɪˌlekˈtrɑːnɪk] *adj* electrónico; **~ data processing** procesamiento electrónico de datos; ~ **mail** correo electrónico

electronics [ˌɪlek'trɒniks, Am: ɪˌlek-'trɑ:nɪks] n + sing vb electrónica f

elegance ['elɪgəns, Am: '-ə-] n no pl elegancia f

elegant ['elɪgənt, Am: '-ə-] adj elegante

elegy ['elədʒɪ] n elegía f

element ['elɪmənt, Am: '-ə-] n 1. a. CHEM, MAT elemento m 2. ELEC resistencia f

elementary [ˌelɪ'mentərɪ, Am: -ə-'ment̬ə-] adj elemental; (course) básico; ~ **school** Am escuela f (de enseñanza) primaria

elephant ['elɪfənt] n elefante m

elevate ['elɪveɪt] vt 1. (raise) elevar; (prices) aumentar 2. (in rank) ascender

elevation [ˌelɪ'veɪʃn] n 1. (rise) elevación f; (of person) ascenso m 2. (height) altura f

elevator ['elɪveɪtə', Am: -t̬ə-] n Am ascensor m, elevador m AmL

eleven [ɪ'levn] adj once; inv s. a. **eight**

elevenses [ɪ'levnzɪz] npl Brit, inf **to have** ~ tomar las once

eleventh [ɪ'levnθ] adj undécimo

elf [elf] <elves> n duende m

elicit [ɪ'lɪsɪt] vt obtener

eligible ['elɪdʒəbl] adj 1. elegible; ~ **to vote** con derecho a voto 2. (desirable) deseable

eliminate [ɪ'lɪmɪneɪt] vt 1. (eradicate) eliminar 2. (exclude from consideration) descartar

elite [er'li:t] n élite f

elm [elm] n olmo m

elocution [ˌelə'kju:ʃn] n no pl elocución f

elongated adj alargado

elope [ɪ'ləʊp, Am: -'loʊp] vi fugarse

elopement [ɪ'ləʊpmənt, Am: -'loʊp-] n fuga f

eloquent ['eləkwənt] adj elocuente

El Salvador [el'sælvəˌdɔːr, Am: -dɔːr] n El Salvador

else [els] adv más; **anyone** ~? ¿alquien más?; **anything** ~?, **everybody** ~ (todos) los demás; **every-**

thing/all ~ todo lo demás; **someone/something** ~ otra persona/cosa, ¿algo más?; **or** ~ si no

elsewhere [ˌels'weə', Am: 'elswer] adv en otro sitio; **let's go** ~! ¡vamos a otra parte!

ELT [ˌiːel'tiː] n abbr of **English language teaching** enseñanza de inglés

elude [ɪ'luːd] vt eludir; (blow) esquivar

elusive [ɪ'luːsɪv] adj 1. (evasive) evasivo; (personality) esquivo 2. (difficult to obtain) difícil de conseguir

elves [elvz] n pl of **elf**

emaciated [ɪ'meɪʃɪeɪtɪd, Am: -t̬ɪd] adj form demacrado, jalado AmL

e-mail ['iːmeɪl] n abbr of **electronic mail** e-mail m

e-mail address n dirección f de correo electrónico

emancipate [ɪ'mænsɪpeɪt] vt emancipar

embankment [ɪm'bæŋkmənt, Am: em-] n (of a road) terraplén m; (by river) dique m

embargo [ɪm'bɑːgəʊ, Am: em-'bɑːrgoʊ] <-goes> n embargo m; **trade** ~ embargo comercial; **to put** [o **lay**] **an** ~ **on a country** imponer un embargo sobre un país

embark [ɪm'bɑːk, Am: em'bɑːrk] I. vi embarcar(se); **to** ~ **on** [o **upon**] **sth** emprender algo II. vt embarcar

embarkation [ˌembɑː'keɪʃn, Am: -bɑːr'-] n embarque m

embarrass [ɪm'bærəs, Am: em-'ber-] vt 1. (make feel uncomfortable) avergonzar 2. (disconcert) desconcertar

embarrassed adj avergonzado; (silence) violento; **to be** ~ pasar vergüenza

embarrassing adj embarazoso

embarrassment [ɪm'bærəsment, Am: em'ber-] n 1. (shame) vergüenza f 2. (trouble, nuisance) molestia f

embassy ['embəsɪ] <-ies> n embajada f

embed [ɪm'bed, Am: em-] <-dd-> vt (fix) hincar; (in rock) incrustar;

(*in memory*) grabar

embellish [ɪmˈbelɪʃ, *Am:* em-] *vt* adornar

embers [ˈembəʳz, *Am:* -bəʳz] *npl* ascuas *fpl*

embezzle [ɪmˈbezl] <-ing> *vt* desfalcar

embezzlement [ɪmˈbezlmənt] *n no pl* desfalco *m*

embitter [ɪmˈbɪtəʳ, *Am:* emˈbɪt̬əʳ] *vt* amargar

emblem [ˈembləm] *n* emblema *m*

embody [ɪmˈbɒdɪ, *Am:* emˈbɑ:dɪ] *vt* 1. (*convey: theory, idea*) expresar 2. (*personify*) personificar 3. (*include*) incorporar

emboss [ɪmˈbɒs, *Am:* emˈbɑ:s] *vt* (*letters*) grabar en relieve; (*leather, metal*) repujar

embrace [ɪmˈbreɪs, *Am:* em-] I. *vt* 1. (*hug*) abrazar 2. (*accept: offer*) aceptar; (*ideas, religion*) incorporarse a 3. (*include*) abarcar II. *vi* abrazarse III. *n* abrazo *m*

embroider [ɪmˈbrɔɪdəʳ, *Am:* emˈbrɔɪdəʳ] *vi, vt* bordar

embroidery [ɪmˈbrɔɪdərɪ, *Am:* em-] *n* bordado *m*

embryo [ˈembrɪəʊ, *Am:* -oʊ] *n* embrión *m*

emcee [ɛmˈsi:] *n Am* presentador(a) *m(f)*

emend [ɪˈmend] *vt form* enmendar

emerald [ˈemərəld] *n* esmeralda *f*

emerge [ɪˈmɜ:dʒ, *Am:* -ˈmɜ:rdʒ] *vi* (*come out*) salir; (*secret*) revelarse; (*ideas*) surgir

emergency [ɪˈmɜ:dʒənsɪ, *Am:* -ˈmɜ:r-] I. <-ies> *n* 1. (*dangerous situation*) emergencia *f*; MED urgencia *f*; ~ **room** sala *f* de urgencias; **in an** ~ en caso de emergencia 2. POL crisis *f inv* II. *adj* (*exit*) de emergencia; (*services*) de urgencia; ~ **cord** *Am* timbre de alarma; ~ **brake** *Am* freno de mano; ~ **exit** salida de emergencia; ~ **landing** aterrizaje forzoso; ~ **service** servicio de urgencia

emergent [ɪˈmɜ:dʒənt, *Am:* -ˈmɜ:r-] *adj* emergente; (*democracy*) joven

emery board *n* lima *f* de esmeril

emery paper *n* papel *m* de lija

emigrant [ˈemɪgrənt] *n* emigrante *mf*

emigrate [ˈemɪgreɪt] *vi* emigrar

emigration [ˌemɪˈgreɪʃn] *n* emigración *f*

eminence [ˈemɪnəns] *n no pl* eminencia *f*

eminent [ˈemɪnənt] *adj* eminente

emission [ɪˈmɪʃn] *n* emisión *f*

emit [ɪˈmɪt] <-tt-> *vt* (*radiation, light*) emitir; (*odour*) despedir; (*smoke*) echar; (*cry*) dar

emotion [ɪˈməʊʃn, *Am:* -ˈmoʊ-] *n* emoción *f*

emotional [ɪˈməʊʃənl, *Am:* -ˈmoʊ-] *adj* 1. (*relating to the emotions*) emocional; (*involvement, link*) afectivo 2. (*moving*) conmovedor 3. (*governed by emotion*) emocionado

emotive [ɪˈməʊtɪv, *Am:* -ˈmoʊt̬ɪv] *adj* emotivo

empathy [ˈempəθɪ] *n no pl* empatía *f*

emperor [ˈempərəʳ, *Am:* -əʳəʳ] *n* emperador *m*

emphasis [ˈemfəsɪs] <emphases> *n* 1. LING acento *m* 2. (*importance*) énfasis *m inv*; **to put** [*o* **lay**] **great ~ on punctuality** hacer especial hincapié en la puntualidad

emphasize [ˈemfəsaɪz] *vt* 1. LING acentuar 2. (*insist on*) poner énfasis en, enfatizar *AmL*; (*fact*) hacer hincapié en

emphatic [ɪmˈfætɪk, *Am:* emˈfæt̬-] *adj* (*forcibly expressive*) enfático; (*strong*) enérgico; (*refusal*) rotundo

emphatically [ˈemfəsaɪli] *adv* (*expressively*) con énfasis; (*strongly*) enérgicamente; (*forcefully*) categóricamente

empire [ˈempaɪəʳ, *Am:* -paɪəʳ] *n* imperio *m*

employ [ɪmˈplɔɪ, *Am:* em-] *vt* 1. (*person*) emplear 2. (*object*) utilizar

employee [ˌɪmplɔɪˈiː, *Am:* ˈem-] *n* empleado, -a *m, f*

employer [ɪmˈplɔɪəʳ, *Am:* emˈplɔɪəʳ] *n* empresario, -a *m, f*

employment [ɪmˈplɔɪmənt, *Am:*

'em-] *n no pl* empleo *m;* **to be in ~**
Brit, form tener trabajo

employment agency *n* agencia *f* de
empleo

empower [ɪmˈpaʊəʳ, *Am:* emˈpaʊɚ] *vt* **to ~ sb to do sth** (*give
ability to*) capacitar a alguien para
hacer algo; (*authorise*) autorizar a alguien a hacer algo

empress [ˈemprɪs] *n* emperatriz *f*

emptiness [ˈemptɪnɪs] *n no pl*
vacío *m*

empty [ˈemptɪ] **I.** <-ier, -iest> *adj*
1. (*with nothing inside*) vacío
2. (*useless*) inútil; (*words*) vano
II. <-ie-> *vt* (*pour*) verter; (*deprive
of contents*) vaciar **III.** <-ie-> *vi* vaciarse; (*river*) desembocar **IV.** <-ies>
n pl envases *mpl* (vacíos)
◆ **empty out** *vt* vaciar

empty-handed [ˌemptɪˈhændɪd]
adj con las manos vacías

EMS [ˌiːemˈes] *n abbr of* **Economic
and Monetary System** SME *m*

EMU [ˌiːemˈjuː] *n no pl abbr of* **Economic and Monetary Union** UME *f*

emulate [ˈemjʊleɪt] *vt* emular

emulsion [ɪˈmʌlʃn] *n* emulsión *f*

enable [ɪˈneɪbl] *vt* **1. to ~ sb to do
sth** permitir a alguien que haga algo
2. INFOR activar

enact [ɪˈnækt] *vt* **1.** (*carry out*) llevar
a cabo **2.** THEAT representar **3.** (*law*)
promulgar

enamel [ɪˈnæml] *n* esmalte *m*

encase [ɪnˈkeɪs, *Am:* en-] *vt* encerrar

enchant [ɪnˈtʃɑːnt, *Am:* enˈtʃænt]
vt encantar

enchanting *adj* encantador

enc(l) *abbr of* **enclosure** recinto *m*

enclose [ɪnˈkləʊz, *Am:* enˈkloʊz] *vt*
1. (*surround*) cercar; **to ~ sth in
brackets** poner algo entre paréntesis
2. (*include*) adjuntar, adosar *AmL*

enclosure [ɪnˈkləʊʒəʳ, *Am:* enˈkloʊʒɚ] *n* **1.** (*enclosed area*) recinto *m*
2. (*action*) cercamiento *m* **3.** (*letter*)
documento *m* adjunto

encompass [ɪnˈkʌmpəs, *Am:* en-]
vt abarcar

encore [ˈɒŋkɔːʳ, *Am:* ˈɑːŋkɔːr] **I.** *n*
repetición *f* **II.** *interj* otra

encounter [ɪnˈkaʊntəʳ, *Am:* enˈkaʊntɚ] **I.** *vt* encontrar; **to ~ sb**
encontrarse con alguien (por casualidad) **II.** *n* encuentro *m*

encourage [ɪnˈkʌrɪdʒ, *Am:* enˈkɜːr-] *vt* (*give confidence*) alentar;
(*give hope*) dar ánimos a; **to ~ sb
to do sth** animar a alguien a hacer
algo

encouragement [ɪnˈkʌrɪdʒmənt,
Am: enˈkɜːr-] *n no pl* estímulo *m*

encroach [ɪnˈkrəʊtʃ, *Am:* enˈkroʊtʃ] *vi* **to ~ on** [*o* **upon**] **sth**
(*intrude*) invadir algo; *fig* usurpar
algo

encyclop(a)edia [ɪnˌsaɪkləˈpiːdɪə,
Am: en-] *n* enciclopedia *f*

end [end] **I.** *n* **1.** (*last, furthest
point*) final *m* **2.** (*finish*) fin *m;* **in
the ~** a fin de cuentas; **it's not the ~
of the world** no es el fin del mundo
3. (*extremities*) extremo *m* **4.** *pl*
(*aims*) fin *m;* (*purpose*) intención *f;*
to achieve one's ~s conseguir los
propios objetivos **5.** (*piece remaining*) resto *m* **6.** SPORTS lado *m* **II.** *vt*
1. (*finish*) acabar **2.** (*bring to a stop:
reign, war*) poner fin a **III.** *vi* **to ~ in
sth** terminar en algo
◆ **end up** *vi* terminar; **to ~ doing
sth** terminar haciendo algo

endanger [ɪnˈdeɪndʒəʳ, *Am:* enˈdeɪndʒɚ] *vt* poner en peligro; **an
~ed species** una especie en peligro
de extinción

endearing *adj* entrañable

endeavor *Am,* **endeavour** [ɪnˈdevəʳ, *Am:* enˈdevɚ] *Brit* **I.** *vi* **to ~
to do sth** esforzarse por hacer algo
II. *n* esfuerzo *m*

ending [ˈendɪŋ] *n* fin *m;* LING terminación *f*

endive [ˈendɪv, *Am:* ˈendaɪv] *n Am*
endibia *f*

endorse [ɪnˈdɔːs, *Am:* enˈdɔːrs] *vt*
1. (*declare approval for*) aprobar;
(*product*) promocionar **2.** FIN endosar

endorsement *n* **1.** (*support: of a
plan*) aprobación *f;* (*recommendation*) recomendación *f* **2.** FIN en-

doso *m*

endow [ɪn'daʊ, *Am:* en-] *vt* dotar; **to be ~ed with sth** estar dotado de algo

endurance [ɪn'djʊərəns, *Am:* en-'dʊrəns] *n no pl* resistencia *f*

endure [ɪn'djʊəʳ, *Am:* en'dʊr] **I.** *vt* **1.** (*tolerate*) soportar, aguantar **2.** (*suffer*) resisitir **II.** *vi form* durar

ENE *abbr of* **east-northeast** ENE

enema ['enɪmə, *Am:* -ə-] <-s *o* enemata> *n* enema *m*

enemy ['enəmɪ] *n* enemigo, -a *m*, *f*

energetic [ˌenə'dʒetɪk, *Am:* -ə-'dʒet̬-] *adj* enérgico

energy ['enədʒɪ, *Am:* -ə-] <-ies> *n* energía *f*

enforce [ɪn'fɔːs, *Am:* en'fɔːrs] *vt* aplicar; (*law*) hacer cumplir

engage [ɪn'geɪdʒ, *Am:* en-] **I.** *vt* **1.** *form* (*hold interest*) atraer **2.** (*put into use*) activar **3.** TECH (*cogs*) engranar; **to ~ the clutch** embragar **II.** *vi* **1.** MIL trabar batalla **2.** TECH engranar

engaged *adj* **1.** (*occupied*) ocupado; **to be ~** (*telephone*) estar comunicando **2.** (*to be married*) prometido; **to get ~ (to sb)** comprometerse (con alguien)

engagement [ɪn'geɪdʒmənt, *Am:* en-] *n* **1.** (*appointment*) compromiso *m* **2.** MIL combate *m* **3.** (*marriage*) compromiso *m*

engagement ring *n* anillo *m* de compromiso

engaging *adj* atractivo

engender [ɪn'dʒendəʳ, *Am:* en-'dʒendə-] *vt form* engendrar

engine ['endʒɪn] *n* **1.** (*motor*) motor *m* **2.** *Brit* RAIL máquina *f*

engineer [ˌendʒɪ'nɪəʳ, *Am:* -'nɪr] *n* **1.** (*with a degree*) ingeniero, -a *m*, *f* **2.** (*technician*) técnico, -a *m*, *f* **3.** *Am* RAIL maquinista *mf*

engineering [ˌendʒɪ'nɪərɪŋ, *Am:* -'nɪr-] *n no pl* ingeniería *f*

England ['ɪŋglənd] *n* Inglaterra *f*

English ['ɪŋglɪʃ] *adj* inglés; **~ speaker** anglófono, -a *m*, *f*

English Channel *n* Canal *m* de la Mancha **Englishman** <-men> *n*

inglés *m* **English-speaker** *n* persona *f* de habla inglesa **English-speaking** *adj* de habla inglesa **Englishwoman** <-women> *n* inglesa *f*

engraving [ɪn'greɪvɪŋ, *Am:* en-] *n* grabado *m*

engross [ɪn'grəʊs, *Am:* en'groʊs] *vt* absorber; **to be ~ed in sth** estar absorto en algo

engulf [ɪn'gʌlf, *Am:* en-] *vt* hundir

enhance [ɪn'hɑːns, *Am:* -'hæns] *vt* realzar; (*improve or intensify: chances*) aumentar; (*memory*) refrescar

enigma [ɪ'nɪgmə] *n* enigma *m*

enjoy [ɪn'dʒɔɪ, *Am:* en-] **I.** *vt* **1.** (*get pleasure from*) disfrutar de; **to ~ doing sth** disfrutar haciendo algo; **~ yourselves!** ¡que lo paséis bien! **2.** (*have: health*) poseer **II.** *vi Am* pasarlo bien

enjoyable [ɪn'dʒɔɪəbl, *Am:* en-] *adj* agradable; (*film, book, play*) divertido

enjoyment [ɪn'dʒɔɪmənt, *Am:* en-] *n no pl* disfrute *m*

enlarge [ɪn'lɑːdʒ, *Am:* en'lɑːrdʒ] **I.** *vt* **1.** (*make bigger*) agrandar; (*expand*) extender **2.** PHOT ampliar **II.** *vi* extenderse

enlargement *n* aumento *m*; (*expanding*) extensión *f*; PHOT ampliación *f*

enlighten [ɪn'laɪtn, *Am:* en-] *vt* **1.** REL iluminar **2.** (*explain*) instruir

enlightened *adj* (*person*) progresista; REL iluminado; (*age*) ilustrado

enlightenment [ɪn'laɪtnmənt, *Am:* en-] *n no pl* **1.** REL iluminación *f* **2.** PHILOS **the (Age of) Enlightenment** el Siglo de las Luces

enlist [ɪn'lɪst, *Am:* en-] **I.** *vi* MIL alistarse **II.** *vt* MIL alistar; (*support*) conseguir

enmity ['enmətɪ] <-ies> *n* enemistad *f*

enormity [ɪ'nɔːmətɪ, *Am:* -'nɔːr-mət̬ɪ] <-ies> *n* enormidad *f*

enormous [ɪ'nɔːməs, *Am:* -'nɔːr-] *adj* enorme

enough [ɪ'nʌf] **I.** *adj* (*sufficient*) suficiente, bastante **II.** *adv* bastante; **to**

be experienced ~ (to do sth) tener la suficiente experiencia (para hacer algo); **to have seen** ~ haber visto demasiado **III.** *interj* basta **IV.** *pron* bastante; **that's** (**quite**) ~! ¡basta ya!; **that should be** ~ eso debería ser suficiente; ~ **is** ~ basta y sobra

enquire [ɪnˈkwaɪər, *Am:* enˈkwaɪə·] **I.** *vi* preguntar; **to** ~ **for sb** preguntar por alguien; **to** ~ **about sth** pedir información sobre algo; **to** ~ **into a matter** indagar en un asunto **II.** *vt* preguntar; **to** ~ **the reason** preguntar por qué

enrage [ɪnˈreɪdʒ, *Am:* en-] *vt* enfurecer

enrich [ɪnˈrɪtʃ, *Am:* en-] *vt* enriquecer

enrol *Brit,* **enroll** [ɪnˈrəʊl, *Am:* enˈroʊl] *Am* **I.** *vi* inscribirse **II.** *vt* inscribir; (*on a course*) matricular

enrollment *n Am,* **enrolment** [ɪnˈrəʊlmənt, *Am:* enˈroʊl-] *n* inscripción *f;* (*on a course*) matriculación *f*

en route [ˌɒnˈruːt, *Am:* ˌɑːn-] *adv* en el camino

ensue [ɪnˈsjuː, *Am:* enˈsuː] *vi form* seguirse

ensure [ɪnˈʃʊər, *Am:* enˈʃʊr] *vt* asegurar

entail [ɪnˈteɪl, *Am:* en-] *vt* acarrear; **to** ~ **doing sth** implicar hacer algo

entangle [ɪnˈtæŋgl, *Am:* en-] *vt* enredar; **to get** ~**d in sth** quedar enredado en algo; *fig* verse envuelto en algo

entanglement *n* enredo *m;* (*situation*) embrollo *m*

enter [ˈentər, *Am:* -ţə·] **I.** *vt* **1.** (*go into*) entrar en; (*penetrate*) penetrar **2.** (*insert*) introducir; (*into a register*) inscribir **3.** (*join*) hacerse socio de **4.** (*make known*) anotar; (*claim*) presentar; (*plea*) formular **II.** *vi* THEAT entrar

♦ **enter into** *vi* (*form part of*) tomar parte en; **to** ~ **discussion** meterse en una discusión; **to** ~ **negotiations** iniciar negociaciones

♦ **enter up** *vt* asentar; (*in accounts*) registrar

♦ **enter upon** *vi* emprender

enterprise [ˈentəpraɪz, *Am:* -ţə·-] *n* **1.** (*firm*) empresa *f* **2.** (*initiative*) iniciativa *f*

enterprising *adj* emprendedor

entertain [ˌentəˈteɪn, *Am:* -ţə·-] *vt* **1.** (*amuse*) entretener **2.** (*guests*) recibir **3.** (*consider*) considerar; **to** ~ **doubts** abrigar dudas

entertainer [ˌentəˈteɪnər, *Am:* -ţə·ˈteɪnə·] *n* artista *mf*

entertaining *adj no pl* entretenido; (*person*) divertido

entertainment [ˌentəˈteɪnmənt, *Am:* -ţə·-] *n* **1.** *no pl* (*amusement*) diversión *f* **2.** (*show*) espectáculo *m*

enthral [ɪnˈθrɔːl] <-ll-> *vt,* **enthrall** *vt Am* cautivar

enthrone [ɪnˈθrəʊn, *Am:* enˈθroʊn] *vt form* entronizar

enthusiasm [ɪnˈθjuːziæzəm, *Am:* enˈθuː-] *n* entusiasmo *m*

enthusiast [ɪnˈθjuːziæst] *n* entusiasta *mf*

enthusiastic [ɪnˌθjuːziˈæstɪk, *Am:* enˌθuː-] *adj* entusiasta; **to be** ~ **about sth** estar entusiasmado con algo

entice [ɪnˈtaɪs, *Am:* en-] *vt* tentar

entire [ɪnˈtaɪər, *Am:* enˈtaɪə·] *adj* **1.** (*whole*) todo; (*total*) total **2.** (*complete*) entero

entirely *adv* enteramente; **to agree** ~ estar completamente de acuerdo

entirety [ɪnˈtaɪə·ətɪ, *Am:* enˈtaɪrəţɪ] *n* **in its** ~ en su totalidad

entitle [ɪnˈtaɪtl, *Am:* enˈtaɪţl] *vt* **1.** (*give right*) autorizar; **to** ~ **sb to act** autorizar a alguien para actuar **2.** (*book*) titular

entitled *adj* **1.** (*person*) autorizado **2.** (*book*) titulado

entity [ˈentətɪ, *Am:* -ţəţɪ] <-ies> *n form* entidad *f*

entourage [ˈɒntʊrɑːʒ, *Am:* ˌɑːn-tʊˈrɑːʒ] *n* séquito *m form*

entrance[1] [ˈentrəns] *n* (*way in*) entrada *f;* (*door*) puerta *f;* **front** ~ entrada *f* principal

entrance[2] [ɪnˈtrɑːns, *Am:* enˈtræns] *vt* encantar

entrance examination [ˈentrəns ɪgˌzæmɪˈneɪʃn] *n* examen *m* de ingreso **entrance fee** n cuota f de entrada [o de inscripción]

entrant ['entrant] n participante mf

entrepreneur [ˌɒntrəprə'nɜːʳ, Am: ˌɑːntrəprə'nɜːr] n empresario, -a m, f

entrust [ɪn'trʌst, Am: en-] vt confiar; **to ~ sth to sb** confiar algo a alguien

entry ['entrɪ] <-ies> n **1.** (act of entering) entrada f; (joining an organization) ingreso m **2.** (entrance) acceso m

entry form n formulario m de inscripción **entryphone** n Brit portero m automático

E-number ['iːnʌmbəʳ, Am: -bɚ] n número m E

enunciate [ɪ'nʌnsɪeɪt] vt **1.** (sound) pronunciar **2.** (theory) enunciar

envelop [ɪn'veləp, Am: en-] vt envolver

envelope ['envələʊp, Am: -loʊp] n sobre m, cierro m Chile

enviable ['envɪəbl] adj envidiable

envious ['envɪəs] adj envidioso

environment [ɪn'vaɪərənmənt, Am: en'vaɪ-] n entorno m; **the ~** ECOL el medio ambiente

environmental [ɪnˌvaɪərən'mentl, Am: enˌvaɪrən'menṭl] adj ambiental; ECOL medioambiental; **~ pollution** contaminación f ambiental

environmentalist n ecologista mf

environmentally-friendly adj ecológico

envisage [ɪn'vɪzɪdʒ, Am: en-] vt, **envision** vt Am **1.** (expect) prever **2.** (imagine) formarse una idea de

envoy ['envɔɪ, Am: 'aːn-] n enviado, -a m, f

envy ['envɪ] **I.** n no pl envidia f **II.** <-ie-> vt envidiar

EPA [ˌiːpiː'eɪ] Am abbr of **Environmental Protection Agency** Agencia f del Medio Ambiente

epic ['epɪk] **I.** n epopeya f **II.** adj épico

epicenter n Am, **epicentre** ['epɪsentəʳ, Am: -ṭɚ] n Brit, Aus epicentro m

epidemic [ˌepɪ'demɪk, Am: -ə'-] **I.** n epidemia f **II.** adj epidémico

epilepsy ['epɪlepsɪ] n no pl epilepsia f

epileptic [ˌepɪ'leptɪk] n epiléptico, -a m, f

epilog n Am, **epilogue** ['epɪlɒg, Am: -əlɑːg] n Brit epílogo m

episode ['epɪsəʊd, Am: -əsoʊd] n episodio m

epitome [ɪ'pɪtəmɪ, Am: -'pɪṭ-] n **1.** (embodiment) personificación f **2.** (example) arquetipo m

epitomise vt Aus, Brit, **epitomize** [ɪ'pɪtəmaɪz, Am: -'pɪṭ-] vt personificar

epoch ['iːpɒk, Am: 'epək] n form era f

equal ['iːkwəl] **I.** adj (the same) igual; (treatment) equitativo; **to be ~ to a task** ser capaz de realizar una tarea **II.** n igual mf **III.** <Brit: -ll-, Am: -l-> vt **1.** pl MAT ser igual a **2.** (match) igualar

equality [ɪ'kwɒlətɪ, Am: -'kwɑːləṭɪ] n no pl igualdad f

equalize ['iːkwəlaɪz] **I.** vt nivelar **II.** vi Aus, Brit SPORTS empatar

equally ['iːkwəlɪ] adv igualmente; **to divide sth ~** dividir algo equitativamente

equanimity [ˌekwə'nɪmətɪ, Am: -əṭɪ] n no pl ecuanimidad f

equate [ɪ'kweɪt] **I.** vt equiparar **II.** vi **to ~ to sth** ser equivalente [o igual] a algo

equation [ɪ'kweɪʒn] n ecuación f

equator [ɪ'kweɪtəʳ, Am: -tɚ] n no pl ecuador m

Equatorial Guinea n Guinea f Ecuatorial

equilibrium [ˌiːkwɪ'lɪbrɪəm] n no pl equilibrio m

equip [ɪ'kwɪp] <-pp-> vt **1.** (fit out) equipar; **to ~ sb with sth** proveer a alguien de algo **2.** (prepare) preparar

equipment [ɪ'kwɪpmənt] n no pl equipo m

equities ['ekwətɪz, Am: -ṭɪz] n pl, Brit acciones fpl ordinarias

equivalent [ɪ'kwɪvələnt] **I.** adj equivalente; **to be ~ to sth** equivaler a algo **II.** n equivalente m

equivocal [ɪ'kwɪvəkl] adj equívoco

ER [ˌiːˈɑːʳ, *Am:* -ˈɑːr] *n abbr of* **Elizabeth Regina** Reina *f* Isabel

era [ˈɪərə, *Am:* ˈɪrə] *n* era *f*

eradicate [ɪˈrædɪkeɪt] *vt* erradicar

erase [ɪˈreɪz, *Am:* -ˈreɪs] *vt a.* INFOR borrar

eraser [ɪˈreɪzəʳ, *Am:* -ˈreɪsɚ] *n Am* goma *f* de borrar

erect [ɪˈrekt] **I.** *adj* erguido; ANAT erecto **II.** *vt* eregir; (*construct*) construir; (*put up*) levantar

erection [ɪˈrekʃn] *n* **1.** *no pl* ARCHIT construcción *f* **2.** ANAT erección *f*

ERM [ˌiːɑːrˈem] *abbr of* **Exchange Rate Mechanism** SME *m*

erode [ɪˈrəʊd, *Am:* -ˈroʊd] *vt* erosionar

erosion [ɪˈrəʊʒn, *Am:* -ˈroʊ-] *n no pl* erosión *f*

erotic [ɪˈrɒtɪk, *Am:* -ˈrɑːt̬ɪk] *adj* erótico

err [ɜːʳ, *Am:* ɜːr] *vi* errar

errand [ˈerənd] *n* recado *m;* **to run an ~** (salir a) hacer un recado

erratic [ɪˈrætɪk, *Am:* -ˈræt̬-] *adj* **1.** GEO errático **2.** MED (*pulse*) irregular

error [ˈerəʳ, *Am:* -ɚ] *n* error *m;* **to do sth in ~** hacer algo por equivocación

erupt [ɪˈrʌpt] *vi* **1.** (*explode: volcano*) entrar en erupción; *fig* estallar **2.** MED salir

eruption [ɪˈrʌpʃn] *n* erupción *f; fig* estallido *m*

escalate [ˈeskəleɪt] *vi* (*increase*) aumentar; (*incidents*) intensificarse

escalator [ˈeskəleɪtəʳ, *Am:* -t̬ɚ] *n* escalera *f* mecánica

escapade [ˌeskəˈpeɪd] *n* aventura *f*

escape [ɪˈskeɪp] **I.** *vi* escaparse; (*person*) huir de; **to ~ from** escaparse de; **to ~ from a program** INFOR salir de un programa **II.** *vt* escapar a; (*avoid*) evitar; **to ~ sb('s attention)** pasar desapercibido a alguien; **a cry ~d him** se le escapó un grito **III.** *n* **1.** (*act*) fuga *f;* **to have a narrow ~** salvarse por muy poco **2.** (*outflow*) escape *m*

escapism [ɪˈskeɪpɪzəm] *n no pl* escapismo *m*

eschew [ɪˈstʃuː, *Am:* es-] *vt form* evi-

tar

escort [ˈeskɔːt, *Am:* -kɔːrt] **I.** *vt* acompañar; (*politician*) escoltar **II.** *n* **1.** (*companion*) acompañante *mf* **2.** *no pl* (*guard*) escolta *f*

ESE *n abbr of* **east-southeast** ESE *m*

Eskimo [ˈeskɪməʊ, *Am:* -kəmoʊ] <-s> *n* esquimal *mf*

ESL [ˌiːesˈel] *n abbr of* **English as a second language** inglés *m* como segunda lengua

esophagus [iːˈsɒfəgəs, *Am:* ɪˈsɑːfə-] *n Am* esófago *m*

ESP [ˌiːesˈpiː] *n abbr of* **extrasensory perception** percepción *f* extrasensorial

esp. *abbr of* **especially** especialmente

especial [ɪˈspeʃl] *adj* especial

especially [ɪˈspeʃəlɪ] *adv* **1.** (*particularly*) especialmente **2.** (*in particular*) en particular

espionage [ˈespɪɑːʒ] *n no pl* espionaje *m*

espouse [ɪˈspaʊz] *vt* apoyar

Esq. *abbr of* **Esquire** Sr. *m*

Esquire [ɪˈskwaɪəʳ, *Am:* ˈeskwaɪɚ] *n Brit* (*special title*) Señor *m*

essay¹ [eˈseɪ] *n* **1.** LIT ensayo *m* **2.** SCHOOL redacción *f*

essay² [ˈeseɪ] *vt* **1.** (*try*) intentar hacer **2.** (*test*) probar

essence [ˈesns] *n* **1.** *no pl* esencia *f;* **time is of the ~ here** el tiempo es de vital importancia aquí **2.** (*in food*) esencia *f*, extracto *m*

essential [ɪˈsenʃl] **I.** *adj* esencial; (*difference*) fundamental **II.** *n pl* **the ~s** los elementos básicos [*o* esenciales]

essentially [ɪˈsenʃəlɪ] *adv* esencialmente

est. **1.** *abbr of* **estimated** est. **2.** *abbr of* **established** fundado

establish [ɪˈstæblɪʃ] **I.** *vt* **1.** (*found*) fundar **2.** (*begin: relationship*) entablar **3.** (*set: precedent*) sentar; (*priorities, norm*) establecer **4.** (*determine*) determinar; (*facts*) verificar; (*truth*) comprobar; **to ~ that ...** comprobar que... **II.** *vi* establecerse

established [ɪˈstæblɪʃt] *adj*

1. (*founded*) fundado **2.** (*fact*) comprobado; (*procedures*) establecido
establishment [ɪ'stæblɪʃmənt] *n* **1.** (*business*) empresa *f* **2.** (*organization*) establecimiento *m;* **the Establishment** POL la clase dirigente
estate [ɪ'steɪt] *n* **1.** (*piece of land*) finca *f* **2.** LAW patrimonio *m;* **housing** ~ urbanización *f;* **industrial** ~ polígono *m* industrial
estate agent *n* Brit agente *mf* de la propiedad inmobiliaria **estate car** *n* Brit coche *m* familiar
esteem [ɪ'stiːm] **I.** *n no pl* estima *f;* **to hold sb in high/low** ~ tener a alguien en gran/poca estima **II.** *vt* estimar
esthetic [iːs'θetɪk] *adj* estético
estimate ['estɪmeɪt, *Am:* -mɪt] **I.** *vt* calcular; **to** ~ **that ...** calcular que... **II.** *n* cálculo *m* (aproximado); **rough** ~ *inf* cálculo aproximado
estimation [,estɪ'meɪʃn] *n no pl* opinión *f;* **in my** ~ a mi juicio
Estonia [es'təʊniə, *Am:* es'toʊ-] *n* Estonia *f*
Estonian [es'təʊniən, *Am:* es'toʊ-] *adj* estonio
estranged *adj* separado
et al. [et'æl] *abbr of* **et alii** et al
etc. *abbr of* **et cetera** etc.
et cetera [ɪt'setərə, *Am:* -'set̬ə-] *adv* etcétera
etching *n* aguafuerte *m*
eternal [ɪ'tɜːnl, *Am:* -'tɜːr-] *adj* eterno
eternity [ɪ'tɜːnətɪ, *Am:* -'tɜːrnət̬ɪ] *n no pl* eternidad *f*
ethical *adj* ético
ethics *n* + *sing vb* ética *f*
Ethiopia [,iːθi'əʊpɪə, *Am:* -'oʊ-] *n no pl* Etiopía *f*
Ethiopian [,iːθi'əʊpɪən, *Am:* -'oʊ-] *adj* etíope
ethnic ['eθnɪk] *adj* étnico; ~ **cleaning** limpieza étnica
ethos ['iːθɒs, *Am:* -θɑːs] *n no pl* espíritu *m*
etiquette ['etɪket, *Am:* 'et̬ɪkɪt] *n no pl* etiqueta *f*
EU [,iː'juː] *n abbr of* **European Union** UE *f*

Eucharist ['juːkərɪst] *n no pl* REL **the** ~ la Eucaristía
euphemism ['juːfəmɪzəm] *n* eufemismo *m*
euphoria [juː'fɔːrɪə] *n no pl* euforia *f*
EUR *n s.* **Euro** EUR *m*
Eurasia [jʊə'reɪʒə, *Am:* jʊ'-] *n no pl* Eurasia *f*
Eurasian [jʊə'reɪʒn, *Am:* jʊ'-] *adj* euroasiático
euro ['jʊərəʊ, *Am:* 'jʊroʊ] *n* euro *m*
euro cent *n* céntimo *m* de euro **euro coins** *n* monedas *fpl* de euro **euro-currency** *n* eurodivisa *f* **euro notes** *n* billetes *mpl* de euro
Europe ['jʊərəp, *Am:* 'jʊrəp] *n no pl* Europa *f*
European [,jʊərə'pɪən, *Am:* jʊrə-] *adj* europeo
European Central Bank *n* Banco *m* Central Europeo **European Community** *n* Comunidad *f* Europea **European Council** *n* Consejo *m* Europeo **European Court of Justice** *n* Tribunal *m* de Justicia Europeo **European Investment Bank** *n* Banco *m* Europeo de Inversiones **European Monetary System** *n* Sistema *m* Monetario Europeo **European Parliament** *n* Parlamento *m* Europeo **European Union** *n* Unión *f* Europea
euthanasia [,juː θə'neɪzɪə, *Am:* -ʒə] *n no pl* eutanasia *f*
evacuate [ɪ'vækjʊeɪt] *vt* (*people*) evacuar; (*building*) desocupar
evacuation [ɪ,vækjʊ'eɪʃn] *n* evacuación *f*
evacuee [ɪ,vækjuː'iː] *n* evacuado, -a *m, f*
evade [ɪ'veɪd] *vt* (*responsibility, person*) eludir; (*police*) escaparse de; (*taxes*) evadir
evaluate [ɪ'væljʊeɪt] *vt* (*value*) tasar; (*result*) evaluar; (*person*) examinar
evangelist [ɪ'vændʒəlɪst] *n* evangelista *mf*
evaporate [ɪ'væpəreɪt] **I.** *vt* evaporar; ~**d milk** leche evaporada **II.** *vi* evaporarse; *fig* desaparecer

evaporation [ɪˌvæpəˈreɪʃən] *n* eva-poración *f*

evasion [ɪˈveɪʒn] *n* evasión *f*

evasive [ɪˈveɪsɪv] *adj* evasivo

eve [iːv] *n no pl* víspera *f;* **on the ~ of** en vísperas de; **Christmas Eve** Nochebuena *f;* **New Year's Eve** Nochevieja *f*

even [ˈiːvn] **I.** *adv* **1.**(*indicates the unexpected*) incluso; **not ~** ni siquiera **2.**(*despite*) **~ if ...** aunque...; **~ so ...** aun así... **3.**(*used to intensify*) hasta **4.** **+** *superl* (*all the more*) aún **II.** *adj* **1.**(*level*) llano; (*surface*) liso **2.**(*equalized*) igualado; **to get ~ with sb** ajustar cuentas con alguien **3.**(*of same size, amount*) igual **4.**(*constant, regular*) uniforme; (*rate*) constante **III.** *vt* **1.**(*make level*) nivelar; (*surface*) a-llanar **2.**(*equalize*) igualar

◆ **even out I.** *vi* (*prices*) nivelarse **II.** *vt* igualar

◆ **even up** *vt* igualar

evening [ˈiːvnɪŋ] *n* (*early*) tarde *f;* (*late*) noche *f;* **good ~!** ¡buenas tardes/noches!; **every Monday ~** cada lunes por la noche; **all ~** toda la noche

evening class *n* clase *f* nocturna

evening dress *n* traje *m* de noche

event [ɪˈvent] *n* **1.**(*happening*) evento *m;* **sporting ~** acontecimiento *m* deportivo **2.**(*case*) caso *m;* **in any ~, at all ~s** *Brit* en cualquier caso

eventful [ɪˈventfl] *adj* accidentado

eventual [ɪˈventʃuəl] *adj* final

eventuality [ɪˌventʃuˈæləti, *Am:* -t̮i] <-ies> *n inv* eventualidad *f*

eventually [ɪˈventʃuəli] *adv* **1.**(*finally*) finalmente **2.**(*some day*) con el tiempo

ever [ˈevər, *Am:* -ə-] *adv* **1.**(*on any occasion*) alguna vez; **have you ~ been to Barcelona?** ¿has estado alguna vez en Barcelona?; **for the first time ~** por primera vez; **better than ~** mejor que nunca **2.**(*in negative statements*) nunca, jamás; **nobody has ~ heard of him** nadie ha oído nunca hablar de él; **never ~** nunca

jamás **3.**(*always*) **~ after** desde entonces; **~ since ...** desde que...; **~ since** (*since then*) desde entonces **4.** *Brit, inf* (*very*) **I'm ~ so grateful** se lo agradezco profundamente; **your're ~ so kind!** ¡usted es (siempre) tán amable!

evergreen [ˈevəgriːn, *Am:* -ə-] *n* árbol *m* de hoja perenne

everlasting [ˌevəˈlɑːstɪŋ, *Am:* -ə-ˈlæstɪŋ] *adj* **1.**(*undying*) imperecedero; (*gratitude*) eterno *f* **2.**(*incessant*) interminable

every [ˈevri] *adj* **1.**(*each*) cada; **~ time** cada vez **2.**(*all*) todo; **in ~ way** de todas las maneras **3.**(*repeated*) **~ other week** en semanas alternas; **~ now and then** [*o* **again**] de vez en cuando

everybody [ˈevriˌbɒdi, *Am:* -ˌbɑːdi] *pron indef, sing* todos, todo el mundo; **~ else** todos los demás

---

! **everybody** y **everyone** (= cada uno, todos) están siempre en singular: "Everybody enjoys a sunny day; as everyone knows."

---

everyday [ˈevrideɪ] *adj* diario; (*clothes*) de diario; (*event*) ordinario; (*language*) corriente; (*life*) cotidiano

everyone [ˈevriwʌn] *pron s.* **everybody**

everything [ˈevriθɪŋ] *pron indef, sing* todo; **is ~ all right?** ¿está todo bien?; **wealth isn't ~** la riqueza no lo es todo

everywhere [ˈevriweər, *Am:* -wer] *adv* en todas partes; **to look ~ for sth** buscar algo por todas partes

evict [ɪˈvɪkt] *vt* desahuciar

eviction [ɪˈvɪkʃən] *n* desahucio *m*

evidence [ˈevɪdəns] *n* **1.** *no pl* (*sign*) indicios *mpl* **2.**(*proof*) prueba *f* **3.**(*testimony*) testimonio *m;* **to give ~** (**on sth/against sb**) prestar declaración (sobre algo/contra alguien)

evident [ˈevɪdənt] *adj* evidente; **it is ~ that ...** está claro que...

evidently *adv* evidentemente
evil ['i:vl] **I.** *adj* malo; **to have an ~ tongue** tener una lengua afilada **II.** *n* mal *m*
evoke [ɪ'vəʊk, *Am:* -'voʊk] *vt* evocar
evolution [,i:və'lu:ʃn, *Am:* ,evə-] *n no pl* evolución *f; fig* desarrollo *m*
evolve [ɪ'vɒlv, *Am:* -'vɑ:lv] **I.** *vi* (*gradually develop*) desarrollarse; (*animals*) evolucionar **II.** *vt* desarrollar
ewe [ju:] *n* oveja *f*
ex [eks] <-es> *n inf* ex *mf*
exact [ɪg'zækt] **I.** *adj* exacto; **the ~ opposite** justo el contrario **II.** *vt* exigir; **to ~ sth from sb** exigir algo a alguien
exacting *adj* exigente
exactly [ɪg'zæktlɪ] *adv* exactamente; **not ~** no precisamente; **~!** ¡exacto!
exaggerate [ɪg'zædʒəreɪt] *vi, vt* exagerar
exaggeration [ɪg,zædʒə'reɪʃn] *n* exageración *f*
exalted [ɪg'zɔːltɪd, *Am:* -t̬ɪd] *adj* **1.** (*elevated*) elevado **2.** (*jubilant*) exaltado
exam [ɪg'zæm] *n* examen *m*
examination [ɪg,zæmɪ'neɪʃn] *n* **1.** (*exam*) examen *m* **2.** (*investigation*) investigación *f;* **medical ~** reconocimiento *m* médico **3.** LAW interrogatorio *m*
examine [ɪg'zæmɪn] *vt* **1.** (*test*) **to ~ sb** (*in sth*) examinar a alguien (de algo) **2.** (*study*) estudiar **3.** LAW interrogar **4.** MED hacer un reconocimiento médico de
examiner [ɪg'zæmɪnəʳ, *Am:* -ɚ] *n* examinador(a) *m(f)*
example [ɪg'zɑːmpl, *Am:* ɪg'zæm-] *n* ejemplo *m;* **for ~** por ejemplo; **to follow sb's ~** seguir el ejemplo de alguien; **to set a good ~** dar un buen ejemplo
exasperate [ɪg'zɑːspəreɪt] *vt* exasperar
exasperation [ɪg,zɑː'speɪʃn] *n no pl* exasperación *f*
excavate ['ekskəveɪt] *vt* excavar
excavation [,ekskə'veɪʃn] *n* excavación *f*

exceed [ɪk'siːd] *vt* exceder; (*outshine*) sobrepasar
exceedingly *adv* excesivamente
excel [ɪk'sel] <-ll-> **I.** *vi* sobresalir **II.** *vt* **to ~ oneself** lucirse
excellence ['eksələns] *n no pl* excelencia *f*
Excellency ['eksələnsɪ] *n* Excelencia *f;* **His ~** Su Excelencia
excellent ['eksələnt] *adj* excelente
except [ɪk'sept] **I.** *prep* **~ (for)** excepto, salvo, zafo *AmL* **II.** *vt form* exceptuar
exception [ɪk'sepʃn] *n* excepción *f;* **to make an ~** hacer una excepción; **with the ~ of ...** con excepción de...; **the ~ proves the rule** *prov* la excepción confirma la regla *prov*
exceptional [ɪk'sepʃənl] *adj* excepcional
excerpt ['eksɜːpt, *Am:* -sɜːrpt] *n* extracto *m*
excess [ɪk'ses] <-es> *n* exceso *m;* **in ~ of** superior a
excess baggage *n,* **excess luggage** *n* exceso *m* de equipaje **excess charge** *n* suplemento *m*
excessive [ɪk'sesɪv] *adj* excesivo
exchange [ɪk'stʃeɪndʒ] **I.** *vt* **1.** (*trade for the equivalent*) cambiar **2.** (*interchange*) intercambiar; **to ~ words** discutir **II.** *n* **1.** (*interchange, trade*) intercambio *m;* **in ~ for sth** a cambio de algo **2.** FIN, ECON cambio *m;* **foreign ~** divisas *fpl*
exchange rate *n* tipo *m* de cambio
exchequer [ɪks'tʃekəʳ, *Am:* -ɚ] *n no pl* erario *m;* **the Exchequer** Hacienda
excise ['eksaɪz] *n no pl* FIN impuestos *mpl* interiores
excite [ɪk'saɪt] *vt* **1.** (*move*) emocionar; **to be ~d about an idea** estar entusiasmado ante una idea **2.** (*stimulate*) estimular; **to ~ sb's curiosity** despertar la curiosidad de alguien
excitement [ɪk'saɪtmənt] *n* emoción *f*
exciting [ɪk'saɪtɪŋ, *Am:* -t̬ɪŋ] *adj* emocionante
excl. 1. *abbr of* **exluding** excepto,

salvo **2.** *abbr of* **exclusive** exclusive
exclaim [ɪk'skleɪm] *vi, vt* exclamar
exclamation [ˌeksklə'meɪʃn] *n* exclamación *f*
exclamation mark *n* signo *m* de exclamación
exclude [ɪk'sklu:d] *vt* **1.** (*shut out*) expulsar; **to be ~d from school** ser expulsado de la escuela **2.** (*leave out*) excluir; (*possibility*) descartar
excluding [ɪk'sklu:dɪŋ] *prep* excepto, salvo
exclusion [ɪk'sklu:ʒn] *n* exclusión *f*; **to the ~ of** con exclusión de
exclusive [ɪks'klu:sɪv] **I.** *adj* exclusivo; **~ interview** entrevista *f* en exclusiva; **~ of** sin; **to be ~ of** not include **II.** *n* exclusiva *f* **III.** *adv* **from 5 to 10 ~** del 5 al 10 exclusive
excommunicate [ˌekskə'mju:nɪkeɪt] *vt* excomulgar
excrement ['ekskrəmənt] *n no pl* excremento *m*
excruciating [ɪk'skru:ʃɪeɪtɪŋ, *Am:* -t̬ɪŋ] *adj* agudísimo; (*pain*) atroz
excursion [ɪk'skɜ:ʃn, *Am:* -'skɜ:rʒn] *n* excursión *f*
excuse [ɪk'skju:z] **I.** *vt* **1.** (*justify: behaviour*) justificar; (*lateness*) disculpar **2.** (*forgive*) perdonar; **~ me!** ¡perdone! **3.** (*allow not to attend*) **to ~ sb from sth** dispensar a alguien de algo **4.** (*leave*) **after an hour she ~d herself** después de una hora se disculpó y se fue **II.** *n* **1.** (*explanation*) excusa *f*, agarradera *f AmL* **2.** (*pretext*) pretexto *m*; **poor ~** mal pretexto
ex-directory [ˌeksdɪ'rektərɪ] *adj Aus, Brit* **to be ~** no figurar en la guía
execute ['eksɪkju:t] *vt* **1.** *form* (*carry out*) realizar; (*manoeuvre*) efectuar; (*plan*) llevar a cabo; (*order*) cumplir **2.** (*put to death*) ejecutar
execution [ˌeksɪ'kju:ʃn] *n* **1.** *no pl* (*carrying out*) realización *f* **2.** (*putting to death*) ejecución *f*
executioner [ˌeksɪ'kju:ʃnə', *Am:* -ə'] *n* verdugo *m*
executive [ɪg'zekjʊtɪv, *Am:* -t̬ɪv] **I.** *n* **1.** (*senior manager*) ejecutivo, -a

m, f **2.** + *sing/pl vb* POL poder *m* ejecutivo; ECON órgano *m* ejecutivo **II.** *adj* ejecutivo
executor [ɪg'zekjʊtə', *Am:* -t̬ə'] *n* albacea *mf*
exemplary [ɪg'zemplərɪ] *adj* ejemplar
exemplify [ɪg'zemplɪfaɪ] <-ie-> *vt* ejemplificar
exempt [ɪg'zempt] **I.** *vt* eximir **II.** *adj* exento; **to be ~ from sth** estar exento de algo
exemption [ɪg'zempʃn] *n no pl* exención *f*
exercise ['eksəsaɪz, *Am:* -sə'-] **I.** *vt* **1.** (*muscles*) ejercitar; (*dog*) llevar de paseo; (*horse*) entrenar **2.** (*apply: authority, control*) ejercer; **to ~ caution** proceder con cautela **II.** *vi* hacer ejercicio **III.** *n* ejercicio
exercise bike *n* bicicleta *f* de ejercicio **exercise book** *n* cuaderno *m*
exert [ɪg'zɜ:t, *Am:* -'zɜ:rt] *vt* ejercer; (*apply*) emplear; **to ~ oneself** esforzarse
exertion [ɪg'zɜ:ʃn, *Am:* -'zɜ:r-] *n* esfuerzo *m*
exhale [eks'heɪl] **I.** *vt* espirar; (*gases, scents*) despedir **II.** *vi* espirar
exhaust [ɪg'zɔ:st, *Am:* -'zɑ:-] **I.** *vt a. fig* agotar; **to ~ oneself** agotarse **II.** *n* **1.** *no pl* (*gas*) gases *mpl* de escape **2.** *Aus, Brit* (*pipe*) tubo *m* de escape
exhausted *adj* agotado
exhausting *adj* agotador
exhaustion [ɪg'zɔ:stʃn, *Am:* -'zɑ:-] *n no pl* agotamiento *m*
exhaustive [ɪg'zɔ:stɪv, *Am:* -'zɑ:-] *adj* exhaustivo
exhibit [ɪg'zɪbɪt] **I.** *n* **1.** (*display*) objeto *m* expuesto **2.** LAW documento *m* **II.** *vt* **1.** (*show*) enseñar; (*work*) presentar **2.** (*display character traits*) mostrar; (*rudeness*) manifestar
exhibition [ˌeksɪ'bɪʃn] *n* exposición *f*
exhilarating [ɪg'zɪləreɪtɪŋ, *Am:* -t̬ɪŋ] *adj* estimulante
exile ['eksaɪl] **I.** *n* **1.** *no pl* (*banishment*) exilio *m*; **to go into ~** e-

xiliarse **2.**(*person*) exiliado, -a *m, f*
II. *vt* exili(a)r

exist [ɪgˈzɪst] *vi* existir

existence [ɪgˈzɪstəns] *n* existencia *f*

existing [ɪgˈzɪstɪŋ] *adj* existente;
the ~ laws la actual legislación

exit [ˈeksɪt] **I.** *n* salida *f;* (*of road*)
desvío *m;* **emergency ~** salida de
emergencia; **to make an ~** salir
II. *vt* salir de **III.** *vi* **1.** *a.* INFOR salir
2. THEAT hacer mutis

exodus [ˈeksədəs] *n* éxodo *m*

exonerate [ɪgˈzɒnəreɪt, *Am:* -ˈzɑ:
nə-] *vt form* exonerar

exotic [ɪgˈzɒtɪk, *Am:* -ˈzɑ:t̬ɪk] *adj*
exótico

expand [ɪkˈspænd] **I.** *vi* **1.**(*increase*) expandirse; (*trade*) desarrollarse **2.**(*spread*) extenderse **3.** SO
CIOL explayarse **II.** *vt* **1.**(*make
larger*) ampliar; (*wings*) extender;
(*trade*) desarrollar **2.**(*elaborate*)
desarrollar

expanse [ɪkˈspæns] *n* extensión *f*

expansion [ɪkˈspænʃn] *n* **1.** *no pl*
(*spreading out*) expansión *f;* (*of a
metal*) dilatación *f* **2.**(*elaboration*)
desarrollo *m*

expect [ɪkˈspekt] *vt* esperar; (*imagine*) imaginarse; **to ~ sb to do sth**
esperar que alguien haga algo; **to ~
sth of sb** esperar algo de alguien; **I
~ed better of you than that** esperaba algo más de ti que eso; **I ~ so**
me lo imagino; **to ~ that** esperar que
+*subj*

expectancy [ɪkˈspektəntsi] *n no pl*
esperanza *f;* **life ~** esperanza *f* de
vida

expectant [ɪkˈspektənt] *adj* expectante; (*look*) de esperanza; **~
mother** futura madre

expectation [ˌekspekˈteɪʃn] *n*
1.(*hope*) esperanza *f* **2.**(*anticipation*) expectativa *f;* **in ~ of sth** en
espera de algo

expedient [ɪkˈspi:dɪənt] **I.** *adj*
1.(*advantageous*) conveniente
2.(*necessary*) necesario; (*measure*)
oportuno **II.** *n* recurso *m*

expedition [ˌekspɪˈdɪʃn] *n* expedición *f;* **to go on an ~** ir de expedi-

ción

expel [ɪkˈspel] <-ll-> *vt* expulsar

expend [ɪkˈspend] *vt form* dedicar;
(*money*) gastar

expenditure [ɪkˈspendɪtʃəʳ, *Am:*
-tʃɚ] *n no pl* (*money*) gasto *m*

expense [ɪkˈspens] *n* gasto(s) *m(pl);*
all ~(s) paid con todos los gastos pagados; **at sb's ~** *a. fig* a costa de alguien; **at the ~ of sth** *a. fig* a costa
de algo

expense account *n* cuenta *f* de gastos de representación

expensive [ɪkˈspensɪv] *adj* caro

experience [ɪkˈspɪərɪəns, *Am:*
-ˈspɪrɪ-] **I.** *n* experiencia *f;* **to know
sth from ~** saber algo por experiencia; **to learn by ~** aprender a través
de la experiencia **II.** *vt* experimentar

experienced [ɪkˈspɪərɪənst, *Am:*
-ˈspɪrɪ-] *adj* experimentado

experiment [ɪkˈsperɪmənt] **I.** *n* experimento *m* **II.** *vi* experimentar

expert [ˈeksp3:t, *Am:* -sp3:rt] **I.** *n*
experto, -a *m, f* **II.** *adj* **1.**(*skilful*) experto **2.** LAW pericial; **~ report** informe *m* pericial

expertise [ˌeksp3:ˈti:z, *Am:* -sp3:r-]
n no pl pericia *f;* (*knowledge*) conocimientos *mpl*

expire [ɪkˈspaɪəʳ, *Am:* -ˈspaɪɚ] *vi*
(*terminate*) finalizar; (*contract, licence*) expirar; (*passport, food*) caducar

expiry [ɪkˈspaɪəri, *Am:* -ˈspaɪ-] *n no
pl* terminación *f;* COM vencimiento *f,*
caducidad *f*

explain [ɪkˈspleɪn] **I.** *vt* explicar; **to
~ how/what ...** explicar cómo/
qué...; **that ~s everything!** ¡eso lo
aclara todo! **II.** *vi* explicar
◆ **explain away** *vt* justificar

explanation [ˌekspləˈneɪʃn] *n* explicación *f*

explanatory [ɪkˈsplænətrɪ, *Am:*
-ətɔ:rɪ] *adj* explicativo

explicit [ɪkˈsplɪsɪt] *adj* explícito

explode [ɪkˈspləʊd, *Am:* -ˈsploʊd]
I. *vi* (*blow up*) explotar; (*bomb*) estallar; (*tyre*) reventar; **to ~ with
anger** montar en cólera **II.** *vt*
1.(*blow up: bomb*) hacer explotar;

(*ball*) reventar **2.** (*discredit: rumours*) desmentir; (*theory*) refutar; (*myth*) destruir

exploit ['eksplɔɪt] **I.** *vt* explotar, pilotear *Chile* **II.** *n* hazaña *f*

exploitation [,eksplɔɪ'teɪʃn] *n no pl* explotación *f*

exploration [,eksplə'reɪʃn, *Am:* -splɔ:'-] *n* **1.** *a.* MED exploración *f* **2.** (*examination*) estudio *m*

exploratory [ɪk'splɒrətrɪ, *Am:* -'splɔ:rətɔ:rɪ] *adj* (*voyage*) de exploración; (*test*) de sondeo; (*meeting*) preliminar

explore [ɪk'splɔ:ʳ, *Am:* -'splɔ:r] *vt* **1.** *a.* MED, INFOR explorar **2.** (*examine*) analizar

explorer [ɪk'splɔ:rəʳ, *Am:* -ɚ] *n* explorador(a) *m(f)*

explosion [ɪk'spləʊʒn, *Am:* -'splou-] *n* explosión *f*

explosive [ɪk'spləʊsɪv, *Am:* -'splou-] *adj* explosivo

exponent [ɪk'spəʊnənt, *Am:* -'spou-] *n* **1.** (*person*) exponente *mf* **2.** MAT exponente *m*

export [ɪk'spɔ:t, *Am:* -'spɔ:rt] **I.** *vt* exportar **II.** *n* **1.** (*product*) artículo *m* de exportación **2.** *no pl* (*selling*) exportación *f*

exporter [ɪk'spɔ:təʳ, *Am:* -'spɔ:rtɚ] *n* exportador(a) *m(f)*

expose [ɪk'spəʊz, *Am:* -'spoʊz] *vt* **1.** (*uncover*) enseñar **2.** (*leave vulnerable to*) exponer **3.** (*reveal: person*) descubrir; (*plot*) desvelar

exposed [ɪk'spəʊzd, *Am:* -'spoʊzd] *adj* **1.** (*vulnerable*) expuesto **2.** (*uncovered*) descubierto **3.** (*unprotected*) desprotegido

exposure [ɪk'spəʊʒəʳ, *Am:* -'spoʊ-ʒɚ] *n* **1.** (*contact*) exposición *f* **2.** *no pl* MED hipotermia *f* **3.** *a.* PHOT revelación *f* **4.** (*revelation*) descubrimiento *m*

exposure meter *n* PHOT exposímetro *m*

express [ɪk'spres] **I.** *vt* **1.** (*convey: thoughts, feelings*) expresar; **to ~ oneself** expresarse **2.** *inf* (*send quickly*) enviar por correo urgente **3.** *form* (*squeeze out*) exprimir

II. *adj* **1.** (*rapid*) rápido; **by ~ delivery** por correo urgente **2.** (*precise*) explícito; **by ~ order** por orden expresa **III.** *n* (*train*) expreso *m* **IV.** *adv* **to send sth ~** enviar algo por correo urgente

expression [ɪk'spreʃn] *n* expresión *f*; **as an ~ of thanks** en señal de agradecimiento

expressive [ɪk'spresɪv] *adj* expresivo

expressway [ɪk'spreswei] *n Am, Aus* autopista *f*

expulsion [ɪk'spʌlʃn] *n* expulsión *f*

exquisite ['ekskwɪzɪt] *adj* exquisito

ext. TEL *abbr of* **extension** Ext.

extend [ɪk'stend] **I.** *vi* extenderse; **to ~ to una discussion** llegar a una discusión **II.** *vt* **1.** (*enlarge: house*) ampliar; (*street*) alargar **2.** (*prolong: deadline*) prorrogar; (*holiday*) prolongar **3.** (*offer*) ofrecer; **to ~ one's thanks to sb** dar las gracias a alguien

extension [ɪk'stenʃn] *n* **1.** (*increase*) extensión *f*; (*of rights*) ampliación *f* **2.** (*of a deadline*) prórroga *f* **3.** (*appendage*) apéndice *m* **4.** TEL extensión *f*, supletorio *m AmL*

extensive [ɪk'stensɪv] *adj* **1.** *a. fig* extenso; (*experience*) amplio **2.** (*large: repair*) importante

extensively *adv* intensamente

extent [ɪk'stent] *n no pl* **1.** (*size*) extensión *f* **2.** (*degree*) alcance *m*; **to a great ~** en gran parte; **to some ~** hasta cierto punto; **to such an ~ that …** hasta tal punto que…; **to what ~ …?** ¿hasta qué punto…?

extenuating *adj form* atenuante

exterior [ɪk'stɪərɪəʳ, *Am:* -'stɪrɪɚ] *adj* exterior

exterminate [ɪk'stɜ:mɪneɪt, *Am:* -'stɜ:r-] *vt* exterminar

external [ɪk'stɜ:nl, *Am:* -'stɜ:r-] **I.** *adj* **1.** (*exterior*) externo; (*influence*) del exterior; (*wall*) exterior; **~ world** mundo *m* exterior **2.** (*foreign*) exterior **3.** MED tópico **II.** *npl* las apariencias

extinct [ɪk'stɪŋkt] *adj* (*practice*) extinto; (*volcano*) apagado

extinction [ɪkˈstɪŋkʃn] *n no pl* extinción *f*

extinguish [ɪkˈstɪŋgwɪʃ] *vt* (*candle, cigar*) apagar; (*love, passion*) extinguir

extinguisher [ɪkˈstɪŋgwɪʃə', *Am:* -ɚ] *n* extintor *m*

extol [ɪkˈstəʊl] <-ll-> *vt*, **extoll** [ɪkˈstəʊl] *vt Am* alabar

extort [ɪkˈstɔːt, *Am:* -ˈstɔːrt] *vt* extorsionar; (*confession*) arrancar

extortion [ɪkˈstɔːʃn, *Am:* -ˈstɔːr-] *n no pl* extorsión *f*

extortionate [ɪkˈstɔːʃənət, *Am:* -ˈstɔːr-] *adj* excesivo; **~ prices** precios *mpl* exorbitantes

extra [ˈekstrə] **I.** *adj* adicional; **to work an ~ two hours** trabajar dos horas más; **it costs an ~ £2** cuesta dos libras más; **meals are ~** el precio no incluye las comidas **II.** *adv* (*more*) más; (*extraordinarily*) extraordinariamente; **to charge ~ for sth** cobrar algo aparte **III.** *n* **1.** ECON suplemento *m;* AUTO extra *m* **2.** CINE extra *mf*

extract [ɪkˈstrækt] **I.** *vt* **1.** (*remove*) extraer **2.** (*obtain: information*) sacar **II.** *n* **1.** (*concentrate*) extracto *m* **2.** (*excerpt*) fragmento *m*

extraction [ɪkˈstrækʃn] *n* **1.** (*removal*) extracción *f* **2.** (*descent*) origen *m;* **he's of American ~** es de origen americano

extracurricular [ˌekstrəkəˈrɪkjʊlə', *Am:* -jələ'] *adj* extraescolar

extradite [ˈekstrədaɪt] *vt* extraditar

extradition [ekstrəˈdɪʃn] *n no pl* extradición *f*

extramarital [ˌekstrəˈmærɪtl, *Am:* -ˈmerət̮l] *adj* extramatrimonial

extramural [ˌekstrəˈmjʊərəl, *Am:* -ˈmjʊrəl] *adj Brit* (*course*) para estudiantes externos

extraneous [ɪkˈstreɪnɪəs] *adj* extraño

extraordinary [ɪkˈstrɔːdnrɪ, *Am:* -ˈstrɔːr-] *adj* **1.** *a.* POL extraordinario **2.** (*astonishing*) asombroso

extra time [ˈekstrətaɪm] *n no pl, Aus, Brit* SPORTS prórroga *f*

extravagance [ɪkˈstrævəgəns] *n no pl* **1.** (*wastefulness*) derroche *m* **2.** (*luxury*) lujo *m* **3.** (*elaborateness*) extravagancia *f*

extravagant [ɪkˈstrævəgənt] *adj* **1.** (*wasteful*) despilfarrador **2.** (*luxurious*) lujoso **3.** (*exaggerated: praise*) excesivo **4.** (*elaborate*) extravagante

extreme [ɪkˈstriːm] **I.** *adj* extremo; **with ~ caution** con sumo cuidado; **in the ~ north** en la zona más septentrional **II.** *n* extremo *m;* **to go to ~s** llegar a extremos; **in the ~** sumamente

extremely *adv* extremadamente

extremist [ɪkˈstriːmɪst] *n* extremista *mf*

extremity [ɪkˈstremətɪ, *Am:* -t̮ɪ] *n* **1.** (*furthest point*) extremo *m* **2.** (*situation*) situación *f* extrema **3.** *pl* ANAT extremidades *fpl*

extricate [ˈekstrɪkeɪt] *vt form* sacar; **to ~ oneself from sth** lograr salir de algo

extrovert [ˈekstrəvɜːt, *Am:* -vɜːrt] *adj* extrovertido

exuberant [ɪgˈzjuːbərənt, *Am:* -ˈzuː-] *adj* **1.** (*luxuriant*) exuberante **2.** (*energetic*) desbordante

exude [ɪgˈzjuːd, *Am:* -ˈzuːd] *vt* exudar; *fig* rezumar; **to ~ confidence** irradiar confianza

eye [aɪ] **I.** *n* **1.** ANAT ojo *m;* **to not believe one's ~s** no dar crédito a sus ojos; **to catch sb's ~** llamar la atención de alguien; **to have a good ~ for sth** tener (buen) ojo para algo; **to keep one's ~s open** mantener los ojos abiertos; **visible to the naked ~** visible a simple vista **2.** BOT yema *f* **II.** <-ing> *vt* mirar; (*observe*) observar

eyeball [ˈaɪbɔːl] *n* globo *m* ocular

eyebrow *n* ceja *f* **eyebrow pencil** *n* lápiz *m* de cejas **eyedrops** *npl* gotas *f* para los ojos *pl* **eyelash** <-es> *n* pestaña *f* **eyelid** *n* párpado *m* **eyeliner** *n no pl* lápiz *m* de ojos **eyeshadow** *n* sombra *f* de ojos **eyesight** *n no pl* vista *f* **eyesore** [-sɔːr] *n* monstruosidad *f* **eyewitness** <-es> *n* testigo *mf* ocular

eyrie [ˈaɪərɪ, *Am:* ˈerɪ] *n* aguilera *f*

e-zine ['iːziːn] *n* revista *f* electrónica

Ff

F, f [ef] *n* **1.**(*letter*) F, f *f;* ~ **for Frederick** *Brit,* ~ **for Fox** *Am* F de Francia **2.** MUS fa *m*

FA [ˌefˈeɪ] *n Brit abbr of* **Football Association** *federación inglesa de fútbol*

fable ['feɪbl] *n* fábula *f*

fabric ['fæbrɪk] *n no pl* tejido *m*

fabricate ['fæbrɪkeɪt] *vt* **1.**(*manufacture*) fabricar **2.** *fig* (*invent*) **to ~ an excuse** inventar(se) una excusa

fabulous ['fæbjʊləs, *Am:* -jə-] *adj* fabuloso

facade [fəˈsɑːd] *n a. fig* fachada *f*

face [feɪs] **I.** *n* **1.** *a.* ANAT cara *f;* **on the ~ of it** a primera vista; **to make a long ~** poner cara larga; **to tell sth to sb's ~** decir algo a la cara de alguien **2.**(*front: of building*) fachada *f;* (*of coin*) cara *f;* (*of clock*) esfera *f,* carátula *f Méx;* (*of mountain*) pared *f* **3.**(*respect, honour*) prestigio *m;* **to lose ~** desprestigiarse; **to save ~** guardar las apariencias **II.** *vt* **1.**(*turn towards*) mirar hacia **2.**(*confront*) hacer frente a; **to ~ the facts** enfrentarse a los hechos

◆**face up to** *vi* **to ~ sth** hacer frente a algo

facecloth ['feɪsklɒθ, *Am:* 'feɪsklɑːθ] *n* toallita *f* **face cream** *n no pl* crema *f* facial **facelift** *n* lifting *m* **face powder** *n no pl* polvos *mpl* (para la cara)

facet ['fæsɪt] *n a. fig* faceta *f*

facetious [fəˈsiːʃəs] *adj* chistoso, faceto *Méx*

face value *n* **1.** ECON valor *m* nominal **2.** *fig* **to take sth at ~** creer algo a pie juntillas

facile ['fæsaɪl, *Am:* -ɪl] *adj* simplista

facilitate [fəˈsɪlɪteɪt] *vt* facilitar

facility [fəˈsɪləti, *Am:* -t̬i] *n* <-ies> **1.**(*services*) servicio *m;* **credit facilities** facilidades *fpl* de pago **2.**(*ability, feature*) facilidad *f*

facing ['feɪsɪŋ] *n* **1.** ARCHIT revestimiento *m* **2.** *no pl* (*cloth strip*) vuelta *f*

facsimile [fækˈsɪməli] *n* facsímil *m*

fact [fækt] *n* hecho *m;* **to stick to the ~s** atenerse a los hechos; **in ~** de hecho

faction ['fækʃn] *n* POL facción *f*

factor ['fæktər, *Am:* -tər] *n a.* MAT, BIO factor *m*

factory ['fæktəri] <-ies> *n* fábrica *f*

factual ['fæktʃʊəl, *Am:* -tʃuːəl] *adj* basado en hechos reales

faculty ['fæklti, *Am:* -t̬i] <-ies> *n* facultad *f; Am* (*teachers*) cuerpo *m* docente

fad [fæd] *n inf* moda *f*

fade [feɪd] **1.** (*lose colour*) desteñirse **2.**(*lose intensity: light*) apagarse; (*hope, optimism, memory*) desvanecerse

◆**fade away** *vi* (*sound, love, grief*) apagarse

◆**fade in** **I.** *vi* (*picture*) aparecer progresivamente; (*sound*) subir gradualmente **II.** *vt* (*picture*) hacer aparecer progresivamente; (*sound*) subir gradualmente

◆**fade out** *vi* (*picture*) desaparecer gradualmente; (*sound*) desvanecerse

faeces ['fiːsiːz] *npl form* heces *fpl*

fag [fæg] *n inf* **1.**(*cigarette*) pitillo *m* **2.** *Am, pej* (*homosexual*) marica *m*

fail [feɪl] **I.** *vi* **1.**(*not succeed: person*) fracasar; (*attempt, plan, operation*) fallar; **to ~ to do sth** no conseguir hacer algo **2.** TECH, AUTO (*brakes, steering*) fallar; (*engine*) averiarse **II.** *vt* (*exam, pupil*) suspender **III.** *n* **without ~** (*definitely*) sin falta; (*always*) sin excepción

failing ['feɪlɪŋ] **I.** *n* defecto *m* **II.** *prep* a falta de

failure ['feɪljər, *Am:* 'feɪljə'] *n* **1.** *no pl* (*lack of success*) fracaso *m* **2.** TECH, ELEC fallo *m*

faint [feɪnt] **I.** *adj* **1.**(*scent, odour, taste*) leve; (*line, outline, scratch*) apenas visible **2.** (*slight: resemblance, sign, suspicion*) vago; **not to have the ~est idea** *inf* no tener ni idea **3.** (*weak*) **to feel ~** sentirse mareado **II.** *vi* desmayarse **III.** *n* desmayo *m*

fair¹ [feəʳ, *Am:* fer] **I.** *adj* **1.** (*just: society, trial, wage*) justo; **a ~ share** una parte equitativa; **~ enough** está bien **2.** *inf* (*quite large: amount*) bastante **3.** (*reasonably good: chance, prospect*) bueno **4.** (*light in colour: skin*) blanco, güero *AmL;* (*hair*) rubio **5.** METEO **~ weather** tiempo *m* agradable **II.** *adv* **to play ~** jugar limpio

fair² [feəʳ] *n* feria *f;* **trade ~** feria comercial

fair game *no pl n* caza *f* legal; *fig* objeto *m* legítimo

fairground ['feəɡraʊnd, *Am:* 'fer-] *n* parque *m* de atracciones

fair-haired [ˌfeə'heəd, *Am:* ˌfer-'herd] *adj* rubio

fairly ['feəli, *Am:* 'fer-] *adv* **1.** (*quite*) bastante **2.** (*justly*) con imparcialidad

fairness *n no pl* justicia *f;* **in (all) ~ …** para ser justo…

fairy ['feəri, *Am:* 'feri] <-ies> *n* hada *f*

fairytale *n* cuento *m* de hadas; *fig* cuento *m* chino

faith [feɪθ] *n a.* REL fe *f;* **to have/lose ~ in sb/sth** tener/perder la fe en alguien/algo

faithful ['feɪθfəl] *adj a.* REL fiel

faithfully *adv* **1.** (*loyally*) lealmente; **Yours ~** *Brit, Aus* (le saluda) atentamente **2.** (*exactly*) fielmente

fake [feɪk] **I.** *n* **1.** (*painting, jewel*) falsificación *f* **2.** (*person*) impostor(a) *m(f)* **II.** *adj* ~ **jewel** joya falsa **III.** *vt* **1.** (*counterfeit*) falsificar **2.** (*pretend to feel*) fingir

falcon ['fɔːlkən, *Am:* 'fæl-] *n* halcón *m*

Falkland Islands ['fɔːklændˌaɪləndz] *npl* **the ~** las (Islas) Malvinas

fall [fɔːl] <fell, fallen> **I.** *vi* **1.** (*drop down*) caerse; (*rain, snow*) caer; **to ~ flat** (*joke*) no tener gracia; (*plan, suggestion*) no tener éxito; **to ~ flat on one's face** caerse de morros **2.** (*decrease: prices*) bajar; **to ~ sharply** caer de forma acusada, quedar vacante **3.** (*enter a particular state*) **to ~ madly in love (with sb/sth)** enamorarse perdidamente (de alguien/algo) **II.** *n* **1.** (*drop from a height*) caída *f* **2.** (*decrease*) disminución *f* **3.** *Am* (*autumn*) otoño *m*

◆ **fall about** *vi Brit, Aus, inf* troncharse, partirse

◆ **fall back** *vi* quedarse atrás

◆ **fall back on** *vt,* **fall back upon** *vt* echar mano de

◆ **fall behind** *vi* **1.** (*become slower*) quedarse atrás **2.** (*fail to do sth on time*) retrasarse

◆ **fall down** *vi* **1.** (*person*) caerse; (*building*) derrumbarse **2.** (*be unsatisfactory: person, plan*) fallar

◆ **fall for** *vt* **to ~ sb** enamorarse de alguien; **to ~ a trick** caer en la trampa

◆ **fall in** *vi* **1.** (*collapse: roof, ceiling*) venirse abajo **2.** MIL formar filas

◆ **fall in with** *vt insep* **1.** (*agree to*) aceptar **2.** (*become friendly with*) **to ~ sb** juntarse con alguien

◆ **fall off** *vi* **1.** (*become detached*) desprenderse **2.** (*decrease*) reducirse

◆ **fall out** *vi* **1.** (*drop out*) caer **2.** MIL romper filas

◆ **fall over** *vi insep* caerse

◆ **fall through** *vi* fracasar

fallacy ['fæləsi] <-ies> *n* falacia *f*

fallible ['fæləbl] *adj* falible

fallout ['fɔːlaʊt] *n no pl* PHYS lluvia *f* radiactiva

fallow ['fæləʊ, *Am:* -oʊ] *adj* (*ground, field*) en barbecho

false [fɔːls] *adj* **1.** (*untrue: idea, information*) falso; **~ teeth** dientes *mpl* postizos **2.** (*artificial: beard, eyelashes*) postizo **3.** *liter* (*disloyal*) **a ~ friend** un amigo traicionero

false alarm *n* falsa alarma *f*

falsehood ['fɔːlshʊd] *n* **1.** *no pl* (*untruth*) falsedad *f* **2.** (*lie*) mentira *f*

false teeth *npl* dientes *mpl* postizos

falsify ['fɔːlsɪfaɪ] *vt* falsificar

falter ['fɔːltə^r, *Am:* -ṭə·] *vi* vacilar

fame [feɪm] *n no pl* fama *f*

familiar [fə'mɪliə^r, *Am:* -jə·] *adj*
1. (*well-known*) familiar **2.** (*acquainted*) familiarizado **3.** (*friendly*) de familiaridad; **to be on ~ terms** (**with sb**) tener un trato de confianza (con alguien)

familiarity [fə,mɪli'ærəti, *Am:* -'e-rəṭi] *n no pl* familiaridad *f*

familiarize [fə'mɪliəraɪz, *Am:* -jə-raɪz] *vt* acostumbrar; **to ~ oneself with sth** familiarizarse con algo

family ['fæməli] *n + sing/pl vb* familia *f*

! **family** se puede utilizar tanto en singular como en plural: "Maria's family comes from Italy; Are your family all well?"

---

family planning *n no pl* planificación *f* familiar **family tree** *n* árbol *m* genealógico

famine ['fæmɪn] *n* hambruna *f*

famished ['fæmɪʃt] *adj inf* **to be ~** estar muerto de hambre

famous ['feɪməs] *adj* famoso

famously *adv* **to get on ~** llevarse divinamente

fan¹ [fæn] **I.** *n* **1.** (*hand-held*) abanico *m* **2.** (*electrical*) ventilador *m* **II.** <-nn-> *vt* **1.** (*cool with fan*) abanicar **2.** *fig* (*heighten: passion, interest*) avivar

fan² [fæn] *n* (*of person*) admirador(a) *m(f)*; (*of team*) hincha *mf*; (*of music*) fan *mf*

fanatic [fə'nætɪk, *Am:* -'næṭɪk] *n pej* fanático, -a *m, f*

fanatical *adj* fanático

fan belt *n* AUTO correa *f* del ventilador

fanciful ['fænsɪfəl] *adj* **1.** (*idea, notion*) descabellado **2.** (*design, style*) imaginativo

fan club *n* club *m* de fans

fancy ['fænsi] **I.** <-ie-> *vt* **1.** *Brit* (*want, like*) **to ~ doing sth** tener ganas de hacer algo **2.** *Brit* (*be attracted to*) **he fancies you** le gustas

3. (*imagine*) **to ~** (**that**) … imaginarse (que)… **II.** *n* <-ies> **1.** *no pl* (*liking*) **to take a ~ to sth/sb** quedarse prendado de algo/alguien **2.** *no pl* (*imagination*) fantasía *f* **3.** (*whimsical idea*) capricho *m;* **whenever the ~ takes you** cuando se te antoje **III.** *adj* <-ier, -iest> **1.** (*elaborate: decoration, frills*) de adorno **2.** *inf* (*expensive*) carísimo

fancy dress *n no pl, Brit, Aus* disfraz *m*

fang [fæŋ] *n* colmillo *m*

fantasize ['fæntəsaɪz, *Am:* -ṭə-] *vi* **to ~ about sth** fantasear sobre algo

fantastic [fæn'tæstɪk] *adj* fantástico

fantasy ['fæntəsi, *Am:* -ṭə-] <-ies> *n a.* MUS fantasía *f*

fanzine ['fænziːn] *n* fanzine *m*

FAQ *n* INFOR *abbr of* **frequently asked questions** FAQ *f*

far [fɑː^r, *Am:* fɑːr] <farther, farthest *o* further, furthest> **I.** *adv* **1.** (*a long distance*) lejos; **~ away** muy lejos; **~ from doing sth** lejos de hacer algo; **~ from it** todo lo contrario **2.** (*distant in time*) **as ~ back as I remember …** hasta donde me alcanza la memoria… **3.** (*in progress*) **to not get very ~ with sb/sth** no llegar muy lejos con alguien/algo; **to go too ~** ir demasiado lejos **4.** (*much*) **~ better** mucho mejor; **to be the best by ~** ser el/la mejor con diferencia **5.** (*connecting adverbial phrase*) **as ~ as I know …** que yo sepa…; **as ~ as I'm concerned …** en lo que a mí se refiere… **II.** *adj* **1.** (*distant*) lejano; **in the ~ distance** a lo lejos **2.** (*further away*) **the ~ left/right** (**of a party**) la extrema izquierda/derecha (de un partido)

faraway ['fɑːrəweɪ] *adj* **a ~ land** una tierra lejana

farce [fɑːs, *Am:* fɑːrs] *n* farsa *f*

farcical ['fɑːsɪkl, *Am:* 'fɑːr-] *adj* absurdo

fare [feə^r, *Am:* fer] *n* **1.** (*for journey*) tarifa *f;* **single/return ~** billete sencillo/de ida y vuelta **2.** (*taxi passenger*) pasajero, -a *m, f* **3.** *no pl* GASTR

F_f

comida *f*

Far East *n* the ~ el Extremo Oriente

farewell [ˌfeəˈwel, *Am:* ˌfer-] *interj form* adiós

farm [fɑːm, *Am:* fɑːrm] **I.** *n* (*small*) granja *f,* hacienda *f AmL,* chacra *f CSur, Perú;* (*large*) hacienda *f* **II.** *vt* cultivar

◆ **farm out** *vt* **to** ~ **work** subcontratar

farmer [ˈfɑːməʳ, *Am:* ˈfɑːrmə·] *n* granjero, -a *m, f,* hacendado, -a *m, f,* chacarero, -a *m, f CSur, Perú*

farmhand *n* mozo *m* de labranza

farmhouse *n* <-s> casa *f* de labranza **farmland** *n* terreno *m* agrícola **farmyard** *n* corral *m*

far-reaching [ˌfɑːˈriːtʃɪŋ, *Am:* ˌfɑːr-] *adj* de grandes repercusiones

fart [fɑːt, *Am:* fɑːrt] *inf* **I.** *n* pedo *m* **II.** *vi* tirarse un pedo

farther [ˈfɑːðəʳ, *Am:* ˈfɑːrðə·] **I.** *adv comp of* **far** más allá **II.** *adj comp of* **far** más lejano

farthest [ˈfɑːðɪst, *Am:* ˈfɑːr-] **I.** *adv superl of* **far** más lejos **II.** *adj superl of* **far** (*distance*) más lejano; (*time*) más remoto

fascinate [ˈfæsɪneɪt, *Am:* -əneɪt] *vt* fascinar

fascinating [ˈfæsɪneɪtɪŋ, *Am:* -ṭɪŋ] *adj* fascinante

fascination [ˌfæsɪˈneɪʃən, *Am:* -ə'-] *n no pl* fascinación *f*

fascism *n,* **Fascism** [ˈfæʃɪzəm] *n no pl* fascismo *m*

fascist, Fascist [ˈfæʃɪst] *n* fascista *mf*

fashion [ˈfæʃən] **I.** *n* **1.** (*popular style*) moda *f;* **to be in** ~ estar de moda; **to be out of** ~ estar pasado de moda **2.** (*manner*) manera *f;* **after a** ~ si se le puede llamar así **II.** *vt form* dar forma a; (*create*) crear

fashionable [ˈfæʃənəbl] *adj* (*clothes, style*) moderno; (*nightclub, restaurant*) de moda; (*person, set*) a la moda

fashion show *n* desfile *m* de moda

fast¹ [fɑːst, *Am:* fæst] **I.** <-er, -est> *adj* **1.** rápido; **the ~ lane** el carril de adelantamiento **2.** (*clock*) **to be ~** ir adelantado **3.** (*firmly fixed*) fijo

II. *adv* **1.** (*quickly*) rápidamente **2.** (*firmly*) firmemente **3.** (*deeply*) profundamente; **to be ~ asleep** estar profundamente dormido

fast² [fɑːst, *Am:* fæst] **I.** *vi* ayunar **II.** *n* ayuno *m*

fasten [ˈfɑːsən, *Am:* ˈfæsən] *vt* **1.** (*do up*) atar **2.** (*fix securely*) fijar

◆ **fasten on** *vt* fijarse en; **to ~ an idea** aferrarse a una idea

fastener [ˈfɑːsənəʳ, *Am:* ˈfæsənə·] *n* cierre *m;* **zip ~** cremallera *f*

fast food *n no pl* comida *f* rápida

fastidious [fəˈstɪdɪəs] *adj* escrupuloso

fat [fæt] **I.** *adj* **1.** gordo **2.** (*thick*) grueso **3.** (*large*) grande **II.** *n* **1.** *no pl* (*meat tissue*) carnes *fpl* **2.** (*fatty substance*) grasa *f;* **to live off the ~ of the land** vivir a cuerpo de rey

fatal [ˈfeɪtəl, *Am:* -təl] *adj* **1.** (*causing death*) mortal **2.** (*disastrous*) desastroso **3.** *liter* (*consequences*) funesto

fatality [fəˈtæləti, *Am:* -ṭi] <-ies> *n* fatalidad *f*

fate [feɪt] *n no pl* (*destiny*) destino *m;* (*one's end*) suerte *f*

fateful [ˈfeɪtfəl] *adj* fatídico

fat-free *adj* sin grasas

father [ˈfɑːðəʳ, *Am:* -ðə·] *n* padre *m*

Father Christmas *n Brit* Papá *m* Noel

fatherhood [ˈfɑːðəhʊd, *Am:* -ðə·-] *n no pl* paternidad *f*

father-in-law [ˈfɑːðərɪnlɔː, *Am:* -ðə·ɪnlɑː] <fathers-in-law *o* father-in-laws> *n* suegro *m*

fatherly [ˈfɑːðəli, *Am:* -ðə·li] *adj* paternal

fathom [ˈfæðəm] **I.** *n* NAUT braza *f* **II.** *vt* (*mystery*) desentrañar

fatigue [fəˈtiːɡ] *n no pl* (*tiredness*) cansancio *m,* fatiga *f*

fatten [ˈfætən] *vt* engordar

fatty [ˈfæti, *Am:* ˈfæṭ-] **I.** *adj* **1.** (*food*) graso **2.** (*tissue*) adiposo **II.** <-ies> *n inf* gordinflón, -ona *m, f*

fatuous [ˈfætʃʊəs, *Am:* ˈfætʃu-] *adj* fatuo

faucet [ˈfɔːsɪt, *Am:* ˈfɑː-] *n Am* grifo *m,* bitoque *m Méx, RíoPl*

fault [fɔ:lt] **I.** n **1.** no pl (*responsibility*) culpa f; **to be sb's ~ (that ...)** ser culpa de alguien (que...); **to be at ~** tener la culpa; **to find ~ with sb** criticar a alguien **2.** (*character weakness*) debilidad f **3.** (*defect*) fallo m **4.** GEO falla f **II.** vt encontrar defectos en

faulty ['fɔ:lti, Am: -t̬i] adj defectuoso

fauna ['fɔ:nə, Am: 'fɑ:-] n fauna f

favor ['feɪvə', Am: -və'] n, vt Am, Aus s. **favour**

favorable ['feɪvərəbl] adj Am, Aus s. **favourable**

favorite ['feɪvərɪt] adj, n Am, Aus s. **favourite**

favoritism n Am, Aus s. **favouritism**

favour ['feɪvə', Am: -və'] Brit, Aus **I.** n **1.** no pl (*approval*) favor m, aprobación f; **to be in ~ of sb/sth** estar a favor de alguien/algo; **to find ~ with sb** caer en gracia a alguien **2.** (*helpful act*) favor m, valedura f Méx; **to ask sb a ~** pedir un favor a alguien; **to do sb a ~** hacer un favor a alguien **3.** Am (*small gift*) detalle m **II.** vt **1.** (*prefer*) preferir **2.** (*give advantage to*) favorecer

favourable ['feɪvərəbl] adj favorable

favourite ['feɪvərɪt] adj favorito

favouritism n no pl favoritismo m

fawn¹ [fɔ:n, Am: fɑ:n] **I.** n cervato m **II.** adj beige

fawn² [fɔ:n, Am: fɑ:n] vi **to ~ on sb** elogiar a alguien

fax [fæks] **I.** n no pl fax m **II.** vt mandar por fax

FBI [ˌefbiːˈaɪ] n abbr of **Federal Bureau of Investigation** FBI m

fear [fɪə', Am: fɪr] **I.** n miedo m; **to be in ~ of sth** temer algo **II.** vt **1.** (*be afraid of*) tener miedo de **2.** form (*feel concern*) **to ~ (that ...)** temer (que... +subj)

fearful ['fɪəfəl, Am: 'fɪr-] adj temeroso; **~ of doing sth** temeroso de hacer algo

fearless ['fɪələs, Am: 'fɪr-] adj intrépido

feasibility [ˌfiːzəˈbɪləti, Am: -t̬i] n

no pl viabilidad f

feasible ['fiːzəbl] adj factible

feast [fiːst] **I.** n **1.** (*meal*) banquete m **2.** REL festividad f **II.** vi **to ~ on sth** darse un banquete con algo

feat [fiːt] n hazaña f

feather ['feðə', Am: -ə'] **I.** n pluma f **II.** vt **to ~ one's own nest** barrer hacia dentro

feature ['fiːtʃə', Am: -tʃə'] **I.** n **1.** (*distinguishing attribute*) característica f; (*speciality*) peculiaridad f **2.** pl (*facial attributes*) facciones fpl **3.** (*article*) reportaje m **II.** vt (*have as performer, star*) presentar **III.** vi figurar; **to ~ in ...** figurar en...

feature film n largometraje m

February ['februəri, Am: -eri] n febrero m; s. a. **April**

feces ['fiːsiːz] npl Am s. **faeces**

fed [fed] pt, pp of **feed**

Fed abbr of **federal** fed.

federal ['fedərəl] adj federal

federation [ˌfedəˈreɪʃn] n federación f

fed up [ˌfedˈʌp] adj inf harto; **to be ~ with sth/sb** estar harto de algo/alguien

fee [fiː] n (*for doctor, lawyer*) honorarios mpl; (*membership*) cuota f de miembro; (*for school, university*) tasas fpl de matrícula

feeble ['fiːbl] adj débil

feed [fiːd] <fed, fed> **I.** vt **1.** (*give food to: person, animal*) alimentar; (*plant*) nutrir; (*baby*) amamantar **2.** (*provide food for: family, country*) dar de comer a **II.** vi alimentarse; (*baby*) amamantar **III.** n **1.** no pl (*for farm animals*) pienso m **2.** inf (*meal*) comida f **3.** TECH tubo m de alimentación

◆ **feed back** vt proporcionar

◆ **feed in** vt (*information*) introducir

◆ **feed on** vt insep, a. fig alimentarse de

feedback ['fiːdbæk] n **1.** no pl (*information*) reacción f **2.** no pl ELEC realimentación f

feeding bottle n biberón m

feel [fiːl] <felt, felt> **I.** vi + adj/n

sentir; **to ~ well** sentirse bien; **to ~ hot/cold** tener calor/frío; **to ~ hungry/thirsty** tener hambre/sed; **to ~ like a walk** tener ganas de dar un paseo **II.** *vt* **1.** (*experience*) experimentar **2.** (*think, believe*) **to ~** (*that*) … creer (que)… **3.** (*touch*) tocar; (*pulse*) tomar **III.** *n* **1.** *no pl* (*texture*) textura *f* **2.** *no pl* (*act of touching*) tacto *m*

feeler ['fiːlər, *Am:* -lər] *n* zool antena *f;* **to put out ~s** tantear el terreno

feeling ['fiːlɪŋ] *n* **1.** (*emotion*) sentimiento *m;* **to hurt sb's ~s** herir los sentimientos de alguien **2.** (*sensation*) sensación *f* **3.** (*impression*) impresión *f;* **to have the ~** (**that**) … tener la impresión (de que)…

feet [fiːt] *n pl of* **foot**

feign [feɪn] *vt liter* fingir

fell[1] [fel] *pt of* **fall**

fell[2] [fel] *vt* cortar

fell[3] [fel] *n* (*mountain*) montaña *f*

fell[4] [fel] *adj* HIST feroz; **at one ~ swoop** de un solo golpe

fellow ['feləʊ, *Am:* -oʊ] **I.** *n* **1.** *inf* (*man*) tío *m* **2.** UNIV profesor(a) *m(f)* **II.** *adj* **~ student** compañero, -a *m, f* de clase

fellow citizen *n* conciudadano, -a *m, f* **fellow countryman** *n* compatriota *m*

fellowship ['feləʊʃɪp, *Am:* -oʊ-] *n* **1.** *no pl* (*comradely feeling*) compañerismo *m* **2.** UNIV **research ~** beca *f* de investigación

felony ['feləni] <-ies> *n Am* crimen *m*

felt[1] [felt] *pt, pp of* **feel**

felt[2] [felt] *n no pl* fieltro *m*

felt-tip (**pen**) [ˌfelt'tɪp (pen)] *n* rotulador *m*

female ['fiːmeɪl] **I.** *adj* femenino; ZOOL, TECH hembra **II.** *n* (*woman*) mujer *f;* zool hembra *f*

feminine ['femənɪn] *adj* femenino

feminism ['femɪnɪzəm] *n no pl* feminismo *m*

feminist ['femɪnɪst] *n* feminista *mf*

fence [fens] **I.** *n* cerca *f;* **to sit on the ~** ver los toros desde la barrera **II.** *vi* SPORTS esgrimir **III.** *vt* (*enclose*)

cercar

fencing *n no pl* esgrima *f*

fend for ['fendˌfɔːr, *Am:* 'fendˌfɔːr] *vt* **to ~ oneself** arreglárselas

◆ **fend off** *vt* apartar; **to ~ a question** esquivar una pregunta

fender ['fendər, *Am:* -dər] *n* **1.** (*around fireplace*) guardafuego *m* **2.** *Am* AUTO guardabarros *m inv*

ferment[1] [fə'ment, *Am:* fər-] *vi* CHEM fermentar

ferment[2] ['fɛːment, *Am:* 'fɛːr-] *n no pl, form* agitación *f*

fern [fɜːn, *Am:* fɜːrn] *n* helecho *m*

ferocious [fə'rəʊʃəs, *Am:* -'roʊ-] *adj* feroz

ferocity [fə'rɒsəti, *Am:* -'rɑːsəti] *n no pl* ferocidad *f*

ferret ['ferɪt] *n* hurón *m*

ferry ['feri] <-ies> **I.** *n* (*ship*) ferry *m;* (*smaller*) balsa *f* **II.** *vt* llevar en barca

fertile ['fɜːtaɪl, *Am:* 'fɜːrtl̩] *adj a. fig* fértil

fertility [fə'tɪləti, *Am:* fər'tɪləti] *n no pl* fertilidad *f*

fertilize ['fɜːtəlaɪz, *Am:* 'fɜːrtə-] *vt* **1.** BIO fertilizar **2.** AGR abonar

fertilizer ['fɜːtəlaɪzər, *Am:* 'fɜːrtəl-] *n* fertilizante *m*

fervent ['fɜːvənt, *Am:* 'fɜːr-] *adj*, **fervid** ['fɜːvɪd, *Am:* 'fɜːr-] *adj form* ferviente

fester ['festər, *Am:* -tər] *vi* enconarse

festival ['festɪvəl] *n* **1.** REL festividad *f* **2.** (*special event*) festival *m*

festive ['festɪv] *adj* festivo; **to be in ~ mood** estar muy alegre

festivity [fe'stɪvəti, *Am:* -ti] <-ies> *n pl* festejos *mpl*

festoon [fe'stuːn] *vt* adornar

fetch [fetʃ] *vt* **1.** (*bring back*) traer **2.** (*be sold for*) venderse por

fetching ['fetʃɪŋ] *adj* atractivo

fête [feɪt] *n Brit, Aus* fiesta *f*

fetish ['fetɪʃ, *Am:* 'fet-] *n a.* PSYCH fetiche *m*

fetus ['fiːtəs, *Am:* -təs] *n Am s.* **foetus**

feud [fjuːd] *n* enemistad *f* (heredada); **a family ~** una enemistad entre familias

feudal ['fju:dəl] *adj* HIST feudal
fever ['fi:vər, *Am:* -vɚ] *n* fiebre *f*
feverish ['fi:vərɪʃ] *adj* febril
few [fju:] <-er, -est> **I.** *adj def*
1. (*small number*) pocos, pocas; **one
of her ~ friends** uno de sus pocos
amigos; **quite a ~ people** bastante
gente **2.** (*some*) algunos, algunas;
they left a ~ boxes dejaron algunas
cajas **II.** *pron* pocos, pocas; **a ~** unos
pocos
fewer ['fju:ər, *Am:* -ɚ] *adj, pron*
menos
fewest ['fju:ɪst] *adj, pron* los menos,
las menos
fiancé [fɪ'ɒnseɪ, *Am:* ˌfi:ɑ:n'seɪ] *n*
prometido *m*
fiancée [fɪ'ɒnseɪ, *Am:* ˌfi:ɑ:n'seɪ] *n*
prometida *f*
fiasco [fɪ'æskəʊ, *Am:* -koʊ] <-cos *o*
-coes> *n* fiasco *m*
fib [fɪb] *inf* **I.** <-bb-> *vi* decir men-
tirijillas **II.** *n* mentirijilla *f*, pepa *f And*
fiber ['fɪbər, *Am:* -ɚ] *n Am*, **fibre**
['faɪbər, *Am:* -bɚ] *n* fibra *f*
fibreglass ['faɪbəglɑ:s, *Am:* -bɚ-
glæs] *n* fibra *f* de vidrio
fickle ['fɪkl] *adj* inconstante
fiction ['fɪkʃn] *n no pl a.* LIT ficción *f*
fictional ['fɪkʃənl] *adj* ficticio
fictitious [fɪk'tɪʃəs] *adj* ficticio
fiddle ['fɪdl] **I.** *vt Brit, inf* (*fraudu-
lently change*) falsificar **II.** *n inf*
1. *Brit* (*fraud*) trampa *f* **2.** (*violin*)
violín *m*
fiddler ['fɪdlər, *Am:* -lɚ] *n inf* **1.** (*violinist*) violinista *mf* **2.** *Brit*
(*fraudster*) tramposo, -a *m, f*
fiddly ['fɪdli] <-ier, -iest> *adj inf* difícil
fidelity [fɪ'deləti, *Am:* -t̬i] *n no pl* fidelidad *f*
fidget ['fɪdʒɪt] *vi* agitarse (nerviosamente)
field [fi:ld] *n* **1.** *a.* ELEC, AGR, SPORTS
campo *m;* (*meadow*) prado *m* **2.** +
sing/pl vb (*contestants*) competi-
dores *mpl;* **to lead the ~** ir en cabeza **3.** (*sphere of activity*) esfera *f;* **it's
not my ~** no es de mi competencia
fieldwork ['fi:ldwɜ:k, *Am:* -wɜ:rk]
n trabajo *m* de campo

fiend [fi:nd] *n* demonio *m*
fiendish ['fi:ndɪʃ] *adj* diabólico
fierce [fɪəs, *Am:* fɪrs] *adj* <-er, -est>
(*competition, opposition*) intenso;
(*debate, discussion*) acalorado;
(*fighting*) encarnizado; (*wind*) fuerte
fiery ['faɪəri, *Am:* 'faɪri] <-ier, -iest>
adj **1.** (*heat*) abrasador **2.** (*passionate*) apasionado
fifteen [ˌfɪf'ti:n] *adj* quince *inv; s. a.*
eight
fifteenth *adj* decimoquinto
fifth [fɪfθ] *adj* quinto
fiftieth ['fɪftiəθ] *adj* quincuagésimo
fifty ['fɪfti] *adj* cincuenta *inv; s. a.*
eighty
fig [fɪg] *n* higo *m*
fight [faɪt] **I.** *n* **1.** (*physical*) pelea *f;*
(*argument*) disputa *f* **2.** MIL combate
m **3.** (*struggle*) lucha *f* **II.** <fought,
fought> *vi* **1.** (*exchange blows*) pelear; MIL combatir; **to ~ with sb**
(*against*) luchar contra alguien; (*on
same side*) luchar junto a alguien
2. (*dispute*) discutir **3.** (*struggle to
overcome*) luchar; **to ~ for/against
sth** luchar por/contra algo **III.** *vt*
1. (*exchange blows with, argue
with*) pelearse con **2.** (*wage war, do
battle*) luchar con **3.** (*struggle to
overcome*) combatir; **to ~ a case**
LAW negar una acusación
◆ **fight back I.** *vi* (*counter-attack*)
contraatacar; (*defend oneself*) defenderse **II.** *vt* **to ~ one's tears** contener las lágrimas
◆ **fight off** *vt* (*repel*) rechazar;
(*master, resist*) resistir
fighter ['faɪtər, *Am:* t̬ɚ] *n* **1.** (*person*) luchador(a) *m(f)* **2.** AVIAT caza
m
fighting ['faɪtɪŋ, *Am:* -t̬ɪŋ] *n no pl*
lucha *f;* (*battle*) combate *m*
figment ['fɪgmənt] *n* **a ~ of the
imagination** un producto de la imaginación
figurative ['fɪgjərətɪv, *Am:* -jɚə-
t̬ɪv] *adj* **1.** LING figurado **2.** ART figura-
tivo
figure ['fɪgər, *Am:* -jɚ] **I.** *n*
1. (*shape*) figura *f* **2.** ART estatua *f*

F
f

3. (*numeral*) cifra *f* **4.** (*diagram*) figura *f* **II.** *vt* **1.** *Am* (*think*) figurarse **2.** (*in diagram*) representar **III.** *vi* (*feature*) figurar; **that ~s** *Am* es natural

◆**figure out** *vt* (*comprehend*) entender; (*work out*) resolver

figurehead ['fɪgəhed, *Am:* -jɚ-] *n* NAUT mascarón *m* de proa

Fiji ['fiːdʒiː] *n* **the ~ Islands** las Islas Fiji

Fijian [fɪ'dʒiːən] **I.** *adj* de Fiji **II.** *n* habitante *mf* de (las Islas) Fiji

file¹ [faɪl] **I.** *n* **1.** (*folder*) carpeta *f* **2.** (*record*) expediente *m;* **to open a ~** abrir un expediente **3.** INFOR fichero *m*, archivo *m* **4.** (*row*) fila *f* **II.** *vt* **1.** (*record*) archivar, failear *AmC, RíoPl* **2.** (*present: claim, complaint*) presentar

file² [faɪl] *n* lima *f*
◆**file in** *vi* entrar en fila
◆**file out** *vi* salir en fila

filing ['faɪlɪŋ] *n* no pl clasificación *f*

filing cabinet *n* archivador *m*

Filipino [fɪlɪ'piːnəʊ, *Am:* -noʊ] *adj* filipino

fill [fɪl] **I.** *vt* **1.** (*make full*) llenar; (*space*) ocupar; **to ~ a vacancy** cubrir una vacante **2.** (*seal*) empastar, emplomar *AmL* **II.** *n* **to drink/eat one's ~** hartarse de beber/comer
◆**fill in** *vt* rellenar; **to fill sb in on the details** poner a alguien al corriente de los detalles
◆**fill out** *vt* rellenar
◆**fill up I.** *vt* llenar; (*completely*) colmar **II.** *vi* llenarse

fillet ['fɪlɪt] *n* filete *m*

fillet steak *n* solomillo *m*

filling *n* **1.** (*substance*) relleno *m* **2.** (*in tooth*) empaste *m*, emplomadura *f AmL*

filling station *n* gasolinera *f*, bencinera *f Chile*, grifo *m Perú*

fillip ['fɪlɪp] *n* estímulo *m*

film [fɪlm] **I.** *n* PHOT película *f* **II.** *vt* filmar **III.** *vi* rodar

film star *n* estrella *f* de cine

filter ['fɪltər, *Am:* -t̬ɚ] **I.** *n* filtro *m* **II.** *vt* filtrar

filter lane *n* carril *m* de giro

filth [fɪlθ] *n* no pl mugre *f*

filthy ['fɪlθi] *adj* **1.** (*very dirty*) inmundo **2.** *inf* (*obscene*) obsceno

fin [fɪn] *n* aleta *f*

final ['faɪnl] **I.** *adj* **1.** (*last*) final **2.** (*irrevocable*) definitivo **II.** *n* **1.** SPORTS final *f* **2.** *pl* UNIV examen *m* de fin de carrera

finale [fɪ'nɑːli, *Am:* -'næli] *n* final *m*

finalist ['faɪnəlɪst] *n* finalista *mf*

finalize ['faɪnəlaɪz] *vt* ultimar

finally ['faɪnəli] *adv* **1.** (*at long last*) finalmente; (*expressing impatience*) por fin **2.** (*irrevocably*) definitivamente; (*decisively*) de forma decisiva

finance ['faɪnænts] *vt* financiar

finances ['faɪnæntsɪz] *npl* finanzas *fpl*

financial [faɪ'næntʃəl] *adj* financiero

financial year *n* año *m* fiscal

find [faɪnd] **I.** <found, found> *vt* **1.** (*lost object, person*) encontrar **2.** (*locate*) localizar, hallar **3.** (*conclude*) **to ~ sb guilty/innocent** declarar a alguien culpable/inocente **II.** *n* hallazgo *m*
◆**find out I.** *vt* descubrir; (*dishonesty*) desenmascarar **II.** *vi* **to ~ about sth/sb** informarse sobre algo/alguien

finding ['faɪndɪŋ] *n* **1.** LAW fallo *m* **2.** (*recommendation*) recomendación *f*

fine¹ [faɪn] **I.** *adj* **1.** (*slender, light*) fino; (*feature*) delicado **2.** (*good*) bueno **II.** *adv* **1.** (*all right*) muy bien; **to feel ~** sentirse bien **2.** (*fine-grained*) fino; **to cut it ~** dejar algo para el último momento

fine² [faɪn] **I.** *n* multa *f*, boleta *f AmS* **II.** *vt* multar

fine arts *n* bellas artes *fpl*

finery ['faɪnəri] *n* no pl **in all one's ~** con las mejores galas

finger ['fɪŋgər, *Am:* -gɚ] **I.** *n* ANAT dedo *m;* **little ~** dedo meñique **II.** *vt* manosear

fingernail *n* uña *f* **fingerprint I.** *n* huella *f* dactilar **II.** *vt* **to ~ sb** tomar las huellas dactilares a alguien **fin-**

gertip *n* punta *f* del dedo; **to have sth at one's ~s** tener algo a mano; *fig* saber(se) algo al dedillo

finicky [ˈfɪnɪki] *adj* (*person*) melindroso

finish [ˈfɪnɪʃ] **I.** *n* **1.** (*end*) final *m*, fin *m*; SPORTS meta *f* **2.** (*sealing, varnishing*) acabado *m* **II.** *vi* terminar(se), acabar(se); **to ~ doing sth** terminar de hacer algo **III.** *vt* **1.** (*bring to end*) terminar, acabar; **to ~ school** terminar los estudios **2.** (*make final touches to*) acabar

◆ **finish off** *vt* **1.** (*end*) terminar, acabar **2.** (*defeat*) acabar con **3.** *Am, inf* (*murder*) liquidar

◆ **finish up I.** *vi* **to ~ at** ir a parar en **II.** *vt* terminar

finishing line *n*, **finishing post** *n* línea *f* de meta

finite [ˈfaɪnaɪt] *adj a.* LING finito

Finland [ˈfɪnlənd] *n* Finlandia *f*

Finn [fɪn] *n* finlandés, -esa *m, f*

Finnish [ˈfɪnɪʃ] *adj* finlandés

fir [fɜːᵣ, *Am:* fɜːr] *n* abeto *m*

fire [ˈfaɪəᵣ, *Am:* ˈfaɪɚ] **I.** *n* **1.** (*flames*) fuego *m*; (*in fireplace*) lumbre *f*; (*accidental*) incendio *m*; **to set sth on ~** prender fuego a algo; **to catch ~** encenderse **2.** MIL **to be under ~** MIL estar en la línea de fuego; *fig* ser criticado **II.** *vt* **1.** (*set fire to*) encender **2.** (*weapon*) disparar **3.** *inf* (*dismiss*) despedir, botar *AmL*, fletar *Arg* **III.** *vi* **1.** (*with gun*) disparar **2.** AUTO encenderse

fire alarm *n* alarma *f* contra incendios **firearm** *n* arma *f* de fuego **fire brigade** *n* Brit, **fire department** *n* Am cuerpo *m* de bomberos **fire engine** *n* bomba *m* de incendios **fire extinguisher** *n* extintor *m* de incendios **fireman** <-men> *n* bombero *m* **fireplace** *n* chimenea *f*, hogar *m*

fireproof [ˈfaɪəᵣpruːf, *Am:* ˈfaɪɚ-] *adj* a prueba de incendios

fireside *n* hogar *m* **fire station** *n* parque *m* de bomberos **firewood** *n* no pl leña *f* **firework** *n* fuego *m* artificial

firing squad *n* pelotón *m* de fusila-

miento

firm¹ [fɜːm, *Am:* fɜːrm] **I.** *adj* firme; (*strong*) fuerte; **a ~ offer** una oferta en firme **II.** *adv* firmemente; **to stand ~** mantenerse firme

firm² [fɜːm, *Am:* fɜːrm] *n* empresa *f*

first [fɜːst, *Am:* fɜːrst] **I.** *adj* (*earliest*) primero; **for the ~ time** por primera vez; **at ~ sight** a primera vista; **the ~ December** el primero de diciembre **II.** *adv* primero; (*firstly*) en primer lugar; **at ~** al principio; **to go head ~** meterse de cabeza **III.** *n* **the ~** el primero, la primera; **from the (very) ~** desde el principio

first aid *n* primeros auxilios *mpl*

first aid box *n* botiquín *m* de primeros auxilios

first-class *adj* de primera clase

first-hand [ˌfɜːstˈhænd, *Am:* ˌfɜːrst-] *adj* de primera mano

first lady *n* Am **the ~** la Primera Dama

firstly [ˈfɜːstli, *Am:* ˈfɜːrst-] *adv* en primer lugar

first name *n* nombre *m* (de pila)

first-rate [ˌfɜːstˈreɪt, *Am:* ˌfɜːrst-] *adj* de primer orden

fish [fɪʃ] **I.** <-(es)> *n* **1.** ZOOL pez *m* **2.** no pl GASTR pescado *m* **II.** *vi* pescar **III.** *vt* pescar

fisherman [ˈfɪʃəmən, *Am:* -ɚ-] <-men> *n* pescador *m*

fishfinger *n* palito *m* de merluza

fishing line *n* sedal *m* **fishing rod** *n* Brit, Aus caña *f* de pescar

fishmonger [ˈfɪʃmʌŋɡəᵣ, *Am:* -ɡɚ] *n* Brit pescadero, -a *m, f*

fishy [ˈfɪʃi] <-ier, -iest> *adj inf* dudoso

fist [fɪst] *n* puño *m*

fit¹ [fɪt] **I.** <-tt-> *adj* **1.** (*apt, suitable*) apto, apropiado; (*competent*) capaz; **~ to eat** bueno para comer **2.** (*ready*) listo **3.** SPORTS en forma **II.** <-tt-> *vt* **1.** (*adapt*) ajustar **2.** (*clothes*) sentar bien **3.** (*facts*) corresponder con **4.** TECH caber en, encajar en **III.** *vi* <-tt-> **1.** (*be correct size*) ir bien **2.** (*correspond*) corresponder

◆ **fit in I.** *vi* **1.** (*conform*) encajar

2. (*get on well*) llevarse bien **II.** *vt* tener tiempo para

◆ **fit out** *vt* equipar

fit² [fɪt] *n* **1.** MED ataque *m;* **coughing** ~ acceso *m* de tos **2.** *inf* (*outburst of rage*) arranque *m;* **in ~s and starts** a empujones

fitment ['fɪtmənt] *n Brit* mueble *m*

fitness ['fɪtnɪs] *n no pl* **1.** (*competence, suitability*) conveniencia *f* **2.** (*good condition*) (buena) condición *f* física; (*health*) (buena) salud *f*

fitted ['fɪtɪd, *Am:* 'fɪt̮-] *adj* (*adapted, suitable*) idóneo; (*tailor-made*) a medida; ~ **kitchen** cocina *f* empotrada

fitter ['fɪtər, *Am:* 'fɪt̮ər] *n* técnico, -a *m, f*

fitting ['fɪtɪŋ, *Am:* 'fɪt̮-] **I.** *n* **1.** *pl* (*fixtures*) accesorios *mpl* **2.** (*of clothes*) prueba *f* **II.** *adj* apropiado

five [faɪv] *adj* cinco *inv; s. a.* **eight**

fiver ['faɪvər, *Am:* -vər] *n Brit, inf* billete *m* de 5 libras; *Am, inf* billete *m* de 5 dólares

fix [fɪks] **I.** *vt* **1.** (*fasten*) sujetar; **to ~ sth in one's mind** grabar algo en la memoria **2.** (*determine*) fijar **3.** (*repair*) arreglar **4.** *Am, inf* (*food*) preparar **II.** *n inf* (*dilemma*) aprieto *m;* **to be in a ~** estar en un aprieto

◆ **fix on** *vt* (*make definite*) fijar

◆ **fix up** *vt* **1.** (*supply with*) **to fix sb up** (**with sth**) proveer a alguien (de algo) **2.** (*arrange*) organizar

fixation [fɪk'seɪʃən] *n* fijación *f*

fixed *adj* fijo; **to be of no ~ abode** LAW no tener domicilio permanente

fixture ['fɪkstʃər, *Am:* -tʃər] *n* **1.** (*furniture*) instalación *f* fija **2.** *Brit, Aus* SPORTS partido *m*

fizzy ['fɪzi] <-ier, -iest> *adj* (*bubbly*) efervescente; (*carbonated*) gaseoso

flabby ['flæbi] <-ier, -iest> *adj pej* **1.** (*body*) fofo **2.** (*weak*) débil

flag¹ [flæg] **I.** *n* (*national*) bandera *f;* (*pennant*) estandarte *m* **II.** <-gg-> *vi* flaquear

flag² [flæg] *n* (*stone*) losa *f*

flagpole ['flægpəʊl, *Am:* -poʊl] *n* asta *f*

flagrant ['fleɪgrənt] *adj* descarado

flagship ['flægʃɪp] *n* buque *m* insignia

flagstaff ['flægstɑːf, *Am:* -stæf] *n s.* **flagpole**

flair [fleər, *Am:* fler] *n no pl* estilo *m*

flak [flæk] *n* **1.** MIL fuego *m* antiaéreo **2.** (*criticism*) críticas *fpl*

flake [fleɪk] **I.** *vi* (*skin*) pelarse; (*paint*) desc100ncharse **II.** *n* (*peeling*) hojuela *f;* (*shaving, sliver*) viruta *f;* (*of paint, wood*) lámina *f;* (*of skin*) escama *f;* (*of snow*) copo *m*

flamboyant [flæm'bɔɪənt] *adj* (*manner, person*) exuberante; (*air, clothes*) vistoso

flame [fleɪm] *n* **1.** llama *f;* **to burst into ~** estallar en llamas **2.** (*lover*) (**old**) ~ antiguo amor *m*

flamingo [flə'mɪŋgəʊ, *Am:* -goʊ] <-(e)s> *n* flamenco *m*

flammable ['flæməbl] *adj Am* inflamable

flan [flæn] *n* tarta *f* (de frutas)

Flanders ['flɑːndəz] *n* Flandes *m*

flank [flæŋk] **I.** *n* (*of person*) costado *m;* MIL flanco *m* **II.** *vt* flanquear

flannel ['flænl] *n* **1.** (*material*) franela *f* **2.** *Brit* (*facecloth*) toallita *f* **3.** *pl* (*trousers*) pantalones *mpl* de franela

flap [flæp] **I.** <-pp-> *vt* (*wings*) batir; (*shake*) sacudir **II.** <-pp-> *vi* (*wings*) aletear; (*flag*) ondear **III.** *n* **1.** (*of cloth*) faldón *m;* (*of pocket, envelope*) solapa *f;* (*of table*) hoja *f* **2.** AVIAT flap *m* **3.** (*of wing*) aleteo *m*

flare [fleər, *Am:* fler] *n* **1.** (*blaze*) llamarada *f* **2.** MIL bengala *f* **3.** (*of clothes*) vuelo *m*

flare-up ['fleərʌp, *Am:* 'fler-] *n* estallido *m fig*

flash [flæʃ] **I.** *vt* (*light*) enfocar **II.** *vi* **1.** (*lightning*) relampaguear **2.** (*move swiftly*) **to ~ by** pasar como un rayo **III.** *n* **1.** (*burst*) destello *m;* ~ **of light**(**ning**) relámpago *m;* **in a ~** en un instante **2.** PHOT flash *m*

flashbulb ['flæʃbʌlb] *n* bombilla *f* de flash

flashlight ['flæʃlaɪt] *n* linterna *f* eléctrica

flashy ['flæʃi] <-ier, -iest> *adj inf* ostentoso, llamativo

flask [flɑ:sk, *Am:* flæsk] *n* CHEM matraz *m*; (*thermos*) termo *m*

flat¹ [flæt] **I.** *adj* <-tt-> **1.** (*surface*) llano, plano **2.** (*drink*) sin gas **3.** (*tyre*) desinflado **4.** *Aus, Brit* (*battery*) descargado **5.** MUS desafinado **II.** *n* **1.** (*level surface*) plano *m* **2.** (*low level ground*) llanura *f* **3.** *Aus, Brit* (*tyre*) pinchazo *m* **4.** MUS bemol *m*

flat² [flæt] *n Aus, Brit* (*apartment*) piso *m*, apartamento *m Ven, Col*, departamento *m Méx, CSur*

flatly *adv* rotundamente

flatmate ['flætmeɪt] *n Aus, Brit* compañero, -a *m, f* de piso

flatten ['flætn] *vt* allanar

flatter ['flætə^r, *Am:* 'flæt̮ə[,]] *vt* **1.** (*gratify vanity*) adular **2.** (*make attractive*) favorecer

flattering *adj* **1.** (*clothes, portrait*) que favorece **2.** (*remark, description*) halagador

flattery ['flætəri, *Am:* 'flæt̮-] *n no pl* adulación *f*

flaunt [flɔ:nt, *Am:* flɑ:nt] *vt* hacer alarde de

flavor ['fleɪvə^r, *Am:* -və[,]] *Am* **I.** *n, vt* s. **flavour II.** *n* s. **flavouring**

flavour ['fleɪvə^r, *Am:* -və[,]] *Brit, Aus* **I.** *n* **1.** (*taste*) gusto *m*; (*ice cream, fizzy drink*) sabor *m* **2.** *fig* sabor *m* **II.** *vt* sazonar

flavouring ['fleɪvərɪŋ] *n Brit, Aus* condimento *m*, aromatizante *m*

flaw [flɔ:, *Am:* flɑ:] *n* defecto *m*

flawless ['flɔ:lɪs, *Am:* 'flɑ:-] *adj* intachable

flax [flæks] *n no pl* lino *m*

flea [fli:] *n* pulga *f*

fleck [flek] **I.** *n* mota *f* **II.** *vt* salpicar

flee [fli:] <fled, fled> **I.** *vt* (*run away from*) huir de **II.** *vi* (*run away*) escaparse; *liter* desaparecer

fleece [fli:s] **I.** *n* **1.** (*of sheep*) vellón *m* **2.** (*clothing*) borreguillo *m* **II.** *vt* esquilar

fleet¹ [fli:t] *n* **1.** NAUT flota *f* **2.** (*of aeroplanes*) escuadrón *m*

fleet² [fli:t] <-er, -est> *adj* veloz

fleeting ['fli:tɪŋ, *Am:* -t̮ɪŋ] *adj* fugaz

Flemish ['flemɪʃ] *adj* flamenco

flesh [fleʃ] *n no pl* (*body tissue*) carne *f*; (*pulp*) pulpa *f*; **to be (only) ~ and blood** ser (sólo) de carne y hueso

flesh wound *n* herida *f* superficial

flew [flu:] *pt of* **fly**

flex [fleks] **I.** *vt* flexionar **II.** *n* ELEC cable *m*

flexibility [ˌfleksə'bɪləti, *Am:* -t̮i] *n no pl* flexibilidad *f*

flexible ['fleksəbl] *adj* **1.** (*pliable*) flexible **2.** (*arrangement, policy, schedule*) adaptable

flexitime ['fleksɪtaɪm] *n no pl* horario *m* flexible

flick [flɪk] **I.** *vt* (*with finger*) chasquear **II.** *n* **1.** (*sudden movement, strike*) golpecito *m* **2.** **the ~s** *pl, inf* (*cinema*) el cine

flicker ['flɪkə^r, *Am:* -ə[,]] **I.** *vi* parpadear **II.** *n* parpadeo *m*

flier ['flaɪə^r, *Am:* -ə[,]] *n* aviador(a) *m(f)*

flight [flaɪt] *n* **1.** (*act*) vuelo *m* **2.** (*retreat*) escape *m* **3.** (*series: of stairs*) tramo *m*

flight attendant *n* auxiliar *mf* de vuelo **flight deck** *n* cabina *f* de pilotaje

flight path *n* trayectoria *f* de vuelo

flimsy ['flɪmzi] <-ier, -iest> *adj* **1.** (*light: dress, blouse*) ligero **2.** (*argument, excuse*) poco sólido

flinch [flɪntʃ] *vi* (*in pain*) rechistar

fling [flɪŋ] <flung, flung> **I.** *vt* lanzar **II.** *n inf* aventura *f* (amorosa)

flint [flɪnt] *n* pedernal *m*

flip [flɪp] <-pp-> *vt* dar la vuelta a; **to ~ a coin** echar a cara o cruz

flippant ['flɪpənt] *adj* poco serio

flipper ['flɪpə^r, *Am:* -ə[,]] *n* aleta *f*

flirt [flɜ:t, *Am:* flɜ:rt] **I.** *n* (*woman*) coqueta *f*; (*man*) galanteador *m* **II.** *vi* flirtear

flit [flɪt] <-tt-> *vi* **to ~ (about)** revolotear

float [fləʊt, *Am:* floʊt] **I.** *vi* **1.** (*in liquid, air*) flotar, boyar *AmL* **2.** (*move aimlessly*) moverse sin rumbo **3.** ECON fluctuar **II.** *vt* **1.** (*keep afloat*) poner a flote **2.** (*air*) **to ~ an idea/a plan** sugerir una idea/un plan III. *n* **1.** NAUT flotador *m* **2.** (*vehicle*) carroza *f* **3.** *Aus, Brit* (*cash*) fondo *m*

flock [flɒk, *Am:* flɑːk] *n* (*of goats, sheep*) rebaño *m;* (*of birds*) bandada *f,* parvada *f AmL;* (*of people*) multitud *f*

flog [flɒg, *Am:* flɑːg] <-gg-> *vt* **1.** (*punish*) azotar; *fig* flagelar **2.** *Brit, inf* (*sell*) vender

flood [flʌd] **I.** *vt* inundar; AUTO ahogar un motor **II.** *n* **1.** METEO inundación *f* **2.** (*outpouring*) torrente *m*

floodlight ['flʌdlaɪt] **I.** *n* foco *m* **II.** *vt irr* iluminar (con focos)

floor [flɔːʳ, *Am:* flɔːr] **I.** *n* **1.** (*of room*) suelo *m;* **dance** ~ pista *f* de baile **2.** (*level in building*) piso *m* **II.** *vt* (*knock down*) tumbar

floorboard ['flɔːbɔːd, *Am:* 'flɔːr-bɔːrd] *n* tabla *f* del suelo

floor show *n* espectáculo *m* de cabaret

flop [flɒp, *Am:* flɑːp] <-pp-> **I.** *vi inf* (*fail*) fracasar **II.** *n inf* (*failure*) fracaso *m*

floppy ['flɒpi, *Am:* 'flɑːpi] **I.** <-ier, -iest> *adj* caído **II.** <-ies> *n* diskette *m*

floppy disk *n* diskette *m*

flora ['flɔːrə] *n no pl* flora *f*

floral ['flɔːrəl] *adj* floral

Florida ['flɒrɪdə, *Am:* 'flɔːr-] *n* Florida *f*

florist ['flɒrɪst, *Am:* 'flɔːr-] *n* florista *mf;* **the ~'s** la floristería

flotation [fləʊ'teɪʃn, *Am:* floʊ-] *n* ECON, FIN salida *f* a Bolsa

flounder¹ ['flaʊndəʳ, *Am:* -dɚ] *vi* sufrir

flounder² ['flaʊndəʳ, *Am:* -dɚ] *n* (*flatfish*) platija *f*

flour ['flaʊəʳ, *Am:* -ɚ] *n no pl* harina *f*

flourish ['flʌrɪʃ, *Am:* 'flɜːr-] **I.** *vi* florecer **II.** *n* **with a** ~ con un gesto ceremonioso

flout [flaʊt] *vt* **to ~ a law/rule** incumplir una ley/regla

flow [fləʊ, *Am:* floʊ] **I.** *vi* fluir, correr **II.** *n no pl* (*of water, ideas*) flujo *m;* (*of goods*) circulación *f*

flowchart *n,* **flow diagram** *n* organigrama *m*

flower ['flaʊəʳ, *Am:* 'flaʊɚ] **I.** *n* flor *f;* **to be in** ~ estar en flor **II.** *vi* florecer, florear *AmL*

flowerbed *n* arriate *m* de flores

flower pot *n* maceta *f*

flowery ['flaʊəri] <-ier, -iest> *adj* florido

flown [fləʊn, *Am:* floʊn] *pp of* **fly¹**

flu [fluː] *n no pl* gripe *f,* gripa *f Col*

fluctuate ['flʌktʃʊeɪt] *vi* fluctuar

fluency ['fluːəntsi] *n no pl* fluidez *f*

fluent ['fluːənt] *adj* (*style, movement*) con fluidez; **to speak ~ English** hablar inglés con soltura

fluff [flʌf] *n no pl* pelusa *f*

fluffy ['flʌfi] <-ier, -iest> *adj* lanudo

fluid ['fluːɪd] **I.** *n* fluido *m* **II.** *adj* líquido

flung [flʌŋ] *pt, pp of* **fling**

fluoride ['flʊəraɪd, *Am:* 'flɔːraɪd] *n no pl* fluoruro *m*

fluorine ['flʊəriːn, *Am:* 'flɔːriːn] *n no pl* flúor *m*

fluorocarbon [,flʊərə'kɑːbən, *Am:* ,flɔːrə'kɑːr-] *n* fluorocarburo *m*

flurry ['flʌri, *Am:* 'flɜːr-] <-ies> *n* agitación *f;* (*of snow*) ráfaga *f;* **a ~ of excitement** un frenesí

flush¹ [flʌʃ] **I.** *vi* (*blush*) ruborizarse **II.** *vt* **to ~ the toilet** tirar de la cadena **III.** *n no pl* rubor *m*

flush² [flʌʃ] *adj* llano

flushed ['flʌʃt] *adj* emocionado

flute [fluːt] *n* MUS flauta *f*

flutter ['flʌtəʳ, *Am:* 'flʌtɚ] **I.** *n* **1.** *no pl, Aus, Brit, inf* (*bet*) apuesta *f* **2.** *fig* **to be all of a** ~ ser un manojo de nervios **II.** *vi* **1.** (*quiver*) temblar **2.** (*flap*) agitarse

flux [flʌks] *n no pl* **1.** (*change*) cambio *m* continuo; **to be in a state of** ~ estar continuamente cambiando **2.** MED flujo *m*

fly¹ [flaɪ] <flew, flown> **I.** *vi* volar; (*travel by aircraft*) viajar en avión **II.** *vt* **1.** (*aircraft*) pilotar **2.** (*make move through air*) hacer volar; **to ~ a flag** enarbolar una bandera

fly² [flaɪ] *n* mosca *f*

◆ **fly away** *vi* irse volando

◆ **fly in** *vi* to ~ **from somewhere** llegar (en avión) desde algún sitio

◆ **fly off** *vi* irse volando

flying ['flaɪɪŋ] *n no pl* el volar

flying saucer *n* platillo *m* volante **flying squad** *n* brigada *f* móvil **flying start** *n* SPORTS salida *f* lanzada; **to get off to a ~** entrar con buen pie

flyover ['flaɪˌəʊvəʳ, *Am:* -ˌoʊvɚ] *n Brit* paso *m* elevado

flysheet *n Brit* doble techo *m* (*de una tienda de campaña*)

flyweight ['flaɪweɪt] *n* SPORTS peso *m* mosca

FM [ˌefˈem] PHYS *abbr of* **frequency modulation** FM

FO [ˌefˈəʊ, *Am:* -oʊ] *n Brit abbr of* **Foreign Office** Ministerio *m* de Asuntos Exteriores

foal [fəʊl, *Am:* foʊl] *n* potro, -a *m, f*

foam [fəʊm, *Am:* foʊm] **I.** *n no pl* (*bubbles, foam rubber*) espuma *f* **II.** *vi* to ~ **with rage** echar espuma de (pura) rabia

fob [fɒb, *Am:* fɑːb] *n* cadena *f* de reloj

focal ['fəʊkl, *Am:* 'foʊ-] *adj* focal; ~ **point** punto *m* central

focus ['fəʊkəs, *Am:* 'foʊ-] <-es *o* foci> **I.** *n* foco *m;* **to be in/out of ~** estar enfocado/desenfocado **II.** <-s *o* -ss-> *vi* enfocar; **to ~ on sth** (*concentrate*) concentrarse en algo

fodder ['fɒdəʳ, *Am:* 'fɑː-dɚ] *n no pl* forraje *m;* ~ **crop** cereal-pienso *m*

foe [fəʊ, *Am:* foʊ] *n* enemigo, -a *m, f*

foetus ['fiːtəs, *Am:* -təs] *n* feto *m*

fog [fɒg, *Am:* fɑːg] *n* niebla *f*

foggy ['fɒgi, *Am:* 'fɑːgi] <-ier, -iest> *adj* nebuloso

foglamp *n,* **foglight** *n* faro *m* antiniebla

foil[1] [fɔɪl] *n* 1.(*metal paper*) papel *m* de aluminio 2.(*sword*) florete *m*

foil[2] [fɔɪl] *vt* frustrar

fold[1] [fəʊld, *Am:* foʊld] **I.** *vt* plegar **II.** *n* pliegue *m*

fold[2] [fəʊld, *Am:* foʊld] *n* redil *m*

◆ **fold up** *vt* doblar

folder ['fəʊldəʳ, *Am:* 'foʊldɚ] *n* carpeta *f,* fólder *m Col, Méx*

folding ['fəʊldɪŋ, *Am:* 'foʊld-] *adj* plegable

foliage ['fəʊlɪɪdʒ, *Am:* 'foʊ-] *n no pl* follaje *m*

folk [fəʊk, *Am:* foʊk] *npl* pueblo *m*

folklore ['fəʊklɔːʳ, *Am:* 'foʊklɔːr] *n no pl* folklore *m*

folk music *n* música *f* folk **folk song** *n* canción *f* popular

follow ['fɒləʊ, *Am:* 'fɑːloʊ] **I.** *vt* seguir **II.** *vi* 1.(*take same route as*) seguir 2.(*happen next*) suceder

◆ **follow on** *vi* seguir

◆ **follow through** *vi, vt* terminar

◆ **follow up** *vt* 1.(*consider, investigate*) investigar 2.(*do next*) **to ~ sth by** [*o* **with**] ... hacer algo después de...

follower *n* seguidor(a) *m(f)*

following **I.** *n inv* seguidores, -as *m, f pl* **II.** *adj* siguiente

follow-up ['fɒləʊʌp, *Am:* 'fɑːloʊ-] *n* seguimiento *m*

folly ['fɒli, *Am:* 'fɑːli] *n* locura *f*

fond [fɒnd, *Am:* fɑːnd] <-er, -est> *adj* **to be ~ of sb** tener cariño a alguien; **he is ~ of ...** le gusta...

fondle ['fɒndl, *Am:* 'fɑːn-] <-ling> *vt* acariciar

food [fuːd] *n* comida *f*

food poisoning *n no pl* envenenamiento *m* por alimentos **foodstuff** *n* artículo *m* alimenticio

fool [fuːl] **I.** *n* idiota *mf;* **to make a ~ of sb** poner a alguien en ridículo **II.** *vt* engañar; **you could have ~ed me!** *inf* ¡no me lo puedo creer!

◆ **fool about** *vi* hacer payasadas

foolhardy ['fuːlˌhɑːdi, *Am:* -hɑːr-] *adj* temerario

foolish ['fuːlɪʃ] *adj* tonto

foolproof ['fuːlpruːf] *adj* a toda prueba

foot [fʊt] **I.** <feet> *n* 1.(*of person*) pie *m;* (*of animal*) pata *f;* **to find one's feet** acostumbrarse al ambiente; **to put one's ~ down** acelerar 2.(*unit of measurement*) pie *m* (*30,48 cm*) 3.(*bottom or lowest part*) **at the ~ of one's bed** al pie de la cama; **at the ~ of the page** a pie de página **II.** *vt inf* **to ~ the bill** pagar

F **f**

footage ['fʊtɪdʒ, *Am:* 'fʊt̬-] *n no pl* CINE, TV secuencias *fpl*, imágenes *fpl*

football ['fʊtbɔ:l] *n no pl* **1.** *Brit* (*soccer*) fútbol *m* **2.** *Am* (*American football*) fútbol *m* americano **3.** (*ball*) balón *m*

football player *n* futbolista *mf*

footbridge ['fʊtbrɪdʒ] *n* puente *m* peatonal

foothills ['fʊthɪlz] *n* estribaciones *fpl*

foothold ['fʊthəʊld, *Am:* -hoʊld] *n* asidero *m* para el pie

footing ['fʊtɪŋ, *Am:* 'fʊt̬-] *n no pl* **1.** to lose one's ~ resbalar **2.** (*basis*) posición *f*; **on an equal** ~ en un mismo pie de igualdad

footlights ['fʊtlaɪts] *npl* candilejas *fpl*

footman ['fʊtmən] <-men> *n* lacayo *m*

footnote ['fʊtnəʊt, *Am:* -noʊt] *n* nota *f* a pie de página

footpath ['fʊtpɑ:θ, *Am:* -pæθ] *n* sendero *m*

footprint ['fʊtprɪnt] *n* huella *f*

footstep ['fʊtstep] *n* paso *m*

footwear ['fʊtweəʳ, *Am:* -wer] *n no pl* calzado *m*

for [fɔ:ʳ, *Am:* fɔ:r] **I.** *prep* **1.** (*destined for*) para; **this is** ~ **you** esto es para ti **2.** (*to give to*) por; **to do sth** ~ **sb** hacer algo por alguien **3.** (*intention, purpose*) ~ **sale/rent** en venta/alquiler; **it's time** ~ **lunch** es hora del almuerzo; **to wait** ~ **sb** esperar a alguien; **to go** ~ **a walk** ir a dar un paseo; **what's that** ~? ¿para qué es eso? **4.** (*to acquire*) **to search** ~ **sth** buscar algo; **to apply** ~ **a job** solicitar un trabajo **5.** (*towards*) **to make** ~ **home** dirigirse hacia casa; **to run** ~ **safety** correr a ponerse a salvo **6.** (*time*) ~ **now** por ahora; ~ **a while/a time** por un rato/un momento **7.** (*on date of*) **to set the wedding** ~ **May 4** fijar la boda para el 4 de mayo **8.** (*in support of*) **is he** ~ **or against it?** ¿está a favor o en contra?; **to fight** ~ **sth** luchar por algo **9.** (*employed by*) **to work** ~ **a company** trabajar para una empresa **10.** (*the task of*) **it's** ~ **him to say/do ...** le toca a él decir/hacer... **11.** (*price*) **I paid £10** ~ **it** pagué £10 por ello **12.** (*cause*) **excuse me** ~ **being late** discúlpame por llegar tarde **13.** (*as*) ~ **example** por ejemplo **II.** *conj form* pues

forage ['fɒrɪdʒ, *Am:* 'fɔ:r-] *n no pl* forraje *m*

foray ['fɒreɪ, *Am:* 'fɔ:r-] *n* correría *f*

forbid [fə'bɪd, *Am:* fəʳ-] <forbade, forbidden> *vt* prohibir; **to** ~ **sb from doing sth** prohibir a alguien hacer algo

force [fɔ:s, *Am:* fɔ:rs] **I.** *n* **1.** fuerza *f*; ~ **of gravity** PHYS fuerza de la gravedad; **to combine** ~s unir esfuerzos **2.** (*large numbers*) **in** ~ en grandes cantidades **3.** (*influence*) influencia *f*; **the** ~s **of nature** *liter* las fuerzas de la naturaleza **4.** (*validity*) validez *f*; **to come into** ~ entrar en vigor **5.** MIL **armed** ~s fuerzas *fpl* armadas **II.** *vt* **1.** (*use power*) forzar **2.** (*oblige to do*) obligar; **to** ~ **sb to do sth** obligar a alguien a hacer algo

force-feed [,fɔ:s'fi:d, *Am:* 'fɔ:rsfi:d] *vt* dar de comer a la fuerza

forceful ['fɔ:sfəl, *Am:* 'fɔ:rs-] *adj* enérgico

forceps ['fɔ:seps, *Am:* 'fɔ:r-] *npl* MED fórceps *mpl*

forcibly *adv* a la fuerza

ford [fɔ:d, *Am:* fɔ:rd] **I.** *n* vado *m*, botadero *m Méx* **II.** *vt* vadear

fore [fɔ:ʳ, *Am:* fɔ:r] *n no pl* **to be to the** ~ ir delante; **to come to the** ~ destacar

forearm ['fɔ:rɑ:m, *Am:* -ɑ:rm] *n* antebrazo *m*

foreboding [fɔ:'bəʊdɪŋ, *Am:* fɔ:r-'boʊ-] *n liter* presentimiento *m*

forecast ['fɔ:kɑ:st, *Am:* 'fɔ:rkæst] <forecast *o* forecasted> **I.** *n* predicción *f*; **weather** ~ previsión *f* meteorológica **II.** *vt* pronosticar

forecourt ['fɔ:kɔ:t, *Am:* 'fɔ:rkɔ:rt] *n* explanada *f*

forefathers ['fɔ:,fɑ:ðəʳ, *Am:* 'fɔ:r-,fɑ:ðɚ] *npl liter* antepasados *mpl*

forefinger ['fɔ:fɪŋgəʳ, *Am:* 'fɔ:r-fɪŋgɚ] *n* índice *m*

forefront ['fɔ:frʌnt, *Am:* 'fɔ:r-] *n no pl* primer plano *m;* **to be at the ~ of sth** estar en la vanguardia de algo

forego [fɔ:'gəʊ, *Am:* fɔ:r'goʊ] <forewent, foregone> *vt s.* **forgo**

foreground ['fɔ:graʊnd, *Am:* 'fɔ:r-] *n no pl* **the ~** el primer plano

forehand ['fɔ:hænd, *Am:* 'fɔ:r-] *n (tennis shot)* derechazo *m*

forehead ['fɒrɪd, *Am:* 'fɔ:red] *n* frente *f*

foreign ['fɒrɪn, *Am:* 'fɔ:r-] *adj* **1.** *(from another country)* extranjero **2.** *(involving other countries)* exterior

foreign currency *n* divisa *f*

foreigner ['fɒrɪnər, *Am:* 'fɔ:r-] *n* extranjero, -a *m, f*

foreign exchange *n no pl* **1.** *(system)* cambio *m* de divisas **2.** *(currency)* divisa *f* **Foreign minister** *n* ministro, -a *m, f* de Asuntos Exteriores, canciller *mf AmL* **Foreign Office** *n no pl, Brit* Ministerio *m* de Asuntos Exteriores **Foreign Secretary** *n Brit* ministro, -a *m, f* de Asuntos Exteriores

foreman ['fɔ:mən, *Am:* 'fɔ:r-] <-men> *n* **1.** *(in factory)* capataz *m* **2.** *(head of jury)* presidente *m* (del jurado)

foremost ['fɔ:məʊst, *Am:* 'fɔ:rmoʊst] *adj* principal

forename ['fɔ:neɪm, *Am:* 'fɔ:r-] *n form* nombre *m* (de pila)

forensic [fə'rensɪk] *adj* forense; **~ medicine** medicina *f* forense

foreplay ['fɔ:pleɪ, *Am:* 'fɔ:r-] *n no pl* juegos *mpl* eróticos preliminares

forerunner ['fɔ:rʌnər, *Am:* 'fɔ:r,rʌnə-] *n* precursor(a) *m(f)*

foresee [fɔ:'si:, *Am:* fɔ:r-] *irr vt* prever

foreseeable *adj* previsible; **in the ~ future** en el futuro inmediato

foreshadow [fɔ:'ʃædəʊ, *Am:* fɔ:r-'ʃædoʊ] *vt* anunciar

foresight ['fɔ:saɪt, *Am:* 'fɔ:r-] *n* previsión *f*

foreskin ['fɔ:skɪn, *Am:* 'fɔ:r-] *n* prepucio *m*

forest ['fɒrɪst, *Am:* 'fɔ:r-] *n* bosque *m*

forestall [fɔ:'stɔ:l, *Am:* fɔ:r-] *vt* anticiparse a

forestry ['fɒrɪstri, *Am:* 'fɔ:r-] *n no pl* silvicultura *f*

foretaste ['fɔ:teɪst, *Am:* 'fɔ:r-] *n no pl* anticipo *m*

foretell [fɔ:'tel, *Am:* fɔ:r-] <foretold> *vt* predecir

forever [fə'revər, *Am:* fɔ:r'evə-] *adv,* **for ever** *adv Brit* para siempre

forewent [fɔ:'went, *Am:* fɔ:r-] *past of* **forego**

foreword ['fɔ:wɜ:d, *Am:* 'fɔ:r-wɜ:rd] *n* prefacio *m*

forfeit ['fɔ:fɪt, *Am:* 'fɔ:r-] **I.** *vt* perder el derecho a **II.** *n pl (game)* **to play ~s** jugar a las prendas

forgave [fə'geɪv, *Am:* fə-] *n pt of* **forgive**

forge [fɔ:dʒ, *Am:* fɔ:rdʒ] **I.** *vt* **1.** *(make illegal copy)* falsificar **2.** *(metal)* forjar **II.** *n* **1.** *(furnace)* fragua *f* **2.** *(smithy)* herrería *f*

◆ **forge ahead** *vi* avanzar rápidamente

forger ['fɔ:dʒər, *Am:* 'fɔ:rdʒə-] *n* falsificador(a) *m(f)*

forgery ['fɔ:dʒəri, *Am:* 'fɔ:r-] <-ies> *n* falsificación *f*

forget [fə'get, *Am:* fə-] <forgot, forgotten> **I.** *vt* olvidar; **to ~ (that)** ... olvidar (que)... **II.** *vi* olvidarse

forgetful [fə'getfəl, *Am:* fə-] *adj* olvidadizo

forgive [fə'gɪv, *Am:* fə-] <forgave, forgiven> *vt* perdonar; **to ~ sb (for) sth** perdonar algo a alguien; **to ~ sb for doing sth** perdonar a alguien por hacer algo

forgiveness *n* perdón *m*

forgo [fɔ:'gəʊ, *Am:* fɔ:r'goʊ] *irr vt* privarse de

forgot [fə'gɒt, *Am:* fə-'gɑ:t] *pt of* **forget**

forgotten [fə'gɒtn, *Am:* fə-'gɑ:tn] *pt of* **forget**

fork [fɔ:k, *Am:* fɔ:rk] **I.** *n* **1.** *(cutlery)* tenedor *m* **2.** *(tool)* horca *f* **3.** *(in road)* bifurcación *f* **4.** *(in bicycle)* horquilla *f* **II.** *vi* bifurcarse

F
f

fork-lift (**truck**) [ˌfɔːklɪft('trʌk), Am: ˌfɔːrklɪft('trʌk)] n carretilla f elevadora

forlorn [fə'lɔːn, Am: fɔːr'lɔːrn] adj (person) triste; (place) abandonado; (hope) vano

form [fɔːm, Am: fɔːrm] I. n 1. (type, variety) tipo m; **in any** (**shape or**) ~ de cualquier modo; **in the** ~ **of sth** en forma de algo 2. (outward shape) forma f; (of an object) bulto m 3. (document) formulario m 4. no pl SPORTS **to be in** ~ estar en forma 5. Brit (class) clase f II. vt formar; **to** ~ **part of sth** formar parte de algo; **to** ~ **a queue** formar una cola

formal ['fɔːməl, Am: 'fɔːr-] adj (official, ceremonious) formal; ~ **dress** traje m de etiqueta

formality [fɔː'mæləti, Am: -ti] <-ies> n formalidad f

formally adv formalmente

format ['fɔːmæt, Am: 'fɔːr-] I. n formato m II. <-tt-> vt INFOR formatear

formation [fɔː'meɪʃən, Am: fɔːr-] n formación f

formative ['fɔːmətɪv, Am: 'fɔːr-mətɪv] adj formativo; **the** ~ **years** los años de formación

formatting n INFOR formateo m

former ['fɔːmə', Am: 'fɔːrmə˞] adj anterior; **in a** ~ **life** en una vida anterior

formerly adv antes

formidable ['fɔːmɪdəbl, Am: 'fɔːr-mə-] adj extraordinario

formula ['fɔːmjʊlə] <-s o -lae> pl n fórmula f

forsake [fə'seɪk, Am: fɔːr-] <forsook, forsaken> vt (abandon) abandonar; (give up) renunciar a

fort [fɔːt, Am: fɔːrt] n fortaleza f

forte[1] ['fɔːteɪ, Am: fɔːrt] n no pl (strong point) fuerte m

forte[2] ['fɔːteɪ, Am: fɔːrt-] adv MUS forte m

forth [fɔːθ, Am: fɔːrθ] adv form **to go** ~ irse; **back and** ~ de acá para allá

forthcoming [ˌfɔːθ'kʌmɪŋ, Am: ˌfɔːrθ-] adj 1. (happening soon) ve-nidero 2. (available) **to be** ~ (**from sb**) venir (de alguien)

forthright ['fɔːθraɪt, Am: 'fɔːrθ-] adj directo

forthwith [ˌfɔːθ'wɪθ, Am: ˌfɔːrθ-] adv form en el acto

fortieth ['fɔːtiəθ, Am: 'fɔːrti-] adj cuadragésimo

fortify ['fɔːtɪfaɪ, Am: 'fɔːrtə-] <-ie-> vt MIL fortificar

fortitude ['fɔːtɪtjuːd, Am: 'fɔːrtə-tuːd] n no pl, form fortaleza f

fortnight ['fɔːtnaɪt, Am: 'fɔːrt-] n no pl, Brit, Aus quince días mpl; (business) quincena f; **in a** ~**'s time** dentro de una quincena

fortnightly ['fɔːtnaɪtli, Am: 'fɔːrt-] I. adj quincenal II. adv cada quince días

fortress ['fɔːtrɪs, Am: 'fɔːr-] n forta-leza f

fortunate ['fɔːtʃənət, Am: 'fɔːr-] adj afortunado; **it is** ~ **for her that ...** tiene la suerte de que...

fortunately adv afortunadamente

fortune ['fɔːtʃuːn, Am: 'fɔːrtʃən] n 1. (money) fortuna f; **to make a** ~ hacer una fortuna 2. no pl, form (luck) suerte f

fortune teller n adivino, -a m, f

forty ['fɔːti, Am: 'fɔːrti] adj cuarenta inv; s. a. **eighty**

forum ['fɔːrəm] n foro m

forward ['fɔːwəd, Am: 'fɔːrwəd] I. adv hacia adelante; **to lean** ~ in-clinarse hacia adelante II. adj 1. (to-wards the front) hacia adelante 2. (in a position close to front) en la parte delantera 3. (over-confident) descarado III. vt 1. (send) remitir; **please** ~ por favor, hacer seguir 2. form (help to progress) promover

forwards ['fɔːwədz, Am: 'fɔːr-wədz] adv s. **forward**

forwent [fɔː'went, Am: fɔːr-] pt of **forgo**

fossil ['fɒsəl, Am: 'fɑːsəl] n GEO fósil m

fossil fuel n combustible m fósil

foster ['fɒstə', Am: 'fɑːstə˞] vt 1. (look after) acoger 2. (encourage) fomentar

foster child *n* hijo, -a *m, f* acogido, -a

fought [fɔ:t, *Am:* fɑ:t] *pt, pp of* **fight**

foul [faʊl] **I.** *adj* sucio; (*smell*) fétido; (*weather*) pésimo; (*language*) ordinario **II.** *n* SPORTS falta *f,* penal *m AmL* **III.** *vt* **1.** (*pollute*) ensuciar **2.** SPORTS **to ~ sb** cometer una falta contra alguien

foul play *n* SPORTS juego *m* sucio

found¹ [faʊnd] *pt, pp of* **find**

found² [faʊnd] *vt* (*establish*) fundar

foundation [faʊn'deɪʃən] *n pl* cimientos *mpl;* **to lay the ~(s) (of sth)** poner los cimientos (de algo)

foundation cream *n no pl* maquillaje *m* de base

founder¹ ['faʊndər, *Am:* -dɚ] *n* fundador(a) *m(f)*

founder² ['faʊndər, *Am:* -dɚ] *vi* hundirse

foundry ['faʊndri] <-ries> *n* fundición *f,* fundidora *AmS*

fountain ['faʊntɪn, *Am:* -tən] *n* fuente *f*

fountain pen *n* pluma *f* estilográfica

four [fɔ:ʳ, *Am:* fɔ:r] **I.** *adj* cuatro *inv* **II.** *n* cuatro *m;* (*group of four*) cuarteto *m;* **to go on all ~s** andar a gatas; *s. a.* **eight**

four-letter word *n* palabrota *f*

foursome ['fɔ:səm, *Am:* 'fɔ:r-] *n* grupo *m* de cuatro personas

fourteen [fɔ:'ti:n, *Am:* ˌfɔ:r-] *adj* catorce *inv; s. a.* **eight**

fourteenth *adj* decimocuarto

fourth [fɔ:θ, *Am:* fɔ:rθ] **I.** *adj* cuarto **II.** *n* MUS cuarta *f*

fourth gear *n* AUTO cuarta marcha *f*

Fourth of July *n no pl, Am* Día *m* de la Independencia de Estados Unidos

⸻

[?] El **Fourth of July** o **Independence Day** es el día de fiesta americano no confesional más importante. En este día se conmemora la **Declaration of Independence** (declaración de independencia), mediante la cual las colonias americanas se declaran independientes de Gran Bretaña. Esto ocurrió el 4 de julio de 1776. Esta festividad se celebra con meriendas campestres, fiestas familiares y partidos de baseball. Como broche de oro el día se cierra con unos vistosos fuegos artificiales.

⸻

F *f*

four-wheel drive [ˌfɔ:'hwi:l'draɪv, *Am:* ˌfɔ:r-] *n* tracción *f* a cuatro ruedas

fowl [faʊl] <-(s)> *n* ave *f* de corral

fox [fɒks, *Am:* fɑ:ks] **I.** *n* (*animal*) zorro *m* **II.** *vt* mistificar

foyer ['fɔɪeɪ, *Am:* -ɚ] *n* vestíbulo *m*

fracas ['frækɑ:, *Am:* 'freɪkəs] <-(ses)> *n* gresca *f*

fraction ['frækʃn] *n* fracción *f*

fracture ['fræktʃər, *Am:* -tʃɚ] **I.** *vt* MED fracturar **II.** *n* MED fractura *f*

fragile ['frædʒaɪl, *Am:* -əl] *adj* frágil

fragment ['frægmənt, *Am:* 'frægment] *n* fragmento *m*

fragrance ['freɪgrəns] *n* fragancia *f*

fragrant ['freɪgrənt] *adj* fragante

frail [freɪl] *adj* (*person*) endeble; (*thing*) frágil

frame [freɪm] **I.** *n* **1.** (*for door, picture*) marco *m* **2.** *pl* (*spectacles*) montura *f* **3.** (*supporting structure*) armazón *m o f* **II.** *vt* **1.** (*picture*) enmarcar **2.** (*act as a surround to*) servir de marco **3.** (*put into words*) formular

framework ['freɪmwɜ:k, *Am:* -wɜ:rk] *n* armazón *m o f*

France [frɑ:ns, *Am:* fræns] *n* Francia *f*

franchise ['fræntʃaɪz] **I.** *n* franquicia *f* **II.** *vt* conceder en franquicia

frank [fræŋk] **I.** *adj* franco; **to be ~, …** sinceramente,… **II.** *vt* franquear

frankly *adv* sinceramente

frantic ['fræntɪk, *Am:* -t̬ɪk] *adj* (*hurry, activity*) frenético

fraternity [frə'tɜ:nəti, *Am:* -'tɜ:rnət̬i] <-ies> *n* **1.** *no pl* (*brotherly feeling*) fraternidad *f* **2.** *Am* UNIV club *m* de estudiantes

fraud [frɔːd, *Am:* frɑːd] *n* **1.** *no pl a.* LAW fraude *m* **2.** (*person*) impostor(a) *m(f)*

fraught [frɔːt, *Am:* frɑːt] *adj* tenso; **to be ~ with difficulties/problems** estar lleno de dificultades/ problemas

fray[1] [freɪ] *vi* deshilacharse; **tempers were beginning to ~** la gente estaba perdiendo la paciencia

fray[2] [freɪ] *n* **the ~** la lucha

freak [friːk] **I.** *n* **1.** (*abnormal person, thing*) monstruo *m* **2.** (*enthusiast*) fanático, -a *m, f* **II.** *adj* anormal

freckle ['frekl] *n pl* peca *f*

free [friː] **I.** <-r, -st> *adj* **1.** (*not constrained: person, country, elections*) libre; ~ **and easy** despreocupado; **to break ~ (of sth)** soltarse (de algo); **to be ~ to do sth** no tener reparos para hacer algo **2.** (*not affected by*) **to be ~ of sth** no estar afectado por algo **3.** (*not attached*) **to get sth ~** liberar algo **4.** (*not occupied*) libre; **to leave sth ~** dejar algo libre **5.** (*costing nothing*) gratis; **to be ~ of customs/tax** estar libre de aranceles/impuestos **6.** (*generous*) **to be ~ with sth** dar algo en abundancia **II.** *adv* gratis; ~ **of charge** gratis; **for ~** *inf* gratis **III.** *vt* **1.** (*release: person*) poner en libertad **2.** (*make available*) permitir

freedom ['friːdəm] *n* libertad *f*; ~ **of speech/thought** libertad *f* de expresión/pensamiento

freehold ['friːhəʊld, *Am:* -hoʊld] *n* plena propiedad *f*

free kick *n* SPORTS tiro *m* libre

freelance ['friːlɑːns, *Am:* 'friːlæns] **I.** *adj* autónomo **II.** *adv* por cuenta propia

freely *adv* **1.** (*without obstruction*) libremente **2.** (*generously*) generosamente

Freemason ['friːˌmeɪsən] *n* francmasón, -ona *m, f*

Freephone [ˌfriːˈfəʊn, *Am:* -foʊn] *n* *Brit* número *m* gratuito

free-range [ˌfriːˈreɪndʒ] *adj* de granja

free speech *n no pl* libertad *f* de expresión **free trade** *n no pl* librecambio *m* **freeway** *n Am, Aus* autopista *f* **free will** *n no pl* libre albedrío *m*

freeze [friːz] <froze, frozen> **I.** *vi* (*liquid*) helarse; (*food*) congelarse **II.** *vt* (*liquid*) helar; (*food, prices*) congelar **III.** *n* **1.** METEO ola *f* de frío **2.** ECON congelación *f*

◆ **freeze up** *vi* helarse

freezer *n* congelador *m*, congeladora *f AmS*

freezing *adj* glacial; **it's ~** hiela

freezing point *n* punto *m* de congelación

freight [freɪt] *no pl n* **1.** (*type of transportation*) flete *m* **2.** (*goods*) mercancías *fpl* **3.** (*charge*) porte *m*

freight train *n Am* tren *m* de mercancías

French [frentʃ] *adj* francés; ~ **speaker** francófono, -a *m, f* **French bean** *n Brit* judía *f* verde **French doors** *npl* puertaventana *f* **French dressing** *n no pl* vinagreta *f* **French fried potatoes** *npl*, **French fries** *npl* patatas *fpl* fritas **French horn** *n* trompa *f* de llaves **Frenchman** <-men> *n* francés *m* **French windows** *npl Am s.* **French doors Frenchwoman** <-women> *n* francesa *f*

frenzy ['frenzi] *n no pl* frenesí *m*

frequency ['friːkwəntsi] <-cies> *n no pl* frecuencia *f*

frequent[1] ['friːkwənt] *adj* frecuente, tupido *Méx*

frequent[2] [frɪˈkwent] *vt* frecuentar

frequently ['friːkwəntli] *adv* con frecuencia

fresco ['freskəʊ, *Am:* -koʊ] <-s *o* -es> *n* fresco *m*

fresh [freʃ] *adj* **1.** (*not stale: air, water, food*) fresco **2.** (*new*) nuevo; **to make a ~ start** volver a empezar

freshen ['freʃən] **I.** *vt* refrescar **II.** *vi* (*wind*) soplar más recio

freshman ['freʃmən] <-men> *n* UNIV novato *m*, estudiante *m* de primer año

> ? Con el nombre de **Freshman** se conoce en los EE.UU. a un alumno

de la clase novena, con el de **Sophomore** a uno de la décima, con el de **Junior** al alumno de la decimoprimera clase y con el de **Senior** al de la decimosegunda. Estos términos se utilizan corrientemente para los alumnos de secundaria, aun incluso en el caso de aquellas **High Schools** en las que los alumnos sólo se incorporan a partir de la décima clase. Esta terminología es empleada también por los alumnos universitarios durante sus cuatro años de college.

---

freshness *n no pl* frescura *f*
fresh water *n* agua *f* dulce
fret [fret] <-tt-> *vi* inquietarse
friar ['fraɪəʳ, *Am:* -ɚ] *n* fraile *m*
friction ['frɪkʃn] *n no pl* fricción *f*
Friday ['fraɪdi] *n* viernes *m inv;* **on ~s** los viernes; **every ~** todos los viernes; **this (coming) ~** este (próximo) viernes; **on ~ mornings** los viernes por la mañana; **on ~ night** el viernes por la noche; **last/next ~** el viernes pasado/que viene; **every other ~** un viernes sí y otro no; **on ~ we are going on holiday** el viernes nos vamos de vacaciones
fridge [frɪdʒ] *n* nevera *f,* refrigeradora *f AmS*
fried [fraɪd] *adj* frito
friend [frend] *n* amigo, -a *m, f*
friendly ['frendli] <-ier, -iest> *adj* simpático, entrador *Arg*
friendship ['frendʃɪp] *n* amistad *f*
frieze [friːz] *n* friso *m*
fright [fraɪt] *n* terror *m;* **to take ~ (at sth)** asustarse (por algo)
frighten ['fraɪtən] *vt* asustar
  ◆ **frighten away** *vt* espantar
frightened *adj* asustado
frightening *adj* aterrador
frightful ['fraɪtfəl] *adj* espantoso
frigid ['frɪdʒɪd] *adj* frígido
frill [frɪl] *n* **1.** (*cloth*) volante *m* **2. no ~s** sin excesos

frilly ['frɪli] *adj* (*dress*) de volantes; (*style*) recargado
fringe [frɪndʒ] *n* **1.** *Brit, Aus* (*hair*) flequillo *m,* pava *f AmC, And* **2.** (*edge*) margen *m*
fringe benefits *npl* ECON beneficios *mpl* complementarios
frisk [frɪsk] *vt* cachear
frisky ['frɪski] <-ier, -iest> *adj inf* juguetón
fritter ['frɪtəʳ, *Am:* 'frɪt̬ɚ] *n* buñuelo *m,* picarón *m AmL*
frivolous ['frɪvələs] *adj* frívolo; (*not serious*) poco formal
frizzy ['frɪzi] *adj* (*hair*) encrespado
fro [frəʊ, *Am:* froʊ] *adv* **to and ~** de un lado a otro
frock [frɒk, *Am:* frɑːk] *n* vestido *m*
frog [frɒg, *Am:* frɑːg] *n* rana *f;* **to have a ~ in one's throat** *fig* tener carraspera
frogman ['frɒgmən, *Am:* 'frɑːg-] <-men> *n* hombre-rana *m*
frolic ['frɒlɪk, *Am:* 'frɑːlɪk] <-ck-> *vi* juguetear
from [frɒm, *Am:* frɑːm] *prep* **1.** (*as starting point*) de; **where is he ~?** ¿de dónde es?; **to fly ~ New York to Tokyo** volar de Nueva York a Tokio; **shirts ~ £5** camisas desde £5; **~ inside** desde dentro; **to drink ~ a cup/the bottle** beber de una taza/la botella **2.** (*temporal*) **~ day to day** día tras día; **~ time to time** de vez en cuando **3.** (*at distance to*) **100 metres ~ the river** 100 metros del río **4.** (*one to another*) **to go ~ door to door** ir de puerta en puerta **5.** (*originating in*) **~ my point of view** en mi opinión **6.** (*in reference to*) **~ what I heard** según lo que he escuchado; **translated ~ the English** traducido del inglés **7.** (*caused by*) **~ experience** por experiencia; **weak ~ hunger** débil de [o por] hambre
front [frʌnt] **I.** *n* **1.** *no pl* (*forward-facing part*) frente *f;* (*of building*) fachada *f* **2.** (*outside cover*) cubierta *f* exterior; (*first pages*) principio *m* **3.** (*front area*) parte *f* delantera; **in ~ of** delante de **4.** POL frente *m;* **a**

united ~ un frente común **5.** *no pl* (*promenade*) paseo *m* marítimo **6.** METEO frente *m* **II.** *adj* **1.** (*at the front*) delantero **2.** (*first*) primero **III.** *vi* estar enfrente de; **the flat ~s north** el piso da al norte; **to ~ for** servir de fachada [*o* tapadera]

frontage ['frʌntɪdʒ, *Am:* -t̬ɪdʒ] *n* fachada *f*

front bench *n Brit* POL los ministros del gobierno o sus homólogos en la oposición **front door** *n* puerta *f* principal

frontier [frʌn'tɪər, *Am:* frʌn'tɪr] *n a. fig* frontera *f*

front page *n* primera página *f* **front-wheel drive** *n* tracción *f* delantera

frost [frɒst, *Am:* frɑːst] **I.** *n* escarcha *f* **II.** *vt Am* escarchar

frostbite ['frɒstbaɪt, *Am:* 'frɑːst-] *n no pl* congelación *f*

frosty ['frɒsti, *Am:* 'frɑːsti] <-ier, -iest> *adj* **1.** (*with frost*) escarchado **2.** (*unfriendly*) frío

froth [frɒθ, *Am:* frɑːθ] *n no pl* espuma *f*

frothy ['frɒθi, *Am:* 'frɑːθi] <-ier, -iest> *adj* espumoso

frown [fraʊn] **I.** *vi* fruncir el ceño; **to ~ at sb/sth** mirar con el ceño fruncido a alguien/algo **II.** *n* ceño *m* fruncido

froze [frəʊz, *Am:* froʊz] *pt of* **freeze**

frozen ['frəʊzn, *Am:* 'froʊzn] **I.** *pp of* **freeze II.** *adj* congelado

frugal ['fruːgl] *adj* frugal

fruit [fruːt] *n no pl* fruta *f*

fruitful ['fruːtfl] *adj* provechoso

fruition [fruː'ɪʃən] *n no pl* **to come to ~** realizarse

fruitless ['fruːtləs] *adj* infructuoso

fruit salad *n no pl* macedonia *f*

frustrate [frʌs'treɪt, *Am:* 'frʌstreɪt] <-ting> *vt* frustrar

frustrated *adj* frustrado

frustrating *adj* frustrante

frustration [frʌs'treɪʃən] *n* frustración *f*

fry[1] [fraɪ] <-ie-> *vt* freír

fry[2] [fraɪ] *n Am*, **fry-up** *n Brit* frita-da *f*

frying pan *n* sartén *f*, paila *f AmL*

ft *abbr of* **foot, feet** pie

FT [ˌef'tiː] INFOR *abbr of* **formula translation** TF

fuddy-duddy ['fʌdi,dʌdi] *pej, inf* **I.** <-ies> *n* persona *f* chapada a la antigua **II.** *adj* chapado a la antigua

fudge [fʌdʒ] **I.** *n no pl* dulce *m* de azúcar **II.** <-ging> *vt* (*issue*) esquivar

fuel ['fjuːəl] **I.** *n no pl* combustible *m* **II.** <*Brit:* -ll-, *Am:* -l-> *vt* aprovisionar de combustible

fugitive ['fjuːdʒətɪv, *Am:* -t̬ɪv] *n* fugitivo, -a *m, f*

fulfil <-ll-> *vt Brit*, **fulfill** [fʊl'fɪl] *vt Am, Aus* (*ambition, task*) realizar; (*condition, requirement*) cumplir; (*function, role*) desempeñar

fulfilment *n Brit*, **fulfillment** *n Am, Aus no pl* (*of condition, requirement*) cumplimiento *m;* (*of function, role*) desempeño *m;* (*satisfaction*) realización *f*

full [fʊl] **I.** <-er, -est> *adj* **1.** (*container, space*) lleno; (*vehicle*) completo **2.** (*total*) total; (*recovery*) completo; **to be in ~ flow** estar en pleno discurso **3.** (*maximum*) máximo; (*employment*) pleno; **at ~ speed** a toda velocidad **4.** (*busy and active*) ocupado **II.** *adv* **to know ~ well** (**that ...**) saber muy bien (que...) **III.** *n* **in ~** sin abreviar

full-fledged [ˌfʊl'fledʒd] *adj Am s.* **fully fledged**

full-length *adj* **1.** (*for entire body*) de cuerpo entero **2.** (*not short*) extenso **full moon** *n* luna *f* llena

full-scale *adj* **1.** (*original size*) de tamaño natural **2.** (*all-out*) a gran escala **full stop** *n Brit, Aus* punto *m* **full-time** *adj* de horario completo

fully ['fʊli] *adv* **1.** (*completely*) completamente **2.** (*at least*) al menos

fully-fledged [ˌfʊli'fledʒd] *adj Brit* (*bird*) plumado; (*person*) hecho y derecho

fume [fjuːm] *vi* humear

fun [fʌn] *n no pl* diversión *f;* **to do sth for ~** hacer algo por placer; **to**

have (**a lot of**) ~ divertirse (mucho); **to make** ~ **of sb** reírse de alguien
function ['fʌŋkʃən] **I.** *n a.* MAT función *f* **II.** *vi* funcionar
functional ['fʌŋkʃənl] *adj a.* LING funcional
fund [fʌnd] *n* fondo *m;* **to be short of** ~**s** ir mal de fondos
fundamental [ˌfʌndə'mentəl, *Am:* -t̬əl] **I.** *adj* fundamental **II.** *n* **the** ~**s** los principios básicos
fundamentalism [ˌfʌndə'mentəlɪzəm, *Am:* -t̬əl-] *n no pl* fundamentalismo *m*
fundamentalist *n* integrista *mf*
funding *n* financiación *f*
fundraising ['fʌndˌreɪzɪŋ] *n* recaudación *f* de fondos
funeral ['fju:nərəl] *n* entierro *m*
funeral director *n* director(a) *m(f)* de funeraria **funeral parlour** *n* funeraria *f*
funfair ['fʌnfeəʳ, *Am:* -fer] *n Brit* **1.** (*amusement park*) parque *m* de atracciones **2.** (*fair*) feria *f*
fungus ['fʌŋgəs] *n* (*wild mushroom*) hongo *m;* (*mould*) moho *m*
funnel ['fʌnəl] *n* **1.** (*implement*) embudo *m* **2.** NAUT chimenea *f*
funny ['fʌni] <-ier, -iest> *adj* **1.** (*amusing*) divertido **2.** (*odd, peculiar*) raro; **to feel** ~ no encontrarse bien
fur [fɜːʳ, *Am:* fɜːr] *n* **1.** (*animal hair*) piel *f* **2.** *no pl* CHEM, MED sarro *m*
fur coat *n* abrigo *m* de piel
furious ['fjʊəriəs, *Am:* 'fjʊri-] *adj* **1.** (*very angry*) furioso, enchilado *Méx*, caribe *Ant;* **to be** ~ **about sth** estar furioso por algo **2.** (*intense, violent*) violento
furlong ['fɜːlɒŋ, *Am:* 'fɜːrlɑːŋ] *n Brit: medida de longitud equivalente a 200 metros aproximadamente*
furlough ['fɜːləʊ, *Am:* 'fɜːrloʊ] *n* MIL permiso *m*
furnace ['fɜːnɪs, *Am:* 'fɜːr-] *n a. fig* horno *m*
furnish ['fɜːnɪʃ, *Am:* 'fɜːr-] *vt* **1.** (*supply*) proporcionar **2.** (*provide furniture*) amueblar
furnished ['fɜːnɪʃt, *Am:* 'fɜːr-] *adj* amueblado
furnishings ['fɜːnɪʃɪŋz, *Am:* 'fɜːr-] *npl* muebles *mpl*
furniture ['fɜːnɪtʃəʳ, *Am:* 'fɜːrnɪtʃɚ] *n no pl* mobiliario *m;* **piece of** ~ mueble *m*

> ⚠ **furniture** (= muebles, mobiliario) nunca se utiliza en plural:
> "Their furniture was rather old."

furore [fjʊə'rɔːri, *Am:* 'fjʊrɔːr] *n* furor *m*
furrow ['fʌrəʊ, *Am:* 'fɜːroʊ] **I.** *n* arruga *f* **II.** *vt* arrugar
furry ['fɜːri] <-ier, -iest> *adj* **1.** peludo **2.** (*looking like fur*) peloso; ~ **toy** peluche *m*
further ['fɜːðəʳ, *Am:* 'fɜːrðɚ] **I.** *adj comp of* far **1.** (*greater distance*) más lejano; **nothing could be** ~ **from his mind** estará pensando en cualquier cosa menos en eso **2.** (*additional*) otro; **until** ~ **notice** hasta nuevo aviso **II.** *adv comp of* far **1.** (*greater distance*) más lejos; **we didn't get much** ~ no llegamos mucho más allá; ~ **on** más adelante **2.** (*more*) más; **I have nothing** ~ **to say** no tengo (nada) más que decir **III.** *vt* fomentar; **to** ~ **sb's interests** favorecer los intereses de alguien
furthermore [ˌfɜːðə'mɔːʳ, *Am:* 'fɜːrðɚmɔːr] *adv* además
furthest ['fɜːðɪst, *Am:* 'fɜːr-] *adj, adv superl of* far
furtive ['fɜːtɪv, *Am:* 'fɜːrt̬ɪv] *adj* furtivo
fury ['fjʊəri, *Am:* 'fjʊri] *n no pl* furor *m*
fuse [fjuːz] **I.** *n* **1.** ELEC fusible *m;* **the** ~ **has gone** *Brit, Aus* han saltado los plomos **2.** (*ignition device, detonator*) espoleta *f;* (*string*) mecha *f* **II.** *vi* **1.** ELEC fundirse **2.** (*join together*) fusionarse **III.** *vt* **1.** ELEC fundir **2.** (*join*) fusionar
fuse box <-es> *n* caja *f* de fusibles
fusion ['fjuːʒən] *n* fusión *f*
fuss [fʌs] **I.** *n* alboroto *m;* **to make a** ~ armar un escándalo **II.** *vi* preocu-

parse III. *vt* molestar

fusspot ['fʌspɒt, *Am:* -pɑːt] *n inf* quisquilloso, -a *m, f*

fussy ['fʌsi] <-ier, -iest> *adj* puntilloso; **I'm not** ~ *Brit, inf* no me importa

fusty ['fʌsti] <-ier, -iest> *adj pej* rancio

futile ['fjuːtaɪl, *Am:* -t̬əl] *adj* inútil

future ['fjuːtʃəʳ, *Am:* -tʃɚ] I. *n* 1. *a.* LING futuro *m;* **the distant/near** ~ el futuro lejano/próximo 2. (*prospects*) porvenir *m* II. *adj* futuro

fuze [fjuːz] *Am* I. *n* (*ignition device, detonator*) espoleta *f;* (*string*) mecha *f* II. *vt* molestar

fuzzy ['fʌzi] *adj* 1. (*unclear*) borroso 2. (*hair*) rizado

G

G *n,* **g** [dʒiː] *n* g *f;* ~ **for George** G de Granada

g *abbr of* **gram** g.

gab [ɡæb] <-bb-> *vi inf* estar de palique

gabble ['ɡæbl] *vi* hablar atropelladamente

gable ['ɡeɪbl] *n* ARCHIT aguilón *m;* ~ **roof** tejado *m* de dos aguas

gadget ['ɡædʒɪt] *n* artilugio *m*

Gaelic ['ɡeɪlɪk] *adj* gaélico

gag [ɡæɡ] I. *n* 1. (*cloth*) mordaza *f* 2. (*joke*) chiste *m* II. <-gg-> *vt* amordazar

gage [ɡeɪdʒ] *n, vt Am s.* **gauge**

gaiety ['ɡeɪəti, *Am:* -t̬i] *n no pl* alegría *f*

gain [ɡeɪn] I. *n* 1. (*increase*) aumento *m* 2. (*profit*) beneficio *m* II. *vt* 1. (*obtain*) ganar 2. (*acquire*) adquirir; **to** ~ **success** conseguir el éxito; **to** ~ **weight** engordar; **to** ~ **the upper hand** tomar ventaja III. *vi* (*increase*) aumentar; (*prices, numbers*) subir; (*clock, watch*) adelantarse

gait [ɡeɪt] *n* paso *m*

gala ['ɡɑːlə, *Am:* 'ɡeɪ-] *n* gala *f*

galaxy ['ɡæləksi] <-ies> *n* galaxia *f*

gale [ɡeɪl] *n* tormenta *f*

Galicia [ɡə'lɪsiə] *n* Galicia *f*

Galician *adj* gallego

gall [ɡɔːl] I. *n* bilis *f inv;* **to have the** ~ **to do sth** tener la cara de hacer algo II. *vt* mortificar

gall. *abbr of* **gallon** gal.

gallant ['ɡælənt] *adj* 1. (*chivalrous*) galante 2. (*brave*) valiente

galleon ['ɡæliən] *n* galeón *m*

gallery ['ɡæləri] <-ries> *n* 1. (*public*) museo *m;* (*private*) galería *f* 2. ARCHIT tribuna *f*

galley ['ɡæli] *n* 1. (*kitchen*) cocina *f* 2. (*ship*) galera *f*

gallon ['ɡælən] *n* galón *m* (*Brit 4,55 l, Am 3,79 l*)

gallop ['ɡæləp] I. *vi* galopar II. *n* galope *m;* **at a** ~ *fig* al galope

gallows ['ɡæləʊz, *Am:* -oʊz] *npl* **the** ~ la horca

gallstone ['ɡɔːlstəʊn, *Am:* -stoʊn] *n* cálculo *m* biliar

galore [ɡə'lɔːʳ, *Am:* -'lɔːr] *adj* en cantidad

gamble ['ɡæmbl] I. *n* jugada *f* II. *vi* jugar III. *vt* (*money*) jugar; (*one's life*) arriesgar; **to** ~ **one's future** jugarse el futuro

gambler ['ɡæmbləʳ, *Am:* -blɚ] *n* jugador(a) *m(f)*

gambling *n no pl* juego *m*

game[1] [ɡeɪm] I. *n* 1. (*unit of sports*) juego *m* 2. (*unit of play*) partida *f;* ~ **of chance** juego de azar; **to give the** ~ **away** *fig* descubrir las cartas; **to be on the** ~ *Brit, inf* hacer la calle; **the** ~ **is up** *fig* todo se acabó; **what's your** ~? *fig* ¿qué pretendes? II. *adj* **to be** ~ (**to do sth**) animarse (a hacer algo)

game[2] [ɡeɪm] *n no pl* (*in hunting*) caza *f*

gamekeeper *n* guardabosque *mf*

game show *n* concurso *m* de televisión

gaming ['ɡeɪmɪŋ] *n no pl* juego *m*

gang [ɡæŋ] I. *n* 1. (*criminal group*) banda *f* 2. (*organized group*) cuadrilla f; (of workers) brigada f; inf (of friends) pandilla f, barra f AmL, trinca f And, CSur II. vi to ~ up on sb unirse contra alguien

gangrene ['gæŋgri:n] n no pl gangrena f

gangster ['gæŋstə^r, Am: -stə·] n gángster m

gaol [dʒeɪl] n Brit s. **jail**

⚠ La grafía **gaol** para **jail** (= prisión, cárcel) se utiliza tan sólo en inglés británico en textos oficiales: "The criminal spent ten years in gaol."

gap [gæp] n 1. (opening) abertura f; (empty space) hueco m; (in text) laguna f; **to fill a ~** llenar un espacio en blanco 2. (break in time) intervalo m 3. (difference) diferencia f

gape [geɪp] vi abrirse

gaping adj (hole) enorme

garage ['gæra:ʒ, Am: gə'ra:ʒ] n (of house) garaje m; (for repair) taller m

garbage ['ga:bɪdʒ, Am: 'ga:r-] n no pl, Am, Aus basura f

garbage can n Am cubo m de la basura, tacho m para la basura AmL

garbage truck n Am, Aus camión m de la basura

garble ['ga:bl, Am: 'ga:r-] vt distorsionar

garden ['ga:dn, Am: 'ga:r-] n jardín m

gardener ['ga:dnə^r, Am: 'ga:rdnə·] n jardinero, -a m, f

gardening ['ga:dnɪŋ, Am: 'ga:r-] n no pl jardinería f

garland ['ga:lənd, Am: 'ga:r-] I. n guirnalda f II. vt adornar con guirnaldas

garlic ['ga:lɪk, Am: 'ga:r-] n no pl ajo m

garment ['ga:mənt, Am: 'ga:r-] n prenda f de vestir

garnish ['ga:nɪʃ, Am: 'ga:r-] GASTR I. vt aderezar II. <-es> n aderezo m

garret ['gærət, Am: 'ger-] n buhardilla f

garrison ['gærɪsn, Am: 'gerə-] n

guarnición f

garter ['ga:tə^r, Am: 'ga:rtə·] n liga f

gas [gæs] I. <-s(s)es> n 1. a. CHEM gas m 2. no pl, Am (fuel) gasolina f; **to step on the ~** acelerar II. <-ss-> vt asfixiar con gas

gas chamber n cámara f de gas

gash [gæʃ] I. <-es> n raja f II. vt rajar

gasket ['gæskɪt] n junta f

gasmask n máscara f antigás

gasoline, gasolene ['gæsəli:n] n Am gasolina f, nafta f CSur

gasp [ga:sp, Am: gæsp] I. vi jadear; **to ~ for air** hacer esfuerzos para respirar; **to be ~ing for sth** Brit, inf morirse por algo; I ~ed in amazement di un grito ahogado de asombro II. n jadeo m; **he gave a ~ of astonishment** dio un grito ahogado de asombro; **to be at one's last ~** estar en las últimas; **to do sth at the last ~** hacer algo en el último momento

gas station n Am gasolinera f

gastric ['gæstrɪk] adj gástrico

gastroenteritis [ˌgæstrəʊˌentə'raɪtɪs, Am: -troʊˌentə'raɪtəs] n no pl gastroenteritis f inv

gastronomy [gæ'strɒnəmɪ, Am: -'stra:nə-] n no pl gastronomía f

gate [geɪt] n puerta f; RAIL barrera f; AVIAT puerta f de embarque

gatecrasher n intruso, -a m, f

gatehouse n casa f del guarda

gateway n a. fig puerta f

gather ['gæðə^r, Am: -ə·] I. vt 1. (collect) juntar; (flowers) recoger; (information) reunir; (harvest) cosechar; **to ~ speed** ganar velocidad; **to ~ one's strength** cobrar fuerzas 2. (infer) deducir; **to ~ that ...** sacar la conclusión de que... II. vi juntarse; (people) reunirse

gathering n reunión f

GATT [gæt] n abbr of **General Agreement on Tariffs and Trade** GATT m

gaudy ['gɔ:dɪ, Am: 'ga:-] <-ier, -iest> adj llamativo

gauge [geɪdʒ] I. n 1. (instrument) indicador m 2. RAIL ancho m de vía II. vt 1. (measure) medir 2. (assess) determinar

gaunt [gɔːnt, *Am:* gɑːnt] *adj*
1. (*very thin*) flaco; (*too thin*) demacrado **2.** (*desolate*) lúgubre

gauntlet ['gɔːntlɪt, *Am:* 'gɑːnt-] *n*
to throw down the ~ arrojar el
guante; **to run the** ~ correr baquetas

gauze [gɔːz, *Am:* gɑːz] *n no pl* gasa *f*

gave [geɪv] *pt of* **give**

gavel ['gævl] *n* mazo *m*

gay [geɪ] **I.** *adj* **1.** (*homosexual*) gay
2. (*cheerful*) alegre **II.** *n* gay *mf*

gaze [geɪz] **I.** *vi* mirar; **to** ~ **at sth**
mirar algo fijamente **II.** *n* mirada *f*
fija

gazelle [gəˈzel] *n* gacela *f*

gazette [gəˈzet] *n* gaceta *f*

GB [ˌdʒiːˈbiː] *n* **1.** *no pl abbr of* **Great
Britain** GB **2.** INFOR *abbr of* **gigabyte**
GB

GCE [ˌdʒiːsiːˈiː] *n Brit abbr of* **General Certificate of Education** GCE
m (*título que permite el acceso a los
estudios universitarios*)

GCSE [ˌdʒiːsiːesˈiː] *n Brit abbr of*
**General Certificate of Secondary
Education** *título de enseñanza secundaria que se consigue dos años
antes que el GCE*

❓ Para obtener el **GCSE** (**General
Certificate of Secondary Education**), antiguamente el **O-level**
(**Ordinary Level**), los alumnos
ingleses, galeses y nordirlandeses
de 16 años deben realizar un examen. Es posible examinarse de
una única asignatura, pero la
mayoría de los alumnos prefieren
examinarse de siete u ocho. En Escocia este examen se conoce como
Standard Grade.

GDP [ˌdʒiːdiːˈpiː] *n abbr of* **gross domestic product** PIB *m*

gear [gɪər, *Am:* gɪr] *n* **1.** TECH engranaje *m* **2.** AUTO marcha *f* **3.** *no pl*
(*equipment*) equipo *m*

gearbox <-es> *n* caja *f* de cambios

gear lever *n Brit,* **gear shift** *n Am*
palanca *f* de cambios

gee ['dʒiː] *interj Am, inf* caramba

gel [dʒel] *n* gel *m*

gelatin(e) ['dʒelətɪn] *n no pl* gelatina *f*

gem [dʒem] *n* piedra *f* preciosa; *fig*
joya *f*

Gemini ['dʒemɪnɪ] *n* Géminis *m inv*

gender ['dʒendər, *Am:* -dər] *n* BIO
sexo *m*; LING género *m*

gene [dʒiːn] *n* gen *m*

genealogical [ˌdʒiːnɪəˈlɒdʒɪkl, *Am:*
-ˈlɑːdʒɪ-] *adj* genealógico

genealogy [ˌdʒiːnɪˈælədʒɪ] *n no pl*
genealogía *f*

general ['dʒenrəl] **I.** *adj* general; **as
a** ~ **rule** por regla general **II.** *n* MIL
general *mf*

general anaesthetic *n* anestesia *f*
general **general assembly** <-ies>
n asamblea *f* general **general election** *n* elecciones *fpl* generales

generality [ˌdʒenəˈrælətɪ, *Am:* -t̬ɪ]
<-ies> *n* generalidad *f*

generalization [ˌdʒenərəlaɪzˈeɪʃn,
Am: -ɪ-] *n* generalización *f*

generalize ['dʒenərəlaɪz] *vi, vt* generalizar

generally ['dʒenrəlɪ] *adv* **1.** (*usually*) generalmente; ~ **speaking** hablando en términos generales
2. (*mostly*) en general

general manager *n* director(a) *m(f)*
general **general practitioner** *n
Brit, Aus, Can* médico, -a *m, f* de cabecera **general store** *n Am* tienda *f*
general strike *n* huelga *f* general

generate ['dʒenəreɪt] *vt* generar

generation [ˌdʒenəˈreɪʃn] *n* generación *f*

generative ['dʒenərətɪv, *Am:* -t̬ɪv]
adj generativo

generator ['dʒenəreɪtər, *Am:* -t̬ər]
n generador *m*

generic [dʒɪˈnerɪk] *adj* genérico

generosity [ˌdʒenəˈrɒsətɪ, *Am:*
-ˈrɑːsət̬ɪ] *n no pl* generosidad *f*

generous ['dʒenərəs] *adj* generoso,
rangoso *AmS*

genesis ['dʒenəsɪs] *n no pl* génesis *f*

inv

genetic [dʒɪˈnetɪk, *Am:* -ˈneṭɪk] *adj* genético

geneticist [dʒɪˈnetɪsɪst, *Am:* -ˈneṭə-] *n* genetista *mf*

genetics *n* + *sing vb* genética *f*

Geneva [dʒəˈniːvə] *n* Ginebra *f*

genial [ˈdʒiːnɪəl] *adj* afable

genie [ˈdʒiːni] <-nii *o* -ies> *n* genio *m*

genitals [ˈdʒenɪtlz, *Am:* -əṭlz] *npl* genitales *mpl*

genitive [ˈdʒenətɪv, *Am:* -əṭɪv] *n* genitivo *m*

genius [ˈdʒiːnɪəs] *n* <-ses> genio *m*

genocide [ˈdʒenəsaɪd] *n no pl* genocidio *m*

genre [ˈʒɑ̃ːrə] *n* género *m*

gent [dʒent] *n Brit, Aus, iron, inf* caballero *m;* **the ~s** el servicio de caballeros

genteel [dʒenˈtiːl] *adj* distinguido

gentle [ˈdʒentl] *adj (kind)* amable; *(calm)* suave; *(moderate)* moderado

gentleman [ˈdʒentlmən, *Am:* -ṭl-] <-men> *n (man)* señor *m;* *(well-behaved)* caballero *m*

gentleness [ˈdʒentlnɪs] *n no pl* delicadeza *f*

gentry [ˈdʒentrɪ] *n no pl, Brit* alta burguesía *f*

genuine [ˈdʒenjʊɪn] *adj* genuino

genus [ˈdʒiːnəs] <-nera> *n* género *m*

geographer [dʒɪˈɒɡrəfəʳ, *Am:* -ˈɑːɡrəfɚ] *n* geógrafo, -a *m, f*

geographic(al) [ˌdʒɪəˈɡræfɪk(l), *Am:* -əˈ-] *adj* geográfico

geography [dʒɪˈɒɡrəfɪ, *Am:* -ˈɑːɡrə-] *n no pl* geografía *f*

geological [ˌdʒɪəˈlɒdʒɪkl, *Am:* -əˈlɑːdʒɪk-] *adj* geológico

geologist [dʒɪˈɒlədʒɪst, *Am:* -ˈɑːlə-] *n* geólogo, -a *m, f*

geology [dʒɪˈɒlədʒɪ, *Am:* -ˈɑːlə-] *n no pl* geología *f*

geometric(al) [ˌdʒɪəˈmetrɪk(l), *Am:* -əˈ-] *adj* geométrico

geometry [dʒɪˈɒmətrɪ, *Am:* -ˈɑːmətrɪ] *n no pl* geometría *f*

? La **George Cross** y la **George Medal** son dos condecoraciones británicas introducidas en 1940 que reciben su nombre del Rey George VI. Con estas condecoraciones se distingue a aquellos civiles que han sobresalido por su valentía.

Georgia [ˈdʒɔːdʒə, *Am:* ˈdʒɔːr-] *n* Georgia *f*

geranium [dʒəˈreɪnɪəm] *n* geranio *m*, malvón *m Arg, Méx, Par, Urug*

germ [dʒɜːm, *Am:* dʒɜːrm] *n* **1.** MED microbio *m* **2.** *(plant, principle)* germen *m*

German [ˈdʒɜːmən, *Am:* ˈdʒɜːr-] *adj* alemán

Germanic [dʒəˈmænɪk, *Am:* dʒɚ-] *adj* germánico

German measles *n* + *sing vb* rubeola *f*

Germany [ˈdʒɜːmənɪ, *Am:* ˈdʒɜːr-] *n* Alemania *f*

germinate [ˈdʒɜːmɪneɪt, *Am:* ˈdʒɜːrmə-] *vi, vt* germinar

gerund [ˈdʒerənd] *n* gerundio *m*

gestation [dʒeˈsteɪʃn] *n no pl* gestación *f*

gesticulate [dʒeˈstɪkjʊleɪt, *Am:* -jə-] *vi form* gesticular

gesture [ˈdʒestʃəʳ, *Am:* -tʃɚ] I. *n* gesto *m; fig* muestra *f* II. *vi* hacer un ademán

get [get] I. <got, got, *Am, Aus:* gotten> *vt inf* **1.** *(obtain)* obtener; *(take)* coger; **to ~ a surprise** llevarse una sorpresa; **to ~ the impression that ...** tener la impresión de que... **2.** *(catch: plane, train)* coger **3.** *inf (hear, understand)* comprender **4.** *(cause to be)* **to ~ sth done** hacer algo; **to ~ sb to do sth** hacer que alguien haga algo **5.** *inf (annoy)* fastidiar **6.** *inf (start)* **to ~ going** poner en marcha II. *vi* **1.** + *adj/n (become)* volverse; **to ~ married** casarse; **to ~ upset** enfadarse; **to ~ used to sth** acostumbrarse a algo; **to ~ to like sth** coger afición a

algo **2.** (*have opportunity*) **to ~ to
do sth** llegar a hacer algo; **to ~ to
see sb** lograr ver a alguien **3.** (*travel*)
llegar; **to ~ home** llegar a casa
◆ **get about** *vi* desplazarse
◆ **get along** *vi* **1.** (*have good relationship*) llevarse bien **2.** (*manage*)
arreglárselas
◆ **get around** **I.** *vt insep* (*avoid*)
evitar **II.** *vi* **1.** (*spread*) llegar a
2. (*travel*) viajar mucho
◆ **get at** *vt insep, inf* **1.** (*suggest*)
apuntar a **2.** *Aus, Brit* (*criticize*) meterse con
◆ **get away** *vi* marcharse
◆ **get back** **I.** *vt* recuperar **II.** *vi*
volver
◆ **get behind** *vi* quedarse atrás
◆ **get by** *vi* arreglárselas
◆ **get down** *vt always sep* (*disturb*)
deprimir
◆ **get in** **I.** *vt* **1.** (*say*) decir **2.** (*bring
inside*) llevar dentro **II.** *vi* **1.** (*be
elected*) ser elegido **2.** (*enter*) entrar
◆ **get into** *vt insep* **1.** (*become interested*) interesarse por **2.** (*enter*)
entrar en
◆ **get off** *vi* **1.** (*avoid punishment*)
librarse **2.** (*depart*) marcharse
◆ **get on** *vi* **1.** (*be friends*) llevarse
bien **2.** (*manage*) arreglárselas
◆ **get out** **I.** *vt* sacar **II.** *vi* salir
◆ **get over** *vt insep* (*recover from*)
recuperarse de
◆ **get round** *vt* (*avoid*) evitar
◆ **get through** **I.** *vi* **to ~ to sb** comunicarse con alguien **II.** *vt* (*survive*) pasar
◆ **get together** *vi* reunirse
◆ **get up** **I.** *vt* **1.** (*organize*) organizar **2.** *always sep, Brit, inf* (*wake*)
levantar **II.** *vi* levantarse
◆ **get up to** *vt* llegar a
getaway ['getəweɪ, *Am:* 'geṭ-] *n inf*
fuga *f;* **to make a ~** fugarse
Ghana ['gɑːnə] *n* Ghana *f*
Ghanaian [gɑːˈneɪən, *Am:* -ˈniː-]
adj ghanés
ghastly ['gɑːstlɪ, *Am:* 'gæst-] <-ier,
-iest> *adj* **1.** (*frightful*) horroroso
2. (*unpleasant*) desagradable
ghetto ['getəʊ, *Am:* 'geṭoʊ] <-s o

-es> *n* gueto *m*
ghost [gəʊst, *Am:* goʊst] *n* fantasma *m,* espanto *m AmL,* azoro *m
AmC;* **the ~ of the past** los fantas-
mas del pasado; **to give up the ~**
(*die*) exhalar el último suspiro; (*stop
working*) dejar de funcionar
ghostly ['gəʊstlɪ] <-ier, -iest> *adj*
fantasmal
ghoul [guːl] *n* espíritu *m* demoníaco
G.I. [ˌdʒiːˈaɪ] *n inf* soldado *m* norteamericano (*especialmente en la II
Guerra Mundial*)
giant ['dʒaɪənt] **I.** *n* gigante *m*
II. *adj* gigantesco
gibbon ['gɪbən] *n* gibón *m*
Gibraltar [dʒɪˈbrɔːltəʳ, *Am:* -ˈbrɑːl-
təʳ] *n* Gibraltar *m*
giddy ['gɪdɪ] <-ier, -iest> *adj* mareado
gift [gɪft] *n* **1.** (*present*) regalo *m;* **to
be a ~ from the Gods** ser un regalo
caído del cielo **2.** (*talent*) don *m;* **to
have a ~ for languages** tener talento para los idiomas; **to have the
~ of the gab** *inf* tener mucha labia
gifted *adj* de (gran) talento
gift shop *n* tienda *f* de regalos
gig [gɪg] *n inf* MUS concierto *m*
gigabyte ['gɪgəbaɪt] *n* INFOR gigabyte *m*
gigantic [dʒaɪˈgæntɪk, *Am:* -ṭɪk]
adj gigantesco
giggle ['gɪgl] **I.** *vi* reír(se) tontamente **II.** *n* **1.** (*laugh*) risita *f* **2.** *no
pl, Aus, Brit, inf* (*joke*) broma *f;* **to
do sth for a ~** hacer algo para reírse
un rato **3.** *pl* **to get (a fit of) the ~s**
tener un ataque de risa
gill¹ [gɪl] *n* ZOOL agalla *f*
gill² [dʒɪl] *n* (*measure*) ≈ cuartillo *m*
gilt [gɪlt] *adj* dorado
gimmick ['gɪmɪk] *n* truco *m* (*para
vender más o para atraer la atención*)
gin [dʒɪn] *n* ginebra *f;* **~ and tonic**
gin tonic *m*
ginger ['dʒɪndʒəʳ, *Am:* -dʒəʳ] **I.** *n
no pl* **1.** (*spice*) jengibre *m* **2.** (*colour*) rojo *m* anaranjado **II.** *adj* rojizo;
(*person*) pelirrojo
gingerly ['dʒɪndʒəli, *Am:* -dʒəli] *adv*

con cautela

gipsy ['dʒɪpsɪ] *n s.* **gypsy**

giraffe [dʒɪ'rɑ:f, *Am:* dʒə'ræf] *n* <-(s)> jirafa *f*

girder ['gɜ:dəʳ, *Am:* 'gɜ:rdəʳ] *n* viga *f*

girdle ['gɜ:dl, *Am:* 'gɜ:r-] *n* (*belt*) cinturón *m*; (*corset*) faja *f*

girl [gɜ:l, *Am:* gɜ:rl] *n* niña *f*; (*young woman*) joven *f*, piba *f Arg*

girlfriend ['gɜ:lfrend, *Am:* 'gɜ:rl-] *n* (*of woman*) amiga *f*; (*of man*) novia *f*, polola *f And*

giro ['dʒaɪrəʊ, *Am:* -roʊ] *n no pl* FIN giro *m* bancario

girth [gɜ:θ, *Am:* gɜ:rθ] *n no pl* circunferencia *f*

gist [dʒɪst] *n* **the** ~ lo esencial; **to get the** ~ **of sth** entender lo básico de algo

give [gɪv] I. *vt* <gave, given> 1. (*offer*) dar, ofrecer; (*kiss, signal*) dar; **given the choice ...** si pudiera elegir...; **to** ~ **sb something to eat** dar a alguien algo de comer; **to not** ~ **much for sth** *fig* no dar mucho por algo; **don't** ~ **me that!** *inf* ¡venga ya, tú me la quieres dar con queso! 2. (*lecture, performance*) dar; (*speech*) pronunciar; (*headache, trouble*) producir, dar; **to** ~ **sb a call** llamar a alguien (por teléfono); **to** ~ **sth a go** intentar algo 3. (*organize*) dar, organizar 4. (*pass on*) contagiar II. *vi* <gave, given> (*stretch*) dar de sí III. *n* elasticidad *f*

◆**give away** *vt* 1. (*reveal*) revelar; **to give sb away** delatar a alguien 2. (*offer for free*) regalar

◆**give in** I. *vi* rendirse; **to** ~ **to sth** acceder (finalmente) a algo II. *vt* entregar

◆**give out** *vt* 1. (*distribute*) repartir 2. (*emit*) emitir

◆**give up** I. *vt* **to** ~ **doing sth** dejar de hacer algo II. *vi* rendirse

given ['gɪvn] I. *pp of* **give** II. *adj* determinado; **to be** ~ **to do sth** ser dado a hacer algo III. *prep* ~ **that** dado que +*subj*

glacial ['gleɪsɪəl, *Am:* -ʃəl] *adj* glacial

glacier ['glæsɪəʳ, *Am:* 'gleɪʃəʳ] *n* glaciar *m*

glad [glæd] <gladder, gladdest> *adj* contento; **to be** ~ **about sth** alegrarse de algo

glade [gleɪd] *n* claro *m* (de un bosque)

gladiator ['glædɪeɪtəʳ, *Am:* -t̬əʳ] *n* gladiador *m*

gladly ['glædlɪ] *adv* con mucho gusto

glamor ['glæməʳ, *Am:* -əʳ] *n no pl, Am, Aus s.* **glamour**

glamorous ['glæmərəs] *adj* glamoroso

glamour ['glæməʳ, *Am:* -əʳ] *n no pl* glamour *m*

glance [glɑ:ns, *Am:* glæns] I. *n* mirada *f*; **to take a** ~ **at sth** echar una mirada a algo; **at first** ~ a primera vista; **at a** ~ de un vistazo II. *vi* **to** ~ **at sth** echar una mirada a algo

gland [glænd] *n* glándula *f*

glare [gleəʳ, *Am:* gler] I. *n* 1. (*look*) mirada *f* (fulminadora) 2. *no pl* (*reflection*) resplandor *m* II. *vi* 1. (*look*) fulminar con la mirada 2. (*shine*) resplandecer

glaring *adj* 1. (*blinding*) deslumbrante 2. (*obvious*) que salta a la vista

glass [glɑ:s, *Am:* glæs] <-es> *n* 1. *no pl* (*material*) vidrio *m*, cristal *m*; **pane of** ~ hoja *f* de vidrio 2. (*for drinks*) vaso *m*; (*for wine*) copa *f* 3. *pl* gafas *fpl*, lentes *fpl AmL*

glasshouse ['glɑ:shaʊs, *Am:* 'glæs-] *n* invernadero *m*

glaze [gleɪz] *vt* poner vidrios a

glazier ['gleɪzɪəʳ] *n* vidriero, -a *m, f*

gleam [gli:m] I. *n* reflejo *m*; ~ **of hope** rayo *m* de esperanza II. *vi* brillar

glean [gli:n] *vt* **to** ~ **sth from sb** deducir algo (de las palabras) de alguien

glee [gli:] *n no pl* júbilo *m*

glen [glen] *n Scot* valle *m*

glib [glɪb] <glibber, glibbest> *adj* simplista

glide [glaɪd] I. *vi* 1. (*move smoothly*) deslizarse 2. AVIAT planear II. *n* 1. (*sliding movement*) deslizamiento *m* **2.** AVIAT planeo *m*

glider ['glaɪdə', *Am:* -dəˈ] *n* planeador *m*

glimmer ['glɪmə', *Am:* -əˈ] **I.** *vi* brillar tenuemente **II.** *n* (*light*) luz *f* tenue; ~ **of hope** atisbo *m* de esperanza

glimpse [glɪmps] **I.** *vt* (*signs*) vislumbrar **II.** *n* **to catch a** ~ **of** vislumbrar

glint [glɪnt] **I.** *vi* destellar **II.** *n* destello *m*

glisten ['glɪsn] *vi* brillar

glitter ['glɪtə', *Am:* 'glɪt̬əˈ] **I.** *vi* brillar **II.** *n no pl* **1.** (*sparkling*) brillo *m* **2.** (*shiny material*) purpurina *f*

glittering *adj* brillante

gloat [gləʊt, *Am:* gloʊt] *vi* **to** ~ **over sth** manifestar (gran) satisfacción por algo

global ['gləʊbl, *Am:* 'gloʊ-] *adj* **1.** (*worldwide*) a nivel mundial **2.** (*complete*) global

global warming *n* calentamiento *m* de la atmósfera terrestre

globe [gləʊb, *Am:* gloʊb] *n* **1.** (*map of world*) globo *m* terráqueo **2.** (*shape*) globo *m*

gloom [glu:m] *n no pl* **1.** (*pessimism*) pesimismo *m* **2.** (*darkness*) oscuridad *f*

gloomy ['glu:mɪ] <-ier, -iest> *adj* **1.** (*pessimistic*) pesimista **2.** (*dark*) oscuro

glorify ['glɔ:rɪfaɪ, *Am:* ˌglɔ:rə-] <-ie-> *vt* glorificar; REL alabar

glorious ['glɔ:rɪəs] *adj* **1.** (*illustrious*) glorioso **2.** (*splendid*) espléndido

glory ['glɔ:rɪ] **I.** *n no pl* **1.** (*honour*) gloria *f* **2.** (*splendour*) esplendor *m* **II.** <-ie-> *vi* **to** ~ **in sth** vanagloriarse de algo

gloss [glɒs, *Am:* glɑ:s] *n no pl* **1.** (*shine*) brillo *m;* **to take the** ~ **off sth** *fig* desmejorar algo **2.** (*paint*) pintura *f* esmalte

glossy ['glɒsɪ, *Am:* 'glɑ:sɪ] <-ier, -iest> *adj* brillante; (*paper*) satinado

glove [glʌv] *n* guante *mpl;* **a pair of** ~**s** unos guantes; **to fit sb like a** ~ venir a alguien como anillo al dedo

glow [gləʊ, *Am:* gloʊ] **I.** *n* **1.** (*light*) luz *f* **2.** (*warmth*) calor *m* **3.** (*good feeling*) sensación *f* grata **II.** *vi* **1.** (*illuminate*) brillar **2.** (*be hot*) arder **3.** (*look radiant*) estar radiante

glowing *adj* ardiente; (*praise*) efusivo

glucose ['glu:kəʊs, *Am:* -koʊs] *n no pl* glucosa *f*

glue [glu:] **I.** *n no pl* cola *f,* pegamento *m* **II.** *vt* encolar; **to** ~ **sth together** pegar algo; **to be** ~**d to sth** *fig* estar pegado a algo

glum [glʌm] <glummer, glummest> *adj* **1.** (*downcast*) taciturno **2.** (*drab*) monótono

glut [glʌt] *n* **a** ~ **of sth** una superabundancia de algo

gluten ['glu:tən] *n no pl* gluten *m*

glutton [glʌtn] *n* glotón, -ona *m, f*

glycerin *n Am,* **glycerine** ['glɪsəri:n] *n no pl* glicerina *f*

GMT [ˌdʒi:em'ti:] *abbr of* **Greenwich Mean Time** hora *f* de Greenwich

gnarled [nɑ:ld, *Am:* nɑ:rld] *adj* (*twisted*) retorcido; (*knotted*) nudoso

gnaw [nɔ:, *Am:* nɑ:] **I.** *vi* **to** ~ **at** [*o* **on**] **sth** roer algo **II.** *vt* (*chew*) roer; **to be** ~**ed by doubt** ser asaltado por las dudas

gnome [nəʊm, *Am:* noʊm] *n* gnomo *m*

GNP [ˌdʒi:en'pi:] *n no pl abbr of* **Gross National Product** PNB *m*

go [gəʊ, *Am:* goʊ] **I.** <went, gone> *vi* **1.** (*proceed*) ir; **to** ~ **(and) do sth** ir a hacer algo; **to have to** ~ tener que irse; **to** ~ **home** irse a casa; **to** ~ **on holiday** irse de vacaciones **2.** (*do*) hacer; **to** ~ **shopping** ir de compras; **to** ~ **swimming** ir a nadar **3.** + *adj/n* (*become*) volverse; **to** ~ **bald** quedarse calvo; **to** ~ **to sleep** dormirse; **to** ~ **wrong** salir mal **4.** + *adj* (*exist*) **to** ~ **hungry/thirsty** pasar hambre/sed; **to** ~ **unnoticed** pasar desapercibido **5.** (*happen*) **to** ~ **badly/well** ir mal/bien; **to** ~ **from bad to worse** ir de mal en peor **6.** (*pass*) pasar **7.** (*belong*) pertenecer **8.** (*fit*) quedar bien; **two ~es into eight four times** MAT ocho entre dos da cuatro **9.** (*extend*) extenderse; **those numbers ~ from 1 to 10** esos números van del 1 al 10 **10.** (*function*) funcionar; **to get sth to ~** hacer que algo funcione; **to keep a conversation ~ing** mantener una conversación **11.** (*be sold*) venderse; **to ~ for £50** venderse por 50 libras **12.** (*sound*) sonar; **the ambulance had sirens ~ing** la ambulancia hacía sonar las sirenas **13.** *fig* **what he says ~es** lo que él dice va a misa; **anything ~es** cualquier cosa vale II.<went, gone> *vt* **1. to ~ it alone** hacerlo solo **2.** *inf* (*say*) **ducks ~ 'quack'** los patos hacen 'cuac' III.<-es> *n* **1.** (*turn*) turno *m*; **it's my ~** me toca a mí **2.** (*attempt*) intento *m*; **to have a ~ at sth** intentar algo; **to have a ~ at sb about sth** tomarla con alguien por algo **3.** (*activity*) **to be on the ~** trajinar

◆ **go about** *vt insep* **to ~ one's business** ocuparse de sus asuntos

◆ **go after** *vt insep* seguir; **to ~ sb** ir detrás de alguien

◆ **go ahead** *vi* seguir adelante

◆ **go around** *vi* andar (de un lado para otro); **to ~ and see sb** ir a ver a alguien

◆ **go at** *vt insep* acometer

◆ **go away** *vi* marcharse

◆ **go back** *vi* (*return*) volver, regresarse *AmL*

◆ **go beyond** *vt* (*exceed*) superar

◆ **go by** *vi* (*pass*) transcurrir; **in days gone by** *form* en tiempos pasados

◆ **go down** I. *vt insep* bajar II. *vi* **1.** (*set*) ponerse; (*ship*) hundirse; (*plane*) estrellarse **2.** (*decrease*) disminuir **3.** (*be received*) **to ~ well/badly** ser bien/mal recibido

◆ **go far** *vi fig* llegar lejos

◆ **go for** *vt insep* **1.** (*fetch*) ir a buscar **2.** (*try to achieve*) intentar conseguir **3.** (*choose*) elegir **4.** (*attack*) atacar

◆ **go in** *vi* (*enter*) entrar

◆ **go into** *vt insep* **1.** (*enter*) entrar

en **2.** (*examine*) examinar

◆ **go off** *vi* **1.** (*leave*) irse **2.** (*spoil*) estropearse **3.** (*explode*) estallar **4.** (*stop liking*) **I went off it** dejó de gustarme **5.** (*happen*) **to ~ badly/well** salir mal/bien

◆ **go on** *vi* **1.** (*continue*) seguir **2.** (*go further*) ir más allá

◆ **go out** *vi* **1.** (*leave*) salir; **to ~ with sb** salir con alguien **2.** (*light*) apagarse

◆ **go over** *vt insep* **1.** (*examine*) examinar **2.** (*cross*) atravesar **3.** (*exceed*) exceder

◆ **go through** *vt insep* **1.** (*pass*) pasar por **2.** (*experience*) experimentar

◆ **go up** *vi* subir; **to ~ to sb** acercarse a alguien

◆ **go with** *vt insep* **1.** (*accompany*) acompañar a **2.** (*harmonize*) armonizar con

◆ **go without** *vt insep* pasar sin

go-ahead *n no pl* **to give sth the ~** dar luz verde a algo

goal [gəʊl, *Am:* goʊl] *n* **1.** (*aim*) objetivo *m*; **to achieve/set a ~** conseguir/fijar un objetivo **2.** (*scoring area*) portería *f*; **to keep ~** defender la portería; **to play in ~** *Brit* ser portero **3.** (*point*) gol *m*; **to score a ~** marcar un gol

goalie ['gəʊlɪ, *Am:* 'goʊ-] *n inf*, **goalkeeper** *n* SPORTS portero, -a *m, f*

goat [gəʊt, *Am:* goʊt] *n* cabra *f*; **to act the ~** *Brit, inf* hacer el imbécil; **to get sb's ~** *fig* sacar de quicio a alguien

gobble ['gɒbl, *Am:* 'gɑ:bl] I. *vi* (*make noise*) gluglutear II. *vt inf* jalar

goblet ['gɒblɪt, *Am:* 'gɑ:blət] *n* cáliz *m*

goblin ['gɒblɪn, *Am:* 'gɑ:blɪn] *n* duende *m*

god [gɒd, *Am:* gɑ:d] *n* REL dios *m*; **God** Dios; **God bless** que Dios te/le bendiga; **God knows** quien sabe; **for God's sake!** ¡por el amor de Dios!

god-awful ['gɒd'ɔ:fl, *Am:* ˌgɑ:d-'ɑ:-] *adj inf* horrible **godchild**

['ga:d-] *n* ahijado, -a *m, f* **goddam(ned)** ['ga:d-] *adj inf* maldito
goddaughter ['ga:d,da:tə⁻] *n* ahijada *f*
goddess ['gɒdɪs, *Am:* 'ga:dɪs <-es> *n* diosa *f*
godfather ['gɒd,fa:ðə(r), *Am:* 'ga:d,fa:ðə⁻] *n* padrino *m* **god-forsaken** ['ga:dfə⁻-] *adj* dejado de la mano de Dios
godly ['gɒdlɪ, *Am:* 'ga:d-] *adj* piadoso
godmother ['gɒd,mʌðə(r), *Am:* 'ga:d,mʌðə⁻] *n* madrina *f* **godson** ['ga:d-] *n* ahijado *m*
goes [gəʊz, *Am:* goʊz] *3rd pers sing of* **go**
go-getter [,gəʊ'getə⁻] *n* persona *f* emprendedora
goggle ['gɒgl, *Am:* 'ga:gl] **I.** *vi inf* **to ~ at sth** mirar algo con ojos desorbitados **II.** *n pl* (*glasses*) gafas *fpl*
going ['gəʊɪŋ, *Am:* 'goʊ-] *n* **1.** (*act of leaving*) ida *f;* (*departure*) salida *f* **2.** (*conditions*) **easy/rough ~** condiciones *fpl* favorables/adversas; **while the ~ is good** mientras las condiciones lo permitan
goiter *n Am*, **goitre** ['gɔɪtə⁻, *Am:* -ʈə⁻] *n Brit, Aus no pl* bocio *m*
gold [gəʊld, *Am:* goʊld] *n no pl* (*metal*) oro *m;* **to be good as ~** *fig* portarse como un ángel; **to be worth one's weight in ~** valer su peso en oro **gold digger** *n fig* buscador(a) *m(f)* de oro, cazafortunas *mf inv* **gold dust** *n* oro *m* en polvo; **to be like ~** *fig* ser muy cotizado
golden ['gəʊldən, *Am:* 'goʊl-] *adj* de oro; (*colour*) dorado
golden age *n* edad *f* de oro **golden wedding** *n* bodas *fpl* de oro
goldfish *n inv* pez *m* de colores **gold medal** *n* SPORTS medalla *f* de oro **goldmine** *n* mina *f* de oro; *fig* filón *m* **goldsmith** *n* orfebre *m*
golf [gɒlf, *Am:* ga:lf] *n no pl* golf *m;* **to play ~** jugar al golf
golf ball *n* pelota *f* de golf **golf club** *n* **1.** (*stick*) palo *m* de golf **2.** (*association*) club *m* de golf **golf course** *n* campo *m* de golf

golfer ['gɒlfə⁻, *Am:* 'ga:lfə⁻] *n* golfista *mf*
golly ['gɒlɪ, *Am:* 'ga:lɪ] *interj inf* **by ~!** ¡vaya!
gone [gɒn, *Am:* ga:n] *pp of* **go**
gong [gɒŋ, *Am:* ga:ŋ] *n* gong *m*
gonorrh(o)ea [,gɒnə'rɪə, *Am:* ,ga:nə'-] *n no pl* gonorrea *f*
good [gʊd] **I.** <better, best> *adj* **1.** (*of high quality*) bueno; **a ~ time to do sth** un buen momento para hacer algo; **to be capacitado para (hacer) algo; to be ~ for sb** ser bueno para alguien; **to be as ~ as new** estar como nuevo; **to be ~ and ready** estar listo; **to be in ~ shape** estar en buena forma; **to be a ~ thing that …** ser bueno que… +*subj;* **to do a ~ job** hacer un buen trabajo; **to have the ~ sense to do sth** tener el sentido común para hacer algo; **to have a ~ time** pasar(se)lo bien; **~ thinking!** ¡buena idea! **2.** (*appealing to senses*) **to feel ~** sentirse bien; **to look ~** tener buen aspecto; **to smell ~** oler bien **3.** (*valid*) válido; **to be ~ for nothing** ser completamente inútil **4.** (*substantial*) sustancial **II.** *n no pl* bien *m;* **for one's own ~** en beneficio propio; **to do ~** hacer bien; **for ~** definitivamente
goodbye *interj* adiós; **to say ~ (to sb)** decir adiós (a alguien); **to say ~ to sth** *inf* olvidarse definitivamente de algo
good-for-nothing ['gʊd fə,nʌθɪŋ, *Am:* -fə⁻,-] *n* inútil *mf*
Good Friday *n* Viernes *m* Santo
good-humoured [,gʊd'hju:məd, *Am:* -məd], **good-humored** *adj Am* afable
good-looking [,gʊd'lʊkɪŋ] *adj* guapo
good looks *n no pl* buen parecer *m* **good-natured** [-'neɪtʃəd] *adj* afable
goodness ['gʊdnɪs] *n no pl* **~ knows** quién sabe; **for ~' sake** ¡por Dios!; **thank ~!** ¡gracias a Dios!
goods [gʊdz] *npl* mercancías *fpl;* **to deliver the ~** *fig* dar la talla

goods train *n Brit* tren *m* de mercancías

good-tempered [-'tempəd, *Am:* -pə·d] *adj* afable

goodwill [ˌgʊd'wɪl] *n no pl* buena voluntad *f*; **a gesture of ~** un gesto de buena voluntad

goofy ['guːfɪ] <-ier, -iest> *adj Am, inf* bobo

goon [guːn] *n inf* imbécil *mf*

goose [guːs] <geese> *n* ganso, -a *m, f*

gooseberry ['gʊzbərɪ, *Am:* 'guːsberɪ] <-ies> *n* GASTR grosella *f* espinosa; **to play ~** *Brit, inf* hacer de carabina **goose-flesh** *n no pl*, **goose-pimples** *npl* carne *f* de gallina

gore [gɔːʳ, *Am:* gɔːr] I. *n* sangre *f* derramada II. *vt* cornear

gorge [gɔːdʒ, *Am:* gɔːrdʒ] I. *n* GEO cañón *m* II. *vt* **to ~ oneself on sth** atracarse de algo

gorgeous ['gɔːdʒəs, *Am:* 'gɔːr-] *adj* precioso

gorilla [gə'rɪlə] *n* gorila *m*

gormless ['gɔːmlɪs, *Am:* 'gɔːrm-] *adj Brit, inf* idiota

gorse [gɔːs, *Am:* gɔːrs] *n no pl* aulaga *f*

gory ['gɔːrɪ] <-ier, -iest> *adj* sangriento

gosh [gɒʃ, *Am:* gɑːʃ] *interj inf* dios mío

gosling ['gɒzlɪŋ, *Am:* 'gɑːz-] *n* ansarino *m*

go-slow *n Brit* huelga *f* de celo

gospel ['gɒspl, *Am:* 'gɑːs-] *n* evangelio *m*

gossip ['gɒsɪp, *Am:* 'gɑːsəp] I. *n* **1.** *no pl* (*rumour*) chismorreo *m*; **to have a ~ about sb** cotillear sobre alguien **2.** (*person*) chismoso, -a *m, f* II. *vi* cotillear

got [gɒt, *Am:* gɑːt] *pt, pp of* **get**

Gothic ['gɒθɪk, *Am:* 'gɑːθɪk] *adj* gótico

gotten ['gɒtən, *Am:* 'gɑːtən] *Am, Aus pp of* **get**

gouge [gaʊdʒ] *vt* **to ~ a hole into sth** hacer un agujero en algo

goulash ['guːlæʃ, *Am:* -lɑːʃ] *n no pl* puchero *m* (húngaro)

gourd [gʊəd, *Am:* gɔːrd] *n* calabaza *f* (*para beber*)

gourmet ['gʊəmeɪ, *Am:* 'gʊr-] *n* gastrónomo, -a *m, f*

gout [gaʊt] *n no pl* gota *f*

Gov. *abbr of* **Governor** gobernador(a) *m(f)*

govern ['gʌvn, *Am:* -ə·n] I. *vt* **1.** (*country*) gobernar; (*organization*) dirigir **2.** (*regulate*) regular; (*contract*) regir II. *vi* gobernar

governess ['gʌvənɪs, *Am:* -ə·nəs] <-es> *n* institutriz *f*, gobernanta *f AmL*

governing *adj* directivo

government ['gʌvənmənt, *Am:* -ə·n-] *n* gobierno *m*, administración *f Arg*; **to form a ~** formar gobierno; **to be in ~** estar en el gobierno

governmental [ˌgʌvn'mentl, *Am:* -ə·n'mentl̩] *adj* gubernamental

governor ['gʌvənəʳ, *Am:* -ə·nə·] *n* gobernador(a) *m(f)*; **the board of ~s** el consejo de dirección

Govt. *abbr of* **Government** gobno.

gown [gaʊn] *n* traje *m*; UNIV, LAW toga *f*

GP [ˌdʒiː'piː] *n Brit, Aus abbr of* **general practitioner** médico, -a *m, f* de cabecera

GPO [ˌdʒiː.piː'əʊ, *Am:* -'oʊ] *n Brit* ADMIN *abbr of* **General Post Office** Administración *f* General de Correos

grab [græb] I. *n* **to make a ~ for sth** hacerse con algo; **to be up for ~s** *inf* estar libre II. <-bb-> *vt* **1.** (*snatch*) quitar; **to ~ sb's attention** captar la atención de alguien; **to ~ a chance** aprovechar una oportunidad; **to ~ some sleep** dormir un rato; **to ~ sth (away) from sb** arrebatar algo a alguien; **to ~ sth out of sb's hands** quitar algo a alguien de las manos; **how does this ~ you?** *inf* ¿qué te parece esto? **2.** (*take hold of*) asir, coger, hacerse con; **to ~ hold of sth** hacerse con algo

grace [greɪs] I. *n* **1.** *no pl* (*movement*) elegancia *f*, gracia *f* **2.** *no pl* REL gracia *f*; **divine ~** gracia divina; **by the ~ of God** por la gracia de

Dios; **to fall from** ~ *fig* caer en desgracia **3.** *no pl* (*politeness*) cortesía *f;* **to do sth with good/bad** ~ hacer algo de buen grado/a regañadientes; **to have the (good)** ~ **to do sth** tener la cortesía de hacer algo **4.** (*prayer*) bendición *f* (de la mesa); **to say** ~ bendecir la mesa **II.** *vt* honrar

graceful ['greɪsfl] *adj* elegante; (*movement*) grácil

gracious ['greɪʃəs] **I.** *adj* afable **II.** *interj* ~ (**me**)! Dios mío

grade [greɪd] **I.** *n* **1.** (*rank*) rango *m* **2.** *Am* SCHOOL curso *m;* **to skip a** ~ perder un curso **3.** (*mark*) nota *f* **4.** (*level of quality*) clase *f;* **high/low** ~ alta/baja calidad; **to make the** ~ *fig* alcanzar el nivel deseado **5.** *Am* GEO pendiente *f* **II.** *vt* **1.** (*evaluate*) evaluar **2.** (*categorize*) clasificar

gradient ['greɪdɪənt] *n* pendiente *f*

> [?] El sistema de calificación que se utiliza en los EE.UU. recibe el nombre de **grading system**. Este sistema emplea las siguientes letras para expresar las distintas calificaciones: A, B, C, D, E y F. La letra E, sin embargo, no se suele utilizar. La A representa la máxima calificación, mientras que la F (**Fail**) significa suspenso. Las notas además pueden ir matizadas por un más o un menos. Quien obtiene una A+ es que ha tenido un rendimiento verdaderamente sobresaliente.

gradual ['grædʒʊəl] *adj* gradual

gradually ['grædʒʊlɪ] *adv* gradualmente

graduate¹ ['grædʒʊət] *n* **1.** UNIV licenciado, -a *m, f* **2.** *Am* SCHOOL graduado, -a *m, f*

graduate² ['grædʒʊeɪt] *vi* **1.** UNIV licenciarse; *Am* SCHOOL graduarse **2.** (*move to higher level*) subir de categoría

graduation [ˌgrædʒʊ'eɪʃn, *Am:* ˌgrædʒu'-] *n* SCHOOL, UNIV graduación *f,* egreso *m Arg, Chile*

graffiti [grə'fiːtɪ, *Am:* -ˌtɪ] *npl* graffiti *m*

graft [grɑːft, *Am:* græft] **I.** *n* BOT, MED injerto *m* **II.** *vt* BOT, MED injertar

Grail [greɪl] *n* **the Holy** ~ el Santo Grial

grain [greɪn] *n* **1.** (*smallest piece*) grano *m;* **a** ~ **of hope** una pequeña esperanza; **a** ~ **of truth** una pizca de verdad; **to take sth with a** ~ **of salt** *fig* no creerse algo del todo **2.** *no pl* (*cereal*) cereal *m* **3.** (*of wood*) fibra *f;* (*of meat*) veta *f*

grammar ['græməʳ, *Am:* -ɚ] *n no pl* gramática *f*

grammarian [grə'meərɪən, *Am:* -'merɪ-] *n* gramático, -a *m, f*

grammar school *n* **1.** *Am* (*elementary school*) colegio *m* **2.** *Brit* HIST (*upper level school*) *colegio de enseñanza secundaria al cual se accede por medio de un examen*

> [?] Las antiguas **grammar schools** (que más o menos se corresponden con los institutos) fueron fundadas hace muchos siglos en Gran Bretaña para el estudio del latín. Hacia 1950 el alumno que quería acceder a esta escuela debía aprobar el **eleven-plus examination**. Pero sólo un 20% del alumnado aprobaba este examen. El resto continuaba su intinerario educativo en una **secondary modern school** (escuela secundaria de grado inferior). Estos dos tipos de escuela fueron reorganizados durante los años 60 y 70 como **comprehensive schools** (escuelas integradas).

grammatical [grə'mætɪkl, *Am:* -'mæʈɪ-] *adj* gramatical

gram(me) [græm] *n* gramo *m*

gramophone ['græməfəʊn, *Am:* -foʊn] *n* gramófono *m*, vitrola *f AmL*

gran [græn] *n inf abbr of* **grandmother** abuela *f*

granary ['grænərɪ] <-ies> *n* granero *m*

granary bread *n no pl,* **granary loaf** <- loaves> *n Brit* pan *m* con granos enteros

grand [grænd] **I.** *adj* magnífico; ~ **ideas** grandes ideas; **on a ~ scale** a gran escala; **in ~ style** de estilo sublime; **the ~ total** el importe total; **to make a ~ entrance** hacer una entrada triunfal; **the Grand Canyon** el Gran Cañón **II.** *n inv, inf* (*dollars*) mil dólares *mpl;* (*pounds*) mil libras *fpl*

grandchild <-children> *n* nieto, -a *m, f* **grand(d)ad** *n inf* abuelo *m*

granddaughter *n* nieta *f*

grandeur ['grændʒər, *Am:* -dʒɚ] *n no pl* magnificencia *f*

grandfather *n* abuelo *m*

grandiose ['grændɪəʊs, *Am:* -oʊs] *adj* grandioso

grand jury <- -ies> *n Am* gran jurado *m*

grandly *adv* majestuosamente

grandma *n inf* abuelita *f* **grandmother** *n* abuela *f* **grandpa** *n inf* abuelito *m* **grandparents** *npl* abuelos *mpl* **grand piano** *n* piano *m* de cola **grandson** *n* nieto *m* **grandstand** *n* tribuna *f;* **a ~ view** *fig* una vista que abarca todo el panorama

grange [greɪndʒ] *n Brit* casa *f* solariega

granite ['grænɪt] *n no pl* granito *m*

granny ['grænɪ] *n inf* abuela *f*

grant [grɑːnt, *Am:* grænt] **I.** *n* **1.** UNIV beca *f* **2.** (*subsidy*) subvención *f* **II.** *vt* **1.** (*allow*) otorgar; **to ~ sb a permit** conceder a alguien un permiso; **to take sth for ~ed** dar algo por sentado; **to take sb for ~ed** no valorar a alguien como se merece **2.** (*transfer*) ceder; **to ~ sb sth** conceder algo a alguien; **to ~ sb a favour** hacer un favor a alguien; **to ~**

sb a pardon conceder un indulto a alguien; **to ~ sb a request** acceder a la petición de alguien; **to ~ sb a wish** conceder un deseo a alguien **3.** (*admit to*) reconocer, admitir; **to ~ that ...** estar de acuerdo en que... +*subj*

granule ['grænjuːl] *n* gránulo *m*

grape [greɪp] *n* uva *f*

grapefruit ['greɪpfruːt] *n inv* pomelo *m*

grape juice *n no pl* mosto *m*

grapevine *n vid f;* **to hear sth on the ~** saber algo por los rumores que corren

graph [grɑːf, *Am:* græf] *n* gráfica *f*

graphic ['græfɪk] *adj* gráfico; **to describe sth in ~ detail** describir algo de forma gráfica

graphic design *n no pl* diseño *m* gráfico

graphics *n + sing vb* **1.** (*drawings*) artes *fpl* gráficas **2.** INFOR gráficos *mpl;* **computer ~** gráficos de ordenador

graphics card *n* tarjeta *f* gráfica

graphite ['græfaɪt] *n* grafito *m*

grapple ['græpl] *vi* **to ~ with sth** luchar a brazo partido con algo

grasp [grɑːsp, *Am:* græsp] **I.** *n no pl* **1.** (*grip*) agarre *m;* **to be beyond sb's ~** *fig* estar fuera del alcance de alguien **2.** (*understanding*) comprensión *f* **II.** *vt* **1.** (*take firm hold*) agarrar; **to ~ sb by the arm** coger a alguien del brazo **2.** (*understand*) entender **III.** *vi* intentar coger; **to ~ at sth** *fig* sacar provecho de algo

grass [grɑːs, *Am:* græs] <-es> *n* hierba *f;* (*lawn*) césped *m;* **to cut the ~** cortar el césped; **to put sb out to ~** *inf* jubilar a alguien; **the ~ is (always) greener on the other side (of the fence)** *prov* (siempre) parece mejor lo de los demás

grasshopper ['grɑːshɒpər, *Am:* 'græshɑːpɚ] *n* saltamontes *m inv,* chapulín *m AmC, Méx,* saltagatos *m inv AmC, Méx* **grassroots** [,græs-] *npl* (*of organization*) base *f* popular; **~ opinion** opinión *f* del pueblo **grass snake** *n* culebra *f* de collar

grassy ['grɑːsɪ, *Am:* 'græsɪ] <-ier, -iest> *adj* cubierto de hierba, pastoso *AmL*

grate¹ [greɪt] *n* rejilla *f* de la chimenea

grate² [greɪt] I. *vi* 1. (*annoy: noise*) rechinar; **to ~ on sb** molestar a alguien 2. (*rub together*) rozar; **to ~ against each other** rozar uno con otro II. *vt* GASTR rallar

grateful ['greɪtfl] *adj* agradecido; **to be ~ (to sb) for sth** agradecer algo (a alguien)

gratification [ˌgrætɪfɪˈkeɪʃn, *Am:* ˌgrætə-] *n* gratificación *f*

gratify ['grætɪfaɪ, *Am:* 'grætə-] <-ie-> *vt* gratificar

gratifying *adj* gratificante

gratis ['greɪtɪs, *Am:* 'grætəs] I. *adj* gratuito II. *adv* gratis

gratitude ['grætɪtjuːd, *Am:* 'grætətuːd] *n no pl, form* gratitud *f*; **as a token of my ~** como muestra de mi gratitud

gratuitous [grəˈtjuːɪtəs, *Am:* -ˈtuːətəs] *adj* innecesario

gratuity [grəˈtjuːətɪ, *Am:* -ˈtuːətɪ] <-ies> *n form* propina *f*

grave¹ [greɪv] *n* (*burial place*) tumba *f*; **mass ~** fosa *f* común; **from beyond the ~** desde el más allá

grave² [greɪv] *adj* 1. (*serious*) serio 2. (*bad*) grave

grave-digger ['greɪvˌdɪgəʳ, *Am:* -ɚ] *n* sepulturero, -a *m, f*

gravel ['grævəl] *n* gravilla *f*

gravestone *n* lápida *f* sepulcral

graveyard *n* cementerio *m*

gravitate ['grævɪteɪt] *vi* **to ~ towards sth** tender hacia algo

gravity ['grævətɪ, *Am:* -t̬ɪ] *n no pl* gravedad *f*

gravy ['greɪvɪ] *n no pl* salsa hecha con el jugo de la carne

gray [greɪ] *adj Am s.* **grey**

graze¹ [greɪz] I. *n* roce *m* II. *vt* rozar

graze² [greɪz] *vi* pastar

grease [griːs] I. *n* grasa *f*; (*lubricant*) lubricante *m* II. *vt* engrasar; (*in mechanics*) lubricar

greasepaint *n* maquillaje *m* teatral

greaseproof paper *n* papel *m* encerado

greasy ['griːsɪ] <-ier, -iest> *adj* grasiento

great [greɪt] *adj* 1. (*very big*) enorme; **a ~ amount** una gran cantidad; **a ~ deal of time** muchísimo tiempo; **the ~ majority of people** la gran mayoría (de la gente) 2. (*very good*) grande; **to be ~ at doing sth** *inf* ser bueno en algo; **it's ~ to be back home again** es maravilloso estar de nuevo en casa; **the ~ thing about him is ...** lo mejor de él es...; **~!** ¡estupendo! 3. (*emphatic*) ~ **big** muy grande; **they're ~ friends** son muy amigos; **you ~ idiot!** ¡pedazo de idiota!

great aunt *n* tía *f* abuela

Great Britain *n* Gran Bretaña *f*

? **Great Britain** (Gran Bretaña) se compone del reino de Inglaterra, el de Escocia y el principado de Gales. (El rey Eduardo I de Inglaterra se anexionó Gales en 1282 y en 1301 nombró a su único hijo **Prince of Wales**. El rey Jacobo VI de Escocia heredó en 1603 la corona inglesa convirtiéndose en Jacobo I y en 1707 se unieron los parlamentos de ambos reinos.) Estos países forman, junto con Irlanda del Norte, el **United Kingdom** (Reino Unido). El concepto geográfico de **British Isles** (Islas Británicas) incluye no sólo a la isla mayor que es Gran Bretaña, sino también a Irlanda, la Isla de Man, las Hébridas, Orkney, Shetland, las Islas Scilly y las **Channel Islands** (Islas del Canal de la Mancha).

Greater London *n* la ciudad de Londres y su área metropolitana

great-grandchild *n* bisnieto, -a *m, f*

great-grandparents *npl* bisabuelos *mpl*

Great Lakes *n* Grandes Lagos *mpl*

greatly ['greɪtlɪ] *adv form* sumamente; **to improve** ~ mejorar mucho

greatness ['greɪtnɪs] *n no pl* grandeza *f*

great uncle *n* tío *m* abuelo

Greece [griːs] *n* Grecia *f*

greed [griːd] *n no pl* codicia *f*; (*for food*) gula *f*; (*for money*) avaricia *f*

greedy ['griːdɪ] <-ier, -iest> *adj* (*wanting food*) glotón; (*wanting money*) avaricioso; ~ **for success** ávido de éxito

Greek [griːk] *adj* griego; **it's all ~ to me** eso me suena a chino

green [griːn] **I.** *n* **1.** (*colour*) verde *m* **2.** *pl* (*green vegetables*) verduras *fpl* **3.** (*lawn*) césped *m* **II.** *adj* **1.** *a.* POL verde; ~ **with envy** muerto de envidia; **to have ~ fingers** *Brit, Aus,* **to have ~ thumbs** *Am* tener habilidad para la jardinería **2.** (*unripe*) verde, tierno *Chile, Ecua, Guat* **3.** (*inexperienced*) novato; (*naive*) ingenuo

greenback *n Am, inf* billete *m* (de banco) **green belt** *n* zona *f* verde (*zona en las afueras de las ciudades en la que no se permite construir*) **green card** *n* **1.** *Brit* AUTO carta *f* verde **2.** *Am* (*residence and work permit*) permiso *m* de residencia y de trabajo

greenery ['griːnərɪ] *n no pl* vegetación *f*

greenfly <-ies> *n* pulgón *m*

greengrocer [-ˌgroʊsə·] *n Brit* verdulero, -a *m, f* **greenhorn** [-hɔːrn] *n Am* novato, -a *m, f* **greenhouse** *n* invernadero *m*

Greenland ['griːnlənd] *n* Groenlandia *f*

? El **Royal Observatory** (observatorio astronómico) de **Greenwich** fue construido en 1675 para obtener datos exactos sobre la posición de las estrellas con vista a la creación de cartas de navegación. El **Greenwich meridian** (meridiano de Greenwich) no se fijó oficialmente como el grado cero de longitud con validez universal hasta 1884. Las 24 franjas horarias del planeta se fijan a partir de la hora local del meridiano que es conocida como **Greenwich Mean Time** o **Universal Time**.

G
g

greet [griːt] *vt* saludar; **to ~ each other** saludarse; **to ~ sth with applause** recibir algo con un aplauso; **to ~ sth with delight** sentir gran placer ante algo; **a scene of joy ~ed us** se mostró ante nosotros una escena de alegría

greeting *n* saludo *m*

gregarious [grɪ'geərɪəs, *Am:* -'gerɪ-] *adj* sociable

Grenada [grə'neɪdə] *n* Granada *f*

grenade [grɪ'neɪd] *n* granada *f*

grew [gruː] *pt of* **grow**

grey [greɪ] **I.** *n no pl* gris *m* **II.** *adj* gris; (*grey-haired*) canoso

greyhound *n* galgo *m*

grid [grɪd] *n* parrilla *f*

griddle ['grɪdl] *n* plancha *f*, burén *m* *Cuba*

gridlock *n no pl* paralización *f* del tráfico; *fig* inactividad *f* **grid square** *n* cuadrícula *f*

grief [griːf] *n no pl* dolor *m*; **to come to ~** fracasar; **to give sb (a lot of)** ~ hacer sentir (muy) mal a alguien

grievance ['griːvns] *n* **1.** (*complaint*) queja *f*; **to harbour a ~ against sb** presentar una queja contra alguien **2.** (*sense of injustice*) injusticia *f*

grieve [griːv] **I.** *vi* sufrir; **to ~ for sb** llorar por alguien **II.** *vt* causar dolor

grievous ['griːvəs] *adj form* (*pain*) fuerte; (*danger*) serio

grill [grɪl] **I.** *n* **1.** (*for cooking*) parrilla *f* **2.** *Am* (*restaurant*) asador *m* **II.** *vt* asar a la parrilla

grille [grɪl] *n* rejilla *f*

grilling ['grɪlɪŋ] *n inf* to give sb a ~ interrogar a alguien

grim [grɪm] *adj* **1.** (*very serious*) severo **2.** (*unpleasant*) desagradable

grimace [grɪ'meɪs, *Am:* 'grɪməs] **I.** *n* mueca *f* **II.** *vi* hacer muecas; **to ~ with pain** hacer muecas de dolor

grime [graɪm] *n* mugre *f*

grimy ['graɪmɪ] <-ier, -iest> *adj* mugriento

grin [grɪn] **I.** *n* ancha sonrisa *f* **II.** *vi* sonreír de oreja a oreja; **to ~ and bear it** poner al mal tiempo buena cara

grind [graɪnd] **I.** *n inf* trabajo *m* pesado; **the daily ~** la rutina diaria **II.** <ground, ground> *vt* **1.** (*crush*) aplastar; (*mill*) moler **2.** *Am, Aus* (*chop finely*) picar **3.** (*sharpen*) afilar

◆**grind down** *vt* **1.** (*mill*) moler **2.** (*wear down*) desgastar **3.** (*oppress*) oprimir

grinder ['graɪndər, *Am:* -dɚ] *n* molinillo *m*

grindstone ['graɪndstəʊn, *Am:* -stoʊn] *n* muela *f*; **to keep one's nose to the ~** *inf* trabajar como un enano

grip [grɪp] **I.** *n* **1.** (*hold*) agarre *m*; *fig* control *m*; **to keep a firm ~ on the bag** agarrar fuertemente la bolsa; **to be in the ~ of sth** *fig* estar en poder de algo; **to get a ~ on one-self** *fig* controlarse; **to get to ~s with sth** *fig* enfrentarse con algo **2.** (*bag*) maletín *m* **II.** <-pp-> *vt* agarrar; **to be ~ped by emotion** estar embargado por la emoción; **he was ~ped by fear** el miedo le invadió

gripe [graɪp] *vi inf* quejarse

gripping ['grɪpɪŋ] *adj* emocionante

grisly ['grɪzlɪ] <-ier, -iest> *adj* espeluznante

gristle ['grɪsl] *n no pl* cartílago *m*

grit [grɪt] **I.** *n no pl* **1.** (*small stones*) arenilla *f* **2.** (*courage*) valor *m* **II.** <-tt-> *vt* **to ~ one's teeth** *a. fig* apretar los dientes

gritty ['grɪtɪ, *Am:* 'grɪʈi] <-ier, -iest> *adj* **1.** (*stony*) con arenilla

2. (*brave*) valiente

grizzle ['grɪzl] *vi inf* gimotear

grizzly ['grɪzlɪ] <-ies> *n* oso *m* pardo americano

groan [grəʊn, *Am:* groʊn] **I.** *n* gemido *m* **II.** *vi* gemir; (*floorboards*) crujir; **to ~ about sth** quejarse de algo; **to ~ in pain** gemir de dolor; **to ~ inwardly** lamentarse para sus adentros

grocer ['grəʊsər, *Am:* 'groʊsɚ] *n* **1.** (*shopkeeper*) tendero, -a *m, f* **2.** (*shop*) tienda *f* de ultramarinos

grocery ['grəʊsərɪ, *Am:* 'groʊ-] <-ies> *n* tienda *f* de ultramarinos

groin [grɔɪn] *n* ingle *f*

groom [gruːm] **I.** *n* **1.** (*person caring for horses*) mozo *m* de cuadra **2.** (*bridegroom*) novio *m* **II.** *vt* **1.** (*horse*) almohazar **2.** *fig* (*prepare*) preparar

groove [gruːv] *n* ranura *f*

groovy ['gruːvɪ] <-ier, -iest> *adj inf* guay

grope [grəʊp, *Am:* groʊp] **I.** *vi* ir a tientas; **to ~ for sth** buscar algo a tientas; **to ~ for the right words** buscar las palabras **II.** *vt inf* (*sexually*) sobar

gross¹ [grəʊs, *Am:* groʊs] <-sses> *n* gruesa *f*; **by the ~** en gruesas

gross² [grəʊs, *Am:* groʊs] *adj* **1.** LAW grave; (*neglect*) serio **2.** (*fat*) muy gordo **3.** *Am* (*offensive*) grosero; (*revolting*) asqueroso **4.** (*total*) total; (*without deductions*) bruto

grossly *adv* (*extremely*) enormemente; **to be ~ unfair** ser completamente injusto

grotesque [grəʊ'tesk, *Am:* groʊ-] *n* grotesco

grotto ['grɒtəʊ, *Am:* 'grɑːtoʊ] <-oes *o* -os> *n* gruta *f*

grotty ['grɒtɪ, *Am:* 'grɑːʈi] <-ier, -iest> *adj Brit, inf* chungo

ground¹ [graʊnd] **I.** *n* **1.** *no pl* (*Earth's surface*) suelo *m*; **above ~** sobre el nivel del suelo; **below ~** bajo tierra; **to be on one's own ~** estar en su elemento; **to give ~** ceder terreno; **to stand one's ~** mantenerse firme **2.** *no pl* (*soil*) suelo *m* **3.** (*area of land*) terreno *m* **4.** (*sports field*) campo *m* **5.** (*reason*) **to have ~s to do sth** tener motivos para hacer algo; **on the ~s that ...** porque... **II.** *vt Am, Aus, inf* no dejar salir

ground² [graʊnd] *vt pt, pp of* **grind**

groundbreaking ['graʊnd,breɪkɪŋ] *adj* pionero

ground floor *n Brit* planta *f* baja
  ground fog *n* niebla *f* baja
  ground frost *n no pl* escarcha *f*

grounding ['graʊndɪŋ] *n no pl* rudimentos *mpl*, base *f*

groundkeeper *n* cuidador(a) *m(f)* del terreno de juego

groundnut *n* cacahuete *m*, maní *m AmS* **ground rules** *npl* directrices *fpl* **groundsheet** *n* tela *f* impermeable

groundwork ['graʊndwɜ:k, *Am:* -wɜ:rk] *n no pl* trabajo *m* preparatorio

group [gru:p] **I.** *n* grupo *m;* MUS conjunto *m* musical **II.** *vt* agrupar

grouping ['gru:pɪŋ] *n* agrupamiento *m*

grouse¹ [graʊs] *n* **black ~** gallo *m* lira; **red ~** urogallo *m* escocés

grouse² [graʊs] **I.** *n* **1.** (*complaint*) queja *f* **2.** (*complaining person*) cascarrabias *mf inv* **II.** *vi* quejarse

grove [grəʊv, *Am:* groʊv] *n* arboleda *f;* **olive ~** olivar *m;* **orange ~** naranjal *m*

grovel ['grɒvl, *Am:* 'grɑ:vl] <*Brit:* -ll-, *Am:* -l-> *vi* **to ~** (**before sb**) humillarse (ante alguien)

grow [grəʊ, *Am:* groʊ] <grew, grown> **I.** *vi* **1.** (*increase in size*) crecer; **to ~ taller** crecer en estatura **2.** (*increase*) aumentar; **to ~ by 2%** aumentar un 2% **3.** (*develop*) desarrollarse **4.** (*become*) volverse; **to ~ old** hacerse viejo; **to ~ to like sth** llegar a querer algo **II.** *vt* **1.** (*cultivate*) cultivar **2.** (*let grow*) dejar crecer; **to ~ a beard** dejarse crecer la barba

  ◆ **grow into** *vt insep* acostumbrarse a

  ◆ **grow up** *vi* crecer; **when I ~ I'd**

like to ... cuando sea mayor me gustaría...

grower ['grəʊə^r, *Am:* 'groʊ-] *n* cultivador(a) *m(f)*

growing ['grəʊɪŋ, *Am:* 'groʊ-] *adj* que aumenta

growl [graʊl] **I.** *n* **1.** (*of dog*) gruñido *m;* (*of person*) refunfuño *m* **2.** (*rumble*) ruido *m* sordo **II.** *vi* (*dog*) gruñir; (*person*) refunfuñar

grown [grəʊn, *Am:* groʊn] *pp of* **grow**

grown-up *n* adulto, -a *m, f*

growth [grəʊθ, *Am:* groʊθ] *n* **1.** *no pl* (*increase in size*) crecimiento *m;* **to reach full ~** alcanzar su plenitud **2.** *no pl* (*increase*) aumento *m;* **rate of ~** tasa *f* de crecimiento **3.** (*lump*) bulto *m*

growth rate *n* ECON tasa *f* de crecimiento

grub [grʌb] **I.** *n* **1.** ZOOL larva *f* **2.** *no pl, Brit, inf* GASTR rancho *m* **II.** <-bb-> *vi* **to ~ about** (**for sth**) remover la tierra (buscando algo)

grubby ['grʌbɪ] <-ier, -iest> *adj inf* roñoso

grudge [grʌdʒ] **I.** *n* rencor *m*, roña *f Cuba, Méx, PRico;* **to have a ~ against sb** guardar rencor a alguien **II.** *vt* **to ~ sb sth** envidiar algo a alguien

grudging *adj* poco generoso

grudgingly ['grʌdʒɪŋlɪ] *adv* de mala gana

gruel ['gru:əl] *n no pl* gachas *fpl*

gruelling ['gru:əlɪŋ, *Am:* 'gru:lɪŋ] *adj* duro

gruesome ['gru:səm] *adj* horripilante

gruff [grʌf] *adj* brusco

grumble ['grʌmbl] *vi* quejarse

grumpy ['grʌmpɪ] <-ier, -iest> *adj* gruñón

grunt [grʌnt] **I.** *n* gruñido *m* **II.** *vi* gruñir

guarantee [ˌgærən'ti:, *Am:* ˌger-] **I.** *n* **1.** (*a promise*) promesa *f;* **to give sb one's ~** hacer una promesa a alguien; **there's no ~ that** no es seguro que +*subj* **2.** COM garantía *f* **II.** *vt* **1.** (*promise*) prometer; **to ~**

that asegurar que +*subj* **2.** COM **to be ~d for three years** tener una garantía de tres años

guard [gɑːd, *Am:* gɑːrd] **I.** *n* **1.** (*person*) guardia *mf;* **to be on ~** estar de guardia; **to be on one's ~** (**against sth**) estar en alerta (contra algo); **to be under ~** estar bajo guardia y custodia; **to drop one's ~** bajar la guardia; **to keep ~ over sth** vigilar algo **2.** (*device*) resguardo *m* **3.** *Brit* RAIL jefe, -a *m, f* de tren **II.** *vt* (*protect*) proteger; (*prevent from escaping*) vigilar; (*keep secret*) guardar

> **?** A las **Household Troops** de la monarquía británica pertenecen siete regimientos de los **Guards** (Guardia). Dos regimientos de **Household Cavalry** (caballería): los **Life Guards** y los **Blues and Royals.** Y cinco regimientos de infantería: los **Grenadier Guards,** los **Coldstream Guards,** los **Scots Guards,** los **Irish Guards** y los **Welsh Guards.** La ceremonia del cambio de guardia tiene lugar cada dos días a las 11:30 en el **Buckingham Palace.**

◆**guard against** *vt always sep* (*protect from*) **to guard sb against sth** proteger a alguien de algo

guarded ['gɑːdɪd, *Am:* 'gɑːrd-] *adj* cauteloso

guardian ['gɑːdɪən, *Am:* 'gɑːr-] *n* guardián, -ana *m, f*

Guatemala [ˌgwɑːtɪ'mɑːlə, *Am:* -t̬ə'-] *n* Guatemala *f*

Guatemala City *n* ciudad *f* de Guatemala

Guatemalan [ˌgwɑːtɪ'mɑːlən, *Am:* -t̬ə'-] *adj* guatemalteco

guerrilla [gə'rɪlə] *n* guerrilla *f*

guess [ges] **I.** *n* conjetura *f;* **a lucky ~** un acierto afortunado; **to have a ~, to take a ~** *Am* adivinar; **at a ~** por decir algo; **it's anybody's ~**

¿quién sabe? **II.** *vi* **1.** (*conjecture*) adivinar; **to ~ right** adivinar; **to ~ wrong** equivocarse; **to keep sb ~ing** tener a alguien en suspense **2.** *Am* (*believe*) suponer **III.** *vt* adivinar; **~ what?** ¿sabes qué?

guesswork ['geswɜːk, *Am:* -wɜːrk] *n no pl* conjeturas *fpl*

guest [gest] *n* invitado, -a *m, f;* (*hotel customer*) cliente *mf;* **be my ~** *inf* ¡adelante!

guesthouse *n* casa *f* de huéspedes **guestroom** *n* habitación *f* de invitados

guffaw [gə'fɔː, *Am:* -'fɑː] **I.** *n* carcajada *f* **II.** *vi* reírse a carcajadas

guidance ['gaɪdns] *n no pl* consejo *m*

guide [gaɪd] **I.** *n* **1.** (*person*) guía *mf;* **tour ~** guía turístico **2.** (*book*) guía *f* **3.** (*help*) orientación *f* **4.** (*girls' association*) **the Guides** las exploradoras **II.** *vt* **1.** (*show*) guiar **2.** (*instruct*) orientar **3.** (*steer*) dirigir; **to be ~d by one's emotions** dejarse llevar por los sentimientos

guidebook *n* guía *f* **guide dog** *n* perro-guía *m*

guided tour ['gaɪdɪd-] *n* excursión *f* con guía

guideline *n* directriz *f*

guild [gɪld] *n* (*of merchants*) corporación *f;* (*of craftsmen*) gremio *m*

guile [gaɪl] *n no pl, form* astucia *f*

guillotine ['gɪlətiːn] *n* guillotina *f*

guilt [gɪlt] *n no pl* **1.** (*shame*) culpabilidad *f* **2.** (*responsibility for crime*) culpa *f;* **to admit one's ~** confesarse culpable

guilty ['gɪltɪ, *Am:* -t̬ɪ] <-ier, -iest> *adj* culpable; **to be ~ of a crime** ser culpable de un delito; **to have a ~ conscience** tener un sentimiento de culpabilidad; **to feel ~ about sth** sentirse culpable por algo; **to plead ~ to sth** declararse culpable de algo

guinea ['gɪnɪ] *n Brit* guinea *f*

Guinea ['gɪnɪ] *n* Guinea *f*

guinea pig *n* conejillo *m* de Indias, cuy *m AmS*

guise [gaɪz] *n no pl* **under the ~ of sth** bajo el disfraz de algo

guitar [gɪ'tɑːʳ, *Am:* -'tɑːr] *n* guitarra *f;* **to play the ~** tocar la guitarra

guitarist [gɪ'tɑːrɪst] *n* guitarrista *mf*

gulch [gʌltʃ] <-es> *n Am* barranco *m*

gulf [gʌlf] *n* **1.** (*area of sea*) golfo *m* **2.** *fig* abismo *m*

gull [gʌl] *n* gaviota *f*

gullet ['gʌlɪt] *n* esófago *m*

gullible ['gʌləbl] *adj* crédulo

gully ['gʌlɪ] <-ies> *n* barranco *m*

gulp [gʌlp] **I.** *n* (*large swallow*) trago *m;* **a ~ of air** una bocanada de aire; **to take a ~ of milk** beber un trago de leche; **in one ~** de un trago **II.** *vt* tragar; (*liquid*) beber; (*food*) engullir **III.** *vi* **to ~ for air** respirar hondo

gum[1] [gʌm] *n* ANAT encía *f*

gum[2] [gʌm] **I.** *n* **1.** *no pl* (*sticky substance*) goma *f* **2.** *no pl* (*glue*) pegamento *m* **3.** (*type of sweet*) gominola *f* **II.** *vt* pegar

gumtree ['gʌmtriː] *n* árbol *m* de caucho, gomero *m AmL;* **to be up a ~** *fig* estar en un aprieto

gun [gʌn] *n* arma *f* de fuego; (*cannon*) cañón *m;* (*pistol*) pistola *f;* (*rifle*) fusil *m;* **to stick to one's ~s** *fig* mantenerse en sus trece **gunfire** *n no pl* disparos *mpl* **gunman** <-men> *n* pistolero *m*

gunner ['gʌnəʳ, *Am:* -ɚ] *n* artillero *m*

gunpoint *n no pl* **at ~** a punto de pistola **gunpowder** *n no pl* pólvora *f*

gunshot ['gʌnʃɒt, *Am:* -ʃɑːt] *n* disparo *m*

gurgle ['gɜːgl, *Am:* 'gɜːr-] *vi* **1.** (*baby*) gorjear **2.** (*water*) borbotear

guru ['gʊru, *Am:* 'guːruː] *n* gurú *mf*

gush [gʌʃ] **I.** <-es> *n* chorro *m; fig* efusión *f* **II.** *vi* chorrear; *fig* deshacerse en elogios

gushing *adj* (*excesivamente*) efusivo

gust [gʌst] *n* racha *f*

gusto ['gʌstəʊ, *Am:* -toʊ] *n no pl* entusiasmo *m*

gut [gʌt] **I.** *n* **1.** (*intestine*) intestino *m;* **a ~ feeling** un instinto visceral; **to bust a ~** *inf* echar los bofes **2.** *pl, inf* (*bowels*) entrañas *fpl* **3.** *pl* (*cour-*

age) valor *m* **II.** <-tt-> *vt* destripar

gutless [gʌtlɪs] *adj inf* cobarde

gutsy ['gʌtsɪ] <-ier, -iest> *adj* valiente

gutter ['gʌtəʳ, *Am:* 'gʌtɚ] *n* alcantarilla *f;* (*on roof*) canalón *m*

guttural ['gʌtərəl, *Am:* 'gʌt̬-] *adj* gutural

guy [gaɪ] *n inf* **1.** (*man*) tío *m* **2.** (*rope*) viento *m*

Guyana [gaɪ'ænə] *n* Guyana *f*

guzzle ['gʌzl] *vt inf* jalar

gym [dʒɪm] *n inf* **1.** *no pl* (*gymnastics*) gimnasia *f* **2.** (*gymnasium*) gimnasio *m*

gymnasium [dʒɪm'neɪzɪəm] *n* gimnasio *m*

gymnast ['dʒɪmnæst] *n* gimnasta *mf*

gymnastics [dʒɪm'næstɪks] *npl* gimnasia *f*

gyn(a)ecology [ˌgaɪnɪ'kɒlədʒɪ, *Am:* -'kɑːlə-] *n*, **gynecology** *n Am, Aus no pl* ginecología *f*

gypsy ['dʒɪpsɪ] <-ies> *n* gitano, -a *m, f*

gyrate [ˌdʒaɪ'reɪt] *vi* girar

gyroscope ['dʒaɪrəskəʊp, *Am:* -skoʊp] *n* giroscopio *m*

H h

H, h [eɪtʃ] *n* H, h *f;* **~ for Harry** *Brit*, **~ for How** *Am* H de Huelva

ha [hɑː] *interj* ajá

habit ['hæbɪt] *n* **1.** (*customary practice*) hábito *m*, costumbre *f;* **to be in the ~ of doing sth** tener por costumbre hacer algo; **to get into the ~ of doing sth** acostumbrarse a hacer algo **2.** (*dress*) hábito *m;* **riding ~** traje *m* de montar

habitat ['hæbɪtæt, *Am:* '-ə-] *n* hábitat *m*

habitation [ˌhæbɪ'teɪʃn] *n* **1.** *no pl* (*occupancy*) **unfit for human ~** inhabitable **2.**(*dwelling*) morada *f*

habitual [həˈbɪtʃʊəl] *adj* habitual; ~ **drug use** consumo frecuente de drogas

hack¹ [hæk] **I.** *vt* **1.** *Brit* (*football*) dar una patada a **2.**(*chop violently*) cortar a tajos **3.** *Am, Aus, inf* (*cope with*) aguantar **II.** *vi* hacer tajos; **to ~ at sth** cortar algo a tajos **III.** *n* **1.**(*journalist*) periodista *mf* de pacotilla **2.**(*writer*) escritorzuelo, -a *m, f*

hack² [hæk] *vt* INFOR **to ~ (into) a system** introducirse ilegalmente en un sistema

hacker [hækəʳ, *Am:* -ɚ] *n* INFOR hacker *mf*

had [həd, *stressed:* hæd] *pt, pp of* **have**

haggard [ˈhægəd, *Am:* -ɚd] *adj* macilento

haggle [ˈhægl] *vi* regatear; **to ~ over sth** regatear el precio de algo

Hague [heɪg] *n* **the ~** la Haya

hail¹ [heɪl] **I.** *n no pl* METEO granizo *m* **II.** *vi* granizar

hail² [heɪl] **I.** *vt* **1.**(*call*) llamar; **to ~ a taxi** parar un taxi **2.**(*acclaim*) aclamar **II.** *vi* **to ~ from** ser de

hair [heəʳ, *Am:* her] *n* **1.**(*on skin*) pelo *m*; (*on human head*) cabello *m*; **to have one's ~ cut** cortarse el pelo; **keep your ~ on!** *Brit, Aus, iron, inf* ¡no te sulfures!; **to split ~s** buscarle tres pies al gato **2.**(*of body*) vello *m*

haircut *n* corte *m* de pelo; **to get a ~** cortarse el pelo **hairdresser** *n* peluquero, -a *m, f*; **the ~'s** la peluquería **hairstyle** *n* peinado *m*

hairy [ˈheəri, *Am:* ˈheri] <-ier, -iest> *adj* **1.**(*having much hair*) peludo **2.** *inf* (*frightening*) espeluznante

Haiti [ˈheɪti, *Am:* -t̬ɪ] *n* Haití *m*

Haitian [ˈheɪʃən] *adj* haitiano

hale [heɪl] *adj* robusto; **~ and hearty** fuerte como un roble

half [hɑːf, *Am:* hæf] **I.** <halves> *n* mitad *f*; **~ an apple** media manzana; **in ~** por la mitad; **~ and ~** mitad y mitad; **a kilo and a ~** un kilo y medio; **my other ~** *fig* mi media naranja; **to be too clever by ~** pasarse de listo **II.** *adj* medio; **~ a pint** media

pinta; **~ an hour, a ~ hour** media hora **III.** *adv* **1.**(*partially*) a medias; **~ done** a medio hacer; **~ empty/full** medio vacío/lleno **2.**(*by fifty percent*) **~ as many/much** la mitad **3.** *inf* (*most*) la mayor parte; **~ (of) the time** la mayor parte del tiempo **4.**(*thirty minutes after*) **~ past three** las tres y media

half-dozen *adj* media docena *f* **half-time** *n* SPORTS descanso *m* **halfway** **I.** *adj* medio; **~ point** punto medio **II.** *adv* a mitad de camino; **to be ~ between … and …** estar entre… y…; **to be ~ through sth** ir por la mitad de algo

hall [hɔːl] *n* **1.**(*room by front door*) vestíbulo *m* **2.**(*large public room*) sala *f*; **concert ~** sala *f* de conciertos; **town ~, city ~** *Am* ayuntamiento *m* **3.** UNIV colegio *m* mayor; **~ of residence** residencia *f* universitaria

hallmark [ˈhɔːlmɑːk, *Am:* -mɑːrk] *n* **1.** *Brit* (*engraved identifying mark*) contraste *m* **2.**(*identifying symbol*) distintivo *m*; **her ~** su sello personal

hallo [həˈləʊ, *Am:* -ˈloʊ] <-s> *interj Brit* hola

Hallowe'en [ˌhæləʊˈiːn, *Am:* -oʊˈ-] *n* víspera *f* de Todos los Santos

---

? La fiesta de **Hallowe'en** se celebra el día 31 de octubre, el día antes de **All Saints' Day**, también llamado **All Hallows** (Todos los Santos). Desde hace mucho tiempo en esta festividad cobran un protagonismo destacado los espíritus y las brujas. Los niños hacen **turnip lanterns** (farolillos hechos con calabazas vaciadas), y en Escocia hacen **guising** (esto es, se disfrazan y van de casa en casa cantando o recitando poemas para que los dueños de la casa les den dinero). En los EE.UU. los niños se disfrazan al atardecer y van de puerta en puerta con un saco en la mano.

Cuando el dueño de la casa abre la puerta los niños gritan: 'Trick or treat!'; el inquilino elige entonces entre darles un **treat** (dulce) o sufrir un **trick** (susto). Hoy en día los sustos prácticamente han desaparecido, pues los niños sólo se acercan a aquellas casas en las que las luces de fuera están encendidas, lo cual funciona como señal de bienvenida.

---

halo [ˈheɪləʊ, Am: -loʊ] <-s o -es> n a. fig aureola f

halt [hɒlt, Am: hɔ:lt] I. n no pl parada f; **to bring sth/sb to a** ~ detener algo/a alguien II. vi, vt parar

halve [hɑ:v, Am: hæv] vt 1. (lessen) reducir a la mitad; (number) dividir por dos 2. (cut in two equal pieces) partir por la mitad

halves [ha:vz, Am: hævz] n pl of **half**

ham [hæm] n no pl (cured) jamón m (serrano); (cooked) jamón m (cocido); **a slice of** ~ una loncha de jamón

hamburger [ˈhæmbɜːɡəʳ, Am: -bɜːrɡɚ] n hamburguesa f

hamlet [ˈhæmlɪt] n aldea f

hammer [ˈhæməʳ, Am: -ɚ] I. n martillo m; ~ **blow** a. fig martillazo m; **the** ~ **and sickle** POL, HIST la hoz y el martillo II. vt 1. (hit with tool: metal) martillear; (nail) clavar 2. (book, film, team) machacar; **to** ~ **sb for sth** criticar duramente a alguien por algo III. vi martillear; **to** ~ **at sth** dar martillazos a algo

hamper¹ [ˈhæmpəʳ, Am: -pɚ] vt dificultar; **to** ~ **sb/sth** poner trabas a alguien/algo

hamper² [ˈhæmpəʳ, Am: -pɚ] n 1. (picnic basket) cesta f 2. Am (for dirty linen) cesto m de la ropa

hamster [ˈhæmstəʳ, Am: -stɚ] n hámster m

hamstring [ˈhæmstrɪŋ] n tendón m de la corva

hand [hænd] I. n 1. ANAT mano f; **to be good with one's** ~**s** ser mañoso; **to do sth by** ~ hacer algo a mano; **to shake** ~**s with sb** estrechar la mano a alguien; ~**s up!** ¡manos arriba! 2. (handy, within reach) **at** ~ muy cerca 3. (what needs doing now) **the problem in** ~ el problema que nos ocupa; **to get out of** ~ (things, situation) irse de las manos; (person) descontrolarse 4. pl (responsibility, authority, care) **to be in good** ~**s** estar en buenas manos; **to fall into the** ~**s of sb** caer en manos de alguien 5. (assistance) **to give sb a** ~ **with sth** echar a alguien una mano con algo 6. **on the one** ~ **... on the other** (~) ... por un lado..., por otro (lado)...; **second** ~ de segunda mano II. vt dar; **will you** ~ **me my bag?** ¿puedes pasarme mi bolso?

◆ **hand in** vt entregar
◆ **hand out** vt repartir
◆ **hand over** vt 1. (give, submit) entregar 2. (transfer) transferir

handbag [ˈhændbæɡ] n bolso m, cartera f AmL **handbook** n manual m **handbrake** n Brit freno m de mano **handcuffs** npl esposas fpl; **a pair of** ~ unas esposas

handful [ˈhændfʊl] n no pl (small amount) puñado; **to be a real** ~ (child) ser un bicho; (adult) ser de armas tomar

handicap [ˈhændɪkæp] I. n 1. (disability) discapacidad f; **mental** ~ discapacidad f mental; **physical** ~ invalidez f 2. (disadvantage) desventaja f 3. SPORTS hándicap m II.<-pp-> vt perjudicar; **to be** ~**ped** estar en una situación de desventaja

handkerchief [ˈhæŋkətʃɪf, Am: -kɚtʃɪf] n pañuelo m

handle [ˈhændl] I. n 1. (of pot, basket, bag) asa f; (of drawer) tirador m; (of knife) mango m 2. (knob) pomo m II. vt 1. (touch) tocar; ~ **with care** frágil 2. (machine, tool, weapon) manejar; **I don't know how to** ~ **her** no sé cómo tratarla 3. (direct) ocuparse de

handlebar n manillar m

handling *n no pl* manejo *m;* (*of goods*) manipulación *f*

handout ['hændaʊt] *n* **1.** (*leaflet*) folleto *m* **2.** (*money*) limosna *f*

handshake *n* apretón *m* de manos

handsome ['hænsəm] *adj* **1.** (*man*) guapo; (*animal, thing*) bello **2.** (*large*) considerable

hands-on [,hændz'ɒn, *Am:* -'ɑ:n] *adj* práctico; ~ **approach** enfoque práctico

handwriting *n no pl* letra *f*

handwritten [,hænd'rɪtn] *adj* manuscrito

handy ['hændi] <-ier, -iest> *adj* **1.** (*skilful*) hábil; **to be ~ with sth** ser mañoso para algo; **to be ~ about the house** ser un manitas **2.** (*convenient*) práctico; (*useful*) útil; **to come in ~** venir bien

hang [hæŋ] **I.** <hung, hung> *vi* **1.** (*be suspended*) colgar; (*picture*) estar colgado; **to ~ by/on/from sth** colgar de algo **2.** (*lean over or forward*) inclinarse **3.** (*fit, drape: clothes, fabrics*) caer; **to ~ well** tener buena caída **II.** <hung, hung> *vt* **1.** (*attach*) colgar; (*washing*) tender **2.** (*execute*) ahorcar
◆**hang around** **I.** *vi* **1.** *inf* (*waste time*) perder el tiempo **2.** (*wait*) esperar **3.** (*idle*) no hacer nada **II.** *vt insep* rondar; **to ~ a place** andar rondando por un sitio
◆**hang on** **I.** *vi* **1.** (*wait briefly*) esperar; ~**!** *inf* ¡espera un momento! **2.** (*hold on to*) **to ~ to sth** agarrarse a algo; ~ **tight** agárrate fuerte **II.** *vt insep* **1.** (*depend upon*) depender de **2.** (*give attention*) estar pendiente de; **to ~ sb's every word** estar pendiente de lo que dice alguien
◆**hang out** **I.** *vt* tender **II.** *vi* **1.** (*dangle*) colgar **2.** *inf* (*frequent*) andar; **where does he ~ these days?** ¿por dónde anda estos días?

hangar ['hæŋəʳ, *Am:* -ɚ] *n* hangar *m*

hanger ['hæŋəʳ, *Am:* -ɚ] *n* percha *f*

hanging ['hæŋɪŋ] **I.** *n* **1.** (*act of execution*) ejecución *f* (en la horca) **2.** *no pl* (*system of execution*) horca

f **II.** *adj* colgante

hangover *n* **1.** (*sickness*) resaca *f*, goma *f AmL* **2.** (*left-over*) vestigio *m*

haphazard [hæp'hæzəd, *Am:* -ɚd] *adj* **1.** (*badly planned*) hecho de cualquier manera **2.** (*random, arbitrary*) caprichoso

happen ['hæpən] *vi* **1.** (*occur*) pasar; **whatever ~s** pase lo que pase **2.** (*chance*) **I ~ed to be at home** dio la casualidad de que estaba en casa; **he/it ~s to be my best friend** pues resulta que es mi mejor amigo

happening ['hæpənɪŋ] *n* **1.** (*events*) suceso *m* **2.** (*performance*) happening *m*

happily ['hæpɪli] *adv* felizmente; **they lived ~ ever after** fueron felices y comieron perdices

happiness ['hæpɪnɪs] *n no pl* felicidad *f*

happy ['hæpi] <-ier, -iest> *adj* **1.** (*feeling very good*) feliz; **to be ~ that ...** estar contento de que... +*subj;* **to be ~ to do sth** estar encantado de hacer algo; ~ **birthday!** ¡feliz cumpleaños!; **many ~ returns (of the day)!** ¡que cumplas muchos más! **2.** (*satisfied*) contento; **to be ~ about sb/sth** estar contento con alguien/algo; **are you ~ with the idea?** ¿te parece bien la idea?

harass ['hærəs, *Am:* hə'ræs] *vt* acosar; (*with cares*) abrumar

harassment ['hærəsmənt, *Am:* hə-'ræs-] *n no pl* acoso *m;* **sexual ~** acoso sexual

harbor ['hɑ:rbəʳ] *Am, Aus,* **harbour** ['hɑ:bəʳ] *n* puerto *m;* **fishing ~** puerto pesquero

hard [hɑ:d, *Am:* hɑ:rd] **I.** *adj* **1.** duro; ~ **luck!**, ~ **lines!** *Brit* ¡mala suerte! **2.** (*intense, concentrated*) **to be a ~ worker** ser muy trabajador **3.** (*difficult, complex*) difícil; **to be ~ to please** ser difícil de contentar; **to learn the ~ way** *fig* aprender a base de errores [*o* palos] **II.** *adv* fuerte; **to press/pull ~** apretar/tirar fuerte; **to study/work ~** estudiar/trabajar mucho

hardback ['hɑ:dbæk, *Am:* 'hɑ:rd-]

n libro *m* de tapa dura; **in** ~ con tapa dura **hard currency** <-ies> *n* moneda *f* fuerte **hard disk** *n* INFOR disco *m* duro

harden ['hɑ:dn, *Am:* 'hɑ:r-] **I.** *vt* **1.** (*make more solid, firmer*) endurecer **2.** (*make tougher*) curtir; **to** ~ **oneself to sth** acostumbrarse a algo **II.** *vi* **1.** (*become firmer*) endurecerse **2.** (*become inured*) **to** ~ **to sth** acostumbrarse a algo

hardly ['hɑ:dli, *Am:* 'hɑ:rd-] *adv* apenas; ~ **anything** casi nada; ~ **ever** casi nunca

hardness ['hɑ:dnɪs, *Am:* 'hɑ:rd-] *n no pl* dureza *f*

hardship ['hɑ:dʃɪp, *Am:* 'hɑ:rd-] *n* (*suffering*) penas *fpl;* (*adversity*) adversidad *f;* **to suffer great** ~ pasar muchos apuros **hardware** *n no pl* **1.** (*household articles*) ferretería *f* **2.** INFOR hardware *m*

hardy ['hɑ:di, *Am:* 'hɑ:r-] <-ier, -iest> *adj* fuerte

hare [heəʳ, *Am:* her] *n* liebre *f*

harm [hɑ:m, *Am:* hɑ:rm] **I.** *n no pl* daño *m;* **to do** ~ **to sb/sth** hacer daño a alguien/algo; **there's no** ~ **in trying** no se pierde nada con intentarlo **II.** *vt* hacer daño

harmful ['hɑ:mfl, *Am:* 'hɑ:rm-] *adj* dañino; **to be** ~ **to sth** ser perjudicial para algo

harmless ['hɑ:mlɪs, *Am:* 'hɑ:rm-] *adj* inofensivo

harmonic [hɑ:'mɒnɪk, *Am:* hɑ:-'mɑ:nɪk] *adj* armónico

harmonious [hɑ:'məʊnɪəs, *Am:* hɑ:r'moʊ-] *adj* armonioso

harmony ['hɑ:məni, *Am:* 'hɑ:r-] <-ies> *n a.* MUS armonía *f;* **in** ~ (**with sb/sth**) en armonía (con alguien/algo)

harness ['hɑ:nɪs, *Am:* 'hɑ:r-] **I.** *n* arnés *mpl;* **security** ~ arnés de seguridad **II.** *vt* poner los arreos a

harp [hɑ:p, *Am:* hɑ:rp] **I.** *n* arpa *f* **II.** *vi* **to** ~ **on about sth** (*talk about*) insistir sobre algo

harrow ['hærəʊ, *Am:* 'heroʊ] **I.** *n* grada *f* **II.** *vt* **1.** AGR gradar **2.** (*disturb*) atormentar

harrowing *adj* desgarrador

harsh [hɑ:ʃ, *Am:* hɑ:rʃ] *adj* **1.** (*severe: education, parents*) severo; (*punishment*) duro **2.** (*unfair: criticism*) cruel

harvest ['hɑ:vɪst, *Am:* 'hɑ:r-] **I.** *n* (*of crops*) cosecha *f;* (*of grape*) vendimia *f* **II.** *vt a. fig* cosechar; (*grape*) vendimiar **III.** *vi* cosechar

has [həz, *stressed:* hæz] *3rd pers sing of* **have**

hash¹ [hæʃ] *n no pl* **1.** GASTR picadillo *m* **2.** *no pl, inf* lío *m;* **to make a** ~ **of sth** armarse un lío con algo

hash² [hæʃ] *n no pl, inf* chocolate *m*

hassle ['hæsl] **I.** *n no pl, inf* (*bother*) lío *m;* **to give sb** ~ fastidiar a alguien **II.** *vt inf* fastidiar; **to** ~ **sb to do sth** estar encima a alguien para que haga algo

haste [heɪst] *n no pl* prisa *f;* **more** ~ **less speed** *prov* vísteme despacio, que tengo prisa *prov*

hasten ['heɪsn] *vi* apresurarse; **to** ~ **to do sth** apresurarse a hacer algo

hasty ['heɪsti] <-ier, -iest> *adj* **1.** (*fast*) rápido; **to beat a** ~ **retreat** *a. fig* retirarse a toda prisa **2.** (*rashly*) precipitado; **to make** ~ **decisions** tomar decisiones irreflexivamente

hat [hæt] *n* sombrero *m*

hatch¹ [hætʃ] **I.** *vi* salir del cascarón **II.** *vt* **1.** (*chick*) incubar, empollar **2.** (*devise in secret*) tramar; **to** ~ **a plan** urdir un plan

hatch² [hætʃ] <-es> *n* trampilla *f;* NAUT escotilla *f*

hatchet ['hætʃɪt] *n* hacha *f* (pequeña); **to bury the** ~ enterrar el hacha de guerra

hate [heɪt] **I.** *n* odio *m* **II.** *vt* odiar; **to** ~ **sb's guts** *inf* odiar a alguien a muerte

hatred ['heɪtrɪd] *n no pl* odio *m;* ~ **of sb/sth** odio a [*o* hacia] alguien/algo

hat-trick ['hættrɪk] *n* SPORTS *tres goles marcados por un mismo jugador*

haul [hɔ:l, *Am:* hɑ:l] **I.** *vt* arrastrar; **to** ~ **up the sail** izar la vela **II.** *n* **1.** (*distance*) trayecto *m;* **long** ~ **flight** vuelo *m* intercontinental

H h

2. (*quantity caught: of fish, shrimp*) redada *f;* (*of stolen goods*) botín *m*
haunt [hɔːnt, *Am:* hɑːnt] *vt* **1.** (*ghost*) rondar **2.** (*plague, bother*) perseguir; **to be ~ed by sth** estar obsesionado por algo
haunted *adj* **1.** (*frequented by ghosts*) embrujado **2.** (*troubled*) angustiado
haunting *adj* **1.** (*disturbing*) **a ~ fear/memory** un miedo/recuerdo recurrente e inquietante **2.** (*memorable*) **to have a ~ beauty** tener una belleza evocadora
Havana [həˈvænə] *n* La Habana
have [həv, *stressed:* hæv] **I.** <has, had, had> *vt* **1.** (*own*) tener, poseer; **she's got two brothers** tiene dos hermanos; **to ~ sth to do** tener algo que hacer **2.** (*engage in*) **to have a walk** pasear; **to ~ a bath/shower** bañarse/ducharse; **to ~ a game** echar una partida **3.** (*eat*) **to ~ lunch** comer; **to ~ some coffee** tomar café **4.** (*give birth to*) **to ~ a child** tener un hijo **5.** (*receive*) tener, recibir; **to ~ visitors** tener visita **II.** <has, had, had> *aux* (*indicates perfect tense*) **he has never been to Scotland** nunca ha estado en Escocia; **we had been swimming** habíamos estado nadando; **to ~ got to do sth** *Brit, Aus* tener que hacer algo; **what time ~ we got to be there?** ¿a qué hora tenemos que estar allí?
◆ **have in** *vt always sep* invitar; **they had some experts in** llamaron a algunos expertos
◆ **have on** *vt always sep* **1.** (*wear: clothes*) llevar (puesto); **he didn't have any clothes on** estaba desnudo **2.** *Brit, inf* (*fool*) tomar el pelo a **3.** (*plan*) **have you got anything on this week?** ¿tienes planes para esta semana?
haven [ˈheɪvn] *n* refugio *m*
havoc [ˈhævək] *n no pl* estragos *mpl;* **to play ~ with sth** trastocar [*o* desbaratar] algo
Hawaii [həˈwaɪiː, *Am:* həˈwɑːiː-] *n* Hawai *m*
Hawaiian [həˈwaɪjən, *Am:* hə-

'waː-] *adj* hawaiano
hawk [hɔːk, *Am:* hɑːk] *n a.* POL halcón *m*
hay [heɪ] *n no pl* heno *m;* **to hit the ~** *inf* acostarse; **to make ~ while the sun shines** *prov* aprovechar la oportunidad cuando se presenta *prov*
hazard [ˈhæzəd, *Am:* -ɚd] *n* **1.** (*danger*) peligro *m* **2.** *no pl* (*risk*) riesgo *m;* **fire ~** peligro de incendio; **health ~** riesgo para la salud
hazardous [ˈhæzədəs, *Am:* -ɚ-] *adj* (*dangerous*) peligroso; (*risky*) arriesgado
haze [heɪz] *n* (*mist*) neblina *f;* **heat ~** calina *f*
hazel [ˈheɪzl] **I.** *adj* color avellana **II.** *n* avellano *m*
hazelnut [ˈheɪzlnʌt] *n* BOT avellana *f*
hazy [ˈheɪzi] <-ier, -iest> *adj* **1.** (*with bad visibility*) neblinoso **2.** (*confused, unclear*) vago
he [hiː] *pron pers* **1.** (*male person or animal*) él; **~'s my father** es mi padre; **~'s gone away but ~'ll be back soon** se ha ido, pero volverá pronto **2.** (*unspecified sex*) **if somebody comes, ~ will buy it** si alguien viene, lo comprará
head [hed] **I.** *n* **1.** ANAT cabeza *f;* **to nod one's ~** asentir con la cabeza; **to have one's ~ in the clouds** tener la cabeza llena de pájaros; **to be ~ over heels in love** estar locamente enamorado; **to be off one's ~** *inf* (*crazy*) estar mal de la cabeza; **to laugh one's ~ off** desternillarse de risa **2.** *no pl* (*unit*) cabeza *f;* **a** [*o* **per**] **~** por cabeza **3.** (*mind*) **to clear one's ~** aclararse las ideas; **to get sth/sb out of one's ~** sacarse algo/a alguien de la cabeza **4.** *pl* (*coin face*) cara *f;* **~s or tails?** ¿cara o cruz? **5.** (*boss*) jefe, -a *m, f* **II.** *vt* (*lead*) encabezar; (*a firm, organization*) dirigir
◆ **head back** *vi* volver, regresar
◆ **head for** *vt insep* ir rumbo a; **to ~ the exit** dirigirse hacia la salida
◆ **head off I.** *vt* (*get in front of sb*) cortar el paso a **II.** *vi* **to ~ towards** salir hacia
headache [ˈhedeɪk] *n* dolor *m* de

cabeza

heading ['hedɪŋ] *n* (*of chapter*) encabezamiento *m;* (*letterhead*) membrete *m*

headlight *n,* **headlamp** *n* faro *m* **headline** *n* titular *m* **headmaster** *n* director *m* de colegio **headquarters** *n* + *sing/pl vb* MIL cuartel *m* general; (*of company*) oficina *f* central; (*of party*) sede *f* **headrest** *n* reposacabezas *f inv* **headway** *n no pl* progreso *m;* **to make** ~ hacer progresos

heady ['hedi] <-ier, -iest> *adj* **1.** (*intoxicating*) embriagador **2.** (*exciting*) emocionante

heal [hiːl] I. *vt* curar II. *vi* cicatrizar

health [helθ] *n no pl* salud *f;* **to drink to sb's** ~ beber a la salud de alguien

health insurance *n no pl* seguro *m* médico **health service** *n Brit* servicio *m* sanitario

healthy ['helθi] <-ier, -iest> *adj* **1.** MED sano **2.** FIN próspero

heap [hiːp] I. *n* pila *f,* montón *m;* **to collapse in a** ~ *fig* (*person*) caer desplomado II. *vt* amontonar, apilar

hear [hɪəʳ, *Am:* hɪr] <heard, heard> I. *vt* **1.** (*perceive*) oír **2.** (*be told*) enterarse de; **to** ~ **that ...** enterarse de que..., oír que... **3.** (*listen*) escuchar; **Lord,** ~ **our prayers** REL escúchanos, Señor II. *vi* **1.** (*perceive*) oír; **to** ~ **very well** oír muy bien **2.** (*get news*) enterarse

hearing ['hɪərɪŋ, *Am:* 'hɪr-] *n* **1.** *no pl* (*sense*) oído *m* **2.** LAW vista *f*

heart [hɑːt, *Am:* hɑːrt] *n* **1.** ANAT corazón *m;* **by** ~ de memoria; **to break sb's** ~ *fig* partir el corazón a alguien **2.** *no pl* (*centre*) centro *m;* **to get to the** ~ **of the matter** llegar al fondo de la cuestión **3.** *pl* (*card suit*) corazones *mpl;* (*in Spanish pack*) copas *fpl*

heart attack *n* ataque *m* al corazón **heartbeat** *n* latido *m* (del corazón) **heart disease** *n no pl* enfermedad *f* coronaria

hearth [hɑːθ, *Am:* hɑːrθ] *n* chimenea *f*

heartily *adv* con efusividad; **to eat** ~ comer con ganas

hearty ['hɑːti, *Am:* 'hɑːrti] *adj* <-ier, -iest> **1.** (*enthusiastic*) entusiasta; ~ **welcome** bienvenida calurosa **2.** (*large, strong*) fuerte; **a** ~ **breakfast** un desayuno opíparo

heat [hiːt] I. *n no pl* **1.** (*warmth, high temperature*) calor **2.** *no pl* ZOOL celo *m;* **to be on** ~ estar en celo II. *vi, vt* calentar(se)

◆ **heat up** *vi, vt* calentar(se)

heated *adj* **1.** (*pool*) climatizado **2.** (*argument*) acalorado

heater ['hiːtəʳ, *Am:* - t̬ə-] *n* calefactor *m*

heat exchanger *n* (inter)cambiador *m* térmico **heat gauge** *n* termostato *m*

heath [hiːθ] *n* brezal *m*

heathen ['hiːðn] I. *n* pagano, -a *m, f;* **the** ~ los infieles II. *adj* pagano

heather ['heðəʳ, *Am:* -ə-] *n no pl* brezo *m*

heating *n no pl* calefacción *f*

heave [hiːv] I. *vi* (*pull*) tirar; (*push*) empujar II. *vt* (*pull*) tirar; (*push*) empujar; **he** ~**d the door open** abrió la puerta de un empujón III. *n* (*push*) empujón *m;* (*pull*) tirón *m*

heaven ['hevən] *n* cielo *m;* **to go to** ~ ir al cielo; **it's** ~ *inf* es divino [*o* fantástico]

heavenly ['hevənli] *adj* <-ier, -iest> **1.** (*of heaven*) celestial; ~ **body** cuerpo *m* celeste **2.** (*wonderful*) divino

heavy ['hevi] *adj* <-ier, -iest> **1.** (*weighing a lot*) pesado; ~ **food** comida pesada **2.** (*difficult*) difícil **3.** (*strong*) fuerte; ~ **fall** *a.* ECON fuerte descenso **4.** (*abundant*) abundante; ~ **frost/gale** fuertes heladas/ chubascos **5.** (*excessive*) ~ **drinker/smoker** bebedor/fumador empedernido

heavy metal *n* **1.** (*lead, cadmium*) metal *m* pesado **2.** MUS heavy *m* (metal) **heavyweight** SPORTS I. *adj* (de la categoría) de los pesos pesados II. *n* peso pesado *m*

Hebrew [hiːˈbruː] *adj* hebreo

H h

heck [hek] *interj inf* caramba; **where the ~ have you been?** ¿dónde demonios has/habéis estado?

hectare ['hekteəʳ, *Am:* -ter] *n* hectárea *f*

hectic ['hektɪk] *adj* ajetreado; **~ pace** ritmo intenso

hedge [hedʒ] *n* seto *m* vivo

heed [hi:d] *n* **to pay** (**no**) **~ to sth** (no) prestar atención a algo

heel [hi:l] *n* **1.** (*of foot*) talón *m;* **to be at sb's ~s** pisar los talones a alguien **2.** (*of shoe*) tacón *m*, taco *m AmL*

hefty ['hefti] *adj* <-ier, -iest> (*person*) corpulento; (*profit, amount*) cuantioso

held [held] *pt, pp of* **hold**

height [haɪt] *n* (*of person*) estatura *f;* (*of thing*) altura *f;* **to be afraid of ~s** tener vértigo

heighten ['haɪtn] *vt* aumentar; **to ~ the effect of sth** acentuar el efecto de algo

heir [eəʳ, *Am:* er] *n* heredero *m; ~* **to the throne** heredero del trono

heiress ['eərɪs, *Am:* 'erɪs] *n* heredera *f*

helicopter ['helɪkɒptəʳ, *Am:* -kɑ:ptəʳ] *n* helicóptero *m*

hell [hel] I. *n no pl* **1.** (*place of punishment*) infierno *m;* **to make sb's life ~** *fig, inf* hacer la vida imposible a alguien **2.** *inf* (*as intensifier*) **as cold as ~** un frío de mil demonios; **to run like ~** correr (uno) que se las pela II. *interj* demonios; **what the ~ …!** ¡qué diablos…!

hello [hə'ləʊ, *Am:* -'loʊ] I. <hellos> *n* hola *m;* **a big ~** un gran saludo II. *interj* **1.** (*greeting*) hola; **to say ~ to sb** saludar a alguien **2.** (*beginning of phone call*) diga, dígame, aló *AmC, AmS*

helm [helm] *n* timón *m;* **to be at the ~** llevar el timón; *fig* llevar el mando

helmet ['helmɪt] *n* casco *m*

help [help] I. *vi* **1.** (*assist*) ayudar **2.** (*make easier*) facilitar **3.** (*improve situation*) mejorar II. *vt* **1.** (*assist*) ayudar; **can I ~ you?** (*in shop*) ¿en

qué puedo servirle? **2.** (*prevent*) evitar; **to not be able to ~ doing sth** no poder dejar de hacer algo; **I can't ~ it** no puedo remediarlo III. *n no pl* ayuda *f;* **to be a ~** ser una ayuda IV. *interj* socorro

◆ **help out** *vt* ayudar

helper ['helpəʳ, *Am:* -əʳ] *n* ayudante *mf*

helpful ['helpfl] *adj* **1.** (*willing to help*) servicial **2.** (*useful*) útil

helping ['helpɪŋ] I. *n* ración *f*, porción *f AmL* II. *adj* **to give sb a ~ hand** echar una mano a alguien

helpless ['helplɪs] *adj* indefenso

helpline ['helplaɪn] *n* teléfono *m* de asistencia

hem [hem] *n* dobladillo *m*, basta *f AmL;* **to take the ~ up/down** meter/sacar el dobladillo

hemisphere ['hemɪsfɪəʳ, *Am:* -sfɪr] *n a.* MED hemisferio *m*

hen [hen] *n* (*female chicken*) gallina *f;* (*female bird*) hembra *f*

hence [hens] *adv* **1.** (*therefore*) de ahí **2.** *after n* (*from now*) dentro de; **two years ~** de aquí a dos años

henceforth [ˌhens'fɔ:θ, *Am:* -'fɔ:rθ] *adv, adv* de ahora en adelante

hepatitis [ˌhepə'taɪtɪs, *Am:* -t̬ɪs] *n no pl* hepatitis *f inv*

her [hɜːʳ, *Am:* hɜːr] I. *adj poss* su; **~ dress/house** su vestido/casa; **~ children** sus hijos II. *pron pers* **1.** (*she*) ella; **it's ~** es ella; **older than ~** mayor que ella; **if I were ~** si yo fuese ella **2.** *direct object* la; *indirect object* le; **look at ~** mírala; **I saw ~** la vi; **he told ~ that …** le dijo que…; **he gave ~ the pencil** le dio el lápiz (a ella) **3.** *after prep* ella; **it's for/from ~** es para/de ella

herald ['herəld] I. *vt* presagiar II. *n* presagio *m*

herb [hɜːb] *n* hierba *f*

herd [hɜːd, *Am:* hɜːrd] *n + sing/pl vb* (*of animals*) manada *f;* (*of sheep*) rebaño *f*

here [hɪəʳ, *Am:* hɪr] *adv* **1.** (*in, at, to this place*) aquí; **over ~** acá; **give it ~** *inf* dámelo; **~ and there** aquí y allá **2.** (*introduce*) here is ... aquí está... **3.** (*show arrival*) they are ~ ya han llegado **4.** (*next to*) my colleague ~ mi colega que está aquí **5.** (*now*) where do we go from ~? ¿dónde vamos ahora?; ~ you are (*giving sth*) aquí tienes

hereabouts [ˌhɪərəˈbaʊts, *Am:* ˌhɪrəˈbaʊts] *adv* por aquí

hereafter [hɪərˈɑːftəʳ, *Am:* hɪrˈæftəʳ] **I.** *adv* en lo sucesivo **II.** *n* the ~ el más allá

hereditary [hɪˈredɪtri, *Am:* həˈredɪtər-] *adj* hereditario

heredity [hɪˈredəti, *Am:* həˈredɪ-] *n no pl* herencia *f*

heresy [ˈherəsi] <-ies> *n* herejía *f*

heretic [ˈherətɪk] *n* hereje *mf*

heritage [ˈherɪtɪdʒ, *Am:* -t̬ɪdʒ] *n no pl* patrimonio *m*

hermit [ˈhɜːmɪt, *Am:* ˈhɜːr-] *n* eremita *mf*

hero [ˈhɪərəʊ, *Am:* ˈhɪroʊ] <heroes> *n* **1.** (*brave man*) héroe *m* **2.** (*main character*) protagonista *m* **3.** (*idol*) ídolo *m*

heroic [hɪˈrəʊɪk, *Am:* hɪˈroʊ-] *adj* heroico; ~ deed hazaña *f*

heroin [ˈherəʊɪn, *Am:* -oʊ-] *n no pl* heroína *f*

heroine [ˈherəʊɪn, *Am:* -oʊ-] *n* (*of film*) protagonista *f*; (*brave woman*) heroína *f*

heroism [ˈherəʊɪzəm, *Am:* -oʊ-] *n no pl* heroísmo *m*

heron [ˈherən] <-(s)> *n* garza *f* (real)

herring [ˈherɪŋ] <-(s)> *n* arenque *m*

hers [hɜːz, *Am:* hɜːrz] *pron poss* (el) suyo, (la) suya, (los) suyos, (las) suyas; it's not my bag, it's ~ no es mi bolsa, es la suya; this house is ~ esta casa es suya; this glass is ~ este vaso es suyo; a book of ~ un libro suyo

herself [hɜːˈself, *Am:* həʳ-] *pron* **1.** *refl* se; *after prep* sí (misma); she lives by ~ vive sola **2.** *emphatic* ella misma; she hurt ~ se hizo daño

hesitate [ˈhezɪteɪt] *vi* vacilar; to (not) ~ to do sth (no) dudar en hacer algo

hesitation [ˌhezɪˈteɪʃn] *n* vacilación *f*; without ~ sin titubear

heterogeneous [ˌhetərəˈdʒiːnɪəs, *Am:* ˌhet̬əroʊ-] *adj* heterogéneo

heterosexual [ˌhetərəˈsekʃʊəl, *Am:* ˌhet̬əroʊ-] *adj* heterosexual

hey [heɪ] *interj inf* eh, oye, órale *Méx*

hi [haɪ] *interj* hola

hid [hɪd] *pt of* hide²

hidden [ˈhɪdn] *adj pp of* hide²

hide¹ [haɪd] *n* piel *f*

hide² [haɪd] <hid, hidden> **I.** *vi* esconderse, escorarse *Cuba, Hond* **II.** *vt* (*person, thing*) esconder; (*emotion, information*) ocultar; to ~ one's face taparse la cara

hideous [ˈhɪdɪəs] *adj* **1.** (*very unpleasant, ugly*) espantoso **2.** (*terrible*) terrible

hiding¹ [ˈhaɪdɪŋ] *n* paliza *f*

hiding² [ˈhaɪdɪŋ] *n no pl* to be in ~ estar escondido; to go into ~ ocultarse

hierarchic(al) [ˌhaɪəˈrɑːkɪk(l), *Am:* ˌhaɪˈrɑːr-] *adj* jerárquico

hierarchy [ˈhaɪərɑːki, *Am:* ˈhaɪrɑːr-] <-ies> *n* jerarquía *f*

high [haɪ] **I.** *adj* **1.** (*elevated*) alto; one metre ~ and three metres wide un metro de alto y tres metros de ancho **2.** (*above average*) superior; to have a ~ opinion of sb estimar mucho a alguien **3.** (*important, eminent*) elevado; of ~ rank de alto rango; to have friends in ~ places tener amigos en las altas esferas; (*regarding job*) tener enchufe **4.** (*under influence of drugs*) colocado **5.** (*of high frequency, shrill*) agudo; a ~ note una nota alta **II.** *n* punto *m* máximo; an all-time ~ un récord de todos los tiempos; to reach a ~ alcanzar un nivel récord

higher education *n no pl* enseñanza *f* superior

[?] El **Higher Grade** es el nombre de un examen que hacen los alumnos escoceses que están en el quinto curso (un año después del

GCSE). Los alumnos pueden elegir examinarse de una única asignatura, aunque lo normal es que
ellos prefieran hacer aproximadamente cinco **Highers**.

[?] El **Highland dress** o **kilt** es el
nombre que recibe el traje tradicional escocés. Procede del siglo
XVI y en aquel entonces se compo-
nía de una única pieza. A partir del
siglo XVII esta pieza única se convierte en dos distintas: el **kilt**
(falda escocesa) y el **plaid** (capa de
lana). De esta época procede también el **sporran** (una bolsa que
cuelga del cinturón). Hasta el siglo
XVIII no se diseñan los diferentes
tartans (modelos de diseños escoceses) para cada familia o clan.
Muchos hombres siguen ponién-
dose el **kilt** en acontecimientos especiales, como por ejemplo, una
boda.

highly ['haɪli] *adv* **1.** (*very*) muy
2. (*very well*) **to speak ~ of someone** hablar muy bien de alguien
high-pitched *adj* agudo; **a ~ voice**
una voz aflautada **high-powered**
adj poderoso **high-ranking** *adj* de
categoría **high-risk** *adj* de alto riesgo **high school** *n Am* ≈ instituto *m;*
junior ~ centro *m* de enseñanza secundaria

[?] El término **high school** se uti-
lizaba antiguamente en Gran Bretaña para designar una **grammar
school** (escuela secundaria superior), pero hoy en día se emplea
con el significado de **secondary
school** (escuela secundaria inferior).

high-tech *adj* de alta tecnología
highway ['haɪweɪ] *n* carretera *f*
hijack ['haɪdʒæk] **I.** *vt* secuestrar
II. *n* secuestro *m*
hike [haɪk] **I.** *n* **1.** (*long walk*) caminata *f;* **to go on a** ~ dar una caminata **2.** *Am, inf* (*increase*) aumento *m*
II. *vi* ir de excursión (a pie) **III.** *vt*
Am, inf (*prices, taxes*) aumentar
hilarious [hɪ'leərɪəs, *Am:* -'lerɪ-]
adj divertidísimo
hilarity [hɪ'lærəti, *Am:* -'lerət̬ɪ] *n*
no pl hilaridad *f*
hill [hɪl] *n* colina *f;* (*slope*) cuesta *f*
hillside ['hɪlsaɪd] *n* ladera *f* **hilltop**
['hɪltɒp, *Am:* -tɑːp] *n* cumbre *f*
hilly ['hɪli] <-ier, -iest> *adj* montañoso
hilt [hɪlt] *n* empuñadura *f;* (**up**) **to
the** ~ totalmente, hasta el cuello *inf*
him [hɪm] *pron pers* **1.** (*he*) él; **it's ~**
es él; **older than** ~ mayor que él; **if I
were** ~ yo en su lugar **2.** *direct object* lo, le; *indirect object* le; **she
gave** ~ **the pencil** le dio el lápiz (a
él) **3.** *after prep* él; **it's for/from** ~
es para/de él **4.** (*unspecified sex*) **if
somebody comes, tell** ~ **that ...** si
viene alguien, dile que…
himself [hɪm'self] *pron* **1.** *refl* se;
after prep sí (mismo); **for** ~ para él
(mismo); **he lives by** ~ vive solo
2. *emphatic* él mismo; **he hurt** ~ se
hizo daño
hind [haɪnd] *adj* trasero
hinder ['hɪndər, *Am:* -dɚ] *vt* estorbar; **to** ~ **progress** frenar el progreso; **to** ~ **sb from doing sth** impedir
a alguien hacer algo
hindrance ['hɪndrəns] *n* obstáculo
m
hindsight ['haɪndsaɪt] *n no pl* percepción *f* retrospectiva; **in** ~ en
retrospectiva
Hindu ['hɪnduː] *adj* hindú
hinge [hɪndʒ] **I.** *n* bisagra *f* **II.** *vi* **to
~ on** [*o* **upon**] **sb/sth** depender de
alguien/algo
hint [hɪnt] **I.** *n* **1.** (*trace*) indicio *m*
2. (*allusion*) indirecta *f;* **to drop a** ~
lanzar una indirecta **3.** (*practical tip*)
consejo *m;* **a handy** ~ una indica-

ción útil **II.** *vt* **to ~ sth to sb** insinuar algo a alguien

hip [hɪp] **I.** *n* **1.** ANAT cadera *f* **2.** BOT escaramujo *m* **II.** *adj inf* (*fashionable*) moderno

hippie ['hɪpi] *n* hippy *mf*

hippopotamus [ˌhɪpə'pɒtəməs, *Am:* -'paːʈə-] <-es *o* -mi> *n* hipopótamo *m*

hippy ['hɪpi] <-ies> *n* hippy *mf*

hire ['haɪəʳ, *Am:* 'haɪr] **I.** *n no pl* alquiler *m;* **'for ~'** 'se alquila' **II.** *vt* **1.** (*rent*) alquilar, fletar *AmL* **2.** (*employ*) contratar; **to ~ more staff** ampliar la plantilla

his [hɪz] **I.** *adj poss* su; **~ car/house** su coche/casa; **~ children** sus hijos **II.** *pron poss* (el) suyo, (la) suya, (los) suyos, (las) suyas; **it's not my bag, it's ~** no es mi bolsa, es la suya; **this house is ~** esta casa es suya; **this glass is ~** este vaso es suyo; **a book of ~** un libro suyo

Hispanic [hɪs'pænɪk] **I.** *adj* hispánico **II.** *n* hispano, -a *m, f*

hiss [hɪs] **I.** *vi,* *vt* silbar; **to ~ at sb** silbar a alguien **II.** *n* silbido *m*

historian [hɪ'stɔːriən] *n* historiador(a) *m(f)*

historic [hɪ'stɒrɪk, *Am:* hɪ'stɔːrɪk] *adj* histórico; **this is a ~ moment ...** este es un momento clave...

historical *adj* histórico

history ['hɪstəri] *n no pl* historia *f;* **a ~ book** un libro de historia; **sb's life ~** la vida de alguien

hit [hɪt] **I.** *n* **1.** (*blow, stroke*) golpe *m* **2.** (*success*) éxito *m* **II.** <-tt-, hit, hit> *vt* **1.** (*strike*) golpear, pepenar *Méx;* **to ~ sb hard** *a. fig* pegar a alguien con fuerza **2.** (*crash into*) chocar contra

◆ **hit on** *vt* dar con

hitch [hɪtʃ] **I.** <-es> *n* obstáculo *m;* **technical ~** problema *m* técnico **II.** *vt* **1.** (*fasten*) atar; **to ~ sth to sth** atar algo a algo **2.** *inf* (*hitchhike*) **to ~ a lift** hacer dedo **III.** *vi inf* hacer dedo

hitch-hiking *no pl n* autostop *m*

hitherto [ˌhɪðə'tuː, *Am:* -ə˞'-] *adv form* hasta ahora; **~ unpublished**

no publicado por ahora

HIV [ˌeɪtʃaɪ'viː] *abbr of* **human immunodeficiency virus** VIH *m*

hive [haɪv] *n* colmena *f;* **to be a ~ of business** ser un punto neurálgico de negocios

HMS [ˌeɪtʃem'es] *abbr of* **Her/His Majesty's Service** el Servicio de S.M.

ho [həʊ, *Am:* hoʊ] *interj inf* (*expresses scorn, surprise*) oh; (*attracts attention*) oiga; **land ~!** NAUT ¡tierra a la vista!

HO [ˌeɪtʃ'əʊ, *Am:* -'oʊ] **1.** *abbr of* **head office** oficina *f* principal **2.** *abbr of* **Home Office** Ministerio *m* del Interior

hoard [hɔːd, *Am:* hɔːrd] **I.** *n* acumulación *f* **II.** *vt* acumular; (*food*) amontonar

hoarse [hɔːs, *Am:* hɔːrs] *adj* ronco

hoax [həʊks, *Am:* hoʊks] **I.** <-es> *n* engaño *m* **II.** *vt* engañar

hobby ['hɒbi, *Am:* 'haːbɪ] <-ies> *n* hobby *m*

hockey ['hɒki, *Am:* 'haːkɪ] *n no pl* hockey *m;* **ice ~** hockey sobre hielo

hog [hɒg, *Am:* haːg] **I.** *n Am* (*pig*) puerco *m,* chancho *m AmS* **II.** <-gg-> *vt inf* acaparar; **to ~ sb/ sth** (*all to oneself*) acaparar a alguien/algo (para uno mismo)

hoist [hɔɪst] *vt* (*raise up*) alzar; (*flag*) enarbolar

hold [həʊld, *Am:* hoʊld] **I.** *n* **1.** (*grasp, grip*) agarre *m;* **to take ~ of sb/sth** asirse de [*o a*] alguien/algo **2.** (*control*) dominio *m;* **to have a (strong/powerful) ~ over sb** tener (mucha/gran) influencia sobre alguien **3.** NAUT, AVIAT bodega *f* **II.** <held, held> *vt* **1.** (*keep*) tener; (*grasp*) agarrar; **to ~ hands** agarrarse de la mano; **to ~ sth in one's hand** sostener algo en la mano; **to ~ sb in one's arms** estrechar a alguien entre los brazos **2.** (*keep, retain*) mantener; **to ~ sb's attention/interest** mantener la atención/el interés de alguien **3.** (*delay, stop*) detener; **~ it!** ¡para! **4.** (*contain*) contener **5.** (*possess, own*) poseer; (*land, town*) ocupar; **to ~ the** (**absolute**) **majority** contar con la mayoría (absoluta) **6.** (*make happen*) **to ~ an election/a meeting/ a news conference** convocar elecciones/una reunión/una rueda de prensa; **to ~ talks** dar charlas **III.** *vi* **1.** (*continue*) seguir; **to ~ still** pararse; **~ tight!** ¡quieto! **2.** (*stick*) pegarse **3.** (*believe*) sostener

◆**hold back I.** *vt* (*keep*) retener; (*stop*) detener; **to ~ information** ocultar información; **to ~ tears** contener las lágrimas **II.** *vi* refrenarse; **to ~ from doing sth** abstenerse de hacer algo

◆**hold in** *vt* contener

◆**hold on** *vi* **1.** (*affix, attach*) agarrarse bien; **to be held on by/with sth** estar sujeto a/con algo **2.** (*manage to keep going*) **to ~** (**tight**) aguantar **3.** (*wait*) esperar

◆**hold onto** *vt insep* **1.** (*grasp*) agarrarse bien a **2.** (*keep*) guardar

◆**hold out I.** *vt* extender **II.** *vi* resistir; **to be unable to ~** no poder aguantar

◆**hold up** *vt* **1.** (*raise*) levantar; **to ~ one's hand** levantar la mano **2.** (*delay*) atrasar **3.** (*rob with violence*) atracar

holder ['həʊldəʳ, *Am:* 'hoʊldəʳ] *n* **1.** (*device*) soporte *m* **2.** (*person: of shares, of account*) titular *mf*

holding *n* **1.** *pl* (*tenure*) tenencia *f* **2.** ECON participación *f*; **~s** valores *mpl* en cartera

holding company *n* holding *m*

hole [həʊl, *Am:* hoʊl] *n* **1.** (*hollow space*) agujero *m* **2.** (*in golf*) hoyo *m*

holiday ['hɒlədeɪ, *Am:* 'hɑ:lə-] *n Brit, Aus* vacaciones *fpl*; **on ~** de vacaciones

holidaymaker *n* turista *mf*; (*in summer*) veraneante *mf*

holiness ['həʊlɪnɪs, *Am:* 'hoʊ] *n no pl* santidad *f*; **His/Your Holiness** Su Santidad

Holland ['hɒlənd, *Am:* 'hɑ:lənd] *n* Holanda *f*

hollow ['hɒləʊ, *Am:* 'hɑ:loʊ] **I.** *adj* hueco **II.** *n* hueco *m*; *Am* (*valley*)

hondonada *f* **III.** *vt* **to ~** (**out**) vaciar

holly ['hɒli, *Am:* 'hɑ:lɪ] *n no pl* acebo *m*

holocaust ['hɒləkɔ:st, *Am:* 'hɑ:lə-kɑ:st] *n* holocausto *m*

holy ['həʊli, *Am:* 'hoʊ-] <-ier, -iest> *adj* (*sacred*) santo; (*water*) bendito

Holy Spirit *n* Espíritu *m* Santo

homage ['hɒmɪdʒ, *Am:* 'hɑ:mɪdʒ] *n* homenaje *m*; **to pay ~ to sb** rendir homenaje a alguien

home [həʊm, *Am:* hoʊm] **I.** *n* **1.** (*residence*) casa *f*; **at ~** en casa; **to leave ~** salir [*o* irse] de casa; **away from ~** fuera de casa; **make yourself at ~** ponte cómodo, estás en tu casa **2.** (*family*) hogar *m* **3.** (*institution*) asilo *m*; (*for old people*) residencia *f*; **children's ~** orfanato *m* **II.** *adv* **to be ~** estar en casa; **to go/ come ~** ir/venir a casa **III.** *adj* **1.** (*from own country*) nacional **2.** (*from own area*) local; (*team*) de casa; **the ~ ground** el campo de casa

[?] En los EE.UU. se utiliza el término **Homecoming** para referirse a una importante fiesta que tiene lugar en la High School y la universidad. Ese día el equipo de fútbol local juega en su propio campo. Se celebra una gran fiesta y se erige **homecoming queen** a la alumna más popular.

home-grown *adj* **1.** (*vegetables*) de cosecha propia **2.** (*local*) local

homeland *n* tierra *f* natal **homeless I.** *adj* sin hogar **II.** *npl* **the ~** los sin techo

homely ['həʊmli, *Am:* 'hoʊm-] <-ier, -iest> *adj Brit, Aus* casero

home-made [ˌhəʊm'meɪd, *Am:* ˌhoʊm-] *adj* casero **homemaker** *n Am* ama *f* de casa **home town** *n* ciudad *f* natal, pueblo *m* natal

homeward ['həʊmwəd, *Am:* 'hoʊmwəʳd] **I.** *adv* de camino a casa **II.** *adj* (*journey*) de regreso **homewards** *adv s.* **homeward I.**

homework ['həʊmwɜːk, *Am:* 'hoʊmwɜːrk] *n* SCHOOL deberes *mpl*
homicide ['hɒmɪsaɪd, *Am:* 'hɑː-mə-] I. *n Am, Aus* 1. (*crime*) homicidio *m* 2. (*criminal*) homicida *mf* II. *adj* ~ **squad** *Am, Aus* homicidios *mpl*
homogeneous [ˌhɒmə'dʒiːnɪəs, *Am:* ˌhoʊmoʊ-] *adj*, **homogenous** *adj* homogéneo
homosexual [ˌhɒmə'sekʃʊəl, *Am:* ˌhoʊmoʊ-] *adj* homosexual
homosexuality [ˌhɒməsekʃʊ'æləti, *Am:* ˌhoʊmoʊsekʃʊ'æləti] *n no pl* homosexualidad *f*
Hon. *abbr of* **Honorary** Hon.
Honduran [hɒn'djʊərən, *Am:* hɑːn'dʊr-] *adj* hondureño
Honduras [hɒn'djʊərəs, *Am:* hɑːn'dʊr-] *n* Honduras *f*
hone [həʊn, *Am:* hoʊn] *vt* (*sharpen*) afilar; *fig* (*refine*) afinar
honest ['ɒnɪst, *Am:* 'ɑːnɪst] *adj* 1. (*trustworthy*) honesto 2. (*truthful*) sincero; **to be ~ with oneself** ser sincero consigo mismo
honestly *adv* (*truthfully*) sinceramente; (*with honesty*) honradamente
honesty ['ɒnɪsti, *Am:* 'ɑːnɪ-] *n no pl* 1. (*trustworthiness*) honestidad *f* 2. (*sincerity*) sinceridad *f*; **in all ~** para ser sincero
honey ['hʌni] *n no pl* 1. GASTR miel *f* 2. (*darling*) cariño *m*
honeymoon *n* luna *f* de miel
honor ['ɑːnəʳ] *n Am, Aus s.* **honour**
honorary ['ɒnərəri, *Am:* 'ɑːnərer-] *adj* 1. (*conferred as an honour: title*) honorario; (*president*) de honor 2. (*without pay*) no remunerado
honour ['ɒnəʳ] I. *n Brit* 1. (*respect*) honor *m*; **in ~ of sb/sth** en honor de alguien/algo 2. LAW **Her/His/Your Honour** Su Señoría 3. *pl* (*distinction*) honores *mpl*; **last ~s** honras *fpl* fúnebres II. *vt* 1. (*fulfil: promise, contract*) cumplir (con) 2. (*confer honour*) honrar; **to be ~ed** sentirse honrado
honourable ['ɒnərəbl] *adj Brit* 1. (*worthy of respect: person*) honorable 2. (*honest*) honrado 3. *Brit* POL

the Honourable member for ... el Ilustre Señor Diputado de...
hood [hʊd] *n* 1. (*for head*) capucha *f* 2. *Am* AUTO capó *m*
hoof [huːf, *Am:* hʊf] *n* casco *m*, pezuña *f* <hooves *o* hoofs> casco *m*, pezuña *f*
hook [hʊk] *n* (*device for holding*) gancho *m;* (*for clothes*) percha *f;* (*fish*) anzuelo *m;* **to leave the phone off the ~** dejar el teléfono descolgado
hooker ['hʊkəʳ, *Am:* -ɚ] *n Am, Aus, inf* prostituta *f*
hooligan ['huːlɪgən] *n* hooligan *mf*
hoop [huːp] *n* aro *m*
hoot [huːt] I. *vi* (*owl*) ulular; (*with horn*) tocar la bocina II. *n* (*of owl*) ululato *m;* (*of horn*) bocinazo *m*
hoover® ['huːvəʳ, *Am:* -vɚ] *n Brit, Aus* aspirador *m*
hop¹ [hɒp, *Am:* hɑːp] *n* BOT lúpulo *m*
hop² [hɒp, *Am:* hɑːp] <-pp-> I. *vi* saltar II. *n* salto *m;* (*using only one leg*) salto *m* a la pata coja, brinco *m* de cojito *Méx*
hope [həʊp, *Am:* hoʊp] I. *n* esperanza *f;* **to give up ~** perder la(s) esperanza(s); **to not have a ~ in hell** no tener ni la más remota posibilidad II. *vi* esperar
hopeful ['həʊpfəl, *Am:* 'hoʊp-] *adj* (*promising*) esperanzador; **to be ~** (*person*) ser optimista
hopefully *adv* ~! ¡ojalá!; **~ we'll be in Sweden at 6.00 pm** si todo sale bien estaremos en Suecia a las 6 de la tarde
hopeless ['həʊpləs, *Am:* 'hoʊp-] *adj* desesperado; **to be ~** *inf* (*person*) ser inútil; (*service*) ser un desastre
hopelessly *adv* sin esperanzas; **~ lost** totalmente perdido
horde [hɔːd, *Am:* hɔːrd] *n* multitud *f*
horizon [hə'raɪzn] *n a. fig* horizonte *m*
horizontal [ˌhɒrɪ'zɒntl, *Am:* ˌhɔːrɪ'zɑːn-] *adj* horizontal
hormone ['hɔːməʊn, *Am:* 'hɔːrmoʊn] *n* hormona *f*

H
h

horn [hɔːn, *Am:* hɔːrn] *n* **1.** ZOOL cuerno *m* **2.** MUS trompa *f* **3.** AUTO bocina *f*

hornet ['hɔːnɪt, *Am:* 'hɔːr-] *n* ZOOL avispón *m*

horoscope ['hɒrəskəʊp, *Am:* 'hɔːrəskoʊp] *n* horóscopo *m*

horrendous [hɒ'rendəs, *Am:* hɔː'ren-] *adj* terrible

horrible ['hɒrəbl, *Am:* 'hɔːr-] *adj*, **horrid** ['hɒrɪd, *Am:* 'hɔːr-] *adj* horrible

horrific [hə'rɪfɪk, *Am:* hɔː'rɪf-] *adj* horroroso

horrify ['hɒrɪfaɪ, *Am:* 'hɔːr-] <-ie-> *vt* horrorizar

horror ['hɒrəʳ, *Am:* 'hɔːrəʳ] *n* horror *m*, espantosidad *f AmC, Col, PRico*; ~ **film** película *f* de terror

horse [hɔːs, *Am:* hɔːrs] *n* caballo *m*; **to ride a** ~ montar a caballo; **to eat like a** ~ *inf* comer como una lima; **don't look a gift** ~ **in the mouth** *prov* a caballo regalado, no le mires el dentado *prov*

◆**horse about** *vi*, **horse around** *vi* hacer el tonto

horse racing *n* carreras *fpl* de caballos **horseshoe** *n* herradura *f*

horticultural [ˌhɔːtɪ'kʌltʃərəl, *Am:* ˌhɔːrtə'kʌltʃəʳ-] *adj no pl* hortícola

hose [həʊz, *Am:* hoʊz] *n* manguera *f*

hospice ['hɒspɪs, *Am:* 'haːspɪs] *n* **1.** (*house of shelter*) hospicio *m* **2.** (*hospital*) residencia *f* para enfermos terminales

hospitable [hɒ'spɪtəbl, *Am:* 'haːspɪtə-] *adj* hospitalario

hospital ['hɒspɪtəl, *Am:* 'haːspɪtəl] *n* hospital *m*

hospitality [ˌhɒspɪ'tæləti, *Am:* ˌhaːspɪ'tæləti] *n no pl* hospitalidad *f*

hospitalize ['hɒspɪtəlaɪz, *Am:* 'haːspɪtəl-] *vt* hospitalizar

host [həʊst, *Am:* hoʊst] I. *n* **1.** (*person who receives guests*) anfitrión, -ona *m*, *f* **2.** BIO huésped *m* II. *vt* (*party*) dar; (*event*) ser la sede de

hostage ['hɒstɪdʒ, *Am:* 'haːstɪdʒ] *n* rehén *mf*

hostel ['hɒstl, *Am:* 'haːstl] *n* (*cheap hotel*) hostal *m*; **student** ~ residencia *f* de estudiantes; **youth** ~ albergue *m* juvenil

hosteller ['hɒstələʳ, *Am:* 'haːstələʳ] *n* alberguista *mf*

hostess ['həʊstɪs, *Am:* 'hoʊ-] <-es> *n* **1.** AVIAT azafata *f* **2.** (*woman who receives guests*) anfitriona *f*

hostile ['hɒstaɪl, *Am:* 'haːstl] *adj* hostil; ~ **aircraft** avión enemigo

hostility [hɒ'stɪləti, *Am:* haː'stɪləti] <-ies> *n* hostilidad *f*

hot [hɒt, *Am:* haːt] *adj* **1.** (*food, water*) caliente; (*day, weather*) caluroso; (*climate*) cálido; **it's** ~ hace calor **2.** (*spicy*) picante, bravo *AmL*

hotel [həʊ'tel, *Am:* hoʊ-] *n* hotel *m*

hotline *n* TEL línea *f* directa; **to set up a** ~ poner una línea directa

hound [haʊnd] I. *n* perro *m* de caza II. *vt* perseguir

hour ['aʊəʳ, *Am:* 'aʊr] *n* **1.** (*60 minutes*) hora *f*; **to be paid by the** ~ cobrar por horas **2.** (*time of day*) **at all** ~**s of the day and night** noche y día; **ten minutes to the** ~ diez minutos para en punto **3.** (*time for an activity*) **lunch** ~ hora de comer; **opening** ~**s** horario *m* (comercial)

hourly *adv* (*every hour*) cada hora; (*pay*) por horas

house [haʊs] I. *n* **1.** (*inhabitation*) casa *f*; **to move** ~ mudarse; **to set one's** ~ **in order** *fig* poner sus cosas en orden **2.** (*family*) familia *f*; **the House of Windsor** la casa de Windsor II. *vt* **1.** (*give place to live*) alojar **2.** (*contain*) albergar

household ['haʊshəʊld, *Am:* -hoʊld] I. *n* hogar *m* II. *adj* doméstico **housekeeper** ['haʊsˌkiːpəʳ, *Am:* -pəʳ] *n* ama *f* de llaves **housewife** <-wives> *n* ama *f* de casa, huarmi *f AmS* **housework** *n no pl* tareas *fpl* del hogar

housing ['haʊzɪŋ] *n* vivienda *f*

housing benefit *n Brit* subsidio *m* para la vivienda

hover ['hɒvəʳ, *Am:* 'hʌvəʳ] *vi* **1.** (*stay in air*) cernerse **2.** (*be in an uncertain state*) estar vacilante

how [haʊ] *adv* **1.** (*in this way*) como; (*in which way?*) cómo; ~ **do you mean?** ¿cómo dices? **2.** (*in what condition?*) ~ **are you?** ¿qué tal?; ~ **do you do?** encantado de conocerle **3.** (*for what reason?*) ~ **come ...?** *inf* ¿cómo es que...? **4.** (*suggestion*) ~ **about ...?** ¿qué tal si... ?

however [haʊ'evəʳ, *Am:* -ɚ] **I.** *adv* **1.** (*no matter how*) por más que +*subj;* ~ **hard she tries ...** por mucho que lo intente... **2.** (*in whichever way*) como; **do it** ~ **you like** hazlo como quieras **II.** *conj* (*nevertheless*) sin embargo

howl [haʊl] **I.** *vi* **1.** (*person, animal*) aullar; (*wind*) silbar; **to** ~ **in** [*o* **with**] **pain** dar alaridos de dolor **2.** (*cry*) chillar **II.** *n* **1.** (*person, animal*) aullido *m* **2.** (*cry*) chillido *m;* **to give a** ~ **of pain** soltar un alarido de dolor

hp [ˌeɪtʃ'piː] *abbr of* **horsepower** CV

HP [ˌeɪtʃ'piː] *n Brit, inf abbr of* **hire purchase** compra *f* a plazos

HQ [ˌeɪtʃ'kjuː] *abbr of* **headquarters** sede *f* central

hub [hʌb] *n* **1.** (*of wheel*) cubo *m* **2.** *fig* (*centre*) centro *m*

hubcap [hʌbkæp] *n* tapacubos *mpl*

huckleberry ['hʌklbəri, *Am:* -'ber-] <-ies> *n Am* BOT arándano *m*

huddle ['hʌdl] *vi* apiñarse

hue [hjuː] *n no pl* (*shade*) tonalidad *f*

huff [hʌf] **I.** *vi* **to** ~ **and puff** jadear **II.** *n inf* enfado *m;* **to be in a** ~ estar de morros

hug [hʌg] **I.** <-gg-> *vt* abrazar **II.** *n* abrazo *m*

huge [hjuːdʒ] *adj* enorme

hugely *adv* enormemente

hull [hʌl] *n* NAUT casco *m*

hum [hʌm] <-mm-> **I.** *vi* **1.** (*bee*) zumbar **2.** (*sing*) tararear **II.** *vt* tararear **III.** *n* zumbido *m*

human ['hjuːmən] *adj* humano

humane [hjuː'meɪn] *adj* humanitario

humanism ['hjuːmənɪzəm] *n no pl* humanismo *m*

humanistic [ˌhjuːmə'nɪstɪk] *adj* humanista

humanitarian [hjuːˌmænɪ'teəriən,

Am: hjuːˌmænə'teri-] *adj* humanitario; ~ **aid** ayuda humanitaria

humanity [hjuː'mænəti, *Am:* -t̬i] *n no pl* humanidad *f*

humanize ['hjuːmənaɪz] *vt* humanizar

human rights *npl* derechos *mpl* humanos

humble ['hʌmbl] *adj* humilde; **in my** ~ **opinion, ...** en mi modesta opinión,...

humid ['hjuːmɪd] *adj* húmedo

humidity [hjuː'mɪdəti, *Am:* -t̬i] *n no pl* humedad *f*

humiliate [hjuː'mɪlieɪt] *vt* (*shame*) avergonzar, achunchar *AmC;* (*humble*) humillar

humiliation [hjuːˌmɪlɪ'eɪʃən] *n* humillación *f*

humility [hjuː'mɪləti, *Am:* -t̬ɪ] *n no pl* humildad *f*

humor ['hjuːməʳ, *Am:* -məɚ] *n Am, Aus s.* **humour**

humorous ['hjuːmərəs] *adj* (*speech*) humorístico; (*situation*) divertido; ~ **story** historia graciosa

humour ['hjuːməʳ, *Am:* -məɚ] *n no pl* humor *m;* **sense of** ~ sentido *m* del humor

hump [hʌmp] *n* joroba *f,* petaca *f AmC*

Hun [hʌn] *n* **1.** HIST huno, -a *m, f* **2.** *pej* (*German*) alemán, -ana *m, f*

hunch [hʌntʃ] <-es> *n* presentimiento *m;* **to have a** ~ **that ...** tener la corazonada de que...

hundred ['hʌndrəd] **I.** *adj* ciento; (*before a noun*) cien **II.** <-(s)> *n* cien *m;* ~**s of times** cientos de veces

hung [hʌŋ] *pt, pp of* **hang**

Hungarian [hʌŋ'geəriən, *Am:* -'geri-] *adj* húngaro

Hungary ['hʌŋgəri] *n* Hungría *f*

hunger ['hʌŋgəʳ, *Am:* -gɚ] *n no pl* hambre *f*

hungry ['hʌŋgri] <-ier, -iest> *adj* hambriento; **to go** ~ pasar hambre

hunk [hʌŋk] *n* **1.** (*piece*) trozo *m* **2.** *inf* (*man*) cachas *m inv*

hunt [hʌnt] **I.** *vi, vt* cazar **II.** *n* (*chase*) cacería *f*

hunter *n* cazador(a) *m(f)*

Hh

hunting *n no pl* caza *f*
hurdle ['hɜːdl, *Am:* 'hɜːr-] *n*
1. (*fence*) valla *f* **2.** (*obstacle*) obstáculo *m*
hurl [hɜːl, *Am:* hɜːrl] *vt* lanzar
hurricane ['hʌrɪkən, *Am:* 'hɜːrɪ-
keɪn] *n* huracán *m*
hurry ['hʌri, *Am:* 'hɜːr-] <-ie-> **I.** *vi*
darse prisa, apurarse *AmL* **II.** *vt*
meter prisas, apurar *AmL* **III.** *n* prisa
f, apuro *m AmL;* **what's (all) the ~?**
¿a qué viene tanta prisa?
hurt [hɜːt, *Am:* hɜːrt] **I.** <hurt,
hurt> *vi* doler **II.** <hurt, hurt> *vt*
herir; **it ~s me** me duele **III.** *adj* (*in
pain, injured*) dañado; (*grieved, distressed*) dolido **IV.** *n no pl* **1.** (*pain*)
dolor *m* **2.** (*injury*) herida *f*
husband ['hʌzbənd] *n* marido *m*
hush [hʌʃ] **I.** *n no pl* silencio *m* **II.** *interj* chitón **III.** *vi* callarse **IV.** *vt* hacer
callar
husky[1] ['hʌski] <-ier, -iest> *adj*
(*voice*) ronco
husky[2] ['hʌski] <-ies> *n* ZOOL perro
m esquimal
hustle ['hʌsl] **I.** *vt* dar prisa a **II.** *n*
ajetreo *m*
hut [hʌt] *n* cabaña *f*
hybrid ['haɪbrɪd] *n* híbrido, -a *m, f*
hydraulic [haɪ'drɒlɪk, *Am:* -'drɑː-
lɪk] *adj* hidráulico
hydrocarbon [ˌhaɪdrə'kɑːbən, *Am:*
-droʊ'kɑːr-] *n* hidrocarburo *m*
hydrogen ['haɪdrədʒən] *n no pl* hi-
drógeno *m*
hygiene ['haɪdʒiːn] *n no pl* higiene
f, salubridad *f AmL*
hymn [hɪm] *n* himno *m*
hype [haɪp] *n no pl* COM bombo *m*
publicitario
hyperbole [haɪ'pɜːbəli, *Am:* -'pɜːr-]
n no pl LIT hipérbole *f*
hypnosis [hɪp'nəʊsɪs, *Am:* -'noʊ-]
n no pl hipnosis *f inv;* **to be under ~**
estar hipnotizado
hypnotic [hɪp'nɒtɪk, *Am:* -'nɑːt̬ɪk]
adj hipnótico
hypocrisy [hɪ'pɒkrəsi, *Am:* -'pɑː-
krə-] *n no pl* hipocresía *f*
hypocrite ['hɪpəkrɪt] *n* hipócrita *mf*
hypocritical [ˌhɪpə'krɪtɪkl, *Am:*

-'krɪt̬-] *adj* hipócrita
hypothesis [haɪ'pɒθəsɪs, *Am:*
-'pɑːθə-] *n* <-es> hipótesis *f inv*
hypothetical [ˌhaɪpə'θetɪkl, *Am:*
-poʊ'θet̬-] *adj* hipotético
hysteria [hɪ'stɪəriə, *Am:* -'sterɪ-] *n
no pl* histeria *f*
hysterical *adj* histérico

I, i [aɪ] *n* I, i *f;* **~ for Isaac** *Brit,* **~ for
Item** *Am* I de Italia
I [aɪ] *pron pers* yo; **~'m coming** ya
voy; **~'ll do it** (yo) lo haré; **am ~
late?** ¿llego tarde?
IAEA *n abbr of* **International
Atomic Energy Agency** OIEA *f*
ibid. [ɪ'bɪd] *adv abbr of* **ibidem** ibid.
ice [aɪs] *n no pl* hielo *m;* **to be skating on thin ~** andar sobre terreno
peligroso; **to break the ~** *inf* romper
el hielo; **to put sth on ~** posponer
algo
Ice Age *n* época *f* glacial **iceberg** *n*
iceberg *m;* **the tip of the ~** *fig* la
punta del iceberg **ice cream** *n* helado *m*, nieve *f AmC* **ice cube** *n* cubito *m* de hielo **ice hockey** *n no pl*
hockey *m* sobre hielo
Icelander ['aɪsləndər, *Am:* -də-] *n*
islandés, -esa *m, f*
Icelandic [aɪs'lændɪk] *adj* islandés
ice rink *n* pista *f* de patinaje **ice-
-skating** *n no pl* patinaje *m* sobre
hielo
icicle ['aɪsɪkl] *n* carámbano *m*
icing ['aɪsɪŋ] *n* glaseado *m*
icing sugar *n no pl* azúcar *m* glas
icon ['aɪkɒn, *Am:* -kɑːn] *n* icono *m*
icy ['aɪsi] <-ier, -iest> *adj* helado;
(*unfriendly*) frío
ID [ˌaɪ'diː] *abbr of* **identification**
identificación *f*
idea [aɪ'dɪə, *Am:* -'diːə] *n* idea *f;* **to
get an ~ of sth** hacerse una idea de

algo

ideal [aɪˈdɪəl, *Am:* -ˈdiː-] *adj* ideal

idealism [aɪˈdɪəlɪzəm, *Am:* aɪˈdiː-ə-] *n no pl* idealismo *m*

idealist [aɪˈdɪəlɪst, *Am:* -ˈdiː-ə-] *n* idealista *mf*

idealistic [ˌaɪdɪəˈlɪstɪk] *adj* idealista

idealize [aɪˈdɪəlaɪz, *Am:* -ˈdiː-ə-] *vt* idealizar

identical [aɪˈdentɪkl, *Am:* -t̬ə-] *adj* idéntico, individual *CSur*

identifiable [aɪˈdentɪˌfaɪəbl, *Am:* -ˌdent̬ə-] *adj* identificable

identification [aɪˌdentɪfɪˈkeɪʃən, *Am:* -t̬ə-] *n no pl* identificación *f*

identify [aɪˈdentɪfaɪ, *Am:* -t̬ə-] <-ie-> *vt* identificar

identity [aɪˈdentəti, *Am:* -t̬ət̬i] <-ies> *n* identidad *f*

ideological [ˌaɪdɪəˈlɒdʒɪkl, *Am:* -ˈlɑːdʒɪ-] *adj* ideológico

ideology [ˌaɪdɪˈɒlədʒi, *Am:* -ˈɑːlə-] <-ies> *n* ideología *f*

idiom [ˈɪdɪəm] *n* LING **1.** (*phrase*) modismo *m* **2.** (*style of expression*) lenguaje *m*

idiomatic [ˌɪdɪəˈmætɪk, *Am:* -ˈmæt̬-] *adj* idiomático

idiosyncratic [ˌɪdɪəʊsɪŋˈkrætɪk, *Am:* -oʊsɪnˈkræt̬-] *adj* idiosincrático

idiot [ˈɪdɪət] *n* idiota *mf*

idiotic [ˌɪdɪˈɒtɪk, *Am:* -ˈɑːt̬ɪk] *adj* tonto

idle [ˈaɪdl] *adj* (*lazy*) holgazán; (*with nothing to do*) desocupado; (*machine*) parado; (*fear*) infundado

idol [ˈaɪdl] *n* ídolo *m*

idolize [ˈaɪdəlaɪz] *vt* idolatrar

idyll [ˈɪdɪl, *Am:* ˈaɪdəl] *n* idilio *m*

idyllic [ɪˈdɪlɪk, *Am:* aɪ-] *adj* idílico

i.e. [ˌaɪˈiː] *abbr of* **id est** i.e.

if [ɪf] *conj* si; ~ **it snows** si nieva; **as ~ it were true** como si fuera verdad; ~ **he needs me, I'll help him** si me necesita, le ayudaré; **I wonder ~ he'll come** me pregunto si vendrá; **cold ~ sunny weather** clima soleado aunque frío

ignite [ɪgˈnaɪt] *vi, vt* incendiar(se)

ignition [ɪgˈnɪʃən] *n no pl* AUTO encendido *m*

ignorance [ˈɪgnərəns] *n no pl* ignorancia *f*

ignorant [ˈɪgnərənt] *adj* ignorante; **to be ~ about sth** desconocer algo

ignore [ɪgˈnɔːʳ, *Am:* -ˈnɔːr] *vt* no hacer caso de, ignorar

iguana [ɪˈgwɑːnə] *n* iguana *f*, basilisco *m Méx*

ill [ɪl] *adj* enfermo; **an ~ omen** un mal presagio

illegal [ɪˈliːgəl] *adj* ilegal

illegality [ˌɪlɪˈgæləti, *Am:* -t̬i] <-ies> *n* ilegalidad *f*

illegible [ɪˈledʒəbl] *adj* ilegible

illegitimate [ˌɪlɪˈdʒɪtɪmət, *Am:* -ˈdʒɪt̬ə-] *adj* ilegítimo

ill-fated *adj* desafortunado

illicit [ɪˈlɪsɪt] *adj* ilícito

illiteracy [ɪˈlɪtərəsi, *Am:* -ˈlɪt̬-] *n no pl* analfabetismo *m*

illiterate [ɪˈlɪtərət, *Am:* -ˈlɪt̬-] *adj* analfabeto

illness [ˈɪlnɪs] <-es> *n* enfermedad *f*

illogical [ɪˈlɒdʒɪkl, *Am:* -ˈlɑːdʒɪ-] *adj* ilógico

illuminate [ɪˈluːmɪneɪt, *Am:* -mə-] *vt* iluminar

illumination [ɪˌluːmɪˈneɪʃən, *Am:* -ˌluː-] *n* **1.** *no pl* a. ART iluminación *f* **2.** *pl, Brit* luces *fpl*

illusion [ɪˈluːʒən, *Am:* -ˈluː-] *n* ilusión *f*; **to have no ~s (about sth)** no tener esperanzas (en algo); **to be under the ~ that ...** estar equivocado creyendo que...

illustrate [ˈɪləstreɪt] *vt* ilustrar

illustration [ˌɪləˈstreɪʃən] *n* ilustración *f*; **by way of ~** a modo de ejemplo

illustrative [ˈɪləstrətɪv, *Am:* ɪˈlʌstrətɪv] *adj form* ilustrativo

illustrator [ˈɪləstreɪtəʳ, *Am:* -t̬ɚ] *n* ilustrador(a) *m(f)*

illustrious [ɪˈlʌstrɪəs] *adj form* ilustre

image [ˈɪmɪdʒ] *n* **1.** (*likeness*) imagen *f* **2.** (*reputation*) reputación *f*

imagery [ˈɪmɪdʒəri] *n no pl* imágenes *fpl*

imaginable [ɪˈmædʒɪnəbl] *adj* imaginable

imaginary [ɪˈmædʒɪnəri, *Am:* -əner-] *adj* imaginario

imagination [ɪˌmædʒɪˈneɪʃən] *n* imaginación *f*; (*inventiveness*) inventiva *f*

imaginative [ɪˈmædʒɪnətɪv, *Am:* -t̬ɪv] *adj* imaginativo

imagine [ɪˈmædʒɪn] *vt* **1.** (*form mental image*) imaginar **2.** (*suppose*) figurarse

imbalance [ˌɪmˈbæləns] *n* desequilibrio *m*

imbecile [ˈɪmbəsiːl, *Am:* -sɪl] *n* imbécil *mf*

IMF [ˌaɪemˈef] *n no pl abbr of* **International Monetary Fund** FMI *m*

imitate [ˈɪmɪteɪt] *vt* imitar

imitation [ˌɪmɪˈteɪʃən] *n* **1.** (*mimicry*) imitación *f* **2.** (*copy*) reproducción *f*

imitator [ˈɪmɪteɪtəʳ, *Am:* -t̬ɚ] *n* imitador(a) *m(f)*

immaculate [ɪˈmækjʊlət] *adj* inmaculado

immaterial [ˌɪməˈtɪərɪəl, *Am:* -ˈtɪrɪ-] *adj* **1.** (*intangible*) inmaterial **2.** (*not important*) irrelevante

immature [ˌɪməˈtjʊəʳ, *Am:* -ˈtʊr] *adj* inmaduro; (*fruit*) verde

immediate [ɪˈmiːdɪət, *Am:* -diːt] *adj* inmediato; **the ~ family** la familia directa; **in the ~ area** en las inmediaciones

immediately *adv* inmediatamente; ~ **after ...** justo después de...

immense [ɪˈmens] *adj* inmenso

immensely *adv* enormemente

immerse [ɪˈmɜːs, *Am:* -ˈmɜːrs] *vt* sumergir; **to ~ oneself in sth** *fig* sumirse en algo

immigrant [ˈɪmɪɡrənt] *n* inmigrante *mf*

immigrate [ˈɪmɪɡreɪt] *vi* inmigrar

immigration [ˌɪmɪˈɡreɪʃən] *n no pl* inmigración *f*

imminent [ˈɪmɪnənt] *adj* inminente

immobilize [ɪˈməʊbəlaɪz, *Am:* -ˈmoʊ-] *vt* inmovilizar

immoral [ɪˈmɒrəl, *Am:* -ˈmɔːr-] *adj* inmoral

immortal [ɪˈmɔːtl, *Am:* -ˈmɔːrt̬l] *adj* inmortal

immortality [ˌɪmɔːˈtæləti, *Am:* -ɔːrˈtæləti] *n no pl* inmortalidad *f*

immune [ɪˈmjuːn] *adj* inmune

immunity [ɪˈmjuːnəti, *Am:* -t̬i] *n no pl* inmunidad *f*

impact [ˈɪmpækt] *n no pl* impacto *m*

impair [ɪmˈpeəʳ, *Am:* -ˈper] *vt* (*weaken*) debilitar; (*health*) perjudicar

impart [ɪmˈpɑːt, *Am:* -ˈpɑːrt] *vt form* impartir

impartial [ɪmˈpɑːʃl, *Am:* -ˈpɑːr-] *adj* imparcial

impasse [ˈæmpɑːs, *Am:* ˈɪmpæs] *n no pl* callejón *m* sin salida

impassioned [ɪmˈpæʃnd] *adj* apasionado

impatience [ɪmˈpeɪʃns] *n no pl* impaciencia *f*

impatient [ɪmˈpeɪʃnt] *adj* impaciente

impeachment *n* acusación *f* (*proceso de incapacitación presidencial*)

impeccable [ɪmˈpekəbl] *adj* impecable

impede [ɪmˈpiːd] *vt* impedir

impediment [ɪmˈpedɪmənt] *n* impedimento *m*

impending *adj* inminente

impenetrable [ɪmˈpenɪtrəbl] *adj* impenetrable; (*incomprehensible*) incomprensible

imperative [ɪmˈperətɪv, *Am:* -t̬ɪv] *n* imperativo *m*

imperceptible [ˌɪmpəˈseptəbl, *Am:* -pɚˈseptə-] *adj* imperceptible

imperfect [ɪmˈpɜːfɪkt, *Am:* -ˈpɜːr-] *adj* imperfecto; (*flawed*) defectuoso

imperfection [ˌɪmpəˈfekʃən, *Am:* -pɚˈ-] *n* imperfección *f*

imperial [ɪmˈpɪərɪəl, *Am:* -ˈpɪr-] *adj* imperial

imperialism [ɪmˈpɪərɪəlɪzəm, *Am:* -ˈpɪr-] *n no pl* imperialismo *m*

imperialist [ɪmˈpɪərɪəlɪst, *Am:* -ˈpɪri-] *n* imperialista *mf*

imperious [ɪmˈpɪərɪəs, *Am:* -ˈpɪrɪ-] *adj* imperioso

impersonal [ˌɪmˈpɜːsənl, *Am:* -ˈpɜːr-] *adj* impersonal

impersonate [ɪmˈpɜːsəneɪt, *Am:* -ˈpɜːr-] *vt* hacerse pasar por; (*imitate*) imitar

impertinent [ɪmˈpɜːtɪnənt, *Am:*

-'pɜːrt̩n-] *adj* impertinente
impervious [ɪm'pɜːvɪəs, *Am:* -'pɜːr-] *adj* impermeable; (*not affected*) inmune
impetuous [ɪm'petʃʊəs, *Am:* -'petʃu-] *adj* impetuoso
impetus ['ɪmpɪtəs, *Am:* -təs] *n no pl* 1. (*driving force*) ímpetu *m* 2. *fig* impulso *m*
impinge [ɪm'pɪndʒ] *vi* to ~ on sth afectar a algo
implacable [ɪm'plækəbl] *adj* implacable
implant [ɪm'plɑːnt, *Am:* -'plænt] *vt* implantar
implausible [ɪm'plɔːzɪbl, *Am:* -'plɑː-] *adj* inverosímil
implement ['ɪmplɪmənt] I. *n* (*tool*) instrumento *m*; (*small tool*) utensilio *m* II. *vt* implementar
implementation [ˌɪmplɪmen'teɪʃən] *n no pl* implementación *f*
implicate ['ɪmplɪkeɪt] *vt* implicar
implication [ˌɪmplɪ'keɪʃən] *n no pl* (*hinting at*) insinuación *f*; by ~ implícitamente
implicit [ɪm'plɪsɪt] *adj*, **implied** [ɪm'plaɪd] *adj* implícito
implore [ɪm'plɔːr, *Am:* -'plɔːr] *vt* implorar; to ~ sb to do sth suplicar a alguien que haga algo
imply [ɪm'plaɪ] <-ie-> *vt* 1. (*suggest*) insinuar 2. *form* (*require*) implicar
impolite [ˌɪmpə'laɪt] *adj* descortés
import [ɪm'pɔːt, *Am:* -'pɔːrt] I. *vt* importar II. *n* ECON producto *m* de importación
importance [ɪm'pɔːtns, *Am:* -'pɔːr-] *n no pl* importancia *f*
important [ɪm'pɔːtənt, *Am:* -'pɔːr-] *adj* importante
importantly *adv* significativamente
impose [ɪm'pəʊz, *Am:* -'poʊz] I. *vt* imponer II. *vi* to ~ on sb aprovecharse de alguien
imposing [ɪm'pəʊzɪŋ, *Am:* -'poʊ-] *adj* imponente
imposition [ˌɪmpə'zɪʃən] *n* 1. *no pl* (*forcing*) imposición *f* 2. (*inconvenience*) molestia *f*
impossibility [ɪmˌpɒsə'bɪləti, *Am:*

-ˌpɑːsə'bɪləti] *n no pl* imposibilidad *f*
impossible [ɪm'pɒsəbl, *Am:* -'pɑːsə-] *adj* imposible; (*person*) insoportable
impotence ['ɪmpətəns, *Am:* -təns] *n no pl* impotencia *f*
impotent ['ɪmpətənt, *Am:* -tənt] *adj* impotente
impound [ɪm'paʊnd] *vt* incautar
impractical [ɪm'præktɪkl] *adj* poco práctico
imprecise [ˌɪmprɪ'saɪs] *adj* impreciso
impress [ɪm'pres] *vt* impresionar; to ~ sth on sb inculcar algo a alguien
impression [ɪm'preʃən] *n* 1. (*general opinion*) impresión *f*; to be of the ~ that ... tener la impresión de que...; to make an ~ on sb causar impresión a alguien 2. (*imitation*) imitación *f*
impressionable [ɪm'preʃənəbl] *adj* impresionable
impressionist [ɪm'preʃnɪst] *n* ART impresionista *mf*
impressive [ɪm'presɪv] *adj* impresionante
imprint [ɪm'prɪnt] I. *vt* imprimir; (*in memory*) grabar II. *n* (*mark*) marca *f*
imprison [ɪm'prɪzən] *vt* encarcelar
imprisonment [ɪm'prɪzənmənt] *n no pl* encarcelamiento *m*
improbable [ɪm'prɒbəbl, *Am:* -'prɑːbə-] *adj* improbable
impromptu [ɪm'prɒmptjuː, *Am:* -'prɑːmptuː] *adj* de improviso
improper [ɪm'prɒpər, *Am:* -'prɑːpɚ] *adj* incorrecto; (*immoral*) indecente
improve [ɪm'pruːv] *vt, vi* mejorar
◆**improve on** *vi* superar
improvement [ɪm'pruːvmənt] *n* mejora *f*; (*progress*) progreso *m*; (*of patient*) mejoría *f*
improvisation [ˌɪmprəvaɪ'zeɪʃən, *Am:* ɪmˌprɑːvɪ'-] *n* improvisación *f*
improvise ['ɪmprəvaɪz] *vi, vt* improvisar
impudent ['ɪmpʊdənt] *adj* impertinente

impulse ['ɪmpʌls] *n* impulso *m*; **to do sth on** (**an**) ~ hacer algo por impulso

impulsive [ɪm'pʌlsɪv] *adj* impulsivo

impunity [ɪm'pjuːnəti, *Am:* -ṭi] *n no pl* impunidad *f*

impurity [ɪm'pjʊərəti, *Am:* -'pjʊrəṭi] <-ies> *n* impureza *f*

in¹ [ɪn] **I.** *prep* **1.** (*place*) en; (*inside*) dentro de; **to be** ~ **bed** estar en la cama; **there is sth** ~ **the drawer** hay algo dentro del cajón; ~ **town** en la ciudad; ~ **the country** en el país; ~ **Spain** en España; ~ **the picture** en el cuadro; **the best** ~ **Scotland** lo mejor de Escocia **2.** (*position*) ~ **the beginning/end** al principio/final; **right** ~ **the middle** justo en medio **3.** (*time*) ~ **the twenties** en los (años) veinte; **to be** ~ **one's thirties** estar en los treinta; ~ **May** en mayo; ~ **the afternoon** por la tarde; ~ **a week** en una semana; ~ (**the**) **future** en el futuro; **to do sth** ~ **4 hours** hacer algo en 4 horas; **he hasn't done that** ~ **years** no ha hecho eso desde hace años **4.** (*situation*) ~ **fashion** de moda; **dressed** ~ **red** vestido de rojo; ~ **your place** *fig* en tu lugar **5.** (*concerning*) **to be interested** ~ **sth** estar interesado en algo; **to have confidence** ~ **sb** tener confianza en alguien; **to have a say** ~ **the matter** tener algo que decir al respecto; **a change** ~ **attitude** un cambio de actitud; **a rise** ~ **prices** un aumento de precios **6.** (*by*) ~ **saying sth** al decir algo **7.** (*taking form of*) **to speak** ~ **English** hablar en inglés; ~ **wood** de madera; **to speak** ~ **a loud voice** hablar en voz alta; **2 metres** ~ **length** 2 metros de largo **8.** (*ratio*) **two** ~ **six** dos de cada seis; **to buy sth** ~ **twos** comprar algo de dos en dos; ~ **tens** en grupos de diez **9.** (*as conseqence of*) ~ **return** a cambio; ~ **reply** como respuesta **II.** *adv* dentro, adentro; **to go** ~ entrar; **to put sth** ~ meter algo (dentro); **to be** ~ *inf* (*at home*) estar en casa; (*popular*) estar de moda; **to be** ~ **on sth** estar enterado de algo **III.** *adj* de moda **IV.** *n* ~**s and outs** recovecos *mpl*

in² *abbr of* **inch** pulgada *f*

inability [ˌɪnə'bɪləti, *Am:* -ṭi] *n no pl* incapacidad *f*

inaccessible [ˌɪnæk'sesəbl] *adj* inaccesible

inaccuracy [ɪn'ækjʊrəsi, *Am:* -jɚə-] <-ies> *n* **1.** (*fact*) error *m* **2.** *no pl* (*quality*) imprecisión *f*

inaccurate [ɪn'ækjərət, *Am:* -jɚət] *adj* **1.** (*inexact*) inexacto **2.** (*wrong*) equivocado

inaction [ɪn'ækʃən] *n no pl* inacción *f*

inactive [ɪn'æktɪv] *adj* inactivo

inadequacy [ɪn'ædɪkwəsi] <-ies> *n* **1.** (*insufficiency*) insuficiencia *f* **2.** *no pl* (*quality of being inadequate*) falta *f* de adecuación

inadequate [ɪn'ædɪkwət] *adj* inadecuado

inadmissible [ˌɪnəd'mɪsəbl] *adj* inadmisible

inane [ɪ'neɪn] *adj* estúpido

inanimate [ɪn'ænɪmət] *adj* inanimado

inappropriate [ˌɪnə'prəʊprɪət, *Am:* -'proʊ-] *adj* inapropiado

inaudible [ɪn'ɔːdəbl, *Am:* -'ɑː-] *adj* inaudible

inaugural [ɪ'nɔːdʒʊrəl, *Am:* -'nɑːg-] *adj* inaugural

inaugurate [ɪ'nɔːdʒʊreɪt, *Am:* -'nɑːg-] *vt* inaugurar

inauguration [ɪˌnɔːdʒʊ'reɪʃən, *Am:* -ˌnɑːg-] *n* inauguración *f*

inauspicious [ˌɪnɔː'spɪʃəs, *Am:* -ɑː'spɪʃ-] *adj* poco propicio

in-between *adj* intermedio

Inc. [ɪŋk] *abbr of* **Incorporated** Inc.

incapability [ɪnˌkeɪpə'bɪləti, *Am:* -ṭi] *n no pl* incapacidad *f*

incapable [ɪn'keɪpəbl] *adj* incapaz; **to be** ~ **of doing sth** no ser capaz de hacer algo

incapacity [ˌɪnkə'pæsəti, *Am:* -ṭi] *n no pl* incapacidad *f*

incarcerate [ɪn'kɑːsəreɪt, *Am:* -'kɑːr-] *vt* encarcelar

incarnate [ɪn'kɑːneɪt, *Am:* -'kɑːr-]

adj encarnado

incarnation [ˌɪnkɑːˈneɪʃən, *Am:* -kɑːrˈ-] *n* encarnación *f*

incense¹ [ˈɪnsents] *n* incienso *m*

incense² [ɪnˈsents] *vt* indignar

incentive [ɪnˈsentɪv, *Am:* -t̬ɪv] *n* incentivo *m*

inception [ɪnˈsepʃən] *n no pl* inicio *m*

incessant [ɪnˈsesnt] *adj* incesante

incest [ˈɪnsest] *n no pl* incesto *m*

inch [ɪntʃ] <-es> *n* pulgada *f;* **she knows every ~ of Madrid** conoce cada centímetro de Madrid; **give someone an ~ and they'll take a mile** *prov* les das la mano y te cogen el brazo *prov*

◆ **inch forward** *vi* avanzar lentamente

incidence [ˈɪntsɪdənts] *n no pl* incidencia *f*

incident [ˈɪntsɪdənt] *n* incidente *m*

incidental [ˌɪntsɪˈdentəl, *Am:* -t̬əl] *adj* secundario

incidentally *adv* por cierto

incinerator [ɪnˈsɪnəreɪtəʳ, *Am:* -t̬ɚ] *n* incinerador *m*

incisive [ɪnˈsaɪsɪv] *adj* incisivo

incisor [ɪnˈsaɪzəʳ, *Am:* -zɚ] *n* incisivo *m*

incite [ɪnˈsaɪt] *vt* instigar

inclement [ɪnˈklemənt] *adj* inclemente

inclination [ˌɪnklɪˈneɪʃən] *n* (*tendency*) propensión *f;* **to have an ~ to do sth** tener inclinación a hacer algo

incline [ɪnˈklaɪn] *vi* **1.** (*tend*) tender **2.** (*lean*) inclinarse

inclined [ɪnˈklaɪnd] *adj* **to be ~ to do sth** estar dispuesto a hacer algo

include [ɪnˈkluːd] *vt* incluir; (*in letter*) adjuntar

including [ɪnˈkluːdɪŋ] *prep* incluso; **~ tax** impuesto incluido

inclusion [ɪnˈkluːʒən] *n no pl* inclusión *f*

inclusive [ɪnˈkluːsɪv] *adj* incluido

incognito [ˌɪnkɒgˈniːtəʊ, *Am:* ˌɪnkɑːgˈniːtoʊ] *adv* de incógnito

incoherent [ˌɪnkəʊˈhɪərənt, *Am:* -koʊˈhɪrənt] *adj* incoherente

income [ˈɪŋkʌm, *Am:* ˈɪn-] *n no pl* ingresos *mpl*

income tax *n no pl* impuesto *m* sobre la renta

incoming [ˈɪnˌkʌmɪŋ] *adj* entrante

incomparable [ɪnˈkɒmprəbl, *Am:* -ˈkɑːm-] *adj* incomparable

incompatibility [ˌɪnkəmˌpætəˈbɪlɪti, *Am:* -ˌpæt̬əˈbɪlət̬i] <-ies> *n no pl* incompatibilidad *f*

incompatible [ˌɪnkəmˈpætəbl, *Am:* -ˈpæt̬-] *adj* incompatible

incompetence [ɪnˈkɒmpɪtənts, *Am:* -ˈkɑːmpət̬ənts] *n no pl* incompetencia *f*

incompetent [ɪnˈkɒmpɪtənt, *Am:* -ˈkɑːmpət̬ənt] *adj* incompetente

incomplete [ˌɪnkəmˈpliːt] *adj* incompleto; (*not finished*) inacabado

incomprehensible [ɪnˌkɒmprɪˈhensəbl, *Am:* ˌɪnkɑːm-] *adj* incomprensible

inconceivable [ˌɪnkənˈsiːvəbl] *adj* inconcebible

inconclusive [ˌɪnkənˈkluːsɪv] *adj* inconcluyente

incongruous [ɪnˈkɒŋgrʊəs, *Am:* -ˈkɑːŋ-] *adj* incongruente

inconsequential [ɪnˌkɒnsɪˈkwenʃl, *Am:* -ˈkɑːn-] *adj* **1.** (*illogical*) inconsecuente **2.** (*unimportant*) intrascendente

inconsiderate [ˌɪnkənˈsɪdərət] *adj* desconsiderado

inconsistency [ˌɪnkənˈsɪstəntsi] <-ies> *n* **1.** (*lack of consistency*) falta *f* de coherencia **2.** (*discrepancy*) contradicción *f*

inconsistent [ˌɪnkənˈsɪstənt] *adj* **1.** (*changeable*) incoherente **2.** (*lacking agreement*) contradictorio

inconspicuous [ˌɪnkənˈspɪkjʊəs] *adj* desapercibido

inconvenience [ˌɪnkənˈviːnɪəns] *n* inconveniencia *f*

inconvenient [ˌɪnkənˈviːnɪənt] *adj* inconveniente; (*time*) inoportuno

incorporate [ɪnˈkɔːpəreɪt, *Am:* -ˈkɔːr-] *vt* **1.** (*integrate*) incorporar; (*work into*) integrar; (*add*) añadir **2.** (*include*) incluir **3.** *Am* LAW, ECON constituir

incorporation [ɪnˌkɔːpəˈreɪʃən, *Am:* -ˌkɔːr-] *n no pl* **1.** (*integration*) incorporación *f;* (*working into*) integración *f* **2.** LAW, ECON constitución *f*

incorrect [ˌɪnkəˈrekt] *adj* **1.** (*wrong, untrue*) incorrecto; (*diagnosis*) erróneo **2.** (*improper*) inapropiado

increase **I.** [ɪnˈkriːs, *Am:* ˈɪn-] *vi* incrementar; (*grow*) crecer **II.** *vt* incrementar; (*make stronger*) intensificar **III.** [ˈɪnˈkriːs] *n* incremento *m;* **to be on the** ~ ir en aumento

increasing *adj* creciente

incredible [ɪnˈkredɪbl] *adj* increíble

incredibly *adv* increíblemente

incredulity [ˌɪnkrɪˈdjuːləti, *Am:* -ˈduːləti] *n no pl* incredulidad *f*

incredulous [ɪnˈkredjʊləs, *Am:* -ˈkredʒʊ-] *adj* incrédulo

increment [ˈɪŋkrəmənt] *n* incremento *m*

incubator [ˈɪŋkjʊbeɪtəʳ, *Am:* -t̬ɚ] *n* incubadora *f*

inculcate [ˈɪnkʌlkeɪt] *vt* inculcar

incur [ɪnˈkɜːʳ, *Am:* -ˈkɜːr] <-rr-> *vt* (*costs*) incurrir en; (*losses*) sufrir; **to** ~ **the anger of sb** provocar el enfado de alguien

incursion [ɪnˈkɜːʃən, *Am:* -ˈkɜːr-] *n* intrusión *f;* MIL incursión *f*

indebted [ɪnˈdetɪd, *Am:* -ˈdet̬-] *adj* **to be** ~ **to sb for sth** estar en deuda con alguien por algo

indecent [ɪnˈdiːsənt] *adj* indecente

indecision [ˌɪndɪˈsɪʒən] *n no pl* indecisión *f*

indecisive [ˌɪndɪˈsaɪsɪv] *adj* indeciso

indeed [ɪnˈdiːd] **I.** *adv* **1.** (*really*) realmente; **to be very rich** ~ ser verdaderamente rico **2.** (*affirmation*) en efecto **II.** *interj* ya lo creo

indefinite [ɪnˈdefɪnət, *Am:* -ənət] *adj* indefinido

indelible [ɪnˈdeləbl] *adj* indeleble

indemnity [ɪnˈdemnəti, *Am:* -t̬i] <-ies> *n form* **1.** *no pl* (*insurance*) indemnidad *f* **2.** (*compensation*) indemnización *f*

independence [ˌɪndɪˈpendəns] *n no pl* independencia *f*

independent [ˌɪndɪˈpendənt] *adj* independiente

in-depth *adj* exhaustivo

indeterminate [ˌɪndɪˈtɜːmɪnət, *Am:* -ˈtɜːr-] *adj* indeterminado

index [ˈɪndeks] *n* <-ices *o* -es> índice *m*

index finger *n* dedo *m* índice

India [ˈɪndɪə] *n no pl* la India *f*

Indian [ˈɪndɪən] *adj* **1.** (*of India*) indio, hindú **2.** (*of America*) indio, indígena

Indian Ocean *n no pl* Océano *m* Índico

indicate [ˈɪndɪkeɪt] *vt* indicar

indication [ˌɪndɪˈkeɪʃən] *n* indicio *m*

indicative [ɪnˈdɪkətɪv, *Am:* -t̬ɪv] *adj* indicativo

indicator [ˈɪndɪkeɪtəʳ, *Am:* -t̬ɚ] *n Brit* AUTO intermitente *m*

indict [ɪnˈdaɪt] *vt* **to** ~ **sb of sth** LAW acusar a alguien de algo

indictment [ɪnˈdaɪtmənt] *n* LAW acusación *f; fig* crítica *f*

Indies [ˈɪndiz] *npl* Indias *fpl*

indifference [ɪnˈdɪfrəns] *n no pl* indiferencia *f*

indifferent [ɪnˈdɪfrənt] *adj* mediocre

indigenous [ɪnˈdɪdʒɪnəs] *adj* indígena

indigestion [ˌɪndɪˈdʒəstʃən] *n no pl* indigestión *f*

indignant [ɪnˈdɪɡnənt] *adj* indignado; **to become** ~ indignarse

indignation [ˌɪndɪɡˈneɪʃən] *n no pl* indignación *f*

indignity [ɪnˈdɪɡnɪti, *Am:* -nət̬i] <-ies> *n no pl* indignidad *f*

indirect [ˌɪndɪˈrekt] *adj* indirecto

indiscipline [ɪnˈdɪsɪplɪn] *n no pl, form* falta *f* de disciplina

indiscreet [ˌɪndɪˈskriːt] *adj* indiscreto

indiscriminate [ˌɪndɪˈskrɪmɪnət] *adj* **1.** (*uncritical*) sin criterio **2.** (*random*) indiscriminado

indispensable [ˌɪndɪˈspensəbl] *adj* indispensable

indistinguishable [ˌɪndɪˈstɪŋɡwɪʃəbl] *adj* indistinguible

individual [ˌɪndɪˈvɪdʒuəl] **I.** *n* individuo, -a *m, f* **II.** *adj* individual

individualism [ˌɪndɪˈvɪdʒuəlɪzəm] *n no pl* individualismo *m*
individualist *n* individualista *mf*
individualistic [ˌɪndɪˌvɪdʒuəˈlɪstɪk] *adj* individualista
individuality [ˌɪndɪˌvɪdʒuˈæləti, *Am:* -ˌvɪdʒuˈæləti] *n no pl* individualidad *f*
Indochina [ˌɪdəʊˈtʃaɪnə] *n* Indochina *f*
indoctrinate [ɪnˈdɒktrɪneɪt, *Am:* -ˈdɑːk-] *vt* adoctrinar
indolent [ˈɪndələnt] *adj* indolente
Indonesia [ˌɪndəʊˈniːziə, *Am:* -dəˈniːʒə] *n* Indonesia *f*
Indonesian *adj* indonesio
indoor [ˈɪndɔːʳ, *Am:* ˌɪnˈdɔːr] *adj* interior; (*pool*) cubierto
indoors [ˌɪnˈdɔːz, *Am:* -ˈdɔːrz] *adv* dentro
induce [ɪnˈdjuːs, *Am:* -ˈduːs] *vt* **1.** (*persuade*) inducir **2.** (*cause*) provocar
inducement [ɪnˈdjuːsmənt, *Am:* -ˈduːs-] *n* incentivo *m*
induction [ɪnˈdʌkʃən] *n* iniciación *f*
indulge [ɪnˈdʌldʒ] *vt* (*person*) consentir; (*desire*) satisfacer
indulgence [ɪnˈdʌldʒəns] *n* (*treat*) placer *m;* (*satisfaction*) satisfacción *f*
indulgent [ɪnˈdʌldʒənt] *adj* indulgente
industrial [ɪnˈdʌstriəl] *adj* industrial; (*dispute*) laboral
industrial estate *n* polígono *m* industrial
industrialization [ɪnˌdʌstriəlaɪˈzeɪʃən, *Am:* -lɪˈ-] *n no pl* industrialización *f*
industrial park *n Am* polígono *m* industrial **Industrial Revolution** *n* Revolución *f* Industrial
industrious [ɪnˈdʌstriəs] *adj* trabajador
industry [ˈɪndəstri] *n* **1.** industria *f;* (*branch*) sector *m* **2.** *no pl* (*diligence*) laboriosidad *f*
inedible [ɪnˈedəbl] *adj* no comestible
ineffective [ˌɪnɪˈfektɪv] *adj*, **ineffectual** [ˌɪnɪˈfektʃuəl] *adj* ineficaz
inefficiency [ˌɪnɪˈfɪʃənsi] *n no pl*

ineficiencia *f*
inefficient [ˌɪnɪˈfɪʃnt] *adj* ineficiente
ineligible [ɪnˈelɪdʒəbl] *adj* inelegible; **to be ~ to do sth** no tener derecho a hacer algo
inept [ɪˈnept] *adj* (*unskilled*) inepto; (*inappropriate*) inoportuno
inequality [ˌɪnɪˈkwɒləti, *Am:* -ˈkwɑːləti] <-ies> *n* desigualdad *f*
inequity [ɪnˈekwəti, *Am:* -ti] <-ies> *n* injusticia *f*
inert [ɪˈnɜːt, *Am:* -ˈnɜːrt] *adj* inerte; *fig* inmóvil
inertia [ɪˈnɜːʃə, *Am:* ˌɪnˈɜːr-] *n no pl* inercia *f*
inescapable [ˌɪnɪˈskeɪpəbl] *adj* ineludible
inevitable [ɪnˈevɪtəbl, *Am:* -t̬ə-] *adj* inevitable
inexcusable [ˌɪnɪkˈskjuːzəbl] *adj* imperdonable
inexorable [ɪnˈeksərəbl] *adj form* inexorable
inexpensive [ˌɪnɪkˈspensɪv] *adj* económico
inexperience [ˌɪnɪkˈspɪəriənts] *n no pl* falta *f* de experiencia
inexperienced [ˌɪnɪkˈspɪərɪənst, *Am:* -ˈspɪrɪ-] *adj*, **inexpert** [ɪnˈekspɜːt, *Am:* -spɜːrt] *adj* inexperto
inexplicable [ˌɪnɪkˈsplɪkəbl, *Am:* ˌɪnˈək-] *adj* inexplicable
infallible [ɪnˈfæləbl] *adj* indefectible
infamous [ˈɪnfəməs] *adj* infame
infancy [ˈɪnfəntsi] *n no pl* infancia *f*
infant [ˈɪnfənt] *n* bebé *m*
infantile [ˈɪnfəntaɪl] *adj* infantil
infantry [ˈɪnfəntri] *n + sing/pl vb* MIL infantería *f*
infatuated [ɪnˈfætʃʊeɪtɪd, *Am:* -ueɪt̬ɪd] *adj* **to become ~ with sb** encapricharse por alguien
infect [ɪnˈfekt] *vt* infectar; *a. fig* (*person*) contagiar
infection [ɪnˈfekʃən] *n* infección *f; fig* contagio *m*
infectious [ɪnˈfekʃəs] *adj* infeccioso; *a. fig* contagioso
infer [ɪnˈfɜːʳ, *Am:* -ˈfɜːr] <-rr-> *vt* inferir

inference ['ɪnfərəns] *n form* to draw the ~ that ... sacar la conclusión de que...; by ~ por inferencia

inferior [ɪn'fɪərɪəʳ, *Am:* -'fɪrɪɚ] *adj* inferior

inferiority [ɪnˌfɪərɪ'ɒrəti, *Am:* -ˌfɪri'ɔːrəti] *n no pl* inferioridad *f*

inferno [ɪn'fɜːnəʊ, *Am:* -'fɜːrnoʊ] *n* infierno *m*

infertile [ɪn'fɜːtaɪl, *Am:* -'fɜːrt̬l] *adj* estéril

infest [ɪn'fest] *vt* infestar

infidelity [ˌɪnfɪ'deləti, *Am:* -fə'deləti] *n no pl* infidelidad *f*

infiltrate ['ɪnfɪltreɪt, *Am:* ɪn'fɪl-] *vt* infiltrarse en

infinite ['ɪnfɪnət, *Am:* -fənɪt] *adj* infinito

infinitely *adv* infinitamente

infinitive [ɪn'fɪnətɪv, *Am:* -t̬ɪv] *n* infinitivo *m*

infinity [ɪn'fɪnəti, *Am:* -t̬i] <-ies> 1. *no pl* MAT infinito *m* 2.(*huge amount*) infinidad *f*

infirmary [ɪn'fɜːməri, *Am:* -'fɜːr-] <-ies> *n* 1.(*hospital*) hospital *m* 2.*Am* (*sick room*) enfermería *f*

inflame [ɪn'fleɪm] *vt a.* MED inflamar; to ~ sb with passion desatar la pasión de alguien

inflammable [ɪn'flæməbl] *adj* inflamable; (*situation*) explosivo

inflammation [ˌɪnflə'meɪʃən] *n* MED inflamación *f*

inflammatory [ɪn'flæmətəri, *Am:* -tɔːr-] *adj* 1.MED inflamatorio 2.(*speech*) incendiario

inflatable [ɪn'fleɪtəbl, *Am:* -t̬ə-] *adj* hinchable

inflate [ɪn'fleɪt] *vi, vt* hinchar(se)

inflation [ɪn'fleɪʃən] *n no pl* inflación *f*

inflationary *adj* inflacionario

inflection [ɪn'flekʃən] *n* inflexión *f*

inflexible [ɪn'fleksəbl] *adj* inflexible

inflict [ɪn'flɪkt] *vt* (*wound*) infligir; (*damage*) causar

infliction [ɪn'flɪkʃən] *n no pl* imposición *f*

influence ['ɪnfluəns] I. *n* influencia *f*; to bring one's ~ to bear on sb ejercer presión sobre alguien; to be

under the ~ *fig* estar borracho II. *vt* influir

influential [ˌɪnflʊ'enʃl] *adj* influyente

influenza [ˌɪnflʊ'enzə] *n no pl* gripe *f*

influx ['ɪnflʌks] *n no pl* influjo *m*

inform [ɪn'fɔːm, *Am:* -'fɔːrm] I. *vt* informar; to be ~ed about sth estar enterado de algo II. *vi* to ~ against sb delatar a alguien

informal [ɪn'fɔːml, *Am:* -'fɔːr-] *adj* informal

informant [ɪn'fɔːmənt, *Am:* -'fɔːr-] *n* informante *mf*

information [ˌɪnfə'meɪʃən, *Am:* -fɚ'-] *n no pl* 1.(*data*) información *f*; to ask for ~ pedir informes 2.INFOR datos *mpl*

⚠ **information** no se utiliza en plural: any/some **information** significa informaciones.

information science *n* ciencias *fpl* de la información **information superhighway** *n* autopista *f* de la información **information technology** *n no pl* tecnologías *fpl* de la información

informative [ɪn'fɔːmətɪv, *Am:* -'fɔːrmət̬ɪv] *adj* informativo

informer [ɪn'fɔːməʳ, *Am:* -'fɔːrmɚ] *n* denunciante *mf*

infotainment [ɪnfəʊ'teɪnmənt, *Am:* 'ɪnfoʊteɪn-] *n* infotainment *m*

infrared ['ɪnfrə'red] *adj* infrarrojo

infrastructure ['ɪnfrəˌstrʌktʃəʳ, *Am:* -tʃɚ] *n* infraestructura *f*

infrequent [ɪn'friːkwənt] *adj* poco frecuente

infringe [ɪn'frɪndʒ] *vt* LAW infringir; to ~ sb's right vulnerar un derecho de alguien

infringement [ɪn'frɪndʒmənt] *n* LAW infracción *f*; (*of a rule*) violación *f*

infuriate [ɪn'fjʊərɪeɪt, *Am:* -'fjʊrɪ-] *vt* enfurecer

infusion [ɪn'fjuːʒən] *n* infusión *f*

ingenious [ɪn'dʒiːnɪəs, *Am:* -njəs]

adj ingenioso

ingenuity [ˌɪndʒɪˈnjuːəti, *Am:* -t̬i] *n no pl* ingenuidad *f*

ingenuous [ɪnˈdʒenjʊəs] *adj form* ingenuo

ingrained [ˌɪnˈgreɪnd] *adj* **1.** (*dirt*) incrustado **2.** (*prejudice*) arraigado

ingratiate [ɪnˈgreɪʃɪeɪt] *vr* **to ~ oneself with sb** congraciarse con alguien

ingratitude [ɪnˈgrætɪtjuːd, *Am:* -ˈgrætətuːd] *n no pl* ingratitud *f*

ingredient [ɪnˈgriːdɪənt] *n* ingrediente *m*

inhabit [ɪnˈhæbɪt] *vt* habitar

inhabitant [ɪnˈhæbɪtənt] *n* habitante *mf*

inhale [ɪnˈheɪl] *vi, vt* inhalar

inherent [ɪnˈhɪərənt, *Am:* -ˈhɪr-] *adj* inherente

inherit [ɪnˈherɪt] *vt* heredar

inheritance [ɪnˈherɪtəns] *n* herencia *f*

inhibit [ɪnˈhɪbɪt] *vt* (*hinder*) impedir; (*impair*) inhibir

inhibition [ˌɪnɪˈbɪʃən] *n* inhibición *f*

inhospitable [ˌɪnhɒˈspɪtəbl, *Am:* ɪnˈhɑːspɪt̬ə-] *adj* inhospitalario; (*attitude*) poco amistoso

in-house *adv* COM dentro de la empresa

inhuman [ɪnˈhjuːmən] *adj* inhumano

inhumane [ˌɪnhjuːˈmeɪn] *adj* inhumano

inimitable [ɪˈnɪmɪtəbl, *Am:* -t̬ə-] *adj* inimitable

iniquitous [ɪˈnɪkwɪtəs, *Am:* -t̬əs] *adj* inicuo

iniquity [ɪˈnɪkwəti, *Am:* -t̬i] <-ies> *n* (*wickedness*) iniquidad *f*; (*unfairness*) injusticia *f*

initial [ɪˈnɪʃəl] **I.** *n* inicial *f* **II.** *adj* inicial **III.** <*Brit:* -ll-, *Am:* -l-> *vt* marcar con las iniciales

initially [ɪˈnɪʃəli] *adv* en un principio

initiate [ɪˈnɪʃɪeɪt] *vt* iniciar

initiation [ɪˌnɪʃɪˈeɪʃən] *n* **1.** *no pl* (*start*) inicio *m* **2.** (*introduction*) iniciación *f*

initiative [ɪˈnɪʃətɪv, *Am:* -t̬ɪv] *n* iniciativa *f*; **to take the ~** tomar la

iniciativa; **to show ~** demostrar iniciativa; **to use one's ~** obrar por cuenta propia

inject [ɪnˈdʒekt] *vt* inyectar

injection [ɪnˈdʒekʃən] *n* inyección *f*

injunction [ɪnˈdʒʌŋkʃən] *n* interdicto *m*

injure [ˈɪndʒəʳ, *Am:* -dʒɚ] *vt* herir, victimar *AmL*

injury [ˈɪndʒəri] <-ies> *n* lesión *f*, herida *f*; **a back ~** una lesión de espalda; **to do oneself an ~** *Brit, Aus, iron* hacerse daño

injustice [ɪnˈdʒʌstɪs] *n* injusticia *f*

ink [ɪŋk] *n* tinta *f*

ink-jet printer *n* impresora *f* de chorro de tinta

inkling [ˈɪŋklɪŋ] *n* sospecha *f*; **to have an ~ that ...** tener la sospecha de que...

inland [ˈɪnlənd] *adj* interior

Inland Revenue *n Brit* Hacienda *f*

in-laws *npl* suegros *mpl*

inlet [ˈɪnlet] *n* **1.** GEO ensenada *f* **2.** *Brit* TECH entrada *f*

inmate [ˈɪnmeɪt] *n* residente *mf*; (*prison*) preso, -a *m, f*

inn [ɪn] *n* posada *f*

innards [ˈɪnədz, *Am:* -ɚdz] *npl inf* tripas *fpl*

innate [ɪˈneɪt] *adj* innato

inner [ˈɪnəʳ, *Am:* -ɚ] *adj* **1.** (*interior*) interior **2.** (*feeling*) íntimo

inner tube *n* cámara *f* de aire

innings [ˈɪnɪŋ] *n + sing vb, Brit* (*cricket*) turno *m* de entrada; **to have a good ~s** *Brit, fig* tener una vida larga

innocence [ˈɪnəsns] *n no pl* inocencia *f*

innocent [ˈɪnəsnt] *adj* inocente

innocuous [ɪˈnɒkjʊəs, *Am:* -ˈnɑːk-] *adj* inocuo

innovate [ˈɪnəveɪt] *vi* innovar

innovation [ˌɪnəˈveɪʃən] *n* innovación *f*

innovative [ˈɪnəvətɪv, *Am:* -veɪt̬ɪv] *adj* (*product*) novedoso; (*person*) innovador

innuendo [ˌɪnjuˈendəʊ, *Am:* -doʊ] <-(e)s> *n* indirecta *f*

innumerable [ɪˈnjuːmərəbl, *Am:*

-'nu:-] *adj* innumerable

inoculation [ɪˌnɒkjʊ'leɪʃən, *Am:* -ˌnɑːkjə'-] *n* inoculación *f*

inoffensive [ˌɪnə'fensɪv] *adj* inofensivo

inopportune [ˌɪn'ɒpətjuːn, *Am:* -ˌɑːpəˈtuːn] *adj* inoportuno

inorganic [ˌɪnɔː'gænɪk, *Am:* -ɔːr'-] *adj* inorgánico

input ['ɪnpʊt] *n* (*contribution*) aportación *f*; INFOR entrada *f*

input device *n* INFOR dispositivo *m* de entrada

inquest ['ɪnkwest] *n* LAW investigación *f* judicial

inquire [ɪn'kwaɪəʳ, *Am:* -'kwaɪr] *vi Brit* preguntar; **to ~ about sth** pedir información sobre algo; **to ~ into a matter** indagar en un asunto

inquiry [ɪn'kwaɪəri, *Am:* -'kwaɪri] *n Brit* **1.** (*question*) pregunta *f* **2.** (*investigation*) investigación *f*

inquisition [ˌɪnkwɪ'zɪʃən] *n* inquisición *f*

inquisitive [ɪn'kwɪzətɪv, *Am:* -t̬ɪv] *adj* curioso; **to be ~ about sth** sentir curiosidad sobre algo

insane [ɪn'seɪn] *adj a. fig* loco; **to go ~** volverse loco

insanity [ɪn'sænəti, *Am:* -t̬i] *n no pl* **1.** (*mental illness*) demencia *f* **2.** *a. fig* (*craziness*) locura *f*

insatiable [ɪn'seɪʃəbl] *adj* insaciable

inscription [ɪn'skrɪpʃən] *n* inscripción *f*; (*dedication*) dedicatoria *f*

inscrutable [ɪn'skruːtəbl, *Am:* -t̬ə-] *adj* (*look*) enigmático; (*person*) insondable

insect ['ɪnsekt] *n* insecto *m*

insecticide [ɪn'sektɪsaɪd] *n* insecticida *m*

insecure [ˌɪnsɪ'kjʊəʳ, *Am:* -'kjʊr] *adj* inseguro

insecurity [ˌɪnsɪ'kjʊərəti, *Am:* -'kjʊrət̬i] <-ies> *n* inseguridad *f*

insensible [ɪn'sensəbl] *adj form* insensible; **to be ~ to sth** ser indiferente a algo

insensitive [ɪn'sensətɪv, *Am:* -t̬ɪv] *adj* insensible

inseparable [ɪn'seprəbl] *adj* inseparable

insert [ɪn'sɜːt, *Am:* -'sɜːrt] *vt* insertar; (*coins*) introducir; (*within text*) intercalar

inside [ɪn'saɪd] **I.** *adj* interno **II.** *n* interior *m*; **on the ~** por dentro; **to turn sth ~ out** volver algo del revés **III.** *prep* ~ (**of**) dentro de; ~ **three days** en menos de tres días **IV.** *adv* dentro; **to go ~** entrar

insidious [ɪn'sɪdɪəs] *adj* insidioso

insight ['ɪnsaɪt] *n* perspicacia *f*; **to gain an ~ into sth** entender mejor algo

insignificant [ˌɪnsɪg'nɪfɪkənt] *adj* insignificante

insincere [ˌɪnsɪn'sɪəʳ, *Am:* -'sɪr] *adj* poco sincero

insinuate [ɪn'sɪnjʊeɪt] *vt* insinuar

insipid [ɪn'sɪpɪd] *adj* (*food, drink*) insípido; (*person*) soso

insist [ɪn'sɪst] *vi, vt* insistir; **to ~ on doing sth** obstinarse en hacer algo

insistence [ɪn'sɪstəns] *n no pl* insistencia *f*; **to do sth at sb's ~** hacer algo por insistencia de alguien

insistent [ɪn'sɪstənt] *adj* insistente

insolent ['ɪnsələnt] *adj* insolente

insolvent [ɪn'sɒlvənt, *Am:* -'sɑːl-] *adj* insolvente

insomnia [ɪn'sɒmnɪə, *Am:* -'sɑːm-] *n no pl* insomnio *m*

inspect [ɪn'spekt] *vt* inspeccionar

inspection [ɪn'spekʃən] *n* inspección *f*

inspector [ɪn'spektəʳ] *n* inspector(a) *m(f)*

inspiration [ˌɪnspə'reɪʃən] *n* inspiración *f*

inspire [ɪn'spaɪəʳ, *Am:* -'spaɪr] *vt* inspirar

instability [ˌɪnstə'bɪləti, *Am:* -t̬i] *n no pl* inestabilidad *f*

instal <-ll-> *Brit*, **install** [ɪn'stɔːl] *vt* instalar

installation [ˌɪnstə'leɪʃən] *n* instalación *f*

installment *n Am*, **instalment** [ɪn'stɔːlmənt] *n* **1.** RADIO, TV entrega *f* **2.** COM plazo *m*

instance ['ɪnstəns] *n* caso *m*; **for ~** por ejemplo; **in the first ~** primero

instant ['ɪnstənt] **I.** *n* instante *m*;

for an ~ por un momento; **in an** ~ al instante **II.** *adj* **1.** (*immediate*) inmediato **2.** GASTR instantáneo

instantaneous [ˌɪnstən'teɪnɪəs] *adj* instantáneo

instantly ['ɪnstəntli] *adv* al instante

instead [ɪn'sted] **I.** *adv* en cambio **II.** *prep* ~ **of** en vez de; ~ **of him** en su lugar; ~ **of doing sth** en lugar de hacer algo

instep ['ɪnstep] *n* empeine *m*

instigate ['ɪnstɪgeɪt] *vt* instigar

instil [ɪn'stɪl] <-ll-> *vt*, **instill** *vt Am* **to** ~ **sth** (**into sb**) infundir algo (a alguien)

instinct ['ɪnstɪŋkt] *n* instinto *m;* **to do sth by** ~ hacer algo por instinto

instinctive [ɪn'stɪŋktɪv] *adj* instintivo

institute ['ɪnstɪtjuːt, *Am:* -tuːt] **I.** *n* instituto *m* **II.** *vt form* (*system, reform*) instituir; (*steps, measures*) iniciar; (*legal action*) emprender

institution [ˌɪnstɪ'tjuːʃən, *Am:* -'tuː-] *n* institución *f*

institutional [ˌɪnstɪ'tjuːʃənəl, *Am:* -'tuː-] *adj* institucional

institutionalize [ˌɪnstɪ'tjuːʃənəlaɪz, *Am:* -'tuː-] *vt* institucionalizar; (*person*) ingresar

instruct [ɪn'strʌkt] *vt* instruir; **to** ~ **sb to do sth** ordenar a alguien hacer algo

instruction [ɪn'strʌkʃən] *n* **1.** *no pl* (*teaching*) instrucción *f* **2.** (*order*) **to give sb** ~**s** dar órdenes a alguien

instructive [ɪn'strʌktɪv] *adj* instructivo

instructor [ɪn'strʌktər, *Am:* -tɚ] *n* instructor(a) *m(f)*

instrument ['ɪnstrʊmənt, *Am:* -strə-] *n* instrumento *m*

instrumental [ˌɪnstrʊ'mentl, *Am:* -strə'mentl] **I.** *adj* **1.** MUS instrumental **2.** *fig* **to be** ~ **in doing sth** jugar un papel clave en algo **II.** *n* MUS pieza *f* instrumental

insubordinate [ˌɪnsə'bɔːdɪnət, *Am:* -'bɔːrdənɪt] *adj* insubordinado

insubstantial [ˌɪnsəb'stænʃl] *adj* insustancial

insufferable [ɪn'sʌfrəbl] *adj* insufrible; (*person*) inaguantable

insufficient [ˌɪnsə'fɪʃənt] *adj* insuficiente

insular ['ɪntsjələr, *Am:* -sələ] *adj* **1.** GEO insular **2.** (*person*) de miras estrechas

insulate ['ɪntsjəleɪt, *Am:* -sə-] *vt* aislar

insulation [ˌɪntsjə'leɪʃən, *Am:* -sə'-] *n no pl* aislamiento *m*

insulin ['ɪntsjʊlɪn, *Am:* -sə-] *n no pl* insulina *f*

insult ['ɪnsʌlt] **I.** *vt* insultar **II.** *n* insulto *m*, insultada *f AmL;* **to add** ~ **to injury ...** y por si fuera poco...

insurance [ɪn'ʃʊərəns, *Am:* -'ʃʊrəns] *n no pl* seguro *m;* **to take out** ~ (**against sth**) hacerse un seguro (contra algo)

insurance company <-ies> *n* compañía *f* de seguros **insurance policy** <-ies> *n* póliza *f* de seguros

insure [ɪn'ʃʊər, *Am:* -'ʃʊr] *vt* asegurar

insurer [ɪn'ʃʊərər, *Am:* -'ʃʊrɚ] *n* (*company*) aseguradora *f*

insurmountable [ˌɪnsə'maʊntəbl, *Am:* -sə'maʊntə-] *adj* insuperable

insurrection [ˌɪnsə'rekʃən, *Am:* -sə'rek-] *n* insurrección *f*

intact [ɪn'tækt] *adj* intacto

intake ['ɪnteɪk] *n* **1.** (*action of taking in*) toma *f;* ~ **of breath** aspiración *f* **2.** (*amount taken in*) consumo *m*

intangible [ɪn'tændʒəbl] *adj* intangible

integral ['ɪntɪgrəl, *Am:* -tə-] *adj* **1.** (*part of the whole*) integrante **2.** (*central, essential*) esencial; **to be** ~ **to sth** ser de vital importancia para algo **3.** (*complete*) integral

integrate ['ɪntɪgreɪt, *Am:* -tə-] *vi, vt* integrar(se)

integrated ['ɪntɪgreɪtɪd, *Am:* -tɪd] *adj* integrado

integration [ˌɪntɪ'greɪʃən, *Am:* -tə'-] *n no pl* integración *f*

integrity [ɪn'tegrəti, *Am:* -ti] *n no pl* integridad *f*

intellect ['ɪntəlekt, *Am:* -tə-] *n no pl* intelecto *m*

intellectual [ˌɪntəˈlektʃʊəl, *Am:* -ˈt̬ə-] *adj* intelectual
intelligence [ɪnˈtelɪdʒəns] *n no pl* inteligencia *f*
intelligent [ɪnˈtelɪdʒənt] *adj* inteligente
intelligible [ɪnˈtelɪdʒəbl] *adj* inteligible
intend [ɪnˈtend] *vt* pretender; **to ~ to do sth** tener la intención de hacer algo; **to be ~ed for sth** estar destinado a algo
intended [ɪnˈtendɪd] *adj* intencional
intense [ɪnˈtents] *adj* intenso
intensify [ɪnˈtentsɪfaɪ] <-ie-> *vi, vt* intensificar(se)
intensity [ɪnˈtentsəti, *Am:* -ˈt̬i] *n no pl* intensidad *f*
intensive [ɪnˈtentsɪv] *adj* intensivo
intent [ɪnˈtent] I. *n* propósito *m;* **a declaration of ~** una declaración de intenciones; **to all ~s and purposes** prácticamente II. *adj* atento; **to be ~ on doing sth** estar resuelto a hacer algo
intention [ɪnˈtentʃən] *n* intención *f;* **to have no ~ of doing sth** no tener ninguna intención de hacer algo; **with the best of ~s** con la mejor intención
intentional [ɪnˈtentʃənəl] *adj* intencional
interact [ˌɪntərˈækt, *Am:* ɪntə̬ˈækt] *vi* interaccionar
interaction [ˌɪntəˈrækʃən, *Am:* -tə̬ˈ-] *n* interacción *f*
interactive [ˌɪntəˈræktɪv, *Am:* -tə̬ˈæk-] *adj* interactivo
interbreed [ˌɪntəˈbriːd, *Am:* -tə̬ˈ-] *irr vi* cruzarse
intercept [ˌɪntəˈsept, *Am:* -tə̬ˈ-] *vt* interceptar
interchange [ˌɪntəˈtʃeɪndʒ, *Am:* -tə̬ˈ-] I. *n* 1. *form* intercambio *m* 2. *Brit* (*of roads*) enlace *m* II. *vt* intercambiar
interchangeable [ˌɪntəˈtʃeɪndʒəbl, *Am:* -tə̬ˈ-] *adj* intercambiable
intercourse [ˈɪntəkɔːs, *Am:* -tə̬-kɔːrs] *n no pl* (**sexual**) **~** relaciones *fpl* sexuales; **social ~** *form* trato *m* social

interdependence [ˌɪntədɪˈpendəns, *Am:* -tə̬diː-] *n no pl* interdependencia *f*
interdependent [ˌɪntədɪˈpendənt, *Am:* -tə̬diː-] *adj* interdependiente
interest [ˈɪntrəst, *Am:* -trɪst] I. *n* (*hobby, curiosity*) a. FIN interés *m;* **to take an ~ in sth** interesarse por algo; **to lose ~ in sth** perder el interés por algo; **out of ~** por curiosidad; **a conflict of ~s** un conflicto de intereses; **it's in your own ~ to do it** te conviene hacerlo por tu propio interés; **~ rate** tipo *m* de interés II. *vt* interesar
interested [ˈɪntrəstɪd, *Am:* -trɪst-] *adj* interesado; **to be ~ in sth** estar interesado en algo
interest-free *adj* FIN sin intereses
interesting [ˈɪntrəsˈtɪŋ] *adj* interesante
interface [ˈɪntəfeɪs, *Am:* -tə̬-] *n* 1. (*point of contact*) punto *m* de contacto 2. INFOR interfaz *f*
interfere [ˌɪntəˈfɪər, *Am:* -tə̬ˈfɪr] *vi* interferir; **to ~ in sth** inmiscuirse en algo; **to ~ with sb** (*molest*) abusar de alguien
interference [ˌɪntəˈfɪərəns, *Am:* -tə̬ˈfɪr-] *n no pl* 1. intromisión *f* 2. RADIO, TECH interferencia *f*
interim [ˈɪntərɪm, *Am:* -tə̬-] I. *n no pl* ínterin *m* II. *adj* provisional
interior [ɪnˈtɪərɪər, *Am:* -ˈtɪrɪə̬] I. *adj* interno II. *n* interior *m*
interject [ˌɪntəˈdʒekt, *Am:* -tə̬-] *vt form* interponer
interjection [ˌɪntəˈdʒekʃən, *Am:* -tə̬-] *n* interjección *f*
interlude [ˈɪntəluːd, *Am:* -tə̬luːd] *n* (*interval*) intervalo *m*
intermediary [ˌɪntəˈmiːdɪəri, *Am:* -tə̬ˈmiːdɪer-] <-ies> *n* intermediario, -a *m, f*
intermediate [ˌɪntəˈmiːdɪət, *Am:* -tə̬-] *adj* intermedio
interminable [ɪnˈtɜːmɪnəbl, *Am:* -ˈtɜːr-] *adj* interminable
intermission [ˌɪntəˈmɪʃən, *Am:* -tə̬-] *n* intermedio *m;* CINE, THEAT

descanso *m*

intermittent [ˌɪntəˈmɪtnt, *Am:* -t̬ə-] *adj* intermitente

intern I. [ɪnˈtɜːn, *Am:* -ˈtɜːrn] *vt* recluir **II.** *vi* MED trabajar como interno; SCHOOL hacer (las) prácticas **III.** [ˈɪntɜːn, *Am:* -tɜːrn] *n Am* estudiante *mf* en prácticas; **hospital** ~ médico *m* interno

internal [ɪnˈtɜːnl, *Am:* -ˈtɜːr-] *adj* interno

international [ˌɪntəˈnæʃnəl, *Am:* -t̬ə-] *adj* internacional

International Court of Justice *n* Tribunal *m* Internacional de Justicia

International Monetary Fund *n* Fondo *m* Monetario Internacional

internee [ˌɪntɜːˈniː, *Am:* -tɜːrˈ-] *n* interno, -a *m, f*

Internet [ˈɪntənet, *Am:* -t̬ə-] *n* internet *f*

Internet access *n* acceso *m* a internet **Internet-based learning** *n no pl* aprendizaje *m* por Internet [*o* en línea] **Internet café** *n* ciber café *m* **Internet search engine** *n* motor *m* de búsqueda en la red **Internet user** *n* internauta *mf*

internment [ɪnˈtɜːnmənt, *Am:* -ˈtɜːrn-] *n no pl* internamiento *m*

interplay [ˈɪntəpleɪ, *Am:* -t̬ə-] *n no pl* interacción *f*

interpret [ɪnˈtɜːprɪt, *Am:* -ˈtɜːrprət] **I.** *vt* **1.** (*decode, construe*) interpretar **2.** (*translate*) traducir **II.** *vi* interpretar

interpretation [ɪnˌtɜːprɪˈteɪʃən, *Am:* -ˌtɜːrprəˈ-] *n* interpretación *f;* **to put an ~ on sth** interpretar algo

interpreter [ɪnˈtɜːprɪtəʳ, *Am:* -ˈtɜːrprət̬ɚ] *n* intérprete *mf*

interpreting [ɪnˈtɜːprɪtɪŋ, *Am:* -ˈtɜːrprət-] *n no pl* interpretación *f*

interrelate [ˌɪntərɪˈleɪt, *Am:* -t̬ɚrɪ-] *vi* interrelacionarse

interrogate [ɪnˈterəgeɪt] *vt* interrogar

interrogation [ɪnˌterəˈgeɪʃən] *n* interrogación *f;* LAW interrogatorio *m*

interrogator [ɪnˈterəgeɪtəʳ, *Am:* -t̬əˈrɑːgət̬ɚ] *n* interrogador(a) *m(f)*

interrupt [ˌɪntəˈrʌpt, *Am:* -t̬ə-] *vi, vt* interrumpir

interruption [ˌɪntəˈrʌpʃən, *Am:* -t̬ə-] *n* interrupción *f;* **without ~** sin interrupciones

intersect [ˌɪntəˈsekt] *vi* cruzarse

intersection [ˌɪntəˈsekʃən] *n* **1.** (*of lines*) intersección *f* **2.** *Am, Aus* (*junction*) cruce *m*

intersperse [ˌɪntəˈspɜːs, *Am:* -t̬ɚˈspɜːrs] *vt* intercalar

interstate [ˌɪntəˈsteɪt, *Am:* ˈɪnt̬ɚ-] *adj Am* interestatal

intertwine [ˌɪntəˈtwaɪn, *Am:* -t̬ɚ-] *vi, vt* entrelazar(se)

interval [ˈɪntəvl, *Am:* -t̬ə-] *n a.* MUS intervalo *m;* THEAT entreacto *m;* **at ~s** de vez en cuando

intervene [ˌɪntəˈviːn, *Am:* -t̬ə-] *vi* intervenir; **to ~ on sb's behalf** interceder por alguien

intervening *adj* **in the ~ period** en el ínterin

intervention [ˌɪntəˈvenʃən, *Am:* -t̬əˈ-] *n* intervención *f*

interview [ˈɪntəvjuː, *Am:* -t̬ə-] **I.** *n* entrevista *f;* **to give an ~** conceder una entrevista **II.** *vt* entrevistar

interviewer [ˈɪntəvjuːəʳ, *Am:* -t̬ə-vjuːɚ] *n* entrevistador(a) *m(f)*

interweave [ˌɪntəˈwiːv, *Am:* -t̬ə-] *vt irr* entretejer

intestine [ɪnˈtestɪn] *n* intestino *m*

intimacy [ˈɪntɪməsi, *Am:* -t̬ə-] <-ies> *n* intimidad *f*

intimate [ˈɪntɪmət, *Am:* -t̬ə-] *adj* íntimo; (*knowledge*) profundo; **to be on ~ terms with sb** tener intimidad con alguien

intimidate [ɪnˈtɪmɪdeɪt] *vt* intimidar; **to ~ sb into doing sth** coaccionar a alguien para que haga algo

intimidating *adj* intimidante

intimidation [ɪnˌtɪmɪˈdeɪʃən] *n no pl* intimidación *f*

into [ˈɪntʊ, *Am:* -tə] *prep* **1.** (*to the inside of*) en; (*towards*) hacia; **to walk ~ a place** entrar en un sitio; **to get ~ bed** meterse en cama; **~ the future** hacia el futuro **2.** (*against*) contra; **to drive ~ a tree** chocar contra un árbol; **to bump ~ a friend**

tropezar con un amigo **3.** (*to the state or condition of*) **to grow ~ a woman** convertirse en una mujer; **to translate from English ~ Spanish** traducir del inglés al español **4.** *inf* (*interested in*) **she's really ~ her new job** está entusiasmada con su nuevo trabajo **5.** MAT **two ~ ten equals five** diez entre dos es igual a cinco

intolerable [ɪn'tɒlərəbl, *Am:* -'tɑː- lə-] *adj* intolerable

intolerance [ɪn'tɒlərəns, *Am:* -'tɑː- lə-] *n no pl* intolerancia *f*

intolerant [ɪn'tɒlərənt, *Am:* -'tɑː- lə-] *adj* intolerante

intonation [ˌɪntə'neɪʃən, *Am:* -toʊ'-] *n* entonación *f*

intoxicate [ɪn'tɒksɪkeɪt, *Am:* -'tɑːk-] *vt* embriagar

intoxicating [ɪn'tɒksɪkeɪtɪŋ, *Am:* -'tɑːksɪkeɪtɪŋ] *adj* embriagador

intoxication [ɪnˌtɒksɪ'keɪʃən, *Am:* -ˌtɑːksɪ-] *n no pl, a. fig* (*drunkenness*) embriaguez *f*

intractable [ˌɪn'træktəbl] *adj form* (*person*) obstinado; (*problem*) insoluble

Intranet [ˌɪntrə'net] *n* intranet *f*

intransigent [ɪn'trænsɪdʒənt, *Am:* -sə-] *adj* intransigente

intransitive [ɪn'trænsətɪv, *Am:* -ţɪv] *adj* intransitivo

intravenous [ˌɪntrə'viːnəs] *adj* MED intravenoso

intrepid [ɪn'trepɪd] *adj* intrépido

intricate ['ɪntrɪkət] *adj* intrincado

intrigue [ɪn'triːg] I. *vi, vt* intrigar; **to be ~d by sth** estar intrigado con algo II. *n* intriga *f*

intriguing [ɪn'triːgɪŋ] *adj* intrigante

intrinsic [ɪn'trɪnsɪk] *adj* intrínseco

introduce [ˌɪntrə'djuːs, *Am:* -'duːs] *vt* **1.** (*person*) presentar; **to ~ sb to sth** iniciar a alguien en algo **2.** (*bring in*) introducir

introduction [ˌɪntrə'dʌkʃən] *n* **1.** (*of person*) presentación *f* **2.** (*bringing in*) introducción *f* **3.** (*preface*) prólogo *m*

introductory [ˌɪntrə'dʌktəri] *adj* **1.** (*elementary, preparatory*) de in-

troducción **2.** (*beginning*) introductorio

introspection [ˌɪntrə'spekʃən, *Am:* -troʊ'-] *n no pl* introspección *f*

introverted *adj* introvertido

intrude [ɪn'truːd] *vi* entrometerse

intruder [ɪn'truːdəʳ, *Am:* -ɚ] *n* intruso, -a *m, f*

intrusion [ɪn'truːʒən] *n* intrusión *f*

intrusive [ɪn'truːsɪv] *adj* (*question*) indiscreto; (*person*) entrometido

intuition [ˌɪntjʊ'ɪʃən, *Am:* -tuː'-] *n no pl* intuición *f*

intuitive [ɪn'tjuːɪtɪv] *adj* intuitivo

inundate ['ɪnʌndeɪt, *Am:* -ən-] *vt* inundar

invade [ɪn'veɪd] *vt, vi* invadir

invader [ɪn'veɪdəʳ, *Am:* -ɚ] *n* invasor(a) *m(f)*

invalid[1] ['ɪnvəlɪd] *n* minusválido, -a *m, f*

invalid[2] [ɪn'vælɪd] *adj a.* LAW nulo

invalidate [ɪn'vælɪdeɪt] *vt a.* LAW anular

invaluable [ɪn'væljʊəbl, *Am:* -juə-] *adj* inestimable

invariable [ɪn'veəriəbl, *Am:* -'ve- rɪ-] *adj* invariable

invasion [ɪn'veɪʒən] *n* invasión *f;* **~ of privacy** violación de la intimidad

invent [ɪn'vent] *vt* inventar

invention [ɪn'venʃən] *n* **1.** (*gadget*) invención *f,* invento *m AmL* **2.** *no pl* (*creativity*) inventiva *f*

inventive [ɪn'ventɪv, *Am:* -ţɪv] *adj* inventivo

inventiveness [ɪn'ventɪvnɪs, *Am:* -ţɪv-] *n no pl* inventiva *f*

inventor [ɪn'ventəʳ, *Am:* -ţɚ] *n* inventor(a) *m(f)*

inventory ['ɪnvəntri, *Am:* -tɔːr-] <-ies> *n* **1.** (*catalogue*) inventario *m* **2.** *Am* (*stock*) stock *m*

inverse [ɪn'vɜːs, *Am:* -'vɜːrs] *adj* inverso

inversion [ɪn'vɜːʃən, *Am:* -'vɜːrʒən] *n no pl* inversión *f*

invert [ɪn'vɜːt, *Am:* -'vɜːrt] *vt* invertir

invertebrate [ɪn'vɜːtɪbrət, *Am:* -'vɜːrţəbrɪt] *n* invertebrado *m*

invest [ɪn'vest] *vt, vi* invertir

investigate [ɪn'vestɪɡeɪt] *vt* investigar

investigation [ɪnˌvestɪ'ɡeɪʃən] *n* investigación *f*

investigator [ɪn'vestɪɡeɪtəʳ, *Am:* -t̬ɚ] *n* investigador(a) *m(f)*

investment [ɪn'vestmənt] *n* inversión *f*; **to be a good ~** ser una buena inversión

investor [ɪn'vestəʳ, *Am:* -t̬ɚ] *n* inversionista *mf*

invigorating [ɪn'vɪɡəreɪtɪŋ, *Am:* -t̬ɪŋ] *adj* vigorizante

invincible [ɪn'vɪnsəbl] *adj* invencible

invisible [ɪn'vɪzəbl] *adj* invisible

invitation [ˌɪnvɪ'teɪʃən] *n* invitación *f*

invite [ɪn'vaɪt] *vt* invitar; **to ~ offers** solicitar ofertas; **to ~ trouble** buscar problemas

inviting [ɪn'vaɪtɪŋ, *Am:* -t̬ɪŋ] *adj* atractivo

invoice ['ɪnvɔɪs] **I.** *vt* facturar **II.** *n* factura *f*

invoke [ɪn'vəʊk, *Am:* -'voʊk] *vt* invocar

involuntary [ɪn'vɒləntəri, *Am:* -'vɑːləntɚ-] *adj* involuntario

involve [ɪn'vɒlv, *Am:* -'vɑːlv] *vt* **1.** *(implicate)* implicar; **to be ~d in sth** estar metido en algo; **to get ~d in sth** meterse en algo **2.** *(entail)* comportar

involved [ɪn'vɒlvd, *Am:* -'vɑːlvd] *adj* complicado

involvement [ɪn'vɒlvmənt, *Am:* -'vɑːlv-] *n no pl* implicación *f*

inward ['ɪnwəd, *Am:* -wɚd] *adj* interior

inwardly *adv* interiormente

inwards ['ɪnwədz, *Am:* -wɚdz] *adv* hacia adentro, para dentro

I/O INFOR *abbr of* **input/output** E/S

IOC *n abbr of* **International Olympic Committee** COI *m*

iodine ['aɪədiːn, *Am:* -daɪn] *n no pl* yodo *m*

ion ['aɪən] *n* ión *m*

iota [aɪ'əʊtə, *Am:* -'oʊt̬ə] *n no pl, fig* ápice *m*

IQ [ˌaɪ'kjuː] *n abbr of* **intelligence**

quotient CI *m*

IRA [ˌaɪɑː'ʳeɪ, *Am:* -ɑːr'-] *n no pl abbr of* **Irish Republican Army** IRA *m*

Iran [ɪ'rɑːn, *Am:* -'ræn] *n* Irán *m*

Iranian [ɪ'reɪnjən] *adj* iraní

Iraq [ɪ'rɑːk] *n* Irak *m*

Iraqi [ɪ'rɑːki] *adj* iraquí

irate [aɪ'reɪt] *adj* airado

Ireland ['aɪələnd, *Am:* 'aɪr-] *n* Irlanda *f*

iris ['aɪərɪs, *Am:* 'aɪ-] <-es> *n* **1.** BOT lirio *m* **2.** ANAT iris *m inv*

Irish ['aɪərɪʃ, *Am:* 'aɪ-] *adj* irlandés

Irishman ['aɪərɪʃmən, *Am:* 'aɪ-] <-men> *n* irlandés *m*

Irishwoman ['aɪərɪʃwʊmən, *Am:* 'aɪ-] <-women> *n* irlandesa *f*

iron ['aɪən, *Am:* 'aɪən] **I.** *n* **1.** *no pl* *(metal)* hierro *m*, fierro *m AmL* **2.** *(for pressing clothes)* plancha *f* **II.** *vi, vt* planchar

Iron Age *n* edad *f* de hierro **Iron Curtain** *n* HIST, POL Telón *m* de Acero

ironic [aɪ'rɒnɪk, *Am:* aɪ'rɑːnɪk] *adj* irónico

ironing ['aɪənɪŋ, *Am:* 'aɪɚn-] *n no pl* **to do the ~** planchar

ironing board *n* tabla *f* de planchar

ironmonger's *n* ferretería *f*

iron ore *n no pl* mineral *m* de hierro

irony ['aɪərəni, *Am:* 'aɪ-] <-ies> *n* ironía *f*

irrational [ɪ'ræʃənəl] *adj* irracional

irrefutable [ˌɪrɪ'fjuːtəbl, *Am:* ɪ're-fjət̬ə-] *adj* irrefutable

irregular [ɪ'reɡjələʳ, *Am:* -lɚ] *adj* irregular; *(surface)* desigual; *(behaviour)* anómalo

irregularity [ɪˌreɡjə'lærəti, *Am:* ɪˌreɡjə'lerət̬i] <-ies> *n* irregularidad *f*; *(of behaviour)* anormalidad *f*

irrelevance [ɪ'reləvənts, *Am:* ɪr'-] *n* irrelevancia *f*

irrelevant [ɪ'reləvənt, *Am:* ɪr'-] *adj* irrelevante; **to be ~ to sth** no ser relevante para algo

irreplaceable [ˌɪrɪ'pleɪsəbl] *adj* irreemplazable

irrepressible [ˌɪrɪ'presəbl] *adj* irrefrenable

irresistible [ˌɪrɪ'zɪstəbl] *adj* irresistible

irresolute [ɪ'rezəluːt] *adj* irresoluto

irrespective [ˌɪrɪ'spektɪv] *prep* ~ of aparte de

irresponsible [ˌɪrɪ'spɒnsəbl, *Am:* -'spɑːn-] *adj* irresponsable

irreverent [ɪ'revərənt] *adj* irreverente

irreversible [ˌɪrɪ'vɜːsəbl, *Am:* -'vɜːr-] *adj* irreversible

irrigate ['ɪrɪgeɪt] *vt* **1.** AGR regar **2.** MED irrigar

irrigation [ˌɪrɪ'geɪʃən] *n no pl* AGR riego *m*

irritable ['ɪrɪtəbl, *Am:* -t̬ə-] *adj* irritable

irritate ['ɪrɪteɪt] *vt a.* MED irritar

irritating *adj* irritante

irritation [ˌɪrɪ'teɪʃən] *n* irritación *f*

is [ɪz] *vt, vi 3rd pers sing of* **be**

Islam [ɪz'lɑːm] *n no pl* Islam *m*

Islamic [ɪz'læmɪk, *Am:* -'lɑː-] *adj* islámico

island ['aɪlənd] *n* isla *f*

islander ['aɪləndəʳ, *Am:* -ə·] *n* isleño, -a *m, f*

isolate ['aɪsəleɪt] *vt* aislar

isolated ['aɪsəleɪtɪd, *Am:* -t̬ɪd] *adj* **1.** (*remote*) aislado **2.** (*lonely*) apartado

isolation [ˌaɪsə'leɪʃən] *n no pl* **1.** (*separation*) aislamiento *m* **2.** (*loneliness*) soledad *f*

isotope ['aɪsətəʊp, *Am:* -toʊp] *n* isótopo *m*

Israel ['ɪzreɪl, *Am:* -riəl] *n* Israel *m*

Israeli [ɪz'reɪli] *adj* israelí

Israelite ['ɪzrɪəlaɪt] *n* israelita *mf*

issue ['ɪʃuː] **I.** *n* **1.** (*problem, topic*) cuestión *f*; **family ~s** asuntos *mpl* familiares; **the point at ~** el punto en cuestión; **to force an ~** forzar una decisión; **to make an ~ of sth** convertir algo en un problema **2.** PUBL número *m* **3.** (*of shares*) emisión *f* **II.** *vt* emitir; (*passport*) expedir; (*newsletter*) publicar; (*ultimatum*) presentar; **to ~ a statement** hacer una declaración

it [ɪt] **I.** *pron dem* la, le, lo (*in many cases, 'it' is omitted when referring to information already known*);

who was ~? ¿quién era?; ~'s in my bag está en mi bolso; ~ was in London that ... fue en Londres donde... **II.** *pron pers* **1.** él, ella, ello; *direct object:* lo, la; *indirect object:* le; ~ **exploded** estalló; **I'm afraid of** ~ le tengo miedo **2.** (*time*) **what time is** ~? ¿qué hora es? **3.** (*weather*) ~'s **cold** hace frío; ~'s **snowing** está nevando **4.** (*distance*) ~'s **10 km to the town** hay 10 km hasta el pueblo **5.** (*empty subject*) ~ **seems that ...** parece que... **6.** (*passive subject*) ~ **is said that ...** se dice que...

IT [ˌaɪ'tiː] *n no pl* INFOR *abbr of* **Information Technology** tecnología *f* de la información

Italian [ɪ'tæljən] *adj* italiano

italics [ɪ'tælɪks] *npl* cursiva *f*

Italy ['ɪtəli, *Am:* -'ɪt̬-] *n* Italia *f*

itch [ɪtʃ] **I.** *vi* picar; **to ~ to do sth** *fig, inf* morirse por hacer algo **II.** *n* comezón *f*, rasquiña *f Arg*

itchy ['ɪtʃi] <-ier, -iest> *adj* **my leg is** ~ me pica la pierna

item ['aɪtəm, *Am:* -t̬əm] *n* **1.** (*thing*) artículo *m*; ~ **of clothing** prenda *f* de vestir; **news** ~ noticia *f* **2.** (*topic*) asunto *m*; ~ **by** ~ punto por punto

itinerant [aɪ'tɪnərənt] *adj* intinerante

itinerary [aɪ'tɪnərəri, *Am:* -ərer-] <-ies> *n* itinerario *m*

its [ɪts] *adj poss* su; ~ **colour/ weight** su color/peso; ~ **mountains** sus montañas; **the cat hurt ~ head** el gato se lastimó la cabeza

itself [ɪt'self] *pron refl* él mismo, ella misma, ello mismo; *direct, indirect object:* se; *after prep:* sí mismo, sí misma; **the place** ~ el sitio en sí; **in** ~ en sí

ITV ['aɪtiː'viː] *n Brit abbr of* **Independent Television** cadena de televisión británica

ivory ['aɪvəri] <-ies> *n no pl* marfil *m*

Ivory Coast *n* Costa *f* de Marfil

ivy ['aɪvi] <-ies> *n* hiedra *f*

J j

J, j [dʒeɪ] *n* J, j *f;* ~ **for Jack** *Brit,* ~ **for Jig** *Am* J de Juan

jab [dʒæb] **I.** *n* **1.** (*with the elbow*) codazo *m* **2.** (*in boxing*) (*golpe m*) corto *m* **II.** <-bb-> *vt* **to ~ a needle in sth** pinchar algo con una aguja **III.** <-bb-> *vi* **to ~ at sb/sth** (**with sth**) dar a alguien/algo (con algo)

jack [dʒæk] *n* **1.** AUTO gato *m* **2.** (*in cards*) jota *f* **3.** (*in bowls*) boliche *m*
♦ **jack in** *vt Brit, inf* dejar
♦ **jack up** *vt* (*object*) levantar

jackal ['dʒækɔːl, *Am:* -əl] *n* chacal *m*

jackdaw ['dʒækdɔː, *Am:* -daː] *n* grajilla *f*

jacket ['dʒækɪt] *n* **1.** (*short coat*) chaqueta *f,* chapona *f RíoPl* **2.** (*of a book*) sobrecubierta *f*

jacket potato *n* patata *f* asada (*con piel*)

jack-in-the-box ['dʒækɪndəbɒks, *Am:* -baːks] <-es> *n* caja *f* de sorpresas

jackknife ['dʒæknaɪf] *vi* plegarse

jack plug *n Brit* enchufe *m* de clavija

jackpot ['dʒækpɒt, *Am:* -paːt] *n* (premio *m*) gordo *m*

jaded ['dʒeɪdɪd] *adj* **to be ~ with sth** estar harto de algo

jagged ['dʒægɪd] *adj* irregular

jail [dʒeɪl] **I.** *n* cárcel *f* **II.** *vt* encarcelar

jam¹ [dʒæm] *n* GASTR mermelada *f*

jam² [dʒæm] **I.** *n* **1.** *inf* (*awkward situation*) aprieto *m;* **to get into a ~** meterse en un lío **2.** *no pl* (*crowd*) gentío *m* **3.** AUTO atasco *m* **II.** <-mm-> *vt* **1.** (*cause to become stuck*) atascar; (*door*) obstruir; **to ~ sth into sth** embutir algo en algo **2.** RADIO interferir **III.** <-mm-> *vi* atrancarse; (*brakes*) bloquearse

Jamaica [dʒəˈmeɪkə] *n* Jamaica *f*

Jamaican *adj* jamaicano

jamb [dʒæm] *n* jamba *f*

jangle ['dʒæŋgl] *vi* tintinear

janitor ['dʒænɪtəʳ, *Am:* -ət̬ɚ] *n Am, Scot* conserje *mf*

January ['dʒænjuəri, *Am:* -jueri] <-ies> *n* enero *m; s. a.* **April**

Japan [dʒəˈpæn] *n* Japón *m*

Japanese [ˌdʒæpəˈniːz] *adj* japonés

jar¹ [dʒaːʳ, *Am:* dʒaːr] *n* (*container*) tarro *m*

jar² [dʒaːʳ, *Am:* dʒaːr] <-rr-> *vi* chirriar; (*colours, design*) desentonar

jargon ['dʒaːgən, *Am:* 'dʒaːr-] *n no pl* jerga *f*

jaundice ['dʒɔːndɪs, *Am:* 'dʒaːn-] *n no pl* ictericia *f*

jaundiced ['dʒɔːndɪst, *Am:* 'dʒaːn-] *adj* **1.** MED ictérico **2.** (*bitter*) negativo

Java ['dʒaːvə] *n* Java *f*

javelin ['dʒævlɪn] *n* jabalina *f*

jaw [dʒɔː, *Am:* dʒaː] *n* **1.** ANAT mandíbula *f* **2.** *pl* TECH mordazas *fpl*

jay [dʒeɪ] *n* arrendajo *m*

jaywalker ['dʒeɪwɔːkəʳ, *Am:* -waːkɚ] *n* peatón *m* imprudente

jazz [dʒæz] *n no pl* jazz *m*
♦ **jazz up** *vt inf* animar

JCB® [ˌdʒeɪsiːˈbiː] *n Brit:* máquina usada para cavar y mover tierra

jealous ['dʒeləs] *adj* **1.** (*envious*) envidioso; **to feel/be ~** sentir/tener envidia **2.** (*fiercely protective*) celoso

jealousy ['dʒeləsi] <-ies> *n* **1.** *no pl* (*envy*) envidia *f* **2.** (*possessiveness*) celos *mpl*

jeans [dʒiːnz] *npl* (pantalones *mpl*) vaqueros *mpl*

jeer [dʒɪəʳ, *Am:* dʒɪr] *vi* mofarse; **to ~ at sb** burlarse de alguien

jelly ['dʒeli] <-ies> *n* gelatina *f*

jellyfish <-es> *n* medusa *f*

jeopardise *vt,* **jeopardize** ['dʒepədaɪz, *Am:* '-ɚ-] *vt* poner en peligro

jeopardy ['dʒepədi, *Am:* '-ɚ-] *n no pl* peligro *m;* **to put sth in ~** poner algo en peligro

jerk [dʒɜːk, *Am:* dʒɜːrk] **I.** *n* **1.** (*jolt*) sacudida *f* **2.** (*movement*) tirón *m* **3.** *pej, inf* (*person*) estúpido, -a *m, f* **II.** *vi* sacudirse **III.** *vt* **1.** (*shake*) sacudir **2.** (*pull*) tirar bruscamente de

jersey ['dʒɜːzi, *Am:* 'dʒɜːr-] *n* **1.** (*garment*) jersey *m* **2.** *no pl* (*cloth*) tejido *m* de punto

Jesus ['dʒiːzəs] *interj infpor* Dios, híjole *AmL*

Jesus Christ *n* Jesucristo *m*

jet [dʒet] *n* **1.** (*aircraft*) jet *m* **2.** (*stream*) chorro *m*

jet-black *adj* negro azabache

jet engine *n* motor *m* a reacción **jet lag** *n no pl* jet lag *m*

jettison ['dʒetɪsən, *Am:* 'dʒeṭə-] *vt* deshacerse de

jetty ['dʒeti, *Am:* 'dʒeṭ-] *n* embarcadero *m*

Jew [dʒuː] *n* judío, -a *m, f*

jewel ['dʒuːəl] *n* **1.** (*piece of jewellery*) joya *f* **2.** (*watch part*) rubí *m*

jeweler *n Am,* **jeweller** ['dʒuːələʳ, *Am: -*lə*ʳ*] *n* joyero, -a *m, f;* ~'s (**shop**) joyería *f*

jewellery *n,* **jewelry** ['dʒuːəlri] *n Am no pl* joyas *fpl*

Jewess ['dʒuːes, *Am: -*ɪs] *n* judía *f*

Jewish ['dʒuːɪʃ] *adj* judío

jibe [dʒaɪb] *n* burla *f*

jiffy ['dʒɪfi] *n no pl, inf* **in a** ~ en un santiamén

jigsaw ['dʒɪgsɔː, *Am: -*sɑː] *n* **1.** (*tool*) sierra *f* de vaivén **2.** (*puzzle*) puzzle *m,* rompecabezas *m inv*

jilt [dʒɪlt] *vt* dejar plantado

jingle ['dʒɪŋgl] **I.** *vi* tintinear **II.** *n* (*in advertisments*) jingle *m*

jinx [dʒɪŋks] *n no pl* gafe *f;* **there's a** ~ **on this computer** este ordenador está gafado

jitters ['dʒɪtəz, *Am:* 'dʒɪṭəʳz] *npl inf* nervios *mpl;* **he got the** ~ le entró el canguelo

jittery ['dʒɪtəri, *Am:* 'dʒɪṭ-] <-ier, -iest> *adj inf* nervioso

job [dʒɒb, *Am:* dʒɑːb] *n* **1.** (*piece of work, employment*) trabajo *m;* **to make a good/bad** ~ **of sth** hacer algo bien/mal **2.** *no pl* (*duty*) deber *m;* **to do one's** ~ cumplir con su deber; **it's not her job** no es asunto suyo **3.** *no pl* (*problem*) tarea *f* difícil **4.** *fig* **to be just the** ~ *inf* venir

como anillo al dedo; **it's a good** ~ **that ...** menos mal que...

job centre *n Brit* oficina *f* de empleo

jobless ['dʒɒblɪs, *Am:* 'dʒɑːb-] **I.** *adj* desocupado **II.** *npl* **the** ~ los parados *mpl*

jockey ['dʒɒki, *Am:* 'dʒɑːki] **I.** *n* jockey *mf* **II.** *vi* **to** ~ **for position** disputarse un puesto

jocular ['dʒɒkjʊləʳ, *Am:* 'dʒɑːkjələʳ] *adj form* jocoso

jog [dʒɒg, *Am:* dʒɑːg] **I.** <-gg-> *vi* correr **II.** <-gg-> *vt* empujar; **to** ~ **sb's memory** refrescar la memoria de alguien

♦**jog along** *vi inf* ir tirando

jogger ['dʒɒgəʳ, *Am:* 'dʒɑːgəʳ] *n* persona *f* que hace footing

jogging ['dʒɒgɪŋ, *Am:* 'dʒɑːgɪŋ] *n no pl* footing *m*

join [dʒɔɪn] **I.** *vt* **1.** (*connect*) juntar, unir; **to** ~ **hands** tomarse de la mano **2.** (*come together with sb*) reunirse [*o* juntarse] con; **they'll** ~ **us after dinner** vendrán después de cenar **3.** (*become member of: club*) hacerse miembro de; (*army*) alistarse en **II.** *vi* unirse **III.** *n* unión *f,* juntura *f*

♦**join in** **I.** *vt insep* participar en **II.** *vi* participar

♦**join up** *vi* unirse; MIL alistarse

joiner ['dʒɔɪnəʳ, *Am: -*nəʳ] *n* carpintero, -a *m, f*

joint [dʒɔɪnt] **I.** *adj* conjunto **II.** *n* **1.** (*connection*) unión *f,* juntura *f* **2.** ANAT articulación *f* **3.** TECH conexión **4.** BOT nudo *m* **5.** (*meat*) asado *m*

joint account *n* cuenta *f* conjunta

joist [dʒɔɪst] *n* viga *f*

joke [dʒəʊk, *Am:* dʒoʊk] **I.** *n* chiste *m;* (*trick, remark*) broma *f;* **to make a** ~ gastar una broma; **to play a** ~ **on sb** gastar una broma a alguien **II.** *vi* bromear

joker ['dʒəʊkəʳ, *Am:* 'dʒoʊkəʳ] *n* **1.** (*one who jokes*) bromista *mf* **2.** *inf* (*annoying person*) idiota *m* **3.** (*playing card*) comodín *m*

jolly ['dʒɒli, *Am:* 'dʒɑːli] **I.** <-ier, -iest> *adj* **1.** (*happy*) alegre **2.** (*en-*

joyable) agradable **II.** *adv Brit, inf* muy; ~ **good** estupendo **III.** *vt* to ~ **sb along** animar a alguien

jolt [dʒəʊlt, *Am:* dʒoʊlt] **I.** *n* **1.** (*sudden jerk*) sacudida *f* **2.** (*shock*) impresión *f* **II.** *vt* sacudir

Jordan ['dʒɔːdn, *Am:* 'dʒɔːr-] *n* **1.** (*country*) Jordania *f* **2.** (*river*) Jordán *m*

Jordanian [dʒɔːˈdeɪnɪən, *Am:* dʒɔːr-] *adj* jordano

jostle ['dʒɒsl, *Am:* 'dʒɑːsl] *vt* empujar

jot [dʒɒt, *Am:* dʒɑːt] *n no pl* **there's not a ~ of truth in it** eso no tiene ni pizca de verdad

jotter ['dʒɒtəʳ, *Am:* 'dʒɑːtə·] *n Aus, Brit* cuaderno *m*

journal ['dʒɜːnəl, *Am:* 'dʒɜːr-] *n* **1.** (*periodical*) revista *f* especializada **2.** (*diary*) diario *m*

journalism ['dʒɜːnlɪzəm, *Am:* 'dʒɜːr-] *n no pl* periodismo *m*, diarismo *m AmL*

journalist ['dʒɜːnlɪst, *Am:* 'dʒɜːr-] *n* periodista *mf*

journey ['dʒɜːni, *Am:* 'dʒɜːr-] **I.** *n* viaje *m* **II.** *vi liter* viajar

joy [dʒɔɪ] *n* gozo *m*

joyful ['dʒɔɪfəl] *adj* feliz

joystick ['dʒɔɪstɪk] *n* **1.** AVIAT palanca *f* de mando **2.** INFOR joystick *m*

JP [ˌdʒeɪˈpiː] *Brit abbr of* **Justice of the Peace** Juez *mf* de Paz

Jr *abbr of* **Junior** Jr.

jubilant ['dʒuːbɪlənt] *adj* jubiloso

judge [dʒʌdʒ] **I.** *n* juez *mf* **II.** *vi* juzgar; (*give one's opinion*) opinar **III.** *vt* **1.** juzgar; (*question*) decidir; (*assess*) valorar; (*consider*) considerar; **to** ~ **that ...** opinar que... **2.** (*as a referee*) arbitrar; (*in a jury*) actuar como miembro del jurado de

judg(e)ment ['dʒʌdʒmənt] *n* **1.** LAW fallo *m* **2.** (*opinion*) opinión *f* **3.** (*discernment*) criterio *m*

judicial [dʒuːˈdɪʃl] *adj* judicial

judiciary [dʒuːˈdɪʃəri, *Am:* -ier-] *n no pl, form* poder *m* judicial

judo ['dʒuːdəʊ, *Am:* -doʊ] *n no pl* judo *m*

jug [dʒʌg] *n Aus, Brit* jarra *f*

juggernaut ['dʒʌgənɔːt, *Am:* -ə·-nɑːt] *n* camión *m* grande

juggle ['dʒʌgl] *vi a. fig* hacer juegos malabares

juggler *n* malabarista *mf*

juice [dʒuːs] *n* **1.** *no pl* (*drink*) zumo *m* **2.** (*of meat*) jugo *m* **3.** *no pl, Am, inf* (*petrol*) combustible *m*

juicy ['dʒuːsi] <-ier, -iest> *adj* jugoso

jukebox ['dʒuːkbɒks, *Am:* -bɑːks] *n* máquina *f* de discos

July [dʒuːˈlaɪ] *n* julio *m*; *s. a.* **April**

jumble ['dʒʌmbl] **I.** *n no pl* revoltijo *m* **II.** *vt* mezclar

jumble sale *n* bazar *m* benéfico

jumbo ['dʒʌmbəʊ, *Am:* -boʊ] *n inf* jumbo *m*

jump [dʒʌmp] **I.** *vi* **1.** (*leap*) saltar **2.** (*skip*) brincar **3.** (*jerk*) sobresaltarse **4.** (*increase suddenly*) subir de golpe **II.** *vt* saltar; **to** ~ **a queue** colarse **III.** *n* **1.** (*leap*) salto *m* **2.** (*hurdle*) obstáculo *m*

◆ **jump about** *vi* dar saltos

◆ **jump at** *vt* (*opportunity*) no dejar escapar; (*offer*) aceptar con entusiasmo

◆ **jump down** *vi* bajar de un salto

◆ **jump up** *vi* ponerse de pie de un salto

jumper ['dʒʌmpəʳ, *Am:* -pə·] *n* **1.** (*person, animal*) saltador(a) *m(f)* **2.** *Aus, Brit* (*pullover*) suéter *m* **3.** *Am* (*dress*) pichi *m*

jump lead *n Brit* cable *m* de arranque **jump-start** *vt* hacer arrancar (*empujando o haciendo un puente*)

jumpy ['dʒʌmpi] <-ier, -iest> *adj inf* nervioso

junction ['dʒʌŋkʃən] *n* (*road ~*) cruce *m*; (*motorway ~*) salida *f*

juncture ['dʒʌŋktʃəʳ, *Am:* -tʃə·] *n no pl, form* coyuntura *f*; **at this** ~ en este momento

June [dʒuːn] *n* junio *m*; *s. a.* **April**

jungle ['dʒʌŋgl] *n* selva *f*

junior ['dʒuːnɪəʳ, *Am:* '-njə·] **I.** *adj* **1.** (*younger*) más joven **2.** SPORTS juvenil **3.** (*lower in rank*) subalterno **II.** *n* **1.** (*younger person*) **which is the** ~? ¿quién es el más joven?

J

2. (*low-ranking person*) subalterno, -a *m, f*

junior school *n Brit* escuela *f* primaria

junk¹ [dʒʌŋk] **I.** *n no pl* trastos *mpl*, tiliches *mpl AmC, Méx* **II.** *vt inf* tirar a la basura

junk² [dʒʌŋk] *n* (*vessel*) junco *m*

junk food *n* comida *f* basura

junkie ['dʒʌŋki] *n inf* yonqui *mf*

junk shop *n* tienda *f* de trastos viejos

Jupiter ['dʒu:pɪtə', *Am:* -ṭə·] *n* Júpiter *m*

jurisdiction [ˌdʒʊərɪs'dɪkʃən, *Am:* ˌdʒʊrɪs-] *n no pl* jurisdicción *f;* **to have ~ in sth** tener competencia en algo

jurisprudence [ˌdʒʊərɪs'pru:-dənts, *Am:* ˌdʒʊrɪs-] *n no pl* jurisprudencia *f*

juror ['dʒʊərə', *Am:* 'dʒʊrə·] *n* miembro *mf* del jurado

jury ['dʒʊəri, *Am:* 'dʒʊri] *n* jurado *m*

juryman ['dʒʊərimən, *Am:* 'dʒʊri-] *n* miembro *m* del jurado

just [dʒʌst] **I.** *adv* **1.** (*very soon*) enseguida; **we're ~ about to leave** estamos a punto de salir **2.** (*now*) precisamente; **to be ~ doing sth** estar justamente haciendo algo **3.** (*very recently*) **~ after 10 o'clock** justo después de las 10; **she's ~ turned 15** acaba de cumplir 15 años **4.** (*exactly, equally*) exactamente, justo; **~ like that** exactamente así; **~ as I expected** tal y como yo esperaba; **~ now** ahora mismo; **not ~ yet** todavía no **5.** (*only*) solamente; **~ a minute** espera un momento **6.** (*simply*) simplemente; **~ in case it rains** por si llueve **7.** (*barely*) **~ (about), (only) ~** apenas; **~ in time** justo a tiempo; **it's ~ as well that ...** menos mal que... **8.** (*very*) muy; **you look ~ wonderful!** ¡estás maravillosa! **II.** *adj* (*fair*) justo

justice ['dʒʌstɪs] *n* justicia *f*

justification [ˌdʒʌstɪfɪ'keɪʃən, *Am:* -t̬ə-] *n no pl* justificación *f*

justify ['dʒʌstɪfaɪ] *vt* justificar; **to ~ oneself** disculparse

jut [dʒʌt] <-tt-> *vi* **to ~ out** sobresalir

juvenile ['dʒu:vənaɪl, *Am:* -nl] *adj form* juvenil

K, k [keɪ] *n* K, k *f;* **~ for King** K de Kenia

K *abbr of* **kilobyte** K *m*

Kampuchea [ˌkæmpʊ'tʃi:ə, *Am:* -puː'-] *n* Kampuchea *f*

Kampuchean *adj* kampucheano

kangaroo [ˌkæŋgə'ruː] <-(s)> *n* canguro *m*

karate [kə'raːti, *Am:* kæ'raːt̬i] *n no pl* kárate *m*

Kazakhstan [kaːzaːk'stæn] *n* Kazajstán *m*

kebab [kə'bæb, *Am:* -'baːb] *n* kebab *m*

keel [kiːl] *n NAUT* quilla *f*
♦ **keel over** *vi* volcarse; (*person*) desplomarse

keen [kiːn] *adj* **1.** (*intent, eager*) entusiasta; (*student*) aplicado; **to be ~ to do sth** tener ganas de hacer algo; **to be ~ on sth** ser aficionado a algo **2.** (*perceptive: intelligence*) agudo **3.** (*extreme*) fuerte **4.** *liter* (*sharp*) afilado

keep [kiːp] **I.** *n* **1.** *no pl* (*livelihood*) subsistencia *f* **2.** HIST (*castle tower*) torre *f* del homenaje **3.** *fig* **for ~s** para siempre **II.** <kept, kept> *vt* **1.** (*have: shop*) tener; (*guesthouse*) dirigir **2.** (*store: silence, secret*) guardar; **~ me a place** guárdame un sitio; **~ the change** quédese con el cambio **3.** (*maintain*) mantener; **to ~ one's eyes fixed on sth/sb** no apartar los ojos de algo/alguien; **to ~ sth going** mantener algo a flote *fig;* **to ~ sb waiting** hacer esperar a alguien **4.** (*fulfil*) cumplir; **to ~ an appointment** acudir a una cita **5.** (*re-*

cord: diary) escribir; (*accounts*) llevar; **to ~ time** marcar la hora **III.**<kept, kept> *vi* **1.** *a. fig* (*stay fresh*) conservarse **2.** (*stay*) mantenerse; **~ quiet!** ¡cállate!

◆ **keep away I.** *vi* mantenerse alejado; **keep medicines away from children** mantenga los medicamentos fuera del alcance de los niños **II.** *vt always sep* mantener alejado

◆ **keep back I.** *vi* (*stay away*) **to ~ from sth/sb** mantenerse alejado de algo/alguien **II.** *vt* **to keep sth back** quedarse con algo; **to ~ one's tears** contener las lágrimas

◆ **keep down** *vt* **to keep sb down** oprimir a alguien; **to keep prices down** controlar los precios

◆ **keep in I.** *vt* (*person*) no dejar salir; (*emotions*) contener **II.** *vi* **to ~ with sb** tener buena relación con alguien

◆ **keep off I.** *vi* (*stay off*) mantenerse alejado; **'~ the grass'** 'prohibido pisar el césped' **II.** *vt* **1.** mantener alejado; **keep your hands off!** ¡no lo toques! **2.** (*avoid*) evitar

◆ **keep on** *vi* seguir

◆ **keep out** *vi* no entrar; **~!** ¡prohibido el paso!

◆ **keep up I.** *vt* mantener alto **II.** *vi* **1.** (*prices*) mantenerse estable; (*moral*) no decaer **2.** (*continue*) seguir; **to ~ with sb** mantener el contacto con alguien

keeper ['kiːpəʳ, *Am:* -pɚ] *n* (*in charge*) guarda *mf*; (*museum*) conservador(a) *m(f)*; (*jail*) carcelero, -a *m, f*

keeping ['kiːpɪŋ] *n no pl* **1.** (*guarding*) cargo *m* **2. in ~ with sth** de acuerdo con algo

keepsake ['kiːpseɪk] *n* recuerdo *m*

keg [keg] *n* barril *m*

kennel ['kenl] *n* perrera *f*

Kenya ['kenjə] *n* Kenia *f*

Kenyan ['kenjən] *adj* keniano

kept [kept] *pt, pp of* **keep**

kerb [kɜːb, *Am:* kɜːrb] *n Brit, Aus* bordillo *m*, cordón *m CSur*

kernel ['kɜːnl, *Am:* 'kɜːr-] *n*

1. (*centre of fruit*) almendra *f* **2.** (*essential part*) **a ~ of truth** una pizca de verdad

kerosene ['kerəsiːn] *n no pl, Am, Aus* queroseno *m*

ketchup ['ketʃəp] *n no pl* ketchup *m*

kettle ['ketl, *Am:* 'ket-] *n* tetera *f*, pava *f AmL*

key [kiː] **I.** *n* **1.** (*doors*) llave *f* **2.** *a.* INFOR tecla *f* **3.** *no pl* (*essential point*) clave *f* **4.** (*list*) clave *f*; (*map*) lista *f* de símbolos convencionales **5.** MUS tono *m* **II.** *adj* clave **III.** *vt* **to ~ in** teclear

◆ **key in** *vt* INFOR picar, teclear

◆ **key up** *vt* emocionar; **to be keyed up** estar emocionado

keyboard ['kiːbɔːd, *Am:* -bɔːrd] *n* teclado *m*

keyhole ['kiːhəʊl, *Am:* -hoʊl] *n* ojo *m* de la cerradura

keynote ['kiːnəʊt, *Am:* -noʊt] *n* **1.** MUS nota *f* tónica **2.** (*central idea*) idea *f* fundamental

keypad ['kiːpæd] *n* INFOR teclado *m* numérico **key ring** *n* llavero *m*

kg *abbr of* **kilogram** kg

khaki ['kɑːki, *Am:* 'kæki] *n no pl* caqui *m*

kick [kɪk] **I.** *n* **1.** (*person*) patada *f*; (*horse*) coz *f*; (*in football*) tiro *m*; (*in swimming*) movimiento *m* de las piernas **2.** (*exciting feeling*) placer *m*; **to do sth for ~s** hacer algo para divertirse **3.** (*gun jerk*) culatazo *m* **II.** *vt* dar una patada **III.** *vi* (*person*) dar patadas a; (*horse*) dar coces; SPORTS chutar

◆ **kick about, kick around I.** *vi inf* (*hang about*) andar por ahí; (*thing*) andar rodando **II.** *vt* **1.** (*a ball*) dar patadas a **2.** (*treat badly*) maltratar

◆ **kick off I.** *vi* (*begin*) empezar; (*in football*) hacer el saque de centro **II.** *vt* quitar de un puntapié

kid [kɪd] **I.** *n* **1.** (*child*) niño, -a *m, f*, pipiolo, -a *m, f*; *Am, Aus* (*young person*) chico, -a *m, f* **2.** ZOOL cría *f*; (*young goat*) cabrito *m* **3.** (*goat leather*) cabritilla *f* **II.** <-dd-> *vi* bromear

kidnap ['kɪdnæp] **I.** <-pp-> *vt* secuestrar, plagiar *AmL* **II.** *n* secuestro *m*, plagio *m AmL*

kidnapper ['kɪdnæpə^r, *Am:* -ɚ] *n* secuestrador(a) *m(f)*

kidnapping *n* secuestro *m*

kidney ['kɪdni] *n* riñón *m*

kidney bean *n* judía *f*, poroto *m CSur*

kill [kɪl] **I.** *n no pl* matanza *f* **II.** *vt* **1.** (*cause to die*) matar **2.** (*destroy*) acabar con; **to ~ the flavour of sth** quitar el gusto a algo
  ♦ **kill off** *vt* exterminar; (*a disease*) erradicar

killer ['kɪlə^r, *Am:* -ɚ] *n* asesino, -a *m, f*

killing ['kɪlɪŋ] *n* (*of a person*) asesinato *m*; (*of an animal*) matanza *f*; **to make a ~** *fig, inf* hacer su agosto

killjoy ['kɪldʒɔɪ] *n* aguafiestas *mf inv*

kiln ['kɪln] *n* horno *m*

kilo ['kiːləʊ, *Am:* -oʊ] *n* kilo *m*

kilobyte ['kɪləʊbaɪt, *Am:* -oʊ-] *n* kilobyte *m*

kilogram *n Am*, **kilogramme** ['kɪləʊgræm, *Am:* -oʊ-] *n* kilogramo *m*

kilometre *n Brit, Aus,* **kilometer** [kɪ'lɒmɪtə^r, *Am:* kɪ'lɑːmət̬ɚ] *n Am* kilómetro *m*

kilowatt ['kɪləʊwɒt, *Am:* -oʊwɑːt] *n* kilovatio *m*

kilt [kɪlt] *n* falda *f* escocesa

kin [kɪn] *n no pl* **next of ~** parientes *mpl* más cercanos

kind¹ [kaɪnd] *adj* amable; **he was ~ enough to ...** tuvo la amabilidad de...; **would you be ~ enough to ...?** ¿me haría usted el favor de...?; **with ~ regards** (*in a letter*) muchos recuerdos

kind² [kaɪnd] *n* **1.** (*type*) clase *f*; **what ~ of ...?** ¿qué clase de...?; **they are two of a ~** son tal para cual **2.** (*sth similar to*) especie *f*

kindergarten ['kɪndəgɑːtn, *Am:* -dɚgɑːr-] *n* jardín *m* de infancia, jardín *m* de infantes *RíoPl*

kind-hearted [ˌkaɪnd'hɑːtɪd, *Am:* -'hɑːrt̬ɪd] *adj* bondadoso

kindle ['kɪndl] *vt a. fig* encender

kindly ['kaɪndli] **I.** <-ier, -iest> *adj* amable; (*person*) bondadoso **II.** *adv*

1. (*in a kind manner*) amablemente **2.** (*please*) **~ put that book away!** ¡haz el favor de guardar ese libro!

kindness ['kaɪndnɪs] <-es> *n* **1.** *no pl* (*act of being kind*) amabilidad *f* **2.** (*kind act*) favor *m*

kindred ['kɪndrɪd] **I.** *npl* parientes *mpl* **II.** *adj* afín; **~ spirits** almas *fpl* gemelas

kinetic [kɪ'netɪk, *Am:* -'net̬-] *adj* PHYS cinético

king [kɪŋ] *n* rey *m*

kingdom ['kɪŋdəm] *n* reino *m*

kingfisher ['kɪŋˌfɪʃə^r, *Am:* -ɚ] *n* martín *m* pescador

king-size ['kɪŋsaɪz] *adj* gigante; **~ cigarettes** cigarrillos *mpl* largos

kinky ['kɪŋki] <-ier, -iest> *adj* **1.** (*twisted*) retorcido **2.** (*with tight curls*) ensortijado **3.** (*unusual*) raro

kiosk ['kiːɒsk, *Am:* -ɑːsk] *n* **1.** (*stand*) quiosco *m* **2.** *Brit, form* (*telephone box*) cabina *f* (telefónica)

kipper ['kɪpə^r, *Am:* -ɚ] *n* arenque *m* ahumado

kiss [kɪs] **I.** <-es> *n* beso *m*; **~ of life** respiración *f* boca a boca **II.** *vt* besar; **to ~ sb goodnight/goodbye** dar un beso de buenas noches/despedida a alguien

kit [kɪt] *n* **1.** (*set*) utensilios *mpl*; **tool ~** caja *f* de herramientas **2.** (*parts to put together*) kit *m*

kitchen ['kɪtʃɪn] *n* cocina *f*

kitchen sink *n* fregadero *m*, pileta *f RíoPl*

kite [kaɪt] *n* (*toy*) cometa *f*, volantón *m AmL*

kith [kɪθ] *npl* **~ and kin** familiares *mpl* y amigos

kitten ['kɪtn] *n* gatito, -a *m, f*

kitty ['kɪti, *Am:* 'kɪt̬-] <-ies> *n* **1.** *childspeak* (*kitten or cat*) gatito, -a *m, f* **2.** (*money*) fondo *m*

kiwi ['kiːwiː] *n* **1.** ZOOL, BOT kiwi *m* **2.** *inf* (*New Zealander*) neozelandés, -esa *m, f*

km *abbr of* **kilometre** km

km/h *abbr of* **kilometres per hour** km/h

knack [næk] *n no pl* habilidad *f*; **to get the ~ of sth** coger el tranquillo a

algo, tomar la mano a algo *AmL*
knackered ['nækəd, *Am:* -ɚd] *adj*
Brit, Aus, inf hecho polvo
knapsack ['næpsæk] *n Brit, Am* mochila *f,* tamuga *f AmC*
knead [ni:d] *vt* **1.** GASTR amasar; (*clay*) modelar **2.** (*massage*) dar masajes a
knee [ni:] *n* rodilla *f*
kneecap ['ni:ˌkæp] **I.** *n* rótula *f* **II.** <-pp-> *vt* disparar en la rodilla/en las piernas
kneel [ni:l] <knelt *Am:* kneeled, knelt *Am:* kneeled> *vi* arrodillarse
knew [nju:, *Am:* nu:] *pt of* **know**
knickers ['nɪkəz, *Am:* -ɚz] *npl Brit* bragas *fpl*
knife [naɪf] <knives> *n* cuchillo *m*
knife-edge *n* filo *m;* **to be (balanced) on a ~** *fig* pender de un hilo
knight [naɪt] *n* **1.** HIST caballero *m* **2.** (*chess figure*) caballo *m*
knighthood *n* título *m* de Sir; **to give sb a ~** conceder a alguien el título de sir

[?] En Gran Bretaña, las personas que se han distinguido por sus méritos en favor de su país, son distinguidas con el honor de pasar a formar parte de la **knighthood** (nobleza) y reciben el título de **Sir** delante de su nombre, por ejemplo, **Sir John Smith.** La mujer de un **Sir** recibe el tratamiento de **Lady,** por ejemplo, **Lady Smith** (y se tiene que dirigir uno a ella de esta manera). Si se les quiere nombrar simultáneamente entonces se utilizaría la fórmula de **Sir John and Lady Smith.** A partir del año 1917 también una mujer puede ser distinguida por sus méritos. En ese caso recibe el título de **Dame,** por ejemplo, **Dame Mary Smith.**

knit [nɪt] **I.** *vi* (*wool*) hacer punto; (*with a machine*) tejer **II.** *vt* (*wool*)

tejer
◆ **knit together I.** *vi* **1.** (*combine or join*) unirse **2.** (*mend*) soldarse **II.** *vt* **1.** (*bones*) soldar **2.** *fig* (*join*) unir
knitting *n no pl* labor *f* de punto
knitting-needle *n* aguja *f* de hacer punto, aguja *f* de tejer *AmL*
knitwear ['nɪtweəʳ, *Am:* -wer] *n no pl* géneros *mpl* de punto
knives *pl of* **knife**
knob [nɒb, *Am:* nɑ:b] *n* **1.** (*of a door*) pomo *m* **2.** (*small amount*) pedazo *m;* (*of butter*) trocito *m* **3.** (*lump*) bulto *m*
knock [nɒk, *Am:* nɑ:k] **I.** *n* **1.** (*blow*) golpe *m* **2.** (*sound*) llamada *f* **II.** *vi* golpear; **to ~ on the window/at the door** llamar a la ventana/puerta **III.** *vt* **1.** (*hit*) golpear **2.** *inf* (*criticize*) criticar
◆ **knock down** *vt* **1.** (*cause to fall*) derribar; (*with a car*) echar por tierra **2.** (*reduce*) rebajar
◆ **knock off I.** *vt* **1.** (*cause to fall off*) hacer caer **2.** (*reduce*) rebajar; **to knock £5 off the price** rebajar 5 libras el precio **3.** *inf* (*steal*) robar **II.** *vi inf* terminar
◆ **knock out** *vt* **1.** (*render unconscious*) dejar sin sentido; SPORTS dejar K.O. **2.** (*eliminate*) eliminar
◆ **knock over** *vt* atropellar; (*objects*) volcar
knockdown *adj* **~ price** precio *m* de saldo
knocker ['nɒkəʳ, *Am:* 'nɑ:kɚ] *n* (*on door*) aldaba *f; inf* (*person*) detractor(a) *m(f)*
knockout *n* K.O. *m*
knot [nɒt, *Am:* nɑ:t] **I.** *n* nudo *m;* **to tie/untie a ~** hacer/deshacer un nudo **II.** <-tt-> *vt* anudar
knotty ['nɒti, *Am:* 'nɑ:t̪i] <-ier, -iest> *adj* **1.** (*lumber, wood*) nudoso; (*hair*) enredado **2.** (*difficult*) difícil
know [nəʊ, *Am:* noʊ] <knew, known> **I.** *vt* **1.** (*have information*) saber; **to ~ how to do sth** saber hacer algo; **to ~ that ...** saber que...; **do you ~ ...?** ¿sabes...?

K k

2. (*be acquainted with*) conocer; **to get to** ~ **sb** llegar a conocer a alguien **II.** *vi* saber; **as far as I** ~ por lo que sé; **to** ~ **of** [*o* about] **sth** saber de algo, estar enterado de algo; **I** ~**!** (*I've got an idea!*) ¡lo tengo!; (*said to agree with sb*) ¡lo sé!

know-all ['nəʊɔːl, *Am:* 'noʊ-] *n Brit, Aus, inf* sabelotodo *mf* **know--how** *n no pl* know-how *m*

knowing ['nəʊɪŋ, *Am:* 'noʊ-] *adj* astuto; (*grins, look, smile*) de complicidad

knowingly *adv* **1.** (*meaningfully*) con conocimiento **2.** (*with full awareness*) a sabiendas

knowledge ['nɒlɪdʒ, *Am:* 'nɑːlɪdʒ] *n no pl* **1.** (*body of learning*) conocimiento *m;* **to have (some)** ~ **of sth** tener (algún) conocimiento de algo **2.** (*acquired information*) saber *m;* **to have (no)** ~ **about sth/sb** (no) saber de algo/alguien; **to my** ~ que yo sepa; **to be common** ~ ser de dominio público **3.** (*awareness*) conocimiento *m;* **to bring sth to sb's** ~ poner a alguien en conocimiento de algo

knowledgeable ['nɒlɪdʒəbl, *Am:* 'nɑːlɪ-] *adj* entendido

known [nəʊn, *Am:* noʊn] **I.** *vt, vi pp of* **know II.** *adj* (*expert*) reconocido; (*criminal*) conocido

knuckle ['nʌkl] *n* nudillo *m*
♦ **knuckle down** *vi* ponerse a hacer algo con ahinco
♦ **knuckle under** *vi* darse por vencido

KO [ˌkeɪ'əʊ, *Am:* -'oʊ] *abbr of* **knockout** K.O.

Koran [kə'rɑːn, *Am:* -'ræn] *n no pl* **the** ~ el Corán

Korea [kə'rɪə] *n* Corea *f;* **North/ South** ~ Corea del Norte/Sur

Korean [kə'rɪən] *adj* coreano

kosher ['kəʊʃəʳ, *Am:* 'koʊʃə·] *adj* autorizado por la ley judía

kudos ['kjuːdɒs, *Am:* 'kuːdoʊz] *n no pl* gloria *f*

Kurd [kɜːd, *Am:* kɜːrd] *n* kurdo, -a *m, f*

Kurdish *adj* kurdo

Kurdistan [ˌkɜːdɪ'stɑːn, *Am:* ˌkɜːrdɪ'stæn] *n* Kurdistán *m*

Kuwait [kʊ'weɪt] *n* Kuwait *m*

Kuwaiti *adj* kuwaití

kw *abbr of* **kilowatt** KW

L, l [el] *n* L, l *f;* ~ **for Lucy** *Brit,* ~ **for Love** *Am* L de Lisboa

l *abbr of* **litre** l.

L **1.** *Brit abbr of* **Learner** L **2.** *abbr of* **large** G

LA [ˌel'eɪ] *n abbr of* **Los Angeles** Los Ángeles

lab [læb] *n abbr of* **laboratory** laboratorio *m*

label ['leɪbl] **I.** *n* **1.** (*on bottle, clothing*) etiqueta *f* **2.** (*brand name*) marca *f* **II.** <*Brit:* -ll, *Am:* -l> *vt* etiquetar

labor ['leɪbə·] *Am, Aus s.* **labour**

laboratory [lə'bɒrətrɪ, *Am:* 'læbrəˌtɔːrɪ] <-ies> *n* laboratorio *m*

laborer *n Am, Aus s.* **labourer**

laborious [lə'bɔːrɪəs] *adj* **1.** (*task*) laborioso **2.** (*style*) farragoso

labour ['leɪbəʳ, *Am:* -bə·] **I.** *n* **1.** (*work*) trabajo *m;* **manual** ~ trabajo manual **2.** *no pl* (*workers*) mano *f* de obra **3.** *no pl* (*childbirth*) parto *m;* **to be in** ~ estar de parto **II.** *vi* **1.** (*work*) trabajar **2.** (*do sth with effort*) esforzarse; **to** ~ **on sth** esforzarse en algo **III.** *vt* insistir en

Labour Day *n no pl, Am* Día *m* del Trabajo **labour dispute** *n* conflicto *m* laboral

labourer ['leɪbərəʳ] *n* peón *m*

Labour Exchange *n Brit* HIST bolsa *f* de trabajo

labour force *n* (*of country*) mano *f* de obra; (*of company*) plantilla *f* **Labour Party** *n no pl, Brit, Aus* POL **the** ~ el Partido Laborista **labour relations** *npl* relaciones *fpl* laborales **labour union** *n Am* sindicato *m*

Labrador ['læbrədɔːr (rɪ'triːvəʳ), *Am:* -dɔːr (-ɚ)] *n*, **Labrador retriever** *n* labrador *m*

labyrinth ['læbərɪnθ, *Am:* -ɚ-] <-es> *n* laberinto *m*

lace [leɪs] I. *n* 1. *no pl* (*cloth*) encaje *m;* (*edging*) puntilla *f* 2. (*cord*) cordón *m;* **shoe** ~s cordones *mpl* de zapatos; **to do up one's** ~s atarse los cordones II. *vt* (*fasten*) atar

◆ **lace up** *vt* atar

laceration [ˌlæsə'reɪʃn] *n* laceración *f*

lack [læk] I. *n no pl* falta *f;* **for** ~ **of** ... por falta de... II. *vt* carecer de

lacking ['lækɪŋ] *adj* **he is** ~ **in talent/experience** le falta talento/experiencia

lacquer ['lækəʳ, *Am:* -ɚ] *n* (*for wood, hair*) laca *f;* (*for nails*) esmalte *m*

lad [læd] *n Brit, inf* (*boy*) chico *m*

ladder ['lædəʳ, *Am:* -ɚ] I. *n* 1. (*for climbing*) escalera *f* (de mano) 2. *Brit, Aus* (*in stocking*) carrera *f* II. *vt* hacerse una carrera en

laden ['leɪdn] *adj* cargado; **to be** ~ **with** ... estar cargado de...

ladle ['leɪdl] *n* cucharón *m*

lady ['leɪdɪ] <-ies> *n* señora *f;* (*aristocratic*) dama *f;* **young** ~ señorita *f;* **ladies and gentlemen!** ¡señoras y señores!

ladybird ['leɪdibɜːd, *Am:* -bɜːrd] *n Brit, Aus,* **ladybug** ['leɪdibʌg] *n Am* mariquita *f* **ladylike** *adj* femenino **ladyship** *n form* **her/your** ~ Su Señoría

LAFTA *n abbr of* **Latin American Free Trade Association** ALALC *f*

lag¹ [læg] <-gg-> *vi* rezagarse; **to** ~ **behind** (**sb/sth**) quedarse detrás (de alguien/algo)

lag² [læg] <-gg-> *vt* (*insulate*) revestir con aislantes

lag³ *n Brit, inf* **old** ~ presidiario *m*

lager ['lɑːgəʳ, *Am:* -gɚ] *n no pl* cerveza *f* rubia

lagoon [lə'guːn] *n* laguna *f,* cocha *f AmS*

laid [leɪd] *pt, pp of* **lay¹**

laid-back [ˌleɪd'bæk] *adj inf* tranquilo

lain [leɪn] *pp of* **lie²**

lair [leəʳ, *Am:* leɪr] *n* 1. (*of animal*) cubil *m* 2. (*of criminal*) guarida *f*

laity ['leɪətɪ] *n no pl* **the** ~ el laicado

lake [leɪk] *n* lago *m*

lamb [læm] *n* cordero *m;* (*meat*) (carne *f* de) cordero *m*

lamb chop *n* chuleta *f* de cordero

lame [leɪm] *adj* 1. (*person, horse*) cojo 2. (*argument*) flojo; (*excuse*) débil

lament [lə'ment] I. *n* MUS, LIT elegía *f* II. *vt* lamentar III. *vi* **to** ~ **over sth** lamentarse de algo

laminated ['læmɪneɪtɪd, *Am:* -t̬ɪd] *adj* (*glass, wood*) laminado; (*document*) plastificado

lamp [læmp] *n* lámpara *f*

lamppost *n* farola *f* **lampshade** *n* pantalla *f* (de lámpara)

LAN [læn] *n* INFOR *abbr of* **local area network** RAL *f*

lance [lɑːns, *Am:* læns] I. *n* MIL lanza *f* II. *vt* MED abrir con lanceta

lancet ['lɑːnsɪt, *Am:* 'lænsɪt] *n* MED lanceta *f*

land [lænd] I. *n* 1. *no pl* GEO, AGR tierra *f;* **to travel by** ~ viajar por tierra; **to have dry** ~ **under one's feet** pisar tierra firme 2. (*area: for building*) terreno *m* 3. (*country*) país *m* II. *vi* 1. (*plane, bird*) aterrizar 2. (*arrive by boat*) llegar en barco 3. (*person, ball*) caer III. *vt* 1. (*bring onto land: aircraft*) hacer aterrizar; (*boat*) amarrar 2. (*unload*) desembarcar 3. (*cause*) **to** ~ **sb in trouble** meter a alguien en un lío

landfill site ['lændfɪl saɪt] *n* vertedero *m* de basuras

landing ['lændɪŋ] *n* 1. (*on staircase*) rellano *m* 2. AVIAT aterrizaje *m* 3. NAUT desembarco *m*

landing gear *n* AVIAT tren *m* de aterrizaje **landing strip** *n* pista *f* de aterrizaje

landlady ['lændˌleɪdi] <-ies> *n* (*of house*) propietaria *f;* (*of pub, hotel*) dueña *f;* (*of boarding house*) patrona *f* **landlord** *n* 1. (*of house*) propietario *m;* (*of pub, hotel*) dueño *m;* (*of boarding house*) patrón *m* 2. (*landowner*) terrateniente *m* **landmark** [-mɑ:rk] *n* 1. (*object serving as a guide*) mojón *m;* (*point of recognition*) punto *m* destacado 2. (*monument*) monumento *m* histórico

landowner *n* terrateniente *mf*

landscape ['lændskeɪp] *n no pl* paisaje *m*

landscape architect *n,* **landscape gardener** *n* arquitecto, -a *m, f* de jardines

landslide ['lændslaɪd] *n* 1. GEO corrimiento *m* de tierras 2. POL victoria *f* arrolladora

lane [leɪn] *n* 1. (*narrow road: in country*) vereda *f;* (*in town*) callejón *m* 2. (*marked strip: on road*) carril *m;* SPORTS calle *f* 3. AVIAT vía *f* aérea; NAUT ruta *f* marítima

language ['læŋgwɪdʒ] *n* 1. *no pl* (*system of communication*) lenguaje *m;* **bad** ~ palabrotas *fpl* 2. (*of particular community*) idioma *m;* **native** ~ lengua *f* materna

language laboratory *n* laboratorio *m* de idiomas

languid ['læŋgwɪd] *adj liter* lánguido

languish ['læŋgwɪʃ] *vi* languidecer

lank [læŋk] *adj* 1. (*hair*) lacio 2. (*person*) larguirucho

lanky ['læŋkɪ] *adj* desgarbado

lantern ['læntən, *Am:* -ţən] *n* linterna *f;* (*light*) farol *m*

Laos [laʊs] *n* Laos *m*

lap¹ [læp] *n* falda *f*

lap² [læp] *n* SPORTS vuelta *f*

lap³ [læp] <-pp-> *vt* 1. (*drink*) beber dando lengüetazos 2. (*waves*) acariciar

◆ **lap up** *vt* 1. (*drink*) beber dando lengüetazos 2. *fig, inf* aceptar entusiasmado

lapdog ['læp,dɒg, *Am:* -dɑ:g] *n* perro *m* faldero

lapel [lə'pel] *n* solapa *f*

Lapland ['læplænd] *n* Laponia *f*

Laplander ['læplændə^r, *Am:* -ə·] *n,* **Lapp** [læp] *n* lapón, -ona *m, f*

lapse [læps] **I.** *n* 1. *no pl* (*period*) lapso *m* 2. (*failure*) lapsus *m inv;* ~ **of memory** lapsus de memoria **II.** *vi* 1. (*deteriorate*) deteriorarse 2. (*end*) terminar; (*contract*) vencer; (*subscription*) caducar 3. (*revert to*) **to** ~ **into sth** reincidir en algo; **to** ~ **into silence** quedar(se) en silencio

laptop (**computer**) ['læptɒp, *Am:* -tɑ:p] *n* (ordenador *m*) portátil *m*

larceny ['lɑ:sənɪ, *Am:* 'lɑ:r-] <-ies> *n Am* hurto *m*

lard [lɑ:d, *Am:* lɑ:rd] *n no pl* manteca *f* de cerdo

larder ['lɑ:də^r, *Am:* 'lɑ:rdə·] *n* (*room*) despensa *f;* (*cupboard*) alacena *f*

large [lɑ:dʒ, *Am:* lɑ:rdʒ] *adj* grande; **a** ~ **number of people** un gran número de gente; **to be at** ~ andar suelto; **by and** ~ por lo general

largely ['lɑ:dʒlɪ, *Am:* 'lɑ:rdʒ-] *adv* en gran parte

large-scale [ˌlɑ:dʒ'skeɪl, *Am:* ˌlɑ:rdʒ-] *adj* a gran escala

lark¹ [lɑ:k, *Am:* lɑ:rk] *n* (*bird*) alondra *f*

lark² [lɑ:k, *Am:* lɑ:rk] **I.** *n* 1. *Brit, inf* (*joke*) broma *f* 2. *Brit, inf* (*business*) asunto *m* **II.** *vi Brit, inf* **to** ~ **about** hacer tonterías

larva ['lɑ:və] <-vae> *n* larva *f*

laryngitis [ˌlærɪn'dʒaɪtɪs, *Am:* ˌlerɪn'dʒaɪţɪs] *n no pl* laringitis *f inv*

larynx ['lærɪŋks, *Am:* 'ler-] <-ynxes *o* -ynges> *n* laringe *f*

laser ['leɪzə^r, *Am:* -zə·] *n* láser *m*

laser beam *n* rayo *m* láser **laser printer** *n* impresora *f* láser

lash¹ [læʃ] <-shes> *n* (*eyelash*) pestaña *f*

lash² [læʃ] **I.** <-shes> *n* 1. (*whip*) látigo *m* 2. (*stroke of whip*) latigazo *m* **II.** *vt* azotar

◆ **lash down** *vt* atar firmemente

◆ **lash out** *vi* 1. (*attack*) **to** ~ **at sb** atacar a alguien; (*verbally*) arremeter contra alguien 2. *inf* (*spend*) **to** ~ **on sth** gastarse mucho dinero en algo

lass [læs] <-sses> *n,* **lassie** ['læsɪ] *n Scot, inf* (*girl*) chica *f*

lasso [læ'su:, *Am:* 'læsoʊ] **I.** <-os *o* -oes> *n* lazo *m* **II.** *vt* lazar
last[1] [lɑ:st, *Am:* læst] *n* horma *f*
last[2] [lɑ:st, *Am:* læst] **I.** *adj* **1.** (*final: time, opportunity*) último; **this will be the ~ time** esta será la última vez **2.** (*most recent*) último; **~ night** anoche **II.** *adv* **1.** (*coming at the end*) por último **2.** (*most recently*) por última vez **III.** *n* **the ~ but one** el penúltimo; **at** (**long**) **~** al fin
last[3] [lɑ:st, *Am:* læst] *vi* durar
last-ditch [ˌlɑ:st'dɪtʃ, *Am:* ˌlæst-] *adj*, **last-gasp** [ˌlɑ:st'gɑ:sp, *Am:* ˌlæst'gæsp] *adj* desesperado
lasting ['lɑ:stɪŋ, *Am:* ˌlæst-] *adj* duradero
lastly ['lɑ:stlɪ, *Am:* 'læst-] *adv* por último
last-minute [ˌlɑ:st'mɪnɪt, *Am:* ˌlæst-] *adj* de última hora
latch [lætʃ] <-ches> *n* pestillo *m*
◆ **latch on** *vi inf* **to ~ to sb/sth** agarrarse a alguien/algo
late [leɪt] **I.** *adj* **1.** (*after appointed time*) retrasado; **the train was an hour ~** el tren llegó con una hora de retraso **2.** (*occurring after the usual time*) tardío; **in ~ summer** a finales del verano **3.** (*deceased*) fallecido **4.** (*recent*) reciente **II.** *adv* **1.** (*after usual time*) tarde; **to work ~** trabajar hasta (muy) tarde **2.** (*at advanced time*) **~ in the day** a última hora del día; **~ at night** muy entrada la noche **3.** (*recently*) **of ~** últimamente
latecomer ['leɪtˌkʌməʳ, *Am:* -ɚ] *n* persona o cosa que llega tarde
lately ['leɪtlɪ] *adv* (*recently*) últimamente, ultimadamente *Méx*
latent ['leɪtnt] *adj* latente
later ['leɪtəʳ] **I.** *adj comp of* **late** posterior; (*version*) más reciente **II.** *adv comp of* **late** más tarde; **~ on** después
latest ['leɪtɪst] *adj superl of* **late** último; **his ~ movie** su última película; **at the ~** a más tardar
lathe [leɪð] *n* torno *m*
lather ['lɑ:ðəʳ, *Am:* 'læðɚ] **I.** *n no pl* espuma *f* **II.** *vt* enjabonar
Latin ['lætɪn, *Am:* -ən] **I.** *adj* latino

II. *n* latín *m*
Latin America *n* América *f* Latina
Latin American *adj* latinoamericano
Latino [lə'ti:nəʊ, *Am:* -noʊ] *n* (*person*) latino, -a *m, f*
latitude ['lætɪtju:d, *Am:* 'læt̬ətu:d] *n* **1.** GEO latitud *f* **2.** *form* (*freedom*) libertad *f*
latter ['lætəʳ, *Am:* 'læt̬ɚ] *adj* **1.** (*second of two*) **the ~** el último **2.** (*near the end*) hacia el final
latterly *adv* últimamente
Latvia ['lætvɪə] *n* Letonia *f*
Latvian *adj* letón
laudable ['lɔ:dəbl, *Am:* 'lɑ:-] *adj form* loable
laugh [lɑ:f] **I.** *n* (*sound*) risa *f* **II.** *vi* reír(se); **to ~ at sb** reírse de alguien; **to ~ aloud** reírse a carcajadas; **to make sb ~** hacer reír a alguien
◆ **laugh off** *vt* tomar a risa
laughable ['lɑ:fəbl, *Am:* 'læfə-] *adj* de risa
laughing I. *n* risas *fpl* **II.** *adj* de risa; **this is no ~ matter** no es cosa de risa
laughing stock *n* hazmerreír *m*
laughter ['lɑ:ftəʳ, *Am:* 'læftɚ] *n no pl* risa(s) *f(pl)*
launch [lɔ:ntʃ, *Am:* lɑ:ntʃ] **I.** <-ches> *n* **1.** (*boat*) lancha *f* **2.** (*of missile*) lanzamiento *m* **II.** *vt* **1.** (*set in the water*) botar **2.** (*send forth: missile*) lanzar **3.** (*investigation*) emprender; (*exhibition*) inaugurar
launching ['lɔ:ntʃɪŋ, *Am:* 'lɑ:ntʃ-] *n* **1.** (*act of setting in the water*) botadura *f* **2.** (*of missile*) lanzamiento *m* **3.** (*of exhibition, campaign*) inauguración *f*
launderette [lɔ:n'dret, *Am:* lɑ:ndə'ret] *n Brit* lavandería *f* (automática)
laundry ['lɔ:ndrɪ, *Am:* 'lɑ:n-] *n* **1.** *no pl* (*dirty clothes*) ropa *f* sucia; **to do the ~** hacer la colada **2.** *no pl* (*washed clothes*) ropa *f* lavada
laureate ['lɒrɪət, *Am:* 'lɔ:riːɪt] *n* **Nobel ~** premio *mf* Nobel; **poet ~** poeta *m* laureado (*en Gran Bretaña, poeta elegido por la reina para escribir poemas en ocasiones especiales*)

L

laurel ['lɒrəl, *Am:* 'lɔːr-] *n* laurel *m*
lava ['lɑːvə] *n* lava *f*
lavatory ['lævətrɪ, *Am:* -tɔːrɪ] <-ies> *n* lavabo *m*, lavatorio *m AmL*
lavender ['lævəndəʳ, *Am:* -dɚ] *n* lavanda *f*
lavish ['lævɪʃ] **I.** *adj* abundante **II.** *vt* **to ~ sth on sb** prodigar algo a alguien
law [lɔː, *Am:* lɑː] *n* **1.** *a.* PHYS ley *f* **2.** (*legal system*) derecho *m*; (*body of laws*) ley *f*; **~ and order** la ley y el orden; **to be against the ~** ser ilegal **3.** (*court*) **to go to ~** recurrir a los tribunales
law-abiding ['lɔːəˈbaɪdɪŋ, *Am:* 'lɑː-] *adj* observante de la ley **law court** *n* tribunal *m* de justicia
lawful ['lɔːfl, *Am:* 'lɑː-] *adj form* (*legal*) legal; (*demands*) legítimo
lawless ['lɔːlɪs, *Am:* 'lɑː-] *adj* sin leyes; (*country*) anárquico
lawn [lɔːn, *Am:* lɑːn] *n* (*grass*) césped *m*, pasto *m AmL*
lawnmower *n* cortacésped *m* **lawn tennis** *n* tenis *m* sobre hierba
law school *n Am* facultad *f* de derecho **lawsuit** *n* proceso *m*; **to bring a ~ against sb** presentar una demanda contra alguien
lawyer ['lɔːjəʳ, *Am:* 'lɑːjɚ] *n* abogado, -a *m, f*
lax [læks] *adj* **1.** (*lacking care*) descuidado **2.** (*lenient*) indulgente; (*rules*) poco severo
laxative ['læksətɪv, *Am:* -t̬ɪv] *n* laxante *m*
lay¹ [leɪ] <laid, laid> *vt* **1.** (*place*) poner **2.** (*install*) colocar; (*cable*) tender; (*carpet*) poner, extender; (*pipes*) instalar **3.** (*prepare*) preparar; **to ~ the table** *Brit* poner la mesa **4.** (*egg*) poner **5.** (*state*) presentar; **to ~ one's case before sb/ sth** presentar su caso ante alguien/ algo
◆ **lay aside** *vt*, **lay away** *vt* **1.** (*put away*) guardar; **to ~ one's differences** dejar de lado las diferencias **2.** (*save: food*) guardar; (*money*) ahorrar
◆ **lay by** *vt* reservar

◆ **lay down** *vt* **1.** (*put down*) poner a un lado; (*arms*) deponer; (*life*) sacrificar **2.** (*establish*) estipular; (*law*) dictar
◆ **lay in** *vt* proveerse de
◆ **lay into** *vt* **1.** *inf* (*assault*) atacar **2.** (*criticize*) arremeter contra
◆ **lay off** *vt* despedir (temporalmente)
◆ **lay on** *vt* **1.** (*instal*) instalar **2.** (*provide: food, drink*) proveer de
◆ **lay out** *vt* **1.** (*organize*) organizar **2.** (*spread out*) extender **3.** *inf* (*money*) gastar
◆ **lay up** *vt* **1.** (*store*) guardar; (*money*) ahorrar **2.** (*ship*) desarmar; (*car*) dejar en el garaje **3.** (*in bed*) **to be laid up** guardar cama
lay² [leɪ] *adj* **1.** (*not professional*) lego; **in ~ terms** en términos profanos **2.** (*not of the clergy*) laico
lay³ [leɪ] *pt of* **lie²**
layabout ['leɪə,baʊt] *n inf* vago, -a *m, f*
lay-by ['leɪbaɪ] *n Brit* apartadero *m*
layer¹ ['leɪəʳ, *Am:* -ɚ] *n* capa *f*; **ozone ~** capa de ozono
layer² ['leɪəʳ, *Am:* -ɚ] *n* (*hen*) gallina *f* ponedora
layman ['leɪmən] <-men> *n* lego *m*
layout ['leɪaʊt] *n* **1.** (*of letter, magazine*) diseño *m*; (*of town*) trazado *m* **2.** TYPO maquetación *f*
layover ['leɪəʊvəʳ, *Am:* -oʊvɚ] *n Am* (*on journey*) parada *f*; AVIAT escala *f*
laywoman ['leɪwʊmən] <-women> *n* lega *f*
laze [leɪz] <-zing> *vi* holgazanear
laziness ['leɪzɪnɪs] *n no pl* holgazanería *f*
lazy ['leɪzɪ] <-ier, -iest> *adj* (*person*) vago; (*day*) perezoso
lb *abbr of* **pound** libra *f* (=0,45 kg)
LCD [ˌelsiːˈdiː] *n abbr of* **liquid crystal display** pantalla *f* de cristal líquido
lead¹ [liːd] **I.** *n* **1.** *no pl* (*front position*) delantera *f*; **to be in the ~** estar a la cabeza; **to take (over) the lead** tomar la delantera **2.** (*example*) ejemplo *m*; (*guiding*) iniciativa *f*

3. THEAT papel *m* principal **4.** (*clue*) pista *f* **5.** (*connecting wire*) cable *m*, conductor *m* **6.** Brit, Aus (*for dog*) correa *f* **II.**<led, led> *vt* **1.** (*be in charge of*) dirigir; (*discussion, inquiry*) conducir **2.** (*conduct*) conducir, llevar **3.** (*induce*) inducir; **to ~ sb to do sth** llevar a alguien a hacer algo; **to ~ sb to believe that ...** hacer creer a alguien que... **4.** COM, SPORTS encabezar **5.** (*live a particular way: life*) llevar; **to ~ a quiet/hectic life** llevar una vida tranquila/ajetreada **III.**<led, led> *vi* **1.** (*be in charge*) dirigir **2.** (*guide followers*) guiar **3.** (*conduct*) llevar **4.** (*be ahead*) liderar

◆ **lead aside** *vt* llevar a un lado

◆ **lead astray** *vt* llevar por mal camino

◆ **lead away** *vt* llevar

◆ **lead back** *vt* hacer volver

◆ **lead off I.** *vt* (*person*) llevar afuera; (*room*) comunicar con **II.** *vi* empezar

◆ **lead on** *vt* (*trick, fool*) engañar; (*encourage*) incitar a

◆ **lead to** *vt* llevar a

◆ **lead up to** *vi* conducir a

lead² [led] *n* **1.** *no pl* (*metal*) plomo *m* **2.** (*in pencil*) mina *f*

leaded ['ledəd] *adj* emplomado; **~ fuel** gasolina *f* con plomo

leaden ['ledn] *adj* **1.** (*dark*) plomizo **2.** (*heavy*) pesado

leader ['li:dəʳ, *Am:* -dɚ] *n* **1.** (*of group*) líder *mf* **2.** (*guide*) guía *mf* **3.** *Am* MUS director(a) *m(f)* **4.** Brit (*in newspaper*) editorial *m*

leadership ['li:dəʃɪp, *Am:* -dɚ-] *n no pl* **1.** (*ability*) liderazgo *m*; **~ qualities** dotes *fpl* de mando **2.** (*leaders*) dirección *f* **3.** (*function*) mando *m*

lead-free ['ledfri:] *adj* sin plomo

leading¹ ['ledɪŋ] *n no pl, Brit* emplomado *m*

leading² ['li:dɪŋ] *n no pl* mando *m*

leading lady *n* actriz *f* principal

leading light *n inf* **to be a ~ in sth** ser una figura de referencia en algo

leading man *n* actor *m* principal

lead up *n* tiempo *m* preparatorio

leaf [li:f] <leaves> *n* hoja *f*; **to take a ~ from sb's book** seguir el ejemplo de alguien

◆ **leaf through** *vt* hojear

leaflet ['li:flɪt] *n* folleto *m*

league [li:g] *n* **1.** *a.* SPORTS liga *f*; **to be in ~ with sb** estar confabulado con alguien **2.** (*measurement*) legua *f*

leak [li:k] **I.** *n* (*of gas, water*) fuga *f*; (*of information*) filtración *f*; (*in roof*) gotera *f* **II.** *vi* **1.** (*let escape*) tener una fuga; (*tyre*) perder aire; (*hose, bucket*) perder agua; (*pen*) perder tinta; (*tap*) gotear **2.** (*information*) filtrarse **III.** *vt* **1.** (*let escape*) derramar **2.** (*information*) filtrar

leakage ['li:kɪdʒ] *n* **1.** (*leak*) fuga *f* **2.** *no pl* (*of information*) filtración *f*

lean¹ [li:n] **I.**<leant *Am:* leaned, leant *Am:* leaned> *vi* inclinarse; **to ~ against sth** apoyarse en algo **II.**<leant *Am:* leaned, leant *Am:* leaned> *vt* apoyar; **to ~ sth against sth** apoyar algo contra algo

lean² [li:n] *adj* **1.** (*thin*) flaco; (*meat*) magro; (*face*) enjuto **2.** (*efficient: company*) eficiente

◆ **lean back** *vi* reclinarse

◆ **lean forward** *vi* inclinarse hacia adelante

◆ **lean out** *vi* asomarse

◆ **lean over** *vi* inclinarse

leaning ['li:nɪŋ] *n* inclinación *f*

leant [lent] *pt, pp of* **lean¹**

leap [li:p] **I.**<leapt *Am:* leaped, leapt *Am:* leaped> *vi* saltar; **to ~ to do sth** abalanzarse a hacer algo **II.** *n* salto *m*

◆ **leap up** *vi* **1.** (*jump up*) ponerse en pie de un salto; **to ~ to do sth** apresurarse a hacer algo **2.** (*rise quickly*) subir de pronto

leapfrog [ˌli:pfrɒg, *Am:* -frɑ:g] **I.** *n no pl* pídola *f* **II.**<-gg-> *vt* pasar por encima de

leapt [lept] *vt, vi pt, pp of* **leap**

leap year *n* año *m* bisiesto

learn [lɜ:n, *Am:* lɜ:rn] **I.**<learnt *Am:* learned, learnt *Am:* learned> *vt* aprender; **to ~ to do sth** aprender a hacer algo; **to ~ that** enterarse de que II. <learnt *Am:* learned, learnt *Am:* learned> *vi* aprender; **to ~ from one's mistakes** aprender de los propios errores

learned ['lɜ:nɪd, *Am:* 'lɜ:r-] *adj* erudito

learner ['lɜ:nəʳ, *Am:* 'lɜ:rnɚ] *n* aprendiz *mf*

learning ['lɜ:nɪŋ, *Am:* 'lɜ:r-] *n no pl* 1. (*acquisition of knowledge*) aprendizaje *m* 2. (*extensive knowledge*) saber *m*

learnt [lɜ:nt, *Am:* lɜ:rnt] *pt, pp of* **learn**

lease [li:s] I. *vt* alquilar II. *n* (*act*) arrendamiento *m;* (*contract*) contrato *m* de arrendamiento

leash [li:ʃ] *n Am* correa *f*

least [li:st] I. *adj* mínimo; (*age*) menor II. *adv* menos III. *n* lo menos; **at (the) ~** por lo menos, al menos; **to say the ~** para no decir más

leather ['leðəʳ] *n no pl* cuero *m*

leave¹ [li:v] I. <left, left> *vt* 1. (*depart from*) salir de; (*school, university*) abandonar; (*work*) dejar; **to ~ home** irse de casa 2. (*not take away with*) dejar; (*forget*) olvidar; **to ~ sth to sb** dejar algo a alguien II. <left, left> *vi* marcharse, despabilarse *AmL* III. *n* partida *f;* **to take (one's) ~ (of sb)** despedirse (de alguien)

◆**leave behind** *vt* 1. (*not take along*) dejar 2. (*forget*) olvidar 3. (*progress beyond*) dejar atrás

◆**leave off** *vt* 1. (*give up*) dejar de 2. (*omit*) omitir

◆**leave on** *vt* dejar puesto; (*light*) dejar encendido

◆**leave out** *vt* 1. (*omit*) omitir 2. (*exclude*) excluir

◆**leave over** *vt* dejar

leave² [li:v] *n* permiso *m;* **to go/be on ~** MIL salir/estar de permiso

leaves [li:fz] *n pl of* **leaf**

Lebanese [ˌlebə'ni:z] *adj* libanés, -esa

Lebanon ['lebənən, *Am:* -nɑ:n] *n* (**the**) ~ el Líbano

lecherous ['letʃərəs] *adj* lascivo

lectern ['lektən, *Am:* -tɚn] *n* atril *m;* REL facistol *m*

lecture ['lektʃəʳ, *Am:* -tʃɚ] I. *n* a. UNIV conferencia *f;* **a ~ on sth** una conferencia acerca de algo II. *vi* (*give a lecture*) dar una conferencia; (*teach*) dar clases III. *vt* 1. (*give a lecture*) dar una conferencia a; (*teach*) dar clases a 2. *fig* (*reprove*) sermonear

lecturer ['lektʃərəʳ, *Am:* -ɚ] *n* 1. (*person giving lecture*) conferenciante *mf* 2. UNIV profesor(a) *m(f)* universitario, -a

lecture room *n* UNIV sala *f* de conferencias **lecture theatre** *n* aula *f* magna

led [led] *pt, pp of* **lead¹**

LED [ˌeli:'di:] *n abbr of* **light-emitting diode** diodo *m* electroluminiscente

ledge [ledʒ] *n* (*shelf*) repisa *f;* (*on building*) cornisa *f;* (*on cliff*) saliente *m*

ledger ['ledʒəʳ, *Am:* -ɚ] *n* COM libro *m* mayor

lee [li:] *n* sotavento *m*

leech [li:tʃ] <-es> *n* sanguijuela *f,* saguaipé *m Arg*

leek [li:k] *n* puerro *m*

leer [lɪəʳ, *Am:* lɪr] *vi* mirar lascivamente

leeway ['li:weɪ] *n no pl* flexibilidad *f*

left¹ [left] *pt, pp of* **leave¹**

left² [left] I. *n* 1. *no pl* (*direction, sight*) izquierda *f;* **the ~** la izquierda; **on/to the ~** en/a la izquierda 2. *no pl* POL izquierda *f* II. *adj* izquierdo III. *adv* a [*o* hacia] la izquierda

left-hand [ˌleft'hænd] *adj* a la izquierda; **~ side** lado *m* izquierdo

left-handed *adj* zurdo; **~ scissors** tijeras *fpl* para zurdos

left-luggage office *n Brit* consigna *f,* consignación *f AmC*

leftovers ['leftˌəʊvəz, *Am:* -ˌoʊvɚz] *npl* 1. (*food*) sobras *fpl* 2. (*remaining things*) restos *mpl*

left wing *n* POL izquierda *f*

left-wing [ˌleft'wɪŋ] *adj* POL de izquierda

leg [leg] *n* 1. (*of person*) pierna *f;* (*of*

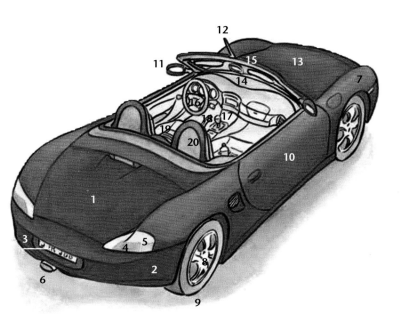

The car

1	boot *Brit*, trunk *Am*	maletero *m*
2	rear bumper	parachoques *m inv* trasero
3	number plate *Brit*, license plate *Am*	matrícula *f*
4	rear light *Brit*, tail light *Am*	luz *f* trasera
5	indicator *Brit*, turn signal *Am*	(luz *f*) intermitente *m*
6	exhaust pipe *Brit*, tailpipe *Am*	tubo *m* de escape
7	wing *Brit*, fender *Am*	guardabarros *m inv*
8	hubcap	tapacubos *m inv*
9	tyre *Brit*, tire *Am*	neumático *m*
10	door	puerta *f*

El coche

11	wing mirror *Brit*, side mirror *Am*	(espejo *m*) retrovisor *m* exterior
12	aerial *Brit*, antenna *Am*	antena *f*
13	bonnet *Brit*, hood *Am*	capó *m*
14	rear-view mirror	(espejo *m*) retrovisor *m*
15	windscreen *Brit*, windshield *Am*	parabrisas *m inv*
16	steering wheel	volante *m*
17	gear lever [*o* stick] *Brit*, gearshift *Am*	palanca *f* de cambio
18	handbrake *Brit*, emergency brake *Am*	freno *m* de mano
19	driver's seat	asiento *m* del conductor
20	headrest	reposacabezas *m inv*, apoyacabezas *m inv*

animal, furniture) pata *f;* **to pull sb's ~** tomar el pelo a alguien **2.** GASTR (*of lamb, pork*) pierna *f;* (*of chicken*) muslo *m* **3.** (*segment*) etapa *f*

legacy ['legəsɪ] <-ies> *n* legado *m;* (*inheritance*) herencia *f*

legal ['li:gl] *adj* **1.** (*in accordance with the law*) legal **2.** (*concerning the law*) jurídico

legalise *vt Brit, Aus,* **legalize** ['li:gəlaɪz] *vt* legalizar

legally ['li:gəlɪ] *adv* legalmente

legate ['legɪt] *n* legado *m*

legation [lɪ'geɪʃn] *n* legación *f*

legend ['ledʒənd] *n* leyenda *f*

leggings ['legɪŋz] *npl* mallas *fpl*

legible ['ledʒəbl] *adj* legible

legion ['li:dʒən] *n* legión *f*

legionnaire [ˌli:dʒə'neər, *Am:* -'ner] *n* legionario *m*

legislation [ˌledʒɪs'leɪʃn] *n* no pl legislación *f*

legislative ['ledʒɪslətɪv, *Am:* -sleɪtɪv] *adj* legislativo

legislator ['ledʒɪsleɪtər, *Am:* -t̬ə·] *n* legislador(a) *m(f)*

legislature ['ledʒɪsleɪtʃər, *Am:* -sleɪtʃə·] *n* cuerpo *m* legislativo

legitimacy [lɪ'dʒɪtɪməsɪ, *Am:* lə-'dʒɪt̬ə-] *n* no pl legitimidad *f*

legitimate [lɪ'dʒɪtɪmət, *Am:* lə'dʒɪt̬ə-] *adj* legítimo

legitimise *vt Brit, Aus,* **legitimize** [lɪ'dʒɪtəmaɪz, *Am:* lə'dʒɪt̬ə-] *vt* **1.** (*make legal*) legitimar **2.** (*justify*) justificar

legless ['legləs] *adj* **1.** (*without legs*) sin piernas **2.** *Brit, inf* (*drunk*) borracho, rascado *Col, Ven,* untado *RíoPl*

legroom ['legrʊm, *Am:* -ru:m] *n* no pl espacio *m* para las piernas

leisure ['leʒər, *Am:* 'li:ʒə·] *n* no pl ocio *m;* **at one's ~** cuando quiera uno

leisure activities *n* actividades *fpl* recreativas **leisure centre** *n* centro *m* recreativo

leisured *adj* (*comfortable*) acomodado

leisurely *adj* pausado

lemon ['lemən] *n* limón *m*

lemonade [ˌlemə'neɪd] *n* **1.** (*still*) limonada *f* **2.** *Brit* (*fizzy*) gaseosa *f*

lemon tea *n* té *m* con limón

lend [lend] <lent, lent> *vt* **1.** (*give temporarily*) prestar; **to ~ money to sb** prestar dinero a alguien **2.** (*impart, grant*) dar

lender ['lendər, *Am:* -də·] *n* FIN prestamista *mf*

length [leŋθ] *n* **1.** no pl (*measurement*) longitud *f;* **it's 3 metres in ~** tiene 3 metros de largo **2.** (*piece: of pipe, string*) trozo *m* **3.** (*of swimming pool*) largo *m* **4.** no pl (*duration*) duración *f;* **at ~** al fin, finalmente; **to go to great ~s to do sth** dar el máximo para hacer algo

lengthen ['leŋθən] **I.** *vt* alargar **II.** *vi* alargarse

lengthways ['leŋθweɪz] *adv, adj,* **lengthwise** ['leŋθwaɪz] *adv, adj* a lo largo

lengthy ['leŋθɪ] <-ier, -iest> *adj* prolongado; **a ~ wait** una larga espera

lenient ['li:nɪənt] *adj* (*judge*) indulgente; (*punishment*) poco severo

lens [lenz] <-ses> *n* **1.** (*of glasses*) lente *m o f;* (*of camera*) objetivo *m* **2.** ANAT cristalino *m*

lent [lent] *pt, pp of* **lend**

Lent [lent] *n* no pl Cuaresma *f*

lentil ['lentl, *Am:* -t̬l] *n* lenteja *f*

Leo ['li:əʊ, *Am:* -oʊ] *n* Leo *m*

leopard ['lepəd, *Am:* -əd] *n* leopardo *m*

leotard ['li:ətɑ:d, *Am:* -tɑrd] *n* malla *f*

leper ['lepər, *Am:* -ə·] *n* **1.** (*leprosy sufferer*) leproso, -a *m, f* **2.** (*disliked person*) marginado, -a *m, f*

leprosy ['leprəsɪ] *n* no pl lepra *f*

lesbian ['lezbɪən] *n* lesbiana *f*

lesion ['li:ʒn] *n* lesión *f*

Lesotho [lə'su:tu:, *Am:* lə'soʊtoʊ] *n* Lesoto *m*

less [les] *comp of* **little I.** *adj* (*in degree, size*) menor; (*in quantity*) menos **II.** *adv* menos; **to drink ~** beber menos **III.** *pron* menos; **~ than ...** menos que...; **~ and ~** cada vez menos

! **less** (= menos) se utiliza para cantidades: "In your glass there is less juice than in my glass; Lisa has eaten less than her brother;"

fewer (= menos) se utiliza para cosas contables o personas: "There are fewer pages in this book than in that one."

lessen ['lesn] I. vi reducirse II. vt disminuir; (risk) reducir

lesser ['lesə', Am: -ə·] adj comp of **less** menor; **to a ~ extent** en menor grado

lesson ['lesn] n 1. SCHOOL clase f 2. fig lección f; **to learn one's ~** aprenderse la lección

lest [lest] conj liter 1. (for fear that) no sea que +subj 2. (if) en caso de que +subj

let [let] <let, let> vt dejar; **to ~ sb do sth** dejar a alguien hacer algo; **to ~ sb know sth** hacer saber algo a alguien; **~'s go!** ¡vámonos!; **~'s see** veamos

◆ **let down** vt 1. (disappoint) decepcionar 2. (lower) bajar; (hair) soltar 3. FASHION alargar 4. Brit, Aus (deflate) desinflar

◆ **let in** vt (person) dejar entrar; (light) dejar pasar; **to let oneself in for sth** meterse en algo

◆ **let off** vt 1. (forgive) perdonar 2. (gun) disparar; (bomb, firework) hacer explotar

◆ **let on** vi inf (divulge) **to ~ about sth** revelar algo

◆ **let out** vt 1. (release) dejar salir 2. FASHION ensanchar 3. (rent) alquilar

◆ **let up** vi 1. (become weaker, stop) debilitarse; (rain) amainar; (cold) suavizarse; (fog) desvanecerse 2. (relent) aflojar

lethal ['li:θl] adj letal; (poison) mortífero; (weapon) mortal

lethargic [lɪ'θɑ:dʒɪk, Am: lɪ'θɑ:r-] adj 1. (lacking energy) letárgico 2. (drowsy) somnoliento

letter ['letə', Am: 'letə·] n 1. (mess-age) carta f 2. (symbol) letra f

letter bomb n carta f bomba **letter-box** n Brit, Aus buzón m de correos

lettering ['letərɪŋ] n no pl caracteres mpl

lettuce ['letɪs, Am: 'let-] n lechuga f

leukaemia n, **leukemia** [lu:'ki:-miə] n Am leucemia f

level ['levəl] I. adj 1. (horizontal) horizontal; (flat) plano 2. (having same height) **to be ~ with sth** estar a la misma altura que algo 3. Brit, Aus (in same position) **to be ~ with sb/sth** estar a la par de alguien/algo 4. (of same amount) igual II. adv a nivel III. n nivel m; **to be on the ~** (business, person) ser serio IV. <Brit: -ll-, Am: -l-> vt 1. (smoothen, flatten) nivelar 2. (demolish completely) derribar

◆ **level off** vi, **level out** vi (aircraft) nivelarse; (inflation) equilibrarse

level crossing n Brit, Aus paso m a nivel **level-headed** adj sensato

lever ['li:və', Am: 'levə'] I. n palanca f II. vt apalancar, palanquear AmL

leverage ['li:vərɪdʒ, Am: 'levə·-] n no pl 1. (using lever) apalancamiento m 2. fig influencia f

levity ['levətɪ, Am: -t̬ɪ] n no pl ligereza f

levy ['levɪ] I. <-ies> n tasa f II. <-ie-> vt imponer

lewd [lju:d, Am: lu:d] adj (person) lascivo; (gesture, remark) obsceno

lexicographer [ˌleksɪ'kɒgrəfə', Am: -kɑ:'grəfə·] n lexicógrafo, -a m, f

lexicography [ˌleksɪ'kɒgrəfɪ, Am: -kɑ:'grə-] n no pl lexicografía f

liability [ˌlaɪə'bɪlətɪ, Am: -t̬ɪ] n no pl responsabilidad f

liable ['laɪəbl] adj 1. (prone) propenso 2. LAW responsable; **to be ~ for sth** ser responsable de algo

liaise [lɪ'eɪz] vi **to ~ with sb/sth** servir de enlace con alguien/algo

liaison [li'eɪzn, Am: 'li:əzɑ:n] n 1. no pl (contact) enlace m; (coordination) coordinación f 2. (affair) aventura f

liar ['laɪə', Am: -ə·] n mentiroso, -a m, f

libel ['laɪbl] I. n LAW libelo m; PUBL difamación f II.<Brit: -ll-, Am: -l-> vt LAW, PUBL difamar

libellous adj, **libelous** ['laɪbələs] adj Am LAW, PUBL difamatorio

liberal ['lɪbərəl] I. adj 1.(tolerant) a. POL liberal 2.(generous) generoso II. n liberal mf

liberalise vt Brit, Aus, **liberalize** ['lɪbərəlaɪz] vt liberalizar

liberate ['lɪbəreɪt] vt liberar; (slaves) manumitir

liberation [ˌlɪbər'eɪʃən] n no pl liberación f

Liberia [laɪ'bɪərɪə] n Liberia f

Liberian adj liberiano

liberty ['lɪbətɪ, Am: -ə-tɪ] n no pl, form libertad f; **to be at ~ to do sth** tener el derecho de hacer algo; **to take the ~ of doing sth** tomarse la libertad de hacer algo

Libra ['li:brə] n Libra m

Libran ['li:brən] I. n Libra mf II. adj de Libra

librarian [laɪ'breərɪən, Am:-'brer-] n bibliotecario, -a m, f

library ['laɪbrərɪ, Am: -brer-] n <-ies> biblioteca f

libretto [lɪ'bretəʊ, Am:-'breṭoʊ] n libreto m

Libya ['lɪbɪə] n Libia f

Libyan ['lɪbɪən] adj libio

lice [laɪs] npl s. **louse 1.**

licence ['laɪsənts] n 1.(document) licencia f, permiso m; **driving ~, driver's ~** Am carnet m de conducir; **under ~** con licencia 2. no pl, form (freedom) libertad f

licence number n AUTO número m de matrícula **licence plate** n AUTO matrícula f

license ['laɪsənts] I. vt autorizar II. n Am s. **licence**

licensed adj autorizado; **a ~ restaurant** un restaurante con licencia de licores

licensee [ˌlaɪsənt'si:] n form concesionario, -a m, f

lick [lɪk] I. n 1.(with tongue) lamedura f 2.(light coating) **a ~ of paint** una mano de pintura II. vt 1.(with tongue) lamer 2. inf (beat) dar una paliza a

licorice ['lɪkərɪs, Am: -ə-ɪʃ] n no pl, Am regaliz f

lid [lɪd] n 1.(for container) tapa f, tape m Cuba, PRico; **to keep the ~ on sth** ocultar algo 2.(eyelid) párpado m

lie¹ [laɪ] I.<-y-> vi mentir II. n mentira f, guayaba f AmL, boleto m Arg; **to be an outright ~** ser de una falsedad total

lie² [laɪ] <lay, lain> vi 1.(be lying down: person) estar tumbado; form (be buried) estar enterrado 2.(be positioned) hallarse

◆**lie about** vi 1.(be somewhere) estar por ahí 2.(be lazy) holgazanear

◆**lie back** vi recostarse

◆**lie down** vi (act) acostarse; (state) estar acostado

◆**lie up** vi Brit esconderse, enconcharse Ven, Perú

lie detector n detector m de mentiras

lieu [luː] n no pl, form **in ~ of** en lugar de

lieutenant [lef'tenənt, Am: luː-] n 1. MIL teniente mf 2.(assistant) lugarteniente mf

life [laɪf] <lives> n vida f; **to breathe (new) ~ into sth** infundir (nueva) vida a algo; **to draw sth/sb from ~** ART copiar algo/a alguien del natural; **to get ~** ser condenado a cadena perpetua

life assurance n no pl, Brit seguro m de vida **lifebelt** n salvavidas m inv **lifeboat** n bote m salvavidas **life buoy** n salvavidas m inv **life expectancy** <-ies> n esperanza f de vida **lifeguard** n socorrista mf, salvavidas mf inv AmL **life insurance** n no pl seguro m de vida **life jacket** n chaleco m salvavidas

lifeless ['laɪfləs] adj 1.(dead) sin vida 2. fig flojo

lifelike ['laɪflaɪk] adj natural

lifeline n 1. NAUT cuerda f salvavidas 2. fig cordón m umbilical

lifelong [ˌlaɪf'lɒŋ, Am: ˌlaɪf'lɑːŋ] adj de toda la vida

life peer n Brit: miembro vitalicio de

la Cámara de los Lores **life pre-server** *n Am* salvavidas *m inv*
lifer ['laɪfə', *Am:* -fɚ] *n inf* condena-do, -a *m, f* a cadena perpetua
life sentence *n* condena *f* a cadena perpetua **life-size** *adj,* **life-sized** *adj* de tamaño natural **lifespan** *n* (*of animals*) tiempo *m* de vida; (*of people*) longevidad *f;* **the average ~** el promedio de vida; (*of machines*) la vida útil **lifestyle** *n* estilo *m* de vida **life-support system** *n* sistema *m* de respiración artificial **lifetime** *n no pl* (*of person*) vida *f;* **in my ~** durante mi vida; **the chance of a ~** (**for sb**) la oportunidad de su vida; **to happen once in a ~** suceder una vez en la vida
lift [lɪft] **I.** *n Brit* ascensor *m,* eleva-dor *m AmL;* **to give sb a ~** llevar (en coche) a alguien **II.** *vi* levantarse **III.** *vt* **1.** (*move upwards*) levantar; (*slightly*) alzar **2.** *inf* (*plagiarize*) pla-giar
 ◆ **lift off** *vi* AVIAT despegar
 ◆ **lift up** *vt* alzar
lift-off ['lɪftɒf, *Am:* -ɑːf] *n* AVIAT, TECH despegue *m*
ligament ['lɪgəmənt] *n* ligamento *m*
light [laɪt] **I.** *n* **1.** *no pl* (*energy, brightness*) luz *f* **2.** *no pl* (*daytime*) luz *f* (de día) **3.** (*source of bright-ness*) luz *f;* (*lamp*) lámpara *f;* **to put a ~ off/on** apagar/encender una luz; **to cast** [*o* shed] **~ on sth** arrojar luz sobre algo; **to come to ~** salir a la luz **4.** *no pl* (*flame*) fuego *m;* **do you have a ~?** ¿tienes fuego? **II.** *adj* **1.** (*not heavy*) ligero **2.** (*not dark: colour*) claro; (*skin*) blanco; (*room*) luminoso **3.** (*not serious*) ligero **4.** (*not intense: breeze, rain*) leve **III.** *adv* ligeramente; **to make ~ of sth** no dar importancia a algo **IV.** *vt* <lit *Am:* lighted, lit *Am:* lighted> **1.** (*illuminate*) iluminar **2.** (*start burning*) encender, prender *AmL*
 ◆ **light up I.** *vt* alumbrar, iluminar **II.** *vi* **1.** (*become bright*) iluminarse **2.** (*start smoking*) encender un ci-garrillo

light bulb ['laɪtbʌlb] *n* bombilla *f,* foco *m AmL*
lighten ['laɪtən] **I.** *vi* **1.** (*become brighter*) clarear **2.** (*become less heavy*) aligerarse; (*mood*) alegrarse **II.** *vt* **1.** (*make less heavy*) aligerar **2.** (*bleach, make paler*) aclarar
lighter ['laɪtə', *Am:* -t̬ɚ] *n* mechero *m,* encendedor *m AmL*
light-headed *adj* **1.** (*faint*) marea-do **2.** (*excited*) delirante **light-hearted** [-'hɑːrt̬ɪd] *adj* (*carefree*) despreocupado; (*happy*) alegre
lighthouse *n* faro *m*
lighting ['laɪtɪŋ, *Am:* -t̬ɪŋ] *n* ilumi-nación *f*
lightly ['laɪtlɪ] *adv* ligeramente; (*to rest, touch*) levemente; **to get off ~** salir bien parado
lightness ['laɪtnɪs] *n no pl* **1.** (*of thing, touch*) ligereza *f* **2.** (*bright-ness*) claridad *f*
lightning ['laɪtnɪŋ] *n no pl* relámpa-go *m*
lightning conductor *n Brit,* **light-ning rod** *n Am* pararrayos *m inv*
light pen *n* lápiz *m* óptico
lightweight I. *adj* (*clothing, materi-al*) ligero **II.** *n* SPORTS peso *m* ligero
light year *n* año *m* luz
likable ['laɪkəbl] *adj Am, Aus s.* **likeable**
like¹ [laɪk] **I.** *vt* **1.** (*find good*) **she ~s apples** le gustan las manzanas; **I ~ swimming** me gusta nadar; **I like it when/how ...** me gusta cuando/cómo... **2.** (*desire, wish*) querer; **would you ~ a cup of tea?** ¿quieres un té?; **I would ~ a steak** querría un filete **II.** *n pl* gustos *mpl*
like² [laɪk] **I.** *adj* semejante **II.** *prep* **to be ~ sb/sth** ser como alguien/algo; **what was it ~?** ¿cómo fue?; **what does it look ~?** ¿cómo es? **III.** *conj inf* como si +*subj*
likeable ['laɪkəbl] *adj* simpático
likelihood ['laɪklɪhʊd] *n no pl* pro-babilidad *f;* **in all ~** con toda pro-babilidad
likely ['laɪklɪ] <-ier, -iest> *adj* pro-bable; **to be quite/very ~** ser bas-tante/muy probable; **not ~!** *inf* ¡ni

hablar!

liken ['laɪkən] *vt* comparar; **to ~ sb to sb** comparar alguien con alguien

likeness ['laɪknɪs] <-es> *n* **1.** (*similarity*) semejanza *f* **2.** (*painting*) retrato *m*

likewise ['laɪkwaɪz] *adv* de la misma forma, asimismo

liking ['laɪkɪŋ] *n no pl* afición *f;* (*for particular person*) simpatía *f;* **to develop a ~ for sb** tomar cariño a alguien; **to be to sb's ~** *form* ser del agrado de alguien

lilac ['laɪlək] *adj* lila

lilo® ['laɪləʊ, *Am:* -loʊ] *n Brit* colchoneta *f* inflable

lily ['lɪlɪ] <-ies> *n* lirio *m*

limb [lɪm] *n* **1.** BOT rama *f* **2.** ANAT miembro *m;* **to be/go out on a ~ (to do sth)** estar/ponerse en una situación arriesgada (para hacer algo)

limber ['lɪmbəʳ, *Am:* -bɚ] *adj* (*person*) ágil; (*material*) flexible

♦ **limber up** *vi* hacer ejercicios de precalentamiento

limbo ['lɪmbəʊ, *Am:* -boʊ] *n no pl* limbo *m;* **to be in ~** estar en el limbo

lime¹ [laɪm] *n* **1.** (*fruit*) lima *f* **2.** (*tree*) limero *m*

lime² [laɪm] *n no pl* CHEM cal *f*

lime³ [laɪm] *n* (*linden tree*) tilo *m*

limelight ['laɪmlaɪt] *n no pl* foco *m* proyector; **to be in the ~** estar en el candelero

limerick ['lɪmərɪk, *Am:* -ɚ-] *n* quintilla *f* humorística

limestone ['laɪmstəʊn, *Am:* -stoʊn] *n no pl* caliza *f*

limit ['lɪmɪt] **I.** *n* límite *m;* (*speed*) ~ AUTO límite *m* de velocidad; **within ~s** dentro de ciertos límites **II.** *vt* limitar

limitation [ˌlɪmɪ'teɪʃn] *n no pl* restricción *f;* (*of pollution, weapons*) limitación *f*

limited ['lɪmɪtɪd, *Am:* -t̬ɪd] *adj* limitado; **to be ~ to sth** estar limitado a algo

limited company *n* sociedad *f* (de responsabilidad) limitada

limousine ['lɪməziːn] *n* limusina *f*

limp¹ [lɪmp] **I.** *vi* cojear **II.** *n no pl*

cojera *f;* **to walk with a ~** cojear

limp² [lɪmp] *adj* flojo

limpet ['lɪmpɪt] *n* lapa *f*

line¹ [laɪn] <-ning> *vt* revestir; (*clothes*) forrar

line² [laɪn] **I.** *n* **1.** (*mark*) a. MAT línea *f* **2.** *Am* (*queue*) fila *f,* cola *f AmL;* **to be in ~ for promotion** tener muchas posibilidades de ascender; **to stand in ~** hacer cola **3.** (*cord*) cuerda *f* **4.** TEL línea *f;* **hold the ~!** ¡no cuelgue! **5.** (*transport company*) línea *f;* **rail/shipping ~** línea de transporte ferroviario/marítimo **6.** (*of text*) línea *f,* renglón *m* **7.** (*field, pursuit, interest*) especialidad *f;* **what ~ are you in?** ¿a qué se dedica?; **to come out with a new ~** *Am* FASHION sacar una nueva línea **II.** <-ning> *vt* **to ~ the streets** ocupar las calles

♦ **line up** *vi, vt* alinear(se)

linen ['lɪnɪn] *n no pl* lino *m*

liner ['laɪnəʳ, *Am:* -nɚ] *n* **1.** (*lining*) forro *m;* **dustbin ~** bolsa *f* de la basura **2.** (*ship*) transatlántico *m*

linesman ['laɪnzmən] <-men> *n* SPORTS juez *mf* de línea

lineup ['laɪnʌp] *n* alineación *f*

linger ['lɪŋgəʳ, *Am:* -gɚ] *vi* entretenerse; (*film*) hacerse largo; **to ~ over sth** tomarse tiempo para (hacer) algo

lingerie ['lænʒəriː, *Am:* ˌlɑːnʒə'reɪ] *n no pl* lencería *f*

lingo ['lɪŋgəʊ, *Am:* -goʊ] <-goes> *n inf* **1.** (*foreign language*) idioma *m* (extranjero) **2.** (*jargon*) jerga *f*

linguist ['lɪŋgwɪst] *n* lingüista *mf*

linguistic [lɪŋ'gwɪstɪk] *adj* lingüístico

linguistics [lɪŋ'gwɪstɪks] *n* lingüística *f*

lining ['laɪnɪŋ] *n* **1.** (*of boiler, pipes*) revestimiento *m;* (*of coat, jacket*) forro *m* **2.** ANAT pared *f*

link [lɪŋk] **I.** *n* **1.** (*in chain*) eslabón *m* **2.** (*connection*) conexión *f;* **rail ~** enlace *m* ferroviario **3.** INFOR vínculo *m,* enlace *m* **II.** *vt* **1.** (*connect*) conectar **2.** (*associate*) relacionar

linoleum [lɪ'nəʊlɪəm, *Am:* -'noʊ-]

n, **lino** ['laɪnəʊ] *n* *no pl* linóleo *m*
lion ['laɪən] *n* león *m*
lioness [laɪə'nes] <-sses> *n* leona *f*
lip [lɪp] *n* **1.** ANAT labio *m* **2.** (*rim: of cup, bowl*) borde *m*; (*of jug*) pico *m*
lip-read *vi* leer los labios
lip salve *n* *no pl* crema *f* de cacao
lip service *n* *no pl* jarabe *m* de pico; **to pay ~ to sth** apoyar algo sólo de boquilla
lipstick *n* barra *f* de labios
liqueur [lɪ'kjʊəʳ, *Am:* -'kɜːr] *n* licor *m*
liquid ['lɪkwɪd] **I.** *n* líquido *m* **II.** *adj* líquido
liquidation [ˌlɪkwɪ'deɪʃn] *n* liquidación *f*; **to go into ~** ECON entrar en liquidación
liquidise ['lɪkwɪdaɪz] *vt* *Brit, Aus* *s.* **liquidize**
liquidiser ['lɪkwɪdaɪzəʳ] *n* *Brit, Aus* *s.* **liquidizer**
liquidize ['lɪkwɪdaɪz] *vt* licuar
liquidizer ['lɪkwɪdaɪzəʳ, *Am:* -zəʳ] *n* licuadora *f*
liquor ['lɪkəʳ, *Am:* -əʳ] *n* *no pl* licor *m*
liquorice ['lɪkərɪs, *Am:* -əʳ-] *n* *no pl* regaliz *m*
Lisbon ['lɪzbən] *n* Lisboa *f*
lisp [lɪsp] *n* *no pl* ceceo *m*
list[1] [lɪst] **I.** *n* lista *f*; **shopping ~** lista de la compra **II.** *vt* **1.** (*make a list*) listar **2.** (*enumerate*) enumerar
list[2] [lɪst] NAUT **I.** *vi* escorar **II.** *n* escora *f*
listen ['lɪsən] *vi* **1.** (*hear*) escuchar; **to ~ to sth/sb** escuchar algo/a alguien **2.** (*pay attention*) estar atento
listener ['lɪsnəʳ, *Am:* -əʳ] *n* oyente *mf*
listeria [lɪ'stɪərɪə, *Am:* -'stɪrɪ-] *npl* listeria *f*
listing ['lɪstɪŋ] *n* **1.** (*list*) lista *f*, listado *m* **2.** (*entry in list*) entrada *f*
listless ['lɪstlɪs] *adj* **1.** (*lacking energy: person*) apagado; (*economy*) débil **2.** (*lacking enthusiasm*) apático; (*performance*) deslucido
lit [lɪt] *pt, pp of* **light**
litany ['lɪtəni] <-ies> *n* letanía *f*
liter ['liːtəʳ, *Am:* -t̬əʳ] *n* *Am* litro *m*
literacy ['lɪtərəsi, *Am:* 'lɪt̬əʳ-] *n* *no*

pl alfabetización *f*; **~ rate** índice *m* de alfabetización
literal ['lɪtərəl, *Am:* 'lɪt̬əʳ-] *adj* literal
literally ['lɪtərəlɪ, *Am:* 'lɪt̬əʳ-] *adv* literalmente; **to take sth/sb ~** tomar algo/a alguien al pie de la letra
literary ['lɪtərərɪ, *Am:* 'lɪt̬ərer-] *adj* literario
literate ['lɪtərət, *Am:* 'lɪt̬əʳ-] *adj* **1.** (*able to read and write*) que sabe leer y escribir **2.** (*well-educated*) culto
literature ['lɪtrətʃəʳ, *Am:* 'lɪt̬əʳətʃəʳ] *n* *no pl* **1.** (*novels, poems*) literatura *f* **2.** (*promotional material*) material *m* informativo
lithe [laɪð] *adj* ágil
Lithuania [ˌlɪθjʊ'eɪnɪə, *Am:* ˌlɪθʊ-] *n* Lituania *f*
Lithuanian *adj* lituano
litigate ['lɪtɪgeɪt, *Am:* 'lɪt̬-] *vi* litigar
litigation [ˌlɪtɪ'geɪʃn, *Am:* ˌlɪt̬-] *n* *no pl* litigio *m*
litmus paper *no pl* *n* papel *m* de tornasol
litre ['liːtəʳ, *Am:* -t̬əʳ] *n* litro *m*
litter ['lɪtəʳ, *Am:* 'lɪt̬əʳ] **I.** *n* **1.** *no pl* (*refuse*) basura *f* **2.** ZOOL camada *f* **3.** MED camilla *f* **II.** *vt* esparcir; **the floor was ~ed with clothes** el suelo estaba cubierto de ropa
little ['lɪtl] **I.** *adj* **1.** (*size, age*) pequeño; **the ~ ones** *inf* los niños **2.** (*amount*) poco; **a ~ something** alguna cosita; **a ~ bit (of sth)** un poco (de algo); **~ by ~** poco a poco **3.** (*duration*) breve; **for a ~ while** durante un ratito **II.** *adv* poco; **~ more than an hour** poco más de una hora
liturgy ['lɪtədʒi, *Am:* 'lɪt̬əʳ-] <-ies> *n* REL liturgia *f*
live[1] [laɪv] *adj* **1.** (*living*) vivo **2.** RADIO, TV en directo; THEAT en vivo **3.** ELEC que lleva corriente; (*wire*) conectado **4.** (*cartridge*) cargado; (*bomb*) con carga explosiva
live[2] [lɪv] *vt* vivir; **to ~ a happy life** llevar una vida feliz
◆ **live down** *vt* lograr superar
◆ **live on** *vi* vivir; (*tradition*) seguir vivo

♦ **live out** *vt* vivir; (*dreams*) realizar
♦ **live up** *vt* **to live it up** vivir a lo grande
♦ **live up to** *vt* vivir conforme a; **to ~ expectations** estar a la altura de lo esperado
livelihood ['laɪvlɪhʊd] *n* sustento *m*
lively ['laɪvlɪ] *adj* (*person, conversation*) animado; (*imagination, interest*) vivo
liven up ['laɪvən ʌp] *vt* animar
liver ['lɪvə', *Am:* -ə·] *n* hígado *m*
livestock ['laɪvstɒk, *Am:* -stɑːk] *n no pl* ganado *m*
livid ['lɪvɪd] *adj* 1. (*discoloured*) lívido 2. (*furious*) furioso
living ['lɪvɪŋ] I. *n no pl* vida *f*; **to work for one's ~** trabajar para ganarse la vida; **to make a ~** ganarse la vida *f* II. *adj* vivo
living conditions *npl* condiciones *fpl* de vida **living room** *n* cuarto *m* de estar, living *m AmL* **living wage** *no pl n* salario *m* digno
lizard ['lɪzəd, *Am:* -ə·d] *n* lagarto *m*; (*small*) lagartija *f*
llama ['lɑːmə] *n* llama *f*
load [ləʊd, *Am:* loʊd] I. *n* carga *f*; **~s** [*o* **a ~**] **of ...** un montón de... II. *vt a.* AUTO, PHOT, INFOR cargar
loaded ['ləʊdɪd, *Am:* 'loʊd-] *adj* 1. (*filled*) cargado 2. (*unfair: question*) tendencioso 3. *Brit, inf* (*rich*) forrado
loaf[1] [ləʊf, *Am:* loʊf] <loaves> *n* pan *m*; **a ~ of bread** un pan
loaf[2] [ləʊf, *Am:* loʊf] *vi* gandulear
loan [ləʊn, *Am:* loʊn] I. *vt* prestar II. *n* préstamo *m*, avío *m AmS*
loath [ləʊθ, *Am:* loʊθ] *adj form* reacio; **to be ~ to do sth** resistirse a hacer algo
loathe [ləʊð, *Am:* loʊð] *vt* (*thing*) detestar; (*person*) odiar
loaves [ləʊfz, *Am:* loʊfz] *n pl of* **loaf**[1]
lob [lɒb, *Am:* lɑːb] <-bb-> *vt* SPORTS hacer un globo a
lobby ['lɒbi, *Am:* 'lɑːbi] I. <-ies> *n* 1. ARCHIT vestíbulo *m* 2. POL grupo *m* de presión II. <-ie-> *vt* presionar
lobbyist ['lɒbiɪst, *Am:* 'lɑːbi-] *n*

miembro *m* de un grupo de presión
lobe [ləʊb, *Am:* loʊb] *n* lóbulo *m*
lobster ['lɒbstə', *Am:* 'lɑːbstə·] *n* langosta *f*; (*with claws*) bogavante *m*
local ['ləʊkəl, *Am:* 'loʊ-] I. *adj* local II. *n* 1. (*inhabitant*) lugareño, -a *m, f* 2. *Brit* (*pub*) taberna *f* (*del barrio, pueblo, etc.*)
local anaesthetic *n* anestesia *f* local **local authority** *n* municipio *m*, ayuntamiento *m* **local call** *n* llamada *f* local **local government** *n* administración *f* municipal
locality [ləʊ'kæləti, *Am:* loʊ'kælə-ti] <-ies> *n* localidad *f*
locate [ləʊ'keɪt, *Am:* 'loʊ-] *vt* 1. (*find*) localizar 2. (*situate*) situar
location [ləʊ'keɪʃn, *Am:* loʊ'-] *n* posición *f*; **to film sth on ~** rodar algo en exteriores
loch [lɒx, *Am:* lɑːk] *n Scot* 1. (*lake*) lago *m* 2. (*inlet*) brazo *m* de mar
lock[1] [lɒk, *Am:* lɑːk] *n* (*of hair*) mechón *m*
lock[2] [lɒk, *Am:* lɑːk] I. *n* 1. (*fastening device*) cerradura *f*, chapa *f Arg, Méx* 2. (*on canal*) esclusa *f* 3. *fig* **~, stock and barrel** completamente, por completo II. *vt* 1. (*fasten with lock*) cerrar con llave; (*confine safely: thing*) guardar bajo llave; (*person*) encerrar 2. (*make immovable*) bloquear III. *vi* cerrarse con llave
♦ **lock away** *vt* (*document*) guardar bajo llave; (*person*) encerrar
♦ **lock out** *vt* impedir la entrada a; **to lock oneself out** dejarse las llaves dentro
♦ **lock up** *vt* (*document*) guardar bajo llave; (*person*) encerrar
locker ['lɒkə', *Am:* 'lɑːkə·] *n* (*at railway station*) consigna *f* automática; (*at school*) taquilla *f*
locket ['lɒkɪt, *Am:* 'lɑːkɪt] *n* guardapelo *m*
locksmith ['lɒksmɪθ, *Am:* 'lɑːk-] *n* cerrajero, -a *m, f*
lockup ['lɒkʌp, *Am:* 'lɑːk-] *n inf* 1. (*cell*) calabozo *m* 2. (*storage space*) garaje *m*
locum ['ləʊkəm, *Am:* 'loʊ-] *n Aus,*

L

Brit interino, -a *m, f*
locust ['ləʊkəst, *Am:* 'loʊ-] *n* langosta *f*, chapulín *m Méx*
locution [lə'kju:ʃn, *Am:* loʊ'-] *n* locución *f*
lodge [lɒdʒ, *Am:* lɑ:dʒ] I. *vi* alojarse II. *vt* (*objection, protest*) presentar III. *n* 1. (*for hunters*) refugio *m* 2. *Brit* (*at entrance to building*) portería *f* 3. (*of freemasons*) logia *f*
lodger ['lɒdʒəʳ, *Am:* 'lɑ:dʒə-] *n* inquilino, -a *m, f*
lodging ['lɒdʒɪŋ, *Am:* 'lɑ:dʒɪŋ] *n* 1. *no pl* (*accomodation*) alojamiento *m*; **board and ~** pensión *f* completa 2. *pl, Brit* (*room to rent*) habitación *f* de alquiler
loft [lɒft, *Am:* lɑ:ft] *n* 1. (*space under roof*) buhardilla *f* 2. (*upstairs living space*) loft *m*
lofty ['lɒftɪ, *Am:* 'lɑ:f-] <-ier, -iest> *adj* 1. *liter* (*tall*) altísimo 2. (*noble*) noble 3. (*haughty*) altivo
log¹ [lɒg, *Am:* lɑ:g] I. *n* 1. (*tree trunk*) tronco *m* 2. (*firewood*) leño *m* II. <-gg-> *vt* talar III. <-gg-> *vi* talar árboles
log² [lɒg, *Am:* lɑ:g] *inf abbr of* **logarithm** log.
log³ [lɒg, *Am:* lɑ:g] I. *n* registro *m*; **ship's ~** cuaderno *m* de bitácora II. *vt* 1. (*record*) registrar 2. (*achieve, attain*) alcanzar
◆ **log in** *vi* INFOR entrar en el sistema
◆ **log off** *vi* INFOR salir del sistema
◆ **log on** *vi s.* **log in**
◆ **log out** *vi s.* **log off**
logarithm ['lɒgərɪðəm, *Am:* 'lɑ:gə-] *n* logaritmo *m*
log book ['lɒgbʊk, *Am:* 'lɑ:gbʊk] *n* NAUT diario *m* de navegación; AVIAT diario *m* de vuelo
logger ['lɒgəʳ, *Am:* 'lɑ:gə-] *n* leñador(a) *m(f)*
loggerheads ['lɒgəhedz, *Am:* 'lɑ:gə-] *npl* **to be at ~** (**with sb/over sth**) estar en desacuerdo (con alguien/sobre algo)
logic ['lɒdʒɪk, *Am:* 'lɑ:dʒɪk] *n no pl* lógica *f*
logical ['lɒdʒɪkl, *Am:* 'lɑ:dʒɪk-] *adj* lógico

login [lɒgɪn, *Am:* lɑ:g-] *n* INFOR inicio *m* de sesión
logjam *n* atolladero *m*
logo ['lɒgəʊ, *Am:* 'loʊgoʊ] *n* logotipo *m*
logoff [lɒgɒf, *Am:* lɑ:gɑ:f] *n* INFOR fin *m* de sesión
logon *n s.* **login**
loin [lɔɪn] I. *n* 1. (*body area*) bajo vientre *m* 2. GASTR lomo *m* II. *adj* de lomo
loiter ['lɔɪtəʳ, *Am:* -ţə-] *vi* 1. (*linger*) entretenerse 2. *a.* LAW merodear
loll [lɒl, *Am:* lɑ:l] *vi* colgar; **to ~ about** holgazanear
lollipop ['lɒlipɒp, *Am:* 'lɑ:lipɑ:p] *n* chupachups® *m inv*
lollipop lady, lollipop man *n Brit, inf:* persona que detiene el tráfico para permitir que los escolares crucen la calle
lolly ['lɒlɪ, *Am:* 'lɑ:lɪ] <-ies> *n* 1. *Aus, Brit* (*lollipop*) chupachups® *m inv* 2. *no pl, Brit, inf* (*money*) pasta *f*
London ['lʌndən] *n* Londres *m*
Londoner *adj* londinense
lone [ləʊn, *Am:* loʊn] *adj* solitario
loneliness ['ləʊnlɪnɪs, *Am:* 'loʊn-] *n no pl* soledad *f*
lonely ['ləʊnlɪ, *Am:* 'loʊn-] <-ier, -iest> *adj* (*person*) solo; (*life*) solitario; (*place*) aislado
loner ['ləʊnəʳ, *Am:* 'loʊnə-] *n* solitario, -a *m, f*
long¹ [lɒŋ, *Am:* lɑ:ŋ] I. *adj* (*distance, time, shape*) largo; **it's a ~ while since ...** hace mucho tiempo desde que... II. *adv* mucho (tiempo); **~ after/before** mucho después/antes; **~ ago** hace mucho (tiempo); **to take ~** (**to do sth**) tardar mucho (en hacer algo); **all day ~** todo el día; **as ~ as** mientras +*subj* III. *n* mucho tiempo *m*; **the ~ and the short of it is that ...** en resumidas cuentas...
long² [lɒŋ, *Am:* lɑ:ŋ] *vi* **to ~ for sth** estar deseando algo
long. *abbr of* **longitude** long.
long-distance [ˌlɒŋ'dɪstənts, *Am:* ˌlɑ:ŋ-] *adj* (*bus, flight*) de largo recorrido; (*race, runner*) de fondo;

(*negotiations, relationship*) a distancia; ~ **call** conferencia *f*

longhand *n no pl* escritura *f* normal (*donde las palabras tienen todas sus letras*)

longing ['lɒŋɪŋ, *Am:* 'lɑːŋɪŋ] **I.** *n* **1.** (*nostalgia*) nostalgia *f* **2.** (*strong desire*) vivo deseo *m* **II.** *adj* anhelante

longitude ['lɒŋgɪtjuːd, *Am:* 'lɑːndʒətuːd] *n* longitud *f*

long jump *n no pl* salto *m* de longitud, salto *m* largo *AmL* **long-lost** *adj* perdido hace mucho tiempo **long-range** *adj* (*missile*) de largo alcance; (*aircraft*) transcontinental; (*policy*) a largo plazo **long-sighted** *adj* **1.** (*having long sight*) hipermétrope **2.** *Am* (*having foresight*) previsor **long-standing** *adj* antiguo **long-suffering** *adj* sufrido **long-term** *adj* (*care*) prolongado; (*loan, memory, strategy*) a largo plazo **long wave** *n* onda *f* larga **long-winded** [ˌlɑːŋ-] *adj* prolijo

loo [luː] *n Aus, Brit, inf* váter *m*

look [lʊk] **I.** *n* **1.** (*at person, thing*) mirada *f*; (*of book, face*) ojeada *f*; **to take** [*o* **to have**] **a ~ at sth** echar un vistazo a algo; **to have a ~ for sth/sb** buscar algo/a alguien **2.** (*appearance*) aspecto *m* **3.** (*style*) look *m* **II.** *vi* **1.** (*use sight*) mirar **2.** (*search*) buscar; **to ~ for sth/sb** buscar algo/a alguien **3.** (*appear, seem*) parecer **III.** *vt* mirar a; **to ~ north** mirar al norte

◆ **look after** *vi* **1.** (*tend, care for*) cuidar **2.** (*take responsibility for*) encargarse de

◆ **look around** *vi s.* **look round**

◆ **look back** *vi* **1.** (*look behind oneself*) mirar (hacia) atrás **2.** (*remember*) recordar

◆ **look down** *vi* **1.** (*from above*) mirar hacia abajo; (*lower eyes*) bajar la vista **2.** (*feel superior*) **to ~ on sth/sb** menospreciar algo/a alguien

◆ **look for** *vt* **1.** (*seek*) buscar **2.** (*expect*) esperar

◆ **look forward** *vi* **to ~ to sth** tener muchas ganas de algo

◆ **look in** *vi Brit, Aus* **to ~ on sb** ir a ver a alguien

◆ **look into** *vi* investigar

◆ **look on** *vi*, **look upon** *vi* **1.** (*watch*) mirar **2.** (*view*) ver

◆ **look out** *vi* tener cuidado; **to ~ for** tener cuidado con; (*look for*) buscar

◆ **look over** *vt* (*report*) revisar; (*house*) inspeccionar

◆ **look round** *vi* **1.** (*look behind oneself*) girarse **2.** (*look in all directions*) mirar alrededor **3.** (*search*) **to ~ for** buscar

◆ **look through** *vt* **1.** (*look*) mirar por **2.** (*examine*) revisar **3.** (*peruse*) **to ~ sth** echar un vistazo a algo

◆ **look to** *vi* **1.** (*attend to*) mirar por **2.** (*depend on*) depender de **3.** (*count on*) contar con

◆ **look up I.** *vt* **1.** (*consult*) buscar **2.** (*visit*) ir a ver **II.** *vi* mirar hacia arriba; **to ~ to sb** *fig* tener a alguien como ejemplo

loom¹ [luːm] *n* telar *m*

loom² [luːm] *vi* **1.** (*come into view*) surgir **2.** (*threaten*) amenazar

loony ['luːnɪ] **I.** <-ier, -iest> *adj inf* (*person*) chiflado; (*idea*) disparatado **II.** <-ies> *n inf* loco, -a *m, f*, chiflado, -a *m, f*

loop [luːp] *n* **1.** (*bend*) curva *f*; (*of string*) lazada *f*; (*of river*) meandro *m* **2.** ELEC circuito *m* cerrado **3.** INFOR bucle *m* **4.** (*contraceptive coil*) espiral *f*

loophole ['luːphəʊl, *Am:* -hoʊl] *n fig* escapatoria *f*

loose [luːs] **I.** *adj* **1.** (*not tight: clothing*) holgado; (*knot, rope, screw*) flojo; (*skin*) flácido **2.** (*not confined*) suelto **3.** (*discipline*) relajado **II.** *vt* soltar

loosely ['luːslɪ] *adv* libremente

loosen ['luːsn] *vt* (*belt*) aflojar; (*tongue*) desatar

loot [luːt] **I.** *n no pl* botín *m* **II.** *vt, vi* saquear

looting *n no pl* saqueo *m*

lopsided [ˌlɒp'saɪdɪd, *Am:* ˌlɑːp-] *adj* **1.** (*leaning to one side*) torcido, chueco *AmL* **2.** (*biased*) parcial

L

lord [lɔːd, *Am:* lɔːrd] *n* **1.** *Brit* (*British peer*) lord *m* **2.** (*aristocrat*) señor *m*

lordship [ˈlɔːdʃɪp, *Am:* ˈlɔːrd-] *n no pl, form* **His Lordship** *Brit* Su Señoría

lore [lɔːʳ, *Am:* lɔːr] *n no pl* sabiduría *f*

lorry [ˈlɒrɪ, *Am:* ˈlɔːr-] <-ies> *n Brit* camión *m*

lorry driver *n Brit* camionero(a) *m(f)*

lose [luːz] <lost, lost> **I.** *vt* perder; **to get lost** (*person*) perderse; (*object*) extraviarse **II.** *vi* perder

loser [ˈluːzəʳ, *Am:* -zɚ] *n* perdedor(a) *m(f)*

loss [lɒs, *Am:* lɑːs] <-es> *n* pérdida *f;* **to be at a ~** no saber cómo reaccionar

lost [lɒst, *Am:* lɑːst] **I.** *pt, pp of* **lose** **II.** *adj* perdido; **to be ~ in a book** estar enfrascado en la lectura de un libro

lost property *no pl n* objetos *mpl* perdidos

lost property office *n Brit, Aus* oficina *f* de objetos perdidos

lot [lɒt, *Am:* lɑːt] *n* **1.** (*destiny*) destino *m* **2.** *Brit* (*large quantity*) **a ~ of, ~s of** mucho(s); **I like it a ~** me gusta mucho **3.** (*in auction*) lote *m*

lotion [ˈləʊʃn, *Am:* ˈloʊ-] *n no pl* loción *f*

lottery [ˈlɒtərɪ, *Am:* ˈlɑːt̬ɚ-] <-ies> *n* lotería *f,* quiniela *f CSur*

loud [laʊd] **I.** *adj* **1.** (*voice*) alto; (*shout*) fuerte **2.** (*noisy*) ruidoso **II.** *adv* alto; **to laugh out ~** reír a carcajadas

loudhailer [ˌlaʊdˈheɪləʳ, *Am:* -lɚ] *n Brit, Aus* megáfono *m*

loudspeaker [ˌlaʊdˈspiːkəʳ, *Am:* ˌlaʊdˈspiːkɚ] *n* altavoz *m*

Louisiana [luˌiːziˈænə] *n* Luisiana *f*

lounge [laʊndʒ] **I.** *n* salón *m* **II.** *vi* **1.** (*recline*) repanchigarse **2.** (*be idle*) hacer el vago
  ◆ **lounge about** *vt,* **lounge around** *vt* holgazanear

lounge bar *n Brit* bar *m* **lounge suit** *n Brit* traje *m* (de calle)

louse [laʊs] *n* **1.** <lice> (*insect*)

piojo *m* **2.** <-es> *inf* (*person*) canalla *mf*

lousy [ˈlaʊzɪ] <-ier, -iest> *adj inf* **1.** (*infested with lice*) piojoso **2.** (*contemptible*) asqueroso

lout [laʊt] *n* patán *m,* jallán *m AmC*

lovable [ˈlʌvəbl] *adj* adorable

love [lʌv] **I.** *vt* querer, amar; **I ~ swimming, I ~ to swim** me encanta nadar **II.** *n* **1.** *no pl* (*affection*) amor *m;* **to be in ~** (**with sb**) estar enamorado (de alguien); **to make ~ to sb** hacer el amor con alguien **2.** *no pl* (*in tennis*) cero *m*

love affair *n* aventura *f,* romance *m*

love life *n inf* vida *f* amorosa [*o* sentimental]

lovely [ˈlʌvlɪ] <-ier, -iest> *adj* (*house, present*) bonito; (*weather*) precioso; (*person*) encantador; **to have a ~ time** pasarlo estupendamente

lover [ˈlʌvəʳ, *Am:* -ɚ] *n* amante *mf*

lovesick [ˈlʌvsɪk] *adj* locamente enamorado, volado *AmL*

loving [ˈlʌvɪŋ] *adj* cariñoso

low¹ [ləʊ, *Am:* loʊ] **I.** *adj* **1.** (*not high, not loud*) bajo; **to be ~** (**on sth**) tener poco (de algo) **2.** (*poor: opinion, quality*) malo; (*self-esteem*) bajo; (*visibility*) poco **II.** *adv* bajo **III.** *n* **1.** METEO depresión *f* **2.** (*minimum*) mínimo *m*

low² [ləʊ, *Am:* loʊ] *vi* mugir

low-alcohol *adj* bajo en alcohol **low-calorie** *adj* bajo en calorías **low-cost** *adj* económico **low-cut** *adj* escotado

lower [ˈləʊəʳ, *Am:* ˈloʊɚ] *vt* bajar; (*flag, sails*) arriar; (*lifeboat*) echar al agua; **to ~ oneself to do sth** rebajarse a hacer algo

Lower House *n* **the ~** la Cámara Baja

low-fat *adj* bajo en calorías; (*milk*) desnatado

lowland *npl* tierras *fpl* bajas, bajío *m AmL*

lowly [ˈləʊlɪ, *Am:* ˈloʊ-] <-ier, -iest> *adj* humilde

low-tech *adj* de baja tecnología

loyal [ˈlɔɪəl] *adj* leal

loyalist [ˈlɔɪəlɪst] *n* partidario, -a *m,*

f del régimen

loyalty ['lɔɪəltɪ, *Am:* -t̬ɪ] <-ies> *n* lealtad *f*

lozenge ['lɒzɪndʒ, *Am:* 'lɑːzəndʒ] *n* pastilla *f*

LP [ˌel'piː] *n abbr of* **long-playing record** LP *m*

Ltd ['lɪmɪtɪd, *Am:* -ət̬ɪd] *abbr of* **Limited** SA

lubricant ['luːbrɪkənt] *n no pl* lubricante *m*

lubricate ['luːbrɪkeɪt] *vt* lubricar

lucid ['luːsɪd] *adj* 1. (*rational*) lúcido 2. (*easily understood*) claro

luck [lʌk] *n no pl* suerte *f*; **good/bad** ~ buena/mala suerte; **to wish sb** (**good**) ~ desear a alguien (buena) suerte; **a stroke of** ~ un golpe de suerte

lucky ['lʌkɪ] <-ier, -iest> *adj* afortunado

lucrative ['luːkrətɪv, *Am:* -t̬ɪv] *adj* lucrativo

ludicrous ['luːdɪkrəs] *adj* absurdo

lug [lʌg] <-gg-> *vt inf* arrastrar

luggage ['lʌgɪdʒ] *n no pl* equipaje *m*

luggage rack *n Brit* baca *f*

lukewarm [ˌluːk'wɔːm, *Am:* -'wɔːrm] *adj* 1. (*liquid*) tibio 2. (*unenthusiastic*) poco entusiasta

lull [lʌl] I. *vt* calmar II. *n* período *m* de calma; (*in fighting*) tregua *f*

lullaby ['lʌləbaɪ] <-ies> *n* nana *f*

lumbago [lʌm'beɪgəʊ, *Am:* -goʊ] *n no pl* lumbago *m*

lumber¹ ['lʌmbə', *Am:* -bɚ] *vi* moverse pesadamente

lumber² ['lʌmbə', *Am:* -bɚ] I. *vt Aus, Brit, inf* **to ~ sb with sth** endilgar algo a alguien II. *n no pl* 1. *Am, Aus* madera *f* 2. (*junk*) trastos *mpl*

lumberjack *n* leñador *m*

luminous ['luːmɪnəs, *Am:* 'luːmə-] *adj* luminoso

lump [lʌmp] I. *n* 1. (*solid mass*) masa *f*; (*of coal*) trozo *m*; (*of sugar*) terrón *m*; ~ **sum** cantidad *f* única 2. (*swelling: in breast, on head*) bulto *m* II. *vt* 1. (*combine*) agrupar 2. (*endure*) aguantar

lumpy ['lʌmpɪ] <-ier, -iest> *adj*

(*custard, sauce*) grumoso; (*surface*) desigual

lunacy ['luːnəsɪ, *Am:* 'luː-] *n no pl* locura *f*

lunar ['luːnə', *Am:* 'luːnɚ] *adj* lunar

lunatic ['luːnətɪk] I. *n* loco, -a *m, f* II. *adj* lunático

lunch [lʌntʃ] I. *n* comida *f*; **to have** ~ comer II. *vi* comer

lunch break *n* descanso *m* para comer

luncheon ['lʌntʃən] *n form* comida *f*

luncheon meat *n* fiambre de cerdo en conserva **luncheon voucher** *n Brit* vale *m* de comida

lunchtime *n* hora *f* de comer

lung [lʌŋ] *n* pulmón *m*

lunge [lʌndʒ] *vi* **to ~ at sb** arremeter contra alguien

lurch [lɜːtʃ, *Am:* lɜːrtʃ] I. *vi* (*people*) tambalearse; (*car, train*) dar sacudidas II. <-es> *n* sacudida *f*; **to leave sb in the** ~ *inf* dejar a alguien colgado

lure [lʊə', *Am:* lʊr] I. *n* 1. (*attraction*) atractivo *m* 2. (*bait*) cebo *m*; (*decoy*) señuelo *m* II. *vt* atraer

lurid ['lʊərɪd, *Am:* 'lʊrɪd] *adj* 1. (*details*) escabroso; (*language*) morboso 2. (*extremely bright*) chillón

lurk [lɜːk, *Am:* lɜːrk] *vi* esconderse

luscious ['lʌʃəs] *adj* 1. (*fruit*) jugoso 2. *inf* (*girl, curves*) voluptuoso; (*lips*) carnoso

lush [lʌʃ] *adj* exuberante

lust [lʌst] *n* 1. (*sexual desire*) lujuria *f* 2. (*strong desire*) anhelo *m*

lusty ['lʌstɪ] <-ier, -iest> *adj* (*person*) sano; (*voice*) potente

lute [luːt] *n* laúd *m*

Luxembourg ['lʌksəmbɜːg, *Am:* -bɜːrg] *n* Luxemburgo *m*

Luxembourger *n* luxemburgés, -esa *m, f*

luxurious [lʌg'ʒʊərɪəs, *Am:* -'ʒʊrɪ-] *adj* lujoso

luxury ['lʌkʃərɪ, *Am:* -ʃɚ-] <-ies> *n* lujo *m*; ~ **flat** piso *m* de lujo

LW *n abbr of* **long wave** OL *f*

Lycra® ['laɪkrə] *n* licra® *f*

lying ['laɪɪŋ] I. *n* mentiras *fpl* II. *adj* mentiroso

lyric ['lɪrɪk] I. *adj* lírico II. *n pl* letra *f*
lyrical ['lɪrɪkl] *adj* lírico

Mm

M, m [em] *n* M, m *f*; ~ **for Mary**
Brit, ~ **for Mike** *Am* M de María
m 1. *abbr of* **metre** m **2.** *abbr of* **mile**
milla *f* **3.** *abbr of* **million** millón *m*
mac [mæk] *n Brit, inf* impermeable
m
macabre [məˈkɑːbrə] *adj* macabro
macaroni [ˌmækəˈrəʊni, *Am:*
-əˈroʊ-] *n* macarrones *mpl*
Macedonia [ˌmæsɪˈdəʊniə, *Am:* -ə-
ˈdoʊni-] *n* Macedonia *f*
Macedonian *adj* macedonio
machine [məˈʃiːn] *n* máquina *f*
machine gun *n* ametralladora *f*
machinery [məˈʃiːnəri] *n no pl, a.
fig* maquinaria *f*
macho ['mætʃəʊ, *Am:* 'mɑːtʃoʊ]
adj machista
mackerel ['mækrəl] <-(s)> *n* caballa *f*
mackintosh ['mækɪntɒʃ, *Am:* -tɑːʃ]
<-es> *n Brit* impermeable *m*
macroeconomics [ˌmækrəʊiːk-
əˈnɒmɪks, *Am:* -roʊˌekəˈnɑːmɪks]
n macroeconomía *f*
mad [mæd] *adj Brit* loco; **to go ~**
volverse loco; **to be ~ about sb**
estar loco por alguien
Madagascar [ˌmædəˈɡæskəʳ, *Am:*
-kɚ] *n* Madagascar *m*
madam ['mædəm] *n no pl* señora *f*
madden ['mædən] *vt* enfurecer
made [meɪd] *pt, pp of* **make**
madman ['mædmən] <-men> *n*
loco *m*
madness ['mædnɪs] *n no pl* locura *f*,
loquera *f AmL*
maestro ['maɪstrəʊ, *Am:* -stroʊ] *n*
maestro *m*
Mafia ['mæfiə, *Am:* 'mɑː-] *n* mafia *f*
magazine [ˌmægəˈziːn, *Am:* 'mæ-
gəziːn] *n* **1.** (*periodical publication*) revista *f* **2.** MIL recámara *f*
magic ['mædʒɪk] I. *n no pl* magia *f*
II. *adj* mágico
magical *adj* **1.** (*power*) mágico
2. (*extraordinary, wonderful*) fabuloso
magician [məˈdʒɪʃn] *n* mago, -a
m, f
magistrate ['mædʒɪstreɪt] *n Brit:
juez que se ocupa de los delitos menores*
magnate ['mægneɪt] *n* magnate *m*
magnet ['mægnɪt] *n* imán *m*
magnetic [mægˈnetɪk, *Am:* -ˈneṭ-]
adj **1.** (*force*) magnético **2.** (*personality*) atrayente
magnetism ['mægnətɪzəm, *Am:*
-ṭɪ-] *n no pl* magnetismo *m*
magnificent [mægˈnɪfɪsnt] *adj*
magnífico
magnify ['mægnɪfaɪ] <-ie-> *vt* ampliar
magnitude ['mægnɪtjuːd, *Am:*
-tuːd] *n no pl* envergadura *f*
mahogany [məˈhɒɡəni, *Am:* -ˈhɑː-
ɡən-] *n no pl* caoba *f*
maid [meɪd] *n* **1.** (*female servant*)
criada *f*, mucama *f AmL* **2.** *liter* doncella *f*
maiden ['meɪdən] *n liter* doncella *f*
mail[1] [meɪl] I. *n no pl a.* INFOR correo
m; **electronic ~** INFOR correo electrónico II. *vt* mandar [*o* enviar] por
correo
mail[2] [meɪl] *n no pl* (*armour*) malla *f*
mailbox *n* **1.** *Am* (*postbox*) buzón *m*
2. INFOR (**electronic**) ~ buzón *m*
electrónico
maim [meɪm] *vt* lisiar
main [meɪn] I. *adj* (*problem, reason, street*) principal; **~ cable** cable
m principal II. *n pl, Brit* ELEC, TECH
red *f* de suministro
mainland ['meɪnlənd] *n no pl*
continente *m*
mainly ['meɪnli] *adv* principalmente
mainstream I. *n no pl* corriente *f*
dominante II. *adj* **1.** (*ideology*) dominante **2.** (*film, novel*) comercial
maintain [meɪnˈteɪn] *vt* **1.** (*preserve, provide for*) mantener

2. (*claim*) sostener
maintenance ['meɪntənəns] *n no pl* **1.** (*keeping, preservation*) mantenimiento *m* **2.** (*alimony*) pensión *f* alimenticia
maize [meɪz] *n no pl* maíz *m*, milpa *f AmL*, capi *m AmS*
Maj. *abbr of* **Major** comandante *mf*
majestic [mə'dʒestɪk] *adj* majestuoso
majesty ['mædʒəsti] <-ies> *n no pl* majestuosidad *f;* **Her/His/Your Majesty** Su Majestad
major ['meɪdʒəʳ, *Am:* -dʒɚ] **I.** *adj* **1.** (*important*) muy importante, fundamental; **a ~ problem** un gran problema **2.** MUS mayor; **in C ~** en do mayor **II.** *n* **1.** MIL comandante *mf* **2.** *Am, Aus* UNIV especialidad *f*
Majorca [mə'jɔ:kə, *Am:* -jɔ:r-] *n* Mallorca *f*
majority [mə'dʒɒrəti, *Am:* -'dʒɔ:rətɪ] <-ies> *n* mayoría *f;* **a narrow/large ~** POL un margen estrecho/amplio
make [meɪk] **I.** *vt* <made, made> **1.** (*produce: coffee, soup, supper*) hacer; (*product*) fabricar; **to make sth out of sth** hacer algo con algo; **to ~ time** hacer tiempo **2.** (*cause*) causar; **to ~ noise/a scene** hacer ruido/una escena **3.** (*cause to be*) **to ~ sb sad** poner triste a alguien; **to ~ sth easy** hacer que algo sea fácil **4.** (*perform, carry out*) **to ~ a call** hacer una llamada; **to ~ a decision** tomar una decision **5.** (*force*) obligar; **to ~ sb do sth** hacer que alguien haga algo **6.** (*earn, get*) **to ~ friends** hacer amigos; **to ~ money** hacer [*o* ganar] dinero; **to ~ profits/losses** tener beneficios/pérdidas **II.** *vi* (*amount to, total*) **today's earthquake ~s five since the beginning of the year** el terremoto de hoy es el quinto de este año **III.** *n* (*brand*) marca *f*
◆ **make for** *vt insep* **1.** (*head for*) dirigirse a **2.** (*help to promote*) **to ~ sth** contribuir a algo
◆ **make of** *vt* **what do you ~ this book?** ¿qué te parece este libro?

◆ **make out I.** *vi* **1.** *inf* (*succeed, cope*) arreglárselas **2.** *vulg* (*have sex*) **to ~ with sb** tirarse a alguien **II.** *vt* **1.** *inf* (*pretend*) **he made himself out to be rich** se hizo pasar por rico **2.** (*discern*) distinguir **3.** (*write out*) **to ~ a cheque** extender un cheque
◆ **make up I.** *vt* **1.** (*invent*) inventar **2.** (*compensate*) **to ~ for sth** compensar algo **3.** (*decide*) **to ~ one's mind** decidirse **II.** *vi* reconciliarse
maker ['meɪkəʳ, *Am:* -kɚ] *n* fabricante *mf*
makeshift ['meɪkʃɪft] *adj* provisional
make-up ['meɪkʌp] *n no pl* maquillaje *m;* **to put on ~** maquillarse
making ['meɪkɪŋ] *n no pl* producción *m*
malaria [mə'leərɪə, *Am:* -'lerɪ-] *n no pl* malaria *f*
Malawi [mə'lɑ:wi] *n* Malaui *m*
Malawian *adj* malauiano
Malaysia [mə'leɪzɪə, *Am:* -ʒə] *n* Malaisia *f*
Malaysian [mə'leɪzɪən, *Am:* -ʒən] *adj* malaisio
malfunction [ˌmæl'fʌŋkʃn] **I.** *vi* fallar **II.** *n* fallo *m*
Mali ['mɑ:li] *n* Mali *m*
Malian *adj* malinés, -esa
malice ['mælɪs] *n no pl* malicia *f*
malicious [mə'lɪʃəs] *adj* malicioso
malign [mə'laɪn] **I.** *adj form* maligno **II.** *vt* calumniar
malignancy [mə'lɪgnənsi] <-ies> *n a.* MED malignidad *f*
malignant [mə'lɪgnənt] *adj* maligno
mall [mɔ:l] *n Am* centro *m* comercial
malnutrition [ˌmælnju:'trɪʃn, *Am:* -nu:'-] *n no pl* desnutrición *f*
malpractice [ˌmæl'præktɪs] *n* mala práctica *f;* **medical ~** negligencia *f* médica
malt [mɔ:lt] *n no pl* malta *f*
Malta ['mɔ:ltə, *Am:* -t̬ə] *n* Malta *f; s. a.* **Republic of Malta**
Maltese [ˌmɔ:l'ti:z] *adj* maltés; **~ cross** cruz *f* de Malta

M

mammal ['mæməl] *n* mamífero *m*

mammoth ['mæməθ] *n* mamut *m*

man [mæn] **I.** *n* <men> **1.** (*male human*) hombre *m* **2.** (*the human race*) ser *m* humano **II.** *vt* <-nn-> (*operate*) encargarse de; **to ~ a factory** contratar personal para una fábrica

manage ['mænɪdʒ] **I.** *vt* **1.** (*accomplish*) lograr; **to ~ to do sth** conseguir hacer algo **2.** (*be in charge of*) dirigir **II.** *vi* **to ~ on sth** arreglárselas con algo

manageable ['mænɪdʒəbl] *adj* (*vehicle*) manejable; (*person, animal*) dócil

management ['mænɪdʒmənt] *n* **1.** *no pl* (*direction*) manejo *m* **2.** *no pl a.* ECON dirección *f*; **to study ~** estudiar administración de empresas

manager ['mænɪdʒəʳ, *Am:* -dʒɚ] *n* administrador(a) *m(f)*; (*of business unit*) gerente *mf*

managerial [ˌmænə'dʒɪəriəl, *Am:* -'dʒɪri-] *adj* directivo; **~ skills** dotes *fpl* de mando

managing director *n Brit* director(a) *m(f)* general

mandarin ['mændərɪn, *Am:* -dɚ-] *n* mandarina *f*

Mandarin ['mændərɪn, *Am:* -dɚ-] *n no pl* LING mandarín *m*

mandarin (orange) ['mændərɪn, *Am:* 'mændəɹɪn] *n* mandarina *f*

mandate ['mændeɪt] *n a.* POL mandato *m*

mandatory ['mændətri, *Am:*-tɔːrɪ] *adj form* obligatorio; **to make sth ~** imponer algo

mane [meɪn] *n* (*of horse*) crin *f*; (*of person, lion*) melena *f*

man-eater ['mæniːtəʳ, *Am:* -t̬ɚ] *n inf* devorador(a) *m(f)* de hombres

maneuver [mə'nuːvəʳ, *Am:* -vɚ] *n, vi, vt Am s.* **manoeuvre**

maneuverability [məˌnuːvərə'bɪləti, *Am:* -ət̬i] *n Am s.* **manoeuvrability**

mango ['mæŋɡəʊ, *Am:* -ɡoʊ] *n* <-gos *o* -goes> mango *m*

manhood ['mænhʊd] *n no pl* **1.** (*adulthood*) edad *f* adulta **2.** (*mas-*

culinity) masculinidad *f*

mania ['meɪnɪə] *n* manía *f*

maniac ['meɪnɪæk] *n* maníaco, -a *m, f*; **football ~** fanático del fútbol

manifest ['mænɪfest] **I.** *adj form* manifiesto; **to make sth ~** poner algo de manifiesto **II.** *vt form* declarar; **to ~ symptoms of sth** manifestar síntomas de algo

manifestation [ˌmænɪfe'steɪʃn] *n form* manifestación *f*

manifesto [ˌmænɪ'festəʊ, *Am:* -toʊ] <-stos *o* -stoes> *n* manifiesto *m*

manipulate [mə'nɪpjʊleɪt, *Am:* -jə-] *vt* manipular

manipulation [məˌnɪpjʊ'leɪʃn, *Am:* -jə-] *n* manipulación *f*

mankind [ˌmæn'kaɪnd] *n no pl* humanidad *f*

manky [ˌmæŋki] <-ier, -iest> *adj Brit, inf* sucio

manly ['mænli] <-ier, -iest> *adj* varonil

manner ['mænəʳ, *Am:* -ɚ] *n no pl* **1.** (*way, fashion*) manera *f*; **in the ~ of sb** al estilo de alguien; **in a ~ of speaking** por así decirlo **2.** (*behaviour*) ~s modales *mpl*; **to teach sb ~s** enseñar a alguien a comportarse **3.** *form* (*kind, type*) clase *f*; **what ~ of man is he?** ¿qué tipo de hombre es?; **all ~ of …** toda clase de…

mannerism ['mænərɪzəm] *n* amaneramiento *m*

manoeuvrability [məˈnuːvrəbɪləti] *n no pl, Brit, Aus* maniobrabilidad *f*

manoeuvre [mə'nuːvəʳ, *Am:* -vɚ] *Brit, Aus* **I.** *n a.* MIL maniobra *f*; **army ~s** maniobras militares **II.** *vt* hacer maniobrar; **to ~ sb into doing sth** embaucar a alguien para que haga algo **III.** *vi* maniobrar

manor ['mænəʳ, *Am:* -ɚ] *n* (*house*) casa *f* solariega

manpower ['mænpaʊəʳ, *Am:* -ɚ] *n no pl* mano de obra *f*

mansion ['mænʃn] *n* mansión *f*

manslaughter ['mænslɔːtəʳ, *Am:* -slɑːt̬ɚ] *n no pl* homicidio *m* involuntario

mantelpiece ['mæntlpiːs] *n* repisa *f* de la chimenea

manual ['mænjʊəl] **I.** *adj* manual; ~ **dexterity** habilidad manual **II.** *n* manual *m;* **instructions** ~ manual de instrucciones

manufacture [ˌmænjʊ'fæktʃər, *Am:* -tʃər] **I.** *vt* fabricar **II.** *n no pl* manufactura *f*

manufacturer [ˌmænjʊ'fækʃərər, *Am:* -ɚɚ] *n* fabricante *mf*

manufacturing [ˌmænjʊ'fæktʃə-rɪŋ, *Am:* -jə'-] *adj* industrial; ~ **industry** industria *f* manufacturera

manure [mə'njʊər, *Am:* -'nʊr] *n no pl* abono *m*

manuscript ['mænjʊskrɪpt] *n* manuscrito *m*

many ['meni] <more, most> **I.** *adj* muchos, muchas; ~ **flowers** muchas flores; ~ **books** muchos libros; **how** ~ **bottles?** ¿cuántas botellas?; **too/so** ~ **people** demasiada/tanta gente; **one too** ~ uno de más; ~ **times** muchas veces; **as** ~ **as ...** tantos como... **II.** *pron* muchos, muchas; ~ **think that ...** muchos piensan que...; **so** ~ tantos/tantas; **too** ~ demasiados/demasiadas **III.** *n* **the** ~ la mayoría; **a good** ~ un gran número

> [!] **many** se utiliza para cosas contables, animales y personas: "Many people make that mistake." **much** se utiliza para cosas no contables y cantidades: "Norman has eaten too much ice-cream."

map [mæp] **I.** *n* (*of region, stars*) mapa *m;* (*of town*) plano *m;* ~ **of the world** mapamundi *m;* **road** ~ mapa de carreteras; **to put a town on the** ~ dar a conocer a un pueblo **II.** <-pp-> *vt* trazar un mapa de

maple ['meɪpl] *n* arce *m*

mar [mɑːr, *Am:* mɑːr] <-rr-> *vt* aguar

marathon ['mærəθən, *Am:* 'merə-θɑːn] *n a. fig* maratón *m*

marble ['mɑːbl, *Am:* 'mɑːr-] *n* **1.** *no pl* (*stone*) mármol *m;* ~ **table** mesa *f* de mármol **2.** (*glass ball*) canica *f*, bolita *f CSur*, metra *f Ven;* **to play** ~**s** jugar a las canicas

march [mɑːtʃ, *Am:* mɑːrtʃ] **I.** <-es> *n a.* MIL marcha *f;* **funeral** ~ marcha fúnebre; **a 20 km** ~ una marcha de 20 km **II.** *vi a.* MIL marchar; (*parade*) desfilar; **to** ~ **into a country** invadir un país

March [mɑːtʃ, *Am:* mɑːrtʃ] *n* marzo *m; s. a.* **April**

Mardi Gras [ˌmɑːdi'grɑː, *Am:* 'mɑːrdiˌgrɑː] *n* Martes *m* de Carnaval

> [?] **Mardi Gras** es el equivalente americano del Carnaval. Esta fiesta la trajeron los colonizadores franceses de New Orleans (en lo que posteriormente será el estado de Louisiana). Aunque la mayoría de las personas piensan en New Orleans cuando escuchan la expresión **Mardi Gras**, lo cierto es que también se celebra en otros lugares como Biloxi/Mississippi y Mobile/Alabama. En New Orleans los **krewes** (agrupaciones de carnaval) celebran muchas fiestas y bailes durante estos días y el martes de carnaval salen en cabalgata.

mare ['meər] *n* yegua *f*

margarine [ˌmɑːdʒəriːn, *Am:* ˌmɑːrdʒɚɪn] *n no pl* margarina *f*

marge [mɑːdʒ, *Am:* mɑːrdʒ] *n Brit, inf abbr of* **margarine** margarina *f*

margin ['mɑːdʒɪn, *Am:* 'mɑːr-] *n* margen *m;* **profit** ~ margen de ganancia; **narrow** [*o* **tight**] ~ margen reducido

marginal ['mɑːdʒɪnl, *Am:* 'mɑːr-] *adj* marginal; **to be of** ~ **interest** ser de interés secundario

M m

marginalise *vt Brit, Aus,* **marginalize** ['mɑːdʒɪnəlaɪz, *Am:* 'mɑːr-] *vt* marginar

marihuana *n,* **marijuana** [ˌmærɪ'wɑːnə, *Am:* ˌmerɪ'-] *n no pl* marihuana *f*

marina [mə'riːnə] *n* puerto *m* deportivo

marinade [ˌmærɪ'neɪd, *Am:* ˌmer-] *n* escabeche *m*

marine [mə'riːn] I. *adj* marino II. *n* infante *m* de marina

marital ['mærɪtəl, *Am:* 'merɪt̬əl] *adj* marital; ~ **bliss** felicidad *f* marital

maritime ['mærɪtaɪm, *Am:* 'mer-] *adj form* marítimo

maritime law *n* código *m* marítimo

marjoram ['mɑːdʒərəm, *Am:* 'mɑːrdʒəˈəm] *n no pl* mejorana *f*

mark [mɑːk, *Am:* mɑːrk] I. *n* 1. (*spot, stain*) mancha *f;* (*scratch*) marca *f;* **to leave one's ~ on sth/ sb** *fig* dejar sus huellas en algo/alguien 2. (*written sign*) raya *f* 3. SCHOOL nota *f;* **to get full ~s** *Brit, Aus* obtener las máximas calificaciones 4. *no pl* (*required standard*) norma *f;* **to be up to the ~** ser satisfactorio; **to not feel up to the ~** no sentirse a la altura de las circunstancias 5. (*target*) blanco *m;* **to hit the ~** dar en el blanco II. *vt* 1. (*make a spot, stain*) manchar 2. (*make written sign, indicate*) marcar; **I've ~ed the route on the map** he señalado la ruta en el mapa 3. (*commemorate*) conmemorar; **to ~ the beginning/end of sth** conmemorar el principio/final de algo; **to ~ the 10th anniversary** celebrar el 10º aniversario

marked [mɑːkt, *Am:* mɑːrkt] *adj* marcado

market ['mɑːkɪt, *Am:* 'mɑːr-] I. *n* mercado *m,* recova *f And, Urug;* **job ~** mercado de trabajo; **stock ~** bolsa *f* de valores II. *vt* comercializar

marketing *n no pl* marketing *m*

marketplace *n* 1. ECON mercado *m* 2. (*square*) plaza *f* (del mercado)

market research *n no pl* estudio *m*

de mercado

marking *n* señal *f;* (*on animal*) pinta *f*

marmalade ['mɑːməleɪd, *Am:* 'mɑːr-] *n no pl* mermelada *f* (*de cítricos*)

maroon¹ [mə'ruːn] *adj* granate

maroon² [mə'ruːn] *vt* abandonar

marquee [mɑː'kiː, *Am:* mɑːr-] *n Brit, Aus* carpa *f*

marriage ['mærɪdʒ, *Am:* 'mer-] *n* 1. (*wedding*) boda *f* 2. (*relationship, state*) matrimonio *m*

married *adj* (*person*) casado; ~ **couple** matrimonio *m;* ~ **life** vida *f* conyugal

marrow¹ ['mærəʊ, *Am:* 'merəʊ] *n Brit, Aus* calabacín *m*

marrow² ['mærəʊ, *Am:* 'merəʊ] *n* MED médula *f*

marry ['mæri, *Am:* 'mer-] <-ie-> I. *vt* 1. (*become husband or wife*) **to ~ sb** casarse con alguien 2. (*priest*) casar II. *vi* casarse; **to ~ above/beneath oneself** casarse con alguien de clase superior/inferior

marsh [mɑːʃ, *Am:* mɑːrʃ] <-es> *n* ciénaga *f*

marshal ['mɑːʃl, *Am:* 'mɑːr-] I. <*Brit:* -ll-, *Am:* -l-> *vt* ordenar II. *n* 1. MIL mariscal *m;* **field ~** mariscal de campo 2. *Am* (*police or fire officer*) comisario *m*

martial ['mɑːʃəl, *Am:* 'mɑːr-] *adj* marcial

martial law *n* ley *f* marcial; **to impose ~ on a country** imponer la ley marcial en un país

Martian ['mɑːʃn, *Am:* 'mɑːr-] *adj* marciano

Martinique [ˌmɑːtɪ'niːk, *Am:* ˌmɑːrtən'iːk] *n* Martinica *f*

martyr ['mɑːtər, *Am:* 'mɑːrt̬ə-] I. *n* mártir *mf* II. *vt* martirizar

martyrdom ['mɑːtədəm, *Am:* 'mɑːrt̬ə-] *n no pl* martirio *m*

marvel ['mɑːvl, *Am:* 'mɑːr-] I. *n* maravilla *f* II. <*Brit:* -ll-, *Am:* -l-> *vi* **to ~ at sb/sth** maravillarse de alguien/ algo

marvellous ['mɑːvələs, *Am:* 'mɑːr-] *adj Brit,* **marvelous** *adj Am* maravilloso; **to feel** ~ sentirse espléndido

Marxism ['mɑːksɪzm, *Am:* 'mɑːrk-] *n no pl* marxismo *m*

Marxist ['mɑːksɪst:, *Am:* 'mɑːrk-] *adj* marxista

masculine ['mæskjəlɪn] *adj a.* LING masculino

masculinity [ˌmæskjə'lɪnəti, *Am:* ˌmæskjə'lɪnəti̬] *n* masculinidad *f*

mash [mæʃ] *vt* machacar; **to** ~ **potatoes** hacer puré de patatas

mask [mɑːsk, *Am:* mæsk] I. *n a. fig* máscara *f;* (*only covering eyes*) antifaz *m;* **oxygen** ~ máscara de oxígeno II. *vt* enmascarar; **to** ~ **the statistics** ocultar las estadísticas

mason ['meɪsn] *n* 1. *Am* (*bricklayer*) albañil *m* 2. (*freemason*) masón, -ona *m, f*

masonry ['meɪsnri] *n no pl* 1. (*stonework*) mampostería *f* 2. (*freemasonry*) masonería *f*

masquerade [ˌmɑːskə'reɪd] I. *n* mascarada *f* II. *vi* **to** ~ **as sth** hacerse pasar por algo

mass [mæs] *n no pl* 1. *a.* PHYS masa *f* 2. (*large quantity*) montón *m;* **to be a** ~ **of contradictions** estar lleno de contradicciones

Mass [mæs] *n* misa *f;* **to attend** ~ ir a misa; **to celebrate a** ~ oficiar una misa

massacre ['mæsəkəʳ, *Am:* -kɚ] I. *n* masacre *f* II. *vt* masacrar

massage ['mæsɑːdʒ, *Am:* mə'-] I. *n* masaje *m;* **water** ~ hidromasaje *m* II. *vt* dar masajes a; *fig* manipular

massive ['mæsɪv] *adj* enorme; ~ **amounts of money** grandes cantidades de dinero

mass media *n* **the** ~ los medios de comunicación de masas

mast [mɑːst, *Am:* mæst] *n* NAUT mástil *m*

master ['mɑːstəʳ, *Am:* 'mæstɚ] I. *n* 1. (*of house*) señor *m;* (*of slave*) amo *m* 2. (*one who excels*) maestro *m;* ~ **craftsman** maestro 3. (*instructor*) instructor *m;* **dancing/singing** ~ instructor de baile/canto 4. (*master copy*) original *m* II. *vt* 1. (*cope with*)

vencer; **to** ~ **one's fear of flying** superar el miedo a volar 2. (*become proficient at*) dominar

mastermind ['mɑːstəmaɪnd, *Am:* 'mæstɚ-] I. *n* cerebro *m* II. *vt* planear

masterpiece *n* obra *f* maestra

Master's *n,* **Master's degree** *n* máster *m*

> **?** En Gran Bretaña se llama **Master's degree** al grado académico que se obtiene al finalizar una carrera tras la defensa de una tesina (**dissertation**). El **Master's degree** recibe distintos nombres según las disciplinas: **MA (Master of Arts), MSc (Master of Science), Mlitt (Master of Letters)** y **Mphil (Master of Philosophy).** Sin embargo en Escocia con la expresión **MA** se designa un primer grado académico.

Mₘ

mastery ['mɑːstəri, *Am:* 'mæstɚ-] *n no pl* (*skill*) maestría *f*

masturbation [ˌmæstə'beɪʃn, *Am:* -tɚ'-] *n no pl* masturbación *f*

mat [mæt] *n* (*on floor*) estera *f;* (*decorative*) tapiz *m;* **bath** ~ alfombra *f* de baño

match¹ [mætʃ] <-es> *n* cerilla *f,* cerillo *m* Méx

match² [mætʃ] I. *n* 1. (*competitor*) contrincante *mf;* **to be a good** ~ **for sb** poder competir con alguien; **to meet one's** ~ encontrar la horma de su zapato 2. SPORTS partido *m* 3. (*similarity*) **to be a good** ~ combinar bien II. *vi* armonizar III. *vt* 1. (*have same colour*) hacer juego con 2. (*equal*) igualar

mate¹ [meɪt] I. *n* 1. ZOOL (*male*) macho *m;* (*female*) hembra *f* 2. *Brit, Aus* (*friend*) amigo, -a *m, f* 3. *Brit, Aus, inf* (*form of address*) compadre *m* 4. NAUT oficial *m* de abordo; **first/second** ~ primer/segundo oficial II. *vi* aparearse III. *vt* aparear

mate² n GAMES mate m
material [mə'tɪərɪəl, Am: -'tɪrɪ-]
I. n 1. (physical substance) material
m; **raw** ~ materia f prima 2. (textile)
tejido m 3. pl (equipment) materia-
les mpl II. adj material; ~ **damage**
daño material
materialise [mə'tɪərɪəlaɪz] vi Brit,
Aus s. **materialize**
materialism [mə'tɪərɪəlɪzəm, Am:
-'tɪri-] n no pl materialismo m
materialist n materialista mf
materialistic [mə,tɪərɪə'lɪstɪk, Am:
-,tɪri-] adj materialista
materialize [mə'tɪərɪəlaɪz, Am:
-'tɪri-] vi materializarse
maternal [mə'tɜːnl, Am: -'tɜːr-] adj
1. (feeling) maternal 2. (relative)
materno
maternity [mə'tɜːnəti, Am: -'tɜːr-
nət̬i] n no pl maternidad f
mathematical [,mæθə'mætɪkl,
Am: -'mæt̬-] adj matemático
mathematician [,mæθəmə'tɪʃn] n
matemático, -a m, f
mathematics [,mæθə'mætɪks, Am:
-'mæt̬-] n matemáticas fpl
maths [mæθs] n Brit, Aus, inf abbr
of **mathematics** mates fpl
matrimonial [,mætrɪ'məʊnɪəl,
Am: -rə'moʊ-] adj form matrimonial
matrix ['meɪtrɪks] <-ices> n a. MAT
matriz f
matron ['meɪtrən] n 1. (middle-
-aged woman) matrona f 2. (nurse)
enfermera f jefe
matter ['mætər, Am: 'mæt̬ər] I. n
1. (question, affair) asunto m; **the ~
in hand** el asunto del que se trata;
it's a ~ of life or death fig es un
asunto de vida o muerte 2. pl (situation) situación f 3. (wrong) problema m; **what's the ~ with you?**
¿qué te pasa? 4. no pl (substance)
materia f II. vi importar; **what ~s
now is that ...** lo que importa ahora
es que...
matter-of-fact [,mætəˈr'əv'fækt,
Am: ,mæt̬ə-] adj 1. (practical) práctico 2. (emotionless) prosaico
mattress ['mætrɪs] n colchón m

mature [mə'tjʊəʳ, Am: -'tʊr] I. adj
1. (person, attitude) maduro; (animal) adulto; **to be ~ beyond one's
years** ser muy maduro para su edad
2. (fruit) maduro 3. FIN vencido II. vi
1. a. fig madurar 2. FIN vencer III. vt
1. (cheese, ham) curar 2. (person)
hacer madurar
maturity [mə'tjʊərəti, Am: -'tʊrə-
t̬i] n <-ies> 1. no pl (of person, attitude) madurez f; **to come to ~** llegar a la madurez 2. FIN vencimiento
m; **to reach ~** tener vencimiento

❓ **Maundy Thursday** es el
nombre que recibe el Jueves Santo
dentro de la **Holy Week** (Semana
Santa). Ese día el monarca reparte
a unas cuantas personas pobres
previamente escogidas el **Maundy
money**. El número de personas a
las que se dispensa esta limosna
está en relación con la edad del
monarca. Cada una de estas personas recibe además un set de
monedas de plata acuñadas especialmente para la ocasión.

Mauritania [,mɒrɪ'teɪnɪə, Am:
,mɔːrɪ'-] n Mauritania f
Mauritanian adj mauritano
Mauritian adj mauriciano
Mauritius [mə'rɪʃəs, Am: mɔː'rɪ-
ʃɪəs] n Mauricio m
mauve [məʊv, Am: moʊv] adj
malva
maverick ['mævərɪk, Am: 'mævə-]
n inconformista mf
max. inf abbr of **maximum** máx.
maxim ['mæksɪm] n máxima f
maximum ['mæksɪməm] I. n máximo m; **to do sth to the ~** hacer algo
al máximo II. adj máximo; **this car
has a ~ speed of 160 km/h** este
coche alcanza una velocidad máxima
de 160 km/h
may [meɪ] <might> aux 1. (be
allowed) poder; ~ **I come in?**
¿puedo pasar?; ~ **I ask you a ques-**

tion? ¿puedo hacerte una pregunta? **2.** (*possibility*) ser posible; **it ~ rain** puede que llueva **3.** (*hope, wish*) ~ **she rest in peace** que en paz descanse

---

⚠ **may** significa poder, tener permiso: "May I finish the pudding, please?" **can** significa poder o ser capaz: "Can you tell me the time, please?"

May [meɪ] *n* mayo; *s. a.* **April**
maybe ['meɪbi:] *adv* (*perhaps*) quizás
mayday ['meɪdeɪ] *n* S.O.S. *m*
May Day *n* Primero *m* de mayo

❓ El **May Day** (1 de mayo) se celebra en algunas partes de Gran Bretaña con el **morris dancing**. En algunos patios de colegios y pueblos se levanta una **maypole** (árbol de mayo) que es adornado con cintas de colores. Cada persona baila cogida a una de esas cintas unos detrás de otros, formándose así un bonito dibujo en torno al árbol.

---

mayhem ['meɪhem] *n no pl* caos *m inv;* **it was** ~ era un caos total
mayonnaise [,meɪə'neɪz] *n* mayonesa *f*
mayor [meəʳ, *Am:* meɪɚ] *n* alcalde *m*
maze [meɪz] *n* laberinto *m*
MBA [,embi:'eɪ] *n abbr of* **Master of Business Administration** máster *m* en administración de empresas
MD [,em'di:] *n abbr of* **managing director** director(a) *m(f)* gerente
me [mi:] *pron* **1.** me; **look at** ~ mírame; **she saw** ~ me vió; **he told** ~ **that ...** me dijo que...; **he gave** ~ **the pencil** me dió el lápiz **2.** (*after verb 'to be'*) yo; **it's** ~ soy yo; **she is older than** ~ ella es mayor que yo **3.** (*after prep*) mí; **is this for** ~? ¿es

para mí esto?
meadow ['medəʊ, *Am:* -oʊ] *n* pradera *f*
meager *adj Am,* **meagre** ['mi:gəʳ, *Am:* -gɚ] *adj* escaso
meal¹ [mi:l] *n* comida *f;* **a heavy/ light** ~ una comida pesada/liviana
meal² [mi:l] *n* (*flour*) harina *f*
mean¹ [mi:n] *adj* **1.** (*miserly*) tacaño, amarrado *Arg, Par, PRico, Urug* **2.** (*unkind*) vil; **to be** ~ **to sb** tratar mal a alguien
mean² [mi:n] <meant, meant> *vt* **1.** (*signify*) significar; **does that name** ~ **anything to you?** ¿te suena ese nombre? **2.** (*express, indicate*) querer decir; **what do you** ~? ¿a qué te refieres? **3.** (*intend for particular purpose*) destinar; **to be meant for sth** estar destinado a algo **4.** (*intend*) pretender; **to** ~ **to do sth** tener la intención de hacer algo; **to** ~ **well** tener buenas intenciones
meander [mɪ'ændəʳ, *Am:* -dɚ] *vi* **1.** (*flow*) serpentear **2.** *fig* (*wander*) vagar
meaning ['mi:nɪŋ] *n* significado *m;* **what is the** ~ **of this?** ¿qué significa esto?; **if you take my** ~ ya me entiendes
meaningful ['mi:nɪŋfəl] *adj* significativo
meaningless ['mi:nɪŋləs] *adj* sin sentido
means [mi:nz] *n* **1.** (*instrument, method*) medio *m;* ~ **of communication/transport** medio de comunicación/transporte **2.** *pl* (*resources*) medios *mpl;* ~ **of support** medios de subsistencia; **by** ~ **of sth** por medio de algo **3.** *pl* (*income*) recursos *mpl;* **a person of** ~ una persona acaudalada
meant [ment] *pt, pp of* **mean**²
meantime ['mi:ntaɪm] *n* **in the** ~ mientras tanto
meanwhile ['mi:nwaɪl] *adv* mientras tanto
measles ['mi:zlz] *n* sarampión *m*
measure ['meʒəʳ, *Am:* -ɚ] **I.** *n* **1.** (*size*) medida *f;* **to get the** ~ **of sb** tomar la medida a alguien

Mm

2. (*measuring instrument*) metro *m*
3. *pl* (*action*) medidas *fpl;* **to take
~s to do sth** tomar medidas para
hacer algo **II.** *vt* medir; **to ~ sth in
centimetres/weeks** calcular algo
en centímetros/semanas **III.** *vi*
medir; **the box ~s 10cm by 10cm
by 12cm** la caja mide 10 cm por 10
cm por 12 cm
measured *adj* comedido
measurement ['meʒəmənt, *Am:*
'meʒɚ-] *n* **1.** *no pl* (*act of measuring*) medición *f* **2.** (*size*) medida *f;*
to take sb's ~s tomar a alguien las
medidas
meat [mi:t] *n no pl* carne *f;* **one
man's ~ is another man's poison**
prov lo que es bueno para unos es
malo para otros *prov*
mechanic [mɪ'kænɪk] *n* mecánico,
-a *m, f*
mechanical *adj* mecánico
mechanism ['mekənɪzəm] *n* mecanismo *m*
med. *adj abbr of* **medium** mediano
medal ['medl] *n* medalla *f*
medallion [mɪ'dæliən, *Am:*
mə'dæljən] *n* medallón *m*
medal(l)ist ['medəlɪst] *n* medallista
mf
meddle ['medl] *vi* **to ~ in sth** meterse en algo
media ['mi:diə] *n* **1.** *pl of* **medium
2. the ~** los medios; **the mass ~** los
medios de comunicación de masas
mediaeval [ˌmedi'i:vəl] *adj* s.
medieval
mediate ['mi:dɪeɪt] **I.** *vi* **to ~ between two groups** mediar entre
dos grupos; **to ~ in sth** mediar en
algo **II.** *vt* **to ~ a settlement** hacer
de intermediario en un acuerdo
mediation [ˌmi:dɪ'eɪʃən] *n no pl*
mediación *f*
mediator ['mi:dɪeɪtəʳ, *Am:* -t̬ɚ] *n*
mediador(a) *m(f)*
medic ['medɪk] *n* **1.** *inf* (*doctor*)
médico, -a *m, f* **2.** (*student*) estudiante *mf* de medicina
medical ['medɪkəl] **I.** *adj* médico
II. *n inf* reconocimiento *m* médico
medicament [mɪ'dɪkəmənt] *n* me-

dicamento *m*
medication [ˌmedɪ'keɪʃən] <-(s)>
n medicamento *m*
medicinal [mə'dɪsɪnəl] *adj* medicinal
medicine ['medsən, *Am:* 'medɪ-
sən] *n* **1.** (*substance*) medicamento
m **2.** *no pl* (*medical knowledge*)
medicina *f*
medieval [ˌmedɪ'i:vl, *Am:* ˌmi:dɪ-]
adj medieval
mediocre [ˌmi:dɪ'əʊkəʳ, *Am:* -'oʊ-
kɚ] *adj* mediocre
mediocrity [ˌmi:dɪ'ɒkrəti, *Am:* -'ɑ:-
krət̬ɪ] *n no pl* mediocridad *f*
meditate ['medɪteɪt] *vi* **1.** (*engage
in contemplation*) meditar **2.** (*think
deeply*) reflexionar; **to ~ on sth** reflexionar sobre algo
meditation [ˌmedɪ'teɪʃn] *n no pl*
meditación *f*
Mediterranean [ˌmedɪtə'reɪniən]
I. *n* Mediterráneo *m* **II.** *adj* mediterráneo
medium ['mi:diəm] **I.** *adj* mediano
II. *n* **1.** <*media* *o* -*s*> (*method*)
medio *m;* **through the ~ of** por
medio de **2.** *no pl* INFOR soporte *m;*
data ~ soporte de datos **3.** <-*s*>
(*spiritualist*) médium *mf*
medley ['medli] *n* **1.** (*mixture*) mezcla *f* **2.** MUS popurrí *m*
meek [mi:k] *adj* manso
meet [mi:t] <met, met> **I.** *vt* **1.** (*encounter*) encontrarse con; (*inten-
tionally*) reunirse con; (*for first
time*) conocer a; **to arrange to ~ sb**
quedar con alguien **2.** (*fulfil*) cumplir
II. *vi* **1.** (*encounter*) encontrarse; (*in-
tentionally*) reunirse; (*for first time*)
conocerse; **to arrange to ~** quedar
2. (*join*) unirse
◆**meet with** *vt insep* reunirse con;
to ~ an accident sufrir un accidente; **to ~ success** tener éxito
meeting ['mi:tɪŋ, *Am:* -t̬ɪŋ] *n*
1. (*gathering*) reunión *f;* **to call a ~**
convocar una reunión **2.** (*casual*) a.
SPORTS encuentro *m*
melancholy ['melənkɒli, *Am:* -kɑ:-
li] **I.** *n no pl* melancolía *f* **II.** *adj* melancólico

? La **Melbourne Cup** es una de las competiciones hípicas más populares entre los australianos. Siempre tiene lugar el primer martes del mes de noviembre. Las apuestas alcanzan varios millones de dólares. Ese día todo el país se pone sus mejores galas y a mediodía se sirve pollo con champán.

mellow ['meləʊ, *Am:* -loʊ] I. *adj* <-er, -est> 1. (*light*) suave 2. (*relaxed*) tranquilo II. *vi* suavizarse

melodrama ['melədrɑːmə, *Am:* -oʊ-] *n* melodrama *m*

melodramatic [ˌmelədrəˈmætɪk, *Am:* -oʊdrəˈmæt̬-] *adj* melodramático

melody ['melədi] <-ies> *n* melodía *f*

melon ['melən] *n* melón *m;* (*watermelon*) sandía *f*

melt [melt] I. *vt* (*metal*) fundir; (*ice, chocolate*) derretir II. *vi* 1. (*metal*) fundirse; (*ice, chocolate*) derretirse 2. *fig* enternecerse

member ['membər, *Am:* -bɚ] *n* miembro *mf;* (*of society, club*) socio, -a *m, f*

membership *n* 1. (*state of belonging*) calidad *f* de miembro; (*to society, club*) calidad *f* de socio; **to apply for ~ of a club** solicitar ingreso en un club; ~ **dues** cuotas *fpl* de socio 2. (*number of members*) número *m* de miembros

membrane ['membreɪn] *n* membrana *f*

memo ['meməʊ, *Am:* -oʊ] *n abbr of* **memorandum** memorándum *m*

memoir ['memwɑːr, *Am:* -wɑːr] *n* 1. (*record of events*) memoria *f* 2. *pl* (*autobiography*) memorias *fpl*

memorable ['memərəbl] *adj* memorable

memorandum [ˌmeməˈrændəm] <-s *o* -anda> *n* memorándum *m*

memorial [məˈmɔːriəl] *n* monumento *m* conmemorativo

memorize ['meməraɪz] *vt* memorizar

memory ['meməri] <-ies> *n* 1. (*ability to remember*) memoria *f;* **if my ~ serves me correctly** si la memoria no me falla 2. (*remembered event*) recuerdo *m;* **to bring back memories** evocar recuerdos 3. INFOR memoria *f;* **random access ~** memoria de acceso directo

menace ['menəs] I. *n* amenaza *f* II. *vt* amenazar

menacing *adj* amenazador

mend [mend] I. *vt* reparar II. *vi* mejorar

menial ['miːniəl] *adj* de baja categoría

meningitis [ˌmenɪnˈdʒaɪtɪs, *Am:* -t̬ɪs] *n no pl* meningitis *f*

menopause ['menəpɔːz, *Am:* -pɑːz] *n no pl* menopausia *f*

menstruate ['menstrʊeɪt, *Am:* -stru-] *vi* menstruar

menstruation [ˌmenstrʊˈeɪʃən, *Am:* -stru'-] *n no pl* menstruación *f*

mental ['mentəl, *Am:* -t̬əl] *adj* 1. (*of the mind*) mental 2. *Brit, inf* (*crazy*) chiflado

mentality [menˈtæləti, *Am:* -t̬i] <-ies> *n* mentalidad *f*

mentally *adv* mentalmente; ~ **disturbed** trastornado

mention ['menʃn] I. *n* mención *f* II. *vt* mencionar; **don't ~ it!** ¡no hay de qué!

menu ['menjuː] *n* 1. (*list of dishes*) carta *f;* (*fixed meal*) menú *m* 2. INFOR menú *m;* **context/pull-down ~** menú contextual/desplegable

MEP [ˌemiːˈpiː] *n abbr of* **Member of the European Parliament** eurodiputado, -a *m, f*

mercenary ['mɜːsɪnəri, *Am:* 'mɜːr-sənər-] *n* <-ies> mercenario, -a *m, f*

merchandise ['mɜːtʃəndaɪz, *Am:* 'mɜːr-] *n no pl* mercancía *f*

merchant ['mɜːtʃənt, *Am:* 'mɜːr-] *n* comerciante *mf*

merciful ['mɜːsɪfl, *Am:* 'mɜːr-] *adj* misericordioso

merciless ['mɜːsɪlɪs, *Am:* 'mɜːr-] *adj*

Mm

despiadado

mercury ['mɜːkjʊri, *Am:* 'mɜːrkjərɪ] *n no pl* mercurio *m*

Mercury ['mɜːkjʊri, *Am:* 'mɜːrkjərɪ] *n no pl* Mercurio *m*

mercy ['mɜːsi, *Am:* 'mɜːr-] *n no pl* **1.** (*compassion*) compasión *f;* **to have ~ on sb** tener compasión de alguien **2.** (*forgiveness*) misericordia *f;* **to be at the ~ of sb** estar a merced de alguien

mere [mɪəʳ, *Am:* mɪr] *adj* mero; **a ~ detail** un simple detalle

merely ['mɪəli, *Am:* 'mɪr-] *adv* solamente

merge [mɜːdʒ, *Am:* mɜːrdʒ] **I.** *vi* unirse; ECON, POL fusionarse; **to ~ into sth** fundirse con algo **II.** *vt* unir; ECON, POL, INFOR fusionar

merger ['mɜːdʒəʳ, *Am:* 'mɜːrdʒɚ] *n* ECON fusión *f*

meridian [məˈrɪdɪən] *n* meridiano *m*

merit ['merɪt] **I.** *n* cualidad *f* **II.** *vt* merecer

mermaid ['mɜːmeɪd, *Am:* 'mɜːr-] *n* sirena *f*

merry ['meri] <-ier, -iest> *adj* **1.** (*happy*) alegre **2.** *Brit, inf* (*slightly drunk*) achispado

mesh [meʃ] *n no pl* malla *f;* **wire ~** red *f* de alambrado

mess [mes] <-es> *n* **1.** *no pl* (*disorganized state*) desorden *m* **2.** *no pl* (*trouble*) lío *m,* merengue *m Arg* **3.** *Brit* (*dining hall*) comedor *m*

message ['mesɪdʒ] *n* mensaje *m*

messenger ['mesɪndʒəʳ, *Am:* -dʒɚ] *n* mensajero, -a *m, f*

messiah [məˈsaɪə] *n* mesías *m inv*

messy ['mesi] <-ier, -iest> *adj* **1.** (*untidy*) desordenado **2.** (*unpleasant*) desagradable; **~ business** asunto *m* turbio

met [met] *vi, vt pt, pp of* **meet**

met. *abbr of* **meteorological** meteor.

metabolic [ˌmetəˈbɒlɪk, *Am:* ˌmet̬əˈbɑːlɪk] *adj* metabólico

metabolism [mɪˈtæbəlɪzəm] *n* metabolismo *m*

metal ['metl, *Am:* 'met̬-] *n* (*element*) metal *m*

metallic [mɪˈtælɪk, *Am:* məˈ-] *adj* metálico

metalworker *n* metalista *mf*

metamorphosis [ˌmetəˈmɔːfəsɪs, *Am:* ˌmet̬əˈmɔːrfə-] <-es> *n* metamorfosis *f inv*

metaphor ['metəfəʳ, *Am:* 'met̬əfɔːr] *n* metáfora *f*

metaphorical [ˌmetəˈfɒrɪkl, *Am:* ˌmet̬əˈfɔːr-] *adj* metafórico

metaphysical [ˌmetəˈfɪzɪkl, *Am:* ˌmet̬-] *adj* metafísico

metaphysics [ˌmetəˈfɪzɪks, *Am:* ˌmet̬-] *n* metafísica *f*

meteorite ['miːtiəraɪt, *Am:* -t̬i-] *n* meteorito *m*

meteorological [ˌmiːtiərəˈlɒdʒɪkəl, *Am:* -t̬iərəˈlɑːdʒɪ-] *adj* meteorológico

meteorology [ˌmiːtiəˈrɒlədʒi, *Am:* -əˈrɑːlə-] *n no pl* meteorología *f*

meter¹ ['miːtəʳ, *Am:* -t̬ɚ] *n* contador *m,* medidor *m AmL;* (**parking**) **~** parquímetro *m*

meter² ['miːtəʳ, *Am:* -t̬ɚ] *n Am s.* **metre**

methane ['miːθeɪn, *Am:* 'meθeɪn] *n* metano *m*

method ['meθəd] *n* método *m*

methodical [mɪˈθɒdɪkl, *Am:* məˈθɑːdɪk-] *adj* metódico

methodology [ˌmeθəˈdɒlədʒi, *Am:* -ˈdɑːlə-] <-ies> *n* metodología *f*

meticulous [mɪˈtɪkjʊləs] *adj* meticuloso

metre ['miːtəʳ, *Am:* -t̬ɚ] *n Brit, Aus* metro *m*

metric ['metrɪk] *adj* métrico

metropolis [məˈtrɒpəlɪs, *Am:* -ˈtrɑːpəl-] <-es> *n* metrópoli *f*

metropolitan [ˌmetrəˈpɒlɪtən, *Am:* -ˈpɑːlə-] *adj* metropolitano

Mexican ['meksɪkən] *adj* mexicano

Mexico ['meksɪkəʊ, *Am:* -koʊ] *n no pl* México *m;* **New ~** Nuevo México

Mexico City *n* Ciudad *f* de México

microcosm ['maɪkrəʊkɒzəm, *Am:* -kroʊkɑːzəm] *n* microcosmos *m inv*

microfilm ['maɪkrəʊfɪlm, *Am:* -kroʊ-] *n* microfilm *m*

microphone ['maɪkrəfəʊn, *Am:*

-foʊn] *n* micrófono *m;* **to speak into a** ~ hablar por micrófono

microscope [ˈmaɪkrəskəʊp, *Am:* -skoʊp] *n* microscopio *m*

microscopic [ˌmaɪkrəˈskɒpɪk, *Am:* -ˈskɑːpɪk] *adj* microscópico

microwave [ˈmaɪkrəʊweɪv, *Am:* -kroʊ-] I. *n* 1. (*wave*) microonda *f* 2. (*oven*) microondas *m inv* II. *vt* poner en el microondas

mid [mɪd] *prep* en medio de

midday [ˌmɪdˈdeɪ] *n no pl* mediodía *m;* **at** ~ a mediodía

middle [ˈmɪdl] *n* medio *m;* **in the ~ of sth** en medio de algo; **in the ~ of the night** en plena noche

middle age *n* mediana edad *f*
middle-aged *adj* de mediana edad
Middle Ages *npl* Edad *f* Media
middle-class [ˌmɪdlˈklɑːs, *Am:* -ˈklæs] *adj* de la clase media
Middle East *n* Oriente *m* Medio
midget [ˈmɪdʒɪt] *n* enano, -a *m, f*
midnight [ˈmɪdnaɪt] *n no pl* medianoche *f*
midst [mɪdst] *n no pl* **in the ~ of** en medio de
midsummer [ˌmɪdˈsʌmər, *Am:* -ə˞] *n no pl* pleno verano *m*
midway [ˌmɪdˈweɪ] *adv* a mitad del camino
might[1] [maɪt] *pt of* **may: it** ~ **be that ...** podría ser que... +*subj;* **how old** ~ **she be?** ¿qué edad tendrá?; ~ **I open the window?** ¿podría abrir la ventana?
might[2] [maɪt] *n no pl* fuerza *f*
mighty [ˈmaɪti, *Am:* ˈmaɪt̬i] <-ier, -iest> *adj* fuerte
migraine [ˈmiːgreɪn, *Am:* ˈmaɪ-] <-(s)> *n* migraña *f*
migrant [ˈmaɪgrənt] *n* 1. (*person*) emigrante *mf* 2. ZOOL ave *f* migratoria
migrant worker *n* trabajador(a) *m(f)* emigrante
migrate [maɪˈgreɪt, *Am:* ˈ--] *vi* emigrar
migration [maɪˈgreɪʃn] <-(s)> *n* emigración *f*
migratory [ˈmaɪgrətri, *Am:* -tɔːr-] *adj* migratorio

mild [maɪld] <-er, -est> *adj* 1. (*not severe*) moderado 2. (*not strong tasting*) suave
mildly [ˈmaɪldli] *adv* 1. (*gently*) suavemente 2. (*slightly*) ligeramente; **to put it** ~ por no decir algo peor
mildness [ˈmaɪldnɪs] *n no pl* 1. (*placidity*) apacibilidad *f* 2. (*softness*) suavidad *f*
mile [maɪl] *n* milla *f* (*1,61 km*); **to stick out a** ~ verse a la legua; **to walk for ~s** andar kilómetros y kilómetros
mileage [ˈmaɪlɪdʒ] *n no pl* AUTO kilometraje *m*
milestone [ˈmaɪlstəʊn, *Am:* -stoʊn] *n* 1. (*marker*) mojón *m* 2. *fig* hito *m*
militant [ˈmɪlɪtənt] *n* militante *mf*
militarism [ˈmɪlɪtərɪzəm, *Am:* -tə˞-] *n no pl* militarismo *m*
military [ˈmɪlɪtri, *Am:* -ter-] I. *n* **the** ~ los militares II. *adj* militar
militia [mɪˈlɪʃə] *n* milicia *f*
milk [mɪlk] I. *n no pl* leche *f;* **there's no use crying over spilt** ~ *prov* a lo hecho pecho *prov* II. *vt* ordeñar
milkman <-men> *n* lechero *m*
milkshake *n* batido *m* de leche, malteada *f Méx*
milky [ˈmɪlki] <-ier, -iest> *adj* lechoso
Milky Way *n no pl* **the** ~ la Vía Láctea
mill [mɪl] I. *n* 1. (*for grain*) molino *m* 2. (*factory*) fábrica *f* (de tejidos) II. *vt* moler
millennium [mɪˈleniəm] <-s *o* -ennia> *n* milenio *m*
miller [ˈmɪlər, *Am:* -ə˞] *n* molinero, -a *m, f*
million [ˈmɪlɪən, *Am:* -jən] <-(s)> *n* millón *m;* **two** ~ **people** dos millones de personas; ~**s of** millones de

M
m

> ❗ **million**, después de una cifra, se utiliza en singular: "Fifty million people watched the World Cup Final."

millionaire [ˌmɪljəˈneəʳ, Am: -ˈner] n millonario, -a m, f

mime [maɪm] I. n pantomima f II. vi actuar de mimo III. vt imitar

mimic [ˈmɪmɪk] I. <-ck-> vt imitar II. n imitador(a) m(f)

min. 1. abbr of **minute** min. 2. abbr of **minimum** mín.

mince [mɪns] n no pl, Aus, Brit carne f picada

mind [maɪnd] I. n 1. (brain) mente f; **to be out of one's ~** estar fuera de juicio; **to change one's ~** cambiar de parecer; **to make up one's ~** decidirse 2. (thought) pensamiento m; **to bear sth in ~** tener algo presente II. vt 1. (be careful of) tener cuidado con; **~ the step!** ¡cuidado con la escalera! 2. (bother) sentirse molesto por; **I don't ~ the cold** el frío no me molesta; **would you ~ opening the window?** ¿haces el favor de abrir la ventana? 3. (look after) estar al cuidado de; **don't ~ me** no te preocupes por mí III. vi **never ~!** ¡no importa!; **I don't ~ me** es igual

mine¹ [maɪn] pron poss (el) mío, (la) mía, (los) míos, (las) mías; **it's not his bag, it's ~** no es su bolsa, es la mía; **this glass is ~** este vaso es mío; **these are his shoes and those are ~** estos zapatos son suyos y estos (son) míos

mine² [maɪn] n MIN, MIL mina f; **a ~ of information** fig una fuente abundante de información

miner [ˈmaɪnəʳ, Am: -nɚ] n minero, -a m, f

mineral [ˈmɪnərəl] I. n mineral m II. adj mineral

mingle [ˈmɪŋgl] vi mezclarse; **to ~ with the guests** mezclarse con los invitados

miniature [ˈmɪnɪtʃəʳ, Am: -iətʃɚ] I. adj de miniatura II. n miniatura f

minimal [ˈmɪnɪml] adj mínimo

minimize [ˈmɪnɪmaɪz] vt minimizar

minimum [ˈmɪnɪməm] I. n mínimo m II. adj mínimo; **~ requirements** requisitos mpl básicos

minister [ˈmɪnɪstəʳ, Am: stɚ] n 1. POL ministro, -a m, f 2. REL pastor m

ministerial [ˌmɪnɪˈstɪəriəl, Am: -ˈstɪri-] adj ministerial

ministry [ˈmɪnɪstri] <-ies> n 1. POL ministerio m 2. REL sacerdocio m

mink [mɪŋk] n no pl visón m

minor [ˈmaɪnəʳ, Am: -nɚ] I. adj (not great) pequeño; (role) secundario; **~ offence** delito m de menor cuantía; **B ~** MUS si m menor II. n (person) menor mf de edad

Minorca [mɪˈnɔːka, Am: -ˈnɔːr-] n Menorca f

Minorcan adj menorquín

minority [maɪˈnɒrəti, Am: -ˈnɔːrətɪ] I. <-ies> n minoría f II. adj minoritario; **~ sport** deporte de minorías

minstrel [ˈmɪnstrəl] n HIST juglar m

mint¹ [mɪnt] n 1. no pl (herb) hierbabuena f 2. (sweet) caramelo m de menta

mint² [mɪnt] I. n (coin factory) casa f de la moneda II. vt acuñar; **to ~ a word** fig acuñar una palabra III. adj **in ~ condition** en perfecto estado

minus [ˈmaɪnəs] prep a. MAT menos; **5 ~ 2 equals 3** 5 menos 2 igual a 3; **~ ten Celsius** diez grados bajo cero

minuscule [ˈmɪnəskjuːl, Am: -ɪ-] adj minúsculo

minute¹ [ˈmɪnɪt] n 1. (sixty seconds) minuto m; **in a ~** ahora mismo; **any ~** de un momento a otro; **at the last ~** a última hora 2. pl (of meeting) acta(s) f(pl)

minute² [maɪˈnjuːt, Am: -ˈnuːt] adj diminuto

miracle [ˈmɪrəkl] n milagro m; **by a ~** por milagro

miraculous [mɪˈrækjʊləs, Am: -jə-] adj milagroso

mirage [ˈmɪrɑːʒ] n espejismo m

mire [maɪəʳ, Am: maɪr] n 1. (swamp) fango m 2. fig berenjenal m

mirror [ˈmɪrəʳ, Am: -ɚ] I. n espejo m II. vt reflejar

miscarriage [ˌmɪsˈkærɪdʒ, Am: ˈmɪsˌker-] n aborto m (espontáneo)

miscellaneous [ˌmɪsəˈleɪnɪəs] *adj* diverso; ~ **expenses** gastos *mpl* varios

mischief [ˈmɪstʃɪf] *n* 1. (*naughtiness*) travesura *f;* **to keep sb out of** ~ impedir a alguien hacer travesuras 2. (*wickedness*) malicia *f*

mischievous [ˈmɪstʃɪvəs, *Am:* -tʃə-] *adj* 1. (*naughty*) travieso 2. (*malicious*) malicioso; ~ **rumours** rumores *mpl* malintencionados

misconception [ˌmɪskənˈsepʃn] *n* idea *f* equivocada; **a popular** ~ un error común

misconduct [ˌmɪskənˈdʌkt, *Am:* -ˈkɑːn-] *n no pl* mala conducta *f*

misdemeanor *n Am*, **misdemeanour** [ˌmɪsdɪˈmiːnər, *Am:* -nər] *n Brit* falta *f*

miser [ˈmaɪzər, *Am:* -zə-] *n* avaro, -a *m, f*

miserable [ˈmɪzrəbl] *adj* 1. (*unhappy*) triste; **to make life** ~ **for sb** hacer insoportable la vida a alguien 2. (*poor*) mísero; **a** ~ **amount** una miseria

misery [ˈmɪzəri] *n* 1. (*unhappiness*) infelicidad *f;* **to make sb's life a** ~ amargar la vida a alguien 2. (*extreme poverty*) miseria *f*, lipidia *f AmC*

misfortune [ˌmɪsˈfɔːtʃuːn, *Am:* -ˈfɔːrtʃən] *n no pl* infortunio *m;* **to suffer** ~ sufrir una desgracia

misgiving [ˌmɪsˈɡɪvɪŋ] *n* recelo *m;* **to be filled with** ~ estar lleno de dudas

misguided [mɪsˈɡaɪdɪd] *adj* desencaminado; ~ **idea** desacierto *m*

mishap [ˈmɪshæp] *n form* percance *m;* **a series of** ~**s** una serie de contratiempos

mislead [ˌmɪsˈliːd] *vt irr* 1. (*deceive*) engañar 2. (*lead into error*) hacer caer en un error; **to let oneself be misled** dejarse engañar

misleading *adj* engañoso

misplace [ˌmɪsˈpleɪs] *vt* extraviar

misread [ˌmɪsˈriːd] *vt irr* interpretar mal

miss¹ [mɪs] *n* (*form of adress*) señorita *f;* **Miss Spain** Miss España

miss² I. <-es> *n* fallo *m* II. *vi* fallar III. *vt* 1. (*not hit*) fallar 2. (*not catch*) perder; **to** ~ **a deadline** no cumplir con una fecha límite 3. (*not go*) **to** ~ **a meeting** faltar a una reunión 4. (*regret absence*) echar de menos

◆ **miss out** I. *vt* 1. (*omit*) omitir 2. (*overlook*) saltarse II. *vi* **to** ~ **on sth** perderse algo

missile [ˈmɪsaɪl, *Am:* ˈmɪsəl] *n* misil *m*

missing [ˈmɪsɪŋ] *adj* desaparecido; **to report sth** ~ dar parte de la pérdida de algo

mission [ˈmɪʃən] *n* misión *f;* **rescue** ~ operación *f* de rescate; ~ **accomplished** misión cumplida

missionary [ˈmɪʃənəri, *Am:* -əner-] <-ies> *n* misionero, -a *m, f*

mist [mɪst] *n* neblina *f*

mistake [mɪˈsteɪk] I. *n* error *m;* **to learn from one's** ~**s** aprender de los propios errores; **to make a** ~ cometer un error; **by** ~ por error II. *vt irr* confundir

mistaken [mɪˈsteɪkən] I. *pp of* **mistake** II. *adj* (*belief*) equivocado; (*identity*) confundido; **unless I'm very much** ~ ... si no me equivoco...

mistreat [ˌmɪsˈtriːt] *vt* maltratar

mistress [ˈmɪstrɪs] *n* 1. (*sexual partner*) amante *f* 2. (*woman in charge*) ama *f;* **the** ~ **of the house** la dueña de la casa

mistrust [ˌmɪsˈtrʌst] I. *n no pl* desconfianza *f;* **to have a** ~ **of sb/sth** recelar de alguien/algo II. *vt* **to** ~ **sb/sth** recelar de alguien/algo

misty [ˈmɪsti] <-ier, -iest> *adj* neblinoso

misunderstand [ˌmɪsˌʌndəˈstænd, *Am:* -dəʳ-] *vt irr* entender mal

misunderstanding *n* malentendido *m;* **there must be some** ~ debe haber un malentendido

misuse¹ [ˌmɪsˈjuːs] *n* mal uso *m*

misuse² [ˌmɪsˈjuːz] *vt* manejar mal

mitigate [ˈmɪtɪɡeɪt, *Am:* -ˈmɪt̬-] *vt form* mitigar

mix [mɪks] I. *n* mezcla *f;* **a** ~ **of people** una mezcla de gente II. *vi*

M

1. (*combine*) mezclarse **2.** (*socially*)
to ~ **with sb** frecuentar a alguien; **to**
~ **well** llevarse bien **III.** *vt* **1.** GASTR
mezclar **2.** (*combine*) combinar; **to**
~ **business with pleasure** combinar el placer con los negocios

mixed *adj* **1.** (*containing various elements*) mezclado; (*team*) mixto; ~
marriage matrimonio *m* mixto
2. (*contradictory*) contradictorio; ~
feelings sentimientos *mpl* contradictorios

mixer ['mɪksəʳ, *Am:* -səʳ] *n* (*machine*) batidora *f*

mixture ['mɪkstʃəʳ, *Am:* -tʃəʳ] *n*
mezcla *f*

mm *abbr of* **millimetre** mm

moan [məʊn, *Am:* moʊn] **I.** *n*
1. (*sound*) gemido *m* **2.** (*complaint*)
quejido *m* **II.** *vi* **1.** (*make a sound*)
gemir; **to** ~ **with pain** gemir de
dolor **2.** (*complain*) lamentarse; **to**
~ **about sth** lamentarse de algo; **to**
~ **that** ... lamentarse de que...
+*subj*

mob [mɒb, *Am:* mɑːb] **I.** *n + sing/
pl* *vb* **1.** (*crowd*) muchedumbre *f*
2. *Brit, inf* (*gang*) pandilla *f*
II. <-bb-> *vt* acosar; **he was ~bed
by his fans** sus fans se aglomeraron
en torno a él

mobile ['məʊbaɪl, *Am:* 'moʊbəl]
I. *n* *a.* TEL móvil *m* **II.** *adj* **1.** (*able to
move*) móvil; (*shop, canteen*) ambulante **2.** (*movable*) movible

mobility [məʊ'bɪləti, *Am:* moʊ'bɪ-
ləṭi] *n no pl* movilidad *f;* **social** ~
Brit movilidad social

mobilization [ˌməʊbɪlaɪˈzeɪʃən,
Am: -bəlɪˈ-] *n a.* MIL movilización *f*

mobilize ['məʊbɪlaɪz, *Am:* -bə-] *vt*
movilizar

mock [mɒk, *Am:* mɑːk] **I.** *adj*
1. (*imitation*) artificial; ~ **leather**
polipiel *f* **2.** (*practice*) ~ **exam** examen *m* de prueba **II.** *vi* burlarse; **to** ~
at sb burlarse de alguien **III.** *vt*
1. (*ridicule*) mofarse de **2.** (*imitate*)
remedar

mockery ['mɒkəri, *Am:* 'mɑːkəʳ-] *n*
1. (*ridicule*) mofa *f* **2.** (*subject of derision*) hazmerreír *mf;* **to make a** ~

of sb/sth ridiculizar a alguien/algo

MOD *n* *Brit s.* **Ministry of Defence**
Ministerio *m* de Defensa

modal ['məʊdəl, *Am:* 'moʊ-] *adj*
modal

modal verb *n* verbo *m* modal

mode ['məʊd, *Am:* 'moʊd] *n* modo
m; ~ **of life** modo de vida; ~ **of
transport** medio *m* de transporte

model ['mɒdəl, *Am:* 'mɑːdəl] **I.** *n*
(*version, example*) *a.* ART modelo *m;*
(*of car, house*) maqueta *f* **II.** <-ll->
vt **1.** (*make figure, representation*)
modelar; **to** ~ **sth in clay** modelar
algo en barro **2.** (*show clothes*) desfilar

modem ['məʊdem, *Am:* 'moʊ-
dəm] *n* INFOR módem *m*

moderate¹ ['mɒdərət, *Am:* 'mɑː-
dəʳ-] *adj* **1.** (*neither large nor small*)
mediano **2.** *a.* POL moderado

moderate² ['mɒdəreɪt, *Am:* 'mɑː-
dəʳ-] **I.** *vt* moderar; **to** ~ **an examination** presidir un examen **II.** *vi*
(*act as moderator*) moderar

moderation [ˌmɒdəˈreɪʃn, *Am:*
ˌmɑːdə-] *n no pl* moderación *f;* **to
drink in** ~ beber con moderación

moderator ['mɒdəreɪtəʳ, *Am:*
'mɑːdəʳeɪtəʳ] *n form* **1.** (*mediator*)
mediador(a) *m(f)* **2.** *Am* (*of discussion*) moderador(a) *m(f)*

modern ['mɒdən, *Am:* 'mɑːdəʳn]
adj moderno

modernize ['mɒdənaɪz, *Am:* 'mɑː-
dəʳ-] *vt* modernizar

modest ['mɒdɪst, *Am:* 'mɑːdɪst]
adj **1.** (*not boastful*) modesto; **to be**
~ **about sth** ser modesto en algo
2. (*moderate*) moderado; **a** ~ **wage**
un sueldo modesto

modesty ['mɒdɪsti, *Am:* 'mɑːdɪst-]
n no pl modestia *f*

modification [ˌmɒdɪfɪˈkeɪʃn, *Am:*
ˌmɑːdɪ-] *n* modificación *f*

modify ['mɒdɪfaɪ, *Am:* 'mɑːdɪ-]
<-ie-> *vt* modificar

module ['mɒdjuːl, *Am:* 'mɑːdʒuːl]
n módulo *m*

moist [mɔɪst] *adj* húmedo

moisture ['mɔɪstʃəʳ, *Am:* -tʃəʳ] *n*
humedad *f*

moisturizer n hidratante m
molasses [məˈlæsɪz] n melaza f
mold [məʊld, Am: moʊld] n, vi Am s. **mould²**
Moldavia [mɒlˈdeɪviə, Am: mɑːl-] n s. **Moldova**
Moldavian adj moldavo
Moldova [mɒlˈdəʊvə, Am: mɑːlˈdoʊ-] n Moldavia f
Moldovan adj moldavo
mole¹ [məʊl, Am: moʊl] n ZOOL topo m
mole² n ANAT lunar m
molecule [ˈmɒlɪkjuːl, Am: ˈmɑːlɪ-] n molécula f
molest [məˈlest] vt 1. (pester) importunar 2. (sexually) abusar (sexualmente) de
moment [ˈməʊmənt, Am: ˈmoʊ-] n momento m; **the ~ of truth** la hora de la verdad; **at the ~** por el momento; **at any ~** en cualquier momento; **at the last ~** en el último momento; **in a ~** enseguida; **not for a ~** ni por un momento
momentary [ˈməʊməntri, Am: ˈmoʊmənter-] adj momentáneo
momentous [məˈmentəs, Am: moʊˈmentəs] adj trascendental
momentum [məˈmentəm, Am: moʊˈmentəm] n no pl PHYS momento m; fig impulso m; **to gather ~** tomar velocidad
Monaco [ˈɒnəkəʊ, Am: ˈmɑːnəkoʊ] n Mónaco m
monarch [ˈmɒnək, Am: ˈmɑːnəʳk] n monarca mf
monarchy [ˈmɒnəki, Am: ˈmɑːnəʳ-] <-ies> n monarquía f
monastery [ˈmɒnəstri, Am: ˈmɑːnəster-] <-ies> n monasterio m
Monday [ˈmʌndi] n lunes m inv; **Easter** [o **Whit**] **~** lunes de Pascua; s. a. **Friday**
monetary [ˈmʌnɪtəri, Am: ˈmɑːnəteri] adj monetario
money [ˈmʌni] n no pl dinero m; **to be short of ~** ir escaso de dinero; **to change ~** cambiar dinero; **to raise ~** recolectar fondos; **~ is the root of all evil** prov el dinero es la fuente de todos los males prov; **~ talks** prov

poderoso caballero es don Dinero prov
Mongolia [mɒŋˈgəʊlɪə, Am: mɑːŋˈgoʊ-] n Mongolia f
Mongolian [mɒŋˈgəʊlɪən, Am: mɑːŋˈgoʊ-] adj mongol
monitor [ˈmɒnɪtəʳ, Am: ˈmɑːnɪtəʳ] **I.** n **1.** INFOR monitor m; **15-inch ~** monitor de 15 pulgadas **2.** (person) supervisor(a) m(f) **II.** vt controlar; **to ~ sth closely** seguir algo de muy cerca
monk [mʌŋk] n monje m
monkey [ˈmʌŋki] n mono, -a m, f
  ◆ **monkey about** vi inf hacer el indio
monologue [ˈmɒnəlɒg, Am: ˈmɑːnəlɑːg] n monólogo m
monopoly [məˈnɒpəli, Am: -ˈnɑːpəl-] <-ies> n monopolio m
monotonous [məˈnɒtənəs, Am: -ˈnɑːtən-] adj monótono
monotony [məˈnɒtəni, Am: -ˈnɑːtən-] n no pl monotonía f
monsoon [mɒnˈsuːn, Am: mɑːn-] n monzón m
monster [ˈmɒnstəʳ, Am: ˈmɑːnstəʳ] n monstruo m
monstrous [ˈmɒnstrəs, Am: ˈmɑːn-] adj **1.** (awful) monstruoso **2.** (very big) enorme
month [mʌnθ] n mes m; **not in a ~ of Sundays** ni por casualidad
monthly [ˈmʌnθli] **I.** adj mensual **II.** adv mensualmente **III.** n publicación f mensual
monument [ˈmɒnjʊmənt, Am: ˈmɑːnjə-] n monumento m
monumental [ˌmɒnjʊˈmentl, Am: ˌmɑːnjəˈmentl̩] adj (very big) monumental; (error) garrafal
mood¹ [muːd] n humor m; **in a good/bad ~** de buen/mal humor; **to not be in the ~ to do sth** no tener ganas de hacer algo
mood² n Am LING modo m
moody [ˈmuːdi] <-ier, -iest> adj voluble
moon [muːn] n no pl luna f; **full/new ~** luna llena/nueva; **once in a blue ~** de Pascua a Ramos
moor¹ [mɔːʳ, Am: mʊr] n (area)

M
m

páramo *m*

moor^2 [mɔːʳ, *Am:* mʊr] *vt* NAUT amarrar

moose [muːs] *n* alce *m* americano

mop [mɒp, *Am:* mɑːp] I. *n* fregona *f*; **a ~ of hair** una mata de pelo II. <-pp-> *vt* fregar

moral ['mɒrəl, *Am:* 'mɔːr-] I. *adj* moral; **to give sb ~ support** dar apoyo moral a alguien II. *n* 1. (*message*) moraleja *f* 2. *pl* (*standards*) moralidad *f*

morale [məˈrɑːl, *Am:* -ˈræl] *n no pl* moral *f*

morality [məˈræləti, *Am:* mɔːˈrælətɪ] <-ies> *n* moralidad *f*

morbid ['mɔːbɪd, *Am:* 'mɔːr-] *adj* morboso

morbidity [mɔːˈbɪdəti, *Am:* mɔːrˈbɪdətɪ] *n no pl* morbosidad *f*

more [mɔːʳ, *Am:* mɔːr] *comp of* **much, many** I. *adj* más; **~ wine/grapes** más vino/uvas; **a few ~ grapes** unas pocas uvas más; **some ~ wine** un poco más de vino II. *adv* más; **~ beautiful than me** más bello que yo; **to drink (a bit/much) ~** beber (un poco/mucho) más; **~ than 10** más de 10 III. *pron* más; **the ~ you eat, the ~ you get fat** cuanto más comes, más gordo te pones; **what ~ does he want?** ¿qué más quiere?

moreover [mɔːˈrəʊvəʳ, *Am:* -ˈrouvə-] *adv* además

morning ['mɔːnɪŋ, *Am:* 'mɔːr-] *n* mañana *f*; **good ~!** ¡buenos días!; **in the ~** por la mañana; **that ~** esa mañana; **the ~ after** la mañana después; **every ~** cada mañana; **6 o'clock in the ~** las 6 de la mañana; **from ~ till night** de la mañana a la noche

Moroccan [məˈrɒkən, *Am:* -ˈrɑːkən] *adj* marroquí

Morocco [məˈrɒkəʊ, *Am:* -ˈrɑːkou] *n* Marruecos *m*

morphology [mɔːˈfɒlədʒi, *Am:* mɔːrˈfɑːlə-] *n* morfología *f*

? El **Morris dancing** existe desde hace mucho tiempo, pero sus orígenes son desconocidos. El nombre procede de 'Moorish' (árabe). Este baile cobra su principal significado en el **May Day** (1 de mayo) y en **Whitsuntide** (Pentecostés). Los **Morris dancers** son, la mayoría de las veces, grupos de hombres vestidos de blanco; algunos llevan campanillas en las pantorrillas y cada uno de ellos porta un bastón, un pañuelo o una corona en la mano. El baile está lleno de movimiento; los bailarines brincan, dan saltos y golpean el suelo con los pies.

morsel ['mɔːsl, *Am:* 'mɔːr-] *n* bocado *m*

mortal ['mɔːtl, *Am:* 'mɔːrtl] *adj* mortal; **~ danger** peligro *m* de muerte

mortality [mɔːˈtæləti, *Am:* mɔːrˈtælətɪ] *n no pl* mortalidad *f*

mortar ['mɔːtəʳ, *Am:* 'mɔːrtə-] *n a.* MIL, TECH mortero *m*

mortgage ['mɔːgɪdʒ, *Am:* 'mɔːr-] I. *n* hipoteca *f* II. *vt* hipotecar

mosaic [məʊˈzeɪɪk, *Am:* moʊ-] *n* mosaico *m*

Moscow ['mɒskəʊ, *Am:* 'mɑːkaʊ] *n* Moscú *m*

Moses ['məʊzɪz, *Am:* 'moʊ-] *n* Moisés *m*

Moslem ['mɒzləm, *Am:* 'mɑːzlem] *adj* musulmán

mosque [mɒsk, *Am:* mɑːsk] *n* mezquita *f*

mosquito [məˈskiːtəʊ, *Am:* -toʊ] <-(e)s> *n* mosquito *m*, zancudo *m* *AmL*

moss [mɒs, *Am:* mɑːs] <-es> *n* musgo *m*

most [məʊst, *Am:* moʊst] *superl of* **many, much** I. *adj* la mayoría de; **~ people** la mayoría de la gente; **for the ~ part** en su mayor parte II. *adv* más; **the ~ beautiful** el más bello, la más bella; **~ of all** más que nada; **~**

likely my probablemente **III.** *pron* la mayoría; **at the (very)** ~ a lo sumo; ~ **of them/of the time** la mayor parte de ellos/del tiempo

mostly ['məʊstli, *Am:* 'moʊst-] *adv* principalmente

MOT [ˌeməʊ'tiː, *Am:* -oʊ'-] *n abbr of* **Ministry of Transport** Ministerio *m* de Transportes

motel [məʊ'tel, *Am:* moʊ-] *n* motel *m*, hotel-garaje *m AmL*

moth [mɒθ, *Am:* mɑːθ] *n* polilla *f*

mother ['mʌðəʳ, *Am:* -ɚ] *n* madre *f*

motherhood *n* maternidad *f* **mother-in-law** *n* suegra *f*

motif [məʊ'tiːf, *Am:* moʊ-] *n* ART motivo *m*

motion ['məʊʃən, *Am:* 'moʊ-] **I.** *n* (*movement*) movimiento *m;* **in slow** ~ a cámara lenta **II.** *vt* indicar con un gesto; **to** ~ **sb to do sth** indicar a alguien que haga algo

motivate ['məʊtɪveɪt, *Am:* 'moʊtə-] *vt* motivar

motivation [ˌməʊtɪ'veɪʃn, *Am:* ˌmoʊtə'-] *n no pl* motivación *f*

motive ['məʊtɪv, *Am:* 'moʊtɪv] *n* motivo *m*

motor ['məʊtəʳ, *Am:* 'moʊtɚ] *n* motor *m*

motorbike *n inf* moto *f* **motor car** *n Brit* automóvil *m* **motorcycle** *n form* motocicleta *f* **motor vehicle** *n form* automóvil *m* **motorway** *n Brit* autopista *f*

motto ['mɒtəʊ, *Am:* 'mɑːtoʊ] <-(e)s> *n* lema *m*

mould[1] [məʊld, *Am:* moʊld] *n no pl, Brit* BOT moho *m*

mould[2] *Brit* **I.** *n* (*for metal, clay, jelly*) molde *m;* **to be cast in the same** ~ estar cortado por el mismo patrón **II.** *vt* moldear

mouldy ['məʊldi, *Am:* 'moʊl-] <-ier, -iest> *adj Brit* mohoso *f*

mount [maʊnt] **I.** *vt* **1.** (*get on: horse*) montar **2.** (*organize*) organizar **3.** (*fix for display*) fijar **II.** *vi* montarse

mountain ['maʊntɪn, *Am:* -ʈən] *n* montaña *f;* **to make a** ~ **out of a molehill** ahogarse en un vaso de agua, hacer de la camisa un trapo *Col, Ven*

mourn [mɔːn, *Am:* mɔːrn] **I.** *vi* lamentarse; **to** ~ **for sb** llorar la muerte de alguien **II.** *vt* llorar la muerte de

mourner ['mɔːnəʳ, *Am:* 'mɔːrnɚ] *n* doliente *mf*

mournful ['mɔːnfl, *Am:* 'mɔːrn-] *adj* **1.** (*grieving*) afligido **2.** (*gloomy*) triste

mourning ['mɔːnɪŋ, *Am:* 'mɔːrn-] *n no pl* luto *m;* **to be in** ~ estar de luto

mouse [maʊs] <mice> *n* ZOOL, INFOR ratón *m*

mousemat *n Brit,* **mousepat** *n Am* alfombrilla *f* para el ratón

moustache [mə'stɑːʃ, *Am:* 'mʌstæʃ] *n* bigote *m*

mousy ['maʊsi] *adj* **1.** (*shy*) apocado; **she is very** ~ es muy poquita cosa **2.** (*brown*) pardo

mouth[1] [maʊθ] *n* **1.** (*of person, animal*) boca *f;* **to shut one's** ~ *inf* callarse; **to be born with a silver spoon in one's** ~ *fig* nacer con un pan debajo del brazo **2.** (*opening*) abertura *f*

mouth[2] [maʊð] *vt* articular

move [muːv] **I.** *n* **1.** (*movement*) movimiento *m;* **to get a** ~ **on** darse prisa **2.** (*change of abode*) mudanza *f* **3.** GAMES jugada *f;* **it's your** ~ te toca a ti **4.** (*action*) paso *m;* **to make the first** ~ dar el primer paso **II.** *vi* **1.** (*change position*) moverse **2.** (*change abode*) mudarse **III.** *vt* **1.** (*change position*) mover **2.** (*cause emotions*) conmover; **to be** ~**d by sth** estar afectado por algo

◆ **move away I.** *vi* mudarse de casa **II.** *vt* apartar

◆ **move back I.** *vi* retirarse **II.** *vt* colocar más atrás

◆ **move forward I.** *vi* avanzar **II.** *vt* mover hacia adelante; (*time*) adelantar

◆ **move in** *vi* (*move into abode*) instalarse

◆ **move out** *vi* (*stop inhabiting*) dejar la casa

M m

movement ['muːvmənt] *n* movimiento *m*

movie ['muːvi] *n Am, Aus* película *f;* **the ~s** el cine

movie star *n* estrella *f* de cine

moving ['muːvɪŋ] *adj* **1.** (*that moves*) móvil; **~ stairs** escaleras mecánicas **2.** (*causing emotion*) conmovedor

mow [məʊ, *Am:* moʊ] <mowed, mown *o* mowed> *vt* cortar

mower ['məʊəʳ, *Am:* 'moʊəʳ] *n* cortacésped *m*

mown [məʊn, *Am:* moʊn] *pp of* **mow**

MP [ˌemˈpiː] *n Brit abbr of* **Member of Parliament** diputado, -a *m, f*

mph [ˌempiˈeɪtʃ] *abbr of* **miles per hour** m/h

Mr ['mɪstəʳ, *Am:* -təʳ] *n abbr of* **Mister** Sr.

Mrs ['mɪsɪz] *n abbr of* **Mistress** Sra.

Ms [mɪz] *n abbr of* **Miss** *forma de tratamiento que se aplica tanto a mujeres solteras como casadas*

MS [ˌemˈes] *abbr of* **multiple sclerosis** esclerosis *f inv* múltiple

Mt *abbr of* **Mount** mte.

much [mʌtʃ] <more, most> **I.** *adj* mucho, mucha; **too ~ wine** demasiado vino; **how ~ milk?** ¿cuánta leche?; **too/so ~ water** demasiada/tanta agua; **as ~ as** tanto como **II.** *adv* mucho; **~ better** mucho mejor; **thank you very ~** muchas gracias **III.** *pron* mucho; **~ of the day** la mayor parte del día

muck [mʌk] *n no pl, Brit, inf* **1.** (*dirt*) suciedad *f* **2.** (*manure*) estiércol *m*

mud [mʌd] *n no pl* **to drag sb's name through the ~** ensuciar el nombre de alguien

muddle ['mʌdl] **I.** *n no pl* desorden *m*, desparpajo *m AmL;* **to get in a ~** liarse **II.** *vt* confundir

muddy ['mʌdi] <-ier, -iest> *adj* fangoso

muffin ['mʌfɪn] *n ≈* mollete *m*

muffle ['mʌfl] *vt* amortiguar

mug [mʌg] **I.** *n* **1.** (*for tea, coffee*) tazón *m* **2.** *Brit, inf* (*fool*) bobo, -a *m, f* **3.** *pej* (*face*) jeta *f*, escracho *m*

RíoPl **II.** <-gg-> *vt* atracar

mugger ['mʌgəʳ, *Am:* -əʳ] *n* atracador(a) *m(f)*

muggy ['mʌgi] <-ier, -iest> *adj* bochornoso

mule [mjuːl] *n* (*animal*) mulo, -a *m, f*

mull [mʌl] *vt* **to ~ sth over** meditar algo

multicultural [ˌmʌltɪˈkʌltʃərəl, *Am:* -t̬ɪ-] *adj* multicultural

multilateral [ˌmʌltɪˈlætərəl, *Am:* -t̬ɪˈlæt̬-] *adj* POL multilateral

multimedia [ˌmʌltimiːdiə, *Am:* -t̬ɪ-] *adj* multimedia *inv*

multinational [ˌmʌltɪˈnæʃnəl, *Am:* -t̬ɪ-] *n* multinacional *f*

multiple ['mʌltɪpl, *Am:* -t̬ə-] *adj* múltiple

multiply ['mʌltɪplaɪ, *Am:* -t̬ə-] <-ie-> **I.** *vt* multiplicar **II.** *vi* multiplicarse

multiracial [ˌmʌltɪˈreɪʃl, *Am:* -t̬ɪ-] *adj* multirracial

multitude ['mʌltɪtjuːd, *Am:* -t̬ətuːd] *n* **1.** (*of things, problems*) multitud *f* **2.** (*crowd*) muchedumbre *f*

mum¹ [mʌm] *n Brit, inf* mamá *f*

mum² *adj* **to keep ~** *inf* guardar silencio

mumble ['mʌmbl] *vi* hablar entre dientes

mummy¹ ['mʌmi] <-ies> *n Brit, inf* (*mother*) mami *f*, mamita *f AmL*

mummy² <-ies> *n* (*preserved corpse*) momia *f*

munch [mʌntʃ] *vi, vt* ronzar

mundane [mʌnˈdeɪn] *adj* prosaico

municipal [mjuːˈnɪsɪpl, *Am:* -əpl] *adj* municipal

municipality [mjuːˌnɪsɪˈpæləti, *Am:* -əˈpælət̬i] <-ies> *n* municipio *m*

mural ['mjʊərəl, *Am:* 'mjʊrəl] *n* mural *m*

murder ['mɜːdəʳ, *Am:* 'mɜːrdəʳ] **I.** *n* (*killing*) asesinato *m;* LAW homicidio *m;* **to commit ~** cometer un asesinato **II.** *vt* (*kill*) asesinar, ultimar *AmL*

murderer ['mɜːdərəʳ, *Am:* 'mɜːrdəʳ] *n* (*killer*) asesino, -a *m, f;* LAW homicida *mf*, victimario, -a *m, f AmL*

murky ['mɜːki, *Am:* 'mɜːr-] <-ier, -iest> *adj* turbio

murmur ['mɜːmər, *Am:* 'mɜːrmər] **I.** *vi, vt* murmurar **II.** *n* murmullo *m*

muscle ['mʌsl] *n* ANAT músculo *m*

muscular ['mʌskjʊlər, *Am:* -kjələ˞] *adj* **1.** (*pain, contraction*) muscular **2.** (*arms, legs*) musculoso

muse [mjuːz] **I.** *vi* to ~ (**on sth**) cavilar [*o* reflexionar] (sobre algo) **II.** *n* musa *f*

museum [mjuːˈzɪəm] *n* museo *m*

mushroom ['mʌʃrʊm, *Am:* -ruːm] *n* (*wild*) seta *f*, callampa *f Col, Chile, Perú;* (*button mushroom*) champiñón *m*

mushy ['mʌʃi] *adj* <-ier, -iest> **1.** (*soft*) blando **2.** (*film, book*) sensiblero

music ['mjuːzɪk] *n* música *f*; **it was ~ to her ears** le sonó a música celestial

musical ['mjuːzɪkəl] *n* musical *m*

musician [mjuːˈzɪʃən] *n* músico, -a *m, f*

Muslim ['mʊzlɪm, *Am:* 'mʌzləm] *adj* musulmán

mussel ['mʌsl] *n* mejillón *m*

must [mʌst] *aux* **1.** (*obligation*) deber; **~ you leave so soon?** ¿tienes que irte tan pronto?; **you ~n't do that** no debes hacer eso **2.** (*probability*) deber de; **I ~ have lost it** debo de haberlo perdido; **you ~ be hungry** supongo que tendrás hambre; **you ~ be joking!** ¡estarás bromeando!

mustache ['mʌstæʃ] *n Am* bigote *m*

mustard ['mʌstəd, *Am:* -tə˞d] *n no pl* mostaza *f*

muster ['mʌstər, *Am:* -tə˞] *vt* reunir; **to ~ the courage to do sth** armarse de valor para hacer algo

mustn't ['mʌsnt] = **must not** *s.* **must**

mutation [mjuːˈteɪʃn] *n* mutación *f*

mute [mjuːt] **I.** *n* **1.** (*person*) mudo, -a *m, f* **2.** MUS sordina *f* **II.** *vt* poner

sordina a **III.** *adj* mudo; **to remain ~** permanecer mudo

mutiny ['mjuːtɪni] **I.** <-ies> *n no pl* motín *m* **II.** *vi* <-ie-> amotinarse

mutter ['mʌtər, *Am:* 'mʌt̬ə˞] *vi, vt* murmurar

mutton ['mʌtən] *n no pl* carne *f* de oveja

mutual ['mjuːtʃuəl] *adj* común

mutually *adv* mutuamente; **it was ~ agreed** se decidió de común acuerdo

muzzle ['mʌzl] **I.** *n* **1.** (*for dog*) bozal *m* **2.** (*of gun*) boca *f* **II.** *vt* poner un bozal a

my [maɪ] *adj poss* mi; **~ dog/house** mi perro/casa; **~ children** mis hijos; **this car is ~ own** este coche es mío; **I hurt ~ foot/head** me he hecho daño en el pie/la cabeza

myriad ['mɪrɪəd] *n* miríada *f*

myself [maɪˈself] *pron refl* **1.** (*direct, indirect object*) me; **I hurt ~** me hice daño **2.** *emphatic* yo (mismo/misma); **I did it (all) by ~** lo hice (todo) yo solo **3.** *after prep* mi (mismo/misma); **I said to ~** me dije (a mí mismo/misma)

mysterious [mɪˈstɪərɪəs, *Am:* -ˈstɪrɪ-] *adj* misterioso

mystery ['mɪstəri] <-ies> *n* misterio *m*

mystic ['mɪstɪk] *adj* místico

mystical ['mɪstɪkl] *adj* místico

mysticism ['mɪstɪsɪzəm] *n no pl* misticismo *m*

mystification [ˌmɪstɪfɪˈkeɪʃn] *n* **1.** (*mystery*) misterio *m* **2.** (*confusion*) perplejidad *f*

mystify ['mɪstɪfaɪ] <-ie-> *vt* desconcertar

mystique [mɪsˈtiːk] *n* mística *f*

myth [mɪθ] *n* mito *m*

mythical ['mɪθɪkl] *adj* mítico

mythological [ˌmɪθəˈlɒdʒɪkl, *Am:* -ˈlɑːdʒɪk-] *adj* mitológico

mythology [mɪˈθɒlədʒi, *Am:* -ˈθɑːlə-] <-ies> *n* mitología *f*

M
m

N n

N, n [en] *n* N, n *f;* ~ **for Nelly** *Brit,* ~ **for Nan** *Am* N de Navarra

N *abbr of* **north** N *m*

nab [næb] <-bb-> *vt inf (person)* coger, pescar; *(thing)* coger

NAFTA ['næftə] *n abbr of* **North Atlantic Free Trade Agreement** TLC *m*

nag¹ [næg] *n (horse)* jamelgo *m*

nag² [næg] <-gg-> *vt* regañar, dar la lata a

nagging ['nægɪŋ] I. *n no pl* quejas *fpl* II. *adj (pain, ache)* persistente

nail [neɪl] I. *n* 1. *(tool)* clavo *m* 2. ANAT uña *f* 3. *fig* **to pay on the ~** pagar a toca teja II. *vt* 1. *(fasten)* clavar 2. *inf (catch: police)* coger

nail brush <-es> *n* cepillo *m* de uñas **nail enamel remover** *n Am* quitaesmalte *m* **nail file** *n* lima *f* **nail polish** *n no pl, Am* quitaesmalte *m* **nail scissors** *npl* tijeras *fpl* para uñas **nail varnish** *n no pl* esmalte *m* de uñas

naive, naïve [naɪˈiːv, *Am:* naːˈ-] *adj* ingenuo

naked ['neɪkɪd] *adj* 1. *(unclothed)* desnudo, encuerado *Cuba, Méx* 2. *(uncovered: blade)* desenvainado; **to the ~ eye** a simple vista

name [neɪm] I. *n* 1. *(surname)* nombre *m;* *(surname)* apellido *m;* **by ~** de nombre; **in the ~ of freedom and justice** en nombre de la libertad y de la justicia; **to call sb ~s** llamar a alguien de todo 2. *(reputation)* fama *f;* **to give sb/sth a good ~** dar buena fama a alguien/algo; **to make a ~ for oneself** hacerse un nombre II. *vt* 1. *(call)* poner nombre a, bautizar 2. *(list)* nombrar

nameless ['neɪmlɪs] *adj* indescriptible; *(author)* anónimo

namely ['neɪmli] *adv* a saber

namesake ['neɪmseɪk] *n* tocayo, -a *m, f*

Namibia [næˈmɪbɪə, *Am:* nəˈ-] *n* Namibia *f*

Namibian [næˈmɪbɪən, *Am:* nəˈ-] *adj* namibio

nanny ['næni] <-ies> *n* niñera *f,* nurse *f AmL*

nap [næp] *n* cabezadita *f;* *(after lunch)* siesta *f;* **to have a ~** echarse una siesta

nape [neɪp] *n* nuca *f,* cogote *m*

napkin ['næpkɪn] *n* servilleta *f*

nappy ['næpi] <-ies> *n* pañal *m*

narcissus [naːˈsɪsəs, *Am:* naːrˈ-] <-es *o* narcissi> *n* narciso *m*

narcotic [naːˈkɒtɪk, *Am:* naːrˈkaːt̬-] *n* narcótico *m*

narrate [nəˈreɪt, *Am:* ˈnereɪt] *vt* narrar, relatar

narrative ['nærətɪv, *Am:* 'neret̬ɪv] *n no pl* narración *f,* relato *m*

narrator [nəˈreɪtə', *Am:* 'nereɪt̬ə] *n* narrador(a) *m(f);* TV comentarista *mf*

narrow ['nærəʊ, *Am:* 'neroʊ] I. <-er, -est> *adj* 1. *(thin)* estrecho 2. *(small: margin)* escaso II. *vi* 1. estrecharse; *(gap)* reducirse 2. *(field)* limitarse, restringirse

narrowly *adv* por poco

narrow-minded [ˌnærəʊˈmaɪndɪd, *Am:* ˌneroʊˈ-] *adj* de mentalidad cerrada; *(opinions, views)* cerrado

NASA ['næsə] *n Am abbr of* **National Aeronautics and Space Administration** NASA *f*

nasal ['neɪzl] *adj* nasal; *(voice)* gangoso

nasty ['naːsti, *Am:* 'næsti] <-ier, -iest> *adj* 1. *(bad)* malo; *(smell, taste)* asqueroso, repugnante; *(surprise)* desagradable 2. *(dangerous)* peligroso

nation ['neɪʃən] *n* nación *f*

national ['næʃənəl] I. *adj* nacional II. *n* súbdito, -a *m, f*

national anthem *n* himno *m* nacional **national costume** *n* traje *m* nacional **national debt** *n* deuda *f* nacional

> **?** El **national emblem** (emblema nacional) de Inglaterra es la **Tudor**

rose, una rosa blanca y plana de la casa real de York sobre la rosa roja de la casa de Lancaster. El emblema nacional de Irlanda es la **shamrock**, una especio de trébol, que fue utilizado, al parecer, por el patrón de Irlanda, St. Patrick, para ilustrar el misterio de la Santísima Trinidad. El **thistle** (cardo) de Escocia fue elegido por el rey Jaime III en el siglo XV como símbolo nacional. El **dragon** de Gales fue utilizado desde hace mucho tiempo como emblema en las banderas de guerra. Los galos tienen también al **leek** (puerro) como símbolo, el cual, según Shakespeare, fue llevado en la batalla de Poitiers contra los franceses en 1356. La **daffodil** (campana pascual) es un sustituto del siglo XX más bonito.

National Guard *n Am* Guardia *f* Nacional **National Health (Service)** *n Brit* (servicio *m* de) asistencia *f* sanitaria de la Seguridad Social **National Insurance** *n no pl, Brit* Seguridad *f* Social

nationalism ['næʃnəlɪzəm] *n no pl* nacionalismo *m*

nationalist ['næʃnəlɪst] *adj* nacionalista

nationality [ˌnæʃə'næləti] <-ies> *n* nacionalidad *f*

nationalization [ˌnæʃənəlaɪ'zeɪʃən, *Am:* -ɪ'-] *n* nacionalización *f*

nationalize ['næʃənəlaɪz] *vt* nacionalizar

national service *n no pl, Brit, Aus* servicio *m* militar

nationwide [ˌneɪʃən'waɪd] *adj* nacional

native ['neɪtɪv, *Am:* -t̬ɪv] **I.** *adj* **1.** (*indigenous*) indígena **2.** (*original*) nativo; (*innate*) innato; (*language*) materno; ~ **country** patria *f* **II.** *n* (*indigenous inhabitant*) nativo,

-a *m, f,* natural *mf;* **to speak English like a** ~ hablar el inglés como un nativo

native American I. *n* indígena *mf* americano, -a **II.** *adj* indígena **native speaker** *n* hablante *mf* nativo, -a

nativity [nə'tɪvəti, *Am:* -t̬i] <-ies> *n* natividad *f;* **the Nativity** la Navidad

nativity play *n* auto *m* de Navidad

NATO ['neɪtəʊ, *Am:* -t̬oʊ] *n abbr of* **North Atlantic Treaty Organisation** OTAN *f*

natural ['nætʃərəl, *Am:* -ə-əl] *adj* natural; **to die from** ~ **causes** morir de causas naturales

natural gas *n no pl* gas *m* natural **natural history** *n no pl* historia *f* natural

naturalize ['nætʃərəlaɪz, *Am:* -ə-əl-] *vt Am* naturalizar

naturally *adv* naturalmente

nature ['neɪtʃəʳ, *Am:* -tʃɚ] *n* naturaleza *f;* **things of this** ~ cosas de esta índole; **to be in sb's** ~ estar en la naturaleza de alguien

naughty ['nɔːti, *Am:* 'nɑːt̬i] <-ier, -iest> *adj* **1.** (*badly behaved: children*) desobediente, travieso **2.** *iron* (*adults*) pícaro **3.** *iron, inf* (*sexually stimulating*) picante

nausea ['nɔːsɪə, *Am:* 'nɑːzɪə] *n no pl* náusea *f*

nauseate ['nɔːsɪeɪt, *Am:* 'nɑːzɪ-] *vt form* asquear

naval ['neɪvəl] *adj* naval

naval commander *n* comandante *mf* naval

nave [neɪv] *n* nave *f*

navel ['neɪvl] *n* ombligo *m*

navigate ['nævɪgeɪt] **I.** *vt* **1.** (*steer*) llevar; AUTO guiar **2.** (*sail*) navegar por **II.** *vi* NAUT, AVIAT navegar; AUTO guiar

navigation [ˌnævɪ'geɪʃən] *n no pl* navegación *f*

navvy ['nævi] <-ies> *n Brit, inf* peón *m*

navy ['neɪvi] **I.** <-ies> *n* **the Navy** la Marina **II.** *adj* ~ (**blue**) azul marino

Nazi ['nɑːtsi] *n* nazi *mf*

NB [ˌen'biː] *abbr of* **nota bene** N.B.

N
n

NBC [ˌenbiːˈsiː] *n abbr of* **National Broadcasting Company** *cadena de televisión*

NE [ˌenˈiː] *abbr of* **northeast** NE *m*

near [nɪəʳ, *Am:* nɪr] **I.** *adj* **1.** (*spatial*) cercano **2.** (*temporal*); **in the ~ future** en un futuro próximo **3.** (*similar*) **the ~est thing to sth** lo más parecido a algo **II.** *adv* (*spatial or temporal*) cerca **III.** *prep* **1.** (*in proximity to*) ~ (**to**) cerca de **2.** (*almost*) **it's ~ midnight** es casi medianoche **IV.** *vt* acercarse a; **it is ~ing completion** está casi terminado

nearby [ˈnɪəbaɪ, *Am:* ˌnɪrˈ-] **I.** *adj* cercano **II.** *adv* cerca

Near East *n* Oriente *m* Próximo

nearly [ˈnɪəli, *Am:* ˈnɪr-] *adv* casi; ~ **certain** casi seguro; **to be ~ sth** estar cerca de algo

nearside [ˈnɪəsaɪd, *Am:* ˌnɪrˈ-] *Brit, Aus* **I.** *n* lado *m* cercano al arcén **II.** *adj* **the ~ lane** (*right-hand drive*) el lado derecho; *Brit* (*left-hand drive*) el lado izquierdo

near-sighted [ˌnɪəˈsaɪtɪd, *Am:* ˌnɪrˈsaɪtɪd] *adj a. fig* miope

neat [niːt] *adj* **1.** (*well-ordered*) cuidado, ordenado **2.** (*deft*) cuidadoso **3.** *Am, Aus, inf* (*excellent*) guay *inf*

neatly *adv* **1.** (*with care*) cuidadosamente **2.** (*deftly*) con estilo

neatness [ˈniːtnəs] *n no pl* pulcritud *f*, limpieza *f*

necessarily [ˈnesəsərəli] *adv* necesariamente; **not ~** no necesariamente

necessary [ˈnesəsəri, *Am:* -ser-] *adj* necesario; **to do what is ~** hacer lo que es necesario; **if ~** cuando sea necesario

necessity [nɪˈsesəti, *Am:* nəˈsesəti] <-ies> *n no pl* necesidad *f*; **in case of ~** en caso de necesidad; **bare ~** primera necesidad

neck [nek] **I.** *n* cuello *m*; (*nape*) cogote *m*; **to be up to one's ~ in** *inf* estar (metido) hasta el cuello en algo **II.** *vi Am, inf* besuquearse

necklace *n* collar *m* **neckline** *n* escote *m* **necktie** *n* corbata *f*

née [neɪ] *adj* de soltera

need [niːd] **I.** *n no pl* necesidad *f*; **basic ~s** necesidades básicas; ~ **for sb/sth** necesidad de alguien/algo; **to be in ~ of sth** necesitar (de) algo; **if ~(s) be** si es necesario; **there's no ~ to shout so loud** no hace falta gritar tan alto **II.** *vt* **1.** (*require*) necesitar **2.** (*ought to have*) **not to ~ sth** no necesitar (de) algo **3.** (*must, have*) **to do sth** tener que hacer algo **4.** (*should*) **you ~n't laugh! – you'll be next** ¡no deberías reír! – tú serás el siguiente

needle [ˈniːdl] **I.** *n* aguja *f* **II.** *vt* pinchar, provocar

needless [ˈniːdlɪs] *adj* innecesario; ~ **to say ...** no hace falta decir...

needlework [ˈniːdlwɜːk, *Am:* -wɜːrk] *n no pl* labor *f* de aguja

needn't [ˈniːdənt] = **need not** *s.* **need**

needy [ˈniːdi] <-ier, -iest> *adj* necesitado

negative [ˈnegətɪv, *Am:* -tɪv] **I.** *adj* negativo **II.** *n* **1.** (*rejection*) negativa *f* **2.** (*making use of negation*) negación *f* **3.** PHOT negativo *m*

neglect [nɪˈglekt] **I.** *vt* desatender; **to ~ to do sth** descuidar hacer algo **II.** *n no pl* negligencia *f*; (*poor state, unrepaired state*) deterioro *m*

negligee *n,* **negligée** [ˈneglɪʒeɪ, *Am:* ˌnegləˈʒeɪ] *n* salto *m* de cama

negligence [ˈneglɪdʒənts] *n no pl* negligencia *f*

negligible [ˈneglɪdʒəbl] *adj* insignificante

negotiable [nɪˈgəʊʃiəbl, *Am:* -ˈgoʊ-] *adj* negociable; **not ~** no negociable

negotiate [nɪˈgəʊʃieɪt, *Am:* -ˈgoʊ-] **I.** *vt* **1.** (*discuss*) negociar **2.** (*convert into money*) **to ~ a cheque** cobrar un cheque **II.** *vi* negociar; **to ~ with sb** negociar con alguien

negotiating table *n fig* mesa *f* de negociaciones

negotiation [nɪˌgəʊʃiˈeɪʃən, *Am:* -ˌgoʊ-] *n* negociación *f*; ~ **for sth** negociación de algo

negotiator [nɪˈgəʊʃieɪtəʳ, *Am:* -ˈgoʊʃieɪt̬ɚ] *n* negociador(a) *m(f)*

negro <-es> *n*, **Negro** ['niːgrəʊ, *Am:* -groʊ] *n* negro *m*

neigh [neɪ] **I.** *n* relincho *m* **II.** *vi* relinchar

neighbor ['neɪbɚ] *n Am s.* **neighbour**

neighborhood ['neɪbɚhʊd] *n Am s.* **neighbourhood**

neighboring ['neɪbərɪŋ] *adj Am s.* **neighbouring**

neighborly ['neɪbɚli] *adj Am s.* **neighbourly**

neighbour ['neɪbəʳ, *Am:* -bɚ] *n* vecino, -a *m, f*

neighbourhood ['neɪbəhʊd, *Am:* -bɚ-] *n* (*smallish localized community*) vecindario *m*; (*people*) vecinos *mpl*

neighbourhood watch *n* vigilancia *f* vecinal

neighbouring ['neɪbərɪŋ] *adj* (*nearby*) cercano; (*bordering*) adyacente

neighbourly ['neɪbəli, *Am:* -bɚli] *adj* amable

neither ['naɪðəʳ, *Am:* 'niːðɚ] **I.** *pron* ninguno; **which one? – ~** (**of them**) ¿cuál? – ninguno (de los dos) **II.** *adv* ni; **~ ... nor ...** ni... ni... **III.** *conj* tampoco; **if he won't eat, ~ will I** si él no come, yo tampoco **IV.** *adj* ningún, ninguna; **in ~ case** en ningún caso

neologism [niːˈɒlədʒɪzəm, *Am:* -ˈɑːlə-] *n form* neologismo *m*

neon ['niːɒn, *Am:* -ɑːn] *n no pl* neón *m*

neon lamp *n*, **neon light** *n* luz *f* de neón

nerd [nɜːd, *Am:* nɜːrd] *n Am* lerdo, -a *m, f*

nerve [nɜːv, *Am:* nɜːrv] *n* **1.** (*fibre*) nervio *m* **2.** (*high nervousness*) **to be in a state of ~s** estar nervioso **3.** *no pl* (*courage, bravery*) valor *m*; **to hold/lose one's ~** mantener/perder el valor

nerve center *n Am*, **nerve centre** *n Aus, Brit* **1.** (*group of closely connected nerve cells*) centro *m* nervioso **2.** *fig* (*centre of control*) centro *m* neurálgico

nerve-racking ['nɜːvrækɪŋ, *Am:* 'nɜːrv-] *adj* perturbador

nervous ['nɜːvəs, *Am:* 'nɜːr-] *adj* (*jumpy*) nervioso; (*edgy*) ansioso

nervous breakdown *n* ataque *m* de nervios

nervy ['nɜːvi, *Am:* 'nɜːr-] <-ier, -iest> *adj Brit* nervioso

nest [nest] **I.** *n* (*animal's home*) nido *m* **II.** *vi* anidar

nest egg *n* (*money saved*) ahorros *mpl*

nestle ['nesl] *vi* acomodarse; **to ~ up to sb** arrimarse a alguien

net¹ [net] **I.** *n* **1.** (*material with spaces*) malla *f*; (*fine netted fabric*) tul *m* **2.** (*device for trapping fish*) red *f* **3.** SPORTS red *f* **4.** (*final profit*) beneficio *m* neto; (*final amount*) importe *m* neto **II.** <-tt-> *vt* (*fish*) pescar; (*criminals*) capturar

net² [net] *adj* ECON neto; **~ income** [*o* **earnings**] beneficio *m* neto

netball ['netbɔːl] *n no pl, Brit: juego semejante al baloncesto y practicado mayoritariamente por mujeres*

net curtain *n* visillo(s) *m(pl)*

Netherlands ['neðələndz, *Am:* -ɚləndz] *n* **the ~** los Países Bajos, Holanda

nett [net] *adj, vt s.* **net¹ II.**, **net²**

netting ['netɪŋ, *Am:* 'net̬ɪŋ] *n no pl* **1.** (*net*) malla *f* **2.** SPORTS red *f*

nettle ['netl, *Am:* 'net̬-] *n* ortiga *f*

network ['netwɜːk, *Am:* -wɜːrk] *n* INFOR, TEL red *f*; **telephone ~** red telefónica

neurological [ˌnjʊərəˈlɒdʒɪkəl, *Am:* ˌnʊrəˈlɑː-] *adj* neurológico

neurosis [njʊəˈrəʊsɪs, *Am:* nʊˈroʊ-] <-es> *n* neurosis *f inv*

neurotic [njʊəˈrɒtɪk, *Am:* nʊˈrɑːtɪk] *adj* neurótico

neuter ['njuːtəʳ, *Am:* 'nuːt̬ɚ] **I.** *adj* neutro **II.** *vt* castrar

neutral ['njuːtrəl, *Am:* 'nuː-] **I.** *adj* **1.** (*uninvolved*) neutral **2.** *a.* CHEM, ELEC neutro **II.** *n* (*part of gears system*) punto *m* muerto

neutralize ['njuːtrəlaɪz, *Am:* 'nuː-] *vt* neutralizar

neutron ['njuːtrɒn, *Am:* 'nuːtrɑːn]

n neutrón *m*

never ['nevə^r, *Am:* -ə-] *adv* 1.(*at no time, on no occasion*) nunca, jamás; **I ~ forget a face** nunca olvido una cara 2.(*under no circumstances*) jamás; **~ ever** nunca jamás; **~ mind** no importa, tanto da

never-ending [ˌnevər'endɪŋ, *Am:* 'nevə-] *adj* interminable

nevertheless [ˌnevəðə'les, *Am:* ˌnevə-] *adv* sin embargo, con todo, no obstante

new [njuː, *Am:* nuː] *adj* 1.(*latest, recent*) nuevo, reciente; (*word*) de nuevo cuño 2.(*in new condition*) nuevo; **brand ~** completamente nuevo

New Age *n* New Age *m*

newborn *adj* reciente

New Brunswick *n* Nueva Brunswick *f* **New Caledonia** *n* Nueva Caledonia *f*

newcomer *n* recién llegado, -a *m, f*

New England *n* Nueva Inglaterra *f*

newfangled *adj* novedoso **new-found** *adj* recién descubierto

New Foundland ['njuːfəndlənd, *Am:* 'nuːfəndlənd] *n* Terranova *f*

newly ['njuːli, *Am:* 'nuː-] *adv* recientemente

newly-wed ['njuːlɪwed, *Am:* 'nuː-] *npl* recién casados *mpl*

new moon *n* luna *f* nueva

New Orleans *n* Nueva Orleans *f*

news [njuːz, *Am:* nuːz] *n + sing vb* noticias *fpl*; **the ~ media** los medios de comunicación; **bad/good ~** buenas/malas noticias; **to be ~** ser noticia

⚠️ **news** se utiliza en singular:
"The news is good; Is there any news of Norman?"

news agency <-ies> *n* agencia *f* de noticias **newsagent** *n Brit, Aus* vendedor(a) *m(f)* de periódicos **newscaster** *n Am* locutor(a) *m(f)* de un informativo **news dealer** *n Am* vendedor(a) *m(f)* de periódicos **newsflash** <-es> *n* ≈ noticia *f* de última

hora, flash *m* informativo **newsletter** *n* nota *f* de prensa **newspaper** *n* periódico *m*; **~ clipping** recorte *m* de periódico **newsprint** *n no pl* papel *m* de periódico **newsreader** *n Brit, Aus* locutor(a) *m(f)* de un informativo **newsreel** *n* noticiario *m* documental **newsroom** *n* sala *f* de redacción **newsstand** *n* quiosco *m* **newsworthy** *adj* de interés periodístico

newt [njuːt, *Am:* nuːt] *n* tritón *m*

New Year *n* año *m* nuevo; **Happy ~** feliz año nuevo; **to celebrate ~** celebrar el año nuevo

New Year's Day *n no pl* día *m* de año nuevo **New Year's Eve** *n no pl* nochevieja *f*

New York I. *n* Nueva York *f* II. *adj* neoyorquino **New Yorker** *n* neoyorquino, -a *m, f* **New Zealand** I. *n* Nueva Zelanda *f* II. *adj* neozelandés, -esa **New Zealander** *n* neozelandés, -esa *m, f*

next [nekst] I. *adj* 1.(*nearest in location*) siguiente 2.(*following in time*) próximo, que viene; **the ~ day** el día siguiente; **~ month** el mes que viene; **(the) ~ time** la próxima vez 3.(*following in order*) siguiente; **to be ~** ser el siguiente II. *adv* 1.(*afterwards, subsequently*) después, luego 2.(*almost as much*) **~ to** después de 3.(*almost*) casi; **~ to nothing** casi nada

next door [ˌneks'dɔː^r, *Am:* ˌnekst-'dɔːr] I. *adv* al lado II. *adj* de al lado **next of kin** *n no pl* pariente *mf* cercano, -a

NHS [ˌenəɪtʃ'es] *Brit abbr of* **National Health Service** servicio *m* de asistencia sanitaria de la Seguridad Social

Niagara Falls [naɪˌægərə'fɔːlz] *n* **the ~** las cataratas del Niágara

nib [nɪb] *n* punta *f*; (*of a pen*) plumilla *f*

nibble ['nɪbl] *vt* mordisquear

Nicaragua [ˌnɪkə'rægjʊə, *Am:* -ə'rɑːgwə] *n* Nicaragua *f* **Nicaraguan** *adj* nicaragüense

nice [naɪs] *adj* 1.(*pleasant, agree-*

able) bueno **2.** (*amiable*) simpático; (*kind*) amable **3.** (*subtle*) sutil, delicado; (*fine*) fino

nicely ['naɪsli] *adv* bien; **to do very ~** quedar muy bonito

niceties ['naɪsətɪz, *Am:* -t̬iz] *npl* detalles *mpl*

niche [niːʃ, *Am:* nɪtʃ] *n* nicho *m*

nick [nɪk] **I.** *n* **1.** (*chip in surface*) mella *f* **2.** *fig* **in the ~ of time** por los pelos **II.** *vt* **1.** (*chip*) mellar; (*cut*) cortar **2.** *Brit, Aus, inf* (*steal*) mangar, chingar *Méx*, pispear *Arg* **3.** *Brit, inf* **to ~ sb** (*arrest*) trincar a alguien; (*catch*) echar el guante a alguien

nickel ['nɪkl] *n* **1.** *no pl* CHEM níquel *m* **2.** *Am* (*coin*) moneda *f* de cinco centavos

nickname ['nɪkneɪm] **I.** *n* apodo *m* **II.** *vt* apodar

nicotine ['nɪkəti:n] *n no pl* nicotina *f*

nicotine patch <-es> *n* parche *m* de nicotina

niece [ni:s] *n* sobrina *f*

Niger ['naɪdʒəʳ, *Am:* -dʒɚ] *n* Níger *m*

Nigeria [naɪ'dʒɪəriə, *Am:* -'dʒɪri-] *n* Nigeria *f* **Nigerian** *adj* nigeriano

niggling ['nɪglɪŋ] *adj* **1.** (*irritating, troubling*) molesto **2.** (*needing very precise work*) meticuloso

night [naɪt] *n* noche *f*; **good ~!** ¡buenas noches!; **last ~** anoche; **the ~ before** la noche anterior; **during the ~** durante la noche

nightcap *n* (*drink*) bebida *f* (*que se toma antes de acostarse*) **nightclub** *n* club *m* (nocturno) **nightdress** <-es> *n* camisón *m* **nightfall** *n no pl* atardecer *m* **nightgown** *n Am,* **nightie** *n inf* camisón *m* **nightingale** *n* ruiseñor *m* **night life** *n no pl* vida *f* nocturna

nightly ['naɪtli] **I.** *adv* cada noche **II.** *adj* de todas las noches

nightmare ['naɪtmeəʳ, *Am:* -mer] *n* pesadilla *f*

night-porter *n* portero *m* nocturno **night school** *n* escuela *f* nocturna **night watchman** *n* vigilante *m* nocturno, nochero *m CSur*

nil [nɪl] *n no pl* **1.** (*nothing, nought*) nada *f* **2.** *Brit* (*no score*) cero *m*

Nile [naɪl] *n* **the ~** el Nilo

nimble ['nɪmbl] *adj* (*agile*) ágil; (*quick and light in movement*) diestro; (*quick-thinking*) listo

nine [naɪn] *adj* nueve *inv;* **~ times out of ten** casi siempre; *s. a.* **eight**

nineteen [ˌnaɪn'ti:n] *adj* diecinueve *inv; s. a.* **eight**

nineteenth *adj* decimonoveno

ninetieth ['naɪntiəθ, *Am:* -t̬i-] *adj* nonagésimo

ninety ['naɪnti, *Am:* -t̬i] *adj* noventa *inv; s. a.* **eighty**

ninth [naɪnθ] *adj* noveno

nip¹ [nɪp] <-pp-> **I.** *vt* **1.** (*bite*) morder **2.** (*pinch, squeeze*) pellizcar **II.** *vi Brit, Aus, inf* apresurarse; **to ~ along** correr

nip² [nɪp] *n Brit, inf* chupito *m*

nipple ['nɪpl] *n* ANAT pezón *m;* (*teat*) tetilla *f,* tetera *f AmL*

nippy ['nɪpi] <-ier, -iest> *adj Brit, Aus, inf* (*quick*) rápido; (*nimble*) ágil

nit [nɪt] *n* **1.** *Brit, Aus, pej, inf* (*stupid person*) imbécil *mf* **2.** ZOOL liendre *f*

nitrogen ['naɪtrədʒən] *n no pl* nitrógeno *m*

NNE *abbr of* **north-northeast** NNE *m*

NNW *abbr of* **north-northwest** NNO *m*

no [nəʊ, *Am:* noʊ] **I.** *adv* no; (*emphasises previous statement's falsity*) en absoluto; **~ parking** prohibido estacionar; **~ way** de ninguna manera **II.** <-(e)s> *n* (*denial, refusal*) no *m;* **to not take ~ for an answer** no admitir un no como respuesta **III.** *interj* (*word used to deny*) no; (*emphasises distress*) qué me dices

no, No. *abbr of* **number** núm., nº

Nobel prize [ˌnəʊbel'praɪz, *Am:* ˌnoʊbel'praɪz] *n* premio *m* Nobel

nobility [nəʊ'bɪləti, *Am:* noʊ'bɪləti] *n no pl* nobleza *f*

noble ['nəʊbl, *Am:* 'noʊ-] *adj* noble

nobody ['nəʊbədi, *Am:* 'noʊbɑ:di] *pron indef, sing* nadie

nod [nɒd, *Am:* nɑ:d] **I.** *n* cabezada

f, inclinación *f* de cabeza **II.** <-dd->
vt **to ~ one's head** asentir con la
cabeza; **to ~ a farewell to sb** saludar a alguien con una inclinación de
cabeza **III.** <-dd-> *vi* asentir con la
cabeza

◆ **nod off** *vi* dormirse

noise [nɔɪz] *n* ruido *m*; (*loud, unpleasant*) estruendo *m*

noisy ['nɔɪzi] <-ier, -iest> *adj* ruidoso; (*very loud, unpleasant*) estrepitoso

nominal ['nɒmɪnl, *Am:* 'nɑːmə-]
adj nominal

nominate ['nɒmɪneɪt, *Am:* 'nɑː-
mə-] *vt* **1.** (*propose*) proponer
2. (*appoint*) nombrar

nomination [ˌnɒmɪ'neɪʃən, *Am:*
ˌnɑːmə-] *n* **1.** (*proposal*) propuesta
f **2.** (*appointment*) nombramiento
m

nominee [ˌnɒmɪ'niː, *Am:* ˌnɑːmə-]
n candidato, -a *m, f*; (*for an award*)
nominado, -a *m, f*

non-alcoholic [ˌnɒnælkə'hɒlɪk,
Am: ˌnɑːnælkə'hɑːlɪk] *adj* sin alcohol

non-committal [ˌnɒnkə'mɪtəl, *Am:*
ˌnɑːnkə'mɪt̬-] *adj* evasivo

nondescript ['nɒndɪskrɪpt, *Am:*
'nɑːndɪ-] *adj* sin nada de particular;
(*person*) anodino; (*colour*) indefinido

none [nʌn] **I.** *pron* **1.** (*nobody*)
nadie, ninguno; ~ **of them** ninguno
de ellos **2.** (*not any*) ninguno, ninguna; ~ **of my letters arrived** ninguna
de mis cartas llegó **3.** (*not any*) nada;
~ **of that!** ¡déjate de eso! **II.** *adv* ~
the less sin embargo; **to be ~ the
wiser** seguir sin entender nada

⚠ **None** se puede utilizar tanto en
singular como en plural: "None of
my friends smoke(s)."

---

nonentity [nɒ'nentəti, *Am:* nɑː-
'nentət̬i] <-ies> *n* **1.** (*person*) cero
m a la izquierda **2.** *no pl* (*insignificance*) insignificancia *f*

non-event [ˌnɒnɪ'vent, *Am:* ˌnɑːnɪ-

'vent] *n inf* fiasco *m*

non-existent [ˌnɒnɪg'zɪstənt, *Am:*
ˌnɑːnɪg'zɪs-] *adj* inexistente

non-fiction [ˌnɒn'fɪkʃən, *Am:*
ˌnɑːn-] *n no pl* no ficción *f*

no-no ['nəʊnəʊ, *Am:* 'noʊnoʊ] *n*
it's a ~ *inf* de eso ni hablar

nonplus [ˌnɒn'plʌs, *Am:* ˌnɑːn-]
<-ss-> *vt* **to be ~sed** quedarse sor-
prendido

nonsense ['nɒnsənts, *Am:* 'nɑː-
nsents] **I.** *n no pl* tonterías *fpl*; **to
talk ~** *inf* decir tonterías **II.** *interj*
tonterías

nonsensical [ˌnɒn'sentsɪkl, *Am:*
ˌnɑːn-] *adj* absurdo

non-smoker [ˌnɒn'sməʊkəʳ, *Am:*
ˌnɑːn'smoʊkə] *n* persona *f* que no
fuma

non-smoking *adj* no fumador

non-starter [ˌnɒn'stɑːtəʳ, *Am:*
ˌnɑːn'stɑːrt̬ə] *n inf* **that proposal
is a ~** esa propuesta es imposible

non-stick [ˌnɒn'stɪk, *Am:* ˌnɑːn-]
adj antiadherente

non-stop [ˌnɒn'stɒp, *Am:* ˌnɑːn-
'stɑːp] **I.** *adj* sin parar; (*flight*) directo **II.** *adv* sin pausa

noodle ['nuːdl] *n* fideo *m*

nook [nʊk] *n liter* rincón *m*; ~**s and
crannies** todos los rincones

noon [nuːn] *n no pl* mediodía *m*

no one ['nəʊwʌn, *Am:* 'noʊ-] *pron
indef, sing* nadie

noose [nuːs] *n* soga *f*

nor [nɔːʳ, *Am:* nɔːr] *conj* **1.** (*and
also not*) tampoco **2.** (*not either*) ni

norm [nɔːm, *Am:* nɔːrm] *n* norma *f*

normal ['nɔːml, *Am:* 'nɔːr-] *adj*
1. (*not out of the ordinary*) normal
2. (*usual*) corriente; **as** (**is**) ~ como
es normal

normalcy ['nɔːməlsi, *Am:* 'nɔːr-]
Am, **normality** [nɔː'mæləti, *Am:*
nɔːr'mælət̬i] *n Brit no pl* normalidad *f*

normally ['nɔːməli, *Am:* 'nɔːr-] *adv*
normalmente

Normandy ['nɔːməndi, *Am:* 'nɔːr-]
n Normandía *f*

north [nɔːθ, *Am:* nɔːrθ] **I.** *n* norte
m; **in the ~ of Spain** en el norte de

España **II.** *adj* del norte, septentrional **III.** *adv* al norte

North Africa *n* África *f* del Norte

North African *adj* norteafricano

North America *n* América *f* del Norte **North American** *adj* norteamericano

North Carolina *n* Carolina *f* del Norte **North Dakota** *n* Dakota *f* del Norte

northeast [ˌnɔːθˈiːst, *Am:* ˌnɔːrˈθ-] **I.** *n* nor(d)este *m* **II.** *adj* del nor(d)este **III.** *adv* al nor(d)este

northeasterly *adj* del nor(d)este; **in a ~ direction** hacia el nor(d)este

northeastern [ˌnɔːˈθiːstən, *Am:* ˌnɔːrˈθiːstɚn] *adj* del nor(d)este, nororiental

northeastward(s) *adj* hacia el nor(d)este

northerly [ˈnɔːðəli, *Am:* ˈnɔːrðɚli] **I.** *adj* del norte; **in a ~ direction** en dirección norte **II.** *adv* (*towards*) hacia el norte; (*from*) del norte

northern [ˈnɔːðən, *Am:* ˈnɔːrðɚn] *adj* del norte; **the ~ part of the country** la parte norte del país

Northern Marianas *n* Marianas *fpl* del Norte **Northern Territory** *n* territorio *m* norte

North Pole [ˈnɔːθpəʊl, *Am:* ˈnɔːrθpoʊl] *n* **the ~** el polo norte **North Sea** *n* Mar *m* del Norte **North-South divide** *n* ECON división *f* Norte-Sur **North Star** *n* Estrella *f* Polar

northward(s) [ˈnɔːθwəd(z), *Am:* ˈnɔːrθwɚd(z)] *adv* hacia el norte

northwest [ˌnɔːˈθwest, *Am:* ˌnɔːrˈθ-] **I.** *n* noroeste *m* **II.** *adj* del noroeste **III.** *adv* al noroeste

northwesterly [ˌnɔːˈθwestəli, *Am:* ˌnɔːrˈθwestɚli] *adj* del noroeste; **in a ~ direction** hacia el noroeste

Northwest Territories *n pl* territorios *mpl* del noroeste

northwestward(s) *adj* hacia el noroeste

Norway [ˈnɔːweɪ, *Am:* ˈnɔːr-] *n* Noruega *f*

Norwegian [nɔːˈwiːdʒən, *Am:* nɔːrˈ-] *adj* noruego

nose [nəʊz, *Am:* noʊz] **I.** *n* **1.** (*smelling organ*) nariz *f*; **to blow one's ~** sonarse la nariz **2.** AVIAT morro *m* **II.** *vt* **to ~ one's way in/out/up** entrar/salir/pasar lentamente

◆ **nose about, nose around** *vi inf* fisgonear

nosebleed *n* hemorragia *f* nasal

nosedive *n* descenso *m* en picado

nosey [ˈnəʊzi, *Am:* ˈnoʊ-] <-ier, -iest> *adj* fisgón

nostalgia [nɒˈstældʒə, *Am:* nɑːˈ-] *n no pl* nostalgia *f*

nostril [ˈnɒstrəl, *Am:* ˈnɑːstrəl] *n* ventana *f* de la nariz

nosy [ˈnəʊzi, *Am:* ˈnoʊ-] <-ier, -iest> *adj s.* **nosey**

not [nɒt, *Am:* nɑːt] *adv* no; **why ~?** ¿por qué no?; **~ at all** (*nothing*) en absoluto; (*no need to thank*) de nada; **~ only ... but also ...** no sólo... sino también; **~ just** [*o* **simply**] no sólo; **~ much** no demasiado

notable [ˈnəʊtəbl, *Am:* ˈnoʊt̬ə-] *adj* notable

notably [ˈnəʊtəbli, *Am:* ˈnoʊt̬ə-] *adv* notablemente

notary [ˈnəʊtəri, *Am:* ˈnoʊt̬ɚ-] <-ies> *n* **~ (public)** notario, -a *m, f*

notation [nəʊˈteɪʃən, *Am:* noʊ-] *n* MAT, MUS notación *f*

notch [nɒtʃ, *Am:* nɑːtʃ] <-es> *n* muesca *f*

note [nəʊt, *Am:* noʊt] **I.** *n* **1.** (*annotation*) nota *f*; **to take ~** tomar nota **2.** LIT apunte *m* **3.** MUS nota *f*; (*sound*) tono *m* **4.** *Brit, Aus* (*piece of paper money*) billete *m* **5.** (*importance*) **of ~** *form* notable **II.** *vt form* anotar; (*mention*) observar

notebook [ˈnəʊtbʊk, *Am:* ˈnoʊt-] *n* cuaderno *m*

noted [ˈnəʊtɪd, *Am:* ˈnoʊt̬ɪd] *adj* célebre; **to be ~ for sth** ser conocido por algo

notepad [ˈnəʊtpæd, *Am:* ˈnoʊt-] *n* bloc *m*

notepaper [ˈnəʊtˌpeɪpəʳ, *Am:* ˈnoʊtˌpeɪpɚ] *n no pl* papel *m* de carta

N ₙ

noteworthy ['nəʊtˌwɜːði, *Am:* 'noʊtˌwɜːr-] *adj form* de interés

nothing ['nʌθɪŋ] **I.** *pron indef, sing* **1.** (*no objects*) nada; **we saw ~ (else/more)** no vimos nada (más); **~ new** nada nuevo **2.** (*not anything*) **there is ~ to laugh at** no tiene nada de gracioso **3.** (*only*) **~ but** tan sólo **II.** *n* **1.** nada *f* **2.** MAT, SPORT cero *m*

notice ['nəʊtɪs, *Am:* 'noʊtɪs] **I.** *vt* ver; (*perceive*) fijarse en; **to ~ (that)** ... darse cuenta de (que)... **II.** *vi* percatarse **III.** *n* **1.** *no pl* (*attention*) interés *m;* **to take ~ of sb/sth** prestar atención a alguien/algo; **to come to sb's ~ (that ...**) llegar al conocimiento de alguien (que...); **to escape one's ~** no percatarse de algo **2.** (*in a newspaper, magazine*) anuncio *m* **3.** *no pl* (*warning*) aviso *m;* **at short ~** a corto plazo; **until further ~** hasta nuevo aviso

noticeable ['nəʊtɪsəbl, *Am:* 'noʊtɪ-] *adj* evidente; (*difference*) notable

notice board *n Aus, Brit* tablón *m* de anuncios

notification [ˌnəʊtɪfɪˈkeɪʃən, *Am:* ˌnoʊtə-] *n* notificación *f*

notify ['nəʊtɪfaɪ, *Am:* 'noʊtə-] <-ie-> *vt* informar; **to ~ sb of sth** notificar algo a alguien

notion ['nəʊʃən, *Am:* 'noʊ-] *n* noción *f*

notoriety [ˌnəʊtəˈraɪəti, *Am:* ˌnoʊtəˈraɪəti] *n no pl* mala fama *f*

notorious [nəʊˈtɔːrɪəs, *Am:* noʊˈtɔːrɪ-] *adj* de mala reputación; (*thief*) bien conocido

notwithstanding [ˌnɒtwɪθˈstændɪŋ, *Am:* ˌnɑːt-] *adv form* no obstante

nougat ['nuːgɑː, *Am:* 'nuːgət] *n no pl* ≈ turrón *m*

nought [nɔːt, *Am:* nɑːt] *n* **1.** *Brit* nada *f* **2.** MAT cero *m*

noun [naʊn] *n* nombre *m;* LING sustantivo *m*

nourish ['nʌrɪʃ, *Am:* 'nɜːr-] *vt* **1.** (*provide with food*) alimentar **2.** *fig, form* (*cherish*) fomentar

nourishing ['nʌrɪʃɪŋ, *Am:* 'nɜːr-] *adj* nutritivo; (*rich*) rico

nourishment *n no pl* alimento *m*

Nova Scotia [ˌnəʊvəˈskəʊʃə, *Am:* ˌnoʊvəˈskoʊ-] *n* Nueva Escocia *f*

novel[1] ['nɒvl, *Am:* 'nɑːvl] *n* novela *f*

novel[2] ['nɒvl, *Am:* 'nɑːvl] *adj* nuevo

novelist ['nɒvəlɪst, *Am:* ˌnɑːvə-] *n* novelista *mf*

novelty ['nɒvəlti, *Am:* 'nɑːvlti] <-ies> *n no pl* novedad *f*

November [nəʊˈvembə[r], *Am:* noʊˈvembɚ] *n* noviembre *m; s. a.* **April**

novice ['nɒvɪs, *Am:* 'nɑːvɪs] *n* novato, -a *m, f;* REL novicio, -a *m, f*

now [naʊ] **I.** *adv* **1.** (*at the present time*) ahora; **just ~** ahora mismo **2.** (*currently*) actualmente **3.** (*then*) entonces; **(every) ~ and then** de vez en cuando **II.** *n* (*present*) presente *m;* **by ~** ahora ya; **for ~** por ahora **III.** *conj* **~ (that)** ... ahora que...

nowadays ['naʊədeɪz] *adv* hoy en día

nowhere ['nəʊweə[r], *Am:* 'noʊwer] *adv* en ninguna parte; **to appear from ~** aparecer de la nada

nozzle ['nɒzl, *Am:* 'nɑːzl] *n* tobera *f;* (*of a petrol pump*) inyector *m;* (*of a gun*) boquilla *f*

nth *adj* **for the ~ time** *inf* por enésima vez

nuclear ['njuːklɪə[r], *Am:* 'nuːklɪɚ] *adj* nuclear

nucleus ['njuːklɪəs, *Am:* 'nuː-] <-ei *o* -es> *n* núcleo *m*

nude [njuːd, *Am:* nuːd] **I.** *adj* desnudo **II.** *n* **1.** ART, PHOT desnudo *m* **2.** (*naked*) **in the ~** desnudo

nudge [nʌdʒ] *vt* dar un codazo a

nudist ['njuːdɪst, *Am:* 'nuː-] *n* nudista *mf*

nudity ['njuːdəti, *Am:* 'nuːdəti] *n no pl* desnudez *f*

nuisance ['njuːsns, *Am:* 'nuː-] *n* molestia *f,* camote *m AmL;* **to make a ~ of oneself** *inf* dar la lata

null [nʌl] *adj* nulo; **~ and void** sin efecto

numb [nʌm] **I.** *adj* entumecido; **to go ~** entumecerse **II.** *vt* entumecer; (*desensitize*) insensibilizar

number ['nʌmbər, *Am:* -bɚ] **I.** *n* **1.** MAT número *m;* (*symbol*) cifra *f;* **telephone** ~ número de teléfono **2.** (*amount*) cantidad *f;* **for a ~ of reasons** por una serie de razones; **to be 3 in** ~ ser 3 **3.** PUBL, MUS, THEAT número *m* **II.** *vt* **1.** (*assign a number to*) poner número a **2.** (*count*) contar **3.** (*amount to*) sumar

---

? El **Number 10 Downing Street** es la residencia oficial del **prime minister** (primer ministro). La casa data del siglo XVII y fue construida por Sir George Downing, político, especulador inmobiliario y espía. El primer ministro vive en el piso más alto y en el resto del edificio se encuentran las oficinas y las salas de reuniones del gabinete de gobierno. El **Chancellor of the Exchequer** (ministro de Hacienda) vive en la casa de al lado, en el **Number 11**. En la misma calle se encuentran además otras dependencias del gobierno.

---

number plate *n Brit* matrícula *f*
numeral ['nju:mərəl, *Am:* 'nu:-] *n* número *m*
numerate ['nju:mərət, *Am:* 'nu:-] *adj* competente en matemáticas
numerical [nju:'merɪkl, *Am:* nu:-] *adj* numérico
numerous ['nju:mərəs, *Am:* 'nu:-] *adj* numeroso
numskull ['nʌmskʌl] *n* idiota *mf*
nun [nʌn] *n* monja *f*
nunnery ['nʌnəri] <-ies> *n* convento *m* de monjas
nurse [nɜːs, *Am:* nɜːrs] **I.** *n* **1.** MED enfermero, -a *m, f* **2.** (*nanny*) niñera *f* **II.** *vt* **1.** (*care for*) cuidar **2.** (*nurture*) nutrir **3.** (*breast-feed*) amamantar
nursery ['nɜːsəri, *Am:* 'nɜːr-] <-ies> *n* **1.** (*school*) guardería *f* **2.** (*bedroom*) cuarto *m* de los niños **3.** BOT

vivero *m*
nursery rhyme *n* canción *f* infantil
nursery school *n* parvulario *m*
nursery slopes *npl Brit* SPORTS pistas *fpl* para principiantes
nursing *n no pl* enfermería *f*
nursing home *n* asilo *m* de ancianos
nurture ['nɜːtʃər, *Am:* 'nɜːrtʃɚ] *vt* alimentar; (*a plant*) cuidar
nut [nʌt] *n* **1.** BOT nuez *f* **2.** TECH tuerca *f*
nutcracker ['nʌtˌkrækər, *Am:* -ɚ] *n* cascanueces *m inv* **nutmeg** *n no pl* nuez *f* moscada
nutrition [njuːˈtrɪʃən, *Am:* nuː-] *n no pl* nutrición *f*
nutritionist [njuːˈtrɪʃənɪst, *Am:* nuː-] *n* nutricionista *mf*
nutritious [njuːˈtrɪʃəs, *Am:* nuː-] *adj*, **nutritive** ['njuːtrətɪv, *Am:* 'nuːtrəˌtɪv] *adj* nutritivo
nuts [nʌts] *adj* **to be** ~ estar chiflado
nutshell ['nʌtʃel] *n no pl* cáscara *f* de nuez; **in a** ~ en resumidas cuentas
nutty ['nʌti, *Am:* 'nʌt̬-] <-ier, -iest> *adj* **1.** (*cake*) con nueces; (*ice cream*) de nueces; (*taste*) a nueces **2.** *inf* (*crazy*) loco, revirado *Arg, Urug*
NW [ˌen'dʌbljuː] *abbr of* **northwest** NO *m*
NY [ˌen'waɪ] *abbr of* **New York** Nueva York *f*

O, o [əʊ] *n* **1.** (*letter*) O, o *f;* ~ **for Oliver** *Brit,* **O for Oboe** *Am* O de Oviedo **2.** (*zero*) cero *m*
oak [əʊk, *Am:* oʊk] *n* roble *m*
oar [ɔːʳ, *Am:* ɔːr] *n* remo *m*
oath [əʊθ, *Am:* oʊθ] *n* juramento *m;* **under** [*o* **upon**] ~ *Brit* bajo juramento
oats [əʊts, *Am:* oʊts] *npl* avena *f;* **to**

sow one's wild ~ andar de picos pardos *inf*

obedience [əˈbiːdɪəns, *Am:* oʊˈ-] *n no pl* obediencia *f*

obedient [əˈbiːdɪənt, *Am:* oʊˈ-] *adj* obediente; **to be ~ to sb/sth** obedecer a alguien/algo

obesity [əʊˈbiːsəti, *Am:* oʊˈbiːsəti] *n no pl* obesidad *f*

obey [əˈbeɪ, *Am:* oʊˈ-] *vt* obedecer

obituary [əˈbɪtʃuəri, *Am:* oʊˈbɪtʃueri] <-ies> *n*, **obituary notice** *n* necrología *f*, obituario *m AmL*

object¹ [ˈɒbdʒɪkt, *Am:* ˈɑːb-] *n* **1.** (*unspecified thing*) objeto *m* **2.** (*purpose, goal*) propósito *m*, objetivo *m*; **the ~ of the exercise is** ... el objeto del ejercicio es...

object² [əbˈdʒekt] **I.** *vi* oponerse **II.** *vt* objetar; **to ~ that** ... objetar que...

objection [əbˈdʒekʃən] *n* objeción *f*; **to raise ~s** poner reparos

objective [əbˈdʒektɪv] *adj* objetivo

objectivity [ˌɒbdʒɪkˈtɪvəti, *Am:* ˌɑːbdʒekˈtɪvəti] *n no pl* objetividad *f*

obligation [ˌɒblɪˈgeɪʃən, *Am:* ˌɑːbləˈ-] *n no pl* obligación *f*; **to be under an ~ to do sth** tener la obligación de hacer algo

oblige [əˈblaɪdʒ] **I.** *vt* **1.** (*force*) obligar **2.** (*perform service for*) hacer un favor a **II.** *vi* **to be happy to ~** estar encantado de ayudar

obliterate [əˈblɪtəreɪt, *Am:* -ˈblɪt̪-] *vt* eliminar

oblivion [əˈblɪvɪən] *n no pl* olvido *m*; **to fall into ~** caer en el olvido

oblivious [əˈblɪvɪəs] *adj* inconsciente; **~ of sth** inconsciente de algo

oblong [ˈɒblɒŋ, *Am:* ˈɑːblaːŋ] **I.** *n* rectángulo *m*, oblongo *m* **II.** *adj* rectangular, oblongo

obnoxious [əbˈnɒkʃəs, *Am:* -ˈnɑːk-] *adj* detestable

oboe [ˈəʊbəʊ, *Am:* ˈoʊboʊ] *n* oboe *m*

obscene [əbˈsiːn] *adj* obsceno, bascoso *Col, Ecua*

obscenity [əbˈsenəti, *Am:* -t̪i] <-ies> *n* obscenidad *f*, bascosidad *f Col, Ecua*

obscure [əbˈskjʊəʳ, *Am:* -ˈskjʊr] **I.** *adj* oscuro **II.** *vt* **1.** (*make difficult to see*) oscurecer **2.** (*make difficult to understand*) complicar

obscurity [əbˈskjʊərəti, *Am:* -ˈskjʊrəti] *n no pl* oscuridad *f*

observance [əbˈzɜːvəns, *Am:* -ˈzɜːr-] *n* observancia *f*

observant [əbˈzɜːvənt, *Am:* -ˈzɜːr-] *adj* observador

observation [ˌɒbzəˈveɪʃən, *Am:* ˌɑːbzɚˈ-] *n* observación

observatory [əbˈzɜːvətri, *Am:* -ˈzɜːrvətɔːr-] *n* observatorio *m*

observe [əbˈzɜːv, *Am:* -ˈzɜːrv] **I.** *vt* **1.** (*watch closely*) observar **2.** (*remark*) comentar **II.** *vi* **1.** (*watch*) observar **2.** (*remark*) **to ~ (up)on sth** hacer una observación sobre algo

observer [əbˈzɜːvəʳ, *Am:* -ˈzɜːrvɚ] *n a.* MIL, POL observador(a) *m(f)*

obsess [əbˈses] *vt* obsesionar; **to be ~ed by sb/sth** obsesionarse por alguien/algo

obsession [əbˈseʃn] *n a.* PSYCH obsesión *f*; **to have an ~ with sb/sth** estar obsesionado con alguien/algo

obsessive [əbˈsesɪv] *adj* obsesivo

obsolete [ˈɒbsəliːt, *Am:* ˌɑːb-] *adj* obsoleto

obstacle [ˈɒbstəkl, *Am:* ˈɑːbstə-] *n* obstáculo *m*

obstinate [ˈɒbstɪnət, *Am:* ˈɑːbstə-] *adj* obstinado; **to be ~ about sth** ser terco en algo

obstruct [əbˈstrʌkt] *vt* **1.** (*block*) obstruir **2.** (*hinder*) dificultar

obstruction [əbˈstrʌkʃn] *n* **1.** (*action*) *a.* MED, POL obstrucción *f* **2.** (*impediment*) obstáculo *m*

obtain [əbˈteɪn] *vt* obtener

obvious [ˈɒbvɪəs, *Am:* ˈɑːb-] *adj* obvio; **it is ~ to me that** ... me doy perfecta cuenta de que...; **the ~ thing to do** lo que hay que hacer

obviously *adv* obviamente, claramente; **~, ...** como es lógico,...

occasion [əˈkeɪʒən] *n* **1.** (*particular time*) ocasión *f*; **on ~** de vez en cuando; **on one ~** en una ocasión

2. (*event*) acontecimiento *m;* **to rise to the** ~ estar a la altura de las circunstancias

occasional [əˈkeɪʒənəl] *adj* ocasional; **I have the** ~ **cigarette** fumo un cigarrillo de vez en cuando

occasionally *adv* ocasionalmente, de vez en cuando

occidental [ˌɒksɪˈdentəl, *Am:* ˌɑ:-ksəˈdentəl] *adj* occidental

occult [ɒˈkʌlt, *Am:* əˈ-] **I.** *adj* oculto **II.** *n no pl* **the** ~ las ciencias ocultas

occupancy [ˈɒkjəpəntsi, *Am:* ˈɑ:-kjə-] *n no pl* ocupación *f*

occupant [ˈɒkjəpənt, *Am:* ˈɑ:kjə-] *n form* (*of building, vehicle*) ocupante *mf;* (*tenant*) inquilino, -a *m, f*

occupation [ˌɒkjəˈpeɪʃən, *Am:* ˈɑ:kjə-] *n* **1.** *a.* MIL ocupación *f;* **to take up** ~ **of a house** tomar posesión de una vivienda **2.** (*profession*) profesión *f*

occupational [ˌɒkjʊˈpeɪʃənəl, *Am:* ˌɑ:kjə-] *adj* profesional

occupier [ˈɒkjʊpaɪəʳ, *Am:* ˈɑ:kjə-paɪɚ] *n* (*of territory, building*) ocupante *mf;* (*tenant*) inquilino, -a *m, f*

occupy [ˈɒkjʊpaɪ, *Am:* ˈɑ:kju:-] <-ie-> *vt* **1.** (*room, position*) ocupar; **to** ~ **space** ocupar espacio; **the bathroom's occupied** el lavabo está ocupado **2.** (*engage*) **to** ~ **oneself** entretenerse; **the whole process occupied a week** todo el proceso llevó una semana **3.** (*dwell in*) **the house hasn't been occupied for a long time** nadie ha vivido en la casa durante mucho tiempo

occur [əˈkɜ:ʳ, *Am:* -ˈkɜ:r] <-rr-> *vi* **1.** (*happen*) ocurrir; **don't let it** ~ **again!** ¡que no vuelva a suceder! **2.** (*come into mind*) **to** ~ **to sb** ocurrirse a alguien; **it** ~**d to me that ...** se me ocurrió que...

occurrence [əˈkʌrəns, *Am:* -ˈkɜ:r-] *n* acontecimiento *m;* **an unexpected** ~ un suceso inesperado; **to be an everyday** ~ ser cosa de todos los días

ocean [ˈəʊʃən, *Am:* ˈoʊ-] *n* océano

m

o'clock [əˈklɒk, *Am:* -ˈklɑ:k] *adv* **it's one** ~ es la una; **it's two/seven** ~ son las dos/las siete

October [ɒkˈtəʊbəʳ, *Am:* ɑ:kˈtoʊbɚ] *n* octubre *m; s. a.* **April**

octopus [ˈɒktəpəs, *Am:* ˈɑ:k-] <-es *o* -pi> *n* pulpo *m*

odd [ɒd, *Am:* ɑ:d] *adj* **1.** (*strange*) extraño; **how** (**very**) ~! ¡qué raro!; **it is** ~ **that ...** es raro que +*subj* **2.** (*not even: number*) impar **3.** (*approximately*) **he is about 50** ~ tiene unos 50 y tantos años **4.** (*occasional*) ocasional; **she does the** ~ **teaching job** da alguna que otra clase

oddly *adv* **1.** (*in a strange manner*) de forma extraña **2.** (*curiously*) curiosamente; ~ **enough** por extraño que parezca

odds [ɒdz, *Am:* ɑ:dz] *npl* probabilidades *fpl;* **the** ~ **against/on sth** las probabilidades en contra/a favor de algo; **the** ~ **are against us** tenemos todo en contra; **against all** (**the**) ~ a pesar de las circunstancias adversas

ode [əʊd, *Am:* oʊd] *n* oda *f*

odor *n Am, Aus,* **odour** [ˈəʊdəʳ, *Am:* ˈoʊdɚ] *n Brit* olor *m*

OECD [ˌəʊi:si:ˈdi:, *Am:* ˌoʊ-] *n abbr of* **Organization for Economic Cooperation and Development** OCDE *f*

of [əv, *stressed:* ɒv] *prep* de; **a friend** ~ **mine/theirs** un amigo mío/de ellos; **free** ~ **charge** sin cargo; **to cure sb** ~ **a disease** curar a alguien de una enfermedad; **a city** ~ **wide avenues** una ciudad con amplias avenidas; **the 4th** ~ **May** el 4 de mayo; **to smell/to taste** ~ **cheese** oler/saber a queso; **because** ~ **sth/sb** a causa de algo/alguien; **two** ~ **the five** dos de los cinco

off [ɒf, *Am:* ɑ:f] **I.** *prep* **1.** (*away from*) **keep** ~ **the grass** prohibido pisar el césped **2.** (*down from*) **to fall/jump** ~ **a ladder** caer/saltar de una escalera; **to get** ~ **the train** bajarse del tren **3.** (*from*) **to eat** ~ **a plate** comer de un plato; **to take**

$10 ~ **the price** rebajar $10 del precio **II.** *adv* **1.** (*not on*) **to switch/ turn sth** ~ apagar algo **2.** (*away*) **it's time I was** ~ ya debería haber salido **3.** (*removed*) **the lid is** ~ la tapa no está puesta **4.** (*free from work*) **to get a day** ~ tener un día libre **5.** (*bad: food*) **to go** ~ pasarse **III.** *adj* **1.** (*not on: light*) apagado; (*tap*) cerrado **2.** (*bad: milk*) cortado **3.** (*free from work*) **to be** ~ **at 5 o'clock** salir del trabajo a las 5

offence [əˈfents] *n* **1.** (*crime*) delito *m*; **minor** ~ infracción *f* **2.** (*affront*) atentado *m*

offend [əˈfend] *vi, vt* ofender; **to be ~ed at sth** ofenderse por algo

offender [əˈfendər, *Am:* -ɚ-] *n* infractor(a) *m(f)*

offense [əˈfens] *n Am s.* **offence**

offensive [əˈfensɪv] **I.** *adj* ofensivo **II.** *n* MIL ofensiva *f*; **to go on the** ~ pasar a la ofensiva

offer [ˈɒfər, *Am:* ˈɑːfɚ] **I.** *vt* ofrecer; **can I ~ you a drink?** ¿quiere tomar algo?; **to** ~ **oneself for a post** presentarse para un puesto **II.** *vi* (*present itself: opportunity*) presentarse **III.** *n* (*proposal*) propuesta *f*; (*of job*) oferta *f*; **an** ~ **of marriage** una proposición de matrimonio

offering [ˈɒfərɪŋ, *Am:* ˈɑːfɚ-] *n* **1.** (*thing given*) ofrecimiento *m*; **as an** ~ **of thanks** en señal de agradecimiento **2.** REL ofrenda *f*

office [ˈɒfɪs, *Am:* ˈɑːfɪs] *n* **1.** (*of company*) oficina *f*; (*room in house*) despacho *m*, archivo *m Col*; **lawyer's** ~ bufete *m* (de abogado) *Brit* POL **the Home Office** el Ministerio del Interior británico **3.** (*position*) cargo *m*

officer [ˈɒfɪsər, *Am:* ˈɑːfɪsɚ] *n* **1.** MIL oficial *mf*; **naval** ~ oficial de marina **2.** (*policeman*) policía *mf*; **police** ~ agente *mf* de policía

official [əˈfɪʃl] **I.** *n* funcionario, -a *m, f* **II.** *adj* oficial

officially [əˈfɪʃəli] *adv* oficialmente

off-line [ˌɒfˈlaɪn, *Am:* ˌɑːf-] *adj* INFOR desconectado, fuera de línea

off-season [ˈɒfˌsiːzən, *Am:* ˈɑːf-] *n* temporada *f* baja

offset [ˈɒfset, *Am:* ˈɑːf-] <offset, offset> *vt* compensar

offshore [ˌɒfˈʃɔːr, *Am:* ˌɑːfˈʃɔːr] **I.** *adj* **1.** (*from the shore: breeze, wind*) terral **2.** (*at sea*) a poca distancia de la costa; ~ **fishing** pesca de bajura; ~ **oilfield** yacimiento *m* petrolífero marítimo **II.** *adv* mar adentro; **to anchor** ~ anclar a cierta distancia de la costa

offside [ˌɒfˈsaɪd, *Am:* ˌɑːf-] *adj* SPORTS fuera de juego

offspring [ˈɒfsprɪŋ, *Am:* ˈɑːf-] *n inv* **1.** (*animal young*) cría *f* **2.** *pl* (*children*) prole *f*

often [ˈɒfən, *Am:* ˈɑːfən] *adv* a menudo; **we** ~ **go there** solemos ir allí; **how ~?** ¿cuántas veces?

oh [əʊ, *Am:* oʊ] *interj* oh; ~ **dear!** ¡Dios mío!; ~ **no!** ¡ay, no!

oil [ɔɪl] **I.** *n* **1.** (*lubricant*) aceite *m*; **sunflower** ~ aceite de girasol **2.** *no pl* (*petroleum*) petróleo *m*; **to strike** ~ encontrar petróleo; *fig* encontrar una mina de oro **3.** (*grease*) grasa *f* **4.** *pl* (*oil-based paint*) óleo *m*; **to paint in ~s** pintar al óleo **II.** *vt* engrasar

oil company *n* empresa *f* petroquímica **oil painting** *n* óleo *m*

oily [ˈɔɪli] <-ier, -iest> *adj* **1.** (*oil-like*) oleoso **2.** (*greasy: hands*) grasiento; (*food*) aceitoso; (*skin, hair*) graso **3.** (*manner*) empalagoso

ointment [ˈɔɪntmənt] *n* MED pomada *f*

OK, okay [ˌəʊˈkeɪ, *Am:* ˌoʊ-] *inf* **I.** *adj* **1.** (*acceptable*) **is it** ~ **with you if …?** ¿te importa si…? **2.** (*not bad*) **to be** ~ no estar mal; **her voice is ~, but it's nothing special** no tiene mala voz, pero tampoco es nada del otro mundo **II.** *interj* vale *inf*, okey *AmL*, *inf*, órale *Méx* **III.** *adv* bastante bien

old [əʊld, *Am:* oʊld] *adj* **1.** (*not young*) viejo; ~ **people** la gente mayor; **to grow ~er** envejecer **2.** (*not new*) viejo; (*food*) pasado; (*wine*) añejo; (*furniture, house*) antiguo **3.** (*age*) **how ~ are you?**

¿cuántos años tienes?; **he's five years** ~ tiene cinco años; **she's three years** ~**er than me** me lleva tres años **4.** (*former: job*) antiguo; ~ **boyfriend** ex-novio *m*

old age *n* vejez *f;* **to reach** ~ llegar a viejo

old-fashioned [ˌəʊld'fæʃənd, *Am:* ˌoʊld-] *adj* **1.** (*not modern: clothes*) pasado de moda; (*views*) anticuado; **to be** ~ estar chapado a la antigua **2.** (*traditional*) tradicional; **it has an** ~ **charm** tiene el encanto de lo antiguo

olive oil *n* aceite *m* de oliva

Olympic [ə'lɪmpɪk, *Am:* oʊ'-] *adj* olímpico; **the Olympic Games** SPORTS los Juegos Olímpicos

Oman [əʊ'mɑːn, *Am:* oʊ'-] *n* Omán *m*

Omani [əʊ'mɑːni, *Am:* oʊ'-] *adj* omaní

ombudsman ['ɒmbʊdzmən, *Am:* 'ɑːmbədz-] <-men> *n* POL defensor(a) *m(f)* del pueblo

omelet(te) ['ɒmlɪt, *Am:* 'ɑːmlət] *n* tortilla *f*

omen ['əʊmen, *Am:* 'oʊ-] *n* augurio *m*

ominous ['ɒmɪnəs, *Am:* 'ɑːmə-] *adj* ominoso

omission [ə'mɪʃn, *Am:* oʊ'-] *n* omisión *f*

omit [ə'mɪt, *Am:* oʊ'-] <-tt-> *vt* (*person, information*) omitir; (*paragraph, passage*) suprimir

omnibus ['ɒmnɪbəs, *Am:* 'ɑːm-] <-es> *n* **1.** (*bus*) ómnibus *m* **2.** (*anthology*) antología *f*

omnipotence [ɒm'nɪpətəns, *Am:* ɑːm'nɪpətəns] *n no pl* omnipotencia *f*

omnipotent [ɒm'nɪpətənt, *Am:* ɑːm'nɪpətənt] *adj* omnipotente

on [ɒn, *Am:* ɑːn] **I.** *prep* **1.** (*place*) sobre, en; ~ **the table** sobre la mesa; ~ **the wall** en la pared **2.** (*by means of*) **to go** ~ **the train** ir en tren; **to go** ~ **foot** ir a pie **3.** (*spatial*) ~ **the right/left** a la derecha/izquierda **4.** (*temporal*) ~ **Sunday** el domingo; ~ **Sundays** los domingos; ~ **the**

evening of May the 4th el cuatro de mayo por la tarde **5.** (*at time of*) **to leave** ~ **time** salir a tiempo; ~ **her arrival** a su llegada **6.** (*about*) sobre; **to be there** ~ **business** estar ahí por negocios **7.** (*through medium of*) ~ **TV/video/CD** en TV/vídeo/CD; **to speak** ~ **the radio/the phone** hablar en la radio/por teléfono **8.** (*in state of*) ~ **sale** en venta; **to go** ~ **holiday/a trip** ir de vacaciones/de viaje **II.** *adv* **1.** (*covering one's body*) **to put a hat** ~ ponerse un sombrero **2.** (*connected to sth*) **make sure the top's** ~ **properly** asegúrate de que esté bien tapado **3.** (*aboard*) **to get** ~ **a train** subir a un tren **4.** (*not stopping*) **to keep** ~ **doing sth** seguir haciendo algo **5.** (*in forward direction*) hacia adelante; **to move** ~ avanzar; **later** ~ más tarde **6.** (*in operation*) **to turn** ~ encender **III.** *adj* **1.** (*functioning*) encendido **2.** (*scheduled*) **what's** ~ **at the cinema this week?** ¿qué dan en el cine esta semana?

once [wʌnts] **I.** *adv* **1.** (*one time*) una vez; ~ **a week** una vez por semana; **at** ~ (*simultaneously*) al mismo tiempo; (*immediately*) en seguida **2.** (*at one time past*) hace tiempo; ~ **upon a time there was ...** *liter* érase una vez... **II.** *conj* una vez que +*subj;* **but** ~ **I'd arrived, ...** pero una vez que llegué...

one [wʌn] **I.** *n* (*number*) uno *m* **II.** *adj* **1.** *numeral* un, uno; ~ **hundred** cien; **it's** ~ **o'clock** es la una; *s. a.* **eight 2.** *indef* un, uno; **we'll meet** ~ **day** nos veremos un día de estos; ~ **winter night** una noche de invierno **3.** (*single*) mismo, único; **all files on the** ~ **disk** todos los archivos en un único disco **III.** *pron pers* **1.** *impers, no pl* **what** ~ **can do** lo que uno puede hacer; **to wash** ~**'s face** lavarse la cara **2.** (*person*) **no** ~ nadie; **every** ~ cada uno **3.** (*particular thing or person*) **any** ~ cualquiera; **this** ~ éste; **which** ~? ¿cuál (de ellos)?; **the** ~ **on the table** el que está en la mesa

one-off [ˌwʌnˈɒf, *Am:* ˈwʌnɑːf] I. *n*
Aus, Brit **to be a** ~ ser un fuera de
serie II. *adj* excepcional; ~ **payment**
pago *m* extraordinario

oneself [wʌnˈself] *pron refl* 1. se;
emphatic sí (mismo/misma); **to deceive** ~ engañarse a sí mismo; **to express** ~ expresarse 2. (*same person*)
uno mismo

ongoing [ˈɒngəʊɪŋ, *Am:* ˈɑːngoʊ-]
adj en curso; ~ **state of affairs** situación que sigue en curso

onion [ˈʌnɪən] *n* cebolla *f*

on-line *adj* INFOR en línea; ~ **data service** servicio *m* de datos en línea; ~
information service servicio *m* de
información en línea; ~ **shop** comercio *m* en línea

onlooker [ˈɒnlʊkəʳ, *Am:* ˈɑːnlʊkɚ]
n espectador(a) *m(f)*

only [ˈəʊnli, *Am:* ˈoʊn-] I. *adj* único;
the ~ **glass he had** el único vaso
que tenía II. *adv* sólo, nomás *AmL;*
not ~ **... but** no solamente…sino; I
can ~ **say ...** sólo puedo decir…; **he
has** ~ **two** sólo tiene dos

onset [ˈɒnset, *Am:* ˈɑːn-] *n no pl* comienzo *m*

onslaught [ˈɒnslɔːt, *Am:* ˈɑːnslɑːt]
n ataque *m* violento; *fig* crítica *f* violenta

onto [ˈɒntuː, *Am:* ˈɑːntuː] *prep*, **on
to** *prep* 1. (*in direction of*) sobre; **to
put sth** ~ **the chair** poner algo
sobre la silla 2. (*connected to*) **to
hold** ~ **sb's arm** aferrarse al brazo
de alguien

onward [ˈɒnwəd, *Am:* ˈɑːnwɚd]
adj, adv hacia adelante; **from today**
~ de hoy en adelante

ooze [uːz] I. *vi* 1. (*seep out*) exudar;
to ~ **from sth** rezumar(se) de algo;
to ~ **with sth** rezumar algo; **to** ~
away acabarse 2. *fig* (*be full of*) rebosar de; **to** ~ **with confidence**
irradiar seguridad II. *vt* rezumar; **to**
~ **pus** supurar

opal [ˈəʊpl, *Am:* ˈoʊ-] *n* ópalo *m*

opaque [əʊˈpeɪk, *Am:* oʊ-] *adj*
opaco

OPEC [ˈəʊpek, *Am:* ˈoʊ-] *n abbr of*
Organization of Petroleum Ex-

porting Countries OPEP *f*

open [ˈəʊpən, *Am:* ˈoʊ-] I. *adj*
1. (*not closed*) abierto; **wide** ~ completamente abierto 2. (*undecided*)
sin concretar; **to keep one's op-
tions** ~ dejar abiertas todas las alter-
nativas 3. (*not secret, public*) público; **an** ~ **secret** una cosa sabida
4. abierto; **to have an** ~ **mind** tener
una actitud abierta II. *n* 1. *no pl* (*outdoors, outside*) (**out**) **in the** ~ al aire
libre 2. (*not secret*) **to get sth** (**out**)
in the ~ sacar algo a la luz III. *vi*
1. (*door, window, box*) abrirse
2. (*shop*) abrir IV. *vt* 1. (*door, box,
shop*) abrir; **to** ~ **the door to sth** *fig*
abrir la puerta a algo; **to** ~ **sb's eyes**
fig abrir los ojos a alguien 2. (*reveal
feelings*) **to** ~ **one's heart to sb**
abrir el corazón a alguien

◈**open up** I. *vi* 1. (*shop*) abrir
2. (*shoot*) abrir fuego II. *vt* abrir

open-air [ˌəʊpənˈeəʳ, *Am:* ˌoʊpən-
ˈer] *adj* al aire libre; ~ **swimming
pool** piscina *f* descubierta

opener [ˈəʊpənəʳ, *Am:* ˈoʊpənɚ] *n*
abridor *m*, destapador *m AmL;*
bottle ~ abrebotellas *m inv;* **can** ~
abrelatas *m inv*

opening [ˈəʊpnɪŋ, *Am:* ˈoʊp-] *n*
1. (*gap, hole*) abertura *f* 2. (*beginning*) apertura *f* 3. (*ceremony*) inauguración *f*

openly [ˈəʊpənli, *Am:* ˈoʊ-] *adv*
1. (*frankly*) honestamente 2. (*publicly*) abiertamente

openness [ˈəʊpənnəs, *Am:* ˈoʊ-] *n
no pl* franqueza *f*

opera [ˈɒprə, *Am:* ˈɑːpr-] *n* ópera *f*

operate [ˈɒpəreɪt, *Am:* ˈɑːpər-] I. *vi*
1. (*work, run*) funcionar 2. (*have or
produce an effect*) actuar 3. (*perform surgery*) operar; **to** ~ **on sb**
operar a alguien II. *vt* 1. (*work*)
manejar 2. (*run, manage*) llevar

operating [ˈɒpəreɪtɪŋ, *Am:* ˈɑːpə-
reɪt̬-] *adj* 1. ECON (*profit, costs*) de
explotación 2. TECH (*speed*) de funcionamiento 3. MED de operaciones;
~ **room**, ~ **theatre** [*o* **theater** *Am*]
quirófano *m*

operation [ˌɒpəˈreɪʃn, *Am:* ˌɑːpə-]

n **1.** *no pl* (*way of working*) funcionamiento *m* **2.** *a.* MED, MIL, MAT, COM operación *f*

operational [ˌɒpəˈreɪʃənl, *Am:* ˌɑːpə-] *adj* **1.** (*relating to operations*) operativo; ~ **commander** MIL jefe *mf* de operaciones **2.** (*working*) **to be** ~ estar en funcionamiento

operator [ˈɒpəreɪtə', *Am:* ˈɑːpəreɪtə̃] *n* (*person*) operador(a) *m(f)*; **machine** ~ maquinista *mf*; **he's a smooth** ~ *inf* sabe conseguir lo que quiere

opinion [əˈpɪnjən] *n* opinión *f*

opinion poll *n* encuesta *f* de opinión

opium [ˈəʊpiəm, *Am:* ˈoʊ-] *n no pl* opio *m*

opponent [əˈpəʊnənt, *Am:* -ˈpoʊ-] *n* **1.** POL opositor(a) *m(f)* **2.** SPORTS contrincante *mf*, rival *mf*

opportunism [ˌɒpəˈtjuːnɪzəm, *Am:* ˌɑːpəˈtuː-] *n no pl* oportunismo *m*

opportunity [ˌɒpəˈtjuːnəti, *Am:* ˌɑːpəˈtuːnəti] <-ies> *n* oportunidad *f*; **at the earliest** ~ lo antes posible

oppose [əˈpəʊz, *Am:* -ˈpoʊz] *vt* oponerse a, estar en contra de

opposed *adj* opuesto; **to be** ~ **to sth** oponerse a algo, estar en contra de algo

opposing *adj* contrario

opposite [ˈɒpəzɪt, *Am:* ˈɑːpə-] **I.** *n* contrario *m*; **quite the** ~! ¡todo lo contrario! **II.** *adj* **1.** (*absolutely different*) contrario; **the** ~ **sex** el sexo opuesto **2.** (*facing*) de enfrente; ~ **to/from sth** enfrente a/de algo **III.** *adv* (*facing*) enfrente; **he lives** ~ vive enfrente **IV.** *prep* enfrente de, frente a

opposition [ˌɒpəˈzɪʃn, *Am:* ˌɑːpə-] *n no pl* **1.** *a.* POL oposición *f* **2.** (*opponent*) adversario, -a *m, f*

oppress [əˈpres] *vt* oprimir

oppression [əˈpreʃn] *n no pl* opresión *f*

oppressive [əˈpresɪv] *adj* opresivo

opt [ɒpt, *Am:* ɑːpt] *vi* optar; **to** ~ **to do sth** optar por hacer algo; **to** ~ **for sth** optar por algo

optic [ˈɒptɪk, *Am:* ˈɑːp-] **I.** *n inf* ojo *m* **II.** *adj* óptico

optical [ˈɒptɪkl, *Am:* ˈɑːp-] *adj* óptico

optician [ɒpˈtɪʃn, *Am:* ɑːp-] *n* óptico, -a *m, f*

optics [ˈɒptɪks, *Am:* ˈɑːp-] *npl* óptica *f*

optimal [ˈɒptɪml, *Am:* ˈɑːp-] *adj* óptimo

optimism [ˈɒptɪmɪzəm, *Am:* ˈɑːptə-] *n no pl* optimismo *m*

optimist [ˈɒptɪmɪst, *Am:* ˈɑːptə-] *n* optimista *mf*

optimistic [ˌɒptɪˈmɪstɪk, *Am:* ˌɑːptə-] *adj* optimista

optimize [ˈɒptɪmaɪz, *Am:* ˈɑːptə-] *vt* optimizar

optimum [ˈɒptɪməm, *Am:* ˈɑːptə-] *adj* óptimo

option [ˈɒpʃn, *Am:* ˈɑːp-] *n* opción *f*; **to have no** ~ **but to do sth** no tener más remedio que hacer algo

optional [ˈɒpʃənl, *Am:* ˈɑːp-] *adj* opcional; (*subject*) optativo

opulent [ˈɒpjʊlənt, *Am:* ˈɑːpjə-] *adj* opulento

or [ɔː', *Am:* ɔːr] *conj* o; (*before o, ho*) u; (*between numbers*) ó; **seven** ~ **eight** siete u ocho; **either ...** ~ **...** o... o...

oracle [ˈɒrəkl, *Am:* ˈɔːr-] *n* oráculo *m*

oral [ˈɔːrəl] *adj* oral

orange [ˈɒrɪndʒ, *Am:* ˈɔːrɪndʒ] *n* naranja *f*; ~ **drink** naranjada *f*

orange juice *n* zumo *m* de naranja

orator [ˈɒrətə', *Am:* ˈɔːrətə̃] *n* orador(a) *m(f)*

orbit [ˈɔːbɪt, *Am:* ˈɔːr-] **I.** *n* órbita *f* **II.** *vi* orbitar **III.** *vt* orbitar alrededor de

orbital [ˈɔːbɪtl, *Am:* ˈɔːrbɪtḷ] *adj* orbital

orchard [ˈɔːtʃəd, *Am:* ˈɔːrtʃə̃d] *n* huerto *m*; **cherry** ~ cerezal *m*

orchestra [ˈɔːkɪstrə, *Am:* ˈɔːrkɪstrə] *n* orquesta *f*

orchestrate [ˈɔːkɪstreɪt, *Am:* ˈɔːr-] *vt* **1.** MUS orquestar **2.** *fig* (*arrange*) organizar

o

ordeal [ɔːˈdiːl, *Am:* ɔːrˈ-] *n* calvario *m*

order [ˈɔːdəʳ, *Am:* ˈɔːrdɚ] **I.** *n* **1.** *no pl (sequence)* orden *m;* **to put sth in** ~ poner en orden algo; **to leave sth in** ~ dejar ordenado algo; **in alphabetical** ~ en orden alfabético **2.** *(instruction) a.* LAW, REL orden *f;* **to give/receive an** ~ dar/recibir una orden; **by** ~ **of sb** por orden de alguien **3.** *(satisfactory arrangement)* orden *m;* **to be out of** ~ no funcionar; **are your immigration papers in** ~? ¿tienes los papeles de inmigración en regla? **4.** *(request)* pedido *m;* **made to** ~ hecho por encargo **II.** *vi* pedir; **are you ready to** ~? ¿ya han decidido qué van a tomar [*o* pedir]? **III.** *vt* **1.** *(command)* **to** ~ **sb to do sth** ordenar a alguien que haga algo **2.** *(request goods or service)* pedir **3.** *(arrange)* ordenar, poner en orden

orderly [ˈɔːdəli, *Am:* ˈɔːrdɚli] <-ies> **I.** *n* celador(a) *m(f)* **II.** *adj* ordenado; *(well-behaved)* disciplinado

ordinary [ˈɔːdənəri, *Am:* ˈɔːrdəner-] *adj* normal, corriente

ordnance [ˈɔːdnənts, *Am:* ˈɔːrd-] *n* artillería *f*

ore [ɔːʳ, *Am:* ɔːr] *n* mena *f;* **iron/copper** ~ mineral *m* de hierro/cobre

organ [ˈɔːgən, *Am:* ˈɔːr-] *n* órgano *m*

organic [ɔːˈgænɪk, *Am:* ɔːrˈ-] *adj* **1.** *(disease, substance, compound)* orgánico **2.** *(produce, farming method)* biológico

organisation *n s.* **organization**

organism [ˈɔːgənɪzəm, *Am:* ˈɔːr-] *n* organismo *m*

organist [ˈɔːgənɪst, *Am:* ˈɔːr-] *n* organista *mf*

organization [ˌɔːgənaɪˈzeɪʃən, *Am:* ˌɔːrgənɪˈ-] *n* organización *f*

organizational [ˌɔːgənaɪˈzeɪʃənəl, *Am:* ˌɔːrgənɪˈ-] *adj* organizativo

organize [ˈɔːgənaɪz, *Am:* ˈɔːr-] *vi, vt* organizar(se)

organized *adj* organizado

orgasm [ˈɔːgæzəm, *Am:* ˈɔːr-] *n* orgasmo *m*

orgy [ˈɔːdʒi, *Am:* ˈɔːr-] <-ies> *n* orgía *f*

orient [ˈɔːriənt] *vt Am* **to** ~ **oneself** orientarse

oriental [ˌɔːriˈentəl] *adj* oriental

orientate [ˈɔːriənteɪt, *Am:* ˈɔːrien-] *vr* **to** ~ **oneself** orientarse

orientation [ˌɔːriənˈteɪʃən, *Am:* ˌɔːrienˈ-] *n* orientación *f*

origin [ˈɒrɪdʒɪn, *Am:* ˈɔːrədʒɪn] *n* origen *m*

original [əˈrɪdʒənəl, *Am:* əˈrɪdʒɪ-] *adj* original

originality [əˌrɪdʒənˈæləti, *Am:* əˌrɪdʒɪˈnæləti] *n no pl* originalidad *f*

originate [əˈrɪdʒəneɪt, *Am:* əˈrɪdʒɪ-] *vi* originarse

ornament [ˈɔːnəmənt, *Am:* ˈɔːr-] *n* adorno *m*

ornamental [ˌɔːnəˈmentl, *Am:* ˌɔːrnəˈmentl̩] *adj* ornamental, decorativo

ornamentation [ˌɔːnəmenˈteɪʃn, *Am:* ˌɔːr-] *n no pl, form* ornamentación *f*, decoración *f*

orphan [ˈɔːfn, *Am:* ˈɔːr-] *n* huérfano -a *m, f,* guacho, -a *m, f Arg, Chi*

orphanage [ˈɔːfnɪdʒ, *Am:* ˈɔːr-] *n* orfanato *m*, orfelinato *m*

orthodox [ˈɔːθədɒks, *Am:* ˈɔːrθədɑːks] *adj* ortodoxo

orthodoxy [ˈɔːθədɒksi, *Am:* ˈɔːrθədɑːk-] <-ies> *n* ortodoxia *f*

oscillation [ˌɒsɪˈleɪʃn, *Am:* ˌɑːsɪˈleɪ-] *n a.* PHYS oscilación *f;* *(of prices)* fluctuación *f*

ostensible [ɒˈstensəbl, *Am:* ɑːˈsten-] *adj* aparente, pretendido

ostrich [ˈɒstrɪtʃ, *Am:* ˈɑːstrɪtʃ] *n* avestruz *f*

other [ˈʌðəʳ, *Am:* -ɚ] **I.** *adj* **1.** *(different)* otro; **some** ~ **way of doing sth** alguna otra forma de hacer algo **2.** *(remaining)* **the** ~ **one** el otro; **the** ~ **three** los otros tres; **any** ~ **questions?** ¿alguna otra pregunta? **3.** *(being vague)* **some** ~ **time** en algún otro momento; **the** ~ **day** el otro día **II.** *pron* **1.** *(people)* **the** ~**s** los otros **2.** *(different ones)* **each** ~ uno a(l) otro, mutuamente; **there might be** ~**s** puede haber otros

3. *sing* (*either, or*) **to choose one or the** ~ escoger uno u otro; **not to have one without the** ~ no tener uno sin el otro **4.** (*being vague*) **someone or** ~ alguien

otherwise ['ʌðəwaɪz, *Am:* '-ə-]
I. *adv* de otro modo; ~, **...** por lo demás,... **II.** *conj* si no

otter ['ɒtər, *Am:* 'ɑːt̬ə] *n* nutria *f*

OU [ˌəʊ'juː, *Am:* ˌoʊ-] *n Brit abbr of*
Open University ≈ UNED *f*

ought [ɔːt, *Am:* ɑːt] *aux* **1.** (*have as duty*) deber; **you** ~ **to do it** deberías [*o* tendrías que] hacerlo **2.** (*be likely*) tener que; **he** ~ **to be here** tendría que [*o* debería] estar aquí; **they** ~ **to win** merecerían ganar **3.** (*probability*) **she** ~ **to have arrived by now** debe haber llegado ya

ounce [aʊns] *n* onza *f* (*28,4 g*)

our ['aʊər, *Am:* 'aʊə] *adj poss* nuestro; ~ **house** nuestra casa; ~ **children** nuestros hijos

ours ['aʊəz, *Am:* 'aʊə-z] *pron poss* (el) nuestro, (la) nuestra; **it's not their bag, it's** ~ no es su bolsa, es nuestra; **this house is** ~ esta casa es nuestra; **a book of** ~ un libro nuestro; ~ **is bigger** el nuestro es mayor

ourselves [aʊə'selvz, *Am:* aʊə-] *pron refl* **1.** nos; *emphatic* nosotros mismos, nosotras mismas; **we hurt** ~ nos lastimamos **2.** *after prep* nosotros (mismos), nosotras (mismas)

oust [aʊst] *vt* (*rival*) desbancar; (*president*) derrocar

out [aʊt] **I.** *adj* **1.** (*absent*) fuera **2.** (*released*) publicado **3.** (*finished*) **before the week is** ~ antes de que acabe la semana **4.** (*not functioning*) apagado **5.** (*not possible*) **it is** ~ eso es imposible **II.** *adv* **1.** (*not inside*) fuera, afuera; **to go** ~ salir fuera; **get** ~! ¡fuera! **2.** (*away*) **to be** ~ no estar; **to be** ~ **at sea** estar mar adentro; **the tide is going** ~ la marea está bajando **III.** *prep* **1.** (*towards outside*) ~ **of** fuera de; **to take sth** ~ **of a box** sacar algo de una caja; **to look/lean** ~ **of the window** mirar por/apoyarse en la ventana **2.** (*outside from*) ~ **of**

sight/of reach fuera de la vista/del alcance; **to drink** ~ **of a glass** beber de un vaso **3.** (*away from*) **to be** ~ **of town/the country** estar fuera de la ciudad/del país; ~ **of the way!** ¡fuera del camino! **4.** (*without*) **to be** ~ **of money/work** estar sin dinero/trabajo; ~ **of breath** sin aliento; ~ **of order** averiado **5.** (*from*) **made** ~ **of wood** hecho de madera; **in 3 cases** ~ **of 10** en 3 de cada 10 casos

outbreak ['aʊtbreɪk] *n* (*of flu, violence*) brote *m*; (*of war*) estallido *m*

outburst ['aʊtbɜːst, *Am:* -bɜːrst] *n* arrebato *m*

outcast ['aʊtkɑːst, *Am:* -kæst] *n* paria *mf*; **social** ~ marginado, -a *m, f* de la sociedad

outcome ['aʊtkʌm] *n* resultado *m*

outcry ['aʊtkraɪ] <-ies> *n* gran protesta *f*

outdated [aʊt'deɪtɪd, *Am:* -t̬ɪd] *adj* pasado de moda

outdo [aʊt'duː] *vt irr* superar

outdoor ['aʊtdɔːr, *Am:* ˌaʊt'dɔːr] *adj* al aire libre

outdoors [ˌaʊt'dɔːz, *Am:* ˌaʊt'dɔːrz] *n* **the great** ~ el aire libre

outer ['aʊtər, *Am:* -t̬ə] *adj* exterior; ~ **ear** oído *m* externo

outfit ['aʊtfɪt] *n* **1.** (*set of clothes*) conjunto *m* **2.** (*team, organization*) equipo *m*

outgoing ['aʊtgəʊɪŋ, *Am:* 'aʊtgoʊ-] *adj* **1.** (*sociable, extrovert*) sociable **2.** (*retiring*) saliente

outgrow [ˌaʊt'grəʊ, *Am:* -'groʊ] *vt irr* **1.** (*habit*) pasar de la edad de; **she's ~n her trousers** le quedan pequeños los pantalones **2.** (*become bigger than*) crecer más que

outing ['aʊtɪŋ, *Am:* -t̬ɪŋ] *n* excursión *f*; **to go on an** ~ ir de excursión

outlandish [aʊt'lændɪʃ] *adj* extravagante

outlaw ['aʊtlɔː, *Am:* -lɑː] **I.** *n* forajido, -a *m, f* **II.** *vt* prohibir

outlay ['aʊtleɪ] *n* desembolso *m*

outlet ['aʊtlet] *n* **1.** (*exit*) salida *f* **2.** (*means of expression*) válvula *f* de escape **3.** ECON punto *m* de venta

outline ['aʊtlaɪn] I. n 1. (*shape*) perfil m 2. (*general description*) resumen m II. vt 1. (*draw outer line of*) perfilar 2. (*describe*) resumir

outlive [ˌaʊt'lɪv] vt sobrevivir a

outlook ['aʊtlʊk] n perspectivas fpl

out-of-date [ˌaʊtəv'deɪt, Am: ˌaʊt-] adj (*clothes*) anticuado, pasado de moda; (*ticket*) caducado; (*person*) desfasado

outpatient ['aʊtˌpeɪʃənt] n paciente mf externo, -a

outpost ['aʊtpəʊst, Am: -poʊst] n 1. MIL puesto m de avanzada 2. fig reducto m

output ['aʊtpʊt] n no pl ECON producción f; (*of machine*) rendimiento m

outrage ['aʊtreɪdʒ] n (*atrocity*) atrocidad f; (*terrorist act*) atentado m; **to feel a strong sense of ~ at sth** sentirse ultrajado por algo

outrageous [aʊt'reɪdʒəs] adj 1. (*cruel, violent*) atroz 2. (*shocking*) escandaloso

outright ['aʊtraɪt] adj total

outside [ˌaʊt'saɪd] I. adj exterior; **the ~ d... la puerta exterior II.** n exterior m; **judging from the ~** a juzgar por el aspecto exterior III. prep 1. (*not within*) fuera de; **to play ~** jugar fuera 2. **~ business hours** fuera de horas de oficina IV. adv fuera, afuera; **to go ~** salir afuera

outsider [ˌaʊt'saɪdər, Am: -dər] n persona f de fuera

outskirts ['aʊtskɜːts, Am: -skɜːrts] npl afueras fpl

outstanding [ˌaʊt'stændɪŋ] adj 1. (*excellent*) destacado 2. FIN (*account*) por pagar

outward ['aʊtwəd, Am: -wəd] I. adj exterior II. adv hacia afuera

outweigh [ˌaʊt'weɪ] vt tener más peso que

oval ['əʊvəl, Am: 'oʊ-] I. n óvalo m II. adj ovalado, oval

ovary ['əʊvəri, Am: 'oʊ-] <-ies> n ovario m

ovation [əʊ'veɪʃən, Am: oʊ-] n ovación f; **to get an ~** ser ovacionado

oven ['ʌvən] n horno m

over ['əʊvər, Am: 'oʊvər] I. prep 1. (*above*) encima de, por encima de; **to hang the picture ~ the desk** colgar el cuadro encima del escritorio 2. (*on*) **to hit sb ~ the head** golpear a alguien en la cabeza 3. (*across*) **to go ~ the bridge** cruzar el puente; **the house ~ the road** la casa de enfrente; **famous all ~ the world** famoso en todo el mundo 4. (*behind*) **to look ~ sb's shoulder** mirar por encima del hombro de alguien 5. (*during*) **~ the winter** durante el invierno; **to stay ~ the weekend** quedarse a pasar el fin de semana 6. (*more than*) **to speak for ~ an hour** hablar durante una hora; **children ~ 14** niños de más de 14 (años) 7. (*through*) **I heard it ~ the radio** lo oí por la radio II. adv 1. (*moving above: go, jump*) por encima; **to fly ~ the city** volar sobre la ciudad 2. (*distance*) **to move sth ~** apartar algo; **~ here** acá; **~ there** allá; **~ the road** cruzando la calle 3. (*moving across*) **to come ~ here** venir para acá; **to go ~ there** ir para allá 4. (*downwards*) **to fall ~** caerse; **to knock sth ~** tirar algo III. adj acabado; **it's all ~** se acabó

overall¹ [ˌəʊvər'ɔːl, Am: ˌoʊ-] n pl (*one-piece protective suit*) mono m; **a pair of ~s** un peto

overall² ['əʊvərɔːl, Am: 'oʊ-] I. adj global II. adv en conjunto

overboard ['əʊvəbɔːd, Am: 'oʊvəbɔːrd] adv al agua; **to fall ~** caer al agua; **to go ~** inf exagerar

overcoat ['əʊvəkəʊt, Am: 'oʊvəkoʊt] n abrigo m

overcome [ˌəʊvə'kʌm, Am: ˌoʊvə'-] vt irr superar

overcrowded [ˌəʊvə'kraʊdɪd, Am: ˌoʊvə'-] adj abarrotado

overdo [ˌəʊvə'duː, Am: ˌoʊvə'-] vt 1. **to ~ things** pasarse 2. inf (*exaggerate*) exagerar

overdose ['əʊvədəʊs, Am: 'oʊvədoʊs] n sobredosis f inv

overdraft ['əʊvədrɑːft, Am: 'oʊvədræft] *n* FIN descubierto *m;* **to have an ~** tener un saldo deudor

overdue [ˌəʊvəˈdjuː, *Am:* ˌoʊvə-ˈduː] *adj* **1.** (*late*) atrasado **2.** FIN por pagar

overestimate [ˌəʊvərˈestɪmeɪt, *Am:* ˌoʊvəˈestə-] *vt* sobreestimar

overflow [ˌəʊvəˈfləʊ, *Am:* ˌoʊvə-ˈfloʊ] *vi* rebosar

overhaul [ˌəʊvəˈhɔːl, *Am:* ˌoʊvə-ˈhɑːl] I. *n* revisión *f* II. *vt* revisar

overhead [ˌəʊvəˈhed, *Am:* ˌoʊvə-ˈ-] I. *n Am* gastos *mpl* generales II. *adj* de arriba, encima de la cabeza; **~ cable** cable *m* aéreo; **~ light** luz *f* de techo III. *adv* en lo alto, por encima de la cabeza

overhear [ˌəʊvəˈhɪə, *Am:* ˌoʊvə-ˈhɪr] *irr vt* oír por casualidad

overlap [ˌəʊvəˈlæp, *Am:* ˌoʊvə-ˈ-] <-pp-> I. *vi* superponerse II. *vt* solapar

overload [ˈəʊvələʊd, *Am:* ˈoʊvə-loʊd] *n* **1.** ELEC sobrecarga *f* **2.** (*of work*) exceso *m*

overlook [ˌəʊvəˈlʊk, *Am:* ˌoʊvə-ˈ-] *vt* **1.** (*look out onto*) tener vistas a **2.** (*not notice*) pasar por alto

overly [ˈəʊvəli, *Am:* ˈoʊvə-li] *adv* demasiado

overnight [ˌəʊvəˈnaɪt, *Am:* ˌoʊvə-ˈ-] I. *adj* de noche; **~ bag** bolsa *f* de fin de semana II. *adv* durante la noche; **to stay ~** pasar la noche

overpower [ˌəʊvəˈpaʊə, *Am:* ˌoʊ-vəˈpaʊə] *vt* dominar

override [ˌəʊvəˈraɪd, *Am:* ˌoʊvə-ˈ-] *vt* anular

overrule [ˌəʊvəˈruːl, *Am:* ˌoʊvə-ˈ-] *vt* anular; **to ~ an objection** LAW rechazar una objeción

overrun [ˌəʊvəˈrʌn, *Am:* ˌoʊvə-ˈ-] *vt irr* **1.** (*invade*) invadir; **to be ~ with sth** estar plagado de algo **2.** (*budget*) exceder

overseas [ˌəʊvəˈsiːz, *Am:* ˌoʊvə-ˈ-] I. *adj* extranjero; (*trade*) exterior II. *adv* **to go/travel ~** ir/viajar al extranjero

oversee [ˌəʊvəˈsiː, *Am:* ˌoʊvə-ˈ-] *irr vt* supervisar

overshadow [ˌəʊvəˈʃædəʊ, *Am:*

ˌoʊvəˈʃædoʊ] *vt* eclipsar

oversight [ˈəʊvəsaɪt, *Am:* ˈoʊvə-] *n* descuido *m;* **by an ~** por equivocación

overstate [ˌəʊvəˈsteɪt, *Am:* ˌoʊvə-ˈ-] *vt* exagerar

overstep [ˌəʊvəˈstep, *Am:* ˌoʊvə-ˈ-] *irr vt* sobrepasar; **to ~ the mark** *fig* pasarse de la raya

overt [ˈəʊvɜːt, *Am:* ˈoʊvɜːrt] *adj* declarado

overtake [ˌəʊvəˈteɪk, *Am:* ˌoʊvə-ˈ-] *irr* I. *vt* adelantar; **events have ~n us** los acontecimientos se nos han adelantado II. *vi* adelantar

over-the-counter [ˌəʊvədə-ˈkaʊntə, *Am:* ˌoʊvə-ðəˈkaʊntə] *adj* sin receta

overthrow [ˌəʊvəˈθrəʊ, *Am:* ˌoʊ-vəˈθroʊ] *vt irr* derrocar

overtime [ˈəʊvətaɪm, *Am:* ˈoʊvə-] *n* **1.** (*work*) horas *fpl* extra **2.** *Am* SPORTS prórroga *f*

overtone [ˈəʊvətəʊn, *Am:* ˈoʊvə-toʊn] *n* trasfondo *m*

overture [ˈəʊvətjʊə, *Am:* ˈoʊvə-tʃə] *n* **1.** MUS obertura *f* **2.** (*show of friendliness*) acercamiento *m;* **to make ~s towards sb** intentar acercarse a alguien

overturn [ˌəʊvəˈtɜːn, *Am:* ˌoʊvə-ˈtɜːrn] I. *vi* volcar, voltearse *AmL* II. *vt* volcar; POL derrumbar

overweight [ˌəʊvəˈweɪt, *Am:* ˌoʊ-vəˈ-] *adj* **to be ~** pesar demasiado

overwhelm [ˌəʊvəˈwelm, *Am:* ˌoʊ-vəˈ-] *vt* **1.** **to be ~ed by sth** estar agobiado por algo **2.** (*swamp*) inundar

overwhelming [ˌəʊvəˈwelmɪŋ, *Am:* ˌoʊvə-ˈ-] *adj* abrumador

owe [əʊ, *Am:* oʊ] I. *vt* deber II. *vi* tener deudas

owing [ˈəʊɪŋ, *Am:* ˈoʊ-] *adj* por pagar

owing to *prep* debido a

owl [aʊl] *n* búho *m*, tecolote *m AmC, Méx;* **barn ~** lechuza *f*

own [əʊn, *Am:* oʊn] I. *adj* propio; **to see sth with one's ~ eyes** ver algo con los propios ojos II. *vt* poseer

owner [ˈəʊnə, *Am:* ˈoʊnə] *n* pro-

pietario, -a *m, f;* **to be the ~ of sth**
ser el dueño de algo

ownership ['əʊnəʃɪp, *Am:* 'oʊnɚ-]
n no pl posesión *f;* **to be under private/public** ~ ser de propiedad privada/pública

ox [ɒks, *Am:* ɑːks] <-en> *n* buey *m*

OXFAM ['ɒksfæm, *Am:* 'ɑːks-] *n Brit abbr of* **Oxford Committee for Famine Relief** *organización benéfica contra el hambre*

oxidation [ˌɒksɪ'deɪʃən, *Am:* ˌɑː-ksɪ'-] *n* oxidación *f*

oxygen ['ɒksɪdʒən, *Am:* 'ɑːksɪ-] *n no pl* oxígeno *m*

oyster ['ɔɪstəʳ, *Am:* -stɚ] *n* ostra *f*

ozone ['əʊzəʊn, *Am:* 'oʊzoʊn] *n no pl* ozono *m*

ozone layer *n* capa *f* de ozono

P

P, p [piː] <-'s> *n* P, p *f;* ~ **for Peter** P de París

p 1. *abbr of* **page** pág. *f* 2. *abbr of* **penny** penique *m*

PA [ˌpiː'eɪ] *n* 1. *abbr of* **personal assistant** ayudante *mf* personal 2. *Am abbr of* **Pennsylvania** Pensilvania *f*

pace [peɪs] I. *n* 1. *no pl* (*speed*) velocidad *f;* **to set the ~** marcar el ritmo 2. (*step*) paso *m;* **to put sb through his ~s** poner a alguien a prueba II. <pacing> *vt* **to ~ oneself** controlarse el tiempo III. <pacing> *vi* **to ~ up and down** pasearse de un lado para otro

pacemaker ['peɪsˌmeɪkəʳ, *Am:* -kɚ] *n* MED marcapasos *m inv*

pacific [pə'sɪfɪk] *adj* pacífico

Pacific [pə'sɪfɪk] *n* **the ~** el Pacífico; **the ~ Ocean** el Océano Pacífico

pacifist ['pæsɪfɪst, *Am:* 'pæsə-] *n* pacifista *mf*

pacify ['pæsɪfaɪ, *Am:* 'pæsə-] <-ie->

vt pacificar

pack [pæk] I. *n* 1. (*bundle*) fardo *m;* (*rucksack*) mochila *f;* (*packet*) paquete *m* 2. (*of wolves*) manada *f* II. *vi* hacer las maletas; **to send sb ~ing** *fig* largar a alguien con viento fresco III. *vt* 1. (*fill: box, train*) llenar 2. (*wrap*) envasar; **to ~ one's suitcase** hacer la maleta

package ['pækɪdʒ] *n* paquete *m*

package holiday *n Brit* viaje *m* organizado

packaging *n no pl* embalaje *m*

packer ['pækəʳ, *Am:* -ɚ] *n* empaquetador(a) *m(f)*

packet ['pækɪt] *n* paquete *m;* (*of cigarettes*) cajetilla *f*

packing *n no pl* embalaje *m*

pact [pækt] *n* pacto *m*

pad¹ [pæd] I. *n* 1. (*cushion*) almohadilla *f* 2. (*of paper*) bloc *m* II. <-dd-> *vt* acolchar

pad² [pæd] <-dd-> *vi* andar silenciosamente

padded *adj* acolchado

padding *n no pl* relleno *m*

paddle ['pædl] I. *n* (*oar*) canalete *m* II. *vi* (*walk, swim*) chapotear

paddling pool *n Brit, Aus* estanque *m* para chapotear

paddock ['pædək] *n* corral *m*

padlock ['pædlɒk, *Am:* -lɑːk] *n* candado *m*

paediatric [ˌpiːdɪ'ætrik] *adj Brit* pediátrico

paediatrician [ˌpiːdɪə'trɪʃn] *n Brit* pediatra *mf*

paedophile ['piːdəʊfaɪl] *n* pederasta *m*

pagan ['peɪgən] *n* pagano, -a *m, f*

page¹ [peɪdʒ] *n* página *f;* (*sheet of paper*) hoja *f*

page² [peɪdʒ] I. *n* HIST paje *m* II. *vt* llamar por el altavoz

pageant ['pædʒənt] *n* **beauty ~** concurso *m* de belleza

pageantry ['pædʒəntri] *n no pl* pompa *f*

pagoda [pə'gəʊdə, *Am:* -'goʊ-] *n* pagoda *f*

paid [peɪd] *pt, pp of* **pay**

pail [peɪl] *n* cubo *m*

pain [peɪn] n dolor m; **to be in ~** estar sufriendo; **to be at ~s to do sth** esmerarse en hacer algo; **on ~ of sth** so pena de algo; **to be a ~ in the neck** fig, inf ser un coñazo

pained adj afligido

painful ['peɪnfəl] adj doloroso; (emotionally) angustioso

painkiller ['peɪnˌkɪləʳ, Am: 'peɪnˌkɪlɚ] n analgésico m

painless ['peɪnləs] adj indoloro; fig fácil

painstaking ['peɪnzˌteɪkɪŋ] adj (research) laborioso; (search) exhaustivo

paint [peɪnt] I. n no pl pintura f II. vi, vt pintar; **to ~ a picture of sth** fig describir algo

paintbrush ['peɪntbrʌʃ] <-es> n (for pictures) pincel m; (for walls) brocha f

painted ['peɪntɪd, Am: -t̮ɪd] adj pintado

painter ['peɪntəʳ, Am: -t̮ɚ] n pintor(a) m(f)

painting n 1. (picture) cuadro m 2. no pl (art) pintura f

pair [peəʳ, Am: per] n 1. (two items) par m; **a ~ of scissors** unas tijeras; **a ~ of trousers** un pantalón 2. (group of two) pareja f; **in ~s** de dos en dos

pajamas [pə'dʒɑːməz] npl Am pijama m

Pakistan [ˌpɑːkɪ'stɑːn, Am: 'pækɪstæn] n Paquistán m

Pakistani [ˌpɑːkɪ'stɑːni] adj paquistaní

pal [pæl] n inf amigo, -a m, f

palace ['pælɪs, Am: -əs] n palacio m

palatable ['pælətəbl, Am: -ət̮ə-] adj sabroso

palate ['pælət] n paladar m

pale [peɪl] I. adj (lacking colour) pálido; (not dark) claro II. vi **to ~ into insignificance** verse insignificante

Palestine ['pælɪstaɪn, Am: -ə-] n Palestina f

Palestinian [ˌpælə'stɪnɪən] adj palestino

palette ['pælɪt] n ART paleta f

palisade [ˌpælɪ'seɪd, Am: -ə'-] n empalizada f

pallet ['pælɪt] n paleta f

palm¹ [pɑːm] n (of hand) palma f

palm² n (tree) palmera f

Palm Sunday n Domingo m de Ramos

palpable ['pælpəbl] adj palpable

paltry ['pɔːltri] <-ier, -iest> adj insignificante

pamper ['pæmpəʳ, Am: -pɚ] vt mimar

pamphlet ['pæmflɪt] n folleto m

pan [pæn] n (cooking container) cazuela f; (of scales) platillo m; (of lavatory) taza f

panacea [ˌpænə'sɪə] n panacea f

panache [pə'næʃ] n no pl brío m

Panama [ˌpænə'mɑː, Am: 'pænəmɑː] n Panamá m

Panamanian [ˌpænə'meɪnɪən] adj panameño

pancake ['pænkeɪk] n crep m, panqueque m AmL

pancreas ['pæŋkrɪəs] n páncreas m inv

panda ['pændə] n panda m

pane [peɪn] n cristal m

panel ['pænəl] n 1. (wooden) tabla f; (metal) placa f; **control ~** panel de control 2. (team) panel m

pang [pæŋ] n **~s of remorse** remordimientos mpl; **~s of guilt** sentimiento m de culpabilidad

panic ['pænɪk] I. n pánico m; **to be in a ~** estar nervioso II. <-ck-> vi ponerse nervioso

panorama [ˌpænə'rɑːmə, Am: -'ræmə] n panorama m

pansy ['pænzi] <-ies> n 1. (flower) pensamiento m 2. pej marica m

pant [pænt] vi jadear

panther ['pænθəʳ, Am: -θɚ] n 1. (black leopard) pantera f 2. Am (puma) puma m

pantomime ['pæntəmaɪm, Am: -t̮ə-] n 1. Brit (play) comedia musical navideña basada en cuentos de hadas 2. fig farsa f

pantry ['pæntri] <-ies> n despensa f

pants [pænts] npl 1. Brit (underpants) calzoncillos mpl 2. Am

P
p

(*trousers*) pantalones *mpl*

pap [pæp] *n no pl* **1.** (*food*) papilla *f* **2.** *fig, inf* chorrada *f*

papa [pə'pɑ:] *n Am, form* papá *m*

papacy ['peɪpəsi] *n no pl* pontificado *m*

papal ['peɪpl] *adj* papal

paper ['peɪpəʳ, *Am:* -pəˣ] *n* **1.** *no pl* (*for writing*) papel *m;* **a sheet of ~** una hoja de papel; **to put sth down on ~** poner algo por escrito **2.** (*newspaper*) periódico *m* **3.** (*document*) documentación *f;* **~s** papeles *mpl*

paperback ['peɪpəbæk, *Am:* -pəˣ-] *n* libro *m* de bolsillo; **in ~** en rústica

paper clip *n* sujetapapeles *m inv;* clip *m* **paperweight** *n* pisapapeles *m inv* **paperwork** *n no pl* trabajo *m* administrativo

papier-mâché [ˌpæpɪeɪ'mæʃeɪ, *Am:* ˌpeɪpəˣmə'ʃeɪ] *n no pl* cartón *m* piedra

paprika ['pæprɪkə, *Am:* pæp'ri:-] *n no pl* pimentón *m* dulce

Papua New Guinea [ˌpæpuənju:-'gɪni, *Am:* ˌpæpjuənu:'gɪni] *n* Papua-Nueva Guinea *f*

par [pɑːʳ, *Am:* pɑːr] *n no pl* **1.** (*standard*) **to be on a ~ with sb** estar al mismo nivel que alguien; **to feel below ~** no sentirse del todo bien **2.** SPORTS par *m;* **to be ~ for the course** *fig* ser lo que uno se esperaba

parable ['pærəbl, *Am:* 'per-] *n* parábola *f*

parabolic [ˌpærə'bɒlɪk, *Am:* ˌperə-'bɑːlɪk] *adj* parabólico

parachute ['pærəʃuːt, *Am:* 'per-] *n* paracaídas *m inv*

parade [pə'reɪd] **I.** *n* desfile *m* **II.** *vi* desfilar

paradigm ['pærədaɪm, *Am:* 'per-] *n* paradigma *m*

paradigmatic [ˌpærədɪg'mætɪk, *Am:* ˌperədɪg'mæṭ-] *adj* paradigmático

paradise ['pærədaɪs, *Am:* 'per-] *n* paraíso *m*

paradox ['pærədɒks, *Am:* 'perə-dɑːks] <-es> *n* paradoja *f*

paradoxical [ˌpærə'dɒksɪkəl, *Am:*

ˌperə'dɑː-k-] *adj* paradójico

paradoxically *adv* paradójicamente

paraffin ['pærəfɪn, *Am:* 'per-] *n no pl* **1.** *Brit* (*fuel*) queroseno *m* **2.** (*wax*) parafina *f*

paragon ['pærəgən, *Am:* 'perə-gɑːn] *n* arquetipo *m*

paragraph ['pærəgrɑːf, *Am:* 'perə-græf] *n* párrafo *m*

Paraguay ['pærəgwaɪ, *Am:* 'perə-gweɪ] *n* Paraguay *m*

Paraguayan [ˌpærə'gwaɪən, *Am:* ˌperə'gweɪ-] *adj* paraguayo

parakeet ['pærəkiːt, *Am:* 'per-] *n* periquito *m*

parallel ['pærəlel, *Am:* 'per-] **I.** *adj* paralelo; **in ~** en paralelo **II.** *n* MAT paralela *f;* GEO paralelo *m;* **to draw a ~** *fig* establecer un paralelismo

paralyse ['pærəlaɪz, *Am:* 'per-] *vt Brit, Aus s.* **paralyze**

paralysis [pə'ræləsɪs] <-ses> *n* parálisis *f inv*

paralytic [ˌpærə'lɪtɪk, *Am:* ˌperə-'lɪṭ-] *adj* MED paralítico; **to be ~** *inf* (*drunk*) estar como una cuba

paralyze ['pærəlaɪz, *Am:* 'per-] *vt* paralizar

paramedic [ˌpærə'medɪk, *Am:* ˌper-] *n* paramédico, -a *m, f*

parameter [pə'ræmɪtəʳ, *Am:* -əṭəˣ] *n* parámetro *m*

paramilitary [ˌpærə'mɪlɪtri, *Am:* ˌperə'mɪləter-] *adj* paramilitar

paramount [ˌpærə'maʊnt, *Am:* 'per-] *adj form* supremo

paranoia [ˌpærə'nɔɪə, *Am:* ˌper-] *n* paranoia *f*

paranoid ['pærənɔɪd, *Am:* 'perə-nɔɪd] *adj* PSYCH paranoico; **to be ~ about sth** estar obsesionado por algo

parapet ['pærəpɪt, *Am:* 'perəpet] *n* parapeto *m*

paraphernalia [ˌpærəfə'neɪlɪə, *Am:* ˌperəfəˣ'neɪljə] *npl* parafernalia *f*

paraphrase ['pærəfreɪz, *Am:* 'per-] *vt* parafrasear

paraplegic [ˌpærə'pliːdʒɪk, *Am:* ˌper-] *n* parapléjico, -a *m, f*

parasite ['pærəsaɪt, *Am:* 'per-] *n* parásito *m*

parasitic [ˌpærəˈsɪtɪk, *Am:* ˌperə-ˈsɪt̮-] *adj* parásito

parasol [ˈpærəsɒl, *Am:* ˈperəsɔːl] *n* sombrilla *f*

paratrooper [ˈpærətruːpəʳ, *Am:* ˈperətruːpɚ] *n* paracaidista *mf*

paratroops [ˈpærətruːps, *Am:* ˈper-] *npl* paracaidistas *mpl*

parcel [ˈpɑːsəl, *Am:* ˈpɑːr-] **I.** *n* (*packet*) paquete *m;* (*of land*) terreno *m* **II.** <*Brit:* -ll-, *Am:* -l-> *vt* dividir; (*land*) parcelar

◆ **parcel out** *vt* repartir en porciones; (*land*) parcelar

parched *adj* seco; **to be ~** *inf* (*thirsty*) estar muerto de sed

parchment [ˈpɑːtʃmənt, *Am:* ˈpɑːrtʃ-] *n* pergamino *m*

pardon [ˈpɑːdn, *Am:* ˈpɑːr-] **I.** *vt* (*forgive*) disculpar; (*prisoner*) indultar; **to ~ sb for sth** perdonar a alguien por algo; (**I beg your**) **~?** ¿cómo dice? **II.** *n* indulto *m*

pare [peəʳ, *Am:* per] *vt* mondar; *fig* (*costs*) recortar; **to ~ one's nails** cortarse las uñas

parent [ˈpeərənt, *Am:* ˈperənt] *n* (*father*) padre *m;* (*mother*) madre *f;* **~s** padres *mpl*

parental [pəˈrentəl] *adj* de los padres

parenthesis [pəˈrentθəsɪs] <-ses> *n* paréntesis *m inv*

parenthood [ˈpeərənthʊd, *Am:* ˈperənt-] *n no pl* paternidad *f*

parish [ˈpærɪʃ, *Am:* ˈper-] <-es> *n* parroquia *f*

parishioner [pəˈrɪʃənəʳ, *Am:* -ɚ] *n* feligrés, -esa *m, f*

parish priest *n* párroco *m*

parity [ˈpærəti, *Am:* ˈperət̮i] <-ies> *n* igualdad *f*

park [pɑːk, *Am:* pɑːrk] **I.** *n* parque *m* **II.** *vt, vi* aparcar, estacionar *AmL*

parking *n no pl* aparcamiento *m*, estacionamiento *m AmL*

parking lights *n Am, Aus* luces *fpl* de estacionamiento **parking lot** *n Am* aparcamiento *m* **parking meter** *n* parquímetro *m* **parking place** *n*, **parking space** *n* aparcamiento *m*, estacionamiento *m AmL*

Parkinson's disease [ˈpɑːkɪŋsənz-dɪˌziːz, *Am:* ˈpɑːr-] *n no pl* enfermedad *f* de Parkinson

parkway [ˈpɑːkweɪ, *Am:* ˈpɑːrk-] *n Am, Aus* avenida *f* ajardinada

parliament [ˈpɑːləmənt, *Am:* ˈpɑːrlə-] *n* parlamento *m*

[?] Las dos **Houses of Parliament** se encuentran en el **Palace of Westminster** de Londres. La cámara baja, elegida por el pueblo, y de la que proceden la mayoría de los ministros, se llama **House of Commons**. Sus diputados reciben el nombre de **members of parliament** o **MP**s. La cámara alta, **House of Lords**, sólo puede aprobar determinadas leyes. Los diputados, **peers of the realm**, se pueden dividir en tres grupos. Los que tienen un escaño en la cámara alta por razón de su trabajo, bien por ser jueces, los **law lords**, o bien por ser obispos de la iglesia anglicana, la **Church of England**. En segundo lugar los que tienen un escaño vitalicio, los **life peers**, y en tercer lugar los que han heredado el escaño junto con su título nobiliario. Un comité de jueces de la **House of Lords** constituye el máximo tribunal de justicia del Reino Unido.

parliamentary [ˌpɑːləˈmentəri, *Am:* ˌpɑːrləˈment̮ɚ-] *adj* parlamentario

parlor *n Am,* **parlour** [ˈpɑːləʳ, *Am:* ˈpɑːrlɚ] *n Brit* salón *m*

parochial [pəˈrəʊkɪəl, *Am:* -ˈroʊ-] *adj fig* de miras estrechas

parody [ˈpærədi, *Am:* ˈper-] <-ies> *n* parodia *f*

parole [pəˈrəʊl, *Am:* -ˈroʊl] *n no pl* LAW libertad *f* condicional

parquet ['pɑːkeɪ, *Am:* pɑːr'keɪ] *n no pl* parqué *m*

parrot ['pærət, *Am:* 'per-] *n* loro *m*

parry ['pæri, *Am:* 'per-] <-ie-> *vt* desviar

parsimonious [ˌpɑːsɪ'məʊniəs, *Am:* ˌpɑːrsə'moʊ-] *adj form* parco

parsley ['pɑːsli, *Am:* 'pɑːr-] *n no pl* perejil *m*

parsnip ['pɑːsnɪp, *Am:* 'pɑːr-] *n* chirivía *f*

parson ['pɑːsən, *Am:* 'pɑːr-] *n* REL pastor *m*

parsonage ['pɑːsənɪdʒ, *Am:* 'pɑːr-] *n* rectoría *f*

part [pɑːt, *Am:* pɑːrt] **I.** *n* **1.** (*not the whole*) parte *f;* (*component*) pieza *f;* **the hard** ~ lo difícil; **in** ~ en parte; **in large** ~ en gran parte; **for the most** ~ en la mayor parte; **in these** ~s *inf* en estas zonas; **to be** ~ **and parcel of sth** ser parte esencial de algo **2.** THEAT, CINE papel *m* **II.** *vt* separar; **to** ~ **sth in two** partir algo en dos; **to** ~ **company** tomar direcciones distintas **III.** *vi* separarse

partial ['pɑːʃəl, *Am:* 'pɑːr-] *adj* **1.** (*incomplete*) parcial **2. she is** ~ **to ...** tiene debilidad por...

partiality [ˌpɑːʃi'æləti, *Am:* ˌpɑːrʃi-'ælə̩ti] *n no pl* **1.** (*bias*) parcialidad *f* **2.** (*liking*) afición *f*

partially *adv* en parte

participant [pɑː'tɪsɪpənt, *Am:* pɑːr'tɪsə-] *n* participante *mf*

participate [pɑː'tɪsɪpeɪt, *Am:* pɑːr'tɪsə-] *vi* participar

participation [pɑːˌtɪsɪ'peɪʃn, *Am:* pɑːrˌtɪsə'-] *n no pl* participación *f*

participle ['pɑːtɪsɪpl, *Am:* 'pɑːrtɪ-sɪ-] *n* participio *m*

particle ['pɑːtɪkl, *Am:* 'pɑːrt̬ə-] *n* partícula *f*

particular [pə'tɪkjələr, *Am:* pə-'tɪkjələ-] *adj* **1.** (*special*) particular, especial; (*specific*) concreto, específico; **in** ~ en especial **2.** (*meticulous*) quisquilloso

particularly [pə'tɪkjʊləli, *Am:* pə-'tɪkjələ-] *adv* especialmente

parting ['pɑːtɪŋ, *Am:* 'pɑːrt̬ɪŋ] *n* **1.** (*separation*) separación *f* **2.** (*say-ing goodbye*) despedida *f* **3.** *Brit, Aus* (*in hair*) raya *f*

partisan [ˌpɑːtɪ'zæn, *Am:* 'pɑːrt̬ɪ-zən] *n* MIL partisano, -a *m, f*

partition [pɑː'tɪʃən, *Am:* pɑːr'-] **I.** *n* tabique *m;* (*of country*) división *f* **II.** *vt* (*room*) dividir con un tabique; (*country*) dividir

partly ['pɑːtli, *Am:* 'pɑːrt-] *adv* en parte

partner ['pɑːtnər, *Am:* 'pɑːrtnə-] *n* (*in relationship, dance*) pareja *f;* COM socio, -a *m, f;* ~ **in crime** cómplice *mf*

partnership ['pɑːtnəʃɪp, *Am:* 'pɑːrtnə-] *n* (*association*) asociación *f;* COM sociedad *f* (comanditaria)

partridge ['pɑːtrɪdʒ, *Am:* 'pɑːr-] *n* perdiz *f*

part-time [ˌpɑːt'taɪm, *Am:* ˌpɑːrt-] *adv, adj* a tiempo parcial

party ['pɑːti, *Am:* 'pɑːrt̬i] *n* <-ies> **1.** (*social gathering*) fiesta *f* **2.** + *sing/pl vb* (*group*) grupo *m;* POL partido *m* **3.** LAW parte *f*

party leader *n* líder *mf* del partido

pass [pɑːs, *Am:* pæs] **I.** <-es> *n* **1.** (*mountain road*) paso *m* **2.** (*in rugby, soccer*) pase *m;* **to make a** ~ **at sb** *fig* insinuarse a alguien **3.** *Brit* (*in exam*) aprobado *m* **4.** (*authorisation*) pase *m* **II.** *vt* **1.** (*go past*) pasar **2.** (*exceed*) sobrepasar **3.** (*exam*) aprobar **4.** (*approve*) aprobar **5.** (*utter*) **to** ~ **a comment** hacer un comentario; **to** ~ **sentence** LAW dictar sentencia **III.** *vi* **1.** (*move by*) pasar; **to** ~ **unnoticed** pasar desapercibido; **it'll soon** ~ se olvidará pronto **2.** SPORTS pasar la pelota **3.** (*in exam*) aprobar **4.** (*elapse*) transcurrir

◆ **pass away** *vi* fallecer

◆ **pass by** *vi* **1.** (*elapse*) pasar **2.** (*go past*) pasar de largo

◆ **pass down** *vt* transmitir

◆ **pass on I.** *vi* (*die*) fallecer **II.** *vt* (*information*) pasar; (*disease*) contagiar

◆ **pass out I.** *vi* perder el conocimiento **II.** *vt Am* (*distribute*) repartir

◆ **pass over** *vt* pasar por alto

◆ **pass up** vt desperdiciar
passage ['pæsɪdʒ] n 1.(corridor) pasillo m 2. LIT, MUS pasaje m
passageway ['pæsɪdʒweɪ] n pasillo m
passenger ['pæsəndʒəʳ, Am: -ən-dʒɚ] n pasajero, -a m, f
passing I. adj (fashion) pasajero; (remark) de pasada **II.** n **in** ~ al pasar
passion ['pæʃən] n pasión f
passionate ['pæʃənət, Am: -ənɪt] adj apasionado
passive ['pæsɪv] **I.** n no pl LING voz f pasiva **II.** adj pasivo
passivity [pæs'ɪvəti, Am: pæs'ɪvə-ţi] n no pl pasividad f
Passover ['pɑːsəʊvəʳ, Am: 'pæs,oʊ-vɚ] n no pl Pascua f judía
passport ['pɑːspɔːt, Am: 'pæs-pɔːrt] n pasaporte m
password ['pɑːswɜːd, Am: 'pæs-wɜːrd] n INFOR contraseña f
past [pɑːst, Am: pæst] **I.** n pasado m **II.** adj pasado **III.** prep ten ~ two dos y diez **IV.** adv por delante
pasta ['pæstə, Am: 'pɑːstə] n no pl pasta f
paste [peɪst] **I.** n no pl 1.(glue) pegamento m 2. GASTR pasta f **II.** vt (stick) pegar
pastel ['pæstəl, Am: pæ'stel] **I.** n pastel m **II.** adj pastel
pasteurize ['pæstʃəraɪz] vt pasteurizar
pastime ['pɑːstaɪm, Am: 'pæs-] n pasatiempo m
pastor ['pɑːstəʳ, Am: 'pæstɚ] n pastor m
pastoral ['pɑːstərəl, Am: 'pæs-] adj REL pastoral
past participle n participio m pasado
pastry ['peɪstri] <-ies> n 1. no pl (dough) masa f 2.(cake) pastel m
pasture ['pɑːstʃəʳ, Am: 'pæstʃɚ] n AGR pasto m; **to put sb out to** ~ inf jubilar a alguien
pat [pæt] **I.** <-tt-> vt dar palmaditas a; **to** ~ **sb on the back** fig felicitar a alguien **II.** n palmadita f
patch [pætʃ] **I.** n 1.(of land) parcela f de tierra; (of criminal) territorio m

2.(piece of cloth) parche m; **to be not a** ~ **on sb** Brit, Aus, inf no tener ni punto de comparación con alguien **II.** vt remendar
◆ **patch up** vt hacer un arreglo provisional a; **to patch things up** fig hacer las paces
patchwork ['pætʃwɜːk, Am: -wɜːrk] n no pl patchwork m; fig mosaico m; ~ **quilt** edredón m de retazos
patchy ['pætʃi] <-ier, -iest> adj (performance) desigual; (results) irregular
pâté ['pæteɪ, Am: pɑːˈteɪ] n paté m
patent ['peɪtənt, Am: 'pætənt] **I.** n LAW patente f; **to take out a** ~ **on sth** patentar algo **II.** adj form (unconcealed) evidente **III.** vt LAW patentar
patent leather n charol m
paternal [pə'tɜːnəl, Am: -'tɜːr-] adj paternal
paternalistic [pə,tɜːnəl'ɪstɪk, Am: -,tɜːr-] adj pej paternalista
paternity [pə'tɜːnəti, Am: -'tɜːrnə-ţi] n no pl, form paternidad f
path [pɑːθ, Am: pæθ] n camino m; (of bullet) trayectoria f; **to cross sb's** ~ tropezar con alguien
pathetic [pə'θetɪk, Am: -'θeţ-] adj **1.**(arousing sympathy) conmovedor **2.** pej (arousing scorn) patético
pathological [,pæθə'lɒdʒɪkl, Am: -'lɑːdʒɪk-] adj inf patológico
pathologist [pə'θɒlədʒɪst, Am: -'θɑːlə-] n patólogo, -a m, f
pathology [pə'θɒlədʒi, Am: -'θɑː-lə-] n no pl patología f
pathos ['peɪθɒs, Am: -θɑːs] n patetismo m
pathway ['pɑːθweɪ, Am: 'pæθ-] n camino m
patience ['peɪʃns] n no pl **1.** paciencia f; **to have the** ~ **of a saint** tener más paciencia que un santo **2.** Brit, Aus GAMES solitario m
patient ['peɪʃnt] **I.** adj paciente **II.** n MED paciente m f
patio ['pætɪəʊ, Am: 'pæţɪoʊ] <-s> n área pavimentada contigua a una casa
patriarch ['peɪtrɪɑːk, Am: -ɑːrk] n

patriarca *m*

patriarchal [ˌpeɪtrɪˈɑːkl, *Am:* -ˈɑːr-] *adj* patriarcal

patriarchy [ˈpeɪtrɪɑːki, *Am:* -ɑːrki] <-ies> *n* patriarcado *m*

patrician [pəˈtrɪʃən] *adj* patricio

patriot [ˈpætrɪət, *Am:* ˈpeɪ-] *n* patriota *mf*

patriotic [ˌpætrɪˈɒtɪk, *Am:* ˌpeɪtrɪˈɑːtɪk] *adj* patriótico

patriotism [ˈpætrɪətɪzəm, *Am:* ˈpeɪtrɪ-] *n no pl* patriotismo *m*

patrol [pəˈtrəʊl, *Am:* -ˈtrəʊl] **I.** <-ll-> *vt* patrullar por **II.** *n* patrulla *f;* **to be on ~** patrullar

patron [ˈpeɪtrən] *n* patrocinador(a) *m(f)*

patronage [ˈpætrənɪdʒ, *Am:* ˈpeɪtrən-] *n no pl* patrocinio *m*

patronize [ˈpætrənaɪz, *Am:* ˈpeɪtrən-] *vt* **1.** *form* (*be customer*) ser cliente de **2.** (*treat condescendingly*) tratar con condescendencia

patronizing [ˈpætrənaɪzɪŋ, *Am:* ˈpeɪtrən-] *adj* condescendiente

> **[?]** Inglaterra, Irlanda, Escocia y Gales tienen cada una sus propios **patron saints** (santos patrones). La festividad de **St George** de Inglaterra se celebra el 23 de abril; **St Patrick** de Irlanda el 17 de marzo; **St Andrew** de Escocia el 30 de noviembre y **St David** de Gales el 1 de marzo.

patter [ˈpætər, *Am:* ˈpætər] *n no pl* **1.** (*clever talk*) labia *f* **2.** (*of rain*) golpeteo *m*

pattern [ˈpætən, *Am:* ˈpætərn] *n* (*model*) modelo *m;* ART diseño *m;* FASHION patrón *m*

patterned *adj* estampado

paunch [pɔːntʃ, *Am:* pɑːntʃ] *n* panza *f*

pauper [ˈpɔːpər, *Am:* ˈpɑːpər] *n* indigente *mf*

pause [pɔːz, *Am:* pɑːz] **I.** *n* pausa *f;* **to give sb ~ for thought** *form* dar que pensar a alguien **II.** *vi* hacer una

pausa

pave [peɪv] *vt* pavimentar; **to ~ the way for sth** *fig* preparar el terreno para algo

pavement [ˈpeɪvmənt] *n* **1.** *Brit* (*beside road*) acera *f,* vereda *f AmL,* banqueta *f Guat, Méx* **2.** *Am, Aus* (*road covering*) calzada *f*

pavilion [pəˈvɪljən] *n* pabellón *m*

paving stone *n Brit* losa *f*

paw [pɔː, *Am:* pɑː] *n* pata *f;* (*of cat*) garra *f;* (*of lion*) zarpa *f*

pawn[1] [pɔːn, *Am:* pɑːn] *n* GAMES peón *m; fig* títere *m*

pawn[2] [pɔːn, *Am:* pɑːn] *vt* empeñar

pawnbroker [ˈpɔːnˌbrəʊkər, *Am:* ˈpɑːnˌbrəʊkər] *n* prestamista *mf* (sobre prenda), agenciero, -a *m, f Chile*

pay [peɪ] **I.** *n* paga *f;* **to be in the ~ of sb** estar a sueldo de alguien **II.** <paid, paid> *vt* pagar; **to ~ attention (to sth)** prestar atención (a algo); **to ~ sb a compliment** hacer un cumplido a alguien; **to ~ respects to sb** presentar los respetos a alguien **III.** <paid, paid> *vi* pagar

◆ **pay back** *vt* devolver

◆ **pay in** *vt* ingresar

◆ **pay off** *vt* liquidar

◆ **pay out** *vi* pagar

◆ **pay up** *vi* pagar (lo que se debe)

payable [ˈpeɪəbl] *adj* pagadero

paycheck *n Am,* **paycheque** *n Brit* cheque *m* de salario **payday** *n no pl* día *m* de pago

payer [ˈpeɪər, *Am:* -ər] *n* pagador(a) *m(f)*

paying *adj* rentable

payment [ˈpeɪmənt] *n* pago *m*

payoff [ˈpeɪɒf, *Am:* -ɑːf] *n* **1.** (*payment*) pago *m* **2.** *fig* beneficios *mpl*

payout *n* FIN desembolso *m*

pay packet *n Brit, Aus* sobre *m* de paga **payroll** *n* nómina *f* **payslip** *n* nómina *f*

PBS [ˌpiːbiːˈes] *n no pl, Am abbr of* **Public Broadcasting System** *organismo americano de producción audiovisual*

PC [ˌpiːˈsiː] **I.** *n* **1.** *abbr of* **personal**

computer PC m **2.** Brit abbr of **Police Constable** agente mf de policía **II.** adj abbr of **politically correct** políticamente correcto

PE [ˌpiːˈiː] abbr of **physical education** educación f física

pea [piː] n guisante m, arveja f Col, Chile; **to be like two ~s in a pod** ser como dos gotas de agua

peace [piːs] n no pl **1.** (absence of war) paz f **2.** (social order) orden m público; **to keep the ~** mantener el orden; **to make one's ~ with sb** hacer las paces con alguien **3.** (tranquillity) tranquilidad f; **~ of mind** tranquilidad de ánimo; **~ and quiet** paz y tranquilidad; **to be at ~** estar en paz; **to leave sb in ~** dejar a alguien en paz; **(may he) rest in ~** que en paz descanse

peaceful ['piːsfəl] adj tranquilo

peacekeeping ['piːsˌkiːpɪŋ] n no pl mantenimiento m de la paz

peacemaker ['piːsˌmeɪkəʳ, Am: -kɚ] n pacificador(a) m(f)

peace march <-es> n marcha f por la paz **peace movement** n movimiento m pacifista **peace settlement** n acuerdo m de paz **peace sign** n señal f de paz **peacetime** n no pl tiempo m de paz **peace treaty** <-ies> n tratado m de paz

peach [piːtʃ] <-es> n melocotón m, durazno m Arg, Chile; **a ~ of a day** un día encantador

peacock ['piːkɒk, Am: -kɑːk] n pavo m real; **as proud as a ~** orgulloúso como un pavo real

peak [piːk] **I.** n **1.** (of mountain) cima f; fig punto m máximo **2.** Brit (of cap) visera f **II.** vi (career) alcanzar el apogeo; (figures) alcanzar el máximo

peak capacity <-ies> n capacidad f óptima

peak hours npl horas fpl punta **peak level** n no pl nivel m máximo **peak period** n período m de máxima actividad **peak season** n temporada f alta

peal [piːl] n (of bell) repique m; **a ~**

of thunder un trueno; **a ~ of laughter** una carcajada

peanut ['piːnʌt] n cacahuete m, maní m AmL, cacahuate m Méx; **to pay ~s** inf pagar una miseria

pear [peəʳ, Am: per] n pera f

pearl [pɜːl, Am: pɜːrl] n perla f; **a string of ~s** un collar de perlas; **~s of sweat** gotas de sudor

pearl barley no pl n cebada f perlada **pearl diver** n, **pearl fisher** n pescador(a) m(f) de perlas **pearl-fishing** n no pl pesca f de perlas

pear tree n peral m

peasant ['pezənt] n campesino, -a m, f

peasantry ['pezəntri] n no pl campesinado m

peat [piːt] n no pl turba f

pebble ['pebl] n guijarro m

pecan [pɪˈkæn, Am: pɪˈkɑːn] n pacana f

peck [pek] **I.** n **1.** (of bird) picotazo m **2.** (kiss) besito m **II.** vt **1.** (bird) picar **2.** (kiss) besar **III.** vi picar

pecking order n jerarquía f

peckish ['pekɪʃ] adj **1.** Brit, Aus hambriento **2.** Am (irritable) irritable

peculiar [pɪˈkjuːlɪəʳ, Am: -ˈkjuːljɚ] adj extraño; **to feel a little ~** no sentirse del todo bien; **to be ~ to sb** ser propio de alguien

peculiarity [pɪˌkjuːlɪˈærəti, Am: -ˈerəti] <-ies> n **1.** (strangeness) singularidad f **2.** (idiosyncrasy) peculiaridad f

peculiarly [pɪˈkjuːlɪəli, Am: -ˈkjuːljɚ-] adv **1.** (strangely) de forma rara **2.** (especially) particularmente

pedal ['pedəl] **I.** n pedal m **II.** <Brit: -ll-, Am: -l-> vi pedalear

pedal bin n cubo m de la basura (con pedal) **pedal boat** n patín m a pedal

pedant ['pedənt] n pedante mf

pedantic [pɪˈdæntɪk, Am: pədˈæn-] adj pedante

peddle ['pedl] vt pej **1.** (sell) vender (de puerta en puerta); **to ~ drugs** traficar con drogas **2.** (idea, lies) difundir

pedestal ['pedɪstəl] n pedestal m; **to knock sb off their ~** bajar los humos a alguien

pedestrian [pɪ'destrɪən, *Am:* pə'-] *n* peatón, -ona *m, f*

pediatric [ˌpiːdi'ætrɪk] *adj Am s.* **paediatric**

pediatrician [ˌpiːdiə'trɪʃən] *n Am s.* **paediatrician**

pedigree ['pedɪɡriː] *n* pedigrí *m*

pedlar ['pedlər, *Am:* -lər] *n Brit, Aus* **1.** (*salesperson*) vendedor(a) *m(f)* ambulante **2.** (*drug dealer*) traficante *mf* de drogas

pedophile ['piːdəʊfaɪl] *n Am s.* **paedophile**

pee [piː] *inf* **I.** *n* no pl pis *m;* **to have a ~** hacer pis **II.** *vi* hacer pis **III.** *vt* **to ~ oneself** mearse encima

peek [piːk] *vi* **to ~ at sth** echar una mirada furtiva a algo

peel [piːl] **I.** *n* (*skin*) piel *f;* (*of fruit*) cáscara *f;* (*peladuras*) mondas *fpl* **II.** *vt* (*fruit*) pelar

peeler ['piːlər, *Am:* -lər] *n* pelapatatas *m inv*

peep¹ [piːp] **I.** *n* (*sound: of bird*) pío *m;* (*of car horn*) pitido *m* **II.** *vi* piar

peep² [piːp] **I.** *n* **to have a ~ at sth** echar una ojeada a algo **II.** *vi* **to ~ at sth** echar un vistazo a algo

◆ **peep out** *vi* asomar

◆ **peephole** ['piːphəʊl, *Am:* -hoʊl] *n* mirilla *f*

peer¹ [pɪər, *Am:* pɪr] *vi* **to ~ at sth** escudriñar algo

peer² [pɪər, *Am:* pɪr] *n* **1.** (*equal*) igual *mf* **2.** *Brit* (*lord*) noble *mf*

peerage ['pɪərɪdʒ, *Am:* 'pɪrɪdʒ] *n* **to be given a ~** recibir un título nobiliario

peerless ['pɪəlɪs, *Am:* 'pɪr-] *adj form* sin par

peg [peɡ] **I.** *n* (*for coat*) colgador *m;* (*in furniture, for tent*) estaquilla *f;* (*in mountaineering, on guitar*) clavija *f;* **clothes ~** pinza *f* de tender la ropa, broche *m* de tender la ropa *Arg;* **to take sb down a ~** or **two** bajar los humos a alguien; **to feel like a square ~ in a round hole** sentirse fuera de lugar **II.** <-gg-> *vt* enclavijar

pejorative [pɪ'dʒɒrətɪv, *Am:*

-'dʒɔːrəṭɪv] *adj form* despectivo

pelican ['pelɪkən] *n* pelícano *m*

pellet ['pelɪt] *n* bolita *f;* (*gunshot*) perdigón *m*

pelt¹ [pelt] *n* (*skin*) pellejo *m*

pelt² [pelt] **I.** *n* **at full ~** a todo correr **II.** *vt* **to ~ sb with stones** tirar piedras a alguien **III.** *vi* **to ~ after sb** salir disparado tras alguien

pelvis ['pelvɪs] <-es> *n* pelvis *f inv*

pen¹ [pen] *n* **1.** (*fountain pen*) pluma *f* estilográfica, pluma *f* fuente *AmL* **2.** (*ballpoint*) bolígrafo *m,* birome *f Arg,* pluma *f* atómica *Méx;* **to put ~ to paper** ponerse a escribir

pen² [pen] *n* (*enclosure*) corral *m*

penal ['piːnəl] *adj* penal

penalise *vt Brit, Aus,* **penalize** ['piːnəlaɪz] *vt Am* penalizar

penalty ['penəlti, *Am:* -ṭi] <-ies> *n* **1.** LAW pena *f;* **to pay a ~ for sth** ser penalizado por algo **2.** (*punishment*) castigo *m* **3.** SPORTS penalti *m*

penalty area *n* SPORTS área *f* de penalti **penalty clause** *n* cláusula *f* penal **penalty kick** *n* SPORTS tiro *m* de penalti

penance ['penəns] *n* no pl REL penitencia *f*

pence [pens] *n pl of* **penny**

penchant ['pɑːnʃɑːn, *Am:* 'pentʃənt] *n* **to have a ~ for sth** tener inclinación por algo

pencil ['pentsəl] *n* lápiz *m*

◆ **pencil in** *vt* apuntar (de forma provisional)

pencil case *n* estuche *m* (para lápices), chuspa *f Col,* cartuchera *f Arg* **pencil sharpener** *n* sacapuntas *m inv,* tajalápiz *m Col*

pendant ['pendənt] *n* colgante *m*

pending ['pendɪŋ] *prep* **~ further instructions** hasta nuevo aviso

pendulum ['pendjələm, *Am:* -dʒə-ləm] *n* péndulo *m*

penetrate ['penɪtreɪt] *vt* penetrar

penetrating *adj* penetrante

penetration [ˌpenɪ'treɪʃən] *n* penetración *f*

penguin ['peŋɡwɪn] *n* pingüino *m*

penicillin [ˌpenɪ'sɪlɪn] *n no pl* penicilina *f*

peninsula [pə'nɪnsjʊlə, *Am:* -sələ] *n* península *f*

peninsular [pə'nɪnsjʊlə^r, *Am:* -sələ^r] *adj* peninsular

penis ['pi:nɪs] <-nises *o* -nes> *n* pene *m*

penitence ['penɪtəns] *n no pl* REL penitencia *f*

penitent ['penɪtənt] *adj* penitente

penitentiary [,penɪ'tentʃəri] *n Am* prisión *f* penitenciaria

penknife ['pennaɪf] <-knives> *n* navaja *f*

pennant ['penənt] *n* banderín *m*

penniless ['penɪlɪs] *adj* **to be** ~ no tener un duro

Pennsylvania [pensɪl'veɪniə] *n* Pensilvania *f*

penny ['peni] <pennies *o* pence> *n* **1.** *Brit* penique *m* **2.** *Am* centavo *m* **3.** *fig* **they're ten a** ~ los hay a patadas

> ⚠ La forma plural de **penny** es **pence**: "The newspaper costs 50 pence."; pero si se quiere decir varias monedas de penique, se usa **pennies**: "There are ten pennies in my purse."

penny-pinching ['peni,pɪntʃɪŋ] *adj* tacaño

pen pal *n* amigo, -a *m, f* por correspondencia **pen pusher** *n Aus, Brit, pej, inf* chupatintas *mf inv,* suche *mf Chile*

pension ['pentʃən] *n* FIN pensión *f*

pensioner ['pentʃənə^r, *Am:* -ʃənə^r] *n Brit* pensionista *mf*

pension fund *n* fondo *m* de pensiones **pension plan** *n,* **pension scheme** *n Aus, Brit* plan *m* de pensiones

pensive ['pentsɪv] *adj* pensativo; **to be in a** ~ **mood** estar meditabundo

pentagon ['pentəgən, *Am:* -ṭə-gɑ:n] *n* pentágono *m*

penthouse ['penthaʊs] *n* (*flat*) ático *m* de lujo

pent-up [,pent'ʌp] *adj* (*emotion*) contenido; (*energy*) acumulado

penultimate [pen'ʌltɪmət, *Am:* pɪ'nʌltə-] *adj* penúltimo

people ['pi:pl] *n* **1.** *pl* (*plural of person*) gente *f;* **the beautiful** ~ la gente guapa, la gente linda *AmL* **2.** *no pl* (*nation, ethnic group*) pueblo *m;* ~**'s republic** república *f* popular

pepper ['pepə^r, *Am:* -ə^r] *n* **1.** *no pl* (*spice*) pimienta *f* **2.** (*vegetable*) pimiento *m*

peppercorn ['pepəkɔ:n, *Am:* -ə-kɔ:rn] *n* grano *m* de pimienta

pepper mill *n* molinillo *m* de pimienta

peppermint ['pepəmɪnt, *Am:* -ə-] *n* **1.** *no pl* (*mint plant*) menta *f* **2.** (*sweet*) caramelo *m* de menta

peppery ['pepəri] *adj* GASTR picante

pep pill *n inf* estimulante *m* **pep talk** *n inf* **to give sb a** ~ dar ánimos a alguien

per [pɜ:^r, *Am:* pɜ:r] *prep* por; **£5** ~ **kilo** £5 por kilo; **100 km** ~ **hour** 100 km por hora; **as** ~ **usual** como siempre

per annum *adv form* al año **per capita** *adv form* per cápita

perceive [pə'si:v, *Am:* pə^r-] *vt* **1.** (*sense*) percibir **2.** (*understand*) comprender

per cent *n Brit,* **percent** [pə'sent, *Am:* pə^r-] *n Am* **25** ~ 25 por ciento

percentage [pə'sentɪdʒ, *Am:* pə-'sentɪdʒ] *n* porcentaje *m*

perceptible [pə'septəbl, *Am:* pə^r-] *adj* perceptible

perception [pə'sepʃn, *Am:* pə^r-] *n* **1.** percepción *f* **2.** (*insight*) perspicacia *f*

perceptive [pə'septɪv, *Am:* pə^r-] *adj* perspicaz

perch[1] [pɜ:tʃ, *Am:* pɜ:rtʃ] **I.** <-es> *n* percha *f;* **to knock sb off his** ~ bajar los humos a alguien **II.** *vi* posarse

perch[2] [pɜ:tʃ, *Am:* pɜ:rtʃ] *n* ZOOL perca *f*

percussion [pə'kʌʃən, *Am:* pə^r-] *n no pl* percusión *f*

percussionist *n* MUS percusionista *mf*

perennial [pər'eniəl, *Am:* pə'ren-] **I.** *n* planta *f* perenne **II.** *adj* perenne

perfect¹ ['pɜːfɪkt, *Am:* 'pɜːr-] *adj* perfecto; (*calm*) total; (*opportunity*) ideal; **a ~ gentleman** todo un señor; **a ~ idiot** un tonto de remate; **to be a ~ stranger** ser completamente desconocido; **to be far from ~** estar (muy) lejos de ser perfecto; **to be a ~ match for sth** ir de maravilla con algo

perfect² [pə'fekt, *Am:* pɜːr-] *vt* perfeccionar

perfection [pə'fekʃən, *Am:* pɚ'-] *n no pl* perfección *f*

perfectionist *n* perfeccionista *mf*

perfectly *adv* perfectamente; **~ clear** completamente claro; **to be ~ honest, ...** para serte sincero,...

perfidious [pə'fɪdiəs, *Am:* pɚ'-] *adj liter* pérfido

perforate ['pɜːfəreɪt, *Am:* 'pɜːr-] *vt* perforar; (*ticket*) picar

perforation [ˌpɜːfər'eɪʃən, *Am:* ˌpɜːrfə'reɪ-] *n* perforación *f*

perform [pə'fɔːm, *Am:* pɚ'fɔːrm] **I.** *vt* **1.** MUS, THEAT, TV interpretar **2.** (*do, accomplish*) realizar; **to ~ one's duty** cumplir con su deber; **to ~ miracles** hacer milagros; **to ~ a task** llevar a cabo una tarea **II.** *vi* THEAT actuar; MUS tocar

performance [pə'fɔːməns, *Am:* pɚ'fɔːr-] *n* (*of play*) representación *f*; (*by individual actor*) actuación *f*; **to make a ~ about sth** *Brit, fig* montar un jaleo por algo

performer [pə'fɔːmər, *Am:* pɚ'fɔːrmɚ] *n* THEAT artista *mf*

perfume ['pɜːfjuːm, *Am:* 'pɜːr-] *n* perfume *m*

perhaps [pə'hæps, *Am:* pɚ'-] *adv* quizá(s)

peril ['perəl] *n form* peligro *m*; **to be in ~** correr peligro; **at ~ of sth** en peligro por algo

perilous ['perələs] *adj form* peligroso

perimeter [pə'rɪmɪtər, *Am:* pə'rɪmətɚ] *n* perímetro *m*

period ['pɪəriəd, *Am:* 'pɪri-] *n* **1.** (*time*) período *m*; ECON plazo *m* **2.** SCHOOL hora *f* **3.** (*menstruation*) regla *f*; **to have one's ~** tener la regla **4.** *Am* LING punto *m* final

periodic [ˌpɪəri'ɒdɪk, *Am:* ˌpɪri'ɑːdɪk] *adj* periódico

periodical [ˌpɪəri'ɒdɪkl, *Am:* ˌpɪri'ɑːdɪ-] *n* revista *f*

periodic table *n* tabla *f* de elementos

peripheral [pə'rɪfərəl] *adj* periférico

periphery [pə'rɪfəri] <-ies> *n* periferia *f*

periscope ['perɪskəʊp, *Am:* -skoʊp] *n* periscopio *m*

perish ['perɪʃ] *vi* **1.** *liter* (*die*) perecer; **~ the thought!** ¡Dios nos libre! **2.** *Aus, Brit* (*deteriorate*) deteriorarse

perishable ['perɪʃəbl] *adj* perecedero

perishing *adj* (*as intensifier*) dichoso; **it's ~!** *inf* ¡hace un frío que pela!

perjury ['pɜːdʒəri, *Am:* 'pɜːr-] *n* perjurio *m*

perk [pɜːk, *Am:* pɜːrk] *n* (*advantage*) ventaja *f*
◆ **perk up** *vi* (*cheer up*) alegrarse; (*improve*) mejorar

permanence ['pɜːmənənts, *Am:* 'pɜːr-] *n*, **permanency** *n no pl* permanencia *f*

permanent ['pɜːmənənt, *Am:* 'pɜːr-] *adj* (*job*) fijo; (*damage*) irreparable; (*situation*) permanente

permeable ['pɜːmɪəbl, *Am:* 'pɜːr-] *adj* permeable

permeate ['pɜːmɪeɪt, *Am:* 'pɜːr-] *vt* impregnar

permissible [pə'mɪsəbl, *Am:* pɚ'-] *adj* (*permitted*) permisible; (*acceptable*) tolerable

permission [pə'mɪʃn, *Am:* pɚ'-] *n no pl* permiso *m*

permissive [pə'mɪsɪv, *Am:* pɚ'-] *adj pej* permisivo

permit¹ ['pɜːmɪt, *Am:* 'pɜːr-] *n* permiso *m* (por escrito)

permit² [pə'mɪt, *Am:* pɚ'-] <-tt-> *vt* permitir; **I will not ~ you to go there** no te permito que vayas allí

permitted [pə'mɪtɪd, *Am:* pɚ'mɪt̬-] *adj* permitido

pernicious [pə'nɪʃəs, *Am:* pɚ'-] *adj*

pernicioso

perpendicular [ˌpɜːpənˈdɪkjʊləʳ, *Am:* ˌpɜːrpənˈdɪkjuːlɚ] *adj* perpendicular

perpetrate [ˈpɜːpɪtreɪt, *Am:* ˈpɜːrpə-] *vt form* perpetrar

perpetrator [ˈpɜːpɪtreɪtəʳ, *Am:* ˈpɜːrpətreɪtɚ] *n form* autor(a) *m(f)* (*de un delito*)

perpetual [pəˈpetʃʊəl, *Am:* pɚˈpetʃu-] *adj* perpetuo

perpetuate [pəˈpetʃʊeɪt, *Am:* pɚˈpetʃu-] *vt* perpetuar

perpetuity [ˌpɜːpɪˈtjuːəti, *Am:* ˌpɜːrpəˈtuːəti] *n no pl, form* perpetuidad *f*; **for ~** LAW a perpetuidad

perplex [pəˈpleks, *Am:* pɚˈ-] *vt* desconcertar

perplexed [pəˈplekst, *Am:* pɚˈ-] *adj* perplejo

persecute [ˈpɜːsɪkjuːt, *Am:* ˈpɜːrsɪ-] *vt* perseguir

persecution [ˌpɜːsɪˈkjuːʃən, *Am:* ˌpɜːrsɪ-] *n* persecución *f*

persecutor *n* perseguidor(a) *m(f)*

perseverance [ˌpɜːsɪˈvɪərəns, *Am:* ˌpɜːrsəˈvɪr-] *n no pl* perseverancia *f*

persevere [ˌpɜːsɪˈvɪəʳ, *Am:* ˌpɜːrsəˈvɪr] *vi* perseverar

Persia [ˈpɜːʃə, *Am:* ˈpɜːrʒə] *n no pl* Persia *f*

Persian *adj* persa

persist [pəˈsɪst, *Am:* pɚˈ-] *vi* (*cold, rain*) continuar; (*doubts*) persistir; (*person*) insistir

persistence [pəˈsɪstəns, *Am:* pɚˈ-] *n no pl* (*of cold, belief*) persistencia *f*; (*of person*) insistencia *f*

persistent [pəˈsɪstənt, *Am:* pɚˈ-] *adj* (*cold, belief*) persistente; (*person*) insistente

person [ˈpɜːsən, *Am:* ˈpɜːrs-] <people *o* plural -s> *n* persona *f*; **about one's ~** encima; **first ~** LING primera persona

personable [ˈpɜːsənəbl, *Am:* ˈpɜːrs-] *adj* agradable

personal [ˈpɜːsənəl, *Am:* ˈpɜːrs-] *adj* (*property, matter, life*) privado; (*belongings, account, letter*) personal; (*appearance*) en persona; (*question*) indiscreto; (*comment, remark*) ofen-

sivo; (*hygiene*) íntimo; **to get ~** llevar las cosas al plano personal; **it's nothing ~** no es nada personal

personal assistant *n* ayudante *mf* personal **personal computer** *n* ordenador *m* personal, computadora *f* personal *AmL*

personality [ˌpɜːsənˈæləti, *Am:* ˌpɜːr-] *n* <-ies> personalidad *f*

personally *adv* personalmente; **to take sth ~** ofenderse por algo

personification [pəˌsɒnɪfɪˈkeɪʃən, *Am:* pɚˌsɑːnɪ-] *n* personificación *f*; **he is the ~ of kindness** es la amabilidad personificada

personify [pəˈsɒnɪfaɪ, *Am:* pɚˈsɑː-nɪ-] *vt* personificar

personnel [ˌpɜːsənˈel, *Am:* ˌpɜːr-] *n* **1.** *pl* (*staff, employees*) personal *m* **2.** *no pl* (*department*) departamento *m* de personal

personnel manager *n* jefe, -a *m, f* de personal

perspective [pəˈspektɪv, *Am:* pɚˈ-] *n* perspectiva *f*

perspiration [ˌpɜːspəˈreɪʃn, *Am:* ˌpɜːr-] *n no pl* transpiración *f*

perspire [pəˈspaɪəʳ, *Am:* pɚˈspaɪɚ] *vi* transpirar

persuade [pəˈsweɪd, *Am:* pɚˈ-] *vt* convencer; **to ~ sb to do sth** convencer a alguien de que haga algo

persuasion [pəˈsweɪʒn, *Am:* pɚˈ-] *n* **1.** (*act*) persuasión *f* **2.** (*conviction*) creencia *f*

persuasive [pəˈsweɪsɪv, *Am:* pɚˈ-] *adj* (*person, manner*) persuasivo; (*argument*) convincente

pert [pɜːt, *Am:* pɜːrt] *adj* respingón

pertain [pəˈteɪn, *Am:* pɚˈ-] *vi form* **to ~ to sth** concernir algo

pertinent [ˈpɜːtɪnənt, *Am:* ˈpɜːrt-nənt] *adj form* pertinente

perturb [pəˈtɜːb, *Am:* pɚˈtɜːrb] *vt form* perturbar

Peru [pəˈruː] *n* Perú *m*

peruse [pəˈruːz] *vt form* leer detenidamente

Peruvian [pəˈruːvɪən] *adj* peruano

pervade [pəˈveɪd, *Am:* pɚˈ-] *vt form* (*attitude*) dominar; (*smell*) invadir

P
p

pervasive [pə'veɪsɪv, *Am:* pə'-] *adj*
form (*influence*) omnipresente;
(*smell*) penetrante

perverse [pə'vɜ:s, *Am:* pə'vɜ:rs] *adj*
1. (*stubborn*) obstinado **2.** (*unreasonable, deviant*) perverso

perversion [pə'vɜ:ʃən, *Am:* pə-
'vɜ:rʒən] *n* perversión *f;* ~ **of justice** deformación *f* de la justicia

pervert[1] ['pɜ:vɜ:t, *Am:* 'pɜ:rvɜ:rt] *n*
pervertido, -a *m, f*

pervert[2] [pə'vɜ:t, *Am:* pə'vɜ:rt] *vt*
pervertir; **to ~ the truth** distorsionar
la verdad

perverted *adj* pervertido

pessimism ['pesɪmɪzəm, *Am:* 'pe-
sə-] *n no pl* pesimismo *m*

pessimist *n* pesimista *mf*

pessimistic [ˌpesɪ'mɪstɪk, *Am:* ˌpe-
sə'-] *adj* pesimista; **to be ~ about
sth** ser pesimista con respecto a algo

pest [pest] *n* **1.** (*insect, animal*)
plaga *f* **2.** *inf* (*person*) pesado, -a *m, f*

pester ['pestə', *Am:* -ə-] *vt* molestar

pesticide ['pestɪsaɪd, *Am:* 'pestə-]
n pesticida *m*

pet[1] [pet] **I.** *n* animal *m* doméstico;
he's the teacher's ~ es el mimado
del profesor **II.** *adj* **1.** (*animal*) doméstico **2.** (*theory*) favorito

pet[2] [pet] <-tt-> *vt* acariciar

petal ['petl, *Am:* 'peţl] *n* pétalo
m

peter ['pi:tə', *Am:* -ţə-] *vi* **to ~ out**
(*path*) desaparecer; (*conversation*)
decaer

petite [pə'ti:t] *adj* menudo

petition [pɪ'tɪʃən, *Am:* pə'-] **I.** *n*
1. POL petición *f* **2.** LAW demanda *f*
II. *vi* LAW **to ~ for divorce** presentar
una demanda de divorcio

pet name *n* apodo *m*

Petri dish ['petri-, *Am:* 'pi:tri-] *n*
plato *m* de Petri

petrified *adj* aterrorizado

petrify ['petrɪfaɪ] <-ies> *vt* aterrorizar

petrochemical [ˌpetrəʊ'kemɪkəl,
Am: -roʊ'-] *adj* petroquímico

petrol ['petrəl] *n no pl, Aus, Brit* gasolina *f,* nafta *f RíoPl,* bencina *f Chile*

petroleum [pɪ'trəʊliəm, *Am:* pə-
'troʊ-] *n* petróleo *m,* canfín *m AmC*

petrol pump *n Aus, Brit* surtidor *m*
de gasolina **petrol station** *n Aus,
Brit* gasolinera *f,* bomba *f And, Ven,*
estación *f* de nafta *RíoPl,* bencinera *f
Chile,* grifo *m Perú* **petrol tank** *n
Aus, Brit* depósito *m* de gasolina

pet shop *n* ≈ pajarería *f*

petticoat ['petɪkəʊt, *Am:* 'peţɪ-
koʊt] *n* enagua *f,* fondo *m Méx*

petty ['peti, *Am:* 'peţ-] <-ier, -iest>
adj **1.** *pej* (*detail*) trivial; (*person*)
mezquino **2.** LAW menor

petulant ['petjələnt, *Am:* 'petʃə-]
adj enfurruñado

pew [pju:] *n* banco *m* (de iglesia)

pewter ['pju:tə', *Am:* -ţə-] *n no pl*
peltre *m*

pH [ˌpi:'eɪtʃ] pH

phallic ['fælɪk] *adj* fálico

phantom ['fæntəm, *Am:* -ţəm] **I.** *n*
fantasma *m* **II.** *adj* (*imaginary*) ilusorio

pharaoh ['feərəʊ, *Am:* 'feroʊ] *n* faraón *m*

pharmacist ['fɑ:məsɪst, *Am:* 'fɑ:r-]
n farmacéutico, -a *m, f,* farmaceuta
mf Col, Ven

pharmacology [ˌfɑ:mə'kɒlədʒi,
Am: ˌfɑ:rmə'kɑ:lə-] *n no pl* farma-
cología *f*

pharmacy ['fɑ:məsi, *Am:* 'fɑ:r-]
<-ies> *n* farmacia *f*

phase [feɪz] **I.** *n* (*stage*) fase *f;* (*period*) etapa *f;* **to be in ~** estar sincroni-
zado; **to be out of ~** estar desfasado
II. *vt* **1.** (*do in stages*) realizar por
etapas **2.** (*coordinate*) sincronizar

◆**phase in** *vt* introducir paulatina-
mente

◆**phase out** *vt* retirar progresivamente

PhD [ˌpi:eɪtʃ'di:] *n abbr of* **Doctor of
Philosophy** doctorado *m*

pheasant ['fezənt] <-(s)> *n* faisán
m

phenomenal *adj* espectacular

phenomenon [fɪ'nɒmɪnən, *Am:*
fə'nɑ:mənɑ:n] <phenomena *o*
-s> *n* fenómeno *m*

philanthropic [ˌfɪlən'θrɒpɪk, *Am:*
-æn'θrɑ:pɪk-] *adj* filantrópico

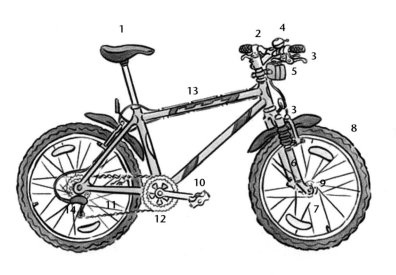

The bicycle

1	saddle *Brit,* seat *Am*	sillín m
2	handlebars	manillar m
3	brake	freno m
4	bell	timbre m
5	front light	luz f delantera, faro m delantero
6	fork	horquilla f
7	spoke	radio m

La bicicleta

8	tyre *Brit,* tire *Am*	neumático m, rueda f
9	hub	cubo m, buje m
10	pedal	pedal m
11	chain	cadena f (de la bicicleta)
12	sprocket	plato m
13	crossbar	barra f transversal
14	gear lever *Brit,* gear *Am*	cambio m de marchas

philanthropist [fɪ'lænθrəpɪst, Am: fə'-] n filántropo, -a m, f
philanthropy [fɪ'lænθrəpi, Am: fə'-] n no pl filantropía f
Philippines ['fɪlɪpiːnz, Am: 'fɪlə-] npl **the ~** las Filipinas
philistine ['fɪlɪstaɪn, Am: -stiːn] n pej ignorante mf
philology [fɪ'lɒlədʒi, Am: fɪ'lɑːlə-] n no pl filología f
philosopher [fɪ'lɒsəfəʳ, Am: -'lɑːsəfəʳ] n filósofo, -a m, f
philosophic(al) [ˌfɪlə'sɒfɪk(əl), Am: -ə'sɑːfɪk-] adj filosófico
philosophy [fɪ'lɒsəfi, Am: -'lɑːsə-] n no pl filosofía f
phlegmatic [fleg'mætɪk, Am: -'mæt̬-] adj flemático
phobia ['fəʊbiə, Am: 'foʊ-] n PSYCH fobia f
phoenix ['fiːnɪks] n fénix m
phone [fəʊn, Am: foʊn] I. n teléfono m; **by ~** por teléfono; **to be on the ~** Brit estar hablando por teléfono II. vt, vi llamar (por teléfono)
◆ **phone back** vt volver a llamar (por teléfono)
◆ **phone up** vt llamar (por teléfono)
phone book n guía f telefónica, directorio m Col, Méx **phone box** <-es> n Brit cabina f telefónica **phone call** n Brit llamada f (telefónica) **phonecard** n tarjeta f telefónica
phone-in n programa de radio o televisión en el que el público participa por teléfono
phoneme ['fəʊniːm, Am: 'foʊ-] n fonema m
phone number n número m de teléfono
phonetic [fə'netɪk, Am: foʊ'net̬-] adj fonético
phonetics [fə'netɪks, Am: foʊ'net̬-] n fonética f
phoney ['fəʊni, Am: 'foʊ-] <-ier, -iest> adj inf (person, address) falso; (documents) falsificado; **to be as ~ as a two-dollar bill** Am ser más falso que un duro sevillano, ser más falso que un billete de tres pesos Méx

phonic ['fɒnɪk, Am: 'fɑːnɪk] adj LING fónico
phonology [fə'nɒlədʒi, Am: -'nɑː-lə-] n no pl fonología f
phony ['fəʊni, Am: 'foʊ-] adj Am s. **phoney**
phosphate ['fɒsfeɪt, Am: 'fɑːs-] n fosfato m
phosphorescent [ˌfɒsfər'esənt, Am: ˌfɑːsfə'res-] adj fosforescente
phosphorus ['fɒsfərəs, Am: 'fɑːs-] n no pl fósforo m
photo ['fəʊtəʊ, Am: 'foʊt̬oʊ] <-s> n inf abbr of **photograph** foto f
photocopier ['fəʊtəʊˌkɒpiəʳ, Am: ˌfoʊt̬oʊ'kaːpiəʳ] n fotocopiadora f
photocopy ['fəʊtəʊˌkɒpi, Am: 'foʊt̬oʊˌkaːpi] I. <-ies> n fotocopia f II. vt fotocopiar
photogenic [ˌfəʊtəʊ'dʒenɪk, Am: ˌfoʊt̬oʊ'-] adj fotogénico
photograph ['fəʊtəɡrɑːf, Am: 'foʊt̬oʊɡræf] I. n fotografía f; **to take a ~ of sb** sacar una fotografía de alguien II. vt fotografiar
photograph album n álbum m de fotos
photographer [fə'tɒɡrəfəʳ, Am: -'tɑːɡrəfəʳ] n fotógrafo, -a m, f
photographic [ˌfəʊtə'ɡræfɪk, Am: ˌfoʊt̬ə'-] adj fotográfico
photography [fə'tɒɡrəfi, Am: -'tɑː-ɡrə-] n no pl fotografía f
photon ['fəʊtɒn, Am: 'foʊtaːn] n fotón m
photosensitive [ˌfəʊtəʊ'sensɪtɪv, Am: ˌfoʊt̬oʊ'sensə-] adj fotosensible
photosynthesis [ˌfəʊtəʊ'sɪntθɪsɪs, Am: ˌfoʊt̬oʊ'-] n no pl fotosíntesis f
phrasal verb [ˌfreɪzəl'vɜːb, Am: ˌfreɪzəl'vɜːrb] n LING verbo m con partícula
phrase [freɪz] I. n frase f; (idiomatic expression) expresión f; **noun phrase** sintagma nominal; **to have a good turn of ~** ser muy elocuente II. vt **to ~ sth well/badly** expresar algo bien/mal
phrasebook ['freɪzbʊk] n libro m de frases
physical ['fɪzɪkəl] adj físico

P
p

physical education *n* educación *f* física

physician [fɪ'zɪʃən] *n Am* médico, -a *m, f*

physicist ['fɪzɪsɪst] *n* físico, -a *m, f*

physics ['fɪzɪks] *n no pl* física *f*

physiological [ˌfɪziə'lɒdʒɪkəl, *Am:* -'lɑ:dʒɪk-] *adj* fisiológico

physiologist *n* fisiólogo, -a *m, f*

physiology [ˌfɪzi'ɒlədʒi, *Am:* -'ɑ:lə-] *n no pl* fisiología *f*

physiotherapist *n* fisioterapeuta *mf*

physiotherapy [ˌfɪziəʊ'θerəpi, *Am:* -oʊ'-] *n no pl* fisioterapia *f*

physique [fɪ'zi:k] *n* físico *m*

pianist ['pɪənɪst, *Am:* 'pi:nɪst] *n* pianista *mf*

piano ['pjɑ:nəʊ, *Am:* pi'ænoʊ] <-s> *n* piano *m*

piazza [pɪ'ætsə, *Am:* -'ɑ:t-] *n* plaza *f*

pick [pɪk] I. *vt* 1. (*select*) elegir 2. (*fruit, vegetables*) recoger 3. (*touch*) **to ~ one's nose** hurgarse la nariz; **to ~ one's teeth** limpiarse los dientes con un mondador; **to ~ holes in sth** *fig* encontrar fallos a algo; **to ~ a lock** forzar una cerradura; **to ~ sb's pocket** robar algo del bolsillo de alguien; **to ~ sb's brain** *fig* aprovecharse de los conocimientos de alguien II. *vi* **to ~ and choose** tardar en escoger III. *n* 1. (*selection*) selección *f*; **to take one's ~** eligir; **the ~ of the bunch** el mejor 2. (*pickaxe*) pico *m*

◆**pick at** *vt insep* picotear

◆**pick off** *vt* (*shoot*) abatir (a tiros)

◆**pick on** *vt insep* meterse con

◆**pick out** *vt* 1. (*choose*) elegir 2. (*recognize*) distinguir

◆**pick up** I. *vt* 1. (*lift*) levantar; **to ~ the phone** coger el teléfono; **to ~ the pieces** *fig* empezar de nuevo 2. (*conversation*) captar; **to ~ an illness** contagiarse con una enfermedad; **to ~ speed** coger velocidad 3. (*collect*) recoger; **to pick sb up** (*sexually*) ligarse a alguien 4. (*learn*) aprender II. *vi* (*improve*) mejorar; **to ~ where one left off** reanudar donde uno lo dejó

pickax *n Am*, **pickaxe** ['pɪkæks] *n*

Brit, Aus pico *m*

picket ['pɪkɪt] *n* MIL piquete *m*

pickings ['pɪkɪŋz] *npl* sobras *fpl*

pickle ['pɪkl] I. *n* encurtido *m;* **to be in a (pretty) ~** *inf* estar en un (buen) berenjenal II. *vt* (*vegetables*) conservar en vinagre; (*fish*) conservar en escabeche

pickled *adj* (*vegetables*) encurtido, (*fish*) en escabeche; **to get ~** *fig, inf* emborracharse

pickpocket ['pɪkpɒkɪt, *Am:* -ˌpɑ:kɪt] *n* carterista *mf*, bolsista *mf* *AmC, Méx*

pick-up ['pɪkʌp] *n* 1. (*part of record player*) brazo *m* del tocadiscos 2. (*vehicle*) camioneta *f* con plataforma

pick-up point *n* punto *m* de recogida

picnic ['pɪknɪk] *n* picnic *m;* **to be no ~** *fig* no ser nada agradable

pictorial [pɪk'tɔ:riəl] *adj* pictórico

picture ['pɪktʃəʳ, *Am:* -tʃɚ] I. *n* 1. (*image*) imagen *f*; (*painting*) pintura *f*; (*drawing*) ilustración *f*; **to draw a ~** hacer un dibujo; **to paint a ~** pintar un cuadro; **to paint a ~ of sth** *fig* representar algo; **to get the ~** *fig* entender; **to put sb in the ~** *fig* poner a alguien en antecedentes 2. (*photo*) fotografía *f*; **to take a ~** sacar una fotografía 3. (*film*) película *f;* **to go to the ~s** ir al cine II. *vt* imaginarse

picture book *n* libro *m* ilustrado

picture gallery *n* galería *f* de arte

picture postcard *n* tarjeta *f* postal

picturesque [ˌpɪktʃə'resk] *adj* pintoresco

piddle ['pɪdl] *vi inf* mear

pie [paɪ] *n* tarta *f*, pay *m AmS;* **it's ~ in the sky** es como prometer la luna

piece [pi:s] *n* 1. (*bit: of wood, metal, food*) trozo *m*; (*of text*) sección *f*; **a ~ of advice** un consejo; **a ~ of clothing** una prenda de vestir; **a ~ of news** una noticia; **a ~ of paper** (*scrap*) un trozo de papel; (*sheet*) una hoja; **a 50p ~** una moneda de 50 peniques; **in one ~** en una sola pieza; **in ~s** en pedazos; **to break**

sth to ~ hacer algo pedazos; ~ **by** ~ pieza por pieza; **to come to** ~**s** (*shatter*) hacerse añicos; (*made to be disassembled*) ser desmontable; **to take sth to** ~**s** *Brit* desmontar algo; **to go all to** ~**s** (*trauma*) sufrir un ataque de nervios; (*collapse, break*) venirse abajo; **to be a** ~ **of cake** *fig, inf* ser pan comido; **to give sb a** ~ **of one's mind** *inf* decir cuatro verdades a alguien **2.** GAMES, ART, MUS pieza *f*

♦ **piece together** *vt* reconstruir

piecemeal ['piːsmiːl] *adv* poco a poco

piece rate *n* precio *m* por unidad

piecework ['piːswɜːk, *Am:* -wɜːrk] *n no pl* trabajo *m* a destajo

pier [pɪəʳ, *Am:* pɪr] *n* muelle *m*

pierce [pɪəs, *Am:* pɪrs] *vt* perforar; **to** ~ **a hole in sth** agujerear algo

piercing *adj* (*wind*) cortante; (*gaze*) penetrante; (*wit*) punzante

piety ['paɪəti, *Am:* -t̬i] *n no pl* piedad *f*

pig [pɪg] *n* **1.** ZOOL cerdo *m;* **to make a** ~**'s ear of sth** *Brit, inf* hacer algo fatal **2.** *pej, inf* (*person*) cochino, -a *m, f*

♦ **pig out** *vi inf* ponerse morado

pigeon ['pɪdʒən] *n* paloma *f*

pigeonhole ['pɪdʒənhəʊl, *Am:* -hoʊl] **I.** *n* casilla *f* **II.** *vt* **to** ~ **sb** encasillar a alguien

piggy bank *n* hucha *f* (*en forma de cerdito*)

pigheaded [ˌpɪg'hedɪd] *adj* testarudo

piglet ['pɪglət, *Am:* -lɪt] *n* cochinillo *m*

pigment ['pɪgmənt] *n* pigmento *m*

pigmentation [ˌpɪgmen'teɪʃən] *n no pl* pigmentación *f*

pigmy ['pɪgmi] <-ies> *n* pigmeo, -a *m, f*

pigsty ['pɪgstaɪ] *n* pocilga *f*

pigswill ['pɪgswɪl] *n no pl* bazofia *f*

pigtail ['pɪgteɪl] *n* coleta *f*

pike[1] [paɪk] *n* (*fish*) lucio *m*

pike[2] [paɪk] *n* (*weapon*) pica *f*

pile [paɪl] **I.** *n* montón *m;* **to have** ~**s of sth** *inf* tener montones de

algo; **to make a** ~ *fig, inf* hacer fortuna **II.** *vt* amontonar

♦ **pile up I.** *vi* acumularse **II.** *vt* amontonar

pile-driver ['paɪlˌdraɪvəʳ, *Am:* -vɚ] *n* martinete *m*

piles *npl inf* almorranas *fpl*

pilfer ['pɪlfəʳ, *Am:* -fɚ] *vt* ratear

pilgrim ['pɪlgrɪm] *n* peregrino, -a *m, f*

pilgrimage ['pɪlgrɪmɪdʒ] *n* peregrinación *f*

pill [pɪl] *n* pastilla *f;* **the** ~ (*contraception*) la píldora

pillar ['pɪləʳ, *Am:* -ɚ] *n* pilar *m;* **a** ~ **of smoke** una columna de humo; **to be a** ~ **of strength** ser firme como una roca; **to chase sb from** ~ **to post** acosar a alguien

pillory ['pɪləri] <-ie-> *vt* **to** ~ **sb** poner en ridículo a alguien

pillow ['pɪləʊ, *Am:* -oʊ] *n* **1.** (*for bed*) almohada *f* **2.** *Am* (*cushion*) cojín *m*

pillowcase ['pɪləʊkeɪs, *Am:* -oʊ-] *n* funda *f* de almohada

pilot ['paɪlət] **I.** *n* piloto *mf* **II.** *vt* pilotar

pilot light *n* piloto *m* **pilot study** *n* estudio *m* piloto

pimp [pɪmp] *n* chulo *m*

pimple ['pɪmpl] *n* grano *m*

pin [pɪn] *n* **1.** (*needle*) alfiler *m;* **to have** ~**s and needles** sentir un hormigueo **2.** *Am* (*brooch*) prendedor *m*

♦ **pin down** *vt* **1.** (*define*) precisar **2.** (*locate*) concretar

pinball ['pɪnbɔːl] *n* **to play** ~ jugar al flíper

pincers ['pɪntsəz, *Am:* -sɚz] *npl* ZOOL pinzas *fpl;* (*tool*) tenazas *fpl*

pinch [pɪntʃ] **I.** *vt* **1.** (*nip, tweak*) pellizcar; **to** ~ **oneself** *fig* pellizcarse para ver si no se está soñando **2.** (*be too tight*) apretar **3.** *inf* (*steal*) birlar **II.** *n* **1.** (*nip*) pellizco *m;* **at a** ~, **in a** ~ *Am* si realmente es necesario; **to feel the** ~ pasar apuros **2.** (*small quantity*) pizca *f;* **to take sth with a** ~ **of salt** tomar algo con cierto escepticismo

pincushion ['pɪnˌkʊʃn] *n* acerico *m*
pine¹ [paɪn] *n* pino *m*
pine² [paɪn] *vi* to ~ (away) languidecer
pineapple ['paɪnæpl] *n* piña *f*
pine cone *n* piña *f*
ping [pɪŋ] I. *n* (*of bell*) tintín *m;* (*of glass, metal*) sonido *m* metálico II. *vi* tintinear
ping-pong ['pɪŋˌpɒŋ, *Am:* -ˌpɑːŋ] *n no pl, inf* ping-pong *m*
pinion¹ ['pɪnjən] *vt* inmovilizar
pinion² ['pɪnjən] *n* TECH piñón *m*
pink [pɪŋk] I. *n* rosa *m;* to be in the ~ rebosar de salud II. *adj* rosado
pinnacle ['pɪnəkl] *n* pico *m; fig* cúspide *f*
pinpoint ['pɪnpɔɪnt] *vt* indicar con toda precisión
pint [paɪnt] *n* pinta *f* (*Aus, Brit* = 0,57 l, *Am* = 0,47 l)
pin-up ['pɪnʌp] *n* 1. (*poster*) póster *m* (*de una celebridad*) 2. (*man*) chico *m* de póster; (*girl*) pin-up *f*
pioneer [ˌpaɪə'nɪəʳ, *Am:* -'nɪr] *n* pionero, -a *m, f*
pioneering *adj* innovador
pious ['paɪəs] *adj* piadoso
pip¹ [pɪp] *n* BOT pepita *f*
pip² [pɪp] *n pl, Brit* (*sound*) pitido *m*
pipe [paɪp] *n* 1. (*tube*) tubo *m;* (*smaller*) caño *m;* (*for gas, water*) cañería *f* 2. (*for smoking*) pipa *f*, cachimba *f AmL*
◆ **pipe down** *vi inf* callarse
pipe cleaner *n* limpiapipas *m inv*
pipeline *n* tubería *f;* to be in the ~ *fig* estar tramitándose
piper ['paɪpəʳ, *Am:* -pəʳ] *n* gaitero, -a *m, f;* he who pays the ~ calls the tune *prov* quien paga, manda
piracy ['paɪərəsi, *Am:* 'paɪrə-] *n no pl* piratería *f*
pirate ['paɪərət, *Am:* 'paɪrət] *n* pirata *m*
pirouette [ˌpɪrʊ'et, *Am:* -u'et] *n* pirueta *f*
Pisces ['paɪsiːz] *n* Piscis *m inv*
piss [pɪs] *vulg* I. *n no pl* to have a ~ mear; to take the ~ (out of sb) *Brit* cachondearse (de alguien) II. *vi* mear; it's ~ing with rain *Brit, Aus*

estar lloviendo a cántaros III. *vt* to ~ oneself laughing mearse de risa
pissed [pɪst] *adj inf* to be ~ 1. *Brit, Aus* (*drunk*) estar borracho 2. *Am* (*angry*) estar de mala leche
pistachio [pɪ'stɑːʃiəʊ, *Am:* -'stæʃiʊ] <-s> *n* pistacho *m*, pistache *m Méx*
pistol ['pɪstəl] *n* pistola *f*
piston ['pɪstən] *n* pistón *m*
pit¹ [pɪt] *n* hoyo *m;* (*mine*) mina *f; inf* (*untidy place*) lobera *f;* the ~s *pl, fig, inf* lo peor
pitch¹ [pɪtʃ] I. *n* 1. *Brit, Aus* (*playing field*) campo *m* 2. *Am* (*baseball*) lanzamiento *m* 3. MUS, LING tono *m;* to be at fever ~ estar muy emocionado 4. *fig* sales ~ labia *f* para vender II. *vt* lanzar
◆ **pitch in** *vi inf* contribuir
pitch² [pɪtʃ] *n no pl* (*bitumen*) brea *f*
pitch-black [ˌpɪtʃ'blæk] *adj* negro como la boca de un lobo
pitcher¹ ['pɪtʃəʳ, *Am:* -əʳ] *n* (*large jug*) cántaro *m; Am* (*smaller*) jarra *f*
pitcher² ['pɪtʃəʳ, *Am:* -əʳ] *n* lanzador(a) *m(f)*
pitchfork ['pɪtʃfɔːk, *Am:* -fɔːrk] *n* horca *f*
pitfall ['pɪtfɔːl] *n pl* escollo *m*
pith [pɪθ] *n no pl* médula *f*
pithy ['pɪθi] <-ier, -iest> *adj* sucinto
pitiful ['pɪtɪfəl, *Am:* 'pɪt̬-] *adj* lamentable
pittance ['pɪtənts] *n no pl* miseria *f*, pavada *f CSur*
pituitary gland [pɪ'tjuːɪtəri-, *Am:* -'tuːətəʳ-] *n* glándula *f* pituitaria
pity ['pɪti, *Am:* 'pɪt̬-] I. *n no pl* 1. (*compassion*) compasión *f;* in ~ por piedad; to feel ~ for sb compadecerse de alguien; to take ~ on sb apiadarse de alguien; for ~'s sake ¡por piedad! 2. (*shame*) to be a ~ ser una pena; more's the ~! ¡desgraciadamente!; what a ~! ¡qué pena! II. <-ies, -ied> *vt* compadecerse de
pivot ['pɪvət] I. *n* eje *m* II. *vi* to ~ round girar
pixel [pɪksəl] *n* INFOR pixel *m*
pizza ['piːtsə] *n* pizza *f*

placard ['plækɑːd, *Am:* -ɑːrd] *n* pancarta *f*

placate [plə'keɪt, *Am:* 'pleɪkeɪt] *vt* aplacar

place [pleɪs] **I.** *n* **1.** (*location, area*) lugar *m*; ~ **of birth** lugar de nacimiento; ~**s of interest** lugares de interés; **to be in** ~ estar en su sitio; *fig* estar listo; **in** ~ **of sb** en vez de alguien; **to fall into** ~ encajar; **to feel out of** ~ sentirse fuera de lugar; **to go** ~**s** *inf* llegar lejos; **to know one's** ~ saber cuál es el lugar de uno; **to put sb in his** ~ poner a alguien en su sitio; **all over the** ~ por todas partes **2.** (*position*) posición *f*; **to lose one's** ~ (*book*) perder la página; **to take first/second** ~ quedar en primer/segundo lugar; **in the first** ~ primero; **in the second** ~ segundo **3.** (*seat*) sitio *m*; **to change** ~**s with sb** cambiar el sitio con alguien **4.** (*in organization*) plaza *f* **II.** *vt* **1.** (*put*) colocar; **to** ~ **one's hopes on sth** poner sus esperanzas en algo; **to** ~ **the emphasis on sth** hacer énfasis en algo; **to** ~ **one's faith in sb** depositar su confianza en alguien; **to** ~ **an order for sth** hacer un pedido de algo; **to** ~ **a bet** hacer una apuesta; **to** ~ **sb in charge (of sth)** poner a alguien a cargo (de algo); **to** ~ **sb under surveillance** poner a alguien bajo vigilancia; **to** ~ **sth under the control of sb** poner algo bajo el control de alguien; **I can't** ~ **him** su cara me suena, pero no la puedo situar **2.** (*impose*) imponer; **to** ~ **a limit on sth** poner un límite a algo

placebo [plə'siːbəʊ, *Am:* -boʊ] <-s> *n* placebo *m*

placement ['pleɪsmənt] *n* colocación *f*

placenta [plə'sentə, *Am:* -t̬ə] <-s *o* -ae> *n* placenta *f*

placid ['plæsɪd] *adj* plácido

plagiarism ['pleɪdʒərɪzəm, *Am:* -dʒɚ-ɪ] *n no pl* plagio *m*

plague [pleɪg] **I.** *n* plaga *f*; **the** ~ HIST la peste; **to avoid sb like the** ~ huir de alguien como de la peste

II. *vt* **to** ~ **sb for sth** acosar a alguien por algo

plaice [pleɪs] *inv n* platija *f*

plaid [plæd] *n no pl, Am* tela *f* a cuadros

plain [pleɪn] **I.** *adj* **1.** sencillo; (*one colour*) de un solo color; **the** ~ **truth** la pura realidad; **a** ~ **girl** una chica más bien fea **2.** (*uncomplicated*) fácil; ~ **and simple** liso y llano **3.** (*clear, obvious*) evidente; **to make sth** ~ dejar algo claro; **to make oneself** ~ **(to sb)** hacerse entender (a alguien) **II.** *adv inf* (*downright*) y punto **III.** *n* GEO llanura *f*

plain clothes *adj* de paisano

plainly ['pleɪnli] *adv* **1.** (*simply*) simplemente **2.** (*obviously*) evidentemente

plain sailing *n fig* **to be** ~ ser cosa de coser y cantar

plaintiff ['pleɪntɪf, *Am:* -t̬ɪf] *n* demandante *mf*

plaintive ['pleɪntɪv, *Am:* -t̬ɪv] *adj* lastimero

plait [plæt] **I.** *n* trenza *f* **II.** *vt* trenzar

plan [plæn] **I.** *n* (*scheme, diagram*) plano *m*; **savings** ~ plan *m* de ahorro; **street** ~ plano *m* de calles; **to draw up a** ~ elaborar un plan; **to go according to** ~ ir de acuerdo con lo previsto; **to make** ~**s for sth** hacer planes para algo **II.** <-nn-> *vt* planificar; (*prepare*) preparar; **to** ~ **to do sth** proponerse hacer algo **III.** *vi* hacer proyectos

plane¹ [pleɪn] *n* MAT plano *m*

plane² *n* (*tool*) cepillo *m*

plane³ *n* AVIAT avión *m*; **by** ~ en avión

plane crash *n* accidente *m* de aviación

planet ['plænɪt] *n* planeta *m*; ~ **Earth** la Tierra

planetary ['plænɪtəri, *Am:* -teri] *adj* planetario

plane tree *n* plátano *m*

plank [plæŋk] *n* tabla *f*

plankton ['plæŋktən] *n no pl* plancton *m*

planner *n* planificador(a) *m(f)*

planning *n no pl* planificación *f*; **at the** ~ **stage** en la etapa de planifica-

P p

ción

planning permission *n* permiso *m* de construcción

plant [plɑːnt, *Am:* plænt] I. *n* 1. BOT planta *f* 2. (*factory*) fábrica *f* 3. *no pl* (*machinery*) maquinaria *f* II. *vt* 1. AGR plantar 2. (*put*) colocar; **to ~ a bomb** poner una bomba

plantation [plæn'teɪʃn] *n* plantación *f*

plaque [plɑːk, plæk, *Am:* plæk] *n* 1. (*on building*) placa *f* 2. *no pl* MED sarro *m*

plasma ['plæzmə] *n no pl* plasma *m*

plaster ['plɑːstər, *Am:* 'plæstər] I. *n* 1. *no pl* ARCHIT, MED yeso *m* 2. Brit (*sticking plaster*) tirita *f* II. *vt* 1. ARCHIT enyesar 2. *inf* (*put all over*) llenar

plasterboard ['plɑːstəbɔːd, *Am:* 'plæstərbɔːrd] *n no pl* cartón *m* de yeso (y fieltro)

plaster cast *n* MED escayola *f*

plastered *adj inf* **to get ~** emborracharse

plastic ['plæstɪk] I. *n* plástico *m* II. *adj* de plástico

plastic bag *n* bolsa *f* de plástico

plastic bullet *n* bala *f* de goma

Plasticine® ['plæstɪsiːn] *n no pl* plastilina *f*

plastic surgery *n* cirugía *f* plástica

plate [pleɪt] *n* 1. (*dinner plate*) plato *m*; **to give sth to sb on a ~** *fig* servir algo a alguien en bandeja; **to have a lot on one's ~** *fig* tener muchos asuntos entre manos 2. (*panel*) lámina *f*

plateau ['plætəʊ, *Am:* plæt'oʊ] <*Brit:* -x, *Am, Aus:* -s> *n* meseta *f*

plateful ['pleɪtfʊl] *n* plato *m*

plate glass *n* luna *f*

platelet ['pleɪlət] *n* plaqueta *f*

plate rack *n* portaplatos *m inv*

platform ['plætfɔːm, *Am:* -fɔːrm] *n* plataforma *f*; Brit, Aus RAIL andén *m*

platinum ['plætɪnəm, *Am:* 'plætnəm] *n no pl* platino *m*

platitude ['plætɪtjuːd, *Am:* 'plætətuːd] *n pej* perogrullada *f*

platonic [plə'tɒnɪk, *Am:* -'tɑːnɪk] *adj* platónico

platoon [plə'tuːn] *n* MIL pelotón *m*

platter ['plætər, *Am:* 'plætər] *n* fuente *f*

plausibility [ˌplɔːzə'brlɪti, *Am:* ˌplɑːzə'brləʤi] *n no pl* plausibilidad *f*

plausible ['plɔːzəbl, *Am:* 'plɑː-] *adj* plausible

play [pleɪ] I. *n* 1. *no pl* (*recreation*) juego *m;* **foul ~** juego sucio; **to be at ~** estar en juego; **to be in/out of ~** estar dentro/fuera de juego; **to bring sth into ~** poner algo en juego; **to give sth full ~** dar rienda suelta a algo; **to make a ~ for sth** intentar conseguir algo 2. THEAT obra *f* de teatro II. *vi* 1. jugar; **to ~ fair** jugar limpio 2. MUS tocar III. *vt* 1. (*participate in game*) jugar; **to ~ football** jugar al fútbol 2. THEAT interpretar; **to ~ the fool** hacer el payaso 3. MUS tocar; **to ~ a CD** poner un compact disc 4. (*perpetrate: joke*) gastar

◆ **play along** *vi* **to ~ with sb** seguir la corriente a alguien

◆ **play down** *vt* quitar importancia a

◆ **play on** *vt* **to ~ sb's weakness** aprovecharse de la debilidad de alguien

◆ **play up** *vi* Aus, Brit dar guerra

◆ **play upon** *vt s.* **to play on**

play-act *vi fig* hacer teatro

playboy *n* playboy *m*

player ['pleɪər, *Am:* -ər] *n* jugador(a) *m(f)*

playfellow *n* compañero, -a *m*, *f* de juego

playful ['pleɪfəl] *adj* juguetón

playground *n* (*of school*) patio *m;* (*in park*) campo *m* de recreo **playgroup** *n* guardería *f* **playhouse** *n* (*theatre*) teatro *m*

playing card *n* carta *f* **playing field** *n* campo *m* de deportes

playmate *n* compañero, -a *m*, *f* de juego **play-off** *n* desempate *m* **playpen** *n* parque *m* **playroom** *n* cuarto *m* de jugar **plaything** *n* juguete *m* **playtime** *n no pl* recreo *m* **playwright** ['pleɪraɪt] *n* dramaturgo, -a *m, f*

plaza ['plɑːzə] *n* plaza *f;* (shopping)
~ centro *m* comercial

plc [ˌpiːelˈsiː] *n Brit abbr of* **public
limited company** S.A. *f*

plea [pliː] *n* 1. (*appeal*) petición *f;* to
make a ~ for mercy pedir clemen-
cia 2. LAW alegato *m;* to **enter a ~ of
not guilty** declararse inocente

plead [pliːd] <pleaded *Am:* pled,
pleaded *Am:* pled> I. *vi* implorar;
to ~ for forgiveness suplicar perdón; **to ~ with sb (to do sth)** suplicar (hacer algo) a alguien; **to ~ innocent (to a charge)** declararse inocente (de un cargo) II. *vt* pretextar;
to ~ ignorance of sth pretextar su
ignorancia en algo; **to ~ sb's cause**
defender la causa de alguien

pleasant ['plezənt] *adj* agradable;
have a ~ journey! ¡buen viaje!; **to
be ~ (to sb)** ser amable (con alguien)

please [pliːz] I. *vt* gustar; **to be hard
to ~** ser difícil de contentar; ~ **yourself** haz lo que te parezca II. *vi*
eager to ~ deseoso de agradar; **to
do as one ~s** hacer lo que uno quiera III. *interj* por favor; **if you ~** *form*
con su permiso

pleased *adj* satisfecho; **to be ~ that
...** estar contento de que +*subj;* **I'm
very ~ to meet you** encantado de
conocerle; **to be ~ to do sth** estar
encantado de hacer algo; **to be as ~
as Punch (about sth)** estar más contento que unas Pascuas (con algo)

pleasing *adj* agradable

pleasurable ['pleʒərəbl] *adj* grato

pleasure ['pleʒəʳ, *Am:* -ɚ] *n* placer
m; **to take ~ in sth/in doing sth**
disfrutar de algo/haciendo algo;
with ~ con mucho gusto

pleat [pliːt] *n* pliegue *m*

plebiscite ['plebɪsɪt, *Am:* -əsaɪt] *n*
plebiscito *m*

pled [pled] *Am, Scot pt, pp of* **plead**

pledge [pledʒ] I. *n* promesa *f;* **to fulfil a ~** cumplir un compromiso; **to
make a ~ that ...** prometer solem-
nemente que...; **a ~ of good faith**
una garantía de buena fe II. *vt* **to ~
loyalty** jurar lealtad; **to ~ to do sth**

prometer hacer algo; **I've been ~d to
secrecy** he jurado guardar el secreto

plenary ['pliːnəri] *adj* plenario

plentiful ['plentɪf(ʊ)l, *Am:* -t̬ɪ-] *adj*
abundante

plenty ['plenti, *Am:* -t̬i] I. *n no pl* ~
of money/time dinero/tiempo de
sobra II. *adv* ~ **more** mucho más

pliable ['plaɪəbl] *adj* 1. (*supple*)
flexible 2. *fig* dócil

pliers ['plaɪəz, *Am:* 'plaɪɚz] *npl* alicates *mpl;* **a pair of** ~ unos alicates

plight [plaɪt] *n* apuro *m*

PLO [ˌpiːelˈəʊ, *Am:* -ˈoʊ] *n abbr of*
**Palestine Liberation Organiz-
ation** OLP *f*

plod [plɒd, *Am:* plɑːd] <-dd-> *vi*
andar con paso pesado; **to ~
through a book** leer un libro lentamente

plonk [plɒŋk, *Am:* plʌŋk] I. *n inf*
ruido *m* sordo II. *vt inf* dejar caer pesadamente

plop [plɒp, *Am:* plɑːp] I. *n* plaf *m*
II. <-pp-> *vi* caerse haciendo plaf

plot [plɒt, *Am:* plɑːt] I. *n* 1. (*conspiracy*) conspiración *f;* **to hatch a ~**
tramar una intriga 2. (*story line*) argumento *m;* **the ~ thickens** *iron* el
asunto se complica 3. (*small piece of
land*) terreno *m;* **a ~ of land** un terreno; **building ~** solar *m* II. <-tt->
vt 1. (*conspire*) tramar 2. (*graph*)
trazar; **to ~ a course** planear una
ruta III. <-tt-> *vi* **to ~ against sb**
conspirar contra alguien; **to ~ to do
sth** planear hacer algo

◆ **plot out** *vt* trazar

plough [plaʊ] I. *n* arado *m* II. *vt*
arar; **to ~ one's way through sth**
abrirse paso por algo; **to ~ money
into a project** invertir mucho dinero en un proyecto

◆ **plough up** *vt* roturar

plow [plaʊ] *n Am s.* **plough**

ploy [plɔɪ] *n* táctica *f*

pluck [plʌk] I. *n* (*courage*) valor *m;*
to have a lot of ~ tener agallas II. *vt*
(*remove*) arrancar; **to ~ a chicken**
desplumar un pollo; **to ~ one's eyebrows** depilarse las cejas

◆ **pluck up** *vt* **to ~ the courage to**

do sth armarse de valor para hacer algo

plucky ['plʌki] <-ier, -iest> *adj* valiente

plug [plʌg] I. *n* (*connector*) enchufe *m*; (*socket*) toma *f* de corriente; (*stopper*) tapón *m*; **to give sth a ~** *inf* dar publicidad a algo II. <-gg-> *vt* **1. to ~ a hole** tapar un agujero; **to ~ a leak** taponar un escape **2.** (*publicize*) anunciar

◆ **plug in** *vt* conectar; ELEC enchufar

plughole ['plʌghəʊl, *Am:* -hoʊl] *n* desagüe *m*; **to go down the ~** *fig* irse al garete

plug-in *n* INFOR plug-in *m*

plum [plʌm] *n* (*fruit*) ciruela *f*; (*tree*) ciruelo *m*; **a ~ job** un trabajo fantástico

plumage ['pluːmɪdʒ] *n no pl* plumaje *m*

plumb [plʌm] I. *vt* sondar; **to ~ the depths** *fig* estar muy deprimido II. *adv* **he hit me ~ on the nose** me dio de lleno en la nariz

◆ **plumb in** *vt* **to plumb sth in** instalar algo

plumber ['plʌməʳ, *Am:* -ɚ] *n* fontanero, -a *m, f*, plomero, -a *m, f AmL*, gasfitero, -a *m, f Chile, Perú*

plumbing ['plʌmɪŋ] *n no pl* fontanería *f*

plume [pluːm] *n* pluma *f*; (*of smoke, gas*) nube *f*

plummet ['plʌmɪt] *vi* caer en picado

plump [plʌmp] *adj* (*person*) rollizo; (*animal*) gordo

◆ **plump for** *vt inf* optar por

plumpness ['plʌmpnəs] *n no pl* gordura *f*

plum pudding *n Brit* budín *m* de pasas **plum tree** *n Brit* ciruelo *m*

plunder ['plʌndəʳ, *Am:* -dɚ] I. *n no pl* saqueo *m* II. *vt* saquear

plunge [plʌndʒ] I. *n* caída *f*; **to take the ~** dar el paso decisivo II. *vi* precipitarse; **to ~ to one's death** tener una caída mortal; **we ~d into the sea** nos zambullimos en el mar; **to ~ into sth** *fig* emprender algo III. *vt* hundir; **to ~ a knife into sth** clavar un cuchillo en algo

◆ **plunge in** *vi* lanzarse

plunger ['plʌndʒəʳ, *Am:* -dʒɚ] *n* (*of syringe*) émbolo *m*; (*for drain, sink*) desatascador *m*

plunk [plʌŋk] *n Am s.* **plonk**

plural ['plʊərəl, *Am:* 'plʊrəl] *n* plural *m*; **in the ~** en plural

pluralism ['plʊərəlɪzəm, *Am:* 'plʊrəl-] *n no pl* pluralismo *m*

plurality [plʊə'ræləti, *Am:* plʊ'ræləti] <-ies> *n* pluralidad *f*

plus [plʌs] I. *prep* más; **5 ~ 2 equals 7** 5 más 2 igual a 7 II. <-es> *n* **1.** (*symbol*) signo *m* más **2.** (*advantage*) punto *m* a favor III. *adj* (*above zero*) positivo; **~ 8** más 8; **200 ~** más de 200; **the ~ side** (**of sth**) el lado positivo (de algo)

plush [plʌʃ] *adj* lujoso

Pluto ['pluːtəʊ, *Am:* -t̮oʊ] *n* Plutón *m*

plutonium [pluː'təʊniəm, *Am:* -'toʊ-] *n no pl* plutonio *m*

ply [plaɪ] <-ie-> I. *vt* **to ~ one's trade** ejercer su profesión; **to ~ sb with questions** acosar a alguien con preguntas; **to ~ sb with wine** no parar de servir vino a alguien; **to ~ a route** hacer un trayecto II. *vi* **to ~ for business** ofrecer sus servicios

plywood ['plaɪwʊd] *n no pl* contrachapado *m*

p.m. [ˌpiː'em] *abbr of* **post meridiem** p.m.; **one ~** la una de la tarde; **eight ~** las ocho de la noche

PM [ˌpiː'em] *n abbr of* **Prime Minister** primer ministro *m*, primera ministra *f*

pneumatic [njuː'mætɪk, *Am:* nuː-'mæt̮-] *adj* neumático

pneumonia [njuː'məʊnɪə, *Am:* nuː'moʊnjə] *n no pl* neumonía *f*

PO [ˌpiː'əʊ, *Am:* -'oʊ] *n Brit abbr of* **Post Office** Correos *m*

poach[1] [pəʊtʃ] *vt* (*eggs*) escalfar; (*fish*) cocer

poach[2] [pəʊtʃ] I. *vt* cazar en vedado; (*fish*) pescar en vedado; **to ~ someone's ideas** birlar las ideas de alguien; **to ~ a manager from a company** apropiarse de un director de una empresa II. *vi* (*catch il-*

legally) cazar furtivamente; (*fish*) pescar furtivamente

poacher ['pəʊtʃəʳ, *Am:* 'poʊtʃɚ] *n* (*hunter*) cazador(a) *m(f)* furtivo; (*fisherman*) pescador(a) *m(f)* furtivo

poaching ['pəʊtʃɪŋ, *Am:* 'poʊtʃ-] *n no pl* caza *f* furtiva; (*fishing*) pesca *f* furtiva

POB *n abbr of* **Post-Office Box** apdo. *m* de correos

PO Box [ˌpiːˈəʊbɒks, *Am:* -ˈoʊbɑːks] <-es> *n abbr of* **Post Office Box** apartado *m* de correos

pocket ['pɒkɪt, *Am:* 'pɑːkɪt] I. *n* bolsillo *m*, bolsa *f AmC, Méx;* (*in billiard table*) tronera *f;* ~ **edition** edición *f* de bolsillo; **a** ~ **of resistance** un foco de resistencia; ~ **of turbulence** AVIAT, METEO racha *f* de turbulencias; **to be out of** ~ salir perdiendo; **to have sb in one's** ~ tener a alguien en el bolsillo; **to line one's** ~**s** forrarse (de dinero); **to pay for sth out of one's own** ~ pagar algo de su bolsillo II. *vt* **to** ~ **sth** meterse algo en el bolsillo; (*steal*) apropiarse de

pocketbook *n* **1.** *Am* (*woman's handbag*) bolso *m*, cartera *f AmL* **2.** (*wallet*) monedero *m*

pocket calculator *n* calculadora *f* de bolsillo

pocketful ['pɒkɪtfʊl, *Am:* 'pɑːkɪt-] *n* **a** ~ **of sth** un puñado de algo

pocketknife <-knives> *n* navaja *f*

pocket money *n no pl* (*for personal expenses*) dinero *m* para gastos personales; *Brit* (*from parents*) paga *f*

pod [pɒd, *Am:* pɑːd] *n* **1.** BOT vaina *f* **2.** AVIAT tanque *m*

POD *abbr of* **pay on delivery** pago *m* contra entrega

podgy ['pɒdʒi, *Am:* 'pɑːdʒi] <-ier, -iest> *adj* gordinflón

podium ['pəʊdiəm, *Am:* 'poʊ-] <-dia> *n* podio *m*

poem ['pəʊɪm, *Am:* poʊəm] *n* poema *m*

poet ['pəʊɪt, *Am:* poʊət] *n* poeta *mf*

poetic [pəʊˈetɪk, *Am:* poʊˈeṭ-] *adj* poético

poetry ['pəʊɪtri, *Am:* 'poʊə-] *n no pl* poesía *f*

poignant ['pɔɪnjənt] *adj* conmovedor

point [pɔɪnt] I. *n* **1.** (*sharp end*) punta *f* **2.** (*promontory*) cabo *m* **3.** (*particular place*) punto *m* **4.** (*particular time*) momento *m;* **boiling/ freezing** ~ punto *m* de ebullición/ congelación; **starting** ~ punto de partida; **to do sth up to a** ~ hacer algo hasta cierto punto; **at this** ~ **in time** en este momento **5.** (*significant idea*) cuestión *f;* **to be beside the** ~ no venir al caso; **to get to the** ~ ir al grano; **to get the** ~ (*of sth*) entender (algo); **to make one's** ~ expresar su opinión; **to make a** ~ **of doing sth** procurar de hacer algo; **to miss the** ~ no captar lo relevante; **to take sb's** ~ aceptar el argumento de alguien; ~ **taken** de acuerdo; **that's just the** ~**!** ¡eso es lo importante!; **what's the** ~**?** ¿qué sentido tiene? **6.** (*in score*) punto *m;* **decimal** ~ coma *f*, punto *m* decimal *AmL;* **to win on** ~**s** ganar por puntos II. *vi* señalar; (*indicate*) III. *vt* apuntar; **to** ~ **sth at sb** apuntar con algo a alguien; **to** ~ **a finger at sb** *a. fig* señalar con el dedo a alguien; **to** ~ **sth toward sth** dirigir algo hacia algo; **to** ~ **sb toward sth** indicar a alguien el camino hacia algo

◆ **point out** *vt* indicar; **to point sth out to sb** (*inform*) advertir a alguien de algo

◆ **point up** *vi form* destacar

point-blank *adv* a quemarropa; **to refuse** ~ negarse rotundamente

pointed ['pɔɪntɪd, *Am:* -t̬ɪd] *adj* **1.** (*implement, stick*) puntiagudo **2.** *fig* (*criticism*) mordaz; (*question*) directo

pointer ['pɔɪntəʳ, *Am:* -t̬ɚ] *n* puntero *m;* (*of clock*) aguja *f*

pointless ['pɔɪntləs] *adj* inútil

point of view <points of view> *n* punto *m* de vista

poise [pɔɪz] I. *n no pl* aplomo *m;* **to lose one's** ~ perder la serenidad II. *vt* **to be** ~**d to do sth** estar a punto de hacer algo

poison ['pɔɪzən] **I.** n veneno m; **to take** ~ envenenarse; **what's your** ~**?** iron ¿qué tomas? **II.** vt envenenar; fig emponzoñar; **to** ~ **sb's mind** (**against sb**) indisponer a alguien (contra alguien)

poisoning n no pl envenenamiento m

poisonous ['pɔɪzənəs] adj venenoso

poke [pəʊk, Am: poʊk] **I.** n (push) empujón m; (with elbow) codazo m **II.** vt (with finger) dar con la punta del dedo en; (with elbow) dar un codazo a; **to** ~ **a hole in sth** hacer un agujero en algo; **to** ~ **holes in an argument** echar un argumento por tierra; **to** ~ **one's nose into sb's business** meter las narices en los asuntos de alguien

poker¹ ['pəʊkər, Am: 'poʊkɚ] n (card game) póquer m

poker² ['pəʊkər, Am: 'poʊkɚ] n (fireplace tool) atizador m

Poland ['pəʊlənd, Am: 'poʊ-] n Polonia f

polar ['pəʊlər, Am: 'poʊlɚ] adj polar

polar bear n oso m polar **polar ice cap** n no pl casquete m polar

polarisation [ˌpəʊlərɑɪ'zeɪʃən] n no pl, Brit, Aus s. **polarization**

polarise ['pəʊlərɑɪz] vt, vi Brit, Aus s. **polarize**

polarity [pəʊ'lærəti, Am: poʊ'lerəti] n no pl polaridad f

polarization [ˌpəʊlərɑɪ'zeɪʃən, Am: ˌpoʊlɚ'-] n no pl polarización f

polarize ['pəʊlərɑɪz, Am: 'poʊ-] vi, vt polarizar(se)

pole¹ [pəʊl, Am: poʊl] n palo m; **fishing** ~ caña f de pescar; **telegraph** ~ poste m telegráfico

pole² [pəʊl, Am: poʊl] n GEO, ELEC polo m; **to be** ~**s apart** fig ser polos opuestos

Pole [pəʊl, Am: poʊl] n (person) polaco, -a m, f

polemic [pə'lemɪk] **I.** n polémica f **II.** adj polémico

pole position n no pl **to be in** ~

estar en cabeza

Pole Star n estrella f polar

pole vault n salto m con pértiga **pole vaulter** n saltador(a) m(f) de pértiga

police [pə'liːs] **I.** npl policía f **II.** vt **to** ~ **an area** vigilar una zona; **to** ~ **a process** supervisar un proceso

> **!** **police** (= la policía) se utiliza en plural: "The police are coming."

police car n coche m de policía **police constable** n Brit policía m, guardia m **police department** n Am departamento m de policía **police dog** n perro m policía **police force** n cuerpo m de policía

policeman [pə'liːsmən] <-men> n policía m

police officer n agente mf de policía **police station** n comisaría f

policewoman <-women> n mujer f policía

policy¹ ['pɒləsi, Am: 'pɑːlə-] <-ies> n POL, ECON política f; **company** ~ política de empresa; **my** ~ **is to tell the truth whenever possible** tengo por norma decir la verdad siempre que sea posible

policy² ['pɒləsi, Am: 'pɑːlə-] <-ies> n FIN póliza f

policyholder n asegurado, -a m, f **policy maker** n responsable mf de los principios políticos de un partido **policy-making** n no pl formulación f de principios políticos

polio [ˌpəʊliəʊ, Am: ˌpoʊlioʊ] n no pl MED polio f

polish ['pɒlɪʃ, Am: 'pɑːlɪʃ] **I.** n no pl **1.** (for furniture) cera f; (for shoes) betún m; (for silver) abrillantador m; (for nails) esmalte m; **to give sth a** ~ dar brillo a algo **2.** (sophistication) refinamiento m **II.** vt (furniture) sacar brillo a; (shoes, silver) limpiar; fig pulir

◆**polish off** vt (food) despacharse; (opponent) liquidar

Polish ['pəʊlɪʃ, Am: 'poʊ-] adj polaco

polished adj **1.** (shiny) pulido **2.** fig

distinguido; **a ~ performance** una actuación impecable

polite [pə'laɪt] *adj* **1.** (*courteous*) atento; **~ refusal** declinación *f* cortés **2.** (*cultured*) educado; **~ society** buena sociedad *f*

politeness *n no pl* cortesía *f*

political [pə'lɪtɪkəl, *Am:* -'lɪt̬ə-] *adj* político

politician [ˌpɒlɪ'tɪʃən, *Am:* ˌpɑːlə'-] *n* político, -a *m, f*

politicize [pe'lɪtɪsaɪz, *Am:* -'lɪt̬ə-] *vt* politizar

politics *n pl* **1.** (*activities of government*) política *f*; **to talk ~** hablar de política **2.** *Brit* (*political science*) ciencias *fpl* políticas

poll [pəʊl, *Am:* poʊl] **I.** *n* encuesta *f*; **opinion ~** sondeo *m* de la opinión pública; **to conduct a ~** hacer una encuesta; **to go to the ~s** acudir a las urnas **II.** *vt* sondear

pollard ['pɒləd, *Am:* 'pɑːləd] *vt* desmochar

pollen ['pɒlən, *Am:* 'pɑːlən] *n no pl* polen *m*

pollen count *n* índice *m* de polen en el aire

pollinate ['pɒlɪneɪt, *Am:* 'pɑːlə-] *vt* polinizar

polling *n no pl* votación *f*

polling booth *n Brit, Aus* cabina *f* electoral **polling day** *n Brit, Aus* día *m* de elecciones **polling place** *n Am*, **polling station** *n Brit, Aus* colegio *m* electoral

pollster ['pəʊlstər, *Am:* 'poʊlstər] *n* encuestador(a) *m(f)*

pollutant [pəl'uːtənt] *n* contaminante *m*

pollute [pə'luːt] *vt* contaminar; **to ~ sb's mind** corromper la mente de alguien

polluter [pə'luːtər, *Am:* -t̬ər] *n* contaminador(a) *m(f)*

pollution [pə'luːʃn] *n no pl* contaminación *f*

polo ['pəʊləʊ, *Am:* 'poʊloʊ] *n no pl* SPORTS polo *m*

polo shirt *n* polo *m*

poly ['pɒli, *Am:* 'pɑːli] *n Brit, inf abbr of* **polytechnic** escuela *f* poli-

técnica

polyester [ˌpɒli'estər, *Am:* ˌpɑːli'estər] *n no pl* poliéster *m*

polygamy [pə'lɪgəmi] *n no pl* poligamia *f*

polygon ['pɒlɪgən, *Am:* 'pɑːlɪgɑːn] *n* polígono *m*

Polynesia [ˌpɒlɪ'niːʒə, *Am:* ˌpɑːlə'niːʒə] *n* Polinesia *f*

polyp ['pɒlɪp, *Am:* 'pɑːlɪp] *n* pólipo *m*

polystyrene [ˌpɒlɪ'staɪəriːn, *Am:* ˌpɑːlɪ-] *n no pl, Brit, Aus* poliestireno *m*

polytechnic [ˌpɒlɪ'teknɪk, *Am:* ˌpɑːlɪ-] *n* escuela *f* politécnica

polythene ['pɒlɪθiːn, *Am:* 'pɑːlɪ-] *n no pl* polietileno *m*

polythene bag *n Brit, Aus* bolsa *f* de polietileno

polyunsaturated fats [ˌpɒliʌn'sætʃəreɪtɪd-, *Am:* ˌpɑːliʌn'sætʃəreɪt̬ɪd-] *npl* grasas *fpl* poliinsaturadas

polyurethane [ˌpɒlɪ'jʊərəθeɪn, *Am:* ˌpɑːlɪ'jʊrə-] *n no pl* poliuretano *m*

pomegranate ['pɒmɪgrænɪt, *Am:* 'pɑːmˌgræn-] *n* (*fruit*) granada *f*; (*tree*) granado *m*

pomp [pɒmp, *Am:* pɑːmp] *n no pl* **~ and circumstance** pompa y solemnidad

pomposity [pɒm'pɒsəti, *Am:* pɑːm'pɑːsət̬i] *n no pl* pomposidad *f*

pompous ['pɒmpəs, *Am:* 'pɑːm-] *adj* pomposo

ponce [pɒns, *Am:* pɑːns] *n* **1.** *Brit, Aus, pej* (*effeminate man*) mariquita *m* **2.** *Brit, inf* (*pimp*) chulo *m*

pond [pɒnd, *Am:* pɑːnd] *n* (*natural*) charca *f*; (*artificial*) estanque *m*; **duck ~** estanque de patos; **fish ~** vivero *m*

ponder ['pɒndər, *Am:* 'pɑːndər] **I.** *vt* considerar **II.** *vi* **to ~ on sth** meditar sobre algo; **to ~ whether ...** preguntarse si ...

ponderous ['pɒndərəs, *Am:* 'pɑːn-] *adj* (*movement*) pesado; (*style*) laborioso

pong [pɒŋ, *Am:* pɑːŋ] *inf* **I.** *n Brit*,

Aus peste *f* **II.** *vi Brit, Aus, pej* **to ~ of sth** apestar a algo

pontificate [pɒn'tɪfɪkeɪt, *Am:* pɑ:n-] *vi pej* pontificar

pontoon [pɒn'tu:n, *Am:* pɑ:n-] *n* **1.** (*floating device*) pontón *m* **2.** *no pl, Brit* (*card game*) veintiuna *f*

pony ['pəʊni, *Am:* 'poʊ-] <-ies> *n* poni *m*

ponytail *n* coleta *f*

poo [pu:] *s.* **pooh**

poodle ['pu:dl] *n* caniche *m*

poof [pu:f] *n Brit, Aus, pej* maricón *m*

pooh [pu:] *n Brit, Aus, childspeak* caca *f;* **to do a ~** hacer caca

pool[1] [pu:l] *n* **1.** (*of water*) charca *f;* (*artificial*) estanque *m;* (*of oil, blood*) charco *f;* **a ~ of light** un foco de luz; **swimming ~** piscina *f,* pileta *f RíoPl*

pool[2] [pu:l] **I.** *n* **1.** (*common fund*) fondo *m* común; **car ~** parque *m* de automóviles; **gene ~** acervo *m* genético **2.** SPORTS billar *m* americano **3.** *pl, Brit* (*football*) **~s** quiniela *f* **II.** *vt* (*money, resources*) hacer un fondo común de; (*information*) compartir

pool hall *n* sala *f* de billar **pool table** *n* mesa *f* de billar

poor [pʊəʳ, *Am:* pʊr] **I.** *adj* **1.** (*lacking money*) pobre; **you ~ thing!** ¡pobrecito! **2.** (*attendance, harvest*) escaso; (*memory, performance*) malo; **~ visibility** visibilidad *f* escasa; **to be ~ at sth** no estar fuerte en algo; **to be in ~ health** estar mal de salud; **to be a ~ loser** no saber perder; **to be a ~ excuse for sth** ser una mala versión de algo; **to have ~ eyesight** tener mala vista; **to have ~ hearing** ser duro de oído **II.** *n* **the ~** los pobres

poorhouse *n* HIST asilo *m* de los pobres

poorly ['pʊəli, *Am:* 'pʊr-] **I.** *adv* **1. to be ~ off** andar escaso de dinero **2.** (*inadequately*) mal; **~ dressed** mal vestido; **to think ~ of sb** tener mala opinión de alguien **II.** *adj* **to feel ~** encontrarse mal

pop[1] [pɒp, *Am:* pɑ:p] *n no pl* MUS pop *m*

pop[2] *n inf* (*father*) papá *m*

pop[3] **I.** *n* **1.** (*small explosive noise*) pequeña explosión *f* **2.** (*drink*) gaseosa *f;* **fizzy ~** bebida *f* gaseosa **II.** <-pp-> *vi* **1.** (*explode*) estallar; (*burst*) reventar **2.** (*go, come quickly*) **to ~ upstairs** subir un momento; **to ~ out for sth** salir un momento a por algo **III.** <-pp-> *vt* **1.** (*make burst*) hacer estallar **2.** (*put quickly*) **to ~ sth on** ponerse algo
♦ **pop up** *vi* (*appear*) aparecer

pop concert *n* concierto *m* pop

popcorn *n no pl* palomitas *fpl* de maíz, pororó *m CSur,* cacalote *m AmC, Méx*

pope [pəʊp, *Am:* poʊp] *n* papa *m*

pop group *n* grupo *m* pop

pop gun *n* pistola *f* de juguete

poplar ['pɒpləʳ, *Am:* 'pɑ:plɚ] *n* álamo *m*

pop music *n no pl* música *f* pop

poppy ['pɒpi, *Am:* 'pɑ:pi] <-ies> *n* amapola *f*

pop singer *n* cantante *mf* pop **pop song** *n* canción *f* pop **pop star** *n* estrella *f* del pop

populace ['pɒpjʊləs, *Am:* 'pɑ:pjəlɪs] *n no pl* **the ~** el pueblo

popular ['pɒpjʊləʳ, *Am:* 'pɑ:pjələʳ] *adj* popular; **he is ~ with girls** tiene éxito con las chicas; **~ front** frente *m* popular; **by ~ request** a petición del público

popularity [ˌpɒpjʊ'lærəti, *Am:* ˌpɑ:pjə'lerət̬i] *n no pl* popularidad *f*

popularize ['pɒpjʊləraɪz, *Am:* 'pɑ:pjə-] *vt* popularizar

popularly ['pɒpjʊləli, *Am:* 'pɑ:pjəlɚ-] *adv* generalmente

populate ['pɒpjəleɪt, *Am:* 'pɑ:pjə-] *vt* poblar

population [ˌpɒpjə'leɪʃən, *Am:* ˌpɑ:pjə'-] *n* población *f;* **the working ~** la población activa

populous ['pɒpjʊləs, *Am:* 'pɑ:pjə-] *adj form* populoso

porcelain ['pɔ:səlɪn, *Am:* 'pɔ:r-] *n no pl* porcelana *f*

porch [pɔ:tʃ, *Am:* pɔ:rtʃ] *n* **1.** (*over*

entrance) porche *m* **2.** *Am* (*verandah*) veranda *f*

porcupine ['pɔːkjʊpaɪn, *Am:* 'pɔːr-] *n* puercoespín *m*

pore [pɔːʳ, *Am:* pɔːr] *n* poro *m*
♦ **pore over** *vi* **to ~ a book/map** estudiar detenidamente un libro/mapa

pork [pɔːk, *Am:* pɔːrk] *n no pl* (carne *f* de) cerdo *m*, (carne *f* de) puerco *m Méx*, (carne *f* de) chancho *m Chile, Perú*

porky <-ier, -iest> *adj pej, inf* gordinflón

porn [pɔːn, *Am:* pɔːrn] *n abbr of* **pornography** porno *m*

pornographic [ˌpɔːnəˈgræfɪk, *Am:* ˌpɔːrnəˈ-] *adj* pornográfico

pornography [pɔːˈnɒgrəfi, *Am:* pɔːrˈnɑːgrə-] *n no pl* pornografía *f*

porous ['pɔːrəs] *adj* poroso

porpoise ['pɔːpəs, *Am:* 'pɔːr-] *n* marsopa *f*

porridge ['pɒrɪdʒ, *Am:* 'pɔːr-] *n no pl* ≈ gachas *fpl* de avena

port¹ [pɔːt, *Am:* pɔːrt] *n* NAUT, INFOR puerto *m*; **~ of call** puerto de escala; **to come into ~** tomar puerto; **to leave ~** zarpar; **any ~ in a storm** *prov* en tiempos de guerrra cualquier hoyo es trinchero

port² [pɔːt, *Am:* pɔːrt] *n no pl* AVIAT, NAUT babor *m*; **to ~ a babor**

port³ [pɔːt, *Am:* pɔːrt] *n no pl* (*wine*) oporto *m*

portable ['pɔːtəbl, *Am:* 'pɔːrt̬ə-] *adj* portátil

portal ['pɔːtəl, *Am:* 'pɔːrt̬əl] *n* portal *m*

portcullis [ˌpɔːtˈkʌlɪs, *Am:* ˌpɔːrt-] <-es> *n* rastrillo *m*

porter ['pɔːtəʳ, *Am:* 'pɔːrt̬ɚ] *n* RAIL mozo *m* de equipajes; (*in hospital*) camillero *m*; (*on expedition*) porteador *m*; *Brit* (*doorkeeper*) portero *m*; **~'s lodge** conserjería *f*

portfolio [pɔːtˈfəʊliəʊ, *Am:* pɔːrtˈfoʊlioʊ] *n* **1.** (*case*) portafolio(s) *m* (*inv*) **2.** (*drawings, designs*) carpeta *f* de trabajos **3.** FIN, POL cartera *f*

porthole ['pɔːθəʊl, *Am:* 'pɔːrthoʊl] *n* portilla *f*

portico ['pɔːtɪkəʊ, *Am:* 'pɔːrt̬ɪkoʊ] <-es *o* -s> *n* pórtico *m*

portion ['pɔːʃən, *Am:* 'pɔːr-] *n* (*part*) parte *f*; (*of food*) ración *f*

portly ['pɔːtli, *Am:* 'pɔːrt-] <-ier, -iest> *adj* corpulento

portrait ['pɔːtrɪt, *Am:* 'pɔːrtrɪt] *n* retrato *m*; **to paint a ~ of sb** retratar a alguien

portray [pɔːˈtreɪ, *Am:* pɔːrˈ-] *vt* (*person*) retratar; (*scene, environment*) representar; *fig* describir

portrayal [pɔːˈtreɪəl, *Am:* pɔːrˈ-] *n* ART retrato *m*; *fig* descripción *f*

Portugal ['pɔːtjʊgəl, *Am:* 'pɔːrtʃə-gəl] *n* Portugal *m*

Portuguese [ˌpɔːtjʊˈgiːz, *Am:* ˌpɔːrtʃəˈ-] *adj* portugués

pose¹ [pəʊz, *Am:* poʊz] *vt* (*difficulty, problem*) plantear; (*question*) formular; **to ~ a threat to sb** representar una amenaza para alguien

pose² [pəʊz, *Am:* poʊz] **I.** *vi* ART, PHOT posar; **to ~ as sth** hacerse pasar por algo **II.** *n* **it's all a ~** es todo fachada

poser ['pəʊzəʳ, *Am:* 'poʊzɚ] *n* **1.** *inf* (*question*) pregunta *f* difícil; (*problem*) dilema *m* **2.** *pej* (*person*) **he's a ~** se hace el interesante

posh [pɒʃ, *Am:* pɑːʃ] *adj inf* **1.** (*stylish: area*) elegante; (*car, hotel, restaurant*) de lujo **2.** *Brit* (*person, accent*) pijo, cheto *CSur*

posit ['pɒzɪt, *Am:* 'pɑːzɪt] *vt form* postular

position [pəˈzɪʃn] **I.** *n* **1.** (*situation*) posición *f*; **to be in ~** estar en su sitio; **to be out of ~** estar fuera de lugar; **to take up a ~ on sth** *fig* adoptar una postura sobre algo; **financial ~** situación económica; **to be in a ~ to do sth** estar en condiciones de hacer algo; **to be in no ~ to do sth** no estar en condiciones de hacer algo; **to put sb in a difficult ~** poner a alguien en un aprieto **2.** *Brit, Aus* (*rank*) posición *f*; **the ~ of director** el cargo de director; **a ~ of responsibility** un puesto de responsabilidad **II.** *vt* colocar

positive ['pɒzətɪv, *Am:* 'pɑːzət̬ɪv]

adj **1.** *a.* MAT positivo; ~ **criticism** crítica *f* constructiva; **to think** ~ ser positivo **2.** (*certain*) definitivo; **to be** ~ **about sth** estar seguro de algo

positively *adv* positivamente; **to answer** ~ contestar afirmativamente; **to** ~ **refuse to do sth** negarse rotundamente a hacer algo

posse ['pɒsi, *Am:* 'pɑːsi] *n* banda *f*

possess [pə'zes] *vt* poseer; **to** ~ **sb** (*anger, fear*) apoderarse de alguien; **what** ~**ed you to do that?** ¿cómo se te ocurrió hacer eso?

possessed [pə'zest] *adj* poseído; **to be** ~ **with sth** estar obsesionado con algo

possession [pə'zeʃn] *n* **1.** *no pl* (*having*) posesión *f;* **to take** ~ **of sth** tomar posesión de algo; **to gain** ~ **of sth** apoderarse de algo; **to be in sb's** ~ estar en poder de alguien; **to have sth in one's** ~ *form* tener algo en su poder **2.** (*item of property*) bien *m*

possessive [pə'zesɪv] *adj* posesivo

possessor [pə'zesəʳ, *Am:* -ɚ] *n* poseedor(a) *m(f)*

possibility [ˌpɒsə'bɪləti, *Am:* ˌpɑːsə'bɪləti] *n* <-ies> posibilidad *f;* **within the bounds of** ~ dentro de lo posible; **is there any** ~ (**that**) …? *form* ¿hay alguna posibilidad de que +*subj*…?; **to have possibilities** tener posibilidades

possible ['pɒsəbl, *Am:* 'pɑːsə-] *adj* posible; **as clean as** ~ lo más limpio posible; **as far as** ~ en lo posible; **as soon as** ~ lo antes posible; **if** ~ si es posible

possibly ['pɒsəbli, *Am:* 'pɑːsə-] *adv* **1.** (*perhaps*) quizás; **could you** ~ **help me?** ¿sería tan amable de ayudarme? **2.** (*by any means*) **we did all that we** ~ **could** hicimos todo lo posible

possum ['pɒsəm, *Am:* 'pɑːsəm] <-(s)> *n* zarigüeya *f*

post¹ [pəʊst, *Am:* poʊst] **I.** *n no pl, Brit* correo *m;* **by** ~ por correo **II.** *vt Brit, Aus* echar (al correo); **to** ~ **sb sth** enviar algo por correo a alguien

post² [pəʊst, *Am:* poʊst] *n* (*job*) puesto *m;* **to take up a** ~ entrar en funciones; **to desert one's** ~ MIL desertar del puesto

post³ [pəʊst, *Am:* poʊst] **I.** *n* poste *m; inf* (*goalpost*) poste *m* (de portería) **II.** *vt Brit, Aus* **to** ~ **sth** (**on sth**) fijar algo (en algo); **to** ~ **sth on the noticeboard** poner algo en el tablón de anuncios

postage ['pəʊstɪdʒ, *Am:* 'poʊ-] *n no pl* franqueo *m;* ~ **and packing** gastos *mpl* de envío

postage meter *n Am* (máquina *f*) franqueadora *f,* estampilladora *f AmL*

postage paid *adj* con franqueo pagado **postage stamp** *n form* sello *m,* estampilla *f AmL*

postal ['pəʊstəl, *Am:* 'poʊ-] *adj* postal

postal order *n* giro *m* postal

postbag *n Brit* **1.** (*bag*) saca *f* (postal) **2.** (*letters*) correspondencia *f* **postbox** <-es> *n Brit, Aus* buzón *m* **postcard** *n* (tarjeta *f*) postal *f* **postcode** *n Brit* código *m* postal

poster ['pəʊstəʳ, *Am:* 'poʊstɚ] *n* (*notice*) cartel *m;* (*picture*) póster *m*

posterity [pɒ'sterəti, *Am:* pɑː'-] *n no pl, form* posteridad *f;* **to preserve sth for** ~ guardar algo para la posteridad

postgraduate [ˌpəʊst'grædʒuət, *Am:* ˌpoʊst'grædʒuwɪt] **I.** *n* postgraduado, -a *m, f* **II.** *adj* de postgrado

posthumous ['pɒstjəməs, *Am:* 'pɑːstʃəməs] *adj form* póstumo

posting ['pəʊstɪŋ, *Am:* 'poʊ-] *n* destino *m*

postman <-men> *n Brit* cartero *m* **postmark** *n* matasellos *m inv* **postmaster** *n* jefe *m* de la oficina de correos

post-modern *adj* posmoderno

postmortem [ˌpəʊst'mɔːtəm, *Am:* ˌpoʊst'mɔːrtəm] *n* autopsia *f*

postnatal [ˌpəʊst'neɪtəl, *Am:* ˌpoʊst'neɪtəl] *adj* postnatal; ~ **depression** depresión *f* posparto

Post Office *n* (oficina *f* de) correos *m* **postpone** [pəʊst'pəʊn, *Am:* poʊst'poʊn] *vt* aplazar, postergar *AmL*

postponement *n* aplazamiento *m,*

postergación *f AmL*

postscript ['pəʊstskrɪp, *Am:* 'poʊs-] *n* posdata *m; fig* epílogo *m*

postulate ['pɒstjəleɪt, *Am:* 'pɑːstʃə-] *vt form* **1.** (*hypothesize*) postular **2.** (*assume*) presuponer

posture ['pɒstʃəʳ, *Am:* 'pɑːstʃɚ] *n no pl* postura *f*

postwar *adj* de la posguerra

pot [pɒt, *Am:* pɑːt] *n* **1.** (*container*) bote *m;* (*for cooking*) olla *f;* (*of food*) tarro *m;* (*for coffee*) cafetera *f;* (*for tea*) tetera *f;* (*for plants*) maceta *f;* ~**s and pans** cacharros *mpl;* ~**s of money** *inf* montones de dinero; **to go to** ~ *inf* echarse a perder; **it's** (**a case of**) **the** ~ **calling the kettle black** dijo la sartén al cazo, apártate que me tiznas **2.** *no pl, inf* (*marijuana*) hierba *f,* mota *f Méx*

potassium [pə'tæsiəm] *n no pl* potasio *m*

potato [pə'teɪtəʊ, *Am:* -t̮oʊ] <-es> *n* patata *f,* papa *f AmL*

potato chips *npl Am, Aus,* **potato crisps** *npl Brit* patatas *fpl* fritas (en bolsa), papas *fpl* chip *AmL* **potato peeler** *n* pelapatatas *m inv,* pelapapas *m inv AmL*

potency ['pəʊtənsi, *Am:* 'poʊ-] *n no pl* fuerza *f*

potent ['pəʊtnt, *Am:* 'poʊ-] *adj* potente

potential [pə'tenʃl, *Am:* poʊ'-] *n no pl* potencial *m*

potentially [pə'tenʃəli, *Am:* poʊ'-] *adv* potencialmente

pothole ['pɒt̮həʊl, *Am:* 'pɑːt̮hoʊl] *n* **1.** (*in road*) bache *m,* pozo *m CSur* **2.** (*underground*) sima *f*

potion ['pəʊʃən, *Am:* 'poʊ-] *n* poción *f*

potter¹ ['pɒtəʳ, *Am:* 'pɑːt̮ɚ] *n* alfarero, -a *m, f*

potter² *vi Brit, fig* entretenerse

pottery ['pɒtəri, *Am:* 'pɑːt̮ɚ-] *n* **1.** *no pl* (*art*) cerámica *f* **2.** <-ies> (*workshop*) alfarería *f*

potty ['pɒti, *Am:* 'pɑːt̮i] I. <-ier, -iest> *adj Brit, inf* chiflado; **to go** ~ chiflarse; **to drive sb** ~ volver loco a alguien; **to be** ~ **about sb** estar loco

por alguien II. <-ies> *n* orinal *m*

pouch [paʊtʃ] *n* bolsa *f*

poultry ['pəʊltri, *Am:* 'poʊl-] *n pl* aves *fpl* de corral

pounce [paʊns] *vi* saltar; **to** ~ **on sth** abalanzarse sobre algo; **to** ~ **on an opportunity** no dejar escapar una oportunidad

pound¹ [paʊnd] *n* **1.** (*weight*) libra *f* (*454 g*) **2.** (*currency*) libra *f;* ~ **sterling** libra esterlina

pound² [paʊnd] *n* (*for cars*) depósito *m;* (*for dogs*) perrera *f*

pound³ [paʊnd] I. *vt* **1.** (*beat*) golpear **2.** (*crush*) machacar II. *vi* (*heart*) latir con fuerza; **my head is** ~**ing!** ¡me estalla la cabeza!

pounding ['paʊndɪŋ] *n* (*noise*) golpeteo *m;* **to take a** ~ *a. fig* recibir una paliza

pour [pɔːʳ, *Am:* pɔːr] I. *vt* vertir; (*money, resources*) invertir; **to** ~ **wine** echar vino; **to** ~ **scorn on sth** burlarse de algo II. *vi* (*water*) fluir; **it's** ~**ing** (**with rain**) llueve a cántaros

♦ **pour in** *vi* llegar en abundancia

♦ **pour out** I. *vt* vertir II. *vi* (*liquid*) salir; (*people*) salir en tropel

pout [paʊt] *vi* hacer un mohín

poverty ['pɒvəti, *Am:* 'pɑːvɚt̮i] *n no pl* pobreza *f*

poverty line *n* **to live below the** ~ carecer de lo necesario para vivir

POW [ˌpiːəʊ'dʌbljuː, *Am:* -oʊ'-] *n abbr of* **prisoner of war** prisionero *m* de guerra

powder ['paʊdəʳ, *Am:* -dɚ] I. *n no pl* polvo *m* II. *vt* empolvar; **to** ~ **one's nose** *fig* ir al servicio

powdered *adj* en polvo

powder keg *n fig* polvorín *m* **powder puff** *n* borla *f,* cisne *m RíoPl* **powder room** *n* tocador *m*

powdery ['paʊdəri] *adj* como de polvo

power ['paʊəʳ, *Am:* 'paʊɚ] I. *n* **1.** *no pl* (*ability to control*) poder *m;* (*strength*) fuerza *f* **2.** (*country, organization*) potencia *f;* **the** ~**s that be** las autoridades **3.** (*right*) derecho *m* **4.** *no pl* (*electricity*) electricidad *f*

II. *vt* impulsar

powerboat *n* lancha *f* fuera borda

power cable *n* cable *m* de transmisión **power cut** *n* Brit, Aus apagón *m*

power-driven *adj* eléctrico

powerful ['pauəfəl, *Am:* 'pauɚ-] *adj* **1.** (*influential*) poderoso; (*emotionally*) intenso **2.** (*strong*) fuerte

powerfully ['pauəfəli, *Am:* 'pauɚ-] *adv* con potencia; (*argue*) de forma convincente

powerhouse *n* **to be a ~ of ideas** *fig* ser una fuente inagotable de ideas

powerless ['pauələs, *Am:* 'pauɚ-] *adj* impotente; **to be ~ against sb** no poder hacer nada contra alguien

power plant *n* central *f* eléctrica

power station *n* central *f* eléctrica

PR [piːˈɑːʳ, *Am:* -ˈɑːr] *n no pl abbr of* **public relations** relaciones *fpl* públicas

practical ['præktɪkl] *adj* práctico

practicality [ˌpræktɪˈkæləti, *Am:* - t̬i] *n* <-ies> viabilidad *f;* **the practicalities of sth** los detalles prácticos de algo

practically ['præktɪkəli, *Am:* -kli] *adv* **1.** (*almost*) casi **2.** (*of practical nature*) **to be ~ based** basarse en la práctica

practice ['præktɪs] I. *n* **1.** *no pl* (*act of practising*) práctica *f;* **to be out of ~** estar desentrenado; **~ makes perfect** *prov* se aprende con la práctica **2.** (*custom*) costumbre *f;* **to make a ~ of sth** tener algo como norma **3.** *no pl* (*of profession*) ejercicio *m* II. *vt Am s.* **practise**

practiced ['præktɪst] *adj Am s.* **practised**

practise ['præktɪs] *Brit, Aus* I. *vt* **1.** (*carry out*) practicar; **to ~ what one preaches** predicar con el ejemplo **2.** (*improve skill*) hacer ejercicios de **3.** (*profession*) ejercer II. *vi* **1.** (*improve skill*) practicar; SPORTS entrenar **2.** (*work in profession*) ejercer

practised ['præktɪst] *adj Brit, Aus* experto

practising ['præktɪsɪŋ] *adj Brit, Aus*

(*professional*) en ejercicio; REL practicante

practitioner [prækˈtɪʃənəʳ, *Am:* -ɚ] *n form* (*doctor*) médico, -a *m, f*

pragmatic [prægˈmætɪk, *Am:* -ˈmæt̬-] *adj* pragmático

pragmatism ['prægmətɪzəm] *n* pragmatismo *m*

prairie ['preəri, *Am:* 'preri] *n* pradera *f*

praise [preɪz] I. *vt* (*express approval*) elogiar; (*worship*) alabar II. *n no pl* (*approval*) elogio *m;* (*worship*) alabanza *f*

pram [præm] *n Brit, Aus* cochecito *m*

prank [præŋk] *n* broma *f*

prattle ['prætl, *Am:* 'præt̬-] *vi pej* parlotear

prawn [prɔːn, *Am:* prɑːn] *n* gamba *f*

pray [preɪ] *vi* REL rezar; **to ~ for sth** rogar algo

prayer [preəʳ, *Am:* prer] *n* REL oración *f;* **to say a ~** rezar

prayer book *n* devocionario *m* **prayer rug** *n* alfombra *f* de oración

praying mantis [-ˈmæntɪs, *Am:* -t̬ɪs] *n* mantis *f inv* religiosa

preach [priːtʃ] *vi, vt* predicar

preacher ['priːtʃəʳ, *Am:* -ɚ] *n* predicador(a) *m(f)*

preamble [priːˈæmbl] *n form* preámbulo *m*

prearrange [ˌpriːəˈreɪndʒ] *vt* organizar de antemano

precarious [prɪˈkeəriəs, *Am:* -ˈkeri-] *adj* precario

precaution [prɪˈkɔːʃn, *Am:* -ˈkɑː-] *n* precaución *f*

precede [prɪˈsiːd] *vt* preceder

precedence ['presɪdəns, *Am:* 'presə-] *n no pl* prioridad *f;* **to take ~ over sb** tener prioridad sobre alguien

precedent ['presɪdənt, *Am:* 'presə-] *n* precedente *m;* **to set a ~** sentar un precedente

preceding [prɪˈsiːdɪŋ] *adj* precedente

precept ['priːsept] *n form* precepto *m*

precinct ['pri:sɪŋkt] *n* **1.** *Brit* (*enclosed area*) recinto *m* **2.** *Am* distrito *m*

precious ['preʃəs] I. *adj* **1.** (*of great value*) precioso **2.** (*affected*) afectado II. *adv inf* ~ **few** muy pocos

precipice ['presɪpɪs, *Am:* 'presə-] *n* precipicio *m*

precipitate [prɪ'sɪpɪteɪt] *vt* precipitar

precipitous [prɪ'sɪpɪtəs, *Am:* -ţəs] *adj* **1.** (*very steep*) empinado **2.** (*rapid*) apresurado

precise [prɪ'saɪs] *adj* (*measurement*) exacto; (*person*) meticuloso

precisely *adv* **1.** (*exactly*) precisamente **2.** (*carefully*) meticulosamente

precision [prɪ'sɪʒən] *n no pl* **1.** (*accuracy*) precisión *f* **2.** (*care*) exactitud *f*

preclude [prɪ'klu:d] *vt form* excluir

precocious [prɪ'kəʊʃəs, *Am:* -'koʊ-] *adj* precoz

preconceived [ˌpri:kən'si:vd] *adj* preconcebido

preconception [ˌpri:kən'sepʃən] *n* idea *f* preconcebida

precondition [ˌpri:kən'dɪʃən] *n* condición *f* previa

precursor [ˌpri:'kɜ:səʳ, *Am:* prɪ'kɜ:r-səʳ] *n form* precursor(a) *m(f)*

predate [pri:'deɪt] *vt form* preceder

predator ['predətəʳ, *Am:* -ţəʳ] *n* depredador *m*

predatory ['predətri, *Am:* -tɔ:ri] *adj* depredador

predecessor ['pri:dɪsesəʳ, *Am:* 'predəsesəʳ] *n* predecesor(a) *m(f)*

predicament [prɪ'dɪkəmənt] *n form* apuro *m*

predicate ['predɪkeɪt] *vt form* **to be ~d on sth** estar basado en algo

predict [prɪ'dɪkt] *vt* predecir

predictable [prɪ'dɪktəbl] *adj* previsible

prediction [prɪ'dɪkʃən] *n* pronóstico *m*

predisposition [ˌpri:dɪspə'zɪʃn] *n* predisposición *f*

predominance [prɪ'dɒmɪnəns, *Am:* -'dɑ:mə-] *n no pl* predominio *m*

predominant [prɪ'dɒmɪnənt, *Am:* -'dɑ:mə-] *adj* predominante

predominate [prɪ'dɒmɪneɪt, *Am:* -'dɑ:mə-] *vi* predominar

pre-eminent [ˌpri:'emɪnənt] *adj form* preeminente

pre-empt [ˌpri:'empt] *vt form* adelantarse a

prefabricated *adj* prefabricado

preface ['prefɪs] *n* prefacio *m*

prefect ['pri:fekt] *n* prefecto *m*

prefer [prɪ'fɜ:ʳ, *Am:* prɪ'fɜ:r] <-rr-> *vt* **1.** (*like better*) preferir **2.** *Brit* LAW **to ~ charges (against sb)** presentar cargos (en contra de alguien)

preferable ['prefrəbl] *adj* preferible

preferably ['prefrəbli] *adv* preferentemente

preference ['prefrəns] *n* preferencia *f*

preferential [ˌprefə'renʃl] *adj* preferente

preferred [prɪ'fɜ:d, *Am:* prɪ:'fɜ:rd] *adj* preferido

prefigure [ˌpri:'fɪgəʳ, *Am:* -'fɪgjəʳ] *vt form* prefigurar

prefix ['pri:fɪks, *Am:* 'pri:fɪks] <-es> *n* prefijo *m*

pregnancy ['pregnəntsi] *n no pl* embarazo *m*; ZOOL preñez *f*

pregnant ['pregnənt] *adj* **1.** (*woman*) embarazada; (*animal*) preñado; **to become ~** quedarse embarazada **2.** *fig* (*silence, pause*) muy significativo

prehistoric [ˌpri:hɪ'stɒrɪk, *Am:* -'stɔ:r-] *adj* prehistórico

prehistory [ˌpri:'hɪstri] *n no pl* prehistoria *f*

prejudge [ˌpri:'dʒʌdʒ] *vt* prejuzgar

prejudice ['predʒʊdɪs] I. *n* prejuicio *m* II. *vt* **to ~ sb against sth** predisponer a alguien contra algo

prejudiced ['predʒʊdɪst] *adj* (*person*) lleno de prejuicios; (*attitude*) parcial; **to be ~ against sb** estar predispuesto contra alguien

preliminary [prɪ'lɪmɪnəri, *Am:* prɪ'lɪmənər-] I. *adj* preliminar II. <-ies> *n* preparativos *mpl*; SPORTS preliminares *mpl*

P
p

prelude ['prelju:d] *n* preludio *m*

premarital [,pri:'mærɪtl, *Am:* -'merətl] *adj* prematrimonial

premature ['premətʃəʳ, *Am:* ,pri:mə'tʊr] *adj* prematuro

premeditated [,pri:'medɪteɪtɪd, *Am:* -teɪt̬ɪd] *adj* premeditado

premenstrual [,pri:'mentstruəl, *Am:* -strəl] *adj* premenstrual

premier ['premɪəʳ, *Am:* prɪ'mɪr] **I.** *n* POL primer ministro *m* **II.** *adj* primero

premise ['premɪs] *n* **1.** (*of argument*) premisa *f* **2.** *pl* (*shop*) local *m*

premium ['pri:miəm] **I.** *n* (*insurance payment*) prima *f;* (*extra charge*) recargo *m* **II.** *adj* de primera calidad

premium bond *n* Brit bono *m* del Estado (*que participa en un sorteo nacional*)

premonition [,pri:mə'nɪʃn] *n* premonición *f;* **to have a ~ that ...** tener el presentimiento de que...

prenatal [,pri:'neɪtl, *Am:* -t̬l] *adj* prenatal

preoccupation [,pri:ɒkjʊ'peɪʃn, *Am:* pri:ɑːkjuː'-] *n* preocupación *f*

preoccupied [prɪ'ɒkjʊpaɪd, *Am:* pri:'ɑːkjuː-] *adj* **to be ~ about sth** inquietarse por algo; **to be ~ with sth** estar absorto en algo

preoccupy [pri:'ɒkjʊpaɪ, *Am:* pri:-'ɑːkjuː-] <-ie-> *vt* preocupar

prepaid [,pri:'peɪd] *adj* pagado por adelantado

preparation [,prepə'reɪʃn] *n* **1.** *no pl* (*getting ready*) preparación *f* **2.** (*substance*) preparado *m*

preparatory [prɪ'pærətəri, *Am:* -'perətɔːr-] *adj* preliminar

preparatory school *n* Brit escuela *f* privada (*imparte enseñanza primaria*)*; Am* colegio *m* privado (*imparte enseñanza secundaria*)

prepare [prɪ'peəʳ, *Am:* -'per] **I.** *vt* preparar **II.** *vi* prepararse

prepared [prɪ'peəd, *Am:* -'perd] *adj* **1.** (*ready*) listo **2.** (*willing*) dispuesto; **to be ~ to do sth** estar preparado para hacer algo

preponderance [prɪ'pɒndərənts,

Am: -'pɑːn-] *n no pl, form* predominio *m*

preposition [,prepə'zɪʃən] *n* preposición *f*

prepossessing [,pri:pə'zesɪŋ] *adj* agradable, atractivo

preposterous [prɪ'pɒstərəs, *Am:* -'pɑːstɚ-] *adj* ridículo

prerequisite [,pri:'rekwɪzɪt] *n form* **to be a ~ for sth** ser una condición sine qua non para algo

prerogative [prɪ'rɒgətɪv, *Am:* -'rɑːgət̬ɪv] *n form* (*right, privilege*) prerrogativa *f*

Presbyterian [,prezbɪ'tɪəriən, *Am:* -'tɪri-] *adj* presbiteriano

pre-school ['pri:sku:l] *adj* preescolar

prescribe [prɪ'skraɪb] *vt* MED recetar

prescribed [prɪ'skraɪbd] *adj* prescrito

prescription [prɪ'skrɪpʃən] *n* MED receta *f*

prescriptive [prɪ'skrɪptɪv] *adj* preceptivo

presence ['prezənts] *n* presencia *f;* **~ of mind** presencia de ánimo; **in my ~** delante de mí; **to make one's ~ felt** hacerse notar

present¹ ['prezənt] **I.** *n no pl* presente *m;* **at ~** en este momento; **for the ~** por ahora **II.** *adj* **1.** (*current*) actual; **at the ~ moment** en este momento; **up to the ~ time** hasta la fecha **2.** (*in attendance*) presente; **to be ~ at sth** asistir a algo

present² ['prezənt] *n* (*gift*) regalo *m;* **to give sb a ~** hacer un regalo a alguien

present³ [prɪ'zent] *vt* **1.** (*give*) presentar; **to ~ sth (to sb)** entregar algo (a alguien) **2.** (*introduce*) presentar; **to ~ a bill** presentar un proyecto de ley; **to ~ sb with sth** (*confront*) enfrentar a alguien con algo; **to ~ a problem for sb** significar un problema para alguien

presentation [,prezən'teɪʃən] *n* presentación *f;* (*of prize, award*) entrega *f;* **to make a ~** hacer una exposición

present-day [,prezəntdeɪ] *adj* actual

presenter [prɪ'zentə^r, *Am:* prɪ'zen-ţɚ] *n* presentador(a) *m(f)*

presently ['prezəntli] *adv* (*soon*) pronto; (*now*) ahora

preservation [ˌprezə'veɪʃən, *Am:* -ɚ'-] *n no pl* (*of building*) conservación *f*; (*of species, custom*) preservación *f*

preservative [prɪ'zɜːvətɪv, *Am:* -'zɜːrvəţɪv] *n* conservante *m*

preserve [prɪ'zɜːv, *Am:* -'zɜːrv] **I.** *vt* (*customs, peace*) mantener; (*dignity*) conservar; (*silence*) guardar; (*food*) conservar; **to ~ sb from sth** proteger a alguien de algo **II.** *n* **1.** (*jam*) confitura *f* **2.** (*reserve*) coto *m*; **to be the ~ of the rich** ser dominio exclusivo de los ricos

preserved *adj* conservado; (*food*) en conserva

preside [prɪ'zaɪd] *vi* **to ~ over sth** presidir algo

presidency ['prezɪdənsi] *n* POL presidencia *f*; (*of company*) dirección *f*

president ['prezɪdənt] *n* POL presidente, -a *m, f*; (*of company*) director(a) *m(f)*

presidential [ˌprezɪ'dentʃəl] *adj* presidencial

press [pres] **I.** *vt* **1.** (*button*) pulsar; (*grapes, olives*) prensar; **to ~ sb to do sth** presionar a alguien para que haga algo; **to ~ sb for sth** exigir algo de alguien; **to ~ sth on sb** imponer algo a alguien; **to ~ a claim** insistir en una petición; **to ~ charges** LAW presentar cargos **2.** (*iron*) planchar **3.** (*album, disk*) imprimir **II.** *vi* apretar; **time is ~ing** el tiempo apremia; **to ~ for sth** insistir para conseguir algo **III.** *n* **1.** (*push*) presión *f*; **at the ~ of a button** apretando un botón **2.** (*machine*) prensa *f*; **printing ~** imprenta *f*; **to go to ~** (*newspaper, book*) ir a imprenta; **the ~** PUBL la prensa; **to have a good ~** tener buena prensa

◆ **press on** *vi* seguir adelante

press agency *n* PUBL agencia *f* de prensa **press conference** *n* PUBL

rueda *f* de prensa

press-gang *vt* **to ~ sb into doing sth** forzar a alguien a hacer algo

pressing *adj* urgente

press office *n* oficina *f* de prensa **press officer** *n* encargado, -a *m, f* de prensa **press release** *n* PUBL comunicado *m* de prensa

press-stud *n* Aus, Brit broche *m* automático

press-up *n* Brit SPORTS flexión *f* de brazos

pressure ['preʃə^r, *Am:* -ɚ] **I.** *n* presión *f*; MED tensión *f*; **to be under ~** *a. fig* estar bajo presión; **to put ~ on sb** (**to do sth**) presionar a alguien (para que haga algo) **II.** *vt* **to ~ sb to do sth** presionar a alguien para que haga algo

pressure cooker *n* olla *f* a presión, olla *f* presto *Méx* **pressure group** *n* POL grupo *m* de presión

prestige [pre'stiːʒ] *n no pl* prestigio *m*

prestigious [pre'stɪdʒəs] *adj* prestigioso

presumably [prɪ'zjuːməbli, *Am:* prɪ'zuːmə-] *adv* presumiblemente

presume [prɪ'zjuːm, *Am:* prɪ'zuːm] *vt* suponer; **to ~ that ...** imaginarse que...; **to ~ to do sth** (*dare*) atreverse a hacer algo

presumption [prɪ'zʌmpʃn] *n* **1.** (*assumption*) suposición *f* **2.** *no pl, form* (*arrogance*) presunción *f*

presumptuous [prɪ'zʌmptjʊəs, *Am:* -tʃuːəs] *adj* impertinente

presuppose [ˌpriːsə'pəʊz, *Am:* -'poʊz] *vt form* suponer

presupposition [ˌpriːsʌpə'zɪʃən] *n* presuposición *f*

pre-tax *adj* antes de impuestos, bruto

pretence [prɪ'tents, *Am:* 'priːtents] *n no pl* pretensión *f*; **to make no ~ of sth** no disimular algo; **under** (**the**) **~ of ...** con el pretexto de...

pretend [prɪ'tend] **I.** *vt* **1.** (*make believe*) fingir; **to ~ to be interested** fingir interés; **to ~ to be sb** hacerse pasar por alguien **2.** (*claim*) pretender; **I don't ~ to know** no pretendo saber **II.** *vi* fingir

pretended *adj* fingido

pretender *n* pretendiente *mf*

pretense [prɪ'tents, *Am:* 'pri:tents] *n no pl, Am s.* **pretence**

pretension [prɪ'tentʃən] *n* pretensión *f*

pretentious [prɪ'tentʃəs] *adj pej* pretencioso

pretext ['pri:tekst] *n* pretexto *m;* **under the ~ of doing sth** so pretexto de hacer algo *form*

pretty ['prɪti, *Am:* 'prɪt̬-] **I.** *adj* <-ier, -iest> (*thing*) bonito, lindo *AmL;* (*child, woman*) guapo, lindo *AmL;* **not a ~ sight** nada agradable de ver; **a ~ mess** *inf* menudo lío **II.** *adv* (*quite*) bastante; **~ much** más o menos

prevail [prɪ'veɪl] *vi* predominar; **to ~ over sb** triunfar sobre alguien; **to ~ upon sb to do sth** *form* convencer a alguien para que haga algo

prevailing *adj* predominante

prevalence ['prevələnts] *n no pl* preponderancia *f*

prevalent ['prevələnt] *adj* extendido

prevaricate [prɪ'værɪkeɪt, *Am:* prɪ'verɪ-] *vi form* andarse con rodeos

prevent [prɪ'vent] *vt* prevenir; **to ~ sb from doing sth** impedir que alguien haga algo

prevention [prɪ'ventʃən] *n no pl* prevención *f*

preventive [prɪ'ventɪv, *Am:* -t̬ɪv] *adj* preventivo

preview ['pri:vju:] *n* CINE, THEAT preestreno *m;* (*of programme, exhibition*) adelanto *m*

previous ['pri:viəs] *adj* anterior; **without ~ notice** sin previo aviso

previously *adv* previamente; **to have met sb ~** haber visto a alguien antes

pre-war *adj* de antes de la guerra

prey [preɪ] *n no pl* (*animal*) presa *f;* (*person*) víctima *f;* **to fall ~ to** (*animal*) ser presa de; (*person*) ser víctima de

♦ **prey (up)on** *vt* **1.** (*feed on*) alimentarse de **2.** (*exploit*) aprovecharse de

price [praɪs] **I.** *n* precio *m;* **to go up/down in ~** subir/bajar de precio; **not at any ~** *fig* por nada del mundo; **to pay a heavy ~** *fig* pagarlo caro; **at a ~** *fig* a un precio muy alto **II.** *vt* poner precio a

priceless ['praɪslɪs] *adj* **to be ~** no tener precio; **that's ~!** *fig* ¡eso es para partirse de risa!, ¡eso es un plato! *AmL*

price level *n* nivel *m* de precios

price war *n* guerra *f* de precios

pricing ['praɪsɪŋ] *n* fijación *f* de precios

prick [prɪk] **I.** *vt* (*jab*) pinchar; (*mark with holes*) agujerear; **to ~ sb's conscience** hacer que a alguien le remuerda la conciencia **II.** *vi* pinchar **III.** *n* **1.** (*of pin, sensation*) pinchazo *m* **2.** *vulg* (*penis*) polla *f,* pija *f RíoPl* **3.** *vulg* (*idiot*) gilipollas *m inv*

prickly ['prɪkli] <-ier, -iest> *adj* (*plant*) espinoso; (*animal*) con púas; (*fabric*) que pica; **~ sensation** picor *m*

pride [praɪd] **I.** *n* **1.** *no pl* (*proud feeling*) orgullo *m;* **to be sb's ~ and joy** ser el orgullo de alguien; **to have ~ of place** ocupar el lugar de honor; **to take ~ in sth** enorgullecerse de algo; **~ comes before a fall** *prov* más dura será la caída **2.** *no pl* (*self-respect*) amor *m* propio; **to swallow one's ~** tragarse el orgullo **3.** ZOOL manada *f* **II.** *vt* **to ~ oneself on** (**doing**) **sth** enorgullecerse de (hacer) algo

priest [pri:st] *n* REL cura *m*

priesthood ['pri:sthʊd] *n no pl* **1.** (*position*) sacerdocio *m* **2.** (*priests*) clero *m*

priestly ['pri:stli] *adj* sacerdotal

priggish ['prɪgɪʃ] *adj pej* mojigato

prim [prɪm] <-mm-> *adj* **1.** *pej* remilgado **2.** (*appearance*) escrupuloso

primacy ['praɪməsi] *n no pl, form* primacía *f*

primaeval [praɪ'mi:vəl] *adj s.* **primeval**

primarily ['praɪmərɪli, *Am:* praɪ'merəl-] *adv* principalmente

primary ['praɪməri, *Am:* -mer-]

I. *adj* **1.** (*principal*) fundamental **2.** (*basic*) *a.* SCHOOL primario; (*industry*) de base **II.** <-ies> *n Am* POL elecciones *fpl* primarias

primate ['praɪmeɪt, *Am:* -mɪt] *n* **1.** ZOOL primate *m* **2.** REL primado *m*

prime [praɪm] **I.** *adj* principal; **of ~ importance** de importancia primordial; **in ~ condition** en perfecto estado **II.** *n no pl* apogeo *m elev;* **to be in one's ~** estar en la flor de la vida; **to be past one's ~** no ser ya ningún jovencito **III.** *vt* (*surface*) aplicar una capa de base sobre; (*gun, pump*) cebar; **to ~ sb for doing sth** preparar a alguien para hacer algo

prime minister *n* POL primer(a) ministro, -a *m, f* **prime number** *n* MAT número *m* primo

primeval [praɪ'mi:vəl] *adj* primigenio

primitive ['prɪmɪtɪv, *Am:* -t̬ɪv] *adj* primitivo

primordial [praɪ'mɔ:diəl, *Am:* -'mɔ:r-] *adj form* primigenio

primrose ['prɪmrəʊz, *Am:* -roʊz] *n* prímula *f*

prince [prɪnts] *n* príncipe *m;* **Prince Charming** príncipe azul

princess [prɪn'ses, *Am:* 'prɪntsɪs] *n* princesa *f*

principal ['prɪntsəpl] **I.** *adj* principal **II.** *n Aus, Am* (*headmaster*) director(a) *m(f);* (*of university*) rector(a) *m(f)*

principality [ˌprɪntsɪ'pæləti, *Am:* -sə'pælət̬i] *n* principado *m*

principally *adv* principalmente

principle ['prɪntsəpl] *n* principio *m*

print [prɪnt] **I.** *n* **1.** TYPO texto *m* impreso; **to appear in ~** publicarse; **to go out of ~** agotarse **2.** (*engraving*) grabado *m;* PHOT positivo *m* **II.** *vt* imprimir; (*publish*) publicar

printer ['prɪntə^r, *Am:* -t̬ə] *n* **1.** (*person*) impresor(a) *m(f)* **2.** INFOR impresora *f*

printing *n* **1.** *no pl* (*art*) imprenta *f* **2.** (*action*) impresión *f*

printing press *n* prensa *f*

print-out *n* INFOR impresión *f*

print run *n* tirada *f*

prior ['praɪə^r, *Am:* 'praɪə] **I.** *adv form* ~ **to ...** antes de... **II.** *adj form* previo

prioritize [praɪ'ɒrɪtaɪz, *Am:* -'ɔ:rə-] *vt* priorizar

priority [praɪ'ɒrəti, *Am:* -'ɔ:rət̬i] <-ies> *n no pl* prioridad *f;* (*in time*) anterioridad *f;* **to get one's priorities right** establecer un orden de prioridades

priory ['praɪəri] *n* priorato *m*

prise [praɪz] *vt Brit, Aus s.* **prize²**

prism [prɪzəm] *n* prisma *m*

prison ['prɪzən] *n* prisión *f;* **to put sb in ~** encarcelar a alguien

prisoner ['prɪzənə^r, *Am:* -ə] *n* preso, -a *m, f;* MIL prisionero, -a *m, f;* **to hold sb ~** detener a alguien; **to take sb ~** hacer prisionero a alguien

prisoner of war *n* prisionero, -a *m, f* de guerra

pristine ['prɪsti:n] *adj form* prístino

privacy ['prɪvəsi, *Am:* 'praɪ-] *n no pl* intimidad *f*

private ['praɪvɪt, *Am:* -vət] **I.** *adj* **1.** (*not public*) privado **2.** (*confidential*) confidencial **II.** *n* MIL soldado *m* raso

privately ['praɪvɪtli, *Am:* -vət-] *adv* **1.** (*in private*) en privado **2.** (*secretly*) en secreto

privation [praɪ'veɪʃən] *n no pl, form* privación *f;* **to suffer ~** pasar apuros

privatization [ˌpraɪvɪtaɪ'zeɪʃən, *Am:* -vət̬ɪ-] *n no pl* privatización *f*

privatize ['praɪvɪtaɪz, *Am:* -və-] *vt* privatizar

privet ['prɪvɪt] *n no pl* alheña *f*

privilege ['prɪvəlɪdʒ] **I.** *n* privilegio *m* **II.** *vt* **to be ~d to do sth** tener el privilegio de hacer algo

privileged ['prɪvəlɪdʒd] *adj* **1.** (*special*) privilegiado **2.** (*confidential*) confidencial

privy ['prɪvi] *adj form* **to be ~ to sth** estar al tanto de algo

prize¹ [praɪz] **I.** *n* premio *m* **II.** *adj inf* de primera; **a ~ idiot** un tonto de remate **III.** *vt* apreciar

prize² *vt* **to ~ sth open** abrir algo por la fuerza

P
p

prize money n SPORTS premio m en metálico

prizewinning adj premiado

pro¹ [prəʊ, Am: proʊ] n inf abbr of **professional** profesional mf

pro² n **the ~s and cons of sth** los pros y los contras de algo

proactive [ˌprəʊˈæktɪv, Am: ˌproʊˈ-] adj con iniciativa

probability [ˌprɒbəˈbɪləti, Am: ˌprɑːbəˈbɪləţi] n probabilidad f; **in all ~** sin duda

probable [ˈprɒbəbl, Am: ˈprɑːbə-] adj probable

probably adv probablemente

probation [prəʊˈbeɪʃən, Am: proʊˈ-] n no pl (in job) período m de prueba; LAW libertad f condicional

probationary [prəʊˈbeɪʃənəri, Am: proʊˈ-] adj de prueba

probe [prəʊb, Am: proʊb] I. vi, vt investigar II. n investigación f; MED, AVIAT sonda f

problem [ˈprɒbləm, Am: ˈprɑː-bləm] n problema m

problematic [ˌprɒbləˈmætɪk, Am: ˌprɑːbləˈmæţ-] adj problemático

procedure [prəˈsiːdʒər, Am: -dʒɚ] n procedimiento m

proceed [prəˈsiːd, Am: proʊˈ-] vi form (move along) seguir; (continue) continuar; **to ~ with sth** (make progress) avanzar con algo; (begin) empezar con algo; **to ~ from** provenir de; **to ~ to do sth** ponerse a hacer algo

proceeds [ˈprəʊsiːdz, Am: ˈproʊ-] n ingresos mpl

process [ˈprəʊses, Am: ˈprɑː-] I. n proceso m; **to be in the ~ of doing sth** estar en vías de hacer algo II. vt procesar; PHOT revelar

processing [ˈprəʊsesɪŋ, Am: ˈprɑː-] n no pl procesamiento m; PHOT revelado m

procession [prəˈseʃən] n desfile m

processor [prəʊˈsesər, Am: prɑː-] n INFOR procesador m

proclaim [prəˈkleɪm, Am: proʊˈ-] vt form proclamar; **to ~ war** declarar la guerra

proclamation [ˌprɒkləˈmeɪʃən,

Am: ˌprɑːklə-] n form proclamación f

procreate [ˈprəʊkrieɪt, Am: ˈproʊ-] vi form procrear

procure [prəˈkjʊər, Am: proʊˈkjʊr] vt form obtener

procurement [prəˈkjʊəmənt, Am: proʊˈkjʊr-] n no pl, form adquisición f

prod [prɒd, Am: prɑːd] I. n golpe m; (with elbow) codazo m; (with sharp object) pinchazo m II. <-dd-> vt golpear; (with elbow) dar un codazo; (with sharp object) pinchar; **to ~ sb (into doing sth)** estimular a alguien (para que haga algo)

prodigal [ˈprɒdɪgl, Am: ˈprɑːdɪ-] adj form pródigo

prodigious [prəˈdɪdʒəs] adj form (size, height) ingente; (achievement, talent) prodigioso

prodigy [ˈprɒdɪdʒi, Am: ˈprɑːdə-] n prodigio m; **child ~** niño, -a m, f prodigio

produce¹ [prəˈdjuːs, Am: -ˈduːs] vt producir; (manufacture) producir; CINE, THEAT, TV realizar; **to ~ a knife** sacar un cuchillo; **to ~ one's passport** enseñar el pasaporte; **to ~ results** producir resultados

produce² [ˈprɒdjuːs, Am: ˈprɑːduːs] n no pl AGR productos mpl agrícolas

producer [prəˈdjuːsər, Am: -ˈduːsɚ] n productor(a) m(f)

product [ˈprɒdʌkt, Am: ˈprɑːdʌkt] n producto m

production [prəˈdʌkʃən] n no pl (of goods) fabricación f; CINE, THEAT, TV producción f

production costs npl costes mpl de producción **production line** n cadena f de montaje

productive [prəˈdʌktɪv] adj productivo

productivity [ˌprɒdʌkˈtɪvəti, Am: ˌproʊdəkˈtɪvəţi] n no pl productividad f

Prof. [prɒf, Am: prɑːf] abbr of **Professor** prof. m, profa. f

profanity [prəˈfænəti, Am: proʊˈfænəţi] n form 1. (blasphemy) blasfemia *f* **2.** (*obscene word*) palabrota *f*

profess [prə'fes] *vt* profesar; **to ~ oneself satisfied** (**with sth**) declararse satisfecho (con algo)

professed [prə'fest] *adj* declarado

profession [prə'feʃn] *n* **1.** (*occupation*) profesión *f* **2.** (*declaration*) declaración *f*

professional [prə'feʃənəl] *adj* profesional

professionalism [prə'feʃənəlɪzəm] *n no pl* profesionalidad *f*

professor [prə'fesə^r, *Am:* -ə-] *n Brit* UNIV catedrático, -a *m, f; Am* SCHOOL profesor(a) *m(f)*

professorship [prə'fesəʃɪp, *Am:* '-ə-] *n* cátedra *f*

proffer ['prɒfə^r, *Am:* 'prɑ:fə^r] *vt form* ofrecer

proficiency [prə'fɪʃnsi] *n no pl* competencia *f*

proficient [prə'fɪʃnt] *adj* competente

profile ['prəʊfaɪl, *Am:* 'proʊ-] *n* **1.** (*side view*) perfil *m*; **in ~** de perfil; **to keep a low ~** *fig* tratar de pasar inadvertido **2.** (*description*) descripción *f*

profit ['prɒfɪt, *Am:* 'prɑ:fɪt] **I.** *n* FIN beneficio *m* **II.** *vi* **to ~ by sth** sacar provecho de algo

profitability [ˌprɒfɪtə'bɪləti, *Am:* ˌprɑ:fɪtə'bɪləti] *n no pl* rentabilidad *f*

profitable ['prɒfɪtəbl, *Am:* 'prɑ:fɪtə-] *adj* rentable

profit margin *n* margen *m* de beneficio

profligate ['prɒflɪgət, *Am:* 'prɑ:flɪgɪt] *adj form* derrochador

profound [prə'faʊnd] *adj* profundo

profuse [prə'fju:s] *adj* profuso

profusion [prə'fju:ʒən] *n no pl, form* profusión *f*

prognosis [prɒg'nəʊsɪs, *Am:* prɑ:g'noʊ-, -] *n form* pronóstico *m*

program, programme ['prəʊgræm, *Am:* 'proʊ-] *Aus, Brit* **I.** *n* programa *m* **II.** <-mm-> *vt* programar

programmer *n* programador(a) *m(f)*

programming *n* programación *f*

progress¹ ['prəʊgres, *Am:* 'prɑ:-] *n no pl* progreso *m*; **to make ~** avanzar; **to be in ~** estar en curso

progress² [prəʊ'gres, *Am:* proʊ-] *vi* progresar

progression [prəʊ'greʃn] *n no pl* progresión *f*

progressive [prə'gresɪv] *adj* progresivo; MED degenerativo; POL progresista

prohibit [prə'hɪbɪt, *Am:* proʊ'-] *vt* prohibir

prohibition [ˌprəʊɪ'bɪʃn, *Am:* ˌproʊ-] *n* prohibición *f*; **the Prohibition** *Am* HIST la Ley Seca

prohibitive [prə'hɪbətɪv, *Am:* proʊ'hɪbət̬ɪv] *adj* prohibitivo

project¹ ['prɒdʒekt, *Am:* 'prɑ:-dʒekt] *n* proyecto *m*; SCHOOL, UNIV trabajo *m*

project² [prəʊ'dʒekt, *Am:* prə-] **I.** *vt* (*forecast*) pronosticar **II.** *vi* sobresalir

projectile [prəʊ'dʒektaɪl, *Am:* prə-'dʒektəl] *n* proyectil *m*

projection [prəʊ'dʒekʃən, *Am:* prə-] *n* **1.** (*forecast*) pronóstico *m* **2.** (*protrusion*) saliente *m*

projector [prə'dʒektə^r, *Am:* -'dʒektə-] *n* proyector *m*

proletarian [prəʊlɪ'teərɪən, *Am:* ˌproʊlə'teri-] *adj* proletario

proletariat [ˌprəʊlɪ'teərɪət, *Am:* ˌproʊlə'teri-] *n no pl* proletariado *m*

proliferate [prə'lɪfəreɪt, *Am:* proʊ'-] *vi* proliferar

proliferation [prəˌlɪfə'reɪʃn, *Am:* proʊ,-] *n no pl* proliferación *f*

prolific [prə'lɪfɪk, *Am:* proʊ'-] *adj* prolífico

prolog *n Am*, **prologue** ['prəʊlɒg, *Am:* 'proʊlɑ:g] *n Brit* prólogo *m*; **to be a ~ to sth** ser un preámbulo de algo

prolong [prə'lɒŋ, *Am:* proʊ'lɑ:ŋ] *vt* prolongar

prom [prɒm, *Am:* prɑ:m] *n* **1.** *Am* (*school dance*) baile *m* **2.** *Brit* (*seafront*) paseo *m* marítimo

promenade [ˌprɒmə'nɑ:d, *Am:*

P
p

‚prɑːməˈneɪd] n Brit (seafront) paseo m marítimo

prominence [ˈprɒmɪnəns, Am: ˈprɑːmə-] n no pl prominencia f; **to give ~ to sth** hacer resaltar algo

prominent [ˈprɒmɪnənt, Am: ˈprɑːmə-] adj **1.** (conspicuous) prominente; (teeth, chin) saliente **2.** (important) importante

promiscuous [prəˈmɪskjuəs] adj pej promiscuo

promise [ˈprɒmɪs, Am: ˈprɑːmɪs] I. vt, vi prometer; **to ~ to do sth** prometer hacer algo II. n **1.** (pledge) promesa f; **to make a ~** prometer **2.** no pl (potential) posibilidad f; **to show ~** demostrar aptitudes

promising adj prometedor

promote [prəˈməʊt, Am: -ˈmoʊt] vt **1.** (in organization) ascender; SPORTS subir **2.** (encourage) promover; COM promocionar

promoter n promotor(a) m(f)

promotion [prəˈməʊʃən, Am: -ˈmoʊ-] n **1.** (organization) ascenso m; **to get a ~** subir en el escalafón **2.** (encouragement) a. COM promoción f

prompt [prɒmpt, Am: prɑːmpt] I. vt **to ~ sb to do sth** estimular a alguien para que haga algo II. adj (quick) rápido; **to be ~** ser puntual

promptly [ˈprɒmptli, Am: ˈprɑːmpt-] adv **1.** (quickly) rápidamente **2.** inf (immediately afterward) puntualmente

promulgate [ˈprɒmlgeɪt, Am: ˈprɑːml-] vt form (theory, belief) divulgar; LAW promulgar

prone [prəʊn, Am: proʊn] I. adj **to be ~ to do sth** ser propenso a hacer algo II. adv form boca abajo

prong [prɒŋ, Am: prɑːŋ] n (of fork) diente m; (of antler) punta f

pronoun [ˈprəʊnaʊn, Am: ˈproʊ-] n pronombre m

pronounce [prəˈnaʊnts] vt **1.** (speak) pronunciar **2.** (declare) declarar; **to ~ that ...** afirmar que...

pronounced adj pronunciado

pronouncement [prəʊˈnaʊntsmənt, Am: ˈprə-] n declaración f; **to**

make a ~ pronunciarse

pronunciation [prəˌnʌntsɪˈeɪʃən] n no pl pronunciación f

proof [pruːf] I. n no pl prueba f; **the burden of ~** el peso de la demostración II. adj **to be ~ against sth** estar a prueba de algo

proofread [ˈpruːfˌriːd] irr vt corregir

prop [prɒp, Am: prɑːp] n **1.** (support) apoyo m **2.** THEAT objeto m de atrezzo

propaganda [ˌprɒpəˈgændə, Am: ˌprɑːpə-] n no pl propaganda f

propagandist [ˌprɒpəˈgændɪst, Am: ˌprɑːpə-] n propagandista mf

propagate [ˈprɒpəgeɪt, Am: ˈprɑːpə-] vt BOT propagar; (lie, rumour) difundir

propagation [ˌprɒpəˈgeɪʃn, Am: ˌprɑːpə-] n no pl BOT propagación f

propel [prəˈpel] <-ll-> vt propulsar

propeller [prəˈpelər, Am: -ə-] n hélice f

propensity [prəˈpensəti, Am: -t̬i] n no pl, form propensión f

proper [ˈprɒpər, Am: ˈprɑːpə-] adj verdadero; (time, method) apropiado; **to be ~ to do sth** ser debido hacer algo

properly [ˈprɒpəli, Am: ˈprɑːpə-li] adv correctamente; **~ dressed** vestido apropiadamente

proper name n, **proper noun** n nombre m propio

property [ˈprɒpəti, Am: ˈprɑːpə-t̬i] <-ies> n propiedad f; LAW bien m inmueble

property developer n ECON promotor(a) m(f) inmobiliario **property market** n no pl mercado m inmobiliario **property owner** n propietario, -a m, f **property tax** n impuesto m sobre la propiedad

prophecy [ˈprɒfəsi, Am: ˈprɑːfə-] <-ies> n profecía f

prophesy [ˈprɒfɪsaɪ, Am: ˈprɑːfə-] <-ie-> vt predecir

prophet [ˈprɒfɪt, Am: ˈprɑːfɪt] n REL profeta, -isa m, f; **~ of doom** catastrofista mf

prophetic [prəˈfetɪk] adj profético

proponent [prəˈpəʊnənt, Am:

-'poʊ-] n defensor(a) m(f)

proportion [prə'pɔːʃən, Am: -'pɔːr-] n 1. (relationship) proporción f; **to be out of ~ to sth** estar desproporcionado con algo; **to be in ~ to sth** estar en proporción con algo; **to keep a sense of ~** mantener un sentido de la medida 2. (part) parte f proporcional 3. pl (size) dimensiones fpl

proportional [prə'pɔːʃənəl, Am: -'pɔːr-] adj, **proportionate** [prə'pɔːʃənət, Am: -'pɔːrʃənɪt] adj proporcional

proposal [prə'pəʊzəl, Am: -'poʊ-] n propuesta f; (offer of marriage) declaración f

propose [prə'pəʊz, Am: -'poʊz] I. vt proponer; (nominate) nombrar; **to ~ a toast** proponer un brindis; **to ~ to do sth** tener la intención de hacer algo II. vi **to ~ (to sb)** declararse (a alguien)

proposition [ˌprɒpə'zɪʃn, Am: ˌprɑːpə'-] n proposición f

propound [prə'paʊnd] vt form proponer

proprietary [prə'praɪətri, Am: -teri] adj propietario; ECON registrado

proprietor [prə'praɪətər, Am: prəʊ'praɪətər] n propietario, -a m, f

propriety [prə'praɪəti, Am: -ti] <-ies> n no pl corrección f

propulsion [prə'pʌlʃən] n no pl propulsión f

pro rata [ˌprəʊ'rɑːtə, Am: ˌprəʊ'reɪtə] I. adj prorrateado II. adv proporcionalmente

prosaic [prə'zeɪɪk, Am: prəʊ'-] adj form prosaico

proscribe [prə'skraɪb, Am: prəʊ'-] vt proscribir

prose [prəʊz, Am: prəʊz] n no pl prosa f

prosecute ['prɒsɪkjuːt, Am: 'prɑːsɪ-] vt LAW procesar

prosecution [ˌprɒsɪ'kjuːʃən, Am: ˌprɑːsɪ'-] n no pl **the ~** la acusación f

prosecutor ['prɒsɪkjuːtər, Am: 'prɑːsɪkjuːtər] n fiscal mf

proselytise vi, **proselytize** ['prɒsəlɪtaɪz, Am: 'prɑːsəlɪ-] vi hacer

proselitismo

prospect ['prɒspekt, Am: 'prɑːspekt] n 1. (possibility) posibilidad f 2. pl (chances) perspectivas fpl

prospective [prə'spektɪv] adj posible; (candidat) futuro

prospectus [prə'spektəs] n prospecto m; UNIV folleto m informativo

prosper ['prɒspər, Am: 'prɑːspər] vi prosperar

prosperity [prɒ'sperəti, Am: prɑː'sperəti] n no pl prosperidad f

prosperous ['prɒspərəs, Am: 'prɑːspər-] adj próspero

prostate (**gland**) ['prɒsteɪt, Am: 'prɑːsteɪt] n próstata f

prostitute ['prɒstɪtjuːt, Am: 'prɑːstətuːt] I. n prostituta f II. vt a. fig **to ~ oneself** prostituirse

prostitution [ˌprɒstɪ'tjuːʃn, Am: -'tʃuː-] n no pl prostitución f

prostrate ['prɒstreɪt, Am: 'prɑːstreɪt] vt **to ~ oneself** postrarse

protagonist [prə'tægənɪst, Am: prəʊ'-] n protagonista mf

protect [prə'tekt] vt proteger

protection [prə'tekʃən] n no pl protección f

protectionism [prə'tekʃənɪzəm] n no pl proteccionismo m

protectionist adj proteccionista

protective [prə'tektɪv] adj protector

protector [prə'tektər, Am: -ər] n protector(a) m(f)

protectorate [prə'tektərət, Am: -ɪt] n protectorado m

protein ['prəʊtiːn, Am: 'prəʊ-] n proteína f

protest¹ ['prəʊtest, Am: 'prəʊtest] n protesta f; (demonstration) manifestación f de protesta; **in ~** en señal de protesta; **to do sth under ~** hacer algo que conste como protesta

protest² [prə'test, Am: prəʊ'-] I. vi protestar; **to ~ against sth** protestar en contra de algo II. vt **to ~ that ...** declarar que...

Protestant ['prɒtɪstənt, Am: 'prɑːtə-] n protestante mf

Protestantism n no pl protestantismo m

protestation [ˌprɒtesˈteɪʃən, *Am:* ˌprɑːˌtesˈteɪ-] *n pl* protesta *f*

protester *n* manifestante *mf*

protest march *n* marcha *f* de protesta **protest vote** *n* voto *m* de protesta

protocol [ˈprəʊtəkɒl, *Am:* ˈproʊtəkɑːl] *n* protocolo *m*

proton [ˈprəʊtɒn, *Am:* ˈproʊtɑːn] *n* protón *m*

prototype [ˈprəʊtətaɪp, *Am:* ˈproʊtə-] *n* prototipo *m*

protracted [prəˈtræktɪd, *Am:* proʊˈ-] *adj* prolongado

protrude [prəˈtruːd, *Am:* proʊˈ-] *vi* sobresalir

protuberance [prəˈtjuːbərəns, *Am:* proʊˈtuː-] *adj form* protuberancia *f*

proud [praʊd] *adj* orgulloso; **to be ~ of sth** enorgullecerse de algo; **to be ~ to do sth** tener el honor de hacer algo

proudly *adv* orgullosamente

prove [pruːv] <proved *o Am:* proven> I. *vt* (*theory*) probar; (*innocence, loyalty*) demostrar; **to ~ sb innocent** probar la inocencia de alguien II. *vi* **to ~ to be sth** resultar ser algo

provenance [ˈprɒvənənts, *Am:* ˈprɑːvən-] *n no pl, form* procedencia *f*

proverb [ˈprɒvɜːb, *Am:* ˈprɑːvɜːrb] *n* refrán *m*

proverbial [prəʊˈvɜːbiəl, *Am:* prəˈvɜːr-] *adj* proverbial

provide [prəʊˈvaɪd, *Am:* prə-] *vt* **1.** proveer; **to ~ sb with sth** proporcionar algo a alguien **2.** *form* LAW estipular

provided *conj* **~ that ...** con tal que... +*subj*

providence [ˈprɒvɪdənts, *Am:* ˈprɑːvə-] *n no pl* providencia *f*

provider *n* **1.** (*person*) proveedor(a) *m(f)* **2.** INFOR proveedor *m;* **Internet Service ~** proveedor de servicios Internet

providing *conj* **~ (that) ...** con tal que... +*subj*

province [ˈprɒvɪnts, *Am:* ˈprɑː-

vɪnts] *n* provincia *f*

provincial [prəʊˈvɪntʃəl, *Am:* prə-ˈvɪntʃəl] *adj* **1.** POL, ADMIN provincial **2.** *pej* (*unsophisticated*) provinciano

provision [prəʊˈvɪʒən, *Am:* prə-] *n* **1.** (*act of providing*) suministro *m;* **to make ~ for sth** tomar medidas de previsión para algo **2.** (*thing provided*) provisión *f* **3.** LAW disposición *f*

provisional [prəʊˈvɪʒənəl, *Am:* prə-] *adj* provisional

provocation [ˌprɒvəˈkeɪʃən, *Am:* ˌprɑːvə-] *n* provocación *f*

provocative [prəˈvɒkətɪv, *Am:* -ˈvɑːkətɪv] *adj* provocador; (*sexually*) provocativo

provoke [prəˈvəʊk, *Am:* -ˈvoʊk] *vt* provocar; (*interest*) despertar; (*crisis*) causar; **to ~ sb into doing sth** provocar a alguien para que haga algo

provost [ˈprɒvəst, *Am:* ˈproʊvoʊst] *n* **1.** *Brit* UNIV rector(a) *m(f)* **2.** *Scot* POL alcalde(sa) *m(f)*

prow [praʊ] *n* NAUT proa *f*

prowess [ˈpraʊɪs] *n no pl, form* destreza *f*

prowl [praʊl] I. *n inf* **to be on the ~** estar merodeando II. *vt* **to ~ the streets** merodear por las calles

proximity [prɒkˈsɪməti, *Am:* prɑːkˈsɪməti] *n no pl, form* proximidad *f*

proxy [ˈprɒksi, *Am:* ˈprɑːk-] <-ies> *n* apoderado, -a *m, f;* **to do sth by ~** hacer algo por poderes

prude [pruːd] *n pej* mojigato, -a *m, f*

prudence [ˈpruːdns] *n no pl* prudencia *f*

prudent [ˈpruːdnt] *adj* prudente

prudish [ˈpruːdɪʃ] *adj pej* mojigato

prune[1] [pruːn] *vt* BOT podar

prune[2] [pruːn] *n* GASTR ciruela *f* pasa

Prussia [ˈprʌʃə] *n* Prusia *f*

Prussian [ˈprʌʃən] *adj* prusiano

pry[1] [praɪ] <pries, pried> *vi pej* **to ~ into sth** entrometerse en algo

pry[2] *vt s.* **prize**[2]

PS [ˌpiːˈes] *abbr of* **postscript** P.D.

psalm [sɑːm] *n* salmo *m*
pseudonym ['sjuːdənɪm, *Am:* 'suː-] *n* seudónimo *m*
psyche ['saɪki] *n* psique *f*
psychedelic [ˌsaɪkɪ'delɪk, *Am:* -kə'-] *adj* psicodélico
psychiatric [ˌsaɪkɪ'ætrɪk] *adj* psiquiátrico
psychiatrist [saɪ'kaɪətrɪst] *n* psiquiatra *mf*
psychiatry [saɪ'kaɪətri] *n no pl* psiquiatría *f*
psychic ['saɪkɪk] *adj* psíquico
psychoanalyse [ˌsaɪkəʊ'ænəlaɪz, *Am:* -koʊ'-] *vt* psicoanalizar
psychoanalysis [ˌsaɪkəʊə'næləsɪs, *Am:* -koʊə'-] *n no pl* psicoanálisis *m inv*
psychoanalyst [ˌsaɪkəʊ'ænəlɪst, *Am:* -koʊ'-] *n* psicoanalista *mf*
psychoanalytic(al) [ˌsaɪkəʊˌænəl'ɪtɪk(əl), *Am:* -koʊˌænə'lɪtɪk(əl)] *adj* psicoanalítico
psychoanalyze [ˌsaɪkəʊ'ænəlaɪz, *Am:* -koʊ'ænəlaɪz] *vt Am s.* **psychoanalyse**
psychological [ˌsaɪkə'lɒdʒɪkəl, *Am:* -kə'lɑːdʒɪ-] *adj* psicológico
psychologist *n* psicólogo, -a *m, f*
psychology [saɪ'kɒlədʒi, *Am:* -'kɑː-lə-] <-ies> *n* psicología *f*
psychopath ['saɪkəʊpæθ, *Am:* -kə-pæθ] *n* psicópata *mf*
psychopathic [ˌsaɪkəʊ'pæθɪk, *Am:* ˌsaɪkə'-] *adj* psicopático
psychosis [saɪ'kəʊsɪs, *Am:* -'koʊ-] <-ses> *n* psicosis *f inv*
psychosomatic [ˌsaɪkəʊsə'mætɪk, *Am:* -koʊsoʊ'mæt-] *adj* psicosomático
psychotherapist [ˌsaɪkə'θerəpɪst, *Am:* -koʊ'-] *n* psicoterapeuta *mf*
psychotherapy [ˌsaɪkəʊ'θerəpi, *Am:* -koʊ'-] *n no pl* psicoterapia *f*
psychotic [saɪ'kɒtɪk, *Am:* -'kɑːtɪk] *adj* psicótico
PT [ˌpiː'tiː] *n abbr of* **physical training** educación *f* física
pt *n abbr of* **pint** pinta *f* (≈ *0,67 litros, Am:* ≈ *0,47 litros*)
pto *abbr of* **please turn over** ver al dorso

pub [pʌb] *n Aus, Brit, inf* bar *m*
puberty ['pjuːbəti, *Am:* -bɚ̩ti] *n no pl* pubertad *f*
pubic ['pjuːbɪk] *adj* pubiano
public ['pʌblɪk] **I.** *adj* público; **to go ~ with sth** revelar algo **II.** *n* público *m*; **in ~** en público
public affairs *npl* asuntos *mpl* públicos **public assistance** *n Am* ayuda *f* estatal
publication [ˌpʌblɪ'keɪʃən] *n no pl* publicación *f*
public defender *n Am* LAW defensor(a) *m(f)* de oficio **public domain** *n* dominio *m* público **public expenditure** *n*, **public expense** *n* gastos *mpl* estatales **public funds** *npl* fondos *mpl* públicos **public health** *n no pl* sanidad *f* pública **public holiday** *n* fiesta *f* oficial **public house** *n Brit, form* bar *m* **public interest** *n* interés *m* público
publicist ['pʌblɪsɪst] *n* publicista *mf*
publicity [pʌb'lɪsəti, *Am:* -ţi] *n no pl* publicidad *f*; **to attract ~** atraer la atención
publicize ['pʌblɪsaɪz] *vt* promocionar
public library <- libraries> *n* biblioteca *f* pública
publicly *adv* en público; **~ owned** de propiedad pública
public opinion *n* opinión *f* pública **public relations** *npl* relaciones *fpl* públicas **public school** *n* **1.** *Brit* (*private*) colegio *m* privado **2.** *Am, Aus* (*state-funded*) escuela *f* pública **public sector** *n* sector *m* público **public-spirited** *adj* solidario **public telephone** *n* teléfono *m* público **public transport** *n* transporte *m* público **public works** *npl* obras *fpl* públicas
publish ['pʌblɪʃ] *vt* publicar; (*information*) divulgar
publisher *n* **1.** (*company*) editorial *f* **2.** (*person*) editor(a) *m(f)*
publishing *n no pl* industria *f* editorial
publishing house *n* editorial *f*
puck [pʌk] *n* SPORTS disco *m*

pudding ['pʊdɪŋ] *n* postre *m*
puddle ['pʌdl] *n* charco *m*
pudgy ['pʊdʒi] <-ier, -iest> *adj* rechoncho
Puerto Rican ['pwɜːtəʊ'riːkən, *Am:* ˌpwertə'-] *adj* portorriqueño
Puerto Rico ['pwɜːtəʊ'riːkəʊ, *Am:* ˌpwertə'riːkoʊ] *n* Puerto Rico *m*
puff [pʌf] I. *vi* (*be out of breath*) jadear II. *vt* 1. (*smoke*) soplar; (*cigarette smoke*) echar 2. (*praise*) dar bombo a 3. (*say while panting*) resoplar III. *n* (*breath, wind*) soplo *m*; **to be out of ~** *Brit, inf* quedarse sin aliento
◆ **puff up** I. *vt* inflar II. *vi* hincharse
puffin ['pʌfɪn] *n* frailecillo *m*
puff pastry *n* hojaldre *m*
puffy ['pʌfi] <-ier, -iest> *adj* hinchado
puke [pjuːk] *vi inf* vomitar
pull [pʊl] I. *vt* 1. (*draw*) tirar de, jalar *AmL*; (*trigger*) apretar; (*gun, knife*) sacar; (*tooth*) extraer; (*muscle*) forzar; **to ~ a fast one** *inf* hacer una jugarreta 2. (*attract*) atraer II. *vi* tirar III. *n* 1. (*action*) tirón *m* 2. *inf* (*influence*) influencia *f*
◆ **pull ahead** *vi* tomar la delantera
◆ **pull apart** *vt insep* 1. hacer pedazos 2. (*criticize*) poner por el suelo
◆ **pull back** *vi* dar marcha atrás
◆ **pull down** *vt* (*demolish*) tirar abajo
◆ **pull in** *vi* llegar
◆ **pull off** *vt inf* **to pull it off** lograrlo
◆ **pull out** *vi* (*to overtake*) salirse; (*drive onto road*) meterse
◆ **pull over** I. *vt* (*police*) parar II. *vi* hacerse a un lado
◆ **pull through** *vi* reponerse
◆ **pull up** I. *vt inf* (*reprimand*) reprender II. *vi* parar
pulley ['pʊli] <-s> *n* polea *f*
pullover ['pʊləʊvəʳ, *Am:* -oʊvəʳ] *n* jersey *m*
pulp [pʌlp] *n* pasta *f*; (*of fruit*) pulpa *f*; (*for making paper*) pulpa *f* de papel; **to beat sb to a ~** *inf* hacer papilla a alguien
pulpit ['pʊlpɪt] *n* púlpito *m*

pulsate [pʌl'seɪt, *Am:* 'pʌlseɪt] *vi* palpitar
pulse¹ [pʌls] *n* ANAT pulso *m*; (*single vibration*) pulsación *f*
pulse² [pʌls] *n* GASTR legumbre *f*
pulverize ['pʌlvəraɪz] *vt* pulverizar
puma ['pjuːmə] *n* puma *m*
pumice ['pʌmɪs] *n* ~ (**stone**) piedra *f* pómez
pummel ['pʌml] <*Brit:* -ll-, *Am:* -l-> *vt* aporrear
pump [pʌmp] I. *n* bomba *f*; (*for fuel*) surtidor *m* II. *vt* bombear
pumpkin ['pʌmpkɪn] *n* calabaza *f*, zapallo *m* *CSur, Perú*
pun [pʌn] *n* juego *m* de palabras, albur *m Méx*
punch¹ [pʌntʃ] I. *vt* 1. (*hit*) pegar 2. (*pierce*) perforar, ponchar *Méx*; (*ticket*) picar; **to ~ holes in sth** hacer agujeros a algo II. <-es> *n* 1. (*hit*) puñetazo *m*; (*in boxing*) golpe *m*; **to pull one's ~es** *fig* no emplear toda su fuerza 2. (*tool*) punzón *m*
punch² [pʌntʃ] *n* GASTR ponche *m*
punch bag *n Brit,* **punching bag** *n Am* saco *m* de arena
punchline *n* gracia *f* (de un chiste)
punch-up *n Brit, inf* pelea *f*
punctual ['pʌŋktʃʊəl] *adj* puntual
punctuate ['pʌŋktʃʊeɪt] *vt* LING puntuar
punctuation [ˌpʌŋktʃʊ'eɪʃən] *n* no *pl* puntuación *f*
puncture ['pʌŋktʃəʳ, *Am:* -tʃəʳ] I. *vt* pinchar, ponchar *Méx*; (*lung*) perforar II. *vi* (*tyre, ball*) pincharse, poncharse *Méx*; (*car*) pinchar III. *n* pinchazo *m*, ponchadura *f Méx*
pundit ['pʌndɪt] *n* experto, -a *m, f*
pungent ['pʌndʒənt] *adj* punzante; (*smell*) acre; (*criticism*) cáustico
punish ['pʌnɪʃ] *vt* castigar
punishing *adj* duro
punishment ['pʌnɪʃmənt] *n* castigo *m*; **to take a lot of ~** *fig* estar muy baqueteado
punitive ['pjuːnɪtɪv, *Am:* -t̬ɪv] *adj form* punitivo
punk [pʌŋk] *n* 1. (*person*) punk *mf* 2. *Am, pej* (*troublemaker*) gambe-

rro, -a *m, f*

punt¹ [pʌnt] SPORTS **I.** *vt, vi* despejar **II.** *n* patada *f* de despeje

punt² **I.** *vi* **to go ~ing** salir de paseo en batea **II.** *n* (*boat*) batea *f*

punter ['pʌntəʳ, *Am:* -t̬ɚ] *n Brit, inf* (*gambler*) jugador(a) *m(f)*

puny ['pjuːni] <-ier, -iest> *adj* enclenque

pup [pʌp] *n* cachorro, -a *m, f*

pupil¹ ['pjuːpl] *n* SCHOOL alumno, -a *m, f*

pupil² ['pjuːpl] *n* ANAT pupila *f*

puppet ['pʌpɪt] *n* títere *m*

puppy ['pʌpi] <-ies> *n* cachorro, -a *m, f*

purchase ['pɜːtʃəs, *Am:* 'pɜːrtʃəs] **I.** *vt form* comprar **II.** *n* **1.** (*act of buying*) compra *f* **2. to get a ~ on sth** agarrarse a algo

purchaser *n* comprador(a) *m(f)*

purchasing power *n* poder *m* adquisitivo

pure [pjʊəʳ, *Am:* pjʊr] *adj* puro; **~ and simple** simple y llano

purée ['pjʊəreɪ, *Am:* pjʊ'reɪ] *n* puré *m*

purely ['pjʊəli, *Am:* 'pjʊrli] *adv* puramente; **~ and simply** simple y llanamente

Purgatory ['pɜːgətri, *Am:* 'pɜːrgətɔːri] *n no pl* REL Purgatorio *m*

purge [pɜːdʒ, *Am:* 'pɜːrdʒ] **I.** *vt* purgar **II.** *n* purga *f*

purification [ˌpjʊərɪfɪ'keɪʃən, *Am:* ˌpjʊrə-] *n no pl* purificación *f*; (*of water*) depuración *f*

purify ['pjʊərɪfaɪ, *Am:* 'pjʊrə-] *vt* purificar; (*water*) depurar

purist ['pjʊərɪst, *Am:* 'pjʊrɪst] *n* purista *mf*

puritan ['pjʊərɪtən, *Am:* 'pjʊrɪ-] *n* puritano, -a *m, f*

puritanical [ˌpjʊərɪ'tænɪkəl, *Am:* ˌpjʊrɪ-] *adj* puritano

Puritanism *n no pl* puritanismo *m*

purity ['pjʊərəti, *Am:* 'pjʊrɪt̬i] *no pl n* pureza *f*

purple ['pɜːpl, *Am:* 'pɜːr-] **I.** *adj* (*reddish*) púrpura; (*bluish*) morado **II.** *n* (*reddish*) púrpura *m;* (*bluish*) morado *m*

purport ['pɜːpət, *Am:* pɜːr'pɔːrt] *vi form* **to ~ to be sth** pretender ser algo

purpose ['pɜːpəs, *Am:* 'pɜːrpəs] *n* (*goal*) intención *f*; (*use*) utilidad *f*; **for practical ~s** a efectos prácticos; **to have a ~ in life** tener una meta en la vida; (**strength of**) **~** resolución *f*; **to no ~** inútilmente; **to serve a ~** servir de algo; **on ~** a propósito

purposeful ['pɜːpəsfəl, *Am:* 'pɜːr-] *adj* decidido

purposely ['pɜːpəsli, *Am:* 'pɜːr-] *adv* a propósito

purr [pɜːʳ, *Am:* pɜːr] *vi* (*cat*) ronronear; (*engine*) zumbar

purse [pɜːs, *Am:* pɜːrs] **I.** *n* **1.** *Am* (*handbag*) bolso *m*, cartera *f AmL*, bolsa *f Méx* **2.** *Brit* (*wallet*) monedero *m;* **public ~** erario *m* público **II.** *vt* (*lips*) apretar

pursue [pə'sjuː, *Am:* pɚ'suː] *vt* perseguir; (*goals*) luchar por; (*rights*) reivindicar; **to ~ a matter** seguir un caso; **to ~ a career** dedicarse a una carrera profesional

pursuer [pə'sjuːəʳ, *Am:* pɚ'suːɚ] *n* perseguidor(a) *m(f)*

pursuit [pə'sjuːt, *Am:* pɚ'suːt] *n* **1.** (*chase*) persecución *f;* **to be in ~ of sth** ir tras algo **2.** (*activity*) actividad *f;* **leisure ~s** pasatiempos *mpl*

purveyor [pə'veɪəʳ, *Am:* pɚ'veɪɚ] *n* proveedor(a) *m(f)*

pus [pʌs] *n* MED *no pl* pus *m*, postema *f Méx*

push [pʊʃ] **I.** *vt* **1.** (*shove*) empujar; (*button*) apretar; **to ~ the door open** abrir la puerta de un empujón; **to ~ sb out of the way** apartar a alguien a empujones; **to ~ one's luck** tentar a la suerte; **to ~ sb too far** sacar a alguien de quicio; **to ~ sb into doing sth** presionar a alguien para que haga algo; **to ~ oneself** exigirse demasiado; **to be ~ed to do sth** tener dificultad para hacer algo; **to be ~ed for money** andar escaso de dinero; **to be ~ing 30** rondar los 30 años **2.** *inf* (*promote*) promover

P
p

II. *vi* empujar; (*press*) apretar; **to ~ for sth** presionar para (conseguir) algo **III.** <-es> *n* empujón *m;* **at the ~ of a button** apretando un botón; **to give sb a ~** *fig* dar un empujón a alguien; **to give sb the ~** *inf* (*partner*) dejar a alguien; (*employee*) echar a alguien; **at a ~ ...** si me apuras...; **if ~ comes to shove** en caso de apuro

◆**push around** *vt* mangonear *inf*

◆**push off** *vi inf* largarse

◆**push on** *vi* **to ~ (with sth)** seguir adelante (con algo)

◆**push through** *vt* (*legislation, proposal*) hacer aceptar

◆**push up** *vt* (*price*) hacer subir

pushchair [-tʃer] *n Brit* sillita *f* de paseo

push-up *n* SPORTS flexión *f*

pushy ['puʃi] *adj* (*ambitious*) ambicioso; (*arrogant*) prepotente

pussy ['pusi] <-ies> *n* (*cat*) minino, -a *m, f*

put [put] <-tt-, put, put> **I.** *vt* **1.** (*place*) poner; (*in box, hole*) meter; **to ~ salt in sth** echar sal a algo; **to ~ energy/time into sth** dedicar energía/tiempo a algo; **to ~ money on sth** jugarse dinero a algo; **to ~ sb in danger** poner a alguien en peligro; **to ~ a stop to sth** poner fin a algo; **to ~ a tax on sth** gravar algo con un impuesto; **to ~ a high value on sth** valorar mucho algo; **to ~ a question** plantear una pregunta; **I ~ it to you that ...** mi opinión es que...; **I ~ the number of visitors at 2,000** calculo que debe haber recibido unos 2.000 visitantes **2.** (*express*) decir; **to ~ one's feelings into words** expresar sus sentimientos con palabras **II.** *vi* NAUT **to ~ to sea** zarpar

◆**put aside** *irr vt* **1.** (*save*) ahorrar **2.** (*ignore*) dejar de lado

◆**put away** *irr vt* **1.** (*save*) ahorrar **2.** (*remove*) guardar

◆**put back** *irr vt* **1.** (*return*) volver a poner en su sitio **2.** (*postpone*) posponer

◆**put by** *irr vt* ahorrar

◆**put down** *irr vt* **1.** (*set down*) dejar **2.** (*attribute*) **to put sth down to sb** atribuir algo a alguien **3.** (*write*) escribir; **to put sb down for sth** (*register*) inscribir a alguien en algo **4.** (*rebellion, opposition*) reprimir **5.** *inf* (*humiliate*) menospreciar **6.** (*animal*) sacrificar

◆**put forward** *irr vt* **1.** (*propose*) proponer **2.** (*advance*) adelantar; **to put the clock forward** adelantar el reloj

◆**put in** *irr* **I.** *vt* **1.** (*place inside*) meter **2.** (*claim, request*) presentar **II.** *vi* NAUT hacer escala

◆**put into** *irr vt* meter

◆**put off** *irr vt* **1.** (*delay*) posponer **2.** (*repel*) alejar; (*food, smell*) dar asco a **3.** (*discourage*) desanimar **4.** (*distract*) distraer

◆**put on** *irr vt* **1.** (*place*) **to put sth on sth** poner algo sobre algo; **to put sb on to sth** *fig* dar a alguien información sobre algo **2.** (*wear*) ponerse **3.** THEAT poner en escena **4.** (*pretend*) fingir; (*accent*) afectar **5.** (*weight*) engordar

◆**put out** *irr* **I.** *vt* **1.** (*extend*) extender; **to ~ one's hand** tender la mano; **to put the dog out** sacar al perro **2.** (*extinguish: fire*) extinguir; (*cigarette*) apagar **3.** (*turn off*) apagar **4.** (*inconvenience*) molestar a **II.** *vi* NAUT zarpar

◆**put through** *irr vt* **1.** (*bill*) hacer aprobar **2.** TEL **to put sb through to sb** pasar a alguien con alguien **3.** (*make endure*) **to put sb through sth** someter a alguien a algo

◆**put together** *irr vt* juntar; (*model*) montar; (*facts, clues*) relacionar

◆**put up** *irr vt* **1.** (*hang up*) colgar; (*notice*) fijar **2.** (*raise*) levantar; (*umbrella*) abrir **3.** (*build*) construir; (*tent*) armar **4.** (*prices*) subir **5.** (*give shelter*) alojar **6.** (*provide*) **to ~ the money for sth** poner el dinero para algo; **to put sth up for sale** poner algo en venta; **to ~ opposition** oponerse

◆ **put up with** *irr vt* soportar

putative ['pjuːtətɪv, *Am:* -t̬ət̬ɪv] *adj form* supuesto

putrefy ['pjuːtrɪfaɪ, *Am:* -trə-] <-ie-> *vi form* pudrirse

putrid ['pjuːtrɪd] *adj form* podrido

putt [pʌt] SPORTS I. *vi* tirar al hoyo II. *n* tiro *m* al hoyo, put *m AmL*

putty ['pʌti, *Am:* 'pʌt̬-] *n no pl* masilla *f*

puzzle ['pʌzl] I. *vt* dejar perplejo II. *n* (*game*) rompecabezas *m inv*; (*mystery*) misterio *m*

puzzled *adj* perplejo

puzzling *adj* desconcertante

PVC [ˌpiːviːˈsiː] *n abbr of* polyvinyl chloride PVC *m*

pygmy ['pɪgmi] *n* <-ies> pigmeo, -a *m, f*

pyjamas [pəˈdʒɑːməz] *npl Aus, Brit* pijama *m*; **a pair of** ~ un pijama

---

⚠️ **pyjamas** (= pijama) se utiliza en plural: "Where are my pyjamas?" Pero **a pair of pyjamas** (= pijama) se utiliza en singular: "Is this my pair of pyjamas?"

---

pylon ['paɪlɒn, *Am:* -lɑːn] *n* torre *f* de alta tensión

pyramid ['pɪrəmɪd] *n* pirámide *f*

pyre ['paɪə', *Am:* 'paɪə-] *n* pira *f*

Pyrenees [pɪrəˈniːz] *npl* the ~ los Pirineos

python ['paɪθən, *Am:* -θɑːn] <-(ons)> *n* pitón *f*

Q q

Q, q [kjuː] *n* Q, q *f;* ~ **for Queenie** *Brit,* ~ **for Queen** *Am* Q de Quebec

Q *abbr of* **Queen** reina *f*

Qatar [kəˈtɑː', *Am:* 'kɑːtɑːr] *n* Qatar *m*

QC [ˌkjuːˈsiː] *n Brit abbr of* **Queen's Counsel** título de abogacía de categoría superior

qua [kwɑː] *prep form* como

quack¹ [kwæk] I. *n* (*sound*) graznido *m* II. *vi* graznar

quack² [kwæk] *n inf* (*doctor*) matasanos *m inv*

quad [kwɒd, *Am:* kwɑːd] *n* 1. *inf* (*quadruplet*) cuatrillizo, -a *m, f* 2. (*quadrangle*) cuadrángulo *m*

quadrangle ['kwɒdræŋgl, *Am:* 'kwɑːdræŋ-] *n form* cuadrángulo *m*

quadrilateral [ˌkwɒdrɪˈlætərəl, *Am:* ˌkwɑːdrɪˈlæt̬-] *n* cuadrilátero *m*

quadruped ['kwɒdrʊped, *Am:* 'kwɑːdrʊ-] *n* cuadrúpedo *m*

quadruple ['kwɒdruːpl, *Am:* 'kwɑːdruː-] *vi* cuadruplicarse

quadruplet ['kwɒdruːplət, *Am:* kwɑːˈdruːplɪt] *n* cuatrillizo, -a *m, f*

quail¹ [kweɪl] <-(s)> *n* codorniz *f*

quail² [kweɪl] *vi* acobardarse

quaint [kweɪnt] *adj* (*charming*) pintoresco; (*strange*) extraño

quake [kweɪk] I. *n* 1. temblor *m* 2. *inf* (*earthquake*) terremoto *m* II. *vi* temblar; **to ~ with cold/fear** temblar de frío/miedo

Quaker ['kweɪkə', *Am:* -kə-] *n* Cuáquero, -a *m, f*

qualification [ˌkwɒlɪfɪˈkeɪʃən, *Am:* ˌkwɑːlɪ-] *n* 1. (*document*) título *m* 2. (*limiting criteria*) restricción *f;* **without** ~ sin reservas 3. SPORTS clasificación *f*

qualified ['kwɒlɪfaɪd, *Am:* 'kwɑːlɪ-] *adj* 1. (*trained*) titulado 2. (*competent*) capacitado 3. (*limited*) **to be a ~ success** tener cierto éxito

qualify ['kwɒlɪfaɪ, *Am:* 'kwɑːlɪ-] <-ie-> I. *vt* **to ~ sb to do sth** dar derecho a alguien para hacer algo; **to ~ a remark** matizar un comentario II. *vi* 1. (*complete training*) titularse, recibirse *AmL;* **to ~ for sth** (*have qualifications*) estar acreditado para algo; (*be eligible*) tener derecho a algo 2. SPORTS clasificarse

qualitative ['kwɒlɪtətɪv, *Am:* 'kwɑːlɪteɪt̬ɪv] *adj* cualitativo

quality ['kwɒləti, *Am:* 'kwɑːləṭi] <-ies> *n* **1.** *no pl* (*excellence*) calidad *f* **2.** (*characteristic*) cualidad *f*
quality control *n* control *m* de calidad
qualm [kwɑːm] *n* **to have** ~**s** (**about sth**) tener escrúpulos (respecto a algo); **to have no** ~**s about doing sth** no tener escrúpulos para hacer algo
quandary ['kwɒndəri, *Am:* 'kwɑːn-] <-ies> *n* **to be in a** ~ estar en un dilema
quantify ['kwɒntɪfaɪ, *Am:* 'kwɑːnṭə-] <-ie-> *vt* cuantificar
quantitative ['kwɒntɪtətɪv, *Am:* 'kwɑːnṭəteɪṭɪv] *adj* cuantitativo
quantity ['kwɒntəti, *Am:* 'kwɑːnṭəṭi] <-ies> *n* cantidad *f*
quantum mechanics ['kwɒntəm-, *Am:* 'kwɑːnṭəm-] *n + sing vb* mecánica *f* cuántica
quarantine ['kwɒrəntiːn, *Am:* 'kwɔːrən-] **I.** *n* cuarentena *f* **II.** *vt* poner en cuarentena a
quark [kwɑːk, *Am:* kwɑːrk] *n* PHYS quark *m*
quarrel ['kwɒrəl, *Am:* 'kwɔːr-] **I.** *n* disputa *f* **II.** <-ll-> *vi* pelearse
quarry[1] ['kwɒri, *Am:* 'kwɔːr-] **I.** <-ies> *n* (*rock pit*) cantera *f* **II.** <-ie-> *vt* extraer
quarry[2] ['kwɒri, *Am:* 'kwɔːr-] <-ies> *n* presa *f*
quart [kwɔːt, *Am:* kwɔːrt] *n* cuarto *m* de galón
quarter ['kwɔːtəʳ, *Am:* 'kwɔːrṭəʳ] **I.** *n* **1.** (*one fourth*) cuarto *m;* **three** ~**s** tres cuartos; **a** ~ **of the British** una cuarta parte de los británicos; **a** ~ **of an hour** un cuarto de hora; **a** ~ **to three** las tres menos cuarto, un cuarto para las tres *AmL;* **a** ~ **past three** las tres y cuarto **2.** *Am* (*25 cents*) cuarto de dólar **3.** (*neighbourhood*) barrio *m;* **at close** ~**s** *fig* de cerca; **in certain** ~**s** *fig* en ciertos círculos **II.** *vt* **1.** (*cut into four*) cuartear **2.** (*give housing*) alojar
quarterback *n* mariscal *mf* de campo **quarterfinal** *n* cuarto *m* de final

quarterly ['kwɔːtəli, *Am:* 'kwɔːrṭəli] **I.** *adv* trimestralmente **II.** *adj* trimestral
quartet [kwɔː'tet, *Am:* kwɔːr-] *n* MUS cuarteto *m*
quartz [kwɔːts, *Am:* kwɔːrts] *n no pl* cuarzo *m*
quash [kwɒʃ, *Am:* kwɑːʃ] *vt* (*rebellion*) sofocar; (*rumour*) acallar; LAW (*verdict*) anular
quaver ['kweɪvəʳ, *Am:* -vəʳ] **I.** *vi* temblar **II.** *n Aus, Brit* MUS corchea *f*
quay [kiː] *n* muelle *m*
queasy ['kwiːzi] <-ier, -iest> *adj* mareado; **to feel** ~ **about sth** *fig* sentir desasosiego acerca de algo
Quebec [kwɪ'bek, *Am:* kwiː'bek] *n* Quebec *m*
queen [kwiːn] *n* reina *f*
Queen Mother *n* Reina *f* Madre
queer [kwɪəʳ, *Am:* kwɪr] <-er, -est> *adj* **1.** (*strange*) extraño; **to have** ~ **ideas** tener ideas raras; **to feel rather** ~ sentirse algo extraño **2.** *pej, inf* (*homosexual*) maricón
quell [kwel] *vt* (*rebellion*) sofocar; (*doubts*) disipar
quench [kwentʃ] *vt* (*thirst*) saciar; **to** ~ **the fire** apagar el incendio
query ['kwɪəri, *Am:* 'kwɪri] **I.** <-ies> *n* pregunta *f;* **to raise a** ~ plantear un interrogante; **to settle a** ~ resolver un interrogante **II.** <-ie-> *vt* **1.** *form* (*dispute*) cuestionar; (*doubt*) poner en duda **2.** (*ask*) preguntar; **to** ~ **whether ...** preguntar si...
quest [kwest] *n* búsqueda *f;* **in** ~ **of sth** en busca de algo
question ['kwestʃən] **I.** *n* **1.** (*inquiry*) pregunta *f;* **to put a** ~ **to sb** hacer una pregunta a alguien **2.** *no pl* (*doubt*) duda *f;* **without** ~ sin duda; **to be beyond** ~ estar fuera de duda **3.** (*issue*) cuestión *f;* **it's a** ~ **of life or death** *a. fig* es un asunto de vida o muerte; **to be a** ~ **of time** ser una cuestión de tiempo **II.** *vt* **1.** (*interrogate*) interrogar **2.** (*doubt*) poner en duda
questionable ['kwestʃənəbl] *adj* discutible

questioner *n* interrogador(a) *m(f)*
questioning I. *n no pl* interrogatorio *m* II. *adj* inquisidor
question mark *n* signo *m* de interrogación
questionnaire [ˌkwestʃəˈneəʳ, *Am:* ˌkwestʃəˈner] *n* cuestionario *m*
queue [kjuː] I. *n Aus, Brit a.* INFOR cola *f;* **to stand in a ~** hacer cola II. *vi* hacer cola
quibble [ˈkwɪbl] I. *n* pega *f* II. *vi* **to ~ over sth** quejarse por algo
quiche [kiːʃ] *n* quiche *f,* quiche *m AmL*
quick [kwɪk] I. <-er, -est> *adj* 1. *(fast)* rápido; **~ as lightning** (veloz) como un rayo; **in ~ succession** uno detrás del otro; **to be ~ to do sth** hacer algo con rapidez; **to have a ~ mind** tener una mente vivaz; **to have a ~ temper** tener mal genio 2. *(short)* corto; **the ~est way** el camino más corto; **to give sb a ~ call** hacer una llamada corta a alguien II. <-er, -est> *adv* rápidamente III. *n* **to cut sb to the ~** *fig* herir a alguien en lo más vivo
quicken [ˈkwɪkən] *vi, vt* apresurar(se)
quick-freeze *vt irr* congelar rápidamente
quickly [ˈkwɪkli] *adv* rápidamente
quickness [ˈkwɪknɪs] *n no pl* rapidez *f*
quicksand *n no pl* arenas *fpl* movedizas **quick-tempered** *adj* irascible **quick-witted** *adj* perspicaz
quid [kwɪd] *inv n Brit, inf (pound)* libra *f*
quid pro quo *n form* compensación *f*
quiet [ˈkwaɪət] I. *n no pl* 1. *(silence)* silencio *m* 2. *(lack of activity)* sosiego *m;* **peace and ~** paz y tranquilidad; **on the ~** a escondidas II. <-er, -est> *adj* 1. *(not loud)* silencioso 2. *(secret)* secreto; **to keep ~ about sth** mantenerse callado respecto de algo
quieten down [ˈkwaɪətn-] *vi* 1. *(quiet)* callarse 2. *(calm)* calmarse
quietly [ˈkwaɪətli] *adv* silenciosa-

mente; **to speak ~** hablar en voz baja
quietness [ˈkwaɪətnɪs] *n no pl* tranquilidad *f*
quill [kwɪl] *n* 1. *(feather, pen)* pluma *f* 2. *(of porcupine)* púa *f*
quilt [kwɪlt] *n* edredón *m*
quince [kwɪns] *n no pl* membrillo *m*
quintessential [ˌkwɪntəˈsenʃəl, *Am:* -teˈ-] *adj form* por antonomasia
quip [kwɪp] *n* pulla *f*
quirk [kwɜːk, *Am:* kwɜːrk] *n* excentricidad *f;* **a ~ of fate** un capricho del destino
quirky [ˈkwɜːki, *Am:* ˈkwɜːr-] <-ier, -iest> *adj* excéntrico
quit [kwɪt] <quit *o* quitted, quit *o* quitted> I. *vi* 1. *(stop)* parar 2. *(resign)* dimitir II. *vt (stop)* parar; **to ~ smoking** dejar de fumar
quite [kwaɪt] *adv* 1. *(fairly)* bastante; **~ a bit** considerablemente, bastantito *Méx;* **~ a distance** una distancia considerable 2. *(completely)* completamente; **not ~ as clever/rich as ...** no tan inteligente/rico como...
quits [kwɪts] *adj inf* **to be ~ (with sb)** estar en paz con alguien; **to call it ~** hacer las paces
quiver [ˈkwɪvəʳ, *Am:* -ɚ] *vi* temblar
quiz [kwɪz] I. <-es> *n* concurso *m* II. *vt* interrogar
quiz show *n* programa *m* concurso
quizzical [ˈkwɪzɪkəl] *adj* interrogante
quorum [ˈkwɔːrəm] *n form* quórum *m*
quota [ˈkwəʊtə, *Am:* ˈkwoʊt̬ə] *n* cuota *f*
quotation [kwəʊˈteɪʃən, *Am:* kwoʊˈ-] *n* LIT cita *f*
quotation marks *npl* comillas *fpl*
quote [kwəʊt, *Am:* kwoʊt] I. *n* 1. *inf (quotation)* cita *f* 2. *pl, inf (quotation marks)* comillas *fpl* 3. *inf (estimate)* presupuesto *m* II. *vt* 1. citar 2. FIN cotizar III. *vi* **to ~ from sb** citar a alguien; **to ~ from memory** citar de memoria

R

R, r [ɑːʳ, *Am:* ɑːr] r, R *f;* ~ **for Roger** R de Ramón
R. 1. *abbr of* **River** r. *m* 2. *Am abbr of* **Republican** republicano
rabbi [ˈræbaɪ] *n* rabino *m*
rabbit [ˈræbɪt] I. *n* conejo, -a *m, f*
II. *vi Brit, Aus, inf* parlotear
rabbit hutch *n* conejera *f*
rabble [ˈræbl] *n no pl* muchedumbre *f*
rabies [ˈreɪbiːz] *n* rabia *f*
RAC [ˌɑːʳeɪˈsiː, *Am:* ˌɑːr-] *n Brit abbr of* **Royal Automobile Club** ≈ Real Automóbil Club *m* de España
race¹ [reɪs] I. *n* carrera *f* II. *vi* 1. (*move quickly*) correr; SPORTS competir 2. (*engine*) acelerarse III. *vt* 1. (*compete against*) competir con 2. (*horse*) hacer correr
race² [reɪs] *n no pl* 1. (*ethnic grouping*) raza *f* 2. (*species*) especie *f*
racecourse [ˈreɪskɔːs, *Am:* -kɔːrs] *n* hipódromo *m*
racehorse [ˈreɪshɔːs, *Am:* -ˌhɔːrs] *n* caballo *m* de carreras
racetrack [ˈreɪstræk] *n* hipódromo *m*
racial [ˈreɪʃəl] *adj* racial
racing *n* carreras *fpl*
racing car *n* coche *m* de carreras
  racing driver *n* piloto *mf* de carreras
racism [ˈreɪsɪzəm] *n no pl* racismo *m*
racist [ˈreɪsɪst] *n* racista *mf*
rack [ræk] I. *n* estante *m;* **luggage ~** portaequipajes *m inv* II. *vt* atormentar
racket [ˈrækɪt] *n* 1. SPORTS raqueta *f* 2. *no pl, inf* (*loud noise*) barullo *m,* balumba *f AmS* 3. (*scheme*) chanchullo *m,* transa *f Méx*
racy [ˈreɪsi] <-ier, -iest> *adj* atrevido
radar [ˈreɪdɑːʳ, *Am:* -dɑːr] *n no pl* radar *m*
radial [ˈreɪdiəl] *adj* radial; TECH en estrella

radiant [ˈreɪdiənt] *adj* radiante
radiate [ˈreɪdieɪt] *vi, vt* irradiar
radiation [ˌreɪdiˈeɪʃən] *n no pl* radiación *f*
radiator [ˈreɪdieɪtəʳ, *Am:* -t̮əʳ] *n* radiador *m*
radical [ˈrædɪkəl] *adj* radical
radii [ˈreɪdiaɪ] *n pl of* **radius**
radio [ˈreɪdiəʊ, *Am:* -oʊ] I. *n* radio *f,* radio *m AmC* II. *vt* (*information*) radiar; (*person*) llamar por radio
radioactive [ˌreɪdiəʊˈæktɪv, *Am:* -oʊˈ-] *adj* radioactivo
radioactivity [ˌreɪdiəʊəkˈtɪvəti, *Am:* -oʊækˈtɪvət̮i] *n no pl* radiactividad *f*
radio station *n* emisora *f* de radio, estación *f* de radio *AmL*
radiotherapy [ˌreɪdiəʊˈθerəpi, *Am:* -oʊˈ-] *n no pl* radioterapia *f*
radish [ˈrædɪʃ] <-es> *n* rábano *m*
radius [ˈreɪdiəs] <-dii> *n* radio *m*
RAF [ˌɑːʳeɪˈef, *Am:* ˌɑːr-] *n abbr of* **Royal Air Force the -** la fuerza aérea británica
raffle [ˈræfl] *n* rifa *f*
raft [rɑːft, *Am:* ræft] *n* balsa *f*
rafter [ˈrɑːftəʳ, *Am:* ˈræftəʳ] *n* viga *f*
rag [ræg] I. *n* 1. (*old cloth*) trapo *m* 2. *pl* (*worn-out clothes*) harapos *mpl* 3. *pej* (*newspaper*) periodicucho *m* II. <-gg-> *vt inf* tomar el pelo a
rage [reɪdʒ] I. *n no pl* furia *f;* **to be in a ~** estar hecho una furia II. *vi* 1. (*express fury*) enfurecerse 2. (*storm*) bramar
ragged [ˈrægɪd] *adj* 1. (*clothes*) hecho jirones 2. (*wearing worn clothes*) andrajoso 3. (*irregular*) irregular
raid [reɪd] I. *n* 1. MIL incursión *f* 2. (*attack*) ataque *m* 3. (*robbery*) asalto *m* 4. (*by police*) redada *f* II. *vt* invadir, atacar
rail [reɪl] *n* 1. (*part of fence*) valla *f;* (*bar*) baranda *f* 2. *no pl* (*railway system*) ferrocarril *m;* **by ~** en tren 3. (*track*) raíl *m,* riel *m AmL*
railcard [ˈreɪlkɑːd, *Am:* -kɑːrd] *n* tarjeta para obtener descuentos en el tren

railing ['reɪlɪŋ] *n* verja *f*

railroad ['reɪlrəʊd, *Am:* -roʊd] *n Am* **1.** (*system*) ferrocarril *m* **2.** (*track*) línea *f* de ferrocarril

railway ['reɪlweɪ] *n Brit* **1.** (*tracks*) vía *f* férrea **2.** (*system*) ferrocarril *m*

railway line *n* vía *f* del tren **railwayman** <-men> *n* ferroviario *m*, ferrocarrilero *m Méx* **railway station** *n* estación *f* del ferrocarril

rain [reɪn] **I.** *n no pl* lluvia *f* **II.** *vi* llover

rainbow *n* arco *m* iris **raincoat** *n* gabardina *f*, piloto *m Arg* **raindrop** *n* gota *f* de lluvia **rainfall** *n no pl* precipitación *f* **rain forest** *n* selva *f* tropical **rainstorm** *n* tormenta *f* de lluvia **rainwater** *n no pl* agua *f* de lluvia

rainy ['reɪni] *adj* <-ier, -iest> lluvioso

raise [reɪz] **I.** *n Am, Aus* aumento *m* **II.** *vt* **1.** (*lift*) levantar; (*flag*) izar; (*anchor*) levar **2.** (*doubts*) suscitar **3.** (*wages, awareness*) aumentar **4.** (*subject, problem*) plantear **5.** FIN recaudar **6.** (*bring up*) cultivar **7.** (*end: embargo*) levantar

raisin ['reɪzn] *n* pasa *f*

rake¹ [reɪk] *n* (*dissolute man*) vividor *m*

rake² [reɪk] **I.** *n* (*tool*) rastrillo *m* **II.** *vt* rastrillar

◆ **rake in** *vt inf* amasar

rally ['ræli] <-ies> **I.** *n* **1.** (*race*) rally *m* **2.** (*in tennis*) peloteo *m* **3.** POL mitin *m* **II.** *vi* MED mejorar; FIN repuntar **III.** *vt* apoyar

◆ **rally round** *vt* apoyar

ram [ræm] **I.** *n* **1.** (*male sheep*) carnero *m* **2.** (*implement*) maza *f* **II.** *vt* <-mm-> **1.** (*hit*) embestir contra **2.** (*push*) **to ~ sth into sth** embutir algo en algo

RAM [ræm] *n abbr of* **Random Access Memory** RAM *f*

ramble ['ræmbl] **I.** *n* caminata *f* **II.** *vi* divagar

rambler ['ræmblər, *Am:* -blə·] *n* **1.** (*walker*) excursionista *mf* **2.** BOT rosa *f* trepadora

rambling ['ræmblɪŋ] *adj* **1.** (*building*) laberíntico **2.** (*plant*) trepador **3.** (*talk*) divagante

ramp [ræmp] *n* **1.** (*sloping way*) rampa *f* **2.** *Am* AUTO carril *m* de incorporación/salida

rampage [ræm'peɪdʒ, *Am:* 'ræmpeɪdʒ] *n* destrozos *mpl;* **to be on the ~** ir arrasando todo

rampant ['ræmpənt] *adj* (*disease, growth*) exhuberante

rampart ['ræmpɑːt, *Am:* -pɑːrt] *n* muralla *f*

ramshackle ['ræmʃækl] *adj* desvencijado

ran [ræn] *pt of* **run**

ranch [rɑːntʃ, *Am:* ræntʃ] <-es> *n* hacienda *f*, rancho *m Méx*, estancia *f RíoPl*

rancher ['rɑːntʃər, *Am:* 'ræntʃə·] *n* hacendado, -a *m, f*, ranchero, -a *m, f Méx*

rancid ['rænsɪd] *adj* rancio

rancor *n Am, Aus,* **rancour** ['ræŋkər, *Am:* -kə·] *n no pl* rencor *m*

random ['rændəm] **I.** *n no pl* **at ~** al azar **II.** *adj* aleatorio

randy ['rændi] <-ier, -iest> *adj inf* cachondo, birriondo *Méx*

rang [ræŋ] *pt of* **ring²**

range [reɪndʒ] **I.** *n* **1.** (*area*) área *m;* (*for shooting*) campo *m* de tiro **2.** (*row*) hilera *f* **3.** *Am* (*pasture*) pradera *f* **4.** (*field*) ámbito *m*, campo *m* **5.** (*scale*) gama *f* **6.** GEO cadena *f* **7.** (*maximum capability*) alcance *m;* **within ~** al alcance **II.** *vi* **1.** (*vary*) variar **2.** (*rove*) deambular **3.** (*extend*) extenderse **III.** *vt* alinear

ranger ['reɪndʒər, *Am:* -dʒə·] *n* guardabosque *mf*

rank¹ [ræŋk] *adj* **1.** (*absolute*) total **2.** (*smelling unpleasant*) fétido

rank² [ræŋk] **I.** *n* **1.** *no pl* (*status*) rango *m* **2.** MIL graduación *f* **3.** (*row*) fila *f;* **cab ~** parada *f* de taxis, sitio *m* de taxis *Méx* **II.** *vi* clasificarse; **to ~ as sth** figurar como algo

◆ **rank among** *vi* situarse entre

rankle ['ræŋkl] *vi* doler

ransack ['rænsæk] *vt* **1.** (*search*) revolver **2.** (*plunder*) saquear

ransom ['rænsəm] *n* rescate *m;* **to**

hold sb to ~ secuestrar a alguien y pedir rescate; *fig* chantajear a alguien

rant [rænt] *vi* despotricar

rap [ræp] *vt* golpear

rape¹ [reɪp] **I.** *n* violación *f* **II.** *vt* violar

rape² [reɪp] *n* BOT, AGR colza *f*

rapeseed oil *n* aceite *m* de colza

rapid ['ræpɪd] *adj* **1.** (*quick*) rápido **2.** (*sudden*) súbito

rapids ['ræpɪdz] *n* rápidos *mpl*

rapist ['reɪpɪst] *n* violador(a) *m(f)*

rapport [ræ'pɔːr, *Am:* -'pɔːr] *n no pl* compenetración *f*

rapture ['ræptʃər, *Am:* -tʃər] *n no pl* éxtasis *m inv*

rapturous ['ræptʃərəs] *adj* extasiado; (*applause*) entusiasta

rare¹ [reər, *Am:* rer] *adj* raro

rare² [reər, *Am:* rer] *adj* GASTR poco hecho

rarely ['reəli, *Am:* 'rer-] *adv* raramente, raras veces

raring ['reərɪŋ, *Am:* 'rerɪŋ] *adj inf* **to be** ~ **to do sth** tener muchas ganas de hacer algo

rascal ['rɑːskl, *Am:* 'ræskl] *n* granuja *mf*

rash¹ [ræʃ] *n* **1.** MED sarpullido *m* **2.** *no pl* (*outbreak*) racha *f*

rash² [ræʃ] *adj* precipitado, impulsivo

rasher ['ræʃər, *Am:* -ər] *n* loncha *f* (de beicon), rebanada *f* (de tocino) *AmC*

raspberry ['rɑːzbəri, *Am:* 'ræzˌber-] <-ies> *n* **1.** (*fruit*) frambuesa *f* **2.** *inf* (*sound*) pedorreta *f*, trompetilla *f* *AmL*

rasping ['rɑːspɪŋ, *Am:* 'ræsp-] *adj* áspero

rat [ræt] *n* rata *f*

ratchet ['rætʃɪt] *n* TECH trinquete *m*

rate [reɪt] **I.** *n* **1.** (*speed*) velocidad *f* **2.** (*proportion*) índice *m*, tasa *f*; **at any** ~ de todos modos; **unemployment** ~ índice *m* de desempleo **3.** (*price*) precio *m* **II.** *vt* **1.** calificar; **to** ~ **sb/sth as sth** considerar algo/a alguien como algo **2.** *Aus, Brit* FIN tasar

rateable ['reɪtəbl, *Am:* -t̬ə-] *adj Brit* tasable; ~ **value** valor *m* catastral

rather ['rɑːðər, *Am:* 'ræðər] *adv* **1.** (*somewhat*) ~ **sleepy** medio dormido **2.** (*more exactly*) más bien **3.** (*very*) bastante **4.** (*in preference to*) **I would** ~ **stay here** prefiero quedarme aquí

ratify ['rætɪfaɪ, *Am:* 'ræt̬ə-] *vt* ratificar

rating ['reɪtɪŋ, *Am:* -t̬ɪŋ] *n* **1.** *no pl* (*estimation*) evaluación *f* **2.** *pl* TV, RADIO índice *m* de audiencia **3.** *Brit* MIL marinero *m*

ratio ['reɪʃiəʊ, *Am:* -oʊ] *n* proporción *f*

ration ['ræʃən] **I.** *n* **1.** (*fixed allowance*) ración *f* **2.** *pl* MIL víveres *fpl* **II.** *vt* racionar

rational ['ræʃənəl] *adj* **1.** (*able to reason*) racional **2.** (*sensible*) razonable

rationale [ˌræʃə'nɑːl, *Am:* -'næl] *n* razón *f* fundamental

rationalize ['ræʃənəlaɪz] *vt* racionalizar

rat race *n* **the** ~ la lucha para sobrevivir

rattle ['rætl, *Am:* 'ræt̬-] **I.** *n* **1.** *no pl* (*noise*) ruido *m*; (*of carriage*) traqueteo *m* **2.** (*for baby*) sonajero *m*, cascabel *m AmL* **II.** *vt* **1.** (*making noise*) hacer sonar **2.** (*make nervous*) poner nervioso

rattlesnake ['rætlsneɪk, *Am:* 'ræt̬-] *n* serpiente *f* de cascabel, víbora *f* de cascabel *Méx*

ratty ['ræti, *Am:* 'ræt̬-] <-ier, -iest> *adj inf* malhumorado

raucous ['rɔːkəs, *Am:* 'rɑː-] *adj* estridente

raunchy ['rɔːntʃi, *Am:* 'rɑːn-] <-ier, -iest> *adj* atrevido

ravage ['rævɪdʒ] *vt* hacer estragos en

rave [reɪv] *vi* desvariar; **to** ~ **against sb/sth** despotricar contra alguien/algo; **to** ~ **about sth/sb** poner algo/a alguien por las nubes

raven ['reɪvn] *n* cuervo *m*

ravenous ['rævənəs] *adj* hambriento

ravine [rə'viːn] *n* barranco *m*

raving ['reɪvɪŋ] *adj* **a** ~ **madman** un

loco de remate

ravioli [ˌrævɪˈəʊli, *Am:* -ˈoʊ-] *n* ravioles *mpl*

ravish [ˈrævɪʃ] *vt liter* **1.**(*please greatly*) cautivar **2.**(*rape*) violar

ravishing *adj* encantador

raw [rɔː, *Am:* rɑː] *adj* **1.**(*unprocessed*) ~ **material** materia prima; **to get a ~ deal** sufrir un trato injusto **2.**(*sore*) en carne viva **3.**(*uncooked*) crudo **4.**(*inexperienced*) novato

rawhide [ˈrɔːhaɪd, *Am:* ˈrɑː-] *n* cuero *m* sin curtir

Rawlplug® [ˈrɔːlplʌg, *Am:* ˈrɑːl-] *n Brit* taco *m* (de plástico)

rawness [ˈrɔːnɪs, *Am:* ˈrɑː-] *n no pl* **1.**(*harshness*) crudeza *f* **2.**(*inexperience*) inexperiencia *f*

ray [reɪ] *n* **1.**(*of light*) rayo *m* **2.**(*trace*) resquicio *m*

raze [reɪz] *vt* arrasar

razor [ˈreɪzər, *Am:* -zɚ] *n* maquinilla *f* de afeitar, rasuradora *f Méx;* (*open*) navaja *f* de afeitar, barbera *f Col*

razor blade *n* hoja *f* de afeitar

RC [ˌɑːrˈsiː, *Am:* ˌɑːr-] **1.** *abbr of* **Roman Catholic** católico, -a *m, f* **2.** *abbr of* **Red Cross** Cruz *f* Roja

Rd *abbr of* **road** c/

RE [ˌɑːrˈiː, *Am:* ˌɑːr-] *Brit abbr of* **Religious Education** educación *f* religiosa

re [riː] *prep* con relación a

reach [riːtʃ] **I.** *n* **1.** *no pl* (*range*) alcance *m;* **to be out of** (**sb's**) ~ *a. fig* estar fuera del alcance (de alguien) **2.**(*of river*) tramo *m* **II.** *vt* **1.**(*stretch out*) alargar, extender **2.**(*arrive at*) llegar a; (*finish line*) alcanzar **III.** *vi* **to ~ for sth** alargar la mano para tomar algo

◆**reach down** *vi* **to ~ to** llegar hasta

◆**reach out** *vi* alargar la(s) mano(s); **to ~ for sth** alargar la mano para a-garrar algo

react [riˈækt] *vi* reaccionar

reaction [riˈækʃn] *n* reacción *f*

reactionary [riˈækʃənri, *Am:* -eri] *adj* reaccionario

reactor [riˈæktər, *Am:* -tɚ] *n* reactor

m

read¹ [riːd] <read, read> **I.** *vt* **1.**(*text*) leer **2.**(*decipher*) descifrar **3.**(*understand*) entender **II.** *vi* leer

◆**read out** *vt* leer en voz alta

◆**read over** *vt* releer

◆**read through** *vt* leer de principio a fin

◆**read up** *vi* repasar

read² [red] *adj* leído; **to take sth as ~** dar algo por hecho

readable [ˈriːdəbl] *adj* **1.**(*legible*) legible **2.**(*easy to read*) ameno

reader [ˈriːdər, *Am:* -dɚ] *n* **1.**(*person*) lector(a) *m(f)* **2.**(*book*) libro *m* de lectura **3.** *Brit* UNIV profesor(a) *m(f)* adjunto, -a

readership [ˈriːdəʃɪp, *Am:* -dɚ-] *n no pl* lectores *mpl*

readily [ˈredɪli] *adv* **1.**(*promptly*) de buena gana **2.**(*easily*) fácilmente

readiness [ˈredɪnɪs] *n no pl* **1.**(*willingness*) (buena) disposición *f* **2.**(*preparedness*) preparación *f*

reading [ˈriːdɪŋ] *n* **1.** *no pl* lectura *f* **2.**(*interpretation*) interpretación *f* **3.** TECH medición *f*

readjustment [ˌriːəˈdʒʌstmənt] *n* TECH reajuste *m*

read only memory *n* INFOR memoria *f* ROM

ready [ˈredi] **I.** *adj* <-ier, -iest> **1.**(*prepared*) listo, pronto *Urug;* **to be ~** estar listo; **to get ~** (**for sth**) prepararse (para algo) **2.**(*willing*) dispuesto **3.**(*available*) disponible **II.** *n* **at the ~** a punto **III.** *vt* preparar

ready-made [ˌrediˈmeɪd] *adj* pre-cocinado

ready-to-wear [ˌreditəˈweər, *Am:* -ˈwer] *adj* prêt-à-porter

reaffirm [ˌriːəˈfɜːm, *Am:* -ˈfɜːrm] *vt* reafirmar

real [rɪəl, *Am:* riːl] *adj* real, auténtico

real estate *n no pl, Am, Aus* bienes *mpl* raíces

realism [ˈrɪəlɪzəm, *Am:* ˈriːlɪ-] *n no pl* realismo *m*

realist [ˈrɪəlɪst, *Am:* ˈriːlɪst] *n* realista *mf*

realistic [ˌrɪəˈlɪstɪk, *Am:* ˌriːə-] *adj* realista

reality [rɪˈælətɪ, *Am:* -ṭi] *n no pl* realidad *f*; **in** ~ en realidad

realization [ˌrɪəlaɪˈzeɪʃən, *Am:* ˌriːəlɪˈ-] *n* **1.** (*awareness*) comprensión *f* **2.** *no pl a.* FIN realización *f*

realize [ˈrɪəlaɪz, *Am:* ˈriːə-] *vt* **1.** (*become aware of*) darse cuenta de **2.** (*achieve*) realizar **3.** FIN realizar

really [ˈrɪəli, *Am:* ˈriːə-] **I.** *adv* en realidad **II.** *interj* ¿de veras?

realm [relm] *n* **1.** (*kingdom*) reino *m* **2.** (*area of interest*) campo *m*

realtor [ˈrɪəltər, *Am:* ˈriːəltər] *n Am, Aus* agente *mf* inmobiliario, -a, corredor(a) *m(f)* de propiedades *Chile*

reap [riːp] *vi, vt* cosechar

reappear [ˌriːəˈpɪər, *Am:* -ˈpɪr] *vi* reaparecer

reappraisal [ˌriːəˈpreɪzl] *n* FIN revaluación *f*

rear[1] [rɪər, *Am:* rɪr] **I.** *adj* trasero **II.** *n* parte *f* trasera

rear[2] [rɪər, *Am:* rɪr] **I.** *vt* (*child, animals*) criar **II.** *vi* (*horse*) encabritarse

rearguard [ˈrɪəgɑːd, *Am:* ˈrɪrgɑːrd] *n no pl* retaguardia *f*

rearrange [ˌriːəˈreɪndʒ] *vt* reorganizar

rear view mirror *n* retrovisor *m*

reason [ˈriːzn] **I.** *n* **1.** (*motive*) motivo *m*; **the ~ why ...** el motivo por el que... **2.** (*sanity*) razón *f*; **to listen to** ~ atender a razones **II.** *vi, vt* razonar

reasonable [ˈriːznəbl] *adj* sensato; (*demand*) razonable

reasonably [ˈriːznəbli] *adv* **1.** (*fairly*) razonablemente **2.** (*acceptably*) bastante

reasoning [ˈriːznɪŋ] *n no pl* razonamiento *m*

reassurance [ˌriːəˈʃʊərəns, *Am:* -ˈʃʊrəns] *n* **1.** (*comfort*) palabras *fpl* tranquilizadoras **2.** *no pl* FIN reaseguro *m*

reassure [ˌriːəˈʃʊər, *Am:* -ˈʃʊr] *vt* tranquilizar

rebate [ˈriːbeɪt] *n* **1.** (*refund*) reembolso *m*; **tax** ~ devolución *f* de impuestos **2.** (*discount*) rebaja *f*

rebel[1] [ˈrebl] *n* rebelde *mf*

rebel[2] [rɪˈbel] <-ll-> *vi* rebelarse

rebellion [rɪˈbelɪən, *Am:* -ˈbeljən] *n no pl* rebelión *f*

rebellious [rɪˈbelɪəs, *Am:* -ˈbeljəs] *adj* rebelde; (*child*) revoltoso

rebirth [ˌriːˈbɜːθ, *Am:* -ˈbɜːrθ] *n* renacimiento *m*

rebound [rɪˈbaʊnd, *Am:* riːˈ-] **I.** *vi* rebotar **II.** *n no pl* rebote *m*

rebuff [rɪˈbʌf] **I.** *vt* rechazar **II.** *n* rechazo *m*

rebuild [ˌriːˈbɪld] *vt irr* reconstruir

rebuke [rɪˈbjuːk] **I.** *vt* reprender **II.** *n* reprimenda *f*

rebut [rɪˈbʌt] <-tt-> *vt* rebatir

recall [rɪˈkɔːl] **I.** *vt* **1.** (*remember*) recordar **2.** (*call back: ambassador*) retirar **II.** *n* memoria *f*

recant [rɪˈkænt] *vi* retractarse

recap [ˈriːkæp] <-pp-> *vi, vt* recapitular

recede [rɪˈsiːd] *vi* retirarse

receding hairline *n* entradas *fpl*

receipt [rɪˈsiːt] *n* **1.** (*document*) recibo *m* **2.** *pl* COM ingresos *mpl* **3.** (*act of receiving*) recepción *f*; **on** ~ **of ...** al recibo de...

receive [rɪˈsiːv] *vt* recibir; (*proposal*) acoger; (*injury*) sufrir

receiver [rɪˈsiːvər, *Am:* -ər] *n* **1.** TEL auricular *m*, tubo *m AmL*, fono *m Chile* **2.** RADIO receptor *m*

recent [ˈriːsənt] *adj* reciente; **in** ~ **times** en los últimos tiempos

recently *adv* recientemente

receptacle [rɪˈseptəkl] *n* receptáculo *m*

reception [rɪˈsepʃən] *n* **1.** *no pl* (*welcome*) acogida *f* **2.** (*in hotel*) recepción *f*

reception desk *n* (mesa *f* de) recepción *f*

receptionist [rɪˈsepʃənɪst] *n* recepcionista *mf*

recess [rɪˈses, *Am:* ˈriːses] <-es> *n* **1.** POL suspensión *f* de actividades, receso *m AmL* **2.** *Am, Aus* SCHOOL recreo *m* **3.** ARCHIT hueco *m* **4.** *pl* (*place*) lugar *m* recóndito

recession [rɪˈseʃn] *n* **1.** (*retreat*) retroceso *m* **2.** ECON recesión *f*

recharge [ˌriːˈtʃɑːdʒ, *Am:* -ˈtʃɑːrdʒ] *vt* recargar

recipe [ˈresəpi] *n* receta *f*

recipient [rɪˈsɪpɪənt] *n* beneficiario, -a *m, f*; (*of letter*) destinatario, -a *m, f*
reciprocate [rɪˈsɪprəkeɪt] I. *vt* corresponder a, reciprocar *AmL* II. *vi* corresponder
recital [rɪˈsaɪtl, *Am:* -t̬l] *n* 1. MUS recital *m* 2. (*description*) relación *f*
recitation [ˌresɪˈteɪʃn] *n* LIT recitación *f*
recite [rɪˈsaɪt] *vt* 1. (*repeat*) recitar 2. (*list*) enumerar
reckless [ˈrekləs] *adj* imprudente; LAW temerario
reckon [ˈrekən] I. *vt* 1. (*calculate*) calcular 2. (*consider*) considerar; **to ~ (that)** ... creer (que)... II. *vi inf* calcular
  ◆ **reckon on** *vt insep* 1. (*count on*) contar con 2. (*expect*) esperar
  ◆ **reckon without** *vt insep* no tener en cuenta
reckoning [ˈrekənɪŋ] *n* cálculo *m*
reclaim [rɪˈkleɪm] *vt* 1. (*claim back*) reclamar 2. (*reuse: land*) recuperar; (*material*) reciclar
recline [rɪˈklaɪn] *vi* apoyarse
reclining seat *n* asiento *m* reclinable
recluse [rɪˈkluːs, *Am:* ˈrekluːs] *n* ermitaño, -a *m, f*
recognition [ˌrekəgˈnɪʃən] *n no pl* a. INFOR reconocimiento *m*; **in ~ of** en reconocimiento de
recognize [ˈrekəgnaɪz] *vt* reconocer
recoil¹ [rɪˈkɔɪl] *vi* echarse atrás; **to ~ from doing sth** rehuir hacer algo
recoil² [ˈriːkɔɪl] *n* retroceso *m*
recollect [ˌrekəˈlekt] *vi, vt* recordar
recollection [ˌrekəˈlekʃn] *n* recuerdo *m*; **to have no ~ of sth** no recordar algo
recommend [ˌrekəˈmend] *vt* recomendar; **it is not to be ~ed** no es recomendable
recommendation [ˌrekəmenˈdeɪʃən, *Am:* -mənˈ-] *n* 1. (*suggestion*) recomendación *f* 2. (*advice*) consejo *m*
reconcile [ˈrekənsaɪl] *vt* (*person*) reconciliar; (*fact*) conciliar; **to become ~d to sth** resignarse a algo
reconciliation [ˌrekənˌsɪlɪˈeɪʃn] *n*

reconciliación *f*
recondition [ˌriːkənˈdɪʃn] *vt* reacondicionar
reconnoiter *Am,* **reconnoitre** [ˌrekəˈnɔɪtəʳ, *Am:* ˌriːkəˈnɔɪt̬əʳ] I. *vt* reconocer II. *vi* reconocer el terreno
reconsider [ˌriːkənˈsɪdəʳ, *Am:* -əʳ] *vt* reconsiderar
reconstruct [ˌriːkənˈstrʌkt] *vt* reconstruir
record¹ [ˈrekɔːd, *Am:* -əʳd] I. *n* 1. (*account*) relación *f*; (*document*) documento *m*; **to say sth off the ~** decir algo extraoficialmente 2. *no pl* (*sb's past*) antecedentes *mpl*; **to have a good ~** tener un buen historial 3. *pl* archivos *mpl* 4. MUS disco *m* 5. SPORTS récord *m* 6. LAW acta *f* 7. INFOR juego *m* de datos II. *adj* récord; **to do sth in ~ time** hacer algo en un tiempo récord
record² [rɪˈkɔːd, *Am:* -ˈkɔːrd] *vt* 1. (*store*) archivar 2. a. INFOR registrar; MUS grabar 3. LAW hacer constar en acta
recorder [rɪˈkɔːdəʳ, *Am:* -ˈkɔːrdəʳ] *n* 1. (*tape recorder*) magnetofón *m* 2. MUS flauta *f* dulce
record holder *n* plusmarquista *mf*
recording [rɪˈkɔːdɪŋ] *n* grabación *f*
recording studio *n* estudio *m* de grabación
record library *n* discoteca *f* **record player** *n* tocadiscos *m inv*
recount¹ [rɪˈkaʊnt] *vt* (*narrate*) contar
recount² [ˈriːkaʊnt] *n* POL recuento *m*
recoup [rɪˈkuːp] *vt* (*losses*) resarcirse de
recourse [rɪˈkɔːs, *Am:* ˈriːkɔːrs] *n no pl* recurso *m*; **to have ~** recurrir a
recover [rɪˈkʌvəʳ, *Am:* -əʳ] *vi, vt* recuperar(se)
recovery [rɪˈkʌvəri, *Am:* -əʳi] <-ies> *n* 1. a. MED, ECON recuperación *f* 2. INFOR reactivación *f*
recreate [ˌriːkriˈeɪt] *vt* recrear
recreation [ˌriːkriˈeɪʃn] *n no pl* recreación *f*
recreational [ˌrekriˈeɪʃənəl] *adj* re-

Rᵣ

creativo

recrimination [rɪˌkrɪmɪˈneɪʃn, *Am:* -əˈ-] *n pl* recriminación *f*

recruit [rɪˈkruːt] I. *vt* reclutar; (*employee*) contratar II. *n* recluta *mf*

recruitment *n no pl* reclutamiento *m*

rectangle [ˈrektæŋgl] *n* rectángulo *m*

rectangular [rekˈtæŋgjʊləʳ, *Am:* -gjələ·] *adj* rectangular

rectify [ˈrektɪfaɪ, *Am:* -tə-] *vt* rectificar

rector [ˈrektəʳ, *Am:* -tə·] *n* **1.** *Brit* REL ≈ párroco *m* **2.** *Am, Scot* SCHOOL director(a) *m(f);* UNIV rector(a) *m(f)*

rectum [ˈrektəm] *n* ANAT recto *m*

recuperate [rɪˈkuːpəreɪt] *vi* recuperarse

recur [rɪˈkɜːʳ, *Am:* -ˈkɜːr] *vi* repetirse

recurrence [rɪˈkʌrəns, *Am:* -ˈkɜːr-] *n* repetición *f*

recurrent [rɪˈkʌrənt, *Am:* -ˈkɜːr-] *adj* repetido

recycle [ˌriːˈsaɪkl] *vt* reciclar

red [red] <-dd-> *adj* rojo; **to be in the** ~ FIN estar en números rojos

red-blooded [ˌredˈblʌdɪd] *adj* fogoso

Red Cross *n no pl* **the** ~ la Cruz Roja

redcurrant *n* grosella *f*

redden [ˈredn] *vi, vt* enrojecer(se)

reddish [ˈredɪʃ] *adj* rojizo

redecorate [ˌriːˈdekəreɪt] *vt* redecorar; (*paint*) volver a pintar

redeem [rɪˈdiːm] *vt a.* REL redimir; (*pawned item*) desempeñar

redeeming [rɪˈdiːmɪŋ] *adj* redentor; **he has no** ~ **features** no tiene ningún punto a su favor

redefine [ˌriːdɪˈfaɪn] *vt* redefinir

redemption [rɪˈdempʃən] *n no pl* redención *f*

redeploy [ˌriːdɪˈplɔɪ] *vt* (*staff*) reorganizar, reubicar *AmL*

redeployment *n* redistribución *f*

red-handed [ˌredˈhændɪd] *adj* **to catch sb** ~ pillar a alguien con las manos en la masa

redhead [ˈredhed] *n* pelirrojo, -a *m, f*

red herring *n fig* pista *f* falsa

red-hot [ˌredˈhɒt, *Am:* -ˈhɑːt] *adj* candente

redirect [ˌriːdɪˈrekt] *vt* (*letter*) reexpedir

redistribute [ˌriːdɪˈstrɪbjuːt] *vt* redistribuir

red light *n* semáforo *m* en rojo **red-light district** *n* barrio *m* chino

redness [ˈrednɪs] *n no pl* rojez *f*

redo [ˌriːˈduː] *vt irr* rehacer

redolent [ˈredələnt] *adj form* **1.** (*smelling of*) ~ **of sth** con olor a algo **2.** (*suggestive of*) **to be** ~ **of sth** hacer pensar en algo

redouble [rɪˈdʌbl] *vt* redoblar; **to** ~ **one's efforts** redoblar los esfuerzos

redraft [ˌriːˈdrɑːft, *Am:* -ˈdræft] *vt* volver a redactar

redress [rɪˈdres] I. *vt* reparar II. *n* reparación *f*

Red Sea *n no pl* **the** ~ el Mar Rojo

redskin *n* piel *mf* roja **red tape** *n no pl* papeleo *m*

reduce [rɪˈdjuːs, *Am:* -ˈduːs] *vt* reducir; (*price*) rebajar; **to** ~ **sb to tears** hacer llorar a alguien; **to be** ~**d to doing sth** verse forzado a hacer algo

reduced [rɪˈdjuːst, *Am:* -ˈduːst] *adj* reducido, rebajado

reduction [rɪˈdʌkʃən] *n* reducción *f;* (*in price*) rebaja *f*

redundancy [rɪˈdʌndəntsi] <-ies> *n* **1.** *no pl* (*uselessness*) superfluidad *f* **2.** (*unemployment*) desempleo *m* **3.** *Brit, Aus* ECON despido *m*

redundant [rɪˈdʌndənt] *adj* **1.** (*superfluous*) superfluo; LING redundante **2.** *Brit, Aus* **to be made** ~ ser despedido

reed [riːd] *n* **1.** (*plant*) junco *m*, totora *f AmS* **2.** *Brit* (*straw*) caña *f* **3.** MUS lengüeta *f*

re-educate [ˌriːˈedʒʊkeɪt] *vt* reeducar

reef [riːf] *n* arrecife *m*

reek [riːk] *vi* apestar; **to** ~ **of corruption** apestar a corrupción

reel¹ [riːl] *n* carrete *m;* (*for film*) bobina *f*

reel² [riːl] *vi* **1.** (*move unsteadily*) tambalearse **2.** (*recoil*) retroceder

ref [ref] *n* **1.** *inf abbr of* **referee** árbitro, -a *m, f* **2.** *abbr of* **reference** referencia *f*

refectory [rɪˈfektəri] <-ies> *n* refectorio *m*

refer [rɪˈfɜːʳ, *Am:* -ˈfɜːr] <-rr-> *vt* remitir; **to ~ a patient to a specialist** mandar a un paciente a un especialista

◆ **refer to** *vt* **1.** (*mention*) referirse a; **refering to your letter/phone call, ...** con relación a su carta/llamada,... **2.** (*consult*) consultar; ~ **page 70** ver página 70

referee [ˌrefəˈriː] I. *n* **1.** SPORTS árbitro, -a *m, f*, referí *m AmL* **2.** *Brit* (*for employment*) persona *f* que da referencias del candidato II. *vi, vt* arbitrar

reference [ˈrefərənts] *n* **1.** (*consultation*) consulta *f* **2.** (*source*) referencia *f* **3.** (*allusion*) alusión *f*; **with ~ to what was said** en alusión a lo que se dijo **4.** (*for job application*) referencias *fpl*

reference book *n* libro *m* de consulta **reference library** *n* biblioteca *f* de consulta

referendum [ˌrefəˈrendəm] <-s *o* -da> *n* referéndum *m*

referral [rɪˈfɜːrəl] *n* remisión *f*

refill¹ [riːˈfɪl] *vt* rellenar

refill² [ˈriːfɪl] *n* recambio *m*

refine [rɪˈfaɪn] *vt* (*oil, sugar*) refinar

refined [rɪˈfaɪnd] *adj* **1.** (*oil, sugar*) refinado **2.** (*very polite*) fino

refinement [rɪˈfaɪnmənt] *n* **1.** (*improvement*) refinamiento *m* **2.** *no pl* (*good manners*) finura *f*

refinery [rɪˈfaɪnəri] <-ies> *n* refinería *f*

refit¹ [riːˈfɪt] <-tt- *o Am* -t-> *vt a.* NAUT reparar

refit² [ˈriːfɪt] *n a.* NAUT reparación *f*

reflect [rɪˈflekt] I. *vt* reflejar II. *vi* **1.** (*cast back light*) reflejarse **2.** (*contemplate*) reflexionar; **to ~ badly on sth** no decir mucho de algo

reflection [rɪˈflekʃən] *n* **1.** (*image*) reflejo *m* **2.** (*thought*) reflexión *f*; **on ~** pensándolo bien

reflector [rɪˈflektəʳ, *Am:* -ɚ] *n* reflector *m*; (*of car*) captafaros *m inv*

reflex [ˈriːfleks] <-es> *n* reflejo *m*

reflexive [rɪˈfleksɪv] *adj* reflexivo

reform [rɪˈfɔːm, *Am:* -ˈfɔːrm] I. *vt* reformar II. *n* reforma *f*

reformation [ˌrefəˈmeɪʃən, *Am:* -ɚˈ-] *n* reforma *f*; **the Reformation** la Reforma

reformatory [rɪˈfɔːmətəri, *Am:* -ˈfɔːrmətɔːri] <-ies> *n Am* reformatorio *m*

refrain¹ [rɪˈfreɪn] *vi form* abstenerse; **to ~ from doing sth** abstenerse de hacer algo

refrain² [rɪˈfreɪn] *n* MUS estribillo *m*

refresh [rɪˈfreʃ] *vt* refrescar

refresher *n* **1.** (*course*) curso *m* de reciclaje **2.** *Brit* LAW honorarios *mpl* suplementarios

refreshing *adj* (*drink*) refrescante; (*change*) reconfortante

refreshment [rɪˈfreʃmənt] *n* refresco *m*

refrigeration [rɪˌfrɪdʒəˈreɪʃn] *n no pl* refrigeración *f*

refrigerator [rɪˈfrɪdʒəreɪtəʳ, *Am:* -ṱɚ] *n* nevera *f*, refrigerador *m AmL*

refuel [ˌriːˈfjuːəl] <-ll-, *Am:* -l-> *vi* repostar combustible

refuge [ˈrefjuːdʒ] *n* refugio *m*; **to take ~ in sth** refugiarse en algo

refugee [ˌrefjʊˈdʒiː] *n* refugiado, -a *m, f*

refugee camp *n* campo *m* de refugiados

refund¹ [ˌriːˈfʌnd] *vt* reembolsar

refund² [ˈriːfʌnd] *n* reembolso *m*

refurbish [ˌriːˈfɜːbɪʃ, *Am:* -ˈfɜːrbɪʃ] *vt* restaurar, refaccionar *AmL*

refusal [rɪˈfjuːzl] *n* negativa *f*

refuse¹ [rɪˈfjuːz] I. *vi* negarse II. *vt* (*request*) rechazar; (*permission*) denegar; **to ~ sb sth** negar algo a alguien

refuse² [ˈrefjuːs] *n form* basura *f*

refuse collection *n* recogida *f* de basuras

regain [rɪˈgeɪn] *vt* recuperar, recobrar

regal [ˈriːgl] *adj* regio

regard [rɪˈgɑːd, *Am:* -ˈgɑːrd] I. *vt* **1.** (*consider*) considerar **2.** *form* (*watch*) contemplar **3.** (*concerning*)

as ~s ... respecto a... **II.** *n form* **1.** (*consideration*) consideración *f;* **to pay no ~ to sth** no prestar atención a algo; **with ~ to ...** en cuanto a... **2.** (*respect*) respeto *m*, estima *f* **3.** (*point*) respecto *m* **4.** *pl* (*in messages*) recuerdos *mpl;* **with kind ~s** muchos saludos

regarding *prep* en cuanto a

regardless [rɪ'gɑːdləs, *Am:* -'gɑːrd-] **I.** *adv* a pesar de todo **II.** *adj* indiferente; **~ of ...** sin tener en cuenta...

regatta [rɪ'gætə, *Am:* -'gɑːtə] *n* regata *f*

reggae ['regeɪ] *n no pl* reggae *m*

regime [reɪ'ʒiːm, *Am:* rə'-] *n* régimen *m*

regiment ['redʒɪmənt, *Am:* -ə-mənt] **I.** *n* regimiento *m* **II.** *vt* reglamentar

region ['riːdʒən] *n* región *f;* **in the ~ of 30** alrededor de 30

regional ['riːdʒənl] *adj* regional

register ['redʒɪstər, *Am:* -stər] **I.** *n* registro *m* **II.** *vt* registrar; (*car*) matricular; (*letter*) certificar **III.** *vi* inscribirse; UNIV matricularse, inscribirse *AmL*

registered ['redʒɪstəd, *Am:* -ərd] *adj* registrado; (*student*) matriculado; (*letter*) certificado

registrar [ˌredʒɪ'strɑːr, *Am:* 'redʒɪstrɑːr] *n* ADMIN secretario, -a *m, f* del registro civil

registration [ˌredʒɪ'streɪʃən] *n* **1.** (*act*) inscripción *f;* UNIV matriculación *f* **2.** (*number*) matrícula *f*

registry ['redʒɪstri] *n Brit* registro *m*

regret [rɪ'gret] **I.** <-tt-> *vt* lamentar; **we ~ any inconvenience to passengers** lamentamos las molestias para los pasajeros **II.** *n* arrepentimiento *m*

regretfully *adv* lamentablemente

regular ['regjʊlər, *Am:* -jələr] **I.** *adj* regular; (*appearance*) habitual **II.** *n* **1.** (*customer*) asiduo, -a *m, f* **2.** MIL soldado *m* regular

regularity [ˌregjʊ'lærəti, *Am:* -'lerəti] *n no pl* regularidad *f*

regularly *adv* con regularidad

regulate ['regjʊleɪt] *vt* **1.** (*supervise*) reglamentar **2.** (*adjust*) regular

regulation [ˌregjʊ'leɪʃn] *n* **1.** (*rule*) regla *f* **2.** *no pl* (*adjustment*) regulación *f*

rehabilitate [ˌriːhə'bɪlɪteɪt, *Am:* '-ə-] *vt* rehabilitar

rehabilitation [ˌriːhəˌbɪlɪ'teɪʃən, *Am:* -ə'-] *n no pl* rehabilitación *f*

rehash [ˌriː'hæʃ] *vt* hacer un refrito de

rehearsal [rɪ'hɜːsl, *Am:* -'hɜːrsl] *n* ensayo *m*

rehearse [rɪ'hɜːs, *Am:* -'hɜːrs] *vt, vi* ensayar

reign [reɪn] **I.** *vi* **1.** (*be monarch*) reinar **2.** *fig* imperar **II.** *n* **1.** (*sovereignty*) reinado *m* **2.** (*rule*) régimen *m*

reimburse [ˌriːɪm'bɜːs, *Am:* -'bɜːrs] *vt* reembolsar

rein [reɪn] *n* rienda *f;* **to give free ~ to sb** dar rienda suelta a alguien

reincarnation [ˌriːɪnkɑː'neɪʃn, *Am:* -kɑːr'-] *n* reencarnación *f*

reindeer ['reɪndɪər, *Am:* -dɪr] *n inv* reno *m*

reinforce [ˌriːɪn'fɔːs, *Am:* -'fɔːrs] *vt* reforzar

reinforcement *n* refuerzo *m*

reinstate [ˌriːɪn'steɪt] *vt form* restituir

reiterate [ri'ɪtəreɪt, *Am:* -'ɪtəreɪt] *vt* reiterar

reject¹ [rɪ'dʒekt] *vt* rechazar; (*proposal*) descartar

reject² ['riːdʒekt] *n* artículo *m* defectuoso

rejection [rɪ'dʒekʃən] *n* rechazo *m*

rejoice [rɪ'dʒɔɪs] *vi* regocijarse

rejuvenate [riː'dʒuːvəneɪt] *vt* rejuvenecer

relapse [rɪ'læps] **I.** *n* MED recaída *f* **II.** *vi a.* MED recaer

relate [rɪ'leɪt] **I.** *vt* **1.** (*establish connection*) relacionar **2.** (*tell*) contar **II.** *vi* (*be connected with*) **to ~ to sb/sth** estar relacionado con alguien/algo

related *adj* **1.** (*linked*) relacionado **2.** (*in same family*) emparentado; **to be ~ to sb** estar emparentado con alguien

relating to *prep* acerca de

relation [rɪˈleɪʃən] *n* **1.** *no pl* (*link*) relación *f*; **in ~ to** en relación a; **to bear no ~ to sb/sth** no tener relación con alguien/algo **2.** (*relative*) pariente *mf* **3.** *pl* (*contact*) relaciones *fpl*

relationship [rɪˈleɪʃənʃɪp] *n* **1.** (*link*) relación *f* **2.** (*family connection*) parentesco *m* **3.** (*between two people*) relaciones *fpl*; **business ~s** relaciones comerciales

relative [ˈrelətɪv, *Am:* -t̬ɪv] **I.** *adj* relativo **II.** *n* pariente *mf*

relatively *adv* relativamente

relax [rɪˈlæks] *vi, vt* relajar(se); **~!** ¡cálmate!

relaxation [ˌriːlækˈseɪʃən] *n* relajación *f*

relaxed *adj* relajado

relay [ˈriːleɪ] **I.** *vt* TV retransmitir **II.** *n* SPORTS carrera *f* de relevos

release [rɪˈliːs] **I.** *vt* **1.** (*set free*) poner en libertad **2.** (*cease to hold*) soltar **3.** (*gas*) emitir **4.** (*film*) estrenar **II.** *n* *no pl* **1.** (*of hostage*) liberación *f* **2.** (*escape*) escape *m* **3.** *no pl* (*of film*) estreno *m*

relegate [ˈrelɪgeɪt, *Am:* ˈrelə-] *vt* relegar

relent [rɪˈlent] *vi* ceder; (*wind, rain*) amainar

relentless [rɪˈlentləs] *adj* implacable

relevance [ˈreləvənts] *n*, **relevancy** *n no pl* pertinencia

relevant [ˈreləvənt] *adj* pertinente

reliability [rɪˌlaɪəˈbɪləti, *Am:* -t̬i] *n no pl* **1.** (*dependability*) seguridad *f* **2.** (*trustworthiness*) fiabilidad *f*

reliable [rɪˈlaɪəbl] *adj* **1.** (*credible*) fidedigno; (*testimony*) verídico **2.** (*trustworthy*) de confianza

reliance [rɪˈlaɪəns] *n no pl* **1.** (*dependence*) dependencia *f* **2.** (*belief*) confianza *f*

relic [ˈrelɪk] *n a. fig* reliquia *f*

relief [rɪˈliːf] *n* **1.** *no pl* (*aid*) socorro *m* **2.** (*relaxation*) alivio *m* **3.** (*replacement*) relevo *m* **4.** *a.* GEO relieve *m*

relieve [rɪˈliːv] *vt* **1.** (*assist*) socorrer

2. (*pain*) aliviar **3.** MIL descercar **4.** (*urinate*) **to ~ oneself** hacer sus necesidades

relieved *adj* aliviado

religion [rɪˈlɪdʒən] *n* religión *f*

religious [rɪˈlɪdʒəs] *adj* religioso

relinquish [rɪˈlɪŋkwɪʃ] *vt* ceder; (*claim, title*) renunciar a

relish [ˈrelɪʃ] **I.** *n* **1.** *no pl* (*enjoyment*) gusto *m* **2.** (*enthusiasm*) entusiasmo *m* **3.** GASTR condimento *m* **II.** *vt* deleitarse en

relocate [ˌriːləʊˈkeɪt, *Am:* -ˈloʊkeɪt] *vi, vt* trasladar(se)

reluctance [rɪˈlʌktəns] *n no pl* desgana *f*

reluctant [rɪˈlʌktənt] *adj* reacio; **to be ~ to do sth** tener pocas ganas de hacer algo

rely [rɪˈlaɪ] *vi* **to ~ on** [*o* **upon**] confiar en; (*depend on*) depender de

remain [rɪˈmeɪn] *vi* **1.** (*stay*) quedar(se) **2.** (*continue*) permanecer; **to ~ seated** quedarse sentado; **the fact ~s that ...** sigue siendo un hecho que...

remainder [rɪˈmeɪndər, *Am:* -dɚ] *n no pl a.* MAT resto *m*

remaining [rɪˈmeɪnɪŋ] *adj* restante

remains [rɪˈmeɪnz] *npl* restos *mpl*

remand [rɪˈmɑːnd, *Am:* -ˈmænd] **I.** *vt* **to ~ sb to prison** [*o* **in custody**] poner a alguien en prisión preventiva **II.** *n* **to be on ~** estar en prisión preventiva

remark [rɪˈmɑːk, *Am:* -ˈmɑːrk] **I.** *vi* **to ~ on sth** hacer observaciones sobre algo **II.** *n* observación *f*

remarkable [rɪˈmɑːkəbl, *Am:* -ˈmɑːr-] *adj* extraordinario; (*coincidence*) singular

remedial [rɪˈmiːdiəl] *adj* SCHOOL recuperativo

remedy [ˈremədi] **I.** <-ies> *n* remedio *m* **II.** *vt* remediar, corregir

remember [rɪˈmembər, *Am:* -bɚ] *vt* **1.** (*recall*) recordar; **I can't ~ his name** no recuerdo su nombre **2.** (*commemorate*) conmemorar

remembrance [rɪˈmembrənts] *n no pl* recuerdo *m*; **in ~ of** en conmemoración de

R
r

? El **Remembrance Day, Re-membrance Sunday** o **Poppy Day** se celebra el segundo domingo de noviembre en conmemoración del armisticio firmado el 11 de noviembre de 1918. Este día se recuerda especialmente con misas y distintas ceremonias a todos aquellos soldados que murieron en las dos guerras mundiales. Las personas llevan unas amapolas de tela, que simbolizan las amapolas florecientes de los campos de batalla de Flandes después de la I Guerra Mundial. A las 11 de la mañana se guardan dos minutos de silencio.

remind [rɪ'maɪnd] vt recordar; **to ~ sb to do sth** recordar a alguien que haga algo; **he ~s me of you** me recuerda a ti; **that ~s me, ...** por cierto,...
reminder [rɪ'maɪndəʳ, Am: -ɚ] n **1.** (note) recordatorio m **2.** (memento) recuerdo m
reminisce [ˌremɪ'nɪs, Am: -ə'-] vi narrar reminiscencias
reminiscent [ˌremɪ'nɪsnt, Am: -ə'-] adj **to be ~ of sb/sth** hacer pensar en alguien/algo
remiss [rɪ'mɪs] adj negligente
remission [rɪ'mɪʃn] n remisión f
remit [rɪ'mɪt] <-tt-> vt form remitir; (money) enviar
remittance [rɪ'mɪtns] n giro m
remnant ['remnənt] n resto m
remorse [rɪ'mɔːs, Am:-'mɔːrs] n no pl remordimiento m
remorseful [rɪ'mɔːsfəl, Am: -'mɔːrs-] adj arrepentido
remorseless [rɪ'mɔːsləs, Am: -'mɔːrs-] adj implacable
remote [rɪ'məʊt, Am: -'moʊt] adj <-er, -est> remoto
remote control n mando m a distancia
remould ['riːməʊld, Am: -moʊld]

n recauchutado m
removable [rɪ'muːvəbl] adj desmontable
removal [rɪ'muːvəl] n **1.** no pl (of stain) eliminación f **2.** (extraction) extracción f **3.** no pl, Brit (move) mudanza f
removal van n camión m de mudanzas
remove [rɪ'muːv] vt **1.** (take away) quitar **2.** (get rid of) eliminar; (entry, name) borrar; (doubts, fears) disipar
remuneration [rɪˌmjuːnə'reɪʃn] n form remuneración f
Renaissance [rɪ'neɪsns, Am: ˌrenə-'sɑːns] n **the ~** el Renacimiento
rename [ˌriː'neɪm] vt poner un nuevo nombre a
render ['rendəʳ, Am: -dɚ] vt form **1.** (make) hacer **2.** (give: thanks) ofrecer; (aid) prestar
rendering ['rendərɪŋ] n MUS interpretación f
rendezvous ['rɒndɪvuː, 'rɒndɪ-vuːz, Am: 'rɑːndeɪ-] **I.** n inv cita f **II.** vi reunirse
rendition [ren'dɪʃn] n interpretación f
renew [rɪ'njuː, Am: -'nuː] vt renovar; (relationship) reanudar
renewable [rɪ'njuːəbl, Am: -'nuː-] adj renovable
renewal [rɪ'njuːəl, Am: -'nuː-] n renovación f
renounce [rɪ'naʊns] vt renunciar a
renovate ['renəveɪt] vt restaurar, refaccionar Ven, Col
renovation [ˌrenə'veɪʃn] n renovación f
renown [rɪ'naʊn] n no pl renombre m
renowned [rɪ'naʊnd] adj renombrado
rent [rent] **I.** n alquiler m **II.** vt alquilar
rental ['rentəl, Am: -təl] n alquiler m
rent boy n Brit, inf chico m de compañía
reopen [riː'əʊpən, Am: -'oʊ-] vt reabrir
reorder [ˌriː'ɔːdəʳ] vt **1.** (reorganize)

reordenar **2.**COM hacer un nuevo pedido de

reorganize [riːˈɔːɡənaɪz, *Am:* -ˈɔːrɡən-] *vt* reorganizar

rep [rep] *n inf* **1.** *abbr of* **representative** representante *mf* de ventas **2.** THEAT *abbr of* **repertory** repertorio *m*

Rep. 1. *abbr of* **Republic** Rep. **2.** *abbr of* **Republican** republicano

repair [riːˈpeəʳ, *Am:* -ˈper] **I.** *vt* reparar, arreglar **II.** *n* reparación *f*, arreglo *m*; **to be under** ~ estar en reparación; **to be in good/bad** ~ estar en buen/mal estado

repair kit *n* caja *f* de herramientas

repatriate [riːˈpætrieɪt, *Am:* -ˈpeɪtriː-] *vt* repatriar

repay [rɪˈpeɪ] <repaid> *vt* (*money*) devolver; (*debts*) liquidar; (*person*) pagar

repayment [rɪˈpeɪmənt] *n* reembolso *m*

repeal [rɪˈpiːl] **I.** *vt* revocar **II.** *n no pl* revocatoria *f*

repeat [rɪˈpiːt] **I.** *vi*, *vt* repetir(se) **II.** *n* repetición *f*

repeatedly *adv* repetidas veces

repel [rɪˈpel] <-ll-> *vt* repugnar

repellent [rɪˈpelənt] **I.** *n* repelente *m* **II.** *adj* repugnante

repent [rɪˈpent] *vi form* arrepentirse

repentance [rɪˈpentəns] *n no pl* arrepentimiento *m*

repercussion [ˌriːpəˈkʌʃən, *Am:* -pɚ-] *n* repercusión *f*

repertoire [ˈrepətwɑːʳ, *Am:* -ɚtwɑːr] *n* repertorio *m*

repertory company [ˈrepətəri ˈkʌmpəni, *Am:* -ɚtɔːri-] *n Brit* compañía *f* de repertorio **repertory theatre** *n Brit* teatro *m* de repertorio

repetition [ˌrepɪˈtɪʃən, *Am:* -əˈ-] *n* repetición *f*

repetitive [rɪˈpetətɪv, *Am:* -ˈpetə-tɪv] *adj* repetitivo

replace [rɪˈpleɪs] *vt* **1.** (*take the place of*) reemplazar **2.** (*put back*) reponer

replacement [rɪˈpleɪsmənt] *n*

1. (*person*) sustituto, -a *m, f*; (*part*) recambio *m* **2.** (*act of substituting*) sustitución *f*

replay [ˈriːpleɪ] *n* SPORTS, TV repetición *f*

replenish [rɪˈplenɪʃ] *vt* rellenar; (*stocks*) reponer

replica [ˈreplɪkə] *n* réplica *f*

reply [rɪˈplaɪ] **I.** <-ied> *vi* **1.** (*verbally*) contestar **2.** (*react*) responder **II.** <-ies> *n* respuesta *f*

reply coupon *n* cupón *m* respuesta

report [rɪˈpɔːt, *Am:* -ˈpɔːrt] **I.** *n* **1.** (*account*) informe *m*; PUBL reportaje *m*; **to give a** ~ presentar un informe **2.** (*explosion*) estallido *m* **II.** *vt* **1.** (*recount*) relatar; **to** ~ **that** ... informar que... **2.** (*denounce*) denunciar **III.** *vi* **1.** (*make results public*) presentar un informe **2.** (*arrive at work*) presentarse

report card *n Am* cartilla *f* escolar

reporter [rɪˈpɔːtəʳ, *Am:* -ˈpɔːrtɚ] *n* reportero, -a *m, f*

repose [rɪˈpəʊz, *Am:* -ˈpoʊz] *n no pl* reposo *m*; **in** ~ de reposo

represent [ˌreprɪˈzent] *vt* **1.** (*act for*) representar **2.** (*state*) declarar

representation [ˌreprɪzenˈteɪʃən] *n* **1.** (*acting for*) representación *f* **2.** (*statement*) declaración *f*

representative [ˌreprɪˈzentətɪv, *Am:* -t̬ət̬ɪv] **I.** *adj* representativo **II.** *n* **1.** *a.* COM representante *mf*, agenciero, -a *m, f* Arg **2.** POL diputado, -a *m, f*

repress [rɪˈpres] *vt* reprimir

repression [rɪˈpreʃn] *n no pl* represión *f*

reprieve [rɪˈpriːv] **I.** *vt* indultar **II.** *n* indulto *m*

reprimand [ˈreprɪmɑːnd, *Am:* -rəmænd] **I.** *vt* reprender **II.** *n* reprimenda *f*

reprint[1] [ˌriːˈprɪnt] *vt* reimprimir

reprint[2] [ˈriːprɪnt] *n* reimpresión *f*

reprisal [rɪˈpraɪzl] *n* represalia *f*; **to take** ~**s** tomar represalias

reproach [rɪˈprəʊtʃ, *Am:* -ˈproʊtʃ] **I.** *vt* reprochar **II.** *n* reproche *m*; **beyond** ~ intachable

reproduce [ˌriːprəˈdjuːs, *Am:*

-'duːs] *vi*, *vt* reproducir(se)
reproduction [ˌriːprə'dʌkʃn] *n* reproducción *f*
reptile ['reptaɪl] *n* reptil *m*
republic [rɪ'pʌblɪk] *n* república *f*
republican [rɪ'pʌblɪkən] **I.** *n* republicano, -a *m*, *f* **II.** *adj* republicano
republication [ˌriːˌpʌblɪ'keɪʃn] *n* *no pl* reedición *f*

? La **Republic of Malta** (República de Malta), que durante los años 1814 al 1947 fue una colonia británica y base naval, se ha dado a conocer en los últimos años como **English language learning centre** (centro de enseñanza del inglés). Jóvenes de toda Europa viajan hasta Malta para participar en sus renombradas escuelas de inglés. La mayoría de las veces los estudiantes se alojan con familias maltesas. Durante el verano se celebran un gran número de actividades en la playa en las que los estudiantes que lo desean pueden participar. Además, al anochecer, la ciudad de Paceville ofrece múltiples posibilidades de diversión para gente joven.

---

repudiate [rɪ'pjuːdɪeɪt] *vt* (*accusation*) negar; (*suggestion*) rechazar
repugnant [rɪ'pʌɡnənt] *adj* repugnante
repulsive [rɪ'pʌlsɪv] *adj* repulsivo
reputable ['repjʊtəbl, *Am:* -t̬əbl] *adj* acreditado
reputation [ˌrepjʊ'teɪʃn] *n* reputación *f;* **to have a good/bad ~** tener buena/mala fama
repute [rɪ'pjuːt] *n* *no pl* reputación *f*
reputed [rɪ'pjuːtɪd, *Am:* -t̬ɪd] *adj* supuesto; **she is ~ to be rich** tiene fama de rica
request [rɪ'kwest] **I.** *n* petición *f;* ADMIN solicitud *f;* **on ~** a petición; **to make a ~ for sth** pedir algo **II.** *vt*

pedir; ADMIN solicitar
requiem ['rekwɪəm] *n,* **requiem mass** *n* réquiem *m*
require [rɪ'kwaɪəʳ, *Am:* -'kwaɪə˞] *vt* **1.** (*need*) necesitar **2.** (*demand*) exigir; **to ~ sb to do sth** exigir a alguien que haga algo
requirement [rɪ'kwaɪəmənt, *Am:* -'kwaɪə˞-] *n* requisito *m*
requisite ['rekwɪzɪt] **I.** *adj* indispensable **II.** *n* requisito *m*
requisition [ˌrekwɪ'zɪʃn] **I.** *vt* requisar **II.** *n* **1.** *no pl* solicitud *f* **2.** MIL requisa *f*
reroute [ˌriː'ruːt] *vt* desviar
rescue ['reskjuː] **I.** *vt* rescatar **II.** *n* rescate *m;* **to come to sb's ~** rescatar a alguien
rescuer ['reskjʊəʳ, *Am:* -ə˞] *n* salvador(a) *m(f)*
research [rɪ'sɜːtʃ, *Am:* 'riːsɜːrtʃ] **I.** *n* investigación *f* **II.** *vi, vt* investigar
researcher *n* investigador(a) *m(f)*
resemblance [rɪ'zembləns] *n* *no pl* parecido *m*
resemble [rɪ'zembl] *vt* parecerse a
resent [rɪ'zent] *vt* **to ~ sth** sentirse molesto por algo
resentful [rɪ'zentfəl] *adj* resentido
resentment [rɪ'zentmənt] *n* resentimiento *m*
reservation [ˌrezə'veɪʃən, *Am:* -ə˞'-] *n* reserva *f;* **to have ~s about sth** tener ciertas dudas sobre algo
reserve [rɪ'zɜːv, *Am:* -'zɜːrv] **I.** *n* **1.** reserva *f;* **to have sth in ~** tener algo en reserva **2.** SPORTS suplente *mf* **3.** MIL **the ~** la reserva **II.** *vt* reservar
reserved *adj* reservado
reservoir ['rezəvwɑːʳ, *Am:* -ə˞vwɑːr] *n* **1.** (*tank*) depósito *m* **2.** (*lake*) embalse *m*
reset [ˌriː'set] *vt irr* INFOR reiniciar
reshuffle [ˌriː'ʃʌfl] *n* reorganización *f*
reside [rɪ'zaɪd] *vi form* residir
residence ['rezɪdənts] *n* **1.** (*home*) domicilio *m* **2.** *no pl* (*act*) residencia *f*
residence permit *n* permiso *m* de residencia
resident ['rezɪdənt] **I.** *n* residente *mf* **II.** *adj* residente

residential [ˌrezɪ'denʃl] *adj* residencial

residue ['rezɪdjuː, *Am:* -ədu:] *n* residuo *m*

resign [rɪ'zaɪn] I. *vi* 1. (*leave job*) renunciar; POL dimitir 2. GAMES abandonar II. *vt* renunciar a; **to ~ one-self to sth** resignarse a algo

resignation [ˌrezɪg'neɪʃn] *n* 1. (*from job*) renuncia *f;* POL dimisión *f* 2. *no pl* (*conformity*) resignación *f*

resigned [rɪ'zaɪnd] *adj* resignado

resilience [rɪ'zɪlɪəns, *Am:* 'zɪljəns] *n no pl* (*of material*) elasticidad *f;* (*of person*) resistencia *f*

resilient [rɪ'zɪlɪənt, *Am:* -'zɪljənt] *adj* (*person*) resistente

resin ['rezɪn] *n no pl* resina *f*

resist [rɪ'zɪst] *vt* resistir

resistance [rɪ'zɪstənts] *n* resistencia *f*

resistant [rɪ'zɪstənt] *adj* resistente

resolute ['rezəluːt] *adj* resuelto

resolution [ˌrezə'luːʃn] *n* resolución *f*

resolve [rɪ'zɒlv, *Am:* -'zaːlv] I. *vt* 1. (*solve*) resolver 2. (*settle*) acordar II. *n* resolución *f*

resolved [rɪ'zɒlvd, *Am:* -'zaːlvd] *adj* resuelto

resort [rɪ'zɔːt, *Am:* -'zɔːrt] *n* 1. *no pl* (*use*) recurso *m;* **as a last ~** como último recurso 2. (*for holidays*) lugar *m* de veraneo; **ski ~** estación *f* de esquí

resound [rɪ'zaʊnd] *vi* resonar

resounding *adj* resonante; (*success*) rotundo

resource [rɪ'zɔːs, *Am:* 'riːsɔːrs] *n* recurso *m;* **natural ~s** recursos *mpl* naturales

resourceful [rɪ'zɔːsfəl, *Am:* -'sɔːrs-] *adj* ingenioso

respect [rɪ'spekt] I. *n* 1. (*relation*) respeto *m* 2. (*esteem*) estima *f;* **with all due ~** con el debido respeto 3. (*point*) respecto *m;* **in all/many/ some ~s** desde todos/muchos/algunos puntos de vista; **in this ~** a este respecto; **with ~ to** con respecto a 4. *pl* (*greetings*) recuerdos *mpl* II. *vt* respetar

respectable [rɪ'spektəbl] *adj* respetable; (*performance*) aceptable

respected [rɪ'spektəd] *adj* respetado

respectful [rɪ'spektfl] *adj* respetuoso

respective [rɪ'spektɪv] *adj* respectivo

respiration [ˌrespə'reɪʃen] *n no pl* respiración *f*

respite ['respaɪt, *Am:* -pɪt] *n no pl* 1. (*pause*) pausa *f* 2. (*delay*) retraso *m*

resplendent [rɪ'splendənt] *adj* resplandeciente

respond [rɪ'spɒnd, *Am:* -'spaːnd] *vi* 1. (*answer*) contestar 2. (*react*) responder

response [rɪ'spɒns, *Am:* -'spaːns] *n* 1. (*answer*) respuesta *f* 2. (*reaction*) reacción *f*

responsibility [rɪˌspɒnsə'bɪləti, *Am:* -ˌspaːnsə'bɪləti] *n* responsabilidad *f*

responsible [rɪ'spɒnsəbl, *Am:* -'spaːn-] *adj* responsable; **to be ~ for sth/to sb** ser responsable de algo/ante alguien

responsive [rɪ'spɒnsɪv, *Am:* -'spaːn-] *adj* sensible

rest¹ [rest] I. *vt* 1. (*cause to repose*) descansar 2. (*support*) apoyar II. *vi* 1. (*cease activity*) reposar, descansar 2. (*remain*) quedar 3. (*be supported*) apoyarse; **to ~ on sth** basarse en algo; **you can ~ assured that ...** esté seguro de que... III. *n* 1. (*period of repose*) descanso *m* 2. MUS pausa *f* 3. (*support*) apoyo *m*

rest² [rest] *n* resto *m;* **the ~** los demás

restaurant ['restərɔ̃ːŋ, *Am:* -təraːnt] *n* restaurante *m*

restaurant car *n Brit* vagón *m* restaurante

restful ['restfəl] *adj* tranquilo, relajante

restitution [ˌrestɪ'tjuːʃen, *Am:* -'tuː-] *n no pl* 1. (*return*) restitución *f* 2. LAW indemnización *f*

restive ['restɪv] *adj,* **restless** ['restlɪs] *adj* inquieto

R
r

restoration [ˌrestəˈreɪʃn] *n no pl* restauración *f*; (*return to owner*) devolución *f*

restore [rɪˈstɔːʳ, *Am:* -ˈstɔːr] *vt* **1.** (*building*) restaurar; (*peace*) reestablecer **2.** *form* (*return to owner*) restituir

restrain [rɪˈstreɪn] *vt* contener; (*temper*) dominar; **to ~ sb from doing sth** impedir que alguien haga algo

restrained [rɪˈstreɪnd] *adj* (*style*) sobrio

restraint [rɪˈstreɪnt] *n* **1.** *no pl* (*self-control*) dominio *m* de sí mismo **2.** (*restriction*) restricción *f*

restrict [rɪˈstrɪkt] *vt* restringir

restriction [rɪˈstrɪkʃən] *n* restricción *f*

rest room *n Am* aseos *mpl*

restructure [ˌriːˈstʌktʃəʳ, *Am:* -tʃɚ] *vt* reestructurar

result [rɪˈzʌlt] I. *n* resultado *m* II. *vi* **to ~ from** ser consecuencia de; **to ~ in** ocasionar

resume [rɪˈzjuːm, *Am:* -ˈzuːm] I. *vt* (*work, journey*) reanudar II. *vi form* proseguir

résumé [ˈrezjuːmeɪ, *Am:* ˈrezʊmeɪ] *n* **1.** (*summary*) resumen *m* **2.** *Am, Aus* (*curriculum vitae*) currículum *m* (vitae)

resumption [rɪˈzʌmpʃən] *n no pl* reanudación *f*

resurgence [rɪˈsɜːdʒəns, *Am:* -ˈsɜːrdʒəns] *f n no pl, form* resurgimiento *m*

resurrection [ˌrezəˈrekʃn] *n no pl* resurrección *f*

resuscitate [rɪˈsʌsɪteɪt, *Am:* -əteɪt] *vt* resucitar

retail [ˈriːteɪl] COM I. *n no pl* venta *f* al detalle II. *vt* vender al detalle III. *vi* venderse al detalle; **this product ~s at £5** el precio de venta al público de este producto es de 5 libras

retailer *n* minorista *mf*, menorista *mf Chile, Méx*

retail price *n* COM precio *m* de venta al público

retain [rɪˈteɪn] *vt* **1.** *form* (*keep*) retener, conservar **2.** (*employ*) contratar

retainer *n* **1.** ECON iguala *f* **2.** (*servant*) criado, -a *m, f*

retaliate [rɪˈtælɪeɪt] *vi* tomar represalias

retaliation [rɪˌtælɪˈeɪʃn] *n no pl* represalias *fpl*

retch [retʃ] *vi* tener arcadas

retentive [rɪˈtentɪv, *Am:* -t̬ɪv] *adj* retentivo

retina [ˈretɪnə, *Am:* ˈretnə] <-s *o* -nae> *n* retina *f*

retire [rɪˈtaɪəʳ, *Am:* -ˈtaɪɚ] *vi* **1.** (*stop working*) jubilarse **2.** *form* (*withdraw*) retirarse

retired *adj* jubilado

retirement [rɪˈtaɪəmənt, *Am:* -ˈtaɪɚ-] *n* jubilación *f*

retiring [rɪˈtaɪərɪŋ, *Am:* -ˈtaɪɚ-] *adj* **1.** (*reserved*) reservado **2.** (*worker, official*) saliente

retrace [riːˈtreɪs] *vt* repasar; **to ~ one's steps** volver sobre sus pasos

retract [rɪˈtrækt] I. *vt* (*statement*) retirar; (*claws*) retraer; (*wheels*) replegar II. *vi* retractarse

retrain [riːˈtreɪn] *vt* reciclar

retread [ˈriːtred] *n* neumático *m* recauchutado

retreat [rɪˈtriːt] I. *vi* retroceder; MIL batirse en retirada II. *n a.* MIL retirada *f*

retrial [ˌriːˈtraɪəl, *Am:* ˈriːtraɪl] *n* nuevo juicio *m*

retribution [ˌretrɪˈbjuːʃn, *Am:* -rə'-] *n no pl, form* castigo *m* justo

retrieval [rɪˈtriːvl] *n no pl a.* INFOR recuperación *f*; **on-line information ~** recuperación de información en línea

retrieve [rɪˈtriːv] *vt a.* INFOR recuperar; (*error*) enmendar; (*situation*) salvar

retriever [rɪˈtriːvəʳ, *Am:* -ɚ] *n* perro *m* cobrador

retrospect [ˈretrəspekt] *n no pl* **in ~** mirando hacia atrás

retrospective [ˌretrəˈspektɪv] I. *adj* **1.** (*looking back*) retrospectivo **2.** *Brit* LAW retroactivo II. *n* ART exposición *f* retrospectiva

return [rɪ'tɜːn, *Am:* -'tɜːrn] **I.** *n*
1. (*going back*) regreso *m*, vuelta *f*
2. (*giving back*) devolución *f;* **by ~**
(**of post**) *Brit, Aus* a vuelta de correo
3. (*recompense*) recompensa *f;* **in ~**
for sth a cambio de algo **4.** FIN ganancia *f* **5.** *fig* **many happy ~s** (**of
the day**)! ¡feliz cumpleaños! **II.** *adj*
1. (*ticket*) de ida y vuelta, redondo
Méx **2.** (*match*) de vuelta **III.** *vi*
1. (*come back*) volver **2.** (*reappear*)
volver a aparecer **IV.** *vt* **1.** (*give back*)
devolver **2.** (*reciprocate*) corresponder a **3.** (*send back*) volver a colocar **4.** *Brit* POL elegir
returning officer *n Can* POL escrutador(a) *m(f)*
return key *n* INFOR tecla *f* de retorno
reunion [ˌriː'juːnɪən, *Am:* -'juːnjən]
n **1.** (*meeting*) reunión *f* **2.** (*after
separation*) reencuentro *m*
reunite [ˌriːjuː'naɪt] *vt* volver a unir;
(*friends*) reconciliar
rev [rev] *n* AUTO revolution *f*
♦ **rev up** *vt* <-vv-> acelerar
revaluation [riːˌvæljʊ'eɪʃən] *n* revaluación *f*
revamp [ˌriː'væmp] *vt inf* modernizar
Revd. *abbr of* **Reverend** Rev.
reveal [rɪ'viːl] *vt* revelar
revealing [rɪ'viːlɪŋ] *adj* revelador
reveille [rɪ'væli, *Am:* 'revli] *n no pl*
MIL diana *f*
revel ['revl] <*Brit:* -ll-, *Am:* -l-> *vi* ir
de juerga
♦ **revel in** <*Brit:* -ll-, *Am:* -l-> *vi* **to
~ sth** deleitarse con algo
revelation [ˌrevə'leɪʃən] *n* revelación *f*
revelry ['revlri] <-ies> *n no pl* jolgorio *m*
revenge [rɪ'vendʒ] **I.** *n no pl* **1.** (*retaliation*) venganza *f* **2.** SPORTS revancha *f* **II.** *vt* vengar; **to ~ oneself on
sb** vengarse de alguien
revenue ['revənjuː, *Am:* 'revənuː]
n ingresos *mpl;* (*of government*)
rentas *fpl* públicas
reverberate [rɪ'vɜːbəreɪt, *Am:*
-'vɜːrbəreɪt] *vi* (*sound*) reverberar
reverence ['revərəns] *n no pl* vene-

ración *f*
Reverend ['revərənd] *adj* reverendo; **the Right Reverend** el obispo;
the Most Reverend el arzobispo
reverent ['revərənt] *adj* reverente
reverie ['revəri] *n liter* ensueño *m*
reversal [rɪ'vɜːsl, *Am:* -'vɜːrsl] *n* (*of
order*) inversión *f;* (*of policy*) cambio *m* completo; (*of decision*) revocación *f*
reverse [rɪ'vɜːs, *Am:* -'vɜːrs] **I.** *vt*
1. (*turn other way*) invertir **2.** *Aus,
Brit* AUTO poner en marcha atrás **II.** *vi*
Aus, Brit AUTO dar marcha atrás **III.** *n*
1. *no pl* **the ~** lo contrario **2.** AUTO
marcha *f* atrás; **to go into ~** dar marcha atrás **3.** (*the back*) reverso *m;* (*of
cloth*) revés *m* **IV.** *adj* **1.** (*inverse*) inverso **2.** (*direction*) contrario
reverse charge call *n* TEL llamada *f*
a cobro revertido
revert [rɪ'vɜːt, *Am:* -'vɜːrt] *vi* volver;
to ~ to type *fig* volver a ser el
mismo de siempre
review [rɪ'vjuː] **I.** *vt* **1.** (*consider*) analizar **2.** (*criticize: book, film*)
hacer una crítica [*o* reseña] de **3.** MIL
pasar revista a **II.** *n* **1.** (*examination*)
análisis *m inv;* **to come under ~** ser
examinado; **to hold a ~** MIL pasar revista **2.** (*criticism: of book, film*)
crítica *f,* reseña *f* **3.** (*magazine*) revista *f*
reviewer [rɪ'vjuːə{^r}, *Am:* -ə{^r}] *n* crítico, -a *m, f*
revise [rɪ'vaɪz] *vt* **1.** (*text*) revisar;
(*opinion*) cambiar de **2.** *Brit, Aus* repasar
revision [rɪ'vɪʒn] *n* **1.** *no pl* (*of text*)
revisión *f;* (*of policy*) modificación *f*
2. *no pl, Brit, Aus* UNIV repaso *m*
revitalize [riː'vaɪtəlaɪz, *Am:* -ţəl-]
vt revitalizar
revival [rɪ'vaɪvəl] *n* **1.** MED reanimación *f* **2.** (*of interest*) renacimiento
m **3.** CINE, THEAT reestreno *m*
revive [rɪ'vaɪv] **I.** *vt* **1.** MED reanimar
2. (*idea, custom*) restablecer **3.** CINE,
THEAT reestrenar **II.** *vi* **1.** (*be restored
to life*) volver en sí **2.** (*be restored:
tradition*) restablecerse
revoke [rɪ'vəʊk, *Am:* -'voʊk] *vt* re-

R{~r}

vocar

revolt [rɪ'vəʊlt, Am: -'voʊlt] POL I. vi rebelarse, alzarse AmL; **to ~ against sb/sth** sublevarse contra alguien/ algo II. vt repugnar a III. n 1. (uprising) revuelta f 2. no pl (rebelliousness) rebeldía f

revolting [rɪ'vəʊltɪŋ, Am: -'voʊltɪŋ] adj repugnante

revolution [ˌrevə'luːʃn] n a. POL revolución f

revolutionary [ˌrevə'luːʃənri] adj revolucionario

revolutionize [ˌrevə'luːʃnaɪz] vt, vt revolucionar

revolve [rɪ'vɒlv, Am: -'vɑːlv] vi girar

revolver [rɪ'vɒlvəʳ, Am: -'vɑːlvɚ] n revólver m

revolving adj giratorio

revue [rɪ'vjuː] n THEAT revista f

revulsion [rɪ'vʌlʃən] n no pl repulsión f

reward [rɪ'wɔːd, Am: 'wɔːrd] I. n recompensa f II. vt recompensar

rewarding adj gratificante

rewind [ˌriː'waɪnd] irr vt (tape) rebobinar; (watch) dar cuerda a

rewire [ˌriː'waɪəʳ, Am: -'waɪɚ] vt renovar la instalación eléctrica de

reword [ˌriː'wɜːd, Am: -'wɜːrd] vt 1. (rewrite) volver a redactar 2. (say again) expresar de otra manera

rewrite [ˌriː'raɪt] irr vt volver a redactar

Rh abbr of **rhesus** Rh

rheumatism ['ruːmətɪzəm] n no pl reumatismo m

rheumatoid arthritis [ˌruːmətɔɪd-ˌɑːˈθraɪtɪs, Am: -ˌɑːrˈθraɪtɪs] n no pl MED artritis f inv reumatoidea

Rhine [raɪn] n **the ~** el Rin

rhinoceros [raɪˈnɒsərəs, Am: -ˈnɑː-sə-] <-(es)> n rinoceronte m

Rhone [rəʊn, Am: roʊn] n **the ~** el Ródano

rhubarb ['ruːbɑːb, Am: -bɑːrb] n no pl ruibarbo m

rhyme [raɪm] I. n 1. (similar sound) rima f; **without ~ or reason** sin ton ni son 2. (poem) poesía f II. vi rimar

rhythm ['rɪðəm] n ritmo m

rhythmic ['rɪðmɪk] adj, **rhythmi-**

cal adj rítmico

RI [ˌɑːˈraɪ, Am: ˌɑːr-] abbr of **religious instruction** religión f

rib [rɪb] I. n costilla f II. <-bb-> vt inf tomar el pelo a

ribbon ['rɪbən] n cinta f

rice [raɪs] n no pl arroz m

rice pudding n arroz m con leche

rich [rɪtʃ] I. <-er, -est> adj rico; (soil) fértil; (food) pesado; **to be ~ in sth** abundar en algo II. n **the ~** los ricos

rickets ['rɪkɪts] n no pl raquitismo m

rickety ['rɪkəti, Am: -ti] adj desvencijado; (steps) tambaleante

rickshaw ['rɪkʃɔː, Am: -ʃɑː] n carro m de culí

rid [rɪd] <rid o ridded, rid> vt **to ~ sth/sb of sth** librar algo/a alguien de algo; **to get ~ of sb/sth** deshacerse de alguien/algo

riddance ['rɪdns] n inf **good ~ (to bad rubbish)!** ¡vete con viento fresco!

ridden ['rɪdn] pp of **ride**

riddle[1] ['rɪdl] n 1. (conundrum) adivinanza f 2. (mystery) misterio m

riddle[2] ['rɪdl] vt acribillar; **to be ~d with mistakes** estar plagado de errores

ride [raɪd] I. n paseo m; **to take sb for a ~** inf tomar el pelo a alguien II. <rode, ridden> vt 1. (sit on) **to ~ a bike** ir en bici; **can you ~ a bike?** ¿sabes montar en bici? 2. Am, inf explotar III. <rode, ridden> vi (on horse, bicycle) montar

♦ **ride out** vt a. fig aguantar

rider ['raɪdəʳ, Am: -dɚ] n (on horse) jinete m; (on bicycle) ciclista mf; (on motorbike) motociclista mf

ridge [rɪdʒ] n 1. GEO cresta f 2. (of roof) caballete m

ridicule ['rɪdɪkjuːl] I. n no pl burlas fpl; **to hold sth/sb up to ~** poner algo/a alguien en ridículo II. vt ridiculizar

ridiculous [rɪ'dɪkjʊləs] adj ridículo

riding n no pl equitación f

riding school n escuela f de equitación

rife [raɪf] adj extendido; **to be ~**

with sth estar plagado de algo
riff-raff ['rɪfræf] *n no pl* chusma *f*
rifle¹ ['raɪfl] *n* fusil *m,* rifle *m*
rifle² ['raɪfl] **I.** *vt* saquear **II.** *vi* **to ~ through sth** rebuscar en algo
rifle range *n* campo *m* de tiro
rift [rɪft] *n fig* ruptura *f*
rig [rɪɡ] <-gg-> **I.** *vt* amañar **II.** *n* **1.** TECH (**oil**) ~ plataforma *f* petrolífera **2.** NAUT aparejo *m*
rigging ['rɪɡɪŋ] *n no pl* NAUT jarcia *f*
right [raɪt] **I.** *adj* **1.** (*correct*) correcto; (*ethical*) justo; **to put sth ~** poner algo en orden; **to be ~** (**about sth**) tener razón (en algo), estar en lo cierto (sobre algo) *AmL;* **to do the ~ thing** hacer lo que se debe hacer; **to put a clock ~** poner el reloj en hora **2.** (*direction*) derecho **3.** POL de derechas **4.** (*well*) bueno **II.** *n* **1.** *no pl* (*entitlement*) derecho *m* **2.** (*morality*) **to be in the ~** tener razón **3.** (*right side*) derecha *f;* SPORTS derechazo *m* **4.** POL **the Right** la derecha **III.** *adv* **1.** (*correctly*) correctamente **2.** (*straight*) directamente; **~ away** inmediatamente **3.** (*to the right*) hacia la derecha **4.** (*precisely*) precisamente; **~ here** justo aquí **IV.** *vt* enderezar **V.** *interj* ¡de acuerdo!, ¡órale! *Méx*
right angle *n* ángulo *m* recto
righteous ['raɪtʃəs] *adj form* (*person*) virtuoso; (*indignation*) justificado
rightful ['raɪtfəl] *adj* legítimo
right-hand [,raɪt'hænd] *adj* **on the ~ side** a la derecha
right-handed [,raɪt'hændɪd] *adj* diestro
rightly *adv* **1.** (*correctly*) correctamente; **if I remember ~** si recuerdo bien **2.** (*justifiably*) con razón
right of way <-rights> *n* servidumbre *f* de paso; (*on road*) preferencia *f*
right-wing [,raɪt'wɪŋ] *adj* POL de derechas
rigid ['rɪdʒɪd] *adj* rígido; (*inflexible*) inflexible
rigmarole ['rɪɡmərəʊl, *Am:* -mə-roʊl] *n no pl* galimatías *m inv*

rigor mortis [,rɪɡə'mɔːtɪs, *Am:* ,rɪ-ɡɚ'mɔːrtɪs] *n no pl* MED rigidez *f* cadavérica
rigorous ['rɪɡərəs] *adj* riguroso
rile [raɪl] *vt inf* irritar
rim [rɪm] *n* **1.** (*of bowl*) canto *m;* (*of spectacles*) montura *f* **2.** GEO borde *m*
rind [raɪnd] *n no pl* (*of fruit*) cáscara *f;* (*of bacon, cheese*) corteza *f*
ring¹ [rɪŋ] *n* **1.** (*small circle*) círculo *m;* (*of people*) corro *m* **2.** (*jewellery*) anillo *m* **3.** (*in boxing*) cuadrilátero *m;* (*in circus*) pista *f*
ring² [rɪŋ] **I.** *n* **1.** *no pl, Brit* llamada *f;* **to give sb a ~** llamar a alguien (por teléfono) **2.** (*of bell*) toque *m* **II.** <rang, rung> *vt* **1.** *Brit* llamar (por teléfono) **2.** (*bell*) tocar; (*alarm*) hacer sonar **III.** <rang, rung> *vi* **1.** *Brit* llamar **2.** (*bell*) sonar
◆ **ring back** *vi, vt* TEL volver a llamar (a)
◆ **ring off** *vi Brit* colgar
ring binder *n* archivador *m* de anillas
ringing *n no pl* repique *m*
ringing tone *n* TEL tono *m* de llamada
ringleader ['rɪŋliːdəʳ, *Am:* -dɚ] *n* cabecilla *mf*
ringlet ['rɪŋlɪt] *n* tirabuzón *m*
ring road *n Brit, Aus* ronda *f* de circunvalación
rink [rɪŋk] *n* pista *f* de patinaje
rinse [rɪns] **I.** *vt* enjuagar; (*hands*) lavar **II.** *n* **1.** *no pl* (*wash*) enjuague *m* **2.** (*hair colouring*) reflejos *mpl*
riot ['raɪət] **I.** *n* disturbio *m;* **to run ~** *fig* desmandarse **II.** *vi* causar disturbios
riot gear *n* uniforme *m* antidisturbios
riotous ['raɪətəs, *Am:* -t̬əs] *adj* descontrolado; (*party*) desenfrenado
riot police *n* policía *f* antidisturbios
rip [rɪp] **I.** <-pp-> *vi* rasgarse **II.** <-pp-> *vt* rasgar **III.** *n* rasgón *m,* rajo *m AmC*
◆ **rip up** *vt* romper
RIP [,ɑːʳaɪ'piː, *Am:* ,ɑːr-] *abbr of* **rest in peace** E.P.D., D.E.P

ripcord ['rɪpkɔːd, *Am:* -kɔːrd] *n* cordón *m* de apertura

ripe [raɪp] *adj* (*fruit*) maduro

ripen ['raɪpən] **I.** *vt* hacer madurar **II.** *vi* madurar

rip-off ['rɪpɒf, *Am:* -ɑːf] *n inf* timo *m*, vacilada *f inf*, *Méx*

ripple ['rɪpl] **I.** *n* onda *f* **II.** *vi, vt* rizar(se)

rise [raɪz] **I.** *n no pl* **1.** (*increase*) subida *f;* **to give ~ to sth** dar lugar a algo **2.** (*incline*) cuesta *f* **II.** <rose, risen> *vi* **1.** (*arise*) levantarse **2.** (*become higher: ground*) subir (en pendiente); (*river*) crecer **3.** (*improve socially*) ascender

rising ['raɪzɪŋ] **I.** *n* levantamiento *m* **II.** *adj* (*in number*) creciente; (*flood-waters*) en aumento; (*sun*) naciente

risk [rɪsk] **I.** *n* **1.** (*chance*) riesgo *m;* **to run the ~ of sth** correr el riesgo de algo **2.** *no pl* (*danger*) peligro *m;* **at one's own ~** bajo su propia responsabilidad; **to be at ~** correr peligro **II.** *vt* arriesgar

risky ['rɪski] <-ier, -iest> *adj* arriesgado, riesgoso *AmL*

risqué ['riːskeɪ, *Am:* rɪˈskeɪ] *adj* atrevido

rissole ['rɪsəʊl, *Am:* -oʊl] *n* croqueta *f*

rite [raɪt] *n* rito *m;* **last ~s** extremaunción *f*

ritual ['rɪtʃʊəl, *Am:* -əl] *n* ritual *m*

rival ['raɪvl] **I.** *n* rival *mf* **II.** *adj* competidor **III.** <*Brit:* -ll-, *Am:* -l-> *vt* competir con

rivalry ['raɪvlri] *n* rivalidad *f*

river ['rɪvəʳ, *Am:* -əʳ] *n* río *m*

rivet ['rɪvɪt] **I.** *n* remache *m* **II.** *vt* **1.** (*join*) remachar **2.** (*interest*) **to be ~ed by sth** quedar absorto con algo

riveting ['rɪvətɪŋ, *Am:* -ɪt̬ɪŋ] *adj inf* fascinante

road [rəʊd, *Am:* roʊd] *n* **1.** (*between towns*) carretera *f;* (*in town*) calle *f;* (*route*) camino *m;* **by ~** por carretera **2.** *fig* sendero *m;* **to be on the ~ to recovery** estar reponiéndose

roadblock *n* control *m* de carretera

road hog *n inf* loco, -a *m, f* del volante **road map** *n* mapa *m* de carreteras **road safety** *n no pl* seguridad *f* vial **roadside I.** *n* borde *m* de la carretera **II.** *adj* de carretera **road sign** *n* señal *f* de tráfico **roadway** *n no pl* calzada *f* **roadworks** *npl* obras *fpl* de carretera

roam [rəʊm, *Am:* roʊm] *vi, vt* vagar (por)

roar [rɔːʳ, *Am:* rɔːr] **I.** *vi* rugir; **to ~ with laughter** reírse a carcajadas **II.** *n* (*of lion*) rugido *m;* (*of engine*) estruendo *m*

roast [rəʊst, *Am:* roʊst] **I.** *vt* asar; (*coffee*) tostar **II.** *n* asado *m*

roaster ['rəʊstəʳ, *Am:* 'roʊstəʳ] *n* asador *m*

roasting ['rəʊstɪŋ, *Am:* 'roʊst-] *n inf* **to give sb a ~** echar una bronca a alguien

rob [rɒb, *Am:* rɑːb] <-bb-> *vt* robar; **to ~ sb of sth** robar algo a alguien; (*deprive*) privar a alguien de algo

robber ['rɒbəʳ, *Am:* 'rɑːbəʳ] *n* ladrón, -ona *m, f*

robbery ['rɒbəri, *Am:* 'rɑːbəʳi] <-ies> *n* robo *m*

robe [rəʊb, *Am:* roʊb] *n* toga *f;* (*dressing gown*) traje *m*

robin ['rɒbɪn, *Am:* 'rɑːbɪn] *n* ZOOL petirrojo *m*

robot ['rəʊbɒt, *Am:* 'roʊbɑːt] *n* robot *m*

robust [rəʊˈbʌst, *Am:* roʊˈ-] *adj* robusto, fuerte

rock[1] [rɒk, *Am:* rɑːk] *n* **1.** GEO roca *f* **2.** *fig* **to be on the ~s** estar sin blanca; **whisky on the ~s** whisky con hielo

rock[2] [rɒk, *Am:* rɑːk] **I.** *vt* **1.** (*swing*) mecer **2.** (*shock*) sacudir **II.** *vi* balancearse

rock bottom *n* fondo *m;* **to hit ~** tocar fondo

rockery ['rɒkri, *Am:* 'rɑːkəʳi] <-ies> *n* jardín *m* rocoso

rocket ['rɒkɪt, *Am:* 'rɑːkɪt] **I.** *n* cohete *m* **II.** *vi* (*prices*) dispararse

Rockies ['rɒkiz, *Am:* 'rɑːkiz] *n* **the ~** las Rocosas

rocking chair ['rɒkɪŋ, *Am:* 'rɑːk-] *n*

mecedora *f*; columpio *m AmL* **rocking horse** *n* caballito *m* mecedor

rocky[1] ['rɒki, *Am:* 'rɑːki] <-ier, -iest> *adj* rocoso

rocky[2] ['rɒki, *Am:* 'rɑːki] <-ier, -iest> *adj* (*unstable*) inestable

Rocky Mountains *n* Montañas *fpl* Rocosas

rod [rɒd, *Am:* rɑːd] *n* varilla *f*; (*fishing rod*) caña *f* de pescar

rode [rəʊd, *Am:* roʊd] *pt of* **ride**

rodent ['rəʊdnt, *Am:* 'roʊ-] *n* roedor *m*

rodeo ['rəʊdɪəʊ, *Am:* 'roʊdɪoʊ] <-s> *n* rodeo *m*

roe[1] [rəʊ, *Am:* roʊ] *n* (*fish eggs*) hueva *f*

roe[2] [rəʊ, *Am:* roʊ] <-(s)> *n* (*deer*) corzo, -a *m, f*

rogue [rəʊg, *Am:* roʊg] *n* **1.** (*rascal*) pícaro, -a *m, f* **2.** (*villain*) bribón, -ona *m, f*

role *n*, **rôle** [rəʊl, *Am:* roʊl] *n a.* THEAT papel *m*

role model *n* modelo *m* a imitar **role play** *n* juego *m* de imitación

roll [rəʊl, *Am:* roʊl] **I.** *n* **1.** (*turning over*) voltereta *f* **2.** *no pl* (*swaying movement*) balanceo *m* **3.** (*of paper*) rollo *m* **4.** (*noise: of drum*) redoble *m* **5.** (*bread*) panecillo *m* **II.** *vt* **1.** (*push*) hacer rodar **2.** (*form into cylindrical shape*) **to ~ sth into sth** enrollar algo en algo **3.** (*make: cigarette*) liar **III.** *vi* rodar

◆ **roll about** *vi* vagar
◆ **roll by** *vi* (*time*) pasar
◆ **roll in** *vi* llegar en abundancia
◆ **roll over** *vi* dar vueltas
◆ **roll up I.** *vi inf* aparecer **II.** *vt* enrollar; (*sleeves*) arremangarse

roll call *n* lista *f*

roller ['rəʊlər, *Am:* 'roʊlə·] *n* rodillo *m*

roller coaster *n* montaña *f* rusa **rollerskate** *n* patín *m* de ruedas

rolling *adj* (*hills*) ondulado

rolling pin *n* rodillo *m* **rolling stock** *n* AUTO material *m* rodante

ROM [rɒm, *Am:* rɑːm] *n no pl abbr of* **Read Only Memory** ROM *f*

Roman ['rəʊmən, *Am:* 'roʊ-] **I.** *adj*

romano; (*alphabet*) latino; (*religion*) católico **II.** *n* romano, -a *m, f*

Roman Catholic *adj* católico

romance [rəʊˈmæns, *Am:* roʊˈmænts] *n* **1.** (*love affair*) romance *m* **2.** (*novel*) novela *f* rosa

Romania [rəˈmeɪnɪə, *Am:* roʊˈ-] *n* Rumanía *f*

Romanian [rəˈmeɪnɪən, *Am:* roʊˈ-] *adj* rumano

romantic [rəʊˈmæntɪk, *Am:* roʊˈmænt̮ɪk] *adj* LIT, ART romántico

Rome ['rəʊm, *Am:* 'roʊm] *n* Roma *f*

romp [rɒmp, *Am:* rɑːmp] **I.** *vi* juguetear; **to ~ home** ganar fácilmente **II.** *n* retozo *m*

rompers ['rɒmpəʳz, *Am:* 'rɑːmpə·z] *npl Am* pelele *m*

roof [ruːf] <-s> **I.** *n* techo *m*; (*of house*) tejado *m*; (*of mouth*) paladar *m* **II.** *vt* techar

roofing *n no pl* techumbre *f*

roofrack *n Brit* baca *f*, parrilla *f AmL*

rook [rʊk] *n* **1.** (*bird*) grajo *m* **2.** (*in chess*) torre *f*

rookie ['rʊki] *n Am, Aus, inf* novato, -a *m, f*

room [ruːm] *n* **1.** (*in house*) habitación *m*, pieza *f AmL*, ambiente *m CSur;* **~ and board** pensión *f* completa **2.** *no pl* (*space*) espacio *m;* **to make ~ for sb/sth** hacer sitio a alguien/algo; **there's no more ~ for anything else** ya no cabe nada más

rooming house *n Am* pensión *f*

roommate *n Am* compañero, -a *m, f* de habitación **room service** *n* servicio *m* de habitaciones

roomy ['ruːmi] <-ier, -iest> *adj* amplio

roost [ruːst] **I.** *n* percha *f* **II.** *vi fig* pasar la noche

rooster ['ruːstəʳ, *Am:* -stə·] *n Am, Aus* gallo *m*

root [ruːt] *n* **1.** *a.* BOT, LING, MAT raíz *f*; **to take ~** *a. fig* arraigar **2.** (*source*) causa *f*; **the ~ of the problem is that ...** el problema radica en que...

◆ **root about** *vi*, **root around** *vi* hozar
◆ **root out** *vt* arrancar

R
r

root beer *n Am: bebida gaseosa hecha con extractos de plantas*
rope [rəʊp, *Am:* roʊp] **I.** *n* cuerda *f;* **to know the ~s** *fig* estar al tanto de todo **II.** *vt* atar con una cuerda
rop(e)y ['rəʊpi, *Am:* 'roʊ-] <-ier, -iest> *adj Brit, Aus, inf* flojo
rosary ['rəʊzəri, *Am:* 'roʊ-] <-ies> *n* rosario *m*
rose[1] [rəʊz, *Am:* roʊz] **I.** *n* **1.** (*flower, colour*) rosa *f* **2.** (*on watering can*) roseta *f* **II.** *adj* rosa
rose[2] [rəʊz, *Am:* roʊz] *pt of* **rise**
rosebud *n* capullo *m* **rosebush** *n* rosal *m* **rosemary** *n no pl* romero *m*
rosette [rəʊ'zet, *Am:* roʊ'-] *n* rosetón *m*
roster ['rɒstəʳ, *Am:* 'rɑːstɚ] *n no pl* lista *f*
rostrum ['rɒstrəm, 'rɒstrə, *Am:* 'rɑːstrəm, 'rɑːstrə] <-s *o* rostra> *n* tribuna *f*
rosy ['rəʊzi, *Am:* 'roʊ-] <-ier, -iest> *adj* **1.** (*rose-colour*) rosado, sonrosado **2.** (*optimistic: future*) prometedor
rot [rɒt, *Am:* rɑːt] **I.** *n no pl* putrefacción *f;* **to stop the ~** acabar con la degeneración **II.** <-tt-> *vi* pudrirse **III.** *vt* pudrir
rota ['rəʊtə, *Am:* 'roʊṭə] *n Brit* lista *f* de turnos
rotary ['rəʊtəri, *Am:* 'roʊṭɚ-] *adj* rotatorio
rotate [rəʊ'teɪt, *Am:* 'roʊteɪt] **I.** *vt* **1.** (*turn round*) dar vueltas a **2.** (*alternate*) alternar; *AGR* cultivar en rotación **II.** *vi* girar
rote [rəʊt, *Am:* roʊt] *n no pl* **by ~** de memoria
rotor ['rəʊtəʳ, *Am:* 'roʊṭɚ] *n* rotor *m*
rotten ['rɒtn, *Am:* 'rɑːtn] *adj* **1.** (*food*) podrido **2.** *inf* (*behaviour*) despreciable
rotund [rəʊ'tʌnd, *Am:* roʊ'-] *adj* redondeado
rough [rʌf] **I.** *adj* **1.** (*road*) desigual; (*surface*) áspero **2.** (*work*) chapucero **3.** (*voice*) bronco **4.** (*imprecise*) aproximado; (*idea*) impreciso **5.** (*person, manner*) tosco **6.** (*sea*)

agitado; (*weather*) tempestuoso **II.** *n no pl* **the ~** el rough **III.** *vt* **to ~ it** *inf* pasar sin comodidades
roughage ['rʌfɪdʒ] *n no pl* fibra *f* (de los alimentos)
rough-and-ready [ˌrʌfənd'redi] *adj* tosco pero eficaz
roughly *adv* **1.** (*approximately*) aproximadamente; **~ speaking** por así decirlo **2.** (*aggressively*) bruscamente
roughness ['rʌfnɪs] *n no pl* **1.** (*of surface*) aspereza *f* **2.** (*unfairness*) dureza *f*
roulette [ruː'let] *n no pl* ruleta *f*
round [raʊnd] **I.** <-er, -est> *adj* redondo **II.** *adv* alrededor; **to come ~** pasar por casa; **~** (*about*) **10 o'clock** a eso de las 10; **the other way ~** al revés; **all ~** por todos lados **III.** *prep* **1.** (*surrounding*) alrededor de; **to go ~ sth** dar la vuelta a algo; **just ~ the corner** justo a la vuelta de la esquina **2.** (*visit*) **to go ~ a museum** visitar un museo **3.** (*here and there*) **all ~ the house** por toda la casa; **to sit ~ the room** estar sentado en la habitación **4.** (*approximately*) alrededor de; **~ 11:00** alrededor de las 11:00; **somewhere ~ here** en algún lugar de por aquí **IV.** *n* **1.** (*circle*) círculo *m* **2.** *pl MED* visita *f* **3.** (*in card games*) mano *f;* (*in boxing*) asalto *m* **4.** (*of drinks*) ronda *f* **5.** (*of ammunition*) bala *f* **V.** *vt* (*corner*) doblar
◆ **round off** *vt* rematar
◆ **round up** *vt* **1.** *MAT* redondear por exceso **2.** (*gather*) reunir; (*cattle*) rodear
roundabout ['raʊndəbaʊt] **I.** *n Aus, Brit* **1.** *AUTO* rotonda *f* **2.** *Brit* tiovivo *m* **II.** *adj* indirecto
rounders ['raʊndəz, *Am:* -dɚz] *n no pl, Brit SPORTS* juego similar al béisbol
roundly *adv* categóricamente, rotundamente
round-shouldered [ˌraʊnd'ʃəʊldəd, *Am:* -'ʃoʊldɚd] *adj* encorvado
round trip *n* viaje *m* de ida y vuelta
round-up ['raʊndʌp] *n* **1.** *AGR* rodeo

m **2.**(*by police*) redada *f* **3.**(*summary*) resumen *m*

rouse [raʊz] *vt* **1.**(*waken*) despertar **2.**(*activate*) provocar

rousing ['raʊzɪŋ] *adj* (*welcome*) caluroso; (*speech*) vehemente

rout [raʊt] **I.** *vt* derrotar **II.** *n* derrota *f* aplastante; (*flight*) huida *f* en desbandada

route [ruːt, *Am:* raʊt] *n* ruta *f;* (*of bus*) recorrido *m;* NAUT rumbo *m*

routine [ruːˈtiːn] **I.** *n* **1.** *a.* INFOR rutina *f* **2.**(*of dancer*) número *m* **II.** *adj* rutinario

row¹ [rəʊ, *Am:* roʊ] *n* **1.**(*line*) hilera *f*, fila *f* **2.**(*succession*) **three times in a ~** tres veces consecutivas

row² [raʊ] *n* **1.**(*quarrel*) pelea *f;* **to have a ~** pelearse **2.**(*noise*) escándalo *m;* **to make a ~** armar jaleo

row³ [rəʊ, *Am:* roʊ] **I.** *vi* remar **II.** *vt* (*boat*) llevar

rowboat ['rəʊbəʊt, *Am:* 'roʊboʊt] *n Am* bote *m* de remos

rowdy ['raʊdi] <-ier, -iest> *adj* **1.**(*noisy*) alborotador **2.**(*quarrelsome*) pendenciero

rowing *n no pl* SPORTS remo *m*

rowing boat *n Brit* bote *m* de remos

royal ['rɔɪəl] *adj* real

royalist ['rɔɪəlɪst] *adj* monárquico

royalty ['rɔɪəlti, *Am:* -t̬i] <-ies> *n* **1.** *no pl* (*sovereignty*) realeza *f* **2.** *pl* (*payment*) derechos *mpl* de autor

RP [ˌɑːˈpiː, *Am:* ˌɑːr-] *n no pl abbr of* **received pronunciation** *pronunciación estándar del inglés británico*

rpm [ˌɑːˈpiːˈem, *Am:* ˌɑːr-] *n abbr of* **revolutions per minute** rpm

RRP [ˌɑːˈɑːˈrˈpiː] *n no pl, Brit abbr of* **recommended retail price** PVP *m*

RSPCA [ˌɑːˈresˌpiːsiːˈeɪ, *Am:* ˌɑːr-] *n Brit abbr of* **Royal Society for the Prevention of Cruelty to Animals** ≈ asociación *f* protectora de animales

Rt Hon. *n Brit* POL *abbr of* **Right Honourable** ≈ Excelentísimo Señor *m*, ≈ Excelentísima Señora *f* (*tratamiento protocolario que se da a los diputados británicos*)

rub [rʌb] **I.** *n* **1.**(*act of rubbing*) fro-

tamiento *m* **2.** *liter* (*difficulty*) dificultad *f* **II.**<-bb-> *vt* frotar; (*one's eyes*) restregarse; **to ~ sth clean** lustrar algo

◆**rub down** *vt* **1.**(*horse*) almohazar **2.**(*dry*) secar frotando

◆**rub in** *vt* **1.**(*spread on skin*) aplicar frotando **2.** *inf* (*keep reminding*) reiterar; *pej* insistir en

◆**rub off** **I.** *vi* **1.**(*become clean*) irse **2.**(*affect*) **to ~ on sb** pegarse a alguien **II.** *vt* quitar frotando

◆**rub out** *vt* borrar

rubber ['rʌbəʳ, *Am:* -ɚ] *n* **1.**(*material*) goma *f*, hule *m Méx* **2.** *Aus, Brit* goma *f* (de borrar), borrador *m Col*

rubber band *n* goma *f* (elástica)

rubber plant *n* planta *f* del caucho

rubbing *n* frotamiento *m*

rubbish ['rʌbɪʃ] **I.** *n no pl, Brit* **1.** *inf* (*waste*) basura *f* **2.** *inf* (*nonsense*) tonterías *fpl* **II.** *vt Aus, Brit, inf* poner verde

rubbish bin *n* cubo *m* de la basura

rubbish dump *n*, **rubbish tip** *n* vertedero *m*, tiradero *m Méx*

rubble ['rʌbl] *n no pl* escombros *mpl*

ruby ['ruːbi] <-ies> *n* rubí *m*

RUC [ˌɑːrˈjuːˈsiː, *Am:* ˌɑːr-] *n abbr of* **Royal Ulster Constabulary** *policía de Irlanda del norte*

rucksack ['rʌksæk] *n Brit* mochila *f*

ruddy ['rʌdi] <-ier, -iest> *adj liter* (*cheeks*) rubicundo

rude [ruːd] *adj* **1.**(*impolite*) grosero, meco *Méx* **2.**(*vulgar*) vulgar

rudimentary [ˌruːdɪˈmentəri, *Am:* -də'-] *adj* rudimentario

rue ['ruː] *vt liter* lamentar

rueful ['ruːfl] *adj* arrepentido

ruffian ['rʌfɪən] *n iron* canalla *mf*

ruffle ['rʌfl] *vt* **1.**(*hair*) alborotar; (*clothes*) fruncir **2.**(*upset*) alterar

rug [rʌɡ] *n* **1.**(*small carpet*) alfombra *f* **2.** *Brit* manta *f*

rugby ['rʌɡbi] *n no pl* rugby *m*

rugged ['rʌɡɪd] *adj* (*landscape*) accidentado; (*construction*) resistente

ruin ['ruːɪn] **I.** *vt* **1.**(*bankrupt*) arruinar **2.**(*destroy*) destruir **3.**(*spoil*) estropear **II.** *n* ruina *f*

rule [ruːl] **I.** *n* **1.**(*law*) regla *f;* (*prin-*

ciple) norma *f*; **a ~ of thumb** una regla general; **it is against the ~s** va contra las normas; **as a ~** por lo general **2.** *no pl* (*control*) gobierno *m* **3.** (*measuring device*) regla *f* **II.** *vt* **1.** (*govern*) gobernar **2.** (*draw*) trazar con una regla **3.** (*decide*) dictaminar **III.** *vi* **1.** (*control*) gobernar **2.** LAW **to ~ for/against sb/sth** fallar a favor/en contra de alguien/algo
♦ **rule out** *vt* descartar

ruler *n* **1.** (*sovereign*) soberano, -a *m*, *f* **2.** (*measuring device*) regla *f*

ruling ['ruːlɪŋ] **I.** *adj* gobernante; (*class*) dirigente **II.** *n* fallo *m*

rum [rʌm] *n* ron *m*

Rumania [ruˈmeɪnɪə, *Am:* roʊ'-] *n s.* **Romania**

Rumanian [ruˈmeɪnɪən, *Am:* roʊ'-] *s.* **Romanian**

rumble ['rʌmbl] **I.** *n no pl* ruido *m* sordo; (*of thunder*) estruendo *m* **II.** *vi* hacer un ruido sordo; (*thunder*) retumbar

rummage ['rʌmɪdʒ] *vi* revolver

rumor *Am*, **rumour** ['ruːməʳ, *Am:* -məʳ] *Brit, Aus* **I.** *n* rumor *m* **II.** *vt* **it is ~ed that …** se rumorea que…

rump [rʌmp] *n* grupa *f*

rump steak *n* filete *m* de lomo de ternera

rumpus ['rʌmpəs] *n no pl, inf* jaleo *m*; **to raise a ~** armar un escándalo

run [rʌn] **I.** *n* **1.** (*jog*) **to go for a ~** salir a correr; **on the ~** deprisa y corriendo **2.** (*series*) racha *f* **3.** (*hole in tights*) carrera *f* **4.** SPORTS carrera *f*; (*ski slope*) pista *f* de esquí **5.** CINE, THEAT permanencia *f* en cartel **6.** *fig* **in the long ~** a la larga **II.** *vi* <ran, run> **1.** (*move fast*) correr; **to ~ for the bus** correr para no perder el autobús **2.** (*operate*) funcionar; **to ~ smoothly** ir sobre ruedas *fig* **3.** (*extend*) extenderse **4.** (*flow: river*) fluir; (*make-up*) correrse **5.** (*enter election*) presentarse, postularse *AmL* **III.** *vt* <ran, run> **1.** (*move fast*) **to ~ a race** participar en una carrera **2.** (*enter in race*) presentar **3.** (*drive*) llevar; **to ~ sb home** llevar a alguien a casa **4.** (*pass*) pasar

5. (*operate*) poner en marcha; **to ~ a household** llevar una casa
♦ **run about** *vi* andar de un lado para otro
♦ **run across** *vt* toparse con
♦ **run away** *vi* escaparse
♦ **run down I.** *vi* (*clock*) parar **II.** *vt* **1.** (*run over*) atropellar **2.** (*disparage*) hablar mal de
♦ **run in** *vt* AUTO rodar
♦ **run into** *vt* dar con; AUTO chocar con
♦ **run off I.** *vi* (*water*) derramarse **II.** *vt* dejar correr
♦ **run out of** *vi* quedarse sin
♦ **run over I.** *vi* irse **II.** *vt* AUTO atropellar a
♦ **run through** *vt* pasar sin parar por
♦ **run up I.** *vi* **to ~ against difficulties** tropezar con dificultades **II.** *vt* **to ~ debts** endeudarse

runaround ['rʌnəraʊnd] *n no pl* **to give sb the ~** traer a alguien al retortero

runaway ['rʌnəweɪ] *adj* (*train*) fuera de control; (*person*) fugitivo; (*horse*) desbocado

rung¹ [rʌŋ] *n* peldaño *m*

rung² [rʌŋ] *pp of* **ring²**

run-in ['rʌnɪn] *n inf* altercado *m*

runner ['rʌnəʳ, *Am:* -əʳ] *n* **1.** (*person*) corredor(a) *m(f)*; (*horse*) caballo *m* de carreras **2.** (*on sledge*) patín *m*

runner bean *n Brit* habichuela *f*

runner-up [,rʌnərˈʌp, *Am:* -əʳ'-] *n* subcampeón, -ona *m, f*

running I. *n no pl* **1.** (*action of a runner*) carrera *f* **2.** *fig* **to be in/out of the ~** tener/no tener posibilidades de ganar **II.** *adj* **1.** (*consecutive*) sucesivo **2.** (*flowing*) que fluye

running costs *npl* gastos *mpl* de explotación

runny ['rʌni] <-ier, -iest> *adj* líquido

run-of-the-mill [,rʌnəvðəˈmɪl] *adj* corriente y moliente

runt [rʌnt] *n* enano *m*

run-up ['rʌnʌp] *n* **1.** SPORTS carrerilla *f* **2.** (*prelude*) período *m* previo; **the ~ to sth** el preludio de algo

runway ['rʌnweɪ] n pista f
rupee [ru:'pi:, Am: 'ru:pi:] n rupia f
rupture ['rʌptʃə', Am: -tʃə-] I. vt romper; **to ~ oneself** herniarse II. n hernia f, relajadura f Méx
rural ['rʊərəl, Am: 'rʊrəl] adj rural
rush[1] [rʌʃ] n BOT junco m
rush[2] [rʌʃ] I. n 1. (hurry) prisa f; **to be in a ~** tener prisa 2. (charge) ataque m; (surge) ola f; **gold ~** fiebre f del oro II. vi ir deprisa III. vt 1. (do quickly) hacer precipitadamente 2. (attack) asaltar
♦ **rush through** vt aprobar urgentemente
rush hour n hora f punta
rusk [rʌsk] n bizcocho m
Russia ['rʌʃə] n Rusia f
Russian ['rʌʃn] adj ruso
rust [rʌst] I. n no pl herrumbre f II. vi oxidarse
rustic ['rʌstɪk] adj rústico
rustle ['rʌsl] I. vi susurrar II. vt 1. (paper) hacer crujir 2. (cattle) robar
rustproof ['rʌstpru:f] adj inoxidable
rusty ['rʌsti] <-ier, -iest> adj oxidado
rut[1] [rʌt] n bache m; **to be stuck in a ~** estar metido en la rutina
rut[2] [rʌt] n no pl ZOOL celo m
ruthless ['ru:θləs] adj despiadado
Rwanda [rʊ'ændə, Am: -'ɑ:n-] n Ruanda f
Rwandan adj ruandés
rye [raɪ] n no pl centeno m

S
S

S, s [es] n S, s; **~ for Sugar** S de Soria
S [es] n no pl 1. abbr of **south** S m 2. Am abbr of **satisfactory** suficiente m
SA 1. abbr of **South Africa** Sudáfrica f 2. abbr of **South America** Sudamérica f

Sabbath ['sæbəθ] n sabat m
sabotage ['sæbətɑ:ʒ] I. vt sabotear II. n sabotaje m
saccharin ['sækərɪn] n no pl sacarina f
sachet ['sæʃeɪ, Am: -'-] n bolsita f
sack[1] [sæk] I. n 1. (large bag) saco m; (paper or plastic bag) bolsa f 2. no pl, inf (dismissal) **to get the ~** ser despedido; **to give sb the ~** despedir a alguien II. vt despedir
sack[2] [sæk] I. n no pl (plundering) saqueo m II. vt (plunder) saquear
sacking ['sækɪŋ] n no pl (sackcloth) arpillera f
sacrament ['sækrəmənt] n (ceremony) sacramento m
sacred ['seɪkrɪd] adj sagrado
sacrifice ['sækrɪfaɪs, Am: -rə-] I. vt sacrificar; **to ~ one's free time** privarse de tiempo libre II. n sacrificio m
sacrilege ['sækrɪlɪdʒ, Am: -rə-] n sacrilegio m
sad [sæd] <-dd-> adj 1. (unhappy) triste 2. (deplorable, shameful) lamentable
saddle ['sædl] I. n silla f de montar; (of bicycle) sillín m II. vt 1. (horse) ensillar 2. inf (burden) **to ~ sb with sth** encajar algo a alguien
saddlebag ['sædlbæg] n alforja f
sadist ['seɪdɪst, Am: 'sæd-] n sádico, -a m, f
sadistic [sə'dɪstɪk] adj sádico
sadly adv 1. (unhappily) tristemente 2. (regrettably) desgraciadamente; **to be ~ mistaken** estar muy equivocado
sadness ['sædnəs] n no pl tristeza f
sae, SAE [ˌeseɪ'i:] n abbr of **stamped addressed envelope** sobre con las señas de uno y con sello
safari [sə'fɑ:ri] n safari m
safe [seɪf] I. adj 1. (free of danger) seguro; **it is not ~ to ...** es peligroso... +inf; **~ journey!** ¡buen viaje!; **~ and sound** sano y salvo; **to be on the ~ side ...** para mayor seguridad... 2. (secure) salvo 3. (certain) seguro II. n caja f de caudales
safeguard ['seɪfgɑ:d, Am: -gɑ:rd]

I. *vt* salvaguardar **II.** *vi* protegerse **III.** *n* salvaguardia *f*

safekeeping [ˌseɪfˈkiːpɪŋ] *n no pl* custodia *f*

safely *adv* sin riesgos; **I can ~ say ...** puedo decir sin temor a equivocarme que...

safe sex [seɪfˈseks] *n* sexo *m* seguro

safety [ˈseɪfti] *n no pl* seguridad *f*

safety belt *n* cinturón *m* de seguridad **safety catch** *n* seguro *m* **safety pin** *n* imperdible *m* **safety valve** *n* válvula *f* de seguridad

sag [sæg] <-gg-> *vi* combarse, achiguarse *Arg, Chile*

saga [ˈsɑːgə] *n* saga *f*

sage[1] [seɪdʒ] *n liter* (*wise man*) sabio *m*

sage[2] [seɪdʒ] *n no pl* (*herb*) salvia *f*

Sagittarius [ˌsædʒɪˈteərɪəs, *Am:* -əˈteri-] *n* Sagitario *m*

Sahara [səˈhɑːrə, *Am:* -ˈherə] *n* **the ~ (Desert)** el Sáhara

said [sed] **I.** *pt, pp of* **say II.** *adj* dicho

sail [seɪl] **I.** *n* (*on boat*) vela *f*; **to set ~** (*for a place*) zarpar (hacia un lugar) **II.** *vi* **1.** (*travel*) navegar **2.** (*start voyage*) zarpar **3.** (*move smoothly*) deslizarse **4.** *fig* (*do easily*) **to ~ through sth** hacer algo con facilidad **III.** *vt* (*manage: boat, ship*) gobernar

sailboat [ˈseɪlbəʊt, *Am:* -boʊt] *n Am* (*sailing boat*) barco *m* de vela

sailing *n* SPORTS vela *f*

sailing ship *n*, **sailing vessel** *n* velero *m*

sailor [ˈseɪləʳ, *Am:* -lɚ] *n* marinero, -a *m, f*

saint [seɪnt, sənt] *n* santo, -a *m, f*

? El **Saint Patrick's Day**, 17 de marzo, es el día en que se celebra el patrón de Irlanda. En los EE.UU., sin embargo, no es día de fiesta oficial. A pesar de ello mucha gente lleva el color verde y se organizan fiestas. En muchas ciudades hay desfiles, de los cuales el más grande y famoso es el que tiene lugar en New York City.

sake [seɪk] *n* **for the ~ of sb/sth** por alguien/algo

salad [ˈsæləd] *n* ensalada *f*; verde *m CSur*

salad bowl *n* ensaladera *f* **salad cream** *n Brit: aliño para la ensalada parecido a la mayonesa* **salad dressing** *n* aliño *m*

salami [səˈlɑːmi] *n no pl* salami *m*, salame *m CSur*

salary [ˈsæləri] *n* sueldo *m*

sale [seɪl] *n* **1.** (*act of selling*) venta *f*; **for ~** se vende; **on ~** en venta **2.** (*reduced prices*) saldo *m*

saleroom [ˈseɪlruːm] *n Am* sala *f* de subastas

sales assistant *n Brit*, **salesclerk** *n Am* dependiente, -a *m, f* **sales conference** *n* conferencia *f* de ventas **sales department** *n* sección *f* de ventas **sales figures** *npl* cifras *fpl* de ventas **sales force** *n* personal *m* de ventas **salesman** *n* (*in shop*) dependiente *m*; (*for company*) representante *m* **saleswoman** *n* (*in a shop*) dependienta *f*; (*for company*) representante *f*

saliva [səˈlaɪvə] *n no pl* saliva *f*

sallow [ˈsæləʊ, *Am:* -oʊ] *adj* <-er, -est> cetrino

sally [ˈsæli] **I.** <-ies> *n* salida *f* **II.** <-ie-> *vi* MIL hacer una salida; **to ~ forth** ponerse en marcha; *fig* salir resueltamente

salmon [ˈsæmən] *n* salmón *m*

saloon [səˈluːn] *n* **1.** *Brit* (*car*) turismo *m* **2.** *Am* (*bar*) bar *m*

salt [sɔːlt] **I.** *n a.* GASTR, CHEM sal *f* **II.** *vt* salar

salt cellar *n* salero *m*

saltwater [ˈsɔːltˌwɔːtəʳ, *Am:* ˈsɔːltˌwɑːt̬ɚ] *adj* de agua salada

salty [ˈsɔːlti, *Am:* ˈsɔːlt̬i] *adj* salado

salute [səˈluːt] **I.** *vt a.* MIL saludar **II.** *n* MIL **1.** (*hand gesture*) saludo *m* **2.** (*firing*) salva *f*

Salvadorian [ˌsælvəˈdɔːrɪən] *adj* salvadoreño

salvage ['sælvɪdʒ] **I.** *vt* salvar **II.** *n* no pl **1.** (*retrieval*) salvamento *m* **2.** (*things saved*) objetos *mpl* salvados

salvation [sæl'veɪʃən] *n no pl a.* REL salvación *f*

Salvation Army *n no pl* Ejército *m* de Salvación

same [seɪm] **I.** *adj* **1.** (*identical*) igual; **the ~** (**as** *sb/sth*) igual (que alguien/algo) **2.** (*not another*) mismo; **at the ~ time** al mismo tiempo **II.** *pron* **1.** (*nominal*) **the ~** el mismo, la misma, lo mismo **2.** (*adverbial*) **it comes to the ~** da lo mismo; **all the ~** de todas formas; **~ to you** igualmente

Samoa [sə'məʊə, *Am:* sə'moʊə] *n* Samoa *f*

Samoan *adj* samoano

sample ['sɑ:mpl, *Am:* 'sæm-] **I.** *n* muestra *f*; **free ~** muestra gratuita **II.** *vt* probar

sanatorium [ˌsænə'tɔ:rɪəm] <-s *o* -ria> *n* sanatorio *m*

sanctimonious [ˌsæŋktɪ'məʊnɪəs, *Am:* -'moʊ-] *adj pej* mojigato

sanction ['sæŋkʃn] **I.** *n* sanción *f* **II.** *vt* sancionar

sanctity ['sæŋktəti, *Am:* -t̬i] *n no pl* santidad *f*

sanctuary ['sæŋktʃʊəri, *Am:* -tʃueri] *n* <-ies> **1.** REL santuario *m* **2.** *no pl* (*refuge*) refugio *m*

sand [sænd] **I.** *n* arena *f*; **the ~s** la playa **II.** *vt* lijar

sandal ['sændl] *n* sandalia *f*, quimba *f AmL*

sandbag *n* saco *m* de arena **sandbox** *n Am s.* **sandpit sandcastle** *n* castillo *m* de arena **sand dune** *n* duna *f* **sandpaper I.** *n no pl* papel *m* de lija **II.** *vt* lijar **sandpit** *n Brit* cajón *m* de arena (*donde juegan los niños*) **sandstone** *n no pl* piedra *f* arenisca **sandstorm** *n* tormenta *f* de arena

sandwich ['sænwɪdʒ, *Am:* 'sændwɪtʃ] **I.** <-es> *n* bocadillo *m*; (*made with sliced bread*) sándwich *m* **II.** *vt* intercalar

sandy ['sændi] *adj* <-ier, -iest> arenoso

sane [seɪn] *adj* **1.** (*of sound mind*) cuerdo **2.** (*sensible*) sensato

sang [sæŋ] *pt of* **sing**

sanitary ['sænɪtəri, *Am:* -teri] *adj* **1.** (*relating to hygiene*) sanitario **2.** (*clean*) higiénico

sanitary towel *n Brit,* **sanitary napkin** *n Am* compresa *f* (higiénica)

sanitation [ˌsænɪ'teɪʃən] *n no pl* saneamiento *m*

sanity ['sænəti, *Am:* -t̬i] *n no pl* cordura *f*; (*of decision*) sensatez *f*

sank [sæŋk] *pt of* **sink**

Santa (**Claus**) [ˌsæntə('klɔ:z), *Am:* 'sæntə(ˌklɑ:z)] *n* Papá *m* Noel

sap¹ [sæp] *n no pl* BOT savia *f*

sap² [sæp] <-pp-> *vt* socavar

sapling ['sæplɪŋ] *n* pimpollo *m*

sapphire ['sæfaɪəʳ, *Am:* -aɪɚ] *n* zafiro *m*

sarcasm ['sɑ:kæzəm, *Am:* 'sɑ:r-] *n no pl* sarcasmo *m*

sarcastic [sɑ:'kæstɪk, *Am:* sɑ:rt'-] *adj* sarcástico

sardine [sɑ:'di:n, *Am:* sɑ:r'-] *n* sardina *f*

Sardinia [sɑ:'dɪnɪə, *Am:* sɑ:r-] *n* Cerdeña *f*

Sardinian *adj* sardo

SAS [ˌeseɪ'es] *n Brit* MIL *abbr of* **Special Air Service** comando de operaciones especiales del ejército británico

sash [sæʃ] <-es> *n* faja *f*

sat [sæt] *pt, pp of* **sit**

Satan ['seɪtən] *n no pl* Satanás *m*

satchel ['sætʃəl] *n* bolsa *f*, busaca *f Col, Ven*

satellite ['sætəlaɪt, *Am:* 'sæt̬-] *n* satélite *m*

satin ['sætɪn, *Am:* 'sætn] **I.** *n* raso *m* **II.** *adj* satinado

satire ['sætaɪəʳ, *Am:* -aɪɚ] *n* sátira *f*

satisfaction [ˌsætɪs'fækʃn, *Am:* ˌsæt̬-] *n no pl* satisfacción *f*; **to do sth to sb's ~** hacer algo para satisfacción de alguien; **to be a ~** (**to sb**) ser una satisfacción (para alguien)

satisfactory [ˌsætɪs'fæktəri, *Am:* ˌsæt̬-] *adj* satisfactorio; SCHOOL suficiente

satisfy ['sætɪsfaɪ, *Am:* -əs-] <-ie-> *vt* **1.** (*person, desire*) satisfacer **2.** (*convince*) convencer; **to ~ sb that ...** convencer a alguien de que... **3.** (*debt*) saldar

satisfying *adj* satisfactorio

satsuma [sæt'su:mə, *Am:* 'sætsəmɑ:] *n Brit, Am* satsuma *f*

saturation [ˌsætʃə'reɪʃən] *n no pl a.* CHEM, ECON saturación *f*

Saturday ['sætədeɪ, *Am:* 'sætɚ-] *n* sábado *m; s. a.* **Friday**

sauce [sɔːs, *Am:* sɑːs] *n* **1.** salsa *f* **2.** (*impertinence*) frescura *f*

saucepan ['sɔːspən, *Am:* 'sɑːs-] *n* cacerola *f*

saucer ['sɔːsər, *Am:* 'sɑːsɚ] *n* platillo *m*

saucy ['sɔːsi, *Am:* 'sɑː-] *adj* <-ier, -iest> descarado

Saudi Arabia [ˌsaʊdɪə'reɪbɪə] *n no pl* Arabia *f* Saudí [*o* Saudita]

Saudi (**Arabian**) [ˌsaʊdi (ə'reɪbɪən)] *adj* saudí, saudita

sauna ['sɔːnə, *Am:* 'saʊ-] *n* sauna *f*

saunter ['sɔːntər, *Am:* 'sɑːntɚ] **I.** *vi* pasear **II.** *n no pl* paseo *m*

sausage ['sɒsɪdʒ, *Am:* 'sɑːsɪdʒ] *n* salchicha *f*; (*cured*) salchichón *m*

sausage roll *n Brit, Aus* empanadilla *f* de salchicha

savage ['sævɪdʒ] **I.** *adj* (*fierce*) salvaje, feroz **II.** *n pej* salvaje *mf* **III.** *vt* (*attack*) atacar salvajemente

save¹ [seɪv] **I.** *vt* **1.** (*rescue*) salvar; **to ~ face** salvar las apariencias **2.** (*keep for future use*) guardar **3.** (*collect*) coleccionar **4.** (*avoid wasting*) guardar **5.** INFOR guardar **II.** *vi* **1.** (*keep for the future*) ahorrar; **to ~ for sth** ahorrar para algo **2.** (*conserve*) **to ~ on sth** guardar algo **III.** *n* SPORTS parada *f*

save² [seɪv] *prep* ~ (**for**) salvo

saving ['seɪvɪŋ] **I.** *n* **1.** *pl* (*money*) ahorros *mpl* **2.** (*economy*) ahorro *m* **II.** *adj* **the ~ grace of ...** el único mérito de...

savings account ['seɪvɪŋzəˌkaʊnt] *n* cuenta *f* de ahorros **savings bank** *n* caja *f* de ahorros

savior *n Am,* **saviour** ['seɪvjər, *Am:* -vjɚ] *n* salvador(a) *m(f)*

savor ['seɪvɚ] *n Am s.* **savour**

savory ['seɪvəri] *n Am s.* **savoury**

savour ['seɪvər, *Am:* -vɚ] **I.** *n* **1.** (*taste*) sabor *m* **2.** (*pleasure*) gusto *m* **II.** *vt* saborear

savoury ['seɪvəri] *adj* **1.** (*salty*) salado **2.** (*appetizing*) sabroso

saw¹ [sɔː, *Am:* sɑː] *pt of* **see¹**

saw² [sɔː, *Am:* sɑː] **I.** *n* sierra *f* **II.** <-ed, sawn *o* -ed> *vt* serrar

sawdust ['sɔːdʌst, *Am:* 'sɑː-] *n no pl* serrín *m*

sawmill ['sɔːmɪl, *Am:* 'sɑː-] *n* aserradero *m*

sawn [sɔːn, *Am:* sɑːn] *pp of* **saw**

sawn-off shotgun [ˌsɔːnɒf'ʃɒtgʌn, *Am:* ˌsɑːnɑːf'ʃɑːtgʌn] *n* escopeta *f* de cañones recortados

Saxon ['sæksən] *adj* sajón

Saxony ['sæksəni] *n no pl* Sajonia *f*

saxophone ['sæksəfəʊn, *Am:* -foʊn] *n* saxofón *m*

say [seɪ] **I.** <said, said> *vt* **1.** (*speak*) decir; **to ~ sth to sb's face** decir algo a alguien en su cara **2.** (*state information*) **to ~** (**that**) ... decir (que)...; **to have something/nothing to ~** (**to sb**) tener algo/no tener nada que decir (a alguien); **when all is said and done** a fin de cuentas **3.** (*think*) opinar; **people ~ that ...** se dice que... **4.** (*indicate*) indicar; **to ~ sth about sb/sth** expresar algo sobre alguien/algo **5.** (*tell*) explicar; **to ~ where/when** explicar dónde/cuándo **6.** (*for instance*) (**let's**) **~ ...** digamos... **II.** <said, said> *vi* **I'll ~!** *inf* ¡ya lo creo!; **I must ~ ...** debo admitir... **III.** *n no pl* parecer *m;* **to have one's ~** expresar su propia opinión; **to have a ~ in sth** tener voz y voto en algo

saying ['seɪɪŋ] *n* dicho *m*

say-so ['seɪsəʊ, *Am:* -soʊ] *n no pl, inf* visto bueno *m*

scab [skæb] *n* **1.** (*over wound*) costra *f* **2.** *inf* (*strikebreaker*) esquirol *mf*

scaffold ['skæfə(ʊ)ld, *Am:* 'skæfld] *n* (*for execution*) patíbulo *m*

scaffolding ['skæfəldɪŋ] *n no pl* andamiaje *m*

scald [skɔːld, *Am:* skɑːld] **I.** *vt* escaldar **II.** *n* escaldadura *f*

scale¹ [skeɪl] **I.** *n* **1.** ZOOL escama *f* **2.** *no pl* TECH, MED sarro *m* **II.** *vt* **1.** (*remove scales*) escamar **2.** TECH, MED quitar el sarro de

scale² [skeɪl] *n* (*weighing device*) platillo *m;* **~s** balanza *f;* (*bigger*) báscula *f*

scale³ [skeɪl] **I.** *n* (*range, magnitude, proportion*) *a.* MUS escala *f;* **on a large/small ~** a gran/pequeña escala; **to draw sth to ~** dibujar algo a escala **II.** *vt* escalar

◆ **scale down** *vt* reducir

scallop ['skɒləp, *Am:* 'skɑːləp] *n* vieira *f;* **~** (**shell**) venera *f*

scalp [skælp] **I.** *n* cabellera *f* **II.** *vt* escalpar

scalpel ['skælpəl] *n* MED escalpelo *m*

scam [skæm] *n inf* timo *m*

scamper ['skæmpəʳ, *Am:* -pɚ] *vi* corretear

scampi ['skæmpi] *npl* gambas *fpl*

scan [skæn] **I.** <-nn-> *vt* **1.** (*scrutinize*) escudriñar **2.** (*look through quickly*) dar un vistazo a **3.** MED explorar **II.** *n* INFOR escaneado *m;* MED escáner *m*

scandal ['skændl] *n* **1.** (*public outrage*) escándalo *m* **2.** *no pl* (*gossip*) chismorreo *m*

scandalize ['skændəlaɪz] *vt* escandalizar

scandalous ['skændələs] *adj* escandaloso

Scandinavia [ˌskændɪ'neɪviə] *n* Escandinavia *f*

Scandinavian *adj* escandinavo

scanner ['skænəʳ, *Am:* -ɚ] *n* INFOR escáner *m*

scant [skænt] *adj* escaso

scanty ['skænti, *Am:* -t̬i] *adj* **1.** (*clothing*) ligero **2.** (*insufficient*) insuficiente

scapegoat ['skeɪpgəʊt, *Am:* -goʊt] *n* cabeza *f* de turco

scar [skɑːʳ, *Am:* skɑːr] **I.** *n* cicatriz *f* **II.** <-rr-> *vt* marcar con cicatriz **III.** <-rr-> *vi* **to ~** (**over**) cicatrizar(se)

scarce [skeəs, *Am:* skers] *adj* escaso

scarcely ['skeəsli, *Am:* 'skers-] *adv* apenas

scare [skeəʳ, *Am:* sker] **I.** *vt* asustar, julepear *AmL;* **to be ~d stiff** estar muerto de miedo **II.** *n* **1.** (*fright*) susto *m*, julepe *m AmL* **2.** (*panic*) pánico *m*

◆ **scare away** *vt*, **scare off** *vt* ahuyentar

scarecrow ['skeəkrəʊ, *Am:* 'skerkroʊ] *n* espantapájaros *m inv*

scarf [skɑːf, *Am:* skɑːrf] <-ves *o* -s> *n* (*round neck*) bufanda *f;* (*round head*) pañuelo *m*

scarlet ['skɑːlət, *Am:* 'skɑːr-] *adj* escarlata

scarlet fever *n no pl* MED escarlatina *f*

scarper ['skɑːpəʳ, *Am:* 'skɑːrpɚ] *vi Brit, Aus, inf* largarse

scarves [skɑːvz, *Am:* skɑːrvz] *pl of* **scarf**

scary ['skeəri, *Am:* 'skeri] *adj* <-ier, -iest> que da miedo; **~ film** película *f* de miedo

scathing ['skeɪðɪŋ] *adj* mordaz; **to be ~ about sb/sth** criticar duramente a alguien/algo

scatter ['skætəʳ, *Am:* 'skæt̬ɚ] **I.** *vt* esparcir **II.** *vi* dispersarse

scatterbrained *adj* atolondrado

scavenge ['skævɪndʒ] *vi* **1.** ZOOL buscar comida **2.** (*search*) buscar cosas en la basura, pepenar *AmC, Méx*

scavenger ['skævɪndʒəʳ, *Am:* -ɚ] *n* **1.** ZOOL animal *m* carroñero **2.** (*person*) persona que hurga en la basura en busca de comida

scenario [sɪ'nɑːriəʊ, *Am:* sə'nerioʊ] *n* **1.** THEAT, LIT guión *m* **2.** (*situation*) escenario *m*

scene [siːn] *n* **1.** THEAT, CINE escena *f;* (*setting*) escenario *m;* **behind the ~s** *a. fig* entre bastidores **2.** (*locality*) lugar *m* **3.** (*view*) vista *f* **4.** (*milieu*) mundo *m;* **to appear on the ~** presentarse; **to set the ~** crear un ambiente **5.** (*embarrassing incident*) escándalo *m;* **to make a ~** montar un número

scenery ['siːnəri] *n no pl* **1.** (*landscape*) paisaje *m* **2.** THEAT, CINE decorado *m*

scenic ['siːnɪk] *adj* pintoresco

scent [sent] **I.** *n* **1.** (*aroma*) olor *m* **2.** (*in hunting*) rastro *m;* **to throw sb off the** ~ despistar a alguien **3.** *no pl, Brit* (*perfume*) perfume *m* **II.** *vt* **1.** (*smell*) oler **2.** (*sense, detect*) intuir **3.** (*apply perfume*) perfumar

sceptic ['skeptɪk] *n* escéptico, -a *m, f*

sceptical *adj* escéptico

schedule ['ʃedjuːl, *Am:* 'skedʒuːl] **I.** *n* **1.** (*timetable*) horario *m;* **to stick to a** ~ seguir un horario; **everything went according to** ~ todo fue según lo previsto **2.** (*plan of work*) programa *m* **II.** *vt* **1.** (*plan*) programar **2.** (*list*) catalogar

scheduled *adj* programado

scheduled flight *n* vuelo *m* regular

scheme [skiːm] **I.** *n* **1.** (*structure*) esquema *m* **2.** *Brit* (*programme*) programa *m;* ECON plan *m* **3.** (*plot*) treta *f* **II.** *vi pej* intrigar

schism ['sɪzəm] *n* cisma *m*

schizophrenia [ˌskɪtsəʊ'friːnɪə, *Am:* -sə'-] *n no pl* esquizofrenia *f*

schizophrenic [ˌskɪtsəʊ'frenɪk, *Am:* -sə'-] *adj* esquizofrénico

scholar ['skɒləʳ, *Am:* 'skɑːlə-] *n* **1.** (*learned person*) erudito, -a *m, f* **2.** (*student*) estudiante *mf* **3.** (*scholarship holder*) becario, -a *m, f*

scholarly *adj* erudito

scholarship ['skɒləʃɪp, *Am:* 'skɑː-lə-] *n* **1.** *no pl* (*learning*) erudición *f* **2.** (*grant*) beca *f* **scholarship holder** *n* becario, -a *m, f*

school¹ [skuːl] **I.** *n* **1.** (*institution*) escuela *f;* **to be in** ~ estar en edad escolar; **to go to** ~ ir al colegio **2.** (*buildings*) colegio *m* **3.** (*university division*) facultad *f* **II.** *vt* enseñar

school² [skuːl] *n* ZOOL banco *m*

school age ['skuːleɪdʒ] *n* edad *f* escolar **schoolbook** *n* libro *m* escolar **schoolboy** *n* colegial *m,* escolero *m Perú* **schoolchild** *n* colegial(a) *m(f),* escolero, -a *m, f Perú* **schoolgirl** *n* colegiala *f,* escolera *f Perú*

schooling *n no pl* enseñanza *f*

school leaver *n Brit, Aus:* alumno que ha finalizado sus estudios

schoolmaster *n* profesor *m*

schoolmistress *n* profesora *f*

❓ Con la expresión **School of the air** se designa una red de difusión por radio para el **outback** de Australia. Esta red funciona en zonas aisladas del país y tiene como finalidad educar a la población en edad escolar. Una docena de estas escuelas cubren un área de 2,5 millones de km y alcanzan a cientos de niños. Los alumnos reciben material didáctico y envían sus deberes hechos de vuelta, hablan por radio con sus profesores y compañeros de clase y la mayoría de las veces son sus padres o un profesor particular quienes los vigilan en casa.

❓ El **school system** (sistema escolar) americano comienza con la **elementary school** (que abarca desde el curso primero hasta el sexto u octavo). En algunos lugares después del **sixth grade**, el sexto curso, los alumnos pasan a otra escuela, la **junior high school** (donde se les imparte la docencia correspondiente a los cursos séptimo, octavo y noveno). Después los alumnos acceden a la **high school** donde permanecen por espacio de tres cursos. En aquellos lugares donde no hay **junior high school** los alumnos pasan directamente de la **elementary school** (donde han estado ocho años) a la **high school**, que, en ese caso, comienza con el **ninth grade**, es decir, el noveno curso. Los alumnos finalizan su itinerario escolar cuando han terminado el **twelfth grade**, el curso decimosegundo.

schoolteacher *n* profesor(a) *m(f)*
schoolyard *n* Am patio *m* del colegio
sciatica [saɪˈætɪkə, Am: -ˈæt̬-] *n no pl* MED ciática *f*
science [ˈsaɪənts] *n* ciencia *f*
science fiction *n* ciencia ficción *f*
scientific [ˌsaɪənˈtɪfɪk] *adj* científico
scientist [ˈsaɪəntɪst, Am: -t̬ɪst] *n* científico, -a *m, f*
sci-fi [ˈsaɪˌfaɪ] *n abbr of* **science fiction** ciencia *f* ficción
Scilly Isles [ˈsɪli aɪls] *n* the ~ las Islas Sorlingas
scissors [ˈsɪzəz, Am: -ɚz] *npl* tijeras *fpl*; **a pair of** ~ unas tijeras
scoff[1] [skɒf, Am: skɑːf] *vi* (*mock*) burlarse
scoff[2] [skɒf, Am: skɑːf] *vt* Brit, inf (*eat*) engullir
scold [skəʊld, Am: skoʊld] *vt* regañar
scone [skɒn, Am: skoʊn] *n* bollo *m*
scoop [skuːp] I. *n* 1. (*utensil*) cucharón *m* 2. (*amount*) cucharada *f* 3. PUBL primicia *f* informativa II. *vt* PUBL adelantarse a
◆ **scoop up** *vt* recoger
scooter [ˈskuːtəʳ, Am: -t̬ɚ] *n* 1. (*toy*) patinete *m* 2. (*vehicle*) (**motor**) ~ escúter *m*, Vespa® *f*
scope [skəʊp, Am: skoʊp] *n no pl* 1. (*range*) alcance *m* 2. (*possibilities*) posibilidades *fpl*
scorch [skɔːtʃ, Am: skɔːrtʃ] I. *vi, vt* chamuscar(se) II. *n* <-es> quemadura *f*
scorching *adj* abrasador
score [skɔːʳ, Am: skɔːr] I. *n* 1. (*number of points*) puntuación *f*; **to keep** (**the**) ~ llevar la cuenta 2. (*goal, point*) gol *m* 3. SCHOOL nota *f* 4. (*twenty*) veintena *f*; ~**s of people** mucha gente 5. (*dispute*) rencilla *f*; **to settle a** ~ ajustar cuentas 6. MUS partitura *f* II. *vt* 1. (*goal, point*) marcar 2. (*cut*) cortar III. *vi* 1. SPORTS marcar un tanto 2. *inf* (*suc-*

ceed) triunfar
◆ **score out** *vt* tachar
scoreboard [ˈskɔːbɔːd, Am: ˈskɔːrbɔːrd] *n* marcador *m*
scorn [skɔːn, Am: skɔːrn] I. *n* desprecio *m* II. *vt* despreciar, ajotar *Cuba*
Scorpio [ˈskɔːpiəʊ, Am: ˈskɔːrpioʊ] *n* Escorpión *m*
scorpion [ˈskɔːpiən, Am: ˈskɔːr-] *n* escorpión *m*
Scot [skɒt, Am: skɑːt] *n* escocés, -esa *m, f*
scotch [skɒtʃ, Am: skɑːtʃ] *vt* 1. (*rumour*) acallar 2. (*plan*) frustrar
Scotch [skɒtʃ, Am: skɑːtʃ] I. *n* whisky *m* (escocés) II. *adj* escocés
scot-free [ˌskɒtˈfriː, Am: ˌskɑːt'-] *adv* 1. (*without punishment*) impunemente; **to get away** ~ librarse del castigo 2. (*unharmed*) sin un rasguño
Scotland [ˈskɒtlənd, Am: ˈskɑːt-] *n* Escocia *f*
Scots [skɒts, Am: skɑːts] *adj s.* **Scottish**
Scotsman [ˈskɒtsmən, Am: ˈskɑːts-] <-men> *n* escocés *m*
Scotswoman [ˈskɒtsˌwʊmən, Am: ˈskɑːts-] <-women> *n* escocesa *f*
Scottish [ˈskɒtɪʃ, Am: ˈskɑːt̬ɪʃ] *adj* escocés
scoundrel [ˈskaʊndrəl] *n pej* sinvergüenza *mf*
scour [skaʊəʳ, Am: skaʊɚ] *vt* 1. (*scrub*) fregar 2. (*search*) recorrer
scourge [skɜːdʒ, Am: skɜːrdʒ] *n a. fig* azote *m*
scout [skaʊt] *n* explorador(a) *m(f)*, scout *mf Méx*
scowl [skaʊl] I. *n* ceño *m* fruncido II. *vi* fruncir el ceño
scrabble [ˈskræbl] *vi* 1. (*grope*) hurgar 2. (*claw for grip*) escarbar
scram [skræm] <-mm-> *vi inf* largarse, rajarse *AmC*
scramble [ˈskræmbl] I. *vi* moverse apresuradamente; **to** ~ **for sth** esforzarse por algo II. *vt* revolver; ~**d eggs** huevos revueltos III. *n no pl* 1. (*rush*) carrera *f*; (*chase*) persecución *f* 2. (*struggle to get*) arrebatiña

f, rebatinga *f Méx*

scrap¹ [skræp] **I.** *n* **1.** (*small piece*) trozo *m* **2.** (*small amount*) pizca *f* **3.** *pl* (*leftover food*) sobras *fpl* **4.** *no pl* (*old metal*) chatarra *f* **II.** <-pp-> *vt* (*get rid of*) desechar; (*abandon*) descartar; (*abolish*) abolir

scrap² [skræp] **I.** *n inf* (*fight*) agarrada *f,* agarrón *m Méx* **II.** <-pp-> *vi* pelearse

scrapbook ['skræpbʊk] *n* álbum *m* de recortes **scrap dealer** *n* chatarrero, -a *m, f*

scrape [skreɪp] **I.** *vt* **1.** (*remove layer*) raspar, rasquetear *Arg* **2.** (*rub against*) rozar **II.** *n* **1.** *no pl* (*act of scraping*) raspado, -a *m, f* **2.** *inf* (*situation*) lío *m*
◆**scrape through** *vi* salvarse por los pelos; SCHOOL aprobar por los pelos

scrapheap ['skræphiːp] *n* montón *m* de basura; **to throw sth on the ~** desechar algo

scrap merchant *n Brit* chatarrero, -a *m, f*

scratch [skrætʃ] **I.** *n* **1.** (*cut on skin*) rasguño *m,* rayón *m AmL* **2.** (*mark*) raya *f* **3.** (*start*) **from ~** desde cero **II.** *vt* **1.** (*cut slightly*) arañar **2.** (*mark*) rayar **3.** (*relieve itch*) rascar **III.** *vi* rascarse **IV.** *adj* improvisado

scrawl [skrɔːl, *Am:* skrɑːl] **I.** *vt* garabatear **II.** *n* garabatos *mpl*

scrawny ['skrɔːni, *Am:* 'skrɑː-] <-ier, -iest> *adj* escuálido, silgado *Ecua*

scream [skriːm] **I.** *n* chillido *m;* **to be a ~** ser la monda **II.** *vi* chillar

screech [skriːtʃ] *vi* chillar

screen [skriːn] **I.** *n* **1.** *a.* TV, FILM, INFOR pantalla *f* **2.** (*framed panel*) biombo *m* **3.** *no pl* (*thing that conceals*) cortina *f* **II.** *vt* **1.** (*conceal*) ocultar **2.** (*shield*) proteger **3.** (*examine*) examinar; (*revise*) revisar **4.** TV emitir; CINE proyectar

screening *n* **1.** (*showing: in cinema*) proyección *f* **2.** MED chequeo *m*

screenplay ['skriːnpleɪ] *n* guión *m*

screw [skruː] **I.** *n* **1.** (*small metal fas-*tener) tornillo *m* **2.** (*propeller*) hélice *f* **II.** *vt* atornillar
◆**screw up** *vt* **1.** (*fasten with screws*) atornillar **2.** *inf* (*make a mess of*) joder

screwdriver ['skruːˌdraɪvəʳ, *Am:* -vɚ] *n* destornillador *m,* desarmador *m AmL*

scribble ['skrɪbl] **I.** *vt* garabatear **II.** *vi* hacer garabatos **III.** *n* garabatos *mpl*

script [skrɪpt] *n* **1.** CINE guión *m* **2.** (*writing*) escritura *f*

Scripture ['skrɪptʃəʳ, *Am:* -tʃɚ] *n* Sagrada Escritura *f*

scroll [skrəʊl, *Am:* skroʊl] **I.** *n* rollo *m* (de papel) **II.** *vi* INFOR desplazarse

scrotum ['skrəʊtəm, *Am:* 'skroʊtəm] <-tums *o* -ta-> *n* escroto *m*

scrounge [skraʊndʒ] **I.** *vt inf* conseguir gorroneando, manguear *Arg;* **to ~ sth off** [*o* **from**] **sb** gorronear algo a alguien **II.** *vi inf* gorronear

scrounger ['skraʊndʒəʳ, *Am:* -ɚ] *n pej, inf* gorrón, -ona *m, f,* pedinche *mf Méx*

scrub¹ [skrʌb] <-bb-> **I.** *vt* **1.** (*clean*) fregar **2.** (*cancel*) cancelar **II.** *n no pl* (*clean*) fregado *m*

scrub² [skrʌb] *n no pl* BOT matorral *m*

scruff [skrʌf] *n* cogote *m;* **to grab sb by the ~ of the neck** coger a alguien por el cogote

scruffy ['skrʌfi] <-ier, -iest> *adj* desaliñado, fachoso *Méx*

scrum ['skrʌm] *n* SPORTS melé *f*

scruple ['skruːpl] *n no pl* escrúpulo *m;* **to have no ~s** (**about doing sth**) no tener escrúpulos (en hacer algo)

scrupulous ['skruːpjʊləs] *adj* escrupuloso

scrutinise *vt Brit, Aus,* **scrutinize** ['skruːtɪnaɪz, *Am:* -tənaɪz] *vt* escudriñar; (*votes*) escrutar

scrutiny ['skruːtɪni, *Am:* -təni] *n no pl* escrutinio *m*

scuba diving ['skuːbəˌdaɪvɪŋ] *n* submarinismo *m*

scuff [skʌf] *vt* raspar

The computer

El ordenador

1	screen	pantalla *f*, monitor *m*
2	keyboard	teclado *m*
3	mouse	ratón *m*
4	mousemat *Brit*, mousepad *Am*	alfombrilla *f* para (el) ratón
5	desktop	escritorio *m*
6	swivel chair	silla *f* giratoria
7	joystick	palanca *f* de mando, joystick *m*

8	scanner	escáner *m*, scanner *m*
9	processor *Brit*, computer *Am*	procesador *m*
10	web camera	cámara *f* web, webcam *f*
11	printer	impresora *f*
12	speaker	altavoz *m*
13	discs *Brit*, disks *Am*	disquetes *mpl*, diskettes *mpl*

scuffle ['skʌfl] I. *n* refriega *f* II. *vi* pelearse

scullery ['skʌləri] *n* antecocina *f*

sculptor ['skʌlptər, *Am:* -tər] *n* escultor *m*

sculpture ['skʌlptʃər, *Am:* -tʃər] I. *n* escultura *f* II. *vt* esculpir

scum [skʌm] *n no pl* 1. (*foam*) espumaje *m* 2. (*evil people*) escoria *f*

scupper ['skʌpər, *Am:* -ər] *vt* 1. (*ship*) hundir 2. *inf* (*plan*) echar por tierra

scurrilous ['skʌrɪləs, *Am:* 'skɜːrɪ-] *adj pej* (*damaging*) difamatorio; (*insulting*) calumnioso

scurry ['skʌri, *Am:* 'skɜːri] <-ie-> *vi* correr

scuttle¹ ['skʌtl, *Am:* 'skʌt̬-] *vi* (*run*) correr

◆**scuttle away** *vi*, **scuttle off** *vi* (*run*) escabullirse

scuttle² ['skʌtl, *Am:* 'skʌt̬-] *vt* (*sink*) hundir

scuttle³ ['skʌtl, *Am:* 'skʌt̬-] *n* cajón *m* para el carbón

scythe [saɪð] I. *n* guadaña *f* II. *vt* (*with a scythe*) guadañar; (*with swinging blow*) segar

SE [ˌesˈiː] *n abbr of* **southeast** SE *m*

sea [siː] *n* mar *m o f;* **by ~** por mar; **by the ~** junto al mar; **out at ~** en alta mar; **a ~ of people** un mar de gente

sea bed *n no pl* lecho *m* marino

seaboard ['siːbɔːd, *Am:* -bɔːrd] *n* litoral *m*

seafood ['siːfuːd] *n no pl* marisco *m*

seafront ['siːfrʌnt] *n* 1. (*promenade*) paseo *m* marítimo, malecón *m Méx* 2. (*beach*) playa *f*

seagoing ['siːˌɡəʊɪŋ, *Am:* -ˌɡoʊ-] *adj* de altura

seagull ['siːɡʌl] *n* gaviota *f*

seal¹ [siːl] *n* zool foca *f*

seal² [siːl] I. *n* (*stamp*) sello *m;* **~ of approval** aprobación *f* II. *vt* 1. (*put a seal on*) sellar 2. (*close: frontier, port*) cerrar

sea level *n no pl* nivel *m* del mar

sea lion *n* león *m* marino

seam [siːm] *n* 1. (*stitching*) costura *f* 2. (*junction*) juntura *f* 3. MIN veta *f,* filón *m*

seaman ['siːmən] <-men> *n* marinero *m*

seance ['seɪɑ̃ːnts, *Am:* 'seɪɑːnts] *n* sesión *f* de espiritismo

seaplane ['siːpleɪn] *n* hidroavión *m*

search [sɜːtʃ, *Am:* sɜːrtʃ] I. *n* búsqueda *f;* (*of building*) registro *m,* cateo *m Méx* II. *vi a.* INFOR buscar; **to ~ for** [*o* **after**] **sth** buscar algo; **~ and replace** INFOR buscar y reemplazar III. *vt* 1. *a.* INFOR buscar en; (*building, baggage*) registrar, catear *Méx* 2. (*examine*) examinar

search engine *n* INFOR motor *m* de búsqueda

searching *adj* (*look*) penetrante

searchlight ['sɜːtʃlaɪt, *Am:* 'sɜːrtʃ-] *n* reflector *m*

search party <-ies> *n* equipo *m* de salvamento **search warrant** *n* orden *f* de registro

seashore ['siːʃɔːʳ, *Am:* -ʃɔːr] *n no pl* 1. (*beach*) playa *f* 2. (*near sea*) costa *f*

seasick ['siːsɪk] *adj* mareado; **to get ~** marearse

seaside ['siːsaɪd] *Brit* I. *n no pl* 1. (*beach*) playa *f* 2. (*coast*) costa *f* II. *adj* costero

season ['siːzən] I. *n* 1. (*period of year*) estación *f* 2. (*epoch*) época *f;* **the** (**fishing/hunting**) **~** la temporada (de pesca/de caza); **to be in ~** estar en sazón; **to be out of ~** estar fuera de temporada 3. SPORTS temporada *f* II. *vt* GASTR sazonar; (*add salt and pepper*) salpimentar

seasonal ['siːzənəl] *adj* estacional

seasoned *adj* 1. (*experienced*) experimentado 2. (*dried: wood*) secado 3. (*spiced*) sazonado

seasoning ['siːzənɪŋ] *n no pl* condimento *m*

season ticket *n Brit, Aus* abono *m* (de temporada)

seat [siːt] I. *n* 1. (*furniture*) asiento *m;* (*on a bicycle*) sillín *m;* (*in the atre*) butaca *f;* (*in a car, bus*) plaza *f;* **is this ~ free/taken?** ¿está libre/ocupado este asiento?; **to take one's ~** sentarse 2. (*buttocks*) trasero *m inf*

S
s

3. POL escaño *m*, banca *f Arg, Par, Urug* **4.** (*centre*) sede *f* **II.** *vt* **1.** (*place on a seat*) sentar **2.** (*have enough seats for*) tener cabida para

seat belt *n* cinturón *m* de seguridad

seawater ['siːˌwɔːtə', *Am:* -ˌwɑːt̬ə'] *n no pl* agua *f* de mar

seaweed ['siːwiːd] *n no pl* algas *fpl*, huiro *m Chile*

seaworthy ['siːˌwɜːði, *Am:* -ˌwɜːr-] *adj* en condiciones de navegar

sec [sek] *abbr of* **second** seg.

secluded [sɪˈkluːdɪd] *adj* solitario

seclusion [sɪˈkluːʒn] *n no pl* aislamiento *m*

second¹ ['sekənd] **I.** *adj* segundo; **to have ~ thoughts about sb/sth** dudar de alguien/algo; **on ~ thoughts** *Brit, Aus,* **on ~ thought** *Am, Aus* pensándolo bien; **the ~ floor** *Brit* el segundo piso, el tercer piso *AmL; Am* el primer piso, el segundo piso *AmL* **II.** *n* **1.** *Brit* (*second-class degree*) *título calificado con la segunda o tercera nota que es posible obtener en el Reino Unido* **2.** *no pl* (*second gear*) segunda *f* **3.** COM artículo *m* con defectos de fábrica **III.** *adv* en segundo lugar **IV.** *vt form* (*back up*) apoyar

second² ['sekənd] *n* (*unit of time*) segundo *m;* **just a ~!** ¡un segundo!

second³ [sɪˈkɒnd, *Am:* -ˈkɑːnd] *vt Brit, Aus* (*officer, staff*) destinar

secondary ['sekəndəri, *Am:* -deri] *adj* secundario

secondary school *n* instituto *m* de enseñanza secundaria, liceo *m Chile, Méx*

second class I. *adv* **to send sth ~** *Brit* enviar algo por correo regular; **to travel ~** viajar en segunda **II.** *adj* de segunda clase **second cousin** *n* primo, -a *m, f* segundo, -a **second- -hand** *adj, adv* de segunda mano **second hand** *n* (*on watch*) segundero *m*

secondly *adv* en segundo lugar

secondment [sɪˈkɒndmənt, *Am:* -ˈkɑːnd-] *n Brit, Aus no pl* traslado *m* temporal por trabajo

second-rate [ˌsekəndˈreɪt] *adj*

mediocre

secrecy ['siːkrəsi] *n no pl* secreto *m*

secret ['siːkrɪt] **I.** *n* secreto *m* **II.** *adj* secreto; **to keep sth ~ (from sb)** ocultar algo (a alguien)

secret agent *n* agente *mf* secreto, -a

secretary ['sekrətəri, *Am:* -rəteri] <-ies> *n* secretario, -a *m, f;* **Secretary of State** *Brit* ministro; *Am* secretario de Estado

secretary-general [ˌsekrətəriˈdʒenərəl, *Am:* -rəteri'-] <secretaries-general> *n* secretario, -a *m, f* general

secrete¹ [sɪˈkriːt] *vt* (*discharge*) segregar

secrete² [sɪˈkriːt] *vt form* (*hide*) ocultar

secretive ['siːkrətɪv, *Am:* -t̬ɪv] *adj* reservado

sect [sekt] *n* secta *f*

sectarian [sekˈteəriən, *Am:* -ˈteri-] *adj* sectario

section ['sekʃn] *n* **1.** (*part*) *a.* MIL, MUS, PUBL sección *f;* (*of object*) parte *f* **2.** (*group*) sector *m* **3.** (*of document*) artículo *m*

sector ['sektə', *Am:* -t̬ə'] *n* sector *m*

secular ['sekjʊlə', *Am:* -lə'] *adj* **1.** (*non-religious*) secular **2.** REL seglar

secure [sɪˈkjʊə', *Am:* -ˈkjʊr] **I.** *adj* <-rer, -est> **1.** (*safe*) seguro; **to make sth ~ against attack** proteger algo contra los ataques **2.** (*confident*) **to feel ~ about sth** sentirse seguro respecto a algo **3.** (*fixed*) firme **II.** *vt* **1.** (*obtain*) obtener **2.** (*make firm*) asegurar; *fig* afianzar **3.** (*guarantee repayment*) garantizar

security [sɪˈkjʊərəti, *Am:* 'kjʊrət̬i] <-ies> *n* **1.** *no pl* (*safety*) seguridad *f;* **~ of employment** estabilidad laboral **2.** *no pl* (*payment guarantee*) fianza *f* **3.** *pl* FIN títulos *mpl;* **securities market** mercado *m* de valores

Security Council *n* Consejo *m* de Seguridad (de las Naciones Unidas) **security forces** *npl* fuerzas *fpl* de seguridad **security guard** *n* guarda *mf* jurado, -a

sedan [sɪˈdæn] *n Am, Aus* AUTO

sedán *m*

sedate [sɪ'deɪt] **I.** *adj* tranquilo **II.** *vt* MED sedar

sedation [sɪ'deɪʃən] *n no pl* MED sedación *f*; **under** ~ sedado

sedative ['sedətɪv, *Am:* -t̬ɪv] *n* sedante *m*

sediment ['sedɪmənt, *Am:* 'sedə-] *n no pl* sedimento *m*

seduce [sɪ'djuːs, *Am:* -'duːs] *vt* seducir

seduction [sɪ'dʌkʃn] *n no pl* seducción *f*

seductive [sɪ'dʌktɪv] *adj* seductor

see¹ [siː] <saw, seen> **I.** *vt* **1.** (*perceive*) ver; **to** ~ **that ...** ver que...; **you were** ~**n to enter the building** se os vio entrar en el edificio; **may I** ~ **your driving licence?** ¿me permite (ver) su permiso de conducir?; **I could** ~ **it coming** lo veía venir; **as I** ~ **it ...** a mi modo de ver... **2.** (*visit*) visitar; ~ **you!** *inf* (*when meeting again later*) ¡hasta luego! **3.** (*have relationship*) **to be** ~**ing sb** salir con alguien **4.** (*investigate*) **to** ~ **how/what/if ...** averiguar cómo/qué/si... **5.** (*ensure*) ~ **that you are ready when we come** procura estar listo cuando vengamos **II.** *vi* **1.** (*use eyes*) ver; **as far as the eye can see** ~ hasta donde alcanza la vista **2.** (*find out*) descubrir; ~ **for yourself!** ¡compruébelo usted mismo!; **let me** ~ ¿a ver? **3.** (*understand*) comprender; **I** ~ ya veo
◆ **see about** *vt inf* encargarse de; (*consider*) pensarse
◆ **see off** *vt* despedir
◆ **see through** *vt* **1.** (*look through*) ver a través de **2.** (*not be deceived by*) calar a *inf*
◆ **see to** *vt* encargarse de

see² [siː] *n* REL sede *f*

seed [siːd] *n* **1.** BOT semilla *f*; (*of fruit*) pepita *f*, pepa *f AmL* **2.** (*beginning*) germen *m*

seedling ['siːdlɪŋ] *n* planta *f* de semillero

seedy ['siːdi] <-ier, -iest> *adj* sórdido; (*place*) de mala muerte

seeing *conj* ~ (**that**) en vista de (que)

seek [siːk] <sought, sought> *vt* **1.** (*look for*) buscar **2.** (*ask for: help, approval*) pedir; (*job*) solicitar
◆ **seek out** *vt* (*person*) ir a buscar

seem [siːm] *vi* **1.** (*appear to be*) parecer; **to** ~ **as if ...** parecer como si... +*subj*; **it is not all what it** ~**s** no es lo que parece **2.** (*appear*) **it** ~**s that ...** parece que...; **so it** ~**s, so would** ~ eso parece

seemingly *adv* aparentemente

seen [siːn] *pp of* **see**

seep [siːp] *vi* filtrarse

seesaw ['siːsɔː, *Am:* -sɑː] *n* balancín *m*

seethe [siːð] *vi* **1.** (*bubble*) borbotar **2.** *fig* (*be angry*) estar furioso; **to** ~ **with anger** hervir de cólera

see-through ['siːθruː] *adj* transparente

segment ['segmənt] *n* segmento *m*

segregate ['segrɪgeɪt, *Am:* -rə-] *vt* segregar

seize [siːz] *vt* **1.** (*grasp*) asir, agarrar **2.** (*take: opportunity*) no dejar escapar
◆ **seize on** *vt* aprovecharse de
◆ **seize up** *vi* (*engine, muscles*) agarrotarse

seizure ['siːʒər, *Am:* -ʒər] *n* **1.** (*of drugs*) incautación *f* **2.** MED ataque *m*

seldom ['seldəm] *adv* rara vez

select [sɪ'lekt, *Am:* sə'-] **I.** *vt* (*candidate, player*) seleccionar; (*gift, wine*) escoger **II.** *adj* (*high-class*) selecto; (*club, restaurant*) exclusivo; **the** ~ **few** los escogidos

selection [sɪ'lekʃən, *Am:* sə'-] *n* **1.** (*choosing*) selección *f* **2.** (*range*) surtido *m* **3.** *no pl* (*choice*) elección *f*

selector [sɪ'lektər, *Am:* sə'lektər] *n* **1.** SPORTS seleccionador(a) *m(f)* **2.** TECH selector *m*

self [self] *n* <selves> uno mismo, una misma; **the** ~ PSYCH el yo

self-assurance *n no pl* seguridad *f* en uno mismo **self-assured** *adj* seguro de sí mismo **self-catering** *adj Aus, Brit* (*apartment*) con cocina individual; (*holiday*) sin servicio de co-

midas **self-centered** *adj Am,* **self- -centred** *adj Brit, Aus* egocéntrico
self-confessed *adj* confeso **self- -confidence** *n no pl* seguridad *f* en uno mismo **self-conscious** *adj* tímido; **to feel** ~ sentirse cohibido **self-contained** *adj* autosuficiente; (*apartment*) con cocina y cuarto de baño **self-control** *n no pl* dominio *m* de sí mismo **self-defence** *n Aus, Brit,* **self-defense** *n Am no pl* defensa *f* propia **self-discipline** *n no pl* autodisciplina *f* **self-employed** *adj* **to be** ~ trabajar por cuenta propia **self-esteem** *n no pl* amor *m* propio **self-evident** *adj* evidente **self-explanatory** *adj* que se explica por sí mismo **self-governing** *adj* autónomo **self-help** *n* autoayuda *f* **self-indulgent** *adj* indulgente consigo mismo **self-inflicted** *adj* autoinfligido **self-interest** *n no pl* interés *m* propio
selfish ['selfɪʃ] *adj* egoísta
selfishness *n no pl* egoísmo *m*
selfless ['selfləs] *adj* desinteresado
self-pity *n no pl* lástima *f* de sí mismo **self-portrait** *n* autorretrato *m* **self-preservation** *n no pl* instinto *m* de conservación **self-respect** *n no pl* amor *m* propio **self-righteous** *adj* farisaico **self-sacrifice** *n no pl* abnegación *f* **self-satisfied** *adj* satisfecho de sí mismo **self-service** *adj* ~ **store** autoservicio *m;* ~ **restaurant** self-service *m* **self-sufficient** *adj* autosuficiente **self- -taught** *adj* autodidacto
sell [sel] **I.** *vt* <sold, sold> **1.** (*exchange for money*) vender **2.** *fig* (*make accepted*) hacer aceptar; **I'm sold on your plan** tu plan me ha convencido **II.** *vi* <sold, sold> venderse; **to** ~ **at** [*o* **for**] **£5** venderse a 5 libras
 ◆ **sell off** *vt* liquidar
 ◆ **sell out I.** *vi* **1.** COM, FIN agotarse **2.** *fig* venderse **II.** *vt* liquidar
 ◆ **sell up** *Aus, Brit* **I.** *vi* liquidar **II.** *vt* vender
sell-by date ['selbaɪˌdeɪt] *n Brit* COM fecha *f* límite de venta

seller *n* vendedor(a) *m(f);* ~**'s market** mercado *m* de vendedores
selling price *n* precio *m* de venta
Sellotape® ['seləteɪp, *Am:* -oʊ-] *n no pl, Brit* celo *m*
sell-out ['selaʊt] *n* **1.** THEAT, CINE éxito *f* de taquilla **2.** (*betrayal*) traición *f*
selves [selvz] *n pl of* **self**
semblance ['sembləns] *n no pl, form* apariencia *f*
semen ['siːmən] *n no pl* semen *m*
semester [sɪ'mestər, *Am:* sə'mestər] *n* semestre *m* (académico)
semi ['semi] *n Aus, Brit, inf* casa *f* pareada
semicircle ['semɪˌsɜːkl, *Am:* -ˌsɜːrkl] *n* semicírculo *m*
semicolon [ˌsemɪ'kəʊ lən, *Am:* 'semɪˌkoʊ-] *n* punto *m* y coma
semiconductor [ˌsemɪkən'dʌktər, *Am:* -tər] *n* ELEC semiconductor *m*
semi-detached [ˌsemɪdɪ'tætʃt] *adj* ~ **house** casa *f* pareada
semifinal [ˌsemɪ'faɪnəl] *n* SPORTS semifinal *f*
seminar ['semɪnɑːr, *Am:* -ənɑːr] *n* UNIV seminario *m*
seminary ['semɪnəri, *Am:* -ner-] *n* REL seminario *m*
semiskilled [ˌsemɪ'skɪld] *adj* semicualificado
Sen. *n Am abbr of* **Senator** senador(a) *m(f)*
senate ['senɪt] *n no pl* POL senado *m*
senator ['senətər, *Am:* -ˌtər] *n* POL senador(a) *m(f)*
send [send] *vt* <sent, sent> **1.** (*message, letter*) enviar, mandar; **to** ~ **sth by post** enviar algo por correo; **to** ~ **one's love to sb** mandar saludos cariñosos a alguien; ~ **her my regards** dale recuerdos de mi parte; **to** ~ **word** (**to sb**) *form* informar (a alguien) **2.** (*propel*) lanzar; **to** ~ **sth flying** hacer saltar algo por los aires **3.** *inf* (*cause*) **to** ~ **sb to sleep** hacer que alguien se duerma
 ◆ **send away** *vt* despedir
 ◆ **send back** *vt* devolver
 ◆ **send for** *vt* (*person*) llamar; (*goods*) encargar

◆ **send in** vt (reinforcements) mandar

◆ **send off** vt **1.** (by post) enviar por correo **2.** Aus, Brit SPORTS expulsar

◆ **send on** vt **1.** (send in advance) mandar por adelantado **2.** (forward: mail) remitir

◆ **send out** vt **1.** (send on errand) mandar **2.** (dispatch) enviar **3.** (emit: signal, rays) emitir

◆ **send up** vt **1.** (drive up: prices, temperature) hacer subir **2.** (caricature) imitar

sender n remitente mf

send-off ['sendɒf, Am: -ɑ:f] n despedida f; **to give sb a good** ~ dar una buena despedida a alguien

send-up n inf parodia f

Senegal [ˌsenɪ'gɔ:l] n el Senegal

Senegalese [ˌsenɪgə'li:z] adj senegalés, -esa

senile ['si:naɪl] adj senil

senior ['si:niəʳ, Am: -njəʳ] I. adj **1.** form (older) mayor; **James Grafton, Senior** James Grafton, padre **2.** (higher in rank) superior II. n mayor mf

senior citizen n jubilado, -a m, f

senior high school n instituto m de bachillerato

seniority [ˌsi:ni'ɒrəti, Am: si:'njɔ:-rəti] n no pl antigüedad f

sensation [sen'seɪʃən] n sensación f

sensational [sen'seɪʃənəl] adj sensacional

sense [sents] I. n **1.** (faculty) sentido m **2.** (ability) sentido m; **to lose all** ~ **of time** perder la noción del tiempo **3.** (way) sentido m; **in every** ~ en todos los sentidos **4.** (sensation) sensación f **5.** pl (clear mental faculties) juicio m; **to come to one's** ~**s** (recover consciousness) recobrar el conocimiento; (see reason) entrar en razón **6.** no pl (good judgment) (**common**) ~ sentido m común **7.** (meaning) significado m, sentido m; **to make** ~ tener sentido II. vt sentir; **to** ~ **that ...** darse cuenta de que...

senseless ['sentsləs] adj **1.** (pointless) sin sentido; (remark) insensato

2. MED inconsciente

sensibility [ˌsentsɪ'brɪləti, Am: -sə-'brɪləti] n no pl sensibilidad f

sensible ['sentsɪbl, Am: -sə-] adj **1.** (having good judgement) sensato **2.** (suitable) práctico

sensibly adv **1.** (wisely) sensatamente **2.** (dress) con ropa cómoda

sensitive ['sentsɪtɪv, Am: -sətɪv] adj **1.** (appreciative) sensible **2.** (touchy) susceptible

sensitiveness n, **sensitivity** [ˌsentsɪ'tɪvəti, Am: -sətɪvəti] n **1.** (touchiness) susceptibilidad f **2.** (understanding) sensibilidad f

sensual ['sentʃʊəl, Am: -ʃʊəl] adj, **sensuous** ['sentsjʊəs, Am: -ʃʊəs] adj sensual

sent [sent] pt, pp of **send**

sentence ['sentəns, Am: -təns] I. n **1.** (court decision) sentencia f; (punishment) condena f; **jail** ~ condena de encarcelamiento **2.** LING frase f II. vt condenar

sentiment ['sentɪmənt, Am: -tə-] n form **1.** (opinion) opinión f **2.** no pl (emotion) sentimiento m

sentimental [ˌsentɪ'mentəl, Am: -tə'mentəl] adj sentimental

sentry ['sentri] n centinela m

separate¹ ['seprət, Am: 'sepəʳt] adj separado

separate² ['sepəreɪt] I. vt separar; **to** ~ **two people** separar a dos personas II. vi separarse

separation [ˌsepə'reɪʃən] n separación f; (division) división f

September [sep'tembəʳ, Am: -bəʳ] n septiembre m; s. a. **April**

septic ['septɪk] adj séptico; **to go** [o turn] ~ infectarse

sequel ['si:kwəl] n **1.** continuación f **2.** (follow-up) desenlace m

sequence ['si:kwəns] n **1.** (order) orden m; (of events) sucesión f **2.** (part of film) secuencia f

sequin ['si:kwɪn] n lentejuela f

sera ['sɪərə, Am: 'sɪrə] n pl of **serum**

Serb [sɜ:b, Am: sɜ:rb] adj serbio

Serbia ['sɜ:bɪə, Am: 'sɜ:r-] n Serbia f

Serbian ['sɜ:bɪən, Am: 'sɜ:r-] n ser-

S

bio, -a *m, f*

Serbo-Croat [ˌsɜːbəʊˈkrəʊæt, *Am:* ˌsɜːrboʊkroʊˈ-] *n* LING serbocroata *mf*

serenade [ˌserəˈneɪd] **I.** *vt* dar una serenata a **II.** *n* serenata *f,* mañanita *f Méx*

serene [sɪˈriːn, *Am:* səˈ-] *adj* **1.** (*calm*) sereno **2.** (*peaceful*) tranquilo

serial [ˈsɪəriəl, *Am:* ˈsɪri-] *n* serial *m;* **TV** ~ telenovela *f*

serial killer *n* asesino, -a *m, f* en serie **serial number** *n* número *m* de serie

series [ˈsɪəriːz, *Am:* ˈsɪriːz] *n inv* serie *f*

> ⚠ **a series** se utiliza con el verbo en singular: "A new television series begins today."

serious [ˈsɪəriəs, *Am:* ˈsɪri-] *adj* **1.** (*earnest, solemn*) serio **2.** (*problem, injury*) grave

seriously *adv* **1.** (*in earnest*) seriamente, en serio; **no,** ~ ... no, en serio... **2.** (*ill, damaged*) gravemente **3.** *inf* (*very*) extremadamente

sermon [ˈsɜːmən, *Am:* ˈsɜːr-] *n a. fig* sermón *m*

serpent [ˈsɜːpənt, *Am:* ˈsɜːr-] *n* serpiente *f*

serum [ˈsɪərəm, *Am:* ˈsɪrəm] <-s *o* sera> *n* suero *m*

servant [ˈsɜːvənt, *Am:* ˈsɜːr-] *n* criado, -a *m, f,* mucamo, -a *m, f AmL*

serve [sɜːv, *Am:* sɜːrv] **I.** *n* SPORTS saque *m* **II.** *vt* **1.** (*attend*) atender **2.** (*provide*) servir **3.** (*be enough for*) ser suficiente **4.** (*work for*) estar al servicio de; **to** ~ **sb's interests** servir a los intereses de alguien **5.** (*complete: sentence, mandate*) cumplir **6.** (*help achieve*) ser útil a; **if my memory** ~**s me right** si la memoria no me falla **7.** *fig* **it** ~**s him/her right!** ¡se lo merece! **III.** *vi* **1.** (*put food on plates*) servir **2.** (*be useful*) servir **3.** SPORTS sacar

◆ **serve out** *vt* GASTR servir

◆ **serve up** *vt* GASTR servir; *fig* ofrecer

service [ˈsɜːvɪs, *Am:* ˈsɜːr-] **I.** *n* **1.** *no pl* servicio *m;* **bus/train** ~ servicio de autobuses/trenes **2.** (*department*) servicio *m;* **the Service** MIL el ejército **3.** SPORTS saque *m* **4.** REL oficio *m;* **to hold a** ~ celebrar una misa **5.** *Brit* TECH mantenimiento *m;* AUTO revisión *f* **6.** (*set*) vajilla *f;* **tea** ~ juego *m* de té **II.** *vt* (*car, TV*) revisar

service charge *n* gastos *mpl* de servicio **serviceman** *n* militar *m* **service station** *n* estación *f* de servicio

serviette [ˌsɜːviˈet, *Am:* ˌsɜːr-] *n Brit* servilleta *f*

session [ˈseʃn] *n* (*meeting*) sesión *f;* **to be in** ~ estar reunido

set [set] **I.** *adj* **1.** (*ready*) listo; **to get** ~ (**to do sth**) prepararse (para hacer algo) **2.** (*fixed*) fijo; **to be** ~ **in one's ways** tener costumbres profundamente arraigadas **3.** (*assigned*) asignado **II.** *n* **1.** (*group: of people*) grupo *m;* (*of kitchen utensils*) batería *f;* (*of stamps*) serie *f;* (*of tools*) set *m;* ~ **of glasses** cristalería *f;* ~ **of teeth** dentadura *f* **2.** (*collection*) colección *f* **3.** CINE plató *m* **4.** (*television*) televisor *m* **5.** (*in tennis*) set *m* **6.** (*musical performance*) actuación *f* **III.** *vt* <set, set> **1.** (*place*) poner, colocar **2.** (*start*) **to** ~ **sth on fire** prender fuego algo **3.** (*adjust*) ajustar; (*prepare*) preparar; **to** ~ **the table** poner la mesa **4.** (*fix*) fijar; **to** ~ **oneself a goal** fijarse un objetivo **IV.** *vi* **1.** (*become firm: cement*) endurecerse; (*jelly, cheese*) cuajar **2.** (*sun*) ponerse

◆ **set about** *vt* emprender; **to** ~ **doing sth** comenzar a hacer algo

◆ **set aside** *vt* reservar; (*time*) guardar; (*money*) ahorrar

◆ **set back** *vt* **1.** (*delay*) retrasar **2.** (*place away from*) apartar

◆ **set down** *vt* **1.** (*drop off*) dejar **2.** (*write*) poner por escrito

◆ **set off I.** *vi* partir **II.** *vt* **1.** accionar **2.** (*detonate*) hacer explotar **3.** (*cause*) causar **4.** (*enhance*) hacer

◆ **set out I.** *vt* **1.** (*display, arrange*)

disponer, colocar **2.** (*explain*) exponer **II.** *vi* partir; **to ~ to do sth** (*intend*) tener la intención de hacer algo
◆ **set up** *vt* establecer
setback ['setbæk] *n* revés *m;* **to experience a** ~ tener un contratiempo
settee [se'ti:] *n* sofá *m*
setting ['setɪŋ, *Am:* 'seṭ-] *n* **1.** (*scenery*) marco *m* **2.** (*frame for jewel*) engaste *m*
settle ['setl, *Am:* 'seṭ-] **I.** *vi* **1.** (*take up residence*) instalarse **2.** (*get comfortable*) ponerse cómodo **3.** (*calm down*) calmarse; (*weather*) serenarse; (*situation*) normalizarse, aconcharse *Chile* **II.** *vt* **1.** (*calm down: stomach*) calmar **2.** (*decide*) acordar; **that ~s it!** ¡ya no hay más que decir! **3.** (*conclude*) finalizar; (*resolve*) resolver **4.** (*pay*) pagar
◆ **settle down** *vi* **1.** (*take up residence*) instalarse **2.** (*calm down*) calmarse
◆ **settle in** *vi* acostumbrarse
◆ **settle up** *vi* ajustar cuentas
settlement ['setlmənt, *Am:* 'seṭ-] *n* **1.** (*resolution*) resolución *f* **2.** (*agreement*) acuerdo *m* **3.** FIN, ECON liquidación *f;* **in ~ of sth** para liquidar algo **4.** (*village, town*) asentamiento *m*
settler ['setlə^r, *Am:* 'seṭlɚ] *n* colono, -a *m, f*
set-up ['setʌp, *Am:* 'seṭ-] *n* estructura *f*
seven ['sevn] *adj* siete *inv; s. a.* **eight**
seventeen [,sevn'ti:n] *adj* diecisiete *inv; s. a.* **eight**
seventeenth [,sevn'ti:nθ] *adj* decimoséptimo
seventh ['sevəntθ] *adj* séptimo
seventieth ['sevəntiθ] *adj* septuagésimo
seventy ['sevənti, *Am:* -ṭi] *adj* setenta *inv; s. a.* **eighty**
sever ['sevə^r, *Am:* 'sevɚ] *vt* cortar; (*relationship*) romper
several ['sevərəl] **I.** *adj* (*some*) varios; (*distinct*) distintos; ~ **times** varias veces **II.** *pron* (*some*) algunos, algunas; (*different*) varios, varias; ~ **of us** algunos de nosotros

severance ['sevərənts] *n no pl, form* ruptura *f*
severance pay *n* indemnización *f* por despido
severe [sɪ'vɪə^r, *Am:* sə'vɪr] *adj* **1.** (*problem, illness*) grave; (*pain*) fuerte **2.** (*criticism, punishment, person*) severo; (*rough*) duro
severity [sɪ'verəti, *Am:* sə'verəṭi] *n no pl* gravedad *f*, severidad *f*
Seville [sə'vɪl] *n* Sevilla *f*
sew [səʊ, *Am:* soʊ] <sewed, sewn *o* sewed> *vi, vt* coser
◆ **sew up** *vt* coser
sewage ['su:ɪdʒ] *n no pl* aguas *fpl* residuales
sewer ['səʊə^r, *Am:* 'soʊɚ] *n* alcantarilla *f*
sewing ['səʊɪŋ, *Am:* 'soʊ-] *n no pl* costura *f*
sewing machine *n* máquina *f* de coser
sewn [səʊn, *Am:* soʊn] *pp of* **sew**
sex [seks] <-es> *n* sexo *m;* **to have** ~ tener relaciones sexuales
sex appeal *n no pl* atractivo *m* sexual **sex education** *n no pl* educación *f* sexual
sexist *adj* sexista
sex life *n no pl* vida *f* sexual
sexual ['sekʃʊəl, *Am:* -ʃəl] *adj* sexual
sexy ['seksi] <-ier, -iest> *adj inf* sexy
Seychelles [seɪ'ʃelz] *n* Islas *fpl* Seychelles
shabby ['ʃæbi] <-ier, -iest> *adj* **1.** (*badly maintained*) deteriorado **2.** (*poorly dressed*) desharrapado, encuerado *Méx, Cuba*
shack [ʃæk] *n* choza *f*, ruca *f Arg, Chile*, jacal *m Méx*
shackles ['ʃæklz] *npl* grilletes *mpl*
shade [ʃeɪd] **I.** *n* **1.** *no pl* (*shadow*) sombra *f;* **in the ~ of** a [*o* en] la sombra de **2.** (*covering*) pantalla *f* **3.** *pl, Am* (*roller blind*) persiana *f* **4.** (*variation*) matiz *m;* (*of colour*) tono *m* **5.** *no pl* (*small amount*) pizca *f* **6.** *pl, inf* (*glasses*) gafas *fpl* de sol **II.** *vt* dar sombra a
shadow ['ʃædəʊ, *Am:* -oʊ] **I.** *n a. fig* sombra *f;* **without a ~ of a doubt**

sin lugar a dudas **II.** vt (follow) seguir

shadowy <-ier, -iest> adj **1.** (containing darker spaces) sombreado; (photograph) oscuro **2.** (vague) impreciso

shady ['ʃeɪdi] <-ier, -iest> adj **1.** (protected from light) sombreado **2.** inf (dubious) turbio; (character) sospechoso

shaft [ʃɑːft, Am: ʃæft] n **1.** (of weapon) asta f **2.** TECH eje m **3.** (ray) rayo m **4.** (for elevator) hueco m; (of mine) pozo m

shaggy ['ʃægi] <-ier, -iest> adj peludo

shake [ʃeɪk] **I.** n (wobble) sacudida f; (vibration) vibración f **II.** <shook, shaken> vt **1.** (joggle) sacudir; (house) hacer temblar; **to ~ hands** darse la mano; **to ~ one's head** negar con la cabeza **2.** (unsettle) debilitar **3.** (make worried) desconcertar **III.** <shook, shaken> vi temblar
◆ **shake off** vt sacudirse; fig librarse de
◆ **shake up** vt sacudir

shake-up ['ʃeɪkʌp] n reorganización f

shaky ['ʃeɪki] <-ier, -iest> adj **1.** (jerky) tembloroso **2.** (wavering) inseguro **3.** (unstable) inestable

shall [ʃæl] aux **we ~ win the match** ganaremos el partido

shallot [ʃə'lɒt, Am: -'lɑːt] n chalote m, cebolleta f AmL

shallow ['ʃæləʊ, Am: -oʊ] adj **1.** (not deep) poco profundo **2.** (superficial) superficial

sham [ʃæm] pej **I.** n (imposture) impostura f; (fake) fraude m **II.** adj falso; (deal) fraudulento **III.** <-mm-> vt fingir

shambles ['ʃæmblz] n inf (place) escombrera f; (situation) confusión f

shame [ʃeɪm] **I.** n no pl **1.** (humiliation) vergüenza f, pena f AmC; **to put sb to ~** avergonzar a alguien **2.** (pity) pena f; **what a ~!** ¡qué pena!; **it's a ~ that ...** es una pena que... +subj **II.** vt avergonzar

shamefaced [ʃeɪm'feɪst, Am: '--]

adj avergonzado, apenado AmC

shameful ['ʃeɪmfl] adj pej vergonzoso, penoso AmC

shameless ['ʃeɪmlɪs] adj pej descarado, conchudo AmL

shampoo [ʃæm'puː] **I.** n champú m; **~ and set** lavar y peinar **II.** vt lavar con champú

shamrock ['ʃæmrɒk, Am: -rɑːk] n trébol m

shandy ['ʃændi] <-ies> n Brit, Aus clara f

shanty town n chabolas fpl, favelas fpl AmL

shape [ʃeɪp] **I.** n forma f; **to take ~** adquirir forma; **in the ~ of sth** en forma de algo; **to get into ~** ponerse en forma **II.** vt **1.** (form) **to ~ sth into sth** dar a algo la forma de algo **2.** (influence) influenciar **3.** (determine) condicionar

shapeless ['ʃeɪpləs] adj informe

shapely ['ʃeɪpli] <-ier, -iest> adj bien proporcionado

share [ʃeə', Am: ʃer] **I.** n **1.** (part) parte f, porción f **2.** (participation) participación f **3.** FIN acción f; **to have ~s in sth** tener acciones en algo **II.** vt **1.** (divide) dividir **2.** (have in common) compartir; **to ~ sb's view** compartir las opiniones de alguien
◆ **share out** vt dividir

share certificate n título m de acción

shareholder ['ʃeə,həʊldə', Am: 'ʃer,hoʊldə'] n accionista mf

share issue n emisión f de acciones

shark [ʃɑːk, Am: ʃɑːrk] <-(s)> n tiburón m

sharp [ʃɑːp, Am: ʃɑːrp] **I.** adj **1.** (cutting) afilado; (pointed) puntiagudo **2.** (angular: feature) anguloso; (curve) cerrado **3.** (severe) severo; (pain) agudo, intenso; **to be ~ with sb** ser mordaz con alguien **4.** MUS sostenido **II.** adv **1.** (exactly) en punto; **at ten o'clock ~** a las diez en punto **2.** (suddenly) de repente; **to pull up ~** frenar en seco **III.** n MUS sostenido m

sharpen ['ʃɑːpən, Am: 'ʃɑːr-] vt

1. (*blade*) afilar; (*pencil*) sacar punta a **2.** (*intensify*) agudizar

sharpener ['ʃɑːpənəʳ, *Am:* 'ʃɑːrpənɚ] *n* afilador *m*, afiladora *f* *Méx;* **pencil** ~ sacapuntas *m inv*

sharp-eyed [ˌʃɑːp'aɪd, *Am:* ˌʃɑːrp'-] *adj* observador

shatter ['ʃætəʳ, *Am:* 'ʃæt̬ɚ] **I.** *vi* hacerse añicos **II.** *vt* **1.** (*smash*) hacer añicos, destrozar **2.** (*disturb*) perturbar; (*unity*) destruir

shave [ʃeɪv] **I.** *n* afeitado *m*, rasurada *f* *Méx;* **to have a** ~ afeitarse **II.** *vi* afeitarse **III.** *vt* afeitar, rasurar *Méx*

shaver ['ʃeɪvəʳ, *Am:* -vɚ] *n* maquinilla *f* de afeitar, rasuradora *f Méx*

shaving brush *n* brocha *f* de afeitar

shaving cream *n* crema *f* de afeitar

shawl [ʃɔːl, *Am:* ʃɑːl] *n* chal *m*

she [ʃiː] *pron pers* ella; **here** ~ **comes** ahí viene

sheaf [ʃiːf, ʃiːvz] *n* (*of wheat*) gavilla *f;* (*of documents*) fajo *m*

shear [ʃɪəʳ, *Am:* ʃɪr] <sheared, sheared *o* shorn> *vt* (*sheep*) esquilar

◆ **shear off** *vi* romperse

shears [ʃɪəz, *Am:* ʃɪrz] *npl* (*for sheep*) tijeras *fpl* de esquilar

sheath [ʃiːθ] *n* **1.** (*for knife*) vaina *f*, funda *f AmL* **2.** *Brit* (*condom*) condón *m*

shed¹ [ʃed] *n* cobertizo *m*, galera *f AmL*

shed² [ʃed] <shed, shed> **I.** *vt* **1.** (*cast off*) quitarse **2.** (*blood, tears*) derramar; (*light*) emitir **II.** *vi* (*snake*) mudar de piel

sheen [ʃiːn] *n no pl* brillo *m*

sheep [ʃiːp] *n* oveja *f*

sheepdog ['ʃiːpdɒg, *Am:* -dɑːg] *n* perro *m* pastor

sheepish ['ʃiːpɪʃ] *adj* tímido

sheepskin ['ʃiːpskɪn] *n* piel *f* de borrego

sheer [ʃɪəʳ, *Am:* ʃɪr] **I.** *adj* **1.** (*unmitigated*) puro; ~ **coincidence** pura coincidencia **2.** (*vertical*) escarpado; ~ **drop** caída *f* en picado **3.** (*thin*) fino **II.** *adv liter* absolutamente

sheet [ʃiːt] *n* **1.** (*for bed*) sábana *f*

2. (*of paper*) hoja *f* **3.** (*of glass*) lámina *f*

sheik(h) [ʃeɪk, *Am:* ʃiːk] *n* jeque *m*

shelf [ʃelf] <shelves> *n* estante *m*

shelf life *n no pl* tiempo *m* de conservación

shell [ʃel] **I.** *n* **1.** (*of nut, egg*) cáscara *f;* (*of shellfish, snail*) concha *f* **2.** TECH armazón *m* **3.** (*gun*) proyectil *m*, cartucho *m AmL* **II.** *vt* **1.** (*remove shell*) pelar **2.** MIL bombardear

◆ **shell out** *vi inf* aflojar; **to** ~ **for sth** apoquinar para algo

shellfish ['ʃelfɪʃ] *n inv* crustáceo *m;* GASTR marisco *m*

shelter ['ʃeltəʳ, *Am:* -t̬ɚ] **I.** *n* refugio *m;* **to take** ~ refugiarse **II.** *vt* resguardar **III.** *vi* refugiarse

sheltered *adj* abrigado

shelve [ʃelv] *vt* posponer; POL postergar

shelves [ʃelvz] *n pl of* **shelf**

shepherd ['ʃepəd, *Am:* -ɚd] **I.** *n a.* REL pastor *m* **II.** *vt* guiar, dirigir

shepherd's pie *n* pastel *m* de carne

sheriff ['ʃerɪf] *n Am* sheriff *mf*

sherry ['ʃeri] <-ies> *n* jerez *m*

Shetland Islands *npl,* **Shetlands** ['ʃetləndz] *npl* Islas *fpl* Shetland

shield [ʃiːld] **I.** *n* **1.** (*armour*) escudo *m* **2.** (*protective layer*) revestimiento *m* **II.** *vt* proteger

shift [ʃɪft] **I.** *vt* **1.** *Am* (*in mechanics*) cambiar **2.** *Brit, Aus, inf* (*dispose of*) quitar **II.** *vi* **1.** (*change, rearrange position*) moverse **2.** *inf* (*move over*) correrse **III.** *n* **1.** (*alteration, change*) cambio *m* **2.** (*period of work*) turno *m*

shiftwork ['ʃɪftwɜːk, *Am:* -wɜːrk] *n no pl* trabajo *m* por turnos

shifty ['ʃɪfti] <-ier, -iest> *adj* sospechoso; (*eyes*) furtivo

Shiite ['ʃiːaɪt] *adj* chiíta

shilling ['ʃɪlɪŋ] *n* HIST chelín *m*

shilly-shally ['ʃɪliʃæli] *vi pej, inf* titubear

shimmer ['ʃɪməʳ, *Am:* -ɚ] **I.** *vi* brillar **II.** *n no pl* brillo *m*

shin [ʃɪn] **I.** *n* espinilla *f* **II.** <-nn-> *vi* **to** ~ **down** deslizarse; **to** ~ **up sth** trepar a algo

S

shine [ʃaɪn] **I.** *n no pl* brillo *m* **II.**<shone *o* shined, shone *o* shined> *vi* brillar, relucir **III.**<shone *o* shined, shone *o* shined> *vt* **1.**(*point light*) **to ~ a torch onto sth** iluminar algo con una linterna **2.**(*brighten by polishing*) sacar brillo a
◆ **shine down** *vi* brillar

shingle ['ʃɪŋgl] *n no pl* guijarros *mpl*

shingles ['ʃɪŋglz] *n no pl* MED herpes *m*

shiny ['ʃaɪni] <-ier, -iest> *adj* brillante

ship [ʃɪp] **I.** *n* barco *m;* **to board a ~** subir a una embarcación, embarcar **II.** *vt* <-pp-> **1.**(*send by boat*) mandar por barco **2.**(*transport*) transportar

shipbuilding *n no pl* construcción *f* naval

shipment ['ʃɪpmənt] *n* **1.**(*quantity*) remesa *f* **2.** *no pl* (*action*) envío *m*

shipper *n* consignador(a) *m(f)*

shipping ['ʃɪpɪŋ] *n no pl* **1.**(*ships*) embarcaciones *fpl* **2.**(*freight dispatch*) transporte *m*

shipwreck **I.** *n* naufragio *m* **II.** *vt* **to be ~ed** naufragar **shipyard** *n* astillero *m*

shire ['ʃaɪəʳ, *Am:* 'ʃaɪɚ] *n* condado *m*

shirk [ʃɜːk, *Am:* ʃɜːrk] *vt* eludir

shirt [ʃɜːt, *Am:* ʃɜːrt] *n* camisa *f*

shirty ['ʃɜːti, *Am:* 'ʃɜːrti] <-ier, -iest> *adj Brit, Aus, pej, inf* borde; **to get ~** (**with sb**) ponerse borde (con alguien)

shit [ʃɪt] *inf* **I.** *n no pl* **1.**(*faeces*) mierda *f* **2.** *pej* (*nonsense*) gilipolleces *fpl*, pendejadas *fpl AmL;* **no ~!** ¡no jodas! **II.** *interj* mierda

shiver ['ʃɪvəʳ, *Am:* -ɚ] **I.** *n* estremecimiento *m* **II.** *vi* temblar

shoal [ʃəʊl, *Am:* ʃoʊl] *n* (*of fish*) banco *m*

shock [ʃɒk, *Am:* ʃɑːk] **I.** *n* **1.**(*unpleasant surprise*) conmoción *f*, batata *f CSur;* **to give sb a ~** dar un disgusto a alguien **2.** *inf*(*electric shock*) descarga *f* **3.** MED shock *m* **4.**(*impact*) choque *m* **II.** *vt* **1.**(*appal*) horrorizar **2.**(*scare*) asustar

shock absorber ['ʃɒkæbˌzɔːbəʳ, *Am:* 'ʃɑːkəbˌsɔːrbɚ] *n* amortiguador *m*

shocking ['ʃɒkɪŋ, *Am:* 'ʃɑːkɪŋ] *adj* **1.**(*causing indignation, distress*) espantoso, horrible **2.**(*offensive*) escandaloso

shock wave *n* PHYS onda *f* expansiva

shod [ʃɒd] *pt, pp of* **shoe**

shoddy ['ʃɒdi, *Am:* 'ʃɑːdi] <-ier, -iest> *adj* de pacotilla

shoe [ʃuː] **I.** *n* zapato *m;* (*for horse*) herradura *f* **II.**<shod *o Am:* shoed, shod *o Am:* shoed> *vt* calzar; (*horse*) herrar, encasquillar *AmL*

shoelace *n* cordón *m* (de zapato), pasador *m Perú* **shoe polish** *n* betún *m*, lustrina *f Chile*

shoeshop *n* zapatería *f*

shoestring ['ʃuːstrɪŋ] *n Am* cordón *m* (de zapato); **to do sth on a ~** *inf* hacer algo con poquísimo dinero

shone [ʃɒn, *Am:* ʃoʊn] *pt, pp of* **shine**

shoo [ʃuː] **I.** *interj inf* fuera **II.** *vt inf* ahuyentar

shook [ʃʊk] *pt of* **shake**

shoot [ʃuːt] **I.** *n* **1.**(*hunt*) cacería *f* **2.** BOT retoño *m* **II.**<shot, shot> *vi* **1.**(*fire weapon*) disparar; **to ~ at sth/sb** disparar a algo/alguien **2.** SPORTS chutar **3.** CINE rodar **4.**(*move rapidly*) volar; **to ~ past** pasar como un rayo **III.**<shot, shot> *vt* **1.**(*bullet*) disparar **2.** CINE rodar, filmar
◆ **shoot down** *vt* (*aircraft*) derribar
◆ **shoot past** *vi* pasar como una bala
◆ **shoot up** *vi* (*expand*) crecer mucho

shooting ['ʃuːtɪŋ, *Am:* -tɪŋ] *n* **1.**(*killing*) asesinato *m* **2.** *no pl* (*firing of gun*) tiroteo *m* **3.** *no pl* (*hunting*) caza *f*

shooting star *n* estrella *f* fugaz

shop [ʃɒp, *Am:* ʃɑːp] **I.** *n* **1.**(*for sale of goods*) tienda *f;* **book ~** librería *f;* **to talk ~** hablar de trabajo **2.**(*for manufacture*) taller *m* **II.**<-pp-> *vi* comprar

shopaholic [ʃɒpəˈhɒlɪk, *Am:*

ʃɑːp-] *n* adicto, -a *m*, *f* a las compras
shop assistant *n Brit* dependiente, -a
m, *f* **shop floor** *n* taller *m* **shopkeeper** *n* comerciante *mf*, des-
pachero, -a *m*, *f Chile* **shoplifter** *n*
ladrón, -ona *m*, *f* (*que roba en tiendas*) **shoplifting** *n* robo *m* (*en tiendas*)

shopper *n* comprador(a) *m(f)*

shopping ['ʃɒpɪŋ, *Am:* 'ʃɑː-p-] *n no
pl* (*purchases*) compras *fpl*

shopping bag *n Brit* bolsa *f* de compras, jaba *f Cuba* **shopping center**
n Am, Aus, **shopping centre** *n*
centro *m* comercial **shopping mall**
n Am, Aus centro *m* comercial

shop steward *n* enlace *mf* sindical
shop window *n* escaparate *m*, vitrina *f AmL*

shore [ʃɔːʳ, *Am:* ʃɔːr] *n* **1.** (*coast*)
costa *f* **2.** (*beach*) orilla *f*; **on** ~ a tierra
◆ **shore up** *vt a. fig* apuntalar

shorn [ʃɔːn, *Am:* ʃɔːrn] *pp of* **shear**

short [ʃɔːt, *Am:* ʃɔːrt] **I.** *adj* **1.** (*not
long*) corto **2.** (*not tall*) bajo
3. (*brief*) breve **4.** (*not enough*) escaso; **to be** [*o* **run**] ~ **on sth** andar escaso de algo **5.** (*brusque*) brusco
II. *n* CINE cortometraje *m* **III.** *adv* **to
cut** ~ interrumpir bruscamente; **to
fall** ~ **of sth** no alcanzar algo; **in** ~
en resumidas cuentas

shortage ['ʃɔːtɪdʒ, *Am:* 'ʃɔːrt̬ɪdʒ] *n*
falta *f*, escasez *f*

shortbread ['ʃɔːtbred, *Am:* 'ʃɔːrt-]
n no pl galleta *f* dulce de mantequilla

short-change [ʃɔːt'tʃeɪndʒ, *Am:*
ʃɔːrt'-] *vt* dar mal el cambio; *fig*
timar

short-circuit [ʃɔːt'sɜːkɪt, *Am:*
ʃɔːrt'sɜːr-] **I.** *n* cortocircuito *m* **II.** *vi*
ponerse en cortocircuito **III.** *vt* poner
en cortocircuito

shortcoming ['ʃɔːtˌkʌmɪŋ, *Am:*
'ʃɔːrt-] *n* defecto *m*

shortcrust ['ʃɔːtkrʌst, *Am:* 'ʃɔːrt-] *n*,
shortcrust pastry *n no pl* pasta *f*
quebradiza

short cut *n* atajo *m*; *fig* fórmula *f*
mágica

shorten ['ʃɔːtən, *Am:* 'ʃɔːr-] *vt* acortar

shortfall ['ʃɔːtfɔːl, *Am:* 'ʃɔːrt-] *n*
deficiencia *f*; ECON déficit *m*

shorthand ['ʃɔːthænd, *Am:* 'ʃɔːrt-]
n no pl, Brit, Aus, Can taquigrafía *f*
shorthand typist *n Aus, Brit, Can*
taquimecanógrafo, -a *m*, *f*

shortlist I. *vt* preseleccionar **II.** *n*
lista *f* de candidatos preselecciona-
dos **short-lived** *adj* efímero

shortly ['ʃɔːtli, *Am:* 'ʃɔːrt-] *adv* dentro de poco

shorts [ʃɔːtz, *Am:* ʃɔːrtz] *npl* pantalones *mpl* cortos; **a pair of** ~ (unos)
pantalones cortes

⚠️ **shorts** se utiliza en inglés
siempre en plural: "Where are my
blue shorts?" Pero **a pair of shorts**
se usa en singular: "This is Peter's
pair of shorts."

---

short-sighted ['ʃɔːrtˌsaɪtɪd] *adj*
1. (*myopic*) miope **2.** (*not prudent*)
corto de miras **short-staffed** *adj
Aus, Brit* falto de personal **short
story** *n* narración *m* corta **short-
-tempered** *adj* irascible **short
wave** *n* onda *f* corta

shot¹ [ʃɒt, *Am:* ʃɑːt] **I.** *n* **1.** (*act of
firing weapon*) tiro *m*, disparo *m*,
baleo *m AmC;* **to fire a** ~ disparar
un tiro **2.** *no pl* (*shotgun pellets*)
perdigones *mpl* **3.** (*person*) tira-
dor(a) *m(f)*; **to be a good/poor** ~
ser un buen/mal tirador **4.** (*photograph*) foto *f*; CINE toma *f* **5.** *inf* (*injection*) inyección *f* **6.** *inf* (*try, stab*)
intento *m*; **to have a** ~ **at sth** probar
suerte con algo **II.** *pt, pp of* **shoot**

shot² [ʃɒt, *Am:* ʃɑːt] *adj inf* (*worn
out*) **to get** ~ **of sth/sb** quitarse
algo/a alguien de encima

shotgun ['ʃɒtɡʌn, *Am:* 'ʃɑːt-] *n*
escopeta *f*

should [ʃʊd] *aux* **to insist that sb** ~
do sth insistir en que alguien debería
hacer algo; **I** ~ **like to see her** me
gustaría verla; **why** ~ **I/you ...?**
¿por qué debería/deberías...?; **I** ~

Sₛ

be so lucky! *inf* ¡ojalá!
shoulder [ˈʃəʊldəʳ, *Am:* ˈʃoʊldɚ]
I. *n* 1. ANAT hombro *m;* **to glance
over one's** ~ mirar por encima del
hombro; **to be sb's** ~ **to cry on** ser
el paño de lágrimas de alguien; **to
rub** ~**s with sb** codearse con alguien 2. (*side of road*) arcén *m* II. *vt*
(*responsibility*) cargar con
shoulder bag *n* bolso *m* de bandolera **shoulder blade** *n* omóplato *m*
shoulder strap *n* tirante *m*
shout [ʃaʊt] I. *n* grito *m* II. *vi, vt* gritar
◆ **shout down** *vt* hacer callar a gritos
shouting *n no pl* griterío *m*
shove [ʃʌv] I. *n* empujón *m*, pechada
f Arg, Chile II. *vt* 1. (*push*) empujar;
to ~ **one's way through** abrirse
paso a empujones 2. (*place*) meter
◆ **shove off** *vi* 1. *inf* (*go away*) largarse 2. (*launch by foot*) desatracar
shovel [ˈʃʌvəl] I. *n* 1. (*tool*) pala *f*
2. (*machine*) excavadora *f* II.<*Brit:*
-ll-, *Am:* -l-> *vt* palear
show [ʃəʊ, *Am:* ʃoʊ] I. *n* 1. (*expression*) demostración *f* 2. (*exhibition*) exposición *f;* **slide** ~ pase
m de diapositivas; **to be on** ~ estar
expuesto; **to run the** ~ llevar la voz
cantante 3. (*play*) espectáculo *m;*
quiz ~ concurso *m* II.<showed,
shown> *vt* 1. (*display*) mostrar
2. (*express*) demostrar 3. (*expose*)
exponer 4. (*prove*) probar; **to** ~ **sb
that ...** demostrar a alguien que...
5. (*escort*) guiar; **to** ~ **sb to the
door** acompañar a alguien a la puerta III. *vi* <showed, shown> 1. (*be
visible*) verse 2. *Am, Aus, inf* (*arrive*)
aparecer 3. (*be shown*) proyectarse
◆ **show in** *vt* hacer pasar
◆ **show off** I. *vt* lucir II. *vi* presumir
◆ **show out** *vt* acompañar a la puerta
◆ **show up** I. *vi* 1. (*be apparent*) ponerse de manifiesto 2. *inf* (*arrive*)
aparecer II. *vt* 1. (*expose*) descubrir
2. (*embarrass*) poner en evidencia
showbiz *n no pl, inf*, **show business** *n no pl* mundo *m* del espec-

táculo
showdown [ˈʃəʊdaʊn, *Am:* ˈʃoʊ-] *n*
enfrentamiento *m*
shower [ˈʃaʊəʳ, *Am:* ˈʃaʊɚ] I. *n* 1. (*of
rain*) chaparrón *m;* (*of sparks, insults*) lluvia *f* 2. (*for washing*) ducha
f, lluvia *f Arg, Chile, Nic* II. *vt* derramar; **to** ~ **compliments on sb** colmar de cumplidos a alguien III. *vi*
ducharse
showery [ˈʃaʊəri, *Am:* ˈʃaʊɚi] *adj*
lluvioso
showing *n* proyección *f*
show jumping [ˈʃəʊˌdʒʌmprɪŋ, *Am:*
ˈʃoʊ-] *n no pl* concurso *m* hípico
shown [ʃəʊn, *Am:* ʃoʊn] *pp of*
show
show-off [ˈʃəʊɒf, *Am:* ˈʃoʊˌɑːf] *n*
fanfarrón, -ona *m, f*
showpiece [ˈʃəʊpiːs, *Am:* ˈʃoʊ-] I. *n*
joya *f* II. *adj* excepcional
showroom [ˈʃəʊrʊm, *Am:*
ˈʃoʊruːm] *n* salón *m* de exposición
shrank [ʃræŋk] *vt, vi pt of* **shrink**
shrapnel [ˈʃræpn(ə)l] *n no pl* metralla *f*
shred [ʃred] I.<-dd-> *vt* (*cut into
shreds*) cortar en tiras; (*document*)
triturar II. *n* 1. (*strip*) tira *f* 2. *no pl*
(*of hope, truth*) pizca *f*
shredder [ˈʃredəʳ, *Am:* -ɚ] *n* tritura-
dora *f*
shrewd [ʃruːd] *adj* astuto
shriek [ʃriːk] I. *n* chillido *m* II. *vt, vi*
chillar
shrill [ʃrɪl] *adj* agudo
shrimp [ʃrɪmp] *n* <-(s)> *Brit* camarón *m*
shrine [ʃraɪn] *n* 1. (*tomb*) sepulcro
m 2. (*site of worship*) santuario *m*
shrink [ʃrɪŋk] <shrank *o Am:*
shrunk, shrunk *o Am:* shrunken>
I. *vt* encoger II. *vi* 1. (*become
smaller*) encoger 2. (*be reluctant to*)
to ~ **from** (**doing**) **sth** rehuir (hacer)
algo
shrinkage [ˈʃrɪŋkɪdʒ] *n no pl* 1. (*of
clothes*) encogimiento *m* 2. (*of
costs*) reducción *f*
shrink-wrap [ˈʃrɪŋkræp] *vt* empaquetar en plástico
shrivel [ˈʃrɪvəl] <*Brit:* -ll-, *Am:* -l->

I. *vi* secarse, arrugarse **II.** *vt* secar, a- rrugar

◆ **shrivel up** *vi* secarse

shroud [ʃraʊd] **I.** *n* sudario *m* **II.** *vt* envolver; **~ed in mystery** envuelto en un halo de misterio

Shrove Tuesday [ˌʃrəʊvˈtjuːzdeɪ, *Am:* ˌʃroʊvˈtuːzdeɪ] *n* martes *m inv* de Carnaval

shrub [ʃrʌb] *n* arbusto *m*

shrubbery [ˈʃrʌbəri] *n no pl* arbus- tos *mpl*

shrug [ʃrʌg] **I.** *n* encogimiento *m* de hombros **II.** <-gg-> *vt, vi* **to ~ one's shoulders** encogerse de hombros

◆ **shrug off** *vt* **1.** (*ignore*) negar im- portancia a **2.** (*overcome*) superar

shrunk [ʃrʌŋk] *pt, pp of* **shrink**

shrunken [ˈʃrʌŋkən] **I.** *pp of* **shrink** **II.** *adj* encogido

shudder [ˈʃʌdər, *Am:* -ɚ] **I.** *vi* es- tremecerse **II.** *n* estremecimiento *m*

shuffle [ˈʃʌfl] *vt* (*cards*) barajar; (*feet*) arrastrar

shun [ʃʌn] <-nn-> *vt* rehuir

shunt [ʃʌnt] *vt* RAIL cambiar de vía

shut [ʃʌt] **I.** <shut, shut> *vt* cerrar **II.** <shut, shut> *vi* cerrarse

◆ **shut down** *vt, vi* **1.** (*shop, fac- tory*) cerrar **2.** (*turn off*) desconectar

◆ **shut off** *vt* **1.** (*isolate*) aislar **2.** (*turn off*) desconectar

◆ **shut out** *vt* **1.** (*block out*) ahuyen- tar; (*thought*) borrar de la memoria **2.** (*exclude*) dejar fuera

◆ **shut up I.** *vt* **1.** (*confine*) encerrar **2.** *inf* (*cause to stop talking*) hacer callar **II.** *vi inf* (*stop talking*) callarse

shutter [ˈʃʌtər, *Am:* -t̬ər] *n* **1.** PHOT obturador *m* **2.** (*of window*) contra- ventana *f*

shuttle [ˈʃʌtl, *Am:* ˈʃʌt̬-] **I.** *n* **1.** (*plane*) puente *m* aéreo **2.** (*sew- ing-machine bobbin*) lanzadera *f* **II.** *vt* transportar **III.** *vi* (*travel regu- larly*) ir y venir

shuttlecock [ˈʃʌtlkɒk, *Am:* ˈʃʌt̬l- kɑːk] *n* volante *m*

shy [ʃaɪ] <-er, -est> *adj* tímido

◆ **shy away from** *vi* **to ~ sth** asus- tarse de algo; **to ~ doing sth** evitar hacer algo

Siamese [ˌsaɪəˈmiːz] **I.** *n inv* **1.** (*per- son*) siamés, -esa *m, f* **2.** (*language*) siamés *m* **II.** *adj* **1.** GEO, HIST siamés, -esa **2.** (*brothers*) ~ **twins** siameses *mpl*

Siberia [saɪˈbɪəriə, *Am:* -ˈbɪri-] *n no pl* Siberia *f*

sibling [ˈsɪblɪŋ] *n form* hermano, -a *m, f*

Sicilian [sɪˈsɪljən] *adj* siciliano

Sicily [ˈsɪsɪli] *n* Sicilia *f*

sick [sɪk] <-er, -est> *adj* **1.** (*ill*) enfer- mo; **to feel ~** sentirse mal; **to fall ~** caer enfermo; **to be off ~** estar de baja (por enfermedad) **2.** (*about to vomit*) mareado **3.** (*angry*) furioso; **to be ~ and tired of sth** estar harto de algo **4.** *inf* (*joke*) de mal gusto

sick bag *n* bolsa *f* para vomitar **sick bay** *n* enfermería *f*

sicken [ˈsɪkən] **I.** *vi* (*become sick*) enfermar; **to ~ for sth** *Brit* estar in- cubando algo **II.** *vt* (*upset*) molestar

sickening [ˈsɪkənɪŋ] *adj* (*repulsive*) repugnante

sickle [ˈsɪkl] *n* hoz *f*

sick leave [ˈsɪkliːv] *n* baja *f* por en- fermedad

sickly [ˈsɪkli] <-ier, -iest> *adj* **1.** (*not healthy*) enfermizo, apolismado *Col, Méx, PRico*, telenque *Chile* **2.** (*very sweet*) empalagoso

sickness [ˈsɪknəs] *n no pl* **1.** (*illness*) enfermedad *f* **2.** (*nausea*) mareo *m*

sick pay *n* subsidio *m* de enfermedad

side [saɪd] *n* **1.** (*vertical surface*) lado *m*; **at the ~ of sth** en el lado de algo; **~ by ~** uno al lado de otro **2.** (*flat surface*) superficie *f*; (*of page*) cara *f* **3.** (*edge*) límite *m* **4.** (*half*) parte *f* **5.** (*cut of meat*) cos- tado *m* **6.** (*direction*) **from ~ to ~** de lado a lado **7.** (*party in dispute*) bando *m*; (*team*) equipo *m*; **to take ~s** tomar partido **8.** (*aspect*) aspecto *m*

sideboard [ˈsaɪdbɔːd, *Am:* -bɔːrd] *n* aparador *m*, bufet *m AmL*

sideburns [ˈsaɪdbɜːnz, *Am:* -bɜːrnz] *npl* patillas *fpl*

side effect *n* efecto *m* secundario

sidelight *n* AUTO luz *f* de posición

Ss

sideline ['saɪdlaɪn] *n* 1. (*activity*) actividad *f* secundaria 2. *Am* SPORTS línea *f* de banda

sidelong ['saɪdlɒŋ, *Am:* -lɑːŋ] *adj* de soslayo

sidesaddle ['saɪd,sædl] *adv* **to ride** ~ montar a asentadillas

sideshow *n* caseta *f*

sidestep ['saɪdstep] <-pp-> I. *vt a. fig* esquivar II. *vi* dar un paso hacia un lado

side street *n* calle *f* lateral

sidetrack ['saɪdtræk] I. *vt* apartar de su propósito, distraer II. *n* vía *f* muerta; *fig* cuestión *f* secundaria

sidewalk ['saɪdwɔːk, *Am:* -wɑːk] *n Am* acera *f*, vereda *f AmL*

sideward ['saɪdwəd], **sideways** ['saɪdweɪz] *adv* de lado

siding ['saɪdɪŋ] *n* RAIL vía *f* muerta

sidle ['saɪdl] *vi* **to** ~ **up to sb** acercarse sigilosamente a alguien

siege [siːdʒ] *n* MIL sitio *m;* **to lay** ~ **to sth** sitiar algo

Sierra Leone [sɪˈerəlɪˈəʊn, *Am:* sɪˌerəlɪˈoʊn] *n* Sierra *f* Leona

Sierra Leonean [sɪˈerəlɪˈəʊnɪən] *adj* sierraleonés, -esa

sieve [sɪv] I. *n* colador *m* II. *vt* colar

sift [sɪft] *vt* 1. (*pass through sieve*) tamizar 2. (*examine closely*) escudriñar

sigh [saɪ] I. *n* suspiro *m* II. *vi* suspirar

sight [saɪt] I. *n* 1. (*view, faculty*) vista *f;* **at first** ~ a primera vista; **to be out of (one's)** ~ no estar a la vista (de uno); **to catch** ~ **of sth** vislumbrar algo; **to know sb by** ~ conocer a alguien de vista; **to lose** ~ **of sth** perder algo de vista; (*to forget*) no tener presente algo 2. *pl* (*attractions*) lugares *mpl* de interés 3. (*on gun*) mira *f* II. *vt* ver

sightseeing ['saɪt,siːɪŋ] *n no pl* turismo *m;* **to go** ~ visitar los lugares de interés

sign [saɪn] I. *n* 1. (*gesture*) señal *f* 2. (*signpost*) indicador *m;* (*signboard*) letrero *m* 3. (*symbol*) símbolo *m* 4. *a.* MAT, ASTR, MUS signo *m* 5. (*trace*) rastro *m* II. *vt* firmar

◆ **sign away** *vt* (*rights*) ceder

◆ **sign off** *vi inf* RADIO, TV terminar la emisión

◆ **sign on** I. *vi* 1. (*agree to take work*) firmar un contrato; **to** ~ **as a soldier** enrolarse como soldado; **to** ~ **for sth** inscribirse en algo 2. *Brit, inf* (*confirm unemployed status*) sellar (en el paro) II. *vt* contratar

◆ **sign out** *vi* firmar en el registro de salida

◆ **sign over** *vt* **to sign sth over to sb** traspasar algo a alguien

◆ **sign up** I. *vi* apuntarse II. *vt* contratar

signal ['sɪgnəl] I. *n* señal *f;* **to give (sb) a** ~ **(to do sth)** hacer una señal (a alguien) (para que haga algo) II. <*Brit:* -ll-, *Am:* -l-> *vt* 1. (*indicate*) indicar 2. (*gesticulate*) hacer señas a III. <*Brit:* -ll-, *Am:* -l-> *vi* hacer una señal; **he** ~**led right** AUTO puso el intermitente derecho

signalman ['sɪgnəlmən] <-men> *n* RAIL guardavía *mf*

signature ['sɪgnətʃəʳ, *Am:* -nətʃəʳ] *n* firma *f*

signet ring ['sɪgnɪt,rɪŋ] *n* anillo *m* de sello

significance [sɪgˈnɪfɪkəns, *Am:* -'nɪfə-] *n no pl* 1. (*importance*) importancia *f* 2. (*meaning*) significado *m*

significant [sɪgˈnɪfɪkənt, *Am:* -'nɪfə-] *adj* significativo

sign language ['saɪn,læŋgwɪdʒ] *n* lenguaje *m* de señas **signpost** I. *n* señal *f* II. *vt* señalizar

silence ['saɪləns] I. *n* silencio *m* II. *vt* (*person*) hacer callar

silencer ['saɪlənsəʳ, *Am:* -səʳ] *n* silenciador *m*

silent ['saɪlənt] *adj* silencioso; LING mudo; ~ **film** película *f* muda; **to fall** ~ callarse

silhouette [ˌsɪluˈet] I. *n* silueta *f* II. *vt* destacar; **to be** ~**d against sth** perfilarse sobre algo

silicon ['sɪlɪkən] *n no pl* silicio *m*

silicon chip *n* chip *m* de silicio

silicone ['sɪlɪkəʊn, *Am:* -koʊn] *n no pl* silicona *f*

silk [sɪlk] *n* seda *f;* ~ **dress** vestido *m* de seda

silky ['sɪlki] <-ier, -iest> *adj* sedoso

silly ['sɪli] <-ier, -iest> *adj* (*person*) tonto; (*idea*) absurdo; **to look** ~ parecer ridículo

silt [sɪlt] *n no pl* sedimento *m*

silver ['sɪlvəʳ, *Am:* -vɚ] **I.** *n no pl* **1.** (*metal*) plata *f* **2.** (*coins*) monedas *fpl* de plata

silver foil *n,* **silver paper** *n* papel *m* de plata

silversmith ['sɪlvəsmɪθ, *Am:* -vɚ-] *n* platero, -a *m, f*

silverware ['sɪlvəweəʳ, *Am:* -vɚ-] *n Am* cubiertos *mpl*

silvery <-ier, -iest> *adj* plateado

similar ['sɪmɪləʳ, *Am:* -əlɚ] *adj* similar

similarity [ˌsɪmə'lærəti, *Am:* -ə'lerəti] *n* parecido *m,* semejanza *f*

simile ['sɪmɪli, *Am:* -əli] *n* LIT, LING símil *m*

simmer ['sɪməʳ, *Am:* -ɚ] *vi* hervir a fuego lento

♦ **simmer down** *vi inf* tranquilizarse

simple ['sɪmpl] *adj* **1.** (*not complex*) sencillo **2.** (*foolish*) simple

simplicity [sɪm'plɪsəti, *Am:* -ţi] *n no pl* **1.** (*plainness*) sencillez *f* **2.** (*ease*) simplicidad *f*

simplify ['sɪmplɪfaɪ, *Am:* -plə-] *vt* simplificar

simply ['sɪmpli] *adv* **1.** (*not elaborately*) sencillamente **2.** (*just*) simplemente

simulate ['sɪmjʊleɪt] *vt* simular

simultaneous [ˌsɪmǝl'teɪnɪəs, *Am:* ˌsaɪml'teɪnjəs] *adj* simultáneo

sin [sɪn] **I.** *n* pecado *m* **II.** *vi* <-nn-> pecar

since [sɪns] **I.** *adv* desde entonces; **ever** ~ desde entonces **II.** *prep* desde **III.** *conj* **1.** (*because*) ya que **2.** (*from the time that*) desde que

⚠ **since** se utiliza con complementos temporales exactos: "Vivian has been waiting since two o'clock; We have lived here since

1998"; **for** se utiliza en cambio para períodos, espacios de tiempo: "Vivian has been waiting for two hours; We have lived here for three years."

sincere [sɪn'sɪəʳ, *Am:* sɪn'sɪr] *adj* sincero

sincerely *adv* sinceramente; **yours** ~ le saluda atentamente

sincerity [sɪn'serəti, *Am:* sɪn'serəţi] *n no pl* sinceridad *f*

sinew ['sɪnju:] *n* ANAT tendón *m*

sinful ['sɪnfəl] *adj* (*person*) pecador; (*thought, act*) pecaminoso

sing [sɪŋ] <sang, sung> **I.** *vt, vi* (*person, bird*) cantar; (*wind, kettle*) silbar **II.** *vt* cantar

Singapore [ˌsɪŋə'pɔːʳ, *Am:* 'sɪŋəpɔːr] *n* Singapur *m*

Singaporean [sɪŋə'pɔːriːən, *Am:* 'sɪŋəpɔːriːən] **I.** *adj* de Singapur **II.** *n* habitante *mf* de Singapur

singe [sɪndʒ] *vt* chamuscar

singer ['sɪŋəʳ, *Am:* -ɚ] *n* cantante *mf*

singing *n no pl* canto *m*

single ['sɪŋgl] **I.** *adj* **1.** (*one only*) único, solo; **not a** ~ **person/thing** nadie/nada; **every** ~ **thing** cada cosa **2.** (*with one part*) simple **3.** (*unmarried*) soltero **II.** *n* **1.** *Brit, Aus* (*one-way ticket*) billete *m* de ida **2.** (*record*) single *m* **3.** SPORTS golpe *m* que marca un tanto

♦ **single out** *vt* señalar

single-breasted [ˌsɪŋgl'brestɪd] *adj* (*suit*) recto, sin cruzar

Single European Market *n* **the** ~ el mercado Único Europeo

single-handed *adv* sin ayuda de nadie **single-minded** *adj* resuelto

singly ['sɪŋgli] *adv* uno por uno

singular ['sɪŋgjələʳ, *Am:* -lɚ] *n no pl* singular *m*

Sinhalese [ˌsɪnhə'liːz, *Am:* ˌsɪnhə-'liːz] *adj* cingalés

sinister ['sɪnɪstəʳ, *Am:* -stɚ] *adj* siniestro

sink [sɪŋk] <sank, sunk> **I.** *n* fre-

gadero m II. vi 1. (in water) hundirse 2. (price, level) bajar III. vt 1. (cause to submerge) hundir 2. MIN excavar
◆ sink in vi (be understood) entenderse
sinner ['sɪnəʳ, Am: -ɚ] n pecador(a) m(f)
sinus ['saɪnəs] n seno m
Sioux [su:] adj sioux
sip [sɪp] I. <-pp-> vi, vt sorber II. n sorbo m
siphon ['saɪfən] I. n sifón m II. vt sacar con sifón
◆ siphon off vt (money) malversar
sir [sɜːʳ, Am: sɜːr] n señor m
siren ['saɪərən, Am: 'saɪrən] n sirena f
sirloin ['sɜːlɔɪn, Am: 'sɜːr-] n no pl solomillo m, diezmillo m Méx
sissy ['sɪsi] <-ies> n inf marica m
sister ['sɪstəʳ, Am: -ɚ] n 1. a. REL hermana f 2. Brit, Aus (nurse) enfermera f
sister-in-law ['sɪstərɪnlɔː, Am: -tɚ-ɪnlɑː] <sisters-in-law o sister-in--laws> n cuñada f, concuña f AmL
sit [sɪt] <sat, sat> I. vi 1. sentarse; (be in seated position) estar sentado 2. (enter exam) presentarse; to ~ for an examination presentarse a un examen 3. (be placed) yacer; (rest unmoved) permanecer quieto 4. (be in office) to ~ in parliament/congress ser diputado 5. (fit) to ~ well/badly caer [o sentar] bien/mal II. vt 1. (put on seat) sentar 2. Brit (take exam) presentarse a
◆ sit about vi Brit, sit around vi estar sin hacer nada
◆ sit back vi (in chair) sentarse cómodamente
◆ sit down vi 1. (take a seat) sentarse 2. (be sitting) estar sentado
◆ sit up vi 1. (sit erect) sentarse derecho 2. (not go to bed) trasnochar
sitcom ['sɪtkɒm, Am: -kɑːm] n inf TV abbr of situation comedy comedia f de situación
site [saɪt] I. n sitio m; building ~ obra f II. vt situar

sit-in ['sɪtɪn, Am: 'sɪt̬-] n sentada f
sitting n sesión f; (for meal) turno m
sitting room n Brit cuarto m de estar
situated ['sɪtʃʊeɪtɪd, Am: 'sɪtʃu-eɪt̬ɪd] adj situado
situation [ˌsɪtʃʊ'eɪʃn, Am: ˌsɪtʃu'-] n situación f
six [sɪks] adj seis inv; s. a. eight
sixteen [sɪk'stiːn] adj dieciséis inv; s. a. eight
sixteenth [ˌsɪk'stiːnθ] adj decimosexto
sixth [sɪksθ, Am: sɪkstθ] adj sexto

? Sixth-form college es el nombre que recibe en Gran Bretaña un college para alumnos de 16–18 años, procedentes de un colegio donde no hay sixth form (sexto curso). En el college pueden examinarse de sus A-levels (algo parecido a la selectividad) o realizar dos cursos equivalentes que les permiten prepararse al acceso a la universidad.

sixtieth ['sɪkstiθ] adj sexagésimo
sixty ['sɪksti] adj sesenta inv; s. a. eighty
size [saɪz] n no pl 1. (of person, thing, space) tamaño m; to be the same ~ as ... ser de las mismas dimensiones que...; to increase/decrease in ~ aumentar/disminuir de tamaño 2. (of clothes) talla f; (of shoes) número m
◆ size up vt evaluar
sizeable ['saɪzəbl] adj bastante grande, considerable
sizzle ['sɪzl] I. vi chisporrotear II. n no pl chisporroteo m
skate¹ [skeɪt] n (fish) raya f
skate² [skeɪt] I. n patín m II. vi patinar
skateboard ['skeɪtbɔːd, Am: -bɔːrd] n monopatín m
skater n patinador(a) m(f)
skating n patinaje m
skating rink n pista f de patinaje
skeleton ['skelɪtən, Am: '-ə-] n

1. ANAT esqueleto *m*, cacastle *m* AmC, Méx **2.** (*framework*) armazón *m* **3.** (*outline*) esquema *m*

skeleton staff *n* personal *m* mínimo

skeptic ['skeptɪk] *n Am, Aus* escéptico, -a *m, f*

sketch [sketʃ] **I.** *n* **1.** ART boceto *m* **2.** (*rough draft*) borrador *m* **3.** (*outline*) esquema *m* **4.** THEAT, TV sketch *m* **II.** *vt* hacer un boceto de

sketchbook ['sketʃbʊk] *n* cuaderno *m* de dibujo

sketchy ['sketʃi] <-ier, -iest> *adj* (*vague*) impreciso; (*incomplete*) incompleto

skewer ['skjʊər, *Am:* 'skjuːə] **I.** *n* pincho *m*, brocheta *f* **II.** *vt* ensartar

ski [skiː] **I.** *n* esquí *m* **II.** *vi* esquiar

ski boot *n* bota *f* de esquí

skid [skɪd] **I.** <-dd-> *vi* patinar, colear *AmC, Ant* **II.** *n* derrape *m;* **to go into a ~** empezar a resbalar

skier ['skiːər, *Am:* -ə] *n* esquiador(a) *m(f)*

skiing *n no pl* esquí *m*

ski jump *n no pl* salto *m* de esquí

skilful ['skɪlfəl] *adj Brit, Aus* hábil, tinoso, a *Col, Ven*

ski lift *n* telesquí *m*

skill [skɪl] *n* **1.** *no pl* (*ability*) habilidad *f* **2.** (*technique*) técnica *f*

skilled *adj* **1.** (*trained*) preparado; (*skilful*) hábil, habiloso *Chile, Perú* **2.** (*requiring skill*) cualificado

skillful ['skɪlfəl] *adj Am s.* **skilful**

skim [skɪm] <-mm-> **I.** *vt* **1.** (*move above*) rozar **2.** GASTR espumar; (*milk*) desnatar **II.** *vi* **to ~ through sth** *fig* hojear algo

skimmed milk *n Brit,* **skim milk** *n Am no pl* leche *f* desnatada

skimp [skɪmp] *vi* escatimar gastos; **to ~ (on sth)** escatimar (algo)

skimpy ['skɪmpi] <-ier, -iest> *adj* **1.** (*meal*) escaso **2.** (*dress*) corto y estrecho

skin [skɪn] **I.** *n* **1.** (*of person*) piel *f;* **to be soaked to the ~** estar calado hasta los huesos **2.** (*of apple, potato, tomato*) piel *f* **3.** (*on milk*) nata *f* **II.** <-nn-> *vt* (*animal*) despellejar

skin-deep *adj* superficial **skin-div-**

ing *n no pl* submarinismo *m*

skinhead ['skɪnhed] *n* cabeza *mf* rapada

skinny ['skɪni] <-ier, -iest> *adj* flaco, charcón *Arg, Bol, Urug*

skintight [skɪn'taɪt] *adj* muy ceñido

skip¹ [skɪp] *n Brit, Aus* (*container*) contenedor *m* de basura

skip² [skɪp] **I.** <-pp-> *vi* **1.** (*take light steps*) brincar **2.** *Brit, Aus* (*with rope*) saltar a la comba **II.** <-pp-> *vt* **1.** (*leave out*) omitir **2.** (*not participate in*) saltarse **III.** *n* brinco *m*

ski pants *npl* pantalones *mpl* de esquí **ski pole** *n* palo *m* de esquí

skipper ['skɪpər, *Am:* -ə] *n* NAUT capitán, -ana *m, f*

skipping rope *n Brit,* **skip rope** *n Am* comba *f*

skirmish ['skɜːmɪʃ, *Am:* 'skɜːr-] *n* escaramuza *f*

skirt [skɜːt, *Am:* skɜːrt] **I.** *n* falda *f*, pollera *f AmL* **II.** *vt* **1.** (*path, road*) rodear **2.** (*avoid*) evitar

skirting (**board**) ['skɜːtɪŋ(bɔːd), *Am:* 'skɜːrtɪŋ(bɔːrd)] *n Brit, Aus* rodapié *m*

ski suit *n* mono *m* de esquí

skittle ['skɪtl, *Am:* 'skɪt-] *n* bolo *m;* **a game of ~s** un partido de bolos

skive [skaɪv] *vi Brit, inf* gandulear

skulk [skʌlk] *vi* esconderse

skull [skʌl] *n* calavera *f;* ANAT cráneo *m*

skunk [skʌŋk] *n* mofeta *f*, zorrino *m CSur*

sky [skaɪ] <-ies> *n* cielo *m;* **to praise sth/sb to the skies** poner algo/a alguien por las nuebes

skydiving ['skaɪ,daɪvɪŋ] *n* caída *m* libre (*en paracaídas*)

sky-high [,skaɪ'haɪ] **I.** *adv a. fig* por las nubes; **to go ~** (*prices*) dispararse **II.** *adj* (*price*) astronómico

skylight ['skaɪlaɪt] *n* tragaluz *m*, aojada *f Col*

skyline ['skaɪlaɪn] *n* **1.** (*city rooftops*) perfil *m* **2.** (*horizon*) horizonte *m*

skyscraper ['skaɪskreɪpər, *Am:* -pə] *n* rascacielos *m inv*

slab [slæb] *n* **1.** (*flat piece: of stone*)

losa *f*; (*of wood*) tabla *f* **2.**(*slice: of cake, of cheese*) trozo *m*

slack [slæk] *adj* **1.**(*loose*) flojo **2.**(*lazy*) vago; (*writing style*) descuidado **3.**(*not busy*) de poca actividad; ~ **demand** poca demanda

slacken ['slækən] *vi, vt* aflojar(se)
♦ **slack off** *vi*, **slacken off I.** *vi* disminuir **II.** *vt* reducir

slag [slæg] *n no pl* escoria *f*

slain [sleɪn] *pp of* **slay**

slam [slæm] <-mm-> **I.** *vt* **1.**(*strike*) golpear; **to** ~ **the door** dar un portazo **2.** *inf* (*criticize*) poner por los suelos **II.** *vi* **1.**(*close noisily*) cerrarse de golpe **2.**(*hit hard*) **to** ~ **against sth** chocar contra algo

slander ['slɑ:ndəʳ, *Am:* 'slændəʳ] **I.** *n no pl* LAW calumnia *f* **II.** *vt* calumniar

slang [slæŋ] **I.** *n no pl* argot *m* **II.** *adj* de argot **III.** *vt Brit, Aus, inf* insultar

slanging match *n Brit, Aus* bronca *f*

slant [slɑ:nt, *Am:* slænt] *n* **1.** *no pl* (*slope*) inclinación *f* **2.**(*perspective*) perspectiva *f*; **to put a favourable** ~ **on sth** dar un sesgo favorable a algo

slanting *adj* inclinado

slap [slæp] **I.** *n* palmada *f*; **a** ~ **in the face** una bofetada; *fig* un insulto **II.**<-pp-> *vt* dar una palmada/una bofetada a **III.** *adv inf* directamente, de lleno

slapdash ['slæpdæʃ] *adj pej, inf* chapucero

slapstick ['slæpstɪk] *n no pl* payasadas *fpl*

slap-up ['slæpʌp] *adj Brit, Aus, inf* **a** ~ **meal** una comilona

slash [slæʃ] *vt* **1.**(*cut deeply*) rajar **2.**(*reduce: prices, spending*) rebajar (drásticamente)

slat [slæt] *n* (*of wood*) listón *m*, tablilla *f*

slate [sleɪt] **I.** *n no pl* pizarra *f* **II.** *vt Brit, Aus, inf* (*criticize*) poner por los suelos

slaughter ['slɔ:təʳ, *Am:* 'slɑ:t̬əʳ] **I.** *vt* matar **II.** *n no pl* matanza *f*

slaughterhouse ['slɔ:təhaʊs, *Am:* 'slɑ:t̬əʳ-] *n* matadero *m*, tablada *f Par*

Slav [slɑ:v] *adj* eslavo

slave [sleɪv] **I.** *n* esclavo, -a *m, f* **II.** *vi* trabajar como un burro

slave driver *n inf* negrero, -a *m, f*

slavery ['sleɪvəri] *n no pl* esclavitud *f*

Slavic ['slɑ:vɪk] *adj* eslavo

slavish ['sleɪvɪʃ] *adj* **1.**(*unoriginal*) poco original **2.**(*servile*) servil

Slavonic [slə'vɒnɪk, *Am:* -'vɑ:nɪk] *adj* eslavo

slay [sleɪ] <slew, slain> *vt liter* matar

sleazy ['sli:zi] <-ier, -iest> *adj* (*area, bar*) sórdido

sledge [sledʒ] *n* trineo *m*

sledgehammer ['sledʒˌhæməʳ, *Am:* -əʳ] *n* almádena *f*

sleek [sli:k] *adj* lacio y brillante

sleep [sli:p] **I.** *n no pl* sueño *m*; **to go** [*o* **get**] **to** ~ dormirse; **to put sb to** ~ dormir a alguien; **to put an animal to** ~ (*kill*) sacrificar un animal **II.**<slept, slept> *vi* dormir; **to** ~ **sound(ly)** dormir profundamente **III.** *vt* alojar
♦ **sleep in** *vi Brit* (*stay in bed*) dormir hasta tarde

sleeper ['sli:pəʳ, *Am:* -pəʳ] *n* **1.**(*person*) persona *f* dormida **2.**(*carriage*) coche *m* cama **3.***Brit, Aus* (*blocks*) traviesa *f*

sleeping bag *n* saco *m* de dormir

sleeping car *n* coche *m* cama

sleeping partner *n Brit* COM socio, -a *m, f* comanditario, -a

sleeping pill *n* somnífero *m*

sleepless ['sli:pləs] *adj* (*night*) en vela

sleepwalk ['sli:pˌwɔ:k, *Am:* -ˌwɑ:k] *vi* caminar dormido

sleepwalker ['sli:pˌwɔ:kəʳ, *Am:* -ˌwɑ:kəʳ] *n* sonámbulo, -a *m, f*

sleepy ['sli:pi] <-ier, -iest> *adj* somnoliento

sleet [sli:t] *n no pl* aguanieve *f*

sleeve [sli:v] *n* **1.**(*of shirt*) manga *f* **2.**(*cover*) manguito *m* **3.**(*for record*) funda *f*

sleigh [sleɪ] *n* trineo *m*

sleight of hand [ˌslaɪtɒf'hænd, *Am:* -ɑ:f-] *n no pl* prestidigitación *f*

slender ['slendəʳ, *Am:* -dəʳ] *adj* delgado; (*majority*) escaso

slept [slept] *pt, pp of* **sleep**

slew [slu:] *pt of* **slay**

slice [slaɪs] **I.** *n* **1.** (*of bread*) rebanada *f;* (*of meat*) tajada *f;* (*of cucumber, lemon*) rodaja *f* **2.** (*tool*) pala *f* **II.** *vt* cortar

sliced bread *n* pan *m* de molde

slick [slɪk] **I.** <-er, -est> *adj* **1.** (*performance*) pulido **2.** (*person*) hábil **II.** *n* (*oil*) marea *f* negra

slide [slaɪd] **I.** <slid, slid> *vi* **1.** (*slip*) resbalar **2.** (*glide smoothly*) deslizarse **II.** <slid, slid> *vt* deslizar **III.** *n* **1.** (*playground structure*) tobogán *m* **2.** PHOT diapositiva *f* **3.** (*for microscope*) portaobjetos *m inv* **4.** *Brit* (*hair clip*) pasador *m*

sliding *adj* (*sunroof*) corredizo; (*door*) corredero

sliding scale *n* escala *f* móvil

slight [slaɪt] **I.** <-er, -est> *adj* **1.** (*small: chance*) escaso; (*error*) pequeño; **not in the ~est** en absoluto; **not to have the ~est** (**idea**) no tener ni la menor idea **2.** (*slim*) delgado **II.** *n* desaire *m* **III.** *vt* despreciar

slightly *adv* un poco

slim [slɪm] <-mm-> **I.** *adj* delgado **II.** <-mm-> *vi* adelgazar

slime [slaɪm] *n no pl* cieno *m*

slimming I. *n no pl* adelgazamiento *m* **II.** *adj* (*pill*) para adelgazar

slimy ['slaɪmi] <-ier, -iest> *adj* **1.** (*covered in slime*) viscoso **2.** (*person*) adulón

sling [slɪŋ] <slung, slung> **I.** *vt* **1.** (*fling*) lanzar **2.** (*hang*) colgar **II.** *n* **1.** (*for broken arm*) cabestrillo *m* **2.** (*weapon*) honda *f*

slip [slɪp] <-pp-> **I.** *n* **1.** (*slipping*) resbalón *m* **2.** (*mistake*) error *m;* ~ **of the tongue** lapsus (linguae) **3.** COM resguardo *m;* **a** ~ **of paper** un trozo de papel **4.** (*women's underwear*) combinación *f* **5.** *fig* **to give sb the** ~ dar esquinazo a alguien **II.** *vi* **1.** (*slide*) resbalarse **2.** (*move quietly*) deslizarse; **to** ~ **into/out of one's pyjamas** ponerse/quitarse el pijama **3.** (*decline*) decaer **III.** *vt* deslizar

◆ **slip away** *vi* escabullirse

◆ **slip in** *vi* colarse

◆ **slip out** *vi* salir un momento

slipper ['slɪpər, *Am:* -ə-] *n* zapatilla *f,* pantufla *f AmL*

slippery ['slɪpəri] <-ier, -iest> *adj* resbaladizo

slip road ['slɪprəʊd, *Am:* -roʊd] *n Brit* vía *f* de acceso

slipshod ['slɪpʃɒd, *Am:* -ʃɑːd] *adj* chapucero

slip-up ['slɪpʌp] *n* desliz *m*

slipway ['slɪpweɪ] *n* NAUT grada *f*

slit [slɪt] **I.** <slit, slit> *vt* cortar; **to** ~ **sb's throat** cortar el cuello a alguien **II.** *n* **1.** (*tear*) raja *f* **2.** (*narrow opening*) rendija *f*

slither ['slɪðər, *Am:* -ə-] *vi* deslizarse

sliver ['slɪvər, *Am:* -ə-] *n* (*of glass, wood*) astilla *f;* (*of lemon*) rodaja *f* fina

slob [slɒb, *Am:* slɑːb] *n inf* patán *m*

slog [slɒg, *Am:* slɑːg] *inf* **I.** *n no pl* esfuerzo *m* **II.** <-gg-> *vi* (*walk*) caminar con gran esfuerzo **III.** <-gg-> *vt* (*hit*) golpear

slogan ['sləʊgən, *Am:* 'sloʊ-] *n* eslogan *m*

slop [slɒp, *Am:* slɑːp] <-pp-> *vi, vt inf* derramar(se)

slope [sləʊp, *Am:* sloʊp] **I.** *n* inclinación *f;* (*up*) cuesta *f;* (*down*) declive *m* **II.** *vi* inclinarse; **to** ~ **down** descender, bajar; **to** ~ **up** ascender, subir

sloping *adj* inclinado

sloppy ['slɒpi, *Am:* 'slɑːpi] <-ier, -iest> *adj* **1.** (*careless*) descuidado **2.** (*loose-fitting*) holgado

slot [slɒt, *Am:* slɑːt] **I.** *n* **1.** (*narrow opening*) ranura *f* **2.** TV espacio *m* **II.** <-tt-> *vt* **to** ~ **sth in** hacer encajar algo

sloth [sləʊθ, *Am:* slɑːθ] *n* **1.** *no pl* (*laziness*) pereza *f* **2.** ZOOL perezoso *m*

slot machine ['slɒtməʃiːn, *Am:* 'slɑːt-] *n* **1.** (*fruit machine*) máquina *f* tragaperras **2.** *Brit, Aus* (*vending machine*) máquina *f* expendedora

slouch [slaʊtʃ] *vi* **1.** (*have shoulders bent*) encorvarse **2.** (*walk*) caminar arrastrando los pies

Slovak ['sləʊvæk, *Am:* 'sloʊvɑ:k] *adj* eslovaco

Slovakia [sləʊ'vækiə, *Am:* sloʊ-'vɑ:ki-] *n no pl* Eslovaquia *f*

Slovakian *n* eslovaco, -a *m, f*

Slovene ['sləʊviːn, *Am:* 'sloʊ-] *adj* esloveno

Slovenia [sləʊ'viːniə, *Am:* sloʊ'-] *n no pl* Eslovenia *f*

Slovenian *n* esloveno, -a *m, f*

slovenly ['slʌvənli] *adj* descuidado

slow [sləʊ, *Am:* sloʊ] **I.** *adj* lento; **to be ~ to do sth** tardar en hacer algo; **to be (10 minutes) ~** ir (10 minutos) retrasado **II.** *vi* ir más despacio **III.** *vt* frenar; (*development*) retardar

◆**slow down I.** *vt* ralentizar **II.** *vi* **1.**(*reduce speed*) reducir la velocidad **2.**(*be less active*) moderar el ritmo de vida

slowly *adv* lentamente; ~ **but surely** lento pero seguro

slow motion *n* cámara *f* lenta; **in** ~ a cámara lenta

sludge [slʌdʒ] *n no pl* lodo *m*

slug¹ [slʌg] *n* ZOOL babosa *f*

slug² [slʌg] <-gg-> *n inf* (*bullet*) bala *f*

sluggish ['slʌgɪʃ] *adj* (*person*) perezoso, conchudo *Méx;* (*progress*) lento; (*market*) flojo

sluice [sluːs] **I.** *n* (*gate*) compuerta *f* **II.** *vt* regar; **to ~ sth down** enjuagar algo

slum [slʌm] *n* (*area*) barrio *m* pobre; (*on outskirts*) suburbio *m*

slump [slʌmp] **I.** *n* ECON depresión *f;* ~ **in prices** descenso *m* repentino de los precios **II.** *vi* desplomarse; (*prices*) bajar notablemente

slung [slʌŋ] *pt, pp of* **sling**

slur [slɜːʳ, *Am:* slɜːr] <-rr-> **I.** *vt* pronunciar con dificultad **II.** *n* calumnia *f*

slurp [slɜːp, *Am:* slɜːrp] *inf* **I.** *vt, vi* sorber (ruidosamente) **II.** *n* sorbo *m* (ruidoso)

slush [slʌʃ] *n no pl* nieve *f* medio derretida

slush fund *n* fondos *mpl* para sobornar

slut [slʌt] *n pej* puta *f*

sly [slaɪ] *adj* **1.**(*secretive*) sigiloso **2.**(*crafty*) astuto, songo *Col, Méx*

smack [smæk] **I.** *vt* **1.**(*slap*) dar un manotazo a **2.**(*hit noisily*) golpear **II.** *n* **1.** *inf* (*slap*) bofetada *f* **2.**(*loud noise*) ruido *m* fuerte **III.** *adv* (*exactly*) exactamente

◆**smack of** *vi* oler a

small [smɔːl] **I.** *adj* **1.**(*not large*) pequeño; (*person*) bajo **2.** TYPO, LIT (*letter*) minúscula **II.** *n no pl* **the ~ of the back** la región lumbar

small ad *n* anuncio *m* breve **small business** <-es> *n* pequeña empresa *f* **small change** *n no pl* calderilla *f* **smallholder** *n Brit* minifundista *mf* **small hours** *npl* madrugada *f* **smallpox** *n no pl* viruela *f* **small talk** *n no pl* cháchara *f*

smarmy ['smɑːmi, *Am:* 'smɑːr-] *adj pej* zalamero

smart [smɑːt, *Am:* smɑːrt] **I.** *adj* **1.**(*clever*) inteligente **2.**(*elegant*) elegante **3.**(*quick*) rápido **II.** *vi* escocer; **my eyes ~** me pican los ojos

smart card *n* INFOR tarjeta *f* electrónica

smash [smæʃ] **I.** *n* **1.**(*sound*) estruendo *m* **2.**(*accident*) colisión *f* **II.** *vt* **1.**(*break: glass*) hacer pedazos; *fig* destruir **2.** SPORTS (*record*) batir **III.** *vi* **1.**(*break into pieces: glass*) hacerse pedazos **2.**(*strike against*) chocar

◆**smash up** *vt* hacer pedazos; (*car*) destrozar

smashing *adj Brit, inf* imponente

smash-up *n* choque *m* violento

smattering ['smætərɪŋ, *Am:* 'smæt̬-] *n* nociones *fpl*

smear [smɪəʳ, *Am:* smɪr] **I.** *vt* **1.**(*spread*) untar **2.**(*attack*) desprestigiar **II.** *n* **1.**(*blotch*) mancha *f* **2.**(*accusation*) calumnia *f* **3.** MED frotis *m* **smear campaign** *n* campaña *f* de desprestigio

smell [smel] **I.** <*Brit, Aus:* smelt, smelt *Am, Aus:* -ed, -ed> *vt, vi* oler **II.** *n* **1.**(*sense of smelling*) olfato *m* **2.**(*odour*) olor *m*

smelly ['smeli] *adj* <-ier, -iest> apestoso, que huele mal

smelt [smelt] *Brit, Aus pt, pp of* **smell**

smile [smaɪl] **I.** *n* sonrisa *f* **II.** *vi* sonreír

smirk [smɜːk, *Am:* smɜːrk] **I.** *vi* sonreírse afectadamente **II.** *n* sonrisa *f* afectada

smock [smɒk, *Am:* smɑːk] *n* bata *f* corta

smog [smɒg, *Am:* smɑːg] *n no pl* smog *m*

smoke [sməʊk, *Am:* smoʊk] **I.** *n no pl* humo *m;* **to go up in** ~ quedarse en agua de borrajas **II.** *vt* (*cigarette*) fumar, pitar *AmS* **III.** *vi* **1.** (*produce smoke*) echar humo **2.** (*smoke tobacco*) fumar, pitar *AmS*

smoked *adj* ahumado

smokeless ['sməʊkləs, *Am:* 'smoʊk-] *adj* sin humo

smoker *n* **1.** (*person*) fumador(a) *m(f)* **2.** RAIL vagón *m* de fumadores

smokescreen *n a. fig* cortina *f* de humo

smoking *n no pl* el fumar; **to give up** ~ dejar de fumar

smoky ['sməʊki, *Am:* 'smoʊ-] *adj* <-ier, -iest> (*filled with smoke*) lleno de humo

smolder ['sməʊldɚ] *vi Am s.* **smoulder**

smooth [smuːð] **I.** *adj* (*not rough*) liso; (*surface*) llano; (*texture*) suave; (*sea*) tranquilo **II.** *vt* allanar
  ◆ **smooth over** *vt* (*difficulty*) solucionar

smother ['smʌðɚ, *Am:* -ɚ] *vt* **1.** (*suffocate*) ahogar **2.** (*suppress*) contener

smoulder ['sməʊldɚ, *Am:* 'smoʊldɚ] *vi* arder sin llama

smudge [smʌdʒ] **I.** *vt* manchar **II.** *n* mancha *f*

smug [smʌg] *adj* <-gg-> presumido

smuggle ['smʌgl] *vt* pasar de contrabando

smuggler ['smʌglɚ, *Am:* -lɚ] *n* contrabandista *mf*

smuggling ['smʌglɪŋ] *n no pl* contrabando *m*

smutty ['smʌti, *Am:* 'smʌt̬-] *adj* <-ier, -iest> obsceno, verde

snack [snæk] *n* bocado *m;* **to have a** ~ tomarse un tentempié

snack bar *n* cafetería *f*

snag [snæg] *n* dificultad *f;* **there's a** ~ hay un problema

snail [sneɪl] *n* caracol *m*

snake [sneɪk] *n* (*small*) culebra *f;* (*large*) serpiente *f*

snap [snæp] <-pp-> **I.** *n* **1.** (*sound*) chasquido *m* **2.** (*photograph*) foto *f* **3.** METEO **a cold** ~ una ola de frío **II.** *adj* repentino; ~ **decision** decisión *f* repentina **III.** *vi* **1.** (*break*) romperse **2.** (*move*) **to** ~ **shut** cerrarse de golpe **3.** (*bite*) **to** ~ **at sb** intentar morder a alguien **4.** (*speak sharply*) contestar con brusquedad; **to** ~ **at sb** contestar a alguien de forma brusca **IV.** *vt* **1.** (*break*) romper **2.** (*make snapping sound*) chasquear; **to** ~ **one's fingers** chasquear los dedos **3.** PHOT tomar un fotografía de
  ◆ **snap up** *vt* lanzarse sobre

snappy ['snæpi] *adj* <-ier, -iest> **1.** *inf* FASHION de lo más elegante **2.** (*quick*) rápido; **look** ~! ¡date prisa!

snapshot ['snæpʃɒt, *Am:* -ʃɑːt] *n* foto *f* instantánea

snare [sneəʳ, *Am:* sner] **I.** *n* trampa *f* **II.** *vt* cazar (con trampa); (*person*) atrapar

snarl [snɑːl, *Am:* snɑːrl] **I.** *vi* gruñir **II.** *n* gruñido *m*

snatch [snætʃ] **I.** <-es> *n* **1.** (*sudden grab*) arrebatamiento *m* **2.** (*theft*) robo *m* **II.** *vt* (*steal*) robar; (*win*) ganar; **to** ~ **sth** (**away**) **from sb** arrebatar algo de alguien **III.** *vi* quitar algo de las manos; **to** ~ **at sth** tratar de arrebatar algo
  ◆ **snatch up** *vt* agarrar

snazzy ['snæzi] <-ier, -iest> *adj inf* de lo más elegante

sneak [sniːk] *Am* **I.** *vi* moverse furtivamente; **to** ~ **in/out** entrar/salir a hurtadillas **II.** *vt* hacer furtivamente; **to** ~ **a look at sth/sb** mirar algo/a alguien con disimulo **III.** *n Brit,* *childspeak* acusica *mf*

sneakers ['sni:kə^rz, *Am:* -kə·z] *npl Am* zapatillas *fpl* de deporte

sneer [snɪə^r, *Am:* snɪr] I. *vi* hacer un gesto de burla y desprecio; (*mock*) mofarse; **to** ~ **at sth/sb** mofarse de algo/alguien II. *n* expresión *f* desdeñosa

sneeze [sni:z] I. *vi* estornudar II. *n* estornudo *m*

sniff [snɪf] I. *vi* sorber; **not to be ~ed at** *fig* no ser de despreciar II. *vt* olfatear

sniffer dog ['snɪfə^rˌdɒg, *Am:* 'snɪfə·ˌdɑ:g] *n* perro *m* rastreador

snigger ['snɪgə^r, *Am:* -ə·] I. *vi* reírse con disimulo II. *n* risa *f* disimulada

snip [snɪp] I. *vt* cortar (con tijeras) II. *n* **1.** (*piece of cloth*) recorte *m* **2.** *Brit, inf* (*cheap item*) ganga *f*

sniper ['snaɪpə^r, *Am:* -ə·] *n* francotirador(a) *m(f)*

snippet ['snɪpɪt] *n* retazo *m*

snivel(l)ing I. *n* no *pl* lloriqueo *m* II. *adj* llorón

snob [snɒb, *Am:* snɑ:b] *n* (e)snob *mf*

snobbery ['snɒbəri, *Am:* 'snɑ:bə·-] *n* (e)snobismo *m*

snobbish ['snɒbɪʃ, *Am:* 'snɑ:bɪʃ] <more, most> *adj* (e)snob

snog [snɒg, *Am:* snɑ:g] *Brit* I. <-gg-> *vi inf* morrearse II. *vt inf* morrear

snooker ['snu:kə^r, *Am:* 'snʊkə·] *n* billar *m* inglés

snoop [snu:p] *pej, inf* I. *n* fisgón, -ona *m, f* II. *vi* fisgonear

snooty ['snu:ti, *Am:* -t̬i] <-ier, -iest> *adj* presumido, pituco *Am*S

snooze [snu:z] *inf* I. *vi* (*nap*) echar una cabezada; (*nap lightly*) dormitar II. *n* cabezada *f*

snore [snɔ:^r, *Am:* snɔ:r] MED I. *vi* roncar II. *n* ronquido *m*

snorkel ['snɔ:kəl, *Am:* 'snɔ:r-] I. *n* tubo *m* snorkel (de respiración) II. <*Brit:* -ll-, *Am:* -l-> *vi* bucear con tubo

snort [snɔ:t, *Am:* snɔ:rt] I. *vi* bufar II. *vt inf* (*cocaine*) esnifar III. *n* bufido *m*

snout [snaʊt] *n* hocico *m*, morro *m*

snow [snəʊ, *Am:* snoʊ] *no pl* I. *n* nieve *f* II. *vi* nevar

◆**snow under** *vt* **to be snowed under** (**with sth**) estar desbordado (de algo)

snowball ['snəʊbɔ:l, *Am:* 'snoʊ-] I. *n* bola *f* de nieve II. *vi fig* aumentar progresivamente

snowbound ['snəʊbaʊnd, *Am:* 'snoʊ-] *adj* embarrancado en la nieve

snowdrift *n Brit* ventisquero *m* **snowdrop** *n* campanilla *f* de invierno **snowfall** *n no pl* nevada *f* **snowflake** *n* copo *m* de nieve **snowman** *n* muñeco *m* de nieve **snowplough** *n Brit,* **snowplow** *n Am* quitanieves *m inv* **snowshoe** *n* raqueta *f* (de nieve) **snowstorm** *n* tormenta *f* de nieve

snowy ['snəʊi, *Am:* 'snoʊ-] *adj* de mucha nieve

SNP [ˌesen'pi:] *n abbr of* **Scottish National Party** Partido *m* Nacional Escocés

snub [snʌb] I. <-bb-> *vt* **to** ~ **sb** desairar a alguien II. *n* desaire *m*

snub-nosed *adj* de nariz respingona

snuff [snʌf] I. *n* rapé *m* II. *vt* (*put out*) apagar

◆**snuff out** *vt* (*candle*) apagar

snug [snʌg] *adj* **1.** (*cozy*) acogedor **2.** (*tight: dress*) ajustado

snuggle ['snʌgl] *vi* acurrucarse; **to** ~ **up to sb** acurrucarse contra alguien

so [səʊ, *Am:* soʊ] I. *adv* **1.** (*in the same way*) tan, tanto; ~ **did/do I** yo también; ~ **to speak** por así decirlo **2.** (*like that*) así; **I hope/think** ~ espero/creo que sí **3.** (*to such a degree*) tan, tanto; ~ **late** tan tarde **4.** (*in order that*) para; **I bought the book** ~ **that he would read it** compré el libro para que lo leyera **5.** (*as a result*) así; **and** ~ **she won** y así ganó II. *conj* **1.** (*therefore*) por (lo) tanto **2.** *inf* (*and afterwards*) ~ (**then**) **he told me ...** y entonces me dijo... **3.** (*summing up*) así que; ~ **what?** ¿y qué?; ~ **now, ...** entonces...

soak [səʊk, *Am:* soʊk] **I.** *vt* **1.** (*keep in liquid*) remojar, ensopar *AmS* **2.** *inf* (*overcharge*) desplumar **II.** *vi* (*lie in liquid*) estar en remojo
◆ **soak in** *vi* penetrar
◆ **soak up** *vt* absorber

so-and-so ['səʊənsəʊ, *Am:* 'soʊənsoʊ] *n inf* (*person*) fulano *m*

soap [səʊp, *Am:* soʊp] *n no pl* jabón *m*

soapbox ['səʊpbɒks, *Am:* 'soʊpbɑːks] *n* tribuna *f* improvisada
soap flakes *npl* jabón *m* en escamas **soap opera** *n* telenovela *f* **soap powder** *n no pl* jabón *m* en polvo

soapy ['səʊpi, *Am:* 'soʊp-] <-ier, -iest> *adj* jabonoso

soar [sɔːʳ, *Am:* sɔːr] *vi* **1.** (*house*) elevarse mucho **2.** (*prices*) ponerse por las nubes; (*hopes*) renacer **3.** (*bird, plane*) remontar el vuelo; (*glide*) planear

sob [sɒb, *Am:* sɑːb] **I.** *n* sollozo *m* **II.** <-bb-> *vi* sollozar **III.** <-bb-> *vt* decir sollozando

sober ['səʊbəʳ, *Am:* 'soʊbɚ] *adj* **1.** (*not drunk*) sobrio **2.** (*serious*) serio **3.** (*plain*) discreto
◆ **sober up** *vi* espabilar la borrachera

sob story *n pej* dramón *m*
so-called [ˌsəʊ'kɔːld, *Am:* ˌsoʊ-'kɑːld] *adj* así llamado, presunto

soccer ['sɒkəʳ, *Am:* 'sɑːkɚ] *n no pl, Am* fútbol *m*

sociable ['səʊʃəbl, *Am:* 'soʊ-] *adj* sociable

social ['səʊʃəl, *Am:* 'soʊ-] *adj* social
socialism ['səʊʃəlɪzəm, *Am:* 'soʊ-] *n no pl* socialismo *m*

socialist *n* socialista *mf*

socialize ['səʊʃəlaɪz, *Am:* 'soʊ-] *vi* alternar con la gente

social science *n* ciencia *f* social **social security** *n no pl, Aus, Brit* seguridad *f* social **social service** *n pl* (*welfare*) servicios *mpl* sociales **social work** *n no pl* asistencia *f* social **social worker** *n* asistente *mf* social

society [sə'saɪəti, *Am:* -ṭi] *n* **1.** (*all people*) sociedad *f*; (**high**) ~ alta so-

ciedad *f* **2.** (*organization*) asociación *f*

sociologist [ˌsəʊʃi'ɒlədʒɪst, *Am:* ˌsoʊsi'ɑːlə-] *n* sociólogo, -a *m, f*

sociology [ˌsəʊʃi'ɒlədʒi, *Am:* ˌsoʊsi'ɑːlə-] *n no pl* sociología *f*

sock [sɒk, *Am:* sɑːk] *n* calcetín *m*, media *f AmL;* **to pull one's ~s up** *inf* hacer un esfuezo

socket ['sɒkɪt, *Am:* 'sɑːkɪt] *n* ELEC enchufe *m*, tomacorriente *m Arg, Perú*

sod¹ [sɒd, *Am:* sɑːd] *n* césped *m*
sod² [sɒd, *Am:* sɑːd] *n Brit, vulg* cabrón, -ona *m, f*
◆ **sod off** *vi Brit, inf* ~! ¡vete a la mierda!

soda ['səʊdə, *Am:* 'soʊ-] *n* **1.** *no pl* CHEM sosa *f* **2.** *Am* (*fizzy drink*) refresco *m* **3.** (*mixer drink*) soda *f*

soda water *n no pl* soda *f*

sodden ['sɒdn, *Am:* 'sɑːdn] *adj* empapado

sodding ['sɒdɪŋ, *Am:* 'sɑːdɪŋ] *adj Brit, vulg* jodido

sodium ['səʊdɪəm, *Am:* 'soʊ-] *n no pl* sodio *m*

sodium chloride *n no pl* cloruro *m* sódico

sofa ['səʊfə, *Am:* 'soʊ-] *n* sofá *m*

soft [sɒft, *Am:* sɑːft] *adj* (*ground, contact lenses*) blando; (*skin, landing*) suave

soften ['sɒfən, *Am:* 'sɑːfən] **I.** *vi* ablandarse, suavizarse **II.** *vt* ablandar, suavizar

softener ['sɒfənəʳ, *Am:* 'sɑːfənɚ] *n* suavizante *m*

softly *adv* **1.** (*not hard*) suavemente **2.** (*quietly*) silenciosamente

softness ['sɒftnɪs, *Am:* 'sɑːft-] *n no pl* **1.** (*not hardness*) blandura *f* **2.** (*smoothness*) suavidad *f*

software ['sɒftweəʳ, *Am:* 'sɑːftwer] *n no pl* software *m*

soggy ['sɒgi, *Am:* 'sɑːgi] <-ier, -iest> *adj* empapado

soil¹ [sɔɪl] *vt form* ensuciar
soil² [sɔɪl] *n no pl* AGR suelo *m*

solace ['sɒlɪs, *Am:* 'sɑːlɪs] **I.** *n no pl* consuelo *m* **II.** *vt* consolar

solar ['səʊləʳ, *Am:* 'soʊlɚ] *adj* solar

Sₛ

solarium [səʊˈleəriəm, *Am:* soʊˈleri-] <-s *o* solaria> *n* solárium *m*

solar panel *n* placa *f* solar **solar power** *n no pl* energía *f* solar **solar system** *n* sistema *m* solar

sold [səʊld, *Am:* soʊld] *pt, pp of* **sell**

solder [ˈsɒldəʳ, *Am:* ˈsɑːdəʳ] I. *vt* soldar II. *n no pl* soldadura *f*

soldier [ˈsəʊldʒəʳ, *Am:* ˈsoʊldʒəʳ] I. *n* (*military person*) militar *mf*; (*non officer*) soldado *mf* II. *vi* servir como soldado

◆ **soldier on** *vi* seguir adelante

sold out [ˌsəʊldˈaʊt, *Am:* ˌsoʊld-] *adj* vendido

sole¹ [səʊl, *Am:* soʊl] *adj* (*unique*) único; (*exclusive*) exclusivo

sole² [səʊl, *Am:* soʊl] *n* (*of foot*) planta *f*; (*of shoe*) suela *f*

sole³ [səʊl, *Am:* soʊl] <-(s)> *n* (*fish*) lenguado *m*

solemn [ˈsɒləm, *Am:* ˈsɑːləm] *adj* solemne

solicit [səˈlɪsɪt] I. *vt form* (*ask for*) solicitar II. *vi* (*prostitute*) abordar clientes

solicitor [səˈlɪsɪtəʳ, *Am:* -t̬əʳ] *n Aus, Brit* procurador(a) *m(f)*

solid [ˈsɒlɪd, *Am:* ˈsɑːlɪd] I. *adj* 1. (*hard*) sólido; (*silver*) macizo 2. (*argument*) sólido 3. (*line*) ininterrumpido II. *n* sólido *m*

solidarity [ˌsɒlɪˈdærəti, *Am:* ˌsɑːləˈderət̬i] *n no pl* solidaridad *f*

solid fuel *n* combustible *m* sólido

solitaire [ˌsɒlɪˈteəʳ, *Am:* ˈsɑːlətəʳ] *n* solitario *m*

solitary [ˈsɒlɪtəri, *Am:* ˈsɑːlətəri] *adj* 1. (*alone, single*) solitario 2. (*isolated*) solo; (*unvisited*) apartado

solitary confinement *n* aislamiento *m*

solitude [ˈsɒlɪtjuːd, *Am:* ˈsɑːlətuːd] *n no pl* soledad *f*

solo [ˈsəʊləʊ, *Am:* ˈsoʊloʊ] *n* MUS solo *m*

soloist [ˈsəʊləʊɪst, *Am:* ˈsoʊloʊ-] *n* solista *mf*

Solomon Islands [ˈsɒləmənˌaɪləndz, *Am:* ˈsɑːlə-] *npl* Islas *fpl* Salomón

solstice [ˈsɒlstɪs, *Am:* ˈsɑːl-] *n* solsticio *m*

soluble [ˈsɒljəbl, *Am:* ˈsɑːl-] *adj* soluble

solution [səˈluːʃən] *n* solución *f*

solve [sɒlv, *Am:* sɑːlv] *vt* resolver

solvency [ˈsɒlvənsi, *Am:* ˈsɑːl-] *n no pl* solvencia *f*

solvent [ˈsɒlvənt, *Am:* ˈsɑːl-] I. *n* disolvente *m* II. *adj* solvente

solvent abuse *n Brit* inhalación *f* de disolventes

Somali [ˌsəˈmɑːli, *Am:* soʊ'-] *adj* somalí

Somalia [ˌsəˈmɑːliə, *Am:* soʊ'-] *n* Somalia *f*

somber *adj Am,* **sombre** [ˈsɒmbəʳ, *Am:* ˈsɑːmbəʳ] *adj* sombrío

some [sʌm] I. *adj indef* 1. *pl* (*several*) algunos; ~ **apples** algunas manzanas; ~ **people think ...** algunos piensan... 2. (*imprecise*) algún, alguna; ~ **day** algún día; ~ **time ago** hace algún tiempo 3. (*amount*) un poco de, algo de; ~ **more tea** un poco más de té; **to have** ~ **money** tener algo de dinero II. *pron indef* 1. *pl* (*several*) algunos; **I would like** ~ quisiera algunos 2. (*part of it*) algo; **I would like** ~ quisiera algo III. *adv* unos, unas; ~ **ten of them** unos diez de ellos

somebody [ˈsʌmbədi, *Am:* -ˌbɑːdi] *pron indef* alguien; ~ **or other** alguien

somehow [ˈsʌmhaʊ] *adv* 1. (*through unknown methods*) de alguna manera 2. (*for an unclear reason*) por algún motivo

someone [ˈsʌmwʌn] *pron s.* **somebody**

someplace [ˈsʌmpleɪs] *adv Am* en algún lugar

somersault [ˈsʌməsɔːlt, *Am:* -əʳsɑːlt] I. *n* salto *m* mortal II. *vi* dar un salto mortal

something [ˈsʌmθɪŋ] I. *pron indef, sing* algo; ~ **else/nice** algo más/ bonito II. *adv* ~ **around £10** alrededor de 10 libras

sometime [ˈsʌmtaɪm] *adv* en algún momento; ~ **soon** pronto

sometimes ['sʌmtaɪmz] *adv* a veces
somewhat ['sʌmwɒt, *Am:* -wɑ:t] *adv* algo
somewhere ['sʌmweəʳ, *Am:* -wer] *adv* (*be*) en alguna parte; (*go*) a alguna parte; **to be ~ else** estar en otra parte; **to go ~ else** ir a otra parte
son [sʌn] *n* hijo *m*
sonar ['səʊnɑ:ʳ, *Am:* 'soʊnɑ:r] *n* sonar *m*
song [sɒŋ, *Am:* sɑ:ŋ] *n* canción *f*
songwriter *n* compositor(a) *m(f)*
sonic ['sɒnɪk, *Am:* 'sɑ:nɪk] *adj* sónico
son-in-law ['sʌnɪnlɔ:, *Am:* -lɑ:] <sons-in-law *o* son-in-laws> *n* yerno *m*
sonnet ['sɒnɪt, *Am:* 'sɑ:nɪt] *n* soneto *m*
sonny ['sʌni] *n no pl, inf* hijito *m*; (*aggressive*) majo *m*
soon [su:n] *adv* pronto, mero *AmC*, *Méx*; **~ after ...** poco después de...; **how ~ ...?** ¿para cuándo...?; **as ~ as possible** tan pronto como sea posible
sooner ['su:nəʳ, *Am:* -ə·] *adv comp of* **soon** más temprano; **~ or later** tarde o temprano; **no ~ ... than** apenas... cuando; **no ~ said than done** dicho y hecho; **the ~er the better** cuanto antes mejor
soot [sʊt] *n no pl* hollín *m*
soothe [su:ð] *vt* calmar; (*pain*) aliviar
sophisticated [sə'fɪstɪkeɪtɪd, *Am:* -təkeɪţɪd] *adj* sofisticado
sophomore ['sɒfəmɔ:ʳ, *Am:* 'sɑ:fəmɔ:r] *n Am* estudiante *mf* de segundo año
soppy ['sɒpi, *Am:* 'sɑ:pi] <-ier, -iest> *adj inf* sensiblero
soprano [sə'prɑ:nəʊ, *Am:* -'prænoʊ] *n* soprano *f*
sorbet ['sɔ:beɪ, *Am:* 'sɔ:r-] *n* sorbete *m*
sorcerer ['sɔ:sərəʳ, *Am:* 'sɔ:rsərə·] *n liter* hechicero *m*
sordid ['sɔ:dɪd, *Am:* 'sɔ:r-] *adj* sórdido
sore [sɔ:ʳ, *Am:* sɔ:r] **I.** *adj* **1.** (*aching*) dolorido **2.** *Am, inf* (*offended*) ofen-

dido **II.** *n* MED llaga *f*; *fig* recuerdo *m* doloroso
sorely ['sɔ:li, *Am:* 'sɔ:r-] *adv form* muy; **to be ~ tempted to do sth** estar casi por hacer algo
sorrow ['sɒrəʊ, *Am:* 'sɑ:roʊ] *n* pena *f*
sorry ['sɒri, *Am:* 'sɑ:r-] **I.** <-ier, -iest> *adj* **1.** triste, apenado; **to be ~ (that)** sentir (que) *+subj;* **to feel ~ for sb** tener lástima de alguien **2.** (*regretful*) arrepentido; **to be ~ about sth** estar arrepentido por algo **3.** (*said before refusing*) **I'm ~ but I don't agree** lo siento, pero no estoy de acuerdo **II.** *interj* perdón
sort [sɔ:t, *Am:* sɔ:rt] **I.** *n* **1.** (*type*) tipo *m;* (*kind*) especie *f;* (*variety*) clase *f;* **something/nothing of the ~** algo/nada por el estilo **2.** *inf* (*to some extent*) **~ of** en cierto modo; **that's ~ of difficult to explain** es algo difícil de explicar **II.** *vt* **1.** (*arrange*) clasificar **2.** INFOR ordenar **3.** *Brit, inf* (*restore to working order*) arreglar
 ◆ **sort out** *vt* **1.** (*arrange*) clasificar **2.** (*tidy up*) arreglar **3.** (*resolve*) aclarar
sorting office *n* oficina *f* de clasificación de correo
SOS [ˌesəʊ'es, *Am:* -oʊ'-] *n abbr of* **Save Our Souls** SOS *m*
so-so ['səʊsəʊ, *Am:* 'soʊsoʊ] *inf* **I.** *adj* regular **II.** *adv* así así
soufflé ['su:fleɪ, *Am:* su:'fleɪ] *n* suflé *m*
sought [sɔ:t, *Am:* sɑ:t] *pt, pp of* **seek**
soul [səʊl, *Am:* soʊl] *n* **1.** (*spirit*) alma *f;* **God rest his/her ~** que en paz descanse **2.** (*person*) alma *f;* **not a ~** ni un alma
soulful ['səʊlfəl, *Am:* 'soʊl-] *adj* conmovedor
sound¹ [saʊnd] **I.** *n* **1.** (*noise*) ruido *m* **2.** LING, PHY sonido *m* **3.** (*idea expressed in words*) **by the ~ of it** según parece; **I don't like the ~ of that** no me gusta nada **II.** *vi* **1.** (*make noise*) sonar **2.** (*seem*) parecer **III.** *vt* (*alarm*) hacer sonar

S

sound² [saʊnd] **I.** *adj* **1.** (*healthy*) sano **2.** (*health*) bueno; (*basis*) sólido **II.** *adv* **to be ~ asleep** estar profundamente dormido

sound³ [saʊnd] *vt* **1.** NAUT sondear **2.** MED auscultar

sound⁴ [saʊnd] *n* (*channel*) estrecho *m*

◆ **sound off** *vi inf* **to ~ about sb/ sth** sentar cátedra sobre algo/alguien

sound barrier *n* barrera *f* del sonido

soundbite *n* frase *f* lapidaria

sound effects *npl* efectos *mpl* de sonido

soundly *adv* **1.** (*completely*) **to sleep ~** dormir profundamente **2.** (*strongly*) **to thrash sb ~** dar una buena paliza a alguien

soundproof ['saʊndpruːf] **I.** *vt* insonorizar **II.** *adj* insonorizado

sound system *n* equipo *m* de sonido

soundtrack *n* CINE banda *f* sonora

soup [suːp] *n no pl* sopa *f*; (*clear*) caldo *m*; **to be in the ~** *inf* estar con el agua hasta el cuello

soup plate *n* plato *m* sopero **soup spoon** *n* cuchara *f* sopera

sour ['saʊəʳ, *Am:* 'saʊɚ] *adj* agrio; (*milk*) cortado; **to go ~** agriarse; (*milk*) cortarse

source [sɔːs, *Am:* sɔːrs] *n a. fig* fuente *f*; **from a reliable ~** de una fuente fiable

south ['saʊθ] **I.** *n* sur *m*; **in the ~ of Spain** en el sur de España **II.** *adj* del sur, meridional **III.** *adv* al sur

South Africa *n* Sudáfrica *f* **South African** *adj* sudafricano **South America** *n* América *f* del Sur **South American** *adj* sudamericano **South Carolina** *n* Carolina *f* del Sur **South Dakota** *n* Dakota *f* del Sur

southeast [ˌsaʊθˈiːst] **I.** *n* sureste *m* **II.** *adj* del sureste **III.** *adv* al sureste **southeasterly** *adj* del sureste; **in a ~ direction** hacia el sureste **southeastern** *adj* del sureste **southeastward(s)** *adv* hacia el sureste

southerly ['sʌðəli, *Am:* -ɚ·li] **I.** *adj* (*location*) del sur; **in a ~ direction** en dirección sur **II.** *adv* (*towards*) hacia el sur; (*from*) del sur

southern ['sʌðən, *Am:* -ɚn] *adj* del sur; **the ~ part of the country** la parte sur del país

southern hemisphere *n* hemisferio *m* sur

South Korea *n* Corea *f* del Sur **South Korean** *adj* surcoreano

South Pole *n* Polo *m* Sur

southward(s) ['saʊθwəd(z), *Am:* -wɚd(z)] *adv* hacia el sur

southwest [ˌsaʊθˈwest] **I.** *n* suroeste *m* **II.** *adj* del suroeste **III.** *adv* al suroeste **southwesterly** *adj* del suroeste; **in a ~ direction** hacia el suroeste **southwestern** *adj* del suroeste **southwestward(s)** *adv* hacia el suroeste

souvenir [ˌsuːvəˈnɪəʳ, *Am:* -ˈnɪr] *n* recuerdo *m*

sovereign ['sɒvrɪn, *Am:* 'saːvrən] *n* soberano, -a *m, f*

soviet ['saʊviət, *Am:* 'soʊviet] **I.** *n* soviet *m* **II.** *adj* soviético

Soviet Union *n* HIST Unión *f* Soviética

sow¹ [saʊ, *Am:* soʊ] <sowed, sowed *o* sown> *vt* sembrar

sow² [saʊ] *n* cerda *f*

sown [saʊn, *Am:* soʊn] *pp of* **sow¹**

soy [sɔɪ] *n Am,* **soya** ['sɔɪə] *n Brit* soja *f*

soya bean *n Brit,* **soy bean** ['sɔɪbiːn] *n Am* soja *f* **soya sauce** *n Brit,* **soy sauce** *n Am* salsa *f* de soja

sozzled ['sɒzld, *Am:* 'saːzld] *adj Brit, Aus, inf* **to be ~** estar mamado

spa [spaː] *n Am* balneario *m*

space [speɪs] **I.** *n a.* ASTR, PHYS, TYPO espacio *m*; **parking ~** plaza *f* de aparcamiento; **in a short ~ of time** en un breve espacio de tiempo **II.** *vt* espaciar

◆ **space out** *vt* espaciar

spacecraft *n* nave *f* espacial **spaceman** <-men> *n* astronauta *m*, cosmonauta *m* **spaceship** *n* nave *f* espacial, astronave *f* **spacewoman** <-women> *n* astronauta *f*

spacing ['speɪsɪŋ] *n no pl* espacio *m*

spacious ['speɪʃəs] *adj* espacioso

spade [speɪd] *n* **1.** (*tool*) pala *f* **2.** (*playing card*) pica *f*

spaghetti [spə'geti, *Am:* -'geṭ-] *n* espaguetis *mpl*

Spain [speɪn] *n* España *f*

span [spæn] **I.** *n* **1.** (*of time*) lapso *m* **2.** (*of arch*) luz *f* **3.** (*of wing*) envergadura *f* **II.**<-nn-> *vt* **1.** (*cross*) atravesar **2.** (*include*) abarcar

Spaniard ['spænjəd, *Am:* -jəˈd] *n* español(a) *m(f)*

spaniel ['spænjəl, *Am:* -jəl] *n* perro *m* de aguas

Spanish ['spænɪʃ] *adj* español; ~ **speaker** hispanohablante *mf*

spank [spæŋk] *vt* dar unos cachetes (en el trasero)

spanner ['spænəʳ, *Am:* -əˈ] *n Brit, Aus* llave *f*

spar¹ [spɑːʳ, *Am:* spɑːr] *n* NAUT palo *m*

spar² [spɑːʳ, *Am:* spɑːr] *vi* <-rr-> (*in boxing*) entrenar

spare [speəʳ, *Am:* sper] **I.** *vt* **1.** (*pardon*) perdonar; **to ~ sb sth** ahorrar algo a alguien; **to ~ no effort** no escatimar esfuerzos **2.** (*do without*) prescindir de **II.** *adj* **1.** (*additional*) de repuesto **2.** (*remaining*) sobrante **III.** *n* repuesto *m*

spare part *n* repuesto *m* **spare time** *n no pl* tiempo *m* libre **spare tire** *n Am*, **spare tyre** *n* AUTO rueda *f* de recambio

sparing ['speəˈɪŋ, *Am:* 'sperɪŋ] *adj* moderado; **to be ~ with one's praise** escatimar los elogios

spark [spɑːk, *Am:* spɑːrk] *n* **1.** (*from fire, electrical*) chispa *f* **2.** (*small amount*) pizca *f*

sparking plug ['spɑːkɪŋplʌg, *Am:* 'spɑːrk-] *n Am* bujía *f*

sparkle ['spɑːkl, *Am:* 'spɑːr-] **I.** *n no pl* destello *m*, brillo *m* **II.** *vi* centellear; (*eyes*) brillar

sparkler ['spɑːkləʳ, *Am:* 'spɑːrkləˈ] *n* bengala *f*

sparkling ['spɑːklɪŋ, *Am:* 'spɑːrkl-] *adj* brillante

spark plug ['spɑːkplʌg, *Am:* 'spɑːrk-] *n Brit* bujía *f*

sparring partner *n* **1.** SPORTS sparring *m* **2.** *fig* antagonista *mf*

sparrow ['spærəʊ, *Am:* 'speroʊ] *n* gorrión *m*

sparse [spɑːs, *Am:* spɑːrs] *adj* escaso

Spartan ['spɑːtən, *Am:* 'spɑːr-] *adj* espartano

spasm ['spæzəm] *n* MED espasmo *m;* (*of anger*) arrebato *m*

spasmodic [spæz'mɒdɪk, *Am:* -'mɑːdɪk] *adj* espasmódico

spastic ['spæstɪk] *n pej* espástico, -a *m, f*

spat¹ [spæt] *pt, pp of* **spit²**

spat² [spæt] *n inf* (*quarrel*) rencilla *f*

spate [speɪt] *n no pl* (*of letters*) aluvión *m;* **to be in full ~** *Brit* (*river*) estar crecido

spatter ['spætəʳ, *Am:* 'spæṭəˈ] *vt* salpicar; **to ~ sb with mud/water** salpicar de barro/agua a alguien

spawn [spɔːn, *Am:* spɑːn] **I.** *n no pl* ZOOL hueva(s) *f(pl)* **II.** *vt* generar, producir **III.** *vi* desovar

speak [spiːk] <spoke, spoken> **I.** *vi* **1.** hablar; **to ~ to sb** hablar con alguien; **so to ~** por así decirlo **2.** + *adv* **broadly ~ing** en términos generales; **strictly ~ing** en realidad **II.** *vt* decir, hablar; **to ~ one's mind** hablar claro [*o* con franqueza]

◆ **speak for** *vi* hablar por; **speaking for myself ...** en cuanto a mí...; **it speaks for itself** habla por sí solo

speaker *n* **1.** hablante *mf* **2.** (*orator*) orador(a) *m(f)* **3.** (*loudspeaker*) altavoz *m*

spear [spɪəʳ, *Am:* spɪr] **I.** *n* lanza *f;* (*for throwing*) jabalina *f;* (*for fishing*) arpón *m* **II.** *vt* atravesar (con una lanza)

spearhead ['spɪəhed, *Am:* 'spɪr-] **I.** *vt* encabezar **II.** *n a. fig* punta *f* de lanza

special ['speʃəl] **I.** *adj* especial; (*aptitude*) excepcional; **nothing ~** *inf* nada en particular **II.** *n* RAIL tren *m* especial

specialist ['speʃəlɪst] *n* especialista *mf*

speciality [ˌspeʃɪ'æləti, *Am:* -ṭi] *n* <-ies> especialidad *f*

specialize ['speʃəlaɪz] *vi, vt* especializar(se)

S_s

specially *adv* especialmente
specialty ['speʃəlti, *Am:* -t̬i] *n Am, Aus s.* **speciality**
species ['spi:ʃiz] *n inv a.* BIO especie *f*
specific [spə'sɪfɪk] *adj* específico
specifically *adv* expresamente; (*particularly*) específicamente
specification [ˌspesɪfɪ'keɪʃən, *Am:* -əfɪ'-] *n* especificación *f*
specify ['spesɪfaɪ, *Am:* -əfaɪ] <-ie-> *vt* especificar
specimen ['spesɪmɪn, *Am:* -əmən] *n* ejemplar *m*; (*of blood, urine*) muestra *f*
speck [spek] *n* punto *m*, mota *f*
speckled *adj* con motitas, moteado
specs [speks] *npl Brit, inf abbr of* **spectacles** gafas *fpl*
spectacle ['spektəkl] *n* espectáculo *m*
spectacular [spek'tækjʊlər, *Am:* -lər] I. *adj* espectacular II. *n* programa *m* especial
spectator [spek'teɪtər, *Am:* -t̬ər] *n* espectador(a) *m(f)*
spectrum ['spektrəm] <-ra *o* -s> *n* espectro *m*
speculate ['spekjʊleɪt] *vi* **to ~ about sth** (*hypothesize*) especular acerca de algo; (*conjecture*) hacer conjeturas acerca de algo
speculation [ˌspekjʊ'leɪʃən] *n* especulación *f*, conjetura *f*
sped [sped] *pt, pp of* **speed**
speech [spi:tʃ] <-es> *n* **1.** *no pl* (*capacity to speak*) habla *f* **2.** (*words*) palabras *fpl* **3.** (*public talk*) discurso *m*
speechless ['spi:tʃləs] *adj* mudo
speed [spi:d] I. *n* **1.** (*velocity*) velocidad *f*; **at a ~ of ...** a una velocidad de... **2.** (*quickness*) rapidez *f* **3.** (*gear*) marcha *f* II. *vi* <sped, sped> **1.** (*go fast*) ir de prisa; **to ~ by** pasar volando **2.** (*exceed speed restrictions*) ir a exceso de velocidad
◆ **speed up** <-ed, -ed> I. *vt* acelerar, expeditar *AmL* II. *vi* acelerarse
speedboat ['spi:dbəʊt, *Am:* -boʊt] *n* lancha *f* motora
speeding *n no pl* exceso *m* de velocidad

speed limit *n* velocidad *f* máxima
speedometer [spi:'dɒmɪtər, *Am:* -'dɑːmət̬ər] *n* velocímetro *m*
speed trap *n* control *m* de velocidad
speedway ['spi:dweɪ] *n* SPORTS pista *f* de carreras
speedy ['spi:di] <-ier, -iest> *adj* veloz
spell[1] [spel] *n a. fig* encanto *m*; **to be under a ~** estar hechizado
spell[2] [spel] *n* **1.** (*period*) temporada *f* **2.** (*turn*) turno *m*
spell[3] [spel] <spelled, spelled *o Brit:* spelt, spelt> *vt* **1.** (*form using letters*) deletrear; **how do you ~ it?** ¿cómo se deletrea? **2.** (*signify*) significar
◆ **spell out** *vt* deletrear
spellbound ['spelbaʊnd] *adj* hechizado; *fig* fascinado
spelling *n no pl* ortografía *f*
spelt [spelt] *pt, pp of* **spell**
spend [spend] <spent, spent> *vt* **1.** (*money*) gastar **2.** (*time*) pasar; **to ~ time** (**doing sth**) dedicar tiempo (a hacer algo)
spending money *n* dinero *m* para gastos personales
spendthrift ['spendθrɪft] *inf* I. *adj* derrochador, botado *AmC* II. *n* derrochador(a) *m(f)*, botador(a) *m(f)* *AmL*
spent [spent] I. *pt, pp of* **spend** II. *adj* (*used*) gastado
sperm [spɜːm, *Am:* spɜːrm] <-(s)> *n* esperma *m o f*
spew [spju:] *vi, vt* vomitar
sphere [sfɪər, *Am:* sfɪr] *n* esfera *f*
spice [spaɪs] I. *n* especia *f*, olor *m* *Chile* II. *vt* condimentar
spick and span [ˌspɪkən'spæn] *adj inf* impecable
spicy ['spaɪsi] <-ier, -iest> *adj* picante
spider ['spaɪdər, *Am:* -dər] *n* araña *f*
spider's web *n Brit,* **spiderweb** ['spaɪdəweb, *Am:* -dər-] *n Am, Aus* telaraña *f*
spiel [ʃpi:l] *n inf* rollo *m*
spike [spaɪk] I. *n* **1.** (*pointed object*) pincho *m* **2.** *pl* (*running shoes*) zapatillas *fpl* con clavos II. *vt* clavar

spill [spɪl] <spilt, spilt *o Am, Aus:* spilled, spilled> *vi, vt* derramar(se)
◆ **spill over** *vi* derramarse
spillage [ˈspɪlɪdʒ] *n* derrame *m*
spilt [spɪlt] *pp, pt of* **spill**
spin [spɪn] I. *n* 1. (*rotation*) vuelta *f* 2. (*in washing machine*) revolución *f* 3. (*drive*) **to go for a ~** dar un paseo (en coche) II. *vi, vt* <spun *Brit:* span, spun> 1. (*rotate*) girar 2. (*make thread*) hilar
◆ **spin out** *vt* prolongar
spina bifida [ˌspaɪnəˈbɪfɪdə] *n no pl* MED espina *f* bífida
spinach [ˈspɪnɪtʃ] *n* espinacas *fpl*
spinal [ˈspaɪnəl] *adj* ANAT espinal
spinal cord *n* médula *f* espinal
spindly <-ier, -iest> *adj* larguirucho
spin doctor *n* POL asesor(a) *m(f)*
spin-dryer *n* secador *m* centrífugo
spine [spaɪn] *n* 1. (*spinal column*) columna *f* vertebral 2. BOT espina *f*
spineless [ˈspaɪnləs] *adj* (*weak*) blando
spinning *n* rotación *f*
spinning top *n* peonza *f* **spinning wheel** *n* rueca *f*
spin-off [ˈspɪnɒf, *Am:* -ɑːf] *n* subproducto *m*
spinster [ˈspɪnstəʳ, *Am:* -stɚ] *n a. pej* solterona *f*
spiral [ˈspaɪərəl, *Am:* ˈspaɪ-] I. *n* espiral *f* II. *adj* espiral; **~ staircase** escalera *f* de caracol III. *vi* <*Brit:* -ll-, *Am:* -l-> (*increase*) aumentar
spire [ˈspaɪəʳ, *Am:* -ɚ] *n* ARCHIT aguja *f*
spirit [ˈspɪrɪt] *n* 1. (*soul*) alma *f* 2. (*ghost*) fantasma *m* 3. *pl* (*mood*) ánimos *mpl;* **to be in high/low ~s** estar animado/desanimado 4. (*character*) carácter *m* 5. (*attitude*) espíritu *m* 6. *pl* (*alcoholic drink*) alcohol *m*
spirited *adj* enérgico; (*discussion*) animado
spirit-level *n* nivel *m* de burbuja
spiritual [ˈspɪrɪtʃuəl] I. *adj* espiritual II. *n* MUS espiritual *m* negro
spiritualism [ˈspɪrɪtʃuəlɪzəm] *n no pl* espiritismo *m*
spit¹ [spɪt] *n* GASTR asador *m*

spit² [spɪt] I. *n inf* saliva *f* II. *vi* <spat, spat> 1. (*expel saliva*) escupir 2. (*crackle*) chisporrotear
spite [spaɪt] I. *n no pl* rencor *m;* **in ~ of** a pesar de II. *vt* fastidiar
spiteful [ˈspaɪtfəl] *adj* rencoroso
spittle [ˈspɪtl, *Am:* ˈspɪt̬-] *n* escupitajo *m,* desgarro *m AmL*
splash [splæʃ] I. *n* 1. (*sound*) chapoteo *m* 2. (*small drops*) salpicadura *f* II. *vi, vt* salpicar
spleen [spliːn] *n* ANAT bazo *m*
splendid [ˈsplendɪd] *adj* espléndido
splint [splɪnt] I. *n* tablilla *f* II. *vt* entablillar
splinter [ˈsplɪntəʳ, *Am:* -t̬ɚ] I. *n* astilla *f* II. *vi* astillarse
split [splɪt] I. *n* 1. (*crack*) grieta 2. (*in clothes*) desgarrón 3. (*division*) división *f* II. *vt* <split, split> 1. (*divide*) dividir 2. (*crack*) agrietar III. *vi* <split, split> 1. (*divide*) dividirse 2. (*form cracks*) agrietarse
◆ **split up** *vi* **to ~ with sb** separarse de alguien
split personality *n* PSYCH doble personalidad *f*
splutter [ˈsplʌtəʳ, *Am:* ˈsplʌt̬ɚ] *vi* chisporrotear; (*person*) farfullar
spoil [spɔɪl] <spoilt, spoilt *Am:* spoiled, spoiled> I. *vt* 1. (*ruin*) estropear 2. (*child*) mimar, engreír *AmL* II. *vi* estropearse
spoilsport [ˈspɔɪlspɔːt, *Am:* -spɔːrt] *n inf* aguafiestas *mf inv*
spoilt I. *pt, pp of* **spoil** II. *adj* mimado, engreído *AmL*
spoke¹ [spəʊk, *Am:* spoʊk] *pt of* **speak**
spoke² [spəʊk, *Am:* spoʊk] *n* radio *m*
spoken *pp of* **speak**
spokesman *n* portavoz *m,* vocero *m AmL* **spokesperson** *n* portavoz *mf,* vocero, -a *m, f AmL* **spokeswoman** *n* portavoz *f,* vocera *f AmL*
sponge [spʌndʒ] I. *n* 1. (*cloth*) esponja *f* 2. GASTR bizcocho *m* II. *vt* limpiar con una esponja
◆ **sponge down** *vt,* **sponge off** *vt* limpiar con una esponja
◆ **sponge on** *vt inf* vivir a costa de

S

sponge bag *n Aus, Brit* neceser *m*
sponsor ['spɒntsəʳ, *Am:* 'spɑ:ntsɚ]
I. *vt* patrocinar II. *n* patrocinador(a)
m(f), propiciador(a) *m(f) AmL*
sponsorship *n no pl* patrocinio *m*
spontaneous [spɒn'teɪnɪəs, *Am:*
spɑ:n'-] *adj* espontáneo
spooky ['spu:ki] <-ier, -iest> *adj inf*
espectral
spool [spu:l] *n* bobina *f;* (*of film*)
carrete *m*
spoon [spu:n] *n* cuchara *f*
spoon-feed ['spu:nfi:d] *vt* 1. (*feed*)
dar de comer con cuchara 2. *pej* to ~
sb dar todo hecho a alguien
spoonful ['spu:nfʊl] <-s *o* spoons-
ful> *n* cucharada *f*
sporadic [spə'rædɪk] *adj* esporádico
sport [spɔ:t, *Am:* spɔ:rt] *n* 1. (*activity*) deporte *m* 2. *inf* (*person*) **to be
a** (**good**) ~ ser buena gente
sporting *adj* deportivo, esportivo
AmL
sports car *n* coche *m* deportivo
sports field *n* campo *m* de deportes
sports jacket *n* chaqueta *f* de sport
sportsman ['spɔ:tsmən, *Am:*
'spɔ:rts-] *n* deportista *m*
sportsmanship *n no pl* deportivi-
dad *f*
sportswear *n no pl* ropa *f* de deporte
sportswoman ['spɔ:ts,wʊmən,
Am: 'spɔ:rts-] *n* deportista *f*
sporty ['spɔ:ti, *Am:* 'spɔ:rti̩] <-ier,
-iest> *adj* deportivo
spot [spɒt, *Am:* spɑ:t] I. *n* 1. (*mark*)
mancha *f* 2. (*pattern*) lunar *m*
3. *Brit* (*on skin*) grano *m* 4. *Brit*
(*little bit*) poquito *m;* **a ~ of rain** una
gota de lluvia 5. (*place*) lugar *m;* **on
the** ~ (*at once*) en el acto 6. (*part of
TV, radio show*) espacio *m* 7. *fig* **to
put sb on the** ~ poner a alguien en
un aprieto II. <-tt-> *vt* (*see*) divisar
spot check *n* control *m* al azar
spotless ['spɒtləs, *Am:* 'spɑ:t-] *adj*
1. (*very clean*) inmaculado 2. (*un-
blemished*) sin manchas
spotlight ['spɒtlaɪt, *Am:* 'spɑ:t-] *n*
foco *m*
spot-on [spɒt'ɒn, *Am:* spɑ:t'ɑ:n]
adj Aus, Brit, inf exacto

spotted *adj* manchado
spotty ['spɒti, *Am:* 'spɑ:ti̩] <-ier,
-iest> *adj Aus, Brit* (*having blemished skin*) con granos
spouse [spaʊz] *n form* cónyuge *mf*
spout [spaʊt] I. *n* (*of jar*) pico *m;*
(*tube*) caño *m* II. *vi* chorrear
sprain [spreɪn] I. *vt* torcer II. *n*
torcedura *f*
sprang [spræŋ] *vi, vt pt of* **spring**
sprawl [sprɔ:l, *Am:* sprɑ:l] *pej* I. *vi*
tumbarse; **to send sb ~ing** derribar
a alguien II. *n* (*of town*) extensión *f*
spray [spreɪ] I. *n* 1. (*mist*) rocío *m*
2. (*device*) atomizador *m* II. *vt* rociar
spread [spred] I. *n* 1. (*act of spreading*) propagación *f* 2. (*range*) gama *f*
3. (*article*) reportaje *m* a toda página
4. *Aus, Brit, inf* (*meal*) comilona *f*
II. <spread, spread> *vi* (*liquid*) extenderse; (*disease*) propagarse;
(*news*) difundirse III. <spread,
spread> *vt* 1. (*disease*) propagar;
(*news*) difundir 2. (*butter*) untar
3. (*map, blanket*) extender
spread-eagled [ˌspred'i:gld, *Am:*
'spred,i:-] *adj* despatarrado
spreadsheet ['spredʃi:t] *n* INFOR
hoja *f* de cálculo
spree [spri:] *n* parranda *f*, tambarria *f*
AmC; **to go** (**out**) **on a drinking** ~ ir
de juerga
sprightly ['spraɪtli] <-ier, -iest> *adj*
vivaz
spring [sprɪŋ] I. *n* 1. (*season*) primavera *f* 2. (*jump*) salto *m* 3. (*metal
coil*) resorte *m* 4. (*elasticity*) elasticidad *f* 5. (*source of water*) manantial
m, yurro *m CRi* II. <sprang,
sprung> *vi* saltar; **to** ~ **to one's
feet** levantarse de un salto
III. <sprang, sprung> *vt* **to** ~ **sth
on sb** soltarle algo a alguien
springboard ['sprɪŋbɔ:d, *Am:*
-bɔ:rd] *n* trampolín *m*
spring-clean *vt* limpiar a fondo
spring onion *n Aus, Brit* cebolleta *f*
spring roll *n* rollito *m* de primavera
springtime *n no pl* primavera *f*
sprinkle ['sprɪŋkl] I. *vt* salpicar II. *n*
salpicadura *f*

sprinkler ['sprɪŋklə', *Am:* -ə-] *n* aspersor *m*

sprint [sprɪnt] SPORTS **I.** *vi* esprintar **II.** *n* esprint *m*

sprinter ['sprɪntə', *Am:* -t̬ə-] *n* velocista *mf*

sprocket ['sprɒkɪt, *Am:* 'sprɑː-] *n* plato *m*

sprout [spraʊt] **I.** *n Brit* (**Brussels**) ~s coles *mpl* de Bruselas **II.** *vi* brotar

spruce¹ [spruːs] *n* BOT picea *f*

spruce² [spruːs] *adj* aseado
  ◆ **spruce up** *vt* to spruce oneself up arreglarse

sprung [sprʌŋ] **I.** *adj Brit* de muelles **II.** *pp of* **spring**

spry [spraɪ] *adj* ágil

spun [spʌn] *pt, pp of* **spin**

spur [spɜː', *Am:* spɜːr] **I.** <-rr-> *vt fig* estimular **II.** *n* **1.** (*device*) espuela *f* **2.** (*encouragement*) estímulo *m;* **on the ~ of the moment** *inf* sin pensarlo

spurious ['spjʊərɪəs, *Am:* 'spjʊrɪ-] *adj* falso

spurn [spɜːn, *Am:* spɜːrn] *vt form* desdeñar

spurt [spɜːt, *Am:* spɜːrt] **I.** *n* esfuerzo *m* supremo; **to put on a ~** acelerar **II.** *vi Am* (*accelerate*) acelerar

spy [spaɪ] **I.** *n* espía *mf* **II.** *vi* espiar; **to ~ on sb** espiar a alguien **III.** *vt* divisar

Sq. *abbr of* **square** Pza.

squabble ['skwɒbl, *Am:* 'skwɑːbl] **I.** *n* riña *f* **II.** *vi* reñir

squad [skwɒd, *Am:* skwɑːd] *n* **1.** (*group*) pelotón *m;* (*of police*) brigada *f;* **anti-terrorist ~** brigada antiterrorista **2.** (*sports team*) equipo *m*

squaddie ['skwɒdi, *Am:* 'skwɑːdi] *n Brit, inf* soldado *m* raso

squadron ['skwɒdrən, *Am:* 'skwɑːdrən] *n* escuadrón *m*

squalid ['skwɒlɪd, *Am:* 'skwɑːlɪd] *adj* sórdido

squall [skwɔːl] **I.** *n* ráfaga *f* **II.** *vi* chillar

squalor ['skwɒlə', *Am:* 'skwɑːlə-] *n no pl* miseria *f*

squander ['skwɒndə', *Am:* 'skwɑːndə-] *vt* (*money*) malgastar

square [skweə', *Am:* skwer] **I.** *n* **1.** (*shape*) cuadrado *m* **2.** (*in town*) plaza *f* **3.** *fig* **to go back to ~ one** volver al punto de partida **II.** *adj* **1.** (*square-shaped*) cuadrado; **four ~ metres** cuatro metros cuadrados **2.** *inf* (*level*) igual; **to be** (**all**) **~** SPORTS estar (todos) empatados **III.** *vt* **1.** (*align*) cuadrar **2.** *inf* (*settle*) acomodar; **I can't ~ this with my principles** no puedo encajar esto con mis principios **3.** MAT elevar al cuadrado
  ◆ **square up** *vi* to ~ with sb ajustar cuentas con alguien

square dance *n* baile *m* de figuras

[?] **Square dance** es el nombre que recibe un popular baile americano. Grupos de cuatro parejas bailan en círculo, en cuadrado o formando dos líneas. Todos ellos llevan a cabo los movimientos que les va indicando un **caller**. El **caller** puede dar las indicaciones cantando o hablando. Estos bailarines suelen bailar acompañados de músicos con violines, bajos o guitarras.

---

squarely *adv* directamente

square root *n* raíz *f* cuadrada

squash¹ [skwɒʃ, *Am:* skwɑːʃ] *n Am* (*vegetable*) calabaza *f*

squash² [skwɒʃ, *Am:* skwɑːʃ] **I.** *n* **1.** *no pl* SPORTS squash *m* **2.** *Aus, Brit* (*drink*) zumo *m* **II.** *vt* aplastar

squat [skwɒt, *Am:* skwɑːt] **I.** <-tt-> *vi* **1.** (*crouch down*) agacharse **2.** (*in property*) ocupar una vivienda sin permiso **II.** <-tt-> *adj* rechoncho

squatter ['skwɒtə', *Am:* 'skwɑːt̬ə-] *n* ocupa *mf*

squawk [skwɔːk, *Am:* skwɑːk] **I.** *vi* graznar **II.** *n* (*sharp cry*) graznido *m*

squeak [skwiːk] **I.** *n* chirrido *m* **II.** *vi* chirriar

squeaky ['skwiːki] <-ier, -iest> *adj* chirriante

squeal [skwiːl] *vi* chillar

S **s**

squeamish ['skwiːmɪʃ] *adj* remilgado

squeeze [skwiːz] I. *n* 1.(*pressing action*) estrujón *m* 2.(*limit*) restricción *f* II. *vt* 1.(*press together*) estrujar 2.(*force*) presionar

squelch [skweltʃ] I. *vi* chapotear II. *vt Am* aplastar III. *n* chapoteo *m*

squid [skwɪd] <-(s)> *n* calamar *m*

squiggle ['skwɪgl] *n* garabato *m*

squint [skwɪnt] I. *vi* bizquear II. *n* estrabismo *m*, bizquera *f AmL*

squirm [skwɜːm, *Am:* skwɜːrm] *vi* retorcerse

squirrel ['skwɪrəl, *Am:* 'skwɜːr-] *n* ardilla *f*

squirt [skwɜːt, *Am:* skwɜːrt] *vi* salir a chorros

Sr *n abbr of* **senior** padre

Sri Lanka [ˌsriːˈlæŋkə, *Am:* -ˈlɑːŋ-] *n* Sri Lanka *m*

Sri Lankan [ˌsriːˈlæŋkən, *Am:* -ˈlɑːŋ-] *adj* esrilanqués

SSW [ˌesesˈdʌblju:] *abbr of* **south-southwest** SSO

St *n* 1. *abbr of* **saint** (*man*) S., Sto.; (*woman*) Sta. 2. *abbr of* **street** c/

stab [stæb] I. <-bb-> *vt* apuñalar, achurar *CSur;* **to ~ sb to death** matar a alguien de una puñalada II. *n* 1.(*blow*) puñalada *f* 2.(*sudden pain*) punzada *f* 3.(*attempt*) **to have a ~ at** (**doing**) **sth** intentar (hacer) algo

stable[1] ['steɪbl] *adj* estable

stable[2] ['steɪbl] *n* cuadra *f*

stack [stæk] I. *vt* apilar II. *n* 1.(*pile*) pila *f* 2. *inf* (*large amount*) montón *m*, ponchada *f CSur*

stadium ['steɪdɪəm] <-s *o* -dia> *n* estadio *m*

staff [stɑːf, *Am:* stæf] I. *n* 1.(*employees*) personal *m*, elenco *m AmL* 2.SCHOOL, UNIV profesorado *m* 3.(*stick*) bastón *m* II. *vt* dotar de personal

stag [stæg] *n* ciervo *m*

stage [steɪdʒ] I. *n* 1.(*period*) etapa *f*, pascana *f AmS;* **to do sth in ~s** hacer algo por etapas 2.THEAT escena *f;* **the ~** el teatro II. *vt* 1.(*produce on stage*) representar 2.(*organize*) organizar

stagecoach ['steɪdʒkəʊtʃ, *Am:* -koʊtʃ] *n* diligencia *f*

stage manager *n* THEAT director(a) *m(f)* de escena; CINE director(a) *m(f)* de producción

stagger ['stægəʳ, *Am:* -ɚ-] I. *vi* tambalearse II. *vt* 1.(*amaze*) asombrar 2.(*work, payments*) escalonar

staggering *adj* (*amazing*) sorprendente

stagnant ['stægnənt] *adj a. fig* estancado

stagnate [stægˈneɪt, *Am:* 'stægneɪt] *vi* estancarse

stag night *n*, **stag party** *n Brit* despedida *f* de soltero

staid [steɪd] *adj* serio

stain [steɪn] I. *vt* 1.(*mark*) manchar 2.(*dye*) teñir II. *n* 1.(*mark*) mancha *f* 2.(*dye*) tinte *m*

stained glass window *n* vidriera *f*

stainless ['steɪnləs] *adj* (*immaculate*) inmaculado; (*that cannot be stained*) que no se mancha

stainless steel *n* acero *m* inoxidable

stain remover *n* quitamanchas *m inv*

stair [steəʳ, *Am:* ster] *n* 1.(*rung*) peldaño *m* 2. *pl* (*set of steps*) escalera *f*

staircase ['steəkeɪs, *Am:* 'ster-] *n*, **stairway** ['steəweɪ, *Am:* 'ster-] *n* escalera *f*

stake [steɪk] I. *n* 1.(*stick*) estaca *f* 2.(*share*) participación *f;* **to have a ~ in sth** tener interés en algo 3.(*bet*) apuesta *f;* **to be at ~** estar en juego II. *vt* 1.(*mark with stakes*) marcar con estacas 2.(*bet*) apostar; **to ~ a claim to sth** reivindicar algo
◆**stake out** *vt Am, inf* poner bajo vigilancia

stalactite ['stæləktaɪt, *Am:* stə-ˈlæk-] *n* estalactita *f*

stalagmite ['stæləgmaɪt] *n* estalagmita *f*

stale [steɪl] *adj* pasado; (*bread*) duro

stalemate ['steɪlmeɪt] *n* tablas *fpl*

stalk[1] [stɔːk] *n* tallo *m*

stalk[2] [stɔːk] I. *vt* (*follow*) acechar II. *vi* **to ~ off** marcharse airadamente

stall [stɔ:l] **I.** *n* **1.** (*for animal*) establo *m* **2.** *Brit, Aus* CINE, THEAT **the ~s** el patio de butacas **3.** (*in market*) puesto *m*, tarantín *m* *Ven* **II.** *vi* **1.** (*stop running: engine*) calarse **2.** *inf* (*delay*) ir con rodeos **III.** *vt* (*engine*) calar

stallion ['stælɪən, *Am:* -jən] *n* semental *m*, padrón *m* *AmL*, padrote *m* *AmC, Méx*

stalwart ['stɔ:lwət, *Am:* -wə·t] *n* *form* partidario, -a *m*, *f* leal

stamina ['stæmɪnə, *Am:* -ənə] *n no pl* resistencia *f*

stammer ['stæmə·, *Am:* -ə·] **I.** *vi* tartamudear **II.** *vt* decir tartamudeando **III.** *n* tartamudeo *m*

stamp [stæmp] **I.** *n* sello *m*, estampilla *f* *AmL*; (*device*) tampón *m*; (*mark*) sello *m* **II.** *vt* **1.** (*place postage stamp on*) pegar un sello en **2.** (*impress a mark on*) estampar **3. to ~ one's foot** patear **III.** *vi* patalear

stamp album *n* álbum *m* de sellos

stamp collector *n* coleccionista *mf* de sellos

stampede [stæm'pi:d] *n* estampida *f*

stance [sta:ns, *Am:* stæns] *n* postura *f*

stand [stænd] **I.** *n* **1.** (*position*) posición *f*; **to take a ~ on** (**doing**) **sth** adoptar una postura con respecto a (hacer) algo; **to make a ~ against sth** oponer resistencia a algo **2.** *pl* (*in stadium*) tribuna *f* **3.** (*support, frame*) soporte *m*; **music ~** atril *m* **4.** (*market stall*) puesto *m*, trucha *f* *AmC* **5.** (*for vehicles*) parada *f* **II.**<stood, stood> *vi* **1.** (*be upright*) estar de pie; **to ~ still** estarse quieto **2.** (*be located*) encontrarse **3.** (*remain unchanged*) mantenerse en vigor **III.**<stood, stood> *vt* **1.** (*place*) poner (de pie), colocar **2.** (*bear*) aguantar; **I can't ~ her** no la puedo ver **3.** (*pay for*) **to ~ sb a drink** invitar a alguien a una copa

◆ **stand aside** *vi* **1.** (*move*) apartarse **2.** (*stay*) mantenerse aparte

◆ **stand by I.** *vi* (*be ready to take action*) estar alerta **II.** *vt* (*support*) apoyar

◆ **stand down** *vi* *Brit, Aus* renunciar

◆ **stand for** *vt* **1.** (*mean*) significar **2.** (*tolerate*) aguantar

◆ **stand in** *vi* **to ~ for sb** suplir a alguien

◆ **stand out** *vi* destacar

◆ **stand up** *vi* (*be upright*) levantarse, arriscarse *Col*

standard ['stændəd, *Am:* -də·d] **I.** *n* **1.** (*level*) nivel *m* **2.** (*norm*) norma *f* **3.** (*flag*) estandarte *m* **II.** *adj* **1.** (*normal*) normal **2.** LING estándar

standardize ['stændədaɪz, *Am:* -də·-] *vt* estandarizar

standard lamp ['stændədlæmp, *Am:* -də·d-] *n* *Brit, Aus* (*floor lamp*) lámpara *f* de pie

standby ['stændbaɪ] *n* **1.** (*of money, food*) reserva *f* **2.** AVIAT lista *f* de espera; **to be** (**put**) **on ~** estar sobre aviso

stand-in ['stændɪn] *n* suplente *mf*; CINE doble *mf*

standing ['stændɪŋ] **I.** *n* **1.** (*status*) posición *f* **2.** (*duration*) **of long ~** desde hace mucho tiempo **II.** *adj* **1.** (*upright*) vertical **2.** (*permanent*) permanente

standing order *n* pedido *m* regular

standoffish [ˌstænd'ɒfɪʃ, *Am:* -'ɑ:fɪʃ] *adj* *inf* distante, estirado

standpoint ['stændpɔɪnt] *n* punto *m* de vista

standstill ['stændstɪl] *n no pl* paralización *f*; **to be at a ~** estar parado

stank [stæŋk] *pt of* **stink**

staple[1] ['steɪpl] **I.** *n* (*product, article*) producto *m* principal **II.** *adj* (*principal*) principal

staple[2] ['steɪpl] **I.** *n* (*fastener*) grapa *f* **II.** *vt* grapar

stapler ['steɪplə·, *Am:* -plə·] *n* grapadora *f*

star [sta:·, *Am:* sta:r] **I.** *n* estrella *f* **II.** *vt* <-rr-> THEAT, CINE tener como protagonista

starboard ['sta:bəd, *Am:* 'sta:r-bə·d] **I.** *n* NAUT estribor *m* **II.** *adj* de estribor

starch [stɑːtʃ, *Am:* stɑːrtʃ] *n no pl* almidón *m*

stardom ['stɑːdəm, *Am:* 'stɑːr-] *n no pl* estrellato *m,* estelaridad *f Chile*

stare [steəʳ, *Am:* steə] I. *vi* mirar fijamente II. *n* mirada *f* fija

starfish ['stɑːfɪʃ, *Am:* 'stɑːr-] <-(es)> *n* estrella *f* de mar

stark [stɑːk, *Am:* stɑːrk] I. *adj* **1.** (*desolate*) severo **2.** (*austere*) austero II. *adv* ~ **naked** en cueros, empelotado *AmL*

starkers ['stɑːkəʳs, *Am:* 'stɑːrkəz] *adj Brit, Aus, inf* (*naked*) en cueros

starling ['stɑːlɪŋ, *Am:* 'stɑːr-] *n* estornino *m*

starry ['stɑːri] <-ier, -iest> *adj* estrellado

starry-eyed [ˌstɑːri'aɪd, *Am:* 'stɑːriˌaɪd] *adj* soñador

Stars and Stripes *n* the ~ *la bandera de EE.UU.*

star sign *n* signo *m* del zodiaco

start [stɑːt, *Am:* stɑːrt] I. *vi* **1.** (*begin*) comenzar; **to ~ to do sth** empezar a hacer algo **2.** (*begin journey*) salir **3.** (*make sudden movement*) sobresaltarse II. *vt* **1.** (*begin*) comenzar **2.** (*set in operation*) poner en marcha **3.** (*establish: business*) abrir III. *n* **1.** (*beginning*) principio *m;* **to make an early/late ~** empezar temprano/tarde **2.** SPORTS salida *f* **3.** (*sudden movement*) sobresalto *m;* **to give sb a ~** dar un susto a alguien

◆ **start off** *vi* **1.** (*begin*) empezar **2.** (*begin journey*) salir

◆ **start up** I. *vt* fundar; (*vehicle*) arrancar II. *vi* empezar; (*vehicle*) arrancar

starter *n* **1.** AUTO arranque *m* **2.** *Brit, inf* GASTR entrante *m*

starting point *n* punto *m* de partida

startle ['stɑːtl, *Am:* 'stɑːrtl] *vt* sobresaltar

startling *adj* (*surprising*) asombroso; (*alarming*) alarmante

starvation [stɑː'veɪʃən, *Am:* stɑːr'-] *n no pl* hambre *m*

starve [stɑːv, *Am:* stɑːrv] I. *vi* pasar hambre, hambrear *AmL;* (*die of hunger*) morir de hambre II. *vt* hacer pasar hambre; (*of love, support*) privar

stash [stæʃ] *vt* ocultar

state [steɪt] I. *n* **1.** (*condition*) estado *m;* ~ **of siege/war** estado de sitio/guerra; ~ **of mind** estado de ánimo; **to be in a ~** *inf* estar nervioso **2.** (*nation*) estado *m* **3.** (*pomp*) **to lie in ~** yacer en la capilla ardiente II. *vt* **1.** (*express*) declarar **2.** (*specify, fix*) exponer

State Department *n no pl, Am* ≈ Ministerio *m* de Asuntos Exteriores

stately ['steɪtli] *adj* majestuoso

statement ['steɪtmənt] *n* **1.** (*declaration*) declaración *f;* **to make a ~** LAW prestar declaración **2.** (*bank statement*) extracto *m* de cuenta

state school *n* escuela *f* pública

statesman ['steɪtsmən] <-men> *n* estadista *m*

static ['stætɪk, *Am:* 'stæt̬-] I. *adj* estático II. *n* PHYS *no pl* electricidad *f* estática

station ['steɪʃən] I. *n* **1.** RAIL estación *f* **2.** (*place*) sitio *m* **3.** RADIO emisora *f* **4.** (*position*) puesto *m;* **action ~s!** MIL ¡a sus puestos! **5.** (*social position*) clase *f* social II. *vt* **1.** (*place*) colocar **2.** MIL destinar

stationary ['steɪʃənəri, *Am:* 'steɪʃəner-] *adj* inmóvil

stationer ['steɪʃənəʳ, *Am:* -ʃənə] *n Brit* dueño, -a *m, f* de una papelería

stationery ['steɪʃənəri, *Am:* 'steɪʃəner-] *n no pl* artículos *mpl* de papelería

station master *n* jefe, -a *m, f* de estación **station wagon** *n Am, Aus* furgoneta *m*

statistics [stə'tɪstɪks] *n* estadística *f*

statue ['stætʃuː] *n* estatua *f*

stature ['stætʃəʳ, *Am:* -ə] *n* **1.** (*height*) estatura *f* **2.** (*reputation*) talla *f*

status ['steɪtəs, *Am:* -t̬əs] *n no pl* **1.** (*official position*) estatus *m* **2.** (*prestige*) prestigio *m*

status quo *n no pl* statu quo *m* **status symbol** *n* signo *m* de prestigio social

statute ['stætjuːt, *Am:* 'stætʃuːt] *n*
LAW ley *f*

statutory ['stætjətəri, *Am:* 'stætʃə-
tɔːr-] *adj* legal

staunch¹ [stɔːntʃ] *adj* incondicional

staunch² [stɔːntʃ] *vt* restañar

stave [steɪv] *n* **1.** MUS pentagrama *m*
2. (*piece of wood*) duela *f*
   ◆ **stave in** <stove in, stove in> *vt*
   romper
   ◆ **stave off** <staved off, staved
   off> *vt* (*postpone*) aplazar; (*prevent*) evitar

stay [steɪ] I. *n* estancia *f*, estada *f*
AmL II. *vi* **1.** (*remain present*) quedarse **2.** (*reside temporarily*) alojarse
   ◆ **stay behind** *vi* quedar atrás
   ◆ **stay in** *vi* quedarse en casa
   ◆ **stay on** *vi* quedarse
   ◆ **stay out** *vi* no volver a casa
   ◆ **stay up** *vi* no acostarse

staying power *n no pl* resistencia *f*

STD [ˌestiːˈdiː] *n* **1.** MED *abbr of* **sexually transmitted disease** ETS *f*
2. *Brit, Aus* TECH *abbr of* **subscriber
trunk dialling** *servicio de transfe-
rencias interurbanas;* ~ **code** prefijo
m

stead [sted] *n no pl* lugar *m;* **in his/
her** ~ en su lugar; **to stand sb in
good** ~ (**for sth**) ser útil a alguien
(para algo)

steadfast ['stedfɑːst, *Am:* -fæst] *adj*
firme

steady ['stedi] I. <-ier, -iest> *adj*
1. (*stable*) fijo, firme **2.** (*regular*)
regular **3.** (*boyfriend*) formal II. *vt*
1. (*stabilize*) estabilizar **2.** (*make
calm*) calmar

steak [steɪk] *n* bistec *m*, bife *m AmL;*
(*of lamb, fish*) filete *m*

steal [stiːl] <stole, stolen> *vt, vi*
robar, cachar *AmC*, apachar *Perú*

stealth [stelθ] *n no pl* sigilo *m;* **by** ~
con sigilo

stealthy ['stelθi] *adj* sigiloso

steam [stiːm] I. *n no pl* **1.** (*water vapour*) vapor *m* **2.** *fig* **to run out of** ~
perder vigor; **to do sth under one's
own** ~ hacer algo por sus propios
medios; **to let off** ~ desahogarse

II. *vi* (*produce steam*) echar vapor
III. *vt* GASTR cocer al vapor
   ◆ **steam up** *vi* **1.** (*become steamy*)
   empañarse **2.** *inf* **to get steamed up**
   (**about sth**) acalorarse (por algo)

steam engine *n* máquina *f* de vapor

steamer ['stiːməʳ, *Am:* -ɚ] *n*
1. (*boat*) vapor *m* **2.** GASTR vaporera *f*

steamroller I. *n* apisonadora *f* II. *vt*
a. fig aplastar **steamship** *n* vapor *m*

steamy ['stiːmi] <-ier, -iest> *adj*
1. (*full of steam*) lleno de vapor
2. (*very humid*) húmedo

steel [stiːl] I. *n no pl* acero *m* II. *adj*
de acero

steelworks ['stiːlwɜːks, *Am:*
-wɜːrks] *n inv* planta *f* siderúrgica

steep¹ [stiːp] *adj* **1.** (*sharply sloping*)
empinado **2.** (*increase, fall*) pronunciado **3.** (*expensive*) exorbitante

steep² [stiːp] *vt* remojar

steeple ['stiːpl] *n* ARCHIT torre *f* con
aguja

steeplejack ['stiːpldʒæk] *n* repa-
rador(a) *m(f)* de torres

steer [stɪəʳ, *Am:* stɪr] I. *vt* dirigir;
(*car*) conducir, manejar *AmL* II. *vi*
conducir, manejar *AmL;* **to** ~ **clear
of sth/sb** evitar algo/a alguien

steering *n no pl* dirección *f*

steering wheel *n* volante *m*, guía *f*
PRico

stem [stem] I. *n* (*of plant*) tallo *m;*
(*of glass*) pie *m* II. <-mm-> *vt* detener; (*blood*) restañar

stench [stentʃ] *n no pl* hedor *m*

stencil ['stensl] I. *n* **1.** (*cut-out pattern*) plantilla *f* **2.** (*picture drawn*)
patrón *m* II. *vt* dibujar utilizando
una plantilla

stenographer [stəˈnɒɡrəfəʳ, *Am:*
-ˈnɑːɡrəfɚ] *n* estenógrafo, -a *m, f*

step [step] I. *n* **1.** (*foot movement*)
paso *m;* ~ **by** ~ paso a paso; **to take
a** ~ **towards sth** *fig* dirigirse hacia
algo; **to be in/out of** ~ llevar/no llevar el paso; *fig* estar/no estar al tanto
2. (*of stair, ladder*) peldaño *m*
3. (*measure*) **to take** ~**s** (**to do sth**)
tomar medidas (para hacer algo)
4. *pl, Brit* (*stepladder*) escalera *f*
II. <-pp-> *vi* pisar

S **s**

◆**step down** *vi* dimitir
◆**step in** *vi* intervenir
◆**step up** *vt* aumentar
stepbrother *n* hermanastro *m* **stepdaughter** *n* hijastra *f* **stepfather** *n* padrastro *m*
stepladder ['step₁lædə', Am: -ə'] *n* escalera *f* de mano
stepmother ['step₁mʌðə', Am: -ə'] *n* madrastra *f*
stepping stone ['stepɪŋstəʊn, Am: -stoʊn] *n* pasadera *f*
stepsister *n* hermanastra *f* **stepson** *n* hijastro *m*
stereo ['steriəʊ, Am: 'sterioʊ] I. *n* 1. *no pl* **in ~** en estéreo 2. (*hi-fi system*) equipo *m* (estéreo) II. *adj* estéreo
stereotype ['steriətaɪp] I. *n pej* estereotipo *m* II. *vt pej* estereotipar
sterile ['steraɪl, Am:'sterəl] *adj* estéril
sterilization [₁sterəlaɪ'zeɪʃən, Am: ₁sterəlɪ'-] *n no pl* esterilización *f*
sterilize ['sterəlaɪz] *vt* esterilizar
sterling ['stɜːlɪŋ, Am:'stɜːr-] I. *n no pl* FIN (**pound**) **~** libra *f* esterlina II. *adj* (*silver*) de ley
stern¹ [stɜːn, Am: stɜːrn] *adj* severo
stern² [stɜːn, Am: stɜːrn] *n* NAUT popa *f*
steroid ['stɪərɔɪd, Am: 'sterɔɪd] *n* esteroide *m*
stethoscope ['steθəskəʊp, Am: -skoʊp] *n* estetoscopio *m*
stew [stjuː, Am: stuː] I. *n* estofado *m*, hervido *m AmS* II. *vt* estofar; (*fruit*) hacer compota de III. *vi* cocer
steward ['stjʊəd, Am: 'stuːəd] *n* 1. AVIAT auxiliar *m* de vuelo 2. (*at concert, demonstration*) auxiliar *mf*
stewardess [₁stjʊə'des, Am: 'stuːə-dɪs] <-es> *n* azafata *f*, aeromoza *f Méx, AmS*
stick¹ [stɪk] *n* palo *m;* **walking ~** bastón *m;* MIL porra *f*
stick² [stɪk] <stuck, stuck> I. *vi* 1. (*adhere*) pegarse 2. (*be unmovable: door, window*) atascarse 3. (*endure*) **to ~ in sb's mind** grabarse a alguien (en la mente) II. *vt* 1. (*affix*) pegar 2. *inf* (*tolerate*) aguantar 3. *inf*

(*put*) poner
◆**stick around** *vi inf* quedarse
◆**stick out** *vi* 1. (*protrude*) sobresalir 2. (*endure*) **to stick it out** aguantar
◆**stick up** *vi* sobresalir
◆**stick up for** *vt* defender
sticker ['stɪkə', Am: -ə'] *n* pegatina *f*
sticking plaster *n Brit* tirita® *f,* curita® *f AmL*
stickler ['stɪklə', Am: -lə'] *n* **to be a ~ for sth** insistir mucho en algo
stick-up ['stɪkʌp] *n inf* atraco *m*
sticky ['stɪki] <-ier, -iest> *adj* (*label*) adhesivo; (*surface, hands*) pegajoso
stiff [stɪf] *adj* 1. (*rigid*) rígido, tieso; (*brush*) duro; **to have a ~ neck** tener tortícolis 2. (*price*) exorbitante
stiffen ['stɪfn] I. *vi* 1. (*become tense*) ponerse tenso; (*muscles*) agarrotarse 2. (*become stronger*) hacerse más duro II. *vt* almidonar; (*exam*) hacer más difícil
stifle ['staɪfl] *vt* sofocar
stigma ['stɪgmə] *n* estigma *m*
stile [staɪl] *n escalones que permiten pasar por encima de una cerca*
stiletto [stɪ'letəʊ, Am: -'letoʊ] <-s> *npl* (*shoes*) zapatos *mpl* de tacón de aguja
stiletto heel *n* tacón *m* de aguja
still¹ [stɪl] I. *n* CINE, PHOT fotograma *m* II. *adj* 1. (*calm*) tranquilo, quieto 2. (*water*) sin gas
still² [stɪl] *adv* 1. (*even*) aún, todavía 2. (*nevertheless*) sin embargo
stillborn ['stɪl₁bɔːn, Am: 'stɪlbɔːrn] *adj* nacido muerto
still life *n* ART naturaleza *f* muerta
stilt [stɪlt] *n* zanco *m*
stilted ['stɪltɪd, Am: -t̬ɪd] *adj* forzado
stimulant ['stɪmjələnt] *n* estimulante *m*
stimulate ['stɪmjəleɪt] *vt* estimular
stimulating *adj* estimulante
stimulation [₁stɪmjə'leɪʃən] *n no pl* estímulo *m*
stimulus ['stɪmjələs] <-li> *n* estímulo *m*
sting [stɪŋ] I. *n* 1. (*organ*) aguijón *m;*

(*injury*) picada *f* **2.** (*pain*) escozor *m* **II.** <stung, stung> *vi* picar; (*eyes*) escocer **III.** <stung, stung> *vt* picar

stingy ['stɪndʒi] <-ier, -iest> *adj inf* tacaño, pijotero *AmL*

stink [stɪŋk] **I.** *n* mal olor *m* **II.** <stank *Am*, *Aus*: stunk, stunk> *vi* apestar, bufar *AmL*

stint¹ [stɪnt] *n* período *m*

stint² [stɪnt] *vt* escatimar; **to ~ one-self of sth** privarse de algo

stir [stɜːᵣ, *Am*: stɜːr] **I.** *n* **1.** (*agitation*) **to give sth a ~** remover algo **2.** (*excitement*) conmoción *f*; **to cause a ~** causar revuelo **II.** <-rr-> *vt* **1.** (*coffee, sauce*) remover; (*fire*) atizar, avivar **2.** (*imagination*) estimular **III.** <-rr-> *vi* moverse

stirrup ['stɪrəp, *Am*: 'stɜːr-] *n* estribo *m*

stitch [stɪtʃ] **I.** <-es> *n* **1.** (*in knitting*) punto *m*; (*in sewing*) puntada *f* **2.** MED punto *m* (de sutura) **3.** (*pain*) flato *m* **II.** *vt* coser

stoat [stəʊt, *Am*: stoʊt] *n* armiño *m*

stock [stɒk, *Am*: stɑːk] **I.** *n* **1.** (*reserves*) reserva *f* **2.** COM, ECON existencias *fpl*; **to have sth in ~** tener algo en stock; **to be out of ~** estar agotado; **to take ~** hacer el inventario; *fig* hacer un balance **3.** FIN acción *f* **4.** ZOOL ganado *m* **5.** *no pl* (*line of descent*) linaje *m* **II.** *adj* (*model*) estándar; (*response*) típico **III.** *vt* **1.** (*keep in supply*) vender **2.** (*supply goods to*) suministrar

stockbroker ['stɒk,brəʊkəᵣ, *Am*: 'stɑːk,broʊkɚ] *n* corredor(a) *m(f)* de bolsa

stock cube *n* cubito *m* de caldo

stock exchange *n* bolsa *f* **stock market** *n* mercado *m* bursátil

stockpile **I.** *n* reservas *fpl* **II.** *vt* almacenar **stockroom** *n* COM almacén *m*, bodega *f Méx* **stocktaking** *n* inventario *m*

stocky ['stɒki, *Am*: 'stɑːki] <-ier, -iest> *adj* bajo y fornido

stodgy ['stɒdʒi, *Am*: 'stɑːdʒi] <-ier, -iest> *adj* pesado

stoke [stəʊk, *Am*: stoʊk] *vt* atizar

stole¹ [stəʊl, *Am*: stoʊl] *pt of* **steal**

stole² [stəʊl, *Am*: stoʊl] *n* estola *f*

stolen [stəʊln, *Am*: stoʊln] *pp of* **steal**

stolid ['stɒlɪd, *Am*: 'stɑːlɪd] *adj* impasible

stomach ['stʌmək] **I.** *n* **1.** (*internal organ*) estómago *m* **2.** (*belly*) vientre *m* **II.** *vt inf* tolerar

stomach ache *n no pl* dolor *m* de estómago

stone [stəʊn, *Am*: stoʊn] **I.** *n* **1.** GEO piedra *f*; **to be a ~'s throw** (**away**) estar a tiro de piedra **2.** (*of fruit*) hueso *m*, carozo *m CSur* **3.** *Brit*: unidad de peso equivalente a 6,35 kg **II.** *adv* ~ **hard** duro como una piedra **III.** *vt* apedrear

stone-cold *adj* helado

stone-deaf [ˌstəʊn'def, *Am*: ˌstoʊn-] *adj* sordo como una tapia

stonework ['stəʊnwɜːk, *Am*: 'stoʊnwɜːrk] *n no pl* cantería *f*

stood [stʊd] *pt, pp of* **stand**

stooge [stuːdʒ] *n* compañero *m*

stool [stuːl] *n* taburete *m*

stoop [stuːp] **I.** *n no pl* **to have a ~** ser cargado de espaldas **II.** *vi* inclinarse; **to ~ to sth** rebajarse a algo

stop [stɒp, *Am*: stɑːp] **I.** *n* **1.** (*break in activity*) pausa *f*; **to put a ~ to sth** poner fin a algo **2.** (*halting place*) parada *f* **3.** *Brit* LING punto *m* **II.** <-pp-> *vt* **1.** (*cause to cease*) parar **2.** (*switch off*) apagar **3.** (*block*) rellenar, tapar **III.** <-pp-> *vi* pararse, detenerse; **to ~ doing sth** dejar de hacer algo

◆ **stop by** *vi* pasar por

◆ **stop off** *vi* detenerse un rato

◆ **stop up** *vt* (*hole*) tapar

stopgap ['stɒpgæp, *Am*: 'stɑːp-] **I.** *n* medida *f* provisional **II.** *adj* provisional

stopover ['stɒpəʊvəᵣ, *Am*: 'stɑːpoʊvɚ] *n* (*on journey*) parada *f*; AVIAT escala *f*

stoppage ['stɒpɪdʒ, *Am*: 'stɑːpɪdʒ] *n* **1.** (*cessation of work*) interrupción *f* **2.** FIN, ECON retención *f*

stopper ['stɒpəᵣ, *Am*: 'stɑːpɚ] **I.** *n* tapón *m* **II.** *vt* taponar

stop press *n* PUBL noticias *fpl* de últi-

Sₛ

ma hora **stopwatch** *n* cronómetro *m*

storage ['stɔ:rɪdʒ] *n no pl* almacenaje *m;* INFOR almacenamiento *m*

storage heater *n Brit* acumulador *m* (de calor) **storage space** *n* espacio *m* para guardar cosas **storage tank** *n* tanque *m* de almacenamiento

store [stɔːʳ, *Am:* stɔːr] **I.** *n* **1.** *Brit* (*storehouse*) almacén *m;* **what is in ~ for us?** *fig* ¿qué nos espera en el futuro? **2.** *Am, Aus* (*shop*) tienda *f* **3.** (*supply*) reserva *f* **4.** *no pl* (*importance*) **to set ~ by sth** dar importancia a algo **II.** *vt* **1.** (*put into storage*) almacenar **2.** (*keep for future use*) guardar **3.** INFOR guardar; (*data*) archivar

storeroom ['stɔːrʊm, *Am:* 'stɔːrruːm] *n* despensa *f*

storey ['stɔːri] *n Brit, Aus* piso *m*

stork [stɔːk, *Am:* stɔːrk] *n* cigüeña *f*

storm [stɔːm, *Am:* stɔːrm] **I.** *n* **1.** METEO tormenta *f* **2.** *fig* trifulca *f;* **to take sth by ~** asaltar algo **II.** *vi* (*speak angrily*) bramar **III.** *vt* asaltar

stormy ['stɔːmi, *Am:* 'stɔːr-] <-ier, -iest> *adj* tempestuoso

story¹ ['stɔːri] <-ries> *n* **1.** (*account*) historia *f;* (*fictional*) cuento *m* **2.** (*news report*) artículo *m*

story² ['stɔːri] *n Am s.* **storey**

storybook ['stɔːribʊk] *n* libro *m* de cuentos

stout [staʊt] **I.** *n* cerveza *f* negra **II.** *adj* (*person*) robusto; (*resistance*) tenaz

stove [stəʊv, *Am:* stoʊv] *n* **1.** (*heater*) estufa *f* **2.** *Am, Aus* cocina *f*

stove in [stəʊv -, *Am:* stoʊv -] *pt, pp of* **stave in**

stow [stəʊ, *Am:* stoʊv] *vt* guardar

stowaway ['stəʊəweɪ, *Am:* 'stoʊ-] *n* polizón *m*

straddle ['strædl] *vt* sentarse a horcajadas sobre

straggle ['strægl] *vi* **1.** (*move in a disorganised group*) avanzar desordenadamente **2.** (*lag behind*) rezagarse

straight [streɪt] **I.** *n* (*straight line*) recta *f* **II.** *adj* **1.** (*not bent*) recto **2.** (*honest*) honrado, franco; **to be ~ with sb** ser sincero con alguien **3.** (*plain*) sencillo; (*undiluted*) solo **4.** (*consecutive*) seguido **5.** THEAT serio **6.** (*traditional*) convencional **7.** *inf* (*heterosexual*) heterosexual **III.** *adv* **1.** (*in a direct line*) en línea recta; **to go ~ ahead** ir todo recto **2.** (*at once*) **to get ~ to the point** ir directo al grano **3.** (*tidy*) en orden; **to put sth ~** ordenar algo

straighten ['streɪtn] *vt* enderezar; (*arm, leg*) estirar

♦**straighten out** *vt* (*problem*) resolver

straightforward [ˌstreɪt'fɔːwəd, *Am:* -'fɔːrwəd] *adj* **1.** (*honest*) honesto **2.** (*easy*) sencillo

strain¹ [streɪn] **I.** *n no pl* **1.** *no pl* (*pressure*) presión *f;* **to be under a lot of ~** tener mucho estrés **2.** *no pl* PHYS deformación *f* **3.** MED torcedura *f* **II.** *vi* esforzarse **III.** *vt* **1.** (*stretch*) estirar **2.** (*overexert*) **to ~ one's eyes** forzar la vista **3.** (*coffee*) filtrar

strain² [streɪn] *n* **1.** (*variety: of animal*) raza *f;* (*of virus*) cepa *f* **2.** MUS tono *m*

strained [streɪnd] *adj* (*relation*) tenso; (*smile*) forzado

strainer *n* colador *m*

strait [streɪt] *n* **1.** GEO estrecho *m* **2.** (*bad situation*) **to be in dire ~s** estar en grandes apuros

straitjacket ['streɪtˌdʒækɪt] *n* PSYCH, MED camisa *f* de fuerza

straitlaced [ˌstreɪt'leɪst, *Am:* 'streɪtleɪst] *adj* mojigato

strand [strænd] *n* (*of wool*) hebra *f;* (*of rope*) ramal *m;* **a ~ of hair** un mechón de pelo

strange [streɪndʒ] *adj* **1.** (*peculiar*) extraño, raro **2.** (*unfamiliar*) desconocido

stranger ['streɪndʒəʳ, *Am:* -dʒɚ] *n* desconocido, -a *m, f*

strangle ['stræŋgl] *vt* estrangular

stranglehold ['stræŋglhəʊld, *Am:* -hoʊld] *n* dominio *m* total

strap [stræp] **I.** *n* correa *f;* (*of dress*) tirante *m* **II.** <-pp-> *vt* atar [*o* sujetar] con una correa

strapping ['stræpɪŋ] **I.** *n* (*bandage*) esparadrapo *m* **II.** *adj inf* robusto

strategic [strə'ti:dʒɪk] *adj* estratégico

strategy ['strætədʒi, *Am:* 'stræt̬-] <-ies> *n* estrategia *f*

straw [strɔ:, *Am:* strɑ:] *n* **1.** *no pl* (*dry stems*) paja *f* **2.** (*for drinking*) pajita *f*, popote *m Méx*, pitillo *m And* **3.** *fig* **to be the last** ~ ser el colmo

strawberry ['strɔ:bəri, *Am:* 'strɑ:-ˌberi] <-ies> *n* fresa *f*, frutilla *f AmL*

stray [streɪ] **I.** *adj* **1.** (*dog, cat*) callejero **2.** (*hair*) suelto; (*bullet*) perdido **II.** *vi* (*wander*) errar; (*become lost*) perderse

streak [stri:k] **I.** *n* **1.** (*stripe*) raya *f* **2.** (*tendency*) vena *f;* **to be on a winning** ~ tener una buena racha **II.** *vt* rayar; **to have one's hair ~ed** hacerse mechas **III.** *vi* ir rápido

streaker *n* persona que corre desnuda en un lugar público

stream [stri:m] **I.** *n* **1.** (*small river*) arroyo *m*, estero *m Chile, Ecua* **2.** (*current*) corriente *f;* **to go against the** ~ *fig* ir a contracorriente; **to come on** ~ (*factory*) entrar en funcionamiento **3.** (*flow*) chorrito *m;* (*of people*) torrente *m* **II.** *vi* fluir **III.** *vt Brit, Aus* SCHOOL dividir en grupos de acuerdo con su aptitud académica

streamer ['stri:mə', *Am:* -mə-] *n* serpentina *f*

streamline ['stri:mlaɪn] *vt* aerodinamizar; (*method*) racionalizar

streamlined *adj* aerodinámico

street [stri:t] *n* calle *f;* **to be on the ~s** hacer la calle

streetcar *n Am* tranvía *m* **streetlamp** *n,* **street light** *n* farola *f*

streetwise ['stri:twaɪz] *adj* espabilado

strength [streŋθ] *n* **1.** *no pl* (*power*) fuerza *f;* (*of alcohol*) graduación *f* **2.** (*number of members*) **to be at full** ~ tener el cupo completo; **to be below** ~ estar corto de personal

strengthen ['streŋθən] *vt* fortalecer, reforzar

strenuous ['strenjʊəs, *Am:* -juəs]

adj (*exercise*) agotador; (*supporter*) acérrimo; (*denial*) rotundo

stress [stres] **I.** *n no pl* **1.** (*mental strain*) estrés *m* **2.** (*emphasis*) énfasis *m inv* **3.** LING acento *m* **4.** PHYS tensión *f* **II.** *vt* **1.** (*emphasise*) recalcar **2.** LING acentuar

stretch [stretʃ] **I.** <-es> *n* **1.** GEO trecho *m* **2.** (*piece*) trozo *m;* (*of road*) tramo *m;* (*of time*) período *m* **II.** *vi* estirarse **III.** *vt* **1.** (*extend*) estirar; **to ~ one's legs** estirar las piernas **2.** (*demand a lot of*) **to ~ sb's patience** poner a prueba la paciencia de alguien

stretcher ['stretʃə', *Am:* -ə-] *n* camilla *f*

stricken ['strɪkən] *adj* **1.** (*distressed*) afligido **2.** (*wounded*) herido **3.** (*afflicted*) **to be ~ with illness** estar enfermo; **she was ~ with remorse** le remordía la conciencia

strict [strɪkt] *adj* (*person*) severo, fregado *AmC;* (*control, orders*) estricto

stride [straɪd] **I.** <strode, stridden> *vi* andar a trancos **II.** *n* **1.** (*long step*) zancada *f* **2.** *fig* **to take sth in one's** ~ tomarse algo con calma

strife [straɪf] *n no pl* lucha *f*

strike [straɪk] **I.** *n* **1.** (*military attack*) ataque *m* **2.** (*withdrawal of labour*) huelga *f* **3.** (*discovery*) descubrimiento *m* **4.** *Am* (*in baseball*) golpe *m* **II.** <struck, struck> *vt* **1.** (*collide with*) golpear; **to ~ a match** encender una cerilla **2.** (*achieve*) conseguir; **to ~ a balance** encontrar un equilibrio; **to ~ a bargain with sb** hacer un trato con alguien **3.** (*manufacture: coin*) acuñar **4.** (*clock*) marcar; **the clock struck three** el reloj dio las tres **III.** <struck, struck> *vi* **1.** (*hit hard*) golpear; (*attack*) atacar **2.** (*withdraw labour*) **to ~ for sth** hacer una huelga para conseguir algo

◆ **strike back** *vi* devolver el golpe

◆ **strike down** *vt* **she was struck down by cancer** fue abatida por el cáncer

◆**strike off** vt Brit, Aus (lawyer, doctor) inhabilitar

◆**strike out** vt borrar

◆**strike up** vt (conversation) entablar; (friendship) trabar

striker ['straɪkə', Am: -kə·] n 1. SPORTS ariete mf 2. (strike participant) huelguista mf

striking ['straɪkɪŋ] adj (beauty) impresionante; (resemblance) sorprendente

string [strɪŋ] I. n 1. (twine) a. MUS cuerda f; (on puppet) hilo m; **to pull ~s** fig mover hilos; **with no ~s attached** sin compromiso alguno 2. pl MUS instrumentos mpl de cuerda 3. INFOR secuencia f II. <strung, strung> vt poner una cuerda a

string bean n Am, Aus habichuela f

stringed instrument n instrumento m de cuerda

stringent ['strɪndʒənt] adj severo, riguroso

strip [strɪp] I. vt 1. (unclothe) desnudar 2. (dismantle) desmontar II. vi desnudarse III. n tira f; (of metal) lámina f; (of land) franja f

strip cartoon n Brit historieta f

stripe [straɪp] n 1. (coloured band) raya f 2. MIL galón m

striped adj, **stripey** adj rayado, a rayas

strip lighting n alumbrado m fluorescente

stripper ['strɪpə', Am: -ə·] n persona f que hace striptease

strip-search [ˌstrɪˈsɜːtʃ, Am: ˈstrɪps-sɜːrtʃ] vt **to ~ sb** hacer desnudar a alguien para registrarle

strive [straɪv] <strove, striven o strived, strived> vi esforzarse; **to ~ to do sth** esmerarse en hacer algo

strode [strəʊd, Am: stroʊd] pt of **stride**

stroke [strəʊk, Am: stroʊk] I. vt acariciar II. n 1. (caress) caricia f 2. MED derrame m cerebral 3. (of pencil) trazo m 4. (in swimming: style) estilo m 5. (bit) **a ~ of luck** un golpe de suerte

stroll [strəʊl, Am: stroʊl] I. n paseo m; **to go for a ~** dar una vuelta II. vi dar un paseo

stroller ['strəʊlə', Am: 'stroʊlə·] n Am, Aus (pushchair) cochecito m

strong [strɒŋ, Am: strɑːŋ] I. adj 1. (powerful) fuerte 2. (physically powerful) robusto II. adj inf **to be still going ~** ir todavía bien

stronghold ['strɒŋhəʊld, Am: 'strɑːŋhoʊld] n (fortified place) fortaleza f; fig baluarte m

strongly adv fuertemente; (criticize) enérgicamente; **to be ~ opposed to sth** estar muy en contra de algo

strongroom ['strɒŋrʊm, Am: 'strɑːŋruːm] n cámara f acorazada

stroppy ['strɒpi, Am: 'strɑːpi] adj Brit, Aus, inf enfadado

strove [strəʊv, Am: stroʊv] pt of **strive**

struck [strʌk] pt, pp of **strike**

structural ['strʌktʃərəl] adj estructural

structure ['strʌktʃə', Am: -tʃə·] I. n estructura f; (building) construcción f II. vt estructurar

struggle ['strʌgl] I. n esfuerzo m; **to be a real ~** suponer un gran esfuerzo II. vi esforzarse

strum [strʌm] <-mm-> vt MUS rasguear

strung [strʌŋ] pt, pp of **string**

strut¹ [strʌt] <-tt-> vi **to ~ about** pavonearse

strut² n puntal m

stub [stʌb] I. n (of cheque) talón m; (of cigarette) colilla f II. <-bb-> vt **to ~ one's toe against sth** tropezar con algo

◆**stub out** vt (cigarette) apagar

stubble ['stʌbl] n no pl 1. (beard growth) barba f de tres días 2. AGR rastrojo m

stubborn ['stʌbən, Am: -ə·n] adj terco

stuck [stʌk] I. pt, pp of **stick²** II. adj (jammed) atascado

stuck-up [ˌstʌkˈʌp] adj inf engreído

stud¹ [stʌd] n 1. (horse) semental m, garañón m AmL 2. (establishment) caballeriza f

stud² [stʌd] n 1. (small metal item) tachón m; **collar ~** gemelo m 2. Brit,

Aus (*on shoe*) taco *m*

student ['stju:dənt, *Am:* 'stu:-] *n* estudiante *mf*

student union *n* (*organization*) asociación *f* de estudiantes; (*meeting place*) club *m* de estudiantes universitarios

studio ['stju:diəʊ, *Am:* 'stu:dioʊ] <-s> *n* estudio *m;* (*of artist*) taller *m*

studious ['stju:diəs, *Am:* 'stu:-] *adj* estudioso

study ['stʌdi] **I.** *vt* estudiar; (*evidence*) examinar **II.** *vi* estudiar **III.** <-ies> *n* estudio *m*

stuff [stʌf] **I.** *n no pl* **1.** *inf* (*things*) materia *f* **2.** (*belongings*) cosas *fpl* **3.** (*material*) material *m;* (*cloth*) tela *f* **II.** *vt* **1.** (*fill*) llenar; **to ~ sth into sth** meter algo en algo **2.** (*preserve: animal*) disecar

stuffing ['stʌfɪŋ] *n no pl* relleno *m*

stuffy ['stʌfi] *adj* (*room*) mal ventilado; (*person*) tieso

stumble ['stʌmbl] *vi* **1.** (*trip*) tropezar **2.** (*while talking*) balbucear

stumbling block *n* obstáculo *m*

stump [stʌmp] **I.** *n* (*of plant*) tocón *m;* (*of arm*) muñón *m* **II.** *vt inf* desconcertar

stun [stʌn] <-nn-> *vt* **1.** (*stupefy*) dejar pasmado **2.** (*render unconscious*) dejar sin sentido

stung [stʌŋ] *pt, pp of* **sting**

stunk [stʌŋk] *pt, pp of* **stink**

stunning ['stʌnɪŋ] *adj* (*surprising*) aturdidor

stunt [stʌnt] *n* **1.** (*acrobatics*) acrobacia *f* **2.** (*publicity action*) truco *m* publicitario

stunted *adj* enano

stuntman ['stʌntmæn] *n* especialista

stupendous [stju:'pendəs, *Am:* stu:-] *adj* estupendo

stupid ['stju:pɪd, *Am:* 'stu:-] *adj* estúpido

stupidity [stju:'pɪdəti, *Am:* stu:'pɪdəti̯] *n no pl* estupidez *f*

sturdy ['stɜ:di, *Am:* 'stɜ:r-] *adj* robusto, fuerte

stutter ['stʌtəʳ, *Am:* 'stʌt̬ə] **I.** *vi* (*stammer*) tartamudear, cancanear,

AmL **II.** *n* tartamudeo *m*

sty[1] [staɪ] *n* (*pigsty*) pocilga *f*

sty[2] [staɪ] *n,* **stye** *n* MED orzuelo *m*

style [staɪl] *n* **1.** *a.* ART, ARCHIT estilo *m* **2.** (*elegance*) elegancia *f* **3.** (*fashion*) moda *f*

stylish ['staɪlɪʃ] *adj* **1.** (*fashionable*) a la moda **2.** (*elegant*) garboso

stylus ['staɪləs] <-es> *n* estilete *m*

suave [swɑ:v] *adj* cortés; *pej* zalamero

sub [sʌb] *n* **1.** *inf abbr of* **submarine** submarino *m* **2.** *Brit, Am, inf abbr of* **subscription** suscripción *f*

subconscious [ˌsʌb'kɒnʃəs, *Am:* -'kɑ:nʃəs] **I.** *n no pl* subconsciente *m* **II.** *adj* subconsciente

subcontinent [ˌsʌb'kɒntɪnənt, *Am:* 'sʌbˌkɑ:ntnənt] *n* GEO subcontinente *m;* **the Indian ~** el subcontinente de la India

subcontract [ˌsʌb'kɒntrækt, *Am:* 'sʌbˌkɑ:n-] *vt* subcontratar

subcontractor [ˌsʌbkən'træktəʳ] *n* subcontratista *mf*

subdue [səb'dju:, *Am:* -'du:] *vt* (*tame*) controlar; (*repress*) reprimir

subdued *adj* (*colour*) suave; (*person*) apagado

subject ['sʌbdʒɪkt] **I.** *n* **1.** (*theme*) tema *m* **2.** SCHOOL, UNIV asignatura *f* **3.** POL súbdito, -a *m, f* **II.** *adj* POL subyugado; **~ to approval** pendiente de aprobación; **to be ~ to sth** estar sujeto a algo

subjective [səb'dʒektɪv] *adj* subjetivo

subject matter *n* tema *m;* (*of letter*) contenido *m*

sublet [sʌb'let] <sublet, sublet> *vt* subarrendar

submarine ['sʌbməˌri:n] *n* submarino *m inv*

submerge [səb'mɜ:dʒ, *Am:* -'mɜ:rdʒ] *vi, vt* sumergir(se)

submission [səb'mɪʃn] *n no pl* **1.** (*acquiescence*) sumisión *f* **2.** *no pl* (*of proposal*) presentación *f*

submissive [səb'mɪsɪv] *adj* sumiso

submit [səb'mɪt] <-tt-> **I.** *vt* entregar; (*proposal*) presentar **II.** *vi* someterse

S

subnormal [ˌsʌb'nɔːml, *Am:* -'nɔːr-ml] *adj* subnormal

subordinate [sə'bɔːdənət, *Am:* -'bɔːrdənɪt] I. *n* subordinado, -a *m, f* II. *adj* (*secondary*) secundario; (*lower in rank*) subordinado

subpoena [sə'piːnə] LAW I. *vt* citar II. *n* citación *f* (judicial)

subscribe [səb'skraɪb] *vi* 1. (*agree*) **to ~ to sth** suscribir algo 2. (*make susbscription*) suscribirse

subscriber [səb'skraɪbə^r, *Am:* -ɚ] *n* (*to magazine*) suscriptor(a) *m(f)*; (*to phone service*) abonado, -a *m, f*

subscription [səb'skrɪpʃn] *n* suscripción *f*; **to take out a ~ to sth** suscribirse a algo

subsequent ['sʌbsɪkwənt] *adj* posterior; **~ to …** después de…

subsequently *adv* después

subside [səb'saɪd] *vi* 1. (*lessen*) disminuir 2. (*sink*) hundirse; (*water*) bajar

subsidence [səb'saɪdns] *n no pl* hundimiento *m*; (*of water*) bajada *f*

subsidiary [səb'sɪdɪəri, *Am:* -əri] I. *adj* secundario II. <-ies> *n* ECON filial *f*

subsidize ['sʌbsɪdaɪz, *Am:* -sə-] *vt* subvencionar

subsidy ['sʌbsədi, *Am:* -sə-] <-ies> *n* subvención *f*

subsistence [səb'sɪstəns] *n* subsistencia *f*

substance ['sʌbstəns] *n* 1. *no pl* (*matter*) sustancia *f* 2. (*essence*) esencia *f* 3. (*main point*) punto *m* más importante; **the ~ of the conversation** el punto esencial de la conversación

substantial [səb'stænʃl] *adj* sustancial; (*difference*) notable

substantially [səb'stænʃəli] *adv* considerablemente

substantiate [səb'stænʃieɪt] *vt* corroborar

substitute ['sʌbstɪtjuːt, *Am:* -stətuːt] I. *vt* sustituir; **to ~ margarine for butter, to ~ butter by** [*o* with] **margarine** sustituir la mantequilla por la margarina II. *n* 1. (*equivalent*) sustituto 2. *a.* SPORTS suplente *mf*

substitution [ˌsʌbstɪ'tjuːʃn, *Am:* -stə'tuː-] *n a.* SPORTS sustitución *f*

subterranean [ˌsʌbtə'reɪnɪən] *adj* subterráneo

subtitle ['sʌbˌtaɪtl, *Am:* 'sʌbˌtaɪt̬l] I. *vt* subtitular II. *n* subtítulo *m*

subtle ['sʌtl, *Am:* 'sʌt̬-] *adj* sutil

subtlety ['sʌtlti, *Am:* 'sʌt̬lt̬i] <-ies> *n* sutileza *f*

subtotal ['sʌbˌtəʊtl, *Am:* -ˌtoʊt̬l] *n* subtotal *m*

subtract [səb'trækt] *vt* sustraer

subtraction [səb'trækʃn] *n no pl* resta *f*, sustracción *f*

suburb ['sʌbɜːb, *Am:* -ɜːrb] *n* barrio *m* periférico; **the ~s** la periferia

suburban [sə'bɜːbən, *Am:* -'bɜːr-] *adj* periférico; (*train*) de cercanías

suburbia [sə'bɜːbɪə, *Am:* -'bɜːr-] *n no pl* barrios *mpl* periféricos

subversive [səb'vɜːsɪv, *Am:* -'vɜːr-] *form* I. *adj* subversivo II. *n* persona *f* subversiva

subway ['sʌbweɪ] *n* 1. *Brit, Aus* (*walkway*) paso *m* subterráneo 2. *Am* (*railway*) metro *m*, subte *m* Arg

succeed [sək'siːd] I. *vi* tener éxito; **to ~ in doing sth** lograr hacer algo II. *vt* suceder a

succeeding *adj* siguiente; **in the ~ weeks** en las próximas semanas

success [sək'ses] *n no pl* éxito *m*

successful [sək'sesfl] *adj* exitoso; **to be ~** (*person*) tener éxito; (*business*) prosperar

succession [sək'seʃn] *n no pl* sucesión *f*; **in ~** sucesivamente

successive [sək'sesɪv] *adj* sucesivo; **six ~ weeks** seis semanas seguidas

successor [sək'sesə^r, *Am:* -ɚ] *n* sucesor(a) *m(f)*

succinct [sək'sɪŋkt] *adj* sucinto

succulent ['sʌkjʊlənt] I. *adj* suculento II. *n* planta *f* carnosa

succumb [sə'kʌm] *vi form* sucumbir

such [sʌtʃ] I. *adj* tal, semejante; **~ great weather/a good book** un tiempo/un libro tan bueno; **~ an honour** tanto honor II. *pron* **~ is life** así es la vida; **people ~ as him**

las personas que son como él; **as ~** propiamente dicho

such-and-such [ˈsʌtʃənsʌtʃ] *adj inf* tal o cual

suchlike [ˈsʌtʃlaɪk] *pron* **cookies, chocolates and ~** galletas, bombones y cosas por el estilo

suck [sʌk] *vt* succionar; (*with straw*) sorber; (*air*) aspirar; (*breast*) mamar

sucker [ˈsʌkəʳ, *Am:* -ɚ] *n* **1.** *Am* (*person*) bobo, -a *m, f* **2.** ZOOL ventosa *f*

suction [ˈsʌkʃən] *n no pl* succión *f*

Sudan [suːˈdæn] *n* Sudán *m*

Sudanese [ˌsuːdəˈniːz] *adj* sudanés

sudden [ˈsʌdən] *adj* (*immediate*) repentino, sorpresivo *AmL*; (*death*) súbito; (*departure*) imprevisto; **all of a ~** *inf* de repente

suddenly *adv* de repente

suds [sʌdz] *npl* jabonaduras *fpl*

sue [sjuː, *Am:* suː] <suing> *vt* demandar; **to ~ sb for damages** demandar a alguien por daños y perjuicios; **to ~ sb for divorce** poner a alguien una demanda de divorcio

suede [sweɪd] *n* ante *m*

suet [ˈsuːɪt] *n no pl* sebo *m*

suffer [ˈsʌfəʳ, *Am:* -ɚ] **I.** *vi* sufrir; **the economy ~ed from ...** la economía se vio afectada por... **II.** *vt* **1.** (*undergo*) sufrir **2.** (*bear*) aguantar **3.** MED padecer

sufferer [ˈsʌfərəʳ, *Am:* -ɚɚ] *n* enfermo, -a *m, f*

suffering [ˈsʌfərɪŋ] *n* sufrimiento *m*

suffice [səˈfaɪs] *vi* bastar

sufficient [səˈfɪʃnt] *adj* suficiente

suffix [ˈsʌfɪks] *n* sufijo *m*

suffocate [ˈsʌfəkeɪt] *vi* asfixiarse

sugar [ˈʃʊgəʳ, *Am:* -ɚ] **I.** *n no pl* azúcar *m* **II.** *vt* echar azúcar a

sugar beet *n* remolacha *f* azucarera

sugar cane *n* caña *f* de azúcar

suggest [səˈdʒest, *Am:* səɡˈ-] *vt* **1.** (*propose*) proponer, sugerir; **to ~ (to sb) that ...** sugerir a alguien que... **+subj 2.** (*hint*) insinuar; **what are you trying to ~?** ¿qué insinúas?

suggestion [səˈdʒestʃən, *Am:* səɡˈdʒes-] *n* sugerencia *f*; **to make the ~ that ...** sugerir que...

suicide [ˈsjuːɪsaɪd, *Am:* ˈsuːə-] *n*

1. (*act*) suicidio *m*; **to commit ~** suicidarse **2.** *form* (*person*) suicida *mf*

suit [suːt] **I.** *vt* **1.** (*be convenient*) convenir; **that ~s me fine** eso me viene bien **2.** (*be right*) ir [*o* sentar] bien; **they are well ~ed** (**to each other**) hacen (una) buena pareja **3.** (*look attractive with*) quedar bien; **this dress ~s you** este vestido te sienta bien **II.** *n* **1.** (*jacket and trousers*) traje *m*; (*jacket and skirt*) traje *m* de chaqueta **2.** LAW pleito *m* **3.** GAMES palo *m*

suitable [ˈsuːtəbl, *Am:* -ṭəbl] *adj* apropiado

suitcase [ˈsuːtkeɪs] *n* maleta *f*, valija *f RíoPl*, petaca *f Méx*

suite [swiːt] *n* **1.** (*set of rooms*) suite *f* **2.** (*set of furniture*) juego *m* **3.** MUS suite *f*

suitor [ˈsuːtəʳ, *Am:* ˈsuːṭɚ] *n a. iron* pretendiente *m*

sulfur [ˈsʌlfəʳ] *n Am* CHEM azufre *m*

sulk [sʌlk] *vi* enfurruñarse

sulky [ˈsʌlki] <-ier, -iest> *adj* enfurruñado

sullen [ˈsʌlən] *adj* malhumorado

sulphur [ˈsʌlfəʳ, *Am:* -fɚ] *n no pl* azufre *m*

sultana [sʌlˈtɑːnə, *Am:* -ˈtænə] *n* pasa *f* de Esmirna

sultry [ˈsʌltri] <-ier, -iest> *adj* **1.** (*weather*) bochornoso **2.** (*sensual*) sensual

sum [sʌm] *n* **1.** (*addition*) suma *f* **2.** (*total*) total *m*

summarize [ˈsʌməraɪz] *vt* resumir

summary [ˈsʌməri] **I.** *n* resumen *m* **II.** *adj* sumario

summer [ˈsʌməʳ, *Am:* -ɚ] **I.** *n* verano *m* **II.** *adj* de verano, veraniego

summerhouse [ˈsʌməhaʊs, *Am:* ˈ-ɚ-] *n* cenador *m*

summertime [ˈsʌmətaɪm, *Am:* ˈ-ɚ-] *n no pl* (*season*) verano *m*; **in the ~** en verano

summit [ˈsʌmɪt] *n* cima *f*; *fig* cumbre *f*

summon [ˈsʌmən] *vt* (*people*) llamar; (*meeting*) convocar; LAW citar

◆**summon up** *vt* **to ~ the courage/strength to do sth** armarse de

S
s

valor/fuerzas para hacer algo

summons ['sʌmənz] *npl* llamamiento *m;* LAW citación *f;* **to serve sb with a** ~ entregar una citación a alguien

sump [sʌmp] *n* AUTO cárter *m*

sun [sʌn] *n* sol *m;* **to do/try everything under the** ~ hacer/probar de todo

sunbathe ['sʌnbeɪð] *vi* tomar el sol

sunburn ['sʌnbɜːn, *Am:* 'sʌnbɜːrn] *n* quemadura *f* de sol

sunburned *adj,* **sunburnt** *adj* quemado (por el sol)

Sunday ['sʌndeɪ] *n* domingo *m; s. a.* **Friday**

Sunday school *n* REL ≈ catequesis *f inv*

sundial *n* reloj *m* de sol **sundown** *n Am, Aus* puesta *f* de sol

sundry ['sʌndri] *adj* varios; **all and** ~ *inf* todo el mundo

sunflower ['sʌnˌflaʊəʳ, *Am:* -ˌflaʊɚ] *n* girasol *m,* maravilla *f Chile*

sung [sʌŋ] *pp of* **sing**

sunglasses ['sʌnˌglɑːsɪz, *Am:* 'sʌnˌglæsɪs] *npl* gafas *fpl* de sol

sunk [sʌŋk] *pp of* **sink**

sunlight ['sʌnlaɪt] *n no pl* luz *f* del sol

sunlit ['sʌnlɪt] *adj* soleado

sunny ['sʌni] <-ier, -iest> *adj* **1.** *(day)* soleado **2.** *(personality)* alegre

sunrise ['sʌnraɪz] *n* amanecer *m*

sunroof ['sʌnruːf] *n* techo *m* corredizo **sunscreen** *n* filtro *m* solar

sunset ['sʌnset] *n* puesta *f* de sol

sunshade ['sʌnʃeɪd] *n* sombrilla *f*

sunshine ['sʌnʃaɪn] *n no pl* sol *m*

sunstroke *n no pl* insolación *f,* asoleada *f Col, Chile, Guat*

suntan ['sʌntæn] *n* bronceado *m*

suntanned *adj* bronceado

suntan oil *n* aceite *m* bronceador

super ['suːpəʳ, *Am:* -pɚ] *adj inf* genial

superannuation ['suːpərˌænjʊ'eɪʃn, *Am:* ˌsuːpərˌænju'-] *n Brit, Aus no pl* pensión *f* (de jubilación)

superb [suːˈpɜːb, *Am:* səˈpɜːrb] *adj* magnífico

superficial [ˌsuːpəˈfɪʃl, *Am:* ˌsuːpɚˈ-] *adj* superficial

superfluous [suːˈpɜːfluəs, *Am:* -ˈpɜːr-] *adj* superfluo

superglue® ['suːpəglu:, *Am:* -pɚ-] *n* superglue® *m*

superhighway [ˌsuːpəˈhaɪweɪ, *Am:* 'suːpɚˈ-] *n Am* autopista *f* (de varios carriles)

superimpose [ˌsuːpərɪmˈpəʊz, *Am:* -pɚɪmˈpoʊz] *vt* PHOT superponer

superintendent [ˌsuːpərɪnˈtendənt, *Am:* ˌsuːpɚ-] *n* **1.** *(person in charge)* director(a) *m(f)* **2.** *Am (head of police department)* superintendente *mf*

superior [suːˈpɪəriəʳ, *Am:* səˈpɪriɚ] **I.** *adj* **1.** *(better, senior)* superior; **to be** ~ **(to sb/sth)** estar por encima de alguien/algo **2.** *(arrogant)* de superioridad **II.** *n* superior *mf*

superiority [suːˌpɪəriˈɒrəti, *Am:* səˌpɪriˈɔːrəti] *n no pl* superioridad *f*

superlative [suːˈpɜːlətɪv, *Am:* səˈpɜːrlətɪv] *n* superlativo *m*

superman ['suːpəmæn, *Am:* -pɚ-] *n* superhombre *m;* CINE Supermán *m*

supermarket ['suːpəmɑːkɪt, *Am:* -pɚˌmɑːr-] *n* supermercado *m*

supermodel ['suːpəˌmɒdəl, *Am:* 'suːpɚˌmɑːdəl] *n* supermodelo *f*

supernatural [ˌsuːpəˈnætʃərəl, *Am:* -pɚˈnætʃɚəl] *adj* sobrenatural

superpower [ˌsuːpəˈpaʊəʳ, *Am:* 'suːpɚˌpaʊɚ] *n* POL superpotencia *f*

supersede [ˌsuːpəˈsiːd, *Am:* -pɚˈ-] *vt* sustituir

supersonic [ˌsuːpəˈsɒnɪk, *Am:* -pɚˈsɑːnɪk] *adj* AVIAT supersónico

superstar ['suːpəstɑːʳ, *Am:* 'suːpɚstɑːr] *n* superestrella *f*

superstition [ˌsuːpəˈstɪʃən, *Am:* -pɚˈ-] *n* superstición *f*

superstitious [ˌsuːpəˈstɪʃəs, *Am:* -pɚˈ-] *adj* supersticioso

superstore ['suːpəstɔːʳ, *Am:* -pɚstɔːr] *n* hipermercado *m*

supervise ['suːpəvaɪz, *Am:* -pɚ-] *vt* supervisar

supervision [ˌsuːpəˈvɪʒn, *Am:*

-pə'-] *n no pl* supervisión *f*

supervisor [ˌsuːpəˈvaɪzəʳ, *Am:* 'suː-pə-vaɪzɚ] *n* **1.** *(person in charge)* supervisor(a) *m(f)* **2.** UNIV director(a) *m(f)* de tesis

supine ['suːpaɪn, *Am:* suː'-] *adj* supino

supper ['sʌpəʳ, *Am:* -ɚ] *n* cena *f*; **to have ~** cenar

supple ['sʌpl] *adj* flexible

supplement ['sʌplɪmənt, *Am:* -lə-] **I.** *n* suplemento *m* **II.** *vt* complementar

supplementary [ˌsʌplɪˈmentəri, *Am:* -ləˈmentɚi] *adj* adicional, suplementario

supplier [səˈplaɪəʳ, *Am:* -ɚ] *n* proveedor(a) *m(f)*

supply [səˈplaɪ] **I.** <-ie-> *vt* **1.** *(provide)* suministrar; *(information)* facilitar **2.** COM proveer **II.** *n* **1.** *(act of providing: of electricity, water)* suministro *m* **2.** *no pl* ECON oferta *f*; **~ and demand** oferta y demanda; **to be in short ~** escasear

support [səˈpɔːt, *Am:* -ˈpɔːrt] **I.** *vt* **1.** *(hold up)* sostener **2.** *(provide for)* mantener; **to ~ oneself** ganarse la vida **3.** *(provide with money)* financiar **4.** *(encourage)* apoyar **5.** *Brit (follow)* ser un seguidor de **II.** *n* **1.** *no pl (backing, help)* apoyo *m*; **in ~ of sth** en apoyo de algo **2.** *(structure)* soporte *m*

supporter *n* **1.** *(of cause)* partidario, -a *m, f* **2.** *Brit* SPORTS seguidor(a) *m(f)*

supporting *adj Brit (role)* secundario

supportive [səˈpɔːtɪv, *Am:* -ˈpɔːrtɪv] *adj* comprensivo; **to be ~ of sth/sb** apoyar algo/a alguien

suppose [səˈpəʊz, *Am:* -ˈpoʊz] *vt* **1.** suponer; **to ~ (that) ...** suponer que... **2.** *(obligation)* **to be ~d to do sth** tener que hacer algo **3.** *(opinion)* **the book is ~d to be very good** dicen que el libro es muy bueno

supposedly [səˈpəʊzɪdli, *Am:* -ˈpoʊ-] *adv* supuestamente

supposing *conj* **~ that ...** suponiendo que...

suppress [səˈpres] *vt* reprimir

supreme [suːˈpriːm, *Am:* sə'-] *adj* supremo; **Supreme Court** Tribunal *m* Supremo

surcharge ['sɜːtʃɑːdʒ, *Am:* 'sɜːrtʃɑːrdʒ] **I.** *n* recargo *m* **II.** *vt* aplicar un recargo a

sure [ʃʊəʳ, *Am:* ʃʊr] **I.** *adj* **1.** *(certain)* seguro; **to be ~ of sth** estar seguro de algo; **to make ~ (that) ...** asegurarse de que...; **I'm not ~ why/ how** no sé muy bien por qué/cómo; **for ~** seguro **2.** *(confident)* **to be ~ of oneself** estar seguro de sí mismo **II.** *adv* seguro; **~ enough** en efecto

surely ['ʃɔːli, *Am:* 'ʃʊrli] *adv (certainly)* sin duda; **~ you don't expect me to believe that?** ¿no esperarás que lo crea?

surety ['ʃʊərəti, *Am:* 'ʃʊrəti] <-ies> *n* **1.** *(person)* fiador(a) *m(f)*; **to stand ~ (for sb)** ser fiador de alguien **2.** *(guarantee)* fianza *f*

surf [sɜːf, *Am:* sɜːrf] *n* olas *fpl*

surface ['sɜːfɪs, *Am:* 'sɜːr-] **I.** *n* superficie *f*; **on the ~** *fig* a primera vista **II.** *vi* salir a la superficie **III.** *vt (road)* revestir

surface mail *n* **by ~** por vía terrestre

surfboard ['sɜːfbɔːd, *Am:* 'sɜːrfbɔːrd] *n* tabla *f* de surf

surfeit ['sɜːfɪt, *Am:* 'sɜːr-] *n no pl, form* exceso *m*

surfer ['sɜːfəʳ, *Am:* 'sɜːrfɚ] *n* surfista *mf*

surfing ['sɜːfɪŋ, *Am:* 'sɜːr-] *n no pl* surf *m*

surge [sɜːdʒ, *Am:* sɜːrdʒ] **I.** *vi* abalanzarse **II.** *n* oleaje *m*

surgeon ['sɜːdʒən, *Am:* 'sɜːr-] *n* cirujano, -a *m, f*

surgery ['sɜːdʒəri, *Am:* 'sɜːr-] *n* **1.** *no pl (medical operation)* cirugía *f*; **to undergo ~** someterse a una intervención quirúrgica **2.** *Brit* POL *sesión durante la que un parlamentario atiende las consultas de sus electores*

surgical ['sɜːdʒɪkl, *Am:* 'sɜːr-] *adj* quirúrgico

Surinam(e) ['sʊənæm, *Am:* ˌsʊrɪˈnɑːm] *n* Surinam *m*

Surinamese [ˌsʊənæˈmiːz] *adj* surinamés

surly ['sɜːli, *Am:* 'sɜːr-] <-ier, -iest> *adj* hosco

surname ['sɜːneɪm, *Am:* 'sɜːr-] *n* apellido *m*

surplus ['sɜːpləs, *Am:* 'sɜːr-] I. *n* excedente *m; FIN* superávit *m* II. *adj* sobrante; **to be ~ to requirements** *Brit* estar de más

surprise [səˈpraɪz, *Am:* sɚ'-] I. *n* sorpresa *f;* **to sb's ~** para sorpresa de alguien II. *vt* sorprender

surprising *adj* sorprendente

surprisingly *adv* sorprendentemente

surrealism [səˈrɪəlɪzəm, *Am:* -'riː-ə-] *n* surrealismo *m*

surrender [səˈrendəʳ, *Am:* -dɚ] I. *vi a. MIL* rendirse II. *vt form* entregar III. *n* 1. *(giving up)* rendición *f* 2. *no pl, form* entrega *f*

surreptitious [ˌsʌrəpˈtɪʃəs, *Am:* ˌsɜːr-] *adj* subrepticio, furtivo

surrogate ['sʌrəgɪt, *Am:* 'sɜːr-] I. *adj (substitute)* sucedáneo II. *n* sustituto, -a *m, f*

surrogate mother *n* madre *f* de alquiler

surround [səˈraʊnd] I. *vt* rodear II. *n (frame)* marco *m*

surrounding *adj* de alrededor

surroundings *npl* alrededores *mpl*

surveillance [sɜːˈveɪləns, *Am:* sɚ'-] *n no pl* vigilancia *f*

survey [səˈveɪ, *Am:* sɚ'-] I. *vt* 1. *(research)* investigar 2. *(look at carefully)* contemplar 3. *Brit (examine)* examinar 5. *GEO* medir 5. *(poll)* encuestar II. *n* 1. *(poll)* encuesta *f* 2. *(report)* informe *m* 3. *(examination)* examen *m*

surveyor [səˈveɪəʳ, *Am:* sɚˈveɪɚ] *n Brit (property assessor)* tasador(a) *m(f)*

survival [səˈvaɪvl, *Am:* sɚ'-] *n no pl* supervivencia *f*

survive [səˈvaɪv, *Am:* sɚ'-] *vi, vt* sobrevivir (a)

survivor [səˈvaɪvəʳ, *Am:* sɚˈvaɪvɚ] *n* superviviente *mf*

susceptible [səˈseptəbl] *adj* susceptible; *MED* propenso

suspect¹ [səˈspekt] *vt* sospechar

suspect² ['sʌspekt] I. *n* sospechoso, -a *m, f* II. *adj* sospechoso

suspend [səˈspend] *vt* suspender

suspender [səˈspendəʳ, *Am:* -dɚ] *n* 1. *Brit (strap)* liga *f* 2. *pl, Am (braces)* tirantes *mpl,* suspensores *mpl AmL,* calzonarias *fpl Col*

suspender belt *n Brit, Aus* liguero *m,* portaligas *m inv AmL*

suspense [səˈspens] *n* 1. *(uncertainty)* incertidumbre *f* 2. *CINE* suspense *m*

suspension [səˈspentʃən] *n no pl* 1. suspensión *f* 2. *SCHOOL, UNIV* expulsión *f* temporal

suspension bridge *n* puente *m* colgante **suspension points** *npl* puntos *mpl* suspensivos

suspicion [səˈspɪʃən] *n* 1. *(belief)* sospecha *f;* **to arrest sb on ~ of sth** arrestar a alguien como sospechoso de algo 2. *no pl (mistrust)* recelo *m,* desconfianza *f* 3. *(small amount)* pizca *f*

suspicious [səˈspɪʃəs] *adj* 1. *(arousing suspicion)* sospechoso 2. *(lacking trust)* desconfiado

sustain [səˈsteɪn] *vt* 1. *(maintain)* sostener 2. *(withstand)* aguantar

sustainable [səˈsteɪnəbl] *adj* sostenible

sustained [səˈsteɪnd] *adj* continuo

sustenance ['sʌstɪnənts, *Am:* -tnəns] *n no pl* sustento *m*

SW [ˌesˈdʌbljuː] *abbr of* **southwest** SO

swab [swɒb, *Am:* swɑːb] I. *n MED* tapón *m,* frotis *m inv* II.<-bb-> *vt* 1. *MED* limpiar (con algodón) 2. *(wash)* fregar

swagger ['swægəʳ, *Am:* -ɚ] I. *vi* pavonearse II. *n* arrogancia *f*

swallow¹ ['swɒləʊ, *Am:* 'swɑːloʊ] I. *vt* tragar, engullir II. *vi* tragar saliva III. *n* trago *m*
◆ **swallow up** *vt (absorb)* tragar

swallow² ['swɒləʊ, *Am:* 'swɑːloʊ] *n ZOOL* golondrina *f*

swam [swæm] *vi pt of* **swim**

swamp [swɒmp, *Am:* swɑːmp] I. *n* pantano *m,* suampo *m AmC,* wampa f Méx **II.** vt (flood) inundar

swan [swɒn, Am: swɑːn] n cisne m

swap [swɒp, Am: swɑːp] **I.** <-pp-> vt cambiar; **to ~ sth (for sth)** cambiar algo (por algo) **II.** n cambio m

swarm [swɔːm, Am: swɔːrm] **I.** vi (move in large group) aglomerarse **II.** n **1.** (of bees) enjambre m **2.** fig multitud f

swarthy ['swɔːði, Am: 'swɔːr-] <-ier, -iest> adj moreno

swastika ['swɒstɪkə, Am: 'swɑːstɪ-] n cruz f gamada

swat [swɒt, Am: swɑːt] <-tt-> vt aplastar

sway [sweɪ] **I.** vi balancearse **II.** vt **1.** (move from side to side) balancear **2.** (persuade) persuadir **III.** n no pl **1.** liter (influence) influencia f **2.** form (control) control m; **to hold ~ over sth/sb** dominar algo/a alguien

Swazi ['swɑːzi] adj swazilandés, -esa

Swaziland ['swɑːzilænd] n Swazilandia f

swear [sweəʳ, Am: swer] <swore, sworn> **I.** vi **1.** (take oath) jurar; **I couldn't ~ to it** inf no pondría la mano en el fuego **2.** (curse) decir palabrotas **II.** vt jurar

◆ **swear in** vt LAW **to ~ sb** tomar juramento a alguien

swearword ['sweəwɜːd, Am: 'swerwɜːrd] n taco m

sweat [swet] **I.** n no pl sudor m **II.** vi sudar

sweat band n (for head) cinta f; (for wrists) muñequera f

sweater ['swetəʳ, Am: 'sweṭɚ] n jersey m

sweatshirt ['swetʃɜːt, Am: -ʃɜːrt] n sudadera f

sweaty ['sweti, Am: 'sweṭ-] <-ier, -iest> adj sudado

swede [swiːd] n Brit, Aus GASTR colinabo m

Swede [swiːd] n sueco, -a m, f

Sweden ['swiːdn] n GEO Suecia f

Swedish ['swiːdɪʃ] adj sueco

sweep [swiːp] <swept, swept> **I.** n **1.** no pl (cleaning action) barrida f **2.** (chimney cleaner) deshollina-

dor(a) m(f) **3.** (movement) **with a ~ of her arm** con un amplio movimiento del brazo **4.** (range) alcance m **II.** vt **1.** (clean with broom) barrer **2.** (remove) quitar **III.** vi barrer

◆ **sweep away** vt **1.** (remove) erradicar **2.** (carry away) arrastrar

◆ **sweep up** vt barrer

sweeper n **1.** (device) barredera f **2.** (person) barrendero, -a m, f

sweeping adj (gesture) amplio; (victory) aplastante

sweet [swiːt] **I.** <-er, -est> adj **1.** (like sugar) dulce **2.** (pleasant) agradable **3.** (smile) encantador; (person) amable **II.** n **1.** Brit, Aus (candy) caramelo m, dulce m Chile **2.** Brit, Aus (dessert) postre m

sweet-and-sour [ˌswiːtənˈsaʊəʳ, Am: -ˌsaʊɚ] adj agridulce

sweetcorn ['swiːtkɔːn, Am: -kɔːrn] n Am maíz m (tierno)

sweeten ['swiːtən] vt endulzar

sweetener n GASTR sacarina f

sweetheart ['swiːthɑːt, Am: -hɑːrt] n **1.** (term of endearment) cariño m **2.** (boyfriend, girlfriend) novio, -a m, f

sweetness n no pl dulzor m

sweet pea n guisante m de olor

swell [swel] <swelled, swollen o swelled> **I.** vt **1.** (size) hinchar **2.** (number) engrosar **II.** vi **1.** (get bigger) hincharse **2.** (increase) aumentar **III.** n no pl (of sea) oleaje m **IV.** <-er, -est> adj Am, inf genial

swelling n hinchazón m

sweltering adj sofocante

swept [swept] vt, vi pt, pp of **sweep**

swerve [swɜːv, Am: swɜːrv] **I.** vi virar bruscamente **II.** n finta f; (of car) viraje m brusco

swift¹ [swɪft] adj (fast-moving) rápido; (occurring quickly) súbito

swift² [swɪft] n ZOOL vencejo m

swig [swɪg] n inf trago m

swill [swɪl] **I.** n no pl bazofia f **II.** vt **1.** (swirl) remover **2.** (rinse) baldear

swim [swɪm] **I.** <swam, swum> vi **1.** (in water) nadar **2.** (be full of water) estar inundado **3.** (whirl) **her head was ~ming** la cabeza le daba

vueltas **II.** <swam, swum> *vt*
1. (*cross*) cruzar a nado **2.** (*do*) **to** ~
a few strokes dar cuatro brazadas
III. *n* nado *m;* **I'm going to have a**
~ voy a nadar

swimmer ['swɪmər, *Am:* -ə·] *n* nada-
dor(a) *m(f)*

swimming *n no pl* natación *f*

swimming cap *n* gorro *m* de natación **swimming costume** *n Brit,*
Aus traje *m* de baño

swimmingly *adv inf* **to go** ~ ir sobre
ruedas

swimming pool *n* piscina *f,* alberca *f*
Méx, pileta *f Arg* **swimming**
trunks *npl* traje *m* de baño (de caballero)

swimsuit ['swɪmsuːt] *n Am* bañador
m

swindle ['swɪndl] **I.** *vt* estafar **II.** *n*
estafa *f*

swine [swaɪn] *n* **1.** *liter* (*pig*) cerdo
m **2.** *inf* (*person*) cabrón, -ona *m, f*

swing [swɪŋ] **I.** *n* **1.** (*movement*)
vaivén *m* **2.** (*hanging seat*) columpio
m, burro *m AmC* **3.** (*sharp change*)
cambio *m* en redondo; POL viraje *m*
4. *no pl* MUS swing *m* **5.** *fig* **to get**
(**back**) **into the** ~ **of things** *inf*
coger el tranquillo a algo
II. <swung, swung> *vi* **1.** (*move*
back and forth) oscilar; (*move circu-*
larly) dar vueltas **2.** (*on hanging*
seat) columpiarse **III.** <swung,
swung> *vt* **1.** (*move back and*
forth) balancear **2.** *inf* (*influence*) influir

swing bridge *n* puente *m* giratorio
swing door *n Brit, Aus* puerta *f* giratoria

swingeing ['swɪndʒɪŋ] *adj Brit*
(*cut*) salvaje; (*criticism*) feroz

swipe [swaɪp] **I.** *vt* **1.** *Brit* (*swat*)
abofetear **2.** *inf* (*steal*) robar
3. (*card*) pasar **II.** *n* golpe *m*

swirl [swɜːl, *Am:* swɜːrl] **I.** *vi, vt* arre-
molinar(se) **II.** *n* remolino *m*

swish [swɪʃ] **I.** *vi* hacer frufrú
II. <-er, -est> *adj inf* elegante **III.** *n*
(*of cane*) silbido *m;* (*of dress*) frufrú
m

Swiss [swɪs] *adj* suizo

switch [swɪtʃ] **I.** <-es> *n* **1.** ELEC interruptor *m,* suiche *m Méx*
2. (*change*) cambio *m* **II.** *vt* cambiar;
to ~ **sth for sth** cambiar algo por
algo

◆ **switch off** *vt* apagar; (*water, elec-*
tricity) cortar

◆ **switch on** *vt* encender

switchboard ['swɪtʃbɔːd, *Am:*
-bɔːrd] *n* TEL centralita *f*

Switzerland ['swɪtsələnd, *Am:*
-səˈlənd] *n* Suiza *f*

swivel ['swɪvəl] **I.** *n* plataforma *f* giratoria **II.** <*Brit:* -ll-, *Am:* -l-> *vt* girar

swollen ['swəʊlən, *Am:* 'swoʊ-]
I. *pp of* **swell II.** *adj* hinchado

swoon [swuːn] *vi* desvanecerse

swoop [swuːp] **I.** *n* **1.** (*dive*) caída *f*
en picado **2.** *inf* (*surprise attack*) redada *f* **II.** *vi* bajar en picado

swop [swɒp, *Am:* swɑːp] <-pp->
vt, vi Brit, Can s. **swap**

sword [sɔːd, *Am:* sɔːrd] *n* espada *f*

swordfish <-(es)> *n* pez *m* espada

swore [swɔː, *Am:* swɔːr] *pt of*
swear

sworn [swɔːn, *Am:* swɔːrn] **I.** *pp of*
swear II. *adj* jurado

swot [swɒt, *Am:* swɑːt] <-tt-> *vi*
Brit, Aus, inf hacer codos, mache-
tearse *Méx*

swum [swʌm] *pp of* **swim**

swung [swʌŋ] *pt, pp of* **swing**

syllabi ['sɪləbaɪ] *n pl of* **syllabus**

syllable ['sɪləbl] *n* sílaba *f*

syllabus ['sɪləbəs] <-es, *form:* sylla-
bi> *n* (*in general*) plan *m* de estudios; (*for specific subject*) programa
m

symbol ['sɪmbl] *n* símbolo *m*

symbolic(al) [sɪmˈbɒlɪk(l), *Am:*
-ˈbɑːlɪk-] *adj* simbólico

symbolism ['sɪmbəlɪzəm] *n no pl*
simbolismo *m*

symbolize ['sɪmbəlaɪz] *vt* simbolizar

symmetrical [sɪˈmetrɪkl] *adj* simétrico

symmetry ['sɪmətri] *n no pl a.* MAT
simetría *f*

sympathetic [ˌsɪmpəˈθetɪk, *Am:*
-ˈθet̬-] *adj* (*understanding*) com-

prensivo; (*sympathizing*) receptivo;
to be ~ towards sb/sth apoyar a alguien/algo

sympathize ['sɪmpəθaɪz] *vi* mostrar comprensión; **to ~ with sb** simpatizar con alguien; (*feel compassion for*) compadecerse de alguien

sympathizer *n* simpatizante *mf*

sympathy ['sɪmpəθi] *n no pl* (*compassion*) compasión *f;* (*understanding*) comprensión *f;* **you have my
deepest ~** le acompaño en el sentimiento

symphony ['sɪmfəni] *n* sinfonía *f*

symposium [sɪm'pəʊziəm, *Am:*
-'poʊ-] <-s *o* -sia> *n form* simposio
m

symptom ['sɪmptəm] *n* síntoma *m*

synagogue ['sɪnəgɒg, *Am:* -gɑ:g]
n sinagoga *f*

syndicate ['sɪndɪkət, *Am:* -dəkɪt] *n*
1. ECON consorcio *m* **2.** PUBL agencia *f*
de noticias

syndrome ['sɪndrəʊm, *Am:*
-droʊm] *n* síndrome *m*

synonym ['sɪnənɪm] *n* sinónimo *m*

synopsis [sɪ'næpsɪs] <-es> *n* sinopsis *f inv*

syntax ['sɪntæks] *n no pl* sintaxis *f
inv*

synthetic [sɪn'θetɪk, *Am:* -'θeṭ-]
adj sintético

syphilis ['sɪfɪlɪs, *Am:* 'sɪflɪs] *n no pl*
sífilis *f inv*

syphon ['saɪfn] *n* sifón *m*

Syria ['sɪriə] *n* Siria *f*

Syrian ['sɪriən] *adj* sirio

syringe [sɪ'rɪndʒ, *Am:* sə'-] *n* jeringuilla *f*

syrup ['sɪrəp] *n no pl* **1.** GASTR almíbar *m*, sirope *m AmC, Col* **2.** MED jarabe *m*

system ['sɪstəm] *n* sistema *m;* **to get
something out of one's ~** *inf* quitarse algo de encima

systematic [ˌsɪstə'mætɪk, *Am:*
-'mæṭ-] *adj* sistemático

systems analyst *n* analista *mf* de sistemas

T t

T, t [ti:] *n* T, t *f;* **~ for Tommy** *Brit,* **~
for Tare** *Am* T de Tarragona

t *abbr of* **tonne** t (*Brit: 1,016 kilos;
Am: 907 kilos*)

ta [tɑ:] *interj Brit, inf* gracias

TA *n Brit abbr of* **Territorial Army**
*ejército voluntario de reservistas
británico*

tab [tæb] *n* **1.** (*flap*) solapa *f;* (*on
file*) lengüeta *f* **2.** (*label*) etiqueta *f;*
to keep ~s on sb *fig* no perder de
vista a alguien

tabby ['tæbi] *n* gato *m* atigrado

table ['teɪbl] *n* **1.** mesa *f;* **to set the
~** poner la mesa **2.** MAT tabla *f*
3. (*list*) lista *f;* **~ of contents** índice
m

tablecloth ['teɪblklɒθ, *Am:* -klɑ:θ]
n mantel *m* **tablespoon** *n* (*spoon*)
cucharón *m;* (*amount*) cucharada *f*

tablet ['tæblɪt] *n* (*pill*) comprimido
m; (*of stone*) lápida *f*

table tennis *n no pl* ping-pong *m*

tabloid ['tæblɔɪd] *n* diario *m* sensacionalista

taboo [tə'bu:] **I.** *n* tabú *m* **II.** *adj*
tabú

tacit ['tæsɪt] *adj* tácito

tack [tæk] **I.** *n* **1.** (*nail*) tachuela *f*
2. (*approach*) **to try a different ~**
intentar un enfoque distinto **II.** *vt*
1. (*nail down*) clavar con tachuelas
2. (*sew*) hilvanar **III.** *vi* NAUT virar

tackle ['tækl] **I.** *vt* **1.** (*in soccer*) entrar a; (*in rugby, US football*) placar
2. (*deal with: issue*) abordar; (*problem*) atacar; **to ~ sb about sth** enfrentarse con alguien por algo **II.** *n
no pl* **1.** (*in soccer*) entrada *f;* (*in
rugby, US football*) placaje *m*
2. (*equipment*) equipo *m*

tacky ['tæki] <-ier, -iest> *adj inf*
(*showy*) vulgar

tact [tækt] *n no pl* tacto *m*

tactful ['tæktfl] *adj* discreto

tactic ['tæktɪk] *n* ~(**s**) táctica *f*

tactical ['tæktɪkl] *adj* táctico

tactile ['tæktaɪl, *Am:* -tl] *adj form*
táctil

tactless ['tæktləs] *adj* falto de tacto

tadpole ['tædpəʊl, *Am:* -poʊl] *n*
renacuajo *m*

tag [tæg] **I.** *n* **1.** (*label*) etiqueta *f;*
(*metal*) herrete *m* **2.** *no pl* (*game*) **to
play** ~ jugar al pillapilla **II.** <-gg->
vt etiquetar

tail [teɪl] **I.** *n* **1.** ANAT, AVIAT cola *f;* (*of
dog, bull*) rabo *m* **2.** *pl* (*side of coin*)
cruz *f* **II.** *vt* seguir

◆ **tail off** *vi* disminuir

tailback ['teɪlbæk] *n Brit* caravana *f*
de coches

tailor ['teɪləʳ, *Am:* -lə] *n* sastre *m*

tailor-made [ˌteɪləˈmeɪd, *Am:*
-ləˈ-] *adj* hecho a medida

tailpipe ['teɪlpaɪp] *n Am* tubo *m* de
escape

taint [teɪnt] *vt* (*food*) contaminar;
(*reputation*) manchar

Taiwan [ˌtaɪˈwɑːn] *n* Taiwán *m*

Tajikistan [tɑːˈdʒiːkɪˌstɑːn] *n* Tayi-
kistán *m*

take [teɪk] **I.** *n* PHOT, CINE toma *f*
II. <took, taken> *vt* **1.** (*accept*)
aceptar; (*advice*) seguir; (*criticism*)
soportar; (*responsibility*) asumir;
(*medicine*) tomar; **to ~ sth seriously** tomar algo en serio; **to ~
one's time** tomarse su tiempo; **to ~
sth as it comes** aceptar algo tal y
como es **2.** (*hold*) coger, agarrar *AmL*
3. (*capture: prisoners*) prender;
(*city*) conquistar; (*power*) tomar; **to
~ office** entrar en funciones
4. (*bring*) llevar **5.** (*require*) requerir
6. (*have: decision, holiday*) tomar;
to ~ a rest descansar **7.** (*feel, assume*) **to ~ (an) interest in sth** interesarse por algo; **to ~ offence**
ofenderse; **to ~ pity on sb** apiadarse
de alguien; **I ~ it that ...** supongo
que... **8.** (*photograph*) sacar **9.** (*bus,
train*) coger, tomar *AmL*

◆ **take after** *vt* parecerse a

◆ **take apart** *vt* **1.** (*disassemble*)
desmontar **2.** (*destroy*) despedazar

◆ **take away** *vt* (*remove*) quitar;
MAT restar

◆ **take back** *vt* **1.** (*return*) devolver

2. (*accept back*) aceptar **3.** (*repos-
sess*) recobrar **4.** (*retract*) retractar

◆ **take down** *vt* **1.** (*remove*) quitar;
(*from high place*) bajar **2.** (*write
down*) apuntar

◆ **take in** *vt* **1.** (*bring inside*) recoger, acoger (en casa) **2.** (*deceive*)
to be taken in by sb ser engañado
por alguien **3.** (*understand*) comprender

◆ **take off I.** *vt* **1.** (*remove from*)
retirar **2.** (*clothes*) quitarse **3.** *Brit*
(*imitate*) imitar **II.** *vi* AVIAT despegar

◆ **take on** *vt* **1.** (*accept*) aceptar
2. (*fight*) enfrentarse a

◆ **take out** *vt* **1.** (*remove*) quitar;
(*withdraw*) retirar **2.** (*bring outside*)
sacar

◆ **take over** *vt* **1.** (*buy out*) comprar
2. (*seize control*) tomar el control de

◆ **take to** *vt* (*start to like*) coger
simpatía a, encariñarse con *AmL;* **to
~ drink** darse a la bebida

◆ **take up I.** *vt* **1.** (*bring up*) subir
2. (*start doing*) comenzar **3.** (*adopt*)
adoptar **II.** *vi* **to ~ with sb** relacionarse con alguien

taken *vt pp of* **take**

take-off ['teɪkɒf, *Am:* -ɑːf] *n* AVIAT
despegue *m*

takeover ['teɪkˌəʊvəʳ, *Am:* -ˌoʊvə]
n POL toma *f* del poder; ECON adquisición *f*

takeover bid *n* oferta *f* pública de
adquisición de acciones

taking ['teɪkɪŋ] *n* **1.** *no pl* **it's yours
for the** ~ es tuyo si lo quieres **2.** *pl*
(*receipts*) ingresos *mpl*

talc [tælk] *n no pl* polvos *mpl* de
talco

tale [teɪl] *n* cuento *m;* **to tell ~s** *fig*
chivarse

talent ['tælənt] *n* talento *m*

talented *adj* talentoso

talk [tɔːk] **I.** *n* **1.** (*conversation*) conversación *f,* plática *f Méx* **2.** (*lecture*)
charla *f* **3.** *pl* (*discussions*) negociaciones *fpl* **II.** *vi* hablar; **look who's
~ing** *inf* ¡mira quién habla!

◆ **talk over** *vt* **to talk sth over** hablar algo

talkative ['tɔːkətɪv, *Am:* - t̬ɪv] *adj*

locuaz

talker *n* hablador(a) *m(f)*

talk show *n* programa *m* de entrevistas

tall [tɔːl] *adj* alto

tally¹ ['tæli] <-ie-> *vi* concordar

tally² <-ies> *n* cuenta *f*

talon ['tælən] *n* garra *f*

tambourine [ˌtæmbə'riːn] *n* pandereta *f*

tame [teɪm] *adj* **1.** (*domesticated*) doméstico; (*not savage*) manso **2.** (*unexciting*) soso

tamper with *vt* manosear

tan [tæn] I. <-nn-> *vi* broncearse II. <-nn-> *vt* **1.** (*make brown*) broncear **2.** (*leather*) curtir III. *n* bronceado *m*

tang [tæŋ] *n* olor *m* penetrante

tangent ['tændʒənt] *n* tangente *f*; **to go off at a ~** salirse por la tangente

tangerine [ˌtændʒə'riːn] *n* mandarina *f*

tangible ['tændʒəbl] *adj* tangible

tangle ['tæŋgl] I. *n* **1.** (*in hair, string*) maraña *f* **2.** *fig* (*confusion*) enredo *m* II. *vt* enredar

tango ['tæŋgəʊ, *Am:* -goʊ] *n* tango *m*

tangy ['tæŋi] <-ier, -iest> *adj* fuerte

tank [tæŋk] *n* **1.** (*container*) depósito *m*; (*aquarium*) acuario *m* **2.** MIL tanque *m*

tanker ['tæŋkər, *Am:* -ɚ] *n* (*lorry*) camión *m* cisterna; (*ship*) buque *m* cisterna; **oil ~** petrolero *m*

tanned [tænd] *adj* bronceado

tanner ['tænər, *Am:* -ɚ] *n* curtidor(a) *m(f)*

tantalizing *adj* tentador

tantamount ['tæntəmaʊnt, *Am:* -t̬ə-] *adj* **to be ~ to sth** equivaler a algo

tantrum ['tæntrəm] *n* berrinche *m*, dengue *m Méx*; **to throw a ~** coger [*o* agarrar *AmL*] una rabieta

Tanzania [ˌtænzə'nɪə, *Am:* -'niːə] *n* Tanzania *f*

tap¹ [tæp] *n* **1.** *Brit* (*for water*) grifo *m*, bitoque *m Méx, RíoPl* **2.** TEL micrófono *m* de escucha

tap² [tæp] *n* golpecito *m*

tap dance ['tæpˌdɑːnts, *Am:* -ˌdænts] *n* claqué *m*

tape [teɪp] I. *n* **1.** (*adhesive strip*) cinta *f* adhesiva; MED esparadrapo *m* **2.** (*measure*) cinta *f* métrica **3.** (*cassette*) cinta *f*, tape *m RíoPl* II. *vt* **1.** (*fasten with tape*) poner una cinta a **2.** (*record*) grabar

tape measure *n* metro *m*

taper ['teɪpər, *Am:* -pɚ] *n* cerilla *f* ◆ **taper off** *vi* disminuir

tape recorder *n* grabadora *f*

tapestry ['tæpɪstri, *Am:* -əstri] *n* **1.** (*art form*) tapicería *f* **2.** (*object*) tapiz *m*

tapeworm ['teɪpwɜːm, *Am:* -wɜːrm] *n* tenia *f*, solitaria *f*

tar [tɑːr, *Am:* tɑːr] *n no pl* alquitrán *m*

target ['tɑːgɪt, *Am:* 'tɑːr-] *n* blanco *m*

tariff ['tærɪf, *Am:* 'ter-] *n* ECON arancel *m*

tarmac® ['tɑːmæk, *Am:* 'tɑːr-] *n no pl, Brit* asfalto *m*

tarnish ['tɑːnɪʃ, *Am:* 'tɑːr-] *vt* deslustrar

tarpaulin [tɑː'pɔːlɪn, *Am:* tɑːr-'pɑː-] *n* lona *f* impermeabilizada

tart¹ [tɑːt, *Am:* tɑːrt] *adj* (*sharp*) agrio; (*acid*) ácido

tart² [tɑːt, *Am:* tɑːrt] *n* GASTR tarta *f*

tartan ['tɑːtn, *Am:* 'tɑːrtn] *n* tartán *m*

task [tɑːsk, *Am:* tæsk] *n* tarea *f*, tonga *f Col*; **to take sb to ~** llamar la atención a alguien

taskforce *n* equipo *m* de trabajo

tassel ['tæsl] *n* borla *f*

taste [teɪst] I. *n* **1.** *no pl* sabor *m*; **to have a ~ of sth** probar algo **2.** (*liking*) gusto *m*; **to get a ~ for sth** tomar el gusto a algo II. *vt* **1.** (*food, drink*) saborear **2.** (*experience*) experimentar III. *vi* **to ~ of sth** saber a algo

tastebud ['teɪstbʌd] *n* papila *f* gustativa

tasteful ['teɪstfəl] *adj* con gusto

tasteless ['teɪstləs] *adj* **1.** (*food*) soso **2.** (*clothes, remark*) de mal

T t

gusto

tasty ['teɪsti] *adj* sabroso

tattered ['tætəd, *Am:* 'tæt̬ə·d] *adj* hecho jirones

tatters ['tætə^rz, *Am:* 'tæt̬ə·z] *npl* jirones *fpl;* **to be in** ~ estar hecho jirones

tattoo [tə'tu:, *Am:* tæt'u:] I. *n* (*on skin*) tatuaje *m* II. *vt* tatuar

tatty ['tæti, *Am:* 'tæt̬-] <-ier, -iest> *adj pej* estropeado

taught [tɔːt, *Am:* tɑːt] *pt, pp of* **teach**

taunt [tɔːnt, *Am:* tɑːnt] *vt* burlarse de

Taurus ['tɔːrəs] *n* Tauro *m*

taut [tɔːt, *Am:* tɑːt] *adj* (*wire, string*) tensado; (*skin*) terso

tautology [tɔː'tɒlədʒi, *Am:* tɑː'tɑːlə-] <-gies> *n* tautología *f*

tavern ['tævən, *Am:* -ə·n] *n* taberna *f,* estanquillo *m Ecua*

tawdry ['tɔːdri, *Am:* 'tɑː-] <-ier, -iest> *adj pej* hortera

tax [tæks] FIN I. <-es> *n* impuesto *m;* **to put a ~ on sth** gravar algo con un impuesto; **free of** ~ exento de impuestos II. *vt* gravar con un impuesto

taxable ['tæksəbl] *adj* imponible

tax allowance *n* desgravación *f* fiscal

taxation [tæk'seɪʃən] *n no pl* impuestos *mpl*

tax avoidance *n* evasión *f* de impuestos **tax collector** *n* recaudador(a) *m(f)* de impuestos **tax evasion** *n* evasión *f* de impuestos **tax-free** *adj* libre de impuestos **tax haven** *n* paraíso *m* fiscal

taxi ['tæksi] *n* taxi *m*

taxi driver *n* taxista *mf,* ruletero, -a *m, f AmC, Méx*

taxing *adj* difícil

taxi rank *n Brit,* **taxi stand** *n Am* parada *f* de taxis

taxonomy [tæk'sɒnəmi, *Am:* -'sɑː-nə-] *n* taxonomía *f*

taxpayer ['tæks,peɪə^r, *Am:* -ə·] *n* contribuyente *mf* **tax relief** *n* exención *f* de impuestos **tax return** *n* declaración *f* de renta **tax year** *n* año *m* fiscal

TB [ˌtiː'biː] *n abbr of* **tuberculosis** tuberculosis *f inv*

tea [tiː] *n* **1.** *no pl* (*drink*) té *m;* **a cup of** ~ una taza de té; **camomile** ~ infusión *f* de manzanilla; **not for all the** ~ **in China** ni por todo el oro del mundo **2.** *Brit* (*afternoon meal*) merienda *f; Aus* (*evening meal*) cena *f*

tea bag *n* bolsita *f* de té

teach [tiːtʃ] <taught, taught> *vt* enseñar; **to** ~ **sb a lesson** *fig* dar una lección a alguien

teacher ['tiːtʃə^r, *Am:* -tʃə·] *n* profesor(a) *m(f)*

teacher training *n* formación *f* de profesorado

teaching *n* **1.** *no pl* (*profession*) docencia *f* **2.** *pl* (*doctrine*) enseñanza *f*

teacup *n* taza *f* de té

teak [tiːk] *n no pl* teca *f*

team [tiːm] *n* equipo *m*

◆ **team up** *vi* **to** ~ **with** asociarse con

team-mate *n* compañero, -a *m, f* **teamwork** *n* trabajo *m* en equipo

teapot ['tiːpɒt, *Am:* -pɑːt] *n* tetera *f*

tear¹ [tɪə^r, *Am:* tɪr] *n* lágrima *f;* **to burst into** ~**s** echarse a llorar

tear² [teə^r, *Am:* ter] I. *n* rotura *f* II. <tore, torn> *vt* rasgar; (*muscle*) distender; **to** ~ **a hole in sth** hacer un agujero en algo; **to be torn between two possibilities** no saber qué posibilidad elegir III. <tore, torn> *vi* rasgarse

◆ **tear apart** *vt* destrozar

◆ **tear down** *vt* derribar

◆ **tear into** *vt* arremeter contra

◆ **tear up** *vt* despedazar

teardrop ['tɪədrɒp, *Am:* 'tɪrdrɑːp] *n* lágrima *f*

tearful ['tɪəfəl, *Am:* 'tɪrfl] *adj* lloroso

tear gas *n* gas *m* lacrimógeno

tea room *n* salón *m* de té

tease [tiːz] I. *vt* **1.** (*make fun of*) tomar el pelo a **2.** (*provoke*) provocar; (*sexually*) tentar **3.** TECH cardar II. *n* bromista *mf;* (*sexually*) provocador(a) *m(f)*

teashop *n Brit* salón *m* de té **teaspoon** *n* (*spoon*) cucharita *f;* (*amount*) cucharadita *f*

teaspoonful ['tiːspuːnfʊl] *n* cucharadita *f*

tea-strainer ['tiːˌstreɪnəʳ, *Am:* -ɚ] *n* colador *m* para el té

teat [tiːt] *n* (*of animal*) teta *f*; (*of bottle*) tetina *f*

teatime ['tiːtaɪm] *n Brit* hora *f* del té

tea towel *n Brit* paño *m* de cocina

technical ['teknɪkəl] *adj* técnico

technicality [ˌteknɪˈkæləti, *Am:* -nəˈkælət̬i] <-ies> *n* (*detail*) detalle *m* técnico

technician [tekˈnɪʃn] *n* técnico, -a *m, f*

technique [tekˈniːk] *n* técnica *f*

technological [ˌteknəˈlɒdʒɪkl, *Am:* -ˈlɑːdʒɪ-] *adj* tecnológico

technology [tekˈnɒlədʒi, *Am:* -ˈnɑːlə-] *n* tecnología *f*

teddy bear ['tedɪ-] *n* osito *m* de peluche

tedious ['tiːdiəs] *adj* aburrido, tedioso

tedium ['tiːdɪəm] *n no pl* tedio *m*

tee [tiː] *n* SPORTS tee *m*

teem [tiːm] *vi* to ~ with sth estar repleto de algo

teeming *adj* muy numeroso

teen ['tiːn] *n* adolescente *mf*

teenage(d) ['tiːneɪdʒ(d)] *adj* adolescente

teenager ['tiːneɪdʒəʳ, *Am:* -dʒɚ] *n* adolescente *mf*

teens [tiːnz] *npl* to be in one's ~ no haber cumplido los veinte años

tee-shirt ['tiːʃɜːt, *Am:* -ʃɜːrt] *n* camiseta *f*

teeter ['tiːtəʳ, *Am:* -t̬ɚ] *vi* to ~ (around) tambalearse; to ~ on the brink of sth estar a punto de algo

teeth [tiːθ] *pl of* **tooth**

teetotal [tiːˈtəʊtl, *Am:* tiːˈtoʊt̬l] *adj* abstemio

tel. *abbr of* **telephone** tel.

telecommunications ['telɪkəˌmjuːnɪˈkeɪʃnz] *npl* telecomunicaciones *fpl*

teleconference ['telɪˌkɒnfərəns, *Am:* -ˌkɑːn-] *n* teleconferencia *f*

telegram ['telɪgræm] *n* telegrama *m*

telegraph ['telɪgrɑːf, *Am:* -græf] *n*

no *pl* telégrafo *m*

telegraph post *n Brit, Aus* poste *m* telegráfico

telepathy [tɪˈlepəθi, *Am:* təˈ-] *n no pl* telepatía *f*

telephone ['telɪfəʊn, *Am:* -əfoʊn] **I.** *n* teléfono *m* **II.** *vt* llamar por teléfono **III.** *vi* telefonear

telephone book *n* guía *f* telefónica **telephone booth** *n,* **telephone box** *n Am* cabina *f* telefónica **telephone call** *n* llamada *f* telefónica **telephone directory** *n* guía *f* telefónica **telephone exchange** *n Brit* central *f* telefónica **telephone number** *n* número *m* de teléfono

telesales ['telɪseɪls] *n no pl* ventas *fpl* por teléfono

telescope ['telɪskəʊp, *Am:* -əskoʊp] **I.** *n* telescopio *m* **II.** *vi* plegarse

televise ['telɪvaɪz, *Am:* 'telə-] *vt* televisar

television ['telɪˌvɪʒən, *Am:* 'teləˌvɪʒ-] *n* televisión *f*

television camera *n* cámara *f* de televisión **television program** *n Am, Aus,* **television programme** *n Brit* programa *m* de televisión **television set** *n* televisor *m*

tell [tel] <told, told> **I.** *vt* **1.** (*say*) decir; to ~ sb of sth comunicar algo a alguien; I told you so te avisé; you're ~ing me! *inf* ¡a mí me lo vas a contar! **2.** (*narrate*) contar **3.** (*command*) to ~ sb to do sth ordenar a alguien hacer algo; do as you're told *inf* haz lo que te mandan **4.** (*distinguish*) to ~ sth from sth distinguir algo de algo **5.** (*know*) there is no telling no hay manera de saberlo **II.** *vi* **1.** hablar; to ~ of sth hablar de algo **2.** (*know*) saber; you never can ~ nunca se sabe; who can ~? ¿quién sabe?

◆ **tell apart** *vt* distinguir

◆ **tell off** *vt* to tell sb off for sth reñir a alguien por algo

◆ **tell on** *vt* to ~ sb chivarse de alguien

teller ['teləʳ, *Am:* -ɚ] *n* **1.** POL escrutador(a) *m(f)* **2.** FIN cajero, -a *m, f*

telling ['telɪŋ] *adj* 1.(*revealing*) revelador 2.(*significant*) contundente

telling-off ['telɪŋ'ɒf, *Am:* ˌtelɪŋ'ɑːf] <tellings-off> *n* **to give sb a ~ for (doing) sth** echar una bronca a alguien por (hacer) algo

telly ['teli] *n Brit, Aus, inf* tele *f*

temp [temp] I. *vi* trabajar temporalmente II. *n* trabajador(a) *m(f)* temporal

temp. *abbr of* **temperature** temperatura

temper ['tempəʳ, *Am:* -pɚ] *n* (*temperament*) temperamento *m*; (*mood*) humor *m*; **good ~** buen humor; **bad ~** mal genio; **to get into a ~** ponerse como una fiera; **to keep one's ~** no perder la calma; **to lose one's ~** perder los estribos

temperament ['temprəmənt] *n* temperamento *m*

temperamental [ˌtemprə'mentl, *Am:* -tl] *adj* caprichoso

temperate ['tempərət] *adj* (*moderate*) moderado; (*climate*) templado

temperature ['temprətʃəʳ, *Am:* -pɚətʃɚ] *n* temperatura *f*; **to have a ~** MED tener fiebre

tempi ['tempiː] *n pl of* **tempo**

template ['templɪt] *n* plantilla *f*

temple ['templ] *n* REL templo *m*

tempo ['tempəʊ, 'tempiː, *Am:* -poʊ, -] <-s *o* -pi> *n* 1. MUS tempo *m* 2.(*pace*) ritmo *m*

temporal ['tempərəl] *adj form* temporal

temporarily ['tempərəli, *Am:* 'tempərerəlɪ] *adv* temporalmente

temporary ['temprəri, *Am:* 'tempərerɪ] *adj* (*improvement*) pasajero; (*staff, accommodation*) temporal; (*relief*) momentáneo

tempt [tempt] *vt* tentar; **to ~ sb into doing sth** tentar a alguien a hacer algo

temptation [temp'teɪʃn] *n* 1. *no pl* (*attraction*) tentación *f*; **to succumb to ~** ceder a la tentación 2.(*tempting thing*) aliciente *m*

tempting ['temptɪŋ] *adj* atractivo; (*offer*) tentador

ten [ten] *adj* diez *inv*; *s. a.* **eight**

tenacious [tɪ'neɪʃəs, *Am:* tə'-] *adj* (*belief*) firme; (*person*) tenaz

tenacity [tɪ'næsəti, *Am:* tə'næsət̬ɪ] *n no pl* tenacidad *f*

tenancy ['tenənsi] <-ies> *n* arrendamiento *m*

tenant ['tenənt] *n* (*of land*) arrendatario, -a *m, f*; (*of house*) inquilino, -a *m, f*

tend¹ [tend] *vi* 1.**to ~ to do sth** tender a hacer algo 2.(*usually do*) soler

tend² *vt* (*look after*) ocuparse de

tendency ['tendənsi] <-ies> *n* tendencia *f*

tender¹ ['tendəʳ, *Am:* -dɚ] *adj* (*not tough*) tierno; (*part of body*) sensible

tender² ['tendəʳ, *Am:* -dɚ] I. *n* COM oferta *f*; **to put sth out for ~** *Brit* sacar algo a concurso II. *vt* (*offer*) ofrecer; (*apology*) presentar III. *vi* **to ~ for sth** hacer una oferta para algo

tenderness ['tendənɪs, *Am:* -ɚ-] *n no pl* 1.(*softness*) blandura *f* 2.(*sensitivity*) sensibilidad *f*

tendon ['tendən] *n* tendón *m*

tenement ['tenəmənt] *n* bloque *m* de pisos

tenet ['tenɪt] *n* principio *m*

tenfold ['tenfəʊld, *Am:* -foʊld] *adv* diez veces

tennis ['tenɪs] *n no pl* tenis *m*

tennis ball *n* pelota *f* de tenis **tennis court** *n* pista *f* de tenis **tennis player** *n* tenista *mf* **tennis racket** *n* raqueta *f* de tenis

tenor ['tenəʳ, *Am:* -ɚ] *n* 1. MUS tenor *m* 2.(*character*) tono *m*

tense¹ [tens] *n* LING tiempo *m*

tense² *adj* (*wire, person*) tenso

tension ['tentʃən] *n no pl* tensión *f*

tent [tent] *n* (*for camping*) tienda *f* de campaña, carpa *f AmL*; (*in circus*) carpa *f*

tentacle ['tentəkl, *Am:* -tə-] *n* tentáculo *m*

tentative ['tentətɪv, *Am:* -t̬ət̬ɪv] *adj* (*person*) vacilante; (*decision*) provisional

tenth [tenθ] *adj* décimo

tenuous ['tenjʊəs] *adj* tenue

tenure ['tenjʊəʳ, *Am:* -jɚ] *n no pl* **1.** (*possession*) posesión *f*, tenencia *f* **2.** (*period*) ejercicio *m*

tepid ['tepɪd] *adj* tibio

term [tɜːm, *Am:* tɜːrm] **I.** *n* **1.** (*label, word*) término *m*; ~ **of abuse** insulto *m*; ~ **of endearment** expresión *f* afectuosa; **in no uncertain ~s** en términos claros **2.** *pl* (*conditions*) condiciones *fpl* **3.** (*limit*) límite *m*; COM plazo *m* **4.** (*period*) **in the short/long** ~ a corto/largo plazo; **prison** ~ sentencia *f* de prisión **5.** *Brit* UNIV, SCHOOL trimestre *m* **6.** *pl* **to be on good/bad ~s with sb** llevarse bien/mal con alguien **II.** *vt* calificar de

terminal ['tɜːmɪnl, *Am:* 'tɜːr-] **I.** *adj* terminal; (*boredom*) mortal **II.** *n* **1.** RAIL, AVIAT, INFOR terminal *f* **2.** ELEC polo *m*

terminate ['tɜːmɪneɪt, *Am:* 'tɜːr-] *form* **I.** *vt* poner fin a; (*contract*) rescindir **II.** *vi* terminarse

termination [ˌtɜːmɪ'neɪʃn, *Am:* ˌtɜːr-] *n no pl* fin *m*; (*of contract*) rescisión *f*

termini ['tɜːmɪnaɪ] *n pl of* **terminus**

terminology [ˌtɜːmɪ'nɒlədʒi, *Am:* ˌtɜːrmɪ'nɑːlə-] *n* terminología *f*

terminus ['tɜːmɪnəs, *Am:* 'tɜːr-] <-es *o* -i> *n* (*station*) estación *f* terminal; (*bus stop*) última parada *f*

termite ['tɜːmaɪt, *Am:* 'tɜːr-] *n* termita *f*

tern [tɜːn, *Am:* tɜːrn] *n* golondrina *f* de mar

terrace ['terəs] *n* **1.** *a.* AGR terraza *f* **2.** *Brit, Aus* (*row of houses*) hilera *f* de casas adosadas

terrain [te'reɪn] *n* terreno *m*

terrapin ['terəpɪn] <-(s)> *n* galápago *m*

terrestrial [tɪ'restrɪəl, *Am:* tə'-] *adj form* terrestre

terrible ['terəbl] *adj* **1.** (*shocking*) terrible **2.** (*very bad*) espantoso

terribly ['terəbli] *adv* **1.** (*very badly*) terriblemente **2.** (*very*) tremendamente

terrier ['terɪəʳ, *Am:* -ɚ] *n* terrier *m*

terrific [tə'rɪfɪk] *adj inf* tremendo

terrified *adj* aterrorizado

terrify ['terɪfaɪ] <-ie-> *vt* aterrar

terrifying *adj* aterrador

territorial [ˌterɪ'tɔːrɪəl, *Am:* -ə'-] *adj* territorial

territory ['terɪtəri, *Am:* 'terətɔːri] <-ies> *n* territorio *m*

terror ['terəʳ, *Am:* -ɚ] *n no pl* terror *m*

terrorism ['terərɪzəm] *n no pl* terrorismo *m*

terrorist ['terərɪst] *n* terrorista *mf*

terrorize ['terəraɪz] *vt* aterrorizar

terse [tɜːs, *Am:* tɜːrs] *adj* lacónico

test [test] **I.** *n* **1.** SCHOOL, UNIV examen *m* **2.** MED prueba *f*; **blood** ~ análisis *m inv* de sangre **3.** (*trial*) **to put sth to the** ~ poner algo a prueba **II.** *vt* **1.** (*examine*) examinar **2.** MED analizar; **to** ~ **sb for sth** hacer a alguien una prueba de algo **3.** (*measure*) comprobar

testament ['testəmənt] *n* **1.** *form* **last will and** ~ testamento y últimas voluntades **2.** REL **the Old/New** ~ el Antiguo/Nuevo Testamento

testicle ['testɪkl] *n* testículo *m*

testify ['testɪfaɪ] <-ie-> **I.** *vi form* **to** ~ **to sth** atestiguar algo **II.** *vt* **to** ~ **that …** declarar que…

testimonial [ˌtestɪ'məʊnɪəl, *Am:* -'moʊ-] *n form* **1.** (*character reference*) referencias *fpl* **2.** (*tribute*) homenaje *m*

testimony ['testɪməni, *Am:* -moʊni] <-ies> *n* testimonio *m*

testing *adj* duro

test-tube baby *n* bebé *m* probeta

tetanus ['tetənəs] *n no pl* tétano *m*

tether ['teðəʳ, *Am:* -ɚ] **I.** *n* **to be at the end of one's** ~ no aguantar más **II.** *vt* amarrar

Teutonic [tjuː'tɒnɪk, *Am:* tuː'tɑː-nɪk] *adj* teutónico

Texan ['teksən] *adj* tejano

Texas ['teksəs] *n* Tejas *m*

text [tekst] *n* texto *m*

textbook ['tekstbʊk] *n* libro *m* de texto

textile ['tekstaɪl] *n pl* tejidos *mpl*

textual ['tekstʃʊəl, *Am:* -tʃu-] *adj* textual

Tt

texture ['tekstʃə', *Am:* -tʃɚ] *n* textura *f*

Thai [taɪ] *adj* tailandés

Thailand ['taɪlənd] *n* Tailandia *m*

Thames [temz] *n no pl* **the** (**River**) ~ el Támesis

than [ðən, ðæn] *conj* que; **you are taller** ~ **she** (**is**) eres más alto que ella; **more** ~ **60** más de 60; **more** ~ **once** más de una vez; **no sooner had she told him,** ~ ... en cuanto se lo dijo...

thank [θæŋk] *vt* agradecer; **to** ~ **sb** (**for sth**) dar las gracias a alguien (por algo); ~ **you** gracias; ~ **you very much!** ¡muchas gracias!; **no,** ~ **you** no, gracias

thankful ['θæŋkfəl] *adj* **to be** ~ **that** ... alegrarse de que... +*subj*

thankfully *adv* afortunadamente

thanks [θæŋks] *npl* gracias *fpl;* ~ **very much** muchísimas gracias; ~ **to** gracias a; **in** ~ **for** ... en recompensa por...; **no** ~ **to him** no fue gracias a él

⏤⏤⏤⏤⏤⏤⏤⏤⏤⏤⏤⏤⏤⏤

❓ **Thanksgiving** (Acción de Gracias) es una de las fiestas más importantes de los EE.UU. Se celebra el cuarto jueves del mes de noviembre. El primer **Thanksgiving Day** fue celebrado en 1621 por los **Pilgrims** en **Plymouth Colony**. Habían sobrevivido a grandes dificultades y querían dar las gracias a Dios por ello. Es costumbre que las familias se reúnan para celebrar este día. La comida principal consiste en **stuffed turkey** (pavo relleno), **cranberry sauce** (salsa de arándanos), **yams** (patatas dulces) y **corn** (maíz).

⏤⏤⏤⏤⏤⏤⏤⏤⏤⏤⏤⏤⏤⏤

that [ðæt, ðət] **I.** *adj dem* <**those**> ese, esa, eso; (*more remote*) aquel, aquella, aquello; ~ **table** esa mesa; ~ **book** ese libro **II.** *pron* **1.** *rel* que; **the woman** ~ **told me** ... la mujer que me dijo...; **all** ~ **I have** todo lo que tengo **2.** *dem* **what is** ~**?** ¿eso qué es?; **who is** ~**?** ¿ése/ésa quién es?; **like** ~ así; **after** ~ después de eso; ~**'s it!** ¡eso es! **III.** *adv* tan; **it was** ~ **hot** hacía tanto calor **IV.** *conj* **1.** que; **I told you** ~ **I couldn't come** te he dicho que no puedo ir **2.** (*in order that*) para que +*subj*

thatch [θætʃ] *n no pl* (*roof*) techo *m* de paja

thaw [θɔː, *Am:* θɑː] **I.** *n* **1.** (*weather*) deshielo *m* **2.** (*in relations*) distensión *f* **II.** *vi* **1.** (*weather*) deshelar; (*food*) descongelarse **2.** (*relations*) volverse más cordial

the [ðə, *stressed, before vowel* ðiː] **I.** *def* art el *m*, la *f*, los *mpl*, las *fpl*; **from** ~ **garden** del jardín; **at** ~ **hotel** en el hotel; **at** ~ **door** a la puerta; **to** ~ **garden** al jardín; **in** ~ **winter** en invierno **II.** *adv* (*in comparison*) ~ **sooner** ~ **better** cuanto antes mejor

theater *n Am,* **theatre** ['θɪətə', *Am:* 'θiːətɚ] *n Brit, Aus* **1.** teatro *m* **2.** *Brit* **operating** ~ quirófano *m*

theatrical [θɪ'ætrɪkl] *adj* teatral

theft [θeft] *n* robo *m*

their [ðeə', *Am:* ðer] *adj poss* su(s); ~ **house** su casa; ~ **children** sus hijos

theirs [ðeəz, *Am:* ðerz] *pron poss* (el) suyo, (la) suya, (los) suyos, (las) suyas; **this house is** ~ esta casa es suya; **they aren't our bags, they are** ~ no son nuestras bolsas, son suyas; **a book of** ~ un libro suyo

them [ðem, ðəm] *pron pers pl* **1.** (*they*) ellos, ellas; **older than** ~ mayor que ellos; **if I were** ~ si yo fuese ellos **2.** *direct object* los, las; *indirect object* les; **look at** ~ míralos; **I saw** ~ yo los vi; **he gave** ~ **the pencil** les ha dado el lápiz **3.** *after prep* ellos, ellas; **it's from/for** ~ es de/para ellos

thematic [ˌθiːm'ætɪk, *Am:* θiː'mæ̣t-] *adj* temático

theme [θiːm] *n a.* MUS tema *m*

theme park *n* parque *m* temático

theme song *n no pl* sintonía *f*
themselves [ðəm'selvz] *pron*
1. *subject* ellos mismos, ellas mismas
2. *object, refl* se; **the children behaved** ~ los niños se portaron bien
3. *after prep* sí mismos, sí mismas;
by ~ solos
then [ðen] **I.** *adj form* (de) entonces
II. *adv* **1.** (*at aforementioned time*)
entonces; **before** ~ hasta entonces;
from ~ **on**(**wards**) a partir de entonces; **since** ~ desde entonces;
until ~ hasta aquel momento;
(**every**) **now and** ~ de vez en cuando **2.** (*after that*) después; **what** ~?
¿y qué? **3.** (*as a result*) por tanto; ~
he must be there entonces debe
estar ahí
thence [ðens] *adv form* de ahí
theologian [ˌθɪə'ləʊdʒən, *Am:*
ˌθiːə'loʊ-] *n* teólogo, -a *m, f*
theological [ˌθɪə'lɒdʒɪkl, *Am:* ˌθiːə-
'lɑːdʒɪ-] *adj* teológico
theology [θɪ'ɒlədʒi, *Am:* -'ɑːlə-]
<-ies> *n* teología *f*
theorem ['θɪərəm, *Am:* 'θiːərəm] *n*
MAT teorema *m*
theoretical [θɪə'retɪkəl, *Am:* ˌθiːə-
'ret-] *adj* teórico
theorist ['θɪərɪst, *Am:* 'θiːərɪst] *n*
teórico, -a *m, f*
theorize ['θɪəraɪz, *Am:* 'θiːə-] *vi*
teorizar
theory ['θɪəri, *Am:* 'θiːə-] <-ies> *n*
teoría *f;* **in** ~ en teoría
therapeutic(al) [ˌθerə'pjuːtɪk(l),
Am: -ˌtɪk-] *adj* terapéutico
therapist ['θerəpɪst] *n* terapeuta *mf*
therapy ['θerəpi] <-ies> *n* terapia *f*
there [ðeə', *Am:* ðer] *adv* allí, allá;
here and ~ aquí y allá; ~ **is/are**
hay; ~ **will be** habrá; ~ **you are!**
¡ahí lo tienes!; ~ **is no one** no hay
nadie; ~ **and then** en el acto
thereafter [ðeər'ɑːftə', *Am:* ðer-
'æftə'] *adv* a partir de entonces
thereby [ðeə'baɪ, *Am:* ðer'-] *adv
form* por eso
therefore ['ðeəfɔː', *Am:* 'ðerfɔːr]
adv por (lo) tanto
therein [ðeər'ɪn, *Am:* ðer'-] *adv
form* ahí dentro

thermal ['θɜːməl, *Am:* 'θɜːr-] *adj*
térmico
thermometer [θə'mɒmɪtə', *Am:*
θə'mɑːmətə'] *n* termómetro *m*
these [ðiːz] *pl of* **this**
thesis ['θiːsɪs] <-ses> *n* tesis *f inv*
they [ðeɪ] *pron pers* **1.** (*3rd person
pl*) ellos, -as; ~ **are my parents/
sisters** (ellos) son mis padres/(ellas)
son mis hermanas **2.** (*people in general*) ~ **say that ...** dicen que...
thick [θɪk] *adj* **1.** (*wall*) grueso;
(*coat*) gordo; (*hair*) abundante;
(*liquid*) espeso; **through** ~ **and thin**
a las duras y a las maduras **2.** (*stupid*) corto; **to be as** ~ **as two short
planks** *inf* no tener dos dedos de
frente
thicken ['θɪkən] **I.** *vt* espesar **II.** *vi*
espesarse
thicket ['θɪkɪt] *n* matorral *m*
thickness ['θɪknɪs] *n no pl* (*of wall*)
grosor *m;* (*of hair*) abundancia *f;* (*of
sauce*) consistencia *f*
thief [θiːf] <thieves> *n* ladrón, -ona
m, f
thigh [θaɪ] *n* muslo *m*
thimble ['θɪmbl] *n* dedal *m*
thin [θɪn] <-nn-> **I.** *adj* (*clothes*)
fino; (*person*) delgado; (*soup,
sauce*) claro; (*hair*) ralo **II.** <-nn->
vt (*dilute*) aclarar
thing [θɪŋ] *n* cosa *f;* **the best** ~ lo
mejor; **one** ~ **after another** una
cosa después de otra; **to be a** ~ **of
the past** ser algo del pasado; **to
know a** ~ **or two** saber algo; **if it's
not one** ~ **it's another** cuando no
es una cosa es otra; **it's the done** ~
es lo que hay que hacer; **the latest** ~
in shoes el último grito en zapatos;
all his ~**s** todas sus cosas; **as** ~**s
stand** tal como están las cosas; **you
lucky** ~**!** ¡qué suerte tienes!; **all** ~**s
being equal** si no sale ningún imprevisto
think [θɪŋk] <thought, thought>
I. *vt* **1.** (*believe*) pensar; **who would
have thought it!** ¡quien lo hubiese
pensado! **2.** (*consider*) **to** ~ **sb** (**to
be**) **sth** considerar a alguien como
algo; ~ **nothing of it!** ¡no merece la

pena mencionarlo! **II.** *vi* pensar; **to ~ aloud** pensar en voz alta; **to ~ for oneself** pensar por sí mismo; **to ~ of doing sth** pensar en hacer algo; **to ~ about sth** pensar en algo
◆**think ahead** *vi* pensar de cara al futuro
◆**think back** *vi* **to ~ to sth** recordar algo
◆**think of** *vi* pensar en
◆**think through** *vt* estudiar detenidamente
◆**think up** *vt* inventar
thinker *n* pensador(a) *m(f)*
thinking I. *n* *no pl* **1.** (*thought process*) pensamiento *m* **2.** (*reasoning*) razonamiento *m* **II.** *adj* inteligente
think tank *n* gabinete *m* estratégico
third [θɜ:d, *Am:* θɜ:rd] *adj* tercero; *before n m sing:* tercer
thirdly *adv* en tercer lugar
third party *n* tercero *m* **Third World** *n* **the ~** el Tercer Mundo
thirst [θɜ:st, *Am:* θɜ:rst] *n* sed *f;* **to quench one's ~** apagar la sed; **~ for power** ansias *fpl* de poder
thirsty [ˈθɜ:sti, *Am:* ˈθɜ:r-] <-ier, -iest> *adj* sediento; **to be ~** tener sed; **to be ~ for sth** *fig* estar ansioso por algo
thirteen [ˌθɜ:ˈti:n, *Am:* θɜ:rˈ-] *adj* trece *inv; s. a.* **eight**
thirteenth [ˌθɜ:ˈti:nθ, *Am:* θɜ:rˈ-] *adj* decimotercero; *before n m sing:* decimotercer
thirtieth [ˈθɜ:tiəθ, *Am:* ˈθɜ:rtɪ] *adj* trigésimo
thirty [ˈθɜ:ti, *Am:* ˈθɜ:rtɪ] *adj* treinta *inv; s. a.* **eighty**
this [ðɪs] **I.** <these> *adj def* este, esta; **~ car** este coche; **~ house** esta casa; **~ one** éste, ésta; **~ day** hoy; **~ morning** esta mañana; **~ time last month** hoy hace un mes **II.** <these> *pron dem* éste, ésta, esto; **who is ~?** ¿éste/ésta quién es?; **~ and that** esto y aquello; **~ is Ana (speaking)** (*on the phone*) soy Ana **III.** *adv* así; **~ late** tan tarde; **~ big** así de grande
thistle [ˈθɪsl] *n* cardo *m*
thorn [θɔ:n, *Am:* θɔ:rn] *n* espina *f*
thorny [ˈθɔ:ni, *Am:* ˈθɔ:r-] <-ier,

-iest> *adj* espinoso, espinudo *AmC, CSur;* (*issue*) peliagudo
thorough [ˈθʌrə, *Am:* ˈθɜ:roʊ] *adj* **1.** (*detailed*) exhaustivo **2.** (*careful*) minucioso
thoroughbred [ˈθʌrəbred, *Am:* ˈθɜ:roʊ-] *n* pura sangre *mf*
thoroughfare [ˈθʌrəfeər, *Am:* ˈθɜ:-roʊfer] *n form* vía *f* pública
thoroughly *adv* a fondo
those [ðəʊz, *Am:* ðoʊz] *pl of* **that**
though [ðəʊ, *Am:* ðoʊ] *conj* aunque; **as ~** como si +*subj;* **even ~** aunque
thought [θɔ:t, *Am:* θɑ:t] **I.** *pt, pp of* **think II.** *n* **1.** *no pl* (*process*) reflexión *f;* **on second ~s** tras madura reflexión; **without ~** sin pensar; **after much ~** tras mucho reflexionar; **to be deep in ~** estar ensimismado **2.** (*idea, opinion*) pensamiento *m;* **that's a ~** es posible
thoughtful [ˈθɔ:tfl, *Am:* ˈθɑ:t-] *adj* **1.** (*pensive*) pensativo **2.** (*considerate*) amable
thousand [ˈθaʊznd] *adj* mil; **three ~** tres mil; **~s of birds** miles de pájaros

> **!** Después de cifras **thousand** se utiliza en singular: "Five thousand inhabitants."

thrash [θræʃ] *vt* **1.** (*beat*) apalear **2.** *inf* (*defeat*) dar una paliza a
thread [θred] **I.** *n* **1.** *no pl* (*for sewing*) hilo *m;* **to hang by a ~** pender de un hilo **2.** (*of screw*) rosca *f* **II.** *vt* (*needle*) enhebrar
threat [θret] *n* amenaza *f*
threaten [ˈθretən] *vt* amenazar
threatening *adj* amenazador
three [θri:] *adj* tres *inv; s. a.* **eight**
three-dimensional *adj* tridimensional
threshold [ˈθreʃhəʊld, *Am:* -hoʊld] *n* **1.** (*doorway*) umbral *m* **2.** (*limit*) límite *m*
threw [θru:] *pt of* **throw**
thrift [θrɪft] *n no pl* ahorro *m*
thrill [θrɪl] **I.** *n* estremecimiento *m* **II.** *vt* emocionar

thriller [ˈθrɪləʳ, *Am:* -ɚ] *n* (*book*) novela *f* de suspense; (*film*) película *f* de suspense

thrilling [ˈθrɪlɪŋ] *adj* emocionante

thrive [θraɪv] <thrived *o* throve, thrived *o* thriven> *vi* (*person, plant*) crecer mucho; (*business*) prosperar

thriving *adj* próspero

throat [θrəʊt, *Am:* θroʊt] *n* (*internal*) garganta *f;* (*external*) cuello *m;* **to be at each other's ~s** estar como el perro y el gato

throb [θrɒb, *Am:* θrɑ:b] <-bb-> *vi* (*engine*) vibrar; (*heart*) palpitar

throes [θrəʊz, *Am:* θroʊz] *npl* **to be in the ~ of sth** estar de lleno en algo

throne [θrəʊn, *Am:* θroʊn] *n* trono *m*

throng [θrɒŋ, *Am:* θrɑ:ŋ] *n* multitud *f*

throttle [ˈθrɒtl, *Am:* ˈθrɑ:t̬l] I. *n* acelerador *m;* **at full ~** a todo gas *inf* II. <-ll-> *vt* estrangular

through [θru:] I. *prep* 1. (*spatial*) a través de, por; **to go right ~ sth** traspasar algo; **to go ~ the door** pasar por la puerta 2. (*temporal*) durante; **all ~ my life** durante toda mi vida 3. *Am* (*until*) **Monday ~ Friday** de lunes a viernes 4. (*by means of*) por (medio de) II. *adv* 1. (*of place*) de un lado a otro; **I read the book ~** leí el libro entero; **to go ~ to sth** ir directo a algo; **~ and ~** de cabo a rabo 2. (*of time*) **all day ~** de la mañana a la noche; **halfway ~** a medio camino 3. TEL **to put sb ~ to sb** poner a alguien con alguien

throughout [θru:ˈaʊt] *prep* 1. (*spatial*) por todas partes de 2. (*temporal*) a lo largo de

throve [θrəʊv, *Am:* θroʊv] *pt of* **thrive**

throw [θrəʊ, *Am:* θroʊ] I. *n* lanzamiento *m; his last ~ fig* su última oportunidad II. <threw, thrown> *vt* 1. (*propel*) tirar; (*ball, javelin*) lanzar; **to ~ oneself at sb** echar los tejos a alguien; **to ~ oneself into sth** entregarse de lleno a algo; **to ~ a**

party dar una fiesta 2. *inf* (*confuse*) desconcertar

◆ **throw away** *vt* tirar

◆ **throw out** *vt* 1. (*person*) echar; (*thing*) tirar 2. (*heat, light*) despedir

◆ **throw up** *vi inf* vomitar, buitrear *CSur,* revulsar *Méx*

throw-in [ˈθrəʊɪn, *Am:* ˈθroʊ-] *n* (*in soccer*) saque *m* de banda; (*in baseball*) lanzamiento *m*

thrown *pp of* **throw**

thrush [θrʌʃ] *n* ZOOL tordo *m*

thrust [θrʌst] I. <-, -> *vt* empujar II. *n no pl* (*propulsion*) propulsión *f*

thud [θʌd] *n* golpe *m* sordo

thug [θʌg] *n* matón *m*

thumb [θʌm] *n* pulgar *m;* **to stand out like a sore ~** cantar como una almeja

thump [θʌmp] I. *vt* golpear II. *n* 1. (*blow*) porrazo *m* 2. (*noise*) golpe *m* sordo

thunder [ˈθʌndəʳ, *Am:* -dɚ] *n no pl* 1. METEO trueno *m*, pillán *m Chile;* **a clap of ~** un trueno 2. (*sound*) estruendo *m* 3. **to steal sb's ~** quitar las primicias a alguien

thunderous [ˈθʌndərəs] *adj* estruendoso

thunderstorm [ˈθʌndəstɔ:m, *Am:* -dɚstɔ:rm] *n* tormenta *f*

thunderstruck [ˈθʌndəstrʌk, *Am:* -dɚ-] *adj form* estupefacto

Thursday [ˈθɜ:zdeɪ, *Am:* ˈθɜ:rz-] *n* jueves *m inv; s. a.* **Friday**

thus [ðʌs] *adv form* 1. (*therefore*) por lo tanto 2. (*like this*) de este modo

thwart [θwɔ:t, *Am:* θwɔ:rt] *vt* frustrar; (*plan*) desbaratar

thy [ðaɪ] *pron poss, liter* tu(s)

thyme [taɪm] *n no pl* tomillo *m*

tic [tɪk] *n* tic *m*

tick¹ [tɪk] *n* garrapata *f*

tick² I. *n* 1. (*sound*) tic-tac *m* 2. (*mark*) visto *m* II. *vi* hacer tic-tac; **I don't know what makes her ~** no acabo de entender su manera de ser III. *vt* marcar

◆ **tick off** *vt* 1. (*mark off*) marcar 2. *Brit, Aus, inf* (*scold*) echar una bronca a 3. *Am, inf* (*exasperate*) dar

T t

la lata a

◆ **tick over** *vi* **1.** TECH ir al ralentí **2.** *fig* ir tirando

ticket ['tıkıt] *n* **1.** (*for bus, train*) billete *m*, boleto *m* AmL; (*for cinema, concert*) entrada *f* **2.** (*tag*) etiqueta *f*; **just the ~** *fig* justo lo que hacía falta

ticket collector *n* revisor(a) *m(f)*

ticket office *n* RAIL ventanilla *f* de venta de billetes; THEAT taquilla *f*

tickle ['tıkl] *vt* hacer cosquillas

tidal ['taıdəl] *adj* de la marea

tidal wave *n* maremoto *m*

tide [taıd] *n* **1.** (*of sea*) marea *f*; **high ~** pleamar *f*; **low ~** bajamar *f* **2.** (*of opinion*) corriente *f*; **to go against the ~** ir contracorriente

tidy ['taıdi] I. *adj* <-ier, -iest> ordenado II. *vt* ordenar

tie [taı] I. *n* **1.** (*necktie*) corbata *f* **2.** (*cord*) atadura *f* **3.** *pl* (*bond*) lazos *mpl*; (*diplomatic*) relaciones *fpl* II. *vt* atar; (*knot*) hacer; **to be ~d by sth** estar limitado por algo

◆ **tie down** *vt* atar; **to tie sb down to sth** *fig* comprometer a alguien a algo

◆ **tie up** *vt* atar; (*hair*) recogerse; **to be tied up** *fig* estar ocupado

tier [tıəʳ, *Am:* tır] *n* (*row*) hilera *f*; (*level*) grada *f*; (*in hierarchy*) nivel *m*

tiger ['taıgəʳ, *Am:* -gɚ] *n* tigre *m*

tight [taıt] I. *adj* **1.** (*screw, knot*) apretado; (*clothing*) ceñido; (*rope, skin*) tirante **2.** (*condition, discipline*) estricto; (*budget*) restringido; (*schedule*) apretado; **to keep a ~ hold on sth** mantener un control riguroso de algo; **to be ~ for time** ir escaso de tiempo **3.** (*hard-fought*) reñido II. *adv* **to close sth ~** cerrar bien algo; **sleep ~!** ¡que duermas bien!

tighten ['taıtn] *vt* **1.** (*make tight*) apretar; (*rope*) tensar **2.** (*restrictions*) intensificar

tight-fitting *adj* ajustado

tightrope ['taıtrəʊp, *Am:* -roʊp] *n* cuerda *f* floja

tights [taıts] *npl* **1.** *Brit* (*leggings*) medias *fpl* **2.** *Am, Aus* (*for dancing*) mallas *fpl*

tile [taıl] I. *n* (*for roof*) teja *f*; (*for walls, floors*) azulejo *m* II. *vt* (*roof*) tejar; (*wall*) poner azulejos a, alicatar; (*floor*) embaldosar

till¹ [tıl] *adv, conj s.* **until**

till² *n* caja *f*

tilt [tılt] I. *n* inclinación *f*; (**at**) **full ~** a toda máquina II. *vt* inclinar III. *vi* inclinarse

timber ['tımbəʳ, *Am:* -bɚ] *n* **1.** *no pl, Brit* (*wood*) madera *f* **2.** (*beam*) viga *f*

time [taım] I. *n* **1.** tiempo *m*; **to kill ~** matar el tiempo; **to make ~** hacer tiempo; **to spend ~** pasar el tiempo; (**how**) **~ flies** el tiempo vuela; **to be a matter of ~** ser cuestión de tiempo; (**only**) **~ can tell** (sólo) el tiempo lo dirá; **in ~** a tiempo; **over ~** con el tiempo; **after a ~** al cabo de un tiempo; **all the ~** continuamente; **a long ~ ago** hace mucho tiempo; **to have a good ~** pasárselo bien; **most of the ~** la mayor parte del tiempo; **in one week's ~** dentro de una semana; **it takes a long ~** se tarda mucho; **to give sb a hard ~** *inf* hacerlas pasar canutas a alguien **2.** (*clock*) hora *f*; **what's the ~?** ¿qué hora es? **3.** (*moment*) momento *m*; **the right ~** el momento oportuno; **at any ~** a cualquier hora; **the next ~** la próxima vez **4.** (*occasion*) vez *f*; **each ~** cada vez; **from ~ to ~** de vez en cuando **5.** (*epoch*) época *f*; **to be behind the ~s** estar anclado en el pasado **6.** SPORTS tiempo *m* II. *vt* **1.** SPORTS cronometrar, relojear *Arg* **2.** (*choose best moment for*) elegir el momento para

time bomb *n* bomba *f* de relojería

time-consuming ['taımkən‚sju:mıŋ, *Am:* -‚su:-] *adj* que exige mucho tiempo

timeless ['taımləs] *adj* eterno

time limit *n* límite *m* de tiempo

timely ['taımli] *adj* <-ier, -iest> oportuno

time-out [‚taım'aʊt] *n* **1.** SPORTS tiempo *m* muerto **2.** (*rest*) descanso *m*

timer ['taıməʳ, *Am:* -ɚ] *n* temporizador *m;* GASTR reloj *m* avisador

timescale ['taɪmskeɪl] *n* escala *f* de tiempo **timeshare** *n* multipropiedad *f* **timetable** I. *n* (*for bus, train*) horario *m;* (*for project, events*) programa *m* II. *vt* programar **time zone** *n* huso *m* horario

timid ['tɪmɪd] *adj* <-er, -est> tímido

timing ['taɪmɪŋ] *n no pl* cronometraje *m;* **that was perfect ~** ha sido el momento oportuno

tin [tɪn] *n* **1.** *no pl* (*metal*) estaño *m;* (*tinplate*) hojalata *f* **2.** (*container*) lata *f;* (*for baking*) molde *m*

tin can *n* lata *f*

tinder ['tɪndəʳ, *Am:* -dəʳ] *n no pl* yesca *f*

tin foil *n* papel *m* de aluminio

tinge [tɪndʒ] I. *n* **1.** (*of colour*) tinte *m* **2.** (*of emotion*) dejo *m* II. *vt* **1.** (*dye*) teñir **2.** *fig* matizar

tingle ['tɪŋgl] I. *vi* estremecerse II. *n no pl* estremecimiento *m*

tinker ['tɪŋkəʳ, *Am:* -kəʳ] I. *n Brit* gitano, -a *m, f* II. *vi* **to ~ with sth** tratar de reparar algo

tinkle ['tɪŋkl] I. *vi* tintinear II. *n* tintineo *m*

tin-opener *n Brit, Aus* abrelatas *m inv*

tinsel ['tɪnsl] *n no pl* oropel *m*

tint [tɪnt] *vt* teñir

tiny ['taɪni] *adj* <-ier, -iest> menudo, chingo *Col, Cuba*

tip¹ [tɪp] *n* punta *f;* **from ~ to toe** de pies a cabeza; **it's on the ~ of my tongue** lo tengo en la punta de la lengua

tip² [tɪp] I. <-pp-> *vt* **1.** *Brit, Aus* (*empty out*) verter **2.** (*incline*) inclinar; **to ~ the balance in favour of sb** inclinar la balanza a favor de alguien II. *n Brit* basurero *m*

tip³ [tɪp] I. *n* **1.** (*for service*) propina *f,* yapa *f Méx* **2.** (*hint*) aviso *m;* **to take a ~ from sb** seguir el consejo de alguien II. <-pp-> *vt* dar una propina a

◆ **tip off** *vt* avisar

◆ **tip over** I. *vt* volcar II. *vi* volcarse

tip-off ['tɪpɒf, *Am:* -ɑːf] *n inf* soplo *m*

tipsy ['tɪpsi] *adj* <-ier, -iest> bebido, achispado *AmL*

tiptoe ['tɪptəʊ, *Am:* -toʊ] *n* **on ~**(**s**) de puntillas

tirade [taɪ'reɪd, *Am:* 'taɪreɪd] *n* diatriba *f*

tire¹ ['taɪəʳ, *Am:* 'taɪɚ] *n Am s.* **tyre**

tire² I. *vt* cansar II. *vi* cansarse

tired ['taɪəd, *Am:* 'taɪɚd] *adj* <-er, -est> (*person*) cansado; (*excuse*) trillado; **to be ~ of sth** estar harto de algo

tiredness ['taɪədnɪs, *Am:* 'taɪɚd-] *n no pl* cansancio *m*

tireless ['taɪəlɪs, *Am:* 'taɪɚ-] *adj* incansable

tiresome ['taɪəsəm, *Am:* 'taɪɚ-] *adj* molesto; (*person*) pesado, molón *Guat, Ecua, Méx*

tiring ['taɪrɪŋ] *adj* agotador, cansador *Arg*

tissue ['tɪʃuː] *n* **1.** *no pl* (*paper*) papel *m* de seda **2.** (*handkerchief*) Kleenex® *m* **3.** *no pl* ANAT, BIO tejido *m;* **a ~ of lies** una sarta de mentiras

tit [tɪt] *n vulg* teta *f*

title ['taɪtl, *Am:* -t̬l] I. *n* **1.** (*name*) título *m* **2.** *no pl* LAW derecho *m* II. *vt* titular

title role *n* papel *m* principal

titter ['tɪtəʳ, *Am:* 'tɪt̬əʳ] I. *vi* reírse disimuladamente II. *n* risa *f* disimulada

tittle-tattle ['tɪtltætl, *Am:* 'tɪt̬l̩ˌtæ-t̬l] *n no pl, inf* chismorreo *m*

TNT [ˌtiːen'tiː] *n abbr of* **trinitrotoluene** TNT *m*

to [tuː] I. *prep* **1.** (*in direction of*) a; **to go ~ Spain/Oxford** ir a España/Oxford; **to go ~ the cinema** ir al cine; **~ the left** a la izquierda **2.** (*until*) hasta; **to count up ~ 10** contar hasta 10; **a quarter ~ five** las cinco menos cuarto **3.** *with indirect object* **to talk ~ sb** hablar con alguien; **to show sth ~ sb** mostrar algo a alguien; **this belongs ~ me** esto es mío; **to be kind ~ sb** ser amable con alguien **4.** (*in comparison*) a; **superior ~ sth** superior a algo **5.** (*by*) por; **known ~ sb** conocido por alguien II. *infin particle*

1. (*infin: not translated*) ~ **do/ walk/put** hacer/caminar/poner; **she wants** ~ **go** quiere irse **2.** (*wish, command*) **I told him** ~ **eat** le dije que comiera; **he wants me** ~ **tell him a story** quiere que le cuente un cuento **3.** (*purpose*) **he comes** ~ **see me** viene a verme; **to phone** ~ **ask sth** llamar para preguntar algo **4.** (*in consecutive acts*) para; **I came back** ~ **find she had left Madrid** volví para descubrir que se había ido de Madrid **5.** (*in ellipsis*) **he doesn't want** ~ **eat, but I want** ~ **eat** él no quiere comer, pero yo sí

toad [təʊd, *Am:* toʊd] *n* **1.** (*animal*) sapo *m* **2.** (*person*) esperpento *m*

toadstool ['təʊdstuːl, *Am:* 'toʊd-] *n* seta *f* venenosa

to and fro *adv* de un lado a otro

toast [təʊst, *Am:* toʊst] **I.** *n* **1.** *no pl* (*bread*) tostada *f;* **a piece of** ~ una tostada **2.** (*drink*) brindis *m inv* **II.** *vt* **1.** (*cook*) tostar **2.** (*drink*) brindar

toaster *n* tostadora *f*

tobacco [tə'bækəʊ, *Am:* -oʊ] *n no pl* tabaco *m*

tobacconist [tə'bækənɪst] *n* estanquero, -a *m, f*

toboggan [tə'bɒgən, *Am:* -'bɑː-gən] *n* tobogán *m*

today [tə'deɪ] *adv* (*this day*) hoy; (*nowadays*) hoy día

toddler ['tɒdlə', *Am:* 'tɑːdlə-] *n* niño, -a *m, f* que empieza a caminar

toddy ['tɒdi, *Am:* 'tɑːdi] <-ies> *n* (**hot**) ~ ponche *m*

toe [təʊ, *Am:* toʊ] *n* ANAT dedo *m* (del pie); (*of sock*) punta *f;* (*of shoe*) puntera *f;* **to keep sb on their** ~**s** mantener a alguien en estado de alerta

toecap *n* puntera *f* **toenail** *n* uña *f* del dedo del pie

toffee ['tɒfi, *Am:* 'tɑːfi] *n* toffee *m*

together [tə'geðə', *Am:* -ə-] *adv* **1.** (*jointly*) juntos, juntas; **all** ~ todos juntos, todas juntas; ~ **with sb** junto con alguien; **to live** ~ vivir juntos; **to get** ~ juntarse; **to get it** ~ *inf* organizarse **2.** (*at the same time*) a la vez

toggle ['tɒgl, *Am:* 'tɑːgl] *n* **1.** INFOR

tecla *f* de conmutación **2.** TECH palanca *f* acodada

toil [tɔɪl] **I.** *n no pl* labor *f* **II.** *vi* (*work hard*) afanarse

toilet ['tɔɪlɪt] *n* **1.** (*room*) cuarto *m* de baño **2.** (*appliance*) váter *m*

toilet bag *n* neceser *m* **toilet paper** *n* papel *m* higiénico

toilet roll *n Brit, Aus* rollo *m* de papel higiénico

token ['təʊkən, *Am:* 'toʊ-] **I.** *n* **1.** (*sign*) señal *f;* (*of affection*) muestra *f;* **by the same** ~ por la misma razón **2.** *Brit, Aus* (*coupon*) bono *m* **3.** (*for machines*) ficha *f* **II.** *adj* (*symbolic*) simbólico

told [təʊld, *Am:* toʊld] *pt, pp of* **tell**

tolerable ['tɒlərəbl, *Am:* 'tɑːlə-] *adj* soportable

tolerance ['tɒlərəns, *Am:* 'tɑːlə-] *n no pl* tolerancia *f*

tolerant ['tɒlərənt, *Am:* 'tɑːlə-] *adj* tolerante

tolerate ['tɒləreɪt, *Am:* 'tɑːləreɪt] *vt* **1.** (*accept*) tolerar **2.** (*endure*) soportar

toleration [ˌtɒlə'reɪʃn, *Am:* ˌtɑːlə-'reɪ-] *n no pl* tolerancia *f*

toll [təʊl, *Am:* toʊl] *n* **1.** AUTO peaje *m* **2.** *Am* TEL tarifa *f* **3.** *no pl* (*damage*) número *m* de víctimas

toll-free *adv Am* gratis

tom [tɒm, *Am:* tɑːm] *n* (*cat*) gato *m* macho

tomato [tə'mɑːtəʊ, *Am:* -'meɪt̬oʊ] <-oes> *n* tomate *m*

tomb [tuːm] *n* tumba *f*, guaca *f AmL*

tombstone ['tuːmstəʊn, *Am:* 'tuːmstoʊn] *n* lápida *f* sepulcral

tome [təʊm, *Am:* toʊm] *n* librote *m*

tomorrow [tə'mɒrəʊ, *Am:* -'mɑː-roʊ] *adv* mañana; **the day after** ~ pasado mañana; **a week from** ~ de mañana en una semana; ~ **morning** mañana por la mañana

ton [tʌn] *n* tonelada *f* (*Brit: 1,016 kilos; Am: 907 kilos*); ~**s of** *inf* montones de

tone [təʊn, *Am:* toʊn] *n* **1.** (*sound*) tono *m;* (*of voice*) timbre *m* **2.** (*style*) clase *f* **3.** (*of colour*) matiz *f*

◆ **tone down** *vt* moderar

◆ **tone up** *vt* poner en forma

toneless ['təʊnləs, *Am:* 'toʊn-] *adj* monótono

toner ['təʊnə^r, *Am:* 'toʊnɚ] *n* 1. (*for skin*) tonificante *m* 2. (*for printer*) tóner *m*

tongs [tɒŋz, *Am:* tɑ:ŋz] *npl* tenazas *fpl*

tongue [tʌŋ] *n* 1. ANAT lengua *f;* **to hold one's ~** callarse; **to stick one's ~ out (at sb)** sacar la lengua (a alguien); **to say sth ~ in cheek** decir algo irónicamente 2. (*language*) idioma *m*

tongue twister *n* trabalenguas *m inv*

tonic ['tɒnɪk, *Am:* 'tɑ:nɪk] *n* (*stimulant*) tónico *m*

tonic water *n* tónica *f*

tonight [tə'naɪt] *adv* (*evening*) esta tarde; (*night*) esta noche

tonnage ['tʌnɪdʒ] *n no pl* tonelaje *m*

tonne [tʌn] *n no pl* tonelada *f* (métrica)

tonsil ['tɒnsl, *Am:* 'tɑ:n-] *n* amígdala *f*

tonsillitis [ˌtɒnsɪ'laɪtɪs, *Am:* ˌtɑ:nsə'laɪtɪs] *n no pl* amigdalitis *f*

too [tu:] *adv* 1. (*overly*) demasiado 2. (*also*) también 3. (*moveover*) además

took [tʊk] *vt, vi pt of* **take**

tool [tu:l] *n* herramienta *f,* implemento *m AmL*

tool box *n* caja *f* de herramientas

tool kit *n* juego *m* de herramientas

toot [tu:t] *vi* pitar

tooth [tu:θ] <teeth> *n* (*of person, animal*) diente *m;* (*molar*) muela *f;* (*of comb*) púa *f;* (*of saw*) diente *m;* **to fight ~ and nail (to do sth)** luchar a brazo partido (para hacer algo)

toothache ['tu:θeɪk] *n* dolor *m* de muelas

toothbrush ['tu:θbrʌʃ] *n* cepillo *m* de dientes

toothpaste ['tu:θpeɪst] *n no pl* pasta *f* dentífrica

toothpick *n* palillo *m,* pajuela *f Bol, Col*

top¹ [tɒp, *Am:* tɑ:p] *n* (*spinning top*) peonza *f*

top² I. *n* 1. (*highest part*) parte *f* superior; (*of mountain*) cima *f;* (*of tree*) copa *f;* (*of head*) coronilla *f;* **to get on ~ of sth** *fig* llegar a lo más alto de algo; **from ~ to bottom** de arriba a abajo; **from ~ to toe** de pies a cabeza; **to be at the ~** *fig* estar en la cima; **at the ~ of one's voice** a grito pelado; **to go over the ~** *fig* exagerar 2. (*surface*) superficie *f;* **on ~ of** encima de 3. (*clothing*) top *m* 4. (*end*) punta *f* superior; (*of table, list*) cabeza *f* 5. (*of bottle*) tapón *m* II. *adj* 1. (*highest, upper*) más alto 2. (*best*) de primera calidad 3. (*most successful*) exitoso 4. (*most important*) mejor 5. (*maximum*) máximo III. <-pp-> *vt* (*be at top of*) encabezar

◆ **top up** *vt* 1. (*fill up again*) recargar 2. (*add to*) completar

top hat *n* sombrero *m* de copa, galera *f AmL* **top-heavy** *adj* inestable

topic ['tɒpɪk, *Am:* 'tɑ:pɪk] *n* tema *m*

topical ['tɒpɪkl, *Am:* 'tɑ:pɪ-] *adj* de interés actual

top-level [ˌtɒp'levəl, *Am:* 'tɑ:pˌlev-] *adj* de alto nivel

topography [tə'pɒgrəfi, *Am:* -'pɑ:-grə-] *n no pl* topografía *f*

topping ['tɒpɪŋ, *Am:* 'tɑ:pɪŋ] *n* GASTR cobertura *f*

topple ['tɒpl, *Am:* 'tɑ:pl] I. *vt* derribar II. *vi* caerse

topsy-turvy [ˌtɒpsi't3:vi, *Am:* ˌtɑ:psi't3:r-] *adj inf* desordenado

torch [tɔ:tʃ, *Am:* tɔ:rtʃ] <-es> *n* 1. *Aus, Brit* (*electric*) linterna *f* 2. (*burning stick*) antorcha *f;* **to put sth to the ~** prender fuego a algo 3. *Am* (*blowlamp*) soplete *m*

torchlight ['tɔ:tʃlaɪt, *Am:* 'tɔ:rtʃ-] *n no pl* (*electric*) luz *f* de linterna; (*burning*) luz *f* de antorcha

tore [tɔ:^r, *Am:* tɔ:r] *vi, vt pt of* **tear**

torment ['tɔ:ment, *Am:* 'tɔ:r-] I. *n* tormento *m* II. *vt* atormentar

torn [tɔ:n, *Am:* tɔ:rn] *vi, vt pp of* **tear**

tornado [tɔ:'neɪdəʊ, *Am:* tɔ:r'neɪ-doʊ] *n* <-(e)s> tornado *m*

torpedo [tɔ:'pi:dəʊ, *Am:* tɔ:r'pi:-

dou] <-es> *n* torpedo *m*

torrent ['tɒrənt, *Am:* 'tɔ:r-] *n* **1.**(*of water*) torrente *m* **2.**(*of complaints*) carga *f*

torrential [təˈrenʃl, *Am:* tɔ:'-] *adj* torrencial, torrentoso *AmL*

torso ['tɔ:səʊ, *Am:* 'tɔ:rsoʊ] *n* torso *m*

tortoise ['tɔ:təs, *Am:* 'tɔ:rtəs] *n* tortuga *f*

tortuous ['tɔ:tjʊəs, *Am:* 'tɔ:rtʃʊəs] *adj* tortuoso; (*reasoning*) enrevesado

torture ['tɔ:tʃəʳ, *Am:* 'tɔ:rtʃəʳ] I. *n* tortura *f* II. *vt* torturar; **to** ~ **oneself with sth** martirizarse con algo

Tory ['tɔ:ri] <-ies> *n Brit:* miembro de los conservadores británicos

toss [tɒs, *Am:* tɑ:s] I. *n* lanzamiento *m;* **to win the** ~ ganar a cara o cruz; **to argue the** ~ *inf* discutir insistentemente; **I don't give a** ~ *inf* me importa un pepino II. *vt* (*throw*) lanzar; **to** ~ **a coin** echar una moneda a cara o cruz

◆ **toss up** *vi* **to** ~ **for sth** echar algo a cara o cruz

tot [tɒt, *Am:* tɑ:t] *n inf* (*child*) niño, -a *m, f* pequeño, -a

◆ **tot up** *vt inf* sumar

total ['təʊtl, *Am:* 'toʊtl] I. *n* total *m* II. *adj* total III. *vt* <*Brit:* -ll-, *Am:* -l-> **1.**(*count*) sumar **2.**(*amount to*) ascender a

totalitarian [ˌtəʊtælɪ'teəriən, *Am:* toʊˌtælə'teri-] *adj* totalitario

totality [təʊ'tæləti, *Am:* toʊ'tæləṭi] *n no pl* totalidad *f*

totally ['təʊtəli, *Am:* 'toʊṭəl-] *adv* totalmente

totem pole ['təʊtəm-, *Am:* 'toʊṭəm-] *n* tótem *m*

totter ['tɒtəʳ, *Am:* 'tɑ:ṭəʳ] *vi* tambalearse

toucan ['tu:kæn] *n* tucán *m*

touch [tʌtʃ] <-es> I. *n* **1.** *no pl* (*sensation*) tacto *m* **2.**(*act of touching*) toque *m* **3.** *no pl* (*communication*) **to be in** ~ (**with sb**) estar en contacto (con alguien); **to lose** ~ **with sb** perder el contacto con alguien **4.** *no pl* (*skill*) **to lose one's** ~ perder la destreza **5.** *no pl* (*small amount*) po-

quito *m;* (*of irony*) pizca *f* **6.** SPORTS **to go into** ~ salir del campo II. *vt* **1.**(*feel*) tocar **2.**(*brush against*) rozar **3.**(*move emotionally*) conmover III. *vi* tocarse

◆ **touch down** *vi* AVIAT aterrizar

◆ **touch up** *vt* PHOT retocar

touchdown ['tʌtʃdaʊn] *n* **1.** AVIAT aterrizaje *m* **2.**(*American football*) touchdown *m;* (*rugby*) ensayo *m*

touching ['tʌtʃɪŋ] *adj* conmovedor

touchstone ['tʌtʃstəʊn, *Am:* -stoʊn] *n* piedra *f* de toque

touchy ['tʌtʃi] <-ier, -iest> *adj* (*person*) susceptible; (*issue*) delicado

tough [tʌf] *adj* **1.**(*fabric, substance*) fuerte; (*meat, skin*) duro **2.**(*person*) resistente **3.**(*strict*) estricto; **to be** ~ **on sb** ser severo con alguien **4.**(*difficult*) difícil; ~ **luck** *inf* mala suerte

toughen ['tʌfən] *vt* endurecer

toughness *n no pl* (*strength*) resistencia *f;* (*of meat*) dureza *f*

toupée ['tu:peɪ, *Am:* tu:'peɪ] *n* peluquín *m*

tour [tʊəʳ, *Am:* tʊr] I. *n* **1.**(*journey*) viaje *m;* **guided** ~ excursión *f* guiada **2.**(*of factory*) visita *f* **3.** MUS gira *f* II. *vt* **1.**(*travel around*) recorrer **2.**(*visit*) visitar

tourism ['tʊərɪzəm, *Am:* 'tʊrɪ-] *n no pl* turismo *m*

tourist ['tʊərɪst, *Am:* 'tʊrɪst] *n* turista *mf*

tourist agency *n* agencia *f* de viajes **tourist guide** *n* **1.**(*book*) guía *f* turística **2.**(*person*) guía *mf* **tourist information office** *n* oficina *f* de turismo

tournament ['tɔ:nəmənt, *Am:* 'tɜ:r-] *n* SPORTS torneo *m*

tour operator *n* operador *m* turístico

tousle ['taʊzl] *vt* revolver

tout [taʊt] I. *n* revendedor(a) *m(f)* II. *vi* **to** ~ **for custom** buscar clientes

tow [təʊ, *Am:* toʊ] I. *n* remolque *m;* **to give sb a** ~ remolcar a alguien; **to have sb in** ~ *fig* llevar a alguien a cuestas II. *vt* remolcar

toward(s) [tə'wɔ:d(z), *Am:*

Fruit and vegetables

1	apple	manzana *f*
2	pear	pera *f*
3	peach	melocotón *m*
4	strawberry	fresa *f*
5	grapes	(racimo *m* de) uvas *fpl*
6	cherries	cerezas *fpl*
7	orange	naranja *f*
8	lemon	limón *m*
9	mandarin, tangerine	mandarina *f*
10	banana	plátano *m*, banana *f AmL*
11	potato	patata *f*, papa *f AmL*
12	tomato	tomate *m*
13	Brussels sprouts	coles *fpl* de Bruselas

14	cabbage	col *f*
15	celery	apio *m*
16	garlic	ajo *m*
17	onion	cebolla *f*
18	cauliflower	coliflor *f*
19	cucumber	pepino *m*
20	aubergine *Brit*, eggplant *Am*	berenjena *f*
21	carrot	zanahoria *f*
22	leek	puerro *m*
23	corn cob, corn *Am*	mazorca *f*, panocha *f*
24	lettuce	lechuga *f*

tɔːrd(z)] *prep* **1.**(*in direction of*) hacia **2.**(*for*) por

towel ['taʊəl] *n* toalla *f;* **to throw in the ~** tirar la toalla

towel rack *n Am*, **towel rail** *n Aus, Brit* toallero *m*

tower ['taʊəʳ, *Am:* 'taʊɚ] *n* torre *f;* **a ~ of strength** un gran apoyo

♦ **tower above** *vi*, **tower over** *vi* **to ~ sb** ser mucho más alto que alguien

tower block *n Brit* edificio *m* de apartamentos

towering *adj* altísimo

town [taʊn] *n* (*large*) ciudad *f;* (*small*) pueblo *m;* **to go out on the ~** salir de juerga

town centre *n Brit* centro *m* de la ciudad **town council** *n Brit* ayuntamiento *m* **town hall** *n* POL ayuntamiento *m* **town planning** *n* urbanismo *m*

township ['taʊnʃɪp] *n* **1.**Am, Can municipio *m* **2.** South Africa distrito *m* segregado

townspeople ['taʊnzˌpiːpl] *npl* ciudadanos *mpl*

tow truck *n Am* grúa *f*

toxaemia [tɒkˈsiːmɪə, *Am:* taːk-] *n*, **toxemia** *n Am no pl* toxemia *f*

toxic ['tɒksɪk, *Am:* 'taːk-] *adj* tóxico

toxin ['tɒksɪn, *Am:* 'taːk-] *n* toxina *f*

toy [tɔɪ] *n* juguete *m;* **cuddly ~** muñeco *m* de peluche

♦ **toy with** *vt* jugar con

toyshop *n* juguetería *f*

trace [treɪs] **I.** *n* **1.**(*sign*) rastro *m;* **to disappear without ~** desaparecer sin dejar rastro **2.**(*slight amount*) pizca *f* **II.** *vt* **1.**(*locate*) localizar **2.**(*draw outline of*) trazar; (*with tracing paper*) calcar

tracing paper *n* papel *m* de calco

track [træk] **I.** *n* **1.**(*path*) senda *f* **2.**(*rails*) vía *f* **3.**Am (*in station*) andén *m* **4.**(*mark*) pista *f;* (*of animal*) huella *f;* **to cover one's ~s** borrar las huellas; **to be on the ~ of sb** seguir la pista a alguien; **to lose/keep ~ (of sb)** perder/no perder de vista (a alguien); **to make ~s** *inf* largarse **5.**(*path*) camino *m;* **to be on**

the right ~ *fig* ir por buen camino; **to be on the wrong ~** *fig* estar equivocado; **to be on ~ (to do sth)** *fig* estar en camino (de hacer algo); **to change ~** *fig* cambiar de rumbo **6.**SPORTS pista *f* **7.**(*song*) canción *f* **II.** *vt* **1.**(*pursue*) seguir la pista de **2.**(*trace*) trazar

♦ **track down** *vt* localizar

track-and-field *n* atletismo *m*

tracking station ['trækɪŋˈsteɪʃn] *n* AVIAT, TECH centro *m* de seguimiento

track record *n* historial *m* **tracksuit** *n* chándal *m*

tract [trækt] *n* **1.**(*of land*) tramo *m* **2.**ANAT, MED sistema *m;* **digestive ~** tubo *m* digestivo; **respiratory ~** aparato *m* respiratorio

tractor ['træktəʳ, *Am:* -tɚ] *n* tractor *m*

trade [treɪd] **I.** *n* **1.**no pl (*buying and selling*) comercio *m* **2.**(*profession*) oficio *m* **3.**(*swap*) intercambio *m* **II.** *vi* comerciar; **to ~ in sth** dedicarse al negocio de algo **III.** *vt* (*exchange*) intercambiar

♦ **trade on** *vt* aprovecharse de

trade agreement *n* acuerdo *m* comercial **trade association** *n* asociación *f* mercantil **trade barrier** *n* barrera *f* arancelaria **trade directory** *n* guía *f* mercantil **trade fair** *n* COM feria *f* de muestras **trade gap** *n* déficit *m* inv de la balanza comercial

trade-in ['treɪdɪn] *n* COM permuta *f*

trademark *n* marca *f*

trade-off ['treɪdɒf, *Am:* -aːf] *n* intercambio *m*

trader ['treɪdəʳ, *Am:* -ɚ] *n* comerciante *mf*

trade route *n* ruta *f* comercial **trade secret** *n* secreto *m* profesional

tradesman ['treɪdzmən] <-men> *n* tendero *m*

trade surplus *n* excedente *m* comercial **trade union** *n* sindicato *m* **trade war** *n* guerra *f* comercial

trading ['treɪdɪŋ] *n no pl* comercio *m*

tradition [trəˈdɪʃən] *n* tradición *f;* **by ~** por tradición

traditional [trə'dɪʃənəl] *adj* tradicional

traditionalism [trə'dɪʃənəlɪzəm] *n no pl* tradicionalismo *m*

traditionalist [trə'dɪʃənəlɪst] *n* tradicionalista *mf*

traffic ['træfɪk] I. *n no pl* 1. (*vehicles*) tráfico *m*; **air** ~ tráfico *m* aéreo 2. (*movement*) tránsito *m*; **drug** ~ tráfico *m* de drogas II. <trafficked, trafficked> *vi pej* **to** ~ **in sth** traficar con algo

traffic jam *n* atasco *m*

trafficker ['træfɪkəʳ, *Am:* -ɚ] *n pej* traficante *mf*

traffic light *n* semáforo *m* **traffic warden** *n Brit* controlador(a) *m(f)* de estacionamientos

tragedy ['trædʒədi] <-ies> *n* tragedia *f*

tragic ['trædʒɪk] *adj* trágico

trail [treɪl] I. *n* 1. (*path*) camino *m* 2. (*track*) pista *f*; **a** ~ **of destruction** una estela de destrucción; **to be on the** ~ **of sb** seguir la pista de alguien II. *vt* 1. (*follow*) seguir la pista de 2. (*drag*) arrastrar
  ♦ **trail behind** *vi* ir detrás
  ♦ **trail off** *vi* esfumarse

trailblazer ['treɪl‚bleɪzəʳ, *Am:* -zɚ] *n* pionero, -a *m, f*

trailer *n* 1. (*wheeled container*) remolque *m* 2. *Am* (*mobile home*) caravana *f* 3. CINE tráiler *m*

trailer park *n Am* cámping *m* de caravanas

train [treɪn] I. *n* 1. RAIL tren *m* 2. (*series*) serie *f*; ~ **of thought** hilo *m* del pensamiento II. *vi* entrenarse III. *vt* formar; (*animal*) amaestrar

train driver *n* maquinista *mf*

trained ['treɪnd] *adj* formado; (*animal*) amaestrado

trainee [treɪ'niː] *n* aprendiz(a) *m(f)*

trainer *n* 1. (*person*) entrenador(a) *m(f)* 2. *Brit* (*shoe*) zapatilla *f* de deporte

training *n no pl* 1. (*education*) formación *f* 2. SPORTS entrenamiento *m*; **to be in** ~ **for sth** estar entrenando para algo

training camp *n* SPORTS campamento *m* de instrucción **training course** *n* curso *m* de formación

trait [treɪt] *n* rasgo *m*

traitor ['treɪtəʳ, *Am:* -ţɚ] *n* traidor(a) *m(f)*

traitorous ['treɪtərəs, *Am:* -ţɚ-] *adj pej, form* traicionero

trajectory [trə'dʒektəri, *Am:* -tɚi] *n* trayectoria *f*

tram [træm] *n Brit, Aus* tranvía *m*

tramp [træmp] I. *vi* andar con pasos pesados II. *n* (*down-and-out*) vagabundo *m*

trample ['træmpl] I. *vt* pisar; **to** ~ **sth underfoot** pisotear algo II. *vi* **to** ~ **on sth** pisar algo

trampoline ['træmpəliːn] *n* trampolín *m*

tramway ['træmweɪ] *n* tranvía *m*

trance [trɑːns, *Am:* træns] *n* trance *m*

tranquil ['træŋkwɪl] *adj* tranquilo

tranquility [træŋ'kwɪləti, *Am:*-əţi] *n Am s.* **tranquillity**

tranquilize ['træŋkwɪlaɪz] *vt Am s.* **tranquillize**

tranquilizer *n Am s.* **tranquillizer**

tranquillity [træŋ'kwɪləti, *Am:* -ţɪ] *n no pl* tranquilidad *f*

tranquillize ['træŋkwɪlaɪz] *vt* MED tranquilizar

tranquillizer *n* tranquilizante *m*

transact [træn'zækt] *vt* tramitar

transaction [træn'zækʃn] *n* COM transacción *f*, transa *f RíoPl*

transatlantic [‚trænzət'læntɪk, *Am:* ‚trænsæt'-] *adj* transatlántico

transcend [træn'send] *vt* trascender

transcendent [træn'sendənt] *adj* trascendente

transcendental [‚trænsen'dentl, *Am:* -ţl] *adj* trascendental

transcontinental ['trænzkɒntɪ'nentl, *Am:* ‚trænskɑːntn'en-] *adj* transcontinental

transcribe [træn'skraɪb] *vt* transcribir

transcript ['trænskrɪpt] *n* transcripción *f*

transcription [træn'skrɪpʃn] *n* transcripción *f*

transept ['trænsept] *n* ARCHIT crucero *m*
transfer [træns'fɜː, *Am:* -'fɜːr]
I. <-rr-> *vt* trasladar; (*power*) transferir; SPORTS traspasar II. *n* 1. traslado
m; SPORTS traspaso *m* 2. (*picture*)
cromo *m*
transferable [træns'fɜːrəbl] *adj*
transferible
transfigure [træns'fɪgəʳ, *Am:* -'fɪg-
jɚ] *vt* transfigurar
transfix [træns'fɪks] *vt form* **to be
~ed by sth** estar totalmente parali-
zado por algo
transform [træns'fɔːm, *Am:*
-'fɔːrm] *vt* transformar
transformation [ˌtrænsfə'meɪʃn,
Am: -fɚ'-] *n* transformación *f*
transformer [træns'fɔːməʳ, *Am:*
-'fɔːrmɚ] *n* ELEC transformador *m*
transfusion [træns'fjuːʒn] *n* transfusión *f*
transgress [trænz'gres] *form* I. *vt*
transgredir; **to ~ a law** infringir una
ley II. *vi* cometer una transgresión
transgression [trænz'greʃn] *n form*
transgresión *f*
transient ['trænzɪənt, *Am:* 'træn-
ʃnt] *adj form* pasajero
transistor [træn'zɪstəʳ, *Am:* -tɚ] *n*
ELEC transistor *m*
transit ['trænsɪt] *n no pl* tránsito *m;*
in ~ de paso
transition [træn'zɪʃn] *n* transición *f*
transitional [træn'zɪʃənl] *adj* (*period*) transitorio; (*government*) de
transición
transitive ['trænsətɪv, *Am:* -ţɪv] *adj*
LING transitivo
transitory ['trænsɪtəri, *Am:* -sətɔː-
rɪ] *adj* pasajero
translate [trænz'leɪt, *Am:* træn-
'sleɪt] I. *vt* LING traducir; **to ~ sth
from English into Spanish** traducir
algo del inglés al español II. *vi* LING
traducir
translation [trænz'leɪʃn, *Am:*
træn'sleɪ-] *n* traducción *f*
translator [trænz'leɪtəʳ, *Am:*
træn'sleɪţɚ] *n* traductor(a) *m(f)*
transliterate [trænz'lɪtəreɪt, *Am:*
træn'slɪţ-] *vt* transliterar

transliteration [ˌtrænzlɪtə'reɪʃn,
Am: træn,slɪţ-] *n* LING *no pl* transli-
teración *f*
translucent [trænz'luːsənt] *adj*
translúcido
transmission [trænz'mɪʃən] *n*
transmisión *f;* **data ~** INFOR transmisión de datos
transmit [trænz'mɪt, *Am:* træn-
'smɪt] <-tt-> *vt* transmitir
transmitter [trænz'mɪtəʳ, *Am:*
træn'smɪţɚ] *n* transmisor *m*
transmute [trænz'mjuːt] *vt form*
transmutar
transparency [træns'pærənsi, *Am:*
træn'sper-] *n* <-ies> transparencia *f*
transparent [træns'pærənt, *Am:*
træn'sper-] *adj* transparente
transpiration [ˌtrænspɪ'reɪʃn] *n no
pl* transpiración *f*
transpire [træn'spaɪəʳ, *Am:* -'spaɪ-
ɚ] *vi* 1. (*happen*) tener lugar; **it ~ed
that ...** ocurrió que... 2. (*emit vapour*) transpirar
transplant [træns'plɑːnt, *Am:*
træn'splænt] I. *vt* trasplantar II. *n*
trasplante *m*
transplantation [ˌtrænsplɑːn'teɪʃn, *Am:* -splæn'-] *n no pl* trasplante
m
transport [træn'spɔːt, *Am:*
-'spɔːrt] I. *vt* transportar; *Brit* HIST
deportar II. *n no pl* transporte *m;* **~
costs** gastos *mpl* de transporte
transportation [ˌtrænspɔː'teɪʃn,
Am: -spɚ'-] *n no pl* transporte *m;
Brit* HIST deportación *f*
transport café <-s> *n Brit* cafetería
f de carretera
transporter [træn'spɔːtəʳ, *Am:*
-'spɔːrţɚ] *n* transportador *m*
transpose [træn'spəʊz, *Am:*
-'spoʊz] *vt* transponer
transsexual [træns'seksjʊəl, *Am:*
-'sekʃuəl] *n* transexual *mf*
transverse ['trænzvɜːs] *adj* transversal
transvestite [trænz'vestaɪt] *n* travestido *m*
trap [træp] I. *n* 1. (*device*) trampa *f;*
(*ambush*) emboscada *f;* **to set a ~**
poner una trampa; **to fall into a ~**

Tₜ

caer en una emboscada **2.** *Brit, inf* **to shut one's** ~ cerrar el pico **II.** *vt* <-pp-> atrapar

trapdoor [ˌtræpˈdɔːʳ, *Am:* ˈtræpdɔːr] *n* escotillón *m*

trapeze [trəˈpiːz, *Am:* træpˈiːz] *n* trapecio *m*

trapezium [trəˈpiːzɪəm] <-s *o* -zia-> *pl Brit, Aus,* **trapezoid** [ˈtræpɪzɔɪd] *n Am* MAT trapecio *m*

trappings [ˈtræpɪŋz] *npl* **the ~ of power** el boato del poder

trash [træʃ] **I.** *n no pl* **1.** *Am* (*rubbish*) basura *f* **2.** *inf* (*people*) gentuza *f*; (*book, film*) basura *f* **3.** *inf* (*nonsense*) **to talk** ~ decir tonterías **II.** *vt inf* **1.** (*wreck*) destrozar **2.** (*criticize*) poner por los suelos

trashcan [ˈtræʃkæn] *n Am* cubo *m* de la basura

trashy [ˈtræʃi] *adj inf* malo

trauma [ˈtrɔːmə, *Am:* ˈtraːmə] *n* trauma *m*

traumatic [trɔːˈmætɪk, *Am:* traːˈmæt-] *adj* traumático

traumatise *vt Aus, Brit,* **traumatize** [ˈtrɔːmətaɪz] *vt* traumatizar

travel [ˈtrævəl] **I.** <*Brit:* -ll-, *Am:* -l-> *vi* **1.** (*make journey*) viajar; **to ~ by air/car** viajar en avión/coche; **to ~ light** viajar con poco equipaje **2.** (*light, sound*) propagarse **3.** (*be away*) estar de viaje **4.** *inf* (*go fast*) ir rápido **II.** <*Brit:* -ll-, *Am:* -l-> *vt* viajar por **III.** *npl* viajes *mpl*

travel agency *n* agencia *f* de viajes

travel agent *n* agente *mf* de viajes

traveler [ˈtrævləʳ, *Am:* -lər] *n Am s.* **traveller**

travel expenses *n* gastos *mpl* de viaje **travel guide** *n* guía *f* turística

traveling *n no pl, Am s.* **travelling**

travel insurance *n* seguro *m* de viaje

traveller [ˈtrævələʳ, *Am:* -ələr] *n Brit* viajero, -a *m, f*

traveller's cheque *n Brit,* **traveler's check** *n Am* cheque *m* de viaje

travelling *n no pl, Brit* viajar *m*

travelling allowance *n* dietas *fpl* **travelling salesman** *n* viajante *mf* de comercio

travel sickness *n no pl* mareo *m*

traverse [ˈtrævɜːs, *Am:* -ərs] *vt* atravesar

travesty [ˈtrævəsti, *Am:* -ɪsti] <-ies> *n pej* parodia *f*

trawl [trɔːl, *Am:* trɑːl] *vi* pescar al arrastre; **to ~ through sth** *fig* rastrear algo

trawler [ˈtrɔːləʳ, *Am:* ˈtrɑːlər] *n* pesquero *m* de arrastre

tray [treɪ] *n* bandeja *f*, charola *f AmS*

treacherous [ˈtretʃərəs] *adj* traicionero; (*road, weather*) peligroso

treachery [ˈtretʃəri] *n no pl* traición *f*

treacle [ˈtriːkl] *n no pl, Brit* melaza *f*

tread [tred] **I.** <trod *Am:* treaded, trodden *Am:* trod> *vi* pisar; **to ~ on/in sth** pisar algo **II.** *n* **1.** (*step*) escalón *m* **2.** AUTO dibujo *m*

treadmill [ˈtredmɪl] *n* rueda *f* de andar; *fig* rutina *f*

treason [ˈtriːzn] *n no pl* traición *f*

treasure [ˈtreʒəʳ, *Am:* -ər] **I.** *n* tesoro *m*; *fig* joya *f* **II.** *vt* atesorar

treasure hunt *n* caza *f* del tesoro

treasurer [ˈtreʒərəʳ, *Am:* -ər] *n* tesorero, -a *m, f*

treasury [ˈtreʒəri] <-ies> *n* tesorería *f*; **the Treasury** Hacienda *f*

Treasury Secretary *n Am* ≈ Ministro, -a *m, f* de Hacienda

treat [ˈtriːt] **I.** *vt* **1.** (*deal with, handle, discuss*) *a.* MED tratar; **to ~ sb badly** tratar mal a alguien **2.** (*pay for*) invitar **II.** *vi* **to ~ with sb** negociar con alguien **III.** *n* **1.** (*present*) regalo *m*; **it's my ~** invito yo **2.** (*pleasure*) placer *m*; **it was a real** ~ ha sido un auténtico placer

treatise [ˈtriːtɪz, *Am:* -tɪs] *n* tratado *m*

treatment [ˈtriːtmənt] *n* **1.** *no pl* trato *m*; **to give sb the ~** *inf* hacer sufrir a alguien; **special ~** tratamiento *m* especial **2.** MED tratamiento *m*

treaty [ˈtriːti, *Am:* -ti] <-ies> *n* tratado *m*; **peace ~** tratado de paz

treble [ˈtrebl] **I.** *n* MUS tiple *mf* **II.** *vt* triplicar **III.** *vi* triplicarse

treble clef *n* clave *f* de sol

tree [triː] *n* árbol *m*

tree house *n* cabaña *f* en un árbol
tree-lined ['triːlaɪnd] *adj* arbolado
treetop *n* **in the ~s** en lo alto de los árboles **tree trunk** *n* tronco *m* del árbol
trek [trek] I. <-kk-> *vi* caminar II. *n* caminata *f* (larga)
trellis ['trelɪs] <-es> *n* espaldera *f*; (*for plants*) enrejado *m*
tremble ['trembl] I. *vi* temblar; **to ~ with cold** tiritar de frío; **to ~ like a leaf** temblar como un azogado II. *n* temblor *m*; **to be all of a ~** *Brit, inf* estar como un flan
tremendous [trɪ'mendəs] *adj* **1.** (*enormous*) enorme; (*crowd, scope*) inmenso **2.** *inf* (*extremely good*) estupendo
tremor ['tremər, *Am:* -ɚ] *n* (*shake*) vibración *f*; (*earthquake*) temblor *m*; (*of fear, excitement*) estremecimiento *m*
tremulous ['tremjʊləs] *adj* trémulo
trench [trentʃ] <-es> *n* zanja *f*; MIL trinchera *f*
trench coat *n* trinchera *f*
trend [trend] *n* **1.** (*tendency*) tendencia *f*; **downward/upward ~** tendencia *f* a la baja/alcista **2.** (*fashion*) moda *f*; **to set a new ~** fijar una nueva moda
trendy ['trendi] <-ier, -iest> *adj* (*clothes, bar*) de moda; (*person*) moderno
trepidation [ˌtrepɪ'deɪʃn] *n no pl* ansiedad *f*
trespass ['trespəs] *vi* LAW entrar ilegalmente
trespasser ['trespəsər, *Am:* -pæsɚ] *n* intruso, -a *m, f*
trestle table ['tresl] *n* mesa *f* de caballete
triad ['traɪæd] *n* tríada *f*
trial ['traɪəl] *n* **1.** LAW proceso *m*; **to stand ~** ser procesado; **to be on ~ for one's life** ser acusado de un crimen capital **2.** (*test*) prueba *f*; **clinical ~s** ensayos *mpl* clínicos; **~ of strength** prueba de fuerza; **to give sb a ~** poner a alguien a prueba **3.** (*source of problems*) suplicio *m*; **~s and tribulations** tribulaciones

fpl
trial period *n* período *m* de prueba
triangle ['traɪæŋgl] *n* triángulo *m*
triangular [traɪ'æŋgjʊlər, *Am:* -lɚ] *adj* triangular
tribal ['traɪbl] *adj* tribal
tribe [traɪb] *n* tribu *f*
tribulation [ˌtrɪbjʊ'leɪʃn, *Am:* -jəˈ-] *n form* tribulación *f*
tribunal [traɪ'bjuːnl] *n* tribunal *m*
tributary ['trɪbjʊt(ə)ri, *Am:* -teri] <-ies> *n* GEO afluente *m*
tribute ['trɪbjuːt] *n* homenaje *m*; **to pay ~ to sb** rendir tributo a alguien; **to be a ~ to sb** hacer honor a alguien
trick [trɪk] I. *n* **1.** (*ruse*) truco *m*; **to play a ~ on sb** tender una trampa a alguien **2.** GAMES mano *f* II. *adj* **a ~ question** una pregunta con trampa III. *vt* engañar
trickery ['trɪkəri] *n no pl* artimañas *fpl*
trickle ['trɪkl] I. *vi* salir en un chorro fino; (*in drops*) gotear; **to ~ out** (*people*) salir poco a poco; (*information*) difundirse poco a poco II. *n* (*of liquid*) hilo *m*; (*of people, information*) goteo *m*
tricky ['trɪki] <-ier, -iest> *adj* **1.** (*crafty*) astuto **2.** (*difficult*) complicado; (*situation*) delicado
tricycle ['traɪsɪkl] *n* triciclo *m*
trident ['traɪdnt] *n* tridente *m*
tried [traɪd] I. *vi, vt pt, pp of* **try** II. *adj* **~ and tested** probado con toda garantía
trifle ['traɪfl] *n* **1.** (*insignificant thing*) bagatela *f* **2.** (*small amount*) **a ~** un poquito **3.** *Brit* (*dessert*) dulce *m* de bizcocho borracho
♦ **trifle with** *vt* jugar con
trifling *adj* insignificante
trigger ['trɪgər, *Am:* -ɚ] I. *n* **1.** (*of gun*) gatillo *m*; **to pull the ~** apretar el gatillo **2.** *fig* detonante *m* II. *vt* (*reaction*) provocar; (*revolt*) hacer estallar
trigonometry [ˌtrɪgə'nɒmətri, *Am:* -'nɑːmə-] *n no pl* trigonometría *f*
trillion ['trɪliən, *Am:* -jən] *n* billón *m*

trilogy ['trɪlədʒi] <-ies> n trilogía f

trim [trɪm] I. n 1. (state) **to be in ~** (**for sth**) estar listo (para algo) 2. (hair) **to give sb a ~** cortar las puntas del pelo a alguien 3. no pl (decorative edge) borde m II. adj (neat) aseado; (lawn) cuidado III. <-mm-> vt 1. (cut) cortar; **to ~ one's beard** cortarse la barba 2. (reduce) reducir
◆ **trim down** vt recortar

Trinidad ['trɪnɪdæd] n Trinidad f; **~ and Tobago** Trinidad y Tobago

Trinity ['trɪnəti, Am: -ţɪ] n no pl Trinidad f; **the** (**holy**) **~** la (Santísima) Trinidad

trinket ['trɪŋkɪt] n baratija f

trio ['triːəʊ, Am: -oʊ] n a. MUS trío m

trip [trɪp] I. n 1. (journey) viaje m; (shorter) excursión f; **business ~** viaje de negocios; **to go on a ~** irse de viaje 2. inf (effect of drugs) viaje m 3. (fall) tropezón m II. <-pp-> vi (stumble) tropezar; **to ~ on sth** tropezar con algo III. <-pp-> vt **to ~ sb** (**up**) hacer tropezar a alguien
◆ **trip over** vi dar un tropezón
◆ **trip up** I. vi tropezar II. vt hacer tropezar

tripe [traɪp] n no pl 1. GASTR callos mpl, guata f Méx 2. pej, inf **to talk ~** decir bobadas

triple ['trɪpl] I. vt triplicar II. vi triplicarse

triple jump n triple salto m

triplet ['trɪplɪt] n (baby) trillizo, -a m, f

triplicate ['trɪplɪkət, Am: -kɪt] adj triplicado; **in ~** por triplicado

tripod ['traɪpɒd, Am: -pɑːd] n trípode m

trite [traɪt] adj tópico

triumph ['traɪʌmf] I. n triunfo m; **a ~ of engineering** un éxito de la ingeniería II. vi triunfar; **to ~ over sb** triunfar sobre alguien

triumphant [traɪˈʌmfnt] adj (victorious) triunfante; (return) triunfal; **to emerge ~ from sth** salir triunfante de algo

trivia ['trɪvɪə] npl trivialidades fpl

trivial ['trɪvɪəl] adj (unimportant) irrelevante; (dispute, matter) trivial

trivialize ['trɪvɪəlaɪz] vt trivializar

trod [trɒd, Am: trɑːd] pt, pp of **tread**

trodden ['trɒdn, Am: 'trɑːdn] pp of **tread**

trolley ['trɒli, Am: 'trɑːli] n 1. Brit, Aus (small cart) carretilla f; **drinks ~** carrito m de bebidas; **luggage ~** carrito m para el equipaje; **shopping ~** carrito m de la compra; **to be off one's ~** estar chiflado 2. Am (trolley-car) tranvía m

trombone [trɒmˈbəʊn, Am: trɑːmˈboʊn] n trombón m

troop [truːp] I. n 1. pl MIL tropas fpl 2. (of people) grupo m II. vi **to ~ in/out** entrar/salir en tropel

troop carrier n avión m de transporte de tropas

trooper ['truːpər, Am: -pɚ] n 1. MIL soldado m de caballería; **to swear like a ~** soltar tacos como un carretero 2. Am (state police officer) policía mf

trophy ['trəʊfi, Am: 'troʊ-] n <-ies> trofeo m

tropic ['trɒpɪk, Am: 'trɑːpɪk] n trópico m; **the ~s** los trópicos

tropical ['trɒpɪkl, Am: 'trɑːpɪk-] adj tropical

trot [trɒt, Am: trɑːt] I. n trote m; **on the ~** seguidos II. vi trotar

trotter ['trɒtər, Am: 'trɑːţɚ] n manita f de cerdo

trouble ['trʌbl] I. n 1. (difficulty) dificultad f, problema m; **engine ~** avería f del motor; **stomach ~** dolor m de estómago; **to have ~** tener dificultades; **to ask for ~** buscarse problemas; **to get into ~** meterse en un lío; **to be in ~ with sb** tener problemas con alguien; **to land sb in ~** meter en un lío a alguien; **to stay out of ~** mantenerse al margen de los problemas 2. no pl (inconvenience) molestia f; **to go to the ~** (**of doing sth**) darse la molestia (de hacer algo); **to put sb to the ~ of doing sth** molestar a alguien pidiéndole que haga algo; **to be not worth the ~** no merecer la pena II. vt

1. *form* (*inconvenience*) molestar; **to ~ sb for sth** molestar a alguien por algo **2.** (*worry*) preocupar **III.** *vi* **to ~ to do sth** molestarse en hacer algo

troubled *adj* **1.** (*period*) turbulento **2.** (*worried*) preocupado

troublemaker ['trʌbl,meɪkəʳ, Am: -kəʳ] *n* alborotador(a) *m(f)*

troubleshooting ['trʌblʃuːtɪŋ] *n* localización *f* de problemas

troublesome ['trʌblsəm] *adj* molesto

trough [trɒf, Am: traːf] *n* **1.** (*receptacle*) abrevadero *m;* **feeding ~** comedero *m* **2.** (*low point*) punto *m* bajo **3.** METEO zona *f* de bajas presiones

troupe [truːp] *n* THEAT compañía *f*

trouser leg *n* pernera *f*

trousers ['traʊzəz, Am: -zəʳz] *npl* pantalones *mpl;* **a pair of ~** un pantalón; **to wear the ~** *fig* llevar los pantalones

trout [traʊt] *n* <-(s)> trucha *f*

trowel ['traʊəl] *n* (*for building*) llana *f;* (*for gardening*) desplantador *m*

truancy ['truːənsi] *n no pl* falta *f* a clase

truant ['truːənt] *n Brit, Aus* **to play ~** hacer novillos

truce [truːs] *n* tregua *f*

truck [trʌk] **I.** *n* **1.** (*lorry*) camión *m;* **pickup ~** camioneta *f* de plataforma **2.** *Brit* (*train*) vagón *m* de mercancías **II.** *vt Am* transportar

trucker *n* camionero, -a *m, f*

truculent ['trʌkjʊlənt] *adj* agresivo

trudge [trʌdʒ] *vi* caminar penosamente

true [truː] *adj* **1.** (*not false*) cierto; **to ring ~** sonar convincente **2.** (*genuine, real*) auténtico; **~ love** amor *m* verdadero; **to come ~** hacerse realidad **3.** (*loyal*) fiel; **to remain ~ to sth** mantenerse fiel a algo; **to be ~ to one's word** mantener su palabra; **to be ~ to oneself** ser fiel a sí mismo **4.** (*accurate*) exacto

truffle ['trʌfl] *n* trufa *f*

truly ['truːli] *adv* **1.** (*sincerely*) sinceramente; **yours ~** un saludo **2.** (*as*

intensifier) realmente

trump [trʌmp] *n* triunfo *m;* **to turn up ~s** *Brit* salvar la situación

trumpet ['trʌmpɪt, Am: -pət] *n* trompeta *f;* **to blow one's own ~** *inf* tirarse flores

trumpeter ['trʌmpɪtəʳ, Am: -pəṭəʳ] *n* trompetista *mf*

truncate [trʌŋ'keɪt] *vt* truncar

truncheon ['trʌntʃən] *n Brit, Aus* porra *f,* macana *f AmL*

trundle ['trʌndl] *vi* rodar

trunk [trʌŋk] *n* **1.** ANAT, BOT tronco *m;* (*of elephant*) trompa *f* **2.** (*for storage*) baúl *m* **3.** Am (*of car*) maletero *f,* baúl *m AmL* **4. a pair of swimming ~s** un bañador

truss up [trʌs-] *vt* atar

trust [trʌst] **I.** *n* **1.** *no pl* (*belief*) confianza *f;* **to place one's ~ in sb** depositar su confianza en alguien; **to take sth on ~** aceptar algo con los ojos cerrados **2.** *no pl* (*responsibility*) responsabilidad *f;* **a position of ~** un puesto de responsabilidad **3.** FIN, COM consorcio *m* **II.** *vt* **1.** (*place trust in*) confiar en; **to ~ sb to do sth** confiar a alguien el hacer algo; **to ~ that ...** esperar que +*subj* **2.** (*rely on*) dar responsabilidad a; **to ~ sb with sth** confiar responsabilidad de algo a alguien **III.** *vi* **to ~ in sb** confiar en alguien

trusted ['trʌstɪd] *adj* (*friend*) leal; (*method*) comprobado

trustee [trʌs'tiː] *n* fideicomisario, -a *m, f*

trusting *adj* confiado

trustworthy ['trʌst,wɜːði, Am: -,wɜːr-] *adj* (*person*) honrado; (*data*) fiable

trusty ['trʌsti] <-ier, -iest> *adj* leal

truth [truːθ] *n* verdad *f;* **a grain of ~** una pizca de verdad; **in ~** en realidad; **to tell the ~, ...** a decir verdad,...

truthful ['truːθfəl] *adj* veraz; (*sincere*) sincero

try [traɪ] **I.** *n* **1.** (*attempt*) intento *m;* **to give sth a ~** intentar algo **2.** (*in rugby*) ensayo *m* **II.** <-ie-> *vi* esforzarse; **to ~ and do sth** *inf* intentar hacer algo **III.** <-ie-> *vt* **1.** (*attempt*) intentar; **to ~ one's best** esforzarse al máximo; **to ~ one's luck** probar suerte **2.** (*test*) experimentar **3.** (*annoy*) cansar **4.** LAW juzgar

◆ **try on** *vt*, **try out** *vt* probar

trying *adj* (*exasperating*) molesto; (*difficult*) difícil

tsar [zɑːʳ, *Am:* zɑːr] *n* zar *m*

T-shirt ['tiːʃɜːt, *Am:* -ʃɜːrt] *n* camiseta *f*, playera *f Guat, Méx*, polera *f Chile*

tub [tʌb] *n* cubo *m*; (*of ice-cream*) tarrina *f*; (*bathtub*) bañera *f*

tuba ['tjuːbə] *n* tuba *f*

tubby ['tʌbi] <-ier, -iest> *adj inf* rechoncho, requenete *Ven*

tube [tjuːb, *Am:* tuːb] *n* **1.** (*cylinder*) tubo *m*; **to go down the ~s** *fig* echarse a perder **2.** *no pl, Brit* RAIL metro *m* **3.** *Am, inf* TV tele *f*

tuber ['tjuːbəʳ, *Am:* 'tuːbəʳ] *n* tubérculo *m*

tuberculosis [tjuːˌbɜːkjʊˈləʊsɪs, *Am:* tuːˌbɜːrkjəˈloʊ-] *n no pl* tuberculosis *f inv*

TUC [ˌtiːjuːˈsiː] *n Brit abbr of* **Trades Union Congress** congreso *m* sindical

tuck in [tʌk-] *vi* comer con apetito

Tuesday ['tjuːzdeɪ, *Am:* 'tuːz-] *n* martes *m inv; s. a.* **Friday**

tuft [tʌft] *n* (*of hair*) mechón *m*; (*of grass*) mata *f*

tug [tʌg] **I.** *n* **1.** (*pull*) tirón *m* **2.** NAUT remolcador *m* **II.** <-gg-> *vt* tirar de; NAUT remolcar

tuition [tjuːˈɪʃən] *n no pl* enseñanza *f*

tulip ['tjuːlɪp, *Am:* 'tuː-] *n* tulipán *m*

tumble ['tʌmbl] **I.** *n* caída *f*; **to take a ~** caerse **II.** *vi* caerse

tumble drier *n*, **tumble dryer** *n* secadora *f*

tumbler ['tʌmbləʳ, *Am:* -bləʳ] *n* vaso *m*

tummy ['tʌmi] <-ies> *n childspeak* barriguita *f*

tumor *n Am*, **tumour** ['tjuːməʳ, *Am:* 'tuːməʳ] *n Brit, Aus* tumor *m*

tumult ['tjuːmʌlt, *Am:* 'tuː-] *n no pl* (*uproar*) tumulto *m*; (*emotional*) agitación *f*

tumultuous [tjuːˈmʌltʃʊəs, *Am:* tuːˈmʌltʃuːəs] *adj* (*noisy*) tumultuoso; (*disorderly*) agitado

tuna ['tjuːnə, *Am:* 'tuː-] *n* <-(s)> atún *m*

tundra ['tʌndrə] *n no pl* tundra *f*

tune [tjuːn, *Am:* tuːn] **I.** *n* **1.** MUS melodía *f* **2.** *no pl* (*pitch*) **to be in ~** estar afinado; **to be out of ~** estar desafinado; **to be in ~ with sth** *fig* armonizar con algo; **to be out of ~ with sth** *fig* desentonar con algo **3.** **to change one's ~** cambiar de parecer **II.** *vt* **1.** MUS afinar **2.** AUTO poner a punto

◆ **tune in** *vi* **to ~ to a station** sintonizar una emisora

tuneful ['tjuːnfəl] *adj* melódico

tuneless ['tjuːnləs] *adj* disonante

tunic ['tjuːnɪk, *Am:* 'tuː-] *n* FASHION casaca *f*; HIST túnica *f*

Tunisia [tjuːˈnɪzɪə, *Am:* tuːˈniːʒə] *n* Túnez *m*

tunnel ['tʌnl] **I.** *n* túnel *m*; MIN galería *f* **II.** <-*Brit:* -l-, *Am:* -ll-> *vi* hacer un túnel

turban ['tɜːbən, *Am:* 'tɜːr-] *n* turbante *m*

turbid ['tɜːbɪd, *Am:* 'tɜːr-] *adj* turbio

turbine ['tɜːbaɪn, *Am:* 'tɜːrbɪn] *n* turbina *f*

turbot ['tɜːbət, *Am:* 'tɜːr-] *n* <-(s)> rodaballo *m*

turbulence ['tɜːbjʊləns, *Am:* 'tɜːr-] *n no pl* turbulencia *f*

turbulent ['tɜːbjʊlənt, *Am:* 'tɜːr-] *adj* turbulento

turd [tɜːd, *Am:* tɜːrd] *n vulg* **1.** (*excrement*) zurullo *m* **2.** (*person*) cerdo, -a *m, f*

turf [tɜːf, *Am:* tɜːrf] <-s *o* -ves> *n* **1.** *no pl* BOT césped *m*; **a (piece of) ~** un tepe **2.** (*territory*) territorio *m*

turgid ['tɜːdʒɪd, *Am:* 'tɜːr-] *adj pej* ampuloso

Turk [tɜːk, *Am:* tɜːrk] *n* turco, -a *m, f*

turkey ['tɜːki, *Am:* 'tɜːr-] *n* **1.** ZOOL pavo *m*; **to talk ~** *Am, inf* hablar claro **2.** *Am, Aus, inf* (*stupid person*) papanatas *mf inv*

Turkey ['tɜːki, *Am:* 'tɜːr-] *n* Turquía *f*

Turkish ['tɜːkɪʃ, *Am:* 'tɜːr-] I. *adj* turco II. *n* turco, -a *m, f*

turmoil ['tɜːmɔɪl, *Am:* 'tɜːr-] *n no pl* caos *m inv;* **to be thrown into** ~ estar sumido en el caos; **to be in a** ~ estar desconcertado

turn [tɜːn, *Am:* tɜːrn] I. *vi* 1. *(rotate)* girar; **to** ~ **on sth** girar sobre algo 2. *(switch direction)* volver; *(tide)* cambiar; *(car)* girar; **to turn around** dar media vuelta, voltearse *AmL;* **to** ~ **right/left** torcer a la derecha/izquierda 3. *(change)* cambiar; *(for worse)* volverse; *(leaves)* cambiar de color; *(milk)* agriarse II. *vt* 1. *(rotate)* hacer girar; *(key)* dar vuelta a 2. *(switch direction)* volver, voltear *AmL;* **to** ~ **one's head** volver la cabeza; **to** ~ **a page** pasar una página 3. *fig* **to** ~ **30** cumplir los 30; **it** ~**ed my stomach** se me revolvió el estómago; **to** ~ **sth upside down** dejar algo patas arriba III. *n* 1. *(change in direction)* cambio *m* de dirección; **to make a** ~ **to the right** girar hacia la derecha; **to take a** ~ **for the worse/better** mejorar/empeorar; **the** ~ **of the century** el cambio de siglo 2. *(period of duty)* turno *m;* **it's your** ~ te toca a ti; **to speak out of** ~ hablar fuera de lugar 3. *(rotation)* rotación *f* 4. *(service)* favor *m;* **one good** ~ **deserves another** *prov* favor con favor se paga 5. *(shock)* **to give sb a** ~ dar un susto a alguien 6. THEAT número *m*

◆**turn away** I. *vi* apartarse II. *vt (refuse entry)* no dejar entrar

◆**turn back** I. *vi* retroceder II. *vt (send back)* hacer regresar

◆**turn down** *vt* 1. *(reject)* rechazar 2. *(reduce volume)* bajar

◆**turn in** *vt (hand over)* entregar

◆**turn into** *vt* transformar en

◆**turn off** *vt* 1. ELEC desconectar; *(light)* apagar; *(motor)* parar; *(gas)* cerrar 2. *inf (be unappealing)* repugnar

◆**turn on** *vt* 1. ELEC conectar; *(light)* encender, prender *AmL;* *(gas)* abrir 2. *(excite)* excitar

◆**turn out** I. *vi* salir; **it turned out**

to be true resultó ser cierto II. *vt (light)* apagar

◆**turn over** *vt (change the side)* dar la vuelta a

◆**turn round** I. *vi* volverse II. *vt* 1. *(move)* girar 2. *(change)* transformar

◆**turn to** *vt* **to** ~ **sb (for sth)** recurrir a alguien (para algo)

◆**turn up** I. *vi (arrive)* llegar II. *vt* 1. *(volume)* subir 2. *(find)* encontrar

turnaround ['tɜːnərˌaʊnd, *Am:* 'tɜːrnɚ-] *n (improvement)* mejora *f*

turning ['tɜːnɪŋ, *Am:* 'tɜːr-] *n (road)* bocacalle *f*

turning point *n* momento *m* decisivo

turnip ['tɜːnɪp, *Am:* 'tɜːr-] *n* nabo *m*

turn-off ['tɜːnɒf, *Am:* 'tɜːrnɑːf] *n* AUTO salida *f* de una calle; **to be a real** ~ *inf* ser repugnante

turnout ['tɜːnaʊt, *Am:* 'tɜːrn-] *n* número *m* de asistentes; POL número *m* de votantes

turnover ['tɜːnˌəʊvəʳ, *Am:* 'tɜːrnˌoʊvɚ-] *n* 1. COM, FIN volumen *m* de negocios; *(sales)* facturación *f* 2. *(in staff)* rotación *f* 3. GASTR empanada *f*

turnpike ['tɜːnpaɪk, *Am:* 'tɜːrn-] *n Am* AUTO autopista *f* de peaje

turnstile ['tɜːnstaɪl, *Am:* 'tɜːrn-] *n* torniquete *m*

turntable ['tɜːnˌteɪbl, *Am:* 'tɜːrn-] *n* 1. MUS plato *m* giratorio 2. RAIL plataforma *f* giratoria

turn-up ['tɜːnʌp, *Am:* 'tɜːrn-] *n Brit* vuelta *f;* **to be a** ~ **for the book(s)** ser una gran sorpresa

turpentine ['tɜːpəntaɪn, *Am:* 'tɜːr-] *n no pl* trementina *f*

turquoise ['tɜːkwɔɪz, *Am:* 'tɜːr-] *n (color)* azul *m* turquesa

turret ['tʌrɪt, *Am:* 'tɜːr-] *n (tower)* torreón *m;* *(of tank, ship)* torreta *f*

turtle ['tɜːtl, *Am:* 'tɜːrt̬l] <-(s)> *n* tortuga *f*

turtledove ['tɜːtldʌv, *Am:* 'tɜːrt̬l-] *n* tórtola *f*

turves [tɜːvz, *Am:* tɜːrvz] *n pl of* **turf**

tusk [tʌsk] *n* colmillo *m*

tussle ['tʌsl] I. *vi* pelearse II. *n* pelea *f*

T
t

tut [tʌt] *interj* ~ ~! ¡vaya, vaya!

tutor ['tjuːtəʳ, *Am:* 'tuːt̬ɚ] *n* profesor(a) *m(f)* (particular)

tutorial [tjuːˈtɔːrɪəl, *Am:* tuːˈ-] *n* clase *f* en grupo reducido

tuxedo [tʌkˈsiːdəʊ, *Am:* -doʊ] *n Am* esmoquin *m*

TV [ˌtiːˈviː] *n abbr of* television TV *f*

tweak [twiːk] I. *vt* pellizcar II. *n* pellizco *m*

tweed [twiːd] *n no pl* tweed *m*

tweezers ['twiːzəz, *Am:* -zɚz] *npl* (a pair of) ~ (unas) pinzas

twelfth [twelfθ] *adj* duodécimo

twelve [twelv] *adj* doce *inv; s. a.* **eight**

twentieth ['twentɪəθ, *Am:* -t̬ɪ-] *adj* vigésimo

twenty ['twenti, *Am:* -t̬i] *adj* veinte *inv; s. a.* **eighty**

twerp [twɜːp, *Am:* twɜːrp] *n inf* imbécil *mf*

twice [twaɪs] *adv* dos veces

twiddle ['twɪdl] *vt* (hacer) girar; **to** ~ **one's thumbs** estar mano sobre mano

twig [twɪg] *n* ramita *f*

twilight ['twaɪlaɪt] *n* crepúsculo *m*

twin [twɪn] I. *n* gemelo, -a *m, f;* **identical** ~**s** gemelos idénticos II. *adj* gemelo III. *vt* <-nn-> hermanar

twine [twaɪn] *n no pl* cordel *m*

twinge [twɪndʒ] *n* punzada *f;* **a** ~ **of conscience** un remordimiento de conciencia

twinkle ['twɪŋkl] *vi* (*diamond, eyes*) brillar; (*star*) centellear

twinkling ['twɪŋklɪŋ] I. *adj* (*diamond, eyes*) brillante; (*star*) centelleante II. *n* **in the** ~ **of an eye** en un abrir y cerrar de ojos

twirl [twɜːl, *Am:* twɜːrl] I. *vi* girar II. *vt* dar vueltas a

twist [twɪst] I. *vt* **1.** (*turn*) dar vueltas a; **to** ~ **sth around sth** enrollar algo alrededor de algo; **to** ~ **sb's arm** *fig* presionar a alguien; **to** ~ **sb round one's little finger** manejar a alguien a su antojo **2.** (*distort: truth*) tergiversar II. *vi* **1.** (*squirm around*) (re)torcerse **2.** (*curve: path, road*)

serpentear; **to** ~ **and turn** dar vueltas III. *n* **1.** (*turn*) vuelta *f* **2.** (*unexpected change*) giro *m*

twisted ['twɪstɪd] *adj* (*cable, logic*) retorcido; (*ankle*) torcido

twit [twɪt] *n inf* imbécil *mf*

twitch [twɪtʃ] I. *vi* ANAT, MED moverse (nerviosamente); (*face*) contraerse II. *n* <-es> **to have a** (**nervous**) ~ tener un tic (nervioso)

two [tuː] I. *adj* dos *inv* II. *n* dos *m;* **that makes** ~ **of us** *inf* ya somos dos; **to put** ~ **and** ~ **together** *inf* sacar conclusiones; *s. a.* **eight**

two-dimensional [ˌtuːdɪˈmentʃənəl] *adj* bidimensional; *fig* superficial **two-faced** *adj pej* falso, falluto *RíoPl*

twofold ['tuːfəʊld, *Am:* -foʊld] *adv* dos veces

two-time *vt inf* poner los cuernos a **two-way** [ˌtuːˈweɪ, *Am:* 'tuː-] *adj* de dos sentidos; (*process*) recíproco

tycoon [taɪˈkuːn] *n* magnate *m*

type [taɪp] I. *n a.* TYPO tipo *m;* **he's not her** ~ no es su tipo II. *vt, vi* escribir a máquina

typesetting ['taɪpˌsetɪŋ, *Am:* -ˌset̬-] *n no pl* composición *f* tipográfica

typewriter ['taɪpˌraɪtəʳ, *Am:* -t̬ɚ] *n* máquina *f* de escribir

typhoid (**fever**) ['taɪfɔɪd] *n no pl* fiebre *f* tifoidea

typhoon [taɪˈfuːn] *n* tifón *m*

typhus ['taɪfəs] *n no pl* tifus *m inv*

typical ['tɪpɪkəl] *adj* típico

typically *adv* típicamente

typify ['tɪpɪfaɪ] <-ie-> *vt* simbolizar

typing ['taɪpɪŋ] *n no pl* mecanografía *f*

typist ['taɪpɪst] *n* mecanógrafo, -a *m, f*

tyrannical [tɪˈrænɪkəl] *adj pej* tiránico

tyranny ['tɪrəni] *n no pl* tiranía *f*

tyrant ['taɪərənt, *Am:* 'taɪrənt] *n* tirano, -a *m, f*

tyre ['taɪəʳ, *Am:* 'taɪɚ] *n Aus, Brit* neumático *m*, caucho *m Col, Ven;* **spare** ~ neumático de repuesto

tzar [zɑːʳ, *Am:* zɑːr] *n* zar *m*

U u

U, u [ju:] *n* U, u *f;* ~ **for Uncle** U de Uruguay

UAE [ˌjuːeɪˈiː] *npl abbr of* **United Arab Emirates** EAU *mpl*

ubiquitous [juːˈbɪkwɪtəs, *Am:* -wətəs] *adj* omnipresente

udder [ˈʌdəʳ, *Am:* -ə·] *n* ubre *f*

UEFA [juːˈeɪfə] *n abbr of* **Union of European Football Associations** UEFA *f*

UFO [ˌjuːefˈəʊ, *Am:* -ˈoʊ] *n abbr of* **unidentified flying object** OVNI *m*

Uganda [juːˈgændə] *n* Uganda *f*

Ugandan *adj* ugandés

ugh [ɜːh] *interj* *inf* uf

ugly [ˈʌɡli] <-ier, iest> *adj* (*person*) feo, macaco *Arg, Méx, Cuba, Chile;* (*mood*) peligroso; (*weather*) horroroso; ~ **duckling** patito *m* feo; **to be ~ as sin** ser más feo que Picio

UHT [ˌjuːeɪtʃˈtiː] *adj abbr of* **ultra heat treated** UHT

UK [ˌjuːˈkeɪ] *n abbr of* **United Kingdom** RU *m*

Ukraine [juːˈkreɪn] *n* Ucrania *f*

Ukrainian *adj* ucraniano

ulcer [ˈʌlsəʳ, *Am:* -sə·] *n* (*stomach*) úlcera *f*, chácara *f* Col; (*in mouth, external*) llaga *f*

Ulster [ˈʌlstəʳ, *Am:* -stə·] *n* *no pl* Ulster *m*

ulterior [ʌlˈtɪərɪəʳ, *Am:* -ˈtɪriə·] *adj* (*motive*) oculto

ultimata [ˌʌltɪˈmeɪtə, *Am:* -t̬əˈmeɪt̬ə] *n pl of* **ultimatum**

ultimate [ˈʌltɪmət, *Am:* -t̬əmɪt] *adj* (*experience*) extremo; (*praise*) supremo; (*cost*) definitivo; (*cause*) primordial

ultimately [ˈʌltɪmətli, *Am:* -t̬əmɪt-] *adv* **1.** (*in the end*) finalmente **2.** (*fundamentally*) fundamentalmente

ultimatum [ˌʌltɪˈmeɪtəm, *Am:* -t̬əˈmeɪt̬əm] <ultimata *o* -tums> *n* ultimátum *m*

ultrasonic [ˌʌltrəˈsɒnɪk, *Am:* -ˈsɑː-

nɪk] *adj* ultrasónico

ultrasound [ˈʌltrəsaʊnd] *n* ultrasonido *m*

ultraviolet [ˌʌltrəˈvaɪələt, *Am:* -lɪt] *adj* ultravioleta

Ulysses [ˈjuːlɪsiːz, *Am:* juːˈlɪs-] *n* Ulises *m*

umbilical cord [ʌmˈbɪlɪkl] *n* cordón *m* umbilical

umbrella [ʌmˈbrelə] *n* paraguas *m inv;* **beach ~** parasol *m;* **to do sth under the ~ of sth** *fig* hacer algo bajo el amparo de algo

umpire [ˈʌmpaɪəʳ, *Am:* -paɪə·] *n* árbitro *mf*

umpteenth [ˈʌmptiːnθ] *adj* enésimo

UN [ˌjuːˈen] *n abbr of* **United Nations** ONU *f*

unable [ʌnˈeɪbl] *adj* incapaz

unabridged [ˌʌnəˈbrɪdʒd] *adj* LIT no abreviado

unacceptable [ˌʌnəkˈseptəbl] *adj* inaceptable

unaccompanied [ˌʌnəˈkʌmpənɪd] *adj* sin compañía

unaccustomed [ˌʌnəˈkʌstəmd] *adj* **to be ~ to doing sth** no tener la costumbre de hacer algo

unacknowledged [ˌʌnəkˈnɒlɪdʒd, *Am:* -ˈnɑːlɪdʒd] *adj* no reconocido

unadventurous [ˌʌnədˈventʃərəs] *adj* poco atrevido

unadvisable [ˌʌnədˈvaɪzəbl] *adj* poco aconsejable

unaffected [ˌʌnəˈfektɪd] *adj* **1.** (*not changed*) inalterado **2.** (*down to earth*) sencillo

unambiguous [ˌʌnæmˈbɪɡjuəs] *adj* inequívoco

unanimity [ˌjuːnəˈnɪməti, *Am:* -t̬i] *n no pl, form* unanimidad *f*

unanimous [juːˈnænɪməs, *Am:* -əməs] *adj* unánime

unanswered [ʌnˈɑːnsəd, *Am:* -ˈænsə·d] *adj* sin contestar

unarmed [ʌnˈɑːmd, *Am:* -ˈɑːrmd] *adj* desarmado

unassuming [ˌʌnəˈsjuːmɪŋ, *Am:* -ˈsuː-] *adj* modesto

unattainable [ˌʌnəˈteɪnəbl] *adj* inasequible

unattractive [ˌʌnəˈtræktɪv] *adj* feo; (*personality*) antipático

unauthorized [ˌʌnˈɔːθəraɪzd, *Am:* -ˈɑː-] *adj* no autorizado

unavailable [ˌʌnəˈveɪləbl] *adj* inasequible

unavoidable [ˌʌnəˈvɔɪdəbl] *adj* inevitable

unaware [ˌʌnəˈweəʳ, *Am:* -ˈwer] *adj* **to be ~ of sth** ignorar algo

unawares [ˌʌnəˈweəz, *Am:* -ˈwerz] *adv* **to catch sb ~** coger a alguien desprevenido

unbalanced [ˌʌnˈbælənst] *adj* desequilibrado

unbearable [ˌʌnˈbeərəbl, *Am:* -ˈberə-] *adj* insoportable

unbeatable [ˌʌnˈbiːtəbl, *Am:* -ˈbiːt̬ə-] *adj* (*team, army*) invencible; (*value, quality*) inmejorable

unbeaten [ˌʌnˈbiːtn] *adj* invicto

unbecoming [ˌʌnbɪˈkʌmɪŋ] *adj* **1.** (*dress, suit*) que sienta mal **2.** (*attitude, manner*) impropio

unbelievable [ˌʌnbɪˈliːvəbl] *adj* increíble

unbiased [ʌnˈbaɪəst] *adj* imparcial

unborn [ʌnˈbɔːn, *Am:* -ˈbɔːrn] *adj* (*baby*) no nacido; (*foetus*) nonato

unbounded [ʌnˈbaʊndɪd] *adj* ilimitado

unbreakable [ʌnˈbreɪkəbl] *adj* indestructible

unbridled [ʌnˈbraɪdld] *adj* desenfrenado

unbroken [ʌnˈbrəʊkən, *Am:* -ˈbroʊ-] *adj* **1.** (*not broken*) no roto **2.** (*continuous*) ininterrumpido **3.** (*record*) imbatible

unburden [ʌnˈbɜːdən, *Am:* -ˈbɜːr-] *vt* **to ~ oneself of sth/to sb** desahogarse de algo/con alguien

unbusinesslike [ʌnˈbɪznɪslaɪk] *adj* poco profesional

unbutton [ʌnˈbʌtən] *vi, vt* desabrochar(se)

uncalled-for [ʌnˈkɔːldfɔːʳ, *Am:* -fɔːr] *adj* gratuito

uncanny [ʌnˈkæni] *adj* <-ier, -iest> **1.** (*mysterious*) misterioso **2.** (*remarkable*) extraordinario

unceremonious [ˌʌnˌserɪˈməʊniəs, *Am:* -ˈmoʊ-] *adj* (*abrupt*) brusco

uncertain [ʌnˈsɜːtən, *Am:* -ˈsɜːr-] *adj* **1.** (*unsure*) dudoso; **to be ~ of sth** no estar seguro de algo; **in no ~ terms** claramente **2.** (*unpredictable*) incierto

uncertainty [ʌnˈsɜːtənti, *Am:* -ˈsɜːrtənt̬i] <-ies> *n* **1.** (*unpredictability*) incerteza *f* **2.** *no pl* (*unsettled state*) incertidumbre *f* **3.** *no pl* (*hesitancy*) indecisión *f*

unchallenged [ʌnˈtʃælɪndʒd] *adj* incontestado; **to go ~** pasar sin protesta

unchanged [ʌnˈtʃeɪndʒd] *adj* inalterado

uncharacteristic [ˌʌnkærəktəˈrɪstɪk, *Am:* -ˌkerɪktə-] *adj* poco característico

unchecked [ˌʌnˈtʃekt] *adj* (*unrestrained*) desenfrenado

uncivil [ʌnˈsɪvl] *adj form* grosero

uncle [ˈʌŋkl] *n* tío *m*

unclean [ˌʌnˈkliːn] *adj* sucio

unclear [ʌnˈklɪəʳ, *Am:* -ˈklɪr] *adj* nada claro; **to be ~ about sth** no estar seguro de algo; **an ~ statement** una afirmación vaga

uncomfortable [ʌnˈkʌmpftəbl, *Am:* ʌnˈkʌmpfɚt̬ə-] *adj* (*situation*) molesto; (*person*) incómodo

uncommon [ʌnˈkɒmən, *Am:* ʌnˈkɑːmən] *adj* (*rare*) extraño

uncommunicative [ˌʌnkəˈmjuːnɪkətɪv, *Am:* ˌʌnkəˈmjuːnɪkət̬ɪv] *adj* poco comunicativo

uncompromising [ʌnˈkɒmprəmaɪzɪŋ, *Am:* ʌnˈkɑːm-] *adj* intransigente

unconcerned [ˌʌnkənˈsɜːnd, *Am:* -ˈsɜːrnd] *adj* (*not worried*) despreocupado; **to be ~ about sth** no preocuparse por algo

unconditional [ˌʌnkənˈdɪʃənl] *adj* incondicional

unconfirmed [ˌʌnkənˈfɜːmd, *Am:* -ˈfɜːrmd] *adj* no confirmado

unconnected [ˌʌnkəˈnektɪd] *adj* desconectado

unconscious [ʌnˈkɒntʃəs, *Am:* ʌnˈkɑːn-] **I.** *adj* inconsciente; **to knock sb ~** dejar a alguien inconsciente; **to**

be ~ of sth (*unaware*) no ser consciente de algo **II.** *n no pl* PSYCH **the ~** el inconsciente

unconsciously *adv* inconscientemente

unconstitutional [ˌʌnˌkɒntstɪˈtjuː-ʃənəl, *Am:* ʌnˌkɑːntstəˈtuː-] *adj* inconstitucional

uncontrollable [ˌʌnkənˈtrəʊləbl, *Am:* -ˈtroʊ-] *adj* incontrolable

uncontrolled [ˌʌnkənˈtrəʊld, *Am:* -ˈtroʊld] *adj* descontrolado

uncontroversial [ˌʌnkɒntrəˈvɜːʃl] *adj* no controvertido

unconvinced [ˌʌnkənˈvɪnst] *adj* **to be ~ of sth** no estar convencido de algo

unconvincing [ˌʌnkənˈvɪnsɪŋ] *adj* poco convincente

uncooked [ʌnˈkʊkt] *adj* crudo

uncorroborated [ˌʌnkərˈɒbəreɪ-tɪd, *Am:* -ˈrɑːbəreɪṭɪd] *adj* no corroborado

uncouth [ʌnˈkuːθ] *adj* basto

uncover [ʌnˈkʌvəʳ, *Am:* -ˈkʌvɚ] *vt* desvelar

uncritical [ʌnˈkrɪtɪkl, *Am:* -ˈkrɪṭ-] *adj* **to be ~ of sth** no criticar algo

unctuous [ˈʌŋktʃuəs] *adj* zalamero

uncut [ʌnˈkʌt] *adj* **1.** (*not cut*) sin cortar; **an ~ diamond** un diamante en bruto **2.** (*not shortened*) sin cortes

undated [ʌnˈdeɪtɪd, *Am:* -ṭɪd] *adj* sin fecha

undaunted [ʌnˈdɔːntɪd, *Am:* -ˈdɑːnṭɪd] *adj* impertérrito; **to be ~ by sth** quedarse impávido ante algo

undecided [ˌʌndɪˈsaɪdɪd] *adj* **1.** (*unresolved*) indeciso; **to be ~ about sth** estar indeciso ante algo **2.** (*not settled*) no decidido

undeclared [ˌʌndɪˈkleəd, *Am:* -ˈklerd] *adj* **1.** FIN no declarado; **~ income** ingresos *mpl* no declarados **2.** (*not official*) no oficial

undefined [ˌʌndɪˈfaɪnd] *adj* indefinido

undemanding [ˌʌndɪˈmɑːndɪŋ] *adj* que exige poco esfuerzo; **to be ~** (*easy-going*) ser poco exigente

undemocratic [ˌʌndeməˈkrætɪk] *adj* antidemocrático

undemonstrative [ˌʌndɪˈmɒn-strətɪv, *Am:* -ˈmɑːnstrəṭɪv] *adj form* reservado

undeniable [ˌʌndɪˈnaɪəbl] *adj* innegable

undeniably *adv* indudablemente

under [ˈʌndəʳ, *Am:* -dɚ] **I.** *prep* **1.** (*below*) debajo de; **~ the bed** debajo de la cama **2.** (*supporting*) bajo; **to break ~ the weight** romperse bajo el peso **3.** (*less than*) **to cost ~ 10 euros** costar menos de 10 euros; **those ~ the age of 30** aquellos con menos de 30 años de edad **4.** (*governed by*) **~ Charles X** bajo Carlos X **5.** (*in category of*) **to classify the books ~ author** clasificar los libros por autor **II.** *adv* debajo

underage [ˌʌndəʳˈeɪdʒ, *Am:* -dɚ-] *adj* menor de edad

undercarriage [ˈʌndəˌkærɪdʒ, *Am:* -dɚˌker-] *n Brit* AVIAT tren *m* de aterrizaje

undercharge [ˌʌndəˈtʃɑːdʒ, *Am:* -dɚˈtʃɑːrdʒ] *vt* **to ~ sb** cobrar de menos a alguien

underclothes [ˈʌndəkləʊðz, *Am:* -dɚkloʊðz] *npl*, **underclothing** [ˈʌndəˌkləʊðɪŋ, *Am:* -dɚˌkloʊ-] *n no pl* ropa *f* interior

undercoat [ˈʌndəkəʊt, *Am:* -dɚkoʊt] *n no pl* primera capa *f* de pintura

undercover [ˌʌndəˈkʌvəʳ, *Am:* -dɚ-ˈkʌvɚ] *adj* secreto

undercurrent [ˈʌndəkʌrənt, *Am:* -dɚkɜːr-] *n* **1.** (*in sea*) corriente *f* submarina **2.** *fig* tendencia *f* oculta

undercut [ˌʌndəˈkʌt, *Am:* -dɚ-] *irr vt* vender más barato

underdeveloped [ˌʌndədɪˈveləpt, *Am:* -dɚdɪ-] *adj* subdesarrollado; **~ country** país *m* subdesarrollado

underdog [ˈʌndədɒg, *Am:* -dɚ-dɑːg] *n* desvalido, -a *m, f*

underdone [ˌʌndəˈdʌn, *Am:* -dɚ-] *adj* poco hecho

underequipped [ˌʌndərˈkwɪpt] *adj* mal equipado

underestimate [ˌʌndərˈestɪmeɪt, *Am:* -dɚˈestə-] *vt* subestimar

U **u**

underfed [ˌʌndəˈfed, *Am:* -dɚ-] *n* desnutrido, -a *m, f*

underfoot [ˌʌndəˈfʊt, *Am:* -dɚ-] *adv* debajo de los pies

undergo [ˌʌndəˈgəʊ, *Am:* -dɚˈgoʊ] *irr vt* **to ~ sth** experimentar algo; **to ~ a change** sufrir un cambio

undergraduate [ˌʌndəˈgrædʒʊət, *Am:* -dɚˈgrædʒuət] *n* estudiante *mf* no licenciado, -a

underground [ˈʌndəgraʊnd, *Am:* -dɚ-] **I.** *adj* subterráneo; *fig* clandestino **II.** *adv* bajo tierra; **to go ~** *fig* pasar a la clandestinidad **III.** *n no pl, Brit* (*subway train*) metro *m*

undergrowth [ˈʌndəgrəʊθ, *Am:* -dɚgroʊθ] *n no pl* maleza *f*

underhand [ˈʌndəhænd, *Am:* ˌʌndɚ-] **I.** *adj Brit* turbio **II.** *adv Am* (*underarm*) por debajo del hombro

underlay [ˌʌndəˈleɪ, *Am:* -dɚ-] *n no pl, Brit, Aus* refuerzo *m*

underlie [ˌʌndəˈlaɪ, *Am:* -dɚ-] *irr vt* **to ~ sth** subyacer a algo

underline [ˌʌndəˈlaɪn, *Am:* -dɚ-] *vt a. fig* subrayar

underlying [ˌʌndəˈlaɪɪŋ, *Am:* -dɚ-] *adj* subyacente

undermanned [ˌʌndəˈmænd, *Am:* -dɚ-] *adj* sin plantilla suficiente

undermine [ˌʌndəˈmaɪn, *Am:* -dɚ-] *vt* socavar; **to ~ sb's confidence** bajar la confianza de alguien

underneath [ˌʌndəˈniːθ, *Am:* -dɚ-] **I.** *prep* debajo de **II.** *adv* por debajo **III.** *n no pl* **the ~** la superficie inferior

undernourished [ˌʌndəˈnʌrɪʃt, *Am:* -dɚˈnɜːr-] *adj* desnutrido

underpaid [ˌʌndəˈpeɪd, *Am:* -dɚ-] *adj* mal pagado

underpants [ˈʌndəpænts, *Am:* -dɚ-] *npl* calzoncillos *mpl*

underpass [ˈʌndəpɑːs, *Am:* -dɚpæs] <-es> *n* paso *m* subterráneo

underpay [ˌʌndəˈpeɪ, *Am:* -dɚ-] *irr vt* pagar un sueldo insuficiente a

underperform [ˌʌndəpəˈfɔːm] *vi* rendir por debajo de lo suficiente

underprivileged [ˌʌndəˈprɪvəlɪdʒd, *Am:* -dɚ-] *adj* sin privilegios

underrate [ˌʌndəˈreɪt, *Am:* -dɚ-] *vt* **to ~ sb** subestimar a alguien; **to ~ the importance of sth** infravalorar la importancia de algo

underscore [ˌʌndəˈskɔːr, *Am:* -dɚˈskɔːr] *vt* subrayar; **to ~ a point** *fig* recalcar un punto

underseal [ˈʌndəsiːl, *Am:* -dɚ-] *n Brit* impermeable *m*

undershirt [ˈʌndəʃɜːt, *Am:* -dɚ-ʃɜːrt] *n Am* camiseta *f*

underside [ˈʌndəsaɪd, *Am:* -dɚ-] *n* superficie *f* inferior

undersigned [ˈʌndəsaɪnd, *Am:* ˈʌndɚsaɪnd] *n form* **the ~** el/la abajofirmante

underskirt [ˈʌndəskɜːt, *Am:* -dɚskɜːrt] *n* enaguas *fpl*

understaffed [ˌʌndəˈstɑːft, *Am:* -dɚˈstæft] *adj* falto de personal

understand [ˌʌndəˈstænd, *Am:* -dɚ-] *irr* **I.** *vt* entender, comprender; **to make oneself understood** hacerse entender; **to ~ sb's doing sth** entender que alguien haga algo; **as I ~ it** según tengo entendido **II.** *vi* entender

understandable [ˌʌndəˈstændəbl, *Am:* -dɚ-] *adj* comprensible

understanding **I.** *n* **1.** *no pl* (*comprehension*) entendimiento *m;* **a spirit of ~** un espíritu de comprensión; **to do sth on the ~ that ...** hacer algo a condición de que...; **to not have any ~ of sth** no tener ni idea de algo **2.** (*agreement*) acuerdo *m;* **to come to an ~** llegar a un acuerdo **II.** *adj* comprensivo

understate [ˌʌndəˈsteɪt, *Am:* -dɚ-] *vt* minimizar

understated *adj* sencillo

understatement [ˌʌndəˈsteɪtmənt, *Am:* ˌʌndɚˈsteɪt-] *n* atenuación *f*

understudy [ˈʌndəˌstʌdi, *Am:* -dɚ-] <-ies> *n* THEAT suplente *mf*

undertake [ˌʌndəˈteɪk, *Am:* -dɚ-] *irr vt* **to ~ a journey** emprender un viaje; **to ~ to do sth** comprometerse a hacer algo

undertaker [ˈʌndəˌteɪkər, *Am:* -dɚˌteɪkɚ] *n* director(a) *m(f)* de pompas fúnebres; **the ~'s** la funeraria

undertaking [ˌʌndəˈteɪkɪŋ, *Am:* ˌʌndəˈteɪ-] *n* **1.** (*project*) empresa *f* **2.** *form* (*pledge*) **to give an ~ that ...** prometer que...

undervalue [ˌʌndəˈvælju:, *Am:* -dəʳ-] *vt* subvalorar

underwater [ˌʌndəˈwɔːtəʳ, *Am:* -dəʳˈwɑːt̬əʳ] *adj* submarino

underwear [ˈʌndəweəʳ, *Am:* -dəˈwer] *n no pl* ropa *f* interior

underweight [ˌʌndəˈweɪt, *Am:* -dəʳ-] *adj* de peso insuficiente

underworld [ˈʌndəwɜːld, *Am:* -dəʳwɜːrld] *n* **1.** *no pl* (*criminal milieu*) hampa *m* **2.** (*afterworld*) **the Underworld** el infierno

underwrite [ˌʌndərˈaɪt, *Am:* ˈʌndəʳaɪt] *irr vt* (*insure*) asegurar

underwriter [ˈʌndərˌaɪtəʳ, *Am:* -dəʳˌraɪt̬əʳ] *n* asegurador(a) *m(f)*

undesirable [ˌʌndɪˈzaɪərəbl, *Am:* -ˈzaɪrəbl] *adj* indeseable

undeveloped [ˌʌndɪˈveləpt] *adj* ECON subdesarrollado

undisclosed [ˌʌndɪsˈkləʊzd, *Am:* -ˈkloʊzd] *adj* no revelado

undiscovered [ˌʌndɪsˈkʌvəd, *Am:* -əʳd] *adj* no descubierto

undisputed [ˌʌndɪˈspjuːtɪd, *Am:* -t̬ɪd] *adj* incontestable

undistinguished [ˌʌndɪˈstɪŋgwɪʃt] *adj* mediocre

undivided [ˌʌndɪˈvaɪdɪd] *adj* íntegro; **sb's ~ attention** toda la atención de alguien

undo [ʌnˈduː] *irr vt* **1.** (*unfasten*) soltar; **to ~ buttons** desabrochar botones; **to ~ a zipper** bajar una cremallera **2.** (*cancel*) anular; **to ~ the good work** deshacer el trabajo bueno

undoing *n no pl, form* ruina *f*

undoubted [ʌnˈdaʊtɪd, *Am:* -t̬ɪd] *adj* indudable

undoubtedly *adv* indudablemente

undress [ʌnˈdres] *vi*, *vt* desnudar(se), desvestir(se) *AmL*

undressed *adj* desnudo, desvestido *AmL;* **to get ~** desnudarse, desvestirse *AmL*

undue [ʌnˈdjuː, *Am:* -ˈduː] *adj form*

indebido

undulating *adj form* ondulante

unduly [ʌnˈdjuːli, *Am:* -ˈduː-] *adv* indebidamente

undying [ʌnˈdaɪɪŋ] *adj liter* imperecedero

unearned [ʌnˈɜːnd, *Am:* -ˈɜːrnd] *adj* inmerecido

unearth [ʌnˈɜːθ, *Am:* -ˈɜːrθ] *vt* desenterrar; **to ~ the truth** descubrir la verdad

unearthly [ʌnˈɜːθli, *Am:* -ˈɜːrθ-] *adj* sobrenatural

unease [ʌnˈiːz] *n no pl* malestar *m*

uneasiness *n no pl* inquietud *f*

uneasy [ʌnˈiːzi] *adj* <-ier, -iest> (*person*) intranquilo; (*relationship*) inestable

uneconomic [ˌʌnˌiːkəˈnɒmɪk, *Am:* -ˌekəˈnɑːmɪk] *adj* poco lucrativo

uneducated [ʌnˈedʒʊketɪd, *Am:* -ˈedʒʊkeɪt̬ɪd] *adj* inculto

unemotional [ˌʌnɪˈməʊʃənəl, *Am:* -ˈmoʊ-] *adj* impasible

unemployable [ˌʌnɪmˈplɔɪəbl] *adj* incapacitado para trabajar

unemployed [ˌʌnɪmˈplɔɪd] **I.** *n pl* **the ~** los desempleados **II.** *adj* parado

unemployment [ˌʌnɪmˈplɔɪmənt] *n no pl* **1.** (*condition*) desempleo *m;* **~ benefit** subsidio *m* de paro **2.** (*rate*) desocupación *f*

unending [ʌnˈendɪŋ] *adj* interminable

unenviable [ʌnˈenviəbl] *adj* poco envidiable

unequal [ʌnˈiːkwəl] *adj* desigual; **to be ~ to sth** no estar a la altura de algo

unequaled *adj Am,* **unequalled** *adj Brit* sin igual

unequivocal [ˌʌnɪˈkwɪvəkəl] *adj* inequívoco; **to be ~ in sth** ser claro en algo

unethical [ʌnˈeθɪkəl] *adj* poco ético

uneven [ʌnˈiːvən] *adj* **1.** (*not flat*) desnivelado **2.** (*unequal*) desigual **3.** (*of inadequate quality*) irregular

uneventful [ˌʌnɪˈventfəl] *adj* sin acontecimientos

unexceptional [ˌʌnɪkˈsepʃənəl] *adj*

corriente

unexciting *adj* **1.**(*commonplace*) trivial **2.**(*uneventful*) aburrido

unexpected [ˌʌnɪkˈspektɪd] *adj* inesperado

unexplained [ˌʌnɪkˈspleɪnd] *adj* inexplicado

unexpressive [ˌʌnɪkˈspresɪv] *adj* inexpresivo

unfailing [ʌnˈfeɪlɪŋ] *adj* indefectible

unfair [ˌʌnˈfeəˈ, *Am:* -ˈfer] *adj* injusto

unfaithful [ˌʌnˈfeɪθʊl] *adj* **1.**(*adulterous*) infiel **2.**(*disloyal*) desleal

unfamiliar [ˌʌnfəˈmɪljəˈ, *Am:* -jɚ] *adj* desconocido

unfashionable [ʌnˈfæʃənəbl] *adj* pasado de moda

unfasten [ˌʌnˈfɑːsən, *Am:* -ˈfæsn] *vt* desatar

unfavorable *adj Am*, **unfavourable** [ʌnˈfeɪvərəbl] *adj Brit, Aus* **1.**(*adverse*) adverso **2.**(*disadvantagous*) desfavorable

unfeeling [ʌnˈfiːlɪŋ] *adj* insensible

unfinished [ʌnˈfɪnɪʃt] *adj* inacabado

unfit [ʌnˈfɪt] *adj* **1.**(*unhealthy*) **I'm** ~ no estoy en forma; **to be** ~ **for sth** no estar en condiciones para algo **2.**(*unsuitable*) no apto

unflagging [ʌnˈflægɪŋ] *adj* incansable

unflappable [ʌnˈflæpəbl] *adj inf* imperturbable

unfold [ʌnˈfəʊld, *Am:* -ˈfoʊld] **I.** *vt* desdoblar; *fig* revelar **II.** *vi* abrirse; *fig* revelarse

unforeseen [ˌʌnfɔːˈsiːn, *Am:* -fɔːrˈ-] *adj* imprevisto

unforgettable [ˌʌnfəˈgetəbl, *Am:* -fɚˈget̬-] *adj* inolvidable

unforgivable [ˌʌnfəˈgɪvəbl, *Am:* -fɚˈ-] *adj* imperdonable

unfortunate [ʌnˈfɔːtʃənət, *Am:* -ˈfɔːrtʃnət] *adj* desafortunado; **to be** ~ **that ...** ser lamentable que... +*subj*

unfortunately *adv* por desgracia

unfounded [ʌnˈfaʊndɪd] *adj* infundado

unfriendly [ʌnˈfrendli] *adj* <-ier, -iest> antipático

unfulfilled [ˌʌnfʊlˈfɪld] *adj* incumplido; (*frustrated*) frustrado

unfurl [ʌnˈfɜːl, *Am:* -ˈfɜːrl] *vt* desplegar

unfurnished [ˌʌnˈfɜːnɪʃt, *Am:* -ˈfɜːr-] *adj* desamueblado

ungainly [ʌnˈgeɪnli] *adj* <-ier, -iest> torpe

ungenerous [ʌnˈdʒenərəs] *adj* tacaño

ungovernable [ʌnˈgʌvənəbl, *Am:* ʌnˈgʌvɚnə-] *adj* ingobernable

ungraceful [ʌnˈgreɪsfəl] *adj* chabacano

ungracious [ˌʌnˈgreɪʃəs] *adj form* descortés

ungrateful [ʌnˈgreɪtfəl] *adj* ingrato

ungrudging [ʌnˈgrʌdʒɪŋ] *adj* generoso

unguarded [ʌnˈgɑːdɪd, *Am:* ʌnˈgɑːr-] *adj* sin vigilancia; **in an ~ moment** en un momento de descuido

unhappy [ʌnˈhæpi] *adj* <-ier, -iest> **1.**(*sad*) infeliz **2.**(*unfortunate*) desafortunado

unharmed [ʌnˈhɑːmd, *Am:* -ˈhɑːrmd] *adj* ileso

UNHCR [ˌjuːenetʃsiːˈɑːˈ] *n no pl abbr of* **United Nations High Commission for Refugees** ACNUR *f*

unhealthy [ʌnˈhelθi] *adj* <-ier, -iest> **1.**(*sick*) enfermizo **2.**(*unwholesome*) nocivo

unheard [ʌnˈhɜːd, *Am:* -ˈhɜːrd] *adj* **1.**(*not heard*) desoído **2.**(*ignored*) desatendido

unhelpful [ʌnˈhelpfʊl] *adj* de poca ayuda

unhurt [ʌnˈhɜːt, *Am:* -ˈhɜːrt] *adj* ileso

UNICEF *n*, **Unicef** [ˈjuːnɪsef] *n abbr of* **United Nations International Children's Emergency Fund** UNICEF *f*

unicorn [ˈjuːnɪkɔːn, *Am:* -kɔːrn] *n* unicornio *m*

unidentified [ˌʌnaɪˈdentɪfaɪd, *Am:* -t̬ə-] *n* **1.**(*unknown*) desconocido **2.**(*not made public*) no identificado

unification [ˌjuːnɪfɪˈkeɪʃən] *n no pl* unificación *f*

uniform [ˈjuːnɪfɔːm, *Am:* -nəfɔ:rm] *n* uniforme *m*

uniformity [ˌjuːnɪˈfɔːməti, *Am:* -nəˈfɔːrməti] *n no pl* uniformidad *f*

unify [ˈjuːnɪfaɪ, *Am:* -nə-] *vt* unificar

unilateral [ˌjuːnɪˈlætrəl, *Am:* -nəˈlæt̬-] *adj* unilateral

unimaginable [ˌʌnɪˈmædʒnəbl] *adj* inimaginable

unimportant [ˌʌnɪmˈpɔːtənt, *Am:* -ˈpɔːr-] *adj* sin importancia

uninformed [ˌʌnɪnˈfɔːmd, *Am:* -ˈfɔːrmd] *adj* desinformado

uninhabitable [ˌʌnɪnˈhæbɪtəbl, *Am:* -t̬əbl] *adj* inhabitable

uninhabited [ˌʌnɪnˈhæbɪtɪd] *adj* desierto

uninhibited [ˌʌnɪnˈhɪbɪtɪd, *Am:* -t̬ɪd] *adj* desinhibido

uninjured [ˌʌnˈɪndʒəd, *Am:* -dʒɚd] *adj* ileso

uninsured [ˌʌnɪnˈʃʊəd, *Am:* -ˈʃʊrd] *adj* no asegurado

unintelligible [ˌʌnɪnˈtelɪdʒəbl] *adj* incomprensible

unintentional [ˌʌnɪnˈtentʃənəl] *adj* involuntario

uninterested [ʌnˈɪntrəstɪd] *adj* indiferente

uninteresting *adj* aburrido

uninterrupted [ʌnˌɪntərˈʌptɪd] *adj* ininterrumpido

union [ˈjuːnjən] *n* unión *f*; (*trade ~*) sindicato *m*

unionist [ˈjuːnjənɪst] *n* unionista *mf*; (*member of a trade union*) sindicalista *mf*

Union Jack *n* bandera del Reino Unido

unique [juːˈniːk] *adj* **1.** (*only one*) único **2.** (*exceptional*) excepcional

uniqueness *n no pl* unicidad *f*

unison [ˈjuːnɪsən, *Am:* -nə-] *n no pl* **to sing in ~** cantar al unísono; **to act in ~ with sb** obrar de acuerdo con alguien

unit [ˈjuːnɪt] *n* **1.** *a.* INFOR, COM unidad *f*; **~ of currency** unidad monetaria **2.** + *sing/pl vb* (*team*) equipo *m* **3.** (*furniture*) módulo *m*

unite [juːˈnaɪt] **I.** *vt* unir **II.** *vi* unirse, juntarse

united *adj* unido

United Arab Emirates *npl* **the ~** los Emiratos Árabes Unidos **United Kingdom** *n no pl* **the ~** el Reino Unido **United Nations** *n no pl* **the ~** las Naciones Unidas **United States** *n* + *sing vb* **the ~** (*of America*) los Estados Unidos (de Norteamérica)

unity [ˈjuːnəti, *Am:* -t̬i] *n no pl* unidad *f*

Univ. *abbr of* **University** Univ.

universal [ˌjuːnɪˈvɜːsəl, *Am:* -nəˈvɜːr-] *adj* universal

universe [ˈjuːnɪvɜːs, *Am:* -nəvɜːrs] *n* **the ~** el universo

university [ˌjuːnɪˈvɜːsəti, *Am:* -nəˈvɜːrsət̬i] <-ies> *n* universidad *f*; **the ~ community** la comunidad universitaria

university education *n no pl* educación *f* universitaria **university lecturer** *n* profesor(a) *m(f)* universitario, -a **university town** *n* ciudad *f* universitaria

unjust [ʌnˈdʒʌst] *adj* injusto

unjustifiable [ʌnˌdʒʌstɪˈfaɪəbl] *adj* injustificable

unjustified [ʌnˈdʒʌstɪfaɪd] *adj* injustificado

unkempt [ʌnˈkempt] *adj* descuidado

unkind [ʌnˈkaɪnd] *adj* desagradable; **to be ~ to sb** tratar mal a alguien

unkindly *adv* cruelmente

unknown [ʌnˈnəʊn, *Am:* -ˈnoʊn] *adj* desconocido

unlawful [ʌnˈlɔːfəl, *Am:* -ˈlɑː-] *adj* ilegal

unleaded [ʌnˈledɪd] *adj* sin plomo

unleash [ʌnˈliːʃ] *vt* soltar

unless [ənˈles] *conj* a no ser que +*subj*; **he won't come ~ he has time** no vendrá a menos que tenga tiempo

unlike [ʌnˈlaɪk] *prep* **1.** (*different from*) diferente **2.** (*in contrast to*) a diferencia de

unlikely [ʌnˈlaɪkli] <-ier, -iest> *adj* improbable; **it's ~ that ...** es difícil que...

unlimited [ʌnˈlɪmɪtɪd, *Am:* -t̬ɪd] *adj* ilimitado

unload [ʌn'ləʊd, *Am:* -'loʊd] *vt* descargar; *inf* (*get rid of*) deshacerse de

unlock [ʌn'lɒk, *Am:* -'lɑːk] *vt* abrir

unlucky [ʌn'lʌki] *adj* desgraciado; (*at cards, in love*) desafortunado; **to be** ~ tener mala suerte

unmarried [ʌn'mærɪd, *Am:* -'mer-] *adj* soltero

unmask [ʌn'mɑːsk, *Am:* -'mæsk] *vt* **to** ~ **sb as sth** desenmascarar a alguien como algo

unmentionable [ʌn'mentʃənəbl] *adj* inmencionable

unmentioned [ʌn'mentʃənd] *adj* indecible

unmistak(e)able [ˌʌnmɪ'steɪkəbl] *adj* inconfundible

unmitigated [ʌn'mɪtɪgeɪtɪd, *Am:* -'mɪt̬əgeɪt̬ɪd] *adj* absoluto; (*disaster*) total

unmoved [ʌn'muːvd] *adj* impasible

unnatural [ʌn'nætʃərəl, *Am:* -ə-əl] *adj* poco natural; (*affected*) afectado

unnecessary [ʌn'nesəsəri, *Am:* -seri] *adj* innecesario

unnerve [ʌn'nɜːv, *Am:* -'nɜːrv] *vt* **to** ~ **sb** poner nervioso a alguien

unnoticed [ˌʌn'nəʊtɪst, *Am:* -'noʊtɪst] *adj* **to go** ~ pasar inadvertido

unobtainable [ˌʌnəb'teɪnəbl] *adj* inalcanzable

unobtrusive [ˌʌnəb'truːsɪv] *adj* discreto

unoccupied [ˌʌn'ɒkjəpaɪd, *Am:* -'ɑːkjə-] *adj* **1.** (*uninhabited*) deshabitado **2.** (*chair, table*) libre

unofficial [ˌʌnə'fɪʃəl] *adj* no oficial

unorthodox [ʌn'ɔːθədɒks, *Am:* -'ɔːrθədɑːks] *adj* poco ortodoxo

unpack [ʌn'pæk] *vi* deshacer el equipaje

unpaid [ʌn'peɪd] *adj* (*work*) no remunerado; (*bill*) pendiente

unpalatable [ʌn'pælətəbl, *Am:* -t̬əbl] *adj* desagradable

unparalleled [ʌn'pærəleld, *Am:* ʌn'per-] *adj form* sin precedentes

unperturbed [ˌʌnpə'tɜːbd, *Am:* ˌʌnpə-'tɜːrbd] *adj* **to be** ~ **by sth** quedarse impertérrito ante algo

unplanned [ʌn'plænd] *adj* espon-

táneo

unpleasant [ʌn'plezənt] *adj* desagradable

unplug [ʌn'plʌg] <-gg-> *vt* desconectar

unpopular [ʌn'pɒpjələ, *Am:* ʌn-'pɑːpjələ] *adj* impopular

unprecedented [ʌn'presɪdentɪd, *Am:* -ədentɪd] *adj* sin precedentes

unpredictable [ˌʌnprɪ'dɪktəbl] *adj* imprevisible

unpretentious [ˌʌnprɪ'tentʃəs] *adj* sin pretensiones

unprincipled [ʌn'prɪntsəpld] *adj* sin principios

unproductive [ˌʌnprə'dʌktɪv] *adj* improductivo

unprofessional [ˌʌnprə'feʃənəl] *adj* poco profesional

unprofitable [ʌn'prɒfɪtəbl, *Am:* ʌn'prɑːfɪt̬ə-] *adj* no rentable

unprovoked [ˌʌnprə'vəʊkt, *Am:* ˌʌnprə'voʊkt] *adj* no provocado

unpublished [ˌʌn'pʌblɪʃt] *adj* inédito

unqualified [ʌn'kwɒlɪfaɪd, *Am:* ʌn'kwɑːlə-] *adj* **1.** (*without qualifications*) sin título **2.** (*unlimited*) incondicional; (*support*) total

unquestionable [ʌn'kwestʃənəbl] *adj* indiscutible

unravel [ʌn'rævəl] <*Brit:* -ll-, *Am:* -l-> **I.** *vt* desenredar, desenmarañar **II.** *vi* deshacerse

unreal [ʌn'rɪəl, *Am:* -'riːl] *adj* irreal

unrealistic [ʌn,rɪə'lɪstɪk] *adj* poco realista

unrealized *adj* sin explotar

unreasonable [ʌn'riːzənəbl] *adj* poco razonable

unreasoning [ʌn'riːzənɪŋ] *adj* irracional

unrecognised [ʌn'rekəgnaɪzd] *adj* no reconocido

unrefined [ˌʌnrɪ'faɪnd] *adj* (*sugar, oil*) sin refinar

unrelated [ˌʌnrɪ'leɪtɪd, *Am:* -rɪ-'leɪt̬ɪd] *adj* no relacionado

unrelenting [ˌʌnrɪ'lentɪŋ, *Am:* -rɪ-'lent̬ɪŋ] *adj* implacable; (*pain, pressure*) incesante

unreliability [ˌʌnrɪlaɪə'bɪlɪti, *Am:*

-rɪlaɪə'bɪlət̮i] n no pl informalidad f

unreliable [ˌʌnrɪ'laɪəbl] adj informal

unremarkable [ˌʌnrɪ'mɑːkəbl, Am: -rɪ'mɑːrk-] adj normal

unremitting [ˌʌnrɪ'mɪtɪŋ, Am: -rɪ'mɪt̮-] adj form sin tregua

unrepeatable [ˌʌnrɪ'piːtəbl, Am: -t̮ə-] adj irrepetible

unresolved [ˌʌnrɪ'zɒlvd, Am: -rɪ'zɑːlvd] adj sin resolver

unrest [ʌn'rest] n no pl descontento m

unrestrained [ˌʌnrɪ'streɪnd] adj incontrolado

unrestricted [ˌʌnrɪ'strɪktɪd] adj ilimitado; (access) libre

unripe [ʌn'raɪp] adj verde

unruly [ʌn'ruːli] <-ier, -iest> adj indisciplinado; (children) revoltoso

unsafe [ʌn'seɪf] adj peligroso

unsatisfactory [ʌnˌsætɪs'fæktəri, Am: ʌnˌsæt̮-] adj insatisfactorio; (answer) poco convincente

unsatisfied [ʌn'sætɪsfaɪd, Am: -'sæt̮-] adj insatisfecho

unscathed [ʌn'skeɪðd] adj ileso

unscrupulous [ʌn'skruːpjələs] adj sin escrúpulos

unseemly [ʌn'siːmli] adj form impropio

unseen [ʌn'siːn] adj sin ser visto

unselfish [ʌn'selfɪʃ] adj generoso

unsettle [ʌn'setl, Am: -'set̮-] vt perturbar

unsettled [ˌʌn'setld, Am: -'set̮-] adj (period) agitado; (weather) inestable; (person) inquieto; (issue) no resuelto

unsettling adj inquietante

unsightly [ʌn'saɪtli] <-ier, -iest> adj feo

unskilled [ʌn'skɪld] adj **1.** (not skilled) no cualificado **2.** (not requiring skill) no especializado

unsociable [ʌn'səʊʃəbl, Am: -'soʊ-] adj insociable

unsold [ʌn'səʊld, Am: -'soʊld] adj sin vender

unsolicited [ˌʌnsə'lɪsɪtɪd, Am: -t̮ɪd] adj no solicitado

unsolved [ʌn'sɒlvd, Am: -'sɑːlvd]

adj sin resolver

unsophisticated [ˌʌnsə'fɪstɪkeɪtɪd, Am: -təkɪtɪd] adj (simple) sencillo; (person) ingenuo

unsound [ʌn'saʊnd] adj (unreliable) de no fiar; **to be of ~ mind** ser mentalmente incapacitado

unspeakable [ʌn'spiːkəbl] adj indecible

unspecified [ʌn'spesɪfaɪd] adj no especificado

unspoken [ʌn'spəʊkən, Am: -spoʊ-] adj tácito

unstable [ʌn'steɪbl] adj inestable; fig voluble

unsubstantiated [ˌʌnsəb'stæntʃieɪtɪd, Am: -'stæntʃieɪtɪd] adj no probado

unsuccessful [ˌʌnsək'sesfəl] adj fracasado; **to be ~ in sth** fracasar en algo

unsuitable [ʌn'suːtəbl, Am: -'suːt̮ə-] adj inapropiado

unsung [ʌn'sʌŋ] adj olvidado

unsure [ʌn'ʃʊəʳ, Am: -'ʃʊr] adj inseguro; **to be ~ about sth** no estar seguro de algo

unsuspecting [ˌʌnsə'spektɪŋ] adj confiado

unsustainable [ˌʌnsə'steɪnəbl] adj insostenible

unsympathetic [ˌʌnsɪmpə'θetɪk, Am: -'θet̮-] adj poco comprensivo

untangle [ʌn'tæŋgl] vt desenredar

untenable [ˌʌn'tenəbl] adj insostenible

untested [ʌn'testɪd] adj no probado

unthinkable [ʌn'θɪŋkəbl] adj inconcebible

unthinking [ʌn'θɪŋkɪŋ] adj irreflexivo

untidy [ʌn'taɪdi] <-ier, -iest> adj (room) desordenado; (appearance) desaliñado

untie [ʌn'taɪ] <-y-> vt desatar; **to ~ a knot** deshacer un nudo

until [ən'tɪl] I. adv temporal hasta; ~ **then** hasta entonces II. conj hasta que +subj; ~ **he comes** hasta que venga

untimely [ʌn'taɪmli] adj **1.** (premature) prematuro **2.** (inopportune)

U u

inoportuno

untold [ˌʌnˈtəʊld, *Am:* -ˈtoʊld] *adj* **1.** (*immense*) incalculable **2.** (*not told*) nunca contado

untouched [ʌnˈtʌtʃt] *adj* **1.** (*not affected*) intacto **2.** (*emotionally unmoved*) insensible

untoward [ˌʌntəˈwɔːd, *Am:* ˌʌnˈtɔːrd] *adj form* desfavorable

untreated [ʌnˈtriːtɪd, *Am:* -ˈtriːt̬ɪd] *adj* no tratado

untried [ʌnˈtraɪd] *adj* no probado

untroubled [ʌnˈtrʌbld] *adj* tranquilo

untrue [ʌnˈtruː] *adj* falso; **to be ~ to sb** ser infiel a alguien

untrustworthy [ʌnˈtrʌstˌwɜːði, *Am:* -ˌwɜːr-] *adj* indigno de confianza

unused [ʌnˈjuːzd] *adj* no usado

unusual [ʌnˈjuːʒəl, *Am:* -ʒuəl] *adj* insólito

unusually *adv* extraordinariamente

unveil [ˌʌnˈveɪl] *vt* (*uncover*) descubrir; (*present*) presentar

unwanted [ʌnˈwɒntɪd, *Am:* -ˈwɑːnt̬ɪd] *adj* no deseado

unwarranted [ʌnˈwɒrəntɪd, *Am:* -ˈwɔːrənt̬ɪd] *adj* injustificado

unwavering [ʌnˈweɪvərɪŋ] *adj* inquebrantable

unwelcome [ʌnˈwelkəm] *adj* (*guest*) importuno; (*information*) desagradable

unwell [ʌnˈwel] *adj* **to feel ~** sentirse mal

unwieldy [ʌnˈwiːldi] *adj* difícil de manejar

unwilling [ʌnˈwɪlɪŋ] *adj* no dispuesto; **to be ~ to do sth** no estar dispuesto a hacer algo

unwind [ʌnˈwaɪnd] *irr vi* (*relax*) relajarse

unwise [ʌnˈwaɪz] *adj* imprudente

unwittingly *adv* **1.** (*without realizing*) inconscientemente **2.** (*unintentionally*) de forma no intencionada

unworkable [ʌnˈwɜːkəbl, *Am:* -ˈwɜːr-] *adj* impracticable

unworthy [ʌnˈwɜːði, *Am:* -ˈwɜːr-] <-ier, -iest> *adj* indigno

unwrap [ʌnˈræp] <-pp-> *vt* desen-

volver .

unwritten [ʌnˈrɪtən] *adj* no escrito

unyielding [ʌnˈjiːldɪŋ] *adj* inflexible

up [ʌp] I. *adv* **1.** (*movement*) (hacia) arriba; **~ here/there** aquí/allí arriba; **to look ~** mirar (hacia) arriba; **to get ~** levantarse; **to come ~** subir; **on the way ~** de subida; **to be ~ all night** no dormir en toda la noche **2.** (*limit*) **~ to** hasta; **~ to here** hasta aquí; **~ to now** hasta ahora; **~ to 100 euros** hasta 100 euros; **time's ~** se acabó el tiempo **3.** (*responsibility of*) **it's ~ to you** tú decides; **it's ~ to me to decide** me toca a mí decidir **4.** SPORTS **to be 2 goals ~** ir ganando por 2 goles **5.** (*phrases*) **to be ~ and about** estar en buena forma; **to be ~ against sth** habérselas con algo; **~ and down** arriba y abajo; **to be ~ for (doing) sth** estar listo para (hacer) algo; **~ for sale** a la venta; **to feel ~ to sth** sentirse capaz de algo; **this isn't ~ to much** esto no vale gran cosa; **what's ~?** ¿qué hay de nuevo?; **what's ~ with him?** ¿qué le pasa? II. *prep* encima de; **to climb ~ a tree** subir arriba de un árbol; **to go ~ the stairs** subir las escaleras; **to go ~ the street** ir por la calle III. <-pp-> *vi inf* **to ~ and do sth** ponerse de repente a hacer algo

upbeat [ˈʌpbiːt] *adj inf* optimista

upbringing [ˈʌpbrɪŋɪŋ] *n no pl* educación *f*

upcoming [ˈʌpˌkʌmɪŋ] *adj* venidero

update [ʌpˈdeɪt] *vt* poner al día; INFOR actualizar

upgrade[1] [ʌpˈgreɪd] *vt* mejorar la calidad de; INFOR mejorar

upgrade[2] [ˈʌpgreɪd] *n* **1.** (*improvement*) mejora *f* **2.** *Am* (*slope*) cuesta *f*; **to be on the ~** *fig* ir mejorando

upheaval [ʌpˈhiːvəl] *n* trastorno *m*

uphill [ʌpˈhɪl] I. *adv* cuesta arriba II. *adj* **1.** (*sloping upward*) ascendente **2.** (*difficult*) difícil

uphold [ʌpˈhəʊld, *Am:* -ˈhoʊld] *irr vt* sostener; **to ~ the law** defender la ley

upholstery *n no pl* tapicería *f*

upkeep [ˈʌpkiːp] *n no pl* mantenimiento *m*

upland ['ʌplənd] *n* the ~s las tierras altas

uplift [ʌp'lɪft] *vt* inspirar

uplifting [ʌp'lɪftɪŋ] *adj* positivo

upon [ə'pɒn, *Am:* -'pɑ:n] *prep* 1. (*on top of*) sobre; **to hang ~ the wall** colgar en la pared 2. (*at time of*) ~ **her arrival** a su llegada; ~ **this** a continuación; **once ~ a time** érase una vez

upper ['ʌpəʳ, *Am:* -ɚ] *adj* (*further up*) superior; **the Upper House** POL la Cámara Alta

upper case *n no pl* TYPO letra *f* mayúscula **upper-class** *adj* de clase alta

uppermost *adj* más alto

upright ['ʌpraɪt] I. *adj* vertical; *fig* recto II. *adv* derecho

uprising ['ʌpraɪzɪŋ] *n* alzamiento *m*

uproar ['ʌprɔːʳ, *Am:* -rɔːr] *n no pl* alboroto *m*, batifondo *m CSur*, tinga *f Méx*

uproot [ʌp'ruːt] *vt a. fig* desarraigar

upset[1] [ʌp'set] I. *vt irr* 1. (*overturn*) derrumbar; (*boat, canoe*) volcar 2. (*unsettle*) trastornar II. *adj* (*distressed*) acongojado; **to get ~ about sth** enfadarse por algo; **to have an ~ stomach** tener el estómago revuelto

upset[2] ['ʌpset] *n no pl* (*trouble*) problema *m;* (*argument, quarrel*) discusión *f;* **stomach ~** trastorno *m* estomacal

upshot ['ʌpʃɒt, *Am:* -ʃɑːt] *n no pl* resultado *m*

upside down *adv* al revés; **to turn sth ~** poner algo del revés

upstage [ʌp'steɪdʒ] *vt* eclipsar

upstairs [ʌp'steəz, *Am:* -'sterz] I. *adj* de arriba II. *adv* arriba; **to go ~** ir arriba III. *n no pl* (**the**) ~ el piso de arriba

upstanding [ʌp'stændɪŋ] *adj form* íntegro

upstart ['ʌpstɑːt, *Am:* -stɑːrt] *n* arribista *mf*

upstream [ʌp'striːm] *adv* aguas arriba

upsurge ['ʌpsɜːdʒ, *Am:* -sɜːrdʒ] *n* aumento *m*

uptake ['ʌpteɪk] *n inf* **to be quick on the ~** cogerlas al vuelo; **to be slow on the ~** ser algo torpe

uptight [ʌp'taɪt] *adj inf* tenso; **to get ~ about sth** ponerse nervioso por algo

up-to-date [ˌʌptə'deɪt] *adj* 1. (*contemporary*) moderno 2. (*informed*) al día

upturn ['ʌptɜːn, *Am:* -tɜːrn] *n* mejora *f*

upward ['ʌpwəd, *Am:* -wɚd] I. *adj* ascendente; ~ **mobility** ascenso *m* social II. *adv* (hacia) arriba

uranium [jʊə'reɪniəm, *Am:* jʊ-] *n no pl* uranio *m*

Uranus ['jʊərənəs, *Am:* 'jʊrənəs] *n* Urano *m*

urban ['ɜːbən, *Am:* 'ɜːr-] *adj* urbano

urbane [ɜː'beɪn, *Am:* ɜːr-] *adj* fino

urbanization [ˌɜːbənaɪ'zeɪʃən, *Am:* ˌɜːrbənɪ'-] *n no pl* urbanización *f*

urchin ['ɜːtʃɪn, *Am:* 'ɜːr-] *n iron* pilluelo, -a *m, f*

urge [ɜːdʒ, *Am:* ɜːrdʒ] I. *n* impulso *m* II. *vt* **to ~ sb to do sth** instar a alguien a hacer algo; **to ~ caution on sb** recomendar precaución a alguien
♦ **urge on** *vt* **to urge sb on to do sth** animar a alguien a hacer algo

urgency ['ɜːdʒənsi, *Am:* 'ɜːr-] *n no pl* urgencia *f*

urgent ['ɜːdʒənt, *Am:* 'ɜːr-] *adj* urgente; **to be in ~ need of sth** necesitar algo urgentemente

urgently *adv* urgentemente

urinal [jʊə'raɪnəl, *Am:* 'jʊrənəl] *n* 1. (*place*) urinario *m* 2. (*vessel*) orinal *m*

urinate ['jʊərɪneɪt, *Am:* 'jʊrəneɪt] *vi* orinar(se)

urine ['jʊərɪn, *Am:* 'jʊrɪn] *n no pl* orina *f*

urn [ɜːn, *Am:* ɜːrn] *n* 1. urna *f* 2. (*for tea*) tetera *f*

Uruguay ['jʊərəgwaɪ, *Am:* 'jʊrəgweɪ] *n* Uruguay *m*

Uruguayan [ˌjʊərə'gwaɪən, *Am:* ˌjʊrə'gweɪ-] *adj* uruguayo

us [əs, *stressed:* ʌs] *pron pers* nos; *after prep* nosotros; **it's ~** somos nosotros; **older than ~** mayores que

nosotros; **he saw** ~ (él) nos vió; **he gave the pencil to** ~ nos dio el lápiz
USA [ˌjuːesˈeɪ] *n abbr of* **United States of America** EE.UU. *mpl*
use I. [juːs] *n* uso *m;* **in** ~ en uso; **to be of** ~ **to sb** ser de utilidad para alguien; **to make** ~ **of sth** utilizar algo; **to put sth to** ~ poner algo en servicio; **to be out of** ~ estar fuera de servicio; **to come into** ~ empezar a utilizarse; **to go out of** ~ quedar en desuso; **it's no** ~ es inútil II. [juːz] *vt* **1.** (*make use of*) (*skills*) usar; hacer uso de; **to** ~ **logic** emplear la lógica; **to** ~ **sth to do sth** utilizar algo para hacer algo; **to** ~ **sth against sb** utilizar algo en contra de alguien; **to** ~ **common sense** emplear el sentido común **2.** (*consume*) consumir **3.** (*manipulate*) utilizar; (*exploit*) explotar III. [juːs] *aux* **he ~d to live in London** vivía en Londres
◆ **use up** *vt* agotar
used [juːzd] *adj* usado
used to [juːst tʊ] *adj* acostumbrado; **to be** ~ **sth** estar acostumbrado a algo; **to become** ~ **sth** acostumbrarse a algo; **to be** ~ **doing sth** tener la costumbre de hacer algo
useful [ˈjuːsfəl] *adj* útil
usefulness *n no pl* utilidad *f*
useless [ˈjuːsləs] *adj* inútil
user *n* usuario, -a *m, f;* (*of gas, electricity*) consumidor(a) *m(f);* **drug** ~ drogadicto, -a *m, f*
user-friendly *adj* INFOR fácil de utilizar
usher [ˈʌʃəʳ, *Am:* -ɚ] I. *n* ujier *m;* CINE, THEAT acomodador(a) *m(f)* II. *vt* **to** ~ **sb in** hacer pasar a alguien
usual [ˈjuːʒəl, *Am:* -ʒʊəl] *adj* usual; **as** ~ como de costumbre
usually *adv* normalmente
usurp [juːˈzɜːp, *Am:* -ˈsɜːrp] *vt* usurpar
utensil [juːˈtensl] *n* utensilio *m*
uterus [ˈjuːtərəs, *Am:* -ţɚ-] <-ri *o* -es> *n* útero *m*
utilitarian [juːˌtɪlɪˈteərɪən, *Am:* -əˈterɪ-] *adj* utilitario
utility [juːˈtɪləti, *Am:* -ţi] <-ies> *n*

1. *form* (*usefulness*) utilidad *f;* ~ **room** trastero *m* **2.** (*public service*) empresa *f* de servicio público
utmost [ˈʌtməʊst, *Am:* -moʊst] I. *adj* mayor II. *n no pl* **the** ~ lo máximo
utopian *adj* utópico
utter¹ [ˈʌtəʳ, *Am:* ˈʌţɚ] *adj* completo
utter² [ˈʌtəʳ, *Am:* ˈʌţɚ] *vt* pronunciar; **without ~ing a word** sin mediar palabra
utterance [ˈʌtərənts, *Am:* ˈʌţ-] *n* enunciado *m*
utterly *adv* completamente
U-turn [ˈjuːtɜːn, *Am:* ˈjuːtɜːrn] *n* giro *m* de ciento ochenta grados
Uzbekistan [ˌʌzˌbekɪˈstɑːn, *Am:* -ˈstæn] *n* Uzbekistán *m*

V

V, v [viː] *n* V *f*
V *abbr of* **volt** V
vacancy [ˈveɪkəntsi] <-ies> *n* **1.** (*room*) habitación *f* vacía **2.** (*job*) vacante *f;* **to fill a** ~ ocupar una vacante
vacant [ˈveɪkənt] *adj* vacío; (*job*) vacante
vacate [vəˈkeɪt, *Am:* ˈveɪkeɪt] *vt form* (*seat*) desocupar; (*room, building*) salir de; (*job*) dejar vacante
vacation [vəˈkeɪʃən, *Am:* veɪ-] I. *n Am* vacaciones *fpl;* **on** ~ de vacaciones II. *vi Am* estar de vacaciones
vaccinate [ˈvæksɪneɪt, *Am:* -səneɪt-] *vt* MED vacunar
vaccine [ˈvæksiːn, *Am:* vækˈsiːn] *n* vacuna *f*
vacillate [ˈvæsəleɪt] *vi* dudar
vacuous [ˈvækjuəs] *adj* bobo
vacuum [ˈvækjuːm] *n* vacío *m*
vacuum cleaner *n* aspiradora *f*
vagabond [ˈvægəbɒnd, *Am:* -bɑːnd] *n* vagabundo, -a *m, f*
vagina [vəˈdʒaɪnə] *n* vagina *f*

vagrant ['veɪgrənt] *n* vagabundo, -a *m, f*

vague [veɪg] *adj* **1.** (*promise*) vago; (*description*) impreciso; (*outline*) borroso **2.** (*absent-minded*) distraído

vain [veɪn] *adj* **1.** (*conceited*) vanidoso **2.** (*fruitless*) vano; **in ~** en vano

Valentine's Day ['væləntaɪn-] *n no pl* día *m* de los enamorados

valiant ['væliənt, *Am:* -jənt] *adj* valiente

valid ['vælɪd] *adj* válido; (*excuse*) legítimo; LAW vigente

validate ['vælɪdeɪt, *Am:* 'vælə-] *vt* **1.** (*ratify*) dar validez a **2.** (*authenticate: document*) validar; (*ticket*) sellar

validity [və'lɪdəti, *Am:* -ṭi] *n no pl* validez *f;* (*of excuse*) legitimidad *f;* (*of law*) vigencia *f*

valley ['væli] *n* valle *m*

valor *n no pl, Am,* **valour** ['vælə^r, *Am:* -ɚ] *n no pl, Brit, Aus, form* valor *m*

valuable ['væljuəbl] **I.** *adj* valioso **II.** *n pl* objetos *mpl* de valor

valuation [ˌvælju'eɪʃən] *n* tasación *f*

value ['vælju:] **I.** *n* valor *m;* **to be of ~ to sb** ser valioso para alguien; **to be good ~ (for money)** estar bien de precio; **to put a ~ on sth** poner precio a algo **II.** *vt* **1.** (*cherish*) apreciar **2.** (*estimate worth*) tasar

value-added tax *n Brit* impuesto *m* sobre el valor añadido

valued *adj form* apreciado

valve [vælv] *n* válvula *f*

vampire ['væmpaɪə^r, *Am:* -paɪɚ] *n* vampiro *m*

van [væn] *n* furgoneta *f*

vandal ['vændəl] *n* vándalo *m*

vandalism ['vændəlɪzəm] *n no pl* vandalismo *m*

vanguard ['vængɑːd, *Am:* -gɑːrd] *n no pl* vanguardia *f*

vanilla [və'nɪlə] *n no pl* vainilla *f*

vanish ['vænɪʃ] *vi* desaparecer

vanity ['vænəti, *Am:* -əṭi] <-ies> *n* vanidad *f*

vanquish ['væŋkwɪʃ] *vt* derrotar

vantage point ['vɑːntɪdʒ-, *Am:* 'vænt̬ɪdʒ-] *n* mirador *m*

vapor *n Am,* **vapour** ['veɪpə^r, *Am:* -pɚ] *n Brit, Aus* (*steam*) vapor *m;* (*on glass*) vaho *m,* vaporizo *m Méx, PRico*

variability [ˌveəriə'bɪləti, *Am:* ˌveriə'bɪləṭi] *n no pl* variabilidad *f*

variable ['veəriəbl, *Am:* 'veri-] **I.** *n* variable *f* **II.** *adj* variable

variance ['veəriənts, *Am:* 'veri-] *n* **1.** *no pl* (*difference*) discrepancia *f;* **at ~** en contradicción **2.** *no pl* (*variation*) variación *f*

variant ['veəriənt, *Am:* 'veri-] **I.** *n* variante *f* **II.** *adj* divergente

variation [ˌveəri'eɪʃən, *Am:* ˌveri'-] *n no pl* variación *f*

varicose veins ['værɪkəʊs-, *Am:* 'verəkoʊs-] *npl* varices *fpl*

varied ['veərɪd, *Am:* 'verɪd] *adj* variado

variety [və'raɪəti, *Am:* -əṭi] <-ies> *n* (*diversity, type*) variedad *f;* **for a ~ of reasons** por varias razones; **~ is the spice of life** *prov* en la variedad está el gusto *prov*

various ['veəriəs, *Am:* 'veri-] *adj* **1.** (*numerous*) varios **2.** (*diverse*) diferentes

varnish ['vɑːnɪʃ, *Am:* 'vɑːr-] **I.** *n no pl* barniz *m;* (*nail*) ~ esmalte *m* de uñas **II.** *vt* barnizar

vary ['veəri, *Am:* 'veri] <-ie-> *vi, vt* variar

varying *adj* variable

vascular ['væskjələ^r, *Am:* -kjəlɚ] *adj no pl* vascular

vase [vɑːz, *Am:* veɪs] *n* (*for flowers*) florero *m;* (*ornamental*) jarrón *m*

vast [vɑːst, *Am:* væst] *adj* (*area, region*) vasto; (*quantity*) enorme; **the ~ majority** la gran mayoría

vat [væt] *n* tanque *m;* (*for wine, oil*) cuba *f*

VAT [ˌviːeɪ'tiː] *n no pl, Brit abbr of* **value added tax** IVA *m*

Vatican ['vætɪkən, *Am:* 'væṭ-] *n no pl* **the ~** el Vaticano

vault¹ [vɔːlt, *Am:* vɑːlt] *n* ARCHIT bóveda *f;* (*under church*) cripta *f;* (*in bank*) cámara *f* acorazada

vault² [vɔːlt, *Am:* vɑːlt] **I.** *n* (*jump*) salto *m* **II.** *vi, vt* saltar

V_v

VCR [ˌviːsiːˈaːʳ, *Am:* -ˈaːr] *n abbr of* **videocassette recorder** vídeo *m*

veal [viːl] *n no pl* ternera *f*

veer [vɪəʳ, *Am:* vɪr] *vi* (*vehicle*) virar; (*wind*) cambiar de dirección; **to ~ towards sth** dar un giro hacia algo

vegetable [ˈvedʒtəbl] *n* verdura *f*

vegetable garden *n* huerto *m* **vegetable oil** *n no pl* aceite *m* vegetal

vegetarian [ˌvedʒɪˈteəriən, *Am:* -əˈteri-] *n* vegetariano, -a *m, f*

vegetate [ˈvedʒɪteɪt, *Am:* ˈ-ə-] *vi* vegetar

vegetation [ˌvedʒɪˈteɪʃən, *Am:* -əˈ-] *n no pl* vegetación *f*

vehement [ˈviːəmənt] *adj* vehemente

vehicle [ˈvɪəkl, *Am:* ˈviːə-] *n* **1.** (*method of transport*) vehículo *m* **2.** (*channel*) medio *m*

veil [veɪl] **I.** *n* velo *m;* **to draw a ~ over sth** *fig* correr un tupido velo sobre algo **II.** *vt* velar

veiled *adj* (*criticism*) velado; **thinly ~** apenas disimulado

vein [veɪn] *n* **1.** ANAT, BOT vena *f;* GEO veta *f,* sirca *f Chile* **2.** *fig* **to talk in a more serious ~** hablar más en serio; **in (a) similar ~** del mismo estilo

velocity [vɪˈlɒsəti, *Am:* vəˈlɑːsəti̯] <-ies> *n form* velocidad *f*

velvet [ˈvelvɪt] *n no pl* terciopelo *m*

vendetta [venˈdetə, *Am:* -ˈdet̬-] *n* vendetta *f*

vendor [ˈvendɔːʳ, *Am:* -dɚ] *n* vendedor(a) *m(f)*

veneer [vəˈnɪəʳ, *Am:* -ˈnɪr] *n* chapado *m*

venerable [ˈvenərəbl] *adj* (*person*) venerable; (*tradition*) ancestral; (*building, tree*) centenario

venereal disease [vəˈnɪəriəl-, *Am:* vəˈnɪri-] *n* enfermedad *f* venérea

Venezuela [ˌvenɪˈzweɪlə, *Am:* -əˈzweɪ-] *n* Venezuela *f*

Venezuelan *adj* venezolano

vengeance [ˈvendʒənts] *n no pl* venganza *f;* **to take ~ on sb** vengarse de alguien; **with a ~** *fig* con ganas

venison [ˈvenɪsən] *n no pl* (carne *f* de) venado *m*

venom [ˈvenəm] *n no pl* veneno *m; fig* malevolencia *f*

venous [ˈviːnəs] *adj* venoso

vent [vent] **I.** *n* **1.** (*outlet*) conducto *m* de ventilación; **to give ~ to sth** *fig* dar rienda suelta a algo **2.** FASHION abertura *f* **II.** *vt* **to ~ one's anger on sb** desahogarse con alguien

ventilate [ˈventɪleɪt, *Am:* -t̬əleɪt] *vt* ventilar

ventilation [ˌventɪˈleɪʃən, *Am:* -t̬əˈleɪ-] *n no pl* ventilación *f*

venture [ˈventʃəʳ, *Am:* -tʃɚ] **I.** *n* **1.** (*endeavour*) aventura *f* **2.** COM empresa *f;* **joint ~** empresa conjunta **II.** *vt* **1.** (*dare*) **to ~ to do sth** atreverse a hacer algo **2.** (*express: an opinion*) aventurar

◆ **venture out** *vi* atreverse a salir

venture capital *n* FIN capital *m* de riesgo

venue [ˈvenjuː] *n* (*of meeting*) lugar *m* (de reunión); (*of concert*) lugar *m* (de celebración); (*of match*) campo *m*

Venus [ˈviːnəs] *n no pl* Venus *m*

veranda(h) [vəˈrændə] *n* veranda *f*

verb [vɜːb, *Am:* vɜːrb] *n* verbo *m*

verbal [ˈvɜːbəl, *Am:* ˈvɜːr-] *adj* **1.** (*oral*) verbal; **~ agreement** acuerdo *m* verbal **2.** (*word for word*) literal

verbally *adv* verbalmente

verbatim [vɜːˈbeɪtɪm, *Am:* vɚˈbeɪt̬ɪm] *adv* literalmente

verdict [ˈvɜːdɪkt, *Am:* ˈvɜːr-] *n* **1.** LAW (*of jury*) veredicto *m;* (*of magistrate, judge*) fallo *m;* **to return a ~** (*jury*) emitir un veredicto; (*magistrate, judge*) dictar sentencia **2.** (*opinion*) juicio *m;* **to give a ~ on sth** dar una opinión sobre algo

verge [vɜːdʒ, *Am:* vɜːrdʒ] *n* margen *m; Brit* (*next to road*) arcén *m;* **to be on the ~ of ...** *fig* estar al borde de...

◆ **verge on** *vt* rayar en

verify [ˈverɪfaɪ, *Am:* ˈ-ə-] <-ie-> *vt* **1.** (*corroborate*) confirmar **2.** (*authenticate*) verificar

veritable [ˈverɪtəbl, *Am:* -ət̬ə-] *adj* auténtico

vermin ['vɜːmɪn, *Am:* 'vɜːr-] *n* **1.** *pl* (*animals*) alimañas *fpl;* (*insects*) bichos *mpl* **2.** *pej* (*people*) gentuza *f*

vernacular [vəˈnækjələ^r, *Am:* vəˈnækjələ] *n* **1.** (*local*) lengua *f* vernácula **2.** (*everyday*) lengua *f* coloquial

verruca [vəˈruːkə] <-s *o* -ae> *n* verruga *f*

versatile ['vɜːsətaɪl, *Am:* 'vɜːrsətəl] *adj* (*tool, device*) versátil; (*person*) polifacético

versatility [ˌvɜːsəˈtɪləti, *Am:* ˌvɜːrsəˈtɪləti] *n no pl* versatilidad *f*

verse [vɜːs, *Am:* vɜːrs] *n* (*of poem*) verso *m;* (*of song*) estrofa *f*

version ['vɜːʃən, *Am:* 'vɜːrʒən] *n* versión *f*

versus ['vɜːsəs, *Am:* 'vɜːr-] *prep* **1.** (*in comparison to*) frente a **2.** SPORTS, LAW contra

vertebra ['vɜːtɪbrə, *Am:* 'vɜːrtə-] <-ae> *n* vértebra *f*

vertebrate ['vɜːtɪbreɪt, *Am:* 'vɜːrtəbrɪt] **I.** *n* vertebrado *m* **II.** *adj* vertebrado

vertical ['vɜːtɪkəl, *Am:* 'vɜːrtə-] *adj* vertical

vertigo ['vɜːtɪgəʊ, *Am:* 'vɜːrtəgoʊ] *n no pl* vértigo *m*

verve [vɜːv, *Am:* vɜːrv] *n no pl* ímpetu *m;* **with ~** con brío

very ['veri] **I.** *adv* muy; **~ much** mucho; **not ~ much** no mucho; **the ~ best** lo mejor de lo mejor; **at the ~ least** por lo menos; **the ~ same** justo lo mismo; **~ well** muy bien **II.** *adj* **the ~ next day** justo al día siguiente; **the ~ fact** el mero hecho

vessel ['vesəl] *n* **1.** (*any kind of boat*) embarcación *f;* (*large boat*) navío *m* **2.** (*container*) recipiente *m*

vest [vest] *n* **1.** Brit (*undergarment*) camiseta *f* **2.** *Am, Aus* (*outergarment*) chaleco *m*

vestige ['vestɪdʒ] *n* vestigio *m*

vestry ['vestri] <-ies> *n* sacristía *f*

vet¹ [vet] *n* veterinario, -a *m, f*

vet² *vt* <-tt-> examinar

veteran ['vetərən, *Am:* 'vetəɹən] *n* veterano, -a *m, f*

veterinarian [ˌvetərɪˈneəriən, *Am:* -ˈneri-] *n Am* veterinario, -a *m, f*

veterinary ['vetərɪnəri, *Am:* -ner-] *adj* veterinario

veto ['viːtəʊ, *Am:* -toʊ] **I.** *n* <-es> veto *m* **II.** *vt* <vetoed> **1.** (*exercise a veto against*) vetar **2.** (*forbid*) prohibir

vex [veks] *vt* **1.** (*annoy*) sacar de quicio **2.** (*upset*) afligir

via ['vaɪə] *prep* por

viability [ˌvaɪəˈbɪləti, *Am:* -əti] *n no pl* viabilidad *f*

viable ['vaɪəbl] *adj* viable

vibrant ['vaɪbrənt] *adj* (*person*) enérgico; (*music*) vibrante; (*economy*) en ebullición; (*colour*) radiante

vibrate [vaɪˈbreɪt, *Am:* 'vaɪbreɪt] *vi* vibrar

vibration [vaɪˈbreɪʃən] *n* vibración *f*

vicar ['vɪkə^r, *Am:* -ə] *n* vicario *m*

vicarage ['vɪkərɪdʒ] *n* vicaría *f*

vice¹ [vaɪs] *n* (*wickedness*) vicio *m*

vice² *n Brit, Aus* (*tool*) torno *m* de banco

vice-chairman <-men> *n* vicepresidente, -a *m, f* **vice-chancellor** *n Brit* UNIV rector(a) *m(f)* **Vice President** *n* vicepresidente, -a *m, f*

vice versa [ˌvaɪsi'vɜːsə, *Am:* -sə-'vɜːr-] *adv* viceversa

vicinity [vɪˈsɪnəti, *Am:* vəˈsɪnəti] <-ies> *n* **in the ~ of ...** en los alrededores de…

vicious ['vɪʃəs] *adj* (*fighting*) salvaje; (*attack*) despiadado; (*pain*) atroz

victim ['vɪktɪm] *n* víctima *f;* **to be the ~ of sth** ser víctima de algo

victimize ['vɪktɪmaɪz, *Am:* -tə-] *vt*

discriminar
victor ['vɪktəʳ, Am: -tɚ] n vencedor(a) m(f)

? La **Victoria Cross** fue creada en el año 1856 por la reina Victoria durante la guerra de Crimea como la condecoración militar más alta de la **Commonwealth**. Se concede a quien haya destacado por su valentía. La inscripción reza: 'For valour' (Por el valor).

Victorian [vɪk'tɔ:rɪən] adj victoriano
victorious [vɪk'tɔ:rɪəs] adj victorioso
victory ['vɪktərɪ] <-ies> n victoria f
video ['vɪdɪəʊ, Am: -oʊ] I. n 1. (machine) vídeo m 2. (tape) cinta f de vídeo II. vt grabar en vídeo
video camera n videocámara f
video conference n videoconferencia f **video game** n videojuego m **videophone** n videoteléfono m **video recorder** n magnetoscopio m
vie [vaɪ] <vying> vi to ~ (with sb) for sth competir (con alguien) por algo
Vietnam [ˌvjet'næm, Am: ˌviːet-'nɑːm] n Vietnam m
Vietnamese [ˌvjetnə'miːz, Am: viˌet-] adj vietnamita
view [vjuː] I. n 1. (opinion) punto m de vista; **exchange of ~s** intercambio m de opiniones; **to express a ~** expresar un parecer 2. (sight) vista f; **to come into ~** aparecer ante la vista; **to disappear from ~** perderse de vista; **to be on ~** estar expuesto; **in ~ of sth** fig en vista de algo; **with a ~ to sth** fig con vistas a algo II. vt 1. (consider) considerar 2. (watch) ver
viewer n 1. (person) telespectador(a) m(f) 2. (device) proyector m de diapositivas
viewpoint n punto m de vista
vigil ['vɪdʒɪl, Am: 'vɪdʒəl] n vela f

vigilance ['vɪdʒɪləns] n no pl vigilancia f
vigilant ['vɪdʒɪlənt] adj vigilante
vigor n Am, Aus, **vigour** ['vɪgəʳ, Am: -ɚ] n no pl vigor m
vigorous ['vɪgərəs] adj enérgico; (growth) pujante
vile [vaɪl] adj (shameful) vil; (weather) asqueroso; **to be ~ to sb** portarse mal con alguien; **to smell ~** apestar
village ['vɪlɪdʒ] n pueblo m
villain ['vɪlən] n villano, -a m, f
vindicate ['vɪndɪkeɪt, Am: -də-] vt 1. (justify) justificar 2. (clear of blame) vindicar
vindictive [vɪn'dɪktɪv] adj vengativo
vine [vaɪn] n vid f; (climbing) parra f
vinegar ['vɪnɪgəʳ, Am: -əgɚ] n no pl vinagre m
vineyard ['vɪnjəd, Am: -jɚd] n viñedo m
vintage ['vɪntɪdʒ, Am: -ţɪdʒ] n cosecha f
vinyl ['vaɪnəl] n no pl vinilo m
viola [vi'əʊlə, Am: vi'oʊ-] n MUS viola f
violate ['vaɪəleɪt] vt violar; **to ~ sb's privacy** entrometerse en la vida privada de alguien
violence ['vaɪələnts] n no pl violencia f
violent ['vaɪələnt] adj (cruel) violento; (argument) acérrimo
violet ['vaɪələt, Am: -lɪt] I. n 1. BOT violeta f 2. (colour) violeta m II. adj violeta
violin [ˌvaɪə'lɪn] n violín m
violinist [vaɪə'lɪnɪst] n violinista mf
VIP [ˌviːaɪ'piː] s. **very important person** VIP mf
viper ['vaɪpəʳ, Am: -pɚ] n víbora f
virgin ['vɜːdʒɪn, Am: 'vɜːr-] n virgen f
virginity [və'dʒɪnəti, Am: vɚ'dʒɪ-nəţi] n no pl virginidad f
Virgo ['vɜːgəʊ, Am: 'vɜːrgoʊ] n Virgo mf
virile ['vɪraɪl, Am: -əl] adj viril
virility [vɪ'rɪləti, Am: və'rɪləţi] n no pl virilidad f

virtual ['vɜːtʃuəl, *Am:* 'vɜːrtʃu-] *adj* virtual

virtually *adv* prácticamente

virtual reality *n* realidad *f* virtual

virtue ['vɜːtjuː, *Am:* 'vɜːrtʃuː] *n* **1.** (*moral quality*) virtud *f* **2.** (*advantage*) ventaja *f*; **by ~ of** *form* en virtud de

virtuous ['vɜːtʃuəs, *Am:* 'vɜːrtʃu-] *adj* virtuoso

virulent ['vɪrʊlənt, *Am:* -jə-] *adj* virulento

virus ['vaɪərəs, *Am:* 'vaɪ-] <-es> *n* virus *m inv*

visa ['viːzə] *n* visado *m*

vis-à-vis [ˌviːzɑːˈviː, *Am:* ˌviːzəˈviː] *prep* con relación a

viscount ['vaɪkaʊnt] *n* vizconde *m*

viscous ['vɪskəs] *adj* viscoso

vise [vaɪs] *n Am s.* **vice²**

visibility [ˌvɪzəˈbɪləti, *Am:* -əbɪləti] *n no pl* visibilidad *f*

visible ['vɪzəbl] *adj* visible

vision ['vɪʒən] *n* **1.** *no pl* (*sight*) vista *f* **2.** (*image*) visión *f*

visit ['vɪzɪt] I. *n* visita *f*; **to pay a ~ to sb** ir a ver a alguien II. *vt* visitar

visitor ['vɪzɪtəʳ, *Am:* -t̬əʳ] *n* visitante *mf*

visualize ['vɪʒuəlaɪz] *vt* visualizar

vital ['vaɪtəl, *Am:* -t̬əl] *adj* vital; **~ ingredient** ingrediente *m* esencial

vitamin ['vɪtəmɪn, *Am:* 'vaɪt̬ə-] *n* vitamina *f*

vitriolic [ˌvɪtriˈɒlɪk, *Am:* -ˈɑːlɪk] *adj* vitriólico

vivacious [vɪˈveɪʃəs] *adj* vivaz

vivid ['vɪvɪd] *adj* (*colour*) vivo; (*imagination*) fértil

vivisection [ˌvɪvɪˈsekʃən, *Am:* -əˈ-] *n no pl* vivisección *f*

vocabulary [vəʊˈkæbjələri, *Am:* voʊˈkæbjələr-] *n* vocabulario *m*

vocal ['vəʊkəl, *Am:* 'voʊ-] *adj* **1.** (*of the voice*) oral **2.** (*outspoken*) vehemente

vocalist ['vəʊkəlɪst, *Am:* 'voʊ-] *n* vocalista *mf*

vocation [vəʊˈkeɪʃən, *Am:* voʊˈ-] *n* vocación *f*

vocational [vəʊˈkeɪʃənəl, *Am:* voʊˈ-] *adj* vocacional

vociferous [vəʊˈsɪfərəs, *Am:* voʊˈ-] *adj* vociferante

vogue [vəʊg, *Am:* voʊg] *n* moda *f*; **in ~** de moda

voice [vɔɪs] I. *n* voz *f*; **in a loud ~** en voz alta; **to raise/lower one's ~** levantar/bajar la voz; **to lose one's ~** quedarse afónico; **to give ~ to sth** expresar algo II. *vt* expresar

void [vɔɪd] I. *n* vacío *m* II. *adj* **1.** inválido **2. to be ~ of sth** estar falto de algo

vol *abbr of* **volume** vol.

volatile ['vɒlətaɪl, *Am:* 'vɑːlət̬əl] *adj* volátil; (*situation*) inestable; (*person*) voluble

volcanic [vɒlˈkænɪk, *Am:* vɑːlˈ-] *adj* volcánico

volcano [vɒlˈkeɪnəʊ, *Am:* vɑːlˈkeɪnoʊ] <-(e)s> *n* volcán *m*

vole [vəʊl, *Am:* voʊl] *n* ratón *m* de campo

volley ['vɒli, *Am:* 'vɑːli] I. *n* **1.** MIL descarga *f*; **a ~ of insults** una sarta de insultos I. **2.** SPORTS volea *f* II. *vi* SPORTS volear

volleyball *n no pl* voleibol *m*

volt [vəʊlt, *Am:* voʊlt] *n* voltio *m*

voltage ['vəʊltɪdʒ, *Am:* 'voʊltɪdʒ] *n* voltaje *m*

volume ['vɒljuːm, *Am:* 'vɑːljuːm] *n no pl* volumen *m*; **to turn the ~ up/down** subir/bajar el volumen; **to speak ~s for sth** ser muy indicativo de algo

voluntary ['vɒləntəri, *Am:* 'vɑːlənteri] *adj* voluntario

volunteer [ˌvɒlənˈtɪəʳ, *Am:* ˌvɑːlənˈtɪr] I. *n* voluntario, -a *m, f* II. *vi, vt* ofrecer(se)

vomit ['vɒmɪt, *Am:* 'vɑːmɪt] I. *vi, vt* vomitar II. *n no pl* vómito *m*

voracious [vəˈreɪʃəs, *Am:* vɔːˈreɪ-] *adj* voraz

vote [vəʊt, *Am:* voʊt] I. *vi* votar; **to ~ for/against sth** votar a favor/en contra de algo; **to ~ on sth** someter algo a votación II. *vt* **to ~ that ...** proponer que... +*subj* III. *n* **1.** (*choice*) voto *m*; **to have the ~** tener derecho al voto **2.** (*election*) votación *f*; **to put sth to the ~**

someter algo a votación
◆ **vote in** *vt* elegir (por votación)
◆ **vote on** *vt* aprobar (por votación)
voter *n* votante *mf*
voting *n* votación *f*
vouch [vaʊtʃ] *vi* **to ~ for sb** responder por alguien
voucher ['vaʊtʃər, *Am:* -tʃər] *n Aus, Brit* **1.** (*coupon*) vale *m* **2.** (*receipt*) comprobante *m*
vow [vaʊ] **I.** *vt* jurar **II.** *n* voto *m*
vowel ['vaʊəl] *n* vocal *f*
voyage ['vɔɪɪdʒ] **I.** *n* viaje *m* **II.** *vi* viajar
vulgar ['vʌlgər, *Am:* -gər] *adj* vulgar
vulgarity [vʌl'gærəti, *Am:* -'gerəti] *n no pl* vulgaridad *f*
vulnerable ['vʌlnərəbl, *Am:* 'vʌlnərə-] *adj* vulnerable
vulture ['vʌltʃər, *Am:* -tʃər] *n* buitre *m*

W, w ['dʌblju:] *n* W, w *f*
w *abbr of* **watt** W
W *n abbr of* **west** O
wad [wɒd, *Am:* wɑːd] *n* (*of cotton*) bola *f*; (*of banknotes*) fajo *m*
waddle ['wɒdl, *Am:* 'wɑːdl] *vi* anadear
wade [weɪd] *vi* **to ~ across sth** vadear algo; **to ~ into sb** *fig, inf* tomarla con alguien
wafer ['weɪfər, *Am:* -fər] *n* **1.** (*biscuit*) galleta *f* de barquillo **2.** REL hostia *f*
waffle¹ ['wɒfl, *Am:* 'wɑːfl] *vi Brit* parlotear; (*in essay*) meter paja *fig*
waffle² *n* GASTR gofre *m*, waffle *m AmL*
waft [wɒft, *Am:* wɑːft] **I.** *vi* llegar (flotando) **II.** *vt* llevar por el aire
wag [wæg] <-gg-> *vt* menear; **to ~ one's finger at sb** amenazar a alguien con el dedo

wage [weɪdʒ] **I.** *vt* **to ~ war against sb** librar una batalla contra alguien; **to ~ a campaign for sth** emprender una campaña por algo **II.** *n* sueldo *m*
wager ['weɪdʒər, *Am:* -dʒər] **I.** *n* apuesta *f* **II.** *vt* apostar
waggle ['wægl] **I.** *vt* mover **II.** *vi* moverse
waggon *n Brit,* **wagon** ['wægən] *n* **1.** (*horse-drawn*) carro *m* **2.** *Brit* RAIL vagón *m*
wail [weɪl] **I.** *vi* gemir **II.** *n* lamento *m*
waist [weɪst] *n* cintura *f*
waistband *n* cinturilla *f* **waistcoat** *n Brit* chaleco *m*
wait [weɪt] **I.** *vi* esperar; **to ~ for sb** esperar a alguien; **to keep sb ~ing** hacer esperar a alguien; **he cannot ~ to see her** está ansioso por verla; **(just) you ~!** ¡vas a ver! **II.** *vt* **to ~ one's turn** esperar su turno **III.** *n no pl* espera *f*; **to lie in ~ for sb** estar al acecho de alguien
◆ **wait about** *vi,* **wait around** *vi* **to ~ for sth** estar a la espera de algo
◆ **wait behind** *vi* quedarse
◆ **wait on** *vt* servir

> **?** El **Waitangi Day** o **New Zealand Day** se celebra el 6 de enero. Ya que fue en ese día del año 1840 cuando 512 jefes de tribu de los **Maori** firmaron un acuerdo con el gobierno británico que significó el comienzo de Nueva Zelanda como nación.

waiter ['weɪtər, *Am:* -tər] *n* camarero *m,* garzón *m AmL,* mesero *m Méx*
waiting list *n* lista *f* de espera **waiting room** *n* sala *f* de espera
waitress ['weɪtrɪs] *n* camarera *f,* garzona *f AmL,* mesera *f Méx*
waive [weɪv] *vt form* renunciar a
wake¹ [weɪk] *n* NAUT estela *f*; **in the ~ of** tras, después de
wake² [weɪk] *n* velatorio *m*
wake³ [weɪk] <woke *o* waked, woken *o* waked> *vt* despertar

◆ **wake up** *vi, vt* despertar(se)
waken ['weɪkən] *vt form* despertar
Wales ['weɪlz] *n* Gales *m*
walk [wɔːk, *Am:* wɑːk] **I.** *n* **1.** (*stroll*) paseo *m;* **to take a ~** ir a dar un paseo; **it's a five minute ~** está a cinco minutos a pie **2.** (*gait*) andar *m* **3.** (*walking speed*) paso *m* **4.** **~ of life** condición *f* **II.** *vt* andar; (*distance*) recorrer a pie; **to ~ sb home** acompañar a alguien a su casa; **to ~ the dog** sacar a pasear el perro **III.** *vi* andar; (*stroll*) pasear
walker ['wɔːkəʳ, *Am:* 'wɑːkə·] *n* paseante *mf;* (*as hobby*) excursionista *mf*
walkie-talkie [ˌwɔːki'tɔːki, *Am:* ˌwɑːki'tɑː-] *n* walkie-talkie *m*
walking *adj* **it is within ~ distance** se puede ir a pie; **to be a ~ encyclopaedia** ser una enciclopedia ambulante
walking-stick *n* bastón *m*
walkman® ['wɔːkmən, *Am:* 'wɑːk-] <-s> *n* walkman® *m*
walkway *n* pasarela *f*
wall [wɔːl] **I.** *n* muro *m;* (*interior surface*) pared *f;* (*enclosing town*) muralla *f;* (*enclosing garden*) tapia *f;* **a ~ of silence** un muro de silencio; **to have one's back to the ~** *fig* estar entre la espada y la pared; **to go to the ~** (*go bankrupt*) quebrar; **to go up the ~** subirse por las paredes **II.** *vt* (*garden*) cercar con un muro; (*town*) amurallar
wall chart *n* gráfico *m* de pared
wallet ['wɒlɪt, *Am:* 'wɑːlɪt] *n* cartera *f,* billetera *f AmL*
wallflower ['wɔːlˌflaʊəʳ, *Am:* -ˌflaʊə·] *n* **1.** BOT al(h)elí *m* **2.** *fig* ≈ patito *m* feo
wallop ['wɒləp, *Am:* 'wɑːləp] *vt inf* (*hit*) dar un golpetazo a
wallow ['wɒləʊ, *Am:* 'wɑːloʊ] *vi* revolcarse; **to ~ in self-pity** sumirse en la autocompasión; **to ~ in money** nadar en el dinero
wallpaper I. *n* papel *m* pintado **II.** *vt* empapelar
walnut ['wɔːlnʌt] *n* **1.** (*nut*) nuez *f* **2.** (*tree*) nogal *m*

walrus ['wɔːlrəs] <walruses *o* walrus> *n* morsa *f*
waltz [wɔːls, *Am:* wɔːlts] <-es> **I.** *n* vals *m* **II.** *vi* valsar
◆ **waltz in** *vi inf* entrar como si nada
◆ **waltz out** *vi inf* salir como si nada
wand [wɒnd, *Am:* wɑːnd] *n* varita *f* mágica
wander ['wɒndəʳ, *Am:* 'wɑːndə·] **I.** *vi* vagar; **to let one's thoughts ~** dejar volar la imaginación **II.** *n inf* paseo *m*
wane [weɪn] **I.** *vi* menguar **II.** *n* **to be on the ~** menguar
want [wɒnt, *Am:* wɑːnt] **I.** *vt* **1.** (*wish*) querer; **to ~ to do sth** querer hacer algo; **to ~ sb to do sth** querer que alguien haga algo **2.** (*need*) necesitar; **he is ~ed by the police** lo busca la policía **II.** *n* **to be in ~ of sth** necesitar algo; **for ~ of sth** por falta de algo
wanting *adj* **to be ~ in sth** estar falto de algo
WAP [wæp] *abbr of* **wireless application protocol** WAP
war [wɔːʳ, *Am:* wɔːr] *n* guerra *f;* **to be at ~** estar en guerra; **to declare ~ on sb** declarar la guerra a alguien; **to go to ~** entrar en guerra
war crime *n* crimen *m* de guerra
war cry *n* grito *m* de guerra
ward [wɔːd, *Am:* wɔːrd] *n* **1.** LAW pupilo, -a *m, f* **2.** (*in hospital*) sala *f* **3.** *Brit* POL distrito *m* electoral
◆ **ward off** *vt* evitar
warden ['wɔːdn, *Am:* 'wɔːr-] *n* guardián, -ana *m, f;* (*of prison*) alcaide *m*
warder ['wɔːdəʳ, *Am:* 'wɔːrdə·] *n* celador *m*
wardrobe ['wɔːdrəʊb, *Am:* 'wɔːrdroʊb] *n* **1.** (*cupboard*) (armario *m*) ropero *m* **2.** (*clothes*) vestuario *m*
warehouse ['weəhaʊs, *Am:* 'wer-] *n* almacén *m*
wares [weəz, *Am:* werz] *npl inf* mercancías *fpl*
warfare ['wɔːfeəʳ, *Am:* 'wɔːrfer] *n no pl* guerra *f*
warhead *n* cabeza *f* de guerra

W
w

warlike ['wɔːlaɪk, *Am:* 'wɔːr-] *adj* belicoso

warlord *n* jefe *m* militar

warm [wɔːm, *Am:* wɔːrm] **I.** *adj* **1.** caliente; (*climate, wind*) cálido; (*clothes*) de abrigo; **to be ~** (*person*) tener calor; (*thing*) estar caliente; (*weather*) hacer calor **2.** (*affectionate*) afectuoso; **~ welcome** calurosa bienvenida; **to be ~** ser efusivo; **you're getting ~** *fig* ¡caliente, caliente! **II.** *vt* calentar

◆ **warm up** *vi* calentarse

warm-blooded *adj* de sangre caliente

warmly *adv* calurosamente

warmth [wɔːmθ, *Am:* wɔːrmθ] *n no pl* **1.** (*heat*) calor *m* **2.** (*affection*) calidez *f*

warm-up *n* (pre)calentamiento *m*

warn [wɔːn, *Am:* wɔːrn] *vt* avisar; **to ~ sb not to do sth** advertir a alguien que no haga algo; **to ~ sb of a danger** prevenir a alguien contra un peligro

warning [wɔːnɪŋ, *Am:* wɔːrnɪŋ] *n* aviso *m;* **a word of ~** una advertencia; **to give sb a ~** advertir a alguien; **without ~** sin previo aviso

warning light *n* luz *f* de advertencia

warp [wɔːp, *Am:* wɔːrp] **I.** *vi* torcerse **II.** *vt* torcer; **to ~ sb's mind** (re)torcer la mente de alguien **III.** *n* deformación *f*

warrant ['wɒrənt, *Am:* 'wɔːr-] **I.** *n* LAW orden *f* **II.** *vt* (*justify*) justificar

warranty ['wɒrənti, *Am:* 'wɔːrən-ti] <-ies> *n* garantía *f*

warren ['wɒrən, *Am:* 'wɔːr-] *n* **1.** ZOOL conejera *f* **2.** *fig* laberinto *m*

warrior ['wɒriəʳ, *Am:* 'wɔːrjɚ] *n* guerrero, -a *m, f*

warship *n* barco *m* de guerra

wart [wɔːt, *Am:* wɔːrt] *n* verruga *f;* **~s and all** *inf* con sus virtudes y defectos

wartime *n no pl* **in ~** en tiempos de guerra

wary ['weəri, *Am:* 'weri] <-ier, -iest> *adj* (*not trusting*) receloso; (*watchful*) cauteloso; **to be ~ of sth** recelar de algo

was [wɒz, *Am:* wɑːz] *pt of* **be**

wash [wɒʃ, *Am:* wɑːʃ] **I.** *vt* lavar; (*dishes, floor*) fregar; **to ~ one's hands** lavarse las manos **II.** *vi* **1.** (*person*) lavarse **2.** (*do the washing*) lavar la ropa **III.** *n* lavado *m;* **to be in the ~** (*clothes*) estar en la lavandería

◆ **wash down** *vt* lavar

◆ **wash up I.** *vt* (*dishes*) fregar **II.** *vi* **1.** (*clean dishes*) fregar los platos **2.** *Am* (*wash*) lavarse (las manos y la cara)

washed-out *adj* **1.** (*bleached*) desteñido **2.** (*tired*) cansado

washer ['wɒʃəʳ, *Am:* 'wɑːʃɚ] *n* **1.** *Am* (*washing-machine*) lavadora *f* **2.** TECH arandela *f*

washing ['wɒʃɪŋ, *Am:* 'wɑːʃɪŋ] *n no pl* lavado *f;* **to do the ~** hacer la colada

washing machine *n* lavadora *f,* lavarropas *m inv Arg* **washing powder** *n no pl, Brit* detergente *m* en polvo

Washington [,wɒʃɪŋtən, *Am:* ,wɑː-ʃɪŋ-] *n* Washington *m*

Washington D.C. *n* Washington D.C.

[?] **Washington's Birthday** es un día de fiesta oficial en los EE.UU. Aunque George Washington en realidad nació el 22 de febrero de 1732, su cumpleaños se celebra desde hace algunos años siempre el tercer lunes del mes de febrero, para que se produzca así un fin de semana largo.

---

washing-up *n Brit* **to do the ~** fregar los platos **washing-up liquid** *n* detergente *m* líquido

washout ['wɒʃaʊt, *Am:* 'wɑːʃ-] *n inf* desastre *m*

washroom ['wɒʃrʊm, *Am:* 'wɑːʃ-ruːm] *n Am* aseos *mpl,* sanitarios *mpl AmL*

wasp [wɒsp, *Am:* wɑːsp] *n* avispa *f*

wastage ['weɪstɪdʒ] *n no pl* desgaste m

waste [weɪst] **I.** *n* **1.** *no pl* (*misuse*) derroche *m;* **it's a ~ of money** es un derroche de dinero; **it's a ~ of time** es una pérdida de tiempo; **to go to ~** echarse a perder; **what a ~!** ¡qué pena! **2.** *no pl* (*unwanted matter*) residuos *mpl* **II.** *vt* malgastar; (*time*) perder; (*opportunity*) desaprovechar; **to ~ one's breath** *fig* hablar inútilmente; **to ~ no time in doing sth** apresurarse a hacer algo **III.** *vi* agotarse; **~ not, want not** *prov* quien guarda, halla *prov*
◆ **waste away** *vi* consumirse
wastebasket *n Am,* **wastebin** *n Brit* papelera *m*
wasteful ['weɪstfəl] *adj* derrochador
wasteland *n* yermo *m*
wastepaper basket *n* papelera *f*
watch [wɒtʃ, *Am:* wɑːtʃ] **I.** *n* **1.** *no pl* (*observation*) vigilancia *f;* **to be on the ~ for sth** estar a la mira de algo; **to keep a close ~ on sb** vigilar a alguien con mucho cuidado; **to be on ~** estar de guardia **2.** (*clock*) reloj *m* (de pulsera) **II.** *vt* mirar; **to ~ a film** ver una película; **to ~ the kids** vigilar a los niños; **to ~ one's weight** cuidar el peso; **~ it!** ¡cuidado! **III.** *vi* **to ~ as sb does sth** fijarse en cómo alguien hace algo
◆ **watch out** *vi* tener cuidado
watchdog *n* **1.** *Am* perro *m* guardián **2.** *fig* guardián, -ana *m, f*
watchful ['wɒtʃfəl, *Am:* 'wɑːtʃ-] *adj* vigilante; **to keep a ~ eye on sb** estar pendiente de alguien
watchmaker *n* relojero, -a *m, f*
watchman <-men> *n* guardián *m* **watchtower** *n* atalaya *f* **watchword** *n* contraseña *f*
water ['wɔːtər, *Am:* 'wɑːtɚ] **I.** *n* agua *f;* **under ~** bajo agua; **by ~** por mar; **to pass ~** orinar; **~ on the brain** MED hidrocefalia *f;* **to be ~ under the bridge** *fig* ser agua pasada; **like ~ off a duck's back** como si oyera llover; **to pour cold ~ on sth** *fig* echar agua fría a algo; **to be in deep ~** *fig* estar metido en un lío; **still ~s run deep** *prov* no te fíes del

agua mansa *prov;* **to hold ~** *fig* ser consistente **II.** *vt* (*plants*) regar; (*livestock*) dar de beber a **III.** *vi* lagrimear
watercolor *Am,* **watercolour** **I.** *n* acuarela *f* **II.** *adj* de acuarela **watercress** *n no pl* berro *m* **waterfall** *n* cascada *f* **waterfront** *n* (*harbour*) puerto *m* **water heater** *n* calentador *m* de agua
watering can *n* regadera *f*
water level *n* nivel *m* del agua **water lily** <-ies> *n* nenúfar *m* **water-logged** *adj* anegado
watermark *n* (*on paper*) filigrana *f* **watermelon** *n* sandía *f* **water pistol** *n* pistola *f* de agua **water polo** *n* waterpolo *m,* polo *m* acuático
waterproof ['wɔːtəpruːf, *Am:* 'wɑːṭɚ-] **I.** *adj* impermeable **II.** *n Brit* impermeable *m*
watershed ['wɔːtəʃed, *Am:* 'wɑːṭɚ-] *n* GEO divisoria *f* de aguas; **to mark a ~** *fig* marcar un punto decisivo
waterside *n no pl* orilla *f*
water-skiing *n no pl* esquí *m* acuático **water tank** *n* cisterna *f*
watertight ['wɔːtətaɪt, *Am:* 'wɑːṭɚ-] *adj* **1.** hermético **2.** *fig* irrecusable; (*agreement*) a toda prueba
waterway *n* canal *m* **waterworks** *n pl* reserva *f* de abastecimiento de agua; **to turn on the ~** *fig* echar a llorar
watery <-ier, -iest> *adj* aguado
watt [wɒt, *Am:* wɑːt] *n* ELEC vatio *m*
wave ['weɪv] **I.** *n* **1.** (*of water*) ola *f;* (*on surface, of hair*) ondulación *f;* PHYS onda *f* **2.** **to make ~s** *fig* causar problemas **3.** (*hand movement*) **to give sb a ~** saludar a alguien con la mano **II.** *vi* **1.** (*make hand movement*) **to ~ at sb** saludar a alguien con la mano; **to ~ goodbye** decir adiós con la mano **2.** (*flag*) ondear **III.** *vt* **1.** (*move*) agitar **2.** **to have one's hair ~d** rizarse el pelo
wave-length *n* **to be on the same ~** *fig* estar en la misma onda
waver ['weɪvər, *Am:* -vɚ] *vi* **1.** (*lose determination*) vacilar **2.** (*be unable*

to decide) titubear

wavy ['weɪvi] <-ier, -iest> *adj* ondulado

wax¹ [wæks] **I.** *n no pl* cera *f*; (*in ear*) cerumen *m* **II.** *vt* **1.** (*polish*) encerar; (*shoes*) lustrar **2.** (*remove hair from*) depilar con cera

wax² *vi liter* (*moon*) crecer

way [weɪ] **I.** *n* **1.** (*route*) camino *m*; **to be on the** ~ estar en camino; **to be out of the** ~ estar en un lugar remoto; **to be under** ~ estar en curso; **on the** ~ **to sth** de camino a algo; **to go out of one's** ~ **to do sth** *fig* tomarse la molestia de hacer algo; **to go one's own** ~ *fig* irse por su lado; **to know one's** ~ **around sth** saber cómo moverse en algo; **to lead the** ~ mostrar el camino; **to lose one's** ~ equivocar el camino; **the right** ~ **round** del derecho; **the wrong** ~ **round** del revés; **all the** ~ (*the whole distance*) todo el trayecto; (*completely*) completamente; **to be a long** ~ **off** estar muy alejado; **to have a** (**long**) ~ **to go** tener aún un (largo) trayecto por recorrer; **to have come a long** ~ *fig* haber llegado lejos; **to go a long** ~ *fig* ir lejos; **to be in sb's** ~ estorbar a alguien; **in the** ~ en el paso; **to get out of sb's/sth's** ~ dejar el camino libre a alguien/algo; **to give** ~ dar paso; *fig* dejar hacer; **to give** ~ **to sth** dar paso a algo; **by the** ~ *fig* por cierto **2.** (*fashion*) manera *f*; **in many** ~s de muchas maneras; **in some** ~s en cierto modo; **there are no two** ~s **about it** no hay otra posibilidad; **the** ~ **to do sth** la manera de hacer algo; **sb's** ~ **of life** el estilo de vida de alguien; **to my** ~ **of thinking** tal como lo veo yo; **either** ~ de cualquier forma; **no** ~! ¡de ninguna manera!; **to get one's own** ~ *inf* salirse con la suya; **in a** ~ en cierto modo **3.** *no pl* (*condition*) **to be in a bad** ~ estar en mala forma **II.** *adv inf* **to be** ~ **past sb's bedtime** haber pasado con mucho de la hora de dormir

waylay [ˌweɪˈleɪ, *Am:* ˈweɪleɪ] <waylaid, waylaid> *vt* acechar

way out *n* salida *f*

way-out *adj inf* (*very modern*) ultramoderno; (*unusual*) fuera de serie

wayside *n* **to fall by the** ~ *fig* quedarse en el camino

wayward ['weɪwəd, *Am:* -wɚd] *adj* díscolo

WC [ˌdʌbljuːˈsiː] *n abbr of* **water closet** WC *m*

we [wiː] *pron pers* nosotros, nosotras; ~'**re going to Paris and** ~'**ll be back here tomorrow** vamos a París y volvemos mañana

weak [wiːk] *adj* **1.** (*not strong*) débil; (*coffee, tea*) claro; **to be** ~ **with hunger** estar sin fuerzas por el hambre; ~ **spot** *fig* flaqueza *f* **2.** (*below standard*) flojo; **to be** ~ **at sth** estar flojo en algo

weaken ['wiːkən] *vi, vt* debilitar(se); (*diminish*) disminuir

weakling ['wiːklɪŋ] *n* enclenque *mf*

weakly ['wiːkli] *adv* **1.** (*without strength*) débilmente **2.** (*unconvincingly*) sin convicción

weak-minded [ˌwiːkˈmaɪndɪd] *adj* **1.** (*lacking determination*) indeciso **2.** (*stupid*) tonto

weakness ['wiːknɪs] <-es> *n* **1.** *no pl* (*lack of strength*) debilidad *f*; **to have a** ~ **for sth** tener debilidad por algo **2.** (*area of vulnerability*) punto *m* débil

weal [wiːl] *n* cardenal *m*

wealth [welθ] *n no pl* **1.** (*money*) riqueza *f* **2.** (*large amount*) abundancia *f*

wealthy ['welθi] **I.** <-ier, -iest> *adj* rico **II.** *the* ~ los ricos

wean [wiːn] *vt* destetar; **to** ~ **sb off sth** *fig* desenganchar a alguien de algo

weapon ['wepən] *n* arma *f*

weaponry ['wepənri] *n no pl* armamento *m*

wear [weə^r, *Am:* wer] <wore, worn> **I.** *vt* (*clothes, jewellery*) llevar **II.** *vi* **to** ~ **thin** desgastarse **III.** *n* **1.** (*clothing*) ropa *f* **2.** (*amount of use*) desgaste *m*; **to be the worse for** ~ (*person*) estar desmejorado
◈ **wear down** *vt* gastar

◆ **wear off** *vi* desaparecer
◆ **wear out** *vi*, *vt* gastar(se)
weary ['wɪəri, *Am:* 'wɪri] I. <-ier, -iest> *adj* (*very tired*) extenuado; (*unenthusiastic*) desanimado; **to be ~ of sth** estar harto de algo II. *vi* (*become tired*) cansarse; (*become bored*) aburrirse
weasel ['wi:zl] *n* comadreja *f*
weather ['weðəʳ, *Am:* -ɚ] I. *n no pl* tiempo *m*; (*climate*) clima *m*; ~ **permitting** si lo permite el tiempo; **to make heavy ~ of sth** complicar algo; **to be under the ~** estar indispuesto II. *vt* **to ~ sth** hacer frente a algo; **to ~ the storm** *fig* capear el temporal
weather-beaten *adj* curtido
weather forecast *n* previsión *f* meteorológica
weatherman *n* hombre *m* del tiempo
weave [wi:v] <wove *Am:* weaved, woven *Am:* weaved> *vi*, *vt* tejer; **to ~ sth together** entrelazar algo
weaver ['wi:vəʳ, *Am:* -vɚ] *n* tejedor(a) *m(f)*
web [web] *n* 1. (*woven net*) tela *f*; **spider('s) ~** telaraña *f* 2. (*on foot*) membrana *f* 3. INFOR **the ~** la red
webaddict *n* INFOR ciberadicto, -a *m, f* **web browser** *n* INFOR navegador *m* de internet **web camera** *n* INFOR cámara *f* web **webmaster** *n* INFOR administrador(a) *m(f)* de web **web page** *n* INFOR página *f* web **website** *n* INFOR sitio *m* web **web surfer** *n* INFOR internauta *mf***webzine** *n* INFOR revista *f* electrónica
wed [wed] <wedded *o* wed, wedded *o* wed> *form* I. *vt* **to ~ sb** casarse con alguien II. *vi* casarse
wedded ['wedɪd] *adj* casado; **to be ~ to sth** *fig* estar unido a algo
wedding ['wedɪŋ] *n* boda *f*
wedding cake *n no pl* tarta *f* nupcial **wedding dress** *n* traje *m* de novia **wedding present** *n* regalo *m* de boda **wedding ring** *n* alianza *f*
wedge [wedʒ] I. *n* cuña *f*; **a ~ of cake** un trozo de pastel II. *vt* **to ~ the door open** mantener la puerta

abierta (con una cuña); **to be ~d between sth** estar apretado entre algo
wedlock ['wedlɒk, *Am:* -lɑ:k] *n no pl* matrimonio *m*; **to be born out of ~** nacer fuera del matrimonio
Wednesday ['wenzdeɪ] *n* miércoles *m inv; s. a.* **Friday**
wee [wi:] I. *adj Scot, a. inf* pequeñito; **a ~ bit** un poquito II. *n no pl, childspeak, inf* pipí *m* III. *vi childspeak, inf*hacer pipí
weed [wi:d] I. *n* 1. (*plant*) mala hierba *f* 2. *Brit, pej, inf*(*person*) enclenque *mf*II. *vt* desherbar
weedkiller *n no pl*herbicida *m*
weedy ['wi:di] *adj* <-ier, -iest> *Brit, inf*flaco
week [wi:k] *n* semana *f*; (*work period*) semana *f* laboral; **last ~** la semana pasada; **once a ~** una vez por semana; **during the ~** durante la semana
weekday *n* día *m* laborable
weekend [,wi:k'end, *Am:* 'wi:kend] *n* fin *m* de semana; **at the ~(s)** *Brit, Aus,* **on the ~(s)** *Am* el fin de semana
weekly ['wi:kli] I. *adj*semanal II. *adv* semanalmente III. *n* <-ies> semanario *m*
weep [wi:p] *vi* <wept, wept> 1. (*cry*) llorar; **to ~ with joy** llorar de alegría 2. (*secrete liquid*) supurar
weeping willow *n* sauce *m* llorón
weigh [weɪ] I. *vt* pesar II. *vt* pesar; **to ~ oneself** pesarse; **to ~ one's words** medir las palabras; **to ~ sth against sth** *fig* contraponer algo a algo
◆ **weigh down** *vt fig* abrumar
◆ **weigh up** *vt* (*calculate*) calcular; (*judge*) juzgar
weight [weɪt] I. *n* 1. (*amount*) peso *m*; (*metal object*) pesa *f*; **to put on ~** engordar; **to lift ~s** levantar pesas; **to be a ~ off sb's mind** ser un alivio para alguien; **to pull one's ~** *inf* poner de su parte 2. *no pl* (*importance*) valor *m*; **to attach ~ to sth** dar importancia a algo II. *vt* cargar
weightlifter *n* levantador(a) *m(f)* de pesas

weight-lifting *n no pl* levantamiento *m* de pesas

weighty ['weɪti, *Am:* -t̬i] *adj* <-ier, -iest> **1.** (*heavy*) pesado **2.** (*important*) importante

weir [wɪəʳ, *Am:* wɪr] *n* presa *f*

weird [wɪəd, *Am:* wɪrd] *adj* misterioso

welcome ['welkəm] **I.** *vt* **1.** (*greet*) dar la bienvenida a **2.** (*support*) aprobar **II.** *n* **1.** (*reception*) bienvenida *f* **2.** (*expression of approval*) aprobación *f*; **to give sth a cautious** ~ dar una acogida contenida a algo **III.** *adj* grato; **to be** ~ ser bienvenido; **a** ~ **change** un cambio esperado; **you are** ~ (*response to thanks*) de nada **IV.** *interj* bienvenido

welcoming *adj* acogedor

weld [weld] *vt* soldar

welder *n* soldador(a) *m(f)*

welfare ['welfeəʳ, *Am:* -fer] *n no pl* **1.** (*well-being*) bienestar *m* **2.** *Am* (*state aid*) asistencia *f* social; **to be on** ~ vivir a cargo de la asistencia social

welfare state *n* estado *m* del bienestar

well¹ [wel] **I.** *adj* <better, best> bien; **to feel** ~ sentirse bien; **to get** ~ recuperarse; **to look** ~ tener buen aspecto **II.** <better, best> *adv* **1.** (*satisfactorily*) bien; ~ **enough** suficientemente bien; ~ **done** bien hecho; **money** ~ **spent** dinero bien gastado; **that's all very** ~, **but ...** está muy bien, pero...; **just as** ~ menos mal **2.** (*thoroughly*) completamente; ~ **and truly** de verdad **3.** (*very*) muy; **to be** ~ **pleased with sth** estar muy satisfecho con algo **4.** (*reasonably*) justamente; **you might (just) as** ~ **tell her the truth** más valdría que le dijeras la verdad; **to leave** ~ **alone** no meterse en algo **5.** (*in addition*) **as** ~ *Brit* también; **as** ~ **as** así como **III.** *interj* (*exclamation*) vaya; **very** ~! ¡muy bien!

well² *n* pozo *m*
◆ **well up** *vi* brotar

well-balanced *adj* bien equilibrado

well-behaved *adj* bien educado

well-being *n no pl* bienestar *m*

well-deserved *adj* merecido **well-developed** *adj* bien desarrollado

well-disposed *adj* **to be** ~ **towards sth** ser favorable a algo

well-earned *adj* merecido **well-educated** *adj* culto **well-founded** *adj* fundado **well-heeled** *adj* ricacho

well-informed *adj* **to be** ~ **about sth** estar bien informado sobre algo

wellington (**boot**) ['welɪŋtən(-)] *n* bota *f* de goma

well-kept *adj* (muy) cuidado **well-known** *adj* conocido; **it is** ~ **that ...** es bien sabido que... **well-meaning** *adj* bienintencionado **well-off** *adj* acomodado **well-organised** *adj* bien organizado **well-paid** *adj* bien pagado **well-proportioned** *adj* bien proporcionado **well-read** *adj* (*knowledgeable*) instruido **well-spoken** *adj* bienhablado **well-to-do** *adj* acaudalado **well-wisher** *n* simpatizante *mf* **well-worn** *adj* **1.** (*damaged by wear*) raído **2.** *fig* (*over-used*) trillado

welly ['weli] *n inf abbr of* **wellington** bota *f* de goma

Welsh [welʃ] *adj* galés

Welshman ['welʃmən] <-men> *n* galés *m*

Welshwoman ['welʃˌwʊmən] <-women> *n* galesa *f*

welt [welt] *n* (*from blow*) cardenal *f*

went [went] *pt of* **go**

wept [wept] *pt, pp of* **weep**

were [wɜːʳ, *Am:* wɜːr] *pt of* **be**

west [west] **I.** *n* oeste *m*; **in the** ~ **of Spain** en el oeste de España; **the West** el Occidente; POL el Oeste **II.** *adj* del oeste, occidental **III.** *adv* al oeste

western ['westən, *Am:* -tə-n] **I.** *adj* del oeste, occidental **II.** *n* CINE western *m*

westerly ['westəlɪ, *Am:* -stə-] **I.** *adj* del oeste **II.** *adv* (*towards*) hacia el oeste; (*from*) del oeste

westward(s) ['westwəd(z), *Am:* -wə-d(z)] *adj* hacia el oeste

wet [wet] **I.** *adj* <-tt-> (*soaked*) mojado; (*not yet dry*) húmedo; **to get** ~

mojarse; ~ **through** mojado hasta los huesos; ~ **weather** tiempo lluvioso; **to be a ~ blanket** *fig* ser un aguafiestas II. <wet, wet> *vt* humedecer; **to ~ oneself** orinarse; **to ~ the bed** mojar la cama; **to ~ one's pants** mearse III. *n no pl* **the ~** (*rain*) la lluvia

wetsuit *n* traje *m* de neopreno

whack [hwæk] I. *vt* golpear II. *n* golpe *m;* **a fair ~** *fig, inf* una parte justa

whale [hweɪl] *n* ballena *f;* **to have a ~ of a time** pasarlo bomba

wham [hwæm] *interj inf* zas

wharf [hwɔːf, *Am:* hwɔːrf] <-ves> *n* muelle *m*

what [hwɒt, *Am:* hwʌt] I. *adj interrog* qué; ~ **kind of book?** ¿qué tipo de libro?; ~ **time is it?** ¿qué hora es?; ~ **an idiot!** ¡qué idiota! II. *pron* 1. *interrog* qué; ~ **can I do?** ¿qué puedo hacer?; ~ **does it matter?** ¿qué importa?; ~**'s up?** ¿qué hay?; ~**'s his name?** ¿cómo se llama?; ~ **about Paul?** ¿y Paul?; ~ **about a walk?** ¿te va un paseo?; **so ~?** ¿y qué? 2. *rel* lo que; ~ **I like is …** lo que me gusta es…; ~ **is more** lo que es más

whatever [hwɒt'evəʳ, *Am:* hwʌt-'evəʳ] I. *pron* 1. (*anything*) (todo) lo que; ~ **happens** pase lo que pase 2. (*any of them*) cualquier(a); ~ **you pick is fine** cualquiera (de los) que elijas está bien; **nothing ~** nada de nada II. *adj* 1. (*being what it may be*) cualquiera que; ~ **the reason** sea cual sea la razón 2. (*of any kind*) de ningún tipo; **there is no doubt ~** no hay ningún tipo de duda

whatsoever [ˌhwɒtsəʊ'evəʳ, *Am:* ˌhwʌtsoʊ'evəʳ] *adv* sea cual sea; **to have no interest ~ in sth** no tener interés alguno en algo

wheat [hwiːt] *n no pl* trigo *m;* **to separate the ~ from the chaff** *fig* separar la cizaña del buen grano

wheatgerm *n no pl* germen *m* de trigo

wheel [hwiːl] I. *n* 1. (*of vehicle*) rueda *f;* **front/rear ~** rueda *f* de- lantera/trasera; **on ~s** sobre ruedas 2. TECH torno *m* 3. (*steering wheel*) volante *m* II. *vt* (*bicycle, pram*) empujar III. *vi* **to ~ and deal** *inf* hacer negocios sucios

◆ **wheel round** *vi* dar media vuelta

wheelbarrow *n* carretilla *f* **wheelchair** *n* silla *f* de ruedas **wheel clamp** *n* cepo *m*

wheeling ['hwiːlɪŋ] *n* ~ **and dealing** *inf* negocios *mpl* sucios

wheeze [hwiːz] I. <-zing> *vi* resollar II. *n Brit, inf* **a good ~** una buena idea

when [hwen] I. *adv* cuándo II. *conj* 1. (*time*) cuando; ~ **it snows** cuando nieva; **I'll tell her ~ she arrives** se lo diré cuando llegue 2. (*considering that*) si

whenever [hwen'evəʳ, *Am:* -əʳ] I. *conj* 1. (*every time that*) siempre que; ~ **I can** siempre que puedo 2. (*at any time that*) **he can come ~ he likes** puede venir cuando quiera II. *adv* cuando sea

where [hweəʳ] *adv* 1. *interrog* dónde 2. *rel* donde; **the box ~ he puts his things** la caja donde pone sus cosas

whereabout(s) ['hweərəbaʊt(s), *Am:* 'hwerə-] I. *n + sing/pl vb* paradero *m* II. *adv inf* dónde

whereas [hweər'æz, *Am:* hwer'-] *conj* 1. (*while*) mientras que 2. LAW considerando que

whereby [hweə'baɪ, *Am:* hwer'-] *conj form* por lo cual

wherein [hweər'ɪn, *Am:* hwer'-] *conj form* en donde

whereupon [ˌhweərə'pɒn, *Am:* 'hwerəˌpɑːn] *conj form* con lo cual

wherever [ˌhweər'evəʳ, *Am:* ˌhwer-'evəʳ] I. *conj* dondequiera que; ~ **I go** dondequiera que vaya II. *adv* ~ **did she find that?** ¿dónde demonios encontró eso?

wherewithal ['hweəwɪðɔːl, *Am:* 'hwer-] *n no pl, liter* recursos *mpl*

whet [hwet] <-tt-> *vt* **to ~ sb's appetite** aguzar el deseo de alguien

whether ['hweðəʳ, *Am:* -əʳ] *conj* si; **she doesn't know ~ to buy it or**

not no sabe si comprarlo o no; **I doubt ~ he'll come** dudo que venga; **~ rich or poor ...** sean ricos o pobres...; **~ I go by bus or bike ...** vaya en autobús o en bicicleta...

which [hwɪtʃ] **I.** *adj interrog* **~ one/ ones?** ¿cuál/cuáles? **II.** *pron* **1.** *interrog* cuál **2.** *rel* (el/la) que, (los/ las) que; **the book ~ I read** el libro que leí

whichever [hwɪtʃˈevəʳ, *Am:* -ɚ] **I.** *pron* cualquiera que; **you can choose ~ you like** puedes escoger el que quieras **II.** *adj* cualquier, el que; **you can take ~ book you like** puedes coger el libro que quieras

whiff [hwɪf] *n* olor *m;* **to catch a ~ of sth** percibir un olorcillo a algo; **a ~ of corruption** una sospecha de corrupción

while [hwaɪl] **I.** *n* rato *m;* **a short ~** un ratito; **after a ~** después de un tiempo; **once in a ~** de vez en cuando **II.** *conj* **1.** (*during which time*) mientras **2.** (*although*) aunque
♦ **while away** *vt* pasar; **to ~ the time** hacer tiempo

whilst [hwaɪlst] *conj Brit s.* **while**

whim [hwɪm] *n* capricho *m;* **to do sth on a ~** hacer algo por capricho

whimper [ˈhwɪmpəʳ, *Am:* -pɚ] **I.** *vi* quejarse **II.** *n* quejido *m*

whine [hwaɪn] *vi* **1.** (*complain*) gemir **2.** (*engine*) zumbar

whinge [hwɪndʒ] *vi inf* quejarse

whip [hwɪp] **I.** *n* **1.** (*lash*) látigo *m,* chicote *m AmL* **2.** POL *persona encargada de la disciplina de partido* **II.** <-pp-> *vt* **1.** (*strike*) azotar **2.** GASTR batir **3.** *Am, fig, inf* (*defeat*) **to ~ sb** dar una paliza a alguien
♦ **whip out** *vt* sacar de repente
♦ **whip up** *vt* (*encourage*) avivar; **to ~ support** conseguir apoyo

whipped cream *n* nata *f* montada

whippet [ˈhwɪpɪt] *n* lebrel *m*

whipping *n* (*punishment*) azotaina *f*

whipping-boy *n* cabeza *f* de turco

whipping cream *n no pl* nata *f* para montar

whirl [hwɜːl, *Am:* hwɜːrl] **I.** *vi* girar

rápidamente **II.** *vt* hacer girar **III.** *n* **to give sth a ~** *fig* probar algo

whirlpool *n* remolino *m*

whirlwind *n* torbellino *m;* **a ~ romance** un idilio relámpago

whirr [hwɜːʳ, *Am:* hwɜːr] *vi* hacer ruido

whisk [hwɪsk] **I.** *vt* **1.** GASTR batir **2.** (*take*) **to ~ sb off somewhere** llevar a alguien a toda prisa a algún sitio **3.** (*sweep*) sacudir **II.** *n* batidora *f*

whisker [ˈhwɪskəʳ, *Am:* -kɚz] *n* **1.** *pl* (*facial hair*) pelo *m* de la barba; (*of animal*) bigotes *mpl* **2.** *fig* **by a ~** por un pelo; **within a ~** (**of sth**) a dos dedos (de algo)

whiskey *n Irish, Am,* **whisky** [ˈhwɪski] *n* <-ies> *Brit, Aus* whisky *m*

whisper [ˈhwɪspəʳ, *Am:* -pɚ] **I.** *vi* susurrar **II.** *vt* susurrar; **it is ~ed that ...** se rumorea que... **III.** *n* susurro *m;* **to speak in a ~** hablar muy bajo; **the ~ of the leaves** el rumor de las hojas

whist [hwɪst] *n no pl* whist *m*

whistle [ˈhwɪsl] **I.** <-ling> *vi* (*of person*) silbar; (*of bird*) trinar **II.** <-ling> *vt* silbar **III.** *n.* **1.** *no pl* (*sound*) silbido *m* **2.** (*device*) pito *m;* **to blow the ~ on sb** *fig* llamar al orden a alguien

whit [hwɪt] *n no pl, form* **not a ~** ni pizca

white [hwaɪt] **I.** *adj* blanco; **~ lie** mentira *f* piadosa **II.** *n* **1.** (*colour*) blanco *m;* (*of egg*) clara *f* **2.** (*person*) blanco, -a *m, f*

whitebait *n inv* chanquetes *mpl*

whitecollar worker *n* oficinista *mf*

white goods *npl* electrodomésticos *mpl* **White House** *n no pl* **the ~** la Casa Blanca **white sauce** *n* besamel *f* **white spirit** *n no pl, Brit* trementina *f*

whitewash **I.** <-es> *n* **1.** *no pl* (*paint*) enjalbegue *m* **2.** (*coverup*) blanqueo *m* **3.** *inf* (*victory*) paliza *f* **II.** *vt* **1.** (*paint*) encalar **2.** (*conceal*) blanquear **3.** *inf* (*defeat*) dar un baño a

whither ['hwɪðəʳ, *Am:* -ɚ] *adv form* adónde

whiting ['hwaɪtɪŋ, *Am:* -t̬ɪŋ] *n* pescadilla *f*

Whitsun ['hwɪtsən] *n no pl* Pentecostés *m*

whittle ['hwɪtl, *Am:* 'hwɪt̬-] <-ling> *vt* tallar
   ◆ **whittle down** *vt fig* reducir gradualmente

whizz [hwɪz] *vi inf* **to ~ by** pasar como una bala

whizz kid *n inf* joven genio *m*

who [hu:] *pron* **1.** *interrog* quién, quiénes **2.** *rel* que; **the people ~ work here** la gente que trabaja aquí; **it was your sister ~ did it** fue tu hermana quien lo hizo

WHO [ˌdʌbljuːˌeɪtʃ'əʊ, *Am:* -'oʊ] *n abbr of* **World Health Organization** OMS *f*

whoever [hu:'evəʳ, *Am:* -ɚ] *pron rel* quien, quienquiera que; **~ said that doesn't know me** el que dijo eso no me conoce

whole [həʊl, *Am:* hoʊl] **I.** *adj* **1.** (*entire*) todo; **the ~ world** el mundo entero **2.** (*in one piece*) entero; **to swallow sth ~** tragarse algo entero **3.** *inf* **a ~ lot of people** mucha gente; **to be a ~ lot faster** ser mucho más rápido **II.** *n* todo *m*; **as a ~** en su totalidad; **on the ~** en general; **the ~ of Barcelona** toda Barcelona

wholefood ['həʊlfu:d, *Am:* 'hoʊl-] *n Brit* alimentos *mpl* integrales

wholegrain ['həʊlgreɪn, *Am:* 'hoʊl-] *adj* integral

whole-hearted [ˌhəʊl'hɑːtɪd, *Am:* ˌhoʊl'hɑːrt̬ɪd] *adj* entusiasta

wholemeal ['həʊlmi:l, *Am:* 'hoʊl-] *adj Brit* integral

wholesale ['həʊlseɪl, *Am:* 'hoʊl-] **I.** *adj* **1.** COM al por mayor **2.** (*large-scale*) a gran escala **II.** *adv* COM al por mayor

wholesaler *n* mayorista *mf*

wholesome ['həʊlsəm, *Am:* 'hoʊl-] *adj* sano

whom [hu:m] *pron* **1.** *interrog* a quién, a quiénes; *after prep* quién,

quiénes **2.** *rel* a quien, que; *after prep* quien, que

whoop [hu:p] **I.** *vi* gritar **II.** *n* grito *m*

whoopee ['hwʊpi, *Am:* 'hwu:pi] *interj* estupendo

whooping cough ['hu:pɪŋkɒf, *Am:* -kɑ:f] *n no pl* tos *f* ferina

whoops [hwʊps] *interj inf* epa

whopper ['hwɒpəʳ, *Am:* 'hwɑ:pɚ] *n* **1.** (*thing*) cosa muy grande; **what a ~!** ¡qué enorme! **2.** (*lie*) embuste *m*

whopping ['hwɒpɪŋ, *Am:* 'hwɑ:pɪŋ] *adj inf* enorme

whore [hɔːʳ, *Am:* hɔːr] *n pej* puta *f*

whose [hu:z] **I.** *adj* **1.** *interrog* de quién, de quiénes **2.** *rel* cuyo, cuya, cuyos, cuyas **II.** *pron poss* de quién, de quiénes

why [hwaɪ] **I.** *adv* por qué; **~ not?** ¿por qué no? **II.** *n* the **~s and wherefores of sth** el porqué de algo

wick [wɪk] *n* mecha *f*; **to get on sb's ~** *Brit, inf* hacer subir a alguien por las paredes

wicked ['wɪkɪd] *adj* malvado; **a ~ sense of humour** un sentido del humor mordaz

wicker ['wɪkəʳ, *Am:* -ɚ] *n no pl* mimbre *m*

wicket ['wɪkɪt] *n* SPORTS palos *mpl*; **to be on a sticky ~** *fig* estar en una situación difícil

wide [waɪd] **I.** *adj* (*broad*) extenso; (*measurement*) ancho; **it is 3 m ~** mide 3 m de ancho; **eyes ~ with fear** ojos muy abiertos de miedo; **a ~ range** una amplia gama; **~ support** gran apoyo; **to be ~ of the mark** no acertar **II.** *adv* extensamente; **to be ~ apart** estar muy lejos (el uno del otro); **~ open** (*eyes*) muy abierto; (*door*) abierto de par en par

widely *adv* extensamente; **~ admired** muy admirado; **~ differing aims** objetivos *mpl* muy diferentes

widen ['waɪdən] **I.** *vt* ensanchar; (*discussion*) ampliar **II.** *vi* ensancharse

wide-open *adj* **1.** (*undecided*) abierto **2.** (*exposed*) expuesto

Ww

widespread ['waɪdspred] *adj* extendido; *fig* general

widow ['wɪdəʊ, *Am:* -oʊ] *n* viuda *f*

widower ['wɪdəʊəʳ, *Am:* oʊəˈ] *n* viudo *m*

width [wɪdθ] *n no pl* anchura *f; (of clothes, swimming pool)* ancho *m;* **to be 3 cm in** ~ medir 3 cm de ancho

wield [wiːld] *vt* manejar; *(weapon)* empuñar; *(power)* ejercer

wife [waɪf] <wives> *n* mujer *f*

wig [wɪg] *n* peluca *f*

wiggle ['wɪgl] *vt* menear; *(toes)* mover

wild [waɪld] **I.** *adj* **1.** *(animal, man)* salvaje; *(flower)* silvestre; *(landscape)* agreste; *(hair)* descuidado **2.** *(undisciplined)* indisciplinado; *(plan)* estrafalario; *(remarks)* delirante; *(guess)* disparatado **3.** *(stormy)* tormentoso **4.** *inf (angry)* furioso; **to drive sb** ~ sacar de quicio a alguien; **to go** ~ ponerse loco **5.** *inf (very enthusiastic)* emocionado **II.** *adv* **to grow** ~ crecer libre; **to let one's imagination run** ~ dejar volar la imaginación **III.** *n pl* **the ~s** la tierra virgen

wild boar *n* jabalí *m* **wild card** *n* comodín *m* **wildcat** *n* ZOOL gato *m* montés

wilderness ['wɪldənəs, *Am:* -dɚ-] *n no pl (desert)* páramo *m;* **to be in the** ~ *fig* estar marginado

wildfire *n* **to spread like** ~ extenderse como un reguero de pólvora **wildlife** *n no pl* fauna *f* y flora

wildly *adv* **1.** *(uncontrolledly)* como loco; **to behave** ~ portarse como un salvaje; **to talk** ~ hablar sin ton ni son **2.** *(haphazardly)* a lo loco **3.** *inf (very)* muy

wilful ['wɪlfəl] *adj Brit* **1.** *(deliberate)* deliberado **2.** *(obstinate)* obstinado

will¹ [wɪl] <would> **I.** *aux* **1.** *(to form future tense)* **I expect they'll come by car** supongo que vendrán en coche; **he'll win** ganará **2.** *(with tag question)* **you won't forget to tell him,** ~ **you?** no te olvidarás de-

círselo, ¿verdad?; **they** ~ **accept this credit card in France, won't they?** aceptarán esta tarjeta de crédito en Francia, ¿no? **3.** *(to express immediate future)* **we'll be off now** ahora nos vamos; **I'll answer the telephone** contesto yo al teléfono **4.** *(to express an intention)* **I** ~ **not be spoken to like that!** ¡no consiento que se me hable así! **5.** *(in requests and instructions)* ~ **you let me speak!** ¡déjame hablar!; **just pass me that knife,** ~ **you?** pásame ese cuchillo, ¿quieres?; ~ **you have a slice of cake?** ¿quiere un pedazo de tarta?; **who'll post this letter for me?** – **I** ~ ¿quién me echa esta carta al buzón? – lo haré yo **6.** *(used to express a fact)* **the car won't run without petrol** el coche no funciona sin gasolina **7.** *(to express persistence)* **he** ~ **keep doing that** se empeña en hacer eso; **they** ~ **keep sending me those brochures** no dejan de mandarme estos folletos **8.** *(to express likelihood)* **they'll be tired** estarán cansados; **she** ~ **have received the letter by now** ya debe haber recibido la carta **II.** *vi form* **as you** ~ como quieras

will² **I.** *n* **1.** *no pl (faculty)* voluntad *f; (desire)* deseo *m;* **the** ~ **of the people** la voluntad del pueblo; **to lose the** ~ **to live** perder las ganas de vivir; **at** ~ a voluntad; **with the best** ~ **in the world** con la mejor voluntad del mundo; **to have a** ~ **of one's own** ser cabezón; **where there's a** ~, **there's a way** *prov* querer es poder *prov* **2.** *(testament)* testamento *m* **II.** *vt* **1.** *(try to cause)* sugestionar; **to** ~ **sb to do sth** sugestionar a alguien para que haga algo **2.** *form (ordain)* ordenar **3.** *(bequeath)* legar

willful *adj Am s.* **wilful**

willing ['wɪlɪŋ] *adj* **1.** *(not opposed)* dispuesto; **to be** ~ **to do sth** estar dispuesto a hacer algo **2.** *(compliant)* servicial

willingness *n no pl* **to show** ~ **to do sth** mostrar buena voluntad para hacer algo

willow ['wɪləʊ, *Am:* -oʊ] *n* sauce *m*

willpower *n no pl* fuerza *f* de voluntad

wilt [wɪlt] *vi* (*plants*) marchitarse; (*person*) languidecer

wily ['waɪli] <-ier, -iest> *adj* astuto

wimp [wɪmp] *n inf* endeble *mf*

win [wɪn] **I.** *n* victoria *f* **II.** <won, won> *vt* **1.** (*be victorious*) ganar; **to ~ first prize** llevarse el primer premio; **to ~ the day** prevalecer **2.** (*promotion, contract*) conseguir; (*recognition, popularity*) ganarse **III.** <won, won> *vi* ganar; **you (just) can't ~ with her** con ella, siempre llevas las de perder; **you ~!** ¡como tú digas!

◆ **win over** *vt* **to win sb over to sth** convencer a alguien para algo

◆ **win round** *vt s.* **win over**

wince [wɪns] *vi* **1.** (*with pain*) hacer un gesto de dolor **2.** (*with embarrassment*) estremecerse

winch [wɪntʃ] <-es> *n* torno *m*

wind¹ [wɪnd] **I.** *n* **1.** (*current of air*) viento *m;* **gust of ~** ráfaga *f;* **to get ~ of sth** enterarse de algo; **to put the ~ up sb** *Brit, Aus* asustar a alguien; **to sail close to the ~** estar a punto de pasarse de la raya; **to take the ~ out of sb's sails** desanimar a alguien **2.** *no pl* (*breath*) aliento *m;* **to get one's ~** recobrar el aliento **3.** *no pl, Brit, Aus* MED gases *mpl;* **to break ~** ventosear **II.** *vt* dejar sin aliento

wind² [waɪnd] <wound, wound> **I.** *vt* **1.** (*coil*) enrollar; (*wool*) ovillar; **to ~ sth around sth** enrollar algo alrededor de algo **2.** (*wrap*) envolver **3.** (*turn: handle*) hacer girar; (*watch*) dar cuerda a **4.** (*film*) hacer correr **II.** *vi* serpentear

◆ **wind down I.** *vt* **1.** (*lower*) bajar **2.** (*gradually reduce*) disminuir progresivamente **II.** *vi* (*relax*) desconectar

◆ **wind up I.** *vt* **1.** (*bring to an end*) acabar; (*debate, meeting, speech*) concluir **2.** *Brit, Aus* COM liquidar **3.** (*watch*) dar cuerda a; **to wind sb up** *Brit, fig* tomar el pelo a alguien

II. *vi* (*come to an end*) finalizar; **to ~ in prison** ir a parar a a la carcel

windbag *n inf* charlatán, -ana *m, f*

wind energy *n no pl* energía *f* eólica **windfall** *n fig* ganancia *f* imprevista **wind instrument** *n* instrumento *m* de viento **windmill** *n* molino *m* de viento

window ['wɪndəʊ, *Am:* -doʊ] *n* (*in building*) *a.* INFOR ventana *f;* (*of shop*) vidriera *f;* (*display*) escaparate *m;* (*of car, train, in envelope*) ventanilla *f;* **a ~ of opportunity** una oportunidad

window box <-es> *n* jardinera *f* **window cleaner** *n* limpiacristales *mf inv* **window display** *n* escaparate *m* **window ledge** *n* alféizar *m* **window-shopping** *n no pl* **to go ~** ir a mirar escaparates **window--sill** *n* repisa *f* de la ventana

windpipe *n* tráquea *f* **wind power** *n no pl* energía *f* eólica

windscreen *n Brit, Aus* parabrisas *m inv* **windscreen wiper** *n* limpiaparabrisas *m inv*

windshield *n Am* parabrisas *m inv* **windsock** *n* manga *f* de viento

windsurfer *n* surfista *mf*

windsurfing *n no pl* windsurf *m*

windswept ['wɪndswept] *adj* azotado por el viento

windy¹ ['wɪndi] <-ier, -iest> *adj* ventoso

windy² ['waɪndi] <-ier, -iest> *adj* sinuoso

wine [waɪn] **I.** *n no pl* vino *m* **II.** *vt* **to ~ and dine sb** dar a alguien muy bien de comer y de beber

wine glass <-es> *n* copa *f* para vino

wing [wɪŋ] **I.** *n* **1.** ZOOL, AVIAT, ARCHIT, POL ala *f;* **to spread one's ~s** *fig* desplegar las alas; **to take sb under one's ~** *fig* hacerse cargo de alguien **2.** (*side of field*) ala *f* exterior; (*player*) extremo, -a *m, f* **3.** *pl* THEAT bastidores *mpl;* **to be waiting in the ~s** *fig* estar esperando su oportunidad **4.** *Brit* AUTO guardabarros *m inv* **II.** *vt* (*wound*) herir en el ala

winger ['wɪŋəʳ, *Am:* -ɚ] *n* SPORTS extremo, -a *m, f*

W
w

wing nut n TECH palomilla f

wingspan n envergadura f

wink [wɪŋk] I. n guiño m; **to give sb a** ~ guiñar el ojo a alguien; **to have forty** ~**s** inf echarse una siestecita; **not to sleep a** ~ no pegar ojo; **in a** ~ en un abrir y cerrar de ojos II. vi **1.** (close one eye) guiñar el ojo; **to ~ at sb** guiñar el ojo a alguien **2.** (flash) parpadear

winner ['wɪnəʳ, Am: -ɚ] n **1.** (person, team) ganador(a) m(f) **2.** inf (goal, point) tanto m decisivo **3.** inf (success) éxito m; **to be on to a ~ with sth** tener mucho éxito con algo

winning ['wɪnɪŋ] I. adj **1.** (team) ganador; (ticket) premiado **2.** (charming) encantador II. n pl (money) ganancias fpl

winter ['wɪntəʳ, Am: -t̬ɚ] I. n invierno m II. vi (animals) invernar; (person) pasar el invierno

winter sports npl deportes mpl de invierno **wintertime** n no pl invierno m

wint(e)ry ['wɪntri] adj invernal

wipe [waɪp] I. n **1.** (act of wiping) limpieza f; **to give sth a ~** limpiar algo **2.** (tissue) toallita f II. vt **1.** (remove dirt) limpiar; (floor) fregar; (one's nose) sonarse; **to ~ sth dry** secar algo **2.** (erase: disk, tape) borrar

◆ **wipe out** vt (population, species) exterminar; (debt) liquidar

◆ **wipe up** vt limpiar

wire ['waɪəʳ, Am: 'waɪɚ] I. n **1.** no pl (metal thread) alambre m; ELEC cable m; **to get one's ~s crossed** inf tener un malentendido **2.** (telegram) telegrama m II. vt **1.** (fasten with wire) sujetar con alambre **2.** ELEC conectar **3.** (send) **to ~ sb money** enviar un giro telegráfico a alguien

wire-cutters npl cortaalambres m inv, pinzas fpl de corte Méx

wireless n Brit no pl radio f

wiring ['waɪərɪŋ, Am: 'waɪɚ-] n no pl ELEC instalación f eléctrica

wiry ['waɪəri, Am: 'waɪɚ-] <-ier, -iest> adj (hair) áspero; (build, person) enjuto y fuerte

wisdom ['wɪzdəm] n no pl sabiduría f; (of decision) prudencia f

wisdom tooth <- teeth> n muela f del juicio

wise [waɪz] adj (person) sabio; (words) juicioso; (decision, choice) inteligente; **the Three Wise Men** los Reyes Magos; **to be ~ to sth** estar al tanto de algo

◆ **wise up** vi **to ~ to sth** ponerse al tanto de algo

wisecrack n **to make a ~ about sth** hacer un chiste sobre algo

wish [wɪʃ] I. <-es> n **1.** (desire) deseo m; **against my ~es** en contra de mi voluntad; **to make a ~** expresar un deseo **2.** pl (greetings) **give him my best ~es** dale muchos recuerdos de mi parte; (with) **best ~es** (at end of letter) un abrazo II. vt **1.** (feel a desire) desear; **I ~ he hadn't come** ojalá no hubiera venido **2.** form (want) **to ~ to do sth** querer hacer algo **3.** (hope) **to ~ sb luck** desear suerte a alguien; **to ~ sb happy birthday** felicitar a alguien por su cumpleaños III. vi desear; **if you ~** como quieras; **to ~ for sth** anhelar algo; (make a wish) desear algo

wishbone n espoleta f

wisp [wɪsp] n (of hair) mechón m; (of straw) brizna f; (of smoke) voluta f; (of cloud) jirón m

wistful ['wɪstfəl] adj melancólico

wit [wɪt] n **1.** no pl (clever humour) ingenio m; **to have a dry ~** ser mordaz **2.** (practical intelligence) inteligencia f; **to be at one's ~s' end** estar para volverse loco; **to frighten sb out of his ~s** dar a alguien un susto de muerte; **to keep one's ~s about one** andar con mucho ojo **3.** (witty person) chistoso, -a m, f

witch [wɪtʃ] <-es> n bruja f

witchcraft n no pl brujería f, payé m CSur **witch doctor** n brujo m, payé m CSur **witch-hunt** n caza f de brujas

with [wɪð] prep con; ~ **me** conmigo; ~ **you** contigo; **to replace sth ~ something else** reemplazar algo por otra cosa; **the man ~ the umbrella** el hombre del paraguas; **~ all his faults** (*despite*) a pesar de todos sus defectos; **to cry ~ rage** llorar de rabia; **to be pleased ~ sth** estar satisfecho con algo; **to fill up ~ fuel** llenar de gasolina; **to be angry ~ sb** estar enfadado con alguien; **he/she took it ~ him/her** lo llevó consigo

withdraw [wɪð'drɔ:, *Am:* -'drɑ:] *irr* **I.** *vt* **1.** (*take out*) quitar; (*money*) sacar **2.** (*take back*) retirar **II.** *vi* **1.** *form* (*leave*) retirarse; **to ~ from public life** retirarse de la vida pública **2.** *fig* (*become unsociable*) recluirse

withdrawal [wɪð'drɔ:əl, *Am:* -'drɑ:-] *n* **1.** *a.* MIL retirada *f;* **to make a ~** FIN sacar dinero **2.** *no pl* (*of consent, support*) supresión *f*

withdrawal symptoms *npl* síndrome *m* de abstinencia

wither ['wɪðə^r, *Am:* -ə[.]] *vi* **1.** (*plants*) marchitarse **2.** *fig* (*lose vitality*) debilitarse; **to allow sth to ~** dejar que algo pierda vida

withering ['wɪðərɪŋ] *adj* **1.** (*heat*) abrasador **2.** (*criticism, glance*) hiriente

withhold [wɪð'həʊld, *Am:* -'hoʊld] *irr vt* (*information*) ocultar; (*support*) negar; (*rent*) retener

within [wɪð'ɪn] **I.** *prep* dentro de; **~ 3 days** en el plazo de tres días; **~ 2 km of the town** a menos de 2 km de la ciudad; **~ the law** dentro de la ley **II.** *adv* dentro; **from ~** desde adentro

without [wɪð'aʊt] *prep* sin; **~ warning** sin previo aviso; **to do ~ sth** apañárselas sin algo

withstand [wɪð'stænd] *irr vt* resistir; (*heat, pressure*) soportar

witness ['wɪtnəs] **I.** *n* **1.** (*person*) testigo *mf;* **to be (a) ~ to sth** presenciar algo **2.** *no pl, form* (*testimony*) testimonio *m;* **to bear ~ to sth** dar fe de algo **II.** *vt* (*see*) ser testigo de; (*changes*) presenciar; **to ~ sb doing sth** observar a alguien haciendo algo

witness box <-es> *n Brit,* **witness stand** *n Am* tribuna *f* (de los testigos)

witty ['wɪti, *Am:* 'wɪt̬-] <-ier, -iest> *adj* gracioso

wizard ['wɪzəd, *Am:* -ə[.]d] *n* mago, -a *m, f*

wizened ['wɪznd] *adj* (*fruit*) marchito; (*face, skin*) arrugado

wobble ['wɒbl, *Am:* 'wɑ:bl] **I.** *vi* tambalearse; (*voice*) temblar **II.** *n* tambaleo *m*

wobbly ['wɒbli, *Am:* 'wɑ:bli] <-ier, -iest> *adj* **1.** (*unsteady*) tambaleante; (*chair*) cojo **2.** (*note, voice*) tembloroso

woe [wəʊ, *Am:* woʊ] *n no pl, liter* desgracia *f*

woeful ['wəʊfəl, *Am:* 'woʊ-] *adj* lamentable

wok [wɒk, *Am:* wɑ:k] *n* puchero *m* chino de metal

woke [wəʊk, *Am:* woʊk] *vt, vi pt of* **wake**

woken ['wəʊkən, *Am:* 'woʊ-] *vt, vi pp of* **wake**

wolf [wʊlf] **I.** <wolves> *n* lobo *m;* **a ~ in sheep's clothing** un lobo disfrazado de cordero; **to cry ~** dar una falsa alarma **II.** *vt inf* engullir

wolf whistle *n* silbido *m* de admiración

woman ['wʊmən] <women> *n* mujer *f*

womanizer *n* mujeriego *m*

womanly ['wʊmənli] *adj* (*not manly*) femenino; (*not girlish*) de mujer adulta

womb [wu:m] *n* útero *m*

womenfolk ['wɪmɪnfəʊk, *Am:* -foʊk] *npl* mujeres *fpl*

won [wʌn] *vt, vi pt, pp of* **win**

wonder ['wʌndə^r, *Am:* -də[.]] **I.** *vt* preguntarse; **I ~ why he said that** me extraña que dijera eso **II.** *vi* preguntarse; **to ~ about sth** preguntarse algo; **to ~ at sth** maravillarse de algo **III.** *n* **1.** (*marvel*) maravilla *f;* **to do ~s** hacer maravillas; **it's a ~ (that)** ... es un milagro que ... +*subj* **2.** *no pl* (*feeling*) asombro *m;* **in ~** con estupefacción

wonderful ['wʌndəfəl, *Am:* -də[.]-] *adj* maravilloso

wont [wəʊnt, *Am:* wɔ:nt] *form* **I.** *adj* to be ~ to do sth soler hacer algo **II.** *n no pl* as is her ~ como suele hacer

woo [wu:] *vt* **1.** (*try to attract*) to ~ **sb** (*customers*) buscar atraer a alguien; (*voters*) buscar el apoyo de alguien **2.** (*court*) cortejar

wood [wʊd] *n* **1.** *no pl* (*material*) madera *f*; (*fuel*) leña *f*; to touch ~, to knock on ~ *Am, fig* tocar madera **2.** (*group of trees*) bosque *m*

woodcutter *n* leñador(a) *m(f)*

wooded ['wʊdɪd] *adj* boscoso

wooden ['wʊdn] *adj* **1.** (*made of wood*) de madera; (*leg, spoon*) de palo **2.** (*awkward*) rígido

woodpecker *n* pájaro *m* carpintero

woodwind *n* instrumentos *mpl* de viento (de madera)

woodwork *n no pl* **1.** (*wooden parts of building*) carpintería *f* **2.** *Brit* (*carpentry*) ebanistería *f* **woodworm** *n inv* carcoma *f*

woody ['wʊdi] <-ier, -iest> *adj* (*plant*) leñoso; (*flavour*) amaderado

wool [wʊl] *n no pl* lana *f*; to pull the ~ over sb's eyes *fig* dar a alguien gato por liebre

woolen *Am*, **woollen** ['wʊlən] *adj Brit* de lana

woolly *adj Brit*, **wooly** ['wʊli] <-ier, -iest> *adj Am* **1.** (*made of wool*) de lana **2.** (*wool-like*) lanoso **3.** (*vague*) vago

word [wɜːd, *Am:* wɜːrd] **I.** *n* **1.** (*unit of language*) palabra *f*; to be a man of few ~s ser hombre de pocas palabras; to not breathe a ~ of sth no decir ni pío de algo; to be too ridiculous for ~s ser tremendamente ridículo; in other ~s en otros términos; ~ for ~ literalmente; a ~ of advice un consejo; a ~ of warning una advertencia; to say the ~ dar la orden; by ~ of mouth de viva voz; to put in a good ~ for sb interceder por alguien; to have ~s with sb discutir con alguien; my ~! ¡caramba! **2.** *no pl* (*news*) to get ~ of sth enterarse de algo; to have ~ that ... tener conocimiento de que... **3.** *no*

pl (*promise*) palabra *f* de honor; to keep one's ~ cumplir su promesa **4.** *pl* (*lyrics*) letra *f* **II.** *vt* expresar

wording *n no pl* términos *mpl*

wordplay *n no pl* juego *m* de palabras

word processing *n no pl* tratamiento *m* de textos **word processor** *n* procesador *m* de textos

wore [wɔːʳ, *Am:* wɔːr] *vt, vi pt of* **wear**

work [wɜːk, *Am:* wɜːrk] **I.** *n* **1.** *no pl* (*useful activity*) trabajo *m*; to set sb to ~ poner a trabajar a alguien; good ~! ¡bien hecho!; to make short ~ of sth despachar algo rápidamente **2.** *no pl* (*employment*) empleo *m*; to be in/out of ~ estar en activo/en paro **3.** *no pl* (*place of employment*) lugar *m* de trabajo **4.** (*product*) *a.* ART, MUS obra *f*; ~ of reference libro *m* de consulta **5.** *pl* + *sing/pl vb* (*factory*) fábrica *f*; steel ~s fundición *f* de acero **II.** *vi* **1.** (*do job*) trabajar; to get ~ing poner manos a la obra; to ~ to do sth dedicarse a hacer algo **2.** (*function*) funcionar; (*be successful*) salir adelante; MED hacer efecto; to ~ against sb obrar en contra de alguien **3.** + *adj* (*become*) to ~ free soltarse; to ~ loose desprenderse **III.** *vt* **1.** (*make sb work*) to ~ sb hard hacer trabajar duro a alguien; to ~ oneself to death matarse trabajando; to ~ one's way through university pagarse la universidad trabajando **2.** (*operate*) hacer funcionar; to be ~ed by sth ser accionado por algo **3.** (*move*) to ~ sth free liberar algo; to ~ sth loose desprender algo **4.** (*bring about*) producir; (*miracle*) lograr **5.** (*shape*) tallar; (*metal*) trabajar **6.** MIN explotar; AGR cultivar

◆ **work off** *vt* (*frustration*) desahogar

◆ **work out I.** *vt* **1.** (*solve*) resolver **2.** (*calculate*) calcular **3.** (*understand*) comprender **II.** *vi* **1.** (*give result*) salir **2.** to ~ for the best salir perfectamente **3.** (*do exercise*) entrenarse

◆ **work over** *vt inf* to work sb over dar una paliza a alguien

◆ **work up** *vt* **1.** (*energy, enthusiasm*) estimular; **to work oneself up** emocionarse **2.** (*develop*) desarrollar

workable ['wɜːkəbl, *Am:* 'wɜːr-] *adj* factible

worker ['wɜːkəʳ, *Am:* 'wɜːrkɚ] *n* trabajador(a) *m(f)*; (*in factory*) obrero, -a *m, f*

work ethic *n* ética *f* del trabajo

workforce *n* + *sing/pl vb* población *f* activa **workhorse** *n* bestia *f* de carga

working *adj* **1.** (*employed*) empleado; (*population*) activo; (*day, week*) laboral **2.** (*functioning*) que funciona; (*moving: model*) móvil; **to have a ~ knowledge of sth** tener conocimientos básicos de algo

working class <-es> *n* **the ~** la clase obrera **working-class** *adj* obrero

workload *n* (volumen *m* de) trabajo *m*

workman <-men> *n* obrero *m*

workmanship ['wɜːkmənʃɪp, *Am:* 'wɜːrk-] *n no pl* **1.** (*skill in working*) destreza *f* **2.** (*quality of work*) confección *f*

work of art *n* obra *f* de arte

workout *n* SPORTS entrenamiento *m*

work permit *n* permiso *m* de trabajo **workplace** *n* lugar *m* de trabajo

works committee *n*, **works council** *n* comité *m* de empresa

worksheet *n* hoja *f* de trabajo **workshop** *n* (*place, class*) taller *m* **work station** *n* INFOR estación *f* de trabajo

worktop *n Brit* encimera *f*

world [wɜːld, *Am:* wɜːrld] *n no pl* mundo *m*; **a ~ authority** una autoridad mundial; **the ~ champion** el campeón del mundo; **the animal ~** el mundo animal; **the best in the ~** el mejor del mundo; **the (whole) ~ over** en el mundo entero; **to see the ~** ver mundo; **to travel all over the ~** viajar por todo el mundo; **to be ~s apart** ser como la noche y el día; **to be out of this ~** *inf* ser fantástico; **to have the best of both ~s** nadar y

guardar la ropa; **to mean the ~ to sb** serlo todo para alguien; **to think the ~ of sb** tener un alto concepto de alguien; **it's a small ~!** ¡el mundo es un pañuelo!; **I wouldn't do such a thing for (all) the ~** no haría algo así por nada del mundo; **what in the ~ ...?** ¿qué demonios...?

World Bank *n* **the ~** el Banco Mundial **world-class** *adj* de clase mundial **World Cup** *n* SPORTS **the ~** la Copa del Mundo **world-famous** *adj* de fama mundial

worldly ['wɜːldli, *Am:* 'wɜːrld-] *adj* mundano

world record *n* récord *m* mundial **world war** *n* HIST guerra *f* mundial **world-wide** I. *adj* mundial II. *adv* por todo el mundo

World Wide Web *n* INFOR Red *f* Mundial

worm [wɜːm, *Am:* wɜːrm] I. *n* gusano *m*; (*insect larva*) oruga *f*; (*earthworm*) lombriz *f* II. *vt* **to ~ oneself under sth** deslizarse por debajo de algo; **to ~ a secret out of sb** sonsacar un secreto a alguien

worn [wɔːn, *Am:* wɔːrn] I. *vt, vi pp of* **wear** II. *adj* desgastado; (*clothing*) raído

worn-out *adj* (*person, animal*) rendido; (*clothing*) raído

worried *adj* preocupado; **to be ~ about sth** estar preocupado por algo; **to be ~ sick about sth** estar preocupadísimo por algo

worry ['wʌri, *Am:* 'wɜːr-] I. <-ies> *n* preocupación *f*; **financial worries** problemas *fpl* económicos; **to be a cause of ~ to sb** dar problemas a alguien II. *vt* <-ie-, -ing> preocupar III. <-ie-, -ing> *vi* **to ~ (about sth)** preocuparse (por algo); **don't ~!** ¡no te preocupes!

worrying *adj* preocupante

worse [wɜːs, *Am:* wɜːrs] I. *adj comp of* **bad** peor; **from bad to ~** de mal en peor; **to get ~** empeorar; **to get ~ and ~** ser cada vez peor; **to make matters ~ ...** por si fuera poco... II. *n no pl* **the ~** el/la peor; **to change for the ~** cambiar para mal;

W

to have seen ~ haber visto cosas peores **III.** *adv comp of* **badly** peor; **to do sth ~ than ...** hacer algo peor que...

worsen ['wɜːsən, *Am:* 'wɜːr-] *vi, vt* empeorar

worship ['wɜːʃɪp, *Am:* 'wɜːr-] **I.** *vt* <-pp-, *Am:* -p-> *a.* REL adorar **II.** *vi* <-pp-, *Am:* -p-> REL hacer sus devociones **III.** *n no pl* adoración *f;* **Your Worship** Su Señoría

worst [wɜːst, *Am:* wɜːrst] **I.** *adj superl of* **bad** the ~ el/la peor; **the ~ soup I've ever eaten** la peor sopa que he comido (nunca); **the ~ mistake** el error más grave **II.** *adv superl of* **badly** peor; **to be ~ affected by sth** ser los más afectados por algo **III.** *n no pl* **the** ~ lo peor; **at** ~ en el peor de los casos; **to fear the** ~ temerse lo peor; **if** (**the**) ~ **comes to** (**the**) ~ en el peor de los casos

worth [wɜːθ, *Am:* wɜːrθ] **I.** *n no pl* (*of person*) valía *f;* (*of thing, money*) valor *m;* **to prove one's** ~ demostrar su valía **II.** *adj* **to be** ~ **...** valer...; **to be** ~ **it** valer la pena; **to be** ~ **millions** *inf* ser millonario; **to be** ~ **a mention** ser digno de mención; **it's not** ~ **arguing about!** ¡no vale la pena discutir por eso!; **it's** ~ **remembering that ...** conviene recordar que...; **it's** ~ **a try** vale la pena intentarlo; **for what it's** ~ *inf* por si sirve de algo

worthless ['wɜːθləs, *Am:* 'wɜːrθ-] *adj* **1.** (*valueless*) sin ningún valor **2.** (*useless*) inútil

worthwhile [ˌwɜːθ'hwaɪl, *Am:* ˌwɜːrθ-] *adj* que vale la pena

worthy ['wɜːði, *Am:* 'wɜːr-] <-ier, -iest> *adj* (*admirable*) encomiable; **a** ~ **cause** una noble causa; **to be** ~ **of sth** ser merecedor de algo

would [wʊd] *aux pt of* **will 1.** (*future in the past*) **he said he** ~ **do it later on** dijo que lo haría más tarde; **we thought they** ~ **have done it before** pensamos que lo habrían hecho antes **2.** (*intention*) **he said he** ~ **always love her** dijo que siempre la querría; **I** ~ **rather have**

beer prefiero beber cerveza; **I** ~ **rather die than do that** antes morir que hacer eso; **why** ~ **anyone want to do something like that?** ¿por qué nadie querría hacer algo así? **3.** (*possibility*) **I'd go myself, but I'm too busy** iría yo mismo, pero estoy demasiado ocupado **4.** (*conditional*) **what** ~ **you do if you lost your job?** ¿qué harías si te quedaras sin trabajo?; **I** ~ **have done it if you'd asked** lo habría hecho si me lo hubieras pedido **5.** (*polite request*) ~ **you mind saying that again?** ¿te importaría repetir eso?; ~ **you like ...?** ¿te gustaría...? **6.** (*regularity in past*) **they** ~ **help each other with their homework** solían ayudarse con los deberes **7.** (*typical*) **the bus** ~ **be late when I'm in a hurry** por supuesto, el autobús siempre llega tarde cuando tengo prisa; **he** ~ **say that, wouldn't he?** era de esperar que lo dijera, ¿no? **8.** (*opinion*) **I** ~ **imagine that ...** me imagino que...; **I** ~**n't have thought that ...** nunca habría pensado que... **9.** (*deduction*) **the guy on the phone had an Australian accent − that** ~ **be Tom, I expect** el chico con quien hablé por teléfono tenía acento australiano − debía de ser Tom

would-be *adj* **1.** (*wishing to be*) aspirante **2.** (*pretending to be*) supuesto

wound[1] [waʊnd] *vi, vt pt, pp of* **wind**[2]

wound[2] [wuːnd] **I.** *n* herida *f* **II.** *vt* herir

wounded *adj* herido

wove [wəʊv, *Am:* woʊv] *vt, vi pt of* **weave**

woven ['wəʊvən, *Am:* 'woʊv-] *vt, vi pp of* **weave**

wow [waʊ] *inf* **I.** *interj* caray **II.** *vt* **to** ~ **sb** volver loco a alguien

wrangle ['ræŋgl] **I.** <-ling> *vi* discutir **II.** *n* riña *f*

wrap [ræp] **I.** *n* (*robe*) bata *f;* **to keep sth under** ~**s** *fig* mantener algo en secreto **II.** *vt* <-pp-> envolver; **to ~ one's fingers around sth** agarrar algo con las manos

wraparound ['ræpəˌraʊnd] *adj* (*skirt*, *dress*) cruzado; (*sunglasses*) envolvente

◆ **wrap up I.** *vt* <-pp-> envolver; **to wrap oneself up against the cold** abrigarse para protegerse del frío; **that wraps it up for today** *fig* eso es todo por hoy **II.** *vi* (*dress warmly*) abrigarse; **to ~ warm** abrigarse bien; **to be wrapped up in sth** *fig* estar absorto en algo

wrapper ['ræpər, *Am:* -ɚ] *n* **1.** (*packaging*) envoltorio *m* **2.** *Am* (*robe*) bata *f*

wrapping paper *n* (*plain*) papel *m* de embalar; (*for presents*) papel *m* de regalo

wrath [rɒθ, *Am:* ræθ] *n no pl, liter* ira *f*

wreak [ri:k] <-ed, -ed *o* wrought, wrought> *vt form* **to ~ damage (on sth)** hacer estragos (de algo); **to ~ vengeance on sb** vengarse de alguien

wreath [ri:θ] <wreaths> *n* (*of flowers*) corona *f*; (*of smoke*) espiral *f*

wreathe [ri:ð] *vt liter* **to be ~d in sth** estar rodeado de algo; **to be ~d in smiles** no dejar de sonreír

wreck [rek] **I.** *vt* destrozar; (*hopes, plan*) arruinar; **to ~ sb's life** destrozar la vida de alguien **II.** *n* NAUT naufragio *m*; AUTO accidente *m*; **an old ~** (*car*) un cacharro; **to feel a complete ~** estar hecho polvo; **to be a nervous ~** tener los nervios destrozados

wreckage ['rekɪdʒ] *n no pl* (*of vehicle*) restos *mpl*; (*of building*) escombros *mpl*

wrecker ['rekər, *Am:* -ɚ] *n Am* AUTO camión-grúa *m*

wren [ren] *n* chochín *m*

wrench [rentʃ] **I.** *vt* arrancar; **to ~ oneself away** soltarse de un tirón; **to ~ one's ankle** torcerse el tobillo; **to ~ sb from sb** *fig* separar a alguien de alguien **II.** *n* **1.** (*jerk*) tirón *m*, jalón *m CSur*; (*injury*) torcedura *f*

2. (*emotional pain*) dolor *m* (*causado por una separación*) **3.** *Am* TECH llave *f* inglesa

wrestle ['resl] <-ling> *vi* luchar

wrestler *n* luchador(a) *m(f)*

wrestling *n no pl* lucha *f*

wrestling bout *n*, **wrestling match** *n* combate *m* de lucha

wretch [retʃ] <-es> *n* infeliz *mf*

wretched ['retʃɪd] *adj* (*life, person*) desdichado; (*house, conditions*) miserable; (*weather*) horrible; **to feel ~** (*sick*) estar muy mal; (*depressed*) estar muy abatido; **my ~ car's broken down again!** ¡este maldito coche se me ha vuelto a estropear!

wriggle ['rɪgl] <-ling> *vi* retorcerse; **to ~ out of sth** *fig, inf* escapar de un apuro

wring [rɪŋ] <wrung, wrung> *vt* retorcer; **to ~ one's hands** retorcerse las manos; **to ~ sb's neck** *inf* retorcer el cuello a alguien; **to ~ water out of sth** escurrir el agua de algo; **to ~ the truth out of sb** sacar la verdad a alguien

wringer ['rɪŋər, *Am:* -ɚ] *n* rodillo *m* para escurrir la ropa

wrinkle ['rɪŋkl] **I.** *n* arruga *f* **II.** <-ling> *vi* arrugarse **III.** <-ling> *vt* arrugar

wrist [rɪst] *n* **1.** ANAT muñeca *f* **2.** (*of shirt*) puño *m*

wristband *n* (*strap*) correa *f*; (*sweatband*) muñequera *f*

wristwatch <-es> *n* reloj *m* de pulsera

writ [rɪt] *n* orden *f* judicial; **to issue a ~ against sb** expedir un mandato judicial contra alguien

write [raɪt] <wrote, written, writing> **I.** *vt* **1.** escribir; **to ~ sb a cheque** extender un cheque a alguien **2.** MUS componer **II.** *vi* escribir; **to ~ to sb** *Brit,* **to ~ sb** *Am* escribir a alguien

◆ **write down** *vt* apuntar

◆ **write off** *vt* **1.** (*give up doing: attempt*) abandonar; (*project*) dar por perdido; **to write sb off as useless** descartar a alguien como inútil **2.** FIN

Ww

(*debt*) cancelar **3.** *Brit* AUTO destrozar
◆ **write out** *vt* escribir
◆ **write up** *vt* poner por escrito; (*article, report*) redactar
write-off *n Brit* **to be a complete ~** (*car*) ser declarado siniestro total; (*project, marriage*) ser un fracaso
writer ['raɪtə^r, *Am:* -t̬ə^r] *n* **1.** (*person*) escritor(a) *m(f)* **2.** INFOR **CD- -ROM/DVD ~** grabador *m* de CD- -ROM/DVD
write-up *n* ART, THEAT, MUS crítica *f*
writhe [raɪð] <writhing> *vi* retorcerse; **to make sb ~ with embarrassment** hacer pasar a alguien por una situación incómoda
writing ['raɪtɪŋ, *Am:* -t̬ɪŋ] *n no pl* **1.** (*handwriting*) letra *f*; **in ~** por escrito; **to put sth in ~** poner algo por escrito **2.** (*action*) **she likes ~** le encanta escribir **3.** (*written work*) obra *f*
writing paper *n* papel *m* de carta
written **I.** *vt*, *vi pp of* **write II.** *adj* escrito
wrong [rɒŋ, *Am:* rɑːŋ] **I.** *adj* **1.** (*not right: answer*) incorrecto; **to be ~ about sth** equivocarse en algo; **to be ~ about sb** juzgar mal a alguien; **to get the ~ number** equivocarse de número; **to prove sb ~** demostrar que alguien se equivoca **2.** (*not appropriate*) inoportuno; **to say the ~ thing** decir lo que no se debe **3.** (*bad*) malo; **is there anything ~?** ¿te pasa algo?; **what's ~ with you today?** ¿qué te pasa hoy?; **something's ~ with the television** el televisor no funciona bien; **it is ~ to do that** está mal hacer eso **II.** *adv* **1.** (*incorrectly*) incorrectamente; **to do sth ~** hacer algo mal; **to get sth ~** equivocarse en algo; **to get it ~** comprender mal; **to go ~** equivocarse; (*stop working*) estropearse, descomponerse *Méx*; (*fail*) salir mal **2.** (*morally reprehensible*) mal; **to do sth ~** hacer algo mal **III.** *n* **1.** *no pl a.* LAW, REL mal *m*; (**to know**) **right from ~** saber distinguir entre lo que está bien y lo que está mal; **to do ~** obrar mal; **he can do no ~** es inca-

paz de hacer nada malo; **to be in the ~** (*mistaken*) estar equivocado **2.** (*injustice*) injusticia *f*; **to right a ~** enderezar un entuerto
wrongful *adj* injusto
wrongly *adv* mal
wrote [rəʊt, *Am:* roʊt] *vi, vt pt of* **write**
wrought [rɔːt, *Am:* rɑːt] *pt, pp of* **work III.4, 5., wreak**
wrought iron *n no pl* hierro *m* forjado
wrought-up *adj* nervioso; **to get ~ about sth** ponerse nervioso por algo
wrung [rʌŋ] *vt pt, pp of* **wring**
wry [raɪ] <wrier, wriest *o* wryer, wryest> *adj* irónico
WW *n abbr of* **World War** Guerra *f* Mundial
WWW *n abbr of* **World Wide Web** INFOR WWW *f*

X, x [eks] *n* X, x *f*
xerox, Xerox® ['zɪərɒks, *Am:* 'zɪrɑːks] *vt Am* fotocopiar
Xmas ['krɪstməs, 'eksməs] *n abbr of* **Christmas** Navidad *f*
X-ray ['eksreɪ] **I.** *n* (*photo*) radiografía *f*; **~s** rayos *mpl* X **II.** *vt* radiografiar
xylophone ['zaɪləfəʊn, *Am:* -foʊn] *n* xilófono *m*

Y, y [waɪ] *n* Y, y *f*
yacht [jɒt, *Am:* jɑːt] *n* (*for pleasure*) yate *m*; (*for racing*) velero *m*

yachting *n no pl* **to go** ~ navegar
yak [jæk] *n* yak *m*
yam [jæm] *n* **1.** (*vegetable*) ñame *m* **2.** *Am* (*sweet potato*) batata *f*, camote *m* *AmL*
yank [jæŋk] **I.** *vt inf* **to** ~ **sth** tirar de algo, jalar de algo *AmL* **II.** *n inf* tirón *m*, jalón *m* *AmL*
Yank [jæŋk] *n*, **Yankee** ['jæŋki] *n pej, inf* yanqui *mf*, gringo, -a *m, f* *AmL*
yap [jæp] <-pp-> *vi* (*bark*) ladrar
yard¹ [jɑ:d, *Am:* jɑ:rd] *n* (*3 feet*) yarda *f* (*0,91 m*)
yard² *n* **1.** (*paved area*) patio *m* **2.** *Am* (*garden*) jardín *m*
yardstick *n fig* criterio *m*
yarn [jɑ:n, *Am:* jɑ:rn] **I.** *n* **1.** *no pl* (*thread*) hilo *m* **2.** (*story*) cuento *m;* **to spin a** ~ inventarse una historia **II.** *vi* inventar historias
yawn [jɔ:n, *Am:* jɑ:n] **I.** *vi* bostezar **II.** *n* bostezo *m*
yeah [jeə] *adv inf* sí
year [jɪəʳ, *Am:* jɪr] *n* **1.** (*twelve months*) año *m;* ~ **in,** ~ **out** año tras año; **all** ~ **round** (durante) todo el año; **happy new** ~**!** ¡feliz año nuevo!; **I'm seven** ~**s old** tengo siete años **2.** school, univ curso *m*
yearly **I.** *adj* anual **II.** *adv* anualmente
yearn [jɜːn, *Am:* jɜːrn] *vi* **to** ~ **to do sth** ansiar hacer algo; **to** ~ **after sth** anhelar algo; **to** ~ **for sth** añorar algo
yeast [ji:st] *n no pl* levadura *f*
yell [jel] **I.** *n* grito *m* **II.** *vi, vt* gritar
yellow ['jeləʊ, *Am:* -oʊ] **I.** *adj* **1.** (*colour*) amarillo **2.** *pej, inf* (*cowardly*) cobarde **II.** *n* **1.** (*colour*) amarillo *m* **2.** *Am* (*of egg*) yema *f* (de huevo)
yelp [jelp] **I.** *vi* aullar **II.** *n* aullido *m*
Yemen ['jemən] *n* Yemen *m*
Yemeni ['jeməni] *adj* yemení
yep [jep] *adv inf* sí
yes [jes] *adv* sí
yesterday ['jestədeɪ, *Am:* -təˑ-] *adv* ayer; ~ **morning** ayer por la mañana, ayer en la mañana *AmL*, ayer a la mañana *CSur;* **the day before** ~ anteayer
yet [jet] **I.** *adv* **1.** (*up to a particular*

time) todavía; **it's too early** ~ **to ...** aún es muy pronto para...; **not** ~ aún no; **as** ~ hasta ahora; **have you finished** ~**?** ¿ya has terminado?; **the best is** ~ **to come** aún queda lo mejor **2.** (*in addition*) ~ **again** otra vez más; ~ **bigger/more beautiful** aún más grande/más bonito; ~ **more food** todavía más comida **3.** (*despite that*) sin embargo; **we'll get there** ~ llegaremos a pesar de todo **II.** *conj* a pesar de todo
yew [ju:] *n* tejo *m*
yield [ji:ld] **I.** *n* com, fin rendimiento *m;* agr producción *f* **II.** *vt* (*results*) dar; agr producir; com, fin proporcionar; **to** ~ **ground** ceder terreno; **to** ~ **responsibility** delegar responsabilidad **III.** *vi* **to** ~ **to temptation** ceder a la tentación; **to** ~ **to sb** (*give priority*) dar prioridad a alguien
◆ **yield up** *vt* entregar
yob [jɒb, *Am:* jɑ:b] *n*, **yobbo** ['jɒbəʊ, *Am:* 'jɑ:boʊ] <-s> *n Brit, Aus, inf* gamberro, -a *m, f*
yoga ['jəʊgə, *Am:* 'joʊ-] *n no pl* yoga *m*
yog(ho)urt ['jɒgət, *Am:* 'joʊgəʳt] *n* yogur *m*
yoke [jəʊk, *Am:* joʊk] *n* **1.** agr yugo *m* **2.** fashion canesú *m*
yokel ['jəʊkl, *Am:* 'joʊ-] *n pej* paleto, -a *m, f*, pajuerano, -a *m, f Arg, Bol, Urug*
yolk [jəʊk, *Am:* joʊk] *n* yema *f* (de huevo)
you [ju:] *pron pers* **1.** *2nd person sing* tu, vos *CSur; pl:* vosotros, vosotras, ustedes *AmL;* **I see** ~ te/os veo; **do** ~ **see me?** ¿me ves/veis?; **it is for** ~ es para ti/vosotros; **older than** ~ mayor que tú/vosotros **2.** *2nd person sing, polite form* usted; *pl:* ustedes; **older than** ~ mayor que usted/ustedes
young [jʌŋ] **I.** *adj* joven; ~ **children** niños *mpl* pequeños; **a** ~ **man** un joven; **my** ~**er brother** mi hermano menor; **to be** ~ **at heart** ser joven de espíritu; **you're only** ~ **once!** ¡sólo se es joven una vez! **II.** *n pl* **1.** (*young*

X
x
Y
y

people) **the** ~ los jóvenes **2.** (*off-spring*) cría *f*

youngster [ˈjʌŋkstəʳ, *Am:* -stɚ] *n* joven *mf*

your [jɔːʳ, *Am:* jʊr] *adj poss* **1.** *2nd pers sing* tu(s); *pl:* vuestro(s), vuestra(s) **2.** *2nd pers sing and pl, polite form* su(s)

yours [jɔːz, *Am:* jʊrz] *pron poss* **1.** *sing:* (el) tuyo, (la) tuya, (los) tuyos, (las) tuyas; *pl:* (el) vuestro, (la) vuestra, (los) vuestros, (las) vuestras, el de ustedes *AmL*, la de ustedes *AmL* **2.** *polite form* (el) suyo, (la) suya, (los) suyos, (las) suyas

yourself [jɔːˈself, *Am:* jʊr-] *pron refl* **1.** *sing:* te; *emphatic:* tú (mismo/misma); *after prep:* ti (mismo/misma) **2.** *polite form:* se; *emphatic:* usted (mismo/misma); *after prep:* sí (mismo/misma)

yourselves *pron refl* **1.** os, se *AmL*; *emphatic, after prep:* vosotros (mismos), vosotras (mismas), ustedes (mismos/mismas) *AmL* **2.** *polite form:* se; *emphatic:* ustedes (mismos/mismas); *after prep:* sí (mismos/mismas)

youth [juːθ] *n* **1.** *no pl* (*period*) juventud *f* **2.** (*young man*) joven *m* **3.** *no pl* (*young people*) jóvenes *mpl*

youth centre *n*, **youth club** *n* club *m* juvenil

youthful [ˈjuːθfəl] *adj* juvenil

youth hostel *n* albergue *m* juvenil

yucky [jʌki] *adj inf* asqueroso

Yugoslavia [ˈjuːgəʊˈslɑːviə, *Am:* -goʊˈ-] *n* HIST Yugoslavia *f*

Yugoslavian *adj* HIST yugoslavo

Z Z

Z, z [zed, *Am:* ziː] *n* Z, z *f*

Zaire [zaɪˈrə, *Am:* -ˈɪr] *n* Zaire *m*

Zairean [zaɪˈrən] *adj* zaireño

Zambia [ˈzæmbɪə] *n* Zambia *f*

Zambian [ˈzæmbɪən] *adj* zambiano

zany [ˈzeɪni] <-ier, -iest> *adj inf* (*person*) chiflado; (*idea*) loco

zeal [ziːl] *n no pl* celo *m*

zealot [ˈzelət] *n* fanático, -a *m, f*

zealous [ˈzeləs] *adj* ferviente

zebra [ˈzebrə, *Am:* ˈziːbrə] *n* cebra *f*

zebra crossing *n Brit, Aus* paso *m* de cebra

zenith [ˈzenɪθ, *Am:* ˈziːnɪθ] <-es> *n* ASTR cenit *m*; **to be at the ~ of sth** *fig* estar en el apogeo de algo

zero [ˈzɪərəʊ, *Am:* ˈzɪroʊ] <-s o -es> *n* cero *m*; **below ~** METEO bajo cero
◆ **zero in on** *vi* **to ~ sth** centrarse en algo

zest [zest] *n no pl* **1.** (*enthusiasm*) entusiasmo *m* **2.** (*rind*) corteza *f*

zigzag [ˈzɪgzæg] **I.** *n* zigzag *m* **II.** <-gg-> *vi* zigzaguear

Zimbabwe [zɪmˈbɑːbweɪ] *n* Zimbabue *m*

Zimbabwean [zɪmˈbɑːbwiən] *adj* zimbabuo

zinc [zɪŋk] *n no pl* cinc *m*, zinc *m*

zip [zɪp] **I.** *n* cremallera *f*, cierre *m* relámpago *Arg* **II.** <-pp-> *vt* **to ~ sth up** subir la cremallera de algo

zip code *n Am* código *m* postal

zip-fastener *n Brit*, **zipper** [ˈzɪpəʳ, *Am:* -ɚ] *n Am* cremallera *f*, cierre *m* relámpago *Arg*

zodiac [ˈzəʊdiæk, *Am:* ˈzoʊ-] *n no pl* zodíaco *m*

zombie [ˈzɒmbi, *Am:* ˈzɑːm-] *n* zombi *mf*

zone [zəʊn, *Am:* zoʊn] *n* zona *f*

zoo [zuː] *n* zoo *m*

zoological [ˌzəʊəʊˈlɒdʒɪkəl, *Am:* ˌzoʊəˈlɑːdʒɪ-] *adj* zoológico

zoologist [zuˈɒlədʒɪst, *Am:* zoʊ-ˈɑːlə-] *n* zoólogo, -a *m, f*

zoology [zuˈɒlədʒi, *Am:* zoʊˈɑːlə-] *n no pl* zoología *f*

zoom [zuːm] **I.** *n* PHOT zoom *m* **II.** *vi inf* **to ~ past** pasar volando
◆ **zoom in** *vi* PHOT **to ~ on sth** enfocar algo en primer plano

zoom lens *n* zoom *m*

zucchini [zʊˈkiːni, *Am:* zuː-] <-(s)> *n inv, Am* calabacín *m*, calabacita *f* *AmL*

Z Z

Apéndice II

Supplement II

▶ LOS VERBOS REGULARES E IRREGULARES ESPAÑOLES
SPANISH REGULAR AND IRREGULAR VERBS

▶ Abreviaturas:

pret. ind.	pretérito indefinido
subj. fut.	subjuntivo futuro
subj. imp.	subjuntivo imperfecto
subj. pres.	subjuntivo presente

▶ Verbos regulares que terminan en -ar, -er e -ir

▶ hablar

presente	imperfecto	pret. ind.	futuro	
hablo	hablaba	hablé	hablaré	**gerundio**
hablas	hablabas	hablaste	hablarás	hablando
habla	hablaba	habló	hablará	
hablamos	hablábamos	hablamos	hablaremos	**participio**
habláis	hablabais	hablasteis	hablaréis	hablado
hablan	hablaban	hablaron	hablarán	

condicional	subj. pres.	subj. imp.	subj. fut.	imperativo
hablaría	hable	hablara/-ase	hablare	
hablarías	hables	hablaras/-ases	hablares	habla
hablaría	hable	hablara/-ase	hablare	hable
hablaríamos	hablemos	habláramos/-ásemos	habláremos	hablemos
hablaríais	habléis	hablarais/-aseis	hablareis	hablad
hablarían	hablen	hablaran/-asen	hablaren	hablen

► comprender

presente	imperfecto	pret. ind.	futuro	
comprendo	comprendía	comprendí	comprenderé	**gerundio**
comprendes	comprendías	comprendiste	comprenderás	comprendiendo
comprende	comprendía	comprendió	comprenderá	
comprendemos	comprendíamos	comprendimos	comprenderemos	**participio**
comprendéis	comprendíais	comprendisteis	comprenderéis	comprendido
comprenden	comprendían	comprendieron	comprenderán	

condicional	subj. pres.	subj. imp.	subj. fut.	imperativo
comprendería	comprenda	comprendiera/ -iese	comprendiere	
comprenderías	comprendas	comprendieras/-ieses	comprendieres	comprende
comprendería	comprenda	comprendiera/ -iese	comprendiere	comprenda
comprenderíamos	comprendamos	comprendiéramos/-iésemos	comprendiéremos	comprendamos
comprenderíais	comprendáis	comprendierais/-ieseis	comprendiereis	comprended
comprenderían	comprendan	comprendiera/ -iesen	comprendieren	comprendan

► recibir

presente	imperfecto	pret. ind.	futuro	
recibo	recibía	recibí	recibiré	**gerundio**
recibes	recibías	recibiste	recibirás	recibiendo
recibe	recibía	recibió	recibirá	
recibimos	recibíamos	recibimos	recibiremos	**participio**
recibís	recibíais	recibisteis	recibiréis	recibido
reciben	recibían	recibieron	recibirán	

condicional	subj. pres.	subj. imp.	subj. fut.	imperativo
recibiría	reciba	recibiera/-iese	recibiere	
recibirías	recibas	recibieras/-ieses	recibieres	recibe
recibiría	reciba	recibiera/-iese	recibiere	reciba
recibiríamos	recibamos	recibiéramos/-iésemos	recibiéremos	recibamos
recibiríais	recibáis	reciebierais/-ieseis	recibiereis	recibid
recibirían	reciban	recibieran/-iesen	recibieren	reciban

▶ Verbos con cambios vocálicos

▶ <e → ie>   pensar

presente	imperfecto	pret. ind.	futuro	
pienso	pensaba	pensé	pensaré	**gerundio**
piensas	pensabas	pensaste	pensarás	pensando
piensa	pensaba	pensó	pensará	
pensamos	pensábamos	pensamos	pensaremos	**participio**
pensáis	pensabais	pensasteis	pensaréis	pensado
piensan	pensaban	pensaron	pensarán	

condicional	subj. pres.	subj. imp.	subj. fut.	imperativo
pensaría	piense	pensara/-ase	pensare	
pensarías	pienses	pensaras/-ases	pensares	piensa
pensaría	piense	pensara/-ase	pensare	piense
pensaríamos	pensemos	pensáramos/-ásemos	pensáremos	pensemos
pensaríais	penséis	pensarais/-aseis	pensareis	pensad
pensarían	piensen	pensaran/-asen	pensaren	piensen

▶ <o → ue>   contar

presente	imperfecto	pret. ind.	futuro	
cuento	contaba	conté	contaré	**gerundio**
cuentas	contabas	contaste	contarás	contando
cuenta	contaba	contó	contará	
contamos	contábamos	contamos	contaremos	**participio**
contáis	contabais	contasteis	contaréis	contado
cuentan	contaban	contaron	contarán	

condicional	subj. pres.	subj. imp.	subj. fut.	imperativo
contaría	cuente	contara/-ase	contare	
contarías	cuentes	contaras/-ases	contares	cuenta
contaría	cuente	contara/-ase	contare	cuente
contaríamos	contemos	contáramos/-ásemos	contáremos	contemos
contaríais	contéis	contarais/-aseis	contareis	contad
contarían	cuenten	contaran	contaren	cuenten

▶ <u → ue>   jugar

presente	imperfecto	pret. ind.	futuro	
juego	jugaba	jugé	jugaré	**gerundio**
juegas	jugabas	jugaste	jugarás	jugando
juega	jugaba	jugó	jugará	
jugamos	jugábamos	jugamos	jugaremos	**participio**
jugáis	jugabais	jugasteis	jugaréis	jugado
juegan	jugaban	jugaron	jugarán	

condicional	subj. pres.	subj. imp.	subj. fut.	imperativo
jugaría	juegue	jugara/-ase	jugare	
jugarías	juegues	jugaras/-ases	jugares	juega
jugaría	juegue	jugara/-ase	jugare	juegue
jugaríamos	juguemos	jugáramos/-ásemos	jugáremos	juguemos
jugaríais	juguéis	jugarais/-aseis	jugareis	jugad
jugarían	jueguen	jugaran/-asen	jugaren	jueguen

► <e → i>   pedir

presente	imperfecto	pret. ind.	futuro	
pido	pedía	pedí	pediré	**gerundio**
pides	pedías	pediste	pedirás	pidiendo
pide	pedía	pidió	pedirá	
pedimos	pedíamos	pedimos	pediremos	**participio**
pedís	pedíais	pedisteis	pediréis	pedido
piden	pedían	pidieron	pedirán	

condicional	subj. pres.	subj. imp.	subj. fut.	imperativo
pediría	pida	pidiera/-iese	pidiere	
pedirías	pidas	pidieras/-ieses	pidieres	pide
pediría	pida	pidiera/-iese	pidiere	pida
pediríamos	pidamos	pidiéramos/-iésemos	pidiéremos	pidamos
pediríais	pidáis	pidierais/-ieseis	pidiereis	pedid
pedirían	pidan	pidieran/-iesen	pidieren	pidan

▶ Verbos con cambios ortográficos

▶ <c → qu>   atacar

presente	imperfecto	pret. ind.	futuro	
ataco	atacaba	ataqué	atacaré	**gerundio**
atacas	atacabas	atacaste	atacarás	atacando
ataca	atacaba	atacó	atacará	
atacamos	atacábamos	atacamos	atacaremos	**participio**
atacáis	atacabais	atacasteis	atacaréis	atacado
atacan	atacaban	atacaron	atacarán	

condicional	subj. pres.	subj. imp.	subj. fut.	imperativo
atacaría	ataque	atacara/-ase	atacare	
atacarías	ataques	atacaras/-ases	atacares	ataca
atacaría	ataque	atacara/-ase	atacare	ataque
atacaríamos	ataquemos	atacáramos/-ásemos	atacáremos	ataquemos
atacaríais	ataquéis	atacarais/-aseis	atacareis	atacad
atacarían	ataquen	atacaran/-asen	atacaren	ataquen

▶ <g → gu>   pagar

presente	imperfecto	pret. ind.	futuro	
pago	pagaba	pagué	pagaré	**gerundio**
pagas	pagabas	pagaste	pagarás	pagando
paga	pagaba	pagó	pagará	
pagamos	pagábamos	pagamos	pagaremos	**participio**
pagáis	pagabais	pagasteis	pagaréis	pagado
pagan	pagaban	pagaron	pagarán	

condicional	subj. pres.	subj. imp.	subj. fut.	imperativo
pagaría	pague	pagara/-ase	pagare	
pagarías	pagues	pagaras/-ases	pagares	paga
pagaría	pague	pagara/-ase	pagare	pague
pagaríamos	paguemos	pagáramos/-ásemos	pagáremos	paguemos
pagaríais	paguéis	pagarais/-aseis	pagareis	pagad
pagarían	paguen	pagaran/-asen	pagaren	paguen

▶ <z → c>   cazar

presente	imperfecto	pret. ind.	futuro	
cazo	cazaba	cacé	cazaré	**gerundio**
cazas	cazabas	cazaste	cazarás	cazando
caza	cazaba	cazó	cazará	
cazamos	cazábamos	cazamos	cazaremos	**participio**
cazáis	cazabais	cazasteis	cazaréis	cazado
cazan	cazaban	cazaron	cazarán	

condicional	subj. pres.	subj. imp.	subj. fut.	imperativo
cazaría	cace	cazara/-ase	cazare	
cazarías	caces	cazaras/-ases	cazares	caza
cazaría	cace	cazara/-ase	cazare	cace
cazaríamos	cacemos	cazáramos/-ásemos	cazáremos	cacemos
cazaríais	cacéis	cazarais/-aseis	cazareis	cazad
cazarían	cacen	cazaran/-asen	cazaren	cacen

▶ <gu → gü> averiguar

presente	imperfecto	pret. ind.	futuro	
averiguo	averiguaba	averigüé	averiguaré	**gerundio**
averiguas	averiguabas	averiguaste	averiguarás	averiguando
averigua	averiguaba	averiguó	averiguará	
averiguamos	averiguába-mos	averiguamos	averiguare-mos	**participio**
averiguáis	averiguabais	averiguasteis	averiguaréis	averiguado
averiguan	averiguaban	averiguaron	averiguarán	

condicional	subj. pres.	subj. imp.	subj. fut.	imperativo
averiguaría	averigüe	averiguara/-ase	averiguare	
averiguarías	averigües	averiguaras/-ases	averiguares	averigua
averiguaría	averigüe	averiguara/-ase	averiguare	averigüe
averiguaría-mos	averigüemos	averiguára-mos/-ásemos	averiguáre-mos	averigüemos
averiguaríais	averigüéis	averiguarais/-aseis	averiguareis	averiguad
averiguarían	averigüen	averiguaran/-asen	averiguaren	averigüen

▶ <c → z>   vencer

presente	imperfecto	pret. ind.	futuro	
venzo	vencía	vencí	venceré	**gerundio**
vences	vencías	venciste	vencerás	venciendo
vence	vencía	venció	vencerá	
vencemos	vencíamos	vencimos	venceremos	**participio**
vencéis	vencíais	vencisteis	venceréis	vencido
vencen	vencían	vencieron	vencerán	

condicional	subj. pres.	subj. imp.	subj. fut.	imperativo
vencería	venza	venciera/-iese	venciere	
vencerías	venzas	vencieras/-ieses	vencieres	vence
vencería	venza	venciera/-iese	venciere	venza
venceríamos	venzamos	venciéramos/-iésemos	venciéremos	venzamos
venceríais	venzáis	vencierais/-ieseis	venciereis	venced
vencerían	venzan	vencieran/-iesen	vencieren	venzan

▶ <g → j>   coger

presente	imperfecto	pret. ind.	futuro	
cojo	cogía	cogí	cogeré	**gerundio**
coges	cogías	cogiste	cogerás	cogiendo
coge	cogía	cogió	cogerá	
cogemos	cogíamos	cogimos	cogeremos	**participio**
cogéis	cogíais	cogisteis	cogeréis	cogido
cogen	cogían	cogieron	cogerán	

condicional	subj. pres.	subj. imp.	subj. fut.	imperativo
cogería	coja	cogiera/-iese	cogiere	
cogerías	cojas	cogieras/-ieses	cogieres	coge
cogería	coja	cogiera/-iese	cogiere	coja
cogeríamos	cojamos	cogiéramos/-iésemos	cogiéremos	cojamos
cogeríais	cojáis	cogierais/-ieseis	cogiereis	coged
cogerían	cojan	cogieran/-iesen	cogieren	cojan

▶ <gu → g>   distinguir

presente	imperfecto	pret. ind.	futuro	
distingo	distinguía	distinguí	distinguiré	**gerundio**
distingues	distinguías	distinguiste	distinguirás	distinguien-do
distingue	distinguía	distinguió	distinguirá	
distinguimos	distinguía-mos	distinguimos	distinguire-mos	**participio**
distinguís	distinguíais	distinguisteis	distinguiréis	distinguido
distinguen	distinguían	distinguieron	distinguirán	

condicional	subj. pres.	subj. imp.	subj. fut.	imperativo
distinguiría	distinga	distinguiera/-iese	distinguiere	
distinguirías	distingas	distinguieras/-ieses	distinguieres	distingue
distinguiría	distinga	distinguiera/-iese	distinguiere	distinga
distinguiría-mos	distingamos	distinguiéra-mos/iésemos	distinguiére-mos	distingamos
distinguiríais	distingáis	distinguierais/-ieseis	distinguiereis	distinguid
distinguirían	distingan	distinguieran/-iesen	distinguieren	distingan

▶ <qu → c>   delinquir

presente	imperfecto	pret. ind.	futuro	
delinco	delinquía	delinquí	delinquiré	**gerundio**
delinques	delinquías	delinquiste	delinquirás	delinquiendo
delinque	delinquía	delinquió	delinquirá	
delinquimos	delinquíamos	delinquimos	delinquire-mos	**participio**
delinquís	delinquíais	delinquisteis	delinquiréis	delinquido
delinquen	delinquían	delinquieron	delinquirán	

condicional	subj. pres.	subj. imp.	subj. fut.	imperativo
delinquiría	delinca	delinquiera/-iese	delinquiere	
delinquirías	delincas	delinquieras/-ieses	delinquieres	delinque
delinquiría	delinca	delinquiera/-iese	delinquiere	delinca
delinquiríamos	delincamos	delinquiéramos/-iésemos	delinquiéremos	delincamos
delinquiríais	delincáis	delinquierais/-ieseis	delinquiereis	delinquid
delinquirían	delincan	delinquieran/-iesen	delinquieren	delincan

► Verbos con desplazamiento en la acentuación

► <1. pres: envío>   enviar

presente	imperfecto	pret. ind.	futuro	
envío	enviaba	envié	enviaré	**gerundio**
envías	enviabas	enviaste	enviarás	enviando
envía	enviaba	envió	enviará	
enviamos	enviábamos	enviamos	enviaremos	**participio**
enviáis	enviabais	enviasteis	enviaréis	enviado
envían	enviaban	enviaron	enviarán	

condicional	subj. pres.	subj. imp.	subj. fut.	imperativo
enviaría	envíe	enviara/-iase	enviare	
enviarías	envíes	enviaras/-iases	enviares	envía
enviaría	envíe	enviara/-iase	enviare	envíe
enviaríamos	enviemos	enviáramos/-iásemos	enviáremos	enviemos
enviaríais	enviéis	enviarais/-iaseis	enviareis	enviad
enviarían	envíen	enviaran/-iasen	enviaren	envíen

▶ <1. pres: continúo> continuar

presente	imperfecto	pret. ind.	futuro	
continúo	continuaba	continué	continuaré	**gerundio**
continúas	continuabas	continuaste	continuarás	continuando
continúa	continuaba	continuó	continuará	
continuamos	continuába-mos	continuamos	continuare-mos	**participio**
continuáis	continuabais	continuasteis	continuaréis	continuado
continúan	continuaban	continuaron	continuarán	

condicional	subj. pres.	subj. imp.	subj. fut.	imperativo
continuaría	continúe	continuara/-ase	continuare	
continuarías	continúes	continuaras/-ases	continuares	continúa
continuaría	continúe	continuara/-ase	continuare	continúe
continuaría-mos	continuemos	continuára-mos/-ásemos	continuáre-mos	continuemos
continuaríais	continuéis	continuarais/-aseis	continuareis	continuad
continuarían	continúen	continuaran/-asen	continuaren	continúen

▶ Verbos que pierden la *i* átona

▶ <3. pret: tañó> tañer

presente	imperfecto	pret. ind.	futuro	
taño	tañía	tañí	tañeré	**gerundio**
tañes	tañías	tañiste	tañerás	tañendo
tañe	tañía	tañó	tañerá	
tañemos	tañíamos	tañimos	tañeremos	**participio**
tañéis	tañíais	tañisteis	tañeréis	tañido
tañen	tañían	tañeron	tañerán	

condicional	subj. pres.	subj. imp.	subj. fut.	imperativo
tañería	taña	tañera/-ese	tañere	
tañerías	tañas	tañeras/-eses	tañeres	tañe
tañería	taña	tañera/-ese	tañere	taña
tañeríamos	tañamos	tañéramos/-ésemos	tañéremos	tañamos
tañeríais	tañáis	tañerais/-eseis	tañereis	tañed
tañerían	tañan	tañeran/-esen	tañeren	tañan

▶ <3. pret: gruñó> gruñir

presente	imperfecto	pret. ind.	futuro	
gruño	gruñía	gruñí	gruñiré	**gerundio**
gruñes	gruñías	gruñiste	gruñirás	gruñendo
gruñe	gruñía	gruñó	gruñirá	
gruñimos	gruñíamos	gruñimos	gruñiremos	**participio**
gruñís	gruñíais	gruñisteis	gruñiréis	gruñido
gruñen	gruñían	gruñeron	gruñirán	

condicional	subj. pres.	subj. imp.	subj. fut.	imperativo
gruñiría	gruña	gruñera/-ese	gruñere	
gruñirías	gruñas	gruñeras/-eses	gruñeres	gruñe
gruñiría	gruña	gruñera/-ese	gruñere	gruña
gruñiríamos	gruñamos	gruñéramos/-ésemos	gruñéremos	gruñamos
gruñiríais	gruñáis	gruñerais/-eseis	gruñereis	gruñid
gruñirían	gruñan	gruñeran/-esen	gruñeren	gruñan

▶ Los verbos irregulares

▶ abolir

presente	subj. pres.	imperativo	
–	–		**gerundio**
–	–	–	aboliendo
–	–	–	
abolimos	–	–	**participio**
abolís	–	abolid	abolido
–	–	–	

▶ abrir

participio:	abierto

▶ adquirir

presente	imperativo	
adquiero		**gerundio**
adquieres	adquiere	adquiriendo
adquiere	adquiera	
adquirimos	adquiramos	**participio**
adquirís	adquirid	adquirido
adquieren	adquieran	

▶ agorar

presente	
agüero	**gerundio**
agüeras	agorando
agüera	
agoramos	**participio**
agoráis	agorado
agüeran	

▶ ahincar

presente	imperfecto	pret. ind.	imperativo	
ahínco	ahincaba	ahinqué		**gerundio**
ahíncas	ahincabas	ahincaste	ahínca	ahincando
ahínca	ahincaba	ahincó	ahinque	
ahincamos	ahincábamos	ahincamos	ahinquemos	**participio**
ahincáis	ahincabais	ahincasteis	ahincad	ahincado
ahíncan	ahincaban	ahincaron	ahinquen	

▶ airar

presente	
aíro	**gerundio**
aíras	airando
aíra	
airamos	**participio**
airáis	airado
aíran	

▶ andar

presente	pret. ind.	
ando	anduve	**gerundio**
andas	anduviste	andando
anda	anduvo	
andamos	anduvimos	**participio**
andáis	anduvisteis	andado
andan	anduvieron	

▶ asir

presente	imperativo	
asgo		**gerundio**
ases	ase	asiendo
ase	asga	
asimos	asgamos	**participio**
asís	asid	asido
asen	asgan	

▶ aullar

presente	imperativo	
aúllo		**gerundio**
aúllas	aúlla	aullando
aúlla	aúlle	
aullamos	aullemos	**participio**
aulláis	aullad	aullado
aúllan	aúllen	

▶ avergonzar

presente	pret. ind.	imperativo	
avergüenzo	avergoncé		**gerundio**
avergüenzas	avergonzaste	avergüenza	avergonzando
avergüenza	avergonzó	avergüence	
avergonza-mos	avergonza-mos	avergüence-mos	**participio**
avergonzáis	avergonzas-teis	avergonzad	avergonzado
avergüenzan	avergonza-ron	avergüencen	

▶ caber

presente	pret. ind.	futuro	condicional	
quepo	cupe	cabré	cabría	**gerundio**
cabes	cupiste	cabrás	cabrías	cabiendo
cabe	cupo	cabrá	cabría	
cabemos	cupimos	cabremos	cabríamos	**participio**
cabéis	cupisteis	cabréis	cabríais	cabido
caben	cupieron	cabrán	cabrían	

▶ caer

presente	pret. ind.	
caigo	caí	**gerundio**
caes	caíste	cayendo
cae	cayó	
caemos	caímos	**participio**
caéis	caísteis	caído
caen	cayeron	

▶ ceñir

presente	pret. ind.	imperativo	
ciño	ceñí		**gerundio**
ciñes	ceñiste	ciñe	ciñendo
ciñe	ciñó	ciña	
ceñimos	ceñimos	ciñamos	**participio**
ceñís	ceñisteis	ceñid	ceñido
ciñen	ciñeron	ciñan	

▶ cernir

presente	imperativo	
cierno		**gerundio**
ciernes	cierne	cerniendo
cierne	cierna	
cernimos	cernamos	**participio**
cernís	cernid	cernido
ciernen	ciernan	

▶ cocer

presente	imperativo	
cuezo		**gerundio**
cueces	cuece	cociendo
cuece	cueza	
cocemos	cozamos	**participio**
cocéis	coced	cocido
cuecen	cuezan	

▶ colgar

presente	pret. ind.	imperativo	
cuelgo	colgué		**gerundio**
cuelgas	colgaste	cuelga	colgando
cuelga	colgó	cuelgue	
colgamos	colgamos	colgamos	**participio**
colgáis	colgasteis	colgad	colgado
cuelgan	colgaron	cuelguen	

▶ crecer

presente	imperativo	
crezco		**gerundio**
creces	crece	creciendo
crece	crezca	
crecemos	crezcamos	**participio**
crecéis	creced	crecido
crecen	crezcan	

▶ dar

presente	pret. ind.	subj. pres.	subj. imp.	subj. fut.
doy	di	dé	diera/-ese	diere
das	diste	des	dieras/-eses	dieres
da	dio	dé	diera/-ese	diere
damos	dimos	demos	diéramos/-ésemos	diéremos
dais	disteis	deis	dierais/-eseis	diereis
dan	dieron	den	dieran/-esen	dieren

imperativo

da	**gerundio**
dé	dando
demos	
dad	**participio**
den	dado

► decir

presente	imperfecto	pret. ind.	futuro	
digo	decía	dije	diré	**gerundio**
dices	decías	dijiste	dirás	diciendo
dice	decía	dijo	dirá	
decimos	decíamos	dijimos	diremos	**participio**
decís	decíais	dijisteis	diréis	dicho
dicen	decían	dijeron	dirán	

condicional	subj. pres.	subj. imp.	subj. fut.	imperativo
diría	diga	dijera/-ese	dijere	
dirías	digas	dijeras/-eses	dijeres	di
diría	diga	dijera/-ese	dijere	diga
diríamos	digamos	dijéramos/-ésemos	dijéremos	digamos
diríais	digáis	dijerais/-eseis	dijereis	decid
dirían	digan	dijeran/-esen	dijeren	digan

► desosar

presente	imperativo	
deshueso		**gerundio**
deshuesas	deshuesa	desosando
deshuesa	deshuese	
desosamos	desosemos	**participio**
desosáis	desosad	desosado
deshuesan	deshuesen	

▶ dormir

presente	pret. ind.	imperativo	
duermo	dormí		**gerundio**
duermes	dormiste	duerme	durmiendo
duerme	durmió	duerma	
dormimos	dormimos	durmamos	**participio**
dormís	dormisteis	dormid	dormido
duermen	durmieron	duerman	

▶ elegir

presente	pret. ind.	imperativo	
elijo	elegí		**gerundio**
eliges	elegiste	elige	eligiendo
elige	eligió	elija	
elegimos	elegimos	elijamos	**participio**
elegís	elegisteis	elegid	elegido
eligen	eligieron	elijan	

▶ empezar

presente	pret. ind.	imperativo	
empiezo	empecé		**gerundio**
empiezas	empezaste	empieza	empezando
empieza	empezó	empiece	
empezamos	empezamos	empecemos	**participio**
empezáis	empezasteis	empezad	empezado
empiezan	empezaron	empiecen	

▶ enraizar

presente	pret. ind.	imperativo	
enraízo	enraicé		**gerundio**
enraízas	enraizaste	enraíza	enraizando
enraíza	enraizó	enraíce	
enraizamos	enraizamos	enraicemos	**participio**
enraizáis	enraizasteis	enraizad	enraizado
enraízan	enraizaron	enraícen	

▶ erguir

presente	pret. ind.	subj. pres	subj. imp.	subj. fut.
yergo	erguí	irga/yerga	irguiera/-ese	irguiere
yergues	erguiste	irgas/yergas	irguieras/-eses	irguieres
yergue	irguió	irga/yerga	irguiera/-ese	irguiere
erguimos	erguimos	irgamos	irgiéramos/-ésemos	irguiéremos
erguís	erguisteis	irgáis	irguierais/-eseis	irguiereis
yerguen	irguieron	irgan/yergan	irguieran/-esen	irguieren

imperativo

yergue	**gerundio**
yerga	irguiendo
yergamos	
erguid	**participio**
yergan	erguido

▶ errar

presente	pret. ind.	imperativo	
yerro	erré		**gerundio**
yerras	erraste	yerra	errando
yerra	erró	yerre	
erramos	erramos	erremos	**participio**
erráis	errasteis	errad	errado
yerran	erraron	yerren	

▶ escribir

participio :	escrito

▶ estar

presente	imperfecto	pret. ind.	futuro	
estoy	estaba	estuve	estaré	**gerundio**
estás	estabas	estuviste	estarás	estando
está	estaba	estuvo	estará	
estamos	estábamos	estuvimos	estaremos	**participio**
estáis	estabais	estuvisteis	estaréis	estado
están	estaban	estuvieron	estarán	

condicional	subj. pres.	subj. imp.	subj. fut.	imperativo
estaría	esté	estuviera/ -ese	estuviere	
estarías	estés	estuvieras/ -eses	estuvieres	está
estaría	esté	estuviera/ -ese	estuviere	esté
estaríamos	estemos	estuviéra- mos/-ésemos	estuviéremos	estemos
estaríais	estéis	estuvierais/ -eseis	estuviereis	estad
estarían	estén	estuvieran/ -esen	estuvieren	estén

▶ forzar

presente	pret. ind.	imperativo	
fuerzo	forcé		**gerundio**
fuerzas	forzaste	fuerza	forzando
fuerza	forzó	fuerce	
forzamos	forzamos	forcemos	**participio**
forzáis	forzasteis	forzad	forzado
fuerzan	forzaron	fuercen	

▶ fregar

presente	pret. ind.	imperativo	
friego	fregué		**gerundio**
friegas	fregaste	friega	fregando
friega	fregó	friegue	
fregamos	fregamos	freguemos	**participio**
fregáis	fregasteis	fregad	fregado
friegan	fregaron	frieguen	

▶ freír

presente	pret. ind.	imperativo	
frío	freí		**gerundio**
fríes	freíste	fríe	friendo
fríe	frió	fría	
freímos	freímos	friamos	**participio**
freís	freísteis	freíd	freído
fríen	frieron	frían	frito

► **haber**

presente	pret. ind.	futuro	condicional	subj. pres.
he	hube	habré	habría	haya
has	hubiste	habrás	habrías	hayas
ha	hubo	habrá	habría	haya
hemos	hubimos	habremos	habríamos	hayamos
habéis	hubisteis	habréis	habríais	hayáis
han	hubieron	habrán	habrían	hayan

subj. imp.	subj. fut.	imperativo	
hubiera/-iese	hubiere		**gerundio**
hubieras/ -ieses	hubieres	he	habiendo
hubiera/-iese	hubiere	haya	
hubiéramos/ -iésemos	hubiéremos	hayamos	**participio** habido
hubierais/ -ieseis	hubiereis	habed	
hubieran/ -iesen	hubieren	hayan	

► **hacer**

presente	pret. ind.	futuro	imperativo	
hago	hice	haré		**gerundio**
haces	hiciste	harás	haz	haciendo
hace	hizo	hará	haga	
hacemos	hicimos	haremos	hagamos	**participio**
hacéis	hicisteis	haréis	haced	hecho
hacen	hicieron	harán	hagan	

► **hartar**

participio :	hartado – *saturated*
	harto (*only as attribute*): estoy harto – *I've had enough*

▶ huir

presente	pret. ind.	imperativo	
huyo	huí		**gerundio**
huyes	huiste	huye	huyendo
huye	huyó	huya	
huimos	huimos	huyamos	**participio**
huís	huisteis	huid	huido
huyen	huyeron	huyan	

▶ imprimir

participio :	impreso

▶ ir

presente	indefinido	pret. ind.	subj. pres.	subj. imp.
voy	iba	fui	vaya	fuera/-ese
vas	ibas	fuiste	vayas	fueras/-eses
va	iba	fue	vaya	fuera/-ese
vamos	íbamos	fuimos	vayamos	fuéramos/-ésemos
vais	ibais	fuisteis	vayáis	fuerais/-eseis
van	iban	fueron	vayan	fueran/-esen

subj. fut.	imperativo	
fuere		**gerundio**
fueres	ve	yendo
fuere	vaya	
fuéremos	vayamos	**participio**
fuereis	id	ido
fueren	vayan	

▶ jugar

presente	pret. ind.	subj. pres.	imperativo	
juego	jugé	juegue		**gerundio**
juegas	jugaste	juegues	juega	jugando
juega	jugó	juegue	juegue	
jugamos	jugamos	juguemos	juguemos	**participio**
jugáis	jugasteis	juguéis	jugad	jugado
juegan	jugaron	jueguen	jueguen	

▶ leer

presente	pret. ind.	
leo	leí	**gerundio**
lees	leíste	leyendo
lee	leyó	
leemos	leímos	**participio**
leéis	leísteis	leído
leen	leyeron	

▶ lucir

presente	imperativo	
luzco		**gerundio**
luces	luce	luciendo
luce	luzca	
lucimos	luzcamos	**participio**
lucís	lucid	lucido
lucen	luzcan	

▶ maldecir

presente	pret. ind.	imperativo		
maldigo	maldije		**gerundio**	
maldices	maldijiste	maldice	maldiciendo	
maldice	maldijo	maldiga		
maldecimos	maldijimos	maldigamos	**participio**	
maldecís	maldijisteis	maldecid	maldecido	*cursed*
maldicen	maldijeron	maldigan	maldito	*noun, adjective*

▶ morir

presente	pret. ind.	imperativo	
muero	morí		**gerundio**
mueres	moriste	muere	muriendo
muere	murió	muera	
morimos	morimos	muramos	**participio**
morís	moristeis	morid	muerto
mueren	murieron	mueran	

▶ oír

presente	pret. ind.	imperativo	subj. imp.	subj. fut.
oigo	oí		oyera/-ese	oyere
oyes	oíste	oye	oyeras/-eses	oyeres
oye	oyó	oiga	oyera/-ese	oyere
oímos	oímos	oigamos	oyéramos/-ésemos	oyéremos
oís	oísteis	oid	oyerais/-eseis	oyéreis
oyen	oyeron	oigan	eyeran/-esen	oyeren

gerundio	participio
oyendo	oído

▶ oler

presente	imperativo	
huelo		**gerundio**
hueles	huele	oliendo
huele	huela	
olemos	olamos	**participio**
oléis	oled	olido
huelen	huelan	

▶ pedir

presente	pret. ind.	imperativo	
pido	pedí		**gerundio**
pides	pediste	pide	pidiendo
pide	pidió	pidas	
pedimos	pedimos	pidamos	**participio**
pedís	pedisteis	pedid	pedido
piden	pidieron	pidan	

▶ poder

presente	pret. ind.	futuro	condicional	
puedo	pude	podré	podría	**gerundio**
puedes	pudiste	podrás	podrías	pudiendo
puede	pudo	podrá	podría	
podemos	pudimos	podremos	podríamos	**participio**
podéis	pudisteis	podréis	podríais	podido
pueden	pudieron	podrán	podrían	

▶ podrir (pudrir)

presente	imperfecto	pret. ind.	futuro	condicional
pudro	pudría	pudrí	pudriré	pudriría
pudres	pudrías	pudriste	pudrirás	pudrirías
pudre	pudría	pudrió	pudrirá	pudriría
pudrimos	pudríamos	pudrimos	pudriremos	pudriríamos
pudrís	pudríais	pudristeis	pudriréis	pudriríais
pudren	pudrían	pudrieron	pudrirán	pudrirían

imperativo

	gerundio
pudre	pudriendo
pudra	
pudramos	**participio**
pudrid	podrido
pudran	

▶ poner

presente	pret. ind.	futuro	condicional	imperativo
pongo	puse	pondré	pondría	
pones	pusiste	pondrás	pondrías	pon
pone	puso	pondrá	pondría	ponga
ponemos	pusimos	pondremos	pondríamos	pongamos
ponéis	pusisteis	pondréis	pondríais	poned
ponen	pusieron	pondrán	pondrían	pongan

gerundio	**participio**
poniendo	puesto

▶ prohibir

presente	imperativo	
prohíbo		**gerundio**
prohíbes	prohíbe	prohibiendo
prohíbe	prohíba	
prohibimos	prohibamos	**participio**
prohibís	prohibid	prohibido
prohíben	prohíban	

▶ proveer

presente	pret. ind.	
proveo	proveí	**gerundio**
provees	proveíste	proveyendo
provee	proveyó	
proveemos	proveímos	**participio**
proveéis	proveísteis	provisto
proveen	proveyeron	proveído

▶ querer

presente	pret. ind.	futuro	condicional	imperativo
quiero	quise	querré	querría	
quieres	quisiste	querrás	querrías	quiere
quiere	quiso	querrá	querría	quiera
queremos	quisimos	querremos	querríamos	queramos
queréis	quisisteis	querréis	querríais	quered
quieren	quisieron	querrán	querrían	quieran

gerundio	participio
queriendo	querido

▶ raer

presente	pret. ind.		
raigo/rao/ rayo	raí	**gerundio**	
raes	raíste	rayendo	
rae	rayó		
raemos	raímos	**participio**	
raéis	raísteis	raído	
raen	rayeron		

▶ reír

presente	pret. ind.	imperativo	
río	reí		**gerundio**
ríes	reíste	ríe	riendo
ríe	rió	ría	
reímos	reímos	riamos	**participio**
reís	reísteis	reíd	reído
ríen	rieron	rían	

▶ reunir

presente	imperativo	
reúno		**gerundio**
reúnes	reúne	reuniendo
reúne	reúna	
reunimos	reunamos	**participio**
reunís	reunid	reunido
reúnen	reúnan	

▶ roer

presente	pret. ind.	subj. pres.	subj. imp.	subj. fut.
roo/roigo	roí	roa/roiga	royera/-ese	royere
roes	roíste	roas/roigas	royeras/-eses	royeres
roe	royó	roa/roiga	royera/-ese	royere
roemos	roímos	roamos/ roigamos/ royamos	royéramos/ -ésemos	royéremos
roéis	roísteis	roáis/roigáis/ royáis	royerais/ -eseis	royereis
roen	royeron	roan/roigan	royeran/ -esen	royeren

imperativo

	gerundio
roe	royendo
roa/roiga	
roamos/ roigamos roed roan/roigan	**participio** roído

▶ saber

presente	pret. ind.	futuro	condicional	subj. pres.
sé	supe	sabré	sabría	sepa
sabes	supiste	sabrás	sabrías	sepas
sabe	supo	sabrá	sabría	sepa
sabemos	supimos	sabremos	sabríamos	sepamos
sabéis	supisteis	sabréis	sabríais	sepáis
saben	supieron	sabrán	sabrían	sepan

imperativo

	gerundio
sabe	sabiendo
sepa	
sepamos	**participio**
sabed	sabido
sepan	

▶ salir

presente	futuro	condicional	imperativo	
salgo	saldré	saldría		**gerundio**
sales	saldrás	saldrías	sal	saliendo
sale	saldrá	saldría	salga	
salimos	saldremos	saldríamos	salgamos	**participio**
salís	saldréis	saldríais	salid	salido
salen	saldrán	saldrían	salgan	

▶ seguir

presente	pret. ind.	subj. pres.	subj. imp.	subj. fut.
sigo	seguí	siga	siguiera/-ese	siguiere
sigues	seguiste	sigas	siguieras/-eses	siguieres
sigue	siguió	siga	siguiera/-ese	siguiere
seguimos	seguimos	sigamos	siguéramos/-ésemos	siguiéremos
seguís	seguisteis	sigáis	siguierais/-eseis	siguiereis
siguen	siguieron	sigan	siguieran/-esen	siguieren

imperativo

	gerundio
sigue	siguiendo
siga	
sigamos	**participio**
seguid	seguido
sigan	

▶ sentir

presente	pret. ind.	subj. pres.	subj. imp.	subj. fut.
siento	sentí	sienta	sintiera/-ese	sintiere
sientes	sentiste	sientas	sintieras/-eses	sintieres
siente	sintió	sienta	sintiera/-ese	sintiere
sentimos	sentimos	sintamos	sintiéramos/-ésemos	sintiéremos
sentís	sentisteis	sintáis	sintierais/-eseis	sintiereis
sienten	sintieron	sientan	sintieran/-esen	sintieren

imperativo

	gerundio
siente	sintiendo
sienta	
sintamos	**participio**
sentid	sentido
sientan	

► ser

presente	imperfecto	pret. ind.	futuro	
soy	era	fui	seré	**gerundio**
eres	eras	fuiste	serás	siendo
es	era	fue	será	
somos	éramos	fuimos	seremos	**participio**
sois	erais	fuisteis	seréis	sido
son	eran	fueron	serán	

condicional	subj. pres.	subj. imp.	subj. fut.	imperativo
sería	sea	fuera/-ese	fuere	
serías	seas	fueras/-eses	fueres	sé
sería	sea	fuera/-ese	fuere	sea
seríamos	seamos	fuéramos/-ésemos	fuéremos	seamos
seríais	seáis	fuerais/-eseis	fuereis	sed
serían	sean	fueran/-esen	fueren	sean

► soltar

presente	imperativo	
suelto		**gerundio**
sueltas	suelta	soltando
suelta	suelte	
soltamos	soltemos	**participio**
soltáis	soltad	soltado
sueltan	suelten	

▶ tener

presente	pret. ind.	futuro	condicional	imperativo
tengo	tuve	tendré	tendría	
tienes	tuviste	tendrás	tendrías	ten
tiene	tuvo	tendrá	tendría	tenga
tenemos	tuvimos	tendremos	tendríamos	tengamos
tenéis	tuvisteis	tendréis	tendríais	tened
tienen	tuvieron	tendrán	tendrían	tengan

gerundio	participio
teniendo	tenido

▶ traducir

presente	pret. ind.	imperativo	
traduzco	traduje		**gerundio**
traduces	tradujiste	traduce	traduciendo
traduce	tradujo	traduzca	
traducimos	tradujimos	traduzcamos	**participio**
traducís	tradujisteis	traducid	traducido
traducen	tradujeron	traduzcan	

▶ traer

presente	pret. ind.	imperativo	
traigo	traje		**gerundio**
traes	trajiste	trae	trayendo
trae	trajo	traiga	
traemos	trajimos	traigamos	**participio**
traéis	trajisteis	traed	traído
traen	trajeron	traigan	

► valer

presente	futuro	imperativo	
valgo	valdré		**gerundio**
vales	valdrás	vale	valiendo
vale	valdrá	valga	
valemos	valdremos	valgamos	**participio**
valéis	valdréis	valed	valido
valen	valdrán	valgan	

► venir

presente	pret. ind.	futuro	condicional	imperativo
vengo	vine	vendré	vendría	
vienes	viniste	vendrás	vendrías	ven
viene	vino	vendrá	vendría	venga
venimos	vinimos	vendremos	vendríamos	vengamos
venís	vinisteis	vendréis	vendríais	venid
vienen	vinieron	vendrán	vendrían	vengan

gerundio	participio
viniendo	venido

▶ ver

presente	imperfecto	pret. ind.	subj. imp.	subj. fut.
veo	veía	vi	viera/-ese	viere
ves	veías	viste	vieras/-eses	vieres
ve	veía	vio	viera/-ese	viere
vemos	veíamos	vimos	viéramos/-ésemos	viéremos
veis	veíais	visteis	vierais/-eseis	viereis
ven	veían	vieron	vieran/-esen	vieren

gerundio	participio
viendo	visto

▶ volcar

presente	pret. ind.	imperativo	
vuelco	volqué		**gerundio**
vuelcas	volcaste	vuelca	volcando
vuelca	volcó	vuelque	
volcamos	volcamos	volquemos	**participio**
volcáis	volcasteis	volcad	volcado
vuelcan	volcaron	vuelquen	

▶ volver

presente	imperativo	
vuelvo		**gerundio**
vuelves	vuelve	volviendo
vuelve	vuelva	
volvemos	volvamos	**participio**
volvéis	volved	volvido
vuelven	vuelvan	

▶ yacer

presente	subj. pres.	imperativo	
yazco/yazgo/ yago	yazca/yazga/ yaga		**gerundio** yaciendo
yaces	yazcas/ yazgas/yagas	yace/yaz	
yace	yazca/yazga/ yaga	yazca/yazga/ yaga	
yacemos	yazcamos/ yazgamos/ yagamos	yazcamos/ yazgamos/ yagamos	**participio** yacido
yacéis	yazcáis/ yazgáis/ yagáis	yaced	
yacen	yazcan/ yazgan/ yagan	yazcan/ yazgan/ yagan	

▶ VERBOS INGLESES IRREGULARES
ENGLISH IRREGULAR VERBS

Infinitive	Past	Past Participle
abide	abode, abided	abode, abided
arise	arose	arisen
awake	awoke	awaked, awoken
be	was *sing*, were *pl*	been
bear	bore	borne
beat	beat	beaten
become	became	become
beget	begot	begotten
begin	began	begun
behold	beheld	beheld
bend	bent	bent
beseech	besought	besought
beset	beset	beset
bet	bet, betted	bet, betted
bid	bade, bid	bid, bidden
bind	bound	bound
bite	bit	bitten
bleed	bled	bled
blow	blew	blown
break	broke	broken
breed	bred	bred
bring	brought	brought
build	built	built
burn	burned, burnt	burned, burnt
burst	burst	burst
buy	bought	bought
can	could	–
cast	cast	cast

Infinitive	Past	Past Participle
catch	caught	caught
chide	chided, chid	chided, chidden, chid
choose	chose	chosen
cleave[1] *(cut)*	clove, cleaved	cloven, cleaved, cleft
cleave[2] *(adhere)*	cleaved, clave	cleaved
cling	clung	clung
come	came	come
cost	cost, costed	cost, costed
creep	crept	crept
cut	cut	cut
deal	dealt	dealt
dig	dug	dug
do	did	done
draw	drew	drawn
dream	dreamed, dreamt	dreamed, dreamt
drink	drank	drunk
drive	drove	driven
dwell	dwelt	dwelt
eat	ate	eaten
fall	fell	fallen
feed	fed	fed
feel	felt	felt
fight	fought	fought
find	found	found
flee	fled	fled
fling	flung	flung
fly	flew	flown
forbid	forbad(e)	forbidden
forget	forgot	forgotten
forsake	forsook	forsaken
freeze	froze	frozen

Infinitive	Past	Past Participle
get	got	got, gotten *Am*
gild	gilded, gilt	gilded, gilt
gird	girded, girt	girded, girt
give	gave	given
go	went	gone
grind	ground	ground
grow	grew	grown
hang	hung, JUR hanged	hung, JUR hanged
have	had	had
hear	heard	heard
heave	heaved, hove	heaved, hove
hew	hewed	hewed, hewn
hide	hid	hidden
hit	hit	hit
hold	held	held
hurt	hurt	hurt
keep	kept	kept
kneel	knelt	knelt
know	knew	known
lade	laded	laden, laded
lay	laid	laid
lead	led	led
lean	leaned, leant	leaned, leant
leap	leaped, leapt	leaped, leapt
learn	learned, learnt	learned, learnt
leave	left	left
lend	lent	lent
let	let	let
lie	lay	lain
light	lit, lighted	lit, lighted
lose	lost	lost

Infinitive	Past	Past Participle
make	made	made
may	might	–
mean	meant	meant
meet	met	met
mistake	mistook	mistaken
mow	mowed	mown, mowed
pay	paid	paid
put	put	put
quit	quit, quitted	quit, quitted
read [ri:d]	read [red]	read [red]
rend	rent	rent
rid	rid	rid
ride	rode	ridden
ring	rang	rung
rise	rose	risen
run	ran	run
saw	sawed	sawed, sawn
say	said	said
see	saw	seen
seek	sought	sought
sell	sold	sold
send	sent	sent
set	set	set
sew	sewed	sewed, sewn
shake	shook	shaken
shave	shaved	shaved, shaven
stave	stove, staved	stove, staved
steal	stole	stolen
shear	sheared	sheared, shorn
shed	shed	shed
shine	shone	shone

Infinitive	Past	Past Participle
shit	shit, *iron* shat	shit, *iron* shat
shoe	shod	shod
shoot	shot	shot
show	showed	shown, showed
shrink	shrank	shrunk
shut	shut	shut
sing	sang	sung
sink	sank	sunk
sit	sat	sat
slay	slew	slain
sleep	slept	slept
slide	slid	slid
sling	slung	slung
slink	slunk	slunk
slit	slit	slit
smell	smelled, smelt	smelled, smelt
smite	smote	smitten
sow	sowed	sowed, sown
speak	spoke	spoken
speed	speeded, sped	speeded, sped
spell	spelled, spelt	spelled, spelt
spend	spent	spent
spill	spilled, spilt	spilled, spilt
spin	spun	spun
spit	spat	spat
split	split	split
spoil	spoiled, spoilt	spoiled, spoilt
spread	spread	spread
spring	sprang	sprung
stand	stood	stood
stick	stuck	stuck

Infinitive	Past	Past Participle
sting	stung	stung
stink	stank	stunk
strew	strewed	strewed, strewn
stride	strode	stridden
strike	struck	struck
string	strung	strung
strive	strove	striven
swear	swore	sworn
sweep	swept	swept
swell	swelled	swollen
swin	swam	swum
swing	swung	swung
take	took	taken
teach	taught	taught
tear	tore	torn
tell	told	told
think	thought	thought
thrive	throve, thrived	thriven, thrived
throw	threw	thrown
thrust	thrust	thrust
tread	trod	trodden
wake	woke, waked	woken, waked
wear	wore	worn
weave	wove	woven
weep	wept	wept
win	won	won
wind	wound	wound
wring	wrung	wrung
write	wrote	written

► FALSOS AMIGOS
FALSE FRIENDS

Para más información el usuario debe de consultar la entrada en el diccionario. En los casos en los que la palabra inglesa está fuera del orden alfabético ésta aparece en *cursiva*.

Readers should consult the main section of the dictionary for more complete translation information. When the English term appears out of alphabetical order, it is shown in *italics*.

Meaning(s) of the Spanish word:	falso amigo false friend		Significado(s) de la palabra inglesa:
	español	English	
1) enormous	abismal	abysmal	pésimo
1) present 2) current	actual	actual	verdadero
at the moment	actualmente	actually	en realidad
1) appropriate 2) fitting, suitable	adecuado, -a	adequate	1) suficiente 2) idóneo
1) diary 2) notebook 3) agenda	agenda	agenda	1) orden del día 2) agenda
bedroom	alcoba	alcove	nicho
1) entertainment 2) enjoyment	amenidad	amenities	comodidades
1) to attend (*vi*) 2) to help (*vt*)	asistir	to assist	ayudar
1) audience 2) (JUR) hearing, courtroom	audiencia	audience	1) público 2) audiencia
1) to notify 2) to warn 3) to call	avisar	*to advise*	aconsejar, asesorar
billion	billón	billion	mil millones
1) white 2) light 3) pale	blanco, -a	blank	1) en blanco 2) vacío 3) absoluto, completo

Meaning(s) of the Spanish word:	falso amigo false friend		Significado(s) de la palabra inglesa:
	español	English	
1) soft 2) mild 3) weak 4) gentle	blando, -a	bland	1) suave, blando 2) afable 3) insípido, insulso
1) excellent 2) brave 3) wild 4) rough	bravo, -a	brave	valiente
1) countryside 2) field 3) camp	campo	camp	1) campamento 2) grupo
1) shameless 2) cynical	cínico, -a (adj)	*cynical*	1) escéptico 2) cínico
1) shamelessness 2) cynicism	cinismo	cynicism	1) escepticismo 2) cinismo
1) understanding 2) tolerant 3) comprehensive	comprensivo, -a	comprehensive	exhaustivo, completo
1) commitment 2) promise 3) agreement 4) awkward situation	compromise	compromise	1) transigencia 2) arreglo
1) leader 2) driver	conductor	conductor	1) (MUS) director 2) (PHYS, ELEC) conductor 3) cobrador, interventor
1) lecture 2) conference 3) talk 4) call	conferencia	conference	congreso
estar constipado: to have a cold	constipado, -a	constipated	estreñido
1) to build 2) to construe	construir	to construe	interpretar
1) to check 2) to control	controlar	to control	1) dominar 2) controlar 3) erradicar

Meaning(s) of the Spanish word:	falso amigo false friend		Significado(s) de la palabra inglesa:
	español	English	
1) habit 2) custom	costumbre	costume	traje
disappointment	decepción	deception	1) engaño 2) fraude
to disappoint	decepcionar	*to deceive*	engañar
1) request 2) (COM) demand 3) (JUR) action	demanda	demand	1) exigencia 2) reclamación de un pago 3) demanda
1) to ask for 2) (JUR) to sue	demandar	to demand	1) reclamar 2) requerir 3) preguntar
1) to displease 2) to anger, to offend	disgustar	to disgust	1) dar asco 2) repugnar
1) displeasure 2) suffering 3) quarrel	disgusto	disgust	1) repugnancia 2) indignación
1) to divert 2) to entertain 3) to embezzle	distraer	to distract	distraer
1) pregnant 2) awkward	embarazado, -a	embarassed	avergonzado
1) escape 2) excursion	escapada	escapade	aventura
1) stage 2) scene	escenario	*scenery*	1) paisaje 2) decorado
1) possible 2) extra	eventual	eventual	1) final 2) posible
fortuitously, possibly	eventualmente	eventually	1) finalmente 2) con el tiempo
1) to incite 2) to irritate 3) to arouse	excitar	*to excite*	1) emocionar 2) estimular
success	éxito	exit	1) salida 2) desvío

Meaning(s) of the Spanish word:	falso amigo false friend		Significado(s) de la palabra inglesa:
	español	English	
1) strangeness 2) eccentricity	extravagancia	extravagance	1) derroche 2) lujo 3) prodigalidad 4) extravagancia
1) odd 2) eccentric	extravagante	extravagant	1) despilfarrador 2) lujoso 3) excesivo 4) extravagante
1) factory 2) masonry 3) building	fábrica	fabric	1) tejido 2) estructura
1) to manufacture 2) to build 3) to fabricate	fabricar	to fabricate	1) inventar 2) fabricar 3) falsificar
crème caramel	flan	flan	1) (*Brit*) tartaleta de frutas 2) (*Am*) flan
1) sentence 2) expression, saying 3) style 4) (MÚS) phrase	frase	*phrase*	1) locución 2) expresión
1) study 2) dressing room 3) office 4) (POL) cabinet	gabinete	*cabinet*	1) armario, vitrina 2) gabinete de ministros
1) brilliant 2) funny 3) great	genial	genial	afable
1) genius 2) stroke of genius	genialidad	geniality	afabilidad
1) pagan 2) dashing, elegant 3) considerate	gentil (adj)	genteel	distinguido
1) to be ignorant of 2) to ignore	ignorar	to ignore	no hacer caso a
uninhabitable	inhabitable	inhabitable	habitable

Meaning(s) of the Spanish word:	falso amigo false friend		Significado(s) de la palabra inglesa:
	español	English	
uninhabited	inhabitado, -a	inhabited	habitado
insult, harm	injuria	injury	1) lesión 2) herida
to insult, to injure	injuriar	*to injure*	1) herir 2) estropear 3) perjudicar
poisoning	intoxicación	intoxication	1) embriaguez 2) (MED) intoxicación
to poison	intoxicar	*to intoxicate*	1) embriagar 2) (MED) intoxicar
1) to insert 2) to put in	introducir	to introduce	1) presentar 2) iniciar 3) abordar 4) introducir
1) long 2) lengthy 3) shrewd	largo, -a	large	grande
1) reading 2) reading material 3) knowledge 4) interpretation	lectura	lecture	1) discurso, conferencia 2) sermón 3) consejo
1) bookshop 2) stationer's 3) library 4) bookcase	librería	library	1) biblioteca 2) collección
1) mask 2) fancy dress party 3) masquerade	máscara	mascara	rímel
1) poverty 2) pittance 3) stinginess 4) misfortune	miseria	misery	tristeza
to inconvenience, to annoy	molestar	to molest	1) atacar 2) agredir
1) slow to pay up 2) slow	moroso, -a	morose	taciturno, malhumorado

Meaning(s) of the Spanish word:	falso amigo false friend		Significado(s) de la palabra inglesa:
	español	English	
piece of news	noticia	notice	1) interés 2) letrero, anuncio 3) aviso
1) well-known 2) obvious	notorio, -a	notorious	de mala reputación
obvious	ostensible	ostensible	aparente
relative	pariente	parent	padre, madre
pretentious	pedante	pedantic	puntilloso
newspaper	periódico	periodical	1) boletín 2) revista
1) arrogant, conceited 2) insolent	petulante	petulant	enfurruñado
condom	preservativo	preservative	conservante
conceited	presuntuoso, -a	presumptuous	1) impertinente 2) osado
to aspire to to expect to mean to to try	pretender	to pretend	1) fingir 2) pretender
teacher	profesor	professor	1) (*Brit*) catedrático 2) (*Am*) profesor de universidad
1) to make real, to fulfil 2) to carry out, to make 3) (ECON) to realize 4) to produce	realizar	to realize	1) ser consciente de 2) realizar 3) cumplir
container, vessel	recipiente	recipient	destinatario
1) to remember 2) to remind	recordar	to record	1) archivar 2) registrar, grabar
saying	refrán	refrain	estribillio
importance	relevancia	relevance	1) pertinencia 2) importancia

Meaning(s) of the Spanish word:	falso amigo false friend		Significado(s) de la palabra inglesa:
	español	English	
1) important 2) outstanding	relevante	relevant	1) pertinente 2) importante 3) oportuno
to summarize	resumir	to resume	1) reanudar, proseguir con 2) volver a ocupar
1) insinuating 2) reluctant	reticente	reticent	reservado
reward, remuneration	retribución	retribution	castigo justo
health	sanidad	sanity	cordura
1) healthy 2) intact 3) wholesome	sano, -a	*sane*	1) cuerdo 2) sensato
1) sensitive 2) noticeable	sensible	sensible	1) sensato, prudente 2) práctico 3) consciente 4) notable
1) liking 2) friendliness	simpatía	*sympathy*	1) compasión, comprensión 2) simpatía
friendly	simpático, -a	*sympathetic*	1) comprensivo, receptivo 2) cordial 3) simpatizante
1) to stand 2) to support	soportar	to support	1) sostener, aguantar 2) ayudar 3) mantener
1) smooth 2) soft 3) gentle 4) mild	suave	suave	afable, cortés
1) poor suburb 2) slum area	suburbio	suburb	barrio periférico

Meaning(s) of the Spanish word:	falso amigo false friend		Significado(s) de la palabra inglesa:
	español	English	
1) to happen (*vi*) 2) to succeed (*vi*) 3) to follow on (*vi*) 4) to inherit (*vt*)	**suceder**	**to succeed**	1) tener éxito 2) suceder
1) event, incident 2) outcome	**suceso**	**success**	éxito
1) evocative 2) thought-provoking 3) attractive	**sugestivo, -a**	**suggestive**	1) indecente 2) sugestivo
1) commonplace 2) cliché	**tópico**	**topic**	tema
1) cruel 2) gruesome	**truculento, -a**	**truculent**	agresivo
1) dissolute 2) habit-forming 3) defective 4) spoilt	**vicioso, -a**	**vicious**	1) malo, salvaje 2) despiadado 3) feroz 4) atroz

► LOS NUMERALES NUMERALS

► Los numerales cardinales
 Cardinal numbers

cero	0	zero
uno (*apócope* un), una	1	one
dos	2	two
tres	3	three
cuatro	4	four
cinco	5	five
seis	6	six
siete	7	seven
ocho	8	eight
nueve	9	nine
diez	10	ten
once	11	eleven
doce	12	twelve
trece	13	thirteen
catorce	14	fourteen
quince	15	fifteen
dieciséis	16	sixteen
diecisiete	17	seventeen
dieciocho	18	eighteen
diecinueve	19	nineteen
veinte	20	twenty
veintiuno (*apócope* veintiún), -a	21	twenty-one
veintidós	22	twenty-two
veintitrés	23	twenty-three
veinticuatro	24	twenty-four
veinticinco	25	twenty-five
treinta	30	thirty
treinta y uno (*apócope* treinta y un) -a	31	thirty-one
treinta y dos	32	thirty-two
treinta y tres	33	thirty-three

cuarenta	40	forty
cuarenta y uno (*apócope* cuarenta y un) -a	41	forty-one
cuarenta y dos	42	forty-two
cincuenta	50	fifty
cincuenta y uno (*apócope* cincuenta y un) -a	51	fifty-one
cincuenta y dos	52	fifty-two
sesenta	60	sixty
sesenta y uno (*apócope* sesenta y un) -a	61	sixty-one
sesenta y dos	62	sixty-two
setenta	70	seventy
setenta y uno (*apócope* setenta y un) -a	71	seventy-one
setenta y dos	72	seventy-two
setenta y cinco	75	seventy-five
setenta y nueve	79	seventy-nine
ochenta	80	eighty
ochenta y uno (*apócope* ochenta y un) -a	81	eighty-one
ochenta y dos	82	eighty-two
ochenta y cinco	85	eighty-five
noventa	90	ninety
noventa y uno (*apócope* noventa y un) -a	91	ninety-one
noventa y dos	92	ninety-two
noventa y nueve	99	ninety-nine
cien	100	one hundred
ciento uno (*apócope* ciento un) -a	101	one hundred and one
ciento dos	102	one hundred and two
ciento diez	110	one hundred and ten
ciento veinte	120	one hundred and twenty
ciento noventa y nueve	199	one hundred and ninety-nine
dos cientos, -as	200	two hundred
dos cientos uno (*apócope* doscientos un) -a	201	two hundred and one